SPORTS

Babe Ruth (*The New York Times*)

SPORTS

AS REPORTED BY
The New York Times

Edited by

Gene Brown

and

Arleen Keylin

ARNO PRESS

New York • 1976

A Note to the Reader

Original copies of *The New York Times* were not available to the publisher. This volume, therefore, was created from 35mm microfilm.

Library of Congress Cataloging in Publication Data
Main entry under title:

Sports.

1. Sports—History—Miscellanea. 2. Sports stories. I. Brown, Gene. II. Keylin, Arleen. III. New York Times.
GV576.S62 796'.09 76-2450
ISBN 0-405-06689-9

Assistant to the Editors: Eve Nelson

Editorial Assistant: Sandra Jones

Manufactured in the United States of America

2 3 4 5 6 7 8 9 10

CONTENTS

Hockey

Horse Racing

Skiing

Swimming

Tennis

Track and Field

INTRODUCTION

Sports—a world of excitement, glamour, skill, winning and losing, of fantasy and superstars. Sports gives us heroes to identify with and worship—and provides escape from the problems and concerns of modern life.

It is difficult to overestimate the importance of sports in the lives of Americans over the past eighty years or so. From the time of the earliest story in this book—Corbett beats Sullivan for the heavyweight title in 1892—sports have steadily gained an ever larger role as multi-media events and as multi-million dollar businesses.

There is a great deal that can be said and argued about the economic, social, and even political aspects of sports. This book, however, concentrates on the people and events themselves. You are invited to enjoy 175 major events as reported at the time they took place. Here is a sampler of some of the best sports reporting available in print.

CORBETT NOW IS CHAMPION

SULLIVAN MEETS HIS MATCH AT NEW-ORLEANS.

THE CALIFORNIAN KEPT AWAY FROM THE BIG FELLOW'S BLOWS, AND FINALLY FORCED THE FIGHTING—THE BOSTON PUGILIST KNOCKED OUT IN THE TWENTY-FIRST ROUND.

NEW-ORLEANS, La., Sept. 7.—John L. Sullivan, the heavyweight champion pugilist who has held the honor so long, was defeated to-night by James Corbett of California. The fight lasted for twenty-one rounds and took place before a crowd of over 10,000 persons in the arena of the Olympic Club.

Corbett came out of the fight fresh and without a mark. Sullivan was badly punished. It was a contest between science and strength. Corbett's expert boxing and his agility in dodging the big fellow's blows and eluding his rushes won him the fight. Corbett was given a great ovation at the close when he had given the Boston pugilist a knock-down and knock-out blow. Sullivan soon recovered and was able to make a short speech in which he said that he was glad the championship would remain in this country.

It was the old generation against the new. It was the gladiator against the boxer. Sullivan represented the first stage in the evolution of the American pugilist, and swept away old methods and old traditions. The old style was severe training and bloody battles, fights under difficulties in secluded spots, which the contestants performed for little money before the most objectionable classes. Although Sullivan has thrice defended the championship with bare knuckles, under London prize-ring rules, he was the virtual inventor of the modern glove contest.

He did better with the gloves than all his predecessors with naked fists, and did as much execution with padded hands in four rounds as the old-time fighters with ungloved battering rams. He Americanized the manly art, deprived it of much of its brutality, and made it possible to decide championships before athletic clubs under the best auspices before classes of people who formerly took little interest in the sport. Nature intended him for a gladiator, and although he abused nature to a considerable extent, not even the best trained rivals could defeat him. In England and America he defended the title of champion, and when anywhere near his true self there was no doubt as to the result. He stood out a central figure in the history of pugilism and attracted to him a following from every corner of the country.

Wherever Sullivan fought people flocked to see him, and no matter what his condition, no matter who his rival, no matter what the odds, the crowd was for Sullivan. It was so in to-night's battle. Whatever the attraction of the other two contests forming the triple event, the name of Sullivan contained the magic power.

The crowd which came before Monday night had the gladiator chiefly in mind. Those who did not arrive in time to see the other battles came with a rush before the hour for the heavyweights to meet. All day long Tuesday special trains arrived, and even yesterday hundreds of people from almost every State, from California to New-York and from Minnesota to Texas, came pouring into the city. Canal Street and St. Charles Streets had a look of carnival season. Hotels, saloons, and all places of resort were crowded. Men of high and men of low degree mingled freely, and nearly all said Sullivan.

At night the streets were very animated. There was no rush to the other fights, but to the heavyweight contest the visitors and local admirers of the sport felt impressed with the necessity of starting early. Carriages, cabs, wagonettes, wagons turned into pleasure vehicles, and street cars began bearing spectators to the Olympic arena. And the rush kept up until nearly the hour for the call of time.

Everybody recognized the necessity of going early, for it was known that the arena would be packed to its utmost capacity, and those who had not secured reserved seats would have to struggle for a point of vantage.

The betting was not very heavy. The principal reason was the large majority which built its hopes upon Sullivan. The champion of champions was a strong favorite in the pool rooms. The morning odds were 1 to 4 Sullivan and 3 to 1 Corbett.

The night before, in banter between the backers of the men, Wakeley and Brady each deposited $50 to bind the bet of $2,000 to $1,000. This was at odds of 2 to 1, and the money was to have been put up at 1 o'clock P. M. yesterday. When Brady came down town and found 3 to 1 Corbett posted, he forfeited the $50 and turned over $1,000 to Harrison's turf exchange, getting $3,000 against it. There was another bet of $1,000 on Corbett, and D. B. Mitchell, New-York Commissioner, telegraphed $500 at the odds. Although $1,000 went in on Sullivan at 1 to 4, the Corbett bets forced a change in the odds, 3 to 10 being laid against Sullivan, 5 to 2 against Corbett. At those odds a large local cotton house placed $1,000 on Corbett, and a Californian sport made a similar bet. The Sullivan men, although Wakeley, Johnson, and the leading backers demurred at the odds, did not delay to back their favorite. Men formed in line and played from $100 to $500 each on the champion, and up to about 3 o'clock Harrison's room stood to pay out $26,000 on Corbett and $22,000 on Sullivan.

On combinations the room stood to pay out $14,000 if Sullivan won, and $9,000 if Corbett proved the victor. At the Crescent the betting on Sullivan was marked, $5,000 coming in within a short space of time, one bet being for $2,000. A rush of Corbett money in the morning also forced a drop in the odds from 3 to 1 to 5 to 6.

The Sullivan contingent was so confident of the champion's ability to win with ease that they made a number of bets on the duration of the affair. Hurd bet $500 that Sullivan would win inside of fifteen rounds, and Honest John Kelly laid a wager of $300 with "Alf" Kennedy, "Billy" Myer's backer, that Sullivan would win in thirteen rounds.

The great battle between Sullivan and Corbett for the pugilistic championship of the world was the culmination of interest and excitement to-night. All the streets leading from the business portion of the city to the Olympic Club were brilliantly lighted and every one was crowded with enthusiasts, male and female, adult and infantile. Every car and carriage was greeted with huzzas and the atmosphere was infused with a suppressed excitement as if some stupendous event, some gigantic casualty was about to occur.

If there was excitement on the streets, there was something beyond that in the club itself. Every square inch of the stupendous structure was occupied. No seat was vacant, no box empty. In every direction there was a solid mass of men. Although the figures 10,000 is an immense number, it would be no overstatement to say that there were 1,500 more than that number who saw the great heavyweight battle to-night.

This huge assemblage comported itself faultlessly. There were enthusiastic and encouraging cheers for each man, but no disagreeable personalities. New-Orleans notables were well represented. Mayor John Fitzpatrick, who refereed the Sullivan-Kilrain contest at Richburg with eminent satisfaction, was an interested spectator. Chief of Police Dexter Gaster sat in a box in citizen's clothes. District Attorney Butler and Assistant Lowel Adams, both sporting enthusiasts, were awarded reserved seats, while the City Council and the Orleans Parish delegations to the State Senate and Hosue had each more than a quorum present.

The participants in the previous battles—McAuliffe, Myer, Dixon, Skelly—and the horde of famed pugilistic visitors to the city all had good points of vantage. The entrance of "Bob" Fitzsimmons, the middle-weight champion, and "Joe" Choyinski, Corbett's thrice-defeated heavy-weight opponent, gave the audience an opportunity to do some cheering during the wait for the appearance of the champions. A sensation was produced by a very innocent cause. At 8:30 in order to make the arena cool and comfortable. The tarpaulins which covered the place were pulled back from over all parts of the amphitheatre, save the ring itself. Therefore when a light shower fell there was a decided commotion in the assemblage. There were very few umbrellas in

Gentleman Jim whips the Boston Strong Boy at New Orleans on September 7, 1892.

Gentleman Jim whipping John L. Sullivan at New Orleans.

the crowd, but as the rain soon ceased and the tarpaulins were replaced over the roof, the disturbance subsided, and the spectators patiently awaited the approach of 9 o'clock and the entrance of the gladiators.

Ex-Mayor Guillotte entered the ring at 8:50 and made the address advising perfect quiet and fair treatment to each man without personal remarks. He was interrupted by the appearance of Sullivan, and a moment later by Corbett, both of whom were greeted with tremendous cheering. Sullivan was attired in green trunks with legs bare, his feet being covered with black socks and fighting shoes. Corbett wore the fancy mascot belt his wife knit for him, but detached it before the fight began and left it exposed to view only a gray pair of trunks; his legs were also bare. On behalf of the club, Capt. Barrett of the police force presented Prof. Duffy a handsome punch bowl of silver as a token of the appreciation by the club of his services as referee. Sullivan showed up in splendid shape, massive in proportions, and showing every sign of good training. Corbett, taller and slighter, looked equally well trained, but not as strong. He looked happy and confident, and chatted with friends outside of the ring while he waited for his gloves to be adjusted.

Sullivan, on the contrary, was cautious, and submitted to a little rubbing from McAuliffe without a word. When fighters and seconds were called up for final directions from the referee, he said hardly a word, while Corbett asked questions and gesticulated pleasantly. Agreeably to his promise, expressed early in the afternoon, Sullivan did not wear the plasters over his stomach to which Corbett had objected.

Sullivan experienced great difficulty in putting on the five-ounce gloves, and it took several powerful tugs and assistances from McAuliffe to put the giant's hands into the mittens. Corbett's shapely hands slipped into his pair with ease. Behind the gigantic form of the Boston man were "Charley" Johnson, "Jack" McAuliffe, "Joe" Lannon, and "Phil" Casey. Corbett's seconds were "Billy" Delaney, "Jim" Daley, and "Prof." John Donaldson. Prof. "Mike" Donovan, who had received instructions from the New-York Athletic Club not to go behind either man, could not resist the temptation to help. He lay outside Corbett's corner and fanned him industriously during each intermission. Sullivan's form was massive; his structure, so often described, was at its best. The big muscles behind his shoulders bulged out hard and heavy and his arms were embodiment of power. There was just a suggestion of heaviness about him. The flesh about his stomach was white, and that portion of his body was not at all as flat as prize fighters usually is. His weight just before entering the ring was 212 pounds.

Corbett was clotted with muscles. He was slight, but all the flesh on him was muscle. His stomach was covered with knots of sinew. His chest was hard but flexible. His back, while no ways as ponderous as Sullivan's, was hard, firm, and deep with muscle. His large arms were a mass of sinew molded into ideal athletic form. His weight, taken for record before he stepped into the ring, was 187 pounds.

Corbett from the beginning was confident, and he showed his ability to stop Sullivan and avoid his blows. He was happy and smiling. His tactics at first were purely defensive and he ducked, he sprang, he even ran out of Sullivan's reach; but it was by no means a walking-around match. Even at the beginning he faced his adversary, countered, stopped, and swung, and was away with lightning quickness before return could be administered. His early campaign was to tire and blow Sullivan. With this view he kept bothering the big man into following him, swinging heavily at him and not finding him there. Then, when he drew blood in the fifth, he made a target of Sullivan's nose and mouth, jabbed him alternately in the stomach and the nose, and battered his man badly.

About this time Sullivan began to appreciate the fact that it was the next thing to the impossible for him to reach the Californian. Nevertheless, he rushed at him and would only desist when his nose came up short against Corbett's left.

In the tenth Sullivan rushed the fighting in a vain attempt to finish the fight then. None of the big bets depended on a result in that round.

When the end came it was unexpected. John L. had been bleeding from the nose, and his lips were swollen and sore, but even Corbett men expected him to stay in the ring as many rounds more, but Corbett's finishing strokes were lightning in speed and force. Three times the left went into Sullivan's face. Four times the right smashed on the swollen nose and mouth. Then Sullivan collapsed. He went down hands first, then knees, then shoulders. He tried to push himself up, and did get his hands off the ground. The referee then began counting the ten seconds, but Sullivan had not really risen from the ground. The idol had fallen; the huzzas of the crowd greeted the new pugilist king.

The battle commenced at 9:10. Both men stepped lightly to the centre of the ring. Sullivan immediately became the aggressor. He made a left lead and was stopped. Corbett danced all about his opponent, eyeing him closely. Sullivan made a rush, but Jim backed away; he also attempted a left-hander, but Jim would not bite. Sullivan looked vicious as he played for an opening; he attempted a right-hand stomach punch, but the blow fell short. Sullivan tried to corner Jim, but the latter slipped away. The gong sounded and not a blow had been landed by either man.

Sullivan was still the aggressor in the second. He attempted a left for the head and missed it, Jim slipping neatly away from a left-hand swing. A moment later the men came to a clinch and Jim aimed a left-hander. Sullivan upper-cut Jim in a duck and touched him again with his left hand a little later. Jim eyed his man closely, and when Sullivan would rush the Californian would slip away. Sullivan landed a heavy right on the shoulder, but received a stomach punch in return.

Corbett ducked away in the third from a heavy lunge. Sullivan followed him about the ring, trying for stomach. Jim's head missed a heavy left-hander, and Sullivan looked vicious. Jim landed two heavy stomach punches, and duly missed a vicious right; both hit each other on the head. Corbett stepped out of harm's way. He came back quickly and landed his left on the stomach. He also planted heavy left on the champion's ear, sending his head back. Both men were fighting hard when the gong sounded. Sullivan was ringing wet from perspiration.

Sullivan missed his left again in the fourth, but he chased Jim around the ring. Sullivan landed a light left, Corbett stepped up close, attempting to punch the stomach, but John was guarding that member with his right hand. The champion followed his opponent all over the ring and received a heavy left-hand swing on the head for his pains. Corbett was standing well up in this round against the great gladiator with whom he was fighting. Jim landed both hands on Sullivan's head as the round ended, and the champion went to his corner with a sneering smile.

In the fifth round Sullivan stepped to the centre with a smile and Corbett touched his nose with a left. The champion tried to land a left on the stomach and the men clinched, Sullivan landing his first heavy right. Sullivan missed a fearful left hand, and staggered forward from the force of the blow. The men boxed cautiously for an opening and the champion seemed eager for hot work. He followed his antagonist all around the ring and first blood came from Sullivan's nose. The fight was fast and furious and Sullivan nearly fell on the ropes from left hand jabs on the head. As the round ended Corbett landed a heavy right on the champion's head.

Both men landed light lefts in the sixth, and Sullivan's nose was bleeding again. The champion was beginning to look tired, for he missed a heavy right aimed for the jaw. Corbett took plenty of time and used the entire ring to manœuvre in. He landed a light left on the stomach and punched the champion on the face. A little later there was heavy exchange of lefts on the head; Sullivan seemed to be angry, and slapped his opponent with his left hand. Corbett landed with blows on the head and ran away. The men were in the centre of the ring, and it began to look like some of the fight was out of Sullivan. Jim landed a heavy left on Sullivan's head, and the champion went to his corner looking tired.

Corbett in the seventh walked right up to Sullivan and barely avoided a left-hand punch. The champion was trying his hardest for the right on the jaw, but foxy Corbett was not there. The champion landed two light blows on the head and Corbett sent in a hot shot for the left on the nose. He jabbed Sullivan continually on the nose in this round and blood flowed freely. Jim was cheered to the echo for his skillful fighting. Sullivan's only hope was looked for from his heavy right. Sullivan was forced on the ropes by a heavy right on the jaw, and as the gong sounded he received a heavy left on the jaw.

On the eighth Sullivan landed light left on the stomach, and received the left on the mouth. Jim was now the aggressor, forcing the champion toward the post, and Sullivan, attempting a left-hand stomach punch, slipped away. Sullivan hit Corbett in a clinch and the audience yelled "foul:" both exchanged heavy lefts, but Jim's head missed the mighty right. Jim barely escaped the right and sent his left in the champion's stomach, forcing him to the ropes. Jim landed heavy left on the mouth, which brought blood and a smile from the champion. Sullivan looked very tired as the gong sent them to their corners.

The men got in the middle of the ring in the ninth and Jim's head barely missed two swings. Sullivan was puffing and both exchanged good lefts. Sullivan received a light one on the ear and got another on the nose, but evened up matters a little with his right. Jim landed a heavy left on the nose and both men hugged each other in the clinch. Sullivan was missing many blows now, though when he did land, it was twice as heavy as his antagonist's. Both men landed light lefts, but the Californian landed heavy on the stomach; as the gong sounded Jim had all the best of Sullivan and went to his corner looking like the victor.

Sullivan attempted to land his left in the tenth, but the blow was very short. He followed his opponent, however, and both exchanged lefts. Corbett's right found the champion's head and his left got there a moment later, but the champion landed on the head in return. This was a great fight so far, and Corbett apparently had the admiration of the crowd, as he was doing most of the hitting. When the round ended Corbett was lustily cheered.

Both landed good blows in the eleventh, and Sullivan got twisted around from the force of his left. Corbett showed great ability, even at clinching his more bulky opponent. Sullivan was extremely cautious, though he got a crushing blow on the nose. Jim tried to deliver a heavy right-hand blow, and the champion was forced to the ropes to avoid it. Sullivan received a punch in the stomach from the left and got it again a moment later.

In the twelfth Sullivan was last to respond, and when he did he got a left in the stomach. He got it again very heavily and a repetition a moment later. Sullivan landed a fairly good blow with his right, though he got the left in the stomach in return. Jim landed another left in the stomach and ran away smiling. The Californian landed a good left on the head, but the champion stopped the right with his shoulder. Sullivan made a vicious rush, and Corbett clipped him in the stomach with his left. The champion's head was forced back twice from two heavy left-handers, and the round wound up with both Corbett's hands in Sullivan's stomach.

Round thirteen found Jim first up again. Dodging the usual left lead from the champion, he slipped away from the left a moment later, and the men boxed scientifically for an opening. Sullivan could not draw his antagonist on with left-hand feints, but he barely touched his body with the left; the men's toes touched, they stood so close, and Sullivan never attempted to land the right, his left was short, Corbett stepping away. Sullivan was now forcing matters, but carefully. He got a left on the nose that sent his head far back, though the champion landed light on the head.

In the fourteenth the Californian's stock was sky-high, and he stepped to his opponent, though he got a left on the nose for his pains. Both men landed good blows. Corbett landed the left and Sullivan the right; both men got heavy blows on the head and Sullivan was pushed back with the left. Again both men got in good lefts, though the first blow was the heavier of the two. Jim landed a left on Sullivan's face and slipped away. Sullivan landed on the forehead, but in attempting to land his left fell into a corner, standing closely to his man. Honors were easy.

Corbett was first to the centre in the fifteenth. Sullivan made his famous rush and forced his man all over the ring, though he was nearly knocked down with a right. The men clinched and separated, Sullivan receiving a right on the ear. The latter landed his left on Jim's nose, but his stomach was uncoved and he received a heavy blow. Jim landed the usual left on the head, but he got the right on the body in return. Both men landed lefts, Sullivan missed his vicious right for the body. Both men received light lefts, though Jim recorded a heavy stomach punch as the round ended.

The sixteenth round commenced with a rally. Sullivan received the left on his dial; he attempted a left lead for the head, and Jim saved himself by pulling away.

The champion's head was pushed back once more. Sullivan landed heavily on the nose and stomach a moment later. Jim looked very fresh as he punched the champion in the head and stomach. Sullivan received two good punches, and Jim clinched. During the lock Sullivan hit his opponent and the audience yelled "foul," though Corbett refused to have the victory that way.

Jim was first up again, in the seventeenth round, looking none the worse for wear. Sullivan landed a good left, though his right for the body was short. Sullivan was breathing hard. Jim neatly avoided a left for the face, but sent his own fist home a moment later on Sullivan's head. Sullivan's face was very red, and he received a left-hand swing in the stomach for coming too close. Both exchanged light lefts and boxed for an opening for the right. No severe punishment was administered to either man in this round.

Jim Corbett was, as usual, first to respond in the eighteenth. A beautiful rally took place in the centre of the ring. Jim landed two stomach punches, but got two light punches on the head. A fearful left-hand jab on the nose was presented to John and he got a hot one on the head for being too familiar. Jim's left found the champion's stomach and face, and also the head; later, John L. landed a right punch on the ribs that sounded all over the house, though he got a left swing in the stomach a moment later. Sullivan was extremely cautious, although he got four heavy rights on the face. This was all Corbett's round.

In the nineteenth round both men were quick to respond. They boxed cautiously, Sullivan landing, and "Jim" retaliated on the stomach and then stepped away from a heavy right, and the champion looked tired. Sullivan's left was continually in motion, seemingly from the rattles. The Californian looked too clever for him and he laughed sarcastically at the champion as he leisurely boxed for an opening. Corbett landed two quick lefts in the stomach and Sullivan lost his temper from a staggering right, rushed at his opponent, but he looked like a beaten man.

Sullivan looked tired for the twentieth round, and his left was very short; he was blowing hard and seemed very cautious, but he was the same resolute, ferocious man of yore. Both exchanged rights, and Sullivan was beaten to the ropes with a right and left. The champion was nearly knocked down with the left on the stomach and right on the head. Corbett was dead game and unhurt so far. Sullivan tried a right, and received five clips on the head and stomach. The champion's knees were shaking, and he seemed unable to defend himself. Sullivan was fought to the ropes with heavy rights and lefts, and the gong seemed his only safety.

The twenty-first round was the last. Corbett was the first to respond to time. Sullivan's left lead was very weak, and he seemed anxious to wait. His opponent was with him, however, saw the championship bee in his bonnet, and the champion received a left on the nose. Sullivan was trying for the right, though he made little attempt to send it home. Sullivan was beaten down with heavy rights and lefts, falling to the ground. He attempted to rise and fight, but nature gave way and he fell and was counted out, and Corbett was proclaimed the champion of America by Referee Duffy.

The ovation that Corbett received was something tremendous, and he walked around the ring kissing and hugging his friends. Sullivan afterward made a speech in the centre of the ring, saying that he was glad America got the championship. He had fought once too often in the ring.

WITH THE CITY CROWDS.

A great many men of this town, young, middle-aged, and old, endured a lot of physical discomfort last night to get the tidings from New-Orleans as fast as telegraph wires could bring the bulletins and strong-voiced announcers tell the story thus spread out in chapters. Up town the centre of interest in the fight was on the stretch of Broadway from Twenty-fourth to Thirty-fourth Street, and in the neighboring streets where all the resorts for sporting men had the advantages of the telegraphed bulletins, and that part of the city looked almost as animated as on an election night.

JEFFRIES WINS FROM FITZSIMMONS

Youth and Muscle Overmatch Science and Pluck.

CONTEST ENDS IN 11TH ROUND

Boxers Get About $25,000 Cash and Contingent Profits.

The Winner Is Now Champion of the World — Great Crowds Gather to Obtain News of the Event.

The long-heralded prizefight, known by a pleasant fiction of New York law as a boxing contest, between Robert Fitzsimmons, who held the championship of the world, and James J. Jeffries, the aspiring boilermaker from California, was fought last night in the building of the New Coney Island Sporting Club.

It resulted in an indisputable victory for Jeffries in the eleventh round. Consequently the world has a new champion pugilist this morning, and Fitzsimmons, who knocked out Corbett, who knocked out Sullivan, has taken his place in the long procession of fistic heroes known in ring circles as "back numbers" or "has beens."

The work of changing champions occupied a little less than forty-four minutes. How much the two men gained in money nobody knows. On a rough estimate it is said that Fitzsimmons, whose dignity demanded large pecuniary inducements to tempt him to display his prowess upon a comparatively unknown man, will receive about $25,000 of the gate receipts as his share, besides contingent profits from the vitascope, which took photographs of the fight and will reproduce them indefinitely.

Jeffries will do as well and is probably richer by a comfortable amount in side bets, to say nothing of gratuities from winners, who are naturally all his enthusiastic friends.

The room in which the battle was fought is 200 feet long by 100 wide, and is 40 feet high. Ceilings, walls, and rafters are stained a light brown. From the arena tiers of seats arise to within fifteen feet of the ceiling.

In the centre of the arena rises the square platform, with the three stout manila ropes inclosing the square in which the fighting was done. Over the ring, up among the rafters, four strong arc lamps were hung. Twenty other arc lamps, equidistant, hang alongside the arena. High above the ring hung a square, flying gallery, suspended from the rafters by iron rods.

At 9 o'clock all the arena seats were occupied, and the tiers of seats banked at each side and the ends presented masses of white faces and shirt fronts. There was a clamor of thousands of tongues and a cloud of tobacco smoke drifting up and gathering in a haze against the roof.

A WELL-DRESSED CROWD.

It was a well-dressed gathering. There was not a shabby man in sight anywhere, nor were there many whose dress indicated the sporting man. Immediately about the ring there were rows of middle-aged and elderly men, some of them with white hair and beards. These had a distinctively well-fed and well-groomed appearance, and diamonds flashed from their fingers and shirt fronts in the electric light. But for the diamonds and the formidable cigars at which many of them pulled, they might have been taken for vestrymen waiting for the opening of a religious service, so tranquil was their demeanor, so calm were their countenances and the peace of their attitudes.

There were old and young men who had traveled more than a thousand miles and spent hundreds of dollars to reach the ringside, and they were content to be there. Some of them had thousands and ten of thousands of dollars at stake, but it is against sporting ethics to display emotion and the prevalent face was impassive, even though it might sometimes pale or flush.

Only the newspaper men and the police seemed to be busy or interested. A casual observer, dropping in through the roof from some distant country, would have thought the crowd had gathered for an evening which it expected to be rather a bore.

The preliminary demonstration was all from the seats looking down upon the arena. The younger men there were more restless and eager and alert than the veterans below, and vented their feelings in cheers and handclapping on trivial provocations.

JEFFRIES LOOKED ANGRY.

There was a great cheer and a rattle of applause when Jeffries walked in a little after 9 o'clock, pushing his way through the men packed along the arena. He looked huge and rather angry than pleased, and,

Jeffries

Fitzsimmons

with his red sweater under a sack coat, and a flimsy cap on the back of his head resting on his thick black hair, was the most carelessly dressed and the roughest-looking man in the room. There was a fainter cheer as Fitzsimmons was announced, and after his disappearance there were symptoms of impatience and cries and hoots began to sound from around the house.

The rumor that there was a dispute over the rules had gone abroad, and it caused impatience and dissatisfaction. The uncertainty of Chief of Police Devery's intentions added to the uneasy feeling. The men there had not come to see whether Fitzsimmons or Jeffries was the better boxer. They wanted to see which was the "best man," which could hit hardest, endure the most pain and fatigue, keep his head, and use his skill the better when breath was coming hard and short and the body was sore and the muscles tired and resenting the fearful strain upon them.

At 10 o'clock there were yet vacant patches in the expanses of reserved seats opposite the ring on each side. The crowd amused itself watching workmen on the flying platform patch a broken railing and put the finishing touches on the rows of black vitascope machines, which looked like mortars trained on the ring below. Stamping in imitation of drum beats, whistles and cat calls, and ironical cheers relieved the monotony.

FLOWERS FOR FITZSIMMONS.

But the annoyance of waiting seemed to be forgotten when a cheer began at the eastern end of the great building, and the men there were seen to rise in their seats. The mass of humanity surged up like a great wave as a mound of roses appeared moving through the throng down on the floor. This was a gigantic horseshoe of pink, white, and crimson roses, with American flags above it, and bearing the inscription, "Good Luck to the Champion."

Behind this aesthetic proclamation, which was carried by two men, Fitzsimmons stalked solemnly, like the chief figure in a classic spectacle. His bearing was solemn, like that of a man who felt that he was about to perform a rite with the eyes of an admiring world concentrated upon him. He wore a bath robe of pale blue, gathered at the waist, and his head was bare. His three attendants, in white flannel undershirts and long trousers, followed him, two of them bearing galvanized iron buckets and broad palm-leaf fans, one of them with a long bottle driven into his hip pocket.

Jeffries was more on the rough-and-ready order. He moved briskly and swung his shoulders and wore a red sweater, with suspenders over it, and the breeches of ordinary, commonplace humanity; but his three seconds carried the galvanized iron buckets and the bottles and fans and were also in their undershirts.

AN AESTHETIC FEATURE.

A stray wounded moth had been fluttering about the padded surface of the ring, and as the big floral piece was carried in many of the roses tumbled to pieces. Therefore, it was another aesthetic feature of the affair that the first actual preliminary was to clear the ring of moth and rose leaves, which was done with one of the big fans.

Fitzsimmons, sitting on his wooden stool in his corner, watched this operation with interest. Jeffries, from his stool in his corner, twisted his neck and peered between the men who surrounded him, trying to catch a view of his antagonist.

Then came the referee, George Siler, in blue and white striped undershirt, collarless and bareheaded. He leaned negligently against the ropes in an unoccupied corner while the seconds inspected the gloves and other seconds fitted them on.

Fitzsimmons rubbed his hands together before he submitted to be gloved, his air being that of a man who rather expected to enjoy himself. Jeffries leaned over and rubbed his palms on the floor to get resin upon them. Billy Brady leaned against the ropes opposite the press stalls, and bit the top one idly. Nobody in or around the ring was excited or hurried. One of the seconds held a fan over Fitzsimmons's head as Eastern attendants hold umbrellas of state above potentates.

By this time the spectators had all arrived and it was seen that men of several classes were elbow to elbow and cheek by jowl. There were sporting men and business men, financiers and actors, society men and jockeys, and distributed among them all were the denizens of South Brooklyn, who always can afford to buy a front seat at a prize fight in or around New York.

MRS. FITZSIMMONS PRESENT.

Mrs. Fitzsimmons got into the clubhouse, and was in her husband's dressing room while he was preparing for the battle, but she decided not to attempt to witness the fight. She saw William A. Brady, the manager of Jeffries, shook hands with him, and remarked:

"We will beat your man again to-night, as we did the other at Carson City."

Brady smiled and replied that he hoped not, and Mrs. Fitzsimmons, after seeing that her husband was properly equipped for the fray, kissed him, and wishing him good luck, sent him out into the arena.

George E. Smith, ("Pittsburg Phil,") a man who never in his career on the turf, even when a decision of $100,000 depended on an inch of ground, was known to betray excitement, caused some surprise by becoming one of the most enthusiastic of the shouters. He was a Jeffries man, and his excitement was in marked contrast to the cool demeanor of some of the others.

About 10:17 Jeffries's seconds, with serious demeanor, began to withdraw his trousers, and a hundred pencils in the press stalls were instantly busy with the chronicle of this portentous fact.

Two journalists with split second watches had quite an energetic dispute as to whether the ceremony began at 10:17 or 10:17¼. There was also a solemn drawing of corks from the bottles and an unfolding and laying aside of large towels. About the same time Fitzsimmons untied and put away his pale-blue robe and revealed himself naked but for trunks and shoes with black stockings turned down nearly to his ankles. The trunks were ornamented with rosettes of red, white, and blue. Jeffries also wore trunks, shoes, and stockings. His trunks were plain white.

A PERFUNCTORY HANDSHAKE.

Then they gargled their throats from the bottles and met each other at the centre of the ring, where they shook hands coldly and perfunctorily.

There was silence throughout the house by this time. The contrast between the two was startling. Fitzsimmons looked little and white confronting his antagonist. Jeffries is a dark man. His eyes and hair are black and his skin almost a tan. Fitzsimmons is light-eyed and what hair he has is pale red. No woman has a skin whiter or smoother than his.

The word was given and the men rose from the stools to which they had returned. Neither looked cheerful. Jeffries swallowed hard; Fitzsimmons moistened his lips with his tongue, and as he faced his man and they slowly and cautiously circled about, feinting, advancing, and retreating, never within arm's length, their eyes intently fastened on each other, he began to work his lips nervously.

THEY FACE EACH OTHER.

If the crowd had been a crowd of dead men, the stillness could not have been deeper than it was. The two pugilists trod softly as cats. Nothing could be heard but the gentle thud, thud of their ever restless, shifting feet as they circled.

Then there was a sudden rush and the sharp slap of a glove landing, a gleaming of arms and twisting and violent motion of white bodies in the ring, a storm of cries, with applause and some roaring laughter from arena and encompassing seats.

Jeffries had led. He was not afraid to fight. That was one point settled.

Fitzsimmons's light blue eyes opened wide and blazed angrily. Jeffries crouched low, keeping his tremendous left arm well thrust out, his head down, looking from under his eyebrows.

In the second round the cheering and shouting began again. The crowd then felt that it would see what it had gathered to see—a fight with hard knocks. The two men in the ring smiled at each other as both missed and they came together in a clinch, but the big muscles in their thighs were already quivering and they did not relax their watchfulness the fraction of a second.

The crowd was evidently with Jeffries, and after Fitzsimmons had tumbled on his back, looking a much-surprised man, joy was unrestrained. It was evident then that the ideas of Chief of Police Devery on slugging were liberal, and that there would be no interference. The older sporting men around the ring, their last fear removed, settled down more placidly and calmly than ever and looked entirely and supremely happy.

After the sixth round a new change came into Fitzsimmons's face. He had looked furious at times and amused at times, as he felt that he had scored a point or that his antagonist had missed one.

FITZSIMMONS WORRIED.

Now he looked old and worn and anxious. Wrinkles seemed to come into his cheeks. He was aggressive, crafty, watchful, always moving, his rather cruel lips working and working as if he would like to bite; but he seemed like a man who is hunted. Once or twice thereafter his lips broke into a smile. When he and Jeffries broke out of a clinch and separated at the end of the eighth round, their mutual grins were almost affable. But as he sat on his stool and breathed fast and his seconds fanned him furiously with towels and fans and gave him from the bottle to gargle, he looked harassed.

When the end came it seemed very quick and easy. The blow that really did the work was given with Jeffries's left glove. After it was delivered Fitzsimmons stood an instant, his hands hanging by his side, his knees bowed. The knock-out with the right came swiftly. It was given from the hip, much like a quick slap. It was not like one of the long, hard swings Jeffries had aimed at him several times, and which had gone over his head.

When it landed Fitzsimmons fell and turned on his right side. There was no need to count. His body was limp and doubled up. He passed the back of his hand wearily over his bald forehead and straightened out on his back, his lower lip hanging foolishly, his long upper lip scarlet.

Jeffries looked at him an instant and walked to his corner, breathing hard. A thousand men were storming and swirling about the ringside then.

Hats were waving and the big hall was ringing with yells and cheers and exultant laughter.

Fitzsimmons was dragged to his stool, his heels trailing helplessly on the floor. It was all over.

DEVERY AND SILER TALK.

After the knockout blow had been dealt Chief of Police Devery jumped to the outer edge of the ring and waited for the referee to count the fatal tenth second. He stepped into the ring then and his men surrounded it. He was asked in the ring by a reporter for THE NEW YORK TIMES whether, in accordance with his declaration of a few days ago, he would arrest the principals.

"Wait a few moments and we will see," he replied. And then as he saw that Fitzsimmons had recovered sufficiently to sit up and answer the greeting and hand-shake Jeffries offered him, he added:

"No, there will be no arrests. Fitzsimmons is all right now, and the law has not been violated. He is as well as when he entered the ring, according to the report of Dr. Creamer, who examined him; so an arrest is not necessary."

"I wish it to be said, and said distinctly, that neither Mr. McLaughlin nor any other man made me change my opinion regarding the stand I took two days before the fight. I would have stopped the fight in a minute if I had seen anything that was a violation of the law."

George Siler, the referee, and Chief Devery had a short talk, and then the referee declared to a reporter for THE NEW YORK TIMES that the fight was one of the best he had ever witnessed.

"It was Jeffries's fight from start to finish," he said, "and if the fight had been stopped at any time previous to the knockout, the decision would have to have been in Jeffries's favor. Several times during the fight it looked as if one or the other was tired, and some little hugging was attempted, but I stepped in and stopped this. There were positively no fouls in this fight."

SCENES ON THE OUTSIDE.

When Fitzsimmons emerged from his quarters preparatory to the start to the scene of the fight his carriage was surrounded by a crowd numbering several thousand persons who escorted him to the big pavilion. As the procession moved along it gained in size, and by the time the clubhouse was reached it was almost large enough to block the fighter's way into the building. Into the throng dashed headlong the ticket speculator with his cry of "They're cheap at seven," meaning that five-dollar seats had advanced in price.

Shortly after Fitzsimmons's carriage had reached the clubhouse a small figure enveloped in a long mackintosh slipped down the avenue toward the pavilion. Some one in the crowd set up the cry, "It's Bob's wife—there goes Mrs. Fitzsimmons." The cry caused a rush to set in toward the clubhouse.

A dozen ball players early in the evening gathered around "Tim" Hurst, the ex-umpire, noted as a referee of boxing matches, and who was advising his hearers to bet on Fitzsimmons. Actors made another group, while politicians, brokers, and business men generally were also in evidence. The usual number of hangers-on strolled around selling badges, flags, chewing gum, and trinkets of all kinds. It was such a sight, indeed, as has seldom been seen even on Coney Island.

BLUNDER COSTS GIANTS VICTORY

Merkle Rushes Off Base Line Before Winning Run Is Scored, and Is Declared Out.

CONFUSION ON BALL FIELD

Chance Asserts That McCormick's Run Does Not Count—Crowd Breaks Up Game.

UMPIRE DECLARES IT A TIE

Singular Occurrence on Polo Grounds Reported to President Pulliam, Who Will Decide Case.

Censurable stupidity on the part of player Merkle in yesterday's game at the Polo Grounds between the Giants and Chicagos placed the New York team's chances of winning the pennant in jeopardy. His unusual conduct in the final inning of a great game perhaps deprived New York of a victory that would have been unquestionable had he not committed a breach in baseball play that resulted in Umpire O'Day declaring the game a tie.

With the score tied in the ninth inning at 1 to 1 and the New York's having a runner, McCormick, on third base waiting for an opportunity to score and Merkle on first base looking for a similar chance, Bridwell hit into centre field. It was a fair hit ball and would have been sufficient to win the game had Merkle gone on his way down the base path while McCormick was scoring the winning run. But instead of Merkle going to second base to make sure that McCormick had reached home with the run necessary to a victory, Merkle ran toward the clubhouse, evidently thinking that his share in the game was ended when Bridwell hit the ball into safe territory.

Manager Chance of the Chicago Club quickly grasped the situation and directed that the ball be thrown to second base, which would force out Merkle, who had not reached that corner.

Manager Chance, who plays first base for the Chicago club, ran to second base and the ball was thrown there, but immediately Pitcher McGinnity interfered in the play and a scramble of players ensued, in which, it is said, McGinnity obtained the ball and threw it into the crowd before Manager Chance could complete a force play on Merkle, who was far away from the base line. Merkle said that he had touched second base, and the Chicago players were equally positive that he had not done so.

Manager Chance then appealed to Umpire O'Day, who was head umpire of the game, for a decision in the matter. The crowd, thinking that the Giants had won the game, swarmed upon the playing field in such a confusion that none of the "fans" seemed able to grasp the situation, but finally their attitude toward Umpire O'Day became so offensive that the police ran into the crowd and protected the umpire, while arguments were being hurled pro and con on the point in question by Manager Chance and McGraw and the umpire.

Umpire O'Day finally decided that the run did not count, and that inasmuch as the spectators had gained such large numbers on the field that the game could not be resumed O'Day declared the game a tie. Although both Umpires O'Day and Emslie, it is claimed, say that they did not see the play at second base, Umpire O'Day's action in declaring that McCormick's run did not count was based upon the presumption or fact that a force play was made on Merkle at second base. The rule covering such a point is as follows:

One run shall be scored every time a base runner, after having legally touched the first three bases, shall legally touch the home base before three men are put out, provided, however, that if he reach home on or during a play in which the third man be forced out or

Fred Merkle

be put out before reaching first base a run shall not count. A force-out can be made only when a base runner legally loses the right to the base he occupies and is thereby obliged to advance as the result of a fair hit ball not caught on the fly.

The singular ending of the game aroused intense interest throughout the city, and everywhere it was the chief topic of discussion. Early in the evening a report was widely circulated that President Pulliam had decided the game was a tie and must be played again. When this rumor reached Mr. Pulliam he authorized the following statement:

"I made no decision in the matter at all and I will not do so until the matter is presented to me in proper form. The statement on the 'ticker' that I had decided the game a tie is entirely unauthorized."

But according to Umpire O'Day the game is a tie and will remain so until either the National League or the National Commission decides the matter. Last night Umpire O'Day made an official report of the dispute to President Pulliam. Manager Chance declared that the game was a tie, and the management of the Giants has recorded the game as a 2 to 1 victory.

The result of this game may prove to be the deciding factor in the championship race, and inasmuch as it is a serious matter to be dealt with President Pulliam may ask the league to act upon the question or go still further and place it in the hands of the National Commission—the supreme court of baseball.

In any event there will be no double-header this afternoon, and it may be several days before the problem will be decided. The official reporter of the league in New York credits the Giants with a victory, but, of course, this is subject to any action President Pulliam or the league may take in the matter.

President Murphy of the Chicago Club last night entered formal claim to yesterday's Chicago-New York game in behalf of Chicago. President Murphy bases his claim on the ground that Merkle of the New York team, who was at first when the ball was hit safely to centre by Bridwell in the ninth inning, had failed to continue to second when his team mate scored the winning run from third. President Murphy entered his claim in a letter to President Harry C. Pulliam of the National League, wherein Mr. Murphy cites in support of his contention the decision rendered in the game at Pittsburg, Sept. 4, between Pittsburg and Chicago, in which precisely the same contingency, he asserts, arose. The Chicago club protested the game, but the protest was not allowed, because the single umpire who officiated declared that he had not seen the play. In yesterday's game the omission of Merkle to continue to second, Mr. Murphy declares, was noted by Umpire O'Day.

CLASSY AND THRILLING BALL.

Third Battle of Leading Teams Produces Sensational Sport.

Well, anyway, it was a classy baseball game from the time in the first inning when Roger Bresnahan makes an entrance, accompanied by a dresser, who does him and undoes him in his natty mattress and knee pads, till the end of the ninth, when Bridwell singles safely to centre, bringing in what looks like the winning run.

And, from a spectacular point of view, that mix-up at the finish was just the appropriate sensation to a bang-up, all-a-quiver game. They all know they have seen a mighty snappy game of ball; that New York has brought over one more run than the enemy, whether the run counts or not; that McGinnity in holding on to the ball after the ninth-inning run, has done so with the idea that it belongs to the home team, and that good Master O'Day has said, as he exits: "I didn't see the play on second—the run doesn't count."

Up to the climactic ninth it was the toss of a coin who would win. For here is our best-beloved Mathewson pitching as only champions pitch, striking out the power and the glory of the Cubs, numbering among his slain Schulte in the first, Pfeister in the third, Steinfeldt in the fourth, Pfeister in the fifth, Haydon and Schulte in the sixth, Hayden in the eighth, and Evers and Schulte in the ninth—these last in one-two order. Proper pitching, and for this and other things we embrace him.

But then, Pfeister is pitching good ball, too. Not so good as the Matty article, for this isn't to be expected, or desired, even. Pfeister doesn't strike anybody out, and Pfeister gives an occasional base on balls, and once he hits a batter, but aside from these irregularities Pfeister must be accounted in the king row of Wednesday matinée pitchers. The gentleman who feels the weight of the delivery, and thereafter takes his base, is the plodsome McCormick. It is in the second inning, and Pfeister whirls up a curve that doesn't break right. In fact, it breaks directly in McCormick's tummy, and Pfeister is forced to figure that the joke's on him. After the heroic Dr. Creamer has emptied half a hydrant on the prostrate McCormick the latter walks wanly to first, but he has to wait to walk home till the ninth inning.

Meantime, the game has progressed swiftly, remarkable for excellent plays by a number of us on either side, and remarkable also for the in-and-out work of Evers at second for Chicago.

It is in the fifth that the Cubs, or one of them, find the solitary run that represents the day's work. Hofman has been thrown out at first by Bridwell, and then the admirable Tinker takes his bat in his hand and faces Matty with determination writ large on his expressive features. Mr. Tinker drives the ball away out to right centre for what would be a two-bagger if you or I had made it, gentle reader—and this is no disparagement of the Tinker, for he is well seeming in our sight. As the ball approaches Master Donlin this good man attempts to field it with his foot. It's a home run all right, when you get down to scoring, but if this Donlin boy was our boy we'd have sent him to bed without his supper, and ye mind that, Mike.

We found the stick all right in the sixth, and tied the score. Herzog—and, by the way, he led the batting list yesterday in the absence of Tenney; that is, the playing absence, for Fred was among those present in the stand—Herzog, then, belts boldly to Steinfeldt, and it's a hit all right, but the throw that Steinfeldt makes to first is particularly distressing, and Herzy goes on to second. Bresnahan yields up a sacrifice bunt. Donlin hits over second base, Herzog scores, and 18,000 people go out of their minds.

It is at this stage of the game that reputable prophets speak confidently of ten innings, mayhap eleven, or so many thereof as may be pulled off before day becomes night. But darkness never stops this Wednesday game at the Polo Grounds. It goes the limit without interference by the dimming skies. We fancy ourselves mightily in the ninth, after Devlin has made a clean single to centre. To be sure, Seymour has just gone out at first on a throw by Evers, but we have a chance. Devlin is on first, and the start is splendid. But here is McCormick, with a drive over to Evers, who throws out Devlin at second, and we're not very far advanced—and two are down and out. Merkle, who failed us the day before in an emergency is at bat, and we pray of him that he mend his ways. If he will only single we will ignore any errors he may make in the rest of his natural life.

On this condition, Merkle singles. McCormick advances to third, and everybody in the inclosure slaps everybody else and nobody minds. Perfect ladies are screaming like a batch of Coney barkers on the Mardi Gras occasion, and the elderly banker behind us is beating our hat to a pulp with his gold-handled cane. And nobody minds. Aided by these indications of the popular sentiment, Master Bridwell hits safely to centre, McCormick trots home, the reporter boys prepare to make an asterisk under the box score of the game with the line—"Two out when winning run was scored"—the merry villagers flock on the field to worship the hollow where the Mathewson feet have pressed, and all of a sudden there is a doings around second base. McGinnity, walking off the field with the ball, as is the custom of some member of the winning team, is held up by Tinker and Evers, who insist that the run does not count, as Merkle has not touched second. And then begins the argument which will keep us in talk for the rest of the season, and then some. Certainly the Cubs have furnished us sport. W. W. AULICK.

Bewildering biography of a grizzly—

CHICAGO.	AB	R	H	PO	A	NEW YORK.	AB	R	H	PO	A
Hayden, rf.	4	0	0	1	0	Herzog, 2b.	8	1	1	1	1
Total...	30	1	5*	27	15	Bres'h'n, c.	3	0	0	10	0
Schulte, lf.	4	0	0	1	0	Donlin, rf.	4	0	1	2	0
Chance, 1b.	4	0	1	11	1	Seymour, cf.	4	0	1	1	0
St'nf'dt, 3b.	2	0	0	1	0	Devlin, 3b.	4	0	2	0	2
Hofman, cf.	3	0	1	0	0	McC'm'k, lf.	3	0	0	1	0
Tinker, ss.	3	1	1	8	6	Merkle, 1b.	3	0	1	10	1
Kling, c.	3	0	1	0	1	B'dwell, ss.	4	0	1	2	3
Pfeister, p.	3	0	0	1	0	M'th's'n, p.	3	0	0	0	2
Total...	30	1	5	27	15	Total...	31	1	7	27	9

Errors—Steinfeldt, Tinker, (2.)

Chicago	0	0	0	0	1	0	0	0	0	—1
New York	0	0	0	0	0	1	0	0	0	—1

Home run—Tinker. Sacrifice hits—Steinfeldt, Bresnahan. Double plays—Tinker and Chance, (2;) Evers and Chance; Mathewson, Bridwell, and Merkle. Left on bases—New York, 7; Chicago, 3. First base on balls—Off Pfeister, 2. First base on errors—New York, 2. Hit by pitcher—By Pfeister, 1. Struck out—By Pfeister, none; by Mathewson, 9. Time of game—One hour and thirty minutes. Umpires—Messrs. O'Day and Emslie.

AUTO CASE HELD OVER.

Racing Board Fails to Act on Disqualification of Drivers.

For more than three hours the Racing Board of the American Automobile Association wrestled with the recalcitrant Motor Racing Association yesterday afternoon without coming to any decision in reference to the disqualification of the entrants and participants in the recent unsanctioned twenty-four-hour race at Brighton Beach which the Motor Racing Association promoted. C. G. Wyckoff, President of the Motor Racing Association, and Harry S. Houpt, Treasurer of the association, appeared before the board informally and discussed the situation. While the meeting was harmonious, the subject was handled on both sides without gloves, but the atmosphere was probably slightly cleared by the plain speaking. Because of the unofficial character of the visit of the Motor Racing Association officials, the whole matter was laid over until next Saturday, when it will probably be taken up by the Racing Board for final settlement.

The actions of the board taken at yesterday's meeting concerned the Vanderbilt Cup race details. Arrangements were made with the owners of property at the junction of Jericho Turnpike and Woodbury Road, where the Flatiron turn occurs, so that the embankment can be razed to make the turn safe and several trees removed. It was also arranged that a three-quarter-mile stretch of the Jericho Pike should be resurfaced, while all the State and county roads will be treated with oil, beginning Oct. 1. There will be 2,200 gallons of oil spread under pressure to insure a dustless course. The building of a mile road eighteen feet wide has been begun, joining the Old Country Road and the beginning of the Parkway. It will be completed Oct. 1. Work was started by 200 men yesterday.

A change was made in the rules for the Vanderbilt Cup race whereby the clause declaring that a "car in each and every one of its parts and equipment must be entirely constructed in the country which it represents" shall not be considered to include tires. American cars may use foreign tires, or vice versa.

The members of the board present were Chairman Thompson and Messrs. Pardington, Graves, Budlong, Batchelder, Webb, Owen, Swain, and Elliott.

MERCEDES IN GRAND PRIZE.

Two German Cars Entered in the Race Under A. C. A. Sanction at Savannah.

The Automobile Club of America announced yesterday the receipt, through the Kaiserlicher Automobile Club of Germany, of two entries of Mercedes cars in the Grand Prize race at Savannah. The cars are to be driven at Savannah by Salzer and Poggie, who drove two of the three cars in the Grand Priz at Dieppe. Lautenschlager, the winner of the Grand Prix, will not consent to come to America. The two entries make ten cars entered thus far for the event, three Fiats, three Benz, a B. L. M., and an Acme car are the others. Twenty foreign cars are pledged and three other American cars.

The entries thus far secured for the twenty-four hour race at Brighton Beach include two Loziers, two Thomases, a Garford, Fiat, Renault, Simplex, Stearns, A-K, Acme, Pullman, and Cleveland for the big event, and of a Mercedes, Isotta, Fiat, Simplex, Stearns, Thomas, Moon, and A-K cars in the short races.

TRUBE CHAMPION RUNNER.

Run-Off of National Event Won Easily by New York A. C. Man.

The one-mile run for the senior championship of the Amateur Athletic Union, which was declared "no race" by Referee Sullivan on last Saturday, owing to the bungling of the judges in miscalling the number of laps to be run, was finally decided at Travers Island yesterday over a perfect track. As in the race on Saturday, Harry L. Trube of the New York Athletic Club finished in the lead, but this time he won with comparative east, leading Harvey Cohn of the Irish-American Athletic Club, the second man, by something like thirty-five yards, while J. H. Wright of the New West Side Athletic Club was fifteen yards back of Cohn. J. Murphy of the Irish-Americans was fourth, while Walter Becker and W. O'Connell of the New York Athletic Club did not finish. Trube covered the distance in 4:25, two and two-fifths seconds slower than the best time ever made over the track.

When the men were called on the track there were two absentees—W. Hay of Montreal and M. T. Morris of Brooklyn.

"All the News That's Fit to Print."

The New York Times.

THE WEATHER.
Fair to-day and to-morrow; continued cool; northerly winds.

VOL. LIX...NO. 19,155. * * * NEW YORK, TUESDAY, JULY 5, 1910.—EIGHTEEN PAGES. ONE CENT, In Greater New York, Jersey City, and Newark. { Elsewhere, TWO CENTS.

EIGHT KILLED IN FIGHT RIOTS

Clashes Between Races in Many Cities Follow Contest—Negroes the Victims.

A BATTLE IN GEORGIA

Armed Force Evicts Blacks from a Uvaldia Construction Camp, Slaying Three.

MANY FIGHTS OCCUR HERE

San Juan Hill and Hell's Kitchen Districts Prolific of Trouble—Gang Organized to Beat Up Colored Folk.

Riots between negroes and white men, attacks upon the former by the latter, and in many instances upon the whites by the blacks, occurred in all parts of the country yesterday evening as a result of Johnson's victory over Jeffries at Reno, Nev. Scores of negroes were injured seriously, and eight negroes were killed outright. One killing occurred in Houston, Texas. The negro's throat was slashed by a white man on a trolley car on which both were riding, and the negro bled almost to death before he could be taken to a hospital, where he died later. He had jeeringly proclaimed Johnson's victory. Three others were slain at Uvaldia, Ga., in a gang fight at a construction camp; one in Omaha, two in Little Rock, and a negro Constable was killed in Mounds, Ill., by rioters of his own race whom he tried to arrest.

In this city fights between whites and blacks were frequent throughout the night. Gangs of men and boys formed apparently for the sole purpose of beating up whatever negroes they could get their hands upon, and in many instances the negroes retaliated in part. Riot calls came into the West Thirty-seventh Street Police Station constantly throughout the evening. The centres of the local trouble were the districts known as Hell's Kitchen and San Juan Hill and in Harlem. Fifty-third Street, a negro section, was another source of almost constant trouble.

In St. Joseph, Mo., feeling ran so high that a mob attacked a white man who had taken the part of a negro against it, and the white victim was saved only by the intervention of the police. In Pittsburg the blacks stopped street cars and evicted the white passengers, ursurping their places. Four were sent to the hospital there.

From Washington, Philadelphia, Baltimore, New Orleans, Atlanta, Cincinnati, Louisville, Roanoke, St. Louis, St. Joseph, Macon, Little Rock, and Pueblo also came reports of conflicts between whites and blacks.

In Little Rock the conductor of a railroad train was shot by rioters who fought all over his train.

Probably the worst fight was that at Uvaldia. The conduct of the negroes in the construction camp near there so enraged the whites that an armed force marched against the camp to "clean it out." The invaders were met by volley after volley of pistol and rifle shots from the negroes, but none of the whites was injured. Their return fire, however, killed three negroes and wounded five others. The rest fled into the woods, where they are being hunted now by the whites.

MANY NEGROES LOCKED UP.

Whites Also Arrested After Race Fights Over Reno Contest.

Fights which in some instances assumed the proportions of a riot occurred in various sections of the city last night between white men and negroes over the outcome of the Jeffries-Johnson fight at Reno. In some cases the white man was at fault; in others the blame was put on the negroes, while in some it was hard to decide which was at fault.

In the "Hell's Kitchen" district, the "San Juan Hill" section on the west side, and the negro district of Harlem there were frequent encounters. Trouble was reported from other quarters also.

Assaults Reported Up to Midnight.

BRADLEY, WILLIAM, negro, 148 East Thirty-first Street; assaulted by white boys at Thirty-eighth Street and Ninth Avenue.

DUNCANSON, THOMAS V., West Indian negro; assaulted at Fortieth Street and Ninth Avenue, and badly beaten.

EDELIN, JOHN H., negro, 523 West Forty-eighth Street; assaulted by an unidentified white man; five scalp wounds and lacerated lips; assaulted at Forty-ninth Street and Eleventh Avenue; attended by Flower Hospital surgeon.

FANDANIKER, JAMES, white, of 552 West 120th Street; arrested for fighting with four negroes, who escaped.

GOLDBURN, EDMUND, a West Indian negro, 416 West Thirty-sixth Street; charged with attempting to assault James A. Graffe, white, of 241 West 111th Street; the negro was badly beaten; Goldburn had a pistol on him when arrested.

HENNION, ARTHUR, white, of 2,213 Eighth Avenue; arrested for fighting with four negroes, who escaped, over the result of the Jeffries-Johnson fight.

LEWIS, CHARLES, negro, Glenwood Avenue, East Orange, N. J.; found unconscious as a result of an assault at Thirty-eighth Street and Ninth Avenue; attended by New York Hospital surgeon.

O'FLAHERTY, NEIL, white; arrested for creating disturbance as a result of his failure to find a negro he could whip.

REYNOLDS, JOHN H., negro, 341 West Sixty-third Street; arrested on a charge of being concerned in the assault on Eugene O'Keefe; locked up in the West Thirty-seventh Street Station.

RICE, ABRAHAM, negro, cook, 480 West Thirty-sixth Street; charged with assaulting Eugene O'Keefe, white, with a bottle; locked up in the West Thirty-seventh Street Station.

SHETTLIN, WILFRED, negro laborer, 324 West Thirty-seventh Street; beaten over the head; attended by a New York Hospital surgeon.

TURNER, NELSON, a negro, 47 East 132d Street; arrested for carrying concealed weapons at Thirty-ninth Street and Ninth Avenue.

UNIDENTIFIED NEGRO found by Policeman Pritchard of West Forty-seventh Street Station at Fifty-ninth Street and Eleventh Avenue; taken to Flower Hospital, where it was said his skull was fractured; he will probably die.

WHITE, ALPHONSE, negro boy, 216 West Fortieth Street; arrested for carrying a

Continued on Page 4.

RAILWAY MEN'S HIGHER PAY.

Increases in Southeastern Territory—Pennsylvania's Employes Voting.

WASHINGTON, July 4.—F. P. Curtiss, Vice President of the Order of Railway Conductors, has announced the basis of the increase of pay to be given to conductors, flagmen, brakemen, and traveling baggage masters of railroads in Southeastern territory involved in the wage controversy just settled by the commission under the Erdman act. The increases will be allowed in two installments. The first is dated back to take effect from July 1 and the other is to go into effect next April 1.

The following is the increased new scale on the basis of 100 miles:

Conductors of passenger trains from $2.20 to $2.50, and on April 1, 1911, $2.75.
Traveling baggage masters from $1.10 to $1.35, and later, $1.55.
Passenger flagmen and brakemen from $1 to $1.32; later, $1.50.
Conductors of through freights from $3.18 to $3.55; later, $3.75.
Brakemen and flagmen on through freights from $1.75 to $2.35; later, $2.50.
Conductors on local freights from $3.80 to $4.15; later, $4.25.
Brakemen and flagmen on local freights from $2.30 to $2.63; later, $2.75.

PHILADELPHIA, July 4.—There were no developments to-day in the situation regarding the demands of the trainmen employed on the Pennsylvania Railroad lines east of Pittsburg, Erie, and Buffalo for increased wages.

Balloting on the strike proposition submitted by the Order of Railway Conductors and the Brotherhood of Railroad Trainmen to the 15,500 men involved was begun yesterday at the various headquarters of the railroaders, and will be continued until the men have voted. The trainmen demanded an increase of from 5 to 20 per cent., but the company, in refusing the demands, declares that they virtually amount to an increase of 18 to 20 per cent. above the wages paid by the Pennsylvania's competitors.

HALF HOUR ON A LIVE WIRE.

Boy and Brother Who Tried to Save Him May Die.

CHICAGO, July 4.—Stretched across live wires of the sanitary district power plant with 12,000 volts of electricity passing through his body and blue flames shooting from his extremities, Nicholas Maronich, 19 years old, of Evanston, lay for half an hour yesterday while efforts were made to rescue him. He was taken down finally burned so badly that both of his legs had to be amputated.

His sixteen-year-old brother Joseph, who had attempted to lift him and had fallen from the top of the fifty foot pole as the result of shock, also was taken in charge by physicians. It is not believed the older boy will live. The younger has a chance for recovery.

No one knows how Nicholas happened to climb the pole to the perilous position. Both the police and fire departments were notified and men hurried to the scene. A large crowd gathered and witnessed the attempts of the fire department to raise its longest ladder. It failed to reach the hanging legs of the boy.

A half hour had passed since the boy had been discovered on the wires. Suddenly his body was seen to relax and hang limp. This was the first signal to the crowd underneath that the current had been shut off.

The boy was lowered then with ropes to the ground and removed to a hospital along with his brother. He had not lost consciousness, the doctors declared, until the current was shut off.

TWO KILLED IN SHOOTING.

Discharged Bartender Shoots Saloon Keeper and Is Killed by a Policeman.

Special to The New York Times.

HAVERSTRAW, N. Y., July 4.—Revolver in hand, Herman Zipple, a bartender, discharged three days ago by Leo Hirschfeld, a saloon keeper of Main Street, Haverstraw, walked into Hirschfeld's bottling house, on Fairmount Avenue early this afternoon, and without a word began firing at the proprietor and a workman known as John. He fired five shots in all, one of which struck Hirschfeld in the left side of the neck and another in the left temple, killing him instantly. A third bullet inflicted a flesh wound in the shoulder of the helper. Then Zipple turned and fled up Fairmount Avenue.

Policeman Sheridan, hearing the shots from his post near by, gave chase for two blocks. At the top of the hilly street near Hudson Avenue Zipple turned and fired his remaining shot at the policeman, now only ten paces away. The bullet went wild. A moment later the policeman had fired four shots from his revolver at Zipple, who fell to the street with a bullet in the right side, one in his left arm, and two in the left leg. He was taken to the home of Dr. E. B. Laird, where he died half an hour later.

ROOSEVELT ON A PICNIC.

He and His Family Have Their Annual Outing at Lloyd's Neck.

Special to The New York Times.

OYSTER BAY, N. Y., July 4.—Col. Theodore Roosevelt spend his usual quiet Fourth of July. He had no visitors, and politics was tabooed. He had arranged to go in the evening to Sea Cliff to review the Sea Cliff Separate Company, the military organization which took part in his reception at Oyster Bay when he returned from abroad, but at the last moment he sent word that he would be unable to keep the engagement.

During the day Col. Roosevelt and his family went on their annual picnic to Lloyd's Neck. In the evening there were fireworks on the Roosevelt lawn. The former President is not an exponent of a safe and sane Fourth, and there was plenty of noise all day long in his vicinity. No casualties were reported.

About the time Col. Roosevelt returned from the picnic excursion an inquiry came from Sagamore Hill regarding the Jeffries-Johnson fight. No news had been received at that time, and a few minutes later the telephone at the telegraph office rang again. This time the announcement of Johnson's victory was made and the operator who communicated the news to Sagamore Hill said later that he distinctly heard a noise like an exploding expletive. No information could be obtained as to who actually made the inquiry about the fight, but the voice, the operator said, sounded much like Col. Roosevelt's.

Politics will be taken up again at Sagamore Hill to-day, when Representative Poindexter, a militant insurgent from Washington, arrives. Gov. Hughes did not put in an appearance to-day, but it was said that he was expected here this week.

Bridgehampton's 250th Birthday.

BRIDGEHAMPTON, L. I., July 4.—The two hundred and fiftieth anniversary of the settlement of the village of Bridgehampton was celebrated to-day by the unveiling of a monument, a parade, and a public meeting, at which addresses were made by prominent residents and others. A conspicuous figure in the celebration was "Judge" Henry P. Hedges, who is 92 years old, and said to be the oldest living graduate of Yale. Addresses were also made by Charles Gardiner, a member of an old Long Island family, and the Rev. Arthur Newman, pastor of the Bridgehampton Presbyterian Church.

HUGHES PUT FIRST FOR CHIEF JUSTICE

Said at Beverly to be Practically Certain to Succeed Late Chief Justice.

NO ACTION TILL DECEMBER

Taft Will Wait for Congress to Name Both New Chief Justice and One or More Associate Justices.

BEVERLY, Mass., July 4.—While the President declines definitely to commit himself in any way, it is regarded here to-night as practically certain that Gov. Hughes of New York will be the next Chief Justice of the United States Supreme Court, in succession to Chief Justice Fuller, who died to-day near Bar Harbor. Gov. Hughes has already accepted an appointment as an Associate Justice and his nomination to that place has been confirmed by the Senate. Unlooked for developments may cause a change in the President's attitude, but as matters stand at present, Gov. Hughes is foremost in the President's eye.

No appointment of a successor to Chief Justice Fuller, whose death came as a great shock to the President, will be made until Congress meets in December next. By that time it is believed that the President may have to appoint also a successor to Justice Moody, in whose behalf a retirement bill was passed at the session of Congress just closed.

Early in his Administration, Mr. Taft announced that only under the most exceptional circumstances would he make a recess appointment to any one of the Federal benches. He believes that no Judge of a United States court should act in a case until confirmed by the Senate. He regards this as holding especially true in the case of the United States Supreme Court, for which tribunal no one has a deeper respect than Mr. Taft. In fact it has never been denied that Mr. Taft's original ambition was to become the Chief Justice himself.

In the selection of an Associate Justice President Taft will take plenty of time for deliberation. It is believed that the President will be definitely informed as to Justice Moody's intentions as to retirement within the next month or two, so the Chief Executive is practically casting about for two men. It is the President's well-known method to listen with earnest patience and interest to all suggestions that come from reputable sources regarding a vacant judgeship. He will weigh the matter over carefully and unquestionably is looking forward to hearing from the more representative of the bar associations and attorneys of prominence the country over.

Both privately and publicly President Taft has declared that a Chief Magistrate of the Nation has no duty more solemn or higher than the appointment of Justices of the United States Courts, and especially of the Supreme Court. His views on this subject are pretty thoroughly known by now.

The probable retirement of Justice Moody will make the fourth vacancy in less than two years. It is not unlikely that before his term of four years has expired President Taft will have been called upon to appoint six out of the nine Justices forming the supreme tribunal. Probably no other President has ever been faced with such a serious duty. President Taft told some of his friends recently that he was anxious above almost everything else that his Administration might be known for the character of his appointments to the Federal bench.

The President also said recently that Gov. Hughes to his mind was almost an ideal man for the Supreme Court bench. He regards Gov. Hughes as a broad-minded man of affairs, a man of wide experience in the law, as an Executive, and as a publicist. It was said to-night that in offering the Associate Justiceship to Gov. Hughes the President pointed out to the distinguished New Yorker that he was at the parting of the ways. Down one road led a political career with an excellent chance for the Presidency at the end. Down the other led a long journey of usefulness on the Supreme Court bench, with the Chief Justiceship of the greatest tribunal in the world as the ultimate achievement.

It can be positively stated that the President is entirely open-minded as to the Supreme Court vacancies. One of the most likely candidates spoken of here to-night is Justice Swayze of the New Jersey Supreme Court. He has been strongly recommended to the President, and is said to have had an excellent chance for appointment to succeed the late Justice Peckham had Gov. Hughes declined.

President Taft, it is said, is anxious to secure for the Supreme Court men between 40 and 50 years of age. The appointment of Justice Lurton was an exception, and it is not believed he would again select a man of that age. For this reason there is but little talk of Senator Root of New York and Secretary of War Dickinson, who were prominently regarded as Supreme Court possibilities. Attorney General Wickersham's prominence in the trust cases seems to preclude any thought of him.

TALK OF BOWERS AND HOYT.

Washington Hears Little of Hughes as Chief Justice Fuller's Successor.

Special to The New York Times.

WASHINGTON, July 4.—Chief Justice Fuller's death caused a great shock to Washington when the news became known about noon to-day. None of the Chief Justice's associates are in town, but J. M. Wright, Marshal of the Supreme Court, expects them to assemble for the funeral as soon as Mr. Fuller's family has expressed its desires. The Vice President will appoint a committee of Senators, and the Speaker a committee of members of the House to do honor on behalf of Congress to the dead Chief Justice.

Rarely has the Supreme bench been left in so crippled a condition as now by the death of its presiding Justice. Gov. Hughes, who was appointed to succeed the late Justice Brewer, has not yet taken the oath of office. Justice Moody is still critically ill, and under a special act of Congress may retire with full pay within five months.

Mr. Hughes will of course be sworn in when the October term of the court convenes, so that will leave only two vacancies, but even should the President issue his commission now, he could take no part in the deliberations of the court on cases already heard. As things stand now, should the six associate Juticces remaining actively on duty decide pending cases, except those in regard to which a fair degree of unanimity exists, there is a likelihood of the decision being reached by a vote of four to three, which, though standing as a majority of the Justices, is not a majority of the full court.

Mr. Fuller was a Democrat, and was appointed by Mr. Cleveland twenty-two years ago to the post his death leaves vacant. There remain but two Democrats

Continued on Page 5.

JERSEY WINDS TOSS CURTISS IN BIPLANE

Opens Atlantic City Meet with Short Flight, but Is Forced to Descend.

PLANE ROCKED LIKE A BOAT

Test Satisfies Aviator, Who May Try To-day to Make a Fifty-Mile Flight Over the Ocean.

Special to The New York Times.

ATLANTIC CITY, N. J., July 4.—Cheered by nearly 100,000 spectators, Glenn H. Curtiss opened this afternoon the Atlantic City aviation meet with a spectacular flight. He only flew for a half mile, but that dash was fraught with danger, for the stiff wind which blew down the side streets between the high hotels caused his airship to rock as though it was being tossed on the ocean.

As Curtiss flew down the beach, about twent-five feet in the air, toward the million-dollar pier, a bather and a small child broke from the crowd and ran out on the beach almost on the spot the aviator had selected to land. Screams of terror arose from the crowd, but Curtiss raised his forward planes, skimmed over the pair, and dropped in the sand 100 feet from the pier.

Police and firemen were impressed to keep back the throng, but it was with the greatest difficulty that a lane was cleared wide enough to enable Curtiss to try out his motor and his ability to fly and land. While he was preparing to fly the wind increased from a gentle sea breeze to a stiff northwest wind, and, although the managers of the meet said they would not insist on a flight under the conditions, Curtiss said he would "take a shy at it."

"It was the most dangerous flight I ever have made," said Curtiss. "When I found I was caught in eddies that threatened to overturn my plane or drive me into the ocean, I was strongly tempted to turn out to sea and go up in the air, but the fear that I might be forced to drop in the water or imperil the lives of the spectators in landing caused me to stick close to the beach.

"At several points I was caught in swirls that proved to me that my machine will stand the strongest wind. I therefore shall stick to my contract to make daily flights and to try for both the altitude and distance speed prizes.

Curtiss said that if the conditions were favorable he would try to cover the fifty-mile speed course over the ocean to-morrow. He stood by his machine all the afternoon, in the hope that the wind either would change or die down, that he might make a real flight, but he was forced to be satisfied with one little flight.

Because of the difficulty with the crowd and the narrow escapes, the Aero Club and police officials decided to-night to clear the beach of bathers and strollers to-morrow morning and keep it clear for the balance of the meet, using police, firemen, and the Atlantic City troop of cavalry for this purpose.

Despite the disappointment to Curtiss and the people, the short flight demonstrated that he could land and get away from the sand without difficulty.

"This is my first attempt to land in sand and I find it ideal," said Curtiss. "The wheels sink in deep enough to stop headway without using the brakes, and when the beach is cleared I believe I shall be able to start or finish without trouble.

"I do not believe the air currents will bother me materially, and once I get clear of the land I shall be able to carry out the over-the-ocean trials without difficulty. No wind will be worse than that I passed through this morning, and with reasonably still air there will be a chance of smashing some of the present records."

Dr. Francis L. Sweeney of Philadelphia represented the Pennsylvania Aero Club, and Henry M. Neely, Chairman of the Contest Committee of the National Council of Aero Clubs, witnessed the flight. He is preparing to measure the course for the distance races to-morrow.

Fears that Curtiss might attempt an ocean flight and meet with an accident caused the assembling of a fleet of speedy yachts just off the beach—Fred Burke of Philadelphia, with the Corinthia; Col. Thomas Potter of Philadelphia, with the Olive; Col. Brown of Pittsburg, with the Skiboo. All were prepared to aid the aviator should he drop into the ocean.

The machine used by Curtiss to-day was the same in which he made his flight from Albany to New York. Another plane, which arrived to-day, will be used by Hamilton to-morrow. Kleckner, a Curtiss pupil, will fly during the latter part of the week, and Capt. Baldwin is expected to-morrow.

Word was received to-night that the Wright machines, with Brookins and Coffyn, will arrive to-morrow or Wednesday, and the big events in which the two makes of machines will be pitted against each other will start Thursday.

Interest in the flights led people to gather on the Boardwalk shortly after daylight. Many refused to believe there would be no further attempts at flight and stuck to the Boardwalk until dark.

SHOT DOWN AS HE RAN.

Youth Fatally Wounded After Quarreling Over a Trifle.

As a result of a quarrel, Louis Ludwig, 17 years old, of 130 Pennington Street, Newark, N. J., was shot yesterday, probably fatally, by Nikolai Popel, also 17 years old, of Elizabeth, N. J., in Newark. Popel was arrested.

The trouble started Saturday, when Popel and Ludwig quarreled over a trifle. Ludwig struck Popel in the face. Ludwig's hat fell off. Popel picked it up and tore it to pieces. Ludwig then fled.

Popel yesterday saw Ludwig in front of a saloon with a stone in his hand. Popel drew a pistol and fired at Ludwig, who fled pursued by Popel, firing as he ran. One of the bullets went through Ludwig's breast and another went through his back.

New Danish Cabinet.

COPENHAGEN, July 4.—A new Cabinet has been formed, with Klaus Bernstein, who was Minister of the Interior in the Holstein-Ledrebord Cabinet, in 1909, as Premier and Minister of Defense. The other members of the Cabinet include Count Ahlefeldt-Laurvig, Minister of Foreign Affairs; M. Neergaard, Minister of Finance; A. Nielsen, Minister of Agriculture, and M. Svenderup, Minister of the Interior.

19 DEAD IN WRECK OF BIG FOUR FLIER

Head-on Collision Piles Cincinnati Section of Twentieth Century Limited Upon Freight.

FAST TRAIN DETOURED

Was Running on C., H. & D. Tracks and Crashed Into Freight Near Middletown, Ohio—Many Injured.

MIDDLETOWN, Ohio, July 4.—Nineteen persons were killed outright, three probably fatally hurt, and many seriously injured in a head-on collision between a freight train and the Cincinnati secton of the Twentieth Century Limited, southbound, on the tracks ofg the Cincinnati, Hamilton & Dayton Railroad here to-day. Of the killed, eighteen were passengers, the other victim being a member of the passenger train crew.

The dead are:

BAKER, S. P., Cincinnati.
SMITH, H. A., Dayton.
KIRK, J. SMITH, Dayton.
FROHLE, GEORGE, Dayton.
GOLDEN, FRANK, passenger train brakeman
COOLEY, JOHN W., McCutcheonsville, Ohio.
DAUBENMIRE, Miss FAY H., Pleasantville, Ohio.
SNYDER, RAY B., London, Ohio.
GARRIGUS, A. S., Columbus, Ohio.
VAN HORNE, RICHARD, Dayton.
MOULTON, CHARLES H., Youngstown, Ohio.
BODEY, Mrs. JESSE D., Dayton, Ohio.
DUNLEAVY, WILLIAM, Dayton, Ohio.
KING LEN YUEN, Columbus, Ohio.
GRANT, C. B., Springfield, Ohio.
Unidentified woman about 40 years of age.
Unidentified man, initials W. A. on clothing.
Two unidentified men, supposed to be from Dayton.

The injured are:

Mrs. J. Smith Kirk, Dayton, perhaps fatally; Peter Jennings, engineer Big Four passenger train, badly injured; W. B. Lamm, fireman Big Four passenger train, internal injuries, recovery doubtful; Train Pilot Wald of the C., H. & D., seriously injured; Samuel Wayne Garrigus, 829 West Towne Street, Columbus, arms and several ribs broken; John J. White, livery man, Dayton, not dangerously hurt; James L. H. Konneny, Louisville, Ky., right leg and ribs broken; W. S. Erskine, Memphis, Tenn., back injured, serious; Will Litz, Harroudsburg, Ky., badly burned, contusions; Oscar Cubanissy, colored, Cincinnati, head and side injured; William Weisner, Cincinnati, head, elbows, and shoulders injured, serious; W. D. White, Cleveland, head cut; A. F. Dayton, Latonia, Ky., condition serious; Jerry Ferguson, Dayton, side hurt, not serious; Mrs. Emma Lindy, Caledonia,, Ohio, thigh and hips injured, serious; John Rankin, Springfield, right leg dislocated, hip injured; C. E. Doty, Bellefontaine, right leg broken; Frank Edwards, Latonia, Ky.; Will Hallor, Dayton; Joe Davis, Cleveland, Ohio; Wilbur Greenwood, Springfield, Ohio; James Heragan, Dayton.

The freight train, which was a second section, was attempting to make a siding to give the Chicago, Cleveland, Cincinnati & St. Louis Railway's passenger train a clear track, when the Big Four's limited, traveling at a speed of fifty miles an hour, flashed around a curve and crashed into it.

The Big Four train, which is the one which connects at Cleveland with the Lake Shore Twentieth Century Limited, had been detoured to avoid a blocked track on that road at Genoa, a few miles south of here, caused by a freight wreck earlier in the day. In addition to its regular crew it carried a pilot engineer of the Cincinnati, Hamilton & Dayton Road, who was practically in charge of the train.

A misunderstanding of orders caused the disaster. Pilot Engineer George Wald had received orders to wait at Post Town, a siding station three miles north of this city, according to railroad officials. The freight train was to have passed him there, but was late in pulling out of Middletown. Instead of the seven minutes' margin which Wald thought he had to reach Middletown the time was less than five minutes.

The first section of the frieght had taken the siding here, and Conductor John Weaver, in charge of the second section, tried to reach the north end of the same siding. Before his train had cleared the switch points the passenger train rounded a curve screened by the thickly wooded lots on each side of the track. The engine crews had time to jump, but not all escaped serious injury.

The crash when the trains met was terrific. The freight was made up of gondola cars, flat cars, and box cars loaded with lumber. Directly behind the passenger locomotive and the tender was a combination baggage and smoking car, followed by a day coach and a chair car. All the dead and injured were in the first two cars, there being six passengers in the smoker and twenty-one in the day coach.

The engines locked into a mass of smashed steel and iron, the heavy passenger locomotive telescoping its smaller fellow as far as the cab. First in the freight train were a steel coal car and a box car loaded with six-inch timbers.

The heavy gondola car ripped the floor out of the combination car and tossed it and the locomotive tender down a ten-foot embankment into a cornfield. The timbers in the car following were driven with terrific force into the day coach, which mounted the gondola car and split it in twain.

Every seat in this coach was torn from its fastenings, the roof was thrown to one side, and the heavy weight of massive timbers, hurled with awful force, struck among the men and women in the coach. Even before the crash came rescuers were running to the wreck from the Middletown station of the Cincinnati, Hamilton & Dayton Railroad, 300 yards south of the accident.

Every surgeon in town was summoned to the place, which is a mile or more from the city proper, and calls for assistance were sent to Dayton and Hamilton.

Relief trains were made up at each of these places and the injured were placed upon them and sent to hospitals in those cities, there being no such institution in Middletown.

Coroner J. A. Burnett was summoned from Hamilton and immediately began an inquiry into the cause of the wreck. He was unwilling to-night to offer any conclusions on the result of his investigations.

Vernon Wallace, fireman of the freight train, declared that the passenger train was running ahead of schedule. "We had seven minutes to make the siding when we left the Middletown yards, just below the city," he said. "That must have given us fully five minutes' margin as we passed the station. Yet we hardly cleared the station with our rear flags when the flier came around the curve. I yelled to the engineer and jumped, and he did the same."

Wald, the pilot on the passenger engine, is said to have declared that he was strictly on schedule.

'MOTHER WOODS' FOUND SLAIN

Philanthropic Lodging House Keeper Dead from a Wound in the Breast.

Hannah Woods, 65 years old, a widow, of 390½ Water Street, who runs a lodging house at that address and is known as "Mother Woods" because of her practice of giving lodging to old and homeless women of the neighborhood, was murdered last night. The police have not determined whether she was shot or stabbed.

Dr. Brown of Hudson Street Hospital said a gash in the woman's left breast probably had been caused by a bullet. No arrest has been made. The police of Oak Street Station are at work on the case.

AMERICANS HURT IN FRANCE.

Two Women Seriously Injured in an Automobile Accident.

CHALONS-SUR-SAONE, France., July 4.—An automobile in which five Americans were driving was overturned in a ditch to-day in an attempt to avoid a bull. Two of the women passengers were seriously injured.

The members of the party have not yet been identified.

ESCAPE FROM BURNING BOAT.

Crew of Seven Take to Dinghy, Two Having to Cling to It and Swim.

BLOCK ISLAND, R. I., July 4. The power boat Bashi Basouk of New York with seven men on board, caught fire five miles off here at 5 A. M. to-day, and was destroyed.

All hands escaped by jumping into a small dinghy, which held them until a local fisherman rescued them and brought them here.

The dinghy was so small that two of the party could not get on board and they had to stay in the water, hanging to the rail.

BALLOON LOST IN THE PARK.

Broke Away While Leo Stevens Was Giving Boys an Aeronautic Lesson.

A big balloon belonging to Leo Stevens broke away yesterday afternoon from its moorings in Central Park and had not been recovered late last night by the aeronaut.

Stevens was showing the boys of Public School 77 how a big balloon is inflated and manoeuvred. The gas was made and the balloon partly filled at 97th Street in the Park.

After moving it to 106th Street, Stevens allowed the balloon to rise 1,000 feet, when suddenly the rope snapped. John Kilpatrick, one of Stevens's helpers, was thrown about thirty feet and badly cut over the eye. Edward Durant, one of the boys from the school who also was holding the rope, was also thrown.

The balloon broke away about 5 o'clock and was seen over Long Island City an hour after. Later it was seen heading toward Manhattan.

DYING AFTER STOLEN RIDE.

Three Men Stole Steel Man's Auto and Upset It—One May Live.

PITTSBURG, July 4.—While Col. H. P. Bope, Vice President of the Carnegie Steel Company, was attending the ball game this afternoon, three men jumped into his automobile, which, was parked across Forbes Field, and started on a joy ride. They crossed the river to the south side, where two motor cycle policemen raced after them.

The high-speed car was leaving the police behind when it crashed into a pile of smokestacks lying in the street. The car turned turtle and the three men were dragged from beneath the car and hurried to a hospital.

John Miller has a fractured skull, and A. G. Lucas has an injured spine. Both men will die. Charles Hays is seriously cut and bruised, but may recover. The machine was wrecked.

SAVE WOMAN FROM SUICIDE.

Three Members of St. Louis's Crew Leap in the River and Pull Her Out.

Matthew Teale and Robert Patterson, engineers, and Robert McIntee, a sailor of the Steamship St. Louis of the American Line, saved last night from drowning in the North River at the foot of Twenty-fourth Street Belle Williams, 34 years old, of South Missouri Street, Atlantic City, N. J. She was removed to Bellevue Hospital, a prisoner charged with attempted suicide. She was unable to make any statement.

The engineers, sitting on Pier 64, say the woman leap into the water, and a moment later they were in the river struggling with her. She fought their efforts to save her until McIntee heard their cries and dived into aid them. By their combined efforts the woman was lifted to the pier.

NO MORE $10 HOGS.

Armour Thinks They'll Keep Around $9—South America Getting Beef Trade

CHICAGO, July 4.—J. Ogden Armour, the packer, who returned yesterday from a two months' trip to Europe, does not believe that this country will "see $10 hogs" again. Speaking of meat prices, he said:

"If there is a bountiful wheat, corn, and oats crop this year we may hope for lower prices. If the grain is short the supply of cattle and hogs will be short. I do not believe the country will see $10 hogs again. Hogs normally should range around $9.

"Meat export business from the United States to Europe is dead," continued Mr. Armour. "South America is furnishing the meat that Europe consumes. The United States cannot compete to advantage with the country south of the equator. Cattle conditions there are as they were in the West twenty-five years ago. As a cattle producer South America is rapidly outdistancing the United States."

AUTO FALLS INTO LAKE.

One Man Drowned and Six Other Persons Have Narrow Escapes.

Special to The New York Times.

WILKESBARRE, July 4.—Joseph H. Callahan of Wilkesbarre was killed to-night in an automobile accident at Harvey's Lake, eighteen miles from here, and six other persons had narrow escapes.

They were in a sightseeing automobile, of which the steering gear had broken and which was being hauled back to the Hotel Oneonta. The rope of the hauling machine broke and the disabled machine ran into the lake, turning over as it fell down an embankment and into ten feet of water.

Callahan, who was at the steering wheel, was caught under the machine and drowned and the others were thrown into the water. Some could swim and the others were rescued by persons in boats.

Callahan was a foreman at the Wilkesbarre Lace Mills.

JOHNSON WINS IN 15 ROUNDS; JEFFRIES WEAK

"I Couldn't Come Back," Says Former Champion, Helpless After Third Knockdown.

POOR FIGHT, SAYS SULLIVAN

White Man Outclassed by His Opponent from the First Tap of the Gong.

CROWD'S SYMPATHY AROUSED

Yells to Referee to Save Jeffries from a Knockout and His Seconds Jump Into the Ring.

JOHNSON'S SHARE, $70,600

While Jeffries Takes $50,400 from the Purse—The Moving-Picture Rights Bring Them More Thousands.

By JOHN L. SULLIVAN.
Special to The New York Times.

RENO, Nev., July 4.—The fight of the century is over and a black man is the undisputed champion of the world.

It was a poor fight as fights go, this less than fifteen-round affair betweeen James J. Jeffries and Jack Johnson. Scarcely ever has there been a championship contest that was so one-sided.

All of Jeffries's much-vaunted condition and the prodigious preparations that he went through availed him nothing. He wasn't in it from the first bell tap to the last, and as he fell bleeding, bruised, and weakened in the twenty-seventh second of the third minute of the fifteenth round no sorrier sight has ever gone to make pugilistic history. He was practically knocked out twice in this round.

Johnson's deadly left beat upon his unprotected head and neck, and he went down for the count just before the second minute had gone in the fifteenth round. As Johnson felled him the first time he was conscious, but weakened. He tactfully waited for the timekeeper's call of nine before he rose. When he did Johnson caught him flush on the jaw again, and he fell almost in the same spot, but further out, and as he leaned against the lower rope his great bulk crashed through outside the ring.

His seconds and several newspaper men hauled him into the ring again, and he staggered weakly over to the other side. Johnson slowly followed him, measured his distance carefully, and as Jeff's head always hangs forward, struck him hard in the face, and again that terrible left hand caught him, sending him reeling around to a stooping posture.

Johnson pushed his right hand hard as Jeffries wheeled around, and quick as a flash whipped his left over again, and Jeff went down for the last time. His seconds had given it up.

They didn't wait for the ten seconds to be counted, but jumped into the ring after their man. Billy Delaney, Johnson's chief second, always watchful for the technicalities, yelled his claim for the fight for his man on the breach of the rules by Jeff's handlers. Tex Rickard, in the meantime, was trying to make himself heard, and he was saying that the fight was Johnson's.

Result Left the Crowd Dazed.

By this time the crowd was realizing that Johnson had won out, but there was very little cheering. Jeff had been such a decided favorite they could hardly believe that he was beaten and that there wouldn't still be a chance for him to reclaim his lost laurels. The crowd was not even willing to leave the arena, and as poor old Jeff sat in his corner being sprayed with water and other resuscitating liquids he was pitied from all sides.

The negro had few friends, but there was no real demonstration against him They could not help but admire Johnson, because he is the type of prize fighter that is regarded highly by sportsmen. He played fairly at all times and fought fairly. He gave in wherever there was a contention and he demanded his rights only up to their limit, but never beyond them.

Had Picked Johnson to Win.

I have never witnessed a fight where I was in such a peculiar position. I all along refused to announce my choice as to the winner. I refused on Jeff's account, because he was sensitive and I wanted to be with him some time during his training. I refused on Johnson's account, because of my well-known antipathy to his race, and I didn't want him to think that I was favoring him from any other motive than a purely sporting one. He might have got this impression, although since I know him better, in the last few weeks, I am rather inclined to believe that he hasn't many of the petty meannesses of human character.

You will deduce from the foregoing that I really had picked Johnson as the winner. My personal friends all know it, and even Jeffries accused me of it one day, but I denied it in this way. I said:

"Jeff, I have picked the winner, but I haven't done it publicly. A few personal friends know who I think will win, and I am not going to tell you before the fight. I don't want you to get any wrong impression."

However, the fact remains that three weeks ago I picked Johnson to win. It seems almost too much to say, but I did say inside of fifteen rounds. It's all over now, and it does not matter who I picked to win to either Jeff or Johnson, but the main theory I based my decision on was the old one that put me out of the game. Jeff could not come back. Jeffries was a mere shell of his former self. All the months of weight reducing, involving great feats of exercise, had come to naught.

The experts who figured that a man must receive his reward for such long, conscientious, muscle-wearing and nerve-racking work, figured that he must get it even providentially.

It seemed only just to human nature that Jeffries must win, even in the face of all the features resting on the other side of the argument. For it is true, and probably would only be denied by Johnson himself, that the big colored champion did not train conscientiously. As subsequent events proved he didn't have to train more than he did, but nevertheless he took a chance, and, by his manner and deportment, seemed perfectly willing to stand the consequences, whatever they were. The result was success for him in its fullest meaning.

Johnson got scarcely a hard knock during the whole encounter, and was never bothered by Jeffries's actions one little bit. He came out of the fray without a mark, if one except the cut lip he got in the third round, which proved to be only the opening of the old cut that George Cotton gave him the other day when Gov. Dickerson was out at his training quarters.

Never before has there been a fight for the championship of the world with so many peculiar ends to it, because never before has a black man been a real contender for the championship. Johnson, of course, was the credited champion even before to-day's fight by virtue of his defeat of Tommy Burns, but just the same the rank and file of sporting people never gave him the full measure of his title. Jeffries has always been the bugaboo of Johnson's championship career, and it seemed to many that if only the big boilermaker would go back into the fighting game and get himself into condition he could obliterate this so-called blot on the pugilistic map.

Jeffries was persuaded against his will, and he went to work with a willingness and determination that brought about wonderful results, but that couldn't bring back outraged old nature.

Johnson Never in Doubt.

Probably never before was a championship so easily won as Johnson's victory to-day. He never showed the slightest concern during the fifteen rounds and from the fourth round on his confidence was the most glaring thing I ever saw in any fighter. He was the one person in the world at that moment who knew that Jeffries's best blow was packed away in his last fight and on the road and by the running brooks from which he lured the fish during his preliminary training for his fight.

He was a perfect picnic for the big negro, who seemed to be enjoying himself rather than fighting for 60 per cent. of a $101,000 purse. It could not have been all assumed, either, as his remarks during the contest to me, while I sat below and near him at the ringside, showed that he had honestly a good opinion of himself.

Once in the interval between the fifth and sixth rounds he leaned over and said: "John, I thought this fellow could hit."

I said: "I never said so, but I believe he could have six years ago."

Johnson continued with conversation when he should have been paying attention to the advice his seconds were giving him, and said: "Yes; five or six years ago ain't now, though."

By that time the bell had rung and he was up and at it again.

My, what a crafty, powerful, cunning left hand he has. He leads with it, of course, but he does most of his work in close, and some of his blows look as though he were trying to lead with his right while his left is traveling to its goal. He is one of the craftiest, cunningest boxers that ever stepped into the ring, and poor old Jeffries could not get set or anywhere near him for an effective punch.

As a matter of fact, he didn't have any. They both fought closely all during the fifteen rounds. It was just the sort of a fight that Jeffries wanted. There was no running around and ducking like Corbett did with me in New Orleans.

Jeffries didn't miss so many blows, because he hardly started any. Johnson was on top of him all the time, and he scarcely attempted a blow that didn't land. There wasn't a full swing during the whole fifteen rounds, something unusual in this latter-day fighting.

The only thing that wasn't actual fighting to-day was the many clinches that occurred, and here, instead of Jeff getting in the fatal work, it was Johnson. None of the plans that all of the experts and critics have been talking about for the last six months materialized.

Jeffries's fearful rushes were not there. The awful wallops that he was going to land on Johnson's body, where were they?

Johnson didn't receive a blow during the whole encounter that would have hurt a 16-year-old boy. From the time Jeff got his right eye closed in the sixth round it was all over as far as I was concerned. I felt then that if Jeffries had all this power behind that had been claimed for him, he would get mad and he would at least take a desperate chance. Probably he had some such idea in mind himself, for he did step in viciously in the next round, but a gloved fist always stopped his onward way.

When I saw Johnson throw Jeffries away from him in one of the many clinches in the eighth or ninth round I was still further convinced that the negro was the winner.

This had been one of his favorite stunts during his training, and he was expected to at least attempt it here. He didn't get gay at all with Jeffries in the beginning, and it was always the white man who clinched, but Johnson was very careful, and he backed away and took no chances, and was good-natured with it all.

Probably the Last Big Fight Here.

There were those in the throng to-day who will probably say it was the greatest fight the world ever saw, but that is because it was the most peculiar fight crowd the world ever saw, for half of them never saw a fight before. It was the greatest fight this class ever saw, but, as a matter of fact, it was about the poorest fight that has ever been fought for the championship. It will probably be the last big fight in this country, notwithstanding the crowd's enthusiastic reception of Billy Muldoon's sentimental speech, "Let us give three cheers for the great, broad-minded State of Nevada and its great, broad-minded Governor," because it will be hard to work up the fervor that has existed all through the arrangements for this fight.

It will go down in history as the greatest fight that ever took place in some respects, and from a purely sporting point of view the very worst.

Nevertheless, the best man won, and I was one of the first to congratulate him, and also one of the first to extend my heartfelt sympathy to the beaten man.

JOHN L. SULLIVAN.

United Press International

Jack Johnson (right) knocks out Jim Jeffries.

EIGHT KILLED IN FIGHT RIOTS

Continued from Page 1.

pistol which he fired at Thirty-ninth Street and Ninth Avenue; locked up in West Thirty-seventh Street Station.

The Storm Centre.

The West Thirty-seventh Street Police Station seemed to be the storm centre, so far as the police were concerned, and within half an hour after Johnson was declared the winner over Jeffries the mix-ups in that precinct started. Although every policeman in the precinct was on "fight duty," it was impossible to prevent the clashes between the races which followed each other at quick intervals. Between 9 and 11 o'clock a wounded negro was taken to that station on an average of one for every fifteen minutes.

Most of the trouble centred in Ninth Avenue between Thirty-eighth and Forty-second Streets, where a gang of men and boys had formed for the purpose of attacking every negro that ventured into that section.

In most cases this gang was directly responsible for all that occurred, although in some instances the negro was the offender. Edmund Goldburn, a negro, of 416 West Thirty-sixth Street, and James A. Graffe, a white man, of 241 West 111th Street, were among the first to get into a mix-up.

Graffe said he was walking through Thirty-eighth Street, and as he neared Ninth Avenue Goldburn approached him and remarked that "any cullud man can whip any white man." When he demurred Goldburn jerked a pistol out of his pocket and threatened to shoot him. The two grappled, and a moment later Policeman Smith of the West Thirty-seventh Street Station came up on the run. A crowd of about 1,000 men and boys had gathered in the meantime, and Smith had to fight his way to the place where Graffe and the negro were struggling. Goldburn was locked up.

In a few minutes there came a report of a riot from Ninth Avenue and Thirty-seventh Street, and the police got there just as Wilfred Shettlin, a negro, of 324 West Thirty-seventh Street, fell to the sidewalk as the result of a severe beating he had received at the hands of white men and boys. Shettlin did not know any of his assailants. He was permitted to go home.

The next fight was in West Thirty-sixth Street, and was a direct outcome of an argument over the respective merits of the white and negro races. In this case two white men, Eugene and Charles O'Keefe, brothers, of 411 West Thirty-sixth Street, were on their way home when they met Abraham Rice of 408 West Thirty-sixth Street and John Reynolds of 461 West Sixty-first Street, both colored.

Mob Quickly Gathered.

One of the negroes remarked to the white men as they passed that a negro was always a better fighter than the white man, and then either Rice or Reynolds struck Eugene O'Keefe over the head with an empty bottle. In a moment the block was filled with a howling mob of men and boys. Policemen Thorpe and Thompson ran to the scene, and the two negroes started to run. Rice ran into his own apartments, while Reynolds darted up the stairs of No. 408 and tried to escape by the roof. Both were caught and locked up on charges of assault.

A little later Charles Lewis, a negro, of Glenwood Avenue, East Orange, was brought into the West Thirty-seventh Street Station. He was found unconscious at Thirty-eighth Street and Ninth Avenue. When he regained consciousness he said he remembered being set upon by a gang.

This caused the police to go through the section of which Ninth Avenue and Thirty-ninth Street is the centre and order the tenants in the houses to remain in doors. Most of them readily promised to do so, but the rowdies who were making most of the trouble ignored the order. The boys who made up most of this gang, it was said, were armed with clubs, which they wielded with terrible effect. Every attack drew a crowd, but the gang always managed to scatter and make good their escape before the police could interfere.

William Bradley of 148 East Thirty-first Street, a North Carolina negro, who has been in New York only a few weeks, was walking down Ninth Avenue when the gang at Thirty-eighth Street got him. They beat him unmercifully. Thomas V. Duncanson, of 300 West Fortieth Street, got similar treatment and he too said he did not know why he had been attacked. In the attack on Duncanson several shots were fired but nobody was hit.

Some Victims May Die.

The West Forty-seventh Street Station police were out in full force, and they reported many clashes between the races. The most serious case was that of an unidentified negro who was taken with a fractured skull to the Flower Hospital. Policeman Pritchard found him at Fifty-eighth Street and Eleventh Avenue. Beside him was an open knife.

John Edelin was another negro whose serious injury was reported by the West Forty-seventh Street Station. He had five bad wounds in his head, besides other injuries. He was assaulted, he said, following a fight argument, by men he did not know. The assailants, according to the negro, were all white.

Edwin Cilley, a negro, was set upon and beaten over the head with a lead pipe, receiving injuries from which it is said he may die. The negro took refuge in the vestibule of the home of Dr. Alexander Brown, at 16 West Sixty-fifth Street, and when the gang tried to get him Dr. Brown went to Cilley's aid, holding his assailants off with a revolver. The negro was removed later to the Flower Hospital. None of his assailants was captured.

The "Pearl Button Gang," a coterie of tough young white men in the neighborhood of Ninety-ninth Street and Columbus Avenue, resented the result of the fight, and were soon mixed up with about ten negroes from the tenement houses in Ninety-eighth, Ninety-ninth, and 100th Streets, which are almost entirely occupied by colored tenants.

Capt. Zimmerman and his reserves from the West 100th Street Station hastened to the scene. The mob, now numbering over 1,500, scattered, and the negroes made their escape through adjacent hallways. Four of the white men were captured and locked up on charges of disorderly conduct.

A cry of "Let's lynch the first 'nigger' we meet!" started a riot in front of a saloon in Eighth Avenue near 135th Street soon after Johnson was reported the winner over Jeffries. The cry was taken up and within a few minutes a crowd had gathered. Then an Eighth Avenue car came along and somebody shouted, "There's a nigger!" and a moment later a middle-aged man was pulled out of the car and badly beaten. The police reserves were hurried to the scene and arrested several men, who were charged with being the ringleaders in the riot. During the row one negro fired a pistol three times, but got away.

THREE KILLED IN UVALDIA.

Armed Party of Whites Attack Negro Camp and Drive Out Occupants.

Special to The New York Times.

UVALDIA, Ga., July 4.—Three negroes were killed and many wounded in a clash with whites at a construction camp near this place to-day.

The negroes at the camp have been insolent in their remarks about Jeffries for some time, and to-day were boasting that Johnson would kill the white man. The negroes were drinking, and their conduct so enraged the white people of Uvaldia that a party was formed to clean out the camp.

As they approached the camp, the white men were met by volley after volley of shots from the negroes, but no one was wounded. The white people immediately returned the fire, killing three negroes and wounding five others. The fire of the whites was so deadly that the negroes fled from the camp into the woods, where they are being hunted by the whites.

Constant shots are being exchanged between the negroes and the pursuing whites, and late this afternoon the whites sent into town for more ammunition.

The feeling is very bitter, and the whites say they intend to run the negroes out of the county. Conservative citizens have asked Gov. Brown to send troops to stop the rioting.

MANY FIGHTS IN WASHINGTON.

Reserves Called Out to Quell Several Disturbances in Pennsylvania Ave.

WASHINGTON, July 4.—Race riots were prevented with difficulty by the police here to-night. Many fistic enounters between negroes and white men occurred in the streets in arguments over the Reno battle, and several fights threatened to precipitate serious disorder and endangered pedestrians.

In Pennsylvania Avenue, near the Post Office Building, three white men chased a negro who had been shouting "Hurrah for Johnson, champion of the world!" In a few seconds the wide thoroughfare was alive with rushing men and women, and fight after fight followed in quick succession.

THE FIGHT BY ROUNDS.

Negro Champion Led All the Way—Jeffries Slow and Clumsy.

By JOHN L. SULLIVAN.

Special to The New York Times.

RENO, Nev., July 4.—This is the story of the fight by rounds:

FIRST ROUND.

They approached each other, and Jeffries walked around to the opposite side, which was Johnson's corner. They circled around for fully ten seconds. Johnson led with left, and landed lightly on Jeffries's nose. They kept close to each other and seemed unwilling to break away. Jeffries feinted, and Johnson stood on his toes as he forced his man away with a left push and a light left punch on the jaw. In the clinch which followed both worked their left hands for the body. They were unwilling to break. Jeff was doing all the clinching. As they sparred again Jeffries tried to land his left on Johnson, but Johnson threw his head aside. Another clinch, and they slowly walked about, hugging each other, Jeffries the while calmly chewing gum. They sparred around each other again after the break. Johnson got in a left-hand blow which just scraped Jeffries's chin. They jostled again and clinched. They were still clinching when the gong sounded. There wasn't anything but just cold water used during the intermission on both men.

SECOND ROUND.

Johnson led as Jeffries feinted for him. As they fiddled around Johnson stepped in and landed twice on Jeff's chin. The second blow was harder than the first, but a clinch followed it. As they circled around, holding each other tightly, Johnson threw up his right and caught Jeffries on the chin. Here Rickard took a hand, and it was his first interference. He told the men that they must break. Johnson feinted with his left, and Jeffries came in and landed a light right on Johnson's ribs. As they were going to a clinch Johnson put both hands lightly on Jeffries's chin. They sparred around after breaking. Johnson feinted a left and Jeffries ducked. Another clinch, and Johnson used his favorite blow, a right-hand uppercut in close. Another clinch followed, and both men were careful on breaking away. Jeffries feinted, and as he came in with his usual crouch, Johnson landed a right on his eye which caused it to flush. At this stage it was seen that one of the early blows of Jeffries had drawn blood from Johnson's lip. Johnson was as jovial as he has ever been, and laughed outright just before the round ended. Nothing was needed during the rest but some cold water.

THIRD ROUND.

Johnson appeared the more careless of the two. He talked to Jeff and derided him as he made feints for his head. When he essayed another feint they came together in a clinch and held on to each other. Johnson came up with his left hand on Jeffries's nose. He repeated it instantly, and in the clinch which followed brought left and right up to Jeffries's jaw. Then there was another clinch, and shortly after breaking away Johnson stepped in again and landed a right and left on Jeff's neck. In the next passage of arms Jeffries landed his left on Johnson's upper arm and Johnson brought his right down on Jeffries's neck. They were not damaging blows, but they showed that Johnson had the better judgment of distance. Johnson, in the sparring which followed, landed another left on Jeffries's chin. Jeffries was getting the punching right along, but seemed to be not at all worried. His face was flushed, and he looked sarcastic as Johnson struggled around with him. Johnson brought up his hand in attempting to uppercut again, and it went past Jeffries's face. Johnson's wide grin was apparent to all in the vast throng. Johnson had done all the hitting so far, and he chuckled as he went to his corner. He was in perfect good humor, because his feints had brought nothing like a showdown from Jeff, and he was beginning to think the big fellow hadn't anything to show.

FOURTH ROUND.

Jeffries feinted with his left, but Johnson guarded with his right arm. Johnson landed on Jeffries's right ear, and in the clinch brought his right hand up, but didn't do any damage. He kept joshing Jeffries all the time, and Rickard admonished him that it was a fight and not a talkfest. Jeffries led and caught Johnson with a hard right on the chin. Johnson brought his hands around Jeff's neck. The blood was trickling from Johnson's mouth here, and they clinched. In the next sparring Jeffries led low, and Johnson called attention to it. Corbett, from Jeff's corner, was trying to disconcert Johnson, but the latter answered with a right on Jeff's chin as they came to a clinch. Johnson stuck out another left straight for Jeff's head, and it landed good and hard. In the clinch which followed Johnson caught Jeff and dared him to bring forth those demon punches he was famous for. Johnson caught Jeffries with a left hard on the jaw. While Johnson was being handled in his corner during the interval he looked down at me and said that Jeffries couldn't hit hard.

FIFTH ROUND.

Jeffries came away from his corner for this round in a low crouch. Johnson feinted. As Jeff stepped away Johnson kidded and said: "I will straighten him up in a minute." The crowd heard it and said, "He will straighten you up. Johnson led again with his left and landed on Jeffries's stomach. In the clinch which followed the big black looked over Jeffries's shoulders and grinned. Johnson tried to get in his short rights, and one which caught Jeff's mouth cut his upper lip. Jeffries led, but fell short Johnson met him and caught him with a straight left and right on the forehead. Johnson while in close brought his right hand up again on Jeff's mouth. Johnson caught Jeffries's left lead, and Jeff seemed bothered because he couldn't find an opening. As they stood off, Jeffries crouched, jumped to his toes, and landed the first straight blow to his credit during the fight, a straight left on Johnson's forehead.

SIXTH ROUND.

As they advanced to the centre of the ring, they both kept to their own sides, Johnson was the first to start hostilities with a hard one to Jeffries's body. He landed a left on Jeffries's cheek, and the blood trickled down the white man's face. Johnson brought his left back, shooting it again into Jeffries's stomach. They broke away and sparred around. Johnson backed Jeffries with a left feint, but Jeffries stepped out of the way. Johnson was showing all the cleverness, but Jeffries did not seem a bit disturbed, except that he constantly chewed his gum. In the next passage Johnson caught him, probably the hardest blow so far, a straight left, a walloping hard one, on Jeffries's jaw as the latter rushed in. The fiercest fighting so far followed this, but Johnson's blows were quicker and oftener. In the clinch which followed, they hugged persistently, Johnson working his short-arm deadeners. A hard left landed on Jeffries's eye. Johnson's blows were harder than they seemed. Jeffries was bleeding from the nose and his damaged right eye was getting blacker and blacker each second. They worked hard over Jeffries's body during the intermission, but it seemed to irritate him more than it did him good. He motioned them to let him alone.

SEVENTH ROUND.

Jeffries's right eye was closing as he came up for this round. Johnson was first to lead again. As they clinched Johnson said: "Come on, you Jeff." They fiddled around for fully twenty seconds. Jeffries was more careful. Johnson was grinning, and as Jeffries came forward the negro would step back. Finally Jeffries came in, but his left lead went around Johnson and landed on his neck. Jeffries's nose still kept bleeding all during the round. Johnson feinted with a left and landed a right counter on Jeffries's left shoulder. Then another clinch followed and Rickard told them to break. Rickard was having very little to do up to this time, as both men were fighting very squarely and fairly. In the next passage Johnson landed the most effective blow that had come across so far. It was a left on the chin, but it was mighty powerful. He followed this by a right on Jeffries's face. Jeff was beginning to show the effects of the punishment. The hot sun beat down on the fighters, and they perspired freely about the head, though Jeffries was exuding water pretty much from every pore in his body. In the clinch which followed Johnson struck up his left hand and landed it on Jeffries's damaged face. While Johnson was being wiped and rubbed during the interval he "kidded" Corbett, who was watching what was being done in his corner with an idea of rattling the champion. Johnson eyed him this time and yelled: "Too late now to do anything, Jim; your man's all in."

EIGHTH ROUND.

Johnson kept after Jeffries all the time, and as Jeffries led Johnson would stop him, coming in with a left on the chest. Jeffries led again, and caught a right on his ear and a hard left on his face. In the next lead, Johnson led a scoring blow; it was a terrific straight punch on Jeffries's nose. Then Jeffries got in on Johnson's stomach a hard one, but it did not disturb Johnson, and they hugged. When they broke away again, Johnson punched another left in Jeffries's face. Another clinch, and Johnson grinned over Jeffries's shoulder, and winking to the newspaper men, kept his left hand busy. It generally found a resting place. The referee here admonished them to break. Jeffries attempted to land a left on Johnson's head, but Johnson stepped away and then he stepped in again and landed a left on Jeffries's chin. They hugged around the ring, and took their time about breaking. As they sparred for another opening, Jeffries led and landed lightly on Johnson's jaw. In the clinch Johnson whipped his right half across and just grazed Jeffries's chin. They were clinching as the bell rang. On points and effectiveness, the fight was going all Johnson's way. There was no hard work in Johnson's corner during the minute rest, while Jeffries's handlers were busy as bees.

NINTH ROUND.

Jeffries started to lead and landed a light left on Johnson's body. A clinch followed, with Jeffries doing the holding. Johnson led on the breakaway, and landed lightly on the chest. Another clinch followed. As they broke away Johnson landed a left on the chin and a right on the jaw. As they stepped in again Johnson's left found Jeffries's stomach, and another clinch followed. Jeffries hugging to save himself. Johnson led a left, shooting it across lightly on Jeffries's face, but Jeffries stepped away and did not try to come back. Jeffries guarded his stomach safely from two lefts Johnson tried to put in. Two straight lefts found Jeffries's chin, and stopped him completely. As they broke away Johnson stepped quickly in and landed his left in Jeff's stomach. Johnson "kidded" the big boilermaker again as they passed each other going to their corners, and Jeffries was looking very much the worse for wear.

TENTH ROUND.

Both fiddled and Johnson feinted, but Jeffries didn't come in. Johnson tried another left, but Jeff stepped away. On his next attempt he landed straight on Jeffries's face and then they clinched. Jeffries all this time had not landed a real blow. Jeffries tried a right counter, but it didn't go through, then they clinched. Jeffries was half-hearted in his lead, and it brought nothing more than a clinch. Johnson shot over a straight right and landed on Jeffries's face. It was a clean blow, starting just as Jeffries came in. Johnson landed a hard left on Jeffries's stomach, and all that Jeffries could do was to plant both his hands on the negro's ribs. In the clinch which followed this Johnson did effective work with his short-arm punches, landing left and right on Jeffries's face. Jeffries essayed another lead when they came to the clinch. Jeffries appeared tired as he went to his corner and his handlers looked worried. Johnson, on the other hand, was keeping cool, and nobody in his corner was the least bit flustered. Mrs. Johnson, from about the sixth row on the west side of the arena, signaled to Johnson that he was doing great work. "Keep it up, Jack!" she shouted.

ELEVENTH ROUND.

They fiddled for an opening and Johnson landed a light right on Jeffries's cheek as they clinched. In the clinch Johnson landed a hard left on Jeff's chin. As Jeff broke away Johnson was right on top of him with left and right, but Jeff's attempts were like pawing the air. He got all the worst of it in this encounter, but he made an attempt to get back. It did not seem to worry the negro one bit. Johnson was working his close blows to perfection, and in every clinch he managed to land a right-hand uppercut or left. Jeffries's judgment of distance was pitiful to look at. He was spitting quantities of blood and breathing laboriously. Johnson was worrying him greatly and he was holding on. Johnson was working his famous short-arm punches like piston rods, and as they broke away he turned Jeffries's head clear around with a left on the jaw. A clinch followed, with Jeffries doing it all. He did not seem to have the punch, and Johnson was landing almost as he pleased. A straight right on the chin caught Jeffries and he wabbled. He pushed his hands out before him trying to hit the big negro, but Johnson banged a left on the bleeding mouth just as the round closed. It was all Johnson's round, and there was no betting against him anywhere.

TWELFTH ROUND.

Jeff was worried, for, try as he could, he could not reach Johnson, but he must feint, and every time he came in he caught a left or right somewhere where it hurt. In the clinches that followed, Johnson put three more rights on Jeffries's jaw, and Jeff clung to him. He was showing his punishment very plainly and was weakening fast. He did not try to hit Johnson. He was hugging all the while, Johnson meantime landing hard lefts and rights on Jeffries's nose, mouth, and jaw. Jeffries was getting very tired and his face was covered with blood. As he fiddled around from a breakaway, Johnson caught him with another hard right and a straight left, and he clinched again. As they broke, Johnson landed another left in the face and brought his right over on the jaw for good measure. Johnson went to his corner smiling and Jeffries was very tired.

THIRTEENTH ROUND.

Jeffries worked slowly toward Johnson and essayed a left hand feint which produced a clinch. Here Johnson called to a friend in the crowd over Jeff's shoulder: "Hello, Tom," Jeffries's efforts were very clumsy. In the next passage, Johnson planted another left on Jeffries's nose and also brought his right over. One left followed another from Johnson and they landed where he aimed them. Then there was clinching. Jeffries was not nearly as steady on his feet as the negro was. In the clinches he brought his left into Johnson's stomach and Johnson looked over his shoulder and never made an attempt to resist the punch aimed at his ribs. This looked like the beginning of the end. Johnson landed a left and right on Jeffries's face. Jeffries clinched and Johnson mercilessly beat away at him. Jeff was a sight to behold; his face was cut in six places and he was still going after Johnson. Johnson brought some lefts across and they always caught Jeffries on the face. Jeffries's arms seemed like lead and he could scarcely raise them, let alone hit Johnson. As the gong sounded, Jeff walked away slowly. He seemed all broken up and refused to be encouraged by his seconds. Johnson was jovial at all times.

FOURTEENTH ROUND.

Johnson lost no time in this round and planted that ever-ready left in Jeff's face and Jeff hugged. As he stepped away he caught another left on his face. In the clinch that followed he tried to bring his right up on Johnson's jaw and landed lightly, but it never bothered the big negro. Jeffries tried a right swing, but Johnson anticipated it and landed a left on Jeff's face. Jeff straightened, the crowd yelling. He tried a straight left for Johnson's face. He landed, but it made no impression only to bring a laugh from Johnson, who in the next clinch dared Jeff to hit, just to see how hard he could do it. Jeffries started to use his great strength, and put all his weight into a body blow while he was clinching with Johnson. Johnson pushed him away and brought his left around on Jeffries's jaw. Jeffries tried two ineffectual lefts, but Johnson got in close. Johnson "kidded" all his attempts. During the minute's rest only water was being used in Johnson's corner, while in Jeffries's they were bringing everything into play that they had.

FIFTEENTH ROUND.

Johnson met Jeff in the centre of the ring and sent a left on Jeff's eye, and then they clinched. Johnson broke quickly and shot a left from his hip straight into Jeffries's face. Jeff tottered and went down on the west side of the ring. He fell on both knees, and as the timekeeper and referee yelled at him the number of seconds, he turned around and rested one foot on the floor, looking the while toward the timekeeper. Johnson walked about the centre, craftily eyeing his big opponent. Jeff waited for nine and then arose. Johnson stepped in as he got on his feet and whipped another left full on the face, and Jeff went down again almost in the same place, but this time he crashed through the ropes. Several of his seconds and some newspaper men helped to get him back in the ring again, and Johnson coolly watched the proceedings for more than half way across the ring.

When Jeff landed inside again, he was reeling, but not nearly as far gone as lots of fellows who have been down twice for the count. He staggered over to the east side and Johnson stepped in to him as he came over and sent him reeling with a right on the ear. As he turned around, ready to close down, Johnson's left again found the already battered and beaten face. As Jeff sank sideways to the floor the immense crowd was on its feet, some yelling and some cheering. Johnson calmly walked around his big opponent toward his own corner. His seconds were already getting his chair ready to push through the ropes for him to sit on. Timekeeper Hartig was yelling at the top of his voice the enumerated seconds. About eight seconds from the time Jeff went down one of his handlers broke into the ring.

He was closely followed by two more. That was sufficient to end the fight, according to the rules. Billy Delaney, always Johnny-on-the-spot for transgressions like these, broke through the ropes and made his way to Tex Rickard, loudly demanding the fight for his man. Tex in the meanwhile was trying to make himself heard to the effect that he had already decided Johnson the winner.

Johnson was the winner, the fight was over, and Jeff was being dragged to his corner. Johnson walked over ostensibly to shake hands with his beaten foe, but the crowd in the ring was too much for him, and he was dragged away by his seconds. Jeffries stayed there for fully ten minutes after the final gong, with his seconds fussing over him and trying to bring him to some kind of presentable shape.

The round lasted, according to Timekeeper Harting, two minutes and twenty-five seconds. JOHN L. SULLIVAN.

JEFFRIES GOING HOME.

Plans to Return to His California Ranch at Once.

JEFFRIES'S TRAINING CAMP, July 4.—Jeffries, the pugilist, left the camp early this morning. Jim Jeffries, farmer, returned. He will never enter the ring again. That was settled once and for all to-day.

Mrs. Jeffries arrived at the camp half an hour before the car from the ringside appeared. She was weeping, but endeavored to restrain her sobs. When Jeffries's car stopped in front of the cottage she rushed out to him, and together they passed from sight through the door.

There were few to witness the return of the vanquished fighter. Two or three automobiles stood in the road where fifty had been crowded in the morning. Jeffries's personal friends were there, eager to do something to aid him, but unable to find words. Jeffries stepped from the house a few moments after he entered it and went to the rubbing room. He walked a little unsteadily and seemed a bit dazed. His trainers accompanied him, and after a bath he was rubbed down and partook of a glass or two of wine. It was then he made his first statement after leaving the ring, and he said he was sorry for his friends. Jeffries also was puffed from the blows, but the flow of blood had been stopped.

His right eye, to the blinding of which his trainers attributed his defeat in so few rounds, was swollen almost shut, but not injured seriously.

There have been no changes in Jeffries's plans. He purposes to return to his home in Southern California at once. He will leave with his wife and a few friends to-morrow.

LARGE SUMS WAGERED.

RENO, Nev., July 4.—It is estimated that over $250,000 was won and lost in Reno alone on the outcome of to-day's fight. Betting Commissioner Corbett announced to-night that three wagers of $10,000 each and several approximating $5,000 were intrusted to him at the ringside to-day by men of National prominence. The Pari mutuels paid $20.90 to $1 on Johnson to win in from fourteen to nineteen rounds.

George Considine of New York bet $5,000 on Jeffries at odds of 10 to 6½, and announced that he had more at the same price.

At 11 o'clock the betting was 2 to 1 on Jeffries, with plenty of money in sight to back the white man. On twenty rounds the figures were even money, with more Johnson cash than Jeffries money in sight.

At noon the betting had gone back to 10 to 6. When the word went around that 2 to 1 was to be had the Johnson money came in with a rush and quickly forced the odds back to where they had stood since yesterday

LONDON NOT SURPRISED.

Special Cable to THE NEW YORK TIMES.

LONDON, Tuesday, July 5.—Johnson's victory was received here with mingled feelings. Although it was almost midnight when the news came through, excited crowds thronged the leading hotels and gathered around the newspaper offices anxiously awaiting the result. When it did come it cannot be said to have caused so much surprise as regret, for, truth to tell, the English had all along pinned their faith on the negro, believing it impossible for Jeffries to "come back."

At the National Sporting Club, where hundreds of leading sportmen awaited the result, the feeling prevailed that it at least showed Americans capable of sinking racial feeling in allowing a colored man to win, grave doubt having been freely expressed beforehand that this would be the case. Thus the negro's victory has raised the English opinion of American fair play.

SAD CROWD AT RINGSIDE.

Sympathy with Jeffries in Defeat—Not the Fighter of Old.

By Associated Press.

RENO, Nev., July 4.—John Arthur Johnson, a Texas negro, the son of an American slave, to-night is the undisputed heavyweight champion of the world.

James J. Jeffries of California, winner of twenty-two championship fights, the man who never was brought to his knees before by a blow, to-night passed into history as a broken idol. He met utter defeat at the hands of the black champion.

While Jeffries was not actually counted out, he was saved only from this crowning shame by his friends pleading with Johnson not to hit the fallen man again, and the towel was brought into the ring from his corner. At the end of the fifteenth round Referee Tex Rickard raised the black arm, and the great crowd filed out, glum and silent.

Jeffries was dragged to his corner, bleeding from nose and mouth and a dozen cuts on the face. He had a black, closed eye and swollen features, and he held his head in his hands, dazed and incoherent.

Johnson walked out of the ring without a mark on his body except a slight cut on his lip, which was the opening of a wound received in training.

Ring experts agree that it was not even a championship fight. Jeffries had a chance in the second round, perhaps, but after the sixth it was plain that the undefeated one was weakening and outclassed in every point, and after the eleventh round it was hopeless.

Not the Old Jeffries.

It was the greatest demonstration the ring has ever seen of the failure of a fighter to "come back" after years of retirement. The youth and science of the black man made Jeffries look like a green man.

The great Jeffries was like a log. The reviled Johnson was like a black panther, beautiful in his alertness and defensive tactics.

Jeffries fought by instinct, it seemed, showing his gameness and his great fighting heart in every round, but he was only a shell of his old self. The old power to take a terrible beating and bore in until he landed the knockout blow was gone.

After the third round Johnson treated his opponent almost as a joke. He smiled and blocked playfully, warding off the rushes of Jeffries with a marvelous science, now tucking a blow under his arm, again plucking it out of the air as a man stops a baseball.

The battle was honestly fought. Of that there was no doubt after the first round. There was no evidence or hint of the famous "yellow streak" on the part of Johnson.

Johnson proved himself so absolutely Jeffries's master that experts, such as W. Corbett, the Australian sporting writer and ring expert, declared that Tommy Burns had put up a better fight against Johnson, and that the black man was only playing with the other man.

The end was swift and terrible. It looked as though Johnson had been holding himself under cover all the rest of the time, and now that he had measured Jeffries in all his weaknesses he had determined to stop it quick.

Jeffries had lost the power of defense. A series of right and left uppercuts, delivered at will, sent him staggering to the ropes. He turned and fought back by instinct and because he was dying hard.

With the exception of a few fast rounds the fight was tame. Jeffries did not have the power in his punch to hurt Johnson after he had received blow after blow on the jaw, and his vital power was ebbing. But even before this stage came Jeffries could not reach the black man effectively. The blows landed with nearly all the speed taken out of them. It was like hitting a punching bag.

The Jeffries crouch was in evidence at times, but during most of the fight Jeffries fought standing straight and working with something of his old aggressiveness.

When the Finish Came.

The fifteenth round started with a clinch after Jeffries had failed to land on the body. Johnson then tore loose, and before the spectators were prepared for the finish he had sent Jeffries down with lightninglike left and right blows to the jaw. Jeffries fell half way through the ropes on the west side of the ring.

Those under him saw that he had lost his sense of surroundings and that the faces at the ringside were a blur to him. His time had come. He was feeling what he had caused others to feel in the days of his youth and power.

Johnson came over and stood poised over his adversary, his body ready for a left hook if Jeffries regained his feet.

Jim Corbett, who stood in Jeffries's corner all during this fight, telling Johnson what a fool he was and how he was in for the beating of his life, now ran forward with outstretched arms, crying, "Oh, don't, Jack; don't hit him!"

Jeffries painfully raised himself to his feet. His jaw had dropped. His eyes were nearly shut and his face was covered with blood. With trembling legs and shielding arms he tried to put up a defense, but he could not stop a terrific right smash on the jaw, followed by two left hooks. He went down again. Jeffries's physician and other friends jumped toward the ring.

"Stop it!" they cried. "Don't put the old fellow out!"

Sam Berger ran along the ring calling to Bob Armstrong, "Bring that towel—you know what I mean—don't let him get hit."

From Johnson's corner his seconds were calling to him to quit. Then the referee stopped the time keeper, and it was all over.

Soothing lotions were applied to the fallen champion's bruised face, but his heart was something that could not be reached. He bowed his head in his hands and groaned:

"I was too old to come back."

Corbett, Choynski, Jack Jeffries, and the others were ready to cry, but they united in trying to cheer the defeated man.

"It's all off with you, Jim," said Corbett, "but you did the best you could."

"Cheer up, we'll go fishing to-morrow," said Frank Gotch, the wrestling champion.

In an instant after the crowd realized that the fight was over the ring was stampeded by a wild throng. The short-end betting men were hilarious, but in the great mass of the spectators there was a feeling of personal loss. Hope had lived in thousands of breasts until the last minute, and now their idol had crumbled and this black man stood peerless. They could not help admire him, and there was little animosity shown toward him. For the most part the people were silent, just readjusting things to their minds. Hundreds swallowed the bitter pill of heavy financial loss.

Arrival of the Fighters.

Little enthusiasm for anything was shown before the fight began until Jack Johnson and his crew were seen stringing down the aisle. Then the crowd stood up and cheered, as much from pent-up excitement as anything else.

This was 2:28 o'clock, an hour after the scheduled time for the fight. Four minutes later Jeffries loomed out of the crowd on the other side of the arena, and then the cheering broke loose again.

The ring was quickly crowded with trainers and seconds. Jeffries laughed as he passed through the ropes and jumped up and down on the platform for a moment, satisfying himself that it was strong enough. He wore his old soft cap and an old suit of clothes, and chewed gum. Johnson wore a bathrobe with violet lining.

Berger walked up to Johnson and asked him to toss for corners.

"Take any corner you want," said Johnson; "it's all the same to me."

Berger took the southwest corner and gave Johnson the northeast. This placed the sun in Johnson's eyes.

Behind the fighters as the bandages were being fastened stood Corbett and Billy Delaney.

The veteran Delaney made the match of keener interest to the sporting men. He was in Johnson's corner as an open enemy of Jeffries. Delaney picked up Jeffries at Carson City when Corbett met Fitzsimmons, and made him a great fighter. At that time Delaney was Corbett's trainer and manager and later acted for years in the same capacity for Jeffries. A quarrel made this situation possible.

With no preliminary handshaking or picture posing the men faced each other at 2:45 o'clock. Johnson wore blue tights and an American flag as his belt. There was a sign of involuntary admiration as his naked body stood in the white sunlight. Jeffries in his purple trunks stood out as a hairy giant.

Jeers at Johnson.

There was no open attempt on the part of Jeffries and his men to frighten the negro. They figured he would be trembling with fear at the sight of the white monster and there were many cries of "Cold feet, Johnson" when his entrance in the ring was delayed.

Now when the men stood up at last to fight it out, each on their own resources, it was plain that the negro was very nervous.

"Now, you will get it, you black coward," yelled Jeffries's admirers.

"Don't talk to them, give them a square deal," said the majority of the men at the ringside.

Johnson Soon Gained Confidence.

The men smiled at each other. Jeffries feinted, Johnson glided away. Johnson tried out a straight left and tapped Jeffries's face. They clinched and worked cautiously for body blows, but there was little snap in either and they were still waltzing when the round ended.

"Cut out the motion pictures," yelled the crowd. Johnson turned and tapped Jeffries lightly on the shoulder as he went to his corner and smiled.

At the opening of the second round Jeffries came up with his old crouch, with his left arm stuck out like a scantling. This was the blow and the attitude that carried him to glory in the early days of his fighting career. But there was a change in the negro. He had found himself. This was no terror of the mountains to be afraid of. Here was a simple boxer and in his heart of hearts Jack Johnson believed he was master. Six years ago when Johnson whipped Jack Jeffries he walked up to Jim, who was in his brother's corner, and said: "I can whip you, too."

And this conviction was uppermost in him when the second round began. The slight indecision and trembling of Johnson's mouth and the glint of trouble in his eyes were gone. He forced the fighting and in a clinch made his first attempt at his carefully developed right uppercut.

Jeffries took it without flinching. He tried another but missed. The men wrestled and Johnson showed that he was as strong as Jeffries.

"All right, Jim, I'll love you if you want me to," said Johnson as they clinched just after the gong rang.

Between the whisking of towels and the dashing of water and hasty gargling, Delaney poured into Johnson's ear his words of advice. He know now—probably knew long before the battle—just how it would end. Did he not know every inch of Jim Jeffries's body and the limitations of his brain? Each blow taught him what had happened in five years of easy life of the former champion.

In the second, third and fourth rounds Jeffries had his chance if he ever had one. The first showed that he could not stay long.

His friends claim now that if he had started in with his entire force he could have reached Johnson with a sleeping blow. On the other hand, men whose opinions are valued on these matters say Johnson could have beaten Jeffries at any time in Jeffries's career.

At any rate, Jeffries passed by his chance. Jeffries kept walking in, missing body blows and taking face punishment. Up to this point, however, the fight was little more than a wrestling bout. The men refused to break in clinches and at times half a minute passed without a blow being struck.

The Start Was Slow.

At the beginning of the fourth round Rickard became disgusted with the way things were going, and when Corbett told Jeffries to take it easy as he started for the centre of the ring the referee said:

"Quit this motion work; get busy, boys."

Jeffries assumed his crouch and started for Johnson as if he would mow him down with one blow. But the black was not there. His shadow fell across the spot where Jeffries's blow was aimed. They came together and Johnson missed for the fourth time a damaging right uppercut. Here he began to try out his new blow, a left uppercut, testing it out first.

Johnson kept up a fire of jokes and repartee, sometimes with Jeffries, often with Corbett, and again with sporting writers.

"He'll kill you, Jack," yelled a sporting man who had bet $10,000 on Jeffries.

"That's what they all say," retorted Johnson, and for answer he shot a snappy left to Jeffries's face and they came to a clinch. In this round Jeffries landed the only blow that came near hurting Johnson. It was a body blow that made the black man wince. It was the only round in which Jeffries had an advantage, and the opening of the fifth Johnson came up as good as new. The pace up to and through this round was slow. Neither man was badly hurt.

"That left was a joke. You big stiff, I always knew you were a faker," shouted Corbett as Johnson stung Jeffries in the face. Jeffries brought cheers at this point by a left to the head, but a clinch and the gong ended it.

The tide of battle from this time on flowed into the Johnson corner, and Delaney was hopping in glee.

"Go in and finish him," was the advice whispered to Johnson.

"It's all over for you, Jim," said Johnson, as he came up. Jeffries laughed and chewed his gum. In this round Jeffries's eye was closed, and he started in to take a severe lacing in order to land the stomach blow which he and his backers depended upon. Jeffries missed a right and took a right and left to the head. His nose was bleeding when the gong struck.

Corbett walked to the end of the ring and looked at Johnson. The negro was smiling and breathing easy.

"It's got a long time to go," he said to the sporting men and those who had bet money on the seven-round end. The fighting in the seventh was somewhat faster, but at no time did Jeffries live up to expectations. His eye was swollen, and he rubbed it as he leaned on the glistening black shoulder in the clinches. He was beginning to look more like a wounded bull than a clever thinking man. As they rushed each other around, Johnson sent in lefts to the face twice at close range. Jeffries drew a lead and put in a left to the face that covered Johnson's golden teeth with blood, but Jack laughed and in a mix-up sent in two lefts to the face, and Jeffries's mouth was streaked with blood.

Crowd Begins to Fear for Jeffries.

"It looks bad for Jeffries," said the sports as a slight indecision in Jeffries's walk was noticed.

"Remember how much he took from Fitzsimmons and then landed," said the hopeful ones.

Jeffries got a left in the face at the opening of the eighth.

"Did you see that one, Jimmy?" said Johnson to Corbett as he leaned over Jeffries's shoulder and grinned. Johnson's blows became quicker and harder during this round, but Jeffries was not badly hurt, only tiring faster than the spectators realized. He leaned forward, his eyes fixed on a vital spot on Johnson's body, trying again and again to reach it. Johnson tried to put his uppercut through, but Jeffries still possessed the quickness to snap his head out of danger.

"Stand up and fight, you coward," yelled Corbett as Johnson tucked away a body blow in the ninth.

"Just wait," said Jack. He waited for a lead, and then put a hard left to the body, but Jeffries stopped it with his glove. As the round ended he hit Johnson in the ribs in a way that was not relished. After this round George Little, Johnson's ex-manager, placed several hundred dollars at ten to nine on Jeffries.

The tenth was rather slow. Jeffries brushing away the head blows as he would brush away flies and trying always for that terrible body punch. Jeffries also tried to wear down Jack by his weight in the clinches. But Johnson did about an equal amount of shoving and succeeded in getting in his new left uppercut to the face several times.

The eleventh opened carefully. Johnson let loose and kept his man's head bobbing constantly. In a clinch Johnson landed three uppercuts and Jeffries began to show distress. He was slowing down. A hard right to the nose sent the blood spattering.

One of Jeffries's friends left the ringside crying. Men looked and sighed as they saw the old champion's legs shaking on his way to his corner.

"Watch him! Get him!" called Delaney as Johnson met Jeffries's slow lead in the twelfth.

"I will," said Johnson and smiled. He waited, drew back, and hooked Jeffries hard in the face. Jeffries looked tired, but whacked away at the body, drawing forth only a pretty exhibition of boxing on the part of the black that set the crowd cheering. Jeffries spat out a great quantity of blood as he walked to his corner and Johnson fairly beamed confidence.

The thirteenth showed rapid dissolution on Jeffries's part. Following Corbett's advice he stuck to the clinch until he was forced away. Then he received two lefts and a right uppercut to the face. After that Johnson played with him. Holding Jeffries with his right on the shoulder Johnson fairly rained left blows to the face and Jeffries wilted. He continued to come on, however, with his eye almost closed and his legs sinking.

The crowd waited silently for the fourteenth and watched hopelessly when Jeffries walked into a left and then failed to get his own left home. The wonderful work of the negro was never in better evidence than here. He was simply unhittable

"How do you like 'em, Jim?" he asked of the sober and silent Jeffries. To the end of the round he continued to give more of them.

Johnson opened up his heavy battery at the opening of the fifteenth round. It seemed no great effort for him to finish it all. There was only one side to it.

Less than an hour of fighting had served to bring to an end the career of the man hitherto believed invincible, and had solved the question that had been agitating the world since Johnson won the championship belt from Tommy Burns.

CROWD GATHERS AT ARENA.

About 20,000 See the Fight at a Cost of $360,000.

Special to The New York Times.

RENO, July 4.—Between midnight and 9 o'clock this morning fifteen special trains from San Francisco, Sacramento, Los Angeles, Vancouver, Seattle, Portland, Spokane, and other points landed their heavy loads of perspiring humanity on the streets of Reno, which became so congested that all traffic was stopped for a time. The cooks and porters on the Pullmans came up and staked their dollars on Johnson and then went back to the station to await the result.

By 10 o'clock the crowd, which was estimated to number 25,000, had commenced to wend its way to the arena, which was about three-quarters of a mile east from the station and close to the railroad tracks. They went in automobiles and all kinds of horse vehicles, but the majority walked along the railroad tracks or the dusty road that led to the arena.

I OUTCLASSED HIM, JOHNSON DECLARES

Says He Won Because He Was Jeffries's Superior in Ever Point of Fighting.

RICKARD PICKED JEFFRIES

But Johnson Won as He Pleased—First Knockdown Settled Contest

RENO, July 4.—Jack Johnson made the following statement after the fight:

"I won from Mr. Jeffries because I outclassed him in every department of the fighting game. Before I entered the ring I was certain I would be the victor. I never changed my mind at any time.

"Jeffries's blows had no steam behind them. So, how could he hope to defeat me? With the exception of a slight cut on my lower lip, which was really caused by an old wound being struck, I am unmarked. I heard people at the ringside remark about body blows being inflicted upon me. I do not recall a single punch in the body that caused me any discomfort. I am in shape to battle again tomorrow if it were necessary.

"One thing I must give Jeffries credit for is the game battle he made. He came back at me with the heart of a true fighter. No man can say he did not do his best.

"I believe we both fought fairly. There was nothing said between us which was rough. He joked me and I joked him. I told him I knew he was a bear but I was a gorilla and would defeat him.

"For the next few weeks I shall play in vaudeville. Then I shall go to my home in Chicago to rest I do not think I shall fight for several months, because I do not know a man now who could give me a good battle. No attention will be paid to Sam Langford's challenges by me. I do not consider he could give me a fight that would draw."

Johnson's first words after Jeffries went down were:

"I could have fought for two hours longer. It was easy. Where is my lucky bathrobe? I'm going to give one of my gloves to Jeffries and the other to Corbett. I guess Jeff won't be so grouchy now. Somebody wire to my mother. I wish it was some longer. I was having lots of fun. Not one blow hurt me. He can't hit. He won't forget two punches I landed on him. He was only half the trouble Burns was."

Tex Rickard, the referee and promoter of the fight, said:

"Jack Johnson is the most wonderful fighter that ever pulled on a glove. He won as he pleased from Jeff and was never in danger. I could not help but feel sorry for the big white man as he fell beneath the champion's blows. It was the most pitiable fight I ever saw. As a matter of fact, I thought away down in my heart that Jeffries would be the winner of the fight.

"All the News That's Fit to Print."

The New York Times.

THE WEATHER.

Generally fair and continued warm to-day and to-morrow; moderate south winds.

☞ For full weather report see Page 17.

VOL. LXI...NO. 19,889. * * * NEW YORK, MONDAY, JULY 8, 1912.—EIGHTEEN PAGES. ONE CENT In Greater New York, Jersey City, and Newark. | Elsewhere, TWO CENTS.

ARMED PRISONER AT BAY IN TOMBS

Knocks Down Keeper After Attempt to Escape Is Discovered and Takes His Pistol.

THEN STANDS OFF GUARDS

687 Prisoners Groan in Chorus as Shots Are Fired at Fugitive Hiding in Jail Cellar.

THOUSANDS AROUND PRISON

Police Reserves Guard Tombs Wall and Keep Back Throng—Man in Hiding a Dangerous Burglar.

Somewhere in the unlighted passages of the cellars beneath the Tombs and the old building from which runs the Bridge of Sighs, now known as the Annex, a man was hiding early this morning, listening, it may be imagined, to the footsteps of guards who were searching for him. The man, George Wilson, an ex-convict and a burglar whose exploits have won him the nickname of "Raffles" from the police, clutched a revolver in his hand, a six-shooter, from which he had fired just one shot. Five shots were left in his weapon, and though several times uneasy keepers had let fly a bullet at his shadow as he slipped from hiding place to hiding place in the dim recesses of the cellar, Wilson, up to midnight, had hoarded his ammunition. Not one shot after the first one had been drawn from him.

In the small hours of this morning Night Warden Jones, with his twenty-five keepers and the reserves of the Elizabeth Street Police Station were still conducting the search for the fugitive, but it seemed likely, even to the searchers, that they would get no trace of Wilson until daylight came to their aid. Through the building a rumor swept that Wilson long before had scaled the wall about the Tombs and had escaped with the aid of a confederate, who might have thrown a rope over the wall from the outside. Warden Jones and several keepers, who had taken shots at what they thought was Wilson's form dimly outlined in the darkness of the cellar, were convinced, however, that at midnight Wilson still lay hidden somewhere beneath the prison, and that there he had a good chance of staying undiscovered until daylight disclosed his hiding place.

However, they searched the Criminal Court building also on the chance that he had crossed the Birdge of Sighs.

Escape from His Cell Unexplained.

How Wilson escaped from his cell is not known, though Warden Jones has a theory that he slipped from the line while the prisoners were exercising in the corridors of the jail yesterday afternoon, and then slid down a pipe in a two-foot shaft which carries steam and water pipes throughout the building.

That he was missing was discovered when Warden Jones and Keeper Kelly went through the seventh and eighth tiers of the prison taking the roll for the night. That was at 9:30 o'clock. The Warden counted 121 prisoners, that many of the 688 in jail being lodged in these tiers. Kelly's count was only 120, and a second count showed that Wilson was missing. Instantly the alarm was given, and every one of the twenty-five keepers, armed with revolvers, began the search for Wilson.

At first no one got trace of him, but then Keeper William Hollihan went into the yard. He saw no one there, and was passing from the new building to the annex when he was felled by a heavy blow on the head. A man bent over him, wrested his revolver from his hand, and then ran as the keeper, dazed, but still conscious, staggered to his feet.

Wilson—it was he who had struck the keeper and grabbed the revolver—turned to see Hollihan stumbling after him, and fired one shot at the man. It flew wild, but Hollihan ducked instinctively, glancing up again just in time to see Wilson disappear into a manhole which gave into a bin near the kitchen, where potatoes and other vegetables are dropped down a chute. The fact that Hollihan ducked, and so was not positive that he had seen Wilson disappear, led to the rumor that the fugitive had scaled the wall. Hollihan was so sure, however, that he saw Wilson go down the manhole that Warden Jones and the other keepers were convinced that Wilson was in the jail buildings somewhere.

The report of the shot which Wilson fired resounded through the jail, and an instant afterward there came a hurried telephone call from Engineer L. J. Daly, asking Warden Jones to come to the engine room at once, armed with his revolver. The engineer had heard a noise in the coal just an instant after he had heard the report of the revolver shot.

Keepers Fire at Fugitive.

Warden Jones hurried to the engine room, but he found no trace of Wilson. He was still hunting when there came the report of a second shot from another part of the extensive cellars, and presently an excited keeper ran up to say that he thought he had seen Wilson and had fired but thought he had not hit him.

At the report of the shot there rose through every corridor of the Tombs a long-drawn, mournful groan or wail, the cry which prisoners in every jail give whenever one of their number is being sought by the guards. The wailing cry and the shots were heard clearly in the streets, and presently crowds began to collect in Centre, Lafayette, Franklin, and Leonard Streets, which surround the Tombs.

Within the prison the guards ran about excitedly, and one of them, it was said, fired two shots at a terrified prison chef who crouched on the cellar stairs, too frightened to explain that he was not Wilson. Then Warden Jones sent for the police.

Lieut. McCormick and Sergt. McGuire with the reserves of the Elizabeth Street Station House hurried to the prison and the officers went inside after posting

Continued on Page 2.

TAFT AND MacVEAGH CONFER.

On Same Train from Boston—Secretary Denies He'll Quit.

Special to The New York Times.

BOSTON, July 7.—President Taft and Secretary Franklin MacVeagh left Boston to-night for Washington on the Federal limited. Secretary MacVeagh had come down from his Summer home at Dublin, N. H., and President Taft had motored over from Beverly, Mass. John Hays Hammond was in the private car with them.

The meeting between the President and Secretary is thought to have a bearing on the resignation of Arthur Platt Andrew, Assistant Secretary of the Treasury. When informed that Senator Lodge had come out in Andrew's defense, Mr. MacVeagh said that he intended to make no other statement in regard to the matter than the one he already had given out. He declined to comment on Senator Lodge's statement that Mr. Andrew had saved the country a great deal of money during his term in office. He remarked, however, that James F. Curtis, also a Boston man, and an Assistant Secretary of the Treasury, was doing excellent work, and that he felt himself fortunate to have so able an assistant.

Mr. MacVeagh also took occasion to deny reports that he would resign from the Cabinet.

"The matter has never come up in any conversation that I have had with President Taft," said the Secretary, "and you may say that the reports are absolutely untrue."

HEAT CAUSES ONE DEATH.

Temperature Only Five Degrees Lower Than on Hottest Day.

One death and many prostrations were caused by the heat in this city yesterday. The day was not the hottest of the Summer, but it was within five degrees of the record, and those who had to stay in the city did not notice much difference. The maximum register was 84 degrees at 3 P. M., and the minimum 63 degrees at 3:30 A. M. At 8 o'clock last night the mercury had dropped to 72 degrees, but to-day, if the Weather Bureau forecast holds good, it will again soar, and the day will probably be as hot as was yesterday.

Clarence Schorb, 24 years old, of Plainfield, N. J., had been to Coney Island with his wife, and was on his way home when he was taken ill in the ferry house at the foot of Liberty Street. An ambulance was summoned from the Hudson Street Hospital, but Mr. Schorb was dead when the doctor arrived.

The most serious of the cases of heat prostration reported were those of John Duffy, 28 years old, of 184 Wyckoff Street, Brooklyn; Louis Myer, 45 years old, of 30 Henry Street, Manhattan, and John Patterson, 39 years old, of 159 Albany Street, Brooklyn.

In the Central Park Zoo the animals in the lion house suffered greatly from the heat. The big Siberian tiger and the young leopard "Tom" showed their sufferings most pitifully, and Keeper Crowley played the hose upon these two beasts frequently during the afternoon.

To the hippopotami the day was one of unalloyed bliss, and Miss Murphy and her companion left their pool to get the full benefit of the beating sun.

GREAT STORM HITS CHICAGO.

Rainfall Floods Basements and Keeps Fire Department Busy.

Special to The New York Times.

CHICAGO, July 7.—A violent electrical storm, entailing a property loss of many thousand dollars, swept over this city this afternoon. It broke the backbone of the heat wave which has lasted for several days, causing the death of twenty persons.

To-day's storm was accompanied by a peculiarly heavy rainfall. In some sections of the city the rainfall was estimated at from four to six inches. This downpour, during the three hours' duration of the storm, completely choked the sewers in the business district as well as in many of the outlying residential sections. Streets were rendered impassable for hours. The Fire Department was swamped with calls for engines to pump out flooded basements, more than 200 appeals for help being made within the first hour of the storm.

Lightning, which was exceptionally vivid, terrifying the more timid, struck in innumerable places. The Fire Department responded to forty-two alarms of fire while the storm was in progress, all but one or two of the outbreaks being caused by lightning. While many buildings were struck by lightning and some demolished, there was no loss of life, although many narrow escapes were recorded. On Lake Michigan the storm created havoc among pleasure craft, and a number of rescues from drowning were made by the life-saving crew.

FOUR DIE IN LABOR RIOT.

Lumber Mill Force and Union Men Clash in Louisiana.

BATON ROUGE, La., July 7.—Four men were killed in a labor riot at Galloway's mill, three miles from De Ridder, according to a message received to-night by Gov. Hall. The Sheriff of Calcasieu has been authorized to call out troops.

Open warfare is said to exist between union men and the members of the lumber mill force. Many are reported injured and there is much excitement.

De Ridder is on the Kansas City Southern Railroad, fifty-three miles north of Lake Charles.

The dead are Gates Hall, Roy Morton, Edward Brown, and an unidentified Italian. Hall, Morton, and Brown were union men. A party of 200 union men from De Ridder, under the leadership of A. L. Emerson, President of the Brotherhood of Timber Workers, went to Grabow, where a strike is in progress, to hold a meeting. The proprietor of the mill and his non-union employes met them and in a wordy clash that followed some one fired a revolver. This was followed by a fusillade.

Sheriff Reid left in a special train for Grabow, accompanied by the Coroner, and a detachment of the Louisiana National Guard will follow as soon as the men can be assembled.

Trouble has been brewing for some time. The mill at Grabow employs sixty workmen.

AMERICANS CAPTURE FIRST OLYMPIC RACE

Complete Sweep by Yankee Athletes in 100 Meters Sprint Sets the Stadium in Uproar.

PENTATHLON IS ALSO OURS

And Six of the Eight Competitors Left in the 800 Meters Run Carry American Colors.

By Marconi Transatlantic Wireless Telegraph to The New York Times.

STOCKHOLM, July 7.—For the second time in the history of the Olympic games the Stars and Stripes floated today from all three flag poles on which are hoisted the national emblems of the countries obtaining first, second, and third places in final events.

The previous occasion was at Athens, when American athletes won all the points in the standing broad jump. The event to-day in which the Americans made a clean sweep was the final of the 100-meter flat race, which produced a struggle worthy alike of the gallant men competing and of the traditions of the Attic games.

Barely a yard separated the first and fifth men at the finish, and none of the 20,000 present except the judges knew who had won. But a moment later a mighty shout rose when the numbers were posted, showing that Ralph Craig of Detroit was first, Meyer, the New Yorker, second, and Lippincott of Philadelphia third. Patching of South Africa was fourth, and Belote took fifth place.

By this time the American contingent had got their second wind, and the "rahs" that followed the hoisting of the flags high above the roof of the stadium were something not easily to be forgotten. There was a touch of sadness about the rejoicing for those who remembered that sitting in one of the dressing rooms was an American youth who would have given his life almost to have run. This was H. P. Drew of Springfield, Mass., who performed so finely yesterday, but in doing this unfortunately sprained his leg badly. Hoping against hope that he might be able to start, Drew donned his running togs and went out to the starting post, but had to be helped back.

"Tough luck," said a well-known American, who stood near THE TIMES correspondent, and many who heard him answered: "It is."

Drew was a warm favorite in this event until he received his injury.

Scarcely had the cheering over the triple victory in the hundred meter race died away, when L. E. Meredith, the Pennsylvania schoolboy, started them again by winning his heat in the semi-finals of the 800 meters race. The German champion, Braun, was second, with Melvin Sheppard, the American star, third, and Putnam, the Cornell crack, fourth. The first four in each heat are eligible to compete in the final to-morrow.

In the second heat Brock, the Canadian, obtained first place, closely followed by Edmundson of the Pacific Coast. Caldwell provided the surprise of the race, so far as Americans were concerned, by taking third place, while Ira Davenport of Chicago was fourth.

Six of Eight for 800 Meters Final.

Thus out of the eight men who qualified for the final, six are Americans, and many experts think that history will repeat itself in the outcome.

Besides these successes on the cinder path James Thorpe of the Carlisle Indian School won the pentathlon, with J. J. Donoghue of California third. This event is designed to show the all-around ability of athletes, and consists of the running broad jump, throwing the javelin, 200 meters run, throwing the discus, and 1,500 meters run. Thorpe won first place in all except the javelin throw, in which he was third.

Commenting on Thorpe's success, Commissioner Sullivan said to THE TIMES correspondent:

"His all-around work was certainly sensational. It is a complete answer to the charge that is often made, that Americans specialize in athletics. In fact, the pentathlon was added to the games especially for the benefit of foreigners, but we have shown that we can produce all-around men, too. It also answers the allegation that most of our runners are of foreign parentage, for Thorpe is a real American, if there ever was one."

Commenting on the incidents in the 100-meter race, when several false starts were made before the men eventually got away, and in one of these the starter actually fired his pistol and Lippincott and Craig ran the whole course in vain Commissioner Sullivan said that he was glad that the Americans won, for if the result had been different he would surely have lodged an emphatic protest, as the rules say with the firing of the pistol the race is on.

As to the final in the 800 meters race to-morrow the winner is expected to be either Sheppard, Meredith, or Davenport, with the latter the favorite.

Another bit of ill-luck befell the Americans early in the day, when Willie Kramer, while running in a heat of the 10,000 meters race, for which he was much fancied, had a recurrence of a bad strain of a tendon of

Continued on Page 3.

YOUNG MEN IN POLITICS.

This year's campaign has brought to the front a number of strong men of the younger generation. Read about them in

NEXT SUNDAY'S TIMES.

THIRD PARTY CALLED TO CHICAGO AUG. 5

Four of the Seven Roosevelt Governors, Glasscock, Stubbs, Bass, and Hadley, Don't Sign.

CALL OLD PARTIES CORRUPT

Dissatisfied Voters Asked to Join the New—Old Age Pensions and Recall to be in the Platform.

With a flourish of trumpets the call for the convention of the National Progressive Party was sounded yesterday by Senator Joseph M. Dixon of Montana, Chairman of the Provisional National Committee selected by the Roosevelt men at Chicago. The call is addressed, "To the People of the United States," and sets forth that the delegates from the various States shall assemble at Chicago on Monday, Aug. 5, to name candidates for President and Vice President of the United States and to adopt a platform. The document bears the names of sixty-three signers, representing forty different States, and including three Governors, two United States Senators, some Congressmen and ex-Governors, two ex-United States Ministers and jurists, and a college head. Three of the signers are Democrats.

The eight States not represented by signers in the call are North Carolina, South Carolina, Arkansas, Delaware, Nevada, Maine, Idaho, and Mississippi. These States will, however, be represented by delegates, Senator Dixon said last night, with the possible exception of two or three which he would not specify, but in which it was hoped that the third party sympathizers would be able to take over the regular Republican Party machinery. This is the call:

The Call.

To the people of the United States, without regard to past political differences, who through repeated betrayals realize that to-day the power of the crooked political bosses and of the privileged classes behind them is so strong in the two old party organizations that no helpful movement in the real interests of our country can come out of either;

Who believe that the time has come for a National Progressive movement—a Nation-wide movement—on non-sectional lines, so that the people may be served in sincerity and truth by an organization unfettered by obligation to conflicting interests;

Who believe in the right and capacity of the people to rule themselves, and effectively to control all the agencies of their Government, and who hold that only through social and industrial justice, thus secured, can honest property find permanent protection;

Who believe that government by the few tends to become, and has in fact become, government by the sordid influences that control the few;

Who believe that only through the movement proposed can we obtain in the Nation and the several States the legislation demanded by the modern industrial evolution; legislation which shall favor honest business and yet control the great agencies of modern business so as to insure their being used in the interest of the whole people; legislation which shall promote prosperity and at the same time secure the better and more equitable diffusion of prosperity; legislation which shall promote the economic well-being of the honest farmer, wage-worker, professional man, and business man alike, but which shall at the same time strike in efficient fashion—and not merely pretend to strike—at the roots of privilege in the world of industry no less than in the world of politics;

Who believe that only this type of wise industrial evolution will avert industrial revolution;

Who believe that wholesome party government can come only if there is wholesome party management in a spirit of service to the whole country, and who hold that the commandment delivered at Sinai, "Thou shalt not steal," applies to politics as well as to business;

To all in accord with these views a call is hereby issued by the Provisional Committee under the resolution of the mass meeting held in Chicago on June 22 last, to send from each State a number of delegates whose votes in the convention shall count for as many votes as the State shall have Senators and Representatives in Congress, to meet in convention at Chicago on the 5th day of August, 1912, for the purpose of nominating candidates to be supported for the positions of President and Vice President of the United States.

Signers of the Call.

Alabama—Oscar R. Hundley.
Arizona—Dwight B. Heard.
California—Hiram W. Johnson, Chester H. Rowell, Charles S. Wheeler.
Colorado—Ben B. Lindsey.
Connecticut—Joseph W. Alsop, Flavel S. Luther.
Florida—J. H. Gregory, Jr., H. L. Anderson.
Georgia—Julian Harris.
Indiana—Edwin D. Lee, Horace C. Stilwell.
Illinois—Medill McCormick, Chauncey Dewey, La Verne W. Noyes.
Iowa—John L. Stevens.
Kansas—Henry J. Allen.
Kentucky—Leslie Coombs.
Louisiana—John M. Parker, Pearl Wright.
Maryland—Charles J. Bonaparte, E. C. Carrington, Jr.
Massachusetts—C. S. Bird, Matthew Hale.
Michigan—Theodore M. Joslyn.
Minnesota—Milton D. Purdy.
Missouri—W. R. Nelson.
Montana—Joseph M. Dixon.
Nebraska—Arthur G. Ray.
New Hampshire—W. J. Beattie.
New Jersey—Everett Colby, George L. Record, J. Franklin Fort.
New Mexico—George Curry, Miguel A. Otero.
New York—W. A. Prendergast, Oscar S.

Continued on Page 2.

GIRL CUT TO DEATH IN A BRONX FLAT

Stabbed Forty Times, She Accuses "a Man," but Dies Before She Can Describe Him.

VICTIM ELEVEN YEARS OLD

Reported Missing After Going to Confession Saturday Afternoon, Found in Vacant Lot Next Morning.

Julia Connors, eleven years old, who lived with her parents at 3,872 Third Avenue, the Bronx, died yesterday morning in Fordham Hospital, the victim of one of the most brutal murders that the police have had to deal with in years.

Her body was covered with at least forty slashes and stab wounds and her lips were swollen as if she had been gagged or had been forced to drink some powerful drug. The little girl was found about 8:30 o'clock yesterday morning in a lot between Fulton Avenue, Third Avenue, and 172d and 173d Streets, the Bronx. She was alive when found, and was able to murmur her name and say that "a man" had attacked her.

Within half an hour after the police were notified Lieut. Meehan, Lieut. Wines and all the detectives of the Tremont Station were working on the case. Late in the afternoon they found the scene of the attack upon the child, a vacant flat on the third floor, north side, of the four-story apartment house at 3,968 Third Avenue, the back yard of which ends at the lot, and within ten feet of the place where the little girl was found.

A woman looking out of the kitchen window of her apartment, in 542 East 173d Street, noticed what she supposed was the body of a child lying half in a small packing box, about ten feet from the rear fence which separates the apartment houses from the lot.

"There is a child there!" she shouted to some boys who were playing ball in the lot.

Working in his back yard garden was Edward McGarry, who lives on the first floor of No. 542. Hearing the woman's cry he dropped his spade and climbed the low wooden fence to the lot. With the lower part of her body, which was unclothed, stuffed into the box, half hidden by three pieces of old, well-worn oilcloth and covered with blood and dirt, he found little Julia Connors. McGarry called to his little daughter to bring him some water, and soon after the janitor appeared with a bottle of alcohol. McGarry, who is a painter, has studied first aid to the injured, and while the crowd gathered about he put his theories into practice. He washed the child's face with alcohol and water, and then began to massage her above the heart. The shock of the cold mixture revived the child, and while McGarry was bending over her she suddenly opened her eyes and made a feeble motion with her right arm. Policeman Reilly, who had been summoned from his post, bent close to her, as McGarry tried to get her to tell of the attack.

Child Accuses a Man.

"What is your name?" asked McGarry.

A spasm passed over the face of the child in the effort she was making to speak. Once she murmured something, but the two men could not understand what she said. McGarry asked her again.

"Julia Connors," came the reply, so faint that the men could only just hear it.

"Who hurt you?" she was asked.

The swollen lips parted, and then louder than before she said: "A man, a man."

"What man?" they asked her, but though they bent close again they heard no reply. The girl was unconscious, and she remained in that condition until she died. Dr. Herman Cohen of 500 East 173d Street, who had been called, worked over her until the arrival of Dr. McSweeney from Fordham Hospital. It took fifteen minutes to bring the hospital automobile, but the trip back was made at top speed. Nothing could be done for her, and she died at 9:10 A. M., soon after she was carried into the hospital.

The disappearance of the child had been reported to the police on Saturday night, and as soon as the report reached the station that she had been found, the victim of a brutal attack, the detectives began their investigation at the point where she had left her home. Julia was the daughter of Edward Connors, a shipping clerk employed by Baker & Williams, 236 Water Street. She lived with her father and mother and Mary, her fourteen-year-old sister, and her brothers Edward, 10 years old, and Eugene, 7, in a modest flat on the second floor of 3,872 Third Avenue.

About 4 o'clock Saturday afternoon Mr. and Mrs. Connors and the two boys went to Crotona Park, two blocks from their home, to watch a baseball game. The father asked Julia to go with them, but she declined. She was a member of the Holy Angels Society of the Catholic Church of Our Lady of Victory, in Webster Avenue, and she told her parents that she was going to the church and to confession.

She did so and returned home about 5 o'clock. Mary gave her her supper and the child left the house to join her parents. She had promised her mother that she would accompany her to a Third Avenue store to purchase a hat.

Child Was Good-looking and Clever.

Little Julia was a good-looking, blue-eyed, dark-haired child, about five feet tall and weighing about seventy pounds. She was a pupil in Public School No. 4, at 173d Street, was clever and had artistic aspirations. On the walls of the Connors home hang a number of pictures she had drawn. Mrs. Connors described her as a home-loving little girl who was seldom out at night, and it was because of this that the Connors were worried when they returned and 6 o'clock came and little Julia had not come home.

Members of the family went out and looked about the neighborhood and then went to the Tremont Station and told the police that the girl was missing. Lieut. McMahon, according to Mr. Connors, said there was no cause for worry and the girl would soon come home.

When it grew late and their daughter had not returned Connors and his wife became alarmed. With Mrs. John Hicks, the wife of a doctor who lives in the house, Mr. and Mrs. John McCaffery, two boys, and a Miss Riordan they started out in earnest to search. Back and forth through Crotona Park they tramped, armed with lanterns, searching. At intervals they would call Julia's name, but the only answers were the jeers of youths who occupied the benches and grass. They would imitate the calls.

Connors said that he returned to the station at 11:30 o'clock Saturday night and asked the Lieutenant to send policemen to help in the search. The father

Continued on Page 2.

EARTHQUAKE SHAKES ALASKA

Vibrations Last for Forty Seconds—Mine Foreman Killed.

FAIRBANKS, Alaska, July 7.—The most violent earthquake ever felt here took place at 10 o'clock last night, the earth rocking continuously for forty seconds. Less violent shocks occurred throughout the night.

Louis Anderson, foreman of a mine in Dome Creek, was suffocated beneath a huge slab of earth loosened by the quake.

WASHINGTON, July 7.—The heaviest earthquake shocks since the San Francisco disaster of 1906 were recorded to-day on the seismographs at the Georgetown University Observatory. The distance was calculated at 3,000 miles and the direction uncertain.

The tremors continued from 3:07 until 5 A. M. The heaviest shock, at 3:41 A. M., threw two needles completely out of scale and registered 95 millimeters on another dial.

WHALE RAMS A SCHOONER.

Crew Abandons Her and Rows 120 Miles Before Being Rescued.

ST. JOHNS, N. F., July 7.—A collision with a whale on the Grand Banks caused such serious damage to the two-masted schooner Empire, from Oporto for St. Johns, that the vessel was abandoned by her crew of six men and a passenger, who reached here to-day.

The accident happened last Tuesday. After keeping the vessel afloat two days, the crew had to leave her when the pumps became choked. The men rowed 120 miles toward land before they were picked up by a fishing schooner. The Empire was loaded with salt.

BULLDOG ATTACKS BOY.

Animal Had Been Enraged by Children Who Threw Things at It.

Joseph Schwartz, 5 years old, descended by the fire escape into the rear yard of his residence, 161 East 118th Street, yesterday and was attacked by a bulldog which had been angered by a number of children who had been throwing things at it from windows. Jacob kicked it off and tried to run up the fire escape, but the dog got a grip on his leg and pulled him to the ground and attacked him savagely.

The boy's face was badly torn before the owner, Anton Peshar, who is janitor of the building, pulled the dog off. Dr. McKinlay of Harlem Hospital cauterized the wounds and took several stitches.

MAMMOTH CAVE HAS RIVAL.

Wonderful Hole in the Ground Discovered in Southern Arizona.

Special to The New York Times.

NOGALES, Ariz., July 7.—One of the most wonderful caves in the world has been found in Southern Arizona. Unnamed, unexplored and almost unknown is the vast cavern. Only a few persons have dared enter to view its grandeur and to study the wondrous work of nature. This cave lies in the foothills of the Huachuca Mountains, about forty miles northeast of Nogales, Santa Cruz County.

Exploring parties have entered and spent days inside, but none has ever discovered the end. They report passageways, rooms and chambers innumerable. One room has a level and smooth floor and they call it the dance hall, and there are unfathomed pits and chasms.

PRESIDENT LEAVES BEVERLY.

Ends the First Part of His Vacation and Returns to Washington.

Special to The New York Times.

BEVERLY, Mass., July 7.—President Taft ended the first part of his vacation to-night when he departed for Washington, where he will confer to-morrow with the members of the Republican National Committee.

The President, with Mrs. Taft, attended services to-day at the First Unitarian Church at Beverly. There were few outside the church when the President and Mrs. Taft, accompanied by Major T. L. Rhoades, motored up to the church. After the service Mrs. Taft called on Miss Mabel Boardman at Manchester and Mrs. Levi Z. Leiter at The Farms.

The President left in an automobile shortly before 6 o'clock for Boston, where he was to board a train for Washington.

The President hopes to get back to Beverly in two weeks for another week-end visit.

ROCKEFELLER IS 73 TO-DAY.

Plans No Departure from His Daily Routine to Celebrate.

Special to The New York Times.

CLEVELAND, Ohio, July 7.—There will be no birthday cake at Forest Hill to-morrow, although it will be the seventy-third birthday anniversary of its owner. John D. Rockefeller said to-day that no special arrangements had been made to celebrate the day.

"I will pass the day as usual," he said.

Unless Mr. Rockefeller decides at the last minute to depart from his usual daily routine, he will rise at 7:30 o'clock, and, after a light breakfast, will play golf from 9:30 until 11:30. He will then go to his Summer home, where he will take a short nap. At 1 o'clock he will eat a light luncheon. At 3 o'clock he will go driving, either in an automobile or about his estate in a buggy. At 6 o'clock he will eat his dinner, after which he will spend a short time in reading. Often it is his Bible which he reads. He usually retires at 9 o'clock.

The master of Forest Hill bore his seventy-three years lightly as he stepped from his automobile at the Euclid Avenue Baptist Church to-day. He arrived too late to attend Sunday school, and, after greeting friends, took his place in a pew reserved for him. His only birthday benefaction thus far is $3,000 to his church to complete an $11,000 fund for new decorations.

GIFT BY VINCENT ASTOR.

Wins Favor of Rhinebeck Fans by Present of a Baseball Park.

Special to The New York Times.

POUGHKEEPSIE, N. Y., July 7.—Vincent Astor is now a full-fledged citizen of Rhinebeck, and if the baseball fans had anything to say about it he could have any office he wanted in that town. It became known to-day that the young owner of Ferncliffe had presented a park to the ball club within two days after he learned that such a park was needed. The plot is a part of the Astor estate just outside the village, but easy of access. The land is level and very desirable for a baseball diamond.

Young Astor has made a hit with the residents of Rhinebeck. He gives promise of filling the position which his father, Col. Astor, held for so many years. He has told the leading men of the town that he wants to be regarded as a fellow-citizen, and has assured them of his interest in the welfare of the community. He expects to spend most of the Summer at Ferncliffe, supervising the improvements in progress there. Among Mr. Astor's plans is the erection of a new house. This was planned by Col. Astor before he went abroad with his bride last Winter.

FALL RIVER BOAT RAMS WARSHIP

Passenger Liner Commonwealth Smashes the New Hampshire Off Newport.

ACCIDENT DUE TO FOG

Passengers Bound for Boston Awakened by Crash, but Quickly Reassured.

DAMAGE IS ABOVE WATER LINE

Battleship's Stern Badly Torn by Impact, While Liner's Bow Suffers Jagged Hole—Capt. Oliver's Report.

Special to The New York Times.

NEWPORT, R. I., July 7.—The Fall River liner Commonwealth, in command of Capt. W. B. Appleby, Commodore of the Fall River fleet, crept away from her pier here shortly after 4 o'clock this morning to feel her way cautiously through the fog to Fall River, where her 1,000 passengers were to be transferred to trains for Boston and points in New England. About 100 had alighted here, where heavy freight was deposited also, but the rest of the passengers were still asleep.

Through the thick gray mist the Commonwealth poked her way at about twelve knots an hour, a lookout in the bow, and Capt. Appleby himself on watch in the pilot house. All about him, the Captain knew, were ships of the North Atlantic fleet, assembled for the naval manoeuvres next week off Block Island, No Man's Land, and Martha's Vineyard.

From all sides sounded the clanging of fog bells aboard the battleships, cruisers, and the torpedo flotilla, but the sounds came out of a pall of gray through which not a thing could be seen.

Too Late to Avoid Collision.

She was still moving slowly when there came a cry from the lookout, and at the same instant Capt. Appleby saw the gray bulk of a ship looming up close to his bows. He rang the signal to reverse the engines and gave the necessary orders to swing the Commonwealth out of her course in the hope that a collision might be avoided, but so close was his ship to the bulk ahead of it that, though the engines were sent spinning backward at once, there came a crash as the bows of the Commonwealth drove into the stern of the vessel ahead.

The Sound steamer stopped short with a shiver which shook the crockery from the shelves and threw the sleeping passengers from their berths. Instantly there was a rush to the deck. Men, women, and children, few of them clothed in anything but their sleeping garments, clamored to be told what had happened.

Except that he had struck a battleship of some kind, Capt. Appleby himself did not know what had happened. He did not even know the name of the vessel he had struck. But suddenly, so quickly that it seemed as if the message must have been prepared in advance, came a wireless call from Capt. James H. Oliver of the battleship New Hampshire, stating that it was his boat which the Commonwealth had struck, and asking if help were needed.

Capt. Appleby, while the Commonwealth was falling away from the warship, had started men to examine the damage to his steamer. As in response to his orders the Commonwealth backed a few hundred yards from the New Hampshire and came to a stop, members of the crew examined the bows, and presently the report was made that a jagged hole had been torn in the starboard bow, but that the water-tight bulkhead was holding, and that the steamer was in no danger.

Officers and stewards ran among the excited passengers, urging them to keep cool, as there was no danger, and within a few minutes after the collision the Commonwealth was making back to her own pier here, while her passengers, excited still, but not in a panic, hurried into their clothes.

Crew Waits for Accident.

Aboard the New Hampshire even greater damage, apparently, had been done than was done to the Commonwealth, but there was no semblance even of excitement. Lieut. Harry Campbell, who had been on watch, had caught sight of the white hulk of the Commonwealth several seconds before the war gray of the battle ship had been visible aboard the Sound liner. One glance told him that the Commonwealth was going to strike the New Hampshire astern.

So near was the Sound liner when Lieut. Campbell first sighted her that he realized the Commonwealth could not be stopped or turned aside in time to prevent a collision, so instantly he ordered sounded the bells and whistles which call every member of the crew of a warship to their quarters in time of collision. So quickly was the order obeyed that before the Commonwealth struck, a matter of scarcely more than seconds later, every man aboard the New Hampshire whose place was on deck was in that place waiting coolly for the collision.

When the crash came, just astern, as Lieut. Campbell had foreseen, the warship was cut open above the protective deck and through the after compartments of the gun and berth decks, Capt. Oliver's after cabin and the boiler room beneath being wrecked. The starboard armor-plate was driven in about three inches and the light bulkheads about the after compartments were crushed in and torn from the angle irons. The deck beams were torn from the sides of the New Hampshire as far as the after hatch.

Already Capt. Oliver had issued orders which brought the divers on deck prepared to make an examination of the damage, and no sooner had the Commonwealth backed off than these men were making a careful examination of the in

AMERICANS CAPTURE FIRST OLYMPIC RACE

Continued from Page 1.

Achilles. He will not be able to participate further in the games.

Owing to a misunderstanding, three Americans, including the Hawaiian "Duke," who qualified for the semi-finals of the 100-meter swimming race, did not put in an appearance to-night when the heats were contested. Consequently they are barred from further participation.

The American Committee has lodged a protest, which will be decided to-morrow. Permanent debarring of the men would involve a loss of an almost certain three points for America.

[By Cable.]

Altogether to-day the American athletes made sure of eleven more points in the contest for the Olympic championship.

Matt Halpin of New York, a member of the Olympic Committee, told THE TIMES correspondent to-night that he was much delighted over the day's successes. He said:

"Although we expected that Thorpe would win the pentathlon, his great performance exceeded our hopes. Donoghue will show up much better in the decathlon.

"You will find there will be results in other events just as good as the hundred. Every one except those on the injured list is in splendid shape.

"We are unfortunate in having Willie Kramer out of commission, as he stood a good chance in the 5,000-meter race to-morrow."

Mike Murphy, trainer of the American team, is also delighted with the achievements of his charges.

Col. R. M. Thompson and other members of the American Committee gave a luncheon to-day on board the yacht Catania to Americans and newspapermen in Stockholm. In a short speech Col. Thompson spoke of the great feeling of good fellowship existing here between the Americans and the Swedes.

Special Cable to THE NEW YORK TIMES.

LONDON, Monday, July 8.—The Daily Telegraph's correspondent at Stockholm, describing Craig's victory in the final heat of the 100 meters race, says the automatic instrument returned the time as 10 4-5 seconds, but the correspondent's watch made the time three-tenths of a second faster, and he says there is little doubt of its correctness.

With reference to the two semi-finals in the 800 meters race, the correspondent points out that the six Americans who got into the final did not press themselves, and there was really no telling what they might not accomplish. He adds:

"The first impressions of the sturdily-framed Davenport are well confirmed. He may put up a world's record. The Italian, Lunghi, is not so good as he was, and Melvin Sheppard and Braun, like Davenport, were satisfied to remain leisurely among the qualifying four.

"Only the deciding race can tell what these very hot half-milers are capable of. The way they left our men, Mann and Soutter, when the steam was turned on in the first heat, was a real eye-opener."

Fierce Struggle in the Hundred.

By Associated Press.

STOCKHOLM, July 7.—The American athletes continued in winning vein to-day at the Olympic games.

In the final of the 100-meter flat race they succeeded in getting all the points to their credit.

The victory belonged to anybody until ten feet from the tape, when R. C. Craig of Detroit by a great burst of speed crossed a foot ahead. Only inches separated the next three—Meyer of New York, Lippincott of the University of Pennsylvania, and Patching of South Africa. Belote of Chicago was fifth.

Another splendid victory was that of James Thorpe of the Carlisle Indian School, who carried off the Pentathlon, a competition for all-around athletes. The events were the running broad jump, throwing the javelin, best hand; 200 meters flat race, throwing the discus, best hand, and the 1,500 meters flat race.

Thorpe made six points in this contest, his records being: Running broad jump, 7 meters, 7 centimeters; throwing the javelin, 52 meters; 200 meters flat, 23 seconds; throwing the discus, 35 meters, 37 centimeters; 1,500 meters flat, 4:44.

P. R. Bie of Norway was second, with 15 points, Joseph J. Donoghue of the Los Angeles Athletic Club was third with 26 points, and J. A. Menaul of the University of Chicago made 28 points.

The Americans again surprised themselves in the semi-finals of the 800 meters flat race. Six runners of the eight who will toe the mark in the final struggle were more than they had dared to hope for.

United Press International

United States' Jim Thorpe exhibits his style at the Olympics.

J. E. Meredith of Mercersburg Academy made the running throughout the first heat. J. L. Tait of Ontario worked hard for 500 meters, keeping a close second, but lost on the homestretch and finished fifth. Eight started in the heat, the three Britishers bringing up the rear.

Eight also started in the second heat, Ira N. Davenport, University of Chicago; H. W. Holden, Bates College, and E. Bjorn, Sweden, each taking the lead in that order. This was a splendid race. The field was well bunched. The two Latins, Lunghi, Italy, and Cortesac, Portugal, sprinted in the first half. The strength of the Portuguese was not equal to his ambition, however, and he soon fell to the rear. The Italian, also, could not keep up the pace in the last stretch. G. M. Brock, Ontario, and E. J. Henley, England, completed the squad, John Paul Jones of Cornell being reserved for the 1,500 meters race, and therefore not appearing in this race.

The sensational event of the morning was the splendid race between Louis Tewanima, the Indian, and L. Richardson of South Africa, in the second heat of the 10,000 meters flat race, in which eleven runners started. Until the last mile the order was: Stenroos, Finland; Tewanima, and H. Karlsson, Sweden, the little Indian hanging closely on the Finn's heels, with the Swede a yard behind.

About the beginning of the last mile Stenroos dropped back and Richardson pushed forward from 100 yards in the rear and took his place. The tal[illegible]an in green and his little red brother were almost shoulder to shoulder for two laps. On the final circuit Richardson sprinted at a quarter-mile gait. Tewanima once came to the front gamely, but Richardson won by a yard amid great enthusiasm. Both compete in the final heat.

The Indian walked freshly across the field afterward, but his opponent had to be helped away. Two Englishmen, F. N. Hibbins and T. Humphreys, gave up before the race was two-thirds over.

In the first heat of the 10,000-meters Kolehmainen, the Finn, won with ease. Keeper made a fine fight for second place, having a good brush with William J. Kramer in the first half of the race. Kramer, however, was obliged to give up in the eighteenth round, with eight laps still to be covered. The other American runner, Harry E. Hellowell of the New York Athletic Club, ran only four laps, a sore foot compelling him to abandon the race. The failure of the Americans was a great disappointment.

The third heat of the 10,000-meters flat race was a pretty victory for a little Finn, T. Kolehmainen, who outran England's famous ten-miler, W. Scott. For the United States, Louis Scott of South Paterson and U. F. McGuire of North Attleboro, Mass., unattached, were third and fifth, respectively, while Person, a Swede, was fourth. George V. Bonhag of the Irish-American Athletic Club of New York failed to start.

After the sixteenth lap the race became a contest between Kolehmainen and W. Scott, who kept together until the last mile, when the Finn took a long lead. W. Scott drew up in the final lap, but the Finn crossed the tape ten yards ahead.

From time to time throughout the afternoon a cyclist entered the stadium, black, haggard, and dust covered from the 320-kilometer race over the rough roads around Lake Malar. The race, which began at 2 o'clock this morning, was won by Lewis of South Africa, who covered the course in 10 hours 42 minutes. Grubb of England was second, and Carl O. Shutte, Kansas City, attached to the St. Louis Cycling Club, was third. The team race, combined with the individual competition, gave Sweden first place, England second, and the United States third. The Swedes had the advantage of familiarity with the tortuous track.

The semi-finals of the 100-meter swim proved a fiasco, as the American, McGillivray, Huszagh, and Kahanamoku, who had qualified by winning heats in the previous round, remained on the steamer Finland, in the belief that the event was to be contested on Monday. Some competitors protested against the semi-finals being held, saying that they would be valueless without the three fastest competitors. The round, however, was completed. Healy of Australia won the first heat in 1:05 3-5. Bretting of Germany swam over in the second heat in 1:04 3-5.

Through this failure of understanding, whether on the part of the Swedish committee or the American managers, the Americans may lose the final of this event. The Hawaiian, Kahanamoku, whom the republican democracy aboard the Finland call "the Duke," is the talk of the town to-day, not only for what he does but for the easy way in which he does it. He has caught the popular fancy, and the President of the British Life-saving Service has offered him a cup if he swims 100 meters in one minute during the contests.

The athletes of the United Kingdom, whose predecessors taught the world sprinting, long distance running and bicycling, had a bad day. Except for the colonials, Great Britain took a back seat, having no representative in the final of the 100 meters, being shut out of the final in the 800 and having small prospect of winning the 10,000 meters, unless the colonies carry the Union Jack to the front. This, naturally, has depressed all Englishmen, both the athletes and the spectators, but they carried themselves like sportsmen and were prompt to congratulate the victors.

On the other hand, the meeting proves that the Continentals, particularly the Northern races, are not behind the British and Americans in the qualities that go to make athletes. They need only practice in the special sports to hold their own.

The exhibition in the Stadium is as hard for a spectator to follow as a three-ring circus. There was something doing on the cinder track most of the time to-day and within the oval the jumping and pentathlon events took place.

At one end the wrestling contests were in progress. The wrestling includes feather, middle, and heavy weight. In the preliminary bouts all the contestants were Europeans from the Northern and Slav countries. No American or Britisher participated.

"All the News That's Fit to Print."

The New York Times.

THE WEATHER.
Fair, slightly warmer Thursday; Friday, fair, warmer; moderate winds, becoming south.
For full weather report see Page 22.

VOL. LXII...NO. 19,990. ... NEW YORK, THURSDAY, OCTOBER 17, 1912.—TWENTY-FOUR PAGES. ONE CENT In Greater New York, Jersey City, and Newark. | Elsewhere, TWO CENTS.

PUT MURDER PLOT CLOSER TO BECKER

Mass of Testimony Brought in Corroborating the Confessions of the Conspirators.

MRS. ROSENTHAL ON STAND

Husband Told Her Certain Money Was for Rose and Becker, but She Saw No Payment.

TOMBS TALK IN EVIDENCE

Lawyer Now a Convict Swears He Heard Becker Say He'd Yet Get a Pension for Killing Rosenthal.

Lieut. Charles Becker, into whose ears, in the last few days, had thundered the accusing periods of "Billiard Ball" Jack Rose, "Bridgey" Webber, Harry Vallon, and Sam Schepps, listened yesterday to a succession of lighter attacks, a series of blows each less severe than the testimony of the State's important witnesses, but in their cumulative effect as damaging to his case as had proved the testimony of any one man. Sixteen persons, among them Mrs. Lillian Rosenthal, widow of the man whom the State calls Becker's victim, ascended to the witness stand, delivered their fire and made way for Becker's next assailant.

At the end of the day District Attorney Whitman was ready to rest his case—he will do so to-day—confident that whatever might have been the effect on the jury of Sam Schepps, his main dependency as a corroborative witness, the men who are to determine Becker's fate had heard yesterday such corroboration of incidents in the confessions of Rose, Webber, and Vallon, as must persuade them of the truth of the whole narrative.

To corroborate the testimony of the men who are self-confessed accomplices of Becker, is made by law an essential phase of the conviction of the accused Lieutenant. District Attorney Whitman realized this when he first began his preparation of the case against Becker. He realized it when he wrung from Rose his confession, and from Webber and Vallon admissions of the part they had played, and he provided for it in the testimony of Schepps, the dapper, fat little "butter-in," as Rose termed him, the man whom all tolerated, and in whom none confided.

Props for Schepps's Testimony.

Schepps fulfilled the trust thus placed in him. When John F. McIntyre, chief counsel for Becker, finished Schepps's cross-examination on Tuesday the little man had eluded every pitfall and returned to his cell in the West Side Prison still legally unconnected with the murder of Herman Rosenthal. So far Schepps was successful but of his effect on the jury Mr. Whitman was not so sure.

Flippant, arrogant, insolent, his own self-esteem garbing him like a cloak, Schepps cut a figure before the jury at which they laughed at times but a figure, too of a man too sharp, too wily, too versed in the ways of the underworld to have shared in the acts in which he did share, to have listened to the words to which he did listen, to have seen the situations which he did see, and still have no suspicion that murder was being plotted, that the conspirators were his associates, and that the victim was Herman Rosenthal.

Mr. Whitman realized this and his entire effort yesterday was to accomplish that which Schepps might have failed to accomplish. To do this, the wife of the murdered man and the wife of the man on trial as his murderer faced each other yesterday for the first time in court.

Mrs. Rosenthal was dressed in deep mourning, with black hat and long crepe veil. Her face was white and its pallor was accentuated by the warm red of her lips. Her eyes were tired, weary, and there was no lustre in them. Mrs. Becker, clothed hitherto in a suit of blue, might have known, so different was her dress yesterday, that she must face the widow of the dead gambler. The bright-eyed little woman who sits all day taking notes while witness after witness assails her husband, appeared yesterday in a gray dress striped with dark blue and on her head was a dark velvet hat with black wing trimming.

Mrs. Rosenthal was subdued, oppressed by the grief which her appearance in the courtroom and the ordeal of her examination made more poignant. Mrs. Becker was cheerful, more cheerful than she had appeared on other days of the trial, and once or twice she laughed. Becker, too, seemed light-hearted and unruffled. He caught his wife's eye once and smiled happily at her. She returned the greeting.

Overheard Talk in Tombs.

For there was nothing in the testimony yesterday except it be that of James E. Hallon, a disbarred lawyer now serving his second term in Sing Sing, to terrify the Lieutenant by its damning quality. The witnesses told simply of how Becker had visited Rose's home, how he had sat with Rose in the Union Square Hotel, how he had been apprehensive about Rose's health when the bald-headed gambler was in hiding in Harry Pollok's flat.

There was no boldly flung declaration that he had wished "to cut the heart" from Rosenthal, no dramatic recital of how he had demanded that Rosenthal be "croaked," no recollection of his hysterical order to "kill him in front of a policeman if you want to." Becker had to listen to only one statement of anything like this nature, and it came from the lips of the convict from Sing Sing, a

Continued on Page 5.

NEWS IN HIGHEST COURT.

Bathtub Case Waits While Jurists Read Bulletins from Boston.

Special to The New York Times.

WASHINGTON, D. C., Oct. 16.—There was diversion in the session of the United States Supreme Court this afternoon. The Chief Justice and the Associate Justices were listening to argument in the case of the Government against the Bathtub Trust. But there was just a suspicion of uneasiness or distraction on the part of the court—something that suggested expectancy or keen interest in matters not connected with bathtubs or the Sherman anti-trust law.

The court page entered the judicial chamber with some show of excitement, and, hurrying to the bench, handed a slip of paper to Associate Justice Day. It was evident that the Bathtub Trust was forgotten by the Justices as the slip of paper was passed down the line. In groups of two or three the distinguished jurists of the highest court in the land leaned over the paper and read eagerly what was written on it.

This diversion happened at intervals throughout the session of the court. Then it came out that for the first time in its history the Supreme Bench was getting bulletins of a baseball game. Justice Day, the foremost fan of the court, made arrangements for the bulletin service. The progress of the final match in the world's series was made known to the court inning by inning.

BRITISH SHELLS NOT BARRED.

Wickersham Holds That Eight-Hour Labor Law Does Not Apply.

Special to The New York Times.

WASHINGTON, Oct. 16.—Attorney General Wickersham has rendered an opinion on the question sumitted to him by Secretary Meyer of the Navy Department as to whether the Hadfield Foundries Company of Sheffield, England, should have the contract for making projectiles for the United States Navy. The particular legal question involved was whether the statutory requirement that such projectiles should be made in manufactories where the eight-hour law was observed applied to a concern whose works were located in a foreign country. The Attorney General's decision has not been made public, but it is understood that he holds that the eight-hour limitation is, to a certain extent, negligible in a matter of this kind.

The eight-hour law, it is held, would not apply to the operation of the furnaces where the steel was produced, nor to the time of service of managers, clerks, accountants, or employes who give only a part of their time or skill to the work of making the projectiles.

It has been decided by the Navy Department to award a portion of the contract to the English bidders for the purpose of ascertaining the character of their work. At the same time the American bidders will be given an opportunity to have a part of the contract if the price for the work can be agreed on between themselves and the department. There is some expectation that the department will allow the American bidders the contract this time at the figures bid by them, but with the condition that if the Hadfield company's projectiles are satisfactory, the next award will be made absolutely on the merits of the work and the price.

The shells involved in the competition are twelve-inch and fourteen-inch explosive projectiles. Target shells were not bid for by the English bidders. The Hadfield company was the only bidder that offered to carry out the whole contract of 3,500 twelve-inch and 2,000 fourteen-inch projectiles. It proposed to deliver the shells in this country, and its figures were one-third lower than the American bids.

If the Government should give the entire contract to the English firm, it would save $654,500 on the twelve-inch shells and $317,500 on the fourteen-inch shells. But the department takes the view that it is not entirely a matter of saving money at this time. It has always been the policy to give such work to American firms on the ground that domestic workmen and capitalists should be considered first, and because if, for a period of years, American ordnance work were to be done abroad, the United States would be unprepared in time of war.

GIANTS RETURN DOWNCAST.

Snodgrass First Off Train—Mathewson Rides to Grand Central Alone.

Just before midnight the Giants came home. A downcast crew they were met by the subdued enthusiasm of a very small gathering at the West 125th Street Station, where all the players but Mathewson alighted from the Boston train. Snodgrass was the first to step to the platform, looking a little sheepish as his friends crowded around him and told him not to fret.

The welcoming supporters, fewer in number than the crowds that have awaited the former returns from Boston, contented themselves with muffled sympathy, and the originally contemplated band and parade were nowhere to be seen.

In solitude Mathewson rode alone to the Grand Central and from there went his unobserved way.

SAW HER FATHER KILLED.

But Daughter Did Not Learn Until Later Dead Man Was Her Parent.

While Mrs. Nasio Carcagnico was putting the supper on the table last evening in her home at 37 Johnson Avenue, Brooklyn, her little daughter, Mary, told her of a street accident that had just attracted a crowd to the corner next to her home. Engine 116, returning from a false alarm, had turned the corner from Broadway and had run over a man that had got in the way. He had been kicked and trampled on by the horses and the heavy wheels of the engine truck had crushed him. Mary had been jammed far back in the crowd, but she had seen the patrol wagon come and go after the ambulance surgeon had said the man was dead.

Then mother and daughter sat down to supper, for the father would be in from work any minute. The minutes lengthened to an hour, however, and he did not come. By 7:30 o'clock the worried mother went out to make inquiries. These led her to the Stagg Street station, where she found that it was her husband who had been killed by the engine.

YOU MUST REGISTER TO VOTE.

To-morrow and Saturday are the last days to register. If you do not register you cannot vote. Registration booths open from 7 A. M. to 10 P. M.

SOX CHAMPIONS ON MUFFED FLY

Snodgrass Drops Easy Ball, Costing Teammates $29,514, Boston Winning, 3-2.

GIANTS EXPLODE IN TENTH

Bostonians, Angry at Sox Management, Start Boycott, Keeping Crowd Down to 17,000.

LUCK WITH SOX—FULLERTON

Boston Outguessed and Outgeneraled, He Declares—McGraw Blames Nobody—$490,833 Receipts.

Special to The New York Times.

BOSTON, Mass., Oct. 16.—Write in the pages of world's series baseball history the name of Snodgrass. Write it large and black. Not as a hero; truly not. Put him rather with Merkle, who was in such a hurry that he gave away a National League championship. Snodgrass was in such a hurry that he gave away a world championship. It was because of Snodgrass's generous muff of an easy fly in the tenth inning that the decisive game in the world's series went to the Boston Red Sox this afternoon by a score of 3 to 2, instead of to the New York Giants by a score of 2 to 1.

It is the tenth inning of the eighth game of the series. The score of games is 3 to 3, and the score of this contest is 1 to 1. Mathewson, the veteran, has given the lie to his own announcement that he could never again pitch in such a contest by holding the Red Sox enemy at bay for nine innings in decisive fashion. One run has been made off him, but that has been through the fortunate hit of a youngster who has never faced him before. The regular members of the Boston team have been helpless in the face of his speed and his elusive fadeaway. They have been outfought, outgeneraled, outspeeded, and their only hope is that Wood, who has gone in fresh only two innings before, will hold out until the veteran shall give way to the strain.

Murray Breaks the Tie.

And who is this that comes to the bat for the Giants? 'Tis "Red" Murray—once the hitless. And what does he do? He pierces the mark of one of the smokiest of Wood's shoots and puts the ball far over the head of Speaker into the left field stands. It is a home run hit, but ground rules limit it to two bases. Yet what is the difference? Merkle also sees through the smoke, and the ball which Wood has sent so speedily toward him is returned so fast that Wood can hardly see it as it goes toward centre field. So Murray is in with the run that unties the score, and it only remains for Mathewson to hold himself for one more inning and New York has a world championship and the Giant players the lion's share of the big purse hung up for the players, a difference of $29,514.

Is Mathewson apprehensive as he walks to the box? He is not. All the confidence that was his when the blood of youth ran strong in his supple muscles is his now. Even though the mountainous Engle faces him—the Engle who brought in the two runs of the Red Sox on Monday—he shows not a quiver, and he is right. All that Engle can do with the elusive drop served up is to hoist it high between centre and right fields. Snodgrass and Murray are both within reach of it, with time to spare. Snodgrass yells, "I've got it," and sets himself to take it with ease, as he has taken hundreds of the sort. Murray stops, waiting for the play that will enable him to line the ball joyfully to the infield just to show that his formidable right wing is still in working order.

When the Fly Ball Falls.

While the ball is soaring its leisurely way let us pause for a moment to think what hangs upon that fly.

It is not the 2,000 Giant rooters who are gayly waving their blue and white flags and yelling exultantly over the certain downfall of the foe. It is not the 15,000 Boston fans who have groaned and sat silent, as though at a funeral. A President is forgetting the bitter assaults that have been made upon him. A former President is being eased of his pain by his interest in it. A campaign which may mean a change in the whole structure of the Nation's Government has been put into the background. What happens will be flashed by telegraph the length and breadth of the land, and thereby carried over and under the sea, and millions will be uplifted or downcast.

And now the ball settles. It is full and fair in the pouch of the padded glove of Snodgrass. But he is too eager to toss it to Murray and it dribbles to the ground. Before Snodgrass can hurl the ball to second Engle is perching there.

Mathewson stands in the box, stunned for a moment, then swings his gloved hand in a gesture that is eloquent of his wrath. He has lost none of his courage and determination, but it can be seen as he faces Hooper that there is just a bit of uncertainty in his bearing. Proof comes that he has lost some of his cunning, for Hooper hits the ball so hard that Snodgrass has to sprint and reach to pull down his liner. For Yerkes he cannot put them over at all, and two Red Sox are on the bases.

Three Giants Let It Drop.

And now that something which upsets a ball team—which McGraw has called an explosion—becomes evident. Speaker pops up a high foul near first base, and Merkle, Meyers, and Mathewson converge on it with none collected enough to say which shall take it, and it drops among them. The three who have made the muss walk to the box arguing, Mathewson saying

Continued on Page 6.

YOUNG DIAZ RAISES HIS FLAG OF REVOLT

Starts Rising Against Madero by Entering Vera Cruz City—Seizes Arsenal.

ELATION IN MEXICO CITY

Fighting in Vera Cruz Imminent Between Opposing Forces — 3,000 Troops to Attack New Rebel Chief.

MEXICO CITY, Oct. 16.—Gen. Felix Diaz, nephew of Gen. Porfirio Diaz, the deposed President of Mexico, raised the banner of rebellion at Vera Cruz to-day. He entered the city with 500 men and seized the arsenal and garrison. Col. Diaz Ordaz was in command of the garrison, which comprised that number of the Twenty-first Infantry and one six-gun battery. Gen. Diaz then placed men in charge of the two gunboats, Tampico and Bravo, lying in the harbor.

The news of the rising created excitement here, although there were no street demonstrations. Mexicans generally appeared elated at the new developments. According to the reports Gen. Diaz found many adherents when he entered the city, including some of the troops, but the government has been informed that the Nineteenth Infantry remains loyal, as well as the artillery. Col. Gutierrez, commanding the loyal troops, notified the government that he will resist.

The two opposing forces are now in the City of Vera Cruz, and street fighting is imminent. President Madero has ordered the mobilization of 3,000 regulars to proceed against Gen. Diaz. The arrest of alleged partisans of Diaz in Mexico City is expected momentarily.

The government has instructed the railroads into Vera Cruz to withdraw all equipment—the Mexican to Orizaba, the Inter-Oceanic to Jalapa, and the Vera Cruz-Pacific to Tierra Blanca.

Believing that a great portion of the army remains loyal, President Madero, through the War Department, has also ordered every available soldier in the service, both regular and irregular, into the lines which are being drawn about Vera Cruz in an effort to crush, with the least possible delay, the new rebellion begun by Gen. Diaz.

From Santa Ducretia, on the Tehuantepec Isthmus, Gen. Zozaya has been ordered to move to the north, and even from the northern part of the republic, where remnants of Orozco's army are still raiding in large bands, Gen. Blanquet has been summoned to the capital with the greater part of his forces to join the campaign against Diaz, whom the Government regards as a greater menace than any other revolutionist.

EL PASO, Texas, Oct. 16.—A Felix Diaz rebel junta has been organized here. It is generally admitted to-day among refugees here that the nephew of the former President of Mexico would be most acceptable to the revolutionary element as a provisional President.

PAY RANSOM FOR AMERICAN.

McCormick's Friends Send $5,000 to Mexican Rebels for His Release.

Special to The New York Times.

WASHINGTON, Oct. 16.—The friends of Arthur McCormick, the manager of the Palomas ranch, who was kidnapped by a number of Mexican bandits, have forwarded to the bandits the $5,000 demanded as a ransom. The State Department was notified of this action on the part of McCormick's family to-day, and informed the Mexican Government of the seizure of Mr. McCormick. Negotiations are in progress looking to his release.

The delivery of the ransom was without the knowledge of the State Department and was voluntary on the part of the McCormicks. The State Department was advised to-day that Mrs. John T. Cameron had sent a special messenger to meet Gen. Salazar at Cinco de Mayo to get the best terms possible for the release of her husband, for whom the rebel chieftain demanded a ransom of $20,000 Mexican. The original demand was for $15,000. The amount was probably raised, it is said, because of notices appearing in the American newspapers of Cameron's business activities and the efforts of his wife to rescue him.

Ambassador Wilson telegraphed the State Department to-day that Gen. Telles and Gen. Aubert had sent troops to effect the capture of the bandits.

POLICE INVADE HOTEL.

Take Temporary Charge of the Lincoln in Broadway.

Inspector John F. Dwyer and fourteen of his detectives created much excitement in Broadway at midnight this morning, when they walked into the Hotel Lincoln at Broadway and Fifty-second Street and took possession. Broadway was thronged at the time with late theatre parties, and when Inspector Dwyer, who has become a familiar figure along Broadway, was recognized, the crowd followed and stood outside the hotel.

The Inspector announced to the night clerk that he had come "to look things over," and until further notice he was in charge. The Inspector then detailed Detective Anthony, who was formerly a sailor, to be telephone operator, despite the detective's protests that he knew nothing about switchboards. Anthony's instructions were to sit quiet, look wise, and not answer any calls.

The same procedure regarding the elevators was followed. Two detectives were assigned to each elevator, with instructions to allow no one to depart. Each of the six floors of the building had two men watching the halls, while the Inspector in the office below was going over the hotel register to ascertain the number of guests in each room. After he had made out a list for each floor, the Inspector detailed more of his men to go to each room and see that the number in the room corresponded with that on the register. No arrests were made and the police withdrew after seeing that the rooms were occupied by legitimate guests.

Latest Shipping News.

ARRIVED—SS St. Paul, Southampton, Oct. 9.

'NOT I, THE CAUSE,' ROOSEVELT'S MOTTO

So He Gives It from Sick Bed Through Ex-Senator Beveridge to Louisville Audience.

HIS SPEECH ALSO READ

Asks Wilson to Say Why His State Has Not Sued Trusts Incorporated in New Jersey.

COL. ROOSEVELT'S MESSAGE.

It matters little about me, but it matters all about the cause we fight for. If one soldier who happens to carry the flag is stricken another will take it from his hands and carry it on. One after another the standard bearers may be laid low, but the standard itself can never fall. You know that personally I did not want ever to be a candidate for office again. And you know that only the call that came to the men of the sixties made me answer it, in our day, as they did more nobly in their day. And now, as then, it is not important whether one leader lives or dies, it is important only that the cause shall live and win. Tell the people not to worry about me, for if I go down another will take my place. For always the army is true. Always the cause is there, and it is the cause for which the people care, for it is the people's cause.

Special to The New York Times.

LOUISVILLE, Ky., Oct. 16.—Ex-Senator Albert J. Beveridge of Indiana brought the people of Louisville and Kentucky to-night a message from the bedside of Theodore Roosevelt in Chicago telling them not to mind him, but to carry on the battle. Over 5,000 people crowded into the auditorium at Phoenix Hill and heard a masterly address by the candidate for Governor of Indiana on the Progressive ticket, who extolled the views of his wounded chieftain, and asked the people of Kentucky to go to the polls in November and lend their aid in electing a man who would do his best to give the people a Government which would be rid of trusts.

After telling of the condition of Col. Roosevelt and that the leader of the Progressive Party was not concerned about his own troubles but was looking forward to a great victory in November, the speaker reviewed the record of Gov. Woodrow Wilson, the Democratic nominee for President, charging him with failure to keep his word regarding prosecuting of the big trusts incorporated in New Jersey.

More enthusiasm marked to-night's meeting that has been shown before at any gathering of the Bull Moose Party in this State. There was a scarcity of negroes present, which was considered a good indication by the Republican leaders who attended the meeting.

At the close of his address ex-Senator Beveridge, when asked if he would fill any other engagements for Col. Roosevelt in the campaign, said he would only make one other speech.

"I am needed in the Indiana campaign," he added, "and will not have any time to devote to work outside of that State."

The ex-Senator said in his speech here:

Beveridge's Speech.

"Not a man, but a cause; not a personality, but a principle. This is the word. Had the shot done the work that it was meant to do, yet it would not have stayed the cause. Had it laid the great leader low, still the principle would have marched onward. But our leader is spared still to lead that forward movement in American life which God meant him to lead to final victory. Over slander and abuse, over falsehood and libel, over craft and cunning, over plot for his ruin by criminal wealth and the crazed mind which was the plot's sure fruit, over all the forces of evil and their workmen, the great American prevails.

"Every American is proud of these fine traits this typical American showed in the hour of real trial. The fires of danger once more prove him pure gold. Such pluck, such calm, such kindness, such thought for others, even for the one who sought his death! With the bullet in his breast, his first thought was to save the poor creature who had fired it. He cried out to the men who were in the very act of killing his crazed assailant: 'Stop; do not hurt him! Bring him to me.' And under this strong arm the madman found safety and protection. He next thought was of the people for whose welfare he is fighting and the word given him to speak to them.

"'Drive on,' he said. 'I will speak to the people of their cause.' And he did it from the moment the shot was fired, of which all mankind even now has heard. Until this very moment never once has he weakened, never once has good cheer left him, never once has his sunny soul been clouded.

"And this is what a century of liberty has done for us; for this is the kind of man every American mother would have her son grow up to be. And this is Theodore Roosevelt.

"Now that it is sure that he will live, he might well think of himself with that pride which his countrymen take in his noble character. But instead he thinks not at all of himself, but only of the cause he stands for.

Message Roosevelt Sends.

"He called me to Chicago, and at his bedside he asked me to say for him these words to all the people:

It matters little about me, but it matters all about the cause we fight for. If one soldier who happens to carry the flag is stricken another will take it from his hands and carry it on. One after another, the standard bearers may be laid low, but the standard itself can never fall.

You know that personally I did not want ever to be a candidate for office again. And you know that only the call that came to the men of the 60's made me answer it in our

Continued on Page 3.

RAISES $300,000 AT DINNER.

Duke of Westminster's Banquet in Aid of Tariff Reform a Success.

Special Cable to THE NEW YORK TIMES.

LONDON, Oct. 16.—The Duke of Westminster's much discussed "£1,000 a head banquet" was given this evening at Grosvenor House, the Duke's London residence.

The Duke conceived the idea of inviting to dine with him some 200 guests, who were expected to contribute £1,000 ($5,000) each to the tariff reform fund.

The subscriptions actually reached £60,000. An anonymous subscriber gave £10,000. The lowest amount donated was a guinea, and there were several checks for £1,000 each, including one from Birch Crisp and another from Waldorf Astor, M. P.

It is expected that the fund will reach £100,000 by next Monday.

DISTRUST OIL PROJECT.

Other Banks Think Deutsche Bank Is Too Favorably Treated.

BERLIN, Oct. 16.—Fear that the proposed petroleum monopoly under the auspices of the German Government will be a one-sided arrangement unduly favoring the interests of the Deutsche Bank was the cause of their refusal to enter the syndicate, according to a statement authorized by the Dresdner Bank, the Disconto Gesellschaft, and the Bleichroeder Bank to-day.

The three banks declare it to be untrue that their refusal was inspired by their relations with the Standard Oil Company. On the contrary, they say, they offered to cancel their contracts with that concern and to enter the monopoly company, and withdrew only when the syndicate refused to give the necessary guarantees for equality of treatment.

APPEAL TO GRAND JURY

To Discover the Circulator of Rumors of a "Murder."

The Brooklyn firm of Abraham & Straus appealed to the Grand Jury yesterday for an inquiry that would assist the house in learning the source of a rumor, current now three weeks, that a young girl employe of the firm's store in Fulton Street, had been attacked, robbed and killed somewhere in the store.

The Brooklyn Detective Bureau, the Coroner and the newspapers have tried for three weeks to discover the origin of this story, which has been persistently circulated, now through anonymous letters, now through telephone messages, always with the same details and always without names to make it definite.

The rumor thus circulated was that a girl employe, returning to the store in the evening to get a pocketbook which she had left behind, was attacked by two men, who after killing her left her body jammed behind the wire meshes of one of the lockers.

This crime, said the anonymous circulator of the rumor, had been "suppressed."

POLICEMAN'S AUTO HITS MAN.

Joseph Sheppard, Who Owns the Car, Once in Becker's Vice Squad.

Joseph Sheppard, a patrolman attached to the Lee Avenue station, in Brooklyn, was driving along Atlantic Avenue last evening in his touring car when, at the dimly lighted corner of Washington Avenue, he ran over a civilian and broke the civilian's leg. The victim of the unavoidable accident was William Annis of 1,359 St. John's Place. He was taken to the Swedish Hospital.

Interested at the discovery of another policemen owner of an automobile, the reporters asked who this Sheppard was and whence he had come. They learned that he had been transferred to the distant Brooklyn precinct some eight months ago, prior to which time he was a detective at Headquarters and connected with the Vice Squad, then operating under the command of Lieut. Charles Becker.

GOVERNMENT CLOSES PORTS.

Foreign Vessels Barred from Harbors to Protect Military Secrets.

WASHINGTON, Oct. 16.—For the protection of military secrets of the United States, President Taft to-day issued an executive order forbidding foreign vessels to enter the following ports without the special authority of the Navy Department:

Tortugas, Fla.; Great Harbor, Culebra; Guantanamo, Cuba; Pearl Harbor, Hawaii; Guam and Subig Bay, Philippine Islands.

These ports are American naval bases. The order declared that they were not sub-ports of entry, and should not be made such. It specifically closes the harbors to commercial and privately owned vessels of foreign register, as well as to the warships of foreign powers, unless the Secretary of the Navy sanctions their entry.

MUST GIVE 'PHONE SERVICE.

Public Service Commission Decides in Favor of Metropolitan Company.

ALBANY, Oct. 16.—The Public Service Commission has ordered the New York Telephone Company to furnish telephone service to the Metropolitan Telegraph and Telephone Company at its offices in New York City.

The New York Telephone Company had refused service, alleging that the Metropolitan Company was created solely for the purpose of selling securities on the credit of a company of the same name which was succeeded by the New York Telephone Company in 1896.

HARVARD'S STRONG MAN.

Hardwick Wins This Year's Test, but Huntington Outpointed Him in 1911.

CAMBRIDGE, Oct. 16.—Huntington R. Hardwick of Quincy is the champion strong man of Harvard, according to the exhaustive tests recently made under the supervision of the physical director.

Hardwick got a total of 1,271.1 points. This mark is lower than that of F. T. Huntington of the class of 1912, who held the championship last year. Huntington's total was 1,303. Hardwick is a player on the 'Varsity football team.

ROOSEVELT GAINS, BULLET LOCATED, LODGED IN RIB

Wound Is Healing Without Infection and He May Be Out of Danger by To-night.

WON'T PROBE FOR BULLET

Broken Rib Will Be Allowed to Heal Without Putting Patient in Plaster Cast.

MAY SOON START HOME

Mrs. Roosevelt in Charge and Anxious to Have Colonel at Oyster Bay.

FEW BESIDES FAMILY SEE HIM

Patient in Good Humor and Continually Jokes with the Doctors.

HOPES TO MAKE SPEECH HERE

Beyond That He Agrees to Take No Active Part in the Campaign—Bulletins Reassuring.

SAYS HE FEELS FIT.

Bulletin from Dr. J. B. Murphy.

By Telegraph to the Editor of THE NEW YORK TIMES.

CHICAGO, Oct. 16, 11:30 P. M.—Col. Roosevelt's pulse, 82; temperature, 98.6; respiration, 20; white blood count, 6,400. He is in much less pain and moves with greater ease. His general condition is good. He says he feels fit.

JOHN B. MURPHY.

ROOSEVELT'S CONDITION EXCELLENT.

By Dr. Alexander Lambert,

Col. Roosevelt's Family Physician.

I am struck with the excellence of Col. Roosevelt's condition after what he has been through. There is no question but that he has a serious wound with serious possibilities, none of which has appeared, and we shall not anticipate nor cross any bridge until we get there.

I shudder when I realize how narrow an escape from instant death Col. Roosevelt had. The bullet struck him from below at an angle such that unless deflected it would have surely passed through the little lobe of his right lung upwards and inwards through the auricles of the heart or the arch of the aorta.

The folded manuscript and heavy steel spectacle case checked and deflected the bullet so that it passed up at such an angle that it went outside the ribs and in the muscles. If this deflection had not occurred and the bullet gone through the arch of the aorta or auricles of the heart, Col. Roosevelt would not have lived sixty seconds.

ALEXANDER LAMBERT.

Special to The New York Times.

CHICAGO, Oct. 16.—Optimism rules about the bedchamber of Col. Roosevelt to-night after a day of steady gain in condition as marked by the tenor of the official bulletins and the cheerful talk of his physicians.

A bulletin issued at 10 o'clock this evening indicated almost a normal state of health, the physicians noting especially the absence of any sign of sepsis or pleural complications. At midnight the Colonel was sleeping soundly.

With the discovery of the bullet from Schrank's revolver imbedded near the fourth rib, which is now found to have been fractured by the impact, the Colonel's medical attendants are relieved of further anxiety on that score.

Already there is talk that the Colonel will be well enough to start for Oyster Bay by Saturday. Mrs. Roosevelt, who arrived this morning and took control of affairs, is very anxious to have him taken out of the midst of so much politics.

The surgeons in response to the insistent demands of Col. and Mrs. Roosevelt say that it is absolutely necessary to keep him under a minute-to-minute examination until to-morrow night at least. By to-morrow night, they say, the seventy-two hours in which blood poison must be guarded against will have elapsed.

That the bullet wound is healing normally without infection was officially announced to-night.

A description of the wound, given to-night by Dr. W. B. McCauley, is the first given to the public by the surgeons. He said that the bullet's path through the muscles of the chest was lacerated to some extent by the battered lead but that there was little contusion and no extensive area of bruised and extravasated surrounding tissue.

Cut a Comparatively Small Hole.

"The bullet did not 'mushroom,' as might have been expected," said Dr. McCauley. "For that reason it cut a comparatively small hole in the skin and did not reduce a large portion of the nearby tissues to a pulp, as is the case in a soft bullet that 'mushrooms' in animal tissue after it hits a bone. I think the bundle of papers in Col. Roosevelt's pocket checked it, and the spectacle case fr-

SOX CHAMPIONS ON MUFFED FLY

Continued from Page 1.

things which he emphasizes with angry gestures.

Now the Boston throng calls for the blood of the veteran—and gets it.

His control is gone, and Speaker, saved by a blunder, hammers the ball hard to right field, and Engle is over the plate. Lewis stands still while four bad ones pass him, and then Gardner steps up and puts all his weight against the ball, and it goes far out to Devore, too far for him to stop Yerkes with the winning run, even though his throw comes true as a bullet.

Too bad! Too bad! The world championship belongs in New York and Boston is perfectly aware of it. Here as well as there admiration is ungrudging for a team that could come from behind, win two decisive victories on its gameness, and deserve to win a third, and sympathy is widespread for a gallant pitcher and his gallant mates, who were cheated of their triumph by a bit of bravado. After the game the Red Sox rooters gave hearty cheers "for the best player on the giants' team—Snodgrass."

Most of all the sympathy is due to Mathewson. Three times he has given prodigally of his waning vigor to bring the world championship to New York, and three times he has deserved victory, but has had it denied because his team has failed to play its real game behind him. What it meant to him to pitch the game to-day he only knows.

As he sat in the corridor of his hotel this morning it could be seen that he had little left to give. The skin was drawn tightly over the bone on his jaw and chin, and in his hollowed cheeks the furrows that have been graven by hard campaigns of recent years were startling in their depth. As he warmed up his gauntness was evident, and the Boston fans gloated over the thought that he could not long stand the rush of their sluggers.

Yet up to that disastrous tenth he was "Big Six" at his best. His fast ball shot with a thud into the glove of Meyers, his drop shot down in front of the batters and his fadeaway had the best of them, breaking their backs. Now and again he seemed in trouble, and the Boston rooters yelled that he was going, but no sign of a crack appeared, and only eight safe hits were made off him in the ten periods.

It was in the first inning that he showed what he meant to do. Yerkes, second up, fanned on a fadeaway. Speaker got to second on an error by Doyle, but Lewis went out on three pitched balls. With two on bases in the second and one out, he made Cady pop up, and Bedient sent a grounder to Doyle. In the third he sent the Red Sox to the field with three pitched balls.

So he went along to the seventh, holding the game as he wished, and it was only in this round that two hits were bunched on him. That luck had some part here cannot be denied. Stahl got on with a pop up, which first eluded the rush of Murray, Snodgrass, and Doyle. Wagner walked, but it seemed as though nothing would come of it when "Big Six" with two out had fooled Henriksen, who was batting for Bedient, twice on strikes and had started a fadeaway over the plate. Henriksen had never faced him before and was not at all familiar with the fadeaway, but his bat happened to connect with the ball as he made a wide swing, and the sphere shot over third base for a double, bringing in Stahl. The ball was rapidly curving over the foul line, and six inches more of this deflection would have made the hit vain.

In the eighth and ninth the Sox hit him hard, but could not place the ball out of reach of the Giant fielders. In the fatal tenth the whole Boston side should have been put out on flies and none should have reached first base.

Yet credit must not be denied to young Bedient. When he went to the box Gardner, Stahl, and Cady were as solicitous for his welfare as though he were an only child with the croup. After each ball in the early innings, Gardner walked in and told him pleasant things and soothed him, and on frequent occasions the others added their attentions. It was made evident before the game had gone very far, however, that others on the Red Sox team were in far greater need of an anchor than he.

Whatever nervousness he might have had at first, it was not long before both his feet were firmly planted on the ground and he refused to let them be lifted. He was dangerously wild at times, but in the pinches he was as cool as the east wind that wafted its chilling way across the field. At first he was exceedingly deliberate in his work, but as the game went on he took things calmly and pitched almost as fast as Mathewson. His departure from the box after the seventh inning was a matter of batting strategy, not of necessity.

The one run scored against him in the third inning had in it elements of luck and misfortune. He let Devore walk to first, but a double play would have been possible had not Gardner, too intent on watching him, fumbled Doyle's swift grounder. Murray's drive to left centre which scored Devore was just missed by Speaker, his fingers touching the ball. In the fourth Bedient showed his class. With Herzog on third and only one out he forced Fletcher, who had made a safe hit the first time up, and Mathewson to send up high flies.

Wood, who went to the box in the eighth, gave promise at first showing the form of the first two games he won. In the ninth, however, the Giants showed that they could find his smoke ball, and in the tenth they made it plainly evident that he could not last long. Murray's drive was one of the hardest hits of the series, and Merkle's fairly sizzled. Meyers sent one of the same sort to the box, and it wa simply good fortun that Wood's bare hand found itself in the way. He gave plain indication of distress and was legally out of the game, Engle having batted for him in the last half of the tenth. Collins was warming up to take his place when the Giants exploded.

At the bat, in the field and in baserunning the Giants excelled. They got nine hits off Bedient and wood to eight off Mathewson. In the error column they showed up two to five, and in the baserunning they were fast, while the Sox at times were slow and blundering.

In the error-making Gardner was the worst offender. He made a bad mess of a slow tap by Meyers in the second, the ball being right in his hand. He was equally bad on an attempted double steal in the same inning when he muffed a perfect throw by Wagner to cut down the Indian. He contributed another on Doyle's drive in the third when he missed the double play.

After that he settled down and was in the game whenever opportunity offered. Wagnr also was an offender, dropping a fine throw by Cady to head off a steal by Snodgrass. Stahl contributed the fifth Red Sox bungle in the seventh, when he badly misjudged a high foul and let it get away from him.

On the Giants' side Doyle erred in the first inning, when he muffed a perfect throw by Devore to catch Speaker, who was trying to stretch a long single. The other was made by Snodgrass. Nothing more need be said. He will miss the $1,283 it cost him.

Mixed in with the errors were some fine plays. The best of all was the catch of Hooper of a high drive from Doyle's bat, which was going for a home run into the bleachers back of right field. He picked it out of the air with a jump and almost fell over the low fence.

Fletcher made a startling play in the second. On a hard hit by Stahl with Wagner on first, Doyle threw wildly to the shortstop on the bag. Fletcher dived forward and retrieved the ball, jamming his foot on the bag just before Gardner rushed into it. On the base paths the worst exhibition was that of Yerkes. He was on third when Speaker started a steal from first. Meyers whipped the ball to Mathewson, and he shot it to Herzog, and Yerkes was nipped by feet.

A peculiar piece of hard luck for the Giants resulted from a protest that had been made by Manager McGraw. In Saturday's game Lewis scored one of the Red Sox runs because of a triple he drove into a blind alley off the left field bleachers. McGraw insisted that thereafter such a hit should be good for only two bases, and the rule was made. Herzog, in the fourth with nobody out, drove a vicious ball into this same alley, and was waved back to second after easily getting to the third sack. He did not get home, as he probably would have except for McGraw's protest. With his run scored the series would have been won by the Giants in the ninth, for there would have been no fatal tenth inning.

The setting for the most stirring finish of a world championship in the history of baseball was not calculated to be inspiring. Little would one have thought that such an event was taking place in one of the best baseball cities in the country. There was an atmosphere of dreariness about the affair. The ramshackle structures of the Boston field, the rusty grass interspersed with dry patches did not look good to one who had been used to the glories of the Brush Stadium. The sun shone brightly, but the east wind was chilly.

The Royal Rooters were not there. Offended by the neglect to recognize their unwavering loyalty by providing seats for them the day before they boycotted the game and their influence was shown by the fact that thousands of others did the same thing.

Then, too, there was a general feeling among the Boston rooters that the series had been lost by the routs of Monday and Tuesday. One could scarcely find one this morning who believed that the Red Sox could stop the rush of the Giants. Mixed with this was some worse feeling. There had been many rumors afloat of trouble among the Red Sox. It was said that Wood on the train coming from New York on Monday had accused O'Brien of deliberately giving his game to the Giants, and that they had engaged in a fight which accounted for the inability of Wood to win his third victory. According to a local newspaper report charges were widely made among fans that the management of the Boston's had deliberately sent O'Brien in to be slaughtered for the purpose of swelling their income from the series. At all such things the persons responsible for baseball here scoffed, but they had their effect in keeping down the attendance.

Of the 17,000 odd who were present, however, many were loyal to the team and were quite willing to show it when the occasion arose. The management of the club helped them to make noise by distributing thousands of rattles, which, when beaten together or on the backs of seats, set up a chorus like that of giant crickets. At times this noise was weird in the extreme.

When the game was over there was no Royal Rooters' band to lead a zigzag procession and no delirious outburst. Hundreds of fans, however, made a rush on the Red Sox bench, where they cooped the players in almost suffocating confinement and insisted on cheering them again and again, not even forgetting Snodgrass of the Giants.

Here the only really violent incident of the hard-fought series occurred. After the game was finished Manager McGraw ran over to the Red Sox bench to shake hands with Manager Stahl and congratulate him on his victory and sportsmanship. A Boston fan, rushing from behind, ran into him and almost tipped him into the bench pit. McGraw turned and in saving himself half pushed, half struck the man. There was a bit of excitement for a moment, but good feeling was running too high for anything serious to happen, and the Giants' manager was able to pay his courtesies and escape.

Boston has shown no great jubilation to-night over the victory. What it wanted was proof of the superiority of the Red Sox, not a championship handed to them as a gift. Fans admit that the Sox were played to a standstill and that no large honor accrues to them. Beyond the cheering at the grounds there has been no demonstration in the city.

Mayor Fitzgerald, however, is determined that the team shall have some recognition. After the game he went to the clubhouse and congratulated Manager Stahl and President McAleer and suggested that a big dinner be given to the team. This was declined because the men were anxious to get away and take up other affairs. There will be instead a parade to-morrow morning from the ball park to Faneuil Hall and addresses there at noon.

SHEER LUCK WON FOR RED SOX—FULLERTON

Boston, Outguessed and Outgeneraled, Never Should Have Captured Decisive Game.

BEDIENT SAVED BY HOOPER

Mathewson, Baseball's Greatest Pitcher, Beat Batters Back All the Way—Nervous Anxiey Broke Giants.

By HUGH S. FULLERTON.

Special to The New York Times.

BOSTON, Mass., Oct. 16.—Boston is tearing down the statues to-night of the Revolutionary leaders and replacing them with those of Tris Speaker, Hugh Bedient, Buck Henriksen, and Jake Stahl.

Never since that memorable night when Kid Revere rode to Lexington and started the tenth inning rally has Boston been so worked up, for the Red Sox are champions of the world by virtue of a victory due more to sheer luck than anything else, and to-night the Tories from New York are fleeing homeward beaten in the toughest luck finish that ever was known in a series of this sort.

With the championship in their hands, whether deserved or not, the Giants exploded in the tenth inning to-day, and a muffed fly, an easy foul permitted to drop safe, a little panic in the ranks, a final rush by the Red Sox, and it was over, and again the American League won the championship.

There is a bitter taste remaining from the greatest series of games ever played, for to-day Boston boycotted its ball club because of the trouble between the management and the royal rooters yesterday, which resulted in the Mayor publicly denouncing Secretary Roy. This reduced the attendance to a little over half what it has been, and those loyal 17,000 witnessed the most thrilling game of the entire series.

It was a battle between youth and experience, and during most of the journey it seemed as if the skill and cunning of the veteran Mathewson would stop the Red Sox. It did until, with the count 1 to 0, with the Red Sox outguessed and outgeneraled at every point, Olaf Henriksen, with two strikes called and another nearly called, caught a curve and drove it over third, evening up the score, and from that on Boston went wild.

Wood Responded Nobly.

Smoky Joe Wood, summoned to redeem himself for yesterday's frightful exhibition, responded nobly, but the Giants were full of fight, and they battled him royally, expecting to rush the assault and win again, but when the ninth came with the teams still on even terms, with both pitchers almost unhittable, it looked as if the finish would be delayed another day. Mathewson, matching his brain and his experience against the driving power of the Red Sox, was out there pitching, lobbing his slow one around the corner, shooting his fast one across at unexpected intervals, while Wood was burning holes in the air. In the first of the ninth Murray caught hold of a fast one and ripped a line double into the left field seats and raced home with what seemed the $1,283-per-man run when Merkle whaled a ball past second.

The victory was within grasp, already New York was World's Champion City, Broadway was World's Champion Street, Harry Stevens was World's Champion, and the greatness of New York was demonstrated and all the dope upset. The gunmen had been summoned to shoot up a few who thought differently. It had been demonstrated that the Knickerbockers had it all over the Pilgrims at any style of going until Engle came to bat and cracked a fly to centre. It wasn't a hard fly, and it was caught squarely in both hands. Snodgrass muffed and let Engle land on second. The luck that has pursued the Giants throughout the year and through the series suddenly deserted them. Snodgrass made a desperate effort to redeem himself by jerking down Hooper's line smash.

Mathewson, the greatest pitcher of all time, faced the crisis of his career. He had responded nobly, with sore and worn-out arm, and he had outwitted, outguessed, and outgeneraled the Red Sox. In the pinch he wavered and passed Yerkes, and the Boston rooters raised a wild yell. For Tris Speaker was coming to bat—Speaker, the hero of the year. Mathewson poised and dropped a slow curve inside the plate. Speaker, who had been outguessed all day—Speaker, the man who, according to American League pitchers, is unfoolable—swung at the bad ball and lofted an easy fly toward first base.

Any one could have caught it. I could have jumped out of the press box and caught it behind my back, but Merkle quit. Yes, Merkle quit cold. He didn't start for the ball. He seemed to be suffering from financial paralysis. Perhaps he was calculating the difference between the winners' and losers' end. He didn't start. Mathewson saw the ball going down. Meyers saw it would fall safe, and they raced toward it, too late, and the ball dented the turf a few feet from first. On the next try Speaker lashed a vicious single to right, the score was tied, men on second and third, and after Lewis had walked and filled the bases Gardner drove a long fly to Devore, out over his head. He caught it and made a desperate heave to the plate, but before the ball came to Meyers Yerkes had crossed the plate, the greatest series of ball games ever played was over, and the Boston Red Sox were World's Champions.

Luck Deserted Giants.

While I still believe Boston ought to have won the championship because it is slightly a better team than New York, the Red Sox never should have won to-day's game. Giving them all due credit, they had all the luck and all the breaks. The luck has been following the Giants all through the series, but to-day it turned upon them utterly. It required a marvelous catch by Hooper, a catch I regard as the greatest of the entire series, to prevent them from beating Bedient by a clear margin. They were outpitched by Mathewson all the way, for the foxy veteran, announcing sadly that he was done forever, and to doleful music singing his swan song, came back and pitched like a two-year-old. He wanted the money, and he put $1,283 worth of thought into everything he pitched until the tenth. Bedient, too, was good. He pitched a clever game of ball all the way, used his speed well, and the run that New York got off him was the result of a pass and hit that just grazed Speaker's fingers. After Bedient was taken out to permit Henriksen to slam a double over third and tie up the score and almost win the game, Joe Wood came back to redeem himself, and although he permitted the Giants to get ahead again in the tenth by clustering two hard hits, he may consider himself redeemed.

The result is psychological rather than baseballic. The Giants broke from nervous anxiety just as the Red Sox did in the two preceding games, and threw it away after they had it won.

From an expert standpoint it was a wonderful game of ball. The pitching was tight, the fielding fast, and at every turn one could see the workings of the brains of the leaders in the movements of their men. Four times Stahl switched his style of attack against Mathewson, first rushing and hitting the first ball, they trying to wait him out. McGraw changed his system twice, and toward the end, after Wood had gone in, he seemed to change instructions to every man who went to bat. Neither could break the defenses of the other until that final round, when panic seized the Giants and let the Red Sox rescue their money and their honors, jerking them from the very grasp of the Giants.

While we made good as a prophet we are not particularly proud of the feat. New York outgamed and outgeneraled the Red Sox through the entire series. The Red Sox showed more batting strength, less speed, less baseball smartness, and Stahl was outgeneraled by McGraw, who came near winning the championship by outguessing him on pitchers.

SERIES RECEIPTS, $490,833.

All Records Smashed in This Year's World's Championship Games.

The attendance and receipts for the world's series this year established new records. Nearly $500,000 will be divided among the owners of the Boston and New York clubs, the players and the National Commission. The total amount taken in at the gates was $490,833, contributed by 252,037 persons. These figures surpass by many thousands the most sanguine expectations of the club owners and National Commission. The series last year between the Giants and the Athletics ended in six games, when the attendance was 179,851 and the receipts $342,364.50.

According to the division of receipts as announced by the National Commission, 10 per cent. of the gross receipts are set apart for the National Commission, 60 per cent. of the net receipts of the first four games go to the players. This amount is subdivided, 60 per cent. going to the winning club and 40 to the losing. The remainder of the money is equally divided between the owners of the two clubs.

Snodgrass's muff of Engle's fly cost each New York player $1,283, as this was the difference between the winners' and the losers' end of the players' purse. The players' share for the first four games only was $147,571. Of this amount each of the twenty-two Red Sox players receives $4,024.68, while twenty-three New York players each receive $2,566.46. The National Commission receives $49,083.60 for its services, which will more than cover the cost of running the commission until next year's series.

The series represented a small fortune for the owners of the two clubs. After deducting the National Commission's and players' share $294,177.70 remained for the clubs. This represented for each club more money than was taken in by some of the major league clubs for the entire season of 154 games, and was more than sufficient to pay the club salaries and ground expenses for the year.

"All the News That's Fit to Print."

The New York Times.

THE WEATHER
Partly cloudy today; local rains, somewhat cooler tomorrow; moderate northeasterly winds.
For full weather report see Page 15.

VOL. LXIV...NO. 20,716. NEW YORK, TUESDAY, OCTOBER 13, 1914.—EIGHTEEN PAGES. ONE CENT In Greater New York, Jersey City and Newark. | Elsewhere TWO CENTS.

GERMANS IN GHENT, PUSH ON TOWARD COAST; ALLIES FIGHT NOW TO CHECK REINFORCEMENTS; GERMAN SUBMARINE SINKS RUSSIAN CRUISER

BOSTON TAKES THIRD GAME, 5-4, IN 12TH INNING

Mack Pitcher's Wild Throw Gives Braves Three Straight in the World's Series.

NERVE-RACKING STRUGGLE

Both Teams Score Twice in the Tenth—Gowdy Again a Hero at the Bat.

FOUL MUFF SAVES BRAVES

Evers, After Tip Is Dropped, Singles, Paving Way for Tying Run—Atones for Bad Play.

35,520 AT FENWAY PARK

Thousands Stand Outside Boston Grounds During Game—Will Make Clean Sweep Today, Evers Says.

Special to The New York Times.

BOSTON, Oct. 12.—A giddy toss to third base by Joe Bush in the twelfth inning brought today's contest at Fenway Park to an abrupt end and gave the Boston Braves the third game of the world's series over the Athletics by a score of 5 to 4. This whimsical throw by Bush was fraught with tragedy for the Mackmen, making a last desperate stand to hold their fading glory. On this foolish bit of a schoolboy's error hinged the most nerve-racking struggle that has ever been played in the national classic.

The purple haze of eventide was gathering over Fenway Park, and the 35,520 persons who had sat for more than three hours were restless and fatigued as they looked down, from all sides of the solid banks of humanity, at the figures which moved about phantomlike in the twilight. The score was 4 to 4, and Boston was at the bat in the last half of the twelfth inning.

The rawboned Texan, Hank Gowdy, the Giant castoff, stepped to the plate, swinging a vicious looking black bat. Hank had already battered Bush's pitching for a home run and a two-bagger. Bush had not only Gowdy to fear. He had a howling, yelling, hostile populace, making his eardrums ache with a raucous clamor. These victory-thirsty thousands demanded the sacrifice of Connie Mack's stalwart flinging youngster to complete a Boston holiday. The ball was hardly visible from the stands. Gowdy swept his bat across the plate as freely as a reaper mowing down the golden grain. The shock of his bat sent the ball soaring into the midst of the Royal Rooters in the left field bleachers. Stallings then rushed Larry Gilbert in as a pinch hitter, and sent Leslie Mann out to second to run for the red-headed Gowdy.

A Battle of Baseball Wits.

The wits of Stallings were matched against the wits of Mack. Bush looked over to the Athletics' bench. Mack wig-wagged for him to pass the pinch hitter. It looked like a good bit of strategy, for it would put a runner on first and second, and enhance the possibilities of a force out at third or a double play. Bush threw out four balls and Gilbert went to first.

Herb Moran was next at the bat, and he did just exactly the thing that the resourceful Mack expected. He dropped a bunt down along the third-base line. It was Bush's play to get the ball to Baker at third and force Mann.

Poor Bush! Cool under fire all afternoon, the strain had been too much for him. He got the ball, whirled about, and made a ghastly throw to third which was out of Baker's reach and Mann rushed home with the victory. The crowd went wild. All the feeling and enthusiasm, which had been bottled up as the game seesawed one way and then the other, burst forth with unrestrained fury. The mob jammed down to the field and smothered the Boston players in a demonstration of fanatical joy which has rarely been seen at a baseball game.

A heart-broken youth, his eyes blurred with tears, slunk away under the big stands as the pæans of victory rang in his ears. His had been a great responsibility. His team mates, the fading world's champions, had played masterful ball behind him, and they were all fighting shoulder to shoulder to try to stem the relentless onslaught of an all-powerful enemy.

Then, by one tragic throw, he had knocked the foundation from under the Mackian machine and it came tumbling down in ruins. There was no comfort for Bush. Not even the soft, fatherly forgiveness of the Athletic leader could push back that strangling lump which lodged in the youngster's throat. O fickle fame! A year ago praise of this strapping boy from the backwoods of Minnesota was on every baseball fan's lips from Maine to Texas as the iron-nerved hero who had downed the slugging Giants.

The Unconquerable Braves.

But what of the Boston Braves? They must go down in baseball annals as the team which doggedly refused to be defeated. They played great ball today. Toward the end of the game, when the Mackmen suddenly found themselves and played as brilliantly as they ever played in their hour of greatest glory, the Braves stuck to their task, surmounting all the obstacles

Continued on Page 8.

KAISER'S EYES SHINE WITH PRIDE FOR ARMY

Is Sure of Victory and Discusses With Chancellor a New Map of Europe.

Special Cable to THE NEW YORK TIMES.

ROME, Oct. 12, (Dispatch to The London Daily News.)—The famous Berlin painter, Vollbehr, who has just seen the Kaiser, says that his Imperial Majesty is in the highest spirits. His pride in his valorous army is so great that it shines through his eyes, which are phosphorescent with happiness. The Mayor of Weimar says that the Kaiser, addressing his troops, said:

"My boys, the leaves are falling, but we shall all return to our beloved homes."

Both the Kaiser and the German Chancellor, who is accompanying him at the front, are certain of victory. They spoke about changing the map of Europe after the war.

$1,200 FOR 11 PEARS TO HELP BELGIANS

And a German at British Fruit Sale Buys Auction Hammer for Ten Guineas.

Special Cable to THE NEW YORK TIMES.

LONDON, Oct. 12.—Remarkable scenes were witnessed in the fruit auction salesrooms at Hull today, when $1,200 was paid for eleven ordinary French pears, the proceeds to be devoted to the Belgian Relief Fund. Many purchasers paid $50 for a single pear, and the first purchaser at that price was a German fruit merchant, who also gave 10 guineas ($52.50) for the auctioneer's hammer. At the close of the day the auctioneer sold his second hammer.

Some purchasers bought their pears several times over, and one man who paid $100 had no pear at the end of the sale.

PRUSSIA'S LOSSES NOW PUT AT 211,000

Amsterdam Total From Casualty Lists Does Not Include Those of Other German States.

LONDON, Tuesday, Oct. 13.—The forty-four lists of losses in the Prussian Army, which have been published, contain a total of 211,600 killed, wounded, and missing, according to a Reuter dispatch from Amsterdam.

The lists do not include losses among the Bavarians, Saxons, and Württembergers.

A Rome dispatch on Oct. 7 said that the German casualty lists showed 117,000 killed and missing, but that the Berlin authorities admitted that the total losses to date reached 300,000.

EARL'S WAR 'DON'TS' FOR BRITISH BOYS

One of Them Against Dividing Up Germany 'Before You Have Got Hold of It.'

Special Cable to THE NEW YORK TIMES.

LONDON, Oct. 12.—Lord Curzon of Kedleston tonight delivered a rousing speech at Harrow to an audience which included the masters and boys of Harrow School.

He said he knew of the anticipation of European statesmen of the highest rank who had prophesied for years that it would be in 1914 that Germany would strike the blow at Europe. Some people, he remarked, were of the opinion that it would be over by Christmas. He went on, speaking with great gravity:

"In my judgment more than one Christmas will pass before the soldiers return home."

Lord Curzon concluded with the following "Don'ts":

"Don't think the war does not affect you individually. It touches every man, woman, and child in this country.

"Don't be overjoyed at a victory. Don't be downhearted at a defeat.

"Don't be unnerved by personal or family bereavements.

"Don't be frightened at casualty lists, so long and sometimes so distressing.

"Don't think that you know how to wage the campaign and that the War Office does not.

"Don't write to the newspapers telling Generals and Admirals what they ought to do, but if you have an opinion that you could do it much better tell it to as few people as possible.

"Don't get nervous because the progress of the war is slow. It can only be slow in these stages.

"Don't underrate the enemy.

"Don't waste breath in attempting to ascertain what is to happen to the German Emperor in this world or the next.

"Don't begin to divide up the German Empire before you have got hold of it.

"Don't listen to any one who cries 'halt' before we have carried out the full purpose for which we are fighting.

"And, when the war is over, don't throw away the lessons of the war."

Earl Curzon also said:

"Germany has taken Antwerp to fortify it, to keep it, to make a great naval port of it, to use it as a great jumping-off place for her future attempts upon this country. It is no temporary occupation, unless we make it so."

WILSON BLOCKED ONE-TERM BILL

Letter He Wrote to A. Mitchell Palmer in 1913 Said to Have Sidetracked It.

IN PIGEON HOLE EVER SINCE

Develops That House Committee Filed Senate Measure on Advice of President-Elect.

SILENT ON BALTIMORE PLANK

Limit of Presidential Tenure Never Mentioned in Any of Mr. Wilson's Campaign Speeches.

Special to The New York Times.

WASHINGTON, Oct. 12.—It has been learned here that President Wilson is opposed to the plank in the Baltimore platform limiting the President of the United States to one term. It was ascertained today that Mr. Wilson, then President-elect but still Governor of New Jersey, expressed his views on this subject in February, 1913, in a letter to Representative A. Mitchell Palmer of Pennsylvania.

On Feb. 1, 1913, the Senate by the necessary two-thirds vote adopted a joint resolution submitting to the States a constitutional amendment limiting the Presidency to a single term of six years. The resolution was then sent to the House, where it was pigeon-holed in the Judiciary Committee. Had it been adopted by the House and ratified by three-fourths of the States during the incumbency of President Wilson, he, like Mr. Roosevelt and Mr. Taft, would have been disqualified for further service in the White House.

Upon receipt of the letter from Mr. Wilson, Representative Palmer, so the story goes, submitted the communication, which was ten pages in length, to Chairman Henry D. Clayton of the House Judiciary Committee and to other leading Democratic members of that committee. Republican members of the committee were not taken into the secret. The resolution had been introduced in the Senate as a result of the widespread criticism of Mr. Roosevelt's third-term aspirations in 1912, but the strong opposition of President-elect Wilson was sufficient, it was said, to cause the Democratic leaders of the House to sidetrack the measure.

The plank in the Baltimore platform, which is generally understood to have been inserted at the request of William J. Bryan, now Secretary of State in President Wilson's Cabinet, reads:

> We favor a single Presidential term, and to that end urge the adoption of an amendment to the Constitution making the President of the United States ineligible for re-election, and we pledge the candidate of this convention to this principle.

During the Presidential campaign Mr. Wilson refused to comment on the one-term plank. It was not known until today, except by a few of the President's more intimate advisers and the members of the Judiciary Committee, to whom the President's letter to Representative Palmer was shown, that Mr. Wilson ever had commented one way or the other on the plank.

The resolution adopted by the Senate on Feb. 1, 1913, proposed to alter the first two sentences of Section 1, Article II., of the Constitution, as follows:

> The Executive power shall be vested in a President of the United States of America. The term of the office of President shall be six years, and no person who has held the office by election or discharged its powers or duties or acted as President under the Constitution and laws made in pursuance thereof shall be eligible to hold again the office by election.

After a debate lasting for three days the final vote on the amendment was one of the most exciting in the history of the Senate. A change of one vote from the affirmative to the negative would have killed the measure. The deciding vote was cast by Senator Robert L. Owen of Oklahoma, who came into the Senate Chamber just in time to be recorded. Senator Shively of Indiana was the only Democrat who voted against the resolution. Seventeen Republicans, who were desirous of eliminating Mr. Roosevelt as a future Presidential possibility, voted with the Democrats.

At the time the Senate voted favorably on the resolution the sentiment in the House was overwhelmingly in favor of limiting the Presidential term. From that day to this many of the Democratic leaders have been puzzled over the failure of the House to act on the resolution. These members, of course, were not aware of the President-elect's communication to Representative Palmer.

Special to The New York Times.

PHILADELPHIA, Oct. 12.—Representative A. Mitchell Palmer, who lives at Sunbury, Penn., is on campaign tour in the rural sections of the State and could not be reached tonight.

ARRESTED AT WHITE HOUSE.

William Wayne Belvin Disturbs the Executive Mansion.

Special to The New York Times.

WASHINGTON, D. C., Oct. 12.—William Wayne Belvin, said by the police to be the former New York broker, was arrested at the executive offices of the White House today after he had made an attempt to see President Wilson.

Policeman Dalrymple, on duty at the executive offices, thought that Belvin acted peculiarly and persuaded him to go away. Belvin started to leave the building, but before doing so was said to have raised a disturbance and was arrested by James Sloan, the chief secret service operative of the force engaged in guarding the President.

He was taken to a police station.

HEARS GHENT IS OCCUPIED

Amsterdam Dispatch Passed by British Censor Without Confirmation.

BIG CAPTURE OF STORES

Berlin Tells of the Booty Found When the Army Entered Antwerp.

20,000 PRISONERS TAKEN

13,000 English Fled Into Holland, Says the Official Report—Cavalry Victory Near Lille.

The Kaiser's Message on Antwerp's Surrender

Special Cable to THE NEW YORK TIMES.

ROTTERDAM, Oct. 12, (Dispatch to The London Daily News.)—It is announced that the Kaiser has telegraphed to his aunt, the Dowager Grand Duchess of Baden, as follows:

> Antwerp was occupied this afternoon without fighting. God be thanked in deepest humility for this glorious result! To Him be all honor!

LONDON, Tuesday, Oct. 13.—The Daily News correspondent at Rotterdam, wiring on Monday at 3:24 P. M., says:

"It is reported here that the Germans have entered Ghent."

This message has been passed for publication by the British Press Bureau, which takes no responsibility for it.

LONDON, Oct. 13, 2:40 A. M.—The Belgian town of Ghent is now occupied by the Germans, according to an Amsterdam dispatch to Reuter's Telegram Company.

Uhlans have arrived at Selzaete, a short distance from Ghent, and the commander announced that 6,000 soldiers must be quartered on the village.

On Sept. 7 a German force was in the vicinity of Ghent. Its commander and the Burgomaster, M. Braun, entered into an agreement by which the enemy would not then enter the city provided certain supplies were forthcoming. These consisted of 10,000 litres of benzine, 1,000 litres of mineral water, 150,000 kilos of oats, 100 bicycles, 10 motor cycles, and 25 compressed-air cylinders for motor cars. In addition, there was to be supplied a quantity of material for bandages and 100,000 cigars. The goods required by the Germans were delivered on Sept. 9. That night two German officers entered the city and were shot—one of them killed and the other wounded. The latter was held as a prisoner of war. This incident did not cause either party to break the agreement.

Ghent, with a population of nearly 200,000, is at the vertex of a spreading letter V formed by railways running to Ostend and to Antwerp, each about forty miles away. The city, which is the capital of East Flanders, has long been famous in the history and culture of the Low Countries. Here it was in 1576, by an interprovincial agreement known as the Pacification of Ghent, that the country united to drive out the Spanish soldiers. Here, also, on Dec. 24, 1814, the treaty was signed ending the war of 1812-14 between the United States and Great Britain.

BIG CAPTURE OF STORES.

German Report Tells of the Conditions in Antwerp.

LONDON, Oct. 12, 10:20 P. M.—The following official statement has been received from Berlin by the Marconi Wireless Telegraph Company:

"Enormous quantities of provisions of all kinds were captured in Antwerp. The garrison of the northern forts and 13,000 English fled to Holland when they were disarmed. The English themselves are said to have blown up ten of the Antwerp forts. The Belgians estimate that they lost 20,000 men as prisoners.

"When the fall of Antwerp was made known to the Allies the French cavalry was withdrawn in the direction of Arras.

"The interrupted artillery engagement in the Woevre region was resumed Oct. 11. At the same time the German right wing and centre resumed the bombardment of Rheims. On the whole the situation for the Germans is favorable.

"Before his departure for the front Emperor William promoted Prince Joachim (youngest son of the Emperor) to the rank of cavalry Captain.

"It is reported that a Russian fleet of eight large vessels and ten small ships was sighted on Saturday near Kustendje, (a seaport of Rumania on the Black Sea,) steaming in a southerly direction."

Report Cavalry Victory.

A Reuter dispatch from Berlin, via Amsterdam, gives this bulletin, issued last night by the General Staff:

> Our cavalry on Saturday completely routed a French cavalry division west of Lille, and near Habebrouck we inflicted severe losses on another French cavalry division. Until now the engagements on the front in the western theatre did not lead to a decision.
>
> In the eastern theatre we repulsed in the north all attacks of the First and Tenth Russian armies on Oct. 9 and 10. The Russian outflanking efforts by way of Schirwindt (East Prussia) were equally repulsed, and the Russians lost 1,000 prisoners.
>
> In South Poland the advance guards of our armies have reached the Vistula. Near Grojeo, south of Warsaw, we captured 2,000 men of the Second Siberian Army Corps.
>
> The Russian official communications about a great Russian victory at Augustowo and Suwalki (Russian Poland) are invented. The fact that no official Russian communication has been published about the tremendous defeats at Tannenberg and Insterberg vouches a lack of reliable official information.

Says Antwerp Defense Collapsed.

BERLIN, Oct. 12, (by wireless to Sayville, L. I.)—The General Staff of the German Army announces today that in the beginning a very strong garrison defended Antwerp with great energy, but that after the attack by German infantry and marine divisions the defenders fled in full rout. Among the Antwerp garrison was one British marine brigade.

The complete collapse of the Anglo-Belgian defense of Antwerp was shown by the fact that no military authority could be found with which to treat concerning the surrender of the city. This surrender was finally negotiated with the Burgomaster.

It is impossible to give as yet the number of prisoners taken with Antwerp. Many of the defenders who fled to Holland were interned.

Gen. von Beseler, who has been decorated with the Order of Merit for his capture of Antwerp, has issued a proclamation, addressed to the people, saying that no one would be harmed unless they committed hostilities upon the Germans. "Resistance," he announced, "will cause the destruction of your beautiful city." Private property in Antwerp was spared.

A Dutch paper and Sir Sven Anders Hedin, the Swedish geographer, are quoted as stating that the damage caused by the bombardment of Antwerp was insignificant. They state that the museums and churches were not harmed.

A copy of The London Morning Post, received here, declares that the Germans during the bombardment of Antwerp, were most careful to spare churches and museums.

Welcomes Our Red Cross.

The American Red Cross unit which is to serve among German and Austrian wounded has arrived here. The coming of the Americans has been gratefully acknowledged by the Government. Two groups will go to Vienna and two other groups to Breslau, whence they will proceed to the field hospitals.

The return for last week issued by the Reichsbank shows an increase of 544,000,000 marks ($136,000,000) in specie notes, while circulation shows a decrease of 292,000,000 marks, ($73,000,000.)

The following information has been given out for publication:

"Reports received from Vienna set forth that the Russian siege of the Przemysl fortress has been abandoned. Austrian troops have defeated six Russian divisions near Lanout. They also routed one division of Cossacks east of Nymao.

"The Japanese have occupied the Shantung Railroad, in Shantung Province, China. This is a Chinese State railroad and was built by Germans. China has protested against this action.

"The Politiken, a newspaper published in Copenhagen, in a recent issue declares that Japan's cause of action, especially in the occupation of German islands in the Pacific, is difficult of comprehension, as such steps have no military connection with the attack on the German territory of Kiao-Chau.

"The Corriere della Sera, published at Stampa, Switzerland, reports revolting atrocities on the part of the French Senegalese troops.

"The German press, referring to the late King Charles of Rumania, lays particular stress upon his political ability, his great statesmanship, and his efficiency as a military leader."

Summary of War News.

A news dispatch from Rotterdam states that the Germans have entered Ghent. The British censor passed this message for publication, but refused to take the responsibility for it.

The French War Office announces that violent attacks by the Germans have occurred along the entire front, resulting in the gaining of ground by the Allies at some points, while they have not yielded at any part of the line. The report issued earlier in the day stated that desperate fighting was taking place in the vicinity of Lassigny and Lens, and that cavalry engagements continued in the region of Lille.

The French Embassy in Washington received a dispatch telling of four desperate attacks made by the Germans between Aprémont and the Meuse. Trenches were taken by the Germans and retaken by the French several times, finally remaining in the possession of the French.

German Army Headquarters reports that the situation in France is favorable. The interrupted artillery engagement in the Woevre region was resumed on Sunday, and at the same time the German centre resumed the bombardment of Rheims.

Further detail of the fall of Antwerp is given in the German report. Enormous quantities of provisions of all kinds were captured. The garrison of the northern forts and 13,000 British fled to Holland, where they were disarmed, the report says. The English are reported to have blown up ten of the Antwerp forts before they left.

The Austrians announce that the siege of Przemysl has been abandoned by the Russians. The strongly reinforced garrison completely overwhelmed the opposing army, and the Russians are now said to be fleeing from Galicia and north to the Vistula River, pursued by the German-Austrian Army, which has already captured many prisoners.

The Russian Ministry of Marine announces that the armored cruiser Pallada was torpedoed by a German submarine in the Baltic on Sunday, and was sunk with her entire crew.

German aeroplanes again appeared over Paris yesterday and six bombs were dropped into the city. None of the missiles exploded.

GUARDING ANTWERP FROM PLUNDERERS

Germans Police the City and Put Out Fires Caused by the Bombardment.

Special Cable to THE NEW YORK TIMES.

AMSTERDAM, Oct. 12, (Dispatch to The London Daily Chronicle.)—I have been able to get details of the German occupation of Antwerp from Dutch friends who have been there since Friday. As neutrals they can go there with little risk, though for an English journalist to make the trip would be to invite execution as a spy.

The German soldiers left here have done no plundering, and the city is well policed by armed guards. The soldiers are using the city's brigade appliances to extinguish the fires that still smolder in buildings wrecked by shells, but the water supply seems inadequate.

Many instances of hurried flight are to be found in bundles of clothing and other property left in the streets by refugees who found that they had brought from home more than they could carry away. In the streets on the outskirts are Belgian guns still in position at hastily formed barricades.

The Germans seem very anxious for the population to return, and promise their safety if they behave peacefully. Some of the people have already returned, but there does not appear to be any general tendency in that direction.

The German soldiers entered the town singing. Many were decorated with flowers, having nosegays in their tunics, in the muzzles of their rifles, and in their horses' bridles; but this triumphant entry was only for spectacular purposes, and most of the troops afterward marched out again to encamp on the outskirts. There are now few German soldiers in the city except in the square before the Hotel de Ville.

As regards the damage inflicted by the shells, I am able to furnish the following details from the testimony of observers, but the list must not be taken as being complete. Among the buildings destroyed were the Palais de Justice, the synagogue, St. Joseph's Church, the Hippodrome, the Minerva Motor Works, the house 810 in the Avenue des Arts, and Tinchant's Cigar Factory in the Place de Meir. Very serious damage was done in the Avenue Moretus, the Avenue du Sud, the Rue de l'Esplanade, the Rue de la Justice, and the Avenue Quentin Matsys. Other damage was done chiefly in the southern part of the town and in the suburbs of Berchem and Zurenberg.

It was a pathetic experience while compiling this list to be surrounded by a group of refugees anxiously asking what news there was of the streets in which their homes had once been.

WASHINGTON, Oct. 12.—An official report received here today describes the efforts of German military authorities at Brussels to send word through the American Legation to the people of Antwerp of the intended bombardment of that city.

German officials asked Minister Whitlock to transmit the notification which, under Article 26 of The Hague Convention, an invading force is obliged to give to the people of a city about to be bombarded. Mr. Whitlock refused to present the communication, desiring, in view of the strict neutrality of the United States, not to be the bearer of military messages to any of the belligerents. The Germans insisted that all other means of communication had failed. The Spanish Minister, who was in conference with Mr. Whitlock when the representations were made, finally decided to send the Spanish Naval Attaché to Antwerp with the notification.

ADMITS GERMANS' GAINS.

British Expert Says They Obtained All They Strove For at Antwerp.

Special Cable to THE NEW YORK TIMES.

LONDON, Tuesday, Oct. 13.—The military expert of The Standard says:

"It would be very foolish to attempt to ignore the fact that the successful German operations against Antwerp have resulted in considerable material and military value for the enemy. The possession of the city is a moral asset

Continued on Page 2.

RUSSIAN CRUISER SUNK BY GERMAN SUBMARINE

Pallada Torpedoed in Baltic Fight—All Her Crew Lost; Carried 570 Men.

Special Cable to THE NEW YORK TIMES.

PETROGRAD, Oct. 12—(Dispatch to The London Morning Post.)—The naval staff announces that yesterday during the usual scouting operations in the Baltic the Russian armored cruiser Pallada was sunk by a German submarine with all on board.

German submarines were seen about the Baltic last Saturday and were fired upon by Russian cruisers. They launched torpedoes at the armored cruiser Admiral Makarov, but without success, and were beaten off. The Makarov had put out to overhaul a suspicious-looking trading vessel sailing under the Dutch flag. While engaged in this routine work of sea scouting she caught sight of a submarine's periscope and opened fire. The Makarov was not hit, although several torpedoes, it is believed, were fired at her.

Next day the Russian cruisers Bayan and Pallada went out scouting and located the German submarines, but, notwithstanding their rapid artillery attack, one of the submarines succeeded in firing a torpedo at the Pallada, which went to the bottom with all hands. The Bayan, so far as known here, returned in safety to her base. No German losses are reported.

The Pallada had a displacement of 7,775 tons and a normal complement of 570 officers and men.

The Pallada, Bayan, and Admiral Makarov were sister ships, all commissioned about seven years ago. The Bayan, erroneously, it now appears, was reported lost several weeks ago when she went aground in the Baltic.

The Pallada carried 570 officers and men. The cruiser was one of the fastest in the Russian Navy and under forced draught had made as high as twenty-three knots an hour. She was 443 feet long and carried a main battery of two eight-inch and eight six-inch guns.

HOLLAND REPORTS ON THE INTERNED TROOPS

20,000 Belgians, 1,500 British Prisoners There—Marines Who Escaped Welcomed Home.

LONDON, Tuesday, Oct. 13.—Altogether 22,000 British and Belgian soldiers are interned at different points in Holland. About 1,500 of these men are British. This statement has been made by the Dutch War Office, according to a dispatch from the Rotterdam correspondent of The Times.

Special Cable to THE NEW YORK TIMES.

LONDON, Oct. 12.—The return of the Naval Brigade from Antwerp to Deal this evening produced unparalleled scenes of enthusiasm. Long before the arrival of the trains thousands of people thronged the approaches to the station, and when the men, headed by a full brass band of the Royal Marines, marched out to the strains of patriotic music, the streets of the old seaport town vibrated with cheers. Hundreds of flags and handkerchiefs fluttered in the men's faces as they passed.

The marines, all wearing khaki, looked somewhat grizzled but hardy. As they marched on mothers, wives, and sweethearts mixed with them in their ranks, and one tall marine had his little son hoisted on his shoulder beside his rifle, while his wife hung on his free arm, a proud woman. The men, numbering more than 3,000, came in two batches.

All day long, too, streams of Belgian refugees poured into Deal. Considerable difficulty is being experienced in finding accommodation for them as they arrive in trains from Folkstone. Many of them have gone into the surrounding country districts.

ALLIED LEFT BEGINS ATTACK

Moving in Northwest France to Prevent Aid to Von Kluck.

GERMAN FORCES RETIRING

But Are Reported Massing Around Ypres in Preparation for a Big Battle.

MAY BE AIMING AT OSTEND

Extensive Movements of Troops Suggest a Definite Project to Gain a Seaport.

Special Cable to THE NEW YORK TIMES.

NORTHWEST FRANCE, Oct. 11, (Dispatch to The London Daily Telegraph.)—All the heavy fighting by the Allies' armies is taking place in Northwest France.

There are violent engagements over a wide area and the Allies are taking the initiative before there is a possibility of the German army corps released by the fall of Antwerp reinforcing von Kluck's right.

For this reason it may be predicted that the issue will be decided before many hours have elapsed.

Reports German Flank Failed.

Special Cable to THE NEW YORK TIMES.

BEHIND THE LEFT WING IN FRANCE, Oct. 11, (Dispatch to The London Daily Mail.)—Since I sent my last dispatch Thursday night the course of the great battle of Arras has changed for the worse and then again for the better. As I write the position of the Allies is stronger than ever.

At certain points the Allies were forced to give ground on Friday, but since then they have recaptured the lost terrain and have driven the Germans back still further.

The line, which the Germans intended as a net for Lille, has been bent back between La Bassée and Tournai. There is no real resistance and we hold the country safe.

The fighting around Arras has been exceedingly severe since last Tuesday, and Lens has changed hands at least three times in as many weeks.

The Germans are heavily massed in the triangle of Douai-Bethune-Arras, and if they could succeed in bursting the ring at Lens some part of their desperate programme might be realized, but so far they have failed. They have got their forces hopelessly scattered.

It would be absurd to say that they are for that reason negligible. They lie in considerable numbers on the east of Hazebrouck, separated, though they be, from their main body by at least twenty miles. They are in some force between Bethune and La Bassée and in the country surrounding Orchies.

All these members, divorced from their proper body, which was to have marched triumphantly from a captured Lille straight on Arras and the rear of our left wing at Peronne, are being gradually swept up into a general retreat north and east of Lille.

GERMANS MASSING FOR FIGHT.

Calais Sees Signs of Possible Movement Toward the Coast.

By Marconi Transatlantic Wireless Telegraph to The New York Times.

CALAIS, Oct. 12, (Dispatch to The London Times.)—The arrival at Calais of a hundred refugees is one of the indications of the extension of the fighting area in northern France.

I am informed that there is a great movement of German troops from the neighborhood of Lille in the direction of Courtrai, (Belgium,) and that this is preliminary to an impending great battle on the other side of the Belgian frontier.

At the same time, however, there is increasing activity on the part of the Germans between Lille and the French coast. Indeed, it is by no means unlikely that the Germans are contemplating an effort to establish themselves on the coast—a move which, although attended with obvious dangers, might, if successful, seriously hamper the operations of the Allies.

Concentrating Around Ypres.

By Marconi Transatlantic Wireless Telegraph to The New York Times.

NORTH OF FRANCE, Oct. 12, (Dispatch to The London Times.)—The latest information I have been able to obtain speaks still of strong German columns of all arms passing through

BOSTON WINS THIRD SERIES GAME IN TWELFTH INNING

BOSTON TAKES THIRD GAME, 5-4

Continued from Page 1.

which were placed in their path by the tall tactician and his players. On the Boston bench Stallings held the whip and he lashed his players on with an overwhelming discipline.

There were moments in this game that have never been equaled on the diamond for dramatic intensity. The setting itself was fitting for one of the greatest spectacles in American sports. Beautiful Fenway Park was filled to its last seat. The first impression as one glanced over the banks of faces which surrounded the field on every side was that there must be a million onlookers. Handsomely gowned women were there in great numbers. Men of all walks of life, from the Boston banker to the big, good-natured stevedore, who was enjoying his Columbus Day holiday, forgot all toil and care, and were rooting vociferously for Jim Gaffney's Boston Braves.

The Royal Rooters, some of them in war paint and feathers, with bowie knife and tomahawk, were the life of the party. There are cities in this country which will never know what a fourteen-carat baseball fan is until they see Boston raving about its baseball team. The Royal Rooters are not all men. Their wives and families strung along in the long line yesterday and helped the men cheer Stallings's men on to victory. Their band played "Tammany," and Jim Gaffney was about the happiest man in the world.

Gates Opened at 9 A. M.

Many of the fans had been waiting from the time the gates opened at 9 o'clock this morning. They chewed sandwiches and drank bottles of pop to while the time away. At 12 o'clock there were thousands packed outside the park, and the police were at their wits' end to keep them quiet. This mob wouldn't budge an inch. It waited patiently right up to the end of the game and got the news about what was going on from the boys on the top of the bleachers, who cheerfully yelled down the glad tidings from their lofty perches. On the big tall flagpole in centre field two boys hung on and watched the game. Sometimes they were hanging on with one hand and sometimes only by their feet entwined about the pole. They yelled down the news to the crowd in the street which watched them pop-eyed. For three hours their necks were worth about a nickel, but they didn't fall.

"Honey Fitz," Boston's ex-Mayor, led the Royal Rooters, and although Mayor Curley was present, "Fitz" stole most of his thunder. There were a lot of frills before the game started. Johnny Evers got his automobile and took the Boston team tearing around the field on a joy ride. Stallings received half a dozen presents, and Gowdy and Evers received other gifts. "Honey Fitz" made one presentation speech, and not to be outdone Mayor Curley came back strong with another. tI was just like Christmas morning for the Braves as the gifts showered on them.

Large batteries of camera men trained their 24-centimeter siege cameras on all the notables, and for once in his life William Klem, the greatest umpire who never made a mistake, declined to have his picture taken. What's the matter with Klem? When he turned his back to the cameras even his best friends said that Harry Stevens giving away his peanuts wouldn't occasion more surprise. This is the age of wonders! "Honey Fitz" wore his stove pipe hat. No occasion is complete up here without that gorgeous silk "Kelly" shining out like a lighthouse in a fog. Some say that John F. Fitzgerald sleeps in that dicer, but he doesn't.

Most of the way it was an even thing between Tyler and Bush. The Braves' southpaw made the Mackian hitters appear amateurish time and again. The Braves got nine hits and the Athletics eight, but the Bostons made their hits do the most good.

Gowdy's Terrific Hitting.

Gowdy hit with all the fury of a Ty Cobb against a weak pitcher. He crashed out a homer and two doubles. What team could stand up in front of that long range artillery fire? Echo answers, "No team." Gowdy was the main incentive for three of Boston's five runs. If Hank doesn't watch out he'll be done in bronze on the Boston Common. A whale of a hitter is Hank, even if the New York Giants didn't discover it. The best of it is Hank is one of those happy-go-lucky cusses that doesn't know he has done anything out of the ordinary. Butch Schmidt made a great play in the eighth inning when he made an almost impossible stop of Bush's drive, and blocking the ball in its wild flight he turned about, scooped it out of the dust, and threw Bush out at first.

The tenth inning with the Athletics at bat gave the crowd a thrill it will never forget. Two out, the bases full, and "Home Run" Baker at the bat.

For once in the game the multitude was still. It was so quiet that one could hear the big fat man sitting next to him breathing hard. Boston's fans clutched tightly to the arms of their seats. The tireless drummer held his drumsticks suspended above his drumhead. Thirty-five thousand pairs of eyes were glued on Baker. Thirty-five thousand bodies swayed with him as he swung at the ball.

The batting Hercules waved his ashen club with fury. A sputtering bouncer burned the grass on its way between first and second base. Evers boldly attempted to arrest it and his hands were badly blistered for his trouble. Smartly Schang, set at third, romped home with the run which broke the 2 to 2 tie and put Philadelphia in the lead.

Evers Asleep at the Switch.

Then something unbelievable happened. Johnny Evers was rubbing his burning hands and the ball was tucked under his arm. Eddie Murphy, who had traveled from second to third on the hit, watched him like a cat. Not only Evers, but all the other Boston players stood stupidly in their tracks dumbfounded as they saw the White Elephants scurry into the lead. Murphy at third was forgotten. Cautiously, step by step, he edged nearer home, and then made one wild dash for the plate while the ball was still caressed under Evers's arm.

Evers, the smartest and sharpest player in the game, caught fast asleep! Tomorrow Stallings will pin alarm clocks all around him, and tonight he will send him to bed early to get enough sleep.

Quickly the Braves were able to tie the score, and all because of the muff of a foul tip by Wallie Schang. It's a small thing to hang a ball game on, but in this case it was all important. In this tenth after Gowdy had punched a great hole in the centre field atmosphere with his home run, Devore, batting for Tyler, Stallings's last resort to retrieve those two Mackian runs, struck out and the Boston leader was in a torrid frenzy on the bench. Moran outguessed Bush and got a pass. Evers was at the bat. Bush got two strikes and a ball on him, and then shot one over the outside of the pan. Evers reached for it and just tipped it foul. The ball bounced into Schang's mitt and out again. Unlucky muff! If Schang had held that ball it would have been the second out, and a moment later Connolly lifted to Walsh for what would have been the third out.

As it was, Evers got another crack at the ball and this time whanged a single to right centre which sent Moran to third base. Connolly's long fly gave Herbie ample time to score the tying run.

Athletics First to Score.

The American Leaguers were the first to score, sending a run across the plate in the opening inning on Murphy's two-base salute off Tyler's delivery. He moved to third on Oldring's sacrifice, and scored when Connolly dropped Collins's high fly. The Braves tied the score in the second inning on Maranville's walk, steal of second, and sprint to the plate on Gowdy's double into the left-field bleachers.

In the fourth each team added another run. For the Athletics McInnis doubled in the same spot and scored on Walsh's single to left. Schmidt responded for the home team with a single over second, advanced on Deal's out, and counted on Maranville's single to right. With the score 2 to 2, the play continued without advantage one way or the other until the tenth inning.

Today the Athletics showed the best they had, and the Braves more than matched them. Athletic sympathizers, and they are legion, for many a tidy sum of money which would more than buy the Winter's coal has been bet on the Mackian machine, are about ready to throw up the sponge.

The Braves are dead sure that they will accomplish something that has never been done before in a world's series, take four games straight: And if you saw them today you'd be confident that they will do it, too.

Three to one was being offered here tonight that Boston would win the series, with few takers. There were several bets made, however, on tomorrow's game at even money and 10 to 8 in favor of Boston.

WORLD'S SERIES, 1914.

First Game—Boston, 7; Philadelphia, 1.

Second Game—Boston, 1; Philadelhia, 0.

Third Game—Boston, 5; Philadelphia, 4.

THIRD GAME.	
Attendance, (paid) ...	35,520
Receipts	$63,808.00
Nat. Com.'s share.....	6,380.80
Players' share	34,456.32
Clubs' share	22,970.88
Each club's share	11,485.44
TOTAL FOR THREE GAMES.	
Attendance (paid)	76,653
Receipts	$163,086.00
Nat. Com's share	16,308.60
Players' share	88,066.32
Clubs' share	47,223.64
Each club's share.....	29,355.54
ATTENDANCE AND RECEIPTS, 1913.	
First game, attendance	36,291
Receipts	$75,255.00
Second game, att'nd'ce	20,563
Receipts	$49,640.00
Third game, att'nd'ce..	36,888
Receipts	$75,763.00
ATTENDANCE AND RECEIPTS, 1912.	
First game, attendance	35,730
Receipts	$75,127.00
Second game, att'nd'ce	30,148
Receipts	$42,962.00
Third game, att'nd'ce..	34,624
Receipts	$63,142.00

FOUR STRAIGHT, EVERS PREDICTS

With Rudolph in Box, Braves' Captain Expects Boston to Win Series Today.

By JOHN J. EVERS,
Captain of the Boston Braves.

Special to The New York Times.

BOSTON, Oct. 12.—For the first time in twelve years, for the first time since I have been in big league baseball, I let my head hang in a game of baseball today, and the "bone" nearly cost us the contest. If I had not done this, we would have won the game in the tenth inning instead of the twelfth.

I want everybody to understand that I am not trying to spring any alibis for letting Murphy sneak home with a run in the tenth inning, a run that the Athletics should never have had except for my mistake. I am anxious to make it plain that I am assuming all the blame, for I have called so many other fellows in my time for pulling "bones" that I don't want to put myself in a position where they can say: "Well, when Evers kicked one himself he was there with the alibi after bawling all of us."

It looked as if that mistake of mine was going to cost the game, and perhaps the series, for a time. I would have felt it very deeply and keenly if my mistake had stopped us from winning. It would have been a desperate blow to me.

"It was my mistake," I said when I went to the bench after the inning. "I pulled a 'bone' and I am to blame."

"It's all right, Johnny," said the players. "We will get those two back."

I am glad to be able to say that I did something toward getting back those two runs with my hit in our half of the tenth inning. But what I want to lay particular emphasis upon in this story is that our club has one of the gamest bunches of ball players that I ever saw in uniform, and I played with the old Cubs, which were a fighting crowd.

The gameness is not confined to the men on the field playing the game, but the men on the bench are also game. They did a lot to win the game today with their encouragement in the times when we needed it. Every time a man goes up to the bat they are all behind you there with encouraging remarks. "Come on now," they will yell. "We know you can do it. We are all pulling for you here."

The Spirit That Wins.

It is this spirit on the field and on the bench which makes a club play ball and keeps everybody hustling. George Stallings has fostered it. How many ball clubs in the game which would have come back after the Athletics had counted two runs in the tenth inning? Gowdy led the assault, and he led it in a way to put new life into all of us.

"He's been trying to slip a fast one over on me with the first pitch," declared Gowdy as he went to the bat. "If he tries it this time I am going to cock myself and kiss it. You watch that ball go."

Gowdy made good and drove the ball into the grandstand. After we got those two runs and tied the score we knew the Athletics were beaten, and they knew it themselves. In fact, they acted like a beaten club when they first went to work today, for their heads and hearts seemed to be down. They were inclined to be friendly and chatty, and this is always a sign of nervousness and loss of heart. But they did not receive any encouragement from us along these lines, because we were out there to play ball and not to chat. Therefore we adopted the same tactics as we have in the preceding games, and went after them as hard as we could in batting, fielding, and talking. We figured that we had them beaten from the start when we saw how they felt about it. We should have won the game long before we did.

I don't consider the Athletics have a chance now, and I look to see them beaten tomorrow. This club of ours is in the mood now where it can't be stopped. The players are full of success, and every batter that goes up there to the plate feels that he can hit any pitcher in the world, and he can. We don't care whom they start against us. To show the versatility of the hitting—Gowdy smashed a fast ball into the centre-field stand for a home run and a slow ball into the left-field seats for two bases on his next time up. He is supposed to be a fast-ball hitter, or so the Athletics think; and Bush was trying to get him off his balance with a slow one.

Not Bothered by Speed.

I guess that we have shown the Athletics in this series that we can hit speed. Both Bender and Bush tried to beat us with fast balls, and Bender had to quit, while we beat Bush's fast ball after the dusk had set in, when it should have improved in its effectiveness.

Before I go any further I want to call attention to the prediction made by "Hank" O'Day, once—or, in fact, twice—an umpire and now manager of the Chicago Cubs, just before the present series opened.

"The Boston Club," said 'Hank,' "won't win a game, and I don't care if you quote me."

Hank does not predict any better than he does some other things which he has tried.

I also want to say something about the Royal Rooters who have followed this club through the series and who have done so much to keep us on our toes with their real, sincere rootings. It helps a team when it is in there fighting to have a bunch yelling their throats out and pulling their heart strings loose for it to win. The Royal Rooters took up a collection on the train on the way from Philadelphia to Boston on Saturday to buy Stallings a scarfpin which carried a diamond about as big as the little finger nail. This sort of encouragement that this crowd, headed by former Mayor Fitzgerald, pulls would help any team. I guess the Giants and McGraw might have done better if they had received a little of that same sort of support from the New York fans when they were fighting for world's championships.

Both the Boston pitchers showed wonderful ball. James went into the box in the eleventh inning almost cold because things were happening so fast about that time that he had little chance to warm up. He did not go out to the "pen" until Whitted took his place at the plate, and instead of taking one or two and stalling, Whitted hit at the first ball and popped up a fly to Baker.

You can't blame a man for overlooking some things in an inning of stress like that. I know I was blind mad when I went to the plate, determined to do something to make up for my "bone." Whenever I make a mistake it always gets my temper and causes me to fight back harder. We all stalled as long as we could, while changing from the bat to the field, but James was pretty cold when he went to the box. He pitched superbly, and was never in danger. Don't think that Tyler did not pitch a very heady game, too, and it was only the necessity of putting a pinch hitter into the game that caused Stallings to remove him. Tyler got caught only once when the Athletics sprang the hit-and-run in the tenth inning when we were not looking for it—one of the few plays pulled by that club in the series that we have not been set for. Schang was away from first base with the pitch, and Tyler's toss of Murphy's roller to second arrived too late for the force out.

Tomorrow we will have Dick Rudolph in the box, and he knows the Athletic hitters down to hair lines when it comes to their likes and dislikes at the plate, as he showed in his first game, which was really the toughest of the series to pitch, because the first one always puts every one under the big strain. Rudolph should be as good or better tomorrow than he was last Friday.

The way these games have broken has been a great thing for our pitchers. We have had a good man in reserve all the time. If we should lose tomorrow, James will be fresh for Wednesday, since the two innings he worked today won't amount to more than a workout, but I don't think we are going to need James, because I believe tomorrow will settle it.

"Hank" Gowdy will be in there with his fighting spirit and talk and pep, and so will "Rabbit" Maranville and the rest, and "Hank" will probably hit a few, too, which are liable to end it.

The Official Score

AB, at bat; R, runs; H, hits; TB, total bases; SH, sacrifice hits; SB, stolen bases; SO, struck out; BB, bases on balls; PO, put out; A, assists; E, errors.

BOSTON.

	AB	R	H	2B	3B	HR	TB	SH	SB	SO	BB	PO	A	E
Moran, rf	4	1	0	0	0	0	0	0	0	0	1	2	0	0
Evers, 2b	5	0	3	0	0	0	3	0	1	0	0	3	5	0
Connolly, lf	4	0	0	0	0	0	0	1	0	0	0	1	0	1
Whitted, cf	5	0	0	0	0	0	0	0	0	1	0	2	0	0
Schmidt, 1b	5	1	1	0	0	0	1	0	0	1	0	17	1	0
Deal, 3b	5	0	1	1	0	0	2	0	0	0	0	2	3	0
Maranville, ss	4	1	1	0	0	0	1	0	2	0	1	2	3	0
Gowdy, c	4	1	3	2	0	1	8	0	0	0	0	6	0	0
Tyler, p	3	0	0	0	0	0	0	0	0	1	0	1	5	0
James, p	0	0	0	0	0	0	0	0	0	0	0	0	2	0
*Devore	1	0	0	0	0	0	0	0	0	1	0	0	0	0
†Gilbert	0	0	0	0	0	0	0	0	0	0	1	0	0	0
‡Mann	0	1	0	0	0	0	0	0	0	0	0	0	0	0
Totals	40	5	9	3	0	1	15	1	3	4	3	36	19	1

*Batted for Tyler in tenth inning.
†Batted for James in twelfth inning.
‡Ran for Gowdy in twelfth inning.

ATHLETICS.

	AB	R	H	2B	3B	HR	TB	SH	SB	SO	BB	PO	A	E
Murphy, rf	5	2	2	2	0	0	4	0	1	0	1	2	0	0
Oldring lf	5	0	0	0	0	0	0	1	0	1	0	1	0	0
Collins, 2b	4	0	1	0	0	0	1	1	1	0	1	1	4	0
Baker, 3b	5	0	2	1	0	0	3	0	0	2	1	4	4	0
McInnis, 1b	5	1	1	1	0	0	2	0	0	0	1	18	0	0
Walsh, cf	4	0	1	0	0	0	1	0	0	0	1	1	0	0
Barry, ss	5	0	0	0	0	0	0	0	0	0	0	0	7	0
Schang, c	4	1	1	0	0	0	1	0	0	0	1	6	1	1
Bush, p	5	0	0	0	0	0	0	0	0	2	0	0	5	1
Totals	42	4	8	4	0	0	12	2	2	5	6	33	21	2

BOSTON													
Runs	0	1	0	1	0	0	0	0	0	2	0	1	—5
Hits	1	1	0	2	1	1	0	0	0	2	0	1	—9
ATHLETICS.													
Runs	1	0	0	1	0	0	0	0	0	2	0	0	—4
Hits	1	0	0	2	1	1	0	0	1	2	0	0	—8

Hits—Off Tyler, 8 in 10 innings; off James, none in two innings. Struck out—By Tyler, 4; by James, 1; by Bush, 4. First base on errors—Philadelphia, 1. Double play—Maranville, Evers and Schmidt. Left on bases—Boston, 6; Philadelphia, 10. Umpires—Mr. Klem behind the plate; Mr. Dineen on the bases; Mr. Hildebrand in right field; Mr. Byron in left field. Time of game—Three hours and six minutes.

THRONG AT TIMES SQUARE.

The fickleness of baseball crowds was illustrated in Times Square yesterday when another record-breaking throng of fans watched the reproduction of the third game for the world's championship between the Boston Braves and the Philadelphia Athletics on THE TIMES's scoreboard. For nine innings, during which time the rival teams engaged in a struggle that was filled with thrills, the spectators showed a decided partiality for the National League champions, but when the Philadelphians went into the lead in the tenth inning with two runs the majority of the vast crowd forgot their loyalty to the Braves and cheered the Athletics. In the second half of the tenth the Boston players, led by Gowdy, again tied the score, and the sentiment underwent another rapid change, and Boston was returned to its former position of favorite. This feeling was in evidence until the end of the game.

Admirable police arrangements relieved the congestion, which was so marked on the first day of the series, and, despite the fact that the holiday augmented the crowd, there was no unpleasant incident to mar the event. Although the first two games indicated an almost certain victory for Boston, and a crowd of about 14,000 witnessed the contest between the Giants and Yankees at the Polo Grounds, more persons watched the progress of the game at Fenway Park reproduced on THE TIMES's scoreboard than at any time during the series. It was a remarkable tribute to the national game.

For three hours nearly 20,000 excited fans waited with fevered expectancy for the result. It mattered not to the spectator that two outside cities were battling for the championship, while the Giants were facing the Yankees in the city series, and it is doubtful whether more enthusiasm could have been aroused had McGraw's men been the contenders instead of the Braves. It was baseball they wanted, and the brand they got was of a sufficiently inspiring quality to bring out all the latent enthusiasm.

"All the News That's Fit to Print."

The New York Times.

THE WEATHER
Partly cloudy, somewhat warmer today; fair tomorrow; moderate south winds.
For full weather report see Page 18.

VOL. LXIV...NO. 20,891. . . . NEW YORK, TUESDAY, APRIL 6, 1915.—TWENTY PAGES. ONE CENT In Greater New York, Jersey City and Newark. | Elsewhere TWO CENTS.

WILLARD VICTOR; JOHNSON RETIRES FROM PRIZE RING

Black Fistic Champion Knocked Out in 26th Round by Giant Young Kansan.

NEGRO'S FIGHT FOR A TIME

Wore Himself Out Battering a Younger, Stronger Adversary, Who Thrived on Punishment.

WILL RETURN TO FRANCE

Plans to Turn Farmer and Never Enter Ring Again—Willard to Tour United States.

Special Cable to THE NEW YORK TIMES.

HAVANA, April 5.—"It was a clean knockout and the best man won. It was not a matter of luck. I have no kick coming."

Such were the words of ex-champion Jack Johnson when he had recovered from Jess Willard's terrific left jab to the heart and right swing to the jaw in the twenty-sixth round of the championship fight that restored puglistic supremacy to the white race and made Willard champion this afternoon at Oriental Park.

To those who watched the battle and longed for the white man to win the day looked dark in the earlier stages because the negro outgeneraled the younger man and appeared to hit him as he willed. As Johnson's terrific blows rained on Willard he appeared to be suffering, but as the fight continued and Willard found that the champion's blows were not able to put him out he appeared to gain confidence, which he had seemed to lack when the battle started, and, under the coaching of Tom Jones, he began to look more cheerful.

Johnson's old-time ring smile continued throughout these early rounds, but as time sped and he found that, although he landed his blows, they never appeared to have much effect, the smile disappeared, and from the tenth to the twentieth round Johnson exercised every art in his power to put out the challenger. After that twentieth round there was little doubt among those at the ringside as to how the fight was going. It was too plain that once more youth was showing. Johnson was tiring so fast that he tried to hold Willard in clinches, but his strength, which was able to do that earlier, was unable then, and Willard always got the best of the infighting, continually landing terrific blows to the body.

Sent Word to Wife to Leave.

Johnson realized in the twenty-second round that his hold on the championship was growing short and asked for Jack Curley. The latter was at the gate at the time, but appeared shortly before the last round.

"Tell my wife I'm tiring, and I wish you'd see her out," said Jack. Curley understood and carried out Johnson's wish.

It was only a little time after that when Willard landed his terrific body blow, followed by the blow to the jaw that spelled defeat to Johnson and turned bedlam loose among the thousands of spectators, who could hardly realize, so quickly did it happen, that Johnson was prostrate in the ring and that Jack Welsh was counting the fateful ten. The decisive blow landed about the middle of the round.

At the end Johnson made a movement as if to grab Willard, but the latter stepped back and Johnson fell full length upon the floor and lay there until his seconds had assisted him to his feet.

At first after his defeat Johnson appeared dazed, but he quickly recovered, and his smile reappeared as he explained that the best man had won.

Willard played a game in the ring that was declared necessary to beat Johnson, namely, to make the latter act as aggressor. Both realized the necessity of caution. Johnson showed skill and cunning in blocking his more husky opponent.

Youth Must Be Served.

As the fight wore on and Willard had received all the blows in Johnson's collection and had found their capacity to do damage grow less, he became more and more aggressive, while despair began to dawn on the countenance of the champion. Willard's blows were not so numerous and Johnson clearly outpointed him, except toward the last, but these early blows that the Kansas giant did land would have spelled a knockout for almost any one but Johnson.

When the fight ended there was no doubt as to which was the better man. Willard had fought his own fight and overcome the older master by the sheer force of youth; the thirties had to retire in favor of the twenties.

Willard appears to be a most unassuming champion. There was no boastfulness on his part afther the fight. The same quiet modesty was in evidence which he displayed for days before the fight while training in Havana, and which won for him many friends and caused the Cubans to look upon prizefighters in an entirely different light from that to which they had been accustomed.

The scene of the fight was a picture. Squadrons of Cuban cavalry sat their horses in perfect alignment near the ringside, while the great grandstand was filled with a crowd representative of the Cuban Republic, including Cabinet members, army officers, Governors of provinces, and Ministers of various nations. Many women, mostly American tourists, but with quite a sprinkling of Cubans, added color to the scene, while many other women, members of Cuba's aristocracy, from the seclusion of the racetrack clubhouse trained their glasses on the battling gladiators.

Women as Enthusiastic as Men.

The tremendous enthusiasm which the Cubans displayed over the match is thought generally here to augur well for the sport, and, as one prominent Cuban official said, causes Cuban boys

Continued on Page 8.

CONSUL'S YOUNG WIFE SEEKS DEATH IN POISON

Says Husband Deserted Her on Family's Plea, to Explain Mercury Draught.

Mrs. Joseph Gonzalez, a young woman who says she is the second wife of Z. Manuel Gonzales, Consul General for Costa Rica, was made prisoner yesterday afternoon in her apartment at 320 Manhattan Avenue, near 113th Street, on a charge of attempted suicide.

The young woman's mother called in neighbors, who got Dr. Emanuel Reinhardt of 112 Cathedral Parkway and the police yesterday afternoon after her daughter had run to her crying: "I have taken bichloride of mercury."

Dr. Reinhardt gave immediate treatment, but said he could not tell at once whether she had taken poison or not. The police found no mercury in the house, though they found several empty bottles in a medicine closet which might have contained the poison.

The young woman persisted in the declaration that she had taken poison, and said she had done it because her husband had left her. She said they had been married last Aug. 8 after a courtship of three and a half years, and that none of his family had called on her until December, when one of Gonzalez's three daughters made a visit.

Mrs. Gonzalez said she realized that none of her husband's family liked her, but she and he were happy until about five weeks ago, when he became irritable, due to the constant efforts of his family to estrange him from her. Four weeks ago, she said, they quarreled, and he left her to live with his sister, Mrs. Lewis Chable of Ridgewood Heights, N. J.

Since then, she said, she had called often at his office, 2 Rector Street, to beg him to return, but he would not be reconciled, and a few days ago sent her word that she must leave the flat. Then she decided to kill herself.

Over the telephone Mr. Gonzalez said last night he had heard of his wife's attempt on her life, but preferred to say nothing.

SHIP HITS HELL GATE ROCK.

The Frank Somers, Adrift with Hole in Side, Saved by Tugs.

The steam fishing boat reported by the police to be the Frank Somers of the Atlantic Fishing Company, en route to Newport from Tuckerton, N. J., struck a rock while avoiding a tug and tow off the Sunken Meadows, near Hell Gate late last night, staving a large hole in her side. With water pouring into the hold, Captain T. C. Sawyer put her about and headed south under full steam, blowing the whistle frantically for help. The working of her pumps could be heard on either side of the East River.

The fireboat Abram S. Hewitt, in answer to the Somers' whistles, came racing over from Greenpoint. With the aid of two tug boats the Frank Somers was steered south, in search of a suitable place to tie up. Off Twenty-eighth Street a number of boats are anchored in the East River, and more than one dangerous collision was narrowly averted. At Tenth Street the smaller boats led the steamer to the Manhattan side of the river, where she tied up.

HELD, CRUSHED, FOR AN HOUR

Firemen Called to Cut Wall to Free Victim Caught by Elevator.

William Dennan of 538 Fifty-sixth Street, Brooklyn, slipped and fell yesterday between the wall of the elevator well and the edge of the freight elevator car in Dannemiller's coffee roasting works at 116 Thirty-ninth Street, Brooklyn. His cries roused the place, but no one could stop the elevator until its pressure upon Dennan's body stopped it between the third and second floors.

Then no one dared slide down the rope to it lest he set it in motion again, and Dennan, held fast and still conscious, could not be reached. Dr. Salzberg of the Holy Family Hospital was lowered down on a rope and administered opiates to Dennan, but he could not free him, and word was sent to Fire Truck 114, in Fifth Avenue, near Fifty-second Street.

Capt. Dennis J. Cahill and his men responded, and finally decided they would have to cut away the wall. This they did, and after an hour freed the injured man. Dr. Salzberg hurried him to the hospital, but he was crushed so badly that it was said he probably would die.

DRYS GAIN IN MICHIGAN.

Eight Counties Switch and 265 Saloons Will Close.

DETROIT, Mich., April 5.—Returns received up to midnight indicated sweeping victories for the "drys" in the local option contests, which were noteworthy features of the Michigan State election today. Incomplete returns also showed large majorities for the Republican State ticket. All of the four "dry" counties—Eaton, Lenawee, Genesee, and Sanilac—which voted on the saloon question, remained in the "dry" column with comfortable majorities.

At least eight of the "wet" counties, where local option was at stake, apparently went over to the "drys." They are Berrien, Calhoun, Emmett, Kalamazoo, Lapeer, Mason, Oakland, and Tuscola. Grand Traverse remained "wet," and Chippewa and Iron Counties are thought to have retained their saloons, although the result is close.

The apparent victory of the "drys" meant the closing of at least 265 saloons throughout the State.

H. P. WHITNEY BUYS LAND.

May Build Country Home on Tract of 165 Acres at Greenville, L. I.

MINEOLA, L. I., April 5.—Harry Payne Whitney, banker and sportsman of 871 Fifth Avenue, New York City, has purchased for $132,500 165 acres of land at Greenville, L. I., from the Valley Land Company of 49 Wall Street. A deed conveying the property was filed in the County Clerk's office today.

The property is on the corner of the North Hempstead Turnpike and the Valley Road and lies near the Piping Rock field and clubhouse. The deed conveys the right to the purchaser to place wires and pipes for gas and water on the property. It is rumored that Mr. Whitney will build a country home on the property.

HIGHWAYS BILLS SIGNED.

Mayor Mitchel Files Too Late a Request for a Hearing.

Special to The New York Times.

ALBANY, April 5.—Gov. Whitman this afternoon signed bills appropriating $4,100,000 for repair and maintenance of highways for the next fiscal year. The bills were opposed by Democrats in both houses on the ground that the amount they carried was too large.

Mayor Mitchel filed a request for a hearing on the bills with Senator Henry M. Sage, Chairman of the Senate Finance Committee, but not until after they had been sent to the Governor.

FINDS PLOT TO AID ALLIES' WARSHIPS

Collector Malone Says He Has Evidence That Supplies Are Sent to British Secretly.

WANTS GRAND JURY ACTION

More Vessels Asked For at Washington to Protect the Harbor's Neutrality.

NIGHT SCOUTING IN HARBOR

Destroyer's Trip and Man with a Telescope in Highland Light Figure in Investigation.

Dudley Field Malone, Collector of the Port, announced last night that he had found evidence of a widespread conspiracy to violate the neutrality proclamation of President Wilson through the establishment here of an agency to supply the British warships lying outside the three-mile zone with food and fuel. He said his evidence would be presented to the Federal Grand Jury within a day or two.

The facts on which he is prepared to base such an allegation were collected by Mr. Malone in a series of spectacular midnight tours of the waters surrounding New York, which he made aboard the torpedo boat destroyer Parker, one of the fastest ships of this type in the service.

With a powerful searchlight to guide him, Mr. Malone has scoured the docks along the Hoboken and New York waterfronts, and has dashed out to sea in search of carriers which he has suspected of violating the laws.

Grand Jury to Act.

The Collector made his last tour this morning on board the MacDougal, following a long conference with United States District Attorney Marshall. He said, just before starting, that he expected to ask the Grand Jury to act without further delay.

Coincident with these developments it became known that Mr. Malone had called upon the Government for additional ships and was planning effectually to seal the Port of New York to the British vessels. He now has under his direction for that purpose the torpedo boat destroyers MacDougal and Parker, each capable of a speed of 33 knots; the destroyer Drayton, which is of an older type; the Dolphin, Secretary Daniels's ship, which carries four six-inch guns, and a naval tug. Two more torpedo boat destroyers are expected to arrive here within a few days for scout duty in connection with Mr. Malone's plans.

All of these ships are equipped with wireless, and Mr. Malone explained that he was in touch by telephone also with the naval stations at Tompkinsville, Kill van Kull, and Whitestone.

Scouting Trips by Night.

Co-operating with Mr. Malone in the work of breaking up the alleged conspiracy are the members of the Neutrality Squad, headed by George F. Lamb and a score or more of Secret Service agents who were sent her from Washington at the Collector's request. They have been working day and night for more than a month, scouring the waterfront and accompanying Mr. Malone on his mysterious and exciting scouting trips about the harbor and in the open sea.

In this way they have covered every wharf and pier in the port of New York from Newark Bay to Whitestone, the territory under the jurisdiction of the Collector, and have sought to detect sea-going tugs and other vessels upon which suspicion rested.

A Secret Service agent has been stationed at the Highland Light at Navesink, N. J., every morning, and it has been his duty to scan the horizon with a powerful telescope for vessels carrying supplies to the British warships. Whether any vessels actually had been caught in the act of violating the neutrality proclamation by transshipping supplies Mr. Malone would not say, inferring that such information would come out only when the case was placed before the Federal Grand Jury.

Headquarters in a Hotel.

The investigations of Mr. Malone's agents on land and sea have disclosed, he asserts, that part of a downtown hotel, said to be well below Forty-second Street, was engaged as a headquarters by the alleged conspirators, and that there the plans were formulated and orders issued.

An organization of great power and influence was formed, Mr. Malone says, and negotiations were opened by its agents with dozens of Captains and owners of vessels who live in this city, Philadelphia, and the New England States. The services of many Captains were engaged, it is said, and a fleet of big tugboats was put into service to move supplies from various points to the British warships. Experienced crews were engaged quietly to operate the tugs, and were impressed with the necessity of silence.

According to Mr. Malone, evidence has been presented to him that the principal operatives of a private detective agency, which is known all over the country, have been working with the agents of the organization. So much information has been obtained that Mr. Malone has been able to outline his case and his tour this morning was made to obtain a few details which, he believes, will insure action by the Grand Jury.

Story of Malone Trips.

While Mr. Malone would not discuss the case in detail he admitted making the trips in the torpedo boats and did not attempt to deny that he had obtained evidence which had astounded him.

Mr. Malone has boarded the Parker

Continued on Page 2.

JAIL YAWNS FOR 102 ACCUSED BY PRIEST

Metuchen Authorities Put to It to House Men Father Csmadia Says Libeled Him.

NOT CELLS ENOUGH FOR ALL

Wholesale Arrests Follow Charge That Pastor Drank Too Much at a Pig Roast.

Special to The New York Times.

METUCHEN, N. J., April 5.—Unless there is a big supply of ready cash on hand tomorrow, Metuchen will have to build a lean-to to the town jail to accommodate the 102 members of the Hungarian Roman Catholic Church of South River, who are charged with having libeled criminally their pastor, the Rev. Father Paul Csmadia. Fifteen of the parishioners were arrested today. The others will be apprehended tomorrow.

Furthermore, the order has gone forth to lock them up if they can't furnish bail. Among the accused are some of the most prominent citizens of Metuchen. The town jail hasn't nearly enough room for so many prisoners. Justice of the Peace William B. Black signed so many warrants today that his hand became cramped and Chief of Police Eberwin said it would be an all-day job to serve the warrants on the South River congregation.

The trouble started over a pig roast some weeks ago. Some of the congregation charge that Father Csmadia became "intoxicated and hilarious," and proceeded to sing songs and strike persons in the street. They drew up a petition to this effect and sent it to Bishop John F. McFaul at Trenton. Whereupon Bishop McFaul sent it to Father Csmadia.

The priest asserted that the charges were untrue. On the question of pig roasts, rum, duck suppers, and the like he has ideas akin to those of the Rev. Billy Sunday, and he even preached a sermon, he said, denouncing such things. Then he took the petition to court. The warrants followed.

"The petition which the congregation signed is so libelous," said Justice Black today, "that Father Csmadia is justified in taking drastic action. Prosecutor William E. Florance is co-operating with me. Those who cannot furnish bail will be locked up."

And that isn't all. Father Csmadia went before the Middlesex Grand Jury today as complaining witness against his sexton and organist and another member of the congregation. He complained that they had broken up a service in the church on Feb. 28 by removing an emblem from the church and putting it in a saloon at Drury Hill.

The troubles of the South River folk have torn Metuchen in two. Father Csmadia gave a parade and picnic tonight, and his followers turned out in force. Their rivals also got up a celebration. The police were ready to do their part if called on.

LIFTS IN NERO'S PALACE.

Income Tax, Hobble Skirts, Shorthand, and Trusts Known to Ancients

Special to The New York Times.

PHILADELPHIA, April 5.—The palace of Nero had three elevators.

In the year 6 A. D. an income tax was established in Rome on all incomes in excess of $4,000.

The hobble skirt was one of dame fashion's decrees in the days of Moses.

These and many other interesting facts going to show that life among the ancients was not so different from that of today were brought out by Prof. Camden M. Cobern, explorer and archaeologist, who has just returned from a trip to Palestine. He began a series of lectures upon his archaeological discoveries today in the Arch Street Methodist Episcopal Church.

Professor Cobern pointed out that the Jews had three different systems of shorthand reporting in the first century and that in every Jewish court a shorthand reporter or clerk sat on each side of the Judge. Many of the Roman aristocrats took "stenographers" with them on their travels.

Other advantages enjoyed by the ancients, according to Professor Cobern, follow:

In St. Paul's time there were seventy labor unions in Rome; hence a struggle between capital and labor must have been waged even then.

There were several great monopolies in the first century, the greatest of all being the oil business. The "trust" dealt in olive oil and the like.

There also were monopolies in eggs, perfumes, and bricks.

As to homes, Professor Cobern says he has read in manuscripts dug from ancient tombs and houses of a Roman who spent the equivalent of $12,000,000 upon decorations for his house. Another plutocrat spent $90,000,000 in one year. Nero on one occasion spent $175,000 for roses on his banquet tables. The roses were brought from Egypt.

BOY PINNED UNDER AN AUTO.

Crowd Lifts Wheel from Head of Lad Hurt Mortally.

James Fitzsimmons, 11 years old, of 405 West Forty-ninth Street, and Robert Fitzpatrick, the same age, of 407 West Forty-ninth Street, who were playing tag at 8:35 o'clock last night in the street at Eighth Avenue and Forty-second Street, were knocked down by an auto driven by Henry L. Bergh, a chauffeur of 312 West Forty-ninth Street.

Bergh stopped his auto suddenly, and when he got out he found that one of the rear wheels was resting partly on the head and shoulders of Fitzpatrick. He and several men who ran to his aid lifted the auto and released the lad, who was unconscious. The boys were taken in the auto to the Polyclinic Hospital, where it was found that Fitzpatrick was suffering from a fractured skull. He will probably die. Fitzsimmons was not injured seriously.

Bergh said that he had been one day in the employ of Charles M. Aguirre of 235 West 113th Street, ex-Chief of Police of Havana, who is now living in this city.

EXPEL PINCHOT FROM BELGIUM

Germans Force ex-Forester, Going as a Relief Agent, to Leave the Country.

BANNED FOR HIS SISTER?

She Is Wife of British Diplomat—Washington to Aid, but Denies Pinchot Has Official Status.

Special Cable to THE NEW YORK TIMES.

THE HAGUE, April 5, (Dispatch to The London Daily Mail.)—I learn from Antwerp that Gifford Pinchot, who recently came to Europe to superintend the work of providing relief for the stricken people of Northern France, has been expelled from Belgium by order of the German military authorities.

Mr. Pinchot came to Holland several days ago, bearing the title of special attaché, and was formally accredited to Holland and Luxemburg. His particular mission was to visit that part of France now under German occupation and pave the way for relief measures similar to those already undertaken in Belgium.

According to reports, he was stopped at Antwerp by the German authorities and both he and his wife, who accompanied him, were subjected to a rigid examination. He was finally ordered to return to Holland. No reason for the action of the German authorities has thus far been ascertainable. Mr. Pinchot has arrived at The Hague and is staying at the United States Legation as the guest of the Minister, Dr. van Dyke.

Special to The New York Times.

WASHINGTON, D. C., April 5.—The report from The Hague that Gifford Pinchot, ex-Chief Forester of the United States, who was seeking to enter northern France to serve the International Belgium Relief Commission in the distribution of supplies, had been expelled from Belgium by the German authorities, was partly confirmed by a high Government official tonight. But the statement was made that "expelled" was probably too strong a word to use in Mr. Pinchot's case and the belief was expressed that the matter would be adjusted.

It was made plain, however, that Mr. Pinchot did not go upon his mission as an agent of the United States Government, as stated in a press dispatch from The Hague. On the contrary, the United States Government, while recognizing and doing all it can to assist the International Relief Commission in its work, has no official connection with the movement, and Mr. Pinchot is an agent of that commission, not of the Government. He wanted to take charge of the distribution of relief supplies to Belgians who had crossed the border into northern France. The territory in which Mr. Pinchot wishes to go is controlled by German military authorities.

A dispatch received by the State Department from Dr. van Dyke, Minister to The Hague, informed officials here that there was some hitch over Mr. Pinchot's credentials.

The dispatch further indicated, however, that one objection to Mr. Pinchot was that his sister was the wife of Sir Alan Johnstone, formerly British Minister to Denmark, who is still in the British Diplomatic Service. The German Government has reserved the right to refuse to recognize any neutral agents who are even remotely connected with persons in the service of Germany's enemies.

It was pointed out that if the German officials objected to Mr. Pinchot personally it might be difficult to persuade them to allow him to proceed. He would be in the position of a suggested appointee as Ambassador, who might be regarded as persona non grata. But if the hitch over his credentials involves only proper identification it may be possible to straighten the difficulty. The matter has been taken up with the German Government by the State Department in behalf of the International Relief Committee.

A dispatch from The Hague, dated March 29, told of Gifford Pinchot's being presented to the Dutch Foreign Minister that day on the eve of his departure for Brussels. The dispatch went on:

"Mr. Pinchot reported today at the American Legation as a special attaché for Holland and Luxemburg, and spent several hours in obtaining the necessary papers and permits from the various legations. The German permit, after referring to Mr. Pinchot's diplomatic mission, asks that every facility be given him in the performance of his task of distributing relief among the French people in the portions of France now occupied by the German Army."

CAN SAVE 50,000 LIVES

But Dr. Biggs Says State Death Rate Must Equal City's to Do It.

Dr. Herman M. Biggs, State Commissioner of Health, predicted last night that 50,000 lives would be saved in New York State in the next five years if the up-State death rate was brought down to the rate in this city. This, he explained, would be twice the number that the State Health Department had set as its goal in its campaign against disease and unhealthful conditions.

In a telegram to Gov. Whitman from the office of the State Health Department in this city last night, Dr. Biggs said that for the eight months ending on March 1, the general death rate was 13.5, the lowest for any consecutive eight months in the State's history. Each month had shown a decrease, he said, and a total of 8,000 lives had been saved outside New York City in the last eight months.

Figures received here from the Division of Vital Statistics at Albany convinced Dr. Biggs that the campaign could easily double the record it had set out to make, judging from the results thus far obtained.

RELIEF GRAIN HELD UP.

Report of Trouble Between American Committee and Germans.

Special Cable to THE NEW YORK TIMES.

AMSTERDAM, April 5 (Dispatch to the London Morning Post).—The steamer Strathtay has arrived at Rotterdam with 13,000 sacks of grain for the American Relief Committee in Belgium.

Yesterday morning when three elevators began to unload it orders were given for the work to stop. It is said difficulties have arisen between the committee and the German Government.

DRIVE AUSTRIANS BACK IN HUNGARY

Russians Pushing On to Heads of Two Railroads Leading Southward.

STORM CISNA, IN GALICIA

Austrian Mountain Base Taken, with Great Stock of War Munitions and Provisions.

AUSTRIAN LOSSES GREAT

German Official Report Shows Czar's Forces Have Made Substantial Advance in Poland.

LONDON, Tuesday, April 6.—The attention of the public for the time being is directed toward the great struggle for the Carpathians passes, where the Russians apparently are making very steady progress despite the obstinate resistant offered by the Austrian and German troops.

The Russians are on the Hungarian side of both the Dukla and Lupkow Passes, and, with the aid of continual reinforcements, are gaining the heights which dominate Uzsok Pass. Even the Austrian official report admits that fighting is now taking place in the Laborcza Valley, which is south of Lupkow Pass, while the Russians announce the capture of Cisna, an important station on the Galician side of the high mountains between Lupkow and Uzsok Passes, where they captured a great stock of war munitions and provisions.

The Russians also are advancing from Dukla Pass on Bartfeld, which is at the head of the line of railway running south into Hungary, and fighting not far from Mezo Laborcz, another important railroad head. On Saturday and Sunday they captured in the Carpathians upward of 3,000 prisoners. They claim further success in Bukowina, and the capture of another thousand prisoners, but the Austrians assert that they repulsed a Russian force which attempted to cross the Dniester River.

The Russians are making progress in Northern Poland, a German official report telling of the repulse of a Russian attack on Mariampol, which is considerably west of the region which a few days ago was in the possession of the Germans.

Official Report of Operations.

PETROGRAD, April 5.—The following official report of the operations in the Carpathians was issued this evening:

"In the Carpathians during the night of April 3-4 and during the whole of the following day in the region to the north of Bartfeld there was fierce fighting with artillery and the bayonet. We took took 20 officers and more than 1,200 soldiers prisoners and captured 2 machine guns. At the same time we continued to make progress on the front between Mezo Laborez and Uzsok. In the course of the day we captured about twenty-five officers and more than 2,000 soldiers and took three guns.

"Having occupied the railway station at Cisna, we captured engines and coaches as well as a great stock of ammunition and a part of a provision train.

"There was desperate fighting Wednesday and Thursday near the village of Okna, to the north of Czernowitz (Bukowina,) as a result of which we took more than a thousand prisoners whom the Austrians had left behind."

Lost More Than 15,500 in a Day.

GENEVA, April 5, (via Paris, April 6.)—Dispatches received here tonight from Budapest state that a serious battle started in the Carpathians on Saturday evening, extending from Dukla to Eperies, Hungary.

The dispatches state that the fighting was the severest around Saros and that the Austrian and German armies were repulsed. The new young Bavarian troops suffered heavily, it is said, and the Austrian losses on Sunday alone were over 15,500.

The battle continues and reinforcements are being hurried up to assist the Austro-German forces.

CAPTURE 2,020 RUSSIANS.

Austrians Report Attacks in the Carpathians Repulsed.

WASHINGTON, April 5.—A dispatch from the Vienna Foreign Office to the Austro-Hungarian Embassy here tonight said:

"In the Carpathians engagements continue on the heights on both sides of the Laborcz Valley. The enemy, who until now has made violent attacks, was repulsed from several positions by a counter-attack yesterday, directed against the eastern neighboring heights. Also at Virava, a strong Russian attack was repulsed and 2,020 Russian prisoners taken yesterday.

"North of the Uzsok Pass the situation is unchanged. A renewed Russian attack failed after a short struggle.

"On the other fronts there is nothing of importance to report."

A later dispatch to the Austro-Hungarian Embassy said:

"On the front in the Beskibenkiden section of the Carpathians it is generally quiet, since all Russian attacks of the past few days have been repulsed. In the neighboring east sections of the Carpathians strong Russian attacks continue.

"On the front between the Pruth and Dniester Rivers we repulsed a superior Russian attack. The enemy advanced in ten to fifteen 'echelons' at several places, and engagements continued until night, with heavy losses to the enemy, who were everywhere repulsed and retreated in flight in the southern section.

"In Poland and West Galicia the situation is unchanged. A Russian night attack on the Lower Nida failed under the efficient fire from our positions.

"From the war press headquarters

Continued on Page 4.

NO MOVE BY EITEL; MANY CONFERENCES

Crisis in the Affairs of the German Cruiser Believed to be Near.

Special to The New York Times.

NEWPORT NEWS, Va., April 5.—The fate of the Prinz Eitel Friedrich tonight is rapidly approaching a crisis. Though clearance was granted certain British ships this afternoon, including the merchantman Horseley, it was learned tonight that the cleared ships were still in port. It was suggested that this might mean that they had been requested not to leave so as to avoid all complications arising from the Prinz Eitel's possible departure in the near future.

A flurry of excitement was caused this morning, when two big Pennsylvania Railroad tugs came up to the head of the pier at which the Prinz Eitel is moored, and after reporting to the navy tug on guard there, took up positions near the German cruiser. But it was said afterward that the presence of the tugs had nothing to do with the plans of the Eitel, as the tugs had reported to the navy tug Patuxent only to get permission to approach the piers near which the Prinz Eitel was lying.

Broken wire communications with Washington have delayed the final negotiations as to the ship's fate, but today activity in this direction was renewed. When Collector of Customs Hamilton, who is in charge of both the port of Norfolk and the port of Newport News, left his office this morning he called on Rear Admiral Beatty, in command of the Norfolk Navy Yard. Then in his launch he went to see Rear Admiral Helm on board the battleship Alabama. After dinner this evening he called on Commander Thierichens on the Prinz Eitel, and following that conference he put off in his launch in the direction of the Alabama. Earlier in the day Commander Thierichens visited Admiral Helm on the Alabama.

WAR NOW FOR DEFENSE, SAYS GERMAN WRITER

Dreams of Swift Victory Gone, Asserts Paul Michaelis—Must Preserve the Empire.

Special Cable to THE NEW YORK TIMES.

ROTTERDAM, April 5, (Dispatch to The London Daily News.)—Paul Michaelis in his weekly review of the war in the Berlin Tageblatt is in gloomy mood regarding the present position of the German armies, and he speaks of the spirit of modesty that now reigns in Germany. He says:

"We only see how tremendously difficult it is made for us to preserve our national unity and freedom. Many dreamed too easily of our victory over our enemies. People thought to gather in the harvest when really the first preparations for the final result still had to be created. In the meantime we have become more modest, and it becomes clear to us that, even with the greatest self-sacrifice, it will only be with difficulty that we shall be able to conquer the opposition of the world of enemies.

"Everybody has long since abandoned the expectation that between today and tomorrow the world could be healed by the German spirit. We have had to be convinced unwillingly and by hard facts that in this war it is not a question of putting through a fantastic world policy, but a question of protecting our house and home. So little as the war was begun to lay a new yoke upon the world, it certainly will have to be carried on for the self-preservation of the German Empire.

"It would be idle to try to fix the details of what the final peace will be, but in any case our object must be the making certain of our national existence for the longest possible time."

After referring to the course of the submarine war, the writer concludes:

"We are confident that this Winter of our discontent will be followed by a glorious Summer."

SUBMARINE U-31 SINKS TWO SMALL VESSELS

Takes Place of the U-28 and Destroys a Russian Bark and British Steamer Olivine.

LONDON, April 5.—The German submarine U-31 has replaced the U-28 off the west coast of England. Today reports were received of the sinking of the Russian bark Hermes and the steamer Olivine, both small vessels. They were destroyed by the U-31.

The crews of the two vessels took to their boats and were rescued by a British torpedo boat destroyer.

GERMAN FLEET CUT OFF BY OWN MINE FIELD

Returning Baltic Warships Find Coast So Perilous They Can't Reach Base.

Special Cable to THE NEW YORK TIMES.

COPENHAGEN, April 5, (Dispatch to The London Daily Mail.)—German naval activity, in the Baltic which began with the attack on Libau, came to a dramatic climax yesterday. The German fleet was returning from its Russian expedition when suddenly it found itself caught in its own minefield, had gone adrift.

The weather has been very bad during the last week and it is supposed that the mines must have got loose and floated into neutral waters. As a result of these drifting mines all maritime traffic has been stopped and it is reported that no fewer than six big German steamers have been sunk by them. I crossed to Sweden yesterday and during the journey several mines were seen floating in the sea, making the passage most dangerous.

The German squadron has, it seems, been prevented from returning to its naval base and in the meantime has taken refuge between the Islands of Gothland and Oeland until the passage has been cleared.

STOCKHOLM, April 5.—The Dagblad states that it learns from the Swedish naval authorities that Russian ships have laid a large number of mines along the Baltic coast of Germany from Ruegen Island to Barnhol Island. It is stated that the Swedish naval officials have stationed torpedo boats in the Baltic to warn shipping of the mines.

NOTE TO ALLIES CRITICISES TERMS OF BLOCKADE

United States Insists Upon Right to Trade with Germany Through Neutral Ports.

FIRM BUT FRIENDLY STAND

Wilson Holds That to Admit the Entire Proposed Embargo Would Be Unneutral.

CITES LAW AND PRECEDENTS

Expresses Hope That England Will Modify Order in Council with Regard to Seizures.

ADMITS NEW WAR PHASES

Use of Submarines and Aircraft Necessitate Change in Form of Blockade.

Special to The New York Times.

WASHINGTON, April 5.—Secretary Bryan today made public the text of the identic notes sent by this Government to the British and French Governments protesting against the invasion of neutral rights involved in the recent British Order in Council establishing a long-range blockade of European waters.

Generally speaking, the American note voices the confident expectation "that the Order in Council will not be carried out harshly with respect to neutral shipping," basing this expectation on the wide latitude given to prize courts and other bodies in applying the order. Great Britain is warned that "heavy responsibilities" will be imposed on her by a strict enforcement of the order, and that she should be prepared to make full reparation for every act in violation of neutral rights, but the note concludes with assurances that the American statement is made in the most friendly spirit. The apparent purpose of the note is to place this Government on record as objecting to the new rules of international law laid down by Great Britain.

The American note, which has been made public in London and Paris, insists on the right of innocent shipments "to be freely transported to and from the United States through neutral countries to belligerent territory without being subjected to the penalties of contraband traffic, or breach of blockade, much less detention, requisition, or confiscation."

While the United States indicates its readiness to admit that the old form of "close blockade, with its cordon of ships in the immediate offing of the blockaded ports, is no longer practicable in the face of an enemy possessing the means and opportunity to make effective defense by submarines, mines, and air craft," it is insisted that whatever form of effective blockade be established it must conform to the spirit and rules of international law.

Defends Non-contraband Trade.

The United States Government admits the right of the Allies, in strict accordance with the rules of international law, to blockade the German ports and coast, but insists that neutral ships carrying innocent shipments, and not contraband of war, must have the right to pass through the blockading cordon to neutral countries, even if the shipments are destined to pass through those countries into Germany. This is regarded by the United States as a clear right to which its citizens are entitled under international law, and the British Government is informed that "no claim on the part of Great Britain of any justification for interfering with these clear rights of the United States and its citizens as neutrals could be admitted."

For the United States to admit that England had any right to stop neutral shipments of non-contraband bound through neutral countries into Germany, the American note declares, would amount to the assumption by the United States of an "attitude of un-neutrality" toward the present enemies of Great Britain. For England to set up any such claim of right to disregard established rights under international law would be for the British Government to fling to the winds "the principles for which she has consistently and earnestly contended in other times and circumstances."

The text of the note fully bears out the exclusive forecast of its contents contained in a Washington dispatch printed in THE NEW YORK TIMES on March 19, four days after the British Order in Council was printed. That forecast reported the Government as taking the stand that "even if a blockade be proclaimed and effectively maintained along the whole German coast, (and it is admitted that the Allies have a perfect right to adopt such a course,) the United States does not admit the right of the Allies to stop non-contraband shipments carried in neutral ships to neutral ports when destined to the enemy."

This forecast is fully borne out by the basic statement of the note made public today, which says: "It is confidently assumed that his Majesty's Government will not deny that it is a rule sanctioned by general practice that, even though a blockade should exist and the doctrine of contraband as to unblockaded territory be rigidly enforced, innocent shipments may be freely transported to and from the United States through neutral countries to belligerent territory without being subject to the penalties of contraband traffic or breach of blockade, much less to detention, requisition, or confiscation."

Firm, but Cordial.

The tone of the American note is firm, but cordial. There is no threat of drastic action or, in fact, threat of any sort. What the American note says about the unusual features of the new British form of long-range blockade is important as indicating that care for the future has been exercised. The United

WILLARD VICTOR; JOHNSON RETIRES

Continued from Page 1.

and even men to yearn for skill in the manly art of defending themselves with their fists instead of with knives and pistols.

The enthusiasm of the women present grew as it became apparent that Willard probably would win. They groaned as Johnson appeared to outclass the white man, but as Willard's chances improved they grew wildly excited and vied with the men in striving to make their shouts of cheer reach the man who was battling for the pugilistic supremacy of their race.

Hardly any disorder occurred during the match, except when the great crowd charged into the ring as Johnson laid prostrate. The rural guards beat back the intruders with their machetes flat. One man was painfully, although not seriously, hurt.

Citizens of Havana will tender a reception to Willard tomorrow night, at which either the Governor of the province or the Mayor of Havana will present a gold watch as a souvenir to the victor. Willard had planned to leave Havana tomorrow, but yielded to requests to remain another day.

STORY OF THE BATTLE.

Crowd Jeered at Johnson When His Strength Began to Wane.

By The Associated Press.

HAVANA, April 5.—Jack Johnson, exile from his own country, today lost the heavyweight championship of the world to Jess Willard, the Kansas cowboy, the biggest man who ever entered the prize ring and a "White Hope" who at last has made good. The negro was knocked out in the twenty-sixth round with a smashing right swing to the point of the jaw.

The day after tomorrow Johnson, his wife, and a little group of friends will sail for Martinique, there to await passage back to France, where Johnson purposes to settle down and lead the life of a farmer, raising pigs and chickens. There is no doubt that he is through with the ring.

Willard is going back to the United States to win the fortune which was denied him today, when Johnson got $30,000 before the fight started, Willard taking only a small share of the net receipts. Just what his share was is not known.

For twenty rounds Johnson punched and pounded Willard at will, but his blows grew perceptibly less powerful as the fight progressed, until at last he seemed unable or unwilling to go on. Johnson stopped leading and for three or four rounds the battle was little more than a series of plastic poses of the white and the black gladiators.

So it was until the twenty-fifth round, when Willard got one of his wildly swinging windmill right-hand smashes to Johnson's heart. This was the beginning of the end.

When the round closed Johnson sent word to his wife that he was all in, and told her to start for home. She was on the way out and was passing the ring in the twenty-sixth round when a cyclonic right to the jaw caused Johnson to crumple on the floor of the ring, where he lay, partly outside the ropes, until after the referee had counted ten and held up Willard's hand in token of the cowboy's newly won laurels.

Johnson was slow in responding to the gong for what proved to be the final round, while Willard seemed fresh. Willard delivered four blows in this round—a left to the face, a right to the stomach, a left to the body, and the final right swing to the jaw that stretched the negro out for the count. Johnson seemed powerless to make any defense. He was shaky from the start of the round.

Actual Knockout Doubted.

There is much discussion tonight as to whether Johnson really was knocked out. In the sense of being smashed into unconsciousness, he certainly was not put out. The consensus of opinion is that Johnson felt that there was no possibility of his winning, and when knocked down chose to take the count rather than rise and stand further punishment. Johnson often has stated that fighting is a business, and that he would not foolishly submit to repeated knockdowns when he found he had met his master.

A second or two after Jack Welsh, the referee, had counted ten Johnson quickly got up. It was well that he did so, for a moment later a rush of spectators to the fighting platform all but smothered the pugilists. For an instant it seemed as if trouble was threatened, and some fifty or more of the several hundred soldiers stationed about the fight arena jumped into the ring and formed circles around vanquished and victor.

Under escort of the soldiers Willard and Johnson went to their dressing rooms, while the crowd cheered and broke into wild discussion. Willard was out of his dressing room in a few moments and in an automobile on his way back to Havana. He was escorted half way to the city from the Marianao race track, where the fight was held, by a troop of Cuban cavalry.

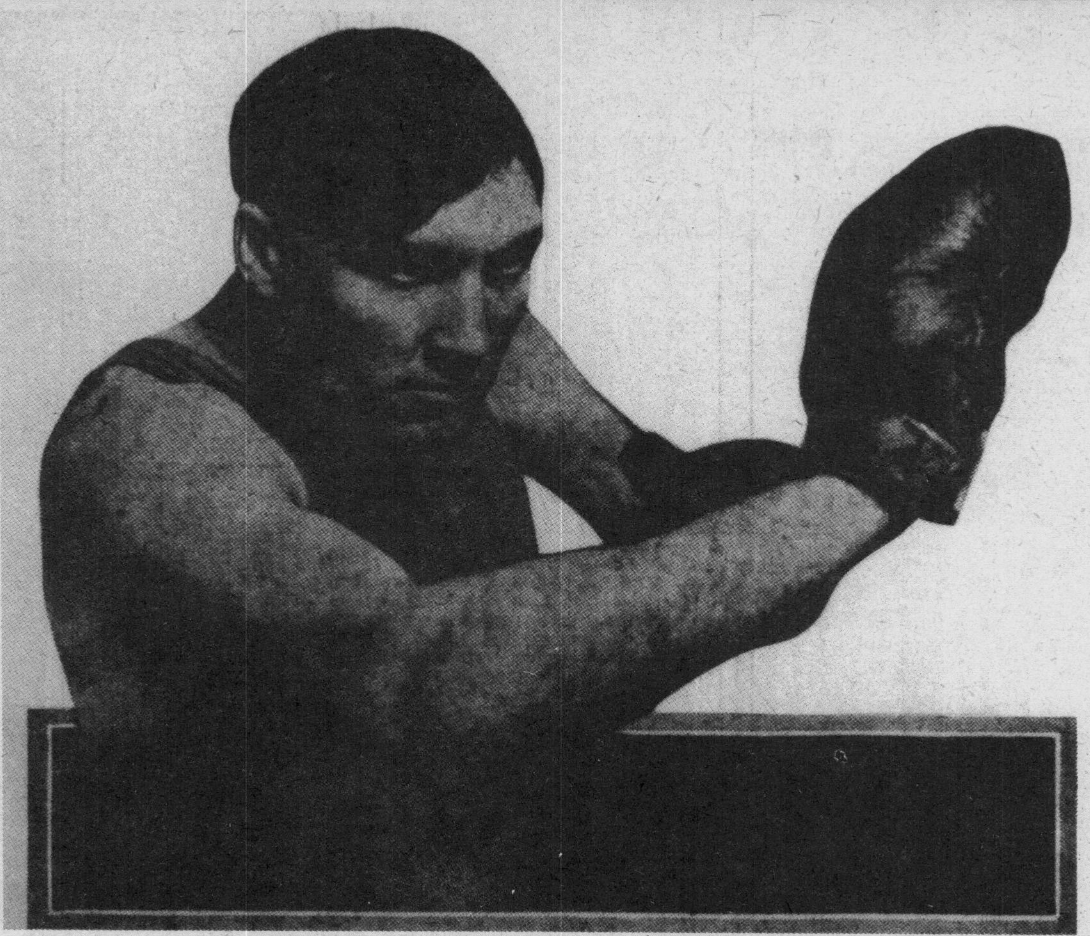

Jess Willard, the New Heavyweight Champion.

Crowds lined the streets and narrow roadways, and the new white champion was loudly cheered. He was decidedly the favorite of the crowd all through the fight, and tonight is the hero of the Island.

Automobiles returning to the city from the fight flew white flags, and thus the news spread far and wide that the white challenger had beaten the negro champion. As Willard came along, the crowds in the streets waved flags and linen handkerchiefs tied to sticks. At one point a group of negro children, who evidently had heard that Johnson was the victor, waved black flags at the white champion, who was much amused.

Neither Man Badly Marked.

Willard is a modest champion, taking his victory as philosophically as he had looked forward to the fight. Neither he nor Johnson showed much evidence of having been engaged in a heavyweight championship battle. The new champion's lip, right ear and left cheek showed slight cuts, but at no time was there more than a drop or two of blood in evidence.

In this respect the fight was in great contrast to the Johnson-Jeffries fight at Reno five years ago, when Jeffries was cut to pieces and blood splashed over the spectators at the ringside. Evidently thinking that this condition might prevail again today, Johnson, just before the start of the fight, objected to the presence of a white woman in the newspaper seats just outside the ropes, and she was relegated to a place out of possible range.

No fight between heavyweights that has gone to a finish was cleaner or less brutal. Johnson's left eye was partly closed in the early rounds, but not sufficiently to interefre with his fighting. His lip also was cut inside, and his famous golden smile flashed from a very red setting.

The end of the fight came with a suddenness that dazed the spectators. It followed two or three rounds of almost complete idleness on the part of the contestants, and the crowd settled down to a long-drawn-out struggle, believing that it would go the full limit of the forty-five rounds without either man being able to register a knock-out.

The early rounds were filled with flashes of Johnson's former wonderful speed, when he would rain rights and lefts to Willard's body and face, delivering ten blows to one from the big white challenger. Through all this time Willard was strictly on the defensive, and on occasion Johnson played with him, once standing with guard down and letting Willard swing at him only to dodge and laugh at the awkwardness of his opponent.

The fight resulted just as many had predicted, Willard and his friends particularly prophesying that if the battle lasted twenty rounds Johnson could not win. This was based partly on the belief that Willard could stand all the punishment Johnson could inflict and partly on the doubt as to Johnson's condition and his ability at his age to fight a long battle against the odds of superior height, weight, and reach and fewer years.

A Glutton for Blows.

Willard said before entering the ring that he expected to take a beating for ten or fifteen rounds at the hands of his faster and more skilled opponent, and had trained to withstand it. As a matter of fact, he took twenty rounds of severe punishment, but laughed the blows aside and kept standing up against the rushes of the negro, who numerous times in the earlier rounds swept Willard before him to the ropes. Willard's back showed many welts raised by the ropes as he fell into them.

In the rushes Johnson would attack Willard in the body, and when the latter's hands and arms came down to guard that part of his anatomy Johnson would swing rights and lefts to the unprotected jaw and face. After each of these attacks Willard would come cheerfully back for more.

Johnson's grin through the early rounds began to change to a look of wonderment as the battle turned into the twenties, and it was evident when the negro had come to the conclusion that it was useless for him to try to knock out the young Western giant he seemed to know that he was in no condition to fight forty-five rounds. His blows lacked the force which sent Jeffries toppling from the topmost rung of the pugilistic ladder at Reno. Time had done its work. It had been the opinion of Johnson and many of his friends that he did not have to be in the best condition to whip Willard, underrating the latter's splendid condition and youthful stamina.

The fight was all Johnson's during the first twenty rounds, Willard only once or twice taking the aggressive, and then swinging clumsily and wildly. Meanwhile his body was growing pink under the blows that flashed from Johnson.

In these rounds Willard took a beating which would have put an ordinary fighter down and out. The crowd got used to seeing him throw off the negro's slashing blows and expected to see Johnson do the same thing when Willard swung his right to the negro's chin in the fatal twenty-sixth round. They expected to see Johnson jump up and continue fighting, just as Willard had come back, but the old champion knew that he had fought his last championship fight.

Slow After Twentieth Round.

In the twentieth round to the final, the fight looked slow and the crowd began to hoot and ask that somebody do something. There was a single cry of "fake," but it was not taken up by the other spectators. The reason it looked slow was because Johnson, who had been doing all the fighting, suddenly stopped and began sparring for time. It was some time before Willard or one of his seconds realized that Johnson was through and only needed a blow or two to send him to pugilistic oblivion.

During the early part of the fight Johnson carried all his old-time confidence and self-assertiveness. He was constantly bandying words with the spectators about the ring and talked steadily at Willard, who heeded the negro's chatter about as little as he did his blows.

Willard's seconds were after Johnson all the time, tauntingly warning him to keep away from Willard's terrific right. It was in the sixteenth round that one of Willard's seconds shouted: "Jack, you run into Jess's right. We will pick you up right over here."

"Be sure you take good care of me," said Johnson. It so happened that when Johnson went down for the count it was in Willard's corner.

When a spectator called out, "Johnson, you will get yours today," Johnson replied: "Well, there is good money in it, isn't there?"

Willard probably will take his own time in accepting any challenges. He already had announced that if he won he would not fight another negro. There is no doubt that today's fight will do the new champion a world of good. Today he was palpably nervous, and at first was afraid to go at Johnson. He constantly jabbed or lunged and then backed away, instead of following up an advantage when it came to him.

It can hardly be said at present that Willard is a great fighter, but he is a wonderful specimen of physical manhood, and is likely to develop an aggressiveness and skill that may make him invincible for years to come.

Willard Clumsy in Ring.

Willard looked very clumsy against Johnson today. A more skillful man might have knocked Johnson out after the twelfth round, for after that the negro was going on speed and nerve and skill.

Throughout the fight the Cubans kept shouting words of encouragement to Willard, such as "Kill the black bear!" and "Knock him out and let us go home!" When one spectator shouted at Johnson that he was an old man, the negro replied, "You just watch the old man," and with that he chased Willard twice across the ring, knocking his head first to the right and then to the left with a series of cross-blows.

Throughout the twenty-first, twenty-second, twenty-third, and twenty-fourth rounds Johnson hardly struck a blow. He kept feinting at Willard, who was ever ready to break ground. When Johnson finally went down in the twenty-sixth round he rolled over on his back. The sun was beating down with torrid intensity, and his arms drew up as though to shield his eyes from the glare, while the referee counted him out.

There was virtually no big betting down here on the fight. The odds for small wagers today varied from 8 to 5 to 6 to 5 on the negro.

The crowd looked to number between 15,000 and 20,000. In addition fully 5,000 persons viewed the fight from the distant slopes and hills. The Cubans, who made up a large percentage of the crowd, were much excited. Many women, both Cuban and American, were present, as well as all the notables in the island.

Havana itself was deserted during the battle, a half holiday having been declared informally. Tonight, however, the streets are ablaze with lights and the Cubans are celebrating Willard's victory. Several thousands of them blocked the Plaza in front of Willard's quarters at the hotel, when the new champion returned triumphantly from the battle. The police had to clear a passage through the cheering crowd of men and women. Willard was wearing the same old sweater, blue trousers, and felt hat which had become familiar through his training work on the road.

The demonstration was something new to Willard who had been going quietly about the streets for the last two weeks, and he grinned like an embarrassed schoolboy. The giant was slapped and mauled and pelted with flowers as, with his training partners, he shoved his way through the throngs. Once in his own room he was his quiet self again, chatting as if he had just returned from a training bout, instead of being victor in a championship battle.

One of Jack's Blows Did Hurt.

Willard said that none of Johnson's blows hurt more than momentarily, except a slash over the heart about the twentieth round, which made him gasp for breath during the rest of the round. He declared he was not sore about the body, but one of the toes of his left foot was slightly sprained and swollen from a twist. Johnson during the fight kept extending his left foot until he could just press down on Willard's left toes.

The new champion said: "I have no immediate plans for fights in the future. I am obligated to the syndicate which promoted the fight, and would like to rest at home after an exhibition tour, which I understand is projected.

"The blow that actually brought the fight to a quick conclusion was a right-hand smash to Johnson's body early in the last round. I felt Johnson grow limp in the next clinch and knew I had the championship within my reach. A left to the body and a right smash to the jaw put Johnson down for the count."

LITTLE BETTING ON FIGHT.

HAVANA, April 5.—The day broke with overcast skies and a cool wind from the sea, but the skies cleared later and the weather for the fight was clear and bright. Early in the day the downtown fight headquarters were crowded with ticket buyers, and the morning saw the arrival in Havana of wealthy Cubans from all over the island to witness the contest.

Johnson and Willard both were up early. Johnson prepared coolly to defend his title. His only nervousness seemed to be over the $30,000 cash he was to receive at 11 o'clock. He chatted and laughed while preparing for the trip to the ring.

Willard had had a refreshing sleep. He said he proposed to go slow in the ring, and that he expected to take a good deal of punishment during the first ten rounds, hoping to wear Johnson down and get an opportunity to land a knockout blow. Willard said that never in his ring career had he felt any discomfort from any blow delivered on his body, and he did not fear Johnson's jabs.

Johnson, one of the largest men who ever stepped into a prizering, faced an opponent measurably larger and ten years younger than himself. The negro is 38 years old. Willard is 28, weighs normally 20 pounds more than Johnson, and tops him five and one-half inches, being 6 feet 6 inches in height. Not within the history of the prizefight had two such giants been brought together before.

Records of the Boxers.

Jess Willard.

Born Dec. 19, 1887, Pottawatomie County, Kan.

1911.	Rounds.
Feb. 15—Louis Fink, lost; Suppulpa, Ohio	10
March 7—Ed. Burke, k. o.; El Reno, Okla.	3
March 25—Louis Fink, k. o.; Oklahoma City, Okla	3
March 25—John Young, k. o.; Fort Wayne, Ind.	6
June 29—Frank Bowers, k. o.; St. Charles, Ind.	3
July 29—Arthur Pelky, no dec.; New York City	10
Aug. 19—Luther McCarthy, no dec.; New York City	10
Dec. 3—Sailor White, k. o.; Buffalo, N. Y.	1
Dec. 27—Sailor Kearns, k. o.; New York City	8
1913.	
March 20—Gunboat Smith, lost; San Francisco	20
Nov. 17—George Rodel, no dec.; Milwaukee	10
Dec. 3—Carl Morris, won; New York City	10
Dec. 12—George Davis, k. o.; Buffalo, N. Y.	2
Dec. 29—George Rodel, k. o.; New Haven, Conn.	9
1915.	
April 5—Jack Johnson, k. o.; Havana.	26

Jack Johnson.

Born March 31, 1878, Galveston, Texas.

1901.	Rounds.
Feb. 25—Joe Choynski, k. o. by; Galveston	3
1903.	
Feb. 3—Denver Ed. Martin, won; Los Angeles	20
Feb. 27—Sam McVey, won; Los Angeles	20
1905.	
March 28—Marvin Hart, lost; San Francisco	20
April 25—Jim Jeffords, k. o.; Philadelphia	4
May 9—Joe Jeannette, no dec.; Philadelphia	6
July 15—Morris Harris, k. o.; Philadelphia	3
Dec. 1—Young Peter Jackson, won; Baltimore	12
1906.	
April 26—Sam Langford, won; Chelsea	15
Nov. 6—Jim Jeffords, won; Lancaster, Penn.	6
Nov. 26—Joe Jeannette, draw; Portland, Me.	10
1907.	
Feb. 19—Peter Felix, k. o.; Sydney, N. S. W.	1
March 4—Bill Lang, k. o.; Melbourne.	9
July 17—Bob Fitzsimmons, k. o.; Philadelphia	2
Nov. 22—Jim Flynn, k. o.; San Francisco	11
1908.	
Dec. 26—Tommy Burns, won; Sydney, N. S. W.	14
1909.	
Sept. 19—Al Kaufman, no dec.; San Francisco	10
Oct. 16—Stanley Ketchel, k. o.; Colma, Cal.	12
1910.	
July 4—Jim Jeffries, k. o.; Reno, Nev.	15
1912.	
July 4—Jim Flynn, won; Las Vegas, N. M.	9
Dec. 19—Jim Johnson, draw; Paris...	8
1914.	
July 4—Frank Moran, won; Paris....	20
1915.	
April 5—Jess Willard, lost; Havana..	26

"All the News That's Fit to Print."

The New York Times.

THE WEATHER
Fair, continued warm Saturday; showers and lower temperature at night and Sunday.
For full weather report see Page 19.

VOL. LXVIII...NO. 22,442. NEW YORK, SATURDAY, JULY 5, 1919. TWENTY-TWO PAGES TWO CENTS Metropolitan District 50 Mile Radius | THREE CENTS Within 200 Miles | FOUR CENTS Elsewhere

R-34, DUE TONIGHT, PASSED BY HANDLEY-PAGE AT 97-MILE SPEED; AIRPLANE MAY STOP HERE, OR GO ON TO ATLANTIC CITY; DEMPSEY WINS RING CHAMPIONSHIP IN THREE ROUNDS

WILLARD BEATEN IN EASY FASHION IN TOLEDO ARENA

Smashing Attack by Young Challenger Nearly Ends Battle in First Round.

SIX KNOCKDOWNS AT START

Willard Takes More Punishment, but at End of Third Round Decides to Quit.

PAY $1,000,000 TO SEE FIGHT

45,000 Spectators Suffer in the Intense Heat—New Yorkers Backed Willard at 5 to 4.

Special to The New York Times.

TOLEDO, Ohio, July 4.—Jack Dempsey won the heavyweight championship of the world this afternoon in an affair which was not a battle, but a slaughter. Never in the history of the American ring has a heavyweight champion offered such a spectacle in defense of his title as that of Willard today. From sixty seconds after the fight began Dempsey punched Willard virtually at will.

The end of the fight came thirty seconds after the finish of the third round, when Willard's seconds threw two towels into the middle of the canvas, signifying that their man was unable to come up for the fourth round. While Willard was not actually counted out by Referee Pecord, the result constitutes a technical knockout, and will be so recorded.

When the towels flashed through the air Willard's face was a mass of blood, while Dempsey was spattered on his breast and his back with the blood of his opponent. Jess's right eye was completely closed, there was a freely bleeding cut beneath this eye, his mouth was bleeding profusely, six teeth were out, and the whole right side of his face was swollen to almost twice its normal size. Dempsey had not one mark.

So terrific was the punishment which Willard received, so weak was he, so incapable of defense, that during the third round shouts of "Stop it! Stop it!" rose from many parts of the arena, in which were 45,000 spectators of one of the poorest fights in the history of boxing, the onlookers including 500 women. It was a fight which was unpleasant to watch, which brought none of the thrills of fine strife, and which gave no satisfaction to any one except those who had bet on Dempsey, and even these thought little of the spectacle except as a kind of pugilistic murder.

Mrs. Willard Happy.

Mrs. Jess Willard arrived in Toledo yesterday without the news being made known. She was in the arena and saw her husband beaten. Tonight she declared herself entirely happy because of his announcement that he is through and will never fight again. This was the first time she had seen her husband in action in the ring.

The spectators, indeed, were rather dazed with the complete collapse of the champion and the amazing speed with which the beginning of the end came. The battle opened with a feeling-out process by both men. Willard managed to get two punches to Dempsey's face. Then Jack let out. He put over a smashing right to the jaw and a left to the stomach. Willard's 245 pounds of weight crashed to the canvas. His title was gone right there.

A roar rose that could have been heard out in Lake Erie. Willard was near the edge of the north side of the ring, and struggled to a sitting posture. He seemed utterly dazed, but there was a fatuous smile upon his lips. At the count of six, he staggered to his feet. The remaining two minutes of the round saw the champion knocked down five more times, and battered twice to the ropes, helpless. He could not defend himself; he could not hit back; his immense bulk was almost as helpless as if he had been a child.

It was the whistle which saved Willard in this round from a knockout, for at this fight a whistle was used, military fashion, instead of the time-honored gong. Seven seconds before the round ended Dempsey knocked Willard down for the sixth time. The champion was in the southwest corner of the ring, having landed on the floor from the ropes. Pecord began to count, "one, two, three, four, five, six, seven," he counted, amid bedlam. Then the whistle, inaudible except to those at the immediate ringside, sounded. Jess was saved for a few minutes longer.

Willard a Chopping Block.

As Willard was taken to his corner the Dempsey crowd shrieked in ecstacy, not having heard the whistle and thinking that the fight had ended by a knockout. Some enthusiasts burst over the sixty-dollar seats and clambered into the ring to shake Jack's hands, but they were

Continued on Page Four.

Hindenburg Regime Passes with End of Supreme Command

BERLIN, July 3, (Associated Press.)—Field Marshal von Hindenburg left Kolberg, Prussia, today.

His departure marked the dissolution of the supreme army command.

DUTCH TO GIVE UP KAISER FOR TRIAL

Allies Receive Assurances, Though Rights of Sovereignty Will Be Maintained.

SUMNER TO BE CHIEF JUDGE

White May Represent America on the Tribunal—Hewart to be Prosecutor.

LONDON, Saturday, July 5.—The Allies, according to The Daily Mail, have received assurances that the Dutch Government in the last resort will not refuse to surrender the former German Emperor for trial.

The newspaper says that the necessary formal objections will doubtless be raised to maintain the rights of Dutch sovereignty, but as the demand for the ex-Kaiser's person can be made in the name of the League of Nations, national rights will not be infringed and there is no doubt that the Dutch Government will be quite ready to get rid of the unwelcome guest.

It is not considered likely, The Mail continues, that the matter will come before the Dutch courts, despite certain statements at The Hague.

The chief count in the former Kaiser's indictment, The Mail understands, will be his action in causing the violation of Belgium and Luxemburg. The proceedings will be conducted in English, but a translation will be made into several languages simultaneously.

Sumner to Preside at Trial.

John Andrew Hamilton, Lord Sumner, will preside over the five judges representing the United States, Great Britain, France, Italy, and Japan, at the trial of the ex-Kaiser, according to The Evening News.

Sir Gordon Hewart, Solicitor General of Great Britain, will lead for the prosecution.

William Hohenzollern, it is said, will be defended by German counsel, assisted by British lawyers if he wishes them.

The decision to bring the former Emperor to London, with other prominent accused persons, has been a well-kept secret, and it is understood that Premier Lloyd George was responsible for the proposal.

Commission to Fix Procedure.

Great state trials in England, of which there have been none in many years, have been held in Westminster Hall, but it is not believed that William Hohenzollern will receive that honor. The procedure for his trial will be laid down by a commission which will be appointed by a committee that the Allies will soon set up to execute the provisions of the Peace Treaty.

Of the five judges who will be chosen by the British, American, French, Italian, and Japanese Governments, Edward Douglass White, Chief Justice of the Supreme Court of the United States, is regarded as the logical choice of the American Government. Parliamentary gossip holds that the former Emperor certainly should not have a privileged position in court, but should be put in the dock like any other man charged with a crime.

The trial is looked for this Autumn, and steps for the ex-Kaiser's extradition are expected to be taken soon, if not already begun.

Dutch newspapers have discussed his extradition ever since he took refuge in Holland. Their general sentiment seems to be that it would be a humiliation for Holland to surrender the former monarch at the demand of the Powers, which demand would be untenable under the law, since the Kaiser's case does not come under extradition treaties, and the charge of "a supreme offense against international morality and the sanctity of treaties" is not covered by existing laws.

Hint Demand for Neutral Judges.

The Nieuwe Rotterdamsche Courant, in an article which is reputed to have been inspired, recently said that the Dutch Government might be prepared to make the necessary changes in its constitutional law on being given certain guarantees as to the constitution of the court and the character of the trial. The guarantees specified by the newspaper were that impartial judges who would not be of accusing nationalities would preside, and that the former Emperor might receive the right to produce all available evidence in his defense.

The Handelsblad of Amsterdam recently said, regarding the former Emperor and Crown Prince:

"Both of them have been admitted to this country as a matter of fact, not

Continued on Page Three.

Progress of the R-34 from Scotland to Long Island

MOBS SACK SHOPS IN ITALIAN CITIES

Riots Against High Cost of Living Occur in Florence, Bologna, and Other Places.

TROOPS SHOOT AT IMOLA

Four Killed When Mob Is Fired Upon—Almost Soviet Rule in Some Towns.

FLORENCE, July 4, (Associated Press.)—Following serious riots here yesterday against the high cost of living, during which mobs sacked several shops in the outskirts of the city, order has been restored everywhere as the result of measures taken by the authorities, assisted by the labor organizations. The prices of goods are being fixed according to the desire of the population.

At the gates of the city yesterday rioters held up merchants coming in with their produce, and fixed their own prices.

The rioters were quieted in certain places by the Prefect of the district, who requisitioned all fruits and vegetables, which in the Summer form the staple foods of the poor. He fixed prices 40 per cent. less than those currently charged. Where the crowds met merchants with their own produce, eggs which had been selling from 8 to 10 cents each were sold at 4 cents.

The mobs backed camions up to the entrances of the stores, sacked and loaded the vehicles with foodstuffs. Then the camions were whirled to strike headquarters, where the provisions were distributed. Only the food stores were looted, the clothing shops not being touched.

During the afternoon crowds of strikers congregated in the Piazza Victor Emmanuel, but were dispersed by police and carabineers. There were many spirited incidents. It was necessary for the carabineers to charge the crowds several times before the square was cleared. Many arrests were made.

In the evening armed guards occupied strategic points throughout the city.

Military camions are still going out from Florence to the regions stricken by the earthquake, where conditions now have almost been restored. Tomorrow the military authorities intend to transport from Florence portable barracks which formerly were used by the army in the field. These will replace the tents now in use in the Mugello Valley.

ROME, July 4, (Havas.)—Four persons were killed today when troops fired on a crowd at Imola, twenty-two miles from Bologna, as a result of demonstrations against the high cost of living.

Newspaper dispatches report the agitation to be particularly strong at Bologna, Ravenna, Florence, and Forli. Stores have been pillaged.

The Giornale d'Italia yesterday said that in Imola and other towns in the Romagna district of Central Italy the authorities had virtually handed over their administrative powers to Socialist, Syndicalist, and anarchist organizations, which had taken control of the region as Soviets.

The Government has ordered that the price of frozen meat be reduced throughout Italy to 50 cents a pound.

The greater part of this city will be left in darkness and the cars will stop running if the threatened strike at the Central Power Station at Terni, 49 miles northeast of Rome, is carried out. This station provides the hydraulic power for Romes electric current.

SOCIALISTS IN CONTROL.

In Bologna They Take Over City Government and Fix Prices.

Special Cable to THE NEW YORK TIMES.

ROME, July 4.—All the shopkeepers in Bologna, alarmed at the news of sacking and palliging of shops in Forli, Imola, and Faenza, sold their goods at half the ordinary prices today. An immense crowd invaded the markets, buy-

Continued on Page Three.

Giant Plane Off from Newfoundland For New York and Atlantic City

Handley-Page Machine with a Crew of Six Men Makes a Perfect "Hop Off"—The Transatlantic Flight Project Abandoned.

Airplane Reports Going Well at 97 Miles an Hour.

By Wireless to The New York Times.

AIRPLANE ATLANTIC.

12:30 A. M., G. M. T., July 5, (8:30 P. M., July 4, New York Time.)

VIA NORTH SYDNEY, N. S.

All going well; making 85 knots, approaching North Sydney.

HANDLEY-PAGE PLANE ATLANTIC.

The above message shows that the airplane had traveled 350 miles in the first four hours, an average of nearly ninety miles an hour. At the time the message was sent she was making 85 knots, or 97 miles an hour, at which rate she should reach New York at 5 o'clock this morning, and Atlantic City, if she goes there, about 6:30 A. M.

Airplane 120 Miles East of Halifax at 11:45 P. M.

HALIFAX, N. S., July 4.—The Handley-Page airplane, bound from Harbor Grace, N. F., for New York, passed over Antigonish, Nova Scotia, at 11:45 tonight, local time.

The plane was traveling at high speed and at a great height. Antigonish is 120 miles east of Halifax.

Special to The New York Times.

HARBOR GRACE, N. F., July 4.—The Handley-Page biplane Atlantic is on her way to the United States. The world's biggest airplane left here at 20:25 Greenwich mean time, (4:25 New York time,) bound direct for New York or Atlantic City. Early rising New Yorkers may see her cut diagonally across the city from Long Island before 7 o'clock tomorrow morning.

More than 1,200 miles lie before her and her crew hopes that she will clip them off at an average rate of eighty an hour.

When the biplane left Harbor Grace it was the announced intention to sail directly to Atlantic City, avoiding a landing in the vicinity of New York. At 11 o'clock tonight, however, Lieut. Col. Stedman, the business representative here of the Handley-Page firm, wired Mr. Workman, the New York representative, to look for the biplane in New York at daybreak, and said that she would make a landing there if a field could be found.

It was a desire that the monster land plane should get to the United States before the slower dirigible that led the Handley-Page firm in England to induce the crew in Newfoundland to abandon the long planned transatlantic crossing and set out upon the first international flight starting from Newfoundland, and the first from there destined to end, if all goes well, in the United States.

The Atlantic's course, as it was planned momentarily before her departure, differs much from that plotted last night when the biplane was on the very verge of setting out upon the journey calculated to bring her into the United States in time to participate in the Independence Day celebration. She steered about 285 degrees magnetic from Harbor Grace, planning to cross Placentia Bay near its upper end and then to take a course which would cut Miquelon Island and Cape Breton Island about in the middle.

Thence she is to be flown straight down the backbone of Nova Scotia on the opposite side of the coast from Halifax, probably not passing within miles of that city, since she is due in that vicinity about midnight.

Once clear of Nova Scotia, the plotted line of travel starts near the mouth of the Bay of Fundy and leads direct to Boston, which city may get a glimpse of the British visitor soon after daylight.

If Boston proves in fact to be the landfall of the arrival in the United States, the Atlantic's course thenceforward is mostly overland, cutting diagonally down through Rhode Island and Connecticut, across Long Island and thence over New York City.

Fog Delays Early Start.

Aboard the Atlantic are six men—Major Herbert George Brackley, Royal

Continued on Page Two.

Projected Course of the Handley-Page Machine from Newfoundland to This City.

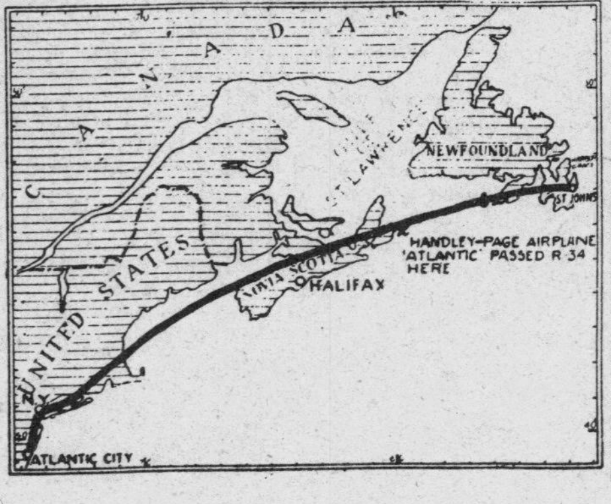

AMERICANS WOULD SINK FOE'S SHIPS

Maintain Old Contention in Discussing Fate of Interned War Craft.

ALWAYS VETOED SURRENDER

Americans Opposed British Project for That of Grand Fleet at Scapa Flow.

By RICHARD V. OULAHAN.

Special Cable to THE NEW YORK TIMES.

PARIS, July 3.—The allied naval experts are now considering the disposition of the German warships in the German ports which, under the terms of the Versailles Treaty, are to be turned over to the Allies. The assertion that if the German fleet had been delivered by the enemy to the British at Scapa Flow in accordance with the terms of the armistice of Nov. 11 the ships would not have been sunk by their German crews, being, in that case, considered as surrendered property instead of delivered for internment subject to the future disposition of the Allies, has considerable influence on the present discussion in the allied counsels.

Since Horatio Bottomley asked in the House of Commons, soon after the sinking of the fleet, if President Wilson had not been responsible for preventing the outright surrender of the ships, there has been more or less talk suggesting that the President or his representatives in the Peace Conference insisted upon the internment policy. The point of the criticism is that if the ships had been surrendered outright they would have been placed in charge of British crews, and it would not have been possible for the Germans to sink them. Under conditions of internment ships remain in the care of their own crews. Heretofore internment has been applied only to vessels in neutral ports, where they were subject to the regulation and control of neutral Governments, but retained their crews. It was a new policy to intern ships in a belligerent country, but the practices governing neutral internment were followed.

It is now possible to say what was the attitude of the American representatives concerning the decision to intern the German warships at Scapa Flow instead of treating them as surrendered enemy property. In the conferences of the allied naval experts the British representatives argued for outright surrender. The American experts took the contrary view. They had been insisting that the only feasible method of disposing of the German fleet was an agreement among the Allies to sink it. The reasons for this have been stated many times, the main reason being that the distribution on the basis of shipping losses in the war or in proportion to naval effort against the enemy would so increase the British fleet as to give it undue preponderance and compel the United States and perhaps other nations to go to tremendous expense to build up their naval strength in order to preserve the former ratio to the British fleet. It was also contended that an increase of naval armaments was contrary to allied principles.

In line with this argument the American experts, the leading one of whom was Admiral Benson, held that it would be unfair to surrender the German warships to the British, as this would give the British a prior claim to their permanent possession. It is not known whether that argument was advanced quite so strongly as here stated, but that was the impression the American experts intended to convey.

The upshot was that the American view prevailed, and the German warships were interned under British care at Scapa Flow, subject to future agreement among the Allies as to how they should be disposed of after they were formally surrendered by Germany.

The American attitude that German warships ought to be sunk instead of distributed among the allied navies has not been modified. It is still maintained on the ground that with the Allies bound by the principle that armaments should be reduced it would be inconsistent with the spirit of the times and with that principle to augment the fleet of any power.

DIRIGIBLE WAS OFF SYDNEY AT 8:40 O'CLOCK

British Flier Heads for New York After Giving Up Attempt to Reach St. John's.

LOST IN THE FOG FOR HOURS OVER TRINITY BAY

Big Airship Reached Newfoundland at 6 o'Clock Yesterday Morning, and Was Later Held Up By Bad Weather.

SYDNEY, N. S., July 4.—The British dirigible R-34, on her way to Mineola, L. I., from East Fortune, Scotland, and the Handley-Page bombing plane, which started southward from Harbour Grace, N. F., to New York or Atlantic City, this afternoon, were both about fifty miles off Sydney at 8:40 o'clock, New York times, (12:40 Greenwich mean time,) according to wireless reports received here.

HARBOR GRACE, N. F., July 4.—A message received at the Admiralty wireless station here tonight stated that the R-34 was headed for the Canadian mainland and making good progress. Officers estimated that the dirigible should reach Mineola about noon tomorrow.

ST. PIERRE, Miquelon, July 4.—The R-34 was sighted by officials of the Colonial Administrator's office at 4 P. M., local time, crossing slowly between Little Miquelon, or Langley Island, and the Island of St. Pierre.

HALIFAX, N. S., July 5.—The dirigible R-34 was in communication with the wireless station at Barrington Passage at 2 o'clock this morning, local time, but her position was not given. Barrington is on the west coast of Nova Scotia, 175 miles from Halifax.

Abandons Attempt to Reach St. John's.

ST. JOHN'S, N. F., July 4.—At 9 o'clock, Greenwich mean time, the wireless station at Mount Pearl reported that the R-34 had abandoned her attempt to reach St. John's, and was proceeding westward from Trinity Bay, headed in the direction of New York.

The British wireless received a report from the R-34 saying she expected to cross Newfoundland far north of St. John's, passing over the southern extremity of Notre Dame Bay., thence proceeding to Bonne Bay, on the west coast, going down the Gulf of St. Lawrence, and reaching the Canadian mainland from the direction of Cape Breton or Prince Edward Island.

The airship, it was said in earlier radio advices, had been obliged to take the northerly track because of atmospheric depression here, due to a heavy rainstorm and a thick fog.

The R-34 reached Notre Dame Bay at 6 A. M., and it was announced at that time that the dirigible was to pass over St. John's at noon.

Lost in Fog in Trinity Bay.

At 6:30 o'clock, Greenwich mean time, (2:30 P. M., New York time,) the British naval station reported that the R-34 was lost in a dense fog north of Trinity Bay.

The dirigible was unable to reach Cape Race with its wireless, but gave its position to the warship Cornwall in Bonavista Bay, whence it was relayed to the wireless station here.

The customs collector at Clarenville, at the lower end of Trinity Bay, 66 miles in an air line from this city, later reported the passage of the R-34, headed west and plainly visible.

LONDON, July 4.—The position of the R-34, according to a report received by the Air Ministry at 3 o'clock this morning, was 51.20 north latitude and 48.40 west longitude. This gives the position of the dirigible as just east of Newfoundland.

Big Crowd Expected to Welcome R-34; Seaplanes and 'Blimp' to Meet Her at Sea

Special to The New York Times.

ROOSEVELT AVIATION FIELD, L. I., July 4.—"When will the giant British dirigible, R-34, arrive at Roosevelt Field?" is the question army and navy officers, both American and British, are asking tonight. On one point everybody is agreed and that is, barring unusual weather conditions, the dirigible will arrive off the Mineola aviation fields some time tomorrow. A few officers are of the opinion that the airship may appear early in the morning, while others, and they are of greater number, are of the opinion that it will be noon or later before the largest of all airships is sighted.

If the R-34 arrives before 8 o'clock she will probably descend immediately to her prepared anchorage. If she arrives after that hour—and this is the one best bet according to officers in a position to know—she will probably circle above the clouds until late in the afternoon before she is brought to earth and towed to her concrete anchorage blocks by the 500 American bluejackets and soldiers who are here to aid in safeguarding the British airship during the short time she will remain in America.

The last definite word received concerning the progress of the R-34 was relayed to the wireless station at Mineola tonight from Newport. It was a message from St. Pierre, Miquelon, which stated that at 9 o'clock the R-34 was off Sydney, N. S. The speed the dirigible was making, which must be known to predict the hour of arrival, was not given in the message. Immediately following the receipt of this message, Lieut. Colonel Frederick W. Lucas of the Royal Air Force, who is the Air Service Attaché of the British Embassy in Washington, sent a wireless to the commander of the R-34 asking him to wireless when he expected to arrive at Roosevelt Field. At 11 o'clock no answer had been received.

One thing is certain and that is that the R-34 will not be anchored during the hot hours. As soon as she is made fast to the anchorage blocks the big job of refilling her gas compartments will begin and the officers in charge said tonight that no hydrogen gas will be pumped into the compartments while the great 634-foot long bag is hot. To do so during the hot hours, it was pointed out, would mean the loss of thousands of cubic feet of much needed buoyancy fuel and neither the British nor the American authorities care to run the chance of losing any of the gas that will be needed in the homeward journey, which will probably start within ten hours after the airship is made secure on Roosevelt Field.

Prepare Cordial Welcome.

Furthermore, it is probable that should the R-34 arrive tomorrow night she will remain aloft until early Sunday morning, when she will be brought down and her officers and crew taken in hand "for the time of their life," as one of the American officers here expressed it tonight. It is the intention of the Americans to give the British fliers a welcome that none will ever forget. Secretary of the Navy Daniels, probably Assistant Secretary Franklin D. Roosevelt, Rear Admiral J. J. Glennon, commanding the Third Naval District; Brigadier-Gen. William Mitchel, of the Army Air Force; Captain T. T. Craven, U. S. N., Chief of the naval air organization; Colonel Thomas De Witt Milling, who commanded the American aviators in the First Army of the A. E. F., a personal representative of Secretary Baker and of General March, the Chief of Staff, Colonel Charles De F. Chandler, the pioneer of ballooning in the American Army, and a score of other well-known officers of the army and navy will be on hand as the official representatives of the United States. Immediately after the R-34 is landed a dinner will be given to the

WILLARD BEATEN IN EASY FASHION

Continued from Page 1, Column 1.

waved back and shooed out of the ring. "It's not over," the officials yelled, and then the whistle blew for the second round.

Dempsey backed Willard into the ropes almost at once and began to pump his deadly left into Willard's countenance. In a few seconds the Dempsey heavy artillery showed its effect, and Jess's right eye became completely closed. Then came the opening of the cut on Willard's right cheek. Willard made a feeble attempt to fight back, but had nothing. He was too weak and tried to save himself by hanging on in the clinches. Pecord kept prying the men apart.

Dempsey himself seemed rather tired in this round from the effect of the constant hitting of Willard's bulk and from the heat, which was 110 degrees at the ringside during the fight. The round ended without Willard having been kocked down, but he was one of the worst battered champions ever beheld.

When the third round began Willard showed the least iota of an attempt to fight back, but he could not land on Dempsey. Then Jack opened up the artillery again. He made nothing more or less than a chopping block of the champion. He punched Willard four times in succession in the face. These blows smashed up Willard's mouth pretty badly and knocked out some of the six teeth which Jess lost during the fracas. Willard's face could hardly be seen for blood. Dempsey continued to uppercut Willard with his left, and cries of "Stop it! Stop it!" rose in ever-increasing volume. But Willard weathered the round without being knocked down. If it had not been for his immense reserve of strength he would have been knocked out in the first round. In the third round Dempsey again showed fatigue from his own exertions.

Seconds Give Up Fight.

Then came the whistle for the end of the round. In another thirty seconds Ray Archer threw one towel from Willard's corner, followed at once by another towel thrown by Monahan. The crowd shrieked. Dempsey's friends rushed toward the ring, and the world had another heavyweight champion.

The spectators had two different views of Willard's behavior as far as pluck is concerned. Some gave him praise for coming up for the last two rounds in the condition he was in and taking the frightful beating which Dempsey gave him. Others declared he showed lack of heart by not coming up to the scratch for the fourth round and losing his title by standing on his feet until the last.

"How did he ever beat Johnson?" was the general question. Certain it is that Willard was in no condition to enter a ring. When he first stepped on the canvas it was noted that he showed not one trace of pink. His skin had a peculiar olive-drab hue. Dempsey was as brown as an Indian. Willard's paucity of fighting since he won the title from Johnson in Havana in April, 1915, his age, and his lack of hard training for the bout tell the story of his poor condition. The fight he made was pitiful for a world's champion. The Jamaica Kid, Dempsey's sparring partner, undoubtedly could have put up an infinitely better battle than did Big Jess.

For their nine minutes of fighting the battlers received a fortune. Willard drew down $160,000 from Tex Rickard, the promoter of the bout; something like $20,000 from admissions to his training camp, and a percentage of the moving picture receipts. Dempsey received $27,500 from Rickard, about $20,000 from admissions to his training camp, and a percentage of the movie receipts.

$500,000 Profit for Rickard.

The crowd which witnessed the sad affair was not up to expectations. Along the upper sides of the great hectagonal arena, where were the $10 seats, there was but a mere sprinkling of spectators. The $15 seats, that come in next toward the ring, were not occupied any better than the cheaper locations. Even the choicer seats were not all taken, and, just before the start of the bout those in the cheap seats, in mass formation, plunged into the better seats.

The arena, which has a total capacity of 80,000, was not much more than half filled. Tex Rickard could not give an accurate estimate tonight, but he thought that the attendance was 45,000. The total receipts are estimated at about $1,000,000. If this estimate of receipts, which is the best obtainable, is correct, this leaves the promoter a net profit of about $500,000, as the expenses of the bout reached half a million.

Fighting Face of the New Champion

Jack Dempsey, World's Champion
Wins the Title at 24.

What the crowd lacked in numbers, according to these estimates, it made up in quality. There were sporting men and club men and society men and business men and hotel men there who are known from one end of the country to the other. The visitors came from all the big cities, from as far south as New Orleans and as far west as San Francisco. There was a big contingent of New Yorkers.

Probably more women saw this fight than have ever witnessed a heavyweight battle in the United States. There was a section on the southwest side of the arena reserved for them. It was well filled. There was also a scattering of women throughout the arena.

$2,000,000 Placed in Bets.

The betting on the fight was light for a championship battle. Early this morning the odds were at even money. Then came the New York and other contingents with Willard coin, and Willard again became the favorite. The prevailing odds when the men entered the ring were 5 to 4 on Willard. It is estimated about $2,000,000 was wagered in all.

The day's proceedings at the arena started at 11 o'clock, when the first preliminary, of which there were six, was staged. The amusement ended at 4:20½, when the towels acted as a curtain to the event. The main bout started at 4:09, the fighters having entered the ring shortly before 4 o'clock. Dempsey was the first to appear, climbing into his corner, the northwest, at 3:57. He got a big cheer. At 3:58 Willard took his corner, the southeast. His reception was not quite as uproarious as that for his rival.

The champion wore blue trunks, with a belt of red, write and blue. Dempsey wore white trunks, with a belt also of red, white and blue. Both men entered the ring with their hands already bandaged. Dempsey sat down on a stool beneath a big umbrella in his corner. He looked slightly worried. Willard stood up in his corner, also under an umbrella, and seemed much at his ease. He waved his hand to friends near the ringside and shouted greetings to some of them.

The champion walked across the ring to Dempsey's corner. He shook hands with Demsey and said: "Hello, Jack, how are you, Jack? All right?"

Dempsey grinned, and responded: "You bet."

In Willard's corner were Ray Archer, Jack Hempel and Walter Monahan. In the Dempsey corner were Jack Kearns, Jimmie De Forest and Bill Tate.

At 4:07 o'clock the fighters went to the centre of the ring. They were photographed shaking hands and then were cautioned by Referee Pecord. Tex Rickard, one of the judges, took his place in the press seats, at the north side of the ring, while Major A. J. Drexel Biddle, second judge, was seated in the press stand on the south side of the ring. Then the fight began.

One Thermometer at 120.

The moving picture machines were installed to the west of the ring on a platform about thirty feet high. The day was clear and excessively hot throughout. At 1:30 P. M. a thermometer at the ringside registered 120 degrees. A slight breeze occasionally stirred, and every time it did it was greeted by cheers from the fans. Once a cloud obscured the sun for a minute and it was also applauded. Nearly every man in the arena had his coat off and his handkerchief tucked under his hat. It was a white crowd sartorially, and to look over the shimmering masses of silk shirts, with the sun beating on them, was to risk eye trouble from the reflection.

One hundred enthusiasts reached the arena as early as 5 o'clock in the morning, although the gates did not open until 8:30. These were holders of ten-dollar tickets for rush seats, who were afraid they would not get their choice, but they need not have worried.

At 11 o'clock there were 8,000 persons in the arena. The best of the preliminaries was the semi-final, a bout of eight rounds, between Frankie Mason of Fort Wayne, Ind., and Carl Tremaine of Detroit, bantams. Billy Rooks of Detroit gave the decision to Tremaine, a verdict which was roundly hissed.

Another preliminary which attracted some attention was the eight-round go between Jock Malone of St. Paul and Navy Ralston of Joliet, Ill. They fought at 146 pounds, and the decision went to Malone.

Although there was not as great a crowd at the arena as had been expected, Toledo was jammed. Many persons slept last night in their automobiles and in hotel rotundas. It was difficult to get anything to eat this morning, because of the crowds in the hotels and restaurants.

Willard and Dempsey spent a quiet day until they left for the ring. Dempsey was up at 6:30 o'clock and had a breakfast of oranges, poached eggs, and coffee. He ate dinner at noon. Willard got up at 9 o'clock, and at 10 ate a heavy breakfast, his only meal before the fight.

Tonight Toledo is wild with joy over the result of the fight, as Dampsey has made himself extremely popular here. Enthusiastic rooters are parading the town, and jollification is in the air.

WILLARD HELPLESS AFTER FIRST ROUND

Challenger's Terrific Attack Sends Kansan to Floor Six Times Within Two Minutes.

FIGHT IS ALL DEMPSEY'S

Special to The New York Times.

AT THE RINGSIDE, TOLEDO, Ohio, July 4.—The punch which started Jess Willard on his way to pugilistic oblivion came about a minute after the start of the first round. It was a sharp, short right crack on the jaw, following a left which Dempsey buried in the Champion's stomach. This short right, which traveled not more than fifteen inches, shook the massive frame as Willard was backing toward the ropes on the north side of the ring. He went down with a crash, but was soon up in a sitting posture with face toward the east. Dempsey's terrific right punch had turned him half-way around as he went down.

That blow was the beginning of the end, for when Jess got up he ran headlong into a frenzied, wild-eyed battler, who knew that victory was within his grasp. Until that punch, the opening round had been tame. Dempsey fooled Willard at the start, when he came from his corner quietly and cautiously. Willard and his backers had expected the same kind of a football rush which Jack had used in all his fights. They expected that Dempsey would rush at the champion just as he had rushed at big Fred Fulton.

Dempsey came out of his corner the personification of a calculating fighter. His step was springy, and he glided around softly, waiting for the champion to make his lead. Willard stuck out his long, left arm and jabbed Dempsey lightly in the face. He then tried to follow with a right to the body, and the fighters came to a clinch. At the order of Referee Pecord, Willard stepped away with both arms free, and Dempsey did the same. It was plain that both men were determined to live up to the rules.

Again Dempsey glided around the towering plainsman, Willard sticking to the centre of the ring. With head down, Jack rushed his opponent and shot a hard right to Willard's body at close quarters. He repeated the blow before he backed away. Jess grinned his silly grin and did not appear to be disturbed. Perhaps he wasn't, but those two rib roasters looked as if they hurt.

Dempsey Tears In.

Again the boxers clashed, and Jess tried to send in two uppercuts, but Dempsey did not appear to be bothered. Jess again tried his left jab. By this time Dempsey evidently knew that there was no sting in Willard's punches. None of them, except one left jab, had even sent his head out of position. He held his head low, the jaw a shining target for Willard's attack. This brief minute of sparring, during which the men had come to clinch three times and Dempsey had learned that there was no steam in Willard's punches, worked like a tonic on the challenger.

Again Jack, with head down, bored into his massive opponent. His left, and then his right, shook the champion all over. Willard began to back away now, and again Dempsey's left shot to the stomach. As big Jess bent over under the pain of this crack to the body, Dempsey's right came up like a flash and caught him flush on the jaw. The champion dropped his left arm, groping for the ropes as he went down.

As his 245 pounds hit the canvas, the whole platform shook, and there was a sickening grin on the champion's face. He was going to get up as Referee Pecord leaned down to count over him, but Monahan yelled from Willard's corner not to hurry. Jess got up on one knee and then rose to his feet. Little did the crowd know what was coming, no one ever dreamed that they were going to witness two long drawn-out minutes of the worst punishing a champion ever received in the ring. As soon as Willard was on his feet again, Dempsey's rush at the dazed, wavering title-holder, almost carried him off the floor. The crowd seemed to be all for Dempsey, who now made a target of Willard's face, and chopped and scraped the right side of the champion's head and face with his left and rocked his jaw with his right.

Down went Willard again. He struggled to his feet, and amid scenes of the wildest excitement Dempsey continued the bull-like rushes and another terrific right toppled over the tottering Willard. He saved himself from a hard bump on the canvas by hanging on to the ropes. He was still on both feet, and while he was draped over the ropes Dempsey shot two terrific rights to his body and straightened him up. Relentlessly, Dempsey went at him. He hit him when and where he pleased. Willard, bewildered, staggering, and on the verge of a knockout, groped blindly about the ring, while Dempsey chopped the left side of his face until it was red and bruised.

The gruelling battering opened up a cut under the champion's eye. Blood was flowing down his cheek. Down Willard went again under the punishment.

The crowd, at first dumfounded, finally awoke to what Dempsey was doing, and the whole arena flew up with wild clamor. "Finish him, Jack," "Knock him out," were shouts heard above the tumult. Dempsey worked as fighter never worked before. Willard by this time was unable to lift his hands from his sides. Six times Willard hit the floor, and twice besides he was knocked off his feet, only to hang on the ropes to save himself from a fall. Dempsey's arms worked like piston rods. He put in every ounce of strength he had to finish the champion. To Jess and his handlers the round seemed an age long. Monohan was frantic and waved his arms in excitement each time Jess went down. He entreated and implored his pal to get up. It seemed to the Willard crowd as if the round would never end.

The last time Dempsey bowled the champion over on the ropes, they were in a neutral corner. The sun beat down on the bloodstained champion. Dempsey's energy seemed limitless. As the great soft frame was sprawled over the ropes, Dempsey shot pitiless smashes into his body, and then, when Jess straightened up on his feet, another shower of rights and lefts banged Willard's head back and forth. Then, putting all he had into one desperate effort, Jack drove his right against the bruised left jaw and Willard tumbled over in a heap in a corner.

Under the terrific smashing the champion's brain was dulled. Pecord began to count over him as he sat up under the entreaties of his seconds. There was a glassy stare in his eyes and a meaningless grin on the cut and battered face.

"One, two, three, four, five, six, seven," counted Pecord, and the shout which rent the air was so great that the spectators heard no more. As Pecord counted "seven" Timer W. Warren Barbour blew his whistle, which ended the round and saved Willard from a one-round defeat.

The crowd thought Willard had been knocked out. The great arena became a scene of wild disorder. Men left their seats, struggled over the backs of the men in front of them, and jumped over the press benches into the ring. They grabbed Dempsey and they kissed him. They slapped him on the back and fought savagely with one another to shake his hand. From Willard's corner Monahan and Hempel jumped, with the blast of the timer's whistle, and fairly dragged Willard to his corner. They threw the pail of ice water into his face. They put strong ammonia to his nostrils and did everything possible in that minute of rest to bring him back to consciousness.

The officials had a hard time clearing the ring. The referee ordered Jack Kearns, Dempsey's manager, out of the ring. Kearns thought the fight was over and started to take Dempsey through the ropes with him. Pecord told him that the bell had saved Willard, and he called Dempsey out for the second round.

"That's all wrong," yelled Kearns. "They are going to make us win this fight twice."

DEMPSEY'S RECORD.

Opponents.	Result.	Rds.
1915-'16—Kid Hancock	K	1
Billy Murphy	K	1
Chief Gordon	K	6
Johnny Berson	K	7
Animus Campbell	K	7
Joe Lyons	K	9
Fred Woods	K	4
George Copelin	K	7
Andy Malloy	K	3
Two-round Gilligan	K	1
Battling Johnson	K	1
George Christian	K	1
Jack Koehn	K	1
Joe Bonds	K	10
Dan Ketchell	K	5
Bob York	K	4
Johnny Suddenberg	W	10
Terry Kellar	W	10
Andy Malloy	W	10
Jack Downey	L	4
1917—Jim Flynn	K by	1
Willie Meehan	D	4
Al Norton	K	1
Willie Meehan	D	4
Charlie Miller	K	1
Bob McAllister	W	4
Gunboat Smith	W	4
Carl Morris	W	4
1918—Homer Smith	K	1
Carl Morris	W F	6
Jim Flynn	K	1
Bill Brennan	K	6
Bull Sadee	K	1
Tom Riley	K	1
Billy Miske	N D	10
Dan Ketchell	K	2
Arthur Pelky	K	1
Kid McCarthy	K	1
Bob Devere	K	1
Dan (Porky) Flynn	K	1
Fred Fulton	K	1
Terry Kellar	K	5
Willie Meehan	L	4
Jack Moran	K	1
Battling Levinsky	K	3
Dan (Porky) Flynn	K	1
Billy Miske	N D	8
Carl Morris	K	1
Gunboat Smith	K	[illegible]
1919—Jess Willard	K	3

W—Won. L—Lost. W F—Won on foul. K by—Knocked out by. K—Knockout. D—Draw. N D—No decision.

45,000 SEE FIGHT IN SIZZLING HEAT

Crowd Broils and Steams in Sun-Baked Arena for Hours Waiting for Big Bout.

500 WOMEN IN MULTITUDE

Expensive Seats in Arena Well Occupied, but "Bleacher" Places Go Begging.

MERCURY AT 110 DEGREES

Throng Leaves the Scene Disappointed in the Spectacle Provided and Glad to Get Away.

Special to The New York Times.

TOLEDO, Ohio, July 4.—At twenty minutes past 4 o'clock this afternoon 45,000 persons who had stewed, broiled, and steamed, most of them for hours, under the most torrid rays that ever invaded the temperate zone, rose mournfully, yet gladly, from the pine boards on which they had perched in the Willard-Dempsey fight arena, and with scarcely a backward glance at the platform below where a bruised and bleeding ex-champion sat dazed, and where a little crowd of friends or would-be friends slapped the brawny back of a new champion, plodded their stolid way from the parched amphitheatre.

They were mournful because the spectacle which they had anticipated with such eagerness had proved so unworthy the name of a battle. They were glad because they were going away, and in all the broad world there was no better place to go away from than the stricture in Bay View Park in the City of Toledo.

There were, as has been mentioned above, some 45,000 of them. There might have been, as had been prophesied that there would be, about 80,000 spectators for the clash of the heavyweights, but the good geniuses of the other 35,000 led them to stay away. There were thereby spared the expenditure of much money, the endurance of much suffering, and the dismal sight of the much-heralded encounter.

Of the multitude, which emerged in packed, slowly moving masses from the four great entrances, something more than 1 per cent. were women. About 500 of the recently emancipated sex were scattered about the sides of the gently sloping saucer. They were chiefly early-comers, and they had enjoyed, apparently, some of the innocuous bouts which preceded the ultimate one.

The little affair in which Jack Dempsey starred, absolutely unsupported, had been too much for them, however. "It was awful. Never again," seemed to be the keynote of the remarks of those who had anything to say. Most of the women, though, went forth in silence, with lips drawn into a line which expressed no joy whatever.

Crowd Disperses Quickly.

The bad taste which the feature of the afternoon had left in the mouths of the crowd vanished almost entirely when it emerged and discovered that not all the world was the inferno of heat which that monstrous building was today. Little wandering breezes which had been almost entirely barred from the interior by the high walls of the arena crept fitfully about and strayed refreshingly over scorched faces outside the structure. Down by the ringside the temperature had averaged 110 degrees throughout the afternoon, and it had been little, if any, cooler even up on the rim of the vast platter. Outside, however, in the shade of the scattered trees, conditions were much more tolerable, and groups stood for awhile to revive their energies before taking up the rest of the little journey to automobiles and trolley cars.

The distribution of the great throngs to the hotels and houses of Toledo or near-by towns, and to the railway stations was effected with surprising celerity and lack of friction. Automobiles were parked outside by thousands, limousines and roadsters, runabouts and touring cars, and also, most valuable of all in the eyes of the trudging multitude, hundreds of taxicabs, or cars doing duty for the day in that capacity. Most of the latter had been preserved by far-sighted persons, but there were a few cruisers, which were snapped up with avidity by perspiring wayfarers.

Then, too, sad as is the light in which the narrative reveals poor human nature, it must be recorded that the waving of large bills in the faces of desperate men served to so weaken the memories of many taxi pilots that they totally forgot that their cars had been reserved by persons still churning their way through the crowd.

HEAVYWEIGHT CHAMPIONS.	
John L. Sullivan	1882 to 1892
James J. Corbett	1892 to 1894
Robert Fitzsimmons	1897 to 1899
James J. Jeffries	1899 to *1905
Marvin Hart	1905
Tommy Burns	1906 to 1908
Jack Johnson	1908 to 1915
Jess Willard	1915 to 1919
Jack Dempsey	1919

*Retired.

The trolley cars massed in serried lines near by were charged and instantaneously loaded. They were burdened, indeed, to an extent which makes the word "capacity" seem feeble, and they put out for the city at half-minute intervals with heads and heels protruding from all apertures. Within less than an hour the vast assemblage had been separated into its component units, and absorbed into thousands of faraway niches.

The crowd was much longer in collecting than in departing. In fact, it gathered slowly throughout the five hours preceding the bout for the world's title. By noon a smattering of spectators dotted the bowl, and from then onward there was a steady growth in bulk of the human sea, which ultimately filled the gigantic saucer more than half way to its periphery.

The Wait for the Big Event.

There wasn't much to engage attention until the preliminary bouts began, and there wasn't very much until after they finished. A brass band or two made spasmodic efforts to elevate the spirits of the multitude, but there didn't seem to be much pep in their jazz, and their reception was apathetic.

Far otherwise was it with the vendors of ginger ale, pop, lemon shrub, and other mild, tepid beverages, who buzzed up and down the aisles. They were almost embraced by loving strangers, who asked no questions about what the bottles commanded, but merely said "Give me some of that; how much," and poured the contents down.

As noon drew near the drops of humanity oozing into the great entrances, north, south, east and west, began to merge into rivulets and to flow instead of saunter down the inclined passageways, from whose inner ends the seats descended in a slow incline to the ringside, and ascended to the outer rim of the vast amphitheatre. At the entrances it was necessary for the would-be member of the Pine Seat Club inside to run the gauntlet of countless peddlers of this, that, and the other commodity.

The venders of cushions, componnded of flabby straw, were peculiarly persistent and eloquent in their salesmanship: "Here y'are, here y'are," they shouted. "Protect yourself. Nobody else is goin' to look out for you. Get a nice, soft, luxurious cushion. The tar oozing out of the pine boards inside will stick to you like a brother if you don't. Here y'are, here y'are."

Cooling Drinks in Demand.

The distributers of cooling drinks found it unnecessary to urge the merits of their wares. They were constantly surrounded by thirsty men, already superheated by even the short walk from automobile or trolley car. Some pedlers had gone to the unecessary trouble of coloring their anaemic lemonade or shrub or pop some vivid hue or other, usually red, in accord with circus traditions. It may have been a labor of love with them. In any event, it was wasted effort, for this half-broiled crowd would have gulped down beverages colored like a crow's wing or a mustard plaster without even a glance.

Once inside, there was no confusion among the early crowds. Plenty of youths—soldiers recently discharged from service—were on hand in each passageway and at each turning to direct the inquirer to the seat for which his pasteboard called. Once there, he settled down with his cushion, if he had fallen for it, or with a couple of newspapers to do duty as a pedestal, adjusted the edge of the plank behind or the toes of the man perched thereon in the small of his back, and set himself with such patience as his parents had transmitted to him to watch the preliminary bouts.

By 12:30 o'clock the great bowl, mounting, it seemed to those at the ringside, to empyrean distant heights, was about one-third filled. Occasionally a splash of color, in the form of a parasol, a gown, or a bit of millinery, stood out, revealing the presence of femininity in the sweltering mass of shirt-sleeved men. A "Jenny Wren" section, set apart for the women, seemed to have comparatively small attraction for the early comers of the fairer sex, who evidently had decided to sit where they would be certain of plenty of answers to their plenty of questions about the proceedings on the little roped platform below.

"Bleachers" Slow to Fill.

Peculiarly enough, and in contradistinction to that other sporting classic, a world's series baseball game, the bleachers, as the mile or so of rows of $10 seats up at the far-flung rim of the saucer were dubbed, were last to fill. Seats there were not reserved. It was a case of first come first served, and it had been expected that the genuine but not plutocratic enthusiasts would arrive early to select their perches. Yet, with the $40 and $25 regions closely inhabited as early as 1 o'clock, the popular price localities showed row upon row of empty planks gleaming yellow in the lavish July sunlight.

It was already obvious that the holders of medium price seats had decided not to miss any item of the pugilistic menu. They were on hand to scan the preliminary bouts, with a view to whetting their appetities for the royal dish of wild boar which they expected later. All over the amphitheatre the humble handkerchief was serving divers purposes. It was dropped in sunbonnet fashion over thousands of heads; it was used as a mop for thousands of perspiring brows and cheeks; it was swayed by hot hands as a sort of futile fan.

For this was a hot day; let there be no misunderstanding about that. Still more, it was a hot day in Toledo. That is the last word in caloric north of Nashville. The mercury bubbled and sizzled several degrees on the wrong side of 90, even on a shaded corner downtown. In the sun-soaked arena of pine boards up in Bay View Park, with nothing whatever intervening between Old Sol and a multitude which had learned to detest him, degrees of Fahrenheit heaped up until they were beyond count.

Breeze Taunts Broiling Crowd.

Occasionally—say once every ten minutes—the flicker of a breeze fanned the crowd for a second or so, and a sigh of gratitude arose, made more fervent each time by the hope that the cooling touch was the forerunner and prophet of a change in conditions. But this always proved to be merely airy persiflage.

From 2 o'clock onward the hitherto spasmodic hum of motors outside the structure merged into a steady chorus. The Time for the piéce de résistance to be served was drawing near, and the gilded or blaseé fans who scorned the minor preliminaries and were determined to swelter no longer than was necessary began to fill the ringside seats and the section immediately behind.

By this time the less interesting six-round bouts between unknowns had ceased, and eight-round matches between boxers of somewhat more than local repute were holding the boards. The wise ones had had this all figured out, and they arrived almost coincidentally with the departure from the ring of the last frail member of the Toledo Athletic Club. They were rewarded, therefore, by seeing some real action throughout their stay.

As the newspapermen, packed about the ring, glanced around to scan the new arrivals, their eyes caught the gleam of an occasional uptilted silver flask. No visions of "search and seizure" marred the simple pleasure of these foresighted men. They had considered the temperature, diagnosed their own cases, and had brought with them such remedies as they believed to be beneficial.

At Last the Stage Is Set.

The sports writers gazed an instant upon the sparkling flasks and then with a unanimous impulse called wildly for the noble personage who had been circulating among them with a bucket of quite moist water, from which they drank copiously and gratefully without the medium of cups or mugs. They remembered others days—days in Braves' Field in Boston, for instance—when an October breeze played about them and was cursed for its pains. They blushed at the recollection, and vowed if they ever met another breeze they would atone to it for their rudeness to its Boston brother.

At 3 o'clock the crowd was there. It was a solid mass of humanity from the ringside up to the extreme limits of the $25 seats. Beyond that, in the $15 reserved seats and the $10 bleachers, there were comparatively few persons. The fact that the arena was a structure of magnificent distances had helped to keep them away. As a matter of fact, only a pair of keen eyes glued to a pair of field glasses would have been able to distinguish more than a pair of gyrating figures across the hundred yards or so separating those seats from the ring.

The sun made brief but welcome disappearances behind tiny, fleecy clouds as the afternoon drew to the half-way mark, and the little flirting breeze increased the frequency of its overtures. A captive balloon, with its occasional trips overhead, and a pair of capering acrobatic airplanes helped the apathetic gathering to stir to a semblance of interest. The massed thousands thus far were enduring, they were not enjoying. They were there for one purpose only, and they were prepared to gasp, perspire, and suffer until the dawning of the great moment.

DEMPSEY'S RISE LIKE FLASH OF METEOR

New Champion Battled His Way to Pugilistic Fame in Period of Three Years.

WILLARD HIS ANTITHESIS

Probably no championship prize ring battle—certainly none in recent years—has brought together two men more dissimilar in personality, character, or methods of fighting than that at Toledo yesterday, in which Jack Dempsey dethroned Jess Willard as heavyweight champion of the world.

Dempsey's rise to pugilistic fame has been unusually rapid. In a little more than three years he has sprung from obscurity to be the premier pugilist of the world. As a boxer he has attracted attention mainly through his ability to hit effectively. He has not a great amount of cleverness. His advantage has depended on his battering ram punches. He hits with destroying power, as his record of quick and decisive knockouts will attest. Although he lays no particular claim to knowledge of the finer points of the game, he repeatedly and consistently has shown that he is, withal, a cool, heady, and resourceful ring general.

Dempsey was born June 24, 1895, in Salt Lake City. He is of Scotch-Irish extraction, with a touch of Indian blood in his veins, according to Jack Kearns, his manager. This combination argues for a natural fighting instinct, which Dempsey admittedly has.

Dempsey was brought up in the rough ways of the plains. He has lived an out-of-doors life since childhood, and was guided by no particular plan in life until he entered on his ring career. Yielding early to the promptings of a roving disposition, he knocked about the country, until one day he brought up in a gymnasium conducted by Jack Kearns in the West. His boxing activities really began there, and his success since that time he modestly shares with Kearns, who has piloted him through all his battles.

Dempsey a Powerful Hitter.

Dempsey's ring activities were not impressive enough to demand attention in the official record books until the season of 1915-16. The records from then on vividly portray his rapid rise. His blows have laid low nearly all who have faced him, and others who half-heartedly clamored for a meeting with him were deterred by a realization of what might happen if they were to face the heavy-hitting boxer in the ring.

The match which gave Dempsey front rank prominence was the bout in which he disposed of Fred Fulton. Dempsey knocked out the Minnesota title-pretender in the remarkably short space of twenty-three seconds, at Harrison, N. J., July 27, 1918. This victory stirred the boxing world. Praise was heaped on him, and he was heralded by many as the next champion of the class.

Previous to this encounter, Dempsey had knocked out numerous other heavyweights, but none of them had been conceded the prominence accorded to Fulton. Among his victims Dempsey includes the names of Carl Morris, original "White Hope"; Battling Levinsky, Bill Brennan, Bob Devere, Jim Flynn, Dan ("Porky") Flynn, Bob McAllister, Al Norton, Homer Smith, and a host of others.

Through all his ring career, Dempsey has attracted popularity. He is modest, and, with boyish simplicity, refuses to indulge in braggadocio, as have many ring exponents both of the present and the past. His life is an open book. He hides nothing and embellishes nothing. He has a personality which attracts one to him as a model of clean living, and reflects the disposition of a gentleman from head to heels.

Dempsey is a lover of children. He is one of a large family. During his training camp life on Maumee Bay the Utah heavyweight attracted no end of attention and publicity by his play with neighbors' children. He would take them on the beach, to sing and dance with, and have an all-around good time. At Long Branch, where he makes his home while in training for important bouts, he lavishes his fondness for children on the little ones of his boarding mistress.

Willard's Age Camouflaged.

The direct antithesis of Dempsey is Willard. According to boxing records, he was born in Pottawatomie County, Kansas, December 29, 1887. This would make him less than thirty-two years old. But a recent investigation of the age he gave when he applied for a license to marry disclosed that he should now be thirty-seven.

Willard's mother came from Kentucky, and his father from Illinois. From his youth he was attracted to the life of the plains. He followed the calling of a cowboy until he entered his ring career. This happened when he became too heavy for the saddle, for from early manhood he was endowed with a massive physique. To this day Willard likes the outdoors, where he has spent most of his life, and he prefers the quiet of the plains to the noise and bustle of the city. He is a skillful horseman and an expert pistol and rifle shot.

Willard has no great fondness for the boxing game. He has demonstrated this many times since he won the heavyweight title from Jack Johnson in Havana April 5, 1915. He has hated training and everything that training entails. He demonstrated this while preparing for the combat with Dempsey. Many of his critics and friends complained over his very apparent lack of interest in training, and had misgivings as to the outcome of the contest. Willard pursued his own course, however, taking no advice but his own, and mapping his camp life to suit his own tastes.

The Kansan's career contains really but one great bout—his clash with Jack Johnson. It wasn't until 1911 that he gave serious thought to becoming a boxer. The "white hope" clamor at that time awakened in the Kansas giant visions of his own potential ability. His first bout offered little encouragement to his admirers. In fact, he was so awkward that some of his friends deserted him, disgusted. But Willard persevered, shaping his career with the one object in view to obtain a match with Johnson for the heavyweight title. He got his chance and realized his ambition.

Willard was the largest champion in the history of the ring. He is a stickler for home life. He spends most of his time when not on the road with his wife and five children on their farm at Lawrence, Kan. He is reputed to be worth half a million dollars, being the ring's richest champion. All this money he has made since he won the title. He has been successful in oil investments and has realized a handsome income from this source.

NEW YORKERS LOST MUCH ON WILLARD

Made Him a Favorite in the Betting When They Reached Scene of the Battle.

Thousands Won on Freak Bets—Defeated Champion Fooled Followers on His Condition.

Special to The New York Times.

TOLEDO, Ohio, July 4.—Toledo is ringing tonight with the joyous shouts of the host of bettors who cleaned up on Jack Dempsey. While early today there was a rush of Dempsey money which brought the odds to even, the arrival of the big bettors on the special trains which came in about noon swung the betting the other way. The appearance of the Willard money flung the odds back to 5 to 4, and there they remained up to the time of the fight.

In the last two hours before the crowd started out to the arena the betting was brisk, and the race track followers from New York and the Wall Street representatives went down on the champion strong. When the odds were in sight the Dempsey admirers began to bet heavily, and cleaned up with a vengeance.

The happiest crowd, however, is made up of those who made the freak bets. One man who bet $50 to $1,000 that Dempsey would win on a knockout before the fourth round is a person of renown here tonight. He is pointed out in the hotels and on the streets. Others who bet on odds that Willard wouldn't come up in the sixth round also made a killing.

Those who bet $75 to $1,000—and there were many of these bets—that there would be a knockout are happy.

There were wild betting scenes in the jammed lobbies of the hotels and on the streets this morning. No one molested the gamblers, and they worked openly to their hearts' content. Just before the fight started there was some betting at the arena, but this was small compared with other fights, as the bets had already been made.

Dempsey "Hated to Have to Hit Him"; Willard Saw "It Was Useless to Continue"

By JACK DEMPSEY.

I told you I would knock him out in the first round, and to all intents and purposes that is what I did. He took a lot of punishment in the next two rounds, but was so feeble that I hated to have to hit him.

By JESS WILLARD.

In the first round, when Dempsey hit me with a left hook, I tried hard to continue, but I was rapidly losing my strength. My eye was closed at the end of the third round, and I realized that it would be useless for me to continue, as I could hardly see. It is hard to admit defeat, but Dempsey is the hardest puncher I ever faced.

By JACK KEARNS,
(Dempsey's Manager.)

Jack is a real champion. He knocked Willard out twice. They gave us the fight in the first round, then brought us back with the bell, and Jack got him again in the third. Dempsey will be a popular champion.

RUTH WALLOPS OUT HIS 28TH HOME RUN

Terrific Crash Over the Polo Grounds Stands Sets New World's Record.

YANKS SPLIT WITH RED SOX

Lose the First by 4 to 0, but Take the Second Game, 2 to 1, After 13 Innings.

A new world's batting record was made up at the Polo Grounds yesterday, when Babe Ruth, Boston's superlative slugger, boosted his twenty-eighth home run of the season high over the right field grand stand into Manhattan Field, which adjoins the Brush Stadium. This smashes the thirty-five-year-old record made by Ed Williamson of Chicago, who was credited with twenty-seven homers in 1884.

Ruth's glorious smash yesterday was the longest drive ever made at the Polo Grounds. It came in the ninth inning of the second game of a double-header with the Yankees and tied the score at 1 to 1. Bob Shawkey was doing the pitching and he heaved over a slow curve, hoping to fool Ruth as he has done before.

Ruth stood firmly on his sturdy legs like the Colossus of Rhodes, and, taking a mighty swing at the second ball pitched to him, catapulted the pill for a new altitude and distance record. Several seasons ago Joe Jackson hit a home run over the top of the right field stand but the ball landed on the roof. Ruth's bang yesterday cleared the stand by many yards and went over into the weeds in the next lot.

The Boston mauler not long ago made his twenty-sixth home run at the Polo Grounds, smashing the modern home run record made by Buck Freeman. Then it was discovered in the dusty archives of the game that Williamson had made twenty-seven in one season. Ruth's mark now surpasses all home run achievements, ancient or modern. Ruth got a great reception from the crowd of 5,000 or more fans, and throughout the afternoon he was hailed with cheers every time he came up to bat.

Yanks Need Thirteen Innings to Win.

Ruth's homer tied the score, and it wasn't until the thirteenth inning of this second game that the Yanks finally won out by 2 to 1. In the thirteenth, with two out, Wallie Pipp pasted a triple against the front of the bleachers in right field and trotted home with the winning run when Del Pratt boomed a hiih sacrifice fly out to Ruth in left field.

This belated victory gave the Yanks an even break on the day's pastime, for Boston shut out Huggins's men in the first game by a score of 4 to 0. Waite Hoyt, the Brooklyn schoolboy, pitched for the Red Sox in the second and Bob Shawkey officiated for the Yanks. Hoyt gave a remarkable performance of his pitching skill, and from the fourth inning to the thirteenth he did not allow a hit and not a Yankee runner reached first base. In these nine hitless innings the youngster was at the top of his form and pitched with the coolness and skill of a veteran.

Shawkey came through the seething fray with flying colors after one of the hardest battles he ever entered. There were times when the Red Sox had victory within their grasp, only to be baffled at the last moment by Shawkey's wonderful generalship. The menace of Ruth's mighty bat was always a shadow in Shawkey's path. In the sixth inning Ruth shot a mighty blow to right centre field for three bases. It looked like a home run, but Ruth in his anxiety to break the record cut second base by a few feet and was declared out by the watchful umpire Tommy Connolly.

Again in the twelfth inning, Ruth brought the crowd to its feet by thumping a tremendous slam to deep right centre which for a moment looked as if it were going to clear the centre field bleaches. Young Chick Fewster then covered himself with glory by romping back at top speed to snare the ball just as it was geeting away.

Stuffy McInnis to the Fore.

This second game bristled with brilliant fielding, the star of the defensive work being Stuffy McInnis, the Boston first baseman. There were times yesterday when he covered the territory around first base with all the brilliancy of Hal Chase in his hey-day. There was one play which fans will not soon forget. It came in the tenth inning when Duffy Lewis slammed a red hot grounder to short. Scott speared it with his usual skill and made a low, wide throw to first. McInnis reached out as if he were made of India rubber and pinched the ball between his thumb and index finger. There the ball stuck and Lewis was out. The crowd gave McInnis a howling reception when he walked to the bench after that inning.

The Yankees played a listless game in the first affair, and although Sam Jones was so wild that he gave nine bases on balls, the Yanks couldn't harvest a single run. Twice—in the third and in the fourth—they had the bases full and failed to produce a tally. No less than fourteen of the Yanks were left stranded and opportunities to score came so fast that they couldn't keep track of them.

Jack Quinn was also inclined to be wild, and his few passes were costly. Bases on balls figured in both innings in which the Red Sox got their runs. Joe Wilhoit, who used to be with the Giants and before that with the Boston Braves, played in right field in place of Harry Hooper. Wilhoit set the Western League afire in Wichita by batting over .300 and he has come back to the majors to try his hand again. He nailed the first ball that Quinn pitched to left for a Texas Leaguer, but didn't do much after that.

Jack Quinn Tames Ruth in First.

All eyes were on Babe Ruth in this first game but he failed to do anything. Quinn walked him purposely in the first inning and when the home-run king came to bat in the third inning, Quinn struck him out. There was much commotion in the fifth when Babe fanned again. On his fourth trip to the plate Ruth skied to Fewster.

Joe Wilhoit welcomed Quinn in the first inning of the opening game with a Texas Leaguer to left. He sailed along on Vitt's sacrifice and Bill Lamar hoisted one to Fewster. Quinn walked Ruth intentionally and Schang got a pass, filling the bases. McInnis streaked a single to the right field wall, and Wilhoit and Ruth scrambled over the plate. McInnis and Schang then tried to launch a double steal and Schang died in the attempt.

Pipp and Lewis got aboard on singles in the second inning with one out but Fewster and Ruel both died at the hands of Scott. Scotty made a great catch of Ruel's foul over near the boxes back of third. In the third Jones was as wild as a Fiji but the Yanks couldn't take advantage of it. With one out, Vick ambled and went to second on a wild pitch. Peck also got a pass and Baker skied to Wilhoit. Pipp got a pass and the bases were loaded up with dead head passengers. It was up to Del Pratt to clean the corners, but the very nicest that Del could produce was a foul fly to Vitt.

The Red Sox grabbed another brace of tallies in the fourth. McInnis walked and Shannon was safe on Peck's fumble, while Scotty pushed them along with a sacrifice. After Jones fanned, Wilhoit cracked a single to right centre and encouraged McInnis and Shannon over the platter.

Yanks Crowd Bases, Then Quit.

In the Yankees' half of this same inning Jones was still wild, and again the three corners were profusely decorated with New York citizens. Peckinpaugh had a chance to do something for his country, but fell down on the job. With two out in this stanza, Ruel singled and Quinn got a pass. Vick also got a free ticket, and there they were, three of them all ready and willing to race home. Peckinpaugh lofted a foul or two into the stand and then struck out, to the mournful chorus of 5,000 moans.

Peckinpaugh opened the ninth with a single to left and Baker soaked a liner to Shannon, who made a great catch. Shannon tried to double Peck off first and threw the ball into the grand stand. Peck, instead of coming back to touch first, went right on to third but the ball was out of play and Peck had to come back to first. Pipp rocketed to Wilhoit and Jones tossed Pratt out at first and the lifeless affair was ended.

The Yanks showed a little more gumption early in the second game and culled a run in the second inning off Hoyt. Pipp beat out an infield tap between first and second and raced to third on Pratt's single to left, Del going to second on the throw to catch Pipp. Duff Lewis knocked a single to centre, scoring Pipp, while Pratt scooted to third. Fewster was thrown out by Vitt and Ruel hammered a hot liner to McInnis, who tossed to Vitt, and Pratt was doubled before he could get back to third.

The Red Sox nicked Shawkey for three hits in the fifth, but could not get a run. After Peck tossed McNally out at first, McNeil singled to right. Scott singled to left, McNeil halting at second. Hoyt banged a single to centre and filled the bases. Gilhooley cracked a hot grounder to Pipp, who soaked the ball home, forcing McNeil. Oscar Vitt skied to Vick and Shawkey was saved from an embarrassing situation.

The scores:

FIRST GAME.

BOSTON. (A.)	Ab	R	H	Po	A	NEW YORK. (A.)	Ab	R	H	Po	A
Wilhoit,rf	5	1	2	4	0	Vick,rf	3	0	1	1	0
Vitt,3b	4	0	0	1	3	Peck'p'gh,ss	4	0	1	3	3
Lamar,cf	4	0	1	0	0	Baker,3b	5	0	0	6	2
Ruth,lf	3	1	0	0	0	Pipp,1b	3	0	1	11	3
Schang,c	3	0	1	3	0	Lewis,lf	4	0	1	2	0
McInnis,1b	3	1	1	13	0	Pratt,2b	5	0	0	1	3
Shannon,2b	4	1	0	3	4	Fewster,cf	3	0	0	3	0
Scott,ss	3	0	0	2	1	Ruel,c	3	0	1	6	2
Jones,p	3	0	1	1	5	Quinn,p	2	0	0	0	4
						Thorm'len,p	0	0	0	0	0
Total....	32	4	6	27	31	aGleich	0	0	0	0	0
						Total....	32	0	5	27	14

Errors—McInnis, Shannon, Peckinpaugh Pratt.

a Batted for Quinn in eighth.

Boston ....2 0 0 2 0 0 0 0 0—4
New York................0 0 0 0 0 0 0 0 0—0

Stolen base—Fewster, Schang. Sacrifice hit—Scott. Left on bases—New York, 14; Boston, 6. First base on errors—New York, 0; Boston, 2. Bases on balls—Off Quinn, 4; Jones, 9. Hits—Off Quinn, 6 in 8 innings; Thormahlen, 0 in 1. Struck out—By Quinn, 3; Thormahlen, 1; Jones, 3. Wild pitch—Jones. Losing pitcher—Quinn.

SECOND GAME.

NEW YORK. (A.)	Ab	R	H	Po	A	BOSTON. (A.)	Ab	R	H	Po	A
Vick,rf	5	0	0	3	0	Gilhooley,rf	6	0	2	3	0
Peck'p'gh,ss	5	0	1	2	7	Vitt,3b	6	0	1	2	3
Baker,3b	5	0	0	2	1	Lamar,cf	6	0	2	1	0
Pipp,1b	5	2	2	14	2	Ruth,lf	4	1	2	2	0
Pratt,2b	5	0	1	4	5	McInnis,1b	5	0	0	19	2
Lewis,lf	4	0	1	2	0	McNally,2b	5	0	1	1	3
Fewster,cf	4	0	0	5	2	McNeill,c	4	0	2	3	1
Ruel,c	4	0	0	6	2	Scott,ss	5	0	1	2	5
Shawkey,p	4	0	0	1	1	Hoyt,p	5	0	1	1	4
						Schang,c	3	0	1	1	0
Total....	41	2	5	39	20	Total...	49	1	13	*37	18

a Batted for McNeil in eleventh.

*Winning run scored with one out.

Error—Fewster.

New York.....0 1 0 0 0 0 0 0 0 0 0 0 1—2
Boston ....0 0 0 0 0 0 0 0 1 0 0 0 0—1

Two-base hit—Pratt. Three-base hit—Schang. Home run—Ruth. Stolen bases—Gilhooley, Ruth, Scott. Sacrifice fly—Pratt. Double play—McInnis and Vitt. Left on bases—New York, 2; Boston, 13. Bases on balls—Off Shawkey, 4; Hoyt, 6. Struck out—By Shawkey, 4; Hoyt, 3. Wild pitch—Shawkey.

GIANTS-YANKS SERIES OFF.

McGraw Doesn't Think Fans Are Clamorous for Encounter.

The Giants and the Yankees will not play a city series this season. President Charles A. Stoneham of the local National League Club, yesterday sent a letter to President Jacob Ruppert of the Yankees, declining the suggestion made by the owners of the Yankees for a post-season series. Mr. Stoneham stated in his letter that on account of the forced absence of Manager McGraw in Texas, it would not be advisable to play the series. He also stated in his letter that it was the opinion of Manager McGraw that there was no demand on the part of the fans for such a series and added that during the last few weeks the Giants had been experimenting with new players and were in a somewhat disorganized condition.

Another reason why the New York National League Club is not particularly anxious to play is because the players will share in the world's series receipts anyhow and the Yankees will also get a share if they finish in third place in the American League.

WHITE SOX ARE 1919 CHAMPIONS

Win American League Pennant by Victory Over the Browns, 6 to 5.

IN FRONT SINCE JULY 10

Chicago Team Out of Lead Only a Short Time Since Opening Day of Season.

CLEARLY OUTCLASSED FIELD

Gleason Scores Triumph with Players Whom Rowland Led to Victory Two Years Ago.

For the second time within the space of three years, and the fourth time in the nineteen years of American League history, the pennant in the junior major league goes to the Chicago White Sox. By their victory yesterday over the Browns at Chicago, 6 to 5, the peppery players led by Kid Gleason put themselves in a position where they may lose all the remaining games of the season, while the Cleveland Indians, leading contender for the championship, can win all their games without making any change in the relative position of the two clubs.

The White Sox have four more games to play, one with the Browns and three with the Tigers. The Indians have one more game to play with the Tigers and two with the Browns. If the White Sox lose all their remaining games and the Indians win their remaining three, the standing at the end of the season would be:

	W.	L.	P.C.
Chicago	88	52	.629
Cleveland	86	53	.619

Steady and consistent play from the opening days of the season has stamped the Chicago club as the best balanced team in the American League. For a time the Yankees flashed to the front from late June until mid-July, but at no time during the leadership of the Huggins clan was there any indication that the Sox would be distanced. On July 1 the White Sox were 3½ games behind the league leaders and this was the widest gap that separated the Comiskey crowd from the top since the season opened last April. Seldom has a club held the lead for such a great part of the season as the Sox of 1919 have held their lead.

For less than thirty days of the championship campaign which began on April 23 last, the White Sox have been out of first place. Gleason's team won five of its first six games and led the league at the close of the first week. Throughout the entire month of May the advantage was maintained and after the Decoration Day games the Sox held a four-game lead over Cleveland in second place.

During the first eleven days of June Chicago continued to set the pace, and on June 12 the Yankees stepped into the lead, holding first place until June 15, when the Sox regained the position. Gleason's team held undisputed title to first place for three days, or until June 18, when the Indians came on even terms. This tie continued for two days and then the Sox went in front for two more days. On June 22 the Yankees regained first place and held it for a space of seventeen consecutive days, or until July 10. During this period the White Sox dropped to third place, trailing the Indians for a few days, but never were far from the top. Third place was the lowest berth of the White Sox during the year.

On July 10 the Sox passed the Yankees, went into first place and every other club has been taking their dust since that date. Exactly one week after regaining the lead the Chicagoans were four and one-half games ahead of the field and from July 17 to the present time no other club has been within four games of first place. The advantage of the leaders has stretched at times to eight games. First the Comiskey crowd beat down the lead which the Yankees had picked up. Then the Indians began to make considerable noise, but not enough to cause any serious trouble for the leaders. In August the Detroit Tigers made their bid and climbed from a second division berth until they were within four games of first place. Never could the Jennings troupe get any closer to first place. From Aug. 9 to 23 the margin between White Sox and Tigers never exceeded five games, was never less than four. Then the Sox put on a spurt, and soon ran the difference up to eight games over the Indians who took the place after the Tigers had wilted. The difference dwindled to four games before the White Sox settled the championship yesterday.

The players have justified many complimentary things said about them by the critics last Spring. When Gleason brought about the return of Jackson, Felsch, Williams and Lynn, four players whom Comiskey had openly denounced, at the same time adding that none ever would wear a White Sox uniform again, the critics picked the White Sox to win. Practically the same team had outclassed the field in 1917, and the doings in the majors during 1918 were generally discounted. The White Sox, Yankees, Indians and Red Sox were rated as the class of the field and Chicago more than lived up to the predictions. The White Sox of 1919 have played a better brand of ball than the Sox of 1917, and none can say that they won their honors because some other contender was unfortunate.

One Change Since 1917.

The club which Gleason led past the wire a winner yesterday differs but slightly in the regular lineup from the team which Rowland led home first two years ago. The difference is on the left side of the infield. Weaver played shortstop in 1917 and McMullin held down third base, while Risberg was a substitute. This year McMullin is the substitute infielder, Weaver is at third base and Risberg at shortstop. This infield is as strong a combination as that of two seasons back.

The other regulars—Schalk, Gandil, Eddie Collins, Jackson, Felsch, Leibold, and John Collins—are playing the same positions as before. Cicotte is still the star of the pitching force, but he has a new Lieutenant. Claude Williams, a southpaw, has succeeded to the place that Urban Faber held in 1917. Faber has had a poor season and probably will not be seen in the world's series. Kerr, a newcomer in the majors this season, ranks next to Cicotte and Williams. Of the pitchers with the club in 1917 Benz, Wolfgang, and Danforth are gone, and their places are now filled by Bill James, Grover Lowdermilk, and Erskine Mayer.

The White Sox lead the American League in team batting and base running, and will compare favorably from a fielding standpoint with any major league club of years. In teamwork the club also shines, and there is no disputing the fact that the Sox clearly outclassed the other American League pennant chasers in a season when four clubs made bids for the leadership after the season was two months old.

Kid Gleason is the fourth manager to bring a pennant to Chicago's South Side, where the White Sox have made their home since the American League was expanded in the Fall of 1900 into a major organization, with clubs in both East and West. Clark Griffith managed the winners of the 1901 championship, Fielder Jones turned the trick in 1906, Clarence Rowland repeated in 1917, and now Gleason joins the list.

GIANTS DIVIDE TWIN BILL WITH BRAVES

Take Opening Game Easily, 6 to 1, but Suffer 3-2 Defeat in 10-Inning Finale.

BOSTON, Sept. 24.—The Giants got an even break in today's double header with the Braves, winning the first game with ease by the score of 6 to 1, and dropping the second section of the twin bill by the score of 3 to 2 in ten innings. The visitors pounded Dick Rudolph and Al Demaree hard in the opener, and in the second they were next to helpless before Dana Fillingim, only two runners reaching second base after the first inning.

The victory in the first game was the twenty-fourth which Jess Barnes has registered this season, and the ex-Brave hopes to reach the quarter-century mark in the series with the Phillies, which begins at the Polo Grounds on Saturday. Barnes was hit much harder than usual, but he kept the blows so well scattered that he would probably have scored a shut-out but for a fumble by Doyle in the first inning. The error spoiled a chance to make a double play. The Braves collected eight hits from the second inning to the ninth, but could not send another runner over the plate.

The Giants drove Rudolph from the mound in the second inning of the opening game. Ten Giants faced the veteran boxman, and collected six hits and a pass. Then Demaree was sent to the hill, and he was able to keep down the scoring, but could not stop the hitting. The Giants collected sixteen hits off the two home hurlers, Fletcher leading in the assault with four, while George Kelly got three.

Frisch's Fine Base Running.

The Giants put over a run in the first inning. Burns doubled, but was out at third when Young grounded to Pick. Frisch followed with a single, reached third while Young was being retired between third and the plate on Doyle's roller to Rudolph, and then came a double steal by Frisch and Doyle, the former scoring when Ford made a bad return.

The Braves matched this run in their first inning on Christy's single, an error by Doyle on Pick's grounder, and a single by Carroll.

New York put the game beyond the reach of the Braves in the second inning by chalking up three runs. Statz singled and scored on a double by Kelly. The latter reached third when Smith bunted safely and Barnes followed with a double which scored Kelly and put Smith on third. A pass to Burns filled the bases and brought about the retirement of Rudolph, Demaree replacing him. Young grounded to Ford and into a double play, Smith crossing the plate while the double killing was being completed.

The scoring ended in the Giants' fourth inning, when two more runs were pushed over the plate. Barnes opened with a single, Burns lined to Christy. Young walked and was forced at second by Frisch. The ex-collegian stole second and Doyle shot a single to centre which scored Barnes and Frisch.

Hubbell Makes Debut.

Wilbur Hubbell, who worked out with the Giants at Gainesville last Spring and has spent the recent season in the International League, pitched his first game for New York in the closing section of the double header. The youngster gave a fine account of himself, but was unfortunate in being in a game in which the Giants were so completely tamed with the stick. He held the Braves to two runs in nine innings, but this only carried him into an extra session, and the Braves put over the deciding marker in the tenth.

The Giants made an impressive start against Fillingim, but subsided after one good inning. Burns singled to left, Young drew a pass, and Frisch bunted safely, filling the bases. Doyle forced Burns at the plate with a bounder to Fillingim. Cooney went out on a grounder to Holke, both Young and Frisch scoring on the out. It was a fine exhibition of base running by Frisch, who raced in from second on the infield out.

From this time to the end of the game the Giants were tame. Kelly reached second base in the second inning on Powell's error and an infield out, but was left. In the ninth Doyle walked, and Cooney sacrificed him to second. These were the only Giants to reach second base after the first inning. In the third frame Young and Doyle got singles, but Young died stealing before Doyle made his hit, and Larry was forced at second. The Giants got only five hits off Fillingim—two in the first inning, two in the third, and a single by Burns in the eighth.

DODGERS WIN TWO GAMES.

Beat Phillies as Robinson Agrees to Manage Brooklyn Again.

PHILADELPHIA, Sept. 24.—By way of celebrating the announcement that Wilbert Robinson had agreed to manage the Brooklyn club again next season, the Dodgers made a total of twenty-seven hits and eighteen runs while defeating the Phillies in a double header this afternoon. The Robins grabbed the first game by a score of 4 to 1, and romped to an easy victory in the second by 14 to 7.

The Dodgers won the first game by coming from behind in the closing innings. They were being beaten 1 to 0 up to the seventh inning, when the Brooklyn hitsmiths finally got the range of Meadows's curves and bunched their hits in the last three rounds for a total of four runs. Jeff Pfeffer managed to keep the Quaker hits fairly well scattered, except in the second inning, when doubles by Bancroft and Tragesser produced a run.

In the seventh inning the Robins tied up the game. Baird was safe on Luderus's error, stole second and scored on Pfeffer's single. They took the lead in the eighth on Griffith's double and Zach Wheat's single. Two Brooklyn runs were chased over the plate in the ninth when Baird singled, Pfeffer walked, and Olson cracked out a triple.

WORLD RECORD IS SET BY MAN O' WAR

Riddle's Speed Miracle Shatters All Previous Marks for Mile and Three Furlongs.

WINS BELMONT BY A BLOCK

Finishes Half Furlong Before Donnacona in 2:14 1-5, Clipping Former Figures 2 3-5s.

GREAT THRONG IS AMAZED

Experts Who See Flying Heels of Fair Play's Great Son Spurn Distance Dub Him Horse of Ages.

Samuel D. Riddle's marvelous race horse, Man o' War, gave at Belmont Park yesterday what was beyond a doubt the greatest exhibition of speed ever witnessed on any race track when he shattered the world's record for a mile and three furlongs in winning the $10,000 Belmont Stakes, while a crowd of 25,000 sat stunned by the almost unbelievably brilliant performance. The champion did not just clip the mark, but literally shattered it, for he ran the distance in 2:14 1-5, which is two and three-fifths seconds faster than any horse had ever run it before.

The world's record was previously held by Dean Swift, which ran a mile and three furlongs in 2:16 4-5, at Liverpool, England, in 1908. The next lowest mark was made in the running of the Belmont last year when Sir Barton set a new American record for the distance of 2:17 2-5. The Canadian and Australian records do not even closely approach the English and American marks, which stood until yesterday afternoon.

When the figures were posted there was a hum of amazement in the packed stands. Every one had been expecting Man o' War to lower the record made by Sir Barton last year, but no one was quite ready to believe it would be lowered to the extent of several seconds and take the world's mark with it. Not even his owner had thought he would stage such a performance, for he had not sent his colt out with the expectation of making such wonderful time.

Best of All Times and Climes.

The race left no doubt in the minds of all turfmen present that they had seen the greatest horse of this or any other age. Up to this time they had been content to say that he was America's finest product, but after he crossed the line in the Belmont and his time was flashed there were none among the veterans of the turf who could think of a horse that compared with him. It is safe to say that Man o' War is the superhorse of the ages as far as records go back; a horse the like of which will probably never be seen by the present generation of horsemen. Man o' War would seem to typify the final goal of breeders, the perfect race horse, gifted with all the essentials of greatness. The son of Fair Play has set a mark which all horses save himself are likely to shoot at vainly for many years to come.

The Belmont Stakes did not, of course, provide a real contest. No one in the great throng had expected that it would. The public as well as horsemen have given up any idea that any three-year-old in the country can make Man o' War get out of a gallop. It was not a race but an exhibition by a great horse and as such it more than satisfied every one who saw the colt in action. There is pleasure enough for those present in the thought that they have seen the world's greatest race horse and moreover have been witnesses of his record-making performance. Man o' War finds himself in the position of Alexander of yore, seeking new worlds to conquer, and as there are no horses of his age to race with him he has only the reduction of records for various distances as a stimulus.

David Harum Is Withdrawn.

It was the original intention to send two horses against the Fair Play colt in the Belmont Stakes, but W. R. Coe's David Harum was withdrawn and only G. W. Loft's Donnacona was left to act as a running mate. Donnacona is a high class colt, one of the best of his age and it is something of a measure of the greatness of Man o' War that Donnacona finished a sixteenth of a mile back of the winner though doing his best to the end.

There was scarcely any speculation on the race. Man o' War was quoted at the prohibitive odds of 1 to 20, as against 12 to 1 for the Loft colt. Practically the only wagers made were by persons who wanted, for the sake of sentiment, to say that they had made a bet on Man o' War.

The start for the Belmont is made from a chute which leads across the straightaway track into the training track. From this latter the horses turn into the main track at the turn which leads to the stretch.

As the barrier went up Man o' War popped to the front and Jockey Clarence Kummer, wearing his gold stirrups again, let the Fair Play colt run with a fine flight of speed from the beginning. Man o' War never waits for a pace maker. His habit of running races is to go to the front and bid his rivals to come on and catch him.

Through the training track course Man o' War maintained a lead of about two lengths, and was still under restraint, while Donnaconna was moving along at a fast clip and apparently had something left. As the horses reached that point where they turned into the main track Donnaconna moved up resolutely until he closed the gap of daylight which had appeared between the horses since the start. From the stands it appeared that he was right at the heels of the champion, and the Loft horse was moving with fine speed.

Flashes Away from Rival.

Kummer looked back and, seeing Donnacona, he gave Man o'War his head. The son of Fair Play developed a new rate of speed in half a dozen strides. He began to move away from his rival as though the latter was anchored. At the turn into the stretch Man o' War was four lengths in front, and he had not yet been permittd to run as it was quite evident he wished to. When Man o' War reached the stretch the crowd began to yell to Kummer to let him run, for it was the desire of every one to see anew record made. Kummer did as they desired. Instead of taking a pull on his mount, as he had done in his previous race, he let Man o' War step along all through the

Continued on Page Three.

Riddle Refuses an Offer of $260,000 for Man o' War

Just a short time before Man o' War stepped out on the track at Belmont Park yesterday to shatter the world's record for a mile and three furlongs, his owner, Samuel D. Riddle of Philadelphia, refused an offer of $260,000 for this great colt. In doing so he was not seeking to establish a price for Man o' War, for he declared emphatically that he would not set a sum on this son of Fair Play. As far as the Philadelphia sportsman is concerned, no amount of money could buy his prize racer, which he intends to retire to the stud after the 1921 season. The offer was made by Joseph L. Murphy, also of Philadelphia.

UPSET WINS DERBY BY NECK IN DRIVE

Whitney's Fleet Three-Year-Old Captures Rich Latonia in Duel with Gladiator.

LOUISVILLE, Ky., June 11.—Harry Payne Whitney's Upset, one of the best of the three-year-olds owned by the New York sportsman, captured the $15,000 Latonia Derby over a route of a mile and a half at Latonia this afternoon in a stirring finish with the Redstone Stable's Gladiator. Upset won by only a neck after a hard drive through the final furlong. Montfort Jones's Ethel Gray was third, three lengths back of the second horse. There were eight starters, three of the original number named, including Paul Jones, winner of the Kentucky Derby and the Suburban, being withdrawn. The time for the race was 2:32. The record is 2:30 2-5, held by Governor Gray and John Gund.

It was a remarkably well-contested race, and Upset had to be hustled along at times to win. He was very cleverly handled by Jockey Rodriguez, who saved much ground at the turns and kept in a contending position throughout. Gladiator, on the other hand, seemed to be bothered by the turns and repeatedly lost ground, but closed with such a rush that he was rapidly gaining on the winner as he neared the finish line.

Ethel Gray Shows Stamina.

Gladiator gave a remarkably fine exhibition of both speed and endurance and was easily the best of all the others. Ethel Gray lasted better than it was thought she would and easily took the measure of a number of the colts which left the barrier with her.

The victory was worth $16,300 to the winner, while $2,000 went to the second horse and $800 to the third.

R. F. Folson's fleet Peace Pennant set a fast pace after he left the barrier to take the lead. For a mile he seemed to have all the speed, and with his stablemate, Rouleau, he did his best as far as he could go. In the meantime Upset was running third, with Rodriguez hugging the rail at the turns and taking every advantage he could for his mount. Gladiator was close on the heels of the Whitney horse for half a mile, but he went slightly wide at the turns and was in fifth position when he neared the turn into the stretch.

By this time Peace Pennant and Rouleau had retired and Upset was leading. The Whitney colt bore out a trifle at the last turn, where he experienced his only bit of adverse luck. But he straightened out in the lead. Gladiator began to move up with a rush in the stretch and Rodriguez had to put Upset to a hard drive to win.

Gladiator's Great Finish.

The Whitney colt stood the drive gamely, gave up his best, and just lasted. Gladiator made such an impressive finish that it was the opinion of some he might have won but for the ground lost at the turns earlier in the race. He at least proved that he is a colt of greater promise than was generally believed.

There was some regret that Ral Parr's Paul Jones did not start, as this would have been a test of his ability over a fast track. While there is been no question of his ability, there is a desire to see him run over a fast track against the same kind of horses he has defeated in the mud. Both of his big victories this year were scored in the mud. Paul Jones was too lame to start today, and his trainer, William Garth, announced his withdrawal early in the day. Kinburn and Sterling were the others that were scratched.

The summaries:

FIRST RACE—Purse $1,200; two-year-old maiden fillies; five furlongs. Julia N., 115 pounds (Lunsford), $4.60, $2.50, $2.50, first; Present, 115 (Robinson), $2.80, $2.70, second; Mary Gaffney, 115 (Wida), $11.20, third. Time—1:01 3-5. Romper, Mary C., Majorie McKay, Millersburg, Sahara, Zade, Alberta S., Horkyte and Cozette also ran.

SECOND RACE—Purse $1,200; claiming; three-year-olds and upward; six furlongs. Green Grass, 115 pounds (Pool), $51.30, $8.90, $3, first; Bullion, 115 (Morrissey), $2.90, $2.20, second; Jack Hare, Jr., 110 (Wilson), $2.20, third. Time—1:13 3-5. Rapid Stride, Basil and B. B. Johnson also ran.

THIRD RACE—Purse $2,000; Paulin Handicap; three-year-olds and upward; one mile and a sixteenth. Drastic, 105 pounds (Pool), $6, $4.40, $2.60, first; Baigneur, 102 (Wida), $4.40, $3, second; Minto II., 102 (Wida), $4.30, third. Time—2:32. Rouleau, Courtship and Breeze also ran.

FOURTH RACE—Purse $1,600; two-year-olds; colts and geldings; five furlongs. Brunswick, 108 pounds (Garner), $6.30, $3.70, $2.60, first; Greenland, 108 (Rodriguez), $5.20, $2.80, second; Eastside, 113 (Lunsford), $2.40, third. Time—1:00 2-5. Some Baby, Redlegs and Runzaf also ran.

FIFTH RACE—The Latonia Derby; for three-year-olds; $15,000 added; one mile and a half. Upset 126 pounds (Rodriguez), $3.30, $2.80, $2.40, first; Gladiator 126 (Johnson), $4.20, $3.60, second; Ethel Gray 112 (Lunsford), $4.30, third. Time—2:32. Douleau, Captain Mac, Peace Pennant, Prince Pal and Make Up also ran.

SIXTH RACE—Metropolitan Handicap; for three-year-olds and upward; purse $1,800; six furlongs. Westwood 101 pounds (Garner), $18.90, $6.70, $5.10, first; Marjorie Hynes 102 (Kererls), $4.20, $3.10, second; Blue Paradise 101 (Wida), $4, third. Time—1:12 2-5. Jorice, Lady Fairplay, Colonel Taylor, Marie Miller, Tacola also ran.

SEVENTH RACE—For four-year-olds and upward; claiming; purse $1,200; one mile and three-sixteenths. Star Realm 104 pounds (Hunt), $7, $3.70, $2.40, first; Sun God 109 (Carmody), $3.20, $2.20, second; Lazy Lou 104 (Wida), $2.20, third. Time—1:58 4-5. Sir John Vergne and Bourbon Green also ran.

Weather clear; track fast.

BECKETT TO MEET BURNS.

Articles Signed for Match in Albert Hall, London, on July 16.

LONDON, June 12.—Joe Beckett, heavyweight champion of England, and Tommy Burns, the French Canadian pugilist, will box twenty rounds at Albert Hall on July 16. Articles for the match were signed by the two men today.

Burns will put in two weeks' training at Hampstead Heath and then go to Bournemouth for a short time.

Pentathlon Winner Track Captain.

LAWRENCE, Kan., June 12.—Everett L. Bradley, winner of the pentathlon at the Penn relay games, has been elected Captain of the track team of Kansas University for 1921. Bradley is a sophomore in the university.

FAST SPURT WINS MILE FOR CURTIS

Midshipman Furnishes Sensation at N. Y. A. C. Games by Spectacular Victory.

MEREDITH FAILS IN 440

Former Star Not Able to Qualify in Trial Heat—Besgeir Takes Quarter Mile.

The fastest mile race that has been recorded on the famous old cinder path in several years was yesterday furnished by William Curtis, a tall, lithe midshipman who carried the United States Naval Academy's emblem to victory in the mile handicap run, one of the stellar attractions at the one hundred and fourth games of the New York Athletic Club, held at Travers Island. The Annapolis student, who has been a consistent performer in the dual meets in which the midshipmen have participated this season, started from scratch, and with a wonderful burst of speed over the last half lap showed the way to the tape in 4:21.

Curtis was making his début as a prize seeker in open A. A. U. competition, and from start to finish he ran a spectacular race, which had a crowd of about 6,000 cheering madly. The midshipman numbered among his victims the redoubtable Mike Devaney of the Millrose A. A. and Bob Crawford, sensational Lafayette College miler, both of whom started with him from the back mark. Pat Flynn, Celtic runner of the Paulist A. C., finished second, about fifteen yards back of the navy runner, and Devaney was third, five yards in the rear of the Winged F wearer. Crawford failed to approach the first three.

The naval student made all his running in the closing lap. Flynn, in receipt of forty-five yards, made most of the early pace for a field which numbered twenty-three starters and right up to the bell lap he appeared to have an excellent chance of winning. With the bell sounding the start of the closing eclipse, however, Curtis raced like a scared rabbit, with Devaney following gamely as the midshipman started to cut down on his rivals in front. Round the first turn of the closing lap Curtis raced, picking up ground with every stride, with Devaney five yards back of him. Entering the backstretch the midshipman overhauled Flynn and for a time they raced shoulder to shoulder.

Navy Man Draws Away.

Flynn, however, did not possess the necessary strength to hold the flying Curtis and as the turn was made into the homestretch the naval student gradually began to open up a winning lead. Devaney here began to weaken and as Curtis shot away in a burst of speed the crowd sent up a din which carried out to the Sound. Flynn gave chase with every bit of his remaining strength, but Curtis continued to the tape without slackening speed and at the finish had worked up a lead of fifteen yards.

The race was but one installment of an attractive series of competitions, which drew a crowd of 6,000 to the historic Travers Island athletic field. Surrounding the field on three sides the spectators made a picturesque scene. Fashionably gowned girls and women were conspicuously in evidence as in pre-war days when the annual Spring games were a fixture in the lives of Mercury Foot members. The weather was favorable, although there were early fears that rain would again interfere with this meet, originally scheduled for last Saturday. Old Sol in all his radiance shone down on the picturesque scene from end to end of the program, however, and lent his aid in making the affair one of the most successful ever conducted by the New York A. C.

Particular interest centred about the comeback effort of James E. (Ted) Meredith, former University of Pennsylvania middle-distance crack, and a hero of the last Olympic games at Stockholm in 1912. Meredith, out of competition for several years, made the quarter-mile handicap run the medium for his return to competition for the purpose of seeking a berth on the Olympic team this Summer. The redoubtable Ted, however, did not quite measure up to the task of retrieving handicaps allotted against him, and failed to qualify in the trial heats.

Meredith Weakens in Stretch.

Meredith was the scratch starter with James W. (Jake) Driscoll, Boston runner, who sported the emblem of the U. S. Navy, in the two-furlong race. The former Red and Blue wearer showed traces of his once famous form in the early stages of the heat, but in the dash down the homestretch Meredith weakened perceptibly and was shut out of the qualification places by Harold Finley, a Mercury Foot wearer, who was allowed a start of nine yards. Driscoll won the heat from the honor mark in 50 2-5 seconds, and was trailed by R. Besgeir of the Glencoe A. C., who was allowed a start of 13 yards.

Andy B. Kelly of the New York A. C., former Holy Cross College star and 300-yard record holder, was another veteran to start in this race. Kelly managed to qualify in the first trial heat, finishing third, back of James M. Roche, New Haven, Harriers, and C. D. Rogers, Meadowbrook Club, Philadelphia.

In the final Besgeir made good use of his handicap allowance and managed to break the tape a winner despite a determined spurt by Roche. Besgeir led by less than a yard in 50 seconds. Driscoll carried off third position, close on the heels of Roche.

The most spectacular victory of the day came in the half-mile run, in which Bob Crawford literally threw himself to an eyelash victory over Allan B. Helffrich, New York A. C. runner. Tommy Campbell, Yale runner, finished third. The time for the test was 1:56 2-5.

Large Field in Half-Mile.

A field of forty runners answered the call for this race and made a dense pack through which the scratch men, Crawford, Campbell, Homer Baker, of the Glencoe A. C., and Jack Sellers of the New York A. C. could make no progress until the last lap. Helffrich, who was allowed eighteen yards, was a contender over the greater part of the distance and carried the field around at a good pace. The scratch starters sought time and again to get through the thickly bunched field, but without success until the last turn before the home stretch, when Crawford's strong, sturdy legs carried him to almost even terms with Helffrich. A few strides down the straightaway to the worsted and the runners were running as a team, Helffrich fighting doggedly to retain the lead while Crawford fought with all that was in him to displace his rival. Right up to the finish line the two battled for supremacy, Crawford just managing to throw himself over the line a victor. Baker finished fourth, seven yards back of Campbell, while Sellers was fifth, five yards back of Baker.

Loren Murchison, the crack New York A. C. sprinter, flashed a brilliant burst of speed carrying off the 100-yard dash against a formidable field. Murchison went through the qualifying and semi-final heats with flying colors and in the final test thrilled the crowd with a century in ten seconds flat. Young Bernie Wefers followed his clubmate over the line and Harry Appel was third.

Ivan C. Dresser of the New York A. C., former intercollegiate two-mile and cross-country champion, gave an impressive demonstration of form in capturing the three-mile run from scratch against a field of eleven rivals. Dresser contented himself with following the pace set alternately by Frank Titterton, Glencoe, A. C.; Jack Costello and Al

Continued on Page Three.

American Olympic Committee Revises Dates for More Than Twenty Tryouts

With trials, both sectional and final, in track and field athletics, boxing, wrestling, swimming, cycling and numerous other contests which are included in the program for the seventh Olympic Games at Antwerp, Belgium, this Summer, athletes in all sections of the country will soon enter upon an intensive period of competitive preparation for the international classic.

The revised schedule of tryouts, as announced yesterday by Frederick W. Rubien, Secretary to the American Olympic Committee, shows more than twenty elimination competitions scheduled for various parts of the country, from coast to coast, and from the Canadian border to the Gulf.

The schedule of dates and places follows:

June 1-15—Preliminary pistol tryout in 100 shooting centres.
June 13—Buffalo, N. Y., cycle road race.
June 13—Cycling eliminations.
June 20—New York cycling road race.
June 21-23—Final pistol tryouts, Quantico, Va.
June 26—Track and field tryouts: Eastern, Franklin Field, Philadelphia; Central, Stagg Field, Chicago; Coast, Pasadena, Cal.; Southern, New Orleans, La.
June 26-27—Swimming tryouts, men and women: Pacific Coast, San Francisco, Neptune Beach.
July 1-2—Wrestling and boxing tryouts: Coast, Portland.
June 28, 29, 30, July 1—Boxing tryouts, Metropolitan Association.
Not Fixed—Wrestling tryouts: Southern, Birmingham, Ala.
Not Fixed—Boxing tryouts: Southern, Atlanta.
July 1—Final cycling eliminations.
July 2-3—Army finals, track, swimming, wrestling and boxing, at St. Louis.
July 4—Final pentathlon tryouts, Brooklyn.
July 5—Tug-of-war final tryouts in conjunction with army finals, at St. Louis.
July 6-7—Wrestling tryouts: Middle West, Gary, Ind.
Not Fixed—Boxing tryouts: Middle West, Pittsburgh.
July 8—Modern pentathlon tryouts, West Point, N. Y.
July 9-10—Final tryouts steeplechase, decathlon and 10,000-metre walk, N. Y. A. C.
July 10-11—Final swimming tryouts, men, Chicago.
July 10-14—Final swimming tryouts, women, Manhattan Beach, N. Y.
*July 12-13—Final boxing tryouts, New York.
July 17—Final tryouts, track and field, national A. A. U. championships, Harvard Stadium, Cambridge, Mass. (July 16, junior A. A. U. championships).
July 23-24—Final rowing tryouts and N. A. A. O. championships, Worcester, Mass.
July 28—Final gymnastic tryouts, New York.
*July 28-29—Final wrestling tryouts, New York.
*Dates not definite.

PUBLIC SCHOOL 10 WINS TRACK TITLE

Leads Large Field in Struggle for P. S. A. L. Elementary Championship.

Athletes of Public School 10, Manhattan, carried off the elementary schools track and field championship title in the annual struggle under the auspices of the Public Schools Athletic League at Brooklyn Athletic Field yesterday. The youngsters representing this school accounted for the winning total of 33 points, a margin of eight in excess of the total compiled by the representatives of Public School 14, Manhattan, to which institution the title has fallen in the two previous annual meets.

Public School 40, Manhattan, finished third with 23 tallies; P. S. 184, Manhattan, fourth, with 19, P. S. 37, Bronx, fifth, with 16; P. S. 10, Bronx, sixth, with 12; P. S. 27, Manhattan, seventh, with 10, and P. S. 128, Brooklyn, eighth, with 9.

One record went by the boards in the course of the title struggle. In the half-mile relay, unlimited weight class, Public School 27's fast traveling quartet clipped three seconds off the P. S. A. L. mark, which has stood since 1906. The "27" youngsters negotiated the distance in 1:45, against the old record of 1:48. The victorious quartet led throughout the race, but was hard pressed by the P. S. 40 team, which finished second. P. S. 10 carried off third laurels and P. S. 184 was fourth.

The summaries:

Track Events.

40-Yard Dash, 75-Pound Class—Won by J. Unger, P. S. 184, Manhattan; V. Petibone, P. S. 40, Manhattan, second; R. Young, P. S. 50, Brooklyn, third; F. Christenfeld, P. S. 16, Brooklyn, fourth. Time—0:06.

50-Yard Dash, 85-Pound Class—Won by J. Roberts, P. S. 10, Manhattan; M. Felix, P. S. 62, Manhattan, second; R. Krivohlavy, P. S. 70, Manhattan, third; L. Novick, P. S. 10, Manhattan, fourth. Time—0:07 1-5.

60-Yard Dash, 100-Pound Class—Won by S. Hetietze, P. S. 61, Manhattan; L. Kaufman, P. S. 37, Bronx, second; P. Recein, P. S. 43, Brooklyn, third; F. Tempro, P. S. 184, Manhattan, fourth. Time—0:07 4-5.

70-Yard Dash, 115-Pound Class—Won by W. Fine, P. S. 171, Manhattan; G. Sarna, P. S. 10, Manhattan, second; J. Henry, P. S. 5, Manhattan, third; N. Williams, P. S. 69, Manhattan, fourth. Time—0:08 4-5.

100-Yard Dash, Unlimited Weight Class—Won by R. Kimbrough, P. S. 69, Manhattan; J. Gallagher, P. S. 10, Manhattan, second; C. Andeill, P. S. 10, Bronx, third; R. Carlier, P. S. 127, Brooklyn, fourth. Time—0:11 4-5.

Relay Races.

220-Yard Relay, 70-Pound Class—Won by P. S. 27, Manhattan (Healy, Kinde, Finlayson and Kimble); P. S. 10, Bronx (Petrol, Ginsberg, Lauren and Briskman), second; P. S. 40, Manhattan (M. Dubner, Strotz, C. Lahara and F. Vaiveri), third; P. S. 19, Manhattan (Silver, Fletcher, Gottadanker and Fineglass), fourth. Time—0:30 2-5.

360-Yard Relay, 85-Pound Class—Won by P. S. 40, Manhattan (Perillo, Farbman, Hackl and Riccobono); P. S. 62, Manhattan (W. Applebaum, Glitter, Charkes and Scheine), second; P. S. 184, Manhattan (Hare, Cohen, Marcus and Harris), third; P. S. 82, Manhattan (E. Smola, E. Holecek, J. Kilian and J. Kovatsky), fourth. Time—0:45 2-5.

440-Yard Relay, 100-Pound Class—Won by P. S. 62, Manhattan (Sandack, Slobotsky, Klein and Hecht); P. S. 10, Manhattan (Moskowitz, Ablacott, Silberstein and Carr), second; P. S. 184, Manhattan (Cantor, Goldberg, Peterfreund and Eisenberg), third; P. S. 25, Manhattan (J. Hirsh, H. Goldberg, J. Drummond and J. Dahl), fourth. Time—0:54.

440-Yard Relay, 115-Pound Class—Won by P. S. 184, Manhattan (Unger, Peskin, Lehrman and Modesky); P. S. 40, Manhattan (F. Kushnick, D. Rosa, J. Della and A. Romer), second; P. S. 10, Manhattan (Steingold, Romaine, Losquadro and Langdon); third; P. S. 89, Brooklyn (Kumansky, Schwartz, Rubin and Pelter), fourth. Time—0:52 4-5.

880-Yard Relay, Unlimited Weight Class—Won by P. S. 27, Manhattan (Gordon, Burrose, Marchini and Harrison); P. S. 40, Manhattan (Miraglia, Gambordella, Balducci and Egelhofer), second; P. S. 10, Bronx (Bruno, Haas, Mussbaum and Weiner), third; P. S. 184, Manhattan (Skurnick, Lenenger, Napoli and Sultan), fourth. Time—1:45. (New Record.)

Field Events.

Running High Jump (85-pound Class)—Won by R. Johnson, P. S. 128, Brooklyn, with 4 feet 3 inches; L. Morgenstern, P. S. 20, Manhattan, 4 feet 2½ inches, second; M. Eiman, P. S. 10, Manhattan, 4 feet 2 inches, third; E. Doorak, P. S. 82, Manhattan, 4 feet 1 inch, fourth.

Running Broad Jump (100-pound Class)—Won by S. Goldstein, P. S. 62, Manhattan, with 16 feet 6 inches; E. Homa, P. S. 89, Brooklyn, 15 feet 10 inches, second; G. De Stasio, P. S. 37, Bronx, 15 feet 8 inches, third; M. Johnson, P. S. 184, Manhattan, 15 feet 6 inches, fourth.

Running High ump (100-pound Class)—Won by L. Morasco, P. S. 40, Manhattan, with 4 feet 1 0inches; J. O'Connor, P. S. 37, Bronx, 4 feet 10 inches, second; William Cox, P. S. 160, Brooklyn, 4 feet 9 inches, third; S. Port, P. S. 10, Manhattan, 4 feet 8 inches, fourth. (Morosco outjumped O'Connor on jump-off).

Putting 8-pound Shot (115-pound Class)—Won by N. Ercolano, P. S. 10, Bronx, with 35 feet 4 inches; C. Azzara, P. S. 128, Brooklyn, 31 feet 8 inches, second; V. Bulgalski, P. S. 40, Manhattan, 31 feet 2 inches, third; S. Mehler, P. S. 37, Bronx, 30 feet 11½ inches, fourth.

Running Broad ump (115-pound Class)—Won by F. Care, P. S. 37, Bronx, with 16 feet 3¼ inches; H. Cohen, P. S. 62, Manhattan, 15 feet 9 inches, second; L. Cohen, P. S. 184, Manhattan, 15 feet 1¼ inches, third; R. Hellerman, P. S. 128, Brooklyn, 14 feet 5 inches, fourth.

Running Broad Jump, 85-Pound Class—Won by W. Linton, P. S. 152, Brooklyn, with 15 feet 8 inches; C. Lenitsky, P. S. 40, Bronx, 15 feet 6½ inches, second; H. Mathies, P. S. 37, Bronx, 14 feet 11 inches, third; M. Rubin, P. S. 52, Bronx, 14 feet 9 inches, fourth.

Putting Eight-Pound Shot, Unlimited Weight Class—Won by H. Rosen, P. S. 10, Manhattan, with 41 feet 5 inches; R. Bury, P. S. 72, Queens, 41 feet, second; M. Siegel, P. S. 55, Bronx, 38 feet 11 inches, third; J. Goldstein, P. S. 66, Brooklyn, 37 feet 7½ inches, fourth.

Running High Jump, Unlimited Weight Class—Won by L. Simon, P. S. 10, Manhattan, with 5 feet 2 inches; H. Pionet, P. S. 10, Manhattan, 5 feet 1 inch, second; W. Rennie, P. S. 127, Brooklyn, 5 feet ½ inch, third; J. Spigler, P. S. 167, Brooklyn, 5 feet, fourth.

Point Score.

P. S. 10, Manhattan, 33 points; P. S. 62, Manhattan, 25; P. S. 40, Manhattan, 23; P. S. 184, Manhattan, 19; P. S. 37, Bronx, 16; P. S. 10, Bronx, 12; P. S. 27, Manhattan, 10; P. S. 128, Brooklyn, 9.

MISS WAGNER AND MISS CASSEL WIN

Capture Women's State Tennis Doubles Championship in Hard-Fought Match.

Miss Marie Wagner and Miss Clare Cassel yesterday won the women's tennis doubles championship of New York State, defeating Miss Margaret Grove and Mrs. L. G. Morris on the clay courts of the New York Tennis Club in as close a final as has ever been played in a women's event, the sets going at 6—3, 4—6, 14—12. The completion of the singles, in which Miss Wagner meets Miss Grove for the title, was indefinitely postponed after a series of misunderstandings and much argument on the part of the committee and the players. It is hoped that the disagreement will be finally settled some time during the coming week.

Under the circumstances, the three-set match in which Miss Wagner and Miss Cassel acquired their title was far from an afternoon tea party. All four contestants played with something more than the mere enjoyment of the game in mind, and it must be confessed that Miss Grove, on the losing side, easily carried off the honors of the day. She covered a tremendous lot of ground, generally leaving her partner at the net, and taking care of everything that came past or over her. Her strokes were good and her judgment was even better. She knew when to lob and when to drive, and as often as she got close to the net herself her volleying was good for a point.

Neither Miss Wagner nor Miss Cassel seemed up to form, the latter showing a distinct lack of practice and hitting far more softly and safely than is her custom, while the former single champion indicated an uncertainty of the outcome, which frequently affected her usually dependable shots. Mrs. Morris stuck to her habitual net-play, and did some splendid volleying, anticipating her opponents' shots with rare judgment. But in the pinches she did not always have the finality to her kills that would have settled the rallies, and this slight weakness may have cost her side the match.

The losers were within one point of victory no less than five times in the rubber. Leading at 8—7, with Miss Wagner serving, they had the score at 0—40 in their favor, but three attempts failed to finish the argument, and two vantage points after deuce had been called were cancelled in similar fashion. Again at 11—10 only two points were needed by Miss Grove and her partner to bring a well-deserved victory, but once more the fighting spirit of their rivals, combined with their own over-anxiety to score, averted a decision.

At 12—11 the losers were ahead for the last time, and after the games had been squared on service, Miss Wagner and Miss Cassel broke through for the odd and finished up at 14—12 on their own delivery.

TENNIS FIXTURES AT HAND.

Several Important Tournaments on This Week's List.

The coming week will be an exceedingly active one in tennis circles, with every day devoted to important tournaments both in the metropolitan district and elsewhere. Tomorrow afternoon, at the Orange Lawn Tennis Club, Mountain Station, N. J., play begins in the New York State championship, on turf, with a simultaneous event on clay for the women's New Jersey title. Ichiya Kumagae is the present New York State champion, having won the McLoughlin Challenge Cup outright at Utica last season. He will be entered again at South Orange, with a number of worthy contenders to challenge him for his title. Entries closed with Allen C. Bragaw last Friday, and with Mrs. David C. Mills for the women's event. George Miles is the official referee of the tournament.

At the New Haven Lawn Club, another open tourney begins tomorrow, and here also the entry list promises to be unusually strong. Most of the leading players of New England will take part, with some contestants also from the Metropolitan District.

More distant tournaments that run through the week include the Pennsylvania State championship at the Merion Cricket Club, Philadelphia; the Maryland championship at Baltimore, the Southern championship and sectional doubles at New Orleans and the women's championship of Rhode Island at the Agawam Hunt Club, Providence.

On Thursday, June 17, the Massachusetts singles will open at the Longwood Cricket Club, Boston, and the Southern California Handicap Tournament is scheduled for the same day at Los Angeles. Next Saturday marks the opening of the Metropolitan singles and doubles championships at the New York Tennis Club, titles at present held by S. Howard Voshell and Vincent Richards and Allen Behr respectively. There will also be the annual Husbands and Wives tournament, under the direction of Miss Marie Wagner. Entries for the Metropolitan singles will close with A. J. Ostendorf, Chairman of the committee, on Thursday, June 17. Bird W. Stair is the official referee of the tournament.

MISS ZINDERSTEIN WINS.

Beats Miss Townsend for Delaware Women's Tennis Title.

WILMINGTON, Del., June 12.—Miss Marion H. Zinderstein, Boston, won the women's lawn tennis championship of Delaware by defeating Miss Ann B. Townsend, Philadelphia, in the challenge round here today, 6—1, 7—5. The winner played brilliantly. Her service and cross court shots stood out conspicuously.

Antipodes to Send Scullers.

Hadfield will represent New Zealand and Baynes Australia in the single sculling races at Brussels in the Olympic regatta.

JERSEY TITLE GOES TO THROCKMORTON

Champion Retains State Tennis Premiership by Beating Botsford, 6-3, 6-2, 6-4.

WINS BY SUPERIOR SPEED

Pace and Variety of Holder's Shots Puzzle Challenger — Letson and Anderson Advance in Doubles.

Harold Throckmorton successfully defended his title of tennis champion of New Jersey on the clay courts of the Montclair Athletic Club yesterday afternoon, defeating Willard Botsford in the final round of the singles in straight sets by 6—3, 6—2, 6—4. Two matches were played in the doubles, filling the remaining semi-final brackets. Ben Letson and Fred C. Anderson scored in unexpectedly decisive style over the former Manhattan champions, Alrick H. Man, Jr., and Cedric Major, while Gerald Emerson and Willard Botsford, after winning the opening set lost a hard-fought struggle to Alfred D. Hammett and Embree H. Henderson of the University Heights Club. Those already in the semi-finals are Throckmorton and Kumagae and the Vandeventer brothers and these teams will appear with yesterday's winners in the finish of the event this afternoon, beginning at 2:30.

The singles final was somewhat disappointing, as Botsford, after his hard matches of the earlier rounds, most of which had gone to three sets, seemed to lack the necessary agility and energy to cope with the champion's dazzlingly fast game. The loser often appeared anchored in midcourt, while Throckmorton shot clean placements past him, both from deep court and from the net position.

Whether or not he was weary from his previous efforts, and particularly from the grueling semi-final against Alrick Man, Jr., it was evident that Throckmorton's speed of stroke and foot was far too great for the challenger. Botsford had defeated softer games by his own steadiness and accuracy, and by comparison with such players as Kashio, for example, his hitting seemed sufficiently severe.

Speed and Versatility Win.

But Throckmorton yesterday flashed a brand of tennis that was far in advance of anything that Botsford has faced since he played Kumagae in the Chevy Chase tournament, and while the Japanese star has a rifle-shot forehand drive, his volleying game is still negligible. It was versatility of shots as well as consistent speed and pace that beat the English youngster yesterday.

Throckmorton's game was going so well that he could afford to take chances, and as a result he often scored in more brilliant style than was absolutely necessary, frequently ignoring the more obvious shots for the sake of trying experiments which in a closer match might have proved dangerous.

In the long run, however, his reckless hitting won its reward, for in the pinches the title-holder always had an irresistible shot under control, whereas Botsford's efforts in the crucial rallies were largely defensive. Throckmorton also had a powerful weapon in service, which proved exceedingly effective all through the match. His total of clean aces was unusually large, and only three times in the entire three sets did he fail to win on his delivery.

At the very outset Throckmorton gave a spectacular display of service, rushing through the opening game with four straight points to his credit. The next was a terrific deuce session, which Botsford barely managed to win after a total of eighteen rallies had been played. The champion again won easily on service, but Botsford this time equalized almost as decisively.

With a lead of 3—2 on his own infallible delivery, Throckmorton put the set on ice by breaking through in a deuce game, but seemed to lose his advantage when Botsford returned the compliment, playing the cannon-ball offerings with confidence for the first time in the set.

Throckmorton, however, increased his speed, and, after another deuce game, succeeded in increasing his lead to 5—3. He had difficulty in putting away the set on his own service, but after two more calls of deuce emerged victorious at 6—3.

Starts with Love Game.

Botsford began the second set impressively by serving a love game and holding his rival close on the second game. After that, however, he went rather to pieces, losing his delivery with bad errors twice in succession and eventually trailing at 1—5. He won his service by a belated effort, but Throckmorton cleaned up at 6—2 with the loss of only one more point.

The champion kept up his overwhelming speed through the first three games of the final set, twice breaking through Botsford's service. He lost his own, however, and the challenger pulled up to within a game of him at 3—2. Service made it 4—2 for Throckmorton, and after Botsford had reciprocated he made a last effort for a set by breaking through again and tying up the games at 4 all.

Throckmorton, however, dashed the youngster's hopes by upsetting his service in turn with a brilliant display of hitting and then ran out the match as he had begun it, with a love game, for a 6—4 decision.

The score by points follows:

FIRST SET.		Total Pts.	G.
Throckmorton	[illegible]	42	6
Botsford	[illegible]	32	3
SECOND SET.			
Throckmorton	0 6 4 4 8 4 1 4	31	6
Botsford	4 4 1 1 6 1 4 1	22	2
THIRD SET.			
Throckmorton	8 4 4 2 1 4 2 2 4 4	35	6
Botsford	6 2 1 4 4 1 4 4 2 0	28	4

Youngsters Beat Veteran Pair.

Ben Letson and Fred Anderson made good their claim to a place among the best of the new doubles teams when they went through the veteran combination of Alrick H. Man, Jr., and Cedric Major in straight sets, 6—4, 6—3. Both youngsters were very steady and severe overhead and did not hesitate to hit the ball hard all the time, whereas the older players were inclined to be cautious at their own expense. After winning the opener by a single break in service, the second came more easily to Letson and Anderson, who finished in a blaze of good volleying and smashing.

Hammett and Henderson, an exceedingly steady though not at all showy team, surprised their young opponents with a great uphill fight after losing the opener at 8—6. For half of the second set the University Heights pair looked like sure losers, lobbing short and seeming unable to volley the hard drives of Emerson and Botsford. Trailing at 1—3, after a double break in service, however, the choppers gradually came to life and actually took five games in a row for the set which squared the match, 6—3, both of the losers making inexcusable errors on easy chances close up. Having settled down to their normal game, Hammett and Henderson simply chopped and lobbed their opponents to death and let them beat themselves again by the same score.

The summaries:

SINGLES—Final Round—Harold Throckmorton defeated Willard Botsford, 6—3, 6—2, 6—4.

DOUBLES—Fourth Round—Ben Letson and Fred C. Anderson defeated Alrick H. Man, Jr., and Cedric Major, 6—4, 6—3; Alfred D. Hammett and Embree H. Henderson defeated Gerald Emerson and Willard Botsford, 6—8, 6—3, 6—3.

Golf Tournament Will Help In Princeton Infirmary Drive

Golf is to contribute its bit in the campaign for funds for Princeton University. The women's committee raising money for a new infirmary will hold a tourney at the Arcola Country Club on June 25, in which the events are a men's foursome, a mixed foursome and a putting contest. The work of raising $350,000 for the new hospital is beng conducted by Prnceton women entirely, including wives, mothers, sisters and friends of graduates and under graduates, and is not a part of the general endowment campaign for $14,000,000.

ACCLAIM GARDNER AS GREAT GOLFER

British Experts Write, Too, of Popularity American Has Gained Over There.

Special Cable to THE NEW YORK TIMES.

LONDON, June 12.—The Morning Post's golf expert, writing today of the Gardner-Tolley match in the final of the British amateur title tourney, says:

"Had Gardner won his victory would have been as popular as that of any foreigner could have been. A good fellow that, and a good golfer."

The Daily Mail's correspondent, describing the scene after Tolley's winning putt, says:

"The crowd seized him and in spite of his 14 stone, 6 pounds, bore him shoulder high toward the clubhouse amid a storm of cheering and stampede of 3,000 excited spectators. Poor Gardner, his splendidly plucky effort in the last four holes knocked out by a heart-breaking putt that he could hardly have expected his opponent to hole, slipped quietly to the back of the crowd. It was some time before he met Tolley again and congratulated him with the happy smile and spontaneous large-heartedness that have made the American so popular wherever he has gone in this country."

The London Daily Mail in an editorial says:

"Every one will congratulate Gardner on the splendid game he played, and his popularity was shown by the cheers with which the sportsmanlike crowd followed his earlier victories."

Gardner "Won All Hearts."

A Daily Express editorial says:

"Very naturally and quite properly we are glad Tolley won, but our satisfaction would have been but little less if Gardner had triumphed. He has won all our hearts not only by the quality of his game, but by the spirit in which he played it. American golf, as represented by Gardner, has a great future."

The Daily Graphic says: "Gardner proved himself an opponent worthy of any player."

The Daily Mirror's golf correspondent says: "Hagen and Barnes traveled through the night to 'see Gardner win.' That was how they put it, and also to tell us how they defeated Duncan and Mitchell. To hear these two professionals talk, the Open Championship Cup is already as good as in America."

His Personality Praised.

The Times says editorially: "Gardner's personality has made him deservedly popular since his arrival in this country. 'If he wins,' wrote our golfing correspondent the day before the final, 'it is impossible to think of any invader whose victory would give half so much pleasure.' In his match with Lockhart on the previous day Gardner had already had a taste of the whole-hearted sympathy and good feeling of his fellow players and the big crowd of Scottish enthusiasts that followed the game. When he ran down the long and difficult putt that secured his entry into the semi-final round the spectators, we are told, though they naturally longed for Lockhart to win, broke into tempestuous applause. This is as it should be. It is the right spirit of all international sport."

The Times golfing correspondent says today: "It would be difficult to praise Gardner too highly. One had to wish him to be beaten, but it was hateful to have to do so. No American golfer has made so many friends here or made them so quickly, and he is not only a very gallant and modest fighter but a fine and accomplished player. May he come back soon again."

GOLF CHAMPION LOSES.

Herron Is Beaten by Fownes in Invitation Tournament, 3 and 2.

Special to The New York Times.

PITTSBURGH, June 12.—Making his first start of the season in a tournament, S. Davidson Herron, national amateur golf champion, was beaten in the final round of the Allegheny Country Club invitation fixture here today by W. C. Fownes, Jr., a fellow member of the Oakmont Country Club, 3 up and 2 to play. Fownes led at the end of the first round, 2 up.

Herron was not at his best. He drove in true form, getting great distance from the tee, but was off in the rest of his game. Fownes, on the other hand, played his best, beating par by two strokes on his first round.

Fownes, a veteran player and himself a former national champion and captain of the United States international team, also was the medalist, with a card of 151 for the thirty-six holes.

Herron qualified third, with 155. In today's semi-final round, played in the morning, Fownes disposed of Eben M. Myers, of the home club, an old rival and also a former national champion, 4 and 2, after being 1 down at the turn.

CLUB NET TEAMS TO MEET.

N. Y. T. C. Champions Will Play Terrace-Kings County Organization.

On Sunday, June 20, the Inter-City Club champion tennis team of the New York Tennis Club will play a team match consisting of eight singles and four doubles with the Terrace-Kings County Tennis Association at the latter's grounds, Avenue I, Flatbush.

The New York Lawn Tennis Team will be the same one which won the Metropolitan League championship last year and defeated the Philadelphia champions. This team will be composed of Vincent Richards, holder of the National junior championship; Harry Steinkampf, Henry Bassford, Allen Behr, Ingo Hartman, Leon Croley and Elliott H. Binzen.

The team of the Terrace-Kings County will include S. Howard Voshell, whose match with Richards should tell who is the greatest player in the Metropolitan district at the present time. The team will also include Frank and Fred Anderson, Cecil and Gerald Donaldson, and the veterans, Royal D. Ritchey, Henry Mollenhauer and Charles Chambers.

SAWYER IS WINNER IN 37-HOLE MATCH

Takes Metropolitan Amateur Golf Title from White on Links at Apawamis.

10-FOOT PUTT DECIDES IT

Siwanoy Linksman Is Hard Pressed All the Way, with Rival Getting the Breaks.

POOR DRIVES ARE COSTLY

Loser Pulls His Tee Shots Out of Line Repeatedly—White 1 Up After the Morning Round.

A ten-foot putt that hesitated on the lip of the cup for a fraction of a second and then toppled into the thirty-seventh hole won the metropolitan golf championship for Ned Sawyer of Siwanoy yesterday afternoon on the Apawamis course at Rye. This grand finale of one of the closest and most strenuous matches ever played for a local title defeated Gardiner W. White of Nassau. It was an extraordinarily exciting finish of a day of brilliant golf. The performers were worn out from the strain, caddy boys were exhausted, and six or seven hundred spectators, of whom many had seen the morning round and all of whom had accompanied the afternoon round from the first tee, had been ready to quit long before, but had been attracted hole after hole by a match that never seemed to be near the end.

Sawyer should have won by a wider margin. That's the bewildering part of the great battle. His golf was sounder, steadier, more consistent and altogether more deserving. But against Gardiner White's poorer playing Sawyer was strangely unable to make progress. At the end of the morning round White led by 1 up, lost this when Sawyer squared the match at the first hole on the afternoon circuit, and then seven straight holes were halved in succession. Thenceforth White played anything but commendable golf. Hardly a tee shot was straight. Most of them were pulled far off the line, and were Apawamis not a course of parallel holes most of the drives would have been out of bounds. On most links fully half of his drives would have landed over the boundary fence. But with the fairways running side by side White's ball kept on clear ground and, by approach shots that were really his only long suit, he was able time and again to recover lost distance and break even with Sawyer.

Safety Play Rules.

Still another remarkable feature and one that is true of not one match in a hundred was the absence of long putting. Sawyer's ten-footer on the extra hole that won was the longest tap of the afternoon round. Both men played safely as a rule. They tried for halves and not for wins, and ran their approach putts up to striking distance so that the second putts could go down easily. Except for White's miserable driving neither man ever gave the other an opening. And because of this the match became all the more interesting as it progressed. Spectators couldn't help thinking about Bob Gardner's great event on Friday at Muirfield, where he lost on the thirty-seventh hole after apparently enjoying a big advantage in earlier periods of play.

In the gallery were practically all the victims of last week's tournament. Jerry Travers, looking as gloomy as his sombre brown golf clothes, never missed a thing. White had put Jerry out on Friday. A. L. Walker, Jr., the intercollegiate champion, was there wishing he were in the finals, as he was last year at Brooklawn. Two other champions, W. M. Reekie of Jersey and J. S. Worthington of Westchester, were not quite good enough when the entire metropolitan field assembled as one group, and they, too, were intent on seeing every last bit of yesterday's great final.

And here's what they saw: Sawyer, the Western amateur champion in 1905, when he was rated as one of Chicago's "big three," using extreme care, gauging and measuring every shot before playing it, and scarcely ever making the slightest mistake; and White, a younger man, still in his twenties, who got more nervous as the end drew near, who was disturbed by the faintest movement of a spectator or a camera man, and who was playing in his greatest match of a career which began when he was a high school boy in 1910 and which carried him along near but never at the top ever since.

White Favorite With Gallery.

White unquestionably was the favorite with the crowd. He was applauded at every opportunity, and at times when there was actually no incentive. As he played some shots, notably on the seventh, a clapping of hands followed his swing while the ball was in mid-air, yet not one man living could have foretold where the little white pellet was to land.

Not only was the final putt the longest of the afternoon, but on only one hole was more than the regulation number of putts taken. This was at the twelfth, a hole that Sawyer simply threw away. He was on the green, whereas White was short and only half way up the hill, but took three putts to go down, taking a half instead of a win which should and could have been his. Other than this, putting was always accurate, although short.

If any one thing could be pointed to as having prevented Sawyer from winning by a wider margin it was his downright misfortune on the greens. Sawyer won the medal with 148, and had had defeated in the earlier rounds of the tourney such a string as Harry Scharff, C. Eddie Van Vleck, Jr., Oswald Kirkby, last year's champion, and W. P. Seeley. His matches were distinguished by his putting. Yesterday, to save himself from overrunning the hole, he tapped his ball too weakly, and the result left him always struggling. In the afternoon round his ball ran to the very lip of the cup on the eleventh, twelfth and fifteenth holes. On the second, seventh and tenth it rimmed the hole, and on the ninth, the hardest hole at Apawamis, his putt stopped less than two inches short of going down for a birdie 4.

Even the winning putt on the thirty-seventh came within an ace of following the same fate as earlier ones. His ball seemed to hop in staccato-like jumps for the hole, and then seemed to rest momentarily on the edge of the cup. Sawyer's caddy was snapping his fingers as

Continued on Page Three.

WORLD RECORD IS SET BY MAN O' WAR

Continued from Page One.

stretch, although at no time urging him. He simply let the colt run reely, and then it became evident how uh he outclasses the others of his age. He not only left a wide margin between him and Donnacona, but he made a joke of the race, as such. He gained a length with every two strides, and, though his head was still held high in the air, he increased his lead by a sixteenth of a mile in the distance of the stretch. Man o' War was around the turn and being pulled up when Donnacona crossed the finish line.

There was great cheering for the champion when he came back to the stands and general congratulations for Mr. Riddle for the establishment of the new world's record. Horsemen who watched the race thought the Fair Play colt could have reduced the mark by at least another fraction of a second had he been in the least extended. Though he was fairly flying through the stretch, he was not running at his top speed. Kummer sat perfectly still on him, neither urging or restraining him, and perhaps one touch of the whip would have taken another two-fifths from the time. This was the first time that Man o' War had ever raced at such a distance, but when he pulled up he was not even breathing hard.

Cleopatra Sets Track Mark.

Not all of the record-making was left to Man o' War. W. R. Coe's Cleopatra set a new track record for a mile and three furlongs over the main course in winning the Coaching Club American Oaks from P. A. Clark's La Rablee and Ral Parr's Oceanna. She covered the distance in 2:18 4-5, and at that had only to gallop to score her victory by three lengths.

These were the high lights of a program which included no less than three distinct features, but which brought out such small fields as to provide rather poor contests. Cleopatra, which is easily the best three-year-old filly of the year, had almost as easy a time winning the Oaks as did Man o' War in his race. She outclassed her field, and it was just a question of how far she would win by. She was not extended at any time to gain the victory by the margin of three lengths, and was just galloping through the stretch.

This race was run over the main course, the start being made just below the clubhouse. Oceanna and La Rablee broke in front and set the pace to the head of the stretch, while McAtee kept Cleopatra in the rear, but always close enough so she could move up when ready. The pacemakers gave a pretty exhibition. They ran head and head for six furlongs and showed fine speed. After the first mile Cleopatra began to move up gradually, and at the turn into the stretch she assumed command, to win as her rider pleased. Meantime Oceanna had tired, finding the distance and the pace too much for her, and La Rablee took second by fifteen lengths.

Thrift Is First Home.

The Amateur Cup handicap, at a mile, in which gentlemen riders had the mounts, was one of the best contests of the day, and was won by Thrift, ridden by Mr. Tucker, which finished a head in front of Super, ridden by Mr. Alpers, with The Decision third. Thrift was disqualified, however, for bumping both Genevieve B. and The Decision.

Super and Thrift raced head and head nearly the entire distance. Alpers turned into the stretch on the rail, and Thrift came up beside him. The two fought it out all the way to the finish. Super seemed to be in rather close quarters, but weakened right at the end. The bumping which caused the disqualification occurred at the far turn and at the turn into the stretch.

W. S. Kilmer's Our Flag won the final event, the one which brought the Belmont meeting to a close. This son of Cock o' the Walk defeated a field of twelve in the five-furlong dash for maiden two-year-olds. He won by a length and a half from Dough Girl, with Sammy Jay close up for third. Dough Girl led to the head of the stretch, where the winner moved up and took command, to win handily.

The summaries:

FIRST RACE.

For three-year-olds and upward; purse $1,169. Six and a half furlongs, main course.

Horse.	Wt.	Jockey.	Odds.	Fin.
Sugarmint	104	Ponce	9-2	1no
Flibbertygibbet	108	Murray	9-10	2^{s}
Thistle Queen	107	Turner	30-1	3^{1½}
Marmon	115	Zoeller	15-1	4
Pibroch	118	Rice	8-1	5
Prim III	110	Longo	100-1	6
Basilius	112	Fator	4-1	7
Elma Johnson	110	Buxton	50-1	8
Millrace	102	Campbell	30-1	9

Time—1:21.

Start good; won driving; place easily. Sugarmint, b. f., by McGee—Mint Blossom; owned and trained by J. H. McDonald.

SECOND RACE.

The Amityville Steeplechase Handicap, for four-year-olds and upward; $1,200 added. About two and a quarter miles.

Horse.	Wt.	Jockey.	Odds.	Fin.
Decisive	135	Cheyne	12-1	1^{1}
Hibler	142	Parretta	8-1	2^{8}
Royal Arch	144	Crawford	3-1	3^{8}
Doublet	150	Byers	13-5	4
Lytle	140	Kennedy	6-5	*

*Fell.

Time—4:43.

Start good; won ridden out; place same. Decisive, ch. g., by Marathon—Lottie Dorr; owned by W. H. Maxwell and trained by M. Brady.

THIRD RACE.

The Coaching Club American Oaks, for fillies three years old; $5,000 guaranteed. One mile and three furlongs.

Horse.	Wt.	Jockey.	Odds.	Fin.
Cleopatra	117	McAtee	2-9	1^{8}
La Roblee	111	Kummer	4-1	2^{15}
Oceanna	111	Schuttinger	20-1	3

Time—2:18 4-5.

Start good; won galloping; place easily. Cleopatra, ch. f., by Corcyro—Gallice; owned by W. R. Coe and trained by W. Karrick.

FOURTH RACE.

The Belmont, for three-year-olds; $10,000 guaranteed. One mile and three furlongs.

Horse.	Wt.	Jockey.	Odds.	Fin.
Man o' War	126	Kummer	1-20	1^{20}
Donnacona	126	Barrett	15-1	2

Time—2:14 1-5.

Start good; won galloping. Man o' War, ch. c., by Fair Play—Mahuba; owned by Glen Riddle Farm and trained by L. Feustel.

FIFTH RACE.

The Amateur Cup Handicap, for three-year-olds and upward. One mile.

Horse.	Wt.	Jockey.	Odds.	Fin.
†Thrift	150	Mr. Tucker	8-5	1^{h}
Super	145	Mr. Alpers	3-5	2^{15}
The Decision	157	Mr. Wright	15-1	3^{30}
Genevieve B.	148	Mr. Wildey	20-1	4

†Disqualified.

Time—1:42 3-5.

Start good; won driving; place same. Super, b. c., by Superman—Sister Jeannie; owned by Dosoris Stable and trained by J. Fitzsimmons.

SIXTH RACE.

For two-year-old maidens; purse $1,169. Five furlongs.

Horse.	Wt.	Jockey.	Odds.	Fin.
Our Flag	115	Davies	5-2	1^{1½}
Dough Girl	112	Ambrose	5-1	2^{½}
Sammy Jay	115	Turner	6-1	3^{½}
Mlle. Cadeau	112	Gordon	25-1	4
Idle Dell	112	Moore	7-1	5
Jamaica Belle	112	Fator	15-1	6
H'p o' the North	115	Rice	12-1	7
Chevalier	115	Schuttinger	3-1	8
Sobrigade	115	Zoeller	5-2	9
Smarty	115	Swart	40-1	10
The Swell	115	Hamilton	25-1	11
Jacobean	115	Fairbrother	20-1	12

Time—0:54 3-5.

Start good; won easily; place driving. Our Flag, ch. c., by Cock o' the Walk—Private Flag; owned by W. S. Kilmer and trained by J. S. Healy.

Weather clear; track fast.

TRIAL RACES LEAVE EXPERTS IN DOUBT

Results Thus Far in Resolute-Vanitie Series Are the Reverse of Conclusive.

CHALLENGER IS A MYSTERY

Many Yachtsmen View Shamrock IV. with Respect and Accord Her a Chance to Lift Trophy.

As the result of the trial races off Newport between Resolute and Vanitie for the honor of defending the America's Cup there is considerably more doubt in the minds of most yachtsmen today as to which craft should have the honor of representing this country in the great international contest than there was a week or a month ago.

To date there have been seven trial races off Newport, and of these Resolute has been awarded four decisions, but two of the seven races were flukes, one, owing to lack of breeze and the other to an approach to a fog, in which navigation rather than the skill of skipper and crew or the merit of the vessels themselves counted. Of the five contests that had the actual requirement on which to base a decision on the relative merits of the two sloops Vanitie has three to her credit and Resolute has two, of which one was on her allowance, while Vanitie defeated Resolute, boat for boat, in five out of the entire seven contests off old Brenton Reef light vessel.

Also, there is greater doubt as to whether that old silver mug which has been here since 1851 will continue to remain in the custody of the New York Yacht Club or be transferred overseas to the keeping of the Royal Ulster Yacht Club. Yachtsmen, having seen the Shamrock IV. under sail, are more in the dark than they were before as regards her latent possibilities. She is a real mystery ship and becomes more so each day. Real experts who know a lot about designing yachts as well as the sailing of them have veered in their judgment, first opining that she had no chance, then that she was a winner and so on, back and forth at frequent intervals; and today they know no more than they did when she first arrived in this country six years ago.

Lipton's Craft Finds Favor.

Public interest in the race has started to develop with the near approach of the big contest and, while the average layman in no way lacks patriotism and a desire to see America pre-eminent in everything it undertakes, still there appears to be a very large tide of public opinion in favor of the challenger. Sir Thomas Lipton is popular with the vast masses who admire his pluck in coming back smiling and never giving up in despair. He appeals to the people as a good sportsman. Aside from that the public interest in the race has caused the fact that the challenger is a "mystery" craft to become known, and the people like mysteries.

As between Resolute and Vanitie, except in certain regions such as Boston, public sentiment is more largely with Vanitie. How one yacht may come in first and still not win is a puzzle to many who do not understand handicapping and who believe that the speedier craft is the better. By this same token, should Shamrock IV. be beaten on allowance, there will be many who will still pass her the palm though she may not take the cup.

Such public sentiment might result in future contests being between craft built to the limit of certain dimensions or conditions and racing without handicap—first home the winner.

A grizzled old skipper who has seen every cup race held during the last fifty years, after looking the defense candidates and the challenge over, remarked that the one that could carry her spars would be the one to win. So far this year we have had numerous illustrations of the common sense of that remark. Resolute has met with several mishaps, including the carrying away of a mast, a topmast and a gaff, as well as other defects which have been cared for without attracting public attention. It is safe to say that one of the chief reasons for the trials being held off Newport was that it is convenient to the Herreshoff shops at Bristol, and Resolute has spent much of her time there, in addition to which workmen from there have been within easy call of that contender at all times.

Can Resolute Stand the Gaff?

Will Resolute be able to stand a severe pummeling such as she might receive, and still be fit to defend the cup, or is it possible that something like that which happened to the one-horse chaise might happen to her?

Shamrock IV. is a great, over-rigged creation. She has loftier spars than either Resolute or Vanitie. The tip of her club pierces the sky, and her spread of canvas is enormous. So far she has carried away a gaff and her spreaders were found to be too weak to insure safety, but they were spreaders made here after the original ones were destroyed by fire. The newest spreaders are supposed to be as sturdy as the old ones. However, it is quite evident that the chief concern of Mr. Nicholson, her designer, is as to whether she can carry her spread of canvas without carrying away something, and, from Sir Thomas Lipton's first remark when he landed here, to the effect that he had great hopes, providing she "held together," all of which demonstrates that the coming contests off Sandy Hook will afford a perfect demonstration of the successful application of scientific principles to a very interesting problem, that of a frail craft, lightly sparred and rigged, carrying an immense spread of canvas, or, on the other hand, the unsuccessful application of those same scientific principles.

Before the challenger came to this country she is reported to have been thoroughly tried out in breezes of greater velocity than either of the defenders have met with so far this year and to have stood the test. Time may have had some unknown effect upon some one part of the entire structure, as for instance the glue used in constructing the mast or other spars. Only time and severe trials will tell that, and that is why the Lipton menage is so anxious to get busy down off Sandy Hook.

Vanitie a Sturdy Craft.

Vanitie has gone through the season so far like a seasoned old campaigner. Not a spar has carried away and nothing of consequence has happened to her structurally although, at the commencement of the season her usefulness came very near being destroyed when it was found that an injurious solution was being used for polishing her beautiful bronze plating. That was discovered in time, however, and today she is sturdier than either Resolute or Shamrock IV.

While Resolute has made a slightly better showing as regards winnings on corrected times, still Vanitie has won a large majority of her contests on actual time, and a fair share even after allowing the Bristol craft the allotted one minute and forty-two seconds. In fact, eliminating two of the races which were largely flukes, one because of a lack of breeze and the other because of what approximated to a fog, and Vanntie's showing is quite as good as Resolute's.

It is true that the Corinthian skipper aboard the Resolute has subjected that craft to much more heavy handling than has Commodore Nichols the Vanitie. Rounding marks Resolute has often—almost always—been driven to the uttermost, and frequently to such an extent as to lose most if not all the advantage gained in one direction by killing her headway momentarily. If it has been done for the purpose of discovering her weak points, then it certainly accomplished its purpose, as the mishaps attest.

During the last week one of the officials of the contests remarked that conditions to be met with off Sandy Hook were entirely different from those off Newport and that the yachts might make a different showing off there. In so much as the big races are to be held off the Hook, where tidal and wind conditions are such an important factor, so much so that more than one international race has been won on a knowledge of local conditions there, then why were the trials not held there—where the two defense candidates would be subjected to th exact conditions to be met in the mig races, and so that the skippers and navigators of her might become more familiar with those mystifying tidal and wind conditions?

A Matter of Propinquity.

The official referred to did not volunteer an answer. It was not necessary, or at least one good reason was apparent to all who are at all familiar with conditions. That reason is that the shops at Bristol are much nearer Brenton Reef than Sandy Hook, and Resolute has found that a decided and necessary advantage. Vanitie has not needed any great assistance in that direction and could as well have been racing off Sandy Hook, or the Isle of Wight for that matter. She has been the old reliable and has always been at the starting line, as well as the finishing line, and undamaged.

Commodore Nichols's handling of Vanitie has shown marked and daily improvement. He has remembered and taken advantage of every earlier error in judgment or actual helmsmanship, and this is making him a more and more formidable adversary for Resolute's skipper. Vanitie's crew has improved, too, and the afterguard is most capable.

SAWYER IS WINNER IN 37-HOLE MATCH

Continued from Page One.

if calling for a seven with his dice, and Sawyer himself had bent into a crouching position as if to urge the ball on just a fraction of an inch. Perhaps both of these urgings helped. At any rate, the ball continued and slipped ever so easily in, while White rushed to congratulate his opponent, and the spectators breathed for the first time in more than a minute. The silence which had hung over Apawamis while the putt was being made was broken by loud cheers and thunderous applause.

White's ability to win holes and halve them completely mystified the throng of onlookers. The Nassau star was among friends and probably was picked as the winner by fully half of the crowd, but how a golfer who continually pulled his tee shots off the course could remain a contender was cause for wonderment. His morning round was hardly the less replete with atrocious drives than his afternoon. This was especially true during the last half of the first eighteen holes. White took a commanding lead at the start, which should have served the average man in good stead for the rest of the round, but his driving simply took away all his advantage gained early. White won the third, fourth, lost the fifth, then won the seventh, lost the eighth and took the ninth. He went out in 39 to Sawyer's 40 and was 2 up at the turn. The next two were halved, then he went to 3 up by winning the short uphill twelfth, halved the next two and lost the fifteenth. His old enemy—a pulled drive—began its work and he needed five strokes to Sawyer's four.

This brought White down to 2 up, and after halving the next he went to 1 up when Sawyer won the difficult seventeenth. Here White again pulled his ball to the rough, gaining little distance on his second and pulling his htird 'way out int othe first fairway. He was on in four strokes whereas Sawyer landed on the green in two with a magnificent brassie wallop, and the hole went to the Siwanoy man. The last was halved.

The morning cards:

Out—
Par .... 4 4 4 4 3 4 4 3 5—35
Sawyer .... 5 5 5 4 3 4 5 3 6—40
White .... 5 5 4 3 4 4 4 5 5—39

In—
Par .... 4 4 3 4 5 4 4 5 4—37—72
Sawyer .... 4 4 4 3 6 4 3 4 4—36—76
White .... 4 4 3 3 6 5 3 6 4—38—77

By the starting time for the afternoon round, Secretary A. H. Pogson of the M. G. A. had recruited a battalion of ran smack against a rude beginning of the second half of the strenuous journey, for Sawyer promptly won the first hole and squared the match. White, his old pulled drive working in the worst form, walloped his tee shot into a sand trap to the left, was out only forty yards on his second and on the green in three whereas Sawyer had landed within ten feet of the pin on two course marshals and had strung out a rope to keep the crowd away from the field of play. White leading by 1 up, and needed the regulation pair of putts.

Then some of the closest golf that this Metropolitan district has ever seen was played. Seven straight holes, from the second to the eighth inclusive, were halved. But on all this journey, White rarely drove a straight ball from the tee. He sliced to the rough on the second, pulled on the third, drove well on the fourth, fifth and sixth, sliced on the seventh and pitched on to the green on the short downhill eighth.

More of last week's tournament players met trouble on the Apawamis ninth than on any other hole. White pulled his drive to the middle of the fifteenth fairway, pulled his second shot to rough grass behind the fifteenth teeing ground, the ball skimming through trees, got out on the course on his third, and near the edge of the green on four. Sawyer, meanwhile, had banged two perfectly straight balls down the course and was on this long 600-yard hole green in three. His first putt stopped only a couple of inches short, and he just missed a birdie. As it was Sawyer won the hole, 5 strokes to 6.

This put him 1 up for the first time in the whole match, but the new prosperity seemed too much for him to stand, and he sliced his drive on the tenth hole to the woods and out of bounds. His second attempt, however, was straight, and he was on the green in three. White again pulled his drive, and the ball landed on the same peninsula in the pond where his similar pulled tee shot had stopped on Friday. He made a remarkably good approach—approaches being White's best art—and he gained the green. He was down in 4 to Sawyer's 5, and again the match was all even.

White straightway won the eleventh, to go to 1 up again when Sawyer's second was off the edge, and he took 3 to get on and 3 to get down while White was negotiating the hole in par figures. At the twelfth, which was halved, the only poor putting of the day took place. Sawyer drove the green, whereas White was short, but took three taps with his putter to sink his ball.

Sawyer won the next when White sliced far off the line of direction and his ball came to rest on the tenth fairway. White's second barely missed the brook and he took five to Sawyer's four. The fourteenth was halved, White's approaching again saving him, for his second shot played with a brassie was sliced to the ninth fairway. At the sixteenth White once again pulled his drive—it was getting to be a habit with him—but he approached with a magnificent loft and needed only four strokes to Sawyer's five. This put him 1 up again. They halved the sixteenth.

At the difficult seventeenth White pulled—always the pull—his drive to another fairway, pulled his second shot to the rough left of the green and chipped on with his third shot, but Sawyer had laid his second almost dead and took 4 to White's 5. This squared the match. By this time the gallery was on tiptoe with excitement and a deep circle of spectators completely surrounded the home hole, which was halved.

White's drive on the thirty-seventh was his best of the day, straight down the alley. His second was just short of the green, while Sawyer's was nicely on, ten feet from the flag. White ran his approach up and then Sawyer's brilliant putt ended the match.

The cards follow:

Out—
Sawyer .... 4 4 4 4 3 4 4 3 5—35
White .... 5 4 4 4 3 4 4 3 6—37

In—
Sawyer .... 5 5 4 4 5 5 4 4 4—40—75
White .... 4 4 4 5 5 4 4 5 4—39—76

The summary:

Championship Division.

Final—D. E. Sawyer, Siwanoy, defeated Gardner W. White, Nassau, 1 up (37 holes.) White led at end of first round by 1 up.

For President's Cup.

BEATEN SIXTEEN.

Final—J. Simpson Dean, Princeton, defeated H. K. Kerr, Greenwich, 7 and 5. Dean led at end of first round by 4 up.

Third Sixteen.

Final—T. V. Bermingham, Wykagyl, defeated Eddie H. Driggs, Jr., Engineers, 1 up. Bermingham led first round by 1 up.

Fourth Sixteen.

Final—C. H. Brown, Hudson River, defeated A. E. Ranney, Greenwich, 3 and 2. First round ended all square.

Club Pairs Tourney.

Won by Engineers' Country Club team, Harry K. B. Davis and R. W. Thompson, with 35, 37—72.

Metropolitan Handicap.

Low Gross—Won by A. F. Kammer, Baltusrol, 34, 40—74.

Low Net—Won by W. M. Reekie, Upper Montclair, on the play-off after a tie with Ray Twyeffort at 72.

FAST SPURT WINS MILE FOR CURTIS

Continued from Page One.

Hulsebosch of the Paulist A. C. until two laps from the finish, when the former Cornell runner forged to the front and remained in the van thereafter. Dresser's margin of victory at the finish line amounted to thirty-five yards and his time was 14:51 1-5, a sterling performance considering that Dresser has been out of competition for more than a year.

Plant Fails Against Handicap.

Willie Plant, national walking champion, failed to redeem handicaps in the one-mile walk. The Morningside A. C. pedestrian attained equal position with Tom Moroney, St. Amselm's A. C., on the final lap, but the latter had enough strength left to lead the title-holder in a ding-dong battle to the finish.

The summaries:

Track Events.

100-Yard Dash, Handicap—Won by Loren Murchison, New York A. C. (scratch); Bernard D. Wefers, New York A. C. (1 yard), second; Harry Appel, unattached (6 yards), third. Time—0:10.

880-Yard Run, Handicap—Won by R. Crawford, Lafayette College (scratch); Allan B. Helffrich, New York A. C. (18 yards), second; Thomas Campbell, Yale University (scratch), third. Time—1:58 2-5.

120-Yard High Hurdles Race, Handicap—Won by Harold E. Barron, Meadowbrook Club, Philadelphia (5 yards); A. Perry Roberts, New York A. C. (6 yards), second; Thomas H. Farrell, New York A. C. (6 yards), third. Time—0:16.

Three-Mile Run, Handicap—Won by Ivan C. Dresser, New York A. C. (scratch); Al Hulsebosch, Paulist A. C., (75 yards), second; George Cornetta, New York A. C. (25 yards), third. Time—14:51 1-5.

220-Yard Dash, Handicap—Won by Ramon W. Georgi, New York A. C. (5 yards); Bernard D. Wefers, New York A. C. (2 yards), second; Ellis Perlman, New York A. C. (4 yards), third. Time—0:23 2-5.

One-Mile Walk, Handicap—Won by Thomas A. Marone, St. Anselm's A. C. (30 seconds); William Plant, Morningside A. C. (scratch), second; Joseph D. Pearman, New York A. C. (scratch), third. Time—7:04 1-5.

One-Mile Run, Handicap—Won by William Curtis, U. S. Navy (scratch); Patrick Flynn, Paulist A. C. (45 yards), second; Michael A. Devaney, Millrose A. A., third. Time—4:21.

440-Yard Run, Handicap—Won by R. Beszeir, Glencoe A. C. (13 yards); James M. Roche, New Haven Harriers' A. C. (5 yards), second; James W. Driscoll, U. S. Navy (scratch), third. Time—0:50.

Field Events.

Putting Sixteen-Pound Shot, Handicap—Won by A. F. Makay, Mohawk A. C. (7 feet), 39 feet 6½ inches; Patrick J. McDonald, New York A. C. (scratch), 46 feet 4 inches, second; Herbert S. Elsey, Mohawk A. C. (2 feet 6 inches), 43 feet 4¼ inches, third.

Running High Jump, Handicap—Won by A. Abromit, Morningside A. C. (3 inches), 6 feet; Fred J. Seifert, New York University (5 inches), 5 feet 8 inches, second; E. J. Benzinger, St. Anselm's A. C. (5 inches), 5 feet 8 inches, third. (Seifert won second place on jump-off.)

Throwing the Discus, Handicap—Won by Robert G. Walker, New York A. C. (10 feet), 128 feet 8¾ inches; P. O'Connor, Loughlin Lyceum (12 feet), 117 feet 11 inches, second; Thomas J. Anderson, Jr., St. Christopher Club (10 feet), 119 feet 9¼ inches, third.

Pole Vault, Handicap—Won by R. M. Burtt, New York A. C. (18 inches), 11 feet 6 inches; George Plamas, unattached (15 inches), 11 feet 6 inches, second; Ralph Runyan, New York A. C. (6 inches), 12 feet, third.

Throwing 56-Pound Weight, Handicap—Won by Matthew J. McGrath, New York A. C. (scratch), with 39 feet 3½ inches; Thomas J. Anderson, Jr., St. Christopher Club (5 feet 6 inches), 32 feet 2¼ inches, second; Patrick J. McDonald, New York A. C. (scratch), 36 feet 4 inches, third.

Section 1

"All the News That's Fit to Print."

The New York Times.

THE WEATHER
Generally fair and warmer today; Monday, cloudy, probably thunder showers; southwesterly winds.
For full weather report see Page 19.

Section 1

VOL. LXX....No. 23,171. NEW YORK, SUNDAY, JULY 3, 1921. In Eight Parts, Including Rotogravure Picture Sections, Book and Magazine Section. FIVE CENTS In Manhattan, Bronx, and Brooklyn } Elsewhere TEN CENTS

DEMPSEY KNOCKS OUT CARPENTIER IN THE FOURTH ROUND; CHALLENGER BREAKS HIS THUMB AGAINST CHAMPION'S JAW; RECORD CROWD OF 90,000 ORDERLY AND WELL HANDLED

HARDING ENDS WAR; SIGNS PEACE DECREE AT SENATOR'S HOME

Thirty Persons Witness Momentous Act in Frelinghuysen Living Room at Raritan.

DROPS BLOT ON SIGNATURE

Joint Resolution of Congress Made Effective at 4:10 P. M., Daylight Saving Time.

TEXT OF THE RESOLUTION

Steel Pen Used to Be Given to Representative Porter, Author of Historic Document.

Special to The New York Times.

RARITAN, N. J., July 2.—War with Germany ended as it began, by Congressional declaration and Executive signature on American soil.

At 4:10 P. M., local daylight saving time, in the living room of "The Hill," Senator Joseph S. Frelinghuysen's home here, President Harding placed his signature to the Porter joint Congressional resolution declaring peace with Germany and Austria, just two years and four days after the ill-fated Treaty of Versailles was signed.

By a coincidence, a year ago to the day, Warren G. Harding, United States Senator from Ohio and Republican nominee for President, left Washington for his Marion front porch to prepare his speech of acceptance containing the promise of "formal and effective peace so quickly as a Republican Congress can pass its declaration for a Republican Executive to sign."

Scarcely thirty persons in a country home in the hills of Somerset County witnessed the last act that concluded the World War, while a few minutes before, fifty miles away in another part of the State, 90,000 persons saw a wartime riveter in a shipyard knock to the floor of the ring a former French enlisted man and aviation pilot.

Blot on Signature.

"That's all," said President Harding as he held his pen above his signature on a broad vellum typewritten page. The ink dripped from the pen and made a blot the size of a 5-cent piece on the page, almost effacing the "G." of the President's signature.

More ceremony has been connected with making an entry in the family Bible or a débutante's memory book than that accompanying the signature that ended a war that called to the colors 4,800,000 young Americans. And yet the very informality of the occasion heightened its impressiveness. Except for the four cameramen—there were no movies—not one of the witnesses spoke or moved while the President signed the peace resolution. The thirty-odd Government officials and their wives, secret service men, county officers, reporters, butlers, maids, chauffeurs and gardeners that were in Senator Frelinghuysen's living room were busy with their own thoughts, and the modest Frelinghuysen ancestral home will have a place in history long after an international heavyweight championship is forgot.

While President Harding, Senators Frelinghuysen, Hale and Kellogg and Speaker Gillett played golf over the Somerset Hills County Club at Bernardsville this morning, E. W. Smithers, a White House attaché, was on his way from Washington with a leather pouch containing the Porter resolution that the Senate passed yesterday afternoon. "Doc" Smithers reached "The Hill" at 2 o'clock and sat on the Frelinghuysen porch, his pouch between his knees, waiting for the President and his party, who arrived at 3:45.

Receives Papers on Porch.

President Harding, wearing a Palm Beach suit, white shoes, white socks with black clocks, a white shirt, buttoned by removable gold studs, and a green and red bow tie, climbed briskly out of the automobile, and as he sat down in a wicker chair on the porch took a sheaf of papers from the hands of the Washington messenger. Spectators remained a few feet away wondering whether the peace resolution was to be signed there and thereby make another front porch famous.

The President read through the document carefully and then examined some routine papers that had been brought from Washington for his attention. Patsy, a white, wire-haired Irish terrier, sniffed inquiringly at one of the Presidential shoes, while Emily and Joseph Jr., two of the Frelinghuysen children, vainly tried to entice the puppy to their swing seat. For five or ten minutes the President concentrated over official papers and then went indoors.

In the Frelinghuysen living room, an addition to the original house, a small mahogany table, a family heirloom, had been swept bare of its ornaments and was placed in the southwest corner of the room. Two windows, south and west, shed light on the table and to the right was a broad carved wooden mantel of severe lines that would delight a col-

Continued on Page Fifteen.

President Harding Asks, 'Was It a Good Fight?'

RARITAN, N. J., July 2.—President Harding showed little interest when informed late today that Jack Dempsey had defeated Georges Carpentier, French challenger, with a knockout in the fourth round.

"Was it a good fight?" he asked of newspaper men when told the result.

He made no further comment and changed the conversation into other channels.

WIFE AND MOTHER BOTH TAKE POISON

Women Go to Hotel Commodore, Swallow Mercury, and Elder One Phones Physician.

FOUND CLASPING BABY SHOE

Young Woman Was Worried Because Husband Took Child to His Mother—Both May Die.

An attempt is being made to unravel the mystery of why Mrs. Mortimer Weiss, 20 years old, of 46 Fort Washington Avenue, and her mother, Mrs. Frances Weiss, who lived at the Hotel Remington, attempted to commit suicide in the Hotel Commodore by taking bichloride of mercury. They were found there yesterday noon, having taken the poison thirty-six hours before and only let word of their condition get to the outside when their suffering became too great to be borne, and the elder Mrs. Weiss telephoned to a physician.

The only explanation yet given is that the younger Mrs. Weiss had quarreled with her husband, who had taken their baby girl to his mother's home. Clasped in the woman's hand when their room was opened yesterday was a baby's shoe and under her pillow a little rubber dog, such as babies cut their teeth on. She was nearly unconscious and her mother barely able to speak, and neither of them would tell why they tried to die. The daughter is in Bellevue Hospital and the mother in Flower Hospital. Little hope is entertained for the recovery of either, owing to the fact that blood poisoning, also treated immediately, is difficult to check.

Mrs. Frances Weiss is a nurse who has been employed by Dr. Arthur Greenburg, who has offices in the Hotel Remington.

She is about 40 years old. The younger Mrs. Weiss is the wife of Mortimer Weiss, 26 years old, who is associated with his mother, Mrs. Carryl Weiss, in a millinery business at 647 Madison Avenue. They have been married about three years and have a baby a year and a half old. Their married life has not been happy, and on Wednesday Weiss took the baby and went to his mother's home. What the final cause of the break was only the four members of the two Weiss families know, and they would not talk yesterday.

Took Poison From Doctor's Office.

Late Thursday night mother and daughter went to Dr. Greenburg's office in the Hotel Remington. He was out, but the mother opened the office with her key and they remained there for nearly two hours. They apparently took the bichloride tablets from a shelf in his laboratory, for he missed his supply when he went to look for it yesterday, and in the room at the Commodore was found an envelope bearing Dr. Greenburg's name which contained two of the fourteen tablets they had taken.

When they left the Remington they took a cab and drove to the Commodore,

Continued on Page Fifteen.

CROWD EARLY AT GATES

Thousands Wait Through Morning Hours for Opening of Arena

POLICE IN PERFECT CONTROL

Handle Entrance and Exit of Huge Throng Without Difficulty —1,000 Firemen on Guard.

CHEER NOTABLES ON ENTRY

Spectators Eat Lunches in Streets—Bootleggers and Crooks Noticeably Absent.

More than 90,000 men and women, the biggest crowd that ever saw a sporting event in the United States, saw Jack Dempsey knock out Georges Carpentier yesterday.

Such a crowd had never been assembled in this country. It is possible that more persons may have seen some of the championship football matches in England, but there have never been that number seated as spectators of a sporting event. In another way, Tex Rickard, promoter of the fight, achieved a new record. The gate receipts, estimated at approximately $1,600,000 by Mr. Rickard, were far above all previous records.

All day long the crowd had been gathering for the championship battle. From 9 o'clock in the morning, when the gates were opened, until a few minutes before three in the afternoon, when the event of the day was scheduled to begin, a steady stream of men with a noticeable sprinkling of women marched steadily across the muddy fields leading to the saucer-shaped arena, until it seemed as though the latter, large as it was, could hold no more.

This mass of humanity, piled tier on tier in the wooden saucer, was released suddenly by the blow which sent Carpentier to the floor of the ring and retained the championship for Dempsey. Every one started for the exits at once. The pressure increased until the crush became terrific. The policemen and firemen, at least ten of whom were stationed in each section, handled the mass rushing for the exits with the same calm efficiency that they had displayed throughout the day. Regular traffic rules were enforced, the spectators in one aisle being held to let those in another aisle proceed, thus avoiding the cross-currents which usually add to the confusion.

Arena Quickly Emptied.

In one minute after Carpentier had been counted out, streams of men and women were pouring from a hundred exits, though many stayed to see the bout between Miske and Renault, which, though scheduled as a preliminary, was put on after the championship fight.

The last of the huge crowd departed silently and without confusion after the bell and clanged on the Miske-Renault bout. Seven minutes after this had ended the huge arena was empty, except for a few hundred curious ones who clustered around the ringside, watching the newspaper men at work. Policemen quickly had this crowd on the move and the arena was emptied of its non-working spectators at 4:35.

The crowd did not have the expected difficulty in getting out of Jersey City. About one-third of the number went by way of the Hudson Tubes, which carried 60,000 more than the usual number of Saturday passengers and ran its trains on a ninety-second schedule practically all day. Others regained New York by the ferries, which carried 30,000 more back from the fight.

The street cars, taxicabs and motor buses running from Boyd's Thirty Acres were too few to take care of more than a very small percentage of the depart-

Continued on Page Five.

Give Notice of Coming Marriage of Col. Balsan To Consuelo, Duchess of Marlborough

Special Cable to THE NEW YORK TIMES.

LONDON, July 2.—Notice has been given at the Westminster Registry office in Covent Garden of the marriage of Consuelo, Duchess of Marlborough, and Colonel Jacques Balsan.

Louis Jacques Balsan, who himself gave the notice, described himself as a Lieutenant Colonel in the French Army, retired, and gives his age as 52, while the age of the bride-elect is given as 44.

Colonel Balsan is well known in London, where he was a member of the French Aeronautical Mission during the war. He is possessed of considerable wealth, and is a member of a firm which manufactures uniforms and blankets for the French Army.

PARIS, July 2.—The Duchess of Marlborough will be married to J. Balsan at the London Registry office in a few days, it is said by the Continental edition of The Daily Mail. Reports that the Duchess was to marry M. Balsan have been current for several months, but have been frequently denied.

M. Balsan holds a high place in French society. He has been identified with major sports, owning a large racing stable and being an expert pilot of dirigible balloons and airplanes. He distinguished himself in the war, and was promoted to the rank of Lieutenant Colonel just before the armistice was signed.

The Duchess of Marlborough, formerly Consuelo Vanderbilt, was reported last January to be planning her marriage to the French sportsman, Jacques Balsan, when she purchased a magnificent estate at Eze, near Monte Carlo. Rumors of her approaching marriage to Balsan were revived when her divorced husband, the Duke, married Miss Gladys Deacon, formerly of Boston, in Paris, on June 25. The Duchess and Balsan were seen almost daily at tennis in Paris at the same time that the Duke and Miss Deacon were seen continually at dances.

The Duchess of Marlborough is the daughter of the late William K. Vanderbilt and the present Mrs. O. H. P. Belmont. Her marriage to the Duke of Marlborough took place in 1895. They had two children, the Marquis of Blandford, heir to his father's title, and Lord Ivor Churchill. The estrangement of the Duke and Duchess became known in 1907 when they decided to live apart for two years. Temporary reconciliations were effected largely through the intercession of the King in 1919, and the Duke and Duchess took up their residence again at Crowhurst until February, 1920, when they separated for the last time. The following March the Duchess started suit to establish conjugal rights and in May she obtained a final divorce.

Dempsey's First Thought Is Telegram to His Mother

Jack Dempsey's first thought as he came victorious from the ring was of his mother. He took a pencil and wrote her the following telegram:

Mrs. C. Dempsey, 3,572 South State St., Salt Lake City, Utah.

Dear Mother: Won in the fourth round. Received your wire. Will be home soon as possible. Love and kisses. JACK.

REFORMERS DEMAND ARREST OF DEMPSEY

Police Refuse Without Warrant, and They Fail to Get Plea Before Any Judge.

NEW MOVE EXPECTED TODAY

Assault and Battery Charged in Complaint—Not So "Brutal" as They Anticipated.

Herbert Clark Gilson, attorney for the International Reform Bureau, and two other representatives of that organization were among the thousands at the ringside when Dempsey knocked out Carpentier yesterday afternoon. They sat in $50 seats so that they could see everything that went on, but they did not root for either the champion or the challenger, and failed to join in the tumult when the Frenchman was knocked to the floor and counted out.

The reformers were present as witnesses to see whether the law was violated, and they decided that it was. Immediately after the fight Mr. Gilson went to the temporary police station beneath the grand stand and filed a complaint with Lieutenant Michael A. Martin, charging Dempsey with assault and battery and with violating the New Jersey Crimes act, which prohibits prizefighting. He told the police that the knockout was sufficient evidence that the law against prizefighting had been violated.

"Lieutenant," said Mr. Gilson, "I want you to place on the blotter here a complaint against Jack Dempsey, the prizefighter, charging him with assault and battery on Georges Carpentier of France, in this arena a few minutes ago."

Lieutenant Martin made the entry in the blotter, but refused to make an arrest without a warrant. Mr. Gilson wanted quick action and scouted around Jersey City until he found Chief of Police Battersby, who had attended the fight.

The Chief, who had thoroughly enjoyed himself and was busily engaged in discussing the knockout with his friends, could not be found for some time. Then he flatly refused to order Dempsey's arrest without a warrant.

Insist On Prompt Arrest.

"But we want him arrested before he leaves this State and we may not be able to find a Judge to issue a warrant today," said Mr. Gilson.

"That makes no difference," the Chief replied. "I must have a warrant."

"You don't need a warrant," Mr. Gilson argued. "You were at the fight and witnessed the violation of the law yourself. You saw the knockout."

"You must get a warrant first," said the Chief with finality.

Mr. Gilson then attempted to find one of the three County Judges, but was unable to do so last night. He said that he would continue his efforts today and was determined to go through with the reformer's intention of punishing violators of the law.

"Did you see all the fight?" Mr. Gilson was asked.

"Yes," he replied, "I saw it all. Dr. Wilbur F. Crafts, Superintendent of the International Reform Bureau, asked me to attend for the specific purpose of seeing whether the law was violated."

Asked to tell his impressions of the fight, Mr. Gilson said:

"I sat pretty well up front, in one of the $50 seats. A ringside seat? I don't know. There were a number of seats in front of me, but I suppose, as it was a $50 seat, you would call it at the ringside. I could see very well.

"I went in during the next to the last preliminary before the championship bout. This was a brutal affair, but I did not pay so much attention to it or the next fight, in which a man named Tunney clearly outclassed his opponent. Tunney's opponent was groggy long before the fight was stopped by the referee, who should have acted sooner than he did to stop the brutal punishment the loser was receiving.

Called Obvious Prize Fight.

"As to my impressions of the fight between Dempsey and Carpentier, it was obviously a prize fight in violation of the law. There can be no question about it. It was a prize fight, not a boxing exhibition, from the moment the two men entered the ring and put up their hands until the knockout punch was delivered. Both men showed they were out to win by a knockout, not on points or a newspaper decision.

"It was not as brutal as I had expected, however. It was not such a bloody, brutal fight as the fight between Dempsey and Willard at Toledo, for example. I did not see that fight, but I read in the newspapers that Dempsey knocked Willard down seven times

Continued on Page Twelve.

COBB FIGHTS IT OVER AGAIN

Calls Carpentier Soul of the Fray, Dempsey the Body.

ALL WHO'S BALLYHOO THERE

Arts, Science, Drama, Politics, Bar, Bench and Commerce Are Represented.

BOYLE'S 30 ACRES FERTILE

If There Is No New War, He Thinks Jack Will Be Best Fighter for a While.

By IRVIN S. COBB.

It is recorded that, once upon a time, Aaron Burr, being challenged by Alexander Hamilton, bade Hamilton to meet him over in Jersey and there destroyed his enemy. Yesterday afternoon, also New Jersey history, in a way of speaking, repeated itself, which is a habit to which history is addicted. Challenger and challenged met, and again the challenger lost the issue.

Posterity has appraised the loser of that first duel as of more value than the winner who survived. One is moved, to wonder whether in the present instance the analogy will continue. Carpentier, an alien, a man who does not speak our language, was the favorite of the crowd before the fight started and while it progressed, and, if I am one to judge, was still its favorite when he came out of it summarily defeated though he was. Dempsey, a native born, will never forget, I am sure, the vast roar of approbation which arose from thirty acres of close-packed humanity about him when for a half-minute it seemed that he was slipping toward defeat. The thing never happened before when an American champion fought before an American audience. But then we never had for a champion a man whose war record—his lack of one rather—was stained with a taint.

Even so, and to the contrary notwithstanding, he showed himself a better man, as a fighter, than the Dempsey who whipped Willard two years ago at Toledo. Carpentier was the soul of the fight, but Dempsey was the body of it. Considering the thing purely in its pugilistic aspects, he won on merit—won because he was bigger and stronger, because he had more endurance than the Frenchman, and because, as it turned out, he was almost as fast upon his feet, when the needs of the moment demanded speed, and almost as clever a boxer as his opponent was. And to top all, he had a short arm blow, using either arm at will to deliver it, the like of which has not been seen on this Continent since Stanley Ketchel passed out.

Loses Like a Gentleman.

It was that drum-fire on his body which wasted Carpentier's substance of resistance, so that when the decisive jolts reached his jaw he had naught left in him with which to weather the blast. He fought fairly, did Carpentier, and like a gentleman he was licked fairly and like a gentleman. As a gentleman and a fighter he bulks tonight as the man the majority of the audience hoped to win and for whom, as a gallant soldier and a brave man, they wish good luck through all his days.

As for Dempsey, unless this country should go to war again, it seems probable that he will continue to be our leading fighter for quite some time to come.

Let us consider the matter chronologically, as it were.

At noon of the day when a championship battle is to be fought two hours later almost anything that happens is news. A prominent music hall performer, entering unostentatiously, accompanied only by his private photographer, his personal press agent and his official announcer—one such just came in as I did—constitutes a thrill. A slew-jawed functionary sowing powdered resin broadcast upon the canvas carpet of the ring amounts to a positive sensation. The sight of a near or Hudson seal society leader eating a proletariat ham sandwich in a box is worth a bulletin. And the mere appearance of a moving picture star is a riot. Such being the case, one begins one's preliminary story thus:

Not since the good old days when the courtesies of the press always were extended to the profession with food and drinks free and no questions asked, have I seen so many distinguished journalists gathered in one spot. We sit, we in whose hands the present destiny of English literature rests, in concentric rows about the fighting platform, like so many drops that have coagulated at the bottom of a huge funnel. Terracing up beyond and behind and on every side of us rise the banked tiers of the biggest ampitheatre this world has seen since the Caesars sat in the Circus Maximus having their Christian martyrs fried on one side. It is the biggest arena ever built of match work and pine planking. Assuredly were the weather as sultry as usually it is in these latitudes it would be the hottest. But the whimsical gods of the weather have been mighty good to us this July day. Under a London-colored sky, as gray and almost as thick as a fog, the centre of population of the United States

Continued on Page Nine.

Dempsey Says He Won Just as He Thought He Would; Carpentier Asserts He Staked His All in the Second

"Carpentier is a good, game fellow, but I think I've got it on him," Jack Dempsey remarked as he entered his dressing room after defending his title. The champion was as happy as a schoolboy and bore no marks to show the effect of the Frenchman's punches.

"I won just as I thought I would," the champion said. "It was a good fight and I think the public was satisfied. They say Carpentier staggered me with a right-hand punch in the second round. I never even remember being hit hard enough to shake me up.

"Perhaps he caught me off balance and it looked as though I was staggering. Perhaps I could have finished him sooner, but I was taking no chances. Carpentier is the heavyweight champion of Europe and I had my own title at stake and wanted to take no unnecessary chance of losing it."

"You've got to hand it to Carpentier; he was surely game," Dempsey said on several occasions.

Georges Carpentier took his defeat gamely and praised Dempsey as a great champion. In his dressing room after the fight Carpentier dictated this statement:

"I staked my all to win in the second round. I hit him hard, but could not drop him. I tried again in the third, but a right to my neck seemed to daze me. I do not know how he got through my guard in the fourth.

"America should be proud of Dempsey. He is a great champion."

CARPENTIER BROKE HIS THUMB IN FIGHT

He Also Sprained His Right Wrist on Dempsey's Jaw in Second Round.

NOT OFFERED AS EXCUSE

Carpentier Cables to Wife That He Is Uninjured and Was Beaten Fairly.

Special to The New York Times.

CARPENTIER'S TRAINING CAMP, MANHASSET, L. I., July 2.—Georges Carpentier returned to his training camp here this afternoon and informed a representative of THE NEW YORK TIMES that he knows no man in the world who is in the same class with Dempsey. He said he put forth every ounce of his strength in the fight and fel that when the American people read their newspapers tomorrow they would believe he had done his best and had not shown the white feather.

On Carpentier's behalf, however, his old friend Thierry Mallet, acting as spokesman, said that an injury to Carpentier's thumb eight days ago, which led to the breaking of the thumb in the second round today, was a contributing cause toward his defeat. Mallet did not attribute the defeat of the Frenchman to this cause, however.

Carpentier's external injuries appeared to be a slight cut under the eye, a slightly swollen nose and a badly swollen right hand, due to the fracture of a bone in the thumb. The injury to the thumb, it was said, was the most serious damage he sustained. In this connection Dr. Joseph B. Connolly, at the training camp here, gave out the following statement:

"This is to certify that I, Dr. Joseph B. Connolly, examined Georges Carpentier after his fight with Jack Dempsey and found him suffering from a fracture of the right metacarpal bone of his thumb, which rendered his right hand useless."

The doctor also said that the wrist was sprained from the blow landed on Dempsey's jaw. The hand has swollen to three times its normal size.

Mallet said that Georges received the injury eight days ago while working Carpentier lost the battle. His trainer, did not care to say anything about it at the time as they felt the announcement might be taken as preparing the groundwork for an excuse in the event Carpentier lost the battle. His manager, Gus Wilson, and the personnel in the camp were anxious to make the point that they did not attribute their man's defeat to the fractured thumb.

Mallet said to THE TIMES representative that Carpentier was a light heavyweight, and was not in the same class as Dempsey, who was a heavyweight. He said:

"On his return Georges said to me, 'You believe that I am a wonder as a light heavyweight. I am. You and I believed Dempsey was not a wonder as a heavyweight. But he is. A very good little man cannot hope to equal a very good big man.'"

"The handicap was too great, that's all," said Mallet. "Carpentier is the best man in the world in his class today, in 170 to 172 pounds weight, the light heavyweight class, but he is not in the same class as Dempsey, who is twenty pounds heavier."

"Georges was further handicapped, in addition to his fractured thumb, by the use of eight-ounce gloves to which he was unaccustomed," added Mallet. "His method is to strike with what may be described as a recoiling blow, but that sort of blow was neutralized by the weight of the glove. He always used four-ounce gloves in previous battles. Georges depended on speed to overcome Dempsey's weight, but in this case speed was overcome by power."

"Who will be your successor as a challenger of Dempsey?" THE TIMES representative asked Carpentier, who appeared cheerful as he walked about under the trees playing with a white rabbit.

"I don't know any man in the world in Dempsey's class," responded the defeated challenger.

"How did Dempsey control himself in the ring?" he was asked.

"His conduct was all that could be

Continued on Page Seven.

BLOW TO THE JAW ENDS THE CONTEST

Story of the Fight by Rounds Shows the Superiority of Dempsey.

ONLY ONCE IN DISTRESS

Carpentier Showed Well in Second Round, but After That Was Beaten Down.

FIRST ROUND.

The gong clanged to start the bout at 3:16 P. M. As the men advanced to the centre of the ring they were both smiling; Dempsey, a sardonic grin which was half sneer; Carpentier, a smile which reflected confidence. There were no preliminaries. Carpentier was the first to lead. He speared the champion with a left jab to the face. A clinch followed in which Carpentier worked his right in an inside uppercut to the champion's chin. Dempsey's head bobbed with the blow. The crowd roared its encouragement of the frail-looking challenger, who wasted no time in his supreme effort. The men were parted and Carpentier again leaped to the attack with characteristic springiness, bounding at the flat-footed champion with a wicked right which curled harmlessly past Dempsey's neck. Carpentier tried again with his right for the jaw, and this time landed on the champion's face with enough force to make Dempsey blink. Dempsey dug a left to the stomach and another clinch followed. Dempsey clubbed his right to the back of Carpentier's head in the clinch. Carpentier hooked a left to the stomach as Dempsey, his left shoulder raised in protection of his jaw and with right poised for immediate use, forced the pace. Carpentier missed a right for the face and in a clinch which followed Dempsey punished his rival severely about the stomach. Dempsey blocked Carpentier's right lead for the stomach and missed with a left hook for the head. Dempsey went in past the challenger's extended, guarding left and jabbed his left to the face. In a clinch the champion battered Carpentier severely about the stomach with rights and lefts. Dempsey missed a right for the jaw and Carpentier grazed the champion's chin with a right. Carpentier led a right which glanced off the champion's hunched left shoulder and landed on Dempsey's guarding left glove. Dempsey, forcing a fast pace, crowded Carpentier continually. In a clinch the champion cuffed Carpentier with rights and lefts and jolted the challenger with a left which shook him. As the men emerged from the clinch Carpentier's nose was bleeding. The skin on the bridge of the nose had been ripped with Dempsey's jolts in close, and the blood trickled down the challenger's face. Carpentier, crouching low, tried a right for the jaw. The blow landed high on Dempsey's temple. Both boxers tried with rights for the jaw. Carpentier missed. Dempsey landed with a glancing blow. A clinch followed in which Dempsey forced Carpentier to the ropes and there pounded the challenger hard about the stomach. Carpentier tried to cover against the blows. He couldn't. Dempsey, the stronger of the two, easily roughed his rival around and landed heavily to the mid-section. As the men were being broken Carpentier was off balance, and with the added weight of a recalcitrant right to the body sprawled over the second strand of the ring, where he hung momentarily doubled up, his glove tips supporting him outside the ropes. Dempsey stepped back as Carpentier quickly came erect without a count. The body punishment plainly hurt Carpentier. Carpentier tried a right and missed before the bell ended the round. Dempsey's round.

SECOND ROUND.

Crouching low, swaying his head from side to side and with his arms drawn protectingly against his jaw, Dempsey forced Carpentier around the ring. Carpentier retreated carefully, slowly, his left extended as he danced back on his toes and his right poised, ready to strike. Suddenly Carpentier leaped in with a left jab and followed with a right high on the head. Dempsey disregarded the blows and shuffled steadily

Continued on Page Two.

DEMPSEY PROVES PROWESS

Forces Carpentier Down With Incessant Rain of Terrific Blows.

TWICE FLOORS OPPONENT

But Frenchman Is Courageous After First Knockdown and Fights Until Knocked Out.

NO "ACCIDENTAL CHAMPION"

Great Throng That Gave Louder Cheer for Georges at Start Acclaims Jack at the End.

Jack Dempsey is still heavyweight champion of the world—it might almost be said that for the first time he is really the champion. Georges Carpentier, in many respects the most serious opponent Dempsey has ever met, stood up against him yesterday afternoon in Tex Rickard's stadium in Jersey City and could not last through the fourth round. And at that, Carpentier fought better than most American critics believed possible.

His end came at a few seconds after 3:30, when the fourth round had been going on one minute and sixteen seconds. Dempsey found the Frenchman's face with his left and followed it up with a hard right just in front of the ear. Carpentier went down, but on the count of nine leaped to his feet and seemed in shape to give the champion more trouble. But he never had the chance.

Dempsey led a light left to the face, and then as Carpentier swayed aside from the blow Dempsey drove a tremendous smash with his right hand into Carpentier's ribs, below the heart. This was quickly followed by a smashing right to the jaw.

The blow to the body was a hard enough blow in itself, because that spot had already been hammered and weakened by a score of fierce short-arm jolts in the desperate in-fighting of the previous rounds, but at the blow to the jaw Carpentier dropped again—dropped on his right side and lay there while Referee Harry Ertle swung his arm above him and counted. At the count of eight Carpentier stirred and made a desperate effort to rise; but he could not move. Nine, ten—and Dempsey's championship was secure.

Witnessed by 90,000 Persons.

So ended the "battle of the century," fought before 90,000 people—a fight which had aroused more interest, in all probability, than any other in all history.

Perhaps this interest had been enhanced by the futile efforts of moral reformers to stop the fight, but there were other elements which made it unique.

When the New World met the Old in the persons of Heenan and Sayers, when Jim Jeffries's gallant effort to come back against Jack Johnson roused the slumbering bitterness of racial feeling, millions of people who had never hitherto paid any attention to prizefighting found themselves roused by a new stimulus and found in the meeting of two boxers an interest such as they would never have supposed could be attached to a mere sporting event.

Yesterday's fight was international, too; it drew a bigger crowd than had ever seen a prizefight. It brought forward for the first time a real heavyweight contender from the Continent of Europe in a sport where heretofore the English-speaking world has had no serious competition.

There was novelty not only in the size of the crowd, but in the composition of it. The throng included thousands of women and a considerable number of public officials such as have rarely been seen in this country at a professional boxing bout. The fight aroused an intensity of interest that would have been impossible but for the still living emotions roused by the war.

No Accidental Champion.

Dempsey was in many ways the most unpopular of white champions. Those who know him best say that this unpopularity is largely undeserved; but the fact remained that millions of people in Dempsey's own country were hoping that the foreign challenger could beat him. The crowd, though it gave the champion a vociferous welcome, seemed to prefer Carpentier by a considerable majority—before the fight. Its speedy end found thousands cheering the winner who, ten minutes before, had been shouting for Carpentier. Dempsey had shown that whatever else might be said about him, he was no accidental champion. He can fight.

He had, to be sure, a big advantage in size. He had a reach longer by an inch than the challenger; he weighed 188 pounds as he stepped into the ring, while Carpentier weighed only 172. To the eye the difference was greater than this. Carpentier seemed fragile, a thing of mere nerves and desperate determination against Dempsey's huge bulk.

But Dempsey was no slow-moving leviathan. At long-range Carpentier had the better of him, but from half-way through the first round, when the infighting really began, Dempsey had been steadily hammering the Frenchman's body, and occasionally his face, with short but terrifically violent punches which broke Carpentier's defense all to

United Press International

Dempsey (L) vs. Carpentier (R)

pieces and left him a ready victim to the final blows.

So long as the fighting was at arm's length Carpentier had the advantage. His right, flashing with incredible speed, found Dempsey's jaw once in the second round, and shook him badly. Dempsey said after the fight that he couldn't remember being hit hard enough to unsettle him. But to the eyes of spectators at the ringside he looked unsettled through all the rest of that round: and the blow was hard enough to break Carpentier's thumb and sprain his wrist.

Carpentier's Right Failed.

Yet this one fierce smash was the only one that seriously disturbed the champion. He was able, after this shock, to drive Carpentier away from him with one or two fierce swings. The challenger's deadly right—the right that had knocked out most of the men who stood between Carpentier and the championship of Europe—never landed after that.

Again and again Carpentier swung—long, fast, powerful swings—with his right hand; but Dempsey always kept out of the way. Sooner or later he always brought Carpentier to close range; and once clinched, Dempsey began again the terrible pounding that a man of Carpentier's build could not long withstand.

No doubt the much-discussed moral factor had its effect on both fighters. Carpentier could not fail to be buoyed up, perhaps set on edge, perhaps even somewhat overstrained, by the knowledge that not only everybody in his own country and in England, but millions of men and women in the strange land where he had come to contest the championship with a native son, were hoping he would win.

Dempsey perhaps was settled into a fierce sullenness by the knowledge that his victory would be bad news to most of the world. But whatever the moral factor may have done to the dispositions of the fighters, it had nothing to do with the outcome of the fight. Carpentier lost because he could not keep Dempsey from hitting him and because he had not the strength to endure Dempsey's blows.

16 Minutes Late in Starting.

Rickard, the promoter, had promised the crowd that the big fight would start at 3 o'clock, daylight saving time, and, so far as was humanly possible, he kept his word. It was, in fact, sixteen minutes past 3 when the fight actually began, and to get it away as promptly as that it was necessary to defer the last of the six preliminaries, a match between Billy Miske and Jack Renault, until the big fight was over. It served as a sort of after-dinner consolation for the late comers, who had missed the other preliminaries, or for the exigent persons whose demand for action had not yet been satisfied.

Most of the women spectators, it was observed, came in rather late, filing through the alleys and aisles of the huge wooden arena during the fifth preliminary, between Gene Tunney and Soldier Jones.

Few of the masculine spectators were so deliberate as that. At 8 o'clock in the morning, when the arena was opened to the ushers and to the 1,600 Jersey City police and firemen, who kept excellent order throughout the day and were always vigilantly on guard against accidents that never happened, there were already hundreds of spectators gathered outside the ropes surrounding the stadium.

At 9 o'clock, when the doors were opened to the public, the hundreds had become thousands, and all through the rest of the morning more spectators were pouring in—across the ferries, from the tube stations, by surface cars, in automobiles and by train. Before the first preliminary bout began, at 12:50, the arena was almost full.

Not an Untoward Incident.

Any number of mishaps might have occurred, and with ninety thousand people gathered in a hastily-constructed lumber arena a mishap might have meant a catastrophe. But nothing untoward happened.

The arena had been soaked in water every day during its construction. The boards were still damp. The ground underneath—Boyle's Thirty Acres, in a dismal, unprepossessing section of Jersey City just below the eastward slope of the hill crowned by the Boulevard—was an almost stagnant pool. At every exit, at every gate opening into the various sections of the huge enclosure, firemen were stationed, alert for the first spark from a cigar stub or a carelessly discarded match. But though a blue haze of tobacco smoke hung over the arena all day, a fire would have had no chance to get started.

Policemen, two, were everywhere. Thanks to them the crowd was kept moving, ushered to the proper seats, and held pretty well in the seats. Conflicts over tickets which had been duplicated by forgers were few, and only here and there developed into sufficient importance to call for the subduing appearance of a policeman. Airplanes flew over the arena throughout the fight and some of them flew dangerously low; but by good luck none of them met with accidents.

Even the weather was surprisingly favorable. All day long gray clouds hung low over Jersey City, but only once, for a few minutes during the second preliminary fight, did rain fall, and then only a few scattering drops which had no more effect than to make thousands of perspiring men fight their way into raincoats which they presently discarded.

Breeze for the Big Fight.

A hot sun would have been as bad as rain, or worse, but the sun stayed behind the clouds except for a minute or two just after 2 o'clock, and during the big fight there was a light breeze which made the arena unexpectedly comfortable.

It might have been expected that, since a crowd which had been gathering all day would want to go away all at once, there would be some disorder. But there was none, nor any serious congestion. Thousands walked out after the big fight was settled, and the other thousands which waited for the postponed fight between Miske and Renault were able to get away at their leisure, for the afternoon was not yet ended and there was plenty of time to get home for dinner.

It was a rather apathetic crowd that sat through the preliminaries, eating the sandwiches and drinking the soft drinks that were distributed at two or three times the Polo Ground prices. What the price might be nobody cared, for it was a long wait while the early comers sat on their damp benches and watched the unimportant battling of minor fighters. The lunches were at least sufficient to sustain life in thousands of men who had dashed away from home after an early and hurried breakfast and had spent most of the middle part of the day in wishing that the Volstead act had not suppressed those corner dispensaries of first aid.

Crowd Patiently Waits.

The crowd seemed but little interested in the band and the song "pluggers," and its hopes of excitement from incipient fights over seating were disappointed. Its enthusiasm began to awaken, however, with the first knockdown, and the hard fighting in some of the later preliminaries whipped up the appetite of men and women who had come to see somebody damaged, and were beginning to be rather bored with the wait.

The fifth preliminary was ended at 2:50 by the referee's decision that ended by the referee's decision that Gene Tunney had given Soldier Jones as much punishment as was good for him, and the crowd was rather impatiently waiting for Miske and Renault, who stood, wrapped in towels, just beyond the ringside waiting their turn. Then Joe Humphries, the scarlet-faced announcer, who has been introducing champions, challengers and any extraneous celebrities who might be present at all the championship fights of recent history and who had been exercising his cracked voice through the amplifier on the unimportant names of the fighters in the preliminary, took up the transmitter, not unlike a desk telephone, connected with the three big megaphones that stood in the press seats just below the ring.

"Everybody sit down!" he shouted. The crowd, standing as it had stood after every bout to stretch weary muscles and ease aching bones, responded to this order in rather half-hearted manner. Everywhere men were still standing up in spite of the irritable entreaties of those behind them, while officials crowded into the ring and attendants sprinkled rosin over the dampened corners where fighters in earlier bouts had been sponged between rounds.

"Everybody sit down!" Humphreys repeated. And then, when his appeal seemed to have only partial effect, he added, "The big bout is next."

Then everybody stood up. Down an eastward aisle there was a confused swirling, and a thin blue thread of policemen, marked out sharply in the gray mass, tried desperately to clear the corridor. All about men stood on seats looking down for the entrance of the combatants. Humphreys was shouting again into the megaphone, announcing that a collection would be taken for St. Francis's Hospital in Jersey City—"the hospital that does good without any money," he added in an aside to those near the ring—and that there were only ten minutes left for the collection as the big fight began at 3.

But the collection got rather inadequate attention. The eyes of the crowd were drawn to that corridor where the police were trying to clear a passage to the ringside, where other police were pushing back the principals and seconds of the last unregarded preliminary, forcing out the hangers-on who had no right so near the ropes, compelling the telegraph messengers and the miscellaneous functionaries of the fight to sit down and clear the view for those behind them. Above two airplanes swung over the arena, lower than those which had circled about it earlier in the day.

Into the ring came a huge floral horseshoe—red roses, red and white carnations, and gladiolas—with the word "success" picked out in red letters. It was for Dempsey, from friends in Jersey City.

A swarm of photographers and movie camera men poured into the ring and began to take pictures of the horseshoe and the crowd, tearing the air with their cries of "Sit down!" flung fiercely at one another.

A Picture of Carpentier.

Then, while the ring was still crowded with photographers milling evcitedly and falling over one another's tripods, Carpentier suddenly appeared, followed by his seconds. Wrapped in his gray dressing gown, bordered in midnight blue, he came lightly into his corner—the southeastern one—and then as the crowd stood up and cheered with a flutter of waving straw hats he went to the ropes on each side of the ring and held aloft his clasped hands, shaking them in greeting, while the band played the Marseillaise.

A moment later he was back on his stool, talking to his manager and chief of staff, François Descamps. Carpentier has muscles, and formidable muscles; but it was hard to pay attention to the muscles or to remember that this was the man who had knocked out heavyweights who outweighed him thirty or forty pounds.

For those who were near enough to see them, the centre of attraction was his eyes—gray eyes, rather eager, rather excited, in a gray face with blond hair brushed back above it; a face that had more than ever the curious girlish quality that would hardly be looked for in an aspirant to the heavyweight championship. Eagerness and enthusiasm were there, but more than all an apparent realization of the fact that he represented France; that he represented millions of soldiers who had fought in the trenches as well as inside the ropes; and that this day was the climax of his whole career. His eager intensity, his fiery slightness, gave to some of the onlookers a curious sense of resemblance between Georges Carpentier and another French champion of old. He suggested Joan of Arc.

And over this slender, eager, almost devout personage hovered the crafty Descamps. A fat, excitable man, wrapped in a gray sweater trimmed in a dark cream color, a light brown cap on his head and a pink-striped towel swinging from his belt, he talked to the champion, then passed about the ring and chatted with the officials, then came back to Carpentier once more.

A new focus of interest. At 3 o'clock exactly, four minutes after Carpentier had entered, Jack Dempsey came in. He, too, had come up the crowded aisle almost unseen, except by those just beside him; and his entrance into the ring brought a much louder cheer than the challenger had evoked.

Dempsey nodded and smiled slightly, but only for a moment. His famous scowl, the scowl that has entered into tradition as part of a personality, was on his browned, unshaven face. Under black eyebrows and curling black hair he glowered stolidly, sullenly.

Underneath his old maroon sweater showed his white trunks, and the end of a red, white and blue ribbon, which for some reason he had put on in place of a belt. He, too, sat down, but in a moment he was up, standing in front of the floral horseshoe for a photograph, and then crossing the ring to shake hands with Carpentier under fire of the movie cameras.

Object to Dempsey's Tape.

They stood there a moment, the eager gray-eyed blonde and the scowling dark fighter who had come out to defend his right to the championship before a public which seemed inclined to give him no credit for anything but ability to fight. Then they separated, back to their corners once more, and Dempsey, with a sombre, preoccupied air, danced up and down lightly on his tiptoes. Then he sat down and held out his hands to be wound with bandages and adhesive tape.

In a moment the vigilant Descamps was in Dempsey's corner.

"No, no, no!" he shouted, and tore the rolls of tape out of the hands of Dempsey's seconds. The belief that Dempsey's terrific pounding of Willard had been made possible in some degree by his tape-wound hands was strong in the Frenchman's camp, and Descamps was determined that only the soft gauze bandages permitted by the New Jersey Boxing Commission should be used. He thrust one of Dempsey's seconds aside rather roughly, and after a brief but bitter argument gained his way. Dempsey held out his hands to be wound with the strips of gauze, with Descamps leaning against the ropes, almost over him, and following every movement with the vigilance of suspicion.

Meanwhile Jack Kearns, the man behind Dempsey, was showing no interest in Carpentier's hands, nor very much in Dempsey's. Coatless, with a long dark four-in-hand tie over his white shirt and his thinning hair brushed up from his forehead, he could have posed better than Carpentier for a shirt advertisement, and would not have seemed wholly out of place as an illustration of what the well dressed man will wear.

Then there was an interlude while Humphries introduced the distinguished guests—first Mayor Frank Hague of Jersey City, then Governor Edward I. Edwards. Each in his turn shook hands with both fighters and both managers, and then the two shook hands with each other, outside the ropes, before they climbed down out of range of the cameras. Then followed introductions of the State Boxing Commissioners—Robert Doherty, Charles McNair and Charles Lyons—and of Bill Brennan, who was indulging in the popular outdoor sport of challenging the winner.

Referee Harry Ertle, looking rather strained and careworn, but resplendent in white shirt and flannel trousers, was next introduced.

Then a browned man in blue serge, carrying a light stick and a half-burned cigar in an amber holder, came in and allowed himself to be introduced as "the world's premier promoter, Tex Rickard," which he undoubtedly is. The weights were announced and the public was informed that Joe Bannon was timekeeper.

Meanwhile the seconds of each fighter had been solicitously inspecting the big eight-ounce gloves and had found them satisfactory. The principals had sat silently in their corners; Dempsey glum and grim, Carpentier glancing about him alertly—at his antagonist, at the crowd, finally, with the interest of a veteran military aviator, at the gray airplanes circling against the gray sky overhead.

The gloves fitted on, Carpentier shed his dressing gown and stood out in white jersey trunks, with a light blue stripe down the side. He sat down and let his seconds fan him, while Dempsey, the gloves securely fitted, once more danced on his toes and then spat with an air of satisfaction.

Once more Humphreys got the attention of the crowd. Going over to Dempsey's corner, where Descamps still stood alertly watching the champion, the announcer drew Dempsey out and presented him to the crowd as "the champion, Jack Dempsey, on whom every redblooded American pins his hopes this day." A cheer, a bow, and then Carpentier came forward to be introduced as "the heavyweight champion of the Old World, the idol of his people, and a soldier of France."

The roar that came from the crowd at that made its cheer for Dempsey seem like nothing but a hoarse whisper. All over the arena men stood on their seats and waved their straw hats while they shouted frantically.

Carpentier bowed, shook his clasped hands and then turned to the centre of the ring where principals and seconds gathered for the final instructions of the referee. Now Kearns stepped to Dempsey's side and let his arm linger across the champion's bare brown back, his fingers pinching Dempsey affectionately.

Back to the corners once more, where both men were sponged and Carpentier sank, then rose, flexing his knees. Then the seconds tumbled out of the ring and at 3:16 the gong signaled the beginning of the fight.

PRINCETON RALLIES AND BEATS CHICAGO

Avenges Defeat of Last Year With Brilliant 21-18 Victory at Stagg Field.

TRIUMPH IN LAST PERIOD

Tigers Pull Game From Fire by Scoring Two Touchdowns After Fumble Turns Tide.

FINAL ASSAULT IS HALTED

Easterners Make Great Stand on One-Yard Line as Battle Ends —32,000 See Contest.

Special to The New York Times.

CHICAGO, Oct. 28.—The Princeton football team avenged its defeat at the hands of Chicago last season by beating the Maroon eleven at Stagg Field this afternoon in the most sensational intersectional battle of football history. Apparently beaten beyond all hope of even their most enthusiastic admirers at the end of the third period when they were trailing by 18 to 7, the fighting Tigers staged a desperate rally and rose to a glorious triumph by the score of 21 to 18. The immense throng of 32,000 which filled every available space within the confines of the limited enclosure, was stunned by the sudden change in the fortunes of battle.

With the Princeton line ripped and literally torn to pieces by the powerful line plunging of the Thomas boys and Sorn, the turning point came shortly after the start of the final period. Princeton was in possession of the ball on her own 1-yard line. Cleaves, standing fully 10 yards beyond the goal, pulled the unexpected by shooting a forward pass to Gorman, who sprinted to his own 40-yard mark before he was brought to earth. The Tigers failed to gain and Cleaves punted to Chicago's 42-yard line. Pyott, the Maroon left halfback, was stopped and then came the "break" of the game that eventually was to lead to Princeton's victory.

Zorn, a Chicago back, fumbled the ball on the next play and then Gray picked up the rolling spheroid and made a brilliant run for a touchdown. Smith kicked the goal and the Tigers were now within striking distance of their opponents. The score at this point was 18 to 14 in favor of the Maroon eleven. Before the stunned Chicago players could recover from this sudden change in the aspect of the battle, the Tigers uncorked another desperate assault which again carried the ball across the Maroon goal line. This touchdown gave the Tigers their victory, but the most thrilling and dramatic moment of this battle of battles was still to come.

Despite the fact that within several minutes more the game would pass into history, the Chicago players refused to concede defeat. In the closing minutes of the terrific struggle they fought brilliantly and desperately. On the other hand, the Tigers fought with equal brilliancy and with equal desperation to maintain their slim lead until the final whistle would assure them of their hard-earned victory.

Tigers Hold at Goal Line.

Shortly after the final kick-off, Chicago, with the help of two well-executed forward passes, advanced the ball to Princeton's twenty-five yard line. Another forward pass brought the pigskin to the six-yard mark and Chicago's followers still held out hope for a victory. Twice the Maroon assault was halted with a net gain of only three and a half yards. The brilliant John Thomas made another yard and with the ball scarcely more than a yard from the goal line Princeton stopped another charge by the same Thomas and it was the Tigers' ball just two feet from the goal. Princeton then kicked out of danger and before the teams could line up again the whistle blew and the great battle between the East and the West had ended.

Chicago outplayed Princeton both on the attack and on the defense in the first half of the contest. Although the Thomas boys made some spectacular runs these were due in no small measure to the magnificent line opening of Ponderlik and Rorke. Yet Princeton was playing what the East for years had called Western football—passing and running in open and risky style. It was this method of play which eventually gave the Tigers their triumph.

The Chicago players uncorked a whirlwind attack shortly after the start of the game and got off to an early lead. Several minutes after the opening whistle the Maroons were in possession of the ball on their own forty-yard line. Then they began a steady advance toward the Princeton goal. Brilliant line plunging and end running by John Thomas and Pyott brought the pigskin to the four-yard line. Two more plunges by Thomas put it across the line for the first score of the game. Pyott's try for the goal was partly blocked and Chicago was leading by 6 to 0.

Shortly before the close of the first period a brilliant forward pass from Snively to Gray for 45 yards put the ball on Chicago's 7-yard line. A penalty moved it up to the 5-yard mark just as the quarter ended. When the second period opened Cleaves went across for the Tigers' first touchdown on the fourth down, but not until after the Chicago players had fought desperately to halt the Tigers' advance. Ken Smith booted the ball between the uprights, and Princeton was leading by 7 to 6.

Chicago Resumes Lead.

The Tigers' advantage was short-lived, however, as several minutes later the Maroons crashed through for another touchdown. Chicago marched steadily down the field to gain this score and advanced the ball to the Princeton 10-yard line on brilliant line plunging by Harry and John Thomas. The Princeton line was wavering badly at this point, and on two more plays John Thomas crashed across the goal line. Smith tried to kick a field goal for Princeton from the 25-yard mark later in the period, but the kick was blocked. Princeton advanced the ball as far as Chicago's 20-yard line toward the close of the period, but lost the spheroid on a fumble. The first half ended with the ball in midfield.

In the third period Princeton was held for downs on Chicago's 13-yard line. Later in the quarter, with the help of a Princeton penalty of half the distance to the goal line, Chicago advanced well into the Tigers' territory. With the ball on the Princeton 20-yard line John Thomas crashed through for fifteen yards, and in two more plays went across for Chicago's third touchdown. Pyott failed to kick the goal and the period ended with the score at 18 to 7 in favor of the Maroons. What occurred in the final quarter has been told above.

The crowd was slow in assembling, although at 12:30 when the gates of Stagg Field were thrown open thousands of optimists who hoped to buy tickets were lined around the gates, to disperse slowly when the megaphone trumpeters announced no tickets were for sale.

The police regulations held the curious back for blocks from the stadium, and the gathering army of fans marched in comfort to the scene of combat, massing in colorful sections.

There was not much life until just an hour before game time, when a stocky [illegible]

Continued on Page Twenty-eight.

Play-by-Play Story of Penn Game Brings Gloom to Navy

Special to The New York Times.

ANNAPOLIS, Md., Oct. 28.—Gloom and surprise were mingled when the Naval Academy contingent received the news of the defeat of its team by the University of Pennsylvania, at Philadelphia, this afternoon. It was entirely unexpected, and many thought the Navy would win by a big score. The only saving element is the belief that the Navy players will work all the harder to defeat Pennsylvania State and the Army, thus redeeming the season. The story of the game was received by plays while the Navy plebes were playing the eleven of Staunton Military Academy and the local youths were badly defeated.

HARVARD DEFEATS DARTMOUTH, 12-3

Jenkins Intercepts Forward Pass in Final Period and Scores Only Touchdown.

GREEN HAS NO ATTACK

Hanover Team's Sole Tally Comes on 48-Yard Goal From Placement by Neidlinger.

Special to The New York Times.

CAMBRIDGE, Mass., Oct. 28.—Harvard defeated Dartmouth, 12 to 3, in the stadium this afternoon, but the game was well worth ten years of waiting. The battle was witnessed by more than 50,000 spectators and excitement ran high, for every moment of the two hours the teams were on the field thrill followed thrill and one of the cleanest-fought games in the stadium was marked by as desperate play as possibly could be imagined.

Harvard could not cross the big Green team's goal line by rushing from scrimmage, but the New Hampshire eleven, which could make no dangerous approach for itself with the running attack, twice took the ball away from Bob Fisher's varsity men on downs, and then backed into the shadow of the Hanover goal. But these defenses could not stand off the drop and placement kicking of Charlie Buell and George Owen, the pair who made last year's victory over Yale possible, and while the giant Neidlinger drove a placement goal for Dartmouth, and almost from middle field, this could not meet the Harvard edge.

Still, with things moving so that a sudden break might have cost Harvard its lead, and another field goal tied the score, Dartmouth suddenly saw its hopes for victory or a tie broken into the proverbial smithereens. With the count 6 to 3, with Harvard leading and with the last quarter of the game half way along, Harris, the Dartmouth kicker, went back to position. He did not kick, but tried to get away a forward pass. He received the ball in form and drew back to make his pass. Harris even got the ball away, but so suddenly had Percy Jenkins rushed in from the Crimson flank that Harris found himself smothered too late to hold the ball.

Jenkins leaped as the pass was made, driving his arm upward and hitting the ball with the palm of his hand. He hit it just right to send it upward and immediately over his own head, not far, just a foot or two. Another Harvard player crashed into Harris just as Jenkins hit the ball, and when the leather descended it was into Jenkins's arms, four other Crimson players were through with Jenkins, and all were between him and the Harvard goal, which was far behind. For Jenkins it was simply a matter of legging it for more than 45 yards up the field and tagging the ball down behind the Dartmouth posts.

Jenkins Shines Again.

The spectacular effort of Jenkins shortly was followed by another burst of quick thinking and action on the part of the Harvard wing. Not more than thirty seconds after he had made his score, Jenkins pounced on the ball again, this time following a fumble by Calder, a Hanover substitute back, providing the Crimson with a first down just inside Dartmouth's 30-yard line, but here, even with the game out of reach, Dartmouth stood its ground, took the ball from Harvard on downs and then cut loose with an end-running attack which carried the ball across the middle field and for the finest advance made by either team during the game.

The Harvard eleven was entered in approximately the same marching order as against Centre a week ago, except that Hartley's place at right end was taken by Dan Holder. The Crimson's front was unchanged. Half of the men in the line-up, however, had played no football for a week, and it took them a long time to get going. Dartmouth was on its toes from the start. The Green had no attack except that shown in desperation at the finish, and when the chance to win had passed.

Harvard's line was never threatened, although Neidlinger had two chances for placement shots and scored on one of them. His 48-yard boot and with the ball teed as high, almost, as on a kick-off, carried as true as the crow flies. But the splendid effort was made when the Green was six points behind.

In the first period the match quickly developed into a kicking duel between Gehrke of Harvard and Harris of Dartmouth. Harvard's punting was done against the wind, but Gehrke held his own and Harvard got the benefit of runbacks. Very early the Crimson started its rushing game, and after receiving the ball on Dartmouth's 45-yard line gained one first down and was helped further by an opponent's off-side. But with the ball on its own 25-yard mark Dartmouth simply ripped Harvard's attack wide open in one play, one forward pass failing, and another being completed for only a short gain before Captain Buell tried for a drop-kick field goal from the 31-yard line, missing from an angle.

Dartmouth Has a Chance.

Before the end of the period Dartmouth also had a chance to score. One of Harris's kicks had carried to Harvard's 9-yard line, and the Crimson return was short, Mills getting under way behind some fine interference and dashing to within 27 yards of Harvard's goal. Dartmouth was never closer to the Harvard posts than this. There was no gain, however, and after a forward pass failed, Neidlinger missed a placement shot, started from Harvard's 32-yard line and not far from the side of the field.

In the second period Harvard made the most of the wind. Twice in the second fifteen minutes of play Captain Buell signalled for fair catches, and each time Dartmouth interfered. The first of the 15-yard penalties provided Harvard with a first down on its opponents' 21-yard line, two plays gaining only slightly and then Buell missing a drive for goal when immediately in front of the posts and when he had splendid protection.

The other penalty for Dartmouth's interference on a Harvard fair catch put Harvard within 25 yards of its objective. The Crimson then pushed forward for a first down but after getting just inside the 10-yard line on fourth down and with about a yard to go Buell dropped back for the third time, and then put Harvard three points in the lead with a pretty drop kick on which the ball had to carry only 18 yards.

The score was 3 to 0 at the end of the first half, and early in the second the Cambridge boys started into Hanover territory again. Dartmouth's defense against the Crimson's running

Continued on Page Twenty-nine.

QUAKERS OVERCOME NAVY LEAD TO WIN

New Pennsylvania Stadium Dedicated With Unexpected Triumph Over Middies, 13-7.

MAKES BRILLIANT SHOWING

After Gaining Only Twenty-One Yards in First Half Red and Blue Is Invincible in Second.

Special to The New York Times.

PHILADELPHIA, Pa., Oct. 28.—Massed in a section of the new Penn Stadium, 600 blue-coated midshipmen saw their Navy eleven, a team that had ridden rough shod over Western Reserve, Bucknell and Georgia Tech, defeated by the Pennsylvania team by a score of 13 to 7, Penn sweeping from behind to win one of the greatest victories in its history.

Tonight Philadelphia is filled with a joyous band of students and alumni, who are singing the praises of Heisman and his associates and of the members of the Quaker eleven, from end to end and from centre to fullback. Not within the last two decades has Penn's cup of joy been as full as it is at this very moment.

All told it was a great day for the Red and Blue. Not only were their football heroes victorious over a team coached by a former Pennsylvania mentor, Bob Folwell, but in doing so they overcame an old-time hoodoo. They dedicated their $750,000 stadium, seating some 50,000 persons, and demonstrated to the football world at large that dedications and defeats are not synonymous.

Victory Is Unexpected.

Most gratifying of all to the warriors of the Red and Blue was the fact that the Penn team blazed out a victory when it was least expected. Before the game started today, Pennsylvanians were only hopeful that Heisman had at least finally succeeded in working out something that would hold the middies in check.

During the first half of the battle Penn's fears proved well founded for the Navy backs ripped the Red and Blue line into bits, using a fake forward pass formation that seemed to leave the Heisman eleven totally at sea. Beginning at the middle of the first quarter, the Navy backs, McKee, Cullen, Norris and Conroy began a march that threw consternation into the Penn stands. With steady smashes through the line and off the tackles, the midshipmen carried the ball from the centre and guard for the first and what proved to be the last Navy score.

The second quarter was a repetition of the first, with the Navy in complete domination of the situation. Time and time the midshipmen threatened the Penn goal line. Once they reached the Red and Blue 23-yard mark after a march of 50 yards. Once they were checked by an off-side play by one of the Navy forwards.

The way the Navy backs were going it seemed certain that the Midshipmen would score once more, but John Thurman, Penn's 200-pound quarterback and tackle, intercepted a forward pass and delayed what seemed to be the inevitable. Again the Navy took up the march down the field, but when they got to the Penn's 10-yard line the Red and Blue line braced and held for downs.

Navy Held for Downs.

Undaunted, the Middies began all over again, with short dashes through the line and runs around the Penn flanks. The Middies reached the Penn 15-yard line only to be checkmated for the second time by the frenzied Pennsylvanians, who held them for downs in the shadow of the goal posts. Then came the end of the half, a résumé of which showed that the Red and Blue had the ball in its possession for just exactly eight plays, four of them rushes which netted a total of 21 yards and four punts.

But something transpired in the Pennsylvania quarters during the intermission. Heisman must have used alchemy on his cohorts, for when they returned to the field they were a different team. Captain "Pos" Miller, the little 160-pound Red and Blue leader, danced about the field like a Comanche. Catching the spirit of their captain the other ten Pennsylvanians followed suit. The Quaker team was nothing but a bunch of waving arms and dancing legs before the kick-off.

Heisman had shifted his line-up, taking Thurman out of the quarterback position and replacing him with Langdon. Thurman was shifted back to his old tackle position, relieving the weakened Graf, against whom the Middies had concentrated their attack in the opening half.

Miller Opens Attack.

No sooner had Cullen kicked off than the transformation of the Penn team was evident. Miller ran over and grabbed the descending oval out of a mate's hands, running it back fifteen yards to Penn's 34-yard line. Twisting and pulling himself out of the grasp of Navy tacklers, he reeled off two first downs just outside the Navy tackles. In a hole, he dropped back and deftly threw a forward pass into the awaiting arms of Rae McGraw, his fellow halfback, for a gain of nine yards, taking the ball to the Navy's 30-yard line. Another first down and then Penn started what looked like an innocent end run.

McGraw stepped back out of the way of the charging Navy linemen and then hurled the ball on a line to Miller, clear of his man. With a great catch, the youngster wheeled and was on his way toward the Navy goal line. Cullen and Conroy made desperate efforts to bring the fleet Pennsylvanian down, but he plunged headlong across the line and then "Ted" Hamer sent the Red and Blue cohorts into a state akin to frenzy by booting a goal from placement, tying up the score at 7-all.

Norris brought Hamer's kick-off back to the 35-yard line, but a Navy penalty, one of the many inflicted against the Middies, set them back 15 yards and forced a surrender of the ball, Cullen punting to McGraw, who dodged a Navy end and returned 10 yards. Unable to gain by running plays, Penn again punted.

Navy Kick Blocked.

An incompleted Navy pass forced the Middies to punt. Cullen, depending a little too much on his own forward wall and underestimating Penn's, failed to get back quite as far as usual. With the snap of the ball the three Penn men ripped through the line, and some unknown hero, his identity lost in the jumping mass of red and blue striped bodies, blocked the ball.

It bounced over toward the side lines with one Navy player and three Penn men after it. The Pennsylvanians won the race, both Tally and Fairchild clutching it in a death embrace on the Navy's 45-yard line. After Miller had wriggled his way for 7 yards through the line, McGraw, with a headlong dive over a mass at centre, gave Penn a first down on the Navy 32-yard line.

Then Penn worked its masterpiece, faking the same play over again. With Langdon streaking down the right side of the field and drawing the midshipmen's secondary defense to that side of the gridiron, Miller passed the ball to the left to Ertresvaag, the Red and Blue right end, who snatched it out of the grasp of a Navy back and staggered to the 9-yard line before he was hauled to earth. Miller broke through Bolles and Parr for 8 yards, carrying the ball to the Navy 1-yard line, when the whistle blew for the quarter.

On the first play after the teams had changed goals, Miller smashed between Mathews and Lentz for the remaining yard. Hamer's try for a goal was blocked, but the failure meant little to

Continued on Page Twenty-eight.

Princeton Undergrads Celebrate Chicago Victory With Bells, Bonfires and Parade

Special to The New York Times.

PRINCETON, N. J., Oct. 28.—With bells tolling and bonfires burning on several parts of the campus, the Princeton undergraduates celebrated their team's victory over Chicago in enthusiastic manner here tonight. Never in the history of football at Princeton has an early season game created so much interest among students and townspeople as the intersectional classic in the Windy City today. When a Tiger team beats Harvard or Yale in football, the huge bell in the belfry of old Nassau Hall is pressed into service and the undergraduates take turns ringing it. But never has it been known to ring for an early season victory before.

When the news came through by radio and telegraph that Princeton had held the Maroons on their 1-foot line and the game was over, the hundreds of students formed an enthusiastic parade down Nassau Street singing the old Princeton songs, and the famous bell began to ring out the "Glory of Old Nassau."

A play-by-play account of the game came through at University Field during the game between Princeton freshmen and Fordham freshmen; the Western Union main office gave out the same thing; radio sets in the "Tiger Shop" and Palmer Laboratory also reported the game in detail. Each place was crowded with eager students, cheering madly one minute, groaning hoarsely the next. All agreed that never in football history has a game, outside of the big three, created so much fierce interest as this.

When the team and its followers return to jungle land tomorrow, a glorious homecoming is being planned by the undergraduate body. A parade will be formed and the victorious warriors will be escorted from the station to their rooms in state.

PITTSBURGH TRIMS BUCKNELL, 7 TO 0

Panthers Win Hard-Fought Battle, Scoring Only in Final Period of Game.

Special to The New York Times.

PITTSBURGH, Pa., Oct. 28.—The Pittsburgh Panthers this afternoon smashed and ripped the Bucknell line time after time, only to lose the ball either on downs or a punt when a score was in the making, and it was not until the last period of play that the Panthers were able to breach the Orange and Blue, defense and make the score that gave them a 7-to-0 victory.

It was their first victory at home this year and was sweet revenge for the defeats by Bucknell in 1912 and 1913, the two previous contests between the teams. There was not much to choose between the two teams during the first half, both showing sterling qualities in defense when their line was menaced. Bucknell made three first downs to Pittsburgh's two in the first period, and carried the ball to the Blue and Gold five-yard line, but Denton and Dayhoof were unable to batter their way through the Pitt defense and they lost the ball on downs. On the kickout of Flanagan the ball was still on Pittsburgh's 23-yard line in Bucknell's possession when the period ended.

The Orange and Blue was forced to kick as the second quarter opened, and the Panthers, by a series of forward passes, carried the ball to the 20-yard line, where a try at goal was missed by Williams. On the next play Anderson carried the ball to Bucknell's 5-yard line, where a fumble by Colonna was recovered by Bihl for Bucknell, and Jenkins punted out of danger as the half ended.

Bucknell kicked off, and Shuler, who was very good at running back punts, carried the ball 25 yards to his own 45-yard line. Pitt kept edging toward the other end of the field, until suddenly Foster intercepted a Pittsburgh forward pass and ran 15 yards before Sack downed him. Bucknell punted as the quarter ended.

Pitt started to play straight football in the last period, and by reason of Colonna's line bucks and end runs by Anderson and Flanagan, carried the ball to Bucknell's 5-yard line.

Colonna made a yard on the next play, and Bucknell was penalized half the distance to the goal line for offside play. Colonna failed to gain on the next two tries, but another penalty against Bucknell for offside play put the ball on the 1-yard line, from where Colonna was pushed over for the one touchdown of the game.

The line-up:

PITTSBURGH (7).		BUCKNELL (0).
Jordan	L.E.	Julian
Simpson	L.T.	Homan
Clark	L.G.	Merrett
Bowser	C.	Bihl
Sack	R.G.	Reed
Fredette	R.T.	Edgar
Williams	R.E.	Butler
Shuler	Q.B.	Dayhoff
Flanagan	L.H.B.	Wilsbach
Anderson	R.H.B.	Denton
Hewitt	F.B.	Jenkins

SCORE BY PERIODS.

Pittsburgh	0	0	0	7	—7
Bucknell	0	0	0	0	—0

Touchdowns, Colonna. Point after touchdown, Williams.

Substitutions—Bucknell: Morgan for Reed, Foster for Dayhoff, Henning for Jenkins, Starrett for Morrett, Buckovitz for Edgar: Pittsburgh: Colonna for Hewitt, Gourley for Fredette, Sauer for Jordan, Frank for Simpson, Hewitt for Colonna.

Referee—Al Sharpe, Yale. Umpire—Ed Thorpe, De La Salle. Head Linesman—D. W. Merriman, Geneva. Time of periods—15 minutes.

YALE'S CONQUERORS SMOTHER PURDUE, 56-0

Iowa, in Second Conference Game, Scores Almost at Will on Boilermakers.

IOWA CITY, Ia., Oct. 28 (Associated Press).—Tearing great holes in Purdue's line with their smashing interference and hard-hitting backs, Iowa's big ten champions scored almost at will on the Boilermakers, swamping them under a 56-to-0 score in Iowa's second conference game of the season, played on Iowa field here today.

Captain Gordon Locke, playing Parkin's quarterback position, starred for the Hawkeyes in the first two periods, crumbling the Purdue line for gain after gain. Locke was given a rest late in the second period and remained out for the rest of the game. Parkin, who took the pilot's position in the third quarter and part of the fourth, played up to the form he showed at Yale and reeled off run after run for gains of from five to thirty yards.

Coach Jones early in the second half began sending in his second-string men, who kept up the scoring.

TRINITY DOWNS UNION.

Keating Is Star in 7-3 Triumph for New Englanders.

Special to The New York Times.

SCHENECTADY, N. Y., Oct. 28.—Union College, after suffering a number of defeats on the gridiron and playing two tie games, made a desperate attempt to win the home game here today with Trinity, and it was not until the third period that Trinity took the lead and won the contest on Alexander Field by the score of 7 to 3.

Sutton of Union kicked to Keating of Trinity on the 15-yard line in the third quarter and Keating ran the whole length of the field through Union's team for a touchdown. He later kicked the goal. Just previously Captain Heldorf made a place kick from the 25-yard line after a series of line plunges.

The score:

TRINITY (7.)		UNION (3.)
Miller	L.E.	Kruse
Noble	L.T.	Cotton
Anderson	L.G.	Bellinger
Brill	C.	Willetts
O'Connor	R.G.	Glenn
Woolan	R.T.	Deane
Wilcox	R.E.	Welling
Keating	R.B.	Heldorf
Kennedy	R.H.B.	Palmer
Montgomery	L.H.B.	Rich
Artgies	F.B.	Stanley

SCORE BY PERIODS.

Trinity	0	0	7	0	—7
Union	0	0	3	0	—3

Substitutions—Trinity: Hart for Miller, McNally for Woolan, Allen for Montgomery, Daly for Wilcox, Cumford for Daly; Union: R. Myer for Welling, Nitchman for Rich, Welling for R. Meyer.

Referee—Chase. Umpire—Peterson. Head linesman—Delahant.

HOLY CROSS UPSETS VERMONT ELEVEN

Worcester Collegians Score Unexpected 6 to 0 Victory in Hard-Played Game.

Special to The New York Times.

WORCESTER, Mass., Oct. 28.—Holy Cross upset the dope here today, defeating Vermont 6—0. It was a hard played game all the way through. Holy Cross scored early in the opening period.

Glennon kicked off to Captain Johnson, Beck punted. Riopel and Crowley netted ten yards for the Purple. Crowley punted to Driscoll. On a centre play Johnson fumbled and Captain Healey recovered. On a criss cross around Vermont's right end Glennon scored. Riopel missed the goal.

From this point on both teams resorted to a kicking game, looking for a break. Late in the last period Vermont brought the ball to the Holy Cross 20-yard line on four successful passes, but could not score.

Vermont found the Holy Cross line a stone wall on defense and was able to make but two first downs on straight football.

The line-up:

HOLY CROSS (6).		VERMONT (0).
Butler	L.E.	Semansky
McGrath	L.T.	Harnis
Cooney	L.G.	Nowland
Healey	C.	Margolski
Golembemski	R.G.	Masley
Ray	R.T.	Garrety
Mahaney	R.E.	Eastborn
Glennon	Q.B.	Driscoll
Riopel	R.H.B.	Beck
Slmendinger	L.H.B.	Gooch
Crowley	F.B.	Johnson

SCORE BY PERIODS.

Holy Cross	6	0	0	0	—6
Vermont	0	0	0	0	—0

Touchdown—Glennon.

Substitutions—Butler for Young, Broussard for Slmendinger, Young for Butler, Cooney for Ray, Yarnell for Gooch, Gooch for Driscoll, Johnson for Margolski.

Referee—Keegan. Umpire—Kelly. Linesman—Sherlock. Time of periods—15 minutes.

C. C. N. Y. OUTPLAYED BY HOBART ELEVEN

Geneva Team Too Strong for New York Collegians, Winning by Score of 24 to 0.

Special to The New York Times.

GENEVA, N. Y., Oct. 28.—Hobart College's football team outkicked, outran and outplayed City College of New York here this afternoon, winning 24 to 0. A field goal and three touchdowns, one in each of the first three-quarters, was the means by which the Hobart score was obtained. Tannenbaum, husky New York fullback, played a star game for his team. His terrific line bucking netting many yards through the Hobart line.

The local aggregation stiffened when it looked as though New York would score and several times turned a seemingly tight situation for themselves into a critical one for their opponents. There were long, openfield dashes by Gasper, Hobart quarterback, and brilliant forward passing one pass, and a splendid bit of openfield running by Loghry, Hobart end, netting the local team fifty yards and a touchdown.

Hobart scored in the first five minutes of play, Gasper taking advantage of the wind and dropping a field goal. Shortly after, Loghry interrupted a New York forward pass and scored the first touchdown. Gorman kicked the goal. Loghry ran 50 yards in the second quarter and carried the second forward pass over. Again Gorman kicked the goal. New York tried many forward passes, but most of them were intercepted.

Loghry was again given the ball on a forward pass in the third quarter and took the ball within two yards of the line, from where Gasper carried it over. Gorman kicked the goal.

In the last quarter New York threatened, but lost the ball on the 50-yard line when Hobart's line tightened following a series of violent plunges that broke through the centre for gains. The game ended with the ball on New York's 50-yard line, where Dailey intercepted the last New York forward pass.

The line-up:

HOBART (24.)		C. C. N. Y. (0.)
Loghry	L.E.	Garvey
Wilson	L.T.	Brodsky
Scofield	L.G.	Miller
Gorman	C.	Schtterns
Ellinwood	R.G.	Shapiro
Jones	R.T.	[illegible]
Hogan	R.E.	Wasson
Gasper	Q.B.	Rosenwasser
Thibodeau	L.H.B.	Farber
Dailey	R.H.B.	Oshins
Knowles	F.B.	Tannebaum

SCORE BY PERIODS.

Hobart	10	7	7	0	—24
C. C. N. Y.	0	0	0	0	—0

Substitutions—C. C. N. Y.: T. Tannebaum for Farber, Farber for Tannebaum, Vogel for Shapiro, Greenberg for Farber, Rengle for Kudin. Hobart: Skinner for Ellinwood, G. Loghry for Gasper, Barnum for Scofield, Clarke for Loghry, Krause for Scofield, Skinner for Krause, Souhan for Knowles, Knowles for Souhan, Barnum for Gorman, Clarke for Thibodeau, Grosjean for Loghry.

Referee—Benzonia, Rochester. Umpire—Wright, Columbia. Head linesman—Dinan, Syracuse.

VIRGINIA IS VICTORIOUS.

Has Little Difficulty in Defeating Johns Hopkins by 19 to 0.

BALTIMORE, Md., Oct. 28.—Outplaying Johns Hopkins in all angles of the game, University of Virginia won today's game at Homewood Field before a disappointing crowd, 19 to 0. After the first period in which neither team scored, there was no doubt as to the final result.

In the second quarter Virginia rolled up 13 points on touchdowns by Wilson and Arnold. A line plunge brought the initial score and a forward pass the second touchdown, Fenwick kicking one of the two points after the touchdowns. The final Virginia touchdown was made in the last quarter by Wilson.

Scores Twice at Soccer.

A double triumph at soccer was scored by the Riverdale Country School over the Arden School at the latter's grounds at New Brighton, S. I., yesterday, when both the first and second teams of the visitors emerged victorious over their respective opponents by scores of 3-1 and 2-1 respectively.

SYRACUSE BATTLES PENN STATE TO DRAW

Stalwart Defense of Both Teams Marks Contest Which Ends in a Scoreless Tie.

20,000 AT TENSE STRUGGLE

Crowd at Polo Grounds Sees Both Elevens Miss Chances to Score— Frugone and Wilson Star.

Penn State and Syracuse, two of the strongest elevens in the East, met head-on at the Polo Grounds yesterday afternoon, grappled for sixty minutes and finished in a scoreless tie with the ball in mid-field. New York may see more thrilling football battles before the season ends, it may even see a more powerful defense unleashed by some team or other, but it will not see a greater defensive game or a harder, more fiercely played contest if it waits through this and many seasons to come. The 0-0 score, the position of the ball when the game ended and the 20,000 who saw the game will tell you that the two teams were as evenly matched yesterday as the proverbial peas of the same pod.

Each team made seven first downs and not only were they even collectively, but also individually. Frugone's hard and deceptive running offset Harry Wilson's great playing, and Zimmerman and Palm were about on a par except in kicking, where Zimmerman had the edge. Both teams were well supported and the crowd was typical of football, with pretty girls, spirit and colors galore.

If a palm had to be awarded it would go to Syracuse. The Orange entered the fray an under dog, and it was an underdog throughout most of the first half, but it was anything but that through the rest of the contest.

Twice, in fact, the yellow-jersied combination broke loose with sweeping offensives which swept the far-famed Nittany Lions before them, but the end of the first half halted the first one and a costly fumble the second, and the Orange never succeeded in getting going again.

Penn State, too, had its chances to shove across a touchdown, the best one coming early in the opening period, when Simmons fumbled on his own 10-yard line and Bedenk recovered the ball for State. Bezdek's machine had already made one first down, and was full of confidence and drive, but the Orange was not to be so easily scored upon.

Wilson Makes a Yard.

Palm shot Wilson at the line, and Harry squirmed through for one of the coveted 10 yards. Palm essayed an off-tackle smash, but the fiercely charging Orange forwards smothered him and drove him back for a 2-yard loss. Again Wilson hurled himself at the Orange stone wall, and again he came to earth at the line of scrimmage. Then Palm played his ace in the hole, the running pass which has so often crowned Penn State with victory. Palm himself took the ball and ran back toward the end, then he passed straight and true to Wilson, but the receiver, too, was still behind the line of scrimmage, and two Syracuse tacklers downed him in his tracks. The ball went to Syracuse, and Meehan rushed into the fray, a slim youngster who eventually proved to be the salvation of the Salt City team.

This was young Zimmerman, a slight chap who can't weigh much over 155 pounds. He immediately booted the ball out of danger, and, though Penn State and its followers didn't know it at the time, the Nittany Lions' finest chance to score had gone by the board.

The Pennsylvanians were on the offensive throughout the remainder of this period, however, and the jump-shift of Bezdek's bunched, backfield seemed to have the Syracuse team worried. The Blue-clad backs would line up so close together that they seemed to be in almost tandem formation, and then they would go shooting off tackle and around end, or Palm would work Bezdek's new version of the old-fashioned criss-cross and most of these plays would bring gains. When they resorted to the pass in the early part of the game the Keystone team also looked to have the Syracuse defense guessing, and many of these passes, started far behind the line of scrimmage, were successfully completed, but the Orange combination always found a place further than which it would not yield, and then Palm, forced to kick, found himself losing ground on the interchange of punts with Zimmerman.

Syracuse, on the other hand, seemed to have little or no offensive power at the outset of the game. Their tries at the Blue line were always smothered, and they found that attempting to skirt the Penn State ends was an exceedingly unprofitable business.

All this through the first period and the greater part of the second. Then for some inexplicable reason the aspect of the game suddenly changed. Until this time it had been all Penn State, all Bezdek and the infectious chorus of the Pennsylvanian's "Victory" song. Syracuse had shown nothing yet, but a tight defense when its back was to the wall and the courage to fight a good fight no matter what the outcome.

Orange Takes the Offensive.

But here Fivaz intercepted a forward pass which had been thrown by Palm and carried it to the Nittany Lion's 30-yard line. Then Zimmerman attempted a place kick which failed dismally and Penn State recovered. State kicked. Whether this made Frugone, who was running the Syracuse eleven at the time, think that after all the Penn State team was not sure of itself, or not, will never be known. Whatever the reason, he began to drive his team and the Orange line and backs responded in an unexpected manner. They opened up holes, took out their men and literally brushed the powerful Blue defense aside for a time. Frugone himself made first down on a plunge through the centre of the line. Then he hit one tackle for 5 yards and the other for 7, and Meehan's team had made its second first down of the game. Frugone shot Kellog through for 7 yards and Anderson delivered the three that were necessary to make it first down again.

State was alarmed. Bezdek began to warm up a couple of substitutes and the cheer leaders changed their plea from "let's go" to "hold that line." Starting after their fourth successive first down, Bowman made a yard in a smash at the centre of the line and the Orange was sweeping along like a storm which gathers momentum as it goes, when the timekeeper's whistle sounded, ending the half and the rally.

As the second half began Zimmerman kicked off to Wilson on the 10-yard line. It was a beautiful kick, as were nearly all those which Zimmerman got off during the encounter. Wilson, however, by turning and twisting, ran the ball back 15 yards before he was downed. On three plays Penn State failed to make any appreciable gain and Palm kicked to Zimmerman who eluded the first two men down the field and returned almost 20 yards before he was pulled to earth. Penn State held and when Syracuse failed to make the necessary yard on the fourth down, the ball went over to the Lions.

Mike Palm, Bezdek's great field general, began to wave distress signals at this juncture, but the Penn State physician who went out to look him over, was all for leaving Mike in the game. Referee McCarthy was of another mind and came over to the Penn State bench to warn Bezdek that Palm was groggy and in no condition to play. Bezdek immediately relieved him with Patton.

One of the first things that the newcomer did was to let one of Zimmerman's punts get past him and roll inside the Penn State 10-yard line. It looked like a bad break for Bezdek's team and it looked blacker still for the Blue when it was penalized 5 yards for offside play. But Patton retrieved his error and pulled his team out of the hole by a low, but long-carrying punt

Continued on Page Twenty-seven.

First Football Death Here; High School Boy Crushed

The first football death of the year in this city was reported yesterday, when Louis Manilla, 13 years old, of 302 East 101st Street died in Mount Sinai Hospital of injuries received while playing Tuesday with some boys in a lot at 105th Street and Fifth Avenue.

Manilla, who was a pupil of the Patrick Henry Junior High School, went after the ball kicked by one of the boys. He fell on the ball, and others who went after it fell on top of him, crushing his right side.

FORWARD PASS IS COLUMBIA NEMESIS

Williams's Aerial Attack Takes Victory From Lion Eleven in Last Two Minutes.

FINAL SCORE IS 13 TO 10

Fumbling and Weakness in Line Handicaps Each Team—Mallon Is the Individual Star.

A vision of Benny Boynton swept down over South Field yesterday afternoon. Boynton was not in gridiron togs, but the same old spirit that he instilled into the Williams football machinery while he was its star a few years ago came to light again yesterday. It was that characteristic spirit that Boynton always had—the belief that no game is over until the final whistle blows. And so, fighting like a pack of wolves against seemingly uneven odds, the Williams eleven, with only two minutes of play remaining, and the score 10 to 6 against them, broke loose with some brilliant forward passing that completely bewildered the Columbia defense. When the final whistle blew the victory that looked so much like Columbia's had been torn asunder and Williams had won the game by a score of 13 to 10, the first defeat of the season for the Morningside lads.

By the time the first half had ended the game looked as if it might belong to anybody. Neither team had been able to score. On two occasions Mallon of Williams had tried to break the tie by attempts at field goals. But both times his kicks, one from the 40-yard line and the other from the 25-yard line, went far from the goal posts. For the greater part of the time it was an exchange of punts, with Williams having a slight edge.

The big Columbia line continued to show its lack of power. The backfield seemed to be a weakened thing, too. Lack of effective interference was holding up possible gains and, on the whole, the team was showing a rather unimpressive kind of football. Williams, at the same time, had not reached her maximum style of play and was willing, if not eager, to continue the exchange of punts. During the half, with everything looking about even, Williams managed to make one more first down than Columbia, 5 to 4.

After the Morningside Heights team had built up its four-point lead near the end of the game, its confidence seemed to increase with its lead, the brilliant work of the third quarter passed and O'Neill's combination had reverted to the indifferent brand of ball that is displayed in the first half.

Williams Pass Accurate.

Mallon, who along with Dickey were worthy men to act in the role of understudies for the great Benny Boynton, was quick to take advantage of the Blue and White's relapse. One after another Mallon's forward passes swept the ball down the field. And each time as his powerful right arm caught hold of the ball it was whirled with the speed and accuracy of a bullet from a gun into the hands of one of his teammates.

The Columbia players seemed to take the forward passing attack as something that could not last until the goal line was reached. But it did last. With the ball on Columbia's 28-yard line Monjo dropped back and tossed a pass to Mallon for an 8-yard gain. The next forward was broken up. Then Mallon caught the ball well back from the line and threw it straight over the centre of the line into the outstretched arms of Parker. Without an opponent near Parker stepped over the goal line with the score that added another Columbia scalp to the belt of the New Englanders.

After Columbia had failed to score in the first half, it began the second half with an outburst of pep that brought back memories of early season triumphs. Coach Buck O'Neill must have more than whispered words of meaning to his warriors during the intermission. Right at the start Williams tried some line bucking and forward passing but failed to gain ground. Then Columbia, getting the ball in Williams territory on the 23-yard line, swept down the field as though there wasn't any force that could stop them and in two plays had the ball across the goal line. First Roderick dashed around left end for 25 yards, and then on the next play dropped back and threw the ball for 30 yards to Bob Burtt who ran the remaining 20 for the Columbia score.

Koppisch's Fumble Costly.

A short time later in that quarter, with Columbia again in possession of the ball on its own 18-yard line, Koppisch fumbled and Williams got the ball. Dickey made two yards through the line. Mallon sprinted around right end on the next play for a touchdown. When Mallon failed at the goal Columbia was bubbling with enthusiasm and Williams was inclined to think that maybe that point meant more than it really did.

Near the middle of the final quarter, when the Blue and White thought that the victory had been snugly tied up, Bob Burtt hoisted the ball between the goal posts from the 25-yard line for three more points. But a few minutes later came Williams's all-powerful drive that upset Columbia's hopes for victory.

It was the first defeat of the season for the Lion after a series of four straight victories. From a technical point of view Columbia was barely outplayed. Williams made nine first downs and the Blue and White made eight. But it was a superior brand of aerial work that accounted largely for the New Englander's victory. The passes were the nucleus for the attack and as each one that was successful passed through the air Columbia became a trifle more riled. They couldn't do anything—there was too much protection and cleverness to the Williams forward pass. In the second half the ground gained on forward passes was enough to carry Williams from one end of the field to the other. In all, out of fifteen tries nine of the passes were successful and netted a total of 101 yards.

Mallon Individual Star.

The man who stood out as the hero of the Williams triumph was Mallon. Not only was he able to play football from the standpoint of brawn, but he supplied the greater part of the brainy element as well. From his position at quarterback he directed the team in almost flawless fashion. And in carrying the ball, kicking it or throwing it, he displayed an equal degree of proficiency. Almost equal praise is due Dickey, an open field runner of more than usual ability.

Columbia's hero is missing. No man stood out above his mates yesterday for the Blue and White. Bob Burtt probably comes closest to the honor, scoring every point that the Blue and

Continued on Page Twenty-seven.

ARMY HOLDS YALE TO TIE AT 7 TO 7

Both Elevens Fail to Realize Opportunities in Colorful Game at New Haven.

ELIS ARE FIRST TO SCORE

Forward Pass Paves Way for Touchdown in Third Period— Cadets in Quick Comeback.

76,000 SPECTATORS ATTEND

Spectacular Struggle Is Staged in Bowl—Poor Generalship Costs Blue a Possible Triumph.

Special to The New York Times.

NEW HAVEN, Conn., Oct. 28.—Floundering like a ship without a rudder, playing with the air of a team which knew it ought to do something but didn't know how to do it, Yale this afternoon couldn't even score one of those moral victories which used to make life in New Haven worth living. The Army held the Elis even, 7 to 7, but it is doubtful if the West Pointers were as good a team as the Tad Jones eleven.

True, Yale escaped defeat, which is something in these days of football upsets, but the tie game caused nobody to throw his hat into the air and give three cheers for the dear old Blue. The result, as a matter of fact, pleased nobody. The Cadets had had a sneaking notion that they might win. Yale had been favored in the betting. When they retired from the field of battle, the decision was still in the lap of the gods.

No game could well have been more colorful than today's battle. As a football game it was interesting and hard fought, though indecisive. As a spectacle it left even the Yale-Harvard conflict far in its wake. The Bowl held about 76,000 people, with parading cadets, dignified generals and pretty girls in expensive furs to lend atmosphere. It was everything that a college football game ought to be on a crisp day in Autumn.

The only thing missing was in the intellectual efforts that might reasonably have been expected of young college men. It is doubtful if either team could have reached a passing mark in brain work. The Elis had at least one excellent chance to win, and lost because their heads were not as nimble as their feet. The Army passed up a fine opportunity in the first quarter because Quarterback Smythe would not take half a loaf—would not take three points when he felt there was a chance for seven.

First Half Is Scoreless.

In the first half, the Army mule and the bulldog sparred without a score. In the third period, Yale began opening up its attack. The Elis reached upon the shelf, got down the forward pass and dusted it off. A fling from Whitey Neale to "Memphis Bill" Mallory caught the Army napping. Mallory staggered to the four-yard line before he was downed. On the next play Neale took the ball, faked a sweep around the Army's left end and then cut in rapidly outside tackle. He fell over the line with a touchdown which made it look like Yale's game.

But the mule still had a kick left. He lashed out in the final minutes of the third period and marched right down the field from Yale's 43-yard mark to the goal line. From midfield, Smythe dropped back and threw a pass to Wood, who traveled 25 yards to the Yale 28-yard cross-bar. Smythe lunged through left tackle for 4 more yards. With the ball on the 19-yard line, Smythe threw another pass to Wood. The Yale defense was wide open. Doc Jordan, the Yale captain, failed to protect his territory, and Wood, catching the ball with the ease of a baseball player, sprinted 15 yards. Wight dragged him to earth only 3 yards away from the goal line.

A touchdown was inevitable. Wood tried the line and picked up 2 yards. On the next play he simply fell over the Blue line, plunging like a fancy diver in a swimming meet. When he landed on terra firma, it was behind the goal line. Smythe kicked the goal which tied the score.

Even then it was not too late for Yale. In the same period—the fourth—Yale tried another forward pass. It was strange how the Elis antiquated aerial attack was fooling the soldiers. This time Wight threw and Neidlinger received. He plunged on and for twelve yards. A fifteen-yard penalty against the Army also helped immensely. By the time the referee had finished pacing off the fatal distance the pigskin was only thirty-six yards from the Army goal posts.

Golden Opportunity Departs.

Yale then prodded the cadet line twice, battering tactics which yielded slightly more than four yards on the third down. Neidlinger decided to go back to that strangely successful forward pass offensive. It was poor generalship, and Neale made matters worse by flinging a high, long pass which gave the Army defense plenty of time to get up and knock the ball to the ground.

Fourth down now, and still five yards to go. There was nothing else to do but drop kick, but Wight's effort, although well aimed, was low. It sailed beneath the cross-bar from the 42-yard line, and with it went Yale's best chance.

Second guessing is a popular indoor amusement, but, nevertheless, there was no valid reason why Yale should have tried a long, aimless pass at that moment. A short throw to uncovered territory at the side might have gained the 5 yards needed. Then it would have been first down on the 27-yard mark. If line plays had then failed, Wight would have been within range of the goal, and his drop kick would have carried far enough to give Yale the 3 points.

Neidlinger, the quarterback, realized that he had failed. He was taken out soon after, and he looked like a broken-hearted young man as he ran from the field. His head was bent. Now and then he shook it in a peculiarly pathetic manner, and struck the palm of one hand with his fist, like a man who has made a big mistake and realizes, after it is all over, what might have been. Nobody could console him. He brushed past coaches and fellow-players, and, still shaking his head in that helpless manner, rushed for the dressing room.

Not Neidlinger's Fault.

But it wasn't Neidlinger who was to blame. He isn't a quarterback, and does not claim to be one. It was a Yale failure, and the team, without a directing head, played as if it was not sure what ought to be done next. While the Elis faltered, victory slipped from their grasp.

However, the indictment can be broadened enough to include young Mr.

Continued on Page Twenty-nine.

PRINCETON RALLIES AND BEATS CHICAGO

Continued from Page Twenty-six.

the side lines and of a sudden the Maroon side of the field arose with a wild cheer. Hats came off and Chicago paid its tribute to Stagg, the beloved "old man," who did not hear, but walked quickly to the station from which he was to direct practice.

Maroon Welcomes Its Heroes.

Ten minutes later the Maroon first squad bounded out from the southwest of the stadium and the Chicago sections rose again, seething with noise and enthusiasm as the Maroon welcomed its heroes.

Half an hour later the Princeton squad, thirty-five strong, rushed onto the scene, and the same instant the blue and maroon clad band, escorting the biggest drum in the college world, marched around the field, and, while the teams practiced kicking, the band stood before the west stands and played "Wave the Flag of Old Chicago." The stands by that time were packed, masses of humanity banked the field in the boxes and, with the sun shining through a slight haze, a hint of a chill commenced to creep through the air. With the Black and Orange of the Tigers massed in the east stand, the Maroon of Chicago lending its color to the west stand, and with the great temporary stands at the ends of the field occupied by neutrals, the scene was set for the struggle between the East and the West.

The field was cleared while the teams retired for the final sessions with the coaches, and the cheer leaders took charge. Chicago sang "Go, Chicago-Go-Go!" and gave the Maroon "Fight" and the massed crowd in the west stand formed a great "C" of maroon and white. Then suddenly from the east stand came the scream of the Tiger, the famous "Tiger, Tiger, Tiger!" of Princeton. The hosts of the East and West were battling in war of sound, sending their cheers, wave upon wave, across the field.

Between halves the Maroon band paraded, and marching to midfield, formed a huge "P" in honor of Princeton and played the Princeton hymn and then formed the "C" of Chicago. During the interim President Judson of Chicago crossed the field to call upon President Hibben, who accompanied him back to call at the Chicago official box.

United Press International

John Thomas (with ball) of Princeton making 1st touchdown in 1st quarter against Chicago.

STORY OF THE GAME TOLD PLAY BY PLAY

Chicago Takes Early Lead, but Princeton Rallies to Win in Final Quarter.

Special to The New York Times.

CHICAGO, Oct. 28.—Following is the detailed description of the Princeton-Chicago football game played here today:

FIRST PERIOD.

Baker of Princeton kicked off over the Maroon goal line. Chicago lined up on the 20-yard mark and Strohmeier kicked to midfield. Princeton was off-side and penalized five yards. Crum smashed into the Maroon tackle for four yards. Cleaves failed at Chicago's right end. Cleaves tried a long forward pass and Pyott intercepted the pass on the 15-yard line.

Chicago kicked immediately to Princeton's 45-yard line and on a fake pass Cleaves was driven back and lost fifteen yards. Both teams were off-side and the ball was brought back. Cleaves plunged for four yards, but Princeton was penalized five yards for King being off-side.

On a fake on-side kick, Princeton tried a double pass and Cleaves passed to Snively, who lost twelve yards. Princeton kicked across field to Chicago's 40-yard line where Pyott was dropped. John Thomas shot straight through Princeton's centre for eight yards and Harry Thomas smashed right tackle for six more, landing on Princeton's 44-yard line. John Thomas tore the tackle open again and ripped through to Princeton's 36-yard line. John Thomas smashed through from a bad shift for seven yards, then Pyott got loose through tackle and end for four yards and was fourteen yards from the Tiger goal.

John Thomas tried right end for a small gain. Pyott was held without gain on a try at right end. Lewis was hurt, and, although objecting to quitting, was taken out and Rohrke sent in. John Thomas smashed the Tiger line for six yards for a first down on Princeton's 4-yard line, and John Thomas smashed in for two yards. Chicago held a short consultation, and John Thomas ripped straight through for the line.

Pyott's Kick Blocked.

Pyott's try for goal after touchdown was half blocked and low, and Chicago lost the point. Score—Chicago 6, Princeton 0.

Baker kicked off to Harry Thomas, who was thrown on the 24-yard line without gain. Harry Thomas was stopped in a crash into right tackle. Strohmeier kicked to Chicago's 45-yard line, where Cleaves caught the ball and raced around Chicago's left end to Chicago's 23-yard line. Crump lunged out of bounds for a 2-yard gain. Gorman, on a fake kick, made a plunge for a yard. A forward pass from Cleaves was grounded. Baker tried for a drop kick from the 32-yard line and missed.

Pyott kicked to Gorman, who made a fair catch on Princeton's 45-yard line. Cleaves went through Chicago's left tackle for 4 yards. A forward pass, Snively to Cleaves, gained a yard only. Crum, on a fake double pass, gained 4 yards and gave Princeton first down. Crum fumbled, but recovered and gained a yard. Snively shot a forward pass to Gray for 45 yards and put the ball on Chicago's 7-yard line. The ball was moved to the 5-yard line on a penalty. Crum plunged at centre for a scant yard gain, and the quarter ended. Score—Chicago 6, Princeton 0.

SECOND PERIOD.

Only several yards from her own goal line, Chicago put up a terrific fight to halt the Tigers' rush. Crum plunged for two yards, gained half a yard and with a yard to go Princeton sent Cleaves in and on the fourth down he smashed through the Chicago line for the touchdown. Ken Smith kicked the goal. Score: Princeton 7, Chicago 6.

King kicked off to Cleaves, who came back to the 25-yard line. Van Gerbig replaced Crum. Princeton tried to kick, was blocked and the ball went out of bounds on Princeton's 31-yard line. John Thomas gained two yards at left tackle, then smashed through the Tiger right side for six and, sprinting around left end on a double pass, gained first down on the 17-yard line. Harry Thomas gained five through the line. Princeton's line would not hold and John Thomas landed on the 10-yard line. John Thomas ripped through Princeton's left tackle for four yards. On a fake end run the Tiger line was pulled all to pieces and John Thomas poured through and over the secondary defense for the touchdown. Caruso went in for Harry Thomas but he failed at the try for goal, the pass being bad. Score: Chicago 12, Princeton 7.

Cleaves Makes Forward Pass.

Zorn replaced John Thomas. Chicago was penalized for taking out time and Baker, kicking off from Chicago's 45-yard line, made an on-side kick and Cleaves got the ball at Chicago's 35-yard line. Gorman made a plunge for one yard. Cleaves gained three at right end. A forward pass, Cleaves to Smith, put the ball on Chicago's 11-yard line. Gorman was thrown for a loss. Van Gerbig tried a run, was thrown for a loss and was hurt, Beattie replacing him. Cleaves faked a drop-kick, then ran and lost two yards, forcing Princeton to kick.

Princeton tried to drop-kick from the 25-yard line, but when Smith kicked Fletcher blocked and it was Chicago's ball on the 25-yard line. Strohmeier punted to midfield, where Cleaves signaled for a fair catch on the 45-yard line. Beattie plunged through tackle for six yards. Beattie plunged for three more on a feint at a double pass. Beattie mauled his way through centre for eight yards and first down on the 31-yard line. Cleaves was stopped in a try at right end. Beattie gained three yards on a plunge and a forward pass, Beattie to Cleaves, and took the ball to Chicago's 21-yard line. On the next play Beattie fumbled after plunging through the line and Gowdy recovered for Chicago. Zorn failed to gain. Zorn failed again to find a hole and Pyott kicked to Gorman, who was downed on Princeton's 47-yard line and there the half ended with the ball in Princeton's possession. Score—Chicago 12, Princeton 7.

THIRD PERIOD.

Lewis returned to the game, replacing Rohrke. Burgess went in at quarterback for Chicago, Strohmeier going to end. Dickson went out and Emery went in for Princeton.

King kicked-off, and after a fumble Gorman came back to Chicago's 35-yard line. Beattie gained a yard at tackle. Cleaves kicked to Pyott, who was thrown on Chicago's 29-yard line. Zorn gained a yard and Chicago kicked, Gorman coming back to Princeton's 39-yard line. Cleaves kicked to Pyott, who was thrown on Chicago's 17-yard line. Byler went in at right half for Caruso. Zorn opened Princeton's line for seven yards. Byler failed and Pylott kicked to Gorman, who came back five yards. The ball was called back, and Princeton was penalized five yards for off-side.

Zorn dived through the line for three yards. Zorn failed to gain and Pyott dropped back to kick. Gray blocked the kick and recovered out of bounds on Chicago's 22-yard line. Beattie plunged at centre for two yards, then on a fake at forward, passing Cleaves, cracked through for three more. A well-planned double pass, Snively to Cleaves, failed.

Chicago Holds for Downs.

Princeton spread again for a pass on the fourth down and completed the same play, failing by inches to gain first down. Chicago got the ball on its own 13-yard line, and Pyott kicked to Cleaves, who made a fair catch on Chicago's 40-yard line. Beattie plunged for two yards. Snively threw a 40-yard pass, which failed. Princeton shot a forward pass over the line, and Burgess recovered after the ball bounded off a Princeton receiver's hand. Zorn took two plunges for ten yards and a first down. Then he was stopped at the line. Zorn and Byler were stopped for short gains and Pyott kicked to Gorman who twisted and wrestled back to Princeton's 50-yard line. Rohrke replaced Lewis.

Cleaves kicked to Pyott on Chicago's 25-yard line and he returned six yards before being dragged down. Zorn plunged twice and gained five yards and Pyott kicked to Gorman, who was tackled on Princeton's 22-yard line. Princeton was penalized half the distance for using hands in interference. Cleaves kicked to his own 28-yard line and Chicago went wild when John Thomas was sent in for Byler. On the first play Zorn smashed through centre for six yards and John Thomas made two yards, then failed.

On the fourth down, with one yard to go and the ball on the 20-yard line, John Thomas ripped a hole straight through the Tiger defense for fifteen yards and landed on the 6-yard line. Zorn failed to gain. John Thomas plunged to within two yards of the goal line and then dived at Princeton's right end. He was over the line and was hurled back, but the goal was allowed. Pyott again failed to kick the goal. Score—Chicago 18, Princeton 7.

Baker kicked off to Pyott, who came back twenty yards to Chicago's 34-yard line just as the quarter ended. Score—Chicago 18, Princeton 7.

FOURTH PERIOD.

Miller replaced Pondelik for Chicago. Zorn plunked through tackle for three yards. Then Pyott raced around left end for fourteen yards before King was dragged down by Gorman. John Thomas gained a yard. A forward pass, John Thomas to Pyott, gained three yards. It was the first pass Chicago had completed. Pyott kicked and Gorman, catching the ball on the 20-yard line, passed to Cleaves, who came back to midfield. Princeton was heavily penalized. The ball was called back and put on the Tiger 1-yard line for holding in interference.

From ten yards behind his own goal line Cleaves shot a forward pass to Gorman, who ran back to Princeton's 40-yard line and was almost clear when dragged down. Dawson replaced King at centre. Princeton tried a reverse forward pass, Cleaves to Gorman, and lost five yards. Wingate went in for Gorman. Cleaves kicked and the ball came to rest on Chicago's 42-yard line. Pyott failed to gain, and on the next play Zorn fumbled and Gray grabbed the ball and, outsprinting the Maroons, scored a touchdown. Smith kicked the goal. Score—Chicago 18, Princeton 14.

Baker kicked to Zorn, who fumbled, recovered and came back to the 25-yard line. John Thomas gained two yards at centre. Pyott gained three by cutting in on an end run. McMasters replaced Burgess. Griffin replaced Alford. John Thomas was stopped at centre, and on the fourth down Chicago kicked to Cleaves, who was dropped on the 42-yard line. Cleaves shot a long forward pass to Smith, who was downed on Chicago's 32-yard line.

Another forward pass by Cleaves was grounded. Chicago had interfered with the catch and it was the Tiger's ball on the Chicago's 18-yard line. Cleaves tore through Chicago's centre for three yards. Rohrke was off-side and the 5-yard penalty put the Tigers on Chicago's 7-yard line. Cleaves battered his way through centre for three yards and then for one. Ewer was thrown back. Crum went in for Ewer. Crum was called on to plunge and took a heavy smash. The ball was so close to the goal line that the officials had to tear the tangle of humanity apart, but it was over the line and Princeton led by 20 to 18. Smith kicked the goal. Score—Princeton 21, Chicago 18.

Baker kicked o McMasters, who came back to the 34-yard line. A forward pass, Thomas to Pyott, was completed, but failed to gain. Christiansen replaced Gowdy. A forward pass, Pyott to McMasters, gained 15 yards. The same play landed the ball on Princeton's 45-yard line. Zorn gained a yard at tackle. A long pass over the line was grounded, but Princeton had interfered this time, and it was Chicago's ball on Princeton's 25-yard line.

Chicago could not gain, and ran the ball out to the centre of the field, where a long forward pass, Pyott to Strohmeier, put the ball on the Tiger 6-yard line. Twice the Maroon assault was hurled back, and there were 2½ yards of ground between the ball and the line. John Thomas was held for a yard gain, and on his last dying effort found the Tiger line unbreakable, and it was Princeton's ball two feet from the goal line.

Princeton kicked out of danger just as the whistle blew, and Chicago went down in the most sensational defeat of the year, leaving the East triumphant. Final Score—Princeton 21, Chicago 18.

The line-up:

PRINCETON (21).		CHICAGO (18).
Gray	L. E.	[illegible]
Treat	L. T.	Fletcher
Dickenson	L. G.	Pondelik
Alford	C.	King
Snively	R. G.	[illegible]
Baker	R. T.	[illegible]
Tillson	R. E.	[illegible]
Gorman	Q. B.	Strohmeier
Caldwell	L. H. B.	[illegible]
Crum	R. H. B.	H. Thomas
Cleaves	F. B.	J. Thomas

SCORE BY PERIODS.

Princeton	0	7	0	14	—21
Chicago	6	6	6	0	—18

Touchdowns—J. Thomas (3), Crum (2), Gray. Points after touchdown—Smith (3), Beattie (substitute for Crum).

Referee—Schwartz, Brown. Umpire—[illegible] Backett, West Point. Head linesman—[illegible] Eldridge, Michigan. Field judge—[illegible] Dartmouth. Time of periods—15 minutes.

"All the News That's Fit to Print."

The New York Times.

THE WEATHER
Fair and warmer today and Friday; moderate winds.
Temperature Yesterday—Max., 49; Min., 37.
☞ For weather report see next to last page.

VOL. LXXII....No. 23,826. *** NEW YORK, THURSDAY, APRIL 19, 1923. TWO CENTS In Greater New York | THREE CENTS Within 200 Miles | FOUR CENTS Elsewhere

74,200 SEE YANKEES OPEN NEW STADIUM; RUTH HITS HOME RUN

Record Baseball Crowd Cheers as Slugger's Drive Beats Red Sox, 4 to 1.

25,000 ARE TURNED AWAY

Gates to $2,500,000 Arena Are Closed Half an Hour Before Start of Game.

MANY NOTABLES ATTEND

Governor Smith Throws Out First Ball—Shawkey, in Great Form, Allows Only Three Hits.

Governors, generals, colonels, politicians and baseball officials gathered together solemnly yesterday to dedicate the biggest stadium in baseball, but it was a ball player who did the real dedicating. In the third inning, with two team mates on the base lines, Babe Ruth smashed a savage home run into the right field bleachers, and that was the real baptism of the new Yankee Stadium. That also won the game for the Yankees, and all the ceremony which had gone before was only a trifling preliminary.

The greatest crowd that ever saw a baseball game sat and stood in this biggest of all baseball stadia. Inside the grounds, by official count, were 74,200 people. Outside the park, flattened against doors that had long since closed, were 25,000 more fans, who finally turned around and went home, convinced that baseball parks are not nearly as large as they should be.

The dream of a 100,000 crowd at a baseball game could easily have been realized yesterday if the Yankee Colonels had only piled more concrete on concrete, more steel on steel, and thus provided the necessary space for the overflow. In the face of this tremendous outpouring all baseball attendance records went down with a dull thud. Back in 1916, at a world's series game in Boston, some 42,000 were present, and wise men marveled. But there were that many people in the Yankee Stadium by 2 o'clock yesterday, and when the gates were finally closed to all but ticket holders at 3 o'clock the Boston record had been exceeded by more than 30,000.

Shawkey Pitches Fine Game.

It was an opening game without a flaw. The Yankees easily defeated the Boston Red Sox, 4 to 1. Bob Shawkey, war veteran and oldest Yankee player in point of service, pitched the finest game of his career, letting the Boston batters down with three scattered hits. The Yankees raised their American League championship emblem to the top of the flagpole—the chief feature of an opening-day program that went off perfectly. Governor "Al" Smith, throwing out the first ball of the season, tossed it straight into Wally Schang's glove, thus setting another record. The weather was favorable and the big crowd was handled flawlessly.

Only one more thing was in demand, and Babe Ruth supplied that. The big slugger is a keen student of the dramatic, in addition to being the greatest home run hitter. He was playing a new rôle yesterday—not the accustomed one of a renowned slugger, but that of a penitent, trying to "come back" after a poor season and a poorer world's series. Before the game he said that he would give a year of his life if he could hit a home run in his first game in the new stadium. The Babe was on trial, and he knew it better than anybody else.

He could hardly have picked a better time and place for the drive that he hammered into the bleachers in the third inning. The Yankees had just broken a scoreless tie by pushing Shawkey over the plate with one run. Witt was on third base, Dugan on first, when Ruth appeared at the plate to face Howard Ehmke, the Boston pitcher. Ruth worked the count to two and two, and then Ehmke tried to fool him with one of those slow balls that the Giants used successfully in the last world's series.

The ball came in slowly, but it went out quite rapidly, rising on a line and then dipping suddenly from the force behind it. It struck well inside the foul line, eight or ten rows above the low railing in front of the bleachers, and as Ruth circled the bases he received probably the greatest ovation of his career. The biggest crowd in baseball history rose to its feet and let loose the biggest shout in baseball history. Ruth, jogging over the home plate, grinned broadly, lifted his cap at arm's length and waved it at the multitude.

Home Run Settles Outcome.

That homer was useful as well as dramatic and decorative. It drove three runs across the plate, and those runs, as later events proved, were the margin by which the Yankees won. All the New York scoring was in that one inning, and the Red Sox, although they touched Shawkey for one run in the seventh, could not close the gap.

But the game, after all, was only an incident of a busy afternoon. The stadium was the thing. For the Yankee owners it was the realization of a dream long cherished. For the fans it was something which they had never seen before in baseball. It cost about $2,500,000 to build, and eleven months were spent in the construction work. It is the most costly stadium in baseball, as well as the biggest.

First impressions—and also last impressions—are of the vastness of the arena. The stadium is big. It towers high in the air, three tiers piled one on the other. It is a skyscraper among baseball parks. Seen from the vantage point of the nearby subway structure,

Continued on Page Fifteen.

Jim Larkin to Be Deported As an Undesirable Alien

Special to The New York Times.

WASHINGTON, April 18.—James Larkin, who was convicted under the so-called Lusk laws in New York and later pardoned by Governor Smith, is listed by the Federal Government as an undesirable and must leave the country, it was announced today by Assistant Secretary of Labor Robe C. White.

The original order of deportation was approved by the Federal Government on March 16, but a stay was requested. This was granted and Larkin was paroled in the custody of counsel. Today the original order was confirmed and Larkin's deportation directed as soon as he can be located.

BOMB IRISH REBELS IN SEASIDE CAVE

Free State Troops Use Mines, Guns and Smoke in Futile Efforts to Dislodge Them.

THEIR ESCAPE IS CUT OFF

Fugitives Face Starvation in Crevice in Wild Cliff, 100 Feet Above the Shannon Coast.

Copyright, 1923, by The New York Times Company. By Wireless to THE NEW YORK TIMES.

DUBLIN, Arpil 18.—A cave in a perpendicular cliff on the Shannon coast, near the Causeway, in one of the wildest spots in County Kerry, is the scene of a fierce battle between fugitive rebels and besieging national troops. In a cave more than 100 feet from the top of Clashmeelcon Cliff, which rises perpendicularly from the Shannon's shore, prominent insurgents have made their hiding place.

The approach to the cave from the cliffs is by a precipitous path, which even the venturesome Kerry goat would not have the audacity to descend. This winding path by the cliff side, with a yawning chasm underneath, where one false step would mean instant death, did not deter the rebels from adopting it as a place of security from attack.

National troops attempted a descent in the early hours of the morning. One officer and three men accomplishing it successfully. Examining the rocks the intrepid soldiers discovered a crevice barely sufficient to admit one man at a time. Two of them crept through the crevice and encountered a barricade a few feet inside. This was surmounted, but a few yards further in they found another barricade.

While removing it fire was opened on them from inside the cave and Volunteer O'Neill of the Dublin Guards fell mortally wounded and Lieutenant Pyerson of the Engineers was seriously injured.

The firing from the cave continued and the two soldiers outside had to take shelter behind a rock. The shelter was a meagre one, but they manfully replied to the fire from the cave. Seeing their position the troops on the crest of the cliff lowered ropes and the wounded officer and the two other men were safely hauled up under heavy fire from the cave. Volunteer O'Neill's body was thrown to the beach beneath and attempts to recover it were beaten off by a hot fire from the cave.

Reinforcements of National troops arrived and called on the men in the cave to surrender. An attempt was then made to smoke the garrison out by means of burning sacks of hay and turf. This plan being ineffective two mines were lowered and exploded at the mouth of the cave. This also failed to bring out the occupants and machine gun and rifle fire were directed against the stronghold.

Throughout the night lamps were lowered from the crest of the cliff to discover any attempt to escape during the darkness. The lamps were fired on and stoned from the cave without effect. There was no attempt by the entrapped irregulars to escape.

Yesterday morning more mines were exploded and machine gun and rifle fire maintained by the troops, but the irregulars have made no attempt to come from their fastness.

Two Red Cross men pluckily descended the path from the cliff to the shore yesterday morning and recovered the body of O'Neill, which had been buffeted about by the tide and was in danger of being washed out to sea.

The cave where the irregulars are entrenched gives shelter from attack, but there is no chance of escape from surrender, or from death from starvation.

LEAGUE RECOGNIZES IRELAND.

Agrees to Invite Free State to Customs Conference Oct. 15.

GENEVA, April 18 (Associated Press).—The Irish Free State having established a customs régime, the Council of the League of Nations today voted to add Ireland to the non-members of the League which will be invited to the

Continued on Page Two.

PANIC IN MARKS HITS CUNO CABINET, SHAKING ITS POLICY

Government's Passive Resistance Plan in the Ruhr Imperilled by Drop in Exchange.

ALARM IN OCCUPIED DISTRICT

Sudden Collapse Carries the Mark to 33,000 to the Dollar Despite Efforts to Peg It.

SOCIALISTS URGE PEACE

Their Spokesman in the Reichstag Calls on the Government to Make a Concrete Offer.

By CYRIL BROWN.

Copyright, 1923, by The New York Times Company. By Wireless to THE NEW YORK TIMES.

BERLIN, April 18.—There was a mark panic on the Boerse between noon and 1 o'clock today which utterly eclipsed all political discussions. Opening around 23,000 paper marks to the dollar this morning, the mark was fluctuating between 31,000 and 33,000 tonight.

The Reichsbank was impotent to check the onslaught for the first time since the Cuno Goverment's stabilization action started.

So hopeless was the outlook that the bank did not even try to intervene by dumping dollars and pounds sterling on the market.

This dramatic collapse came as a shock to the Government and political circles. Stabilization around 20,000 marks to the dollar is an important factor in the Government's strategy of Ruhr resistance. The crash has accordingly upset all Chancellor Cuno's calculations. The Cabinet early this afternoon held a hurried session to discuss the situation and later a conference took place between the members of the Government and the Reichsbank.

Reports are current of grave differences between Reichsbank President Havenstein and Finance Minister Hermes. The question at issue is said to be whether the mark should be supported to the limit, meaning to the limit of the Reichsbank's gold holdings, or allowed to take an appreciable drop and then again be pegged. Powerful business and industrial interests have been urging the Government to withdraw Reichsbank support and let the mark drop to 25,000 so as to stimulate export business. At the same time, the Socialists are bringing pressure on the Government to conserve its holding of foreign exchange for the inevitable resumption of reparation payments rather than use them up in what they call futile attempts to stabilize the mark.

The opposite view, namely, to keep the mark pegged at all costs as long as the Ruhr struggle lasts, was expressed by the German Nationalist, Dr. Helfferich, in the Reichstag this afternoon, as follows:

"We expect action to support the mark will be continued even if the Reichsbank's gold is placed at stake thereby. In this battle the Reichsbank's gold is our powder, which we must shoot off."

Opposes Inquiry by Experts.

BERLIN, April 18 (Associated Press).—On the resumption of debate in the Reichstag today on the recent address of Baron von Rosenberg, the Foreign Minister, Herr Breitscheidt, speaking in behalf of the Socialists, strongly urged that the Government should make a definite concrete offer to France for a settlement of the reparations question.

"Our duty," said the Deputy, "is to bring about a speedy end of the Ruhr adventure. We have no friends in the world. America and England will not intervene."

While not saying that it was acceptable, Herr Breitscheidt suggested that the plan of Louis Barthou, on behalf of France, and M. Delacroix, on behalf of Belgium, for the payment of 35,000,000,000 gold marks by Germany had the merit of definiteness. "What we object to in the plan," he added, "is the stipulation for the progressive evacuation of the Ruhr, and its failure to reimburse Germany for the costs of maintaining the armies of occupation.

Herr Breitscheidt expressed the opinion that Germany probably would be far better off by making a direct offer than to risk the verdict of a board of experts, which procedure he believed France and the other Allies would not accept.

"We are not affiliated with or related to this Government," declared the Deputy, "but nevertheless we desire to see it remain in office to liquidate the Ruhr conflict, which occurred during its régime."

In urging the Government to come forward with a precise offer Herr Breitscheidt suggested that it peruse the

Continued on Page Three.

Orchestra at Musical Comedy Walks Out; Composer Plays Piano and Saves the Show

The audience at the Astor Theatre last night sat through the performance of "Lady Butterfly," a musical comedy, and apparently enjoyed it, although the pit was without an orchestra. The piano furnished the only accompaniment, played by Werner Jansen, composer of the show, who stepped into the breach when trouble developed among the musicians.

The difficulty resulted from the recent resignation from the American Federation of Musicians of Abraham Nussbaum, cornetist. The management, under instructions from the Federation, returned Nussbaum's last quarter's dues after the matinee performance yesterday and told him that the Federation, which had held his resignation in abeyance, had decided to accept it.

Last night Nussbaum insisted on taking his place in the orchestra. He was ordered out, and six others, members of the Musical Mutual Protective Union, also walked out in sympathy, as they were subject to fines if they refused to follow Nussbaum. To avoid trouble with the Federation, Mr. Jansen insisted that the other eleven members of the orchestra leave. They did so, and Frank Dobson, the comedian, announced to the audience that the management had nothing to do with the row and promised to refund the money to those who wished to leave. The audience applauded, but nobody walked out. The curtain went up a few minutes late. A new orchestra will be on hand tonight, it was announced.

Nussbaum, it is said, is one of the extremists in the Musical Mutual Protective Union, and bitterly fought the compromise proposal of F. Paul A. Vaccarelli, under which the union would have been reinstated in the Federation, from which it was suspended two years ago.

Edward Lissman, the musicians' contractor, who ordered Nussbaum to leave, said he was acting under instructions from J. J. Shubert and that Mr. Shubert declared he would do business only with members of the Federation, which has an agreement with the theatre managers.

SUGAR PRICES JUMP TO HIGHEST OF YEAR

Cuban Raws Advance to 6¼ Cents, Refined to 9.50 and 9.85.

BRITISH TOLD OF SHORTAGE

Chancellor of the Exchequer Warns House of Commons That Prices May Go Higher.

Raw and refined sugars yesterday took the biggest jump since the Government investigation into the price of sugar started. Cuban raw sugars advanced to 6¼ cents per pound in a violent market, a price which was a full quarter of a cent above the previous high for the year. Practically all of the big refiners advanced their price of refined sugar to 9.50 cents, and one, the Pennsylvania Sugar Refining Company, advanced to 9.85 cents for prompt shipment in bulk bags.

The market was extremely violent all day, but it was the consensus in the trade that it was not a particularly speculative one. Many small speculators who were in the market for sugar at the time of the recent rise had been frightened out by the Government's investigation, and the present trading, it is said, is largely confined to dealers and professional operators.

There were two outstanding developments in the sugar trade yesterday which served to accelerate the market. One was a prediction from Cuba that the complete outturn of sugar this year would be 3,500,000 tons, comparing with predictions of 4,000,000 to 4,100,000 tons which had been made recently by the sugar companies here.

Another factor was the purchase of 23,000 bags of Cuban sugar by the American Sugar Refining Company at 6 cents a pound, plus freight, a new record for 1923. Operators previously had bought sugar at this figure, but for a refiner to do so was regarded as extremely significant as to the future course of the market. After this announcement was made the market fairly boiled.

Production of sugar in Cuba up to April 1 of this year was 2,755,785 tons. This compares with 1,985,956 tons in the corresponding period of last year. In connection with the predictions by Cubans that the total outturn for the year would reach only 3,500,000 tons, it was noted by many interests in the trade that to reach the latest Cuban estimate production for the remainder of the year would have to be only about 750,000 tons, whereas in the corresponding period of last year it was 2,009,233 tons.

The season in Cuba now is being wound up, and about forty-six centrals have finished grinding, out of 182 that operated during the season. At this time in 1922 there were still 170 centrals operating and in 1921 there were 196. Cabled reports yesterday to some of the leading operators here brought word of heavy rains which had retarded crop operations in some parts of Cuba, and this tended to further accelerate the market for both refined and raw sugar.

Shortage, Says Chancellor.

LONDON, April 18 (Associated Press).—The House of Commons, by a vote of 244 to 100, refused tonight to consider a private bill introduced by Captain John H. Thorpe, Conservative, proposing to follow the custom of France, Spain and other countries and permit Ministers, whether belonging to the House of Lords or the Commons, to speak in either House.

The Chancellor of the Exchequer, Stanley Baldwin, replying to criticisms of his budget, gave details of the manner in which the Dominions are paying their debts to England. The Australian and New Zealand debts are funded and interest amounting to about £6,000,000 yearly is being received regularly. A substantial portion of the South African debt had been paid off and the remainder funded. The Canadian debt had practically been settled. Therefore the House would see that the country was receiving exactly the same treatment from the Dominions that Great Britain gave to those to whom she was indebted.

Mr. Baldwin also went into elaborate details about the sugar trade in reply to labor criticisms of his failure to reduce the duty. He pointed out that American consumption of sugar was increasing by leaps and bounds owing to prohibition and to increase in population and wealth. He humorously advised the people of England to wait for prohibition until there was again a great surplus of sugar; otherwise, by giving up alcohol and taking to sugar, they might feel they were casting a real burden on the masses of the people.

The Chancellor expressed his belief that the rise in sugar to 30 shillings a hundredweight, or thrice the price in January, 1922, was caused entirely by

Continued on Page Eight.

POLICE POST GUARDS IN BUCKETING TRIAL

Prosecutor Charges E. M. Fuller's Lawyer With Kidnapping a State Witness.

$6,612,000 STOCKS MISSING

Accountant Reports List to Referee in Bankruptcy—Creditors Demand Books.

Five detectives and five uniformed policemen were summoned yesterday to guard the State's witnesses in the trial of Edward M. Fuller, head of the brokerage firm of E. M. Fuller & Co., which went into the hands of a receiver last June with liabilities of more than $5,000,000. The posting of the guard followed Assistant District Attorney Hugo Wintner's statement to Judge Nott in General Sessions that one of his witnesses had been spirited out of his office a week before by Eugene F. McGee, one of Fuller's lawyers.

Mr. Wintner added that the Grand Jury had been requested to investigate his charge that an attempt was being made to obstruct justice by interfering with witnesses needed by the prosecution, and when he told the Court that McGee had taken one of Fuller's clerks in a taxicab from his office, McGee declared: "That is absolutely false: it is a lie." The Court advised Mr. Wintner not to begin the Grand Jury proceeding until Fuller's trial on an indictment charging him with bucketing had been finished.

While a jury was being selected for the broker's trial, an attorney for the trustee in the bankruptcy inquiry appeared before Harold P. Coffin, Federal referee, in his office at 217 Broadway, and presented a petition of the creditors requesting that the books of Fuller & Co. be turned over to their lawyers for examination.

No Trace of Millions in Stocks.

An accountant, on the witness stand told the referee that he had been unable to find $6,612,000 in securities which Fuller & Co. were believed to have had in its possession at the time of the failure on June 26 last. He said that he had found that $4,000,000 was owed to the firm and that some securities had been recovered, but they were not part of those which he was unable to trace, and that his investigation indicated that, deducting the $4,000,000 in debts, the liabilities of the firm would total about $2 000,000. The referee reserved decision on the application for the delivery of the books to the creditors' lawyers.

Fuller was placed on trial in General Sessions yesterday on the complaint of Franklin B. Link of Westmoreland, Tenn., who charged that in May, 1922, Fuller and his partner W. Frank McGee, bucketed his order to sell $1,500 worth of Middle States Oil stock. It was the basis of one of thirteen indictments returned by the Grand Jury in July last.

Fuller has been tried twice on this indictment. The jury disagreed in the first trial, and Judge Johnston declared a mistrial on the second occasion, when the prosecution reported that J. Harold Braid, a broker, one of the witnesses for the State, had disappeared. Braid later surrendered and was held in $2,500 bail as a material witness.

Wintner Accuses McGee.

Fuller came to court yesterday with his lawyers, Eugene F. McGee and William J. Fallon. A few minutes before the trial opened Mr. Wintner announced that a week before he had summoned to his office Lawless West, who formerly was a blotter clerk for E. M. Fuller & Co., and that while West was waiting to be questioned by him, Attorney McGee appeared and took West away in a taxicab.

West was in court when the trial began. John Markey, a process server in the District Attorney's office, had just handed him a "John Doe" subpoena when Mr. Wintner noticed McGee talking to him. Walking over to the lawyer Mr. Wintner said: "Stop talking to my witness."

"Where do you get that stuff?" retorted McGee.

West then showed the subpoena to Fallon, who was heard to say: "Pay no attention to it. You are under subpoena for the defense."

Mr. Wintner then walked up to Judge Nott, closely followed by McGee, and said: "Your honor, the Grand Jury is investigating a conspiracy in which this man McGee and the witness West are concerned. McGee kidnapped him out of my office."

When McGee replied that the accusation was a falsehood, Judge Nott announced that he would not then pass on the matter of placing West as a witness before the Grand Jury, and added that he thought it advisable to defer such action until the Fuller trial had been finished. A few minutes before another

LIKELY TO RAILROAD CLEAN BOOK BILL; STRIFE AT HEARING

Senators Hear Publishers Fight Censorship Urged by Religious Leaders.

JUSTICE FORD HITS EDITORS

Gertrude Atherton Says Ban Would Only Result in Publication in Other States.

SAY BILL WOULD BAR BIBLE

Gallatin Asks Year's Delay—Mgr. Lavelle Among Those Urging Adoption of Measure.

Special to The New York Times.

ALBANY, April 18.—With the Democratic Party committed through platform pledges to the abolition of film censorship, the Democratic Senate is most likely to railroad to final passage the Cotillo-Jesse "Clean Book" bill, which would establish a censorship over printed matter so severe in its character that if it should be rigidly enforced, it was asserted, the Bible, Shakespeare, the Encyclopaedia Britannica, practically every dictionary, the classics with few exceptions and even some works by the early fathers of the Catholic Church would come under the ban.

A week ago there was not the slightest expectation that this bill, advocated chiefly by the Society for the Suppression of Vice and especially directed against a handful of recent works of fiction which the courts have refused to suppress, would go through. Then, after a hearing held on short notice before an Assembly committee, at which no one appeared to oppose the bill, it was rushed through the Assembly. It is on the order of third reading in the Senate now.

Authors and publishers appeared before the Senate Judiciary Committee today at a hastily arranged hearing, given at their request, to oppose the bill. They pleaded for delay for another year before any legislation was enacted and pledged themselves to get together with those advocating the bill, which they condemned as anti-American and anti-religious, and evolve some compromise measure.

Could Convict on One Word.

The advocates of the measure, outnumbering the opponents two to one at the hearing and counting among their number Justice John Ford of the Supreme Court, Mgr. Lavelle of St. Patrick's Cathedral, who appeared as the spokesman of Archbishop Hayes, and Henry L. Bowlby of the Lord's Day Alliance, did not manifest a spirit of compromise. Gertrude Atherton, the author, and Horace S. Liveright of the firm of Boni & Liveright were among the prominent spokesmen for the opposition.

Objection to the bill was centred on a clause under which it would be possible to segregate a word, phrase or sentence which to a jury might appear objectionable from its contevt in a book written for an entirely laudable purpose and make it the basis of conviction that would carry with it suppression of the book and fine and imprisonment for author and publisher. The full text of the clause which the opponents regard as objectionable follows:

"The words obscene, lewd, lascivious, filthy, indecent and disgusting, and each of them, as used in this section, shall be taken and construed with full force and effect in their commonly and generally accepted meaning and signification. An indictment, information, complaint or other charge may be based upon the whole or exclusively upon a part or parts of any publication or written or printed matter; and if the prosecution be based exclusively upon a part or parts, only such part or parts shall be admissible in evidence or considered for any purpose upon any hearing, examination or trial. Whether the matter set out in the indictment, complaint, information or other charge offends against this section shall be a question of fact to be decided by the trier or triers of fact. Opinion or expert testimony shall not be received for any purpose whatever upon any hearing, examination or trial under this section; nor shall it be a necessary constituent element of the crime charged that the matter on which the prosecution is based have a tendency to excite lustful or lecherous desire."

Dr. Max Fleischer, an editorial writer

Continued on Page Four.

Saves $141,019 in Year By Paying War Bills Promptly

Special to The New York Times.

WASHINGTON, April 18.—Secretary Weeks today authorized the announcement that through prompt settlement of bills and resort to rediscounting the War Department has saved $141,019.22 during the present fiscal year, and $13,158.07 during February alone. This saving was effected by putting into practice the policy of settling bills within the ten-day period ordinarily allowed for 2 per cent. discounts.

Director of the Budget H. M. Lord has written to Secretary Weeks a letter complimenting him upon the excellent showing made by his department, declaring this is a remarkable record which he does not think has been ever equaled by "any private business concern."

MARINE UNION PLANS A FLEET OF ITS OWN

Engineers' Beneficial Association Offers Shipping Board $300,000 for Three Vessels.

SEES PROFIT IN OPERATION

Intend Ultimately to Put 110 Steamships on Seas—Lasker Asked to Take Up Proposal.

Inspired by recent trade union ventures in capitalistic enterprises, the Marine Engineers' Beneficial Association 33 has offered the United States Shipping Board $300,000 cash for three ships. Thomas D. Healey, business manager of the union, in a letter to Chairman Albert D. Lasker of the Shipping Board, said he was confident that the union could operate the ships at a profit, and asked that the offer be placed before President Harding and the officials of the Shipping Board.

Mr. Healey said the union contemplated a steady growth of business, beginning in the coastwise trade and developing eventually until it had under its control a fleet of 110 ships operating all over the world. The union had no intention, he said, of swelling its overhead costs with high-salaried officials.

Mr. Healey's letter to Mr. Lasker said:

"The announcement contained in the daily papers to the effect that it is the intention of the United States Shipping Board, with the President's approval, that in the event it is impossible to dispose of the Government-owned ships on fair terms, to have the Government operate them. In the event this plan is decided upon I want to offer you my assurances that I will cooperate in every way possible, both personally and in my official capacity, to make Government operation successful. As a marine engineer, as business manager of this organization and as an American citizen, I am for an American merchant marine with my whole heart and soul.

"In my twenty-eight years' experience as a marine engineer American ship owners have always blamed their failure to compete with foreign ship owners upon the supposedly high wages paid to American crews. But statistics will show the only time wages were really high was during the war, when profits of 1,000 per cent. or more a voyage were not uncommon. It is generally admitted that the wages of the crew average about 8 per cent. of the operating expenses of a ship, and probably much less when the overhead is figured in.

"We feel that American ships can be profitably operated, and that is one of the reasons for our offer, contained in letter dated April 12, to purchase the steamships Hanley, Hannawa and Pomona for $100,000 cash each. These ships and other ships which we expect to purchase later are at present a liability to the Government and costing money whether laid up or operated under an M. O.-4 agreement. Under our plan, it will mean, instead of a constant drain upon the Treasury, an immediate accession to the United States Treasury of $300,000 and an example to the world that Americans can compete with them on even terms.

"We intend to have satisfied crews, pay high wages and instill into the men operating them that they are their ships and they are not working to enrich individuals who, despite their claims of losing money, have about them all the marks and signs of affluence.

"I trust you will therefore bring our offer to the President and your colleagues on the board, and advocate favorable consideration of our offer, in view of its obvious advantage to the Government, to the men who earn their living by going to sea, and to the citizens engaged in agriculture and in manufacture who need an American merchant marine available to ship their products at reasonable rates."

Replying to the offer, Commissioner Lissner of the Shipping Board wrote:

"As you know, ordinary matters concerning ship sales are handled by the Ship Sales Committee of this board, and I have no doubt your proposal will take its usual course and receive such consideration as it deserves."

DETECTIVE TOOK $600, WOMAN SAYS, NOT TO ARREST HER

Boarding House Keeper Testifies Raider Got All She Had After Asking $1,000.

ACCUSED BLAMES CORRIGAN

McAllister Charges "Frame-Up" Due to Magistrate's Animosity.

HEARING IN A TUMULT

Rival Witnesses Indulge in Rapid-Fire Exchange at Hirshfield Inquiry.

Commissioner of Accounts Hirshfield's challenge to the public to come forward and tell of a single incident of police liquor grafting was met in stirring fashion at the Commissioner's inquiry yesterday when a woman accused a detective to his face of having demanded and received $600 from her.

The woman, keeper of a sailors' boarding house, named and identified Robert McAllister of the Headquarters Staff assigned to enforce the State prohibition law. In a stormy session, marked by a tumult of accusation, denial and incrimination she stuck to her story, giving time and place and insisting that the bribe was handed over in consideration that she be spared the shame of arrest.

She swore that when McAllister and his fellow-detectives descended upon her boarding house she gave him the money—all she had—after he had demanded $1,000, and that in return McAllister arrested her brother instead of herself and promised that the case would "not amount to much."

Mrs. Mary Castro, the day's sensational witness, was mistress of herself and of the situation. When Commissioner Hirshfield scoffed at her story and said that no sane man would believe it, she took an oath on her God and the lives of her children.

McAllister, leaping from the chair where he sat with other members of his squad, hearing all the testimony, characterized the charge as "a lie and a frame up." Mrs. Castro insisted upon questioning the detective when he in turn took the stand, and she brandished the word "lie" as vociferously as did he.

When he was asked how he accounted for the accusations McAllister cried: "Judge Corrigan has it in for me because I arrested a woman who said she was his niece."

Magistrate Joseph E. Corrigan, whose charges of bootleg grafting on the part of the police were partially responsible for Mayor Hylan's order for the investigation, said last evening that he had no niece over 14 years old and that neither of them—the youngest is 1 year old—had ever been in New York. The woman was sailing under false colors if she pretended to any relationship or even acquaintanceship, Magistrate Corrigan asserted.

Police Stories Tally.

Five of McAllister's brother policemen who accompanied him on the raid at Mrs. Castro's house corroborated his testimony and declared that no money had been passed. All of them told the same story as McAllister, even to minor details. Most of them said that McAllister was in their sight during their entire stay in the house and that no money could have passed without their knowledge.

"I don't believe her story. I don't believe her testimony," Mr. Hirshfield declared after McAllister had testified. "I don't believe that any sane or sensible person does believe it."

After all the other witnesses had been called Commissioner Hirshfield recalled Mrs. Castro. "You still maintain that you gave up $600?" he asked.

"I did, so help me God," was the reply. "My three children may die—he took the six $100 bills from me."

The raid on Mrs. Castro's was on Dec. 4. With McAllister were Patrolmen Coonan, Plagge, Yost, Passini and Reed. Two other detectives from the neighborhood, O'Leary and O'Hara, joined them while the raid was in progress. The police took twenty-one quarts of whisky and placed under arrest Thomas McCarthy, Mrs. Castro's brother, also known as Foley. Foley was discharged on the ground that the police had broken into the room where the liquor was, and that the liquor belonged to a sailor.

"They went upstairs in one of the sailors' rooms—all the rooms were locked," Mrs. Castro testified. "I never had anything to do with the rooms. They broke in the doors and found something there.

"When McAllister came downstairs into my room I told him: 'I am ashamed to be arrested. I was never arrested before in my life.' So he began talking to me, and then—"

"What did he say?" said Commissioner Hirshfield.

Wanted $1,000, She Says.

"He said he would not arrest me if I would give him something?"

"What did he mean by something?"

"Money."

"Did he says money?"

"Yes, he did. So I told him I did not have as much as he wanted, and I opened my safe and showed him what I had"

"How much did he ask?"

"I think he wanted a thousand dollars."

"Did he ask you for a thousand dollars."

"Yes, he did."

"Where was he?"

"In my room."

Commissioner Hirshfield asked whether when McAllister was talking to her the other policemen were there, too.

"I don't remember if they [illegible] I think they were [illegible] only my [illegible]

"[illegible]

Statue of Chac-Mool, Tiger King of the Mayas, Is Discovered in the Ruins of Chichen-Itza

Special Cable to THE NEW YORK TIMES.

MERIDA, Yucatan, April 17.—One of the most important Maya discoveries of the century was made today in the ruined city of Chichen-Itza by Miguel Angel Fernandez, an artist of Merida, when he found a statute of Chac-Mool, the famous Tiger King of the ancient Mayas. The statue, which differs in attitude from the other recumbent representations of this deified ruler, measures more than five feet in length.

According to these measurements, the Chac-Mool discovered by Fernandez is larger than the famous statue of Chac-Mool now in the National Museum of Mexico City. This reclining figure of the Tiger King, said to have been the greatest of the rulers of the Itzaes, is a monolith, 4¾ feet long, 2½ feet wide and is 3½ feet high. It was discovered in 1874 by the French savant, Dr. Auguste Le Plongeon, twenty-five feet below the surface of tangled undergrowth.

When found, the funeral urn at the back of the head is said to have contained the heart of Chac-Mool, some primitive ornaments, and the knife of light colored obsidian with which he was assassinated. The statue is regarded as the most perfect example of ancient Mayan art.

Florida House Votes to End All Flogging In Convict Camps, But Keeps Leasing Plan

TALLAHASSEE, Fla., April 18.—The House today voted 63 to 15 to abolish corporal punishment in this State in the handling of county prisoners. The action came on the adoption of an amendment, offered by Representative Savis of Leon, to the measure which would abolish the county convict lease system.

It would be physically impossible for a man to receive 100 lashes with a strap and survive, Dr. T. C. Jones, convict camp physician employed by the Putnam Lumber Company at Clara, today told the legislative committee inquiring into the death of Martin Tabert of North Dakota, and other reported brutalities in prison camps.

Dr. Jones attributed the primary cause of Tabert's death to pneumonia, contracted after he had treated him for a disease which caused gland enlargements, ulcers and splotches on the body. The physician said that he entered on the burial permit that death was caused by pneumonia and a complication of malaria but in reality the complication was the disease as outlined. This was said to have been done to save any embarrassment to the boy's family although at the time he did not know whether Tabert had any relatives.

The camp doctor testified he had been employed by the Putnam Lumber Company for three years and a half and that the convicts were treated humanely, were well fed and that he never heard any general complaint. Dr. Jones said he was graduated from the medical college at Memphis, Tenn., in 1903, and that he had devoted his practice to convict and free labor camps in this and other States.

Other witnesses testified that Tabert had received more than a hundred lashes from a whipping boss named Walter Higginbotham.

A. B. Shivers, a former guard recalled, said that the convicts were fed on hot water, bacon and corn bread for breakfast six times a week.

The funeral of Tabert, with a small group of townspeople singing hymns, wide-eyed school children looking on and an itinerant preacher officiating, was described before the Legislative Investigating Committee.

B. Duffet, an employee of the Putnam Lumber Company, which had Tabert under lease, said he asked two women of the town to attend and on the way to the burial-grounds, the two women testified, they met the preacher and asked him to deliver the funeral sermon. The women asserting that they knew nothing at the time of the identity of the lad but endeavored to give a Christian burial to him.

GIANTS BAT HARD; BEAT BRAVES, 7-4

Scott Hits Homer and Pitches Well for Six Innings, but Weakens Toward Close.

JESS BARNES STOPS RALLY

Retires Side After Gowdy Walks With None Out in Ninth—O'Connell Makes Triple.

Special to The New York Times.

BOSTON, April 18.—Jack Scott all but went the route for the Giants today in a game which the champions won from the Braves by a score of 7 to 4. Having pitched six innings in fine fashion, Jack staggered a bit in the seventh and staggered some more at the start of the Braves' half of the ninth. He was quickly taken out and Jess Barnes was sent in to replace him. Jess checked effectively the contemplated assault by the Braves and the victory was preserved.

A pass to Hank Gowdey, first man at bat for the Braves in the ninth, was the signal for Scott's removal. Felix was put on to run for Gowdy and Walton Cruise was ordered to bat for Joe Genewich when Barnes entered the box. Jess made short work of Cruise, and of Powell, who followed him. Cruise hit into a double play and Powell fanned. Perhaps the exertion of running out a home-run swat which he delivered in the fourth inning caused Scott to weaken. The big pitcher hit the ball to the fence in right centre in that round, and, much to his discomfort, had to run the circuit of the bases.

Genewich, who retired to permit Cruise to hit into the ninth inning double play, was the third Boston pitcher to face the Giants, having been preceded by John Watson and Joe Oeschger. Watson was withdrawn under fire in the fourth inning and his successor was taken out for a pinch hitter in the eighth.

Giants Score in Second.

An error by Ford in the second inning gave the Giants an opening and they took advantage of it to the extent of scoring one run. Meusel had been retired when Young reached first base on Ford's wild toss of his grounder. Kelly poked a single to right centre and Young dashed to third. A pass to O'Connell filled the bases and Snyder sent a long sacrifice fly to Powell on which Young scampered home.

In the third inning the Giants made another run, and but for faulty coaching at third base they would have made at least one more. Bancroft opened with a single to left, and after Groh had lifted to Southworth, Frisch walked. Meusel drove a long fly to Southworth, who muffed the ball. Bancroft dashed to third base, was halted there by Hughie Jennings and then sent on again. By this time Southworth had pegged to Conlon, who threw Banny out at the plate. However, Young singled sharply to left and Frisch counted.

Scott checked in with his homer in the fourth inning. Snyder walked, following the demise of O'Connell, and big Jack slammed the ball between Powell and Southworth. The pellet didn't stop rolling until it reached the fence, and Jack puffed around the sacks and over the plate behind Snyder.

Scott's wallop marked the beginning of the end for Watson. Bancroft was thrown out by Boeckel, who made a fine play on his torrid smash, but Groh walked and Frisch singled to centre, Groh stopping at second. Here Watson passed from the scene and Oeschger came in. Groh pilfered third base, but a moment later, when Frisch dashed for second, Conlon took a short throw from Gowdy and ran Frisch down when Frank darted back toward first base.

A run for the Braves and a pretty double play by the Giants marked the home half of this inning. Boeckel opened with a single to right centre, but was forced at second on McInnis's rap to Groh. Bagwell singled to right, McInnis pulling up at second. Conlon singled to centre, scoring McInnis and putting Bagwell on second. Ford followed with a hot shot to Groh, who tagged Bagwell on the line between second and third and then threw to Kelly in time to double up Ford.

Three-bagger for O'Connell.

Two were out in the fifth inning when Kelly drew a base on balls and scored on O'Connell's three-base smash to right centre. Jimmy would have made a home run on this blow but for smart fielding by Southworth.

In the seventh inning a misunderstanding between Bagwell and Ford enabled Young to get a two-base hit and paved the way for the scoring of two runs by the Giants. Young lifted a fly to short left field just inside the foul line. Either Bagwell, who came in for the ball, or Ford, who went for it, could have caught it, but each stepped back to permit the other to make the catch, with the result that the ball struck the turf between them and Young got to second base. Kelly hit to Ford, who had a play on Young at third base in front of him but didn't realize it, for he retired Kelly with a throw to McInnis, Young reaching third. O'Connell walked and flashed over the plate behind Young when Snyder doubled to right centre.

Scott experienced some difficulty in the last half of this inning, the Braves getting to him for three runs. Conlon singled to centre, Ford strolled and Gowdy rapped the ball to the left field corner of the big lot for three bases, scoring both men. Henry, sent up to bat for Oeschger, perished on strikes and Powell was thrown out by Frisch, but Gowdy scored while this play was in motion.

With Genewich pitching for the Braves in the eighth inning the Giants made threatening gestures but didn't score. Bancroft walked and, after Groh and Frisch had flied out, Meusel singled to right. Young, however, couldn't get the ball past Genewich, who tossed him out.

McInnis doubled to left when the Braves went to bat in this inning, but Scott got rid of Bagwell on strikes. McInnis got to third while Bancroft and Kelly were disposing of Conlon but was left there when Ford lifted to Meusel.

The score:

NEW YORK (N.)	Ab	R	H	Po	A
Bancroft.ss	4	0	1	1	4
Groh.3b	4	0	0	2	2
Frisch.2b	4	1	1	3	6
Meusel.lf	5	0	1	3	0
Young.rf	5	2	2	1	0
Kelly.1b	4	1	1	8	0
O'Connell.cf	3	1	1	1	0
Snyder.c	3	1	1	7	1
Scott.p	4	1	2	1	0
J. Barnes.p	0	0	0	0	0
Total	36	7	10	27	13

BOSTON (N.)	Ab	R	H	Po	A
Powell.cf	5	0	0	3	0
Sou'worth.rf	3	0	0	4	1
Boeckel.3b	4	0	1	0	1
McInnis.1b	4	1	1	12	0
Bagwell.lf	4	0	2	2	0
Conlon.2b	4	1	2	1	4
Ford.ss	3	1	0	2	1
Gowdy.c	3	1	2	3	2
Watson.p	1	0	0	0	0
Oeschger.p	1	0	0	0	2
Genewich.p	0	0	0	0	1
aHenry	1	0	0	0	0
bCruise	1	0	0	0	0
Total	33	4	8	27	12

a Batted for Oeschger in seventh.
b Batted for Genewich in ninth.
Errors—Southworth, Ford.

New York ....0 1 1 2 1 0 2 0 0—7
Boston ....0 0 0 1 0 0 3 0 0—4

Two-base hits—Young, Snyder, Bagwell, McInnis. Three-base hits—O'Connell, Gowdy. Home run—Scott. Stolen base—Groh. Sacrifice—Snyder. Double plays—Groh and Kelly; Bancroft, Frisch and Kelly. Left on bases—New York 10, Boston 5. Bases on balls—Off Scott 4, Watson 4, Oeschger 2, Genewich 1. Struck out—By Scott 4, Watson 1, Oeschger 1. Hits—Off Scott 8 in 8 innings (none out in ninth), J. Barnes none in 1, Watson 5 in 3 2-3, Oeschger 4 in 3 1-3, Genewich 1 in 2. Winning pitcher—Scott. Losing pitcher—Watson. Umpires—Klem and Derr. Time of game—2:02.

BASEBALL

YESTERDAY'S RESULTS.

AMERICAN LEAGUE.
New York 4, Boston 1.
Philadelphia 3, Washington 1.
Cleveland 6, Chicago 5.
Detroit 9, St. Louis 6.

NATIONAL LEAGUE.
New York 7, Boston 4.
Brooklyn 6, Philadelphia 5.
Chicago 7, Pittsburgh 2.
St. Louis 4, Cincinnati 2.

STANDING OF THE CLUBS.

AMERICAN LEAGUE.

	Won.	Lost.	P.C.
New York	1	0	1.000
Philadelphia	1	0	1.000
Cleveland	1	0	1.000
Detroit	1	0	1.000
Boston	0	1	.000
Washington	0	1	.000
Chicago	0	1	.000
St. Louis	0	1	.000

NATIONAL LEAGUE.

	Won.	Lost.	P.C.
New York	2	0	1.000
Brooklyn	1	0	1.000
Chicago	1	1	.500
Pittsburgh	1	1	.500
St. Louis	1	1	.500
Cincinnati	1	1	.500
Philadelphia	0	1	.000
Boston	0	2	.000

WHERE THEY PLAY TODAY.

AMERICAN LEAGUE.
Boston at New York.
(Game starts at 3:30 P. M.)
Washington at Philadelphia.
Chicago at Cleveland.
Detroit at St. Louis.

NATIONAL LEAGUE.
New York at Boston (Two Games).
Philadelphia at Brooklyn.
(Game starts at 3:30 P. M.)
St. Louis at Cincinnati.
Pittsburgh at Chicago.

TWO HOMERS MARK DETROIT'S TRIUMPH

Williams and Heilmann Get Circuit Drives as Tigers Trounce Browns, 9-6.

ST. LOUIS, April 18.—With George Sisler on the sick list, the Browns lost the opening game of the season to Detroit here today, 9 to 6.

Kenneth Williams started his home run slugging of the season by lifting the ball into the right field stands in the seventh, with Francis on the mound for the Tigers. In the preceding inning, Heilmann hit into the right field stands for a home run, scoring Cobb, who had singled ahead of him. Heilmann's four-bagger was off Danforth.

Mayor Kiel twirled the first ball. The attendance was estimated at 20,000.

The score:

DETROIT (A.)	Ab	R	H	Po	A
Blue.1b	5	1	1	10	1
Jones.3b	3	0	0	0	2
Haney.3b	1	0	0	1	0
Cobb.cf	4	3	3	1	0
Veach.lf	3	2	2	0	0
Goth'g'l.lf	0	0	0	1	0
Heilm'n.rf	5	2	4	2	2
Cutshaw.2b	4	0	2	6	2
Rigney.ss	4	0	1	2	4
Bassler.c	5	0	0	4	0
W. C'lins.p	2	3	2	0	3
Francis.p	3	0	0	0	0
aPratt	0	1	0	0	0
Total	39	9	15	27	15

ST. LOUIS (A.)	Ab	R	H	Po	A
Rob'tson.3b	4	1	2	1	1
Gerber.ss	4	1	0	1	1
Tobin.rf	4	1	2	3	0
Williams.lf	5	2	3	4	0
McManus.2b	4	0	1	2	1
Severeid.c	3	0	0	6	1
Jacobson.cf	4	0	0	7	0
Durst.1b	2	0	0	7	0
Schulte.1b	0	0	0	1	0
Shocker.p	0	0	0	0	1
Danforth.p	0	1	0	0	2
Wright.p	0	0	0	0	2
Root.p	0	0	0	0	0
bP. Collins	1	0	0	0	0
cWhaley	1	0	0	0	0
dVan Gilder	1	0	1	0	0
eRice	0	0	0	0	0
Total	33	6	9	27	9

a—Batted for Jones in sixth.
b—Batted for Danforth in sixth.
c—Batted for Durst in eighth.
d—Batted for Wright in eighth.
e—Ran for Vangilder in eighth.
Errors—Cobb, Gerber.

Detroit .... 3 0 1 0 0 4 0 1 0—9
St. Louis .... 2 0 0 2 0 0 1 0 0—6

Two-base hits—McManus, W. Collins, Heilmann. Home runs—Heilmann, Williams. Sacrifices—Danforth, Cutshaw, Fothergill (2). Left on bases—Detroit 10, St. Louis 7. Bases on balls—Off W. Collins 4, Danforth 1, Wright 1. Struck out—By W. Collins 1, Danforth 1, Francis 2, Wright 2, Root 1. Hits—Off Shocker 6 in 1 inning; Danforth 7 in 5, Wright 2 in 2, Root 0 in 1, Collins 5 in 3 2-3, Francis 4 in 5 1-3. Hit by pitcher—By W. Collins, Robertson, Tobin. By Danforth, Blue, Pratt. Winning pitcher—Francis. Losing pitcher—Danforth. Umpires—Dinneen and Ormsby. Time of game—2:30.

GREAT CROWD SEES INDIANS WIN OPENER

Cleveland Rallies in Ninth and Beats White Sox, 6-5, Before 20,372.

CLEVELAND, April 18.—One of the largest opening-day crowds that ever witnessed an American League game here saw Cleveland make a ninth-inning rally and defeat Chicago, 6 to 5, today. After the White Sox had gone into the lead, 5 to 4, in the eighth inning, Wambsganss led off in the ninth for the Indians with a double. Speaker fouled out, but Guisto walked and Summa and Sewell singled, two runs scoring.

Kamm made his American League début by handling his two assists cleanly and getting a double out of four times at bat.

Faber, who started the game for Chicago, retired in favor of Pinch-Hitter Strunk, who started a rally in the eighth which resulted in Coveleskie being knocked from the box.

The official attendance was 20,372, about 350 less than the opening-day record.

The score:

CLEVELAND (A.)	Ab	R	H	Po	A
Jamieson.lf	5	0	1	1	1
W'gans.2b	5	3	3	1	2
Speaker.cf	5	1	2	1	0
Guisto.1b	3	1	0	11	2
Summa.rf	5	0	3	2	0
J. Sewell.ss	4	1	2	3	2
Lutzke.3b	3	0	0	1	2
O'Neill.c	4	0	2	5	2
Coveleskie.p	3	0	0	1	1
Uhle.p	0	0	0	0	0
Boone.p	0	0	0	1	0
aBrower	1	0	1	0	0
Total	38	6	14	27	12

CHICAGO (A.)	Ab	R	H	Po	A
Hooper.rf	5	1	3	1	0
Johnson.ss	3	0	1	3	5
Collins.2b	4	1	2	3	5
Mostil.cf	5	1	1	2	0
Sheely.1b	4	0	2	10	0
Kamm.3b	4	0	1	0	2
Falk.lf	3	1	0	0	0
Schalk.c	4	0	1	6	0
Faber.p	2	0	0	0	1
Mack.p	1	0	0	0	0
bStrunk	1	1	1	0	0
Total	37	5	12	*25	13

*One out when winning run was scored.
aBatted for Uhle in eighth.
bBatted for Faber in eighth.
Errors—J. Sewell, Lutzke, Johnson.

Cleveland ....0 0 1 1 2 0 0 0 2—6
Chicago ....0 0 0 0 1 0 0 4 0—5

Two-base hits—Kamm, Hooper (2), Speaker (2), J. Sewell, Wambsganss. Stolen bases—Wambsganss, J. Sewell. Sacrifice—Johnson. Double plays—Collins, Johnson and Sheely; O'Neill and Guisto. Left on bases—Chicago 8, Cleveland 11. Bases on balls—Off Faber 3, Mack 1, Boone 2. Hits—Off Faber 10 in 7 innings; Mack, 4 in 1 1-3; Coveleskie, 10 in 7 1-3; Uhle, 1 in 2-3; Boone, 1 in 1. Struck out—By Faber 4, Mack 1, Coveleskie 2, Boone 1. Wild pitch—Uhle. Passed ball—Schalk. Winning pitcher—Boone. Losing pitcher, Mack. Umpires—Hildebrand, Moriarty and Rowland. Time of game—2:20.

Southern Association.

Mobile 3, New Orleans 6.
Little Rock 4, Memphis 3.
Atlanta 8, Nashville 7.
Chattanooga 5, Birmingham 4.

ROBINS MAKE FIVE IN 9TH, WIN BY 6-5

Olson's Hit Drives In Deciding Run in Thrilling Finish Against Phillies.

WHEAT STARTS THE RALLY

Opens Final Inning With Homer, Which Upsets Pitcher Head and Paves Way for Triumph.

Some player on the Phillies baseball team must have walked inadvertently under a ladder recently or allowed an ebony-hued cat to streak across his path, for after Art Fletcher's Quaker athletes had the game neatly sewed up with a four-run lead in the ninth inning at Ebbets Field yesterday afternoon, the Robins came to bat in their half of the frame and batted out a triumph. Uncle Robbie's warriors staged a one-man rally, started by Zach Wheat, the first man up, who lifted a home run over the right field fence, which resulted in five runs being scored—enough to win by the count of 6 to 5. No one was out when Hank DeBerry scampered in on Ivy Olson's single with the winning tally. About 3,000 hardy fans witnessed the spectacular victory.

Ralph Head, the Phillies recruit pitcher from Hartford, went along smoothly, allowing only three hits and one run until the ninth. Brooklyn's lone tally had been scored on a couple of walks, an infield out and a sacrifice fly. But in the last frame the storm broke. The Phillies had scored two runs in their half of the ninth when Heine Sand, the $40,000 recruit from Salt Lake, poled a home run over the right field barrier, scoring Walker who had singled.

Not to be outdone, Zach Wheat started the Robins' half with a circuit clout in the same direction. And then the fun began. Fred Schliebner singled to right and Barber drew a walk. At this juncture Head was relieved by Wilbur Hubbell. Dutch Ruether was sent in to bat for Andy High. He was walked, filling the bases, and Nels was delegated to run for him. Schliebner was safe at the plate on Hank DeBerry's scratch hit along third, and the Phillies decided that a new pitcher was necessary.

Fletcher commissioned Lee Meadows to silence the Brooklyn attack but he failed. He walked Burley Grimes, forcing in Barber with a run. And then served one to Ivy Olson that was very much to his liking. Olsen crashed a single to centre field, and Nels and DeBerry crossed the plate, ending a successful and glorious game for Squire Ebbets's organization.

Grimes Makes Poor Start.

Burley Grimes was Robinson's choice as pitcher. He allowed the Phillies ten hits. He made a poor start, for in the first inning he was reached for three singles and a triple that resulted in three runs. After that slip Grimes held them scoreless until the ninth inning, when two more runs ambled over the plate by virtue of Sand's homer.

The Robins made a single run in the fifth inning. Hank DeBerry walked and went to second when Grimes drew another pass. Both advanced when Head threw Olsen out at first. Jimmy Johnston lifted a long fly to Curt Walker and DeBerry had plenty of time to come in with the run.

Goldie Rapp opened the first inning for Philadelphia with a single to right, and went to second when Holke bounced a single off Ivy Olson's shoe. Both runners scored on Williams's triple which took a freak bounce off the sloping right field fence. Williams came home when Olson threw out Curt Walker at first. Then Grimes tightened up, striking out four batters and allowing one hit in the next three innings.

A number of excellent catches were made by the outfielders of both the Phillies and Robins. Tom Griffith made a beautiful running catch of Holke's long fly in the fifth inning, and Williams returned the compliment in the other half of the frame when he grabbed Griffith's hard-hit fly after a long run.

Set Date for Play-Off of Tie.

The fourteen-inning game Tuesday which resulted in a 5-to-5 tie will be played off between the Brooklyn and Philadelphia Clubs at Ebbets Field on Saturday, June 23, as part of a double-header.

The score:

BROOKLYN (N.)	Ab	R	H	Po	A
Olson.2b	5	0	1	2	4
Johnston.ss	3	0	0	5	2
T Griffith.rf	3	0	0	6	0
Wheat.lf	4	1	2	1	0
Schl'bner.1b	4	1	2	7	3
Barber.cf	3	1	0	0	0
High.3b	3	0	0	1	1
DeBerry.c	3	2	2	4	1
Grimes.p	2	0	0	1	0
aRuether	0	0	0	0	0
bNels	0	1	0	0	0
Total	30	6	7	27	11

PHILADELPHIA (N.)	Ab	R	H	Po	A
Rapp.3b	4	1	1	1	2
Holke.1b	4	1	2	9	0
Williams.cf	4	1	1	5	0
Walker.lf	4	1	2	4	0
Lee.rf	4	0	1	1	0
Sand.ss	4	1	1	1	3
Park'son.2b	4	0	1	2	3
Henline.c	4	0	1	1	0
Head.p	3	0	0	0	0
Hubbell.p	0	0	0	0	0
Meadows.p	0	0	0	0	0
Total	35	5	10	*24	8

* None out when winning run was scored.
a Batted for High in ninth.
b Ran for Ruether in ninth.
Errors—Wheat, Walker.

Brooklyn .... 0 0 0 0 1 0 0 0 5—6
Philadelphia .... 3 0 0 0 0 0 0 0 2—5

Three-base hit—Williams. Home runs—Sand, Wheat. Sacrifice—Johnston. Double plays—Olson, Johnston and Schliebner; Parkinson, Sand and Holke. Left on bases—Philadelphia 3, Brooklyn 7. Bases on balls—Off Head 4, Hubbard 1, Meadows 1. Struck out—By Grimes, 4. Hits—Off Head, 3 in 8 innings (none out in ninth), Hubbell 1 in none (none out in ninth), Meadows 1 in none (none out in ninth). Wild pitch—Head. Winning pitcher—Grimes. Losing pitcher—Meadows. Umpires—Hart and McCormick. Time of game—2 hours.

ATHLETICS BEGIN WELL.

Open American League Season With Victory Over Senators.

PHILADELPHIA, April 18.—Philadelphia opened the American League season here today by defeating Washington, 3 to 1.

A home run by Dykes in the second inning with a teammate on the sacks was the blow that sent Walter Johnson down to defeat.

Harris twirled fine ball for the Athletics holding the Senators to four widely scattered hits. Miller's sensational catch in the eighth was the fielding feature. More than 20,000 persons saw the game.

The score:

PHILADELPHIA (A)	Ab	R	H	Po	A
Matthews.cf	3	0	2	1	0
Perkins.c	4	0	0	4	0
Hale.3b	4	0	0	0	0
Hauser.1b	3	0	0	11	0
Miller.lf	4	1	1	7	0
Galloway.ss	4	1	1	1	1
Welch.rf	3	0	1	0	0
Dykes.2b	2	1	1	3	1
B. Harris.p	2	0	0	0	5
Total	29	3	6	27	7

WASHINGTON (A.)	Ab	R	H	Po	A
Rice.rf	4	0	0	0	0
Evans.cf	4	0	0	4	0
Judge.1b	4	1	1	12	0
Goslin.lf	4	0	1	1	0
S. Harris.2b	3	0	0	1	3
Conroy.3b	4	0	0	2	0
P'k'paugh.ss	4	0	1	1	1
Ruel.c	4	0	1	3	1
Johnson.p	2	0	0	0	5
Total	33	1	4	24	12

Errors—Hale, Galloway, Rice, Peckinpaugh.

Philadelphia .... 0 2 0 1 0 0 0 0 .—3
Washington .... 1 0 0 0 0 0 0 0 0—1

Two-base hits—Judge, Galloway, Peck. Home run—Dykes. Stolen base—S. Harris. Sacrifices—Dykes, B. Harris. Double plays—S. Harris, Peckinpaugh and Judge. Left on bases—Washington 7, Philadelphia 6. Bases on balls—Off Johnson 2, B. Harris 1. Struck out—By Johnson 2, B. Harris 3. Hit by pitcher—By B. Harris (S. Harris). Umpires—Nallin and Owen. Time of game—1:43.

Yale Freshmen Triumph, 5-2.

Special to The New York Times.

NEW HAVEN, Conn., April 18.—The Yale freshmen defeated the Collegiate Preparatory School nine this afternoon by 5 to 2. Lindley of Yale made two home runs.

Brown Wins at Net.

PROVIDENCE, R. I., April 18.—Brown opened the tennis season with a victory over Holy Cross, 4 matches to 2, here this afternoon. Cold weather hindered the contestants.

Connecticut House Defeats Bill Legalizing Sunday Ball

HARTFORD, Conn., April 18.—For the first time this session House Leader John Buckley of Union lost the house when his bill which would legalize Sunday football and baseball was defeated by a vote of 139 to 86. Republicans and Democrats split on the issue, 124 Republicans and 15 Democrats voting against the bill and 56 Republicans and 30 Democrats voting for it. While the prevailing opinion of the House was against legalizing Sunday baseball it is not believed that the House would be willing to go to the other extreme of strictly enforcing the present law. Governor Templeton, in declaring that he would veto the original bill if it were passed, has expressed himself as being in favor of "leaving things as they are."

JERSEY CITY OPENS WITH 6-1 VICTORY

Zellars Holds Toronto While Skeeters Pound Reynolds for Inaugural Triumph.

More than 7,000 fans turned out to see Ben Egan's Jersey City nine turn in a 6 to 1 victory over Toronto in the opening game of the International League championship season in Jersey City yesterday afternoon. Rube Zellars, the Skeeters' star southpaw, was in excellent form, and aside from the fourth inning, when the Maple Leafs bunched one of their six hits with a base on balls and a sacrifice, he never was in danger.

Reynolds was on the mound for Toronto, and while he pitched good ball at times, he weakened when hits meant runs. The Skeeters reached him for a brace of tallies in the first inning, registered two more in the sixth and so counted for the final pair of runs in the seventh. Reynolds was taken out with two men retired in the seventh and was relieved by Lynch, who pitched effectively during his one and one-third innings of work.

The only run made by Toronto, which came in the fourth, was the result of a base on balls to Kelly, a two-base hit by R. Gonzales and Hill's sacrifice fly to Donelson.

Donelson started the Skeeters on the way to victory in the first inning. With one out he singled and Jacobs walked. Cobb grounded to R. Gonzales at short, and when Gonzales made a wild throw in trying to force Jacobs at second Donelson and Jacobs reached home before the ball was returned.

In the seventh the Skeeters brought their total to four. Jacobs walked again, Cobb doubled and Wagner singled, accounting for two runs. The final Jersey City runs came across in the seventh when Moran and Freitag singled, both coming home on a triple by Jacobs. It was the timely blow by Jacobs that resulted in the withdrawal of Reynolds.

John Jacobs was the star on the attack for the Skeeters. He walked on his first three trips to the plate and scored twice, and on his fourth time he connected for the triple which drove in two runs. Holt contributed the fielding feature when with two Toronto men on base and two out he made a sensational one-hand stop of a hard drive, retiring the side.

Mayor Hague was late in reaching the ball park and the opening ceremony of tossing out the first ball was dispensed with.

The score:

JERSEY CITY.	Ab	R	H	Po	A
Moran.2b	4	1	1	1	1
Donelson.rf	4	1	1	3	0
Jacobs.lf	1	2	1	5	0
Holt.1b	4	0	0	6	1
Cobb.cf	4	1	1	3	0
Wagner.3b	4	0	1	1	3
Ray.ss	4	0	1	2	1
Freitag.c	4	0	1	5	0
Zellars.p	3	1	0	1	2
Total	32	6	7	27	8

TORONTO.	Ab	R	H	Po	A
M.G'zales.3b	4	0	0	0	1
O'Rourke.2b	5	0	2	4	3
Wingo.lf	4	0	0	1	0
Maisel.cf	4	0	0	3	0
Onslow.1b	4	0	1	8	0
Kelly.rf	2	1	1	0	0
R.G'zales.ss	3	0	1	3	0
Hill.c	3	0	1	5	1
Reynolds.p	3	0	0	0	4
Lynch.p	0	0	0	0	1
aCapes	1	0	0	0	0
Total	33	1	6	24	10

a Batted for Lynch in ninth.
Errors—Cobb, O'Rourke, R. Gonzales.

Jersey City ....2 0 0 0 0 2 2 0 x—6
Toronto ....0 0 0 1 0 0 0 0 0—1

Two-base hits—O'Rourke, R. Gonzales, Cobb. Three-base hits—Jacobs. Stolen base—Jacobs. Sacrifice—Hill. Left on bases—Jersey City 5, Toronto 10. Bases on balls—Off Zellars 4, Reynolds 3. Struck out—By Zellars 4, Reynolds 4. Hits—Off Reynolds 6 in 6 2-3 innings, Lynch 1 in 1 1-3. Wild pitch—Reynolds. Umpires—Gaston and Magerkirth. Time, 1:50.

CARDS EVEN UP SERIES.

Toney Outpitches Rixey as St. Louis Defeats Reds, 4 to 2.

CINCINNATI, April 18.—Toney outpitched Rixey in the second game of the season here today and the St. Louis Cardinals evened up the series by beating the Cincinnati Reds, 4 to 2. Rixey was wild and was hit safely in every inning but one. Mann made the first home run of the local season on a long drive to right centre inside the grounds in the third inning.

The score:

ST. LOUIS (N.)	Ab	R	H	Po	A
Blades.lf	5	1	3	1	0
Mann.cf	5	1	2	4	0
Hornsby.2b	3	0	1	0	0
B'tomley.1b	5	0	0	8	2
Stock.3b	4	1	3	1	3
Schultz.rf	4	0	0	3	0
Freigau.ss	4	0	2	3	1
Clemons.c	3	0	0	6	0
aSmith	0	1	0	0	0
Ainsmith.c	1	0	0	1	0
Toney.p	4	0	1	0	3
Total	38	4	12	27	11

CINCINNATI (N.)	Ab	R	H	Po	A
Burns.rf	4	0	3	1	0
Harper.cf	3	1	0	3	0
Duncan.lf	3	0	1	3	0
Bohne.2b	3	0	0	3	5
Fonseca.1b	3	1	1	12	0
Hargrave.c	4	0	1	2	0
Pinelli.3b	4	0	2	1	1
Caveney.ss	3	0	0	2	6
bRoush	1	0	0	0	0
Rixey.p	2	0	0	0	3
cWingo	1	0	0	0	0
Total	31	2	8	27	15

a Ran for Clemons in seventh.
b Batted for Caveney in ninth.
c Batted for Rixey in ninth.
Errors—Blades, Freigau.

St. Louis ....0 0 1 0 0 0 1 1 1—4
Cincinnati ....0 0 0 0 0 2 0 0 0—2

Two-base hits—Burns, Duncan, Blades (2). Home run—Mann. Stolen base—Fonseca. Sacrifices—Duncan, Bohne, Rixey, Schultz. Left on bases—St. Louis 11, Cincinnati 7. Base on balls—Off Rixey 3, Toney 2. Struck out—By Rixey 2, Toney 6. Wild pitch—Toney. Umpires—Quigley and Pfirman. Time of game—2:02.

CUBS BEAT PIRATES, 7-2.

Victors Pound Boehler for Six Hits in Eighth Inning.

CHICAGO, April 18.—Boehler weakened in the eighth inning, and the Chicago Cubs pounded out six hits, including two doubles and a triple, broke a tie score, and defeated the Pittsburgh Pirates, 7 to 2, in the second game of the series here today. Johnny Kelleher of Chicago knocked the ball into the newly erected left bleachers for a home run, the first in the new park. Grimm of Pittsburgh duplicated the feat a little later. Alexander pitched in fine form.

The score:

CHICAGO (N.)	Ab	R	H	Po	A
Statz.cf	5	0	2	2	0
Heathcote.rf	2	1	1	3	0
Granth'm.2b	4	1	2	1	6
Grimes.1b	3	1	1	15	1
Friberg.3b	2	1	1	0	2
Miller.lf	4	1	1	0	0
Kelleher.ss	3	1	1	3	6
Hartnett.c	4	0	1	2	1
Alexander.p	3	1	1	1	2
Total	30	7	11	27	18

PITTSBURGH (N.)	Ab	R	H	Po	A
Maranv'le.ss	4	0	1	2	5
Carey.cf	4	0	0	4	1
Bigbee.lf	4	0	0	0	1
Russell.rf	4	1	1	1	0
Tierney.2b	4	0	0	2	2
Traynor.3b	2	0	2	3	0
Grimm.1b	3	1	1	0	1
Gooch.c	3	0	0	3	1
Boehler.p	3	0	0	0	3
Total	31	2	5	24	14

Errors—Kelleher, Russel, Maranville.

Chicago ....0 0 1 0 1 0 0 5 .—7
Pittsburgh ....0 0 0 0 0 0 2 0 0—2

Two-base hits—Russell, Heathcote, Grimes. Three-base hits—Alexander, Friberg. Home runs—Kelleher, Grimm. Stolen base—Statz. Sacrifices—Traynor, Kelleher, Alexander. Double plays—Boehler, Maranville and Grimm; Maranville, Tierney and Grimm. Left on bases—Pittsburgh 3, Chicago 6. Bases on balls—Off Boehler 5. Struck out—By Boehler 2, Alexander 2. Umpires—Sentelle and Moran. Time of game—1:30.

HUGE CROWD FAILS TO FILL EVERY SEAT

Fans Prefer to Stand Five Deep in Covered Section Rather Than Go in Bleachers.

THRONG SWARMS ON FIELD

Game Interrupted Near Finish Until Police Clear Grounds—Other Yankee Sidelights.

Although a crowd of 74,200 persons witnessed the dedication of the Yankees' gigantic new stadium yesterday afternoon not every seat in the enclosure was occupied. In the far reaches of the bleachers, both in right field and in left field, there were small stretches of empty seats. This does not mean, however, that the stadium was not filled beyond its total seating capacity. Not only was every seat in the grand stand occupied but the fans were standing four and five deep behind the seats in all of the three tiers. There were far more than enough standees to fill the comparatively few empty seats in the bleachers, but these chose to witness the game while standing in the grand stand rather than while sitting in the bleachers.

Despite the vast throngs in the grand stand no confusion prevailed and the crowd was well handled. With few exceptions the aisles were kept remarkably clear in view of the vastness of the throng. Many who were unable to obtain seats in the grand stand chose various points of vantage on the ramps from which to view the game.

Shortly before the game ended many fans poured out onto the field from the bleachers. Many of them surrounded Ruth and the game was halted momentarily while the field was being cleared. As soon as the game had been completed many surrounded the dugout of the Yankees through which the passageway leads to the players' club house and some of the athletes had difficulty in making their way from the field.

More than 200 members of the New York Kiwanis Club and their friends attended the game. The delegation occupied a section in the mezzanine on the first-base side of the stands. Before leaving for the stadium the members of the club held a luncheon at the Hotel McAlpin, where resolutions were adopted calling for courtesy to ball players on New York and visiting clubs when on the field and extending the courtesy of the club to players of the major leagues. The resolutions were adopted as the result of "Courtesy Week," which is being observed by the club at its various branches throughout the United States. The resolutions also called upon the public to co-operate with the club in extending courtesy at all times to the players, particularly when on the field. The resolutions were introduced by James Steedman, former President of the organization.

Despite the elaborate ceremonies, everything went along smoothly and the game started only one minute after the scheduled time. It was just 3:31 P. M. when Shawkey tossed up the first ball to Chick Fewster.

Contrary to the usual order of things, Governor Smith did not make a wild throw when he tossed out the first ball to Wally Schang. Wally caught the pellet without much difficulty and then ran over and returned the ball to the Governor.

Governor Warms Up.

Before starting the game officially, Governor Smith indulged in a few practice tosses for the benefit of the army of photographers who surrounded his box.

Frank Chance, once manager of the Yankees in the days when the local American League club never thought of winning a pennant, made his début as manager of the Red Sox. The Peerless Leader, attired in a natty red and gray uniform, occupied one of the coaches' boxes while his team was at bat.

Eleven members of the Boston club took part in the game and of these four had once worn the uniform of the Yankees. Chick Fewster played shortstop for the Sox, Camp Skinner was in centre field, Norman McMillan was at second base and Al Devormer behind the bat. All four of these were members of the Yankees when the American League champions opened their season last year.

The only double play of the game came in the eighth inning and was made by Scott, Ward and Pipp. It was made on Fewster and Collins after the former had been hit by a pitched ball.

Although President Ban Johnson of the American League had previously announced that Billy Evans would be umpire-in-chief of the game, Tommy Connolly, the veteran arbiter, took up his position behind the plate just before the game started. Evans was at first base and Homes at third. One more umpire would have given the event a real world's series aspect in this regard.

Although Ruth hit the first home run ever made in the new stadium, George Burns of the Red Sox had the honor of making the first hit. It was a single in the second inning and came with none on the bases and one out.

Shawkey had the honor of pitching the first ball as well as the first strike. Shawkey also registered the first strike out while Ehmke gave the first base on balls. Scott made the first assist and Pipp was credited with the first put out. Shano Collins was the first outfielder to catch a fly in the new park when he grabbed Ruth's hoist in the first inning. Meusel made the first two-base hit, while McMillan made the first three-bagger. The first stolen base in the new arena has still to be made. Burns attempted the stunt in the second inning and was thrown out. Pipp also tried in the third but met a similar fate.

Scott Plays 987th Straight As Yanks Win in New Stadium

By playing in his regular position at shortstop in yesterday's game as the Yankees won in their new stadium, Everett Scott increased his string of consecutive games to 987. Scott recently suffered an injury to his ankle while playing in an exhibition at Springfield, Mo., and it was feared at the time that he would not be able to keep his record intact by playing in the opening game of the season. Scott's ankle came around nicely, and there was little evidence of his recent injury shown in his playing yesterday. Unless any of the Yankees' next thirteen games are postponed because of rain, the star shortstop will reach his coveted mark of 1,000 consecutive games on May 2.

TICKET SPECULATORS ARRESTED AT STADIUM

Two Are Taken Into Custody for Offering Pasteboards at Excessive Prices.

The opening of the American League baseball season here yesterday also witnessed the inauguration of the Police Department's open war on ticket speculators at baseball games. Two pasteboard brokers were arrested yesterday by Detective Andrew M. O'Connor of Inspector Ryan's Fifth Inspection District staff, charged with offering grand stand seats at prices in excess of the face value of the tickets. The men were taken into custody outside the new Yankee Stadium before the Yankee-Red Sox game started. They described themselves as Abraham Cohen, 28 years old, of 547 Howard Avenue, Brooklyn, and Sebastian Calabrese, 35 years old, of 235 East Twenty-seventh Street.

In Night Court, before Magistrate Bernard E. Douras, Detective O'Connor charged Cohen with offering his $1.10 grand stand seat for $1.25, and Calabrese with offering his ticket for sale at $1.50. The charge involves a violation of Section 1,534 of the Penal law, the maximum punishment for which is a fine of $500 or one year in jail, or both. Cohen and Calabrese pleaded guilty to the charge and were held in $500 bail each for trial in Special Sessions. In default of bail both prisoners were locked up in the Night Court prison.

SIZE OF STADIUM IMPRESSES CROWD

Few Had Previously Realized Magnitude of New Monument to Baseball.

PLANT COVERS TEN ACRES

When Triple Deck Stand Is Completed Capacity Will Be Approximately 85,000

Although many facts and figures had been published in advance to give baseball fans some idea of the massiveness of the Yankees' Stadium it was not until the formal opening yesterday that the fans really had an opportunity to grasp what a gigantic edifice Colonels Ruppert and Huston have caused to be erected as a monument to baseball. Figures of such a nature are impressive, but to the average person they are not nearly so impressive as seeing the structure itself.

Upward of 100,000 visited the stadium yesterday for the opening game of the local American League season. More than 70,000 of them succeeded in cramming their way inside. The others encountered closed gates, for, big as it is, there is a limit to what the Yankees' new home can hold and it was filled to capacity a half an hour before the game time. The official attendance figures showed that the capacity of the place at present is 74,200. When the triple deck stand is completed it will entirely surround the field and it is estimated that the capacity then will be increased to approximately 85,000.

The stadium now covers about ten acres of ground—property that was purchased from the William Waldorf Astor estate in February, 1921, for about $600,000. This money and the cost of construction represent an outlay of about $2,500,000. Before the actual work of building the stadium could be started it was necessary to fill in and level the ground. To accomplish this 45,000 cubic yards of earth were used. Then it was necessary to excavate 25,000 cubic yards of earth to lay the foundation for the grand stand and bleachers.

In building the grand stand and bleachers 2,500 tons of structural steel and 1,000 tons of reinforcing steel, 2,000,000 board feet and 600,000 lineal feet of lumber, 4 miles of piping for rails and 500 tons of iron were used.

With a maximum force of 500 workmen it required eleven months to construct the stadium. The work of leveling the ground was completed toward the close of 1921 and the work of building the big triple deck grand stand was started last Spring. The distance around the outer edge of the grand stand and bleachers is 2,501 feet and the extreme length inside is 700 feet. To sod the infield and the outfield a special type of grass was selected, necessitating transporting 116,000 square feet of sod from Long Island.

The plans for the stadium were not drawn until every baseball park of account in the country had been thoroughly inspected. The best features of these structures were molded together to make the Yankees' home. With what success this was accomplished every fan who was fortunate enough to squeeze inside yesterday will attest.

The drainage system is one of the best to be found anywhere. Eleven large pipes have been laid around the outfield and a network of twenty-four pipes has been laid under the infield as well as a concrete gutter in front of the grandstand.

In short, the Yankees' Stadium is just about the last word in baseball plants.

OTHER INTERNATIONAL GAMES.

At Reading.

		R.	H.	E.
Buffalo	0 0 0 0 1 0 3 0 0	4	6	1
Reading	0 1 0 0 1 0 1 0 0	3	8	0

Batteries — Mohart and Urban; Martin, Carts and Clarke.

At Baltimore.

		R.	H.	E.
Syracuse	0 0 0 0 0 0 3 0 0	3	9	1
Baltimore	0 0 0 0 2 0 1 0 0	3	[illegible]	1

(Game called; darkness.)

Batteries—Reinhardt and Niebergall; Ogden, Thomas and McAvoy.

STANDING OF THE CLUBS.

	Won.	Lost.	P. C.
Jersey City	1	0	1.000
Buffalo	1	0	1.000
Rochester	1	0	1.000
Newark	0	1	.000
Toronto	0	1	.000
Reading	0	1	.000
Baltimore	0	0	.000
Syracuse	0	0	.000

WHERE THEY PLAY TODAY.

Toronto at Jersey City.
Rochester at Newark.
Syracuse at Baltimore.
Buffalo at Reading.

ROCHESTER CAPTURES OPENER FROM NEWARK

More Than 10,000 See the Bears Drop Ten-Inning Game by 9 to 7.

Special to The New York Times.

NEWARK, N. J., April 18.—George Stallings's Rochester Hustlers defeated Mickey Devine's Newark Bears in the opening game of the International League season at Harrison Field here today. The score was 9 to 7 and it took ten innings to decide the contest.

Ten thousand fans saw the contest, unmindful of the chilly weather and the rain which fell during the last half of the game. Frederick C. Breidenbach, Mayor of Newark, tossed the first ball from the pitchers' mound, with Mayor Riordan of Harrison catching it. The two Mayors marched to the centre field fence with the players of both teams behind them and a troop of Boy Scouts. The Boy Scouts fired a salute as the flag was hoisted to the top of the pole.

Beall, who went in the box for Rochester after Wisner had been hammered off the mound, did a lot to win his own game. He hammered out a home run and, in the tenth inning, with the score tied, drove out a single which scored Lunte. Barnes in the same inning singled to centre, scoring McQuinn and Beall.

The game bristled with brilliant plays. There were three, however, which stood out. The first came in the sixth inning, when Billy Zeitman, Newark's star left fielder, made a great one-hand running catch of a drive made by Archdeacon. Pitt, Rochester's right fielder, made a catch almost as sensational in the same inning off a drive by Altenberg. Newark executed a great double play in the eighth inning. Rochester had scored once and had the bases loaded. Archdeacon drove a line drive to See in right field. After making the catch, See shot the ball on a line to Devine at the plate, and Mickey touched out Jenkins.

Rochester was first to score, getting two runs in the opening inning. Archdeacon drew a pass, but was forced at second by Pitt. Benes tried for a double play and threw wild to first, Pitt going to second. Barnes walked, and Merkle smashed the ball against the left-field fence. Pitt and Barnes scored. Merkle was run down after trying to stretch his hit into a triple.

Newark pounded Wisner for five safeties in the second inning and scored four runs. Anderson led off with a home run. Zeitman beat out a bunt. Miller sacrificed and Devine drove Zeitman home with a single to left. Benes tripled to left, scoring Devine, while Mickey counted on Baldwin's three-base smash to the same territory. Newark accounted for two more runs in the third inning. See doubled to centre, and Anderson advanced him with a sacrifice. Zeitman tripled to left, and See counted. Zeitman scored while Miller was being thrown out at first.

Rochester came back with three runs in the fifth and tied the score in the eighth. A home run by Beall, a pass to Archdeacon, Pitt's double and Kommand's single gave Rochester three runs. The run that tied the score was made by Kommand, who singled, took second on a sacrifice, and scored when Smith, batting for Womack, singled.

The score:

ROCHESTER (I.)	Ab	R	H	Po	A
Archd'con.cf	3	1	0	0	0
Pitt.rf	5	2	1	3	0
Barnes.2b	5	1	3	2	1
Merkle.1b	4	0	1	11	0
Kommand.lf	6	1	3	3	2
Lunte.3b	4	1	1	2	1
Jenkins.ss	5	0	2	1	3
Lake.c	2	0	0	3	1
Wisner.p	1	0	0	0	1
aGriffin	0	0	0	0	0
Beall.p	3	2	2	0	2
Womack.c	2	0	0	2	0
bSmith	1	0	1	0	0
McQuinn.c	1	1	1	3	2
cYordy	1	0	0	0	0
Keenan.p	0	0	0	0	0
Total	41	9	15	30	13

NEWARK (I.)	Ab	R	H	Po	A
Altenberg.cf	[illegible]				
Sheridan.ss	[illegible]				
See.rf	[illegible]				
Anderson.3b	[illegible]				
Zitman.lf	[illegible]				
Miller.1b	[illegible]				
Devine.c	[illegible]				
Benes.2b	[illegible]				
Baldwin.p	[illegible]				
Fileshifter.p	[illegible]				
Kneisch.p	[illegible]				
dKnothe	[illegible]				
eManley	[illegible]				
Total	35	7	13	30	14

a Ran for Lake in sixth.
b Batted for Womack in eighth.
c Batted for Pitt in tenth.
d Batted for Kneisch in tenth.
e Batted for Altenberg in tenth.
Errors—Sheridan, Benes.

Rochester ....2 0 0 0 3 0 0 1 0 [illegible]
Newark ....0 4 2 0 0 0 0 0 0 [illegible]

Two-base hits—Merkle, See, Pitt. Three-base hits—Benes, Baldwin, Zitman, See. Home runs—Anderson, Beall. Stolen bases—Griffin, Devine. Sacrifices—Miller, Anderson (2), Lunte, Merkle, Benes. Double plays—Lunte, Barnes and Merkle; See, Benes and Devine. Left on bases—Rochester 10, Newark 8. Bases on balls—Off Baldwin 2, Beall 6, Fileshifter 1, Kneisch 2. Struck out—By Wisner 2, Fileshifter 1, Kneisch 1, Baldwin 4. Hits—Off Baldwin 6 in 4 innings, Wisner 8 in 2 1-3, Fileshifter 7 in 4 1-3, Kneisch 2 in 1 2-3, Beall 4 in 7 2-3. Hit by pitcher—By Fileshifter (Lake). Wild pitch—Beall. Winning pitcher—Beall. Losing pitcher—Fileshifter. Umpires—Carpenter, James, Hett. Time of game—3:00.

74,200 SEE YANKEES OPEN NEW STADIUM

Continued from Page 1, Column 1.

the mere height of the grandstand is tremendous. Baseball fans who sat in the last low of the steeply sloping third tier may well boast that they broke all altitude records short of those attained in an airplane.

Once inside the grounds, the sweep of the big stand strikes the eye most forcibly. It throws its arms far out to each side, the grandstand ending away over where the bleachers begin. In the centre of the vast pile of steel and concrete was the green spread of grass and diamond, and fewer ball fields are greener than that on which the teams played yesterday.

The Yankees' new home, besides being beautiful and majestic, is practical. It was emptied yesterday of its 74,000 in quicker time than the Polo Grounds ever was. Double ramps from top to bottom carried the stream of people steadily and rapidly to the lower exits, which are many and well situated. Fans from the bleachers and far ends of the grand stand poured out onto the field and were swept through gates in left field. The grandstand crowd passed through exits opening on both Doughty Avenue and 157th Street, which lies along the south side of the stadium.

Throng Handled Without Confusion.

The record-breaking throng was handled with almost no confusion at all. Transportation facilities were strained before the game because of the big flow of people from downtown points, but the subway, elevated and surface lines handled the heavy traffic without a break after the game. There was little congestion in the 161st Street station of the Lexington Avenue subway, much of the crowd walking to nearby elevated and surface lines.

The fans were slow in coming to the stadium. When the gates were thrown open at noon only about 500 persons were in line before the ticket windows. But by 1 o'clock the guardians of law and order in front of the main entrance began finding their hands full. The supply of 50,000 unreserved grand stand and bleacher seats began dwindling rapidly, and by 2 o'clock the huge grand stand was beginning to bulge at the sides. Ten minutes later the gates to the main stand were ordered closed, and patrons who arrived more than an hour before game time were greeted with the "Standing Room Only" sign and the gentle announcement that bleacher seats only were available. When 3 o'clock came around even the bleachers were packed solidly with humanity, and after that there was nothing to do but close the gates and padlock them.

Inspector Thomas Riley, in charge of police arrangements outside the grounds, estimated that 25,000 fans were turned away, and officials of the club agreed with this estimate.

Kenesaw M. Landis, High Commissioner of Baseball, travelled to the scene in democratic style. He disembarked from an Interborough train shortly before 2 and was caught up in the swirl before the main entrance, being rescued finally by the police and escorted inside the stadium.

Preceding him by an hour was the Seventh Regiment Band, which arrived at 1 o'clock and immediately launched on a musical program. Just about the same time the Yankees and Red Sox deployed on the scene, the champions looking neat and natty in new home uniforms of white. The Bostonians were a symphony in red—red sweaters, red-peaked caps, red striped stockings. At their head was Frank Chance, Peerless Leader of the old-time Cubs, returned now to lead the Red Sox out of the baseball wilderness.

Governor Greeted Warmly.

Then at 3 o'clock the spotlight shifted from the players to the celebrities of opening day. Governor Smith moved down to his box, accompanied by Mrs. Smith, and got a rousing greeting. Judge Landis, in gray overcoat, doffing his wide brimmed hat in greeting, came on to the field and immediately strode out to centre field, where the American League flag was waiting. The Seventh Regiment Band assembled near the Yankee bench on the third base side, and John Philip Sousa, in bandmaster's uniform, took his baton in hand and moved to the head of the musicians. The two teams clustered into platoon formation and the parade began.

Once out at the flagpole, the old traditional ritual of opening day began. While the band played "The Star-Spangled Banner," the Stars and Stripes were pulled slowly to the peak of the flagpole. After it fluttered the red, white and blue American League pennant, and as the last note of the national anthem died away and the halyards were made fast, the big crowd let loose a roar that floated across the Harlem and far beyond.

That wasn't the end of it, by any means. Back to the home plate came the band and the players and the notables. In the front line of march were the Yankee Colonels, Ruppert and Huston, side by side and beaming broadly; Judge Landis, Mrs. Smith, the Governor and Harry Frazee, the Boston club owner. It was noticed for the first time that Mayor Hylan was absent, and club officials explained that the city's chief executive was unable to attend because of illness. Byron Bancroft Johnson, President of the American League, was also missing because of a sudden attack of influenza.

Major Gen. Robert Lee Bullard, commander of the Department of the East, and his staff took part in the exercises, and other prominent military men present were Major Gen. Frank T. Hines, Director of the Veterans' Bureau; Major Gen. F. W. Sladen, Superintendent of West Point; Major Gen. William Weigle of Governors Island and Major Charles D. Daley and Captain M. B. Ridgway of West Point. State Commander Callan represented the American Legion and Captain Robert Woodside the Veterans of Foreign Wars.

Governor Smith and Judge Landis were escorted to their boxes along the third base side, and the photographers then got in their deadly work. Mr. Smith was snapped throwing an imaginary first ball. Judge Landis had to take off his hat and have his white locks photographed. Somebody stepped up and presented a big floral horseshoe to the Yankee club, and Colonel Ruppert and Managers Huggins and Chance were lined up for a picture in front of this. Charles A. Stoneham, President of the Giants, was taken in friendly converse with the Yankee owners.

Babe Ruth Receives Gift.

Then the teams converged around the plate again, and Babe Ruth was presented with a case containing a big bat—a delicate hint to the slugger, possibly. After Babe had blushingly mumbled his thanks, Governor Smith stood up in his box, took a shiny white ball between thumb and first finger and threw it carefully at Wally Schang.

Now here was the first deviation from a decent and proper opening day program. Tradition demands that the thrower miss the objective by several feet. But the Governor, unwinding the official arm, hit Schang's glove as well as Bob Shawkey ever did. Old-time baseball men considered it a distinct social error.

After that there was nothing to do but to play the game. Frank Chance walked out on the coaching line. The Yankees scattered briskly to their positions, Everett Scott going to shortstop as a signal to the world that the record of 986 consecutive games would not be broken yet. Umpire Tommy Connolly, dean of the American League staff, who unexpectedly appeared to take charge of the game, mumbled something to the effect that the contest might begin, and Shawkey, twirling his red sleeved arms, pitched "Ball One" to the first batter, Chick Fewster, who used to play with the Yankees. The season was started.

As events turned out, the game was an easy one for the Yankees. After the third inning they were never seriously extended, that one concentrated burst of gunfire being the undoing of the long and lanky Ehmke, who was pitching the game for Frank Chance. In all his career Shawkey never pitched a finer game. Although slightly shy on control, the sailor worked carefully and shrewdly, and kept the three Boston hits sparsely scattered throughout the nine innings.

Burns Gets First Hit.

The first hit off him—in fact, the first hit in the new stadium—came from the bat of first baseman George Burns in the second inning, but Burns was cut down trying to steal and the rally died down. In the sixth Emhke singled to centre with none out, and that was the second hit. In the seventh, after Burns walked, Norman McMillan, traded by the Yanks last Winter, prodded a triple to right centre, and that was the third hit. It was the only one which did any damage, for Burns scampered home from first with the sole Boston run of the game.

The Yanks' big third inning started with Ward's single to left, the first Yankee hit. Scott bunted him to second, but Ward was nipped at third on Shawkey's grounder straight at Ehmke. Shawkey moved up to second while Ward was being run down. Witt coaxed a pass out of Ehmke, and Shawkey came in from second when Dugan dropped a single in short centre. Witt trotted to third, and the stage was set for Ruth's blast into the right-field bleachers.

In the fourth the Yanks got after Ehmke again, but lost a run because of bad work on the bases. To start the inning Bob Meusel got a two-bagger out of a Texas League fly to short left, Fewster barely getting his glove under the ball. But Schang bunted to Ehmke and Meusel was nailed by a shade at third base. Ward then fanned, but Scott rammed a hard hit double between Collins and Skinner. Schang tried to come all the way from first on the drive and was out for his pains, a fast relay from Collins to Burns to Devormer slaying the catcher at the plate.

Ruth got his first walk in the fifth, and the crowd joined in a chorus of boos and jeers that smacked of the good old days of 1921. The Yanks went out in order in the sixth, and Shawkey's single was the only incident in the seventh, which was Ehmke's last inning. Menosky batted for him, and Fullerton finished up for Chance's team. He walked Ruth again in the eighth and was heartily hooted by the assembled citizenry.

Shawkey's only sign of weakening came in the seventh, when he passed Burns and McMillan tripled. There was still only one out, but Sailor Bob fanned the veteran Shanks and Dugan made a clever play on DeVormer's hard grounder for the third out. Fine support helped Shawkey again in the eighth. Fewster was hit with none out, but Scott got in front of Collins's ground ball and started a fast double play through Ward and Pipp. This was the last time the Red Sox showed signs of life.

Ruth Makes Error.

Everything wasn't milk and honey for Ruth. To start the fifth he muffed Harris's high fly to short right, juggling the ball twice and then letting it hit the turf. This faux pas placed Harris on second, and Shawkey passed McMillan after fanning Burns. With runners on second and first and only one out the Yankee veteran settled down, outwitted Shanks on a third strike and made DeVormer roll gently to Pipp.

The Yanks looked like a new team on their own ball field. They hustled every minute, kept their heads up and slugged hard when the time came to strike. Aaron Ward played one of the best games of his life at second base, and his stop of Ehmke's fast grounder behind second in the third inning was by all odds the finest fielding play of the game.

Everett Scott, who sprained his ankle last week, was not the fastest athlete on the field, but he showed little effects from the injury. He handled five chances deftly at shortstop and wasted no time in getting around the bases when he doubled to right centre in the fourth. It was Scott's 987th consecutive game; only thirteen more and he will be up to the 1,000 mark.

The score:

NEW YORK (A.)	Ab	R	H	Po	A
Witt.cf	3	1	1	3	0
Dugan.3b	4	1	1	1	1
Ruth.rf	2	1	1	3	0
Pipp.1b	3	0	0	12	0
Meusel.lf	4	0	1	0	0
Schang.c	4	0	0	4	2
Ward.2b	3	0	1	3	3
Scott.ss	2	0	1	1	4
Shawkey.p	3	1	1	0	0
Total	29	4	7	27	12

BOSTON (A.)	Ab	R	H	Po	A
Fewster.ss	[illegible]				
Collins.rf	[illegible]				
Skinner.cf	[illegible]				
Harris.lf	[illegible]				
Burns.1b	[illegible]				
McMillan.2b	[illegible]				
Shanks.3b	[illegible]				
Devormer.c	[illegible]				
Ehmke.p	[illegible]				
aMenosky	[illegible]				
Fullerton.p	[illegible]				
Total	[illegible]				

aBatted for Ehmke in eighth.

New York ....0 0 4 0 0 0 0 0 [illegible]
Boston ....0 0 0 0 0 0 1 0 [illegible]

Two-base hits—Meusel, Scott. Three-base hit—McMillan. Home run—Ruth. [illegible] Scott. Double play—Scott, Ward and Pipp. Left on bases—New York [illegible], Boston [illegible]. Bases on balls—Off Shawkey [illegible] [illegible] ton 1. Struck out—By Shawkey [illegible] 4, Fullerton 1. Hits—Off Ehmke [illegible] innings, Fullerton none in 1. Hit by pitcher—By Shawkey (Fewster). Losing pitcher—Ehmke. Umpires—Connolly, [illegible] and Holmes. Time of game—[illegible].

"All the News That's Fit to Print."

The New York Times.

THE WEATHER
Fair and cool today; Sunday fair and warmer.
Temperature yesterday—Max., 65; min., 54.
For weather report see next to last page.

VOL. LXXII....No. 23,975. ••••• NEW YORK, SATURDAY, SEPTEMBER 15, 1923. TWO CENTS in Greater New York | THREE CENTS Within 200 Miles | FOUR CENTS Elsewhere

DEMPSEY WHIPS FIRPO IN SECOND ROUND OF FIERCEST OF HEAVYWEIGHT BATTLES; 90,000 IN POLO GROUNDS, 25,000 RIOT OUTSIDE

ARMY DIRECTORATE WINS FULL POWER IN SPANISH REVOLT

King Accepts Resignation of Cabinet and Invites Primo Rivera to Take Charge.

MARTIAL LAW PROCLAIMED

Country Everywhere Is Calm, With the Army Directing Work of Officials.

MIXED CABINET PLANNED

Army Men and Some Civilian Ministers Will Attempt to Carry Out Reform Program.

MADRID, Sept. 14 (Associated Press).—The revolt started by Captain General Primo Rivera at Barcelona and which spread with great rapidity through various sections of the country culminated today in the resignation of the Spanish Cabinet and the setting up of a military directorate.

King Alfonso, who returned to Madrid today, was besought by Premier Alhucemas to provide methods for the punishment of the revolting military men, but he declined to do so, and Alhucemas immediately handed in his own resignation and that of his Ministers.

Captain General Primo Rivera is on his way to Madrid, there to take charge, at least for the time being, of the directorate, which is now composed of Generals Cavalcanti, Saro, Daban, and Federico Berenguer, and presided over by General Munoz Cobo, Captain General of Madrid.

It is stated that General Primo Rivera tomorrow probably will substitute a mixed military and civil cabinet for the directorate and that he will designate the following as Ministers:

President of the Council of Ministers—MUNOZ COBO.
Foreign Minister—Marquis DE VILLA URRUTIA or Senor FEDERICO PINA.
Minister of Marine—Admiral CARRANZA.
Minister of War—General BERMUDEZ DE CASTRO.
Minister of Justice and Cults—Magistrate MENA or HITA.
Minister of Finance—General ALTOLAGUIRRE.
Minister of Interior—General MARTINEZ ANIDO.
Minister of Labor—General MARVA.
Minister of Commerce—Senor MONTERO.

General Primo Rivera before leaving Barcelona declared that it was not his intention to give up his post of Captain General of Catalonia.

Country Quiet Under Martial Law.

Although martial law has been proclaimed throughout the realm no disturbances have been reported from any place. The people everywhere are said to be carrying out their usual daily routing, and there is scarcely anywhere any indication that there has been a successful coup d'état in Spain.

Primo Rivera, has instructed the military judges to institute proceedings against Santiago Alba, former Foreign Minister, and has issued a proclamation inviting all Spaniards to declare themselves on the political morality of the former Minister. It is reported that Señor Alba is a refugee in Biarritz.

At a meeting of the Municipal Council today the Mayor forbade a Socialist interpellation regarding the military movement. One of the councilors in the name of his party approved of the militarist coup, and the session had to be suspenced to prevent disorders.

The Socialist Party repudiates a manifesto issued by the Communists and anarchists in which they claim to be heading the workers.

The military authorities have ordered all Government officials and functionaries to carry on their duties under the direction of the military. All justices and magistrates were notified that they were subject to military orders.

General Francisco de Aguilera, former Minister of War, arrived in Madrid today and announced himself as conforming with the military movement.

Admiral Juan Bautista Aznar, Minister of Marine in the Alhucemas Cabinet, has placed himself at the disposal of the new government of General Primo Rivera.

Captain General Munoz Cobo of Madrid, has appointed Millan de Priego, Director General of Public Safety, as Minister of the Interior ad interim.

King Returns to the Capital.

The King reached the city at 9:15 A. M. He was greeted at the railway station by the Captain General of Madrid, the members of the Cabinet, prominent members of the military establishment and other notables.

On leaving the station the King proceeded direct to the palace, where he had a conference with Premier Alhucemas.

It is understood that the Premier requested his Majesty to grant the Government facilities for punishment of the military revolters in Barcelona and elsewhere. The King refused and the Premier there upon submitted the resignation of the entire Cabinet.

At the conclusion of his conversation with King Alfonso, Premier Alhucemas announced he had proposed to the King the immediate dismissal of the Captains General of Barcelona, Saragossa and all the other military officers associated with the present movement. He also recommended the immediate summoning of Parliament to discuss the situation and establish the responsibility not only of the members of the Government, but also of those who had prevented the Cabinet from governing.

King Alfonso replied it was indispensable that he have time to consider the situation. Thereupon the Premier handed his Majesty the resignation of the entire Cabinet.

A semi-official statement says:

"In view of the fact that the words

Continued on Page Four.

Spanking Machine Proposed For First Offenders in Canada

WINNIPEG, Sept. 14.—A spanking machine, which would have instruments varying from a broad paddle to a cat-of-nine tails and so geared as to be administered with different degrees of severity, was advocated to take the place of jail sentences for first offenders under the Criminal Code by Crown Prosecutor R. B. Graham today.

Mr. Graham strongly advocated the use of some sort of a machine to take the place of corporal punishment by the human hand and said he believed such an innovation would materially reduce the crime record.

2 MORE DESTROYERS WENT ON THE ROCKS

Belated Report of Additional Disasters Rouses Denby, Who Orders Full Inquiry.

PROCEEDINGS TO BE PUBLIC

San Diego Dispatch Says the Marcus, Besides the Farragut and Somers, Was Damaged.

Special to The New York Times.

WASHINGTON, Sept. 14.—Two other destroyers—the Farragut and Somers—of the squadron wrecked off the coast of Santa Barbara Saturday also ran on the rocks and were slightly damaged, according to a belated message received by the Navy Department today.

This makes nine destroyers damaged, seven of them almost complete wrecks, in the still unexplained accident, details of which are lacking at the Navy Department, to the annoyance of Secretary Denby.

In direct disobedience of the regulations, the report of the injury to the Farragut and Somers was delayed an unreasonable time, and this and the failure of the officials on the scene to furnish the Navy Department with full information have caused the accident to be shrouded in mystery and brought the navy under public criticism.

Navy officials were without any explanation at all for the belated message coming today.

Secretary Denby had maintained a very calm, judicial temperament up until this very latest development. While the inadequate information convinced navy officers that either an abnormal natural phenomenon caused the accident or gross inefficiency and lack of caution were responsible, Secretary Denby quietly announced that he would suspend judgment until the Board of Inquiry had made its report.

Officers to Be Exposed.

He waited two days for fuller details and then sent a brusque message for them. They came yesterday. But today, when this belated message added to the mystery, he immediately ordered that the board of inquiry at San Diego should conduct its inquiry into the disaster in the open. This was done so that those responsible for the disaster should be fully exposed in the public press, an unusual procedure.

In addition to the Farragut and Somers being injured in the Saturday night wreck, another destroyer, the J. F. Burns, had an accident on the Pacific Coast about the same time, according to the message received today by the Board of Inspection and Survey, from the San Diego Naval District.

The regulations require that all accidents be reported immediately. The first report, that of the wreckage of the seven vessels of the squadron, was received by the Communications Division Saturday. This belated message today should also have gone to that division, but instead was sent to the Board of Inspection and Survey, which sent it at once to the Secretary.

The inquiry now in progress at San Diego, it was announced, will not only establish the cause of the accident, but will determine why the officers in charge violated the regulations by withholding information six days and then sending it to the wrong bureau in the Navy Department.

Text of Belated Report.

The mysterious, belated message telling of the injury to two other members of the destroyer squadron follows:

"To Board of Inspection and Survey:

"Completed inspection of J. F. Burns

Continued on Page Three.

ENRIGHT NOW ACTS ON GRAFT CHARGES AFTER LONG SILENCE

Orders Trial of 2 Detectives Accused of Taking Bribe in Liquor Seizure.

JUSTIFIES ACTS TO HYLAN

'Score of Newspaper Buzzards' Acted as Jury at Inquiry, He Says in Letter.

5 PROMOTIONS UNDER FIRE

Taxpayers' Suits Expected as Result of Civil Service Reform Investigation.

Official cognizance of the cumulative evidence of graft by policemen in liquor cases, brought out during the inquiry before Judge Crain, was taken by Police Commissioner Richard E. Enright yesterday, when departmental charges were filed against Detective Sergeants William Morrison and David Lambert, accusing them of failing to prevent the transportation of liquor and demanding and receiving a $2,500 bribe.

The accusations against the two detectives were the same as were made two years ago and which were the occasion for two departmental investigations, both of which came to naught. Magistrate Corrigan, in his defense of the criminal libel action brought by Commissioner Enright, produced evidence to show that the Commissioner was kept informed of the progress of these previous inquiries.

Commissioner Enright, following the announcement of the action against the two detectives, broke his long silence with regard to developments in the Crain inquiry, and for the first time since the inquiry was resumed last month issued a statement in justification of his course in the form of a letter to Mayor Hylan. The Commissioner at the beginning of the letter launched abruptly into an attack on the newspapers, referring to the "score of newspaper buzzards occupying the jury box as a jury" in the Crain inquiry. The rest of the letter is devoted to the Commissioner's version of the retirement of Captain Patrick J. Randles and Lieutenant Moriarty and his course in the Petrucci investigations.

Detectives Face New Charges.

Lambert and Morrison, already under suspension as a result of their admission that they testified falsely before Judge Crain, were summoned to headquarters yestrday. They were taken to the office of Chief Inspector Lahey and reinstated so that the additional charge could be preferred against them.

The new charge is neglect of duty "in that they stopped an automobile containing alleged liquor on West Thirty-seventh Street and failed to bring to the station and put under arrest the person or persons transporting the alleged liquor, and demanded and received $2,500 for failing to put said perron or persons under arrest."

Lambert, before his suspension, was attached to the East Twenty-second Street Station, and Morrison to the West 100th Street Station. After the filing of the new charge they were suspended again. When their cases will be called for trial at Police Headquarters has not yet been decided.

The charges against the two detectives related to the now famous Petrucci liquor seizure on May 28, 1921. Evidence introduced by John D. Lindsay, counsel for Magistrate Corrigan, disclosed that two departmental inquiries into the case had been conducted, one by Sergeant Frederick C. Kruse, confidential investigator for Commissioner Enright, and the other by Chief Inspector William J. Lahey. Both said that they kept the Commissioner informed of developments.

Both Detectives Confer.

The witnesses called before Inspector Lahey, with one important exception, were the same as those Mr. Lindsay produced. One after another denied making certain statements before Inspector Lahey, until Mr. Lindsay put in evidence a record of the Lahey hearing obtained by chance from a source outside of the Police Department. Lam-

Continued on Page Five.

Illinois Labor Repudiates Foster in Pleas For Soviet Russia and One Big Union

DECATUR, Ill., Sept. 14 (Associated Press).—Recognition of Soviet Russia, the subject of a third proposal supported by William Z. Foster, followed the "labor party" and "amalgamation" issues into the discard late today at the convention of the Illinois Federation of Labor. The eighty delegates who voted with Foster for "amalgamation" in the morning stayed with him throughout. The vote against the proposal was 350.

Amid cries of "steam roller" and threats of a break the resolution for "amalgamation" was defeated by a vote of 313 to 30.

William Z. Foster, against whom the administration fight had been directed rather than against "amalgamation" itself, was on his feet as the vote was put, demanding a hearing. President Lynal of the Peoria Trades and Labor Council yelled, "You will either play fair or we will do something else."

Victor Olander, Secretary-Treasurer of the federation, spoke for nearly two hours this morning, "laying bare" what he declared "the true record of William Z. Foster." He made his chief argument against the miners' delegates who compose the majority of Foster's following, waving in his hand the reports issued this week by the United Mine Workers of America, identifying Foster as the leader of the movement which would disrupt their union.

"If you have any doubt what is in these reports," he shouted, "come up and look at them. Come up and get them, Foster."

Before the Secretary-Treasurer spoke, Foster defended himself against what he said was "every foul accusation save wife-beating."

Matthew Woll, Vice President of the American Federation of Labor, yesterday challenged Foster to tell where he obtained the money with which he carried on the Trade Union Educational League. He accused Foster of stealing the name of the Farmer-Labor Party and asserted that the amalgamation movement advocated by Foster was an attempt to take control of the political power of the State and represented an effort to destroy the leadership of the American Federation of Labor.

"You heard," Foster said, "Mr. Woll's speech yesterday. The books of the Trade Educational League are open for inspection. I challenge them to examine them. Only one charge touched me, that I am bent on breaking up the labor movement. I risked my life in the steel strike and spent time in nearly every jail in the Pittsburgh district. I appeal to your intelligence. Don't fall for Woll's contemptible ruse. If you believe in amalgamation, be a man and vote for it."

Olander in reply called Foster a Communist and a member of the I. W. W. and maintained the "amalgamation" plan was in reality the "one big union" idea. He said that the Communists were behind Foster and that his challenge to open his books was empty, as the books of the Communists were the books that would show his support.

Harding Executor Named, With Bond at $750,000

Special to The New York Times.

MARION, Ohio, Sept. 14.—Charles D. Schaffner of this city was appointed executor of the estate of President Harding by the Probate Court this morning and his bond was fixed at $750,000.

This is probably the largest bond ever required in any estate settled in the Marion County Probate Court. No exact estimate of the estate has been made, but court attachés say the amount of the bond indicates that it will exceed $500,000.

CALL WARD'S WIFE AS STATE WITNESS

Subpoena Is Served at Murder Trial, and Sheriff Seeks Father of Accused.

TEN ACCEPTED FOR JURY

Defense Springs Surprise, but State Challenges Man Who Believes in Death Sentence.

The process of finding a jury to try Walter S. Ward for the murder of Clarence M. Peters dragged along slowly yesterday, and when court adjourned until Monday ten jurors were in the box. At one point Ward offered to accept a juror who admitted that he believed in the death sentence but had scruples about voting it. Mrs. Beryl Curtiss Ward, again at her husband's side, wept when the defense counsel announced Ward's waiver, but brightened when the talesman was excused.

Forty-eight veniremen were tested for jury service during the day, and when the session ended the first panel of 121 talesmen had been exhausted. Supreme Court Justice Wagner ordered a new panel of seventy-five prospective jurors to report on Monday. Juror No. 4, Michael Doherty, selected on Wednesday, was excused when the State informed Justice Wagner that Deputy Attorney General Dwyer was a personal friend of Doherty. In his place Napoleon Major, Tarrytown haberdasher, was accepted.

The three additional jurors accepted yesterday were Ivan P. Flood of White Plains, Secretary of the Westchester Chamber of Commerce; David Horton of Hawthorne, tool manufacturer, and Stephen W. Batcheler, a Peekskill grocer. George Kibbe Turner, short story writer, qualified as a juror, but was excused by the Court when he pleaded that he was under contract to supply fiction within a specified time.

State to Call Mrs. Ward.

It developed during the day that Attorney General Carl Sherman had subpoened Mrs. Ward as a witness and did not intend to have her appear before the Extraordinary Grand Jury when that body resumes its investigations into conspiracy allegations on Tuesday. It was predicted that any effort to force Mrs. Ward to testify against her husband, even to facts not covered by the prohibition against a wife's evidence, would precipitate a sharp legal battle.

A second step against Ward's family was the delivery of a subpoena to Sheriff George J. Werner for George S. Ward, father of the defendant. This will be served if the elder Ward ventures within the State. Mr. Sherman admitted that he knew where George Ward is, but refused to tell. The father of the accused has been absent from the State for several months.

The first talesman examined by Mr. Sherman was Thomas J. Sherwood, a carpenter of Ossining. He was excused. Two talesmen were then challenged by the prosecution because they opposed the death penalty, and William Brundage, a farmer, was barred in a peremptory challenge by Mr. Mills. During the day the State ran its total of such challenges up to twenty-four and the defense fifteen. Each is allowed thirty peremptory challenges. Mr. Flood, chosen as Juror No. 8, was acceptable to the State although he announced a personal prejudice against the imposition of the death setence.

Farmer Is Rejected.

During the questioning of James B. Parry, a Yorktown farmer, Mr. Sherman asked if the man had been talking to Edward Matthews, one of the confidential investigators employed by the Ward attorneys. Mr. Sherman asked if Matthews had not spoken to Parry on the Court House steps. The farmer denied this and reiterated his denial after the prosecutor had singled Matthews out of the spectators and had Parry look at him. Mr. Campbell protested against what he called "a play" by the State, and then issued a peremptory challenge against Parry.

Mr. Horton was chosen quickly, and after the next two talesmen had been rejected by Mr. Sherman in peremptory challenges, Mr. Batcheler was accepted. When he was asked if he knew the Wards, he said that he knew the man who delivered bread to his store, but not his name. Walter Ward smiled broadly at this.

Frank Brannigan, a hotel man of Mamaroneck, aroused the ire of the defense counsel by some of his replies, and Mr. Mills banned him because he seemed to have made up his mind about the case.

Ward's offer to accept a juror who frankly said he would, if pressed, vote for the electric chair penalty, came during the testing of the next talesman. He was Marcellus B. Parsons, a paper exporter, living in Rye. Mr. Parsons said that he would "not be a party to finding a man guilty of murder," but would perform his duty as a citizen if the evidence indicated no other way out. Counsel for the defense went into conference, joined by Ward and his wife.

"Mr. Parsons," said Mr. Campbell, finally, "if the defendant says to you that he is willing to waive his misgivings, will you put aside your feelings and act as a juror?"

Mr. O'Neill at once interposed an objection. Ward and his wife leaned forward to catch the talesman's reply, but before it came Justice Wagner sustained the State's protest. Mr. O'Neill then challenged the venireman for cause.

MAYOR'S DOCTORS ADMIT CONDITION IS NOW CRITICAL

Infection in Left Lung Rises, Threatening Spread of Pleurisy to That Region.

TWO NURSES AT BEDSIDE

Dr. Monaghan Says the Heart Is Strong Despite the Strain of Hard Breathing.

PATIENT IN INTENSE PAIN

Bears Up Without Opiates, However, When Told They Are Bad for Him.

Mayor Safely Through Night.

Special to The New York Times.

SARATOGA SPRINGS, N. Y., Saturday, Sept. 15.—Mayor Hylan's condition was unchanged at 5 o'clock this morning. He was sleeping at that hour and seemed to have passed safely through the night.

Special to The New York Times.

SARATOGA SPRINGS, N. Y., Sept. 14.—Mayor John F. Hylan of New York City, who has been ill here for three weeks, reached a probable crisis today. For the first time the attending physicians admitted in an official bulletin that the Mayor's condition was critical.

The area of pneumonia infection in the left lung did not "spread," according to the physicians, but was "rising" from the original point of infection in the inner cells to the surface of that lung, threatening to cause a pleurisy similar to that on the right side.

Mayor Hylan's condition as described in the late afternoon bulletin, which admitted that his state was critical, had become no worse when the physicians completed their examination of the patient at 9 o'clock tonight. The bulletin issued after that examination read:

"Mayor Hylan is holding his own since the last bulletin. Although his temperature has risen, this is not, in the opinion of his attending physicians, a grave sign because temperature in pneumonia is a measure of the patient's resistance, and is, in its essentials, a protective reaction. The pneumonic processes have not extended. Temperature, 103; pulse, 108; respiration, 30.

"CHARLES E. NAMMACK, M. D.,
"GEORGE F. COMSTOCK, M. D.,
"FRANK J. MONAGHAN, M. D."

Afternoon Bulletin Gloomy.

The bulletin issued in the late afternoon was the least encouraging of any put out by the physicians. Mayor Hylan has been suffering intense pain from the new infection of the pleura surrounding the left lung. He was informed that it would aid his recovery if he could endure the pain without the administration of opiates, which have a tendency to retard the absorption of the pneumonic infection, and he courageously declared that he would make the fight without opiates. Reports from the Mayor's bedside were that he was making a brave fight for life, and had borne the pain without flinching but at the cost of considerable strain.

The sharp increase in pulse and respiration between the morning and afternoon examinations indicated that he was having trouble in breathing because of the decrease in his effective lung capacity and that an increasing strain was being placed on his heart.

Dr. Monaghan said that the Mayor's heart was strong and steady and that the heart apparently was standing the strain without sign of weakening. The quality of Mayor Hylan's pulse was reported to be very satisfactory. His stomach, kidneys and intestines were also reported to be functioning properly.

There is no disposition tonight to disguise the fact that the Mayor is in a very critical condition. An indication of this was the engagement of another nurse from the Saratoga Hospital, to have two nurses on duty at night. Mrs. Elsie Thompson, considered one of the best nurses in the New York City Health Department, sleeps in the cottage which Mayor and Mrs. Hylan occupy with their son-in-law and daughter, Mr. and Mrs. John F. Sinnott, so that there will be three nurses on duty or on immediate call.

Doctors Within Easy Call.

Dr. Nammack, who is in charge of the case with Dr. George F. Comstock, is staying at the Schuyler Inn, a short distance from the Hylan home, with Grover A. Whalen, Commissioner of Plant and Structures, the Mayor's most intimate friend among the New York City Commissioners. Arrangements have been made to get Dr. Nammack, Dr. Comstock and Dr. Monaghan within a few minutes' time.

Although the evening bulletin stated that Mayor Hylan was "holding his own" since the last preceding bulletin, this was not taken to mean that the

Continued on Page Four.

West Speeds Harvest as Frost Nips Crops; Wisconsin Loses $300,000 on Tobacco Alone

CHICAGO, Sept. 14.—Farmers of the Central West urged on by the heavy frosts and, in some sections, snow and ice of the last few days, are beginning to house all crops still standing in the fields that might be injured by early Winter weather.

Tobacco growers of Wisconsin have suffered a loss in one county alone of $300,000, it was estimated. Hampered by a shortage of labor many are encountering difficulty in getting the cut plants under cover and repetition of the heavy frosts tonight is expected to raise this total damage.

Weather forecasts by Henry Cox, in charge of the Government Bureau here, were for more frosts tonight over the greater portion of the Northern Plains States with warmer weather in prospect for tomorrow and the week-end.

He predicted temperatures up to 80 degrees were probable within a few days and declared confidently that Indian Summer will hold its usual session before real Winter sets in.

WASHINGTON, Sept. 14.—The present cold wave is classified by the Government Weather experts as definitely a part of the new Winter.

The Summer sluggishness of air pressure movements, the Weather Bureau announced today, has passed, and the quicker succession of areas of high and low bringing more marked and rapid changes in temperatures, has begun.

The eastward movement from North Dakota last night of a centre of high pressure brought record low temperatures for this time of the year at Lacross, where the thermometer registered 30 degrees; at Milwaukee, where it was 38 and at Cincinnati with 40. Lower temperatures are expected tonight in the Atlantic States and there will be frost in the Ohio valley, lower lake region, North Atlantic States and the mountain districts of the Middle Atlantic section. Rising temperatures are forecast for the Ohio valley and the lower lake region tomorrow, but the cold weather is expected to continue to the eastward over Sunday.

MOB FIGHTS FOR TICKETS

Crowd Seeking $3.30 Admissions Sweep Police Aside in Rush

WOMEN HURT IN CRUSH

Many Injuries Reported in Effort to Restore Order Outside the Polo Grounds.

FANS BAIT SPECULATORS

Police Arrest Twelve Men Charged With Profiteering in Tickets.

Never has such a crowd gathered at an arena for the purpose of either witnessing the fight inside or waiting outside for bits of information of the progress of the battle as that which stormed the Polo Grounds last night.

Just before Dempsey and Firpo entered the ring, the police estimated that there were as many milling about the entrances and extending in mass formation in all directions for a distance of a quarter of a mile as there were inside the ball grounds. Police officials agreed that 150,000 persons would be a conservative estimate of fight fans whose mecca was the Polo Grounds.

From 4 o'clock on, when some 25,000 fans broke into a riot as the few remaining $3.30 seats were put on sale until shortly after the main bout went on, the 485 patrolmen and twenty-five mounted police under Inspector Thomas McDonald and Captain Edward P. Mulroney had their hands full in bringing about a semblance of order before the entrances. The crowd was divided into three groups—those who had tickets, those who wanted to buy tickets and those who were there to see what was going on. Each group collided with the other with a resultant chaos which tested the wits of patrolmen experienced in traffic control. Added to their troubles in handling the pedestrians, nightfall brought more trouble in the form of several thousand motor cars and sightseeing buses.

Ticket Van Appears.

Only prompt action on the part of the police prevented serious consequences which followed the appearance of the ticket van containing 3,500 of the lower priced $3.30 seats. Extending east on 155th Street, under the viaduct, as far as the Harlem River, was a long line of humanity, sidewalk deep. This line formed the night before, had grown in proportions from 4,000 at 10 o'clock yesterday morning to an estimated number of 20,000 at 4:30 in the afternoon. At the head of this line was Mrs. R. B. Zinser of 63 East 183d Street, who had taken her place at 8:30 yesterday morning to buy a ticket. She was flanked by Charles O'Brien, a Boston laborer, and John Farman, an oil driller of Port Arthur, Texas, both of whom had arrived for the long wait Thursday night supplied with food and soap boxes.

At 4:30 an auto ticket van moved in from Eighth Avenue and stopped in front of the Manhattan Casino just inside 155th Street. The sight of the wagon was the signal for about 5,000 late comers who had gathered in Eighth Avenue. They made a dash for the wagon, sweeping patrolmen off their feet and overturning a Ford car which was parked close by. The thousands of fight fans, who had waited long hours, angered by the turn of affairs, swarmed forward to mob the intruders. Hats and clothes were torn, women in the crowd were crushed and hand to hand encounters followed. Mounted police, augmented by scores of patrolmen, rushed to the spot and battled with the frenzied men.

Police Forced to Use Nightsticks.

When some semblance of order had been restored, only through the frequent use of nightsticks on recalcitrants, the ticket sellers tried to serve the fans. The crowd surged about the van in waves, so close were the men to each

Continued on Page Two.

85,800 Pay to See Big Fight; Receipts Put at $1,250,000

A crowd of 85,800 persons paid $1,250,000 to see the bout at the Polo Grounds last night, according to the official figures announced by Promoter Tex Rickard. It is estimated that approximately 5,000 more were inside the park, this number including policemen, firemen, ushers, pop vendors and other employes.

The fighters divided 50 per cent. of the total receipts, and Dempsey's share, 37½ per cent. of the $1,250,000 amounts to $468,750. Firpo, whose share was 12½ per cent., will draw down about $156,250.

FIRPO HAD THE TITLE WITHIN HIS GRASP

Slow Thinking Cost Him Crown in First Round, When Champion Was in Distress.

DEMPSEY'S HEADWORK WON

Dazed and Injured, He Evaded the Argentine's Punches Until He Recovered.

The latest battle for the world's heavyweight title proved one thing above everything else — that brute strength alone will not avail in a clash between a pair of two-fisted fighting men. If Luis Angel Firpo had the brain power in proportion to his tremendous strength, there is no denying that he and not Jack Dempsey would be world's heavyweight champion this morning.

Endowed with the mentality which would enable him to think and think quickly in emergencies, Firpo could afford to be slow moving and cumbersome. But Firpo with all his great strength to give and take punishment, lacked that one essential—a fighting brain. He had Dempsey on the verge of pugilistic oblivion. He had the world's heavyweight title, the ring's richest honor, within his grasp. Twice he floored Dempsey in that tense, pulse-quickening first round and on one of the knockdowns Firpo had the champion knocked completely out of the ring. When Dempsey was assisted back by writers in the first row of ringside seats, he was in a sad plight.

As a cold matter of fact he was a beaten man, had it been a man with a fighting brain he was facing—a man who could hold his head and meet the situation coolly. But there was nothing cool about the infuriated, wild-eyed giant who saw Dempsey assisted back into the ring and saw Dempsey stand there swaying groggily, his back to the ropes, his jaw an open target. Dempsey did not have sense enough to cover his chin. His brain was dulled for the moment under the pile-driving power of Firpo's terrific rights to the head and jaw.

But Firpo was not quick enough to realize the golden opportunity there before him in the canvas-covered ring, nor was he quick enough to act, once his lethargic brain brought to him a full realization of the chance that awaited him. One more mighty swing of his crushing right, a carefully delivered blow, accurately landed to that unprotected jaw of Dempsey, would have witnessed the crowning of a new champion.

But Firpo did not send over the blow and right there Firpo lost his only chance.

Dempsey Recovers Quickly.

This emergency over, the danger for him past because of his rival's lack of a fighting head, Dempsey quickly recovered. His faculties soon were restored and he once more was the fearless fighting man, the man with a fighting heart, a fighting head and undying courage. Dempsey once again was the easy-moving, lightning-fast, crushing hitter of old. He was, in a word, Dempsey, the man-killer, and he killed with the destructive fury that only those who have felt the full force of his blows can tell.

Dempsey's speed, agility, rapid and accurate hitting, his shifty, weaving, swaying method of advancing upon an opponent, and the dynamic force back of his blows were the combinations which brought victory to the champion at a time when the title was dangling from his brow by a slim thread.

Dempsey needed all of his faculties to win. He showed that he possessed them, and, what is more, he knew exactly how to employ all his fighting resources when the necessity arose. He battered Firpo to the floor of the ring seven times in that first round. Five of these knock-downs were clean-cut crashes to the floor and Firpo was forced to take the benefit of the count each time before arising. Twice, too, Dempsey drove his rival to his knees, but Firpo got up in these two instances without taking a count.

In that second round Dempsey twice drove his rival to the floor before putting him down for the final count. The first time Firpo got up at a count of two. The second time the giant Argentine boxer regained his feet after a count of five had been tolled over him. By that time his resistance was reduced to an extent where one finishing punch would end the bout.

Dempsey Lands Finishing Punch.

His spirit was strong but the flesh was weak. He came rumbling in at Dempsey and the champion hooked over

Continued on Page Two.

FIRPO FELLED TEN TIMES

Champion Downed Twice and Punched Through Ropes at Outset.

CROWD IS SPORTSMANLIKE

Argentine Receives Striking Tribute of Cheers and Prolonged Handclapping.

RECEIPTS ARE $1,250,000

Dempsey's Share Is $468,750, and About $156,250 Will Go to the Challenger.

In the shortest and fiercest battle ever fought between heavyweights, Jack Dempsey last night knocked out Luis Angel Firpo before a crowd of 90,000 people at the Polo Grounds 57 seconds after the second round began.

But no champion ever had a closer call. In the first round, after Firpo had gone down seven times, one of his long, smashing rights caught Dempsey fairly and knocked him clear through the ropes. The champion's head disappeared over the edge of the ring, his white-clad legs shot up in the air, and it seemed that a new world's champion was about to enter into his glory.

On the count of nine Dempsey managed to stagger back into the ring, but the end of the round found him obviously badly shaken, and staggering as he had never staggered before.

To the spectators at the ringside it looked as if Dempsey was all gone, but his heart and his head were still there, and enough punching power to carry him through to victory in the second round. Firpo's right was too slow to reach the champion, who was striking in with all his power. He caught Firpo with a right and put him down. Two seconds later the challenger was up but a moment more and Dempsey had him down again for the count of five.

Dempsey Instantly Upon Him.

Once more the "Wild Bull of of the Pampas" staggered to his feet, but Dempsey was on him instantly, caught him with a left to the jaw and then toppled him with a right as he sank. Bleeding slightly at the mouth, the huge brown man from the Argentine turned slowly over, striving vainly to rise as the referee's pumping arm marked the counts of eight and nine, and stiffened helplessly as the tenth count ended his championship hopes for the time.

In less than four minutes of fighting the champion had been knocked down twice and the challenger ten times. From the first instant the fight had been a fight, a fierce exchange of wallops unbroken by any strategic manoeuvres. Dempsey won because he could hit faster and oftener, but above all because he could keep going and cash in on his advantages when he had them.

As for Firpo, he is not champion this morning by the slimmest of margins, but those who saw him fight last night were not inclined to predict that he never will be champion. He put up a terrific fight and at the end of the first round had ninety thousand more or less patriotic fans practically resigned to the loss of the championship. After the fight Firpo complained that he hadn't got an even break from Referee Jimmy Gallagher.

Firpo asserted that Gallahgher had warned the fighters before the bout began that after a knockdown the man on his feet must move away to a neutral corner. Dempsey, he protested, stood over him and was on him instantly when he got off the canvas.

Dempsey Fought With His Head.

Whatever the justice in this complaint, there is no doubt that Dempsey won because he fought with his head as well as with hands, and Firpo had nothing but his hands and his courage. The question as to whether the Argentine fighter can "take it" is answered. He took a worse hammering even than Jess Willard took at Toledo, and if his brain had been as quick as his arm was powerful he would have survived it to win. He can also "give it."

But Dempsey outweighed by twenty-four pounds, shorter and with less reach, won because he had a super-fighting brain and a coolness which enabled him to hang on when everything seemed lost and to use all his powers in the desperate and successful effort to hold his time.

Firpo has at least a certain consolation in his 12½ per cent. of the gate receipts. Promoter Tex Rickard, who always puts on a good show and always brings out the customers, reported that the ticket sale amounted to $1,250,000. Of this Dempsey got $468,750, and the challenger's share will come to about $156,250, not to mention the incidental profits of moving pictures.

85,800 Paid Admissions.

There were 85,800 paid admissions, and police, firemen, ushers, newspaper men, telegraph operators, refreshment vendors and so on will probably raise the total to 90,000, a figure surpassed only by the Willard-Firpo fight in the history of prize fighting. The receipts fell short of the $1,600,000 brought in by the Dempsey-Carpentier fight only because of the limit imposed in this State on the price of the ringside seats.

What might have happened had Dempsey utilized his superior boxing ability to stand off and take few chances until he had felt out Firpo no one can say. But he didn't do that. Realizing that most of his followers expected him to get in and fight, he rushed in furiously at the sound of the bell, and partly slipping, partly caught by one of Firpo's smashes, he dropped to one knee before the round was five seconds old. Yet he still stuck to his aggressive tactics and thereby showed the crowd that both he and Firpo were better men than anybody knew. It is a rare fight which enables both victor and vanquished to feel that they have surpassed themselves, all in the space of three minutes and fifty-seven seconds.

Good Sportsmanship Shown.

In one other respect the fight offered a pleasant surprise. The display of bad sportsmanship which had been feared, in view of the way a Polo Grounds crowd hissed Eugene Criqui, and the obvious hostility to Firpo displayed by the crowds which came to see him train at Atlantic City, was not in evidence. There were a few, a very few, boos and groans when announcer Joe Humphreys told the crowd that Firpo weighed 216½ pounds, 24 pounds more than Dempsey, but when Firpo came into the ring he was greeted with considerable applause, and when Humphreys introduced him he received the tribute of prolonged cheers and handclapping.

It was exactly the note that comes from a college crowd when it gets up to give the conventional rah-rah for the visiting football team before the game begins. It was, of course, far surpassed by the roar of applause for Dempsey a moment later. But, at least, it may and should have saved the North American reputation for sportsmanship, which had seemed in considerable danger of being visibly and disreputably lost. The crowd was for Dempsey, of course, except for a tiny minority of Latin Americans, and it was tremendously relieved and delighted when he won. How it would have received a victory by Firpo no one can say, but at least it lived up to its opportunities and behaved much better than some other crowds of recent memory.

Forty Thousand Watts of Light.

At half-past 7 the lights were turned on in the stands, and shortly afterward the great battery of thousand-watt lamps, thirty-six white and four blue, to give a scientifically blended synthetic daylight, flooded the ring and showed the long, unending lines of customers streaming into the tier of upper and lower stands. Ringside seat-holders were coming in by that time, and the lights showed the first scattering arrivals of women near the ring, good-looking women too, these early comers, as Meleager said of Sappho's poems, only a few but roses. They had to be good-looking to stand the harsh revealing glare of those ring lights.

Yet, though the unending lines of ticket-holders filed in at every entrance, the arena did not seem more than half full when the first preliminary fighters stepped into the ring at 8 o'clock. It was a relief to the veterans of the long wait when the bell-like voice of Joe Humphreys, world's champion announcer, rang out over the click of telegraph instruments and portable typewriters and the insistent shuffling murmur of arriving feet, and announced that 415 pounds of British Empire beef, almost equally divided between Joe Bright of England and Louis Brown of Australia, would mix it up for six rounds.

Inside of a minute, however, the mother country was vindicated when Joe Bright flattened the representative of the Dominions for the count and the bloodthirsty crowd roared with elation and the first casualty of the evening.

This entitled the spectators to an extra, and Frankie Koebele, who has been dodging Firpo's slow swings in his Atlantic City camp, came into the ring for a four-round struggle with Charlie Nashert. When Koebele went down half way through the first round it looked optimistic for those who expected an evening of one-round finishes, but he got up again and proceeded to demonstrate that being Mr. Firpo's sparring partner is not the best sort of boxing practice.

Mr. Koebele lost the decision, being saved twice by the gong; giving meanwhile an exhibition of club swinging that greatly amused the crowd. The ancient Greeks in their dramatic festivals liked a whole day of tragedy topped off by a swift knockabout farce. Spectators who come in time for the preliminaries of a big championship fight seem to prefer the comedy first, and they were much delighted with this bout. It probably was not so funny to Mr. Koebele.

Mike Burke from Greenwich Village stood up against Al Roberts of Staten Island in the next contest. This one really was a contest and the rapid thump-bump of gloves on bodies held the crowd's attention despite the distracting drumming of an airplane circling over the stadium, an electric sign on its groundward side advertising one of the big taxi companies. By this time the seats were nearly all occupied and 90,000 people shouted their approval of the vicarious bloodshed. Roberts, though cut to pieces, stayed to the end of the rounds and drew much applause from the sporting populace.

Then came the semi-final between Leo Gates, the Mohawk Indian strayed off the reservation and now resident in Harlem, and Bartley Madden of the west side. Each of them, in contrast to the preceding fighters, fulfilled the Poet Herrick's ideal of beauty in being white and hairless as an egg. But before the first round was over Gates, the noble red man, was getting pinked up about the eye. The Mohawks have gone back since the days of Joseph Brant, for Gates took a good deal of hammering

Wide World Photo.

THE KNOCKOUT IN THE SECOND ROUND.

in the twelve rounds. The populace paid little attention to the last round of the fight, for just as it began Luis Angel Firpo with an escort of policemen came down to the ringside and diverted everybody's attention. Half a minute later Dempsey entered, and after that nobody paid much attention to the end of the semi-final, or the expected decision in favor of Madden.

Crowd Waiting Two Hours.

Most of the crowd had been gathered in the Polo Grounds for nearly two hours, watching a series of preliminaries, when the fighters appeared during the last round of the semi-final, at 9:55. A cold wave, the first of Winter or the last of this wintry Summer as the case may be, had not chilled their anticipations, which had been whetted by some bloody fighting in one of the earlier preliminaries and then allowed to slump during the long-drawn-out and slowly fought semi-final. In the centre of the baseball diamond was the ring in which Bartley Madden was working through the last of twelve rounds to a decision over Leo Gates, a ring flooded with light from forty big lamps overhead, blended into something that is supposed to be as near like daylight as possible, though it was not much nearer than near-beer.

The flood of light from these lamps, swung from a network of wires sixteen feet above the floor of the ring, spread out in a slowly dimming circle over the rows of benches placed in the playing field, falling on masses of upturned faces, glinting back in a hundred double reflections from pairs of eyeglasses. Around the field on all sides rose a great elliptical mass, buried in darkness—the double grandstand of the Polo Grounds, packed with people, pitch black save for the feeble red lamps marking exits here and there and the firefly flashes of smokers' matches sparking out for an instant here and there all over the blank wall.

Firpo Appears With Escort.

Peering into the blackness, one could see here, too, the faint double flash of the ring lights reflected from eyeglasses, blinking this way and that as spectators tried to see into other portions of the crowd rather than watch the dull proceedings in the ring.

Suddenly, a rippling cheer began in one corner of the grandstand and slowly progressed down one of the diagonal aisles toward the ring side. A file of policemen was moving toward the ring, and a step behind the leader a towering figure, brown-faced, with matted hair, Luis Angel Firgo, coming up for the fight in which most of the experts, and even most unprofessional observers, among whom this writer to his shame must be included, thought he hadn't the ghost of a chance.

Firpo Fierce in Approach.

A few steps behind him came the porty bulk of Dan Washington, his negro rubber, and clustering in the rear his three seconds, Hughie Gartland, Guillermo Widmer and Horatio Lavalle, the [illegible] Argentine sportsman, who has [illegible] his right-hand man in preparation for the fight. The cheering grew as Firpo neared his corner, the southeastern one, and all over the stadium people stood up, despite the protesting cries of those behind them, to get a look at the man who had been called "the wild bull of the pampas," and who, according to the experts, had nothing to entitle him to the name but his looks.

He looked fierce and dangerous as he approached the ring. He always does. But he was frowning with a faraway, nervous, almost wistful look—the sort of look that comes over the face of even the least wistful of men as he prepares to get into the ring with Jack Dempsey. As he stopped outside the ring the unconsidered semi-final ended, and there was another and louder cheer, coming down from the grand stand, heralding the progress of the champion toward the ring of light.

Firpo a Troubled Giant.

Firpo climbed into his corner and sat down on the swinging stool wrapped in a dressing gown of big checks of black and lemon yellow, with cuffs and collar of a deep purple. It was in character like all of this strange man's habits. Whether intentionally or not, it fits into the public character he has built up for himself, opulent, exotic, and contrasting boldly with the simple white sweater wrapped around the champion's shoulders.

Beside this troubled giant Dempsey looked slight and boyish as he came into the ring in white silk trunks and white sweater, boyishly simple against the other's splendor. The moment he entered the ring he crossed quickly, smiling, to the challenger's corner and shook hands with the opponent he had never seen before. It seemed a simple and spontaneous gesture, and was certainly an effective one. Firpo shook hands, of course, but he didn't smile. As Dempsey returned to his corner Firpo, still on his feet, moved his huge head about slowly and almost bewildered. He looked like a man who didn't know where he was. He certainly didn't look like the man who was about to give one of the best of heavyweight champions the hardest fight of his life.

Ritnals of the Ring.

Then the usual formalities. Both boxers had put on their gloves before entering the ring, so that delay was obviated. But there had to be the usual poses of the two fighters, their managers and the referee before the cameras. There had to be the usual impassioned appeals of Joe Humphreys for sufficient quiet to enable him to tell the crowd that Johnny Gallagher was going to referee and that George Partrich and Billy McPartland would be the judges. This finished, the hardly repressed crowd began buzzing noisily again. Once more Humphreys appealed for quiet and announced that following the championship fight there would be another eight-round bout. A chorus of groans drowned out the names of the fighters. This crowd was in no mood for an afterpiece with the big fight still to come.

Firpo, seated in his corner, still looked about, frowning and puzzled, as Humphreys got Dempsey on his feet and proudly proclaimed him to the crowd, "The champion of champions, our own champion, Jack Dempsey."

Dempsey Small in Comparison.

The shouts that greeted the champion were partly, no doubt, the product of the natural tendency of most crowds to be with the man on top; partly to a genuine sympathy with the native son; partly, too, to the increased liking which Dempsey has won in the past few years. Then, stilling the crowd as best he could, Humphreys introduced "the pugilistic marvel of Argentine, the recognized champion of all South America, Luis Angel Firpo." A cheer adequate to the demands of courtesy; then the fighters were back in their corners for the last consultation with their seconds. Around Dempsey gathered Joe Benjamin, his brother John and his manager and dominant spirit, Jack Kearns; and by this time the champion, too, was serious, though even when frowning, even with his famous fighting face, he could look like nothing but a small boy beside this sombre giant from the Argentine.

Strikes Up Firpo's Guard.

Final consultation of boxers and seconds with the referee, and then all but three men piled out of the ring as the gong sounded. Quick as a flash Dempsey rushed across the ring, struck up Firpo's guard or the place where his guard might have been and wasn't, but the challenger didn't go down. Instead, the champion, half slipping, half knocked over by Firpo's right-hand counter, was down on one knee, down for the first time since that ancient fight with Jim Flynn, the Pueblo fireman, long before he won the title. He was up again before they could more than start counting, and as he got up on his feet 90,000 people got up on their feet, too, and not one of them sat down before the round was over. Ninety thousand people realized in one breath that they were about to see one of the classic fights of all history.

They came into a clinch, and, breaking, Dempsey caught him on the jaw with his fierce left hook—a blow that looks hard and is in reality still harder. Firpo was jolted, but he lashed out with the famous pile-driver right. It must be feared that he was covering up that right, to some extent, in his training. Certainly last night it moved with none of the dismal slowness of those training punches at Atlantic City. It caught Dempsey in the ribs, caught him fair and square. The champion was apparently unshaken. Had the right been overestimated? Apparently, for a moment later, as they were breaking from a brief clinch, Dempsey again whipped a left hook to the jaw and the Argentine challenger tumbled to the floor.

Gets Dempsey Again.

But he, too, was up in an instant and once more that long right shot out and caught Dempsey in the body. Dempsey came back with a right to the jaw. Down went Firpo again. One, two, and again he was up. Dempsey's left struck his jaw and he went down again. One, two, three, and up again. The roaring crowd was beginning to think that here was another Jess Willard when that long right flashed out again. Dempsey, on the offensive, hadn't covered it. It caught him in the ribs. Another instant and it had caught him again.

The two huge fighters, huge and swift, doubly swift to the eyes of those who for an hour and a half had been watching the slow fighters of the preliminaries, closed again. In furious infighting Dempsey hammered a series of rights and lefts to the body. With a thump Firpo dropped again. This time he seemed to be gone, but on the count of seven he got to his knees and two seconds later he was on his feet. Dempsey kept at him. Three times in quick succession Firpo was hammered down, rising each time before the count was started. Jess Willard had never done this. The man could take it. He could take the best, the frantically repeated best, of the greatest heavyweight of the age, and still bounce back to his feet to go on fighting. Could he be beaten at all?

Thought Championship Gone.

And then, as Dempsey came toward him again, his right toward the right field stands, Firpo's long driving right caught him on the point of the jaw, and head first, feet pointed in air, the heavyweight champion shot out through the ropes and to all appearance out of his championship. The referees arm waved while ninety thousand people howled frantically and inarticulately, but Dempsey, pushed back from the heads and shoulders of the sporting writers in the front row of ringside seats, crawled weakly through the ropes and was on his feet again with just one single second to spare. Leaning against the ropes for an instant more, he was an easy target, but Firpo, excited, swung that right again and again and missed.

Dempsey Falls Into Clinch.

Dempsey fell into a clinch and they were clinched against the ropes when the bell ended the first round. And out of 90,000 people about 88,000 thought that Dempsey was through. Jack Kearns, in his corner, rubbing his head, rubbing his body, patting him, constantly talking to him in an undertone, worried in all probability as he has never been worried before, did what he could for him, and Dempsey came up for the second round.

He came out a beaten man to all appearance, but his head and his heart were not beaten and he had enough strength left to fight through on the plan that his lightning-quick fighting brain told him was the only one that could win. Firpo came out slowly—too slowly to gather in that championship. He was worried for, after all, he had hit the canvas seven times in three minutes and had got such a pounding as no other man had ever received and kept on his feet. Dempsey came in, hooked over a left and put Firpo down; but in two seconds he was up again. Then a moment of in-fighting, always Dempsey's best game, and Firpo sank under a right to the body and a left to the jaw. This time he was down for four seconds, rising on the fifth as game as ever. But Dempsey lost no time. This was the decisive moment. The champion's left caught the Wild Bull on the jaw, the champion's right caught him as he was going down, and this time Luis Angel Firpo did not get up. He had lost. But he had lost about the greatest fight in the history of pugilism.

Though there was nothing to attract early comers except a program of run-of-the-mine music and the spectacle of sunset and nightfall over Washington Heights, a good many spectators insisted on arriving in the latter part of the afternoon. Naturally, those who meant to rush into the few unreserved seats in that small portion of uncovered bleachers left in the reconstructed stadium were on hand long before sunset, and the battalions of policemen, firemen, ushers newspaper men and others whose early arrival might be regarded as an occupational disease increased the number of early comers. Those who held reserved seats, as a rule, stayed downtown for dinner before coming to the fight, yet even among these the early arrivals were fairly numerous, and by 6 o'clock the long lines of men waiting their turn at the lunch counters in the rear of the grandstand were massing like a bread line of Japanese earthquake refugees.

Outside the stadium there were other spectators who had to come early to avoid the rush. Clinging to the rocky slopes of Coogan's Bluff, hundreds of hardy mountaineers peered anxiously through the narrow space between upper and lower tiers of the grandstand, which gave them a precarious and distant view of the ring. More distant still were the standees on the roof of a tall apartment house on Edgecombe Avenue, on top of the hill, who were able to look over both stands and down into the centre of the arena, though it seemed that they could hardly see anything but the network of wires supporting the forty lights hung above the canvas.

Elevated Pours In Crowds.

Inside, meanwhile, the crowd gradually increased by trickles, a fresh surge pouring through the gates with the arrival of each elevated train. In the great closed horseshoe of the double grandstand dark spots of spectators gradually took shape against the green slope of the seats. The yellow expanse of temporary board seats in the playing field, extending like the sands of a Roman arena inside the amphitheatre, was more sparsely populated in the early hours, for ringside seat holders were more apt to be of the type who dined well and carefully downtown before taking a taxi to the arena.

So the slowly gathering crowd amused itself by listening to the alternate offerings from a battery of three amplifiers at each corner of the ring. The sun went down, and for a period there was no light in the gathering dusk but the occasional golden reflection from one of Mr. Hedley's yellow elevated trains as it drew up into the parking space to the north of the Polo Grounds. Meanwhile the knots of yawning policemen and firemen clustered about the ring, more and more newspaper men and telegraph operators crowded their way into the narrow accommodations of the press benches, and clouds of tobacco smoke began to turn this outdoor arena into the semblance of an orthodox interior fight scene.

Resin Brought for the Arena.

The ropes were stretched and tightened, boxes of resin were emptied on the new canvas and trodden in. Various citizens, prominent or obscure, were paged from the ringside through the amplifiers and those who had come early tried to pretend that they were diverted by these pastimes, while newspaper men squeezed in tighter and tighter.

SARAZEN TRIUMPHS OVER HAGEN ON 38TH

Captures Thrilling Extra-Hole Match and Retains Pro Golf Title at Pelham.

LOSER MAKES GREAT FIGHT

Is Three Down at Twenty-eighth, but Evens Score at the Thirty-fifth.

For the second successive time, Gene Sarazen, Briarcliff Lodge professional, is the P. G. A. champion. After one of the most thrilling matches ever played, a match that held even his fellow-pros spellbound by its tenseness, Sarazen successfully defended his one remaining title by defeating Walter Hagen on the thirty-eighth green at the Pelham Country Club yesterday afternoon.

The perpetration of one of the cardinal sins of golf, lifting the head, was the ultimate cause of Hagen's downfall, although a wonderful recovery from the rough by Sarazen played a powerful part.

Sarazen, having seen his three-hole lead dwindle to nothing between the tenth hole and the eighteenth in the afternoon round and having had to get down a nervy four-foot putt to save his half at the first extra hole, went boldly for the second hole. He had watched Hagen's tee shot cut the corner of the trees, knowing by the shout of the crowd banked around the green that his rival was somewhere near. There was no indecision on his part when he struck the ball. He pulled the shot a trifle and it just cleared the trees, landing in the heavy rough quite a distance from the green.

Hagen's ball had just escaped a trap and was perched up, leaving him but an easy chip to the hole. Sarazen studied his shot carefully, told his caddy that he was going to put the ball up close and did. It was a magnificent shot that stopped dead, not more than two feet from the hole.

Hagen Misses Chance.

It was now up to Hagen, and instead of having the upper hand, as he had before Gene played his shot, Walter's back was against the wall with the most critical moment of the match at hand, he looked up and flubbed his ball into the trap just ahead. Then, however, as if to prove that he would go down fighting, he almost holed out on his next shot. Sarazen still had his putt to make before his title was safe, but he holed it without wasting more than a second in studying the line.

By defeating Hagen today, Sarazen not only won the P. G. A. title but he also demonstrated that he is the outstanding match play golfer among the professionals. It was the third time that he had defeated Hagen in match play in this country and it transferred to his sturdy shoulders the title that Hagen has enjoyed for several years.

Gene played the course in seventy-three strokes during the afternoon, one under par, the same as did Hagen, but the little champion had birdies at the two extra holes, while Hagen had only one. The little Italian star was a stroke higher than Hagen in the morning round, having a 77 to 76.

The story of the match hinges on the final round, for at the end of the first eighteen holes the two golf giants were all even.

Starting out the afternoon round with two birdies on the first nine holes and nothing worse than par figures on the others, Gene was 3 up on Hagen by the time the seventh hole was played. He took three putts on the first green in the afternoon. He was short on his approach putt and left himself open for Hagen to lay him a partial stymie so that the hole was halved.

Sarazen Wins Third Hole.

Sarazen made a great recovery from a trap to save his half on the second, but he broke the spell with a birdie at the third hole, where he was home with two beautiful wooden shots, while Hagen was in the rough to the left of the green. After pitching onto the green, Hagen hit the cup on his try for a 4, but his ball failed to drop in.

After halving the fourth in par 3s Sarazen holed two fine putts on the next two greens, a thirty-footer for a win at the fifth and a four-yarder for a half at the sixth. Hagen became 3 down by taking three putts at the seventh. The eighth and ninth were halved in par figures.

Hagen rimmed the cup for a 2 at the ninth and his first win came at the seventh, where he played a fine approach and holed a six-foot putt. He was lucky to get his half at the twelfth, for he overplayed the green and his ball was in the rough. He chipped back to five feet and got down the putt. Gene was on in two but could not hole his putt for a 3. Both were close to getting their 3s at the thirteenth, but halved the hole in birdie 4s. The next hole also was halved, as was the fifteenth, at which Hagen almost ran down his putt for a 3.

Sarazen lost the sixteenth, where he was trapped at the side of the green, and Hagen squared the match by taking the seventeenth, 5 to 6. Here Sarazen, first to play, sliced to the rough, while Walter hooked out of bounds. Walter then played a great shot to the green and Gene pitched short into a trap, from where he played his next to the green and took two putts. Hagen, although trapped, saved a half at the home hole when he laid Sarazen a partial stymie.

Morning Round.

In the morning round Sarazen lost a chance to square the match at the eighth, which was halved in 5s, by taking three putts. He was home with a line brassie second while Walter pushed his second off to the rough at the right of the green. The latter pitched out too strong but got down in two putts while Gene was two yards short and then missed his try for a birdie.

Hagen had all the better of the first two shots at the ninth but missed a four-footer for a win, giving Sarazen a half in 4. Gene had a chance to get down a six-foot putt for a win at the tenth but missed it, but he squared the match a hole later when he played a great stop-shot ten feet short of the flag and Hagen overplayed to the rough over the green and then missed his next stroke completely. He conceded the hole when he failed to get his next down while Sarazen was up dead for a sure four.

Hagen blundered when he attempted to cut the trees too finely going to the long fourteenth and it cost him the hole, for his ball hit an overhanging branch and dropped dead. His next attempt did the same thing. But he finally played a superb shot and reached the green. Sarazen was safely home on his third, and Hagen conceded the hole.

Hagen became 1 up by taking the fifteenth with a 4, his second stopping hole high to the left of the pin, two yards away. Gene's second ran over the green into a rough patch, and he overplayed the cup or his recovery, and then failed to hole a four-yarder for a half. Both got down good putts to halve the short sixteenth in threes, Sarazen's recovery from a trap being superbly played.

The seventeenth was halved in fives, but Gene squared the match by winning the home hole, 3 to 4, when Walter's drive found a trap and was so close to the bank that he did well in getting it out at all. He made a bold try for his 3, but overran the cup. Gene was only a few yards from the cup with a great tee shot and had an easy birdie 3.

The cards:

MORNING ROUND.

Out—
Sarazen ....4 5 5 3 4 5 4 5 4—39
Hagen ....5 4 5 3 4 4 4 5 4—38
In—
Sarazen ....3 4 4 6 5 5 3 5 3—38—77
Hagen ....3 5 4 4 6 4 3 5 4—38—76

AFTERNOON ROUND.

Out—
Sarazen ....3 4 4 3 3 4 4 4 4—35
Hagen ....3 4 5 3 4 4 5 4 4—38
In—
Sarazen ....3 4 4 4 5 4 4 6 4—38—73
Hagen ....3 5 4 4 5 4 5 5 4—35—73
Extra holes:
Sarazen 4 3
Hagen 4 4

Giant-Orioles Series Here; Benefit Game for Pioneers

The Giants and the Baltimore Orioles, five-time pennant winners in the International League, will play a series of three exhibition games at the Polo Grounds next Wednesday, Thursday and Friday. The receipts of the Thursday contest will go to a benefit fund for John B. Day and Jim Mutrie, the pioneers of National League baseball in New York. Day was owner and President of the first New York club in 1883 and Mutrie was his manager. An effort is being made to have Babe Ruth and perhaps one other Yankee play with the Giants that day, Colonel Jacob Ruppert, it is said, already having given his permission. Both teams will turn over their share of the gate receipts to the benefit fund.

YANKS LOSE TWO TO THE RED SOX

Boston Team Closes Home Season With Double Victory, 5-4 and 3-2.

Special to The New York Times.

BOSTON, Sept. 29.—More than 10,000 persons saw the Boston Red Sox close the local American League season today by defeating the champion Yankees in both games of a double-header. They won the opener, 5 to 4 in the regulation nine innings, but had to battle sixteen innings to win the second, 3 to 2.

The Yankees made fourteen hits off Quinn in the opening engagement, but failed to bunch them except in the seventh and eighth innings. They scored two runs in each of these innings and wiped out a four run lead which errors by Dugan and Schang had given the Red Sox in the first and fourth.

Waite Hoyt was Quinn's opponent on the mound and the perennial boy wonder was only so-so. Eleven hits were made off him and four of them came in the first inning, while Dugan and Schang were mussing things up by muffing easy throws at third base and the plate respectively.

Red Sox Score Again.

Three runs resulted and the enemy bagged another in the fourth when Collins beat out a single to Dugan, advanced to second on Dugan's wild throw past first, went to third on an infield out and scored on a wild pitch. Perfect support behind Hoyt would have prevented all of Boston's first four runs.

The Yankees did not ring the bell until the seventh, and then they were stopped after scoring two runs on singles by Lou Gehrig, Elmer Smith, Aaron Ward and Ernie Johnson, who succeeded Everett Scott at short in the fourth. They resumed their attack on Quinn in the eighth and tied the count by scoring two more runs on singles by Dugan, Ruth and Smith and an infield out.

Hoyt, meantime, had settled into a steady, effective stride, never yielding more than one hit an inning. With one out in the eighth, however, Menosky got hold of one and smacked it against the centre field bleacher wall for a triple, and scored the winning run a moment later on Collins's sacrifice fly.

The sunset engagement produced a masterly pitching duel between Battling Bob Shawkey on the one hand and George Murray, himself a former Yankee, on the other. Both were lucky to escape being scored on in the first few innings, but both were well supported, and it wasn't until the fifth that the Yankees scored the first run of the game on Hofmann's single to left and Witt's double past Mike Monosky.

McMillian's triple to centre and doubles by Johnny Mitchell and Val Picinich gave the Sox two runs and a lead in their half of the fifth, but in the seventh the Yankees tied it up on Hofmann's double and two long flies, each of which advanced the runner.

Neither side threatened in the eighth or ninth inning, but in the second half of the tenth Shank's single to right, an infield error and a sacrifice put runners in second and third with only one out. Shanks was caught at the plate, however, and the next batsman grounded to Mike Gazella for the third out.

Yankees Miss Chance.

In the twelfth the Yankees filled the bases with two out, but failed to score, and in the following round they missed another chance by failing to extract a run out of two passes, a sacrifice and an infield hit.

Shawkey had had enough by the end of the fourteenth inning, and in the following round George Pipgras assumed the pitching burden for the Yanks. A marvelous throw by Ruth, which caught Collins going from first to third on McMillan's blast to left, saved the young right-hander in the fifteenth, but in the sixteenth the Sox broke through and scored the winning run on a pass to Mitchell, Picinich's sacrifice, a wild pitch and Burns's single to centre.

The score:

FIRST GAME.

BOSTON (A.)	Ab	R	H	Po	A
Mitchell,ss	4	0	1	3	3
Walters,c	4	0	2	5	1
Donoghue,rf	4	1	0	1	0
Burns,1b	4	1	2	9	0
Menosky,lf	4	2	2	2	1
Collins,cf	3	1	2	3	0
Shanks,3b	4	0	2	1	1
McMillan,2b	4	0	0	3	5
Quinn,p	3	0	0	0	2
Total	34	5	11	27	13

NEW YORK (A.)	Ab	R	H	Po	A
Witt,cf	5	0	1	0	1
Dugan,3b	5	1	1	2	3
Ruth,lf	4	1	1	1	0
Gehrig,1b	4	1	2	12	0
Smith,rf	4	1	2	1	0
Ward,2b	4	0	2	3	5
Schang,c	4	0	0	2	0
Scott,ss	1	0	0	1	4
Johnson,ss	3	0	2	2	2
Hoyt,p	3	0	2	0	0
aHendrick	1	0	1	0	0
Total	38	4	14	24	15

a Batted for Hoyt in ninth.
Errors—Boston 0, New York 2 (Dugan 2).

Boston ....3 0 0 1 0 0 0 1 ..—5
New York ....0 0 0 0 0 0 2 2 0—4

Two-base hit—Burns. Three-base hit—Menosky. Sacrifice—Collins. Double play—McMillan, Mitchell and Burns. Left on bases—New York 7, Boston 6. Struck out—By Hoyt 1, Quinn 3. Wild pitch—Hoyt. Umpires—Dinneen, Rowland and Connolly. Time of game—1:03.

SECOND GAME.

NEW YORK (A.)	Ab	R	H	Po	A
Witt,cf	4	0	2	4	0
Gazella,3b	6	0	0	1	4
Ruth,lf	6	0	1	4	2
Gehrig,1b	6	0	2	11	1
Smith,rf	6	0	0	3	0
Ward,2b	7	0	1	7	4
Hofmann,c	7	2	3	12	2
Scott,ss	1	0	0	1	2
Johnson,ss	5	0	0	2	3
Shawkey,p	5	0	1	1	5
Pipgras,p	0	0	0	0	0
Total	53	2	10	*46	23

BOSTON (A.)	Ab	R	H	Po	A
Mitchell,ss	7	2	3	8	8
Picinich,c	6	0	1	4	2
Donaghue,rf	5	0	1	8	1
Burns,1b	7	0	1	17	1
Menosky,lf	4	0	1	5	0
Collins,cf	5	0	0	2	0
Shanks,3b	5	0	1	2	0
McMillan,2b	5	1	2	6	6
Murray,p	5	0	0	1	4
Total	49	3	10	48	22

* One out when winning run was scored.
Errors—Boston 0, New York 1 (Gehrig).

Boston—
0 0 0 0 2 0 0 0 0 0 0 0 0 0 0 1—3
New York—
0 0 0 0 1 0 1 0 0 0 0 0 0 0 0 0—2

Two-base hits—Mitchell, Picinich, Hofmann. Three-base hits—Gehrig, McMillan. Sacrifices—Shawkey, Gehrig, McMillan, Murray, Picinich. Double plays—McMillan, Mitchell and Burns (2); Ward, Scott and Gehrig. Left on bases—New York 11, Boston 9. Bases on balls—Off Shawkey 3, Pipgras 3, Murray 8. Struck out—By Shawkey 7, Pipgras 1, Murray 3. Hits—Off Shawkey, 8 in 14 innings; Pipgras, 2 in 2. Wild pitches—Shawkey, Pipgras. Losing pitcher—Pipgras. Umpires—Rowland, Connolly and Dinneen. Time of game—2:33.

On Near-By Links.

M. R. White was the winner in the Class A sweepstakes at the Dunwoodie Country Club yesterday. White turned in a score of 80, 16—64, while A. Walling was runner-up with 78, 12—66. In class B, N. J. Horan led the field with 97, 25—72 and J. J. Quencer and Frank Devoe tied for second with net 74 each. Their scores were: Quencer 100, 26—74, Devoe 100, 26—74.

J. P. Downey and M. G. MacDonald also won their way to the finals in the club championship division yesterday. Downey defeated Lee Stewart, 6 and 5 and MacDonald defeated W. S. Johnston, 1 up.

A. L. Walker Jr. won the George Hunter medal in the qualifying round of eighteen holes for the club championship at the Richmond County Country Club yesterday. Walker easily led the field by turning in a 75, while the runner-up was Gerald Henderson who had a score of 80.

The following men qualified in the first sixteen and have been matched as follows: Fred Gilmer and Gerald Henderson, F. G. and W. F. Van Clief, David [illegible] and Henry Miller-Jones, J. A. Fuller and D. W. Mufford, A. D. Holland and W. H. Rachau, William Pannock and Philip Thell, Robert C. Stanley and A. L. Walker.

GIANTS ARE BEATEN BY THE ROBINS, 5-1

Champions, With Many Changes in Line-Up, Get Only Three Blows Off Ruether.

HUNTZINGER MAKES DEBUT

Former Penn Star Yields Only Three Hits in First Five Innings —Is Relieved by Barnes.

The Giants didn't hurt their own cause any by losing to the Robins yesterday at the Polo Grounds and they did help the cause of Brother Dutch Ruether, who pitched the game and won and now needs only one more victory to gain that bonus of $1,000 from Charles H. Ebbets, the Brooklyn President. In such matters ball players must stick together, and since Ruether will have still another crack at the champions, it looks like a fair prediction that the athlete will win and the club President lose.

The score was 5 to 1. Reuther, facing a conglomeration of new Giants, old Giants, first-string Giants and second-string Giants, allowed only three widely spaced singles. After the third frame, when McGraw's languid warriors scored their lone run without a hit, no Giant got beyond first base and only five got that far. In Reuhter's educated hands the champs were as pliant as putty, but Frank Frisch was not in the game, and Bill Cunningham didn't stay very long, nor Hank Gowdy.

As a further indication that the Giants' pennant struggle is over, McGraw sent against the Dodgers Walter Huntzinger, the collegian from the University of Pennsylvania who was purchased last June and reported only recently. The new man looks something like Solemn John Watson, and yesterday pitched like Watson at his best. Huntzinger, cool and determined, pitched three hitless innings, allowed only three hits and one run in the next two and was honorably discharged at the end of the fifth with the score tied at 1-1. On the whole, a neat performance by a lad who never pitched to anything more robust than college batters before.

Virgil Barnes followed him to battle with the bonus-seeking Reuther, and in the seventh a single and three errors, two of them horrible throws by Kelly and Alex Gaston, gave the Robins two runs and the game. Jack Fournier, the French first baseman, faced Jack Scott in the eighth and hit his twenty-seond homer of the season into the lower right field stand. Three singles and a forceout manufactured another and the last Brooklyn run in tne ninth, while the Giants' only run came in the third on Kelly's walk and steal and two outs.

Travis Jackson spelled Frisch at second base. When Cunningham withdrew a young man by the name of Wilson, a broad-shouldered and wide-beamed outfielder from the Virginia League, played centrefield, hit the ball hard but not safely and committed an error in the seventh that let in two runs. Gaston got his long deferred chance to catch after Gowdy had quit. They say that McGraw will give "Hickory Mose" Solomon, the home run hitter from Hutchinson, Kan., a chance at first base this afternoon. It's now the open season for rookies, and for the remaining days of the season the Giants will look as patched as grandma's quilt.

The score:

BROOKLYN (N.)	Ab	R	H	Po	A
Bailey,cf	3	0	1	5	0
Johnston,ss	5	0	0	1	5
B. G'ffith,lf	5	0	2	1	0
Fournier,1b	4	2	2	12	0
T. G'ffith,rf	4	1	2	1	0
H'greaves,c	4	1	1	2	1
Olson,2b	4	1	2	4	3
High,3b	3	0	0	1	2
Ruether,p	4	0	2	0	3
Total	36	5	12	27	14

NEW YORK (N.)	Ab	R	H	Po	A
Bancroft,ss	4	0	0	2	3
Groh,3b	3	0	0	0	0
aMaguire	1	0	0	0	0
Jackson,2b	4	0	0	4	8
Young,rf	3	0	0	1	1
Meusel,lf	3	0	1	2	0
Cun'gham,cf	1	0	0	3	0
Wilson,cf	2	0	0	2	0
Kelly,1b	2	1	1	12	0
Gowdy,c	1	0	0	0	0
Gaston,c	2	0	1	0	0
H'tzinger,p	1	0	0	0	1
Barnes,p	1	0	0	0	1
Scott,p	1	0	0	1	0
Total	29	1	3	27	16

aBatted for Groh in ninth inning.
Errors—Brooklyn 2 (Johnston, Hargreaves). New York 3 (Wilson, Kelly, Gaston).

Brooklyn ....0 0 0 0 1 0 2 1 1—5
New York ....0 0 1 0 0 0 0 0 0—1

Home run — Fournier. Sacrifice — High. Double plays—Bancroft, Jackson and Kelly (2); Ruether, Olson and Fournier. Left on bases—New York 2, Brooklyn 7. Bases on balls—Off Barnes 2, Ruether 1. Struck out—By Ruether 2. Hits—Off Huntzinger, 3 in 5 innings; Barnes, 4 in 2; Scott, 5 in 2. Losing pitcher—Barnes. Umpires—McCormick, Klem, Finneran. Time of game—1:18.

AT ST. LOUIS.

FIRST GAME.

ST. LOUIS (A.)	Ab	R	H	Po	A
Gerber,ss	5	0	0	0	2
Ezzell,3b	4	1	2	1	2
Tobin,rf	4	1	2	1	0
Williams,lf	3	2	2	4	0
McManus,2b	4	1	2	1	3
Severeid,c	3	1	1	6	0
Jacobson,cf	4	0	3	4	1
Schl'bner,1b	2	0	0	10	0
Kolp,p	2	0	0	0	0
Wright,p	2	0	0	0	2
Total	33	6	12	27	10

CHICAGO (A.)	Ab	R	H	Po	A
A'deacon,cf	5	1	2	2	0
Hooper,rf	4	3	3	2	0
Collins,2b	5	1	[illegible]	[illegible]	[illegible]
Sheely,1b	4	0	1	7	3
Barrett,lf	4	0	1	6	0
Kamm,3b	4	0	0	1	2
McClellan,ss	4	0	0	3	4
Crouse,c	4	0	0	1	0
Bl'k'ship,p	3	0	0	0	2
aMostil	1	0	0	0	0
Total	38	5	10	24	11

a Batted for Blankenship in ninth.
Errors—St. Louis 3 (McManus, Jacobson, Schliebner); Chicago 2 (Barrett, McClellan).

St. Louis ....0 1 0 2 1 0 2 0 ..—6
Chicago ....0 0 1 0 3 0 1 0 0—5

Two-base hits—Jacobson, Barrett, Collins. Home runs—Hooper, Williams. Stolen bases—Collins, McManus. Sacrifices — Severeid, Schliebner 2. Double plays—Sheely, McClellan and Sheely; Jacobson, McManus and Schliebner. Left on bases—Chicago 7, St. Louis 7. Bases on balls—Off Blankenship 1, Wright 1. Struck out—By Kolp 1, Wright 3. Hits—Off Kolp 8 in 4 2-3 innings, Wright 2 in 4 1-3. Wild pitch—Blankenship. Balk—Blankenship. Winning pitcher—Wright. Umpires—Ormsby and Moriarty. Times of game—1:38.

SECOND GAME.

CHICAGO (A.)	Ab	R	H	Po	A
A'deacon,cf	2	1	0	0	0
Mostil,cf	3	0	0	0	0
Hooper,rf	5	0	2	1	0
Collins,2b	4	1	2	5	2
Sheely,1b	3	1	0	12	0
Barrett,lf	3	0	1	2	1
Kamm,3b	2	0	0	3	3
McClellan,ss	4	1	1	1	7
Schalk,c	4	0	1	3	0
Robertson,p	3	1	2	0	2
Leverette,p	0	0	0	0	1
aCrouse	0	0	0	0	0
bElsh	0	1	0	0	0
Total	33	6	9	27	16

ST. LOUIS (A.)	Ab	R	H	Po	A
Gerber,ss	4	0	1	3	2
Ezzell,3b	5	1	2	0	1
Tobin,rf	4	1	1	4	0
Williams,lf	4	2	1	1	0
McManus,2b	5	0	0	3	5
Severeid,c	3	1	3	4	2
Jacobson,cf	3	0	2	2	0
Schl'bner,1b	4	0	2	7	1
Van Gilder,p	2	0	0	0	2
Root,p	1	0	0	0	0
cDurst	1	0	0	0	0
Total	35	5	12	27	12

a Batted for Robertson in ninth.
b Ran for Crouse in ninth.
c Batted for Van Gilder in sixth.
Errors—Chicago 4 (Archdeacon 2, Hooper, Collins); St. Louis 1 (Ezzell).

Chicago ....0 0 2 0 0 2 1 0 1—6
St. Louis ....0 0 0 1 0 1 2 1 0—5

Two base hits—Robertson, Jacobson, Schalk, Ezzell. Home runs—Collins, Tobin. Stolen bases—Barrett, McClellan, Elsh. Sacrifices—Kamm, Barrett, Jacobson, Tobin. Double plays—Kamm, Collins and Sheely; McClellan, Kamm, McClellan and Sheely. Left on bases—Chicago 5, St. Louis 9. Bases on balls—Off Robertson 4, Van Gilder 2, Root 1. Struck out—By Robertson 2, Van Gilder 2. Hits—Off Robertson 11 in 8 innings, Leverette 1 in 1, Van Gilder 7 in 6, Root 2 in 3. Winning pitcher—Robertson. Losing pitcher—Root. Umpires—Moriarty and Ormsby. Time of game—1:40.

AT WASHINGTON.

PHILADELPHIA (A.)	Ab	R	H	Po	A
Matthews,cf	4	0	0	0	0
Bruggy,c	4	0	0	6	2
Hale,3b	5	0	3	2	0
Hauser,1b	3	1	0	13	0
Welch,lf	2	0	1	2	0
Galloway,ss	4	0	1	1	4
Dykes,2b	4	0	0	1	5
McGowan,rf	4	0	3	2	0
Hasty,p	1	0	0	0	1
Rommel,p	1	0	0	0	0
B.Harris,p	1	1	0	0	1
aFrench	1	0	0	0	0
Total	34	2	8	27	13

WASHINGTON (A.)	Ab	R	H	Po	A
Leibold,cf	4	0	1	2	0
P'paugh,ss	3	0	1	2	7
Goslin,lf	4	0	2	0	0
Rice,rf	3	0	0	0	0
Judge,1b	2	0	0	15	2
Ruel,c	3	0	1	5	2
S.Harris,2b	4	0	1	1	3
Prothro,3b	3	0	0	2	6
Zahniser,p	3	0	0	0	4
bWade	1	0	0	0	0
cGharrity	1	0	0	0	0
Total	31	0	6	27	24

aBatted for Rommel in seventh.
bBatted for Prothro in ninth.
cBatted for Zahniser in ninth.
Errors—Philadelphia 0, Washington 2 (Peckinpaugh, Judge).

Philadelphia ....0 0 0 0 0 0 0 1 1—2
Washington ....0 0 0 0 0 0 0 0 0—0

Two-base hits—Welch, McGowan. Three-base hit—Goslin. Sacrifice—Peckinpaugh. Left on bases—Philadelphia 9, Washington 10. Bases on balls—Off Rommel 2, B. Harris 3, Zahniser 4. Struck out—By Rommel 2, B. Harris 2, Zahniser 4. Hits—Off Hasty 4 in 3 innings, Rommel 1 in 3, B. Harris 1 in 3. Wild pitch—Zahniser. Passed ball—[illegible] Winning pitcher—B. Harris. Umpires—Nallin and Evans. Time of game—1:50.

Baseball Today, Ebbets Field. Brooklyn vs. Phila., 3 P. M.—Advt.

BASEBALL

YESTERDAY'S RESULTS.

NATIONAL LEAGUE.
Brooklyn 5, New York 1.
Cincinnati 11, St. Louis 1.
Chicago 5, Pittsburgh 4. (Ten innings.)
Philadelphia 4, Boston 2.

AMERICAN LEAGUE.
Boston 5, New York 4. (First game.)
Boston 3, New York 2 (16 innings). (Second game.)
Detroit 3, Cleveland 0.
Philadelphia 2, Washington 0.
St. Louis 6, Chicago 5. (First game.)
Chicago 6, St. Louis 5. (Second game.)

STANDING OF THE CLUBS.

NATIONAL LEAGUE.

	Won.	Lost.	P.C.
New York	94	56	.627
Cincinnati	91	60	.603
Pittsburgh	85	66	.563
Chicago	81	69	.540
St. Louis	76	73	.510
Brooklyn	72	77	.483
Boston	52	96	.351
Philadelphia	48	102	.320

AMERICAN LEAGUE.

	Won.	Lost.	P.C.
New York	96	52	.649
Cleveland	76	68	.528
Detroit	77	69	.527
St. Louis	73	71	.507
Washington	71	74	.490
Chicago	65	80	.448
Philadelphia	64	80	.444
Boston	60	88	.405

WHERE THEY PLAY TODAY.

NATIONAL LEAGUE.
Boston at New York.
(Game starts at 3 P. M.)
St. Louis at Cincinnati.
Pittsburgh at Chicago.
Philadelphia at Brooklyn.

AMERICAN LEAGUE.
Cleveland at Detroit.
Chicago at St. Louis.
Philadelphia at Washington.
Other clubs not scheduled.

INDIANS BLANKED BY TIGER RECRUIT

Whitehill Yields 2 Hits, Detroit Creeps Within Point of Second Place—Score 3-0.

DETROIT, Mich., Sept. 29.—Earl Whitehill, a recruit pitcher formerly of the Birmingham club of the Southern Association, held the Cleveland Indians to two hits today and won his game for Detroit, 3 to 0. Whitehill took up the pitching burden in the first inning when Dauss walked Jamieson. He retired the side and pitched splendidly thereafter, Speaker and Uhle being the only Cleveland players to get a hit off his delivery. This victory enabled the Tigers to land within one point of second place now occupied by the Indians.

The score:

CLEVELAND (A.)	Ab	R	H	Po	A
Jamieson,lf	1	0	0	1	1
Summa,rf	0	0	0	0	0
Connolly,rf	4	0	0	2	0
Speaker,cf	4	0	1	2	0
Sewell,ss	4	0	0	1	1
S'phenson,2b	3	0	0	2	4
Lutzke,3b	2	0	0	0	3
Wamby,3b	1	0	0	1	0
Knode,1b	2	0	0	10	1
Brower,1b	0	0	0	1	0
O'Neill,c	2	0	0	3	1
Myatt,c	0	0	0	1	0
Uhle,p	3	0	1	0	3
aShaner	1	0	0	0	0
Total	27	0	2	24	14

DETROIT (A.)	Ab	R	H	Po	A
Blue,1b	2	0	0	11	0
Jones,3b	3	0	2	0	2
Cobb,cf	4	0	0	1	0
Manush,lf	4	0	0	1	0
Veach,lf	0	0	0	1	0
Heilmann,rf	3	2	2	4	1
Pratt,2b	3	0	1	3	3
Rigney,ss	4	0	1	2	3
Bassler,c	3	0	1	4	2
Dauss,p	0	0	0	0	0
Whitehill,p	3	1	2	0	1
Total	29	3	9	27	12

a Batted for Knode in eighth.
Errors—Detroit 3 (Jones, Manush, Rigney). Cleveland 1 (O'Neill).

Detroit ....0 0 0 1 1 0 0 1 ..—3
Cleveland ....0 0 0 0 0 0 0 0 0—0

Two-base hits—Jones, Uhle. Sacrifices—Jones, Pratt, Whitehill, Blue. Double plays—Pratt, Rigney and Blue; Heilmann and Rigney; Jones, Pratt and Blue. Left on bases—Cleveland 4, Detroit 9. Base on balls—Off Dauss 1, Uhle 3, Whitehill 2. Struck out—By Whitehill 3, Uhle 1. Hits—Off Dauss, 0 in no innings; Whitehill, 2 in 9. Hit by pitcher—By Whitehill (Jamieson). Passed ball—O'Neill. Winning pitcher—Whitehill. Umpires—Holmes, Hildebrand and Owens. Times of game—2:05.

AT CINCINNATI.

CINCINNATI (N.)	Ab	R	H	Po	A
Burns,rf	4	4	3	2	0
Daubert,1b	4	0	1	8	1
Kimmick,2b	4	2	3	3	3
Roush,cf	5	0	1	3	0
Duncan,lf	5	1	3	3	0
Wingo,c	5	0	1	4	1
Pinelli,3b	4	1	2	1	1
Fowler,ss	4	2	2	2	4
Luque,p	3	1	1	1	1
Total	38	11	17	27	11

ST. LOUIS (N.)	Ab	R	H	Po	A
Flack,rf	3	0	0	1	0
Smith,lf	3	1	1	3	0
B'tomley,1b	3	0	1	8	0
Mueller,cf	4	0	0	3	0
Stock,3b	4	0	1	0	1
Toporcer,2b	2	0	0	2	2
McCurdy,c	2	0	0	2	2
Bell,ss	3	0	1	3	5
Toney,p	2	0	0	0	0
Stuart,p	0	0	0	0	2
aSherdel	1	0	0	0	0
North,p	0	0	0	0	0
bDouthitt	1	0	0	0	0
Total	31	1	4	24	12

a Batted for Stuart in seventh.
b Batted for North in ninth.
Errors—Cincinnati 1 (Roush); St. Louis 2 (Smith, Toporcer).

Cincinnati ....1 0 2 4 3 1 0 0 ..—11
St. Louis ....1 0 0 0 0 0 0 0 0—1

Two-base hits—Burns, Duncan. Three-base hits—Burns, Pinelli, Fowler. Stolen bases—Burns, Daubert, Kimmick 2, Smith 2. Sacrifices—Kimmick, Luque. Double plays—Fowler and Daubert; Fowler and Kimmick; Toporcer, Bell and Bottomley. Left on bases—St. Louis 9; Cincinnati 8. Bases on balls—Off Luque 6; Toney 2; Stuart 1. Struck out—By Luque 4. Hits—Off Toney, 7 in 3 1-3 innings; Stuart 8 in 2 2-3; North 2 in 2. Passed balls—Wingo, McCurdy. Losing pitcher—Toney. Umpires—Moran, Hart and Wilson. Time of game—1:37.

AT CHICAGO.

CHICAGO (N.)	Ab	R	H	Po	A
Statz,cf	4	1	3	2	0
Adams,ss	5	1	1	2	6
Grantham,2b	4	0	1	1	5
Grimes,1b	5	1	4	17	1
Friberg,3b	2	0	1	1	1
Miller,lf	4	0	1	2	0
Grigsby,rf	4	0	1	2	0
Hartnett,c	4	0	0	2	0
bCallaghan	0	1	0	0	0
Alexander,p	3	1	0	1	5
aO'Farrell	1	0	1	0	0
cVogel	0	0	0	0	0
Total	36	5	13	30	18

PITTSBURGH (N.)	Ab	R	H	Po	A
Moore,ss	5	0	1	4	8
Carey,cf	5	0	1	1	0
Traynor,3b	4	0	1	0	5
Barnhart,rf	4	0	0	2	0
Russell,lf	4	0	1	2	0
Rawlings,2b	3	1	1	4	3
Grimm,1b	3	2	1	13	3
Schmidt,c	4	1	0	2	1
Meadows,p	4	0	1	1	2
Total	36	4	7	*29	22

*Two out when winning run scored.
a Batted for Alexander in tenth.
b Ran for Hartnett in tenth.
c Ran for O'Farrell in tenth.
Errors—Chicago 2 (Grantham, Hartnett); Pittsburgh 2 (Rawlings, Schmidt).

Chicago ....0 1 0 0 0 1 0 0 0 3—5
Pittsburgh ....0 0 0 0 0 0 0 2 0 2—4

Two-base hits—Rawlings, Statz. Home run—Grimm. Stolen base—Carey. Sacrifices—Friberg (2), Rawlings. Double plays—Moore and Grimm; Grimm, Moore and Grimm; Grantham, Adams and Grimes. Left on bases—Pittsburgh 4, Chicago 5. Bases on balls—Off Meadows 1, Alexander 1. Struck out—By Alexander 2, Meadows 1. Umpires—O'Day, Pfirman and Quigley. Time of game—1:29.

AT PHILADELPHIA.

PHILADELPHIA (N.)	Ab	R	H	Po	A
Metz,ss	4	0	1	1	5
Williams,cf	4	0	1	6	0
Walker,rf	4	0	1	3	0
Parkinson,2b	4	0	1	2	3
Lee,lf	4	2	2	2	0
Holke,1b	4	2	2	8	1
Woehrs,3b	2	0	2	2	1
Wilson,c	[illegible]	0	0	3	0
Betts,p	3	0	0	0	0
Total	31	4	10	27	10

BOSTON (N.)	Ab	R	H	Po	A
Nixon,cf	4	0	1	4	0
Felix,lf	5	0	2	2	0
So'worth,rf	5	1	4	1	1
McInnis,1b	4	1	3	7	1
Boeckel,3b	4	0	1	1	2
Ford,2b	3	0	0	3	1
R.Smith,ss	4	0	2	1	2
O'Neil,c	3	0	1	4	1
Genewich,p	3	0	1	1	1
E.Smith,c	1	0	0	0	0
aPowell	1	0	0	0	0
Bachelder,p	0	0	0	0	0
bEmmerich	0	0	0	0	0
Total	37	2	15	24	9

a Batted for Genewich in seventh.
b Ran for McInnis in ninth.
Errors—Philadelphia 1 (Wilson); Boston 0.

Philadelphia ....0 2 0 2 0 0 0 0 ..—4
Boston ....0 0 0 2 0 0 0 0 0—2

Two-base hits — Southworth 2, Boeckel, Holke. Three-base hit—Lee. Sacrifices—Wilson, Ford. Double plays—Metz, Parkinson and Holke; Woehrs, Parkinson and Holke. Left on bases — Boston 11, Philadelphia 5. Bases on balls—Off Genewich 1, Betts 2. Struck out—By Genewich 4, Betts 2. Hits—Off Genewich, 10 in 7 innings, Bachelder, 0 in 1. Losing pitcher—Genewich. Umpires—Powell and McCormick. Time of game—1:48.

TICKET SALE OPENS FOR WORLD SERIES

Both New York Clubs Ready to Receive Reservations for Six Games by Mail Only.

THREE GAMES FOR $16.50

Upper Stands at Stadium and Polo Grounds to Be Unreserved—No Orders for Single Game.

Following immediately on the heels of the clinching of the pennant by the Giants, both New York clubs announced yesterday in an official statement that they are now ready to accept applications for world series reserved seat tickets. The applications can be made by mail only, and the price for one reserved seat for three games will be $16.50, including war tax. The lower grand stand will be reserved at both the Yankee Stadium and the Polo Grounds.

How to buy tickets for the big series starting Oct. 10 is told in the following statement issued by Edward G. Barrow of the Yankees and James J. Tierney of the Giants:

"Both New York clubs are now accepting applications for seats for the world series. It is requested that the following instructions be complied with in making application for tickets in order to eliminate all unnecessary correspondence in filling orders:

"Applications to be made to the American League Baseball Club of New York (Yankees) at their office, 226 West Forty-second Street, for tickets for games 1, 3, 5 to be played at the Yankee Stadium.

"Applications to be made to the National Exhibition Company (Giants) at their office, 15 West Forty-fourth Street, for tickets for games 2, 4, 6 to be played at the Polo Grounds.

"Applications will be received by mail only, accompanied by money order or certified check.

"The whole lower grand stand will be reserved at both the Yankee Stadium and Polo Grounds.

"Tickets will be sold for a series of three games only—no orders for tickets for single games will be accepted. The prices, including war tax, are $16.50 each (one ticket for three games).

"The whole upper stand and mezzanine at the Yankee Stadium and the whole upper stand at the Polo Grounds will be thrown open to the purchasers of general admission tickets. General admission and bleacher tickets go on sale at the grounds at 10 A. M. on the day of the game. Prices as follows: General admission, $3.30 (unreserved); bleacher seats, $1.10 (unreserved)."

VAN RYN WINS 2 MATCHES.

Gains Third Round in Essex County Tennis With Dunham.

Special to The New York Times.

WEST ORANGE, N. J., Sept. 29.—The annual Essex County lawn tennis championship for men opened today on the courts of the Essex County Country Club with a field of thirty-two contenders for the title. Philip and Ludlow Vandeventer of Plainfield, James D. Ewing of the Amackassin Club, Yonkers, and S. Onda of New York are the seeded players.

All but three of the matches in the first round were completed today and two players gained their third round bracket. Mason Kirkland disposed of John Van Ryn at 6—2, 7—5, and K. K. Carter at 7—5, 6—1. Lindsey Dunham advanced to the second round through the default of Frank Rogers and then defeated Charles Cameron at 6—1, 6—4. Six defaults in all were registered during the day.

Play will be resumed tomorrow morning under the direction of Richard P. Bennett, and the field will be brought down to the semi-finals during the week. The semi-finals and final will be played Saturday and Sunday.

The summaries:

First Round—Philip Vandeventer won from Alfred Walters by default; E. G. Oelsner won from D. C. Dunn by default; Richard P. Bennett defeated George Groesbeck, 6—8, [illegible]; James D. Ewing defeated J. G. Hall, 6—4, 5—7, 6—2; K. K. Carter won from Ira Kip Jr. by default; Mason Kirkland defeated John Van Ryn, 6—2, 7—5; Ludlow Vandeventer won from A. E. Feaver by default; B. L. George defeated G. C. Thomas Jr., 6—4, 6—2; H. D. Ewing defeated H. T. Greenwood, 6—1, 6—2; S. Brabans defeated Earl Bache, 6—4, 6—4; F. Bellows won from W. E. Knowles by default; Lindsey Dunham won from Frank Rogers by default; Charles Cameron defeated W. C. Lenz, 8—6, 6—1.

Second Round—Kirkland defeated Carter, 7—5, 6—1; Dunham defeated Cameron, 6—1, 6—4.

WALKER INJURES HAND.

Bout With Jones Is Postponed Until Night of Oct. 8.

The Mickey Walker-Jimmy Jones bout for the world's welterweight championship, which was scheduled for Dreamland Park in Newark tomorrow night has been postponed one week because of an injury to Walker's right hand. The bout, which is scheduled as a twelve-round contest, will be held on the evening of Oct. 8.

Jones is already holder of the world's welterweight title by virtue of a ruling by the New York State Athletic Commission, but outside New York State Walker is recognized as the titleholder. Thus the approaching bout will bring together two boxers who hold the same title, and an interesting encounter should result.

LONDON SEEKS BIG BOUT.

May Offer £65,000 Purse for Heavyweight Battle.

LONDON, Sept. 29.—The Central News learns that arrangements have been made in London to offer a purse of £65,000 for a match at London about the end of January between Jack Dempsey and the winner of the Carpentier-Beckett fight. The promoter of the scheme, it is declared, offers to deposit £10,000 in a New York bank as a guarantee, and also offers to pay the transportation of Dempsey and his manager and trainer and all training expenses in England.

FORT WORTH WINS AGAIN.

Takes Third Game of Dixie Series From New Orleans, 3-1.

NEW ORLEANS, La., Sept. 29.—Fort Worth drove Winn off the mound in the first inning today and won the third game of the Dixie Series, from New Orleans, 3 to 1. The series now stands two victories for the Texas League champions and one for the Southern Association team.

Boxing Show Starts Oct. 17.

The next amateur boxing tournament of the Metropolitan A. A. U. to be conducted at Madison Square Garden is scheduled for the nights of Oct. 17 and 18. Bouts will be contested in six classes, the weights being 112, 126, 135, 147, 160 pounds and heavyweight division.

THE LEADING BATSMEN.

National League.

Player and Club.	G.	A.B.	R.	H.	P.C.
Hornsby, St. Louis	107	424	89	163	.385
Wheat, Brooklyn	96	344	62	129	.374
Bottomley, St. Louis	130	507	75	186	.367
Frisch, New York	148	631	116	221	.350
Fournier, Brooklyn	128	494	85	173	.350

American League.

Player and Club.	G.	A.B.	R.	H.	P.C.
Heilmann, Detroit	138	515	114	206	.400
Ruth, New York	148	506	145	196	.387
Speaker, Cleveland	141	542	119	201	.371
Collins, Chicago	137	476	81	170	.357
Sewell, Cleveland	144	515	89	183	.355

American Association.

Minneapolis 7, Louisville 6.
Indianapolis 5, St. Paul 0.
Kansas City 9, Columbus 0.
Milwaukee 7, Toledo 1 (first game).
Toledo 2, Milwaukee 1 (second game).

Baseball Today, Polo Grounds, 3 P. M. Giants vs. Boston. Grdstd $1.10.—Advt.

$10,000 Havre de Grace Race Is Captured by Enchantment

HAVRE DE GRACE, Md., Sept. 29.—The $10,000 Havre de Grace Handicap for three-year-olds and up, the feature event on today's racing program, was captured by Enchantment. Exodus finished second and Vigil third. The time for the mile and one-eighth was 1:50 4-5. Enchantment is owned by H. P. Whitney.

MURPHY SWEEPS CLOSING DAY CARD

Wins Both Grand Circuit Races at Columbus With Peter Etawah and Mary Ann.

COLUMBUS, Ohio, Sept. 29 (Associated Press).—Thomas W. Murphy, the New York horseman, made a clean sweep of the two events on today's Grand Circuit card, the final of the local meeting.

With Peter Etawah, a favorite, he won the 2:05 pace, although he was nosed out in the second heat by Peter Daphne. In the third mile Peter Etawah outraced Peter Daphne in the stretch for the decision.

With Mary Ann, Murphy won a straight-heat victory in the 2:09 trot. Jean Axworthy, driven today by Stokes, was second in each mile. Practically all of the horses which raced here have been shipped to Lexington, Ky., for the next two weeks' racing.

The summaries:

2:05 PACE.
Purse $1,000.

Peter Etawah, b. g., by Etawah (Murphy) 1 2 1
Peter Daphne, br. g. (Shively) 8 1 2
Easter Bell, b. m. (McMahon) 2 3 8
Neita Patch, b. m. (Eagan) 3 8 4
Miss Marie, b. m. (H. Thomas) 4 6 5
Jane R., George, Volo and Raven's Direct Heir also started.
Time—2:04¼, 2:04¾, 2:05.

2:09 TROT.
Purse $1,000.

Mary Ann, b. m., by Belwin (Murphy) 1 1 1
Jean Axworthy, b. m. (Stokes) 2 2 2
The Consequence, b. g. (McMahon) 6 3 3
Eleanor Worthy, b. m. (Loomis) 3 4 4
Supreme Justice, b. h. (Best) 4 5 5
San Pedro Girl also started.
Time—2:05¾, 2:06, 2:07.

LATONIA ENTRIES.

FIRST RACE — Purse, $1,400; claiming; three-year-olds and upward; fillies and mares; six furlongs. *Queen Esther 105 pounds, *Karo, *Winter Blossom and *Mildred Ruth 105, *Orlovo and *Ruby 109 each, Miss Meise, Telma K., Red Wood, Little Hope and Spring Showers 110 each, Georgette 114. Also eligible—*Modesty 109, *Punta Gorda 105, Miss Beulah 110, *Irish Rose 105, *Reliability 109.

SECOND RACE—Purse, $1,400; claiming; two-year-olds; maidens, colts and geldings; [illegible] furlongs. **Coley McDevitt 113 pounds, [illegible]trutter 118, Business Like 118, Frontiersman 118, Rambler 118, New Pink 118, Eminent 118, Liege 118, Black Ruler 118, Say It 118, Program 118, Star Beck 118. Also eligible—Poland 118, Firetoma 118, Melbourne 118, *Double T 113, Boss Man 118, Rockwork 118.

THIRD RACE—Purse, $1,400; claiming; three-year-olds and upward; one mile and seventy yards. King Charming 99 pounds, *Golden Billows 99, *Courtship 100, Sunny Ducrow 100, *Hoy 102, Romping Mary 103, Jake Feld 105, Mayor Carrel 105, *Claymore 106, Trooper 108, Vanishing Boy 110, Neddam 116. Also eligible—Glencolonko 118, *Fred Kinney 103, *Jupiter 101, Miss Maize 102, *Winner Take All 107, *Flower Shop 102.

FOURTH RACE—Purse $1,400; claiming; for four-year-olds and upward; one mile and seventy yards. *Tulalip 102 pounds, *Queen High 102, *Cautious 104, *Fincastle 105, Parish Maid, Sister Flo 107 each, *Ben Valet 112, Fancy Free 114, *Attorney 115, Widgeon 117, Westwood 120. Also eligible: Tony Beau, *Brother John 115 each, *Oo La La 109, *Simpleton 112, Sagamack, Baladin 110 each.

FIFTH RACE—Purse $1,700; allowances, "The Rosedale"; for two-year-olds; five and a half furlongs. Rip 102 pounds, Main Spring 102, Margaret Lawrence 104, Deronda, Hunter, Beau Butler, Earl Pool 107 each.

SIXTH RACE—Purse $1,400; claiming; for three-year-olds and upward; fillies and mares; six furlongs. *Antonia 105 pounds, *Tokiheme 105, *Winding Through 109, *Gem 109, *Martha Fallon 109, *Batty H. 109, *Palladium 110, Finday 110, Put and Take 110, May Prosper 110, Purple and White 110, Dimples 114. Also eligible: *Modna 109, *Fly Cast 109, Jou Jou 115, *Sister Josella 105.

SEVENTH RACE—Purse $1,500; claiming; for three-year-olds and upward; one mile and a sixteenth. *Lady Astor 101 pounds, Post Haste 105, Huonec 107, Dream Maker 107, Hold Me 108, Mavourneen 108, Fantoche 109, Precious Lula 110, Wood Trap 111.

*Apprentice allowance of five pounds claimed.

LATONIA RESULTS.

FIRST RACE—For three-year-olds and upward; claiming; purse $1,400; one mile and seventy yards. King Charming, 105 pounds (Parke), $4.60, $3.10, $2.50; Taylor Hay, 105 (Fronk), $5.60, $3.40, second; Bosh, 105 (Byrne), $3.90, third. Time—1:44 1-5. Tulalip, Kewpie O'Neil, Kirklevington, Chaplet, Mart O'Hara and Rey de Ada also ran.

SECOND RACE—For two-year-olds, fillies, maidens; purse $1,400; five and one-half furlongs. Pearl Mesta, 115 pounds (Scobie), $7.60, $3.30, $2.50, first; Lady Longridge, 115 (Pool), $3.80, $3.20, second; Medina, 115 (Connelly), $3.80, third. Time—1:07 4-5. Waukulla, Nell McChord, Bona Vera, Howdy, Benigna, Virginia Queen, Dusty Mary, Ocerina and Rose Estill also ran.

THIRD RACE—For three-year-olds and upward; allowances; the Autumn Inaugural; purse $1,600; six furlongs. Translate, 108 pounds (Pool), $6.40, $3.70, $3.00, first; Marvin May, 111 (Garner), $5.70, $4.70, second; Lord Granite, 106 (Fronk), $7.20, third. Time—1:12 1-5. Great Luck, Right On Time, Heremon, Bradley's Toney, Betty Beall, Pegasus, Wida and Pyx also ran.

FOURTH RACE — For three-year-olds and upward; the Cincinnati Auto Club Handicap; purse $1,800; six furlongs. Braedalbane, 115 pounds (Garner), $13.10, $7.60, $3.00, first; Pindar Peel, 105 (Heupel), $9.00, $3.00, second; Fair Phantom, 120 (Scobie), $2.20, third. Time—1:11 3-5. Nassau and Dr. Clark also ran.

FIFTH RACE—For three-year-olds and upward; the Covington Handicap; $5,000 added; one mile and a sixteenth. In Memoriam, 108 pounds (Barrett), $15.20, $6, $3.90, first; Actuary, 108 (Pool), $4.80, $3.40, second; Hopeless, 102 (Heupel), $4, third. Time—1:44. Chacolet, Lady Madcap, Barracuda, Best Pal, Cherry Tree, Surf Rider, Triumph and Prince K also ran.

SIXTH RACE—For two-year-olds; claiming; purse, $1,400; six furlongs. Sanola, 111 pounds (Fronk), $8, $4.30, $3.80, first; Postillion, 113 (Graner), $4.80, $8.50, second; Phoebe Snow, 114 (Pevic), $3.40, third. Time—1:13. Defiant, Boots and Shoes, Pearl Boots, Red Wood, Wong Bok, Shindy and Markiluna also ran.

SEVENTH RACE—For three-year-olds and upward; claiming; purse, $1,400; one mile and a sixteenth. Tippo Sahib, 113 pounds (Gennerson), $57.70, $18.50, $9.40, first; Make Up, 113 (Parke), $3.40, $2.90, second; Tender Seth, 108 (Pevic), $4.60, third. Time—1:48. Huonec, Sway, Grand Dame, Resting Time, Who Knows Me, Plus Ultra and Normal also ran.

Weather clear; track fast.

AQUEDUCT ENTRIES.

FIRST RACE—For maiden three-year-olds and upward; claiming; six and a half furlongs. Whirligig 105 pounds, *Bigger Still 103, Wilton Flanna 102, High Commander 105, *Irene Sweeney 103, Sister Sue 112, Tikeh 105, Baby Boy 105, Plentycoos 114, Patsy B. 106, Sylvan Spring 113, Uranus 112, H. Warren 105.

SECOND RACE—The Pickpocket Handicap; for three-year-olds and upward; one mile and a sixteenth. Flannel Shirt 118 pounds, Episode 112, McKee 109, Maryland Belle 104, High Prince 105.

THIRD RACE—For two-year-olds; claiming; five furlongs. First Lady Harding 108 pounds, Mad Trooper 104, East Wind 106, Vulnad 104, Mitau 109, Aggravating Papa 104, Flitlow 104, Houri 109, Praiseworthy 104, Sieivebloom 101, Escoba D'Oro 106, Hilarity 107.

FOURTH RACE—The Junior Champion; for two-year-olds; one mile. Sun Pal, Bracadale, Briggs Buchanan, Mr. Mutt, Stanwix, Bonaparte, Comic Artist McAuliffe, Aga Khan 105 pounds each.

FIFTH RACE—For three-year-olds and upward; claiming; one mile. Lady Inez 111 pounds, Carmen Pentages 105, King's Belle 103, Trite 106, Whirligig 106, *Maize 102, *Diversity 106, Scare Crow 100, Rekab 106, *Dan Boiling 101, Red Legs 112.

SIXTH RACE—For filly two-year-olds; conditions; five furlongs. Janet Blair 107 pounds, Exploit 116, Miss Domino 116, Starab 107, Stardrift 101, Nellie Gray 107, Broadcast 101, Rinkey 101, Lady Belle 116.

*Apprentice allowance claimed.
Weather clear, track fast.

LITTLE CHIEF BEATS ONLY OTHER STARTER

Captures Edgemere Handicap From High Chief—Brainstorm and Athelstan Scratched.

WALKOVER IN THE 'CHASE

Two That Go to the Post Belong to J. E. Widener—Sande Scores Double at Aqueduct.

Little Chief, bay son of Wrack-Medora II., raced to an almost uncontested victory in the Edgemere Handicap, which was scheduled as the feature at the Aqueduct track yesterday afternoon. Only High Chief of the other three horses entered accepted the issue, and for all the chance the Riviera Stable's colt had with Little Chief he also might have been left in his stall. However, $1,000 of the $5,000 added money purse went to the second horse, so there was some balm in the defeat for his owner.

A crowd of 10,000 persons was on hand for the final Saturday of racing at the Queens County Jockey Club course, but it found nothing to be enthusiastic about in the competition. Besides the two horse race in the feature there was a walkover for J. E. Widener in the steeplechase and the four remaining contests were also damaged by scratches.

With Brainstorm and Athelstan out of the way Little Chief had only to gallop to take down the $5,450 which went to the winner of the featured contest. Sande, who was in the saddle, took a tight hold on the Rancocas colt when the barrier lifted and rated him behind the other horse until the stretch turn was passed, then he let out a wrap and his mount came away to win cantering by four lengths. Naturally, the winner was an overwhelming favorite. From the time the scratches went up on the board it was only a question of by how much Sande would let the Wrack colt win.

The Rancocas Stable and Sande made it a double for the afternoon when they put Sheridan over in The Belle Harbor, a six-furlong dash for two-year olds which closed the program. This was also a hollow victory in which the green and white silks, borne by both Sheridan and Eaglet, were greatly favored. The winner had a margin of three lengths at the judges' stand while Eaglet was just a length back of Bonaparte for the place.

There was nothing at stake in the Queensboro Steeplechase, second on the card, for F. S. von Stade's Domingo, the only entry outside the Widener Stable, was scratched. The crowd did not take kindly to this lack of competition and each time the two horses came past the grandstand during their two and one-half mile journey there was a chorus of boohs and derisive cheering. Withal, it was a pretty and well-run race, with Grenadier a half-length winner over his stable mate Houdini. The time, 5:30, was slow. On account of the race being a walk-over the first and second money was cut in half, the value to the first horse being $1,525 and to the second $350.

The summaries:

FIRST RACE.

For three-year-olds and upward; claiming; purse $1,000; six and a half furlongs.

Horse.	Wt.	Jockey.	Odds.	Fin.
Runviso	108	L. Fator	9-5	1[1]
Poe	108	Schuttinger	2-2	2[h]
Mutiny	113	Kummer	18-5	3[h]
Hyperion	113	Collins	10-1	4[1½]
Wilton Flanna	98	Milner	2,500-1	5

Place and show—Runviso, 3-5, 1-5; Poe, 1-2, 1-6; Mutiny, 6-5, 1-3.
Time—1:18 2-5.

Start good; won ridden out; place driving. Runviso, ch. c., 3, by Runnymede—Mieco; owned by the Oak Ridge Stable and trained by J. Loftus.

SECOND RACE.

The Queensboro Steeplechase Handicap; purse $3,500 added; about two and a half miles.

Horse.	Wt.	Jockey.	Odds.	Fin.
*Grenadier	145	Byers	..	1[½]
*Houdini	135	Jones	..	2

*J. E. Widener entry.
Time—5:30.

Start good; won galloping. Grenadier, b. g., 5, by Fair Play—Mission; owned by J. E. Widener and trained by J. H. Lewis.

THIRD RACE.

For maiden two-year-olds; claiming; purse $1,000; five furlongs.

Horse.	Wt.	Jockey.	Odds.	Fin.
Deputy	107	Hernandez	6-1	1[1]
The Reaper	104	Stutts	11-5	2[1]
Belcross	107	Accardy	8-1	3[1]
Fausto	114	Rice	50-1	4[½]
Kerry Girl	107	Fator	15-1	5[½]
Blue Miss	104	Thurber	12-1	6[1]
AggravatingPapa	110	Legere	10-1	7[1]
Ebony Belle	109	Carroll	2½-1	8[1]
Spontaneous	104½	Collins	20-1	9[2]
Star Man	107	Wa off	20-1	10[2]
Moon Dream	104	Matthews	100-1	11[11]
Blend	111	McTaggart	100-1	12

Place and show—Deputy, 2½-1, 6-5; The Reaper, 4-5, 1-3; Belcross, 3-1, 8-5.
Time—0:59 4-5.

Start good; won ridden out; place driving. Deputy, b. g., 2, by Ambassador IV.—Blue Ballot; owned by the Quincy Stable and trained by J. Fitzsimmons.

FOURTH RACE.

The Edgemere Handicap; for three-year-olds and upward; purse $5,000 added; one mile and an eighth.

Horse.	Wt.	Jockey.	Odds.	Fin.
Little Chief	124	Sande	1-30	1[4]
High Chief	96	Milner	25-1	2

Time—1:52 3-5.

Start good; won easily; place driving. Little Chief, b. c., 4, by Wrack—Medora II.; owned by the Rancocas Stable and trained by S. C. Hildreth.

FIFTH RACE.

For three-year-olds and upward; purse $1,000; one mile.

Horse.	Wt.	Jockey.	Odds.	Fin.
Red Legs	115	Legere	1-2	1[½]
Fusee	109	Accardy	9-5	2[4]
Rekab	117	Frey	20-1	3[10]
Cork Elm	103	Thurber	40-1	4

Place and show—Red Legs, out, out; Fusee, out, out; Rekab, 4-1, 2-5.
Time—1:40 3-5.

Start good; won ridden out; place driving. Red Legs, ch. g., 5, by Rock View—Starcadia; owned by J. A. Coburn and trained by G. W. Coburn.

SIXTH RACE.

The Belle Harbor; for two-year-olds; non-winners of $2,500; purse $1,000; six furlongs.

Horse.	Wt.	Jockey.	Odds.	Fin.
*Sheridan	110	Sande	4-5	1[3]
Bonaparte	119	Turner	11-5	2[1]
*Eaglet	110	L. Fator	4-5	3[h]
Sleepy Head	105	Thurber	20-1	4[4]
All in All	116	McTaggart	20-1	5[h]
Cano	113	Kummer	5-1	6

*Rancocas Stable entry.
Place and show—Sheridan, 1-6, out; Bonaparte, 1-2, out; Eaglet, 1-6, out.
Time—1:12 3-5.

Start good; won easily; place driving. Sheridan, br. c., 2, by Sweep—Iridescence; owned by the Rancocas Stable and trained by S. C. Hildreth.

Weather clear, track fast.

HAVRE DE GRACE RESULTS.

FIRST RACE—For two-year-olds; claiming; purse $1,300; five and one-half furlongs. Donaghee, 112 pounds (Marinelli), $6.80, $5.20, $3.30, first; Byron, 103 (Lee), $20.50, $7.70, second; Fredericktown, 100 (McAtee), $3.20, third. Time—1:06 3-5. Snow Maiden, Gay Ben, Anna Horton, Bramton, Elsbeth, Idle Thoughts and Wrackhorn also ran.

SECOND RACE—For two-year-olds and upward; claiming; purse $1,300; six furlongs. Wellfinder, 111 pounds (Thorndike), $7.90, $3, $2.80, first; Mainmast, 121 (Marinelli), $3, $2.60, second; May Blossom, 112 (McLane), $4.80, third. Time—1:12 4-5. Leatherwood, Reprisal, Glentilt and Salt Peter also ran.

THIRD RACE—For three-year-olds and upward; claiming; purse $1,300; one mile and one-sixteenth. Trevelyan, 108 pounds (Corcoran), $5.60, $4.80, $3.80, first; Yoshimi, 112 (Bonham), $22.80, $12.40, second; Hobey Baker, 111 (Marinelli), $4.80, third. Time—1:46 2-5. Valentia, Commie Cl, Flint, Coscorron, May Roberts, Bar Coy, Cote d'Or, Tingling, Hickory and On High also ran.

FOURTH RACE—For three-year-olds and upward; claiming; purse $1,300; one mile and one-sixteenth. Buddie Keen, 111 pounds (Costello), $13.80, $7.30, $3.80, first; Bendita, 102 (Kessner), $15.10, $6.70, second; Ticacey, 113 (Marinelli), $2.70, third. Time—1:46 4-5. South Breeze, The Foreigner, Bonfire, Cordelier and Avalanche also ran.

FIFTH RACE—For three-year-olds and upward; The Havre de Grace Handicap; $10,000 added; one mile and one-eighth. Enchantment, 118 pounds (McAtee), $3.50, $3.20, $2.40, first; Exodus, 109 (Corcoran), $7.40, $3.90, second; Vigil, 107 (Marinelli), $3.20, third. Time—1:50 4-5. Ten Minutes, Blazes and Dunlin also ran.

SIXTH RACE—For three-year-olds and upward; The Fade Out Claiming Handicap; purse $1,600; one mile and seventy yards. Forest Love, 103 pounds (Marinelli), $10.20, $4.10, $3, first; Lady Myrz, 95 (Callahan), $6.30, $3.90, second; Faith, 98 (Chalmers), $4.80, third. Time—1:42 3-5. Thimble and Wrangle also ran.

SEVENTH RACE—For three-year-olds and upward; claiming; purse $1,300; one mile and one-sixteenth. Advocate, 105 pounds (Roach), $21.30, $8.30, $3.90, first; Pastoral Swain, 113 (Babin), $3.70, $3.20, second; Night Raider, 103 (Lee), $6.60, third. Time—1:45 1-5. Royal Duck, Bellsolar, Bastille, King John and Poor Sport also ran.

Weather clear, track fast.

HURLINGHAM BEATS SHELBURNE, 15 TO 7

British Team Reaches Final in Polo Series for Monty Waterbury Cup.

MEADOW BROOK ADVANCES

Defeats Orange County, 9 to 7, and Will Meet the Foreign Stars Tomorrow.

As a result of yesterday's polo games at the Meadow Brook Club, Westbury, L. I., the Hurlingham four of England and the Meadow Brook Club of this country, the two leading polo organizations of the two nations, will meet in the final for the Monty Waterbury Cup. Meadow Brook defeated the Orange County horsemen, 9 to 7, on International Field, in the first game, and Hurlingham eliminated Tommy Hitchcock's Shelburne riders, winners of the trophy last year, on Cochran Field in the second contest, by the convincing score of 15 to 7.

Hurlingham's victory came somewhat as a surprise, as the team in its previous performances in this country this year has shown nothing of the power exhibited yesterday. Captain Frederick E. Guest at No. 1 and Earle W. Hopping at No. 2 for the British combination rode around, through and past the Shelburne defense practically at will, despite the fact that the great Tommy Hitchcock, international star, was at back for the losers. Guest scored seven times, while Hopping contributed four more to his team's total.

In the meantime only Hitchcock was able to penetrate the goal so well guarded by the Marquis of Cholmondeley with any consistency. He galloped up from his position at the other end of the field and, with brilliant attacks single-handed, amassed four goals for Shelburne. His teammates were of little assistance, C. P. Beadleston counting twice and Howard Phipps once, for Shelburne's total of seven goals.

Invaders Receive Two Points.

The Hurlingham four carried an aggregate handicap of 23, while Shelburne totaled 25, so the invading four received two points at the start of the contest. However, the Hurlingham soon demonstrated that this allowance was entirely unnecessary, for in the first period Hopping scored on a clever drive from a hazardous angle and Major F. W. Barrett, who was at No. 3 for the British four, added another before Shelburne could even threaten. Before the period ended, Beadleston took a pass from Stephen Sanford and registered, bringing the score to 4-1.

In the second chukker Hopping again broke loose and swept down the field with long, accurate strokes to add to Hurlingham's count. Phipps and Hitchcock each scored in this frame, but Shelburne was unable to gain on its opponents, as Hopping registered again before the bell. Still Shelburne trailed by three points.

In the third period, however, Cholmondeley and Guest came into action, each scoring, while the former held the Shelburne riders completely in check. When Hitchcock's goal in the fourth chukker was equaled by another by Guest, the half ended with the British representatives well in the lead, 9 to 4.

Hitchcock brought all his daring forward at the start of the second half, deserting his post to dash up the field, carrying the ball straight toward its [illegible], sharp drives, and sending it between the posts twice; but his [illegible] efforts were useless, for Guest [illegible] a free road when he secured the ball a short time before the period ended, and sent it home.

Beadleston added one more to Shelburne's total in the sixth period, but that proved to be the last for the Americans. Guest then started a drive that was uncheckable, scoring four times in the last three periods, while Hopping rode off the opposition to make the way clear for his teammate.

Score Tied at Three Goals.

The Meadow Brook four caught the Orange County combination, which started with a three-goal handicap, in the second period, but they did not stay on equal terms for long. Webb was the first to register. In the opening chukker he dribbled through the entire Orange County defense and in the second he outraced Stevenson in a brilliant dash down the field, sending the ball hurtling through the posts from a difficult angle. Smith was the next to count, receiving a pass from Webb and tying the score at 3 to 3.

The brilliant defense of Milburn had kept the Orange County team from adding to its handicap up to this point, but suddenly it started a rally that resulted in two successive goals by Heckscher and the period ended with Orange County still leading by two points.

A foul by Strawbridge gave Meadow Brook a free try from the sixty-yard line at the opening of the third period, and Milburn's powerful drive cleared the upraised mallets of the Orange horsemen by several feet, going squarely between the posts. The brilliant mallet work of Strawbridge kept the play in Meadow Brook's territory for the greater part of the rest of the period, but as the bell rang Milburn finally broke loose and carried the ball the length of the field, tying the score again 5 to 5.

Milburn sent Meadow Brook in the lead for the first time in the fourth period, scoring his third successive goal with a strong, accurate drive from the offside which carried a distance of seventy-five yards before entering the posts. Steady work by Milburn and Webb for Meadow Brook and Strawbridge for Orange County prevented further scoring in the half, which ended 6 to 5, in favor of Meadow Brook.

But even the strong right arm of Strawbridge could not withstand the assault of the famous international pair, Milburn and Webb. In the fifth period Webb and Penn Smith added two more goals to the Meadow Brook score. At the start of the sixth Webb added another, putting his team safely ahead, for they were never again caught by Orange County, and when the final gong rang led at 9 to 7.

Hurlingham and Meadow Brook will meet in the final contest for the Monty Waterbury Cup on International Field tomorrow.

The line-up:

HURLINGHAM (15).	SHELBURNE (7).
1—Capt. F. E. Guest	1—Stephen Sanford
2—E. W. Hopping	2—C. P. Beadleston
3—Maj. F. W. Barrett	3—H. C. Phipps
Back—Marquis of Cholmondeley	Back—Thos. Hitchcock Jr.

Goals—Hurlingham: Guest 7, Hopping 4, Barrett 1, Marquis of Cholmondeley 1, by handicap 2. Shelburne: Beadleston 2, Phipps 1, Hitchcock 4.

Referee—J. C. Cooley. Time of periods—7½ minutes.

MEADOW BROOK (9).	ORANGE COUNTY (7).
1—R. Penn Smith	1—G. M. Heckscher
2—J. Watson Webb	2—R. Belmont
3—F. S. von Stade	3—M. Stevenson
Back—Devereux Milburn	Back—R. E. Strawbridge Jr.

Goals—Meadow Brook: Smith 2, Webb 4, Milburn 3. Orange County: Heckscher 3, Stevenson 1, by handicap 3.

Referee—Major Vivien Lockett. Time of periods—7½ minutes.

RUMSON FOUR DEFEATED.

Fail to Overcome Whippany River's Handicap and Lose, 10-8.

Special to The New York Times.

MORRISTOWN, N. J., Sept. 29.—The Whippany River polo team, aided by a three-goal handicap, defeated the Rumson four here today by a score of 10 to 8. The game was fast and cleanly played throughout, Rumson outscoring the victors, eight holes to seven, but failing to overcome the handicap.

Burden playing at No. 2 starred for the Rumson team with four goals, while Albright, at No. 2, and Grainiff, at back, played best for the victors.

HARTZ WINS AUTO RACE.

Captures San Joaquin Valley 150-Mile Classic in 1:26:50.

FRESNO, Cal., Sept. 29.—Harry Hartz won the annual 150-mile speed classic of the San Joaquin Valley from a fast field today in one hour, 26 minutes, 50 seconds. His average of 103.65 miles an hour was a shade behind Bennett Hill's 1922 track record of 103.70. Eddie Hearne was second. His time was 1:27.6 4-5. Jerry Wonderlich was third.

67,000 SEE ILLINOIS BEAT MICHIGAN, 39-14

Red Grange Makes Five of Six Touchdowns Registered by Victors at Urbana.

SCORES ON FIRST KICKOFF

Races 90 Yards and Crosses Goal Line in the First Ten Seconds of Play.

ALSO GOES 65, 55, 45 YARDS

Spectators Scream in Delight as Noted Athlete Tallies Four Times in First Quarter.

URBANA, Ill., Oct. 18 (Associated Press).—A flashing, red-haired youngster, running and dodging with the speed of a deer, gave 67,000 spectators jammed into the new $1,700,000 Illinois Memorial Stadium the thrill of their lives today, when Illinois vanquished Michigan, 39 to 14, in what probably will be the outstanding game of the 1924 gridiron season in the West.

Harold (Red) Grange, Illinois phenomenon, all-American halfback, who attained gridiron honors of the nation last season, was the dynamo that furnished the thrills. Grange doubled and redoubled his football glory in the most remarkable exhibition of running, dodging and passing seen on any gridiron in years—an txhibition that set the dumfounded spectators screaming with excitement.

Individually, Grange scored five of Illinois' six touchdowns in a manner that left no doubt as to his ability to break through the most perfect defense. He furnished one thrill after another. On the very first kick-off Grange scooped up the ball bounding toward him on the Illinois five-yard line and raced ninety yards through the Michigan eleven for a touchdown in less than ten seconds after the starting whistle blew.

Grange Plays Sensationally.

Before the Michigan team could recover from its shock, Grange had scored three more touchdowns in rapid succession, running sixty-five, fifty-five and forty-five yards, respectively, for his next three scores. Coach Zuppke took him out of the line-up before the first quarter ended. He returned later to heave several successful passes and score a fifth touchdown in the last half.

Michigan, bewildered by the catastrophe, unleashed a rain of forward passes, in an attempt to recoup, but most of them grounded when the receiver was covered by the Illinois defense.

Michigan was unable to stage a sustained rally and Illinois' lead was never in danger. This was largely due to the failure of the Wolverines to complete their passes, nine of their thirteen heaves being grounded and one intercepted. Michigan's three successful passes of the thirteen attempted were good for a total of 37 yards. Illinois completed five passes for a total of 70 yards, two others grounding.

Grange surpassed all of his former exploits in every department. He handled the ball twenty-one times, gained 402 yards and scored five touchdowns. Unbiased experts agree that his performance was among the greatest ever seen on an American gridiron.

Grange Again Surprises.

Running through a labyrinth of interference and tacklers, he crossed the field twice to gain the open on his first play. Britton made the point after touchdown. On the second kick-off, Grange received the ball and raced 10 yards before he was downed. Illinois lost the ball on downs but recovered by the same method on the 33-yard line. While the crowd was still breathless from cheering his first touchdown, Grange tore off 65 yards for a second, around right end.

A moment later, on the same play, he ran fifty-five yards for a touchdown and shortly after scored his fourth of the quarter from Michigan's 44-yard line. In each instance he started behind perfect interference and side-stepped Michigan's safety men in the final spring. He has a way of dodging, almost coming to a dead stop before whirling in another direction, that leaves his tacklers flat-footed and amazed.

The game was won and lost in the first thrill packed moment when Grange, extricating himself repeatedly from seemingly hopeless tangles of tacklers, crossed the goal line and permanently shook the Wolverine morale. The shock which his four touchdowns produced on the highly keyed Michigan team, dazed the Michigan crowd and team, and when the game was over many were still attempting to explain the defeat.

Steger scored Michigan's first touchdown in the second quarter after Britton's short punt had given Michigan the ball on Illinois's 25-yard line. Three drives at the line and a penalty for Illinois put the ball on the 15-yard line. Steger crashed off left tackle for the touchdown. Rockwell kicked goal.

Grange re-entered the game in the third period, and after an exchange of punts had given Illinois the ball, he passed 23 yards to Britton, who was downed on Michigan's 24-yard line. Leonard made six and Grange eight. On the next play Grange circled end for 10 yards and his final touchdown. Illinois obtained the ball on Michigan's territory shortly after the final quarter opened and Grange tossed the ball 23 yards to Leonard, who scored Illinois's final touchdown.

Michigan's opportunity for a rally came on the next kick-off, when an Illinois man clipped the kicker and the ball was given to Michigan on Illinois's 20-yard line. Steger gained 5 and Heath made it first down with 3 yards to go. Rockwell and Steger were held to 1-yard gains, but on the next play Rockwell smashed across for Michigan's final touchdown.

Encouraged by this Michigan threw passes to all sections of the field without avail, and the game ended with Michigan holding the ball on her own 20-yard line.

The line-up:

ILLINOIS (39).		MICHIGAN (14).
Rokusek	L.E.	Marion
C. A. Brown	L.T.	Babcock
Slimmer	L.G.	Slaughter
Roberts	C.	Brown
Roy Miller	R.G.	Steele
R. L. Hall	R.T.	Hawkins
Kassell	R.E.	Grube
H. A. Hall	Q.B.	Rockwell
Grange	L.H.B.	Steger
McIlwain	R.H.B.	Parker
Britton	F.B.	Miller

SCORE BY PERIODS.

Illinois	27	0	6	6—39
Michigan	0	7	0	7—14

Touchdowns—Grange (5), Leonard (substitute for McIlgain), Steger, Rockwell. Points afte. touchdowns—Britton (3), Rockwell (2).

Referee—C. J. Masker, Northwestern. Umpire—J. J. Schommer, Chicago. Linesman—N. E. Kearns, Depau. Field judge—J. M. Nichols, Oberlin. Time of periods—15 minutes.

Wide World Photos

Red Grange grabs ball after first kickoff of game with Michigan and gets away for 95-yard gain and a touchdown for Illinois.

United Press International

Harold "Red" Grange

SWARTHMORE A WINNER.

Defeats Ursinus, 13 to 6, in Hard Game at Collegeville.

Special to The New York Times.

COLLEGEVILLE, Pa., Oct. 18.—The Ursinus College football team was defeated by Swarthmore's eleven today in one of the most gruelling games ever witnessed on Patterson Field. The Garnet scored early in the first period after a series of end runs and forward passes. The score was 13 to 6.

FORDHAM WINS, 26-0, FROM ST. STEPHEN'S

Maroon Scores Easy Victory, While Its Own Goal Line Is Never in Danger.

WOERNER SCORES TWICE

Graham Also Notable Ground Gainer for Winners, Making Two Long Runs During Game.

Fordham won its third game of the season yesterday by beating St. Stephen's easily by a score of 26 to 0. It was Fordham's game throughout and the Maroon goal line was never in danger. Coach Gargan's defense did not permit the up-Staters to make a single first down, while the Fordham backs made enough points to insure a Maroon victory. The running of Graham and Woerner gave the visitors plenty of trouble, Woerner scoring twice and Graham once. Zakszewski made the other touchdown for the winners when he intercepted a forward pass and ran twenty-five yards for an easy score. Fordham was without the services of Manning and Leary.

Fordham threatened to march down the field after the initial kick-off, but the St. Stephen's defense forced them to kick. Bissel then blocked Noble's punt and Smead fell on the oval on the fifteen-yard line, but the Maroon was held on downs. After Noble kicked, Graham opened up the Fordham attack and resorted to an aerial game. Three successful passes put the Maroon in scoring position and Graham took it over the line for the seven-yard mark for the first score of the game. Graham also kicked the ball over for the seventh point.

St. Stephen's received the kick-off, but Graham intercepted a pass, giving the ball to Fordham. A series of kicks ended with the ball in the visitors possession, but Graham caught another enemy pass and ran thirty-five yards before being tackled. Another intercepted pass and a kick pushed the Maroon back to midfield, and the half ended with both sides engaged in a kicking game. This punting encounter continued, with Fordham getting the better half. Graham then changed tactics and took to a running attack. Zakszewski and Woerner made a first down and Graham gained thirty-five yards around left end. Woerner then shot through tackle and scored another touchdown.

Graham's forty-yard run-back of a punt once more threatened the visitors' goal posts, but they managed to hold the Maroon on downs. However, clever running by Graham and Woerner again brought the ball within scoring distance and Woerner took the ball around left end for a touchdown. Zakszewski intercepted a forward pass on the St. Stephen's twenty-five yard line and raced through a broken field for the final touchdown. Gargan put in the second team and the tilt ended with both elevens again in a kicking game.

The work of Deloria stood out for the losers, but he was able to do little with the Maroon tacklers. The St. Stephen's defense held well at times, stopping the Maroon attack several times when it looked as though they would score. They completed a few passes, but they were lateral and little ground was gained. On the attack they failed to move past midfield and only twice did they come out of their thirty-yard line.

The line-up:

FORDHAM (26).		ST. STEPHEN'S (0).
Stanford	L.E.	Rogen
Bissel	L.T.	Leupke
Bruce	L.G.	Smith
Brennen	C.	Urguhart
Smead	R.G.	Harvey
Bill	R.T.	Schlafly
Fitzgerald	R.E.	Harding
Graham	Q.B.	Noble
Delaney	L.H.B.	Kennedy
Slane	R.H.B.	Deloria
Malone	F.B.	Carlton

SCORE BY PERIODS.

Fordham	7	0	7	12—26
St. Stephens	0	0	0	0—0

Touchdowns—Woerner (2), Graham, Zakszewski. Points after touchdown—Graham (2).

Substitutions — Fordham: Stevenson for Brennen, Woerner for Delaney, Obester for Smead, Howley for Graham, Feaster for Bill, Buckley for Malone, Rose for Stevenson, Irwin for Bissel, Bissel for Fitzgerald, Simonetti for Bruce, Conroy for Stanford, Roberts for Fitzgerald. St. Stephens: McKean for Schafly, Murray for Kennedy, Kennedy for Schlafly, Murray for Carlton.

Referee—Bent, Trinity. Umpire—Hennessy, Brown. Linesman — Shearer, Dickinson. Time of periods—12 minutes.

YALE WINS AT SOCCER.

Beats Dartmouth, 3-0, in Opener of Season for Both Teams.

Special to The New York Times.

NEW HAVEN, Conn., Oct. 18.—Yale defeated Dartmouth at soccer football here today by 3 to 0. In the first half Hiram Bingham Jr., son of the Lieutenant Governor of Connecticut, kicked a short side goal for the only score previous to intermission.

In the second half Milliken kicked a goal, his effort covering twenty feet past Forrest, Dartmouth goal defender. Wyzga kicked the third goal.

The New York Times.

SUNDAY, SEPTEMBER 27, 1925. ***

SPORTS Section 9

COLUMBIA WARRIORS FLATTEN HAVERFORD

Tide of Touchdowns Sweeps Over Pennsylvanians, Who Lose by 59 to 0.

LONG RUNS THRILL 15,000

Pease, Madden and Norris Tear Off Big Gains in Impressive Victory.

VISITORS' LINE CRUMBLES

Smashes by Kirchmeyer and Sesit Break Defense in Opening Game at Baker Field.

By SEABURY LAWRENCE.

Showing all the power of a successful football team in the making, Columbia opened its season at Baker Field yesterday before 15,000 spectators by running roughshod over the Haverford eleven, defeating the lighter Pennsylvania team by 59 to 0. If comparisons can be made through last year's score against Haverford, then Columbia is about twice as good as she was in the opening clash last year, when the tally was 29 to 3.

After watching his strenuous young men crash through the Haverford line and romp around the ends until they had rolled up such a big score, Coach Crowley was encouraged last night in the belief that he is working with the groundwork of a winning eleven. Time and again the line of the Pennsylvanians crumbled before the fierce plunges of the Columbia backs, and Kirchmeyer, Pease, Madden and Sesit skirted the ends until the Haverford lads were dizzy and staggering.

There is undoubted power in the Columbia team, but its speed cannot be measured until the opposition is stronger and there is more of what might be termed "kick" to the game. On both defense and attack the Haverford eleven was practically helpless against the Blue and White players, so that the game did not give as much of a line on Columbia's future achievements as it might have. Beginning slowly, the Morningside eleven worked up to a fast pace with the entrance of Madden, Norris and Kaplan into the game, and in the second half was going strong in all departments. However, they were guilty of considerable fumbling early in the game.

Long Runs Thrill Fans.

The deer-like speed of Walter Koppisch was missing from the picture, but the flashing runs of Madden, Pease and Norris gave the spectators whatever thrills they absorbed from a contest so one-sided. It was a great day for the lookers-on, who basked in a placid Autumn sunshine, but not so good for the players, who got very steamed up after a few minutes of action on the green gridiron. The warm sunshine may have been one reason why Coach Crowley used so many substitutes. New men were running on the field every few minutes and it was almost impossible to keep track of the changes. At any rate, the head coach must have had a chance to get a look at every man in his squad.

The game was played in four periods, two of fifteen minutes and two of twelve minutes. After backing and filling in midfield, with the red and black sweatered Haverford line holding fairly well, Madden at right halfback, took the ball and flashed around the right end for a brilliant run of thirty-five yards and then went around the same way for twenty more. With the ball on Haverford's 10-yard line, Madden fumbled and Columbia lost the ball and probably a touchdown.

Haverford's attack crumbled against Columbia's strong line and they punted out. After some line plunging Kirchmeyer swirled around the right end for a run of twenty yards and the first score of the game. Sesit missed the kick.

Following this Captain Pease continued to work Kirchmeyer and the fullback kept on making gains through centre and added ten yards around the right end. He also fumbled a pass and Haverford recovered the ball. Haverford could not gain and when the period ended it was Columbia's ball on Haverford's 3-yard line.

Kirchmeyer Over the Line.

Columbia opened the second period at an increased pace. On a forward pass, Pease to Madden, there was a gain of ten yards. Another long pass followed but Pease could not hold it. The Columbia captain tried a place kick from the 40-yard line but it went wide. Haverford was thrown for a loss and on an off-tackle play Pease carried the ball to Haverford's 10-yard line. On two line plunges Kirchmeyer carried it over but Sesit again missed the goal.

The Blue and White team began to roll down the field easily and some substitutes went in, French understudying for Schimetitsch at centre, Williams going in for Raphael, Jaeger for Kirchmeyer and Shaw for Osnato. On a beautiful forward pass from Pease to Jaeger the ball landed on Haverford's 5-yard line and Madden took it over in two plunges, making the score 19-0, when Pease kicked the goal.

Columbia's third score of this period was made after Madden skirted left end for twenty-five yards and after some line plunges made the touchdown. Pease kicked the goal, making the score 26-0, as it stood at the end of the half.

After a 15-minute rest the teams ran out on the field again. Haverford kicked off and Columbia brought it back to her own 36-yard line. Madden gained six yards through the line and then five more the same way. Kirchmeyer had returned to the game and finally landed the ball on Haverford's 20-yard line. On a perfect forward pass Pease ran the remaining distance for a goal and the score stood 32-0.

Norris now went in for Kirchmeyer and the first thing he did was to put over a beautiful forward pass to Pease, who was downed on Haverford's 15-yard line. This was Norris's first play in major league football and it was a good one.

Norris Shows His Heels

On a fake pass Norris made a further gain and then Sesit tore through right tackle for a touchdown. Norris kicked the goal and the score stood Columbia 39, Haverford 0. Norris then came through with some good twisting runs and the quarter ended with the ball on Haverford's 7-yard line and their goal threatened again.

Columbia quickly worked the ball down the field after the fourth period started.

Continued on Page 3, This Section.

Wide World Photos.

Madden of Columbia Making Ten-Yard Gain Against Haverford at Baker Field Yesterday

Wall Street Commissioners Are Quoting 6 to 5 on Pittsburgh to Win World Series

Wall Street betting commissioners have made the Pittsburgh Club favorites over the Washington Club in the forthcoming World Series. Several sums of money have been placed with the various commissioners to bet at odds ranging from 11 to 10 to 12 to 10 that Pittsburgh will win the series. R. C. Fabb of 67 Exchange Place, said that he had $5,000 to wager at these odds. G. B. De Chadenedes & Co., 20 Broad Street, announced that they have $10,000 to bet on Pittsburgh at 6 to 5.

So far the greatest interest appears to be in the first game, according to J. S. Fried & Co. of 20 Broad Street. They reported yesterday that they had placed $6,000 to $5,000 on the Pirates to take the initial contest. At the end of the day they announced they had $12,000 still uncovered to be wagered against $10,000 that Pittsburgh will win the series.

W. L. Darnell & Co. of 44 Broad Street said that they had bet $6,000 to $5,000 on the Pirates to win the series from the Senators, and that they have placed $3,000 to $2,500 on the Pirates to capture the first game. The Darnell firm reported that most of the interest in the outcome of the series has come from Pittsburgh fans.

N.Y.U. BEATS NIAGARA IN 4TH PERIOD, 14-0

Connors Goes Around End and Briante Through Centre Near End of Close Contest.

10,000 WATCH TEAMS PLAY

Captain O'Neill Sits on Sideline, While Fay Calls Signals—Winners' Line Shows Strength.

A series of rallies in the last quarter of the game on Ohio Field gave the New York University eleven its initial victory over Niagara University yesterday by the score of 14 to 0. A record breaking opening game crowd of 10,000 marked the inauguration of a "new football régime" under Head Coach Meehan.

For three and a half quarters the game appeared as though it would end in a scoreless tie, with N. Y. U. on the aggressive. A series of end runs and centre plunging from midfield for the three first downs brought the ball to Niagara's eight-yard line, where Connors made a left-end run for the first touchdown. Fine forward passing between Kelly and Connors for the first scoring, and passing from Connors to Briante paved the way for the second touchdown, with the ball on Niagara's seven-yard line. Briante plunged through centre for the second touchdown.

Captain John O'Neill, because of injuries, watched the game from the side lines, while Fay took his place at quarterback. Connors starred for the Violet with his 50-yard punts and long, well-handled forward passes. Fay, Roselle and Briante played a stellar game, with big gains through centre and around end, which netted N. Y. U. its fourteen first downs. Bierling, Turner and Mullin starred for the up-State eleven.

The N. Y. U. line held strongly throughout the game, Niagara's gains being made by forward passes and punting. Both teams resorted to punting frequently.

N. Y. U. Wins the Toss.

New York University won the toss and elected to defend the south goal and receive the ball. Playing an offensive game, the Violet team rushed the ball down to its opponents' 25-yard line on the kick-off, but lost the ball on a fumble. Following this, Connors and Mullin engaged in a punting duel. Mullin tried for a placement kick from centre field but missed the goal by inches. With the ball on its 10-yard line, Niagara made a desperate attempt to get down the field but failed, and the quarter ended.

The second quarter was marked by several fine forwards from Connors to Kelly. With the ball on the Niagara 35-yard line, Connors's attempt at a goal went wild. At this point Niagara began to show some speed and made two long gains around end, aided by Bierling's fast footwork. On an exchange of punts both sides failed to gain and the half ended with the ball in possession of the Violet on its own 5-yard line.

Connors kicked off for N. Y. U., opening the second half. A number of fumbles lost considerable ground for the Heights eleven. Fay and Briante made three first downs through centre and around right end, but failed to take the ball to the posts as the quarter ended.

Perlman Recovers Fumble.

A recovered fumble by Perlman in the fourth quarter started a rally for the Meehan's charges. Following Briante's

Continued on Page 3, This Section.

FOLEY'S GREAT RUNS DOWN HOBART, 32-0

Syracuse Captain Goes 90 Yards on First Kick-Off for the Initial Touchdown.

COVERS 55 YARDS TWICE

Reynolds's Eleven Shows Speed and Ruggedness—10,000 Spectators See Game.

By ALLISON DANZIG.

Special to The New York Times.

SYRACUSE, N. Y., Sept. 26.—The first Syracuse football team under the new régime of Coach Pete Reynolds got away to a brilliant start today when Captain Jim Foley took the opening kick-off from Hobart and carried the ball ninety yards down the centre of the field behind strong interference for a touchdown. Before the afternoon was over Foley had made two other runs of fifty-five yards each, and Syracuse won the game at 32-0.

A point a minute was the goal the team set for itself and that was exactly what it made, for the periods in deference to the wishes of Hobart were cut down to eight minutes each instead of the customary fifteen. Last year Syracuse won at 35-0.

Ten thousand spectators gathered at Archbold Stadium to witness the inauguration of the season and to see what Reynolds had been able to accomplish in his first year as the successor of Chick Meehan. They saw a fast, rugged eleven, smartly directed by its brilliant captain, break loose with an attack that in its variety and spiritedness was superior to the initial showing of the 1924 machine.

Six first downs followed in rapid succession in the first quarter, five of which were made through the line and around the ends and the other through the air. The attack slowed down at times during the rest of the game, but there was evidence enough that in spite of the loss of McBride, Simmons and Bowman from the backfield, Waldorf and Starobin, a great pair of tackles, and Fivaz, centre, and Noble, end, Coach Reynolds has built a team worthy of the best traditions of Syracuse.

Co-Eds Cheer Lustily.

Syracuse goes in strong for atmosphere and there were fitting ceremonies to mark the opening of the 1925 season. Three girl cheer leaders, attired in orange sweaters and white skirts, brought forth vocal efforts from the co-eds to vie in power with those of the males, while a thousand schoolboys, admitted free, outdid every one else.

The university band of sixty pieces, headed by a color detail from the R. O. T. C., marched around the field, and players and spectators stood at attention as the national anthem was played. As usual, the campus cannon was on the field to boom out at every touchdown and the detonations were frequent during the afternoon.

Hobart was at no time able to cope with the heavier and more powerful Orange machine. In the first quarter the visitors did not have the ball until the last minute, when they received the kick following Syracuse's second touchdown. On two subsequent occasions Hobart was in possession of the ball in

Continued on Page 3, This Section.

25,000 SEE MARS BEAT CHANCE PLAY

Victor's 1:37 for Mile in the Junior Champion Believed Record for Two-Year-Olds.

FURIOUS DRIVE TO WIRE

But Man o' War Colt Leads by Half a Length at Aqueduct—Dazzler Takes Handicap.

By HENRY R. ILSLEY.

By running a mile in the remarkable time of 1:37 flat Walter M. Jeffords's two-year-old colt Mars captured the third running of the Junior Champion Stakes at the Aqueduct course yesterday afternoon, and it is believed that he covered the distance in as fast time as has ever been recorded for a two-year-old. It was only a second slower than the record for the course, established by H. P. Whitney's John P. Grier in 1921.

Mars, a 6-to-1 shot, won the race in a furious drive with the odds-on favorite, the Log Cabin Stud's Chance Play, getting up to score by half a length at the wire. Harry Richards, recently graduated from the apprentice ranks, had the mount on the son of Man o' War and Christmas Tree, which earned $[illegible]550 for his owner and breeder. He was saddled by T. A. Smith and carried 108 pounds, being in receipt of six and one-half pounds from the favorite.

A big half-holiday crowd turned out to witness the best card of the meeting, and 25,000 cheered Mars and Richards as the two came back to the scales. The weather was made to order and the spectators were rewarded by some thrilling finishes. It was a tough day for the players of form, only one favorite being first at the wire.

Only Three in Handicap.

The Aqueduct Handicap, another $5,000 stake, shared the honors of the afternoon with the Champion, but the latter held the public interest. Only three ran in the handicap, which was for three-year-olds and upward, at a mile and five sixteenths. It was the sixteenth running of the stake and the winner was the Greentree Stable's four-year-old colt Dazzler, by Whisk Broom II-Masda, ably ridden by Bernie Thompson, who became a full-fledged jockey through his fortieth victory.

Dazzler, carrying only ninety-eight pounds, was the outsider of the trio, held at 6 to 1. He ran the distance in

Continued on Page 5, This Section.

HARRIMAN'S FOUR WINS OPEN TITLE

Springs Surprise by Overcoming Milburn's Meadow Brook Team 11 Goals to 9.

SHOWS UNEXPECTED DASH

Orange County Quartet Comes From Behind Three Times, Thrilling 3,000 Spectators.

Special to The New York Times.

WESTBURY, L. I., Sept. 26.—W. Averell Harriman's Orange County polo team sprung a surprise today by winning the open championship on International Field here by defeating Devereux Milburn's vaunted Meadow Brook four, 11 goals to 9.

The victory of Orange County was scored in the fastest and most thrilling game of the tournament and saw the eventual victors come from behind three times before the Meadow Brook opposition was overcome. Harriman's four played a galloping game from the start and the scrimmages resulted in lost and battered helmets, dropped and broken mallets and some surpassing polo which brought repeated cheering from the 3,000 spectators.

By coming through victorious in the final this afternoon Orange County added a new name to the seven which have been recorded as winners of America's polo classic in the twenty-two years of its existence, and prevented Meadow Brook from adding another to its five previous triumphs.

The team which upset the favorite today consisted of Harriman, No. 1; J. Watson Webb, No. 2; Malcolm Stevenson, No. 3, and J. Cheever Cowdin, back. All of them played a brand of polo that was too much for Devereux Milburn and Thomas Hitchcock Jr., considered America's greatest internationalists, and C. V. Whitney and Elmer J. Boseke.

The weather was clear and cold when the eight riders rode out with Louis E. Stoddard and Lord Wodehouse officiating as umpire and referee, respectively. At the throw-in Meadow Brook got the jump and put its teamwork into play in one of the few opportunities offered during the contest.

Meadow Brook Scores First.

A quick passing of the ball from Milburn to Hitchcock resulted in the first score being chalked up for Meadow Brook before the game was two minutes

Continued on Page 5, This Section.

Results of Football Games Played Yesterday

East.

Columbia 59, Haverford 0.
N. Y. U. 14, Niagara 0.
Syracuse 32, Hobart 0.
Pennsylvania 32, Ursinus 0.
Cornell 80, Susquehanna 0.
Dartmouth 59, Norwich 0.
Brown 33, Rhode Island State 0.
Rutgers 19, Alfred 3.
Pittsburgh 28, Washington and Lee 0.
Penn State 14, Lebanon Valley 0.
Colgate 28, Canisius 0.
Holy Cross 41, Manhattan 0.
Washington and Jefferson 20, Geneva 12.
Lafayette 20, Muhlenberg 14.
West Virginia 18, Allegheny 0.
Bucknell 17, Western Maryland 0.
Williams 13, Hamilton 0.
Amherst 23, Rochester 6.
Connecticut Aggies 7, Wesleyan 3.
Union 68, St. Michaels 0.
Georgetown 25, Drexel 0.
Bowdoin 7, St. Stephens 6.
Lowell Textile 18, Bates 0.
Franklin and Marshall 15, Albright 0.
Maryland 13, Washington College 0.
George Washington 45, Blue Ridge 0.
Pennsylvania Military College 39, Prospect Park (Pa.) F. C. 0.
Gettysburg 40, St. John's (Md.) 0.
St. Lawrence 19, Upsala 0.
Vermont 7, Clarkson 0.
Syracuse Freshmen 51, Oswego H. S. 7.
Princeton Varsity 7, Princeton Second 0.
West Virginia Wesleyan 7, Waynesburg 0.
Main 33, Fort William 0.
Villanova 33, Loyola (Baltimore) 0.
East Stroudsburg Normal 59, Mining and Mechanical Institute 0.
Thiel 7, Broaddus 6.

West.

Notre Dame 41, Baylor 0.
Western Reserve 14, Toledo 0.
Oberlin 7, Albion 3.
Ohio Wesleyan 41, Capitol 0.
Wittenberg 13, Akron 3.
Case 15, Baldwin-Wallace 7.
Denison 0, Hillsdale 0.
Wooster 17, Ashland 0.
Detroit U. 26, Alma 0.
Michigan Aggies 16, Adrian 0.
Butler 28, Earlham 0.
Mount Vernon 13, Slippery Rock 0.
Muskingum 7, Rio Grande 0.
Western State Normal 20, Bowling Green 0.
Iowa State 28, Simpson 0.
Marquette 10, Loyola (Chicago) 0.
Carroll 73, Great Lakes Training 0.
Creighton 33, Midland 8.
Kansas Aggies 26, Emporia Normal 7.
Colorado College 6, Western State 0.
MacAlester 12, River Falls Normal 12.
Nebraska Normal 3, Colorado University 0.
Grinnell 27, Penn College 13.
Regis 14, Colorado Mines 0.

West

Haskell Institute 35, Fairmont 0.
Lombard 32, Mount Morris 0.
Dakota Wesleyan 7, South Dakota State 0.
St. Thomas 6, Upper Iowa 6.
St. Olaf 51, Luther Phalen 0.
Transylvania 21, Cincinnati 13.
North Dakota Aggies 47, Jamestown College 0.
Gustavus Adolphus 12, Bottineau A. C. 6.
South Dakota 45, Yankton 0.

Far West.

Southern California 74, Whittier 0.
California 28, Santa Clara 0.
Olympic Club 9, Stanford 0.
Washington 108, Willamette 0.
California (Southern Branch) 7, San Diego Teachers' 0.

South.

Virginia Mil. Inst. 46, Emory and Henry 0.
South Carolina 33, Erskine 0.
Davidson 7, Wofford 0.
Georgia 32, Mercer 0.
Alabama 53, Union 0.
Georgia Tech 13, Oglethorpe 7.
Virginia 40, Hampden Sidney 0.
Wake Forest 6, North Carolina 0.
William and Mary 44, Lenoir-Rhyne 0.
Virginia Poly 0, Roanoke 0.
Duke 36, Suffolk 0.
Citadel 7, Paris Island Marines 0.
Presbyterian College 14, Clemson 9.
Furman 27, Newberry 10.
Kentucky 13, Maryville 6.
Sewanee 14, Bryson 0.
University of Chattanooga 40, Jacksonville Normal 0.
Alabama Poly 26, Birmingham Southern 0.
Vanderbilt 27, Teachers' College 0.
Southwest Louisiana 17, Loyola (La.), 0.
Louisiana State 27, Louisiana Normal 0.
Tulane 77, Louisiana College 0.
Monmouth 12, Hedding 12.
Fort Benning 49, Stetson 7.
Southern Methodist 48, Texas Teachers' 0.
Texas Christian U. 31, East Texas Teachers' College 0.
Texas U. 33, Southwestern U. 0.
Southern Methodist 48, Denton Teachers' College 0.
Rice Institute 43, Stephen Austin Normal 0.
Simmons U. 35, Stewards U. 0.

Schools.

Blair Academy 13, Barringer H. S. 9.
Mercersburg 20, En Haut Club 0.
New York Military 26, St. Stephen's 6.
Mackenzie School 31, Port Jervis H. S. 0.
Harrisburg Tech 7, Mahoney City H. S. 0.
Lansdale Prep. 7, Colvert Hall 1.
Lawrenceville 6, Haverford Prep. 3.
Beckley 2, Lancaster H. S. 0.

British Golfers Oppose U. S. Ball, 5 to 1; One Who Supports It Is Called a Bolshevist

By Wireless to THE NEW YORK TIMES.

LONDON, Sept. 26.—Heated controversy has been provoked in British golf circles by the proposal to adopt as compulsory the new ball of American size for next year's championships. The question recently was debated at the annual meeting of the Royal and Ancient Association at St. Andrews, and golfers are described as astounded over the news.

A recent plebiscite taken on the proposal to change the balls in size and weight was defeated by the approximate majority of five to one. British golfers point out that the balls made by British manufacturers on the new American dimensions have lessened the driving power to the equivalent of about ten yards and are more difficult to control in the short game.

A. C. C. Roome, well-known British expert, who is among those sponsoring the adoption of the new ball, is likened to a "golf Bolshevist, anxious to spread confusion." Whence this sudden desire on the part of America for the limitation of the power of golf? asks one observer, who adds that it is true that everything America has introduced has been directed to make golf easier.

Another golf expert, writing in The Evening Star, has this biting comment to make: "A large majority of the leading American players use Dunlop and Silver King golf balls, both made in England. That, no doubt, is distasteful to the Middle West, which seems to exercise the same sinister influence on American golf opinion in regard to profit arising from recreation as it did on demanding its pound of flesh on the war loans."

PIRATE FANS GLUM AS GIANTS WIN TWO

25,000 Pittsburgh Boosters See Their New Champions Beaten by 4-3 and 3-0.

BARNES TAKES THE OPENER

Outhurls Aldridge in Bristling Duel, While Fitzsimmons Holds Rivals to 4 Hits.

By HARRY CROSS.

Special to The New York Times.

PITTSBURGH, Sept. 26.—Boosters' Day for the Pirates at Forbes Field this afternoon wasn't what one would exactly call a howling success. Some 25,000 fans came out to boost the new champion and saw the Giants boost the ball. The Giants took two games of the double-header and made a clean sweep of the series. What little consolation there was for the Giants, the New York players enjoyed their revenge.

The Giants took the first game, 4 to 3, when Zeke Barnes outpitched Vic Aldridge in a seething tossing duel. The Giants hit Victor only in the first two innings, but that was enough. The only damage done off Barnes was Earl Smith's two-bagger in the fourth, which sent over two runs.

Aldridge is regarded here as the Pirates' best bet to pitch the first game of the world's series against Washington. He had up to today won nine games straight and wanted to make it ten.

Fred Fitzsimmons completely outhurled Johnny Morrison in the second game, which went to the Giants, 3 to 0. He gave the Buccaneers only four hits. New York bunched hits on Morrison in the seventh and eighth and inserted them just where they would do the most good.

Sad Day for Boosters.

It was not a joyful occasion for the Pirate fans to see their champions spanked by the arrogant Giants. The boosters came in droves and made plenty of noise before the first game. They had a brass band and distributed jazz tunes all over the pleasant Oakland district, where Forbes Field nestles near Schenley Park. Vendors walked through the stands dressed as real pirates, selling Pittsburgh's latest song, "The Peppy Pirates." No one had a chance to sing it today.

The great shock to the Pittsburghers was that their hero, Kiki Cuyler, failed to get a hit during the afternoon. He is the man they expect will thump the Senator pitchers out of the world title.

Glenn Wright at shortstop did some high and fancy fielding. Pie Traynor got a day off and Eddie Moore played third, while at second was a young Manhattanite named Lafayette Thompson, who used to play ball for George Washington High School up in the Dyckman section. He looks as if he was on the way to become quite a ball player.

The Giants were gayly familiar with the pitching of Vic Aldrich in the first inning of the opening tilt. After Young died at first Frisch singled to centre

Continued on Page 4, This Section.

N. Y. A. C. RELAY FOUR SETS WORLD RECORD

Goodwin, Scholz, Tierney, Marsters Smash 1⅞-Mile Medley Mark at Travers Island.

PAULEN BEATS HELFFRICH

Holland Star, in U. S. Debut, Wins Special 600—Payne Takes National 'Chase Title.

By JAMES P. DAWSON.

A crowd of 5,000 athletic fans saw athletic history made yesterday on the New York A. C. playground at Travers Island, where the Mercury Foot club conducted its 115th track and field meet. The large crowd thrilled to the sight of a fleet-footed New York A. C. relay quartet shattering the sixteen-year-old record of the Irish-American A. C. for the one and seven-eighths mile medley relay race; saw Adrian Paulen, Holland's great middle-distance runner, score a spectacular victory in his first American competitive effort, and cheered Russell Payne, stout-hearted, strong-limbed distance runner of the Illinois A. C. of Chicago, on the road to victory in an exciting two-mile steeplechase event for the Amateur Athletic Union's national championship.

The outstanding event was the sensational running of the four Mercury Foot standard bearers, Willie Goodwin, Jackson V. Scholz, Joe Tierney and George Marsters, in the record-breaking medley relay. Running in this order, the quartet sped to victory over a second New York A. C. team and a Loughlin Lyceum four in a handicap medley, in the unprecedented time of 7 minutes 25 4-5 seconds. The performance eclipsed the long-standing record of the old Irish-American A. C. team by 18 3-5 seconds, casting into the discard the mark of 7 minutes 44 2-5 seconds, made at Boston by Jimmy Archer, Jim Rosenberger, Abel Kiviat and Joe Bromilow.

Tierney Runs 0:47 1-5 Quarter.

The record came after one of the most consistent relay races ever run here. Goodwin, the lead-off man, started with a cracking mile leg in 4:21 3-5 and this performance was matched by the furlong leg of Scholz, who sprinted the 220 yards in 22 seconds flat. Then Tierney took the baton and sped over the quarter-mile leg in the remarkable time of 47 1-5 seconds and to round out the race Marsters, with the chance for a record urging and the cheers of the crowd driving him, raced over the closing half-mile leg in 1:55.

Paulen's triumph was well-earned. Opposed by the great Alan B. Helffrich, Marsters and Johnny Holden, in a special 600-yard scratch race, Paulen came through to victory in one of the most thrilling finishes seen here in recent years. He broke the tape a yard and a half ahead of Helffrich and covered the 600 yards in 1:12 4-5. Marsters closed strongly and managed to wrest third position from Holden.

For the entire race until the field hit the stretch, Paulen followed the pace. He was off fourth and last when Helffrich dashed to the front, moved into third position rounding the first turn and after three-quarters of a lap was second. Then on the backstretch of the last lap Holden sprinted with Marsters, and together they passed the

Continued on Page 7, This Section.

HAGEN WINS, 6 AND 5; RETAINS P. G. A. TITLE

Beats Mehlhorn After Great Battle in Chicago and Is Over Par Only Once.

HAS A 67 IN THE MORNING

But Rival Comes Home in Par 70 and Is Just 3 Down After Brilliant Playing.

VICTOR THEN TURNS IN 33

And Is One Under 4s for the Last Four Holes—Chicagoan Has 34, but Fails to Take an Outgoing Hole.

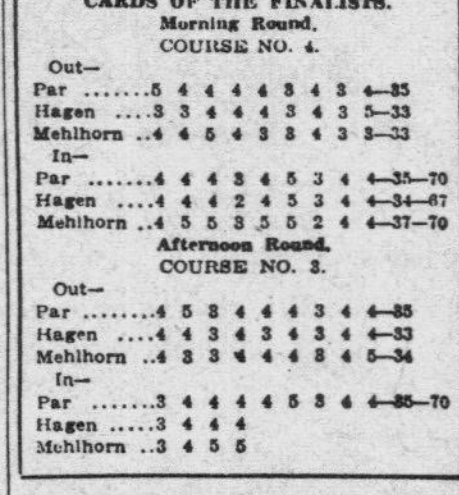

CARDS OF THE FINALISTS.

Morning Round.
COURSE NO. 4.

Out—										
Par	5	4	4	4	4	3	4	3	4	—35
Hagen	3	3	4	4	4	3	4	3	5	—33
Mehlhorn	4	4	5	4	3	3	4	3	3	—33
In—										
Par	4	4	4	3	4	5	3	4	4	—35—70
Hagen	4	4	4	2	4	5	3	4	4	—34—67
Mehlhorn	4	5	5	3	5	5	2	4	4	—37—70
Afternoon Round. COURSE NO. 3.										
Out—										
Par	4	5	3	4	4	4	3	4	4	—35
Hagen	4	4	3	4	3	4	3	4	4	—33
Mehlhorn	4	3	3	4	4	4	3	4	5	—34
In—										
Par	3	4	4	4	4	5	3	4	4	—35—70
Hagen	3	4	4	4						
Mehlhorn	3	4	5	5						

By WILLIAM D. RICHARDSON.

Special to The New York Times.

CHICAGO, Sept. 26.—Walter Hagen today terminated the greatest week of his golfing career by defeating William Mehlhorn of Chicago, former Western open champion, 6 up and 5 to play, in the final thirty-six hole round of the 1925 P. G. A. championship, played over the Olympia Fields links. By his victory Hagen continues his ownership of the professional golfers' trophy which he was defending and which he has now won three times since 1916, the year it was put up for competition.

Never in his life was Hagen more of a machine than he was against Mehlhorn this morning and again this afternoon. Only once in the thirty-one holes of play was he over par figures at any hole. In the morning round he was 67 against the par of 70, and he might even be conceded a 66, for he didn't hole out on the ninth green, where Mehlhorn sank a twenty-five foot putt for a birdie 3. He was again out in 33 on the No. 3 course in the afternoon and one under 4's for the four holes played after the turn.

Mehlhorn wasn't guilty of many errors, playing the No. 4 course in par during the morning round but finding himself 3 down just the same. He almost matched Hagen for the first eleven holes in the afternoon round, playing the first nine holes in 34, yet failing to take a single hole from Hagen's lead. He finally collapsed under the strain and permitted Hagen to capture two holes in a row with par figures. Rain, which had been threatening, came down hard as the last four holes were played.

Records of the Finalists.

In the course of the tourney Hagen defeated Al Watrous, Grand Rapids, 1 up, 39 holes, in the first round; Mike Brady, Winged Foot, 7 and 6, in the second round; Leo Diegel, Glen Oaks, 1 up, 40 holes, in the third round, and Harry Cooper, Dallas, Texas, 3 and 1, in the semi-final.

Mehlhorn defeated Emmett French, Youngstown, Ohio, 5 and 4, in the first round; Al Espinosa, Chicago, 1 up, in the second round; Tommy Kerrigan, Siwanoy, 7 and 6, in the third round, and Morte Dutra, Aberdeen, Washington, 8 and 6, in the semi-final.

In spite of what appears to be a crushing defeat, viewed solely from the final score, Mehlhorn fought a great battle today and lost a duel that no one in the world could have won. Not only was Hagen in one of his greatest scoring moods, with putts going into the hole from all angles and distances, with his mashie and mashie-niblick sending the ball soaring up close to the pin and his driver behaving the best it has all week, but he had almost every break in the luck. Time and again Mehlhorn had at least reasonable expectation of getting a win or a half when Hagen would kill his hope with some sort of a golfing miracle.

The deciding hole was the third in the afternoon round. Having just won the second with a 30-foot putt for an eagle 3, Mehlhorn reduced Hagen's lead to only two holes. His iron shot to the 235-yard third was a gem, a trifle past the hole, but apparently good for a win after Hagen had missed his tee shot, sending his ball through a trap and up on the fringe of a bunker, still far away from the green and from the pin. Hagen's next shot, a chip, was almost as bad, for he failed to reach the near edge of the green.

Hagen Gets 70-Footer.

Every one, Mehlhorn included, thought that it would be a win for the Middle Westerner, but instead of that the best he got was a half, for Hagen holed a putt that was fully 70 feet, and nearly 80, in length. Mehlhorn almost succeeded in dropping his down hill for a putt, but it curled off at the end of its journey and left him 2 down when he might have been only 1 down.

That stroke of fortune, good for Hagen, bad for Mehlhorn, settled the issue then and there. Had he succeeded in winning the hole, as he would have except for Hagen's miraculous putt, the outcome might have been different. It seemed to have tremendous effect on Mehlhorn's subsequent play. To him it must have been conclusive evidence that he was playing against an unbeatable foe. It gave Hagen the mental edge. It made the vast difference between being 2 up and 1 up. Had Mehlhorn won that hole he would have been a much more dangerous foe than he was after the hole was played.

Hagen practically clinched his victory two holes later when he pitched out of the rough to within a foot of the hole for a birdie 3. Mehlhorn, in a furrow on his tee shot, played a spectacular recovery to the green—a stroke that ordinarily would have been good for a half had it not been for the fact that Hagen's ball was snuggling so close to the pin. Hagen was again back to 3 up.

Impending disaster had been avoided and from there on he never once gave his opponent a chance to break through, except on the twelfth, where he sliced his tee shot. By then, however, Mehlhorn was at a point where it was im-

Continued on Page 3, This Section.

Hagen Triumphs Over Mehlhorn in Chicago by 6 and 5

Continued from Page 1, This Section.

possible for him to take advantage of any opening.

It is doubtful whether, for sheer golf, there ever has been a match that compared with this one over thirty-one holes. Hagen's start in the morning was one that would taken the heart out of almost any one, for he holed a thirty-foot putt for an eagle 3 on the first hole and a forty-footer for a birdie 3 on the second. That made him 2 up right off the tee and then Mehlhorn took three putts on the next green, presenting Hagen with an unearned hole, for Walter was short on his approach.

Mehlhorn's Takes Fifth Hole.

The first rift in Mehlhorn's clouds came at the fifth, where he holed a twelve-footer for a 3, reducing Hagen's lead to two holes. Hagen's first putting error came at the short sixth, where, with mud on his ball, he missed a one-yarder.

After winning the ninth and losing the eleventh through a badly hooked tee shot—his first one off the fairway—Mehlhorn had another glorious chance to get back to only 1 down playing to the twelfth. Here Walter's mashie was badly shanked, headed apparently for the rough. Instead of hitting the bank of the green and bouncing off to the right, however, it hit a spectator squarely in the back and kicked on to the green, enabling him to get a good position which he did not deserve. Seeing that things were breaking so nicely for him, Hagen then pitched to within eight feet of the pin on the next hole, dropped the putt for a birdie 2, and was again 3 up.

It took Mehlhorn two holes to forget that incident and he lost one of them to become 4 down. He managed to get one of them back, but he finished the round 3 down when his golf didn't deserve that fate. After the fifth hole in the afternoon round he was generally struggling, forcing his game, and failing to get anywhere against the sort of golf that Hagen kept turning on against him.

The figures of the match showed that Hagen had four one-putt greens in the morning against five for Mehlhorn, but Hagen's were more opportune than Mehlhorn's. Mehlhorn was inside Hagen on six holes going out and Hagen inside Mehlhorn on six holes coming in. Hagen played the odd at six holes on the outgoing nine in the morning and at five holes coming in. Mehlhorn played the odd at one hole out and two holes in.

Hehlhorn was in the rough only, four times in the morning and in only one trap: Hagen was in the rough on three. In the afternoon Hagen and Mehlhorn each had three one-putt greens, but Mehlhorn had one three-putt green. Hagen was in the rought on four holes and Mehlhorn on six. Hagen played the odd after ten tee shots, Mehlhorn after only one. Hagen was inside on eight greens, Mehlhorn on five.

Walter Hagen Watching Leo Diegel

HOLE-BY-HOLE DETAIL OF FINAL IN PRO GOLF

Detailed Description Shows How Hagen Retained His Title by Defeating Mehlhorn.

Special to The New York Times.

CHICAGO, Sept. 26.—The hole-by-hole description of the final match in the P. G. A. championship between Walter Hagen and William Mehlhorn at Olympia Fields here today follows:

Morning Round.

COURSE NO. 4.

No. 1, 515 Yards, Par 5—Mehlhorn had the honor and hooked into the rough. Hagen was straight and a trifle ahead. Both used woods and reached the green, Mehlhorn playing a fine shot out of the long grass. Hagen, putting first, holed a putt from the back edge of the green for an eagle 3. It was fully 30 feet. Mehlhorn then missed his putt of 25 feet.

Hagen, 3; Mehlhorn, 4; Hagen, 1 up.

No. 2, 435 Yards, Par 4—Hagen went boldly and carried the trap on the right, but was in the rough just off the fairway. Hagen's second reached the green, but was 40 feet past the flag. Mehlhorn was weak with his mashie niblick, and five yards short of the green. He chipped up close for a 4, but Hagen again hit the hole with a putt that was in all the way. It was a birdie 3.

Hagen, 3; Mehlhorn, 4; Hagen, 2 up.

No. 3, 404 Yards, Par 4—Mehlhorn passed Hagen by five yards off the tee, and his shot was better placed, Hagen being to the right. Hagen's approach failed to reach the green. Mehlhorn was only a little better off, just on the near edge, a long way from the pin. Hagen's chip was three feet wide. Mehlhorn failed to hit his putt and left himself a five-foot putt, which he missed, Hagen holing for his third straight win.

Hagen, 4; Mehlhorn, 5; Hagen, 3 up.

No. 4, 367 Yards, Par 4—Both had good drives, Mehlhorn about five yards in front. Hagen's mashie-niblick was dead on the pin, but quite short. Mehlhorn had a fine chance to get well inside, but neglected to take it, his run-up being twenty feet short of the hole. Hagen's ball had mud on it, and, although it started for the right spot, it curled off to the right and stopped near the hole. Mehlhorn's putt hit Hagen's ball, nearly knocking it in.

Hagen, 4; Mehlhorn, 4; Hagen, 3 up.

No. 5, 350 Yards, Par 4—The drives were about even, Mehlhorn's a little better, for the opening of the green. Hagen played a fine approach to within eight feet of the pin. Mehlhorn's pitch was a trifle strong, about twelve feet past the hole. He then holed out for a birdie 3, after which Hagen missed.

Mehlhorn, 3; Hagen, 4; Hagen, 2 up.

No. 6, 150 Yards, Par 3—Mehlhorn played what looked like a great shot, five yards above the hole, but Hagen pitched to within three feet. Mehlhorn was strong with his putt, which ran four feet past. He holed, and then Hagen, with a clod of mud on his ball, generously missed the putt for a win.

Mehlhorn, 3; Hagen, 3; Hagen, 2 up.

No. 7, 400 Yards, Par 4—Mehlhorn passed Hagen by thirty yards off the tee, but there was little to choose between them after the second shots, Hagen being above the hole, Mehlhorn below it. Hagen was about twenty-five feet away and putted a couple of feet short. Mehlhorn's bid for a birdie 3 almost went in, the ball stopping on the lip of the cup. Hagen then holed for his half.

Mehlhorn, 4; Hagen, 4; Hagen, 2 up.

No. 8—180 Yards—Par 3—Mehlhorn was on the green, hole high to the right, forty-five feet away. Hagen was over the back edge in the short rough. Hagen had to play first and his chip nearly went in the hole, stopping a foot away. Mehlhorn putted two feet short, holed and conceded Hagen a half. It was a fine putt, most of it up-hill.

Mehlhorn, 3; Hagen, 3; Hagen, 2 up.

No. 9, 445 Yards, Par 4—Both caught the rough with their drives, it being the first time that Hagen had been off the course. He was worse off than Mehlhorn and missed the green with his second, his ball shooting into the short rough at the left. Mehlhorn got home, twenty-five feet short of the hole. Hagen's chip left him nearly five yards short. Then Mehlhorn putted in for a 3.

Mehlhorn, 3; Hagen, 5; Hagen, 1 up. Both had 33s out.

No. 10, 443 Yards, Par 4—Mehlhorn was on the right, again in front; Hagen on the left perilously near the rough. Both got the green with their seconds, Hagen about twenty feet above the hole, Mehlhorn twenty-five. Mehlhorn had a side-hill putt to make, but his ball stopped about eight inches short. Hagen also was short and the hole was halved.

Mehlhorn, 4; Hagen, 4; Hagen, 1 up.

No. 11, 365 Yards, Par 4—Mehlhorn pushed his drive into a trap—his first excursion into the sand. Hagen purposely played for the left and his ball landed in the fairway of the No. 8 hole. Melhorn had a fine recovery to about five feet off the short edge of the green. Hagen put his second in, thirty-five feet from the hole, and after Mehlhorn had chipped a yard short, Walter hit the cup and his ball hopped out. Mehlhorn then missed his putt, costing him the hole.

Hagen, 4; Mehlhorn, 5; Hagen, 2 up.

No. 12, 390 Yards, Par 4—Both had good drives, Hagen down the centre, Mehlhorn on the left. Hagen got a lucky break when he shanked his mashie shot, only to have his ball hit a spectator and bounce into the green. Otherwise it would have been in the rough. After Mehlhorn had pitched on, Hagen putted up to a foot from the lower edge of the green and Mehlhorn, twenty feet away, hit his ball on the approach putt.

Hagen, 4; Mehlhorn, 5; Hagen, 2 up.

No. 13, 125 Yards, Par 3—Hagen pitched to within eight feet of the hole. Mehlhorn was barely on the green, thirty feet to the left on the top of a mound. He chipped beyond the hole, but Hagen holed his putt for a birdie 2.

Hagen, 2; Mehlhorn, 3; Hagen, 3 up.

No. 14, 420 Yards, Par 4—Hagen, using an iron off the tee, barely got over the first water hazard. Mehlhorn tried to steer his drive and hooked it into the rough. After Hagen had almost reached the green with a brassie, Mehlhorn hit the branch of a tree and his ball dropped into the fairway. He was still a long way from the green, pushed a long iron into a cluster of trees, and was weak on his next, just on the edge in 4, while Hagen was just off in 2. Hagen chipped five feet past and then holed for a par 4, after Mehlhorn just missed his putt for a 5.

Hagen, 4; Mehlhorn, 6; Hagen, 4 up.

No. 15, 550 Yards, Par 5—Hagen's drive was down the middle, Mehlhorn's a rod on the right. Mehlhorn's second hit a tree and dropped in the rough, close to a tree. Hagen played a fine iron second, straight for the opening to the green. Mehlhorn had a great recovery to six yards. Hagen's twenty-foot putt stopped short and the hole was halved.

Hagen, 5; Mehlhorn, 5; Hagen, 4 up.

No. 16, 134 Yards, Par 3—Hagen's pitch was strong and on the back edge of the green. Mehlhorn played a beautiful massie-niblick to within a yard and sank the putt for a birdie after Hagen had pulled up close.

Mehlhorn, 2; Hagen, 3; Hagen, 3 up.

No. 17, 367 Yards, Par 4—Mehlhorn's drive skimmed the trees on the right. Hagen played off to the left and out in front. Neither got close to the pin on their second shots, Hagen being twenty feet to the right and Mehlhorn about three feet inside. Both putted up close and halved the hole.

Mehlhorn, 4; Hagen, 4; Hagen, 3 up.

No. 18, 445 Yards, Par 4—Mehlhorn had a tremendous drive, almost to the creek. Hagen was off to the right. Both fell short on their mashie pitches, just on the front edge of the green, fifteen yards from the pin. Hagen, after running a yard past the hole on his approach putt, holed it down hill and conceded Mehlhorn a putt of two feet or more that was missable.

Mehlhorn, 4; Hagen, 4; Hagen, 3 up. Hagen had a 67 for the round, Mehlhorn a 70.

Afternoon Round.

COURSE NO. 3.

No. 1, 345 Yards, Par 4—Mehlhorn started with a tremendous drive that almost reached the creek. It was nearly 300 yards long and Hagen's wallop, although 250 yards, looked amateurish beside it. Hagen's pitch was short, twenty yards from the hole. Mehlhorn's low running shot also was short by about twenty-five feet. Hagen's approach putt ran a yard past. Mehlhorn had to borrow on his putt and his ball slid past the hole. Hagen holed and picked up Mehlhorn's ball.

Mehlhorn 4, Hagen 4; Hagen 3 up.

No. 2, 516 yards, Par 5—Mehlhorn led Hagen by fully thirty yards from the tee and hit his second on two within thirty feet of the hole after Hagen had failed to reach the green. Hagen chipped up a yard past, his ball almost hitting the flagstick. Mehlhorn's putt ran right for the hole and dropped in for an eagle 3.

Mehlhorn 3, Hagen 4; Hagen 2 up.

No. 3, 335 Yard, Par 3—Mehlhorn reached the green and stopped twelve feet from the pin. Hagen missed his tee shot and his ball stopped on top of a bunker. His second was a feeble effort, but he then holed a putt of about eighty feet for a par 3. Mehlhorn almost sank his second but got only a half after deserving a win.

Mehlhorn 3, Hagen 3; Hagen 2 up.

No. 4, 440 Yards, Par 4—Hagen was back of Mehlhorn off the tee and played a safe approach that barely had legs to get to the green. Mehlhorn went boldly for the pin and his ball went over, stopping in the short rough, a yard off the green. Mehlhorn chipped back to within two inches, his ball almost going in. Hagen took no chances and played safe for a half.

Mehlhorn 4, Hagen 4; Hagen 2 up.

No. 5, 350 Yards, Par 4—Mehlhorn went too boldly for the direct line to the hole and was nearly out of bounds on the left and in a furrow. Hagen came out of the rough with a superb shot that landed on the short edge of the green and rolled up to within two feet of the hole. Mehlhorn played a fine recovery to twenty-five feet, but missed his putt for a 3. Hagen holed.

Hagen 3, Mehlhorn 4; Hagen 3 up.

No. 6—370 Yards—Par 4—Hagen sliced to the rouogh and Mehlhorn passed him by nearly fifty yards. Hagen had another great approach. His ball ran twenty¾five feet beyond. Mehlhorn played a bad approach and failed to get to the green. Mehlhorn played a fine run-up to within a foot, blocking Hagen's line. Walter had to sink a four-foot putt for his half after he ran by the hole on the first putt.

Hagen, 4; Mehlhorn, 4; Hagen, 3 up.

No. 7—163 Yards—Par 3—Hagen was short. Mehlhorn was hole high to the right, twenty feet away. Hagen putted wide, giving Mehlhorn an opening, but Willie failed to seize it, his putt stopping a yard short. Both holed out for pars.

Hagen, 3; Mehlhorn, 3. Hagen, 3 up.

No. 8—373 Yards—Par 4—Hagen was straight and Mehlhorn in the woods when he attempted to cut corners in the dog's leg. He made a miraculous recovoery, hooking a mashie-niblick around the trees to within eighteen feet of the hole. Hagen was also on to ten feet, but the hole was halved, although Mehlhorn nearly holed his putt.

Hagen, 4; Mehlhoron, 4; Hagen, 3 up.

No. 9—408 Yards—Par 4—Hagen was straight down the fairway. Mehlhorn sliced underneath a bush from where he could do nothing more than play out to the fairway. Hagen reached the green with his second, but was short, and Mehlhorn followed with a shot that left his ball above the hole. After Hagen putted past the hole by a few feet, Mehlhorn nearly dropped a fifteen-footer for a 4.

Hagen, 4; Mehlhorn, 5; Hagen, 4 up. Hagen out in 33, Mehlhorn 34.

No. 10—165 Yards—Par 3—Both were on at the right, about twenty feet from the hole, and took two putts from there.

Hagen, 3; Mehlhorn, 3; Hagen, 4 up.

No. 11—365 Yards—Par 4—Hagen drove down the middle. Mehlhorn almost reached the green, but chipped past by about twelve feet, while Hagen's pitch was only ten feet away. Neither could drop their putts, Hagen almost laying Mehlhorn a stymie when he missed.

Hagen, 4; Mehlhorm, 4; Hagen, 4 up.

No. 12—440 Yards—Par 4—Hagen was in the roouth with his drive, while Mehlhorn hit a screamer many yards ahead. Hagen was short on his approach, but Mehlhorn missed the green completely and lost the hoole when Hagen putted up close and got doown his putt for a 4, while Mehlhorn missed his.

Hagen, 4; Mehlhorn, 5. Hagen, 5 up.

No. 13—315 Yards—Par 4—Mehlhorn once more passed Hagen with his drive, his ball being just short of the green, but in the rough, while Hagen was nearly ninety yards from the green. Hagen's pitch stopped thirty feet below the hole. Mehlhorn's effort was almost as feeble. Hagen putted up close and Mehlhorn was seven feet short and then missed, giving Hagen the hole and the match.

Hagen, 4; Mehlhorn, 5; Hagen, 6 up and 5 to play.

HAGEN LEADS ALL IN TITLES CAPTURED

Has Won American and British Open Twice, as Well as a Great Many Others.

Special to The New York Times.

CHICAGO, Sept. 26.—Walter Hagen has won more championships and open tournaments than any other American golfer. His victory here today in the Professional Golfers' Association championship was the third time he has lifted this title. A fourth time he was beaten on the thirty-eighth green in the final by Gene Sarazen.

He repeated this year, as he won at French Lick Springs last year and thus established a record of ten straight match play victories in the event, five in each tournament. This duplicates the feat of Bobby Jones, who for two years straight has won the amateur championship.

Hagen has won the American open championship and the British open championship twice. He is the only American-born golfer who has ever succeeded in winning a major golf championship in Great Britain. He turned the trick at Sandwich and Hoylake and finished one stroke behind the winner at Troon.

He has won the French and the Belgian open, the North and South three times, the Western three times, the Metropolitan twice and a large number of sectional and other open tournaments, such as the Texas open, where the first prize was $1,500.

The professional champion was born in Rochester, N. Y., and learned his game at the Country Club of Rocnester, where he served as caddy, caddy-master, assistant professional and professional. His only other job as a club professional was at Oakland Hills, Detroit. For a number of years he has devoted his time to exhibition and tournament golf and to the Pasadena Golf and Country Club, St. Petersburg, Fla., of which organization he is President.

PRO HOCKY BODY COMPLETES LEAGUE

Approves Applications of New York and Pittsburgh at Meeting Here.

An eight-club international hockey circuit was completed yesterday at the meeting of the National Hockey League in the Biltmore Hotel with the approval of applications for membership in the league by teams of New York and Pittsburgh. With the favorable action on the applications of New York and Pittsburgh, an eight-club circuit with clubs in Montreal, Toronto, Hamilton, Ont.; Ottawa and Boston is to be completed: Montreal is to be represented by two teams, the Canadians and the Wanderers.

New York's games are to be played at the New Madison Square Garden, beginning Dec. 8. Purchase of the players of the Hamilton, Ont., club by local interests was announced by T. P. Gorman, manager of the Garden team, in the course of the meeting. It also was announced that the Pittsburgh club's games and the team's headquarters will be in Duquesne Gardens in Pittsburgh.

The players who are to make up the New York team were announced last night as follows:

Fordes, Randall, Langois, Spring, Roach, McKennon, Bouchard, the Green brothers and Captain Billy Burch, the latter said to have been purchased from the Hamilton, Ont., club by the New York franchise owners, for a sum in excess of $40,000. Twenty-one dates for the Garden have been alloted, but have not yet been finally settled upon.

RICHARD IS BEATEN BY DRIGGS, 6 AND 4

Engineers' Player Loses in the Final Round of Cherry Valley Golf Tourney.

Special to The New York Times.

GARDEN CITY, L. I., Sept. 26.—Playing at a pace much too fast for his opponent, Eddie Driggs of the home club won the invitation golf tournament at the Cherry Valley Club today by defeating Walter Richard of the Engineers, 6 up and 4 to play, in the final.

Earlier in the day Driggs had put an end to the aspirations of Neil Fulgerson of Belleclaire, while Richard unexpectedly won from "Laddie" McMahon of Sleepy Hollow after an up-hill match.

Against Driggs in the final Richard always played at a disadvantage. He lost the first hole when he topped his tee shot, and Driggs became 2 up after Richard pulled to the rough at the second hole. He made amends with a birdie at the next, dropping an eight-footer for his 3. A fine iron shot left Driggs on the green at the sixth, Richard having pulled to the rough and being still shy of the green in 2. Richard reduced his opponent's lead to 2 up by winning the eighth, Eddie having sliced to the ditch, but Driggs came right back with a birdie 4 to take the ninth, Richard again slicing to the rough.

Both made a mess of the tenth, which was halved in 6, and Driggs became 5 up at the twelfth, Richard taking three putts at the eleventh and twelfth. The Engnieers representative managed to prolong the match with a half at the next, but Eddie finished in a spectacular fashion with a birdie 3 to win the fourteenth.

The cards:

Driggs, out............4 4 4 5 4 4 3 5 4—37
Richard, out..........5 5 3 6 4 5 3 4 5—40
Driggs, in............6 4 4 5 3
Richard, in...........6 5 5 5 4

Eleven Holes Halved.

In the morning Driggs had played sixteen holes in two over 4s to beat Neil Fulkerson, who won only a single hole, the short fifteenth. Eleven were halved and the former Princeton man won four. Eddie clearly outplayed the younger golfer. Neil was forced to play the odd at almost every hole. Driggs's second shots were particularly good and this was also true of his approach shots.

In the other semi-final Richard and McMahon had an up and down match to the twelfth. There was never more than two holes' difference between the pair, with Richard in the lead or even practically all the way. Only three of the fifteen holes were halved, the others being won or lost.

McMahon in Trouble.

An approach dead to the pin at the fifth squared accounts for Laddie after he had been two down going to the fourth tee. A twenty-foot putt at the ninth for Richard left him turning for home 1 up. At the twelfth hole he increased his lead to 2 up by laying his approach dead from a distance of fifty yards for a birdie 4, and that was the turning point so far as Laddie was concerned.

At the thirteenth, fourteenth and fifteenth holes, Laddie was in trouble off the edge of the green and Richard won the fourteenth and fifteenth to end the match.

"All the News That's Fit to Print."

The New York Times.

THE WEATHER
Cloudy, with rising temperature, today; tomorrow, rain and warmer.
Temperature yesterday—Max., 29; min., 22.
For weather report see Page 21.

VOL. LXXV....No. 24,861. NEW YORK, WEDNESDAY, FEBRUARY 17, 1926. TWO CENTS In Greater New York | THREE CENTS Within 200 Miles | FOUR CENTS Elsewhere in the U. S.

CITY CROWDS CHEER ROOSEVELT HEROES IN ROUND OF HONORS

Rescuers Parade With Military Escort From Battery to City Hall Ceremony.

DECORATED BY THE MAYOR

Walker Says They Exemplified Spirit of New York When They Helped Fellow-Men.

GIVES MEDALS FOR VALOR

Throng After Throng Pays Honor to Seamen at Luncheon, Dinner and Theatre.

New York City paid homage yesterday to Captain George Fried and his gallant rescue crew of the steamship President Roosevelt, saviors of twenty-five seamen from the stricken British freighter Antinoe.

The city's formal tribute to their outstanding feat of American seamanship was paid by Mayor Walker. He awarded gold medals on behalf of the municipality to the Captain and the seventeen surviving men of the nineteen who manned the lifeboats in the four-day epic of rescue. Taps and the silence of the hundreds at the City Hall ceremonies were the honors to two sailors who died, Master-at-Arms Uno Witanen and Boatswain's Mate Ernest Heitman.

The informal recognition came from the mariners' fellow New Yorkers. Hundreds of thousands, scorning the bitter wind, walled Broadway to cheer and to applaud when the heroes paraded from the Battery to the City Hall. Additional thousands paused to cheer or to wave as the men were carried from the City Hall to a luncheon at the Advertising Club. Still more paid tribute at the Roosevelt, where the rescuers are lodged, or at the Winter Garden, where they were entertained last night.

Parade Up Broadway.

The parade up Broadway began at noon. The municipal boat Macom, with Grover Whalen and other members of the Mayor's Committee aboard, brought the rescuers from the Hoboken pier of the President Roosevelt to the Barge Office. Several thousand persons were in Battery Park when the heroes and their hosts arrived and they gave them a demonstration.

Escorted by a detachment of the Sixteenth Infantry, led by Colonel Stanley Ford, and by details of marines and sailors from the Navy Yard, the men went up Broadway. Captain Fried and Chief Officer Robert Miller walked ahead of their crew, with Rear Admiral C. P. Plunkett on one side and on the other Major Gen. Charles P. Summerall.

As the column filed into Broadway a roar of welcome went up from the persons massed on the sidewalks and from the spectators at every window. Flags and bunting rippled in the stiff breeze and "Welcome Home" pennants, resurrected by street peddlers from the era of returning war veterans, fluttered along the curbs. The sailors received a continuous ovation to the City Hall.

The plaza in front of the hall was jammed. More than 200 policemen were on duty, and busy maintaining lines. Snow heaped high directly across from the entrance to the City Hall was covered with spectators, giving the effect of an amphitheatre. Upon arrival, the soldiers and marines wheeled into place to form an honor guard, while Captain Fried and his men were escorted up the City Hall steps and to the Aldermanic Chamber.

Wives and Relatives There.

Mrs. Fried and Mrs. Miller and a number of relatives of the sailors had been taken to the Aldermanic Chamber earlier. They were seated in the front row, facing Hector Fuller, a member of the Mayor's Committee on Welcome who acted as master of ceremonies. The arrival of the rescuers outside the building had been signaled to those waiting in the Aldermanic Chamber by the burst of applause and cheering.

Mayor Walker, accompanied by a military escort from the Sixty-ninth Regiment and by Joseph V. McKee, President of the Board of Aldermen, and other city officers, entered in advance of the men of the President Roosevelt. A moment later Captain Fried led his company in, while a band in the gallery played "Hail to the Chief."

As each of the sailors came down to the dais Mayor Walker shook hands with him. The officers of the Roosevelt were placed with the Mayor and the members of the crew lined up to his right.

"Mr. Mayor," said Vice Chairman Whalen, "it is with difficulty that your committee has discharged its duty this morning because it found in these sea heroes most modest men. As a matter of fact, it was very difficult to find them on board the ship when your committee went to Hoboken this morning in order to bring them here to be officially received by you.

"However, we are here, and it is my great privilege to present to you Captain George Fried, Chief Officer Miller, Second Officer Sloan, Fourth Officer Upton and the rescue crew of the steamship President Roosevelt."

The spectators in the chamber broke in with applause and cheers. The band launched into "The Star-Spangled Banner."

The Mayor Speaks.

"With the observation of Mr. Whalen" said the Mayor, "about that modesty of yours and of your crew, which I know to be constitutional—in fact, innate—it is not my purpose this morning to make you any long address of welcome.

"You are a native of New York,

Continued on Page Nine.

Odds Quoted in Wall Street On Next New York Governor

Wall Street is showing interest at this early date as to who will be the next Governor of New York. W. L. Darnell & Co., betting commissioners, of 44 Broad Street issued yesterday a slate of the odds which they would lay against Democrats and Republicans who have been mentioned for the office.

The first figure after each of the following names is the odds which the commissioners are willing to lay that the person named will not be the next Governor:

REPUBLICAN.

Nicholas M. Butler, 3 to 1.
Ogden L. Mills, 4 to 1.
Frederick E. Crane, 5 to 1.
Arthur S. Tompkins, 5 to 1.
Nathaniel Elsberg, 7 to 1.
Albert Ottinger, 7 to 1.
Theodore Roosevelt, 7 to 1.
Emory H. Buckner, 10 to 1.

DEMOCRAT.

Alfred E. Smith, 9 to 5.
George V. McLaughlin, 3 to 1.
Mayor W. S. Hackett of Albany, 4 to 1.
Franklin D. Roosevelt, 5 to 1.
John V. McAvoy, 6 to 1.
Victor J. Dowling, 6 to 1.
Carl Sherman, 7 to 1.
George R. Lunn, 10 to 1.

VOTE $660,995,940 FOR ARMY AND NAVY

House Passes War Department Bill and Senate Adopts Naval Measure.

$34,000,000 FOR AVIATION

House Naval Committee Agrees on $100,000,000 More for 5-Year Air Service Program.

Special to The New York Times.

WASHINGTON, Feb. 16.—Congress today voted total appropriations of $660,995,940 for national defense. Of this amount $339,300,000 was carried in the army bill which was passed by the House, and $321,495,940 in the navy bill passed by the Senate.

The army bill included, among other items, an appropriation of $50,000,000 for rivers and harbors. Of the total allowed for the army, $15,236,000 was made available for the army service.

The naval bill, as approved by the Senate, authorized $18,900,000 for aviation construction and maintenance.

A five-year naval aviation building program to cost $100,000,000, at the rate of $20,000,000 a year, has been virtually agreed upon by the House Naval Committee. While the committee has not made any report, it is understood to favor the construction of two dirigibles, each three times the size of the Shenandoah; 1,000 new airplanes and an authorization for a metal-clad dirigible.

Senator Hale, Republican, of Maine, Chairman of the Senate Naval Committee, announced today that his committee disagreed with the House, which had voted to close the Lakehurst lighter-than-air naval station. The Senate committee recommended the restoration of Lakehurst, and this action was approved today by the Senate.

Fund for Lakehurst Urged.

"The House has approved the closing of the Lakehurst lighter-than-air naval station and has made a reduction of $417,000 in the amounts allowed by the budget for naval aviation," says the report of the Senate Naval Committee filed today.

"The approved budget estimates for maintaining Lakehurst were $775,000. The House has allowed $128,000 to maintain Lakehurst as a closed station. The closing of Lakehurst would make necessary the disbanding of the trained personnel there, which is the sole nucleus of rigid airship personnel in the United States.

"The Los Angeles, after six months of such limited preservation as these reduced funds will permit, will need a considerable overhauling before she can again be placed in serviceable condition. The helium repurification plant, the only one of its kind in the world, will be closed. The navy is charged with the development of rigid airships.

"Inasmuch as the question of lighter-than-air craft is now before a legislative committee of Congress it is felt that no action looking toward the closing of Lakehurst should be taken until a definite policy as to the further development and use of lighter-than-air craft is determined.

"Your committee therefore recommends the restoration of the appropri-

Continued on Page Ten.

LENGLEN IS WINNER OVER HELEN WILLS IN FURIOUS BATTLE

French Tennis Star Exhausted After 6-3, 8-6 Victory Over American Girl.

BAD RULING UPSETS LATTER

Probably Cost Her Set—Discouraged, She Lets Down From Brilliant Play.

GREAT OVATION TO VICTOR

She Is Buried Under Roses Before Throng—Faints After Doubles Triumph.

By FERDINAND TUOHY.

Special Cable to THE NEW YORK TIMES

CANNES, Feb. 16.—Some spectacles will remain forever, even in a newspaper man's mind. Such a one was that of Suzanne Lenglen, lying on a bed on the sixth floor of the Carlton Hotel here at noon today, directly after her grueling victory over Helen Wills, 6—3, 8—6, in a simple game of tennis, yet a game which made continents stand still, and was the most important sporting event of modern times exclusively in the hands of the fair sex.

A few minutes before I had left her enthroned in a flowery bower in the middle of the tennis court, like a Broadway favorite after a successful first night.

From a balcony high above the Mediterranean, I next glimpsed her being swept along a side street by a frantically cheering mob.

Then she lay before me in complete whiteness of coat and skirt, capped by her vivid, crimson face.

Quiet While Furore Rages.

Only Mme. Lenglen moved about the room, arranging gifts of dolls and flowers above the furore still arising from the street, as I asked Suzanne how she had won, and waited while she gasped back to breath and then broke into a torrent of French, openly, perhaps challengingly, as if to say "Now, for God's sake, will you English and Americans leave me alone for a moment and accept my supremacy, however much it may be getting boresome!"

In fact, I believe she said something very like that, though her first frantic thoughts were for her stricken father at Nice, while I fought with time to capture every notion, opinion, thought and reaction from the victor of Europe. Nor was Suzanne silent. She rebelled against being forced to play, maintained the champion's right to do what she pleases pleaded for tennis goodwill, explained away her indifferent display by her private worry and the public din during the match, developed praise for her rival, though somewhat grudgingly, and concluded on the defiant note that she, Suzanne, intended to improve "malgre tout" and to remain enthroned for many years more, with her racquet as her sceptre.

Gives Grudging Praise to Helen.

With difficulty I dragged from the prostrate girl such grim, little verbal bouquets as "Helen showed more intelligence than I imagined. She has style and production of strokes. She will improve."

Yet none of this—not even Helen's splendid drives and placings—worried Suzanne, according to Suzanne. A little more magnanimity might have issued from that white couch and its palpitating burden, and with little damage to the truth of the day, as most of those present saw it.

"Elle se defende, la petite," said a French spectator of our amazing courtside champion.

"What a game Helen is putting up!" echoed the serried Anglo-American brigade. "She'll have her yet."

Suzanne might have beckoned to the rising star more fervently without in any way weakening her own puissant case, since today she, too, played like a champion.

For many games in the memorable second set she fell steadily behind, yet she overhauled the challenger, to win fresher than Helen, and this afternoon the French girl gave one of the pluckiest performances ever seen on a tennis court when she was carried in a collapsing state to victory with Vlasto in the women's doubles over Hellen Wills and Contostavos.

She is to leave here later with her mother in an automobile for Nice. She is absolutely all in and is cancel-

Continued on Page Fifteen.

Paris Again Gaily Observes Mardi Gras; Lean 'Ox' Is Burned as High Costs Protest

By Wireless to THE NEW YORK TIMES.

PARIS, Feb. 16.—For the first time in many years Paris today observed with something of the old spirit the ancient feast of Mardi Gras. Not for eight years have students carried an ox through the boulevards, but this year there was a cynical strain in what has always been a joyous celebration, for a lean-faced ox of flimsy cardboard took the place of the fat ox, and the hungry looking replica was later solemnly burned atop Montmartre as a protest against the ever-mounting cost of living.

Despite this semi-serious aspect tens of thousands of Parisians lined the boulevards to watch the students and their girls march behind the pasteboard ox. Thousands of little children dressed in fancy costumes and masked added much color to the day, which for nearly everyone was a half-holiday.

For the students, however, it was a real occasion of protest, although to hear them sing, shout and dance through the boulevards one would not have gathered that the high cost of living was bothering them to any great extent. They assert, however, that boarding-house keepers grow more hard-hearted every month, and that unless something is done they will be forced to reduce their eating to one meal a day.

While there were signs that Paris had again taken up the lively observance of Mardi Gras, nothing like the mad gayety of pre-war Mardi Gras is ever expected again. In those days of cheap living a huge real ox was roasted in a public square and the whole city gave itself over to the spirit of the carnival.

Opposing Groups of Women Besiege Smith And Legislators in 48-Hour Bill Battle

Special to The New York Times.

ALBANY, Feb. 16.—With one group fighting for the measure and another opposing it, the Mastick-Shonk bill providing for a forty-eight hour working week for women and minors in industry has brought about one of the most spirited contests between women that the Capitol has seen in years.

Today a delegation of workers, led by Mrs. Mary A. Murray, Chairman of the Industrial Council of the National Woman's party, called on Governor Smith at the Executive Chamber to voice their protest against the measure. They presented a petition signed by 897 working women from all parts of the State.

"We are united in the opinion," said a statement issued by Mrs. Murray, "that if the Mastick-Shonk bill is passed and the law is enforced, the result will be that in a great many industries women will lose their jobs and be replaced by men.

"We wage-earners believe that to restrict by legislation the hours of the labor of women, but not those of men, perpetuates the idea that women are of a class apart in industry who are classed with children and who only are to be allowed to work at special hours, under special supervision, and subject to special governmental regulations."

Governer Smith, however, strongly favors a forty-eight-hour week for women and has recommended it in his message to the Legislature for several years past. While the bill now before the lawmakers is sponsored by Republicans, it is acceptable to the Governor.

Women favoring the bill made an intensive campaign among the members of the Assembly. They were led by Mary E. Dreier, Chairman of the joint legislative conference, representing fifteen organizations of women.

"It is a pleasure to remind you," read a letter which these women sent to Speaker McGinnies and the Republican Assemblymen, "as a Republican, that you are pledged by your party platform to favor enactment of a forty-eight-hour week for women in industry with suitable provision for safeguarding seasonable employment."

TWO WORLD FLIERS PLAN HOP TO POLE

Wade and Ogden Will Quit the Army to Lead Air Quest for Arctic Continent.

WILL START THIS SUMMER

University Alumni to Finance Flight—Hope to Beat Soviet Aviators.

Lieutenant Leigh Wade, one of the army round-the-world fliers, announced last night that he intended to resign from the army with Lieutenant H. H. Ogden, another round-the-world flier, to lead a polar expedition by air this Summer.

"I am going to resign from the army between now and March 2," said Lieutenant Wade at the Army and Navy Club. "My purpose is to take part in an Arctic expedition. I do not know whether Lieutenant Ogden has resigned or not, but I do know that his resignation has been sent in." An Associated Press dispatch from Washington said that Lieutenant Ogden already had resigned.

Lieutenant Wade denied that his resignation was influenced by the resignation of Brig. Gen. William Mitchell or that he would join the latter in a campaign for a unified air force, although he has been said to favor General Mitchell's ideas.

"I had intended to resign before the Mitchell case," he said. "I have no criticism to make of the service in any way. I am very sorry to leave the service. I like it very much, but I believe there is a better future, for me at least, outside the service."

Lieutenant Wade left last night for Providence, where he will deliver a lecture on his round-the-world flight. He will give a similar lecture at East Orange on Thursday evening and expects to continue his talks until the equipment for the polar flight is assembled and the party is ready to take off.

Another Flier May Quit.

Lieutenant Lowell Smith, who also made the round-the-world flight, was reported ready to resign also, but Lieutenant Wade said he knew nothing of Smith's plans.

In Washington it was said that Wade and Ogden wanted to resign because each had private employment in prospect, and this was confirmed by Lieutenant Wade as true of himself. He added that after the polar flight he would enter the employ of an electric light manufacturing company at New London, his home.

The polar expedition was conceived by Robert A. Pope, a Harvard graduate, during a five-year stay in the Arctic, according to a representative of the proposed expedition. It will probably be known as the All-American University Alumni Polar Exploration Expedition, because it would be backed, it was said, by alumni of Harvard, Yale, Princeton, University of Pennsylvania, Amherst and Dartmouth.

Mr. Pope, who is an engineer, returned from the Arctic about a year ago and at once began to interest influential persons in the project to claim the supposed polar continent for the United States.

Plans were hastened, it was said, when it was learned three weeks ago that Soviet Russia was forming an expedition of eight planes to look for the supposed continent and take it in the name of Soviet Russia for use as an air base.

Mr. Pope was said to feel that the possession of the continent, if there is one, by the United States would give this nation domination of the air in the Western Hemisphere.

Plans of Air Expedition.

Present plans call for the departure of the expedition from Seattle, Wash., on June 8. It is expected that the main base will be established at Point Barrow early in July. In the middle of that month a reconnoissance flight will be made by two of the planes.

If any sight of the supposed continent is discovered search will be made for a suitable base, and on the return of the planes the main expedition will move there. From this base an extensive survey will be made.

The main objective of the expedition, according to the representative, is to claim the supposed Arctic Continent for this country. A trip to the North Pole will undoubtedly be attempted, according to the representative, but

Continued on Page Three.

ANDRUS TO BEQUEATH HUGE SUM TO POOR

'Millionaire Straphanger' Plans to Use $50,000,000 for Home for Westchester Children.

CELEBRATES 85TH BIRTHDAY

His Institution to Provide for Hospital, Recreation Centre and Orphan Asylum.

John E. Andrus of Yonkers, known as the "multi-millionaire straphanger," whose wealth has been estimated at $100,000,000, selected yesterday, his eighty-fifth birthday, to announce that he would leave on his death 45 per cent. of his entire fortune in the form of a trust fund for the endowment of an institution for the poor children of Westchester County. When all of them shall have been taken care of, then the children of other parts of the State and the country also may enjoy similar benefits.

Numerous gifts have been made by Mr. Andrus, but this latest plan tops all his former philanthropic enterprises and will, necessarily, be his last. He was not quite clear, he said, regarding the exact nature of the proposed institution, and knew only that he wanted to leave something that would "help children who need help until they are able to help themselves."

Mr. Andrus's best idea of the nature of the institution he plans is something of a combination hospital, recreation centre and orphan asylum with educational facilities, but the details will be worked out later. The institution will be named for his wife.

Institution to Get Income.

His general plan, as announced yesterday, is to place the large sum, estimated now at perhaps close to $50,000,000, in trust for the proposed institution, to which, each year, the income will be given. He expects, however, that the institution will be able to reinvest part of the income, thus increasing the yield each year.

Mr. Andrus, all his life an economist, wants, he said, to be as sure as he can before he dies that the fund will be handled in a thoroughly businesslike manner so that there will be no waste. To find the proper persons to accomplish this is apparently his greatest worry at present.

In 1917 Mr. Andrus created the Surdna Foundation and in December of that year, when the incorporation papers for the foundation were drawn and approved, he said that his first benefaction under it would be homes for orphan children. To this purpose he said he was going to devote $2,500,000 and that he had 100 acres near Broadway in Hastings on which the homes were to be built.

The Surdna Foundation, which took its name from the reversed spelling of "Andrus," was modeled after the Rockefeller Foundation in its general plan and it was the stated purpose of its founder to make it a vehicle for many future gifts for the benefit of humanity.

Mr. Andrus is head of the Arlington Chemical Company in Yonkers and continues active in its affairs. He made his first dollar seventy-five years ago selling fish to Horace Greeley, he said.

Rode to Office in Subway.

He was for years a member of the House of Representatives and was also for a time Mayor of Yonkers. He became known as the "multi-millionaire straphanger," because he rode daily from his modest home in Yonkers to his downtown office on the subway and said he did so from preference.

Yesterday he celebrated his birthday chiefly by taking a little extra time for luncheon, because members of his family had arranged a small celebration for him at his Hudson Terrace home. There was a birthday cake and Mr. Andrus said he enjoyed it thoroughly.

His associates at the chemical plant said they were not at all surprised to see him at his desk as usual on his eighty-fifth birthday. He plunged into his work as usual, taking a few moments to glance at numerous messages of congratulation.

Just before going to his home for the birthday cake he received a delegation consisting of Mayor William A. Walsh of Yonkers and five former Mayors, who congratulated him. They gave him a big basket of flowers and he posed with them for photographers. He unhesitatingly bared his head at the photographers' request, although the picture was taken in the open and it was cold.

"I feel like a million dollars," he told

Continued on Page Five.

DAVIS MAY RULE COUNTESS CATHCART CAN BE ADMITTED

Consults on the "Semi-Legal" Aspect of the Case and Delays Decision.

AGITATION STIRS OFFICIALS

Possibility of New Interpretation of "Moral Turpitude" as Affecting Divorces.

WOMEN QUESTION CURRAN

Club Delegates in Interview Suggest He Resign—They Also Console the Countess.

Special to The New York Times.

WASHINGTON, Feb. 16.—The possibility that Countess Cathcart, detained at Ellis Island, may, after all, be admitted into the country developed this afternoon, when Secretary Davis, who himself came to this country as an immigrant child, reserved his decision on the case after taking it under advisement.

Secretary Davis spent some time this afternoon at the Department of Justice conferring with officials. On his return to the Department of Labor long after it had closed its offices for the day he was closeted in conference with Assistant Secretary of Labor Robe Carl White, Second Assistant Secretary W. W. Husband and Theodore Risley, Solicitor for the Department of Labor.

The Cathcart case has assumed great importance in the minds of officials of the Administration, and, because of its possible ramifications and consequences, is being handled with particular care. The department is not only aware that the question of what constitutes moral turpitude has been raised, if not altogether differently, at least in sharper lines than ever before, but also realizes that it cannot lightly ignore the protests of women leaders from all parts of the country against any discrimination against a woman that might be tantamount to setting up a "double standard" of morals in handling immigration cases.

If Other Nations Should Retaliate.

While officials insist that they are governed wholly by the law, as construed by certain court decisions to the effect that "adultery" does constitute "moral turpitude," they nevertheless recognize that if foreign nations should once retaliate against the United States, and enact similar laws, applicable to Americans going abroad, a most undesirable situation would be precipitated.

In a conference with newspaper men late this afternoon Mr. Davis asserted that a "certain semi-legal question" is "puzzling" him very much in his study of the record now before him. Before reaching a decision, the Secretary said, he wanted to feel wholly satisfied that he was right in his interpretation of the law, fully recognizing the fact that if the ruling was adverse to the Countess it would have a far-reaching effect in its application to others with the same status seeking admission.

On the other hand, should the decision be to admit the Countess, it would not only be possible for the Earl of Craven, for whom a warrant has been issued, to return, but the whole policy of the Immigration Bureau for two decades in "moral turpitude" cases would be upset.

Secretary's Attitude a Surprise.

Secretary Davis's somewhat cryptic reference to the certain "semi-legal" question that is greatly bothering him in his approach to final judgment in the case came as a surprise. Every indication is that the Board of Review has recommended deportation of the Countess, thereby taking the view of immigration officials who have handled "moral turpitude" cases so long that they possess what has come to be known in the Department of

Continued on Page Four.

Treasury So Sure on Tax Bill It Sends Out Blanks Now

WASHINGTON, Feb. 16 (AP).—The confidence of the Treasury that the Tax bill will be ironed out and passed finally by House and Senate and signed by the President before March 15, is shown in language, used in explanatory matter being sent to taxpayers in the smaller income divisions with the blank forms for their returns.

Distribution of these returns today disclosed that the Treasury was proceeding on the assumption that the taxes on 1925 incomes would be assessed under the provisions of the new law.

"The Revenue act of 1926 has now become a law," said the attached explanation, "and special attention is directed to the following changes in the instructions on this form which must be complied with in making out your return for the calendar year 1925."

PRESIDENT STUDIES NON-VOTING STOCKS

He Confers With Professor Ripley to Learn if Federal Action Is Advisable.

STATES HELD ACCOUNTABLE

Department of Justice Is to Determine Status of Class B Securities.

Special to The New York Times.

WASHINGTON, Feb. 16.—The Federal Government is now studying the question of the organization of enterprises which issue non-voting stock to the public and hold control through a small issue of voting or Class B stock.

President Coolidge is himself looking into the question and the Department of Justice is conducting an inquiry to determine whether interstate commerce laws have been violated.

These studies have reached no conclusion, but there is a probability that the Administration may recommend legislation to meet the alleged abuses, if such correction should be within the purview of the Government.

That he might get expert opinion on the subject, President Coolidge yesterday summoned Professor W. Z. Ripley, the Harvard economist, and discussed with him his articles and speeches upon the Class B and Class A stocks. Professor Ripley's criticism of the system before the American Academy of Political Science some months ago and in subsequent magazine articles, helped focus attention upon voteless stock operations and stirred the New York Stock Exchange to action.

Ripley Holds States Must Act.

Professor Ripley informed the President, it was said at the White House today, that there did not at the present time appear to him anything that the Federal Government could do to stop non-voting stock operations. Professor Ripley holds that a correction must come from the State Governments, as he has not seen any stock issue of this kind which would come under control of Federal laws. In other words, the Federal Government is powerless to act, it was said, until the concern issuing such stock was engaged in interstate commerce, such as a public utility, and even then there may be no opportunity to act.

The activity of the New York Stock Exchange, the Governors of which announced recently that "in the future the committee in considering applications for the listing of securities will give careful thought to the matter of voting control," is expected to influence the States in considering revision of laws chartering corporations.

Since the war scores of big enterprises have been formed on the Class B and Class A stock system. The Supreme Court of Illinois some weeks ago decided that no corporation char-

Continued on Page Six.

Gilpatric Tells How Giving Aid to the Young Caused Him to Embezzle Putnam Bank Funds

HARTFORD, Conn., Feb. 16 (AP).—The efforts of a banker to aid the young people of his home town to get a start in life accounted for some of the funds embezzled by G. Harold Gilpatric, former State Treasurer and former cashier of the wrecked First National Bank of Putnam, he admitted today.

Gilpatric, blinded by a bullet he fired into his head in an attempt at suicide in August, 1924, and now serving a fifteen-year sentence in Atlanta prison, is back in Connecticut to aid his creditors in unscrambling the financial tangle left by his frenzied effort in 1924 to find funds to stave off disgrace and imprisonment. It was at the first of a series of hearings, held before Referee in Bankruptcy Saul Berman here today, that the story of how he had aided Putnam's young men and women came to light.

Explaining notes found in his possession after the financial crash, Gilpatric disclosed that he had aided a young war veteran just back from France to get started in the garage business; he had assisted two young women who desired to open a tea room; he had helped another young man to open a machine shop; he had advanced money to a young man suffering from tuberculosis and in need of food and fuel for his home, and he had loaned additional funds to aid other young persons he considered worthy.

The former banker was questioned for three hours regarding his manipulation of the funds from the Putnam bank, after which the hearing was adjourned until tomorrow at Putnam.

A willing witness, Gilpatric attempted today to explain claims, notes and mortgages as they were read off by Lawrence E. Howard, counsel for the trustee of the Gilpatric bankrupt estate.

Nearly half of the more than $800,000 embezzled by Gilpatric was covered by the former banker in his explanation of four financial transactions. He estimated that the Cobert Machine Company had received from him, or from the First National Bank of Putnam, $100,000; the Monson (Mass.) Worsted Company, or D. J. Cochran Jr., whom he considered as one, received in excess of $100,000; another $150,000 went to meet his transactions with John J. Burns of this city, he said, and another $75,000 was advanced to the Vito Construction Company, road builders, of Thompson.

MINERS, 698 TO 2, RATIFY COAL PEACE; OPEN PITS TONIGHT

Standing Vote to End Strike Brings Burst of Cheering in Scranton Convention.

WORK STARTS TOMORROW

Lewis and Other Chiefs Declare 'Voluntary Conciliation,' Not 'Arbitration,' Conceded.

REED AND PEPPER ASSAILED

Pinchot Is Praised for Settlement Effort—Red Delegate Is Unseated With Unanimous Approval.

From a Staff Correspondent.

SCRANTON, Pa., Feb. 16.—The Tri-District Convention of the United Mine Workers of America this evening ratified the tentative agreement made on Friday by the Joint Negotiating Committee of Miners and Operators in Philadelphia, and voted to lift the strike order at midnight tomorrow and permit the 158,000 mine workers to return Thursday morning to the pits which they deserted on Sept. 1.

The formality of affixing the signatures of the twelve members of the Joint Negotiating Committee to the five-year agreement will take place tomorrow at the office of Major W. W. Inglis, President of the Glen Alden Coal Company, in this city. The first coal shipments will be on their way to market Thursday night, but normal tonnage will not be attained for three or four weeks.

Ratification by a standing vote was all but unanimous. Of the 700 delegates only two voted against the new contract. Their reasons were not disclosed as they did not take the floor, but their action was reported as an incident of the fational struggle within District No. 1, headed by President Rinaldo Cappellini.

Lone Communist Hastily Departs.

The convention was enthusiastically and overwhelmingly in favor of the reports made by the Union leaders and a burst of cheering followed the vote.

One delegate, who admitted being in possession of circulars issued by an organization affiliated with the Communist Party of America, was unseated by the convention when he refused to renounce belief in the Communist propaganda contained in the circular. The incident provoked an uproar, but President John L. Lewis maintained order. A policeman at the door gave the man a two-minute start and saved him from harm at the hands of irate miners who sought to follow him to the street.

The delegates ratified the compact after speeches by the members of the Miners' Negotiating Committee, who declared that it was the result of one of the greatest victories ever acheived by organized labor in the United States.

They explained that the agreement meant the retention of the right to strike, successful resistance to the demands of the operators for compulsory arbitration, elimination of any possibility of a wage reduction for five years, continuance of present wages for that period and the impossibility of a wage decrease before the expiration of the contract.

In its report to the convention the Scale Committee said that the tentative agreement which it proposed be accepted "protects the wages and conditions of the anthracite mine workers, eliminates arbitration, retains the absolute principle of collective bargaining and mutual agreement, and at the same time permits of the solution of many problems in the industry which if disposed of in the proper light will mean much to the anthracite mine workers, our organization and the industry."

Lewis Says Check-Off Is Understood.

President Lewis maintained that in deference to the dislike of the word "check-off" by the operators, the term was not used. Instead a clause was written referring the demands of operators and miners "on the question of cooperation and efficiency" to the Conciliation Board, without the umpire, to work out "a reciprocal program of cooperation and efficiency."

"Whether we wrote check-off in or left it out, that is precisely what it means," declared Mr. Lewis. "The operators understand what we mean when we say in the agreement that we shall work out a reciprocal program of cooperation and efficiency.

"They know that for us to cooperate with them in the reduction of costs and in the increasing of efficiency means the check-off. When they sign that document it means that we shall work it out, not that we may work it out. It is a mandate just as strong as the English language can make it and if it is not worked out, it will be a violation of the contract."

Credit Only to Pinchot and Grant.

The speakers praised the efforts made by Governor Pinchot to settle the strike, and President Cappellini of District 1 said Secretary of Labor James J. Davis, President Coolidge and Senators Reed anad Pepper were "so far away you couldn't get to them with a wireless."

President Andrew Mattey of District 7 credited Richard F. Grant, President of the Susquehanna Collieries Company, with bringing both sides to the adoption of the terms of the contract. Mr. Mattey, whose prediction at the Tri-State District Convention last June that the strike would last six months was greeted with laughter, essayed the rôle of prophet again today when he asserted that the next strike would last ten months, "not because you will want it, but because the other fellow will lock you out."

Vice President Philip Murray criti-

LENGLEN IS WINNER OVER HELEN WILLS

By FERDINAND TUOHY.

Continued from Page 1, Column 3.

ing tonight's celebration held here in her honor.

Helen Exceeds Expectations.

As for the match itself it is already passing into history after one acre, for one hour, had given almost the greatest sporting story of history. The pointage was: First set Helen 17 points, Suzanne 31. Second set, Helen 46, Suzanne 52. In the whole match Helen hit 32 outs and Suzanne 30 while each player double faulted only once each in the match.

As Morpurgo said afterward, Lenglen played far below her form which was confirmed by Suzanne herself saying that she never got a solitary one of her famous shots home—though for that surely, Helen was in some measure responsible.

Helen made her admirers, who are legion, fairly roar with joy as she more than exceeded expectations, playing well within herself, and remaining permanently on the offensive almost throughout the long drawnout second set. The crashed drives with masculine strength and more than masculine precision home along the side and baselines, causing the panting Suzanne to scurry hither and thither as she certainly had never scurried before.

Struggle a Thrilling One.

And Suzanne's incessant, weak returns! How some other day Helen, more experienced, may profit by them with the net crashes entirely absent in this day's battle virtually fought out on the baseline!

Though, perhaps, all honors were even—Helen, for playing so magnificently, Suzanne for so doggedly defending her empire.

"There are other years," ventured Helen, almost imperceptibly. "I play in the singles at Nice. Helen can come there if she likes," throws out Suzanne.

But how thrilling it is to see femininity linked in such a struggle as today's. Suzanne, exquisitely garbed in pink and white, purring her usual approval to admiration as she skipped about the courts cotton clad Helen following behind with her strange, catlike tread as if saying, "I really am quite a modest little girl, much too modest for all this."

Since 8 in the morning the entire social register of the Riviera, flanked by a goodly slice of the Almanac de Gotha and Debrett, had been fighting their way to the Carlton courts in one long procession of automobiles stretching out along the Nice and Monte Carlo road.

And for three hours we sat there in the bleachers, 4,000 strong, just as when we were waiting for Dempsey and Carpentier, laughing hysterically at each trivial incident—as when chic women trod the skyline transparently on the rooftops or when the gendarmes engaged in arboreal pursuits in trying to compel the young locals to descend from the branches of trees.

Then each celebrity would be hailed on his entry as at a first night, and perfidious jokes would be cracked anent the building of stands which went on beneath us until Suzanne sent her first service over.

Turmoil While the Struggle Raged.

At that moment one surely never beheld such a vivid rainbow effect beneath a blazing sun as was afforded by hundreds of the smartest women of Europe all assembled in their Helen and Suzanne frocks specially ordered for the occasion.

Once the game began we ceased to behave. Within we applauded each punch or, rather, stroke while the rally still proceeded, cheering frantically when Helen excelled, while without, demos got a little of his own back in the presence of a thousand strong company of locals, rooting through the uplifted draping for Suzanne and France. From hotel windows and roofs hundreds of yards away little figures signaled their participation in the contest by waving handkerchiefs and flags at each point.

Repeatedly poor, susceptible Suzanne implored for calm, only for the turmoil to break out anew, sending her almost down in defeat before the outwardly unperturbed but inwardly quivering little poker face.

Then when the battle was at the tensest moment came the errors of linesmen, giving three outs against Miss Wills, all of which were in, and ending in letting Suzanne think she had won the match before she actually had. As events turned out Helen proceeded to win two more games before the end. Upon this, of course, the dukes and movie men invaded the court one and all and the limp and gasping Suzanne was held up in the midst of masses of floral offerings, a complete Tetrazzini of tennis, while hundreds of movie men and still men snapped or reeled her for you. Meanwhile the lone little California girl hung practically unsung in the background, not thinking she was wanted.

So ended this epic for the present. To be resumed at a later date when it may be hoped that in addition to acclaiming so obviously and joyously a coming champion we may spare a turn of applause for her who showed us today that she knows how to fight gamely.

As Helen says: "It is always like this; when the public have had a champion for many years they want to see her beaten."

Helen must have studied philosophy in addition to art. Nor would the future going be less difficult if Suzanne, perhaps, took a course in the same school.

Caution Dominates Play.

CANNES, France, Feb. 16 (AP).—Suzanne Lenglen remains undisputed tennis champion of the world by virtue of her victory today over Helen Wills after one of the most dramatic matches in the history of tennis, ending with both very near collapse.

Both seemed conscious of the responsibility resting on them, and for once the emotions of the California girl were not entirely held in check. Care and caution dominated the play, which during the greater part of the time was from the baseline. But as the fight became more bitter extra driving power was put into the strokes, and when finally Mlle. Lenglen had achieved victory she threw her racquet in the air and leaped for very joy.

Surrounded with flowers and showered with congratulations from many of the great of the world, an ovation was given Suzanne such as perhaps she had never experienced in her career. The reaction made the tears flow down her face as friends gathered about her but the cheers of the multitude soon brought back the smile of the victor.

"I told you you would have to congratulate me," she said to one who had previously expressed some doubt as to her ability to win.

Helen Wills, with youth in her favor, took her defeat philosophically. "There will be other tennis matches; other years are coming," was all she would say.

Decision Costs Helen Set.

The California girl took the lead in the first set, as had been hoped by her supporters, and the score stood 2—1 at the end of the third game. But the French champion, playing with oldtime skill and finesse, evened matters in the fourth, and won also the fifth and sixth. Helen took the next game, but Suzanne finished the set with careful placements.

The second set was most dramatic. Miss Wills started by winning her service game at love. She took the next after deuce had been called, and then the third.

Suzanne began to cough, placed a hand over her heart and stepped to the sidelines, where she took a long draught of cognac with water.

Spurred by the stimulant, the French girl won the next three games, evening the count. Miss Wills took the seventh, another deuce game.

The French girl evened it again, and then Helen made it 5—4, needing only one game to take the set. She had run the score up to 40—15 in this game when, with one point to go for the set, an unaccountable decision by the linesman completely upset her.

Suzanne's return struck several inches outside the line, spectators in the stands were firmly convinced, and Helen herself made no attempt to strike at it. Nevertheless it was allowed as a point for Mlle. Lenglen by the linesman, Cyril Tolley, the former British amateur golf champion, who is also a tennis enthusiast.

Miss Wills changed over to receive Suzanne's service, thinking she had won her own, when she was called back.

"What did you call that? she asked Mr. Tolley, showing emotion for the first time.

"Inside," Tolley replied.

Helen threw up both hands in a gesture of despair, while thousands of spectators at her end of the court shouted: "Out!"

From then on the American girl put up a spiritless fight and allowed Mlle. Lenglen to take the initiative. She went down, 6 to 5, and then tied the set at 6-all, but, although she brought the last two games to deuce, the old spirit was missing.

Upon her arrival from Nice Mlle. Lenglen was nearly mobbed by her admirers, and had the greatest difficulty in making her way through the crowds, which were larger outside the courts than in the stands. The roofs of neighboring houses were burdened so so heavily with spectators that they might be expected to crash in at any moment. Periscopes were utilized by men standing outside the high fences to get a view of the play.

The match was contested under the most trying circumstances ever beheld

Point Score, Stroke Analysis, Of Great Contest at Cannes

First Set.

POINT SCORE.

Mlle. Lenglen	4	2	3	4	4	4	1	4	5	—31—6
Miss Wills	0	4	5	0	0	2	4	1	3	—19—3

STROKE ANALYSIS.

	A.	P.	N.	O.	DF.	EP.	E.
Mlle. Lenglen	0	5	3	11	0	5	14
Miss Wills	0	5	14	12	0	5	26

Second Set.

POINT SCORE.

Mlle. Lenglen—
0 5 2 2 4 4 5 4 4 4 4 3 6 5—52—8

Miss Wills—
4 3 4 4 1 1 7 2 6 0 2 5 4 2—46—6

STROKE ANALYSIS.

	A.	P.	N.	O.	DF.	EP.	E.
Mlle. Lenglen	2	12	10	19	1	14	30
Miss Wills	0	16	17	20	1	16	38

Recapitulation.

	A.	P.	N.	O.	DF.	EP.	E.	TP.
Mlle. Lenglen	2	17	13	30	1	19	44	83
Miss Wills	0	21	31	32	1	21	64	65

in tennis. Fully 2,000 spectators from the most varied outside vantage points imaginable kept up a running fire, cheering, talking and commenting, to the intense annoyance of Suzanne, who spoke to the crowd after the manner of a Queen addressing her subjects, ordering them to remain silent. When her orders were ignored she pleaded, "Please be quiet."

Women Faint In Crush.

There was nearly a riot when the gates to the courts opened two hours before the match. Several women, who had stood in line all night, fainted.

One section of the stand was occupied by members of various royal families, including former King Manual of Portugal, Grand Duke Michael of Russia, Prince George of Greece, the Rajah of Pudukota and others.

Two hours after Suzanne and Helen met in the singles combat they again faced one another, but this time attended by their respective partners, Didi Vlasto and Henriette Contoslavos. Again Mlle. Lenglen was victorious, playing until her utter collapse. She with her partner won to the score of 6—4, 8—6.

The California girl, however, dominated the doubles courts and showed much better tennis than any of the others; she had had her injured knee dressed in the interval and opened up a terrific attack, always directed at Suzanne.

Mlle. Lenglen gave signs of her approaching collapse in the middle of the second set. She and Mlle. Vlasto centred their attack upon Mlle. Contoslavos, leaving Helen standing on her side of the court. Every time the ball came near the American girl, however, it was killed for an irretrievable point.

She was cheered as she left the court and surrounded by fans, in strange contrast to her lonely exit after her singles match with Suzanne.

Mlle. Lenglen fainted after the doubles match and had to be assisted off the court. Miss Wills, without a look at Suzanne, shook hands with Mlle. Vlasto and then walked off.

SEES MISS WILLS NEAR TOP.

English Expert Says She Will Soon Equal Mlle. Lenglen.

By PERRY ROBINSON,

Special Correspondent of The London Times.

Copyright, 1926, by The New York Times Company.

Special Cable to THE NEW YORK TIMES

CANNES, Feb. 16.—The result of fourteen games to nine and 83 points to 65 fairly reflects the character of today's match, but Miss Wills made such a strong showing in the second set when she once led by 5—4 that most spectators were convinced it will not be long before she succeeds in playing as well as the present world's champion. Her foot work is already as good as the French girl's. She has some lovely shots and seems to be gaining in generalship each time she plays.

Both pleyars were evidently nervous in starting, but Miss Wills naturally was most affected, and the first set was uninteresting and not brilliant. However, in it Mlle. Lenglen won three love games, two of which were on her own service, and the final result, 6—3, 8—6, was no sensation.

With the second set Miss Wills gained courage. She won the first game at love on her own service and lost the next, then taking two running and went to 3—1.

She lost the next two and then won very gallantly on her own service. The excitement was intense when she led 5—4, at which point Miss Wills was leading in points, winning them by hard and confident tennis. Perhaps she tired.

Mlle. Lenglen was serving with the games 7—6 and 40—15. She was again within a point of winning the match. Miss Wills hit the ball deep into the left-hand corner and both players seemed to consider it out. Miss Wills advanced to the net to congratulate the winner. The umpire called the game and set, and the spectators stod cheering and began to disperse. Suddenly it appeared the lineman had not called the ball out. Everybody resumed their seats and the game was resumed.

The really thrilling moment came when Miss Wills won the point and went to deuce, then to advantage. But it was the end. Mlle. Lenglen, playing with extreme care and perfect judgment, won the next three points and the match was over, 8—6.

BRITISH EXCITED OVER MATCH

Both Miss Wills and Mlle. Lengle Are Acclaimed in the Papers.

Copyright, 1926, by The New York Times Company.

Special Cable to THE NEW YORK TIMES.

LONDON, Wednesday, Feb. 17.—Britishers could not have shown greater interest in the Lenglen-Wills battle if one of the contestants had been their own countrywoman.

The newspapers have been arousing preliminary excitement by detailing columns of the alleged doings and sayings of the two players and all the talk that has been going on round them. The result was watched for here as keenly as the result of the Derby, and the chief feature of this morning's papers are descriptions of the match by special writers sent to Cannes for the purpose.

"The universe can now go on as before," says The Evening News, referring to the advance publicity given to the match. "It seemed as if the earth itself would pause in its rotation, as if all the international excitement would end in an appeal to the League of Nations. Anything might have happened, including a war between the United States and France."

Several papers editorially deplore the "boosting" which has been given to the match as degrading to the game, but it is noticeable that a lot of this publicity stuff found a home in their news columns. The Westminster Gazette admits that the newspapers by no means are free from blame in the matter, adding:

"There is a tendency to magnify the difficulties incidental to all sporting competitions and so turn them into front page sensations."

"Seldom has any sporting event aroused so much interest beforehand," says The Daily Mail, "and seldom has such interest had such a thrilling climax. Both the victor and the vanquished have won fresh laurels."

"Everybody wanted to see Miss Wills make a good show," says The Daily Chronicle, "and that she unquestionably did."

FRANCO-GERMAN MATCH OFF.

Mlle. Lenglen Will Not Play Frau Neppach.

Copyright, 1926, by The New York Times Company.

Special Cable to THE NEW YORK TIMES.

PARIS, Feb. 16.—French tennis fans do not know whether to be annoyed or amused over the startling promptitude with which the woman tennis champion of Germany, Frau Neppach, challenged Suzanne Lenglen immediately after her dramatic victory today over Helen Wills, the American girl contender.

A telegram, timed to reach Cannes soon after today's match was received from Frau Neppach by the Carlton Club officials this morning requesting a meeting with the winner of the Wills-Lenglen contest, adding that the German girl would arrive at Cannes tomorrow personally to press her demand.

Train Beats Two Airplanes To Coast With Tennis Photos

Copyright, 1926, by The New York Times Co.

Special Cable to THE NEW YORK TIMES.

PARIS, Feb. 16.—The fable of the tortoise and the hare was called to mind by an exploit of photographers who thought airplanes would be the quickest way to get the precious tennis match plates to London before competitors who stuck to train travel. Two machines were chartered and shortly after the Cannes tournament ended took off and headed north. The first came down in the Durance Valley, having developed motor trouble, and the second descended near Lyons a little later. Meanwhile a train crawled northward and passed the humbled airmen with its luckier and larger crew of movie men and photographers.

MISS WILLS LAUDED BY ALL STARS HERE

Mrs. Mallory Says She Should Have "Knocked Cover Off the Ball" at Start.

RICHARDS FOR COAST GIRL

Lacoste and Borotra Both Say American Champion Played a Wonderful Game.

Helen Wills and Suzanne Lenglen made the local tennis public almost forget that there was a national indoor championship being played in this city yesterday. One of the largest galleries that ever attended a second day of play in the tournament was gathered at the Seventh Regiment Armory but it seemed that every one came to discuss the match at Cannes, and interest in the championship was secondary.

William Tilden, Vincent Richards, Mrs. Molla Mallory, Jean Borotra and René Lacoste of the French international team and even Georges Carpentier, who left his boxing pursuits to see his countrymen play tennis, were all eagerly besieged throughout the afternoon for expressions of opinion on the match between the American and French champions.

While opinion seemed to be almost unanimous before the match was played that Miss Wills had practically no chance of winning, few of the players mentioned went on record as being greatly surprised by the fine showing made by the Berkeley girl. All of them have seen both Miss Wills and Mlle. Lenglen play numerous times and practically every one of them has played with both of them.

Mersereau Is Satisfied.

Jones W. Mersereau, President of the United States Lawn Tennis Association, said that "Miss Wills must have played exceptional tennis under the conditions. It is a satisfaction to know she put up such a plucky fight against odds and I would look to see her do even better the next time they meet."

Julian S. Myrick, Chairman of the Davis Cup Committee, said: "Helen made a remarkably good showing, considering all the circumstances, and proved she is not far from being Suzanne's equal. I am confident she would do better in another match and possibly defeat the French star."

Mrs. Mallory's observations were perhaps the most interesting, because of the fact that she has been a rival of both Miss Wills and Mlle. Lenglen, defeating the latter here in one set in 1921 and losing her title to the American girl in 1923. Miss Wills, according to Mrs. Mallory, should have won the first set. If she had won it, in her opinion, she probably would have won the match. Miss Wills, stated the New York woman, should have knocked the cover off the ball in that set and never let down for a moment.

What Tilden Told Her.

"I was almost on the point of sending Helen a cable," said Mrs. Mallory, "to knock the cover off the ball. That was what Tilden told me to do when I played Suzanne in 1921. I was inspired by his advice and I played every shot for a placement. That is the only way you can beat Suzanne."

In the former American champion's opinion, Mlle. Lenglen will defeat Miss Wills more decisively should they meet again. Vincent Richards takes the opposite view.

"My money will be on Helen," said Richards, "if Suzanne ever meets her again. She will smother her. Helen has a good tennis head on her. She will know more the next time they meet. Instead of tightening up she will keep on socking the ball."

René Lacoste, who bears the weight of his twenty-one years more seriously than does Miss Wills the burden of twenty, was totally disinclined to lose his poise over the match. He declared that he had expected Mlle. Lenglen to win by a score of perhaps 6—3, 6—2. Miss Wills did unusually well to get nine games from her, he thought, but he declared that Mlle. Lenglen had everything to lose and nothing to gain in the match and so was naturally nervous.

Borotra was deeply impressed by Miss Wills' showing. "I have always had great admiration for Helen," he said. "My admiration is now all the greater. She must have played wonderfully."

Tilden limited himself to the following statement: "I am glad they played. I'm sorry Helen lost."

Carpentier said, "Suzanne is the great artiste."

"All the News That's Fit to Print."

The New York Times.

THE WEATHER
Thundershowers today, cooler at night; tomorrow fair.
Temperatures yesterday—Max., 79; min., 67.
For weather report see Page 25.

VOL. LXXV....No. 25,032. **** NEW YORK, SATURDAY, AUGUST 7, 1926. TWO CENTS in Greater New York | THREE CENTS Within 200 Miles | FOUR CENTS Elsewhere in the U. S.

PLANT'S 'HEARTBEAT' THRILLS SCIENTISTS AT OXFORD MEETING

Hindu Savant Causes Further Sensation by Showing 'Blood' of Plant Flowing.

AUDIENCE SITS ABSORBED

Watches With Rapt Attention as Lecturer Submits Snapdragon to Death Struggle.

WIDE RANGE OF DISCUSSION

Papers on Education, Penal System, Labor and Electricity Read Before British Association.

Special Cable to THE NEW YORK TIMES.

OXFORD, Aug. 6.—Rarely in all its history of nearly a hundred years of scientific achievement has the British Association for the Advancement of Science witnessed a more remarkable scene than this afternoon's, when Sir Jagadis Chandra Bose, the Hindu savant, demonstrated to an audience listening with absorbed interest the experiments by which he says he has proved that plants live lives akin to the lives of human beings.

Using instruments of almost incredible delicacy, one of which he had never exhibited before in public, the Oriental scientist showed his spectators the "heart" of a plant "beating" and the "blood" of a plant "flowing" in a manner which, according to him (and his audience was more than inclined to believe it), was far more similar to the phenomena connected with human life than science was willing to admit.

After explaining his theories by actual experiment, Sir Jagadis declared that present scientific conceptions of plant life were erroneous. One of the changes to be brought about, if his theories are applied, he said, would be the elimination of the vivisection of animals as an aid to scientific investigation.

Program Again Diverse.

The remarkable revelations of the Hindu savant formed only one of the many items on the program of the third session of the British Association at Oxford this afternoon. As was the case yesterday, the program was most diverse, allowing opportunity for experts in various provinces of science to have their innings and advance their views.

Among those men who read papers before sections of the association today were Professor J. Graham Kerr, who predicted dire things if education continues in its now accepted grooves; Dr. James Drever, who spoke on the penal system; Sir Lynden Macassey, who suggested a cure for the present-day "strike fever"; Sir Thomas Holland, who attacked the neglect of civic training in our education, and Sir John F. C. Snell, who discussed the future of electricity.

These and others lavished the results of their long and painstaking study on auditors listening so raptly as never to lose a syllable.

Shows Plants Have "Hearts."

Sensational revelations of Sir Jagadis Chandra Bose concerning the "heart-beats" of plants were followed with breathless interest by his Oxford audience.

It was known that he had brought to Oxford extraordinarily delicate instruments with which he seeks to prove the existence in plants of life closely resembling that of human beings, including one instrument which he never before has shown in public.

Hence both sexes of the audience were on tiptoe with eager anticipation when the world-renowned Hindu scientist appeared this afternoon in the lecture hall.

Before entering he had plucked at random an ordinary snapdragon and with this he made his experiment.

Savants watching him felt like pinching themselves to see if they were dreaming as Sir Jagadis in a matter-of-fact way began to reveal his wonders.

Placing the snapdragon in a tiny tray amid an awe-inspiring array of bottles and instruments, he showed how his apparatus recorded, by a series of continuous lines, the action of the beating "heart" of the plant, the lines being transcribed on a sensitized plate.

Then, to prove that it was indeed a heart he had under observation, he moved the plant slightly to another tray containing bromide. The plant immediately drooped and the "writing" changed perceptibly. Then he moved it into a tray containing musk, which immediately revived it.

He made further experiments with cobra poison and strychnine, obtaining even more startling results, which he declared proved that the nervous reactions of plants are stimulated by certain drugs exactly as in the case of human beings.

Measures Sap Pressure of Plants.

The hitherto unknown instrument revealed by Sir Jagadis today was designed by him for recording and measuring the rate of movement of sap or "blood" in plants and studying how it is modified by the action of drugs which affect the circulation of the life force.

When the circulation of the sap is stimulated by a drug, his recorder showed an upcurve, and when a depressant was used the struggle between the forces of life and death was clearly visible to the absorbed spectators.

They saw the development of a crisis

Continued on Page Six.

Lord Grey Advises British To Keep Their Walking Legs

EPSOM, England, Aug. 6 (AP).—"Keep your legs" was the advice Viscount Grey of Fallodon recently gave to the boys of Epsom College. He warned them against giving up walking and riding bicycles because the means of communication have been so much improved, and said even a middle-aged man is better for walking twenty miles a day or riding fifty on a wheel.

Viscount Grey is doubtful whether all the modern mechanical contrivances which have become part of everyday life are of benefit to humanity and warned his audience against neglecting their minds and bodies because mechanical genius has devised ways of amusing persons without requiring them to make any effort on their own behalf.

HANDS OFF MEXICO, IS COOLIDGE POLICY

He Holds That There Has Been No Cause for Action in Religious Struggle.

NO MOVE ON SOVIET DEBT

President Talks of Fall Campaigns With Tilson—Wades Brook and Lands Trout.

Special to The New York Times.

PLYMOUTH, Vt., Aug. 6.—President Coolidge is watching with great concern the struggle between the Government of Mexico and the Catholic Church, but has not been advised of any developments in Mexico which would justify American intervention, as suggested yesterday by the Supreme Council of the Knights of Columbus at its convention in Philadelphia. The President's policy in the struggle is hands off.

Since coming here the President has not been in touch with the State Department, and, has not been informed of any violation of treaty rights or of violations to American citizens or property rights which would justify any action by the United States in the present domestic problem in Mexico, a problem which has deeply affected Catholics and others in this country.

Sitting on the piazza of his old homestead this afternoon after a day devoted to fishing and calls on relatives, Mr. Coolidge gave his views upon foreign questions that have arisen and have become acute since he began his vacation. The fight between the State and Church in Mexico and other matters concerning American rights have formed the subject of an inquiry by President Coolidge in the last two weeks. He has kept in close touch with reports from Mexico, but it was said here authoritatively that nothing had occurred there that would warrant drastic action by this Government.

No Violence Reported to Him.

While President Coolidge may not accept the action of the Mexican Government as one tending to create a friendly sentiment in the United States, because of the religious issue involved, he has not received any reports of violence against Americans there as the result of the contest. However, he has decided that American rights must be rigidly upheld. The President will act on the protests of the Knights of Columbus and other organizations only if American rights or American property are violated as a result of the conflict.

The Administration policy toward Mexico, which has been one of patience respecting the land and oil laws, would be no more aggressive than at present. It was made clear here today, if treaty rights or the rights of American citizens in that country are violated. President Coolidge is anxious to help that Government, as evidenced in the negotiations on the land and oil troubles and his refusal to lift the arms embargo while the conflict between Church and State was in progress. His patience, it was apparent today, might become exhausted if American rights are not upheld in the present situation.

Concerned with foreign relations as deeply as with domestic affairs, President Coolidge reasserted today the American position in regard to Soviet Russia, as the result of a report that the Soviet Government desires to settle the Russian debt to the United States. He holds that all that the present régime in Russia had to do toward that end was to revoke the ordinance by which it repudiated its debt to the United States. He had not heard that this had been done or that the Soviet Government desired to send agents here to confer on its debt settlement.

Tilson Presents Political Affairs.

President Coolidge had the political situation presented to him in detail today by Representative Tilson of Connecticut, the Republican House leader, who will be in charge of headquarters in New York for the Republican Senate and House campaigns. Offices there will be opened on Aug. 15. Stopping off on his way to his Summer home at Lake Sunapee, Mr. Tilson, accompanied by Mrs. Tilson, had luncheon with the President and Mrs. Coolidge. He told the President that conditions were improving steadily for the Republican Party and that there no longer appeared to be any doubt of Republican control of the next Senate. The Republican majority in the House will be larger, he believed, because of the return of the Farmer-Labor Party voters to the Republican Party in the West.

Mr. Tilson holds that the House majority will be larger, but may be more independent, due to farm relief agitation. He is hopeful that if conditions do not improve this Fall there will be some agreement among the party leaders in the East and West

Continued on Page Two.

FIVE WARRANTS OUT IN HALL-MILLS CASE, BUT ARE NOT SERVED

State to Keep Check on Former Servants, Mrs. Russell and Gorsline.

SIX ARE QUESTIONED AGAIN

Rector's Intrigue Was Known to Many, Maid Says—Denies Call to Mrs. Hall on Murder Night.

HURRY IN BURIAL ALLEGED

Dr. Long Declares Undertaker Seemed in Desperate Rush—Mrs. Riehl Gets Permit to Leave State.

Six witnesses told Assistant Attorney General Alexander Simpson yesterday what they knew about the Hall-Mills case, and the prosecutor and the State troopers, finally in agreement on this phase of the revived investigation, reported that five warrants had been obtained, but would be held unserved.

The examination of the witnesses was conducted at Somerville, N. J. The stories heard included that of Barbara Tough, former maid in the Hall household. She denied that she telephoned to Mrs. Frances Stevens Hall, now at liberty in $15,000 bail charged with the slaying of her husband, the Rev. Dr. Edward W. Hall, and Mrs. Eleanor R. Mills shortly before the clergyman and his choir leader were shot to death four years ago near New Brunswick, N. J.

Tells of Gossip in Parish.

The former servant, however, did add to the voluminous history of the case. She told Senator Simpson, according to his version of her narrative, that the intimacy of Mrs. Mills and the rector was "common knowledge" among his parishioners—a fact that all of those who were questioned have denied. Miss Tough, a slow-spoken but emphatic Scotswoman, doubted whether Mrs. Hall knew about it.

The other witnesses examined were Dr. William H. Long, Somerset County physician; Mrs. Maria Gildea, who was cook for the slain clergyman; Peter Tumulty, gardener-chauffeur for the Hall family; Mrs. Minna Clarke, organist of Dr. Hall's church, who was erroneously reported "missing," and Raymond Schneider, a youth, who found the bodies and who was sentenced to the Rahway Reformatory after he had falsely charged a New Brunswick youth, Clifford Hayes, with the double murder.

The warrants included one for Ralph V. Gorsline, vestryman of the Church of St. John the Evangelist. All the warrants were merely for material witnesses except Gorsline's. This warrant charged him as an "accessory after the fact." The documents were obtained, it was explained, for service only if the persons named showed a disposition to leave the State. None of the witnesses has shown any such disposition.

Others Named in Warrants.

Others named in the warrants were Mrs. Nellie Lo Russell, negress, who discredited the story of the State's chief witness to date, Mrs. Jane Gibson, the "pig woman"; Barbara Tough, Tumulty and Mrs. Gildea. It was made clear that nobody would be arrested and that the issuance of the warrants was merely a precautionary step.

The Assistant Attorney General motored from his office in Jersey City to the State Troopers' headquarters in Main Street, Somerville, at noon. He left after he had received a telephone call informing him that troopers had brought in several witnesses he desired to question. Miss Tough came to the headquarters voluntarily, and so did Mrs. Clarke. The latter explained that she had shuttered her home in New Brunswick in order to shield herself against intrusion, and that she had never been "missing."

The questioning of the witnesses lasted from about 2 o'clock until 7 o'clock last night. Mrs. Gildea, Schneider and Tumulty were the last witnesses to be questioned, the examination in their case being conducted by Major Mark O. Kimberling and Captain John J. Lamb, the prosecutor having returned to Jersey City. In his absence the State Troopers declined to give out the substance of what Mrs. Gildea, Schneider and the chauffeur had to offer.

Simpson Quotes Witnesses.

In substance, Senator Simpson gave as the examination of Miss Tough.

Continued on Page Four.

American Girl Rescues Another At Lausanne, but Refuses Name

By Wireless to THE NEW YORK TIMES.

GENEVA, Aug. 6.—A young American girl on a holiday was walking alone along the shore of Lac de Joux, near Lausanne, yesterday, when she saw a small boat containing a young man and a girl overturn.

The man, who could not swim, was hanging to the keel, shouting for help, but the girl had disappeared in the water. Without hesitating, the American girl swam out to the spot and brought the girl to the shore, where she soon recovered, while a man in a boat rescued the other victim.

The American girl when asked for her name said that it did not matter. The plucky, modest girl then smilingly nodded good-bye to a small crowd and walked away amidst the cheers of "Bravo, l'Americaine."

LONG CHASE ABROAD LANDS BANK THIEVES

Two Men Wanted in Robbery of $109,000 Snared After Hunt Through Seven Countries.

SHOE TREES ARE SOLE CLUE

Reveal Names of Fugitives Who Are Brought Back on Liner—Pair to Be Sent to Coast.

With the arrival here yesterday of the Berengaria two young Poles ended a ten months' holiday at the expense of a couple of San Francisco banks and there was brought to a close a true detective story containing elements such as movies are made of and emphasizing the relentless persistence of surety company investigators.

The young men, brothers, are charged with having stolen $109,000 in securities. They are Ludwig and Julius Busch, respectively 33 and 29 years old, and they came to this country in 1924. But for a pair of shoe trees—articles which are not known ever to have figured prominently in any detective story—the two would still be at liberty.

The men were traced and brought back to this country by Samuel MacCubbin, head of the investigation and claims department of the Fidelity and Deposit Company of Baltimore, which has an office in this city at 55 Liberty Street, and bonds bank employes. The romantic story of the Busch brothers was told yesterday by Vincent Cullen, Vice President of the company, and pieced out by MacCubbin, the detective, when the ship arrived.

Both Got Bank Jobs.

Coming to the land of the free in search of riches, the two young men arrived in San Francisco in July, 1924, and one, Julius, went to work for the Bank of Italy, while Ludwig got a job with the Anglo-California Trust Company. Neither was bonded individually, but each bank carried a blanket policy with the Fidelity and Deposit Company covering defalcations.

Suddenly, in October, 1925, both young men disappeared. At the time not much was thought of their going, but when a check of their books was made in January it was found that securities valued at about $109,000 had disappeared from the Bank of Italy. Investigation disclosed that one brother, apparently, had taken the securities, disposing of them through the brother employed in the other bank.

The San Francisco police could find no trace of the two, but did find that the Buschs had abandoned certain belongings in their lodgings at 1,927 Jackson Street. From all articles of clothing and everything else, however, marks of possible identification had been carefully removed.

MacCubbin started on the case in March, the fugitives having a lead on him then of five and a half months. Diligent work, according to Mr. Cullen, resulted in MacCubbin's finding that at one time one of the men had shipped some baggage to Montreal. So MacCubbin went to Montreal. There, according to Mr. Cullen, the trail was completely lost, MacCubbin, even with the aid of the Montreal police, being unable to find any trace of the two men. MacCubbin even went to the extent of poring over hotel registers for many months back, but to no purpose. So he returned to San Francisco.

The Telltale Shoe Trees.

Going thoroughly through the effects of the two men again, MacCubbin made a very careful examination of

Continued on Page Four.

"The Eel," Noted Paris Criminal, Escapes By Underground Tunnels, Posing as Inspector

Special Cable to THE NEW YORK TIMES.

PARIS, Aug. 6.—In the case of Georges Reme, known as "The Eel," it seems that something like a "master criminal" really does exist.

Reme is wanted for numerous crimes and felonies and may be characterized as a "con man," his career so far being free from murder or common thieving. Two days ago he was brought to the Palais de Justice in Paris in a Black Maria, similar to that from which the fictional Arsene Lupin escaped by lifting the floor boards.

Reme's method was not so crude. He reached the Palais de Justice with a dozen other offenders, but instead of sitting on the bench to which they were conducted in an antechamber, he went to the bench where there were a number of juvenile delinquents waiting to be questioned.

When one of these was called Reme took him by the arm, having concealed his hat under the bench, and marched him out of the room.

Then taking a number of typewritten letters from his pocket, he went ahead into the underground passage which leads from the Juvenile Court and walked coolly to the end of the tunnel, where a policeman challenged him. "I am a secret service inspector," he said, without batting an eyelash, and with a sure step and apparently complete familiarity with his surroundings he passed through the intricate haze of hallways to the outer door, where he passed the guard and went to the street.

Then his trail was lost, but a black automobile which had been noticed hovering about was discovered to have disappeared.

KEHOE FOUND GUILTY OF MILK CONSPIRACY; IS LOCKED IN TOMBS

Jury Out 6 Hours, 12 Minutes; Judge Refuses to Continue Defendant's $10,000 Bail.

AUG. 12 SET FOR SENTENCE

Maximum Penalty Three Years' Imprisonment, Together With $500 Fine.

LAWYER PROMISES APPEALS

Mrs. Kehoe Hysterical at Verdict—Conviction a Warning, Health Commissioner Says.

Three weeks to a day after he had been placed on trial, William H. Kehoe, formerly Assistant Corporation Counsel, was found guilty last night of conspiracy in the bootleg cream graft scandal. After deliberating six hours and twelve minutes, the jury returned its verdict before Judge Max S. Levine in General Sessions at 10:07 P. M.

Kehoe was taken to the Tombs and locked in a cell after the Court had denied the application of Michael M. Edelstein, his counsel, for the continuance of the $10,000 bail under which he has been at liberty since his indictment. Aug. 12 was named as the date for his sentence.

Kehoe and his wife were chatting together in the corridor outside the court room when word was received that the jury was ready to report. Both had looked for a disagreement because of the length of time which the jury had been out. Mrs. Kehoe remained outside as her husband entered and stood at the bar. He gave a glance of swift appraisement at the faces of the jurymen as they filed in and his own face went white.

When the verdict was announced Kehoe leaned heavily forward on the railing with both hands clutching it. He swayed slightly and sought to steady himself. His pedigree was given in a voice little above a whisper. He was 40 years old, he said; born in the United States, lived at 191st Street and Woodall Avenue, Hollis, Queens; was a lawyer, married and of temperate habits.

Wife Informed of Verdict.

A relative who was seated near the door tiptoed out of the court room and approached Mrs. Kehoe, who had been in daily attendance at the trial. When informed of the verdict Mrs. Kehoe became hysterical and her cries could be heard through the building. She was calmed somewhat later and left the building without seeing her husband before he was taken to the Tombs.

After the verdict had been rendered Edward L. Purves of 54 West 106th Street, Juror No. 9, thanked Judge Levine in behalf of the jury for the consideration shown by the Court.

Kehoe was convicted of conspiracy to do an act injurious to the public health, or for the perversion or obstruction of justice, or of the due administration of the laws. It is a misdemeanor punishable by an indeterminate sentence in the penitentiary, the maximum of which is three years, or by a fine of $500, or both.

Mr. Edelstein said no move could be made to obtain Kehoe's release until after his sentence was pronounced. A certificate of reasonable doubt will then be sought and an attempt made to obtain his admission to bail. The case will be fought through the highest courts, Mr. Edelstein said.

Warning, Says Harris.

In commenting on the result of the trial last night Dr. Louis I. Harris, Health Commissioner, said:

"The hands of the guardians of the lives of the children, the sick and all others in the community have been strengthened by this verdict, and it may properly be interpreted as the utterance of a warning by representatives of the citizens of the community that the people of this city will not tolerate a corrupt act that endangers the welfare of any of our people.

"If Mr. Pecora's address to the jury and his appeal for the protection of the public health were studied by every citizen, it would create a sentiment that would insure against a repetition of the scandalous conditions revealed at this trial. Mr. Pecora's address was a brilliant presentation of the basis of public health service."

It was 3:55 P. M. when Judge Levine finished his charge and the jury retired. Kehoe, his coat removed because of the heat, paced back and forth in the gallery about the central rotunda of the Criminal Courts Building, Mrs. Kehoe clinging to his arm.

At the end of three hours it became apparent that there was a division in the jury. Judge Levine, at 7:15 o'clock, ordered a recess until 8:30 and the jurymen had dinner. They returned at 8:40 o'clock. Up to that time they had asked for no instructions.

Pecora Sums Up.

Assistant District Attorney Ferdinand Pecora began his summing up when court opened. He charged that Kehoe was the real ringleader in the bootleg milk graft. He said the respondent had conspired illegally with Samuel Doner, wholesale cream dealer, to levy tribute of $1 on every can of bootleg cream which the latter brought into the city from uninspected sources and to furnish protection for the illicit traffic.

"Kehoe cared more for the $1 a can he collected on bootleg cream brought in by Doner than he did for the lives of the men, women and children of New York City," Mr. Pecora said.

Mr. Pecora told the jury that he had no apology to make for the character of Doner or Harry Danziger, his chief witnesses.

"Honest men don't pay graft for

Continued on Page Eleven.

GERTRUDE EDERLE SWIMS THE CHANNEL IN RECORD TIME OF 14 HOURS 31 MINUTES; AMERICAN IS FIRST WOMAN TO CROSS

"It Had to Be Done, I Did It," Says Miss Ederle; Twice Spurned Burgess's Advice to Give Up

By ALEC RUTHERFORD,
British Expert on Channel Swimming.

Special Cable to THE NEW YORK TIMES.

DOVER, England, Aug. 6.—During the wait on the tug in Dover Harbor and the journey to the hotel after the Channel triumph, I had an opportunity of chatting with Miss Ederle, her father and the rest of the party. Miss Ederle said:

"I just knew if it could be done, it had to be done, and I did it."

Her father said he was never sure until the finish. He was very proud that his daughter had performed the feat, whose achievement he attributed largely to her splendid persistence.

Burgess told me that twice during the swim he wanted Miss Ederle to come out of the water—the first time at noon and the second time at 6 o'clock. It was her father and sister who would not let her come out, he said.

Anyway, Gertrude herself refused and repeatedly declared she had no intention of giving up. She said:

"I am doing it for mummy."

This was in reference to a series of wireless messages urging her to go on sent by her mother in New York during the swim. They were read to Gertrude while she was in the water.

I gather that Gertrude achieved her victory by a margin of only ten minutes. Had she not reached the favorable flood tide when she did she could never have got over.

During the latter half of the swim an amusing dialogue took place between "Pop" Ederle and his daughter. "Pop" continually roared over the side of the boat:

"Trudie, don't forget you won't get that roadster unless you get over."

Gertrude always responded:

"Pop, I will have that roadster."

Aboard the tug on the way back to Dover she constantly reminded her father that the roadster was to be got immediately. After her bath at the hotel when I asked what she was going to do next, she said:

"I shall go to bed and sleep all day. I need it. I am so tired."

I understand she is to return to France tomorrow, then go on to Germany to see her father's people and then go back to Paris to buy some "nice clothes" and presents for "Mum."

She will return to America on the Berengaria on Aug. 21.

MAYOR PICKS KELBY FOR HEALTH INQUIRY

Ex-Justice Will Investigate Conditions in Department as Special Counsel.

TO TAKE UP MILK GRAFT

Centralization of Inquiry in All Boroughs Planned to Help in Prosecutions.

Mayor Walker authorized yesterday the announcement that Charles H. Kelby, former Justice of the Appellate Division of the Supreme Court, Second Department, had accepted appointment as special counsel to take charge of the investigation into the affairs of the Board of Health.

The announcement was made by Charles F. Kerrigan, assistant to the Mayor, after a talk over the telephone with Mayor Walker at Dixville Notch, N. H. Judge Kelby, it was learned, will have charge of a general investigation of conditions in the Health Department and will carry on in each of the five boroughs the inquiry into milk graft, which has already resulted in several indictments, with a view to submitting evidence to the District Attorneys in the several counties.

Judge Kelby has had several conferences with Health Commissioner Louis I. Harris and said he considered it in the public interest to have the whole situation in the Health Department thoroughly investigated and submitted to the prosecuting authorities for action.

The appointment of Judge Kelby, who is a Republican and a law associate of former Controller Charles L. Craig, with offices at 120 Broadway, was the city administration's answer to the demand of the Citizens Union and others, for an investigation of the milk situation by the Attorney General on the ground that an attempt was being made to protect those higher up in milk graft. Governor Smith, it has been said, has been reluctant to put the investigation into the hands of Attorney General Albert Ottinger, a Republican and a candidate for the Republican nomination for Governor, and believes that this would not be the best way to take politics out of the inquiry.

Centralizes the Inquiry.

Mayor Walker, it was said, denied that the centralization of the investigation, which was the chief argument advanced in support of an investigation by the Attorney General, would be obtained by the appointment of Judge Kelby.

The announcement of the selection of Judge Kelby, who will rank as a special aid to the Corporation Counsel, as made at the Mayor's office, read:

"Mayor Walker and Commissioner Harris have agreed that the information collected by the Health Commissioner should be reviewed by a lawyer of high standing who would be able to sift the evidence and prepare cases for prosecution by the District Attorneys in the five counties of the City of New York. Judge Kelby has been assured of the cooperation of all of the District Attorneys in Manhattan, Bronx, Brooklyn, Queens and Richmond.

"Working with Commissioner Harris, it is felt special counsel will be able to develop cases, reinforce those where there are missing links in the evidence

Continued on Page Two.

HUNT JERSEY WOODS FOR ROVING LEOPARD

Scores of Volunteers Aid Posse in Search for Escaped Cat as Fear for Children Spreads.

DOGS PUT ON ITS TRAIL

Animal Reported Seen Twice, but It Eludes Hunters—Reward for Capture Raised to $500.

Special to The New York Times.

RED BANK, N. J., Aug. 6.—In the glare of automobile headlights a posse of State troopers, Monmouth County detectives and farmers, armed with high power rifles and pistols, scoured the woodland coverts on and near the Brookdale farm of Lewis S. Thompson near Lincroft until midnight tonight for the full-grown Indian leopard that escaped yesterday from Oliver W. Holton's Twinbrook zoo at Middletown.

With half a dozen dogs trying to pick up the trail, the posse explored the woods and brush land, using flashlights when beyond the beams of the automobile lights. But when the search was given up at midnight the leopard was still at large. It was said that the hunt would be resumed and continued until the animal was found.

Mr. Holton, who offered a reward of $100 yesterday for the capture of the animal dead or alive, increased the offer today to $500, and it was agreed that no effort was to be made to capture the leopard alive, due to a fear that some one might be injured or killed.

The reward and the fear that spread over the countryside that the roving animal might attack a child brought scores of volunteers to the hunt. The search was centred around the Brookdale farm during the day after Jeremiah Vaughan, a watchman at the Harry Payne Whitney breeding farm, reported that he believed he had seen the leopard fleeing from a dog near a barn early in the morning. Abram Lower, superintendent of Mr. Holton's zoo, hurried to the farm and positively identified tracks in a near-by cornfield and a clump of woods as those of the fugitive animal.

Toward sundown the posse closed in on the clump of woods, believing the leopard was cornered there. As the circle of men became smaller the tension increased and a sudden burst of shots in the wood sent all members of the posse in that direction. They were keenly disappointed to find the shots had been fired by jokers in the posse.

The reported presence of the leopard near the Whitney farm caused persons in charge there to establish a guard to protect 200 blooded horses and a score of foals. Farmers in the neighborhood are apprehensive also of their stock, but even more so of their children.

Margaret Ellison, eight-year-old daughter of a farmer on the Nut Swamp Road, was believed to have seen the animal last night near her home. It was skulking along the edge of a wood.

The girl ran home, telling of the "big white dog with yellow spots on it" that she had seen. Before her father reached the spot the animal had disappeared.

Late in the afternoon Superintendent Lower expressed the belief that the leopard was cornered and would be brought down within a short time.

"We found footmarks along the edge of the cornfield and around rabbit burrows," he said. "We traced them into the woods. We failed to find any tracks leading from the woods and I think the leopard is in there and that we have a good chance of getting it tonight."

The leopard was brought to the Middletown zoo from Singapore, India.

CHEERED AT BRITISH SHORE

She Lands Smiling at Kingsdown After Hard Battle From Gris-Nez.

CONQUERS WIND, RAIN, TIDE

Fights for Three Desperate Hours Off English Coast Till Favoring Current Aids.

BONFIRES LIGHT LAST DASH

Searchlights Also Sweep From Shore as New York Girl Comes In With Strokes Still Strong.

By T. R. YBARRA.

Special Cable to THE NEW YORK TIMES.

DOVER, Aug. 6.—Gertrude Ederle, the plucky little New York girl, swam across the English Channel today in 14 hours 31 minutes, thus winning not only the honor of being the first woman to accomplish this feat but breaking by a goodly margin the best record made by a male cross-Channel swimmer.

The speediest cross-Channel swim made before today was that of the Italian swimmer, Sebastian Tirabocchi, who swam from France to England in 1923 in 16 hours 23 minutes.

Gertrude Ederle's successful swim came fifty-one years after the Channel was first conquered by an English swimmer, Captain Matthew Webb. In 1911, the Channel was crossed by another Englishman, T. W. Burgess, who now has achieved the added glory of having trained the young American girl and of having guided her today from start to finish of her magnificent swim.

Fought to Reach Favoring Current.

Miss Ederle plunged into the water this morning at 7:09 o'clock at Cape Gris-Nez, France. She landed at Kingsdown, near Deal, England, at 9:40 o'clock this evening. For three desperate hours she fought the ebb and flow of the tide, with the British shores looming temptingly before her yet apparently hopelessly out of reach. But she gritted her teeth and stuck to it, putting every ounce of strength and will power into her strokes.

She knew that if she could only stick it out a favorable turn in the tide might let her reach the coveted shore. Instead of making for Shakespeare Cliff or St. Margaret's Bay, as swimmers usually do, Gertrude made toward Deal. And at last the favoring current for which she was praying swept her toward the cliffs of England.

English Cheers Greet Smiling Victor.

Soon after 9 o'clock tonight she was off Kingsdown. Just before 10 o'clock she emerged from the water and walked ashore. Delight at her victory had effaced all memory of the terrible hours through which she had passed.

As she came on to the beach she was happy and smiling. And the crowd who had rushed to Kingsdown from all directions at the news that the game little American was struggling toward the English shore surged around her in mad enthusiasm and sent up cheer after cheer of delirious joy.

Miss Ederle had hardly reached the shore before she was hustled into a rowboat which whisked her to the tug which had accompanied her across the Channel.

During the last few hours of her record-breaking swim, Gertrude Ederle had to buck the wickedest possible combination of obstacles. The sea was rough, the tide was running strongly against her and a stinging spray was hurled into her face as she swam doggedly forward. It was a fine piece of headwork which enabled her to take advantage of the favoring current and reach Kingsdown Beach.

EXPERT'S STORY OF SWIM.

By ALEC RUTHERFORD,
British Expert on Channel Swimming.

Special Cable to THE NEW YORK TIMES.

DOVER, Aug. 6.—Gertrude Ederle, the nineteen-year-old New York champion girl swimmer, is one of the pluckiest swimmers that ever attempted the huge task of swimming the English Channel. I watched this pretty, tiny atom of humanity in her red bathing dress and skull cap, with goggles like a motorist's, battle for fourteen hours today against the merciless elements.

At 6:30 this evening she was facing the white cliffs of Dover, only six miles away from England. She was still battling pluckily, refusing to give in, though faced with over two hours of further battle against the cross-tides before the favorable inshore tide set in and gave her the chance to progress toward victory. At that time there was a squally rain and a heavy, powerful, swamping sea against the swimmer.

Miss Ederle entered the Channel at Cape Gris-Nez at 7:08 this morning amid the wild cheers of the Channel swimmers assembled at the training camp there. She was accompanied by

Continued on Page Three.

Britain and America Thrilled by Great Achievement of New York Girl Swimmer

By ALEC RUTHERFORD.
Continued from Page 1, Column 8.

the tug Alsace, carrying the Stars and Stripes and a wireless apparatus for flashing to America messages during each mile of progress.

Aboard the tug were the father and sister of the swimmer; Burgess, her trainer; Helmi, the Egyptian Channel aspirant; Miss Cannon, another American girl swimmer, and Timson, the Boston swimmer. There also was a second tug, with newspaper men, photographers and movie cameramen.

Legend on Tug Points Way.

Chalked on the lee side of the tug Alsace in front of Miss Ederle's eyes were the words, "This Way, Ole Kid!" with an arrow pointing forward.

The wind at the start was southwest, the temperature was 61 and there was a rough sea. Miss Ederle set off with strong strokes and covered the first four miles in three hours. She was swimming with a strong crawl and she refused to go slow when ordered to by her trainer.

Her party hung over the side of the boat singing American songs, including frequently "The Star-Spangled Banner." Miss Ederle responded from the water.

The swimmer hugged the leeward shelter of the tug. At 10:30 o'clock this morning she had her first meal—beef extract drunk while floating on her back and also chicken eaten during ten minutes of rest.

Her sister Margaret, Helmi and Timson all took turns accompanying Gertrude in the water for long periods. Gertrude shouted back her confidence in victory repeatedly to cheering messages from the tugs. There was no jazz band similar to last year.

Anthem Sung in Midchannel.

Wild enthusiasm, to which Gertrude responded, greeted her arrival in midchannel just about midday. "The Star-Spangled Banner" was again sung. The demonstration lasted several minutes.

At 1:30 o'clock, nine miles from the English coast, rain started, with a strong, fierce wind causing a heavy swell difficult to battle against.

At 3 o'clock the swimmer was drifting toward Dover with the incoming tide and the rain was stronger than ever.

At 5 o'clock the wind was increasing in power and velocity and the sea was choppy and angry. The tug party was now singing "Yes, We Have No Bananas." A second meal of chocolate was now served to the swimmer.

Miss Cannon, another American aspirant, took the water with Gertrude for an hour. Gertrude offered her a drink of chocolate. The weather was becoming worse every moment and the sea rougher.

At 6 o'clock there was talk of giving up, since the weather and the sea were too bad for victory. Miss Ederle seemed to swim more strongly against the terrible conditions and pluckily shouted: "No! No!" On she struggled a few yards, only to fall back twice as many.

At 6:30 o'clock she was still going strong, holding her own against the cross tides. It was a great swim.

It was when Miss Ederle had passed south of Goodwin Lightship that the party for the first time decided that victory seemed possible. The crowds on shore began to gather in thousands all along the beach and automobiles by the hundreds all sounded their horns. Tugs in the Channel hooted their sirens and scores of flares were lit on the beach to guide her in.

As she approached the shallow water, hundreds of people, regardless of their clothes, waded in the water and surrounded her. Miss Ederle walked ashore unaided, quickly followed by her father, who clasped her in his arms and wrapped her in a dressing gown. She had great difficulty in fighting her way back through the cheering and swaying crowd to the rowboat which took her back to the tug.

The tug at once put out to sea toward Dover. Gertrude was on deck wrapped in Trainer Burgess's coat, the only clothing she had besides her swimming costume.

She traveled in this fashion all the way to Dover, chatting cheerfully all the time.

Regrettable Incident Occurs.

But a regrettable anti-climax was to follow, which certainly will cause considerable public resentment. The tug arrived in the harbor at about 11:30 P. M., but could not get near the pier until a large barge had been moved out. It was midnight before the tug came alongside.

Even then the Channel conqueror was not allowed to land. Trouble arose at once in regard to customs and passports, the party aboard the tug having no passports with them. After a long delay an official was found, and it was 12:30 P. M. before he went aboard. Then followed the most curious scene that could possibly have happened. The solemn officer produced an official document and made Gertrude stand up on deck while he cross-examined her for several minutes, demanding her name, her father's name and her whole family history, until at last he came to her age.

Gertrude, who had been replying smilingly to all questions, said "19." The officer began to write down "13," and then suddenly looked up at her and queried if 13 was right.

It took Gertrude several minutes to recover sufficiently to tell the officer her age was "19." The same catechism was put to Miss Ederle's father, Trainer Burgess, the Egyptian swimmer Helmi, the American swimmer Timson and everybody else aboard the tug.

After this long formality a sudden cheer, mixed with the booes and hisses from the somewhat angry crowd ashore, composed mostly of dockmen whose patience had been sorely tried by this demonstration of officialdom, greeted the announcement that Gertrude would be graciously permitted to enter England, but only on condition that she reported promptly to officials the next morning.

Gertrude then descended the gangway and had to walk afoot over half a mile along the dockside lanes before she could reach her waiting automobile. In this she hurried to the Grand Hotel, where she was given a hot soda bath and put abed.

Bonfires Blazed Way to the Shore.

KINGSDOWN, England, Aug. 6 (AP).—Gertrude Ederle, American swimming marvel, tonight won the proud distinction of being the first of her sex to conquer the treacherous waters of the English Channel. Not only did she succeed after a heroic effort and a sensational finish in accomplishing the feat, but she did it in faster time than any of the previous successful men performers.

Starting from the beach at Gris-Nez, France, at 7:09 o'clock this morning, she landed on the beach at Kingsdown, near Deal, at 9:40 o'clock tonight, having taken but 14 hours 31 minutes to make the difficult passage, as against the former record of 16 hours 23 minutes made by the Italo-Argentine swimmer Tirabocchi when he swam the Channel from Calais to Dover three years ago.

"I am a proud woman," was all Miss Ederle would say as she paused just for a moment on English soil after triumphantly walking up the beach, virtually as fresh as when she started on her long grind.

In fact, she was feeling in such fine fettle she wanted to plunge into the water to swim to the tug waiting about 200 yards offshore to take her back to France. She was dissuaded, however, and was rowed out amid acclamations by the large crowd which had come from the seaside resort of Deal and other watering places near by to watch the climax of the momentous event in Channel swimming history.

The swim came to an end in what might be described as a blaze of glory, for, to guide the swimmer as she neared the goal, huge bonfires were kept burning along the beach, lighting up the waters, so that those ashore could see the strong, steady strokes which Miss Ederle kept up until she was able to touch bottom and walk ashore. The glare of torches on the accompanying boats and their strong searchlights added to the brilliancy.

The swimmer refused all offers of help in landing. Waving all aside, she walked out of the surf unaided, amid tremendous outbursts of cheering which completely drowned the tugboats' sirens.

Sets Out Swimming Strongly.

CAPE GRIS-NEZ, France, Aug. 6 (AP).—Gertrude Ederle, the American swimmer, started at 7:09 o'clock this morning in an attempt to swim the English Channel. The weather conditions when she took her plunge were fine.

It was a grim and determined swimmer that entered the water this morning in sharp contrast to last year, when she dove off as if on a holiday. With set face she walked into the Channel from the sandy beach instead of diving from the rocks of the cape, as before.

She barely acknowledged the cheers of the few onlookers, but walked briskly until the water reached her waist, and then launched off with a steady crawl of twenty-eight strokes to the minute, making for the escorting tug Alsace, 500 yards away.

She was going very strong, and her trainer, T. W. Burgess, was already warning her, "Take your time, Miss Ederle!"

Miss Ederle did not come from Boulogne on board the convoying tug, as in her last attempt, but submitted to the greasing operation in the Hotel Sirene at the Cape.

The greasing was done by her sister, Margaret. First a coat of lanoline about an eighth of an inch thick was applied and then a layer of heavy grease. Miss Ederle then donned her swimming suit, cut deeply under the arms, and over this a third layer of grease was applied.

The swimmer displayed some impatience over the long greasing operation, and said to "Old Bill" Burgess, her trainer: "For heaven's sake, let's get started!"

"Gee, but it's cold," were her first words as she struck off. "It's fresher than last year," was her greeting to the Channel water, which registered 61 degrees Fahrenheit as the sun rose over the cliffs.

For the first two miles after she caught up with the tug, Miss Ederle continued mechanically at 28 to 29 strokes a minute, making good progress.

The sea was very calm, and she raised her goggles over her forehead for several hundred yards, saying: "It will be time enough to look through these things when the breeze freshens."

The pilots of both convoying tugs did their best to shield the swimmer from the increasing breeze which arose about noon after Miss Ederle had been in the water five hours. At that time she was nine miles out.

Approximate Route of Miss Ederle's Record Swim.

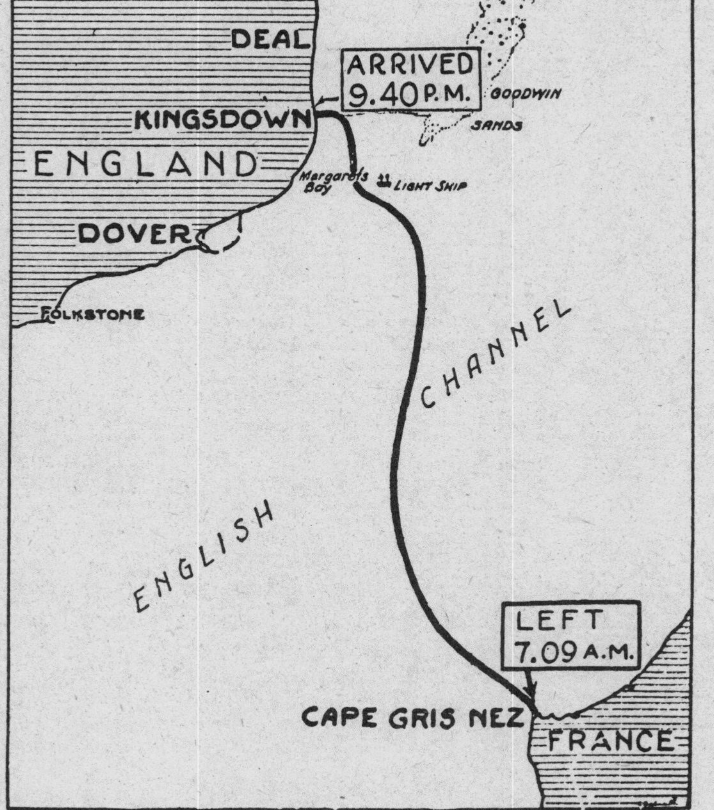

BREAKING RECORDS MISS EDERLE'S FORTE

Girl Swimmer Began Her Winning Career Three Years Ago and Has Kept It Up.

INHERITED FINE PHYSIQUE

Learned to Swim at Nine, but Did Not Become Expert Until She Was Sixteen.

Gertrude Ederle, the first woman swimmer to vanquish the English Channel, has all the qualities that go to make up the kind of heroine whom America will ungrudgingly and freely worship and honor for her splendid accomplishment. The record of her 19 years shows her to be courageous, determined, modest, sportsmanlike, generous, unaffected and perfectly poised. She has, in addition, beauty of face and figure and the abounding health that is the natural result of the normal life she has led of her own volition.

Although of German parentage, she is a child of "the sidewalks of New York." She was born on the west side of the city, reared there and schooled there. Her home today is at 108 Amsterdam Avenue, although she and her parents spend their Summers in a cottage at Highlands, N. J. Miss Ederle's father is a German butcher and her mother is of the sturdy German housewife type. Some of the qualities of endurance and stamina which have been displayed by Miss Ederle were inherited from her parents and improved by the girl's life and training.

Miss Ederle did not "swim before she walked." She knew nothing of swimming until she was nine years old, when she was taught to swim "dog fashion." She liked swimming, however, and steadily improved, though by her own admission, she did not learn to swim correctly until she was fifteen years old and a member of the Women's Swimming Association, the emblem of which she proudly wears on all her record breaking swims.

Her parentage showed early in the sturdy physique. Her shoulders broadened rapidly with her aquatic training under the tutelage of L. De B. Handley, coach of the Women's Swimming Association of New York. She did not consider that she had learned to swim correctly until she had mastered the crawl stroke which has since carried her to many victories.

Her First Bid for Fame.

Miss Ederle made her first bid for aquatic fame three years ago in the three-mile ocean race for the Joseph P. Day cup, which she won easily, defeating Helen Wainwright, then all-round amateur champion, Hilda James, English champion and others. Following that, world's records fell before her on various courses and for distances ranging from 50 yards to half a mile.

June 15, 1925, Miss Ederle shattered the men's record for the classic twenty-one-mile swim from the Battery to Sandy Hook in New York Bay. She covered the course in 7 hours 11 minutes and 30 seconds. No woman ever before had completed that trip.

Miss Ederle enhanced her natural physical strength and ability by taking the best of care of herself. Although, by her own and her mother's admission, the girl loves all normal pleasures, including a jazzy dance now and then, she never yielded to her interest in such things at the cost of her health or her athletic progress. In quite a few sports Miss Ederle excelled many of her sex, but she settled on swimming, and thereafter stuck to her one purpose.

She does not smoke, drink alcoholic beverages of any kind, or attempt the rôle of "life of the party" at any late affairs. She loves home work, is a good cook, milks cows—occasionally—and lives as much of her life as she consistently can in the open air. According to her mother, young men have never been her weakness, and she is today unattached even to the extent of having a regular "boy friend." She has given no thought to marriage, but has devoted all her attention to conquering the art of swimming.

Captured Senior Championship.

At the age of 16 Miss Ederle captured the Metropolitan A. A. U. senior 100-yard swimming championship, free style, for women. Her time was 1:06. From then on she went from victory to victory, with seldom a defeat in contests in the water. In spite of her accomplishments and her popularity she kept herself well in the background and accepted her victories with becoming modesty.

In spite of the records she has shattered, Miss Ederle has referred to herself as a "lazy swimmer," and she said on one occasion that this might be true of her in other matters. She disclosed some time ago that she quit school after her first year in high school. But, in spite of this, Miss Ederle talks well, speaks grammatically, and is well informed on many topics.

One of Miss Ederle's favorite water performances is that of breaking records heretofore held by men. She has done this in her Channel swim, clipping almost two hours off the fastest time in which the crossing was ever made by a man swimmer. In 1922 she smashed a world's record at Hamilton, Bermuda, in the 150-yard free style race, which she won in 1 minute 49 4-5 seconds.

Records held by Miss Ederle today, as listed in Spalding's Official Athletic Almanac, include:

Women's short course records, free style—150 yards, 1 minute 42 1-5 seconds, Miami Beach, Fla., March 1, 1925; 200 meters, 2 minutes 46 4-5 seconds, Brooklyn, April 4, 1923; 220 yards, 2 minutes 46 4-5 seconds, Brooklyn, April 4, 1923; 300 yards, 3 minutes 45 seconds, Miami Beach, Feb. 28, 1925; 400 meters, 5 minutes 53 1-5 seconds, Brighton Beach, Sept. 4, 1922; 440 yards, 5 minutes 54 3-5 seconds, Brighton Beach, Sept. 4, 1922; 500 yards, 6 minutes 45 1-5 seconds, Brighton Beach, Sept. 4, 1922; 500 meters, 7 minutes 22 1-5 seconds, Brighton Beach, Sept. 4, 1922.

Miss Ederle was one of the swimmers in relay races in which records were established for 200, 250, 400 and 500 yards at Miami Beach in February, 1925.

Her records for women's long course, free style, are: 100 metres, 1 minute 12 1-5 seconds, Honolulu, Oct. 11, 1923; 200 meters, 2 minutes 45 2-5 seconds, Honolulu, Oct. 10, 1923; 220 yards, 2 minutes 49 seconds, Rye Beach, N. Y., July 4, 1923; 400 meters, 5 minutes 54 2-5 seconds, Honolulu, Oct. 13, 1923; 440 yards, 6 minutes 1-5 second, New Brunswick, N. J., Sept. 2, 1922.

Miss Ederle's successful swim yesterday was her second attempt to conquer the Channel. Late last Summer the young woman, then under the training of Jabez Wolff, swam from Cape Gris Nez to within six and one-half miles of the English coast. She was in the water on that occasion 8 hours and 46 minutes, and her performance was regarded as one of the best in the Channel. For a time she was ahead of the records of the five men who have successfully accomplished the Channel swim.

On her return to the United States after her first attempt, Miss Ederle said she could have kept going longer, though she was not certain she could have reached shore. She said Wolff touched her, disqualifying her, and ordered her out of the water.

Wolff replied that he had not touched her, or ordered her out, but that she had collapsed as a result of having swallowed a quantity of salt water.

"All the News That's Fit to Print."

The New York Times.

THE WEATHER
Mostly cloudy and possibly showers today and tomorrow.
Temperature yesterday—Max. 77, min. 60.
For weather report see Page 25.

VOL. LXXV....No. 25,073. NEW YORK, FRIDAY, SEPTEMBER 17, 1926. TWO CENTS In Greater New York | THREE CENTS Within 200 Miles | FOUR CENTS Elsewhere in the U. S.

TILDEN VANQUISHED; HIS SIX-YEAR REIGN IN U. S. TENNIS ENDS

Champion Put Out of National Play by Cochet of France, 6-8, 6-1, 6-3, 1-6, 8-6.

FIGHTS FIERCELY TO END

Ignores Hurt Knee, Striving in Vain to Save Day With One of His Famous Rallies.

TWO OTHER FRENCHMEN WIN

Richards Lone U. S. Survivor as Johnston Bows to Borotra and Williams to Lacoste.

By ALLISON DANZIG.

The six-year reign of William Tilden over tennisdom came to an end yesterday, William Johnston also went down to defeat and France placed three men in the semi-finals of the national championship at the West Side Tennis Club, Forest Hills. Six years of American supremacy on the courts crumpled under a French attack that eliminated three of America's Big Four, leaving Vincent Richards as the only hope of the United States to keep the title from going overseas.

Tilden, the invincible, the player whose magic with a racquet has confounded the greatest players of the world and made America supreme in tennis, at last has relinquished his sceptre.

The tall, gaunt Tilden, who has stood challenging all comers, at last has toppled after reigning so absolutely for six years that he had come to be regarded as the most powerful potentate in amateur sports, immune to defeat in national championship play and capable of rising superior to any crisis through the sheer wizardry of his strokes.

Even the injury to his knee that paved the way for his defeat by René Lacoste last Saturday, his first in Davis Cup singles, had been looked upon as a negligible consideration, so supreme was the confidence in Tilden's mastery. But it was that injury that undermined the champion's great playing strength, as Henri Cochet of France fought his way to victory in five sets at 6—8, 6—1, 6—3, 1—6, 8—6.

Falls With Colors Flying.

If ever a champion went down with colors flying William Tilden was that champion yesterday. Fighting from behind all the way during the two hours that the match lasted, the Philadelphian won the hearts of the 9,000 spectators in the stadum as he never won them in victory. He gave himself unsparingly and with reckless disregard for his underpinning in his vain effort to withstand the demoralizing steadiness and craftily placed shots of his opponent.

The climax of the match, the point at which the gallery broke into its wildest demonstrations, was during the final set when Tilden, trailing at 1—4, rallied to volley Cochet dizzy with one of the most sensational exhibitions he ever gave at the net and pull up to 4-all. Every winning shot of the American was greeted with roars of applause and with each successive game in the series of three hearts became lighter with hope for an American victory.

When Tilden won the eighth game there were few who believed that the catastrophe would occur. The champion, it was agreed, was still the old champion, capable of lifting his game in an emergency to unassailable heights. But after leading at 40—15 on Cochet's service in the ninth game, Tilden had reached the end of his rope. The player whose last-minute pull-ups had brought him out of the jaws of defeat so many times in the past finally met his master.

Cochet, playing with the coolness of a veteran of twice his years and absorbing the champion's cannonball service and lightning drives with machinelike steadiness, confounded the American's most desperate efforts and checkmated his every thrust with counter-strokes of craft. Tilden's service enabled him to go into the lead at 6—5, and then the débâcle came as the invader crushed all opposition in the next three games, in which Tilden got only four points.

Let full justice be done Cochet, the player who achieved what had been looked upon as the impossible. Fairness to Tilden necessitated consideration of the bearing his physical condition had upon the match, but fairness to the young Frenchman also calls for due acknowledgment of the fact that Tilden, even with the fullest support of his legs, would have been extended to the limit to prevail over Cochet, and still might well have failed.

Cochet Amazes Onlookers.

Those who last saw Cochet in this country in 1922 were unable to comprehend how he could have beaten Richards abroad twice this year, but satisfactory explanation was furnished yesterday. No French player that ever came to the United States has given a more masterly exhibition than did Cochet against the champion. There was a confidence about this young player that those who have watched him in action abroad looked upon as a foreboding sign. Cochet was at his best for the first time in this country, and went about his task as though he never had any doubt about the outcome.

This 24-year-old youth was coolness personified. In the face of Tilden's most devastating swipes he maintained the even tenor of his way, assimilating speed as though he were brought up on it and eternally getting the ball back as steadily as the patter of rain. Lacoste had come to be regarded as the most mechanically perfect player in

Continued on Page Seventeen.

Policeman Saves Two Girls Near Drowning at Coney

Two girls in danger of drowning were rescued by a policeman at Coney Island yesterday, as crowds on the Boardwalk looked on and cheered.

Patrolman Thomas Kicklichter was on the Boardwalk when he saw two girls in danger beyond the life lines. Miss Virginia Riccardi of 268 Ninety-fifth Street, had been seized with cramps while swimming with her friend Miss Frances Bicertil of 2,767 West Sixteenth Street, Coney Island. The policeman threw off his hat and coat and racing into the water swam toward the pair. Miss Riccardi sank twice before he reached her, and Miss Bicertil was weak from the effort to keep her friend afloat. The policeman brought them both ashore. Miss Riccardi was taken to the Coney Island Hospital.

NUTMEG DEMOCRATS DEMAND DRY REPEAL

State Convention's Platform Calls Prohibition a Blow at Personal Liberty.

NAME TYLER FOR SENATE

Improved Labor Conditions and Wider State and Local Rule Are Advocated.

Special to The New York Times.

NEW HAVEN, Conn., Sept. 16.—Repeal of the prohibition amendment was demanded today by the Democratic State Convention, which nominated candidates for United States Senator, Governor and other State offices and adopted a platform for the State campaign.

The anti-prohibition plank reads as follows:

"The Eighteenth Amendment has no place in the framework of our Government. It is an indefensible curtailment of personal liberty. We believe that it should be repealed and pledge our candidates for office to work for that end. In taking this unequivocal stand we do not countenance non-enforcement. While prohibition is the law of the land, it is the duty of our Government to enforce it. We oppose the return of the saloon."

The plank was adopted by a 10 to 1 vote of the convention.

Vincent Callahan of Branford, a lifelong temperance worker, voicing opposition to the plank, said:

"I oppose any attempt to repeal the Eighteenth Amendment. It has brought peace, happiness and prosperity to homes that never knew them before."

In replying to him Timothy Lynch of Rockville said:

"A Democratic convention is not a prohibition convention and prohibitionists have no place in it. I hope that new rules will be adopted which will prevent their being at the Democratic convention two years hence."

Rollin V. Tyler, Probate Court Judge, of Haddam, was named to oppose Hiram Bingham for the Senate and Charles G. Morris of this city was nominated for the Governorship. The rest of the State ticket follows:

For Lieutenant Governor, Milo R. Waters, Norwich; Secretary of State, David Richman, New Haven; State Treasurer, Peter M. Kennedy, Waterbury; Controller, Joseph F. Brown, Enfield; Attorney General, Frederick M. McCarthy, Ansonia.

The greatest applause of the convention greeted the speech of Judge William E. Thoms of Waterbury, who placed Mr. McCarthy in nomination. Judge Thoms declined the nomination for Governor. His friends stated that an attempt would be made to have him on the State ticket two years hence with Governor Smith of New York for the Presidency.

The platform pledges the candidates and party to work for three changes in the immediate future: First, jury service for women; second, better conditions for employment and shorter hours of labor; third, a thorough legislative investigation of tax burdens so that greater equality may be effected.

The platform calls decentralization the outstanding issue of the campaign and urges shifting of government, except for fundamental functions, from Washington to the States and from State capitals to local communities. It adds:

"We believe that this State should be returned to its citizens. Today the people of Connecticut are ruled, not by themselves, but for the benefit of a Republican machine."

SMITH AND WAGNER HEAD PARTY SLATE FRAMED AT ALBANY

Democratic Leaders Meet With Governor to Make Plans for Syracuse.

TWO SURPRISES ON LIST

Tremaine of Buffalo Named for Controller and Stoltz of Syracuse for Attorney General.

JOHNSON OFFERS PLATFORM

Planks Will Be Devised to Meet Expected Nomination of Mills by Republicans.

Special to The New York Times.

ALBANY, N. Y., Friday, Sept. 17.—At a conference of Democratic State leaders held with Governor Smith at the Executive Mansion here tonight, which adjourned shortly before 1 o'clock this morning, a tentative slate was completed for presentation to the State convention, which is to meet in Syracuse on Sept. 27.

The slate agreed on, which will have to be approved by the convention, is as follows:

For Governor—ALFRED E. SMITH of New York.

For United States Senator—ROBERT F. WAGNER of New York.

For Lieutenant Governor—EDWIN CORNING of Albany.

For State Controller—MORRIS S. TREMAINE of Buffalo.

For Attorney General—BENJAMIN STOLTZ of Syracuse.

The two last mentioned on the list are surprise candidates, for whom not even a semblance of a boom had been launched, and in each case the selection has been made as a matter of political expediency.

In the case of Stultz the determination was not made until a late hour, when it was found that the ticket arranged contained no one of the Jewish faith. At that time Neal B. Brewster of Syracuse and Joseph Kellogg of Glens Falls were the two men being considered for the Attorney Generalship. The substition of Stoltz for Brewster was proposed by William H. Kelley of Syracuse, boss of Onondaga County.

Conference Called Quietly.

Consideration of the names of both Tremaine and Brewster last night furnished the surprise of the conference, which was called very quietly to obviate the necessity of Governor Smith going to New York today to see the leaders there, as had been announced. Instead, there came to this city as imposing an array of Democratic leaders as has been brought together thus far this year.

The list includes George W. Olvany, leader of Tammany Hall; Norman E. Mack of Buffalo, National Committeeman; John H. McCooey, leader in Kings County; Henry M. Naylor, County Chairman of Erie County; Edward J. Flynn, Democratic leader in the Bronx; United States Senator Royal S. Copeland, William H. Kelley of Syracuse, William Bray of Utica, Edwin Corning, the probable candidate for Lieutenant Governor, and Joseph Johnson, Commissioner of Public Works in Manhattan and Chairman of the committee charged with the duty of preparing a tentative platform for presentation to the Syracuse convention.

News of Arrival Leaks Out.

Most of these men arrived in Albany about 7 o'clock and went at once to the Executive Mansion, where they had dinner. No announcement had been made of the gathering, but the news had leaked out. When the Governor greeted his guests he said to the newspaper men, "Pretty nearly everything relating to the welfare of the State of New York and the Democratic Party will be discussed." It was 9 o'clock before the conferees got down to actual business and began drafting the slate, with the prospect of taking up the platform later on.

There was a decided prospect when the conferees met that Corning would not be named for the second place on

Continued on Page Three.

Actress's Son, 5, Decides His Own Custody; Goes to Mother, Janet Beecher, in Court

The preference of Richard Wyndham Hoffmann, five-year-old son of Dr. Richard H. Hoffmann and Janet Beecher, actress, as to his parents decided yesterday a habeas corpus application sued out by Dr. Hoffmann before Supreme Court Justice Valente. The application sought to compel his wife to return their son to him under the terms of the report of former Justice Richard McC. Marsh as referee in the litigation between the Hoffmanns. The boy chose his mother, and under Justice Valente's order she will have him until Justice Lydon decides the application to confirm Referee Marsh's report now pending before him.

After the Hoffmann's had sued each other for the custody of the boy and for a separation, in which Mrs. Hoffmann charged her husband with unkind acts, and he alleged abandonment, Referee Marsh took testimony and decided that the actres had left her husband's home, and that the testimony against him did not justify Miss Beecher in leaving him. While the referee also found as unjustified all charges involving the personal conduct of Miss Beecher, he decided that because of her stage engagements, requiring her to be away from the city most of the year, she should have the custody of their boy only from June 15 to Sept. 15.

Miss Beecher's failure to deliver the boy to her husband on Wednesday caused the physician to sue out the habeas corpus writ yesterday, haling her and the boy before Justice Valente. The boy, dresed in a while sailor suit, with blue trimmings, sat with his mother while the attorneys argued the legal phase of the case. Justice Valente turned to the boy suddenly and, requesting a halt in the argument, said:

"Come here, Richard."

The boy walked to the Justice's chair and faced him calmly as the Court said:

"Richard, whom would you rather live with, your mother or your father?"

As the father leaned forward to catch the reply and the mother half rose from her chair gasping, the child answered:

"My mother."

Miss Beecher stifled an exclamation and sank into her chair. Justice Valente, announcing that he was loath to take the boy from his mother, said that he was to remain with her until the referee's report was acted upon. The father, however, is to see him every day and be with him over the week-ends. Dr. Hoffmann also had his boy for several hours after the court proceeding ended, but was directed to return the boy to Mrs. Hoffmann at 5 P. M.

Quebec Liquor System Yields Record Revenue of $5,339,394

Special to The New York Times.

MONTREAL, Sept. 16.—For the fifth year of its operation the Quebec Liquor Commission has turned into the Provincial Government $3,500,000 on trade account. There is an additional $1,839,394 from the commission, comprising license fees of beer shops, taverns, hotels and restaurants.

This is the largest revenue yielded to date, but the profits will not be known till the commission lays its report before the Quebec Legislature. Though all of the funds are turned over, the Government does not always demand the full profits of the commission.

For example, last year the commission was allowed to hold back $1,000,000 to add to its working capital. The commission began operations on borrowed capital, but each year has created reserves for working capital.

NINE NEW MEMBERS ON LEAGUE COUNCIL

Poland, Czechoslovakia, Holland, Rumania, Colombia, China, Chili, Salvador, Belgium, In.

FRENCH GROUP DOMINANT

Ireland Is Turned Down by the Assembly With Only 10 Votes Out of 48.

BY EDWIN L. JAMES.

Copyright, 1926, by The New York Times Company
By Wireless to THE NEW YORK TIMES.

GENEVA, Sept. 16.—The difficulties attending the admission of Germany to the League of Nations were finally liquidated today when, in accordance with the compromise adopted to settle the dispute over Council seats, the Assembly elected nine non-permanent members of the Council. Of the three non-permanent seats created only one was filled, that for Poland. The other two, created for Spain and Brazil, were left vacant.

The following States were elected:

For three years: Poland, Chile and Rumania.

For two years: Colombia, Holland and China.

For one year: Czechoslovakia, Belgium and Salvador.

Holland was declared by a two-thirds vote re-eligible at the end of her term, which is intended to assure to her a six-year seat. The other members elected today are not re-eligible at the end of their terms. The Council of the League, therefore, now is composed of these nine nations, plus the holders of permanent seats—Britain, France, Germany, Italy and Japan—there being fourteen members in the new Council instead of ten of which the old Council was made up.

French Group Very Strong.

A glance at the composition of the new Council shows that the French group came out exceptionally well. The action of Spain and Brazil in leaving Geneva threatened seriously to reduce the French strength in the Council, since those two nations usually voted with France on important issues. On the Council as it existed France, Belgium, Czechoslovakia, Brazil and Spain formed five of the ten members. But the election of Poland, Rumania, Belgium and Czechoslovakia, all French allies, leaves France in a position relatively as strong as regards the opposite group, led by England, and even stronger if one figures that the Germans with the Dutch will probably be independent.

In the new Council of fourteen members the French group has France, Poland, Rumania, Belgium, Czechoslovakia, Colombia, Salvador and most likely Chile. This places France and her allies in the position of controlling the Assembly and, on most occasions, the Council of the League.

The candidacy of Ireland fell flat, she getting only ten votes out of forty-eight. This defeat was due to two factors—first, the failure of the British Empire votes to back her up, and, secondly, the feeling against the British Empire having two voices on the Council.

Stresemann Declines Chairmanship.

The new Council met this afternoon and on the principle of alphabetical rotation the Chairmanship was offered to Dr. Stresemann. He expressed pleasure at the honor, but, pleading lack of knowledge of French and of League procedure, asked that he be excused and that the Council President take the chair. Thus the Germans added to their newly acquired League reputation that of being shrinking violets. This attitude of modesty has made a great impression because of the predictions that Germany's League membership would bring discord into the League.

However, one should pay attention to the German declarations that they are now feeling their way and next year will be old and adapted members of the League. Dr. Stresemann would be the first to discourage hopes that the Germans will always be as placable as they are at this session of the Assembly.

Although satisfaction at today's settlement of the thorny question was generally expressed, it seems wise to point out that the South American representation on the Council was badly handled. This was due to the use of the bloc system by which the Latin-American republics held caucusses and named their three candidates. It so happened that Argentina, Bolivia, Brazil, Costa Rica, Honduras, Peru and Ecuador were absent from Geneva during this Assembly. Of nineteen South American and Central American delegations this left twelve at Geneva, with the Central Americans voting together six votes. And so Colombia and Salvador were chosen with

Continued on Page Nine.

HALL CRIME WITNESS SAW HENRY STEVENS THERE, SIMPSON SAYS

Grand Jury Acted on Story of Spectator at the Murder Prosecutor Asserts.

HEARING FOR FOUR TODAY

Higher Bail for Widow May Be Asked—State to Apply for a "Foreign" Jury.

TO PRESS PERJURY CHARGES

Indictments for False Affidavits Sought—Simpson Insists That Gorsline Has Not Told All.

Henry Stevens was at the scene when the Rev. Dr. Edward W. Hall and Mrs. Eleanor R. Mills were shot to death four years ago, according to Assistant Attorney General Alexander Simpson. The State, he added, has a witness who will testify to that.

Senator Simpson made this disclosure yesterday in explaining how and why Henry Stevens had been one of four persons accused of the murder by the Somerset County Grand Jury in indictments returned on Wednesday at Somerville. The eyewitness, said the Senator, was one of the thirty witnesses who appeared before the Grand Jury.

The unnamed person is the second to come forward as a spectator of the murder. Mrs. Jane Gibson, "the pig woman," was the first. It was her story and her identifications that caused the arrest and the subsequent indictment of the three others charged with the crime. They are Mrs. Frances Stevens Hall, widow of the minister; her other brother, Willie Stevens, and her cousin, Henry de la Bruyere Carpender.

Hearing Set for Today.

The four defendants are to have a hearing on the indictments at 5 P. M. today at Somerville. Supreme Court Justice Charles W. Parker will preside and with him on the bench will be Common Pleas Judge Frank L. Cleary. Senator Simpson, it was said, would ask that the bail of $15,000 which has given Mrs. Hall her freedom since Aug. 1 be increased substantially.

Francis L. Bergen, Prosecutor for Somerset County, will reconvene the Grand Jury at Somerville on Monday. Evidence of alleged perjury in the Hall-Mills investigation will be laid before the jurors. Indictments for "three or four" persons will be sought, declared Senator Simpson.

The Assistant Attorney General whose feat in obtaining four indictments from a Grand Jury that took only ten minutes to determine upon its course was commented upon widely yesterday, went to Trenton during the day. He conferred informally with Chief Justice William S. Gummere of the Supreme Court. Later, Senator Simpson said that the Chief Justice had set next Thursday at Trenton as the time and place of an application by the State for a "foreign" jury to try the case against the four under indictment.

Jurors From Other Counties.

Under the New Jersey law in criminal cases a change of venue is not permitted. A "foreign" jury, chosen from talesmen designated from any county in the State by the Chief Justice and two Associate Justices, is imported to the county within which the offense was committed. Senator Simpson said he felt it would be difficult to get a jury with open minds in Somerset County. The same was true of a jury that might be drawn from his own county, Hudson.

The special prosecutor said that the trial might not be held until the second week in November. He could not speak definitely on this, however, owing to the many elements entering into the situation. The State has not yet determined whether the four defendants will be tried together or separately.

When Senator Simpson reached his office in Jersey City early yesterday he turned at once to the indictment of Henry Stevens. Some surprise had been expressed over the accusation so suddenly made against Stevens, who had cited six of his neighbors at Lavallette, N. J., as able to support his alibi for the night of the murder, Sept. 14, 1922. Inspector John J. Underwood and other investigators, however, had

Continued on Page Two.

MEXICAN BANDITS MURDER ROSENTHAL TO ESCAPE TRAP TROOPS SET FOR THEM; AMERICA DEMANDS SLAYERS BE PUNISHED

Coolidge Made Anxious by Killing of Rosenthal; State Department Acts Quickly on Murder

Special to The New York Times.

PAUL SMITH'S, N. Y., Sept. 16.—President Coolidge, notified by the State Department late this afternoon of the murder of Jacob Rosenthal of Woodmere, L. I., is watching developments in Mexico and will insist that the State Department demands for the arrest and punishment of the bandits be complied with without delay by the Mexican authorities.

This latest turn in the relations between the United States and Mexico is a source of much anxiety to the President, who hoped that the Mexican Government had reached a point of stability and that order existed in the country.

He hoped, too, that the Calles Government would approach the oil and land law disputes with the intention of making recessions that would be satisfactory to American property owners in Mexico.

WASHINGTON, Sept. 16 (AP).—Secretary Kellogg tonight instructed Mr. Schoenfeld, Chargé at Mexico City, to make representations to the Calles Government to leave no stone unturned in apprehending and punishing the slayers of Jacob Rosenthal of New York.

The Secretary's action shows that the State Department is prepared to exert every effort to establish responsibility for the killing and to take a firm stand in demanding the punishment of those guilty.

While the text of the instructions was not made public, the announcement indicates that the Washington Government feels that such an offense against its nationals warrants prompt action by the Mexican authorities.

Pending further developments, State Department officials refused to forecast what additional steps might be necessary.

NEW YORK MAN STABBED

Body Found by Soldiers After Fight in Which Two Brigands Fall.

DECOYS CARRIED "RANSOM"

Police Refused to Let Friend of Victim Take $10,000 the Kidnappers Demanded.

STRAINED RELATIONS LOOM

Killing of American First in the Coolidge Regime—Widow Cancels Trip to Mexico.

Copyright, 1926, by The New York Times Company.
Special Cable to THE NEW YORK TIMES.

MEXICO CITY, Sept. 16.—Jacob Rosenthal of Woodmere, L. I., was murdered last night by the bandits who kidnapped him on Sunday night while he was on his way in an automobile from Cuernavaca to Mexico City.

Federal troops and police who had been pursuing the kidnappers since Monday found the body of Mr. Rosenthal.

Retarded in their flight by the weakness of their captive, who was more than 60 years old, and having failed to get the $10,000 ransom they demanded, the bandits killed him with machetes and blows from their rifle butts.

The pursuing forces, after a short battle with the bandits, found the body of the American lying on the grass in the deep brush near the Cuatla Road.

The bandits had held their victim for nearly three days before seeking ransom, and yesterday they sent a letter to Joseph Ruff, son-in-law of Mr. Rosenthal, demanding that 20,000 pesos be delivered by two mounted men at a spot on the Cuatla road several miles east of where Mr. Rosenthal was taken captive.

Offer to Pay Bandits Refused.

Joseph Ruff was in Cuernavaca, but Lucien Ruff, a cousin, informed the American Embassy and the police of the letter and asked to be permitted to carry the ransom money to the bandits. But the Chief of Police and the chief of military operations had another plan, and sent two soldiers dressed in civilian clothes as decoys. Instead of the 20,000 pesos ransom demanded by the bandits the disguised soldiers carried a bag filled with iron rings.

As the mounted decoys rode along the road to the spot designated by the bandits the Federal troops made a wide swing around the road in an effort to capture the entire gang.

When the troops approached the spot the bandits opened fire, which was returned by the troops. After a short skirmish the bandits fled, first killing Mr. Rosenthal. His body was found in the brush near the bodies of two dead bandits.

The rest of the band escaped to the mountains.

All three bodies were taken to Cuernavaca.

The American Embassy retained Dr. Priestly to represent the United States at the autopsy on the body of Mr. Rosenthal at Cuernavaca. Dr. Priestly arrived there tonight. The body will be brought to Mexico City tomorrow and forwarded from here to his home.

Rosenthal Wrote Letter.

Part of the letter sent to Mr. Ruff demanding the 20,000 pesos ransom was written in English by Mr. Rosenthal and part of it in Spanish by one of the bandits. Mr. Rosenthal wrote:

"I am held here in the forest about two miles from where we breakfasted. I have slept in the rain. My captors want 20,000 pesos ransom."

The Spanish section of the letter gave directions for sending the money. It read:

"Send the money from Cuernavaca by two mounted men, who will ride along the Cuatla road until they reach a spot where we will meet them and deliver the captive."

After capturing Rosenthal on Sunday evening the bandits crossed the Cuernavaca road and entered the forests to the east near the road which leads to the Summer resort of Cuatla.

The military authorities believe that when the bodies of the bandits are shown to the citizens of Cuernavaca they will be readily identified and that clues will be provided that will insure the prompt capture of the remaining members of the bandit gang.

Plan to Trap Bandits Kept Secret.

Telegrams from Cuernavaca are vague. The Police Department, in the hope of capturing the kidnappers, had requested the American Embassy not to advise the American reporters of the request for ransom lest the bandits learn from the American press details of the plan for their capture.

The death of Mr. Rosenthal, however, caused the American Embassy to give out what few details were

KING CHECKS HELPED TO PAY G. O. P. DEFICIT

Ex-Secretary Tells of $5,000 Gift in 1922 to Daugherty for Ohio Campaign Losses.

$5,000 SENT IN 1920 ALSO

$25,000 Check From Politician to Jess Smith Revealed, but Court Bars It From Evidence.

The late John T. King sent two checks of $2,500 each in 1922 to Harry M. Daugherty, then Attorney General, as contributions to the Republican campaign deficit in Ohio, it was revealed yesterday at the seventh day of the trial in Federal Court in which Mr. Daugherty and Colonel Miller are charged with fraudulent conspiracy. This was testified to by John D. Durkin, formerly Mr. King's private secretary.

Mr. Durkin also testified that Mr. King had sent a check for $5,000 to Mr. Daugherty in 1920, also for the benefit of the Republican Party.

Check Sent in Campaign.

Max D. Steuer, Mr. Daugherty's counsel, showed that the $5,000 check Mr. King had sent to Mr. Daugherty had been dated April 19, 1920, when "the campaign of 1920 was going on, either primary campaigns or preparation for the nomination of President, or the campaign itself."

Mr. Steuer then asked Mr. Durkin:

"Did you ever in your life draw a check, see a check of any kind that was payable to H. M. Daugherty or Harry Daugherty or Harry M. Daugherty intended for this defendant at the bar, that had any relation to or any connection with any bonds, that was drawn by Mr. King?"

"No sir," answered Mr. Durkin, "I never did."

In being thus accounted for, the two 1922 checks, which had been hanging fire since the previous day, were thus disposed of as comparatively irrelevant so far as the criminal issue itself was concerned.

Further interest attached to the testimony of Mr. Durkin when he said that on April 28, 1922, he deposited Liberty Loan bond coupons amounting to $2,125 in Mr. King's bank account in the Guaranty Trust Company. Mr. Durkin identified a photostatic copy of the deposit slip.

Mr. Durkin's admission gained significance from the fact that the con-

Continued on Page Four.

AIMEE M'PHERSON ORDERED ARRESTED

Evangelist With Four Others Accused of Conspiracy to Support Kidnapping Story.

ONE TO MAKE CLEAN BREAST

Ormiston Expected to Clear Up Cottage Mystery—Evangelist's Mother Among the Accused.

LOS ANGELES, Sept. 16 (AP).—The arrest of Aimee Semple McPherson, Angelus Temple evangelist; Mrs. Minnie Kennedy, her mother; Kenneth G. Ormiston, former Angelus Temple radio operator; John Doe Martin and Mrs. Lorraine Wiseman-Sielaff was ordered late today by District Attorney Asa Keyes.

Complaints charging the five persons with conspiracy to defeat justice in connection with Mrs. McPherson's disappearance last Spring were ordered drawn by the District Attorney. The complaints will bear the signature of Charles Reimer, Assistant Chief of Detectives under Keyes.

Ormiston, according to his attorney, S. S. Hahn, will accept service of the warrant here in Los Angeles. Hahn, in conference with District Attorney Keyes, said that he would produce Ormiston immediately. He indicated that he had been in touch with the former radio operator near Alhambra, a suburb of Los Angeles.

Orders for the five arrests grew out of a third official investigation into the strange disappearance of the evangelist on May 18 at Ocean Park, near here, and her reappearance on June 23 at Douglas, Ariz., with a story of having been kidnapped.

Elements of this third investigation were revelations by Mrs. Wiseman-Sielaff that money had been furnished to her from Angelus Temple to produce a woman to be identified as the occupant of a cottage at Carmel, Cal., immediately after the evangelist's disappearance, to show that it was not Mrs. McPherson who occupied the cottage, and revelations by Miss Bernice Morris that money had been paid from the temple in an apparent effort to manufacture evidence to support the kidnapping story.

Counsel for Angelus Temple informed the District Attorney that Mrs. McPherson and her mother would be surrendered as soon as the warrant for their arrest was prepared.

Statement by District Attorney.

District Attorney Keyes issued this statement:

"Legal action to place before the public of this community all of the facts and circumstances of this case and to prosecute before the bar of justice this woman and her associates is imperative.

"As the District Attorney of this county and its chief law enforcement officer, I have proceeded from the beginning with the thought in mind that Mrs. McPherson's position as the religious leader of a considerable number of people and the custodian of their Christian faith entitles her to protection from hasty or ill-considered action.

"From the time that the story of the finding of Mrs. McPherson was broadcast to the country there has been an atmosphere of a gigantic hoax surrounding it. As time progressed this increased with the unbelievable story of the kidnapping and the brazen activities of Mrs. McPherson and her friends to build up a false alibi for her.

"It is my duty and I can do no less than to exert the full power of my office to bring this woman before the bar of justice in order that she may have a fair and public hearing. It is with regret that I take action against a person so high in the religious esteem of many persons, but the community and the upright members of all religions would welcome a fair and open hearing of a situation which has become a national scandal."

Ormiston to Turn State's Evidence.

Ormiston, who has been sought by officials for several months, will turn

Continued on Page Eighteen.

Texas House Votes Ferguson Regime Inquiry; Includes Oil Firms Accused of Tax Evasion

Special to The New York Times.

AUSTIN, Texas, Sept. 16.—By a vote of 104 to 22 the lower house of the Texas Legislature, in special session, today ordered an investigation of the administration of Governor Miriam A. Ferguson.

The resolution, which originally provided for an inquiry into the Highway Commission, the Text Book Board and the Governor's pardon record, was amended just before passage to include oil and sulphur companies. It was charged that the State has been losing $3,000,000 to $7,000,000 a year in taxes because of incompetent reports to the State Controller by some of these companies on their production.

The charge that members of the Legislature have practiced before the Highway Commission and the Pardon Board also will be investigated.

A special committee of nine members of the House will be appointed later by Speaker Lee Satterwhite to conduct the inquiry. It will begin work after the special session adjourns and will report to the next regular session of the Legislature, which will convene on the second Tuesday of January.

The committee is empowered to summon witnesses and to enforce their presence. Its sessions will be public. An appropriation of $25,000 was made to defray its expenses.

The Ferguson supporters in the House were opposed to deferring the inquiry and urged that it begin immediately and report to the special session.

"Jim" Ferguson is keeping a vigilant eye on every move of the Legislature. Just now he is endeavoring to inject the Ku Klux Klan issue into the proceedings. He charges that the Klan is behind every move that is made to discredit the Administration. His action is taken as a further indication that he is preparing to announce himself as a candidate for the United States Senate.

In his latest pronouncement Mr. Ferguson says that "the League of Nations and the World Court are a fool's dream calculated to get this country into more trouble than anything that has ever happened before," and adds that he expects to have plenty to say on this issue later on.

TILDEN VANQUISHED; 6-YEAR REIGN ENDS

By ALLISON DANZIG.

Continued from Page 1, Column 1.

tennis, but Cochet could have given him spades and a couple of racquets yesterday.

At the end of a rally in the seventh game of the third set Major A. P. Simmonds, the umpire, called out "advantage Lacoste." Cochet stopped in his act of serving and looked quizzically at the official, who raised his hat, amid the laughter of the spectators, to apologize for his mistake. But the mistake was easy enough to understand. Major Simmonds, like many another person there, must have been under the delusion this machine-like youth was Lacoste.

But Cochet was more than a machine. There was a tennis brain directing this mechanically perfect player's shots that left Tilden at his wits' end in trying to fathom its workings. It was not Cochet's strokes that were so irresistible, but the craftiness with which they were deployed.

Off the ground the Frenchman was outclassed in speed and depth, for, as regards pase, his strokes for the most part were hardly more than defensive returns, crossing the net at high altitude and bounding high off the turf to afford Tilden the opportunity to get set for his pasting returns. Playing safe against Tilden's blistering shots, Cochet awaited his opportunities to let loose with a forcing stroke—opportunities which [illegible] made himself by the changing direction and varying length he employed. Once he had the champion wide of the court and on the run, then Cochet's shots sought a lower level and deeper territory and usually in the American's backhand corner.

If his ground strokes were lacking in severity, Cochet's volleys were the last word in finality. Any time that the Frenchman came to the net he was a dangerous figure, deadly overhead and sure on the straight volley. As a rule, Tilden can dislodge any opponent who entrenches himself at the net, but he was always worried yesterday when Cochet bearded his forcing shots. Because Cochet is so deft a volleyer and handles his racquet like an artist at close quarters, the champion knew that he must put the ball out of his reach or directly on top of his feet to stump him, and he could not hit the bull's-eye. Lobbing was out of the question, for Cochet handled everything overhead with unfailing precision.

Against an opponent of this calibre, who was a stonewall in his back court and a catapult at close quarters, Tilden never had a moment's peace of mind, except in the fourth set, when he carried all before him by the sheer fury of his attack. The champion appreciated from the very start the size of the task facing him, for Cochet against Hunter had given h[illegible] ling of what to expect, and for the first time in the tournament the gallery saw an aroused Tilden in the very first game—a Tilden who hit out with bludgeon strokes off the ground, capitalized his cannonball service for its full worth, jockeyed with all his cunning for positional advantages and who exploited his volleying game as few have seen him exploit it in all the years that he has held the title.

It is doubtful whether many appreciated how magnificent a volleyer Tilden can be until this match, so seldom has he felt it necessary to seek close grips with his opponents. [illegible] was a reason for his change in tactics yesterday, a change which he adopted on Wednesday also. The strain of plugging up the gaps in his back court called for greater demands upon his knee than the work of holding his position at the net, and for that reason Tilden the driver and chopper became a volleyer.

And what a volleyer the champion was! Even Richards at his best could not have performed more sensationally than did the champion as he twisted and stooped and went through every sort of evolution in bringing off low drop volleys off his feet and smashes in the air.

Frenchman Remains Calm.

There were times, particularly in the fourth set and during the champion's rally in the final chapter when it seemed that human resistance to this sort of shot-making was futile, but Cochet was never worried and in due time put in his oar to take the play away from the champion with shot-making at the net that evoked almost equally thunderous applause. Everything that the champion did well Cochet did also, and he was able to do it over a longer period than Tilden, rising to irresistible heights in the final stages when Tilden was making the last desperate stand of a champion who felt his crown slipping away from him.

So totally absorbed were the officials, as well as the spectators, in this match that all thought of the other contests was forgotten until the last point was played, and as a result the play in the three other matches got away to a late start. Two hours after Tilden walked off the courts a beaten man, Johnston also passed out of the play in five sets, the victim of Jean Borotra.

Borotra, who had never before taken even a set from the Californian and who was subdued in three sets in the Davis Cup challenge round last week, blasted the hopes of Johnston just when it seemed that, with Tilden out of the competition, he had a real chance to break through and regain the title which he held in 1915 and 1919. The score was 3—6, 4—6, 6—3, 6—4, 6—4.

Williams Also Falls.

Long before the Basque had finished his rally, which carried him to victory from the almost hopeless position of 0—2 in sets, René Lacoste had disposed of Dick Williams, captain of the Davis Cup team and No. 4 in the American ranking, at 6—0, 6—3, 8—6, and Richards had eliminated Jacques Brugnon, at 6—2, 6—1, 6—2.

Thus, for the second time this year, the situation developed in which the United States found itself with only one representative left in the semi-finals of a national tennis championship. Last February Tilden and Richards bowed to Borotra and Lacoste, respectively, in the indoor play at the Seventh Regiment Armory, while Brugnon also gained a bracket in the semi-finals, leaving John Van Ryn, a Princeton undergraduate, as America's last entry. The title went to Lacoste and unless Richards reaches his most inspired heights France is likely to carry off the turf court crown also.

There is deep confidence in Richards, however. The New York youth has been playing the best tennis of all the Americans since his return from abroad, and while he did not show to advantage yesterday against Brugnon it may be expected that he will rise to the occasion this afternoon and play in his best form against Borotra while Lacoste and Cochet are having it out in the other semi-final. Lacoste is favored to win over Cochet, though the latter, if he plays in the same form that he showed yesterday, will have an equal chance of winning.

Gallery Is Stunned.

The triumph of Borotra over Johnston was as unexpected as was the defeat of Tilden, but the gallery, dazed by the downfall of the champion, failed to show any great reaction to the upset. Anything was possible after Cochet's victory. Johnston has lost many a heart-breaking match during the six years that he has tried to break up the monopoly Tilden has held on the title, but yesterday's was in a way the most distressing one of all.

Leading at 2—0 in sets, the Californian looked to be a certain winner, and at last it appeared he would have the opportunity to test his strength against Richards in championship play. As he has always beaten Richards in a three-out-of-five-set match, there was reason for him to look forward with confidence to a match with the New York youth, and then would come his big opportunity to regain the crown.

But for the seventh successive year Johnston's dream went up in smoke—the smoke of Borotra's lightning drives and darting volleys, and America's second ranking player passed out of the play along with the world's first.

It was Borotra's volleying that decided the match. The spectacular Basque, unable to collect his forces in the first two sets in the face of the Californian's destructive forehand drives, took to the air in the third set, and out of the air, as he leaped for his volleys and overhead kills, came the shots from his racquet that put the quietus upon Johnston.

The pace set by the Basque in the three last sets at times carried Johnston off his feet. Never for a minute did Borotra cease going to the net and everything that came within his reach there was doomed to destruction. There were times when he faltered in control and volleyed into the net as Johnston gauged his openings accurately, but in general Borotra was irresistible up forward.

Johnston's control in the later stages of the match was not at its best, and his forehand drive found the net with irritating persistency, costing him precious points at times when he had the advantage in position. In the final set the Californian made a tremendous fight for the third game, winning it at 8—6 with a marvelous exhibition of volleying, and when he continued his deadly work at close quarters in the fourth to lead at 3—1 it seemed that Borotra's rally was to be in vain.

Basque Never Loses Smile.

But the Basque, never discouraged and smiling his appreciation of his opponent's shot-making, came back to take the play away from Johnston at the net and ran through three games in a row, earning 7 of his 14 points on placements. This brilliant display of pyrotechnics by the Basque stung Johnston into dynamic action in the eighth and he broke through on three placements to tie the score at 4 all.

That was his last game, though he led at 30—0 in the ninth. Borotra pulled up on even terms on the Californian's errors, lashed out from the net to break through at 5—3 and the play came to an end in the tenth as Johnston's control lapsed in the face of his opponent's ruthless stroking from the net.

The other two matches were tame in comparison to the big two. Williams had one of his erratic days and, except at the start of the second set and in the late stages of the final chapter, practically defeated himself on errors. The Philadelphian redeemed himself in the last set when he pulled up from 2—5 to 5—all, averting defeat four times in the process by the margin of a single stroke and bringing off such bewildering cross-court volleys and drives that Lacoste, for all his steadiness, was helpless. There was nothing the French youth could do when he could not get his racquet on the ball.

In the thirteenth game Williams made another of his pull-ups from 15—40 to deuce and there seemed a good prospect of his winning the set, but he lapsed into his erring ways and dropped the game and Lacoste relentlessly mowed down all opposition in the fourteenth to bring the play to a close.

Brugnon appeared to be tired in his match with Richards, showing the effects of his strenuous match with Dr. George King on Wednesday. Had he been fresher he would have had an excellent opportunity for winning at least a set, for Richards was none too keen himself. The New York youth, realizing that he had nothing to fear, was not taking matters any more seriously than was necessary, conserving his energies for the bigger test today against Borotra. Whenever he needed points he made them, either with beautiful volleys or clean passing shots, and there was no reason to become alarmed over his sluggishness.

Third Set Bitterly Fought.

There was no indication from the way in which the play started in the match between Tilden and Cochet of the startling outcome it was to have. The champion, showing a keenness that he had not manifested in his previous matches, was a rampant figure from the start, and as he bombarded Cochet's back court with murderous swipes that were measured to the inch it seemed that the French youth was up against greater power than he could withstand. His soft returns were set-ups for the American and his control was wavering, and in short order Tilden took the first two games, getting all of his points on errors.

Beginning with the third game Cochet began to find himself, and soon the thought behind his strokes was revealed as he started Tilden on the long run that was to continue to the end of the match. Four games in succession went to the invader, games which Tilden tried his best to win but in vain, as Cochet outguessed him and caught him off balance with confusing changes of direction. Finding the going too rough from back court, Tilden launched a volleying attack and swept through three games to lead at 5—4, bringing off sensational low volleys that were unapproachable.

Now it was Cochet's turn to go to the front again as Tilden faltered in control in the lengthy driving rallies, and then the champion, trailing at 5—6, went forward to hew out his points at the net, taking three games in a row for the set.

The second set found Tilden in a slump. He lost something of his aggressiveness and errors marred his stroking repeatedly. Cochet, on the other hand, was adding pressure to his play with each game and was beginning to reveal the genius of his volley attack. After falling behind at 0—4, Tilden made little effort, preferring to let the set go. Tilden did not make a single placement in this set.

The third set marked the beginning of the real struggle. Tilden brought all of his cunning and resources to bear, and every game in this set was fought for with the most dogged determination. Cochet took the first two games after they had gone to deuce. Tilden tied the score at 2—all and again at 3—all, and then developed a bewildering struggle in the seventh game, which went to 7—5 before Cochet was able to pull it out with a remarkable soft shot down the line off a kill by the champion. He broke through in the eighth on Tilden's errors and outplaced the champion in the ninth for the set.

After the rest period the champion returned to the court to let loose an avalanche of service aces, cannonball drives and volleys that had Cochet reeling. The French youth simply had to wait until the champion's attack had spent itself and then took command again in the final chapter. He won the opening game, 9—7, after a desperate combat that found both players scoring on electrifying strokes, broke through in the fourth to lead at 3—1 on volleys and increased it to 4—1.

Here it was that Tilden staged his rally that carried him to 4—all and ultimately to 6—5, after which Cochet went to the front, taking the last games with three placements in a row as Tilden rushed madly about the court trying to plug up the gaps that Cochet opened with his consummate placing.

The summaries:

Fourth Round.

Henri Cochet defeated William T. Tilden 2d, 6—8, 6—1, 6—3, 1—6, 8—6.

Rene Lacoste defeated R. Norris Williams 2d, 6—0, 6—3, 8—6.

Vincent Richards defeated Jacques Brugnon, 6—2, 6—1, 6—2.

Jean Borotra defeated William Johnston, 3—6, 4—6, 6—3, 6—4, 6—4.

United Press International

Bill Tilden

TILDEN LONG RATED AS GREATEST PLAYER

Mastered Best in World During Reign—Defeat Cost Chance to Tie Record.

The defeat of William Tilden in the national championship yesterday brings to an end one of the most remarkable reigns in the history of not only American but world tennis as well. For six years the Philadelphian has stood out as the unchallenged master of the court, demonstrating his supremacy over the best players of not only this country but also of England, France, Australia and Japan as well. By almost unanimous consensus he has been looked upon as the greatest player of all time.

So great a spell had the wizardry of the champion cast upon the tennis world that it had come to be believed that it was impossible to defeat him when he chose to win, and so, in spite of the numerous defeats that he had suffered this year the tennis public still maintained firm faith that he would successfully defend his crown this week and tie the record of consecutive victories that has stood since 1887, when Richard Sears won the title for the seventh year running. One other player has won the title that many years, but there was a hiatus of several years between the second and third victories of William Larned.

William Tatem Tilden 2d was born in Germantown, Pa. on Feb. 10, 1893. After playing tennis for years on the Philadelphia courts without showing any special aptitude for the game he suddenly achieved some measure of fame by carrying R. Lindley Murray to four sets in the national patriot tournament in 1917.

The following year he reached the final round of the championship, when he lost to Murray again. In 1919 Tilden took his place squarely among the country's best when he fought his way to the final of the championship. There he met William Johnston and then began the rivalry between the two players that has lasted ever since. Tilden was beaten in three sets, but in 1920 he turned the tables on Johnston in five sets and has beaten the Californian every year since, each time in the final except in 1921, when they met in the fourth round.

Tilden and Johnston were named on the American Davis Cup in 1920 and went to Australia to defeat the Antipodeans in the challenge round and bring the trophy back to the United States. Tilden has been the mainstay of every defending team since. In 1920 he also won the Wimbledon championship at England and successfully defended his title there the following year.

COCHET A HEADLINER ABROAD SINCE 1922

Tilden's Conqueror First Gained Fame by Winning World's Hard Court Title.

Henri Cochet of France, who defeated William Tilden yesterday in the national championship, was born in Lyons, Dec. 14, 1901. He first came into wide prominence on the courts in 1922, when he won the world's hard court championship in Europe. He has held that title twice in singles and doubles both and also has won the world's covered court championship in both singles and doubles.

Cochet won the French championship this year, defeating Richards in the process, and again defeated the New York youth in the Wimbledon championship, in which he was put out in the semi-finals by Jean Borotra, the winner of the title. Cochet won the Wimbledon doubles with Jacques Brugnon, conquering Richards and Howard Kinsey in the concluding round.

Cochet came to the United States in 1922 as a member of the French team, but failed to impress as a player of championship possibilities, making an inferior showing. Lack of competition prevented him from improving his game until of late years. He ranked here on a par with Borotra and René Lacoste in 1923 and 1924 and then dropped in the 1925 ranking, only to perform his most sensational feats on European courts this year, leading up to his great victory yesterday.

"All the News That's Fit to Print."

The New York Times.

THE WEATHER
Showers today and tonight, followed by clearing and cooler tomorrow.
Temperatures yesterday—Max. 70, min. 62.
For weather report see Page 46.

VOL. LXXVI....No. 25,080. NEW YORK, FRIDAY, SEPTEMBER 24, 1926. TWO CENTS in Greater New York | THREE CENTS Within 200 Miles | FOUR CENTS Elsewhere in the U.S.

TUNNEY WINS CHAMPIONSHIP, BEATS DEMPSEY IN 10 ROUNDS; OUTFIGHTS RIVAL ALL THE WAY, DECISION NEVER IN DOUBT; 135,000 PAY MORE THAN $2,000,000 TO SEE BOUT IN THE RAIN

FLORIDA CONSCRIPTS ALL ITS UNEMPLOYED TO CLEAR WRECKAGE

Police, Militia and Legion Round Up Men in Streets and Set Them to Work.

CALL ISSUED FOR LABORERS

Miami Wants 25,000 Men and Hollywood and Fort Lauderdale 2,000 Each.

LOSS PUT AT $165,000,000

Known Dead Now 365, With 1,100 Injured, 500 Seriously—Fight on Disease Goes On.

By WARREN IRVIN,
Staff Correspondent of The New York Times.

MIAMI, Fla., Sept. 23.—Conscription of all unemployed persons to aid in clearing away wreckage and to speed the work of rehabilitating the Florida storm-swept area was adopted everywhere in that area today. Militiamen and police, aided by several hundred members of the American Legion who have been specially deputized, patrolled all streets and highways, apprehending all persons who could not show that they were employed and putting them immediately to work.

At the same time the city of Miami sent out a call for 25,000 laborers, and officials of Hollywood and Fort Lauderdale announced that they would employ 2,000 laborers in each city.

Mayor E. C. Romfh of Miami predicted this afternoon that within sixty days every trace of the storm's ravages will have been removed from Miami and the city will be as prosperous as ever.

Death Lists Called Inadequate.

Many here believe that the death list lacks scores of names of persons killed. A local newspaper man declared today that he made a check-up of bodies in the city and temporary morgues last Monday, at which time there were 175, but orders were given, he said, to bury the dead as quickly as possible, and many bodies were buried or shipped North for burial without any record being kept of them.

Even now it is almost impossible to get definite information as to the number of dead. The Police Department in Miami keeps no record of dead or injured and persons who inquire there are directed to the newspaper offices for information. Bodies are being taken to half a dozen different undertaking establishments and the only means of keeping a record is by constant checking up at undertaking establishments.

At Miami Beach the situation is still worse. No record was kept there for several days but yesterday the Publicity Director of the Chamber of Commerce was instructed to compile a list of dead and injured.

Hollywood and Fort Lauderdale are the only cities in which accurate records have been kept from the start.

Four new cases of typhoid at Davie, a village of 300 population five miles west of Fort Lauderdale, were reported today and caused health authorities to order the village evacuated. Sanitary conditions at Davie are very bad. The water there is still several feet deep in spots.

Doctor Rows to Patients.

One doctor who was on duty there without rest for seventy-two hours was compelled to row to a house in which a woman and three children were marooned. He said the demand for medicine liquor in the stricken area has caused the warehouse in Miami jail, where seized liquors are kept, to be emptied for the first time since this city became the bootleg distributing point for Florida.

In other sections, such as Hollywood, the police were sent out to raid all speakeasies and bootleg places, with orders to bring in seized liquors for the sick. A storm of protest arose from the church people when word got out that the doctors were using liquor for medicine.

The same doctor at Davie who rowed out to the home of the marooned woman was reported for "drunkenness," because a woman there said sh smelled liquor on his breath, and in another case when he prescribed liquor for a woman who had been exposed to the wind and rain for several hours the woman's husband threatened to shoot him if "he dared give my wife a drop of liquor."

A flotilla of destroyers arrived today from the navy base at Charleston, bringing all the anti-typhoid serum available in that district. This amounted to several thousand units.

While City Health Officer Claxton of Miami reported an adequate supply on hand today, health officials at Miami Beach said they needed about 3,000 more units of anti-typhoid serum and about 500 units of anti-tetanus serum. Nearly 10,000 persons have been vaccinated in the Miami area.

One case of tetanus developed yesterday in Miami Beach and two in Hollywood. All available tetanus serums

Continued on Page Eleven.

North Carolinians Weave Homespun Suit for Walker

North Carolina mountaineers, reputed by novelists to be a hard-drinking and generally rough lot, are now sitting peacefully in their hillside homes spinning a new suit for Mayor Walker.

The addition to the Mayor's wardrobe will be made of gray homespun and will be presented to him by citizens of Asheville, who arrive on the "Land of the Sky" special train on Oct. 6 on a boosting tour. The color will be gray—chosen by the Mayor himself.

When the delegation reaches the city it will go directly to the City Hall, where, with appropriate ceremony, the suit will be presented.

GENEVA CONFERENCE ADOPTS COURT PLAN

Right of Powers to Withdraw Approval of American Reservations Is Recommended.

NEW PROTOCOL NEXT STEP

United States Will Be Invited to Help Draft It—President's Action in Doub'

By Wireless to THE NEW YORK TIMES.

GENEVA, Sept. 23.—With a single modification, the conference of signatories of the statute of the Permanent Court of International Justice adopted unanimously the conclusions concerning the American reservations which were presented this morning by its committee.

These conclusions were incorporated in "the final act of the conference," which was submitted for signatures.

The single modification concerned the fourth American reservation. The first part of the reservation provided for the withdrawal by the United States of adherence. The committee, to assure equality of treatment to all members, made the provision that the signatory States acting together and by not less than two-thirds majority should have a corresponding right to withdraw consent to the American reservations.

Modified by New Zealander.

On the proposal of Sir Francis Bell of New Zealand this provision was modified so as to extend only to the second paragraph of Reservation 4—by which statute the Court could not be amended without the consent of the United States—and Reservation 5, dealing with advisory opinions. The modification was made after a long debate in which it was agreed that any difficulties which might arise would be confined to the provisions covered by these reservations.

As it stands adopted, a decision by a two-thirds vote against the last points of the American reservations would not in any manner affect America's membership in the Court but only her prerogatives. The United States remains a full member, participating in the election of the Judges, paying her share of Court expenses and possessing the right to withdraw from the Court.

This modification followed a long series of compromises made between national dignity and resentment at the American demands on the one hand and the general desire to extend the influence and jurisdiction of the Permanent Court on the other. The effort made to meet the American demands was stressed by the President tonight in dissolving the conference.

The American reservations, he said, quoting Sir George Foster of Canada, comprised a legislative act by a State outside the League and Court and it would be very easy to say "no." But the conference had considered the difficulties were there to be overcome and nothing had been left undone to give satisfaction to the United States and assure her participation in the Permanent Court.

As to the fate of the conference's work nobody could know what this would be. But the spirit and manner in which the work had been done had proved in obvious manner its sincere desire to find a solution. The only thing that remained to be done was for the Governments to hasten their replies to the United States Government.

This spirit mentioned by the President and which had been evident on the part of the great majority of the delegations persisted in the debates today, though Canada and Sweden stood out against giving the United States more than equality.

Sir Francis Bell at the opening of the reading of the committee's conclusions this morning asked that all the provisions for withdrawing consent to American adherence be dropped. This was not the personal demand of a delegate, he said, but a motion by a Government signatory of the statute of the Court. His Government wanted to see the United States come into the Court and stay in it.

Question of Samoa Raised.

Western Samoa, which was now under the flag of New Zealand, was

Continued on Page Sixteen.

CROWD ARRIVES SMOOTHLY

Throngs Ushered Into Philadelphia Stadium Without Confusion.

MANY NOTABLES ATTEND

Governors of Six States and Mayor Walker Among Long List of Officials.

OVER 75,000 FROM HERE

Trains Alone Carry That Number and Others Make the Trip by Automobile.

Special to The New York Times.

PHILADELPHIA, Sept. 23.—One hundred and thirty-five thousand persons, the largest crowd which ever attended a sports event in America, let out a roar when the referee placed the heavyweight crown on the head of Gene Tunney, which must have made the old Liberty Bell at Independence Hall quiver once more.

As the battle began and the heavyweights set to exchanging their jarring blows which rang with a "plop" audible many rows back of the ring, they followed it with a roaring enthusiasm that only the greatest prize-fight crowd in history could produce.

Shortly before the main bout it was announced that the stadium had been completely sold out, breaking both attendance and receipt records. The paid admissions exceeded 130,000 and the gate receipts were over the two-million mark.

In addition to the paid admissions there were unpaid admissions amounting to $30,000 money value. Tex Rickard announced that he had purposely understated the crowd expected in order not to discourage possible last-minute purchasers of seats.

Crowd Is Well Handled.

Old-timers at the ringside who had seen every big fight since Fitzsimmons defeated Corbett said it was the most perfectly handled bout they had ever seen, for the huge concourse was ushered into the stadium without confusion.

The crowd, which had been cheering the preliminary fighters as they mauled each other to while away the spectators' time, broke into their first real frenzy when Gene Tunney appeared in the path alongside the ring and began climbing up to the square. The cheering was continuous from the moment he appeared. It broke into a single great outburst of yells, with shrill whistles from the thousands of lips sharpening it, as he entered the ring and went to his corner, smiling.

In the ovation for Tunney there was perhaps a note of sympathy.

Dempsey entered a moment after Tunney, and another great roar went up. Rain began falling but nobody seemed to notice it, least of all the fighters as they squared away and the blows began to fly.

They were yelling madly for Gene as he began swinging into the champion with a force they had not dreamed the young challenger possessed. And when the first round ended with Tunney so unmistakably in the lead there was a minute of sheer delirium.

Women Shout Dismay.

They were at it again, and the voices of the women spectators now and again sounded out over all the clamor as Tunney staggered under the blows of the infuriated champion. There were feminine shouts of dismay as well when Tunney shot a hard one at Dempsey.

As the fight settled down into a give and take and the surprise at Tunney's showing waned, the cries of encouragement and warning became an intermittent hum, punctuated by shouts as the blows landed or missed. The crowd was watching for the fine points now.

As one of the thinly padded fists struck its target of flesh with a whack a concerted groan went through the rows of onlookers.

"The nose, the nose," the crowd yelled as one of Gene's uppercuts brought blood on Dempsey's right cheek. "That fancy nose is a goner. Hit that and he's through."

The fourth round passed and the fifth began. The clamor of the crowd quieted a little, for it gave place to admiration that Tunney had lasted so long. The crowd was yelling for a knockout each time Tunney pushed Dempsey into the ropes.

Dempsey was fighting an unexpectedly good man and the crowd was with his enemy. Then the sixth round began, the round which had been set by the experts as the last one possible for Tunney to fight. The crowd was hushed as Tunney went confidently from his corner.

A sigh of relief swept the stadium as Tunney emerged from it shaken but still strong, and there was a burst of applause as he took his seat. The old-time fight followers wagged their heads. "It's not the same old Dempsey," they said.

"He missed his chance right there," said somebody as Dempsey drove with all his dreadful strength at a point in space which Tunney had just left. "If that had landed we'd been on our way home."

And then a burst of women's cries

Continued on Page Three.

Dempsey's Share $850,000; Tunney to Receive $200,000

Special to The New York Times.

PHILADELPHIA, Sept. 23.—The receipts of the Dempsey-Tunney fight tonight were in excess of $2,000,000. On the basis of $2,000,000, the receipts were divided as follows:

Dempsey	$850,000
Tunney	$200,000
Federal Tax	$200,000
State	$100,000
Sesquicentennial	$200,000
Preliminary fights	$40,000
Tex Rickard, promoter	$410,000

AIRPLANE CARRIES TUNNEY TO SCENE

Challenger Is First to Make Way to Heavyweight Title Bout Through Air.

RISK DEPLORED BY MANY

Tunney, However, Is Calm Throughout—Calls Flying Least Trying on Nerves.

Special to The New York Times.

PHILADELPHIA, Sept. 23.—Not content with the prospect of facing Dempsey and destiny, Gene Tunney had to defy death, too. For the first time in the history of heavyweight championships, the challenger flew forth to the field of battle in an airplane.

From Stroudsburg, Pa., where Tunney trained for the three weeks, to Philadelphia the challenger took the shortest route. He winged above the silvery course of the Delaware River, winding through the Pocono Mountains, and landed at the navy yard in plenty of time to weigh in before the astonished eyes of the Pennsylvania State Boxing Commission.

Gene traveled in a red Curtiss Oriole plane, piloted by the expert hands of Casey Jones, noted for his feats of daring. The only other passenger was Wade Morton, driver of racing cars, who finished fourth in the last five-hundred mile classic at Indianapolis.

Challenger Disdains Danger.

The utter distain Tunney displayed for the battle at hand, with the golden goal for which he has striven seven years in the balance, was unusual in itself. He disregarded entirely the fact that a tremendous gate, the greatest financial success in the history of sports, depended upon his appearance in the ring at the proper time. He laughed at the suggestion of danger which he was tempting. He continued in the same unperturbed, undisturbed, confident mood he had displayed from the start.

When the news spread that the challenger had taken to the air with the chance of his life only a few hours away there was a general outcry of disapproval. But there was no opportunity in which to make the challenger change his course. He had decided on his means of travel a week before and he kept it secret from every one, including his manager, Billy Gibson, and Tex Rickard.

The challenger slept late on his morning of destiny, facing the beckoning call of opportunity with the calmness of a child. He arose at 8 o'clock and relished a special breakfast at the Glen Brook Country Club in Stroudsburg, specially prepared by George Ransberry, his private chef. When he came forth into the misty morning he greeted the small crowd waiting to bid him farewell and godspeed in his quest for the coveted crown with the announcement that he was going to fly to Philadelphia.

Cheer Sends Him on Way.

There was gasps of amazement, and after a moment of surprised silence a cheer broke forth from the little knot of well-wishers.

Morton, the race driver, was waiting for the challenger with the motor running in a high powered Duesenberg. Tunney climbed in beside the driver's seat and was speeded to the Shawnee Country Club at Buckwood Inn, about five miles away. There Jones and his Oriole awaited the coming of the precious passenger.

On arriving at the Buckwood Inn Gene was greeted by Reggie Worthington.

"Where's Casey?" asked the challenger.

"Oh, he's out playing golf," Worthington informed him.

"Say, I might play a couple of holes myself before I leave," Gene suggested in his matter-of-fact way, still calm and unexcited.

However, it was decided that the aerial expedition had better get under way, and Casey Jones was summoned from a bunker. He went over to a near-by shed and in a short time taxied out in a blood red sky chariot. Gene walked over to the third tee on the golf course, accompanied by a few friends and a few strangers who had been playing golf but had deserted their game on hearing that the chal-

Continued on Page Two.

TUNNEY ALWAYS MASTER

Challenger Bewilders His Opponent With His Speed, Accuracy.

AGGRESSIVE IN ALL ROUNDS

Sends Rain of Whiplike Lefts Which Champion Cannot Avoid.

OUTCOME IS A SURPRISE

Dempsey Lacks All Evidence of His Old Aggressiveness—Victor Is Acclaimed.

By JAMES P. DAWSON.
Special to The New York Times.

RINGSIDE, SESQUICENTENNIAL STADIUM, Philadelphia, Sept. 23.—Gene Tunney is the new world's heavyweight champion. The ex-marine fought like a marine here tonight in the Sesquicentennial Stadium, when he carried off the decision over Jack Dempsey, once known as the Manassa Mauler and the ring's man-killer, in a ten-round bout which saw the first passing of a heavyweight championship title on a decision.

Through every round of the ten, Tunney battered and pounded Dempsey. He rained rights on the tottering champion's jaw and he bewildered Dempsey with his speed and the accuracy of a whip-like left hand which Dempsey could not evade. When the decision was announced, the crowd let loose a roar of acclaim for "the man of destiny," who had conquered the man-killer, and the countryside sent the roar echoing back.

Confidence Aids Tunney.

The transfer of the title, the ascension of Tunney to the pinnacle in boxing, surprised the majority of those who witnessed the fight and experienced followers of boxing form. It surprised everybody, almost, but Tunney, whose confidence, more than anything else, perhaps, carried him on to a height which the vast majority thought unattainable for him.

He was complete master, from first bell to last. He out-boxed and he outfought Dempsey at every turn. Where it had been expected that Tunney would break and run before the vicious attack of Dempsey, the tiger man, Tunney, the fighting marine, not only failed to back up, but he went forward all the time with the instinct of the true leatherneck and hammered Dempsey in a driving attack which brooked no restraining effort on the part of the champion.

There was no question of the victor at the finish. There was no question even of the winner of each round as the battle progressed, and Dempsey, instead of flashing the fighting fury which was expected of him, instead of surging forward with the tigerish, vicious rushes he has exhibited in previous and more favorable ring engagements, proved himself instead a floundering, weakened, almost helpless fighting machine from which the spark had gone.

All the evidences of the old Dempsey were merely that; only faint evidences, indications, unexpressive flashes save for their expression of futility of helpless hopelessness, of utter ineffectiveness.

They fought this battle in the rain—a driving, torrential downpour which started when the men entered the ring and which increased in fury as the fight progressed. The ring was flooded, the spectators drenched and the gladiators were drenched, but as the fury of the storm increased so did the fighting of Tunney, and Dempsey had nothing with which to meet this Marine attack.

Knockdown Is Lacking.

It was a disappointing transfer of a heavyweight title in one respect. The battle did not end in a knockout. Indeed, through its ten rounds the struggle held not even a knock down. This was due to the fact that Tunney is a weak hitter in the sense that he is not a finishing or destructive hitter.

He is not of the old Dempsey hitting school. But the New York lad is a punishing hitter, a cruel, tantalizing, tormenting puncher and a cool, unruffled boxer at all times. He did about everything else to Dempsey but knock the defending champion down and out. He battered Dempsey to a pulp, until the beaten champion at the finish was a close resemblance to the giant Jess Willard, whom Dempsey pounded and hammered into a helpless hulk out on the shores of Maumee Bay seven years ago when he won the title.

For the first time in his career

Continued on Page Two.

Times Wide World Photo.

GENE TUNNEY, THE NEW CHAMPION

Champion Tunney Praises the Loser; "I Have No Alibis," Asserts Dempsey

Special to The New York Times.

SESQUICENTENNIAL STADIUM, PHILADELPHIA, Sept. 23.—The following statements were made after the bout tonight:

By GENE TUNNEY.

Dempsey fought like the great champion that he was. He had the kick of a mule in his fists and the heart of a lion in his breast. I never fought a harder socker nor do I hope to meet one. Dempsey fought like a gentleman and never took an unfair advantage in the ring. Once or twice he may have hit me a little low, but always it was by accident. He never meant it.

"I'm sorry," he always said following anything close to a foul blow. When the gong rang at the end of the fight he threw his arm over my shoulder and said: "Great fight, Gene; you won." I don't care what they may say about him he is certainly a man in the ring. The hardest blows I felt were two socks on the Adam's apple. That's why I'm so hoarse. I have no plans for the future, but am content to rest a while with the ambition I have nourished for seven years at last realized. The marines, you know, are always first to fight and last to leave. No matter how heavy the going may be you will always find them there in the end.

By JACK DEMPSEY.

I have no alibis to offer. I lost to a good man, an American—a man who speaks the English language. I have no alibis.

Story of the Fight by Rounds

Special to The New York Times.

RINGSIDE, SESQUICENTENNIAL STADIUM, PHILADELPHIA, Sept. 23.—The round by round detail of the Tunney-Dempsey bout fought here tonight follows:

First Round.

Dempsey was attired in blue trunks and Tunney in purple. Dempsey looked rather thin as he stepped forward for a consultation.

As the round started Dempsey, with a scowl on his face, rushed out and drove Tunney to his own corner. Dempsey again rushed. Jack sent a terrific left to the jaw. Dempsey kept rushing in and drove Tunney into his own corner. Dempsey went in and Tunney swung a hard right to Dempsey's chin. Dempsey weaved in again and Tunney was short with a right. They boxed in the centre of the ring for a moment, then Tunney missed a right for the head but ripped two rights to the body. Dempsey jabbed Tunney away, and then Dempsey lunged over the ropes after missing a left swing. Tunney rushed in again and sent a heavy right to the chin. In a terrific exchange Tunney showered left and right swings to Dempsey's jaw and Dempsey was groggy. Gene's only mark in the exchange was a bleeding mouth.

Between rounds Dempsey appeared very tired and his seconds worked hard over him.

Second Round.

Dempsey rushed over to Tunney's corner, trying to get his man. Dempsey swung his right to the jaw, but Tunney got out of the way. They stepped out in the middle of the ring and Tunney swung right and left to the jaw. Dempsey came through with a right to the body and drove Tunney to his corner. Jack drove Gene to a neutral corner and punished him about the head. Tunney sent two lefts to Jack's head. They wrestled across the ring, Dempsey pounding the body. Gene sent short rights and lefts to the jaw. It was now raining heavily. Jack drove Tunney into his own corner with a terrific right to the heart and dazed Tunney. Tunney put over a left and right to the jaw at the bell and the crowd was in an uproar.

Third Round.

Dempsey came out slowly for the third and they met in the middle of the ring. Jack tried a terrific right for the jaw but missed. Gene stood up straight and jabbed lefts and rights to Jack's jaw. Gene put over a heavy right to the head and wrestled Jack back to the ropes. Tunney swung terrific rights and lefts to Jack's jaw. Tunney repeated with a right and had the champion staggering in mid-ring. He graced the champion's jaw and then landed a good right to Jack's jaw. Tunney jumped away and sparred cleverly, but Dempsey kept boring in. Jack came in only to be sent back to the ropes with rights and lefts to the jaw. Tunney sent another left jab to the head, but Jack punished him heavily to the body in return. As Jack came in Tunney ripped lefts and rights to the body at the bell.

Fourth Round.

Dempsey came out with a terrific rush and with a wild right sent Tunney almost over the ropes. Tunney was in bad shape, but he continued to jab Jack away with a left. Jack's eye was cut with one of these lefts. Dempsey went in and sent two lefts to the jaw. Dempsey continued to weave in, trying to land a heavy body blow. Dempsey missed a left to the jaw. Tunney stabbed a left, then swung a heavy right to Jack's jaw. Dempsey's eye was in bad shape and

Continued on Page Three.

VICTORY IS POPULAR ONE

Ex-Marine Gets Ovation as He Enters Ring—Crowd 'Boos' Foe.

BIGGEST IN SPORT HISTORY

Rickard's Luck Turns, However and Distinguished Gathering Is Thoroughly Drenched.

DEMPSEY'S NOSE SUFFERS

Rebuilt for Movies, It Is Target of Challenger as He Piles Up Points for Victory.

By ELMER DAVIS.
Special to The New York Times.

RINGSIDE, SESQUICENTENNIAL STADIUM, PHILADELPHIA, Sept. 23.—While the rain poured down on the greatest crowd that ever saw a sporting event, Gene Tunney beat Jack Dempsey, and captured the world's heavyweight championship in a ten-round fight here tonight.

The champion, in the phrase of one of the ringside critics, lost his title by a synthetic nose. It was by steady pounding away at the built-in beak which Dempsey acquired a couple of years ago that Tunney piled up a heavy lead on points in the early rounds.

Dempsey rallied toward the middle of the fight, but his effort to come back in a last round finish failed. The ex-marine, against whom the experts were betting three and four to one this afternoon, walked off with the title.

Crowd Is With Tunney.

It was the first time in history that the heavyweight championship of the world has changed hands on points, but there was never the slightest doubt after the start that if there were a decision Tunney would get it. The champion's only chance was to win by a knockout, and here his old power had deserted him. He was in somewhat better shape after three years of idleness than when he fought Tom Gibbons at Shelby, Mont., after a two-year layoff in 1923. The swings and hooks that always missed Gibbons occasionally landed on Tunney. But they never landed hard enough. The young fighter from Greenwich Village could stand up and take it.

Though the experts and the gamblers thought, by a heavy majority, that Dempsey would walk off with the fight, about 90 per cent. of the 130,000 people who saw the encounter were for Tunney. There was an uproarious cheer when the challenger entered the ring. He wore the scarlet trimmed blue dressing gown, with the Marine Corps emblem on the back, which was presented to him by old comrades of the Marine Corps. He climbed through the ropes at 9:30, and stood up to let the crowd see him.

Two minutes later the champion of the world came in. There was a scattering round of applause as he entered the ring, but when Joe Griffo, announcer, introduced him as "the heavyweight champion who has defended his title for the past six years," there was a roar of boos that rocked the whole amphitheatre. If ever a fighting champion, as yet undefeated and favored by all the experts to remain undefeated, had such a reception from a crowd, the episode is buried in the obscurity of the past.

The rain began to fall on the crowd in the Sesquicentennial Stadium just as the big fight started. Hitherto the proverbial Rickard luck had held, even against the weather. Though it rained in Philadelphia early this morning and heaps of dark clouds obscured the sky at nightfall when the crowd began to gather in the stadium, the rain held off.

A dozen fight programs have rained out in New York alone this Summer, but it looked as if Rickard, with the biggest fight of the past three years and the biggest fight crowd and biggest gate of all time, was going to get away untouched.

Five preliminary bouts had gone on and the ring had been cleared for the entrance of the principals to the big event when the rain began at last. The amplifier announcers who relayed Joe Griffo's statements to the farthest edges of the huge stadium had just announced, three or four times, that all persons in the audience were requested to keep their seats.

Crowd Came Prepared.

Suddenly all over the huge U-shaped cup of the permanent amphitheatre and the broad wooden expanse of the temporary seats, people stood up by thousands struggling into rain coats. Then they sat down again, grimly determined to stay to the finish, whatever the weather.

At the end, when the bleeding champion and the eager challenger were exchanging wallops before the bell, the ring was splashed and puddled, the crowd was drowned out, but everybody but Dempsey and his friends was happy.

All the predictions and expectations about this fight were upset. Dempsey had hoped to finish his opponent in one punch and expected to do it within two rounds.

The comparatively few last ditch supporters who expected Tunney to win

Tunney Crowned New World's Heavyweight Champion

had been afraid that Dempsey might foul their man. The Pennsylvania boxing regulations forbid the rabbit punch and the kidney punch blows, with which Dempsey has done much execution in clinches in previous fights. The preliminaries, however, showed that these prohibitions were interpreted in practice according to the tendencies of the referee. Some of the preliminary referees were rather broad-minded about these matters.

Dempsey apparently tried at the outset to refrain from these forbidden punches, but toward the end of the fight he used the rabbit punch more and more frequently. Those who know the champion's temperament are prepared to believe that it was the subconscious fighting instinct which animates him in the ring, rather than any deliberate desire to break the rules and use punches which were prohibited by strict interpretation of the law.

Referee Tommy Reilly at first seemed to let the passing champion get away with this, but Frank Weiner of the Pennsylvania Boxing Commission, seated at the ringside, warned him to keep an eye out for them. In the last round when Dempsey made his last stand for the championship Weiner was upon the boxers repeatedly in clinches, seeing that Dempsey's right hand did not forget itself.

How many of the crowd were able to see the fighting in this detail is doubtful, but certainly most of the customers were able to see Tunney's persistent long range battering of the champion's nose. They saw the men rush each other against the ropes and saw the challenger rally again and again after hard punches that would have floored most of the men Dempsey has fought.

And every time he rallied there was a roar from the high-piled tiers of seats, invisible in the darkness behind the bright lights beating on the ring, that heartened Gene Tunney.

The crowd was not only the greatest but the most opulent and most distinguished that ever saw a fight. Mayor W. Freeland Kendrick of Philadelphia was there because it was a Philadelphia show, and Mayor Walker of New York was there because he wouldn't have missed it.

Secretary of the Navy Curtis D. Wilbur, who stopped a navy boxing program at Norfolk the other day because the local clergy had protested against it, was here at the ringside despite protests of the clergy of Pennsylvania. Governor Pinchot and half a dozen other Governors, millionaires estimated at 2,000, though this has not been checked up by census estimators. In fact, almost everybody who professes to be a person of prominence and who was able to get down to Philadelphia at this particular time was on the premises.

The spectators began to gather toward the middle of the afternoon, but by 7 o'clock the big stadium was hardly more than a fourth filled. The bulk of the crowd came late, and so far as could be learned by those who came to the ringside early, there was no serious confusion anywhere. The Philadelphia police seem to have handled the traffic admirably.

Tex Rickard's corps of ushers handled the crowd in the stadium admirably, and even when the transfer of the world's heavyweight title was announced, and a hundred thousand people all tried to get out at once through the streaming rain, there was no confusion more than would ordinarily be expected when a thousand people file out of a theatre at the end of a performance.

As night fell on the stadium and the dozen batteries of big searchlights on the top of the stands blazed out and illuminated the field below, customers were pouring in through dozens of entrances. As they filed down the aisles, many were taking out of their pockets the sandwiches they had brought down to supplement an early dinner or a late lunch, and preparing to be as patient as they could while they waited for the first preliminary to come on at 8 o'clock.

Overhead swooped airplanes, spelling out advertising slogans with colored lights, diving and zooming near the crowd, but, by the luck which seems to attend aviators in the air above fight crowds, never landing.

Up the steeply rising tiers of stands in the permanent stadium the light from the battery lights above fell on the heads of the crowd like moonlight. In these permanent concrete seats alone were seated more people than ever before saw a prize fight, or a baseball game, or a football game. On the chairs and benches placed in the flat ground below had gathered another crowd that has been surpassed only half a dozen times in the history of fighting. Most of them had come out in the hope of seeing Tunney win, and the expectation of seeing Dempsey win. Perhaps it was this conflict between desire and probabilities that kept the crowd fairly quiet as the night wore on.

The first ripples in the crowd were bursts of laughter stirred by the wild

United Press International

Tunney vs. Dempsey

swinging of some of the preliminary fighters. Rickard had assembled several tons of heavyweights for these bouts, but some of them were conspicuous by size rather than merit.

There was an outbreak of local patriotism, however, when Tommy Loughran, the Philadelphia heavyweight, appeared to fight Jimmy Delaney, in the fourth preliminary. Loughran had been one of Dempsey's sparring partners, Delaney one of Tunney's. The fight was accordingly taken by the superstitious as a sort of curtain raiser, the outcome of which would have its ominous bearing on the result of the championship bout.

When Loughran got the decision the Dempsey sentiment, accordingly, was strengthened. Or perhaps it should not be called sentiment. It was calculation, the balance of probability, based not only on Dempsey's record but on the fact that the balance of popular feeling has been against him in most of his big fights and still he had always won.

That nobody allowed his fears to sway his sentiment was proved by the demonstration in favor of Tunney, and against Dempsey, when the contestants came in.

Radio Announcers Busy.

Nobody stepped over the ropes and announced that he would challenge the winner. Instead of that, the radio announcers spread the news from time to time that various prominent or wealthy citizens, with parties of friends, were at the ring side.

Thus boxing changes, as the crowds grow and the gate receipts swell to sums that once would have been inconceivable. The emphasis now is not on the fighters but on the customers. And no wonder, considering that the first fight Tex Rickard promoted, twenty years ago, took in less than 3 per cent. as much money as this battle for the heavyweight championship.

Joe Griffo announced and the amplifying apparatus above him repeated and emphasized his announcement, that Tommy Reilly of Philadelphia would be referee; that Frank Brown of Pittsburgh and Mike Bernstein of Wilkes-Barre would serve as judges and that Jim Hendon and Byron Hayes would supervise the bandaging of the boxers' hands, to make sure that there would be no room for rumors about weights in the bandages, such as clustered about Dempsey's winning of the championship from Jess Willard at Toledo seven years ago.

Then a pause while the crowd struggled into raincoats and waited for the arrival of the fighters. Suddenly there was a swirl down one of the aisles, and the challenger stepped into the ring. His mere appearance brought a roar, which doubled in intensity a moment later when he turned around, on the way to his own corner, and the crowd saw the globe and anchor of the Marine Corps in bright gold on his back.

It was a reminder that Tunney who fought at the front won his first distinction as a fighter when he came through to the light heavyweight championship of the A. E. F., while Dempsey was working in a shipyard. And this, of course, put the capstone on the edifice of popularity which Tunney's pleasing personality has built up.

Dempsey Arrives.

A moment later Dempsey came in, wearing a light white sweater and a towel over his shoulders, with navy blue silk trunks piped in gold. He was clean shaken, the Pennsylvania boxing regulations forbidding the thick growth of wiry beard with which he protects his face when possible. Philadelphia Jack O'Brien, his chief second, had laid out an elaborate program of instructions which aimed for the champion to present an appearance of frightfulness, which it was hoped might scare Tunney into impotence. But Dempsey's fighting face does not show up until he is fighting. He was far from the worst looking champion who has ever stepped into a ring. Though he has never been popular, ringside experts were amazed at the roar of "boos" that greeted his introduction.

The rain came down, luminous streaks in the bright ring; it droned and rattled on thousands of raincoated shoulders in the seats behind. But not till the last round was the ring wet enough to bring serious danger that one of the men might slip and the championship perhaps be retained or lost by accident of the weather.

Dempsey rushed across the ring with the bell, but he failed to finish with one punch. Nor, on the other hand, did he encounter such a disturbing wallop as Luis Angel Firpo handed him in their first exchange at the Polo Grounds three years ago. But in a moment Tunney was thumping his nose and then Dempsey's fighting snarl grew on him.

Unfortunately his fighting ability did not come back with it. He was hitting hard but not accurately, and meanwhile Tunney was beating away at his face. When the bell stopped the first round Tunney fans were delighted that their champion had lasted, had got the better of the fighting, but few of them even yet believed that he could last the distance. But as the fight went on, and the challenger more than held his own, the crowd grew hotter and hotter. Every time Tunney's fists crashed into Dempsey's face there was a howl from the stands of "Finish him off."

Dempsey has heard that often enough before, but never before had he encountered anybody who seemed likely to do it except the foreigner, Firpo.

Tunney Keeps Winning.

Tunney did not finish him off, but he held on, getting the better of round after round, and successfully resisted the champion's final rush in the last forlorn-hope effort to save his title. When the ten-round bell ended the fight, there was hardly room for doubt in anybody's mind about the decision. While the written opinions of judges and referees were being collected, a platoon of Philadelphia policemen jumped into the ring, the usual precaution to surround the champion and keep away too eager enthusiasts who might hamper his exit. They all gathered around Tunney. They knew who was going to be champion.

The judges' opinions were examined, and there was no need to read the referee's. "The judges are agreed," said Announcer Griffo, and the amplifiers repeated his opening, "on giving the decision to Gene Tunney, the new heavyweight champion."

Those words were audible only a few rows back from the ring, but if the amplifier ever repeated them, nobody heard it. The first few rows had begun to cheer and the roar of satisfaction spread all the way back and upward, until the whole stadium was saluting the new champion, a man who had won his good standing in the favor of the public long before he fought his way to the top.

His face immobile, in its usual expression of sullenness which is, as a rule, not more than skin deep, the beaten Dempsey came across the ring and shook hands with his conqueror. Tunney spoke a few words into the radio microphone—for the first time in history a champion talking from the ringside with his title a minute old, to 15,000,000 people; and then a phalanx of policemen made a way for him down the aisle.

They took him out to the car which would cary him off to receive the congratulations of thousands of his friends, and thousands more who would have been Dempsey's friend if he had got the decision.

Jack Dempsey, dethroned after seven years, went out among his handlers to his waiting car. He was driven off in his fighting clothes, with the blood and sweat not yet dry on his body, across the State line to escape still more process servers in the lawsuits brought against him by his former manager and present bitterest enemy, Jack Kearns.

Somewhere in New Jersey the ex-champion was rubbed down and dressed, and had time to think it over, and to remember that the crowd booed him even before he lost. That is a deplorable finish to the career of a man, whatever his mistakes, who has fought some good fights and has deserved more credit than he ever received.

ESTELLE TAYLOR TAKES DEFEAT NEWS CALMLY

Hears Newsboys' Cries at Fort Wayne as Train Brings Her to Join Dempsey.

ABOARD THE PENNSYLVANIA LIMITED, FORT WAYNE, Ind., Sept. 23 (AP).—Mrs. Jack Dempsey, wife of the dethroned champion, learned tonight from the raucous shouts of newsboys on the station platform here the news of her husband's defeat. She took the news stoically, as she had promised her husband she would if the news were bad.

Closeted in her compartment with Mrs. Floyd Fitzsimmons, wife of a fight promoter and one of Jack's friends, Mrs. Dempsey thrust away all proffered details of the fray. Tomorrow afternoon the actress, known to the films as Estelle Taylor, will meet her husband in Philadelphia—and it will be to console him instead of to share in the expected celebration.

She had taken elaborate precautions last night to avoid hearing any news of the combat until she reached him. She ordered officials of the Pennsylvania Limited, which she boarded at Chicago at 5:30 tonight, to admit no messages whatsoever to her compartment. She wired to the fighter to abandon his plan to telephone or telegraph her the result.

News of the first two rounds reached the train at Plymouth, Ind., but they did not penetrate the recesses of Mrs. Dempsey's compartment.

"I don't want to know what hapened until I see Jack," she told the Associated Press. "And when I see him I'll know by looking at him. He won't have to tell me."

She was sitting in her stateroom when the train reached Fort Wayne. Trainmen leaped from the cars with upraised hands cautioning silence.

"Extra! Tunney beats Dempsey by a decision."

She could not help hearing the cry of a newsboy beneath her window.

Mrs. Dempsey would issue no statement. "I shan't capitalize my emotions," she explained to Mrs. Fitzsimmons. "That's so cheap. I am just going to Philadelphia to see Jack—and I want so much to be with him again. That's all."

TUNNEY WAS MASTER IN EVERY ROUND

By JAMES P. DAWSON.

Continued from Page 1, Column 5.

Dempsey felt the sting and cutting pain of a rival's punishing blows. Not even in the long ago when he was knocked out by Fireman Jim Flynn for the only such set-back chalked against Dempsey's record, was the tigerish Dempsey subjected to such painful drilling from a ring foe.

At the finish Dempsey was a sorry, pitiful subject, the object of the sincere sympathy of the crowd as he slumped in his corner to which the clang of the final gong, welcome and a distinct relief, sent him. His mouth and nose spouted blood, his left eye, bruised and battered, was closed tight and bleeding. There was a cut under his left eye about an inch long. And he was all in, absolutely at the end of his tether, through as a fighter if ever a man was.

Like the true fighting man and sportsman, however, Dempsey dragged himself from his corner as the announcer ordered the decision flashed to the crowd through the giant microphones suspended above the ring. "The two judges have agreed on Tunney as the winner and new champion," and lurching forward on unsteady legs, embraced his conqueror for a few fleeting seconds, smiling through his painfully bruised and battered face, which was pounded out of all semblance of normal, and congratulated Tunney through bruised and bleeding lips.

Shakes Hands All Round.

The ring then was the scene of handshaking on all sides. Manager Billy Gibson and Gene Normile, for conqueror and conquered, clasped hands and so did the seconds, but Dempsey wanted nothing to do with this. He carried himself slowly, painfully away, slipped quietly through the ropes with the din of the rain-soaked crowd for the triumphant marine ringing in his ears, and made his way to his dressing room. In the privacy of his quarters Dempsey collapsed, utterly exhausted and completely crushed. It is believed here he may not fight again.

There was everything in this fight but the thrill of the knock down and the knock out. The suspense was sustained and the fight was fought fast and furiously, Tunney doing all the fighting and showing all the speed. The judges who rendered the decision were Mike Bernstein of Wilkes-Barre and Frank Brown of Pittsburgh. The referee was Tom Reilly of Philadelphia, but on the decision his vote was not needed. The judges did their work well. They had no other course, and their decision decided the issue under the Boxing law of Pennsylvania and to the complete satisfaction of the crowd.

Dempsey's time had come. That is the only way to account for this battle and its result. The man who had smashed and crushed all opposition, met his superior in Tunney, a fearless, confident, determined, stronger man, well equipped in every ring essential save finishing punching strength. Dempsey was not the old fighting machine, luxurious living and three years of idleness had done their work. You will hear tales of how this fight was not fought on its merits.

Such tales were circulated before the fight, but they are groundless and a rank injustice to Tunney, a true fighter who undoubtedly will take his place among the ring's greatest champions. Dempsey tried his best, but his best was not good enough. He was no match for the perfectly trained and strongly developed Tunney. He fought his battle. It was a losing one, but he fought on until the last bell sounded. He went down fighting.

Tunney excelled Dempsey in practically every department in which it had been expected that Dempsey would outdo Tunney. The fighting marine was faster, shiftier, more resourceful, more accurate in his fire, cooler at all stages of the fight, deliberate at all times, with an attack which was systematized and varied, but not methodical by any means, and thoroughly effective in its point producing and punishment inflicting propensities. Tunney's footing was steadier and surer. His timing and distance in punching were far superior to those of Dempsey.

In only one respect did Tunney fail to overshadow the defending champion. Dempsey was more aggressive, but with an offensive which was wild and misdirected, weak and ineffective and thoroughly harmless. The sting had gone from the Dempsey punch, the fear-instilling element had gone from the growling, scowling, glowering Dempsey, for these elements in Dempsey's fighting make-up were revealed here tonight in a rain-soaked ring as useless when flashed before a man who refused to be frightened.

Though Tunney failed to surpass Dempsey in aggressiveness the former marine nevertheless made capital by this very shortcoming, for he made Dempsey fight the fight he wanted him to fight—a rushing, tearing fight in which Dempsey was wild, floundered, missed awkwardly and wallowed about the ring.

Tunney, meanwhile, with the skill and precision of the expert fencer, countered this helpless fire with rapier-like lefts and lightning-like rights which cut and punished. Dempsey fooled everybody but himself and Tunney. He was successful in concealing his battle weaknesses in training from the public which watched him and from the critics who inspected him and took his efforts for their surface value. But he must have known himself that the spark was missing and Tunney must have known, too.

Dempsey came into the ring like a man bent on business, not like a fighter come to his doom. He even employed what was either a protection against tender eyebrows and a precaution against their bleeding under a hammering, or the age-old artifice of the ring, coming into the squared circle with both eyes decorated to give the impression of injury. Dempsey's eyebrows were covered with a white substance which was plain grease or zinc salve, not court plaster. There had been no evidence of cuts over either eye up to the time he left Atlantic City yesterday evening, so we must believe this foreign matter was employed as a sort of protection. It failed of its purpose.

Dempsey encountered a situation at the beginning of the fight which was new to him and which he could not overcome at any stage of the battle. He met an upright boxer, light and fleet on his feet, quick and accurate and cutting with his hands, who was unafraid of Dempsey and his rushes.

The defending champion charged as of old, leading to the body with a right and left and after a clinch he rushed again. But this time met the rush with a right, and another, and still another which rattled Jack's teeth and his whole body. Dempsey rushed again, this time landing a left to the body, but Tunney, instead of crumpling under the blow which sent the sent the giant Firpo down, countered with a staggering right to the jaw. Tunney tried another, dancing lightly about Dempsey, sharp-shooting and letting fly with the speed of a bullet. Tunney missed with this one but he landed twice with grazing bolws to the chin and then with a right to the head as Dempsey plunged in headlong, wide open and inviting attack.

It had been predicted and there was basis for the prediction on the strength of the previous records of the rivals. That Dempsey would do just this—invite attack with his corrugated steel jaw as the target, just to get home himself with a destructive blow. But the jaw which withstood the right of Carpentier in that second round five years ago, and the murderous right of the giant Firpo opening that memoriable battle three years ago, did not stand up so well tonight. Or, rather, the recuperative powers of the champion had deserted him, along with all his boxing effectiveness and fighting success. Tunney shot through an opening with another right to the jaw which staggered Dempsey and before the bell the former marine belted Dempsey with rights and lefts to the jaw until the defending champion was groggy as he went to his corner.

Here was something the vast majority of the spectators had not expected—Tunney not only standing fearlessly before the bull-like rushes of Dempsey, the killer, but meeting this attack flat-footed and dealing out his blows with a marksman's accuracy and with staggering force, or dancing away and pecking at the charging human in front of him. The crowd was awed; some of it was distinctly shocked, but the greatest shock was experienced by Dempsey himself.

Dempsey Keeps Up Rushes.

It was the same in the second round, Dempsey rushing and forcing Tunney about the ring, while Tunney, in strategic retreat, countered accurately and solidly with lefts and rights. Dempsey landed a left early which split Tunney's lip and he drove his left and his right to Tunney's body and ribs, but the blows did not disturb Gene, but, on the contrary, made the challenger fight al the harder to beat off this attack.

In the third round Dempsey continued to rush with the old fury, an indomitable will and spirit which commanded admiration, but which lacked direction and which was absolutely ineffective. Tunney's right crosses bounded off Dempsey's face and his right uppercuts smacked against Dempsey's head and face until the defending champion was spitting blood and his renovated nose was bleeding.

Two rights to the jaw staggered Dempsey again, but he survived the ensuing assault because in his eagerness Tunney himself became wild, and then, too, Gene lacks the punch of the true finisher. Dempsey plunged in with a right to the jaw, but, instead of crumpling or backing, Tunney went forward and planted a right uppercut to the face as Dempsey tore in wildly.

Dempsey's greatest exhibition of savageness came with the opening of the fourth round. The defending champion charged like an enraged bull and plunging across the ring, almost drove Tunney out of the ring near Gene's corner, with a swishing left hook to the jaw. Going in close Dempsey pounded the body and they wrestled across the ring to Dempsey's corner, where as they parted from close quarters Tunney wabbled weakly against the ropes. Here, it seemed, was the old Dempsey.

He had Tunney in distress, or so it appeared. But it developed it was only a flash, a desperate effort by Dempsey to overawe his rival and instill in this pretender some respect for the monarch of the ring. Tunney didn't see it that way. He recovered his poise in a jiffy and began boxing. After a few stabbs of his left Tunney opened a cut under Dempsey's right eye from which a crimson stream flowed and flecked the beautiful bronzed body which had been so liberally praised in song, story and picture. More, Tunney stepped in with a right to the jaw which staggered Dempsey and with a succession of left jabs and hooks and right crosses and swings with which he blinded Dempsey in a furious counter assault. Tunney had his rival navigating on unsteady legs and his face blood-smeared at the bell.

Dempsey Cowed at Last.

This treatment cowed Dempsey there and then. If he had had any doubts that he was facing his master, they had been dispelled. As he came up for the fifth round Dempsey, instead of ripping and plunging recklessly at Tunney, was cautious and apprehensive. He tried to box with Tunney, but he was not capable of doing so. Then he started forcing matters again while Tunney danced around, cold and appraising, looking for another opening for a smack with his right. And here it was seen plainly that the sting and force had gone from Dempsey's blows. With them had gone his chances for victory. For he landed to Tunney's jaw with a right as he rushed Tunney to a corner and Tunney came back with a right that was stronger. Again Dempsey lashed out with his right and grazed the jaw and he went close to the ropes and belted Tunney about the body, but Tunney came back with a succession of rights to the jaw which bewildered Dempsey.

Dempsey floundered awkwardly around the ring in the sixth round, but twice managed to hook his left solidly to the jaw, once forcing Tunney across the ring and again sending Tunney backward. But these blows were desperate lunges in a losing cause. The blows were widely separated and, most important of all, they lacked the old Dempsey crushing power. Against this wild attack Tunney set up a varied offensive, fighting all the time, hooking or jabbing with his left or hitting home with left and right to the face and jaw in a one-two combination punch. Under the pace, Tunney was tiring, but Dempsey was practically played out.

The Shift Only a Ghost.

Dempsey tried his shift in the seventh round, the ghost of the famous shift which once meant destruction and which heretofore invariably was well timed and accurate, but it was a pitiful effort last night; a dramatic gesture and nothing more. Against Tunney's jabs Dempsey came in with a left hook which brought the blood from Tunney's eye, the crimson showing as the men separated from a clinch. But Tunney went coolly and deliberately along and with a right to the jaw almost sent Dempsey down.

Tunney pounded home with his right to the face or to the body and Dempsey missed like a novice with a left and right. Tunney pecked away and Dempsey charged in with a left and right to the jaw, which sent Tunney backward on his heels. But Gene rebounded to the attack and clubbed Dempsey about the head with a right. At the bell Dempsey was a sorry looking spectacle, with his left eye blackened and swollen and a cut under his right eye, from which the blood continued to flow.

It was the same through the three succeeding rounds.

Tunney, the master, never overlooked a chance to send home a right to the face, head or jaw of the tottering champion, or a jab or hook with the left which stung and bruised. Dempsey floundered around, fighting doggedly, courageously, aye, recklessly, in the face of his opponent's withering fire, and Tunney fighting just as courageously, determinedly, but with not the recklessness which characterized the work of Dempsey.

Dempsey reached his rival's body with a left and he landed to Tunney's jaw with a right in the eighth round, but he missed more than he landed and the punches which went home had no sting in them. All the time Tunney was jabbing or hooking with his left and crossing his right whenever the opportunity presented for a crash to the jaw or head.

Dempsey's Strength Ebbs.

Dempsey's strength was ebbing in the ninth round. He was weary when the session started, and he was discouraged, too. But he was desperate and he fought on though his task was hopeless by now. Tunney danced around his rival and he continued to dance even when Dempsey crashed home a solid left to the wind, the best body punch of the fight that Dempsey had landed, so far as accuracy was concerned. But Tunney retaliated with a clip of the right on the jaw and after each had missed in an exchange of rights for the jaw, Tunney suddenly started to be the pursuer instead of the pursued. He began chasing Dempsey around the ring.

Tunney closed this round fighting Dempsey in Dempsey's own corner, and battering the champion severely about the face and head with a fusillade of rights and lefts, while Dempsey tore blindly at the body with his right. The crowd sent up a terrific yell for the fighting marine at the end of the round. It was as if the gathering was practicing its shout of acclaim for the victorious Tunney; a sort of rehearsal for the greeting which was to come within the succeeding five minutes. Nobody minded the downpour, which drenched everybody and gave no indication of abating. Here was a new champion on the threshold of being elevated and the thrill overcame the inconvenience and discomfiture of unfavorable weather.

Dempsey Plunges Near End.

They merely touched gloves starting the tenth session and then Dempsey, with the urge of the old Dempsey still upon him, even if the effectiveness was gone, went on the offensive. He rushed blindly, although eagerly, it seemed, only to miss. Then he plunged again, ripping rights and lefts to the body, but Tunney, ignoring the blows, drove home a right which cut Dempsey over the left eye. Another right followed and Dempsey went staggering backward to the ropes.

With another right Tunney closed Dempsey's left eye tightly and the tottering champion clinched. He pawed the air and then suddenly sent a right to the head, but Tunney countered with a left and right to the face and Dempsey's blood smeared his face.

The rest was the picture of the finish of a once great fighter—a human hurricane petered out. Weary of body and mind, wabbling and staggering around, he cut and slashed, blinded and bleeding, his face battered, facing the foe, yes, but helpless. He commanded the admiration of the crowd to the end.

Tunney Appears, Smiling.

Tunney entered the ring first. He received a great reception as he stepped up smiling, wearing a dark robe with a marine insignia on his back. He was followed by his manager, Billy Gibson. Tunney smiled and bowed as he sat down in a swinging chair.

The referee was introduced as Tommy Reilly of Philadelphia, a medium sized but keen-eyed man of 50, wearing the conventional white sweater and white trousers. Then the judges were announced.

Dempsey, wearing a white towel over his shoulders and unshaven, stepped into the ring a few minutes later and received a mixture of cheers and boos. Dempsey wore a white plaster over his right eye. Gene Normile, wearing a white sweater and cap, entered the ring. Dempsey went over to Gene, said "How are you, my boy?" and shook hands. After this Tunney sat down and began wrapping the white bandages around his hands.

Philadelphia Jack O'Brien accompanied Dempsey, acting as his chief second. Jimmy Bronson, Lew Fink and Lou Brix were Tunney's seconds. After the cheering, which marked the entrance of the main bout contenders, quiet maintained over the arena.

As the boxers were bandaging their hands some light drops of rain began to fall and hundreds of the spectators stood up to put on raincoats. It was a tense moment, as it was a question of time if the big bout could go over before the rain began to fall in earnest.

The crowd began to cheer and whistle to hurry the fighters into action.

The boxers continued wrapping their hands as the pattering rain fell harder. Gibson finally began to slip Tunney's gloves on and Jerry the Greek put the gloves on Dempsey.

The weights were announced, Dempsey 190 pounds, Tunney 185½, and the fight was on.

AIRPLANE CARRIES TUNNEY TO SCENE

Continued from Page 1, Column 4.

lenger was about to go forth in quest of fame and fortune.

There were no more than a dozen in the group who saw Tunney make his romantic departure. Gene joked and laughed with his companions continually.

"I had to keep it a secret," he explained, "Gibson would have had a recurrence of hay fever if he knew I was going to fly over and Rickard would have been down here with handcuffs. After all, you know, it's the really sensible thing to do. I shall have a little diversion which will keep my mind off the fight. It will be a much quicker trip than in a train or motor car and there won't be that continuous bumping motion that is hard on the nerves

"If I crash, it won't matter. After all, the longest life is very short. Of course it's Rickard's show, but it's my life, don't forget that."

By the time he had finished his philosophic explanation the plane had taxied into position and Casey Jones was adjusting his parachute paraphernalia.

"I'll promise not to use this, Gene," he laughed as he snapped the buckles into place.

"What shall I do if you break your promise?" asked Gene.

"Just grab hold of my leg," he was instructed.

Jones stepped into the pilot's seat, Tunney climbed into the forward cockpit, known to fliers as "the golden chair," and Morton got in beside him. There was a whir of air as the propeller increased its speed, a flurry of dust and where he had teed off the day before the challenger took off today.

It was 10:05 Daylight Time, when the plane rose like a red fly into the mist that hung over the country. Twice it circled over the Buckwood Inn and then headed south and east toward the City of Brotherly Love.

Less than an hour and a half later it descended at the navy yard, but there were more people to greet the carrier of the challenger than there were to bid it farewell.

The news had spread to Philadelphia and there were a corps of photographers with cameras focused as the plane descended and moved easily and gracefully over the ground until it came to rest, ending its eighty-five-mile journey.

Jones was the first to crawl out of the cockpit.

"Well, how did you like it?" he asked.

"It was grand, Casey," answered Gene. "I enjoyed it a lot."

Hand Trembles a Little.

Then Tunney climbed out, folding his long legs like a jackknife to extricate himself. As he straightened his big form on the ground his face looked sallow under the tan acquired at his Stroudsburg training camp. His hand trembled a little when he thrust it forward to Lieut. Commander J. H. Strong, Flight Commander of League Island Navy Yard, who was the first to welcome Tunney to Philadelphia.

But Gene's mad dash was not yet **over. Twice he was hailed by irate officers of the law as he sped on his way to the offices of the State Boxing Commission to weigh in. His car was not detained but the number of it was noted. Arriving at the Drexel Building Tunney and his party battled their way through a dense crowd packed around the elevators.**

MEXICO CITY ENJOYS FIGHT.

Crowds Fill Plaza to Hear Radio—Americans Lose on Dempsey.

Special Cable to THE NEW YORK TIMES.

MEXICO CITY, Sept. 22.—The Plaza de la Constitution, facing the National Palace, was crowded tonight with interested fans listening to the Dempsey-Tunney fight reurns by radio. The balconies of the City Hall were crowded.

The press gave out bulletins and issued extra editions, receiving the fight news on special wires. The entire city was excited.

The American colony lost heavily, as the majority bet on Dempsey. Clubs were crowded with fight fans.

STORY OF THE FIGHT ROUND BY ROUND

Continued from Page 1, Column 7.

bleeding profusely. Tunney rallied in the centre of the ring and sent two rights to the jaw which had Jack in a bad way. Tunney sent in a fusillade of rights and lefts to Dempsey's jaw and had him staggering. Dempsey was game, however, and was boring in at the bell.

Fifth Round.

Jack came out rather wearily and wove around, looking for an opening. They boxed in the middle of the ring. Tunney put over a right to the head. Dempsey came through with a hard left to the body and a right to the jaw, Gene countering with a left to the bad eye. Dempsey's left eye was going very black. Dempsey kept circling around Gene. Jack worked Tunney into a neutral corner and sent heavy lefts and rights to the body, but Tunney rallied and sent Dempsey back with lefts and rights and had Dempsey going again. Tunney landed another good right to the jaw, Jack missing a wild left. Dempsey seemed to be slowed up, but was still rushing Gene after the bell sounded.

Sixth Round.

Dempsey came out slowly for the sixth. He followed Gene to a neutral corner, missed a left and they clinched. Gene sent several light rights to the jaw. Dempsey rallied and sent several rights to the body and jaw, then went to a neutral corner and held Tunney on the ropes. They fought in the middle of the ring, momentarily, at long range. Then Gene sent a short right to the face. They boxed at long range. Dempsey landed a heavy left to the body, staggering the challenger, but Gene came back with hard lefts and rights to the jaw which staggered the champion. Dempsey kept crowding Tunney, but Gene came back with a hard right which staggered the champion at the bell.

Seventh Round.

Jack came out crouching with his right for Gene's body and they clinched. Dempsey took two swings to the jaw coming in and wrestled Tunney to the ropes. Dempsey sent over a left which cut Tunney's right eye. Jack was rallying and rushed Gene to the ropes, putting heavy lefts to the jaw, and Gene was hanging on. Tunney staggered Jack with a right to the jaw, and Dempsey punished him with heavy rights and lefts to the body. Gene sent a heavy right to the jaw. They stalled for a moment, then Gene landed a right to the side of the head. Jack crouched, then rushed in with a left to the jaw. In a terrific exchange Jack landed a left and right to the jaw and Gene countered with a right and left to the jaw. As Jack came rushing in, Gene hit Jack's bad eye and it began to swell up badly as the round ended.

Eighth Round.

Dempsey began crowding Gene starting the eighth round. Gene retaliated y jabbing two lefts to the face. Dempsey swung two hard lefts to the back of the head. Jack crouched low, looking for an opening, but Gene crashed a heavy right to the side of the head. Gene was too clever for Jack and came in with a hard right swing to the head. As Dempsey rushed in with a wild right swing, Tunney put a hard right to the body which jarred the champion. Tunney jabbed the champion away, and worked Jack into his own corner but could not land. Jack lunged in again but Tunney snapped a hard right to the jaw and Jack backed away. The rain had dropped to a light shower and they were sparring in the middle of the ring as Gene jabbed Jack to the head at the bell.

Ninth Round.

Dempsey danced out as if refreshed but was short with a hard right. Tunney shot a right hook to the jaw. They wrestled to the ropes and then Dempsey missed a wild left and right to the jaw. As Jack came in, Tunney came up with a right uppercut to the jaw. The rain began to fall heavily again. Tunney jabbed Jack lightly with two lefts to the face. Jack missed a wild right, then shot a left to Tunney's body as they clinched. Tunney came over with a high right to Jack's head. Tunney forced Dempsey to his own corner, sent two heavy rights to the jaw and Jack was groggy again. Jack lunged over with a heavy left which did no damage. They wrestled and clinched and the referee broke them. Tunney was forcing Jack in his corner and put over a stiff left and right to the jaw as the bell sounded.

Tenth Round.

The tenth round opened and the rain was falling heavily. The crowd roared for Tunney to finish the champion. The combatants met in the centre of the ring and Tunney sent a right to the head. Dempsey rushed furiously but Tunney came in and sent Dempsey back and closed his eye. Gene sent several right and lef uppercuts to the the head. Tunney delivered two more right and left uppercuts and was doing as he pleased with Dempsey. Tunney was swinging on Dempsey's jaw as the bell rang, ending the bout.

Both judges agreed on Tunney as the winner and the new champion was wildly cheered.

CROWD REACHES STADIUM SMOOTHLY

Continued from Page 1, Column 3.

calling encouragement dominated the stadium as Tunney took the lead with a series of blows against the worried Jack's aching face. The rain was still spattering dawn, but no one noticed it.

There were two great cheers more left in the crowd. One came when the last blow was struck. And it was Gene who struck it. The other, and it was the greatest cheer since that unbelievably exciting battle between Dempsey and Firpo, came when the announcer shouted out to the 135,000 that Tunney was the new world's heavyweight champion.

Since only reserved seat tickets had been sold for the fight, and there were no general admissions, there was not the all-night line waiting to get in which has characterized previous world's championship bouts. But of course there had to be a first arrival, and he appeared with a friend shortly before noon.

The two young men who composed the vanguard of the army of spectators who filled the stadium a few hours later were unshaven and in well-worn clothes. They advanced confidently clear down to the ringside, chose two seats carefully, took off their coats and settled themselves for a ten-hour wait. The ushers had a conference about it, then approached them and gruffly demanded whether they had authorization to be there.

"Yes sir, seven dollars and a half worth" responded one of the young men, displaying two seat stubs.

They were ushered to their proper places far out toward the rim of the bowl by a larger array of ushers than were attending later on to the cabinet ministers, governors and captains of industry.

The earliest arrivals who took up their places on the outer ramparts of the stadium looked down on a great horseshoe tinted in green and gold which even then seemed keyed up with anticipation of the coming drama. From the top of the outer wall fluttered the flags of forty-nine nations. Ten great steel structures supported the hundreds of searchlights which would flood the tiny white roped square down below while the two young men who today were America's foremost citizens pummeled each other upon it.

Second Arrivals at 3 P. M.

The first arrivals sat in unrivaled possession of the entire stadium until 3 o'clock, when the gates were opened and a handful of fight fans with nothing else to do drifted in and lost themselves in the immensity of the arena. Even then there were interesting things to watch.

The hundreds of workmen who have erected the stands for Tex Rickard had left after toiling all night, but a few workmen were putting on the last finishing touches to the ring, lacing its white cover, while others tacked up the final section letters among the stands.

A whole troop of cameramen marched in and began running up and down ladders, inspecting their lofty perches alongside the ring. A whole orchestra of telegraph operators and wire experts were busy around the margin of the Dempsey-Tunney ring tuning up for the millions of words which shortly were to flow over the eighty-six wires radiating out from the ringside. Radio mechanics tinkered with the microphones which were to tell the story of the fight to no one knows how many millions in their homes.

The early arrivals sweltered under a sky covered with dull clouds which did not seem even to filter the sun's rays but weighed down like hot lead. It had been raining at 9 o'clock this morning when the 1,500 ushers recruited largely from Philadelphia schools and colleges reported for duty. But the isolated seat holders studied the sky, smiled with relief, and nodded their heads in approval over the boast of Tex Rickard that it never yet had rained on one of his major contests.

Women began dotting the stands, adding a new touch of color to the gray expanses whose only decoration had been the red collegiate caps of the ushers, the green caps of the hawkers of lemonade, etaosihrdlu aoinhrdlu u cushions, programs and other indispensables of a championship prize fight.

The women of the typical prizefight crowd to which we have become used in Madison Square Garden in these days when social leaders have begun attending them were not the only ones present. There were women who evidently had not come to Philadelphia to see the fight at all, but had decided they might as well see it, since they were here attending the Sesquicentennial anyway.

By 6 o'clock the influx into the stands had grown into a steady march down the long aisles and Tex Rickard's supervisors, veterans of many a Madison Square Garden battle and Boyle's Thirty Acres were darting hither and thither making sure that the machine was functioning.

But before 6 o'clock the confidence of the crowd that the Weather Bureau's threat of rain was only a false alarm was shaken by the deepening of the clouds and a fresh wind, which swept across the stadium bringing a hint of moisture.

Instantly, there appeared, by the same magic which produces the sidewalk umbrella venders when a shower descends on Broadway, hundreds of "keep dry rain hats" ingenious contrivances made of pasteboard in the general shape of an airplane, which when unfolded made an ample covering for the head and shoulders.

It certainly looked like rain, but a little later Tex Rickard himself came sauntering down through the stands to the ringside with his famous smile, and the anxious fans nodded to each other again and averred that once more he was right.

The show, so immeasurably the greatest of its kind on earth, with its crowds of rich men, poor men, beggarmen and maybe even thieves; its clamor, its color, its gayety, its suspense, was on at 7 o'clock, nearly three hours before Dempsey and Tunney clambered through the ropes for those few moments of elemental combat which had drawn ll these thousands.

The Lights Come On.

The lights came on and flooded the horseshoe with a soft radiance. The battery of loud speakers over the ring began distilling dance music from the Broadway successes, and set feet to tapping on the dusty ground of the ringside section in time to the latest song hits of Broadway.

The cries of the barkers proclaiming the necessity for sandwiches and ice cold drinks assumed the dramatic pitch and timbre of the evening, and the great mobs of spectators composed of such diverse human units had become welded into one entity, swinging upward toward its climax of excitement.

Tex Rickard's fifty acres was a vast platter of the 130,000 who had contributed those so-called two million dollars of gate receipts.

They showed fairly yellow under the searchlights and melted away almost into invisibility at the topmost edges of the platter, two hundred yards distant from the ring. Everybody almost, men and women, was smoking. It spread a blue haze of smoke over the arena and through this dusk-like curtain the lights of thousands of matches lighting cigars and cigarettes glowed and went out and reappeared, darting about like fireflies on a Summer evening. Over the arena an airplane, its under wings brilliantly lighted, circled effortlessly like an unearthly hawk.

The crowd was what Rickard had promised it would be—a $250,000,000 crowd, not only the greatest in numbers and in the amount of money they had poured out, but also it included perhaps the greatest group of men and women famous in every conceivable field of endeavor that ever has gathered in one place in this country.

It was world-wide in its scope and as democratic as a national election in the range of classes it drew. The hobo, who had beaten his way to Philadelphia, begged five-fifty and the price of a meal, was not precisely rubbing shoulders with the élite of the world, but he was swaying to the same emotions and shouting and groaning in unison with Governors, leaders of society in half a dozen of our great cities and a few from other countries as well, two thousand reputed millionaires and the stars of the stage and screen.

Long before the champion and the challenger came down the aisle toward the ring the stadium was jammed to capacity.

Notables Gather Early.

The notables had not waited for the last moment to make dramatic entries, but many of them were in their seat an hour and a half before the main bout.

Barney Oldfield was on hand at 6 o'clock, smiling at those who remembered his old triumphs in the days when auto racing was in its prime. At 7 Peggy Joyce, dressed sombrely in black but with a bouquet of orchids on her coat, took her seat in third row from the ring.

A little later a cheer of good fellowship went up as Gertrude Ederle came down to a ringside seat escorted by Dudley Field Malone.

James A. Farley, Chairman of the New York State Boxing Commission, who blocked Tex Rickard's efforts to hold the match in New York and thus sent it to Philadelphia, came in unaccompanied by any audible comment. And a few minutes later William Muldoon, the New York Commissioner who tried to keep the fight in New York, entered and took a seat not far from Farley's.

Tom Donohue, Connecticut Boxing Commissioner, also was close to the ring. Jack Kearns, one time manager of Jack Dempsey, was in a press seat watching his former protégé and present legal adversary joust with Tunney.

John McGraw, Jacob Ruppert, Wilbert Robinson and others famous in the sport world also were present, close to the fighting.

As the hour of the world championship bout itself drew near and the rivers of people flowing down the aisles slowed down to a trickle, the presence of more and more owners of well known names was announced.

William A. Brady, theatrical producer, who in his earlier days managed both Jeffries and Corbett, was here, so was Irene Castle. The Roosevelts entered, Theodore, Kermit and Archie. Jules Mastbaum was on hand with a large party from New York which included both officials and celebrities of the film world. William Fox was present. Charlie Chaplin, Norma Talmadge, Tom Mix, on foot, and Billy Hart, unarmed, were here, overshadowed for once by Jack Dempsey, who used to be in the movies himself.

Tim Mara, New York pro football promoter and a warm friend of Tunney, came in, hoping the challenger would win. William B. Chadbourne, New York attorney, appeared for a moment close to the ring and melted into the crowd. Ambassador Fletcher, America's representative in Mexico, had a ringside seat.

Tex Rickard himself must not be forgotten, for he was an important part of the scenery, glowing as he received congratulations on his latest success as a promoter.

Rickard, in fact, apeared for a moment to be in danger of being thrown out of his own show. Some 3,000 policemen and 700 firemen were faithfully enforcing his rule that ticket holders must get to their seats. Sit down and stay down. While a preliminary bout was in preparation Rickard strolled down to the front and stood beaming a moment.

"Hey, you," bellowed a policeman, "I said sit down, and I meant sit down. Now sit down."

Mr. Rickard turned to him blandly, smiled benignly and sat down in the nearest seat.

Mayor James J. Walker of New York was one of the first officials to arrive.

WASHINGTON SOCIETY GOES TO SEE FIGHT

Planes and Trains Carry Diplomats and High Officials of Government Departments.

Special to The New York Times.

WASHINGTON, Sept. 23.—Hundreds of Washingtonians, many of them nationally prominent, went to Philadelphia today to witness the Dempsey-Tunney fight. Some made the trip by airplane. The first plane carrying passengers to Philadelphia left here at 8:45 o'clock this morning. Among its passengers was William Mooney, Postmaster of Washington, who was boxing partner of Theodore Roosevelt when he was President.

Tunney Shows No Marks; Dempsey in Collapse After Bout

New Champion Has to Battle Way to Dressing Room Through Throng.

Special to The New York Times.

SESQUICENTENNIAL STADIUM, PHILADELPHIA, Sept. 23.—Gene Tunney, wearing his newly acquired crown, had another fight on his hands after he finished with Dempsey. He had to fight his way through the cheering, screaming, back-slapping crowd to his dressing room.

A squad of special police, his manager, Billy Gibson; his trainers and his seconds cleared the way as best they could but it still required a full quarter of an hour to reach the guarded doors.

Only a few very close friends were admitted. Gene immediately jumped into a shower bath and let the cooling waters play over his aching body, while Abe Attell, former featherweight champion of the world, held the floor. When Tunney finally emerged from the shower there were only superficial marks of the battle in evidence.

Gene was asked if his airplane flight this morning had any effect on him.

"Say, I want to tell you now that its over and I won, that I was sick twice and wanted to be a third time. I told the boys when I got out of the plane that I felt fine, but that was only because I wanted to have no excuse if I lost. I'll never try that again, though."

Billy Gibson, the champion's manager, was incoherent, though he had a lot to say for many minutes. His remarks were at last translated to mean that he was satisfied with everything and everybody. Billy said that it was the best handled fight from Tunney's standpoint he had ever seen.

"That's the first time Dempsey ever backed away in his life," Billy declared. "He admitted he was licked and there was nothing questionable or technical about Gene's victory. If it had been fought in New York and there had been five more rounds, Tunney would have won by a knockout."

PHILADELPHIA, Sept. 23 (AP).—Tribute to the sportsmanship and prowess of Jack Dempsey was the first thought of the new champion, Gene Tunney.

After paying his tribute to his defeated opponent, Tunney said he wished to give credit where it was due in his development as the champion—the United States Marines.

"The marines made me," he said, "and I wish to again go on record as saying so and adding 'Thank you' at the same time.

"What did I tell you?" was his greeting to an Associated Press correspondent who had been with him at his training camps in Speculator and Stroudsburg.

Loser Fails to Answer Normile as the Doctors Work on Him.

Special to The New York Times.

SESQUICENTENNIAL STADIUM, PHILADELPHIA, Sept. 23. — Jack Dempsey, ex-heavyweight champion of the world, was in a state of collapse in his dressing room after the bout.

As Dempsey lay back and closed his eyes, Gene Normile, his manager, again encircled the ex-champion's head with his arms. Philadelphia Jack O'Brien stood on his right side soothing him. A doctor in uniform stood on the other side of the table.

The doctor worked over the long gash in Dempsey's left eye. Each time he touched him Dempsey's face twitched and he pulled away. Soon another doctor arrived and both worked on Dempsey.

Big Bill Tate stood at Dempsey's feet. He looked glum and said nothing, nor did Normile say anything. Dempsey was stretched out silent. Only the soothing words of O'Brien and the cautions of the doctor were to be heard.

Dempsey finally grew still under the handling and looked asleep. O'Brien and Normile spoke to him and he didn't answer. They shook him slightly but he did not respond.

Finally the doctor said: "Let him alone. He's tired."

Wants a Return Bout.

PHILADELPHIA, Sept. 23 (AP).—Jack Dempsey broke down and cried like a baby when he reached the seclusion of his hotel and was alone in the room with Jerry the Greek, his faithful little trainer, and Mike rant, his comTpanion. He was tremendously affected by his defeat, but bravely held up while making the trip from the Stadium to the hotel.

Dempsey, his left eye closed shut, and his right eye cut, was a pathetic figure. After burying his face in his hands for a few seconds he regained his composure and stretched himself on the bed for a soothing rub down at the hands of Jerry. This required a half hour, then Dempsey went to bed. He expects his wife, Estelle Taylor, to join him here tomorrow.

Dempsey wants another fight with his conqueror. When he rushed to the centre of the ring to greet Tunney, he asked him for another chance. Dempsey's handlers said that Tunney had agreed.

The defeated champion knew that he would lose as early as the eighth round. He did not want to wait for the verdict of the two judges to be announced before rushing over to greet Tunney, and his handlers had difficulty in keeping him in his seat until the new champion had been acclaimed.

"All the News That's Fit to Print."

The New York Times.

THE WEATHER
Fair today and tomorrow; warmer tomorrow; moderate winds.
Temperature yesterday—Max. 70, min. 60.
For weather report see Page 54.

VOL. LXXVI....No. 25,093. *** NEW YORK, THURSDAY, OCTOBER 7, 1926. TWO CENTS In Greater New York | THREE CENTS Within 200 Miles | FOUR CENTS Elsewhere in the U. S.

RUTH HITS 3 HOMERS AND YANKS WIN, 10-5; SERIES EVEN AGAIN

Babe Breaks Six Records Hitting Two Balls Out of Park, One Into Distant Bleachers.

EVEN ST. LOUIS CHEERS HIM

40,000 See Yankees Get 14 Hits Off Five Pitchers—Hoyt Gives 14, Too, but Survives.

VICTORY CLINCHED IN FIFTH

Five Bases on Balls and a Double Net 4 Runs—Pennock vs. Sherdel Today—Sixth Game Here.

By JAMES R. HARRISON.

Special to The New York Times.

ST. LOUIS, Oct. 6.—Contrary to reports, the king is not dead. Long live the king, for today he hit three home runs and smashed six world's series records as completely as his fellow-Yankees smashed the Cardinals, to tie the world's series at two victories apiece.

After all, there is only one Ruth. He is alone and unique. Tonight he is securely perched on the throne again, and the crown does not rest uneasy on this royal head. For to his record of fifty-nine homers in one season he added today the achievement of three home runs in one world's series game.

Behind his bulky, swaggering figure, the Yankees marched to an overwhelming victory, 10 to 5. When they were going down for the third and almost the last time, Ruth tossed them the rope of three homers. He took personal charge of the world's series and made the game his greatest single triumph. He led the charge of a faltering battalion and turned the tide of battle so much that tonight most of the neutral critics were conceding the championship to the Yankees.

Yanks Find Batting Eye.

Hearing the old familiar ring of Ruth's big bat, the Yankees came out of their coma, made ten runs and fourteen hits and bore the Cardinals to earth with a rugged, slashing attack.

Besides setting world's series records that may stand for all time, George Herman Ruth hit a baseball where only two other men had hit it—into the centrefield bleachers of Sportsmans Park. It is 430 feet to the bleacher fence. The wall is about twenty feet high. Back of it stretches a deep bank of seats, and almost squarely in the middle of this bank Ruth crashed the third homer that made all the history.

It was not one of his longest drives but it was by all odds his best, for it automatically wiped four marks off the record book. It was, as noted above, the first time anybody had hit that many homers in a series game. It made Ruth's number of homers for all series games seven, beating by one the former record of "Goose" Goslin. It made his total bases in one game twelve, three more than Harry Hopper in 1915. His extra bases on long hits amounted to nine. Again three better than any other man had ever done.

Besides those four marks, which were shattered by the one heroic blow, Ruth broke two more. He scored four runs, the most which any player has scored in a world's series game, beating a record of three set by Mike Donlin in 1905, which has been equalled often. Ruth also raised his own record of eighteen extra bases achieved in world series games to a grand total of twenty-seven.

Ruth's first contribution to the gayety of more than 40,000 fans today came in the first inning, when Flint Rhem, the first of five Cardinal pitchers, decided that a fast ball, adroitly served, would fool the king. Ruth swung under the ball and raised it high in the air. The pellet floated out to right field, hugging the foul line and blown by the wind toward foul territory.

Over the Fence It Goes.

At the last moment, with the ball veering closer and closer to the chalk line of extinction, it disappeared over the stand and fell to the broad avenue below—not two feet from the foul line.

In the third, when Ruth came up next, young Mr. Rhem had changed his mind and decided that a fellow who could hit speed that far might be slightly deceived by a pitch of slower pace. So he tossed up a dewdrop slow ball between the waist and shoulder and on the inside corner.

Ruth must have been expecting it, for he leaned back, swung from the floor and, with perfect timing, drove a long, high and hard poke over the bleacher roof in deep right-centre.

In both cases he swung at the first ball. Two pitches and two home runs. Two pitches and the game was practicaly over, with the Yanks inspired and rejuvenated and crowding to the plate to hit with old-time vim.

Two pitches and, who knows, the series was practically over. With his star left-hander, Pennock, thoroughly rested and ready to pitch tomorrow, Miller Huggins has the upper hand once more, with the Yanks finally awake and out of their batting slump.

After the third inning, the Cardinal pitchers treated Mr. Ruth with great aloofness and attempted no familiarities but one. That one was disastrous. In the sixth inning, Herman Bell, a young right-hander, was pitching. Combs opened with a single too deep for Thevenow to handle. Koenig fanned and Bell was so pleased with this conquest that he attempted con-

Continued on Page Twenty.

$150 Postage on One Parcel Sets a Record for Air Mail

PHILADELPHIA, Oct. 6 (AP).—What is believed to be a new record for high postage paid on a single parcel was established here last night, when a package was sent from Philadelphia to San Francisco by air mail carrying $150 in stamps.

Postal regulations prohibited local clerks divulging any description of the package, its contents, or recipient, but the parcel was nearly covered with canceled $5 stamps. The air mail postage across the continent is $4 a pound.

The package went to New York and thence by plane westward.

QUEEN MARIE BUSY FILLING WARDROBE

Rushes From Shops to Luncheon, Then to Tea, Tries on Gowns and Visits Theatre.

SHE MEETS MRS. WILSON

Her Disapproval of Short Skirts Causes a Stir Among the Paris Dressmakers.

By Wireless to THE NEW YORK TIMES.

PARIS, Oct. 6.—Although Queen Marie of Rumania has adopted present-day styles to the extent of shingling her hair and dieting to attain a modish figure, she let it be known today that she does not approve of short skirts.

News came from three leading dressmakers in Paris, where her American gowns are being made, that the Queen refused to recognize the prevailing style of short dresses. Just where the Rumanian Queen will strike a happy medium is a subject of considerable speculation among fashionable women, and it is not impossible that the decision may strike a blow to the extremely short skirts.

Nevertheless her seventeen-year-old daughter, Princess Ileana, wears the customary abbreviated skirt, although somewhat longer than knee length.

The entire wardrobe of Queen Marie has been planned with simple elegance. She will wear three sport costumes on the Leviathan. The remainder of the dresses are all formal in character and there are many of them.

The corridors outside the royal suite at the Ritz are piled high with trunks waiting to be packed with the Queen's Parisian purchases.

Won't Act for the Films.

Americans who had been wondering if Queen Marie, as reported, would go to Hollywood to act for one day in a film production were assured today by the Queen's secretary that she would not consent to become a film star for a day, but would probably visit the motion picture capital. She has been curious to see how pictures are made in America, having already had one of her stories, "Lily of Life," filmed by a French company.

The Queen was the guest of the Maharajah of Kapurthala at luncheon today at the latter's home in the Bois de Boulogne, and afterward she received a visit from Mrs. Woodrow Wilson and Mrs. Wilson's brother, Richard Bolling, who were recently entertained at the royal palace in Bucharest. Mrs. Wilson and her brother are sailing on the Leviathan with the Queen.

The Infanta Beatrice of Orleans-Bourbon, sister of the Queen, who was to have been a member of the royal party, has decided not to sail. No reason is given for the decision, although it is announced that the Infanta will come to Paris to say good-bye to her sister.

Additional interest was given to the party today when it was learned that Prince Hohenlohe-Langenburg, Count Edward Oppersdorf and Auguste Thyssen, German steel manufacturer and financier, have arrived in Paris and will sail on the same ship with the Queen.

Twenty-one packing cases full of beautiful bronzes, marbles, plaster works, earthenware and furniture, destined for the Rumanian Room at Maryhill Museum, Maryhill, Washington, are ready for shipment to the United States. The room will be opened by Queen Marie.

Queen Is Busy All Day.

PARIS, Oct. 6 (AP).—The dual task of being Queen and a prospective American tourist kept Queen Marie on the go today from early morning until late at night. As soon as she had breakfast this morning, she started on another shopping tour to supplement her purchases of yesterday.

She then went to the Bois de Boulogne for luncheon as guest of the Maharajah of Kapurthala. The luncheon was so sumptuous and was served in such a long-drawn-out style that it was almost tea time before the Queen, with her daughter, Princess Ileana, returned to her hotel. On her arrival at her suite she found a num-

Continued on Page Four.

LABOR DENOUNCES DETROIT CHURCHES; REJECTS NEW OFFER

Torrents of Denunciation Also Hit the Y. M. C. A. and Auto Makers in Convention.

ACCUSATIONS ARE RESENTED

Union Chiefs Charge Employers Are Slackers and Profiteers and Assert Plot to Cut Wages.

GREEN IS AGAIN INVITED

But He Declines to Speak at Meeting Arranged by the Federal Council of Churches.

Special to The New York Times.

DETROIT, Oct. 6.—After the convention of the American Federation of Labor had listened for two hours this afternoon to a torrent of denunciation of the employers, the churches and the Young Men's Christian Association of Detroit for the cancellation of addresses to be made by labor leaders on Sunday, President William Green tonight declined an invitation, offered by the Federal Council of Churches, to address a mass meeting in the First Congregational Church.

The invitation was extended late this afternoon, after the attack on the churches, by James Myers of the Federal Council of Churches, under whose auspices the speaking arrangements in the churches had been originally made. He announced that through the courtesy of the Rev. Dr. G. G. Atkins, of the First Congregational Church, an invitation was extended to President Green to speak there Sunday afternoon and that Dr. Lynn Harold Hough promised to preside. A motion to have a labor speaker on Sunday was adopted by a narrow margin by the directors of this church, who rescinded their action because of the opposition expressed to it.

Fourteen speakers, most of them social secretaries of the Federal Council of Churches, will make addresses in local churches on Sunday, it was announced by Mr. Myers, who told the delegates that "the people who were endangering America were those who made it impossible to discuss controversial issues."

The Detroit incident, he said, was not representative of the great Christian forces of America.

Detroit Business Denounced.

During the discussion this afternoon the Detroit Chamber of Commerce was bitterly attacked because of its open letter to ministers who had signified their intention of having labor speakers in their churches. It was charged that the business men's organization had coerced the church boards to withdraw the invitations. A special target of attack was the assertion contained in the open letter, that the speakers originally scheduled to fill the local pulpits were men "who are admittedly attacking our Government and our American plan of employment."

President Green, responding to an inquiry by John P. Frey, President of the Ohio State Federation of Labor, explained that C. D. Van Dusen, President of the Board of Directors of the Young Men's Christian Association, had visited him today and had officially canceled the invitation extended last July asking him to speak at a mass meeting next Sunday. The cause assigned by Mr. Van Dusen, general manager of the S. S. Kresge Company, said Mr. Green, was that the Y. M. C. A. had embarked on a building program which "could be better advanced through the cancellation of the invitation."

Mr. Frey attacked the advocates of the open shop in this city as having waged a campaign forcing the churches and the Y. M. C. A. to withdraw the invitations. He defended the trade union movement and the speakers whose invitations were canceled from the accusations made and ended by saying that if the time ever came "when mammon dominates the altar, then Christianity has passed away."

Mr. Frey charged the employers of this city with taking advantage of the American right to voluntary association, but said they used their association to make it impossible for their employes to unite," and now they are attempting to use their power to compel the disciples of the Carpenter of Nazareth to keep their mouths closed upon the greatest question of the day."

"In this city there is a tablet," he said, "marking the end of the underground railroad which enabled unfortunate slaves to get to Canada. The underground railroad was organized by clergymen of Michigan and Ohio. In those days they were heroic in the face of opposition. Their mouths could not be closed against the injustice of human slavery. That is some-

Continued on Page Six.

Missing Will Made by Guider Is Sought; Cut Sister's Share in Estate, Says Lawyer

Search was begun in Brooklyn yesterday for a will made by the late Borough President Joseph A. Guider on June 2, 1925, which, if found, will make invalid the will already filed with the Surrogate of Kings County making Mrs. Catherine Lubbe, a sister, his heir. That will was drawn in 1916 and besides giving the sister the bulk of the estate named her as executrix.

The missing will is said to have been drawn by Harry E. Shirk, an attorney, of 44 Court Street. Workmen recently renovated his office and upset his files and since that time he has been unable to find it. The 1925 will was witnessed by Mr. Shirk and his sister, Mrs. Frances Johnson. The later document, after bequeathing about $1,500 to a niece, Sister Francis Joseph of the Dominican Order at Whitestone, L. I., gives Mrs. Lubbe, a nephew, Cornelius J. Guider, and a niece, Marie Guider, each one-third of the residuary estate.

Mr. Guider, Mr. Shirk said, went to his office on the day he made his new will to pay respects to the memory of Morris Shirk, his father, who had died a few days previously. Mr. Shirk said he was going over his father's papers when the late Borough President entered the room and in the conversation asked the nature of the papers. Mr. Shirk said that one was a will. Mr. Guider then, according to Mr. Shirk, said he would have to draw up a new will some day.

The attorney said the process was simple and could be done in a few minutes. He said that he prevailed upon Mr. Guider to do it at that time. The Borough President agreed and a form was presented and paragraphs were inserted disposing of the estate. Mr. Guider took the original document with him but left a copy with Mr. Shirk, who placed it in his files. This is the document that has been lost.

A few days later, Mr. Shirk said, he received from Mr. Guider a letter of appreciation of his having drawn the will. This letter also is missing.

Reports that Mr. Guider for several years had been unfriendly with his sister were denied yesterday by Mr. Lubbe. The latter said Mr. Guider's many remembrances to his sister on his numerous trips were sufficient to disprove such a rumor. He said also that he had heard of the existence of the other will and had searched for it without success.

Louis Goldstein, counsel for Mrs. Lubbe, has communicated with Mr. Shirk requesting that a diligent search be made for the missing will.

DEBT RESERVATIONS WILL BE IGNORED

United States Will Not Regard Any French Preamble to Compact as Binding.

HAS INTEREST IN BOND SALE

Rhine Army Costs Must Be Paid From Proceeds of German Rail Securities Issue.

Special to The New York Times.

WASHINGTON, Oct. 6.—Any reservations which members of the French Government or Parliament may attach orally or in the from of a preamble to the ratification of the Mellon-Berenger agreement for the settlement of the French debt will neither concern the American Government nor be regarded as binding it.

In making this point plain today officials at the same time explained that any distribution of proceeds of German railway bonds would naturally and legally involve consultation with and participation by the United States Government. This is provided for in the Paris agreement which the United States signed, even though the United States did not participate in the formulation of nor sign the London agreement relative to the distribution of German reparations.

Stipulation in Paris Agreement.

A clause was inserted in the Paris agreement that if the bonds contemplated under the Dawes plan to enable Germany to pay her treaty charges were sold or distributed the United States would be entitled to her share of the proceeds for application on the debt due from Germany for maintenance of the American Army of Occupation on the Rhine, &c. These distributions, in accordance with agreements concluded several years ago, were to be made after the costs of administration under the Dawes plan, including the costs of the occupational armies, &c., had been taken care of.

So far the American Government has not been approached on this subject by France or other interested powers.

If the German railway bonds are offered to American banking interests it is for the latter to decide whether they care to purchase them, in the opinion of Administration officials, and the bankers will naturally follow the practice of asking whether the State Department considers it wise to so invest American private banking funds.

No Gentlemen's Agreement.

As to the suggestion in press dispatches from France that the Poincaré Government is disposed to accompany ratification of the debt settlement compact with reservations written into a preface, it was intimated in official quarters that they would be disregarded. In other words, there could be no gentlemen's agreement about reservations and the Mellon-Berenger agreement would have to speak for itself so far as the State Department is concerned. Senators might, in their minds, have any reservations they pleased when they ratified an international agreement, but that would make no difference as to the agreement itself.

It is recognized here that the French Government is anxious to satisfy public opinion at home, but it is felt that willingness to make this possible should not permit any juggling with the agreement itself in such manner as to lead to disputes later over its interpretation.

POINCARE EXPECTS SUCCESS.

Is Confident Chambers and Congress Will Accept Reservation Plan.

Special Cable to THE NEW YORK TIMES.

PARIS, Oct. 6.—Premier Poincaré appears to be confident that his scheme for securing ratification of the Mellon-Berenger agreement, with a preface setting forth the French view of circumstances under which revision might be asked, will be approved in America.

To Henry Simon, President of the Chamber Finance Commission, he said yesterday that his information from America was of such a character that he was very optimistic. He felt sure that the American Government and Congress would understand both the character of the step he proposed and its necessity.

M. Simon himself is also optimistic as to acceptance of this form of reservation by the Chamber and by America. The proposed preamble will be in

Continued on Page Five.

'BUD' STILLMAN WILL WED MOTHER'S MAID

Engaged to Canadian Girl Who Once Worked on the Estate in Grande Anse.

PARENTS ARE DELIGHTED

Mrs. Stillman Says She Will Bring Miss Lena Wilson, Her Son's Fiancee, to New York.

James A. (Bud) Stillman Jr. will be married next June to Miss Lena Wilson, who at one time was a servant on the estate of his mother, Mrs. Anna U. Stillman, at Grand Anse, Quebec. Announcement of his engagement was made by young Stillman late last night in his room in Reunion Hall at Princeton. The marriage, he intimated, would take place after his graduation.

Bud's announcement confirmed a copyrighted dispatch to The Daily News from Grand Mere, a point near the Stillman estate in Quebec, in which Mrs. Stillman disclosed the engagement.

Miss Wilson is the daughter of the late William Wilson, a Scotsman who worked as a lumberman in the great timbered area of which the Stillman estate is the heart. Young Stillman met the girl during the months he spent at his mother's Grand Anse home.

Met Her Seven Years Ago.

When asked how he had happened to meet the girl, young Stillman laughed.

"Well, how does a fellow come to meet a girl anyway?" he countered.

"Is she a blonde or a brunette?" Again he laughed and then said somewhat soberly, "a blonde."

Just what did she look like, what was her general appearance, one interviewer wanted to know.

"Oh, I don't think I can tell you that," was the reply.

"Just how was she employed at your mother's home?"

"She just sort of helped my mother around the house," he said.

"What does your mother think of the engagement? Does she think it is all right?"

"Sure. You bet," replied young Stillman, this time with positiveness.

He went on to say that his fiancée would come down from Grand Anse the middle of November with his mother. They were going to try to see the Princeton-Yale game Nov. 13, he said.

"I am delighted with Bud's choice," Mrs. Stillman was quoted as saying in the Grand Mere dispatch." I had often wondered why Bud had not noticed this nice little girl. At last he woke up. I was passing a few days down in New York when Mr. Stillman received a wire from Bud asking us to get him a ring for Lena. I was a little bit surprised, but I was delighted. Mr. Stillman and I shopped for two days for this ring.

"It is a beautiful jewel, but not more beautiful than the jewels that Lena possesses—and by that I refer to her wonderful character. Mr. Stillman is as pleased with Bud's choice as I am. He said, when I told him of the wire, 'We will buy him the nicest ring we can find.' He has not met Lena yet, but he will soon, for I shall take Lena to New York with me shortly. She will pass the Winter there."

Miss Wilson is 18 years old, the dispatch to the Daily News says, and like most of the residents of the timber belt of Quebec, her native tongue is French. She is described as exceedingly attractive.

Helped Mother at Hearings.

Young Stillman, now in his twenties, stood stoutly by his mother's side throughout the long and famous suit of his father. By a coincidence, the brother of Miss Wilson, Johnnie Wilson, was one of the many Canadian witnesses who came forward to aid Mrs. Stillman during the hearings held in the case in Montreal.

"Bud," as he is invariably called by Mrs. Stillman, was a freshman when news of James A. Stillman's suit to divorce his wife and illegitimatize Guy Stillman, then a baby, burst upon the world. He immediately aligned himself with his mother, and when she went to Poughkeepsie, N. Y., to attend the series of hearings held there young Stillman accompanied her.

A tall chap, with an engaging smile

Continued on Page Seven.

APARTMENT HOTELS WORTH $300,000,000 ARE HELD ILLEGAL

W. C. Martin, Tenement Head, Asserts "Serving Pantries" Violate the Law.

ALLEGES COOKING IS DONE

150 New Buildings Hit by Ruling, Among Them Park Lane and Fifth Avenue Hotel.

TEST CASE EXPECTED SOON

Owners Organize to Fight Drastic Decision—Prepare to Take It to the Highest Courts.

Walter C. Martin, Tenement House Commissioner, revealed last night that he had decided that the 150 new apartment hotels in the city with serving pantries, in which some $300,000,000 has been invested and in which thousands of well-to-do families live, were illegal.

Mr. Martin said he based his decision on the discovery that cooking actually was done in the serving pantries, which as a rule were equipped with an electric refrigerator, a sink and an outlet to which an electric stove could be attached. Because cooking is done in these apartments, which are among the costliest and finest in New York, Mr. Martin asserted, they came within the provisions of the Tenement House law, but because they do not actually install stoves or admit that the pantry is used by the tenant as a kitchen they are built without regard to the provisions of the Tenement House law, and hence violate it.

To Seek a Test Case.

Mr. Martin said he would issue an order within a few days to vacate one of the hotels involved, and thus precipitate a test case in the courts.

Among the more conspicuous apartment hotels affected by Mr. Martin's ruling are the Park Lane, the new Fifth Avenue Hotel at Ninth Street and Arthur Brisbane's Ritz Tower.

In addition to the recent popularity of the apartment hotel, one big factor that has led to the construction of so many has been that zoning laws limit the height of apartment houses in relation to the size of their plots much more drastically than they limit the height of hotels. It therefore has been possible to erect a structure of many more stories on a given plot by making it a "hotel" instead of an "apartment house."

Not only would the height of the buildings be affected if it were decided that they were not true hotels, but, once they were held to be regulated by the Tenement House law, various requirements as to exits from suites and other protective features in buildings where there are many kitchens would have to be obeyed if the use of serving pantries as kitchens was continued.

The buildings could, of course, be converted into regular hotels by removing the cooking facilities, but that undoubtedly would affect their popularity in the opinion of real estate men.

To offset the possibility of many additional millions being spent by the owners to meet the requirements under the Tenement House law, which was passed in 1901 and amended in 1909, should Mr. Martin be upheld, these property owners have formed an organization called the Apartment Hotel Owners' Association, it was said last night.

The organization was started last Tuesday when word of Commissioner Martin's ruling reached some of the more prominent of the apartment hotel owners, and a call to all such property owners immediately was sent out for a general meeting. This meeting was held yesterday in the Waldorf, with about forty apartment hotel owners and architects present.

Arthur Brisbane, owner of the forty-two story Ritz Tower apartment hotel; Emory Roth, its architect, and representatives of Bing & Bing and Charles B. Meyers and Rosario Candela, architects, were among those present.

After lengthy discussion of the Tenement House Commissioner's ruling, in which the opinion unanimously was expressed that apartment hotels could not be construed as coming under the requirements of the Tenement House law, the following were elected directors of the new organization:

Harry A. Lanzer, proprietor of the Park Central Hotel; Aron Lapidus of the Lapidus Engineering Corporation, owners of the Beekman, the Park Royal and the Olcott apartment hotels; Max Fishel, who is constructing

Continued on Page Three.

Chile Alone Has Not Assented To Our Pan-American Flight

WASHINGTON, Oct. 6 (AP).—Chile is the only South American Government withholding assent for the crossing of her territory in the projected Pan-American flight sponsored by the army. Until Chile gives the permission requested, the expedition, which plans to cover 18,000 miles, will be held up.

State Department officials are confident the Santiago Government will agree to their request, since the prime object of the flight is to promote friendly relations between the United States and Pan-American republics.

WADSWORTH BAITED BY RURAL W. C. T. U.

Oswego County Convention, Refusing to Hear Him on Prohibition, Endorses Cristman.

SENATOR URGES TOLERANCE

Tour Takes Him Through Dry Territory, Day Ending With Big Meeting at Watertown.

Special to The New York Times.

WATERTOWN, N. Y., Oct. 6.—Senator James W. Wadsworth Jr. entered reputedly dry territory today in his campaign for re-election and at the Village of Mexico, where one of his meetings was held, encountered the Woman's Christian Temperance Union of Oswego County in its forty-ninth annual convention. While Senator Wadsworth at the Town Hall was pleading for modification of prohibition the convention at the First Methodist Church, around the corner, was unanimously adopting a resolution calling for his defeat and the election of Franklin W. Cristman, his dry opponent. The resolution read:

"Whereas James W. Wadsworth, throughout his public life, has consistently and persistently opposed prohibition, woman suffrage and many other principles for which the Woman's Christian Temperance Union has always fought and labored; be it

"Resolved, That we, the Woman's Christian Temperance Union in Oswego County convention assembled, agree for all our respective unions to do all in our power to prevent the election of the said James W. Wadsworth to the office of United States Senator from this State and to that end we pledge ourselves to do all we can to further the election of Franklin W. Cristman to that office."

A copy of the resolution was delivered to Senator Wadsworth just as he was leaving for the next meeting at Pulaski. He read the resolution carefully and smiled.

"The W. C. T. U. has taken that stand many, many times," he said.

Refused to Hear Wadsworth.

C. A. Stone, Oswego County Republican Chairman, upon learning that the convention would be in session while Senator Wadsworth was speaking in Mexico, sent an invitation to the delegates to attend the Wadsworth meeting and listen to the Republican candidate's prohibition views. The invitation was promptly declined, whereupon Chairman Stone suggested that the Senator would be glad to go to the Methodist Church and address the delegates.

"I should say not," was the reply of one of the W. C. T. U. leaders. "Senator Wadsworth's views on prohibition and ours are fundamentally different. We do not care to hear him speak."

Despite this statement, six of the sixty-one women gathered at the Methodist Church walked unobtrusively into the rear part of the town hall while the Senator was speaking and remained until convinced through their own ears of his position on prohibition. Then they left as unobtrusively as they had come and returned to the convention, which immediately went on record as endorsing Mr. Cristman.

"The ministers of the Northern New York Methodist Conference are for Cristman 100 per cent.," said the Rev. E. B. Caldwell, pastor of the church where the convention was held. "All but two of the ministers in the Central New York Conference are for Cristman also. The size of Cristman's vote will be surprising. I believe he will be elected."

Mr. Caldwell admitted regretfully there was "lots of drinking" in Mexico and that the business of bootlegging was thriving there. He personally

Continued on Page Two.

Byrd Will Launch the National Flight Today; Will Fly From Washington Here and Withdraw

Special to The New York Times.

WASHINGTON, Oct. 6.—Lieut. Commander Richard E. Byrd, U. S. N., retired, who flew over the North Pole area in a heavier-than-air machine early in the Summer, will make the first leg of the around-the-country flight sponsored by the Guggenheim Air Foundation, leaving here tomorrow at noon for New York. He will make the hop to New York in the plane that he used in the Arctic flight.

Commander Byrd will pilot the machin himself. He will be accompanied by officers of the Aeronautical Division of the Department of Commerce, two machinists and Charles F. Kunkle of New York, representing the Guggenheim Foundation.

The around-the-country flight from New York will be directed by Floyd Bennett, the naval officer who accompanied Commander Byrd on his polar expedition. Commander Byrd is prevented by lecture engagements from participating in the flight beyond the first leg from Washington to New York.

The purpose of the flight is to arouse public interest in commercial aviation. It has the support of Secretary Hoover, Assistant Air Secretary William P. MacCracken and other Department of Commerce officials concerned with air activities.

Proposed regulations governing aviation within the scope of the law passed by Congress creating a Bureau of Air in the Department of Commerce and the office of Assistant Secretary of Air in the department were considered at a conference today at which Mr. MacCracken presided. Representatives of aeronautical bodies and manufacturers attended.

The conference will continue for several days, following which Assistant Secretary MacCracken and his bureau associates will begin work on the proposed regulations.

GOV. SMITH DEMANDS THAT MILLS SUBMIT DATA ON MILK GRAFT

Insists That Rival Give Him Facts, Figures and Names if Charges Are Not Political.

DEFENDS CONDUCT OF CASES

Says No Evidence of Negligence Was Put Forward to Justify Special Grand Juries.

EAGER TO BEGIN CAMPAIGN

He Withholds Comment on Hearst and on Morris Accusations, but Denies Wasting State's Money.

Taking up without delay the allegations regarding milk graft made on the stump by Congressman Ogden L. Mills, Republican candidate for Governor, Governor Smith, immediately after his arrival in this city from Albany last evening issued a statement answering the questions that Mr. Mills had addressed to him on the subject, and also insisting that if Mr. Mills himself had facts, figures or names, and was not merely using the milk graft subject for political purposes, it was his duty to lay his information, whatever it might be, before the Governor.

The statement was the first campaign utterance of any length from the Democratic camp. The Governor had it ready when he reached the city. As soon as he was asked whether he had anything to say about the Mills charges, the Governor reached for the pile of statements he had prepared and said:

"Here is what I have to say in answer to Mr. Mills on that question."

Governor Smith's Statement.

The statement read:

Congressman Mills publicly asked me why I denied the request of the Citizens Union for Special Grand Juries and the intervention of the Attorney General in the recent milk disclosures in Greater New York. The question is a fair one, and I have never during the many years of my public life failed to answer any question put to me, from no matter what source, regarding my official conduct.

It is not customary for the Governor upon the request of private individuals to call extraordinary sessions of the Grand Jury and set aside properly and legally elected constitutional officers, substituting for them the Attorney General, unless there is good reason given. During my long term of office I set aside the District Attorney in three instances. In one the request came from the District Attorney himself that he be relieved of the prosecution. In two other cases definite and concrete evidence was laid before me tending to show that the District Attorney had failed to act.

Let me relate what happened at a conference between myself and two representatives of the Citizens Union. I asked them if they had any evidence to submit to the District Attorneys and they said no. They made mention of a statement made by a convicted man—that he gave part of the money he received to some other people. I frankly told the representatives that if they could give me any evidence of a failure on the part of any of the District Attorneys in the various counties of Greater New York to act upon evidence, or if they could bring me word from any official that the District Attorneys were not diligently pursuing every lead, I would be glad to comply with their request. The Citizens Union at no time stated to me that they had definitely obtained the Mayor's consent to a request that I supersede the District Attorney. That is just another example of the misleading statements Congressman Mills so often makes.

Says Kelby Is at Work.

Thereafter, the Mayor of the City of New York caused the appointment through the office of the Corporation Counsel of former Justice of the Appellate Division Kelby, who invited everybody with evidence of any kind to lay it before him, and as far as I know has been investigating the whole question of official corruption in the Department of Health. If he is not, I would like to know it.

If Congressman Mills or anybody representing him can lay anything before me tending to show that any or all of the District Attorneys of Greater New York are not diligently performing their duties in this matter, I will be glad to have him do so. I will meet him at the Hotel Biltmore or at any place he desires, and go with him or his representative to the office of such District Attorney.

Congressman Mills further asks me if I know any reason why Justice Kelby should not disclose the results of his investigation, or if there is any real reason why the public should not know of the progress the investigation is making. My answer to that question is that I know of no reason why he should not. His other questions are answered by the answers made to the first question.

If Congressman Mills and his supporters, who profess to have so much information, are as zealous and as sincere in this matter as he would have the people believe, let him bring the facts and information to me. For obvious political reasons he speaks of "men higher up." Who are they? Who does he even suspect them to be? There are two ways of discussing this whole problem—one is for political advantage and the other is for the betterment of conditions in the City of New York. If Congressman Mills is discussing it from the standpoint of the

Yankee Slugging Attack, Led by Ruth's Three Homers, Crushes Cardinals, 10 to 5

By JAMES R. HARRISON.

Continued from Page 1, Column 1.

clusions with Ruth, which was equivalent to tampering with a stick of dynamite.

When the count was finally three and two Mr. Bell did a foolish thing. He drew back his arm and cut loose with a fast ball straight through the middle. When Ruth is hitting as he was today, there is not a pitcher in the world who can afford this gamble. Even a schoolboy pitcher knows better than that.

Ruth waded into the fast ball and put all his shoulders and back behind the 52-ounce bat that has brought more ruin than any other in baseball. He caught the ball as flush as an expert marksman. It was a terrific blow and there was no doubt where it was going.

Douthit ran back as far as he could, and having no scaling irons or ladder, stood by helplessly while the ball shot over the wall and landed in the laps of the St. Louis rooters. It was still going with unabated speed when it arrived. It struck with force and bounced up, and then there came the finest ovation that St. Louis has ever given a visiting athlete.

Babe Gets Ovation.

Three home runs in one world's series game! Only seven men in modern baseball have hit three in any ordinary game. Even the harden partisans of St. Louis had to admit the grandeur of the feat. In Boston or New York or several other cities they would have torn the grandstand down and given Babe the pieces, but for St. Louis it was a gigantic tribute that poured out from more than 40,000 throats.

The folks in the grandstand were inclined to be a bit conservative. A few bitter-enders committed the lèse-majesté of booing the king, but out in the bleachers it was all tumult and uproar. The boys in the sun seats in left, where Ruth was stationed, got to their feet as if one man. They waved papers and programs and Cardinal banners and tossed a few ancient straw hats out on the field.

There have been few more gallant figures than Ruth leading the charge of the Yanks today. It had been a dark hour for the New York gladiators. Before the game, it was reported, Ban Johnson, President of the American League, went to the Yankee dressing room to give the players the sort of talk that a football coach delivers to his men before the big game. There was a general conviction that the Cards were the better team and would win, an opinion that was not changed until the slumbering menace in Babe Ruth's bat awoke and made a new team of the Yanks.

There have been few figures as gallant as Ruth as he strode from the bench to receive the thrice-repeated homage of an enemy crowd—his portly frame swaggering ever so slightly, his face alight with the fire of determination.

If the Babe was going down, he would go down fighting. There was only one man who could jar the Yanks out of their depressing slump. It is still a one-man team and the happy fortune today was that that one man found his batting eye and blazed the trail for his dejected colleagues.

A Lively Ball Game.

With the greatest home-run hitter of them all hitting three homers, it was, naturally enough, a lively occasion. The game was long and one-sided, but it was a good one—a great game, indeed, with attacks and counterattacks, a seesawing score. Twenty-eight hits on both sides and sensation following sensation, even to the almost disastrous collision of two Cardinal outfieldrs.

The paid attendance was 38,825, more than 1,000 above yesterday's first St. Louis game. This number of people paid $166,190 at the gate, bringing the total receipts of the series up to $730,001, a new record.

The previous record for receipts in four games was $723,104, made in 1929. The record for players' share, also made in that year, was $368,783.

With the playing of the fourth game, the players ceased to share in the receipts. However, the players' pool totaled $372,300, a world's series record, surpassing by more than $4,000 the record set in 1923. Of this total the world's series players will share in only 70 per cent., as the remaining 30 per cent. goes to the second, third and fourth place teams in the pennant races of the two leagues.

On this basis the world's series players will divide $260,610. Each club has twenty-five eligible players, which

The New York Times

Babe Ruth at bat.

means that each player for the winning team will receive about $6,254 and each player for the losing team will get $4,168. Both these sums are records in world's series.

The series is sure to go back to New York, and that means a Saturday game at the Stadium, with the two club owners cutting heavily into the net proceeds. With Pennock at hand, refreshed by a four-day rest, and the New York war clubs again playing the music of the solid wallop, the Yanks are favorites here to win, when last night they were poor second-money choices.

It was, until today, a lifeless world's series. Three games had been played, and in none of them was there a great play or a thrilling rally, or hardly an event that the baseball field had not seen dozens of times before.

The Series Awakes.

But today the series awoke and put on its best show. And there was sparkling fielding and the heavy ring of busy bats and enough mistakes to keep the fans on edge from start to finish.

The Cardinals opened brusquely on Waite Hoyt, but fell behind until the fourth. Then four hits and three runs put them one to the good, and raised the grave suspicion that Mr. Hoyt would take an early trip to the clubhouse. But to gain those three runs in the fourth Hornsby had to take out Rhem. Arthur Reinhart, his left-handed successor, threw the game away in the fifth by setting another world's series record, and giving five bases on balls. Four, as a matter of fact, were charged to Reinhart and the fifth to Herman Bell. With only one hit, the Yanks scored four runs, and in the sixth Ruth struck another home run blow and the game was over.

With all this friendly assistance Hoyt was able to stagger through, although he did not pitch a good game. He struck out eight, but was so much in trouble that Urban Shocker pitched almost a complete game in the bull pen, where he was joined later by Shawkey and Pennock, as the Cardinals made their constant threats.

Once Rhem had passed out, Hornsby was at sea and called on four more pitchers in vain. Reinhart, Bell, a young southpaw named William Hallahan and the right-hander, Vic Keen, strayed forth from the bench at odd moments, with Keen showing in the ninth the only flash of ability.

There was one other record tied during the sunny afternoon. Between and among them the five Cardinal pitchers issued ten bases on balls.

In the fourth the exultant fans were frightened speechless as Chick Hafey and Taylor Douthit, two of the outfield guard, crashed together in pursuit of a fly and were knocked groggy. Lazzeri was on first base with one out, when Joe Dugan looped a fly to left centre. Douthit rushed over from centre and Hafey dashed in from left. Eyes glued on the ball, they saw nothing else in the world. Players of more experience would have avoided the crash. Either of them could have caught the ball, but as Douthit touched it he bumped into Hafey, and the ball flew to the ground. Both players were stretched out apparently unconscious.

They were so badly dazed that neither could get up and chase the ball. Bell rushed out from third and retrieved it, but by that time Lazzeri was almost at the plate.

Doctor Rushes Out.

Douthit, as he rushed in, rammed his elbow against Hafey's chest and stomach, and the left fielder was the worse hurt of the two. He went down on his side and lay still. Players of both teams ran out. On their heels came the St. Louis trainer and the club doctor. For a moment it looked like a stretcher case, with the Cardinals out two good ball players, but smelling salts, a dash of cold water and frenzied towel-swinging did the trick and brought them both back to normal.

Douthit did one of the gamest things of the series only a minute later. With Dugan on second, Severeid sliced a pretty single to dead centre. Although only sixty seconds before he had been reclining on his back, Douthit sprinted in and tore loose a wonderful throw which nailed Joe fast at the plate.

It was one of four great throws today. In the second Lazzeri hit against the left field bleachers, but was out at third on Thevenow's fine relay of the ball from Douthit. In the fourth Douthit tried to score from second on a single, but was cut down by Ruth's marvelous line fling straight into Severeid's glove.

Again in the sixth, Meusel singled to right and tried a smart manoeuvre by rounding first base slowly and then suddenly putting on a burst of speed, hoping that Southworth would be taken in by the trick. Billy, however, was wideawake. He erased the big city slicker at second with a throw true and straight.

There was still another interval when the medical talents of the club trainer were needed to resuscitate an athlete. In the fourth, Bob Meusel suddenly stopped the game and walked into the diamond to complain of a dizzy spell and failing eyesight. The fans were not surprised to hear it, for they believed that by that time the Cardinals had knocked all the Yanks dizzy. Expert first-aid ministrations by Trainer Woods restored Robert, and there were no more complaints during the afternoon.

Rhem, in the first inning, struck out Combs and Koenig, but after this gay beginning, he tossed the celebrated fast ball to Mr. Ruth who stowed it away on the outside of the park. Meusel walked and Gehrig singled to right. The Cards had trouble getting hold of the ball and Meusel, smartly, kept on running from first to the plate. That he didn't make it was no fault of the strategy, for a better slide would have landed him safe and sound.

For the Cardinals, Douthit outran a tap to deep short, and Southworth sent him to third with a single through second. Hornsby emulated Ruth to some degree by dashing a rugged hit to right, scoring Douhit and moving Southworth to second.

Cardinals Hitting Fiercely.

The Cardinal hitting was fierce, and Hornsby wisely ordered Bottomley to keep the attack going instead of bunting. Bottomley, however flied to Ruth and Lester Bell did likewise to Combs. Hoyt got out of a very bad hole by fanning Hafey.

Lazzeri's two bagger to left opened the second. Tony thought the ball was going into the stand, and loafed down to first. So was a second late in arriving at third, where Bell did a nice job of touching. Followed Severeid's single, on which Lazzeri could have scored. It was one of three or more runs tossed away by the opulent Yanks.

The second Ruthian product enlivened the third inning. The score was now: Ruth 2, St. Louis 1. The Yanks showed more signs of life in the fourth, when Lazzeri walked and scored during the Hafey-Douthit head-on collision, which also allowed Dugan to reach second. On Severeid's single Joe was tagged out at home, Joe's speed being less than his earnest intentions.

The fourth was almost the end for Waite Hoyt. Up to this time he had done excellent work. Although his curve was nothing to boast about, he had nice control and an effective change of pace, working the corners with low fast balls that were called strikes but were hard to hit.

Koenig charged out to left to make a rattling good catch of L. Bell's fly. Hafey singled and then the Yankee shortstop made up for his good work by fumbling O'Farrell's grounder, an error which nearly cost the game, giving the Cards three unearned runs.

It was a bad break of luck for Hoyt. Thevenow whipped a two-bagger an inch inside first base and Hafey scored while O'Farrell paused at second. Hornsby had no confidence in Rhem and yanked him for Pinch Hitter Toporcer. It was a move that Rogers lived to regret, for Rhem certainly would have done better than the miscellaneous collection of talent which followed him.

Toporcer didn't deliver much at that, though his sacrifice fly to Combs scored O'Farrell with the tying run. Combs's throw was fast, but badly aimed.

Douthit's Two-Bagger.

Here, Douthit sent a rollicking two-bagger out to the bleacher wall in right centre and put his team a run ahead, while the local enthusiasts went crazy with joy. Sportsman's Park was a madhouse for two or three minutes, and the purple-faced rooters went into another spasm when Southworth singled to left. Douthit went for home and Ruth stopped him dead. The vocal storm subsided somewhat.

Back came the Yanks in the fifth to have the game presented to them on a silver platter. Reinhart, a stalwart left-hander with a tricky service like Sherdel's, was nervous and wild. Altogether he gave the most pathetic spectacle of many a world's series. He walked Combs without getting over even one strike, and the Yanks got a break when Koenig popped a fluky double down the right-field line, the ball landing in the one exact spot where no fielder could reach it.

Hornsby slipped when he picked up the ball, and Combs was fast enough to score. With Ruth at bat, Reinhart went on an ascension and neglected to take his parachute with him.

True, he favored Mr. Ruth with a strike, but the other four were balls. Another walk to Meusel filled up the bases and Reinhart went from bad to worse by chucking two bad ones to Gehrig.

Here was the point where Hornsby should have acted. He had Herman Bell warmed up, and it was no secret that Reinhart was now in the clouds. The left-hander steadied a little, but when the count was two and two he walked Gehrig, forcing Koenig in and sending New York ahead.

Bell took up the assignment with the bases still full and no one out, and no one thinking of getting out. Lazzeri's fly to Southworth scored Ruth, while Meusel occupied third after the catch. Dugan's grounder spouted up in the air and during his subsequent demise at the hands of O'Farrell, Meusel raced home with the fourth run.

In the sixth came Combs's single and the third of the Ruth home-run series. The score was now 9 to 4. The Cards in their half of the inning made attempts at reprisals. O'Farrell and Thevenow singled, but Flowers, a hitter for H. Bell fanned. Douthit and Southworth were powerless.

A single by Severeid, Hoyt's sacrifice, and Combs's two-bagger inside third put the Yanks into double figures in the seventh. Protected by his big lead, Hoyt went along in able style now. When O'Farrell led off with a single in the eighth, there was a flutter in the New York bull pen, but it was all a mistake. Hoyt struck out Thevenow and also Holm, who batted for Hallahan. Douthit flied to centre.

Wee Willie Sherdel will come back for the Cards tomorrow and the Cards need that victory very much, for it will be their last home game. Tomorrow night the procession wends back to New York.

SIXTH SERIES GAME HERE NOW ASSURED

Tickets for Seventh Contest, in the Event of a Tie, Will Go to First Applicants.

MUCH TROUBLE EXPECTED

Ed Barrow, Business Manager of Yanks, Looks for Complaints From Reservation Holders.

The world's series took on a new meaning to New York fans yesterday and Babe Ruth's name was on the tip of every one's tongue when his great batting feats of the day became generally known. Last night the thing that seemed to matter most to fans here was the possibility of getting into the Yankee Stadium for the sixth game of the series, Saturday afternoon.

The shift back here, is assured, regardless of who wins today, and the fans who have no reserved seats are contemplating the means whereby they will get into the unreserved sections on Saturday.

There also is another line of thought in the minds of the fans and that has to do with a seventh game if the series should be tied Saturday after the sixth contest. Whereas no more than 38,000 general admissions will be available for the game Saturday, the entire seating and standing room capacity of the park will go on general sale in case a game is played Sunday. That means that 65,000 fans will have a chance to see that combat.

Foresees Trouble at Sale.

However strange it may appear, the Yankee management is hoping that there will be no seventh game.

"A seventh game will mean plenty of trouble for me and for the Yankee business staff," declared Ed Barrow, Business Manager of the Yankees, at his home in Larchmont last night. Barrow was joyful over the Yankee victory and was extremely proud of the home run endeavors of Ruth during the afternoon, but he contemplates a seventh game here with much forboding.

"In the event of a seventh game, it will be played on Sunday, of course," said Barrow last night. "Every ticket will be placed on sale the morning of the game, and that means that the result will be great dissatisfaction, ticket holders for the first three games, and those who were not so lucky, all demanding tickets and, of course, only a part of them being rewarded.

"From a financial point of view, of course, it would mean a great deal to the club, but the club would rather not have to face the situation.

"If the series is tied on Saturday the seats for Sunday's game will be placed on general sale, first come first served. Most of the boxes already are taken, as the majority of these are held by baseball people, such as the Presidents of the league and Judge Landis and their guests. That means that only the grandstand seats, upper mezzanine and lower, and the bleachers, will be on general sale, save where there are boxes not already subscribed for. It will be a gigantic task, the sale of over 60,000 tickets in the time available."

Robinson Proclaims Ruth as Truly Great Player

RUTH REALLY GREAT, ROBINSON DECLARES

Homers and Wonderful Throw Stamp Him as Player Never to Be Forgotten.

PASSES A VITAL FACTOR

Says Ten Bases on Balls Figure Prominently, Even in Face of Yankees' Slugging.

DISAPPOINTED IN RHEM

Asserts Reinhart Was Justifiably Nervous, Considering Situation When He Went to Box.

By WILBERT ROBINSON,
President and Manager of the Brooklyn Robins.

Written for The New York Times.

ST. LOUIS, MO., OCT. 6.—Babe Ruth, bases on balls, and some breaks just ruined the Cardinals today and made it certain that New York would see at least one more game of the World's series.

The old Babe was the backbone of the Yanks as usual with three home runs on all kinds of pitching, making a record for a world's series game. He accounted for four of the Yankees' ten runs with those homers and brought in another on one of his two bases on balls.

He also cut off a run at the plate for the Cardinals in the fourth inning with a wonderful throw from deep left field, and this, I believe, ought to make old Babe a world's series hero nobody should ever forget. He's a really great ball player.

Waite Hoyt, who pitched for the Yanks, pitched good steady ball in every inning except the first and the fourth when the Cardinals made all their runs. He had good control, giving only one base on balls, and although he gave fourteen hits, he kept them well scattered. His good control of a high fast one and a low curve made half of them of no value at all to the Cardinals.

Cards' Pitchers Waver.

Good control was the difference between the pitching the teams received, and the Cardinals lost because their pitchers didn't have it. Rhem, Reinhart, Bell and Hallahan, the first four of the five pitchers the Cardinals used, gave ten bases on balls with fourteen hits.

In the fifth inning, which Reinhart started, he wasted a one-run lead by walking four men and giving a double to Koenig, and the Yankees got four runs on a single hit. In the fourth inning a base on balls by Rhem was followed by a double which brought in a run. Here were five of the Yankees' ten runs following an extraordinary number of bases on balls, which shows that the pitching of the Cardinals was abnormal.

These bases on balls were followed also by hits in which the breaks went to the Yankees. Take the fourth inning. Gehrig was walked by Rhem when one man was down. Joe Dugan hit a pop fly to left centre which should have been an easy catch for Hafey. He and Douthit both raced for it, each yelling he would take it and neither being able to hear the other because of the yelling of the crowd in the bleachers. They collided and knocked each other out and Gehrig scored.

In the fifth inning, after Reinhart had walked Combs, Hornsby ran to the right field foul line in an effort to field a pop fly by Koenig. He couldn't get to it and he slapped the ball just as it hit the ground, knocking it to the boxes built on the field, where he slipped and fell. Combs scored on the hit and Koenig took second.

Run Is Forced In.

Then Reinhart walked three men in a row, forcing in a run, whereupon, although it was the first inning he had pitched, Hornsby had to take him out and put in Bell. With the bases filled Bell was up against a tough

The New York Times

Babe Ruth testing out his bat before today's game.

proposition and he got out of it pretty well by allowing only two runs to come in, one on a sacrifice fly and the other on an infield grounder in front of the plate.

I was surprised at the poor showing of Flint Rhem. He has been one of the Cards' best pitchers, but this was a day when probably any pitcher would have suffered from the Yankee hitting.

Rhem let the Babe hit two homers in the first three innings, and with that base on balls and double in the fourth it was plain he would have to go out soon.

Hornsby did right by putting in a pinch hitter for him in the last half of the fourth when the Cards forged a run in the lead of the Yanks by batting out three runs on four hits and an error by Koenig which I'll refer to later.

He put in Reinhart at the beginning of the fifth and I, for one, thought that in spite of the Yankees' hitting in the first four innings the Cardinals were going to win, for Reinhart ordinarily is a good pitcher. I picked him to beat Pennock in case they worked against each other today, and I was surprised that Rogers didn't start the game with him. The only way I can figure Reinhart's poor showing was that he was nervous. I think the four bases on balls he gave was proof enough of that.

Reinhart's Nerves Natural.

It's not hard to understand why he was nervous. The Yanks are dangerous batters. They had been in a slump and here, suddenly, they were out of it. Babe Ruth had knocked, two home runs off Flint Rhem, a good curve-ball pitcher, in two times at bat.

Reinhart was coming in with the top of the batting order up and Ruth the third man to face him. Would he knock another home run off him? It was a thought to make any pitcher worry, and Reinhart wasn't equal to it, not at least today. It was what the golfers call a mental hazard, which Reinhart couldn't clear, but it's one every pitcher who faces the Yanks has to play. This game shows that the Yanks may be down, but they're never out, not while the old Babe is in the line-up.

This game was a typical Yankee game, where they depended almost altogether on their hitting, and because it was a free hitting game for both sides the crowd for the first time got to see some base running and fielding. In these I think the Yanks looked much worse than the Cardinals.

The base running of the Yanks wasted three runs, two of them in the first two innings, when they needed them. In the first inning Meusel tried to go home from first on a single to right by Gehrig which Southworth seemed a little slow in fielding, and a throw from Southworth relayed by Hornsby caught him at the plate. O'Farrell made a nice play on this by blocking the plate and forcing Meusel to slide inside, where he could tag him out.

Base Running Is Foolish.

In the second inning Lazzeri hit a liner to the left centre field wall which he tried foolishly to stretch to a triple. Douthit was getting his throw started as Lazzeri was turning second and Thevenow relayed it to Bell in time for an easy out. Again in the sixth Meusel tried to stretch a single to right into a double and was caught easily at second on a throw from Southworth to Reinhart. This wasn't smart base running at all, and only the last attempt was justifiable.

Joe Dugan played a good game at third for the Yankees, but the Cardinals' infield outplayed the Yankees, Koenig for the third time in succession made a costly error in the fourth inning, missing an easy grounder while O'Farrell was on first and one man was out. It was a chance for a double play, but he booted the ball and Thevenow, a daugerous hitter in a pinch, came through with a double to right to start the Cardinals' scoring and put them ahead.

I think Hornsby was right not to call on his best pitchers after Reinhart failed so badly in the fifth. He needed his first-string men for the games tomorrow and Saturday, and as the Yankees were then three runs ahead and hitting hard it seemed like good headwork to me to save his best men for the coming game.

Doubts Pennock Will Win.

I guess the pitching choices tomorrow will be Pennock for the Yankees and Sherdel for the Cardinals, the two left-handers who opened the series in New York last Saturday. Pennock won then, but I don't believe he can beat Bill here tomorrow. Bill pitched only seven innings in New York and ought to be in fine condition. Pennock is not very strong, as I have written, and I don't believe he can give his best efforts.

But if the Yanks are hitting the kind of pitching they were today even a good slow ball and curve ball pitcher like Sherdel will have a hard time. The Babe, for instance, hit his first homer off Rhem on a high curve, his second off Rhem on a waist-high slow ball and his third, off Bell, the longest of the three hits, on a low fast one. Still, if Sherdel can keep them low on the corners I believe he can beat Pennock and the Yanks tomorrow.

That would leave Saturday's game to be pitched by old Alexander for the Cardinals and, I believe, Bob Shawkey for the Yanks. Bob looked fine in his relief pitching and I think Huggins plans to give him a chance to start one game.

RUTH'S BIG BAT ROUSES YANKS FROM LETHARGY

Analysis Shows He Inspired Team —Hoyt Improves as Game Progresses.

By RICHARDS VIDMER.

Special to The New York Times.

ST. LOUIS, Oct. 6.—The slumbering Babe awoke today and aroused his Yankee mates out of a dark and dismal slump that had extended through the first three games of the world's series. From the blackness of what looked to be a lost cause, Babe Ruth flashed forth and led the Yankees back to even ground with the Cardinals once more.

Three times the big, broad shoulders of the great Bambino swung rhythmically; three times his long, lean bat lashed forward with synchronized power; three times the ball rode far and farther into the happy hunting grounds of baseballs for home runs and the Yankees followed their leader.

It has been said before, but it was never truer than it was today, "As Ruth goes, so go the Yankees." When the Babe flung his first homer over the right-field bleacher roof his mates opened a sleepy eye and realized that such things were possible. When he blazed away with another the next time up, they stretched themselves, and when he culminated his efforts with a third, longer, harder and further than any of the rest, they were fully aroused to the business at hand and battered and beat the Cardinals, 10 to 5.

Ruth Provides Inspiration.

Ruth's three homers alone weren't enough to win. They accounted for one less run than the Cardinals made all afternoon, but they served as an inspiration to the rest of the Yankees that enabled them to hammer five St. Louis pitchers for fourteen hits, just one less than they made in the first three games combined.

Those three terrific blows that progressively angered, then awed the 40,000 ardent St. Louis fans, lit the fires that burned so brightly in the boilers of the Yankee hitting machine all season. Those mighty gestures of scorn for St. Louis pitching may have proved the turning of the tide in the series.

Three home runs in one world's series is something that has been done seldom before. Three home runs in one world's series game never has been accomplished by any individual since the classic was inaugurated, but that was only one record that fell and was shattered. About every other long-distance hitting mark for a world's series game was broken to bits. As that third mighty drive passed out of view in the far reaches of the farthest central field bleachers the deeds of former heroes passed out with it.

Rhem Starts Out Well.

That trio of mighty drives not only lifted the spirits of the Yankees to a high point of efficiency but shattered the morale of the Cardinals—at least for the day. Flint Rhems, the scion of the South Carolina Rhems, started out in his pitching with a performance that was perfection itself. He fanned the first two men who faced him. Then along came Ruth.

His first jolt didn't help the nerves of the young Southerner any, but the Yankees ran raggedly and with apparent suicidal intent on the bases, wasting runs, and Rhem managed to hold his own until the third when Ruth's second clout shook him again. The Yanks, no longer sleepwalkers but at least half awakened, continued their mad running and wasted more opportunities in the fourth, but Rhem was behind by that time, gave way to a pinch-hitter in the Cards' half of the inning and the bass drum blared for the big parade.

When the Babe hit his third homer, the Yanks' eyes were opened wide and they clouted often and clattered over the plate in single file.

Rhem was bad and got off as lightly as he did because of the Yankees' silly base-running, but Rhem's successors were even worse. Arthur Reinhart pitched to five batters and walked four of them. The other doubled. Herman Bell gave up four hits, including Ruth's third homer, and a base on balls in his two innings before the Yankee battery.

Two hits and three bases on balls off Bill Hallihan didn't increase the Cardinal pitching prestige in the two innings he worked, and only Vic Keen managed to get by unscathed. He hurled the last inning and retired the rampaging Yanks in order. But, then, perhaps they were tired of running around the bases by that time.

Hoyt Strikes Out Eight.

Waite Hoyt, who hurled for the Yankees, couldn't have lasted the full game under his own power alone, but Ruth and the other members of murderers' row supplied the auxiliary. The Cardinals made fourteen hits off Hoyt, but he managed to keep down the scoring as much as he did by not issuing any free transportation whatever and by striking out eight opponents, many at most opportune times.

Through the first four innings Hoyt was weak and wavering, he didn't look as though he could possibly survive the gathering forces of the Cardinal batting order. But he gained courage and incentive when he discovered the support he was getting from his own hitters and he held the Cardinals at his mercy over the last five.

There was a little of everything to stir the hearts of the St. Louis public. Douthit and Hafey collided in chasing a fly and were completely knocked out while the Yankees' third run swept over the plate. Bob Meusel had what appeared to be a dizzy spell, and the game had to be halted again. Lanky Bob resumed his position in right field, but evidently he never fully recovered, for he ran bases as though he was dizzy all afternoon and he played a drive from Douthit's bat badly in the fourth, letting it fall for a double and giving the Cards a run that put them out in front.

Throws Are Valuable.

There were good throws and bad from the outfield, Ruth making the best one when he cut down Douthit at the plate in the fourth and Combs making the worst when he allowed O'Farrell to score on a short fly back of second base in the same inning.

There were wise moves and weird ones. The wise ones being mostly physical and the weird ones entirely mental. Koenig and Gehrig both made nice fielding plays of hard hit balls, but on the backhand stop Gehrig made of Bottomley's drive down the first base line, Hoyt failed to cover first and it didn't do any good.

That lapse of Hoyt's, however, wasn't the worst dim-witted play during the day, and besides it didn't cost anything as Bottomley was forced at second. The best exhibition of a man in a trance was put on by the generally smart and brainy O'Farrell, the Cardinal catcher.

When the Cards were in the deepest throes of their distress, because of Reinhart's wildness, O'Farrell might have saved a run but didn't. Meusel was on third and Gehrig on first. Dugan hit a high-bounding ball in front of the plate. If O'Farrell had let Herman Bell handle it Meusel would have been easily retired at home, but O'Farrell elected to take care of it himself and left the plate unguarded, Meusel scoring easily. Still, what was one run among so many?

And, after all, the Ruth is mighty and will prevail.

RUTH WINS CHEERS OF ST. LOUIS FANS

Bleacherites Rise in Body When Babe Takes Place in Field After His Homers.

BLACK BIRD AN OMEN

Perches on Netting in Front of Press Stand, Boding Ill for Cardinal Prospects.

Special to The New York Times.

ST. LOUIS, Oct. 6.—Brilliant weather and brilliant baseball, much of which was played by the Yanks, fell to the lot of a record-breaking crowd of 40,000 fans who filled Sportsman's Park for the fourth game of the world's series here today. The crowd was bigger and proportionately noisier than that of yesterday, but toward the end of the game, awed perhaps by the power of Babe Ruth's bat and a game gone glimmering, the great turnout of Cardinal rooters became comparatively sane and quiet.

Also, as the time went on, the crowd seemed to take on a deep respect for the wiry right arm of Waite Hoyt. There was a great parade of St. Louis boxmen but Hoyt stayed in the picture to the end and the crowd did not have much to cheer about as far as the Flatbush pitcher was concerned, for he was turning back the big St. Louis sluggers with too much neatness and dispatch for the comfort of the home fans.

Fans Cheer Ruth Freely.

There was a diversity of excitement in the early innings, Babe Ruth being responsible for most of it, with his various home runs and his long throw from left field to nip a man at the plate. The crowd once more crossed the experts by failing to razz or hoot any of the New York players, especially Ruth. After all of the Babe's big hits, when he went out to his position after the side was out, the bleacher fans rose and cheered him.

All sorts of things happened in the long-drawn-out game of 2 hours, 39 minutes, including a knockout, which is not supposed to be included, even in a world's series, and a balk. The knockout was staged when Hafey and Douthit, the St. Louis outfielders, collided and Hafey fell on the grass, apparently unconscious. After some first-aid treatment Hafey jumped up and contributed his best efforts to stem the tide of Yankee hits.

The bleachers basked in a gorgeous brand of Autumn sunshine, but a cool breeze fanned the fevered brows of the great crowd in the grand stand. It was again a colorful gathering, with the cardinal hats worn by the women fans being once more very much in evidence.

The St. Louis folks seemed a bit stunned by the reversal of form staged by the Yanks when it looked as if the Cardinals were coasting along to an easy series victory.

Card Rooters Have One Chance.

The high spot on the afternoon for the Mound City rooters came in the Cardinals' half of the fourth when the home talent put on a rousing rally and scored three runs. Nothing like the bedlam that broke loose at that particular juncture has been heard probably since the time that Jack Dempsey fell through the ropes in the historic battle at the Polo Grounds with Luis Angel Firpo.

It was a wild chorus of cheers, bells, horns and whistles with the human shrieks being augmented by megaphones, without which none of the Missouri rooters would be found at a world's series combat. Even these megaphones, which have been turned out by the million, apparently, to advertise a certain drink, soft, of course, were decorated with the Cardinal bird, which is called by President Sam Breadon of the St. Louis team the "National Bird of Missouri."

Strangely enough, as the afternoon wore along, and Ruth kept poling out his home runs with monotonous regularity, a little bird came and perched on the netting in front of the press stand. Lo and behold it was not a red bird but decidedly black. This was looked upon as not a good sign by the home-bred experts.

Once more the crowd came out to the grounds through the strange and sometimes very rugged St. Louis streets easily and with little confusion. The mounted policemen on the banks of the Mississippi wear olive drab uniforms, helmets such as are affected by African big-game hunters, revolvers and swords. The fearless guardians of the law present such a formidable appearance that few automobile drivers take any liberties with them.

Aided by the foot patrolmen, who are only armed with stars and fancy clubs, the cavalry had the crowd in perfect control, and the grand stand contingent of about 30,000 once more moved through the entrances without a hitch.

The only place that showed any signs of a mob spirit was a ticket office near the grounds, around which hundreds milled as game time approached. The tickets were decidedly scarce, and it was reported that single seats for today's game sold as high as $30.

The bleacher contingent was once more early on the scene of action, hundreds coming at 8:30, when the gates were opened. They once more had a chance to bask several hours in the sunshine, which today was not diversified by showers.

It was a great game for variety and funny stunts, among other good acts being the appearance of a man wearing a fur-lined coat and gloves, who paraded in front of the grand stand blandly swinging a cane. He was loudly cheered, but did not heed the fur-lined coat unless he was starting for the Arctic regions.

'I TOLD YOU SO!' HUGGINS CHORTLES

Yankees Have Started Hitting and Will Keep On to Victory, Manager Says.

HORNSBY BLAMES PITCHERS

Cardinals' Spirits Are Crushed—Better Hurling by Sherdel Promised for Today.

Special to The New York Times.

ST. LOUIS, Oct. 6.—Miller Huggins called the turn yesterday. He said his team wasn't hitting a lick in this series but that the American League champions would get started today. The mite manager was like a schoolboy in the Yankee dressing room after this afternoon's game, which ended with the Ruppert forces all square with the Cardinals.

The Yankee players carried the joy of their abbreviated manager even further, naturally. Theirs was the satisfaction and jubilation of the triumphant team. They were experiencing a sensation which they had not enjoyed since that opening game back in New York. They made the most of it, and Huggins made the most of the fulfillment of his prediction.

But happier than Huggins or any other player was the battering Babe Ruth, hero of this game and idol of baseball fans, young and old.

"I said we weren't hitting, didn't I?" was the greeting of Huggins. "Well, we started today and we won't stop. We battered everything they had to offer us and even then we weren't through. We'll be right back at them tomorrow, hitting now on all six, because the team is hitting again. That spells only one thing, victory.

Gives Ruth Most of the Credit.

"Ruth, more than anything else, accounts for the victory. That's all it was, just Ruth. He deserves every bit of credit that can be heaped on him. He was banging that ball around today in a way that was a caution.

"It was wonderful the way he hit today. Three home runs in as many official times at bat. Five trips to the plate and a run in four of them. A fifth run denied him simply because the other side got a break when he was nailed off third on a stop of a grounder which looked like one of those impossible things. The greatest day ever experienced by a player in a world's series.

"Of course Hoyt pitched good ball, all things considered, and the other players played well and hit well. It was unfortunate that Koenig made that slip in the fourth on O'Farrell's blow, but he tried to do too much; he was trying to scoop the ball up and throw it with the one motion; overeager to make the kill.

"It was fortunate the error was discounted in the rush of the Yankees' attack, otherwise it might have been fatal. But Ruth with his stick showed the way and the rest of the team got solidly behind him.

"I'll use Pennock tomorrow. He's ready for another stab at them and he'll beat them again, too, because the club is going along at the right gait now."

Ruth was praised on all sides. Dressing in front of the locker next to Babe's, Waite Hoyt declined to accept any of the credit for the result, but side-tracked every compliment to the towering form to his left.

Couldn't Lose With Such Aid.

"I did the best I could," said Hoyt, "but Ruth carried the victory. To him goes all the credit—to him and his stick. Any pitcher must win with that combination, Ruth on a hitting rampage."

Times Wide World Photo.

Waite Hoyt, Winning Pitcher in Yesterday's Game.

Ruth was as happy as a boy. He went to the park today more or less mystified with his failure to bang the ball around. He must have found out why and he was tickled beyond belief.

"It just wasn't in the cards that I miss all the time," said Babe with a smile. "I just had to start hitting. I guess I had a pretty fair day today, didn't I?. I can't think right now of anything that has been more welcome to me than that hitting today.

"We're started now, and I don't think there's anything to stop us. The pitching has been no different today from what it has been since the series started. They've been tossing them up there just the same. But we had better results today. Boy, we banged everything everybody had to offer, and they gave us enough pitchers to hit, too.

"I knew all along that when we started hitting we'd get them on the Irun. And we've started hitting."

Quite different was the clubhouse of the Cardinals.

The Cardinals seemed not only depressed in defeat, but actually cowed; conquered thoroughly and completely. Manager Rogers Hornsby was downright sore, principally at the calibre of Cardinals' pitching.

"We lost because of poor pitching," said Hornsby. "It was more than poor. It was miserable pitching. Just ridiculous, no matter from what angle you look at it. There is no other complaint to find with the team. The players in every position but the box did everything that could be asked or expected of them.

"Rhem was a disappointment, but the greatest kick I have with his work was his pitching to Ruth. He just grooved that ball for Ruth every time. The relief pitching was a joke, too. There's no other way to describe it. Ruth got balls that he liked and he socked them. What player wouldn't? And the rest of them got the kind of pitching they can hit and they belted it too.

"Serving them to Ruth that way was a joke to me. He's the biggest reason for our defeat.

"My pitchers either bounced the ball off the Yankee bats, or couldn't see the plate. They issued ten passes and then there was a balk thrown in for good measure.

"We hit just as much as they did and, all things being even, I don't see how we could have missed winning. But nothing can be even with pitching such as we had today.

Times Wide World Photos.

Ruth and Hornsby Before Tuesday's Game in St. Louis.

KLEM INCREASES RECORD.

Veteran Arbiter Now Officiating in His Thirteenth Series.

By officiating in the current baseball classic, William J. Klem has added one more year to his record of having umpired in more world's series than any other arbiter. The present series is the thirteenth in which the dean of the National League staff of umpires has appeared.

Klem officiated in his first world's series in 1908 when the Cubs conquered the Tigers, four games to one. He has been an arbiter in every series since then with the exception of 1910, 1916, 1919, 1921, 1923 and 1925.

Eleven World's Series Records Toppled; Babe Ruth Alone Hangs Up Six of Them

ST. LOUIS, Oct. 6 (AP).—Eleven new world's series records were put on the books tonight by statisticians who found the going as hard in today's game as did the Cardinal pitching corps.

Babe Ruth personally accounted for six of the new marks, as follows:

1. Most homers for one game, 3, breaking former mark of 2 held jointly by Harry Hooper of Red Sox, Benny Kauff of Giants and Ruth.

2. Most homers, total series, 7, breaking old record of 6 set by Goose Goslin in 1924 and 1925. Ruth hit one homer in 1921 and three in 1923.

3. Most total bases in one game, 12, breaking mark of 9 set up by Hooper in 1915.

4. Most extra bases, one game, 9, breaking former record of 6 held jointly by Ruth, Kauff and Hooper.

5. Most runs, one game, 4, breaking record first made by Mike Donlin with Giants in 1905 and equaled by many others.

6. Most extra bases, total series, 27, breaking Ruth's own previous mark of 18.

A seventh record for one club's total bases in a single game was set by the Yankees, whose 14 hits totaled for 28 bases, eclipsing the mark of 27 made by the Giants in 1921.

The other four records were established in the financial sector. The first to fall was the total receipts for the first four world's series games, this year's figure reaching $730,001, against $723,104, made in 1923. Then it was discovered that the players' share, complete, was $372,300.51, against the former mark of $368,783, made in 1923.

Then followed the individual players' share. This year it is approximately $6,254 for each winning player, against $6,143 made in 1923, and $4,168 for the losers, against $4,112 in 1923.

"All the News That's Fit to Print."

The New York Times.

THE WEATHER
Fair today and tomorrow, not much change in temperature.
Temperature yesterday—Max., 68; min., 53.
For weather report see Page 34.

VOL. LXXVII....No. 25,444. NEW YORK, FRIDAY, SEPTEMBER 23, 1927. TWO CENTS In Greater New York | THREE CENTS Within 200 Miles | FOUR CENTS Elsewhere in the U. S.

GENE TUNNEY KEEPS TITLE BY DECISION AFTER 10 ROUNDS; DEMPSEY INSISTS FOE WAS OUT IN 7TH, AND WILL APPEAL; 150,000 SEE CHICAGO FIGHT, MILLIONS LISTEN ON RADIO

LEGIONAIRES ELECT SPAFFORD AS CHIEF, ENDING CONVENTION

New York Man Is Unanimous Choice for National Commander.

GETS OVATION AT SESSION

Veterans in Paris Approve the Stand of Administration at the Geneva Naval Parley.

PASS MITCHELL'S AIR PLAN

Project for Further Immigration Ban Is Tabled—Bissell of New York Heads '40 and 8.'

Copyright, 1927, by The New York Times Company
Special Cable to THE NEW YORK TIMES.

PARIS, Sept. 22.—The convention in France of the American Legion, so long planned and so long heralded, is now history.

The "greatest ever," as the convention is now known to the Legionaires, came to a close this afternoon in a typical burst of fireworks with the election of the new National Commander and other Legion officials. Edward Elwell Spafford of New York City was the man selected for the Legion's highest honor, and he was chosen unanimously, no other name being even offered to the delegates.

When the choice, which represented the wishes of Legion men from all parts of the country, as he was nominated by the North Carolina delegation and the nomination was seconded by Washington, was announced the convention broke into pandemonium.

Paris had never before witnessed such a scene. The Legionaires started shouting and honking horns, while canes rapped applause like the sputter of machine guns.

Mr. Spafford was escorted to the platform amid the blare of bugles, the shrill of fifes and the thunder of the drums of the band of the Buffalo Post, which went "over the top" into the press box so as to be nearer the centre of activities, scattering the astonished newspaper men.

Nearly Mobbed in Congratulations.

Immediately a seething ocean of Legionaires was trying to shake his hands, thump his back and congratulate him in any way, form and manner as it swirled around him. He climbed into the speaker's box, which was almost the only island of safety, but it was fully ten minutes before the noise was sufficiently quieted to allow him to make a short speech of acceptance and thanks.

It was a fitting way in which to end the spectacular convention, for it was marked by the same combination of seriousness of purpose and uproarious good humor and enthusiasm which so impressed the Paris populace in the big parade of last Monday. America's unmistakable, if occasionally boisterous, sincerity is now a French by-word.

It was also the right spirit in which to close the proceedings, as it wiped out any ill feeling which may have been aroused by the vehement discussions which marked the attempts to map out the Legion's policies in the earlier hours of the session.

As the nominations for the Vice Commanders were made the Legionaires resumed their good-natured gayety. The well-known cry of "Never heard of it!" rang out again and again as the various State delegations were called on. But the greatest opportunity for the now renowned humorous sally of the former soldiers came when, on a point of order, a delegate from the Redwood State said, "California yields to Florida."

"What's that?" was heard from every corner of the enormous room amid general laughter, while the Florida delegate cried, "Louder!" and was greeted with cheers.

Election of Vice Commanders.

The five National Vice Commanders chosen represented all sections of the country. They are John T. Lafts of Washington, Paul R. Younts of North Carolina, Daniel W. Spurlock of Louisiana, J. M. Henry of Minnesota and Ralph T. O'Neill of Kansas.

The Rev. Gill Robb Wilson was elected National Chaplain. He comes from Trenton, N. J., and was formerly an aviator in the Lafayette Escadrille.

The session was called to order at 9 o'clock in the morning and lasted, without recess, until nearly 4 in the afternoon. Almost its first official act was to confer on Count Dejean, head of the American Division in the French Department of Foreign Affairs, the distinguished service cross of the Legion in recognition of his valuable services for Legion, to which he was assigned by Foreign Minister Briand to aid in putting on

Continued on Page Two.

Stinson and Schilling Forced Down and Out Of New York to Spokane Non-Stop Air Derby

From a Staff Correspondent of The New York Times.

FELTS FIELD, SPOKANE, Wash., Sept. 22.—The non-stop race from New York to Spokane came to a definite end today when Eddie Stinson was forced down by engine trouble at Missoula, Mont., and C. A. (Duke) Schiller came down at Billings, Mont.

Stinson would have won the race if he had been flying over country where he could have made a landing at any time. When the intake and exhaust valves on one cylinder of his motor went out, he flew around for several hours, trying to get altitude enough to go on with sufficient gliding distance to make a safe landing.

But he could not get up high enough, and after four or five hours went down at the landing field at Missoula. The field is only 200 miles from Spokane and the time he spent flying in circles would have been sufficient for him to get here. But it was too risky and he wisely quit.

Stinson came in with R. E. Dake in a Waco, the last entry in Class A to arrive. He picked Stinson up as a passenger. Stinson has become a philosopher in his attitude toward long-distance flying. "Sometimes you make it and sometimes you don't," is his motto.

"We had good weather most of the way," he said, "although there was some rain and fog over Michigan. We kept to a great circle course which took us through the centre of Lake Erie and over the other lakes. A good part of the time we were out of sight of land. It got dark while we were over Michigan and dawn found us over North Dakota. I think we kept to our course fairly well all the time until I began circling around after engine trouble developed."

There was much disappointment among the 30,000 people at the field, who had been waiting all day for the non-stop fliers to arrive. The enthusiastic crowd, which cheers every pilot who arrives as if he were a favorite son, gave a rousing reception to Stinson.

INDIANAPOLIS MAYOR QUICKLY CONVICTED

Duvall Faces 30 Days in Jail, $1,000 Fine and 4-Year Bar From Office for Corruption.

TAKES VERDICT IN SILENCE

Bitterness Marks Closing Pleas, Defense Laying Charges to a "Malicious Press."

Special to The New York Times.

INDIANAPOLIS, Sept. 22.—Mayor John L. Duvall was found guilty of violation of the Corrupt Practices act in the Marion County Criminal Court tonight. The penalty is thirty days in the Marion County Jail and a fine of $1,000.

The verdict, reported by the jury at 8 o'clock after three hours' deliberation, makes Mayor Duvall ineligible to hold public office for four years after the date of the crime.

Duvall was pale when the verdict was read and his only comment was: "I have nothing to say."

Under the Corrupt Practices act Duvall was specifically charged with promising William H. Armitage, a politician, the privilege of naming three members of the City Administration in exchange for a cash consideration and support in the 1925 mayoralty campaign. The same Grand Jury which acted upon results of a year's inquiry into alleged political corruption in Indiana also indicted Governor Ed Jackson on a charge of attempting to bribe former Governor Warren T. McCray.

Final Pleas Stir Courtroom.

Ralph Inman, defense counsel, and William H. Remy, Marion County Prosecutor, this afternoon held the packed courtroom spellbound during their pleas which at times became so bitter that the audience gasped.

The crowd got so worked up that once, when work upon a new elevator shaft in the courthouse loosened plaster and showered it through an airduct out into the courtroom, half a hundred spectators sprang to their feet in alarm.

Mr. Remy demanded that the jury send Duvall behind the bars for violating the Corrupt Practices act. Mr. Inman denounced the prosecution of Duvall as the result of acts of a malicious press and demanded that the press be "driven out of town."

With Mr. Remy's argument closing about 4:20 and Special Judge Cassius C. Shirley taking about half an hour for instructions, the case went to the jury at about 5 P. M.

Mr. Inman fired broadsides of ridicule at the State attorneys and the chief State witness, William H. Armitage, and Mr. Remy spent about half of his time in reply.

Answering Mr. Inman's charge that the prosecution of Duvall was a matter of political hatred, Mr. Remy pounded upon the railing of the jury box and declared:

"As long as I am in office this fight against political corruption is going to continue and I pledge myself to the jury and to all the people here that this case will not be the end."

Hurling invectives at the prosecution attorneys and the press, Mr. Inman, who defended D. C. Stephenson, the ex-Klan leader, at Noblesville two years ago and lost, proclaimed Duvall the victim of persecution.

Defense Denounces the Press.

Mr. Inman declared that Duvall was the victim of "a sinister influence in Indianapolis which must be satisfied and should be driven out—a malicious press."

"John Duvall isn't the first Indianapolis man made to stand and defend himself solely because he was unfortunate enough to run and be elected to office," he declared.

In his attack on William H. Freeman and William H. Armitage, the State's chief witnesses, Mr. Inman accused Freeman of "willful, corrupt and deliberate" perjury in part of his testimony.

"It is significant that Armitage never talked before his brother was sentenced to jail," he said. "You could tell by the look in his eyes he would tell any kind of a story to save his brother from going to prison for three months."

DARING FLIER, NUMB, AVOIDS CRASH IN CITY

Steve Lacey, on Western Dash, Dazed by Fumes as Gasoline Swirls About His Feet.

MOTOR SPUTTERED AN HOUR

He Fails to Dump Fuel, Fights Back to Field, Lands Safely and Falls Unconscious.

Special to The New York Times.

ROOSEVELT FIELD, L. I., Sept. 22.—A courageous pilot with a sputtering engine fought for an hour to keep his plane under control over New York City and the surrounding area yesterday afternoon, while gasoline swirled four inches deep around his feet and sent up fumes which numbed his hands and his brain. Battling these obstacles, he brought the plane down on the field here and fell over unconscious.

The pilot was Steve Lacey, who had tried so desperately to take part in the non-stop race to the Pacific against C. S. (Duke) Schiller and Eddie Stinson. With his navigator, Louis A. Yancey, he had worked most of the night repairing his blue and silver biplane Air King, which had lost its tail skid in an unsuccessful effort to take off yesterday.

Today, though the New York-Spokane air derby time limit was past and he could not hope to share in the non-stop prize money, he took off again in an endeavor to make good his promise to fly westward "just for fun." The ill luck which balked him yesterday dogged him today. He and Yancey got away perfectly at 12:52 P. M. and soon disappeared from sight. In a few minutes they reappeared and came down with their heavily laden plane, making a perfect landing at 100 miles an hour. Their engine was not functioning properly. It was tuned again and readjusted and up they soared once more.

Saved City From a Disaster.

Then came the mishap unique in aviation, which almost cost both men their lives and only for their heroism would have sent a plane loaded with hundreds of gallons of gasoline roaring in flames into the streets of New York.

Misfortune threatened them from the start of their last flight. It was 2:21 P. M. The Wright Whirlwind motor apparently was functioning perfectly again as Lacey gave the ship the gun and it rolled along the ground. It was running beautifully at 2,000 feet from the starting point

Continued on Page Three.

TREND TOWARD SMITH PLAIN IN FAR WEST AS LEADERS GATHER

Indications Point to First Raising of His Banner at Ogden (Utah) Conference.

11 STATES REPRESENTED

Iowa Democrats at Own Request, Join Gathering, Which Begins Deliberations Today.

TARIFF IS ON THE AGENDA

Most Available Presidential Candidate and Two-thirds Rule Also Topics.

From a Staff Correspondent of The New York Times.

OGDEN, Utah, Sept. 22.—Democrats in the intermountain States, who went to the Democratic National Convention in 1924 for the most part as enthusiastic supporters of William Gibbs McAdoo, are swinging to Governor Alfred E. Smith of New York. There are indications that at a conference which will begin here tomorrow for the discussion of problems vital to the party they will raise the Smith banner and start the first organized movement in the nation to further the Presidential aspirations of New York's Chief Executive, who, as he did in 1924, will enter next year's Democratic national conclave as the favorite son of his party in the Empire State.

At the Hotel Bigelow, where the conference will be held, fifty rooms have been reserve for prospective conferees, and it is probable that fully that many will attend. Nearly all of those who are expected to answer the roll-call when the meeting is called to order at 10 o'clock tomorrow morning are former adherents of Mr. McAdoo. Almost without exception, too, they are at least politically dry, as are the Democratic organizations in the several States that will be represented at the gathering.

Prominent Conferees.

At least two Democratic National Committeemen who wield considerable influence in party councils have accepted invitations to the conference. They are Isidore B. Dockweiler of California and James H. Moyle of Utah. Today, unexpectedly and to the great delight of those who have taken the initiative in calling the intermountain Democrats together, there was added to the number of prominent participants Delbert M. Draper of Salt Lake City, Chairman of the Central Committee, and, it is said here, a real power in the party organization in this State. Another spokesman for Utah will be J. W. Stringfellow, leader of the organization in Salt Lake County, which supplies approximately one-half of the votes cast in the State. He is openly for Governor Smith for President.

Fred W. Johnson of Rock Springs, Wyo., and former State Senator Joseph Chez of Utah, to whose initiative and earnest labors for many months the Democrats in these Far Western States owe their opportunity for coming together to discuss party problems, said today that it should be clearly understood that no one will be asked at the conference to deliver the delegation from his own State to Governor Smith next year.

Purpose of the Meeting.

It is admitted, in fact, that grave doubt exists whether any of the conferees would be in a position to make

Continued on Page Four.

Pope Pius Sends $100,000 to Flood Sufferers; Bishops in Mississippi Area to Distribute It

Pope Pius XI has contributed $100,000 to the relief of the flood sufferers in the Mississippi Valley. The gift was made public here yesterday by the Right Rev. Dr. Edmond A. Walsh, vice president of Georgetown University and President of the Catholic Near East Welfare Association. Dr. Walsh was Director-General of Papal Relief during the post-war famines in Europe.

The Pope's intention to help victims of the flood was first made known by the Pontiff during a recent visit of Dr. Walsh to the Vatican. Dr. Walsh went to Rome to report on the activities of the new association. Joseph F. Moore, General Secretary of the association, was also present when the Pope first spoke of his intention to make the donation.

Dr. Walsh was designated by the Pontiff to bring the gift to America and present it to the hierarchy of the United States. This he did last week in Washington at the annual meeting of the archbishops and bishops in the Catholic University of America.

Announcement of the contribution was made by Cardinal O'Connell of Boston, Chairman of the meeting. A Committee of Bishops from the flood area was formed immediately. On the committee are:

The Most Rev. John W. Shaw, Archbishop of New Orleans; the Right Rev. John B. Morris, Bishop of Little Rock, Ark.; the Right Rev. Cornelius Van de Ven, Bishop of Alexandria, Va.; the Right Rev. Jules V. Jeanmard, Bishop of Lafayette, La.; the Right Rev. Richard O. Gerow, Bishop of Natchez, Miss.

The committee is now drawing up recommendations for the most economical and practical disposal of the money.

"As head of the Catholic Church, Pope Pius desired to do something personal in addition to the help already sent to the stricken areas by the various dioceses in the United States," said Dr. Walsh yesterday at his headquarters, 480 Lexington Avenue. "The only regret of his Holiness was that he could not send more."

GREATEST RING SPECTACLE

Crowd Pays $2,800,000 to Watch Contest at Soldier Field.

THRONG IN SEATS EARLY

Largest Boxing Assemblage in History Handled Smoothly by Police and Ushers.

MANY NOTABLES PRESENT

Senators, Governors and Business Leaders Rub Elbows With Obscure Sport Fans.

By JAMES R. HARRISON.
Special to The New York Times.

CHICAGO, Sept. 22.—Out of the welter and turmoil and clamor of the "fight of the ages" one clear fact stands out—that tonight Tex Rickard unveiled the most beautiful picture in the history of sports here or elsewhere.

One hundred and fifty thousand persons watched in the darkness—the greatest of all boxing crowds by about 35,000. It would fill more than two Yankee Stadiums and almost two Yale Bowls; it would pack the Polo Grounds to capacity and leave 100,000 on the outside.

The total receipts were put at $2,800,000.

Governors and Mayors and United States Senators and millionaires lent the right tone to the occasion and millions listened to the story of the fight as it went out "on the air."

Yet the facts and figures do not seem particularly important as compared to the sheer beauty of a picture that only an artist could paint. This may or may not have been "the fight of the ages," but it most certainly was the "sight of the ages."

The veil of darkness over it all; the rippling sea of humanity stretching out as far as the eye could see; the Doric columns of Soldier Field glowing a soft white along the upper battlements of the arena; and finally the ring itself, where two men fought it out with their fists in a pool of white light—these were the high spots of an unforgettable spectacle.

Impressive in Its Vastness.

It was a picture that should have been seen from the air, from the cockpit of an airplane, where the lights and shadows and the blacks and whites of the panorama could have been viewed in their proper perspective.

The ingredients of the picture were striking. A long, low oval stadium of classic lines, filled to its utmost rim. A gently sloping bank of humanity that seemed to stretch to the horizon, and in the centre of the canvas a twenty-foot ring bathed in the fierce light that beats about a throne.

The vastness of the spectacle was its most impressive quality. It filled the eye and staggered the senses. We have seen the Yale Bowl jammed with people, and last November we saw the same Soldier Field at the Army-Navy game, but this was the crowd of crowds and the spectacle of spectacles, lacking only the natural beauty of Poughkeepsie and New London.

Even though he did not sell all of his 163,000 seats, Tex Rickard reached a long cherished goal in his career as an impresario. The 90,000 of Boyle's Thirty Acres and the 115,000 of the Sesquicentennial were left far behind as Chicago and its influx of fight fans poured through the portals of this sports temple.

There they sat, shoulder to shoulder, from the ring up to the top rim where American flags rippled in a brisk western wind. Not that the stadium was full. The cheaper $5 seats, a few city blocks to the north and south, were sparsely settled, proving that you may lead a boxing fan to water but you can't make him drink.

This will probably stand as the record crowd of ring history, because people will sit only so far away from the scene of activities. And tonight Rickard reached the limit in distances. His $5 patrons were 700 or more feet from the ring, which at the Yankee Stadium would locate them somewhere beyond the centre field fence.

Some Bring Radio Sets.

Time was when a fight fan could buy almost any seat and see the proceedings with the naked eye. But no more. As the citizens flocked through the gates half of them were armed with binoculars, opera glasses and telescopes. Here and there one could see some shrewd lads who had brought portable radios with them. They were the $5 boys, who were going to listen even if they did not see.

The weather man was not fooling when he said fair and warmer, for that was a perfect forecast. The fans brought light coats with them, but they were hardly necessary, especially around the ring, where the heat of the bright lights was very noticeable.

The afternoon was gray and overcast and twilight showed a drab, threatening sky and mist which fore-

Continued on Page Twenty.

GENE TUNNEY, STILL THE CHAMPION.

DEMPSEY TO APPEAL DECISION ON FIGHT

He Says Tunney Was Down for 14 or 15 Seconds in the Seventh Round.

TIMEKEEPER CITES RULE

And Boxing Commissioner Says the Point Was Explained Before Bout Started.

Special to The New York Times.

CHICAGO, Sept. 22.—Jack Dempsey and his manager, Leo Flynn, announced tonight that they intend to appeal to the Illinois Boxing Commission to reverse the decision of the referee and two judges allowing Gene Tunney to retain his world's heavyweight title.

"Intentionally or otherwise, I was robbed of the championship," Dempsey said in his dressing room after the bout. "In the seventh round Tunney was down for a count of fourteen or fifteen. Every stopwatch around the ring caught the time as about fifteen seconds, and the inefficiency of the referee or the timekeeper or both deprived me of the fight.

"Everybody knows I am not a whiner. When Tunney beat me last year I admitted that he was the better man that night. I am not an alibi artist, but I know down in my soul that I knocked Tunney out tonight, and, what's more, chased him all around the ring and should have won on points at least."

Tunney Out, Says Flynn.

Flynn paced up and down the dressing room like a caged lion.

"Everything Jack told you goes double for me," said Flynn. "Before the bout the Boxing Commission said they would see that we got a square deal and would step in and reverse an unfair decision. Now I'm going to take them at their word and make a formal appeal tomorrow to have tonight's verdict reversed.

"Tunney was cleanly knocked out for the count of fifteen in the seventh round. Look at that watch here. It has stopped on the figure fifteen. I have not found a watch yet that got the count under ten. I'm not saying the referee was dishonest. I'm saying that he was inefficient, and it amounts to the same thing as far as we are concerned.

"He failed to take up the timekeeper's count at the start—didn't take it up until the timekeeper had got to four or five. This is the biggest injustice I have ever seen in a ring. Leaving aside the knockout in the seventh round, Jack knocked him down again in the ninth and chased him all around the ring. Why didn't Tunney come out and fight like a champion? Dempsey clearly won on points.

"You can say this for me. Dempsey will fight Tunney any time and any place and knock him out."

Dempsey Wants Another Fight.

"Will I fight him again?" echoed Dempsey. "You bet your life. I beat Tunney tonight and I will beat him again any time he wants to get into the same ring with me. I am not ready to retire, by a long shot—not before I've had another crack at Tunney."

There was plenty of high dudgeoning in the Dempsey dressing room

Continued on Page Eighteen.

STORY OF THE FIGHT TOLD BLOW BY BLOW

Detailed Description of Tunney-Dempsey Bout From the Ringside.

BOTH FIGHTERS AGGRESSIVE

Bout Is Marked by Lively Exchanges—Dempsey Hangs On at the End.

Special to The New York Times.

RINGSIDE, SOLDIER FIELD, CHICAGO, Sept. 22.—The detail of the Tunney-Dempsey bout, which was fought here tonight, follows, round by round:

First Round.

Dempsey rushed Tunney, who sidestepped, and Dempsey again swung a left and clinched and Tunney hooked a left. Tunney hit a right to face as they clinched. Referee pulled them apart. Tunney flashed left to Dempsey's face. Dempsey bobbed and weaved and jabbed to Tunney's jaw. Tunney crossed with a right to Dempsey's jaw. Tunney twice jabbed with lefts to the face and they clinched. Tunney followed with a right to Dempsey's jaw and then dodged away from Dempsey's left hook. Gene hooked to Dempsey's body. Gene again got Jack against the ropes and they clinched. Tunney then jabbed a left to the face.

Second Round.

Tunney jabbed a left to face. Dempsey sent one to chest. They clinched and Tunney held Dempsey's arm. Dempsey put a straight left to the body and Tunney a right to the jaw backing Dempsey to the ropes. Tunney missed a right to the jaw as Dempsey ducked and then Tunney drove a right to the head. Dempsey hooked a left to the head and pounded the body when Tunney left himself open. Tunney drove two rights to the head and clinched. Tunney crossed a right to the jaw and another clinch followed. Dempsey put a left to the body and Tunney a left to the face and they clinched. Tunney hooked a left to the face and in a clinch Dempsey sent a left to the body and head. Tunney drove two rights to Dempsey's head. Dempsey put a left to Tunney's face and another to the body.

Third Round.

They danced about at start of the third and Gene led with a right as Dempsey hooked three lefts to the body. Gene started a right hook to Jack's body, but stopped the blow short as they clinched. Tunney rushed Dempsey and landed with short lefts. Jack drove away at Gene's body, the blows being perilously close to the belt line. They got in at close quarters and Dempsey again hit a low and Judge Lytton shouted "Low" to the referee. Dempsey was short with a left and then Tunney missed a short right and Tunney danced away from a short left. Gene missed a left and came in at close quarters to hook at Demp-

Continued on Page Eighteen.

FIGHT FAST AND FURIOUS

On Verge of Knockout in Seventh Round Tunney Comes Back Strong

FLOORS DEMPSEY IN EIGHTH

Referee and Judges Unanimous in Their Verdict for the Champion.

DISPUTE ON KNOCKDOWN

Challenger Went to Wrong Corner and Thus Delayed Count on Tunney for Few Seconds.

By JAMES P. DAWSON.
Special to The New York Times.

RINGSIDE, SOLDIER FIELD, CHICAGO, Sept. 22.—His refusal to observe the boxing rules of the Illinois State Athletic Commission, or his ignorance of the rules, or both, cost Jack Dempsey the chance to regain the world's heavyweight championship here tonight in the ring at Soldier Field.

By the same token this disregard of rules of ring warfare, or this surprising ignorance, saved the title for Gene Tunney, the fighting ex-marine, who has been king of the ring for just a year.

The bout ended with Tunney getting the decision, and the vast majority in the staggering assemblage of 150,000 people, who paid, it is estimated, $2,800,000 to see this great sport spectacle, approved the verdict.

The decision was given by Referee Dave Barry and Judges George Lytton, wealthy department store owner, and Commodore Sheldon Clark of the Sinclair Oil Company. It was announced as a unanimous decision, but this could not be verified in the excitement attending the finish of the battle. But it should have been unanimous according to all methods of reasoning and boxing scoring, for Tunney won seven of the ten rounds, losing only the third, sixth and seventh, in the last of which, Dempsey made his great mistake. It is known that Judge Lytton voted for Tunney.

Dempsey's Furious Plunge.

In that seventh round Dempsey was being peppered and buffeted about on the end of Tunney's left jabs and hooks and sharp though light right crosses, as he had been in every preceding round, with the exception of the third.

In a masterful exhibition of boxing Tunney was evading the attack of his heavier rival and was countering cleanly, superbly, skillfully, accurately the while for half of the round or so.

Then Dempsey, plunging in recklessly, charging bull-like, furiously and with utter contempt for the blows of the champion, since he had tasted of Tunney's best previously, suddenly lashed a long, wicked left to the jaw with the power of old. This he followed with a right to the jaw, the old "iron mike" as deadly as ever, and quickly drove another left hook to the jaw, under which Tunney toppled like a falling tree, hitting the canvas with a solid thud near Dempsey's corner, his hand reaching blindly for a helping rope which somehow or other refused to be within clutching distance.

Then Dempsey made his mistake, an error which, I believe, cost him the title he values so highly.

Count Begun and Halted.

The knockdown brought the knockdown timekeeper, Paul Beeler, to his feet automatically, watch in hand, eyes glued to the ticking seconds and he bawled "one" before he looked upon the scene in the ring.

There he saw Dempsey in his own corner, directly above the prostrate, brain-numbed Tunney, sitting there looking foolishly serious, his hand finally resting on the middle ring strand. Beeler's count stopped. Referee Barry never started one.

It is the referee's duty to see to it that a boxer scoring a knockdown goes to the corner farthest from his fallen foe and it is the duty of the knockdown timekeeper

Continued on Page Eighteen.

Championship Fight Brings Spectacle to Chicago Unprecedented in Ring History

By JAMES P. DAWSON.

Continued from Page 1, Column 8.

to delay the count from the watch until this rule is obeyed. Beeler was simply observing the rule, which Dempsey either forgot to observe or refused to observe.

The challenging ex-champion stood there, arms akimbo on the top ropes of the ring in his own corner, watching his fallen rival, the characteristic Dempsey snarl o'erspreading his countenance, his expression saying more plainly than words: "Get up and I'll knock you down again, this time for keeps."

Dempsey Finally Moves.

Dempsey had no eyes for Referee Barry, who was waving frantically for the former titleholder to run to a neutral corner, even as he kept an eye on the fallen Tunney. Instead, Dempsey merely looked down at Tunney squatting there, striving instinctively to regain his feet and waiting for his whirling brain to clear.

Finally, Dempsey took cognizance of the referee's frantic motions. He was galvanized into action and sped hurriedly across the ring to a neutral corner, away from Tunney.

If he had observed the rule to the letter, Dempsey should, in fact, have gone to Tunney's corner, which was furthest removed from the fallen champion.

But three or four, or possibly five precious seconds had elapsed before Dempsey realized at all what he should do. In that fleeting time of the watch Tunney got the advantage. No count was proceeding over him, and quickly his senses were returning. When Referee Barry started counting with Timekeeper Beeler, Tunney was in a state of mental revival where he could keep count with the tolling seconds and did, as his moving lips revealed.

Slowly the count proceeded. It seemed an eternity between each downward sweep of the arm of Referee Barry and the steady pounding of the fist of Timekeeper Beeler.

Seconds are like that in a crisis, and here was one if ever one existed.

Tunney's senses came back to him. He got to his feet with the assistance of the ring ropes and with visible effort at the count of "nine." He was groggy, stung, shaken, his head was whirling as so many other heads have whirled under the Dempsey punch.

But Dempsey was wild in this crisis, a floundering, plodding mankiller, as Tunney, back pedaling for dear life, took to full flight, beating an orderly, steady retreat with only light counter moves in the face of the plunging, desperate, vicious Dempsey, aroused now for the kill.

Dempsey plodded on so futilely and ineffectively that he tired from his own exertions. The former champion stopped dead in his tracks in mid-ring and with a smile spreading over his scowling face, motioned disgustedly, daringly, for Tunney to come on and fight.

But Tunney was playing his own game, and it was a winning game. He did not want to expose himself to that deadly Dempsey punch again, and he would not.

Dempsey Wild in Eagerness.

Tunney backed steadily away from Dempsey, pecking and tantalizing with left jabs and grazing right hooks or crosses to the face or jaw. Which meant absolutely nothing to Dempsey. He brushed in against Tunney's blows but, in his eagerness, Dempsey was wild.

After motioning Tunney in, Dempsey backed the champion into the ropes near the challenger's corner and lunged forward savagely with a left and right to the jaw. But Tunney clinched under the blows and held Dempsey for dear life. And Dempsey never again got the chance that round to follow his advantage.

As the bell sounded the end of the round Dempsey was warned for striking low with a left for the body. He was hurling his punches in a blind fury, not particularly concerned over where they landed, so long as they did land.

The crowd which witnessed this dramatic fight, and particularly the critical moments of the seventh round, experienced varying emotions at the crisis. Some yelled themselves hoarse. The shrieks of women mingled with the howls of staid, old business men and the thousands of the purely sporting fraternity clustered about the ringside and extending backward from the battle platform in serried rows of faces.

Gripping Scene at Knockdown.

Society's bluebloods forgot decorum and yelled excitedly. Kings of finance and princes of industry were

TUNNEY AND DEMPSEY IN CHICAGO RING.

Times Wide World Telephoto.

The Champion and Challenger in a Clinch. This Telephotograph Was Taken in One of the Early Rounds of Last Night's Championship Battle.

mingling their yells with those of Governors, mayors, Representatives in Congress, Senators, lawyers, doctors, theatre and movie folk and just plain ordinary people.

It was a scene to grip the observer, a situation to send quickening throbs through the pulses of those at the ringside and in the other sections of Chicago's memorial to her dead heroes. Here was a war hero, a ring hero, a champion, on the floor, and everybody was affected.

Out over the ether wastes some 50,000,000 people who listened to the fight broadcast by the National Broadcast Company over the greatest hook-up ever attempted for sport, had not the advantage of those actually watching the contest.

To those countless listeners it was plain that Dempsey was the victim of something, but just what only those who watched were aware. And there were some watching who did not realize the enormous consequences of this colossal mistake, because they are not versed in boxing rules. But it is safe to say that none among the 150,000 watching or among the 50,000,000 listening, will ever forget that particular elapse of time.

Flynn Will File Protest.

Leo P. Flynn, Dempsey's manager, made no effort after the ight to disguise or conceal his feelings or those of Dempsey. In plain words Flynn said that Dempsey had been robbed of victory because of that seventh-round situation.

"The watch in our corner showed fifteen seconds from the time Tunney hit the floor until he got up at the count of nine," Flynn said. "The legal count over a fallen boxer is ten seconds, not fifteen. Dempsey was jobbed. That's the way I look at it. But I'm going to appeal to the State Athletic Commission to reverse the decision, as is my privilege. Dempsey will fight him again and will knock him out if Tunney ever can be coaxed into meeting him again, just the way he knocked him out tonight."

In the final analysis, however, Dempsey was hoist on his own petard. The rule compelling a boxer to go to the corner furthest removed from a fallen foe is traceable to Dempsey himself. Its adoption followed the Manassa Mauler's battle in 1923 with the giant Firpo when Dempsey stood directly above the fallen Firpo striking the South American just as soon as his knees left the floor without waiting for Firpo to come erect after a knockdown.

Dempsey was permitted to do this then. His attempt to do it tonight was the most expensive mistake he has ever made in his life.

Various Times on Knockdown.

Some watches at the ringside showed twelve seconds on the knockdown, others fourteen, and Flynn holds that Dempsey's corner watch showed fifteen seconds.

But a rule is a rule in boxing as in other big business, adopted to be observed, and the Illinois boxing authorities are to be commended for enforcing their rules without regard to victims or cost. It was unfortunate that Dempsey should have been thus penalized.

It would have been none the less unfortunate, however, if Dempsey had been permitted to remain standing within punching distance of Tunney to strike down the champion before Tunney had actually come erect.

On the strength of that colossal mistake of Dempsey's, it is hard, indeed, to say that Tunney was the better man in the ring tonight. Rather, the seventh round demonstrated what many have always contended despite assertions of Tunney and his associates to the contrary, that the real Dempsey would mow down the best Tunney like a cutting machine at work in a wheat field.

This is not said in an effort to detract from the victory of Tunney. He won and he won cleanly and clearly on points against the best Dempsey available today. But he was knocked down, had the closest call of his career, and, in the end, won only because of his superb boxing skill on defense and the little offense he attempted.

Dempsey Absorbs Tunney Fire.

Tunney peppered Dempsey with a cool, deliberate, two-fisted fire. He blinded him with flurries of punches, cut open old sores over the former champion's two eyes, drew blood from Dempsey's mouth and had Dempsey's face swollen. But it was revealed that Tunney could not hit hard enough nor often enough to keep Dempsey down.

True, Tunney floored Dempsey with a smashing right hook which curled over to the jaw in the eighth round, but Dempsey bobbed right up before a count could be started or before Tunney could be chased to a corner.

And Tunney shook and stung Dempsey times without number with solid right hand smashes to that corrugated steel jaw of the former champion, but, though Dempsey blinked under the punishment, shook from head to heels or went back on his heels, he always charged back in, tirelessly, relentlessly, savagely, viciously, desperately, on legs which were believed to be unsafe and unsound, but which carried him rapidly through ten rounds of persistent chasing in pursuit of the fleeting Tunney.

This Dempsey tonight was, after a manner of speaking, a reincarnation of the old Dempsey with the old spirit, the determination and the purpose. Greatest of all qualifications in this Dempsey of tonight was his courage under fire.

Champion Fights Grimly On.

He fought a typical Dempsey battle to the great delight of hos countless admirers in the vast throng. He was rough and foul at times. He hit Tunney low repeatedly and was warned, and he used the rabbit punch which is barred, and was warned.

In this respect Tunney deserves unstinted praise. He did not crumple like Jack Sharkey under a low blow, though they must have hurt. Instead, he kept grimly on with that determination and supreme confidence in his own ability which are his greatest ring recommendation aside from his superb boxing.

But all things considered, it can not be denied that while Dempsey was defeated, he covered himself with glory. In the light of events it is charitable to attribute Dempsey's fouls to over-anxiety, and wildness in his desperate bid for victory.

That seventh round was but one high light in a thoroughly exciting, thrilling, pulse-stirring battle. Each punch of Tunney's to Dempsey's jaw—and there were many of them—was a thrill in itself as Dempsey recoiled under the blow for a flash only to come charging in again. Those blows which floored Tunney were punches never to be forgotten, and the spectacle of Dempsey down squatting in the eighth round under Tunney's driving right to the jaw recalled the Dempsey-Firpo fight, save that the Tunney punch had not the power behind Firpo's.

And when Dempsey hooked a solid smashing left to the head in the tenth round and then went close and in trying to shake his rival off, wrestled Tunney down, the crowd got another thrill which surpassed that given it by the spectacular manner in which Dempsey piled into his rival fearlessly starting that tenth session. But Dempsey did so only to become exhausted and weakened by his own waning strength and Tunney's desperate blows and to finish the bout groggy, almost falling, but still with strength enough to keep fighting on and on with Tunney after the bell.

For the gong was heard neither by the principals nor the referee. Not until Tunney's seconds scrambled into the ring yelling wildly that the fight was over was the bout over. By then both champion and challenger had struck several blows at close quarters, as if for good measure.

In short, this was a fight worthy the crowd of distinguished men and women who graced it. It would well bear repetition, and possibly will.

Tunney won on his boxing ability alone and Dempsey lost because he could not keep up with the champion. That, in a nutshell, tells the story of the fight on results. Tunney was alert, resourceful, the cool ring general, the master boxer, hitting timely and accurately, and at times desperately in his own defense against the annihilating Dempsey with the revived punch.

Record Figures for Receipts And Attendance at Title Bout

Attendance—150,000.
Receipts—$2,800,000.
Federal tax—$250,000.
State tax—$225,000.
Tunney's share—$1,000,000.
Dempsey's share—$450,000.
Preliminary fighters—$185,000.
Rental of stadium—$100,000.
Incidental expenses—$156,500.
Rickard's profit—$250,000.

DEMPSEY TO APPEAL DECISION ON FIGHT

Continued from Page 1, Column 6.

after the fight. Friends of the Manassa mauler were talking to themselves and walking around in a white heat. One by one they stepped up to slap Jack on the back and tell him what a raw deal he got.

Dempsey was not the picture of blooming health. Both eyes were cut. There was a dark, bluish lump under his right eye. His left ear was cut and swollen and he was bleeding around the mouth. Jerry the Greek had a busy half hour repairing the damage to Jack's features, and it will be several days before Dempsey looks himself again.

John C. Righeimer, Chairman of the Boxing Commission, disappeared after the main bout and coould not be found to comment on the decision or on Flynn's plan to appeal from the verdict.

Timekeeper Beeler announced after the fight that he had counted four seconds over Tunney, when he halted his count, and then began it all over again, having seen Dempsey at least in the neutral corner in accordance with the rule involved. This rule is as follows:

"When a knockdown occurs the timekeeper shall immediately arise and announce the seconds audibly as they elapse. The referee shall first see that the opponent retires to the farthest corner and then, turning to the timekeeper, shall pick up the count in unison with the timekeeper, announcing the seconds to the boxer on the floor. Should the boxer on his feet fail to stay in the corner, the referee and timekeeper shall cease counting until he has so retired."

This rule, while providing for a cessation of a count, makes no specific provision for the resumption of a count or a count's re-start. When this was pointed out to Commissioner Paul Prehn at the ringside, he explained that the regulation providing for a re-start of the count had been adopted an an amendment since the rules were published last year, and added that this ruling was thoroughly explained to, and, it was believed, understood by the principals in tonight's title struggle.

CHAMPION PLACID AFTER THE FIGHT

Special to The New York Times.

SOLDIER FIELD, Chicago, Sept. 22.—Still the champion and a greater champion than ever before, Gene Tunney sat smiling placidly in his dressing room under the concrete stadium after the fight tonight. He had fought a good fight, probably the best fight of his career and he had won. Around him in hoarse excitement thronged his attendants and personal friends, breathless in their joy. But the champion was placid still.

Tunney took his victory as calmly, perhaps, as any champion who ever weathered a fight for the world's greatest pugilistic honor. His lips were swollen, his hands were deathly white and a red smear was on his left cheek where Jack Dempsey's mighty right fist had landed in the seventh round. But his eyes smiled a welcome and his lips echoed their sentiments as best they could.

"Sorry, I can't shake hands, they're frightfully sore," he repeated as each new enthusiast came to offer congratulations."

"Never again will I tape my hands," he explained. "I've always just used gauze on them, tonight they wrapped them with adhesive tape and the circulation was stopped. Look at them."

Calls Dempsey Dangerous.

"It was a great fight," he said. "And don't think that Dempsey isn't dangerous. I made that mistake once and found myself on the floor, for the first time in my life. Jimmy Bronson had just warned me not to get careless when I stepped in for the seventh round, but I thought Dempsey was weak and wabbling. Then he hit me with a left hook and a short right and I looked up to find the referee counting over me.

THE BEGINNING OF THE CHAMPIONSHIP BATTLE.

American Telephone and Telegraph Telephoto.

Dempsey and Tunney Sparring at the Opening of the First Round.

CROWD OF 150,000 WITNESS THE FIGHT

By JAMES R. HARRISON.

Continued from Page 1, Column 5.

boded rain. At 8:30 o'clock a few drops of rain fell, causing veterans of the Sesqui bout to shudder, but the menace passed as quickly as it had come.

Nothing happened to mar the perfection of a superlative spectacle. Police, usher and fire arrangements were perfect; the biggest of all boxing crowds, paying a record gate of about $2,500,000, was handled as quietly and easily as any lesser throng.

Governors in the Crowd.

Tex Rickard acted as host to the most distinguished crowd of his career as a boxing promoter. There were about ten Governors and an equal number of Mayors on the list of ticket buyers. Governor Small of Illinois sat beside Mayor William Hale Thompson of Chicago and William Wrigley Jr., owner of the Cubs.

Elsewhere in the huge assemblage, it was reported, were Governors Ritchie of Maryland, Fisher of Pennsylvania, Moody of Texas, Martin of Florida, Green of Michigan, Moore of New Jersey, Trumbull of Connecticut, Martineau of Arkansas and Hammill of Iowa.

Even royalty was to be found in the lists, for among the ringside watchers were the Princess Xenia, wife of William B. Leeds Jr. The Marquis of Douglas and Clydesdale attended as the guest of Gene Tunney.

Senator James A. Reed of Missouri headed the delegation of Senators and Congressmen. There were dozens of theatrical lights and movie celebrities, a solid phalanx of millionaires, a cordon of financial and business giants and a heavy representation of sporting dignitaries from baseball, boxing, racing and kindred branches.

The most inconspicuous man at the ringside was probably the most important of the 150,000 spectators. He was Graham MacNamee, who talked to more people over the radio than any other man in history. His story went to some 50,000,000 listeners all over the world—a record-breaking "hook-up" that was in keeping with the other angles of this unprecedented and stupendous sporting event.

Righeimer Early at Ringside.

John Righeimer, Chairman of the Illinois Boxing Commission, was an early visitor at the ringside. Asked who would referee the main bout, he remarked mysteriously, "Wait and see."

The front ringside aisles were all cluttered up with celebrities and policemen and the notables had to push through a plebian throng to get to their seats. Rickard had a picked squad of ushers to take care of the select throng, especially the 107 front row seats, where the cream of the cream was concentrated.

Genius of a high order was displayed by Mr. Rickard in cramming two newspaper men into a space that nature intended for only one. Compared to the experts at the bout, sardines live in the great open spaces.

Flood lights on the top of the arena battlements illuminated the scene, while the fans were waiting for the first preliminary fighters to appear. At that moment there were empty spaces in many sections and it did not look as if Mr. Rickard would have a sell-out.

The twilight was gray and forbidding and a west wind was rippling the American flags on the heights of the arena. However, a local weather sharp remarked that a west wind does not mean rain while it is cool.

The local impressarios produced a novelty in the form of a scoreboard bearing the cryptic words "Gene—Jack—Rounds, Down." The last word, it was suspected, was a relic left over from the Army-Navy game.

Every once in a while a flashlight would explode and the experts jumped nervously, fearing that another Chicago gang war had broken out.

Mr. Stillman, the head usher, came along and begged the correspondents in the second row to "move along a couple of niches, boys, and let this writer in." This request was greeted with loud and unfeeling laughter.

The movie boys and photographers were parked on lofty crow's nests to the north of the ring. The movie perch was covered with a canvas awning in case of rain.

Fairbanks Jumps to His Seat.

Doug Fairbanks leaped lightly over three cops, vaulted a railing and landed in his seat at 8:32 P. M. He was followed a minute later by Charlie Chaplin, who looked rather queer without a trick hat and cane.

When the Mayor of Chicago, William Hale Thompson, appeared the cops executed a "right by army corps" and escorted his Honor to his seat.

Governor Fred Green of Michigan was one of the many State Governors present. He did a Lindbergh from Lansing.

The first preliminary hadn't gone one minute before the loud cry of the raspberry could be heard in the outlying sections. The boys were tuning up early.

George M. Cohan waltzed in and felt at home right away when he saw all the American flags that decorated the battlements.

David Belasco was a ringside onlooker, and he admitted that he had never put on as great a show as this. Flo Ziegfeld was near by.

Kenesaw Mountain Landis was horribly handicapped. He had no rail to rest his chin on while he gazed at the proceedings.

A courier dashed up to the press section and announced that Charles M. Schwab, Clarence H. Mackay, Otto Kahn and Bernard Baruch were discovered near the ringside.

Harold Lloyd attempted to slink in disguised without eyeglasses, but he was spotted by a scout.

In the Mayor's section was Kendrick of Philadelphia, who helped to put on the Sesquicentennial party a year ago.

"The only thing I'll hand to Chicago is its weather," he said.

The words were hardly out of his mouth when a few drops of rain fell at 8:30. Mr. Kendrick concealed a chuckle with great difficulty.

STORY OF THE FIGHT TOLD BLOW BY BLOW

Continued from Page 1, Column 7.

sey's head. Again they clinched, with Jack pummeling away at the champion's body.

Fourth Round.

Jack was short with a left hook and Tunney smashed lefts and rights to the head as Jack tried to land a left and they clinched. Gene made him keep his distance. They clinched and traded punches. Dempsey missed a left hook and they wrestled over to the ropes. Gene danced away from Dempsey's left hook and put over a right and followed with a left hook, all blows at Dempsey's face. Gene came over with a right to the head. Tunney led with his right to the jaw and the challenger was somewhat dazed. Tunney got Dempsey against the ropes in Dempsey's corner with a left and then a right. Dempsey was groggy and Gene smashed with a right to the jaw. The bell rang, but so great was the noise the fighters didn't hear. The seconds got into the ring to get them away.

Fifth Round.

Gene opened the fifth with a hook to Jack's chin. Jack went in with a short left. Jack landed with two short lefts. Gene got back with a right to the jaw and followed with a hook to the jaw. Dempsey jabbed with a left, driving another left to Dempsey's head. The champion jabbed with his left to the head and they clinched. Dempsey got in a left and landed a terrific left to the jaw that stopped Tunney momentarily. The stop was short, however. Tunney drove both fists to Jack's head. Gene jabbed with his left and they clinched. Gene unleashed a right which was wide of the mark and then smashed over a right.

Sixth Round.

They danced around each other. Tunney led with a smashing right to the jaw as Jack swung wildly. Gene took a left hook to the body. Gene passed a left to Jack's jaw and they clinched. Gene smashed Jack with a left to the jaw and they clinched. Tunney was a bit wild with a right. Gene hooked a left to the body and Jack let go a smashing left which failed to stagger the champion. Dempsey let go with a right as Gene landed a left hook on Dempsey's head. Gene came right in and backed Dempsey to the ropes with lefts and rights. Dempsey hooked a left to Gene's head. Gene followed with a right to the jaw. Dempsey was wild and Tunney hit a left to the jaw which he followed with a right to the body.

Seventh Round.

Gene missed a left, but got a right to Dempsey's head and jabbed with a left. Dempsey landed two terrific rights and got Tunney against the ropes. Tunney fell to the floor and took a count of nine. Dempsey went to his own corner instead of to a neutral corner thus delaying the starting of the counting. On rising Tunney danced away from Dempsey's wild swings, and he contented himself with defensive tactics. Gene apparently cleared as the round progressed, but Dempsey was chasing him. Dempsey let go with both fists, but none were dangerous. They clinched and Tunney hooked weakly to his head.

Eighth Round.

Gene appeared himself at start of the eighth. He smashed Dempsey with a right to the jaw. When Dempsey let go a left to the jaw Tunney came back to the face. Dempsey missed a left to the head. Gene's jabs opened a small cut over Dempsey's eye. He tried a right but missed and they clinched. Gene kept tapping away at Dempsey's left eye. Tunney missed a left hook and Jack drove home a blow to the body. Gene countered with a right to jaw. Tunney smashed a left to the jaw which sent Jack to his knees but he got up before the counting started. Gene hoked a left to the face and the blood began to fly. They stood in the centre of the ring as the bell ended the round.

Ninth Round.

Jack came dashing out after Tunney. Tunney hooked with his left and landed with a right to Dempsey's head. Tunney drove a right to Jack's head and they clinched. Gene jabbed three lefts to the face and then landed with a right to the face. Dempsey's left eye began to bleed badly and Gene kept smashing with his lefts to the face. Dempsey is bleeding very badly. Gene went at Jack with both fists as he was against the ropes. Gene jabbed with his left and then landed twice with his right as they clinched. Gene smashed a right to the jaw, two more to the jaw and had Dempsey staggering. Dempsey's nose was a red smear as he came to the corner at the end of the round.

Tenth Round.

They shook hands at the start of the tenth round and Jack wrestled Gene to the canvas. Tunney hooked with a right and Jack retaliated with a left. Tunney jabbed with his left. Dempsey feinted with his left and Tunney landed with his right to Dempsey's face and the blood began to flow. Gene hit twice to the face and Jack hung on. Gene hit another left to the face. Gene twice sent a left to the face, then crashed home a right to the jaw and battered Dempsey's head around with both fists. Gene hit Jack with lefts and rights and Jack got in one right to the head in return. Tunney hooked three lefts to the face and drove Dempsey to the ropes with both fists, with Dempsey standing groggily around trying to avoid Tunney's blows.

BOOKS AND FRIENDS FILL TUNNEY'S DAY

Smiling, He Comes to Breakfast, and Chats With Marquis of Douglas as He Eats.

Special to The New York Times.

CHICAGO, Sept. 22.—Gene Tunney weighed in at 189½ pounds at the Illinois Athletic Club here this afternoon at 2:30 o'clock. He stepped on the scales right on schedule before a choking gathering of club members in the gymnasium weighing room after an uneventful ride from his late training quarters overlooking Fox Lake.

Dr. Joseph L. Russell, State Athletic Commission physician, found Tunney's pulse beat to be 30, normal and satisfying, and announced Tunney to be in superb condition and ready for the fight.

The champion and former champion did not meet. Dempsey had weighed in an hour earlier.

The Tunney weighing was attended with the excitement and hubbub usually associated with such ring ceremonies. A crowd of several hundred blocked off Michigan Boulevard, and when Tunney appeared sent up a cheer which echoed out over the broad expanse of Lake Michigan.

In the clubhouse the collection of members eager to get a glimpse of Tunney seemed greater than that in the street.

Ride Thirty Years Ago Recalled.

Following the weighing Tunney repaired with his retinue to the Hotel Sherman, there to await in the seclusion and privacy he so much desires and enjoys the summons to the ring.

It was said this afternoon that Tunney intends to leave Chicago, win or lose, tomorrow, going to Cleveland, where he plans to spend a few days visiting friends.

Then he will slip quietly into New York to pack for a hunting trip of several weeks in the Maine woods. He will be accompanied to Cleveland and New York by Eddie Eagan, former Yale Rhodes scholar and boxer.

There the pair will part company, for Eagan is soon to embark on a tour of the world.

The sixty-odd-mile ride from Fox Lake to the heart of Chicago's Loop recalled a little bit of ring history which made the trip eventful.

A hiatus of thirty years was bridged on that ride by the solemn, portly figure of old Bill McCabe, Tunney's closest friend and adviser. Back in 1897, when the immortal John L. Sullivan went down to defeat before the stabbing, tantalizing gloves of Jim Corbett in New Orleans, McCabe, younger then and the pal and bosom friend of another ring giant, rode with the defending champion in an open barouche to the cheers of the populace.

Protected by Armed Guard.

Today this same McCabe, older, of course, but as keen of mind and as loyal to another ring champion, rode beside Tunney in a high-priced, powerful limousine which was said by its pilot, Eddie Notter, to be armored.

On that ride in the distant past McCabe rode with the slugger going forth to defeat at the hands of the boxer who introduced a new era in pugilism.

Today McCabe rode forth silently with the boxer he hoped was approaching a repetition of ring history in accomplishing the downfall of the slugger, Dempsey.

In the car with Tunney and McCabe were Chief Mike Grady of the Chicago Detective Bureau and Sergeant Bill Smith, husky police bodyguard of Tunney from the time Gene reached Chicago.

Trainer Lou Fink sat with Notter on the front seat. Leading a procession of five cars was a squad car of the Chicago Police Department loaded with detectives, who, in turn, were loaded with ammunition and ready for any emergency.

Behind this car was the limousine in which Tunney made the trip, bundled against the chill blasts in a heavy woolen sweater of scarlet hue, a medium weight topcoat and heavy cap.

Then came another police car, a coupé carrying State troopers who have acted as guards at Tunney's camp, and, finally, a machine with two newspaper men and its photographer-owner, Tommy Howard.

This trip, which started at 12:20 o'clock, was in contrast to the one Tunney made a year ago from Stroudsburg, Pa., to Philadelphia and the title, and to the one he made to camp on his arrival here.

Gene flew in an airplane a year ago and going to camp he traveled at break-neck speed. Today he rode in comfort at a moderate speed, having issued instructions that the speed was not to exceed thirty-five miles an hour. The only variations from this pace came when the procession was going down grade. Then it jumped to forty or forty-five.

There was nothing to interfere with the calm of the champion, no shouts of passing motorists, no blare of klaxons, no shrieking of sirens or whistles. There was only the cheering of a score of little schoolgirls at a corner in Libertyville. The youngsters waved a greeting which the champion smilingly returned.

Tunney enjoyed a good night's rest on the eve of the battle. He was in his room and said to be in bed at 10 o'clock last night.

He breakfasted today on orange juice, prunes, cereal, three boiled eggs, whole wheat bread and boiled milk. Then he repaired to his room to read.

Coming down to breakfast, Tunney was his smiling, modest self, with a cheery word for the camp retinue and the chroniclers who greeted him. He breakfasted with Eddie Eagan, while Dr. Carnes Weeks and Ed Dewing, New York friends who arrived last night with a party including the Marquis of Douglas and Clydesdale, heir of the Duke of Hamilton, chatted with the champion during the meal.

FIGHT CROWDS COME BY AIR, ROAD, RAIL

Michigan Governor, New York Men and St. Louis Browns' Owner Fly to Chicago.

SPECIAL TRAINS BY SCORES

Hotels and Clubs Jammed to Roof and Reservations Are Futile—No Sign of Profiteering.

Special to The New York Times.

CHICAGO, Sept. 22.—The fight-bent throng poured into Chicago today by regular and special trains, automobiles and buses, and a few adventurous souls swooped down out of the sky in airplanes, took off their flying togs and inquired the way to Soldier Field.

"This the the greatest troop movement since the war," said a railroad official as he mopped his clammy brow and watched the hurrying thousands whirl past him through the Union Station.

Special trains were treading on the heels of one another in the yards outside. The regular trains were arriving with extra cars and extra sections, and the hotel people wondered where all the visitors would be accommodated tonight.

Even the private clubs, such as the Illinois A. C., the Chicago A. A., the Hamilton Club and others, were jammed to the roof, and all the little side-street hotels and rooming houses had the "S. R. O." sign out.

During the day the Pennsylvania Railroad alone ran twenty-five special trains into the Windy City, with extra sections of the Broadway Limited, the Manhattan Limited and other regular fliers.

Leeds Flies to the Battle.

The Twentieth Century Limited of the New York Central Lines arrived this morning with a record-breaking human cargo, and three fight specials came in over the Michigan Central—two from New York and one from Newark.

Among those who journeyed to the fight by airplane was Governor Fred W. Green of Michigan. He arrived with a party of friends. Five wealthy New Yorkers landed at Maywood Field here at 5 o'clock this afternoon. William B. Leeds Jr., a flying enthusiast, flew from New York to watch the fight with his wife, the Princess Xenia.

Phil Ball, owner of the St. Louis Browns, chartered a plane and flew here from St. Louis in two and a half hours, arriving this morning. He is going back by the air route tomorrow.

The air cavalcade, however, was not up to expectations. The recent New Jersey disaster cooled the ardor of some of the flying enthusiasts, and many of the proposed air trips were canceled at the last minute.

Among the special trains was one from Hollywood with a detachment of movie folk; another from Tulsa, Okla., over the Santa Fé; two special cars from Oklahoma City, and others from the Pacific Coast. The Baltimore & Ohio ran four special trains from Akron, Ohio, Pittsburgh and New York. The Chicago & Eastern Illinois had four specials, from Texas, St. Louis, Nashville and Florida.

Central's Estimate Is 25,000.

Los Angeles, New Orleans and Milwaukee were other cities to dispatch specials to the "fight of the ages."

A special chartered by James J. Corbett, former world's heavyweight champion, arrived today and brought such celebrities as George M. Cohan, William Collier, David Belasco, Flo Ziegfeld, Harold Lloyd and party, Irving Berlin and Willard Morris.

In addition to the Corbett special there were trains bearing the name of the Madison Square Garden Club, the Old Colony Club, the Bryan Fight Special, the William Duffy Fight Special and the Harris-Turner Special.

L. W. Landman, passenger traffic manager of the New York Central Lines, estimated that his road and subsidiaries carried about 25,000 passengers to the fight.

The hotels in the Loop District turned hundreds of applicants away during the day, and even those who had the foresight to make reservations several weeks ago found that they, too, were out of luck.

"What are we going to do?" asked one hotel manager, with a helpless shrug. "The people who are in the rooms won't get out and we cannot put them out."

Many of the visitors, however, snapped their fingers at the hotels, for they had come on special trains which were scheduled to pull out again within an hour after the fight.

It was a quiet, well-behaved crowd that surged through the Loop district and deployed in the hotel lobbies. There was none of the old prizefight mob spirit about these fans, and, except for a little more bustle, a bit more congestion and an underlying air of excitement, one would hardly have known that anything out of the ordinary was afoot.

Late in the afternoon the Loop was almost deserted, as the fans began swarming toward Soldier Field. The motorists parked their cars on side streets some distance from the stadium and walked the rest of the way.

To the eternal credit of Chicago let it be recorded that there has been no price boosting and profiteering on the part of the hotels, restaurants and clubs. The local merchants reaped a rich harvest, but prices remained the same.

DEMPSEY CHEERFUL AS HE WEIGHS IN

Confident at Pre-Fight Ceremonies in Illinois Athletic Club—Scales 192½ Pounds.

3,000 CROWD THE DOORWAY

Challenger Spends Evening Resting at Hotel—He and Wife Issue Message.

By RICHARDS VIDMER.

Special to The New York Times.

CHICAGO, Sept. 22.—A spontaneous grin spread over the unshaven countenance of Jack Dempsey. His eyes crinkled at the corners with good humor, his chin lifted with confidence, his gaze swept over the assembled gathering of newspaper men who watched every move of the challenger for the world's heavyweight championship.

"So long boys. I'll see you later." Dempsey called, and with a wave of his hand disappeared from the Illinois Athletic Club.

That was the first sight any one outside his official family had of him today. It was the last glimpse the public had of him until he climbed into the ring at Soldier Field about nine hours later and stood face to face with Gene Tunney and the last obstacle on his come-back trail.

At 1:45 o'clock this afternoon Dempsey departed from the Illinois Athletic Club, where before members of the press, of the Illinois Athletic Club and officials connected with the big battle on the banks of Lake Michigan, he weighed in officially at 192½ pounds.

The ceremony was supposed to be private. Not until noon were the newspaper men informed as to the time and place. When the challenger arrived at the club house, however, guarded by a squad of motorcycle policemen and hidden behind the closed doors of a limousine, some 3,000 persons had received the news and were gather about the doorway.

His Stride Is Brisk.

Dempsey mounted the steps with a brisk stride, hastened through the pathway opened for him by uniformed policemen, whisked ten flights upward in an elevator and after stripping stepped on the scales. The scales registered 192½ pounds. Dempsey stepped back into his dressing room, donned his street attire again and reappeared.

He paused before the silent crowd of friends and officials, nodded once or twice as he recognized a familiar face and then, with a smile and his confident call of "So long, boys. I'll see you later," he was gone.

He spent the rest of the afternoon and the early hours of the evening in the bungalow atop the Morrison Hotel, which he had made his official headquarters. It was the same quarters once occupied by President Coolidge.

No one was allowed to see Dempsey and every effort was made by his loyal attendants to see that he was undisturbed in the hours before the big battle. Inquiries brought forth only the response that he was resting.

His only visitor this morning before he was ushered to the Illinois A. C. was Mrs. Dempsey, the former Miss Estelle Taylor. She spent a few minutes in private with her husband and together they released a message for the public.

Dempseys Issue Statement.

The message read:

> We face the issue in calm confidence. May we, from the vantage of our dear fireside, look back on one of life's great satisfactions, the good job well done.
>
> JACK AND ESTELLE.

It was said by his attendants that Dempsey spent a quiet, peaceful and untroubled night at the Morrison Hotel last night. He arose at 9 o'clock this morning after a long sleep, completely rested.

When he appeared at the Illinois Athletic Club he looked in perfect condition to all outward appearances and there was the light of battle in his eyes. As he stepped on the scales he appeared as eager as any one to see what they registered, though it was the eagerness of curiosity, not of nervousness.

The Dempsey who appeared this afternoon bore very little resemblance to the Dempsey who fought and lost in the ring at Philadelphia a year ago. He was ready to win or lose on his merits.

CROWDS ORDERLY ON WAY TO FIGHT

Advance Almost Leisurely Through Streets to the Stadium.

6,000 OFFICERS GUIDE THEM

Gayly Dressed Women Give Color to the Scene—Few Scalpers Appear.

Special to The New York Times.

CHICAGO, Sept. 22.—All the fighting was done inside the grim gray walls of Soldier Field tonight. Outside the crowd that flowed steadily toward the amphitheatre where two modern gladiators fought for world's pugilistic supremacy was quiet, calm, orderly and almost leisurely in their movements.

With some 6,000 men from the Chicago Police Department, the National Guard, the Naval Reserve and the Motorcycle Corps, to maintain order and control, the way was well cleared along the roads that led to the stadium, and all roads seemed to lead there.

As dusk descended on the Windy City and the breeze died down to a gentle zephyr from the direction of Lake Michigan, the human army started its steady march across the bridges that lead to Grant Park. From the North Side the trend was southward, from the South Side the trend was northward. At Seventh and Eighth Streets the streams converged and turned eastward across the bridges.

Michigan Boulevard was filled with a mixture of humanity made kin by reason that each clutched a pasteboard bearing the pictures of Gene Tunney and Jack Dempsey—tickets to the greatest show on earth. The hotels poured out their throngs onto the famous boulevard. Women in gay colors and warm furs, men in mufflers and topcoats, visitors and natives, pushed along the sidewalks of Chicago, elbow to elbow, but there was no jostling or shoving.

In fact there was very little noise. A low murmur of conversation was interrupted only by the calls of greeting when two old friends passed in the parade. Now and then one heard remarks of distress concerning sleeping quarters, but it was good-natured distress, and if one found himself with no place to sleep he seemed to think it a good joke on himself.

The first signs that the scene of battle was near at hand was when the crowd was stopped by a corps of policemen after crossing the bridges which lead to Grant Park.

"Show your tickets, please," and every one suddenly realized that they were on their way to a world's championship prizefight. The realization brought something of a thrill.

A motor corps of taxicabs tore down the street and for a moment the crowd became congested, but a signal from a traffic whistle and motored advance stopped suddenly, letting the human stream flow on.

Large lettered signs and numerous direction arrows showed the way to the gates and there was no confusion or excitement in finding the proper entrance for every ticket-holder. There was a scarcity of scalpers, who usually infest the outskirts of such a sporting spectacle, and all the betting that was on the outcome of the battle must have been done before departing for the scene of the conflict.

As the hour grew later and big lights flared up inside the stadium signaling to the outside world that the preliminary fights had commenced the human stream grew thicker and flowed faster, but still there was no confusion and every one was orderly.

A light drizzle began to fall about 8:30 o'clock and the crowd quickened its pace, seeming to think that there would be protection inside the stadium, but once there they found the rain was just as annoying on the open seats as on the sidewalks outside. The drizzle proved nothing more than that, however, and soon subsided altogether.

During the late afternoon and early part of the evening most of the crowd had made its way to the stadium either on foot or in taxicabs, but as the hours passed the number of limousines and luxurious motor vehicles increased as the social element began to arrive from dinner parties. Their only interest being in the main bout between the champion and his challenger.

The last arrivals went scurrying in and showed far more excitement than any of their predecessors, but their excitement probably was due more to the fear of missing something of the main bout than to their interest in who won. Even the last wave was able to get inside without any trouble as the main part of the army arrived early and already was seated.

On the outside there lingered a few, a very few, who didn't have tickets and had to gain what information they could of the activities inside by translating the spasmodic cheering and the stamping of feet which broke into an uproar when the battle ended. But there was not the milling mob which usually surrounds the arena in which a world's heavyweight championship battle is in progress. Very few managed to slip over the bridges guarded by the bluecoats without holding the necessary pasteboards. Probably very few tried. Most of the crowd outside the stadium was gathered around a radio listening to the details which were transmitted through seven microphones from the ringside.

CHICAGO WAGERING EVEN AT RING TIME

Betting in Fight Centre Active, With More Dempsey Money Than Tunney Reported in Sight.

CHAMPION FAVORITE HERE

Installed a 3 to 4 Choice After Even Money Had Prevailed—$3,000,000 Bet in New York.

Special to The New York Times.

CHICAGO, Sept. 22.—Whether it was an influx of the so-called wise money or merely last-minute sentiment, the odds on the battle for the heavyweight championship went to even money this morning and stayed there until the gong rang.

For the past week Tunney had ruled a favorite at odds of 7 to 5. Yesterday a few bets were made with the title-holder still favored, but the price had slipped to 6 to 5. This morning La Salle Street commission houses were quoting even money, with more Dempsey money offered than Tunney currency.

The Tunney backers seemed more inclined to bet on their man to win by a decision, while the Dempsey supporters were eager to place their bets on a knockout victory. Several bets of the latter nature were reported at 3 to 1.

A tip was circulated in the financial district that Dempsey would win by a knockout in the eighth round and was taken by many as coming from a good source. Many fans placed a little money at odds of 15 to 1 that Dempsey would win in the eighth round and had no trouble getting takers.

Two $50,000 Wagers Reported.

Nick the Greek, noted plunger, was said to have wagered $50,000 on Tunney to win at even money. It also was said that members of Dempsey's retinue had wagered $50,000 on the challenger to win.

From the Tunney camp no money was placed except by Billy Gibson, the champion's manager, so far as could be learned. Gibson was reported to have bet $200,000 on Tunney to win, but made his wager a few days ago and had to give odds.

The prevailing bookmakers' quotations at zero hour were as follows:

Dempsey to win, even money.
Tunney to win, even money.
Dempsey to knock out Tunney, 3 to 1.
Tunney to knock out Dempsey, 6 to 1.
Dempsey to win by a knockout in the first round, 20 to 1.
Tunney to win by a knockout in the first round, 30 to 1.
Dempsey to win in three rounds, 5 to 2.
Tunney to win in five rounds, 10 to 1.
The fight to end a draw, 6 to 5.
Tunney not to be knocked down, 1 to 3.
Dempsey to come up for the ninth round, 5 to 8.
Tunney to stay the limit, 2 to 5.
Dempsey to stay the limit, 1 to 3.

Tunney Money Appears Here.

The expected flow of Tunney money made its appearance in New York yesterday, with the result that long before ring time the price was forced down from even money, as well as 9 to 10 and take your pick, to 3 to 4 with Tunney the favorite. All kinds of last-minute wagering was reported, with the Broadway commissioners bearing the brunt of the drive in the late afternoon and early evening. Just a year ago Dempsey was the favorite at 3½ to 1 with little betting.

SPECULATORS LOSE HEAVILY ON TICKETS

Frantically Cut Prices to Half Face Value, but Fans Fear Counterfeits.

Special to The New York Times.

RINGSIDE, SOLDIER FIELD, CHICAGO, Sept. 22.—Money poured into the Rickard coffers all day long today as the fight-mad fans made a last-minute rush for seats at the Palmer House ticket headquarters, as well as at the temporary booths at Michigan Boulevard and Eleventh Street. The best single day's sales were recorded.

Others of the ticket-selling fraternity did not fare so well. The speculators were running around frantically, unable to dispose of what they expected to be much-demanded pasteboards. Five hours before fight time some were being sold at the price stamped on the tickets, while others were being peddled at a reduced rate. Many of the forty-dollar seats went for $35, with a corresponding decrease in price down the line.

As the time of the fight drew near the prices the speculators demanded grew less and less, and some of the tickets went begging at half the stipulated amount. The speculators mingled in the throngs on Michigan Boulevard, but most of the crowd scurried by, intent on getting to seats already purchased.

Bogus Tickets Frightened Fans.

Two things caused the speculators to be stuck. One was the return of good seats to the regulation box office a few days before the fight and the other was the flood of counterfeit tickets which overran the market.

The fans were reluctant to risk their money on tickets which might be refused at the door, and there was no sense in paying extra prices. That was the attitude of the fan in general, and the speculators suffered accordingly.

Cox Says Tunney Will Quit Ring to Lecture; Hails Him as the 'Cleanest and Finest'

CHICAGO, Sept. 22 (AP).—Gene Tunney will abandon the squared circle of pugilism for the lecture platform of America's young manhood, former Governor James M. Cox of Ohio, once a Presidential candidate, said here today.

"I happen to know that Gene Tunney, perhaps the finest yet most misunderstood man in sports, will devote his future to lecturing young men on how to live," Mr. Cox said. "I have known him for years, as the best son any father could hope for—the cleanest and the finest.

"Gene already has plans for touring Y. M. C. A. buildings, K. of C. halls and everywhere else he can reach young men with his talks on how to live."

The former Governor said the public was suffering from a misunderstanding of the fighter's aloofness.

Home Run Record Falls as Ruth Hits 60th

RUTH CRASHES 60TH TO SET NEW RECORD

Babe Makes It a Real Field Day by Accounting for All Runs in 4-2 Victory.

1921 MARK OF 59 BEATEN

Fans Go Wild as Ruth Pounds Ball Into Stands With One On, Breaking 2-2 Tie.

CONNECTS LAST TIME UP

Zachary's Offering Converted Into Epochal Smash, Which Old Fan Catches—Senators Then Subside.

Babe Ruth crosses the plate after hitting his 60th home run. The Babe is greeted by Lou Gehrig.

Babe Ruth scaled the hitherto unattained heights yesterday. Home run 60, a terrific smash off the southpaw pitching of Zachary, nestled in the Babe's favorite spot in the right field bleachers, and before the roar had ceased it was found that this drive not only had made home run record history but also was the winning margin in a 4 to 2 victory over the Senators. This also was the Yanks' 100th triumph of the season. Their last league game of the year will be played today.

When the Babe stepped to the plate in that momentous eighth inning the score was deadlocked. Koenig was on third base, the result of a triple, one man was out and all was tense. It was the Babe's fourth trip to the plate during the afternoon, a base on balls and two singles resulting on his other visits plateward.

The first Zachary offering was a fast one, which sailed over for a called strike. The next was high. The Babe took a viscious swing at the third pitched ball and the bat connected with a crash that was audible in all parts of the stand. It was not necessary to follow the course of the ball. The boys in the bleachers indicated the route of the record homer. It dropped about half way to the top. Boys, No. 60 was some homer, a fitting wallop to top the Babe's record of 59 in 1921.

While the crowd cheered and the Yankee players roared their greetings the Babe made his triumphant, almost regal tour of the paths. He jogged around slowly, touched each bag firmly and carefully and when he imbedded his spikes in the rubber disk to record officially Homer 60 hats were tossed into the air, papers were torn up and tossed liberally and the spirit of celebration permeated the place.

The Babe's troll out to his position was the signal for a handkerchief salute in which all the bleacherites, to the last man, participated. Jovial Babe entered into the carnival spirit and punctuated his Ringly strides with a succession of snappy military salutes.

Ruth 4, Senators 2.

Ruth's homer was a fitting climax to a game which will go down as the Babe's personal triumph. The Yanks scored four runs, the Babe personally crossing the plate three times and bringing in Koenig for the fourth. So this is one time where it would be fair, although not original, to record Yankee victory 109 as Ruth 4, Senators 2.

There was not much else to the game. The 10,000 persons who came to the Stadium were there for no other purpose than to see the Babe make home run history. After each of Babe's visits to the plate the expectant crowd would relax and wait for his next effort. They saw him open with a base on balls, follow with two singles and then clout the epoch-making circuit smash.

The only unhappy individual within the Stadium was Zachary. He realized he was going down in the records as the historical home run victim, in other words the goat. Zachary was one of the most interested spectators of the home run flight. He tossed his glove to the ground, muttered to himself, turned to his mates for consolation and got everything but that. There is no denying that Zachary was putting everything he had on the ball. No pitcher likes to have recorded after his name the fact that he was Ruth's victim on his sixtieth homer.

The ball that the Babe drove, according to word from official sources, was a pitch that was fast, low and on the inside. The Babe pulled away from the plate, then stepped into the ball, and wham! According to Umpire Bill Dinneen at the plate and Catcher Muddy Ruel the ball traveled on a line and landed a foot inside fair territory about half way to the top of the bleachers. But when the ball reached the bleacher barrier it was about ten feet fair and curving rapidly to the right.

Fan Rushes to Babe With Ball.

The ball which became Homer 60 was caught by Joe Forner of 1,937 First Avenue, Manhattan. He is about 40 years old and has been following baseball for thirty-five, according to his own admission. He was far from modest and as soon as the game was over rushed to the dressing room to let the Babe know who had the ball.

For three innings both sides were blanked. The Senators broke through in the fourth for two runs.

The Yanks came back with one run in their half of the fourth. Ruth opened with a long single to right and moved to third on Gehrig's single to centre. Gehrig took second on the throw to third. Meusel drove deep to Goslin, Ruth scoring and Gehrig taking third after the catch.

With two out in the sicth Ruth singled to right. Gehrig's hit was so fast that it went right through Gillis for a single, Ruth holding second. The Babe tied the score on Meusel's single to centre. Lazzeri was an easy third out.

The box score:

WASHINGTON (A.)	ab.	r.	h.	po.	a.	e.
Rice, rf	3	0	1	2	0	0
Harris, 2b	3	0	0	3	4	0
Ganzel, cf	4	0	1	1	0	0
Goslin, lf	4	1	1	5	0	0
Judge, 1b	4	0	0	8	0	0
Ruel, c	2	1	1	2	0	0
Bluege, 3b	3	0	1	1	4	0
Gillis, ss	4	0	0	2	1	0
Zachary, p	2	0	0	0	1	0
aJohnson	1	0	0	0	0	0
Total	30	2	5	24	10	0

NEW YORK (A.)	ab.	r.	h.	po.	a.	e.
Combs, cf	4	0	0	3	0	0
Koenig, ss		1	1	2	5	0
Ruth, rf		3	3	4	0	0
Gehrig, 1b	4	0	2	10	0	1
Meusel, lf	3	0	1	3	0	0
Lazzeri, 2b	3	0	0	2	2	0
Dugan, 3b	3	0	1	1	1	0
Bengough, c	3	0	1	1	2	0
Pipgras, p	2	0	0	0	2	0
Pennock, p	1	0	0	0	1	0
Total	30	4	9	27	13	1

a Batted for Zachary in ninth.

Washington	0	0	0	2	0	0	0	0	0	—2
New York	0	0	0	1	0	1	0	2		—4

Two-base hit—Rice. Three-base hit—Koenig. Home run—Ruth. Stolen bases—Ruel, Bluege, Rice. Sacrifices—Museul. Double plays—Harris and Bluege; Gillis, Harris and Judge. Left on bases—New York 4, Washington 7. Bases on balls—Off Pipgras 4, Pennock 1, Zachary 1. Struck out—By Zachary 1. Hits—Off Pipgras 4 in 6 innings, Pennock 1 in 3. Hit by pitcher—By Pipgras (Rice). Winning pitcher—Pennock. Umpires—Dineen, Connolly and Owens. Time of game—1:35.

GIANT DEFEAT ENDS THEIR GALLANT RACE

Last Pennant Hope Snuffed as Robins Win by 10-5 at Ebbets Field.

VANCE PROVES BAFFLING

Holds McGrawmen Safely While His Mates Pound Three New York Hurlers.

By JAMES R. HARRISON.

According to every known system of mathematics, including logarithms, the Giants are out of the 1927 pennant race. Their last chance evaporated yesterday afternoon at Ebbets Field when Dazzy Vance and the artful Dodgers plastered a 10-5 defeat on the McGrawmen. Now the Giants haven't got a chance to win the pennant.

For more than two months now the Giants have been in the throes of a nerveracking struggle. At one time they were only half a game out of first place. From a distant point some eight games in the rear they battled forward until they were so close to the Pirates' coat tails that Barney Dreyfuss turned a quaint shade of purple and could not sleep at night.

But it all ended yesterday when Vance baffled our lads while the Messrs. Henry, Barnes and Fitzsimmons were doing no baffling to speak of. In fact, they were not even mildly mysterious. Going into the seventh the score was 4 to 4, but Barnes was knocked out with nobody down, and before Fitzsimmons could apply the brakes the Dodgers were in possession of six runs.

Giants Take the Lead.

The Giants still have a chance to tie the Cardinals for second place, but this is considered most unlikely.

The Dodgers scored four of their runs in the fifth and the six others in the seventh. The efforts of the Giants were more scattered. They rapped Vance for two in the first. Mueller was hit, Reese singled off Vance's glove, and when the Dazzler hurled the ball over Herman's head Mueller scored and Reese went to second, scoring on Roush's single to right.

In the second Harper doubled to centre, took third on Statz's bad return and counted on Cummings's sacrifice fly.

The score was 3-0 for the Giants when the Dodgers suffered a rush of blood to the head and scored four runs in the fifth. Singles by Flowers and Butler and DeBerry's walk filled the bags, with one out. Vance's fly scored Flowers and Statz's double admitted two. The Jigger romped in on Carey's two-bagger.

By dint of much effort the Giants tied the score in their half of the seventh, and this was the exact situation when the Robins went into another trance and scored six runs in their section of the frame.

Barnes, who had relieved Henry at the start of the inning, walked Butler. Reese fumbled DeBerry's bunt and Vance strolled, filling the bases with none out. Whereupon Barnes was given an indefinite sick leave and the good Fitzsimmons wheeled in to take his place. Statz greeted Freddy with a short single to right, scoring Butler.

Harper's Triple Wasted.

With the bases still thickly populated the ancient Carey paddled a double down the left-field foul line and three Robins winged swiftly home. The other details don't matter much. Felix bunted Carey to third and Max scored on Herman's two-bagger. Partridge's base hit sent the Babe home.

MALONEY STOPPED BY HEENEY IN FIRST

By JAMES P. DAWSON.

Jack Dempsey came back to a New York ring last night at Madison Square Garden to a reception which dinned into his ears and must have warmed his heart, and then sat back in his first-row seat to see Tom Heeney, chunky New Zealand heavyweight, knock out Jim Maloney, Boston Irishman, in the first round of what was to have been a ten-round bout featuring a card which attracted 13,000 people to Tex Rickard's arena of sport.

A solid right-hand smash to the jaw sent Maloney nose-diving into the canvas from an exchange at the ropes near a neutral corner and the Hub lad was counted out on his knees after exactly 1 minute 17 seconds of action.

The knockout came as a shock, not in the sense that it was unexpected, but in that it came so suddenly. The men had hardly warmed to their task —were doing little more than sizing each other up, as a matter of fact, and the fans were settling back to enjoy a battle which promised to go a few rounds anyway, when Heeney's finishing right curled over to Maloney's unprotected jaw, and Maloney pitched headforemost to the canvas.

Dempsey was among the most surprised of the big throng. With his wife he entered the arena just as Maloney and Heeney were clambering up to the platform. Mrs. Dempsey went to Promoter Rickard's private box to watch the mêlée, while the former champion, acknowledging the greetings of countless friends clustered in the glare of the powerful ring lights, sat near the ring.

Dempsey Receives Ovation.

The reception Dempsey received was one of the greatest ever accorded anybody in a Garden ring. The man who was making his first public appearance in fight surroundings since the night a little more than a week ago when he failed to wrest the title from Gene Tunney in Chicago was affected by it, too.

James J. Jeffries, world's champion of another generation, was led to the ring by Boxing Commissioner William Muldoon. Jeffries climbed through the ropes to greet the former champion of the present generation and, as these two ring heroes greeted each other, the din of the crowd was terrific.

It would have been a grand climax to have the distinguished guests of the night and the throng which paid $35,930 witness a thrilling, heart-stirring spectacle. But that was not to be. Somehow or other the feeling overtook you as you sat at the ringside that this fight was to be short. It was. And it was the battle which probably means an end to the career of a man who only a year ago was being seriously considered for a fight with Champion Gene Tunney. The knockout by Heeney coming as it did on top of the one-round knockout scored recently by George Godfrey, and the knockout by Jack Sharkey, of which he also was the victim, just about put finis to the career of Maloney.

Decision Against Daley, U. S. Olympic Boxer, Stirs Uproar; Verdict Reversed

U.S. FANS IN UPROAR AT OLYMPIC BOUTS

Rush Toward Ring When Judges Decide Against Daley, but Decision Is Reversed.

BRITISH HOOT THIS ACTION

Holaiko of U. S. Also Gains the Finals but Swedish Followers Boo the Verdict.

ARGENTINA QUALIFIES FOUR

Scandinavian Royalty Roots in Vain for Danish Heavyweight—Five Nations Join Protest.

By The Associated Press.

AMSTERDAM, Aug. 10.—The fighting spirit of the ringside fans at the Olympic boxing events tonight made the action in the ring in the semi-final bouts look like second-rate performances. Not since the Olympics started have such scenes been witnessed in the fighting pavilion.

The uproar started when John L. Daley of Waltham, Mass., American bantamweight entry, was declared the loser in a bout with Isaacs of South Africa, to the great amazement of the boxing fans. Led by Charles Ornstein of Baltimore, manager of the American lacrosse team, the United States fans on the sidelines booed, hissed, yelled and screamed. Even General MacArthur, President of the Olympic Committee, rose excitedly from his seat at the apparent injustice of the decision.

The American rooters rushed into the aisles and tried to crowd up to the ring, and for a while it looked as if there would be a free-for-all between the Dutch police, who were called in to quell the disturbance, and the American rooters.

Meanwhile, the Judges reversed the decision, announcing that they had made a mistake. This sent the British fans and others who favored the South African into a counter-demonstration.

Daley clearly defeated Isaacs in all three rounds, driving him all over the ring with hard right and left hooks to the head. The South African delivered most of his blows with an open glove and was unable to land effectively.

Swedish Fans in Uproar.

The British counter-demonstration had hardly died down when another American, Stephen Holaiko, Auburn, N. Y., lightweight, entered the ring for another bout which stirred up excitement. Holaiko's defeat of Berggren of Sweden brought the Scandinavian fans to their feet, hissing and booing, but the decision stood. Several battles in the audience between Swedish and American adherents were barely averted.

Berggren put up a game battle against Holaiko, making a gallant stand in the final round after the American had gained a wide margin in the first two. The Swedish boxer managed to drive the American to the ropes, but was not scoring cleanly.

The third American who reached the semi-finals got into action before the excitement started and lost a close decision without any protest. This was Harry Devine, Worcester, Mass., featherweight, who was defeated by Van Klaveren of Holland. The victor hit harder and oftener, winning the first and third rounds. The second frame was called a draw when Devine floored his opponent with a left to the jaw but could not keep him down.

After the two American victories the audience remained on the qui vive for the rest of the evening and got plenty of opportunity to cheer in the all-Scandinavian battle between Ramm of Sweden and Sorsdal of Norway, heavyweights. Although bleeding profusely from a blow over the eye received in the first round, Ramm fought back gamely and won the decision.

Italian's Victory Protested.

Further cause for animated discussion at the ringside was furnished by the announcement that Ireland, Germany, Holland, Belgium and Canada had joined in a protest against the decision which declared the Irish bantamweight, Traynor, the loser in a bout with Tamagnini of Italy.

As if to make sure there would be excitement all evening, the brothers of the Swedish King, Princes Charles and Eugene, Prince Olaf of Norway, Princess Axel of Denmark and several other members of Scandinavian royalty appeared at the ringside just in time to see Rodriguez, Argentine heavyweight, whip Michaelsen of Denmark to a standstill. The royal fans got so excited that they yelled like the rest of the ringsiders, Princess Axel urging her compatriot to greater efforts with piercing words in Danish.

The second Argentine to win his way into the final round was Landini, conqueror of the American favorite, Tom Lown, who won a three-round decision over Ray Smillie, last of the Canadian survivors in the tourney. The South American will meet Morgan of New Zealand for the welterweight championship tomorrow.

Landini rushed the Canadian all over the ring in every round, concentrating his attack on Smillie's body. Smillie landed several effective right uppercuts to the head in the third session.

Avendano Gains Final.

Argentina placed her third man in the finals when Avendano won the decision over McCorkindale of South Africa in the semi-finals of the light-heavyweight division. Both fighters scarcely could stand at the close of the battle.

In a final desperate sortie McCorkindale drove the Argentine almost through the ropes twice in the third round, but could not overcome the large margin piled up by Avendano in the first two sessions.

In the other semi-final Peralta of Argentina defeated Biguet of Belgium by decision. The match consisted chiefly of infighting, with the Argentine getting the better of most of the exchanges. Both bled profusely.

Entering the finals, Argentina holds the lead in numbers with four survivors among the sixteen finalists. The Argentines are Peralta, featherweight; Landini, welterweight; Avendano, light-heavyweight and Rodriguez, heavyweight. Italy has three finalists, the United States two, Daley and Holaiko, while Holland, Germany, Sweden, Czechoslovakia, New Zealand, France and Hungary have one each.

The International Amateur Boxing Federation voted today to have a referee in the ring in future Olympics as proposed by Jacob W. Stumpf, manager of the American team.

Rowing Champions Crowned In Olympic Games Regatta

SLOTEN, Holland, Aug. 10 (AP). — Olympic rowing champions crowned today in the finals in the seven classes are:

Eight-oared Shells — United States (University of California).

Double Sculls — United States (Charles McIlvaine and Paul Costello, Penn. A. C., Philadelphia).

Single Sculls—Bob Pearce, Australia.

Fours With Coxswain—Italy.

Fours Without Coxswain—England.

Pairs Without Coxswain — Germany.

Pairs With Coxswain — Switzerland.

MISS OF A JUMP PUTS U. S. EQUESTRIANS OUT

Team, With Victory Near, Disqualified as George, Looking Ahead, Passes Small Obstacle.

HILVERSUM, Holland, Aug. 10 (AP). —With victory almost in sight, the American entries in the three-day Olympic equestrian competition were disqualified today because one member of the team failed to jump a small obstacle in his desire to jump a far greater one ahead.

Under the Olympic rules the disqualification of one member means the disqualification of the whole team.

Until Major C. P. George made this fatal oversight of not noticing the small jump the American had made the best time in today's obstacle jumping test. They seemed sure of ranking first, second and third for the day when Major George failed to take one jump with his horse, Orzella, and was disqualified.

"It is really a tragedy," said Gustavus T. Kirby of the Olympic committee, who stood right next to the obstacle George overlooked. "Our riders and horses were absolutely fit and it looked as if we had smooth sailing. George easily took one difficult jump, then there was an easy low one. Knowing that the hardest jump of all was immediately ahead, he didn't notice the small one, he was so intent on making the difficult grade. I tried to holler to him, but he didn't hear me. We have a slight chance in the individual competition, but not nearly as great as in the team match.

AMERICANS SEVENTH IN TEAM GYMNASTICS

Switzerland Wins Olympic Title —U. S. Fails to Place in Individual Contest.

AMSTERDAM, Aug. 10 (AP).—Switzerland won the Olympic all-round gymnastic team championship today. Czechoslovakia finished second and Yugoslavia third. The United States took seventh place among the fourteen competing nations. France, Finland and Italy also finished ahead of the American team.

According to semi-official calculations, the Swiss team ran up a total of 1,718.62 points to win the championship. A large part of the credit for the Swiss victory was due to the two star individual performers, Miez and Hanggi, who finished first and second in the individual all-round competition. Miez had a total of 247 points to take first place, while Hanggi was close behind with 246.62 points.

The Americans had a total of 1,519.12 points in the team competition, but none of them managed to place in the invididual contest.

M'ARTHUR DEFENDS FOOD SERVED ON SHIP

Says It Was Selected for Athletes by Dietitian—General Calls U. S. Triumph Brilliant.

Special to The New York Times.

WASHINGTON, Aug. 10.—Major Gen. Douglas MacArthur, President of the American Olympic Committee, in a cable from Amsterdam today to T. V. O'Connor, Chairman of the United States Shipping Board, denied charges in British and American newspapers of American failure at the Olympic Games and improper training of the athletes, with particular reference to the food served on the board's steamer, President Roosevelt.

"The American athletes," General MacArthur said, "not only have not failed, but have achieved a brilliant success comparable to those of past Olympics. Guests who were entertained on board the Roosevelt were served the same fare always served to passengers. The athletes had a specially prepared menu prescribed by the dietitian who accompanied the team to Amsterdam.

"The standard of living on American ships is very high—much higher than on competing lines, perhaps. However, this is not a matter of reproach, but one of gratification."

RAIN PUTS OFF BIKE RACES.

Cup Match at Velodrome Will Be Held Next Week.

Rain last night caused the postponement of the bicycle races at the New York Velodrome, and the feature race, which was a 30-mile motor-paced event for the Eddie Leonard Cup, will be held sometime next week.

There will be three feature races on the card for tomorrow night, which will include a 30-mile motor-paced championship, a one-mile team match and a four-cornered match.

Times Wide World Photo.

University of California Crew, Which Won Olympic Title Yesterday by Defeating British Oarsmen.
Left to Right—Marvin Stadler, Bow; John Brinck, No. 2; Francis Frederick, No. 3; William Thompson, No. 4; William Dally, No. 5; James Workman, No. 6; Hubert Caldwell, No. 7; Peter Donlon, Stroke, and Donald Blessing, Coxswain.

CALIFORNIA'S EIGHT WINS OLYMPIC TITLE

By WYTHE WILLIAMS.

Continued from Page 1, Column 1.

tom of all winning crews—namely, ducking their coxswain. Blessing's late galley slaves now became his genial playmates, who gathered him unto themselves and with words of encouragement—such as they hoped he would drown—tossed him almost to the middle of the canal.

An easy victory for America in the double sculls, followed by the triumph of the Californians, made America the winner of the regatta by five points over England, which finished second.

The single sculls, as was expected, resulted in a comparatively easy victory for Bobby Pearce, the Australian giant, over the American, Ken Myers. But as Henry Penn Burke, American team manager, remarked at the end of the race, "This Pearce is not a human being. He should be permitted to race only against motorboats."

Undoubtedly today's performance stamps the Australian as the greatest living oarsman and, as Burke also remarked, Australia, having only one man in the entire regatta, did remarkably well.

California's victory in the eight-oared event kept the Olympic crown for the United States, as the Naval Academy triumphed at Antwerp in 1920 and Yale came home in front in the 1924 regatta in Paris.

Score a Great Victory.

SLOTEN, Holland, Aug. 10 (AP).— California's Golden Bears are now champions of the world. Their blue-tipped oars flashing irrestible power through the narrow waters of the Sloten Canal this afternoon, these brawny native sons of Uncle Sam maintained their unbeaten record and brought the Olympic regatta to a thrilling climax by beating the Thames Rowing Club, Britain's greatest crew, in the eight-oared final.

California's great victory in the final event, following the triumph of the Yankee double scull combination of Charles McIlvaine and Paul Costello over Canada, the latter figuring in his third successive Olympic triumph, saved the day for America. They came after the American single sculling hope, Ken Myers, had been decisively whipped by the 22-year-old Australian marvel, Bobby Pearce, by five lengths, and the Yankee four without coxswain had lost a heart-breaking race to the British four by a bare half-length.

The United States, the only nation winning two events in the seven finals contested, plus a brace of second places and one third which was g ed in the pairs without coxswain, totaled 17 points on a 5—3—1 basis. Britain finished second with 12. Switzerland third with 8, Italy, 6; Germany and Australia each 5; Canada, 4; France, 3; Austria, Belgium and Poland, 1 each.

A crowd of perhaps 10,000 lining the picturesque Sloten banks anticipated the biggest thrill in the eight-oared final, pitting the youthful Yankeen crew from the Golden West against the seasoned British array, and they weren't disappointed.

Stirring Race Is Staged.

From the start until the Americans swept under the finish line amid a din of old-fashioned Yankee cheers, it was a race to quicken pulses. Except for the first 100 meters, when the British got a slight jump, the Californians led all the way, but at no stage was their margin quite a full length nor at any time, except in the last furlong, was the result an apparent certainty. Youthful power and drive and an unconquerable spirit such as they have displayed in all their races this season enabled the Golden Bears to beat the more experienced Britons—a powerful array individually, but lacking the finishing punch in their strokes.

The Californians had the power to overcome a rather poor start and take a commanding lead. Under the vocal lashing of their coxswain, Don Blessing, and the impetuous stroking of Pete Donlon, they had the reserve to withstand a great British challenge in the last half of the race.

The race was won in the first 1,000 meters but saved in the last 1,000, as both put everything into their stroking without their relative positions changing more than six feet at any time.

Blessing did not wave the dirty towel which has been California's battle signal in most of its previous close finishes, but the coxswain beat the sides of "the Golden Gate" ever faster with the tiller handles as he yelled for a higher and higher stroke. Donlon and his mates responded with probably the fastest racing beat they have ever maintained, going up to 40 per minute at the start of the last 500 meters and finishing at 42.

The Californians' time of 6 minutes 3 1-5 seconds was slightly slower than their best mark for the course, 6:02, but today's performance under less favorable conditions represented the fastest race they have rowed. The Britons were clocked at 6:05 4-5.

Ducks Cruise Along Canal.

The Bears thus put the finishing touches to a triumphant campaign which began last April at Seattle and ended in a colorful Holland setting, where the regatta excitement did not disturb the farmers' work or prevent a flock of ducks from cruising their usual course in the path of the oarsmen.

Ky Ebright's broad-backed stalwarts finished the tenth and last race as impressively as the first. They beat all college rivals at home in five races from 2,000 meters to four miles. At the sprint route they won five more races here to establish world supremacy in the field of seventeen countries.

Sloten course records were broken in three of the seven events, while the United States broke even against British Empire competition in four finals.

The Australian, Pearce, won the world's sculling title impressively. He started as favorite, but a five-length margin over Myers was unexpected. The American battled gamely to hold his rangy rival in the first half, but tired and was decisively whipped in the last 1,000 meters.

The American doubles scullers, the veteran Costello and McIlvaine, not only outclassed the Canadians, Wright and Guest, but broke their own course record by winning in 6:41 2-5. Their previous mark was 6:43 4-5.

The Penn Barge Club four without coxswain lost to the British in the most exciting finish. The Americans led for 500 meters, but were unable to stand the spurt of the British quartet from Trinity College, Cambridge, who won by a single second, barely half a length.

Switzerland, Germany and Italy divided the remainder of the regatta honors. The blue-shirted Fascist four with coxswain swamped the Swiss by seven lengths. The Germans conquered the British pair without coxswain by one length, and the Swiss defeated the French pair with coxswain by two and a half lengths in two other record-breaking races. The Germans were clocked at 7:06 2-5, beating the best previous time of 7:12, while the Swiss, in 7:42 3-5, eclipsed the former record of 7:46 4-5.

Fine Weather for Races.

Fine weather prevailed for today's finals of the regatta and the village was gaily decorated. A stiff breeze was blowing down the course, giving promise of improving the oarsmen's times.

Heats for third race positions in the regatta preceded the seven big races for the Olympic titles. The American contingent got off to a good start in the pair oared shells without coxswain, taking third place honors from the Italian crew. John Schmitt and Paul McDowell, the American pair, led from the start and won by 2½ lengths. Their time was 7 minutes 20 2-5 seconds while that of the Italian pair was 7 minutes 24 4-5 seconds.

In the final for pairs with coxswain the Swiss Schochlin brothers beat the French Marcelle brothers by two lengths in 7:42 3-5. This reversed the outcome of the meeting of these same crews just a week ago, when the French won by a foot.

It was the Thames Rowing Club that the California eight beat to take the title. The Bears took the lead early in the race and held it practically all the way. At 250 meters the prows were level, with both eights hitting a high beat. At 500 the Californians were a quarter of a length ahead and the margin was slightly more than this at 1,000 meters, the half way point.

At 1,500 the Golden Bears led by one length and the furious British stretch drive could get back only half of this.

Italy won the first of the seven championships when it defeated Switzerland by seven lengths in the four-oared shells with coxswain, while Germany took the second championship in the pair-oared shells without coxxswain, defeating Great Britain.

The Italian victory in the four-oared shells with coxswain aroused tremendous enthusiasm. The blue-shirted crew outclassed its rivals and finished fresh. The men gave the Fascist salute from their shell and then paddled to the judges' platform with their arms so extended in salute. There they received a big wreath of flowers and the laurel wreath emblematic of their championship.

In the pairs without coxswain the brawny German pair, Kurt Moeschter and Bruno Muller, who eliminated the American crew in this event, led the British pair, O'Brien and Nisbet all the way, winning by a length. The Germans' time was 7 minutes 6 2-5 seconds and the British time was 7 minutes 8 4-5 seconds.

A big German delegation lined the canal banks and went wild, cheering and waving German flags as their compatriots received the laurel wreath, while the bands struck up the German national anthem.

Britain won by half a length in the four without coxswain championship final, being timed at 6 minutes 36 seconds, to the Americans' 6:37.

The Cambridge collegians came from behind to win in a desperate race. After the Americans had led by nearly a length at the halfway point, the British spurted and cut the lead to a half length at 1,250 meters, then nosing up to even terms at 1,500 and forging ahead in the last quarter of the course.

The Trinity College (Cambridge) boys clung to their advantage in a thrilling stretch drive, despite the supreme efforts of the Americans, who, exhausted, keeled over in their shell at the finish. The British likewise were about rowed out, but appeared slightly the fresher.

The American double scullers, Paul Costello and Charles McIlvaine, arrayed against Joe Wright Jr. and Guest, scored a surprise largely because of the decisive fashion in which they won. The Canadians were rowed out completely after the race. Wright said he had rowed his hardest, but could not get any speed out of the shell. Near the halfway mark the Canadian shell seemed to lose life, while the Americans were sculling in great style.

CALIFORNIA LAUDS COACH.

Ebright Met Many Setbacks Before Having a Winning Crew.

SAN FRANCISCO, Aug. 10 (AP).— An unwritten chronology built on faith, perseverance and the habit of taking the knocks and coming up smiling is the real story behind the tremendous triumphs of the University of California crew, Olympic champion.

Just after the war rowing was revived at California. One race after another ended the same way—with the Bears hopelessly outclassed.

Coach Ebright, of slight build and shy, came to Berkeley in 1923. He had been a good coxswain on earlier University of Washington crews. The situation at California was enough to make any veteran coach throw up his hands. The newcomer said nothing, but "pulled off his coat" and went to work. A new system of rowing was introduced. It was founded on the Connibear style, evolved by Hiram Connibear at Washington and now generally used throughout the country.

To the system originated by his former coach Ebright added some of his own technique, one departure being to lengthen the stroke. No new system can be developed in one season. In 1924 his crew lost to Washington by eight lengths. It was a stunning blow to all. The next year brought even more disastrous results and California trailed Washington by eleven lengths.

When 1926 rolled around the gloom was thick, but California surprised by cutting down the margin of the winning crew.

The 1927 outlook was better and Ebright found himself basking in the sunlight of favor. California defeated Washington for the first time in six years and at Poughkeepsie the Blue and Gold shell placed third.

The 1928 curtain rolled up on a new and brilliant period. California's performances this season are engraved permanently in bold letters in the book of records. And Ebright, the slim chap who wouldn't quit, shares honors with the finest oarsmen California has ever produced.

TEN IN ROW FOR CALIFORNIA.

Olympic Champions Have Not Met Defeat This Season.

California's Olympic championship rowing victory over England in the eight-oared final was the tenth straight triumph for the great young college crew from Berkeley this season, The Associated Press reports.

Here is the Golden Bears' record, which shows not a single defeat:

IN UNITED STATES.

Defeated University of Washington by one-half length at three miles, Lake Washington, Seattle.

Defeated Columbia (three-fourths length), Washington, Cornell, Navy, Syracuse and Pennsylvania at four miles at Poughkeepsie.

Defeated Princeton by one-half length, Columbia by one-half length and Yale by one-quarter length in separate 2,000-meter races in Olympic trials, Philadelphia.

AT OLYMPIC GAMES.

Defeated Belgium by eight lengths, Denmark by three lengths, Italy by four lengths, Canada by one-half length and England by three-quarters length in 2,000-meter races on Sloten Canal.

Many Countries Are Pledged to Compete In 1932 Games, Says Garland of Los Angeles

Special Cable to THE NEW YORK TIMES.

AMSTERDAM, Holland, Aug. 10.— William M. Garland of Los Angeles, one of the American members of the International Olympic Committee and Chairman of the American committee for the tenth games, to be held in his home city, has been in Amsterdam throughout the present games trying to get the promise of sufficient cooperation for the 1932 events to assure it being a world competition instead of merely an all-American meeting.

There has been much doubt on this side of the water whether, on account of the length of the trip, many European teams will be able to compete. Garland said: "I am now greatly pleased with the assurances of my colleages, both in Europe and the Far East, as to a big attendance at the Los Angeles games. Realizing the honor and responsibility placed upon her, Los Angeles already has made great preparations.

"The major structures and facilities for the games, costing more than $2,000,000, are completed and the preliminary financing is definitely under way.

"The Olympic idea is steadily progressing as a great world institution along friendly, constructive lines through the increased understanding and confidence among nations in sports. Amsterdam has crowned with success her work in holding the games. America now has her opportunity.

"The tenth games must be made great, and thus America will deserve and win the praise of all nations. Los Angeles looks forward confidently to receiving the sincere help of all persons and organizations in America having to do authoritatively with the athletics that comprise the modern world Olympic Games.

"Such cooperation will have a friendly, appreciative response in Los Angeles, where the main burden will be shouldered."

KELLY PRAISES COSTELLO.

Partner in 1920 and 1924 Insisted He Enter Olympics Again.

Special to The New York Times.

PHILADELPHIA, Aug. 10.—"I'm glad that Paul came through with his third Olympic rowing title, said Jack Kelly, his cousin and 1920 and 1924 Olympic doubles champion partner, when he learned the Penn A. C. veteran and Charles McIlvaine had won at Amsterdam.

"For more than two years I have been after him to go out and beat those fellows. I do not know if Costello will retire after this, but I will be greatly surprised if he does not hang up his oars, except when he rows for exercise."

It is generally understood Bob Pearce's victory over Ken Myers in the single sculls will carry with it the Philadelphia Gold Challenge Cup, emblematic of the world's sculls title. The cup is locked in a bank vault in this city.

TROEH AND TOMLIN TIE IN MARSHALL SHOOT

Each Breaks 148 Out of 150 at Yorklyn Traps—Miss Crothers Leads Women.

Special to The New York Times.

YORKLYN, Del., Aug. 10.—Breaking 148 out of 150 targets, Frank M. Troeh of Portland, Ore., the former national amateur target champion, was deadlocked with Fred H. Tomlin, the national professional titleholder, for high gun honors in the final event of the third day of the T. Clarence Marshall eighth annual registered trap shooting classic here over the hill-top traps of the Yorklyn Gun Club today.

Harry E. Johnson, Haines City, Fla., divided runner-up honors with D. T. Hackett of Atlantic City, each with 147, while Dr. W. G. Cook of Findlay, Ohio, and A. A. Armour of Rising Sun, Md., tied at 146 for third honors.

Of the women entered, Miss Alice M. Crothers, daughter of S. Morris Crothers of Chestnut Hill, Pa., the international titleholder, led with 141 with Mrs. J. S. Murphy of Freehold, the Jersey women's amateur champion, second with 137 and Mrs. Louis R. Slocum of Trenton, N. J., third with 126.

In the award of the class trophies, Troeh led in Class A with Johnson second and Hackett third.

Armour won the honors in Class B while in Class C, Josephs Carr, Freehold, N. J., was first with 145. Howard Brice, Wilmington, won the Class D first prize with 142.

Of the professionals competing, Fred S. Tomlin won the trophy with 148 targets. In the T. Clarence Marshall double target event, Samuel S. Vanzandt of Harrisburg, Mark Arie of Champaign, Ill., the 1920 Olympic amateur titleholder, and Lawrence D. Willis, Wilmington, divided the honors, smashing 45 out of 50 each. In the shoot-off Vanzandt won with Arie second.

GIRL SWIMS CHESAPEAKE.

Lillian Cannon Clips Four Hours From Record for Twelve Miles.

BALTIMORE, Aug. 10 (AP).—Mrs. Edwin M. Day, known in swimming circles as Lillian Cannon, clipped more than four hours from the record for swimming across Chesapeake Bay by winning a race with Clyde Brown in which she made the twelve miles in 5 hours and 25 minutes. Brown, a swimming instructor here, finished six minutes later.

The start was made from Tolchester at 5:05 A. M., and Mrs. Day finished at Bay Shore, near here, at 10:30 A. M. The former record was made two years ago by Laura Louise Calligan, who covered the distance in 9 hours and 40 minutes, to beat the time established by Mrs. Day when she was the first woman to swim the bay.

Silvers Boxes Alger Tonight.

Pal Silvers will meet Billy Alger in the feature six-round bout at the Ridgewood Grove Sporting Club, Brooklyn, tonight. Alger, who comes from the Pacific Coast, has a two-round knockout victory over Ruby Goldstein to his credit. Four more six-rounders and two four-rounders will complete the card.

Rain Halts Rockaway Boxing.

Rain caused the postponement of the boxing program scheduled for the Rockaway's Playland Stadium last night. The card will be held next Friday, with Tommy Jones and Billy Drako engaging in the feature ten-rounder.

Thompson Stops Eddie Dempsey.

CHICAGO, Aug. 10 (AP).—Young Jack Thompson, Pacific Coast welterweight, knocked out Eddie Dempsey of Philadelphia in the fourth round of their scheduled ten-round bout at Englewood Celtic Field here tonight.

MacArthur Highly Excited As California Eight Wins

SLOTEN, Holland, Aug. 10 (AP).— Douglas MacArthur, the Major General who commands the American Olympic forces, was probably more excited than any of the other spectators who watched the spectacular victory of the California crew for America in the Olympic eight-oared final today. The General, sitting on the lowered tonneau of his special automobile, pounded The Associated Press correspondent's back as he alternately yelled at the coxswain, "Come on, Don. Give it to 'em," or to the stroke, "Raise it, Pete. Raise that stroke. Come on, boy. That's the stuff."

U. S. OLYMPIC STARS FACE BRITISH TODAY

50,000 Are Expected to See Meet at Stamford Bridge— New Records Awaited.

CHANCES ARE CALLED EVEN

English Critics Concede Four Field Events to Americans—U. S. Team in Fine Condition.

By J. S. MacCORMAC.

Wireless to THE NEW YORK TIMES.

LONDON, Aug. 10.—The American Olympic team arrived at the Liverpool Street Station today from Amsterdam by special train and will engage in a meet at Stamford Bridge tomorrow with athletes representing the whole British Empire.

Lawson Robertson, United States head coach, said the team did not expect to score so decisive a victory as it did four years ago when only three of the fourteen events were won by the British Empire. He anticipated American successes, however, in all the field events with the exception of the javelin throw.

Major P. J. Walsh, manager of the United States squad, declared that talk about the American team being overfed on the boat coming over was "absolute rot." He said the team was in the best condition, but the results proved that other nations were beginning to produce splendid athletes.

British Concede 4 Field Events.

British experts predict American victories in four of the six field events. The American team in each case will include an Olympic winner, and as Dr. Pat O'Callaghan, Irish winner of the hammer throw at Amsterdam, will be unable to represent the British Empire, a United States victory in this event also is expected.

In the javelin throw with S. A. Lay, New Zealander, who holds the record, and C. G. Weightman-Smith, South Africa, who can throw the javelin over 200 feet, the Empire's chances are considered brighter. On the track the American team for the relay race has been weakened by an injury to Charley Borah, and it is thought that the speed of the Empire runners will more than counterbalance the American superiority in baton changing.

An Empire victory is also thought probable in the 480-yard hurdles relay with a team consisting of S. J. M. Atkinson, Olympic champion; Lord Burghley, Olympic 400-meter hurdles champion; F. R. Gady and G. C. Weightman-Smith. The British runners in the eight-lap steeplechase medley relay and the three-mile team race also form strong combinations, but the American prospects in the one-mile, two-mile and four-mile relays are brighter.

Crowd of 50,000 Expected.

LONDON, Aug. 10 (AP).—With an attendance of 50,000 looked for and with international track and field interest shifted from Amsterdam, the meet between Olympic stars of the British Empire and the United States promises to be the most important athletic contest yet held in England.

Competition is expected to be of an extremely high standard and several new records are awaited.

The rival teams shape up about evenly, according to British sports writers, who freely grant the Americans a certainty of winning five of the fourteen events, all of these in the field, and claim victories in the majority of the track contests. Field events will be calculated on the basis of team averages, which gives America an advantage since the American team includes not only most of the Olympic champions but many of the seconds and thirds.

In the 440-yard relay the Americans are using the team which won in record time at Amsterdam and they also are banking heavily on the running of Ray Barbuti, 400-meter champion, and the only American Olympic winner on the track. One of the finest races is expected to be the 440-yard hurdles, in which all six Olympic finalists including Lord David Burghley, the winner, are participating.

TAILTEANN GAMES WILL BEGIN TODAY

Four Former Irish World Champions to March in Dublin Parade —U. S. Hurlers Play Tomorrow.

DUBLIN, Aug. 10 (AP).—Two small boys in old Irish costumes leading two Irish wolfhounds will head the procession opening the Tailteann games tomorrow, which will last a fortnight. Four Irish world champions of the past—T. F. Kiely, Peter O'Connor, P. J. Ryan and J. J. Flanagan—will be in the parade

J. J. Walsh, director of the games and formerly Postmaster-General of the Free State, will direct the opening ceremony at Croke Park

A picked Irish hurling team will play the United States hurlers Sunday. On Wednesday the international athletic contests begin, for which entries have been received from the United States, South Africa, Australia, Canada, New Zealand, England, Scotland and Wales.

Walsh was greatly disappointed tonight because the American entries apparently will not appear. Irish-Americans, he said, failed to subscribe to bring over their atheltes.

WEISSMULLER SETS NEW OLYMPIC MARK

Wins 100-Meter Free Style Semi-Final in 0:58 3-5—Kojac, Laufer Also Gain Final.

GIRL SWIMMERS ADVANCE

Three U. S. Entrants Reach Finals In 100-Meter Backstroke and Also in 100-Meter Free Style.

AMSTERDAM, Holland, Aug. 10 (AP).—All American athletes, both women and men, with but one exception, survived the final round of trials and eliminations today in the Olympic water sports carnival.

While Miss Clarita Huntzberger, California girl diver from Los Angeles, was eliminated by gaining only a sixth place in the second division of the high diving trials, Johnny Weissmuller, Chicago speedster and defending champion in the 100-meter free-style, set a new Olympic record in the semi-finals of that event. Weissmuller, ace of the American swimming forces, flashed over his favorite distance with huge, space-devouring strokes in 58 3-5 seconds.

Barany, Hungarian, who finished second, gave the American speed king a fight through every inch of the first fifty meters, making the turn with him on even terms. Weissmuller forged ahead with a tremendous burst of speed in the final thirty meters, flailing the water with mighty strokes.

With Weissmuller in the final tomorrow will be George Kojac, the New York schoolboy who won both his preliminary and semi-final heats easily today, and Walter Laufer of Chicago, victor in the morning event but a good second to the Japanese, Takaishi, in his semi-final. Laufer swam faster trailing the Far Easterner than Kojac did in winning his event.

Kojac Outspeeds Zorrilla.

Kojac raced the Argentinian, Zorrilla, 400-meter Olympic champion, to a standstill in the second elimination heat of the 100-meter free-style. The experts believe that Zorrilla, doing too much swimming, was unable to display his best form. He had no sprint left at the close.

Less impressively, the girls of the United States swimming team kept pace with their sturdier brothers. Miss Eleanor Holm, New York schoolgirl, won her heat in the 100-meter backstroke for women and Miss Lisa Lindstrom, even younger along with Miss Marion Gilman of Alameda, Cal., both gained second places to land in the final.

Miss Marie Braun, Dutch star stole most of the applause and left America with little hope of final victory when she stroked this distance in 1 minute 21 3-5 seconds, a new Olympic record. Later Miss King of England did 1:21 flat, lowering Miss Braun's new record.

Victory in the men's 100-meter dash already is conceded Weissmuller with Laufer and Kojac likely to complete the first three names on the board. Zorrilla, the Argentinian, who won the 400-meter championship in spectacular style yesterday; Takaishi the Japanese, and Barany of Hungary, other finalists, appear only as dangerous contenders to Laufer and Kojac. They hold little threat to Weissmuller's supremacy.

Arne Borg, Swedish champion, who came to grief yesterday, losing to Zorrilla and Charlton of Australia in the 400-meter finals, was scratched from the second heat of the 100 meters in which he was scheduled to start. The official reason given was that he was stale.

Withdrawal Causes Talk.

Swimming pool devotees and others said that Borg was none too eager to try conclusions with Weissmuller and risk a second defeat.

In Swedish circles there has been much comment of Weissmuller's being scratched in the 400 meters, and hints were broadly expressed that the American feared Borg.

Weissmuller was being quoted as having promised to give "Mr. Borg a little medicine in the 100 meters."

Weissmuller swam with such apparent carefreeness in his heat that some spectators interpreted his attitude as contemptuous. After permitting Spence, who was swimming in the adjacent lane, to remain head to head with him for seventy-five meters, the American put on a little spurt at the finish and won by about a yard.

Three American women entered in the 100-yard free-style advanced in easy fashion. Miss Albina Osipowich of Worcester, Mass., the girl Weissmuller of the team, is the brightest American hope in this event. Miss Osipowich equaled Ethel Lackie's Olympic record of 1:12 2-5 to defeat Miss Miller of New Zealand.

Miss Eleanor Garratti of San Rafael, Cal., won her heat in 1:14 4 with little opposition, and Miss Susan Laird of Homestead, Pa., swam second to Miss McDowell of Great Britain in her heat. Miss Laird's time was 1:14 1-5. Miss Russell of South Africa, Fräulein Lehmann of Germany, Miss Olsen of Denmark and Miss McDowell will oppose the Americans tomorrow.

Mrs. Betty Pinkston of Detroit led all the qualifiers in the high diving competition with 32.6 points. Miss Georgia Coleman of Los Angeles was second in her division with 31.40 and Miss Onnela of Finland third with 28 points.

Miss Huntzberger was eliminated in the second half of the diving trials when she finished last. The qualifiers were: Miss Sjokviat of Sweden, 29.20 points; Miss Baron, Holland, 28.40 points, and Fräulein Rehborn of Germany, 28.20.

Final tabulation gave the United States eighth place in the water polo series. France defeated the Argentine squad, 8 to 0, to capture third place.

BOYS' CLUB CABLES KOJAC.

Congratulates Swimmer on Feat Breaking Olympic Mark.

Following a meeting of the Executive Committee of the Boys' Club of New York at the clubhouse, Tenth Street and Avenue A, yesterday, the following cablegram was sent to George Kojac, who broke the world record for the 100-meter backstroke in winning that event at the Olympics on Thursday.

"Heartiest congratulations on your magnificent accomplishment."

Kojac, who is 19 years old, has been a member of the Boys' Club since he has 8, and it was in the pool of the clubhouse that he learned to swim. He has represented the club for several years.

Riegels's 60-Yard Run Toward Wrong Goal Helps Georgia Tech Win on Coast, 8-7

CALIFORNIA BEATEN BY GEORGIA TECH, 8-7

60-Yard Run Toward Wrong Goal by Riegels of California Helps Tech Win Before 70,000.

OWN MAN STOPS HIS DASH

But Georgians Tackle Him on 3-Yard Line and Maree Blocks Kick for Safety.

TOUCHDOWN FOR THOMASON

Goes Over in Third Quarter on 15-Yard Gallop—Losers March 98 Yards to Tally in 4th.

Special to The New York Times.

PASADENA, Cal., Jan. 1.—In a thrilling football game before a capacity crowd of 70,000 in the Rose Bowl here today, the Golden Tornado of Georgia Tech defeated the University of California football team by a score of 8 to 7, the victors scoring on a safety and a touchdown. The Western eleven tallied in the fourth quarter after a straight march from its own 2-yard line.

The game was marked by an unusual play, which, it ultimately developed, was of great importance in the final score. It led to Georgia Tech's safety. Captain-elect Riegels of the Golden Bears, playing centre, snatched up a Tech fumble in the second quarter and started toward the Georgia Tech goal. There had been no scoring thus far in the contest and Riegels broke into a dead run.

Tech men sprang up in front of him and in eluding them he cut back across the field. He turned again to escape the opposition and in so doing apparently became confused and started down the field to his own goal, 60 yards away. As he pounded down the side line both California and Tech players stood amazed in their tracks.

Lom Pursues Him.

Benny Lom, halfback for the Golden Bears, sensed the situation almost immediately and sprang into action. Down the field he went after the flying Riegels, who only put on more speed as he heard feet pounding the turf behind him. Finally Lom grabbed hold of his mate at the California 3-yard line and turned him around. Making interference for Riegels, Lom started back down the field, but Tech was alert and a wave of tacklers hit Riegels before he could more than turn around, hurtling him back to the 1-yard line.

California immediately took up the punt formation, but Riegels, at centre, was nervous, and Lom, receiving the ball to kick, was little steadier. As the ball was snapped, Maree, Georgia Tech tackle, stormed through the line and blocked the punt. The ball rolled out of the end zone, but the officials ruled that Breckenridge, California quarterback, had touched it and that a safety would be scored against California.

The annual New Year's Day classic was played under an azure blue sky, with the thermometer standing at 80 degrees and the great crowd in holiday spirit, cheering both teams and the brilliant plays.

Tech's touchdown came in the third period. Shortly after the start of the second half, Lom got off a 60-yard punt that went to Tech's 23-yard line. Mizell punted back and Breckenridge fumbled. Waddey, Tech end, recovered on the Bear 27-yard line.

Jones Blocks Bears' Kick.

Mizell fumbled on the first play and Fitz, California tackle, recovered on the Bear 29-yard line. Lom made half a yard on the first play and on the next Jones broke through to block his kick and recovered the ball on the California 9-yard line.

Four times, Tech smashed the line and wound up just a foot shy of a touchdown. Lom retreated behind his goal line and punted to Thomason, who was downed in his tracks on the California 45-yard line. Mizell blazed around right end for thirty yards to the 15-yard line. On the next play Thomason went through tackle, reversed his field and went over the goal line standing up for a touchdown. As the try for point was missed the score became 8 to 0.

The Bears did not get their passing attack organized until the closing minutes of the final quarter and with just one and a half minutes to play, Captain Irving Phillips took a pass from Lom for a touchdown.

The Bears had advanced the ball from their 2-yard mark, Lom hurling long and accurate passes to Phillips and Eisan in the 98-yard march for the touchdown. Barr kicked goal, making the score 8 to 7.

The contest was marked by an unusual number of breaks in addition to Riegel's dash for his own goal. There also were several fumbles of consequence as in the first quarter when Lom threw a forty-yard pass to Barr, who dropped the ball while standing, all alone on the Tech goal line.

Lom Is Called Back.

Then in the second quarter Lom scooped up a fumble and raced sixty yards to the Tech goal, only to have the ball called back, Referee Dana ruling he had blown his whistle before the fumble.

In the third quarter, Breckenridge fumbled a punt, Waddey recovering for Tech on the California 27-yard line. Mizell fumbled the ball right back into California's possession, only to have Jones block Lom's kick on the 9-yard line, which ultimately led to Tech's touchdown.

In the same quarter Captain Phillips hurled a 40-yard pass to Eisan on a reverse play, only to have the Bear quarterback stumble and fall just as he was about to catch the ball deep in Tech territory.

The fourth quarter saw Rice, racing after another perfect pass from Lom, with a clear field ahead of him, stumble and fall. Eisan took another pass from Lom, took two steps and fumbled, Lumpkin recovering for Tech on the Engineers' 45-yard line.

However, there were shining lights aplenty in the contest. The two rival captains were in brilliant form. Captain Peter Pund was a tower of strength in Tech's hard battling forward wall and Phillips was a hero in defeat at end for the Bears. Warner Mizell and Stumpy Thomason of Tech turned in several sensational dashes. Thomason's runbacks of punts, when he managed to escape Phillips and Avery, were spectacular.

Lom was the outstanding hero for the losers. He played smart football, was in every play and carried the ball on sweeping end runs with dash and vigor. He shot through tackle and over guard, hurled long passes to the ends, or short, snappy passes behind the line of scrimmage to the other backs. His kicking was excellent.

Jones, at end, and Maree, at tackle, were equally good with Pund in the Tech line. Likewise, Steve Bancroft, the bulky Bear tackle, played a rousing game.

How Georgia Tech-California Lined Up for Football Game

Georgia T. (8).		California (7).
Waddey	L.E.	Avery
Maree	L.T.	Fitz
Drennon	L.G.	H. Gill
Pund	C.	Riegels
Westbrook	R.G.	Schwarz
Thrash	R.T.	Bancroft
Jones	R.E.	Phillips
Schulman	Q.B.	Breckenridge
Thomason	L.H.	Lom
Mizell	R.H.	Barr
Lumpkin	F.B.	Schmidt

Score by Periods.

Georgia Tech	0	2	6	0—8
California	0	0	0	7—7

Scoring.

Touchdowns—Thomason, Phillips. Point after touchdown—Barr. Safety—By Georgia Tech on California.

Substitutions.

California—Miller for Riegels, Schlicting for Barr C. Handy for Schwarz, Cockburn for Schmidt, Rice for Schlicting, Norton for Avery, Riegels for Miller, Breckenridge for Eisan, Beckett for Gill.

Georgia Tech—Durant for Schulman, Dunlap for Mizell, Watkins for Maree, Holland for Jones.

Officials.

Referee—Herbert Dana. Umpire—Arthur Badenoch. Linesman—T. M. Fitzpatrick. Field judge—William Streit.

STORY OF THE GAME TOLD PLAY BY PLAY

Detailed Account Shows How the Georgia Tech Football Team Conquered California.

PASADENA, Cal., Jan. 1 (AP).—The following is the play-by-play account of the football game here today between Georgia Tech and California:

FIRST PERIOD.

Captain Pund of Georgia Tech and Phillips of California, a couple of giants, met in midfield with a hearty handclasp as Referee Dana spun a coin for the toss. Phillips was lucky and called the turn. He chose to receive, defending the south goal.

Waddey kicked off, Schmidt receiving and coming back fifteen yards to California's 34-yard line. Barr hit centre for a yard and Lom brought the crowd up cheering with a 37-yard dash after a fake punt. He was downed on Tech's 27-yard line.

Barr made three yards on two plunges. Lom picked left tackle for three yards. Tech regained the ball on the next play when Barr was rushed on a fake place kick and was thrown for a 10-yard loss.

Mizell hit the line for a yard but Tech was penalized five on the next play for having the back field in motion. Mizell kicked and Breckenridge was dropped in his tracks on his 41-yard line.

Barr slashed off four yards at left tackle. Schmidt hit centre for two yards and a 5-yard penalty against Tech for offside gave the Bears first down on Tech's 48-yard line. Lom ripped off six yards at right tackle, was held for no gain on another try and Schmidt added two at centre. Lom kicked, the ball going out of bounds on Tech's 16-yard line.

Thomason made a yard and Mizell punted on the next play. Breckenridge was tackled by Waddey on the 49-yard line. Maree broke through to drop Barr for a 5-yard loss and Lom punted on the next play. Thomason was dropped on Tech's 18-yard line. Tech rooters had a chance to cheer, and did, when Mizell broke loose and ran 33 yards. He was downed on California's 49-yard line.

Lumpkin hit guard for 3 yards and Mizell added 6 at right end. Thomason made it first down on California's 37-yard line. Lumpkin was held for no gain, but Mizell swept around right end for 5 yards. The Bears took the ball on their own 37-yard line when Thomason fumbled and Barr recovered.

Barr hit centre for a yard and added 7 more at left tackle. Schmidt hit centre for a yard as the first period ended.

SECOND PERIOD.

Lom kicked, the ball going out of bounds on Tech's 30-yard line. Mizell went off tackle for 3 yards and Lumpkin chalked up 2 more at centre. Mizell punted to Breckenridge, who returned 3 yards, stopping on California's 49-yard line.

Barr found a hole at right tackle for a yard and Schmidt added two at centre. The Bears made it first down on Tech's 40-yard line when Lom made a short pass to Breckenridge.

The Bears lost five yards for taking too much time out. The Bears made another first down when the officials allowed Lom's pass to Avery, after Shulman, Tech quarter, had interfered with the receiver. It put the ball on Tech's 30-yard line.

Tech recovered the ball on downs after the Bears had rolled up five yards on two line plunges but failed to complete a pass, Lom to Barr, on the fourth down.

Tech went into action on its own 25-yard line. Thomason fumbled and Riegels, centre and captain-elect of the Bears, snatched up the ball and after starting for Tech's goal, suddenly reversed and ran sixty yards to within three yards of his own goal line.

Tech scored a safety on the next play when Lom's attempted kick from behind his goal line was blocked and Barr fell on the ball, making the score, Georgia Tech 2, U. C. 0.

Miller replaced Riegels at centre and Schlicting went in for Barr at right half in the Bear line-up.

Lom kicked from his 20-yard line to put the ball into play. Tech was penalized 15 yards, putting the ball on its own 40-yard line. Lumpkin hit guard for four yards and Mizell kicked, Breckenbridge making a fair catch on the Bear 16-yard line.

Lom kicked after the catch and Lumpkin returned to Tech's 45-yard line. Thomason skirted right end for nine yards, stopping on California's 46-yard line. Dunlap replaced Mizell at Tech's left half. Lumpkin made it first down on California's 44-yard line. Dunlap went around right end for 3 yards and passed to Jones on the next play for a 22-yard gain. It put the ball on California's 14-yard line.

Tech was penalized 5 yards for offside. Cockburn replaced Schmidt at fullback for the Bears.

Durant, who replaced Shulman at quarterback for Tech, was thrown for a 15-yard loss, putting the ball on the 29-yard line. Dunlap's pass was incompleted and he failed to gain at right end. Dunlap's pass fell incompleted in the end zone and the Bears took the ball on their own 20-yard line.

Rice, replacing Schlicting at right half, made three yards. Eisan went in for Breckenridge at quarter. Dunlap gave the crowd a thrill with a 30-yard run back of Lom's kick. Cockburn upset the little Tech man on California's 40-yard line.

California was penalized five yards for taking too much time out. Then California hopes rose to the sky, only to be dropped to earth with a thud when Lom picked up a fumble, ran sixty-eight yards to a supposed touchdown and was called back because the ball had been ruled dead.

Thomason punted out of bounds on California's 22-yard line. Lom skirted end for thirteen yards as the second period ended. The score was Georgia Tech 2, U. C. 0.

THIRD PERIOD.

Lom took Waddey's kick-off on California's 2-yard line and ran it back 20 yards. Riegels was back at centre. Breckenridge was back at quarter and Schlighting at right half in the Bear line-up.

Schmidt hit centre for three yards and Lom punted to Tech's 23-yard line.

Lumpkin went out of bounds and Mizell kicked. Tech recovered the ball on the California 23-yard line when Waddey fell on the oval after Breckenridge had fumbled. The Bears recovered the ball when Fitz recovered Mizell's fumble. Lom's punt was blocked and Mizell recovered for Tech. The ball was on California's 10-yard line.

Tech rooters shouted for a touchdown and Mizell hit centre for four yards. Lumpkin added three more and the ball was on the 3-yard line.

Eisan came in for Breckenridge in the Bear line-up. Lumpkin chopped a hole at centre for 2 yards. Bear rooters sent up a tremendous cheer as Lumpkin was held for no gain and Lom, punting from behind his goal line, sent the ball to midfield.

Dunlap came back 5 yards to California's 45-yard line and Mizell scampered around left end for 30 yards, putting the ball on California's 15-yard line. Tech scored a touchdown when Thomason cut back through tackle and dashed over the line. Thomason's attempted place kick for extra point was wide and the score became Georgia Tech 8, U. C. 0.

Waddey kicked off to Schlicting, who ran the ball back to California's 30-yard line. Lom lost his interference, but pushed ahead for a 7-yard gain around right end. Schmidt made it first down on California's 42-yard line. It was a 5-yard gain. Schmidt was held for no gain and Lom's pass to Phillips fell incomplete.

Lom passed 20 yards to Avery, giving the Bears a first down on Tech's 38-yard line. Lom's pass to Avery was incompleted, but he passed to Eisan on the next play for a yard gain. Phillips's pass to Eisan was incompleted and Tech took the ball on its 37-yard line.

Mizell went around left end for 5 yards. Lumpkin was held for no gain. Cockburn replaced Schmidt at fullback for California. Riegels blocked Mizell's kick and recovered the oval on Tech's 26-yard line.

Lom reversed right end for a 5-yard gain and Schlicting was stopped at the line of scrimmage. Lom's pass was incompleted and Tech took the ball on its 33-yard line. Mizell pushed through centre for 2 yards and Lumpkin added 5 at left guard. Mizell punted to Eisan, who was stopped on California's 28-yard line.

A short pass, Lom to Eisan, netted 3 yards as the period ended with the score Georgia Tech 8, California 0.

FOURTH PERIOD.

Lom's pass was knocked down by Lumpkin. From a pass formation, Lom cut through tackle and ran 26 yards before he was downed. It brought the ball to Tech's 43-yard line. Rice replaced Schlicting at right half for California.

Pund intercepted Lom's pass and Tech snapped into action on its 33-yard line. Thomason ran out of bounds after a yard gain around right end. Lumpkin went through left guard for 4 yards. Mizell kicked to Eisan, who ran out of bounds on California's 49-yard line after a 25-yard return. Rice went through right tackle for 3 yards, but was held for no gain on the next play. After an incompleted pass, Lom kicked.

Thomason fumbled after signaling for a fair catch, but the Tech halfback recovered and dashed back eight yards before he was downed on his 17-yard line.

Tech was penalized five yards for taking too much time out. Mizell kicked to Eisan, who returned five yards. He was stopped on his 47-yard line.

Rice lost two yards at left end. Barr replaced Rice. Eisan fumbled Lom's short pass and Tech took the ball on its 46-yard line.

Mizell hit the line for five yards and was held for no gain on a second try. Lumpkin hit centre for two yards and Mizell punted out of bounds on California's 4-yard line. Lom kicked to Thomason, who was thrown on Tech's 44-yard line by Phillips.

Lumpkin hit left tackle for five yards and Thomason added a yard at centre. Lumpkin made a yard and Mizell punted to Eisan, who ran out of bounds on California's 2-yard line.

Lom carried the ball for three yards and then six yards, both times off tackle. Cockburn made it first down on the 31-yard line.

Lom hit centre for two yards and passed to Phillips for a 37-yard gain, the latter being downed on Tech's 30-yard line. Lom passed to Eisan for a 20-yard gain, Eisan falling on the 10-yard line.

Lom passed over the goal line to Phillips for a touchdown. Barr place-kicked the try for a point and made the score Georgia Tech 8, California 7.

Tech took the ball and Mizell cut through left guard for two yards to stop on Tech's 43-yard line. Thomason and Lumkin hit the line for no gain. The gun sounded before the next play could start.

ANALYSIS OF GAME.

California had the edge in yards gained from scrimmage, making 169 yards to Georgia Tech's 164. California made 13 first downs while the Southerners made six. Of the fifteen passes tried, the Bears completed seven. Tech passed three times and completed once.

California gained 112 yards by aerial plays, Tech gained 35. The Bears punted eight times for a total of 367 yards, averaging 45 yards to the kick. Their opponents punted ten times for a total of 382 yards, averaging 38 yards to the kick.

Mizell proved the best ground gainer of the game, making 136 yards in 11 plays. Lom, the outstanding ball carrier for California took the ball 13 times for a total gain of 121 yards, an average of 9.3 yards to the play.

BIG SIX WINS, 14-6; HOWELL AGAIN STAR

Hero of East's Victory Over West on Saturday Chief Factor in Southwest's Defeat.

SCORES BOTH TOUCHDOWNS

Howell and Rival Player Mix It as Game Nears End—Police Quell Fracas in Dallas.

DALLAS, Tex., Jan. 1 (AP).—Led by Blue Howell, Nebraska fullback, the Big Six Conference all stars defeated the Southwestern all-stars, 14 to 6, in their intersectional game here today. Howell punched the line for both of his team's touchdowns, while Trigg of Southern Methodist University, counted for the Southwest when he recovered a blocked punt on the Big Six 3-yard line and went over. Some 10,000 saw the contest, which was for the benefit of a crippled children's hospital.

Ably abetting Howell today was Bob Mehrle of Missouri. Darting through holes opened by a stalwart line, the corn husker and his aide wasted no time in smashing through a forward wall which the Southwest thought impregnable. In less than four minutes after the kick-off, Howell and Mehrle alternated at their relentless driving for the former to score a touchdown. Mehrle added the extra point with a place-kick.

Southwest Eleven Braces.

The Southwest squad braced momentarily, but early in the second quarter Mehrle knifed through the line, eluded the secondary interference and raced 20 yards before he was brought down on the Southwest's 28-yard line. Behind perfect interference Howell plunged for a first down and then cracked the line for his second touchdown. Again Mehrle accounted for the extra point.

With these two backs on the sidelines, the Southwesterners resisted further forays into their territory and accounted for their lone touchdown soon after the half. King's punt rolled out of bounds on the Big Six team's 8-yard line, and when Haskins attempted to kick, Bartlett, Texas Aggie captain, hurled his huge bulk at the kicker and deflected the punt. Trigg snatched up the ball three yards from the goal line and rolled across under a swarm of tacklers. Love's try for the extra point was short.

Crowd Swarms Onto Field.

All thrills of the contest, Dixie's last of a lengthy season, were not confined to the exploits of Big Six scoring aces. Late in the game, when Howell was chased out of bounds by Burgess, a crowd of several hundred swarmed on the field when the Southwest player apparently swung at his opponent. When the final whistle sounded, Baccus of the Southwestern team was mixing it with Howell and police had to clear the field.

In the East-West game at San Francisco last Saturday, won by the East, Howell scored two of the three touchdowns made by the victors.

King, captain of the Texas University Southwestern Conference championship team, bore the brunt of the losing eleven's attack today in convincing manner.

Thel ine-up:

Big Six (14).		Southwest (6).
Rudi, Iowa State	L. E.	Trigg, S. M. U.
Lyon, Kans. Ags.	L. T.	Williams, T. C. U.
Holm, Neb.	L. G.	Phillips, Texas
James, Neb.	C.	Bartlett, Tex. A.&M.
McMullen, Neb.	R. G.	Baccus, Tex. A.&M.
Smith, Mo.	R. T.	Cowley, Texas
Ashburn, Neb.	R. E.	Ford, Texas
Byars, Mo.	Q. B.	King, Texas
Lindbloom, Ia. S.	L. H.	Burgess, Tex. A&M.
Mehrle, Mo.	R. H.	Love, S. M. U.
Howell, Neb.	F. B.	Hughes, Texas

SCORE BY PERIODS.

Big Six	7	7	0	0—14
Southwest	0	0	6	0—6

Touchdowns—Howell 2, Trigg. Points after touchdown—Mehrle 2.

ALABAMA ALUMNI WIN, 6-0.

Auburn Alumni Loses in First Meeting With Alabama Since 1907.

Special to The New York Times.

MONTGOMERY, Ala., Jan. 1.—Jimmy Johnston plunged over the south goal at Crampton Bowl to give the Alabama Alumni a 6 to 0 victory over Auburn grads football team here today.

The game was the first step to renew athletic relations between the two institutions, which were severed in 1907 due to ill feelings between players of both teams.

The line-up:

Alabama (6).		Auburn (0).
Cardwell	L. E.	Baskin
Perry	L. T.	Carter
Bowdoin	L. G.	Market
Holmes	C.	Patterson
Jones	R. G.	P. Spinks
Pickhard	R. T.	McFaden
McClintock	R. E.	B. Spinks
Hubert	Q. B.	Toxworth
Whitaker	L. H.	Shirley
B. Vandergraff	R. H.	Ford
Johnston	F. B.	Ducote

SCORE BY PERIODS.

Alabama	6	0	0	0—6
Auburn	0	0	0	0—0

Touchdown—Johnston.

TEMPLE FIVE WINS, 42-20.

Pearson Leads Attack Which Beats Washington and Jefferson.

Special to The New York Times.

PHILADELPHIA, Jan. 1.—Temple University in its first athletic meeting with Washington and Jefferson defeated the W. and J. basketball team here this afternoon, 42 to 20.

Red Pearson led the attack for the winners with six field goals and one foul, while Jack Bonner, Willie Stamberg and Grover Wearshing each contributed three field goals for the winners. Temple led at half time, 23 to 8.

The line-up:

Temple (42).	G.	F.	P.
Stamberg, lf	3	0	6
Rothstein	1	0	2
Pearson, rf	6	1	13
Bonner, c	3	1	7
Tomlin	0	0	0
Litwack, lg	2	4	8
Feinberg	0	0	0
Wearshing, rg	3	0	6
Godfrey	0	0	0
Total	18	6	42

W. and J. (20).	G.	F.	P.
Robinson, lf	3	2	8
Hamilton	2	1	5
Hoskins, rf	0	1	1
Sanders, c	2	1	5
McMunn, lg	0	0	0
McKissie	0	0	0
Gilchrist, rg	0	1	1
Total	7	6	20

BASKETBALL RESULTS.

College.

Pennsylvania 24, Rutgers 19.
Temple 42, W. and J. 20.
Michigan 32, Penn State 11.
Purdue 47, De Pauw 24.
Wisconsin 32, Carleton 24.
Butler 43, North Carolina 20.
Pittsburgh 52, Indiana 31.
Iowa State 35, Simpson 16.
Georgia 54, South Carolina 28.
Niagara 29, Cornell 28.
Oklahoma 32, Southern Methodist 13.

School.

Harding (Conn.) 25, Alumni 24.
Patchogue Alumni 29, Varsity 27.

Bennett to Teach Football At U. of Mexico for 2 Weeks

NEW ORLEANS, Jan. 1 (AP).—Dr. M. S. Bennett, director of athletics and former head coach at the University of the South, Sewanee, Tenn., is to teach football at the University of Mexico for two weeks. Sending of an emissary to Mexico for the promotion of football was decided upon at the annual meeting of the National Association of Football Coaches here last week. The selection of Dr. Bennett, who plans to leave tomorrow, was announced by William Roper, president of the association. Faculty members and students of Mexican colleges interested in football will be invited to send representatives to the university for Bennett's lectures. Bennett was football coach at Haverford for several years.

PENN FIVE RALLIES TO BEAT RUTGERS

Red and Blue Quintet Comes From Behind to Triumph by 24 to 19 Count.

Special to The New York Times.

PHILADELPHIA, Jan. 1.—In one of the hardest fought basketball games seen at the Palestra this season, Penn tonight defeated Rutgers, 24 to 19. The New Brunswick five took the place of Syracuse, which canceled the scheduled game last week.

At the request of the Scarlet team the game was divided into four quarters, the visitors leading at half time, 13 to 10. Once again the Red and Blue came through with a dazzling rally in which Don Noble, John Bonniwell and Ed Lobley starred.

Lobley, with three field goals and four fouls, for a total of 10 points, led the attack for Penn. Alton starred for Rutgers with four field goals and one foul.

The line-up:

Penn (24).	G.	F.	P.
Brodieck, lf	0	2	2
Noble	1	2	4
Schaaf, rf	0	2	2
Peterson, c	0	1	1
Bonniwell	2	0	4
Lobley, lg	3	4	10
Lexar, rg	0	1	1
Total	6	12	24

Rutgers (19).	G.	F.	P.
Alton, lf	[illegible]	[illegible]	[illegible]
Preletz, rf	1	1	3
Rohrbach, c	1	1	3
Kish, lg	0	1	1
Boettcher, rg	1	1	3
Guiler	1	0	2
Total	7	5	19

Referee—Tom Thorp, Columbia. Umpire—Kinley, Syracuse. Time of quarters—10 minutes.

MICHIGAN REPULSES PENN STATE, 32 TO 11

Traskowski Leads Attack That Turns Back Easterners—Losers Trail at Half, 17-3.

ANN ARBOR, Mich., Jan. 1 (AP).—The University of Michigan quintet defeated Penn State, 32 to 11, here tonight. The visitors scored first, but soon lost the lead and never again were ahead. Michigan led at half-time, 17 to 3. The Nittany Lions made a complete five-man substitution at the end of fifteen minutes play. Truskowski, with 10 points, led the attack for the winners.

The line-up:

Michigan (32).	G.	F.	P.
Orwig, lf	2	0	4
Dalsamoy	1	0	2
Kanitz, rf	2	2	6
Chapman, c	2	0	4
McCoy, lg	1	2	4
Rose	1	0	2
Trusk'ski, rg	2	4	10
Total	12	8	32

Penn State (11).	G.	F.	P.
Kurine, lf	0	0	0
Jacobson	1	0	2
Meyers, rf	0	0	0
Reinhold	1	0	2
Brownstein, c	0	0	0
Mamas	1	0	2
Mazess, lg	1	1	3
Wilson	0	0	0
Starley, rg	1	0	2
Total	5	1	11

INDIANA FIVE LOSES TO PITTSBURGH, 52-31

Hyatt Leads Attack for Winners, Registering Twelve Field Goals and One Foul.

Special to The New York Times.

PITTSBURGH, Jan. 1.—The University of Pittsburgh five had little difficulty in defeating Indiana here tonight, 52 to 31.

Hyatt, the Pitt star forward, led the attack with twelve goals from the field and one from the foul line for a total of 25 points. Pitt led at half time, 27 to 13.

The line-up:

Pittsburgh (52).	G.	F.	P.
Zehfuss, lf	2	3	7
Arture, lf, rf	0	0	0
Hyatt, rf	12	1	25
L. Cohen, c	1	0	2
Anderson	0	0	0
Wunderlich, lg	3	0	6
Morit	0	0	0
Baker, rg	6	0	12
M. Cohen	0	0	0
Total	24	4	52

Indiana (31).	G.	F.	P.
Wells, lf	0	0	0
Strickland, rf	6	2	14
Ashby	0	0	0
McCracken, c	4	0	8
Jasper	0	0	0
Zeller, lg	1	0	2
Carrell	0	4	4
Schein, rg	0	2	2
Gill	0	1	1
Total	11	9	31

MONTCLAIR A. C. FIVE WINS.

Gains Fifth Straight Victory Beating Warinanco A. C., 39-33.

Special to The New York Times.

MONTCLAIR, N. J., Jan. 1.—The Montclair A. C. basketball team gained its fifth straight victory and kept its record for the season clean by defeating Warinanco A. C. here tonight, 39 to 33.

The line-up:

Montclair A. C. (39).	G.	F.	P.
Wilson, lf	7	1	15
Werner, rf	3	2	8
Gerton	1	0	2
Hattersley, c	3	0	6
Crawford, lg	3	0	6
McCaffrey	0	0	0
Schoen, rg	1	0	2
Total	18	3	39

Warinanco A. C. (33).	G.	F.	P.
Ryan, lf	1	2	4
Wilson, rf	[illegible]	[illegible]	[illegible]
Lange, c	5	2	12
O'Hare, lg	1	0	2
Dressen, rg	6	1	13
Total	14	5	33

BUTLER FIVE VICTOR, 43-20.

Defeats University of North Carolina Quintet at Indianapolis.

Special to The New York Times.

INDIANAPOLIS, Ind., Jan. 1.—Butler defeated the University of North Carolina basketball team here tonight by 43 to 20. The half ended, 21 to 13, with Butler leading.

The line-up:

Butler (43).	G.	F.	P.
White, f	8	3	19
Chandler, f	7	2	16
Fromuth	0	0	0
Hildebrand, c	1	0	2
Allen	0	0	0
Fosier, g	2	0	4
Page	0	0	0
Reynolds	1	0	2
Sale	0	0	0
Total	19	5	43

North Carolina (20).	G.	F.	P.
Satterfield, f	4	0	8
Price, f	2	3	7
Cathy, c	1	0	2
Harper	0	0	0
Hackney, g	0	1	1
Smith, g	1	0	2
Farleigh	0	0	0
Choate	0	0	0
Total	8	4	20

SANGOR OUTPOINTS CHAMPION MORGAN

Wins Newspaper Men's Decision in 10-Round Bout Before 8,500 at Milwaukee.

TITLE NOT AT STAKE

Tod Declines to Quit After Being Fouled in the Fourth—Ryan of Boston Defeats Pall.

MILWAUKEE, Wis., Jan. 1 (AP).—Joey Sangor of Milwaukee, knocked out two weeks ago by an opponent he figured to be a pushover, staged a remarkable come-back by decisively defeating Tod Morgan of Seattle, Wash., junior lightweight champion, in a smashing ten-round battle here this afternoon.

The only reason Sangor is not the new ruler of the 130-pound division is because the Wisconsin law prohibits decisions by a referee or judges. Sangor, however, won the verdict in the opinion of the majority of the newspaper experts, with only one or two dissenting.

The match, fought in the Milwaukee Auditorium, drew a crowd of 8,500, with receipts from \$25,000 to \$30,000. It was the biggest gate in Milwaukee since the days of Ritchie Mitchell.

Morgan had a chance to win the fight in the fourth round, when, during a furious toe-to-toe rally in midring, Sangor cut loose with a sweeping left hook that sunk deep in the foul territory. It was the second foul blow Sangor landed in this session. Morgan sank to his knees, apparently suffering intense pain, but gamely refused to take the fight on a foul and resumed the battle after a short rest.

Sangor weighed 128 pounds, Morgan 128½.

Jack London, Chicago lightweight, had the better of Jackie Nichols of Milwaukee in the six-round semifinal.

Johnny Ryan, a Boston southpaw, defeated Frankie Pall of Toledo in six rounds. Both weighed 122 pounds.

In the opening bout Mitz Minikel, Milwaukee light-heavyweight, knocked out Kid Guepe of Rochester, Minn., in the first round with a right cross to the chin.

Louie New, Milwaukee's newest lightweight, boxed a six-round draw with Vic Walters, a fellow-townsman.

KID KAPLAN IS VICTOR.

Outpoints King in Ten Rounds Before 5,000 at Philadelphia.

Special to The New York Times.

PHILADELPHIA, Jan. 1.—Louis (Kid) Kaplan of Meriden, Conn., former world's featherweight champion, defeated Ritchie King in the main ten-round bout of the Arena holiday card today before a crowd of 5,000 fans. They clashed as lightweights.

Maurice Holtzer of France won from Emory Cabana, French-Canadian lightweight, in ten rounds.

Bucky Boyle of Allentown won a ten-round decision over Gaston Lecadre, French lightweight. The verdict was unpopular.

Johnny Erickson of New York battled to a ten-round draw with Vidal Gregirio of Spain.

PEPPE CONQUERS HALEY.

Gets the Decision in Ten-Round Bout at Philadelphia.

PHILADELPHIA, Jan. 1 (AP).—Johnny Peppe, South Philadelphia, won from Pat Haley, local ring veteran, in the ten-round main event at the Cambria Club today. Peppe weighed 154 and Haley 151. Other bouts resulted as follows:

Buddy Burke, Chester, 167, defeated Battling Willard, Lancaster, 169, in eight rounds.

Tommy Donohue, Philadelphia, 153, won from Joe Boris, Lester, Pa., 155, in six rounds.

Kid Robinson, Virginia, 135, knocked out Frank Little, Philadelphia, 140, in the first round.

Jimmy Smith, Philadelphia, 145, knocked out Frankie Neal, Philadelphia, 137, in the third round.

Bruce Outpoints Mueller.

BUFFALO, Jan. 1 (AP).—Sam Bruce, 142½ pounds, Buffalo, defeated Freddy Mueller, 132½, also of Buffalo, in ten rounds here today. Lou Scozza, 157, Buffalo, won a close decision from Jimmy Mahoney, 168, of Chicago in another ten-rounder. Billy Kowalik and Phil Verdi, featherweights, fought a six-round draw.

Lang Stopped by Roberts.

TACOMA, Wash., Jan. 1 (AP).—Eddie Kayo Roberts of Tacoma, who a year ago was rated among the leaders in the welterweight division, signalized his return to the ring by knocking out Billy Lang, Tacoma, 152-pounder, in the second round of a scheduled six-round main event here today.

McQuillan Defeats Snell.

SEATTLE, Jan. 1 (AP).—Ray McQuillan, Denver, defeated Doc Snell, Tacoma, in six rounds here this afternoon. Snell weighed 135, and McQuillan 139½ pounds. Don Fraser, Spokane junior welterweight, defeated Joe Sielaff, Milwaukee, in a six-round semi-final match.

Rocco Defeats Hartwell.

AKRON, Ohio, Jan. 1 (AP).—Emmett Rocco, Ellwood City (Pa.) heavyweight, defeated Big Bill Hartwell of Kansas City in a ten-round bout here tonight. Sammy Harris, Akron negro lightweight, defeated Chet Smallwood of Terre Haute, Ind., in six rounds.

Yarbo Loses to Hybert.

CLEVELAND, Ohio., Jan. 1 (AP).—Floyd Hybert, Cleveland, won a newspaper decision from Wilson Yarbo, Cleveland, in the six-round main bout of a boxing show here today. Hybert weighed 154½ and Yarbo 160.

Palmer Stops K. O. Leonard.

HAMILTON, Ohio., Jan. 1 (AP).—Frankie Palmer, Cincinnati welterweight, knocked out K. O. Leonard, Nashville, Tenn., in the second round of their ten-round bout here today.

COLLEGE FOOTBALL.

Georgia Tech 8, California 7.
Big Six 14, Southwest 6.
University of Oregon 6, University of Hawaii 0.
Alabama Alumni 6, Auburn Alumni 0.

Stribling Is Knocked Down, Then Stops League in First

KANSAS CITY, Jan. 1 (AP).—After taking a count of four when he was knocked down by Jack League, Texas heavyweight, W. L. (Young) Stribling of Georgia bounded to his feet and knocked out the Texan with a right cross to the jaw in the first round of their scheduled ten-round bout here tonight. The blow that spelled doom for League was the third knockdown punch in two minutes of fighting, Stribling having sent League to the canvas once before ending the bout. Stribling weighed 188 pounds, League 196.

BAN ON SCHMELING NOT LIKELY HERE

State Board Expected to Permit German to Box Sekyra Despite Massachusetts Protest.

A request for the suspension of Max Schmeling made by the Massachusetts Boxing Commission to the State Athletic Commission here yesterday caused apprehension for a time over Friday night's scheduled bout in Madison Square Garden between Schmeling and Joe Sekyra, Dayton, Ohio, heavyweight. But the clouds will disappear today if the commission follows its precedent and acts accordingly.

The Bay State authorities have placed Schmeling on the unavailable list until such time as he consents to meet Ernie Schaaf for Eddie Mack and Tex Rickard's Boston Garden, and have requested the local board to take action against Schmeling in advance of Friday night's scheduled bout. The protest is based on Schmeling's alleged failure to fulfill a contract to box Schaaf. In view of the fact that Schmeling signed to box Sekyra here in advance of the protest from Massachusetts, it is expected the commission today will order the German to box Schaaf in Boston after Friday's encounter.

Joe Jacobs, who is associated with the management of Schmeling, denied yesterday that any contracts had been signed for a bout between the German and Schaaf by any one authorized to obligate Schmeling. He added, however, that Schmeling will fight Schaaf in Boston later.

PETROLLE BEATS POLLOCK.

Floors Rival Four Times—Victor's Brother Also Wins.

SCRANTON, Pa., Jan. 1 (AP).—Pete Petrolle, Schenectady, N. Y., won from Billy Pollock, local lightweight, in ten rounds here this afternoon. Petrolle floored Pollock for counts of nine four times.

In the semi-final Frankie Petrolle, brother of Pete, stopped Billy Oakes of Wilkes-Barre in the second round of a scheduled eight-rounder.

MITCHELL BEATS KAWLER.

Gets Decision From New Yorker in Bout in Allentown, Pa.

ALLENTOWN, Pa., Jan. 1 (AP).—Ray Mitchell of Philadelphia this afternoon won the judge's decision from Nat Kawler of New York in a ten-round bout here. Each scaled 141 pounds.

Mitchell opened a bad gash over the New Yorker's right eye in the sixth round, and it bled freely to the finish.

Miller Victor by Decision.

CINCINNATI, Jan. 1 (AP).—Freddie Miller, Cincinnati featherweight, won the decision from Cecil Payne, Louisville, Ky., in a ten-round bout here today. In the semi-final, Vincent Hambright, Cincinnati junior welterweight, knocked out Paul Anthony, Sioux City, Iowa, in the ninth round.

Webster Wins by Knockout.

SPOKANE, Wash., Jan. 1 (AP).—Al Webster, Billings, Mont., middleweight, stopped Paul Delaney, Spokane, in four rounds here today. Fred Lenhart of Spokane won a six-round decision from Tiger Johnny Cline of Oakland, Cal.

Jones Knocks Out Evans.

NORRISTOWN, Pa., Jan. 1 (AP).—Billy Jones, Pittsburgh, knocked out Bobby Evans, Conshohocken, Pa., in the fourth round of a scheduled ten-round bout today. Joe Parker, Philadelphia, won from Tony Gildo of Camden, N. J., in six rounds.

Brown Wins on a Foul.

INDIANAPOLIS, Jan. 1 (AP).—Norman Brown, Chicago, 147, won on a foul in the fifth round of a scheduled ten-round fight from Meyer Grace, 149, Philadelphia, here tonight. Grace was winning handily at the time of the foul.

Vacca IWns From Cubic.

CHICOPEE, Mass., Jan. 1 (AP).—Johnny Vacca, 118, of Boston, took a close 10-round decision over Willie Cubic, 115¼, of New York, here today.

HAMMOND GETS 200; SETS WORLD'S MARK

Gets Second Straight 200 Score in Cricket Test Match, His 251 Being Made at Sydney.

ENGLAND HAS 365 FOR 6

Only 32 Runs Behind as Australia Scored 397 in Its First Innings at Melbourne.

MELBOURNE, Australia (Wednesday), Jan. 2 (Canadian Press).—Walter Hammond, great Gloucestershire batsman playing today in the first English innings in the third cricket test match against Australia completed a score of 200 runs before being dismissed. As he scored 251 runs at Sydney he thus created a world's record in international cricket by making two consecutive totals of 200 runs in test matches.

England was only 32 runs behind at lunch time today, having 365 runs for six wickets as against Australia's first innings score of 397.

On resuming yesterday morning Hammond wasted no time in getting set and with Sutcliffe doing little more than keeping up his end proceeded to annihilate the Australian bowling. He reached his 50 after an hour and a half's play and went on brilliantly scoring until he reached 99.

Hammond Gets Ovation.

At this point the Australians threw in their best efforts and it was twenty minutes before Hammond got the odd run which completed his century. He had been batting just over three hours. He raised his score to 150 in an hour more and received a tremendous ovation from the crowd, play being suspended for several minutes while Hammond bowed his acknowledgments.

Hammond was thrashing the bowling when play ceased for the day. He gave no chance during his display, though a very confident but unsuccessful appeal for a catch at the wicket was made against him in the last over of the day.

Hammond will make cricket history today if he passes the double century as this would give him two score over 200 in successive innings.

Sutcliffe, who with Hobbs has in the past been a great opening batsman, was only a shade of his best self yesterday. He required three hours and forty minutes to get his 58 and was often in trouble. He hit only three fours.

Jardine With Hammond.

A. P. F. Chapman and P. Hendren, the other English batsmen who are out, looked rather drab in comparison with Hammond, and never settled down. D. R. Jardine batted with more assurance and was with Hammon when stumps were pulled.

The Australian bowling and fielding were very good, the former being brilliant at periods.

The attendance reached 30,000 during the day, which was an unexpected drop from the two previous days' gates.

Scores at the end of the third day's play were:

Australia—First innings	397
England—First innings:	
J. Hobbs, C. Oldirld B. A'Beckett	20
H. Sutcliffe, E. Blackie	58
W. Hammond, not out	169
A. P. F. Chapman, R. Blackie	24
P. Hendern, C. A'Beckett, E. Hendry	19
D. R. Jardine, not out	21
Extra	1
Total (four four wickets)	312

H. Larwood, G. Geary, M. Tate, G. Duckworth and J. C. White to bat.

Fall of wickets: 47 for 1 wicket, 161 for 2, 201 for 3, 238 for four.

NIAGARA BEATS CORNELL.

Wins, 29-28, in Extra-Period Game—Half Time Score, 14-14.

NIAGARA FALLS, N. Y., Jan. 1.—Niagara University won in an extra five-minute period game from Cornell University here tonight, 29-28. The game was tied at the end of the first half, 14 to 14.

The line-up:

Niagara (29).		Cornell (28).
Curran	R.F.	Murphy
Heffernan	L.F.	Layton
Marks	L.F.	Harrington
Schaad	C.	Fisher
Snyder	R.G.	Stein
Meyer	L.G.	Lewis
Scheedy	L.G.	Essemer
——	R.G.	Kass

Referee—Fitting, Erie. Umpire—Greene, Buffalo. Time of halves—20 minutes.

ANDY CALLAHAN WINS.

Drops Kid Wagner Five Times in 12 Rounds in Portland, Me.

PORTLAND, Me., Jan. 1 (AP).—Andy Callahan of Lawrence, Mass., scoring five knockdowns, defeated Eddie Kid Wagner of Philadelphia in the main bout at the Exposition Building tonight. Wagner barely survived the twelfth and final round. One knockdown came in the second, two in the third and two more in the final session. Callahan weighed 140 pounds and Wagner 137.

Malone Wins From Gibbs.

RENO, Nev., Jan. 1 (AP).—Jock Malone, St. Paul middleweight, won a decision in ten rounds from Jack Gibbs of Los Angeles in the feature bout of a New Year's card here this afternoon.

The New York Times.

SUNDAY, OCTOBER 13, 1929.

SPORTS SHIPPING AND MAILS Section 11

ATHLETICS' 10 RUNS IN 7TH DEFEAT CUBS IN 4TH SERIES GAME

Trailing, 8-0, Mackmen Unleash Attack That Beats McCarthy's Men, 10-8, Before 30,000.

15 MEN BAT IN ONE INNING

Four Pitchers, Root, Nehf, Blake and Malone, Used Before Athletics Are Retired.

DYKES'S DOUBLE DECIDES

Simmons, Foxx and Dykes Each Get Two Hits in One Frame—Philadelphians Need One More Game.

By JOHN DREBINGER.

Special to The New York Times.

PHILADELPHIA, Pa., Oct. 12.—Somebody dropped a toy hammer on a stick of dynamite today and touched off an explosion that shook to its heels a continent that Christopher Columbus had discovered 437 years ago to the day.

It happened in the seventh inning of the fourth game of the world's series at a time when more than 30,000 spectators sat in the packed stands of Shibe Park steeped in despair. For all one knows, they may have been the same 30,000 who jammed these same stands the day before, for the number of paid admissions, 29,921, was exactly the same.

The receipts, $140,815, also were the same, making the total for the four games $718,679 and the total paid attendance 160,709. But the feelings of the crowd—all but those of the 500 loyal rooters of Chicago—were infinitely worse.

For the Athletics, beaten in the third game yesterday, were trailing, 8 to 0, and if there is anything at all that can appear certain in this most curious of all possible worlds it was that the Cubs would win this game and square the series at two all.

Chicago Rooters Stunned.

Then started the seventh and it brought in its wake a typhoon, tornado and hurricane, a rush of blood to the head of the spectators and the complete collapse of the 500 loyal rooters from Chicago as a surging Mack attack swept on and flattened all before it to roll up a total of ten runs for the inning.

And so to the Athletics went the fourth game of the series by a score of 10 to 8, and the hopes of the shattered Cub forces tonight are hanging on something slightly thinner than a thread. For the Athletics are now leading in this world's series by a margin of three victories to one, and they need only one more game to conclude the struggle and win for themselves the lion's share of the spoils.

Never in all world series history was there such an inning. Records, large and small, collapsed in wholesale lots, while a crowd, held speechless for hours, howled itself into a perfect delirium and smashed a few more records.

Root Appeared Out for Revenge.

For six innings the bulky, stolid Charlie Root, whom the fates had treated rather unkindly in the first game in Chicago, appeared riding on his way to a merited revenge. Over the period he had held the mightiest of Mack sluggers in a grip of iron, allowing only three scattered hits and mowing them down as though they were men of straw.

And while Charlie was doing this the Cubs, at last thoroughly aroused, cuffed and battered four of Connie Mack's prized hurlers to all sectors of the field. They hammered Jack Quinn, who brought his forty-odd years and his famed spitball into the fray with high hopes only to carry both out badly shattered. They pulverized Rube Walberg and smashed Ed Rommel.

Charlie Grimm hit a homer, Rogers Hornsby hit a single and a triple. Kiki Cuyler hit three singles in a row, and the 500 loyal rooters from Chicago split their 500 throats. The Philadelphians tried hard to ignore them, but it is difficult to ignore 500 loyal rooters from Chicago.

It was warm and sunny, but the great crowd sulked and sat in silence as Al Simmons stepped to the plate to open the Athletic half of the seventh. Two and three-fifths seconds later the storm broke.

Simmons Collects Homer.

Simmons crashed a home-run on top of the roof of the left-field pavilion. It was Al's second circuit clout of the series and the crowd gave him a liberal hand, though the applause was still lacking in enthusiasm.

"Well," they said, "that at least saves us from a shutout."

But the rumbling continued and increased in volume. Jimmy Foxx singled to right. Bing Miller singled to centre and Jimmy Dykes singled to left. The Dykes' hit scored Foxx and when Joe Boley singled to centre Miller raced over the plate.

There was a momentary pause as the veteran George Burns, coming up in the rôle of pinch hitter, popped to Shortstop English but when Max Bishop laced a single to centre, Dykes counted, the Athletics had four runs over and the Cub lead had been cut squarely in half.

By now the crowd had set up a terrifying din. The Cubs began to squirm uneasily and there was much activity on the Chicago bench as Manager Joe McCarthy waved frantically to four or five pitchers warming up furiously in the bull pen. Root was taken out of the box and Arthur Nehf, veteran lefthander, took his place.

There were two on the bases and only one out as George William Haas, called mule for short, stepped to the plate. A moment later there was a roar that almost shook the

Continued on Page Eight.

Hans Wagner Stopped at Gate But He Finally Sees Game

PHILADELPHIA, Oct. 12 (AP).—The gate tenders, who made it a bad day yesterday for any one with a ticket suspected of dealing with speculators, were even more vigilant today.

Old Honus Wagner, the famous Pirate shortstop of two decades ago, one of the greatest players of all time, was stopped at the gate although he protested that a ticket was being held for him inside. It took a delegation of baseball writers to straighten out matters.

FORDHAM CRUSHES N. Y. U. TEAM, 26-0

60,000 at Polo Grounds See Alert Maroon Eleven Score Sterling Victory.

PASSES PLAY MAJOR ROLE

Rivals Miss Touchdown by Inches, but Their Aerial Attack Is Stopped by Winners.

By WILLIAM D. RICHARDSON.

After three years of defeat by N. Y. U., the Fordham Ram rammed its way to a 26-0 victory at the Polo Grounds yesterday, while 60,000 intensely partisan spectators looked down in surprise from the stands. One of the most prominent onlookers was Mayor Walker.

Its first respite since 1925, when it defeated the Violet, 26 to 6, the Maroon now holds a big edge in the ten-game series, having won six times to N. Y. U.'s four.

For only one period was yesterday's game between the two rivals close enough to be exciting. That was in the opening period, when a stone-wall defense by the Maroon linemen was all that prevented N. Y. U. from scoring. Their goal was threatened only once more, another touchdown attack being repelled in the early part of the third period.

Except for those two crises, the Maroon goal was never in danger. The second repulse seemed to take all the strength out of the Violet and from then on it was all Fordham, its line outplaying N. Y. U. decisively and turning the tide.

Finding its efforts to advance the ball along the ground futile against the sturdy, and on two or three occasions thrilling, defense of the Maroons, the Violet took to the air, but even there it met with little success. Follet and Connor, Coach Meehan's star aerial artists, were balked at every turn by the ever-alert Maroon backs and ends.

Of the four touchdowns that Fordham scored, three had their initial impulse in the interception of a pass. But if N. Y. U.'s aerial attack was a failure, Fordham's was a success, the air route being the one that played a huge part in the game.

Tallies on a Pass.

The first Fordham score came early in the second period when Fisher, substituting for Bartos at quarterback, took the N. Y. U. defense men completely by surprise, caught a pass on the Violet 13-yard marker and ran unmolested across the goal line. The toss came from the hand of McMahon and produced a gain of 27 yards.

An intercepted forward started the touchdown, for Murphy, one of the outstanding heroes of the day and a great back in the bargain, hauled down an N. Y. U. pass on the 42-yard line and ran 10 yards before he was hauled down. O'Herin, the Violet back, was fooled by the play, as was Chalmers. Fisher was past them before they realized their mistake.

When the Violet team returned to the field at the beginning of the third period it threw a scare into the Fordham rooters by launching a line attack that resulted in three first downs and carried the ball from the 35-yard line deep into enemy territory before it ran up against a stone-wall defense. Head down, legs working like pistons, La Mark, the Violet fullback, struck time after time and by sheer force drove the Maroon line back.

Responding to his signal, in eight out of nine plays he advanced the ball to his opponents' 32-yard line and then Follet, hero of last year's victory, took up the burden of the attack. Dashing around left end, he raced 31 yards to the corner of the field before he was forced out of bounds.

La Mark Crosses the Line.

The N. Y. U. rooters took hope, confident that the score would be tied, but Follet was to be denied the fruits of his brilliant run. La Mark went across, but the play was called back and N. Y. U. was penalized 5 yards. Three times the N. Y. U. backs hit a stone-wall defense and were turned back. Finally Follet tried to pass to Nemecek on the end zone, but that, too, failed, the ball just grazing his finger tips.

That represented N. Y. U.'s last threat, a similar one having been turned back by an immovable Fordham forward wall in the opening period, when Grant recovered Bartos's fumble on the 15-yard line and N. Y. U. failed to gain the two yards necessary for a touchdown in four attempts.

Late in the third period the Maroon made it 13 to 0 when Elcewicz leaped into the air to receive a pass from Conway and scamper 25 yards to cross the line.

The last two scores came in the final period, the first of them when Pieculewicz intercepted Connor's pass on N. Y. U.'s 35-yard line, and two forwards, one from Fisher to Pieculewicz and the other from Fisher to Elcewicz, brought it to the

Continued on Page Five.

Stephenson of the Cubs Safe at the Plate in Sixth Inning of Yesterday's Game.

Times Wide World Photo.

PRINCETON BEATEN BY BROWN, 13 TO 12

2 Passes, Fogarty to Edwards, in Final 2 Minutes, Cover 59 Yards for Touchdown.

30,000 WITNESS STRUGGLE

Tigers Held on 1-Yard Line by Bruins—Nassau Takes Lead After Bears Score in 2d.

By ARTHUR J. DALEY.

Special to The New York Times.

PRINCETON, N. J., Oct. 12.—Victims of the first upset of the season when they lost to Springfield two weeks ago, Brown's "iron men" were victors in another upset today at Palmer Stadium before a crowd of 30,000 when two needle-like passes from Link Fogarty to Bud Edwards in the last two minutes of play traversed 59 yards and gave Brown the verdict over Princeton, 13 to 12.

Off with a rush that left the notoriously slow-starting Tiger eleven at the post, Brown completely dominated the first period of play to push over a touchdown at the start of the second, when Edwards rolled off centre for a score.

Then the steel-riveted defense of the "iron men" crumpled before an attack launched principally by Trix Bennett and Eddie Wittmer, as Princeton smashed its way to a pair of touchdowns in the second and third quarters.

Brown seemed doomed for an utter rout in the last three quarters, as Princeton's two great ball carriers squirmed and slipped along pretty much as they pleased. The crowning touch in this shattering offensive drive that had netted two touchdowns came when Wittmer cut off tackle for 57 yards and an apparent tally. But some one was holding, and back came the ball and off came six points from the scoreboard.

Penalty Nullifies Touchdown.

Just at the start of the last quarter Princeton was held on the 1-yard line and Edwards kicked out to the 35-yard marker. Bill Scarlett scooped in the ball and shot down the side lines for 35 yards and another apparent touchdown. However, another penalty nullified this.

Edwards was manhandled by an overeager Princeton forward and instead of having a touchdown registered against it, Brown received the ball on its own 20-yard line, a penalty in the end zone being officially interpreted as a touchback.

That was the beginning of the end. Brown's great feat in stopping short the Tigers with a lone yard to go heartened the Providence team which speedily resumed its relentless attitude of the first period. Interspersing off tackle slashes with those bullet-like passes of Fogarty, Brown worked the ball up to midfield, lost it on an intercepted pass and regained it at about the same spot when Fogarty's vicious tackle of Levick forced the Princeton man to drop the ball.

Brown Resorts to Passes.

Then Brown marched down the field, found that it could not gain through the Princeton line and then sought the overhead route for its victory.

Brown's main method of gaining was a tricky reverse play directed at the left side of the Tiger line and then Coach Bill Roper of Princeton withdrew Hockenbury from left tackle, then replaced Lea at left end and finally substituted Levine for Duncan to give the Orange and Black team an entire new left side of the line before the completion of the initial quarter.

Finkie Gurll, Brown quarterback, was the principal factor in the success of reverse plays as he side stepped his way through the weak Princeton left side. He was aided and abetted by Fogarty and Edwards as this pair split the line after Gurll's reverses had opened up the Tiger forward wall.

Brown held the upper hand so completely in the first period that the Bruins registered eight first downs to none for Princeton, but when the Princeton drive got under way midway in the second quarter the Bruin lead in first downs was cut away until the final tabulation, Brown had thirteen first downs to eleven for Princeton.

The Roper team was handicapped a good deal by the absence of Captain Jack Whyte at tackle and Bill Moore at guard. The outstanding player for Princeton was Bill Bar-

Continued on Page Four.

College Football Scores

EAST.

Fordham 26, N. Y. U. 0.
Notre Dame 14, Navy 7.
Harvard 35, New Hampshire 0.
Brown 13, Princeton 12.
Nebraska 13, Syracuse 6.
Columbia 52, Wesleyan 0.
Dartmouth 53, Allegheny 0.
Army 23, Davidson 7.
Holy Cross 20, Rutgers 3.
Colgate 31, Michigan State 0.
Penn State 26, Marshall 7.
Penn 14, V. P. I. 8.
Pittsburgh 27, West Virginia 7.
Georgetown 13, St. Louis U. 0.
Lafayette 23, Manhattan 0.
Williams 27, Bowdoin 6.
Amherst 33, Lowell Textile 25.
St. Lawrence 22, C. C. N. Y. 0.
Cornell 40, Hampden-Sidney 6.
Gettysburg 7, Lehigh 7.
Boston College 7, Villanova 7.
Lebanon Valley 6, F. and M. 0.
W. and J. 14, Bucknell 6.
Union 28, Hobart 13.
Haverford 19, Susquehanna 7.
Drexel 13, Juniata 0.
Delaware 0, Ursinus 0.
Muhlenberg 21, Dickinson 6.
Penn M. C. 7, St. Joseph's 6.
Temple 28, St. Bonaventure 0.
Albright 46, Roanoke 0.
Buffalo 20, Alfred 12.
Clarkson Tech 7, R. P. I. 0.
Broaddus 6, Bethany 0.
Stroudsburg 7, Shippensburg 0.
Smith U. 19, Howard 0.
Davis and Elkins 7, Geneva 0.
Rider 14, Upsala 6.
Catholic U. 18, Baltimore 0.
Conn. Aggies 20, Maine 7.
West. Maryland 12, St. Thomas 6.
Duquesne 18, Albion 0.
Trinity 7, Worcester Tech 6.
Boston U. 27, Vermont 6.
Colby 20, Norwich 7.
Buffalo 20, Alfred 12.
Hamilton 6, Rochester 0.
Tufts 19, Bates 0.
Niagara 19, St. John's (Bklyn.), 14.
Middlebury 14, Mass. Aggies 12.
Brooklyn C. C. 47, Wagner 6.
N. Y. Aggies 24, Conn. Jr. Coll. 0.
Providence 0, Canisius 0.
St. Vincent 7, Mount St. Mary's 6.
Thiel 6, Waynesburg 2.
Yale J. V. 7, Penn J. V. 0.
Yale Fr. 12, Andover 6.
Harvard Fr. 7, Exeter 7.
Dartmouth Fr. 8, Tilton Acad. 6.
Manlius 42, St. Lawrence Fr. 0.
Lehigh Fr. 0, Hill School 0.
Rutgers Fr. 7, Peddie 7.
Trinity Fr. 0, Choate School 0.
Loyola (Baltimore) 31, Washington Coll. 0.
West Chester Teachers 25, Bloomsburg 0.
American U. 8, George Washington 0.
C. C. N. Y. J. V. 2, Stuyvesant High 0.
St. John's (Annapolis) 2, Gallaudet 0.
Coast Guard Acad. 25, Long Island U. 0.
Carnegie Tech Fr. 33, W. and J. Fr. 7.
Wyoming Seminary 25, Ursinus Fr. 0.
Dickinson Fr. 19, Dickinsin Normal 0.
Edinboro 19, California (Pa.) Teachers 0.

SOUTH.

Georgia 15, Yale 0.
Tulane 34, Mississippi A. and M. 0.
Tennessee 52, U. of Mississippi 7.
Centre 60, Morris-Harvey 0.
Virginia 12, Swarthmore 7.
Rice 14, Southwestern Texas 6.
Alabama 46, Chattanooga 0.
Louisiana State 27, Sewanee 14.
Baylor 12, St. Edwards 0.
V. M. I. 13, Citadel 7.
Mississippi Teachers 31, Marion 0.
Richmond 21, Johns Hopkins 7.
Spring Hill 28, Southwestern (La.) 6.
Clark 48, Miles Memorial 0.
Louisiana Coll. 19, Union (Tenn.) 7.
Texas U. 7, Arkansas U. 0.
Kentucky 20, W. and L. 6.
South Carolina 26, Maryland 6.
Texas Christian 28, Centenary 0.
Texas Aggies 19, Kansas Aggies 0.
Daniel Baker 6, Texas Tech 2.
Millsaps 46, Monticello 0.
Auburn Fr. 20, Florida Fr. 7.
Union Coll. 13, Tennessee Wesleyan 13.
Quantico Marines 7, New River State 0.
Southwestern 12, West Kentucky Teachers 6.
Georgetown Coll. 13, Indiana B team 6.
Lenoir Rhyne 6, Atlantic Christian 0.
Alabama Normal 2, Morris Brown 0.

WEST.

Ohio State 7, Iowa 6.
Purdue 30, Michigan 16.
Northwestern 7, Wisconsin 0.
Chicago 13, Indiana 7.
Minnesota 15, Vanderbilt 6.
Illinois 45, Bradley 0.
California 14, Washington State 0.
Stanford 57, California (L.A.Br.) 0.
Grinnell 9, Marquette 7.
Loyola (Chicago) 6, Coe 0.
Illinois Wesleyan 33, Augustana 0.
Monmouth 18, Illinois College 6.
Missouri 19, Iowa State 0.
Kansas 38, Emporia 0.
MacAlester 13, St. John's 6.
Carleton 13, Hamline 6.
Norman 19, Shurtleff 12.
De Pauw 33, Earlham 13.
Danville Normal 25, Valparaiso 0.
Alderson 7, Rio Grande 0.
Wittenberg 20, Denison 0.
Doane 18, Midland 6.
Case 26, Hiram 0.
Akron 12, Wooster 7.
Baldwin-Wallace 39, Capital 6.
Ohio Wesleyan 21, Ohio U. 7.
Mount Union 13, Oberlin 0.
Ohio Northern 36, Cedarville 6.
Cincinnati 18, Kenyon 6.
Dayton 7, Wilmington 0.
Carroll 26, Northwestern Reserves 6.
Iowa Wesleyan 6, St. Ambrose 0.
Ripon 33, Cornell (Iowa) 0.
Regis 13, Mount St. Charles 6.
Iowa Teachers 7, Simpson 0.
Columbia (Iowa) 12, Lacrosse 6.
Oklahoma 26, Creighton 0.
Lombard 7, Rolla Mines 6.
Rose Poly 12, Evansville 7.
Ashland 26, Slippery Rock 7.
Superior 52, Eau Claire Normal 0.
Hibbing 18, Duluth 0.
St. Cloud 31, Rochester (Minn.) 0.
Idaho 19, Montana 0.
Denver 19, Wyoming 6.
Colorado Mines 20, West. State 13.
Brigham Young 12, Montana State 0.
St. Olaf 18, Luther 6.
Pomona 69, Laverne 0.
Eureka 6, Macomb 0.
River Falls 21, Stout Inst. 0.
Parsons 6, Penn College 0.
Abilene 16, West Texas Teachers 0.
Ypsilanti 27, DePaul 0.
Jamestown 65, Mayville 0.
DeKalb Teachers 14, Elmhurst 0.
Colorado U. 19, Colorado Teachers 0.
Oregon 34, Willamette 0.
Oregon State 71, Columbia (Ore.) 7.
Sacramento 21, College of Pacific 7.
Olympic Club 60, Fresno State 0.
Arizona 35, California Tech 0.
Oregon Normal 12, Chigo State 0.
Drake 20, Washington U. (Mo.) 0.
Gonzaga 39, West Coast Army 7.
Whitman 71, Linfield 0.
Santa Clara Fr. 13, Stanford Fr. 0.
Oklahoma A. and M. 18, Oklahoma City U. 0 (night game).
Colorado College 14, Colorado Aggies 13.
Inter-Mountain Union 24, Montana Normal 0.
James Milliken 26, Wabash 6 (night game).
Minot Teachers 32, Dickinson Normal 0.
Pipestone 20, Canton (S. D.) Normal 0.
Western Union 13, Nebraska State Teachers 0.
Southern California 48, Washington 0.
Winona Teachers 20, Red Wing Seminary 0.
Washington U. Fr. 6, Centralia Jr. Coll. 0.
St. Xavier 19, West Va. Wesleyan 12.
Carnegie Tech 33, Western Reserve 6.
Wisconsin B team 6, Michigan B team 0.
Taft High (Berkeley) 19, California (L. A. Br. Fr.) 7.
California Fr. 13, Fullerton Jr. Coll. 0.
Washburn 12, Pittsburg (Kan.) Teachers 7.
Gustavus Adolphus 26, St. Thomas (St. Paul) 0.
Lawrence (Wis.) 26, Northwestern Coll. 6.
Virginia (Minn.) 8, Bemidji Teachers 6.
South Dakota State 38, Morningside 0.
Northern Arizona 13, Loyola (Ariz.) 0.
North Dakota Aggies 21, Moorhead 6.

CANADIAN.

Intercollegiate.

McGill 10, Western U. 7.

Interprovincial.

Hamilton 6, Argonauts 5.
Montreal 3, Ottawa 2.
Sarnia 21, Toronto U. 5.
Kitchener 26, St. Michael's 2.

Intermediate.

Oshawa 25, Guelph 4.
Guelph O. A. C. 7, Varsity 6.

Junior.

Varsity 15, Guelph O. A. C. 9.
Malvern 8, Argonauts 1.
St. Thomas 38, Kitchener 1.

School Scores on Page Six.

NEBRASKA DEFEATS SYRACUSE, 13 TO 6

Sloan Plunges Across Line in Last Quarter to Clinch Odd Game in Series.

ORANGE FIRST TO COUNT

Goes Over in Opening Session, but Victors Gain 7-6 Edge in Next as 20,000 Look On.

By LINCOLN A. WERDEN.

Special to The New York Times.

SYRACUSE, N. Y., Oct. 12.—The Nebraska eleven made a trip here to play an intersectional contest with Syracuse and left Archbold Stadium today a winner by 13 to 6 in one of the most thrilling games of their series.

A crowd of 20,000 sat in to see the Cornhuskers' powerful line finally outplay the Orange stalwarts in a game that was marked by little of the spectacular.

Syracuse employed some of Pop Warner's tricks for the first time, but evidently the Westerners had seen most of them or knew them by heart, for they had no real difficulty in breaking up Syracuse's attack.

Nebraska Has Series Edge.

The victory gave Nebraska an edge in the series that began back in 1917, for the Cornhuskers, having won the past two years, scored their fourth triumph this pleasant Autumn afternoon. Syracuse has won three times.

Syracuse, with four sophomores in the line-up, started with a rush in the opening quarter to push over their only touchdown and though they seemed to be gaining momentum for a stirring climax with less than ten minutes to the final whistle, Greenberg, Nebraska lineman, broke through to intercept a pass and dashed down the field to break up the rally.

Syracuse, seeing a chance to take the lead so quickly taken from them, made a final courageous stand, but was unable to get across the goal line.

In a futile attempt, Syracuse began a forward passing attack in the closing minutes, a method which both teams used only at rare intervals and with slight success.

Syracuse Falls Behind.

Nebraska took the lead in the second period when Peaker made good on a try after Young's touchdown.

The line play that predominated most of the game featured the third period, but at the outset of the fourth quarter Syracuse's hopes were dimmed. The Cornhuskers' powerful fullback, Clair Sloan, who had replaced Young, tossed a 15-yard pass to Farley, who dashed to the 1-yard line, where Stevens brought him down. Then Sloan took the ball over, but he failed to kick the extra point.

In the final minutes Syracuse made one last threat, but its attack was halted. Packer kicked out of bounds to Syracuse's 32-yard line and, after Syracuse accepted the kick and refused a penalty called on Nebraska for holding, the stands were in an uproar.

Greenberg Breaks Through.

Manning, another replacement, went back as though to pass, and the Cornhuskers charged in. Greenberg, right guard, came rushing at Manning, who hurried, tossed the ball, but scarcely had it left his fingers before Greenberg wrapped his arms around it and scampered 25 yards before he was tackled. McBride hammered at the line, but the Orange held and Nebraska lost the ball on downs.

Stevens was away to the first important gain of the game, and the fleet Syracuse back skirted end for a 25-yard run to Nebraska's 40-yard line. Borton went off on another run, this time around left end for 20 yards. A dash by Stevens and a plunge through the line by Sebo for a first down brought the ball to the 10-yard line. Sebo slipped the ball to Borton, who went around left end for the first touchdown. Ellert, sophomore end, failed to kick the extra point.

Relying on a succession of line plays, the Cornhuskers rallied in the second quarter. After the visitors received a kick on their 39-yard-line, steady thrusts by Farley brought the ball down to the 4-yard line. Twice

Continued on Page Two.

Tilden Is Beaten in Two Sets By Borotra on English Court

Special Cable to THE NEW YORK TIMES.

LONDON, Oct. 12.—Jean Borotra conquered Bill Tilden today, 10—8, 9—7, in one of the most bitterly fought indoor tennis matches ever seen at the Queen's Club. Storming the net continuously, the bounding Basque wore down Tilden's tenacious baseline game. Ambassador de Fleuriau was among the celebrities present.

LONDON, Oct. 12 (AP).—William Tilden suffered a reverse in doubles when he and P. D. B. Spence of South Africa were defeated by Borotra and Glasser of France by 6-8, 8-6, 6-1.

France won the series, ten matches to five.

NOTRE DAME DEFEATS NAVY BEFORE 80,000

Comes From Behind in the Last Period to Triumph in Baltimore by 14 to 7.

MULLINS WINS THE GAME

Takes Ball Over as Secretary Adams, Governor Ritchie, Alan Hoover and Others Watch.

By ALLISON DANZIG.

Special to The New York Times.

BALTIMORE, Oct. 12.—Before a record gathering of 80,000 spectators that included Secretary of the Navy Adams, Governor Ritchie of Maryland, Alan Hoover, the son of the President; Admiral Hughes and a host of Senators and other distinguished figures in the official life of Washington, the Notre Dame football team hurdled one of the biggest obstacles on its schedule by defeating Navy today for the third successive year in the Baltimore stadium. The score was 14 to 7.

Getting off to a bad start in the opening period, when the midshipmen passed their way to a touchdown against a second string team, the South Benders rushed their stronger forces into the fray in the second quarter and thereafter were in command of the situation.

A forward pass from the brilliant Carideo to Elder tied the score in the second period and the winning touchdown was carried over in the final quarter by the devastating line-smasher, Mullins.

Crowd Packs the Stadium.

Not since the 1925 game between Navy and Army has such a tremendous crowd filled the municipal stadium here for a football game. There was not a vacant seat in the huge arena and hundreds stood in the aisles. With perfect weather prevailing, the presence of the regiment of 1,700 natty midshipmen and "His Nibs," the Navy goat, tickets were at a premium.

In the fierceness of the conflict and the savageness with which the two stalwart elevens grappled amid a constant din of cheers, the battle fully lived up to the best traditions of the first two of these annual classics, and provided stirring entertainment all the way.

Navy, fortified with the best material it has had since its unbeaten team of 1926, went into the game without being in the least intimidated by the prestige of its opponent, and determined to wipe out the defeats of 1927 and 1928. But as it happened, Notre Dame also boasts exceptionally high-class material, and was much further advanced today in its attack than was Bill Ingram's eleven.

The fact that Knute Rockne lay sick at his home in South Bend gave the Ramblers an additional incentive for wanting to win this game, and an hour's talk with their coach over long-distance telephone before they went out on the field was probably more inspiring to them than any dressing room lecture by Rockne in person could have been.

Well Ahead in Downs.

In the four periods Notre Dame made 20 first downs to 7 for Navy, registering 8 in the second to none for the Midshipmen, and 6 to 2 in the third.

Two thrilling goal line stands by Navy's fighting line in the second period prevented the Rockne men from scoring. On one of these stands Navy took the ball on downs less than two yards from its goal line, where it had been brought by a pass from Elder to Carideo and three line bucks, and a few minutes later Notre Dame was again stopped 12 yards away from the goal line.

It was Crane who helped to pave the way for Navy's touchdown when he took two passes from Joe Bauer that netted 25 yards. Those two passes were followed by a fumble by O'Connor, Notre Dame halfback, which Navy recovered on the opponents' 32-yard line. With the ball on the 7-yard line, Clifton carried it over in two smashes just before the first period ended.

The registering of that score by Navy brought out the Notre Dame first team a few seconds later, and thereafter the ball was always in Navy territory. Bowstrom, the left tackle, was repeatedly called on to kick from behind his goal line. The manner in which the Navy forward rose to the occasion on these difficult assignments was a feature of the game, as also were the quick kicks of Bauer, which Navy sprang right at the start of the play.

A 55-yard march gave Notre Dame its first touchdown. Martin Brill, who transferred from Penn, played a spectacular rôle in this march with two brilliant runs through a broken field. Mullins did his bit and then, with the ball on Navy's 11-yard line, the versatile Carideo passed to Elder over the goal line.

In the third period a 25-yard run around his left end by Brill put the ball on Navy's 8-yard line. This was the last play of the quarter and less than a minute after the final period

Continued on Page Two.

YALE BEATEN, 15-0, BY GEORGIA ELEVEN IN A STIRRING GAME

Blocked Kick, Safety and Long Pass Bring Stunning Defeat in the South.

SMITH IS SCORING STAR

Falls on Blocked Kick for Touchdown and Makes Another After Taking Pass.

35,000 DEDICATE STADIUM

Many Sit in Shirt Sleeves as the Temperature Exceeds 70—Missed Signal Leads to Safety.

By ROBERT F. KELLEY.

Special to The New York Times.

ATHENS, Ga., Oct. 12.—Yale's first football visit to the South ended in disaster on a Summer-like afternoon today as 35,000 persons, some of them in their shirt sleeves, watched the University of Georgia topple the Blue completely and convincingly by the margin of 15 to 0.

A blocked kick on Yale's goal line in the second period and the recovery of it for a touchdown by Vernon Smith, Georgia's left end; a safety after a mixed Yale signal in the third period and a long twisting pass to the same Smith with a following 12-yard run in the fourth period tell the story of the scoring.

But those details fail utterly to tell the story of the hard and decisive tackling that broke the men of Yale this afternoon. Smith kicked the goal after the first score, and missed the second, but none of the thousands of Southerners minded that. The end came a few minutes later with the roaring crowd descending on the field to celebrate Georgia's great victory.

Some Arrive by Plane.

The victory put the crowning touch to a perfect day for Southern football. The biggest crowd this little town ever has held for a game came by special train, airplane and thousands of cars; they saw the ceremonious dedication of the new Sanford Stadium. Then they settled back for the contest in a setting more like baseball than football. The temperature was well over 70 degrees and the sun was hot.

There is no doubt that Yale suffered badly from the heat. The Blue used so many substitutes it was impossible for the scorer to keep track of them, sending them in at times in groups of five or six. But it also was true that Georgia was much the better team today.

The Yale attack was stopped dead in its tracks for the most part by the hard charging of the Georgia forwards, and of thirteen Yale passes six were incomplete and two were intercepted.

Albie Booth, the little quarterback, entered the game halfway in the second period and played into the last period, but Yale never was able to shake him free for a twisting run and only in spots did he turn in the sensational carrying he showed against Vermont in the Bowl.

Leads in First Downs.

On the other hand, Yale did pretty well with Georgia attack, the Southerners gaining six first downs to Yale's seven, but the winners were by far the more alert team and took quick and decisive advantage of the breaks, played smarter football throughout and clearly earned their victory.

Yale kicked off and play stayed pretty well in Georgia's territory during the first period, but never with a Yale attack threatening. It was Yale's punting that kept it there as the teams exchanged kicks.

Yale, at the start, was rushing Smith, who also did his team's punting, and hurrying him. Then came the first break when a low, bounding punt got away from Wilson and Davidson recovered for Georgia on Yale's 46-yard line. Yale held and forced a kick over the line, but play had been shifted to Yale's half of the field.

After an exchange of punts in the second period, things broke suddenly for Georgia. Waugh came back well with a Yale punt that followed a long one by Smith to Yale's 35-yard line, a run of twelve yards. Yale braced strongly, but Kelley, Georgia's other end, made an amazing catch of a forward with two Yale men in front of him on the 20-yard line for a first down there. Then Waugh shot wide around left end to the 8-yard line.

Gallant Stand in Vain.

Yale made a gallant stand with Loeser jamming through and Hikok following him a play or so later to throw men for losses. Yale took the ball on downs on her 7-yard line, but the next play saw the turning of the scales. The Yale line, weakened by its desperate stand, let Georgia sift through. A knot of Southerners blocked McClennan's punt and Smith fell on the ball for the first touchdown.

Yale came back with one of its few real stretches of running, Booth showing well on one run of eighteen yards. But it was stopped on Georgia's 30-yard line and Booth tried a drop from the 35-yard line that fell far short of the mark for a touchback.

It wasn't far into the third period when Smith's fine punting brought another score. He placed one out of bounds on Yale's 12-yard line and on the next play came the safety. Apparently signals were mixed, for Booth was not near the centre's pass, which rolled over the goal line. He picked it up but couldn't get back across the goal line.

Roberts came back well with the free kick that followed and play started pretty much in Yale territory for the rest of the period. Georgia had the ball on Yale's 35-yard line at the start of the final period, but lost it when an incompleted pass came on the fourth down. Booth batting the ball down.

There followed soon after the first

Continued on Page Five.

Athletics' 10-Run Rally in 7th Beats Cubs 10-8

By JOHN DREBINGER.

Continued from Page One.

famed Liberty Bell off its pedestal six miles away.

Haas hit a long high fly to deep centre. The squat Hack Wilson, Cub centrefielder, wheeled about and ran at top speed, his short, stubby legs leaving nothing but a blur as they carried him over the ground. He got under the ball in time to make the catch, but as it came down it crossed the glaring sun. Hack lost sight of it. The ball almost struck him as it landed at his feet, and as it rolled away Boley and Bishop scampered wildly over the plate and Haas, too, completed the circuit for a home run.

The hit had scored three runs and the Athletics were now only one run behind. A sinking feeling must have gripped the Cubs, and as for the five hundred loyal rooters from Chicago, they had passed out long ago. But the assault was not ended yet. Its fury seemed to gain momentum with each succeeding minute.

Cochrane walked and Manager McCarthy unceremoniously yanked Nehf, a world's series hero of another day, and called on Sheriff Blake to stem the surging Mack attack. He stemmed it like a man sticking his head in an electric fan.

Simmons up for 2d Time.

Simmons, up for the second time, singled to left. Foxx singled to centre for his second hit of the inning and Cochrane crossed the plate.

That tied the score at 8-all and the turmoil in the stands was now quite indescribable. A great gathering of staid Philadelphians had suddenly gone completely out of their minds.

McCarthy, fairly beside himself, waved again to his rapidly fading forces in the Chicago bull pen and called on Pat Malone to succeed Blake.

Pat's first effort resulted in Miller getting a crack in the ribs with the ball, and that filled the bases. Then came the concluding stroke.

Dykes, who, it will be remembered, had singled the first time up in this inning, sent a low, hard liner screaming to the left corner of the playing field. Riggs Stephenson, Cub left fielder, chased it desperately, got both hands on the ball, but failed to hold it and, as it bounded away for a two-base hit, Simmons and Foxx scored the two runs that finally put the Mackmen in front.

That was all. It was enough. Malone struck out Boley. He also fanned Burns, who was still in the game as a pinch-hitter, and the crowd fell back in its seats exhausted. No attempts were made to revive the 500 Chicagoans.

All Sorts of Records Toppled.

All sorts of records had been broken as the game collapsed on top of the heads of the stunned Cubs. By scoring ten tallies the Athletics surpassed by two the record for most runs scored in a single inning by a team in a world series game, which was set by the Giants against the Yankees on Oct. 7, 1921.

In that same game and inning the Giants had totaled eight runs, which stood as the record until today, when the Athletics pummeled the four luckless Chicago pitchers for ten in that one tumultuous round.

Again in that same inning eight years ago, the late Ross Young hit safely twice to stand as the only player ever to perform this feat in world series play. Today Simmons, Foxx and Dykes equaled that achievement.

And there was still another record equaled, for after this tempestuous hitting orgy had put the Athletics two runs ahead Connie Mack still had an ace in the hole with which to protect that margin. He trotted out Lefty Grove to pitch the eighth and ninth innings.

Grove Retires Bewildered Cubs.

Lefty Bob, his smoke ball fairly burning down the trail, retired the bewildered Cubs in order in both innings, fanning four of them. And when he fanned the fourth it brought the Cubs' total of strike-outs for the game up to eight and for the series, forty-four.

This enabled the Cubs to tie the rather unenviable record set by the Giants in the series of 1911 in six games and tied by the Yankees in eight games in 1921. The Cubs, it will be noted, have equaled that mark in four.

Up to the moment that that cataclysm descended upon their unsuspecting heads, the Cubs had appeared almost certain winners of this game. Mack had chosen old John Quinn as his pitcher, and though old John skirted safely through the first three innings he plunged into difficulties in the fourth.

Cuyler singled in this round and raced all the way to third when Right Fielder Miller allowed the ball to get away from him. Stephenson's pop fly held the fleet Kiki glued to third, but Grimm walloped the ball over the right-field barrier for a homer and the Cubs were two runs in front.

Quinn's Downfall Comes in Sixth.

Quinn regained his composure in the fifth, but his years and also the Cubs got to him in the sixth and he went down in a heap. Hornsby, who previously had struck out for the seventh time in the series, slashed a single to centre. Wilson and Cuyler also singled, the latter's hit scoring the Rajah. Came another single by Stephenson to drive in Wilson and old John was carted tenderly off the playing field.

Rube Walberg, left-handed ace of the Mack staff, replaced him and added to the confusion. He fielded a tap by Grimm and hurled it wildly past first. It was scored as a hit for Grimm, an error for Walberg and accounted for two more runs, as both Cuyler and Stephenson tallied on the misplay, while Grimm pulled up at third. A moment later Grimm came in with the fifth Chicago run for the round on a sacrifice fly by Zach Taylor to Haas in centre.

Although Walberg succeeded in ending the inning well enough by fanning the next two batters, Mack chose to withdraw him, and when the Cubs came up for the seventh they found the right-handed Ed Rommel opposing them.

Hornsby Triples in Seventh.

This did not seem to displease them at all. With one out, Hornsby tripled to left centre and, after Wilson had walked, Cuyler banged a single to right to score the Rajah. It was Kiki's third straight hit and the entire Cub machine was now clicking perfectly.

Root, in the meantime, was pitching superby and never did he appear greater than in the fifth when Miller beat out an infield hit and Wilson, in some inexplicable manner, muffed a pop fly that fell squarely in his hands in centre.

But a piece of Mack strategy went wrong here and helped the Cubs. Maybe it was the now alert Cub team which caught the sign. In any event Miller and Dykes dashed for second and third as Root wound up to pitch to Boley. It was a hit-and-run play, but there was no hit, as Root pitched wide of the plate and as catcher Taylor whipped the ball to third Miller was thrown out at the post by yards.

Then Wilson redeemed himself by making a spectacular catch of a mighty wallop to right centre by Boley and another Mack rally had been effectually blocked.

In the sixth Root effaced the leaders of the Mack batting order in less time than it takes to tell it. The Cub machine was now moving along magnificently and in all its glistening splendor. Twenty minutes later it lay strewn all over the field, a jangled mass of junk.

Whether McCarthy will be able to patch the broken pieces together is a matter that all Philadelphia is convinced cannot be done. To win the series the Cubs must take three in a row. One more game, the fifth, will be played here on Monday, there being no game tomorrow, and if the Cubs do manage to win that one the series will have to move back to Chicago for completion. But Philadelphia is confident Chicago will not see its Cubs in action again this year.

Times Wide World Photo.

Left to Right—Rogers Hornsby, Hack Wilson, Al Simmons and Jimmy Foxx.

Heavy Hitters of the World's Series Teams, as They Appeared at Shibe Park.

TEN SERIES RECORDS BROKEN OR EQUALED

Athletics' Famous Seventh Inning Brings New Mark in Baseball Classic.

PHILADELPHIA, Oct. 12 (AP).—Ten world's series records were either broken or equaled today by the Athletics in the spectacular seventh inning outburst that gave them their third triumph over the Cubs. This was a record in itself.

One of the marks was equaled twice and another three times, statisticians found after recovering from their dizziness.

Here's what the Athletic's famous seventh did to the record books:

1. Most hits, one club, one inning, 10; beating former record of 8 by Giants against Yankees, Oct. 7, 1921.
2. Most runs, one club, one inning, 10; beating former record of 8 by Giants against Yankees, 1921.
3. Most men at bat, one club, one inning, one club, 6; beating former record of 3 Giants against Yankees, 1921.
4. Most batters up twice in one inning, 6; beating former record of 3 Giants against Yankees, 1921.
5. Most times same pinch-hitter up in one inning, 2; by George Burns.
6. Most home runs, one club, one inning, 2; by Simmons and Haas, equaling record shared by several.
7. Most runs both clubs, one game, 18; equaling total of Giants and Yankees in 1921.
8. Most base hits by one player, one inning, 2 each by Simmons, Foxx and Dykes; equaling record by Ross Young of Giants against Yankees, 1921.
9. Most total bases, one player, one inning, 5; by Simmons (home run and single) equalling record of Young who made double and triple, 1921.
10. Most runs, one player, one inning, 2 each by Simmons and Foxx; equaling record of Frank Frisch of Giants, 1921

ODDS RISE SHARPLY ON THE ATHLETICS

10 to 15 to 1 Offered in Philadelphia and 15 to 20 to 1 in Chicago Betting Circles.

LITTLE CUB MONEY EVIDENT

21 to 1 Is the Price Offered Here—Wagering on Outcome Lightest in Series' History.

Special to The New York Times.

PHILADELPHIA, Oct. 12.—As a result of the Athletics' victory over the Cubs today, giving the American Leaguers a tremendous edge over their National League rivals, practically all the Cubs' money disappeared and the odds on the Athletics, which were on the verge of being eliminated, jumped higher than before.

Nothing that could be called official odds is quotable because of the little betting that has been done on this series, but it is likely that 10 to 15 to 1 on the Athletics for the series would have to be offered tonight to bring a response from any Cub backer.

There are some who would demand even greater odds on what appears to them to be the very slim chance the Cubs have now.

Special to The New York Times.

CHICAGO, Oct. 12.—There was no Cub money in Chicago tonight, the followers of the Philadelphia team offering 15 and 20 to 1 that the Philadelphia team would take down the world's title. There was not even a murmur from the Chicago team's backers.

It is expected that the Athletics will go into the fifth game Monday as the two to one favorites. These odds prevailed tonight.

The New York odds on the Athletics now are 20 to 1 to win the world series. This was the price quoted yesterday after the Athletics came through with their smashing attack to score their third victory With only one game needed, and that to be played on their home field, the Mackmen are decided favorites. This confidence also is reflected in the price of 7 to 5 on the Athletics for the fifth game of the series.

The betting continues light in New York and from a betting point of view this series will go down as the lightest in the history of the Fall classic. From the start the Chicago money has been scarce and even excellent prices failed to bring it out. A few commissioners said that a team that takes a beating such as the Cubs did after holding what looked like a winning lead at the end of six innings is enough to break the morale of the players.

Even at 7 to 5 on the fifth game little money was placed. Much of course will depend upon tomorrow's pitching selection, but after using five pitchers in one game it does not seem as though the Cubs will have much in the way of mound opposition for the Mackmen.

CUBS ATTRIBUTE DEFEAT TO BREAKS

'Can't Beat the Sun,' McCarthy Says, Recalling Haas's Fly Which Got by Wilson.

By ROSCOE McGOWEN.

Special to The New York Times.

PHILADELPHIA, Oct. 12.—Four hundred and thirty-seven years ago Columbus discovered America, in which is located Shibe Park, where Connie Mack's Athletics play ball. It might be assumed that the general feeling around the Cubs' clubhouse after today's disastrous defeat would be that the discovery was an error.

On the contrary, however, your correspondent found the McCarthy men, including their stocky little boss, still as full of fight as a lot of full grown grizzly bears.

"Breaks," said Art Nehf. "I'll say they got 'em. The second hit of Al Simmons in the seventh was a perfect double play ball and it bounced over McMillan's head. We (meaning the Giants) lost a series in the same manner to the Senators in 1924."

"But," added the little southpaw, "we're not done yet. Don't forget that."

McCarthy a Bit Wistful.

Manager McCarthy, dressed for the street, smiled a bit wistfully as he replied to queries from the writer.

"You can't beat the sun, can you?" he counter-questioned, and after watching Old Sol do his worst with Hack Wilson this afternoon, and even doing queer things to the eyes of Art Nehf when he took the mound in the seventh, there could be no argument about that.

Mule Haas, the fleet centre fielder of the Athletics, gave Wilson an alibi—had he asked for one, which he didn't—for missing the drive by Haas that rolled past the Cub outfielder to the centre field wall for a home run, as well as for another fly that Hack lost in the blazing sun.

"I don't blame Wilson a bit," said Haas. "Believe me, that sun was terrible out there and maybe I got a break that I didn't lose one myself."

Wilson had nothing to say to anybody from the press. He obviously felt bad about the unfortunate part he played, albeit helplessly, in the loss of a game that the Cubs seemed safely to have won before Simmons began that weird seventh inning with his home run on the leftfield stand roof.

He rushed from the clubhouse, picked up his three-year-old son and pushed his way rapidly through the thinning crowd out of the park, devoting all of his conversational efforts to the little fellow.

Connie Mack Speechless.

Connie Mack wasn't the purposely reticent old silver fox of the American League when he was encountered after the game. The veteran manager was practically speechless and could only stand and wave his two clenched fists in the air while he sought vainly to swallow an enormous lump in his throat.

He finally did manage to murmur something about a "glorious victory," which probably wasn't what he meant at all. For, although glory may accrue as a result of today's victory, the triumph itself was due much more to a club's debacle than extraordinary playing by the Athletics.

Athletics' Record Rally to Win Followed Double Play

2 FEATURES MARKED ATHLETICS' VICTORY

Sparkling Double Play Checked Third Cub Drive—Record Rally Then Followed.

10 RUNS SET SERIES MARK

Largest Total Ever Made in One Inning—Simmons's Home Run Was Keynote.

AUTUMN SUN PROVED AID

Hindered Wilson in Effort to Catch Haas's Blow, Analysis Shows —Grove Is Effective.

By WILLIAM E. BRANDT.
Special to The New York Times.

PHILADELPHIA, Oct. 12.—Calm retrospect of the helter-skelter spectacle which because of the Athletics' ten-run seventh-inning rally, was in that phase of ball playing the most remarkable game in world's series history focuses two definite points in the mêlée at which the battle tide took a sharp twist.

Those two episodes stand out in sharp demarcation from their context The first swirl of the tide turned the fortunes of war toward the Cubs' cause and carried them so far that before the reverse twist spun the trend in favor of the Mackmen, the Cubs owned an 8 to 0 lead and already foretasted the joy of overwhelming triumph.

The second twist came after the Cub offensive launched its third drive in four innings. The Cubs scored a run in the seventh on a triple and a single. They had two on bases with only one out and prospects of running their tally total to double figures in another few minutes.

Then came the stroke that marked the limit of Cub mastery, a double play, Dykes to Bishop to Foxx, which was a marvel of fielding speed and precision all the way through, the flashiest double play of the series so far. The Cubs were more than merely repulsed in a scoring drive. Within five minutes they were fighting furiously to block a barrage of hits.

Sweeps Cubs Before It.

This second lurch of the tide was the mightiest in world's series history, which details twenty-six hard fought Autumn campaigns. It swept the Cubs before it like driftwood and assembled for the records the hugest offensive total for one inning in a world's series. It overcome an eight-run lead to win the game, 10—8, exalting the Athletics in the space of three put-outs to the name of being the greatest last ditch resurgents a world's series assemblage ever applauded.

After that tide-turning double play was dropped on the Cubs, the keynote for the seventh inning was sounded by Simmons, whose bat unloosed a titanic home-run drive that squirmed across the roof of the two-story left field stand.

Then came a barrage of singles, and Charlie Root, a great pitcher in defeat on Tuesday, a shut-out pitcher for two-thirds of today's game, had to retreat. Nehf and Blake advanced and retreated. Pat Malone it was who finally stopped the onslaught by striking out Boley and Burns.

As happens whenever battle tides run like race horses, that huge inning was crowded with breaks of fortune, all favoring the riders of the tide. For one thing, the Autumn sun slanted over the grand stand from directly behind home plate out to centre field, instead of at its Summer angle, which points straight to right field.

Makes a Desperate Lunge.

Haas's home run was a short hard fly which, because of the sun's direct glare, was first misjudged by Centrefielder Wilson, then was overrun by Wilson's desperate lunge to catch the ball before it fell.

Seven singles there were in this Mack drive and exactly five of them passed through the Cub infield by margins so narrow that one more step by the pursuing player would have caught the ball and stemmed the storm of hitting.

The winning hit, Dykes's double to left, which drove home the ninth and tenth runs, was a long liner which Stephenson held fairly in his glove, only to spill the ball to the grass, probably because the bases were filled and the score tied with only one out. Had he caught the ball he still could not have kept Simmons from scoring from third, but Stephenson, like all his confrères, was in the grip of a deadly current.

The scoring ceased after that, but the force of the tide carried on. In the eighth and ninth the Cubs were feeble fumblers at empty space when they stood up with bats against Grove's fast ball. The agile southpaw struck out Taylor, Hartnett, McMillan and English. The two other batters who faced him, Grimm and Hornsby, offered a grounder to shortstop and a short fly to right respectively.

The strikeout of English, the eighth Chicago strikeout of the day, tied the long-standing record of forty-four for a team in a world's series. Hornsby's fly for the game's final out accomplished at best only the detaining of the club strikeout record breaking until Monday.

STORY OF THE GAME TOLD PLAY BY PLAY

Ten-Run Outburst in the Seventh by the Athletics Brought About Cubs's Downfall.

Special to The New York Times.

PHILADELPHIA, Oct. 12.—The play-by-play description of the fourth game of the world's series follows:

First Inning.

CHICAGO—Quinn couldn't find the plate at the start and walked McMillan on four pitches. With the count two and two, English lifted a foul to Miller just across the line. The count went to three and two on Hornsby and then he went down swinging. It was Hornsby's seventh strikeout of the series. Hack Wilson took one strike and slapped the next pitch to right for a clean single, McMillan stopping at second. Cuyler got one ball, fouled the next three, and watched the third strike go by to even his series total with Hornsby. No runs, one hit, no errors, two left.

PHILADELPHIA—Bishop and Haas went out quickly, the former lifting a short fly to Stephenson and the latter being thrown out by McMillan on his topped roller. Cochrane then popped high to English. No runs, no hits, no errors, none left.

Second Inning.

CHICAGO—Quinn set the Cubs down in order and quickly, Bishop tossing out Stephenson, Cochrane making a fine catch of Grimm's low foul close to the stands near the Athletics' dugout, and Taylor duplicating Stephenson's retirement method. No runs, no hits, no errors, none left.

PHILADELPHIA—Simmons swung at a third strike and Foxx grounded to English, whose throw was off line enough so that Grimm had to tag the runner. McMillan made a fine pick-up of Miller's mean grounder to get him at first. No runs, no hits, no errors, none left.

Third Inning.

CHICAGO—Boley drew a tremendous cheer when he took Root's bounder back of second and threw out the Cub pitcher. McMillan fouled to Foxx, but English worked Quinn for a pass. Boley came far in front of second to take Hornsby's bounder and toss him out. No runs, no hits, no errors, one left.

PHILADELPHIA—Dykes singled to right. Cuyler let the ball get through him for an error and the runner reached second. Boley sacrificed Dykes to third, Grimm unassisted. Root made violent protest to Van Graflan on a third ball, but fanned Quinn on the next pitch. With the count three and two, Bishop grounded to Grimm unassisted. No runs, one hit, one error, one left.

Fourth Inning.

CHICAGO—Wilson flied to Miller near the wall. Cuyler slashed a single past Foxx and Miller let it get through for a two-base error. Stephenson popped to Boley, Cuyler holding third. Miller's error was nullified a moment later when Grimm whacked the ball over the right field wall for a home run, scoring Cuyler ahead of him. Taylor grounded to Boley. Two runs, two hits, one error, none left.

PHILADELPHIA—Haas popped to Taylor, who nearly collided with McMillan, also after the ball. With the count three and two, Cochrane hit a slow, looping double to left. Simmons grounded to McMillan and Cochrane was run down, McMillan to Hornsby, Simmons reaching first. Wilson went almost to the left centre field wall to take Foxx's fly. No runs, one hit, no errors, one left.

Fifth Inning.

CHICAGO—Root got the count to three and two, then grounded to Dykes. McMillan went out easily, Boley to Foxx. Quinn got into another hole with English, but came out of it when the Cub shortstop lined to Bishop. No runs, no hits, no errors, none left.

PHILADELPHIA—Miller slashed a single off Root's glove, the ball rolling slowly toward McMillan. Wilson came in for Dykes's high fly, but muffed it for the second Cub error of the game, and Miller reached second. On a hit and run play Miller was thrown out at third, Taylor to McMillan, and a moment later Wilson redeemed himself by a marvelous running one-hand catch of Boley's long fly toward the scoreboard. Quinn was called out on strikes. No runs, one hit, one error, one left.

Sixth Inning.

CHICAGO—Hornsby opened with a single to centre, and Wilson slapped the first pitched ball for another single between Foxx and Bishop, Hornsby stopping at second. A third single from Cuyler's bat scored Hornsby and sent Wilson to third. Wilson scored on Stephenson's single, which Bishop knocked down but couldn't field. Cuyler took second. Quinn was replaced by Rube Walberg. Grimm's bunt went for a single, and Walberg sent both Cuyler and Stephenson across the plate when he picked up the ball and threw to the stands past Foxx for an error. Taylor's fly to Haas went for a sacrifice, to score Quinn. The play at the plate was close. Haas making a fine throw to Cochrane. Root struck out. McMillan also fanned. Five runs, five hits, one error, none left.

PHILADELPHIA—Root set the Athletics down in order for the third time in the game. Bishop flied to Stephenson. Hornsby tossed out Haas and Wilson took Cochrane's long fly. No runs, no hits, no errors, one left.

Official Box Score of the Fourth World's Series Game

CHICAGO CUBS.

	AB.	R.	H.	TB.	2B.	3B.	HR.	BB.	SO.	SH.	SB.	PO.	A.	E.
McMillan, 3b	4	0	0	0	0	0	0	1	2	0	0	1	3	0
English, ss	4	0	0	0	0	0	0	1	1	0	0	2	1	0
Hornsby, 2b	5	2	2	4	0	1	0	0	1	0	0	1	1	0
Wilson, c	3	1	2	2	0	0	0	1	0	0	0	3	0	1
Cuyler, rf	4	2	3	3	0	0	0	0	1	0	0	0	0	1
Stephenson, lf	4	1	1	1	0	0	0	0	0	0	0	2	1	0
Grimm, 1b	4	2	2	5	0	0	1	0	0	0	0	7	0	0
Taylor, c	3	0	0	0	0	0	0	0	1	1	0	8	1	0
Root, p	3	0	0	0	0	0	0	0	1	0	0	0	0	0
Nehf, p	0	0	0	0	0	0	0	0	0	0	0	0	0	0
Blake, p	0	0	0	0	0	0	0	0	0	0	0	0	0	0
Malone, p	0	0	0	0	0	0	0	0	0	0	0	0	0	0
aHartnett	1	0	0	0	0	0	0	0	1	0	0	0	0	0
Carlson, p	0	0	0	0	0	0	0	0	0	0	0	0	1	0
Total	35	8	10	15	0	1	1	3	8	1	0	24	8	2

PHILADELPHIA ATHLETICS.

	AB.	R.	H.	TB.	2B.	3B.	HR.	BB.	SO.	SH.	SB.	PO.	A.	E.
Bishop, 2b	5	1	2	2	0	0	0	0	0	0	0	2	3	0
Haas, cf	4	1	1	4	0	0	1	0	0	1	0	2	0	0
Cochrane, c	4	1	2	3	1	0	0	1	0	0	0	9	0	0
Simmons, lf	5	2	2	5	0	0	1	0	2	0	0	0	0	0
Foxx, 1b	4	2	2	2	0	0	0	0	0	0	0	10	0	0
Miller, rf	3	1	2	2	0	0	0	0	0	0	0	3	0	1
Dykes, 3b	4	1	3	4	1	0	0	0	0	0	0	0	2	0
Boley, ss	3	1	1	1	0	0	0	0	1	1	0	1	5	0
Quinn, p	2	0	0	0	0	0	0	0	2	0	0	0	0	0
Walberg, p	0	0	0	0	0	0	0	0	0	0	0	0	0	1
Rommel, p	0	0	0	0	0	0	0	0	0	0	0	0	0	0
bBurns	2	0	0	0	0	0	0	0	1	0	0	0	0	0
Grove, p	0	0	0	0	0	0	0	0	0	0	0	0	0	0
Total	36	10	15	23	2	0	2	1	6	2	0	27	10	2

a Batted for Malone in the eighth.
b Batted for Rommel in the seventh.

SCORE BY INNINGS.

Chicago	0	0	0	2	0	5	1	0	0	— 8
Philadelphia	0	0	0	0	0	0	10	0	x	—10

Runs batted in—Cuyler 2, Stephenson 1, Grimm 2, Taylor 1, Bishop 1, Haas 3, Simmons 1, Foxx 1, Dykes 3, Boley 1.

Left on bases—Chicago 4, Philadelphia 6. Bases on balls—Off Quinn 2, Rommel 1, Nehf 1. Struck out—By Quinn 2, Walberg 2, Grove 4, Root 3, Malone 2, Carlson 1. Earned runs—Off Quinn 5, Rommel 1, Root 6, Nehf 2, Blake 2. Hits—Off Quinn, 7 in 5 innings (none out in sixth); Walberg, 1 in 1; Rommel, 2 in 1; Grove, 0 in 2; Root, 9 in 6 1-3; Nehf, 1 in 0 (pitched to two batters); Blake, 2 in 0 (pitched to two batters); Malone, 1 in 2-3; Carlson, 2 in 1. Double plays—Dykes, Bishop and Foxx. Hit by pitcher—By Malone (Miller). Winning pitcher—Rommel. Losing pitcher—Blake. Umpires—Van Graflan (A. L.) at plate, Klem (N. L.) at first base, Dinneen (A. L.) at second base, Moran (N. L.) at third base. Time of game—2:12.

29,991 Persons Paid $140,815 At Fourth World's Series Game

STANDING OF THE CLUBS

	Won	Lost	P.C.
Athletics	3	1	.750
Cubs	1	3	.250

FOURTH GAME STATISTICS

Attendance (paid)	29,991
Receipts (without tax)	$140,815.00
Commissioner's share	14,081.50
Players' share	76,040.10
Each club's share	12,673.35
Each league's share	12,673.35

TOTAL FOR FOUR GAMES

Attendance (paid)	160,709
Receipts (without tax)	$718,679.00
Commissioner's share	71,867.90
Players' share	388,086.66
Each club's share	64,681.11
Each league's share	64,681.11

Last year's fourth game drew a total of 37,331 fans to St. Louis. The receipts were $161,902. For the four games in 1928 the total paid attendance was 199,075 and the receipts were $777,290.

Seventh Inning.

CHICAGO—Rommel went in to pitch for the Athletics. English flied to Haas in short centre, but Hornsby sent the ball far over Haas's head for a triple. Wilson walked. Cuyler slapped his third single of the game to left, scoring Hornsby, but Stephenson hit into a fast double play, Dykes to Bishop to Foxx. One run, two hits, no errors, one left.

PHILADELPHIA—Simmons gave the crowd its first chance to cheer by bouncing the ball on the roof of the left field stands for a homer. Foxx singled to right and Miller got a single to centre when Wilson lost his short fly in the sun. Dykes followed with another single to left that scored Foxx with the second Athletic run. Boley also singled to right to score Miller from second and send Dykes to third. George Burns batted for Rommel and popped to English. Bishop bounced a single over Root's head, scoring Dykes and sending Boley to third. McCarthy removed Root to send the veteran southpaw, Nehf, to the rescue. Haas's hard drive to centre was lost in the sun by Wilson and went past him for a home run. Boley and Bishop scored ahead of Haas and the Athletics were only one run behind. Cochrane drew a pass after taking only one strike and Nehf was taken out, leaving the tying run on first. Blake replaced Nehf. With the count three and one, Simmons, up for the second time, again hit safely when his grounder hopped over McMillan's head for a single, Cochrane stopping at second. Foxx singled for the second time in the inning to score Cochrane with the tying run. McCarthy removed Blake and sent Pat Malone to the mound. Malone's first pitch hit Miller and filled the bases with only one out. Dykes's long fly almost to the left field wall went for a double when Stephenson failed on the catch after a desperate leap. Simmons and Foxx scored to put the Athletics two runs ahead. Boley struck out and Burns, pinch-hitting for the second time, ended the inning by also fanning. Ten runs, ten hits, no errors, two left.

Eighth Inning.

CHICAGO—Grove went to the mound for the Athletics. Boley threw out Grimm. Taylor struck out and Hartnett, batting for Malone, also fanned. No runs, no hits, no errors, none left.

PHILADELPHIA—Carlson went in to pitch for the Cubs. Bishop sent a sinking liner to left for a single. Haas sacrificed, Carlson to Grimm. With the count three and one, Cochrane slapped a single to left and Bishop was out at the plate, Stephenson to Taylor, Cochrane reaching second on the throw. Simmons was called out on strikes. No runs, two hits, no errors, one left.

Ninth Inning.

CHICAGO—McMillan fanned on three pitched balls. Grove's speed under the lengthening shadows of the stands seemed too much for the Cubs. English swung at the first pitch, fouled the next three, and took the third one with his bat on his shoulder. English thereby tied a record for the Cubs for number of strikeouts in a world's series, which is held jointly by the Giants of 1910 and the Yankees of 1921 at forty-four each. Hornsby flied to Miller. No runs, no hits, no errors, none left.

The New York Times.

*** SUNDAY, JUNE 8, 1930.

SPORTS Section 11

GALLANT FOX BEATS WHICHONE 4 LENGTHS IN $81,340 BELMONT

Woodward's Preakness, Derby Winner Ties Sir Barton as Triple Crown Hero.

SANDE IS UP ONCE MORE

Famous Jockey, Face Bandaged From Auto Crash, Carries On to Cheers of 40,000.

SETS RECORD FOR EVENT

Goes Mile and Half in 2:31 3-5—Clinches 3-Year-Old Title in Beating 3-5 Favorite.

BREEDING OF GALLANT FOX

GALLANT FOX, Bay Colt, 1927
- *Sir G'had III
  - Teddy: Ajax, Rondeau
  - Plucky Liege: Spearmint, Concertina
- Marguerite
  - Celt: Commando, *Maid of Erin
  - *Fairy Ring: Radium, Seraph

*Imported.

By BRYAN FIELD.

There no longer exists any doubt about William Woodward's Gallant Fox being the greatest 3-year-old of the year.

At Belmont Park before 40,000 persons, many of whom stood in a drizzling rain, the winner of the Wood Memorial, Preakness and Kentucky Derby added the historic Belmont Stakes to his list of triumphs yesterday, soundly beating Harry Payne Whitney's Whichone, considered by many before the race as the best horse since Man o' War.

The race had a gross value of $81,340 the richest of its kind anywhere in the world—and $66,040 of this went to the winner, bringing the earnings of the 3-year-old son of Sir Gallahad III and Marguerite to $198,730.

The end of the mile and a half test saw Gallant Fox four lengths in front of Whichone and going away further with each jump. James Butler's Questionnaire was four lengths further back, to be third, and Walter J. Salmon's Swinfield brought up the rear. Gallant Fox finished in 2:31 3-5, the fastest time for the race since it was increased to a mile and a half in 1926.

While Gallant Fox set a record for the Belmont over the mile and a half route, the track record for that distance is held by Man o' War, 2:28 4-5, established in 1920. The previous best time for the mile and half in the Belmont was made by Crusader in 1926 when he was clocked in 2:32 1-5.

Sande Grins Through Patches.

Earl Sande rode the winner, kept him in front from start to finish, and grinned through the patches of adhesive tape which marked a motor accident. He gave all the credit to his mount, which by winning the Preakness, Kentucky Derby and Belmont has equaled the feat of Sir Barton.

These two horses are the only ones to win the "triple crown," but Sir Barton's star later was dimmed by a defeat by the great Man o' War. There seems little likelihood of any horse stopping Gallant Fox, and if he goes on to the American Derby and American Classic in Chicago those races apparently will be at his mercy.

Great as he is now, he seems headed for greater glory. Mr. Woodward was warmly congratulated by Joseph E. Widener, president of the Westchester Racing Association, and others of the fashionable throng.

Mr. Woodward led his horse in from the racing strip to a roped off enclosure alongside the stewards' stand so that the spectators might get a good look at the 3-year-old champion. Mr. Woodward was indeed a proud man.

Gallant Fox was a fractious youngster and very nearly stepped on the foot of his owner, but Mr. Woodward held on to his bridle and managed the colt until Jim Fitzsimmons, trainer of Gallant Fox, stepped up and took him in hand. Fitzsimmons was congratulated right and left also, for he has done a great job in keeping the horse in tip top racing condition to beat the best of the East and the West.

Enthusiasm Despite Rain.

Much of the sparkle and glamour was taken from the throng by the rain, but every one went about the business of supporting his choice with vigor and enthusiasm. Despite the prowess of Gallant Fox, the Whitney horse was made the 3-to-5 public choice, while Gallant Fox was as good as 8 to 5.

Therefore, Gallant Fox was beating a very heavily backed favorite when he came down to the line first, but his reception and the roar of welcome were as virile as those in Maryland and Kentucky when he won the greatest classics in those States.

Few races have caused greater excitement in the East, or for that matter, in the country, than the meeting between Gallant Fox and Whichone. The Belmont first was run in 1867 at old Jerome Park, but none of the great duels in its long history aroused as much interest as that yesterday.

And when it came right down to the running, it was not a duel at all because Gallant Fox made a proces-

Continued on Page Five.

Winners of Historic Belmont For the Last Fifteen Years

The last fifteen winners of the Belmont Stakes, a test of a mile and a half for 3-year-olds, which was first run in 1867, when it was captured by Ruthless, follow:

Year.	Winner.	Time.	Value to Winner.
1916	Friar Rock	2:22	$4,100
1917	Hourless	2:17 4-5	5,800
1918	Johren	2:20 2-5	8,950
1919	Sir Barton	2:17 2-5	11,950
1920	Man o' War	2:14 1-5	7,950
1921	Grey Lag	2:16 4-5	8,650
1922	Pillory	2:18 4-5	39,200
1923	Zev	2:19	38,000
1924	Mad Play	2:18 4-5	42,880
1925	Amer. Flag	2:16 4-5	38,500
1926	Crusader	*2:32 1-5	48,550
1927	Chance Shot	2:32 2-5	60,910
1928	Vito	2:33 1-5	63,430
1929	B. Larkspur	2:32 4-5	59,650
1930	Gallant Fox	2:31 3-5	66,040

*Distance increased from 1⅜ to 1½ miles.

OTT'S TWO HOMERS SUBDUE CARDINALS

They Yield Six Runs for Giants, as Each Comes With Two Runners on Base.

SECOND MADE IN SEVENTH

Victors Trail, 7-6, Before Decisive Smash—McGrawmen Take Third Place.

By WILLIAM E. BRANDT.

Sidepocket home-run drives dropping in the lower right-field stands close to the foul line and not very far from home plate provided the chief thrills at the Polo Grounds yesterday when the Giants stretched their winning streak to seven straight and displaced the Pirates from third place.

The final score stood 9 to 7, but for the duration of a depressing half hour immediately after Tayler Douthit's sidepocket homer in the fifth the visiting team held a two-run lead.

Then came the seventh, with its royal rally by the men of McGraw. Four snappy singles served as a prelude for Mel Ott's second homer of the afternoon, his twelfth of the season, and the ball game's winning hit.

This seventh-inning homer by Louisiana Melvin also was a sidepocket shot, the ball dipping into the stands so close to the foul line that the Cardinals disputed Umpire Magerkurth's ruling that it was a fair ball.

Ott's First Homer Goes Far.

Mel's first-inning homer, however, was beyond cavil as to fairness and force. That one sailed so fair and so far that it banged against a chair in the upper story of the right-field stands, way out toward centre field.

The 18,000 fans, most of them driven back from the front rows by the drizzle that fell throughout most of the nine innings, drew their main joy from the Giant batting flurries in the first and seventh innings and from little Mel's big deeds.

The game started as a Southpaw duel between Clarence Mitchell, the ex-Cardinal, and Wild Bill Hallahan. Both pitchers found the ball hard to handle in the first inning. Mitchell walked two cards and he was found for three singles.

It took Ott to get the side out. On Wilson's single to right Little Mel threw a better strike to home plate than Mitchell had been able to pitch. Mel's throw cut down Bottomley trying to score from second and retired the side.

Hallahan passed the first two Giants. Lindstrom's single scored Critz, then Ott's long-range homer yielded three more runs and made the score 4 to 2. Pruett took Mitchell's place and held the Cards safe for three innings.

Cardinals Take Lead.

In the fifth a walk, a single and Douthit's side-pocket homer put the Cards ahead. Blades's double and Wilson's single made the score 6 to 4. Pruett's wild throw in the seventh started the Cards off to their seventh run. The McGraw cause looked dubious at this juncture, for after the first inning the Giants had located Hallahan for nothing more than two scratch hits.

But Marshall came up as a pinch hitter for Pruett starting the home half of the seventh. His line single to centre was the first gun of the winning rally. After Critz was called out on strikes Roettger, Terry and Lindstrom rattled singles to the outfield, two runs scoring, and the tally standing at 7 to 6.

With just a single needed to tie the score, Ott drove his homer down the right-field foul line, and three runs scored.

The Giants needed only a good relief pitcher to hold the Cards through the last two innings, and Joe Heving was the right man. George Fisher, who trained with the Giants last

Continued on Page Six.

Times Wide World Photo.

Gallant Fox Winning the Belmont Stakes by Four Lengths From Whichone.

Times Wide World Photo.

Joseph E. Widener (Left), Sande and William Woodward.

Times Wide World Photo.

Gallant Fox, With Earl Sande Up, Just After the Race.

ROBINS TAME CUBS ON CLARK'S HOMER

Pitcher Connects With Two Men On in 7th and Shatters Chicago's 9-Game Streak.

20,000 CHEER THE VICTORY

Champions Bow Despite Four Circuit Blows—Winners Regain 2-Game Lead.

By ROSCOE McGOWEN.

William Watson Clark, slender Brooklyn southpaw, yesterday shattered the nine-game winning streak of the Chicago Cubs in one of the most fiercely contested battles of the season, which the Robins finally won, 12 to 9, to regain their two-game league lead.

Clark entered the game in the fifth inning as a relief pitcher and performed nicely, but it wasn't his pitching that dislodged the champions from what appeared to be a secure perch of victory. It was his home run over the right-field wall, off Lyn Nelson in the seventh inning, that came with Finn and Lopez on bases and the Robins trailing, 8 to 9.

The hit put the flock into a lead they never relinquished and sent the crowd of 20,000 fans into a joyous outburst of cheering that lasted for many minutes.

Four Chicago home runs were made during the game, two by Woody English and one each by Hack Wilson and Clyde Beck, but none had the stamp of authority that was visible on Clark's smash. The Brooklyn pitcher's circuit blow was no fluke but a ball as well hit as many blasted over the same right field wall by Herman, Ott, Klein, Wilson and other recognized sluggers. All the Cub homers save English's second one bounded into the left field circus seats.

A fine, drizzling rain was falling at 3 o'clock and the game was delayed

Continued on Page Six.

MAJOR LEAGUE BASEBALL

NATIONAL LEAGUE.

YESTERDAY'S RESULTS.

New York 9, St. Louis 7.
Brooklyn 12, Chicago 9.
Boston 6, Pittsburgh 4.
Cincinnati at Philadelphia. (Rain.)

STANDING OF THE CLUBS.

	Won.	Lost.	P.C.
Brooklyn	29	17	.630
Chicago	28	20	.583
New York	24	22	.522
Pittsburgh	22	22	.500
St. Louis	24	24	.500
Boston	19	24	.442
Cincinnati	18	27	.400
Philadelphia	16	24	.400

WHERE THEY PLAY TODAY.

St. Louis at New York (3 P. M.).
Chicago at Brooklyn (3 P. M.).
Pittsburgh at Boston.
Philadelphia at Cincinnati.

AMERICAN LEAGUE.

YESTERDAY'S RESULTS.

New York 12, St. Louis 5.
Chicago 6, Philadelphia 5.
Detroit 6, Boston 0.
Washington at Cleveland. (Rain.)

STANDING OF THE CLUBS.

	Won.	Lost.	P.C.
Philadelphia	31	16	.660
Washington	29	16	.644
Cleveland	27	19	.587
New York	24	19	.558
Chicago	18	24	.429
Detroit	20	27	.426
St. Louis	18	28	.391
Boston	14	32	.304

WHERE THEY PLAY TODAY.

New York at St. Louis.
Boston at Detroit.
Philadelphia at Chicago.
Washington at Cleveland.

JAPAN LEADS SPAIN IN DAVIS CUP PLAY

Takes Two Singles Matches—England Wins in Doubles—Italy Leading.

BARCELONA, June 7 (AP).—Japan took both of the opening singles matches today in its third-round Davis Cup tennis contest with Spain. Yoshiro Ohta defeated Juanico, 6—1, 3—6, 6—2, 6—2 and Takeichi Harada downed Maier, 3—6, 6—2, 6—0, 6—4.

EASTBOURNE, England, June 7 (AP).—England defeated Australia in the doubles match of their third-round Davis Cup tie today, J. C. Gregory and I. G. Collins winning from Jack Crawford and Harry Hopman, 8—6, 10—8, 6—2. The match score now stands at 2—1, Australia leading by virtue of having taken the two opening singles yesterday.

VIENNA, June 7 (AP).—Italy took a lead of two matches to one over Austria today in their third-round Davis Cup tennis contest by winning the doubles match, 9—11, 8—6, 6—1, 1—6, 6—4. The opening singles matches yesterday were divided.

PENN STATE HALTS ONONDAGA TWELVE

Triumphs at Lacrosse by 3-2 Count—Homer of Indians Suffers Broken Arm.

Special to The New York Times.

STATE COLLEGE, Pa., June 7.—Penn State's lacrosse team nosed out the Onondaga Indians today, 3 to 2.

Homer, the Indians' cover point, suffered a broken arm in the second period and had to retire.

The line-up:

Penn State (3).		Indians (2).
Kearl Kaiser	G	Lyons
McMillen	P	Jones
Kaplan	C.P.	Homer
Prizer	F.D.	Williams
Stahley	S.D.	M. Edwards
E. Edwards	T.D.	C. Jones
Weber	C.	Gibson
Anderson	T.A.	W. Powless
Koth	S.A.	I. Powless
Antonson	F.A.	Pierce
Ken Kaiser	O.H.	J. Lewis
D. Lewis	I.H.	A. Lewis

Goals—W. Powless 2, D. Lewis, Koth, Weber.

Substitutions—Penn State: Seubel for Anderson. Onondaga Indians: Waterman for D. Jones, Webster for I. Powless, Lazore for Edwards, Edwards for Homer.

Referee—Korn. Judge of play—Hackett.

GUNN TAKES FINAL IN WILMINGTON GOLF

Atlantan Defeats Larson to Win Invitation Tournament by Score of 1 Up.

Special to The New York Times.

WILMINGTON, Del., June 7.—Watts Gunn of Atlanta, Ga., representing the Oakmont Country Club, defeated Thomas Larson of the Dupont Club to capture the men's golf championship at the Wilmington Country Club invitation tournament today. The score was 1 up.

To enter the final Gunn defeated L. H. Bodeman of St. David's, 7 and 5, while Larson beat C. W. Baker Jr. of Wilmington, 2 up.

In the final Gunn was erratic and it took him 41 strokes to reach the turn. However, on the homeward journey he struck his stride and was 2 below perfect figures on the last nine holes.

The cards:

Out—										
Par	4	3	5	4	4	4	5	3	4	36
Larson	5	4	5	4	4	5	5	4	4	40
Gunn	4	3	6	5	5	5	4	4	5	41
In—										
Par	4	4	3	4	5	4	4	4	3	35
Larson	4	4	3	4	5	4	4	6	3	37
Gunn	5	3	3	4	4	4	4	4	2	38

LAFAYETTE'S NINE BEATS MUHLENBERG

Triumphs in Annual Alumni Day Game at Easton, 7 to 6—Dimmerling Hits Homer.

Special to The New York Times.

EASTON, Pa., June 7.—Lafayette defeated Muhlenberg in the annual Alumni Day game at the Lafayette Stadium today, 7 to 6.

Ross Wiley, on the mound for the Maroon, allowed eight hits. Dimmerling hit a home run.

The box score:

MUHLENBERG.

	ab.	r.	h.	po.	a.	e.
Weber, 2b	5	0	1	3	2	0
Steinh'r, 3b	5	0	1	0	1	0
Smith, c	5	0	1	5	1	0
Snyder, rf	2	3	1	5	1	0
Giltner, cf	4	2	1	0	0	0
Kreischer, ss	4	0	2	1	2	0
Carney, 1b	4	0	0	10	1	0
Stauffer, lf	4	0	0	0	0	0
Tokacs, p	4	1	1	0	2	0
Total	37	6	8	21	10	0

LAFAYETTE.

	ab.	r.	h.	po.	a.	e.
Socolow, 3b	4	1	1	3	3	0
Wilcox, cf	4	1	2	1	1	0
Dim'rl'g, 1b	4	2	2	12	0	1
Tellier, rf	1	1	0	0	0	0
Mundy, lf	2	0	0	2	0	0
Th'mpson, 2b	3	1	2	0	3	0
Besser, c	4	1	1	8	1	1
Custer, ss	3	0	1	1	3	0
Wiley, p	3	0	0	0	5	0
aSfurberg	0	0	0	0	0	0
Total	28	7	9	27	16	2

Muhlenberg	0 0 0	2 0 1	0 2 1	—6
Lafayette	0 0 0	2 0 2	1 2 .	—7

Gallant Fox's Winnings Now Total $198,730; Is Eighth Among Money Earners on U. S. Turf

By his victory in the Belmont Stakes yesterday Gallant Fox added $66,040 to his earnings in the two years of his turf career, bringing his total to $198,730, thus ranking him eighth among the leading money winners of the American turf and in a like position among those of the English turf. He still is $114,909 behind the record earnings of Zev, but, being sound of limb and wind, it is predicted that he will pass Zev's total of $313,639 before he closes his racing career.

If William Woodward's fine thoroughbred also is to achieve greater earnings than the record-holder of the English turf he must reach $291,275, the total won by Isinglass. Donovan, Coronach, Rock Sand, Bayardo and Lemberg are the other English winners which still top Gallant Fox. In France, Ksar, with $335,340, holds the world's record, and Massine and Sardanaple have won more than Gallant Fox and in Australia Gloaming, with $215,500, also heads Gallant Fox's earnings.

Of the American thoroughbreds ahead of Gallant Fox in earnings, only two still are racing, Display, now 7 years old, and Blue Larkspur, 4 years old.

The records and the winnings of the eight American thoroughbreds which have won more than $198,000 follow:

Horse.	Sts.	1st	2d	3d	Amt. Won.
Zev	43	23	8	5	$313,639
Display	99	23	25	26	256,376
Exterminator	100	50	17	17	252,596
Man o' War	21	20	1	0	249,465
Sarazen	55	27	2	6	225,000
Blue Larksp'r	13	8	2	1	220,420
Crusader	42	18	8	4	203,261
Gallant Fox	11	8	2	2	198,730

MILLER-JONES WINS WESTCHESTER TITLE

Defeats R. A. Jones Jr. at 19th Hole in Amateur Golf Tourney at Siwanoy.

SQUARES MATCH AT 18TH

Opponent's Poor Shot Paves Way—Sweetser Victor in Beaten Eight.

By WILLIAM D. RICHARDSON.

Special to The New York Times.

BRONXVILLE, N. Y., June 7.—Making his début in the Westchester amateur championship, Pennington Miller-Jones, former Staten Island golfer, won the district title at Siwanoy today when he defeated R. A. Jones Jr. of Westchester Hills at the nineteenth hole.

One down going to the seventeenth, Miller-Jones came out of a bunker and holed a courageous ten-foot putt to halve the hole and carry the match on. Due to a lucky break when his second shot jumped across the ditch but mostly to his opponent's doubtful judgment in using wood off a poor lie, Miller-Jones squared the match on the eighteenth and then clinched his victory by sinking a ten-yard putt for a birdie 3 on the extra hole.

And so it begins to look as if Jones is stymied in his championship aspirations. This is the second time he has been close enough to touch the cup that cheers the Westchester winner. Some five or six years ago he was runner-up to J. G. Anderson in the Westchester event, losing in a nineteen-hole match on that occasion also.

Jones will never come any closer to winning the title than he did today and as he looks back upon the situation he probably will always

Continued on Page Four.

Record for 100 Has Withstood Attacks of Many Star Runners

The 100-yard running mark has stood the assaults of great runners in surprising fashion through the years. In the records of American champions it is found that ten seconds first was recorded in 1878 by W. C. Wilmer and was not bettered until 1890 and was not further reduced until 1906, when the world's mark of 0:09.6 was recorded by D. J. Kelly.

That time stood until Eddie Tolan ran the distance in 0:09.5 last year. This mark was accepted only a few weeks ago as official. Last year George Simpson, using starting blocks, recorded 0:09.4, but the record was disallowed.

The following table gives an idea of how the time has withstood the assaults:

Year.	Runner.	Time.
*1876	F. C. Saportas	0:10.5
1878	W. C. Wilmer	0:10
1890	J. Owen Jr.	0:09.8
1906	D. J. Kelly	0:09.6
1929	Eddie Tolan	0:09.5
1930	Frank Wykoff	0:09.4

BULLWINKLE LOSES IN BRILLIANT RACE

Trails Maloney, Who Has 65-Yard Handicap, by Less Than 6 Inches in N. Y. A. C. Mile.

BOTH ARE TIMED IN 4:15 4-5

Travers Island Crowd of 5,000 Cheers Sparkling Effort—Sturdy, Beard Win.

By ARTHUR J. DALEY.

A frayed red tape drifted across the chest of George Bullwinkle of City College at the completion of the one-mile run at the 124th track and field games of the New York Athletic Club yesterday. But less than one-tenth of a second before the tired body of the intercollegiate champion had hit the worsted it had been broken and so the greatest mile race in the brief but spectacular career of the Lavender captain was a losing venture.

Not even six inches separated Bullwinkle from his conqueror, Jim Maloney of New York University, as the Violet sophomore crossed the line in 4:15 4-5. So closely locked were they at the finish that Bullwinkle in second place was clocked in the identical figures of Maloney who had started off sixty-five yards in front of him.

Only once in the long and glamorous history of the Winged Foot organization had faster time been made in the picturesque Travers Island setting. That was in 1895, when Tommy Conneff raced to what was then a new world's record, 4:15 2-5.

Glides Through a Drizzle.

When Bullwinkle sped over the Harvard University cinders on a clear, cool day a week ago in 4:18 4-5, his performance was widely heralded as being one of the finest of a meet that was saturated with superfine exhibitions. Yesterday he glided through a dismal drizzle while 5,000 persons, huddled in mackintoshes, cheered him on.

Up Bullwinkle came from the last place, where his scratch rating had arbitrarily placed him. He was fourteenth in a nineteen-man field at one lap, ninth at two circuits, fourth at three and finally second at the gun as the husky figure of Maloney plodded along some six yards ahead of him.

Then up Bullwinkle marched in the backstretch, first by inches and then by feet at a time, until he drew abreast with the leader as they swung around the turn. Two steps he took with the Violet successor to Joe Hickey and he was out in the open ahead, fighting his way along, his eyes staring in front of him as his arms pumped away in rhythmic accord with his driving legs.

For perhaps ten steps it looked as though the intercollegiate champion had the race as good as won. But Maloney was strong and Bullwinkle was not.

Step Separates the Two.

On they came with Coach Emil Von Elling's pupil slowly closing up the gap. Fifty yards from the wire only a step separated the two and ten yards away from the red tape that was strung tautly across the finish Maloney sprinted.

Maloney's Violet jersey drew even with the white one of Bullwinkle

Continued on Page Two.

WORLD MARK FOR 100 BROKEN BY WYKOFF

Beats Simpson 1½ Feet in 0:09.4 Without Using Starting Blocks—Tolan 4th.

COAST TEAM WINS MEET

Southern California Takes National Collegiate A. A. Title—Washington Next.

HURDLES STANDARD TIED

Anderson Equals World's Best Time of 0:14.4—Simpson Takes 220—Six N. C. A. A. Marks Fall.

By The Associated Press.

CHICAGO, June 7.—Frank Wykoff, smiling 20-year-old youngster of the University of Southern California, traveling faster than any human being has galloped 100 yards before, eclipsed the world's record for the century to thrill a crowd of 12,000 today when he won the event in the National Collegiate A. A. track and field championships on Stagg Field in 0:09.4.

Wykoff established his remarkable record without the use of starting blocks, wiping out the existing mark of 0:09.5, held by Eddie Tolan, the University of Michigan's great Negro sprinter. The youth from the Pacific Coast not only eclipsed the record but also defeated George Simpson, the Buckeye Bullet from Ohio State University, who, a year ago, raced to victory in 0:09.4, but whose world's record performance was rejected by the International Amateur Athletic Federation because he made it with starting blocks.

Wykoff's sensational victory was instrumental in helping Southern California carry off the team championship, making the Trojans track and field champions of the entire nation. The Trojans, previous winners of the Eastern Intercollegiate and Pacific Coast titles, annexed 57 27-70 points, with Washington finishing second with 40, giving the Pacific Coast runner-up laurels, too. Iowa was third with 30 1-7, Ohio State fourth with 29 1-10 and Stanford fifth with 28. Forty-three teams broke into the scoring in one of the most spectacular meets ever held in this country.

Meet Record Is Equaled.

Besides Wykoff's world's record another world's mark was tied, six records for the meet were smashed and another meet record was equaled. Only six of the fifteen records established in eight previous N. C. A. A. meets survived the day's assaults, and most of them just by bare fractions.

Wykoff's achievement in cracking the world's mark for the century was a thriller. He was away winging, first out of his holes, and led every foot of the race, with Simpson snapping at his heels after the first thirty yards. With a mighty drive at the tape, Wykoff's chest broke the white string a full eighteen inches ahead of Simpson. The Buckeye flier, defeated for the first time out of doors this year, made one of the worst starts of his career and was last of the eight sprinters off his mark. He overhauled them all except Wykoff, who raced on to victory with the speed of a frightened deer.

Simpson, disappointed in defeat, offered no alibis and blamed only himself for what he regarded as an inexcusably poor start.

Wykoff's victory resulted in a surprising defeat of Tolan. Tolan finished fourth, about four inches back of a comparative unknown, Ed Toppino of Loyola University, New Orleans. The two Texas streaks, Claude Bracey of Rice Institute and Cy Leland of Texas Christian, finished fifth and sixth, respectively.

As Wykoff did not use starting blocks, officials of the meet said there was little doubt that his performance would be acepted internationally as a world's record, since he had no wind advantage. When the sprinters bounded off their marks there was hardly a breeze stirring in the stadium, and the track, rain-soaked for twelve hours previously, had dried out amazingly and was springy and fast.

Sentman Is Defeated.

The spectators had hardly settled back in their seats to watch the first event of the program when a world's record was tied. Stephen Anderson of Washington equalled the world's mark when he ran the 120-yard hurdles in 0:14.4 to defeat Lee Sentman, the hurdling star of Illinois, heretofore undefeated this year. They raced as a team for ninety yards, but the pace was a bit too fast for Sentman and he faltered over the last two barriers, allowing the champion of the far Northwest to draw away and win by a yard. Sentman, however, got revenge in the 220-yard low hurdles, which he won by three yards to equal the meet record of 0:23.2.

Simpson, beaten in the century, left no doubt as to his superiority in the 220-yard dash. He won by at least five yards in 0:20.7, one-tenth of a second slower than the world's record, but a tenth faster than the former N. C. A. A. record which he established a year ago. Leland was second, while Tolan, Farmer of North Carolina, and East and Root of Chicago crossed the line in that order in a blanket finish.

In addition to Simpson's performance in the furlong, new meet records were established in the 880-yard run, two-mile run, pole vault, discus throw and shot-put.

Orval Martin, Purdue's great middle distance runner, wound up his collegate career by winning the 880-yard event in 1:54.1, clipping a tenth of a second off the meet record. Paul Jessup, 6 foot 7 inch football centre from the University of Washington, set a new meet record for the discus with a toss of 160 feet 9¾ inches. Eric Krenz of Stanford, holder of the world's record of 163 feet 8¾

Continued on Page Two

Wyer, Veteran, Scores Surprising Victory In Canadian Marathon, Winning by Half Mile

By The Canadian Press.

TORONTO, June 7.—Percy Wyer, gray-haired veteran of a hundred marathons, today surprised the athletic world by capturing the second national marathon staged by the Monarch Athletic Club.

Wyer, following the torrid pace set by G. Roulsalainen of Montreal, took the lead at the twenty-two-mile mark when the Montreal Finn commenced to falter. From then on he encountered little opposition, to finish a half-mile ahead of Johnny Cuthbert of Guelph. Joe Pearson, Toronto, was third.

Roulsalainen courageously finished out the full distance, but a severe sprain to an ankle forced him to walk the last mile and a half to finish in fifth place. The winner's time was very good, being 2:51 4-5 seconds.

Norman Dack upheld the honor of the Olympic Club of Hamilton by running a heady race to finish fourth, just finishing ahead of the Montrealer.

Johnny Miles, another Hamiltonian, dropped out after running in a contending position for twenty miles. Ezra Lee, Toronto, Claude Turner, Chapleau; Frank Hughes, Hamilton; Bill Spencer, Toronto and Alf Roberts, Toronto, finished in the order named, after Roulsalainen.

The ten runners from United States never were prominently placed during the running of the race and all finished far back in the ruck.

Wyer's victory practically clinches him a place on the team to represent Canada at the British Empire games at Hamilton in August. Three other runners will be recommended by the selection committee. The other two needed to round out the team will be selected, one probably from Eastern and the other from Western Canada.

Cleveland Derby Is Captured by Dixie Lad, With Maya Second and Dark Sea Next

DIXIE LAD TAKES CLEVELAND DERBY

Letellier Stable Entry, an Outsider, First in $15,000 Added Classic.

COE'S MAYA IS SECOND

Dark Sea, Owned by Kilmer, Finishes Third—Gallant Knight, the Favorite, Is Sixth.

CLEVELAND, June 7 (AP).—With 10,000 men and women shouting to their respective riders to come on, Dixie Lad, outsider from the A. B. Letellier stable of New Orleans, saddled by A. Thomas and ridden by Jockey Carl Meyers, won the first running of the $15,000 added Cleveland Derby at Thistledown today. He ran the mile and a quarter in 2:08.

Maya, ridden by Joe Inzelone, and coupled with Cesare as the W. R. Coe entry, which led the parade virtually from the start to the last sixteenth pole, was second in front of Dark Sea, the Kilmer entry, which moved up menacingly at the three-quarter pole, and for a time looked like the winner.

Gallant Knight, the odds-on favorite, finished sixth and only in the early part of the running did he look any part of the colt which ran second to Gallant Fox, winner of the Kentucky Derby and the Belmont Stakes.

Meyers on Dixie Lad soon got his mount into motion and gradually worked his way up to the leaders, the son of Sporting Blue going like a piece of well oiled machinery.

As they neared the far turn Dixie Lad began to move up in earnest and when they hit the head of the home lane it looked as if a different story would be written of the Derby than originally was expected. It was plain that Gallant Knight had had enough, though Schutte kept at work on him, but the son of Bright Knight was through.

Dixie Lad's strides kept getting longer and longer, and Inzelone was riding a great race on Maya, but it was Dixie Lad's day.

The summaries:

FIRST RACE—Purse $800; allowances; 2-year-olds; five furlongs:
Just Believe, 110 (Dough'ty) 3.00 2.60 2.40
Cousin Jo, 107 (Bryant) 3.40 3.20
Anthro, 108 (Gooler) 5.20
Time—1:01 2-5. Ournan, Rising Star and Miss Dinwiddie also ran.

SECOND RACE—Purse $800; claiming; 3-year olds and upward; six furlongs:
Mrs. Foster, 98 (Reeves) 7.00 3.80 3.00
Frank Podesta, 96 (J. Frye) 7.00 3.80
Prancing Step, 106 (Dou'ty) 3.60
Time—1:15. Captain J. S., Woodmont, Bold Robin and Red Leather also ran.

THIRD RACE—The Ohio Handicap; Purse $1,200; 3-year-olds and upward; six furlongs:
Break of Dawn, 110 (Mul'y) 10.00 4.00 2.80
Taddywawa, 108 (Rose) 4.00 2.60
Retort, 96 (Bryant) 2.80
Time 1:14 3-5. High Score and Easter Stocking also ran.

FOURTH RACE—Purse $1,000; claiming; 4-year-olds and upward; one mile and a sixteenth:
Lucky Drift, 103 (Mul'ney) 4.60 3.80 3.60
Happy Hanly, 113 (Berry) 4.60 3.80
Ashburne, 105 (Ross) 6.40
Time 1:50 2-5. Kublai Khan, Checkmate, For Luck, Jasonette, Dingo, Courier and Dynamo also ran.

FIFTH RACE—Purse $1,000; claiming; 4-year-olds and upward; one mile and a sixteenth:
Baby Delhi, 106 (Dell) 5.50 4.00 3.20
Junior C., 105 (Futrell) 11.50 5.40
Coquina, 100 (Cunningham) 6.00
Time—1:51. Lady Basil, Rhubarb, Torrence, St. Matthews and Panorel also ran.

SIXTH RACE—The Cleveland Derby; $15,000 added; 3-year-olds; one mile and a quarter:
Dixie Lad, 114 (C. Meyers) 30.00 8.00 4.60
Maya, 119 (Inzelone) 4.40 3.40
Dark Sea, 114 (Coltiletti) 5.60
Time—2:08. Reveille Boy, Sydney, Cesare, Gallant Knight, Rain or Shine, Miss Bess and Plucky Play also ran.

SEVENTH RACE (Substitute)—Purse $1,000; 3-year-olds and upward; one mile and a sixteenth:
Head Pin, 99 (Carroll) 20.00 9.00 5.20
Mary McClain, 108 (Level) 4.00 3.60
Interior, 100 (Froggatte) 5.80
Time 1:50 1-5. Kamuela, Full Speed, Taystee, Bumpkin and Preander also ran.

EIGHTH RACE (Substitute)—Purse $1,000; claiming; 3-year-olds and upward; one mile and a sixteenth:
Bob Rogers, 112 (Mulrooney) 12.20 5.20 4.20
Cockrill, 106 (Level) 4.60 3.40
Spanflow, 99 (Bryant) 9.00
Time—1:49. Dark Sabre, Full Measure, Miss Bess, Sporting Grit, Aimee Goldsmith, ...

$80,000 Arlington Classic To Be Contested on July 12

CHICAGO, June 7 (AP).—July 12 has been fixed as the date for the second running of the $80,000 Arlington Classic, while the Arlington Cup race, valued at between $25,000 and $30,000, will be held July 19.

The race will be the outstanding feature of Arlington Park's racing season, extending from June 30 through Aug. 2. The purse distribution for the season has been estimated at $600,000.

LOS ANGELES A. C. WINS U. S. GYM TITLE

Heads Swiss Turn Verein of Union City (N. J.) on Revised Count, 87 to 82.

JOCHIM AGAIN GAINS CROWN

New Jersey Star Amasses 3,907 Points to Take the All-Around Championship.

LOS ANGELES, June 7 (AP).—Officials of the National A. A. U., gymnastic division, after revising their count today announced that the Los Angeles Athletic Club had captured the national gymnastic title from the Swiss Turnverein team of Union City, N. J., with a total of 87 points. The New Jersey team, former titleholder, placed second with 82 points. Officials of the meet said they found the results of two events had been overlooked.

The Los Angeles Turnverein took third place with 8 points.

Alfred Jochim of the New Jersey team, five times all-around champion, outstripped the other competitors to collect 3,907 points and win the championship.

New champions were crowned in four of the events, Jochim dropping two of the four titles he carried into the meet. Those he failed to retain were the parallel bars and the flying rings.

THE SUMMARIES.

Free Exercise—Won by Jochim, Swiss Turn Verein; second, Herman Witzig Jr., Swiss Turn Verein; third, Frank Haubold, Swiss Turn Verein.

Club Swinging—Won by Robert Job, Swiss Turn Verein; second, Max Aron, Los Angeles Turn Verein; third, Phil Erenberg, L. A. A. C.

Tumbling—Won by Leo Vandendaele, L. A. A. C.; second, William Herrman Jr., Philadelphia; third, Gary Searl, L. A. A. C.

Horizontal Bar—Won by Jochim, Swiss Turn Verein; second, Glenn Berry, L. A. A. C.; third, Herman Witzig Jr., Swiss Turn Verein.

Side Horse—Won by Frank Haubold, Swiss Turn Verein; second, Jochim, Swiss Turn Verein; third, Glenn Berry, L. A. A. C.

Parallel Bars—Tie for first between Paul Krempel, L. A. A. C., and Herman Witzig Jr., Swiss Turn Verein; third, Haubold, Swiss Turn Verein.

Long Horse—Won by Jochim, Swiss Turn Verein; second, Glenn Berry, L. A. A. C.; third, Herman Witzig Jr., Swiss Turn Verein.

Flying Rings—Won by Paul Krempel, L. A. A. C.; second, Dwight Davis, L. A. A. C.; third, Richard Bishop, L. A. A. C.

Rope Climbing—Won by Leonard Stern, L. A. A. C.; second, James Burton, L. A. A. C.; third, Lester Saltman, Los Angeles, unattached. Best time 0:06 2-5.

Belmont Park Entries.

FIRST RACE—The Priscilla; purse $1,000; claiming; maiden 2-year-olds; four and a half furlongs. (Widener chute).

SCHOONER ANNEXES CURRAN MEMORIAL

Carries Rancocas Silks to Easy Victory in Feature at Washington Park.

RETURNS $11.64 FOR $2

Takes Commanding Lead in Stretch to Defeat Norias—Foreign Exchange Is Third.

CHICAGO, June 7 (AP).—The Rancocas Stable's Schooner won the Thomas Curran Memorial, first 2-year-old stake of the Chicago racing season, at Washington Park today. Schooner ran the five and one-half furlongs over a muddy track in 1:12 1-5 to beat Norias of the Paradise Stock Farm handily. Foreign Exchange, a Kentucky colt, was third. The race carried a gross value of $9,000 of which $7,230 went to the winner. Schooner paid $11.64 in the mutuels.

Schooner was held off the pace for the first three furlongs, but Jockey A. Ayraud found a clear path for the little chestnut son of Bud Lerner as the field entered the stretch and the Rancocas Stable entry rushed into a commanding lead. Norias came with a rush to nose out Foreign Exchange for the place.

The summaries:

FIRST RACE—Purse $1,300; claiming; 3-year-olds and upward; seven furlongs.
Ruane, 111 (Depeso) 10.06 5.18 3.42
Broomshot, 106 (Lennie) ... 9.16 5.20
Shift, 118 (Marinelli) 3.74
Time 1:31. Honi Soit, The Okah, Hy Schneider and Lieutenant Russell also ran.

SECOND RACE—Purse $1,200; maiden 2-year-olds; five furlongs.
Nisia, 113 (Neal) 22.44 9.70 4.84
Hymap, 118 (O'Donnell) ... 6.14 3.58
Port Codine, 116 (Ambrose) 3.46
Time 1:04 1-5. Rest Easy, Brown Hills, Stone Martin, aPangolin, aSilver Lake, bSpring Cleaning, Seguro, Westy's Broom and bSpar also ran.
aField.
bGreentree Stable.

THIRD RACE—Purse $1,200; claiming; 3-year-olds and upward; one mile and a furlong.
Seth's Ballot, 115 (Corbett) 4.24 3.58 2.70
Theo Red, 112 (Keiser) ... 18.44 9.60
Miss Maryland, 112 (Ayraud) 3.56
Time 2:04. Azov, David L., Royal Charge, Helene M., Far Away, John T. D. and Faddy also ran.

FOURTH RACE—Purse $1,400; claiming; 3-year-olds and upward; one mile and seventy yards.
Suntor, 113 (Lennie) 11.48 5.40 4.32
Kingstone, 112 (Marcum) ... 5.40 4.26
Equation, 116 (D. J. Mooney) 7.38
Time 1:51 3-5. Leucite, Portmanteau and Buddy Basil also ran.

FIFTH RACE—The Thomas Curran Memorial, $5,000 added; 2-year-olds; five and a half furlongs.
aSchooner, 119 (Ayraud) 11.64 5.42 2.90
Norias, 111 (Anderson) ... 21.38 5.54
bForeign Exchg., 114 (Hardy) 2.46
Time 1:12 1-5. bHarry Frank, aCharmer, Shining, Jay Walker, Bill Morris, bInsco, Dandy Dan and Chief John also ran.
aRancocas Stable entry. bWatkins-Regan entry.

SIXTH RACE—The Riverdale Handicap; purse $1,800; 3-year-olds and upward; six furlongs.
Cayuga, 111 (Neal) 4.64 3.52 2.62
Club House, 106 (J. Smith) ... 4.66 3.50
Tippy Toe, 102 (Depeso) 3.26
Time 1:13 4-5. Morsun, Nusakan and Silverdale also ran.

SEVENTH RACE—Purse $1,200; claiming; 3-year-olds and upward; one mile and a ...

BELMONT PARK CHART

By The Associated Press.

Saturday, June 7. Twenty-first day. Weather raining; track good.

9736 FIRST RACE—The Glenwood; purse $1,000; claiming; 3-year-olds and upward; seven furlongs. Start good; won driving; place same. Winner, br. c., 3, by Leonardo II—Edna Stack. Trainer, C. Raynor. Time 0:23 1-5, 0:46 4-5, 1:12, 1:26.

Ind.	Starters	Wt.	P.P.	St.	¼	½	¾	Str.	Fin.	Jockeys.	O.	H.	Cl.	Pl.	Sh.
9707	Hacky H.	108	2	3	1^{hd}	$1^{1½}$	1^{2}	1^{2}	$1^{1½}$	K'singer	10	10	10	4	2
9674	Colossal	106½	10	4	2^{2}	2^{2}	2^{1}	$2^{1¼}$	2^{1}	E.Wat's	10	12	12	5	5-2
(6693)	Flying Max	113	4	7	7^{1}	7^{2}	5^{5}	$3^{1½}$	3^{2}	Rob'son	10	10	8	3	8-5
9581	Best Man	103	3	6	$5^{1½}$	3^{hd}	$3^{1½}$	4^{2}	4^{hd}	Rose	6	8	7	5-2	7-5
(5365)	Dangerous	109	5	10	11	11	8^{1}	$6^{1½}$	5^{1}	Eaby	30	30	30	10	5
9693	Imperial Air	110	7	11	$9^{1½}$	$8^{1½}$	7^{2}	8^{hd}	6^{1}	L.Fator	6	8	8	4	2
9575	Black Watch	111	8	8	$8^{1½}$	$6^{1½}$	6^{2}	$7^{1½}$	7^{2}	W.Smith	4	8	8	4	2
9574	Scimitar	111	11	9	10^{2}	10^{1}	$9^{1½}$	9^{2}	8^{2}	Catrone	30	30	30	10	5
9674^{2}	Pennant Lass	112	6	2	4^{2}	$4^{1½}$	$4^{1½}$	$5^{1½}$	9^{2}	Harvey	2	5-2	6-5	2-5	1-4
8269	Agua Caliente	109	1	5	6^{2}	$9^{1½}$	10^{2}	10^{3}	10^{5}	L'hman	15	20	20	8	4
9647^{3}	Stand By	110	9	1	3^{hd}	5^{1}	11	11	11	Kelsay	8	12	12	5	5-2

Scratched—War Saint, Charon, Sun Mission, Sign Off, Buddy Bauer, Infinitus, Perkins, Everytime and Clean Play.

Hacky H proved much the best. He rushed into the lead and, showing good speed, held on gamely. Colossal was kept well up, saved ground, but tired fast. Flying Max broke in a tangle, overcame the interference and finished with a rush. Best Man closed with a rush. Dangerous was outrun to the stretch, where he closed with a rush.

Owners—1, J. P. McGovern; 2, J. E. Davis; 3, Mrs. S. Bennett; 4, Wheatley Stable; 5, Dorwood Stable; 6, Fair Stable; 7, W. E. Martin; 8, Mrs. J. A. Coburn; 9, A. W. Wentzel; 10, W. C. Smith; 11, Brandon Stable.

9737 SECOND RACE—The Woodlark Steeplechase; purse $1,500; allowances; 4-year-olds and upward; about two miles. Start good; won easily; place same. Winner, b. g., 4, by Russley—Acrocephalus. Trainer, P. Green. Time—3:47 4-5.

Ind.	Starters	Wt.	P.P.	St.	M.	1½	Str.	Fin.	Jockeys.	O.	H.	Cl.	Pl.	Sh.
9664^{3}	Actor	132	1	2	1^{1}	1^{1}	1^{8}	1^{4}	*Bst'k	1-2	9-20	9-20	1-5	Out
9664	Beelzebub	152	2	1	2^{10}	2^{20}	2^{30}	2^{15}	Th'dike	2	3	3	1-2	Out
9713^{2}	Le Digard	142	3	4	4^{20}	3^{2}	3^{20}	3^{20}	Veitch	8	8	8	8-5	Out
9719	Volunteer	142	4	3	3^{5}	4^{30}	4	4	Wolke	20	20	20	3	1-2
9725	Melita II	137	5	5	5	5	†		Pinon	30	100	100	20	4

*Gentleman rider. †Refused.

Actor was much the best. He was rated along in front and, racing Beelzebub into defeat, won easing up. Beelzebub handled his heavy impost well and ran a good race. Le Digard was next best. Volunteer had speed for a mile, then quit. Melita II refused.

Owners—1, T. Hitchcock; 2, E. R. Bradley; 3, Eastland Farms Stable; 4, F. Grossman; 5, Flying Horse Farm.

9738 THIRD RACE—The National Stallion Stakes; $5,000 added; 2-year-olds; five furlongs (Widener course). Start good; won easily; place same. Winner, ch. c., 2, by Pennant—Swinging. Trainer, F. Hopkins. Value to winner, $25,400; second, $1,000; third, $500. Time 0:59 3-5.

Ind.	Starters	Wt.	P.P.	St.	¼	Str.	Fin.	Jockeys.	O.	H.	Cl.	Pl.	Sh.
(9678)	aEquipoise	122	7	4	1^{2}	1^{8}	1^{8}	W'man	2-5	2-5	7-20	Out	Out
*(9699)	Polydorus	122	3	2	$2^{1½}$	$2^{1½}$	2^{2}	L.Fator	4	5	9-2	8-5	7-10
9714^{2}	bBaba Kenny	119	1	6	3^{1}	3^{2}	3no	Kelsay	6	7	7	2	1
(9722)	Aknahton	117	4	7	5^{1}	4^{8}	4^{8}	Thurber	10	10	10	3	7-5
9710	Mad Career	122	6	5	7^{1}	5^{1}	5^{2}	Sch'fer	20	20	20	8	4
9691^{2}	aFervor	122	2	1	6^{1}	6^{2}	6^{1}	Rob'son	2-5	2-6	7-20	Out	Out
9699^{2}	bBoys Howdy	117	8	3	$4^{1½}$	7^{2}	7^{1}	Degere	6	7	7	2	1
(9710)	Blue Law	117	5	8	8	8	8	M.Gar'r	20	20	20	8	4

aH. P. Whitney entry. bE. R. Bradley entry. (H. P. Whitney declared to win with Equipoise.)

Scratched—Zelide and Roan Antelope.

Equipoise picked up his weight, broke fast, ran into the lead early and won nicely in hand. Polydorus made a determined bid in the stretch and was next best. Baba Kenny closed gamely and held on well. Aknahton finished with a rush, after being outrun in the early part. Mad Career had no mishap. Boys Howdy ran a good race.

Owners—1, H. P. Whitney; 2, W. R. Coe; 3, E. R. Bradley; 4, M. Field; 5, W. J. Salmon; 6, H. P. Whitney; 7, E. R. Bradley; 8, Greentree Stable.

GALLANT FOX BEATS WHICHONE 4 LENGTHS

By BRYAN FIELD.

Continued from Page One.

sion of it and never gave the others a chance. To stand off three challenges, from each of the horses running against him, and still have left enough speed to come away in fast time under a drizzling rain, is high testimony to his ability.

Gallant Fox may have remembered that he was evening an old score with Whichone, for Mr. Whitney's horse beat him last year in the Futurity on the occasion of their only other meeting.

George Cassidy, who took over the job of starting this Spring, and who is the youngest in the business, got the field of four away in perfect alignment after only a minute and a half at the post. It was a job well done. Sande immediately rushed Gallant Fox to the front, and going around the clubhouse turn Questionnaire dropped into second place, Swinfield into third and Whichone last. That was the order down the backstretch, with Sande having the Fox under a steady hold.

Questionnaire and Swinfield closed threateningly in the middle of the backstretch and it looked as if Gallant Fox might lose the lead, but he let out a notch and the Derby winner drew away.

Once more, on the far turn, Questionnaire and Swinfield closed on the pacemaker, Swinfield particularly looking as if he might do something, but once again Sande let out a notch and again the Fox drew away, with the others beaten off.

Whichone Trails Field.

Whichone all this time had not made a move. He was sawing wood in last place and looked at all times as if he had speed in reserve and was conserving his strength. Here was the horse that never had been turned loose, according to his admirers.

But on the bend he was far enough behind to do his best and no one knew it better than Sonny Workman. He called on his horse and evidently did not get the response he wanted. He went to the whip, and with the first feel of the lash Whichone roused and went up like a flash. At last he was running. The big horse was doing his best.

By this time Gallant Fox was at the top of the stretch, and Sande knew by instinct (for he did'nt look around), what was happening behind. He pressed Gallant Fox for all he had and the horse rushed on.

Whichone was coming with all his great speed, and Sande had deliberately lost ground with Gallant Fox at the turn in order to get him out in the firm footing in the middle of the track.

Whichone gained, but not much. He gained still more and then he was held even. The spectators were on their feet. They were seeing a seemingly invincible horse held even by a colt which was supposed to have beaten only mediocre opposition in the Preakness and Kentucky Derby.

Whitney Horse Distanced.

And then they saw that fine horse, for Whichone is a fine horse, distanced. With Sande hand riding with all his wonted skill, Gallant Fox drew away. Whichone was under the whip and few jockeys can whip the way Workman can, but he was falling steadily back until at the end he was four lengths to the bad, beaten by as great a thoroughbred as ever kicked up the turf.

As the race was run the early pace was slow. The big push came in the last quarter and it was there that Gallant Fox had the speed to run his opposition.

The fractions for the race were: 0:25 1-5, 0:50, 1:15 4-5, 1:40 3-5, 2:06 2-5 and 2:31 3-5.

Mr. Whitney's Equipoise earned his greatest victory when he captured the National Stallion Stakes and $25,400 in hollow fashion. The race was a runaway affair for the son of Pennant and Swinging. The purse was the largest that has been won by a 2-year-old so far this year. Added to previous triumphs and the earlier purses, it gives Equipoise a commanding lead among the juveniles so far as money earned is concerned.

First Six Times.

On racing ability there are few who will put any horse above Equipoise, for he now has raced eight times and has finished in front six times. On one of the occasions when he failed to win he tossed his rider.

Carrying 122 pounds, Equipoise did not show up the others until the race had been half run. Then he came away in such swift fashion and ease that he won by six lengths without half trying.

Equipoise was running coupled with Fervor and the two were the very short price of 7 to 20. Mr. Whitney declared to win with Equipoise and the horse sustained his confidence admirably. There really was no competition in the race for Equipoise, but W. R. Coe's Polydorus ran a good race to be second.

Baba Kenny, one of the best of the E. R. Bradley juveniles, just staved off Aknahton to land the short end of the purse. Equipoise ran the five furlongs of the stake down the Widener chute in 0:59 3-5, very good time considering that the track was not at its best and that Equipoise was not pressed for speed.

Beelzebub Is Second.

The Wood Lark steeplechase, second on the program, saw G. H. (Pete) Bostwick, the amateur rider, add another victory to his long score. He had the leg up on Thomas Hitchcock's Actor which was made the 9 to 20 favorite. With the aid of a twenty-pound weight pull, and Bostwick's good ride, Actor finished four lengths in front at the end of the two miles. Le Digard was a distant third back of Beelzebub which carried 152 pounds, top weight.

Actor did not go to the front until half a mile had been run but then he went into the lead and never lost it. Beelzebub ran an excellent race under the weights but lost ground noticeably on the jumps. Actor cleared these in faultless fashion and between each barrier Beelzebub would have to hurry to again get close. Then would come another jump and again Actor would draw away a length the better of things.

The first race was riddled by scratches, nine horses declining the issue. But even with that many out there were eleven left. A. W. Wentzel's Pennant Lass was made the hot favorite, but she did not land in the money.

The winner turned up in John P. McGovern's Hacky H., which won by a length and a half from Colossal. Both were long shots, the winner paying 10 to 1 to win and Colossal 5 to 1 to place. Flying Max was third, Pennant Lass was ninth.

SANDE REGAINS RANK AS PREMIER JOCKEY

Thirty-one Years Old, He Is Staging Second Come-Back of His Colorful Career.

Once more the stars have been right for Earl Sande. The peerless jockey, staging his second turf comeback at the age of 31, rode into the blinding spotlight of glory at Belmont Park yesterday atop Gallant Fox. It might well have been Gallant Fox and Gallant Sande on the program, for to the crowd one was as gallant as the other.

If Horatio Alger were writing his boys' stories in these days he undoubtedly would have one built around Sande, the poor prairie-born and raised youth who ran away from home to ride on the "bush" tracks of the West and worked and strove until finally he was riding the stars of the turf at $15,000 a year and had accumulated a fortune.

There would be a chapter on that fateful day at Saratoga when he piled up in a nasty spill and was nearly killed. For months he was in a hospital in this city, and it seemed then that he never would ride again and that the premier jockey of the American turf—for he had then achieved that distinction—had gone down into turf history. But he willed otherwise and he came on to renew his conquests for several years.

Then, weight having crept upon him, he decided to retire. Fate had robbed him, in the meantime, of his beloved wife, and he had fought the weight bugaboo as far as he thought he could. He had made something of a fortune and he branched out as owner and trainer and at times rode his own horses. But he reached no great success as owner and trainer and after his ventures in 1928 and 1929 at this he sold his thoroughbreds.

At the start of this year Sande was all but put down in the records as merely the former premier jockey of America. But he decided again that he wasn't through. He signed a contract with William Woodward, owner of Gallant Fox, to ride that fast-going colt in his first Spring engagement on, it is understood, a percentage basis of the winnings. He won with Gallant Fox in the Wood Memorial. Then he went on to win the Preakness and the Kentucky Derby and finally he came up to Thursday night, prepared to ride in the sixty-second Belmont Stakes.

An automobile accident on Thursday night came near stopping Sande in his meteoric comeback. But, despite scratches and bruises, he rode and triumphed with Gallant Fox.

ENGLISH TURF ORIGIN OF THE TRIPLE CROWN

Emblematic of Victories in the Epsom Derby, Two-Thousand Guineas and St. Leger.

In England there are three races in which owners of thoroughbreds spend thousands upon thousands of dollars and years and years of patient waiting. Triumph in these races, which compose the historic Triple Crown, means the highest glory one can achieve upon the turf. The races comprising the Triple Crown are the English Derby, The Two-Thousand Guineas and the St. Leger Stakes.

In America the idea of the Triple Crown being duplicated came when the Preakness, the Kentucky Derby and the Belmont Stakes reached such prominence as to overshadow all other Spring 3-year-old events in this country. And as in England, to win the Triple Crown in America carries with it the utmost that can be won upon our race courses.

The Belmont and the English Derby, the latter run over the famous Epsom Downs course, are both one mile and a half. The Kentucky Derby is at one mile and a quarter and the St. Leger at one mile six furlongs and 132 yards, while the Preakness is at one mile and three-sixteenths and the Two-Thousand Guineas at one mile. All are for 3-year-old colts and fillies excepting the Kentucky Derby, in which geldings also are eligible.

Gallant Fox and Sir Barton are the only winners of the Triple Crown in this country, whereas since the turn of the present century four horses have achieved the honor in England.

The first of these was the Prince of Wales's Diamond Jubilee, which scored in the three races in 1900. Then came Sir J. Miller's Rock Sand in 1904. A long lapse, until 1917, intervened before Gay Crusader achieved the triple honors, but in the very next year Lady James Douglas's Gainsborough triumphed in the three races.

Two of the most famous names of the Brtish turf won triples in the previous century. In 1893 Isinglass turned the trick and in 1899 the Duke of Westminster's Flying Fox won all three races.

Fairmount Park Results.

By The Associated Press.

FIRST RACE—Purse $800; claiming; 3-year-olds and upward; six furlongs.
Cash Play, 106 (Goodrich) 5.10 3.62 2.64
Angel Bright, 97 (Hanford) 4.22 3.04
Blue Blood, 101 (Pegg) 4.82
Time—1:14 1-5. Howard Lee, Rita M., Phi Delta, Philomath, Post Mistress, Avarice and Cherry Blaze also ran.

SECOND RACE—Purse $800; claiming; 3-year-olds and upward; six furlongs.
Mortana, 109 (Root) 4.52 3.32 2.76
Webster, 106 (Hanford) 5.28 3.84
Kind Words, 108 (Cimerak) 3.90
Time—1:14. Ruth Long, Black Alice, ...

SANDS POINT POLO SCHEDULED TODAY

Second of Season's Matches to Be Held on Fleischmann Field at 4 o'Clock.

PHIPPS, IGLEHART TO PLAY

Yale Men Will Be Seen in Action on Hitchcock's Team—Cowdin in Roslyn Line-Up.

By ROBERT F. KELLEY.

With several of the younger players in action, the second game of the new season's weekly polo matches at Fleischmann Field starts at 4 o'clock this afternoon on the famous playing surface of the Sands Point Club.

Of the men who played in last week's opening game, five are to be in the saddle again today. In the place of the three others will be two young college players and one veteran. The veteran is J. Cheever Cowdin, spare player on several international teams, who is to be seen in his first high-goal game of the season.

The two younger players are Michael Phipps and Stewart Iglehart, both of Yale. They are to play with Sands Point and in front of Thomas Hitchcock Jr., captain of the American international teams, and A. Charles Schwartz of the defense committee and regular Sands Point back.

Hitchcock at No. 3.

Iglehart has played pretty much all over a polo team, but for the past couple of seasons he has been most often found in the No. 3 position. It is in this post that he has played with the successful Old Aiken team. But No. 3, for the present and until he changes his mind, belongs to Captain Hitchcock.

Mr. Cowdin is playing with the day's Roslyn team and is to ride at No. 3. In front of him will be W. Averell Harriman and G. H. Bostwick and at back will be Earle A. S. Hopping.

Bostwick is the young steeplechase rider who turned in a good game of polo at Fleischmann Field last week and was invited to join the list of candidates for the American team.

Hopping in Back Position.

The younger Hopping continues to play in the back position, a post new to him this year and one for which he is apparently being groomed with the year's British matches in view, Hopping has been bothered by a sprained back, but this has responded to treatment and he will be in action today.

The Fleischmann Field matches form a part of the general international practice and preparation. Next week's game is expected to see Winston Guest, who is apt to be No. 2 of this year's team, in action. He has been on a fishing trip but is returning this week.

Lorenzo to Meet Rocco.

Tommy Lorenzo and Joe Rocco are scheduled to meet for ten rounds at the Twenty-second Engineers Armory in West 168th Street on Tuesday night. Jimmy Rappoport and Joe Curry are down for eight rounds in the semi-final, while Andy Young will face Augie Vaglica in the opening eight rounder.

Section 10
SPORTS
SHIPPING AND MAILS

The New York Times.

SUNDAY, SEPTEMBER 28, 1930.

SPORTS
SHIPPING AND MAILS
Section 10

JONES WINS, 8 AND 7, SWEEPING TO FOURTH MAJOR TITLE OF YEAR

Beats Homans to Become First to Hold All British and U. S. Crowns at Once.

BREAKS TRAVERS'S RECORD

Closes Match at 29th Green to Capture American Amateur for Fifth Time.

18,000 AT MERION HAIL HIM

Marines Forced to Save Atlantan After Thrilling Climax to His Unexcelled Career.

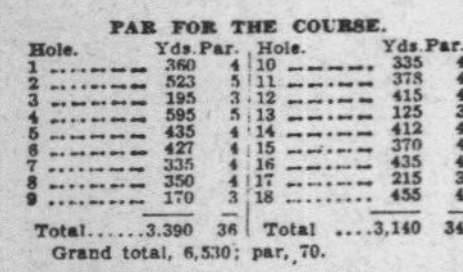

PAR FOR THE COURSE.

Hole.	Yds.	Par.	Hole.	Yds.	Par.
1	360	4	10	335	4
2	523	5	11	378	4
3	195	3	12	415	4
4	595	5	13	125	3
5	435	4	14	412	4
6	427	4	15	370	4
7	335	4	16	435	4
8	350	4	17	215	3
9	170	3	18	455	4
Total	3.390	36	Total	3,140	34

Grand total, 6,530; par, 70.

By WILLIAM D. RICHARDSON.

Special to The New York Times.

ARDMORE, Pa., Sept. 27.—When Gene Homans's ball grazed the side of the cup on the twenty-ninth hole at the Merion Cricket Club today, Bobby Jones not only became the national amateur champion for 1930 but the holder of a record that probably will survive through the ages.

At 28, this rarely-gifted golfer from Atlanta, who defeated Homans 8 up and 7 to play in today's final and who has come closer to mastering the intricacies of the game than any one else, has performed a feat that no one hitherto had considered possible.

Within the short span of five months, Bobby has played in the four major golf events—the British amateur and open championships and the American open and amateur—and won them all, outscoring the professionals at their own game in the two open tournaments and out-stripping all his fellow amateurs in the others.

Moreover he is the first man in the history of American golf to win the National amateur five times, he and Jerry Travers, who was in the gallery that followed the marvelous Atlantan today, having been tied at four victories each until this afternoon.

It was no more than appropriate that all these honors should be spread at Bobby's feet on the same golf course where, as a boy of 14, he made his début in championship golf in 1916 and where, eight years later, he broke his spell of failures in the amateur by beating George von Elm, 9 and 8.

No one in the great throng of fully 18,000 spectators, who made a great human fringe around the green and a solid mass packed in the fairway that Jones had just played from, could help but feel that here was golf history being made.

Wild Demonstration at End.

Regret for Homans, who had put up a resistance that looked weak beside the finished golf of the world's greatest golfer, was overbalanced by the joy of seeing the Southerner make his record, for certainly Bobby will never try to repeat it and almost certainly no one can ever break it.

It was an epochal moment, and the demonstration that came after it was one that will never be forgotten. Playing the hole, a two-shotter with two level fairways and an island green tucked away back in the woods, Jones was dormie 8. But a moment before he had missed a chance to close out the match on the previous hole by misjudging a little pitch shot out of the rough and putting his ball into a bunker alongside Homans's.

Both sides of the fairway were lined with persons ten and twelve rows deep as he and Homans drove off. It was Gene's honor, Bobby having conceded him a birdie 2 on the No. 9 hole. The ex-Princeton star, realizing by now, of course, that it was all over, drove to the left.

Having nothing to lose, Bobby lit into his drive and sent his ball flying down the fairway. It was a long drive, almost reaching the edge of the little stream that runs across the fairway near the 300-yard mark. Homans had to play first and sent a beautiful mashie shot onto the green, a trifle beyond the hole. A moment later Bobby's ball came sailing on, stopping short of the pin.

Onlookers Are Tense.

Despite the fact that all those thousands were standing as close as they could get, the dropping of a pin in the grass would have been heard as Bobby, looking a little haggard and drawn, walked over to his ball after his caddie had handed him his pet putter, known the world over as Calamity Jane. One of those quizzical glances that he gives the hole, the familiar cocking of the Jones head, a slight movement of the wrists as they brought the club back and then forward.

The ball started on its journey up to the hole over the closely cropped grass. He didn't quite have the line, but it stopped so close to the side of the hole that Homans would have had to sink his in order to prevent the match from ending there and then. Knowing full well that it was all over Gene took comparatively little time over his own putt, hit the ball and, almost before it passed by the side of the hole he was over wringing Bobby's hand.

Immediately a great shout was sent up, then the tumult that reverberated for miles. It lasted for several minutes. There was a wild rush

Continued on Page Eight.

Will Not Retire, Says Jones; Declares He May Play in 1931

ARDMORE, Pa., Sept. 27 (AP).—As he accepted the championship cup Bobby Jones paid tribute today to his opponents, to the galleries and to the Merion Club, where in 1916 he first played in the amateur tournament. He has now won five of the last seven.

"I expect to continue to play golf, but just when and where I cannot say now," Bobby told The Associated Press. "I have no definite plans, either to retire or as to when and where I may continue in competition. I might play next year and lay off in 1932. I might stay out of the battle next season and feel like another tournament the following year. That's all I can say about it now."

HEARS LLOYD'S LOST $125,000 ON JONES

London Report Says Atlantans Pooled Bets and Got Odds of 50 to 1.

MYSTERY CLOAKS DEALS

Atlanta Reports Five of Jones's Friends Won $2,500, While 24 Others Also Cashed.

By The Associated Press.

LONDON, Sept. 27.—Any London financiers who may have laid odds of 50 to 1 against Bobby Jones winning four major golf titles in 1930 refrained from making much noise about it after news of Bobby's victory in the American amateur spread tonight.

Such odds were never officially quoted by Lloyd's, for the simple reason that Lloyd's does not conduct an insurance business as a corporation. This is done by individual firms that are members of the historic underwriting organization.

But this story of golfing high finance has cropped up several times this Summer as Bobby pushed on from victory to victory. Lloyd's offices are said to have received inquiries from Atlanta asking for "insurance" against Jones sweeping all the greens of golfdom this year.

Maintain Their Tradition.

It isn't the sort of business that the underwriters could take officially. But various individual members of the firms, who thought they knew a little something about golf, wanted to live up to the tradition that an individual can get insured at Lloyd's against anything from twins and seasickness to earthquakes and avalanches.

These members are understood to have accepted the American proposition as a private deal. Admirers of Bobby in Atlanta are reported to have put up $5 shares to a total of $2,500. This would mean that $125,000, a neat sum to tee up for, is due them from London tonight.

Jones Unaware of Deal.

Bobby knew nothing about the deal this Summer nor had he any idea who were the Atlantans backing him. The identity of the Londoners who accommodated them with a 50-to-1 shot has been hidden in mystery and seemed likely to grow darker in clouds of impenetrable gloom this evening.

The general opinion is that these persons, after spending a Summer of ever-increasing nervousness, finally had complete breakdowns today. Inquiries at leading mental hospitals, however, failed to reveal any unusual increase in the number of golf addicts admitted.

Winners Friends of Jones.

ATLANTA, Ga., Sept. 27 (AP).—The Atlanta Constitution says five Atlanta friends of Bobby Jones will receive $500 each on $10 investments in their belief that he would win all golfdom's major titles this year.

They bet $50 with Lloyd's, at odds of 50 to 1, that Bobby would win the British and American national opens and amateurs. The men are close personal friends of Jones and three of them were at his side today in victory.

Shortly before Jones won the first title in his 1930 campaign the men asked a representative of Lloyd's what odds the well-known house would offer on Bobby winning all four tournaments. Lloyd's offered 50 to 1, so the men cabled $2,000 to England. Lloyd's cabled that $2.500 was the maximum to be paid on the bets, and returned all but $50.

More than twenty-four Atlantans collected various amounts, at odds of 10 to 1 offered against Bobby's winning both the British open and amateur.

Times Wide World Photo.

Bobby Jones Putting on the Fifth Green During Final of National Amateur.

Times Wide World Photo.

Jones Receiving Cup From Findlay S. Douglas, President of U. S. G. A., After Victory Over Homans (Right).

YALE ROUTS MAINE IN OPENER BY 38-0

Record First-Day Crowd of 20,000 Watches McLennan Star With 2 Touchdowns.

BOOTH PLAYS BRILLIANTLY

Passes, Kicks and Runs Spectacularly and Also Crosses Line on a Plunge.

STATISTICS OF THE GAME.

	Yale.	Maine.
First downs	15	4
Lost ball on downs	0	0
Yards gained rushing	279	49
Yards lost rushing	0	29
Forward passes	9	3
Forwards completed	6	0
Yards gained, forwards	61	0
Forwards intercepted	0	2
Lateral passes	3	0
Laterals completed	3	0
Yards gained, laterals	41	0
Laterals intercepted	0	0
Fumbles	1	5
Fumbles recovered	1	4
Penalties	6	1
Yards lost, penalties	40	5

Special to The New York Times.

NEW HAVEN, Conn., Sept. 27.—Yale's football opening today produced a 38-point score for the Blue and the fifth whitewash in succession in the series of games with the University of Maine which began in 1913. Maine has never crossed the Yale goal line since it was assigned the rôle of ringing up the curtain in the Bowl.

Today the crowd of some 20,000, a new record for opening day, sat coatless and hatless under a blistering sun which compelled the rival coaches, Mal Stevens and Fred Brice, to rush replacements into the game in rapid succession. Yale used exactly three complete elevens and the visitors twenty-three players. The reserve camps of both teams were nearly depleted when the contest ended.

Maine's stubborn defense held back the onslaught of the fresh home players to a single touchdown during each period until the fourth, when the weakened Maine ranks allowed three scores to filter across.

Yale Is Never Threatened.

Maine at no time threatened the Yale goal nor did it put on any long marches. The visiting team did not pass the midfield mark, and its only ground gaining adventures were a 17-yard advance by Sims in the third period and an 11-yard gain by Romansky in the first. Blockinger punted well and Captain Borne's rushline play was effective.

Yale's second-string back field was in at the start and Don McLennan's all-round play was the outstanding feature until intermission. His forty-yard run back of a kick, followed by Taylor's forward pass to Snead gaining thirty more, made the scene shift quickly from Yale's thirty-yard line to the Maine five-yard line. McLennan's glancing crash swept the ball across for the opening score and he duplicated his run and his tackle glides in the second period and took the ball across for the second score.

Coach Stevens called a fresh eleven, headed by the first-string back field, into action for the final two minutes of the second period, and hurled it against Maine at the opening of the third.

The crowd, alert to the advent of

Continued on Page Five.

Football Scores

COLLEGES.

East.

Albright 19	Conn. Aggies 0
American U. 14	Shenandoah 12
Amherst 41	Vermont 0
Army 39	Boston U. 0
Bates 26	Mass. Aggies 0
Boston Coll. 54	Catholic U. 7
Brown 7	Rhode Island St. 0
Bucknell 46	Geneva 6
Bucknell Fr. 39	Stroudsburg Tch. 0
Carnegie Tech. 75	Buffalo 2
C. C. N. Y. 44	Long Island 0
Colby 13	Wesleyan 6
Colgate 38	St. Lawrence 0
Columbia 48	Middlebury 0
Cornell 66	Clarkson Tech. 0
Dartmouth 79	Norwich 0
Dickinson 19	Carlisle 7
Drexel 7	Swarthmore 0
Fordham 73	Baltimore 0
Georgetown 14	Mt. St. Mary's 6
Gettysburg 20	Juniata 0
Grove City 90	Morris Harvey 0
Hamilton 0	Alfred 0
Holy Cross 30	St. Bonaventure 0
Lafayette 7	St. Thomas 0
Lehigh 12	Ursinus 0
Lewiston Nor. 13	Cheney Nor. 12
Lowell Text. 14	Arnold 0
Maryland 60	Washington College 6
Muhlenberg 6	St. Joseph's 0
N. Y. U. 35	Hobart 0
Penn. M. C. 13	Prospect Park 0
Penn State 31	Niagara 14
Pittsburgh 52	Waynesburg 0
Providence 12	Rutgers 6
Rider 14	Manhattan 7
Springfield 29	E. Stroudsburg 0
St. John's (Md.) 13	Frank.-Mar. 0
St. Vincent 57	Westinghouse 0
Spring Hill 71	Marion Inst. 0
Syracuse 55	R. P. I. 0
Tufts Fr. 7	Andover 0
Union 32	Cooper Union 0
Villanova 19	Lebanon Valley 0
Wash. and Jeff. 74	Bethany 0
Westminster 19	Edinboro 12
Williams 20	Rochester 0
W. Virginia 26	W. Va. Wesleyan 0
Yale 38	Maine 0

South.

Alabama 43	Howard 0
Arkansas 27	Ozarks 0
Baylor 33	Denton Tech 0
Bowling Green 19	Hope 0
Carson-Newman 12	Mars Hill 0
Catawba 24	Atlantic Chr. 0
Centenary 27	Hendrix 0
Centre 31	Ky. Western Tch. 0
Citadel 13	Erskine 0
Clemson 32	Wofford 0
Florida 45	Southern 6
Georgia 31	Oglethorpe 6
Greenbrier Mil. 7	Emory-Henry Fr. 0
L. S U. 71	Louisiana Tech 0
Millsaps 40	W. Tenn. Tech 0
Miss. College 33	La. College 14
New Mexico 6	N. Mexico Fr. 0
N. Mex. Military 60	Montezuma 0
N. Arizona Tech. 71	N. Mex. Mines 0
New Mexico A. and M. 25	Las Vegas 0

South.

North Carolina U. 13	Wake Forest 7
Presbyterian 9	Mercer 7
Rice 13	Sam Houston 12
St. Xavier 14	Transylvania 0
Sewanee 14	Tenn. Poly. Inst. 0
S. M. U. Reserves 0	Southwestern 0
South Carolina 22	Duke 0
S'thw'tern (Memphis) 14	Miss. A. & M. 0
Tennessee 54	Maryville 0
Texas Aggies 43	Southwestern 0
Texas Christian U. 33	Austin 7
Texas U. 28	El Paso Mines 0
Tulane 88	S. W. La. Inst. 0
Vanderbilt 39	Chattanooga 0
Virginia 48	Rand. Macon 0
V. M. I. 12	Richmond 0
V. P. I. 9	Roanoke 0
W. and L. 15	Hampden-Sydney 0
Wayland 6	Texas Tech. 0

West.

Akron 41	Toledo 0
Albion 26	Detroit Tech 7
Butler 46	Ind. Centenary 0
Carleton 38	Eau Claire Tch. 0
Case 19	Findlay 12
Central Coll. 19	Warrensburg Tch. 0
Cincinnati 46	Cedarville 0
Defiance 6	Hiram 0
Dubuque 12	Wartburg 0
Earlham 14	Bluffton 0
Flint Jr. 6	Michigan Normal 0
Hillsdale 56	Concordia 0
Indiana 14	Miami 0
Iowa 38	Bradley 12
Luther 38	St. Ambrose 0
McAlester 31	St. Ambrose 0
Marquette 27	Lawrence 0
Michigan 33	Denison 0
Michigan 7	Ypsilanti Norm. 0
Michigan State 28	Alma 0
Minnesota 48	S. Dakota St. 0
Monmouth 32	Wheaton 6
Moorhead Tech. 33	Bemidji Tech. 0
N. Mich. Tech. 7	Stevens Pt. Nor. 6
Northland 10	Duluth Tch. 0
Oberlin 25	Kenyon 7
Ohio State 59	Mount Union 0
Ohio University 27	Wilmington 0
Ohio Wesleyan 26	Marshall 6
Olivet 8	Manchester 0
Pittsburg (Kan.) 18	N. E. Okla. Tch. 0
Rose Poly 14	Franklin 0
St. John's (Minn.) 27	St. Paul Luth. 0
St. Louis 27	Cornell Coll 0
St. Olaf 53	Hamline 6
South Dakota 7	Yankton 7
Wooster 13	W. Liberty 0

Far West.

Brigham Young 19	Wyoming 12
California 19	Santa Clara 7
Montana 52	Mount St. Charles 0
Montana State 7	Idaho 6
Occidental 31	Nat. U. of Mexico 6
Oregon 51	Willamette 0
So. California 52	U. C. L. A. 0
Stanford 18	Olympic Club 0
Utah 20	Nevada 7
Utah Aggies 31	Western St. 0
Washington 48	Whitman 0
Wash. State 47	Coll. of Idaho 12

SCHOOLS.

Local.

Alex. Hamilton 27	Stuyvesant 0
Boys High 19	La Salle M. A.
Erasmus Hall 8	Bushwick 0
Far Rockaway 6	Borough Hall Acad. 0
Flushing 0	Hempstead 0
Geo. Washington 12	Brooklyn Prep 6
Jamaica 20	Morris 0
Manual Training 12	Richmond Hill 6
St. Francis Pr. 25	Seward Park 0

Long Island.

Alumni 2	Manhasset 0
Amityville 59	Sayville 0
Baldwin 13	Oceanside 6
Freeport 43	Huntington 0
Great Neck 14	Mineola 0
Rockville Centre B. C. 44	Woodmere 0
Southampton 26	West Hampton 2
Stony Brook 28	East Hampton 0
Valley Stream 6	Alumni 0
Westbury 0	Madison Ave. Pres. 0

Westchester.

Gorton 26	Pelham 0
Rye Neck 21	Chappaqua 7
Mount Vernon 16	Hicksville 0
New Rochelle 7	Middletown 0
Washington Irving 7	Mamaroneck 0
White Plains 6	Pleasantville 0
Yonkers 12	Peekskill High 6

New York State.

Manlius 46	Eastman Bus. Coll. 0
Poughkeepsie 39	Goshen 0

New Jersey.

Asbury Park 14	Alumni 2
Barringer 6	Paterson Central 6
Bloomfield 19	Textile 0
Burlington 0	Collingswood 0
Carteret High 14	Freehold 0
Boonton 12	Alumni 6
Dickinson Evening 6	Alumni 2
Fort Lee 20	Park Ridge 0
Garfield 21	Dover 13
Hackensack 14	Tenafly 0

Continued on Page Three.

Pittsburgh Routs Waynesburg by 52-0, Reserves' 26-Point Drive Featuring Play

Special to The New York Times.

PITTSBURGH, Sept. 27.—Jock Sutherland's latest edition of the Pittsburgh Panthers opened its season today at the stadium with a 52-to-0 victory over Waynesburg.

The locals scored almost at will, the contest's feature being the work of the second and third string players, who made 26 points in the last quarter by virtue of a series of long runs.

Brown, with a 70-yard run off left tackle, and Alpert, with a 50-yard return of a punt, both for touchdowns, made the spectacular offensive plays of the game.

The visitors were helpless against the Panthers and made only one first down, that by the aerial route in the final period.

Particularly pleasing to Panther followers was the display of strength by the reserve players.

Walinchus, a consistent performer last year, began auspiciously this year when he scored two touchdowns when sent into the fray in place of Reider, who had replaced Williams at left half.

Captain Baker displayed booting ability, kicking three goals from placement after touchdowns.

The line-up:

Pittsburgh (52).		Waynesburg (0).
MacMurdo	L.E.	Lofrano
Quatse	L.T.	Berry
H. Morris	L.G.	Wiley
Daugherty	C.	Cummings
Lewis	R.G.	Zaninell
Tully	R.T.	Elliot
Hirschberg	R.E.	Mazza
Baker	Q.B.	Lohr
Williams	L.H.	Patsch
Heller	R.H.	Porter
Hood	F.B.	Rollanson

SCORE BY PERIODS.

Pittsburgh	6	13	7	26—52
Waynesburg	0	0	0	0—0

Touchdowns—Hood, Heller, Baker, Wagner, Walinchus 2, Brown, Alpert. Point after touchdown—Baker (placement) 3, Heller (placement).

Substitutions—Pittsburgh: Reider for Williams, Collins for Heirschberg, Walinchus for Reider, Tormey for Daugherty, Alpert for Baker, Milligan for H. Morris, Siegel for Lewis, Daily for MacMurdo, Basic for Milligan, Wagner for Hood, Luch for Wagner, Kelly for Walinchus, Brown for Alpert, Anderson for Quatse; Waynesburg: Yanosh for Zaninell, Marjas for Derrick, Butterworth for Wiley, Costello for Lohr, Ambrose for Lufrona, Lufrano for Ambrose, Mancuso for Porter, Anderson for Barjas, Costello for Patsch.

Referee—Friesell, Princeton. Umpire—Slack, Pittsburgh. Head linesman—MacFarland, W. and J. Field judge—Robb, Penn State. Time of periods—15 minutes.

FORDHAM TRAMPLES ON BALTIMORE, 73-0

9,000 See Maroon Eleven Flash Irresistible Attack in the Season's Opener.

MURPHY LEADS OFFENSIVE

Scores Five Touchdowns, While Bartos Also Stars—Losers Without First Down.

STATISTICS OF THE GAME.

	Fordham.	Baltimore.
First downs	23	0
Lost ball on downs	0	7
Yards gained rushing	294	16
Yards lost rushing	2	12
Forward passes	18	12
Forwards completed	8	0
Yards gained, forwards	140	0
Forwards intercepted	1	1
Lateral passes	2	0
Laterals completed	2	0
Yards gained, laterals	12	0
Laterals intercepted	0	0
Fumbles	4	3
Fumbles recovered	2	1
Penalties	4	1
Yards lost, penalties	45	15

Led by Jim Murphy, star halfback, who scored five touchdowns, the Fordham University football team opened its season at Fordham Field yesterday afternoon by crushing the University of Baltimore eleven under a 73-0 score before a crowd of more than 9,000.

The score at half-time was 53-0, after which the regulars were taken out. The Maroon substitutes were held to a lone touchdown in the third period. With the return of the varsity in the last quarter Fordham added 13 more points to its total.

The victory was the winners' tenth straight game without a defeat. Major Cavanaugh's machine won seven and tied two in the 1929 season, and it was practically the same team that made such a fine record in the last campaign that was responsible for the overwhelming score yesterday.

The Maryland outfit was unable to make even one first down and was constantly forced to punt after being repulsed by the Maroon's strong defense.

Bartos Stars at Quarterback.

Frank Bartos, who substituted for the injured Jack Fisher at quarterback, ran the Fordham team in a smooth, workmanlike fashion that drew praise from the Maroon mentor. Bartos accounted for one of the Fordham touchdowns, in addition to throwing many passes to Jim Murphy and Bill McMahon for long gains.

The outstanding play of the game was made by Murphy, who battered his way at will through the visitors' line and around the wings. Toward the end of the first half the brilliant Fordham ball carrier caught the visitors' kick-off on his own 15-yard line, ran behind perfect interference down the field to the Baltimore 25-yard mark, where he evaded the outstretched arms of Tierney, Baltimore fullback, and then ran the rest of the distance to score after traveling 85 yards. Johnny Janis also stood out in the winners' relentless attack, and on one occasion ran 40 yards around the Baltimore left end to put the Maroon in a scoring position.

McMahon accounted for the first touchdown in the first five minutes of play. After taking the kick-off,

Continued on Page Three.

London Cheers Bradman As Cricket Star Leaves

LONDON, Sept. 27 (Canadian Press Cable).—England bade farewell today to Don Bradman, the wonderful young cricketer, who has smashed all records in matches in which he has played with the Australian team this season. Hundreds of well-wishers were present at the St. Pancras Railway station when Bradman, with five other members of the team, started on the first stage of his homeward journey. Among them were the Australian girl hockeyites, who have just arrived in England for a series of games. They greeted Bradman with shrill "cooes," the Australian sporting battle cry.

In an interview Bradman said: "I am not saying good-bye, only au revoir; because I hope to see you in 1934, if my cricket is still good enough."

12,000 WATCH N. Y. U. SUBDUE HOBART, 35-0

Sophomore Backs Make Impressive Showing in Opening Game at Ohio Field.

TANGUAY SCORES 3 TIMES

Bill and Bob McNamara Account for Other Tallies—Violet Displays Power in Second.

STATISTICS OF THE GAME.

	N.Y.U.	Hobart.
First downs	5	4
Lost ball on downs	1	0
Yards gained rushing	74	34
Yards lost rushing	4	19
Forward passes	2	2
Forwards completed	2	0
Yards gained, forwards	25	0
Forwards intercepted	1	0
Lateral passes	0	0
Fumbles	2	5
Fumbles recovered	5	1
Penalties	9	1
Yards lost, penalties	90	5

A promising New York University football team made its 1930 début at Ohio Field yesterday and defeated Hobart, 35 to 0. A colorful crowd of 12,000 saw a quintet of violet-jerseyed sophomore ball carriers successfully pass their first test against intercollegiate competition.

Hobart offered the Violet eleven fine opening day opposition, N. Y. U. scoring most of its points in an inspired second quarter and registering its final tally just before the end of the game. But it was during these periods that Coach Chick Meehan kept his varsity eleven in the game, substituting frequently during the other quarters. N. Y. U. lost 90 yards in penalties to Hobart's 5.

Jim Tanguay, dark, curly-haired halfback who runs and punts much in the fashion of his predecessor of 1928, Ken Strong, led the ex-freshman group. Joe La Mark, Jack MacDonald and Bill McNamara also played well, while Bob McNamara, Meehan's latest sophomore find, added a fifth member to this unit.

Tanguay scored three touchdowns and a trio of points after touchdown on placement kicks. Bill and Bob McNamara registered the remaining scores.

Third Team Started.

Coach Meehan started his third team against the up-Staters, keeping the men in action until more than half of the opening period had elapsed before sending in his varsity eleven. During this time the Violet reserves held Hobart to a single first down, but most of the fighting was in N. Y. U. territory.

Chalmers intercepted a Hobart pass thrown by Gohringer on N. Y. U.'s 25-yard line, but an N. Y. U. penalty, its fourth of the period, followed by a poor punt off Tanguay's toe, gave the Orange and Purple the ball on the Violet's 12-yard line. N. Y. U.'s forward wall was too much for the visitors, however, and after two vain attempts in bucking the line, in which Hobart lost considerable ground, a poor pass from the centre was recovered by Hugret on the up-Staters' 43-yard mark.

Tanguay picked up 3 yards off tackle just as the period ended in a scoreless tie. The Violet showed power and drive soon after the second quarter was under way and before the period was brought to a close N. Y. U. had piled up a 28-to-0 margin on a quartet of touchdowns and a similar number of successful

Continued on Page Four.

COLUMBIA CRUSHES MIDDLEBURY, 48-0

20,000 at Baker Field See Lions Open Season Auspiciously Under New Regime.

3 TOUCHDOWNS BY HEWITT

Star Back Passes to Tys for Another Tally—Winners Lead, 19-0, at Half.

VICTOR'S PLAYS DECEPTIVE

Varied Attack Baffles Visitors, Who Fail to Make First Down, Losing 20 Yards Rushing.

STATISTICS OF THE GAME.

	Colum.	Midd'b'y.
First downs	13	0
Yards gained rushing	25	*0
Forward passes	8	7
Forwards completed	5	0
Yards gained, forwards	119	0
Forwards intercepted	0	1
Lateral passes	1	2
Laterals completed	1	2
Yards gained, laterals	15	12
Penalties	8	4
Yards lost, penalties	60	20
Fumbles	3	0
Fumbles recovered	1	2

*Lost 20 yards.

Columbia's football team, new uniforms, new coach, new system and all, got off to an auspicious start yesterday at Baker Field when the Blue and White eleven submerged Middlebury under a 48-0 fusillade of touchdowns.

With 20,000 persons witnessing the début of the Lions under their new coach, Lou Little, former Georgetown mentor, the supporters of the Morningside outfit saw a heavy and fast team that combined a powerful, slam-bang running attack with as deceptive a passing repertoire as has been witnessed at Baker Field in several years.

The performance of Columbia left its alumni and undergraduates with the confident feeling that this season the Lions will start their climb back into the football elect.

Columbia Defense Strong.

So effective was Columbia's defense that Middlebury's attempts to gain by rushing showed a deficit of twenty yards. Try as they did, the visitors could not register a first down and their seven attempts at forward passing went astray, usually because of the alert Blue and White defense.

Not once was Middlebury in Columbia territory and the Lions were forced to punt only once, causing no end of cheering among Blue and White adherents, who filed through the new $25,000 gates given by the class of 1905.

Ralph Hewitt, ace of the Blue and White back field, led the parade across the visitors' goal line, scoring three touchdowns and putting a drop-kick between the bars after one of them. Joe Stanczyk, Remy Tys, Jay Hodupp and Jimmy Sheridan each registered a touchdown.

After banging away at the Middlebury line in the first five minutes of the game, Hewitt slipped around left end, sidestepping, dodging and twisting through would-be tacklers for the first touchdown. Steve Grenda, one of the four sophomores in the starting line-up, kicked the goal from placement for the extra point.

Hewitt's Pass Brings Score.

Columbia's first forward-passing attempt proved successful when Hewitt flipped a 12-yard pass to Tys, who ran thirty-three yards for a touchdown, Tys's teammates providing high class interference.

Late in the second quarter Stanczyk tossed a lateral pass to Manuel Rivero for a 15-yard gain and then Harold Wolkind smashed the line on two plays, bringing the ball to Middlebury's five-yard line. Hewitt went over on the next play, making the score at half time, 19-0.

Hewitt scored again in the third quarter, when he went through left tackle and then cut to the left and eluded the pursuers from Middlebury. Stanczyk broke into the scoring column with a dashing 26-yard run around left end to put the count at 34-0, as the third period closed.

In the fourth quarter Hodupp furnished the longest scoring run of the contest, a 50-yard dash from scrimmage. Sheridan later scored on a line play from the ten-yard line. Hodupp added the extra points on the last two touchdowns.

Bill McDuffee, Columbia centre blocked Huntington's punt in the third period and the ball rolled out of bounds directly behind the goal line, giving the Lions two more points.

The line-up:

Columbia (48).		Middlebury (0).
Tys	L.E.	Hinman
Sherwood	L.T.	Perry
Grenda	L.G.	Whitman
McDuffee	C.	Nelson
Weinstock	R.G.	Duffany
Banko	R.T.	Huntington
Van Voorhees	R.E.	Thrasher
Hewitt	Q.B.	Markowski
Rivero	L.H.	Corliss
Wolkind	R.H.	Bakeman
Stanczyk	F.B.	Hartley

SCORE BY PERIODS.

Columbia	13	6	15	14—48
Middlebury	0	0	0	0—0

Touchdowns—Hewitt 3, Tys, Stanczyk, Hodupp, Sheridan. Points after touchdown—Hodupp 2, Grenda (placement), Hewitt (drop-kick). Safety—Middlebury.

Substitutions—Columbia: Morres for Stanczyk, Barber for Banko, Sheridan for Hewitt, Lippoth for Van Voorhees, Allan for McDuffee, Hall for Rivero, Reilly for Lippoth, Japar for Weinstock, Scott for Wolkind, Ganzle for Barber, Nobiletti for Grenda, Bodtlander for Tys, Stanczyk for Mosser, Japar for Nobiletti, Weinstock for Japar, Banko for Ganzle, Hewitt for Sheridan, Van Voorhees for Reilly, Tys for Bodtlander, McDuffee for Allan, Rivero for Hall, Wolkind for Scott, Mosser for Stanczyk, Ganzle for Banko, Scott for Wolkind, Lippoth for Tys, Hodupp for Rivero, Sheridan for Hewitt, Moss for Sherwood, Allan for McDuffee, Barber for Moss, Hickey for Japar, Hall for Scott, Reilly for Van Voorhees, Gulbransen for Mosser, Britz for Sheridan. Middlebury: Foote for Corliss, Johnson for Whitman, Corliss for Foote, Whitman for Johnson, Johnson for Whitman, Hoyle for Bakeman, Thiele for Hinman, Bram for Markowski, McLean for Perry, Paul for Corliss, Lovell for Nelson, Loveday for Huntington.

Referee—J. C. Hennessey, Brown. Umpire—A. W. Palmer, Colby. Linesman—H. E. Von Kersburg, Harvard. Field judge—F. R. Wallace, Washington College. Time of periods—12 minutes.

City College Scores in Every Period, Winning From Long Island U. by 44-0

C. C. N. Y. opened its football season auspiciously at Lewisohn Stadium yesterday, trampling Long Island University under a barrage of seven touchdowns. The score was 44-0.

An opening-game crowd of 4,000 saw the Lavender score in every period, coming along in the second half with 31 points when the lighter and weaker L. I. U. eleven tired perceptibly.

Schlesinger and Co-Captain Dubinsky each scored two touchdowns for City College, with Hank Berger, Murray Gerenstein and Morris Dulberg carrying the ball across the line for the other scores.

Long Island opened up an effective air attack, completing fifteen out of thirty-one passes for ten first downs, the same number scored by C. C. N. Y., but the visitors were unable to supply a scoring punch when needed.

Schlesinger took a lateral pass from Schneer and sprinted 78 yards for a touchdown in the third quarter. Gerenstein intercepted a pass and ran 80 yards for a touchdown in the same period.

The line-up:

City College (44).		Long Island (0).
Figowitz	L.E.	Klein
Heistein (capt.)	L.T.	Stavisky
Atkins	L.G.	Lucia
Rhodie	C.	Butkus
Rosenbloom	R.G.	(capt.) Grossman
Vance	R.T.	Du Pont
Berger	R.E.	Glaberman
Eisenberg	Q.B.	Roman
Dubinsky (capt.)	L.H.	Finkel
Schneer	R.H.	Goldstein
Schlesinger	F.B.	Marselli

SCORE BY PERIODS.

C. C. N. Y.	7	6	19	12—44
Long Island	0	0	0	0—0

Touchdowns—Berger, Dubinsky 2, Schlesinger 2, Gerenstein, Dulberg. Points after touchdown—Heistein (placement); Berger (drop kick).

Substitutions—C. C. N. Y.: Miller for Schlesinger, Beriad for Atkins, Rubin for Figowitz, Gerenstein for Vance, Tatarsky for Berger, N. Schwartz for Tatarsky, R. Schwartz for N. Schwartz, Vance for Gerenstein, Schlesinger for Miller, Miller for Dubinsky, Figowitz for R. Schwartz, Berger for N. Schwartz, Jacone for Vance, Kaplowitz for Schneer, Gerenstein for Atkins, Tatarsky for Berger, Beriad for Heistein, Klein for Eisenberg, Dulberg for Schlesinger, Rhodie for Shiffman, Yanella for Rosenbloom, Edelson for Jacone, Rubin for Figowitz, Rosenfield for Edelson. Long Island U.: Erdheim for Roman, Braiver for Goldstein, Roman for Erdheim, Mann for Roman, Hansen for Erdheim, Presto for Grossman.

Referee—W. T. Cook, Springfield. Umpire—E. Cragg, Columbia. Linesman—R. J. Shearer, Dickinson. Time of periods—15 minutes.

18,000 See Jones Win U. S. Amateur Title, His Fourth Major Crown of the Year

By WILLIAM D. RICHARDSON.

Continued from Page One.

toward Jones who, had it not been for the presence of a squad of marines, would have been crushed.

It was some moments before order was restored and an opening made through which Jones and Homans could walk over to the number 12 fairway and begin their journey back to the clubhouse. And over the entire distance Jones was cheered on as triumphant a journey as any man ever traveled in sport.

Today's match was far more of a spectacle than it was a contest. As a matter of fact there was not much contest to it. It was merely an exhibition on Jones's part, a parade to victory.

Jones Soon Draws Away.

Starting by winning the very first hole played, Bobby, taking advantage of his opponent's wildness and his proneness to get into bunkers, and likewise his inability to hole winning putts, gradually built up a lead that became three holes at the fourth, eight holes at the sixteenth seven holes at the finish of the morning round, 9 up after the first four holes had been played in the afternoon and, finally, 8 up and 7 to play.

Yesterday, playing against young Charley Seaver, budding Californian, Homans was 5 down at noon, 2 down and 4 to play and yet he pulled the match out of the fire by his sheer nerve.

But it is one thing to start Charley Seaver 5 up and beat him and quite another thing to start Bobby Jones 3 up on the first four holes and 7 up in eighteen. It simply can't be done nowadays. There may have been a time when it could, but those days seem to have gone.

Bobby wasn't flawless today. During the round he was in enough trouble to disprove the generally accepted theory that he is a machine and not a human being, but only on few occasions was Homans able to capitalize on the mistakes.

Gene can play better golf than he played against Jones and Bobby can play better golf than he played against Gene. But what happened to Homans is the same thing that would probably have happened to any one else in his shoes.

None of them, not even the professionals, are able to play their own game against the invincible Atlantan who has carried everything before him this year. His reputation, a reputation that has been earned only after years of bitter experience, seems to overawe them, and is not at all strange.

Homans's Fate Sealed Early.

Jones won the match on the first few holes. When he took 3 over par on the first nine and still was 2 up on Homans no one expected the match to go any further than it did. On the second nine Jones traveled at a par pace and added five more holes to his total. After the fourth hole in the afternoon he was 9 up and the match should have ended even before it did.

Homans got off to a bad start when he was in bunkers on the first three holes. Jones should have been 3 up right there but on the second, after two tremendous wooden shots into the wind up near the green, he played a weak mashie-niblick pitch and took three putts on the terraced green.

Despite the fact that he put his drive into a bunker on the fourth, Bobby got his par 5 and won the hole when Homans took three putts. On the fifth both hooked into the rough, but this time it was Bobby who three-putted to give Homans a half.

Homans got nearer to the hole with his approaches on the sixth and seventh and won the seventh to reduce Bobby's lead from three holes to two when Jones again three-putted. Then, playing the ninth, Homans pitched his tee shot into the water and the penalty stroke cost him the hole, leaving him 3 down at the turn.

Homans Again Finds Bunker.

Homans was bunkered again on the tenth and lost it on Jones's par 4 and then, on the eleventh, Jones holed an eighteen-foot putt for his first birdie in the round. It was right after that that Jones began picking up holes almost as fast as he came to them. Gene got halves on the next two, but Jones won the fourteenth, fifteenth and sixteenth, Homans hooking on the fourteenth, putting his second into a bunker on the fifteenth and taking three putts from an excusable distance on the sixteenth.

The only hole on the last nine which Jones failed to get par on was the seventeenth, where he hooked to the rough and even then almost got his par for he came back to within seven feet and missed the putt. To prevent himself from being 8 down instead of 7 at noontime Gene had to drop a fifteen-foot putt on the last green.

Homans was wild off the tee on the first two holes in the afternoon, but escaped with halves. It looked as if he might win the third when Jones fell short into a bunker while he was on, but he took three putts, and Bobby, coming out almost dead, won the hole. Bobby also won the fourth, Gene's drive going into a bunker. Except for the seventh the next four holes were well played. On the seventh both went over the green on their approaches, but the green was hard to hold.

Bobby was bunkered on the ninth or he might have been dormie. But he failed to get out at all close and Homans, who was nicely on, won the hole to reduce Bobby's advantage back to eight holes instead of nine.

Jones missed a fine opportunity to finish the match on the tenth by pitching into a bunker and taking two to get out. Gene was in the same bunker and pitched out over the green into another, and so the hole was halved in 6s, two over par. Then came the finish.

Solid Jam of Spectators.

Some idea of the size of the crowd may be gathered from the fact that in the afternoon round both sides of the fourth hole from the tee to the green were solidly lined with spectators. The hole is 595 yards in length.

For the first time during the championship the wind was a real element to be considered. It blew across the course from the west, making it a factor in calculating direction on both the first and second holes. Homans found a trap at the first green through making too strong an allowance for this factor. Both players steered a course to the left at the second, even though the wind was sweeping across from right to left.

When Jones missed a putt of less than three feet for his four at the fifth and thus allowed Homans to get a half in 5s, the break seemed to hearten the Englewood boy. He played the next two holes faultlessly, whereas up to that point he had made at least one mistake on each hole.

The fifth hole was supposed to be something of a hoodoo for Jones, but that did not keep him from holing a long curling putt for a par 4 in the afternoon against Homans.

On the other hand the fourth hole, which had been something of a favorite with Homans in his earlier matches, played him false in the final test. He took 6 on both rounds, losing it each time. In the morning he took three putts and in the afternoon he was trapped on his drive and needed four to reach the green.

Jones's three putts on the fifth hole was his first error of the morning round. Up to that point the Atlantan was a perfect golfing machine.

Homans really got into the final through a great tee shot he made at the 215-yard seventeenth in his final round against Seaver on Friday and he duplicated his good work in the morning round against Jones. His tee shot pulled up no more than nine feet from the hole. He didn't have to hole out since Jones missed the green with his tee shot and after pitching on was still away, following which he missed his 3 and conceded the hole.

Generally speaking the crowd was remarkably well handled, but it was inevitable that some mishaps were bound to creep in. Homans was the victim of such a break at the tenth in the morning round. His approach shot rolled just over the green into a trap. Spectators standing along the edge of the green moved out of the way in time to avoid actually stopping the ball which rolled into a heel print, making the recovery very much more difficult. He lost the hole.

In spite of the fact that the wind was more with than against, neither player hit a particularly long drive at the eighteenth in the forenoon Homan's second, a low hit, scurrying shot, struck short of the green but ran over the far side. He holed a good long one for his half in four, after chipping back.

Homans Reveals Spirit.

Homans's tee shot to the ninth in the afternoon revealed his rugged fighting spirit. He was almost hopelessly outdistanced at the time, but when Jones pushed his tee shot into a trap Gene stuck a full iron up within eight feet of the pin. Jones conceded the hole after recovering from the trap and missing his 3.

A small dog was making merry near the green on the tenth hole as Jones drove from the tee far back in the wood across a ravine. The ball struck so near the canine galleryite that it scared him and he scampered for safety.

A narrow sector of a trap to the left of the green at the tenth intervened between Homans's ball and the hole after his drive. At that stage there was nothing for him to do but shoot for the pin. The ball fell short, into a trap. It appeared likely that Jones would wind up the day then and there, but he, too, cut his distance too short and found the trap. An eventful half in 6s sent them on to the eleventh.

The marines and other branches of the constabulary found a man-sized job in rescuing Jones from the mob when the match ended at the eleventh. In spite of the fact that its location makes it most inaccessible, a huge crowd had pushed up as closely as possible, and when Homans, after failing to get his putt for a 3 to win, rushed over to congratulate Jones, the full force of the onrush converged on the two of them about the centre of the green.

An aviator circling overhead near the clubhouse as the players were ready to start the afternoon round, went through his paces with a few loops and other fancy stunts, but he drew scant consideration. The gallery was more intent on jockeying into a position to see what was going to happen on the green turf of that testing first hole.

THE CARDS.

Morning Round.

Out—
Jones ....4 6 3 5 5 4 5 4 3—39
Homans ....5 6 4 6 5 4 4 4 5—43
Jones, 3 up.

In—
Jones ....4 3 4 3 4 3 4 4 4—33—72
Homans ....5 4 4 3 5 5 5 2 4—37—80
Jones, 7 up.

Afternoon Round.

Out—
Jones ....4 5 3 5 4 4 5 4 4—38
Homans ....4 5 4 6 4 4 5 4 2—38

In—
Jones 6 4
Homans 6 4
Jones wins, 8 and 7.

How Jones Won His Fifth National Amateur Golf Title

MONDAY—Scored a 69 to lead field on first round of eighteen holes.

TUESDAY—Returned a 73 to win the qualifying medal with a total of 142.

WEDNESDAY—Defeated C. Ross Somerville and F. G. Hoblitzel, each by 5 and 4, in first and second rounds of match play (eighteen holes).

THURSDAY—Defeated Fay Coleman, 6 and 5, in first thirty-six-hole match.

FRIDAY—Defeated Jess Sweetser, 9 and 8, in semi-final round of thirty-six holes.

YESTERDAY — Defeated Gene Homans, 8 and 7, in final round of thirty-six holes.

Jones's Complete Cards.

QUALIFYING PLAY.

Monday.

Out ....4 5 3 5 4 4 4 4 3—36
In .....3 5 4 2 4 4 4 3 4—33—69

Tuesday.

Out ....4 5 2 5 5 4 4 4 3—36
In .....5 4 4 3 3 5 4 4 5—37—73—142

MATCH PLAY.

Defeated C. Ross Somerville, 5 and 4, Wednesday.

Out ....4 4 3 5 5 4 3 3 2—33
In 4 4 5 3 4

Defeated F. G. Hoblitzel, 5 and 4, Wednesday.

Out ....4 5 4 5 4 6 4 5 4—41
In 4 3 4 3 4

Defeated Fay Coleman, 6 and 5, Thursday (36 holes).

MORNING ROUND.

Out ....5 5 3 6 3 5 4 4 4—39
In .....4 5 4 3 4 6 4 3 4—37—76

AFTERNOON ROUND.

Out ....4 6 3 5 4 4 5 3 3—37
In 4 4 5 3

Defeated Jess Sweetser, 9 and 8, Friday (36 holes).

MORNING ROUND.

Out ....3 5 3 4 4 4 6 4 4—37
In .....5 5 5 3 4 3 4 3 4—36

AFTERNOON ROUND.

Out ....4 5 4 5 3 5 3 4 2—35
In 3

Defeated Gene Homans, 8 and 7, yesterday (36 holes).

MORNING ROUND.

Out ....4 6 3 5 5 4 5 4 3—39
In .....4 3 4 3 4 3 4 4 4—33—72

AFTERNOON ROUND.

Out ....4 5 4 6 4 4 5 4 2—38
In 6 4

Times Wide World Photo.

Crowd Following the Finalists From the First Tee at Merion Cricket Club.

ATLANTA IN GRIP OF VICTORY FEVER

Jones's Home Town Is Tense Till Definite News of Victory Comes From Merion.

MANY WIRE FELICITATIONS

Head of Bank of Which He Is a Director Calls Him Golfing Emperor of All Time.

ATLANTA, Ga., Sept. 27 (AP).—An epidemic of "Bobby Jones fever," which has gripped Atlanta all Summer, came to a climax today.

Home-town friends of the golf champion were almost certain Bobby would win the amateur and increase his season's total to all four of the world's major golf crowns. In fact, rumor said several had placed wagers on that possibility early in the year.

Realizing at the same time the uncertainties of golf, they were beset by a gnawing fear that some last-minute break would deprive him of a final jewel in the four-starred crown that now rests on his touseled head.

Therefore the news that he had come through with one of the most sweeping victories in the history of the American amateur was the signal for an excited series of private and group celebrations.

Accustomed to Victories.

Atlantans, however, are accustomed to Jones victories and to triumphant homecomings of the golf conqueror, and the acclamation of his latest victory was somewhat less boisterous than in years past.

When Bobby went through his 18-hole matches successfully last Wednesday, a great share of the fear for his survival was dispersed.

The fans had little to get excited about in his easy matches with Fay Coleman and Jess Sweetser, and early in his final match with Gene Homans it was apparent he would soon be home with another cup for his big collection. But the suspense was not broken until the very end.

Atlanta newspapers rushed one extra edition after another to the streets to keep the home folks advised of Bobby's progress, and all day long telephones in newspaper offices were busy with the repeated question, "How about Bobby now?"

Out at Eastlake, the country club Jones made famous, the members cluttered around the radio to hear the stroke-by-stroke announcement of Bob's play.

In Bobby's home, four persons sat huddled around the radio. To one he was son, to another husband, and to two youngsters father. Mrs. Jones Sr. and Bobby's wife and two children, Clara Malone and Robert Tyre 3d, probably were more interested in his play than any others.

Many Congratulatory Messages.

Many congratulatory messages were sent to Bobby when news of his victory was received. The first was sent by J. K. Ottley, president of the First National Bank of Atlanta, of which Bobby is a director. It read:

"Your associates on the board of directors of the First National Bank of Atlanta extend heartiest congratulations and join the rest of the world in acclaiming you golfing emperor of all times and all climes."

Although Atlanta probably won't repeat the great welcome it gave Bob when he returned in July with the British and the American open trophies, thousands of his friends will surge around the railroad station when he arrives again Monday morning.

His fellow-members of the Atlanta Atheltic Club plan a private welcoming party for him, but further announcements of a public welcome have not been made. There is little need for such, for Bobby knows he is a king to every one in Atlanta.

High Lights of Jones's Competitive Career

1911 (Age 9)—Won junior championship cup of Atlanta Athletic Club.

1912 (Age 10) — Lost in semi-final round of junior championship of Atlanta Athletic Club.

1913 (Age 11)—Played his first round in 80 strokes at East Lake course.

1915 (Age 13)—Qualified in Southern amateur, but lost in second round.

1916 (Age 14) — Won Georgia State amateur championship. Qualified in playing in his first national amateur tourney, losing in third round, at Merion.

1917 (Age 15)—Won Southern amateur championship.

1918 (Age 16)—Played in Red Cross exhibition matches.

1919 (Age 17) — Finalist in national amateur tourney. Finished in tie for second, Canadian open. Played in first national open, placing with 299, four strokes behind the winner, Ted Ray.

1920 (Age 18)—Won Southern amateur. Tied for eighth place, national open. Medalist in national amateur, beaten in semi-finals.

1921 (Age 19)—Lost in third round, national amateur. Tied for fifth in national open. Withdrew from British open at St. Andrews; lost in fourth round of British amateur.

1922 (Age 20)—Tied for second place, national open. Lost in semi-final, national amateur. Won Southern amateur. Won both matches in Walker Cup contest.

1923 (Age 21)—Won national open, Inwood, after play-off with Bobby Cruikshank. Won medal after play-off in national amateur, but lost in second round.

1924 (Age 22)—Won national amateur at Merion. Runner-up to Cyril Walker in national open. Won singles, lost foursome match in Walker Cup contest.

1925 (Age 23)—Won national amateur at Oakmont. Lost to Willie Macfarlane in play-off for national open.

1926 (Age 24)—Won British open, St. Anne's. Won national open, Scioto. Won medal in national amateur, but lost in final. Won both matches in Walker Cup contest. Lost in quarter-final, British amateur.

1927 (Age 25)—Won Southern open. Finished in quadruple tie for eleventh place in national open. Won national amateur, Minikahda. Won British open, St. Andrews, with record score, 285.

1928 (Age 26)—Won national amateur, Brae Burn. Lost in national open play-off with Johnny Farrell. Won both matches in Walker Cup series.

1929 (Age 27)—Tied for medal in national amateur; lost in first round. Won national open after play-off with Al Espinosa at Winged Foot.

1930 (Age 28)—Won British open at Hoylake. Won British amateur, St. Andrews. Won both matches in Walker Cup series. Won national open, Interlachen. Won national amateur, Merion.

KAESCHE IS VICTOR IN NASSAU C. C. GOLF

Beats McGovern, 4 and 3, and Lee, 3 and 2, to Reach Semi-Finals—White Also Advances.

Special to The New York Times.

GLEN COVE, L. I., Sept. 27.—Max Kaesche of Ridgewood, N. J., reached the semi-final round of the annual invitation golf tournament of the Nassau Country Club today. Winner of the tourney for the last two years, he overcame C. S. Lee of Tuxedo, 3 and 2, in the second round, after defeating C. B. McGovern of Nassau, 4 and 3, in the first.

Gardiner White of Nassau, whose poor putting on Friday barely got him into the first flight, showed improvement on the green in overcoming D. Bowman of Mount Kisco, 2 and 1, in the morning, and James Hewlett, also of Nassau, by 6 and 5 in the afternoon.

The summaries:

First Round—R. D. Pope, Lake Regent, defeated R. M. B. Potter, Nassau, 3 and 2; W. Hoyt, Cherry Valley, defeated F. R. Finlayson, Nassau, 2 and 1; C. S. Lee Jr., Tuxedo, defeated J. D. Cosgrove, Brookville, 5 and 3; Max B. Kaesche, Ridgewood, defeated C. B. McGovern, Nassau, 4 and 3; R. A. Burdick, Nassau, defeated James Sullivan, Brookville, 2 and 1; D. Rockwell, Engineers, defeated K. G. Sheldon, Nassau, 6 and 5; J. A. Hewlett, Nassau, defeated William McCullum, Sonning C. C. (England), 1 up; G. W. White, Nassau, defeated D. Bowman, Mount Kisco, 2 and 1.

Second Round—Hoyt defeated Pope, 4 and 3; Kaesche defeated Lee, 3 and 2; Rockwell defeated Burdick, 3 and 1; White defeated Hewlett, 6 and 5.

Hole-by-Hole Description of National Amateur Golf Final

By The Associated Press.

MORNING ROUND.

Hole 1, 360 Yards, Par 4.

Jones drove with a spoon from the first tee, but was slightly in front of Homans's long tee shot. Bob pitched twenty feet from the cup after Gene put his second in a trap. Homans came out of the sand thirty-five feet from the cup. Gene's long putt for a 4 stayed out. Jones putted close and got his par.

Jones 4, Homans 5. Jones 1 up.

Hole 2, 523 Yards, Par 5.

Jones drove to rough and Homans to a trap at the long second. Gene came out to the rough, and Bob hit a long iron down the fairway. Jones was barely on the green with his third, and Homans was short. Jones's putt ran up the green's bank but rolled back and each was a long way off in 4. They halved in 6's.

Jones 6, Homans 6. Jones, 1 up.

Hole 3, 195 Yards, Par 3.

Jones hit an iron shot to the green, but Homans's spoon shot was on top of a trap to the left. Homans chipped eight feet from the cup. Jones putted short from thirty feet. Homans missed his putt for a 3. Bob holed his par 3.

Jones 3, Homans 4. Jones, 2 up.

Hole 4, 595 Yards, Par 5.

Jones drove into a trip. Homans's tee shot was clear. Bob hit a spoon shot from the sand down the fairway and Gene fired his into rough, although nearer the green. Jones pitched, thirty feet from the pin. Homans, too, pitched on but outside his rival's ball. Homans took three putts while Jones holed his par 5.

Jones 5, Homans 6. Jones, 3 up.

Hole 5, 435 Yards, Par 4.

A stiff cross-wind carried Jones's ball to a bad rough to the left. The wind also carried Homans's ball into a trap. Gene used a spoon from the trap but could not reach the green. Jones went from the rough to the green. Gene made a fine approach, ten feet from the pin. Jones putted within four feet. Homans missed his putt for a four. Jones also missed his putt.

Jones 5, Homans 5. Jones, 3 up.

Hole 6, 427 Yards, Par 4.

The drives at the sixth were practically even; the two second shots just reached the green, with Homans slightly away. Gene's approach putt was short, and so was Bob's. Jones holed his 4. Homans got his half.

Jones 4, Homans 4. Jones, 3 up.

Hole 7, 335 Yards, Par 4.

Jones drove to the edge of a ditch at the seventh and then pitched on. Homans had a straight drive and was well on with his second. Putting from twenty-five feet Bob ran up close. From twenty feet Gene putted within a foot and stymied Jones. Bob could not get by his opponent's ball and took a five.

Homans 4, Jones 5. Jones, 2 up.

Hole 8, 350 Yards, Par 4.

There was little to choose between the drives and both players pitched well on. Each putted close.

Jones 4, Homans 4. Jones, 2 up.

Hole 9, 170 Yards, Par 3.

Homans drove into the water to the right of the green. Jones pitched six yards beyond the flag. Homans had to drop in the rough with a penalty stroke, then pitched out beyond the hole. He missed the next one and then conceded the hole when Bobby laid his putt up almost dead.

Jones 3, Homans 5. Jones, 3 up.

Hole 10, 335 Yards, Par 4.

Homans hooked to rough from the tee after Jones sent a long one down the fairway. Jones played safely to the middle of the green. Gene's ball rolled to a trap beyond the green. He recovered far past the pin and then putted close. Bob was down in two putts for his par 4.

Jones 4, Homans 5. Jones 4 up.

Hole 11, 378 Yards, Par 4.

Preferring accuracy to distance, Jones continued to drive with a spoon. The tee shots at the eleventh were not far apart, but Homans's ball was in front. Bob's second stopped twenty-five feet from the pin. Homans pitched within eight feet. Jones holed the long putt for a birdie 3. Homans just missed his putt and took a par 4.

Jones 3, Homans 4. Jones 5 up.

Hole 12, 415 Yards, Par 4.

Jones had the longer ball at the twelfth but was not in the best position to approach the elevated green. Homans hit a low second shot to the green. Jones pitched high and both second shots finished about twenty-five feet from the cup. Bob pitched close and Gene just missed.

Jones 4, Homans 4. Jones 5 up.

Hole 13, 125 Yards, Par 3.

Both tee shots on the short thirteenth were on the edge of the green on the side on which the cup was placed. Homans putted, from twelve feet, two feet past the cup. From ten feet Jones just missed. They holed their 3s.

Jones 3, Homans 3. Jones 5 up.

Hole 14, 412 Yards, Par 4.

The drives again at the fourteenth were close together, but Gene was away. Homans hit a spoon second shot to the left of the green. Bob was on with a No. 3 iron, fifteen feet from the cup, and putted to the lip. Homans was seven feet short on his third and barely missed his 4. Jones holed his par 4.

Jones 4, Homans 5. Jones 6 up.

Hole 15, 370 Yards, Par 4.

Jones's second was six feet from the pin. Gene's second caught the side of a trap and rolled to the sand. Gene came out and missed his putt for a 4, conceding the hole. Jones knocked his putt for the birdie 3 in with one hand.

Jones 3, Homans 5. Jones 7 up.

Hole 16, 435 Yards, Par 4.

Again at the sixteenth, the "quarry hole," there was no appreciable advantage in the drives, Homans sent a high iron over the cavern to the green. Jones with a No. 4 iron was well inside. From sixty feet, Gene putted four feet short. Jones's putt lipped the cup. Homans missed and took a 5.

Jones 4, Homans 5. Jones 8 up.

Hole 17, 215 Yards, Par 3.

Jones's tee shot at the seventeenth carried to thick rough at the left. Homans drove within seven feet of the cup. Jones approached to within eight feet and missed the putt, taking 4 to a birdie 2 for Homans.

Homans 2, Jones 4. Jones 7 up.

Hole 18, 455 Yards, Par 4.

Both drove to rough at the left. Jones being slightly in front. Homans was over the green with a long iron. Jones pitched eighteen feet from the pin. Gene's third was too strong and he was still away. He holed the twenty-foot putt for the par 4. Jones just missed his birdie 3.

Jones 4, Homans 4. Jones 7 up.

AFTERNOON ROUND.

Hole 19, 360 Yards, Par 4.

Jones again drove with a spoon and was a few yards behind Homans's tee shot, which reached a shallow trap. Bob was just short of the green with his second, while Homans was on. Jones ran up dead and Homans putted close.

Jones 4, Homans 4. Jones, 7 up.

Hole 20, 523 Yards, Par 5.

Gene's tee shot landed in an adjoining fairway, but Bob's was safe. Both were short in two, but Jones put his third ten feet from the pin. Homans's third went over and he putted short. Jones missed and the hole was halved.

Jones 5, Homans 5. Jones, 7 up.

Hole 21, 195 Yards, Par 3.

Neither reached the green from the tee, but Jones almost rolled out from a trap. Homans was just on the edge of the green. Gene slipped two feet past the cup on his first putt and left himself a partial stymie. He missed the putt and took 4 to a 3 for Jones.

Jones 3, Homans 4. Jones, 8 up.

Hole 22, 595 Yards, Par 5.

Homans was trapped from the tee and Jones was in the rough. Homans was short of the green in three and forty feet from the pin on his fourth. Jones pitched twelve feet from the cup in three. Homans was down in six. Jones holed his par 5.

Jones 5, Homans 6. Jones, 9 up.

Hole 23, 435 Yards, Par 4.

Jones was in front by twelve yards on his drive. Each second shot found a resting place on the green, Jones fifty feet from the cup, Homans thirty-five. Jones's putt was four feet short. The hole was halved in 4s.

Jones 4, Homans 4. Jones, 9 up.

Hole 24, 427 Yards, Par 4.

The drives were close together, 230 to 250 yards down the fairway, with Jones in front. Homans used a spoon to get home in two, Jones took a No. 3 iron. Homans putted close from fifty feet so did Jones. They halved in par 4's.

Jones 4, Homans 4. Jones, 9 up.

Hole 25, 335 Yards, Par 4.

Homans's drive was in the fairway while Jones drove into rough. Their second shots rolled past the pin and each had a lengthy putt left for his par. They missed and halved in 5s.

Jones 5, Homans 5. Jones, 9 up.

Hole 26, 350 Yards, Par 4.

Bob nearly drove the green and then chipped to ten feet of the cup. Homans was too strong with his approach, but just missed sinking a 15-footer for a birdie.

Jones 4, Homans 4. Jones, 9 up.

Hole 27, 170 Yards, Par 3 .

Jones missed the green with his tee shot at the twenty-seventh and it landed in a trap. Homans was ten feet from the cup. Jones was eighteen feet short in two and was down in four, conceding Homans his putt and the hole.

Homans 2, Jones 4. Jones, 8 up.

Hole 28, 335 Yards, Par 4.

Jones drove a very long ball from the tee, but it ended in the rough. Homans was in the fairway, thirty yards behind. Gene put his second in a trap to the left. Jones's second found the same trap. Bobby failed to get out on his third, but his fourth was fifteen feet from the pin. Gene went over the green to a trap on the other side. In 4 they were about the same distance from the cup. They halved in 6s.

Jones 6, Homans 6. Jones, 8 up.

Hole 29, 378 Yards, Par 4.

The drives were long, Homans being on the right of the fairway and Jones on the left. Homans pitched onto the green past the cup. Jones was short in two, and each took two putts for a half in par 4.

Jones 4, Homans 4. Jones wins, 8 and 7.

Jones's Walk After Defeat Recalled in Sweetser Match

ARDMORE, Pa., Sept. 27 (AP).—Eight years ago, when Jess Sweetser propelled Bobby Jones out of the amateur championship at Brookline, 8 and 7, the match ended at the eleventh hole, which is about one mile from the clubhouse.

"The longest walk I ever took," Bobby said afterward.

Yesterday after Bobby had beaten Jess, 9 and 8, Sweetser remarked to Jones in the clubhouse:

"I was hoping to carry it to the next green and then if it was 8 and 7 I could say 'Well, Bobby, we're all square now,' but we're not. You're one up."

WOMEN GOLF STARS TO PLAY THIS WEEK

First Fairfield and Westchester Medal Tourney to Start at Rye on Tuesday.

MRS. WHEELER OFFERS CUP

Miss Singer, Miss Jenney, Mrs. Lawlor and Mrs. Jackson Are Among Those Entered.

A field of about 100 women players will take part in the first Fairfield and Westchester County medal play championship tourney that will be held this week at the Westchester Country Club course, Rye, N. Y.

This fifty-four hole affair hereafter will take a regular place on the golfing program, and a handsome trophy donated by Mrs. I. M. Wheeler will be the chief prize at stake. Three victories in the event, however, are necessary to insure permanent possession of the cup.

Miss Catherine Singer, Westchester titleholder; Miss Marie Jenney, former metropolitan champion; Miss Jane Broadwell, Mrs. John D. Chapman, Mrs. B. F. Briggs, Mrs. Joseph Lawlor, Mrs. H. Arnold Jackson, Mrs. Myra D. Paterson and Mrs. L. C. DuBois are among the entrants for the tourney, eighteen holes being scheduled for Tuesday, Wednesday and Thursday. Post entries will be received at the club Tuesday morning.

The pairings and starting times follow:

A. M.
9:00—Mrs. Henry Edson, Round Hill, and Mrs. J. Sterling, Round Hill.
9:05—Mrs. John Chapman, Greenwich, and Mrs. Edgar Arnold, Greenwich.
9:10—Mrs. H. T. Hartwell, Woodway, and Mrs. H. Ridabock, Woodway.
9:15—Mrs. C. Hoffman, Leewood, and Mrs. M. B. McHugh, Leewood.
9:20—Mrs. S. M. Gonda, Leewood, and Mrs. William Macfarlane, Oak Ridge.
9:25—Miss Frances Snyder, Apawamis, and Miss Jane Evans, Siwanoy.
9:30—Mrs. George S. Wallen, Greenwich, and Mrs. Alford, Greenwich.
9:35—Mrs. H. Arnold Jackson, Greenwich, and Mrs. Edward Stevens, Round Hill.
9:40—Mrs. Myra D. Paterson, Greenwich, and Mrs. A. Bassler, Westchester.
9:45—Miss Catherine Singer, Westchester, and Miss Jane Broadwell, Westchester.
9:50—Mrs. L. Lloyd, Greenwich, and Miss Alice Warner, Greenwich.
9:55—Miss Mary Luke, Sleepy Hollow, and Mrs. George Hite, Apawamis.
10:00—Mrs. Benjamin Briggs, Pelham, and Mrs. H. C. Dodge, Westchester.
10:05—Mrs. J. H. Ford, Wykagyl, and Mrs. E. C. Bagg, Wykagyl.
10:10—Miss Betty Pietsch, Tamarack, and Miss Inez Gove, Tamarack.
10:15—Miss Jean Jacques, Leewood, and Miss Anna Hughes, Green Meadow.
10:20—Mrs. D. M. Willard, Winged Foot, and Mrs. L. Jenkins, Westchester Women's Golf and Tennis.
10:25—Mrs. A. Rodney, Quaker Ridge, and Mrs. E. Klauber, Sunningdale.
10:30—Mrs. Irving M. Engel, Mount Vernon, and Mrs. Joseph A. Lawlor, Gedney Farm.
10:35—Mrs. L. Heineman, Quaker Ridge, and Miss Janet Newborg, Quaker Ridge.
10:40—Mrs. A. Leyman, Century, and Mrs. R. P. Limburg, Century.
10:45—Mrs. C. T. Russell, Ardsley, and Mrs. S. S. Laird, Westchester.
10:50—Mrs. A. P. Brush and Mrs. W. B. Miller.
10:55—Mrs. Mary Haney, Bonnie Briar, and Mrs. Estelle, Bonnie Briar.
11:00—Miss Helen Silleck, Greenwich.
11:05—Mrs. George Studwell, Ardsley, and Mrs. Frederick K. Ream, Westchester.
11:10—Mrs. A. Wright, Westchester, and Mrs. Haldenstein, Westchester.
11:15—Mrs. D. Sulzberger, Century, and Mrs. A. Blum, Century.
11:20—Mrs. B. H. Namm, Century, and Miss Adelaide Reckford, Century.
11:25—Mrs. J. C. Quirk, Greenwich, and Miss Marie Jenney, Hudson River.
11:30—Mrs. J. Goldston, Fenimore, and Mrs. L. A. Satz, Fenimore.
11:35—Mrs. T. Murphy, Westchester, and Mrs. Brezovski.
11:40—Mrs. Lewis Young, Hudson River, and Mrs. D. Ford, Siwanoy.
11:45—Mrs. M. E. Singerman, Fenimore, and Mrs. A. Lichtman, Fenimore.
11:50—Mrs. C. W. Howard, Round Hill, and Mrs. J. Seidenberg, Century.
11:55—Mrs. G. O. Suddards, Wykagyl.
12:00—Mrs. J. J. Sinnott, Siwanoy, and Mrs. H. Dunkak, Siwanoy.
12:05—Mrs. I. M. Wheeler, Westchester, and Mrs. L. DuBois, Westchester.
12:10—Mrs. C. Harwood, Westchester, and Miss R. Wise, Westchester.

DUNLAP-BOURNE BEAT PROS

Princeton Captain and Coach Defeat Sarazen and Farrell.

Special to The New York Times.

PRINCETON, N. J., Sept. 27.—George T. Dunlap Jr. and Walter Bourne, captain and coach, respectively, of the Princeton University golf team, defeated Gene Sarazen and Johnny Farrell, professionals, 1 up, in an eighteen-hole match over the Springdale course today.

Dunlap had the best card for the afternoon, a 72. Farrell had a 74, Bourne 76, and Sarazen 77.

Hoppe Wins Two Matches.

Willie Hoppe, who is meeting all comers in fifty-point three-cushion billiard matches at the Strand Billiard Academy, scored two victories yesterday. In the afternoon he defeated Robert Bouche, 50 to 8, in 55 innings, and at night vanquished John Kern, 50 to 16, in 29 innings. High runs were Hoppe 8, Bouche 2; Hoppe 13, Kern 2.

Mineola Trotting Called Off.

Special to The New York Times.

MINEOLA, L. I., Sept. 27.—The scheduled trotting matinee of the Nassau Driving Club at the Fair Grounds today was called off, as there were not enough horses to fill the classes. President Ira L. Terry stated that there would be no other race cards this year.

Cucci Matched With Morro.

Johnny Cucci and Joe Morro are to furnish the action in the principal eight-round bout Thursday night at the 102d Medical Regiment Armory. Joe Kelly and Joe Colucci are paired for the eight-round semi-final.

WESTCHESTER OPEN TO START TUESDAY

67 Golfers Already Entered in 72-Hole Title Tourney at Fenimore Course.

CRUICKSHANK IN THE FIELD

Will Play in Defense of 1929 Crown—Pro-Amateur Event Set for Tomorrow.

A number of the district professionals who have been campaigning in various parts of the country during the last few weeks will compete in the Westchester open golf championship on Tuesday and Wednesday.

Thus far a field of sixty-seven, including a handful of amateurs, is entered for the event, for which Westchester amateurs and professionals are eligible. This limited group, nevertheless, includes a number of players of national prominence as Willie MacFarlane, present metropolitan open titleholder; Bobby Cruickshank, who won the Westchester crown a year ago; Johnny Farrell, former national open champion, and Tony Manero, who triumphed in the Glens Falls open, will compete when play opens at the Fenimore Country Club, White Plains, N. Y.

Before the championship of thirty-six holes of medal play each day starts there will be a pro-amateur tourney as a prelude tomorrow. Entries for this event will be accepted at the first tee. Post entries also will be received for the open championship.

The pairings and starting times follow:

Starting Time.
8:30-12:30—Everitt Smith, Ardsley; Neal Manganello, Westchester Hills; Joseph Donato, unattached.
8:35-12:35—D. T. Williams, Amawalk; Leslie Stubbins, Sleepy Hollow; Joseph Kazimir, unattached.
8:40-12:40—Ben Herb, Dunwoodie; Ed Hansen, Dunwoodie; George Karcher, Green Meadow.
8:45-12:45—John McNamara, Sunningdale; Fred Hunter, Tamarac; Rosi Parina, Broadmoor.
8:50-12:50—John Vacco, Rockwood Hall; B. McDougal, Mount Kisco; Oliver J. Cocke, Metropolis.
8:55-12:55—Nathan Wise, Metropolis; Elmer Voigt, Sunningdale; Joe Rich, Fenimore.
9:00-1:00—Joe Ford, unattached; Jack Patroni, Wykagyl; Frank Novak, St. Andrews.
9:05-1:05—Pat Cercelli, Mount Vernon; F. Grieve, Leewood; Jimmy Farrell, Quaker Ridge.
9:10-1:10—Pat Doyle, New Rochelle; George McLean, Grassy Sprain; Bill Hartman, Gedney Farm.
9:15-1:15—Dave White, Ardsley; Patsy Tiso, unattached; J. A. Cavanaugh, Tamarac.
9:20-1:20—Herman Barron, Tamarack; Tom Creavy, unattached; Tony Manero, unattached.
9:25-1:25—Tom Clancy, Sprain Lake; Phil Turnesa, Elmsford; John Phimister, Tamarack.
9:30-1:30—Willie Macfarlane, Oak Ridge; Mike Turnesa, Elmsford; R. A. Jones Jr., Westchester Hills.
9:35-1:35—Mike Brady, Winged Foot; Jack Sabol, Westchester Hills; Joe Turnesa, Elmsford.
9:40-1:40—Jim Donaldson, Fenimore; Bobby Cruickshank, Progress; Johnny Farrell, Quaker Ridge.
9:45-1:45—John Stevens, Mount Vernon; Bill Goldbeck, Lawrence Park; Dan Galgano, Gedney Farm.
9:50-1:50—Archie Sanderson, Sleepy Hollow; Fred Moore, Dunwoodie; George Kerrigan, Wykagyl.
9:55-1:55—Bob Brown, North Castle; Dugald Blue, Nannaghan; William Fernie, Rockwood Hall.
10:00-2:00—Louis Costello, Broadmoor; Silas Newton, Siwanoy; T. Kerrigan, Siwanoy.
10:05-2:05—H. Logan, Leewood; Paul Nevins, Yonkers; Munzie Fiori, Rye.
10:10-2:10—A. H. McNally; Winged Foot; H. Mahoney Jr., Westchester Country Club; Jack Falito, Yonkers.
10:15-2:15—Victor Arcaro, Rye; J. Sutherland, Green Meadow; Saul Lanzis, Fenimore.
10:20-2:20—Leonard Palumbo, Oak Ridge.

DRIGGS TWICE VICTOR IN CRUMP CUP GOLF

Defeats Perkins by 1 Up to Gain Semi-Final Over Pine Valley Links.

Special to The New York Times.

CLEMENTON, N. J., Sept. 27.—Eddie Driggs of Lakeville, Long Island champion, was among the winners in the first and second round of the Crump Memorial Cup golf tournament over the difficult Pine Valley course here today.

Driggs, after disposing of Emery Stratton of Brae Burn by 1 up in the first round, defeated Phil Perkins by the same score. W. B. (Duff) McCullough of Huntingdon Valley, was eliminated in the second round by Wm. Blaney Jr. of Brae Burn, 2 and 1.

Roland MacKenzie of Wilmington, a Walker Cup player, apparently out of the slump that overtook him in the national amateur at Merion, eliminated J. Walcott Brown of Spring Lake, N. J., 1 up, in the first round, but later lost to J. N. Batchelder of Salem, Mass., in a nineteen-hole match.

E. H. Tipple of London Hunt and Country Club, won from W. H. (Ham) Gardner of Buffalo, 1 up. Tipple will meet Batchelder in the semi-final tomorrow, while Briggs faces Blaney.

The summaries:

First Division.

First Round—Eddie H. Driggs, Lakeville, defeated Emery Stratton, Brae Burn, 1 up; T. P. Perkins, St. Andrews, defeated J. B. Dush, London Hunt, 4 and 3; W. B. McCullough, Huntingdon Valley, defeated John Ayling, St. Andrews, 3 and 2; William Blaney Jr., Brae Burn, defeated Fred Brand Jr., Shannopin, 4 and 3; J. N. Batchelder, Salem, Mass., defeated O. H. Flinn Jr., Allegheny, 4 and 3; Roland Mackenzie, Wilmington, defeated J. W. Brown, Spring Lake, 1 up; J. H. Gardner, Buffalo, defeated Alexander Knapp, Baltimore, 1 up (19 holes); E. H. Tipple, London Hunt, defeated J. W. Yuile, Royal Montreal, 2 up.

Second Round—Driggs defeated Perkins, 1 up; Blaney defeated McCullough, 2 and 1; Batchelder defeated Mackenzie, 1 up (19 holes); Tipple defeated Gardner, 1 up.

The New York Times
***+ SUNDAY, NOVEMBER 22, 1931.

SPORTS Section 10

FIELD GOAL BEATS NOTRE DAME, 16-14, AS 52,000 LOOK ON

Baker's 33-Yard Placement in Final Minute Gives Southern California Triumph.

THREE-YEAR STREAK ENDS

Shaver's Two Touchdowns in Last-Period Rally Precede the Deciding Kick.

BANAS AND SCHWARTZ TALLY

Count After Long Marches in the Second and Third Quarters—Walker Watches Struggle.

STATISTICS OF THE GAME.

	So. Cal.	Notre Dame.
First downs	15	10
Yards gained rushing	117	160
Forward passes	11	10
Forwards completed	2	1
Yards gained, forwards	73	25
Forwards intercepted by	1	2
Laterals	4	3
Laterals completed	4	3
Yards gained, laterals	25	43
Number of punts	5	11
*Distance of punts, yards	229	496
Run-back of punts, yards	75	14
Fumbles	6	0
Own fumbles recovered	4	0
Penalties	0	10
Yards lost, penalties	0	80

*From point where ball was kicked.

By ALLISON DANZIG.

Special to The New York Times.

SOUTH BEND, Ind., Nov. 21.—One of the greatest winning streaks compiled in football since the time of Michigan's point-a-minute teams of a generation ago came to an end with one minute left to play today as Notre Dame's all-conquering horde, unbeaten in three years, went down in stunning defeat before one of the hardest-running, fiercest-tackling elevens that ever stepped upon a gridiron.

With 52,000 spectators looking on thunderstruck in the beautiful new red brick stadium that stands as a monument to Knute Rockne, Southern California, the team that had last defeated the Ramblers in the final game of 1928, performed the almost incredible feat of spotting its opponent a 14-0 lead going into the final period and then proceeding to pile up sixteen points in the space of fifteen minutes to win the game, 16-14.

A 33-yard field goal from placement from the 23-yard line by Johnny Baker in the last sixty seconds of play won this savagely-fought battle just when it seemed that Notre Dame, for the fourth time in six years, was to carry the day by the margin of a point after touchdown.

Stage Two Long Marches.

Two long marches by the rugged, tremendously aggressive Trojans, one for 47 yards and the other for 57 with the brilliant Gaius Shaver carrying the ball over each time, had preceded Baker's electrifying kick, but, in spite of the fact that Southern California was stampeding Notre Dame's defenses with long forward passes and laterals and ripping its heretofore impregnable line to shreds, it looked as though the Trojans were doomed to suffer defeat again through the blocking of Baker's first kick for the extra point by Joe Kurth, the Ramblers' magnificent tackle.

With four minutes left to play after their second touchdown, the Trojans, a desperately inspired team if ever there was one, started another march down the field from deep in their own territory, and in two tremendous passes, one thrown 50 yards by Shaver to Sparling and the other hurled by Shaver to Hall for a 23-yard gain, the first two actually completed by the Californians all day, carried the ball to the 17-yard line.

A 5-yard penalty, one of the many costly setbacks that Notre Dame suffered all afternoon, advanced the ball to the 12-yard mark, but then Notre Dame's powerful line rose up in its might and hurled Sparling back on a reverse to the 15-yard mark, and Clark fumbled Mohler's succeeding pass. Time was fleeting and it seemed that Southern California's dangerous uprising had been squelched and its last chance had gone aglimmering.

Mohler Holds the Ball.

But on third down Orville Mohler, the Trojan quarterback, cunningly called for a field goal, knowing that the Ramblers would be on guard against a pass instead of concentrating entirely on rushing through to block the kick, and big Johnny Baker dropped back to the 23-yard mark, with Mohler holding the ball, and sent the pigskin high and squarely between the uprights.

That pigskin parabola through the air, which gave Southern California its first victory over Notre Dame in three years and a thoroughly deserved one if Leonine courage, berserk tackling on the defense and reckless abandon in running on the offense are football virtues, left the great throng stunned and overwhelmed with despair, save for the handful of Trojan rooters, who were fairly delirious with joy.

It was almost unbelievable. Here was the great Notre Dame team, the most dreaded in the land, a team that had won twenty-five consecutive games, with the single interruption of a tie score against Northwestern in the rain and mud, and which had

SCHERESCHEWSKY OF HARVARD CRASHING THROUGH YALE LINE FOR SMALL GAIN AT CAMBRIDGE YESTERDAY.

Times Wide World Photo.

LAFAYETTE RALLIES TO TOP LEHIGH, 13-7

Scores Twice in Second Half to Triumph in Sixty-fifth Meeting of the Rivals.

LOSERS TAKE EARLY LEAD

Ware Tallies on Pass in First Period—Bugen and Socolow Go Over for Easton Team.

STATISTICS OF THE GAME.

	Lafayette.	Lehigh
First downs	15	3
Yards gained, rushing	227	93
Forward passes	6	6
Forwards completed	0	1
Yards gained, forwards	0	28
Forwards intercepted by	2	0
Lateral passes	1	1
Laterals completed	1	1
Yards, gained, laterals	4	0
Number of punts	11	13
*Distance of punts, yards	413	480
Run back of punts, yards	28	45
Fumbles	0	3
Own fumbles recovered	0	2
Penalties	7	5
Yards lost, penalties	30	25

*From point where ball was kicked.

Special to The New York Times.

BETHLEHEM, Pa., Nov. 21.—Lafayette encountered the most bitter opposition before turning back the courageous Lehigh eleven today. While a crowd of 12,000 persons watched, the doughty little Brown and White aggregation, fighting hard to protect a lead gained early in the battle, wilted as the game drew to a close and bowed to the Maroon-clad visitors from Easton by the score of 13 to 7.

The game, which was the sixty-fifth of the series between the colleges, was bitterly fought, and was productive of many thrills.

Given little chance to win or even hold the powerful Lafayette team to a close score before the battle, the local aggregation surprised its adherents with a gallant stand which forced the visiting players to rise in their fullest strength before emerging triumphant.

Lehigh Kept on Defensive.

There was no doubt concerning the better team, however, regardless of Lehigh's commendable stand, for the Easton players completely outrushed the home eleven, gaining 227 yards on rushing plays as against only 97 for Lehigh.

Following a brilliant sally in the first period, in which it effected a touchdown as the result of a brilliant forward pass, Chick Halsted to Allen Ware, the Lehigh team was forced to play on the defensive for the greater part of the battle. Lafayette's ball carriers chalked up fifteen first downs to three for Le-

Continued on Page Four.

MANHATTAN DOWNS ST. JOHN'S BY 8 TO 7

Centre's Poor Pass in Waning Moments Results in Safety and Defeat for Redmen.

PACE TALLIES ON AERIAL

Owen Scores for Jaspers in the Second Period—Game Last for Indians on Gridiron.

STATISTICS OF THE GAME.

	Manhattan.	St. John's.
First downs	14	7
Yards gained rushing	204	151
Forward passes	13	14
Forwards completed	5	5
Yards gained, forwards	61	83
Forwards intercepted by	1	1
Lateral passes	0	1
Laterals completed	0	1
Yards gained, laterals	0	4
Number of punts	9	9
*Distance of punts, yards	378	256
Run back of punts, yards	26	20
Fumbles	2	1
Own fumbles recovered	0	1
Penalties	3	5
Yards lost, penalties	45	43

*From point where ball was kicked.

Meeting for the last time on the gridiron, Manhattan and St. John's engaged in a thrilling struggle before a crowd of 4,000 at Jasper Field yesterday, the Green emerging victorious, 8—7, by virtue of a safety in the last five minutes of play.

It was a quirk of fate that doomed St. John's last appearance on a college gridiron to fall short of success. Late in the fourth quarter, when the Redmen were protecting a one-point lead, a bad pass from centre sent Arthur Wright, St. John's substitute back, scurrying back into his end zone to retrieve the ball and there he was buried under the charge of Howie Smith and Walt Jacunski.

Gain an Early Lead.

The Redmen got off to an early lead when Captain Babe Pace scored on a forward pass from Mike Stephens. The extra point, gained by a toss from Stephens to Mike Rubinsky, loomed important, for Pete Battle's attempt to convert, after Ken Owen's touchdown in the second period, was blocked by Albert Gallo.

Between the halves the two teams and the spectators stood with bared heads for a moment in silent homage to the late Knute Rockne.

The first quarter revealed the St. John's aerial attack at its best. The Redmen advanced from their 25-yard line on a brilliant succession of passes.

Mike Stephens ran to midfield after receiving a toss from Bob Sheppard. An aerial from Stephens to Rubinsky put the Redmen on the Jasper 26-

Continued on Page Seven.

Lake St. Clair Course of 10 Nautical Miles Adopted for 1932 Harmsworth Trophy Races

By The Associated Press.

DETROIT, Nov. 21—If the Harmsworth Trophy races are held next year they will be run over a new 10-mile triangular course in Lake St. Clair, instead of on the Detroit River, where for ten years Gar Wood has defended the famous plaque.

Officials of the Yachtsmen's Association of America today announced that a course on Lake St. Clair had been approved by the executive and race committees of the association, and would be used for the 1932 events, providing they are run next year.

Designed to meet the requirements of increased speed in the high-powered speedboats, the new course allows gradual curves and lengthy straightaways. The previous course in the Detroit River was only five miles in length.

The officials also said that new Harmsworth rules have lengthened the course, and that next year's race probably would be forty nautical miles instead of thirty, as in the past.

The course which has been approved is triangular, with one straightway of 23,810 feet, or approximately four and a half statute miles, extending approximately parallel to the Grosse Pointe shore of Lake St. Clair from a point just off the Seven-Mile Road Dock easterly to a turn just beyond Gaulker Point.

The triangle's short side, 11,750 feet long, ends near the ship channel and the other long side is parallel to the ship channel for 21,040 feet, or four land miles. Counting the three turns that call for 4,200 feet, the total length of the course is 60,800 feet or ten nautical miles.

Football Scores

COLLEGES

East

- Appalachian Teachers 23 .... Concord 0
- Army 54 .... Ursinus 6
- Boston College 14 .... Boston U. 6
- Brown 19 .... New Hampshire 13
- Bucknell 14 .... Fordham 13
- Catholic University 13 .... Providence 7
- Cheyney Teachers 14 .. Bordentown Inst. 0
- Columbia 0 .... Syracuse 0
- Davis and Elkins 7 .... Quantico Marines 0
- Delaware 31 .... Haverford 0
- Dickinson 14 .... Muhlenberg 6
- Dickinson Semin. 0 ... Lockhaven Teach. 0
- Duquesne 13 .... North Dakota 7
- Gallaudet 0 .... Shepherd 0
- Geneva 38 .... Westminster 0
- Georgetown 13 .... Villanova 6
- Grove City 20 .... Thiel 0
- Hobart 13 .... Rochester 7
- Holy Cross 16 .... Loyola (Md.) 14
- Juniata 26 .... Waynesburg 6
- Lafayette 13 .... Lehigh 7
- Manhattan 8 .... St. John's (Br.) 7
- Massachusetts State 7 .... Tufts 7
- P. M. C. 13 .... Susquehanna 0
- Penn Jr. Var. 21 .... Gettysburg Jr. Var. 6
- Penn 150-Pound 20 .. Princeton 150-Pound 3
- St. John's (Md.) 13 .... Lynchburg 0
- St. Joseph 20 .... Washington College 0
- St. Vincent 13 .... New River 6
- Shippensburg (Pa.) Teach. 7 . Ind. Teach. 6
- Southern Methodist 13 .... Navy 6
- Springfield 38 .... Vermont 0
- Union 7 .... R. P. I. 3
- Upsala 19 .... Brooklyn College 7
- West Chester Teachers 19 ... Millersville 3
- West Virginia 19 .... Penn State 0
- West Virginia State 92 .... Louisville 0
- West Virginia Wesleyan 23 .... Allegheny 7
- Yale 3 .... Harvard 0

South

- Campbell 0 .. William & Mary (Norfolk) 0
- Catawba 39 .... Lincoln Memorial 0
- Centre 75 .... Louisville 0
- Citadel 7 .... Presbyterian 0
- Clark 7 .... Moorehouse 0
- Delta Teachers 27 .. Miss. State Teachers 7
- Duke 0 .... North Carolina 0
- Elon 19 .... Guilford 6
- Fisk 13 .... Talladega 0
- Georgia 12 .... Alabama Poly 6
- Georgia Tech 23 .... Florida 0
- Hampton 25 .... Morgan 0
- High Point 13 .... Lenoir Rhine 6
- Howard 7 .... Birmingham Southern 6
- Howard University 9 .. Virginia Seminary 0
- Howard Payne 20 .... Simmons 0
- Knoxville 0 .... South Carolina Aggies 0
- Louisiana Teach 27 .... Louisiana College 7
- Maryland 13 .... W. & L. 7
- Randolph-Macon 21 .... American 0
- Rice 26 .... Arkansas 12
- Roanoke 7 .... Emory Henry 6
- Rollins 12 .... Bowdon State 6
- South Carolina 21 .. North Carolina State 0
- Southwestern 54 .... Union University 13
- Stetson 20 .... Southern 0
- Tennessee Wesleyan 21 . Alabama Normal 6
- Texas Christian 19 .... Baylor 6
- Texas Mines 20 ..... New Mexico Aggies 0
- Transylvania 18 .... Union College 13
- Tulane 40 .... Sewanee 0
- Tuskegee 32 .... Alabama Teachers 7
- W. Kentucky Teach. 41 .. E. Kentucky T. 7
- Western Maryland 20 ... Mt. St. Mary's 6
- Wilberforce 14 .... Lincoln 6

West

- Arizona 14 .... De Paul 13
- Augustana 7 .... Lake Forest 7
- Baldwin Wallace 19 .... Akron 0
- Bluffton 12 .... Defiance 12
- Bradley 19 .... James Milliken 12
- Carbondale 7 .... DeKalb 6

West

- Colorado University 17 .. Colorado College 7
- De Pauw 13 .... Wabash 7
- Detroit C. C. 0 ...... Wilmington (Ohio) 0
- Detroit 20 .... Michigan State 13
- Drake 6 .... Grinnell 0
- E. Cen. Okla. Tea. 7 .. N'east Okla. Tea. 0
- General Motors Mech 21 .... Assumption 3
- Haskell 51 .... Oglethorpe 6
- Illinois College 12 .... Eureka 0
- Illinois Wesleyan 17 .... Normal 0
- John Carroll 13 .... Otterbein 0
- Kansas 14 .... Missouri 0
- Kansas State 19 ... North Dakota State 6
- Kent State 7 .... Hiram 0
- Monmouth 13 .... Galesburg 7
- Marquette 7 .... Creighton 0
- Michigan 6 .... Minnesota 0
- Midland 0 .... York 0
- Mount Union 32 .... Oberlin 0
- Nebraska 23 .... Iowa State 0
- North Central Teach. 14 . Kalamazoo Col. 7
- Northwestern 19 .... Iowa 0
- Ohio Northern 51 .... Capital 12
- Ohio State 40 .... Illinois 0
- Oklahoma Aggies 14 .... Wichita 6
- Oklahoma City 27 ... Nebraska Wesleyan 0
- Olivet 23 .... Hope 0
- Paine 12 .... Benedict 6
- Pittsburgh Teach. 13 .... Fort Hays State 6
- Purdue 19 .... Indiana 0
- Rio Grande 20 .... Moorehead 13
- St. Olaf 21 .... Concordia (Minn.) 4
- San Francisco 10 .... Nevada 7
- Santa Clara 6 .... Wyoming 0
- Southern California 16 ..... Notre Dame 14
- Temple 16 .... Denver 0
- Valparaiso 27 .. Am. Col. of Phys. Educ. 0
- Virginia State 19 .... St. Paul 0
- Washington & Jefferson 27 . Western Res. 7
- West'n (Mich.) Tch. 7 . Cen. (Mich.) Tch. 6
- Wheaton 15 .... Aurora 0
- Wisconsin 12 .... Chicago 7
- Wittenberg 21 .... Dayton 6
- Wooster 12 .... Denison 6

Far West

- Billings Poly 53 .... Montana Normal 6
- California 6 .... Stanford 0
- College of Puget Sound 25 .... Pacific U. 6
- Flagstaff St. Tea. 13 ... Tempe St. Tea. 7
- Montana Mines 12 .... Intermountain 0
- Oregon 13 .... U. C. L. A. 6
- Pomona 6 .... Occidental 0
- So. Oregon Normal 26 .. Columbia (Ore.) 7
- Washington State 13 .... Gonzaga 6
- Whittier 19 .... Redlands 7

Freshmen

- Bucknell Fr. 13 .... Bellefonte Acad. 0
- Colorado Col. Fr. 20 ... Western State Fr. 0
- Dean Academy 7 ...... Pennsylvania Fr. 6
- Fordham Fr. 37 .... Samuel Johnson 0
- Hun School 12 .... P. M. C. Fr. 0
- Navy Plebes 39 .... Swanley School 13
- New Mexico Fr. 19 .. N. Ariz. Teach. Fr. 6
- Pennington 37 .... Rider Freshmen 0
- Rutgers Fr. 23 .... N. Y. U. Fr. 0
- Villanova Fr. 25 ..... Wyoming Seminary 7
- Virginia Poly Fr. 33 . Oakridge Institute 14
- William & Mary Fr. 14 .. St. John's Fr. 0

Canada

INTERCOLLEGIATE INTERMEDIATE.

- Royal Military 11 .... McMaster 1

C. R. U. SENIOR.

- Western University 7 .. Sarnia Imperials 1

O. R. F. U.

- St. Thomas 11 .... Oshawa 7
- St. Catharines 11 .... Thorold 6

O. R. F. U. JUNIOR.

- Woodstock 32 .... Argonauts 6
- Hamilton D. 13 .... St. Catharines 6

EXHIBITION.

- Montreal A. A. 10 .... Argonauts 0

SCHOOLS

Local

- All Hallows 6 .... Fordham Prep 6
- Bklyn Friends 27 .. Locust Valley Friends 0
- Cleveland 0 .... Tilden Jayvees 0
- George Washington 14 ... James Monroe 0
- John Adams 32 .... Greenport 7
- Manual 7 .... Madison 0
- Morris 12 .... Evander Childs 6
- Poly Prep 7 .... Hamilton 0
- Roosevelt 26 .... Flushing 0
- Textile 6 .... Thomas Jefferson 0
- Samuel Tilden 7 ...... Abraham Lincoln 0
- St. Augustinian 6 .... Boro Hall Academy 0

Long Island

- Amityville 18 .... Patchogue 6
- Baldwin 6 .... Great Neck 0
- Bay Shore 19 .... Babylon 6
- East Hampton 20 .... Smithtown 0
- Glen Cove 31 .... Port Washington 14
- La Salle M. A. 6 .... Chaminade 0
- Lawrence 12 .... Lynbrook 9
- Stony Brook 6 .... Sewanhaka 0
- Valley Stream 31 .... Freeport 9
- Westbury 13 .... Hicksville 6

Westchester

- Concordia Prep 7 .... Xavier 0
- Hackley 24s 7 .... Riverdale 24s 7
- Mamaroneck 0 .... Port Chester 0
- Mount Vernon 12 .... New Rochelle 6
- Peekskill M. A. 19 ..... New York M. A. 7

Westchester

- Riverdale 13 .... Hackley School 7
- Roosevelt (Yonkers) 14 .... Gorton 0
- Tuckahoe 7 .... East Chester 0
- White Plains 2 .... Yonkers 0

New York State

- Albany 13 .... Vincentian (Albany) 0
- Gowanda 19 .... St. Barnard's 0
- Hamburg 0 .... Attica 0
- Ithaca 46 .... Cortland 0
- Keystone Academy 14 ... Cook Academy 7
- Lackawanna 26 .... St. Joseph's 0
- Lafayette 30 .... Technical 0
- Lancaster 20 .... Depew 0
- Mineville 18 .... Granville 6
- Monticello 31 .... Highlands Falls 12
- Niagara Falls 13 .... Lockport 6
- Riverside 7 .... Hutchison 0
- Salamanca 24 .... Fredonia 6
- T. C. A. Prep 19 ... Clark (New Hamp.) 13
- Wellsville 32 .... Nunda 0

New Jersey

- Asbury Park 34 .... West New York 0
- Atlantic City 7 .... Camden 0
- Chatham High 23 .... Bernardsville 0
- Belleville 32 .... Orange 0
- Billingsport 0 .... Woodbury 0
- Boonton 6 .... Madison 0
- Bordentown 6 .... Mount Holly 6
- Camden 7 .... Atlantic City 0

Continued on Page Three.

BUCKNELL TOPPLES FORDHAM, 14 TO 13

Rallies After Trailing, 13-0, to Hand Maroon Its First Setback of the Season.

LOSERS' LATE DRIVE FAILS

Fumble on 7-Yard Line Halts March—Victors Now Only Unbeaten Team in East.

STATISTICS OF THE GAME.

	Bucknell.	Fordham
First downs	8	12
Yards gained rushing	93	124
Forward passes	19	16
Forwards completed	8	8
Yards gained, forwards	172	152
Forwards intercepted by	3	3
Lateral passes	1	0
Laterals completed	0	0
Yards gained, laterals	0	0
Number of punts	11	10
*Distance of punts, yards	395	325
Run back of punts, yards	29	33
Fumbles	1	3
Own fumbles recovered	1	2
Penalties	3	8
Yards lost, penalties	25	50

*From point where ball was kicked.

By LINCOLN A. WERDEN.

Bucknell University's big, smashing team yesterday became the only undefeated eleven in the East by vanquishing Fordham, 14 to 13, at the Polo Grounds.

Not since football was inaugurated at the Lewisburg (Pa.) institution in 1883 has any of its elevens gone through a season without a defeat, but the one on which Clark Hinkle played such a dominant rôle yesterday did another thing—it won after trailing 13 to 0 and thereby tumbled the Maroon from the ranks of the unbeaten.

Attempting to snare victory from the hands of time as the fleeting moments sped by, Fordham began a march from its own 45-yard line to its opponent's 7-yard stripe. Twenty-two thousand persons, with the exception of a small group from the Pennsylvania town, cheered and yelled for one more touchdown with four minutes left to play. But then Ed Danowski, Maroon fullback who had injured his hand earlier in the game, fumbled, and Bucknell recovered the ball.

Thrills at the End.

Fordham's great chance to score was gone, but the last few minutes were packed with a dramatic tenseness that completed a close, fiercely-fought football game.

With the ball on Bucknell's 6-yard line, over-anxiety on the part of the Maroons ruined their chances of damaging the Bucknell attack. Fordham incurred two successive

Continued on Page Six.

COLUMBIA GETS TIE WITH SYRACUSE, 0-0

Both Teams Miss Chances to Tally as 30,000 Look On at Baker Field.

ORANGE LOSES TOUCHDOWN

Moran Runs 82 Yards, but Score Is Nullified by Penalty—Montgomery Stars for Lions.

STATISTICS OF THE GAME.

	Columbia.	Syracuse.
First downs	10	8
Yards gained rushing	168	168
Forward passes	9	6
Forward passes completed	2	3
Yards gained, forwards	32	48
Forwards intercepted by	0	2
Lateral passes	0	1
Laterals completed	0	0
Yards gained, laterals	0	0
Number of punts	11	10
*Distance of punts, yards	463	490
Runback of punts, yards	115	20
Fumbles	2	1
Own fumbles recovered	2	0
Penalties	3	3
Yards lost, penalties	25	50

*From point where ball was kicked.

By WILLIAM D. RICHARDSON.

With Clifford Montgomery, former Kiski star, playing a stellar rôle, Columbia brought the best season it has enjoyed since the days of the immortal Morley and Weekes to a successful close by playing a scoreless tie with the powerful Syracuse eleven at Baker Field yesterday.

Through four hard, but cleanly fought periods, marked by many feats of individual brilliance on the part of the elusive 162-pound back field ace and by sturdy defensive stands on the part of both teams, the wearers of the Blue and White and the Orange battled fiercely but to no avail.

At the outset of the contest, Moran, right halfback on Syracuse, galloped 82 yards for a stunning touchdown only to have the score nullified because of a penalty. That, as it turned out, was the closest Syracuse ever came to scoring against the highly inspired eleven that Coach Lou Little pitted against the up-Staters.

Columbia Misses Chances.

Columbia missed a touchdown in the second period by the thread-like margin of half a yard, failed on an attempted field goal from the 25-yard line in the third period and then let another opportunity slip through its fingers when Mosser, all alone in the clear, let a pass from Montgomery get away from him in the fourth.

On the basis of the foregoing, a great many among the 30,000 spectators who gazed down on the spec-

Continued on Page Three.

Maryland Wins Homecoming Day Game, 13–7; Poppleman Crosses W. and L. Goal Line Twice

Special to The New York Times.

COLLEGE PARK, Md., Nov. 21.—Maryland's eleven celebrated Homecoming Day by defeating Washington and Lee today, 13 to 7.

Poppleman was the outstanding star, scoring both touchdowns for the victors. Sharing the honors with the big fullback were Chalmers, Berger and Hayden.

Sawyers brought the W. and L. supporters to their feet when he intercepted a pass on his own 40-yard line and ran 60 yards for a touchdown.

Maryland gained 277 yards from scrimmage and made seventeen first downs. It attempted fifteen passes, completed six and had one intercepted. It gained 62 yards on completed passes.

The game was remarkably free of misplays, only one fumble being made. That one was made by Maryland, but the ball was recovered by Chalmers.

The line-up:

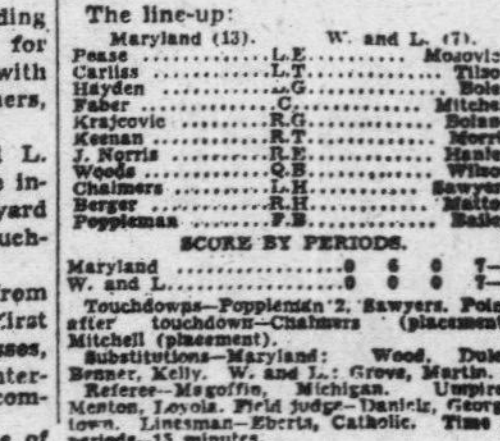

Maryland (13).		W. and L. (7).
Pease	L.E.	Mosovich
Carliss	L.T.	Tilson
Hayden	L.G.	Bolen
Faber	C.	Mitchell
Krajcovic	R.G.	Boland
Keenan	R.T.	Morris
J. Norris	R.E.	Hanley
Woods	Q.B.	Wilson
Chalmers	L.H.	Sawyers
Berger	R.H.	Maltox
Poppleman	F.B.	Bailey

SCORE BY PERIODS.

Maryland	0	6	0	7	—13
W. and L.	0	0	0	7	—7

Touchdowns—Poppleman 2, Sawyers. Points after touchdown—Chalmers (placement), Mitchell (placement).

Substitutions—Maryland: Wood, Duley, Benner, Kelly. W. and L.: Grove, Martin.

Referee—Magoffin, Michigan. Umpire—Menton, Loyola. Field judge—Daniels, Georgetown. Linesman—Eberts, Catholic. Time of periods—15 minutes.

BOOTH'S FIELD GOAL GIVES YALE VICTORY OVER HARVARD, 3-0

Makes Drop-Kick From 14-Yard Line With Three Minutes Left in Last Period.

60,000 SEE VIVID CLIMAX

Eli Captain, in Last Appearance Against Crimson, Ends 3-Year Streak of Rivals.

50TH GAME THRILLS CROWD

Crickard's Long Dash on Opening Kick-Off a Feature—Both Teams Shine on Defense.

By ROBERT F. KELLEY.

Special to The New York Times.

CAMBRIDGE, Mass., Nov. 21.—A little man stood alone on Harvard's 14-yard line with three minutes left to play in the fiftieth football game between Harvard and Yale today. Sixty thousand persons were breathless. The pass came back from centre, the little man took one step, made a drop-kick, and a hysterical outburst of cheering from the Yale stands announced that the Elis had ended Harvard's string of three straight victories over the Blue.

Albie Booth, in his last chance against his ancient rival, had come through. When the shining electrical figures of the scoreboard over the steel stands of Harvard's stadium switched on the final score it read: Yale 3, Harvard 0, and the sons of Eli poured down on the field to strip it bare of goal posts and dance in victory.

That drop-kick which gave the game to Yale was Booth's second chance at a field goal. Early in the second period, from almost the identical distance, he had missed. But this time, coming back to the game midway through the final period, Yale's captain had opened up another chance with a long pass to Barres and when the second opportunity came he seized it with both hands.

Measures Distance Coolly.

Coolly and accurately he measured the distance. There was a bit of an angle, but the ball was fairly close to the middle of the field. It was fourth down, Booth himself having been stopped on the 5-yard line on the previous play.

In Booth's mind there never was a doubt of where that ball was going. He turned his back to walk away even before the hands of Referee Billy Crowell had swung above his head in a signal that meant victory for the Blue.

That play, crisp and clean, put the final seal on one of the greatest battles these ancient rivals ever have staged. It was a game of contrasts, veering from the opening play of the game, when Harvard, on a trick play, very nearly ran the ball for a touchdown, to long periods of close, grinding football in which the running attack of one or the other would be stopped.

Then would come intervals when it seemed as if one of the teams had gained the upper hand, but none of these flashes materialized until that final drop kick of Booth's.

Opportunities there were for both sides, starting with that brilliant opening play, but in the end it was a Yale team which played inspired, great football that earned its victory.

Both Gamble for Chances.

Courageous football studded this game from beginning to end, chance-taking generalship on both sides, exhibitions of amazing defense when threatened, vivid running and passing. But this Blue eleven, rated before the start just a slight underdog, rose to the occasion this afternoon and earned well its triumph.

Not only on the attack, but on the defense, did Yale finally come back from the series of three straight defeats by Harvard. The long, stabbing passes of Barry Wood were covered beautifully for the most part, and when the Crimson tried its lateral pass attack Yale smeared it, often in the back field, and twice recovered the loose ball.

Yale's final gesture in protection of that three-point lead came when Herster Barres and Allen Converse raced through to chase Wood, trying a last-minute, despairing pass, almost to his goal line and smothered him on the 3-yard line as the game ended.

Only a bit more coolness in the air and a slightly drier field could have improved the playing conditions. The weather relented today, after last night's threat of rain and fog, and soon after breakfast, a light, summery breeze from the southwest swept away the overhanging fog and drizzle and revealed a sky like that of an early May morning.

Furs and blankets were thrown aside, and the spectators sat without overcoats throughout the game. The field had been covered, but enough moisture had seeped through to make it a bit muddy at midfield, and the going was slippery here and there.

Now and again during the game, backs would slip when it seemed that they were free, but this sort of thing seemed fairly well divided between both teams.

The crowd itself contributed a tremendous share to the picture in this meeting of the old rivals. Every

Continued on Page Five.

FIELD GOAL BEATS NOTRE DAME, 16-14

By ALLISON DANZIG.

Continued from Page One.

given the impression of having an inexhaustible mine of power as yet untested, humbled on its own playing field.

Only once before in twenty-seven years had the Ramblers tasted defeat on their own turf, in the 1928 game with Carnegie Tech, and never before had they gone down in their new stadium, dedicated in the Navy game a year ago.

Notables in the Throng.

Mayor Walker of New York, who was in the stands with Mayor Cermak of Chicago, Edsel Ford, Mr. and Mrs. John Hertz of Chicago and a host of notables of the stage and screen, was probably as downcast as any one present in the great throng, the largest crowd ever to see a sporting event in this city, for there is no more loyal Notre Dame rooter than New York's Mayor.

It was a stunning disillusionment to see victory that appeared to be within grasp suddenly turned into defeat on a single play, with the final whistle only a minute away. The defeat was all the more galling after the apparently unsurmountable lead that Notre Dame had gained in the second and third quarters. If any one had been so bold as to predict before the game that there was any team that ever wore cleats that could spot the South Benders fourteen points and defeat them in a fourth period he would have been laughed to scorn.

Notre Dame had scored its first seven points in the second period, after being outplayed in the first, on Banas's touchdown, climaxing a 55-yard march, and Jaskwich's place kick. Its next score came with startling abruptness and in the characteristic Notre Dame fashion before the second half was two minutes old.

In just four plays after Schwartz had taken Shaver's kick and run it back to the Notre Dame 37-yard line, the Ramblers had marched sixty-three yards to their second touchdown.

Laterals Figure Prominently.

Brancheau gained nine yards on a reverse. Schwartz, the finest back Notre Dame had on the field, who fully measured up to his All-America laurels of 1930, went around left end for fourteen yards, and then came a lateral pass, one of many of these plays that figured prominently in the game, from Schwartz to Banas.

Going around his left end after taking the lateral, Banas streaked down the field, cut in, evaded tackler after tackler, picked himself up twice after being hurled to the ground, and fought his way to the 2-yard line for a gain of thirty-seven yards. On the next play Schwartz went off his own right tackle, cut back slightly, and went over for the score on the fourth scrimmage of the advance, after which the unfailing Jaskwich again kicked the goal for the extra point.

At the end of this spectacular march, which found the Notre Dame attack functioning in its customary manner in the power of its blocking and the synchronization between the line and backs in working toward the perfect play, the game seemed to have been won and lost.

Probably no one among the 52,000 in the stands thought Southern California had a ghost of a chance and the prospect was that now that the Ramblers had found themselves and their true stride they would run away with the game.

Here was the Notre Dame team that every one had seen or read about for three years, a team so dangerous and powerful that it could strike a fatal blow at any given moment with its flawless technique and precision in the execution of its shift plays. It called for courage of the nth degree to stand up against such a team and to prevent it from turning the game into a rout, but this Southern California team of Howard Jones's had that courage and it showed it by coming back with a surging rush to take command of the game from this point and maintain it all through the rest of the play.

It wasn't any later than the next kick-off that the Trojans, who had shown their mettle by the manner in which they went down under the very first kick-off of the game behind Rosenberg to hurl themselves savagely upon Schwartz, started their amazing comeback.

Before the crowd could get over the startling turn in the situation they had rushed the ball from their own 30-yard mark to Notre Dame's 10-yard line, with Mohler and Shaver ripping through for long gains and Sparling, the end, coming around on reverse plays. Notre Dame stopped this advance of 60 yards and took the ball away on downs.

The Ramblers had stopped the Trojans' advance of 50 yards to their 3-yard line in the first period and had taken the ball away on downs again on the Ramblers' 11-yard mark a minute later. Apparently the Californians lacked a goal-line punch.

Start Another March.

But right after that 60-yard march had come to grief, the Trojans started another that was to lead to their first score on the third play of the final period. A lateral from Mohler to Shaver accounted for 16 yards, a reverse with Sparling picked up 11 more and the rest of the ground was made by the irrepressible, hard-running Shaver, who barely got over the goal line in the very corner of the field.

A damaging penalty played a big part in the Californians' next touchdown. Mohler hurled one of his long passes down the field and the ball was grounded. But the officials ruled that Shaver was interfered with in receiving the pass and the ball was given to Southern California on Notre Dame's 24-yard line for a first down and a gain of 32 yards on the penalty.

There was a storm of protest from the stands, but the decision stood, and in three plays Mohler and Shaver carried the ball to the 10-yard line for another first down. On the next play the lateral pass made its appearance again. Mohler, going into a spin that threw Notre Dame off, suddenly started back and tossed the ball out to the side to Shaver, who thundered around his own left end and fought his way across the goal line, carrying a Notre Dame back with him.

That long penalty was one of ten that were called on Notre Dame during the afternoon, for a total of 89 yards. Many of the penalties were inflicted for interference with the pass receiver and the two passes that the Trojans made for 50 and 23 yards in the closing minutes were the only ones they completed all day out of eleven thrown.

Passer Is Hurried.

Notre Dame completed only one pass out of ten attempted, which seemed almost incomprehensible, the one gaining twenty-five yards in the Ramblers' march to their first score. The reason for this poor showing with the pass was partly because the thrower was hurling the ball too far or his receiver was a step or two short in getting down under it. But the chief reason was the fact that the Southern California ends and tackles were rushing in to hurry the passer.

The Trojan line showed itself to be the equal of Notre Dame's today. It was a line that had tremendous power and all sorts of fight and that went for the Notre Dame line, too. In fact, no game in years has witnessed so ferocious and bruising a battle between lines as took place in the South Bend stadium today.

So great was the wear and tear in this struggle that Hunk Anderson, in the final quarter, was constantly sending in reserves to bolster his line, but fresh troops, even though they were regarded as good as the first line, could do little more than the men they replaced.

The Southern California attack, one of the most mystifying ever exploited by a football team, was much more difficult to solve than Notre Dame probably expected. In practice against their scrubs, the Ramblers had their defense worked out perfectly, but it did not work that way in the game.

The Trojans, going into a huddle, circled around and intermingled, then lined up in three waves, 4—4—3, and then shifted into their starting formation. The starting formation some times found the line balanced, but most of the time unbalanced.

Sometimes there were two men on the short side, sometimes there was only one. The ends were split most of the time, but were spaced in tight from the double wing-back formation, which was used along with the single wing-back alignment.

There were no less than five different bases of the Southern California attack, and with the men shifting around, backs and linemen jumping up and back, the formation changing with almost every play, and the lateral pass thrown in to add to the uncertainty of the defense, it is not to be wondered that the Ramblers failed to diagnose the plays as well as they had expected to.

Weather Clears Unexpectedly.

The ground was firm and dry, for the weather cleared unexpectedly, and the day was perfect for football, so that neither team found any difficulty in executing its plays except the difficulty presented by two fighting lines.

Notre Dame used its conventional 7-2-2 defense, the linemen standing up and some of them a yard back of the line until Southern California had shifted into line, when they would hop up into their places. The Trojans, on the defense, played a six-man line, with the secondary in 3-1-2 or 3-2-1 alignment. Both defenses were stronger against the pass than they weer against the running attack, except that in the final quarter the Notre Dame backs allowed Sparling and Hall to get behind them.

It would hardly be fair to single out men for meritorious service in a game so desperately fought all along the line, but Kurth was certainly a great tackle today in every respect, as was also Krause, and Schwartz was a magnificent back, save that his kicking suffered by comparison with Shaver's at times.

Shaver stood out vividly for the Trojans all the time he was in the game, and Mohler and Sparling did yeoman work, too, while the whole Southern California line covered itself with glory in the manner in which it stood up to Notre Dame's forwards and often outplayed them.

The line-up:

Southern Cal. (16).		Notre Dame (14).
Sparling	L. E.	Kosky
Brown	L. T.	Culver
Rosenberg	L. G.	Harriss
Williamson	C.	Yarr
Stevens	R. G.	Hoffman
Smith	R. T.	Kurth
Arbelbide	R. E.	Devore
Shaver	Q. B.	Jaskwich
Mallory	L. H.	Schwartz
Pinckert	R. H.	Sheeketski
Musick	F. B.	Banas

SCORE BY PERIODS.

Southern California	0	0	0	16—16
Notre Dame	0	7	7	0—14

Touchdowns—Shaver 2, Schwartz, Banas. goal from field—Baker (place kick). Points after touchdown—Jaskwich 2, Baker (all place kicks).

Substitutions—Southern California: Mohler for Shaver, G. Clark for Mallory, Erskine for Smith, Baker for Rosenberg, Rosenberg for Baker, Baker for Rosenberg, Shaver for Mohler, Mohler for Musick, Mallory for Clark, Clark for Mallory, Smith for Erskine, Erskine for Smith, Hall for Brown, Palmer for Arbelbide. Notre Dame—Krause for Culver, Brancheau for Sheeketski, Host for Kosky, Kozak for Kurth, Mahoney for Devore, Wunch for Hoffman, Culver for Krause, Kurth for Kozak, Devore for Mahoney, Hoffman for Wunch, Kosky for Host, Wunch for Hoffman, Leahy for Banas, Krause for Culver, Kozak for Kurth, Leonard for Leahy, Mahoney for Devore, Sheeketski for Brancheau, Culver for Krause, Millheam for Sheeketski, Murphy for Jaskwitch.

Referee—Frank Birch, Earlham. Umpire—H. E. Gillett, Oregon. Linesman—Jay Wyatt, Missouri. Field Judge—Norman Barker, Chicago. Time of periods—15 minutes.

MANHATTAN DOWNS ST. JOHN'S BY 8 TO 7

Continued from Page One.

yard line and then Pace dodged through the Jasper secondaries after snatching Stephens's toss to score the first touchdown of the game.

Manhattan tallied its touchdown in the second period. Thomas ran Pace's punt to the 30-yard line and the Jaspers, with Battle plunging savagely, drove to the 5-yard line. Battle was held twice, but then Owen fought his way over the line through right tackle.

Play slowed up in the third period, as neither Manhattan nor St. John's was able to produce a sustained drive. Forwards were thrown desperately and unsuccessfully as the teams sought a scoring break. Penalties further handicapped the efforts of both teams.

The fourth quarter produced the mosct hectic action of the contest and was crammed with thrills. Manhattan marched to the Indian 9-yard line, but Thomas's pass to Battle was inches short of a first down.

The complexion of things changed when Mike Rubinsky got off a thrilling dash of 56 yards to the Manhattan 27-yard line, only to have Johnny Francis, substitute tackle, recover a fumble by Sheppard.

Again the Jaspers drove into rival territory. Thomas whipped a pass to Owen, who ran to the St. John's 24-yard line. Art Wright of St. John's intercepted a pass deflected by Pendergast on his 25-yard line.

The deciding break of the game then occurred. A bad pass from centre sent Wright into his end zone and the safety that followed gave the Jaspers their winning margin.

The line-up:

Manhattan (8).		St. John's (7).
Del Negro	L. E.	Sullivan
Tepis	L. T.	Moloney
Yuda	L. G.	Mazzolo
Jacunski	C	Halleran
Hartte	R. G.	Johnson
Higgins	R. T.	Dallolio
Moyer	R. E.	Gallo
Thomas	Q. B.	Sheppard
Pendergast	L. H.	Stephens
Owen	R. H.	Rubinsky
Battle	F. B.	Pace

SCORE BY PERIODS.

Manhattan	0	6	0	2—8
St. John's	7	0	0	0—7

Touchdowns—Pace, Owens. Point after touchdown—Rubinsky (pass). Safety—Manhattan.

HARVARD-YALE TIE AT SOCCER, 1 TO 1

Varsity Teams Fail to Break Deadlock at Cambridge After 98 Minutes of Play.

ELI JAYVEES VICTORS, 1-0

Shallenberger's Pass to Smith Beats Crimson Seconds—Harvard Cubs Win, 1-0.

Special to The New York Times.

CAMBRIDGE, Mass., Nov. 21.—The varsity soccer teams of Harvard and Yale played 98 minutes without reaching a decision on the business school field today, the game ending in a 1-1 tie. Harvard scored its goal early in the first period, but Yale tied it up in the final quarter.

Hardly two minutes had elapsed when the Crimson scored. Captain Broadbent worked the ball down the field and near the goal passed out to Jack Wight, who scored on a second shot after the Yale goalie had stopped the first shot.

Yale evened the count late in the fourth period. Don Henry worked the ball from the centre of the field, outwitted the Harvard backs and sent home a sizzling shot. Harvard had the edge in the overtime periods and although in Yale territory all the time, could not break the deadlock.

Shallenberger's Pass Wins.

On Dave Shallenberger's pass to Red Smith late in the second quarter Yale's second varsity soccer team counted the goal that gave the Eli Jayvees a 1-to-0 victory over the Harvard seconds on the business school field.

Harvard threatened desperately throughout the last period but excellent goal guarding by Van Winckle and Avedon frustrated the attempts of the Crimson.

A goal by substitute Bob Russell midway through the first overtime period, gave the Harvard freshmen a 1-0 victory over its Yale rival this morning.

Six Straight for Victors.

The Crimson thereby extended its winning streak to six straight for the season. After an even first half Harvard continually threatened during the second half and overtime sessions. From out of a skirmish around the Eli goal in the first overtime period Russell booted the ball in for the only score of the game.

The line-ups:

Varsity Game.

Harvard (1).		Yale (1).
Powell	G	Van Winckle
Catinella	R.B	Bannion
Wemple	C.B	Hersy
Waters	R.H	Morris
Frame	C.H	Fawcett
Pollard	C.H	Luce
Schumacher	I. R	Henry
Dorman	O. R	Jordan
Gummere	C. F	Noyes
Broadbent	I. L	Knudsen
Wight	O. L	Norris

Goals—Wight, Henry.

Substitutions—Harvard: Caturani for Pollard. Martin for Caturani. Mockin for Gummere. Yale: Curtis for Luce, O'Meara for Noyes.

ST. JOSEPH'S VICTOR AS 20,000 LOOK ON

Conquers Washington College, 20-0, for First Triumph in Two Years.

KANE MAKES 50-YARD RUN

Walker and McNabb Carry the Ball Over the Line for the Other Two Touchdowns.

Special to The New York Times.

PHILADELPHIA, Nov. 21.—St. Joseph's College won its first football victory in two years today by defeating Washington College by a score of 20 to 0 before a crowd of 20,000 rooters. Today's game was the last game of the season on the home grounds. Two years ago St. Joseph's defeated Brooklyn College by a 27-6 score.

After marching the ball down the field on straight football, Joe Walker managed to get the ball across for the first touchdown. McNabb failed to make the extra point when a forward grounded.

The second touchdown came in the second period when Jack Kane scooped up a Washington pass at midfield and dashed 50 yards through the entire Washington team to score. A pass, Doherty to Zuber, made the extra point. After battling to within scoring distance in the fourth period, Charley McNabb carried the ball over for the final touchdown and Morris place-kicked the extra point.

The line-up:

St. Joseph (20).		Washington Col. (0).
Morrow	L.E	Plummer
Slezak	L.T	Lord
McNichol	L.G	Nicholson
Altomare	C	Grosswith
Linaugh	R.G	Dickerson
Conklin	R.T	Blissard
Kane	R.E	Johnson
C. Morris	Q.B	Robinson
Campbell	L.H	Usilton
McNabb	R.H	Dopkins
Walker	F.B	Giraitis

Times Wide World Photo.

ACTION IN MANHATTAN-ST. JOHN'S CONTEST.
Rubinsky, St. John's, Gaining 6 Yards at Jasper Field.

"All the News That's Fit to Print."

The New York Times.

LATE CITY EDITION
WEATHER—Fair today, probably showers tonight or tomorrow.
Temperatures Yesterday—Max., 86; Min., [illegible]

Copyright, 1932, by The New York Times Company.

VOL. LXXXI....No. 27,222. | Entered as Second-Class Matter, Postoffice, New York, N. Y. | NEW YORK, FRIDAY, AUGUST 5, 1932. | * * * * | TWO CENTS In New York City | THREE CENTS Within 200 Miles | FOUR CENTS Elsewhere Except in 7th and 8th Postal Zones

FIREMEN REJECT PAY CUT BY A VOTE OF 4,900 TO 278; BLOCK WALKER ECONOMY

NEXT MOVE IS UP TO STATE

Mayor Held Powerless to Act Without Sanction of the Legislature.

HIS PROGRAM IS ASSAILED

Spokesman for Firemen Scores Failure to Try Berry Plan to Reduce Budget.

SEES WORKERS PENALIZED

Official Count Withheld by Dorman—Returns Based on Duplicate Ballots.

Mayor Walker's plea that the city employes voluntarily yield a month's salary to the city in 1933 has been rejected by the city's Fire Department. The firemen voted against the proposition in a ratio of twenty to one, and if the city wants the month's pay it will have to go to Albany for the authority to get it.

The official poll of the department was placed in the hands of Fire Commissioner Dorman on Wednesday, and up to last night had not been made public. But the Uniformed Firemen's Association, which is virtually a firemen's union, requested every member to fill out a duplicate ballot, showing what his vote had been in the official poll.

The ballots were tallied by a volunteer committee of newspaper men yesterday afternoon in the office of the association in the Pulitzer Building and the result was as follows:

Willing to accept pay cut.....	278
Refusing to accept pay cut...	4,900
Blank ballots	253

The blank ballots are explained by the fact that many firemen are on vacation, it was said by James F. Chambers, executive secretary of the Uniformed Firemen's Association.

The ballots counted yesterday by the newspaper men in the offices of the Uniformed Firemen's Association arrived in sealed envelopes from each of the fire houses in the city, with the exception of two. The results from the two missing houses are expected today.

The ballot, addressed to the association, read as follows: "For the information and records of our association, please be advised that upon the official poll taken regarding the proposed salary refund of one month's salary during 1933, my vote was as follows:"

No Comment From Walker.

Neither Mayor Walker nor Commissioner Dorman was reached for comment last night after the result of the poll became known. The commissioner had already left his office, and the Mayor, on Wednesday, had said he would have no comment to make on the action in the Fire Department, anticipated then, until he had heard the official result from the fire commissioner.

The vote was the most serious blow registered yet against the Mayor's salary cut plea, and all the city can do about it, if it chooses to carry out the threat the Mayor made in his speech to the city employes, asking them to take the cut, is to go to Albany and seek the permission of the Legislature to reduce the salaries of the recalcitrants in the ranks.

Whether this will be done was regarded yesterday as problematical. The general belief at City Hall is that there will be no decision on that, or on the Delaney plan of short-term financing, until the fate of the Mayor himself has been decided by Governor Roosevelt.

If the Mayor should be vindicated, the problem would be his anew. Should he be removed, it would fall into the lap of Joseph V. McKee, President of the Board of Aldermen and the Mayor's successor under the charter, it was pointed out.

Salaries Raised by Legislature.

Some critics of the administration were ready to point out that the salaries of the firemen and police were raised in 1929 by a referendum, authorized by the Legislature, after the city had "passed the buck" to that body, instead of raising the salaries by action of the Board of Estimate, so that the difficulty the city faces now is of its own making. Had the city raised the salaries of its own accord it could cut them also, it is contended.

Vincent J. Kane, president of the

Continued on Page Four.

American Professor Recovers Sancta Sophia Basilian Mosaics

By The Associated Press.

ISTANBUL, Aug. 4.—The recovery of Basilian mosaics, that except for a brief period in 1847 have been hidden from human eyes for four centuries, was announced today by Professor Thomas Whittemore, director of the Byzantine Institute of America.

For months Professor Whittemore and his assistants have been cleaning great mosaics in the inner portico of the mosque of Sancta Sophia.

Basilian art is a school of early Byzantine art characteristic of the monks of St. Basil, once very productive in art and letters.

Islam's taboo against images caused the Byzantine mosaics of Sancta Sophia to be covered with whitewash for centuries. The ban was lifted by the Nationalist Government of President Mustapha Kemal.

MURDER CHARGED TO LIBBY HOLMAN

Ab Walker, Aide of Reynolds, Is Indicted With Widow of the Tobacco Heir for His Death.

FATHER PROTECTS ACTRESS

Declaring Her "Innocence," He Refuses Surrender in Ohio Till 'Proper Time' at Winston-Salem.

Special to THE NEW YORK TIMES.

WINSTON-SALEM, N. C., Aug. 4.—A Forsyth County grand jury this afternoon returned true bills charging that Z. Smith Reynolds, 20-year-old heir to the $15,000,000 R. J. Reynolds tobacco fortune, was murdered by Mrs. Libby Holman Reynolds, the former Broadway "blues" singer, his wife and Albert (Ab) Walker, 20, his boyhood friend and secretary.

Immediately after the indictments were reported to Judge A. M. Stack in Superior Court, capiases were issued for the arrest of the respondents.

Sheriff Transon Scott arrested Walker at 5:15 P. M. at the home of his father, B. B. Walker, a retired real estate man. Accompanied by his lawyer, Bailey B. Liipfert, who is chairman of the county Democratic executive committee, the youth went to the jail, where he was held without bail.

The Sheriff telegraphed to the police of New York City and Cincinnati requesting the arrest of Mrs. Reynolds. From Wyoming, Ohio, a suburb of the latter city, word was received that Albert Holman, the widow's father, charging "a frame-up and a terrible injustice to an innocent young woman," refused to disclose her whereabouts, but said she would be produced "at the proper time."

Sheriff Scott is then understood to have wired a request for an arrest to the Sheriff of Hamilton County, Ohio, where Mrs. Reynolds was reported to be at the Wyoming home of her sister, Mrs. Myron Kohn.

The indictments, handed up by the

Continued on Page Fourteen.

BECCALI OF ITALY WINS 1,500 METERS AT OLYMPIC GAMES

Finishes With Rush to Triumph Before 65,000—Sets Olympic Record of 3:51.2.

TWO WORLD MARKS BROKEN

Nambu, Japan, Betters Hop, Step, Jump Figures—Miss Didrikson, U.S., Cuts Hurdles Time.

FINNISH ATHLETE VICTOR

Matti Jarvinen, Son of Winner in 1906 Games, Surpasses Olympic Javelin Record.

Olympic Point Score.

Un. States	274½	Czech'vakia	19
France	89	Holland	18
Italy	77½	Hungary	16
Germany	59½	Denmark	12
Gt. Britain	59½	Australia	10
Finland	58	South Africa	7
Sweden	43	Latvia	5
Canada	38	Argentina	4
Japan	31	Philippines	4
Poland	25	Belgium	3
Ireland	23	New Zealand	3
Austria	23	Brazil	1

Table includes all events.
Points are unofficial, based on 10 for first place and 5, 4, 3, 2, 1 for the next five places respectively.

By ARTHUR J. DALEY.
Special to THE NEW YORK TIMES.

LOS ANGELES, Aug. 4.—Italy, Japan, Finland and the United States shared the spoils of Olympic competition in the fifth session of the track and field program today as two more world's and two Olympic standards were added to the landslide of falling records before a crowd of 65,000 in the Stadium.

For the first time since the meet got under way, the Green, White and Red of Italy went up on the central mast on the peristyle as the raven-haired Luigi Beccali raced into the ground one of the greatest 1,500-meter fields the games have known, to set a new Olympic mark of 3:51.2 and leave Norman Hallowell of Harvard, America's hope, far in the ruck in sixth place.

Similarly, for the first time, the emblems of Japan and Finland were lofted into the hazy, blue sky alongside the flaming Olympic torch in celebration of the triumphs of Chuhei Nambu and Matti Jarvinen, respectively. The stocky little Nipponese, carrying on in the manner of Mikio Oda, the world's record holder and 1928 champion, not only won the hop, step and jump but set a new universal standard of 51 feet 7 inches, breaking his compatriot's figures by the amazing margin of half a foot.

Scion of Famous Family.

Jarvinen, scion of a family famous for two generations in athletics, hurled the javelin 20 feet further than it had ever been projected before in this great international carnival, launching a prodigious throw of 238 feet 7 inches, only four feet behind his own world's record.

The Olympic record had stood at 218 feet 6⅛ inches, and yet this bespectacled son of the 1906 Olympic discus champion did better than 231 feet every time he whipped the spear out into the turf.

This victory was particularly sweet to Finland, for it had come after Harry Larva, the defending champion, and Eino Purje, looked upon as one of his most formidable rivals, had both failed to place among the first eight in the 1,500-meter run. To make it even more impressive, Finland emulated the example of

Continued on Page Seventeen.

FistThrustThroughWindowBalksGemThieves; Jeweler Used Same Alarm Six Years Before

On an April evening six years ago, Isidore Renner, jeweler, of 132 Rivington Street, shoved his fist through a plate glass window of his shop to raise an alarm when four armed men attempted to rob his store. Yesterday afternoon Renner did exactly the same thing, and again frustrated a robbery.

In 1926 the four men escaped by menacing a crowd with their revolvers. Renner saved $100,000 worth of diamonds and jewelry, however, by smashing the window. The only variation yesterday in the circumstances attending the two incidents was that there were only two robbers this time, but the two men yesterday also escaped after Renner had thrust his fist through the plate glass. And Renner again saved his jewelry.

The jeweler said yesterday that Richard Reece Whittemore, who was hanged Aug. 13, 1926, in Baltimore for the murder of a Maryland penitentiary guard, had participated in the hold-up in 1926 and had threatened to shoot his daughter, Tillie, just before he gave the plate glass alarm. But newspaper accounts at that time had Whittemore in Buffalo awaiting trial on a murder charge.

The two men yesterday were about 22 years old, looked like Italians, and wore dark suits and gray fedora hats. A customer, Samuel Heller of 235 East Fourth Street, was standing at the counter and Renner was replacing jewelry in the showcase. One of the robbers held out a gold watch, but Renner informed him that he did no repair work. He turned to leave, but suddenly whisked around and drew a revolver as the second man ran to the rear where a safe stood, containing $40,000 worth of jewelry.

Renner then shoved his fist through the window, the crash of the glass frightened the two bandits and they ran out of the shop. Heller, who had remained, called Police Headquarters, as Renner nursed a severely lacerated hand. While an ambulance surgeon from Gouverneur Hospital was dressing his wounds, Renner gave a description of the two men to detectives who had arrived in radio cars from the Clinton and East Fifth Street stations, just as Jacob Renner, Isidor's brother and partner, arrived on the scene.

Reich Warns Fighting Must Cease Today; Threatens Special Courts and Death Penalty

By FREDERICK T. BIRCHALL.
Special Cable to THE NEW YORK TIMES.

BERLIN, Aug. 4.—Official warning was given tonight that unless political disorders entirely ceased within eighteen hours, the German Government would issue a Presidential decree providing more drastic penalties for cases of armed assault and the possession of illegal weapons than the law now permits and special emergency courts would be instituted to deal with such offenses.

It is understood that the decree, if issued, will establish the death penalty for certain aggravated cases of this kind, hence the warning.

It came after a special session of the Cabinet had been held to decide what measures should be taken to cope effectively with the acts of terrorism by Communists, National Socialists and unidentified individuals in various parts of the country, more particularly in East Prussia and Silesia. Chancellor von Papen was absent from Berlin, so Baron von Gayl, the Minister of the Interior, presided.

The Cabinet agreed that the situation called for severer penalties than the present penal code provides, if the turbulent sections were to be brought to order.

However, since the proposed decree, which it is understood has already been drafted and has received the approval of the Cabinet, includes the death penalty, and the government is resolved to carry it out relentlessly once it is issued, it was decided to "serve notice" upon all concerned in the recent disturbances in the hope that the warning would be sufficient.

A large section of the press deplores this as indicating more hesitation, but there is no doubt about the Cabinet's firm resolve.

The decree would be issued by President von Hindenburg under Article XLVIII of the Federal Constitution. The declaration of a military state of emergency is not contemplated, but the possibility of instituting a state of civil emergency in certain districts has been considered, and unless the new measure, if re-

Continued on Page Six.

CANADA LISTS BIDS FOR BRITISH MARKET

Estimates at the Ottawa Parley England Would Gain Trade of $100,000,000.

TOTAL CALLED MISLEADING

Dominion Assures Visitors That Figure Is Only Tentative—Many Items Are Involved.

By CHARLES A. SELDEN.
Special to THE NEW YORK TIMES.

OTTAWA, Aug. 4.—Canada told the British delegates to the Imperial Economic Conference today what special tariff preferences or free list entry she was willing to grant on manufactured articles imported from Great Britain and what she demanded in return in the way of preferences in the British market for primary products exported from the Dominion.

After R. B. Bennett, Prime Minister of Canada and president of the conference, had handed his detailed proposals to Stanley Baldwin, head of the British delegation, it was stated officially in behalf of the Canadian Government that its offer "was definite, clear-cut and generous and had been cordially received by the British delegation."

Disagree as to Advantages.

From the same official source came the tentative estimate that the adoption of the program by the United Kingdom would increase the annual sale of British goods in the Canadian market by "anywhere from $100,000,000 to $200,000,000."

When they heard these figures had been made public, the British demurred and courteously intimated to the Canadians that the figures were misleading. Then the Canadians again emphasized to all concerned the tentativeness of what they had said.

British customs and trade experts are now engaged in an examination of all the details of the offer. Until that is finished there will be no decision by Mr. Baldwin and his colleagues. The results of the examination so far, supplemented by the knowledge the British had of the Canadian scheme, has convinced them the offer is not so generous as Mr. Bennett thinks it is.

The minimum estimate of $100,000,000 which the Canadians made of the potential advantage to British exporters is far too high, according to the calculations of the United Kingdom experts. They think that something in the neighborhood of $70,000,000 would be a better guess.

Only Ireland Has No Plan.

The Canadian proposal completes the list from all the dominions except the Irish Free State, which does not yet feel itself in a position to negotiate with the British, although the delegates from both countries are nominally on equal terms at this conference. But, whatever Ireland might ask, it could not be more difficult to meet than the demands of the other British countries.

Canada, Australia, New Zealand and South Africa present programs which would involve a British tariff on food imports from foreign countries. Both Mr. Baldwin and Walter Runciman, President of the Board of Trade, are opposed to food taxes on principle, and they and their fellow-delegates are receiving many messages from England urging them not to yield to the dominions.

But if they do not yield on the question of foodstuffs there is little else that Great Britain can offer. As they came to Ottawa determined to bargain, the only question now is

Continued on Page Six.

FINANCE BOARD BARS PENNSYLVANIA LOAN

Pinchot's Personal Plea Fails as Directors Hold State Has Not Helped Itself.

MICHIGAN GETS $1,800,000

New York Tunnel Plan Study Is Deferred—Red Cross Here Asks 155,960 Barrels of Flour.

Special to THE NEW YORK TIMES.

WASHINGTON, Aug. 4.—In its first adverse decision on appeals by States for unemployment relief aid, the Reconstruction Finance Corporation today declined to lend money at this time to Pennsylvania.

The corporation's refusal was based on the belief that Pennsylvania has not exerted sufficient energy in helping herself, Chairman Atlee Pomerene announced.

It followed personal appeals by Governor Pinchot and other Commonwealth officials for an immediate loan of $10,000,000 from the $300,000,000 corporation funds set aside for this purpose by the unemployment relief act. The corporation has approved comparatively small loans to Illinois and Ohio. Pennsylvania eventually intends to ask for $45,000,000, the maximum loan permitted to any one State under the law.

The corporation announced its decision in the following brief statement:

"The board of directors of the Reconstruction Finance Corporation today heard Governor Pinchot, other officials of the State Government of Pennsylvania and leaders of the Pennsylvania State Legislature in connection with the application of the Governor for funds, under the provisions of Title I of the emergency relief and construction act of 1932, for purposes of relief and work relief in Pennsylvania.

Urges Legislative Action.

"At the conclusion of the meeting Mr. Pomerene, chairman of the board of directors of the corporation, made the following statement to the delegation:

"'It is our belief that, on proper showing, we should extend some relief to the State of Pennsylvania, but it must be borne in mind that we have funds entrusted to our board which are to be expended, not in lieu of State or local relief, but to be supplemental thereto, if, when, and as necessary.

"'After a full hearing we feel persuaded that the Legislature of the State of Pennsylvania, and its several political subdivisions, have not done their full duty with respect to the furnishing of funds for relief purposes.

"'We shall defer action with regard to relief for Pennsylvania until we know what the Legislature will do for the relief of its own people.'"

The Pennsylvania decision was taken as affirmation of the belief heretofore understood unofficially that the corporation will aid States only in the degree in which they have aided themselves.

Otherwise, it has been pointed out, the $300,000,000 might be dissipated without aid reaching to States which have exerted every effort to solve their own problems before applying to the corporation. Among these is New York State, which has not yet applied for a relief loan.

Pinchot Silent on Refusal.

A large number of Pennsylvania officials appeared before the corporation board, in keeping with the request made to Governor Pinchot last Tuesday, when he first appeared, to return today accompanied by responsible officers of the State.

Those with him were Lieut. Gov.

Continued on Page Two.

LEHMAN COMES OUT FOR GOVERNORSHIP; WIDE SUPPORT SEEN

He Plans No Pre-Convention Campaign, Preferring to "Stand on Record."

UP-STATE HELD FRIENDLY

Lieutenant Governor Reports Pledges by "Vast Majority" of Leaders There.

ROOSEVELT PRAISES HIM

Statement Tells of "Deep Personal Affection" and Predicts His Nomination and Election.

From a Staff Correspondent.
Special to THE NEW YORK TIMES.

ALBANY, Aug. 4.—His candidacy for the Governorship was announced today by Lieutenant Governor Herbert H. Lehman, and immediately afterward a warm endorsement came from Governor Roosevelt, who predicted victory for his associate in the contest for the Democratic nomination and later at the polls.

Since Alfred E. Smith, it is known, will back Mr. Lehman, the Lieutenant Governor is regarded by his friends to be in a favorable position already, although several rival candidacies are being advanced.

Mr. Lehman's announcement, which had been expected, was coupled with a statement covering his plan for a ten-day inspection tour of State institutions, beginning Wednesday. The trip will take him into Canada for a first-hand investigation of the St. Lawrence seaway and water power development.

Mr. Lehman's statement on his candidacy follows:

I have been asked by a great many friends, and by the press, whether I intend to run for Governor this Autumn. As it is impossible for me to reply personally to all those who have communicated with me, and in order to avoid any misunderstanding of my position, I make this statement:

I do intend to be a candidate for Governor this Autumn.

I shall not open headquarters, or engage in any pre-convention campaign at the present time.

I prefer to stand on my record of the past three and a half years as a public official.

Governor Roosevelt's Statement.

Governor Roosevelt's statement of endorsement recited Mr. Lehman's record, mentioned his business training as an asset in public office in these "times of financial stress" and spoke of his own "deep personal affection" for the Lieutenant Governor. His statement read:

I believe that Lieut. Gov. Lehman should be the candidate of our party for Governor of New York this Autumn.

Personal experience in and complete familiarity with the affairs of State government in Albany are not only desirable but almost essential qualifications in a candidate.

Forty years ago the executive business of the State could be handled by a Governor spending one or two days a week at the capital. Today the administrative functions are so large and so diversified that the Governorship is a full-time job calling for knowledge of all the details as well as ability. Lieut. Gov. Lehman knows the government of this State inside and out.

As my principal assistant during these four years he has not only cooperated but has given wholehearted support to the important public policies of these years. I

Continued on Page Three.

Four Convicts Killed in Arkansas Break, Three Wounded in Gun Battle With Guards

By The Associated Press.

TUCKER PRISON FARM, Ark., Aug. 4.—Four convicts were killed and three wounded today in a break from the stockade at Camp No. 2 and in a gun battle between the fugitives and officers in a field. One hundred and five prisoners refused to take part in the break.

Archie Jones, a trusty who had won the confidence of the prison authorities, is charged with leading seven prisoners in the attempted escape.

Else Howell, another convict acting as a guard, was shot and killed when he tried to stop the break. Cecil Allen, another trusty guard, was beaten on the head with a pistol and wounded slightly.

Jones and the six other convicts were trailed to a cotton field several miles away by a posse of twenty officers and when the fugitives opened fire, the officers killed three and wounded two others. Two surrendered.

Loy Smith, J. D. Brown and Hershel Chaney were shot dead. Jones was shot in the right arm and Everett Wackerley, serving a life term for murder, was shot in the right knee. They are all young men.

Jones, who had been a trusty guard for fifteen months with a perfect record, originated the plot. Shortly after midnight, he forced another guard to turn over the keys to the stockade, disarmed still another, locked both in a cell and opened the stockade doors. The six other convicts with whom he had plotted the break joined him. They killed a guard and wounded another to get their guns.

The telephone connecting the camp with Tucker Farm headquarters two and a half miles away was put out of commission. The convicts fled on horses.

Hours later the horses were found and bloodhounds were put on the trail. The dogs led the pursuers to the corn field where the fugitives gave battle and were shot down.

MEYER ACTS WITH BANKERS TO AID WHEAT AND COTTON; CUTTEN IN $30,000,000 POOL

Manila Legislators Oppose Roosevelt's Leaving Islands

Wireless to THE NEW YORK TIMES.

MANILA, Aug. 4.—Leaders are planning to present before the Legislature next week a joint resolution opposing Gov. Gen. Theodore Roosevelt's returning to the United States to assist in the election campaign of President Hoover, as it has been rumored that he would do.

The legislators declare that the Governor General is the best friend of the Filipinos in the present troubled times, and insist that his presence here is necessary to help in solving the many problems facing the islands.

Mr. Roosevelt has made no statement in regard to the rumors, but it is believed that he would much prefer to remain in the Philippines because of the pressure of official business.

STEEL MEN APPOINT R.P. LAMONT DICTATOR

Former Commerce Secretary Gets Sweeping Powers for a Drive to Stabilize Industry.

TO BE INSTITUTE PRESIDENT

Will Succeed Schwab as Active Head on Aug. 18—First Aim Is to End 'Concessions.'

Preliminary to the adoption of a more aggressive policy of cooperation to overcome unsettled conditions in the steel industry, Robert P. Lamont, who resigned on Wednesday as Secretary of Commerce, has been chosen to head the American Iron and Steel Institute, which represents about 95 per cent of the steel producers of the country.

Charles M. Schwab, chairman of the Bethlehem Steel Corporation and president of the Steel Institute, will become chairman of the latter body. Mr. Lamont, who will succeed him as the active head of the institute, will devote all of his time to the new duties. The proposed changes were announced in a statement issued at Mr. Schwab's offices yesterday.

To Have Wide Powers.

The selection of Mr. Lamont as executive head of the institute is of special significance at this time since it foreshadows a closer cooperation among the various producing units of what has been one of the most highly competitive industries in the country. Mr. Lamont will, in effect, become the dictator of the industry, although important steel executives expressed distaste yesterday for that term.

Mr. Lamont was for many years president of the American Steel Foundries and as such was one of the leaders of the steel industry. He is considered by other steel men to be peculiarly fitted for the new post. He will be elected to the presidency at a meeting of directors on Aug. 18. In the meantime, he will begin preliminary work looking to the harmonizing of differences among steel producers.

Myron C. Taylor, chairman of the United States Steel Corporation, said yesterday that the plan for the expansion of the executive personnel

Continued on Page Three.

FIRM FARM PRICES SOUGHT

Efforts Will Be Made for Orderly Marketing of Federal Holdings.

GRAIN GROUP ORGANIZING

Action on Cotton to Follow, With Move to Delay Government Sales a Year.

HEAVY TRADING IN STOCKS

3,522,000 Shares Sold in Most Active Day of 1932—Record Rise in Preferred Issues.

As a part of a rounded program designed to hasten the economic recovery, a powerful pool is being organized to strengthen prices of agricultural staples. The project is a private banking enterprise thus far, but it has the active encouragement, if not the sponsorship, of the administration in Washington. Eugene Meyer, Governor of the Federal Reserve Board and until recently chairman of the Reconstruction Finance Corporation, has been conferring with bankers on the general movement, it became known yesterday.

Although the plans are in an embryonic stage, they include the granting of easier credits to large users and consumers of the staple agricultural products as well as the orderly marketing of these products now held by the Farm Board. Through a strong pool, including financial leaders, it is hoped a material improvement in the prices of the leading commodities on the various exchanges of the country can be accomplished.

Stocks Rise in Big Day.

Meanwhile the stock market yesterday had its most active day since last December. The total turnover was 3,522,000 shares, compared with 2,400,000 the day before. Prices rose sharply, with a range of from 2 to 15 points, owing to an enormous investment demand for preferred stocks.

One of the first steps in the economic plan provides for concerted effort to induce industries and manufacturers to purchase materials at present low prices and to provide credit if they should want it. While eventually it may be necessary to form a corporation along the lines of the National Credit Corporation or the American Securities Investing Corporation to carry out the plans, it is understood that at first aid will be given only through the regular banking channels.

Wheat Pool Reported Formed.

The formation of a powerful pool to operate in wheat is reported to have been virtually accomplished. This pool, which will have about $30,000,000 to carry on its operation, in all probability will be managed by Arthur W. Cutten of Chicago, a prominent operator in the grain markets of this country and Canada for many years.

Conditions in wheat are believed such that a substantial betterment in price can be brought about, especially after hedging operations are over, which usually is around Sept. 1. The Farm Board's holdings of wheat have been reduced to around 50,000,000 bushels, including both spot and futures, from the high of around 250,000,000 bushels a little more than a year ago. Part of the plan, it is said, calls for the purchase of remaining holdings of the Farm Board, thus relieving the market from this source of supply, which for more than a year has been keeping it in a semi-demoralized state because the Farm Board has been a heavy seller of wheat on all bulges.

Small Crop in Prospect.

With the Farm Board out of the wheat market, together with prospects of the smallest wheat crop in the United States since 1925, the consensus is that wheat prices could be stabilized at a reasonably higher level. Recent estimates place the Winter wheat crop in this country around 440,000,000 bushels, against 789,000,000 bushels last year, a decline of about 350,000,000 bushels. However, the Spring wheat crop is estimated at more than double the 105,000,000 bushels harvested last year. While Canada is expected to market a much larger wheat crop than in 1931, reports from Europe are to the effect that the wheat harvest there prob-

Continued on Page Two.

Continued from Page One.

scoring a clean sweep; set by the Americans in the 200-meter dash yesterday, as Matti Sippala and Eino Penttila took second and third places.

The only fruits accruing to the United States after its unprecedented harvest of yesterday was the eyelash victory of the versatile Miss Mildred (Babe) Didrikson of Dallas over her team-mate, Mrs. Evelyn Hall of Chicago, in the 80-meter hurdles final.

Following her world's record-breaking exploit in the javelin throw on the opening day, this remarkable young woman athlete from the Southwest showed her gameness in fighting off the determined bid of her Illinois rival to beat her to the tape by a scant two inches and set a new universal mark of 0:11.7.

This victory, of course, did not contribute to the United States point score in the men's track and field competition, but the Americans managed to salvage 8 points during the afternoon as Finland, Japan and Italy made the most impressive additions to the team standing for the unofficial men's championship.

Furth Finishes Sixth.

A fifth place by Lee Bartlett and a sixth by Ken Churchill in the javelin throw, a fourth by Glenn Cunningham and a sixth by Hallowell in the 1,500, and a sixth by Sol Furth of the Millrose A. A., former N. Y. U. captain, in the hop, step and jump, accounted for America's total for the afternoon's proceedings.

Finland, in garnering 19 points, all in the spear-tossing event, lived up, for the first time this week, to the prediction that it would furnish the United States with its chief competition and jumped to second place in the men's track and field standing with 35 points, just ahead of Great Britain with 34.

Canada and Ireland also improved their standing a bit, with totals to date of 23 each. The United States, however, is so far out in the lead in men's track and field with its 158 points that it is practically beyond overtaking.

The Americans, with their leanest day of the games a thing of the past, can wait for another point avalanche in the 400-meter run tomorrow. Bill Carr of Penn, Ben Eastman of Stanford and Jimmy Gordon of the Los Angeles A. C. all qualified with ease for the semi-finals tomorrow as all three won their quarter-final tests.

The 1,500-meter run final, the major event on today's short program, was a big disappointment to the crowd which had been hoping that either Hallowell, Cunningham or Frank Crowley of Manhattan College and the New York A. C. would restore to America the bygone glories of Mel Sheppard's triumph in 1908.

It also was a source of keen regret to Phil Edwards of Canada, third in the 800-meter run, who saw first victory then second place slip from his grasp in the final eighty yards as Jerry Cornes of England nipped him for the runner-up berth.

Wins With Closing Drive.

Beccali won the 1,500-meter run because he had the sprint, not an ordinary sprint, but a closing drive that one might expect from a half-miler but never from a distance runner. Edwards ran just the right kind of race for him, setting a fast pace into the homestretch that left the Canadian with not enough staying power to resist the Italian's finishing burst.

As that brilliant field swept into the last straightaway it was anybody's race. It was apparent that neither Edwards nor Cunningham had enough left. When Cornes, J. E. Lovelock of New Zealand, Erik Ny of Sweden, and Hallowell started to kick for the final drive Beccali had too much for them. And when the Italian let loose with all he had his powerful sprint was enough to carry him to an Olympic championship.

Both Hallowell and Cunningham had good positions when the field lined up for the start of the race. They held the two inside lanes. The Italian was in the middle of the pack and, in his overanxiety to get to that tape first, broke before the gun sounded.

There was a mad scramble for positions in the first fifty yards. Edwards, with his great experience as a half-miler, got the jump on the field, but Lovelock, the Rhodes scholar, was eager to get away from the danger of being pocketed.

Sprints From the Outside.

Hence he sprinted from the outside and cut in ahead of the Canadian Negro, while in back of the two leaders were Beccali, the three Americans, then Ny and Purje and Larva of Finland. In this order they went around the turn, although Ny had moved up far enough to go into the van with three laps more to go.

In the backstretch the Swede dropped out of sight as Cunningham made his initial bid. He went around Edwards and Lovelock, taking Larva with him. Hallowell was in fifth place at this stage and Beccali in sixth position. Cornes was seventh.

They made another circuit of the track and the continual shuffling of places again was evident. The order was Cunningham, Edwards, Lovelock, Beccali, Cornes, Purje, Hallowell, Larva and Crowley.

Miss Mildred Didrikson, United States, 80-Meter Hurdles.

But at this point places meant very little because the entire field was well bunched. As the field swept into the backstretch Cunningham, the burly Kansan, and Edwards had broken away from the rest. The former had a three-yard margin on the Canadian, who, in turn, was ten yards ahead of Beccali, who had advanced to third place.

Run Field Into Ground.

Once more they spun around the du'' gray track, Cunningham and the former N. Y. U. captain running the field into the ground, fifteen yards ahead of their nearest competitors, who were, in order, Cornes, Lovelock, Beccali, Hallowell, Purje and Crowley. The bell sounded for the last lap. The real battle was about to commence.

Edwards started his sprint over on the far side of the field and went ahead of his American rival. Beccali moved up past the fading Lovelock and right into the notch behind Cornes. Hallowell began his pursuit, and he, too, went past the New Zealander. So did Ny.

With his coal-black hair bobbing up and down as his stride lengthened, Beccali came on. He collared Cunningham right at the turn and sailed serenely past the laboring Edwards with 100 yards to go. It was his race from that moment on.

Cornes also was closing in on the two former leaders. Hallowell was through, his head back and his every muscle tightened under the strain. The Briton kept up his pursuit and went by the wilting Cunningham fifty yards from the wire. Then he caught Edwards, beating him by inches. Beccali finished six yards in front of these two, seemingly unaffected by his exertions.

Team-mates rushed over to congratulate the winner. Beccali took his new-won honors very calmly. Remarkably composed, he reached down for his training suit and pulled it on. When he marched to the victory stand the Italian raised his right arm in the Fascist salute as his national anthem was played and as the Ital'an standard shot up to the mast.

As far as close finishes were concerned, however, the final of the women's 80-meter hurdles was quite comparable to the Tolan-Metcalfe 100-meter battle. Miss Didrikson came through with a fighting drive that just edged out her fellow-American, Mrs. Hall.

The Texas girl is all fight from the tip of her toes to the top of her straight black hair. Miss Violet Webb of Great Britain was first over the initial hurdle, a foot ahead of Miss Didrikson and Miss Marjorie Clark of South Africa.

Then the one-woman track team from Dallas began to hurdle. With her left foot extended she sailed over the next stick and was indisputably ahead. But Mrs. Hall was coming along very fast in the adjoining lane, and Miss Clark was stepping over the barriers very well.

With two fences yet left to be cleared, Miss Didrikson had a two-foot advantage. Not quite as finished a timber-topper as Mrs. Hall, the Texas star was much faster between hurdles. Her lead began to slip away as Mrs. Hall advanced and they were absolutely even as their forward feet touched the ground, just before the tape.

Then, with a magnificent closing burst, Miss Didrikson pounced over the last stretch to hit the tape a scant two inches ahead of her teammate in the new world's record time of 0:11.7.

Victory Ceremonies Held.

The start of the day's program was delayed considerably by the victory ceremonies in which the wrestling champions were crowned. The "Star Spangled Banner" was the predominant musical note of this as Bobby Pearce, Jack Van Bebber and Peter Mehringer, all of the United States, were presented with first-place medals.

The initial heat of the 400-meter run presented no difficulties for the favored Alex Wilson of Canada. He just ran fast enough to qualify and cared not whether he was first or third over the line. He permitted Adolf Metzner of Germany to show the way to the line and even did not bother when little Seiken Oki of Japan edged past him for second place. The time of this trial was slow, 0:54.4.

Eastman was the outstanding figure in the second test and he loafed through the distance as only an Eastman can loaf. Traveling as slow as he could, Eastman still won and won by five yards from Joachim Buechner of Germany, much to the delight of the crowd. Despite the calm way he ran, the Stanford wonder was caught in 0:49.

The third heat presented a few anxious moments when Jimmy Ball of Canada, the runner-up by inches to Ray Barbuti for the Olympic crown in 1926, took his time to the last turn when Borj Strandvall of Finland was far out in the lead. But the Dominion ace came on with renewed power in the homestretch, assured himself of second place, and let it go at that. The Finn won in 0:49.8.

Then Carr strolled through his preliminary race. That is all he did and yet the watches caught him in the excellent figures of 0:48.8, time that has been beaten only thrice in the long history of the Olympics. The Penn flier triumphed by almost five yards over George Golding of Australia, practically walking through the last fifty yards.

The great Godfrey Rampling of Great Britain was the cynosure in the fifth heat and he impressed mightily, even though he failed to win. The Briton did not try to do that, but just made certain of qualifying, as he placed second behind Felix Rinner of Austria in the ordinary figures of 0:49.2.

Gordon, third of the Americans, loped his way around the track for 350 meters in the last heat and just accelerated his pace enough to get clear of the three other starters in their scramble to place. The American was clocked in 0:50.6.

The leaders had to step a little faster in the 400-meter quarter-finals, but the casualties were few and far between. The favored ones came through, all three Americans winning the three trials. Carr breezed in in 0:48.4 as he was followed by Walters of South Africa and Golding of Australia; Gordon showed the way to Rampling, the mighty British ace, and Buechner, the German, in 0:48.6, while Eastman strode through his 400 in 0:48.8, ahead of Rinner, the Austrian, and Strandvall, the Finn.

Meanwhile the javelin and the hop, step and jump competitions were getting under way. Matti Jarvinen of Finland was drawing gasps from the crowd as he kept sending the spear out well beyond the Olympic record with every try.

In fact that record was eclipsed in the first throw as Weimann of Germany wiped away the old mark of 218 feet 6⅛ inches with a mighty heave of 223 feet 8⅜ inches. But this stood only for two minutes. Jarvinen came along with a toss of 233 feet 9½ inches which stood for a while as the best throw of the day. The big Finn came close to this on his next throw, which reached out 231 feet ¾ inch.

Point Tabulation for the Olympics

Country.	Weight Lifting.	Track, Men.	Field, Men.	Track, Women.	Field, Women.	Fencing.	Cycling.	Wrestling.	Total.
United States	20	74	84	23½	28	4	1	40	274½
France	36	..	7	..	..	10	26	10	89
Italy	14	18	..	..	..	5	40½	..	77½
Germany	22	13	7	1½	14	2	..	..	59½
Great Britain	..	34	..	5	..	5	15½	..	59½
Finland	..	9	26	..	..	..	..	23	58
Sweden	..	4	11	..	..	..	8	20	43
Canada	..	13	10	6	..	..	4	5	38
Japan	..	1	27	..	3	..	..	..	31
Poland	..	10	..	10	5	..	..	..	25
Austria	9	..	..	..	..	10	..	4	23
Ireland	..	10	13	..	..	..	..	..	23
Czechoslovakia	15	..	4	..	..	..	..	..	19
Holland	..	..	2	..	..	1	15	..	18
Hungary	..	..	3	..	..	4	..	9	16
Denmark	5	..	..	..	..	..	7	..	12
Australia	..	..	..	..	..	..	10	..	10
South Africa	..	3	..	4	..	..	..	..	7
Latvia	..	5	..	..	..	..	..	..	5
Argentina	1	2	1	..	..	..	..	..	4
Philippines	..	..	4	..	..	..	..	..	4
New Zealand	..	3	..	..	..	..	..	..	3
Belgium	..	..	..	..	..	3	..	..	3
Brazil	..	..	1	..	..	..	..	..	1

Points are unofficial, based on 10 for first place and 5, 4, 3, 2, 1 for the next five places respectively.

PAZESI, ITALY, TAKES OLYMPIC BIKE RACE

Leads Team to Victory in 100-Kilometer Road Event—Several Spills Occur.

LOS ANGELES, Aug. 4 (AP).—Over a course which officials described as one of the most difficult in the history of the Olympic road race, Italy made a clean sweep of the long-distance cycling event today, winning individual and team honors.

Attilio Pazesi, youthful Italian ace, led the parade of nearly twoscore cyclists across the finish line with a time of 2 hours 28 minutes 5 3-5 seconds for the 100-kilometer (62.14-mile) course, which stretched across the mountainous road bordering the ocean between Moorpark and Santa Monica. There were several bad spills but no serious injuries.

Speeding into second and fourth places, two team-mates, Guglielmo Segato and Giuseppe Olmo, aided Pazesi in bringing Italy first place in the team event with the fastest combined time, 7 hours 27 minutes 15 1-5 seconds. Segato's time was 2:29:21 2-5 and Olmo's 2:29:48 2-5.

Third place in the individual race was captured by Bernhard Britz, Sweden 2:29:45 1-5, fifth by F. Sorensen, Denmark, 2:30:11 1-5, and sixth by Frank W. Southall, Great Britain, 2:30:16 1-5. Denmark took second place in the team competition with 7:38:50. Sweden was third with 7:39:12, Great Britain fourth with 7:44:53, France fifth with 7:46:31 3-5 and the United States sixth with 7:51:55 3-5.

Champions of the 1932 Games

TRACK AND FIELD.

Men.

Shot-Put—Leo Sexton, United States.
High Jump—Duncan McNaughton, Canada.
Hammer Throw—Dr. Patrick O'Callaghan, Ireland.
10,000-Meter Run—Janusz Kusocinski, Poland.
400-Meter Hurdles—Robert Tisdall, Ireland.
100-Meter Dash—Eddie Tolan, United States.
800-Meter Run—Tom Hampson, Great Britain.
Broad Jump—Ed Gordon, United States.
Pole Vault—Bill Miller, United States.
Discus Throw—John Anderson, United States.
110-Meter Hurdles—George Saling, United States.
200-Meter Dash—Eddie Tolan, United States.
50,000-Meter Walk—Thomas Green, Great Britain.
1,500-Meter Run—Luigi Beccali, Italy.
Javelin Throw—Matti Jarvinen, Finland.
Hop, Step and Jump—Chuhei Nambu, Japan.

Women.

Javelin Throw—Miss Mildred (Babe) Didrikson, United States.
100-Meter Dash—Miss Stella Walsh, Poland.
Discus Throw—Miss Lillian Copeland, United States.
80-Meter Hurdles—Miss Mildred (Babe) Didrikson, United States.

WEIGHT LIFTING.

Featherweight Class—Raymond Suvigny, France.
Lightweight Class—Rene Duverger, France.
Middleweight Class—Rudolf Jsmayr, Germany.
Light Heavyweight Class—Louis Hostin, France.
Heavyweight Class—Jaroslav Skobia, Czechoslovakia.

FENCING.

Foils.

Women—Miss Ellen Preiss, Austria.
Men's Team—France.

WRESTLING.

Catch-as-Catch-Can.

Bantamweight Class—Robert Pearce, United States.
Featherweight Class—Herman Pihlajamaki, Finland.
Lightweight Class—Charles Pacome, France.
Welterweight Class—Jack Van Bebber, United States.
Middleweight Class—Ivar Johansson, Sweden.
Light Heavyweight Class — Peter Mehringer, United States.
Heavyweight Class—Johan Richtoff, Sweden.

CYCLING.

4,000-Meter Pursuit Race—Italy.
1,000-Meter Scratch — Jacobus Van Egmond, Holland.
1,000-Meter Time Trial — Edgar L. Gray, Australia.
2,000-Meter Tandem—Louis Chaillot and Maurice Perrin, France.
100-Kilometer Road Race (team)—Italy.
100-Kilometer Road Race (individual)—Attilio Pazesi, Italy.

INDIAN TEAM SHINES AT FIELD HOCKEY

Baffling Passing Attack Brings 11-to-1 Triumph Over Japanese Olympic Squad.

WINNERS' RECORD MARRED

Went Through 1928 Games Without Being Scored Upon—Other Sidelights on International Meet.

By ALLISON DANZIG.

Special to THE NEW YORK TIMES.

LOS ANGELES, Aug. 4.—The field hockey game between India and Japan, held this morning in Olympic Stadium, drew only a handful of spectators, but those who turned out were rewarded with an exhibition of team play such as is not often seen in any branch of sport. The sunburned stalwarts from the furthest boundaries of the British Empire played circles around the little brown men to defeat them by the overwhelming margin of 11 goals to 1.

It was not for lack of trying that the Nipponese took so bad a beating. Any such statement is superfluous, for it is a racial characteristic of the sons of the Samurai to put their heart and soul into anything and everything they undertake.

They were fighting all over the field, but the baffling team play of their opponents put their efforts to nought. It was almost uncanny the way in which the Indians, without looking up to see where their teammates were, passed the ball straight as a die.

Only the marvelous work of Shunichi Hamada in guarding the Japanese goal prevented the score from being more decisive than it was. Time after time he made spectacular saves with his arms, feet and body that brought shouts of approval from the stands.

The Japanese, though beaten, had the satisfaction of scoring a goal upon their opponents. That was no small feat when it is remembered that in 1928 the Indians went through the Olympics without a single goal being made against them.

The game was played quietly and intensely, with hardly a shout being heard on the field. At the end the players walked off quietly, without any exchange of handshakes or demonstrations, except that they brandished their sticks above their heads and gave a short cheer in the manner of college football teams.

Texas Girl Voices a Lament.

Miss Mildred (Babe) Didrikson, the two-gun girl from Texas who shoots the world's records full of holes, is lamenting because they wouldn't let her compete in more than three events. Already she has lowered the universal standard in both the javelin throw and the 80-meter hurdles and she is all set to put a new record in the books for the high jump on Sunday. "I'd break 'em all if they'd let me," said the pride of the Panhandle.

"All the News That's Fit to Print."

The New York Times.

LATE CITY EDITION
WEATHER—Cloudy and cooler today; tomorrow cloudy.
Temperatures Yesterday—Max., 84; Min., 71.

VOL. LXXXI....No. 27,228. Entered as Second-Class Matter, Postoffice, New York, N. Y. NEW YORK, THURSDAY, AUGUST 11, 1932. ****+ TWO CENTS In New York City | THREE CENTS Within 200 Miles | FOUR CENTS Elsewhere Except in 7th and 8th Postal Zones

RUSSIA TO SELL BONDS HERE; TRADE INCREASE FORECAST, WITH RECOGNITION NEARER

WORLD ISSUE IS PLANNED

10% Securities to Be Paid in Gold or Currency of Nation Where Held.

REVIVAL OF ORDERS IS SEEN

Lack of Credit Held Sole Cause of Huge Drop in Our Exports —Move Spurs Stock Market.

SHIFT BY HOOVER RUMORED

Bank Interests Hope a Trade Commissioner Will Be Sent as Step to Recognition.

With the opening of an international campaign to sell an unlimited amount of Soviet Russian gold bonds redeemable on demand in the currencies of the countries in which they are marketed, it has bcome apparent to banking interests here that a far-reaching change in the relations between this country and Russia is taking place and that this foreshadows the eventual recognition of the Soviet régime by the United States Government.

The financing plan is centred around an issue of internal bonds so arranged as to avoid the difficulties of floating foreign dollar bond issues in this country through established underwriting syndicates. Under the program the sales campaign will be directed from Moscow with the assistance of American consultants. Its sponsors expect that through these bonds international trade, especially with this country, will be given the greatest impetus yet enjoyed.

Two Banks to Act Here.

Arrangements have been made for the Chase National Bank of New York and the International Acceptance Bank to handle the transfer of the funds and the delivery of the bonds in this country.

For many years important banking and commercial interests as well as some government officials have been advocating closer commercial relations with Russia. Recently, Colonel Frederick Pope, president of the Nitrogen Engineering Corporation, urged that the United States send an unofficial observer or commissioner to Russia with a view to facilitating business relations. Because of the non-recognition of Soviet Russia and other trade handicaps, purchases by Soviet Russia in this country have been restricted. Germany and England now get the bulk of the trade.

The possibility that President Hoover might suggest closer trade relations with Russia was widely rumored and discussed in the financial community yesterday. There were definite indications that any such development at the present time would be regarded favorably from a financial standpoint.

Significance was attached to the fact that, in his recent speech, Secretary Stimson referred for the first time since the Russian revolution to the "Government of Russia." This, admitted to be very much of a fine point, was nevertheless considered a straw in the wind, indicative of a changing attitude in Washington.

May Use Bonds to Pay for Goods.

At present, it is felt, any steps that might tend to stimulate this country's foreign trade would be highly beneficial. Observers have pointed out that Russia perhaps presents the greatest potential outlet for American goods abroad, especially as for some years it is likely that Russia would have to buy more from this country than she would sell to us, continuing the present favorable balance of trade for the United States.

Although full details of the bond issue are not available, it is considered likely that the proceeds would be used as part payment for goods purchased in this country. While the bonds are to be redeemable on demand they are to run for a period of ten years. These probably would be more negotiable than notes or acceptances, in view of current banking conditions, and, if manufacturers would accept the bonds as part payment for goods with the understanding that they would not be presented for redemption until the expiration of an agreed period of time, they could go a long way toward stimulating purchases by Russia in this country.

Trade between manufacturers in

Continued on Page Eight.

Rome Officials Welcome Report That Italy May Quit the League

By The Associated Press.

ROME, Aug. 10.—Reports in the European press of a possibility that Italy might withdraw from the League of Nations apparently rather pleased Italian officials and newspapers.

Today's papers characterized the rumor as a recognition of Italy's often-expressed dissatisfaction with world conferences, particularly with the recent disarmament conference.

At its last session the Italian Grand Council made what was regarded by some persons as a veiled threat to withdraw by announcing that it would consider Italy's status with reference to the League in October.

Consequently, no action is expected until then, and responsible quarters think that criticisms of the League by Italy and others may result in enough improvement to make this country's withdrawal unlikely.

SPAIN QUELLS REVOLT OF ARMY ROYALISTS

Gen. Sanjurjo Flees Seville as Republican Troops Close In on Him.

EIGHT KILLED IN MADRID

One Hundred Rebel Leaders Seized After Machine Gun Fight in Capital.

Special Cable to THE NEW YORK TIMES.

SEVILLE, Thursday, Aug. 11.—General José Sanjurjo, the leader of the Royalist revolt, has fled presumably by airplane, and Civil Guards and troops who were supporting him yesterday have declared themselves loyal to the Republic again.

No other forces have entered the city as yet.

A mob stormed the Labradores Club, the headquarters of the landed aristocracy, last night and burned it to the ground. On the whole, the city was calm, however, except for a general strike and shouts of "Death to tyrants." It has been quiet most of the time, with very little violence either at the time it was taken, when the rebel forces were overwhelming, or later when General Sanjurjo fled as the tide turned.

The arrival of Government troops is expected hourly.

Collapse Announced in Madrid.

By FRANK L. KLUCKHOHN.
Special Cable to THE NEW YORK TIMES.

MADRID, Thursday, Aug. 11.—The Royalist revolt which started yesterday collapsed early this morning, according to the Ministry of the Interior, when General José Sanjurjo, its leader, fled from Seville. He is believed to be making for Portugal, with little chance of his being captured.

General Manuel Gonzalez Lopez, the Governor of the Province of Córdoba, who was sent by the Madrid Government to take charge of the province of Seville, has taken command of the rebellious troops in the

Continued on Page Eight.

HITLER IS EXPECTED TO BE CHANCELLOR IN CABINET SHAKE-UP

Every Likelihood Now That Nazi Leader Will Be Appointed Within a Few Days.

CENTRISTS WOULD ACCEPT

Government Seeks Assurance of Moderation and Check on Fascist Leader.

SCHLEICHER TO KEEP POST

Von Papen Likely to Be Foreign Minister—Two More Killings as New Decrees Take Effect.

The text of von Hindenburg's decree on political riots is on page 11.

By FREDERICK T. BIRCHALL.
Special Cable to THE NEW YORK TIMES.

BERLIN, Aug. 10.—There is every likelihood tonight that within a few days Adolf Hitler will be the Chancellor of the German Republic. Thus the impossible of yesterday, in view of the attitude of the present government, has become the best bet of today.

The world's greatest political poker game is being played here. The stake is the actual and not the nominal control of the Reich; the cards are the influences each of the players can bring to bear, either through the voters or by other means, upon the few men who now hold the reins of actual power, and maybe this will be merely a preliminary hand.

The Hitlerites believe they hold the best cards, and undoubtedly they have an ace or two, but there is every reason to believe that the big cards, the ones that will really decide the game, are still in the capable fists of Baron von Gayl, the Minister of the Interior; Chancellor von Papen, President von Hindenburg and, above all, Lieut. Gen. von Schleicher, the Minister of Defense.

The change in the situation today is due chiefly to the attitude of the Centrists, who hold the balance of power in, although they cannot control, the Reichstag.

Have Sought a Showdown.

For weeks the Centrist leaders and the Centrist organs have been calling for a showdown on the National Socialists' pretensions. The Hitlerites, they said, were clamoring for power and had about 14,000,000 voters backing their claim; let them have it.

The Hitlerites themselves were none too eager to enter any Cabinet that they could not dominate. The government, while preferring to have the Hitlerites inside, was quite willing to continue the present status if it could have the support of the Reichstag.

But that meant having the support not only of the Nazis but of the Centrists if the government was to carry on, and the Centrists refused to join with the Nazis in giving it unless the Nazis accepted some share of the responsibility.

The situation was brought to a head a few days ago when the Centrists opened negotiations with the Nazi leaders for a practical coalition both in the Reichstag and the Prussian Diet on certain conditions. The Nazis refused the offer, but they learned in the course of the negotiations that the Centrists were not opposed in principle to the idea of Herr Hitler becoming Chancellor.

At about the same time General von Schleicher and Chancellor von Papen discovered that the Centrists

Continued on Page Eleven.

Reaped Area in Soviet 25% Less Than in 1931; Peasants Won't Harvest Beyond Own Needs

By WALTER DURANTY.
Wireless to THE NEW YORK TIMES.

MOSCOW, Aug. 10.—Harvest figures published today for the five days up to Aug. 5, show 25 per cent less area reaped than at the same date last year and 25 per cent less than for the preceding five-day period.

There was a startling drop in the Black Earth region along the Volga, and the Middle Volga reaped only 172,000 hectares [a hectare is 2.47 acres] compared with 2,250,000 in the preceding five days. There were also poor reports from the Ukraine, where the Spring sowing campaign was unsatisfactory, because many peasants, even in the collectives, ate part of the seed.

Another disquieting factor is contributed by widespread reports that the peasants are not bothering to harvest more grain than for their own needs, beacuse of shortages of goods that they want in return for their surplus grain or money.

The new facilities for marketing offered to individual peasants are producing a certain exodus from the collectives, which, however, is not yet of serious proportions.

In summary the agrarian situation is not rosy, but the freedom with which the press is revealing and discussing facts is the best proof of the authorities' confidence that the difficulties will be overcome.

MOSCOW, Aug. 10 (AP).—A serious lagging in the grain harvest and difficulties by the government in making collections from the peasantry were officially acknowledged today.

The greatest delays were found in the Ukraine and in the North Caucasus, where a devastating drought was experienced last year.

The newspapers attributed the situation to poor organization in the Ukraine, increased activities of the kulaks against collective farmers and insufficient attention paid to individual peasants by Communist party and government officials.

The State farms, which are supposed to be models of Socialist agriculture, showed the lowest percentage of harvesting, which amounted to 33.3 per cent of their sown area.

Crabbe of U. S. Captures Olympic Title Swim; Miss Coleman, Coast Girl, Wins Diving Crown

By ARTHUR J. DALEY,
Special to THE NEW YORK TIMES.

LOS ANGELES, Aug. 10.—Enjoying a complete day of triumph in the swimming competition, the United States marched off with two Olympic titles today. Before a combined crowd of 19,000, Clarence (Buster) Crabbe won the 400-meter free-style crown in a pulsating sprint finish and Miss Georgia Coleman captured the 3-meter springboard diving laurels.

Much to the delight of the California spectators, both Los Angeles aquatic stars came from behind to win. In the morning the graceful blond-haired Miss Coleman, supreme in the voluntary diving where she could call into play the most difficult twists, overhauled her team-mate, Miss Jane Fauntz of Chicago, in the last few dives into the pale blue water.

Miss Katherine Rawls, 14-year-old national champion from Florida, took second honors and Miss Fauntz third, thus giving the United States a clean sweep of the first three places.

However, it remained for the perfectly proportioned six-footer from the Los Angeles A. C., Crabbe, to bring the crowd to its feet with a breath-taking finish in the 400-meter battle in the afternoon. And a grand battle it was!

The bronzed American overtook Jean Taris of France, world's record holder for the distance, with his last few strokes to create a new Olympic record of 4:48.4, just 1 4-10 seconds behind the volatile Frenchman's universal standard.

This was a brilliantly contested race that saw all six finalists cut under the Olympic mark of 5:01.6, as the other times were: Taris, 4:48.5; Tsutomu Oyokata of Japan, 4:52:3; Takashi Yokoyama of Japan, 4:52.5; Noboru Sugimoto of Japan, 4:56.1, and Andrew (Boy) Charlton of Australia, 4:58.6. The first two also bettered Yokoyama's new Olympic standard of 4:51.4, made in a semi-final heat yesterday.

The triumph of the local youth was particularly pleasing to every one in the American camp. It was the first time in the men's swimming events that the Japanese had not met with success, and marked the definite snapping of Nippon aquatic supremacy. Crabbe had not even regained

Continued on Page Nineteen.

GREEN ADVISES FIGHT ON RAIL WAGE CUT

Labor Chief Asserts That the Federation Stands Against Any Reduction of Pay.

HOLDS REPEAL IS DISTANT

But Beer Will Soon Return, He Tells Hotel Workers at Boston Convention.

Special to THE NEW YORK TIMES.

BOSTON, Aug. 10.—President William Green of the American Federation of Labor, here today to attend the convention of the Hotel and Restaurant Employes and Beverage Dispensers International Alliance, declared that railroad employes who have been asked to accept a 15 per cent cut in wages should fight that cut to a finish. He asserted that the federation must adopt a five-day week and a six-hour day to steady the economic structure.

"The entire policy of the American Federation of Labor has been against the reduction of wages during the depression," he said, "and the federation takes its stand now against a cut in the pay of railroad employes.

"It called for the creation of the five-day week on a national basis and upon President Hoover to summon the leaders of labor and the industries to meet in conference and adopt a constructive program to restore buying power and end the depression. The American Federation of Labor will hold its ranks against the destructive policy of wage cutting."

Sees Some Local Improvement.

Discussing the unemployment situation President Green said that he has noticed some spots of local improvement and he feels inspired by hope, but that there is no evidence of general and substantial improvment. He quoted the latest government report that industries had laid off 1,300,000 employes between January and June.

The textile industries show some improvement, he said.

"I want to declare," said Mr. Green, "that in the three years of distress the American Federation of Labor has offered a program, which, if adopted, would have lessened the stress, and which, if adopted now, would soon show improvement."

Summarizing this program, he spoke of the protest against the wage-cutting policy of the industries, which he declared to be short-sighted in that it destroyed the power to buy goods. He touched upon the greater use of machinery which received an impetus after the war, and said he regretted it only because it threw men out of work and put all the savings in the pockets of the employers.

"It is not desirable that the factories should be dismantled of their machinery and the power disconnected and the workers put back on hand labor," he said, "for it is well to go forward, but the industries should divide the profits with labor.

Urges Five-Day Week.

"If with the use of this machinery we can produce enough in five days a week, then give us five days."

President Green was loudly applauded when he declared his belief in the early return of "good wholesome beer."

"A man must be blind and a woman twice blind," he said, "if they cannot see that public opinion is changing tremendously on this subject."

Although he believes that the country is moving inevitably toward the repeal of the Eighteenth Amendment,

Continued on Page Two.

ALL MARKETS SPURT IN NEW BUYING WAVE

Stocks Up 2 to 8 Points to Highs for Rally—Bonds Also Make Substantial Advance.

HEAVY TRADING IN STAPLES

Rail Shares Lead Upswing—Cut in Eastman Dividend Halts It Only Temporarily.

Accompanied by a substantial rise in bonds, the stock market was swept yesterday to the highest level of the month-old rally in the second heaviest trading of the year. A total of 4,430,000 shares changed hands and the net gains ran from 2 points or so in the more sedate stocks to 6 and 8 points in the more volatile ones. The transactions in bonds involved a total of more than $17,000,000, the heaviest since last January, and the advances, among the widest of the year, ranged from 1 to more than 10 points.

Fresh buying enthusiasm was released in all the markets. Cotton jumped $2 a bale at one time and closed almost a dollar a bale higher, while wheat gained 1½ cents a bushel. Other agricultural staples advanced in proportion and the trading was uncommonly heavy. The active demand for securities and commodities reflected the general revival of confidence resulting from the many-sided program of banking interests to hasten the economic recovery.

Gains on Russian Reports.

Yesterday's advance in stocks was widest in the usual group of leaders. J. I. Case, which has been moving up on reports that the United States Government would recognize Russia and that the Soviet Government was preparing to issue gold bonds to finance additional purchases in this country, showed a net gain of 8½ points, closing at the top. International Harvester, also a potential beneficiary of any expansion in Russian business, gained 4½ points. United States Steel common rose 2¾ points and the preferred 1½; Union Pacific 3⅛, Santa Fe 3¾, Western Union 2¼, Reading 3¼, New York Central 2¼, Norfolk & Western 7½, Consolidated Gas 2¾ and American Telephone 3⅞.

Among the stocks with a thin market the gains were much wider, in the average. For instance, International Silver preferred was up 7¾, National Lead preferred B 29¾, Gold Dust preferred 10¾, Adams Express preferred 9⅞, American Zinc preferred 6 and Colorado & Southern 11¼.

Eastman Dividend Is Cut.

There was a sharp break in Eastman Kodak following the announcement that the company had reduced the quarterly dividend rate from $1.25 quarterly to 75 cents. The final quotation, 53, represented a net loss of 7½ points. This break halted for a time the general upswing in the market, but the resumption of the advance brought the main body of stocks up sharply at the close.

The forward movement was led by the railway shares, which benefited from the conferences which began yesterday looking to a revision of the wage scale of organized employes and to the consideration of suggestions that funds be obtained from the Reconstruction Finance Corporation to recondition a great deal of the rolling stock. For a time there was a violent advance in railway shares. The final quotations, however, disclosed a net gain of only $1.61 in the average for twenty-five railway stocks, while twenty-five industrials showed an average appreciation of $3.16. The

Continued on Page Two.

PARTY LEADERS TELL PRESIDENT OF GAINS; HE POLISHES SPEECH

Aides From Over the Nation, Meeting for Notification, See "Sure Success."

BUT SNELL EXPECTS FIGHT

Declares "Real Battle" Will Carry New York State—Sanders Is Cheerful.

ADDRESS IS NEARLY DONE

Hoover Drastically Revises the First Proof of 6,000-Word Speech for Tonight.

Special to THE NEW YORK TIMES.

WASHINGTON, Aug. 10.—President Hoover hurriedly put the finishing touches today to the speech with which he will accept again the Republican nomination for President, while party leaders coming for the notification ceremonies gathered at the capital.

Mr. Hoover's work on the campaign keynote was interrupted time after time by visits of party aides from all sections, bearing tidings either of "sure success" or "changing sentiment" in his favor. These the President received with high pleasure; they added speed and vigor to his pen.

The notification tomorrow night at Constitution Hall, furnishing the occasion for the first campaign utterances of the President, will not only initiate the Republican quest for votes. Finance officials of the national committee are eager to start gathering funds for the party coffers, all open solicitation having been held in check until this occasion is over.

More than 4,000 persons are expected to attend the notification ceremony. The chief guests will be the notification committee of fifty-four, consisting of a member from each State and territory, and headed by Representative Snell of New York, chairman of the Chicago Convention.

Others in the 4,000 will include party officials and leaders from over the nation, members of the administration and the diplomatic corps, Republican Senators and Representatives and their wives, and as many supporters of the Republican cause as can be crowded into the hall.

The notification committee, party officials, Cabinet members, diplomats and Republican Congressmen—numbering in all about 500—will be guests of President and Mrs. Hoover tomorrow afternoon at a buffet luncheon and garden party on the south lawn of the White House.

Hoover Revises Speech Sharply.

The notification ceremony will bepin promptly at 9 P. M., when Everett Sanders, chairman of the national committee, will call the meeting to order. Bishop James E. Freeman of Washington will offer the invocation.

The national chairman will then present Representative Snell, who will formally notify Mr. Hoover of his nomination. The President will reply with his acceptance speech; it will be just four years and a day since he delivered his first acceptance address in the stadium of Leland Stanford University in California.

The benediction by the Rev. W. Coleman Nevils, president of Georgetown University, will conclude the ceremony.

Besides President Hoover those on the stage will be Representative Snell, Chairman Sanders, Senator Dickinson, temporary chairman of the national convention; members of the Cabinet and their wives, officers of the national committee and

Continued on Page Five.

WALKER HAILED IN ALBANY WITH BAND AND FIREWORKS; HAS 'NO FEAR OF REMOVAL'

'I Go With a Clear Conscience,' Asserts Walker, Off to Albany

Among the remarks contained in Mayor Walker's statement before he left for Albany yesterday were the following:

"I wish to say one thing before leaving for Albany—I go with a clear conscience."

"Not one of the complaints contains the statement of any person that I have ever been false to the trust which the people bestowed upon me at two elections by overwhelming majorities."

"Those who are trying to bear false witness against me cannot prevail against the people of the city of New York."

"This is not the case of the joint legislative committee against James J. Walker; it is the case of disappointed but ambitious politicians who are trying to defeat the expressed will of the voters by the use of ouster proceedings instead of ballots."

READY FOR HEARING TODAY

Is Confident of Outcome but Demands Right to a 'Trial' With Witnesses.

MET BY THRONGS AT TRAIN

Mayor Is Gay Under Plaudits Arranged by Politicians—Silent on Court Fight.

ROOSEVELT MAPS PROGRAM

Accusers of Executive Ready to Appear—Mrs. Walker Denounces Charges.

By LLOYD ACUFF.
Special to THE NEW YORK TIMES.

ALBANY, N. Y., Aug. 10.—Mayor James J. Walker arrived in this city tonight prepared to face the crisis of his official life at a removal hearing before Governor Roosevelt at 1:30 P. M. tomorrow.

To the somewhat unexpected blare of a brass band, supplemented by the boom of aerial bombs touched off in his honor, the Mayor reached the Albany station at 6:45 P. M. Through streets lined with persons called out by the express command of the Democratic overlords of Albany, he was driven to his headquarters at the Hotel Ten Eyck, where he at once began work on the defense he will present to the Governor.

Meanwhile, Governor Roosevelt and two of his counsel, Martin Conboy and M. Maldwin Fertig, worked quietly in the study of the Executive Mansion a few blocks away, preparing for their part in the proceedings.

The best information obtainable here was that they would speed the proceedings against Mr. Walker and, regardless of the outcome, do their utmost to deprive the hearing of any tinge of the atmosphere which marked the Mayor's arrival in the city.

Hearing Likely to Be Limited.

Arrangements for the hearing, regarded as one of the most serious chapters in current political history because of its possible effect upon Governor Roosevelt's Presidential aspirations, have been virtually completed. If the Governor carries out his plans, as they are understood at present, Mr. Walker will face Samuel Seabury, his principal accuser, tomorrow and probably on Friday, but will not have an opportunity to cross-examine.

Instead, the Governor will ask for details and explanations which he has noted as desirable in going through the documents in the case, and will limit the statements submitted by both sides to such items as he desires, in the opinion of those familiar with the contemplated procedure.

No prediction as to the outcome has been made in official circles. Friends of the Governor, however, have said he regarded the charges as grave.

The Mayor, on his part, indicated tonight that he approached the hearing in a mood that combined a determination to fight against removal, and confidence.

This spirit was indicated on the steps of the hotel, where the Mayor and Mrs. Walker stepped from their automobile after the parade from the railroad station. Crowded into the narrow street when the Mayor's automobile arrived were perhaps 500 persons, who cheered as Mr. Walker made his appearance.

He stepped from his car, mounted the steps where all could see him, and indicated by the gesture of a clenched fist, shaken at an imaginary adversary, that he expected to make the proceedings a fight to a finish. Then he clasped both hands together, in the manner of a prize-fighter shaking hands with himself in acknowledgment of the plaudits of a crowd, and disappeared into the hotel.

Mayor Hopes to Cross-Examine.

His hopes that he would be cleared at the hearing were expressed by Mr. Walker on the train from New York during an interview with the newspaper men who accompanied him to Albany.

"Do you look forward to the proceedings with confidence?" he was asked.

"Naturally," he replied, and then he reiterated his demand that he was entitled to a trial rather than a hearing.

"I am going prepared to meet any

Continued on Page Three.

WOOLLEN AND BYRD TO RAISE PARTY FUND

Democrats Name Indianapolis Banker and Ex-Governor to Head Finance Committee.

TOBIN IS LABOR CHAIRMAN

$1,500,000 Reported Probable Total of Campaign Chest—State Leaders Confident.

Three major appointments at Democratic national headquarters were announced yesterday. Evans Woollen, Indianapolis banker, was made chairman of the finance committee; former Governor Harry F. Byrd of Virginia chairman of the executive committee of the finance committee, and Daniel J. Tobin, former treasurer of the American Federation of Labor, was appointed chairman of the labor committee. The appointments were revealed by James A. Farley, national chairman.

The selection of Mr. Woollen and Mr. Byrd to have charge of the fund-raising part of the Democratic campaign came after repeated conferences among the leading supporters of Governor Roosevelt for the Presidency. By the selection of Mr. Woollen, who is president of the Fletcher Savings and Trust Company, the largest financial institution in Indiana, and who has been mentioned frequently during the last eight years as a possible candidate for President or Vice President, the nominee has obtained the support of a conservative banker, the naming of whom is expected to offset the belief in certain quarters that Governor Roosevelt is something of a radical.

By the selection of former Governor Byrd, who was a candidate for the Presidential nomination, the Democratic national organization has given recognition to the South and has taken a step to heal some of the wounds that may have been made at the Chicago convention.

Woollen Active in War.

During the World War, Mr. Woollen was in turn Federal Fuel Administrator of Indiana, a member of the

Continued on Page Four.

President Roosevelt's Widow to Fly Today To Washington for Hoover's Notification

Special to THE NEW YORK TIMES.

OYSTER BAY, L. I., Aug. 10.—Mrs. Edith Kermit Roosevelt, widow of President Theodore Roosevelt, will fly to Washington tomorrow morning to attend President Hoover's notification ceremonies as the guest of President and Mrs. Hoover. She had planned originally to make the trip on a train leaving at midnight tonight.

Mrs. Roosevelt's change in plans became known this afternoon at a luncheon she gave at the Sagamore Hill estate in celebration of the fifty-eighth birthday of President Hoover, at which she was hostess to more than 300 women. She felt, according to a member of the family, that after a strenuous day of entertaining and campaigning for the Republican nominee, it would be easier and more enjoyable to travel by plane.

Although she observed her seventy-first birthday anniversary last Saturday, Mrs. Roosevelt confined today's function to celebration of President Hoover's anniversary. She told her guests that "we want to take off our coats, run up our sleeves and elect our President," in a welcoming address that was said to be the longest political speech she had delivered in years.

Mrs. Ethel Roosevelt Derby, daughter of Mrs. Roosevelt and president of the Edith Kermit Roosevelt Republican Club of Oyster Bay, the organization represented at the affair, read a telegram which was sent to the President. The club, the dispatch said, "sends you their congratulations and best wishes in deep appreciation of your record of the last four years and confidence of your success in November, and pledge to you our loyal and enthusiastic support." Mrs. George A. Wyeth and Mrs. Arthur L. Livermore of the Women's National Republican Club discussed national issues.

Mrs. Roosevelt will be accompanied on the flight by her daughter and son-in-law, Dr. Richard Derby of Oyster Bay. They plan to motor to Roosevelt Field at about 10 o'clock.

Times Wide World Photo.

Clarence Crabbe, Who Set Record of 4:48.4 for Event.

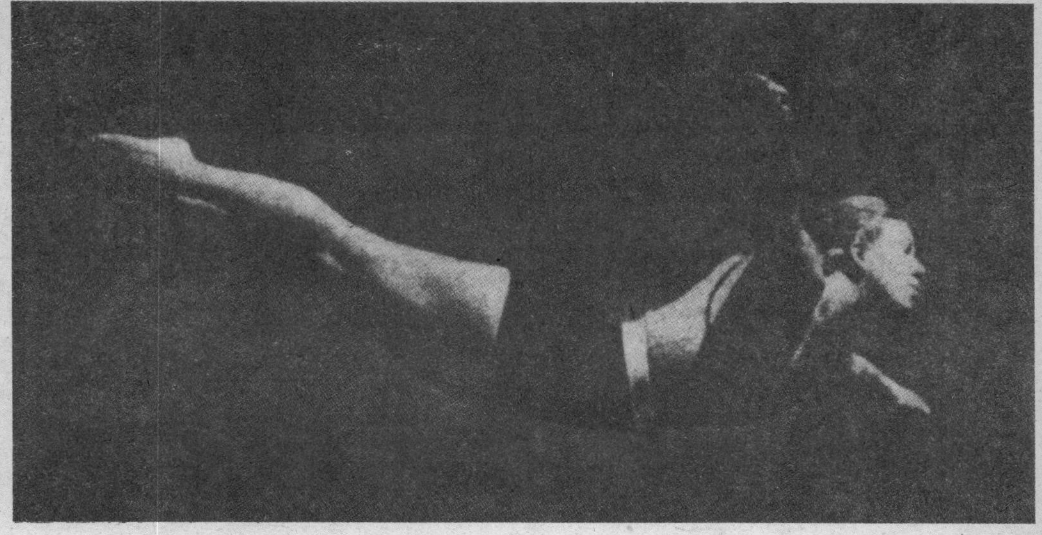

Times Wide World Photo.

Miss Georgia Coleman, Victor in the Three-Meter Springboard Contest with a Total of 87.52 Points.

CRABBE, U. S., FIRST IN OLYMPIC SWIM

By ARTHUR J. DALEY.

Continued from Page One.

his breath before he shouted to a friend in the stands, "Now for the 1,500 meters."

There has not been a race to date that was packed with the thrills that this one had. When Taris and Crabbe came down the homestretch, churning the blue of the water into frothy foam, the spectators grew delirious with excitement.

Rush to Side of Pool.

Swimmers from all countries, standing in the mouth of the tunnel that led to the dressing rooms, rushed to the side of the pool, and the ushers, who had been keeping them in check, forgot their duties as they, too, raced over to the finish line.

The Frenchman, ploughing through the water with stiff-armed strokes, could not withstand the terrific sprinting ability of the dark-haired American, who was stroking smoothly with more and more power. At the halfway mark Taris had led Crabbe by nearly two lengths, and yet the strapping Coast ace beat him to the end wall at the finish by a scant touch.

It was this gallant fight, apparently hopeless at the start, that appealed so much to the crowd. When Crabbe kept recouping more and more territory with every passage down the 50-meter pool, pandemonium broke loose in the stands. Johnny Weissmuller, an Olympic champion himself, could scarcely contain himself in his front-row seat. He leaped over the fence and rushed over for a clear view of the finish.

In his preliminary races Taris had led in the earlier stages and still had been overtaken. It was for such another moment as this that the spectators were waiting. The French ace, off from the end of the plunge with a perfect racing dive, snapped into the lead from the outset.

Taris Draws Away.

At fifty meters he had a one-yard margin on Crabbe, who was having trouble fighting off Oyokata, barely six inches behind. The others were well bunched. As excellent as were his rivals, Taris still was able to draw away a length ahead of the American at seventy-five meters and a length and a half at 100 meters.

Meanwhile Crabbe was shaking off the little Japanese in the lane alongside of him. The lone American entrant was in an inside lane and Taris was over in the outside lane at the far side of the pool. The Frenchman kept moving at his astonishingly fast clip. He had increased his margin to a little more than two lengths at 150 yards. And then Crabbe started to climb up.

The Californian applied more and more power to his arm motions without sacrificing his form. Strange as it seems, Oyokata, the little Japanese automaton, was trying too hard and his easy passage through the water was gone.

Oyokata immediately started to fall back and the race was a clean-cut issue between Crabbe and Taris. These two wheeled at the end of 200 meters an even two lengths apart. But the American's turn was a much better one.

It helped him cut generously into Taris's advantage. At 250 meters the difference between the two was only a length and a half. At 300 meters it was just a length. The cheers of the crowd of 10,000 crew deafening in its proportions. The local boy was making good.

There were just two trips of the course left. Crabbe came up faster until there was no longer any open water between them. Another perfect turn by Crabbe, a less perfect wheel by the tiring Frenchman, and there was just a yard separating them in the final spurt down the tank.

Arms threshing with rhythmic beat, Crabbe came on. Halfway down the pool they were almost even, and then Crabbe gave all he had. His black cap cut through the water like the bow of a fast moving ship and his arms flailed away like a propeller. Buster Crabbe was getting closer and closer to an Olympic championship.

The fast-finishing Japanese were so far to the rear that their whereabouts no longer mattered. This was strictly a two-man battle. But the Parisian had already shot his bolt. He had given too much of his reserve strength in constructing that early lead. In sharp contrast to this, Crabbe had a great deal left.

Three yards away from the dull white concrete wall the two were absolutely abreast. Judges stood crouching over the finish line, waiting eagerly for the first hand to touch. It was Crabbe's. A powerful push with his brawny right arm and his left hand stopped against the wall, a scant tenth of a second before Taris's fingers landed.

Miss Coleman won the diving because she was far more acrobatic and far more skillful in the voluntary dives than any of her rivals. Miss Fauntz set the pace in the compulsory flips into the water. After the second of these the University of Illinois co-ed had a slight margin over her blonde-haired California adversary, 24.32 points to 24.28. Miss Rawls was not far behind with a compilation of 23.64.

Clings to Her Advantage.

The slender mid-Westerner held on grimly to her advantage right up to the fifth dive. Then she executed only a fair running full twist. Miss Coleman was doing beautifully off the board, and in three flights into space she virtually clinched the title.

Miss Rawls came up with some fancy contortions for second place, Miss Coleman winning, with 87.52 points, and the Florida girl compiling 82.56 for runner-up honors. Miss Fauntz was third, with 82.12; Miss Olga Jordan of Germany, fourth, with 77.60; Miss Doris Ogilvie of Canada, fifth, with 70.60, and Miss Magdalene Epply of Austria, sixth, with 63.70.

In an exhibition water polo game the combined German and Hungarian reserves defeated the American reserves, 4 to 3.

JUPITER, U. S., TAKES STAR CLASS TITLE

Gray Sails Craft to Victory, Giving America Its Second Olympic Yachting Crown.

HOLLAND STILL IN LEAD

Shows Way With 77 Points After Three More Races in Monotype Division.

PROTEST MADE BY SWEDEN

Lodges Claim of Foul Against French Boat, First in Day's Contest for Stars.

By The Associated Press.

SAN PEDRO, Cal., Aug. 10.—The United States gave a new twist to Olympic sailboat history today, carrying off major honors in the yachting competition of the international games.

Never before has this country won a championship with its boats. Now it has two of the four titles at stake. Sweden has one of the other two but cannot win the last—so the Yankees take the heavy end of the honors.

The sensational sailor of Lake Pontchartrain, Louisiana, Gilbert Gray, brought the second title to the United States by placing third today in a Star boat race with his sloop Jupiter. This gave him enough points to win, although the seventh and last race is still to be sailed. Owen Churchill's Angelita already had won the eight-meter title, and Tore Holm took six-meters honors yesterday for Sweden with Bissbi.

Chance to Increase Lead.

Gunnar Asther of Sweden charged a foul against the first place finisher, Jean Herbulot of France, in today's Star class race, and if this is allowed Colin Ratsey of England, who finished second, will take first place and Gray, second, increasing the American's winning lead.

After three races today in the monotype division, Jan Maas still held first place for Holland, having 77 points. Italy was second with 69, Spain third with 68, Canada fourth with 58 and Great Britain fifth with 56. The final two races, tenth and eleventh, will be sailed tomorrow.

Four races were to have been sailed today, but the monotype skippers opposed the plan and not one was on the line when the starting gun for the fourth race was fired.

Stage Spectacular Race.

They also refused to sail more than two miles in the third test, splitting this event in half. It turned out to be the most spectacular race of the day, however. The skippers were beset by a fifteen-mile blow. With sails bowled over almost to the water, it seemed, the Canadian entry won in the fast time of 31 minutes 38 seconds.

Maas finished second only 20 seconds later. Germany was less than a minute astern and in 16 seconds Austria came in fourth.

The judges had not ruled on Asther's protest. He charged that the Tramontane, rounding the marker to the windward of the Swedish star, illegally tacked when it had not enough headway to cross the Swedish sloop's bow, causing the latter to bump the Tramontane.

Although already victorious in the series, Holm sailed Bissbi to his sixth straight victory today over the six-meter Gallant, sailed by Ted Conant of the United States.

HINES OF U. S. GAINS IN OLYMPIC BOXING

San Pedro Youth Receives the Decision in Featherweight Battle With Mexican.

MILER, DETROIT, DEFEATED

Eliminated by Murphy of Ireland—Bor, American Lightweight Champion, Scores.

By The Associated Press.

LOS ANGELES, Aug. 10.—Establishing some kind of a record by not listing a knockout in twenty-seven battles over the two day and night period so far, the world's leading boxers waded through another set of preliminaries in their drive today for Olympic championships.

While the bouts have been fast and furious, the contestants have been so evenly matched that only a few knockdowns have been registered.

The net result of today's program saw eight candidates eliminated in the chase for Olympic laurels, while the hopes of the United States and Germany for team titles received setbacks when each nation listed a loser in the skirmishes.

First American Reversal.

The first American reversal came in the light-heavyweight class when John Miler of Detroit lost a close decision to James J. Murphy of Ireland. It was a preliminary bout. The boys mauled each other most of the time, with the judges evidently selecting Murphy on the strenght of a few stiff punches landed during the moments the boys were not locking heads.

Johnny Hines, San Pedro featherweight, had previously kept the United States' slate clean with a decision over Miguel Araico of Mexico. It was one of the best preliminaries of the program, with the boys swinging freely and at all times. Hines was more aggressive, although he was handicapped by a cut over his eye.

The Italian team received its first setback in tonight's opener when Horace Gwynne, swift-punching Canadian bantamweight, scored a well-earned decision over Vito Melis. It was a hard-fouhgt contest, with Gwynne scoring effectively with a neat left hook. In the second round Melis was staggered with a right to the chin. It was a quarter-final bout. Gwynne is Canada's hope in the 118-pound division.

The first casualty of the tournament came to light with the announcement that Carlos Pereyra of Argentina was forced to default in the last quarter final of the bantamweight division to Joe Lang of San Francisco, because of cuts over his eyes suffered in a bout last night with Patrick Hughes of Ireland.

America's amateur lightweight champion, Nat Bor of Fall River, Mass., put on a fine exhibition of boxing to win the decision from Hyman Mizler of Great Britain in a quarter final bout. The British entrant was unable to match the American's skill.

Summaries of the Olympic Games

By The Associated Press.

SWIMMING.

100-METER BACK-STROKE.

Trials.

(First two in each heat and fastest third qualify for semi-finals.)

First Heat—Won by Masoji Kiyokawa, Japan; second, Robert Kerber, United States; third, Robert Halloran, Canada; fourth, Eskil Lundahl, Sweden. Time—1:08.9 (Scratched, Roberto Peper, Argentina.)

Second Heat—Won by Danny Zehr, United States; second, Ernest Kuppers, Germany; third, Kentaro Kawatsu, Japan; fourth, William Francis, Great Britain; fifth, Benevenuto Nunes, Brazil. Time—1:09.9.

Third Heat—Won by Toshio Ire, Japan; second, Munroe Bourne, Canada; third, Jorge Paula, Brazil. Time—1:11.3 (Marcel Noual, France, disqualified for making illegal turn.

Fourth Heat—Won by William Karlsen, Norway; second, Gordon Chalmers, United States; third, Dennis Walker, Canada. Time—1:13.7. (Nilo Medieros, Brazil, scratched.)

Fastest third, Kentaro Kawatsu, Japan.

SPRINGBOARD DIVING—WOMEN.

Final.

Won by Georgia Coleman, United States, 87.52 points; second, Katherine Rawls, United States, 82.56; third, Jane Fauntz, United States, 82.12; fourth, Olga Jordan, Germany, 77.60; fifth, Doris Ogilvie, Canada, 70.60; sixth, Magdalene Epply, Austria, 63.70; seventh, Etsuko Kamakura, Japan, 60.78; eighth, Ingrid Larsen, Denmark, 57.26.

400-METER FREE STYLE.

Final.

Won by Clarence Crabbe, United States; second, Jean Taris, France; third, Tsutomu Oyokata, Japan; fourth, Takashi Yokoyama, Japan; fifth, Noboru Sugimoto, Japan; sixth, Andrew Charlton, Australia. Time—4:48.4. (New Olympic record; old Olympic mark, 4:51.4, held by Yokoyama.)

BOXING.

118-POUND CLASS.

First Preliminaries.

Joe Lang, United States, defeated Sabino Tirado, Mexico.

Carlos Pereyra, Argentina, defeated Patrick Hughes, Ireland.

Quarter Finals.

Horace Gwynne, Canada, defeated Vito Melis, Italy.

Jose Villaneuva, Philippines, defeated Akira Nakao, Japan.

Hans Ziglarski, Germany, defeated Paul Nicolas, France.

Joe Lang, United States, won from Carlos Pereyra, Argentina, by default. (Pereyra suffered severe cuts over eye in bout with Patrick Hughes, Ireland, Tuesday night, and injuries failed to heal sufficiently.)

126-POUND CLASS.

First Preliminaries.

Carl Carlsson, Sweden, defeated Katsuo Kameoka, Japan

Johnny Hines, United States, defeated Miguel Araico, Mexico.

135-POUND CLASS.

First Preliminaries.

Gaston Mayor, France, defeated Manuel Ponce, Mexico.

Frank Genovez, Canada, defeated Eduardo Vargas, Argentina.

Mario Bianchini, Italy, defeated Robert Purdie, New Zealand.

Lawrence Stevens, South Africa, defeated Jose Padilla, Philippines.

Franz Kartz, Germany, defeated Otsu Ko, Japan.

Quarter-Finals.

Nat Bor, United States, defeated Hyman Mizler, Great Britain.

Thure Ahlqvist, Sweden, defeated Gaston Mayor, France.

BOXING.

135-POUND CLASS.

Quarter-Finals.

Mario Bianchini, Italy, defeated Frank Genovese, Canada.

Lawrence Stevens, South Africa, defeated Franz Kartz, Germany.

147-POUND CLASS.

First Preliminaries.

Lucian Laplace, France, defeated Carlos Padilla, Philippines.

Robert Barton, South Africa, defeated John Flood, Ireland.

Eddie Flynn, United States, defeated Luis Sardella, Argentina.

David McCleave, Great Britain, won on foul from Alberto Romero, Mexico, third round.

160-POUND CLASS.

First Preliminaries.

Roger Michelot, France, defeated Louis Lavoie, Canada.

Hans Bernlohr, Germany, defeated Albert Lowe, New Zealand.

175-POUND CLASS.

First Preliminaries.

Gino Rossi, Italy, defeated Nikolaos Mastoridis, Greece.

James J. Murphy, Ireland, defeated John Miler, United States.

Peter Jorgensen, Denmark, defeated Rafael Lang, Argentina.

Davis Carstens, South Africa, defeated Hans Berger, Germany.

HEAVYWEIGHT CLASS.

First Preliminaries.

George Maughan, Canada, defeated Heinz Kohlhaas, Germany.

Santiago Lovell, Argentina, defeated Gunnar Barlund, Finland.

ROWING.

EIGHT-OARED CREWS.

Trials.

First Heat—Won by Italy (Cioni, Garzelli, Del Bimbo, Vestrini, Barsotti, Bracci, Balleri, Barbiere, stroke; Milani, coxswain), 6:28 1-5; second, Great Britain (Haigh-Thomas Payne, Askwith, Sambell, Sergel, Rickett, McCowen, Luxton, stroke; Ranking, coxswain), 6:34 2-5; third, Japan (Hara, Enomoto, Fujiwara, Tanaka, Matsuura, Nishidono, Tamaka, Ikeda, stroke; Sano, coxswain), 6:43 2-5; fourth, Brazil (Mo, Pichler, De Abreu, Rebello, Prevenzano, Pereira, Faria, Carvalho, stroke; de Cunha, coxswain), 6:52 1-5.

Second Heat—Won by United States (Hall, Tower, Chandler, Jastram, Dunlap, Gregg, Blair, Salisbury, stroke; Graham, coxswain), 6:29; second, Canada (Taylor, Boal, Thoburn, Liddell, Fry, Stanyer, Harris, Eastwood, stroke; MacDonald, coxswain), 6:33 1-5; third, Germany (Maier, Flinsch, Von Dusterlho, Heidland, Bender, Hullinghoff, Gaber, Aletter, stroke; Bauer, coxswain), 6:36 4-5; fourth, New Zealand (Solomon, Saunders, Thompson, Jackson, MacDonald, Stiles, Sandos, Cooke, stroke; Gullery, coxswain), 6:38 1-5.

FOUR-OARED CREWS WITHOUT COXSWAIN.

Trials.

First Heat—Won by Great Britain (George, Beresford, Edwards and Babcock, stroke), 7:13 1-5; second, United States (Johnson, Pierie, Mattson and McCosker, stroke), 7:19 2-5; third, Germany (Maier, Flinsch, Gaber and Aletter, stroke), 7:37 4-5.

Second Heat—Won by Italy (Ghiardello, E'Este, Cossu and Provenzani, stroke), 7:06 4-5; second, Canada (Courtney, Herman, Gammon and Pelham, stroke), 7:12.

DOUBLE SCULLS.

Trials.

First Heat—Won by Canada (Demille and Pratt), 7:25; second, Italy (Paroli and Moretti), 7:33; third, Brazil (Goncalves and Tomassini), 7:38 4-5.

Second Heat—Won by United States (Gilmore and Myers), 7:14 3-5; second, Germany (Boetzelen and Buhtz), 7:21 2-5.

"All the News That's Fit to Print."

The New York Times.

LATE CITY EDITION

WEATHER—Fair and much colder today; probably snow tomorrow.
Temperatures yesterday—Max., [illegible]; min., [illegible]

Copyright, 1934, by The New York Times Company.

VOL. LXXXIII....No. 27,737. Entered as Second-Class Matter, Postoffice, New York, N. Y. NEW YORK, TUESDAY, JANUARY 2, 1934. MP TWO CENTS In New York City | THREE CENTS Within 200 Miles | FOUR CENTS Elsewhere Except in 7th and 8th Postal Zones

LAGUARDIA MOVES TO CLEAN UP CITY; STARTS HUNT FOR GRAFT IN BUREAUS; TAMMANY ORGANIZES THE ALDERMEN

COLUMBIA ELEVEN UPSETS STANFORD IN ROSE BOWL, 7-0

40,000 at Pasadena See Lion Team Register Surprising Victory in Rain.

LONE SCORE BY BARABAS

He Races 17 Yards in Second Period on Hidden-Ball Ruse That Baffles Opponents.

MONTGOMERY ALSO SHINES

New Yorkers Rise to Mighty Defensive Heights, Halting Six Cardinal Threats.

Special to THE NEW YORK TIMES.

PASADENA, Calif., Jan. 1.—Those roaring Columbia Lions were sea Lions today and they splashed their way to a surprising and clear-cut victory over the Stanford football team, 7—0, in the annual Tournament of Roses classic.

Thus a season marked by many reverses was climaxed by probably the greatest upset of them all.

Surging through a drizzling, disheartening rain to a one-touchdown lead in the second period, the Lions four times thrust back the furious onslaught of Grayson, Hamilton, Van Dellen and the rest of Stanford's super-backs in a last-half struggle.

Sixteen first downs for Stanford; six for Columbia. Two hundred and seventy-two yards gained for Stanford; 114 yards for Columbia. Six scoring chances for the Cardinals; three for the Lions. But that scoreboard read: Columbia 7, Stanford 0, at the finish.

The bad weather of the last few days cut the attendance considerably. About 40,000 hardy fans showed up for the game. Most of them sat huddled under umbrellas throughout the first half. Former President Herbert Hoover, an alumnus of Stanford, was an interested spectator.

Lions Display Gameness.

No gamer, more determined bunch of football players ever appeared in the Rose Bowl than this furious crew Coach Lou Little loosed on the unsuspecting Indians. Twice turned back from the Cardinal goal line in the first period, they kept on plugging until Al Barabas, left halfback, raced across the line for a touchdown.

Then the visitors clung to this precious margin in the face of the same powerful attack that a scant two months ago had tripped the mighty Trojans of the University of Southern California. The Lions succeeded where the Trojans failed. They stopped Stanford.

Six different times during the contest—twice in the first half and four times in the second—the mighty Red team crashed and drove its way to the shadow of the Columbia goal, and six times Columbia staved off those threats.

Fumbles and penalties contributed to stopping the Indian drives, but the Easterners always were on hand to take advantage of every break offered them.

So magnificent were these defensive stands of the Lions that they overshadowed the lone touchdown of the day, which Barabas scored on a 17-yard dash that still has the California fans baffled—not to mention Stanford.

Starts From Blocked Kick.

It all started from a blocked kick. Alustiza got a bad pass from centre, was hurried, and a trio of Columbians sifted through to block the kick. It was only third down, so when young Bob Reynolds, Stanford tackle, fell on the ball, it was still in Indian possession.

Alustiza, of course, kicked again, and Montgomery returned five yards to the Indian's 45-yard line. Stanford was penalized five yards on the next play, and then Montgomery hurled a pass to Tony Matal.

The end made a leaping catch, came down sliding, and skidded along three more yards before he was stopped, eventually coming to rest on the 17-yard stripe.

On his first try Barabas fumbled, but he recovered for a half-yard loss. On the next effort Montgomery took the ball from centre, wheeled in a deceptive reverse and handed it to Barabas.

Thereupon hostilities seemed to halt for an instant. Every one stood around and looked at every one else. A Columbia back sifted through between right tackle and right end, drawing the secondary away. So Barabas, using the hidden-ball ruse, took off around Stanford's right end. There were no Stanford men in the way and Barabas loped the 17 yards to the goal line.

Amid tremendous jubilation on the part of the Columbia players, Wilder took aim at the uprights

Continued on Page Twenty.

Chain-Gang 'Fugitive' Again in Toils of Law

Special to THE NEW YORK TIMES.

EAST ORANGE, N. J., Jan. 1.—Robert Elliott Burns, whose experiences in a Georgia chain gang induced him to write a book, later dramatized for the films, again came within the clutches of the law today when he was arrested, charged with disorderly conduct, improper registration and no driver's license.

He complained that Patrolman Alois Spaeth, who arrested him, had served him with fifteen summonses during the last year for alleged infractions of the traffic law.

Burns, who operates a toy shop here at 34 Main Street, under the name of R. M. Crane, will have a hearing Thursday before Police Recorder George Grimm Jr.

38 DIE IN FLOODS NEAR LOS ANGELES

Hundreds Are Hurt as Waters From Downpour Rush Off the Denuded Hills.

RAIN UP TO 18½ INCHES

Heaviest on Record—Homes Are Wrecked, Cars Stalled, Streets Turned to Rivers.

Special to THE NEW YORK TIMES.

LOS ANGELES, Jan. 1.—Crushing walls of water raced down out of the Sierra Nevada foothills last night and today as the result of the heaviest rainfall in years and devastated large areas throughout Los Angeles County.

Deaths were estimated from thirty-eight upward, including seven in auto mishaps attributed to the flood, and twenty-seven were listed as missing. They were believed drowned.

Hundreds were injured, and armies of workers combed flood-ravaged areas for other bodies.

Scores of Homes Ruined.

Scores of homes in the higher foothill areas were demolished or badly damaged as the waters hurtled onward to the lower beach areas to spread out and inundate 1,500 homes in the Venice and Long Beach sections.

Los Angeles streets became rivers and the intersection of Seventh and Broadway was converted into a lake.

Thousands of automobiles were strewn along the streets early today, abandoned by their occupants during the night.

The county flood control office reported thirty-nine bridges washed out or closed because of damage.

Train and bus service in and out of Los Angeles was being maintained, but several hours behind schedule. The ridge route into the San Joaquin Valley was closed. Airline passengers were grounded at outlying points and brought in by buses.

A list of dead and missing was compiled tonight by Coroner Frank Nance of Los Angeles County as follows:

The Dead.

PLUMB, ELLWOOD, 55, Long Beach.
GERAGHTY, FRANK, 23, North Hollywood.
GHOSLIN, MARYLIN, 4, Glendale.
MOORE, Mr. and Mrs. J. E., and their daughter, MARTHA, 11, Glendale.
HUBBARD, SHERMAN, and his sister, TOOTS, 18, San Gabriel.
CARTER, Mrs. DOROTHY, 40, Monterey Park.
HERRERA, CHESTER, 12, Los Angeles.

Continued on Page Eleven.

WOODIN QUITS POST; MORGENTHAU MADE HEAD OF TREASURY

Resignation, Sent on Dec. 13 From Arizona, Is Accepted With Regret by President.

NEW SECRETARY IS SWORN

Ceremony in President's Study—No Policy Change Looms, but Bailie Plans to Leave.

Special to THE NEW YORK TIMES.

WASHINGTON, Jan. 1.—Secretary Woodin has resigned from the Cabinet and Henry Morgenthau Jr., Acting Secretary, was sworn in today as head of the Treasury.

The only element of surprise in this first formal change in the Cabinet was that the event had finally taken place.

For months it had been reported that Mr. Woodin would leave the Cabinet because of ill health, and it had long been surmised that Mr. Morgenthau would succeed to his post.

Mr. Woodin's resignation was tendered Dec. 13 on the grounds of continued illness and accepted Dec. 20, to be effective last night.

Without previous intimation of this, however, Mr. Morgenthau was sworn in as Secretary in President Roosevelt's presence this morning.

The White House, in announcing the event, made public the correspondence revealing the Woodin resignation. It was couched in affectionate language similar to that passing between Mr. Woodin and President Roosevelt when the Secretary first tendered his resignation. At that time, some weeks ago, he was persuaded to take an indefinite leave of absence instead.

To Make No Change in Policy.

Mr. Morgenthau, whose monetary program has been both condemned and praised, said this afternoon that there would be no change in Treasury policies.

He made known also that Earle Bailie of New York, now his special assistant, who came here from J. W. Seligman & Co., would not be his Under-Secretary. He said that Mr. Bailie had arranged to serve in Washington only a short time, possibly not more than two months longer.

The word that Mr. Bailie's name would not be offered for Under-Secretary will undoubtedly be acceptable to Senators Johnson and Couzens, who had planned to oppose his confirmation on grounds of past connection with now defaulted South American securities floated in this country.

Neither President Roosevelt nor he had yet decided upon a new Under-Secretary, Mr. Morgenthau asserted, and it was also said at the White House that no consideration had been given to the appointment.

MR. WOODIN'S LETTER.

Mr. Woodin's letter of resignation written in the Southwest, where he has gone for his health, read as follows:

Tucson, Ariz.,
Dec. 13, 1933.

Dear Governor,

It is with great regret that I am compelled to tender you my resignation as Secretary of the Treasury, to take effect at your convenience any time before Jan. 1.

The state of my health will not permit me to remain in this position.

I cannot express what a wrench it is to me to leave your official family and you must know how

Continued on Page Nine.

Roosevelt Spends Day Planning for Congress

By The Associated Press.

WASHINGTON, Jan. 1.—President Roosevelt's New Year's Day was mostly one of work—writing his budget message to Congress and planning for the session that opens Wednesday.

It was after 9 this morning when the Chief Executive arose, and he lost no time in becoming absorbed in his work. It was late this afternoon before he had much free time to spend with his family and guests.

During the morning the President, seated in the Oval Room of the White House, witnessed the swearing in of Henry Morgenthau Jr., the new Secretary of the Treasury. Then he went directly to work on his budget message.

PRESIDENT MAPS HIS BUDGET PLANS

Emergency Appropriations Are Discussed With Senate and House Leaders.

CONFEREES' LIPS SEALED

Robinson Pledges Support to the Executive—Sees 'Simple Course' on Money.

Special to THE NEW YORK TIMES.

WASHINGTON, Jan. 1.—With the Democratic Congressional leaders grouped around him at the White House, President Roosevelt tonight held a final conference on the budget and appropriations before the convening of Congress Wednesday.

The meeting lasted from 8:45 P. M. until 11:25 P. M., but the participants afterward maintained silence as to what transpired. Representative Byrns, majority leader of the House, stated, however, that a "short session" still is in prospect and added, in response to many inquiries, that the monetary question was not discussed.

Those who attended the conference, in addition to Mr. Byrns, were Vice President Garner, Speaker Rainey, Senator Robinson of Arkansas, majority leader of the Senate; Senator Glass and Representative Buchanan, chairmen of the Appropriations Committees; Senator Harrison, chairman of the Senate Finance Committee, and Representative Doughton, chairman of the Ways and Means Committee.

Emergency Expenditures a Topic.

The conference was assumed in informed quarters to be chiefly upon the relationship between the budget and the extraordinary expenditures occasioned by the government's relief and recovery activities, which are expected in some quarters to indicate actual expenditures in the next fiscal year of as much as $6,000,000,000.

When the budget is presented to Congress, probably on Thursday, by the President, it is expected that it will show an anticipated revenue of about $3,400,000,000 for the fiscal year 1935, or some $800,000,000 surplus over the regular departmental appropriations, which are expected to be $2,600,000,000.

Congress may still face the necessity, however, of appropriating in excess of $2,000,000,000 to continue the public works and civil works programs, as well as of extending the authority of the Reconstruction Finance Corporation to expand its activities.

With this possibility in sight, it was thought that tonight's conference revolved at least in part around the question of when and how the relief and recovery appropriations are to be approached, whether in the immediate budget message or at a later date in the session. Whatever decisions may have been arrived at tonight, they apparently bore the approval of the leaders who attended the conference, for there was no evidence either by word or action indicating that the men who apparently control the majorities of the House and Senate disagreed with anything the President proposed.

A few hours before the White House conference the Senate Steering Committee, meeting at the Senate Office Building, had decided upon the desirability of limiting the session to essential legislation, including monetary and banking reforms, stock-exchange regulation and amendment of the Securities

Continued on Page Ten.

DEUTSCH CAUSES CLASH

Aldermanic Head Tells Tammany Men to Stop Being 'Errand Boys.'

HIS REMARKS RESENTED

Sullivan, Vice Chairman, Says It Is Business of Majority to Advance a Program.

MAYOR HURLS CHALLENGE

'I Am Majority,' He Replies—Sets Precedent by Address to the Board.

Battle lines were drawn yesterday between the Republican-Fusion members of the Board of Aldermen and the Tammany majority when they met together for the first time at noon in City Hall.

Bernard S. Deutsch, Fusion president of the board, aroused the ire of the Tammany members by referring to them as "an assemblage of district errand boys." He made the characterization in an appeal to them to revitalize the board so as to obtain popular approval of its functions. He asked them to cooperate with the Fusionists in putting through the constructive reforms of the new administration.

Alderman Timothy J. Sullivan of Manhattan, elected vice chairman of the board at yesterday's meeting over Alderman Joseph Clark Baldwin 3d, set forth Tammany's attitude in one succinct sentence.

"It is the business of the majority to advance a constructive program, and of the minority to criticize," he said. He added the hope that the criticism would continue to be constructive rather than personal.

Mayor Addresses Aldermen.

The Mayor established a precedent by appearing before the Board of Aldermen to address its members. He said he would continue to address them from time to time, in addition to submitting the customary messages. He pleaded with the Tammany majority to cooperate in putting through his economies and administrative reforms.

Informed after his speech that Mr. Sullivan had said, "The majority will institute the reforms," the Mayor said:

"That all depends on who the majority is. I'm the majority in this administration."

The Mayor mentioned the city's financial plight and begged the Aldermen to help restore the municipal credit.

"You know the city's financial condition makes it necessary to balance the budget," he said. "I hope for your cooperation in doing that, but whether I have it or not the budget must be balanced. I'm asking the Legislature to give me power to merge city departments and

Continued on Page Three.

Mayor Takes Athenian Oath of Fealty As Expressing 'Duty and Steadfastness'

The "oath of the young men of Athens" was repeated yesterday by Mayor LaGuardia at the close of his address from the NBC studios. The Mayor said that he could find nothing "more expressive of our duty, our determination and our steadfastness."

The oath follows:

"We will never bring disgrace to this, our city, by any act of dishonesty or cowardice nor ever desert our suffering comrades in the ranks. We will fight for our ideals and sacred things of the city, both alone and with many. We will revere and obey the city's laws and do our best to incite a like respect in those above us who are prone to annul them and set them at naught. We will strive unceasingly to quicken the public sense of civic duty. Thus in all these ways we will transmit this city not only not less but far greater and more beautiful than it was transmitted to us."

The Mayor also pledged his allegiance to President Roosevelt in the following words:

"To the President of the United States, in these times of stress and trouble, I publicly pledge my complete, whole-hearted and individual loyalty and support and that of my administration. To the Governor of New York State I pledge that same loyalty and support."

BLANSHARD TO USE SEABURY'S TACTICS

Accounts Bureau to Be Recast Along Lines Followed in Legislative Inquiry.

TAMMANY TO BE TARGET

Investigation of News-Stand Graft Likely to Be Taken From Levine at Once.

Complete reorganization of the office of the Commissioner of Accounts under its new head, Paul Blanshard, is scheduled to be announced this week, it became known yesterday. Both in purpose and in form the new set-up of the department will resemble the investigating organization maintained by Samuel Seabury for the legislative inquiry into the city government.

In its new form the office is to be purely an investigating body, handling little of the routine work it has done in the past.

Private Hearings Planned.

The procedure to be followed, it is understood, will be for private hearings to be held, with witnesses questioned, and the utmost secrecy preserved. When a case has been prepared, open hearings, with Mr. Blanshard presiding, will follow. It was regarded as likely that in several cases the announcement of the call for the open hearings will be the first intimation that the subject matter of the hearing was being investigated.

It has been an open secret since the appointment of Mr. Blanshard, and the designation of Irving Ben Cooper as counsel to the Commissioner, that the conduct of city departments under Tammany, not covered fully in the city-wide investigation because of the lack of time, will be taken up where the indications warrant the action.

Reorganization of the department

Continued on Page Three.

RID CITY OF GANGS, IS ORDER TO POLICE

LaGuardia Warns Officers No Crook or Racketeer Can Be Tolerated Here Now.

PUTS END TO 'PROTECTION'

Says Those Who Shirk in War on Crime Must 'Get Out'—Abolishes 'Deadlines.'

A police department utterly free of political domination will war upon gangs of criminals that have had official protection, Mayor LaGuardia told 200 ranking officers at Police Headquarters yesterday.

"Drive out the racketeers or get out yourselves," summarizes the warning he gave to the heads of the department after he had sworn in Major Gen. John F. O'Ryan as the new commissioner in the gymnasium where the line-ups are conducted.

His speech, in clipped, crisp sentences, had the ring of sincerity. It was blunt and uncompromising. The men heard it in grim silence.

Says Interference Is Ended.

"There was a time," the Mayor said, "when the Police Department could make or break an administration. That is no longer true. I picked General O'Ryan because I have confidence in him. Remember that.

"There will be no interference in the regular performance of police duty anywhere, any place, any time—and I can't make that too clear.

"This may sound strange to some of you older men, but this time it is going to be true. You have at least four years now in which to do your duty. If you believe that there is any power that can save you if you fail, speak up now—or get out."

Every word was incisive.

"If I did not make myself clear before when I said there will be no interference, I will now. I mean interference by politicians. That statement I shall repeat several times today."

Abolishes Old "Deadlines."

The department has clung to traditional "deadlines" for criminals that were set up in the latter part of the last century by Chief Inspector Byrnes. On that subject the Mayor said:

"I have been told that Fulton Street is considered the deadline for crooks. That deadline is now removed. It is replaced by the Hudson River on the west, the Atlantic Ocean on the south, the Westchester County line on the north and the Nassau County boundary line on the east.

"The crooks and the racketeers must be kept out. That is your job. There are two kinds of crime—the ordinary kind and organized crime. The first you have handled well in the past. The second has caused you much trouble. It thrives only because the men at the head of it enjoy protection. That is the only reason it lives.

"We are removing that protection.

"Now see that that kind of crime is also ably handled. If not—get out!"

The Mayor paused to let the warning sink in.

"If at any time a magistrate will not hold a prisoner," he resumed, "you take your man and your witnesses to headquarters, put all

Continued on Page Two.

MAYOR SWEARS IN AIDES

Tells Each to Remove 'Every One' if Needed to Get Efficiency.

PLEDGES THEM FREE HAND

Politicians No Longer Will Interfere With Prisons or Relief, He Says.

FIRST DAY IS STRENUOUS

New Executive Leaves Home at 8:28 A. M., Does Not Quit City Hall Till 6:30.

With brisk and quiet efficiency F. H. LaGuardia took over the control of city government yesterday and started at once on the housecleaning through which he hopes to establish a financially sound and well-managed community.

Putting aside the traditional ceremony and ostentation of inaugurations, the new Mayor struck a business-like note on his first day in office. A new and faster tempo in the administration of the city appeared with him, in marked contrast to the comfortable ease characteristic of Tammany's methods.

"Clean house and clean it thoroughly," was the keynote of the day. Before darkness fell the Mayor had told all his commissioners how he wanted them to handle the broom.

The Mayor's whirlwind day began when he emerged from his home at 1,274 Fifth Avenue at 8:28 yesterday morning. He wore his customary wide-brimmed black fedora, a well used gray overcoat and a blue serge suit that clung to his stocky figure with the affection of years of companionship.

Cabinet Gets Orders.

He drove directly to Police Headquarters, arriving there on schedule to swear in Major Gen. John F. O'Ryan as Police Commissioner.

In an incisive talk to the higher officers of the department the new Mayor said rackets and racketeers were doomed in this city. Protection for racketeers would be driven out, Mr. LaGuardia promised.

Ten minutes after he finished at Police Headquarters the Mayor was swearing in others of his cabinet in the Municipal Building. Each in turn was told that the new administration would expect efficiency and economy, and a complete absence of political partisanship in operating the government.

After swearing in Paul Blanshard as Commissioner of Accounts, the Mayor said: "I want you to see me as soon as I'm through here. I have a job for you."

It developed that the "job" was several investigations which Mr. Blanshard was ordered to begin at once. The Mayor would not disclose what they were because that might impair their effectiveness. It is known, however, that he has accumulated a good deal of evidence on the graft in newsdealers' licenses and is determined to drive it out of the city. Asked whether prosecutions would result from these investigations, the Mayor said that "would take care of itself."

Free Hand Promised.

The incoming commissioners were promised complete immunity from political interference. Mayor LaGuardia said Tammany had demoralized the Docks and Corrections Departments particularly, and he urged several commissioners to clean house from top to bottom if they found that necessary to straighten out their departments.

After administering the oath to Corporation Counsel Paul Windels, the Mayor said:

"I don't care whether the Law Department is the biggest law office in the world. I want it to be the best. Selection of the right staff will end the practice of hiring special counsel for important litigation. The day of the special counsel is past."

Austin M. MacCormick, receiving the oath of Correction Commissioner, was told that the eyes of the city were upon him because the administration had gone out of town to select him.

"You'll assume office with an absolutely free hand," the Mayor said, "and you'll have no interference of any kind, which unfortunately was not true in the case of your prede-

Continued on Page Two.

Cardinal Assails 'Myths' About Old Teutons; Notes They Kept Slaves and Were Slothful

Wireless to THE NEW YORK TIMES.

MUNICH, Jan. 1.—Cardinal Faulhaber's New Year sermon contained a rebuke of exaggerated Germanism and a message that in "the kingdom of God there are neither favorites nor stepchildren."

Every people is indeed entitled to its racial individuality, he said; but with all respect for "race hygiene," he emphasized "let it not be forgotten that we were saved not by German blood but by the blood of the Saviour."

The Archbishop declared that nationalization of the church would be tantamount to a "regression into Asiatic antiquity." He deprecated the prevalent elaboration of "myths" concerning the ancient Germans. The social organization of these, he said, was very unsatisfactory. They kept slaves, gave rough labor to their women, lived in everlasting intertribal warfare and were slothful and self-indulgent, whereas 2,000 years earlier the Babylonians had, for instance, a regular postal service and the Jews had established a system of schools.

The Cardinal stressed that since the advent of the Hitler government a multitude of new pseudo-religious dogmas had been propounded in Germany, that efforts had been made to found a new confession—a so-called Nordic-Germanic religion—and that this had even been urged for official recognition.

In view of this, he said, he chose the theme of his sermon at the year's turn to emphasize that Jesus had enjoined his disciples to teach and baptize all peoples and unite all nations in a single kingdom of God.

Like its predecessors in the Cardinal's Advent cycle, the sermon was preached at St. Michael's. The church was filled to overflowing and thousands were unable to gain admittance.

Cardinal Faulhaber, a member of a titled family in Germany, has recently launched a series of sharp attacks against Nazi policies and doctrines. He has asked Protestants to join Catholics in defense of Christianity against paganism. He has several times defied the Hitlerites in their own "capital" at Munich. Last June they barred him from a mass for the Catholic Journeymen's conference but afterward apologies were made.

The annual
FINANCIAL REVIEW
and
FORECAST
of
The New York Times
is printed
in this issue

London Darkened by Densest Fog in Years; Men With Torches Precede Street Traffic

Wireless to THE NEW YORK TIMES.

LONDON, Jan. 1.—Britain's New Year's Day was darkened by one of the worst fogs in years, covering an area of some 7,000 square miles.

It caused six deaths and many injuries and seriously crippled all forms of transportation.

Returning revelers first encountered the fog early in the morning. It steadily increased throughout the afternoon, and nightfall came unnoticed amid what is described as a proper old "pea-souper." The long unfamiliar sight of acetylene flares ablaze at London's busiest crossings was again seen, thus belying the modern contention that the dense fogs of Charles Dickens's day were no longer experienced.

Railway trains were delayed, air services were abandoned and road traffic was reduced to a game of follow-the-leader. London bus conductors had to walk along the curbs shouting, as the drivers could not see more than a foot or two ahead.

The main thoroughfare from Hammersmith to Hyde Park was blocked solidly for miles. The police called for volunteers to help control the snail-pace traffic with flashlights.

A man and a woman were drowned in the Wednesfield Canal while walking home from a wedding. Another woman was drowned on falling into the Lea River.

Three cyclists were killed in collisions with automobiles and there were many automobile crashes, resulting in minor injuries.

Shipping was held up both in the Thames and in the English Channel. No air liners arrived at or left Croydon Airdrome. The morning plane from Paris was forced to land at Lympne, on the coast.

By The Associated Press.

LONDON, Jan. 1.—Because of the dense fog today, flares were posted to mark street corners in London, and conductors carrying torches preceded street cars and buses.

A mass of persons in a Wimbledon train, packed like sardines, sang merrily, "Who's Afraid of the Big Black Fog?" A crowd on the Strand was amazed when a duck and drake landed, apparently lost.

An electric train telescoped two coaches tonight when it ran into the rear of another in the Camdentown area. The trains were nearly empty and only a few persons were injured.

Columbia Football Team Upsets Stanford, 7 to 0

Continued from Page One.

and calmly booted the ball from placement for the extra point.

That touchdown was the reward of tremendous valor and determination. Twice in the first period the "Sea Lions" had splashed down to within hailing distance of the Indian goal line, only to be halted by fumbles. Once Barabas was at fault, and later the slippery pigskin eluded Montgomery after he was tackled.

Stanford opened the game with a drive to the Columbia 29-yard line that bogged down when Matal made two consecutive tackles to hold Indian runners for no gain. In the second quarter the Cardinals smashed their way to the 25-yard line before being halted.

In the second half the Indians reached the 15-yard line, where a penalty stopped them; the 14, where they lost the ball on a fumble; the 1-yard stripe, where another fumble halted the attack, and the 8-yard stripe, where Columbia's stalwart line refused to yield.

The game reminded many old-time Rose Bowl veterans of the 1925 contest, in which Knute Rockne's Four Horsemen triumphed over Stanford, 27 to 10. The Indians made all the ground on that day, and Notre Dame made most of the points.

Grayson Likened to Nevers.

Curiously alike, too, were Ernie Nevers, the great fullback of 1925, and Bobby Grayson, Stanford's latest line cracker. Grayson, using that same churning foot motion that Nevers made famous, banged his way over centre, raced through tackle and rushed around end for a total of 160 yards—more than all of Columbia's backs made.

Columbia had two great stars in action today. One was Captain Montgomery, whose shifty swivel hips carried him through the Stanford defense time and time again.

The other was Barabas, who lunged and smashed his way along for frequent gains. And it was a tackle by this sensational sophomore back that halted one Stanford touchdown drive.

Aside from these two, the work of the Columbia ends—McDowell, Matal and Chase—was outstanding. Matal was injured just before the close of the first half and saw no additional action, Chase substituting with more than usual efficiency.

During the third and fourth periods the rain fell only intermittently. The soggy ball made passing almost impossible and the fact that each team completed a long toss at critical times was astonishing.

Stanford tried twelve and completed two for a net gain of 23 yards. The Lions tried only two and made one good—the Montgomery-to-Matal affair.

Punting was exceptionally good, considering the circumstances. Alustiza averaged 30 yards with his boots, while Montgomery turned in a 37-yard average in fourteen attempts. He had the hard luck of twice seeing well-placed efforts roll over the goal line just a foot inside the sidelines.

Game Cleanly Played.

The game was fought savagely, but was cleanly played on the whole. Stanford lost 66 yards on penalties, much of the losses coming from incomplete passes, while the Lions lost 5 yards on four separate occasions.

Columbia's victory today evened up the score somewhat for the Rose Bowl competition. It was the East's seventh victory in the nineteen games played between college teams since Washington State defeated Brown in 1916. The West has won nine contests, while three have ended in ties.

Today's appearance was the first made by Columbia and it was the fourth for Stanford. The Indians have won one, lost two and tied one in their defense of the West's prestige. Columbia also had the distinction of being the first team from New York to play in the Bowl.

After a short exchange of punts, Stanford launched the first real offensive when Maentz, on a reverse, skidded his way deep into Columbia territory, being dragged down on the 26-yard line.

But here Red Matal swung into action, smashed two plays in a row, and Stanford bogged down on the 30-yard stripe, Alustiza punting out of bounds on the 20-yard line.

Times Wide World Photo.
Al Barabas, Who Made Touchdown.

Times Wide World Photo.
Lou Little.

Montgomery swept loose for a ten-yard gain, but the Lions were held. The Lion captain then punted and the slippery pigskin eluded Maentz's grasp. Al Barabas pursued the ball and recovered it on the Stanford 38.

Barabas Runs 26 Yards.

Buoyed by this exhibition of his own skill on a soggy gridiron, Barabas promptly took a reverse from Montgomery and dashed 26 yards before Grayson finally tackled him on the 12-yard line.

However, Barabas fumbled on the next play and Reynolds recovered for Stanford on the 18-yard line. The Cardinals were penalized for holding, but Alustiza got off a terrific kick of 58 yards to Columbia's 39-yard marker.

A short time later Montgomery decided it was time to show the fans that Columbia had other carriers besides Barabas and he sprinted twenty-six yards. Cliff and Barabas then alternated at taking the pigskin, but the drive ended when Montgomery fumbled on the 10-yard line, where Maentz recovered just as the quarter ended.

Alustiza's kick was blocked shortly after play was resumed, but it was only third down and Stanford retained possession of the ball when Reynolds recovered.

New Offensive Starts.

Montgomery returned Alustiza's next effort to the Stanford 45 and another Lion offensive hurriedly got under way. A pass, Montgomery to Matal, put the ball on the 17-yard line.

Barabas almost fumbled on the next play, but recovered and was thrown for a half-yard loss.

This so embarrassed Al that he scored a touchdown on the next play, all of which left Stanford, and the natives, considerably baffled.

Montgomery took the ball, handed it to Barabas, and every one on the Cardinal team stood around looking at one another for a second or two.

Then Al started chugging out around his own left end. Topping, Stanford right end, was flat on his back, and "Bones" Hamilton, right halfback, was nowhere in sight, so Al just galloped along, crossing the goal line without difficulty. Wilder converted the extra point.

Somewhat nettled, Stanford opened up with a terrific drive a few minutes later, smashing 36 yards in seven plays to the Columbia 34, but there the Lions rallied and they had possession of the ball as the half ended.

Stanford opened the second half with a bludgeoning attack that saw Grayson and Hamilton advancing the ball 60 yards in five plays to the Lion 20-yard marker. A 15-yard penalty for holding upset the attack, however, and Alustiza was forced to punt.

After receiving Montgomery's return kick, the Indians cracked right back again, with Grayson passing to Topping for 20 yards. Plunges by Hamilton and Grayson netted a first down on the 13-yard line, but Grayson fumbled and Columbia recovered to stave off the attack on its own 14-yard stripe.

Crashes Over Centre.

Nothing daunted, the Indians drove back a third time when Grayson, on a fake reverse, crashed over centre, bowled right into Referee Tom Louttit and continued on 22 yards to Columbia's 12-yard mark.

In two plays Grayson made it a first down on the 3-yard mark, in three more plays the Cardinals lost a yard and then Grayson fumbled, Brominski recovering on his own 1-yard stripe.

Early in the fourth quarter the Indians launched a fourth drive, with Grayson and Hamilton doing most of the gaining, until they arrived at the 14-yard stripe.

Here Coach Little sent in five substitutes, which time out cost Columbia a 5-yard penalty to its own 8-yard line. But the Columbia line tightened, with McDowell and Chase smashing in to break up plays, and the Stanford march wound up on the 10-yard line.

LIONS JUBILANT IN DRESSING ROOM

Columbia Players and Coaches Dance With Joy

By The Associated Press.

PASADENA, Calif., Jan. 1.—Lou Little stepped on Tiny Thornhill's foot in a pro football game fifteen years ago. He stepped on it again today as Columbia beat Stanford in the classic Rose Bowl game.

"Remember that day I stepped on your foot?" said the Columbia mentor before today's struggle. Tiny did. But today's defeat by Little's Lions will be remembered long after the physical injury of that other time is forgotten.

The Columbia dressing room was a wild scramble of youths who had found victory where only defeat had been expected.

Coaches and players alike were dancing around in circles, hugging each other and shouting unintelligible words through the steam-saturated air.

Barrett Has His Say.

"Oh, boy! Oh, boy! Oh, boy!" shouted Little. "Did the boys play football or did they play football?

"Stanford had a great team. It was the best team we played all year. Clean, hard football from start to finish, that's what it was."

Rise of Football at Columbia Meteoric Under Little Regime

By ARTHUR J. DALEY.

"I did not come here to fail."

That statement was uttered by Lou Little when he signed as Columbia coach after the close of the 1929 season. And his listeners, catching the vibrant personality of the man, felt that he would not fail. He didn't.

When Little shifted from Georgetown to Columbia four campaigns ago, he found the Lion football fortunes at a low ebb. He arrived to find that the Blue and White supporters were hailing a season that showed one major victory as a tremendous success. The squads were small and interest in the gridiron sport practically non-existent.

Swept Out of Doldrums.

That was four years ago. In the interval the Lions have been swept out of the doldrums in which they had stood. They have won twenty-seven games, lost seven and tied two. And four of those seven defeats came in Little's first season as coach. For the past three campaigns one setback a year has been the maximum Columbia has yielded to its opponents, big and small, major and minor.

Cornell turned the trick in 1931 by a 13-0 score; Brown edged out the Lions, 7—6, in 1932 and Princeton vanquished them, 20 to 0, in the third fray of the 1933 campaign. Paradoxical as it seems, that conquest by the Tigers was the turning point of the Columbia fortunes.

The utter rout administered to the New Yorkers in a game that pre-battle predictions had deemed a toss-up proved to be quite a shock to Little. It had its repercussions extended to the squad. In a drastic shake-up the Lion mentor benched five of his regulars and replaced them with substitutes.

From that stage onward Columbia started to click. The new combination made its début against Penn State and it looked like a sorry début for a while. The Nittany Lions made the Columbia variety of Lions look none too well.

Suddenly Comes to Life.

Fearful that the reaction of the Columbia players to the Princeton defeat was a far from favorable one, the Blue and White followers were a bit anxious as Penn State held the Lions scoreless in the first period and on into the second. Then with startling suddenness Columbia's new team came to life to roll up a 33-0 victory before the final whistle.

There was no halting the berserk Lions after that. They went through the rest of the campaign without another loss, looking better and better in each start. Against Navy, as a matter of fact, many experts stated very flatly that in that game the New Yorkers had reached such a peak of perfection that they were close to being the best team in the country.

The entire business of Columbia's march to greatness can be placed almost entirely at the door of Little. He still has the small squads that he inherited when he first came to Morningside Heights. But he is such a master workman in the art of molding whatever material he has into a high-class combination that he takes rank with the old immortals, Rockne, Haughton, Warner, Jones and the others who have contributed so much to the game.

Grounded in Fundamentals.

Little has a system all his own. It has the elements of both Rockne and Warner styles of play and deception as its basis. When Columbia is working properly the Lions have the best-looking offensive manoeuvres seen on any gridiron. Not only is it a spectacular team to watch but it is soundly grounded in the fundamentals. That, after all, is the real secret of the Blue and White success.

When Little is drilling his team in practice sessions at Baker Field he is a driver, a perfect human dynamo. Bustling with energy, alert and keen, Little whips his players with an almost unceasing fire of comment. No fault escapes his watchful eye. He works on a play or a player until he is perfectly satisfied. And Lou Little is not an easy man to satisfy.

This season the Blue and White raced away to a fine start with a 39-to-0 triumph over Lehigh. Then came a scare. Virginia, beaten, 75—0, the week previously by Ohio State, led the overconfident Columbia eleven by 6 to 0 at the half, and it was only by virtue of a stirring rally that the Lions managed to win, 15 to 6.

Then came the game with Princeton. A fumble of the opening kick-off paved the way for the initial Tiger score. The Lions, rocked back on their heels by this mishap, never recovered their poise as the Nassau contingent went on to victory, 20 to 0. Penn State came next and was beaten, 33 to 0.

Brief History of Campaign.

The fray with the Nittany Lions was a mere preliminary to the traditional battle with Cornell. Newt Wilder kicked a field goal that proved to be the margin of victory, 9 to 6. Navy was turned back, 14 to 7, Lafayette 46 to 6 and Syracuse 16 to 0. Stanford was next. That, in brief, was the history of the 1933 Columbia team.

Little's own history goes back before the war. He played on the Leominster (Mass.) High School team for two years and then had one season at Worcester Academy before matriculating at the University of Pennsylvania in 1915. He was an outstanding tackle on the Penn team of 1916.

The war interrupted the career of the Columbia coach. He enlisted and quit the service as a captain in the A. E. F. After the armistice he returned to Penn, again gaining great distinction as a tackle on the Quaker eleven of 1919, a team, which, incidentally, was the Eastern representative in the Rose Bowl tournament.

In 1920 Little coached and played on the Buffalo All-Americans professional eleven. From 1921 to 1923 he coached the Philadelphia Yellow-Jackets and in 1925 he went to Georgetown where his teams compiled a record that showed thirty-seven victories, eight defeats and three ties.

Statistical Chart of Columbia-Stanford Game

	Total.		First Period.		Second Period.		Third Period.		Fourth Period.	
	C.	S.	C.	S.	C.	S.	C.	S.	C.	S.
First downs	6	16	3	1	2	3	0	7	1	5
Net gain by rushing, yards	76	227	64	25	11	65	1	118	0	25
Forward passes attempted	2	12	1	1	1	2	0	1	0	8
Forward passes completed	1	2	0	0	1	1	0	1	0	0
Ground gained by forwards, yards	28	45	0	0	28	8	0	15	0	21
Opponent's forwards intercepted	1	0	0	0	0	0	0	0	1	0
Ground gained on intercepted passes	11	0	0	0	0	0	0	0	11	0
Lateral passes attempted	0	0	0	0	0	0	0	0	0	0
Punts	14	9	5	4	1	3	4	1	4	1
*Distance of punts, yards	513	271	175	117	40	99	136	35	162	20
*Average distance of punts, yards	37	36	35	29	40	33	34	35	41	20
Run-back of punts, yards	48	62	36	31	12	0	0	16	0	15
Run-back of kick-offs, yards	48	20	22	0	0	20	26	0	0	0
Goals from field attempted	0	0	0	0	0	0	0	0	0	0
Blocked kicks	0	1	0	0	0	1	0	0	0	0
Fumbles	4	7	2	1	2	1	0	4	0	1
Own fumbles recovered	2	1	0	0	2	0	0	1	0	0
Opponent's fumbles recovered	5	2	1	2	1	0	3	0	0	0
Penalties	4	8	0	2	1	1	0	2	3	3
Yards lost through penalties	20	70	0	20	5	5	0	30	15	15

*From point where ball was kicked.

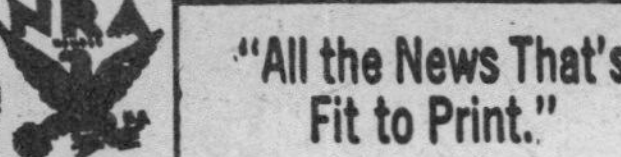

The New York Times.

LATE CITY EDITION
WEATHER—Generally fair today; showers, cooler tomorrow.
Temperatures Yesterday—Max., 75; Min., 60

VOL. LXXXIII....No. 27,901. Entered as Second-Class Matter, Postoffice, New York, N. Y. NEW YORK, FRIDAY, JUNE 15, 1934. PP TWO CENTS In New York City. | THREE CENTS Within 200 Miles | FOUR CENTS Elsewhere Except in 7th and 8th Postal Zones

STEEL UNION VOTES TODAY ON A STRIKE; LABOR BILL FOUGHT

'Rank and File' Win by a Broad Margin in Preliminary Test at Pittsburgh Meeting.

THEY LOOK TO PRESIDENT

Lodges Report That Companies Are Rejecting Their Demand for Recognition.

COMPLAINT IS MADE TO NRA

Green Will Address Convention This Morning—He Shuns Substitute Legislation.

By LOUIS STARK.
Special to THE NEW YORK TIMES.

PITTSBURGH, June 14.—Strike action tomorrow at the convention of the Amalgamated Association of Iron, Steel and Tin Workers will depend largely upon the attitude of William Green, president of the American Federation of Labor, who will address the delegates in the morning.

Mr. Green, it was reported from Washington tonight, was decidedly cool to the substitute for the revised Wagner Bill, which would create a labor board with powers of compulsory investigation that would stop when the board ordered an election.

President Green, it is rumored, has a plan of his own to avert the strike. No details are available here. In some quarters, however, it was said he would limit himself to explaining his attitude on the newly proposed labor board.

The "rank-and-file" delegates are opposed to the new bill on the ground that it would "lead to another Weirton case."

By this they mean that even if the new labor board ordered an election the steel corporations would refuse to assent to such a test, and would bring court action to enjoin the government from obtaining the payrolls, the preliminary step in carrying through an election of spokesmen of employes for collective bargaining.

Insisting on Recognition.

Union delegates want nothing short of an assurance of union recognition. Today spokesmen for 35 out of more than 200 lodges reported on the demand for union recognition served by them on May 31 in accordance with the action of the steel workers' convention in April. Of these thirty-five delegates, thirty-four reported that their demand had been rejected and one announced that a company had withheld an answer.

Michael F. Tighe, the veteran president of the Amalgamated association, who presided when the convention reopened today, said the union committee which visited the office of the Carnegie Steel Corporation, subsidiary of the United States Steel Corporation at Braddock, Pa., had been told to "go to hell and get to hell out of here."

Complaint was made of violation of Section 7-A of the Recovery Act to General Johnson, declared Mr. Tighe.

Federal agents, mediators of the Department of Labor, the National Labor Board and the Pennsylvania State Department of Labor are here as observers, keeping Secretary of Labor Perkins, Governor Pinchot and Senator Wagner up to the minute on important developments.

Steel Corporations Preparing.

The steel corporations are reported to be preparing for eventualities. Plants on the South Side have strung up new barbed wire daubed with black paint as though to resemble old wire. Deputies are being instructed in rifle practice and grenade throwing, it was reported, while cots and supplies of food are being placed in the commissaries.

Additional men to replace employes who may strike are being taken on, and old employes are being canvassed as to their attitude in the event that a walk-out is ordered tomorrow.

Indications of how strongly the "rank and file" leaders were in control of the convention today was shown in a test vote that came on the attempt of the administration leaders to exclude members from the meeting hall. Under the bylaws members may attend conventions.

The administration sought an amendment to exclude them and limit the meeting to delegates only. This required a two-thirds vote for passage. The proposal was defeated by a vote of 96 to 49.

Earl J. Forbeck of McKeesport, Pa., a leader of the "rank-and-file" group, said he was satisfied that the test vote showed the strength of his associates.

"We do not want to strike except as a last resort," he said. "However, I feel that only the personal intervention of President Roosevelt can stop the vote for an immediate

Continued on Page Four.

Baer Knocks Out Carnera To Win Heavyweight Title

Referee Stops Fight in Eleventh Round After Italian Is Floored for Twelfth Time in Bout—56,000 Pay $428,000 Gate.

By JAMES P. DAWSON.

The world's heavyweight championship came back to the United States last night after an absence of a year.

Max Baer, the new Jack Dempsey in every respect save seriousness, knocked out Primo Carnera, Venetian ring giant, in the eleventh round of their scheduled fifteen-round battle in Madison Square Garden's Long Island City Bowl. He triumphed in one of the most sensational encounters ever waged for the ring's richest prize.

The finish came after 2 minutes 16 seconds of the eleventh round when Carnera could not possibly go any further. He had been floored twelve times through the fight, three times in the first round, as many times in the second, once in the third, three times in the tenth and twice in the eleventh.

He fell once under his own weakness and the drive of a languid right he pushed to Baer's face.

Carnera could go no further and he looked appealingly at Referee Arthur Donovan, murmuring a request to the arbiter that the bout be stopped for his own safety. Referee Donovan acted promptly.

"Carnera asked me to stop the fight, just at the second when I was going to stop it anyway," said Donovan after the fight. "He didn't know where he was. He could not have continued, and there was no use letting it go on when he was so helpless."

There was some confusion at the close of the tenth round. Just as the bell rang to terminate the session, Donovan leaped between the men and separated them. Many at the time thought the bout had been stopped.

"I didn't stop the bout in the tenth round," said Donovan. "The bell ended the round just as I stepped between them, and I heard it distinctly."

Notwithstanding, Donovan's action in the closing seconds in the tenth round was interpreted by many at the ringside as an official ending to the fray and surprise was expressed when he announced through the ropes that the bout would proceed.

This surprise was particularly manifest in Baer's corner, where the Californian's seconds had clambered through the ropes before the bell ended the round, in the mistaken belief that Baer had won the fight.

Some 56,000 persons turned out

Continued on Page Twenty-seven.

POLICE SEEK TRUNK IN TUFVERSON CASE

Detectives Here Try to Trace Missing Woman's Luggage Destined for England.

PODERJAY ORDERED HELD

New York Police Ask Vienna to Keep Him in Custody Pending Investigation.

Assistant Chief Inspector John J. Sullivan, in charge of New York detectives, made known yesterday that his office had sent two cable messages to Europe in connection with the case of Ivan Poderjay, reported held by the police in Vienna pending information from New York.

One of the messages asked the Vienna authorities to hold Poderjay, or to keep him under surveillance, until the Missing Persons Bureau here had completed its investigation into the whereabouts of Miss Agnes C. Tufverson, New York attorney, with whom he went through the ceremony of marriage last Dec. 4, when he already had a wife in England, according to his reported statement to the Vienna police.

The other message requested Scotland Yard to investigate whether a large trunk, registered in the name of Poderjay, reached Southampton, England, late last December.

Trunk Sent to Pier.

The police have information that the trunk was shipped from New York via the Hamburg-American Line on Dec. 20, Inspector Sullivan said. Detectives have been informed that it was sent to the Hamburg-American Line pier, but they have been unable to account for its movements after arrival there.

Meanwhile the Yugoslav Consulate General here denied yesterday that Poderjay, as had been reported in the dispatches from Vienna telling of his arrest, was an officer in the Yugoslav Army. He came to the United States several times as a merchant, it was said at the consulate, but was not well known here for the reason that most of his activities centred in London.

A representative of the Tufverson family went to the consulate about six weeks ago, making inquiries concerning Poderjay, it was learned. Subsequently the consulate cooperated with the Missing Persons Bureau in the search for the missing woman and informed detectives that the Yugoslav Legation in London could furnish more information concerning Poderjay.

Inspector Sullivan said that the New York Police Department had received official notice from the Vienna police of their action, together with information that a complete account of the interrogation of Poderjay will be forwarded to New York.

The couple were to have sailed for Europe on the liner Hamburg of the Hamburg-American Line on Dec. 20, and had engaged passage, detectives have learned. For some reason that has not as yet been learned by the New York investi-

Continued on Page Six.

KUNSTLER RESIGNS, STOPPING INQUIRY

In Letter to Referee He Says He Feels His Usefulness as Judge Is Impaired.

ACCUSED OF UNFITNESS

He Plans to Open Law Office—District Attorney Likely to Get Hearing Minutes.

Harold L. Kunstler, Municipal Court Justice in the Second District, resigned yesterday afternoon and put an end to the proceedings by the Bar Association for his removal on the ground of unfitness.

Justice Kunstler announced his action in a letter to Frank C. Laughlin, referee appointed by the Appellate Division to take testimony on the charges and report to the court.

Referee Laughlin accepted the resignation as ending the removal proceedings, which were reopened on Wednesday, ten days after briefs should have been submitted, on the plea of Justice Kunstler that he wanted to try to explain the discrepancy of $126,000 in deposits, as shown by his bank records, in excess of his salary for forty-four months.

After testifying that the excess was due mainly to loans from friends, for most of which he had no records, Justice Kunstler lost his temper during a rigid cross-examination by Thomas E. Dewey, prosecutor for the Bar Association, and the referee adjourned the hearing until yesterday afternoon. The letter of resignation, with a statement by his counsel, was submitted to the referee at the opening yesterday.

Justice Kunstler's resignation leaves a vacancy which Mayor La Guardia has power to fill until the end of the year. A successor will be chosen for a nine-year term at the November election. Mayor La Guardia had no comment to make when told of the resignation. The temporary vacancy must be filled by a resident of the Second District, which centres on Madison Street on the lower East Side.

Letter of Resignation.

The letter of resignation, addressed to the referee and read into the record by Sol Tekulsky, associated with former District Attorney Joab H. Banton in the defense of Justice Kunstler, follows:

Hon. Frank C. Laughlin,
County Court House.

Dear Judge Laughlin:

I am herewith tendering my resignation as a Justice of the Municipal Court of the City of New York, Borough of Manhattan Second District.

I wish to state that I feel that my usefulness as a judge of that court has been impaired and that it is in my own best interests therefore to resign.

I did not wish to take this step until I had an opportunity to submit proofs of the various bank accounts which had been the subject of previous hearings on the charges before you. I wanted particularly to place on record the fact that there were practical-

Continued on Page Four.

ALL DEBTORS TO US EXCEPTING FINLAND TO DEFAULT TODAY

Italy, Hungary, Poland, Latvia, Rumania and Estonia Notify They Will Not Pay.

HOPE PUT IN HULL PLAN

Washington Pins Faith in the Proposal Made to Britain for Payments in Kind.

Special to THE NEW YORK TIMES.

WASHINGTON, June 14.—Out of $477,843,644.45 due tomorrow in war debt payments from fifteen foreign governments, the Treasury is assured of only one payment—$166,538 from Finland. This is recognized as meaning the virtual breakdown of the funding agreements concluded from 1923 to 1925.

It points to an indefinite delay in negotiations for resumption of payments, or more probably the conclusion of new arrangements at some time when conditions will have changed to assure the negotiation of new settlements. It represents the end of the movement begun with the Hoover moratorium in the Summer of 1931.

Hope Put in Hull Plan.

Whether or not new agreements will eventually be concluded along other lines that may take advantage of the partial payment-in-kind suggestion of Secretary Hull in his note to Great Britain cannot be foretold. The immediate British reaction to that suggestion was expected to be unfavorable, but it is hoped that the suggestion will eventually bear fruit.

It is possible that the amount received tomorrow through Finland's full acknowledgment of her due instalment may be increased slightly by a token payment from Lithuania. She had not been heard from today but unofficial reports have indicated a small payment is likely. She made token payments of $10,000 a year ago and of $7,000 last December. Finland has always paid in full.

Yugoslavia was the only country having new obligations due tomorrow that had not been heard from today. On some previous payment dates she has defaulted. During the day the State Department received notices from Italy, Hungary, Estonia, Poland, Rumania and Latvia that no payments would be made.

Previously similar notification had been received from Belgium, Czechoslovakia, France, Great Britain and Rumania. No other governments have new obligations falling due tomorrow, but Austria and Greece are in arrears for previous unpaid instalments which could be received tomorrow. They have not been heard from.

Italy Decides Against Payment.

All of the notices received today were from governments that had defaulted before, except Italy, which in the past had made token payments of $1,000,000 on due dates. She wavered for several days but finally decided against payment, explaining that she would have made a token payment tomorrow except for the Johnson act.

Hungary, as on several occasions in the past, announced that she was depositing to the Foreign Creditors' Account at the Hungarian National Bank a Hungarian Treasury certificate in the pengo equivalent of the amount due, bearing interest at 2 per cent annually. This is not usable by the United States and is not recognized as a payment within the terms of the funding agreement.

Several of the governments in their notes expressed hopes for negotiations of new settlements, an

Continued on Page Six.

MUSSOLINI GREETS HITLER EFFUSIVELY; LONG TALK IS HELD

Chancellor Reaches Venice by Plane—Populace Displays Coolness Toward Him.

CONVERSATION IS SECRET

Other Officials Are Called In After Two Hours—Leaders Have Luncheon Together.

By ARNALDO CORTESI.
Special Cable to THE NEW YORK TIMES.

VENICE, June 14.—The much-advertised first meeting between the Italian and German dictators, from which many expect interesting developments in future European politics, occurred at 10 o'clock this morning at the Lido Civil Airport here.

Both Premier Benito Mussolini and Chancellor Adolf Hitler were smiling amiably as the Chancellor left his airplane and they walked toward each other to shake hands. Their handshake, after an exchange of Roman salutes, was long and friendly—indeed effusive.

When Il Duce turned to introduce his retinue to Der Führer he half threw his right arm around Herr Hitler's shoulders, patting his back with a comradely gesture. On the way to Herr Hitler's hotel the dictators sat side by side in a motor launch, chatting animatedly in German, which was somewhat halting on Signor Mussolini's side.

Conversations Start.

Only a few hours after Herr Hitler's arrival he and Signor Mussolini were already deep in the first of the political conversations that are the principal reason for Der Führer's coming. The occasion for the first talk was afforded by a luncheon of twenty-five covers given by Signor Mussolini in honor of the Chancellor and his retinue in the magnificent Villa Pisani at Stra.

The luncheon was no sooner over than the two leaders retired into one of the rooms adjoining the dining room, where they remained in close conversation for two hours. At the end of that time some of the highest officials of the Italian and German Foreign Offices were admitted and the discussions were continued in their presence for about half an hour longer.

Further occasions for conversation were afforded soon afterward when Signor Mussolini called on Herr Hitler at his hotel and during the course of the afternoon, which the dictators spent together visiting the Venice Biennial Art Exhibition. No inkling of the subject of the discussions was given.

Populace Is Cold.

Great as was the cordiality of the official reception, the Venetian population appeared somewhat cold to Herr Hitler's coming. The crowds lining the banks of the Grand Canal when the Premier and the Chancellor flashed by in their motor boat on the way to Herr Hitler's hotel were not large. This doubtless was partly explainable by the fact that the Italian newspapers only this morning announced Herr Hitler's arrival and were extremely vague about the details. What applause occurred was addressed entirely to Premier Mussolini, the only cries heard being "Viva Mussolini!"

Herr Hitler, however, was warmly cheered by a considerable crowd of Germans standing on the opposite side of the Grand Canal in front of his hotel.

Premier Mussolini had been among the first to reach the airport to receive Chancellor Hitler. He arrived in a launch accompanied by a dozen of his closest collaborators. The airdrome was profusely decorated with

Continued on Page Five.

Blast Reveals a Wide Bomb Plot in France; 'Three Judges of Hell' Threaten President

By The Associated Press.

PARIS, June 14.—The "Three Judges of Hell," who are trying to execute their sentences against various individuals and companies with bombs sent through the mails, became the chief concern of the French police tonight after the fifth bomb had been discovered.

The "three judges" have threatened the lives of the President, the Premier and other high officials and have mailed bombs to the government broadcasting station, an American beauty product company, a food products concern at Nanterre, a book publisher and the Society of Authors.

The bomb sent to the latter exploded in a postoffice yesterday, injuring three clerks. The others were discovered in time to prevent casualties.

The American company involved is Tokalon, controlled by E. Virgil Neal. A fantastic letter to the concern, received three weeks ago, said:

"We will strike the French people without distinction as to age, sex or rank, until they realize their cowardice, before the great pirates deprive them of the right to be severe toward ordinary criminals and stealers of handkerchiefs."

The police believed that the letter and the bombs came from cranks and that the reference was to the lack of results from the Stavisky scandal investigation.

The letter accompanying one bomb was signed "Minos, Eaque, Rhadamante," while the others were inscribed "The Three Judges of Hell."

At the American concern today a girl clerk's life was probably saved by her quick realization that a faint metallic sound as she started to open the package was caused by a spring intended to explode the bomb.

She kept the package closed until police arrived, when it was opened by experts. They found the same kind of powder and loaded mechanism as were in yesterday's machine.

REICH SUSPENDS PAYMENTS ON ALL ITS FOREIGN DEBTS; BRITISH RETALIATION LIKELY

$1,045,582,700 in Dollar Bonds Involved; German Issues Here Higher, Despite Action

The German moratorium will apply to 116 issues of German dollar bonds aggregating a face amount of $1,045,582,700 which were floated in this market.

Of this amount, however, $893,432,800 was already in partial default before yesterday's declaration, only the German Government Dawes Plan 7s and Young Plan 5½s having escaped hitherto the stigma of suspended payments.

American holders of these bonds stand to lose a maximum of about $35,000,000 of interest payments in the six months covered by the moratorium.

Bankers estimate that out of the nominal total of over $1,000,000,000 of German dollar bonds "outstanding" in this market, about $300,000,000 has been repatriated by Germany at bargain prices in the past two years.

In the face of the suspension of service for six months, German bonds listed on the New York Stock Exchange, after early weakness, rallied strongly. The Dawes and Young Plan issues closed with net gains of 2 points and ½ point, respectively. The Reichsmark fell 19 points in foreign exchange to 38.06 cents. Elsewhere in the financial markets there was nothing to indicate that the news had not been discounted in advance.

By classifications, the German dollar bonds outstanding are: State and provincial, $91,985,000; municipal, $75,648,500; corporation, $725,799,300; Dawes Plan, $60,844,300; Young Plan, $91,305,600. Service on the Dawes Plan loan has been fully maintained to date, but sinking fund payments on the Young Plan loan are in default, although interest has been paid.

The so-called "standstill" credits held by American banks are not affected by the moratorium. These credits have been "frozen" under a special agreement since 1931, in which period they have been reduced from more than $600,000,000 to about $230,000,000.

SENATE CONFIRMS TUGWELL BY 53-24

Nine Republican Independents Vote for the Under-Secretary After Hot 6-Hour Debate.

SIX DEMOCRATS OPPOSED

Byrd Leads Fight—Norris Hails Official as Courageous—Black Calls for 'More Tugwells.'

Special to THE NEW YORK TIMES.

WASHINGTON, June 14.—Fifty-one days after President Roosevelt nominated him for Under-Secretary of Agriculture, Dr. Rexford G. Tugwell, chief of the administration's Brain Trust, was confirmed in the Senate today by a vote of 53 to 24.

Six Democrats, Senators Bailey, Byrd, Clark, Dill, Gore and Smith, joined eighteen old-line Republicans in opposition, while nine Progressive Republicans and one Farmer-Laborite united with forty-three Democrats in Dr. Tugwell's support.

Held up in the Senate Agriculture Committee since April 24 through Chairman Smith's stalwart objection the Tugwell nomination was favorably reported by a vote of 16 to 2 Tuesday, but only after the Senate threatened to take the matter forcibly out of the committee's hands.

Although the 2-to-1 majority for Dr. Tugwell had been conceded ever since Monday's hearings, six hours of speech-making and bitter debate preceded the roll-call.

In the first four hours a quartet of Senators occupied the floor, while the time between 3 P. M. and late afternoon was taken up by nine fifteen-minute speeches, some of them by Republican critics of Roosevelt policies.

Glass in Opposition.

Added to the six Democrats who voted "No," Senator Glass was paired against Dr. Tugwell in the roll-call. Senator Borah did not vote, while the position of Senator McNary, the Republican leader, was unstated.

The chief defender of Dr. Tugwell was Senator Norris, Progressive, of Nebraska, and the chief critic was Senator Byrd, Democrat, of Virginia.

Mr. Norris started the day with a speech seriously sponsoring Dr. Tugwell as a "fine man" and deriding Monday's hearing as lacking only the Marine Band to make an entirely successful show. He declared that propaganda such as he had never seen had been used against Dr. Tugwell, and he also accused Senator Byrd of making a "stump speech" at the hearing.

"But Senator Byrd didn't talk to the committee, he talked to the crowd," Mr. Norris continued. "It beat any street-corner crowd I ever saw. He worked them up into a fine furor of patriotism. What he said, however, had no more to do with Dr. Tugwell than the starlings roosting in the Capitol's rafters."

Senator Bailey's cross-examina-

Continued on Page Three.

BRITAIN PLANNING REPRISAL ON REICH

Chamberlain Expected to Urge the Impounding of German Trade Balances Today.

FRANCE READY TO ACT, TOO

MacDonald Calls for German Return to Arms Conference for One More Trial.

By FERDINAND KUHN Jr.
Special Cable to THE NEW YORK TIMES.

LONDON, June 14.—Swift and stern retaliation against Germany was expected tonight to be the British Government's answer to her default on the Dawes and Young loans.

Neville Chamberlain, Chancellor of the Exchequer, intends to make a statement on the moratorium in the House of Commons tomorrow, and there is little doubt that he will recommend severe counter-measures. The most probable method appears to be a compulsory clearing arrangement whereby the government would recoup for British creditors out of Germany's favorable trade balance with Britain.

The German balances here are so substantial that this government could easily take out of them the interest due its citizens on the two loans. Germany sold almost £30,000,000 worth of goods to Britain last year and bought less than £15,000,000. The whole amount of the Dawes loan outstanding in London is a little over £17,000,000 and of the Young loan about £11,000,000.

Warned Reich Two Months Ago.

Two months ago the British Government warned Germany that it would take "a grave view of any proposal to apply a moratorium to the Dawes and Young loans," and at that time the compulsory clearing system was hinted at. Now that the moratorium has come it is generally felt that the government cannot postpone action on behalf of the British creditors any longer.

The Cabinet Ministers are said to be disturbed over the effect their compulsory clearing plan will have on Anglo-American relations. They realize that by impounding German balances here they will be making it more difficult for the American creditors ever to get anything out of Germany. But they feel that no other choice is open unless Germany reconsiders her action before July 1, when the default becomes effective.

Inasmuch as the default had been expected, its effect on the financial market here was slight, though German bonds fell heavily, the mark declined further in terms of sterling and prices of commodities weakened generally.

Far more significant, however, was the shout of rage that arose from the City, even from financial quarters that hitherto have been sympathetic to the Hitler régime. The default was castigated everywhere as a deliberate act of bad faith and as an event that the Ger-

Continued on Page Two.

REPARATION LOANS IN BAN

World Bank Promptly Protests, Charging Broken Contract.

BERLIN BLAMES CREDITORS

Their Policies Wrecked Trade and Drained Off Gold, Schacht Asserts.

ACTION EFFECTIVE JULY 1

Suspension on Dawes and Young Loans Indefinite, on Other Debts for 6 Months.

Statement by Dr. Schacht, World Bank statement, Page. 2.

By OTTO D. TOLISCHUS.
Wireless to THE NEW YORK TIMES.

BERLIN, June 14.—Brushing aside all contractual and treaty obligations, Germany proclaimed today a complete transfer moratorium and suspended cash payments on all her foreign debts, including the Dawes and the Young loans, effective July 1.

This drastic action, which was accompanied by vehement charges that the creditor nations themselves were responsible for it because their commercial and financial policies had wrecked Germany's foreign trade and thus depleted her gold reserves, consisted of two steps.

Schacht Issues Decree.

First, at a meeting of the central committee of the Reichsbank, President Hjalmar Schacht, acting on his own authority, put into effect by decree the compromise formula proposed by the recent transfer conference, although the conditions for its acceptance by a majority of the creditors have not been fulfilled. This formula, affecting all private long and medium term debts, provides for a six months' moratorium and a choice for the creditors in respect to interest payments between 3 per cent funding bonds, available immediately and at full value, or 40 per cent in cash after the six months' moratorium.

Second, the German Finance Minister notified the Bank for International Settlements at Basle that temporarily the debt service on the Dawes and the Young loans would have to be suspended as well because of lack of foreign exchange. Official notes to this effect will be delivered tomorrow to all countries in which these loans were raised, but these notes will also express Germany's willingness to negotiate regarding "practical measures" for resuming payments. They will suggest payment in kind through increased German exports and will appeal to creditor nations to assist in promoting them.

Action Not Unexpected.

The German action was not unexpected. The way had been carefully prepared by the Reichsbank statement showing that Germany's note coverage had dropped to 3.6 per cent and by the foreign trade figures rushed into print yesterday revealing a trade deficit of 178,000,000 marks during the first five months of this year.

Nevertheless, the sweep of the moratorium fulfilled the worst fears of the creditors, some of whom had hoped Germany would pay, at least in part, the interest on the Dawes and the Young loans, first, because France and Great Britain have protested against any tampering with these loans and second, because disregard of this protest hampers validation of the transfer conference's compromise formula by the British, the French and the Spanish delegations. Since the Dutch and the Swiss had previously rejected it and are now negotiating for separate agreements to obtain more favorable terms, the Americans are the only ones still to be heard from.

Of both private and governmental loans by far the largest share is held in the United States.

Fraser Sends Protest.

To protect the rights of holders of Dawes and Young loan bonds, for which he is trustee, Leon Fraser, president of the World Bank, immediately protested to the German Government against the suspension of interest payments on the ground that this violated the

Continued on Page Two.

Crowd of 56,000 Sees Baer Win Title by Knocking Out Carnera in Eleventh

By JAMES P. DAWSON.

Continued From Page One.

for this combat between two of the biggest men ever to fight for the crown. The gross receipts were were $428,000, that sum being paid by a gathering that came from near and far, and represented all walks of life.

One member of the President's Cabinet was in attendance - Postmaster General James A. Farley, who was there with Mrs. Farley. Governors and Mayors from nearby States and cities, including Mayors LaGuardia of New York and Frank Hague of Jersey City, and members of Congress were at the ringside.

The stage and screen were represented, as was the business world, all drawn thither by the promise of an exciting combat that was fulfilled, and the chance to do something for charity. For 10 per cent of the receipts from the show to to the Free Milk Fund for Babies, Inc., of which Mrs. William Randolph Hearst is chairman.

Ex-Champions in Crowd.

Five former wearers of the crown that Baer brought back to America were conspicuous in the gathering. Tommy Burns, Jack Johnson, Jack Dempsey, Gene Tunney and Jack Sharkey thrilled to the spectacle. Undoubtedly they were proud of Baer's achievement.

Certainly Dempsey was. He saw in the ring, triumphant, a man that is nearer to himself than any other heavyweight in existence. It had to be a reminder of the old Manassa Mauler--that was the title of Dempsey at his best—who crushed Carnera in defeat in a battle that rivaled Dempsey's well-remembered duel with Luis Angel Firpo in 1923.

Dempsey, incidentally, has a financial interest in the new champion. He was the first to leap through the ropes and greet this devastating champion, whose padded gloves are mailed fists, piston-like in action and loaded with punching TNT.

He fights in flurries, does this new titleholder, with a style that has made him heretofore unreliable. Outside the ring he is of an easy-going disposition that belies his primitive, fighting fury.

Inside the ring he is tolerant and, to an extent, indulgent. That is why many thought he could not become serious enough to crush the 6-foot, 6½-inch, 263¼ pound giant who held the title until last night.

But when aroused he glories in fighting punch for punch. With him it is a question solely of the survival of the fittest. He demonstrated this amply when he battered Carnera into a figure of abject helplessness with a pitiless, furious assault.

In defeat Carnera crowned himself with the glory of the vanquished fighter who sticks to his guns until he is helpless. Those who said the mammoth Italian could not withstand punishment—could not "take it," in the parlance of the ring—were confounded as the oak-like figure stood up under a battering that would have felled a less determined man.

A Record in Knockdowns.

No heavyweight title defender in the modern history of boxing has been a victim of so many knockdowns in a championship struggle. Even the beating that Jess Willard took at the hands of Dempsey in Toledo back in 1919 paled against that absorbed by Carnera in his desperate but futile attempt to retain the title he won a year ago.

He proved to everybody who saw his losing fight, a battle that was an uphill struggle for him from the outset, that he is thoroughly game and fearless.

Baer, of course, is not the one-punch finisher that Dempsey was. And he does not fight as intently as Dempsey did when he had a foe on the downward path. But he is a terrific hitter, and every serious punch he let fly at Carnera was loaded with dynamite.

The Italian took every blow until he could take no more. Going down twelve times. He also fell once while delivering a punch. And twice in the first round he stumbled drunkenly against and almost through the ropes, helpless and on the brink of defeat.

But he rallied from this harrowing experience and outboxed Baer when the latter became playful in the fourth, seventh, eight and ninth rounds. And he was doing all right until Baer suddenly turned in the tenth round, as he did a year ago against Max Schmeling, and became vicious in the wink of an eye.

Then came what many thought was the end as the bell finished the tenth. At any event, it was unmistakably the finish of Carnera in the eleventh.

A Denial From Carnera.

Carnera denied after the bout that he had appealed to Referee Donovan to stop the fight, but he could have made his appeal without discredit to himself. He had gone further than anybody expected he would after those three knockdowns in the first.

More, on none of the knockdowns did Carnera take advantage of the nine-second count to which he was entitled and which an experienced fighter would use. Maybe this hastened his downfall, but it is doubtful.

Greater even than his survival of the early knockdowns was Carnera's self-confident rally through the fourth, seventh, eighth and ninth rounds. Cumbersome he was, but he fought on gloriously in his own awkward way, waging what he must have felt was a losing battle, but sticking to his guns until he could not go on.

It matters not whether he asked Referee Donovan to stop the fight—the intervention was imminent anyway—but none can dispute that Carnera went down to defeat gloriously, a Spartan to the last.

Baer fought an admirably clean fight, a fact which should be mentioned in view of the widespread suspicion in advance of the battle that he would wage the battle differently. Only one offense was charged against him in the State Athletic Commission's book of fouls, and this was accidental. In the eighth round the Californian was erratic with a sweeping left for the body.

Baer didn't have to resort to objectionable boxing. He tagged Carnera vitally three times in the first three minutes of fighting and from there on knew in his heart that Carnera was his victim whenever he elected to go after him.

Instead of rushing in and finishing the giant, the tolerant husky from California fought and coasted, charged and rested, was furious and easy in changing moods as the fight progressed. But he never withdrew the power from his punch, though at times he withheld the blow.

It followed as a consequence that Carnera was a pitiable sight at the finish. Baer was smiling and unmarked. He leaped over the ropes when his hand had been raised in victory, lithe as a panther and with a broad grin on his face.

"I'm not in condition," he said good-naturedly as he pounded his perfectly formed body on the ring platform.

The fight opened cautiously enough, a surprise for those who had expected Baer to tear out of his corner like a tiger. Carnera was cagey and Baer backed away, sizing up the giant. Short left leads were but feeble forerunners of what was to follow, and a harmless clinch was merely a disguise.

Suddenly, however, Baer leaped in on the attack, transformed in the wink of an eye from the cool strategist to a fighting fury. He led with a left for the body that was merely a feint, and then drove a right to Carnera's huge girth. The Italian winced under the blow and looked startled.

Baer Maintains Attack.

But he had no chance for counter or defense, for like a jiffy, Baer was upon him, lashing out wickedly with a roundhouse right which landed on the jaw, and toppled the giant in his tracks.

Carnera was only slightly more dazed than the crowd that witnessed the fall and the punch that precipitated it. Excitement ran high. Deep-throated words of advice and counsel came from the corner of Baer, clashing with words of encouragement and entreaty from the corner of Carnera.

In the general excitement the giant drew erect before a count could be started or heard above the din. Then Baer leaped after him and the downfall of the giant was under full headway.

In the six-round semi-final Charley Massera of Pittsburgh, 183½, pounded out a decision over Al Ettore, 184, Philadelphia.

James J. Braddock, 180, Jersey City, stopped Corn Griffin, Fort Benning, Ga., in 2:37 of the third round of a scheduled six-rounder.

In a five-rounder, Lou Poster, Pottsville, Pa., defeated Al White, 177½, Greenpoint. Dynamtie Jackson, 208, Los Angeles, defeated Willie McGee, 198, Tampa, Fla., and Eddie Hogan, 216½, Waterbury, outpointed Chester Matan, 208½, Brooklyn, in the other five rounders. The opening four was won by Don Petrin, 177[illegible], Newark, who turned back Ed Karolak, 188, Peekskill.

Estimated Statistics On Championship Fight

Total attendance	56,000
*Paid attendance	52,268
Gross receipts	$428,000
Federal tax	42,800
State tax	21,400
Carnera's share	122,782
Baer's share	40,927
†Dempsey's share	24,556
Milk Fund's share	36,380
Promotion costs	88,600
Garden's profit	50,555

*Official.
†Has contract with Baer.

ACTION IN TITLE BOUT AT THE BOWL LAST NIGHT AND THE NEW HEAVYWEIGHT CHAMPION.

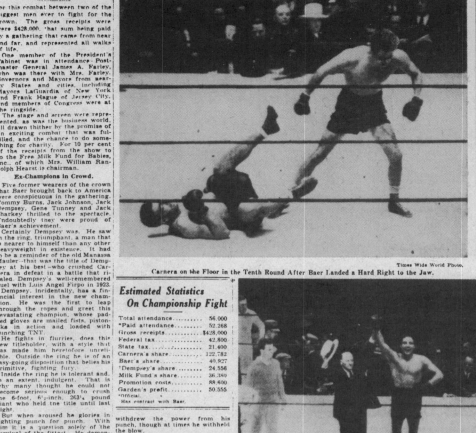

Times Wide World Photo.

Carnera on the Floor in the Tenth Round After Baer Landed a Hard Right to the Jaw.

Times Wide World Photo.

Carnera Down in the Eleventh Round. Referee Donovan Is Holding Baer Off.

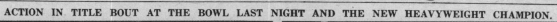

Times Wide World Photo.

Joe Humphreys Announcing Baer the Winner. In the Lower Right-Hand Corner Can Be Seen Carnera.

BAER'S RISE CLIMAX OF FIVE-YEAR DRIVE

Champion's Ascendancy to the Throne Rapid and Studded by Knockout Victories.

Like so many before him in the ring, Max Adelbert Baer—that is his full name—quite accidentally took to boxing. He was pointed to the life of a cattleman in the plans of his parents, but this idea was knocked askew when Max discovered he could punch.

The discovery came at the expense of a cowpuncher with whom Baer differed on some topic no more substantial than the affections of a girl. From that developed the fighter who was to scale the heights as world's heavyweight champion, with the world at his feet.

Baer was born in Omaha, Neb., Feb. 11, 1909, the son of Jacob and Dora Baer. His nationality is German-Jewish-American. His father was a cattle dealer. At the age of 9 the family moved to Livermore, Calif., where Baer Sr. purchased a ranch. The family now makes its home at San Leandro, about eight miles out of Oakland, Calif.

Learned He Could Punch.

Baer had not attained his majority when the knowledge that he could punch launched him on a ring career. He gave up high school after a year for the cattle business, and from this went to boxing.

His first professional opponent was Chief Cariboo in a fight held in Stockton, Calif., which ended in a two-round victory for Baer. This was just five years ago. It was the first of twenty-nine knockouts for Baer in a career that led gradually to the chance at the heavyweight title.

Times Wide World Photo.

Max Baer.

Ray Pelky was associated with the early development of the new champion, and so was Bob McAllister. It was the latter who got Baer his first professional bout. In three other bouts under the direction of McAllister, Baer knocked out Tillie Taverna, Sailor Leeds and Al Ledford.

These conquests attracted attention to the victor, and, after severing relations with McAllister, the young heavyweight signed with J. Hamilton Lorimer.

In his second year as a boxer Baer became associated with Ancil Hoffman, under whose leadership he climbed to fistic heights. Only last year a court battle was waged over the claims of Lorimer and Hoffman to the management of Baer. This litigation ended with Lorimer's managerial claim recognized, and a financial agreement was made.

In his early boxing Baer had the encouragement of his mother. His first complete ring outfit is said to have been purchased out of her funds. He received $40 as his first purse and went on from the Cariboo engagement to purses that were only part of his dream when he started.

Baer first came into prominence when he knocked out Frankie Campbell at San Francisco, Aug. 25, 1930 in five rounds. Campbell died the next day. Baer, noted for his good-natured disposition, was disconsolate and for a time seriously considered retirement from the ring.

Sets Plans for Title.

When he resumed boxing, he definitely set his plans for the title, prematurely, as developments proved. He was not yet ready for the experienced fighters of the ring. Consequently he lost to Les Kennedy, Tiny Abbott and the late Ernie Schaaf in 1930.

These defeats, however, had a steadying effect on the youth who generally regarded boxing as a hobby.

He turned his attention to serious boxing, however, and in 1931, knocked out Tom Heeney, who served as the last opponent for Gene Tunney in the latter's reign as heavyweight champion, and won a decision over Johnny Risko, the man designated by the late Tex Rickard as "the spoiler of championship ambitions."

These bouts led to the meeting last year in which Baer catapulted into the forefront of the challengers. He knocked out Max Schmeling, former titleholder, in ten rounds of fighting that demonstrated the Californian's ability as a puncher.

BEATEN CHAMPION WEEPS LIKE CHILD

'I Didn't Quit,' He Says in His Quarters—Face is Swollen and a Leg Bandaged.

Weeping like a child, Primo Carnera sat propped up on his rubbing table after the bout last night, shaking his head disconsolately minute after minute. His intimates sought to encourage him, to excuse his defeat, but the young giant, his right leg bandaged, seemed completely detached, as if he were far away.

At length he blurted out, "I lose. Don't you see? I lose the championship, that's all." Then he lapsed back into silence, a silence broken only by long, racking sobs. Then, as if it was an afterthought, he said, "but I didn't ask Donovan to stop it. I didn't quit. I'd have fought until I couldn't move, but I'd never give up."

The Italian was a badly beaten figure. The left side of his face was swollen to enormous proportions and his lips were puffed. His ankle was tightly bandaged and caused him obvious pain when he walked to his shower.

Louis Soresi, Carnera's manager, explained the leg injury by saying that the ankle was sprained in the first round, on one of the knockdowns.

"It handicapped him all through the fight," said Soresi, "and was the one thing that cost him the fight. He could have moved away from Baer's right if he had had the full use of the ankle, but the pain was too great."

BAER LOQUACIOUS AFTER THE FIGHT

Says Bout Should Have Ended Sooner as He Talks On and On in Dressing Room.

Max Baer took more punishment on his way to his dressing room than he did in ten and a fraction rounds against Primo Carnera. He was mobbed by delighted fans from the moment he set foot outside of the ring and the police had a terrific task in escorting the new champion to his quarters.

Baer, as usual, was not backward. In a few thousand well-chosen words he discussed the fight, his "lack of condition" and anything else that his interviewers were willing to speak about.

Max had questions popped at him so fast as he sat on a rubbing table that even he could not answer them rapidly enough. Finally he bellowed, "Will you fellows let me talk?"

Since there was no one else in the room with the verbal powers of the loquacious Californian, Max was allowed to talk.

His principal grievance was against Arthur Donovan, the referee, and his failure to stop the fight earlier.

Praise for Carnera.

"Primo's a nice chap," he said, "and he's got lots of heart, a lot more than I thought he had. But I could not hit him near the end of the tenth round. Donovan pushed me away while Carnera was still on his feet, and he stood there with his hands down.

"I pleaded with Donovan to stop the fight. Primo was such a dead cinch to wallop that I was afraid I might crack something back here." At that Baer pointed to the base of his skull.

"Donovan was trying hard enough but I guess he just got excited. I'll bet he never refereed a fight with so many knockdowns in it before." With that remark the champion rolled back his head and started to laugh. He was having a grand time.

Talks About Sharkey.

Some one mentioned the Sharkey-Carnera fight and Baer countered with "Betcha Sharkey's glad he's retired. He's never liked me since that time I came to New York a green 21-year-old kid, and some one asked me to meet Jack Sharkey. I turned to him and said, 'Who is Jack Sharkey?'" Baer had another spasm of laughter.

Ancil Hoffman, Baer's manager, also complained about Donovan's handling of the fight and said that his boxer was willing to meet any one who could draw at the gate. The new champion will remain in the East for seven weeks for the duration of a radio contract, and then will go back to California for a while.

He will keep in condition and will be ready to defend his crown when the Madison Square Garden promoters are ready. Baer has signed with the Garden for his next fight.

MAYOR IS FORCED TO SHOW A TICKET

Ushers Play No Favorites—Old Heroes of Pugilism in Throng at the Fight.

MANY NOTABLES PRESENT

Postmaster General Farley at Ringside—All Sections of Society Are Represented.

By ARTHUR J. DALEY.

Mayor LaGuardia made a triumphant entry into the Madison Square Garden Bowl last night. The vast crowd jumped to its feet and made the welkin ring with its vociferous cheering. Stalwart policemen guarded the smiling Mayor as he bowed to the plaudits of the spectators.

Then he encountered an usher. He was not a big usher as ushers go and he seemed smaller than ever in comparison to the policemen. But he stepped out in front of the chief executive, stared at him coldly and said very crisply, "Ticket, please."

The Mayor looked a bit surprised. He dug into one pocket, then another. Finally he found the pasteboard, presented it and went on his way. But as soon as he reached the ringside who should halt him but another usher. The procedure was the same. He had to produce a ticket. Not until then was he permitted to take his seat.

A Minimum of Delay.

The celebrities could not merely march in on their reputation. The ushers were hard-boiled enough to demand tickets and tickets had to be shown. But they were competent enough and well-drilled enough to place everybody with a minimum of trouble and delay.

This was a typical fight crowd, hailing from all sections of life and all strata of society. There were politicians, bankers, brokers, business men and the old heroes of pugilism. And up in the lower-priced seats along the outer rim of the Bowl were sailors from the fleet and the dyed-in-the-wool fans.

Hidden away in the crowd were five former world's heavyweight champions, one of the largest groups of these former monarchs of the padded mitt ever assembled. Jack Sharkey, Gene Tunney and Jack Dempsey were in the working press section. Further back was Tommy Burns and just within the circle of ringside seats was Jack Johnson.

Representing the lighter divisions there were Benny Leonard, Willie Ritchie, Tony Canzoneri, Jimmy McLarnin and Jack Britton.

Farley a Bit Late.

That inveterate fight goer, Postmaster General Farley, usually at hand for the first preliminary, was a bit late in arriving, but he was there, right up front and not missing a punch.

Others noted at the ringside were Colonel Theodore Roosevelt, Bernard Gimbel, Judge Lester Patterson, George Getz, Bobby Jones, Jim Coffroth, Tiv Kreling, Richard Dix, Will Hays, Vincent Daily, Glenn Cunningham, Major William Kennelly, Jules Brulatour and Hope Hampton.

There were boxing commissioners from California, Illinois and New York. Among them were Dr. Harry I. Martin, Clare Goodwin, Joe Triner, Louis London, Packy McFarland, Major Gen. John J. Phelan, D. Walker Wear and Bill Brown.

Cool But Not Comfortable.

The ushers looked cool, natty and comfortable in their blue shirts and white duck trousers while the sun was shining before the fights. But when darkness came over the arena they appeared much too cool and not at all comfortable.

General Hugh S. Johnson, National Recovery Administration chief, arrived at North Beach Airport, Queens, shortly after 9 P. M. and proceeded from there to the fight by automobile. He flew from Washington in a Curtiss Condor plane, leaving the Capitol at 7:20 P. M.

The crowd witnessed more than a Carnera-Baer battle. It saw Gene Tunney and Jack Dempsey in the squared ring together. Joe Humphreys brought them both within the ropes and the bitter rivals of other years smiled and shook hands like a couple of long-lost friends.

Others introduced were Benny Leonard, Willie Ritchie, Tommy Loughran, Jimmy McLarnin, Steve Hamas, Jack Sharkey and Ray Impellittiere.

Round-by-Round Description of the World's Championship Match

By JOSEPH C. NICHOLS.

Primo Carnera weighed 263¼ pounds for his bout with Max Baer in the Madison Square Garden Bowl last night. The Californian scaled 210. Arthur Donovan was the referee and Charley Lynch and Tommy Shortell the judges.

The round-by-round story of the battle follows:

First Round.

They sparred cautiously and then clinched. Baer tried a left for the face but was wild. Carnera was short with a left to the face but landed a right to the face. Carnera hooked a left to the jaw. Carnera jabbed three stiff rights to Baer's face and the latter rushed in. Carnera held him. Baer sent a solid right to the body and Carnera returned a light left to the face. Carnera grazed Max's face with a long left hand. Baer sent a right to the jaw and floored Carnera for no count. Carnera rolled and floundered about the ring. Carnera fell to the floor twice more in an effort to evade the charging challenger, but arose each time without a count. The champion tottered defenseless in front of his foe, but Baer could not get the range and so the round ended.

Second Round.

Baer swung a right to the jaw and sent Carnera to the ropes. They clinched, and at close quarters Baer landed a right to the jaw. Carnera locked his arms around Baer and fell, dragging his challenger with him. There was no count, and immediately afterward the pair went to the canvas together again. Primo once more grabbing Baer as he received a right on the jaw. Baer then charged the champion and sent a right to the jaw. Carnera fell forward into the Californian's arms, and once more they toppled to the floor. They arose at a count of four.

Third Round.

Carnera hooked a left to the jaw. Baer landed a right to the chin and Carnera held. Baer sent Primo's head back with a long right to the jaw. Carnera stabbed a long left to the face and hooked a left to the face. Baer smashed a left to the body and Carnera held. Carnera hooked a left to the jaw and grazed Baer's chin with a right uppercut. Carnera poked his left into Baer's face several times as Baer boxed, waiting for an opening. They traded long lefts and then lefts and rights to the body at close range. Baer floored Carnera with a right to the temple and charged in in an attempt to strike the champion when he was on the floor. Referee Donovan intervened and Carnera arose without a count.

Fourth Round.

Baer pumped a left into the body and Carnera jabbed three lefts to the head. Carnera was short with a left jab but closed in with a light left and right to the head. Carnera sent a left and right to the head and Baer held. Baer hooked a terrific left to the body but Carnera returned both hands to the midsection. Baer feinted Carnera from a distance of about eight feet and the champion jumped. Baer laughed. Carnera landed several long lefts to Baer's face but Baer rushed into close quarters and smashed both hands to the body. Carnera sent Baer's head back with a hard straight left to the face.

Fifth Round.

Carnera hooked a left to the jaw. Carnera was short with a left to the face and Baer returned a right to the kidneys. Baer landed a right to the jaw and Primo held. Baer was short with a left to the face and dug a left into the body. Carnera reached Baer's jaw with a left hook but missed a right for the head. Baer crouched and shot a left into Carnera's mid-section. Carnera stabbed three lefts to the jaw. Baer landed a right to the jaw that staggered Primo, who held. Baer shot both hands to the body as Carnera tried to maintain his grasp. Baer staggered Carnera again with a wild right to the jaw. The champion fell into his rival's arms and clung desperately, apparently groggy.

Sixth Round.

Baer waltzed to Primo's corner and rubbed his shoes in the resin, almost utterly indifferent to the giant in front of him. Carnera poked a long left into the face and then sent two lefts to the body. Baer hooked a left to the jaw and missed a right for the head. They traded punches toe to toe, with Baer landing on the body and Carnera reaching Baer's head. Carnera brushed Max's face with three lefts and the latter ripped in with a left to the body and a right to the heart. Baer again shook Carnera with a right to the jaw and the champion's knees sagged. Just before the round ended Baer drove a long right to Carnera's jaw.

Seventh Round.

They sparred for several seconds before trading long lefts. Carnera sent a short left to the head and Baer ripped back a left and right to the body. Baer retreated as Carnera stalked him seeking a chance to land a long left. Carnera hooked a left to the jaw and shot a light left and right to the head. Carnera grazed his rival's face with three lefts, and Baer winked at his corner. Carnera sent a left high to the head, but Baer retaliated with two hands to the body. Carnera shot several lefts and rights to the face, but the blows had little effect on Baer.

Eighth Round.

Carnera pawed Baer's face with his left hand. Baer sent a right to the jaw and closed in with a left and right to the body. Carnera missed a left for the face. Carnera landed a heavy right uppercut to the jaw, and Baer smiled and winked at his corner. Baer landed a right to the jaw, and Carnera came in with a left to the face. Baer shot a long right that landed behind Carnera's ears. Carnera rushed Baer to the ropes but could not reach him with a short right uppercut. Carnera landed a right to the jaw and rushed Baer in an effort to follow up the punch. Baer danced out of the way and Carnera tripped to the floor but arose immediately.

Ninth Round.

Primo was short with a left to the face. Baer hooked a left to the jaw and missed a right for the head. Baer landed a light left to the jaw and then held. Carnera drove two long lefts to the face and made Max miss a right for the head. Baer shot a left into Carnera's body. At close quarters Carnera cuffed Baer with both hands. Carnera jabbed a left to the face and Baer sent back a left to the face. Carnera hooked a left to the face. Carnera sent a left and right uppercut to the jaw, but Baer partially blocked the blow. Baer hooked a left to the body at the bell.

Tenth Round.

Baer crouched low and tapped Carnera's body with his right. Carnera clubbed a left to the jaw and sent a right to the midsection. Baer crowded Carnera into a corner and slugged the champion with both hands to the body. Carnera hooked a right uppercut to the body. Carnera landed a left and right to the head but was short with a right to the jaw. Carnera sent Baer's head back with a right uppercut to the jaw. Carnera grazed Baer's face with a left hook and stepped into a hard right to the jaw. Baer landed another hard right to the jaw and Carnera floundered all over the ring. Referee Donovan stepped in front of him and Baer did not know whether to continue. The referee allowed the fight to go on and Baer went after him again landing a series of lefts and rights to the jaw. Carnera sank to the canvas and took a count of four. He arose just as the bell rang when Referee Donovan already had signified that the fight was stopped.

Eleventh Round.

They sparred for a few seconds and Baer dropped Carnera for a count of two with a right to the jaw. Carnera grazed the jaw with a right and then landed squarely with another right to the jaw. Baer stepped into a right to the face but returned a heavy right to he head, making Carnera groggy. The challenger sent another right to the jaw, dropping Carnera for a count of two. Carnera was in poor condition when he arose and Referee Donovan interceded, stopping the fight and sending Carnera to his corner. Baer received credit for the knockout in 2 minutes and 16 seconds of the round.

BAER A 7-TO-5 CHOICE.

Enters Ring the Betting Favorite in Surprising Switch.

Max Baer went into the ring the betting favorite over Primo Carnera. The challenger showed remarkable strength in the closing books, and when he stepped into the ring was the choice at 7 to 5 to dethrone the champion.

Carnera's adherents could get an even play for their money, whereas one had to put up $7 to $5 on Baer.

A last-day rush of Baer money was responsible for Baer's position. A number of California fans with stuffed wallets showed a willingness to back the Coast battler and thus succeeded in switching the quotation.

Hunch players, however, picked Baer merely because he started the day on the short end. They hoped that precedent, which shows that many champions went into the ring odds-on choices only to lose, would support them.

Heavyweight Champions.

John L. Sullivan	1882-92
James J. Corbett	1892-97
Bob Fitzsimmons	1897-99
James J. Jeffries	1899-06
Tommy Burns	1906-08
Jack Johnson	1908-15
Jess Willard	1915-19
Jack Dempsey	1919-26
*Gene Tunney	1926-28
Max Schmeling	1930-32
Jack Sharkey	1932-33
Primo Carnera	1933-34
Max Baer	1934

*Retired undefeated July 21, 1928.

50,000 See American League Triumph Over National All Stars at Polo Grounds

AMERICAN LEAGUE VICTOR AGAIN, 9-7

Launches Six-Run Barrage in Fifth to Beat Nationals in All-Star Classic.

HUBBELL DRAWS ACCLAIM

Fans Ruth, Gehrig, Foxx, Simmons, Cronin and Gomez in First Two Innings.

By JOHN DREBINGER.

Packing thrill upon thrill, the foremost professional ball players of the nation battled for two and three-quarter hours at the Polo Grounds yesterday in the 1934 edition of the ball game of the century, with the forces of the American League demonstrating for the second successive year that at this newly devised form of interleague competition they still hold the edge.

For, by uncorking a devastating six-run rally in the fifth inning, the all-stars of the American League carried the day over Memphis Bill Terry and his carefully chosen National League cast by a score of 9 to 7.

A capacity crowd of 50,000 witnessed the struggle. It was a gathering that occupied every seat in the historic arena, jammed the aisles and roared itself purple.

$52,982 to Players' Fund.

About 15,000 more roared, too, when the gates were locked fifteen minutes before game time, shutting all out who had not already purchased reserved seat tickets. The paid attendance totaled 48,363 and the receipts donated to the players' charity fund were $52,982, net.

It was a crowd, too, which at the outset seemed undecided with which side it was to align itself. The National Leaguers were the home team and they were being bossed by Bill Terry. The American circuit had Joe Cronin, boy pilot of the Senators, at the head, and this sort of gave it a renewed setting of last Fall's world's series.

On the other hand, the American Leaguers also had Babe Ruth and Lou Gehrig and no New Yorker could very well be expected to root against either of these two. Whereupon the crowd simply compromised and bellowed unreservedly for whichever side was showing to advantage for the moment.

In rather sharp contrast with the all-star game in Chicago last year, this conflict developed into a titanic struggle of hitters, during which great names in the pitching industry were rudely jostled about.

Contrast With 1933 Game.

In the 1933 conflict a homer by Babe Ruth won the struggle for the American League, 4 to 2, but while the great Bambino, appearing in only five innings yesterday, was held in more or less restraint, others did some thunderous walloping. Frankie Frisch and Joe Medwick hit homers for the National Leaguers, while Earl Averill banged three runs across with a triple and a double in two successive innings.

Of the eight pitchers to step to the mound, three for the American League and five for the National, only two survived with their prestige intact. One, as can readily be imagined, was the invincible Carl Hubbell, who gave a masterful exhibition of his left-handed talents during his assignment for the first three innings.

The other was Mel Harder, trim right-hander of the Cleveland Indians, who checked a National League rally in the fifth after the Americans had swept to the fore, and hurled scoreless baseball for the remainder of the distance.

Gomez Touched for Four Runs.

Vernon Gomez, ace left-hander of the American circuit, who opposed Hubbell for the first three rounds, fell for four runs during his tenure of office on the wings of the homers hit by the two Cardinals, Frisch and Medwick.

His right-handed Yankee colleague, the burly Charlie Ruffing, was routed summarily from the mound in the fifth, while for the National Leaguers, Lon Warneke of the Cubs and Van Lingle Mungo of the Dodgers came down with a grand crash in the fourth and fifth as the forces of the junior circuit amassed a total of eight runs.

In the minutes before the game there was a respectful silence as a memorial tablet to the late John J. McGraw was unveiled in front of the centre-field clubhouse, and a full-throated, hearty cheer went up as the popular Hubbell received a plaque from the Baseball Writers Association for his services last year as the outstanding player of the campaign.

Excitement Starts at Once.

This done, the spectators warmed quickly to the battle at hand. Nor was there much delay in providing them with plenty of provocation for exercising their vocal accomplishments. Charlie Gehringer, leading off the American League batting order, greeted Hubbell with a single to centre and when Wally Berger momentarily fumbled the ball the fleet Tiger swept down to second. Came a pass to Heinie Manush and there was some uneasiness on the National bench.

Hubbell looked around to his infield, apparently awaiting the familiar Giant huddle. However, for this occasion the lean southpaw was not flanked by Blondy Ryan or Hughie Critz. True, he had his manager, Terry, on one side of him, and behind him, at short, was Travis Jackson, his ailing eye sufficiently improved to permit him to play at the last moment. But at second base was Frisch and at third Pie Traynor of the Pirates, both aliens to him during the regular campaign.

So Hubbell merely bore down to his work with renewed vigor and at this point turned on some of the most magnificent flinging seen in years as he mowed down the best of the American League's batting strength.

Ruth was called out on strikes, the Babe looking decidedly puzzled as a screw ball just clipped the outside corner for the third one. Then Gehrig struck out with a grand flourish, and not even the fact that Gehringer and Manush executed a double steal right under Gabby Hartnett's nose as Lou fished for the third one perturbed the long, lean left-hander.

Amid a deafening uproar Hubbell completed the string by fanning Jimmy Foxx, who at the last moment had been inserted in the American League line-up as the third baseman in place of Frank Higgins.

Scarcely had the furor of this master stroke subsided than the crowd was thrown into an another uproar as Frisch, first up for the Nationals, caught one of Gomez's speed balls and lined it into the densely packed upper right tier. Unmindful of this, Gomez retired the next three, and then all eyes again focused on Hubbell.

And once again the famous southpaw held the crowd and American Leaguers spellbound alike as he continued his sweep down the batting order. He fanned the great Al Simmons and also Cronin, making it five in a row. Bill Dickey, the Yankee catcher, clipped him for a single to left, but Gomez was also swept aside on strikes to make it six strike-outs for the first two innings.

Ovation for Hubbell.

For the third, Gehringer flied to Cuyler in right, Manush grounded out, Ruth drew a pass, Gehrig flied out, and as Hubbell marched to the centre-field clubhouse, his afternoon's assignment completed, he was accorded a tremendous ovation from all sides of the packed arena.

Less fortunate was Gomez, who almost got by with nothing worse than the Frisch homer in the first when trouble overtook him with two out in the third. Frisch walked, Traynor singled and Medwick larruped the ball into the upper left tier to give the National League a 4-0 margin.

With the retirement of Hubbell, however, things suddenly took a turn for the worse for the Terry forces. The tall, angular Warneke came on, and the American Leaguers at once bristled with action.

The Cub righthander retired Foxx on a grounder to start the fourth, but Simmons doubled to left and counted on a single by Cronin. Dickey fanned, then Averill, coming into the battle as pinch hitter for Gomez, hit a tremendous triple which dropped just in front of the bleachers in right centre, and Cronin tallied.

Then came the fifth, in which the fortunes of the National Leaguers toppled like a house of cards. Warneke passed both Ruth and Gehrig, and Terry, after a brief conference with Catcher Hartnett, waved Warneke out and called on Mungo, the ace of Casey Stengel's pitching staff in Brooklyn.

There was no checking the American Leaguers now. Foxx hammered a single to centre and Ruth scored. Jackson made a marvelous stop of Simmons's sharp grounder toward left, but when his hurried toss to second went wide, Simmons received credit for a hit and Gehrig counted, tying the score.

Runs now began to pour over the plate in a torrent. There was a slight pause as Cronin fouled out, but Dickey walked, filling the bases, and Averill, who had remained in the game as the centre fielder, now doubled down the right field foul line, scoring two more.

Gehringer was intentionally passed to fill the bases, again in the hope of enticing Ruffing, now the American League pitcher, to slap into a double play. Ruffing, instead, slapped a single into left and the fifth and sixth runs hustled across the plate.

With Ruth and Gehrig the next hitters, Mungo's troubles loomed almost endless, but at this point the Dodger regained his poise, and ended the inning by retiring the Babe on a grounder and fanning Lou.

National Leaguers Rally.

That seemed to settle the issue quite definitely, but the National League still had a wealth of material on the bench and in this same inning, the fifth, Terry unloaded it. It resulted in a three-run rally that routed Ruffing and was checked just one run short of a tie.

Pepper Martin, the Cardinal thunderbolt, batted for Mungo and walked. Then followed three successive singles by Frisch, Traynor and Chuck Klein, the latter entering the game here as Medwick's successor in the National League outfield.

Two runs had come in during this outburst and Ruffing was asked to withdraw in favor of Harder. The shift brought an abrupt halt to the National charge. For though a third tally was carried in by Traynor on a double steal with Frisch while Paul Waner was striking out, it proved the last marker for the Terry cast.

In the remaining four innings, with Terry hurling all his available man-power into the fray, the National Leaguers obtained just one single off the elusive Cleveland right-hander. That was a double by Billy Herman, Cub second baseman, in the ninth. The sturdy Mel Ott, up twice in the closing stages of the battle, went hitless, as also did Arky Vaughan, who replaced Jackson in the fifth.

One More for the Americans.

As for the American Leaguers, they merely tightened their grip by jamming one more run across off Dizzy Dean in the sixth as this tall and eccentric Cardinal right-hander started on his three innings of labor. A high fly by Simmons in short right which Frisch dropped after a sturdy chase went for a double and a run resulted almost immediately when Cronin pulled a robust two-bagger to left.

The American Leaguers might even have made more, only for the fact that Cronin got himself trapped off second base while Averill was striking out, thereby ending the inning.

Fred Frankhouse, star right-hander of the Braves, went through a commendable ninth for the National League and did his very best to start a rally in the lower half. With no more pinch-hitters available, Terry had to permit Frankhouse to bat for himself in this inning and Fred almost started something with a bunt in front of the plate. But Mickey Cochrane, who had replaced Dickey as the American League catcher, pounced on the ball and caught the Boston pitcher by a step at first.

As a result, the bases were still empty when Billy Herman followed with his double and neither Traynor nor Klein could improve on the situation. Whereupon the crowd filed out well satisfied that it had seen all the baseball that could possibly be crowded into a single afternoon.

Cards Defeat Elmira, 3-1.

ELMIRA, N. Y., July 10 (AP).—The Cardinals defeated the Elmira team of the New York-Pennsylvania League, 3 to 1, in an exhibition game today.

SCENES AT THE ALL-STAR BASEBALL GAME AT THE POLO GROUNDS YESTERDAY.

Times Wide World Photo.

A General View of the Vast Throng Watching the Contest.

Times Wide World Photo.

Mayor LaGuardia and Baseball Commissioner Landis.

Times Wide World Photo.

Averill, American League, Sliding Into Third Base After Hitting Triple in the Fourth Inning. Traynor Is Covering the Bag.

Box Score of the Game

AMERICAN LEAGUE.

	ab.	r.	h.	tb.	2b.	3b.	hr.	bb.	so.	sh.	sb.	po.	a.	e.
Gehringer, Det., 2b	3	0	2	2	0	0	0	3	0	0	1	2	1	0
Manush, Wash., lf	2	0	0	0	0	0	0	1	0	0	1	0	0	0
Ruffing, N. Y., p	1	0	1	1	0	0	0	0	0	0	0	0	0	0
Harder, Cleve., p	2	0	0	0	0	0	0	0	1	0	0	1	0	0
Ruth, N. Y., rf	2	1	0	0	0	0	0	2	1	0	0	0	0	0
Chapman, N. Y., rf	2	0	1	3	0	1	0	0	0	0	0	0	1	0
Gehrig, N. Y., 1b	4	1	0	0	0	0	0	1	3	0	0	11	1	1
Foxx, Phila., 3b	5	1	2	3	1	0	0	0	2	0	0	1	2	0
Simmons, Chi., cf, lf	5	3	3	5	2	0	0	0	1	0	0	3	0	0
Cronin, Wash., ss	5	1	2	3	1	0	0	0	1	0	0	2	8	0
Dickey, N. Y., c	2	1	1	1	0	0	0	2	1	0	0	4	0	0
Cochrane, Det., c	1	0	0	0	0	0	0	0	0	0	0	1	1	0
Gomez, N. Y., p	1	0	0	0	0	0	0	0	1	0	0	0	0	0
Averill, Cleve., cf	4	1	2	5	1	1	0	0	1	0	0	1	0	0
West, St. L., cf	0	0	0	0	0	0	0	0	0	0	0	1	0	0
Total	39	9	14	23	5	2	0	9	12	0	2	27	14	1

NATIONAL LEAGUE.

	ab.	r.	h.	tb.	2b.	3b.	hr.	bb.	so.	sh.	sb.	po.	a.	e.
Frisch, St. L., 2b	3	3	2	5	0	0	1	1	0	0	0	0	1	0
aHerman, Chi., 2b	2	0	1	2	1	0	0	0	0	0	0	0	1	0
Traynor, Pitt., 3b	5	2	2	2	0	0	0	0	0	0	1	1	0	0
Medwick, St. L., lf	2	1	1	4	0	0	1	0	1	0	0	0	0	0
Klein, Chi., lf	3	0	1	1	0	0	0	0	0	0	0	1	0	0
Cuyler, Chi., rf	2	0	0	0	0	0	0	0	0	0	0	2	0	0
Ott, N. Y., rf	2	0	0	0	0	0	0	0	0	0	1	0	1	0
Berger, Bos., cf	2	0	0	0	0	0	0	0	1	0	0	0	0	1
P. Waner, Pitt., cf	2	0	0	0	0	0	0	0	1	0	0	1	0	0
Terry, N. Y., 1b	3	0	1	1	0	0	0	1	0	0	0	4	0	0
Jackson, N. Y., ss	2	0	0	0	0	0	0	0	1	0	0	0	1	0
Vaughan, Pitt., ss	2	0	0	0	0	0	0	0	0	0	0	4	0	0
Hartnett, Chi., c	2	0	0	0	0	0	0	0	0	0	0	9	0	0
Lopez, Brook., c	2	0	0	0	0	0	0	0	1	0	0	5	1	0
Hubbell, N. Y., p	0	0	0	0	0	0	0	0	0	0	0	0	0	0
Warneke, Chi., p	0	0	0	0	0	0	0	0	0	0	0	0	0	0
Mungo, Brook., p	0	0	0	0	0	0	0	0	0	0	0	0	0	0
bMartin, St. L.	0	1	0	0	0	0	0	1	0	0	0	0	0	0
J. Dean, St. L., p	1	0	0	0	0	0	0	0	0	0	0	0	0	0
Frankhouse, Bos., p	1	0	0	0	0	0	0	0	0	0	0	0	0	0
Total	36	7	8	15	1	0	2	3	5	0	2	27	5	1

a Batted for Hubbell in third, but was permitted to replace Frisch in the seventh. b Batted for Mungo in the fifth.

SCORE BY INNINGS.

American League	0	0	0	2	6	1	0	0	0—9
National League	1	0	3	0	3	0	0	0	0—7

Runs batted in—American League: Averill 3, Cronin 2, Ruffing 2, Foxx, Simmons. National League: Medwick 3, Frisch, Traynor, Klein.

Left on bases—American League 12, National League 5. Double play—Lopez and Vaughan. Hits—Off Gomez 3 in 3 innings, Ruffing 4 in 1 (none out in fifth), Harder 1 in 5, Hubbell 2 in 3, Warneke 3 in 1 (none out in fifth), Mungo 4 in 1, Dean 5 in 3, Frankhouse 0 in 1. Struck out—By Gomez 3, Harder 2, Hubbell 6, Warneke 1, Mungo 1, Dean 4. Bases on balls—Off Gomez 1, Ruffing 1, Harder 1, Hubbell 2, Warneke 3, Mungo 2, Dean 1, Frankhouse 1. Winning pitcher—Harder. Losing pitcher—Mungo. Umpires—Pfirman (N. L.) at the plate, Owens (A. L.) at first, Stark (N. L.) at second and Moriarty (A. L.) at third, for the first four and one-half innings; Owens (A. L.) at the plate, Stark (N. L.) at first, Moriarty (A. L.) at second and Pfirman (N. L.) at third, for remainder of game. Time of game—2:44.

WORLD SERIES AIR IMBUES THE FANS

Partisanship Equally Divided at Polo Grounds—15,000 Are Turned Away.

M'GRAW PLAQUE UNVEILED

LaGuardia Among the Onlookers—Landis, Hubbell Occupy Attention.

By ROSCOE McGOWEN.

Lured by the ideal weather and the hope that somehow they might be able to see the all-star classic, 15,000 baseball fans were turned away from the Polo Grounds yesterday. But 50,000 were inside the grounds and had the time of their lives.

They didn't see Babe Ruth hit a home run; they didn't even see him get a single, because for once the great man of baseball had to let the spotlight's glare play over some one else.

Frankie Frisch, not unused to the limelight himself, walloped one of the home runs made during the struggle and Joe Medwick, whose fame is just beginning, was the author of the other one.

Both blows persuaded the National League fans that their circuit would make it an even break with the junior loop. But the American League bats, especially the one swung by Earl Averill, put the crusher on all hopes.

It was a world's series atmosphere, with the exception that the fans paid only the regular prices of admission to see a contest that, in many respects, outdoes the big Autumn show of baseball.

Set Above Grant Monument.

Bunting was draped from the upper and lower box rails, and added to the usual ceremonies was the short but impressive one during which the memorial bronze plaque for the late John J. McGraw was unveiled.

The plaque is set exactly in the middle of the clubhouse in centre field, just above the monument to Captain Eddie Grant.

The unveiling of the McGraw memorial seemed to escape the attention of the crowd in good part, as there was only a scattered bit of applause when the announcer broadcast a description of the plaque and its purpose.

Hubbell figured in a ceremony at the home plate just before he took the mound, when Frank Graham, on behalf of the New York Chapter, Baseball Writers of America, presented him with the most valuable player award voted to him last Winter. A burst of cheering greeted Hubbell on this occasion, but not so great as when he fanned Jimmy Foxx for the third out with two men on bases in the first inning.

Little Trouble Is Caused.

It was a happy and well-behaved throng, with partisanship about equally divided. No one gave the Polo Grounds authorities any trouble with the exception of one ambitious photographer who had to be shooed off the field by Umpire George Moriarty about half way through the game.

Mayor LaGuardia was a distinguished spectator and fans of all degrees were numbered among the crowd.

Billy Evans, Sam Breadon, Judge Fuchs, Charley Stoneham, Steve McKeever and practically every other owner and manager watched the game with keen interest.

Kenesaw Mountain Landis, commissioner of baseball, was much in evidence before the contest started, becoming the usual target for the news photographers, but after Carl Hubbell marched to the mound all eyes thereafter were turned on the pick of the country's diamond stars.

Umpire Pfirman called Warneke's first two pitches to Ruth in the fifth strikes and the Babe put on a pantomime of disgust. He finally drew a pass.

Play-by-Play Description of the All-Star Baseball Game Yesterday

By JAMES P. DAWSON.

The play-by-play description of the American League-National League game at the Polo Grounds yesterday follows:

FIRST INNING.

AMERICAN—It was 1:37 when Hubbell sent the first pitch across the plate and Gehringer fouled it down the first-base line. After two balls Gehringer lined a single past Frisch to right centre and raced to second when Berger momentarily fumbled the ball, sliding in under the throw by a scant margin. Heinie Manush drew a pass, and the entire National League infield, along with Catcher Hartnett, went into a huddle with Hubbell in the box. The crowd cheered when Babe Ruth stepped to the plate with two on and none out, but they groaned when the Bambino was called out on strikes on four pitches. He swung at one. The count went to three and two on Gehrig and when Lou missed a third strike Gehringer stole third and Manush second. The crowd went wild when Hubbell fanned Foxx on five pitches. No runs, one hit, one error, two left.

NATIONAL—Frisch let Gomez's first pitch go by and it was called a ball. He leaned against the next one and crashed the ball high into the upper right-field stand for a home run. A deafening roar greeted Fordham Frankie as he trotted around the base, and Gomez looked dejectedly in the direction the ball had taken. Gehringer made a great stop and a perfect throw to toss out Traynor at first. Medwick fanned. Dickey, after missing the third strike, touched him out at the plate. Cronin scooped up Cuyler's grounder and threw him out at first. One run, one hit, no errors, none left.

SECOND INNING.

AMERICAN—Hubbell fanned Simmons on four pitches. The White Sox ace reached for high and wide ones. So did Joe Cronin, when Hubbell also fanned him on four pitched balls. The count was two strikes and a ball when Dickey rifled a single to left. A new bat he was waving flew out of Gomez's hands as he missed a swing. It was recovered by Manager Terry. Then Gomez missed two more swings to become Hubbell's sixth strike-out victim in two innings. No runs, one hit, no errors, one left.

NATIONAL—Gomez fanned Berger. Simmons raced in from deep centre to pull down Terry's fly. Gomez made it a perfect inning by fanning Jackson. No runs, no hits, no errors, none left.

THIRD INNING.

AMERICAN—Cuyler made a wonderful catch of Gehringer's high, long fly to deep right. Frisch scooped up Manush's grounder and threw him out at first. Ruth walked. Gehrig lined right into the waiting hands of Cuyler for the third out. No runs, no hits, no errors, one left.

NATIONAL—Hartnett grounded to Cronin and was an easy out at first. Billy Herman batted for Hubbell. The American League pilot then raced into short left and pulled down Herman's pop fly. Gomez thought Umpire Pfirman had missed a third strike on Frisch and then Frankie walked. Traynor smashed a single through the box to centre, and Frisch galloped to third. The count was one and one on Medwick when Joe drove a home run into the upper left field stand, scoring Frisch and Traynor ahead of him. Cuyler flied out to Simmons on the first pitch. Three runs, two hits, no errors, none left.

FOURTH INNING.

AMERICAN—Warneke went in to pitch for the Nationals. Jackson easily threw out Foxx. With the count one and one, Simmons crashed a double off the concrete wall in far left. With a little more rise to it the smash would have been a homer. Cronin hit the first pitch for a single off the left-field wall, scoring Simmons. Dickey hit a foul into the upper left-field stand, then was called out on strikes. Averill was sent up to bat for Gomez. After working the count to three and one he lined a triple high over the heads of Cuyler and Berger to the bleacher front in right, scoring Cronin. Gehringer drew a pass on five pitches. Manush fouled out to Traynor. Two runs, three hits, no errors, two left.

NATIONAL—Ruffing took the mound for the Americans. Simmons moved over from centre to left field, replacing Manush, and Averill went to centre. Berger was retired on a high foul fly to Foxx at third. Terry lined a single to left. Jackson lifted a high fly to Averill in short centre. Foxx grabbed Hartnett's bounder and threw him out at first. No runs, one hit, no errors, one left.

FIFTH INNING.

AMERICAN—Ruth didn't like it when Umpire Pfirman called the first two pitches strikes and he looked apprehensively as the next two were called balls. Then Hartnett protested what had been called the third ball. Finally, after Pfirman had examined the ball at the request of Coach Al Schacht, Ruth drew a pass. When Warneke walked Gehrig, Manager Terry and his inner defense conferred in the box with Warneke, looking balefully in the direction of Umpire Pfirman meanwhile. Terry protested to Pfirman, then removed Warneke and summoned Mungo to the mound, while Dizzy Dean was sent to the bull pen to warm up. On Mungo's first pitch, Foxx crashed a single to centre, scoring Ruth and chasing Gehrig to third. Simmons beat out a hit to deep short, Gehrig scoring, while Foxx went to second. He was safe easily when Jackson's toss, made while Travis was in the air after a great stop, was a little high. Cronin tried to sacrifice and fouled out to Hartnett back of the plate. Dickey drew a pass, filling the bases. After two balls, Averill cracked a double down the right-field foul line, scoring Foxx and Simmons and sending Dickey to third. Strategically, on orders from Manager Terry, Mungo intentionally walked Gehringer, again filling the bases. Ruffing worked the count to three and two and then singled sharply to left, scoring Dickey and Averill, and sending Gehringer to second. Ruth, up for the second time, grounded out to Terry, Gehringer and Ruffing advancing. On three pitched balls Gehrig fanned on his second time at bat in the inning. Six runs, four hits, no errors, two left.

NATIONAL—Ruth retired, Chapman replacing him in right field. The game was delayed several minutes while the umpires changed positions, Owens going back of the plate, Stark to first, Moriarty to second and Pfirman to third. During the wait Moriarty forcibly ejected some photographers from the field. Pepper Martin batted for Mungo and drew a pass. Facing a right-handed pitcher, Frisch batted from the left side of the plate for the first time and singled to left centre, chasing Martin to third. Gehringer missed a desperate stab at Traynor's scorching grounder, which went for a single, scoring Martin, while Frisch pulled up at second. Klein batted for Medwick and crashed a single to right, scoring Frisch, while Traynor stopped at second. Ruffing was removed and Harder called to the rescue. Ott batted for Cuyler and lined sharply to right. Chapman missed a catch after dashing in at full speed, but he recovered the ball in time to throw out Klein at second with a rifle peg to Cronin, while Traynor went to third. Paul Waner, batting for Berger, struck out, but on the third strike, Ott stole second, and Traynor raced home from third on Dickey's throw to Gehringer, completing a double steal. Terry walked. Vaughan batted for Jackson and grounded to Cronin, whose throw to Gehringer forced Terry. Three runs, three hits, no errors, two left.

SIXTH INNING.

AMERICAN—Dizzy Dean went to the mound, Paul Waner to centre, Ott to right, Klein to left, Vaughan to shortstop and Lopez caught. Foxx fanned. With the outfield playing deep, Simmons lifted a high fly in short centre, and pulled up safely at second with a two-base hit when Frisch lost the ball in the sun. Cronin banged a double down the left-field foul line, scoring Simmons. The first two pitches to Dickey were strikes, but he waited and got a pass. Cochrane ran for Dickey. Averill struck out and Cronin and Cochrane were caught flat-footed between third and second and second and first. Lopez ran out to short and, after missing Cronin, tossed to Vaughan to complete a double play that retired the side. One run, two hits, no errors, one left.

NATIONAL—Cochrane caught for the Americans. Lopez struck out. Simmons made a glittering catch of Dean's low-flying line drive. Frisch grounded to Cronin, and was an easy out at first. No runs, no hits, no errors, none left.

SEVENTH INNING.

AMERICANS—Herman was permitted to replace Frisch at second base for the Nationals although he had batted for Hubbell in the third inning. Gehringer singled to right, but was out trying to stretch it into a double, Ott to Vaughan. Harder struck out. Chapman stepped into the first pitch and banged a triple to the concrete wall in deep left. Gehrig was called out on strikes. No runs, two hits, no errors, one left.

NATIONAL—Cronin made a nice play in scooping up Traynor's grounder past Foxx and throwing him out at first. Klein bounced to Gehrig, and was safe when Lou's throw to Harder, covering first, was wide. Ott grounded to Cronin, forcing Klein at second, Cronin to Gehringer. Waner popped to Gehrig. No runs, no hits, one error, one left.

EIGHTH INNING.

AMERICAN—Foxx lifted a high fly in short left and pulled up safely at second with a two-base hit when Klein lost the ball in the sun after a hard run. Vaughan raced into left and pulled down Simmons's high fly. Cronin lined into the waiting hands of Waner in centre, Foxx being held at second. Cochrane grounded to Herman, and was out at first on a close play. No runs, one hit, no errors, one left.

NATIONAL—Cronin raced over near second and made a great play on Terry's grounder, throwing the National pilot out at first. He followed with another amazing play on Vaughan's grounder, grabbing a scorcher and tossing Vaughan out at first. Foxx threw out Lopez. No runs, no hits, no errors, none left.

NINTH INNING.

AMERICAN—Frankhouse took the mound for the Nationals. Vaughan raced into left field to catch Averill's high twisting fly for

Continued on Next Page.

Giants Triumph and Strengthen Lead; Dodgers Lose; Yanks Regain First Place

MOORE'S 2 HOMERS HELP GIANTS WIN

He Also Delivers Single and Double in 7 to 6 Victory Over the Pirates.

O'DOUL HITS FOR CIRCUIT

Losers Tally 4 in Ninth, Then Smith Halts Rally—Terrymen Now Lead Cubs by 2 Games.

By JOHN DREBINGER.

With Joe Moore, lead-off man par excellence, stroking the world's champions along at a blistering pace, the Giants sent the Pirates' rapidly fading pennant hopes down to a vanishing point yesterday by coming home in front in the series final at the Polo Grounds, 7 to 6.

That gave the Terry clan the set, three out of four, tossed a ladies' day crowd of 4,000 into a transport of civic enthusiasm and, what was probably most important of all, once again widened the Giants' margin over the second-place Cubs to two full games. For the Chicagoans, on the eve of invading the Harlem, lost a costly battle in Boston.

Moore's contributions to the triumph consisted of four straight hits on his first four turns at bat, two of them sizzling homers into the upper right-field tier. A single and a double rounded out the string and, all told, Texas Joe carted four runs across the plate.

O'Doul Continues His Pace.

Not to be completely overshadowed, Lefty O'Doul also unfurled a homer, his eighth of the campaign, in the general assault on three of the four pitchers Manager Pie Traynor was forced to employ in the battle.

Nor was any of this prodigious stroking ornamental. For with a comparatively simple victory in hand, Freddy Fitzsimmons, shooting for his twelfth pitching victory of the season, suddenly split an oar or something when the infuriated Buccos, with two down in the ninth, blasted four runs over the plate that hurtled Fitz right out of the game.

It took the more placid Al Smith to gather the final out, with the tying run on base and the long-hitting Gus Suhr at bat, thereby saving No. 12 for Fitz.

Until this untoward incident occurred, things moved marvelously well for the champions. They routed Red Lucas inside of three rounds, after counting thrice in the first, and then kept up the fire on Ed Holley and Leon Chagnon until they had run up a margin of 7 to 2, thanks to the extraordinary clouting of Moore, the O'Doul homer and some additional telling shots by Critz and Ott.

Fumble Starts the Inning.

Nothing alarming, therefore, was seen when Blondy Ryan fumbled Lavagetto's sharp grounder to start the ninth and Grace followed with a single. Manager Traynor, having by now run out of pinch-hitters, was forced to allow Birkofer, his fourth pitcher, to bat for himself and Birkie struck out.

Then Lloyd Waner cracked into a force play for the second out and the crowd began to advance in a body toward the exit gates. But one never knows when he is through with these Waners.

Brother Paul, who already had clipped Fitz for three hits, one a double, now laced a single to right and the Pirates had one run in. Jensen larruped a double to right and Lloyd Waner counted. Vaughan shoved a single into left, driving in two more, and the Pirates were now only one run behind, while the crowd was doing some furious back-tracking.

However, at this point the drive got caught on a hook and advanced no further. For our youthful left-hander, Smith, replaced the florid Fitz and the Pirate assault terminated with Suhr, usually a very long hitter, getting no more distance on a terrific cut at the ball than an easy roller to the pitching mound.

A Lively Batting Practice.

Despite the fact that the Giants wound up the nightcap of Thursday's double-header by thumping three Pirate pitchers for sixteen hits, this in no way caused Terry to overlook the fact that in the first game his men were held to six blows and only one run. So all the world's champions were out bright and early yesterday morning doing a lively turn at batting practice.

With Fitz standing 12-5 in games won and lost, Schumacher running 12-4 and Hubbell 13-5, the Giants' one-time big four pitching staff may still be functioning on only three cylinders, but those three are tearing along at a terrific clip.

Today opens the first big "crucial" series of the season at the Polo Grounds, the Cubs dropping in for a five-game series that will run until Wednesday, with Monday an open date and a double-header billed for Tuesday.

The box score:

PITTSBURGH (N.)	ab.	r.	h.	po.	a.	e.
L. Waner, cf	5	1	0	1	0	0
P. Waner, rf	5	1	4	1	0	1
Jensen, lf	5	1	1	2	0	0
Vaughan, ss	4	0	1	3	3	0
Suhr, 1b	5	0	0	9	2	0
Thevenow, 3b	4	0	1	3	3	0
Lavagetto, 2b	2	2	0	2	2	0
Grace, c	3	0	1	2	0	0
Lucas, p	1	0	1	0	1	0
Holley, p	1	0	0	0	0	0
aLindstrom	1	1	0	0	0	0
Chagnon, p	0	0	0	0	0	0
bRoettger	1	0	1	0	0	0
Birkofer, p	1	0	0	0	0	1
Total	36	6	10	24	13	2

NEW YORK (N.)	ab.	r.	h.	po.	a.	e.
Moore, cf	5	4	4	5	0	0
Critz, 2b	3	2	2	3	[illegible]	0
Terry, 1b	2	0	0	10	1	0
Ott, rf	4	0	1	1	0	0
O'Doul, lf	3	1	1	2	0	0
Jackson, ss	4	0	1	2	5	0
Ryan, 3b	3	0	0	1	2	1
Mancuso, c	4	0	2	2	0	0
Fitzsim'ns, p	4	0	0	0	0	0
Smith, p	0	0	0	0	1	0
Total	32	7	11	27	14	1

a Batted for Holley in fifth.
b Batted for Chagnon in seventh.

Pittsburgh .... 0 0 0 0 2 0 0 0 4—6
New York .... 3 0 2 1 0 1 0 0 .—7

Runs batted in—Terry, O'Doul 2, Moore 2, Ott, L. Waner, P. Waner 2, Jensen, Vaughan 2. Two-base hits—Critz, Moore, P. Waner, Thevenow, Jensen. Home runs—O'Doul, Moore 2. Sacrifice—Terry. Double plays—Vaughan, Lavagetto and Suhr; Thevenow, Lavagetto and Suhr; Suhr, Vaughan and Suhr. Left on bases—New York 6, Pittsburgh 8. Bases on balls—Off Holley 2, Fitzsimmons 2. Struck out—By Fitzsimmons 2, Birkofer 1. Hits—Off Lucas 7 in 2 1-3 innings, Holley 1 in 1 2-3, Chagnow 3 in 2, Birkofer 0 in 2, Fitzsimmons 10 in 8 2-3, Smith 0 in 1-3. Hit by pitcher—By Holley (Critz). Winning pitcher—Fitzsimmons. Losing pitcher—Lucas. Umpires—Reardon, Stewart and Klem. Time of game—1:58.

Townsend to Quit Ring.

VICTORIA, B. C., July 13 (AP).—Billy Townsend, once regarded as a strong welterweight prospect, has decided to quit the ring.

Times Wide World Photo.
STARS FOR GIANTS.
Joe Moore.

BRAVES' LATE RUSH DOWNS CUBS, 7-6

Seventh Inning Attack, Marked by Berger's Homer, Nets 4 Runs and Victory.

BOSTON, July 13 (AP).—Wally Berger's twentieth homer of the season started a four-run drive in the seventh that enabled the Braves to defeat the Cubs, 7—6, today in the last game of the series. Bill Lee, who pitched the Cubs to their only other two setbacks this month, was charged with the defeat.

After Berger opened with his circuit drive, singles by Hal Lee and Pinky Whitney brought Bud Tinning to the mound. Randy Moore, batting for Dick Gyselman, singled, and Marty McManus doubled with the bases full, driving in two runs. After Al Spohrer was intentionally passed, filling the bases again, Bill Urbanski went up for Dick Barrett, relief pitcher, and sent over the winning run with an infield single.

Huck Betts started for Boston and gave the Cubs five runs in five innings, including Woody English's first homer of the season and Babe Herman's eighth circuit drive. Barrett held the Cubs to one hit in the sixth and seventh and received credit for the victory.

The box score:

CHICAGO (N.)	ab.	r.	h.	po.	a.	e.
W. Her'n, 2b	5	1	1	3	5	1
English, ss	5	1	1	3	4	0
Cuyler, cf	4	1	1	2	0	0
F. Her'n, rf	4	1	1	3	0	0
Steph'son, lf	4	0	0	1	0	0
Hartnett, c	4	1	1	3	0	0
Grimm, 1b	4	0	2	7	1	0
Hurst, 1b	0	0	0	1	0	0
Hack, 3b	4	1	3	2	1	2
W. Lee, p	3	0	0	0	1	0
Tinning, p	0	0	0	0	1	0
aPhelps	1	0	0	0	0	0
Total	38	6	10	24	13	3

BOSTON (N.)	ab.	r.	h.	po.	a.	e.
Thompson, rf	5	0	1	1	0	0
Jordan, 1b	5	0	0	14	1	1
Berger, cf	5	1	2	2	0	0
H. Lee, lf	4	2	2	2	0	0
Whit'y, ss, 3b	3	2	2	4	1	0
Gyselman, 3b	3	0	0	1	3	1
cR. Moore	1	0	1	0	0	0
dCantwell	0	1	0	0	0	0
Smith, p	1	0	0	0	0	0
McManus, 2b	4	0	2	1	4	0
Spohrer, c	3	0	0	2	0	0
Betts, p	1	0	0	0	2	0
bWorth'gton	1	1	1	0	0	0
Barrett, p	1	0	0	0	1	0
Urbanski, ss	1	0	1	0	1	0
Total	36	7	12	27	13	2

a Batted for Tinning in ninth.
b Batted for Betts in fifth.
c Batted for Gyselman in seventh.
d Ran for R. Moore in seventh.

Chicago .... 0 0 3 0 2 0 0 1 0—6
Boston .... 0 2 0 0 1 0 4 0 .—7

Runs batted in—English 2, F. Herman 2, W. Herman, Grimm, Berger 2, McManus 2, R. Moore, Spohrer, Urbanski. Two-base hits—W. Herman, Grimm, Hack, McManus. Three-base hit—Hack. Home runs—English, F. Herman, Berger. Double plays—English, W. Herman and Grimm; Jordan and Whitney. Left on bases—Chicago 5, Boston 11. Bases on balls—Off W. Lee 2, Tinning 2. Struck out—By W. Lee 2, Barrett 1. Hits—Off W. Lee 9 in 6 1-3 innings, Tinning 3 in 1 2-3, Betts 7 in 5, Barrett 1 in 2, Smith 2 in 2. Winning pitcher—Barrett. Losing pitcher—W. Lee. Umpires—Magerkurth and Quigley. Time of game—1:52.

BUFFALO IN EVEN BREAK.

Downs Syracuse, 11-5, Then Bows, 12-3, Before 15,000.

BUFFALO, N. Y., July 13 (AP).—The Syracuse Chiefs held a two out of three edge on their series with the Buffalo Bisons after gaining an even break in tonight's double-header played before an overflow crowd of more than 15,000.

Buffalo won easily in the first game by 11 to 5. The Chiefs had it a bit easier to win the second, 12 to 3.

Norbert's two homers coupled with a single featured the Syracuse victory. Ollie Tucker also hit his eleventh homer of the year for Buffalo.

The scores by innings:

FIRST NIGHT GAME.

		R.	H.	E.
Syracuse	0 0 2 0 0 0 3 0 0—5	5	12	1
Buffalo	1 5 4 1 0 0 0 0 .—11	11	13	2

Batteries—Pickrel, Fisher, McKeithan and Taylor; Kowalik and Crouse.

SECOND NIGHT GAME.

		R.	H.	E.
Syracuse	4 0 0 0 1 0 2 1 3—12	12	15	1
Buffalo	0 1 0 0 2 0 0 0 0—3	3	8	2

Batteries—Liska, Coombs and Cronin; Perkins, Lisenbee, Elliott and Crouse.

TORONTO IN FRONT, 5-2.

Maple Leafs Defeat Baltimore in Night Game.

TORONTO, July 13 (AP).—Toronto's Maple Leafs scored an International League victory tonight, defeating the Baltimore Orioles, 5—2.

The score by innings:

		R.	H.	E.
Baltimore	0 0 0 0 0 0 0 2 0—2	2	3	0
Toronto	0 2 0 0 0 0 0 3 .—5	5	8	0

Batteries—Lohrman, Richmond, Ogden and Asby; Hilcher, Lucas and Heving.

DODGERS BEATEN BY THE REDS, 8-6

Brooklyn Rally in 9th Falls Short as Victors Earn Even Break in Series.

SLADE CONTINUES HITTING

Gets Triple, Two-Bagger and a Single—Hafey and Lopez Connect for Home Runs.

By ROSCOE McGOWEN.

A ninth-inning Brooklyn drive, its greatest momentum coming from two Cincinnati misplays, fell short of the necessary total and the Reds scored their second straight victory over the Dodgers yesterday, 8 to 6, to even the series.

Casey Stengel's hope of extracting victory from defeat rested chiefly on the possibility that either Tony Piet or Jim Bottomley would add a third error to the Reds' collection for the inning. The Dodger bats had displayed no great power.

With the bases filled, two runs in and two out, Tony Cuccinello hit a tricky bounder over third that Piet, out of position, stopped. His hurried throw struck the dirt in front of Bottomley, but the veteran first-sacker snared the ball half a step ahead of the runner, and that ended the game.

Frey Relieved in Ninth.

Scarcely more than 700 fans were present. Tom Zachary and Benny Frey started the game, but neither was in the box at the finish. Frey lasted until he had retired one man in the ninth. Kolp came to his rescue and contrived to keep the Reds in the lead.

Zachary was driven to cover in the seventh, when a single by Gordon Slade filled the bases with only one out and the visitors leading, 4 to 3. Mark Koenig greeted Dutch Leonard with a triple, giving the Reds an apparently safe margin.

Slade drove home the first run in the opening frame with a three-bagger that followed Piet's single, and in the fifth the former Dodger hit a double off the right-field wall, sending home the third marker. A triple by Schulmerich and Benny Frey's single accounted for the second run in the same inning.

Hafey Continues Attack.

Chick Hafey propelled the ball into the left-field seats in the sixth with nobody on base, and the Reds picked up run No. 8 in the eighth.

A triple by Boyle and Lonnie Frey's fly gave the Dodgers one in the first; Leslie's two-bagger, Cuccinello's sacrifice and a wild pitch scored one in the second, and in the fifth Al Lopez bounced the ball off the left-field upper tier for a homer that tied the score at 3—all. Leonard got a two-bagger in the seventh and scored on Boyle's single.

It was disclosed yesterday that Jimmy Jordan's left foot had been spiked by Slade Thursday. Jimmy was in uniform but didn't play.

Chapman hit Coach Burt Shotton on the right knee in the seventh. He was given first aid with cold towels.

The Cards open a five-game series in Brooklyn today, with a double-header slated for tomorrow.

The box score:

CINCINNATI (N.)	ab.	r.	h.	po.	a.	e.
Piet, 3b	5	2	2	0	2	0
Slade, 2b	5	1	2	2	7	0
Koenig, ss	5	0	1	2	3	2
Hafey, cf	5	1	1	3	0	1
Bot'm'y, 1b	5	0	0	15	1	0
Comor'ky, lf	4	1	3	1	0	0
Lombardi, c	4	0	1	0	0	0
Schulm'h, rf	3	1	2	3	0	0
B. Frey, p	4	2	1	0	2	0
Kolp, p	0	0	0	0	0	0
Total	40	8	14	27	15	3

BROOKLYN (N.)	ab.	r.	h.	po.	a.	e.
Boyle, lf	4	2	2	1	0	0
L. Frey, ss	3	0	0	2	4	0
aWilson	1	0	0	0	0	0
Stripp, ss	1	0	1	1	0	1
Frederick, rf	4	0	1	0	0	0
cSukeforth	0	0	0	0	0	0
Koenecke, cf	4	0	1	3	0	0
Leslie, 1b	4	1	2	8	0	1
Cuccin'o, 3b	4	0	0	1	3	0
Lopez, c	4	1	1	5	1	0
Chap'an, 2b	4	1	1	5	4	0
Zachary, p	2	0	0	0	[illegible]	0
Leonard, p	1	1	1	0	0	0
bTaylor	0	0	0	0	0	0
Total	36	6	9	27	13	2

a Batted for L. Frey in seventh.
b Batted for Leonard in ninth.
c Ran for Frederick in ninth.

Cincinnati .... 1 0 0 0 2 1 3 1 0—8
Brooklyn .... 1 1 0 0 1 0 1 0 2—6

Runs batted in—Slade 2, L. Frey, B. Frey, Lopez, Hafey, Koenig 3, Boyle, Piet, Stripp, Koenecke. Two-base hits—Leslie, Slade, Koenecke, Leonard. Three-base hits—Slade, Boyle, Schulmerich, Koenig. Home runs—Lopez, Hafey. Sacrifice—Cuccinello. Double play—Chapman and L. Frey. Left on bases—Cincinnati 8, Brooklyn 9. Bases on balls—Off B. Frey 4, Leonard 1, Kolp 1. Struck out—By Zachary 2, Leonard 1. Hits—Off Zachary 12 in 6 1-3 innings, Leonard 2 in 2 2-3, B. Frey, 9 in 8 1-3, Kolp 0 in 2-3. Wild pitches—B. Frey, Leonard. Winning pitcher—B. Frey. Losing pitcher—Zachary. Umpires—Pfirman and Moran. Time of game—2:04.

MRS. MALLES ADVANCES.

Tops Miss Roberts to Gain Final in Public Courts Singles.

Mrs. Helen Malles, defending titleholder, gained the final round of the Greater New York public courts tennis tournament by routing Miss Linda Roberts, 6—0, 6—0, yesterday. The match was played at the Kingston Tennis Courts in Brooklyn.

Mrs. Malles, second seeded contestant, will oppose Miss Helen Germaine, former national public parks champion, tomorrow for the championship.

MAJOR LEAGUE BASEBALL

American League.

YESTERDAY'S RESULTS.

New York 4, Detroit 2.
Washington 3, Cleveland 2.
Boston 7, St. Louis 2.
Philadelphia at Chicago, wet grounds.

STANDING OF THE CLUBS.

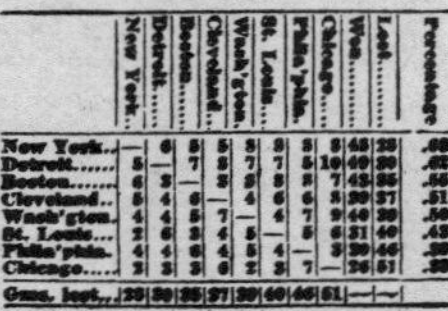

	N. Y.	Det.	Bos.	Clev.	Wash.	St. L.	Phila.	Chi.	Won.	Lost.	Pct.
New York	[illegible]	[illegible]	[illegible]	[illegible]	[illegible]	[illegible]	[illegible]	[illegible]	[illegible]	[illegible]	[illegible]
Detroit	[illegible]	[illegible]	[illegible]	[illegible]	[illegible]	[illegible]	[illegible]	[illegible]	[illegible]	[illegible]	[illegible]
Boston	[illegible]	[illegible]	[illegible]	[illegible]	[illegible]	[illegible]	[illegible]	[illegible]	[illegible]	[illegible]	[illegible]
Cleveland	[illegible]	[illegible]	[illegible]	[illegible]	[illegible]	[illegible]	[illegible]	[illegible]	[illegible]	[illegible]	[illegible]
Wash'gton	[illegible]	[illegible]	[illegible]	[illegible]	[illegible]	[illegible]	[illegible]	[illegible]	[illegible]	[illegible]	[illegible]
St. Louis	[illegible]	[illegible]	[illegible]	[illegible]	[illegible]	[illegible]	[illegible]	[illegible]	[illegible]	[illegible]	[illegible]
Phila'phia	[illegible]	[illegible]	[illegible]	[illegible]	[illegible]	[illegible]	[illegible]	[illegible]	[illegible]	[illegible]	[illegible]
Chicago	[illegible]	[illegible]	[illegible]	[illegible]	[illegible]	[illegible]	[illegible]	[illegible]	[illegible]	[illegible]	[illegible]
Gms. lost	[illegible]	[illegible]	[illegible]	[illegible]	[illegible]	[illegible]	[illegible]	[illegible]			

GAMES TODAY.

New York at Detroit.
Washington at Cleveland.
Philadelphia at Chicago.
Boston at St. Louis.

National League.

YESTERDAY'S RESULTS.

New York 7, Pittsburgh 6.
Cincinnati 8, Brooklyn 6.
Boston 7, Chicago 6.
St. Louis at Philadelphia, rain.

STANDING OF THE CLUBS.

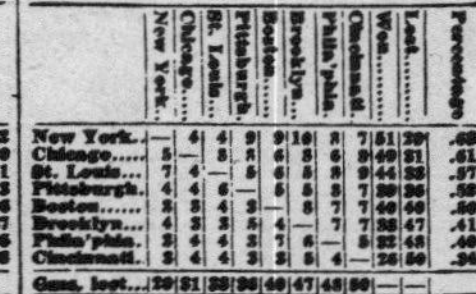

	N. Y.	Chi.	St. L.	Pitts.	Bos.	Bklyn.	Phila.	Cin.	Won.	Lost.	Pct.
New York	[illegible]	[illegible]	[illegible]	[illegible]	[illegible]	[illegible]	[illegible]	[illegible]	[illegible]	[illegible]	[illegible]
Chicago	[illegible]	[illegible]	[illegible]	[illegible]	[illegible]	[illegible]	[illegible]	[illegible]	[illegible]	[illegible]	[illegible]
St. Louis	[illegible]	[illegible]	[illegible]	[illegible]	[illegible]	[illegible]	[illegible]	[illegible]	[illegible]	[illegible]	[illegible]
Pittsburgh	[illegible]	[illegible]	[illegible]	[illegible]	[illegible]	[illegible]	[illegible]	[illegible]	[illegible]	[illegible]	[illegible]
Boston	[illegible]	[illegible]	[illegible]	[illegible]	[illegible]	[illegible]	[illegible]	[illegible]	[illegible]	[illegible]	[illegible]
Brooklyn	[illegible]	[illegible]	[illegible]	[illegible]	[illegible]	[illegible]	[illegible]	[illegible]	[illegible]	[illegible]	[illegible]
Phila'phia	[illegible]	[illegible]	[illegible]	[illegible]	[illegible]	[illegible]	[illegible]	[illegible]	[illegible]	[illegible]	[illegible]
Cincinnati	[illegible]	[illegible]	[illegible]	[illegible]	[illegible]	[illegible]	[illegible]	[illegible]	[illegible]	[illegible]	[illegible]
Gms. lost	[illegible]	[illegible]	[illegible]	[illegible]	[illegible]	[illegible]	[illegible]	[illegible]			

GAMES TODAY.

Chicago at New York (3 P.M.).
St. Louis at Brooklyn (3 P.M.).
Cincinnati at Philadelphia (2).
Pittsburgh at Boston.

Times Wide World Photo.
BABE RUTH.

Ruth's Record of 700 Home Runs Likely To Stand for All Time in Major Leagues

Special to THE NEW YORK TIMES.

DETROIT, July 13.—A record that promises to endure for all time was attained on Navin Field today when Babe Ruth smashed his seven-hundredth home run in a lifetime career. It promises to live, first, because few players of history have enjoyed the longevity on the diamond of the immortal Bambino, and, second, because only two other players in the history of baseball have hit more than 300 home runs.

In his twenty-first year of play, and what is expected to be his farewell season, Ruth rounded out the record he had set for himself before retiring.

He has another mark he is shooting at and which he should attain before the end of the current campaign. He wants to go out with 2,000 bases on balls to his credit, a reflection of the respect rival pitchers have for him. He is only a few short of the mark.

Lou Gehrig and Rogers Hornsby are the only players who have exceeded 300 home runs in their careers. Gehrig boasts 314 and Hornsby 301. The improbability of a parallel to the Ruth mark is appreciated with the knowledge that Gehrig will have to survive ten more years of play, and then average about forty home runs a year, to equal it.

Today a youth was happy and richer by $20. Even before he circled the bases, Ruth was shouting to mates on the field: "I want that ball! I want that ball!" Emissaries were sent scurrying after the youth who recovered the ball after it cleared the fence, and it was restored to Ruth in the Yankee dugout, in exchange for $20.

Ruth paid $20 for his five-hundredth home-run ball, hit in Cleveland, and a similar amount for the home-run ball that touched the 600 mark three years ago. This one was hit in St. Louis.

Ruth had his greatest home-run year in 1927, when he created the modern season's record of 60. He hit 59 in 1921, and 54 in both 1920 and 1928. In 1930 he smashed 49.

Following is a table of the home runs hit by Ruth in championship games and world's series contests:

CHAMPIONSHIP GAMES.

Year.	Team.	Homers.	Year.	Team.	Homers.
1914	Red Sox	0	1926	Yankees	47
1915	Red Sox	4	1927	Yankees	60
1916	Red Sox	3	1928	Yankees	54
1917	Red Sox	2	1929	Yankees	46
1918	Red Sox	11	1930	Yankees	49
1919	Red Sox	29	1931	Yankees	46
1920	Yankees	54	1932	Yankees	41
1921	Yankees	59	1933	Yankees	34
*1922	Yankees	35	1934	Yankees	14
1923	Yankees	41			
1924	Yankees	46		Total	700
†1925	Yankees	25			

*Out until May 20, suspended for barnstorming after 1921 world's series.
†Out until June with illness after collapsing during training trip.

WORLD'S SERIES GAMES.

Yr.	Team Against.	Homers.	Yr.	Team Against.	Homers.
1915	Phillies	0	1926	Cardinals	4
1916	Dodgers	0	1927	Pirates	2
1918	Cubs	0	1928	Cardinals	3
1921	Giants	1	1932	Cubs	2
1922	Giants	0			
1923	Giants	3		Total	15

SENATORS TOP INDIANS.

Victors by 3-2, but Lose Stone With Injured Ankle.

CLEVELAND, July 13 (AP).—The Senators took the first of a four-game series with the Indians, 3 to 2, today at the cost of Right Fielder Jonathan Stone, who suffered a fracture of the left ankle and was carried from the field.

Dr. Edward Castle, the Cleveland club's physician, diagnosed the break as a "Potts fracture." He predicted that it would be many days—perhaps all season—before Washington regains the services of the .300-hitting outfielder.

The box score:

WASHINGTON (A.)	ab.	r.	h.	po.	a.	e.
Myer, 2b	4	0	2	5	2	0
Stone, rf	2	1	2	1	0	0
Harris, rf	1	1	0	1	1	0
Manush, lf	3	1	1	2	0	0
Cronin, ss	3	0	0	0	4	0
Travis, 3b	3	0	1	2	3	0
Schulte, cf	3	0	1	4	0	0
Kress, 1b	4	0	0	7	0	0
Sewell, c	4	0	0	4	1	0
Stewart, p	3	0	0	0	1	0
Total	31	3	7	27	9	0

CLEVELAND (A.)	ab.	r.	h.	po.	a.	e.
Seeds, rf	5	0	2	3	0	0
Knick'er, ss	3	0	1	2	3	0
Averill, cf	4	0	1	2	0	0
Vosmik, lf	4	0	1	2	1	0
Trosky, 1b	4	0	0	10	1	0
Hale, 2b	4	2	4	4	3	0
Kamm, 3b	4	0	1	0	2	0
Pytlak, c	4	0	2	4	0	0
Hil'brand, p	2	0	0	0	1	0
aHolland	1	0	0	0	0	0
Wine'ner, p	1	0	0	0	0	0
Total	36	2	12	27	12	0

a Batted for Hildebrand in seventh.

Washington .... 2 0 1 0 0 0 0 0 0—3
Cleveland .... 0 0 0 0 1 0 0 0 1—2

Runs batted in—Schulte 2, Travis, Pytlak 2. Two-base hits—Stone, Myer, Hale 2, Averill, Manush. Three-base hit—Travis. Sacrifice—Cronin. Double plays—Sewell and Myer; Kamm, Hale and Trosky; Cronin, Myer and Kress; Vosmik and Pytlak. Left on bases—Washington 5, Cleveland 8. Bases on balls—Off Hildebrand 3, Stewart 1. Struck out—By Hildebrand 1, Stewart 3. Hits—Off Hildebrand 6 in 7 innings, Winegarner 1 in 2. Wild pitches—Stewart 2. Losing pitcher—Hildebrand. Umpires—Geisel and Moriarty. Time of game—2:02.

ALBANY BEATS ROCHESTER

Gets Seventeen Hits Off Three Pitchers to Score, 6 to 4.

ROCHESTER, N. Y., July 13 (AP).—Unleashing a strong hitting attack against three Rochester hurlers today, Albany defeated Rochester 6 to 4. The visitors drove Kleinke from the mound in the second frame under a barrage of hits and peppered Kaufmann and Appleton who followed him.

Fifteen Albany runners were left stranded. The Senators made seventeen hits, drew five passes, and one batsman was hit.

The score by innings:

		R.	H.	E.
Albany	1 3 0 0 1 1 0 0 0—6	6	17	2
Rochester	2 0 0 0 1 0 0 1 0—4	4	10	1

Batteries—Chapman and Finney, Klumpp; Kleinke, Kaufmann, Appleton and Florence, Lewis.

Mrs. Bydolek Golf Victor.

ROCHESTER, N. Y., July 13 (AP).—With an 84 that beat the course record for women by three strokes, Mrs. Joseph Bydolek of the Transit Valley Club today defeated Mrs. Charles Hart of Oak Hill, by 2 up in the semi-finals for the championship of the Women's Golf Association of Western New York.

RED SOX TRIUMPH, 7-2.

Beat Browns as W. Ferrell Hits Two Homers and Hurls Well.

ST. LOUIS, July 13 (AP).—Wesley Ferrell's two home runs were more than enough to give the Red Sox a victory over the Browns today, but his team-mates chipped in to run up a 7-to-2 score in the series opener.

The big pitcher's two homers, in the third and fifth innings, were good for four runs, two mates being on base when he made the second one. Max Bishop also hit for the circuit for the visitors.

Ferrell pitched shut-out ball until the ninth, when Bruce Campbell's pinch single drove in two runs.

The box score:

BOSTON (A.)	ab.	r.	h.	po.	a.	e.
Bishop, 2b	4	1	2	3	7	1
Werber, 3b	5	1	1	1	1	0
Morgan, 1b	5	1	2	9	1	0
R. J'nson, lf	5	0	1	3	0	0
Reynolds, cf	4	0	2	1	0	1
Porter, rf	4	0	1	2	0	0
R. Ferrell, c	3	1	2	3	0	0
Lary, ss	3	1	2	4	4	0
W. Ferrell, p	3	2	2	1	1	0
Total	36	7	15	27	14	2

ST. LOUIS (A.)	ab.	r.	h.	po.	a.	e.
Clift, 3b	5	0	1	0	1	0
West, cf	4	0	0	3	0	0
Burns, 1b	4	0	1	7	0	0
Pepper, lf	4	0	0	1	0	0
Garms, rf	4	0	0	3	0	0
Melillo, 2b	4	1	2	5	2	0
Hemsley, c	4	1	2	4	3	1
Strange, ss	3	0	2	4	3	0
Coffman, p	1	0	0	0	0	0
Newsom, p	1	0	0	0	2	0
Andrews, p	0	0	0	0	0	0
aBejma	0	0	0	0	0	0
bCampbell	1	0	1	0	0	0
Total	35	2	9	27	11	1

a Batted for Newsom in eighth.
b Batted for Andrews in ninth.

Boston .... 0 0 1 0 4 0 2 0 0—7
St. Louis .... 0 0 0 0 0 0 0 0 2—2

Runs batted in—W. Ferrell 4, Bishop, Morgan, R. Johnson, Campbell 2. Two-base hits—R. Ferrell, Lary, Hemsley. Three-base hit—Morgan. Home runs—W. Ferrell 2, Bishop. Stolen base—Werber. Sacrifices—Lary, W. Ferrell. Double plays—Strange, Melillo and Burns; Werber, Bishop and Morgan; Lary, Bishop and Morgan; Melillo, Strange and Burns. Left on bases—Boston 7, St. Louis 8. Bases on balls—Off W. Ferrell 2, Newsom 3. Struck out—By W. Ferrell 2, Coffman 1, Newsom 2. Hits—Off Coffman 7 in 4 innings, Newsom 7 in 4, Andrews 1 in 1. Losing pitcher—Coffman. Umpires—Dinneen and Kolls. Time of game—2:08.

Home-Run Hitters.

Yesterday's Homers.

J. Moore, New York Nationals	2
W. Ferrell, Boston Americans	2
O'Doul, New York Nationals	1
Ruth, New York Americans	1
Lopez, Brooklyn	1
Bishop, Boston Americans	1
Berger, Boston Nationals	1
F. Herman, Chicago Nationals	1
English, Chicago Nationals	1
Hafey, Cincinnati	1

The Leaders.

NATIONAL LEAGUE.

Ott, New York	21	Hartnett, Chicago	13
Berger, Boston	20	Camilli, Phila.	11
Klein, Chicago	19	Medwick, St. Louis	11
Collins, St. Louis	12	Cuccinello, Bklyn	10
Jackson, N. York	13		

AMERICAN LEAGUE.

Foxx, Phila.	26	Ruth, New York	14
Johnson, Phila.	26	Simmons, Chicago	13
Gehrig, New York	24	Greenberg, Detroit	11
Bonura, Chicago	18	McNair, Phila.	11
Trosky, Cleveland	16		

League Totals.

National League	395
American League	386
Total	781

RUTH HITS 700TH AS YANKS SCORE, 4-2

Reaches Goal of His Career With Mighty Homer in the Third Against Tigers.

GEHRIG, ILL, FORCED OUT

Consecutive-Game Streak May End—Dickey's Two-Bagger Decides the Contest.

By JAMES P. DAWSON.

Special to THE NEW YORK TIMES.

DETROIT, July 13.—The incomparable Babe Ruth reached his goal today with his 700th home run, a wallop that helped in sending the Yankees back into the lead in the American League pennant race.

It came in the third inning, a drive of about 480 feet high over the right-field wall. Earle Combs was on first when Ruth drove the ball out of the lot, fashioning two runs off Tom Bridges, the Detroit pitcher.

It seemed the blow would carry victory for Charley (Red) Ruffing, who was locked in an intense pitching duel with Bridges as 21,000 looked on.

In the end, however, it was a two-base drive off the bat of reliable Bill Dickey in the eighth inning which brought the triumph by a count of 4 to 2 and restored to the Yankees their slender lead over the Tigers in first place.

Wallop Sends Two Home.

Dickey's hit, one of two for the backstop, chased Ruth and Ben Chapman home with the runs that put the game on the Yankees' side of the ledger.

Tonight the Yanks are happy, and Ruth is the happiest of all. They humbled the ace right-hander of the Tigers' hurling staff with a nine-hit attack and can look forward less apprehensively now to the remaining two games in this crucial series.

Ruffing, hamered to shelter in his last two championship starts and in his all-star game effort as well, selected the right time to return to his winning ways. He gave the Tigers six scant hits.

A pass and a double, with a high fly, brought the first Tiger run in the third, and the only other score came in the eighth, when Ruffing let the Tigers cluster a single and a triple.

Gehrig's Status in Doubt.

Lou Gehrig, playing in his 1,426th consecutive championship game, was involuntarily withdrawn in the second inning, suffering from an attack of lumbago which may very well bring an end to his unique record. Whether he will play tomorrow was undetermined tonight.

With one out in the third, Combs singled. Then, after Saltzgaver had fanned, Ruth, with the count three and two, blasted his fourteenth homer of the season.

That was all the Yankee scoring until the eighth, when, with one out, Ruth drew a pass and took second on Rolfe's single. Rolfe was caught off first, then Chapman walked. Dickey here slashed a double to centre.

Manager McCarthy sent Red Rolfe to short and shifted Saltzgaver to first and Crosetti to third.

The box score:

NEW YORK (A.)	ab.	r.	h.	po.	a.	e.
Combs, cf	3	1	1	4	0	0
Saltz'r, 2b, 1b	4	0	0	7	1	0
Ruth, lf	3	2	1	1	0	0
Byrd, lf	0	0	0	0	0	0
Gehrig, 1b	1	0	1	1	0	0
Rolfe, ss	2	0	1	1	2	0
Chapman, rf	3	1	1	0	0	0
Dickey, c	4	0	2	5	0	0
Crosetti, ss, 3b	3	0	1	2	3	0
Heffner, 2b	4	0	1	6	0	0
Ruffing, p	4	0	0	0	0	0
Total	33	4	9	27	6	0

DETROIT (A.)	ab.	r.	h.	po.	a.	e.
Fox, rf	5	0	0	4	1	0
White, cf	2	1	0	2	0	0
Goslin, lf	4	0	1	1	0	0
Ge'inger, 2b	4	0	1	1	1	0
Rogell, ss	4	1	1	2	4	0
Gr'nberg, 1b	4	0	2	8	0	0
Cochrane, c	3	0	1	5	2	0
Owen, 3b	3	0	0	1	0	0
Bridges, p	3	0	0	0	2	0
aWalker	1	0	0	0	0	0
Total	33	2	6	27	10	0

a Batted for Bridges in ninth.

New York .... 0 0 2 0 0 0 0 2 0—4
Detroit .... 0 0 1 0 0 0 0 1 0—2

Runs batted in—Ruth 2, Gehringer, Dickey 2, Greenberg. Two-base hits—Greenberg, Goslin, Dickey. Three-base hit—Greenberg. Home run—Ruth. Stolen bases—White, Chapman, Cochrane. Double play—Fox and Gehringer. Left on bases—Detroit 8, New York 8. Bases on balls—Off Bridges 4, Ruffing 4. Struck out—By Bridges 8, Ruffing 3. Wild pitches—Bridges 2. Umpires—Donnelly, McGowan and Owens. Time of game—2:12.

Times Wide World Photo.
SHINES ON MOUND.
Charley Ruffing, Yankees.

NEWARK CONQUERS MONTREAL, 5 TO 4

Brown Allows Only 6 Hits in Scoring 12th Victory and Drives Homer.

MONTREAL, July 13 (AP).—Denver Grigsby dropped Dale Alexander's easy fly in right field with two out in the seventh inning today and two Bears scored to give Newark a 5-to-4 victory over the Royals that evened the series.

Orlin Collier allowed ten hits in seven innings, but pitched steadily and might have won but for Grigsby's error. The two tallies tied the score and Newark put over the winning run in the eighth.

Walter Brown limited the Royals to six hits to score his twelfth mound victory and contributed a home run over the scoreboard in the third.

The box score:

NEWARK (I.)	ab.	r.	h.	po.	a.	e.
Neun, 1b	5	1	4	10	1	0
Farrell, ss	4	1	0	0	2	0
Hill, cf	4	0	2	1	0	0
Alex'der, lf	5	0	2	2	0	0
Barton, rf	3	1	2	2	0	0
Muller, 3b	4	0	0	1	1	0
Glenn, c	5	1	3	8	0	0
Schalk, 2b	4	0	0	4	2	0
Brown, p	4	1	1	1	3	0
Total	38	5	14	27	9	0

MONTREAL (I.)	ab.	r.	h.	po.	a.	e.
Walker, lf	4	1	2	2	0	0
Thompson, 2b	2	0	0	1	4	0
King, 3b	3	0	0	0	3	0
Outen, c	3	1	0	4	1	0
Ripple, cf	4	0	0	2	0	0
Grigsby, rf	4	1	1	3	0	1
Sankey, ss	4	0	1	5	2	0
Plummer, 1b	4	1	1	10	1	0
Collier, p	2	0	0	0	1	0
aKimsey	1	0	1	0	0	0
bMyllyk'gas	0	0	0	0	0	0
Smythe, p	0	0	0	0	1	0
cReiber	1	0	0	0	0	0
Total	32	4	6	27	14	1

a Batted for Collier in seventh.
b Ran for Kimsey in seventh.
c Batted for Smythe in ninth.

Newark .... 0 0 1 1 0 0 2 1 0—5
Montreal .... 1 0 0 2 0 0 1 0 0—4

Runs batted in—Outen, Grigsby, Sankey, Kimsey, Neun, Brown, Glenn. Two-base hits—Neun 2, Barton, Kimsey. Three-base hit—Grigsby. Home run—Brown. Sacrifices—Muller, Schalk. Double plays—Thompson, Sankey and Plummer; Farrell, Schalk and Neun. Left on bases—Newark 12, Montreal 5. Bases on balls—Off Collier 2, Brown 4, Smythe 1. Struck out—By Collier 3, Brown 5. Hits—Off Collier 10 in 7 innings, Smythe 4 in 2. Hit by pitcher—By Collier (Farrell). Losing pitcher—Smythe. Umpires—Van Graflan and Parker. Time of game—2 hours.

APPROVES ST. LOUIS BID.

U. S. Football Association Votes to Accept New Member.

Upon recommendation of the National Commission, the delegates attending the twenty-first annual business meeting of the United States Football Association at the Hotel Pennsylvania voted yesterday to accept the application of the St. Louis Professional Soccer League for direct affiliation with the national body. Formerly the Missouri players were recognized through their State association.

Joseph J. Barriskill of Brooklyn, vice president and chairman of the National Cup competition, was elected to the post of presidency of the association by unanimous vote. He succeeded Elmer A. Schroeder of Philadelphia. Other officers were elected as follows: Joseph Triner, Chicago, first vice president; Harold S. Callowhill, Baltimore, second vice president; John J. MacEwen, Cleveland, third vice president; William T. Angus, Cleveland, treasurer.

Minor League Baseball

By The Associated Press.

INTERNATIONAL LEAGUE.

Newark 5, Montreal 4.
Albany 6, Rochester 4.
Buffalo 11, Syracuse 4 (1st night game).
Syracuse 12, Buffalo 3 (second night game).
Toronto 5, Baltimore 2 (night game).

STANDING OF THE CLUBS.

[illegible]

WHERE THEY PLAY TODAY.

Newark at Montreal.
Albany at Rochester.
Baltimore at Toronto.
Syracuse at Buffalo.

AMERICAN ASSOCIATION.

AT MINNEAPOLIS.

[illegible]

AT MILWAUKEE.

[illegible]

AT ST. PAUL.

[illegible]

STANDING OF THE CLUBS.

[illegible]

PACIFIC COAST LEAGUE.

(Night Games Thursday.)

AT SEATTLE.

[illegible]

AT LOS ANGELES.

[illegible]

STANDING OF THE CLUBS.

[illegible]

TEXAS LEAGUE.

(Night Games.)

[illegible]

SOUTHERN ASSOCIATION.

AT CHATTANOOGA.

		R.	H.	E.
New Orleans	0 0 1 0 1 0 0 1 1—4	4	8	0
Chattanooga	0 0 0 0 0 0 1 0 0—1	1	5	2

Batteries—Messenger and George; Linke and Holbrook.

AT ATLANTA.

(First Game.)

[illegible]

AT KNOXVILLE.

[illegible]

AT NASHVILLE.

(Night Game.)

[illegible]

STANDING OF THE CLUBS.

[illegible]

NEW YORK-PENN. LEAGUE.

AT HAZLETON.

[illegible]

AT ELMIRA.

[illegible]

AT WILLIAMSPORT.

[illegible]

AT BINGHAMTON.

(Night Game.)

[illegible]

STANDING OF THE CLUBS.

[illegible]

WESTERN LEAGUE.

(Night games Thursday.)

[illegible]

PACING EVENT GOES TO THE AUCTIONEER

Palin Drives 2-Year-Old to Triumph in Grand Circuit Feature at Toledo.

OUTSIDER WINS FIRST HEAT

Dena Brewer Pays $65.40 for $2 Straight—Whitehead Is Victor With Morley Scott.

TOLEDO, Ohio, July 13 (AP).—A crowd of 5,000 persons, including Governor George White, saw The Auctioneer, owned by E. J. Baker of St. Charles, Ill., and driven by Sep Palin, win the 2-year-old pace, featured event of tonight's Grand Circuit race program. An extra heat was required for a decision.

Holders of $2 straight tickets on Dena Brewer, driven by Jake Mahoney, were pleasantly thrilled in the opening heat, when the bay filly scored and paid $65.40. In the second and third heats Palin took command with his roan colt and triumphed eased up.

The mile and a sixteenth division of the 3-year-old pace was won by Morley Scott, with Ben Whitehead in the sulky. The mile dash for the same age pacers produced another upset with Helen Watts, driven by Stephen Septra, coming home in front to pay $53.20.

The summaries:

THE SUMMARIES.

FIRST EVENT. 2-YEAR-OLD PACE.
Purse $600. Mile Heats. Two in Three.
The Auctioneer, b. c., by Counterpart (Palin) ... 2 1 1
Edna Brewer, b. m. (Mahoney) ... 1 2 2
Duchess Jane, ro. m. (Parshall) ... 3 3 ro
Aunt Ida, ch. f. (Hodson) ... 4 4 ro
Miss Almadale, br. f. (Walton) ... 5 5 ro
Time—2:07¼, 2:11½, 2:09. Ima Patch and The Great Miss Joan also started.

SECOND EVENT. 3-YEAR-OLD PACE.
Purse $150. Mile and a Sixteenth Heat.
Morley Scott, br. g., by Saccharine Boy (White) ... 1
Altamaha, b. f. (Crumrine) ... 2
Doctor H., b. g. (Sipe) ... 3
Rockdale McElwyn, b. h. (Cartnal) ... 4
Anna Part, b. m. (Adams) ... 5
Time—2:15. Helen Watts and Rosindale also started.

THIRD EVENT. 3-YEAR-OLDS.
Purse, $150. Mile and a Sixteenth Heat.
Senator Bedell, l. sor. s., by The Senator (Palin) ... 1
Grace Noon, ch. f. (Valentine) ... 2
Perhaps, gr. g. (Mahoney) ... 3
Harvey Spencer, b. h. (Hodson) ... 4
Branta, b. f. (Gokes) ... 5
Time—2:16½. Flavia and Dr. Lee also started.

FOURTH EVENT. 3-YEAR-OLDS.
Purse, $150. Mile Heat.
Helen Watts, b. m., by General Watts (Stepro) ... 1
Doctor H., b. g. (Sipe) ... 2
Rockdale McElwyn, b. h. (Cartnal) ... 3
Altamaha, b. f. (Crumrine) ... 4
Anna Part, b. m., (Adams) ... 5
Time—2:09. Rosindale and Morley Scott also started.

FIFTH EVENT. 3-YEAR-OLD TROT.
Purse, $150. Mile Heat.
Harvey Spencer, b. h., by Spencer (Hodson) ... 1
Grace Noon, ch. f. (Valentine) ... 2
Perhaps, gr. g. (Mahoney) ... 3
Senator Bedell, sor. s. (Palin) ... 4
Flavia, ch. f. (Thomas) ... 5
Time—2:09½. Dr. Lee and Branta also started.

SIXTH EVENT. THE GOVERNOR. HANDICAP PACE.
Purse $600.
Sombro Hanover, b. g., by Dillon Axworthy (Hodson) ... 1 1
Calumet Calling, b. g (Lacey) ... 2 4
Estrellita, b. m. (Myers) ... 6 2
T. D. Van, blk. g. (Short) ... 3 5
McAllister, b. g. (Crippin) ... 5 3
Time—2:05½, 2:06.
Rip Hanover also started.

SEVENTH EVENT. CLASSIFIED PACE.
Purse $300.
Miss Ontario, b. m., by Grattan Direct (Fleming) ... 1 1
Robert McKinney, b. h. (Hodson) ... 3 2
Hliana, blk. m. (W. Caton) ... 2 3
Bertha B., b. m. (Erskine) ... 3 5
The Patchen Girl, b. m. (Smart) ... 5 4
Time—2:14½, 2:07½.
Worthy Hanover also started.

AUSTRALIAN TEAM VICTOR.

Defeats Derbyshire by 9 Wickets—Other Cricket Results.

LONDON, July 13 (Canadian Press).—The touring Australian cricketers today defeated Derbyshire by nine wickets in a game started Wednesday at Chesterfield. The Australians had a first innings score of 255, then tallied 32 for one after Derbyshire had scored 145 and followed on for 139.

L. O. Fleetwood-Smith, trundling for the visitors, took five wickets for 38.

Results of other first-class matches which ended today were:

Middlesex won on the first innings from Kent at Folkestone; Middlesex, 440; Kent, 188 and 109 for two (Wooley 61 not out).

Gloucestershire defeated Nottinghamshire at Gloucester by an innings and 32; Gloucestershire, 415; Nottinghamshire, 181 and 202 (Walker 90, Sinfield five for 94).

Lancashire defeated Worcestershire by 32 runs at Blackpool; Lancashire, 150 and 229; Worcestershire, 258 and 89 (Hopwood six for 43).

Yorkshire defeated Essex by 12 at Hull; Yorkshire, 337 and 127 for five declared; Essex, 209 and 132 (Bowes four for 43, Douglas five for 48).

Players defeated Gentlemen at the Oval by an innings and 305; Players, 651 for seven declared; Gentlemen, 192 and 154 (Mercer four for 32).

Warwickshire won on the first innings from Leicestershire at Leicester; Warwickshire, 422; Leicestershire, 207 (Payne five for 68, Hollies four for 69) and, following on, 191 for six (Berry 74).

Sussex defeated Northamptonshire by 163 at Hove; Sussex, 287 and 115 for five declared; Northamptonshire, 182 and 57 (Tate 6 for seven).

KENBOY SAILS TO VICTORY.

Leads Wild Cat by 49 Seconds in Larchmont Interclub Race.

Special to THE NEW YORK TIMES.

LARCHMONT, N. Y., July 13.—Arthur Knapp sailed M. O. Grisham's Kenboy to victory in the Larchmont Interclub Friday series yacht race conducted by the Larchmont Yacht Club today. John M. Lovejoy's Wild Cat was forty-nine seconds astern of the winner, followed by Lawrence Marx's Alberta.

The eleven boats which started had a southwest wind for a four-mile beat to Delancey Point and a run back to the finish.

Sheepshead Regatta July 22.

The Sheepshead Bay Yacht Club will hold its first annual regatta on July 22 off the clubhouse in Brooklyn.

Leading Batsmen.

NATIONAL LEAGUE.

[illegible]

AMERICAN LEAGUE.

[illegible]

Cardinals Win Twice on Brilliant Pitching of Dean Brothers; Giants Score

PAUL DEAN, CARDS, HURLS NO-HIT GAME

Stops Dodgers, 3-0, After His Brother, Dizzy, Pitches 3-Hit Shutout, 13-0.

GIVES ONE BASE ON BALLS

Just Misses Perfect Performance—18,000 Thrilled by Baseball Drama.

By ROSCOE McGOWEN.

Those highly publicized Dean brothers lived up to every advance notice as they hurled the Cardinals to a double victory over the Dodgers at Ebbets Field yesterday. The elder brother, Dizzy, allowed three safeties, the first coming in the eighth inning, as the Cards took the opener, 13 to 0.

But good as Dizzy was, he went into eclipse behind the extraordinary feat of his youthful brother, who gave 18,000 fans the thrill that comes once in a baseball lifetime by hurling a no-hit game. The Cards made seven safe blows off Ray Benge to win, 3 to 0.

Paul's work was just one point short of perfection. He issued one pass, drawn by Len Koenecke in the first inning after two were out, but thereafter the Stengel athletes just marched to the plate and right back again with monotonous regularity.

Advance in the Race.

By taking two games while the Giants were winning one from the Braves, the Cardinals advanced to within three games of the league-leading New Yorkers.

The tension among the players on the Cardinal bench and among the fans could almost be felt as Paul went to the mound in the ninth. Thousands of fans rose to their feet and leaned forward to watch every move on the field, while two or three Cardinals in the dug-out could be seen holding their fingers crossed.

Stengel gave Paul no break as the youngster was knocking on the door of baseball's hall of fame. Casey sent Jimmy Bucner, a dangerous southpaw hitter, to bat for Al Lopez, and that youth cut viciously at the first pitch. But Paul slipped both the second and third strikes across the outside corner of the plate, and cheers cascaded from the stands.

Then Johnny McCarthy, another portside swinger, was sent in to bat for Benge. He connected hard with the ball and for a split second the fans held their breath. But the ball went high in the air and nestled into Frankie Frisch's glove for the second out.

Durocher Pounces on Ball.

Now only Ralph Boyle stood between Paul and his goal, and Buzz came closest to spoiling everything. He drove a slashing grounder toward short that sizzled into Durocher's glove on the short hop and Leo couldn't hold it. But he pounced on the ball like a cat and by a lightning throw just beat Boyle to first to end the game.

As Umpire Sears waved high to signify the put-out, thousands of fans swarmed onto the field and engulfed the young pitcher. But his brother Dizzy and several park policemen were there first and managed to clear a way for him off the field through the Brooklyn dug-out.

Aside from Boyle's last-inning smash, there were only two other occasions when the Dodgers came close to hitting Paul safely. In the first inning Lonnie Frey sliced a drive toward left centre and Joe Medwick ran over fast to snare the ball.

In the seventh it was Sam Leslie who hit the ball hard, driving it close to the barrier in left centre, but again Medwick saved the day by racing over and making a gloved-hand catch.

Paul fanned six men, three of them in the last two innings, and thirteen other Dodgers were retired on balls not hit out of the infield.

A Great Day for Deans.

It was the greatest day the Dean brothers ever experienced, a day in which one all-time record was smashed and two amazing predictions by Dizzy were fulfilled.

In winning his twenty-seventh game Dizzy broke a mark established by Cy Young in 1899 as a Cardinal hurler to win the most games in a season. Cy won 26 and lost 15 that season. Dizzy has lost only seven.

When Paul won the nightcap it marked his eighteenth victory, and thus made good Dizzy's boast in the Spring that "Paul and I will win forty-five games for the Cardinals this year."

The dizziest prophecy of all which was made good was voiced in the Cardinals' hotel yesterday morning, when the elder Dean told a St. Louis writer that "Zachary and Benge will be pitching against one-hit Dean and no-hit Dean today." Dizzy fell down only on his own assignment by allowing three hits instead of one.

Field Day at Bat.

As for the run-scoring, which was almost lost sight of in the drama of Paul's performance, the Cardinals had a field day at bat in the opener against Tom Zachary, Lefty Clark, Owen Carroll and Walter Beck.

They amassed seventeen hits, six of them for extra bases, including Jim Collins's thirty-fourth homer of the year, made off Carroll in the fourth. They counted twice in the first and five times in the third, when Zachary was driven to cover. Three more in the fourth, two in the sixth and one in the seventh were made off Carroll. One hit and no runs were counted off Beck in the ninth.

Collins, who drove in six runs in the first encounter, batted in two of the three scored in the nightcap. The other was sent home by Pepper Martin and it was Paul Dean who carried it across.

Paul scored in the sixth for the first run of the contest, paving the way by driving a two-bagger to deep left centre for the second hit off Benge.

Medwick doubled in the seventh and scored on Collins's single, and in the ninth banged a three-bagger to the exit gate. He tallied the final run as Collins grounded sharply to Jordan.

Fine Support for Benge.

Some fine support was accorded Benge, Cuccinello making a remarkable leaping catch of Frisch's line drive in the first inning and Jordan coming up with a sparkling play on Rothrock's grounder in the fourth.

The Brooklyn management announced that Catcher Walter Millies, purchased from Dayton, will report today, as Ray Berres is out with a lame arm.

The box scores:

FIRST GAME.

ST. LOUIS (N.)	ab.	r.	h.	po.	a.	e.
Martin, 3b	4	1	1	1	1	0
Whiteh'd, 2b	1	0	0	0	0	0
Rothrock, rf	4	3	2	2	0	0
Frisch, 2b	4	2	3	0	3	0
Crawford, 3b	0	0	0	0	0	1
Medwick, lf	4	2	2	1	0	0
Collins, 1b	5	3	4	8	1	0
V. Davis, c	3	1	1	7	0	0
Fullis, cf	5	0	1	4	0	0
Durocher, ss	5	0	1	3	1	1
J. Dean, p	5	1	2	1	2	0
Total	40	13	17	27	8	2

BROOKLYN (N.)	ab.	r.	h.	po.	a.	e.
Boyle, rf	4	0	1	2	0	0
Frey, ss	3	0	0	2	4	1
Koenecke, cf	4	0	0	2	0	0
Leslie, 1b	3	0	1	5	1	0
Cuc'nello, 2b	3	0	0	3	1	0
Bucher, 2b	1	0	0	0	0	0
Frederick, lf	4	0	0	1	0	0
Stripp, 3b	4	0	1	0	2	0
Lopez, c	3	0	0	11	0	0
Zachary, p	0	0	0	0	0	1
Clark, p	0	0	0	0	0	0
Carroll, p	1	0	0	0	1	0
aMcCarthy	1	0	0	0	0	0
Beck, p	0	0	0	0	1	0
bTremark	1	0	0	0	0	0
Total	32	0	3	27	10	2

aBatted for Carroll in eighth.
bBatted for Beck in ninth.

St. Louis	2 0 5	3 0 2	1 0 0	—13
Brooklyn	0 0 0	0 0 0	0 0 0	— 0

Runs batted in—Collins 6, Frisch 2, Davis 2, Medwick, Fullis, Durocher.

Two-base hits—Rothrock, Collins 2, Davis. Three-base hit—Martin. Home run—Collins. Stolen base—Frisch. Sacrifice—Rothrock. Double plays—Frey, Cuccinello and Leslie; Frey and Leslie. Left on bases—St. Louis 6, Brooklyn 9. Bases on balls—Off Zachary 2, Carroll 3, J. Dean 4. Struck out—By Zachary 2, Clark 1, Carroll 4, Beck 1, J. Dean 7. Hits—Off Zachary 5 in 2 1-3 innings, Clark 2 in 2-3, Carroll 9 in 5, Beck 1 in 1. Wild pitch—Clark. Losing pitcher—Zachary. Umpires—Rigler, Klem and Sears. Time of game—1:54.

SECOND GAME.

ST. LOUIS (N.)	ab.	r.	h.	po.	a.	e.
Martin, 3b	4	0	1	0	1	0
Rothrock, rf	4	0	0	1	0	0
Frisch, 2b	4	0	0	1	3	0
Medwick, lf	4	2	3	6	0	0
Collins, 1b	4	0	1	9	1	0
DeLancey, c	4	0	1	7	0	0
Orsatti, cf	[illegible]					
Durocher, ss	[illegible]					
P. Dean, p	[illegible]					
Total	[illegible]					

BROOKLYN (N.)	ab.	r.	h.	po.	a.	e.
Boyle, rf	4	0	0	2	0	0
Frey, ss	3	0	0	4	3	0
Koenecke, cf	2	0	0	1	1	0
Leslie, 1b	3	0	0	10	1	0
Cuccin'lo, 2b	3	0	0	3	0	0
Frederick, lf	3	0	0	2	0	0
Total	[illegible]			27	13	1

aBatted for Lopez in ninth.
bBatted for Benge in ninth.

St. Louis	0 0 0	0 0 1	1 0 1	—3
Brooklyn	0 0 0	0 0 0	0 0 0	—0

Runs batted in—Martin, Collins 2. Two-base hits—Medwick, Leslie. Three-base hit—Medwick. Left on bases—St. Louis [illegible]. Bases on balls—Off P. Dean 1. Struck out—By Benge [illegible], P. Dean 6. Umpires—Klem, Sears and Rigler. Time of game—[illegible].

Times Wide World Photo.

PAUL AND DIZZY DEAN.

Dean's Feat Is Outstanding In Last 12 Years of Baseball

Base on Balls Alone Robs Him of Chance to Join the Select Six of the Sport, Who Pitched Perfect Games—Hubbell's Hitless Performance of 1929 Is Eclipsed.

By G. W. DALEY.

While Paul Dean yesterday turned in the first no-hit game in the National League since Carl Hubbell's masterpiece in 1929, and the first since two American League hurlers, Bob Burke and Wesley Ferrell, succeeded in 1931, his performance overshadowed all of the miracle feats of the pitcher's mound in the last twelve years.

For by the margin of a single base on balls the Cardinal yearling missed a perfect game—no hits, no man reaching first base—which has been accomplished only six times in all baseball history. Dean failed to get the ball over for Koenecke, the third man to face him in the opening inning.

Not since Charlie Robertson of the White Sox turned the trick against the Tigers on April 30, 1922, has there been a perfect game in the majors. There have been eight no-hitters since then, but all were marred by passes and errors. None came as close to perfection as Dean did yesterday.

Perfect Games in 1880.

There were two perfect games in 1880, according to the National League records—John Lee Richmond of Worcester against Cleveland and John Montgomery Ward, afterward a manager of the Giants, for Providence against Buffalo. Then there was a lapse until 1904 when Cy Young, for the Red Sox, pitched a perfect performance against the Athletics on May 5 of that year. Addie Joss of the Indians followed in 1908 against the White Sox.

Ernie Shore of the Red Sox is credited with a perfect game, hurled on June 23, 1917, though he did not start the contest. The starting hurler was a temperamental left-hander named Babe Ruth, who was banished from the game by Umpire Owens for disputing a decision which sent Morgan, the first batter of the Senators, to first base on a pass.

Without warming up Shore came to the mound. Morgan was caught stealing and then only twenty-six batsmen faced Shore, there being no hits, no passes and no errors.

There have been 107 no-hit games since 1875, starting with Joseph Borden of Philadelphia against Chicago in the National Association. Since the American League was organized in 1901 there have been sixty-three no-hitters, the National League having twenty-three, the American League thirty-five and the Federal League five.

There were also four pitchers who turned in no-hit performances of ten or more innings—Kimber of Brooklyn in 1884, Harry McIntire of Brooklyn in 1906, George Wiltse for the Giants in 1908 and Fred Toney for the Reds in 1917.

In Class by Itself.

As far as the records show, Dean's feat is in a class by itself in that it is the first time a rookie, or first-year hurler, ever pitched a no-hit game in the majors. The 21-year-old star has made notable progress since joining the Cardinals, winning eighteen battles so far this season, six from the Giants, and he bids fair to become even a better hurler than his brother, the famous Dizzy. The latter modestly says that Paul really is a better pitcher "right now."

Paul won twenty-two games while losing seven with the Columbus club of the American Association last year. His record shows that in 1932 he pitched a no-hit game, performing the feat against Kansas City on Aug. 30 of that year. He is 6 feet 3 inches tall, weighs 192 pounds and his Winter residence is Bradentown, Fla., where the Cardinals trained last Spring.

TORONTO WINS AGAIN, 3-2.

Scores in 13th for Third in Row Over Rochester.

ROCHESTER, N. Y., Sept. 21 (AP).—The Toronto Maple Leafs made it three straight over the Rochester Red Wings in the final International League play-off series tonight, earning a 3-2 decision in thirteen innings. Toronto now needs one more victory to win the series and gain the right to represent the International League in the Little World Series against the American Association champion.

The fourth and fifth games will be played here tomorrow and Sunday afternoons.

The box score:

TORONTO (I.)	ab.	r.	h.	po.	a.	e.
Blakely, cf	5	0	0	3	1	0
Morrissey, 3b	6	1	1	6	4	0
McQuinn, 1b	4	0	1	12	1	1
Boone, rf	4	1	0	1	0	0
Howell, lf	5	1	1	1	0	0
Regan, 3b	6	0	0	4	3	0
Rich'dson, ss	4	0	1	3	3	0
Heving, c	4	0	1	9	2	0
Brennan, p	4	0	0	0	4	0
Total	42	3	5	39	18	1

ROCHESTER (I.)	ab.	r.	h.	po.	a.	e.
Borgm'n, 3b	5	0	3	2	2	3
Toporcer, 2b	4	0	2	4	2	0
Crabtree, cf	6	0	1	4	0	0
Mize, 1b	6	0	3	11	0	0
Winsett, rf	6	0	1	2	0	0
Mills, lf	5	2	3	2	0	0
Carey, ss	5	0	2	2	6	0
Florence, c	6	0	0	12	3	0
Harrell, p	5	0	0	0	2	1
aMoore	1	0	0	0	0	0
Total	49	2	15	39	15	4

aBatted for Harrell in thirteenth.

Toronto	0 0 0	2 0 0	0 0 0	0 0 0	1—3
Rochester	0 1 1	0 0 0	0 0 0	0 0 0	0—2

Runs batted in—Carey, Richardson, Howell. Two-base hits—Carey 2, Mize 2, Heving. Stolen bases—Borgman 2, McQuinn. Sacrifices—Toporcer, Carey. Double plays—Carey and Toporcer; Florence and Carey; Morrissey and McQuinn. Left on bases—Toronto 9, Rochester 13. Bases on balls—Off Harrell 9, Brennan 2. Struck out—By Harrell 8, Brennan 8. Umpires—Van Graflan, Jorda and Parker. Time of game—2:48.

Home-Run Hitters.

Yesterday's Homers.

Collins, St. Louis Nationals 1
Berger, Boston Nationals 1

The Leaders.

AMERICAN LEAGUE.

Gehrig, New York	46	Bonura, Chicago	26
Foxx, Phila.	43	Greenberg, Detroit	25
Trosky, Cleveland	33	Ruth, New York	21
Johnson, Phila.	32	Simmons, Chicago	18
Averill, Cleveland	29	McNair, Phila.	17

NATIONAL LEAGUE.

Ott, New York	35	Hafey, Cincinnati	18
Collins, St. Louis	34	Jackson, N. York	16
Berger, Boston	33	Medwick, S. Louis	16
Hartnett, Chicago	21	Camilli, Phila.	16
Klein, Chicago	19		

League Totals.

American League	663
National League	629
Total	1,292

GIANTS TURN BACK THE BRAVES, 8 TO 1

Hit Hard Behind Fitzsimmons but Lose Ground to Cards, Who Capture Two.

TERRY IS BATTING STAR

Delivers 3 Drives in Leading Barrage on Three Hurlers—Game Clinched in Third.

By JAMES P. DAWSON.
Special to THE NEW YORK TIMES.

BOSTON, Sept. 21.—The Giants overwhelmed the Braves before a handful of onlookers at Braves Field today, but lost ground in the torrid dash for the National League flag nevertheless.

For a change, the champions got behind rotund Freddie Fitzsimmons with some hitting and an 8-to-1 triumph was the result.

But the Terrymen's lead of three and one-half games, with which they opened hostilities here, was cut half a game because while Fitzsimmons was going through the unique experience of having his superb pitching supported with some blasting hitting the Cardinals were taking two games from the Dodgers in Brooklyn.

The combination finds the Giants leading tonight by three games, with seven yet to play. The Cardinals have nine skirmishes facing them and, the way they are going, anything can happen.

A Present to Fitzsimmons.

The Giants gave Fitzsimmons his first run in thirty-four innings today, and it was like a gift from the gods. The victim of three straight shutouts, despite superb pitching, two of them in extra-inning conflicts, the husky knuckle-ball thrower got his first run in the third inning.

The Fitzsimmons bugaboo broken, the Giants went briskly about the task of taming the Braves and giving Fitz his eighteenth victory of the season. They got eleven hits off three of Bill McKechnie's hurlers.

Walter (Huck) Betts was shelled off the mound in the midst of a four-run onslaught in the third. Leo Mangum couldn't stop the Giants and neither could Bob Smith, who pitched the last two innings after Mangum gave way to a pinch-hitter in the seventh.

Not There at Finish.

Fitzsimmons wasn't there at the finish. His determination to field every ball hit at or near him resulted in his getting a crack on the fingers of his pitching hand in the eighth which caused him to falter momentarily. He finished the inning and withdrew. Joe Bowman baffled the Braves in the ninth.

Wally Berger's thirty-third home run of the season was the only count for the Braves. It arrived in the second inning. Thereafter Fitzsimmons was in complete control and he got flawless support.

Three double plays, snappily executed, saved him embarrassment in the third, sixth and eighth. Manager Bill Terry led the Giants' attack with three blows.

The one-run edge that Berger's homer gave the Braves disappeared in the third when Moore opened with a single, Critz sacrificed and Terry's first hit scored Moore. Ott was hit, Mallon let Leiber's roller through him, Mancuso singled and Vergez doubled, all for four runs. After that there was nothing to it.

The box score:

NEW YORK (N.)	ab.	r.	h.	po.	a.	e.
J. Moore, lf	5	1	1	1	0	0
Critz, 2b	4	1	1	4	3	0
Terry, 1b	5	2	3	13	0	0
Ott, rf	3	2	2	0	0	0
Leiber, cf	4	1	0	1	0	0
Mancuso, c	5	0	1	2	0	0
Vergez, 3b	5	1	2	1	4	0
Ryan, ss	4	0	1	4	4	0
Fitzsi'ms, p	4	0	0	1	3	0
Bowman, p	0	0	0	0	0	0
Total	39	8	11	27	14	0

BOSTON (N.)	ab.	r.	h.	po.	a.	e.
Urbanski, ss	4	0	2	2	3	0
Mallon, 2b	4	0	1	2	6	2
Jordan, 1b	3	0	0	14	0	0
Berger, cf	3	1	1	1	0	0
R. Moore, lf	4	0	1	0	0	0
Thompson, rf	4	0	1	5	0	0
Whitney, 3b	4	0	2	0	2	0
Hogan, c	3	0	2	0	1	0
aFletcher	0	0	0	0	0	0
Spohrer, c	0	0	0	1	0	0
Betts, p	0	0	0	0	1	0
Mangum, p	1	0	0	0	2	0
bMcManus	1	0	0	0	0	0
Smith, p	0	0	0	0	1	0
cTyler	1	0	0	0	0	0
dMowry	1	0	0	0	0	0
Total	33	1	9	27	16	2

aRan for Hogan in seventh.
bBatted for Mangum in seventh.
cBatted for Spohrer in ninth.
dBatted for Smith in ninth.

New York	0 0 4	0 2 0	0 0 2	—8
Boston	0 1 0	0 0 0	0 0 0	—1

Runs batted in—Terry, Mancuso 3, Vergez, Ryan, Leiber, Berger.

Two-base hits—Vergez, Ott, Ryan, Whitney. Home run—Berger. Sacrifices—Critz, Leiber. Double plays—Ryan and Terry; Critz, Ryan and Terry; Fitzsimmons, Ryan and Terry. Left on bases—New York 8, Boston 8. Bases on balls—Off Fitzsimmons 3, Smith 1. Struck out—By Fitzsimmons 1, Bowman 1, Smith 1. Hits—Off Fitzsimmons 8 in 8 innings, Bowman 1 in 1, Betts 6 in 2 1-3, Mangum 3 in 4 2-3, Smith 2 in 2. Hit by pitcher—By Betts (Ott). Winning pitcher—Fitzsimmons. Losing pitcher—Betts. Umpires—Magerkurth, Pfirman and Stark. Time of game—1:46.

Leading Batsmen.

AMERICAN LEAGUE.

	G.	A.B.	R.	H.	P.C.
Gehrig, New York	146	555	123	198	.357
Manush, Washington	134	543	89	193	.355
Gehringer, Detroit	144	568	126	200	.352
Simmons, Chicago	130	526	96	180	.342
Foxx, Philadelphia	142	513	116	174	.339

Leader a year ago—Foxx, Phila., .353.

NATIONAL LEAGUE.

	G.	A.B.	R.	H.	P.C.
P. Waner, Pittsburgh	139	575	116	207	.360
Terry, New York	145	575	108	201	.350
J. Moore, Philadelphia	122	458	70	156	.341
Ott, New York	146	554	118	188	.339
Moore, New York	132	550	101	185	.336

Leader a year ago—Klein, Phila., .368.

How the Leading Clubs In Big Leagues Stand

Although the Cardinals gained ground yesterday, they face a tremendous task in their nine remaining games. The St. Louis team can make a clean sweep and still fail in its pennant bid, provided the Giants take six out of seven. In this event, the final standing would be:

	Won.	Lost.	P.C.
Giants	98	55	.641
Cardinals	97	56	.634

In case the Giants capture only three encounters, the Cardinals nevertheless would require eight triumphs to finish in front, furnishing a final standing as follows:

	Won.	Lost.	P.C.
Cardinals	96	57	.627
Giants	95	58	.621

In the American League four victories by the Tigers will decide, even though the Yankees capture eight straight. The final standing would be:

	Won.	Lost.	P.C.
Tigers	98	56	.636
Yankees	97	57	.630

PIRATES CONQUER REDS BY 9-3, 16-3

Pound Four Cincinnati Hurlers for 37 Hits in Both Games of Twin Bill.

PITTSBURGH, Sept. 21 (AP).—Pittsburgh today blasted out a double triumph over Cincinnati, 9 to 3 and 16 to 3, and advanced to within half a game of the first division in the National League.

The Pirates pounded four Red pitchers in both games for a total of thirty-seven hits, while Lucas and Smith tossed steady ball for Pittsburgh.

Tony Freitas worked well for six innings in the opener and stepped out with the score tied. The Pirates then opened up.

Si Johnson was greeted with a barrage of hits as the second game got under way, the Pirates making six runs in the first inning.

The box scores:

FIRST GAME.

CINCINNATI (N.)	ab.	r.	h.	po.	a.	e.
Adams, 2b	4	1	1	4	0	0
Slade, ss	4	0	1	0	2	0
Koenig, 3b	4	0	1	2	0	0
Bott'ley, 1b	4	0	2	4	0	0
Hafey, cf	4	0	0	6	0	0
Pool, rf	4	1	2	1	0	0
Lombardi, c	4	0	0	3	0	0
Com'osky, lf	3	1	1	2	0	0
Freitas, p	2	0	0	1	4	0
aMcCormick	1	0	1	0	0	0
Richmond, p	0	0	0	0	0	0
Kolp, p	0	0	0	0	1	0
Barnes, p	0	0	0	0	0	0
Total	34	3	9	24	8	0

PITTSBURGH (N.)	ab.	r.	h.	po.	a.	e.
L. Waner, cf	2	0	0	0	0	0
Roettger, lf	3	0	0	1	1	0
Jensen, lf, cf	5	2	2	2	0	0
P. Waner, rf	5	2	2	2	0	0
Vaughan, ss	4	2	3	3	5	1
Traynor, 3b	5	3	4	2	1	0
Suhr, 1b	3	0	1	11	2	0
Thevenow, 2b	5	0	3	3	6	0
Padden, c	4	0	1	2	1	0
Lucas, p	5	1	1	1	1	0
Total	40	9	17	27	16	1

aBatted for Freitas in seventh.

Cincinnati	0 0 1	0 0 0	2 0 0	—3
Pittsburgh	1 0 2	0 0 0	2 4 .	—9

Runs batted in—Traynor 4, Koenig, Thevenow 2, McCormick 2, Vaughan 2, P. Waner.

Two-base hits—Vaughan 2, Traynor, Thevenow, P. Waner. Three-base hits—McCormick, Traynor. Stolen bases—Adams, Lucas. Double plays—Vaughan, Thevenow and Suhr; Freitas and Koenig; Traynor, Thevenow and Suhr. Left on bases—Cincinnati 4, Pittsburgh 12. Bases on balls—Off Freitas 2, Richmond 1, Kolp 1. Hits—Off Freitas 8 in 6 innings, Kolp 5 in 1 1-3, Richmond 4 in 1-3, Barnes 0 in 1-3. Hit by pitcher—By Kolp (Suhr). Balk—Freitas. Losing pitcher—Richmond. Umpires—Quigley, Reardon and Barr. Time of game—1:59.

SECOND GAME.

CINCINNATI (N.)	ab.	r.	h.	po.	a.	e.
Adams, 2b	5	1	2	1	2	0
Slade, ss	5	1	4	2	4	1
Koenig, 3b	5	0	1	1	1	0
Bot'mley, 1b	1	0	0	1	1	0
McCor'k, 1b	3	1	1	8	0	0
Hafey, cf	1	0	0	1	0	0
Petoskey, cf	3	0	0	5	1	0
Pool, rf	3	0	2	0	0	0
Manion, c	2	0	0	1	0	0
Lombardi, c	2	0	1	3	0	0
Com'sky, lf	4	0	1	1	0	0
Johnson, p	0	0	0	0	0	0
Kl'nhans, p	0	0	0	0	0	1
aWistert	1	0	0	0	0	0
Grissom, p	1	0	0	0	0	0
Edwards, p	1	0	0	0	1	0
bMarshall	1	0	0	0	0	0
Total	38	3	12	24	10	2

PITTSBURGH (N.)	ab.	r.	h.	po.	a.	e.
Roettger, lf	6	2	3	4	0	0
Jensen, cf	6	2	3	2	0	0
P. Waner, rf	4	3	2	3	0	0
Vaughan, ss	3	2	3	1	2	0
Young, ss	2	0	1	0	0	0
Traynor, 3b	3	2	2	1	0	0
Brub'ker, 3b	1	0	0	0	1	0
Suhr, 1b	4	1	1	7	0	0
Th'v'now, 2b	3	1	2	1	1	0
Lav'gtto, 2b	1	0	0	2	1	0
Grace, c	5	2	1	6	0	0
Swift, p	5	1	2	0	1	0
Total	43	16	20	27	6	0

aBatted for Kleinhans in third.
bBatted for Edwards in ninth.

Cincinnati	0 0 0	0 0 0	0 3 0	— 3
Pittsburgh	6 2 0	7 0 0	0 1 .	—16

Runs batted in—Vaughan, Traynor 2, Suhr, Thevenow 3, Swift 2, Roettger, Jensen 2, McCormick, Petoskey, Pool, P. Waner.

Two-base hits—Slade, Koenig, McCormick, Roettger. Three-base hit—Swift. Stolen base—Jensen. Double plays—Vaughan, Thevenow and Suhr; Petoskey and McCormick. Left on bases—Cincinnati 9, Pittsburgh 9. Bases on balls—Off Johnson 1, Grissom 4, Edwards 1. Struck out—By Swift 4, Edwards 1. Hits—Off Johnson 5 in 1-3 inning, Grissom 7 in 3, Kleinhans 4 in 1 2-3, Edwards 4 in 3. Hit by pitcher—By Swift (Pool). Passed ball—Lombardi. Losing pitcher—Johnson. Umpires—Reardon, Barr and Quigley. Time of game—1:41.

PACIFIC COAST LEAGUE.

By The Associated Press.

AT SACRAMENTO.

					R.	H.	E.
Los Angeles	3 0 0	0 1 0	0 0 0	—	4	10	1
Sacramento	2 0 2	1 1 1	0 4 .	—	11	16	0

Batteries—Garland, Meola, McDougal and Campbell; Koupal and Wirts.

AT HOLLYWOOD.

Portland	0 0 0	3 0 0	0 0 0	—3	8	0
Hollywood	0 2 3	1 0 0	2 2 .	—10	9	1

Batteries—Ulrich and Cox; Shellenback and Bassler.

Portland	0 0 1	0 4 0	1	—6	14	0
Hollywood	1 0 0	2 0 0	0	—3	10	0

Batteries—Smith and H. Doerr; Campbell, Hile, Hebert and Kerr.

AT SAN FRANCISCO.

Seattle	0 1 2	0 0 0	0 0 0	—3	6	2
Missions	1 0 1	0 0 0	0 7 .	—9	14	2

Batteries—Pillette and Bottarini; Lieber and Wolfrom.

STANDING OF THE CLUBS.

	W.	L.	PC.		W.	L.	PC.
L. Angeles	63	30	.677	San Fran.	48	44	.522
Hollywood	51	40	.560	Oakland	42	50	.457
Seattle	50	41	.549	Portland	32	59	.352
Missions	49	42	.538	Sac'mento	32	61	.344

LAFAYETTE SQUAD HIT BY GRADUATION

McCracken and Aides Facing Hard Task in Rebuilding for Football Campaign.

THREE MEN ARE NUCLEUS

Captain Nesi, Bialek and Stabley Counted On to Carry the Chief Burden.

This is the twelfth of a series of articles on Eastern college football teams and their prospects for the coming season.

By ALLISON DANZIG.
Special to THE NEW YORK TIMES.

SAYLORSBURG, Pa., Sept. 21.—Because of the reduction of Lafayette's 1933 football squad through graduation, Coach Herbert McCracken and his aides admittedly face a hard task in preparing for the 1934 campaign.

No less than twenty-two out of thirty-nine men on the 1933 roster were seniors and their replacements consist of six sophomores, five members of the junior varsity squad and five who never played any football before.

The scarcity of sophomores is explained by the fact that last year the freshman team had to call off its game with Muhlenberg because of the lack of sufficient men to undertake the contest.

So skimpy is the material that the coaches have found it necessary to prepare some of the more proficient men to play two or more positions. An idea of their problem may be gained from the fact that candidates who were as far back as fifth or seventh in line for jobs a year ago are now occupying first-string berths.

Coaches' Only Recourse.

In some cases the promotion has been made on worth, on the big improvement shown after a year of experience, but in large it has been the only recourse of the coaches to fill the breach.

However, as discouraging as is the outlook, McCracken is far from overwhelmed by his task. There are a number of players here who are qualified to win a berth on any team, particularly Captain Charley Nesi at left guard, Frank Bialek at fullback and Charley Stabley at left half, and the Lafayette mentor is sure he can put a pretty fair first team on the field that will give a good account of itself.

The spirit of the squad is excellent and its willingness to assimilate any amount of hard work and bumps without complaint has helped to make the coaches forget their troubles. The day after the men arrived in camp here at Saylor's Lake scrimmaging began, and it was continued for the next three days in the toughest sort of going.

Lack of experience and weight are the things that count heaviest against the squad and the drop between the first-string backfield and the next is so marked that the coaches hardly dare entertain the thought of losing any of the regulars through injury. But at the pace the players have been going and the rate some of them have been improving, the situation should be perceptibly improved by the middle of the season.

Men Being Counted On.

The men who are being counted on most are Captain Nesi, Bialek, a big, fast powerhouse of strength of 190 pounds who was held back by a late start in 1933, and Stabley, who can kick and pass as well as carry the ball to town if given any kind of help.

Walter Arnold stands out as an end of considerable promise, Bialkowski is a bundle of energy at right half and Sidney Weiss, who was on the third team last year, needs only more fire to do a good job at quarterback. Pateman, fourth-string tackle last year and the heaviest man on the team, weighing 210 pounds, is also likely to prove a big asset.

For the centre post, Patton, who was third in line a year ago, is leading Chamberlain, Sanzo, sophomore, and Fitzwater, who was a substitute end. Riedman, who was No. 7 among the guards in 1933, is holding down the job on the right side of the line and Bob Duer, freshman captain last year; Jiadosz, who came up from the junior varsity, and Fredericks are the reserves.

The Other Tackles.

The other tackles are Adams, McCaa, Jefferson and Cooke. Fitzwater and Corradino are fighting for the other end job, followed by Updergrove and Peterson and Snyder, sophomores.

Capobianco, Heller and Smith are the reserve quarterbacks. Rusk, Haines, Fulmer and Jones are the replacements for halfback, averaging around 150 pounds, and Peruno is the utility fullback, followed by Smith.

Assisting McCracken are W. Cullen Gourley, Paul Shellenberger and Henry Sage. Charley Soleau, former Colgate star, is the new coach of the freshmen.

The schedule:

Oct. 6, Muhlenberg; 13, F. and M.; 20, N. Y. U. at New York; 27, Albright.
Nov. 3, Pennsylvania at Philadelphia; 10, Rutgers at New Brunswick; 17, Penn State at State College; 24, Lehigh.

NEW ORLEANS VICTOR, 7-2.

Downs Nashville to Gain Lead in Southern Play-Offs.

NEW ORLEANS, Sept. 21 (AP).—The New Orleans Pelicans took the lead in the Southern Association playoffs today, defeating the Nashville Volunteers, 7 to 2.

Clay Bryant, young right-hander, held the Vols to six hits, showing slight weaknesses in the second and seventh innings when, aided by misplays, Nashville pushed across its two runs.

Nashville used three pitchers in an effort to stem the Pelican attack.

The score by innings:

					R.	H.	E.
Nashville	0 1 0	0 0 0	1 0 0	—	2	6	1
New Orleans	4 1 0	0 2 0	0 0 .	—	7	10	2

Batteries—Gaier, Brillheart, Elland and Crouch; Bryant and George.

TEXAS LEAGUE.
Play-off Game.
Galveston 7, San Antonio 2.

MAJOR LEAGUE BASEBALL

National League

YESTERDAY'S RESULTS.

New York 8, Boston 1.
St. Louis 13, Brooklyn 0 (1st).
St. Louis 3, Brooklyn 0 (2d).
Pittsburgh 9, Cincinnati 3 (1st).
Pittsburgh 16, Cincinnati 3 (2d).
Other clubs not scheduled.

STANDING OF THE CLUBS.

	New York	St. Louis	Chicago	Boston	Pittsburgh	Brooklyn	Phila'phia	Cincinnati	Won	Lost	Percentage
New York	—	9	10	14	14	14	15	16	92	54	.630
St. Louis	13	—	9	16	8	15	16	11	88	56	.611
Chicago	11	12	—	10	16	12	12	8	81	61	.570
Boston	5	5	12	—	9	15	13	12	71	71	.500
Pittsburgh	8	12	5	11	—	6	13	15	70	71	.496
Brooklyn	7	6	7	5	16	—	10	14	65	79	.451
Phila'phia	6	5	6	7	9	12	—	8	53	86	.381
Cincinnati	5	6	9	7	7	9	8	—	51	90	.364
Gms. lost	54	56	61	71	71	79	86	90			

GAMES TODAY.

Philadelphia at Brooklyn (2).
(First at 1:30 P. M.)
New York at Boston.
St. Louis at Cincinnati.
Chicago at Pittsburgh (2).

American League

YESTERDAY'S RESULTS.

Detroit at St. Louis, rain.
Other clubs not scheduled.

STANDING OF THE CLUBS.

	Detroit	New York	Cleveland	Boston	Phila'phia	St. Louis	Wash'ton	Chicago	Won	Lost	Percentage
Detroit	[illegible]										
New York	[illegible]										
Cleveland	[illegible]										
Boston	[illegible]										
Phila'phia	[illegible]										
St. Louis	[illegible]										
Wash'ton	[illegible]										
Chicago	[illegible]										
Gms. lost	[illegible]										

GAMES TODAY.

Boston at New York (2 P. M.).
Detroit at St. Louis (2).
Washington at Philadelphia (2).
Cleveland at Chicago.

Football Games Today.

Local.

Home Team.	Opponent.	At.	1933 Score.
*Manhattan	St. Bonaventure	Ebbets Field	6- 0

(Game starts at 8:30 P. M.)

East.

[illegible]

South.

[illegible]

West.

[illegible]

Far West.

Home Team.	Opponent.	At.	1933 Score.
*Fresno	San Fran. Tea.	Fresno	—
*Montana State	Brigham Young	Great Falls	0-25
New Mexico	Freshmen	State Coll.	—
Oregon	Gonzaga	Eugene	14-0
Oregon State	Willamette	Corvallis	21-0
Santa Clara	Nevada	San Fran.	—
So. California	Occidental	Los Ang.	39-0
So. California	Whittier	Los Ang.	51-0
Stanford	San Jose	Palo Alto	27-0
U. C. L. A.	Pomona	Los Ang.	—
U. C. L. A.	San Diego	Los Ang.	13-0
Utah State	Alumni	Logan	33-2

*Denotes night game.

DUQUESNE DEFEATS WAYNESBURG, 39-0

Opens Football Season Before 20,000—Zaneski's 91-Yard Run for Score Features.

Special to THE NEW YORK TIMES.

PITTSBURGH, Sept. 21.—Duquesne University swamped Waynesburg College, 39 to 0, before 20,000 fans in Pittsburgh's intercollegiate football opener at Forbes Field tonight. The Duquesne team made its début under the coaching of Joe Bach, who succeeded Elmer Layden when the latter signed with Notre Dame last Winter.

From the opening kick-off, which Zaneski ran back 91 yards for a touchdown, the Duquesne team dazzled it opponents with a brilliant running and passing attack that netted six touchdowns. Duquesne counted ten first downs to Waynesburg's five.

The line-up:

DUQUESNE (39).		WAYNESBURG (0).
Chapala	L. E.	Holland
Vidoni	L. T.	Coen
Perko	L. G.	Booth
Malkovich	C.	Paul
Kakasic	R. G.	Rozzi
Johnson	R. T.	Sepsi
Disegi	R. E.	McCracken
Gates	Q. B.	Donnelly
Fillingham	L. H.	Currie
Zaneski	R. H.	Worden
Strutt	F. B.	Conroy

SCORE BY PERIODS.

Duquesne	13	13	0	13—39
Waynesburg	0	0	0	0— 0

Touchdowns—Zaneski, Fillingham 2, Airhart, Strutt, Vairo.

Points after touchdowns—Kakasic, Rado, Dillon (placements).

Substitutions—Waynesburg: Parker for Holland, McCone for Coen, McComb for Currie, Larue for Paul, McGlumphy for McCracken, Worden for McGlumphy, Markevina for Worden, Karvasoles for McGlumphy. Duquesne: Cutrona for Gates, Barock for Malkovich, Airhart for Chapala, Burns for Kakasic, Dillon for Zaneski, Nosich for Vidoni, Hefferle for Disegi, Campbell for Strutt, Rado for Skarada, Wiehl for Goodman, Eppler for Barock, Laputka for Nosich, Marin for Dillon, Brinky for Campbell, Cassel for Fillingham, Vairo for Cassel.

Referee—W. H. Friesell, Princeton. Umpire—D. W. Very, Penn State. Linesman—J. J. Gannon. Field judge—O. K. Rebele.

FOOTBALL RESULTS.

COLLEGES.

Ashland 16	Bluffton 6
Birmingham Southern 7	Auburn 0
Drake 6	Simpson 6
Duquesne 39	Waynesburg 0
Lacrosse Teachers 12	Winona Teachers 0
Louisiana Tech. 7	Holmers Jr. Col. 0
Millsaps 21	Delta State Tea. 0
N. Dakota U. 13	Winnipeg All Stars 3
Oglethorpe 12	Newberry 0
St. Thomas (St. Paul) 18	Mankatotea 6
Union 6	Bethel 0
Xavier 41	Transylvania 0

SCHOOLS.

Audubon High 24	Glassboro 13
Germantown Acad. 21	G'ntown High 0
Onondaga Acad. 0	East Wood High 0
Penn Charter 19	La Salle 0

MANHATTAN READY FOR OPENING GAME

Jasper Eleven Slated to Face St. Bonaventure in Night Test at Ebbets Field.

HOLY CROSS ALSO TO PLAY

Considerable Action in the South—So. California and Stanford to Start on Coast.

Football moves into a new season today. The majority of the larger colleges throughout the country still remain in their training grind and it will be two weeks before the season swells to its full flood of hundreds of games on each Saturday. Today, though, finds more than fifty games important enough to be listed in the official guide.

In New York, the first game among the local colleges comes with the opening of Manhattan's season at Ebbets Field. There will be the added interest of a night game, a type of football which has not often been tried in New York, though it has been more or less successful in other parts of the country. Manhattan will face St. Bonaventure in a contest starting at 8:30 P. M.

In New England, Holy Cross will start another season when it meets St. Anselm's at Worcester and Brooklyn College will journey to Kingston to face Rhode Island.

Kentucky to See Action.

In the South there will be considerable activity, with Kentucky facing Maryville, Loyola of New Orleans meeting the Rice team, Southern Methodist starting against the Denton Teachers and, closer at hand, West Virginia playing West Virginia Wesleyan. Washington and Lee also starts, meeting Wofford.

Some of the big fellows start off on the Pacific Coast. Southern California and Stanford both begin. The former plays a double-header at Los Angeles against Occidental and Whittier, teams against which the Trojans rolled up 90 points at the start of last season. Stanford meets San Jose. Further north, Oregon plays Gonzaga and Oregon State will face Willamette.

Of chief interest with the season's start will be the first working of a rule which may make a vital difference in play this season, the rule permitting one incompleted pass into the end zone without loss of the ball. This is designed to increase the scoring threat of teams near the goal line.

To Be Watched With Interest.

Heralded as the strongest team in recent Manhattan football history, John F. (Chick) Meehan's third Jasper eleven will be watched with interest in its début. With seven sophomores in its starting line-up, it is a team of great potentialities.

For the first time in several years, the Jaspers will have a line capable of providing protection for its backs. The Manhattan forward wall this year is a rugged combination, averaging 190 pounds from end to end.

Augmented by the presence of Elmer Taber, sophomore halfback, and Joe Gallagher, an offensive triple threat from left end, Manhattan will this year present a more versatile attack than ever.

The probable line-up:

MANHATTAN.		ST. BONAV'NTURE.
Gallagher	L. E.	Nichols
Bartell	L. T.	Kantakevitch
Wheeler	L. G.	Ventura
Moser	C.	Ganaposki
Pike	R. G.	Klancer
Seick	R. T.	Dorsey
Connell	R. E.	Silk
Downey	Q. B.	Curry
Barkaus	L. H.	Painton
Taber	R. H.	Zayachek
Welch	F. B.	West

Auburn Is Beaten, 7-0.

MONTGOMERY, Ala., Sept. 21.—Birmingham-Southern tonight defeated Auburn, 7—0, before a crowd of 8,500. McKay scored in the second quarter after Wedgeworth, Southern centre, recovered an Auburn fumble on the Auburn 29 yard line. Davis converted with a place kick.

"All the News That's Fit to Print."

The New York Times.

Copyright, 1934, by The New York Times Company.

LATE CITY EDITION
WEATHER—Fair today; tomorrow warmer and possibly rain.
Temperatures Yesterday—Max., 69; min., 56.
Detailed Weather Report, Page 45.

VOL. LXXXIV....No. 28,018. Entered as Second-Class Matter, Postoffice, New York, N. Y. NEW YORK, WEDNESDAY, OCTOBER 10, 1934. P TWO CENTS In New York City. | THREE CENTS Within 200 Miles | FOUR CENTS Elsewhere Except in 7th and 8th Postal Zones

YUGOSLAV KING AND BARTHOU ASSASSINATED BY CROATIAN AS RULER LANDS IN MARSEILLES; EUROPE SHOCKED, FEARS GRAVE COMPLICATIONS

CARDS WIN SERIES, BEAT DETROIT, 11-0; TIGER FANS RIOT

DEAN EASILY THE VICTOR

Six Pitchers Used by the Losers Against Dizzy in Deciding Contest.

7 RUNS SCORED IN THIRD

Frisch's Double With Bases Filled Starts Drive—13 Men Bat in Inning.

WILD SCENES MARK GAME

Landis Banishes Medwick After Aroused Fans Shower Missiles on Player.

By JOHN DREBINGER.
Special to THE NEW YORK TIMES.

DETROIT, Oct. 9.—Amid the most riotous scenes in the history of modern world series play, Frankie Frisch's rip-snorting band of Cardinals today brought an amazing and crushing finish to the seven-game struggle for the world's baseball championship.

The intervention of Commissioner K. M. Landis was made necessary before the Cardinals, who already had achieved unprecedented deeds this year by coming from nowhere to win a pennant in the final leap to the tape, won the crown.

With their inimitable Dizzy Dean back on the firing line once more to give a final display of his matchless pitching skill, the National League champions fairly annihilated the Tigers, led by their wounded but doughty Mickey Cochrane. The score of the seventh and deciding game was 11 to 0.

Smash Clears the Bases.

Figuratively and literally this most astonishing ball club of modern times tore the game apart. In a whirlwind sweep they blasted seven runs across the plate in the third inning, the first three riding home on a base-clearing two-bagger by the indomitable Frisch himself. They routed Elden Auker, Schoolboy Rowe, only a short time ago the pride of all Detroit, and two other pitchers.

For a finish, one of their cast, Jersey Joe Medwick, touched off the spark that sent part of the crowd into a raging demonstration that interrupted the game for twenty minutes and for a time threatened to terminate the battle without further play. Commissioner Landis then took a hand and quelled the disturbance by ordering the Cardinal outfielder from the field.

The uproar got its inception during the upper half of the sixth inning. Medwick bounced a triple off the right-field bleachers and finished his dash around the bases with a slide into third base while the disconsolate gathering looked sullenly on.

Lashes Kick at Owen.

Just what provoked Medwick could not be seen as he crashed into the bag in a cloud of dust, with Marvin Owen, the Tiger third baseman, standing over him. Suddenly the St. Louis player was seen to lift his left foot and strike out with his spikes toward Owen's chest.

Medwick missed his mark, but the flare-up was sufficient to arouse the hostile feeling between the rival teams that had been brewing for several days and players of both sides rushed to the spot. However, the four umpires quickly stepped in between the irate players. When Umpire Bill Klem, dean of the National League staff and the arbiter at that base, decided to take no action, the uproar subsided, with only a few minutes delay.

It looked like the end of the disturbance, but it proved only to be the beginning.

With the end of the Cardinal inning, Medwick started out for left field and was greeted by rounds of boos from the 17,000 fans packed solidly in the huge wooden bleachers that had been constructed especially for the series.

Retreats Toward Infield.

Pop bottles, oranges, apples and anything else that came ready to hand were hurled out on the field and the Cardinal player beat a retreat toward the infield while the umpires called time.

Attendants rushed out to clear away the débris and Medwick returned to his post. The din now

Continued on Page Twenty-eight.

Nazi Offices in Africa Raided by British Police

By The Associated Press

WINDHOEK, Southwest Africa, Oct. 9.—Nazi offices throughout Southwest Africa were raided by the police today without preliminary warning. It was not announced what discoveries had been made.

Southwest Africa was formerly a German colony and since the war has been administered by the British Union of South Africa. Germans still form a large proportion of the population and in recent months have promised to become active politically.

JERSEY DEMANDS LINDBERGH SUSPECT

Lehman Receives Extradition Papers, Expected to Act on Them at Albany Today.

DEFENSE FIGHTS REMOVAL

Will Seek Habeas Corpus Writ—Foley to Delay Trial Here at Moore's Request.

Governor A. Harry Moore of New Jersey signed official papers at Trenton yesterday afternoon for the extradition of Bruno Richard Hauptmann. The papers were handed to Governor Lehman last night at his home, 820 Park Avenue. The New York Executive indicated that he would act on them today, after he returns to Albany.

The extradition papers call upon the authorities in the Bronx, where Hauptmann is held under $100,000 bail awaiting trial for the extortion of $50,000 ransom from Colonel Charles A. Lindbergh to surrender the prisoner to the authorities of Hunterdon County, N. J., where the prisoner was indicted on Monday for the murder of Colonel Lindbergh's infant son two and one-half years ago.

District Attorney Samuel J. Foley of the Bronx, who took part in a conference with Governor Moore and other New Jersey officials at Trenton yesterday, announced that the extortion trial, which had been scheduled to begin tomorrow in the Bronx County Court House, would be adjourned so that the New Jersey authorities could take possession of the prisoner.

Defense to Fight Extradition.

James M. Fawcett, attorney for Hauptmann, said last night that he expected to apply for a writ of habeas corpus in the Bronx County Supreme Court this morning to prevent the extradition of his client to New Jersey. He made this statement after returning from Trenton, where he conferred with New Jersey officials.

The signing of the extradition papers followed a day of official conferences here and in Trenton. Governor Moore, Attorney General David T. Wilentz of New Jersey, Prosecutor Anthony M. Hauck of Hunterdon County and Colonel H. Norman Schwarzkopf, superintendent of the New Jersey State police, conferred yesterday morning in Trenton.

Early in the afternoon Governor Moore telephoned to Governor Lehman, who was attending a luncheon at the Commodore Hotel, notifying him that he expected to sign the papers during the afternoon and asking him where to send them. Governor Lehman asked him to send them directly to his home.

During the luncheon, Governor Lehman familiarized himself with details of the case in a talk with District Attorney Foley, a guest at the same luncheon. Later Mr. Foley went to Trenton, where he joined the conference in Governor Moore's offices.

Ceremony at Signing.

The ceremony at which Governor Moore's signature was affixed to the papers took place in an anteroom of his offices, as cameras clicked and flashlights popped. At 4:3 P. M. the Governor entered the room with John J. Toohey, State Commissioner of Labor. District Attorney Foley took a seat at the Governor's left. Thomas A. Mathis, Secretary of State for New Jersey, who was required by law to add his signature to the Governor's, stood behind the Governor. The ceremony was over within a minute.

Before 5 o'clock, New Jersey and Bronx officials, with Captain John J. Lamb of the New Jersey State

Continued on Page Two.

GOVERNMENT BUYS ONE MILLION ACRES OF WORN-OUT LAND

Tracts Are Obtained Mainly in the Middle and Far West and the Southeast.

FAMILIES ARE RESETTLED

Hopkins Says That Majority Simply Get Up and Go—Work Is Found for Others.

Copyright 1934, by The Associated Press.

WASHINGTON, Oct. 9.—Purchase by the government of a million acres of submarginal farm land, from which whole families have been or will be transplanted, was reported today by Harry L. Hopkins, relief administrator.

Federal buyers are contracting for more of the same type of arid or worn out farm land. It will be turned into parks, forests, game preserves and Indian reservations. Most of the purchasing so far has been in the Middle and Far West and the Southeast.

Obviously enthusiastic about the venture, Mr. Hopkins gave this explanation of its aims:

"Farmers should not be permitted to bump their heads against a stone wall. We might as well use the land for some really social purpose and give the people who have been struggling with it a chance to get going on decent farms."

The interview was the first official word that $25,000,000 of Public Works money, allotted to Mr. Hopkins for the retirement of submarginal farm lands, had been put to work.

"We hope to get between four and five million acres out of that fund," the relief administrator said. "The land is costing around $5 an acre. Some of it—for parks—is costing more because of its nearness to cities."

He reported that buying or option-taking was under way in the Dakotas, Montana, the Southeastern section of the country and the Far West.

Hits Real Estate Dealers.

Declining to tell exactly where purchases were being made, he explained that real estate operators might jump at the chance to boost prices.

"In many instances land companies have taken this poor land and sold it over and over again as fast as the different buyers gave up," he said. "On a lot of these farms nobody ever made any money except the real estate dealers."

The purchase of private land for social purposes is "nothing that the State and the Federal Governments have not done for years," Mr. Hopkins declared. He said land owners were not refusing to participate in the program, although some had declined to take the prices offered.

"It looks now like two-thirds of the families who sell their farms to the government have plans of their own about resettlement," he reported. "They don't want a thing from us—they simply get up and go.

"We do get a resettlement problem with the balance, most of whom already are on relief rolls because the land has busted 'em."

He said relief loans enabled such families to get started on new farms which will produce as much as their abandoned land with less labor and expense.

"Also, we help them to earn some cash in addition to their farm income. We may get preference for them in national forest jobs or work on county highways. Of course, the real hope of this thing is the decentralization of industry."

He said one industry had evi-

Continued on Page Four.

BELGRADE GUARDS BORDER

Rushes Troops to Italian and Hungarian Lines to Avert Invasion.

NEWS OF DEATH HELD UP

Consternation in Capital as People Are Finally Told, but Country Is Quiet Generally.

ONE RIOT AGAINST ITALY

Constitution Makes the Young Crown Prince Yugoslavia's King as Peter II.

Wireless to THE NEW YORK TIMES.

BELGRADE, Oct. 9.—News of the assassination of King Alexander was carefully kept from the Yugoslav people until well into the evening. By 7 P. M. only a few newspaper men had learned that he had been wounded—nothing more—and this news was not allowed to be published.

Troops were quickly mobilized and sent to the Italian and Hungarian frontiers to guard against the possibility of invasion.

At 7:30 a censorship of cables was instituted and all telephonic communications with foreign countries were cut at 8 o'clock.

Announcement of the King's death was made shortly before 8, while movie performances were going on and noisy crowds were enjoying the music of bands in the cafés. The news caused general consternation; mourning flags were hoisted on all public buildings, cafés and movie theatres quickly closed, and bells began to toll in all the churches of the kingdom. Large crowds gathered in the streets of the capital discussing the news.

The Ministerial Council, which had all the functions of the King during his absence, remained in session.

Troops Ordered to Stand By.

First incomplete news from Marseilles arrived at 8 o'clock. Police, gendarmerie and troops were ordered to stand by throughout the country. It was reported at 10 P. M. that there was complete order in all parts of Yugoslavia.

However, when the first news of the murder reached Ljubljana, the capital of Slovenia, it was reported that the assassin was an Italian and anti-Italian demonstrations took place in the streets. This is the only disorder that is known to have occurred thus far.

In view of the general calm in the country, telephonic communication with foreign countries was restored at midnight without censorship.

General Pera Zhivkovitch, the former military dictator, was immediately summoned back to Belgrade by the government.

The question of the succession is settled by the constitution, which makes the 11-year-old Crown Prince Peter ruler of Yugoslavia as Peter II.

The young King, who a few

Continued on Page Fifteen.

Associated Press Photo.

Times Wide World Photo.

VICTIMS OF ASSASSIN'S BULLETS IN FRANCE.
King Alexander of Yugoslavia. Louis Barthou, French Foreign Minister.

GUNMAN FIRES INTO CAR

Shoots General as Well as Alexander and the French Minister.

IS KILLED AFTER ATTACK

Beaten by Crowd Assembled to Welcome Monarch on Arrival for State Visit.

DOZEN IN THRONG WOUNDED

Crime Dims Hope for Accord of Italy and Yugoslavia, an Aim of Journey.

By P. J. PHILIP.
Wireless to THE NEW YORK TIMES.

PARIS, Oct. 9.—Within a few minutes after having stepped ashore at Marseilles today on an official visit to France, King Alexander of Yugoslavia was shot dead by an assassin—apparently one of his own subjects who had obviously come to France for this express purpose.

The French Foreign Minister, Louis Barthou, who had been sitting beside the King in an automobile, was wounded and died less than two hours later after a blood transfusion had failed to arrest a hemorrhage.

Tonight there is not only personal but also political dismay in France and in all Europe over the outrage. For King Alexander, whose eldest son, Peter, 11 years old, is a student in England, not only reigned but ruled over his country. His personality, more than any other single factor, has held together the collection of peoples who were joined under the Serbian crown into the modern Kingdom of Yugoslavia after the World War.

High Hopes Held for Visit.

King Alexander's visit to France was planned months ago when Foreign Minister Barthou went to Belgrade. It was to have been a delicate affair. For while France and Yugoslavia are allies, there was, at least on the French side, an intention to make the visit an occasion for a reconciliation between Yugoslavia and Italy and an attempt to harmonize the aspirations and policies of the three countries.

Now all is lost. The King and M. Barthou are dead and the future is darkly uncertain.

The assassination was the work of one man, or at least only one man participated in it, although many may have planned it. He was Petru Kalemen, a Croat born in Zagreb, and he was killed by the police and the infuriated crowd. His passport, found on his body, showed he had entered France on Sept. 28, having come direct from Zagreb. His crime was carefully planned to the last detail, for as he rushed toward the King's car he shouted "Vive le Roi!" and so gained a few seconds of time while those whose business it was to protect the King hesitated as to whether they had to deal with an assassin or a drunken loyalist.

There was another death—that of Policeman Celestin Galli, who had rushed forward to try to seize the murderer and was shot down in the volley fired by the assassin.

In the fusillade a dozen persons were wounded, including two police inspectors, several women and a press photographer.

King Arrives on Cruiser.

The assassination took place at 4:10 o'clock in the afternoon. Less than an hour before the King, aboard the Yugoslav cruiser Dubrovnik, had steamed into Marseilles Harbor accompanied by a French fleet from Toulon. The ancient port and the city were ablaze with bunting and flags. Hundreds of thousands had massed along the two miles of streets through which the King was to pass on his way to the railway station and Paris.

Telephone messages from two witnesses of the tragedy at Marseilles to your correspondent give the following account of the events:

The King had just landed from a launch at the Quai des Belges in the old port amid immense cheer-

Continued on Page Fifteen.

BOY PRINCE AT PLAY AS HIS FATHER DIED

Peter, 11, Told of Tragedy Only at End of Football Game at British School.

PLANS FOR HIM UNCERTAIN

May Go to France Today With Marie of Rumania After a Short Career as Student.

By CHARLES A. SELDEN.
Special Cable to THE NEW YORK TIMES.

LONDON, Oct. 9.—The new King of Yugoslavia is the 11-year-old Prince Peter, now attending Sandroyd School in Surrey. Although he was Crown Prince Peter when he entered the school two weeks ago his British school fellows had already formed the habit of omitting the title when addressing him or referring to him. They were with him this afternoon on the play-field, where they were initiating him into the mysteries of English football, at the very moment the Prince became "His Majesty" because of the assassination of his father at Marseilles.

News of the tragedy, which was received in London just before 5 o'clock, was immediately telephoned to the school by the Yugoslav Legation. It was after the boys had all trooped in from the field for the traditional afternoon tea that the headmaster called Peter aside to break the news to him.

The Crown Prince came to this country early in September in charge of an English tutor, C. C. Parrott. It was Peter's first trip away from Yugoslavia, although he knows not only English but also three other foreign languages.

He Took In the Sights.

He spent a fortnight in London incognito at the Hotel Claridge and did all of the usual small boy's sight-seeing, visiting the Tower of London, the zoo, watching the Changing of the Guard and, of course, visiting Buckingham Palace, although the British royal family was then in Scotland.

Peter's chief interest here, however, was the radio, and he had a set of his own installed in his hotel room to listen to the broadcast of ceremonies at the launching of the Cunarder Queen Mary. On the day after that event he went down to the village of Cobham, in Surrey, to enter the school.

There, according to the expressed instructions of King Alexander, the boy was placed on even terms with all his schoolmates with reference to living conditions, social status, instruction and discipline. He

Continued on Page Fifteen.

Assassin Too Quick for Guard; Forced Horse Aside, Then Fired

Mounted Escort, Telling His Story, Says He Whirled to Protect King, but Was Too Late—Murderer, Struck Down With Saber, Continued to Discharge Pistol.

Copyright, 1934, by The Associated Press.

MARSEILLES, Oct. 9.—When King Alexander's motor car was driven through a double lane of city police here today at the time of his assassination and that of Foreign Minister Louis Barthou of France two squadrons of mounted Republican Guards with sabers drawn trotted on both sides of the procession. Lieut. Col. Piollet of the horse guards was nearest to the murderer.

This is Colonel Piolett's own description of the assassination:

"The automobile of King Alexander, in which were the King, M. Barthou and General Georges, arrived exactly before the Stock Exchange at the corner of Queen Elizabeth Street when I saw a man leave the crowd, pass by a policeman at the edge of the sidewalk, and start toward my horse.

"He forced my horse around and leaped on the running board of the running automobile. I whirled my horse sharply but so quick was the man that I could not prevent him from putting his arm over the door of the open car. He fired two or three times at the King.

"I lifted my saber and with two slashes knocked down the man, who tumbled to the ground while the chauffeur started ahead.

Continues to Fire.

"The assassin, still on the ground, continued to fire, some bullets hitting policemen and women in the front row of spectators. Police rushed forward while mounted guards surrounded the royal car to hold back the crowd, which was filled with fury.

"The assassin was lifted and the crowd surged forward and would have killed him if the police had not carried him to a news stand."

The chauffeur of the King's car was cut by the saber when the Colonel struck down the assassin.

The chauffeur gave a vivid description of the tragedy.

"Just as the car came into Stock Exchange Square," he said, "a big, fat man ran from the crowd, jumped on the running board of the King's car, and fired four or five shots at the King.

"I immediately grabbed him by the neck while a colonel, just beside the car, began slashing. The assassin tried to kill himself by firing a shot into his mouth but the police by this time closed in and shot him down."

Police List Wounded.

Marseilles police gave out a list of the wounded, as follows:

General Georges, Marius Humbert, Laurent Cartero, Felix Dumazer, Felix Forestier, Emile Ferrier, Mlle. Yolande Parisis and Mme. Justine Dumazer, Mme. Marcelle Harmelin, Mme. Dubrec and Mme. Reynard. The names of two others were not taken by the police. Physicians said all would recover.

Denials were issued that General Alexander Dimitriejevitch, Marshal of the Yugoslav court, had been killed and that Admiral Berthelot, Prefect at Toulon, had been injured.

Almost as soon as the shots were fired the French Government

Continued on Page Sixteen.

ALEXANDER NAMED THREE AS REGENTS

Prince Paul and Two Others to Govern for the Boy King—Cabinet Rules for Present.

By The Associated Press.

BELGRADE, Wednesday, Oct. 10.—The will of King Alexander, found after his assassination, appoints the following as the members of a regency council that is to serve until the boy King, Peter II, comes of age:

Prince Paul of Yugoslavia, cousin of King Alexander.

Former Minister of Education Stankovitch.

Governor Banterovitch of Zagreb.

In the event that any of these are incapacitated, Alexander named as substitutes General Tomitch for Prince Paul, Senator Benjamin for M. Stankovitch and Senator Zet for M. Banterovitch.

The text of the government proclamation issued last night on the death of King Alexander follows:

To the Yugoslavian people:

Our great King Alexander fell heroically on Oct. 9 at Marseilles. He has sealed with his blood the work for peace that was his aim in life, and for which he went to Marseilles and met his death in an allied land.

By virtue of Paragraph 306 of the Constitution, Peter II is now King, and the government, the army and the navy have taken an oath of loyalty to him.

By virtue of Paragraph 45 the Cabinet is now governing the country. The national Parliament has been called for the day after tomorrow.

The King's last words gave a sacred trust, "Guard Yugoslavia," and the government and the nation must be worthy of their King.

The proclamation was signed by the entire Cabinet.

Prince Paul of Yugoslavia, who

Continued on Page Fifteen.

Second Federal Court Bars Price Fixing In Lumber Industry by NRA Code Head

By The Associated Press.

YAZOO CITY, Miss., Oct. 9.—A petition by NRA for an injunction to restrain Mississippi lumber companies from filling orders contracted at prices alleged to be under code figures was denied today by Federal Judge Edwin R. Holmes.

This setback for the price-fixing provisions of the Lumber Industries Code came after an all-day hearing before the District Federal Court. Counsel for State offices of the NRA Compliance Director indicated that the decision would be appealed.

Request for injunctions against the firms today were to have been the first of a series of actions against sixty-two hardwood lumber companies in this State.

The companies sought to be enjoined today were the Gooch Brothers Lumber Company of Yazoo City; T. L. Shannon Brothers of Pickens and Rolling Fork, Miss., and the McGraw Lumber Company of Yazoo City.

The petitions charged specifically that the hardwood manufacturers entered into lumber contracts with the Fisher Corporation, Tennessee division of General Motors, at prices below the minimum set by NRA in its national code for the industry. The injunctions requested halting of execution on these contracts.

It was agreed by counsel that constitutionality of the National Recovery Act was not in argument, nor wage and hour provisions for labor. The defense argued that Congress had not expressly authorized the President, through the NRA, to use price-fixing provisions in codes.

Lumber men of Memphis on Saturday won a decision in the Federal Court which held that price-fixing was not authorized by the Recovery Act. At that time Judge Harry B. Anderson granted an injunction against Federal interference in the sale of 40,000,000 feet of lumber to the Fisher Body Corporation, which the government charged was being sold at 5 to 15 per cent below "cost protection prices" fixed by the Code Authority. The case was brought by 600 manufacturers of hardwoods.

Dizzy Dean Blanks Tigers, 11-0, and Cardinals Capture the World Series

By JOHN DREBINGER.

Continued From Page One.

increased two-fold, more bottles and fruit were showered on the field, and once more the umpires had to call time.

Four times the performance was repeated and each time the anger of the fans, rather than showing any abatement, increased in its intensity. In vain an announcer bellowed through the amplifiers imploring the fans to desist and allow the game to continue. But these Detroit fans were boiling mad and doubtless would have continued the demonstration until the end of time.

Finally, after one more attempt to resume play ended in another deluge of refuse on the playing field, Commissioner Landis rose in his box, a short distance from the Cardinal bench, and waved the umpires to come to him. He ordered Umpire Klem, the two players, Owen and Medwick, and the rival managers, Frisch and Cochrane, to come before him, and there out in full view he held an open court.

Frisch Tries to Protest.

The hearing lasted not more than a minute and the upshot of it was that Landis ordered Medwick to remove himself quickly and quietly from the field. The fiery Frisch attempted to protest, but Landis, with an angry gesture, motioned the St. Louis leader to get out on the field and resume play without further delay.

Chick Fullis, utility outfielder, took Medwick's place in left and the crowd, very much appeased by this turn of events, actually cheered this unassuming St. Louis player as he came trotting out.

Later Commissioner Landis, in explaining his action, stated he primarily ordered Medwick off the field as the only means of continuing the game in the face of the crowd's hostile demonstration.

"Before the series," said baseball's czar, "the umpires are instructed not to put any player off the field unless the provocation is very extreme. I saw as well as everybody what Medwick did, but when Umpire Klem took no action and the players quieted down I hoped the matter was ended.

"But when it became apparent that the demonstration of the crowd would never terminate I decided to take action. I did not call Medwick and Owen in any attempt to patch up the difference between the players.

No Further Action Planned.

"I asked Owen whether he knew of any excuse why Medwick should have made such an attack on him. He said he did not, and with that I ordered Medwick off the field. I do not intend to take any further action."

A few minutes later, after play was resumed, Medwick left the Cardinal bench and crossed over to the Tiger dugout as his only means of exit. There was more jeering, but five policemen rushed out from the boxes in order to discourage any further demonstration on the part of the crowd. This did not prevent one overwrought fan from tossing a final cushion down from the upper tier, the pillow just missing the departing St. Louis player.

The uproar, of course, quite overshadowed all else that happened on the field, even taking the play away from the marvelous Dizzy Dean, who was out to revenge himself in convincing fashion for the beating he had taken in the fifth game in St. Louis last Sunday.

Although he had only one day of rest, the elder Dean was in marvelous form as he shut out the Tigers on six hits to round out the fourth and final victory of the celebrated Dean family. Paul, his 20-year-old brother, had won the third and sixth games of the series. He himself had won the first game, but had suffered a subsequent setback.

Displays Complete Mastery.

Now Dizzy was back to display his complete mastery with the only shutout of the entire series. With his brother he had pitched the Cardinals into a pennant when the entire nation deemed the feat impossible. Together the pair had brought to St. Louis its third world's championship since 1926.

Among other things, Dizzy brought to a dramatic close the sixth million-dollar series since interleague warfare began under present rules in 1905.

The paid attendance was 40,902

Times Wide World Photo.

Paul and Dizzy Dean, who won two games each for Cardinals.

and the receipts were $138,063, bringing the total for the seven games up to $1,031,341. This was less than $200,000 short of the record gate which the Cardinals and Yankees set in 1926 when their seven games drew $1,207,864.

The total attendance for the series just ended was 281,510, the highest since 1926 when the Cards and Yanks set the record of 328,051.

The conclusion of the struggle marked the third time that the Cardinals had engaged in a million-dollar series. It was also their third appearance in a seven-game tussle. Curiously enough, the Cards were returned the victors in all three.

Try to Rally Around Leader

Against the sort of pitching the older and greater Dean turned one the Tigers simply had nothing to offer. They strove valiantly, however, to rally around their leader, the stout-hearted Cochrane. Despite the fact that he had spent the night in a hospital nursing a spike wound in his left leg received yesterday, Mickey insisted on playing behind the bat.

When in that torrid third inning the Tiger pitchers crumbled before the fury of that aroused St. Louis host the entire bottom fell out of the game. In all, Cochrane, who pluckily stuck in the battle until the end of the eighth inning, tossed six hurlers into the fray.

All the Detroit pitchers who had appeared previously in the series passed in review. But there was no restraining this remarkable St. Louis team. Shortly after Labor Day these same Cardinals had trailed the New York Giants by eight games in the National League pennant race, only to rout last year's world champions out of the picture on the final two days. They thus gained the right to give the National circuit its second successive world series triumph over the American League.

The crowd, which had been rather tardy in arriving, was still coming through the gates and climbing over one another in the reserved sections of the upper and lower tiers of the grand stand as the rival forces squared off grimly for the important business at hand.

There was something of an embarrassing moment just before the game began when a delegation of loyal and well-meaning Detroit fans rolled a huge floral horseshoe out toward the plate. But its sponsors sadly underestimated the inherent superstitious characteristics of ball players.

Neither Cochrane nor any other member of the Tiger team could be induced to come out of the Detroit dugout and accept the gift. So, after a deal of futile coaxing, the delegation hauled its offering away in silence.

The crowd, however, did not have to wait long for its first chance to cheer. The opening blast came when Auker, after pitching three straight balls to Martin, fanned the overanxious Pepper on his next three deliveries.

This was followed by a touch of uneasiness as Jack Rothrock rammed a double into deep left centre, but the confidence of the gathering returned when Auker, apparently getting a better grip on himself, retired Frisch on a pop fly to Rogell and Medwick on a foul to Owen.

There was even more cheering in the second as the Cards, though they clipped Auker for two more hits, wound up the inning without a run or a man left on base. After Collins singled, De Lancey wiped him off the bases by grounding into a double play, snappily executed by Owen, Gehringer and Greenberg. Orsatti, after sending a hit into right, finished himself by getting thrown out on an attempted steal.

Crowd Cheers Defensively.

However, there was a rather ominous feeling to all this and the cheering itself, while whole-hearted enough, was entirely of a defensive nature. It seemed as though the crowd, expecting only the Cards to do something on the offensive, was delighted over the success with which their Tigers were holding the invaders in restraint.

The Tigers themselves had been able to make no headway whatsoever against Dean in those first two innings, only one of their cast reaching first base. He got on only because Collins dropped a low throw by Durocher after Leo had made quite a dashing pick-up of Rogell's awkward bounder in the infield.

Then, in the teeth of a lively gale that swept from the northeast over the right-field wall and made it a bit chilly even though the sun shone brightly in a clear sky, the first explosion came.

It came without warning, as most explosions do, with Durocher opening the third inning by lifting a high fly to White in centre. Nothing still threatened as Dizzy strode to the plate.

Dean lifted a high foul behind the plate and right there, had the usually alert Cochrane been himself, a lot of subsequent disaster might have been avoided. The ball dropped just inside the front row of boxes. Cochrane, had he made a try for it, doubtless could easily have caught it. But he never even looked around to see where the ball was going and allowed it to drop harmlessly for a strike.

The next moment the singular Dean person shot a double to left. Martin outsprinted an infield hit to Greenberg, who delayed too long making up his mind what to do with the ball, Dean going to third.

A moment later Martin stole second. Then the charge was on.

Auker, pitching as cautiously as he could, passed Rothrock, filling the bases, and Frisch came up. He ran the count to two and two. He fouled a long shot off to the right, another to the left. Then he hammered a double down the right-field foul line, and as the ball glanced off Fox's glove all the three Cardinals on the bases crossed the plate.

Rowe Replaces Auker.

Frisch's blow finished Auker, and Rowe was called to the mound in an attempt to check the onrushing Cardinals, but didn't stay there long. Schoolboy pitched to three batters and then his day's work was done. He got Medwick on a grounder, but then Collins's sharp single to left chased Frisch across the plate. De Lancey connected for a long two-bagger to right, Collins was in with the fifth run, and Rowe was out.

Elon Hogsett was Cochrane's next selection and the left-hander, too, had a short stay in the box. Orsatti, the first man to face him, walked. Durocher, making his second appearance at the plate during the inning, hit a single to right, and again the bases were filled. Dean scratched a hit along the third-base line and De Lancey came in, leaving the bags still filled.

Martin drew a walk on four straight balls, forcing Orsatti over the plate for the seventh St. Louis run. Now Tommy Bridges, victor over Dizzy Dean in last Sunday's game, relieved Hogsett and managed to bring the inning to a close, Rothrock grounding to Gehringer to force Martin at second for the third out. Thirteen Cardinals came to bat in the inning.

Bridges stopped the scoring until the sixth, although he was clipped for a single by Collins in the fourth.

Martin opened the sixth with a drive to left and raced to second when Goslin handled the ball poorly. Pepper was held at second while Goslin gathered in Rothrock's fly. Frisch then flied to centre, bringing Medwick up and Jersey Joe walloped the triple which brought on his entanglement with Owen after he slid into the base. Martin scored while trouble threatened at third.

Lashes Single to Centre.

After the immediate flare-up had subsided Collins lashed a single to centre, where White fumbled the ball. Medwick came home with the second run of the inning and the ninth of the battle.

Not even the twenty-minute uproar that preceded Medwick's final retirement from the game under orders from Landis interrupted the trend of the engagement. Dizzy, wearing a bright Cardinal windbreaker, stood around the infield while the demonstration was going on in full blast, utterly unmindful of what was going on. Now and then he took a brief warm-up with his catcher.

When play was finally resumed for the last of the sixth the wonder pitcher of the day returned to his task of mowing down the Tigers. Now and then somebody poked him for a hit.

Apparently Dizzy was bent on making this a shutout regardless of how enormous the Cards made the score. Whenever the Tigers threatened Dizzy merely turned on the heat and poured his blazing fast ball and sharp-breaking curve right down the middle.

One could scarcely imagine that this man in the final week of the National League pennant race had pitched his team to victory in three successive starts, that he was making his third appearance in this series and with only forty-eight hours intervening since his last game.

Jokes Through It All.

It was superhuman. Three days ago he had entered a game as a pinch-runner and had received a belt on the head with a thrown ball that might have slain most any other man. But nothing perturbs Dizzy, except when he is in a fit of anger. Then he may tear up uniforms and do all sorts of things. But nothing disturbed his equanimity today. He smiled and joked through it all.

In the seventh the Cards scored two more, probably just for the sheer fun of the thing. Certainly they never needed the runs.

Leo Durocher tripled to the exact spot where he had hit his two-bagger yesterday, the hit which preceded Paul Dean's game-winning blow. Gehringer fumbled Martin's grounder and Leo counted. Martin stole his second base of the day. Then came a long double to left centre by Rothrock and the Wild Horse of the Osage thundered over the plate.

In vain Cochrane tossed in pinch hitters. Fred Marberry pitched the eighth and fell for a hit, but escaped without a score against him. Alvin Crowder, who had started that ill-fated first game when the Tiger infield exploded five errors all around him, pitched the ninth. Perhaps he might have been Cochrane's best bet today. At least, such is the opinion of the vast army of second-guessers.

But what would it have mattered? Crowder at his best could only have obtained a scoreless tie, even though he did retire three Cards in a row in the ninth.

The Tigers had only two scoring chances in the entire battle. They had runners on second and third with only one out in the fifth. They also had runners on first and second with one out in the ninth. Whereupon Dizzy fanned Greenberg for the third time, turning around even before the third strike reached the plate, and Owen ended the battle with a grounder to Durocher.

And so Detroit, faithful to its Tigers to the last, is still seeking its first world's championship. It won three pennants in a row in the days of Ty Cobb and the immortal Hughie Jennings from 1907 to 1909, but lost all three world series clashes. It waited twenty-five years for another chance.

But an amazing ball club, with two of the most remarkable pitchers baseball ever was to see grow up in one family, blocked the path.

Less than a month ago these Cardinals did not appear to have one chance in a thousand of reaching their present goal. But they edged Bill Terry and his Giants right off the baseball map and today they crushed the Tigers.

FANS BLAMELESS, LANDIS DECLARES

Justified in Showing Resentment Over Medwick Incident, Commissioner Says.

DETROIT, Oct. 9 (AP).—Although indicating he contemplated no disciplinary action as a consequence of Joe Medwick's ejection from the final world series ball game today, Commissioner Kenesaw Mountain Landis said tonight that he had reserved decision after hearing all sides of the controversy, which provoked a riotous outburst by the fans.

"I'm going fishing for a few days and then I may have something to say," remarked Landis.

He referred not only to the dispute at third base, involving Medwick and Marvin Owen, Tiger third baseman, but also to controversies in previous games between the umpires and players of both teams, including Hank Greenberg, Goose Goslin and Bill De Lancey.

Calls His Action Right.

"I do not blame the crowd for what happened today," said the commissioner, "although under the circumstances and due to the uncontrollable outburst I felt it was wisest to remove Medwick from the game.

"As I saw the incident at third base, Medwick came sliding hard into the bag, then kicked his feet up at Owen. I did not see Owen make any gesture previously toward Medwick, but I do not say he didn't. I have yet to find two men who agree on exactly what happened or who was to blame.

"When I finally called the players, managers and umpires to my box, I simply asked Medwick if Owen had done anything to him or if there was any reason for his kicking at the Detroit player. To both questions Medwick answered 'No.'

"Thereupon I decided promptly to remove him from the game, particularly as I felt that an even more dangerous outbreak might develop if Medwick continued to play."

COCHRANE PRAISES TRIUMPHANT CARDS

Tiger Pilot Among Celebrities Congratulating the Victors in Clubhouse Demonstration.

FRISCH 'GLAD IT'S OVER'

Terms Series One of Hardest in Career—Medwick Resents Ouster From Game.

By JAMES P. DAWSON.
Special to THE NEW YORK TIMES.

DETROIT, Oct. 9.—"Well, it's all over, and I'm glad."

These were the first words of Frankie Frisch today in the flush of the distinction that is his in having piloted the Cardinals to the world championship and the National League to another demonstration of superiority over the American League.

"I'm glad principally because we won, but I'm tickled also because the series is over," continued Frisch. "It was one of the hardest, toughest series I've ever played in; hard-fought all the way, and cleanly played. At times it was a little rough, but you got to expect a little of that. You can't make baseball a parlor game."

Somebody asked Frisch about the double he had made in the third inning to drive in three runs. "You can take your .880 hitters," he replied. "I'll hit .220, but I'll take that lone hit when it's a winner."

With respect to the Joe Medwick-Marvin Owen incident, Frisch declared "the kid (Medwick) wouldn't hurt anybody."

Offered to Shake Hands.

Medwick was quiet, and a little resentful that he was ordered out of the game by Judge Landis. "I didn't mean to harm anybody, but I don't want anybody taking a kick out of me," he said. "I offered to shake hands with Owen at the time and be refused. What more could I do?"

Owen, incidentally, expressed regret over the removal of Medwick from the game.

When they came from the field, the Cardinals, singing and shouting and tossing things about, celebrated the victory like a group of schoolboys. Trainer Doc Weaver was lifted bodily and tossed under the running shower, clothes and all. Dizzy Dean, a pith helmet on his head, held an inflated rubber tiger by the tail, gripped the tail between his teeth, exerted a Strangler Lewis headlock on the tiger and posed for the clicking cameras.

"The best club in America, and the best manager, too," Dizzy proclaimed for all to hear. "We did it, didn't we? I knew we would from the start. I felt great out there this afternoon. Had a lot of fun. I let them get a couple of hits, then decided to stop fooling around and threw those strikes past them. Boy, was that Greenberg wild! I just had to laugh when he missed those third swings."

Frisch Thanks Durocher.

Manager Frisch looked up from a flood of congratulatory telegrams, stepped over to Leo Durocher and thanked him for his great playing, with a pat on the back. Sam Breadon and Branch Rickey, owner and business manager of the Cardinals, trooped into the clubhouse. Manager Mickey Cochrane of the Tigers came over to offer his congratulations. Will Rogers was there. So was Will Harridge, American League president, who felicitated the victors. Jim Tierney, Giants' secretary, beamed his delight at a National League victory in a series his club had narrowly missed.

Judge Kenesaw M. Landis pushed through the crowd and past a police cordon larger than any ever before assembled here. John A. Heydler, National League president, also offered his congratulations.

The Tigers' clubhouse was quiet. The players were depressed after an 11 to 0 shutout that was thoroughly humiliating.

Praises Dean's Pitching.

The stout-hearted Cochrane, however, forgot his disappointment to praise the victors. "They were too much for us," he said. "We ran against one of those things that happen every now and then and were beaten. As long as we had to be beaten, I'm glad we were well beaten. Dean pitched a great game. He had plenty of stuff. Our fellows simply couldn't get going."

Schoolboy Rowe felt the defeat keenly. "I didn't have a thing," he said. "I warmed up with only about ten pitches and just wasn't there. That's all." Manager Cochrane praised Tom Bridges for an excellent bit of relief hurling.

The Cardinals left tonight at 9 o'clock for St. Louis, where they are to be fêted before disbanding for the season. The Tigers made plans immediately to go their separate ways until summoned for Spring training next year.

EACH OF CARDINALS TO RECEIVE $5,941

Pool for World Series Players Swelled by the Sale of Broadcasting Rights.

DETROIT, Oct. 9 (AP).—Each of the champion St. Louis Cardinals will receive $5,941.19 as his share of the world series receipts, while each of the vanquished Detroit Tigers will get $4,313.90. The shares include receipts from the radio rights, sold to the Ford Motor Company for $100,000.

The Cardinals divided their receipts into twenty-five shares; the Tigers divided theirs into twenty-three shares. The Cardinals also voted $3,000 in donations to club attendants, cutting their actual shares to $5,821.19 each.

The total player pool was $299,785.69 from gate receipts alone. The pool was increased $51,000 by radio receipts. The commissioner received $15,000 from the radio, swelling his share to $169,811.15. Each league and each club received $144,238.57 from the gate and $8,500 each from the radio, or a grand total of $152,738.57 each.

Other shares, including radio receipts, to major league teams finishing from second to fourth, inclusive, in their respective leagues follow:

New York Giants and Yankees, $25,808.92 each.

Chicago Cubs and Cleveland Indians, $17,205.90 each.

Boston Braves and Boston Red Sox, $8,283 each.

Times Wide World Photo.
Mickey Cochrane and Frankie Frisch, the rival managers.

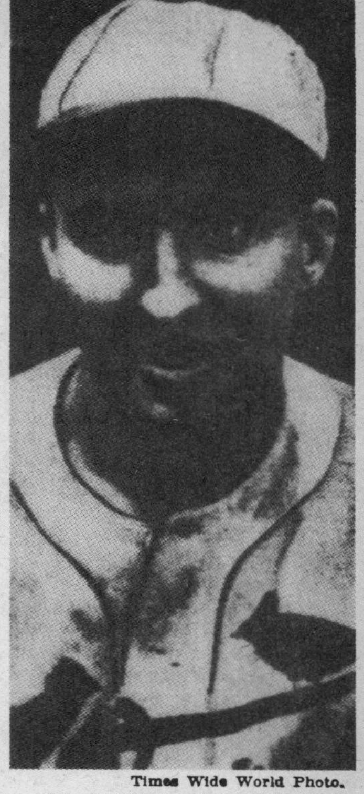

Times Wide World Photo.
Rip Collins, star at bat.

Box Score of the Seventh Game

ST. LOUIS CARDINALS.

	ab.	r.	h.	tb.	2b.	3b.	hr.	bb.	so.	sh.	sb.	po.	a.	e.
Martin, 3b	5	3	2	2	0	0	0	1	1	0	2	0	1	0
Rothrock, rf	5	1	2	4	2	0	0	1	1	0	0	4	0	0
Frisch, 2b	5	1	1	2	1	0	0	0	0	0	0	3	6	0
Medwick, lf	4	1	1	3	0	1	0	0	0	0	0	1	0	0
Fullis, lf	1	0	1	1	0	0	0	0	0	0	0	1	0	0
Collins, 1b	5	1	4	4	0	0	0	0	0	0	0	7	1	1
De Lancey, c	5	1	1	2	1	0	0	0	1	0	0	5	0	0
Orsatti, cf	3	1	1	1	0	0	0	2	0	0	0	2	0	0
Durocher, ss	5	1	2	4	0	1	0	0	0	0	0	3	4	0
J. Dean, p	5	1	2	3	1	0	0	0	1	0	0	1	0	0
Total	43	11	17	26	5	2	0	4	4	0	2	27	12	1

DETROIT TIGERS.

	ab.	r.	h.	tb.	2b.	3b.	hr.	bb.	so.	sh.	sb.	po.	a.	e.
White, cf	4	0	0	0	0	0	0	0	1	0	0	3	0	1
Cochrane, c	4	0	0	0	0	0	0	0	0	0	0	2	2	0
Hayworth, c	0	0	0	0	0	0	0	0	0	0	0	1	0	0
Gehringer, 2b	4	0	2	2	0	0	0	0	0	0	0	3	5	1
Goslin, lf	4	0	0	0	0	0	0	0	0	0	0	4	0	1
Rogell, ss	4	0	1	1	0	0	0	0	0	0	0	3	2	0
Greenberg, 1b	4	0	1	1	0	0	0	0	3	0	0	7	0	0
Owen, 3b	4	0	0	0	0	0	0	0	0	0	0	1	2	0
Fox, rf	3	0	2	4	2	0	0	0	0	0	0	3	0	0
Auker, p	0	0	0	0	0	0	0	0	0	0	0	0	0	0
Rowe, p	0	0	0	0	0	0	0	0	0	0	0	0	0	0
Hogsett, p	0	0	0	0	0	0	0	0	0	0	0	0	0	0
Bridges, p	2	0	0	0	0	0	0	0	1	0	0	0	0	0
Marberry, p	0	0	0	0	0	0	0	0	0	0	0	0	0	0
Crowder, p	0	0	0	0	0	0	0	0	0	0	0	0	0	0
aG. Walker	1	0	0	0	0	0	0	0	0	0	0	0	0	0
Total	34	0	6	8	2	0	0	0	5	0	0	27	11	3

aBatted for Marberry in eighth.

SCORE BY INNINGS.

St. Louis	0	0	7	0	0	2	2	0	0	—11
Detroit	0	0	0	0	0	0	0	0	0	— 0

Runs batted in—St. Louis: Frisch 3, Collins 2, De Lancey, J. Dean, Martin, Medwick, Rothrock.

Left on bases—St. Louis 9, Detroit 7. Struck out—By J. Dean 5, Auker 1, Bridges 2, Crowder 1. Bases on balls—Off Auker 1, Hogsett 2, Marberry 1. Double play—Owen, Gehringer and Greenberg. Hits—Off Auker 6 in 2 1/3 innings, Rowe 2 in 1/3, Hogsett 2 in 0 (none out in third), Bridges 6 in 4 1/3, Marberry 1 in 1, Crowder 0 in 1. Losing pitcher—Auker. Umpires—Geisel (A. L.) at the plate, Reardon (N. L.) at first base, Owens (A. L.) at second base, Klem (N. L.) at third base. Time of game—2:19.

Frisch to Manage Cards Again; 50 Series Games His Record Now

Breadon Calls Him a Great Leader and Pays Warm Tribute to His Courage—Expects to Sign Deans With Little Trouble but Insists Their Fines Will Not Be Refunded.

ST. LOUIS, Oct. 9 (AP).—Frankie Frisch, as every one suspected all along, will manage the St. Louis Cardinals, new world champions, again in 1935.

While the job always has been regarded as safe for the old Fordham Flash, official word from the head man of the front office was not forthcoming until today.

"I think Frisch is a great manager," President Sam Breadon said in Detroit. "I think he has a great deal of courage, and that is the kind of man I want to handle my ball club. I have not talked terms, but he will handle the club next season."

Asked about the current crop of rumors concerning the sale of the club, Breadon said he had received no offers, had made no overtures to any one and that at the present moment did not consider a sale of the team.

Anticipates No Trouble.

Although he phrased it differently, Breadon indicated he expected that signing his star hurlers, Jerome Herman (Dizzy) and Paul (Daffy) Dean, to 1935 contracts would be just a breeze.

"I don't know when I'll sign them for the 1935 season," he said. "All I can say is that it will be taken up in due course. It will be our job to sign them and we'll do it. I don't anticipate any trouble with them. I don't anticipate any trouble with anybody."

Breadon said he had given no thought to bonuses for the Deans, who between them won forty-nine games in the National League and pitched all four of the Cardinals' victories over Detroit in the world series.

He said flatly that fines assessed against Dizzy and Daffy for infractions of the rules some time ago would not be refunded.

"Frisch wouldn't stand for it," he commented.

An Unprecedented Feat.

Added to the glory of piloting his St. Louis Cardinals to their third world championship since Rogers Hornsby first did it in 1926, Manager Frisch bolstered a record unprecedented in baseball annals.

When he took Leo Durocher's throw for the put-out at second base yesterday that ended the bitterly fought 1934 world series, the famous Fordham Flash had completed his fiftieth game in baseball's annual classic.

It is a record that may stand for all time. Not even the great Babe Ruth, who has participated in ten world series to Frisch's eight, can be given much of a chance to surpass it, as the Babe has played in only forty-one series contests, and Ruth's own announcement from the recent battle scene at Detroit indicates that he may never take part in another.

Frisch started his long string of world series contests in 1921, when as the youthful and fiery Fordham Flash he began blazing like a comet across Manhattan's baseball sky. The late John McGraw had tossed the youngster into the line-up earlier in the season and there Frisch stayed.

In that 1921 battle Frisch played at third base in every game and his feats in the opening game turned the spotlight full upon him. Carl Mays, the famous submarine hurler, shut out the McGrawmen with five hits—and young Frisch made four of them, one a three-bagger.

He had no chance to make another because he came to bat only four times.

To prove this hitting was no accident, Frisch completed his slugging in the eight games of the series for an average of .300. In that first series Frankie stole three bases, and his stolen-base total for all series competition is nine.

Still Rated in Forefront.

In the contests just ended he pilfered no bases at all and made only six hits for a mark of .194, but if this is an indication that time is catching up with the Flash, it is ignored by baseball observers, who still rate him the leading second baseman in his league.

Frisch played in world series with the Giants four consecutive years and became the first player to hit .300 or better in a stretch of such games. His average in 1922 was .471; 1923, .400, and 1924, .333. He dropped to .231, .208 and .259 with St. Louis in the series of 1928, 1930 and 1931, but still had a grand average of [illegible]13. H[illegible] all series batting avera[illegible] [illegible]84.

Followi[illegible] [illegible]ation of the World Ser[illegible] [illegible]which Frisch either hol[illegible] [illegible] or shares with other playe[illegible].

Most Series Ga[illegible]—Frisch 50.

Most Times at Bat, Total Series—Frish 197.

Most Times at Bat, Inning—Frisch 2 (shared with fifteen others).

Most Runs, Inning—Frisch 2 (shared with Foxx and Simmons).

Most Base Hits, Total Series—Frisch 58.

Most Hits, Game—Frisch 4 (shared with sixteen others, including Medwick, Collins and Greenberg in Series just ended).

Most Singles, Total Series—Frisch 45.

Section 5 | SPORTS SHIPPING AND MAILS

The New York Times.

SPORTS SHIPPING AND MAILS | Section 5

S | SUNDAY, JUNE 9, 1935. | L++ | S

OMAHA, 7-10, FIRST HOME IN THE $43,980 BELMONT BEFORE 25,000 IN RAIN

VICTOR BY 1½ LENGTHS

Colt Equals Feat of His Sire, Gallant Fox, by Gaining Triple Crown.

FIRETHORN FINISHES NEXT

Trails Woodward's Racer, With Rosemont Third—Triumph Is Worth $35,480.

DELPHINIUM NOSE WINNER

Annexes the National Stallion Stakes—Meadow Brook Chase to Irish Bullet.

By BRYAN FIELD.

Slashing onward through a drenching rain and slippery footing, Omaha yesterday won the historic Belmont Stakes before 25,000 persons in a manner definitely to establish himself as the champion 3-year-old of 1935. He brought to his owner, William Woodward, the distinction of being the one man to have bred and owned two triple crown winners.

To his Kentucky Derby and Preakness victories the son of Gallant Fox now has added the grueling Belmont to duplicate the feat of his sire. It was an easy finish after a testing race. Coming to the line in 2:30 3-5 for the mile and a half, Omaha had Firethorn floundering behind him, only a length and a half back, but as badly beaten as if he were in the ruck.

Firethorn was second in the Preakness. The sloppy footing yesterday favored him, and he gallantly charged at Omaha from the head of the stretch to the sixteenth pole. There his strength was spent and he almost went to pieces, to finish soundly defeated. Eight or ten lengths further back Rosemont came in a tired third, after he had momentarily been in front only to collapse suddenly. Then finished Cold Shoulder and Sir Beverley, stable-mate to Omaha.

Sends Winnings Soaring.

The race grossed $43,980, of which sum $35,480 went to Omaha's credit, sending his winnings soaring past the $100,000 mark. Since his racing career began, the chestnut colt has earned $106,930, but only $3,850 of this was won last year as a juvenile. Omaha's sire is the only thoroughbred to win more than $300,000 in one season, a money record this colt can not hope to surpass, no matter what he does in the way of beating performance marks of Gallant Fox.

Over a track that was not as bad in 1930, Gallant Fox was timed in 2:31 3-5. Once again admirers are prone to say that Omaha is greater than his sire, but Mr. Woodward has yet to join the number, even though time and performance may cause him to do so.

Omaha was a 7-to-10 shot with the big Belmont Park crowd which braved one of the wettest, rawest days of the year. He had Willie Saunders in the saddle and once more the Montana lad was as cold as ice and turned in a faultless performance. His ride was as different from that in the Withers as a ride could be.

Forges On With Power.

Saunders waited so long and he waited so well that some thought Omaha beaten at the top of the stretch. But at the finish the only horse forging on with any show of strength and power was the winner. How much "horse" Saunders had left for the stretch run is shown by the sensational final quarter-mile in 0:25 3-5. This blazing two-furlong effort, after a mile and a quarter had been put behind, was what brought disaster to the others.

Only Firethorn had anything to run against it, and his gallant best was far short of what was necessary.

The start was faultless after half a minute at the post. Wayne Wright, aboard Rosemont, took his horse under restraint as Saunders let Omaha go away easily from the barrier and without urging. Cold Shoulder immediately was sent to the front, his rider's only hope being a front race.

Rounding the first turn, he was two or three lengths in the lead. Straightened away in the backstretch, he was five in front. Another sixteenth and he was eight or ten lengths in front and sending cold shivers down the backs of those who had backed Omaha. Saunders did not give chase but sat tight.

Sir Beverley Drops Back.

Sir Beverley, which had endeavored to force the early pace and found he could not, dropped back and never thereafter was a factor. Wright, in the meantime, had skimmed the rail with Rosemont and was saving ground. Raymond Workman kept within striking distance with Firethorn, and that is the way they moved around the far turn.

On the bend, Rosemont came along the fence, Firethorn further

Continued on Page Eight.

Scottish Soccer Team Routs Canadians, 6-0

TORONTO, June 8 (Canadian Press).—Displaying a brand of soccer that dazzled their less experienced opponents most of the time, the touring Scottish Football Association team defeated an Eastern Canada eleven, 6—0, before 8,000 fans today.

The victory was the tenth for the wearers of the Thistle, who started their tour in Philadelphia, May 18. The Scots scored three goals in each half. David Wilson and Alex Ferguson each scored two goals. The other counters were made by W. Miller and P. Wilson. Tommy Walker played a fine game and his passes led to several goals.

The tourists' short-passing game puzzled the Canadians' defense.

YALE POLOISTS TOP PRINCETON, 3 TO 2

Grace Scores In Last Minute to Break Tie as Play Opens in College Tourney.

TWO TIGER GOALS IN FIRST

Elis Rally to Even Count in the Fifth Period on Slippery Governors Island Field.

By KINGSLEY CHILDS.

Neither rain nor the resultant slippery turf prevented the start of the annual intercollegiate championship polo tournament at Governors Island yesterday, and Yale, waging a gallant uphill fight, conquered Princeton in the final minute by a 3-to-2 count.

Played under conditions anything but conducive to good polo, the contest provided few thrills for the 300 spectators who braved the elements. What spectacular action there was came in the final two periods when Yale made all its three goals.

Off to a 2-to-0 advantage in the first chukker, Princeton appeared headed for a surprise victory when the two-thirds mark was reached. But in the fifth session, the Elis came back to even matters, and then, forty-five seconds before the close of the sixth and final chapter, Peter Grace accounted for the winning tally.

Penalty Shot Decides Contest.

That score by Grace, his second of the afternoon, clicked from his mallet on a free shot about ten yards in front of the Princeton goal mouth. He got the chance when one of his orange-shirted rivals committed a foul in order to prevent a Yale man from tallying.

Grace's penalty drive was virtually a sure goal before he tapped it—so close was the ball to the objective. Then just before the final bell, Julian Peabody, nephew of the internationalist, Thomas Hitchcock Jr., stroke a free shot for Princeton from the 60-yard mark, but the drive, which might have necessitated a "sudden death" overtime session, went wide.

Considering the rain and the treacherous water-soaked field, it was somewhat remarkable that only one spill occurred during the six-period encounter.

That one fall did not come until the final chukker when Peter Dominick of Westchester polo fame slipped from his mount after the pony had stumbled in one of the many holes on the badly churned turf. However, the Yale No. 2 man was uninjured and resumed action within a few moments.

Because of the unfavorable conditions, dashing play and long drives were virtually impossible and it

Continued on Page Nine.

VANDERBILT VICTOR IN YACHT PRESTIGE

Sails His Class M Craft to Triumph Over Windward in Larchmont Regatta.

LUDERS'S BARBARA WINS

Leads Interclub Fleet, With Knapp Fourth in Kenboy—Cantitoe Beats Mouette.

By DANIEL C. McCARTHY.

Special to THE NEW YORK TIMES.

LARCHMONT, N. Y., June 8.—Harold S. Vanderbilt, skipper of Rainbow in the America's Cup races last year, sailed his M boat, Prestige, to victory today in the fifty-first annual Spring regatta of the Larchmont Yacht Club. It was the first appearance since 1931 of Prestige, and she showed to advantage in defeating Windward, owned by George Lauder Jr., by more than six minutes over a 14¼-mile course.

A fleet of seventy-four craft, the largest turnout of the season, competed in the regatta. Conditions were far from ideal for racing, but after a thirty-minute postponement, Race Committee Chairman Hugh Kilmer sounded the gun that sent Prestige and Windward away on the first leg of their race, a six-mile reach to Great Captain Island.

Although Windward held the lead shortly after the boats went over the starting line, Vanderbilt brought his craft out smartly and Prestige soon went ahead. With spinnaker set, the Vanderbilt boat pulled away to a more definite lead on the run to Matinecook Point and then she headed for home far ahead of her rival.

Calm Delays the Racing.

Little or no breeze prevailed when the boats of various classes began to assemble at the starting line. Long Island Sound was as flat as a mill pond. The visibility was close to zero and rain was imminent. After the thirty-minute postponement the race committee hoisted the shortened course signal for all craft.

There were light easterly puffs now and then to give heart to the skippers, but shortly before the second handicap division went over the line the wind shifted around to north-northwest and held quite steadily from that quarter for an hour or so.

In spite of the heavy rain that fell late in the afternoon, the Stars, Wee Scots and Snipes started their competitions.

The winning streak of Arthur Knapp among the Interclubs came to an end when A. E. Luders got his Barbara home ahead of twelve rivals. Knapp, who had sailed M.

Continued on Page Two.

Mrs. Moody, in Old Form, Beats Mrs. Pittman In Final of Tennis at Weybridge, 6-0, 6-4

By The Associated Press.

WEYBRIDGE, England, June 8.—Betting commissioners, who a week ago were offering 4 to 1 against Mrs. Helen Wills Moody's chance at Wimbledon, cut their odds to 2 to 1 today after watching her defeat Mrs. Elsie Goldsack Pittman in the final round of the St. George's Hill tournament, 6—0, 6—4.

Miss Dorothy Round, top-ranking British star, remained the Wimbledon favorite at 11 to 8, with Miss Helen Jacobs, American champion, held at 2 to 1 along with Mrs. Moody.

Returning to competition in the St. George's tournament for the first time since a back injury forced her to default to Miss Jacobs in the American championships two years ago, Mrs. Moody reached the peak of her form in the first set of her match with Mrs. Pittman. Her forehand drives into the back corners had the English star on the defensive from the outset.

Once in command, the Californian seldom bothered even to run after her rival's best returns. Perhaps half of the points Mrs. Pittman won were on placements which Mrs. Moody made no real effort to reach.

Smiling in the clubhouse after her victory, Mrs. Moody said:

"My game seems to be coming back to me. My back? I think we can forget about that."

Mrs. Moody seems to have lost the "killer" instinct which, in former times, bade her win every match, 6—0, 6—0, if she could.

As in other matches this week, she let up in the second set. When she really wanted a decisive point, she simply belted the ball down the sidelines.

Mrs. Moody's only other "warm-up" competition before Wimbledon will come in the Kent championships next week.

Times Wide World Photo.

SAM PARKS JR., THE WINNER, DRIVING FROM TENTH TEE IN U. S. OPEN GOLF.

Six Boats Start in Race Across Ocean to Norway

Vanish Into Fog Off Newport on Hazardous 3,050-Mile Sail—Stormy Weather and Vamarie Lead Fleet Over Line.

By JOHN RENDEL.

Special to THE NEW YORK TIMES.

NEWPORT, R. I., June 8.—With Stormy Weather and Vamarie showing the way, six sailing yachts disappeared into the fog today, bound for Bergen, Norway, in the longest and possibly the rarest of all sporting events, a transatlantic race.

It was the beginning of the seventh race overseas in history, and before them lay 3,050 nautical miles of blue water and three weeks or longer of all that the restless elements hold in store. Their rewards will be fame and prizes given by the King of Norway, the cities of Newport and Bergen, and others.

A spectator fleet of between thirty and forty boats, mostly sailing craft, hovered around Brenton Reef Lightship to watch the start of the Atlantic Derby.

The six smallish yachts sailing eastward in a very large ocean did not present a spectacle of unrivaled magnificence, nor did it arouse a sense of excitement or the feeling of conflict which most great contests do.

Forty-four Men Aboard.

But here was the drama of the waves, the Magellan motif, men against the sea, the perils of the deep, all wrapped up in forty-four men and a few boats starting an event that was more than sport, bigger than a mere test of seamanship and fraught with hardships which few athletes care to face.

And those who watched appreciated quietly. No raucous shouts split the cool air, and only a few deep-throated ships' horns bade them godspeed. Friendly waves of farewell were expressive enough.

For the most part it was a subdued departure. The only vocal cheer was not given by the spectators but by a sailing crew. As the German yawl Stoertebeker, owned by a real seafaring men, Captain Ludwig Schlimbach of Hamburg, manoeuvred for the start, those aboard gave a rousing yell for Herbert L. Stone and the other members of the race committee of the Cruising Club of America, who made the race possible.

Crews Are Cautioned.

Whatever the fortunes of storm and calm might bring in the long watches ahead, this was a gala day and all were cheerful as greetings were called to the prosaic craft left behind.

Smaller yachts have braved the "roaring forties" and have come up smiling and the men on board knew the sea and its ways. As George E. Roosevelt, owner of the black-hulled schooner Mistress, said before sailing, the greatest hazard next to ice was the danger of falling overboard, and the crews were cautioned to maintain a firm grip, especially when working in the bows.

As for the rest, the Coast Guard

Continued on Page Three.

EXETER TURNS BACK ANDOVER BY 8 TO 5

Stages Strong Drive to Overcome Rivals' Early Lead in Annual Contest.

Special to THE NEW YORK TIMES.

EXETER, N. H., June 8.—After trailing at the start, Exeter rallied to take the annual baseball game from Andover today by 8 to 5 before an alumni crowd.

Andover made a splendid opening bid, scoring four runs in the second inning. Whitey MacLean, Ian Viens and Curtis hit safely in this frame after Hurler Arthur Johns had issued two passes.

Johns then was relieved by Captain Everett Woodman, who turned in a brilliant performance. He fanned seven and allowed only two hits during his stay on the mound.

Exeter registered in its half of the second frame and added a counter in the third. Andover scored again in the fourth, but Exeter staged a determined attack to tie the count in the same inning. Four singles in a row, produced by Sam Merrill, Norman Cosby, Woodman and Albert Alter, brought three runs across.

Exeter took the lead in the seventh. Johns tallied on Bill Beard's single to centre, a drive by Cosby providing another run. The winners increased their advantage in the next session when Alter and Johns both singled, the former scoring.

The box score:

ANDOVER.	ab.	r.	h.	po.	a.	e.
MacLean, cf.	2	2	1	0	1	0
Eurenius, 2b.	1	0	0	1	1	1
Woodw'd, 2b.	1	0	0	1	0	1
Viens, c.	5	0	1	10	0	0
Holt, 3b.	3	0	1	6	1	0
Kellog, 3b.	3	1	0	2	1	0
Burdett, rf.	5	0	0	1	0	0
Bacon, lf.p.	1	1	0	1	0	0
Gardner, ss.	4	0	0	2	0	1
Curtis, p.	3	1	2	0	1	1
Poole, lf.	0	0	0	0	0	0
O'Brien, ss.	0	0	0	0	0	0
Total	28	5	5	24	5	4

EXETER.	ab.	r.	h.	po.	a.	e.
Cosby, 2b.	5	1	2	2	3	0
W'dman, ss, p	5	1	1	1	1	0
Alter, rf.	5	2	2	2	0	0
Clark, 1b.	4	0	1	5	0	1
Johns, p.ss.	5	1	2	0	1	0
Bernicle, c.	4	0	1	2	0	0
Beard, c.	5	1	1	14	3	0
Miller, lf.	4	1	2	1	0	0
Merrill, 3b.	3	1	1	0	1	0
Total	40	8	14	27	9	1

Andover .... 0 4 0 1 0 0 0 0 0—5
Exeter .... 0 1 1 3 0 0 2 1 .—8

Stolen bases—Cosby, Alter, Clark 2, Johns 2, Bernicle, Beard, Holt. Sacrifices—Bernicle, Eurenius, Holt. Bases on balls—Off Johns 3, Woodman 6, Curtis 1, Bacon 1. Hit by pitched ball—By Johns (Eurenius). Struck out—By Johns 3, Woodman 7, Curtis 8, Bacon 1. Wild pitch—Curtis. Umpires—Kelleher and Keady.

NEW UTRECHT WINS TITLE TRACK MEET

Stays Unbeaten in P. S. A. L. Games for the Twelfth Successive Year.

By THOMAS J. DEEGAN.

New Utrecht's glory on the track continued undimmed for the twelfth consecutive year as the Green and White amassed 36 points yesterday to capture the thirty-first annual Public Schools Athletic League senior high school track and field championship at Wingate Field, Brooklyn.

Ten and one-half points behind the leaders came Abraham Lincoln, while Haaren set the pace for the Manhattan representatives with a third-place total of 18 markers.

The triumph of the Bensonhurst contingent only served to confirm the general pre-meet speculation that once again New Utrecht would carry off the major honors. For since 1924, when the Brooklyn school first won the title, only once was its supremacy questioned.

Triple Tie Last Year.

A year ago the games resulted in a triple tie for first place among New Utrecht, De Witt Clinton and James Monroe. But yesterday's performance of Coach Barnie Hyman's protégés left no doubt in the minds of the 2,500 spectators that the Green and White had the metropolitan field spread-eagled.

Shortly before the senior meet started, it seemed almost certain that the heavy downpour would necessitate a postponement of the games. The rain stopped, however, for an hour and then, with the meet in full swing, began again. The latter events were run off on a sloppy track.

Just one record was shattered in the senior high school division, the Haaren quartet setting a new mark in the 1,200-yard relay. The team

Continued on Page Three.

PARKS TAKES U. S. OPEN WITH A TOTAL OF 299; THOMSON IS RUNNER-UP

MARGIN IS TWO STROKES

Ex-Captain at Pitt Is Victor in His Second Bid for Golf Title.

HAGEN FINISHES THIRD

Veteran Needs Only a Par Final Round to Win, but Falters and Totals 302.

SARAZEN TIED FOR SIXTH

Is Bracketed With H. Smith, Picard and Krueger at 306 —Dutra Has 308.

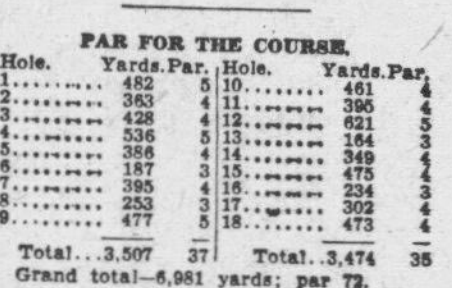

PAR FOR THE COURSE.

Hole.	Yards.	Par.	Hole.	Yards.	Par.
1	482	5	10	461	4
2	363	4	11	395	4
3	428	4	12	621	5
4	536	5	13	164	3
5	386	4	14	349	4
6	187	3	15	475	4
7	395	4	16	234	3
8	253	3	17	302	4
9	477	5	18	473	4
Total	3,507	37	Total	3,474	35

Grand total—6,981 yards; par 72.

By WILLIAM D. RICHARDSON.

Special to THE NEW YORK TIMES.

OAKMONT, Pa., June 8.—Sam Parks Jr., former University of Pittsburgh golf captain, today became the national open golf champion of the United States.

A Pittsburgh boy, only 25 years old and without a single other tournament victory to his credit, added his name to an illustrious list by touring the Oakmont Country Club course four times in a total of 299 strokes.

Starting his last round in a tie with Jimmy Thomson, Pacific Coast siege gun, young Parks outsteadied the Californian, outscoring him by one stroke on each nine, and won the title by that margin.

Walter Hagen, winner in 1914 and again in 1919, finished in third place with a total of 302, which placed him a stroke ahead of Ray Mangrum and Denny Shute, conqueror of Craig Wood in a play-off for the British open crown two years ago.

Defending Champion Has 308.

Gene Sarazen, prime favorite before the tournament started, was tied for sixth with Horton Smith, Henry Picard and Alvin Krueger, their totals being 306. Next in line came Paul Runyan and Dick Metz with 307, and after them Olin Dutra, the defending champion, and Vincent Eldred, tied for twelfth place with a seventy-two-hole total of 308.

Macdonald Smith, Al Watrous, Mortie Dutra, Bobby Cruickshank, Herman Barron and Ted Turner tied at 309 and Victor Ghezzi was twentieth with a score of 311.

Sid Brews, the South African golf ace, tied with Craig Wood, Bill, Ed Dudley, and Gene Kunes, thirteen strokes behind, and Johnny Goodman, winner of the open two years ago, finished far down in the list, failing to lead the amateur division.

That honor fell to Chris Brinke, formerly of Philadelphia and now a resident of Detroit, who led Goodman by a stroke with his total of 315.

Well Deserved Victory.

Although his victory came as a great surprise in view of the fact that Parks started in the championship an unknown, except locally, and against perhaps the greatest field of players ever to play in the national open, it was a deserved triumph, for he was the most consistent of any one in the field.

None of his rounds sparkled as did those of Krueger, the Beloit youth who led the field in the first round with his record breaking 71, which was tied by Turner, Pine Valley professional, on Friday, and then broken by Picard's 70 this morning. But he was consistently good throughout the entire tournament.

Starting with a 77, he had two middle rounds of 73s, and then his closing effort of 76. And where many others, more used to the stresses and strains of championship competition than he, were unable to stand up under them, he did.

There were a few occasions today when he showed signs of cracking up under the terrific load he was carrying on his inexperienced shoulders, but he always managed to straighten himself out and get back on the right path.

Paired With Mac Smith.

By a curious twist of fate Parks, who had won nothing prior to today, played his last three holes with Macdonald Smith, the veteran, who has won everything except the National Open, for which he has tied once and been a contender on numerous occasions.

Thomson, who had been hovering close to the top ever since the tournament started, tied for third at the end of the first round, in the lead for thirty-six holes and still tied with the last eighteen holes to play, lost his chance when

Continued on Page Five.

Miss Wethered Has 76 At Rain-Soaked Merion

Special to THE NEW YORK TIMES.

MERION, Pa., June 8.—Miss Joyce Wethered, British star, gave one of the greatest exhibitions of her golfing career today over the rain-soaked Merion championship east course when she scored a 76, shooting from the men's tees. Women's par for the course is 79.

Paired with George Sayres, Merion pro, the British girl had the best medal score in a foursome that also included Mrs. Glenna Collett Vare, who was teamed with Max Marston, former national titleholder. Miss Wethered and Sayres won the match, 1 up.

Once again the tourist showed her mastery with all clubs.

MANGAN SMASHES U.S. ¾-MILE MARK

Closes With Furious Drive to Defeat Hornbostel in 3:01.4 —Venzke Fourth.

CROWLEY TOPS M'CLUSKEY

Dreyer Betters 178 Feet With Hammer—Peacock and Beard Tie N. Y. A. C. Meet Records.

By ARTHUR J. DALEY.

Amid the pelting rain at Travers Island yesterday, Chuck Hornbostel beat Glen Dawson and Gene Venzke in their heralded three-quarter-mile battle. But ahead of all of them at the tape with a cyclonic finish was Joe Mangan of the New York A. C., unfurling the masterpiece of his career.

Totally overlooked in the pre-race calculations of a remarkably fine crowd of 4,000 that huddled under umbrellas and raincoats at the 134th track and field games of the Winged Foot Club, Mangan outsprinted the mighty Hornbostel in a ding-dong homestretch duel. Not only did he run the puissant Hoosier into the ground but set a new American record in the process.

Eclipses Venzke's Time.

Clocked in the astoundingly fast time of 3:01.4, the amazing Cornell graduate erased from the books Venzke's year-old mark of 3:02.3 as well as eclipsing Tommy Conneff's old track and former world's record of 3:02.8, a figure that had stood for forty years.

It was a remarkable achievement for two reasons. One was the patent class of the men he beat. The other was the truly excellent time he made. And by winning, Mangan undoubtedly ran himself right into the Princeton invitation meet at Palmer Stadium next Saturday. They can't keep him out now.

Only three men in history have ever covered the route in faster time than the determined young Winged Footer did yesterday. One is Bill Bonthron, with 3:00.8 in Sweden; another is Jules Ladoumegue of France, the present world's record holder of 3:00.6, and the third is Jack Lovelock, with an unofficial clocking of 3:00.4.

And Mangan triumphed with a magnificent sprint that even Hornbostel could not match. As overlooked as he had been before the test, the former Cornellian so was overlooked during it. An early laggard, he never broke away from the rear of the procession until a lap from the end, when he climbed to third.

Then he burst past Venzke a half

Continued on Page Four.

YANKS BREAK EVEN, GOMEZ LOSING 7TH

Rout Ferrell in Opener as Gehrig's Seventh Homer Features 12-6 Triumph.

OSTERMUELLER WINS DUEL

Scores for Red Sox, 4-2, Wild Pitch by Southpaw Rival Letting in Two Runs.

By JOHN DREBINGER.

Special to THE NEW YORK TIMES.

BOSTON, June 8.—The Yankees and Red Sox battled each other all over Fenway Park for something like five and a half hours today, but not a fan in a gathering of 20,000 was able to detect where either had gained the slightest advantage.

With Captain Lou Gehrig exploding his seventh home run of the campaign, the McCarthymen captured the opener in a spanking breeze by 12 to 6. But in the afterpiece the Yanks became sadly becalmed as Vernon Gomez lost a left-handers' duel to Fritz Ostermueller, 4 to 2.

That was the good señor's seventh defeat in a season which thus far has seen him win only four engagements and left him feeling very blue indeed.

Figuratively and literally, Gomez tossed this one away in the fifth inning when, with the score tied at 1-all, the bases full and two out, he unfurled a terrific wild pitch.

Adds to McCarthy's Woes.

Bad enough it was to see Ostermueller tear over the plate from third base with one tally. But one can readily imagine the sufferings of Manager Joe McCarthy down in the Yankee dugout when he saw Gomez and his catcher, Arndt Jorgens, commiserating for the oversight. While they were doing this, the fleet-footed Bill Werber, who had come up from second base, also counted.

Those two runs sufficed to give the decision to Ostermueller, who not only pitched well, allowing only six blows, but smacked his adversary for three singles.

The Yanks, who had scored one run in the fourth on Chapman's double and Gehrig's single, came up with another in the sixth on Chapman's second two-bagger and Lazzeri's single. But that was all.

Gomez, who appeared woefully shy on control, walking no fewer than eight batters, fell one run behind in the first inning on a pass, a sacrifice and Almada's hit and, after his lapse in the fifth, he lost one more tally in the seventh on

Continued on Page Six.

Major League Baseball

National League

YESTERDAY'S RESULTS.

Brooklyn 3, Philadelphia 2 (1st, 5 innings.)
(2d game postponed, rain.)
Pittsburgh 14, Cincinnati 8 (1st).
(2d game postponed, rain.)
St. Louis 5, Chicago 4 (1st).
St. Louis 6, Chicago 5. (2d, 11 innings.)
Boston at New York, rain.

STANDING OF THE CLUBS.

	New York	St. Louis	Pittsburgh	Brooklyn	Chicago	Cincinnati	Phila'phia	Boston	Won	Lost	Percentage
New York	—	2	5	3	4	3	5	6	28	11	.718
St. Louis	2	—	3	2	7	5	3	4	26	18	.591
Pittsburgh	2	5	—	4	1	6	5	4	27	20	.574
Brooklyn	1	2	3	—	1	4	7	5	23	20	.535
Chicago	1	4	3	3	—	5	1	4	21	19	.525
Cincinnati	1	1	4	1	3	—	3	4	17	24	.415
Phila'phia	2	3	1	3	2	1	—	2	14	26	.350
Boston	2	1	1	4	1	0	2	—	11	29	.275
Gms. lost	11	18	20	20	19	24	26	29	—	—	

GAMES TODAY.

Boston at New York (3 P. M.).
Brooklyn at Philadelphia.
Cincinnati at Pittsburgh.
Chicago at St. Louis.

American League

YESTERDAY'S RESULTS.

New York 12, Boston 6 (1st).
Boston 4, New York 2 (2d).
Philadelphia 4, Washington 3 (1st).
(2d game postponed, rain.)
Cleveland 3, St. Louis 2.
Chicago 3, Detroit 2.

STANDING OF THE CLUBS.

	New York	Chicago	Cleveland	Detroit	Boston	Wash'gton	Phila'phia	St. Louis	Won	Lost	Percentage
New York	—	2	5	3	5	5	6	2	28	18	.609
Chicago	3	—	1	8	3	3	2	4	24	17	.585
Cleveland	2	3	—	4	2	3	2	8	24	18	.571
Detroit	3	2	4	—	3	4	3	4	23	20	.535
Boston	6	3	3	1	—	4	4	2	23	22	.511
Wash'gton	1	1	2	2	5	—	5	4	20	24	.455
Phila'phia	2	2	2	1	1	5	—	4	17	24	.415
St. Louis	1	4	1	1	3	0	2	—	12	28	.300
Gms. lost	18	17	18	20	22	24	24	28	—	—	

GAMES TODAY.

New York at Boston.
Detroit at Chicago.
St. Louis at Cleveland.
Philadelphia at Washington.

OMAHA TRIUMPHS IN THE BELMONT

Continued From Page One.

out. Omaha, outside of Firethorn, closed on Cold Shoulder. Rosemont saved many lengths as the head of the stretch was reached and there he put Cold Shoulder away. Suddenly he was in the lead, with only a quarter to go, and it looked as if he would score another upset, as he did in the Withers.

Then it was that Saunders turned loose with Omaha. Firethorn had something left and the two went past Rosemont so fast that it seemed almost as if the Withers winner had stepped in a hole. Of course he had not, but he was in the ruck in a twinkling and the race was between the big chestnut from Belair and the son of Sun Briar. They ran head and head for a furlong, with Omaha slowly wearing the other down and slowly drawing off from him. At the sixteenth pole it was all Omaha. Firethorn could do no more. Omaha finished out bull-like, as if he could go on and on, while Firethorn was dead tired.

Leads In the Winner.

In slicker and rain-drenched slouch hat, Mr. Woodward took his colt at the head of the track and stomped through mud and gravel to lead him in as Belmont winners has been led in since 1867. It was a glorious finish to a day which saw many a thrill. And it was a worthy final day to the Belmont Spring meeting. The sport will shift to Aqueduct tomorrow.

The National Stallion Stakes saw a whipping, driving finish with Mrs. Dodge Sloane's Delphinium the winner by a nose over Ogden Phipps's White Cockade, while Mrs. Silas B. Mason's Valevictorian was another nose away. The winner was a 6-to-1 shot, while Valevictorian was an outsider in the betting.

Delphinium was strongly ridden by Johnny Gilbert and flashed a splendid effort, but he was roundly booed after the finish. The cause of this was his swerving dash from the extreme outside post position to the rail position, where he finished.

White Cockade was coupled in the betting with Cascapedia and the two were strongly backed as the second choice at 12 to 5. The favorite was the C. V. Whitney entry of Savings and Triumphant, which finished seventh and eighth as named. Only eight ran and the pair were backed at 6 to 5.

Result Comes as Surprise.

The test grossed $14,720, of which sum $11,720 went to the owner of the winner. The result was a surprise, but many were heard to say that Mrs. Sloane deserved some luck, as a good deal of ill fortune has been the lot of her horses this season. In 1934 she was the country's leading money-winning owner.

The start saw Galsac break inward against Triumphant, but Silvio Coucci pulled him off immediately and it was doubtful if this can be advanced as an excuse for Triumphant's defeat. Delphinium started to bear inward right from the start, but the slight clash between Galsac and Triumphant apparently retarded them enough to be too far back to be interfered with by Delphinium.

Delphinium kept on bearing over and appeared to jostle Bien Joli in the last quarter. Savings made a bid here and ranged alongside of Bien Joli. When Delphinium came from the other side the Colonel E. R. Bradley racer was bounced between. Then Savings faltered.

The main challenge was developing on the outside of Delphinium, where Valevictorian and White Cockade moved as one horse. They swept up on Delphinium, and through the last sixteenth the three strode on as a team. Just at the end Valevictorian faltered slightly, and none knew which of the other two had won, until the judges posted the numbers. The time for the five furlongs was 0:58 1-5.

The 8-year-old steeplechaser, Irish Bullet, bridged a gap from 1917 for F. Ambrose Clark when he won the Meadow Brook Steeplechase Handicap in time which set a new record for the stake. He was caught in 4:44 2-5 at the end of the two and one-half miles.

Favorite in Storng Field.

Mr. Clark won the second running of the Meadow Brook back in 1917 with Falmouth. Yesterday Irish Bullet was made the favorite in a strong field of six and won by five lengths at 8 to 5. Second to him was Joseph E. Widener's Arc Light, which won last year with Irish Bullet second.

Arc Light was making his first start of the season and was just up to take the place by a head with a delayed charge. This edged Jungle King back into third position, two lengths before St. Francis. Rideaway and Spinach completed the field as named.

The long test had a value of $1,755 to the owner of the winner, who watched the race with a party of friends. Irish Bullet shouldered top weight of 156 pounds and was giving a pound to Arc Light. Fred Bellhouse had the leg up and took his mount to the front almost at once. Never thereafter was the lead lost, even though Rideaway made a strong bid in the last half mile. This took so much out of Rideaway that he dropped right off contention in the last 100 yards.

Arc Light was carefully rated for both turns of the field and passed tired horses at the end. He did not menace the winner, but might have made the race closer if Jockey Little had moved sooner. It was a splendid first out for this 11-year-old and he is bound to be a factor of importance in future races.

The day opened with a victory for the favorite when Colonel Bradley's Beanie M. scored by three lengths at 3 to 2. She came out of the press half way through the race to fight it out with Willis Sharpe Kilmer's Sun Dancer. This daughter of Sun Briar appeared the winner a furlong and a half out, but Beanie M. was able to draw off from her in the final drive.

At the finish Beanie M. was going easily, with Sun Dancer driving but still losing ground. A length and a half further back Sweet as Sugar gained the show. This filly might have been closer but for swerving in the stretch. She was right with the lead when she began to bear out and, although she later was straightened away, the move cost her distance. Beanie M. scored in the smart enough time of 0:59 1-5 for the five furlongs down the chute.

Times Wide World Photo.

WILLIAM WOODWARD'S OMAHA BEATING W. M. JEFFORDS'S FIRETHORN IN BELMONT STAKES.

MARY TERRY TAKES CLIPSETTA STAKES

Thompson Filly Beats First Class by Ten Lengths in Feature at Latonia.

LATONIA, Ky., June 8 (AP).—C. R. Thompson's Mary Terry, daughter of Terry and Milfoil, made a show of her opposition to account for the fifty-third running of the Clipsetta Stakes, the feature at Latonia today.

At the conclusion of the five-and-a-half-furlong dash through the slop, Mary Terry was ten lengths in front of her closest rival, First Class. Miss Greenock was a half length further back in third place.

Given an alert ride by the veteran Leo Canfield, Mary Terry followed the early pace of Miss Greenock for a half mile. Turning into the stretch, Canfield gave the filly her head and she went to the front to win in a gallop.

Ten competed for the $2,425 purse, with Mary Terry the favorite. She returned $6.40 for $2 to win and covered the five and a half furlongs in 1:09 2-5.

Top Row Scores by Half Length In Handicap at Washington Park

Baroni Racer Leads Tearout to Wire in Revival of the Great Western, With Count Arthur Third—Victor Covers Mile and Furlong in 1:50 4/5, With Longden in Saddle.

By The Associated Press.

CHICAGO, June 8.—A. A. Baroni's Top Row, which came here recently from California, captured the revival of the Great Western Handicap, at a mile and a furlong, before 17,000 spectators at Washington Park today.

Top Row won by a half length from D. B. Midkiff's Tearout, which took the Latonia Derby a week ago. Count Arthur, from the stable of Mrs. John D. Hertz, was third. The time for the distance was 1:50 4-5, just two-fifths of a second slower than the track record.

Although the winner, a son of Peanuts—Too High, came here wtih a world record of 1:42 for a mile and a sixteenth to his credit, he was second choice in the betting and returned $8.56 for $2 to win, $5.52 to place and $3.52 to show. Tearout paid $8.08 to place and $4.26 to show. Count Arthur, made the favorite with his stable-mate Watch Him, was $2.74 to show. The race had a net value of $4,440 to owner Baroni.

Top Row, packing top weight of 118 pounds and ridden by Jockey J. Longden, followed Biff, the pacesetter, for six furlongs. Biff then surrendered to Count Arthur. Top Row, on the outside, charged into the lead at the head of the stretch and gradually drew away. Tearout was coming fast from far back and the winner was forced to a blistering finish.

In the third race Mrs. E. Haughton's 2-year-old gelding Black Highbrow set a new track record for five furlongs in taking the event from Forever Yours in 0:59 1-5. The previous record was 0:59 2-5, set by Jimmy Moran several years ago.

Aqueduct Track Opens Tomorrow; Queens County Handicap Feature

With the Queens County Handicap as the opening feature, the Summer meeting of the Queens County Jockey Club will get under way at Aqueduct tomorrow to run for twenty-two racing days. John E. Cowdin, president, has announced that the enhanced value in the five featured stakes has so increased the number of entries that one of the most successful meetings in the history of the club is expected.

The $10,000 Brooklyn handicap, to be run June 22, is the richest race of the session and is the third of New York's three major Spring handicaps, the others being the Metropolitan and Suburban already run at Belmont Park. Tomorrow's test has $3,000 in added money. The Carter Handicap carries $5,000, the Great American Stakes $2,500, and the Dwyer Stakes $7,500.

Hurdle Races on Program.

One of the features so popular at Belmont Park which will be strongly continued at Aqueduct is steeplechasing. While the Queens County course may not have as many good jumpers on hand, President Cowdin has aimed to have a race through the field every day. Hurdle races will be substituted when there are not enough steeplechasers on hand.

The support of leaders of the turf for the meeting has been given President Cowdin and his colleagues, through the entry of scores of top-class horses and through the taking of boxes. Some of those who have supported the meeting in both ways are William Woodward, Mrs. R. T. Wilson, W. R. Coe, Robert L. Gerry, Marshall Field and Mrs. Payne Whitney.

Also Alfred Gwynne Vanderbilt, E. R. Bradley, George Atwell Jr., Mrs. Dodge Sloane, Richard F. Howe, C. V. Whitney, Mrs. H. C. Phipps and John Hay Whitney.

Cavalcade, considered the potential champion of the handicap division despite his two defeats this season, is one of the famous horses named for the Aqueduct racing. Whether or not he will be able to keep his engagements, following the mishap in the Suburban, remains to be seen. There he tossed his rider at the start and slightly injured his feet.

Competition to Be Close.

There is certain to be competition of the keenest kind, for John J. Kane, aide to Mr. Cowdin, reports that the Aqueduct barns are well filled and that John Campbell, the general racing secretary, has gotten a good response from horsemen.

Mr. Campbell has just completed a most successful session at Belmont Park, where Joseph E. Widener paid him high praise for the large fields and keen competition which resulted.

The aim in drawing the conditions for the stakes and purses has been to schedule events for all types of horses. The minimum purse will be $900, with overnight events going up to $1,000 and $1,200. For tomorrow's feature horses of three years and upward will be eligible. The distance is a mile.

In the Carter on Saturday horses of the same ages will be eligible, but the distance will be seven furlongs. The Brooklyn is down for decision on June 22 and is one of the East's most famous stakes for older horses. It now is at a mile and a furlong and has been won by many of the best horses on the American turf.

Nominations Total 60.

Sixty nominations have been made for the forthcoming renewal and included are many of the star 3-year-olds as well as the best of the older horses. The final stake of the session, the Great American on July 4, is framed for 2-year-olds. It has attracted an unusually large entry and will be run out of the chute.

The racing strip itself has been carefully gone over by Superintendent Louis Francis and he pronounces the entire mile and a quarter in prime condition. Omaha, the 3-year-old champion, was prepped over the Aqueduct strip.

FEATURE AT SALEM TO WINTER SPORT

By The Associated Press.

SALEM, N. H., June 8.—Alfred Gwynne Vanderbilt's racers dominated today's stake events at Rockingham Park. His two-year-old old bay colt Winter Sport took the $5,000 added juvenile handicap, with a length to spare over Postage Due, his more famous stablemate, while Identify accounted for the first section of the $2,500 White Mountain Handicap for three-year-olds and up.

Knapp in the Saddle.

Winter Sport, with L. Knapp in the saddle, covered the five furlongs in 0:59 4-5 seconds. As the field hustled into the homestretch, it appeared as if the Vanderbilt three-horse entry, which included Speed, would finish in one-two-three order. Speed, however, had to yield to Seabiscuit and Bright and Early, which closed with a rush to capture the third and fourth shares of the purse.

In the other stake, over the mile route, Identify won after a grueling battle with Stocks and Gentle Knight. They put on a blanket finish, with the Vanderbilt star being clocked in 1:38, three-fifths of a second slower than the track record.

VENZKE CAPTURES THE BAXTER MILE; CUNNINGHAM NEXT

Wins Feature at N. Y. A. C. Meet by 3 Yards in 4:10.2 Before 13,000 at Garden.

WORLD MARK FOR O'BRIEN

Timed in 0:57.8 as He Takes the Buermeyer 500—Sprint to Peacock.

TOWNS SHATTERS RECORD

Beats Universal Hurdle Figures —Nordell and Hornbostel Score, Torrance Loses.

By ARTHUR J. DALEY.

Gene Venzke outran his former nemesis, Glenn Cunningham, to win the Baxter Mile which featured the New York A. C. games at Madison Square Garden last night.

This was the first time in more than a score of efforts that Venzke finished first in a mile race against Cunningham, although in the Wanamaker Mile a fortnight ago he was second, with the Kansan third. Joe Mangan was the victor in that contest.

The picture runner from Penn won last night with a surprise sprint at the ninth lap and then fought off two bitter challenges to snap the tape three yards ahead.

Venzke was the king of them all when Cunningham first threatened his reign in 1932. Last night, while a crowd of 13,000 greeted his effort with thunderous applause, the king came back to reclaim his throne. He did it with a magnificent 4:10.2 performance, the fourth fastest eight furlongs ever run indoors.

Runs Brilliant Race.

By a scant two-tenths of a second this climax to the regeneration of Venzke missed equaling the speediest mile he ever unfurled in his odd career that has touched both the top and the bottom. It was a superlative exhibition, sparkling with the confidence, the assurance and the poise that the Penn man has been missing for four long years.

But fate did not relinquish all hold on the runner from Philadelphia. He failed to win outright possession of the Baxter Trophy. Each of those three great foemen finished with a leg on it—Bill Bonthron, Cunningham and Venzke. The Kansan had the fastest time, 4:09.8 a year ago, and that gave the defeated one permanent possession.

For Venzke the long arm of coincidence reached far last night. It was in this same Baxter mile in 1932 that he first rocketed into prominence with the 4:10 exploit that was to constitute the then world's record. And in this self-same race his redemption was completed.

For the first time since then Venzke waged a battle against Cunningham that was shrewdly conceived and expertly run. His defeatist attitude of other days was gone. He ran to win and win he did.

Comes as a Surprise.

Venzke's sprint took the crowd as completely by surprise as it astounded the Kansan. Two laps from the end Cunningham was leading. It looked to be another of those tests where the issue was to hang in the balance until the final circuit.

Then Venzke suddenly darted past the machine from the Corn Belt as though he had been hurled by a catapult. He was a step behind and then he was a step in front. The spectators had the rafters ringing with their frenzied cheers.

When the pair flashed around the oval to the straightaway the strident pealing of the bell was mingled with the thunderous roar of the spectators. Cunningham was making his bid.

Up he came with his lifting drive that has mowed down all before it with the rapacity of a reaper. Up he came to Venzke's shoulder, but he never got further. The Penn man pounded along the boards with a counter-sprint of his own.

For 30 yards Venzke battled bitterly, refusing to yield an inch. One of them had to give in. It was Cunningham. He dropped back and saved himself for his supreme effort that was to come just a bit later.

Around the penultimate turn they streaked, all other starters distanced figures in the background. Then Venzke turned his head, just as he had turned it in the final Olympic tryouts at Palo Alto in 1932.

Crisis of the Battle.

When he looked then he saw Cunningham come hurtling past him for the place that was to force him off the Olympic team. Now Venzke saw that same Cunningham threatening him again. This was the crisis—physical and psychological.

Venzke was equal to it. The straining features of the Kansan were in evidence as he glanced behind, a Cunningham who was at his shoulder ready for the kill as always. But the Jayhawk flier never was able to draw up even with him.

Deep down into his reserve strength Venzke reached and up he came with enough to win. He sprinted like a man possessed—outracing a thousand demons at his heels. Cunningham had nothing to match it.

They rounded the last turn a step apart, the Kansan on the outside

Continued on Page Five.

Fay's Yacht Starlight Wins Honors at Nassau

By Tropical Radio to THE NEW YORK TIMES.

NASSAU, Bahamas, Feb. 15.—A. B. Fay's yacht Starlight captured Governor Bede Clifford's Cup today in a thirty-mile ocean race on corrected time of 2:42:39. Albert D. Phelps's Sonny was second in 2:50:22, and H. M. Matheson's Babe next in 2:59:45.

Harkness Edwards's Winsome Too was placed fourth in 3:05:47, Commodore Wesley Papes's San Cristobal fifth at 3:13:22, and Vadim S. Makaroff's Vamarie sixth at 3:18:35.

Governor Clifford presented this trophy and the cups for the Miami to Nassau race to the victors at a Nassau Yacht Club dinner tonight.

The yacht Caroline, owned and sailed by Harold Bowen of Grants Mills, R. I., arrived here today. She was unreported for more than two days after starting in the race from Miami last Tuesday.

HARVARD SUBDUES YALE SIX, 5 TO 2

Scores Three Times in First Period to Gain a Decisive Lead in Series Opener.

STOCKHAUSEN IS ELI STAR

Makes Many Sensational Stops —Victory Gives Crimson 2d Place Tie in League.

STANDING OF THE TEAMS.

	W.	L.		W.	L.
Dartmouth	3	2	Yale	2	2
Harvard	2	2	Princeton	1	2

Special to THE NEW YORK TIMES.

BOSTON, Feb. 15.—Harvard won the first game of the thirty-sixth hockey series with Yale by handing the Blue a 5-2 defeat tonight before 8,000 partisan spectators in the Garden. The triumph sent Harvard into a second-place tie with the Elis in the Quadrangular League race.

Two goals tallied late in the first frame within twenty-three seconds of each other when two Elis were resting in the penalty box gave the Crimson a lead which it retained throughout the remainder of the game. Yale strived hard in the concluding sessions to overcome the Crimson lead but it was unable to batter down the Harvard defense.

Harvard tallied early in the first period, but Yale tied it up about six minutes later. Then, with Bob Nagle and Bill Moore of Yale in the penalty box on tripping penalties, the Crimson put on the pressure to count twice before the session closed.

Second Period Scoreless.

The second period was scoreless, but Yale tallied before a minute of the third frame had elapsed, only to allow Harvard two more markers before the game ended.

The two Yale markers came off the stick of Captain Mills, but it was sturdy and sensational goal-tending by Tom Stockhausen of New York in the Blue strings that featured the game. Time after time he was called on to make seemingly impossible saves and he made at least twenty difficult stops of terrific Harvard shots from close range.

Louis Carr was the leading goal getter for Harvard with 2 markers, while Captain Moseley scored once and assisted on another. George Roberts also had one and one.

The first period was full of fast skating and stiff body checking, with Harvard taking a 3-1 lead. The Crimson advantage was not secured until late in the session, when the referees sent off two Eli players for tripping within ten seconds, and Harvard made two goals with the Blue two players short.

Crimson Takes Early Lead.

Harvard went into an early lead when Captain Moseley scored the first goal of the game in 2:06, with Ford getting an assist. Yale fought back and tied the game at 8:40 as Badger passed to Mills in front of the Crimson cage to put in the equalizer.

The play was even until Nagel and then Mills of Yale were ruled off, and Harvard got busy at this point. The goal which broke the deadlock was produced by Mechem,

Continued on Page Four.

Winners in Olympics and Part of Crowd at Opening

Associated Press Photo.

Alan Washbond, brake, and Ivan Brown, driver, who scored for U. S.

Chancellor Hitler in foreground among spectators.

Times Wide World Photo.

Miss Sonja Henie of Norway.

Miss Henie Hard Pressed To Defeat Miss Colledge

Wins Third Olympic Figure Skating Title With 424.5 Points to English Girl's 418.1—Miss Vinson Is Fifth.

By The Associated Press.

GARMISCH-PARTENKIRCHEN, Germany, Feb. 15.—Miss Sonja Henie, queen of the figure skaters for ten years, retained the Olympic crown today only after a lanky English girl, Miss Cecilia Colledge, gave the blonde Norwegian the closest contest of her career.

In winning her third Olympic title and beating twenty-two of the world's ranking skaters from twelve nations, Sonja was forced to give an exhibition ranked by experts as her best since she won her first world title in 1926. She entered the free skating with a three-point margin over Miss Colledge and doubled it with a brilliant execution of spins, twirls and jumps.

The final figures gave the titleholder 424.5 points as against 418.1 for the newly risen English star.

Miss Hulten Third.

Miss Maribel Vinson, the American titleholder, moved up one notch from her ranking in the school figures to take fifth with 388.7, behind Miss Vivi-Anne Hulten of Sweden and Miss Liselotte Landbeck of Belgium.

Of the three other Americans, little Miss Audrey Peppe of New York ranked the highest, finishing twelfth. The Weigel sisters of Buffalo were far down the list, Louise placing twenty-first and Estelle twenty-second.

From the start, the event was a battle between the champion and Miss Colledge. The English skater, first of the pair to appear on the ice, kept the crowd of 11,000 in a continuous uproar as she whirled through a program designed to force Sonja to give her best. The judges gave her an average of 5.7 points on both difficulty of program and performance.

Receives a 5.8 Rating.

There was a dead silence when Sonja skated into the arena, appearing slightly nervous. She knew she dared not make one mistake.

Continued on Page Three.

The Complete Results.

By The Canadian Press.

	Points.
1—Sonja Henie, Norway	424.5
2—Cecilia Colledge, Great Britain	418.1
3—Vivi-Anne Hulten, Sweden	394.7
4—Liselotte Landbeck, Belgium	393.3
5—Maribel Vinson, United States	388.7
6—Hedy Stenuf, Austria	387.6
7—Emmy Putzinger, Austria	381.8
8—Viktoria Lindpaintner, Germany	381.4
9—Margarethe Lainer, Austria	373.4
10—Etsuko Inada, Japan	368.1
11—Mollie Phillips, Great Britain	366.2
12—Audrey Peppe, United States	363.3
13—Angela Anderes, Switzerland	355.4
14—Bianca Schenk, Austria	256.4
15—Eva Botond, Hungary	356.1
16—B. Jepson-Turner, Great Britain	352.6
17—Vera Hruba, Czechoslovakia	353.3
18—Yvonne de Ligne, Belgium	348.2
19—Hertha Frey-Dexler, Switzerland	345.4
20—Fritzi Metznerova, Czechoslovakia	339.2
21—Louise E. Weigel, United States	336.4
22—Estelle D. Weigel, United States	324.5
23—Alise Daeguse, Latvia	280.9

BINGHAM ASKS END OF BIG THREE PACT

President Conant of Harvard Urged to Seek Removal of Ban on Early Practice.

Special to THE NEW YORK TIMES.

CAMBRIDGE, Mass., Feb. 15.—William J. Bingham, athletic director and chairman of the committee for the direction of athletic activities at Harvard, in his annual report, submitted today, urges President Conant of Harvard to abrogate the agreement with the presidents of Yale and Princeton whereby the three football squads are not allowed to begin Fall football practice prior to Sept. 15.

Mr. Bingham advocates that the players henceforth be allowed to start practice at least one week earlier than has been the case since 1922, when Harvard, Yale and Princeton took it upon themselves to remove the stress on football by shortening arbitrarily the practice season.

Proper Preparation Needed.

The athletic director points out the inadequacy of this pact, his stand being that the coaches and players have been handicapped. The three universities made their agreement to conform with that in force in the Western Conference. In his

Continued on Page Four.

COLUMBIA DOWNS NAVY FIVE, 40-24

Nash and Casey Pace Victors, Who Roll Up 24-8 Lead in Opening Half.

Special to THE NEW YORK TIMES.

ANNAPOLIS, Md., Feb. 15.—Closing its campaign at home, the Navy five was turned back by Columbia, 40 to 24, today. The visitors rolled up a 24-8 lead in the first half, but were held on even terms in the concluding session.

The Navy led for a brief period at 5 to 1 after the first four minutes of the battle, but was held in check for the rest of the half as the Lions, with Casey showing the way, displayed a powerful attack to gain a comfortable advantage.

The second period was a real contest and the general work of the Midshipmen afforded some hope that they will make a good showing against the Army, which will be met next week.

Casey's playing off the board was the deciding factor in Columbia's strong attack in the first half. With the count 5—1, Casey scored from the foul line and floor, and, after Shamer had put through a 2-pointer for Navy, tallied twice from the field to put the invaders ahead, 8—7.

Nash then recorded a field goal and foul and in the latter part of the stanza was the heaviest scorer. With the score at 18 to 8 favoring Columbia, Nash, Crowley and Casey registered from the field in the last two minutes of the session to make the count 24 to 8.

Navy Wages Hard Fight.

With the last Army-Navy football game as a precedent, today's contest would have been a fine one if only the last half had been played, for the Navy found itself in the closing period.

Schneider scored first, dropping in a field goal for the Navy, which Crowley duplicated, and Nash tallied from the line, to be followed by Fellows, the Navy captain. The scoring then see-sawed to the end.

Nash took scoring honors with 12 points, while Casey came through with 11.

However, Naval Academy athletes made a good day of it, with three victories in four varsity events, while the plebes also were victors in three contests out of four.

Expected defeat on the basketball court was offset by a 16-to-12 triumph over the powerful wrestlers of Washington and Lee, four of whom are Southern Conference champions, a fencing decision over City College of New York and a

Continued on Page Four.

Cavalcade Out of $100,000 Added Handicap; He Did Triumphs in Rich Santa Anita Derby

By The Associated Press.

LOS ANGELES, Feb. 15.—Cavalcade, 3-year-old champion in 1934, was withdrawn today from the $100,000 added Santa Anita Handicap next Saturday.

Trainer Bob Smith said that the pride of the Brookmeade Stable was declared out "because we couldn't get him in shape to win."

To reports around racing circles that Cavalcade was ready to return to stud and was never considered a likely starter in the handicap, Smith declared he hoped to have the horse in shape "by mid-Summer to run in cup races in the East."

Mrs. Silas B. Mason's Head Play also was declared out of the race today because he was not ready. Tommy Taylor, Mrs. Mason's trainer, said continued mud on the track made training of Head Play difficult. Head Play won three handicaps at Santa Anita last year and conquered Discovery in the Suburban Handicap at Belmont last Spring.

In St. Louis, Charles Burke, acting for Tom Kearney, said less than $300 "was bet here on Cavalcade in Winter books," and Jack Doyle in New York said much the same thing. Smith declared:

"He was all right until a little more than a week ago, when he threw a plate covering his old injury, and bruised another part of his hoof. Equipped as he is now, I can't work him out on the muddy track here, and I can't get him in shape by next Saturday. That's why he won't run then."

Withdrawal of Cavalcade from the big race settled once and for all the possibility of a widely heralded renewal of the turf feud

Continued on Page Six.

WISCONSIN OUSTS SPEARS AS COACH

Director Meanwell and Trainer Fallon Also Dismissed by Board of Regents.

By The Associated Press.

MADISON, Wis., Feb. 15.—Dr. Walter E. Meanwell, athletic director, and Dr. Clarence W. Spears, head football coach, storm centers of the University of Wisconsin's athletic department war, were ordered dismissed today, effective July 1, by the Board of Regents.

The ouster of the two doctors, decreed to purge the department of discord, at the same time apparently created a new problem.

The action was taken in defiance of a recommendation by the university athletic board, and a battle between the latter group and the regents appeared in the making.

"Invasion of Authority."

The athletic board had reported, in recommending retention of Meanwell and dismissal of Spears, that it would consider any other action "an invasion of its authority and tantamount to a denial of faculty control" of athletics. It insisted the main issue was whether athletics were to be controlled by the faculty, or be dictated by pressure groups outside the university," rather than the battle between Meanwell and Spears.

The dismissal of Dr. Meanwell precipitated the resignations of the four faculty members of the athletic board. The student member said he also would resign.

Three of the eleven members of the Board of Regents opposed Spears's removal. All voted that Meanwell be ousted.

Along with the ousting of the two doctors, the regents ordered the

Continued on Page Four.

GOYA, 60-1, SCORES IN NURSERY STAKES

Camera Decides Result After Sam Renick's Mount Catches Anglo Saxon at Miami.

By The Associated Press.

MIAMI, Fla., Feb. 15.—In the most bitterrly fought finish in the six runnings of the Nursery States No. 1, the Crescent Stable's virtually unknown brown colt Goya raced to a nose victory at odds of more than 60—1, paying $123,40 for $2 at Hialeah Park today. The camera eye had to be called into play by the judges before the son of Challenger II and Peggy Mac received the $3,190 lion's share of the purse over John C. Clark's Anglo-Saxon.

Willie Crump's Hi-Vic was a close third, a head back of Anglo-Saxon and a length before the Maemere Farm's Maedic. The latter, coupled with Maespur, ruled favorite in the field of eleven 2-year-old colts and geldings.

Sammy Renick drove up on the outside to finish the three furlongs in 0:35 2-5. Goya had started once before, being beaten in a maiden race.

Maedic Falters at End.

In the Nursery, the first of three juvenile stakes on the Miami Jockey Club's forty-six-day calendar, the field got away to a good start and Hi-Vic shot out of the middle of the pack as they began to settle into their respective positions. The young gelding, owned by Crump, a former jockey, stole a narrow lead over Anglo-Saxon, Maedic and Goya.

The front runners were bunched across the track after the fashion of a cavalry charge in the final sixteenth, with Sam Renick's neglect-

Continued on Page Six.

U. S. BOBSLEDDERS WIN AT OLYMPICS; HOCKEY TEAM TIES

Brown Says Discarding Goggles Was a Big Help

GARMISCH - PARTENKIRCHEN, Germany, Feb. 15 (AP).—Ivan Brown attributed his Olympic bobsledding victory today not only to special runners but to two other factors—his comrade's powerful bobbing and the fact he wore no goggles in any of the four heats. Brown exposed his keen woodsman's eyes to the terrific pressure of a fifty-mile-an-hour speed in the belief this might achieve victory.

"Don't tell me those big square goggles don't add wind resistance," he said to The Associated Press correspondent. "I'll bet they would knock off one-hundredth of a second anyway, and we aren't passing up any hundredths in a race like that."

Brown was the only goggleless driver in the field.

BRITISH SIX HOLDS U. S. TO 0-0 DRAW

Olympic Hockey Title Seems Assured for England—Foes Battle 3 Extra Periods.

AMERICANS PRESS ATTACK

But Foster Proves a Giant in His Team's Net—Big Crowd on Hand—Canada Wins, 7-0.

By The Associated Press.

GARMISCH-PARTENKIRCHEN, Germany, Feb. 15.—Great Britain virtually clinched the Olympic ice hockey championship tonight by holding the United States to a scoreless tie.

The game was Britain's last in the final round-robin and gave her a total of 5 points. Only a United States victory over Canada by an unusually large score in the final game tomorrow can prevent Great Britain from taking the title won by Canada since the inception of the Winter Games in 1924.

A triumph over Canada would give America 5 points. The championship then would be decided on total goals, in which the Britons have a wide advantage. Canada, with one triumph and a defeat in two games, can do no better than finish second.

Tie Apparently Britain's Aim.

Today's game saw the teams battle through three extra periods. The Americans carried the attack to their opponents but each drive was turned back either by James Foster, former Winnipeg star playing in the nets for England, or the Britons' strong five-man defense. In contrast, the British made few drives into foreign territory, appearing content to play for a tie.

The Olympic stadium was completely sold out for the game. Almost springlike weather greeted spectators in contrast to the bitter cold of recent days.

Walter Brown, manager and coach of the United States squad, displayed a handful of fan mail from German fans wishing him bad luck saying, "We feel sorry for your boys."

In another final round-robin game Canada swamped Czechoslovakia, 7—0. The winners scored four goals in the first period and then eased up. Hugh Farquharson tallied twice, while Ken Farmer was credited with one goal and three assists.

The victory gave Canada a record of one triumph and one defeat in the finals. The Canadians' surprise 2-1 defeat by Great Britain in the second round was carried over to the finals.

La Batte Plays With Injury.

Phil La Batte of Minneapolis played with a heavily bandaged elbow when the U. S.-Britain game got under way. Both teams started cautiously, with Garrison making the first scoring attempt on a solo dash after two minutes. He nearly counted, the puck hitting Foster's chin and opening a gash.

The Americans' second line went in after six minutes and held an upper hand as Spain and Stubbs almost beat the English goalie twice. England appeared to be playing for a tie, driving long, wild shots down the rink.

In the second period the British forwards made a series of raids during the first three minutes that had Moone, the American goalie, in difficulty. After five minutes the Americans took control again as Garrison nearly blasted Foster from the nets with a shot from six feet out. The goalie just managed to fall on the disk.

Otherwise the period was not exciting, both sides displaying stubborn defensive tactics. Rowe and Garrison combined to get inside the British defense in the closing min-

Continued on Page Three.

BROWN IS HOME FIRST

Riding With Washbond, He Registers Initial American Victory.

COLGATE-LAWRENCE THIRD

Record for Run Is Shattered 22 Times, With Final Heat Deciding the Placings.

MISS HENIE IS ACCLAIMED

Norwegian Girl Gives a Great Performance—Tie Game Adds to Hockey Complications.

POINT STANDING.

Norway	104	Hungary	7
Germany	55	Belgium	5
Sweden	43	Canada	4
Finland	40	Czechoslovakia	4
United States	31½	France	4
Austria	29½	Netherlands	4
Switzerland	23	Italy	3
Great Britain	15	Japan	3

(Points are unofficial, computed on a 10-5-4-3-2-1 basis.)

By ALBION ROSS.

Wireless to THE NEW YORK TIMES.

GARMISCH-PARTENKIRCHEN, Germany, Feb. 15.—The United States won its first gold medal of the fourth Olympic Winter Games this morning when Ivan Brown, guide, caretaker and policeman of Keene Valley, N. Y., drove to victory in the two-man bobsledding competition. Although the United States now has lost completely through these Olympics its short-lived leadership in Winter sports acquired at Lake Placid four years ago, this bobsledding victory is well worth having.

The four heats proved one of the great sporting events of the games. The previous record for the run was broken twenty-two times in the most desperate struggle for places the Winter Olympics have yet provoked in the sixteen years of their existence.

American Lead Reduced.

After bettering the record on his first run yesterday by nearly three seconds and then bettering his own time by another second, Brown found himself this morning nevertheless at a disadvantage in his duel with Fritz Feierabend of Switzerland, who established a final course record yesterday of 1 minute 20.31 seconds. America's position was serious. The run was, as usual, slow until half a dozen sleds had gone down. Brown was drawn in the third starting position and the ambitious Swiss driver in seventeenth place.

The American sled had acquired in the first two heats yesterday a three-second lead. The unfortunate effect of Brown's position in the starting list appeared in the results of the first heat today. Feierabend reduced the American lead to two seconds. This was not so bad. But the situation became acute when Feierabend accomplished a bobbing miracle and established in his second heat a new record of 1 minute 19.88 seconds.

America seemed well on its way to losing its gold medal after it had appeared to be secure. It became necessary for Brown to make the run in 1 minute 21.72 seconds if he were to keep his lead over the Swiss driver.

The spectators held their breath as the American No. 1 sled started down on its fourth and last heat. Brown made the run in 1 minute 20.38 seconds. America had kept its gold medal and Feierabend had to be content with the silver.

Washbond Does His Part.

Gilbert Colgate Jr. of New York won the bronze medal with a time of 5 minutes 33.96 seconds for the four heats.

All the talk about Brown's victory is rather unfair to his rider, Alan Washbond, general store proprietor and bobsled fanatic of Keene Valley. Washbond is not only the proud possessor of some 230 pounds of ballast but he is a living contradiction of the "sack of sand" theory in bobsledding. Like "No Brakes" Bickford of the four-man team, Washbond although a family man and a pillar of Keene Valley society, does not believe in brakes. He does his part, instead, by "bobbing" steadily eight times every 100 yards or so.

Colgate and Brown are old friends and old rivals. Colgate demands that his rider, Richard W. Lawrence of Branchville, N. J., behave literally like the proverbial sack of sand. He is convinced bobbing does more harm than good. The results obtained through Washbond's bobbing efforts this time ought to settle the argument.

Colgate drove a great race but Brown and Washbond not only drove but bobbed their way to the gold medal. As Washbond expressed it in a cablegram to his wife: "We brought home the bacon on the old tin runners."

America is still in the running for a possible second gold medal, as our hockey team played to a 0-0 tie

Continued on Page Three.

MISS HENIE SCORES IN CLOSE CONTEST

Continued From Page One.

The nervousness soon disappeared, however. She swung into a répertoire of difficult figures, at one time executing a brilliant double Axel Paulsen jump, ending in a graceful split, to bring forth cheers from the crowd. At the end of her performance she received a 5.8 rating.

Miss Vinson's program was more conservative but she gave it perfectly to get a maximum rating on performance. Miss Peppe was popular, but, like Miss Vinson, her program was too conventional to gain a higher rating.

Miss Etsuko Inada, little Japanese skater, gave one of the most popular exhibitions as she sprang about the big ice stadium unconcerned and with all the fervor of youth.

U. S. BOBSLEDDERS WIN AT OLYMPICS

Continued From Page One.

with Great Britain in a night game that went three overtime periods and finished after midnight. The game apparently added new complications to the already hopelessly involved system of elimination scoring.

The German broadcaster at the stadium announced at the conclusion of the contest that Britain had clinched the gold medal. The announcement was promptly denied by the British coaches and hockey officials present.

Seen dimly through the smoke engendered by the hockey controversy now raging in every bar and café in the twin towns, it appears that America will have to defeat Canada tómorrow by some such score as 5 or 6 to 0 in order to win the tourney. As there is very little likelihood that the United States will be able to win at all, the stadium announcer was merely somewhat discourteously quick about broadcasting the demise of the American hopes for another gold medal.

It would appear, however, that our chances are excellent for obtaining second place. The United States, in any case, will take the bronze medal, as Czechoslovakia, the other competitor in the fourway finals, already has been eliminated by two painfully thorough defeats.

British Goalie Kept Busy.

Great Britain was kept almost constantly on the defensive tonight, its Anglo-Canadian goalie, James Foster, spending a good deal of his time on his knees struggling with three or even four American players who had gone in a huddle with the puck in front of his cage. Unfortunately, the Americans showed more ability getting into this advantageous position than they did in employing it for the purpose of goal-making.

The American combination fought its way successfully through the elimination round but it is not yet a genuine team with a plan and a technique of its own.

Great Britain, anxious to obtain at least a tie, played a defensive game and made only such raids on American ice as seemed necessary to stem the tide of the American advance.

The day's great event for Olympic guests has been the free figure skating competition for women at the Ice Stadium. Miss Sonja Henie of Norway, who had been so hard pressed by Miss Cecilia Colledge in the compulsory figures that the British enthusiasts were already hailing a new champion, definitely reestablished her threatened prestige by skating as well as she ever has in her long career and retaining her championship. Miss Colledge is the silver medalist and Miss Vivi-Anne Hulten of Sweden the bronze medalist.

Miss Vinson Does Well.

America's national champion, Miss Maribel Vinson, finished in fifth place after successfully presenting a difficult and well arranged program. Today Miss Vinson skated well. She was fast and confident, but apparently she lacked some element of perfection which the judges found in Miss Colledge.

The excitement has been intense here ever since it became known Sonja was in danger of defeat. Her performance today was a revelation to her self-appointed critics. Appearing in a carefully designed white and violet costume, she skated with all the vigor and much of the abandon of a girl just beginning rather than finishing the difficult career of a figure skater who has become a world figure. Opening with a Lutze jump, she performed her Axel Paulsen smoothly and the experts assert she showed in her spins, especially her cross-foot, more smoothness and complete mastery than ever before.

She had, as she always has in Europe, the crowd with her all the way, and her skating brought round after round of applause.

There was no doubt in the minds of the spectators about the identity of the world champion despite all the gossip that has been heard here during the last few days respecting Miss Colledge's chances. The English champion showed again today she is a great acrobat on skates but no dancer.

The Swedes made a clear sweep of the 50-kilometer ski race. They led all the way, taking all three medals. The American competitors fared poorly.

Margin Is 1.35 Seconds.

By The Associated Press.

GARMISCH-PARTENKIRCHEN, Germany, Feb. 15.—Ivan Brown and Alan Washbond successfully fought off the challenge of the great Swiss pilot, Fritz Feierabend, to win the two-man bobsledding competition today by the margin of 1.35 seconds and thus successfully defend the Olympic championship Hubert and Curtis Stevens won for the United States at Lake Placid four years ago.

It was a triumph for American ingenuity as well as speed and skill. A set of $2.48 runners of homemade spring steel they had made in their spare time carried Brown and Washbond to their spectacular victory.

Where Feierabend and other leading rivals were riding on Sheffield steel that set them back as high as $65 a set, the winners placed their faith in their own handicraft.

The total elapsed times for the three leaders were: Brown and Washbond, 5:29.29; Feierabend and Joseph Beerli, 5:30.64; Gilbert Colgate Jr. and Richard W. Lawrence, 5:33.96.

Colgate Praises Winners.

Colgate had nothing but praise for the winners and their sled.

"I think I got everything out of my sled it was built to give," he said, "but it wasn't enough to beat that pair."

Brown, who admitted he didn't sleep a wink after 2 A. M., said he thought he had made only one real mistake in his four runs. In the third run, he said, he misjudged the bend just before the Bavarian horseshoe and as a result hit the big ice wall too late. Fortunately, however, he escaped serious loss of speed.

Although they knew on their last trip just what time they had to make to win, Brown said "We weren't half as nervous then as we were on our first run."

The victory came almost as a birthday present for Brown, who will be 28 tomorrow.

When he went to the breakfast table this morning he found at his place a big cake, inscribed "Good Luck." His team-mates had it baked during the night and found a pastry expert who could write English.

Is Highly Superstitious.

Brown, incidentally, is just about the most superstitious pilot of them all. His pet "mania" takes the form of hunting hairpins. His eyes seldom leave the sidewalk any day until he has found one. Up to today, by actual tabulation, he hadn't failed for twenty-four consecutive days.

Washbond has no superstition except one—he'll ride with no driver except Brown. He never has.

When they originally formed the partnership Washbond was the driver and Brown the bobber. Three years ago, however, Washbond stepped into a hole and injured a knee. So there was nothing for Brown to do but learn to drive. They intend to stick together at least until they have won the 1940 Olympic championship.

Although Reto Capadrutt's chute standard of 1:25:20 took a fearful beating, only one accident marred the record-breaking proceedings. Henri Koch and Gustav Wagner of Luxembourg cracked up on Bavaria Curve today and suffered injuries severe enough to send both to the hospital.

Some of the skiers who helped put Norway into first place.

Times Wide World Photo.

BRITISH SIX HOLDS U. S. TO 0-0 DRAW

Continued From Page One.

utes but three swift shots bounced off Foster's pads. The aggressive Americans looked much the better team.

The crowd, which had expected something better, sat in stony silence as the teams continued to shadow box through the third period. One loud voice urged them to take chairs on the ice. The Americans were willing, but every time they got a scoring chance they ran into a five-man defense. Only Garrison managed to break through now and then for a flying shot.

Just before midway of the period Stubbs suddenly tore in for a couple of shots that forced Foster to making brilliant diving saves. With seven minutes to go, both teams opened up. There was a furious mix-up in front of the British goal, and Garrison was knocked out for a few minutes.

Smith looked as if he had a certain goal, with Foster drawn out of position, but a British player dived in and stopped the puck with his hand. Shaughnessy protested vigorously, but to no avail.

The United States players finally got a big hand as they came out for the first extra period. Foster still was shot with luck, making three sensational saves from off the sticks of Rowe and Smith in the opening minutes. Up to the mid-way point of the period Britain didn't give Moone a single save.

Body checking on both sides was fierce, while just before the period ended La Batte sailed in with the puck, but three Britons helped Foster escape.

At the start of the second extra period both teams began shooting from center ice in desperate hopes of scoring. Both goalies were too good, however.

Erhardt, British defenseman, made the first real shot after four minutes when he staged a one-man invasion. Moone caught the puck on his glove, however. Ross fought in for a close shot soon after but missed. A mixup in front of the British net at the end of the period nearly ended in a free-for-all. The referee sent Shaughnessy and Chappell to the penalty box.

Smith and Garrison opened the final period with two quick attacks that split the British defense. Practically all the play in the final five minutes was in the British end of the rink, with the weary American forwards fighting hard for the goal that wouldn't come. Garrison twice failed from in close as Foster's luck held to the final gun.

Results in Olympics

By The Associated Press.

YESTERDAY'S EVENTS.

Bobsledding.

Two-Man Competition—Won by Ivan Brown and Alan Washbond, United States.

Hockey.

United States 0, Great Britain 0. (Three extra periods.)

Canada 7, Czechoslovakia 0.

Skiing.

Fifty-Kilometer Race—Won by Elis Viklund, Sweden.

Figure Skating.

Women's Championship—Won by Miss Sonja Henie, Norway.

HOCKEY STANDINGS.

Final Round.

	W.	L.	T.	Pts.
Great Britain	2	0	1	5
United States	1	0	1	3
Canada	1	1	0	2
Czechoslovakia	0	3	0	0

(Great Britain and United States credited with victories over Canada and Czechoslovakia, respectively, scored in previous round-robin.)

PREVIOUS EVENTS.

Feb. 7.

Men's Downhill Ski Race (first part of combined competition)—Won by Birger Ruud, Norway.

Women's Downhill Ski Race (first part of combined competition)—Won by Miss Laila Schou Nilsen, Norway.

Feb. 8.

Women's Slalom Ski Race (second part of combined competition)—Won by Miss Christel Cranz, Germany.

Women's Combined Downhill and Slalom Ski Competition—Won by Miss Cranz.

PREVIOUS EVENTS.

Feb. 9.

Men's Slalom Ski Race (second part of combined competition)—Won by Franz Pfnuer, Germany.

Men's Combined Downhill and Slalom Ski Competition—Won by Franz Pfnuer.

Feb. 10.

Men's 40-Kilometer Ski Relay—Won by Finland (Sulo Nurmela, Klaes Karppinen, Matti Lahde and Kalle Jalkanen).

Feb. 11.

Men's 500-Meter Speed Skating Race—Won by Ivar Ballangrud, Norway.

Feb. 12.

Men's 5,000-Meter Speed Skating Race—Won by Ivar Ballangrud, Norway.

Four-Man Bobsledding Competition—Won by Switzerland (Pierre Musy, driver).

Men's 18-Kilometer Ski Race—Won by Erik Larsson, Sweden.

Feb. 13.

Men's Combined 18-Kilometer Ski Race and Jump—Won by Oddbjorn Hagen, Norway.

Men's 1,500-Meter Speed Skating Race—Won by Charles Mathisen, Norway.

Pairs' Figure Skating Competition—Won by Miss Maxi Herber and Ernst Baier, Germany.

Feb. 14.

Men's Figure Skating Championship—Won by Karl Schafer, Austria.

Men's 10,000-Meter Speed Skating Race—Won by Ivar Ballangrud, Norway.

The New York Times.

S Copyright, 1936, by The New York Times Company. SUNDAY, MAY 31, 1936. L++ S

71,754 SEE YANKEES TRIUMPH TWICE; GIANTS LOSE TWO; MEYER FIRST IN AUTO RACE; FIRETHORN TAKES SUBURBAN

166,000 AT INDIANAPOLIS

Coast Star Covers 500 Miles at 109.069 M.P.H. Average.

FIRST TO WIN THREE TIMES

Five Leaders at Finish All Break Record—Horn Second, Trailed by Rose, MacKenzie.

FIFTEEN COMPLETE COURSE

Miller, Hurled From Car After It Hits Guard Rail, Breaks Leg in Only Mishap of Day.

By The Associated Press.

INDIANAPOLIS, Ind., May 30.—Accomplishing what no other driver has done, Louis Meyer of Huntington Park, Calif., roared to his third victory in the 500-mile automobile race over the Indianapolis Motor Speedway today in record-breaking time and with a record-smashing crowd cheering him wildly.

Meyer drove his four-cylinder special the full 500 miles without relief and made only two quick stops. He covered the distance in 4 hours 35 minutes 3.39 seconds, to average 109.069 miles an hour, breaking the previous record of 106.240 miles per hour, hung up by Kelly Petillo, colorful Italian driver, also of Huntington Park, Calif., in winning America's speed classic last year. Meyer won before in 1928 and 1933.

Another Californian, 27-year-old Ted Horn of Los Angeles, finished second, nearly three miles behind Meyer, with Mauri Rose of Dayton, Ohio, third, seven and a half miles back. George (Doc) MacKenzie of Eddington, Pa., was fourth. Petillo, driving the last 125 miles as relief, piloted the car over the finish line for MacKenzie. Chet Miller of Detroit was fifth and Ray Pixley of Fullerton, Calif., sixth. The first five cars to finish broke the old record.

$35,000 Goes to Winner

Fifteen of the original thirty-two starters finished and only five ran out of gasoline, which was restricted to 37.5 gallons for each over the 500 miles.

Meyer's triumph completed the only triple ever made in the event.

As a result of his victory Meyer earned about $35,000, of which $20,000 was first-prize money, with the additional coming from lap prizes and checks from accessory manufacturers. He snatched the lead at the 225-mile mark, when Babe Stapp of Los Angeles and Wilbur Shaw of Indianapolis, at that time the flying leaders, ran into trouble. The car driven by Stapp, tearing along the backstretch at terrific speed, broke a rear axle, forcing him out of the race.

Shaw had to stop at the pits to replenish his fuel supply and then Meyer bounded into the lead. He retained it for only a short time, however, when he was forced to stop for gasoline. He quickly regained it, and with a terrific burst of speed that carried him around the two and one-half-mile brick and asphalt track at a rate of 115 miles per hour, he clung to the lead to the finish.

About seven and one-half miles from the checkered flag he reduced his speed to about 98 miles an hour to save gas. When he brought his car to a stop there were a pint and a half of fuel in his tank and three gallons in his pits.

Most 'Enjoyable' Race

His face smeared with grease, Meyer said today's race was the most enjoyable in which he ever participated because he did not know until the finish that he was going to triumph.

The record-breaking crowd of 166,000 spectators, lured to the track partly as a result of thirty-one deaths since racing was started in 1908, saw only one accident today. Al Miller of Detroit sustained a fractured left leg. Roaring down the stretch in full sight of thousands of spectators in the stands lining the track, he was injured when the front axle broke and his speeding car cracked into a guard rail.

The car swerved back onto the course with Miller's mechanic, Jimmy Jackson of Indianapolis, still sitting in it. The race was immediately slowed down to 60 miles an hour while the wrecked car was hauled off the course. Jackson jumped to safety.

Miller was thrown out of the car and slid across the track. The automobile smashed into the guard rail with terrific force, a piece of the rail piercing the hood and shooting back almost to the seats. Miller lost part of his left leg in a motorcycle accident several years ago and today's fracture was of the same limb.

"I'm pretty lucky," he said as he was being lifted into an ambulance. "I just broke my 'wooden leg.'"

The fracture was between the knee and the hip and may necessitate further amputation.

That was the only accident of the race and the safety of the newly constructed turns, guarded with retaining walls, was proved. It was

Continued on Page Eight

Louis Meyer, Winner at Indianapolis

Times Wide World Photo.

CRAWFORD BEATEN BY BUDGE'S RALLY

Five-Set Victory Gives U. S. Even Break With Australia in Davis Cup Singles.

TWO POINTS FROM DEFEAT

But Californian Makes Brilliant Stand—Quist Downs Allison in the Opener.

By ALLISON DANZIG

Special to THE NEW YORK TIMES.

PHILADELPHIA, May 30.—In the most thrilling Davis Cup match played in this country since 1927, Donald Budge came back from the jaws of defeat today to save an apparently lost cause for the American tennis team at the Germantown Cricket Club.

With a capacity crowd of 7,000 experiencing the same agonizing moments known here when the cup was lost to France nine years ago, the tall, red-headed Californian fought a magnificent uphill battle to defeat Jack Crawford and earn an even division of the opening day's spoils for the United States in the tie with Australia. The score was 6—2, 6—3, 4—6, 1—6, 13—11.

To appreciate how tremendously important a conquest Budge made today, it should be understood that before it was encompassed, the cruelly thin margin of two points was all that stood between his team and practical elimination from the Davis Cup play for the first time in many years in the preliminary competition.

Outlook Appears Dark

Wilmer Allison, the national champion, had gone down before Adrian Quist of Australia in the opening match, 6—3, 5—7, 6—4, 6—1, and when Crawford, rallying after the loss of the first two sets, had reached 5—3 in the fifth chapter, America's hopes seemed irretrievably sunk.

Invincible for the first two sets, Budge had let the match get away from him in the third and from

Continued on Page Eight

OMAHA, 10-11, FIRST IN TWO-MILE EVENT

Woodward Colt Wins by Neck From Bobsleigh for Second Straight in England.

POWERFUL FINISH DECIDES

American Racer Comes From Last Place to Take Queens Plate Before 10,000.

By The Associated Press.

LONDON, May 30.—William Woodward's Omaha, racing two miles for the first time in his gallant career, defeated Lord Derby's Bobsleigh in as thrilling a finish as likely will be seen in England this or any other Summer as he won the Queens Plate at Kempton Park today for his second straight victory on foreign soil.

As 10,000 fans stood in almost paralyzed silence, the magnificent American chestnut, a son of Gallant Fox, and Lord Derby's great runner stepped through the last two furlongs like true champions with Omaha's neck just in front. He kept it there right to the pole as the rival jockeys, Pat Beasley and R. Perryman, flailed Omaha and Bobsleigh, respectively, for all they were worth.

Mrs. C. Rich's Silverlit was six lengths back, third in the field of five.

Stirring Stretch Drive

From the time Omaha, in a few giant strides, came from last place to draw abreast Bobsleigh in the stretch and then thrust his head in front their positions scarcely deviated six inches.

The victory, capped by his finishing sprint, removed any doubt of Omaha's ability to go the two and one-half miles of the Ascot Gold Cup, his chief objective, which will be run June 18. Bobsleigh also is eligible for the race.

"What a colt," said Beasley, his wrists weary from holding Omaha in check the first half-mile while the outsiders set a slow pace. "He does not like that kind of running."

The triumph over Bobsleigh,

Continued on Page Eleven

Major League Baseball

American League

YESTERDAY'S RESULTS

New York 7, Washington 1 (1st).
New York 6, Washington 1 (2d).
Philadelphia 6, Boston 4 (1st).
Boston 6, Philadelphia 2 (2d).
St. Louis 5, Detroit 3 (1st).
St. Louis 5, Detroit 0 (2d).
Cleveland 4, Chicago 3 (1st).
Cleveland 11, Chicago 3 (2d).

STANDING OF THE CLUBS

	New York	Boston	Cleveland	Detroit	Wash'gton	Chicago	Phila'phia	St. Louis	Won	Lost	Percentage
New York	—	4	5	2	6	2	6	4	29	13	.690
Boston	3	—	1	4	5	6	4	3	26	17	.605
Cleveland	0	3	—	4	3	4	2	7	23	17	.575
Detroit	2	1	5	—	4	6	3	2	23	20	.535
Wash'gton	2	5	2	2	—	0	6	4	21	22	.488
Chicago	2	0	1	3	3	—	3	7	19	20	.487
Phila'phia	3	3	1	1	1	1	—	3	13	26	.333
St. Louis	1	1	2	4	0	1	2	—	11	30	.268
Games lost	13	17	17	20	22	20	26	30	—	—	

GAMES TODAY

Boston at New York (3 P. M.).
Washington at Philadelphia.
St. Louis at Detroit.
Chicago at Cleveland.

National League

YESTERDAY'S RESULTS

Brooklyn 9, New York 6 (1st).
Brooklyn 3, New York 0 (2d).
Philadelphia 5, Boston 4 (1st).
Philadelphia 9, Boston 6 (2d).
Pittsburgh 7, Chicago 5 (1st).
Pittsburgh 11, Chicago 7 (2d).
Cincinnati 10, St. Louis 1 (1st).
St. Louis 7, Cincinnati 4 (2d).

STANDING OF THE CLUBS

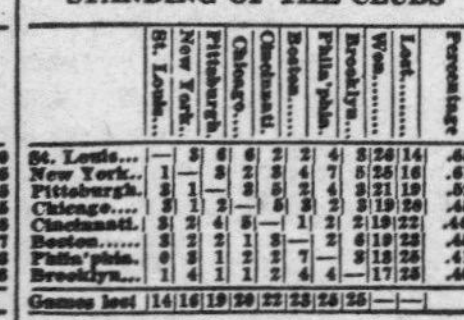

	St. Louis	New York	Pittsburgh	Chicago	Cincinnati	Boston	Phila'phia	Brooklyn	Won	Lost	Percentage
St. Louis	—	3	6	6	2	2	4	3	26	14	.650
New York	1	—	3	2	3	4	7	5	25	16	.610
Pittsburgh	3	1	—	3	5	2	4	3	21	19	.525
Chicago	3	1	2	—	5	3	2	3	19	20	.487
Cincinnati	3	2	4	5	—	1	2	2	19	22	.463
Boston	3	2	2	1	3	—	2	6	19	23	.452
Phila'phia	0	3	1	2	2	7	—	3	18	25	.419
Brooklyn	1	4	1	1	2	4	4	—	17	25	.405
Games lost	14	16	19	20	22	23	25	25	—	—	

GAMES TODAY

New York at Brooklyn (3 P. M.).
Philadelphia at Boston.
Pittsburgh at Chicago.
Cincinnati at St. Louis.

FIRETHORN LEADS GRANVILLE BY NOSE IN 50TH SUBURBAN

Camera Decides $15,625 Race in Favor of Jeffords's Entry Before 25,000 at Belmont.

SCINTILLATOR, 12-1, FIRST

Untermyer Colt Beats Apogee in Juvenile—Richards Rides Both Stake Winners.

By BRYAN FIELD

Closing with a rush that electrified 25,000 persons, Firethorn was up in the last stride at Belmont Park yesterday to nip Granville on the post and win by a nose in one of the most thrilling finishes the famous Suburban Handicap has known in all its fifty runnings. When the photograph of the finish was officially examined, Firethorn's number was displayed to give the Walter M. Jeffords color bearer the second big stake victory of his career.

Granville covered himself with glory, for he is only 3 and under the scale of weights was conceding eleven pounds to Firethorn, which is a 4-year-old. Moreover, he made much of the early pace and held on so gamely that many were found who thought that he might have won.

Whopper Two Lengths Back

Two lengths back of the pair which finished so closely locked, Hal Price Headley's Whopper was third, leading Good Goods by a length. William Woodward, owner of Granville, saw the keen race of his colt and also learned at the park of the victory of his Omaha in England. For this score, as well as the showing of Granville, he was warmly congratulated on all sides.

Granville is preparing for the Belmont Stakes next Saturday and has many admirers who think the colt will go on to become the 3-year-old champion. He shouldered scale weight of 108 pounds against Firethorn's 116. Firethorn paid 6-1.

Harry Richards was the winning rider aboard Firethorn and brought off a stake double in that he also was up on the Juvenile Stakes winner, Scintillator. This 12-to-1 shot is owned by Alvin Untermyer, and Richards brought the colt up with a rush along the rail to score by a scant head in a finish that also called for a photograph to decide.

World Record Holder Fourth

In this test Alfred Gwynne Vanderbilt's three-furlong world record holder, Airflame, ran gamely and well, but met his first defeat when he brought up fourth. The filly Apogee, Fashion Stakes winner and a record breaker at Narragansett Park, was second to Scintillator, leading Billionaire by a length. The five-furlong sprint was run in 1:00 4-5 and the race grossed $7,375, with $6,500 to the winner.

The first of the three stakes fell to Joseph E. Widener, who scored a double. His Bushranger captured the Corinthian Steeplechase Handicap immediately after his home-bred filly, Magic Circle, was first in the curtain raiser.

Bushranger's score marked the ninth time that Mr. Widener's colors have been in front in this test of about two miles through the field. The 6-year-old gelding was first by two lengths at 3 to 4 and was timed in 3:43 3-5.

He earned $1,580 and was handled by Henry Little. Only three ran, Birmingham taking the place by two lengths from Jungle King.

Program Delayed Slightly

The Suburban grossed $15,625, of which the winner's share was $12,125. The running was witnessed by one of the largest crowds to visit Belmont Park in years, the program being delayed slightly so that all might reach seats or points of vantage before the sport began.

There was only a slight post delay for the big race, Identify getting away in front when the word came. Coldsteam and Granville never were far away, and as they ran down the long straightaway of the backstretch, Coldstream took the lead. Granville gained a good position to the outside of Coldstream, and when they went to the far turn Jockey Stout sent the 3-year-old into the lead.

All this time Firethorn was last or next to last, battling for that doubtful distinction with Good Goods. The run around the bend saw Granville pull out to a lead of a couple of lengths, with Whopper now moving to contention and Firethorn making a stern bid on the outside.

Stout Goes to Work

Straightened away for home, it still was Granville in front, with Firethorn now charging fastest of all. He went past Whopper as the effort of Good Goods to stay with him was unavailing.

In the last furlong it appeared that Firethorn would go on to win decisively, but Stout went to work in earnest on Granville and the younger racer hung on grimly and like a keen colt.

Through the last sixteenth there was little to choose between the two and they passed under the wire as a team. Whopper in the meantime had held on to be third, with Good Goods getting fourth money.

The time for the mile and a quarter was 2:04 3-5 over a fast track

Continued on Page Ten

Lazzeri Out at Home in Second Game at Yankee Stadium

Associated Press Photo.

The New York player attempted to score, but was tagged by Bolton, Washington catcher

Cornell's Trackmen Win; Harvard 2d, Dartmouth 3d

Ithacans Register a Decisive Triumph in the I. C. A. A. A. A. Meet—Nine Titles to Sophomores—O'Brien a Victor.

By ARTHUR J. DALEY

Special to THE NEW YORK TIMES.

PHILADELPHIA, May 30.—Riding along on the crest of the inspirational lift that had headed it in the direction of the team championship of the Intercollegiate A. A. A. A. after yesterday's trials, Cornell captured the title today, slamming the door in Harvard's face at the ninth event and nailing it fast from there on.

In the beginning the Crimson rallied its faltering forces to make it close and then the faltering started all over again. Thus as the shadows began to lengthen over Franklin Field exuberant Ithaca graduates were thumping the back of the 72-year-old Jack Moakley, for the Red team had accomplished a feat that had seemed impossible of achievement just two days before.

Cornell had won its tenth intercollegiate crown since that shrewd old master of the coaching art, Moakley, had taken charge at Ithaca thirty-eight years ago. And the Red squad had become the first Eastern winner since 1924.

The triumph was clear-cut and conclusive. Cornell tallied 29½ points and then came in order Harvard with 19 16-21, Dartmouth with 19 3-7, Pitt with 18, Manhattan with 15, Penn with 14 and Princeton with 13.

Only two individual championships dropped into the Cornell basket. One was expected. That was the victory of Walter (Duke) Wood in the discus throw. The other was an astounding surprise that actually clinched top honors for the indomitable brigade from Ithaca.

Herbert Cornell of Cornell brought added fame to a great name by coming up from the ranks of the unheralded to take the 3,000-meter title by inches from Jim Rafferty of Fordham and give the Red a solid block of points that it had had no right even to hope for.

That success broke Cornell away

Continued on Page Three

GOLF TITLE TAKEN BY MRS. DIETRICH

Victor Halts Mrs. Kirkland by 1 Up on 36th Green in Metropolitan Final.

Special to THE NEW YORK TIMES.

HEWLETT HARBOR, L. I., May 30.—By the power of her putter, Mrs. Henry H. Dietrich defeated Mrs. William R. Kirkland Jr., 1 up, on the thirty-sixth hole at Seawane today and became the 1936 women's metropolitan golf champion. Runner-up to Mrs. Jonathan Thorne last year, when she was Miss Betty Pietsch, Mrs. Dietrich acquired the title after a match filled with much spotty play but many dramatic moments.

The victor finished the morning round in 88, with a one-hole advantage over Mrs. Kirkland. She started the afternoon session with a winning streak which left her 5 up at the end of the seventh, and she kept this lead around the turn, which she reached in 42, until she stood 5 up and 5 to play approaching the fourteenth.

Victor Excels on Greens

Here the tide of battle turned, and a match which should have ended on that hole continued, amid growing excitement from the gallery, to the very end. Mrs. Kirkland won four holes in a row until she was only 1 down coming to the home green. Here, after a magnificent approach from the rough, she three-putted, while Mrs. Dietrich, who was on in 4 after a trapped drive, rescued a title which

Continued on Page Eight

FORDHAM RALLIES TO DOWN YALE, 7-6

Palau's Homer With Ladroga on Base in Eighth Settles Hard-Hitting Clash.

Special to THE NEW YORK TIMES.

NEW HAVEN, Conn., May 30.—Fordham three times came from behind Yale today and finally, with an eight-inning rally, sent two runs across the plate for a 7-to-6 victory. The Elis outhit the Rams, 12—7, but failed to make the most of them.

Home runs by Andy Palau and Larry Kelly were outstanding in the heavy hitting game. Palau's drive, sending home ahead of him Bill Ladroga, enabled the visitors to come from behind and win in the eighth.

3,000 in Attendance

Kelley, with four hits, led Yale's attack. Dick Cummins's catch of Proctor's liner over second in the fourth was the most brilliant fielding feature. Both Albie Gurske and Bernie Rankin, who pitched the first seven innings, respectively, for their teams, were fairly effective in the face of terrific bombardments.

About 3,000 spectators saw the game, which added another to a long series of annual defeats of Yale by Fordham.

In the opening inning Cook walked and Cummins singled. Hor-

Continued on Page Two

GIANTS ARE TRIPPED TWICE BY DODGERS

38,000 See Terrymen Outfumble Rivals to Lose Opener, 9 to 6.

BRANDT HURLS SHUT-OUT

Allows 3 Hits as Stengeleers Win Nightcap, 3-0—Only Two Reach Second.

By ROSCOE McGOWEN

For the first time in years the Dodgers won a double header from the Giants at Ebbets Field yesterday and 38,000 fans, jamming the stands beyond seating capacity, were well-nigh overcome by the spectacle. So was Colonel Bill Terry, who saw his infield crack up in each game to let in important runs.

The first game was a 9-6 triumph for Lefty Clark, featuring a second inning, five-run rally on two hits against the hitherto undefeated Harry Gumbert, and home runs by Hank Leiber and Sambo Leslie.

Ed Brandt was the star of the nightcap, allowing only three Giant hits for a 3-0 shutout, during which only two Giants got as far as second base.

Everybody in Flatbush was happy after the two games with the exception of four over-worked groundkeepers, who were kept busy far beyond twilight trying to clear the field of the carpet of torn paper which had begun floating out of the packed stands during the late innings of the finale.

5,000 Turned Away

Perhaps 5,000 persons were turned away before the first game started, as there was no more standing room even that early. Many who had purchased unreserved grandstand seats were much disgruntled because they couldn't find a seat after they got in.

Adding to the general joy of the occasion were bitter arguments in both games that resulted in the banishment of two players. Joe Stripp was majestically thumbed out in the eighth inning of the opener by Umpire Ziggy Sears when he protested too violently that Hank Leiber's two-bagger was foul by a foot.

In the afterpiece Master Melvin Ott was chased away by Umpire Ballanfant when the outfielder denied vehemently he had been tagged out by Jordan in the second inning.

Opener a Game of Fumbles

The first game was pretty much a case of the Giants outfumbling the Dodgers. Junior Frey fumbled grounders by Whitehead in the first and third innings and both misplays were followed shortly by the Leiber and Leslie homers. But even after Sam's clout in the third the Stengelers still led, 5—4.

In the second Frey opened with a high bounding single to Mayo but eventually made the second out at third on Bartell's nice play and things didn't look threatening for the Terrymen. At this point Whitehead chose to fumble Clark's

Continued on Page Six

THRONG JAMS STADIUM

10,000 Turned Away as Yanks Rout Senators, 7-1 and 6-1.

PEARSON AND RUFFING WIN

Monte Scores Eighth Triumph and Charley Gives Only Two Safeties in Nightcap.

NEW YORKERS BAT HARD

Gehrig, Selkirk and Crosetti Hit Homers—DiMaggio Gets Three Straight Doubles.

By JAMES P. DAWSON

The biggest baseball crowd of the year yesterday welcomed the Yankees back to the Stadium and saw a typical exhibition of Yankee hitting strength together with the best pitching performance the club has had as the McCarthymen downed the Senators in both ends of a double-header.

A gathering of 71,754, of whom 70,525 paid, used every available vantage point in the big Bronx ball park to see the Yanks boost their American League lead over the Red Sox to three and one-half games as they stretched their winning streak to four straight.

There have been few larger crowds. Fans stood on runways and ramps and squatted on the stone steps of the aisles in the three-decked stand. It was estimated that more than 10,000 were turned away because of construction work on the bleachers which reduced the park's capacity in this direction. Many others, arriving at the park too late to get a seat or even an advantageous standing place, had their money refunded.

A Perfect Climax

This tremendous gathering saw Charley (Red) Ruffing provide the greatest pitching performance of the Yankee year in the nightcap, when he set Washington down, 6 to 1. In the wake of a stellar performance by Monte Pearson in the opener and in combination with a twenty-six-hit attack that was spread over both games this supplied a perfect climax. Pearson scored his eighth victory in the opener, 7 to 1.

Ruffing held the enemy to two sparse hits, something no other Yankee pitcher has done this year, although Pearson approaches this exhibition of near perfection. Ruffing, in his three previous victories, also boasts a four-hit shut-out over the Indians and a four-hit victory over the Browns.

Seldom in his career has Ruffing pitched so well. Through the nine innings only thirty men faced him, three more than the minimum. The excess was contained in a home run by Joe Kuhel in the fifth, a single by Buddy Myer in the fourth and a pass to Kuhel in the eighth.

Fine Batting Support

Supporting this marvelous hurling was a twelve-hit attack that held the sixth homers of the season for both George Selkirk and Frankie Crosetti, a triple by Selkirk as well, three successive doubles by the irrepressible Joe DiMaggio and some fancy blows by Lou Gehrig and Ben Chapman.

Gehrig also got his seventh homer of the year in the fourth inning of the opener to start the Yanks on the victory road.

Ruffing surpassed Buck Newsom and Fred Marberry, two of his mound rivals, beyond comparison. Neither was there at the finish, as Pete Appleton, who was known as Pete Jablonowski with the Yanks, finished.

DiMaggio's second double opened a four-run attack in the fourth that spelled disaster for Newsom. He scored on Gehrig's single and Selkirk's homer into the right-field bleachers meant two more. A double by Chapman and a single by Tony Lazzeri followed to give New York enough to win.

Another Tally in Fifth

They got another in the fifth, when DiMaggio cracked his third double and scored on Gehrig's second single. Crosetti made his homer in the seventh, a drive into the lower left-field stand, to Nick Marberry for a run.

Pearson romped off with the opener with a masterful exhibition. His hurling went hand in hand with a fourteen-hit attack in which Joe Glenn, Red Robert Rolfe, Crosetti, Chapman and Lazzeri lent able support to Gehrig's circuit blast.

Pearson had two weak moments. Bolton's double and Powell's single fashioned an enemy run in the fifth, tying the count. In the ninth, successive singles by Kuhel, Kress and Bolton jammed the bases with one out, but Chapman and DiMaggio pulled down flies to dismiss the danger.

At the time Pearson could afford to be lenient because he was hugging the five-run lead with which he finished. Four hits, including Rolfe's double, gave the Yanks

Continued on Page Seven

MEYER HOME FIRST IN 500-MILE RACE

Continued From Page One

the first time in years that the race was run without death or a serious accident.

The "tough luck" driver of the race was William (Shorty) Cantlon of Detroit, who was never out of fifth place and always a dangerous challenger after the first 100 miles had been reeled off. With only seven laps to go and clinging tenaciously to third place, Cantlon ran out of gas.

Misfortune hit the pre-race favorites early. Wild Bill Cummings of Indianapolis, winner of the race in 1934, never started. His car balked as the field roared away, because his clutch stuck. He worked frantically over it for half an hour while the other drivers roared on but could not get it started. Then he quit in despair.

Youthful Rex Mays, 23-year-old boy from Los Angeles, one of the pre-race favorites, shot into the lead at the start, but after setting the pace for thirteen laps was forced into the pits by motor trouble and finally ran out of gas in the last stages of the race after he had worked himself back into sixth position. Freddy Frame, Los Angeles, winner in 1932, surrendered after seven and one-half miles, because of a broken spring.

Drives Away in New Car

Meyer, after changing his clothes, rode away from the track in a brand new car. Mrs. Meyer, at the wheel, said she "didn't mind if Louie continued to race as long as he won. I was excited from the start but I knew he would win this time."

Their son, Louis, Jr., 5 years old, remained home in California while his daddy was hanging up the triple victory.

The car in which Mrs. Meyer drove Louis back to his hotel was the one her husband had won as leader at the 200th lap. In the back seat was Meyer's mechanic.

MEYER WILL DRIVE AGAIN

Indianapolis Victor Happy After Third Triumph in Grind.

INDIANAPOLIS, May 30 (AP).—Champion of all Speedway champions, Louis Meyer, 32 years old and the only three-time winner in the history of the 500-mile Indianapolis marathon, said today as he sat in the winner's enclosure:

"Tell every one for me that I am not going to quit just because I won for the third time. I am not through with racing. Racing is what I like most. I am going to be back in there next year to win. Just wait and see."

The average race driver considers his competitive career complete if he once gets the checkered flag at the Speedway. Louis also won in 1928 and 1933, but he described today's grind, in which he set a new speed mark, as the most fun.

"This was the most marvelous race in which I've ever driven and, believe me, I was happier to get the flag than ever before," he said.

"I had darned tough luck before this race, as you know. I had motor trouble and breakdowns galore. If you don't believe I worked to win this race, you should have been in my garage for the last month.

"I'm not kiddin' you. I worked night and day to get the car in shape. But she sure ran when I got her fixed. I didn't figure I had won the race until I got the checkered flag. That was on account of the gasoline. Gasoline was my biggest worry. I was sure of the car, but the gas—I held my breath."

Grimy as he drove off the track, Louis's first request was for a bottle of milk.

"Be sure to give my crew plenty of credit," he said between drinks. "If it wasn't for them I never would have won. Dale Drake, Lawson Harris, Carl Effman, Floyd Gigax and Kenneth Wenz, my crew, had my car in perfect shape. Without that, you know, the best driver in the world cannot win."

Meyer added he would celebrate his triple victory with a "private party" tonight—"just my wife and my friends who have been with me all along."

Meyer said he planned to continue racing through the rest of the current season.

An idea of the confidence his friends had in him came from Harris, his mechanic, who also rode to victory with Louis in 1933. As the winning car came off the track, Harris slapped Meyer repeatedly on the back and yelled:

"What'd I tell you; what'd I tell you!"

How Drivers Finished In 500-Mile Auto Race

INDIANAPOLIS, May 30 (AP).—The finish of the twenty-fourth 500-mile automobile race today, with the speeds:

Driver. Home.	M.P.H.
1—Lou Meyer, Los Angeles	109.069
2—Ted Horn, Los Angeles	108.170
3—Mauri Rose, Dayton, Ohio	107.864
4—Kelly Petillo, Los Angeles, and Doc MacKenzie, Eddington, Pa.	107.460
5—Chet Miller, Detroit	106.919
6—Ray Pixley, Fullerton, Calif.	105.253
7—Wilbur Shaw, Indianapolis	104.233
8—George Barringer, Houston, Tex.	102.630
9—Zeke Meyer, Germantown, Pa.	101.824
10—George Connor, Los Angeles	98.931

CRAWFORD BEATEN BY BUDGE'S RALLY

Continued From Page One

thereon, until Crawford stood at 5—4 and 30-all in the fifth, it seemed that America could reconcile itself to the end of the 1936 campaign in this series.

Allison was so far off his true form in losing to Quist, realizing the worst fears over his inability to find his touch all Spring, that it was unthinkable that he could beat Crawford on Monday, even should the United States win the doubles tomorrow.

A Trying Moment

It was as trying a moment for a young player as could be conceived, particularly when he was opposed to as cunning and experienced an opponent as the giant Australian with the hammer of Thor in his forehand. Those two points that stood between Budge and defeat were all that also separated the United States from its most disheartening setback in the nine years that it has campaigned to reclaim the international trophy.

The indomitable manner in which the gangling, flaming-thatched Californian lifted his game in this dire extremity to turn back an opponent who almost won over the partisan crowd with his gameness redounded even more to his credit than did the great tennis he played in the early stages. It took not only a player with first-class strokes to defeat Crawford but also a player with the heart of a lion and the match temperament that refuses to yield to the vicissitudes of fortune.

Two hours and twenty-five minutes after Levan Richards had got the match under way, the frenziedly happy crowd was storming down from the jammed stands to acclaim the youthful hero, who was stretched out on chairs with a cramp in his leg. One was reminded of the excitement amounting almost to pandemonium that carried away the crowd here in 1927 when the Four Musketeers of France ended America's long reign.

Removes Throng's Despair

For more than an hour during the last three sets today the gallery had sat almost frozen with fear at the thought that the misfortune of 1927 was to be repeated on the return of Davis Cup play to Germantown for the first time in that long interval. Budge's victory lifted the great throng from the depths of despair to delirious joy in the knowledge that the United States was still in the running for the series honors.

With the series tied at 1—all, the doubles match will be held tomorrow afternoon at 3:30 between Crawford and Quist and Budge and Gene Mako of Los Angeles, with an exhibition singles between Vivian McGrath of Australia and Bryan M. Grant Jr. of Atlanta as an added attraction. On Monday, Allison will play Crawford in the first of the final two singles and Budge will engage Quist.

The outcome of the doubles, in which the Australian pair, who hold the Wimbledon championship, rule the slight favorites, may well decide the series. Budge is judged to have a better than even chance of defeating Quist, but before they go on the courts Allison must play Crawford and unless the American champion can woo the muse of inspiration during the next forty-eight hours or Crawford is weakened by the ordeal of playing three successive days, the outlook is none too reassuring for the Americans.

Allison was so far off his game today, except for the second set, that it was difficult to visualize him as the almost perfect player who lowered the colors of Fred Perry at Forest Hills last September. Lacking in confidence, the Texan had neither the control nor the finality of stroke to withstand the coolly discerning and steadfastly deep backcourt attack of the younger Australian.

Quist did not need to show the full strength of his hand with Allison presenting him so much in the way of mistakes. The gallery could only shake its collective head in sad recollection of the great player it saw at Forest Hills last year and which it saw for only a brief spell this afternoon as Allison attacked with his characteristic gusto and elan at the net in the second set.

The opening match put something of a damper on the enthusiasm of the crowd, which, in spite of its effort to be impartial, could not conceal its partisanship with alternate whoops of delight and heavy groans during the following engagement. It was the biggest crowd to turn out for any tennis event in this country, with the exception of the national championships, during the past nine years and it would have been even larger had there been sufficient accommodations.

Not only did it pack every seat in the surrounding stands but it overflowed in hundreds on the turf against the backstops. Scores stood throughout the long afternoon, and neighboring trees and walls enclosing the club grounds offered vantage points for many others.

Included in the throng were the British Ambassador, Sir Ronald Lindsay, and the Russian Ambassador, Alexander A. Troyanovsky.

Puts Rival on Defensive

If enthusiasm was lacking in the opening contest, the crowd more than made up for its apathy in the closing match. Right at the start its mood changed as Budge opened with an attack reminiscent of Ellsworth Vines's to put Crawford on the defensive and keep him straining for the ball in the far corners of the court.

The far-flung attack of the Californian appeared to be more than the stalwart and heavier Crawford could cope with, and the gallery roared its delight as Budge's famed backhand creased the lines and paved the way for his winning assaults from the net.

By the end of the first set, all traces of consternation had disappeared from the stands and as the American opened with a love game in the second set the crowd's gayety bespoke its confidence that the series was as good as squared then and there.

Budge evidently felt pretty much the same way about it, for he now abjured going to the net and met the issue from the back of the court. He was immediately to learn how ambitious an undertaking it is to stand off Crawford from long range, and it was only after he had trailed at 0—30 that he won each of his next two service games.

But from there on the Californian's ground strokes stood forth irresistibly through the set, and the pressure of his drives exacted submission from Crawford, who could not quite withstand the depth and speed of his younger opponent's drives.

With Budge leading, 2 sets to 0, the verdict seemed near at hand. The veteran Crawford apparently had neither the strokes nor the mobility and endurance to cope with the young Californian. But the big man from "Down Under" gave a class exhibition of court tactics in the next two sets. The power and depth of his marvelous, solid forehand and his ever faithful sliced backhand won him the third set, in which Budge unexplainably let up and found himself on the defensive in a back court duel.

It was felt that Budge would realize his mistake during the intermission and come out with his guns blazing for the fourth. It still looked like his match. And so the American did come out fighting, but instead of swarming all over Crawford, Budge now found himself checkmated in the most disheartening manner as the Australian put on a defensive exhibition that was more damaging than any straight forward attack could have been and Budge yielded the chapter at 6—1.

Then came the agonizing fifth set, in which there were five successive breaks through service after the first two games and during which the crowd was alternately torn with such doubts and raised to such ecstasies of relief as to leave it almost as limp and exhausted as were the players at the end.

Times Wide World Photo.

PRESENTATION OF TITLE GOLF TROPHY

Miss Josephine F. Windle, chairman of the tournament, handing trophy to Mrs. Henry H. Dietrich just after latter had defeated Mrs. William R. Kirkland Jr. (left) in final for metropolitan crown.

LINKS HONORS WON BY MRS. DIETRICH

Continued From Page One

for a few bad minutes had seemed to be slipping away from her by calmly holing a five-foot putt.

Throughout the two rounds there was a piquant contrast in the long and short games of the two contenders. Mrs. Kirkland outplayed Mrs. Dietrich both with her drives and long approaches by often as much as forty yards.

But once they neared the green the cup seemed to be a magnet for Mrs. Dietrich's irons and putter. Until she began missing at the fourteenth it seemed she could do no wrong, which Mrs. Kirkland threw away her hitting advantage by under-chipping and inaccurate putting.

The seventh of the second round demonstrated the way the play went. Here both balls were on the far edge of the green in 3, lying side by side. Mrs. Dietrich almost holed out, while Mrs. Kirkland rolled her's past the cup and then missed a two-footer coming back.

At the short holes Mrs. Kirkland was not reaching the green from the tee. At the eighth, when she clubbed up and then holed a 14-foot putt, a loo. of pleased surprise crossed her face. It was the first time she had done that all day.

Again at the twelfth Mrs. Dietrich took her magic putter to hole out from eighteen feet and save a halved 5 after a degree of trap trouble that should in ordinary circumstances have given Mrs. Kirkland the hole. It was clearly discouraging to the loser, and once more at the thirteenth Mrs. Kirkland chipped short to halve in 5 after a substantial driving lead.

At the short fourteenth Mrs. Dietrich gave her first sign of faltering after a tiring week of competition. She trapped her tee shot, failed to get her niblick well out and 2-putted for a 5. Mrs. Kirkland wan with a boggy 4.

At the fifteenth, Mrs. Dietrich played her third shot way short, trapped her fourth, and took 2 to get out. So Mrs. Kirkland took the hole even after losing a stroke on a bunkered drive.

When Mrs. Dietrich's putter also began to falter and she three-putted to lose the sixteenth, even after Mrs. Kirkland had dubbed her iron shot for the water carry, it looked as if it were anybody's match. At the seventeenth Mrs. Kirkland played two tremendous wood shots for a par 5 while Mrs. Dietrich reduced her margin to one by playing her approaches short.

But the denouement at the eighteenth saw a complete return to early form as Mrs. Kirkland lost her hitting advantage by three-putting and Mrs. Dietrich holed out.

By far the best hole of the final was Mrs. Dietrich's seventeenth of the morning round. She followed a dead-straight drive with a spoon shot that curved between two traps. Then taking a No. 3 iron she actually hit the pin from 120 yards and was left with a 2-foot putt for a birdie 4.

CROWN IN BRITAIN GOES TO THOMSON

By The Associated Press.

ST. ANDREWS, Scotland, May 30.—The British amateur golf championship relinquished by Lawson Little today went to 22-year-old Hector Thomson, first home-bred Scot to capture the crown in eleven years.

Thomson, the Scottish amateur champion, defeated James Ferrier, gigantic Australian amateur titleholder, 2 up, winning on the home green, where he hit a long second shot to within six inches of the cup.

After winning, Thomson said he planned to compete in the United States amateur championship at Garden City, L. I., Sept. 14-19.

Play in Rain and Hail

Playing through driving rain and hail today, Thomson fired a 74 at Ferrier in the morning and a 71 in the afternoon. Thomson was 1 down at the end of the first nine holes of the morning round, lost the tenth where he three-putted from 21 feet, and went 3 down at the twelfth when Ferrier hit a perfect pitch and got a birdie 3.

Thomson fought back, however, and won the fourteenth, fifteenth and sixteenth to square the match and so they remained at the end of the first eighteen holes.

The Scottish ace moved out on the first nine of the afternoon round, turning it in 35, one under par, before a gallery of 5,000. He went into the back nine 2 up.

Ferrier cut his advantage to a single hole by winning the twenty-ninth with a 3, but Thomson got it back at the thirty-second, only to lose it at the thirty-fifth, the famous "road hole," where Ferrier played boldly for the green and got a 4 to Thomson's 5.

"All the News That's Fit to Print."

The New York Times.

LATE CITY EDITION
Mostly cloudy, moderate temperature today. Tomorrow mostly cloudy, temperature unchanged.
Temperatures Yesterday—Max., 93; Min., 75

VOL. LXXXV.....No. 28,683. Entered as Second-Class Matter, Postoffice, New York, N. Y. NEW YORK, WEDNESDAY, AUGUST 5, 1936. P TWO CENTS In New York City. | THREE CENTS Within 200 Miles. | FOUR CENTS Elsewhere Except in 7th and 8th Postal Zones.

LEWIS UNIONS FACE DRASTIC PENALTIES IF C. I. O. GOES ON

A. F. of L. Ultimatum Today Is to Order Dissolution or Suspension of Units.

PEACE MOVES ABANDONED

Neither Side Acts to End the Dispute and Compromise Is Opposed at Hearing.

REBEL LEADERS SCORED

Lewis Is Called a 'Mussolini' and Howard a 'Machiavelli' by Frey at Labor Trial.

By LOUIS STARK
Special to THE NEW YORK TIMES.

WASHINGTON, Aug. 4.—Suspension of some of the unions affiliated with the Committee for Industrial Organization by noon tomorrow was indicated as a strong possibility tonight at the close of the second day's session of the executive council of the American Federation of Labor, which has been considering charges that the C. I. O. unions are seeking to build up a rival labor organization.

Unless last-minute developments intervene to brighten the prospects of peace between the craft and industrial groups within the Federation—and there were no peace feelers out tonight on either side—the dissident unions will be told to disband the C. I. O. in a month or to incur the penalty of continuing to remain suspended.

"The executive council will be prepared to render a decision tomorrow morning," said President William Green tonight. "It will decide whether the charges are justified by the weight of evidence and, if the charges are sustained and the unions found guilty, it will decide the penalty to be applied."

Loss of Charters Involved

Temporary suspension would carry with it exclusion from the next convention of the A. F. of L., and if a motion were made there to revoke the charters of the dissident unions it would win overwhelmingly and they would be read out of the federation. This is the assumption if the C. I. O. unions were not allowed to vote at the convention.

If the suspension action is taken, it is unlikely that all the twelve unions which have been summoned to trial would be involved. The International Typographical Union, of which Charles P. Howard is president, has informed the council that Mr. Howard affiliated himself as an individual as a member of and as secretary of the C. I. O. Thus the council would not be expected to punish the entire union for a personal act of its president.

The Hat, Cap and Millinery Workers Union, of which Michael F. Green is president, will also probably not be suspended, for it was only the millinery division, said to comprise most of the union's members, which officially decided to join the C. I. O.

A maximum of ten unions is said to be marked for suspension, but one or two besides the typographical and hat makers' unions may be excepted.

Lewis Unperturbed at Outlook

The unions associated with the C. I. O., of which John L. Lewis is president, may have until about Sept. 1 to signify whether or not they will obey the ruling of the executive council that they dissolve the committee.

That the council has prepared every step of its way, after thoroughly canvassing the legal aspects of the situation, was indicated by the presence of Charlton Ogburn, counsel to the federation, who conferred with Mr. Green at the close of yesterday's and today's sessions.

Mr. Lewis, in his office across the street from the hotel in which the council met today, appeared unperturbed by the possibility of his union's suspension from the federation. He declined to comment on the situation other than to say that he would have to confer with his associates as the council's action may make it necessary.

John P. Frey, president of the metal trades department, completed presentation of his evidence against the C. I. O. unions this morning, assisted by Edward Bieretz, vice president of the International Brotherhood of Electrical Workers.

Mr. Bieretz recalled that the council had voted last Winter that all radio employes should be enrolled in the International Brotherhood of Electrical Workers, which is a craft union. The radio employes had belonged to Federal unions organized on the industrial principle.

He went on to say that the United Radio and Electrical Workers had called a strike at the R. C. A. plant at Camden, N. J. The latter union,

Continued on Page Ten

U. S. Captures 4 Events; Owens Sets Jump Record

Negro Beats 26 Ft. 5 In. to Win 2d Olympic Title—Woodruff, Hardin, Helen Stephens Score—American Team Far in Front.

By ARTHUR J. DALEY
Wireless to THE NEW YORK TIMES.

BERLIN, Aug. 4.—The United States stole away what to date had been distinctly a German show by winning four of the five championships contested this bleak afternoon, as the greatest Olympic Games of them all swung through their third day.

Once again a huge crowd of 90,000 gathered for the morning preliminaries, and once again another capacity throng of 110,000 later packed the Reich Sports Field Stadium. They came to cheer for more German victories, but remained instead to turn their hosannas in the direction of the Americans.

The invincible Jesse Owens won the broad jump at the Olympic record distance of 8.06 meters (26 feet 5 21-64 inches). Miss Helen Stephens walked off with the women's 100-meter final in world record time. Glenn Hardin slammed to victory in the 400-meter hurdles, and John Woodruff, University of Pittsburgh Negro freshman, gave America its first 800-meter triumph in twenty-four years. And topping off the achievement of the Star-Spangled brigade, Owens twice broke the world 200-meter mark around a turn, as well as the Olympic standard, hitting the identical figures of 21.1 seconds in both trials.

Point Score

U. S.	95	Netherlands	4
Germany	76¾	Philippines	4
Finland	30¼	Austria	3
Poland	17	Brazil	2
Japan	16½	Great Britain	2
Canada	9	Argentina	1
Italy	7½	Greece	1
Sweden	6		

Table includes only men's and women's track and field.

Foints are unofficial, based on 10 for first place and 5, 4, 3, 2, 1 for the next five places respectively.

The only championship to evade the eager Americans' grasp was the women's discus crown. And that went to Germany as Miss Gisela Mauermayer broke the Olympic record with a toss of 47.63 meters amid the exuberant shouts of her compatriots.

But Germany's share in the harvest was relatively a minor one. The United States closed so far ahead in the race for the men's track and field team championship that every one else already is lapped at least a full circuit behind. The

Continued on Page Twenty-five

RA PLANS GRANTS TO 125,000 FARMERS

Tugwell Expects That Many in Drought Area to Need Aid Before the Next Crop.

CATTLE BUYING INCREASED

Move Begins to Block Feed Speculation and to Assure Sufficient Seed Supplies.

Special to THE NEW YORK TIMES.

WASHINGTON, Aug. 4.—The Resettlement Administration has put at 125,000 the number of rural families which it expects to aid before another crop can be raised. It is now financing about 32,000 families and the large majority of these have been receiving grants.

Disclosure of these estimates strengthened a belief of some officials that the RA, rather than the WPA, would be the chief drought relief agency. As first outlined by President Roosevelt, the relief program was to be handled by the WPA, which agency was to provide jobs on roads and water conservation projects for needy farmers.

It was estimated by the WPA today that about 40,000 farmers were now employed in the worst drought States of the Middle and Northwest areas. It has authorized the employment of 89,000 men, and although it has indicated that this quota will have to be increased, there has been no guess at what the total employment eventually will be.

With the continued hot weather and general lack of rain gradually diminishing hopes for successful planting of late forage crops for livestock feeding, the AAA added thirty more counties to the emergency area that now embraces 756 counties in nineteen States.

More Cattle Buying Ordered

It also ordered field representatives to speed up the cattle buying program. Purchasing agents at the five principal terminal markets gave immediate effect to the order to buy 2,110 cattle and 225 calves as the day's quota.

Reports to the AAA from its field representatives said that only a little over a fourth of the more than 4,000 head of cattle authorized to be bought yesterday had been actually acquired. This gave rise to suggestions that the agency may have been "bulling the market" for the benefit of farmers with cattle to sell, in announcing the 4,000 head purchase authorization.

The agency ran into difficulty today on its plan to spend $10,000,000 to buy 8,000,000 bushels of wheat, oats, barley and flax to be sold to farmers to be certain of ample seed for Fall and Spring planting. A question arose in the minds of some AAA lawyers as to whether the operation could properly be financed through the Reconstruction Finance and Commodity Credit Corporations.

The RA estimate of 125,000 farm families expected eventually to find their way on its list of clients was believed not to include thousands of Indians on Dakota reservations that the agency has decided to aid. Reports have been coming in to the Bureau of Indian Affairs of appalling conditions on the reserva-

Continued on Page Nine

2,000 IN WILD FIGHT RUSH FOR CITY JOBS

Clothing Torn, Policemen Felled and Desk Smashed in Melee in Municipal Building.

50 RESERVES HALT CRUSH

Futile Hurry for Applications Reflects Huge Demand for Low-Paid Public Posts.

The lure of city jobs with their assured income and promise of pensions incited a crowd of 2,000 men and women to wild disorder yesterday morning in the north lobby of the Municipal Building. The mêlée was so serious that police reserves had to be called to restore order.

When the violent episode was over, the lobby floor was strewn with scraps of clothing and hats. A desk at which James J. McMahon, clerk in charge of the Municipal Civil Service Commission's Application Bureau, had been seated was smashed beyond repair.

The disturbance marked the opening of a fourteen-day period for obtaining applications to take a civil service examination for places on an eligible list for jobs as watchman-attendant and attendant-messenger, which pay $1,200 to $1,800 a year. Applicants must pass written and medical examinations.

The Civil Service Commission had made it plain that early filing of applications was not necessary, but this statement failed to register with the job-seekers, who evidently felt that early filing would be an advantage.

1,000 There at Opening Time

In any event, a group of job-seekers, estimated at 1,000 or more, was outside the Municipal Building at 9 o'clock. They thronged into the elevators and were carried to the commission's offices on the fourteenth floor, where they formed in lines outside the application bureau.

Traffic on the elevators became so congested that the elevator starter urged the commission to transfer the handing out of applications to the north lobby.

For a time, the shift in the scene of operations was effective, although the application-seekers interfered with the arrival and departure of city employes and with WPA workers on a scaffold polishing marble in the lobby.

A few minutes later, however, about 1,000 more applicants suddenly appeared. Building attendants and a few patrolmen attempted in vain to keep order, assuring the crowd, which included about 100 women, that there was no hurry to obtain applications.

Police Felled in Crush

This effort failed. There was a surge of job-seekers, some men climbing over the shoulders of those ahead of them in the densely packed throng. McMahon's desk was crushed to bits. The stock of newspapers of Charles Ginsberg, crippled news dealer in the building, was ripped to pieces. The few patrolmen on duty went down under the crowd.

McMahon broke free and tele-

Continued on Page Six

LANDON GOES HOME TO VOTE IN PRIMARY; CALLS IT PRIVILEGE

Casts Ballot in Independence and Urges All to Use the Right of Suffrage.

FRIENDS GATHER AT POLLS

Nominee Attends a Women's Luncheon and Stag Dinner, Then Returns to Topeka.

By JAMES A. HAGERTY
Special to THE NEW YORK TIMES.

INDEPENDENCE, Kan., Aug. 4.—Governor Landon came back to his home town today and cast his ballot in the State primary election in the same district in which he was beaten for precinct committeeman six years ago. It was his first visit here since his nomination for the Presidency.

In accordance with the Governor's wish there was no demonstration on his arrival, but more than a hundred persons, most of whom were his friends and acquaintances, gathered at the polling place and saw him cast ballot No. 205 in the First precinct of the Third ward.

The first person to greet the Governor as he arrived at the polling place in the agency of the Arnold Motor Company in West Main Street was Charles H. Smith, who defeated him for precinct committeeman and still holds that post.

Mr. Landon's defeat for committeeman was attributed to the influence of the Prairie Oil Company, the heads of which were at that time opposed to Mr. Landon's political advancement because of his activity in seeking legislation to protect independent oil producers, of whom he is one. By party rule the Republican State chairman is selected from the county chairmen and only precinct committeemen are eligible for election as county chairmen. Thus Mr. Landon's defeat blocked a movement to make him State chairman.

Old Opposition Vanishes

This old opposition to Governor Landon among members of his own party in his home city is said to have vanished and the Republicans of Independence are now unanimous in support of their Presidential candidate. Mr. Smith is now an employe of the State Highway Department by appointment of the Governor.

Half a dozen newspaper photographers and one motion picture photographer had their cameras ready when Governor Landon appeared at the polling place soon after 1 o'clock. The judges of the precinct board—for they have two election boards in each precinct in Kansas, one to supervise the voting and the other to count the ballots—were ready for him.

Mr. Landon received his ballot from Mrs. Forriest Wyrick, a judge, who asked: "Which party?"

This question was repeated by Mrs. James Paton, a clerk of the election board.

"The Republican party," Governor Landon replied with a chuckle.

"I see that the old ward is right on the job," he added.

He was registered as "A. M. Landon," with residence at 300 West Maple Avenue, two blocks from the polling place.

The Governor took his ballot and

Continued on Page Twelve

PRESIDENT REBUKES FOES WHO CHARGE 'DROUGHT POLITICS'

Linking of Partisanship to 'Misery' Is Called 'Great Disservice' to the State.

CONFERS ON RELIEF COST

He Finds Increased Outlays in West Partly Offset by Cuts in Industrial Areas.

By CHARLES W. HURD
Special to THE NEW YORK TIMES.

HYDE PARK, N. Y., Aug. 4.—President Roosevelt turned momentarily today from a detailed study of drought relief and its cost to criticize sharply those who have pictured his proposed inspection trip into the West as a political tour.

"It is a very great disservice to the proper administration of any government to link up human misery with partisan politics," the President said at a press conference.

While his statement was a general one, it constituted a reply to charges made yesterday by John D. M. Hamilton, Republican National Chairman, that the Roosevelt administration was making political capital out of its drought-relief program. Mr. Hamilton made this statement in a speech at Bismarck, N. D.

The President's statement, dictated during a talk with newspaper men in the library of his mother's home here, followed a long conference with officials of the Treasury and of the bureaus immediately concerned with relief work.

They had been called here for what Mr. Roosevelt described as a routine conference on fiscal affairs in relation to the new commitments required by the unexpected acceleration of relief activities in the West.

He said that while there had been increases in such expenditures, these were partly offset by savings in industrial areas where a pick-up in business had cut down relief costs. He gave no comparative figures.

The Conferees on Finances

Mr. Roosevelt had called in for the drought study Secretary Morgenthau, Daniel W. Bell Jr., Acting Director of the Budget; Rexford G. Tugwell, Resettlement Administrator, who has just returned from a tour of the drought area; Aubrey Williams, Deputy Works Progress Administrator; Corrington Gill, Assistant Works Progress Administrator, and a group of statistical experts.

All left Hyde Park this afternoon except Mr. Tugwell, who missed his train and returned to join Mr. Roosevelt for a swim at the cottage.

The President received these callers, as he did newspaper men also, attired only in shirt, trousers and slippers, due to the heat, and he invited his guests also to take off their coats.

The fiscal conference supplemented one yesterday with Secretary Wallace and Chester C. Davis, member for agriculture of the Federal Reserve Board.

Replying to questions later at the press conference, the President told newspaper men that the financial condition of the government was

Continued on Page Thirteen

WPA Worker Discovers $1,060 in 'Gold,' Takes Coins From East River Near Park Wall

On his first day of work in two months, Aleck Krunocky, 22-year-old WPA laborer, picked what appeared to be $1,060 in gold coins out of the waters of the East River yesterday.

Krunocky, who is unmarried and lives with his parents at 431 East 122d Street, is employed on work in Carl Schurz Park, which extends along the river front near East Eighty-sixth Street and is separated from the river by a twenty-foot bulkhead. Near this retaining wall yesterday Krunocky saw a Chinese waving excitedly. He investigated and the Chinese pointed to a shiny object on a rocky ledge glittering through about ten inches of murky water.

The tide was low and the East River was down several feet. Aided by another laborer, John Martin, and a stout rope, Krunocky climbed down the retaining wall to a precarious footing on the ledge. He picked up the shiny object.

"It looked like a half dollar, only gold," he said.

He looked further and found two packages wrapped in tarred paper, one of which had soaked through and had broken open. In it he found two more coins and scattered along the ledge a score more, all somewhat dulled with river dirt. Then he opened the second package and discovered enough more to bring the count up to fifty-three, all $20 pieces.

He hurried home with his find, getting away from the growing crowd of spectators as fast as possible, changed his clothes and went to the East 126th Street police station, where he laid the coins in rows before the astonished gaze of Lieutenant William Reidth. They looked like gold to the police officer, but to make sure he called in a pawn broker, who said emphatically that they were genuine.

A dozen policemen examined the money and some said they thought it was good and others declared that it was "light" and must be counterfeit. Today the money will be taken to the Federal experts in the Treasury Building for test.

Lieutenant Reidth called police headquarters and the marine division sent a launch to the point where the money was found. Detectives from the East 102d Street station joined the hunt and the news spread through the neighborhood that gold has been discovered in the WPA diggings in Carl Schurz Park. Hundreds of searchers spent the evening kicking through fresh dirt in the park, but no more gold was found.

Krunocky's discovery will be placed today in the vault of the property clerk at police headquarters to await claimants. If at the end of six months no one has proved ownership the money will be turned over to Krunocky.

Madrid Terror Is Described In an Uncensored Dispatch

Observer Sees Long, Sanguinary Rebellion if Fascists Prevail and End of Liberal Republic if Government Crushes Them.

Wireless to THE NEW YORK TIMES.

LONDON, Aug. 4.—The following is the first full, uncensored account of events in Madrid to reach London since the Spanish civil war began:

MADRID, Aug. 2 (London Times Dispatch).—A fortnight has passed since the first flash of revolt started a conflict that is shaking this republic to its foundations. All is turmoil and strife.

The outlook is a cloud through which two alternatives loom like cliffs. Should the revolt triumph—and, viewed from Madrid, it cannot win without foreign intervention—a Fascist régime would be the result, against which rebellion would continue until drowned in blood. Should the sedition be suppressed—and that certainly will be a long business—the liberal republic of 1931 must perish in the process.

Two extremes are at each other's throats. One must succumb. There is no central force strong enough to separate them. The story of the rising thus far bears out that conviction.

A synopsis of events will show what is occurring. On Saturday night, July 18, as reports came in showing a revolt was spreading to province after province, Premier Santiago Casares Quiroga resigned. The head of the Popular Front government had failed to see and forestall a deep plan of the Union Militar Española. He was "fracasado" (broken); his prestige was gone, and therewith the confidence of the President.

President Manuel Azaña called in the Speaker of the Cortes, Diego Martinez Barrio, who easily formed a Cabinet representing a moderate tendency within republicanism.

The inclusion of Sanchez Roman in the Cabinet was a further guarantee for those who disapproved of the "Bolshevist" associations of the Quiroga Cabinet. Mr. Roman had refused to sign the pre-election Popular Front pact.

The new Cabinet was torpedoed immediately. The Marxist groups would have none of it, and their veto was absolute.

For some fateful hours the ship of state drifted without a helm until President Azaña, proud high priest of pure republicanism, bowed his head to the storm and constitutional prerogative foundered. The Quiroga Cabinet was recalled, but the Prime Minister and Juan Moles, the Minister of the Interior, both

Continued on Page Two

U. S. BIDS GERMANS REVEAL SUBSIDIES

New Treasury Order Requires Full Data on Invoices of the Imports From the Reich.

BERLIN IN A COMPROMISE

Drops the Special Benefits to Shippers—Further Cut in Trade With U. S. Is Seen.

Special to THE NEW YORK TIMES.

WASHINGTON, Aug. 4.—Collectors of customs and American consular officers in Germany were instructed by the Treasury today to give information on invoices of exports from that country as to whether any subsidies or other benefits had been paid on goods shipped to the United States.

The instructions were prepared several days ago and prior to the announcement by the German Government that "aski" marks, which were a special subsidy to German shippers, had been abolished. Abolishment of the "aski" marks, in the opinion of American officials, probably prepared the way for unrestricted trade relations with the United States.

This action by Germany followed a conference of German officials with the State and Treasury Departments which was designed to improve trade relations.

The new orders required that the shipper should specially set out any benefits paid or furnished by the German Government to him on any products exported.

Germany Sent Delegation

On account of the payment of these benefits, which were held to have given an advantage to German exporters to the United States, this government placed certain countervailing duties on products from that country. As a result Germany sent a delegation to confer with the State and Treasury Departments. It was understood that a satisfactory arrangement was made and that the usual trade practices would be resumed.

The regulations issued today require that on goods shipped to the United States the master of the vessel involved should indicate "any benefits or privileges, including marks subject to special exchange" or marks not subject to "any special exchange regulations of the German Government or a department, office or agency thereof."

They further require that the invoices indicate foreign exchange to be converted into marks and the rate of exchange; permission to acquire scrip for redemption at the Konversionskasse; permission to acquire bonds for redemption in Germany and marks acquired from the German Government or any of its agencies in connection with the shipment of goods to the United States "otherwise than in payment of the purchase price of such goods."

"The declaration must be complete, and if any sum, benefit or privilege indicated by the form has not been received or is not to be received, that fact should be indicated in the appropriate place," the

Continued on Page Seven

GREECE IS PLACED UNDER ARMY RULE

Order for a General Strike Is Called a Communist Plot—Chamber Is Dissolved.

WIDE MOVEMENT FEARED

Labor Trouble in Bulgaria, Laid to Russia, Seen as Plot to Upset the Balkans.

By The Associated Press.

ATHENS, Aug. 4.—The Greek Government, confronted by "a Communist plot," tonight proclaimed martial law and dissolved the Chamber.

A twenty-four-hour general strike, scheduled to begin at midnight, was called by Leftist trade unions in protest against a recent law that fixed minimum-wage scales and subjected workers' claims to obligatory arbitration.

The Federation of Conservative Workers declared opposition to the strike in a manifesto.

Labor Meetings Banned

Wireless to THE NEW YORK TIMES.

ATHENS, Aug. 4.—In the face of a call for a twenty-four-hour general strike by the Greek Labor Federation, protesting against a recent government bill instituting compulsory arbitration of labor disputes and forbidding strikes, the authorities have prohibited all workers' meetings, fearing serious disorders.

Tonight, after a long audience with the King, Premier John Metaxas repudiated the government's alleged intention to set up a dictatorship. He insisted the measures the government had taken had no other aim but the maintenance of order.

Economic Unrest Growing

Economic unrest, resulting in strikes and bloody clashes between strikers and the army and police, has been growing steadily in Greece for several months. The strike movement, originating with tobacco workers, started in May and has been marked by attempted general strikes in various cities. The guidance of the campaign has been attributed to Communists, with Deputy Tinakos, a Red, reported as one of the leaders.

Throughout the series of Greek strikes the Greek Government watched the situation in neighboring Bulgaria, where a Communist strike had been sweeping the country. Greek political circles believed that the Bulgarian strike was directed from the Soviet Union and they feared its extension to other parts of the Balkans.

On May 11, after the settlement of a tobacco workers' strike in Saloniki that became a general one and threatened a food shortage, the Greek Labor Federation called a general protest strike of twenty-four hours to start at midnight on May 12. At that time Premier John Metaxas contemplated proclaiming martial law.

Strikes continued in different cities in the ensuing weeks but in the latter part of May it was reported that the movement in Thrace and other parts of Greece

Continued on Page Four

REBELS DEFEATED BY 80,000 LEFTISTS IN MADRID PASSES

Fascists Driven to Northern Side of Mountains, Where Rout Is Expected.

PREMIER STRESSES GAINS

Plane Bombing of Saragossa Aids Four Loyalist Columns, Advancing on City.

LONDON FOR NEUTRALITY

Britain's Full Acceptance of the French Plea Awaits Italy's Reply—Germans See Franco.

Developments in Spain

Madrid Leftists claimed important victories north of that city in an attack launched by 80,000 men. One advanced rebel force was said to have been trapped in Leon Pass by the drive.

Airplanes bombarded Saragossa as four Leftist columns converged on that city and heavy losses were reported on the insurgent side. They, however, reported victories at two points thirty miles from the city.

German naval officers paid a formal call on General Franco at Ceuta. A German ship was forced to leave Larache to escape a government bombardment and was forbidden to land its cargo.

Britain accepted in principle France's plea for neutrality in the civil war, but withheld full acceptance until Italy had acted. Rome's position was still uncertain. Germany was willing to be bound if Russia also would give pledges.

Secretary Hull instructed United States agents in Spain to watch carefully seizures of American property so claims could be presented later.

Drive Goes Past Mountains

By WILLIAM P. CARNEY
Wireless to THE NEW YORK TIMES.

MADRID, Aug. 4 (Passed by the Censor).—Premier José Giral told newspaper men this evening that the government forces had broken through to the other side of the Guadarrama mountains in a new battle against the rebels threatening Madrid.

San Rafael was captured in a drive by the loyalists, he said. This place is forty miles from Madrid.

"A militia column entered the town today," he added. "Some hand-to-hand fighting is still going on with small groups of rebels in the streets or barricaded in ruined buildings, but these will soon be dominated."

[San Rafael is on the road to Segovia, about ten miles from that city, which has been the forward base of one of the columns marching toward Madrid. It is at the northern end of the Leon Pass, the capture of which was announced by the rebels last week. They said they had penetrated to the southern end of the hills and the road to Madrid would no longer be so difficult.

[A dispatch to The Associated Press said officials declared 80,000 men were engaged in a new offensive, that it had been successful and that the drive of the loyalist forces had isolated the rebel defenders of Leon Pass.]

Other Government Gains

Premier Giral also announced that the government forces had had a good day.

"At Huesca [north of Saragossa]," he said, "our forces are at the city gates. The rebel artillery at Cordoba has been silenced since the early morning. We are closing in on Cordoba tonight."

On the Guadarrama heights tonight the forest is afire. Artillery shells and airplane bombs started this blaze.

The correspondent of the newspaper La Libertad with the government forces on the northwestern front reported that from Villalba and from El Escorial to the firing line he had not seen a horse. All transport is motorized. Artillery and other fighting equipment is moved by heavy trucks. The cavalry is outdated, the correspondent believes.

Commander Valderrama of the rebel forces was killed yesterday in fighting on the Somosierra front. An automatic pistol found on him is now the property of one of the leaders of the government army, General Riequelme. Jaime Cobedo, syndicalist leader, was killed yesterday on the same front while inspecting the proletarian militia with Deputy Angel Pestana, also a syndicalist. Deputy Pestana was wounded slightly.

Today's newspapers published a

Continued on Page Two

U. S. Athletes Capture Four Firsts as Owens Wins Again in Olympic Games

Continued From Page One

American total is 83 points to 38¾ for the Reich and 30¼ for Finland.

For three fields of competition, men's track and field, women's track and field and wrestling the Americans' total is 120 points. Germany and Finland are second and third in combined totals, the former having 89¾ points and the latter 48¼.

The German threat is apparently at an end. Smooth lies the path of the United States toward a goal it has always achieved—the Olympic team title.

Yet these Germans have been performing in such astounding fashion all along that counting them out of the running is done reluctantly, even though the ammunition the Teutons have left is of the powder cap variety.

The broad jump had been the one event of his three in these eleventh Olympics that Owens had been most certain of winning. Lutz Long, so unheralded in German sporting circles that he is neither a policeman nor a soldier, tied Owens at 7.87 meters with two leaps remaining and forced this human bullet to catapult out near his own new world record of 26 feet 8¼ inches in order to emerge victorious at all.

Fuehrer Is Delighted

So delighted was Chancellor Hitler by the gallant fight that Long had made that he congratulated him privately just before he himself left the stadium. In fact, his eagerness to receive the youthful German was so great that the Fuehrer condescended to wait until his emissaries had pried Long loose from Owens, with whom he was affectionately walking along the track arm and arm. All the Negro received was his second gold medal, which probably satisfied him well enough at that.

The broad jump was one of the most dramatic events of the entire day, surprising as that may sound. It started with an unusual flourish and ended the same way. In the morning the leapers had to beat 23 feet 5 inches to qualify.

Owens strolled over to the runway and, still in his pullovers, raced to the pit and ran right through, a customary warm-up gesture. But the red flag was raised in a token greatly to the Buckeye Bullet's astonishment. That counted as one of this three jumps. On his second try, which he made in earnest, Jesse hit the take-off board cleanly and sailed through the air. Again the red flag was waved for some mysterious reason.

Has One Jump Left

The situation was getting to be alarming by this time. Owens had only one more jump left to stay in the competition. So, on his last attempt, he sprinted carefully, left the ground with a half-foot clearance at the take-off and went past 25 feet to safety.

In the afternoon Owens had no close calls of that nature. The pressure came from Long. The German, carried along on the wings of superhuman endeavor—the hallmark of every Reich athlete in this meet—was bounding along right at Owens's heels. He was only little more than an inch behind the American's 7.87 meters as they went up for their last three jumps.

On his second in the final Long hit the nail exactly on the head, doing the same distance as the Ohioan and tying him for the championship as the crowd went into frenzied ecstacies of applause. But his jubilation was short-lived. Owens came thundering down the runway and drove out into space a moment later. He had taken the play away at 7.94 meters (26 feet 39-64 inch) and then drove beyond Long's reach with his final jump that cemented the distinction of his becoming the first 26-footer in Olympic history. Incidentally, the German, in second place, also surpassed the Olympic record.

A Strange Race

The secondary feature was the 800-meter final, one of the strangest races ever run in the games. Woodruff had his instructions to go out and run the field into the ground. Instead he was pocketed at the start and buried away in the pack.

The veteran Phil Edwards of Canada was the pace-setter at the get-away, with Woodruff hemmed in along the pole so that he could not escape. The American Negro tried to free himself, but to no avail. At 300 meters he practically stopped in his tracks, an unheard of procedure in high-class competition, and against the world's hand-picked runners, too.

He slowed down to a walk and soon found himself in last place. Then he ran around every one on the outside, a hard way to get ahead, and at the half-way mark was zooming along at full speed out front. But before he could reconcile himself to being off by himself Edwards spurted into the lead once more in the back stretch, and again Woodruff found himself where he had been told not to be.

Lanzi Makes His Bid

Meanwhile a new figure arrived on the scene. He was Mario Lanzi of Italy, running his heart out in an effort to present to Crown Prince Umberto, in Hitler's box, the first Italian championship in these games. Lanzi fled past Kazimierz Kucharski of Poland just before the final turn was reached, and began to climb up Woodruff's back.

The American, startled no end by this unexpected challenge, let go with a withering blast that lifted him past Edwards. He collared the Canadian Negro just as he stepped on the pay dirt of the homestretch. Woodruff suddenly acquired wings. He drew almost four yards in front, then faded rapidly in direct proportion to his approach to the tape. Lanzi, racing frantically, caught Edwards, but missed Woodruff by two yards as the latter was timed in 1:52.9, figures far from extraordinary in this day and age.

One thing was certain, and that was that Woodruff had not traveled just 800 meters. His outside running and singular manoeuvres during the race must have added another fifty meters to his distance. How good this youngster is was indicated by the mere fact that he won. In the last twenty-four years the United States has been sending the best half-milers in the world out after the 800-meter crown. None of them ever made the grade, and yet a college freshman who was entirely unknown two months ago accomplished, after running the worst winning race in history, what none of the others had ever been able to do.

This test and the 400-meter hurdles final were two of the events of the day in which no records were touched. Hardin had the misfortune of the draw, the least satisfactory lane of them all, the outside. He trailed Joe Patterson of the United States right up to the final straightaway and then put on the pressure sufficiently to win by four yards in 0:52.4, a fraction off his own Olympic record. Patterson lost form in the final twenty yards, yielding second place to John Loaring of Canada and third to Miguel White of the Philippines.

There were plenty of marks hit in the 200-meter first and second-round heats, however. Owens registered 0:21.1 twice for a new Olympic mark, while Bobby Packard and Mack Robinson of the United States and Lee Orr of Canada each tied Eddie Tolan's old figures, 0:21.2. All three Americans, by the way, qualified for the semi-finals.

There were two records of sorts in the women's sprint final, too. Miss Stella Walsh, defending her Olympic 100-meter championship, was caught in 11.7 seconds in second place, two-tenths under her own standard, while the great Miss Stephens did 0:11.5 for the second time in the meet. But she did not quite reach her 0:11.4 of yesterday, which will be submitted as a new world record.

Two Break Discus Mark

There were also two records in the women's discus throw. On her first throw Miss Jadwiga Wajsowna beat Miss Lilian Copeland's distance of 40.56 meters and she and Miss Mauermayer continued to practice all afternoon.

The German girl finally won with 47.63 meters (156 feet 3⅜ inches) to the Pole's 46.22 meters (151 feet 7¾ inches).

The 5,000-meter semi-finals saw no records set, but did see two of the three American entrants advance. Don Lash finished third in his heat and Louis Zamperini fifth in his, gaining the last qualifying place by a matter of inches after a cyclonic burst in the last fifty yards. Tommy Deckard missed out with an eighth place.

FOUR OF YESTERDAY'S OLYMPIC WINNERS AND SECOND AND THIRD IN 100-METER DASH

Times Wide World Radiophoto.

Jesse Owens, leaping to Olympic broad jump record

Associated Press Radiophoto.

Miss Kaethe Krauss, who ran third; Miss Helen Stephens, who took the gold medal in the 100 meters, and Miss Stella Walsh, who finished second

Miss Gisela Mauermayer, Olympic discus champion

Times Wide World Radiophoto.

John Woodruff capturing 800-meter run

1936 Olympic Champions

TRACK AND FIELD

Men

100-Meter Dash—Jesse Owens, United States.

800-Meter Run—John Woodruff, United States.

10,000-Meter Run—Ilmari Salminen, Finland.

400-Meter Hurdles—Glenn Hardin, United States.

Shot Put—Hans Woellke, Germany.

Hammer Throw—Karl Hein, Germany.

High Jump—Cornelius Johnson, United States.

Broad Jump—Jesse Owens, United States.

Women

100-Meter Dash—Miss Helen Stephens, United States.

Javelin Throw—Miss Tilly Fleischer, Germany.

Discus Throw—Miss Gisela Mauermayer, Germany.

WRESTLING

Catch-as-Catch-Can

Bantamweight Class—Oedon Zombary, Hungary.

Featherweight Class—Kust Pihlajonalki, Finland.

Lightweight Class—Karoly Karpati, Hungary.

Welterweight Class—Frank Lewis, United States.

Middleweight Class—Emile Poilve, France.

Light-Heavyweight Class—Knut Fridell, Sweden.

Heavyweight Class—Kristjan Paulusalu, Estonia.

WEIGHT-LIFTING

Featherweight Class—Anthony Terlazzo, United States.

Lightweight Class—Mohammed Ahmed Mesbah, Egypt.

*Light Heavyweight Class—Louis Hostin, France.

*Retained title.

Point Tabulation for Olympics

Country.	Track, Men.	Field, Men.	Track, Women.	Field, Women.	Wrestling.	Total.
United States	44	39	12	..	25	120
Germany	2	36¾	8	30	13	89¾
Finland	19	11¼	..	..	18	48¼
Sweden	1	4	..	1	19	25
Hungary	..	..	..	..	20	20
Poland	3	..	5	9	..	17
Japan	3	6½	..	7	..	16½
Estonia	..	..	..	..	15	15
Canada	9	..	..	..	4	13
France	..	..	..	..	10	10
Italy	5	2½	..	..	..	7½
Czechoslovakia	..	..	..	..	5	5
The Netherlands	4	..	..	..	..	4
Philippines	4	..	..	..	..	4
Turkey	..	..	..	..	4	4
Austria	..	..	..	3	..	3
Brazil	2	..	..	..	..	2
Great Britain	2	..	..	..	..	2
Argentina	1	..	..	..	..	1
Greece	1	..	..	..	..	1

Weight-lifting omitted because complete results are not available. Partial results: Egypt 24, United States 13, France 10, Germany 9, Austria 5.

Points are unofficial, based on 10 for first place and 5, 4, 3, 2, 1 for the next five places, respectively.

Program of Events for Today

BERLIN, Aug. 4 (AP).—The program for the fourth day of competition in the eleventh Olympic Games tomorrow (subtract five hours for New York daylight-saving time):

OLYMPIC STADIUM

10:30 A. M.—110-meter hurdles trials; pole vault trials; discus trials.

11:00 A. M.—1,500-meter trials.

1:00 P. M.—50-kilometer walk.

3:00 P. M.—200-meter semi-finals; discus final.

3:30 P. M.—Women's 80-meter hurdles.

4:00 P. M.—Pole vault final.

4:30 P. M.—110-meter hurdles quarter-finals.

5:00 P. M.—1,500-meter semi-finals.

5:30 P. M.—Women's 80-meter hurdles semi-finals.

6:00 P. M.—200-meter final.

6:30 P. M.—Yugoslav gymnastics.

SWIMMING STADIUM

9:00 A. M.—Modern pentathlon, swimming.

FIELD HOCKEY STADIUM

4:30 P. M.—Hockey, United States vs. Japan; India vs. Hungary.

MAY FIELD

2:00 P. M.—Polo, Argentina vs. Mexico.

GYMNASTIC HALL

9:00 A. M.—Fencing, foils, individual.

3:00 P. M.—Fencing, foils, individual; women's foils finals.

6:00 P. M.—Fencing, foils, individual.

POST STADIUM

5:30 P. M.—Soccer, Poland vs. Hungary.

MOMMSEN STADIUM

5:30 P. M.—Soccer, Egypt vs. Austria.

DEUTSCHLAND HALL

8:00 P. M.—Weightlifting, heavyweight and middleweight finals.

OLYMPIC HIGHLIGHTS IN EVENTS YESTERDAY

By The Associated Press.

Track and Field

United States made sweep of first places in three men's finals as Jesse Owens captured the broad jump at new Olympic record distance of 8.06 meters (26 feet 5 21-64 inches), Glenn Hardin took 400-meter low hurdles crown and Johnny Woodruff romped off with 800-meter championships; Miss Helen Stephens eclipsed listed Olympic record in taking women's 100-meter title in 11.5 seconds; Owens, clocked twice in 21.1 seconds, one-tenth of a second under Olympic standard, qualified for 200-meter semi-finals along with Bobby Packard and Mack Robinson; Don Lash and Louis Zamperini qualified for 5,000-meter final, but Tom Deckard was eliminated; Miss Gisela Mauermayer of Germany took women's discus championship with new Olympic record toss of 47.63 meters (156 feet 3⅜ inches) as Miss Stephens and Mrs. Gertrude Wilhelmsen, American representatives, failed to qualify; Chuck Hornbostel and Harry Williamson finished fifth and sixth in 800-meter final, Joe Patterson was fourth in 400-meter hurdles final and Miss Annette Rogers fifth in women's 100-meter final.

Wrestling

Frank Lewis won welterweight gold medal; Ross Flood finished second in bantamweight class; Francis Millard finished second in featherweight division and Dick Voliva took second honors in the middleweight competition. Harley Strong, lightweight; Roy Clemons, light-heavyweight and Roy Dunn, heavyweight, were eliminated.

Soccer

Japan upset Sweden, 3 to 2.

Polo Round Robin

Germany and Hungary played an 8-to-8 tie.

Yachting

American boats fared badly as competition opened in four classes, finishing third in Star Classes, seventh in the six-meter and eight-meter divisions and seventeenth in Monotype Class.

Field Hockey Eliminations

Afghanistan and Denmark played a 6-to-6 tie, the Netherlands and Belgium drew, 2 to 2, and France defeated Switzerland, 2 to 1.

U. S. WOMEN FENCERS BOW

Misses Lloyd and Locke Eliminated in Olympic Games.

BERLIN, Aug. 4 (AP).—Two American women fencers, Miss Marion Lloyd of Richmond Hill, L. I., and Miss Dorothy Locke of Brooklyn, were eliminated in preliminary Olympic foils competition today.

Miss Helene Mayer, the Jewess who left Oakland, Calif., at the invitation of German authorities to compete for Germany in the games, was one of the eight survivors.

Italy captured the men's team foils honors of the day with three victories. France was second and Germany third.

Summaries in Olympics

By The Associated Press.

TRACK AND FIELD

800-METER RUN

Final

Won by John Woodruff, United States, 1:52.9; second, Mario Lanzi, Italy, 1:53.2; third, Phil Edwards, Canada, 1:53.6; fourth, Kazimierz Kucharski, Poland, 1:53.8; fifth, Charles Hornbostel, United States, 1:54.6; sixth, Harry Williamson, United States, 1:55.8; seventh, Gerald Backhouse, Australia; eighth, Brian MacCabe, Great Britain; ninth, Juan Anderson, Argentina.

400-METER HURDLES

Semi-Finals

(Three in each qualify for final)

First Heat—Won by Glenn Hardin, United States, 0:53.2; second, Miguel White, Philippines, 0:53.4; third, Christos Mantikas, Greece, 0:53.6; fourth, Dale Schofield, United States; fifth, Juan Lavenas, Argentina; sixth, Willi Kuerten, Germany.

Second Heat—Won by Joseph Patterson, United States, 0:52.8; second, Johnny Loaring, Canada, 0:53.1; third, Magalhaes Padilha, Brazil, 0:53.3; fourth, Jules Bosmans, Belgium; fifth, Josef Kovacs, Hungary; sixth, Fritz Nottbrock, Germany.

Final

Won by Hardin, United States, 0:52.4; second, Loaring, Canada, 0:52.7; third, White, Philippines, 0:52.8; fourth, Patterson, United States, 0:53; fifth, Padilha, Brazil, 0:54; sixth, Mantikas, Greece, 0:54.2.

200-METER DASH

Trials

(First three in each qualify for quarter finals.)

First Heat—Won by Wynand van Beveren, Netherlands, 0:21.4; second, Thomas Beswick, Argentina, 0:22.1; third, Mutsuo Taniguchi, Japan, 0:22.2; fourth, Jose Almeida, Brazil; fifth, Antonio Salcedo, Philippines.

Second Heat—Won by Martin Osendarp, Netherlands, 0:21.7; second, Egon Schein, Germany, 0:22; third, Alan Pennington, Great Britain, 0:22.1; fourth, Masao Yazawa, Japan; fifth, Francois Dondelinger, France.

Third Heat—Won by Jesse Owens, United States, 0:21.1 (betters Olympic record and world record for distance around turn); second, Lee Orr, Canada, 0:21.6; third, Karl Neckerman, Germany, 0:21.8; fourth, Arthur Sweeney, England; fifth, Nemesio Guzman, Philippines.

Fourth Heat—Won by Arthur Humber, Canada, 0:22.1; second, Gyula Gyenes, Hungary, 0:22.1; third, Felix Rinner, Austria, 0:22.4; fourth, Paul Bronner, France; fifth, King-kwan Chen, China.

Fifth Heat—Won by Paul Haenni, Switzerland, 0:21.9; second, Rennos Frangoudis, Greece, 0:22.1; third, Josef Sir, Hungary, 0:22.2; fourth, Patrick Dannaher, South Africa; fifth, Kim-seng Poh, China.

Sixth Heat—Won by Martin Theunissen, South Africa, 0:21.7; second, Howie MacPhee, Canada, 0:21.8; third, Borje Strandvall, Finland, 0:22.6; fourth, George Fahoum, Egypt; fifth, Chang-chun Liu, China.

Seventh Heat—Won by Robert Packard, United States, 0:21.2 (equals Olympic record); second Eric Grimbeek, South Africa, 0:21.8; third, Albert Steinmetz, Germany, 0:21.9; fourth, Eric Whiteside, India.

Eighth Heat—Won by Matthew Robinson, United States, 0:21.6; second, Aarno Tammisto, Finland, 0:22.2; third, Carlos Hofmeister, Argentina, 0:22.3; fourth, Mario Minai, Hungary; fifth, Dieudonne Devrint, Belgium.

Quarter—Finals

(Three in each qualify for semi-finals.)

First Heat—Won by Orr, Canada, 0:21.2 (equals Olympic record); second, Haenni, Switzerland, 0:21.3; third, Packard, United States, 0:21.3; fourth, Sir, Hungary; fifth, Schein, Germany; sixth, Beswick, Argentina.

Second Heat—Won by Beveren, Netherlands, 0:21.7; second, Theunissen, South Africa, 0:21.9; third, Humber, Canada, 0:22.1; fourth, Frangoudis, Greece; fifth, Hofmeister, Argentina; sixth, Taniguchi, Japan.

Third Heat—Won by Owens, United States, 0:21.1 (betters Olympic record and world record for distance around turn); second, MacPhee, Canada, 0:21.8; third, Grimbeek, South Africa, 0:21.9; fourth, Tammisto, Finland; fifth, Rinner, Austria. (Steinmetz, Germany, disqualified for leaving lane after finishing fourth.)

Fourth Heat—Won by Robinson, United States, 0:21.2 (equals Olympic record); second, Osendarp, Netherlands, 0:21.3; third, Neckermann, Germany, 0:21.6; fourth, Gyenes, Hungary; fifth, Strandvall, Finland.

BROAD JUMP

Final

Won by Jesse Owens, United States, 8.06 meters (26 feet 5 21-64 inches) (betters Olympic record); second, Lutz Long, Germany, 7.87 meters (25 feet 9 27-32 inches); third, Naoto Tajima, Japan, 7.74 meters (25 feet 4 47-64 inches); tied for fourth, Arturo Maffei, Italy, and Wilhelm Leichum, Germany, 7.73 meters (25 feet 4 21-64 inches); sixth, Robert Clark, United States, 7.60 meters (25 feet 1 31-32 inches).

DISCUS THROW—WOMEN

Final

Won by Gisela Mauermayer, Germany, 47.63 meters (156 feet 3⅜ inches) (betters Olympic record); second, Jadwiga Wajsowna, Poland, 46.22 meters (151 feet 7 23-32 inches); third, Paula Mollenhauer, Germany, 39.80 meters (130 feet 6 31-32 inches); fourth, Ko Nakamura, Japan, 38.24 meters (125 feet 5 15-16 inches); fifth, Hide Mineshima, Japan, 37.35 meters (122 feet 6½ inches); sixth, Birgit Lundstrom, Sweden, 35.82 meters (117 feet 6 17-64 inches).

Olympic Records Yesterday

200-Meter Dash—0:21.1, by Jesse Owens, United States; old Olympic record and world record for the distance around a turn, 0:21.2, made by Eddie Tolan, United States, at Los Angeles in 1932. Owens broke record in both trial and quarter-final, while Bobby Packard and Matt Robinson, United States, and Lee Orr, Canada, equaled it.

Running Broad Jump—26 feet 5 21-64 inches, by Jesse Owens, United States; old Olympic record, 25 feet 4¾ inches, made by Edward B. Hamm, United States, at Amsterdam in 1928.

100-Meter Dash, Women—0:11.5, by Miss Helen Stephens, United States. This betters Olympic record of 0:11.9 made at Los Angeles in 1932 and world record of 0:11.8 made at Poznan, Poland in 1933 by Miss Stella Walsh, Poland, but Miss Stephens in trial Monday did 0:11.4.

Discus Throw, Women—156 feet 3⅜ inches, by Miss Gisela Mauermayer, Germany; old Olympic record, 133 feet 2 inches, made by Miss Lilian Copeland, United States, at Los Angeles in 1932.

TRACK AND FIELD

5,000-METER RUN

Trials

(Five in each to qualify for final.)

First Heat—Won by Umberto Cerati, Italy, 15:01; second, Harry Siefert, Denmark, 15:02.8; third, Don Lash, United States, 15:04.4; fourth, Ilmari Salminen, Finland, 15:06.6; fifth, Aubrey Reeve, Great Britain, 15:06.8; sixth, Ake Jansson, Sweden.

Second Heat—Won by Gunnar Hockert, Finland, 15:10.2; second, Frank Close, Great Britain, 15:10.6; third, Josef Noji, Poland, 15:11.2; fourth, Bror Hellstroem, Sweden, 15:12; fifth, Rolf Hansen, Norway, 15:12.6; sixth, Rene Lecuron, France; seventh, Janos Kelen, Hungary; eighth, Tom Deckard, United States; ninth, Hideo Tanaka, Japan.

Third Heat—Won by John Jonsson, Sweden, 14:54; second, Kohei Murakoso, Japan; 14:56.6; third, Peter Ward, Great Britain, 14:59; fourth, Lauri Lehtinen, Finland, 15:00; fifth, Louis Zamperini, United States, 15:02; sixth, Salvatore Mastroienni, Italy; seventh, Roger Rochard, France; eighth, Max Syring, Germany.

100-METER DASH—WOMEN

Final

Won by Helen Stephens, United States, 0:11.5 (betters Olympic and world record); second, Stella Walsh, Poland, 0:11.7; third, Kathe Krauss, Germany, 0:11.9; fourth, Marie Dollinger, Germany; fifth, Annette Rogers, United States; sixth, Emmy Albus, Germany.

WRESTLING

CATCH-AS-CATCH-CAN

Finals

Bantamweight—Won by Oedon Zombory, Hungary; second, Ross Flood, United States; third, Johannes Herbert, Germany.

Featherweight—Won by Kust Pihlajanaeki, Finland; second, Francis Millard, United States; third, Goesta Joensson, Sweden.

Lightweight—Won by Karoly Karpati, Hungary; second, Wolfgang Ehrl, Germany; third, Hermann Pihlajanaeki, Finland.

Welterweight—Won by Frank Lewis, United States; second, Turi Andersson, Sweden; third Joseph Schleimer, Canada.

Middleweight—Won by Emile Poilve, France; second, Dick Voliva, United States; third, Ahmet Kirecci, Turkey.

Light-Heavyweight—Won by Knut Fridell, Sweden; second, August Neo, Estonia; third, Erich Siebert, Germany.

Heavyweight—Won by Kristian Paulusalu, Estonia; second, Joseph Klapuch, Czechoslovakia; third, Nystroem, Finland.

MODERN PENTATHLON

PISTOL SHOOTING

Won by Charles F. Leonard Jr., United States, 200; Lieut. Fred R. Weber, United States, 194, second; Bartha, Hungary, and Gotthardt Handrick, Germany, 192, tied for third; Ceccarelli, Italy, and Sven Trovelt, Sweden, 190, tied for fifth; Grundbacher, Switzerland, Chretien, France, and Von Boisman, Sweden, 189, tied for seventh; Abba, Italy, 188, tenth; Alfred D. Starbird, United States, 181, twenty-third.

THREE-EVENT POINT STANDING

Handrick, Germany, 10.5, first; Trovelt, Sweden, 20, second; Leonard, United States, 26, third; Weber, United States, and Abba, Italy, 26.5, tied for fourth; Edouard Delecourt, Belgium, 27.5, sixth; Ritter Orban, Hungary, 37.5, seventh; Starbird, United States, 40, eighth; Lauri Kettunen, Finland, 42, ninth.

YACHTING

SIX-METER CLASS

Won by Sweden; second, Germany; third, England; fourth, Finland; fifth, Norway; sixth, Argentina; seventh, United States.

EIGHT-METER CLASS

Won by Sweden; second, Italy; third, Norway; fourth, England; fifth, Finland; sixth, Germany; seventh, United States; eighth, Argentina.

STAR CLASS

Won by Germany; second, Sweden; third, United States; fourth, England; fifth, Norway.

MONOTYPE CLASS

Won by England; second, Germany; third, Chile; fourth, Netherlands; fifth, Denmark; sixth, Sweden; seventh, United States.

FIELD HOCKEY

ELIMINATIONS

Afghanistan 6, Denmark 6.

Netherlands 2, Belgium 2.

France 2, Switzerland 1.

POLO

ROUND-ROBIN

*Germany 8, Hungary 8.

*Tie will be played off tomorrow.

SOCCER

ELIMINATION

Japan 3, Sweden 2.

U. S. CREW IN FORM

Hume, in Shape Again, Pacing the Washington Eight Impressively.

BERLIN, Aug. 4 (AP).—American Olympic oarsmen settled into the second week of training today, with of University of Washington crew showing consistent improvement.

Don Hume, stroke of the eight, apparently is completely recovered from his cold and is stroking so well that Coach Al Ulbrickson considers the crew now is equal to its form when it won the trials at Princeton. The Huskies' best time trial was rowed in 6:36 under adverse water and wind conditions.

The British, Hungarian and Italian eights now are regarded as the principal threats, rather than the Swiss crew, which won the Henley Grand Challenge Cup. The Australian all-police crew is considered powerful, but, like the Japanese, erratic.

Cecil Pearce, Australian sculler, has impressed the American sweep-swingers and they predict he will keep the singles title in the family. His cousin, Bobby, won the last two Olympic sculls titles.

FIRST YACHT EVENT DELAYED BY STORM

But Wind Moderates and Race Starts With Olympic Fire Burning on One Ship.

HITLER 'RUNS' RACES TOO

Fuehrer's Mannerisms Recall Those of Jimmy Walker at New York Prize Fights.

By FREDERICK T. BIRCHALL

Wireless to THE NEW YORK TIMES.

BERLIN, Aug. 4.—For a while this morning, the Olympic yachting regatta was in danger of being postponed. There was a storm over the fjord at Kiel at 10:30, when the first race was to have started, and continued stormy weather was feared. However, an hour later the wind moderated, and soon after noon the racing was begun.

The Olympic fire, brought by torch in a relay from the Berlin stadium, burned on the ship von Lubeck, which is a reproduction of the Hanseatic vessels which plied the seas from the twelfth to the fifteenth century.

It seems worth mentioning that the person who is attracting the most attention at the games in Berlin is not an athlete but the German Fuehrer. Hitler is greatly interested in the contests. He is putting in so much time at them that now he can be rated among the most devoted sports fans.

From the time he takes his seat in his box and the Olympic flag and the silver and gold swastika ensigns are raised over him to show he is really there, he is the cynosure of all eyes and the target of thousands of field glasses. If the sun's rays instead of human optics focused through the latter, he would have been burned up long ago.

Not the slightest motion he makes escapes attention, so it has been noted that when a race is in progress he bends forward and runs with the runners, rubbing his hands up and down his legs in unison with their progress. In this respect he has something in common with the eminent James J. Walker, a devotee of the prize ring. It proved a wonderful side show at prize fights in New York when the Hon. James as Mayor was himself throwing punches in great excitement as though to show the lads in the ring how it should be done.

Three Crown Princes Guests

Among the Fuehrer's most attentive satellites are three crown princes who are guests of honor—Crown Prince Umberto of Italy, Paul of Greece and Gustav Adolf of Sweden. The last named is to take an active part in the games at a later stage.

Hitler refuses to use the automobile tunnel for guests of honor, which starts from the Herrstrasse, a quarter of a mile from the stadium, and leads to a private stairway that is right under his box. The squad car bringing him and his escort parks outside the door to government quarters instead.

The police wish he would use the tunnel, which is as high as the cathedral nave, because they have a lot of difficulty keeping people away from the second level railing of the stadium when he is leaving and it would be all too easy to drop something on his head from such a vantage point. Fear, however, never has been one of the Fuehrer's characteristics.

Any good American gate-crasher could walk in the stadium easily. Only the government box is well guarded. At the gates attendants are so afraid of offending an important foreigner that a brisk and important air works wonders.

Next to the Fuehrer, Max Schmeling, whenever he appears in the stadium, gets the most cordial reception. The Propaganda Ministry handed Max free seats for the games the minute he got out of the airplane at Tempelhof after his victory over Joe Louis.

Hitler has not yet shaken hands with a Negro Olympic champion, but the undisguised interest the German populace takes in these exotic visitors and the admiring attention paid to them shows the German people normally have no more race prejudice than any other people, and such as exists has been introduced into German life purely for political purposes. If the Olympics clearly demonstrate this and thus perhaps bring about some amelioration of the racial persecution in Germany, the location of the games in Berlin will have had its advantages.

However, this is almost too much to hope for, because after the tumult and the shouting of the Olympics is over, all the realities of German politics will come to the fore again.

Cuba Runs for Peru

In yesterday's races an athlete named Cuba ran for Peru, and one named Chia for China. Neither scored.

The oldest Olympic competitor is General Artur von Pongracz, Austrian tournament rider. He is 72 and a member of one of the oldest aristocratic families. He competed in the Olympics at Paris and Amsterdam and has taken part in almost every major European riding tournament in thirty-four previous years and has won 400 prizes.

Afoot he is unimpressive. His gait shows his age. Mounted he is quite another person, looking and acting as youthfully as the best.

Austria also has the most distinguished newspaper man present. He is General Ferch, commander in the Austrian Army during the World War. A monument has been built in his honor in Japan, and with his Olympic press badge he wears his Japanese gold medal.

The explanation is that General Ferch introduced skiing in Japan and is regarded there as the founder of Japanese Winter sports.

Continued on Page Twenty-seven

Other News of Sports On Next Three Pages

The New York Times.

SPORTS Section 5

S Copyright, 1937, by The New York Times Company. SUNDAY, JUNE 6, 1937. L+++ S

WAR ADMIRAL WINS BELMONT STAKES FOR TRIPLE CROWN; SCHULTE OF PIRATES INJURED AS GIANTS TRIUMPH, 7-5

PITCH HITS BATTER

Player Unconscious 10 Minutes From Blow on Head by Melton

X-RAYS SHOW NO FRACTURE

Moore, Hurt Friday, Also Is in Hospital—New York Now 10 Points Off Pace

SUHR'S STREAK AT AN END

'Iron Man' Is Forced Out by His Mother's Death After 822 Consecutive Games

By JOHN DREBINGER

Disaster in a variety of forms cracked down on the Pirates yesterday as Pie Traynor's front-running Pittsburghers moved into the Polo Grounds to launch a three-game series with the Giants.

They were forced to enter the contest minus the services of their own iron man first sacker, Gus Suhr, for the first time in six years.

Toward the close of the struggle they lost still another player, Fred Schulte, who was carried from the field unconscious, and at the finish the plucky but sadly riddled and bewildered Corsairs lost the game, 7 to 5.

As a result the Giants pulled themselves into a tie for the National League leadership in the matter of games, though still trailing Pittsburgh by a scant 10 percentage points.

Melton Replaces Smith

Schulte, the Pirates' right-fielder, became a casualty in the eighth inning when Cliff Melton, the Giants' towering left-hander, who had replaced Al Smith in the previous round, cracked the Pittsburgh player on the head with a pitched ball.

The blow landed with terrific force, striking on the left regional front, as it was later described, and Schulte, turned half way around by the impact, landed on his back at the plate.

He was unconscious for more than five minutes while the trainers of both clubs worked over him, and when their efforts failed to revive him a physician who had been sitting in the stands, Dr. C. R. Palmer, rushed out on the field to administer first-aid while a hushed crowd of 15,333 looked on.

Schulte was carried by teammates to the center-field clubhouse, where he regained consciousness after more than ten minutes. Though the stricken player after a few more minutes was able to sit up and talk rationally enough, Dr. Palmer ordered his immediate removal to the Polyclinic Hospital for a more thorough examination.

X-rays taken there revealed no fracture. Physicians said Schulte probably suffered a slight concussion and ordered that the player remain in the hospital two or three days.

Moore and Cochrane Also Hit

The mishap was the second in as many days in which a player suffered a head injury at the Polo Grounds, Joe Moore of the Giants having been a victim on Friday. A week ago last Tuesday Mickey Cochrane, manager of the Tigers, suffered a triple fracture of the skull when he was struck accidentally by a pitch delivered by Bump Hadley of the Yankees.

Suhr's National League endurance record of 822 consecutive games came to a close in the morning when the Pittsburgh first baseman received a wire that his mother died in San Francisco. Following a conference with Manager Traynor, Suhr announced that while it would be impossible for him to travel to the Coast in time for the funeral, he would remain out of the game for three days as a mark of respect.

This unfortunate turn forced the Pirates to take the field with a makeshift line-up that saw Paul Waner, their star outfielder, playing first base, while Schulte replaced Waner in right. Later, when Schulte passed out of the battle, Waner returned to the outfield and Will Brubaker was pressed into service at first.

Joe Bowman opposed the left-handed Smith at the outset. Though he was off to a two-run lead in the first inning when Arky Vaughan [illegible]hed a homer into the upper [illegible] tier with one on, things took [illegible] turn for Joe in the fourth. [illegible] successive hits by Mel Ott, Kiddo Davis, Johnny McCarthy and Gus

Continued on Page Seven

War Admiral Scoring His Third Major Triumph to Take Outstanding Honors Among the 3-Year-Olds

Times Wide World Photo.

Winner of Kentucky Derby and Preakness taking the Belmont Stakes in easy fashion, with Sceneshifter second

YANKS TOP TIGERS, AIDED BY 4 HOMERS

Gehrig Hits Two, Ruffing One in Pinch and DiMaggio Another in 6-5 Victory

MALONE SAVES THE DAY

Stops Walker, Who Had Singled Thrice, With Winning Run on Base in 9th

By JAMES P. DAWSON
Special to THE NEW YORK TIMES.

DETROIT, June 5.—The Yankee home-run guns, silent since last Sunday, burst forth at Navin Field today to pound the Tigers into defeat before a gathering of 27,500.

Battering Lou Gehrig smashed two balls for the circuit to boost his 1937 total to seven. Joe DiMaggio slammed one out of the park to make his total six. Charley Ruffing, in the familiar rôle of pinch-hitter, banged the ball into the distant center-field lower stand for his first of the campaign to round out the biggest home-run day of the year for the champions.

As a consequence, the Yanks sneaked from behind to overhaul Detroit and eke out a 6-to-5 triumph that maintained their lead over the Indians and thrust the Tigers farther off the pace.

Hadley Yields Lead

Feeble Yankee hurling almost wasted this prolific hitting. Irving (Bump) Hadley, in his first start against the Detroiters since he accidentally hit Mickey Cochrane, was not equal to the occasion but, the Yankee pitching staff being what it is at the moment, he hung around for six innings while the enemy held a three-run lead.

When Ruffing's pinch homer tied the count in the seventh, young Frank Makosky went on relief and had the encouragement of successive homers by DiMaggio in the eighth, which chased George Gill, and Gehrig. But in the end it was Pat Malone who saved the day.

Rushed to the rescue in the ninth when the enemy had hammered across a run, a pass and Hank Greenberg's single had the tying run on second and the winning one on first, Malone throttled the Tigers like a master.

He had no easy task. The man he faced was Gerald Walker, who had struck three straight singles against Hadley before Makosky

Continued on Page Seven

Vanderbilt's New Ranger Annexes Third Cup Trial

Defeats Lambert's Yankee by 2 Minutes 5 Seconds Over 28-Mile Windward and Leeward Course Off Newport

By JAMES ROBBINS
Special to THE NEW YORK TIMES.

NEWPORT, R. I., June 5.—Out on a Summer sea, Harold S. Vanderbilt's new yacht Ranger did some slippery work today and defeated Gerard B. Lambert's veteran Yankee by two minutes and five seconds over twenty-eight miles, half of it to windward and the rest down hill. It was Ranger's third straight victory in the first trial series to select a defender of the America's Cup.

While it was light going in a southwest breeze that ranged from seven and one-half to eleven and one-half knots' strength, it was a fairly true breeze with but few soft spots, and the test was a most creditable one for the new racer, which lost her mast before she was ever under sail. She is competing with a makeshift rig. It became evident that despite her large size Ranger does not require much stirring air to make her go.

She led Yankee by five minutes and thirteen seconds over the fifteen miles to windward, and that has been supposed to be Yankee's forte with her enlarged small-boat rig with single headsail. Running back, Yankee picked up three minutes and eight seconds, but Ranger tossed most of that away. She held high of the course with the idea of jibing and reaching for the finish. The trouble was she jibed too soon and wound up with a spinnaker on the other hand.

The pair were sent over to the north bell off Block Island. They went over the line together. Yankee had a Genoa laced in hard as was her mainsail, while Ranger ap-

Continued on Page Eight

PENN NINE BEATS PRINCETON IN 14TH

Wins by 9-8 on Bunt by Diven, Who Sends In Shinn With Deciding Marker

STANDING OF THE TEAMS

	W.	L.		W.	L.
Dartmouth	8	1	Columbia	5	7
Yale	6	2	Princeton	4	6
Harvard	5	3	Cornell	2	10
Penn	6	[illegible]			

Special to THE NEW YORK TIMES.

PHILADELPHIA, June 5.—Before an Alumni Day crowd of 7,000, Pennsylvania finished its Eastern Intercollegiate League baseball and entire athletic campaign by defeating Princeton on Franklin Field in fourteen innings, 9—8, today.

Walter Shinn, who made four of Penn's twelve hits, scored the winning run with one man out. He opened the inning by hitting a single to center, Ed Warwick followed with a single to right and after Dick Field sacrificed, Pitcher George Rusznak walked. That brought up Charley Diven, diminutive shortstop, who bunted safely.

Princeton used four pitchers, Bob

Continued on Page Two

TRACK TITLE KEPT BY LOUGHLIN HIGH

Team Victors in C. H. S. A. A. Meet Score Impressively—Mile Relay Mark Set

Bishop Loughlin Memorial High School scored a convincing team triumph to retain its championship in the eleventh annual City C. H. S. A. A. outdoor track and field meet, held at Boys High Field, Brooklyn, yesterday.

Loughlin's athletes, in winning the trophy for the second successive year, rolled up the impressive total of 70 points, dominating the field. The real battle in the tournament was the struggle for second place, which was won by St. Augustine's with 16 points, as against St. John's with 15.

In the junior midget competition the team trophy went to Mount St. Michael's, with 42 points. Power Memorial was runner-up with 28, and St. Michael's third with 22.

Sets New Standard

One meet record was broken during the afternoon, when the St. Augustine's relay team set a new standard for the mile. The St. Augustine runners negotiated the distance in 3:32.2, shattering the mark of 3:33.2 made by the St. Augustine team of 1933.

Edward Dunham of St. John's Prep carried off the honors in the senior mile run. He ran a steady race, remaining with the pack for the first three laps of the four-lap course.

Dominates Senior Run

Going into the final lap, he gradually stepped up his pace and easily drew ahead, crossing the line about five yards ahead of John Winters of St. Augustine's. The time was 4:43.3.

In the 880-yard senior run Loughlin prevailed, finishing one, two, three. Frank Prine won the event in 1:39.7, showing the way to his team-mates Martin Szmytkowski and Joseph Brachocki.

Prine also captured the senior broad jump, held in the morning at Loughlin Field. He made a leap of 20 feet 9¾ inches to take the

Continued on Page Four

CUNNINGHAM SETS U. S. MARK IN RUN

Takes ¾-Mile Event in 3:00.8 at New York A. C. Games—Close to World Figures

VENZKE TEN YARDS BEHIND

Curb Four Establishes Relay Record—Folwartshny Excels in the Hammer Throw

By ARTHUR J. DALEY

Running with such effortless grace as to give the impression that he could have gone much faster had he so desired, Glenn Cunningham raced to a new American record for three-quarters of a mile at the sixty-ninth annual Spring games of the New York Athletic Club yesterday.

Before a gathering of 5,000, perched high on the encircling knolls at picturesque Travers Island, the Kansas powerhouse covered the six furlongs in 3:00.8 to erase from the books the old figures of 3:01.4 that Joe Mangan posted in this same meet two years ago.

But the Curb Exchange "freshman" paid a heavy penalty for not driving through all the way in the homestretch. He missed by only two-tenths of a second equaling the world record of Jules Ladoumegue and saved for himself the rather empty satisfaction of tying the fastest American-run three-quarters of history, Bill Bonthron's 3:00.8 that was made in Sweden.

Unable to Hold Pace

Gene Venzke, the Cunningham shadow of recent seasons, was Glenn's chief and practically only pursuer. The picture runner from the Winged Foot Club could not hold on to the early fast pace and faded in the face of the bristling last-quarter burst of the Cornhusker to finish ten yards back in second place.

Had Venzke been able to challenge it might well have been a different story. As it was, he lost ground in the backstretch, lost more in the homestretch, and Cunningham, badly in need of some one to push him, lost his world record by his almost imperceptible easing up toward the close.

The Curb flyer was not doing any loafing for that last quarter, since he ripped off the distance in

Continued on Page Three

Times Wide World Photo.

Samuel D. Riddle, owner of victor, with prize which he has just received from Mrs. August Belmont. Jockey Charlie Kurtsinger is in center.

MACCALLUM TAKES NEW JERSEY TITLE

Lightly Regarded Ridgewood Golfer Defeats Scott in Amateur Final, 3 and 2

Special to THE NEW YORK TIMES.

RIDGEWOOD, N. J., June 5.—A 100-to-1 shot came through today to win the New Jersey State amateur golf championship when Ian MacCallum, Ridgewood Country Club player, defeated Paul De B. Scott of the Essex County Country Club, 3 and 2, in the final. The match ended on the 34th hole when MacCallum sank a 6-foot putt for a half.

MacCallum, a rank outsider when this tournament started, came through to the final in a blaze of

Continued on Page Six

TURF FANS IN RIOT AS LONG SHOT WINS

Absent From Original Field, Lassies Mary, 79-1, Takes Rerun Thorncliffe Race

By The Associated Press.

TORONTO, June 5.—Police drove a crowd of about 350 irate racing fans off the racing strip at Thorncliffe Park today after they had delayed the start of the third race for more than two hours.

The riotous scene developed after the second race had been ordered re-run as the result of the absence from the track of one of the entries. Some members of the crowd held tickets on the original winner of the race. They threw stones and pieces of dirt at the horses that came out to run in the third race, driving them back to the barns, and picketed betting booths. No property damage was done.

Special Police Sworn in

After a long delay a detail of fifty special police was sworn in and pushed the protesting mob from the track while the majority of the crowd looked on from the stands. Fist fights between police and members of the crowd developed before the track finally was cleared.

A field of eleven had romped six furlongs for a $700 purse in the second race, a claiming affair for 3-year-olds and upward. Vanished led the field and there was a photo for place and show. The official starter, however, asserted the starting flag had not been dropped because he knew one horse was missing.

The event was ordered re-run and Lassies Mary, the missing horse, a 79-1 shot, came to the post fresh and ready to go and won from a field of tired thoroughbreds. Lassies Mary paid $160.45 for a $2 ticket to

Continued on Page Ten

FIRST BY 4 LENGTHS

35,000 See 9-10 Choice Win $50,020 Race Despite Torn Heel

BREAKS THE TRACK MARK

Runs 1½ Miles in 2:28⅗ to Cut Man o' War's Record and Tie U. S. Time

SCENESHIFTER IS SECOND

Vamoose, 60-1 Shot, Next at Belmont—National Stallion Stakes to The Chief

By BRYAN FIELD

Running with a torn heel, but as easily as if he had wings, War Admiral yesterday clinched the 3-year-old championship before 35,000 persons by winning the sixty-ninth Belmont in time that shattered Man o' War's track record set seventeen years ago.

One of the greatest crowds ever to see a horse race at Belmont Park applauded the chestnut son of Man o' War as he coasted through the stretch to win by four lengths at the end of a mile and a half in 2:28 3-5 over a fast track.

The triumph made War Admiral the fourth horse to win the triple crown of Kentucky Derby, Preakness and Belmont. The earlier three were Sir Barton, Gallant Fox and Omaha.

It was not until after the finish that War Admiral's torn heel was noticed, the blood of the champion staining the tanbark saddling enclosure as the venerable Samuel D. Riddle defied his illness and weakness to come from the roof of the stand to the track level. He wished to lead in his champion as has been traditional in this greatest of all 3-year-old tests since the inaugural running in 1867.

Trainer Takes the Chain

But that other veteran, Trainer George Conway, mindful of his employer as well of War Admiral, took the lead chain, and himself walked War Admiral in amid the applause of the thousands. Conway feared that War Admiral might be too much for his septuagenarian owner to handle, but, as things turned out, the son of Man o' War was as quiet as a mouse and was not blowing enough to douse a candle.

All this was a few minutes after the finish of the $50,020 race in which Maxwell Howard's Sceneshifter was second and the Falaise Stable's 60-to-1 shot Vamoose third.

After that the order was Brooklyn, Flying Scot, Pompoon and Melodist. The winner was a 9-to-10 favorite after once having been as high as even money and he carried scale weight of 126 pounds to earn $38,020 of the total purse. This brings his winnings for the year to $144,620 and more definitely confirms his place as the season's leading money winner.

Work Over Sliced Heel

But it may be many weeks, and perhaps months, before War Admiral runs again to add to his total. In the stall after the finish last night Conway, his grooms, and a veterinarian worked over the sliced heel. Jockey Charlie Kurtsinger said:

"It occurred right at the break. He (War Admiral) was so anxious to get away that he reached too far under with his hind feet, and he clipped his front heels. The steel shoe sheared away a piece of his heel on the back part of the front hoof. The piece was almost as big as a half dollar."

In the heat of battle War Admiral never noticed the injury. And to see him run none would have supposed he was out for more than a gallop. The only time he had to put in any hard licks was in the three-eighths of a mile immediately after the start. Since War Admiral broke from the No. 7 post position on the extreme outside he had to get far enough in front so that he could cross over on his field.

Made Over Rolled Track

Flying Scot, with Johnny Gilbert up, was sent out with a rush to try to prevent War Admiral from getting the lead. Despite the early speed of the Withers winner, he could not outfoot War Admiral even with that fellow's disadvantage of the outside post position. After this brief brush, the race was a procession. It may have been this early bit of dash that accounted for the amazing time which also was equal to the American record set by Handy Mandy under the feather of 109 pounds.

However, that performance made

Continued on Page Eleven

Major League Baseball

National League

YESTERDAY'S RESULTS

New York 7, Pittsburgh 5.
Brooklyn 5, Cincinnati 4.
St. Louis 3, Philadelphia 1.
Chicago 6, Boston 3.

STANDING OF THE CLUBS

	Pittsburgh	New York	Chicago	St. Louis	Brooklyn	Boston	Phila'phia	Cincinnati	Won	Lost	Percentage
Pittsburgh	—	1	3	5	2	5	3	5	24	15	.615
New York	4	—	4	3	5	3	3	4	26	17	.605
Chicago	1	4	—	5	2	4	4	5	25	17	.595
St. Louis	3	2	2	—	3	2	4	4	20	19	.513
Brooklyn	2	2	2	4	—	1	3	4	18	20	.474
Boston	3	3	1	2	4	—	2	2	17	21	.447
Phila'phia	1	3	2	0	3	5	—	2	16	24	.400
Cincinnati	1	2	3	0	1	1	5	—	13	26	.333
Games lost	15	17	17	19	20	21	24	26	—	—	

GAMES TODAY

Pittsburgh at New York (3 P. M.).
Cincinnati at Brooklyn (3 P. M.).
St. Louis at Philadelphia (2).
Chicago at Boston (2).

American League

YESTERDAY'S RESULTS

New York 6, Detroit 5.
Chicago 2, Philadelphia 0.
Cleveland 8, Washington 6.
Boston 11, St. Louis 4.

STANDING OF THE CLUBS

	New York	Cleveland	Chicago	Detroit	Boston	Phila'phia	Wash'gton	St. Louis	Won	Lost	Percentage
New York	—	3	2	5	4	6	2	3	25	14	.641
Cleveland	4	—	2	4	4	3	3	2	22	15	.595
Chicago	3	5	—	1	3	1	3	5	21	17	.553
Detroit	2	2	4	—	2	2	5	5	22	20	.524
Boston	2	1	2	1	—	2	4	5	17	16	.515
Phila'phia	1	0	4	4	0	—	4	3	16	20	.444
Wash'gton	2	2	2	2	3	3	—	4	18	23	.439
St. Louis	0	2	1	3	0	3	2	—	11	27	.289
Games lost	14	15	17	20	16	20	23	27	—	—	

GAMES TODAY

New York at Detroit.
Philadelphia at Chicago (2).
Washington at Cleveland (2).
Boston at St. Louis (2).

Belmont Stakes Chart

By The Associated Press.

The following is the chart showing how the Belmont Stakes was run at Belmont Park yesterday:

6208 FIFTH RACE—The Belmont Stakes; $25,000 added; 3-year-olds; one mile and a half. Start good; won easily; place same. Went to post, 4:22, off 4:29½. Winner, br. c., by Man o' War—Brushup. Trainer, G. Conway. Value to winner, $38,020; second, $5,000; third, $2,500; fourth, $1,000. Time—0:24, 0:48, 1:12 1-5, 1:37, 2:02 1-5, 2:28 3-5. (Equals American record, new track and stake record.) Weather clear; track fast.

Ind.	Starters	Wt.	P.P.	St.	¼	½	¾	Str.	Fin.	Jockeys.	O.	H.	Cl.	Pl.	Sh.
(5923)	War Admiral	126	7	3	1^{2}	1^{4}	1^{4}	1^{4}	1^{4}	Kurtsinger	4-5	1	9-10	1-3	1-8
(6138)	Sceneshifter	126	6	7	3^{4}	2^{2}	2^{3}	2^{10}	2^{10}	Stout	8	10	8	5-2	1
6132	Vamoose	126	1	2	4^{6}	4^{2}	3^{3}	3^{4}	3^{8}	Workman	60	100	60	20	10
(4936)	Brooklyn	126	4	5	7	6^{4}	6^{8}	4^{2}	4^{8}	Wright	6	8	6	2	1
(6132)	Flying Scot	126	5	1	2^{hd}	3^{1}	5^{1}	6^{1h}	5^{hd}	Gilbert	12	15	12	4	7-5
6017	Pompoon	126	3	4	5^{2}	5^{hd}	4½	5^{1}	6^{15}	H. Richards	3	4	7-2	4-5	1-4
6170	Melodist	126	2	6	6^{1}	7	7	7	7	Longden	30	30	20	7	3

War Admiral, very fractious at the stalls, finally got away in full stride and hustled into the lead going into first quarter mile. He was placed under restraint, galloped along saving ground at every stride, drew away in the run through the stretch and won galloping. Sceneshifter began to move up in the run down the backstretch, moved into second place entering the far turn, then set sail for the leader but was no match for the winner. Vamoose, away well, was hustled into a contending position and was hard ridden for the last furlong. Brooklyn made up some ground in the last half mile but never threatened. Flying Scot stopped badly at the end of six furlongs. Pompoon failed to show any speed. Melodist was badly outrun.

Owners—1, Glen Riddle Farms; 2, Maxwell Howard; 3, Falaise Stable; 4, E. R. Bradley; 5, John Hay Whitney; 6, J. H. Louchheim; 7, Wheatley Stable.

WAR ADMIRAL WINS THE RICH BELMONT

Continued From Page One

over a rolled track was not nearly as good a one as Man o' War's 2:28 4-5 over a racing strip that had not been tampered with.

The ceremonies after the finish were participated in by Mr. Riddle, Mrs. August Belmont, widow of the former president of Belmont Park who also was the grandson of the man for whom the Belmont Stakes is named; Conway, Kurtsinger, George H. Bull, president of Saratoga and a director at Belmont Park, and Cornelius Vanderbilt Whitney, vice president of Belmont and senior officer because of the absence of Joseph E. Widener in France.

Mr. Whitney had just seen his fine colt, The Chief, win the twenty-fifth running of the $20,450 National Stallion Stakes, which carried a value of $12,630 to the owner of the winner. The Chief's time for the five furlongs was 0:58 flat, equal to the record for the stake, which was made in 1907 by the unbeaten Colin. With Raymond Workman driving his hardest, The Chief won by a length and a half at 11 to 5 from the filly, Catalysis, who in turn was a length before Transmitter.

Best Son of Man o' War

It was Mr. Whitney who called the significance of the time performance to Mr. Riddle, but that proud owner at the moment had eyes for nothing but his chestnut color-bearer by Man o' War from Brushup, who now has won all five of his starts this year. In his career he has started eleven times and won eight. He has never been out of the money.

It was said at the ceremonies in the unsaddling enclosure that War Admiral is the best son of Man o' War. Previously this distinction had been Crusader's. Now there were none to cavil at giving the palm to War Admiral. He did all asked of him.

At the post he was his usual obstreperous self. Vamoose was as badly behaved, and Melodist was no angel.

The break, when it came after seven and one-half minutes, was an even one with Flying Scot trying to get the lead. But War Admiral was so fleet that he was in front going around the first turn. Flying Scot was second and Sceneshifter and Vamoose close up.

Once straightened away in the backstretch, there was nothing to the race. The leader kept on coasting along and never had to take a challenge from those in back of him. The shifts behind were filled with drama, but rather unknown to most of those present.

Pompoon, worn and tuckered from his earlier efforts, made a half-hearted move, and so did Wayne Wright aboard Edward R. Bradley's Brooklyn. These two had sort of a private war as Messrs. J. H. Louchheim and Bradley, the respective owners, had reinstated their canceled Kentucky Derby wager on a horse for horse basis. Since Brooklyn got fourth money, and thus landed in the Belmont money, Mr. Bradley won this horse for horse wager. It was $10,000 a side, one to be in the money. Technically "in the money" means the first three.

Goes Past Flying Scot

But the only real threat to War Admiral was the move begun at the far turn by Sceneshifter. This former Joseph E. Widener racer, now trained by Earl Sande, went past Flying Scot without trouble. A moment or two later, Vamoose also went past the Withers winner. Both Brooklyn and Pompoon were under the whip to beat each other, but neither was within gunshot of the vanguard.

Turning into the stretch, Sceneshifter came within about three lengths of the flying War Admiral, but that was as close as he got. The Glen Riddle color-bearer stepped blithely through the last quarter to win as he pleased. It is interesting to note that he passed the mile and a quarter mark in 2:02 1-5, faster time than he made in annexing the Kentucky Derby.

The complete fractions follow: 0:24, 0:48, 1:12 1/5, 1:37, 2:02 1/5, 2:28 3/5. Man o' War's old mark was 2:28 4/5, made under 118 pounds. It was not made in the Belmont Stakes. At the time Man o' War won the Belmont in 1920 the race was not at a mile and a half. The performance of War Admiral easily broke the record for the Belmont Stakes, 2:29 1/5, made in 1934 by Peace Chance.

The Glen Riddle establishment now has won four Belmonts—with Man o' War in 1920, and with his three sons, American Flag in 1925, Crusader in 1926 and now War Admiral.

Notables in Crowd

A distinguished gathering saw the race, including Mr. and Mrs. Seth W. Morton, Mrs. William Woodward, John E. Cowdin, Dr. and Mrs. D. Philip McGuire, Mr. and Mrs. John Currie, Alfred Gwynne Vanderbilt, Carter Lee Bowie, Bernard Baruch, Herbert Bayard Swope, Richard Whitney, Joseph E. Davis, Mr. and Mrs. Harry F. Sinclair, Mr. and Mrs. Walter Salmon, John Hay Whitney, Mr. and Mrs. Algernon Daingerfield, Mrs. Payne Whitney, Mrs. Dorothy Harriet Cole-Gill, Miss Mary Mays, Henry W. Bull, George H. Bull, John Sanford, Mr. and Mrs. Parker Corning and Robert Pinkerton.

Those with luncheon reservations in the Turf and Field Club and with the Stevens brothers in the clubhouse included:

J. Henry Alexandre, G. N. Armsby, Mrs. Sherwood Aldrich, J. S. Auerbach, Nelson I. Asiel, Mrs. Paul Abbott, W. F. Armstrong, H. G. Barbe, Miss Beatrice Barnes, Mrs. August Belmont, E. B. Benjamin, A. S. Blodget, Luther L. Blake, William C. L. Breed, Cecil Barret, Charles S. Bromley, C. Perry Boldlestone, F. L. Benson, Mrs. Joseph R. Busk, Jeremiah Beal and W. B. Baldwin.

Also Arthur Broderick, E. H. Carle, G. W. Case, William Gordon Coogan, C. M. Connfelt, R. L. Cerero, Ashley T. Cole, Frederic G. Clarke, B. S. Cutler, William M. Chadbourne, H. Clements, J. M. Ceballos, Lewis L. Clarke, Walter Dunnington, F. B. Davis, H. Mason Day, W. Duryea, William du Pont Jr., William M. Erb, W. H. Erhart, Robert A. Fairbairn, James A. Foley, L. B. Gould, Richard Gibson, Cecil D. Giles and H. Garnett.

Hamersley Has Reservation

Others were Dr. D. L. Gardiner, Mrs. Blanche Gresham Giddeds, H. Maxwell Howard, H. S. Hooker, L. Gordon Hamersley, F. C. Henderson, Heisler Harrington, Frank J. Heller, R. C. Hattersley, Overton Harris, C. L. Jones, Frederick Johnson, H. W. Jackson, Leslie E. Keiffer, Hugh N. Kirkland, Warren Kaine, Shepard Kreoh, J. W. Kilbreth, Charles R. Leonard, Franklin B. Lord, René Leone, G. Leboutillier, R. B. Lanier, George de F. Lord, R. J. Marony, Carl K. Mengal, E. N. Morris, Clifford L. McMillen and Clarence H. Mackay.

There were in addition W. J. McConvill, Charles G. Meyer, H. McCollum, Frank J. Murphy, W. Meikelhan, W. B. Miller, George K. Morrow, Theodore May, R. D. McGrath, James F. Middledith, Phelps Montgomery, Olney B. Mairs, William Maxwell, F. C. Nicodemus Jr., Herbert Neal, J. P. Nicholas, H. I. Nicholas, Leonard Outhwaite, H. W. Phelps, Theodore Pell, George J. Patterson, C. Harvey Pierce, Alexander D. B. Pratt, Martin Quinn, R. K. Rochester, Fred L. Richards, John N. Ryan, D. Rait Richardson, S. D. Ripley, Joseph E. Ridder, G. L. Stevenson, Mrs. D. K. Salmona, John Sloan, Lloyd G. Schultz and Joseph W. Sidenberg.

Also Jack W. Schiffer, Walter Schuttler, W. J. Salmon, George M. Sidenberg Jr., Alexander Stoller, C. H. Thieriot, H. O. Tallmadge, Daniel G. Tendey, E. R. Tinker, Frederick Tilney Jr., Martin Taylor, R. G. Thach, Robert J. Turnbull, Henry J. Topping, Alvin Untermyer, Charles V. Hickox, E. M. Voorhees, Sidney F. Ward, P. A. B. Widener and Elisha Walker.

Mrs. Joseph A. Wade, Charles G. West, Leo F. Wanner, Ira F. Warner, J. T. Winkhaus, J. S. Walsh, M. S. Watts, Charles B. Wiggin, ex-Governor C. S. Whitman, C. H. Young, Charles F. Young, Paul Zuckerman, William Ziegler Jr., Robert G. Johnson, Frederick Sanford Hatch, G. B. Scott and Lawrence Morris were also included.

VARIPAPA STRETCHES LEAD

Takes Fifth Block of Bowling Match With Burton

DALLAS, June 5 (AP).—Andy Varipapa, noted New York bowling star, widened his lead over Nelson Burton of Dallas in the fifth ten-game block of their series last night. Varipapa's advantage went to 258 pins. He won last night by 71 points.

Varipapa and his opponent bowled the first four blocks in New York. Burton and his partner won the American Bowling Congress doubles championship.

AT THE FIFTY-FIRST ANNUAL EXHIBITION OF THE TUXEDO HORSE SHOW ASSOCIATION

Times Wide World Photo.

View during the judging of the five-gaited saddle-horse class on the opening day

PRINCE CHARMING II WINS HUNTER TITLE

Quinn's Entry Also Takes the Sweepstakes and 2 Other Events at Tuxedo

KILCLOUDY GAINS TROPHY

Gives Mrs. Colt Second Challenge Award Score—Miss Arthur Victor

By FRED VAN NESS

Special to THE NEW YORK TIMES.

TUXEDO PARK, N. Y., June 5.—Prince Charming II, a chestnut gelding who in 1933 and 1934 won more hunter championships than any other horse in the country, stamped himself as an important factor in the ring again at the closing session of the fifty-first exhibition of the Tuxedo Horse Show Association today.

Sweeping through with easy victories in the ladies' hunter class and the sweepstakes after he had captured the blue in the model event, he gained the championship of the show, with Miss June Hanes's Molyneux being held in reserve.

Conformation and breeding had much to do with his triumphs. Prince Charming II is a beautiful chestnut by Teddy—Sweet Agnes. Teddy was the sire of Sir Gallahad, who in turn sired Gallant Fox, so that Prince Charming II comes from a noted strain. He was shown by Edward V. Quinn, owner of the Clarreda Farm Stable. It was his first competition this year.

Purchased Last Year

Prince Charming II was purchased by Mr. Quinn last season after he had been out of the show ring for more than a year. He quickly regained his form with his new owner and won three championships in 1936, scoring at Orangeburg, Elberon and Mount Pocono. He went off form after that, but the come-back here has encouraged Mr. Quinn, who will send him to several other exhibitions in the East.

When he was leading the hunters in the country he won championships at Washington, Newport, Westchester Country Club, Fairfield, Conn.; Stamford and Ox Ridge.

By his three victories yesterday Molyneux had become the leading candidate for the hunter championship, but he did not show so well today. He was placed fourth in the hunter sweepstakes, and it was this event that probably decided the championship award.

The closing-day judging was witnessed by a crowd of more than 500, largely members of society, many of whom are among the sponsors of the show.

Modern Rouge Repeats

Modern Rouge, a bay daughter of Baumont and Powder Puff, the latter a champion of several years ago, scored decisively in the champion five-gaited saddle-horse sweepstakes. It was the second time the 4-year-old mare had won for her new owner, Mrs. Fred Wettach, who owns the Trillora Farm. The mare was purchased just before the Devon Show. Second went to Mountain Belle, the property of Moses W. Faitout, and third to Little Sport from the S. K. R. Farm.

James A. Thomas Jr. of White Plains, N. Y., was awarded the trophy in the good-hands event in which there were eleven competitors. The award makes him eligible for the good-hands championship at the next National Horse Show. Miss Elinor Marie Wynne of New York was second and Miss Marion Colt of Tuxedo Park third.

Blackbirder Victor Over Trouper By Length in Massasoit Handicap

Takes Lead in Stretch to Triumph in Mile and Sixteenth Event at Suffolk Downs—The Fighter Captures Sprint—Steelhead and Westy's Duke Run Dead Heat

By The Associated Press.

BOSTON, June 5.—After trailing the field of eight for all but a half mile of the mile and one-sixteenth route, F. L. Flanders's 5-year-old Blackbirder weaved his way through the pack in the stretch to win by a length from Mrs. C. E. Allen's Trouper today in the Massasoit Handicap at Suffolk Downs.

The victor, son of Bostonian, came home in front for the third consecutive time in his four New England starts this season and traveled the route in 1:44 2-5. Mrs. E. I. Wade's Up and Up gained the show spot with a head on Mrs. Walter E. O'Hara's Mucho Gusto, who led through the final turn.

Knocked Off Stride

As he tore down the home stretch, after cutting into the rail to save ground, Blackbirder was bumped hard and knocked off stride. Jockey Carroll Bierman, who rode two previous winners, speedily overcame that mishap and Blackbirder was drawing away as he reached the wire.

The Flanders performer, second choice in the wagering, returned $7.40, $5 and $4.20. Trouper's prices were $27.20 and $11 for place and show and Up and Up's show price was $7.40. The victory was worth $2,645 to the Flanders Stable.

Another star that attempted to repeat was Mrs. Marion Cassidy's Bill Farnsworth, who set a new six-furlong record of 1:10 3-5 here in last Monday's feature.

Finishes in Sixth Place

In the John Hancock Handicap at six furlongs he got off well but weakened and finished sixth. W. F. Morgan's The Fighter won, a length ahead of W. H. Gallagher's Rudie and Miss A. Doris's Lady Higloss. The Fighter was timed in 1:11 4-5 and paid $16, $7.20 and $3.80. Rudie returned $6.60 and $4.40, and Lady Higloss $3.80 for show.

The first dead heat of the meeting occurred in the last race, when the favorite, Steelhead, off last in a field of seven, came with a furious closing rush to divide the honors with Westy's Duke. For the mile and three-sixteenths race they were clocked in 2 minutes flat, a length ahead of Handsome Hal, who took the show award.

Budge Puts Americans in Davis Cup Challenge Round by Defeating von Cramm

U.S. TENNIS TEAM TOPS GERMANY, 3-2

Budge's Fine Rally Halts von Cramm, 6-8, 5-7, 6-4, 6-2, 8-6, at Wimbledon

TENSE FIGHT IN LAST SET

Don Erases Rival's 4-1 Lead —Henkel First Halts Grant to Tie Interzone Final

By THOMAS J. HAMILTON JR.
Wireless to THE NEW YORK TIMES.

WIMBLEDON, England, July 20.—Donald Budge defeated Baron Gottfried von Cramm today, 6—8, 5—7, 6—4, 6—2, 8—6, in a match which will be forever memorable in every land where lawn tennis is played. In doing so, the California redhead not only brought the United States within striking distance of the Davis Cup, for ten long years in alien hands, but vindicated his fighting ability inherited from his Scottish ancestors.

His victory was all the more striking because every one, with the possible exception of a few of the most rabid German supporters of von Cramm, had been sure Budge would win without the slightest difficulty. Bryan M. (Bitsy) Grant of Atlanta lost to Heiner Henkel as expected, 7—5, 2—6, 6—3, 6—4, but connoisseurs of tennis merely murmured among themselves that this was a good thing, because with the score 2—2 in the interzone finals between the United States and Germany von Cramm would be encouraged to play the game of his life and so would succeed in giving at least enough competition to produce an interesting match.

To the surprise and amazement of all von Cramm proceeded to produce tennis that was unbelievable, coming from a player who had been the weaker member of the German doubles team yesterday.

Pate Has Anxious Time

When the German captured the first two sets, Walter Pate, non-playing American captain, from his chair in the shadow of the umpire's stand, merely ordered himself some tea. But when Budge, after coming back in Frank Merriwell style to take the third and fourth sets and even the match, trailed at 1—4 in the final set, then indeed things looked black.

Pate wrung his hands—and so did a small but voluble band of Americans who sought to match the enthusiasm of a larger number of Germans and von Cramm's English supporters.

But Budge was equal to the emergency. He took the next three games and with the score in matches 2—all, in sets 2—2 and in games 4—4, it seemed time for somebody to cry: "Hold, enough."

However, six more games followed, each packed with thrills such as scarcely another sport can produce, before Budge in the fourteenth converted his fifth match point with a forehand placement to von Cramm's backhand, which the game German knew it was hopeless to try for.

America's 3-2 conquest, accounted for by Budge's two singles triumphs and his doubles victory with Mako, settled all controversy concerning Pate's choice of Grant over Frank Parker, who had beaten Henkel in the Wimbledon quarter-finals, for the No. 2 singles berth. Had Pate done so and Parker repeated his victory, at least one of the Americans present would not have been scared out of at least ten years of his mortal existence.

Challenge Round Opens Saturday

But, as it was, the United States did win and there is every prospect of an American victory over Great Britain in the challenge round beginning Saturday. If so much had not depended on the outcome, perhaps the two gallant sportsmen

United Press International

Baron Gottfried Von Cramm, of Germany, and Don Budge of the United States, (R), admiring a racquet before their match.

who contested the deciding match would not have climbed the heights they are capable of scaling and did scale.

"I chose Grant," Pate said afterward, "because after watching him practice for two weeks after Wimbledon I was convinced Bitsy had a better chance against Henkel because of his greater experience."

Parker was the first to congratulate Pate after they had reached the clubhouse of the All-England Club and, with Grant heartbroken over his two defeats, one can leave it at that, along with Pate's summing up of those fifty-eight games between Budge and von Cramm: "I couldn't stand another such two hours."

"How did Budge have such a narrow escape in a match with a player to whom he had lost at Wimbledon in 1935 but had defeated in the interzone Davis Cup finals the same year and again at Wimbledon in the finals only a few weeks ago?" is a query to which there are several answers.

Pate, for instance, pointed out that Budge's shoulder was rather sore from his and Mako's doubles match with von Cramm and Henkel yesterday. But the simplest answer is perhaps the best. Von Cramm was playing inspired tennis, especially in the first two sets, and Budge, though slightly off his game, had the fighting heart which enabled him to come back despite his troubles.

Von Cramm Wins Toss

From the very start, it was evident that Von Cramm was a far different player from yesterday. Winning the toss, he took his opening service at love and although Budge held his it seemed obvious he would have his work cut out for him.

Budge's ground strokes and his service both were giving him trouble, while his volleying lacked decision. Also he showed a curious lethargy which caused him to fail to try for Von Cramm's drop shots and other hard ones that he usually gobbles up.

Later, even another fault developed. On crucial points Budge was misjudging shots, many of which were well within reach and which disconcertingly halted their course on the baseline.

All this may sound as though Von Cramm merely was lucky to force Budge to five sets. Quite to the contrary. His fast service was as fast as Budge's and his "kicker" was forcing Budge to sprint beyond the sidelines on the advantage court. His favorite strategy—manoeuvring for position until he could drive into Budge's backhand corner, then rushing to the net and volleying out of reach of Budge's forehand—came off time and time again.

But with his game gradually catching hold, Budge fought up from 40—0 to two advantages in the fifth only to lose the game on Von Cramm's service ace. Games went with service until the ninth when Budge converted his fifth advantage and broke through to lead 5—4. With a chance for the set, however, Budge missed two easy forehands to drop his service at love.

The next three games went with service Two service aces placed Budge out of danger in the twelfth, but he yielded the fourteenth and the set.

Budge came back in the second set, working up to advantage in the opening game, but von Cramm held fast. The Californian was in difficulties in the sixth when trailing, 15-40, but he also held, and the set went with service until the twelfth game.

Von Cramm still was a most formidable opponent, but with Budge leading, 40 love, it seemed this might go on indefinitely. Instead, von Cramm took the next four points for advantage and set point with bold net play and passing shots which cost Budge heavily the few times he ventured to the net. Von Cramm missed a volley to deuce the game but converted his next advantage for the set on a volley which Budge, misjudging, allowed to light squarely on the left sideline.

Budge Begins Rally

In the third set it was now or never for Budge. Throwing off his lethargy, he attacked with a forcing backhand to the opposite corner to break von Cramm's service in the opening game and hold his own for a 2-0 lead.

Budge had an advantage in the third but failed to handle a drop shot, and von Cramm took the game on a service ace. Then he broke Budge's service at love to draw even.

Budge had lost his service on ground strokes, but in the fifth the situation was reversed, Budge breaking through von Cramm at love. He then took his own service at love for a 4-2 lead.

This, as it turned out, was good enough, von Cramm failing to break through. Budge now was only one set down and it did not take him long to even the score in sets.

Don annexed the first four games of the fourth in five minutes with the loss of only five points. Von Cramm held his next two services, but it was Budge's set handily.

Even during his comeback in the third and fourth sets, Budge got into trouble occasionally, so it seemed his chances of taking the fifth and final one depended upon his ability to hold his own services until von Cramm weakened.

German Breaks Through

The first three games went with service, but in the fourth von Cramm took the best Budge could produce on the rise, rushed to the net and held it to break through. With a 3—1 lead, von Cramm then took own service at love as his supporters went wild.

For the first time a look of anxiety crossed Budge's face, although Pate, who had been coaching him, before he offered Budge a towel as the players changed courts used the towel on himself first. He really needed it more.

Aided perhaps by the fact that his less robust opponent was beginning to lose the benefits of the rest interval after the third set, Budge now threw caution to the winds, rushing to the net behind each return of von Cramm's now weakening service. Helped by a net cord, Budge broke through von Cramm at love, then took his own service at 15 to square the set and match.

This run of three games seemed to promise that the suspense would soon be over. Instead it was just beginning.

Von Cramm led, 40-15, in the next game, but, aided by a double default, Budge fought up to an advantage. Quick to realize his danger, the German drew on his nerves of steel, deuced the game with magnificent volleying, fought off another Budge advantage and went on to capture the game with a service ace.

Budge held his service without difficulty to deuce the set, but von Cramm took his own in the eleventh at love. With it again his turn to take the net Budge squared the match by winning his delivery at love.

Six all! And now the two final games were at hand, although few realized it.

Obviously weakening, the German dropped his service at love but called on his last resources to meet the threat of Budge's service at the net. It was almost the von Cramm of the first two sets who so determinedly was volleying to make it 30-all, but he drove out the next point and Budge had match point in his grasp.

Still von Cramm fought on. After a long rally he scored a placement to Budge's forehand to deuce the game. Then he got two advantages at the net. Each time Budge held, but there were heads shaking over the psychological effect if he should drop this game after all his valiant efforts.

Now Budge got another advantage with a zipping service which von Cramm netted, but lost it on von Cramm's brave placement to the American's forehand. Budge smashed for another, only to send an easy one into the net, smashed again but drove out from his backhand.

German's Charge Fails

But now von Cramm, white with the strain, ended a long rally with an out. After a brief rally the German again charged the net and lost all save honor when he left his backhand open and Budge did not let that opportunity go by.

Budge's triumph meant so much because of the failure of Grant's scarcely less valiant fight to gain an American victory beforehand. The Atlantan's spurt in the first set just fell short, and, although he took the second handily, Henkel broke service at crucial moments for the third and fourth.

With Henkel flashing net play similar to his work in the doubles yesterday, Grant was lucky to get one game of the first six in the opening set. Then, soft-balling Henkel as he does American opponents, he took four straight to deuce the set. But Henkel returned to the net to put shots well out of reach of his diminutive opponent in the next two games with the loss of only two points for the set.

Grant, fighting back valiantly, took five straight games in the second set and squared the match.

In the third set, Henkel was beginning to solve Grant's game. Instead of trying to drive, he chopped hard, concentrating on placements. A three-game run helped him to take the set, but this seemed no cause for too much worry.

Bitsy Returns in Shorts

Returning after the interval in shorts, instead of the flannels he had worn previously, Grant got into trouble immediately. He trailed at love—40, but finally held his service.

Scrambling for gets which other players would be reluctant even to try for, Grant then proceeded to produce the best tennis he has played this season in England. He had four advantages on Henkel's service, but the German finally held his delivery. Although Grant threatened again in both the fourth and sixth games, he still could not break through.

It was clear as the set progressed and Grant's threats to break Henkel weakened that the moment Bitsy lost his own service he would be finished. Perhaps over-conscious of this, Grant tried to play safe in the ninth and Henkel broke his service at love.

Not relenting, Henkel advanced to 40—15. Although Grant bravely fought off two set points to deuce the score, Henkel got another advantage on a placement too far away for Grant to reach, then put over a serve too hot for Grant to handle.

SUTTER IS BEATEN AT NET BY 7-5, 7-5

Notable Clay Court Triumph Is Recorded by Mahoney, Virginia Sophomore

BOWDEN, FISHBACH SCORE

By ALLISON DANZIG

Ernest Sutter of New Orleans, national intercollegiate champion from Tulane and runner-up to Wilmer Allison at Spring Lake, was eliminated from the Eastern clay court championship yesterday at the Jackson Heights Tennis Club, Queens.

Jack Mahoney of the home club, a sophomore at the University of Virginia and a player without a previous notable conquest to his string, caught the stalwart Southerner off his game and eliminated him in sequence sets, 7—5, 7—5.

Sutter, who was beaten in this tournament in his first match a year ago, was so disheartened by the feebleness of his tennis that he was in the mood to go home and put his racquets away for the season when he came off the court.

Lacking in Length

The intercollegiate champion during the past three weeks has not shown anything like the form he displayed on turf at Merion and, although he has a preference for hard courts, he played his poorest match of the year yesterday. His service was pitifully weak and he was guilty of three successive double faults in the fifth game of the second set after he had stood within a point of a 4-1 lead.

Sutter's ground strokes were so lacking in length and sting that he had no safe approach to the net and as a consequence he was forced to stay back and meet his fate at the hands of an opponent who seldom made a mistake.

Vander Meer Hurls Second No-Hit, No-Run Game

Times Wide World

EBBETS FIELD UNDER THE FLOODLIGHTS DURING ITS FIRST NIGHT GAME

DODGERS BOW, 6-0, IN NIGHT INAUGURAL

Vander Meer, Reds' Ace, Makes Baseball History—Hitless String Now 18 1/3 Innings

FILLS BASES IN THE NINTH

By ROSCOE McGOWEN

Last night they turned on the greatest existing battery of baseball lights at Ebbets Field for the inaugural night major league game in the metropolitan area. A record throng for the season there, 40,000, of whom 38,748 paid, came to see the fanfare and show that preceded the contest between the Reds and the Dodgers.

The game, before it was played, was partly incidental; the novelty of night baseball was the major attraction.

But Johnny Vander Meer, tall, handsome 22-year-old Cincinnati southpaw pitcher, stole the entire show by hurling his second successive no-hit, no-run game, both coming within five days, and making baseball history that probably never will be duplicated. His previous no-hitter was pitched in daylight at Cincinnati last Saturday against the Bees, the Reds winning, 3—0. Last night the score was 6—0.

The records reveal only seven pitchers credited with two no-hitters in their careers and none who achieved the feat in one season.

More drama was crowded into the final inning than a baseball crowd has felt in many a moon. Until that frame only one Dodger had got as far as second base, Lavagetto reaching there when Johnny issued passes to Cookie and Dolf Camilli in the seventh.

But Vandy pitched out of that easily enough and the vast crowd was pulling for him to come through to the end.

The Crucial Inning

Johnny mowed down Woody English, batting for Luke Hamlin; Kiki Cuyler and Johnny Hudson in the eighth, fanning the first and third men, and when Vito Tamulis, fourth Brooklyn hurler, treated the Reds likewise in the ninth, Vandy came out for the crucial inning.

He started easily, taking Buddy Hassett's bounder and tagging him out. Then his terrific speed got out of control and, while the fans sat forward tense and almost silent, walked Babe Phelps, Lavagetto and Camilli to fill the bases.

All nerves were taut as Vandy pitched to Ernie Koy. With the count one and one, Ernie sent a bounder to Lew Riggs, who was so careful in making the throw to Ernie Lombardi that a double play wasn't possible.

Leo Durocher, so many times a hitter in the pinches, was the last hurdle for Vander Meer, and the crowd groaned as he swung viciously to line a foul high into the right-field stands. But a moment later Leo swung again, the ball arched lazily toward short center field and Harry Craft camped under it for the put-out that brought unique distinction to the young hurler.

It brought, also, a horde of admiring fans onto the field, with Vandy's team-mates ahead of them to hug and slap Johnny on the back and then to protect him from the mob as they struggled toward the Red dugout.

The fans couldn't get Johnny, but a few moments later they got his father and mother, who had accompanied a group of 500 citizens from Vandy's home town of Midland Park, N. J. The elder Vander Meers were completely surrounded and it required nearly fifteen minutes before they could escape.

Enhances His Record

The feat ran the youngster's remarkable pitching record to eighteen and one-third hitless and scoreless innings and a string of twenty-six scoreless frames. This includes a game against the Giants, his no-hitter against the Bees and last night's game.

Vander Meer struck out seven Dodgers, getting pinch hitters twice, and of the eight passes he issued two came in the seventh and three in the tense ninth.

Added to his speed was a sharp-breaking curve that seldom failed to break over the plate and at which the Dodger batsmen swung as vainly as at his fireball.

On the offense, well-nigh forgotten as the spectacle of Vander Meer's no-hitter unfolded, the Reds made victory certain as early as the third frame, when they scored four times and drove Max Butcher away.

Frank McCormick hit a home run into the left-field stands with Wally Berger and Ival Goodman aboard, while a pass to Lombardi and singles by Craft and Riggs added the fourth run.

Craft's third straight single scored Goodman in the seventh, the latter's blow off Tot Pressnell's right kneecap knocking the knuckleballer out and causing him to be carried off on a stretcher. Berger tripled off Luke Hamlin in the eighth to score Vander Meer with the last run.

The box score:

CINCINNATI (N.)	ab.	r.	h.	po.	a.	e.
Frey, 2b	5	0	1	2	2	0
Berger, lf	5	1	3	1	0	0
Goodman, rf	3	2	1	3	0	0
McC'mick, 1b	5	1	1	9	1	0
Lombardi, c	3	1	0	9	0	0
Craft, cf	5	0	3	1	0	0
Riggs, 3b	4	0	1	0	3	0
Myers, ss	4	0	0	0	1	0
V. Meer, p	4	1	1	2	4	0
Total	38	6	11	27	11	0

BROOKLYN (N.)	ab.	r.	h.	po.	a.	e.
Cuyler, rf	2	0	0	1	0	0
Coscarart, 2b	2	0	0	1	2	0
aBrack	1	0	0	0	0	0
Hudson, 2b	1	0	0	1	0	0
Hassett, lf	4	0	0	3	0	0
Phelps, c	3	0	0	9	0	0
bRosen	0	0	0	0	0	0
Lavagetto, 3b	2	0	0	0	2	2
Camilli, 1b	1	0	0	7	0	0
Koy, cf	4	0	0	4	0	0
Durocher, ss	4	0	0	1	2	0
Butcher, p	0	0	0	0	1	0
Pressnell, p	2	0	0	0	0	0
Hamlin, p	0	0	0	0	1	0
cEnglish	1	0	0	0	0	0
Tamulis, p	0	0	0	0	0	0
Total	27	0	0	27	8	2

aBatted for Coscarat in sixth.
bRan for Phelps in ninth.
cBatted for Hamlin in eighth.

Cincinnati	0 0 4	0 0 0	1 1 0	—6
Brooklyn	0 0 0	0 0 0	0 0 0	—0

Runs batted in—McCormick 3, Riggs, Craft, Berger.

Two-base hit—Berger. Three-base hit—Berger. Home run—McCormick. Stolen base—Goodman. Left on bases—Cincinnati 9, Brooklyn 8. Bases on balls—Off Butcher 3, Vander Meer 8, Hamlin 1. Struck out—By Butcher 1, Pressnell 3, Vander Meer 7, Hamlin 3. Hits—Off Butcher 5 in 2 2-3, Hamlin 2 in 1 2-3, Pressnell 4 in 3 2-3, Tamulis 0 in 1. Losing pitcher—Butcher. Umpires—Stewart, Stark and Barr. Time of game—2:22.

FANS JAM STANDS LONG BEFORE GAME

Night Ball Proves Popular at Ebbets Field—Koy and Brack Beat Owens in Sprints

By LOUIS EFFRAT

They came early and stayed late for the latest of baseball extravaganzas at Ebbets Field last night, and at $1.10 a person considered it a bargain. Of course, the 3,118 bleacherites lucky enough to get into the park at 55 cents each felt it was an absolute "steal."

An hour before Larry MacPhail had the lights turned on there was hardly a vacant seat around, a fact which added to MacPhail's prestige as a master showman. Long before the ball game got under way Brooklyn's entry into the Mazda Belt was proclaimed an artistic as well as a financial success.

There was plenty of music, ably rendered by two fife and drum corps and a band—MacPhail always does things in a big way—flag-lowering ceremonies and a series of sprinting exhibitions by Jesse Owens, the hero of the 1936 Olympics.

Precisely at 8:35 P. M. the lights went on and a terrific roar came from the throng. Turning night into day was something new to Dodger fans and to say that they were pleasantly surprised would be putting it lightly.

Koy Conquers Owens

The initial faux pas came early in the form of a false start by Ernie Koy of the Dodgers as he, Lee Gamble of the Reds and Owens were on the line for their 100-yard handicap dash. Owens, spotting the ball players ten yards, went the distance in 0:09.7, but had to be content with second, behind Koy, who triumphed by a yard. It was a great start for the Dodgers.

After clearing 23 feet 6 inches in a running broad jump exhibition, Owens hooked up with the Dodgers' Gibby Brack in a novel 120-yard race. Owens cleared ten low hurdles while Brack sprinted the distance on the flat. The ball player won by 10 yards, which prompted one fan to remark: "Brack should have given Owens a handicap."

As the Dodgers took infield practice Babe Ruth, perhaps wondering what this national pastime is coming to, made his appearance. He received a royal welcome.

Another Babe, Floyd Caves Herman, who will always be remembered in Brooklyn, also was on hand. Night games, however, are no novelty to him. He plays his share of them for Jersey City.

Quick Approval by Fans

By the time the umpires made their appearance Brooklyn fans already had placed their stamp of approval on the nocturnal game. At this point, not an outfielder had been hit on the head by a fly ball. What would follow was still a matter of conjecture.

After discussing ground rules with the rival captains, the umpires added a few instructions to the crew of photographers who were on the field, it all being new to them, too. Then at 9:45 P. M., Max Butcher tossed the first pitch to Lonnie Frey and history was made at night.

Gehrig Clouts No. 8 at Chicago As Yanks Win Fifth in Row, 6-4

Gordon's Double Features Three-Run Rally Against White Sox in Eighth—Radcliff and Rosenthal Waste Four-Baggers

By JOHN DREBINGER

Special to THE NEW YORK TIMES.

CHICAGO, June 15.—With consuming patience, a crowd of 5,000 Chicagoans waited a long time for the White Sox to give them something of a run for their money at Comiskey Park today.

Finally, in the sixth inning, it came. Lou Gehrig had just hit his eighth homer of the year to help swell the Yankee lead to 3 to 0, which gave the Sox an idea. For Rip Radcliff hit for the circuit with a comrade aboard and that wrenched two runs away from our young Joe Beggs.

In the seventh, Larry Rosenthal, pinch hitting for Johnny Whitehead, who had been pitching a fine game up to then, uncorked another homer with one on and that put the Sox one ahead while the crowd went wild. Jimmy Dykes, for the moment, was easily the craftiest manager on four continents.

Rigney Falls on Mound

But at this point poor Jimmy ran out of numbers, as well as pitchers. The Yanks hopped on Johnny Rigney and Bill Dietrich for three runs in the eighth with the help of Joe Gordon's double, and that gave the McCarthy forces the battle, 6 to 4.

It also gave the world champions their second straight victory of the series and their fifth in a row in their determined bid to regain the lead. In the latter quest, however, they were somewhat stalled as the Indians also won, thereby retaining their half-game margin.

As Beggs, like Whitehead, had to vacate for a pinch hitter in the eighth he, too, was not around at the finish, but the three runs the Yanks scored for him in that round nevertheless gave him his third victory, which Ivy Paul Andrews nailed down for him with a first-class relief job in the last two innings.

Henrich Draws Pass

Asked to protect a one-run margin as he stepped to the mound in the eighth, Rigney immediately got into trouble by passing Tommy Henrich. Jake Powell followed with a single, his third hit, and Gordon doubled, driving in one. George Selkirk, batting for Beggs, was intentionally passed to fill the bases and Dietrich came in to relieve Rigney.

In this he may have succeeded, for it was with considerable relief that Rigney walked out, but Bill brought no great help to the stricken Sox. Frankie Crosetti lifted a long fly to center to score Powell and Red Rolfe smacked a single to right to drive in Gordon. That clinched it.

A trio of singles by Powell, Gordon and Beggs gave the Yanks their first tally off Whitehead in the second and in the sixth, after Gehrig had fired his No. 8 into the lower right pavilion, another tally followed when Powell's double and two passes filled the bases and Beggs emptied one with an infield out.

Luke Appling, slugging Sox shortstop who has been out with a fractured leg ever since the training season, is working out daily, but his return to the line-up still looks a long way off.

Charlie Ruffing likely will seek to make it a clean sweep for the Yanks in the series final tomorrow.

The Box Score

NEW YORK (A.)	ab.	r.	h.	po.	a.	e.
Crosetti, ss	5	0	0	1	2	0
Rolfe, 3b	5	0	1	2	2	0
DiMaggio, cf	5	0	2	2	0	0
Gehrig, 1b	3	1	1	10	0	0
Dickey, c	4	0	0	4	1	0
Henrich, rf	2	2	0	4	0	0
Powell, lf	5	2	3	2	0	0
Gordon, 2b	3	1	2	2	5	1
Beggs, p	3	0	1	0	1	0
bSelkirk	0	0	0	0	0	0
Andrews, p	1	0	0	0	0	0
Total	36	6	10	27	11	1

CHICAGO (A.)	ab.	r.	h.	po.	a.	e.
Berger, ss	5	0	1	3	1	0
Owen, 3b	5	0	1	1	4	0
St'bacher, rf	3	1	1	0	0	0
Kreevich, cf	3	0	1	3	0	0
Radcliff, 1b	3	1	1	12	0	0
Walker, lf	4	0	0	3	0	0
Hayes, 2b	4	0	0	1	6	1
Sewell, c	4	1	1	4	0	0
Whiteh'd, p	2	0	1	0	0	0
aRosenthal	1	1	1	0	0	0
Rigney, p	0	0	0	0	0	0
Dietrich, p	0	0	0	0	0	0
cKuhel	1	0	0	0	0	0
Total	35	4	8	27	11	1

aBatted for Whitehead in seventh.
bBatted for Beggs in eighth.
cBatted for Dietrich in ninth.

New York	0 1 0	0 0 2	0 3 0	—6
Chicago	0 0 0	0 0 2	2 0 0	—4

Runs batted in—Crosetti, Rolfe, Gehrig, Gordon, Beggs 2, Radcliff 2, Rosenthal 2.

Two-base hits—Powell, Gordon. Three-base hit—Owen. Home runs—Gehrig, Radcliff, Rosenthal. Sacrifice—Henrich. Double plays—Gordon, Crosetti and Gehrig; Owen, Hayes and Radcliff. Left on bases—New York 12, Chicago 7. Bases on balls—Off Beggs 2, Andrews 1, Whitehead 4, Rigney 2, Dietrich 2. Struck out—By Beggs 3, Whitehead 3. Hits—Off Beggs 8 in 7 innings; Andrews 0 in 2, Whitehead 7 in 7, Rigney 2 in 0 (pitched to 3 batters in 8th), Dietrich 1 in 2. Winning pitcher—Beggs. Losing pitcher—Rigney. Umpires—Moriarty, Rommel and Kolls. Time of game—2:07.

"All the News That's Fit to Print."

The New York Times.

LATE CITY EDITION
Partly cloudy, possibly scattered showers today and tomorrow; little change in temperature.
Temperatures Yesterday—Max., 80; Min., 66

Copyright, 1938, by The New York Times Company.

VOL. LXXXVII....No. 29,370. Entered as Second-Class Matter, Postoffice, New York, N. Y. NEW YORK, THURSDAY, JUNE 23, 1938. P THREE CENTS NEW YORK CITY and Vicinity | FOUR CENTS Elsewhere Except in 7th and 8th Postal Zones.

LOUIS DEFEATS SCHMELING BY A KNOCKOUT IN FIRST; 80,000 SEE TITLE BATTLE

FIGHT ENDS IN 2:04

Rights Drop the Loser Thrice and Trainer Tosses In Towel

1936 SETBACK AVENGED

Challenger Says He Was Fouled With a Kidney Punch —The Gate Tops $900,000

By JAMES P. DAWSON

The exploding fists of Joe Louis crushed Max Schmeling last night in the ring at the Yankee Stadium and kept sacred that time-worn legend of boxing that no former heavyweight champion has ever regained the title.

The Brown Bomber from Detroit, with the most furious early assault he has ever exhibited here, knocked out Schmeling in the first round of what was to have been a fifteen-round battle to retain the title he won last year from James J. Braddock. He has now defended it successfully four times.

In exactly 2 minutes and 4 seconds of fighting Louis polished off the Black Uhlan from the Rhine, but, though the battle was short, it was furious and savage while it lasted, packed with thrills that held three knockdowns of the ambitious ex-champion, every moment tense for a crowd of about 80,000.

A Representative Gathering

This gathering, truly representative and comparing favorably with the largest crowds in boxing's history, paid receipts estimated at between $900,000 and $1,000,000 to see whether Schmeling could repeat the knockout he administered to Louis just two years ago here and be the first ex-heavyweight champion to come back into the title, or whether the Bomber could avenge this defeat as he promised.

As far as the length of the battle was concerned, the investment in seats, which ran to $30 each, was a poor one. But for excitement, for drama, for pulse-throbs, those who came from near and far felt themselves well repaid because they saw a fight that, though it was one of the shortest heavyweight championships on record, was surpassed by few for thrills.

With the right hand that Schmeling held in contempt Louis knocked out his foe. Three times under its impact the German fighter hit the ring floor. The first time Schmeling regained his feet laboriously at the count of three. From the second knockdown Schmeling, dazed but game, bounced up instinctively before the count had gone beyond one.

On the third knockdown Schmeling's trainer and closest friend, Max Machon, hurled a towel into the ring, European fashion, admitting defeat for his man. The towel sailed through the air when the count on the prostrate Max had reached three.

Ignored in Boxing Here

The signal is ignored in American boxing, has been for years, and Referee Arthur Donovan, before he had a chance to pick up the count in unison with knockdown timekeeper Eddie Josephs, who was outside the ring, gathered the white emblem in a ball and hurled it through the ropes.

Returning to Schmeling's crumpled figure, Donovan took one look and signaled an end of the battle. The count at that time was five on the third knockdown. Further counting was useless. Donovan could have counted off a century and Max could not have regained his feet. The German was thoroughly "out."

It was as if he had been pole-axed. His brain was awhirl, his body, his head, his jaws ached and pained, his senses were numbed from that furious, paralyzing punching he had taken even in the short space of time the battle consumed.

Claims Blurred Vision

Following the bout, Schmeling claimed he was fouled. He said that he was hit a kidney punch, a devastating right, which so shocked his nervous system that he was dazed and his vision was blurred. To observers at the ringside, however, with all due respect to Schmeling's thoughts on the subject, the punches which dazed him were thundering blows to the head, jaw and body in bewildering succession, blows of the old Alabama Assassin reincarnate last night for a special occasion.

Louis wanted to erase the mem-

Continued on Page Fourteen

Bill Introduced in Cuba To Make July 4 a Holiday

Special Cable to THE NEW YORK TIMES.

HAVANA, June 22.—A bill declaring the coming Fourth of July a national holiday was introduced in the House of Representatives last night by Paul de Cardenas, Representative from Havana Province.

The bill is designed to suspend all commercial, industrial and governmental activities to permit attendance at a demonstration being organized for the Fourth of July as homage to the United States.

Plans for the demonstration, which will be held under the auspices of the cultural, social, economic and patriotic groups of the island, were launched last week.

The committee has asserted that homage is being paid to the United States "solely to cultivate and strengthen the sentiment of friendship and close relations that have always existed between the two peoples."

HAUGWITZ DISPUTE RISES OVER CHILD

Former Barbara Hutton Gets Police Guard for Son, 2, but Count Denies Kidnap Threat

Special Cable to THE NEW YORK TIMES.

LONDON, June 22. — Countess Haugwitz-Reventlow, the former Barbara Hutton, Woolworth heiress, broke into the news again today as London buzzed with rumors that her 2-year-old son Lance was under guard against kidnapping.

Late tonight Count Court Haugwitz-Reventlow, who is in Paris, acknowledged in a telephone talk with The Daily Mail that a sharp difference of opinion had arisen between him and the Countess over the future education of their son. According to The Daily Mail, the Danish nobleman also disclosed that the police were anxious to interrogate him should he land in Britain, but he strenuously denied any attempt or threat to kidnap his son.

The gates of Winfield House, the huge Haugwitz-Reventlow mansion, which stands in its own park within Regent's Park, were locked against all comers and policemen patrolled the grounds. Inquirers were referred to a statement issued by W. M. Mitchell, solicitor for the Countess.

Silent for "Legal Reasons"

"I am sure that the press will appreciate that for legal reasons it is impossible for the Countess to make any statement at the present time," he said. "If at a later stage she has anything to say, you may be sure that the press will be informed."

Mr. Mitchell made the statement at the gates of Winfield House, which was a center for reporters and photographers all day. Interest in the statement was heightened by a memorandum from Scotland Yard to the effect that the police had no information about any plot to kidnap the child, although the Countess acknowledged that she had "taken certain precautions."

Later, while Lance was being taken for an airing in the twelve-and-a-half-acre park, the Countess was driven rapidly with Sir Patrick

Continued on Page Ten

REPUBLICANS PLAN CONFERENCE RULE ON CONVENTION VOTE

Party Delegates Agree on a Program to Assure Unity on All Proposals

FIRST SESSION ON MONDAY

Leaders Indicate They Will Welcome Wiretapping as Campaign Issue

By W. A. WARN

Special to THE NEW YORK TIMES.

ALBANY, June 22.—Before the Constitutional Convention adjourned today for the week-end the Republicans took action to insure a firmer control over decisions reached in that body. There will be frequent conferences of all Republican delegates on important pending proposals.

The decision to assure cohesive party action and a united Republican front against the Democratic minority was reached after a discussion held last night at a private dinner given to Chief Judge Frederick F. Crane of the Court of Appeals, president of the convention, by the chairmen of standing committees. All Republican delegates had been invited and all but two or three attended. The conference plan, it was said today, was unanimously approved by all present.

The proposed creation of a steering committee, after having been discussed by Republican delegates for many days, has been definitely dropped.

The conferences, under the plan decided upon, will be held on call from State Senator Perley A. Pitcher, Republican floor leader in the convention. In the event that Senator Pitcher should fail to call a party conference on some important measure, a petition signed by ten of the ninety-two Republican members would compel him to issue the call.

Use of Caucus Barred

Mr. Pitcher stressed the distinction between conferences and caucus action. Where caucus action would bind all participants, conference action would leave a delegate free to vote according to his own convictions, even where that would be in conflict with a decision reached at a conference.

The practice resorted to sometimes at legislative conferences to turn them into a caucus at some critical stage was pronounced taboo by him.

The new plan will have its first application when the convention resumes next week. Senator Pitcher has already issued a call for the first conference, to be held at 4 P. M. Monday. The subject to be discussed is the Dunnigan search and seizure proposal, with its clause forbidding the use in court of evidence obtained through wiretapping or through search and seizure without a court warrant.

The party convention leaders oppose this clause and hope to bring enough persuasive arguments to bear to insure a solid front against the proposal.

Plan Used in the Senate

In establishing its conference plan and its taboo on the caucus, the party has virtually adopted a method which it has followed in the State Senate for fifteen years. It was recalled today that such conferences have demonstrated their effectiveness in keeping party members in line, even though on occasion a Senate leader has had at his command not more than twenty-six Senators, a bare majority.

The Dunnigan search and seizure proposal, and the one favorably re-

Continued on Page Six

Walker Calls on La Guardia at City Hall; Dapper Ex-Mayor Says Visit Is for Clients

Debonair and dapper as ever, former Mayor James J. Walker visited Mayor La Guardia at City Hall yesterday. He said his call was in the interest of several clients who have business dealings with the city.

Tanned and looking healthier than he has in years, Mr. Walker emerged from the Mayor's office after a half-hour chat. Cornered by the City Hall reporters, many of whom he knew, he was asked the nature of his call.

"I could tell you," he smiled, "but why should I? It wasn't anything much—just that I wanted to see the Mayor in the interest of a few clients of mine. Amicus curiae, you might call it—a friend of the court."

The former Mayor hotly denied a hint that he was late for his 2:45 appointment. He swore that he had been in City Hall at 2:40, and had spent the time chatting with Stanley Howe, the Mayor's secretary, until 3 o'clock when Mayor La Guardia was ready to see him. He wore a dark blue suit, a white shirt with a blue tie, Panama hat with the brim turned down, and cornflowers in his buttonhole.

Because there was a hearing going on upstairs on a proposed tax on bookmakers, Mr. Walker was asked if he had any clients who were bookmakers.

"Unfortunately, no," he said with the same eye-crinkling smile. "Taxation," he went on with mock seriousness in his tone, "is a very, very comprehensive subject."

A photographer broke in to ask him to pose "coming through the gate" and shaking hands with Patrolman Charles Stoffers, a veteran police aide in the building.

"Uh-uh," he demurred. "I don't like that coming-through-the-gate business. That picture has been made too many times."

Nevertheless he assumed the pose to satisfy the photographer. Asked if he had discussed a possible successor to the late Senator Copeland with the Mayor, Mr. Walker said:

"Politics? Now what would I know about politics?"

Labor Board Gives C. I. O. Control Of All West Coast Longshoremen

A. F. L. Loses to Bridges Union in Sweeping Decision Setting Up Nation's First Major Geographical Bargaining Agency

By LOUIS STARK

Special to THE NEW YORK TIMES.

WASHINGTON, June 22.—The C. I. O. won a major victory over the A. F. of L. today when its affiliate the International Longshoremen's and Warehousemen's Union, District No. 1, was certified by the National Labor Relations Board as the exclusive bargaining agency for all longshoremen in thirty-one Pacific Coast ports.

The Pacific Coast longshoremen led by Harry Bridges, Australian-born radical leader against whom deportation proceedings have been started on a charge of membership in the Communist party, seceded from the A. F. of L.'s International Longshoremen's Union last year and set up the organization.

In certifying the Bridges union the NLRB made an unprecedented decision in establishing the first major geographical bargaining unit in the marine industry.

The board found that 9,557 of the 12,860 longshoremen on the Pacific Coast had designated the Bridges union as their representative for purposes of collective bargaining.

The decision will affect all longshoremen and warehousemen employed by the Ship Owners Association of the Pacific Coast, Waterfront Employers Association of the Pacific Coast, the Waterfront Employers of Seattle, the Waterfront Employers of Portland, the Waterfront Employers Association of San Francisco and the Waterfront Employers Association of Southern California.

In the course of the hearings, the A. F. of L. protested against the request by Mr. Bridges that his union be designated as the exclusive bargaining agency on the ground that the board had no power to designate a bargaining unit larger than employes of one company.

The board's jurisdiction was protested by the A. F. of L. and its affiliate, the International Longshoremen's Union, because the contract between the employer and the Pacific Coast longshoremen was still in the name of the A. F. of L. organization on behalf of the employes.

The companies also argued that the appropriate bargaining unit for longshoremen must be one restricted to those working for a particular employer at a particular port.

Overruling these objections, the board held that, under the Labor Relations Act, it expressly received authority to decide that the "employer" unit shall be that most appropriate unit for purposes of collective bargaining. The act includes within the term employer "any person acting in the interest of an employer, directly or indirectly," and the term person "includes one or more associations."

The present contract between the employers' associations and the longshoremen is held by the A. F. of L. union, and the board ruled that it was not necessary for it to decide whether the contract now passes to the Bridges organization, because a majority of members had voted to leave the A. F. of L. and to join the C. I. O.

The board declared, however, that

Continued on Page Four

TURROU SPY STORY BARRED IN PRESS

Hardy Gets Writ Halting First Installment—Show-Cause Order Up Today

United States Attorney Lamar Hardy obtained yesterday a court order preventing The New York Post from publishing the revelations of Leon G. Turrou, special agent of the Department of Justice, chief investigator in the German espionage inquiry.

The action was taken about 4:30 P. M., but was not verified in New York City until shortly before 8 P. M. The news had been flashed from Washington about 6:30 P. M., however, which indicated that Mr. Hardy's unusual move had the approval of his chief, Attorney General Homer Cummings.

The effect of the order was to halt scheduled publication today of Mr. Turrou's first installment of a series of articles which were intended to run for about twenty-one days. The show cause order served upon J. David Stern, publisher of The Post, and Mr. Turrou, will be argued this morning before Judge Murray Hulbert at 10:30 A. M., in Room 506 of the Federal Court House in Foley Square.

Seeks to Wait on Inquiry

It was understood that Mr. Hardy's chief objection to the projected articles was that agents have not yet completed investigation of incidents listed in the advertisements and which later must be presented to the grand jury, whose proceedings are secret.

Several items listed for publication, it was learned, for a long time have been a source of grave concern to the War and Navy Departments. If proved true they would overshadow in importance any defense secret thus far known to have been obtained by the spy ring. Officials of the two services had nothing to do with Mr. Hardy's action, but early in the investigation they requested secrecy until the truth was established.

The aim of Mr. Hardy's proceeding is to obtain an injunction which would prevent publication of anything by Mr. Turrou concerning the case until the grand jury, which will be reconvened on Monday, has completed its work.

From Mr. Stern the proceeding drew a challenge to fight for the right to publish the series under sanction of constitutional principles.

"By endeavoring to enjoin this paper from printing the news," declared Mr. Stern, "the government is making an unprecedented attempt to erase the freedom of the press from the Constitution.

"The law places responsibility upon the publisher for news which does any injury. The Constitution protects against the restraint in anticipation of such injury because the exercise of such anticipatory

Continued on Page Two

PRESIDENT NAMES 9 FOR BRITISH SURVEY

He Also Includes Sweden in Investigation of Employer-Employe Conditions

By FELIX BELAIR Jr.

Special to THE NEW YORK TIMES.

HYDE PARK, N. Y., June 22.—President Roosevelt today completed the selection of a study group of nine members representing business, industry, labor, the general public and the law to investigate industrial-labor conditions in Great Britain, and added employer-employe relationships in Sweden to the group's field of inquiry.

The reason for including Sweden in the agenda of the investigation was not explained in the announcement of the personnel of the study group, and suggestions that the President might have in mind a legislative redefinition of labor's responsibility to the public and to management in this country were met with a flat denial by Presidential aides.

Mr. Roosevelt has not the slightest intention of attempting to duplicate in this country the well-defined methods of adjusting industrial disputes practiced in either Great Britain or Sweden, nor does he contemplate a combination of the methods of the two as a means of lessening interruptions to business and industrial operations here, it was explained.

Personnel of the Group

To conduct the inquiry, the President named the following group, for which no chairman was chosen, with each member having an equal voice in the preparation of a final report to the Secretary of Labor:

Lloyd K. Garrison, dean of the University of Wisconsin Law School and former head of the Labor Relations Board.

Robert Watt, representing the American Federation of Labor.

Gerard Swope, president of the General Electric Company.

Henry I. Harriman, former president of the Chamber of Commerce of the United States.

William H. Davis, New York attorney and former NRA deputy administrator.

Mrs. Anna M. Rosenberg, regional director of Social Security for New York.

Charles R. Hook, president of the American Rolling Mills Company.

Marion Dickerman, principal of the Todhunter School for Girls, New York City.

William Ellison Chalmers, assistant United States Labor Commissioner at Geneva, who is to act as general secretary and liaison officer of the group.

Conspicuously absent from the personnel list was a representative for the Committee for Industrial Organization. John L. Lewis, its head, had refused to designate such a representative on invitation of Secretary Perkins. He had agreed to do so but withdrew his agreement when it was hinted several weeks ago that one of the purposes of the inquiry was to pave the way

Continued on Page Three

CUT IN STEEL WAGE BROACHED TO LEWIS AS RECOVERY SPUR

U. S. Corporation Opens Talks on Plan to Make Jobs and Aid Trade by Reducing Pay

PRICE DROP IS EXPECTED

C. I. O. Likely to Face Choice Between Granting Request and Losing Contract

Tentative discussions have been held recently between officials of the United States Steel Corporation and of the Steel Workers Organizing Committee, C. I. O. affiliate, on the possibility of a readjustment of wages that would promote increased production and employment in the steel industry.

These discussions, which thus far have been informal and exploratory, involve the complicated relationships of prices, labor costs and operating volume. Officials of the United States Steel Corporation declined yesterday to comment on the situation beyond saying that conferences had been held at frequent intervals, usually in Pittsburgh, ever since a contract was signed with the C. I. O. affiliate early last year.

John L. Lewis, head of the Committee for Industrial Organization, who personally negotiated the union's contract with Myron C. Taylor, former chairman of the Steel Corporation, declined to comment on the reports that a wage reduction was being discussed.

Corporation Losing Money

United States Steel is operating at about 28 per cent of capacity and is losing money rapidly. Although it has officially maintained its published scale of prices unchanged, price-slashing is rampant in the steel industry and Big Steel is reported in financial circles to be giving serious consideration to the advisability of reducing its published price schedules.

According to the belief in well-informed Wall Street quarters, the corporation has suggested or is about to put up to Mr. Lewis and other C. I. O. officials the proposal that the organized workers and the company should agree to take a cut —one in basic wage rates, the other in prices—in the expectation that this adjustment would lead to larger orders, increased production and employment and a gain in total income for both the workers and the corporation.

The alternative, according to steel experts in the financial district, is likely to be a further diminution of the corporation's business and a further reduction in the amount of employment it can provide.

Should the Steel Workers Organizing Committee agree to a reduction in the basic wage rates, it is probable that some understanding would be reached simultaneously providing that the original wage rates would be restored after a substantial recovery in the corporation's business.

Lewis Faces Dilemma

It is recognized in financial circles that Mr. Lewis and other C. I. O. officials would find it peculiarly difficult to agree to a wage reduction. Organized labor in general has taken the stand that reduction of wages cannot contribute to prosperity.

Philip Murray, chairman of the S. W. O. C., in a speech delivered in Cleveland on Feb. 20, described how the committee in renewing its contract with United States Steel had turned back an effort to link wage rates with operating rates, and he declared that, as a result of the contract, the committee had

Continued on Page Four

Relief Pickets Ride to WPA Office in Autos; Somervell Wonders How They Can Afford It

Lieut. Col. Brehon B. Somervell, local Works Progress Administrator, has watched scores of picketing demonstrations without comment, but when he saw relief workers driving up to his office in automobiles yesterday to picket against wage cuts he decided it was time to do a little protesting on his own account.

"This is the first time I ever saw relief people come up here with automobiles loaded with banners to protest a wage cut," Colonel Somervell told reporters. "If there is anything that would justify a wage cut, it is that."

It all started when the administrator, returning to the WPA building at 70 Columbus Avenue late in the afternoon, found the WPA Teachers Union, Local 453, an A. F. of L. affiliate, organizing a picket line on the block between Sixty-second and Sixty-third Streets.

As he watched, two cars full of signs and pickets appeared. Asked later whether they were WPA cars, Colonel Somervell replied laughingly that he hoped they were not.

The demonstration brought out 610 persons, but most arrived under their own power, according to the police. Most of them were from WPA educational projects, but a sizable delegation represented the five Federal arts projects, which are outside Colonel Somervell's jurisdiction.

Signs carried by the marchers denounced the wage reductions, which range from $4.70 to $14.95 a month. "Up With Recovery—Down With Wage Cuts," one placard said. More than 26,000 clerical and professional workers are included in the groups affected by the cuts.

Deputy Inspector John Challan and thirty patrolmen watched the picket line for two hours. At one point a bag of water came hurtling from an upper window of the WPA building. There was no other incident.

LABOR PARTY THREATENS 3-CORNERED STATE RACE UNLESS TERMS ARE MET

ASKS TWO OFFICES

Would Pick Senator and Lieutenant Governor in Coalition

REPUBLICAN TIE POSSIBLE

Copeland Post for Hillman Is Proposed by Critics of the Democratic Slate

By JOHN L. UNDERHILL

Unless the American Labor party is permitted to name its candidates for the rest of the term of the late Royal S. Copeland in the United States Senate and for Lieutenant Governor in coalition with one of the two major parties, the Labor party will go it alone and name its own slate this Fall.

This was decided yesterday, it was learned, by the board of strategy of the Labor party, meeting to consider the political developments brought about by the announced candidacies of Governor Herbert H. Lehman for the Senate and Attorney General John J. Bennett Jr. for the Governorship.

The Labor party leaders, it was said, are far from satisfied with the tentative Democratic slate of Senator Robert F. Wagner and Governor Lehman for the Senate and Mr. Bennett for Governor. It was indicated that the Labor party leaders feel that Sidney Hillman, president of the Amalgamated Clothing Workers of America, is eminently fitted for the short-term Senate nomination.

Republicans Are Interested

There is a possibility, it was indicated, that if the Democrats fail to come to terms with the Labor party the Republican will. Republican leaders, it was learned, have been in close touch with Labor party heads within the last few days. As yet, however, there has been no formal conference.

Should the Labor party fail to win either major party to a coalition ticket it can support—and the party insists that the whole ticket must be acceptable, even if it wins its two places — consideration will be given to the naming of a separate slate. In any event the party leaders insist that party independence must be maintained on a stronger basis than ever.

Just where Mayor La Guardia, who is dissatisfied with the Lehman candidacy, stands in the Labor party situation was not clear. He did not take part in yesterday's conference of the Labor party leaders and they have, it was learned, heard nothing directly as to his plans. Whether they would be willing to name him as their candidate for the Senate to run against the major party nominee, leaders were not prepared to say. In any event, he is not considered to be in the inner circles of the party.

In connection with the revelation of the Labor party stand, it was recalled that Alex Rose, executive secretary of the Laoor party and its official spokesman, announced earlier in the week that the party would insist on representation before a coalition could be effected. The party choices for Lieutenant Governor, it was learned, are Langdon W. Post, former Tenement House Commissioner, and Frederick F. Umhey, executive secretary of the International Ladies Garment Workers Union.

Mayor Defers Comment

Mayor La Guardia, obviously displeased with the tentative Democratic slate, commented cryptically at City Hall that he would have something to say soon.

"The essential need is for persons who will support good, sound, progressive policies in Washington, Albany and New York," the Mayor said. "I will have something to say on the subject within a few days."

David Dubinsky, president of the International Ladies Garment Workers Union, who had been mentioned as a possible Senate choice, withdrew his name from consideration.

"I am not a candidate for any political office," he said. "I do not believe that the American Labor party will or should make blanket commitments for the support of a slate of candidates of any other political party, Democratic or Republican. The American Labor party is in sympathy with the New Deal and is ready to support outspoken New Dealers, but this is as

Continued on Page Six

Yield of Cigarette Tax Likely to Be $9,000,000

New York City's one-cent tax on each package of cigarettes appeared likely to bring in $9,000,000 a year, three times the estimate of the original yield, when collection figures made public yesterday showed that $1,525.305 had been collected since the tax went into effect on May 1.

City Treasurer Almerindo Portfolio said the city had collected $1,369,224 on the sale of penny stamps, $23,745 on the sale of three-cent stamps, $132,200 from the certification of stamping machines and $135 from various penalties.

The City Council will vote on continuance of this tax, along with others in Mayor La Guardia's program, at its meeting in City Hall tomorrow.

LEHMAN DECLINES TO NAME SENATOR

Says He Will Act on Copeland Vacancy Only If Extra Session Is Called

Special to THE NEW YORK TIMES.

ALBANY, June 22.—Governor Lehman will not appoint a United States Senator to succeed Royal S. Copeland, who died last week, unless President Roosevelt should call a special session of Congress before the vacancy can be filled by election.

The Governor, who yesterday announced his willingness to accept the Democratic nomination for the "short" term of two years which remains of Senator Copeland's six-year term, made this announcement soon after his return to his desk early this evening.

In response to questions by the news correspondents Governor Lehman said he had received a number of messages approving his decision and wishing him well in his venture as a Senate candidate. He said also that he had received no word from President Roosevelt, nor had he an appointment to see the President in the near future.

Mr. Lehman, who, in his capacity as Lieutenant Governor while Mr. Roosevelt was Governor, was looked upon as Mr. Roosevelt's right hand man in the State administration, broke with the President over the latter's proposal to enlarge the Supreme Court.

Denies Talk With Roosevelt

The Governor in reply to questions said he had not discussed with President Roosevelt his proposal to become a Senate candidate. He disclosed his intention to Postmaster General Farley who is State as well as National Democratic chairman, and some other party leaders whom he failed to name.

"What did Mr. Farley say when you told him?" the Governor was asked.

"I am not going to say anything about that; in fact, I have nothing to add to the statement I made yesterday."

"Was former Governor Smith one of the party leaders you told that you were going to run for the Senate?" he was asked.

"No comment," was his reply. Then he added: "I am not going to say with whom I did discuss my plans."

Asked if he had discussed the matter with leaders of the Amer-

Continued on Page Six

Beaten Challenger Says He Was Paralyzed When Louis Sent Right to Kidney

FOUL IS CLAIMED BY GERMAN BOXER

Schmeling Insists Punch to Kidney Caused His Defeat in Short Contest

HE RECUPERATES QUICKLY

Unmarked, He Poses for Group of Photographers—Would Like Another Chance

By JOSEPH C. NICHOLS

In his dressing room after one of the quickest knockouts on record in a heavyweight title fight, Max Schmeling claimed that he had been hit by a foul kidney blow, the second punch that Louis landed.

The German said that the blow paralyzed him and that for a few seconds he could not see. When reminded that there was no foul possible under the rules in this State, Schmeling still insisted that the blow was foul and that it was the cause of his defeat.

"The punch in the kidneys paralyzed me," said Max. "I felt like I had a sharp cramp and I could not move myself around. Then I couldn't see for a little while."

First Punch a Left Hook

According to Max, the first punch Louis landed was a left hook to the jaw, then followed a right to the kidney. The blow did land near the kidney while Schmeling was fighting with his body and left shoulder turned toward Louis and was leaning back behind his own left guard. This position made his left side an easy target.

Schmeling was asked why he got up so soon after the first two knockdowns.

"Was your head clear?" he was asked.

"Sure, my head was clear. I knew what I was doing."

Before that, however, Max had said that he did not know what happened for a minute after he was hit in the kidney. However, it was after that blow connected that Max landed the only really good shot he had in the short fight.

Lands a Short Right

That punch was a short right which caught Louis on the face but apparently did not hurt him. He tried another a second later and it went over Louis's shoulder.

Although he was still groggy as he was taken to his corner, Schmeling had fully recovered before he left the ring and was apparently none the worse for the fight when he reached the dressing room.

Asked if he would fight again, and would he meet Louis again, Max said "Yes" quite positively. Mike Jacobs, promoter of the fight, said that he would use Max in another fight here, but that Max Baer would definitely be the opponent for Louis in September.

Max Machon, Schmeling's trainer, who threw the towel into the ring, explained that he had done so because he could see that Schmeling could not move and did not want him to be seriously hurt.

Schmeling did not have a mark on him and posed for photographers. As soon as he could dress, he said he was going to be examined by his own physician, and departed in company with his American manager, Joe Jacobs.

BRESCIA BEATS KETTLES

Captures Six-Round Semi-Final on Card at Stadium

Jorge Brescia of the Argentine outpointed Al Kettles, South Bend, Ind., heavyweight, in the six-round semi-final at the Yankee Stadium last night. Brescia scaled 211½ pounds and Kettles 205.

Other six-rounders saw Al Bray, 211, Los Angeles, outpoint Abe Simon, 250¼, Richmond Hill; Dave Clark, 175, Detroit, defeat Bud Mignault, 175¼, Brockton, Mass., and Carmen Barth, 163, Cleveland, triumph over Al Coccozza, 165, Harlem.

Bill Poland, 185, Bronx, vanquished Gene Bonin, 194, Willimantic, Conn., and Joe Lubin, 193, Brooklyn, beat Bill Comiskey, 176, Paterson, in the four-round frays.

STREET DANCE IN CHICAGO

Negroes in Gay Celebration of Louis's Triumph

CHICAGO, June 22 (AP).—Chicago's Negro section, with a population of 232,000, staged a gay celebration of Joe Louis's one-round victory over Max Schmeling tonight.

Shots were fired in the air, firecrackers set off, trolley poles jerked from street cars and some windows broken.

Crowds poured into the streets a few moments after Schmeling's defeat was broadcast from New York. Dancing Negroes covered the pavements and tied up traffic. Night clubs in the district reported the liveliest business since New Year's Eve.

Special police details were on duty in the district south of the Loop, but no arrests were reported early in the celebration.

CRITICISM BY MAX BAER

Says He and Schmeling Made the Same Mistake

Max Baer had a very good vest-pocket criticism of Max Schmeling's tactics when the fight was over. In a few thousand well-chosen words the voluble Livermore Larruper discoursed on the battle. The gist of his remarks is found in one sentence.

"The trouble with Schmeling," he said, "was that he fought Louis the way Baer fought him—he did not throw any punches."

Baer revealed that he would sign with Louis today at the commission offices for a fight in September.

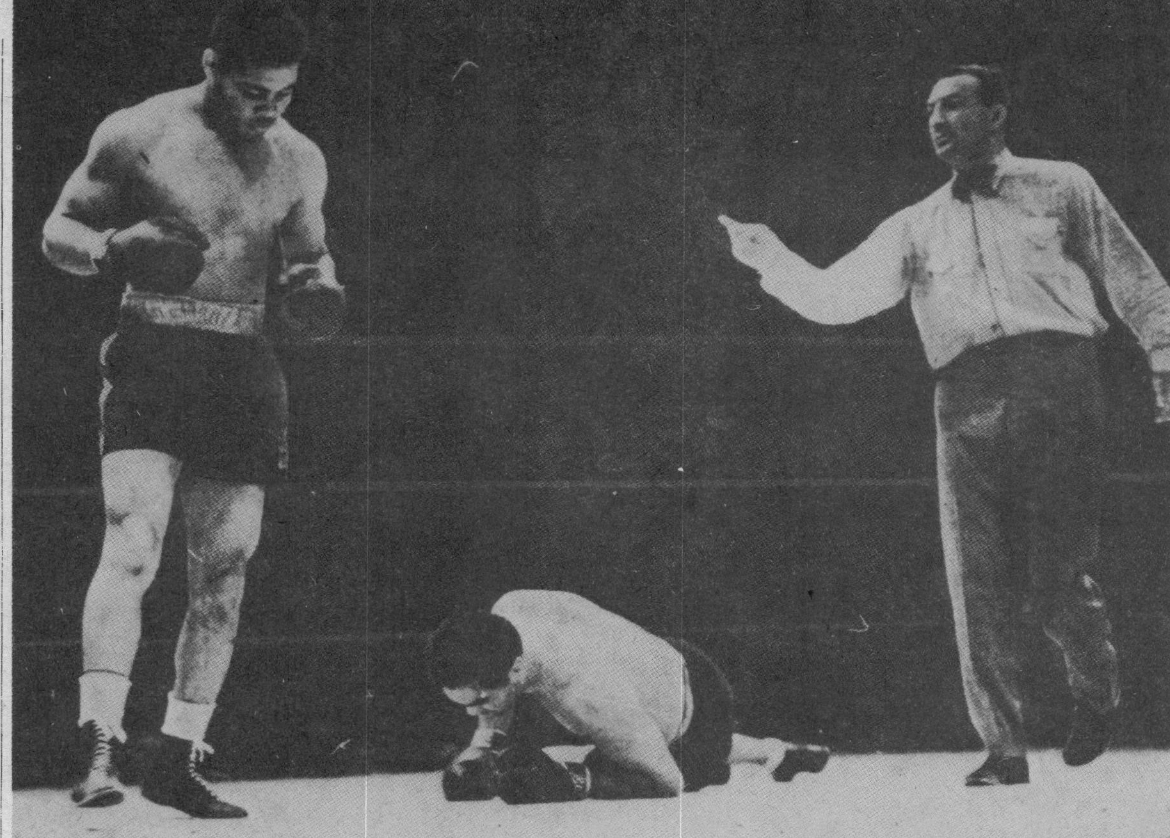

Times Wide World

SCHMELING DOWN WHILE REFEREE DONOVAN WAVES LOUIS TO NEUTRAL CORNER

In this knockdown, the first of three, the German took a count of three. He later took counts of one and five in the one-round fight

LOUIS KNOCKS OUT SCHMELING IN 1ST

Continued From Page One

ory of that 1936 knockout he suffered in twelve rounds. It was the one blot on his brilliant record. He aimed to square the account and he did.

Because of the excitement attending the finish, Louis, in the records, will be deprived of a clean-cut knockout. It will appear as a technical knockout because Referee Donovan didn't complete the full ten-second count over Schmeling. But this is merely a technicality. No fighter ever was more thoroughly knocked out than was Max last night.

Thrilling to the spectacle of this short, savage victory which held so much significance was a gathering that included a member of President Roosevelt's Cabinet, Postmaster General James A. Farley; Governors of several States, Mayors of cities in the East, South and Middle West, Representatives and Senators, judges and lawyers, politicians, doctors, figures of prominence in the professional world, leaders of banking, industry and commerce, stars of the stage and screen, ring champions of the past and present, leaders in other sports and other fields—all assembled eagerly awaiting the struggle whose appeal drew them from distant parts of the country and from Europe.

Millions Hear the Fight

In addition to those looking on at the spectacle, there were millions listening in virtually all over the world, for this battle was broadcast in four languages, English, German, Spanish and Portuguese, so intense was the interest in its outcome.

Louis, hero of one of the greatest stories ever written in the ring, owner of a record of thirty-eight victories in thirty-nine bouts spread over four years, entered the ring the favorite to win at odds of 1 to 2. He won like a 1-to-10 shot. The knockout betting was at even money, take your pick. It could have been on Louis at 1 to 10, for Schmeling never had a chance. His number was up from the clang of the opening gong.

Schmeling, 32-year-old campaigner over a period of fourteen years, aspired to the unparalleled distinction of being the first man to regain the heavyweight crown. He suffered, instead, the fate that overtook Jim Corbett, Bob Fitzsimmons, Jim Jeffries and Jack Dempsey, ring immortals all, who tried and failed.

The fury of Louis's attack explains the result in a nutshell. The defending champion came into the ring geared on high. He never stopped punching until his rival was a crumpled, inert, helpless figure, diving headlong into the resined canvas, rolling over there spasmodically, instinctively, trying to come erect, his spirit willing to return to the attack, his flesh weak, for mind and muscle could not be expected to function harmoniously under the terrific battering Schmeling absorbed in those fleeting two minutes.

Max Throws Two Punches

Emphasizing the savagery with which Louis went after this victory was Schmeling's feeble effort at retaliation. The German ex-champion threw exactly two punches. That is how completely the Bomber established his mastery in this second struggle with the Black Uhlan.

With the opening gong, Louis crept softly out of his corner, pantherlike, eyes alert, arms poised, fists cocked to strike from any angle as he met Schmeling short of the ring's center. Max backed carefully toward his own corner, watching Louis intently, his right, the right which thudded so punishingly against Joe's jaw and temple two years ago, ready to strike over or under a left guard. At least, that was Schmeling's pre-arranged plan.

But Louis wasted only a few seconds in studying his foe, menacing Max meanwhile with a spearing left, before quickly going to work.

Like flashes from the blue, the Bomber's sharp, powerful left started suddenly pumping into Schmeling's face. The blows tilted Max's head back, made his eyes blink, unquestionably stung him. The German's head was going backward as if on hinges.

Max's face was exposed to a left-hook attack and Louis interspersed his onslaught with a few of these blows, gradually forcing Schmeling back to the ropes and preventing the German from making an offensive or counter move, so fast and sharp and true was the opening fire of the defending champion.

Schmeling suddenly shot a right over Louis's left for the jaw, but the blow was short and they went close. At long range again, Joe stuck and stabbed with his left to the face and head, trying to open a lane through Schmeling's protecting arms and gloves for a more forceful shot from the right.

Again Lunges Forward

But the opening didn't come immediately. Instead, Schmeling again lunged forward, his right arching as it drove for Louis's jaw, and it landed on the champion's head as the Schmeling admirers in the tremendous crowd roared encouragement.

Louis, however, only scowled and stepped forward, this time with a terrific right to Schmeling's jaw which banged Max against the ropes, his body partly turned toward the right from Louis.

Schmeling shook to his heels under the impact of that blow, but he gave no sign of toppling. And Joe, like a tiger, leaped upon him, driving a right to the ribs as Schmeling half turned—apparently the blow Schmeling later claimed was foul—swinging with might and main, lefts and rights that thudded against Schmeling's bobbing head, grazed or cracked on Max's jaw and swishing murderous looking left hooks into Schmeling's stomach as the crumpling ex-champion grimaced in pain, his face wearing the expression of a fighter protesting "foul."

Shaken when he first landed against the ropes, Schmeling was rendered groggy under the furious assault to which Louis subjected him while he stood there trying unsuccessfully to avoid the blows or grasp a chance to clinch.

Suddenly the Bomber's right, sharp and true with the weight of his 198¾ pounds back of it as well as his knack of driving it home, landed cleanly on Schmeling's jaw. Max toppled forward and down. He was hurt and stunned, but gamely the German came erect at the count of three.

Louis was on him in a jiffy, with the fury of a jungle beast. After propping the tottering Schmeling with a jolting left to the face, the Bomber's deadly right fist again exploded in Max's face, and under another crack on the jaw, Schmeling went down. This time, however, the German regained his feet before the count progressed beyond one.

Crowd in an Uproar

But Schmeling was helpless. He staggered drunkenly for a few backward steps, the crowd in an uproar as Louis stealthily followed and measured his man. Max was an open target. His jaw was unprotected and inviting. His midsection was a mark for punches. The kill was within Louis's grasp. He lost no time in ceremony.

Spearing Schmeling with blinding straight lefts, numbing Max with powerful left hooks that were sharp, true and destructive, Louis set the stage for one finishing right to the jaw, released the blow and landed in a flash, and the German toppled over in a headlong dive, completely unconscious.

The din of the crowd echoed over the arena, cheers for the conquering Louis, shrieks of entreaty and shouts of advice for Schmeling. But this thunderous roar was unheard by the befogged Schmeling and was ignored by the Bomber, intent only on the destruction of his foe.

In routine fashion, Eddie Josephs, a licensed referee converted into a knockdown timekeeper, started the count over the stricken Schmeling. He counted one, then two, as Referee Donovan went about the duty of signaling Louis to the farthest neutral corner.

Machon Hurls Towel

At "three" a white towel sailed aloft from Schmeling's corner, hurled by the ever-faithful Machon, who realized, as did every one else in the vast gathering, that Schmeling was knocked out, if he was not, indeed, badly hurt.

The towel fell in the ring a few feet from Schmeling. It is the custom in European rings to recognize this gesture as a concession of defeat. It used to be recognized here. But for many years now it has been banned, and Referee Donovan, disregarding the emblem of surrender, tossed it through the ropes and out of the ring.

When he returned to the prostrate figure of Schmeling, moving convulsively on the ring floor doubtless with that instinctive impulse to arise, the count had reached "five." One look was enough for Donovan. Instantly he spread his arms in a signal that meant the end of the bout, although Time-keeper Josephs, as he is duty bound to do, continued counting outside the ring.

This led to confusion at the finish. Some thought the third knockdown count was eight. Actually, the bout was ended at the count of five, the three seconds beyond that time being a gesture against emergency that was superfluous. Schmeling could not have arisen inside the legal ten-second stretch. His hopes were blasted. He was a thoroughly beaten man.

In a few moments, however, as police swarmed into the ring and his handlers worked over him in the corner to which he was assisted, Schmeling returned to consciousness. He was able to smile bravely as he walked across the ring to shake the hand of the conquering Louis, a gesture that carried the impression, somehow, that Max realized at long last that Louis is his master now and for all time.

Bout Described Blow by Blow

Louis came out of his corner quickly and wasted little time springing at his foe. He lashed out with two lefts to the face and cracked a right to the jaw. Schmeling tagged the jaw with a right, but the punch seemingly had no effect on the champion.

The challenger hooked a left to the head and took a left to the body in return. Louis drove Schmeling to the ropes with a fusillade of rights and lefts to the head. The latter was absorbing punishment about the body without being able to lift a hand in his own defense.

Referee Donovan stepped between them, as if to stop the slaughter, but did nothing but wave Louis back to mid-ring.

Puzzled for a second or two, Louis returned to the attack on shouts from his corner and crashed a right to Schmeling's jaw, flooring him for a count of three. The German arose shakily and was submitted to a heavy body fire before taking another right to the jaw, a punch which put him down for only one second.

Rubber-legged and glassy-eyed, the gallant German sought to hold off his tormentor, but Louis shot both hands to the body with crushing force, drove a sharp left hook to the jaw, then fired a right to the chin that felled Schmeling once more. The challenger's instinct drove him to drag himself to all fours, but further he could not move.

The count had reached three when Max Machon, Schmeling's trainer, tossed in the towel to signal defeat. At five Referee Donovan waved his hands to signal the end of the battle. The round had gone 2 minutes 4 seconds.

JOE GLAD HE PROVED A WORTHY CHAMPION

Says He Was a 'Bit Sore' at Max, Explaining Savagery

"Now I feel like the champion."

These were Joe Louis's first words on his arrival in his dressing room.

"I've been waiting a long time for this night," he added, "and I sure do feel pretty glad about everything. I was a little bit sore at some of the things Max said. Maybe he didn't say them, maybe they put those words in his mouth, but he didn't deny them, and that's what made me mad."

What Louis referred to, probably, was the statement attributed to Schmeling a month ago, to the effect that the Negro would always be afraid of him. Something must have rankled Joe, for the savagery with which he battered down the German was never displayed in his other bouts here.

Most of Louis's remarks were addressed to Governor Frank Murphy of Michigan, one of the first admitted to the champion's dressing room.

The Governor admittedly was "full of hero-worship" as he shook hands with the Detroit boxer who, on his own account, was immeasurably pleased with Murphy's visit.

"You'll never know how my heart thumped during that round, Joe," said the Governor.

"I'm glad I made it short for you, sir," responded the champion, who looked exactly like a wool-gathering youngster standing in awe of royalty, instead of a young man who had just earned about $400,000 in 124 seconds.

Louis's managers, Julian Black and John Roxborough, were incensed at Schmeling's claim of foul at first, then laughed it off, saying: "That's for German consumption."

Asked if Schmeling would be considered for a return fight, Black replied, "Certainly not. We've demonstrated tonight that Joe is just too good for Schmeling. We've had enough of him, and he certainly has had enough of us!"

The champion's immediate plans are indefinite. He'll stay around to collect his check today, and probably take in the ball game at the Polo Grounds.

USE PLANE FOR FORECAST

Rain Prediction Follows Tests at 12,000-Foot Level

A new development in fight weather forecasts was introduced yesterday in connection with the Louis-Schmeling fight—and with discouraging results. At the request of Promoter Mike Jacobs, who wanted to allay his fears with a special forecast, the United Air Lines sent W. B. Beckwith, one of its meteorologists, aloft in a plane at noon to the 12,000-foot level, where he could get a forecast based on upper air temperatures and the structure of clouds above this level.

When Beckwith landed he telephoned Jacobs the following:

"Continued overcast, with occasional mist or light rain from 6 P. M. to midnight."

Jacobs decided thereupon he could have gotten along splendidly without this information.

IDOL'S DOWNFALL SADDENS GERMANS

Gay Radio Parties in Berlin Stunned by Louis's Quick Knockout Triumph

BERLIN, Thursday, June 23 (AP).—All Germany, clustered about its short-wave radio sets in the early morning hours, was thunderstruck and almost unbelieving at the unexpected news that "Unser Maxe" Schmeling had failed in his heavyweight comeback try, and failed by the knockout route.

Their high hopes of hearing black-browed Schmeling had fought his way back to the heavyweight championship were dashed so suddenly that the ardor of radio parties and cafe gatherings was quickly dampened.

Heavy-lidded Germans, who had stayed up till 3 A. M. for the short-wave broadcast only to hear a 2:04 minute fight end with dramatic dispatch, climbed into bed a saddened lot at Joe Louis's victory.

All over the Reich they had clustered in homes, restaurants and cafes to hear the fight they hoped would bring the world's championship to Germany.

It was said Adolf Hitler at his Bavarian mountain retreat was among those who heard the disheartening news.

Keeps News From Wife

The maid at Schmeling's Berlin home was so disappointed by the knockout she said she would not awaken Maxie's movie actress wife, Anny Ondra, who left instructions not to be aroused until after the fight.

"I think morning will be time enough to tell her," said the maid, who had stayed up in hope of being able to bear her good news.

The Sportsbar, where Schmeling and his cronies have a regularly reserved table, was "like a tomb," a waiter lamented after the radio told the sad story to patrons looking glumly into their beer steins.

Schmeling's German pals said their only comment was an echo of what the German announcer said at the close of his broadcast from the Yankee Stadium ringside:

"We sympathize with you, Max, although you lost as a fair sportsman.

"We will show you on your return that reports in foreign newspapers that you would be thrown into jail are untrue."

Officials Listen In

K. Metzner, head of the German Boxing Federation, who listened to the broadcast with members of the International European Boxing Federation (FIFA), believed the fight, because of its sudden end, did not give a clear picture of whether Louis or Schmeling was the better fighter.

He said Louis undoubtedly was in excellent form. Schmeling, he thought, watched Louis's left hand too closely, whereas since their last meeting two years ago Louis had developed a powerful right.

He said it was hard to judge whether Trainer Machon's action in throwing in the towel was the proper move, thus making the fight end as a technical knockout.

He added Schmeling could be sure of as hearty a reception at home as ever.

Statistics on Fight

Attendance—80,000.

Estimated gross receipts—$900,000.

Federal tax—$90,000.

State tax—$45,000.

Louis's share (40 per cent of net)—$306,000.

Schmeling's share (20 per cent of net)—$153,000.

Promoter's share, from which all other expenses are deducted—$306,000.

Early Bouts Presage Rough Night, Fans Awaiting the Zero Hour Find

But Crowd Takes Action in Preliminaries Quietly Except for Cannon Cracker Exploded After Poland Wins

By JOHN KIERAN

Breath by breath in the Bronx.

Down in front! The show is about to begin. Major Gen. John J. Phelan has arrived at the ringside wearing a shining straw skimmer and herding a couple of preliminary fighters ing the ring. If anybody cares, their names are Bill Comiskey and Joe Lubin. Wonder what Max and Joe are doing or thinking right at this moment?

Clang! The blond Comiskey moves out to meet the darker Lubin and is greeted with a loud punch on the jaw. Looks like a rough night in the Bronx. Maybe Comiskey was a sailor. He has something tattooed on his left arm. As the scuffle proceeds, he also has something tattooed on his chin—rights and lefts by Lubin.

Upper Stand Fills Early

The upper stand is pretty well filled by this time. The belabored Comiskey probably thinks the ring is pretty well crowded, too. From the pushing around he is getting, he doesn't want to fall down for fear of being trampled to death. He finally saves his life but loses the decision. The crowd and Lubin take it quietly.

Two more heavyweight merry-makers or time-killers enter the ring—Bill Poland and Gene Bonin. Postmaster General James A. Farley saunters into the press section. So does President John Reed Kilpatrick of Madison Square Garden. That's all right. They both used to work here.

Hey! Can that be rain? No, it's one of Poland's seconds giving the neighbors a free shower out of a pail. Bonin goes on a nine-second sit-down strike in the third round. When he gets up he looks as though he would like to picket Poland for brutal oppression of an honest workingman.

Just a Coincidence

Poland wins and a cannon cracker is exploded in the upper right of the grandstand. It turns out that this is just a coincidence, not a celebration of the Poland victory. Schmeling and Louis must be in the Stadium by this time. Dave Clark, a dusky stablemate of Joe Louis, climbs through the ropes to exchange rough pleasantries with a chunky blond named Bud Mignault.

Who's that waving from the rear press row? Well, if it isn't Maximilian Addled-a-Bit Baer himself, the erstwhile Harlequin of Hollywood! He expects to be much closer to the center of the ring in the next big fight Uncle Mike Jacobs stages—for part of the evening anyway.

Dusky Dave Clark carries his mouth protector pushed forward under his upper lip, making him look like one of the Ubangi savages from South Africa. He swings some savage punches, too, and gets the decision. Three or four absent-minded spectators applaud. Schmeling and Louis must be getting ready by this time. Just what time is it? Nine-thirty. It won't be long now.

What! Another preliminary! Well, let this be the last. Abe Simon, 250 pounds, lumbers in to take on Al Bray, a dusky warrior from Los Angeles. They say Bray is a prospect. He's a tall tan gent weighing 211 pounds, but he looks like a slim willow to Simon, who is about as broad as he is long. Hurry up and get it over with, boys. There's something very important coming up soon.

Bray wins a somewhat disorderly brawl and learns something on his travels. He hears the Bronx cheer or full-flowering raspberry for the first time. Bray wasn't that bad. In fact, he was fair to middling, but the crowd was impatient.

Look! Joe Louis is right in this corner. He must have slipped in quietly when nobody was looking. He gets a good cheer. Now Schmeling comes in and gets a bigger cheer. Doc Casey laces on Schmeling's gloves and Jack Blackburn performs the same service for the champion, J. Louis.

Champions Are Cheered

Former champions and ring notables dance in and out as the crowd gives each a round of applause. Gene Tunney, Two-Ton Tony Galento, Jersey James Braddock, Max Addled-a-Bit Baer. The debonair Baer draws mingled cheers and boos.

Now Schmeling is presented. Then the defendant, Shufflin' Joe Louis. They move to the center of the ring with their handlers and gather around Referee Arthur Donovan. Arthur delivers the usual instructions. They part. Clang! It's on.

Well, of all things! It's on and it's over! Just as Joe promised. He stepped in and started a lightning attack. Lefts and rights—Bang! Bang! Bang! Schmeling reeled into the ropes on the first-base side of the ring and clung like a shipwrecked sailor to a lifeline. The Shuffler couldn't have done more damage if he had whacked Max with a baseball bat.

Swaying on the ropes, Max peered about in a bewildered manner. He pushed himself off and Louis struck like dark lightning again. A ripping left and a smashing right. The right was the crusher. Schmeling went down. He was up again and then, under another fusillade, down again. Up once more, barely able to stand, and then down for the third and final time. It was Louis's night and the championship, as John L. Sullivan was once pleased to report, remains in this country.

HARLEM CELEBRANTS TOSS VARIED MISSILES

Thirty Are Slightly Injured—Yorkville Laughs Ruefully

Harlem's celebration of the victory of its hero, Joe Louis, over Max Schmeling started off deliriously but more or less peacefully after the fight ended last night, but wound up early this morning with a wholesale throwing of bottles, tin cans and other missiles from roof tops and windows in the vicinity of Seventh Avenue and 130th Street that resulted in slight injuries to twenty policemen and ten civilians.

Mounted Patrolman Edward Grout was the only one of the casualties who needed special attention, the others suffering minor cuts and bruises. Grout suffered a concussion of the brain when an ash can cover hit him on the head and knocked him off his horse. He received treatment in the West 123d Street station and remained off duty.

The disturbance at Seventh Avenue and 130th Street was quickly quelled by a number of the extra policemen assigned to special duty in Harlem. Meanwhile, all was peaceful in the German-American quarter around East Eighty-sixth Street, where the reaction to the Negro's victory over the German pugilist was one of good-natured "joke-on-us" laughter.

Emmet Smith, a Negro, 23 years old, of 204 West 133d Street, was arrested on a charge of disorderly conduct for tossing a bottle into the air from the sidewalk.

The Harlem streets were almost deserted when the fight began. The Brown Bomber's admirers were all indoors, listening to the radio descriptions of the historic one-round knockout. No sooner was the Schmeling débâcle over than thousands of men, women and children surged out of tenements and radio stores into the Harlem streets, shouting with glee.

Their exuberance at first took the form of hopping upon the running boards and tops of passing taxicabs and private cars, knocking over ash cans and traffic signs and yelling plaudits of their hero.

On his way home from the fight Police Commissioner Valentine stopped at the West 135th Street station to get reports on the Harlem situation. Learning that everything was peaceful, the Commissioner ordered all traffic on Seventh Avenue between 125th and 145th Streets shut off so that the celebrants could cut all the capers they pleased.

"This is their night, let them have their fun," said the Commissioner.

Residents of Yorkville conceded that the better man had won and ruefully counted up their betting losses. Negro bettors had descended on Yorkville for several days offering varying odds on Louis and finding plenty of takers. When the fight began, German-American beer dispensaries and restaurants were crowded with eager radio-listeners. When the fight ended, there was an almost universal silence and then bursts of laughter that sounded sheepish to some observers.

TEAR GAS SCATTERS MOB IN CLEVELAND

Riots Follow Louis Victory—Man Shot, Police Felled

CLEVELAND, June 22 (AP).—Police used tear gas to quell a riotous crowd tonight in the Negro section here celebrating Joe Louis's victory over Max Schmeling.

Charity Hospital was filled with injured and attendants notified police to take others to other hospitals.

One man was shot, probably fatally; two policemen were felled by flying bricks, a street car was stoned, passengers were hurt and sirens screamed at many false alarms.

At one busy intersection jammed with celebrants and spectators general fighting broke out. Knives flashed, clubs swung and missiles flew. All available police squads rushed to the scene and tear gas scattered the melee.

There was only momentary silence after the knockout. Then a din burst loose that could be heard many blocks from the celebration center.

Old men and women did the Big Apple in the streets with the youngsters. Thousands were attracted by the general jamboree and hundreds of police were rushed to the district.

Prominent German clubs were crowded with families drinking beer in silence.

DETROIT NEGROES JOYFUL

Sing and Dance in Streets to Celebrate Louis's Victory

DETROIT, June 22 (AP).—Negro residents of Detroit's "Paradise Valley," who had confidently petitioned the City Council two weeks ago for permission to do so, danced and sang in roped-off streets tonight in celebration of Joe Louis's knockout victory over Max Schmeling.

Police estimated the crowd in the vicinity of St. Antoine and Beacon Streets at 10,000. Celebrations were staged, however, in Negro neighborhoods throughout the city.

Old and young danced in the streets, some in couples and others in rings with locked hands. A swing band played until a late hour.

Albert Pakeman, acting "Mayor of the Valley," said there had not been much betting "because the boys couldn't find any Schmeling money."

Fan Dies After Broadcast

WINCHESTER, Ind., June 22 (AP).—Excitement over the Louis-Schmeling championship fight proved fatal tonight to Richard Hall, 65, Winchester laborer, who suffered a heart attack at the conclusion of a radio broadcast.

Special Trains on Subway

The Independent Subway had special expresses running from Forty-second Street right to the Stadium station, ordinarily a local stop. The same system worked in reverse on the return trip.

Section 5 SPORTS **The New York Times.** SPORTS Section 5

S Copyright, 1938, by The New York Times Company. SUNDAY, JULY 3, 1938. L++ S

MRS. MOODY BEATS HELEN JACOBS, 6-4, 6-0, AT WIMBLEDON; GIANTS ROUT DODGERS, 8-1; KENT CREW WINS THAMES CUP

HUBBELL WINS NO. 9

Scatters 8 Hits, Camilli Driving Homer in Ninth to Prevent Shut-Out

3 RUNS IN THIRD DECIDE

But Giants' Eighth Straight Victory Over Dodgers This Season Is Protested

By JOHN DREBINGER

Carl Hubbell, who had experienced quite a time annexing his 200th victory in the National League, had no trouble at all starting his third hundred yesterday once he found his way to Ebbets Field.

This done, the famous screwball maestro donned his familiar long pants uniform, which in gray looks about the same as in white at the Polo Grounds, and the rest all seemed to come as a matter of course.

The Giants did a lot of things to the Dodgers, the Dodgers did a lot more things to themselves and the result of it all was an 8-to-1 triumph for Colonel Bill Terry's invaders that left the majority in a crowd of 11,241 feeling convinced they had wasted another fine afternoon.

It was an outcome that extended the front-running champions' latest winning streak to six games and gave Hubbell his ninth victory of the campaign in addition to the 201st of his all-time major-league career. Passing hurriedly through Brooklyn, it might also be mentioned that it marked the eighth time in eight starts that the Giants walloped the Dodgers this year, a record which the eminent Babe Ruth was forced to recognize as par for any course he has seen.

Scarcely a Contest

It was, in truth, scarcely a contest at any stage as the Giants reeled off a total of twelve blows, with their former team-mate, the stoutish Freddy Fitzsimmons, the victim of eleven of them, including Harry Danning's fifth homer of the campaign.

In fact, about the only excitement the Dodgers were able to stir came in the sixth, when they gummed things so badly trying to make a double play that they confused even the three umpires, Ballanfant, Klem and Sears. When this turmoil, which lasted some twelve minutes, had been straightened to the satisfaction of every one except the Dodgers, Manager Burleigh Grimes, appearing at a loss to do anything else, announced he was playing the remainder of the game under protest.

Apparently this put Burleigh in accord with the gathering which appeared to view the entire proceedings under stern protest.

As for Hub, he just rolled along with the tide, as he fanned eight and scattered as many hits, although one of these was a homer which Dolf Camilli sent into Bedford Avenue in the ninth. It was Dolf's ninth and was vociferously cheered because it at least enabled the Dodgers to escape a shutout.

Bartell Hits Single

Fitz kept pace with Hubbell for two innings, but ran into his first squall in the third, which Dick Bartell and Alex Kampouris opened with singles. Hubbell tried twice to sacrifice, only to be frustrated each time by the crafty Fitz, but in the end Hub sliced a single to right and a rally was on that presently resulted in three runs, the final two coming home on a double by Jimmy Ripple.

It was directly after the Danning homer in the sixth, a swat that stuck momentarily in the screening above the right-field wall, that a merry rumpus started. With Ripple on second, Hank Leiber on first and one out, Sambo Leslie lifted a fly to short left. Leo Durocher appeared for a moment to have it caught, but dropped the ball as he sprawled on his face. The ball was then hustled to second base, where Fitz caught up with it and proceeded to tag everybody in the arena.

This seemed to convince Umpire Klem it was a double play until the other two arbiters and the Giants reached him. Then the verdict was reversed and only Leiber declared out on a force play which seemed to be beyond all understanding of Grimes, Ruth et al. Very likely it still is, but that was the way it remained.

Fitz stamped himself still one of the best fielding pitchers in that stormy third when he froze to Seeds's hard slam to the mound, held the ball long enough to keep Kampouris glued to third and then

Continued on Page Two

A Play at Second Base in Game at Ebbets Field

Times Wide World

Bartell, Giant shortstop, returning safely to the bag in the third inning when Fitzsimmons tried to pick him off the sack with a snap throw to Durocher.

YANKS SCORE, 12-2, FOR 7TH STRAIGHT

Four Homers Rout Senators—New York 2 Games Behind First-Place Indians

By JAMES P. DAWSON

With no more effort than was required in submerging the fourth-place Senators yesterday, the Yankees vaulted within two games of the league-leading Indians before a gathering of 10,514 at the Stadium. And they encountered little trouble routing Washington, 12 to 2.

Wes Ferrell was pitching high balls and low, fast balls and slow, and some that were so inaccurately or inexpertly heaved that they caused Umpire Johnny Quinn to admonish the big right-hander as early as the fourth inning, when Yankees started hitting the dirt to protect their heads. The temperamental member of the Ferrell family was looking for his eleventh victory, but took his sixth beating instead.

With a blazing fire of fourteen solid thumps that ran the gamut from single to homer, the Yanks blistered Ferrell as they fashioned their seventh straight to touch their season's high in consecutive successes.

Ferrell Works Five Innings

Four homers the McCarthymen stroked, three of them against Ferrell in the five full innings he worked before the realization was borne upon him that his was a futile task indeed. Joe Krakauskas, a southpaw, was the victim of the other round-tripper.

Joe DiMaggio led the attack. He started the scoring with a triple that gave the Yanks a run and the lead in the first.

After that the Californian hit two singles and a homer to send in four runs. Joe's blow for the circuit, his twelfth of the season, was the one struck at the expense of Kra-

Continued on Page Two

Preeminent Defeats Wise Prince In Fleetwing Handicap at Empire

Headley's 7-1 Shot Comes From Last Place in $7,580 Race Before 12,000—Clocks, The Fighter in Dead Heat for Show

By BRYAN FIELD

Coming from last place in a field of eleven, the 6-year-old horse Preeminent, home-bred color bearer of Hal Price Headley, yesterday captured the $7,580 Fleetwing Handicap before 12,000 persons at Empire City. Nick Wall, fresh from his success aboard Mr. Headley's Menow in the Massachusetts Handicap on Wednesday, handled the son of Supremus and skirted the entire field to bring off a three-quarter length victory that was worth $5,850.

Eleven of the sixteen named overnight went to the post, but only ten finished as Jay Jay lost his rider shortly after the break. Preeminent was as high as 8 to 1 and closed at 7 comparatively neglected.

Wise Prince, another who came from far back, was second to the line. The Fighter and Clocks figured in a dead heat for third.

Fading right out of the picture was the Wheatley Stable's fleet filly, Merry Lassie, favored at 11 to 5. She led, but could not carry her speed for even the five-and-three-quarter-furlong dash. The winner was timed in 1:09 2-5 under 123 pounds, which was next to Airflame's top weight of 126.

The first Saturday of the meeting seemed to assure the kind of attendances, which last year amazed so many when new marks were set. James Butler was present as well as Mr. and Mrs. D. Philip MacGuire and Mr. and Mrs. Walter Trabers, all financially interested in the Yonkers course.

Of secondary interest to the vic-

Continued on Page Seven

SHUTE VANQUISHES GULDAHL, 2 AND 1

Brae Burn Pro Cards Par on Last 17 Holes to Take Challenge Match

By The Associated Press.

HINGHAM, Mass., July 2.—Denny Shute, two-time champion of the National P. G. A., today proved again his superiority among the nation's match players as he gained a 2-and-1 victory over Ralph Guldahl, master of medal play, in a thirty-six-hole challenge match for

Continued on Page Four

STORMSCUD VICTOR, WITH THE CHIEF 4TH

16-1 Shot Wins Kent Handicap at Delaware After Favorite Stops Under 126 Pounds

By The Associated Press.

STANTON, Del., July 2.—The climax of a hectic day for favorites at Delaware Park on the next to last Saturday of the meeting came in the running of the $10,000 added one mile and a sixteenth Kent Handicap when Maxwell Howard's The Chief, a 4-to-5 choice, finished fourth in the nine-horse field.

The Chief, carrying top weight of 126 pounds and ridden by Jack Westrope, had no excuse. He was on top and clear of trouble before he weakened midway around the final turn.

Stormscud, a 16-to-1 shot, carrying the Wheatley Stable colors, won with two and one-half lengths to spare over B. F. Whitaker's Mythical King. The latter beat Willis Sharpe Kilmer's Nedayr by a length and The Chief was another length back.

The largest crowd of the meeting, approximately 15,000, saw the Dwyer Stakes and Brooklyn Handicap winner go down to defeat. Stormscud was making his first start since he finished fourth in Havre de Grace's Chesapeake Stakes on April 23, but with one of Trainer Jim Fitzsimmons's famous preps under his belt he was the best horse in the Kent. The colt was neglected in the betting and paid $34.80 for $2.

Stormscud's time of 1:45 4-5 for the mile and a sixteenth was one-fifth of a second slower than the track record. He earned $9,075.

The Wheatley colt broke well and

Continued on Page Seven

Major League Baseball

American League

YESTERDAY'S RESULTS

New York 12, Washington 2.
Boston 6, Philadelphia 5.
St. Louis 13, Detroit 5.
Cleveland at Chicago, wet grounds.

STANDING OF THE CLUBS

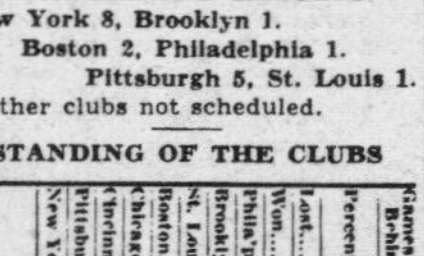

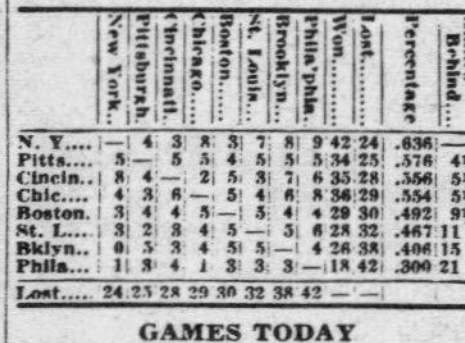

	Cleveland	New York	Boston	Wash'gton	Detroit	Phila'phia	Chicago	St. Louis	Won	Lost	Percentage	Games Behind
Cleve...	—	6	4	7	7	9	3	4	40	22	.645	—
N. Y....	4	—	5	6	7	5	6	6	39	25	.609	2
Boston.	5	4	—	6	5	4	5	8	37	27	.578	4
Wash...	5	2	4	—	4	5	7	7	34	35	.493	9½
Detroit	2	3	7	7	—	5	5	4	33	34	.493	9½
Phila...	2	4	2	2	5	—	4	7	26	35	.426	13½
Chic....	2	3	4	3	2	4	—	6	24	33	.421	13½
St. L....	2	3	1	4	4	3	3	—	20	42	.323	20
Lost.....	22	25	27	35	34	35	33	42	—	—		

GAMES TODAY

Boston at New York (3 P. M.).
Washington at Philadelphia (2).
Cleveland at Chicago (2).
Detroit at St. Louis (2).

National League

YESTERDAY'S RESULTS

New York 8, Brooklyn 1.
Boston 2, Philadelphia 1.
Pittsburgh 5, St. Louis 1.
Other clubs not scheduled.

STANDING OF THE CLUBS

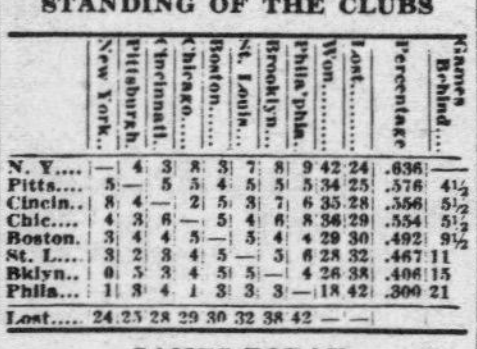

	New York	Pittsburgh	Cincinnati	Chicago	Boston	St. Louis	Brooklyn	Phila'phia	Won	Lost	Percentage	Games Behind
N. Y....	—	4	3	8	3	7	8	9	42	24	.636	—
Pitts....	5	—	5	5	4	5	5	5	34	25	.576	4½
Cincin..	8	4	—	2	5	3	7	6	35	28	.556	5½
Chic....	4	3	6	—	5	4	6	8	36	29	.554	5½
Boston.	3	4	4	5	—	5	4	4	29	30	.492	9½
St. L....	3	2	3	4	5	—	5	6	28	32	.467	11
Bklyn..	0	5	3	4	5	5	—	4	26	38	.406	15
Phila...	1	3	4	1	3	3	3	—	18	42	.300	21
Lost.....	24	25	28	29	30	32	38	42	—	—		

GAMES TODAY

Philadelphia at Brooklyn (2, 2:05 P. M.)
New York at Boston (2).
Chicago at Cincinnati.
St. Louis at Pittsburgh (2).

SCORES BY LENGTH

Kent Conquers London Crew in Final After Beating Yale 150s

NEW RECORD SET BY BURK

U. S. Ace Clips Diamond Sculls Mark by 8 Seconds in Easy Triumph at Henley

By GEORGE A. MOONEY
Wireless to THE NEW YORK TIMES.

HENLEY-ON-THAMES, England, July 2.—Kent School defeated Yale's 150-pound crew and went on to win the prized Thames Challenge Cup by conquering the London Rowing Club in the final as the four-day Royal Henley Regatta came to a close this afternoon. The American singles sculler, Joe Burk of the Penn Athletic Club, Philadelphia, broke the record of 8:10 established thirty-three years ago and annexed the Diamond Sculls event in 8:02.

Kent faced a grim Yale eight in the morning. With seven seniors in the Connecticut school's crew, which averaged about twenty pounds more per man than the Yale boat, the Elis realized they had a difficult task before them. And Kent's flying start did nothing to make that task easier.

Stroking thirty-nine, Kent shot forward to gain a half-length by the first quarter mark. Yale, however, found its stride and, not losing heart, successfully spurted to draw even at the Fawley half-way point.

Weight Begins to Tell

For the next quarter-mile the dogfight was on in earnest and Kent had a tough time shaking off the Elis. The schoolboys' weight was beginning to tell, however. The Elis made one final, valiant challenge for the lead but could not maintain the pace. They gained a yard, but Kent soon overcame them and pressed on to win by two-thirds of a length in the near-record time of 7:06.

Conditions were generally good for records today. The weather was ideal. There was little wind and the current of the placid old Thames was barely noticeable. A strong sun beat down along the picturesque 1 5/16-mile course and, all in all, it was a perfect Henley day.

The size of the crowds along the river banks may not have set a record but it certainly was near it. All day throngs of rowing enthusiasts and fashionably dressed spectators gathered to witness the final events of this annual rowing carnival, now in its ninety-ninth year. Today was a big day and the hucksters and pitchmen were out in full force along the shore. The merry-go-rounds of the carnivals along the river side were in full swing and tonight, with most of the crews released from their rigid training rules, they'll do a brisk business.

Makes the Victory Sweeter

Kent's final race against the London Rowing Club required a terrific effort from the schoolboy crew, which had to work at full power in practically every preliminary race. It was a hard fight, but the difficulty only made the victory sweeter. As one member of the crew put it: "I thought graduation would be the happiest day of my life—but this!"

At the start London jumped in front and, gaining a lead of a half-length, held it, answering spurt for spurt until, well up the course at about the half-way point, Kent made a determined bid, which cut the lead to a deck length. Then, boosting their stroke to thirty-six, the Americans slowly reduced this inch by inch.

Side by side the two shells came

Continued on Page Eight

After the Match at Wimbledon

Times Wide World Radiophoto

Miss Helen Jacobs (left) congratulating Mrs. Helen Wills Moody following the latter's victory. Miss Jacobs, it may be noticed, is favoring her injured ankle.

PENTTI KEEPS TITLE IN NATIONAL GAMES

Retains Senior 10,000-Meter Run Honors—N. Y. A. C. Takes Junior Meet Crown

By ARTHUR J. DALEY
Special to THE NEW YORK TIMES.

BUFFALO, N. Y., July 2.—True to the heritage of his Finnish ancestry, Eino Pentti of the Millrose A. A. won the National 10,000-meter championship in wind-swept Civic Stadium today. It was the lone senior event on the program as the junior title tests opened the fiftieth annual National A. A. U. track and field show.

The American-born and Finnish-bred athlete from New York let go with a withering blast in the last lap to break away from Bob Rankine of Preston, Ont., to win by 100 yards, retaining his crown and winning the distance laurels for the third time.

Marches Off With Crown

Essentially, however, this was a meet for the relatively unheralded youngsters who have not won national or intercollegiate championships or have not been members of Olympic teams. They turned in a well-rounded set of performances that augur well for the pyrotechnics that are promised for the morrow when the seniors swing into action.

Conditions were not ripe for anything extraordinary today because a strong wind swept into the new $2,000,000 stadium off Lake Erie and hamstrung the athletes in their efforts. Still three meet records were smashed in the junior part of the program as the New York Athletic Club, tuning up its sights for bigger game in the senior meet tomorrow, marched off with the team title.

Fittingly enough, Winged Footers contributed two of the new marks as they rolled up 33 points to 19 for the Shore A. C., 15 for the University of North Carolina and 10 for Riverside Junior College.

Two veterans of the distance run-

Continued on Page Six

BOWDEN CONQUERS MURRAY IN 3 SETS

Scores in Nassau Club Tennis by 5-7, 6-2, 6-1—Hunt, Hall and Kovacs Advance

By ALLISON DANZIG
Special to THE NEW YORK TIMES.

GLEN COVE, L. I., July 2.—Taking their cue from their more illustrious compatriots at Wimbledon, American players usurped all four semi-final brackets in the invitation tennis tournament of the Nassau Country Club today as Canada's young Davis Cup representatives were shut out of the action.

Tomorrow at 2:15 P. M. Gilbert Hunt of Washington, the holder of the challenge bowl, will play Frank Bowden of New York, and at 4 o'clock Frank Kovacs of Oakland, Calif., will engage J. Gilbert Hall of South Orange. The final is scheduled for Monday at 3 P. M.

Robert Murray, the ranking player of Canada, and his team-mates, Laird Watt and Douglas Cameron, all found the opposition a little more than they could cope with. They had no illusions to begin with, in view of the late advent of the season up north and their lack of practice on turf, and there was no occasion for them to feel disheartened over their showing.

Canadians' Play Improved

All three of them played crisp, offensive tennis of a standard definitely superior to the Canadian brand of a few years back. Considering the caliber of the opposition, they did all that could have been expected under the circumstances.

The defeat of Murray by Bowden at 5—7, 6—2, 6—1, was the nearest thing to a real disappointment for the Canadians. Watt lost to Kovacs at 6—3, 6—2, joining distinguished company, and Cameron finally yielded to the forehand exemplary of the best form in tennis as wielded by Hall, 7—5, 5—7, 6—2. Ross Wilson, the other member of the team, was eliminated by Hunt Friday.

Bowden had every stroke functioning to perfection at the start, including his booming service, and went ahead at 5—3. Here he fell off in accuracy and began to miss by inches and Murray, getting better length and pace, crowded on pressure to run through four games for the set.

Wages Stubborn Fight

But Bowden was not to be discouraged by the sudden turn of the tide against him. He started all over again in the second set and this time he refused to let down at any point, calling his volleying attack into play to capitalize the openings exacted by his jolting drives.

Cameron, a sturdy left-handed youth with plenty of fight, stood off Hall's superlative forehand for two sets, with little to choose between them, and then tired from the great amount of running he had done. Some of the driving exchanges in this match were extremely brilliant and the young Canadian had good cause to be satisfied with his performance, particularly his salvaging of the second set after Hall had

Continued on Page Eight

Fishbach Halts Kamrath in 3-Set Struggle And Gains College Net Final With Podesta

Special to THE NEW YORK TIMES.

MONTCLAIR, N. J., July 2.—Turning back the threats of Western invaders, Joseph Fishbach of St. John's University, Brooklyn, seeded eighth, and Gerard D. Podesta, Princeton's captain-elect, gained the final of the sixteenth annual Eastern intercollegiate singles tennis championship today on the courts of the Montclair A. C. The pair will meet in the first all-Eastern final since 1935 tomorrow at 2 P. M.

Clashing with Robert Kamrath, second seeded star, of Texas University, Fishbach was victorious in his semi-final match by 6—4, 6—3, 6—2. Outsteadying and outvolleying the tall Texan, Fishbach displayed a brilliant forehand and scored time and again with passing shots.

Displaying the same lasting power that carried him to numerous victories as Princeton's No. 1 man this season, Podesta came through in his battle with Robert Peacock of California, seeded fourth, by 6—3, 2—6, 9—7, 7—5.

Peacock, also entered in the Jersey State event, showed the effects of playing in two singles tournaments at the same time and Podesta outlasted him in a grueling three-hour struggle. Displaying coolness under fire, Podesta invariably sent passing shots down the sidelines as Peacock constantly stormed the net.

Charles T. Mattmann, a Long Island youth representing Miami University, conquered Robert A. Low of Stanford in a torrid five-set engagement to capture the freshman title. Seeded second, Mattmann won from the Pacific Coast star, who hails from the metropolitan dis-

Continued on Page Two

LOSER HURTS ANKLE

Hobbles Through Match as Rival Wins Title for Eighth Time

'TOO BAD,' SAYS VICTOR

Mrs. Moody Was Right to Go On, Opponent States—U. S. Sweep First in Tourney

WIMBLEDON CHAMPIONS

*Men's Singles—J. Donald Budge, Oakland, Calif.
Women's Singles—Mrs. Helen Wills Moody, San Francisco.
*Men's Doubles—Budge and Gene Mako, Los Angeles.
Women's Doubles—Miss Alice Marble, San Francisco, and Mrs. Sarah Palfrey Fabyan, Brookline, Mass.
*Mixed Doubles—Budge and Miss Marble.
*Retained title.

By THOMAS J. HAMILTON
Wireless to THE NEW YORK TIMES.

WIMBLEDON, England, July 2.—After having battled with her inveterate rival on even terms for eight tense games, Miss Helen Jacobs injured her ankle when she seemingly was about to take the lead in her championship match with Mrs. Helen Wills Moody today in the all-England tennis tournament, and was defeated, 6—4, 6—0.

Mrs. Moody's victory therefore lacked the decisiveness of her thrilling fight from behind to win the Wimbledon title from Miss Jacobs three years ago, but there were more than enough of positive results in Don Budge's success in holding all three championships he won last year.

And the victory of Miss Alice Marble and Mrs. Sarah Palfrey Fabyan in women's doubles gave the United States a history-making sweep of all five Wimbledon titles.

The victory was Mrs. Moody's eighth in a Wimbledon women's singles final and set a record for the tournament.

Topic of Long Debate

What would have been the outcome had not this twelfth meeting between the California rivals, Mrs. Moody and Miss Jacobs, been marred by the ankle injury to the latter probably will be debated a long time, as was their historic encounter at Forest Hills in 1933, when Mrs. Moody withdrew because of an injury to her back.

Miss Jacobs, after trailing at 4—2, had evened the score and was within a point of capturing the crucial ninth game when she strained the Achilles tendon in her right ankle in a fruitless attempt to volley Mrs. Moody's beautiful passing shot.

The injury to the ankle, which was weakened in a practice match yesterday, was not immediately apparent, for Miss Jacobs gained an advantage in the next rally and fought hard before finally losing the game. But to the amazement of the huge gallery she then lost the set game without returning a single service and won only three points in the following set, which was over in exactly eight minutes.

Midway through the second set Mrs. Hazel Hotchkiss Wightman, captain of the American Wightman Cup squad, was hurriedly summoned to the court and she pleaded with Miss Jacobs to ask for time to loosen the bandages on her injured ankle. Miss Jacobs, however, refused and calmly continued her brave attempt to play as if nothing had happened.

No Let-up by Mrs. Moody

Mrs. Moody, meanwhile, relentlessly applied pressure, driving first to one sideline, then the other, until a love game, fourth of the set, at long last brought Miss Jacobs's agony to an end.

Unlike most other opponents who have met here this last fortnight, they exchanged not a single smile or remark from the time they appeared on the court until Mrs. Moody ran up to shake hands and tell her defeated rival, "Too bad, Helen."

For this, like the eleven other occasions on which they have met in championship tennis here and in the United States, was the nearest equivalent the game affords to a "grudge fight."

It is possible the Forest Hills gallery will have a chance to see another meeting between the two this Summer, for Miss Jacobs disclosed tonight she will return to the United States to play in the national championships and Mrs. Moody said she hoped to do so.

For a fortnight there was the possibility that the two Helens might meet here—although at first this was most improbable because of Miss Jacobs's shoulder injury, which kept her out of the Wightman Cup matches—and once the encounter was assured the debates on the out-

Continued on Page Eight

Prince Charming II Dominates Hunter Classes in Horse Show at Westport

3-GAITED LAURELS TO MORELAND MAID

Janet Sue, Stablemate, Also Captures Title for Mrs. Weil as Show Ends

MODERNISTIC TOP JUMPER

Carries Off $500 Stake and Championship—Midkiff's Melody Triumphs

From a Staff Correspondent

WESTPORT, Conn., July 2.—Moreland Maid, one of America's greatest saddle horses, added another championship to the long list accumulated in her brilliant show career when she took the title today in the three-gaited division at the final session of the fifteenth annual exhibition of the Fairfield County Hunt Club.

In the presence of a notable gathering of spectators this beautiful chestnut mare, owned by the Fair City Stables of Mrs. L. Victor Weil of Elberon, N. J., was shown to advantage in a small but select field. Mrs. Weil elected to try for the honors with the daughter of American Born and Youth's Charm, scratching Dixie Maid, star of the smaller three-gaited division.

Mr. and Mrs. Reed A. Albee of Larchmont, N. Y., presented their chestnut mare Wild Honey, and the battle for the title was between these two. Wild Honey was placed in reserve.

Large Crowd Present

The afternoon session was favored by one of the largest attendances in recent years, drawn by perfect weather and the promise of scintillating competition in the title events.

Fair City completed a most successful record for the three days by also winning the championship sweepstakes for five-gaited saddle horses, Frank Connors riding the chestnut mare Janet Sue, by Sheridan Acres—Ethel Rex, to take the title. Reserve was the bay gelding American Royal, belonging to Mr. and Mrs. Albee.

The champion hunter was the noted bay gelding Prince Charming II, the property of the Claredda Farm of Mr. and Mrs. E. V. Quinn of Shrewsbury, N. J., and piloted by Joe Molony. Virtually invincible in his division, the veteran gained the laurels by defeating the towering gray gelding Dublin Venture, owned and piloted by Miss Deborah G. Rood of Wilmington, Del.

They also finished in that order in the $500 hunter stake, Prince Charming II earning $250 and Dublin Venture $125.

A large field competed in the $500 jumper stake, the honors and first money of $200 going to Philip J. Bliss of Bronxville, whose Modernistic was ridden by Arthur McCashin. Second went to Morris S. Clark of Orange, Va., riding his own brown gelding, Whoopee.

Whoopee Placed in Reserve

Championship honors among the open jumpers also went to Modernistic, with Whoopee being placed in reserve.

Mrs. Laning Harvey Jr. of Kingston, Pa., annexed the working hunter championship with her chestnut mare, Midkiff's Melody, who also accounted for the Marshall Hall Memorial Trophy. Reserve was the chestnut mare Because, entered by Mr. and Mrs. A. Biddle Duke of Tuxedo Park, N. Y.

The $500 working hunter stake also was captured by Midkiff's Melody. The mare made a fine round of the short course, her pace being evenly sustained. Second was awarded to another Pennsylvania entry, Troop, the big bay gelding which Morris S. Clark rode for Mrs. J. T. Moore Jr. of Reading.

There was a first-class turnout of juniors for the two A. S. P. C. A. horsemanship events. In the Maclay jumping class the field numbered nineteen and performances were excellent. The victor was Michael Daly of Southport, Conn., whose nearest rival was his sister, Madeline.

THE AWARDS

MORNING EVENTS

Class 63. Local Jumpers—First, Miss Barbara W. Thompson's ch. m. Lucy Glitters; second, Miss Peggy Klipstein's ch. g. Red Rock; third, Mrs. John J. Farrell's ch. m. Mermaid; fourth, George S. McCormack's g. g. Blue Blazes.

Class 48. Heavy and Middleweight Hunters—First, Mrs. Charles F. Munson's br. g. Bally Bohill; second, Miss Deborah G. Rood's g. g. Dublin Venture; third, Howard Y. Haffener's (Morris S. Clark agt.) ch. g. Boby E.; fourth, Frederick M. Warburg's br. g. Battle Day.

Class 14. Saddle Horses (three-gaited)—First, Fair City Stables' ch. m. Dixie Maid; second, Mr. and Mrs. Marvin Y. Bell's ch. m. Promenade; third, Miss Jacquelin Ann Hustis's ch. m. Betty Christine; fourth, Glenholme Farm's b. m. Pegy O'My Heart.

Class 40. Ladies' Hunters (up to carrying 165 pounds to hounds)—First, Miss Clare Weber's ch. g. Ballella; second, Miss Deborah G. Rood's g. g. Dublin Venture; third, Mrs. Harry Frank Jr.'s b. g. Our Way; fourth, Mrs. James J. Sexton Jr.'s ch. g. Muffin Man.

Class 15. Three-Gaited—First, Miss May Gardiner's ch. g. Beau Kalarama; second, Fair City Stables' ch. g. Lee Belle Sir Walter.

Class 24. A. S. P. C. A. Good Hand Elimination—First, Mrs. Cary Jackson's ch. g. Mayring; second, Frederick M. Warburg's br. g. Battle Day; third, Miss Deborah G. Rood's g. g. Dublin Venture; fourth, Mrs. Harry Frank Jr.'s b. g. Our Way.

Class 25. Horsemanship—First, Michael Daly; second, Miss Madeleine Daly; third, William Watson; fourth, Miss Ellen Leigh Martin; fifth, Miss Barbara Wahl; sixth, Henry Chase.

Class 58. Knockdown and Out—First, Dudley Brothwell's ch. g. Brookside; second, Philip J. Bliss's (Hubert Moseley Agt.) ch. g. Modernistic; third, Miss Peggy Budd's bl. g. Come On; fourth, Philip J. Bliss's (Hubert Moseley Agt.) b. m. Bay Flight.

AFTERNOON EVENTS

Class 52. $500 Working Hunter Stake—First, Mrs. Laning Harvey Jr.'s ch. m. Midkiff's Melody; second, Mrs. J. T. Moore Jr.'s (Mrs. Cary Jackson Agt.) b. g. Troop; third, Mrs. James J. Sexton Jr.'s br. m. Cleone; fourth, Claredda Farms' br. g. Woodfellow.

Class 20, $500 Championship Three-Gaited Saddle Horse Stake—First, Fair City Stables' ch. m. Moreland's Maid; second, Mr. and Mrs. Reed A. Albee's ch. m. Wild Honey; third, Mr. and Mrs. Marvin Y. Bell's ch. m. Promenade; fourth, Glenholme Farm's b. m. Peg O'My Heart; fifth, Miss May Gardiner's ch. g. Beau Kalarama.

Class 24. Good Hands—First, Miss Barbara Griffiths; second, Henry Chase; third, Alfred W. Van Sinderin; fourth, Miss Elaine Weins; fifth, Miss Elizabeth Farrell; sixth, William Steinkraus.

Class 46, $500 Stake for Hunters—First, Claredda Farm's b. g. Prince Charming II; second, Miss Deborah G. Rood's g. g. Dublin Venture; third, Mrs. Edward Lasker's ch. g. imp. Fair Edgar; fourth, Mrs. James J. Sexton Jr.'s br. m. Cleone.

Class 8, Champion Five-Gaited Saddle Horse Sweepstake—First, Fair City Stables' ch. m. Janet Sue; Mr. and Mrs. Reed A. Albee's b. g. American Royal.

Class 65, $500 Jumper Stake—First, Philip J. Bliss's ch. g. Modernistic; second, Morris S. Clark's br. g. Whoopee; third, Philip J. Bliss's g. g. Grey Flight; fourth, Mrs. Gordon Wright's b. g. Musketeer; fifth, Philip J. Bliss's ch. g. Will Gallop; sixth, May Top Stables' ch. g. Golden Brew.

Class 51. Champion Hunter—First, Claredda Farm's b. g. Prince Charming II; second, Miss Deborah G. Rood's g. g. Dublin Venture.

Class 60. Triple Bars—First, May Top Stables' ch. g. Golden Brew; second, May Top Stables' br. g. Amy's Jim; third, Mrs. James J. Sexton Jr.'s ch. g. Pompeien; fourth, Mrs. Dorothy M. White's g. g. Dancing Pardner.

Class 45. Teams of Three Hunters—First, Miss Deborah G. Rood's g. g. Dublin Venture, Miss Deborah G. Rood's g. g. Grey Mouse, Mrs. Dorothy M. White's g. g. Dancing Pardner; second, Nydrie Stables' ch. g. Lord Benton, Nydrie Stables' ch. g. imp. Lord of Orgile, Howard Y. Haffener's ch. g. Boby E.

Class 67. Championship for Open Jumpers—First, Philip J. Bliss's ch. g. Modernistic; second, Morris S. Clark's br. g. Whoopee.

Class 56. Working Hunter Championship—First, Mrs. Laning Harvey Jr.'s ch. m. Midkiff's Melody; second, Mr. and Mrs. A. Biddle Duke's ch. m. Because.

Class 62. Bareback Jumping—First, Mrs. Harold R. Hull's b. m. Crystal; second, Miss Barbara W. Thompson's ch. m. Lucy Glitters.

The Judges

Saddle Horse and Saddle Ponies—Forest L. Ward.

Horsemanship—Augusten Montulet.

Hunters and Jumpers—Sterling Larrabee, M. F. H.; Frederick H. Bontecou, Lewis L. Bredin and Augusten Montulet.

KENT OARSMEN WHO WON THAMES CHALLENGE CUP AT HENLEY REGATTA

Front Row—Robert K. Awtrey Jr., J. Frederick Requardt Jr., Edmund G. Miller, Philip D. Wilson, Peter H. Conze, Julian Simmons, Charles R. Brothwell Jr. and Henry M. Drinker. Rear Row—James M. Crane Jr., David T. Andrews, assistant manager; John H. Bullock 2d, manager; Evan W. Thomas 2d, Rev. F. H. Sill, headmaster; T. D. Walker, coach, and James E. Hooper Jr.

KENT'S EIGHT, BURK WIN HENLEY FINALS

Continued From Page One

down the course. Reaching the stewards' enclosure well over the mile mark, Kent turned on another cylinder to make its stroke thirty-eight. London answered with a final spurt, but it was hopeless. Kent pulled ahead to win by a length in 7:03—the second fastest time in the history of the Thames Challenge Cup event.

Second Victory for Kent

This was the second time Kent has won the Thames Cup and Father Sill seemed particularly pleased by the success of "his boys" this afternoon.

"Of course I'm proud," he said. "The boys worked hard and they deserve every bit of credit."

Burk, the "robot rower" as he has been called, had another machine-like victory today over L. D. Habbitts of the Reading Rowing Club, calmly knocking eight seconds off the record to finish in 8:02. The previous record of 8:10 was last equaled by H. Buhtz of Germany in 1934.

"It was like rowing against a train," said Habbitts. Burk, the American and Canadian champion, admitted he deliberately set out for the record. With a watch tied at his feet, he paid no attention to his rival and, knowing exactly what he can do, calmly paced himself. The 24-year-old modest Burk protested it was the ideal conditions which were chiefly responsible for his fast time, but most observers agree the conditions were only part of it.

Burk's a powerful man, and although Henley week finishes most scullers for the season, he is returning to America next week to enter the nationals at Red Bank, N. J., later in the month.

Stroking at forty-four, Burk crossed the quarter in 1:22. Habbitts led for the first fifty yards. Meanwhile Burk, mechanically pounding out about forty-five, drew level with the Englishman. As they cleared the 300-yard point, Burk's shell nosed ahead by three or four feet and after that he dropped to forty and finished about 200 yards ahead.

Burk is sold on Henley. "This has been rowing de luxe," he said with enthusiasm. "Many's the time I practiced on Rancocas Creek in New Jersey when the spray would freeze on my sweat shirt. Winning this makes all that worth while."

Toss Coxswain Overboard

HENLEY-ON-THAMES, England, July 2 (AP).—Kent School kept the Thames Cup in America for the third straight year. Tabor Academy won the event the last two years, defeating Kent in the final in 1936. After today's final the Americans gave their school yell and picked up Coxswain Evan W. Thomas and tossed him in the river.

The previous Diamond Sculls record was made by F. S. Kelly in 1905.

The Leander oarsmen successfully defended the Stewards' Cup, defeating Trinity of Oxford easily in 7:33. The Wyfold Cup was retained by the London Club's B oarsmen, who defeated the Royal Chester Rowing Club by four lengths in 7:41.

In the final of the Visitors' Cup, Oriel College, Oxford, stroked by the Dark Blues' varsity stroke, A. B. Hodgson, established a new record for the event, beating Third Trinity, Cambridge, easily in 7:18. The old record of 7:30 was set in 1908 by Magdalene College, Oxford.

The Ladies' Plate went to Radley School in a great performance. It beat Pembroke College, Cambridge, by 1¼ lengths in 6:56.

London won the Grand Challenge Cup over Trinity Hall, Cambridge, by 1 1-3 lengths in 6:58.

Mayor Wilson Cables Burk

PHILADELPHIA, July 2 (AP).—Joe Burk's home town congratulated him today for his record-time sculling victory in the Henley Regatta.

Mayor S. Davis Wilson cabled the champion: "Congratulations on your well-deserved victory. Philadelphia is proud of your achievement."

Henry Penn Burke, president of the National Association of Amateur Oarsmen, which raised the money to send Burk abroad, planned a homecoming welcome and testimonial dinner.

MRS. MOODY'S MOTHER ELATED AT TRIUMPH

But 'Feels Badly' Because of Injury to Miss Jacobs

SAN FRANCISCO, July 2 (AP).—Mrs. Clarence Wills and Mrs. Eula H. Jacobs heard the outcome of the match between their famous tennis playing daughters with mingled emotions today.

Mrs. Wills was happy that her daughter, Mrs. Helen Wills Moody, had set a new Wimbledon record by winning her eighth championship, but she "felt badly" because of Miss Jacobs's injury.

"It would have been so much more satisfactory to have had the match played on even terms," she said. "Helen was confident in her game when she left, but she seemed more jubilant over the prospect of spending the Summer in Europe."

Mrs. Jacobs had hoped her daughter would win, not so much because it would be a victory over Mrs. Moody but because she had played so courageously to reach the final after illness in the early rounds.

"I never thought Helen would do as well as she did to reach the finals," Mrs. Jacobs said. "When she finished so strongly to enter the last round, my hopes were high."

Among the jubilant supporters of Mrs. Moody was Howard Kinsey, former internationalist and instructor here. Kinsey helped train Mrs. Moody last Winter and upon her departure said she was "playing better than ever." At the time he predicted she would win the title.

Women's Swim on Aug. 13

The women's senior metropolitan and New York State long-distance championships will be among the features of the swimming carnival to be conducted by the Associated Swimming Clubs of New York at Playland, Rye, Saturday, Aug. 13. The program will be under the direction of Miss Ethelda M. Bleibtrey, former American Olympic star.

MISS BIXLER GAINS FINAL

Defeats Miss Wandelt in Girls' Metropolitan Tennis

Miss Barbara Bixler, seeded third, eliminated Miss Virginia Wandelt, No. 2, in the girls' metropolitan tennis at the Jackson Heights Tennis Club yesterday and will meet Miss Josephine Sanfilippo, the defending champion, in the final on Tuesday at 10:30 A. M. The scores were 6—3, 5—7, 6—2.

Miss Wandelt put up a spirited battle in the second set when, trailing at 40—love and 5—2, she pulled out the game and set with a brilliant rally, but the pace was too fast in the deciding set.

Arkansas Cards Title Tennis

The ninth annual State tennis tournament, sponsored by the Pine Bluff Park Commission at Oakland Park, Ark., will be played July 15-17, it has been announced by C. C. Beers, secretary. This year a women's bracket will be included. Leading players of the State are expected to be among the entrants.

MRS. MOODY WINS FROM MISS JACOBS

Continued From Page One

come have absorbed all attention here. Even Budge's success in repeating his treble conquest attracted little attention because his success had been taken for granted.

But a little sadly the British tennis world is counting those five vanished titles and wondering how long the American control of Wimbledon will last. The end is nowhere in sight.

That the United States would have both singles titles was already assured by Budge's crushing victory over Henry W. (Bunny) Austin yesterday. This afternoon the Californian regained his doubles championships, he and Gene Mako taking the men's title with a hard-fought victory over the Germans, Henner Henkel and Georg von Metaxa; then he and Miss Marble scoring a brilliant triumph over Henkel and Mrs. Fabyan for the mixed doubles title.

Equally decisively Miss Marble and Mrs. Fabyan showed they are supreme in women's doubles with a victory over Mme. René Mathieu of France and Miss Adeline Yorke of England, champions here last year.

As on so many occasions in the past, Miss Jacobs today opposed her chopped forehand to Mrs. Moody's hard-hit drives. In all the world of women's tennis there is no one to match Mrs. Moody's control, and with her overhead still the only weakness in her game, she stuck close to the baseline and held back her forcing strokes until she had drawn Miss Jacobs out of position.

Miss Jacobs, with less certain control, sought to draw Mrs. Moody to the net with shots to the fourecourt, but much of the time they were not angled sharply enough and left her open to crushing retorts.

Breaks in Service

But Mrs. Moody's game was not quite up to its level of the agonizing semi-final contest with Mme. Hilda Krahwinkel Sperling of Denmark and after the first two games had gone against service, Miss Jacobs held hers for a 2-1 lead. As it turned out, it was the only time in the match that she was ahead, for Mrs. Moody settled down and took the next three games as a result of her steadiness in the long baseline rallies.

It was now that Miss Jacobs, whose unprecedented success in becoming the first unseeded player ever to reach the final had made her the gallery's favorite, embarked on her great fight to rescue the set. Taking advantage of Mrs. Moody's attack of overdriving, she quickly captured the next game and, after a long struggle, annexed the eighth to draw up to 4—4. Then she took to the net in a valiant effort to force the issue.

Actually her volleying brought her little, for she put two valuable balls out of the court. But a series of magnificent chops that landed dead square on the sidelines—Mrs. Moody made no attempt to retrieve them—took her to 40—30, and after a fine placement Miss Jacobs stormed the net for what it seemed might be the turning point of the match.

Instead, it made a crushing defeat certain, for the strain of lunging for Mrs. Moody's tremendous passing shot proved too much for Miss Jacobs's ankle. Few in the gallery saw her stretch to rub the injured ankle, and in fact, although she played thereafter from the baseline, she reached advantage with the next point.

Still Either's Game

Mrs. Moody stiffened and made it her advantage but Miss Jacobs saved the game with a placement, and up to that point it was anybody's game.

But, as it turned out, it was the last point Miss Jacobs was to win in that set. Mrs. Moody gained an advantage when Miss Jacobs's placement was just out and Miss Jacobs, again trying the net, missed a volley. Mrs. Moody took her service like a flash and the set was over.

It was only now that Miss Jacobs's limp became generally noticeable. Although she managed to get two points in the opening game of the second set, the injury clearly was forcing her to overhit most of her strokes.

Less gallant players would have made this limp unmistakable, but Miss Jacobs tried to conceal it, even rushing to the net in the second game in a pretense that all was as before. She was easily passed and the second game went at love.

Two double-faults and two errors disposed of the third, but by this time the tournament officials, sensing what was wrong, had summoned Mrs. Wightman to the court. While Mrs. Moody remained silent on her side of the court, Miss Jacobs and Mrs. Wightman held a quick conference which ended with Miss Jacobs proceeding with the play.

The extent of her perturbation, however, was obvious from the fact that she started moving away after Mrs. Moody's first service went out. But she again went to the net, only to stand helpless as her opponent calmly lobbed over her head.

In the next game Miss Jacobs made her third and last point of the set with a sharply angled shot cross-court. But it was the end.

Wimbledon Winners Since 1900

1900—Mrs. Hillyard	1922—Mlle. Lenglen
1901—Mrs. Sterry	1923—Mlle. Lenglen
1902—Miss Robb	1924—Miss McKane
1903—Miss Douglass	1925—Mlle. Lenglen
1904—Miss Douglass	1926—Mrs. Godfree
1905—Miss Sutton	1927—Miss Wills
1906—Miss Douglass	1928—Miss Wills
1907—Miss Sutton	1929—Miss Wills
1908—Mrs. Sterry	1930—Mrs. Moody
1909—Miss Boothby	1931—Fraeulein Aussem
1910—Mrs. Chambers	
1911—Mrs. Chambers	1932—Mrs. Moody
1912—Mrs. Larcombe	1933—Mrs. Moody
1913—Mrs. Chambers	1934—Miss Round
1914—Mrs. Chambers	1935—Mrs. Moody
1915-18—No matches	1936—Miss Jacobs
1919—Mlle. Lenglen	1937—Miss Round
1920—Mlle. Lenglen	1938—Mrs. Moody
1921—Mlle. Lenglen	

Before the gallery's cheers, which rose as Miss Jacobs changed courts, completely died down, she had lost the sixth game at love, and the match.

Miss Jacobs sat on her racket while Mrs. Moody gave a short interview over a television hook-up, then the conqueror and the defeated one silently walked to the dressing room.

Later, while Mrs. Moody was being presented to Queen Mary, who was present for the second day in succession, Miss Jacobs said she believed her ankle injury was due indirectly to her attempt to save a strain on her injured right shoulder. She explained she had hurt her ankle slightly in a practice match yesterday with Bill Tilden, who has been coaching her the last few weeks, but that she had hoped a strapping would make it last out the match.

"I am more sorry about this than anything in my life," Miss Jacobs said sadly. "I did want to make a game of it and I felt until my ankle went that I had a good chance. I don't mean by that I thought the result a foregone conclusion, but I was absolutely confident I'd play as well as I could, however well that is."

Asked what she thought of Mrs. Moody's determination to finish the match, Miss Jacobs said, "I think Helen did the right thing—she hit shots I couldn't possibly get and I agree the only wise thing to do was to get it over as quickly as possible."

Miss Jacobs, who is sailing for the United States next Saturday to compete in the American championships, recalled that Mrs. Moody's remark at the end of the match was only, "Too bad, Helen," adding, "That's all she said, but please don't rub that in."

Mrs. Moody, who at the age of 31 is two years older than her rival, was a buoyant picture when she emerged after being presented to Queen Mary as the winner of the Wimbledon championship for the eighth time.

"It was too bad about Helen," she said. "But it couldn't be helped, could it?"

Laughing, Mrs. Moody added she felt "just like I always have" over winning the title again, but she declared she had not decided whether she would play here again.

After the excitement of a match like that the other contests fortunately were less of a strain on the gallery's nerves. The men's doubles turned out closer than was expected, for von Metaxa strove gallantly to fill the shoes of the absent Baron Gottfried von Cramm and each of the four sets of the 6—4, 3—6, 6—3, 8—6 match turned on a single service break.

Although a good part of the match was played in a rather heavy drizzle, the volleying duels displayed the American champions at their unbeatable best.

It was a pity that after Miss Marble and Mrs. Fabyan teamed so effectively to beat Mme. Mathieu and Miss Yorke for the women's championship by 6—2, 6—3—the Americans' unified volleying was too much for their opponents, since Mme. Mathieu insisted on staying at the baseline—they had to oppose each other in the mixed doubles.

Henkel's tremendous service did valiant execution in the closing contest, decided by 6—1, 6—4, but Budge and Miss Marble were the stronger team—all the more so since Miss Marble, who in this Wimbledon as in the last has won only this minor prize with her magnificent strokes, was again at the top of her form. Perhaps if she comes to Wimbledon next year she will hold the stage regardless of any return appearance of the two Helens.

Criticism Termed Unfair

WIMBLEDON, England, July 2 (AP).—Mrs. Hazel Hotchkiss Wightman, captain of the American Wightman Cup team, who is a friend of both Mrs. Helen Wills Moody and Miss Helen Jacobs, said today that it was "a shame that everybody seems to be blaming Mrs. Moody for finishing Miss Jacobs off so quickly in the Wimbledon tennis final."

"I think that is unfair," she continued. "It was the only thing to do under the circumstances."

The whole final set of the match had everybody in the stands buzzing about the strange spectacle. Even Queen Mary, in the royal box, appeared to be having an animated discussion about it with former Queen Victoria Eugenie of Spain.

When the excitement was all over Miss Jacobs was a sad and red-eyed girl. She limped to her dressing room with Dr. J. J. Dunning and it was only after a long rest that she would see reporters. But even then she couldn't face them. She fled into the clubhouse and agreed later to receive one American and one English newspaper man.

Then, with her swollen ankle propped on the side of a desk, she told the story of how her ankle was injured. She explained that she first had hurt it in her semi-final round match with Miss Alice Marble on Thursday. After undergoing treatment that night, she injured it again in practice yesterday.

Dr. Dunning explained the ankle condition was the indirect result of the shoulder injury Miss Jacobs suffered some weeks ago, forcing her to withdraw from the Wightman Cup matches and leading to her fainting spell in the Wimbledon clubhouse just before her second-round match. Dr. Dunning said that Miss Jacobs, favoring her injured shoulder, had placed undue strain on her ankle.

THE SUMMARIES

FINAL ROUND

Women's Singles—Mrs. Helen Wills Moody, San Francisco, defeated Miss Helen Jacobs, Berkeley, Calif., 6—4, 6—0.

Men's Doubles—J. Donald Budge, Oakland, Calif., and Gene Mako, Los Angeles, defeated Henner Henkel and Georg von Metaxa, Germany, 6—4, 3—6, 6—3, 8—6.

Women's Doubles—Miss Alice Marble, San Francisco, and Mrs. Sarah Palfrey Fabyan, Brookline, Mass., defeated Mme. Rene Mathieu, France, and Miss Adeline Yorke, England, 6—2, 6—3.

Mixed Doubles—J. Donald Budge, Oakland, Calif., and Miss Alice Marble, San Francisco, defeated Henner Henkel, Germany, and Mrs. Sarah Palfrey Fabyan, Brookline, Mass., 6—1, 6—4.

THE POINT SCORE

MRS. MOODY VS. MISS JACOBS

First Set

(Miss Jacobs Serving)

											Pts.	G.
Miss Jacobs	3	4	5	1	2	5	4	5	5	0	34	4
Mrs. Moody	5	2	3	4	4	7	2	3	7	4	41	6

Second Set

(Miss Jacobs Serving)

							Pts.	G.
Miss Jacobs	2	0	0	0	1	0	3	0
Mrs. Moody	4	4	4	4	4	4	24	6

Stroke Analysis

	S.A.	P.	N.	O.	D.F.
Mrs. Moody	2	8	10	17	0
Miss Jacobs	0	10	18	36	3

	E.	E.P.	T.P.	G.	Sets.
Mrs. Moody	27	8	65	12	2
Miss Jacobs	57	10	37	4	0

RECORDS OF FINALISTS

How Mrs. Moody and Miss Jacobs Advanced at Wimbledon

The records of Mrs. Helen Wills Moody and Miss Helen Jacobs in the Wimbledon tournament:

MRS. MOODY

First Round—Bye.
Second Round—Defeated Mrs. Harry C. Hopman, Australia, 6—3, 6—4.
Third Round—Defeated Mrs. P. F. Glover, England, 6—4, 7—5.
Fourth Round—Defeated Mrs. Bobbie Heine Miller, South Africa, 8—6, 6—4.
Quarter-final—Defeated Miss Kay Stammers, England, 6—2, 6—1.
Semi-final—Defeated Mme. Hilda Krahwinkel Sperling, Denmark, 12—10, 6—4.
Final—Defeated Miss Jacobs, 6—4, 6—0.

MISS JACOBS

First Round—Defeated Miss Mary Whitmarsh, England, 6—0, 6—1.
Second Round—Defeated Miss Joan Ingram, England, 9—7, 6—3.
Third Round—Defeated Miss Freda James, England, 6—4, 6—2.
Fourth Round—Defeated Miss Peggy Scriven, England, 6—3, 6—0.
Quarter-final—Defeated Mlle. Jadwiga Jedrzejowska, Poland, 6—2, 6—3.
Semi-final—Defeated Miss Alice Marble, San Francisco, 6—4, 6—4.
Final—Lost to Mrs. Moody, 6—4, 6—0.

MRS. MOODY STILL AT TOP OF GAME

Now Has Returned to Head of List Twice After Absences From Major Competition

RECORD IS UNPARALLELED

First Scaled Heights in U. S. Tennis in 1923—Roster of Titles a Long One

The victory of Mrs. Helen Wills Moody over Miss Helen Jacobs at Wimbledon yesterday brought to a successful culmination the second big comeback in the career of this unparalleled woman tennis player.

In 1935, after being inactive for the two previous years because of a back injury, she triumphed in the Wimbledon final and now, three years later, she has done it again. She dropped out of tennis in so far as major competition was concerned immediately after her 1935 Wimbledon triumph and stayed out until she hit the comeback trail this year in England.

Mrs. Moody has been a dominant figure in the women's game ever since she won her first United States championship in 1923. Before that, for two years, she was the girls' national titleholder. She took the national singles crown seven times, in 1923, 1924, 1925, 1927, 1928, 1929 and 1931. Since 1927 she has won the Wimbledon singles title eight times, including the present victory.

Add to her record of major triumphs her four French women's championships and her doubles and mixed doubles victories here and abroad and the picture of one of the greatest woman players in history is complete.

Mrs. Moody's record of major championships:

UNITED STATES CHAMPIONSHIPS

1921—Girls' national championship.
1922—Girls' national championship; girls' national doubles championship with Miss Helen Hooker; women's national doubles championship with Mrs. John B. Jessup.
1923—Women's national championship.
1924—Women's national championship; women's national doubles championship with Mrs. George W. Wightman; national mixed doubles championship with Vincent Richards.
1925—Women's national championship; women's national doubles championship with Miss Mary K. Browne.
1927—Women's national championship.
1928—Women's national championship; women's national doubles championship with Mrs. George W. Wightman; national mixed doubles championship with John B. Hawkes.
1929—Women's national championship.
1931—Women's national championship.

ENGLISH CHAMPIONSHIPS

1927—Women's English championship; women's English doubles championship with Miss Elizabeth Ryan.
1928—Women's English championship.
1929—Women's English championship.
1930—Women's English championship; women's English doubles championship with Miss Elizabeth Ryan.
1932—Women's English championship.
1933—Women's English championship.
1935—Women's English championship.
1938—Women's English championship.

FRENCH CHAMPIONSHIPS

1928—Women's French championships.
1929—Women's French championship.
1930—Women's French championship.
1932—Women's French championship; women's French doubles championship with Miss Elizabeth Ryan.

Harness Racing Tomorrow

The third matinee light-harness racing card of the Central New Jersey Horsemen's Association will be presented at the Borough Park track in South Plainfield tomorrow afternoon, starting at 2 o'clock. Three harness races, each with at least four starters, will comprise the card. As an added feature, the Plainfield Wheelmen will stage a championship bicycle race.

Women in Sports

By MAUREEN ORCUTT

One of the greatest fields to take part in a women's one-day invitation golf tournament in the metropolitan district will tee off on the Green Meadow course, Harrison, N. Y., next Friday. It will include stars from Boston, Rhode Island, Syracuse, Lake Placid, Philadelphia and Washington, as well as most of the leaders in the metropolitan section.

Heading the list of out-of-town entrants will be Mrs. Norman Lack of Philadelphia, runner-up in the recent Eastern championship. Others will be Miss Virginia Guilfoil of Syracuse; Miss Helen Detweiller, District of Columbia champion; Miss Jean Bauer, who will defend her Shennecossett title the following week; Miss Rosamond Vahey, runner-up in the Boston championship, and Miss Marjorie Harrison, rising young star from Upper New York State, of whom great things are expected, but who at present is paying more attention to education than to golf.

Mrs. Harb Holds Title

It was hoped that Mrs. Whitney Harb, the former Miss Helen Hicks, might return to defend this title, which she won last year on the Gedney Farm course, but up to the present time she has not announced her intention to compete.

Among the metropolitan stars expected to take part are Mrs. Harry McNaughton, Long Island and New York State champion, who is at the peak of her game; Mrs. William R. Kirkland Jr., runner-up to Mrs. McNaughton in the Long Island championship; Mrs. Charles L. Leichner, the former Mrs. Sylva Annenberg; Mrs. Ray Torgerson and Mrs. Morgan Baker, all from Long Island; Mrs. James Robbins, Westchester champion; Mrs. Henry Dietrich, who will be playing over her home course; Mrs. Russell Holman, Innis Arden star; Mrs. Charles Eastman and Mrs. J. F. Holleran, all of Westchester, and Mrs. Wright G. Goss Jr., recent winner of the New Jersey closed championship, and those fine young golfers, Miss Laddie Irwin and Miss Gail Wild, representing New Jersey.

The tournament will consist of an eighteen-hole medal round, and the committee is so generous in distributing prizes that high handicap as well as low handicap players have a chance of winning awards. Even the mothers of several of the contestants are to be remembered.

An evening of entertainment will follow the tournament.

Shoot Title to Miss Laursen

The tenth annual Great Eastern skeet championship was won last week by Miss Patricia Laursen, 17-year-old high school girl who came from Akron, Ohio, to shoot at Lordship, Conn.

At the end of the women's event the blonde Miss Laursen was tied for first place with Mrs. M. L. Smythe of Cleveland and Mrs. L. S. Webb of Richmond with a score of 95 out of 100. In the shoot-off Miss Laursen broke 25 clays in a row, while Mrs. Smythe and Mrs. Webb could do no better than 24 and 23 respectively.

Miss Laursen, who has been shooting for only a year and a half, represents the Firestone Skeet Club of Akron. An only child, she is carrying on a family tradition, for her father is an enthusiastic shooter. In 1937 she was runner-up in the Ohio State skeet shoot and took similar places in the Midwest junior and women's divisions and in the women's out-of-State division of the Florida State championship.

Wilson Announces Awards

Announcement of athletic awards, traditional climax of Class Day, closed the 1937-38 sports year at Wilson College last week. For the first time in many years, the college tennis championship went to a freshman, Miss Anne Wunderle of Philadelphia. With Miss Gladele Penney, Oyster Bay, N. Y., she also won honorable mention for general excellence in athletics this Spring.

A "W" was given to Miss Barbara Chambers of Cincinnati, who reached the semi-finals of the tournament in which Miss Wunderle was the victor. The runner-up, Miss Jane Little of Wenonah, N. J., president of the Wilson Athletic Association and already a wearer of the "W," received an honorary star.

Pentathlon honors, the greatest athletic recognition that can come to a Wilson girl, were conferred on two members of the graduating class, Miss Frederika Smith of New York and Miss Anna Kratz, Norristown, Pa.

BOWDEN CONQUERS MURRAY IN 3 SETS

Continued From Page One

pulled up to 5—4 and 30—all from 2—4.

Watt stood to his guns gamely against the all-around severity of Kovacs, whose service, volleying and smashing all bear the Californian stamp. It was no small feat to take five games from the towering Oakland youth, who allowed only three to Eugene McCauliff in the next round.

Hunt, winner here a year ago, gained his semi-final bracket after yielding a set to Merritt Cutler, 6—3, 7—9, 6—1.

THE SUMMARIES

Second Round

Merritt Cutler defeated Hunt T. Dickinson, 6—4, 6—4; Frank Bowden defeated E. C. Backe, 6—1, 6—4; Robert Murray defeated Cedric Major, 6—3, 6—2; Frank Kovacs defeated Laird Watt, 6—3, 6—2; E. H. McCauliff defeated E. T. Appleby, 6—2, 6—2.

Quarter-Final Round

Gilbert Hunt defeated Cutler, 6—3, 7—9, 6—1; Bowden defeated Murray, 5—7, 6—2, 6—1; Kovacs defeated McCauliff, 6—2, 6—1; J. Gilbert Hall defeated Douglas Cameron, 7—5, 5—7, 6—2.

Feuer-Hecht Handball Victors

Sam Feuer and Marvin Hecht upset Harry Goldstein and George Baskin, the national champions, in the final of the Metropolitan A. A. U. handball doubles championship at Ravenhall, Coney Island, yesterday. Dave Lerner and Joseph Garber gained the third place medals by beating Walter Cohen and Anthony Racaniello, 21—16, 21—3.

Young Ireland to Test Mayo

The main event at Innisfall Park this afternoon will bring together the Young Ireland and the Mayo Gaelic football teams at 4:30 o'clock. A preliminary hurling contest between Offaly and the New Jersey Rangers is scheduled at 3:15.

The New York Times.

SPORTS Section 5

SUNDAY, SEPTEMBER 25, 1938.

BUDGE AND MISS MARBLE CAPTURE U. S. TENNIS FINALS; ST. BONAVENTURE BEATS MANHATTAN; MAGIC HOUR WINS

JASPERS BOW BY 7-6

Scoring Pass Deflected to Ertle of Bonnies in Last Three Minutes

OWENS KICKS EXTRA POINT

Savage Counts for Manhattan, Which Wastes Big Offensive Advantage in Opener

By KINGSLEY CHILDS

A St. Bonaventure forward pass bounding from a cluster of clawing hands into the arms of Johnny Ertle provided the deciding blow as the scrappy up-Staters shaded Manhattan College, 7 to 6, at Randalls Island Stadium yesterday in New York City's initial intercollegiate football game of the new campaign.

Coming with the suddenness of a sharp lightning bolt from the sky with merely three minutes remaining in the final quarter, the aerial abruptly changed the whole complexion of the proceedings and unfortunately marred Herb Kopf's début as head coach of the Jaspers.

Offensively, as the statistics clearly indicate, Manhattan had a decided edge virtually throughout the encounter, and few, if any, of the 8,000 spectators expected to see the Bonnies prevail. They had made a couple of brilliant defensive stands to thwart enemy scoring attempts, but had finally yielded early in the last quarter, and the resultant Jasper six-point lead seemed safe as the end neared.

Last Desperate Try

But just when the Manhattan rooters were breathing easily, the big break occurred, the up-Staters were back in their territory, trying, as had been the case all afternoon, to get their attack clicking. They had the ball on their 41-yard stripe and elected to take to the air in a last desperate effort.

Henry Bunowski, a commanding figure for the Bonnies at all times, stepped back to his 25 and heaved a high, looping pass. Down around the Manhattan 30, Walt Carew, for whom the aerial was intended, was closely covered by three enemy players, all leaping simultaneously as the ball neared them in its flight.

The pigskin careened sharply to the left, evidently having bounced off the fingertips or a shoulder of a Manhattan man. Ertle, a few feet away from the group, caught the deflected ball and scampered 30 yards for the touchdown while two Jaspers followed in vain pursuit.

Having squared matters at 6-all, the Bonnies concentrated on adding the precious extra point. Al Owens, substitute back, was selected, and with Bunoski holding the ball he calmly and accurately placekicked the goal.

Thus he gave St. Bonaventure its second victory in the eight-game Manhattan series. The up-State college's only previous triumph over the Jaspers was registered ten years ago, when the colleges opened gridiron relations.

In the two minutes and forty-four seconds remaining after Owens had tacked on the deciding tally, Kopf's forces could not function with the same sustained success which they had displayed in rolling up eighteen first downs while their rivals achieved merely three.

Bonnies' Attack Shackled

Until the peculiar twist shattered Manhattan's victory hopes, the Bonnies flashed little offensive effectiveness. The Jaspers held an 8-to-2 advantage in first downs at the intermission.

Two sophomores, Johnny Supulski, a product of La Salle M. A. of Oakdale, L. I., and Ted Mazur, who hails from Bloomfield (N. J.) High, distinguished themselves in their varsity debuts and occupied conspicuous roles in Manhattan's strong downfield drives, especially in the second half.

Supulski was one of the chief ground gainers and also tossed a few good passes which were completed. Mazur reeled off considerable yardage on several end sweeps and when he took over the punting assignment from Joe Mitchell in the second half Manhattan profited by marked improvement in that department.

Late in the third period a pass from Supulski to Mazur furnished the opening wedge in the home team's touchdown advance. Manhattan had obtained the ball on the St. Bonaventure 30, when Bunoski kicked from behind the goal line after the invaders had held for downs on the one-foot line.

The Supulski-Mazur aerial was good for twelve yards. In two ground attempts, Johnny Kopicki plowed along for thirteen more and as he was brought to earth at the

Continued on Page Five

St. Bonaventure Forwards Stop a Manhattan Plunge

Supulski downed in attempting to crash Bonnies' line in game at Randalls Island

Times Wide World

PITT OVERPOWERS W. VIRGINIA, 19 TO 0

35,000 See Goldberg Plunge Across Twice—Panthers Never Threatened

By The Associated Press.

PITTSBURGH, Sept. 24.—Mountaineer hopes of opening the 1938 football season with a staggering upset collapsed on this sunny afternoon as the rebuilt forces of Jock Sutherland's Pittsburgh Panthers crushed West Virginia, 19 to 0, before 35,000 spectators.

Picking up from where they left off last year as the nationally ranked No. 1 team of the college pigskin world, the Panthers drove over touchdowns in the second, third and fourth periods without resorting to a single bit of their famed trickery. So powerless were the vaunted crew from the mountains that they were held to two first downs.

Sophomores Do Well

Not once did the Mountaineers, rated as one of the finest small university elevens in the land, make a serious scoring threat. At the finish, most of the fans paid more attention to the announcer's returns of the Pittsburgh-Cincinnati baseball game than the football game. Sutherland had a full team of sophomores on the field and they were pushing the Mountaineers hard.

Sutherland's "dream backfield," consisting of Marsh Goldberg, Hal Stebbins, Dick Cassiano and Johnny Chickerneo, failed to riddle the Mountaineer defense at will but it was more than enough as it leveled off with drive after drive.

Goldberg, a native of Elkins, W. Va., scored two of the touchdowns, bucking over each time from the 2-yard stripe. The third Panther touchdown came in a freakish way as the ball squirted from Frank Goodell's arms on the goal line

Continued on Page Five

Patty Berg Vanquishes Mrs. Page For National Golf Title, 6 and 5

Minneapolis Girl, 20 Years Old, Dethrones Champion, Shooting Fine Game in Face of Wind—2 Up After 18 Holes

By WILLIAM D. RICHARDSON

Special to THE NEW YORK TIMES.

WILMETTE, Ill., Sept. 24.—Little Patty Berg's fourth attempt to lift the women's national golf crown was successful today.

Playing invincible golf, the best she has shot all week, the 20-year-old Minneapolis redhead avenged the setback she received from Mrs. Estelle Lawson Page of Chapel Hill, N. C., in the final of the championship at Memphis last year by dethroning her opponent, 6 and 5, over the thirty-six-hole route at the Westmoreland Country Club.

Despite the fact that the course was swept by a strong northeast wind that had a chill in it and made the going the roughest it has been all week, Miss Berg played the first eighteen holes in women's par to be 2 up, went out in 37, only two over men's par, in the afternoon and was three strokes under women's par for the day's play when the match ended on the No. 13 green, thirty-first hole of the match.

Miss Berg had a chance to end the unequal contest at 7 and 6, the margin by which Mrs. Page beat her last year, when she teed off to play the thirtieth hole 7 up, but a hooked drive into the rough, a shot into a bunker on the opposite side of the fairway and a mediocre recovery

Continued on Page Seven

MINNESOTA HALTS WASHINGTON, 15-0

Tackle Intercepts Pass and Goes 85 Yards to Score—50,000 Watch Battle

By The Associated Press.

MINNEAPOLIS, Sept. 24.—Minnesota's Golden Gophers hurled another sharp challenge to the football world today, defeating the Washington Huskies, 15 to 0, before 50,000 persons in a game closely fought for the first half only.

The Gophers had a bad scare in the opening period and missed a great chance for scoring in the next quarter. Finally, with a minute of the first-half play remaining, a field

Continued on Page Three

ALABAMA VICTOR ON COAST, 19 TO 7

Southern California Beaten Before 65,000—Tide Gains on Ground and in Air

By The Associated Press.

LOS ANGELES, Sept. 24.—A furious Tide of Crimson from Alabama swept through vast Memorial Coliseum today, carrying before it the hopes of the Southern California football team. The defeat by 19 to 7 once again postponed the Trojans' return to gridiron greatness. A gathering of 65,000 saw the game.

Time and again the stalwart Trojans tried to stem the Tide, plugging a hole off one tackle where George Zivich had ripped through or rushing to the ends to cement a crumbling wing battered by a Holm, a Bardford or a Mosley. But when the Tide stopped pouring through Troy's forward wall, it showered destructive passes.

Everything Southern California tried was to no avail, because the Crimson came out to avenge a defeat administered in the Rose Bowl last New Year's Day by California, and would not be denied.

Two Scores in Second

Twice in the second period Alabama crossed the goal line on lightning passes from slender Herky Mosley. The first touchdown pass went to Billy Slemons, reserve back, and he was tackled just across the goal line.

The next touchdown was the climax of an 80-yard drive. Gene Blackwell, a substitute end, juggled Mosley's pass but held the ball to score.

Southern California, several times failing to cash in on a break, found the 'Bama line almost impregnable and tried to score through the air. Once the Trojans hit Alabama ter-

Continued on Page Five

Football Scores

COLLEGES

East

Alfred 28..........Hartwick 0
Army 32..........Wichita 0
Boston College 63..........Canisius 12
Bklyn. Coll. J. V. 6..St. John's Prep 0
Dartmouth 46..........Bates 0
Holy Cross 28..........Providence 0
Lehigh 16..........Penn M. C. 13
Lowell Textile 20.....New Hampshire 0
Marshall 44..........Carson-Newman 0
Mass. State 12........American I. C. 6
Morris Harvey 25.....West Va. Wes. 6
Navy 26..........W. and M. 0
Panzer 7.......East Stroudsburg Tea. 0
Pittsburgh 19..........West Virginia 0
Richmond 19..........Maryland 6
Rhode Island 14..........Maine 6
Rutgers 20..........Marietta 0
St. Bonaventure 7..........Manhattan 6
Slippery Rock 12...Shippensburg Tea. 7
Upsala 14..........Muhlenberg 13
Wesleyan 27........Coast Guard Ac. 0
Williams 13..........Middlebury 0

South

Arkansas 27.......Oklahoma A. & M. 7
Baylor 33.........Southwestern Tea. 0
Centre 13..........Mississippi College 0
Clemson 13..........Tulane 10
Duke 18..........V. P. I. 0
Georgia 20..........The Citadel 12
Howard Payne 14.........San Marcos 0
Johnson City Tea. 31..........Union 13
Kentucky 46..........Maryville 7
LeMoyne 27..........Tuskegee 6
Mars Hill 6..........Tusculum 6
Mercer 14..........Wofford 0
Mississippi 20..........La. State 7
Mississippi State 19....Howard (Ala.) 0
Miss. State Tea. 39.Arkansas A. & M. 0
Naval Train. Sta. 9..W. and M. (Nor.) 6
North Carolina 14......Wake Forest 6
No. Car. State 19..........Davidson 7
Presbyterian 9..........Oglethorpe 7
Randolph-Macon 6..........Drexel 6
Sam Houston Tea. 15.........Trinity 14
Sou. Methodist 34..North Texas Tea. 7
Stetson 16..........Florida 14
Tennessee 26..........Sewanee 3
Texas A. & M. 52.....Texas A. & I. 0
Texas Christian 13..........Centenary 0
Texas Tech 39..........Wyoming 0
V. M. I. 12..........Virginia 12
West. Ky. Tea. 34..Pitts. (Kan.) Tea. 0
West Texas Tea. 46.....Daniel Baker 7

Continued on Page Three

20,000 AT BELMONT

Roseretter Half Length Back of Magic Hour in $21,250 Realization

DINNER DATE WINS MATRON

Favorite Conquers Ciencia by Head—Ossabaw and Rioter Run One, Two in Chase

By BRYAN FIELD

Magic Hour and Dinner Date captured the Lawrence Realization and Matron Stakes, respectively, before 20,000 persons at Belmont Park yesterday to give both the East and West a share in the main prizes. The 3-year-old son of Sortie, who was first by half a length at the end of the long mile and five furlongs of the Realization, carried the black silks of young Ogden Phipps, of an Eastern racing family.

Dinner Date dashed home in front in the $19,275 Matron to give Mrs. Ethel V. Mars of Illinois and Tennessee her most important score of the Fall season. She was at sea aboard the Cunard White Star liner Queen Mary, but the news was flashed to her by radio. Dinner Date will be pointed for the Selima Stakes at Laurel and the juvenile filly championship.

Magic Hour, who earned $16,800 of the gross of $21,250 in the Realization, afforded one more example of the manner in which 3-year-olds are beating one another this year. The top ones in the division were on the sidelines and at the eleventh hour Cravat, the pre-race favorite, had to be scratched because of an injury suffered in his morning blowout.

Jolly Tar 7-5 Favorite.

Jolly Tar, who had indicated route-running ability at Saratoga, went to the post the 7-to-5 favorite, but finished fourth after being pinched back at the far turn when making his move. Second was the Foxcatcher Farms' Roseretter and Dah He was a distant third. Then came Jolly Tar, Anaflame, Lucky Omen and Purple King.

Magic Hour and Anaflame were coupled and returned 5 to 1 after receding from 7 to 2. Johnny Longden had the leg up on the winner and thereby gained a double, as he earlier had got home first with Sunport.

Magic Hour ran an excellent race for his most noteworthy victory, but he profited from racing luck. At the outset, Purple King made the pace and after half a mile Anaflame joined the leader. All the while the favorite was last and Magic Hour a trailer with him.

The main moves came at the far turn. Harry Richards, aboard Jolly Tar, became aware that he had better get going and sent up the favorite. He tried to slip him through a hole between Dah He, on the outside, and the others nearer the rail. Dah He seemed to come over and pinch back Jolly Tar.

Winner Timed in 2:45

Longden, making his move aboard Magic Hour at about the same time, was not in trouble. Purple King shortened stride badly, while Anaflame was fighting for the lead with Dah He, who moved up fast. Roseretter was yet to be heard from.

When straightened in the stretch Magic Hour sailed past all the others to finish in 2:45 and Roseretter followed him to gain the place easily. Jolly Tar was spent from his efforts and could not even wrest third from the weary Dah He.

Dinner Date had to show class to take the Matron, as Ciencia battled

Continued on Page Nine

After Finals at Forest Hills

Don Budge, who won in four sets, and Gene Mako

Times Wide World

Miss Alice Marble

Times Wide World

BAUERS OF PIRATES SUBDUES REDS, 4-1

Six-Hit Pitching and Rivals' Errors Keep Pittsburgh 2 Games Ahead of Cubs

By The Associated Press.

PITTSBURGH, Sept. 24.—The Pirates preserved their slender two-game advantage in the National League pennant proceedings today by whipping the Reds, 4 to 1, behind Russ Bauers's sparkling six-hit pitching.

With the big scoreboard in left field carrying an inning-by-inning report of Chicago's triumph over St. Louis, the Buccaneers bore down after singles by Billy Myers and Wally Berger, and a fly to deep center by Ernie Lombardi gave Cincinnati its run in the first frame.

The Pirates drove into the lead in the second inning with three runs, two of them charged directly to ragged play, and insured victory in the eighth with another unearned marker.

Vaughan's Walk Starts Rally

Arky Vaughan started the trouble for the Reds by drawing a base on balls off Johnny Vander Meer. He went to second on Gus Suhr's single and moved to third when Pep Young forced Suhr.

Lee Handley made a handle hit to right and Lombardi dropped the throw at the plate, permitting Vaughan to score. Al Todd singled in Young from second and he and Handley advanced to second and third on a passed ball, placing "the Jeep" in position to score on Bauers's long fly to left.

The bases were filled again on a walk and an error before "Double No-Hit" Johnny got the Pirates out.

In the eighth, with two out, Myers booted Lloyd Waner's bounder, Brother Paul Waner walked and Johnny Rizzo singled to give the Pirates their final run.

Bauers struck out four and gave only two passes in winning his twelfth game against thirteen defeats. He was never in hot water after the first inning, giving single hits in the second and fourth and a

Continued on Page Six

Major League Baseball

American League

YESTERDAY'S RESULTS

Boston 7, New York 6.
Washington 7, Philadelphia 3 (10 innings).
Detroit 7, Cleveland 6.
St. Louis 8, Chicago 7 (1st).
Chicago 3, St. Louis 2 (2d)

STANDING OF THE CLUBS

	New York	Boston	Cleveland	Detroit	Wash'ton	Chicago	St. Louis	Phila'phia	Won	Lost	Percentage	Games Behind
N. Y.	—	9	13	14	15	14	15	15	95	50	.655	—
Boston	9	—	12	10	11	12	17	12	83	59	.585	10½
Cleve.	8	10	—	11	12	11	13	18	83	62	.572	12
Detroit	8	12	7	—	13	15	8	14	77	69	.527	18½
Wash.	5	9	9	9	—	11	15	14	72	72	.500	22½
Chic.	8	6	8	7	10	—	10	12	61	77	.442	30½
St. L.	7	5	9	10	7	4	—	9	51	90	.362	42
Phila.	5	8	4	8	4	10	12	—	51	94	.352	44
Lost	50	59	62	69	72	77	90	94	—	—		

GAMES TODAY

Boston at New York (2, 2 P. M.).
Washington at Philadelphia (2).
Chicago at St. Louis (2).
Cleveland at Detroit.

National League

YESTERDAY'S RESULTS

New York 9, Boston 8 (1st).
New York 2, Boston 1 (2d).
Brooklyn 8, Philadelphia 1.
Pittsburgh 4, Cincinnati 1.
Chicago 9, St. Louis 3.

STANDING OF THE CLUBS

	Pittsburgh	Chicago	New York	Cincinnati	Boston	St. Louis	Brooklyn	Phila'phia	Won	Lost	Percentage	Games Behind
Pitts.	—	10	13	10	13	15	11	12	84	58	.592	—
Chic.	9	—	12	11	12	10	11	18	83	61	.576	2
N. Y.	9	10	—	9	12	11	13	15	79	64	.552	5½
Cincin.	7	11	12	—	9	11	13	14	77	65	.542	7
Boston	9	10	6	11	—	13	11	11	71	72	.497	13½
St. L.	7	7	9	8	9	—	12	16	68	75	.476	16½
Bklyn.	9	9	7	9	9	9	—	12	64	77	.454	19½
Phila.	8	4	5	7	8	6	6	—	44	98	.310	40
Lost	58	61	64	65	72	75	77	98	—	—		

GAMES TODAY

Philadelphia at Brooklyn (2, 2:05 P. M.).
New York at Boston (2).
Cincinnati at Pittsburgh.
St. Louis at Chicago.

KILIAN AND VOPEL TAKE SIX-DAY RACE

Germans Annex Bike Grind on Points Before 11,000 at the Garden—Pedens Second

By JOSEPH C. NICHOLS

In a finish so close and thrilling that it caused 11,000 fans to cheer wildly, without restraint, for a full hour, the hardy German team of Gustav Kilian and Heinz Vopel rode through to triumph in the six-day bicycle race which came to an end at Madison Square Garden last night.

With the field closely bunched going into the last hour, and with the prospect of the race being decided on the basis of the points that were to be garnered in the final sixty minutes, the hard-riding Germans pedaled the courageous brother combination of Doug and Torchy Peden into the ground to register a narrow victory over the Maple Leaf combine, on the very basis that they had in mind—points.

The comparatively small matter of 130 points separated the Germans from their second-place rivals, who had a total of 970, as against 1,100 for the victors.

Seven Tied on Distance

As a matter of fact, of the eight teams to finish the grind, seven were tied in the matter of distance covered. They were, besides the first two combinations, the partnerships of Jimmy Walthour and Al Crossley, Jules Audy and Gerard Debaets, Cesare Moretti and Alvaro Georgetti, Giuseppe Olmo and Tino Reboli and Angelo De Bacco and Remigio Saavedra. And trailing this group by the small margin of a single lap was the game duo of Bobby Thomas and Fred Ottevaere.

These combinations pooled their speed resources to provide as tense and hair-raising a spectacle as has been seen in the Garden six-day

Continued on Page Eight

MAKO TAKES A SET

But Bows, 6-3, 6-8, 6-2, 6-1—Budge Wins 4th Main Title in Year

FEAT SETS A PRECEDENT

Miss Marble Disposes of Miss Wynne in 22 Minutes, 6-0, 6-3, Before 12,000

By ALLISON DANZIG

The book was closed yesterday on the greatest record of success ever compiled by a lawn tennis player in one season of national and international championship competition.

J. Donald Budge of Oakland, Calif., stood as the first player in history to win all four of the world's major tennis titles in the same year when he defeated Gene Mako of Los Angeles in the Forest Hills Stadium in the final round of the national championship. The score was 6—3, 6—8, 6—2, 6—1.

The triumph of the 23-year-old red-headed giant, which followed upon the overwhelming victory of Miss Alice Marble of Beverly Hills, Calif., over Miss Nancye Wynne of Australia at 6—0, 6—3, in the shortest women's final on record, completed a campaign of unparalleled achievement on three continents.

Compared With Jones's Slam

No one before him has held at one and the same time the American, British, French and Australian crowns, all of which have fallen in 1938 to the rapacity of Budge's fifteen-ounce racquet for a grand slam that invites comparison with the accomplishment of Bobby Jones in golf.

In this respect, at least, Budge takes precedence over William Tilden, the Frenchmen, Henri Cochet and René Lacoste; Ellsworth Vines, Wilmer Allison, Fred Perry, the Briton, and all the other great modern champions. Jack Crawford of Australia came closest to winning four major crowns when, in 1933, he won three of the titles and led Perry, two sets to one, in the American final.

To complete Budge's record of conquest for the year: He led the United States to victory in the defense of the Davis Cup against Australia at Germantown. He won the British and American doubles and mixed doubles and gained permanent possession of the mammoth Newport Casino Challenge Cup.

Farewell to Forest Hills?

He leaves Forest Hills behind him, possibly for the last time, and heads for the Pacific Southwest championships at Los Angeles with the satisfaction of having won every singles match of consequence in which he started and of establishing a mark that promises to stand for many years. Here, truly, is one of the great competitors of sport and one of the most genuine sportsmen to grace the game.

A gallery of 12,000 looked on under a stinging sun as Budge made history. That the stadium was not filled to capacity was probably attributable to the conviction that the outcome of his meeting with his doubles partner was foreordained. Despite the amazingly fine tennis Mako had produced to concoct the defeat of John Bromwich in the semi-finals, few, if any, conceded the stalwart, blond Los Angeles youth the slightest chance of staying the all-conquering march of the Oakland terror.

But if any had the notion that this was to be a Damon and Pythias act, they were speedily disillusioned. True, the play was animated by friendly manifestations across the net whose contagion was communicated to the gallery, particularly in the third set, when the crowd was roaring with mirth as the doubles champions trapped each other repeatedly with drop shots.

Speed Marks Match

But there was no holding back on either side and there was no trace of amiability in the scorching forehand drives with which Mako caught Budge in faulty position inside the baseline or the murderous backhand and volcanic service which Budge turned loose.

If Mako had the satisfaction of being the only player in the tournament to wrest a set from the champion, it was not because Budge willed it that way. The circumstances under which it was won might have given rise to skepticism as to the validity of the achievement, for it was salvaged from a 2-5 deficit after Mako had slumped badly in the face of Budge's pitilessly raking bombardment.

Possibly at this point Budge, in the security of his commanding lead, may have relented and elected to relax the pressure of his cannonading on his helpless opponent,

Continued on Page Two

BUDGE TOPS MAKO FOR TENNIS TITLE

Continued From Page One

but if he proposed to go further than yield a game or two, his subsequent distress as his strokes got out of hand was a first class bit of acting, and he never pretended to thespian honors.

It would be considerably less than justice not to accord Mako that full measure of praise he deserves for the brilliant tennis he put forth in winning six of the next seven games. His flat forehand was striking like lightning. His backhand slice stood up unwaveringly from any angle. He used the lob and drop shot with his usual aplomb and success and his control was so steadfast that Budge got precious little he did not earn.

The champion, struggling to regain his concentration and accuracy after getting only 3 points in three games, found his touch had deserted him. Nothing would work right for him and his footwork became faulty as he was caught out of position or hit from his heels, while his smash failed glaringly.

It was a worried-looking Budge who stared at Mako's beautiful back-hand drive that went passing by him for the final point of the set as the gallery cheered tumultuously.

With the start of the third set, command of the match reverted to the champion, and he was never seriously challenged again. Possibly Mako was content with taking that set, but whether he was or not, there was not much he could have done to stay the fate that speedily engulfed him.

Budge turned loose a tornado of controlled speed such as had been visited upon no other opponent in the tournament, with his service making the chalk fly on the lines, and Mako found that neither his drop shots nor lobs, nor blistering forehand drives could avail against the sharpshooting that scored 30 earned points for the champion in the last two sets.

When the match ended, Mako received an ovation from the gallery for a performance which, in conjunction with his victories over Bromwich, Franjo Puncec of Yugoslavia and Frank Kovacs, should earn him a high place in the 1938 rankings and possibly serious consideration from the Davis Cup committee in 1939.

Miss Marble's victory over Miss Wynne, restoring her to the championship throne she occupied in 1936, was achieved with one of the most ruthless attacks ever launched by a woman at Forest Hills.

In the almost incredible time of twenty-two minutes the blond Californian had accomplished her task and was walking to the marquee to pose for a score of cameras as she received the cup from President Holcombe Ward of the U. S. L. T. A. after bestowing a kiss upon Umpire Louis W Shaw.

It took just seven minutes for Miss Marble to run out the opening set, in which she allowed her opponent only 8 points. Play started at a terrific pace and it was sustained at that clip to the end. There were no long rallies. Both players were hitting uncompromisingly, throwing caution to the winds, and Miss Wynne, unable to get her strokes under control, was stampeded into summary defeat, as she was in the final at Essex.

Miss Marble has seldom, if ever, had her whole battery of weapons so obedient to her dictates. From both the forehand and the backhand she was hitting with killing pace and length, with her forehand serving her better probably than on any other occasion of her career.

Her service was so strong and deep that Miss Wynne could do little with it, and her volleys, on the few occasions she went forward, were the last word. The Californian's speed of foot was equal to that of her strokes, and from start to finish she flew around the court, attacking unmercifully in a remarkable exhibition of sustained power under almost perfect control.

Miss Wynne, swept off her feet and unable to get her own powerful weapons in hand as she was hurried into faulty timing and execution, made no effort to slow down the pace of the match. Had she changed her methods, she might have broken up the deadly precision of Miss Marble's attack, but the only type of game she knows is the one Miss Marble plays, and so she hastened the end with her mounting streak of over-hit balls.

Henry H. Bassford of Hartsdale is the new veterans' champion. In the final round he defeated Armand L. Bruneau of Brooklyn, 8–6, 4–6, 6–4.

Bruneau led at 4–2 in the first set and 3–1 in the third, and he punished Bassford severely with his drop shots and remarkably accurate lobs, but the Brooklyn veteran's backhand failed to stand up when opportunity called, and Bassford, playing his best tennis when behind, pulled out of the hole each time, to win after Bruneau had stood him off at match point four times.

MARIETTA BEATEN BY RUTGERS, 20-0

Total of 18 First Downs for Scarlet, None for Losers at New Brunswick

TRANAVITCH SCORES FIRST

Gottlieb, Casey Add Touchdowns in Inaugural Test Under Coach Harman

Special to THE NEW YORK TIMES.

NEW BRUNSWICK, N. J., Sept. 24.—Competely outclassing a light Marietta eleven, the Rutgers football team opened its seventieth year of gridiron warfare with a 20-to-0 victory on Neilson Field today before 7,000 persons. The game was the first for Rutgers under its new coach, Harvey Harman.

Neither team clicked in the first period, although Rutgers put on one sustained drive of 36 yards, with Big Bill Tranavitch making most of the yardage on straight line plays.

Midway through the second quarter, Rutgers took the ball on its own 45-yard line when Ray Morrin punted. A sustained drive down the field, with Tranavitch bearing the brunt of the attack, netted a touchdown. Tranavitch scored through left tackle from the 2-yard line three minutes before the half ended. His try from placement for the extra point failed, and the half ended with Rutgers ahead, 6 to 0.

Fails to Score in Third Period

The third period saw Rutgers again dominate the play, although unable to score. Another drive started as the last period opened, but a fumble by Art Gottleib on the 10-yard line temporarily stalled the Scarlet machine.

Morrin punted to the Rutgers' 48, and Moon Mullen and Bert Hasbrouck, substitute for Tranavitch, put the ball on the 16-yard mark in five plays. Gottlieb then scored through right tackle. Len Cooke made good from placement for the extra point.

Cooke's kick-off went out of bounds, and Marietta took the ball on its own 35. Three plays netted no gain. Then Ray Morrin's long pass was intercepted on the 50-yard line by Arny Siegfried, Scarlet quarterback, who raced through the entire Pioneer team to the 12. Siegfried had just gone into the game for Schank.

Reach 3-Yard Line

Gotlieb picked up five yards and a Marietta off-side gave Rutgers a first down on the 3-yard line. Three plays later, Jack Casey carried the ball over the goal on a reverse through left tackle. Cooke again made good the extra point from placement to end the scoring.

Marietta made no first downs and gained only 8 yards from scrimmage, all in the second half. Rutgers made 18 first downs and rolled up 271 yards from scrimmage.

The line-up:

RUTGERS (20)		MARIETTA (0)
Harvey	L.E.	Burger
Cooke	L.T.	Tate
Bednard	L.G.	B. Morrin
Hotchkiss	C.	Varner
Bruyere	R.G.	Howell
Craig	R.T.	Nesha
Staples	R.E.	Cordes
Schank	Q.B.	R. Morrin
Greif	L.H.	Krzykowski
Mullen	R.H.	Duncan
Tranavitch	F.B.	Litman

SCORE BY PERIODS

Rutgers	0	6	0	14—20
Marietta	0	0	0	0— 0

TUFFY LEEMANS, WHO WILL FACE EAGLES TODAY

Falaschi Will Start for Football Giants In League Contest at Philadelphia Today

Hopeful of retaining their position at the top in the Eastern Division of the National Football League and fully aware of the power of the strengthened Eagles, the New York Football Giants will swing into action at Philadelphia this afternoon.

Coach Steve Owen's men, victorious over the Pittsburgh Pirates in their only league start, know, also that while a decision over the Eagles will keep them at the helm, a setback would drop them down to fourth place.

From a New York viewpoint the Philadelphia encounter will have special significance, since it will mark the professional debut of Nello (Flash) Falaschi, the former Santa Clara star. A leg injury forced Felaschi to the sidelines for the games against the All-Stars and the Pirates.

However, his work in recent practice sessions has impressed Owen considerably, and the coach has decided to start him in the backfield, along with Ward Cuff, Tuffy Leemans and Kink Richards. Incidentally, Falaschi will be the only rookie in the Giant starting line-up.

Owen's starting line is likely to include Ray Hanken and Jim Lee Howell at the ends, Kayo Lunday and Tarzan White at the guards, Ed Widseth and Ox Parry at the tackles and Captain Mel Hein at center. The Giants are well fortified with replacements, with Leonard (Feets) Barnum, Hugh Wolfe, Ed Danowski, Dale Burnett, Johnny Gildea and Hank Soar among those who will figure prominently.

Two other contests are listed on today's league schedule. The world champion Redskins will clash with the Cleveland Rams at Griffith Stadium and the Green Bay Packers will oppose the Chicago Cardinals at Milwaukee.

Another game is listed for Wednesday night, when the Packers will pit their strength against the Cardinals in a return engagement, this one to be played under the floodlights at Buffalo, N. Y.

Brooklyn's Dodgers remain idle until next Sunday, when they will battle the Chicago Cardinals at Ebbets Field.

The Giants will open their home season in the Polo Grounds on Monday night, Oct. 3, with the Pirates, it was announced yesterday by John V. Mara, president. The game was originally scheduled for Sunday, Oct. 30, but was moved up by mutual agreement to relieve congestion in the Pittsburgh schedule the latter part of October.

Tickets for the opening game will be available in the office of the New York Football Giants, 11 West Forty-second Street, starting Tuesday morning. The Pirates, who defeated the Dodgers Friday night, have no other league engagement in the meantime.

DARTMOUTH ROUTS BATES ELEVEN, 46-0

HANOVER, N. H., Sept. 24 (AP).—The Dartmouth Indians, as impressive as they were last season when they escaped defeat, opened their football campaign today by swamping a courageous but inexperienced Bates team, 46—0.

The Indians used their star-studded varsity line-up for only twenty minutes of the one-sided action and during that brief interval the regulars accounted for three touchdowns.

Shifty Bob MacLeod, the captain and sparkplug, accounted for most of the yardage before making two scoring plunges from Bates's six-yard line early in the first period. When he and his mates returned for their second tour of duty in the third quarter, Bomber Bill Hutchinson broke loose for a 46-yard touchdown dash.

Coach Earl (Red) Blaik used every member of his fifty-man squad against the garnet-clad youngsters from Maine.

The Dartmouth second-stringers tallied four touchdowns, the most spectacular of which was the 72-yard run-back that Jack Orr, a fullback replacement, made into the Bates end zone with one of Bill Belliveau's punts in the final period.

The remaining counters were provided by Jim Davis, who completed a 20-yard pass from Joe Cottone, Hutchinson's understudy, and by Buford (Cowboy) Hayden and Ray Hall, a third-team back.

Coach Is Not Impressed

In the third period the Indians tossed away three easy scoring chances from the 10-yard line, permitting Hutchinson to attempt placement field goals. Although their performance thrilled the slim crowd of 2,500 students, Blaik was unimpressed by their initial start.

He bewailed the wide gaps between his first-stringers and their immediate replacements and declared he was convinced that Dartmouth's 1938 success depended entirely on the regulars. "We've got plenty of football players here, but only one football team," he said.

The line-up:

DARTMOUTH (46)		BATES (0)
Miller	L.E.	Nichols
Dilkes	L.T.	Bogdanowicz
Young	L.G.	Glover
Gibson	C.	Crooker
Zitrides	R.G.	Clough
Dostal	R.T.	R. Briggs
Wakelin	R.E.	Edminster
Couter	Q.B.	Buccigross
Hutchinson	L.H.	Belliveau
Macleod	R.H.	Wilder
Howe	F.B.	O'Sullivan

LEHIGH TRIUMPHS OVER P. M. C., 16-13

Engineers Turn Back Invaders on Duyckinck's Field Goal in the Third Period

CADETS GAIN EARLY EDGE

Rivals Tie Count at the Half, Then Forge Ahead—7,000 See Bethlehem Game

Special to THE NEW YORK TIMES.

BETHLEHEM, Pa., Sept. 24.—A stubborn cadet football team from Penn Military College was defeated by Lehigh University Engineer's before a crowd of 7,000 in Taylor Stadium this afternoon. The score was 16 to 13.

The Cadets, taking a one-touchdown lead in the first period, fought desperately to defend this advantage, but to no avail, and when the half ended the score was knotted at 7—all.

Boots 37-Yard Goal

What proved to be the Engineers' winning margin was manufactured by Charlie Duyckinck, star placement kicker, who, after Lehigh advanced deep into Cadet territory in the third period, dropped back to his 37-yard stripe and neatly booted a score.

But Lehigh was not through tallying and neither were the Cadets. A pass from Jack Beriont to Jack Kromer gave Lehigh the ball for a first down on the embryo generals' 1-yard mark. A fumble here was recovered by the Engineers, and on the next play Herb Feucht scored around the end.

Air Attack Effective

With a few minutes remaining in the final period, P. M. C. went to the air with effective results. A 42-yard pass, Willie Piff to Hartnett, followed by penalties of fifteen and five yards, for roughing the passer and offside, respectively, advanced the ball to Lehigh's 9-yard mark.

On the first play-off Piff skirted Lehigh's left end and just fell shy of a touchdown. On the next he went across.

The line-up:

LEHIGH (16)		P. M. C. (13)
Simpson	L.E.	Biasiotto
Raboid	L.T.	Montaro
Kirkpatrick	L.G.	Ryan
Famighetti	C.	Chaillingsworth
Thomas	R.G.	O'Malley
Heins	R.T.	Drabkoski
Walton	R.E.	Gardecki
Campbell	Q.B.	Glenn
Cox	L.H.	Piff
Smoke	R.H.	Hartnett
Werthe	F.B.	Derouen

WILLIAMS CONQUERS MIDDLEBURY BY 13-0

Darrell and King Shine for the Victors in Opener

WILLIAMSTOWN, Mass., Sept. 24.—Captain Larry Durrell and the veteran Timmy King led Williams to a 13-to-0 victory over the highly touted Middlebury Panthers on Weston Field today to inaugurate the Williams 1938 season before a crowd of 2,500.

King, the Purple field general, intercepted three passes, kicked brilliantly and was the outstanding blocking back.

Durrell got loose for several long gains and went over for the first Williams score from the 10-yard line. In a battle of linemen the Ephmen forced Middlebury to aerial tactics, but the Panthers threatened only once. That was in the third quarter, when interference on a pass put the visitors on Williams' sixteen.

40,000 Watch Seabiscuit Defeat War Admiral

SEABISCUIT BREAKS TRACK MARK TO WIN

First by 3 Lengths, Howard's Champion Finishes 1 3/16 Miles in 1:56 3/5

EARNINGS REACH $340,480

Outrun at Start, War Admiral Fails in Bid to Pass Rival —Victor Pays 11-5

By BRYAN FIELD
Special to THE NEW YORK TIMES.

BALTIMORE, Nov. 1.—Seabiscuit defeated War Admiral today. Amid scenes of frantic enthusiasm, created by a record crowd of 40,000 persons, that simple fact stood high and alone and it will leave its impression on the American turf. Historic Pimlico never had seen anything like it.

Smashing the track record, beating War Admiral at his own game, the phlegmatic ugly duckling with the lame leg from the Pacific Coast did all, and more, than the son of Man o' War. There was glory enough for the two, but to Charles S. Howard's champion son of Hard Tack and grandson of Man o' War went the distinction and an honor that probably no other thoroughbred in this equine generation will earn.

Thousands rushed the unsaddling enclosure after the finish and all but upset Matchmaker Alfred Gwynne Vanderbilt, owner Howard and the veteran trainer Tom Smith. Answering the pleas of hundreds, Smith grasped a single chrysanthemum for himself, and then thrust the enormous bow of flowers into the reaching hands. In a twinkling ferns, leaves, flowers and even petals were wrenched apart as cheers still rolled forth from the souvenir hunters.

Loser Goes Unnoticed

Virtually unnoticed, blanketed and hooded, out on the middle of the track, War Admiral walked alone toward his stall. But not quite alone—the hot favorite of a few minutes before, who had been made a 1-to-4 shot with the thousands in the stands, still had the faithful Trainer George Conway watching his stride. Scanning his charge's every step for any sign of ailment, Conway then went his way alone.

It was a hard, bitter and punishing race. Until the last furlong it had the thousands on their feet. The time of 1:56 3-5, lowering Pompoon's record by a fifth of a second, surprised few. Both horses were going all out from the fall of the starting flag to the finish and it was Seabiscuit who led, for all except a brief span, when War Admiral tried and failed.

At the end of the mile and three-sixteenths the margin was three lengths, and if they had gone farther the margin would have been greater. The $15,000 which went to the winner brought Seabiscuit's total to $340,480, moving him from fifth to second place among the world's money winners and placing him within striking distance of Sun Beau's record of $376,744. And this sort of horse was neglected in the betting, returning $6.40 for $2, or 11 to 5.

Although both horses appeared to come out of the race in excellent condition, future plans for War Admiral were thrown into confusion. It is possible that he may race again instead of being retired to the stud immediately. Seabiscuit will continue racing, with the Riggs Handicap here Saturday his next start.

Howards Are Congratulated

Mr. and Mrs. Howard were overwhelmed with congratulations as cameras clicked. Police, friends, hostlers and society well-wishers joined in a frenzied outburst produced perhaps by racing only. The Howards hardly had a chance to do more than bow and smile, but the San Franciscans at last got free and paid tribute to Samuel D. Riddle, owner of War Admiral, and Conway.

Smith, asked for a statement, declared: "I said mine on the track!" George Woolf, shouted at and queried before he could even dismount, had his first thought for Red Pollard, Seabiscuit's injured and regular jockey, who heard the race from a hospital bed by radio.

Charlie Kurtsinger, who handled War Admiral, congratulated Woolf, and was able to muster a grin after a finish that must have been as much of a shock to him as to most others. He offered no alibi, nor did anyone else. It was the kind of race in which there could be no alibi.

While all the uproar was going on about him, Seabiscuit stood stolidly. A few minutes before his legs had flown, doubtless as they never had flown before, but now he was at ease. Even flashlight bulbs exploded right under his muzzle caused only a slight toss of his head. And the knee that had forced Smith to scratch him from the $100,000 special at Belmont Park last Spring looked as good after as it had in the race.

United Press International

Seabiscuit beating War Admiral to lower Pompoon's track record by a fifth of a second.

Wired Photo—Times Wide World

Charles S. Howard, owner of the winner; Jockey George Woolf and Alfred Gwynne Vanderbilt, matchmaker, after the contest.

Trainer and Jockey Praised

While the plaudits of the great crowd were for Owner Howard, he was the first to acknowledge his debt to Smith and Woolf. Smith, an old cowhand from the Northwest, who learned the horse business the hard way, bought Seabiscuit as a 3-year-old for $8,500, when the handicap champion virtually was a discard from the Wheatley Stable.

Most of the horse's earnings have been garnered since because Smith has been able to keep in training, and at his fittest, a thoroughbred campaigned up and down the country, from coast to coast, at strange as well as familiar race tracks. Always Seabiscuit has run gamely under heavy weight.

The impost today was 120 pounds for each, and it must have seemed right to the horse who now at 5, is the outstanding thoroughbred in America. As for Woolf, he won the race by taking the track from War Admiral. The wiseacres had said this could not be done.

Woolf accomplished it by whipping Seabiscuit away from the starting post. Turning on a tremendous burst of speed that must have caught Kurtsinger by surprise, Seabiscut jumped a length in front under the sting of the lash.

Passing the stands the first time, Seabiscuit was well enough in front to be able to cross over from the No. 2 post position and take the rail from War Admiral. Then Woolf put in a shrewd touch. Coming to the first turn he deliberately slowed Seabiscuit, so that his mount's churning quarters were right in front of War Admiral's nose. This served the double purpose of giving Seabiscuit a bit of a breather and forcing Kurtsinger to check somewhat to prevent War Admiral from running on the heels of the horse in front.

Around that first turn and into the backstretch Woolf eased his mount a trifle wide, forcing War Admiral wider. These were the same tactics Kurtsinger had worked with War Admiral against Pompoon when those two clashed in the memorable Preakness of 1937 that War Admiral won.

Coming into the backstretch Kurtsinger, always cool and collected, knew that he was getting the worst of things and decided to ask War Admiral for his best in the long, straight run that stretched away to the far turn. He turned loose his holds and slashed with the whip. The Man o' War colt went forward with a bound. Within thirty yards the two were head and head as the deafening roar billowed from the crowd: "There he goes!"

For another furlong the two were head and head. Then War Admiral's nose showed in front. Now Woolf slashed with the whip, and the nose of War Admiral showed no more.

But neither could Seabiscuit draw away. The two went to the far turn as one horse, went around that bend as one horse and headed for the top of the homestretch still with nothing between them.

The Better Horse Wins

Kurtsinger, who stated before the race that he never had had to ask War Admiral for his best, asked now. With all the power that has made him one of the country's first-flight riders he drove forward with War Admiral. Again and again the black-clad arm with the yellow bars rose and fell, but War Admiral could do no more. He had met a better horse.

Woolf, too, was driving. He knew that final turn into the stretch was the last try of the horse justly called Man o' War's greatest son. He, too, flung everything into the drive.

Smith, grizzled and tight-lipped, must have wondered how Seabiscuit's knee was standing the twisting, as well as the pounding, that a turn produces. It is on turns that thoroughbreds' knees give way, when hearts do not.

But Seabiscuit's knee did not give and his courage had been proved in many a racing war. Through the last furlong it was a procession, with the horses speeding like vivid but silent phantoms as the waves of cheering from the stands submerged and overwhelmed the pounding thud of the hoofs.

In all, $754,807 was bet on eight races, $76,811 being waged on the Special. Of this total, $54,898 went in on War Admiral and $21,913 on Seabiscuit.

The fractional times follow: 0:23 3-5, 0:47 3-5, 1:11 4-5, 1:36 4-5 and 1:56 3-5. Although it did not count, the time for the mile was almost a second faster than the track record of 1:37 3-5, made in 1923 by June Grass.

SEABISCUIT 'BEST IN WORLD'

Woolf Gives Mount All Credit—Howard and Smith Elated

BALTIMORE, Nov. 1 (AP).—It was a gloriously happy Georgie Woolf, the pride of Babb, Mont., who finally managed to slip away to the jockey quarters today.

Admirers all but mobbed the chunky little jockey, shouting words of praise at him and demanding yellow flowers from the victory wreath with which Seabiscuit was adorned. But Georgie gave all the credit to his mount.

"He's the best horse in the world," Woolf said. "He proved that today."

This point was not readily yielded, however, by War Admiral's trainer, George Conway, who took the defeat very much to heart. "They'll meet again some day, maybe," said the lanky veteran.

Samuel D. Riddle, owner of War Admiral, was keenly disappointed and slipped away as soon as he could. But Charles S. Howard, owner of Seabiscuit, met all comers with a smile and shout of happiness.

Gehrig Ends Streak at 2,130 Straight Games

LOU, NOT HITTING, ASKS REST ON BENCH

Gehrig's String, Started June 1, 1925, Snapped as Yanks Start Series in Detroit

RETURN OF ACE INDEFINITE

But Iron Man Who Holds Many Records Hopes to Regain Form in Hot Weather

By JAMES P. DAWSON
Special to THE NEW YORK TIMES.

DETROIT, May 2.—Lou Gehrig's matchless record of uninterrupted play in American League championship games, stretched over fifteen years and through 2,130 straight contests, came to an end today.

The mighty iron man, who at his peak had hit forty-nine home runs in a single season five years ago, took himself out of action before the Yanks marched on Briggs Stadium for their first game against the Tigers this year.

With the consent of Manager Joe McCarthy, Gehrig removed himself because he, better than anybody else, perhaps, recognized his competitive decline and was frankly aware of the fact he was doing the Yankees no good defensively or on the attack. He last played Sunday in New York against the Senators.

When Gehrig will start another game is undetermined. He will not be used as a pinch-hitter.

The present plan is to keep him on the bench. Relaxing and shaking off the mental hazards he admittedly has encountered this season, he may swing into action in the hot weather, which should have a beneficial effect upon his tired muscles.

Dahlgren Gets Chance

Meanwhile Ellsworth (Babe) Dahlgren, until today baseball's greatest figure of frustration, will continue at first base. Manager McCarthy said he had no present intention of transferring Tommy Henrich, the youthful outfielder whom he tried at first base at the Florida training camp. Dahlgren had been awaiting the summons for three years.

It was coincidental that Gehrig's string was broken almost in the presence of the man he succeeded as Yankee first baseman. At that time Wally Pipp, now a business man of Grand Rapids, Mich., was benched by the late Miller Huggins to make room for the strapping youth fresh from the Hartford Eastern League club to which the Yankees had farmed him for two seasons, following his departure from Columbia University. Pipp was in the lobby of the Book Cadillac Hotel at noon when the withdrawal of Gehrig was effected.

"I don't feel equal to getting back in there," Pipp said on June 2, 1925, the day Lou replaced him at first. Lou had started his phenomenal streak the day before as a pinch-hitter for Peewee Wanninger, then the Yankee shortstop.

This latest momentous development in baseball was not unexpected. There had been signs for the past two years that Gehrig was slowing up. Even when a sick man, however, he gamely stuck to his chores, not particularly in pursuit of his all-time record of consecutive play, although that was a big consideration, but out of a driving desire to help the Yankees, always his first consideration.

Treated for Ailment

What Lou had thought was lumbago last year when he suffered pains in the back that more than once forced his early withdrawal from games he had started was diagnosed later as a gall bladder condition for which Gehrig underwent treatment all last Winter, after rejecting a recommendation that he submit to an operation.

Lou Gehrig — The New York Times

The signs of his approaching fade-out were unmistakable this Spring at St. Petersburg, Fla., yet the announcement from Manager McCarthy was something of a shock. It came at the end of a conference Gehrig arranged immediately after McCarthy's arrival by plane from his native Buffalo.

"Lou just told me he felt it would be best for the club if he took himself out of the line-up," McCarthy said following their private talk. "I asked him if he really felt that way. He told me he was serious. He feels blue. He is dejected.

"I told him it would be as he wished. Like everybody else I'm sorry to see it happen. I told him not to worry. Maybe the warm weather will bring him around.

"He's been a great ball player. Fellows like him come along once in a hundred years. I told him that. More than that, he's been a vital part of the Yankee club since he started with it. He's always been a perfect gentleman, a credit to baseball.

"We'll miss him. You can't escape that fact. But I think he's doing the proper thing."

Lou Explains Decision

Gehrig, visibly affected, explained his decision quite frankly.

"I decided last Sunday night on this move," said Lou. "I haven't been a bit of good to the team since the season started. It would not be fair to the boys, to Joe or to the baseball public for me to try going on. In fact, it would not be fair to myself, and I'm the last consideration.

"It's tough to see your mates on base, have a chance to win a ball game, and not be able to do anything about it. McCarthy has been swell about it all the time. He'd let me go until the cows came home, he is that considerate of my feelings, but I knew in Sunday's game that I should get out of there.

"I went up there four times with men on base. Once there were two there. A hit would have won the ball game for the Yankees, but I missed, leaving five stranded as the Yankees lost. Maybe a rest will do me some good. Maybe it won't. Who knows? Who can tell? I'm just hoping."

Gehrig's withdrawal from today's game does not necessarily mean the end of his playing career, although that seems not far distant. When that day comes Gehrig can sit back and enjoy the fortune he has accumulated as a ball player. He is estimated to have saved $200,000 from his earnings, which touched a high in 1938, when he collected $39,000 as Yankee salary.

Record of Gehrig's Streak

	G.	AB.	R.	H.	RBI.	HR.	PC.
1925.....	126	437	73	129	68	21	.295
1926.....	155	572	135	179	107	16	.313
1927.....	155	584	149	218	175	47	.373
1928.....	154	562	139	210	142	27	.374
1929.....	154	553	127	166	126	35	.300
1930.....	154	581	143	220	174	41	379
1931.....	155	619	163	211	184	46	.341
1932.....	156	596	138	208	151	34	.349
1933.....	152	583	138	198	139	32	.334
1934.....	154	579	128	210	165	49	.363
1935.....	149	535	125	176	119	30	.329
1936.....	155	579	167	205	152	49	.354
1937.....	157	569	138	200	159	37	.351
1938.....	157	576	115	170	114	29	.295
1939.....	8	28	2	4	1	0	.143
Total..	2,141	7,953	1,880	2,704	1,976	493	.340

*Includes eleven games before consecutive run started.

When Gehrig performed his duties as Yankee captain today, appearing at the plate to give the batting order, announcement was made through the amplifiers of his voluntary withdrawal and it was suggested he get "a big hand." A deafening cheer resounded as Lou walked to the dugout, doffed his cap and disappeared in a corner of the bench.

Open expressions of regret came from the Yankees and the Tigers. Lefty Vernon Gomez expressed the Yankees' feelings when he said:

"It's tough to see this thing happen, even though you know it must come to us all. Lou's a great guy and he's always been a great baseball figure. I hope he'll be back in there."

Hank Greenberg, who might have been playing first for the Yanks instead of the Tigers but for Gehrig, said: "Lou's doing the right thing. He's got to use his head now instead of his legs. Maybe that Yankee dynasty is beginning to crumble."

Scott Former Record Holder

Everett Scott, the shortstop who held the record of 1,307 consecutive games until Gehrig broke it, ended his streak on May 6, 1925, while he was a member of the Yankees. However, Scott began his string, once considered unapproachable, with the Red Sox.

By a strange coincidence, Scott gave way to Wanninger, the player for whom Gehrig batted to start his great record.

With only one run batted in this year and a batting average of .143 representing four singles in twenty-eight times at bat, Lou has fallen far below his record achievements of previous seasons, during five of which he led the league in runs driven home.

Some of his more important records follow:

Most consecutive games—2,130.
Most consecutive years, 100 games or more—14.
Most years, 150 games or more—12.
Most years, 100 runs or more—13.
Most consecutive years, 100 runs or more—13.
Most home runs with bases full—23.
Most years, 300 or more total bases—13.
Most years, 100 runs or more driven in—13.
Most games by first baseman in one season—157.
Most home runs in one game—4 (modern record).
Most runs batted in, one season—184 (American League).

Yanks Overpower Tigers, 22 to 2, With 4 Homers and 13 Other Hits

Dahlgren, Keller, Henrich and Selkirk Make 4-Baggers as Team Bats Around in Three Innings—Ruffing Excels in Box

From a Staff Correspondent

DETROIT, May 2.—Playing for the first time in fifteen years without the services of Lou Gehrig, the Yankees went on a hitting spree today at Briggs Stadium as they launched their first Western invasion against the Tigers.

Making memorable the first game in which Babe Dahlgren has started at first base since he joined the club in 1937, the Yanks pummeled five of Del Baker's flingers, struck seventeen blows of all sizes and varying distances and smothered the Tigers under a 22-to-2 drubbing.

On the impetus of this terrific cannonading the Yanks regained undisputed possession of first place. The Red Sox, who were idle today, dropped to third. They had been tied with the New Yorkers for the No. 1 position.

Tigers Held in Check

Charley (Red) Ruffing coasted to victory as he returned to duty for the first time since he injured his powerful right arm last Tuesday against the Athletics. For six innings Red had a one-hit performance. Then he eased off and the Tigers, to the accompaniment of sarcastic cheers from 11,379 chilled fans, were permitted the luxury of three doubles and as many singles, to boost their hit aggregate to seven.

In the seventeen blows the Yanks struck at the expense of Vernon Kennedy, Harry Eisenstat, Jephat Lynn, Fred Hutchinson and George Gill, in that order, were four rousing home runs and five others for extra bases. All told, the Yanks hit for thirty-five bases. Traffic on the basepaths was further congested by twelve passes the Tiger hurlers gave up.

In three innings the McCarthymen batted around. In one inning, the big seventh when they scored nine runs before chasing the $50,000 Hutchinson in his debut, thirteen club-swingers went to the plate.

Homer No. 2 by Selkirk

Dahlgren hit a homer and a double to drive in two runs. George Selkirk hit his second homer and a double, driving in two runs. Charley Keller hit a homer and a triple to drive in six runs. Tommy Henrich hit a homer with two on. Red Robert Rolfe struck two doubles in the seventh when he batted twice and chased in three runs. Everybody but Henrich hit two blows. Everybody but Frankie Crosetti drove in one or more runs.

Kennedy lasted less than one inning. Eisenstat disappeared after the third, by which time the Yanks had eight runs. Lynn was shelled to cover in the sixth and Hutchinson followed in the seventh, when Keller's homer was the big poke in a nine-run blast. Gill simply had to finish and staggered home without yielding a run.

Dahlgren Fields Well

Dahlgren contributed two fielding gems. His best effort was a foul catch on Greenberg in right.

The home-run harvest brought the Yankee total to ten.

Until the ninth inning the Yanks were near a record for minimum assists, having only two, the first coming after thirteen putouts.

Monte Pearson was to have pitched today, but came up with a lame wrist, the result of being hit by a batted ball. X-ray pictures have been taken to see if any bones are broken.

The Box Score

NEW YORK (A.)	ab.	r.	h.	po.	a.	e.
Crosetti, ss.	5	3	2	5	1	0
Rolfe, 3b.	6	2	2	1	0	0
Henrich, cf.	4	3	1	1	0	0
Dickey, c.	5	2	2	4	0	0
Keller, lf.	5	4	2	3	0	0
Selkirk, rf.	3	2	2	3	0	0
Gordon, 2b.	4	3	2	3	4	0
Dahlgren, 1b	5	2	2	7	0	0
Ruffing, p.	6	1	2	0	0	0
Total	43	22	17	27	5	0

DETROIT (A.)	ab.	r.	h.	po.	a.	e.
McCosky, cf.	5	0	0	3	0	0
Walker, lf.	3	0	0	1	0	0
G'ringer, 2b.	4	0	1	3	1	1
Gr'nberg, 1b.	3	1	0	6	1	0
Fox, rf.	4	0	1	4	0	0
Tebbetts, c.	4	0	1	4	0	0
Rogell, 3b.	3	1	2	2	4	0
Croucher, ss.	3	0	2	3	3	0
Kennedy, p.	0	0	0	0	1	0
Eisenstat, p.	0	0	0	1	0	0
aCullenbine	1	0	0	0	0	0
Lynn, p.	1	0	0	0	0	0
Hutch'son, p.	0	0	0	0	0	0
Gill, p.	1	0	0	0	0	0
bFleming	1	0	0	0	0	0
Total	33	2	7	27	10	1

aBatted for Eisenstat in third.
bBatted for Gill in ninth.

New York ....6 0 2 0 2 3 9 0 0—22
Detroit ....0 0 0 0 0 0 2 0 0— 2

Runs batted in—Keller 6, Gordon, Ruffing 3, Dahlgren 2, Selkirk 2, Henrich 3, Rolfe 3, Dickey, Croucher, Rogell.

Two-base hits—Dahlgren, Tebbetts, Rolfe 2, Rogell, Croucher, Selkirk. Three-base hit—Keller. Home runs—Dahlgren, Selkirk, Henrich, Keller. Sacrifice—Henrich. Double play—Gordon, Crosetti and Dahlgren. Left on bases—New York 7, Detroit 8. Bases on balls—Off Ruffing 4, Lynn 3, Kennedy 2, Eisenstat 1, Gill 1, Hutchinson 5. Struck out—By Ruffing 2, Eisenstat 1, Lynn 2. Hits—Off Kennedy 2 in 1-3 inning, Eisenstat 4 in 2 2-3, Lynn 5 in 2 2-3, Hutchinson 4 in 2-3, Gill 2 in 2 2-3. Balk—Lynn. Passed ball—Tebbetts. Losing pitcher—Kenndey. Umpires—Basil, Ormsby and Summers. Time of game—2:22. Attendance—11,379.

WHITE SOX CHECK ATHLETICS, 4 TO 1

Lyons Pitches Team to Fifth Straight Triumph, Allowing Only Six Safeties

CHICAGO, May 2 (AP).—With the Athletics' erratic defense booting in three runs, the White Sox defeated Philadelphia, 4 to 1, today and climbed into second place over the idle Red Sox. It was Chicago's fifth straight victory and its seventh in the last eight starts.

The veteran Ted Lyons gave only six hits in his first 1939 victory. He was deprived of a shutout when Nick Etten's single followed Bob Johnson's triple in the seventh.

The Athletics made five errors. Miscues by Pitcher Leroy Parmelee and his battery-mate, Frank Hayes, on the same third-inning play let in one run, while poor throws by First Baseman Etten and Third Baseman Dario Lodigiani on another play in the fifth contributed two unearned tallies.

The box score:

PHILADELPHIA (A.)	ab.	r.	h.	po.	a.	e.
Moses, rf.	4	0	1	3	1	0
Gan'bein, 2b.	4	0	0	1	3	0
Miles, cf.	4	0	1	1	0	0
Johnson, lf.	4	1	2	2	0	0
Etten, 1b.	4	0	1	11	1	1
Lod'ani, 3b.	2	0	0	1	2	2
Nagel, 3b.	1	0	0	0	0	0
Hayes, c.	2	0	0	1	0	1
Newsome, ss.	3	0	1	3	2	0
Parmelee, p.	2	0	0	1	2	1
Beckman, p.	1	0	0	0	2	0
Total	31	1	6	24	13	5

CHICAGO (A.)	ab.	r.	h.	po.	a.	e.
Owen, 3b.	2	0	0	4	4	1
Kuhel, 1b.	4	2	2	13	1	0
Walker, lf.	4	1	1	1	0	0
Appling, ss.	4	0	1	4	3	0
McNair, 2b.	4	0	2	3	4	0
Ros'thal, rf.	3	0	0	1	0	0
Kreevich, cf.	3	0	0	0	0	0
Silvestri, c.	3	0	0	1	1	0
Lyons, p.	3	1	2	0	2	0
Total	30	4	8	27	15	1

Philadelphia ....0 0 0 0 0 0 1 0 0—1
Chicago ....0 0 2 0 2 0 0 0 ..—4

Runs batted in—Etten, Appling 2.

Three-base hit—Johnson. Stolen base—Kuhel. Sacrifices—Owen 2, Rosenthal. Double plays—Appling, McNair and Kuhel; Owen, McNair and Kuhel. Left on bases—Philadelphia 4, Chicago 7. Bases on balls—Off Parmelee 2, Lyons 1. Struck out—By Beckman 1, Lyons 1. Hits—Off Parmelee 5 in 6 innings, Beckman 3 in 2. Losing pitcher—Parmelee. Umpires—Geisel, Kolls and Rue. Time of game—1:46. Attendance—1,000.

"All the News That's Fit to Print."

The New York Times.

LATE CITY EDITION
Mostly cloudy, thunder showers this afternoon; little change in temperature. Tomorrow showers.
Temperatures Yesterday—Max., 84; Min., 62

Copyright, 1939, by The New York Times Company.

VOL. LXXXVIII...No. 29,747. Entered as Second-Class Matter. Postoffice, New York, N. Y. NEW YORK, WEDNESDAY, JULY 5, 1939. P THREE CENTS NEW YORK CITY and Vicinity | FOUR CENTS Elsewhere Except in 7th and 8th Postal Zones.

U.S. POLICY ON WAR IS JULY 4 THEME; HOLIDAY TOLL 555

Deaths and Injuries Exceed Last Year's—Millions Get a Four-Day Vacation

ALL TRAVEL LINES CHOKED

Record Crowds at All Near-By Resorts—Nearly 250,000 Visit the World's Fair

As millions of Americans joined yesterday in celebrating the 163d anniversary of our independence, a new note of anxiety for the nation's future was sounded in pronouncements by leaders representing many points of view. United in the belief that there is grave danger of war, they differed widely on how the danger should be dealt with.

While President Roosevelt was renewing at Hyde Park his demand for scrapping the arms embargo, on the theory that the proper objective is to stop a war before it starts, former President Hoover was accusing him, in an article in the American Magazine, of taking a seat in the game of European power politics, and many other speakers were adding to the discussion.

Many millions more of Americans took advantage of the four-day holiday week-end to visit the mountains, the country or the shore. Record crowds were reported from every near-by resort, Coney Island leading with the biggest crowd it has ever had, more than 1,000,000 in number, according to the police. The accidents inevitable in so huge a migration took a heavy toll of life.

More Deaths Than Last Year

Despite the many pleas for safe and sane observance of the holiday, The Associated Press reported that its survey showed 555 fatalities in the country during the four-day period, a figure above the 1938 total of 517. Automobile crashes took 251 lives, drownings 167 and many other kinds of mishaps also figured. There were two deaths listed as due to fireworks.

In New York City the Fourth was not as safe as in recent years. The number of fireworks injuries reported to the police and hospitals here was 1,258, against 846 last year and 1,180 in 1937, when the Fourth fell on Sunday and the celebration was held through Monday. Suburban Westchester, Long Island and New Jersey added their share of firecracker injuries to the total.

As dusk fell last night myriads of the holiday week-enders started home almost simultaneously, placing an almost unbearable strain on transportation facilities of every kind. In the metropolitan area the situation was complicated over past years by the presence of two great mass movements, one of New Yorkers homeward bound and the other of World's Fair visitors heading away from the city.

Auto Traffic Clogs Roads

Automobile traffic congested the principal thoroughfares leading to and from the city far into the night, with the Hudson bridges and tunnels and other key facilities so crowded that their managements said a check-up today might show new week-end and holiday records. All other forms of transportation—bus lines, railroads, ferries, excursion and coastal steamships and air lines—were taxed to the utmost by a vast army of weary men, women and children.

Nearly a quarter million persons spent the day at the World's Fair where Mayor La Guardia, speaking at a huge patriotic mass meeting, compared the dictators to gangsters and urged the people of the world to refuse to kill one another to satisfy the ambitions of any individual. Parades, day and night fireworks and the elaborate Lagoon of Nations show were features of the celebration there.

Distinguished foreigners joined with American residents and visitors in important cities throughout the world in marking the day. William C. Bullitt, American Ambassador to France, speaking at Chalons-sur-Marne, where America's Unknown Soldier fell, said the common ideals of America and France made us equally desirous of maintaining an honorable peace.

In times of tension such as the present the spontaneous outburst of enthusiasm that marked the visit of King George VI and Queen Elizabeth to the United States is of the greatest importance, the Duke of Kent said at the annual Fourth of July dinner of the American Society in London. American Ambassador Joseph P. Kennedy said cordial relations between the United States and Great Britain were taken for granted.

Members of the Cabinet of Eire and other leading figures in the life of the country were guests at a reception at the American legation in Dublin, while in other cities

Continued on Page Ten

Declaration Seen July 4, First Time in 15 Years

By The Associated Press.

WASHINGTON, July 4.—The Declaration of Independence was on display today for the first July 4 in fifteen years. Employes of the Library of Congress agreed to keep the building open so that visitors could see it.

"More and more we notice great crowds come from all over the country at this time of year," said Martin Roberts, chief assistant librarian. "For many it is the trip of a lifetime, and we cannot very well keep them out."

It is believed in some quarters that the Declaration of Independence and the Constitution may soon be moved to the Archives Building. Herbert Putnam, who has just retired as Librarian of Congress, refused to let them be transferred while he was in office.

HUGE HOUSING UNIT IN RED HOOK OPENED

Mayor Questions U. S. Rule on Tenant Income—Heckled by Group in Audience

Mayor La Guardia was mildly booed yesterday when he spoke to 1,500 persons at the official opening of the $13,000,000 Red Hook housing development in Brooklyn, and promptly squelched his hecklers.

As the Mayor rose to speak, the welcoming applause was studded with several isolated but clearly heard boos.

"I appreciate that, too," the Mayor remarked grimly, "and I'll give you proper attention in just a few moments."

After welcoming the eighty families who moved into new quarters in the forty-acre development, the Mayor returned to his hecklers and said:

"I can understand how some people who thrive on maintaining unsafe, unsanitary dwellings which are firetraps can oppose projects of this kind. I am not concerned with them. The satisfaction of housing 2,540 families in a project of this kind more than makes up for the rudeness of any landlords' agents who come here."

USHA Ruling Discussed

With the outburst quelled, the Mayor went on to discuss criticisms of the United States Housing Authority ruling which kept thirty families out of the development because their earnings exceeded the $1,300 a year maximum. Because of this ruling, city authorities believe that at least half the tenants will be on relief, a percentage which they consider far too high for the best interests of the project.

"We must necessarily abide by the rules of the United States Housing Authority," the Mayor remarked. "We have no say in that matter. The Federal Government provides the subsidy and lays down the rules for operation. Personally, I believe that rule is susceptible of amendment.

"I think that the Housing Authority has perhaps set a maximum not compatible with conditions in this city. But the agency is always reasonable and cooperative. New York City can't take the average for other communities and I hope they will bear with us on that. It is only by negotiation and reasoning that we can change the present formula."

At another point the Mayor warned labor that the city would stop its housing program unless it could obtain definite assurances in advance that jurisdictional fights would not be permitted to delay the work. Construction of the Queens midtown tunnel is now tied up because of such a disagreement.

"I have always been for labor,

Continued on Page Two

ROOSEVELT URGES SENATE TO REVERSE THE ARMS EMBARGO

Ready to Have Congress Stay Till Autumn if Necessary to Upset House's Action

BACK IN CAPITAL TODAY

New Dealers Gird for Battle, With Monetary Powers Their Second Major Objective

By FELIX BELAIR Jr.
Special to THE NEW YORK TIMES.

HYDE PARK, N. Y., July 4.—President Roosevelt called on the Senate today to reverse the House action to forbid shipments of arms and munitions to nations at war, and said that he was prepared to see Congress remain in session until September, if necessary, to accomplish that result.

The President departed for Washington on his special train at 11 P. M. (Eastern standard time). He is due to arrive in the capital at 8:30 A. M. Secretary Morgenthau accompanied the President.

On the eve of the scheduled meeting of the Foreign Relations Committee to take up the neutrality issue, Mr. Roosevelt asserted that prevention of war in all parts of the world was the first policy of his Administration.

Puts Issue to the Senate

In the interest of preventing war, the President emphasized repeatedly, it was up to the Foreign Relations Committee to give the executive branch a free hand to determine when and to what countries American materials of war could be exported.

In an impromptu press conference after a lawn party this afternoon, President Roosevelt said he stood for the recommendations sent to Congress months ago by Secretary Hull, in which the Secretary of State asked that the present mandatory arms embargo, which becomes effective on a finding that a state of war existed, should be lifted.

The President's expression of willingness to fight it out with Congress all Summer if necessary was brought out when he was told of reports that the Senate's "isolationist group" was prepared to filibuster on the Administration's amendments through September. That was the privilege of the Senate, Mr. Roosevelt remarked, because its members had full discretion under the rules.

Scoffs at Political Stories

In the course of his press conference remarks, Mr. Roosevelt paused to scoff at published reports that he was contemplating another campaign against reactionary Senators and that this was part of a plan to strengthen his position as a third-term candidate. The reports were typical, the President said, of most political stories written from Washington these days.

In circles close to the White House it was learned yesterday that the President viewed the House rejection of the Administration's neutrality proposals as increasing the chances of war and as adding to his task of keeping this nation and the world at peace. This outline of his position Mr. Roosevelt authenticated today.

Adopting the view attributed to him as his own, the President said he would improve on the published reports of his position in only one respect. He would have emphasized that it was the policy of the Administration to prevent an outbreak of war in all parts of the world. He had nothing to say on the reported

Continued on Page Five

Major Sports Yesterday

BASEBALL

The Yankees routed the Senators, 11 to 1, after dropping the opener of a double-header, 3 to 2, before 61,808 fans who were at the Yankee Stadium for "Lou Gehrig Day." The Giants dropped a twin bill to the Bees at Boston, 3 to 1 and 10 to 2, while the Dodgers annexed two from the Phillies, 6 to 3 and 8 to 6, at Ebbets Field.

TENNIS

Miss Kay Stammers of England eliminated Miss Helen Jacobs of Berkeley, Calif., 6—2, 6—2, in the quarter-finals of the All-England women's tennis singles championship at Wimbledon. However, Miss Alice Marble, the American champion, advanced to the semi-finals along with another entry from the United States, Mrs. Sarah Palfrey Fabyan. Miss Marble defeated Mlle. Jadwiga Jedrzejowska of Poland, 6—1, 6—4, while Mrs. Fabyan vanquished Mme. Rene Mathieu of France, 6—4, 6—2.

GOLF

Jim Bruen, 19-year-old Irish amateur, shot his second 69 in two days for 138 to lead 129 qualifiers in the British open championship at St. Andrews, Scotland. Henry Cotton of Great Britain and Lawson Little of the United States were next with 36-hole totals of 142. Reginald Whitcombe of Great Britain, the defending champion, had a score of 144.

TRACK

Blaine Rideout won the 1,500-meter championship to score the biggest upset of the national A. A. U. meet at Lincoln, Neb. He beat Chuck Fenske by five feet, with Louis Zamperini and Glenn Cunningham following in order. Four records for the games were broken. The Olympic Club of San Francisco dethroned the New York A. C. as the team champion.

RACING

Now What, in the silks of Alfred Gwynne Vanderbilt, took the Demoiselle Stakes and Maxwell Howard's The Chief won the Questionnaire Handicap at Empire City. The Yankee Handicap at Suffolk Downs, worth $15,000 added, went to W. L. Brann's Challedon.

(Complete Details of These and Other Events on Sports Pages.)

YOUTHS CONDEMN RED DICTATORSHIP

But Stand Is Held Not a Reversal of Previous One—Want Roosevelt Again

The American Youth Congress, which on Monday refused to include in its official creed a declaration placing communism on a level with nazism and fascism as contrary to American ideals, adopted by a unanimous vote yesterday a resolution condemning all forms of dictatorship and including communism among them.

The action was taken following Monday's walkout of fourteen organizations of the anti-Communist bloc and charges by their spokesmen that the Congress, frequently in opposition to the policies of Hitler and Mussolini, never had assailed Stalin's regime as dictatorial.

The alternative resolution was presented on the floor of the convention in the Manhattan Center in West Thirty-fourth Street with the unanimous backing of the members of the resolutions committee. James B. Carey, chairman of that body and secretary of the Congress of Industrial Organizations, took the lead in explanation of the seeming self-reversal of the Congress.

Committee's Mind Unchanged

"This committee has not changed its mind by one iota," he told the thousand delegates who attended the general session. "The question was, Could American youth be stampeded into doing something under outside pressure and outside of the proper procedure? I believe this resolution is one you can all stand behind, and I believe the Congress has answered those who tried to use it as a stepping stone to their personal advantage."

Adoption of the resolution came during the final day of formal meetings. The delegates, by an overwhelming majority, favored the reelection of President Roosevelt for a third term, adopted a constitution, elected officers and decided on a national campaign to back a $500,000,000 Federal Loan Fund to further youth in the professions, education and agriculture.

The Dictatorship Resolution

The dictatorship resolution presented by Mr. Carey differed somewhat in form from the creed amendment over which the anti-Communists deserted the Congress. It read:

"Whereas the American Youth is devoted to the principles of true democracy and the great constitutional freedoms of speech, of petition, of the press, of religion and of assembly: Be it resolved that this Congress of youth record its opposition to all forms of dictatorship, regardless of whether they be Communist, Fascist, Nazi or any other type, or bear any other name; that this Congress accord full freedom of speech and discussion to all young people, regardless of race, creed, religion or political label, whether Republican, Democratic, Socialist, Communist, Fascist or any other and that this Congress be open in all its activities and its gatherings to all persons, regardless of race, creed, religion or political label, who are willing to abide by the principles of democratic procedure."

The proposed creed amendment had resolved that: "The American Youth Congress condemns Commu-

Continued on Page Fifteen

61,808 FANS ROAR TRIBUTE TO GEHRIG

Captain of Yankees Honored at Stadium—Calls Himself 'Luckiest Man Alive'

By JOHN DREBINGER

In perhaps as colorful and dramatic a pageant as ever was enacted on a baseball field, 61,808 fans thundered a hail and farewell to Henry Lou Gehrig at the Yankee Stadium yesterday.

To be sure, it was a holiday and there would have been a big crowd and plenty of roaring in any event. For the Yankees, after getting nosed out, 3 to 2, in the opening game of the double-header, despite a ninth-inning home run by George Selkirk, came right back in typical fashion to crush the Senators, 11 to 1, in the nightcap. Twinkletoes Selkirk embellished this contest with another home run.

But it was the spectacle staged between the games which doubtless never will be forgotten by those who saw it. For more than forty minutes there paraded in review two mighty championship hosts—the Yankees of 1927 and the current edition of Yanks who definitely are winging their way to a fourth straight pennant and a chance for another world title.

Old Mates Reassemble

From far and wide the 1927 stalwarts came to reassemble for Lou Gehrig Appreciation Day and to pay their own tribute to their former comrade-in-arms who had carried on beyond all of them only to have his own brillant career come to a tragic close when it was revealed that he had fallen victim of a form of infantile paralysis.

In conclusion, the vast gathering, sitting in absolute silence for a longer period than perhaps any baseball crowd in history, heard Gehrig himself deliver as amazing a valedictory as ever came from a ball player.

So shaken with emotion that at first it appeared he would not be able to talk at all, the mighty Iron Horse, with a rare display of that indomitable will power that had carried him through 2,130 consecutive games, moved to the microphone at home plate to express his own appreciation.

And for the final fadeout, there stood the still burly and hearty Babe Ruth alongside of Gehrig, their arms about each other's shoulders, facing a battery of camera men.

All through the long exercises Gehrig had tried in vain to smile, but with the irrepressible Bambino beside him he finally made it. The Babe whispered something to him and Lou chuckled. Then they both chuckled and the crowd roared and roared.

Late Rally Fails

The ceremonies began directly after the debris of the first game had been cleared away. There had been some vociferous cheering as the Yanks, fired to action by Selkirk's homer, tried to snatch that opener away from the Senators in the last few seconds of the ninth. But they couldn't quite make it and the players hustled off the field.

Then, from out of a box alongside the Yankee dugout there spryly hopped more than a dozen elderly gentlemen, some gray, some shockingly baldish, but all happy to be on hand. The crowd recognized

Continued on Page Twenty-one

NAZIS BEAT PRELATE ON AUSTRIAN TOUR; INNITZER QUITS TRIP

Cardinal Attacked With Eggs and Epithets as He Visits Parishes Near Vienna

STRUCK ON HEAD BY STICK

He Is Called 'Murderer' for Failure to Get Pardons for Slayers of Dollfuss

Wireless to THE NEW YORK TIMES.

VIENNA, July 4.—Theodor Cardinal Innitzer, Archbishop of Vienna, was brutally assaulted in Koenigsbrunn on Sunday following a series of Nazi demonstrations while he was making a tour of rural districts northwest of Vienna, it was learned today. He was pelted with rotten eggs and potatoes by a mob of rural Nazis, who shouted "murderer" and other epithets as he left a Koenigsbrunn church. His biretta (cap) was knocked off by a blow from a stick.

His chauffeur, who had been striving to defend his automobile while the Cardinal was celebrating mass in the church, managed to get his master and a chaplain and secretary inside the car and then drove straight to Vienna. Thus the Cardinal's tour was halted. Both the chaplain and secretary were struck by the mob, and the chauffeur's uniform was ripped.

Cardinal Innitzer has remained in his palace since. No report of the incident has appeared in any Vienna paper. The Cardinal himself has made no statement. The news percolated into Vienna from the districts the Cardinal was visiting.

Women Boo the Prelate

In some villages, it appears, there were such demonstrations as bands of youths marching up and down whistling outside the churches where the Cardinal was celebrating mass. At another place a man tried to spit on the prelate as he passed, while women hissed and booed.

Despite these demonstrations Cardinal Innitzer continued his tour but always slept in the parish priests' houses. At one of them a number of windows were smashed during the night. Each visit was announced in advance by a placard on a church door.

In one village twelve children were to have been confirmed in front of the church, but a threatening crowd gathered and the ceremony was held within the church.

The chief Nazi grievance against Cardinal Innitzer apparently is that he declined to intervene when Planetta and Holzweber, Nazis, were sentenced to death and executed for the murder of Chancellor Engelbert Dollfuss in 1934. Nazis have been taught to believe that Cardinal Innitzer could have saved the lives of the two men, who are now regarded as national heroes, with streets named after them in Vienna and elsewhere.

Since a mob stormed his palace in Vienna last October, Cardinal Innitzer's car has ceased flying a small papal flag as was its custom. The license number also has been changed.

Incidents Began Week Ago

VIENNA, July 4 (AP).—Hostile demonstrations, interpreted as partly a Nazi reaction to the clerical regime under the Dollfuss and Schuschnigg governments of Austria, were disclosed today to have cut short a parish tour by Theodor Cardinal Innitzer, Archbishop of Vienna.

The incidents began last Tuesday in the parish of Nieder Russ-

Continued on Page Six

The European Situation

An investigation of what is going on in Danzig indicated yesterday that the Free City, which may legally have an armed police force of 800, contained between 10,000 and 11,000 armed men; that the recent influx of strangers had boomed business, but that reports of the importation of tanks and field guns had been exaggerated. The best opinion was that the inevitable upheaval was coming in late August or in mid-September. [Page 1.]

Polish representations to Danzig to cease military preparations will not be delivered before the week-end, it was understood in Warsaw. [Page 6.]

That the British and the French are working hand-in-glove was emphasized in a Paris speech by the British War Secretary. [Page 6.] But Russia's cooperation was still in doubt as London reported another hitch in the alliance negotiations. [Page 1.]

SOVIET PACT TALKS ARE SNAGGED ANEW

Moscow Balks at Aid to Small States in West—London and Paris Are Discouraged

By FERDINAND KUHN Jr.
Special Cable to THE NEW YORK TIMES.

LONDON, July 4.—Still another hitch in the negotiations in Moscow became apparent today just as the stock markets here and in Paris were responding joyfully to rumors that a three-power alliance between Britain, France and Russia was about to be signed at last.

The rejoicings in the financial districts were promptly described with typical British understatement as "premature." The signing of a pact is not regarded here as imminent by any means; indeed, official quarters seemed almost more depressed and discouraged over the prospects than at any time since the negotiations began there months ago.

But the British are going to try again. The Cabinet subcommittee on foreign affairs held two long meetings today to discuss the Russian objections to the latest Anglo-French proposals and it finally worked out a possible way of overcoming them.

New Instructions Drafted

Accordingly, still further instructions will be sent tomorrow to Sir William Seeds, the British Ambassador in Moscow, and the long negotiations will drag on while the situation in Danzig continues serious and while the effect of the Russian pact threatens to wear off with every additional week of delay.

Official quarters here today would not disclose the exact points of disagreement. A clue to the nature of the trouble could be found, however, in yesterday's communiqué from The Hague protesting that the Netherlands did not want to be mentioned in any guarantee by the great powers and wanted only to remain neutral.

There is little doubt now that the British and the French asked Russia last week to promise help in the event of aggression against the Netherlands or Switzerland and thus to counterbalance the proposed Anglo-French guarantee of the Baltic States. The smaller States of the East and of the West would have been mentioned by name, but in a separate document that would not have been published.

But the Russians apparently did not take kindly to the idea of guaranteeing little States in the West. For one thing, they have no

Continued on Page Eight

ARMED FORCES PUT AT 10,000 IN DANZIG; FREE CITY IS CALM

Drilling in Barrack Yards Is Seen but There Is No Sign of Massing of Arms

SEPTEMBER CRISIS LIKELY

League Commissioner, Urging Both Sides to Keep Peace, Sets Three Guiding Rules

By FREDERICK T. BIRCHALL
Wireless to THE NEW YORK TIMES.

DANZIG, July 4.—The Free City of Danzig, whose Nazi rulers proclaim its desire and determination to achieve physical reunion with Nazi Germany, is exercising its normal activities and doing its normal business just as if it were not the focus of a bitter political controversy that before long must inevitably produce a new European crisis. The tension is all elsewhere.

Business is better than usual here because in the last few weeks there have been strangers, mostly athletic young men from the Reich, who arrive in civil garb, disappear and presently are met in twos and threes strolling about in the evening in German Elite Guard or Danzig police uniforms, which are scarcely different from German military attire.

As a result there have been some increases in food prices and a scarcity of some kinds of provisions but therewith great benefit to retail trade.

The number of these newcomers cannot be ascertained from any responsible authority. A good guess is that Danzig, which under Versailles treaty and League of Nations guardianship was entitled to an armed police force of 800 men and no soldiers whatever, at present contains armed forces, fully trained or under training, of between 10,000 and 11,000 men.

New Bunks in Barracks

The Langfuhr barracks, which before the last war housed the German Crown Prince's regiment, the Deathhead Hussars, has been newly equipped with three-tier bunks, which appear to be filled. This barracks is reputed to contain at least 2,000 men, but these are described as "police" recruited under the recent Senate decree that established conscription in the Free City and has since authorized the calling up of various classes of the male population.

Similarly, the influx of young men from Germany, many of whom wear the uniform and insignia of the Hitler Elite Bodyguard, is described as comprising former Danzigers who sought service in the Reich and now, under conscription here, prefer to return home.

The Nazi authorities put the number of these newcomers at 500. The Poles say there are 15,000. The fact is that there are probably between 1,000 and 2,000 in addition to the native conscripted Danzigers.

Elite Guards in black uniforms inhabit the Wieden barracks, which also was the home of a German regiment in pre-war days and has been restored and refurbished. There would seem to be between 1,000 and 2,000 of them.

As the airplane from Berlin circles the Free City before making its landing, one can see far below that the parade grounds of these newly established barracks are filled with recruits, some in uniform and some without, doing squad drill, and that they are very busy places indeed. Similarly, as one drives in from the airport one observes through the barred iron gates of another barracks more men doing squad drill. It is quite obvious that Danzig is preparing for more than police duties.

Reports of Imported Guns

From Warsaw have come reports of light tanks and field howitzers being imported into the city. These reports have been echoed in Paris and London and have produced new tension in those capitals.

The artillery is said to have come from Germany by ship and the tanks to have been run across the frontier from East Prussia where Danzig territory has physical contact with Germany, and to have been brought in after the customs houses had been closed for the night and the customs officers had gone home. How they passed the frontier barriers without leaving very obvious wreckage is not explained.

An all-afternoon inquiry by this correspondent failed to disclose a single man who could say that he had personally seen tanks or guns. The Hagelsberg and the Bischofsberg, the hills where they were supposedly housed in earthwork fortifications, proved on investigation to be public parks and playgrounds without visible places where tanks and guns could be concealed.

There are many persons, how-

Continued on Page Six

Atlantic City Fire Razes Boardwalk Area; $110,000 Damage Is Caused in Store Block

Special to THE NEW YORK TIMES.

ATLANTIC CITY, July 4.—A spectacular three-hour fire destroyed an entire block of stores on the Boardwalk here this morning while a crowd of some 50,000 holiday visitors thronged the beach and near-by rooftops to witness the event.

Although nine shops were destroyed on the 160-foot Boardwalk frontage running between Missouri and Columbia Avenues, estimated damage was only $110,000, the buildings being of light construction. All were one or two-story structures. Property damage was set at $75,000 and damage to the merchandise and fixtures at $35,000.

Two firemen were injured of the 120 men who fought the blaze. Both are in the Atlantic City Hospital, Captain Harry Knauff with a broken arm, and Captain Albert Villano with an injured left leg. Knauff was hurt when the roof of one of the buildings collapsed, and Villano when struck by a hose which got out of hand.

The blaze started in a bingo parlor in the middle of the block and the first alarm was turned in at 7:31 A. M., when a Boardwalk stroller noticed the smoke. When firemen arrived a general alarm was turned in, bringing twenty-four pieces of apparatus to the scene. Reinforcements later came in from Pleasantville, Ventnor and Ocean City to be on hand if needed.

It was believed that a lighted cigarette carelessly dropped through a crack in the floor of the bingo parlor started the fire. Whipped by a stiff ocean breeze, the blaze spread rapidly through the sheet metal and wood partitions, and in a short time the entire block was in flames.

The row of buildings was owned by the Perfetti Beachfront Corporation, of which Guilfo Perfetti of Philadelphia is president. It was reported that the Mortgage Guarantee Company of Baltimore held a $300,000 first mortgage on the land and buildings.

Brazil to Buy $18,000,000 in Mexican Oil, Purchasing Refinery Equipment in U. S.

By The Associated Press.

MEXICO CITY, July 4.—Conclusion of an $18,000,000 deal with the Mexican Government Petroleum Agency was announced today by Santo Vahlis, representative of the Brazilian firm of Correa & Castro.

Under the agreement, he said, Mexico will sell approximately 5,500,000 barrels of crude oil annually to Brazil, along with asphalt and refined petroleum products.

The deal is expected to result in trade far in excess of the $18,000,000 figure annually, according to Mr. Vahlis, because it "naturally will open new means of commercial exchange between Mexico and Brazil."

He emphasized that it was a cash, not a barter, transaction. Brazil, being a big purchaser of Mexican oil, naturally hoped to sell Mexico whatever products she might need, it was explained.

Working with Mr. Vahlis was Fernando Saldana Galvan, head of Mexico's government-controlled newsprint agency. Some time ago he was sent by President Lazaro Cardenas to Brazil and elsewhere in South America to seek markets for oil produced by properties of United States, British and Netherlands operators which were expropriated in March, 1938.

"We are going to install a most modern refinery at Rio de Janeiro," Mr. Vahlis said, "costing more than $3,000,000. We are also organizing a direct steamship line between Tampico and Rio de Janeiro for handling the oil."

He said the Rio de Janeiro refinery would handle 10,000 barrels a day, supplemented by a refinery planned at São Paulo to handle 7,000 barrels. The refinery equipment, Mr. Vahlis said, was coming from the United States.

The refineries will be not completed for eight months, but shipment of refined petroleum products already has been started.

61,808 FANS ROAR TRIBUTE TO GEHRIG

Continued From Page One

them at once, for they were the Yanks of 1927, not the first Yankee world championship team, but the first, with Gehrig an important cog in the machine, to win a world series in four straight games.

Down the field, behind Captain Sutherland's Seventh Regiment Band, they marched—Ruth, Bob Meusel, who had come all the way from California; Waite Hoyt, alone still maintaining his boyish countenance; Wally Schang, Benny Bengough, Tony Lazzeri, Mark Koenig, Jumping Joe Dugan, Bob Shawkey, Herb Pennock, Deacon Everett Scott, whose endurance record Gehrig eventually surpassed; Wally Pipp, who faded out as the Yankee first sacker the day Columbia Lou took over the job away back in 1925, and George Pipgras, now an umpire and, in fact, actually officiating in the day's games.

At the flagpole, these old Yanks raised the world series pennant they had won so magnificently from the Pirates in 1927 and, as they paraded back, another familiar figure streaked out of the dugout, the only one still wearing a Yankee uniform. It was the silver-haired Earle Combs, now a coach.

Old-Timers Face Plate

Arriving at the infield, the old-timers strung out, facing the plate. The players of both Yankee and Senator squads also emerged from their dugouts to form a rectangle, and the first real ovation followed as Gehrig moved out to the plate to greet his colleagues, past and present.

One by one the old-timers were introduced with Sid Mercer acting as toastmaster. Clark Griffith, venerable white-haired owner of the Senators and a Yankee himself in the days when they were known as Highlanders, also joined the procession.

Gifts of all sorts followed. The Yankees presented their stricken comrade with a silver trophy measuring more than a foot and a half in height, their thoughts expressed in verse inscribed upon the base.

Manager Joe McCarthy, almost as visibly affected as Gehrig himself, made this presentation and hurried back to fall in line with his players. But every few minutes, when he saw that the once stalwart figure they called the Iron Horse was swaying on shaky legs, Marse Joe would come forward to give Lou an assuring word of cheer.

Mayor La Guardia officially extended the city's appreciation of the services Columbia Lou had given his home town.

"You are the greatest prototype of good sportsmanship and citizenship," said the Mayor, concluding with "Lou, we're proud of you."

Postmaster General Farley also was on hand, closing his remarks with "for generations to come, boys who play baseball will point with pride to your record."

When time came for Gehrig to address the gathering it looked as if he simply would never make it. He gulped and fought to keep back the tears as he kept his eyes fastened on the ground.

But Marse Joe came forward again, said something that might have been "come on, Lou, just rap out another," and somehow those magical words had the same effect as in all the past fifteen years when the gallant Iron Horse would step up to the plate to "rap out another."

Gehrig Speaks Slowly

He spoke slowly and evenly, and stressed the appreciation that he felt for all that was being done for him. He spoke of the men with whom he had been associated in his long career with the Yankees—the late Colonel Jacob Ruppert, the late Miller Huggins, his first manager, who gave him his start in New York; Edward G. Barrow, the present head of baseball's most powerful organization; the Yanks of old who now stood silently in front of him, as well as the players of today.

"What young man wouldn't give anything to mingle with such men for a single day as I have for all these years?" he asked.

"You've been reading about my bad break for weeks now," he said. "But today I think I'm the luckiest man alive. I now feel more than ever that I have much to live for."

The gifts included a silver service set from the New York club, a fruit bowl and two candlesticks from the Giants, a silver pitcher from the Stevens Associates, two silver platters from the Stevens employes, a fishing rod and tackle from the Stadium employes and ushers, a silver cup from the Yankee office staff, a scroll from the Old Timers Association of Denver that was presented by John Kieran, a scroll from Washington fans, a tobacco stand from the New York Chapter of the Baseball Writers Association of America, and the silver trophy from his team-mates.

The last-named present, about eighteen inches tall with a wooden base, supported by six silver bats with an eagle atop a silver ball, made Gehrig weep. President Barrow walked out to put his arms about Lou in an effort to steady him when this presentation was made. It appeared for an instant that Gehrig was near collapse.

On one side of the trophy were the names of all his present fellow-players. On the other was the following touching inscription:

TO LOU GEHRIG

We've been to the wars together,
We took our foes as they came,
And always you were the leader
And ever you played the game.

Idol of cheering millions,
Records are yours by the sheaves,
Iron of frame they hailed you,
Decked you with laurel leaves.

But higher than that we hold you,
We who have known you best,
Knowing the way you came through
Every human test.

Let this be a silent token
Of lasting friendship's gleam,
And all that we've left unspoken,
Your pals of the Yankee team.

As Gehrig finished his talk, Ruth, robust, round and sun-tanned, was nudged toward the microphone and, in his own inimitable, blustering style, snapped the tears away. He gave it as his unqualified opinion that the Yanks of 1927 were greater than the Yanks of today, and seemed even anxious to prove it right there.

"Anyway," he added, "that's my opinion and while Lazzeri here pointed out to me that there are only about thirteen or fourteen of us here, my answer is, shucks, we only need nine to beat 'em."

Then, as the famous home-run slugger, who also has faded into baseball retirement, stood with his arms entwined around Gehrig's shoulders, the band played "I Love You Truly," while the crowd took up the chant: "We love you, Lou."

All Tributes Spontaneous

All given spontaneously, it was without doubt one of the most touching scenes ever witnessed on a ball field and one that made even case-hardened ball players and chroniclers of the game swallow hard.

When Gehrig arrived in the Yankee dressing rooms he was so close to a complete collapse it was feared that the strain upon him had been too great and Dr. Robert E. Walsh, the Yankees' attending physician, hurried to his assistance. But after some refreshment, he recovered quickly and faithful to his one remaining task, that of being the inactive captain of his team, he stuck to his post in the dugout throughout the second game.

Long after the tumult and shouting had died and the last of the crowd had filed out, Lou trudged across the field for his familiar hike to his favorite exit gate. With him walked his bosom pal and team-mate, Bill Dickey, with whom he always rooms when the Yanks are on the road.

Lou walks with a slight hitch in his gait now, but there was supreme confidence in his voice as he said to his friend:

"Bill, I'm going to remember this day for a long time."

So, doubtless, will all the others who helped make this an unforgettable day in baseball.

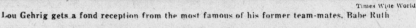

CHIEF FIGURE AT THE STADIUM AND OLD-TIME YANKEES WHO GATHERED IN HIS HONOR

Times Wide World

Lou Gehrig gets a fond reception from the most famous of his former team-mates, Babe Ruth

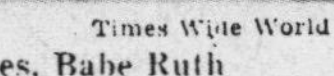

Times Wide World

The erstwhile star receiving a trophy from Manager Joe McCarthy

YANKEES BOW, 3-2, THEN TRIUMPH, 11-1

Stage Five-Run Uprising in Third Inning of Nightcap to Crush Senators

SELKIRK EXCELS WITH BAT

Connects for Circuit in Both Games—Leonard Baffles New Yorkers in Opener

By LOUIS EFFRAT

Something will just have to be done about that former Dodger, Emil (Dutch) Leonard, who seems to have cast a spell over the world-champion Yankees. Yesterday at the Stadium before 61,808 persons, the biggest turnout of the year, Leonard came into the Yankees' own back yard and proceeded to down the McCarthymen for the third time this season for the Senators, 3—2, with a superb six-hitter.

All the fireworks that were so conspicuously absent in the opener made their appearance in the after-piece, in which the home club evened matters with a thirteen-hit attack on Alejandro Carrasquel and Pete Appleton that produced an 11-1 victory for Steve Sundra. Beating the Venezuelan netted the Yanks a Mexican stand-off, but still they lost a game from their lead over the second-place Red Sox.

Leonard Uses Knuckler

Leonard, who throws a perplexing (to the Yankees) knuckler, has won only seven games thus far, but he points with pardonable pride that three of those conquests have been at the expense of the champions. Last week he outlasted Charley (Red) Ruffing in a twelve-inning struggle at Griffith Stadium. Yesterday he did it in regulation time against Monte Pearson and Johnny Murphy.

The first game of the holiday bargain bill was by far the better one from the viewpoint of competition. The Senators, as troublesome as ever, got off to a two-run lead in the first and never were headed. A pass and three successive singles by Taft Wright, Cecil Travis and Buddy Myer did the damage.

In the third Babe Dahlgren doubled, Pearson sacrificed and Frankie Crosetti went out on a grounder to short as the Yankees got one run back. But in the fourth Rick Ferrell's triple and Leonard's single made the count 3—1. It remained that way until Twink Selkirk propelled one into the right-field stands for his thirteenth homer of the campaign.

Dickey Forces DiMaggio

When Joe DiMaggio walked there was a hint of another of those late Yankee rallies, but Leonard took care of that, too. Bill Dickey forced DiMaggio for the second out and Charley Keller rolled to third for the final.

The nightcap became a rout as early as the third, with Selkirk treating himself to another homer, triple and single. Ahead, 1—0, the Yankees fell on Carrasquel for five runs in the third, added three in the fourth and tapered off with single runs in the seventh and eighth, by which time the Senators were completely and definitely subdued.

Sundra, protecting an unbeaten record—he has now won five games—lost his shutout in the second stanza, when he tossed a home-run ball to Wright. There were no runners aboard at the time, so the tremendous blow merely served to tie the score at 1—all. After that, however, it was Sundra's game all the way.

Carrasquel received a diploma from the Venezuelan Baseball Association before he went out to pitch. That might have been the jinx.

The Yanks and Senators now have each won five games this season, proving nothing at all.

War talk, apparently, is as distasteful to Vernon (Lefty) Gomez as to every one else. "Here we are eleven and a half games ahead and they're trying to ring in a war on us," he moaned. "If we were in third place they wouldn't even mention it."

WHITE SOX CAPTURE PAIR FROM BROWNS

Triumph, 7-3 and 7-4, Winning Nightcap With Five in Ninth

ST. LOUIS, July 4 (AP).—The White Sox took a double-header from the Browns today on the strength of one big inning in each contest, 7 to 3 and 7 to 4.

Until the ninth inning of the second game it appeared the Browns might get an even break. At that time the score favored them, 3 to 2. But Ollie Bejma opened the ninth with his second home run of the game, and before the side was retired the Sox had five runs.

Neither team's manager was on the field. Fred Haney of the Browns was suspended for three days following his ejection from yesterday's contest by Umpire Cal Hubbard. Jimmy Dykes of the Sox still was under a three-day suspension imposed after an argument last Sunday at Detroit.

INDIANS BLANKED, 4-0, BY NEWSOM OF TIGERS

56,272, Record Detroit Crowd, See Buck Hurl 3-Hitter

DETROIT, July 4 (AP).—Blustering Buck Newsom slapped a 4-to-0 shut-out on the Indians today to the joy of Detroit's biggest baseball crowd in history, 56,272, but rain intruded to mar the holiday and end the second game of a double-header in the third inning.

While Newsom limited the Indians to three hits and struck out six for his ninth victory of the year, the Tigers grouped their blows off Lefty Al Milnar for two runs in the fifth and two in the seventh and swung back into a virtual third-place tie with the Indians.

One of Newsom's own three singles, Barney McCosky's triple and a one-baser by Roy Cullenbine scored the first two runs. The next pair arrived on Cullenbine's double and singles by Earl Averill and Pinky Higgins.

Today's crowd exceeded the previous record attendance of 54,500 at opening day last year in newly enlarged Briggs Stadium.

Eight Major Penalties Called for Fighting as Rangers Win to Prolong Series

15,692 SEE RANGERS STOP BOSTON, 2 TO 1

Lynn Patrick's Second-Period Tally Wins After Mac Colville Counts in First

FREE-FOR-ALL AT GARDEN

Shore Suffers Broken Nose—Schmidt of Bruins Scores in Opening Minute

By JOSEPH C. NICHOLS

The New York Rangers earned a reprieve last night. Carrying a slam-bang, reckless, teeth-rattling attack to their rivals, the Blue Shirts conquered the Boston Bruins, 2 to 1, in a nerve-tingling battle that produced just about every variety of thrill found in hockey.

By their triumph the New York skaters kept alive their chances of winning the Stanley Cup and its attendant honor, the championship of the world. These chances, though, are slim indeed, with the Bruins still having a tremendous edge. The teams are engaging in a four-out-of-seven game playoff, and Boston already has three games tucked away in the win column, while last night's conquest was the first effected by the New Yorkers.

A wild-eyed crowd of 15,692 left Madison Square Garden after a struggle in which the rival teams tore at each other with a savagery that eclipsed, by far, anything produced in the three previous meetings. The tension which the athletes had been under the past week snapped with a crackling suddenness in the first period and a general fist fight occurred that had all the skaters on the ice at the time engaged. This outbreak set the pitch for the rest of the encounter, played under an electric atmosphere until the final buzzer.

Bruins Lose Little Time

The Rangers had to come from behind, a feat that they accomplished with goals by Mac Colville and Lynn Patrick. The Bruins, prepared to meet a last-stand resistance, lost little time getting the first goal, which is always of tremendous psychological importance. The game was only 49 seconds old when Milt Schmidt batted the puck out of a scramble in front of the Ranger cage for the tally which the Bruins hoped would lead them to a fourth straight victory.

But the Rangers were not at all prepared to succumb supinely. Instead they risked all in a bitter offensive that netted the tying tally in the first period and the winning one in the second.

Even when they had the lead the New Yorkers did not hesitate to attack. They were out to "do or die," and they wanted with all their hearts to score as many goals as possible against young Frank Brimsek.

But Boston accorded its goalie excellent protection, and there was no further scoring. With thirty-one seconds left in the third period, Manager Art Ross pulled Brimsek from the nets, so that his team might attack with six skaters, but so prone were the New Yorkers to rush that Ross had to put Brimsek back with eight seconds left after Neil Colville had fired a disallowed goal from a face-off deep in Ranger ice.

Goalies Are Brilliant

Both goalies, Brimsek and Bert Gardiner, played excellently. Both were called on several times to make almost impossible saves and they came through expertly, on the whole.

The mass fist-fight, which broke out shortly after the midway mark of the first period, with the score tied at 1-all, developed from a situation that seemed mild enough. Phil Watson of the Rangers and Jack Portland, Boston guard, were pushing each other to the boards when suddenly they started swinging.

In a trice the other skaters rushed and blows were exchanged freely. Watson, Murray Patrick and Dutch Hiller did most of the fighting for the New Yorkers, while Eddie Shore, Portland and Gordon Pettinger were the Boston champions.

For some time matters were completely out of hand, but at length the officials managed to restore order and sent the six leading belligerents to the penalty box on majors of five minutes apiece. The deferred penalty rule, providing for substitutes to replace the offending players to insure at least four men from each team on the ice, had to be invoked.

When the game began the Rangers rushed, Hiller skating down the left alley with the disk. He lost it to Milt Schmidt, who quickly carried over New York's line down the center.

Schmidt set the rubber up for Bobby Bauer and Woody Dumart, each of whom fired. Gardiner blocked these shots well enough, and Art Coulter was about to clear when his stick broke, whereupon Schmidt batted the puck into the cords.

This quick tally, of course, was not at all to the Rangers' liking, and they went berserk trying to reach Brimsek. They did so, finally, after a beautiful passing advance made by Bill Carse and Alex Shibicky.

Carse advanced along the center alley and relayed to Shibicky on the left. The latter then flashed a pass back to the center to Mac Colville, who lifted the rubber into the cords in 8:56.

The New Yorkers mantained the offensive and tested Brimsek repeatedly, but with no success. Then occurred the fistic flare-up that threw the Garden into an uproar and resulted in the wholesale banishments. During the absence of most of the belligerents the Rangers led in the rushing and came close to breaking the tie when Clint Smith stick-handled his way to the Boston net, where he was stopped by Brimsek.

Shortly before the end of the period Babe Pratt and Jack Crawford became embroiled in a fight. They, too, received major vacations.

In the second period the Rangers were handicapped by a penalty called on Bryan Hextall. The Bruins could do nothing with this advantage, however, despite their heavy charges.

Then George Allen replaced Hextall in the penalty box and the Bruins attacked again. This strategy did not turn out to their liking, for Clint Smith and Ott Heller worked their way into Boston ice and gave the rubber to Lynn Patrick, who bounced it off Dit Clapper's skate into the cords in 10:02.

For the rest of the period the Patrickmen rushed determinedly, sending many drives at Brimsek's stick. The Boston goalie was alert, however, and turned back everything.

At the start of the third frame the Rangers kept up the same swift, aggressive pace, but they gradually had to give way to the desperate Bruins. Gardiner certainly had his work cut out for him during these closing minutes, but he rose to the occasion manfully.

Shore's Play Brilliant

Eddie Shore, whose work on the Boston backline was truly sensational, suffered most in the fist fighting. His nose was broken, but that did not keep from returning to the game. He was the spearhead of the third-period attack and almost beat Gardiner twice on short drives.

While Brimsek was out of the cage in the last minute, Neil Colville faced off against Shore deep in Ranger ice. The Ranger center got the puck and shot in one motion, and the disk slid the length of the rink into the empty cage. No score was allowed, however, because of an offside move by Murray Patrick.

Eighteen penalties in all were called, ten against the Rangers. The total time assessed against the New Yorkers was 32 minutes and against the visitors 28.

The teams will play the fifth game of the series tomorrow night in Boston. The sixth, if necessary, will be here on Saturday, and the seventh on Sunday in Boston.

In the second period, while the Rangers were conferring among themselves, Linesman Danny McFadyen faced the puck for Gordon Pettinger, who had no one playing against him. The Blue Shirts sprang out of their huddle to spill Pettinger just as he was about to shoot.

The line-up:

RANGERS (2)		BOSTON (1)
Gardiner	Goal	Brimsek
Coulter	Defense	Shore
M. Patrick	Defense	Portland
Watson	Center	Schmidt
Hextall	Wing	Bauer
Hiller	Wing	Dumart
Heller	Spare	Clapper
Shibicky	Spare	Getliffe
M. Colville	Spare	Weiland
N. Colville	Spare	Conacher
L. Patrick	Spare	Cowley
C. Smith	Spare	Pettinger
Pratt	Spare	Hollett
Molyneaux	Spare	Hamill
Allen	Spare	Hill
Carse	Spare	Crawford

AS RANGERS DEFEATED THE BRUINS LAST NIGHT

Times Wide World

Players engaging in fight which brought six major penalties in the first period of game

Times Wide World

Lynn Patrick (No. 9) scoring the winning goal in second session as Frank Brimsek, Boston goalie, goes to his knees in attempt to stop shot.

CANZONERI BEATEN ON POINTS BY BRINK

3,569 See Scranton Fighter Gain a Divided Verdict in Hippodrome Ring

By LOUIS EFFRAT

Tony Canzoneri's comeback campaign received a rude jolt last night at the Hippodrome. The former lightweight champion of the world dropped a ten-round decision to Irish Eddie Brink of Scranton, Pa., with the crowd of 3,569 persons divided on the merits of the verdict.

Canzoneri, slow of foot but still a crafty, ringwise battler, allowed his rugged though weak-punching opponent to take the play away from him in the closing rounds. While the former titleholder was content to bob, weave, duck and dance, Brink continued to toss punches, some of which landed and some of which did not.

Evidently Canzoneri's defensive tactics swayed the opinions of Referee Artie McGovern and Judge George Kelly, both of whom voted in favor of Brink. The other judge, Harold Barnes, ruled for Canzoneri.

Victor Shows Surprise

To most of the spectators who paid a net of $7,560.96, part of which was donated to New York and Brooklyn charities, the announcement of Brink's victory came as a surprise. Canzoneri himself was stunned by the news and Brink appeared to be equally as surprised.

There were times when Brink did have Canzoneri in trouble. The Pennsylvanian, who was beaten in an eight-rounder by Tony three weeks ago, staggered the former champion in the first, sixth and eighth rounds and in the tenth swarmed all over him with numerous though meaningless punches. Perhaps it was that fast finish that impressed the officials.

Canzoneri, on the other hand, landed enough heavy rights to make things interesting for Brink and the customers. Time and again he appeared to have Brink in straits, but each time Tony failed to follow his advantage, and while Brink forced the fighting Canzoneri devoted much time, probably too much time, in displaying his defensive skill.

12th Fight in Comeback

This was Canzoneri's twelfth start in his campaign that he hopes will enable him to return to the heights he once enjoyed. His comeback record now includes ten victories and two setbacks, questionable though last night's upset may be.

Brink weighed 139¾, two pounds less than Canzoneri.

Norment Quarles, 140, Richmond, Va., beat Al Roth, 139, The Bronx, in the bruising ten-round semi-final. It was a hard fight all the way.

Quarles, an accurate left-hooker, kept on top of his man and punished the Bronx boy with powerful body blows. Roth, for a time, blocked the punches with his arms, but the Virginian continued to throw the same punch and recorded his advantage in that manner.

Al Mancini, 124½, Providence (R. I.) featherweight, staged a strong finish to outpoint Benny (Baby) Yack, 121½, Toronto, in a keenly waged eight-round encounter. The decision did not meet with the wholehearted approval of the spectators, many of whom figured Yack, because of his early advantage, was entitled at least to a draw.

The speedy Canadian outboxed his opponent in the first three rounds, staggering him in the second with a heavy overhand right to the head. However, Mancini scored repeatedly at close range and in the eighth round opened a bad cut under Yack's left eye.

Monty Pignatore, 128, Bay Ridge, gained a six-round decision over Tommy Christie, 129½, the Bronx, in a brisk encounter. Pignatore punched fast and was the aggressor most of the time.

In the four-round opener Maxie Migdal, 170¾, the Bronx, registered a victory over Johnny Biele, 176½, Scotia, N. Y.

Bears Overwhelm Redskins by Record Score to Capture World Football Title

VERSATILE DISPLAY MARKS 73-0 ROUT

Bears' Ground Game, Passes and Defensive Power Crush Redskins Before 36,034

11 TOUCHDOWNS ARE MADE

Osmanski Races 68 Yards and Maniaci, Clark Go 42 Each —Interceptions Net Three

By ARTHUR J. DALEY
Special to THE NEW YORK TIMES.

WASHINGTON, Dec. 8 — The weather was perfect. So were the Bears. In the most fearsome display of power ever seen on any gridiron, the Monsters of the Midway won the Ed Thorp Memorial Trophy, which is symbolic of the world football championship, before 36,034 stunned and deriding fans in Griffith Stadium this balmy afternoon.

It being a Sunday, the Washington Humane Society had the day off. So the Bears had nothing to combat in the play-off except the Redskins, who were pretty feebie opposition indeed. Hence it was that the Chicago Bears scalped the Capital Indians, 73 to 0, the highest score in the history of the National Football League.

This was simply dreadful. The only question before the house was whether the Bears could score more points when they were on the offensive or when Washington was on the offensive. It was fairly close competition, Chicago with the ball outscoring the Redskins with the ball, seven touchdowns to four.

Scoring Time Shaved

Before fifty-six seconds had passed the Bears had a tally. Then, when the second half began, they cut that time down, registering another marker in fifty-four seconds. It probably is just as well that the football rules permit only two halves to a game or else George Halas's young men would have been down to fractions of seconds.

There never was anything quite like this. Three weeks ago the Redskins edged out the Bears, 7 to 3. Today it was something else again. Chicago was a perfect football team that played football of such exquisite class that Washington could not have won with a brick wall instead of a line and howitzers instead of backs. The Bears would have battered down everything.

By the time the second half began the Redskins showed a marked improvement. Their defense against points after touchdown had reached such perfection that four out of seven were missed. Washington was the unlucky outfit today. It had the misfortune to have to face a team that could have beaten the other nine elevens in the league just as badly.

Blocking Is Accurate

This was football at its very best. The Bears had the timing for their quick-opening plays down to the hundredth of a second. They riddled the Redskins at will with the overwhelming power of their ground game, rocked them with their infrequent passes and smothered them with their defensive power. The blocking was fiendishly accurate and it almost was a physical impossibility for them to make a mistake.

The Bears registered three touchdowns in the first period, one in the second, four in the third and three in the last. Halas used every eligible man on his squad, thirty-three of them, and fifteen had a share of the scoring. It even reached such a stage that the Bears passed for one point after touchdown by way of variety and by way of adding to Washington's humiliation.

Halas used Sid Luckman, an Old Blue from Columbia, as his first-half quarterback, and no field general ever called plays more artistically or engineered a touchdown parade in more letter-perfect fashion. But the Lion sat out the second half and still the mastodons from the Midwest rolled.

Ray Flaherty's young men were physically in the game, but that was all. After Bill Osmanski had romped 68 yards for the first touchdown, the 'Skins reached the Bear 26, only to have Bob Masterson's 32-yard field-goal effort fail. That was a blow from which George Preston Marshall's lads never recovered. Had they scored, it might have been different.

Go Downhill Speedily

But when they missed they wound up with a minus 10 yards for their first seven passes and went speedily downhill the rest of the way. After a while that descent began to resemble a snowball on the way, picking up power and speed as it heads toward the valley.

The first touchdown was a 75-yard zip to a score. George McAfee picked up 7 yards and then Osmanski, cutting inside Washington's right tackle, went 68 yards more. The tip-off on the Bears came when George Wilson erased two men with the same block to clear the way for the counter.

Then the Bears rolled 80 yards in seventeen plays, the pay-off being Luckman's quarterback sneak from the six-inch line. A moment later Joe Maniaci, the old Fordham Flash, streaked 42 yards for another counter. Jack Manders, Bob Snyder and Phil Martinovich added the extra points and it was 21 to 0.

Redskin fans who had watched their heroes win their first seven games of the league season could not believe their eyes. Yet even they were to become convinced that they were watching one of the greatest football teams of all time in action, a team that had everything.

The Bears reached the 16 in the second quarter and fumbled. Washington made a gesture by going 63 yards to the 18 on ten successive passes, only to lose the ball on downs. The Chicagoans went 56 more to the 24 but Martinovich failed on a field goal try.

Ray Nolting boomed through with one of the eight Bear pass interceptions and the victors were off to the races. Ground plays advanced only 26 yards, so Luckman flipped a 30-yarder to Ken Kavanaugh in the end zone, the freshman from Louisiana State plucking the ball from the grasp of two defenders for another counter. Snyder converted.

The third quarter saw the Redskins give up the ghost. They attempted a pass from the 19, but Hampton Pool, an end, intercepted Sammy Baugh's lateral flick to Jimmy Johnston on the 16 for a marker. Then the Capital crew tried a fourth-down pass from their 33. It was batted down.

So the Bears took over. Nolting gained 10 yards. But he was just warming up. On the next play he burst 23 yards through the middle, feinted Baugh into the middle of the Potomac on the 8 and went across standing up. Dick Plasman missed the conversion, which promptly labeled him an absolute outcast.

Now Stydahar's Turn

Washington took over again and McAfee intercepted a Roy Zimmerman pass for 35 yards of gorgeous broken-field running for a touchdown. It then was Joe Stydahar's turn and he split the bars with a placement.

The Redskins made an effort to score, reaching the 16 only to lose the ball on downs. When the Bears punted Washington assumed the offensive on its 37. A bad pass from center was recovered on the 21 and Zimmerman's pass was intercepted by Bulldog Turner on the 30. He scored, thanks to a block by Pool. Maniaci's placement was blocked and it was 54 to 0.

The league's champions rumbled 74 yards for their next touchdown in the fourth quarter, Harry Clark going 42 yards on a double reverse for the tally. On this he feinted Frank Filchock into Chesapeake Bay. Gary Famiglietti was elected as the point converter, but failed.

The hapless Redskins later saw Filchock fumble in the shadow of his goal posts. Jack Torrance, the reformed shot-put world record-holder, fell on the ball on the 2. He almost crushed the air out of the ball when his 300 pounds landed on it. So Famiglietti burst across on a quick opener. The crusher was a Saul Sherman-Maniaci pass in the end zone for the extra point.

The last touchdown resulted from a 52-yard drive that was culminated by a 1-yard dance by Clark through the middle. He crossed standing up. A Snyder-Maniaci conversion pass missed. And Maniaci intercepted again just as the Redskins gave promise of threatening.

There was no Redskin hero outside of Flaherty, who had to sit on the bench and absorb it all, too much a beating for so fine a gentleman and coach. The Bears had thirty-three heroes. Luckman, Nolting, McAfee, Osmanski and Maniaci in the backfield were outstanding. So were Lee Artoe, Stydahar, Danny Fortmann, Turner and Plasman in the line.

The day was gorgeous. The crowd was representative, with high government officials scattered throughout the stands. Everything was under the control of the Magnificent Marshall, except the Bears.

At the end the Redskin band played "Should Auld Acquaintance Be Forgot?" If said acquaintance is the Chicago Bears, it should be forgot immediately. At the moment the Bears are the greatest football team of all time.

The line-up:

BEARS (73)		REDSKINS (0)
Nowaskey	L. E.	Masterson
Stydahar	L. T.	Wilkin
Fortmann	L. G.	Farman
Turner	C.	Titchenal
Musso	R. G.	Slivinski
Artoe	R. T.	Barber
Wilson	R. E.	Malone
Luckman	Q. B.	Krause
Nolting	L. H.	Baugh
McAfee	R. H.	Justice
Osmanski	F. B.	Johnston

SCORE BY PERIODS

Bears	21	7	26	19—73
Redskins	0	0	0	0—0

Touchdowns—Clark 2, Osmanski, Luckman, Maniaci, Kavanaugh, Nolting, Pool, McAfee, Turner, Famiglietti. Points after touchdown—Manders, Snyder 2, Martinovich, Plasman, Stydahar (placements), Maniaci (pass from Sherman).

SUBSTITUTES

Bears Ends: Siegal, Manske, Plasman, Pool, Kavanaugh. Tackles: Mihal, Kolman, Torrance. Guards: Martinovich, Forte, Baisi. Centers: Bausch, Chesney. Backs: Famiglietti, Clark, Manders, Maniaci, Snyder, Sherman, Masterson, Swisher, McLean.

Redskins — Ends: McChesney, Sanford, Millner. Tackles: Fisher, Russell. Guards: Stralka, Shugart. Centers: Andrako, Parks. Backs: Pinckert, Morgan, Seymour, Zimmerman, Filchock, Moore, Todd, Hare, Hoffman, Farkas, Meade.

Referee—William Friesell, Princeton. Umpire—Harry Robb, Penn State. Linesman—Irving Kupcinet, North Dakota. Field judge—Fred Young, Illinois Wesleyan. Time of periods—15 minutes.

Osmanski away on his 68-yard gallop for a touchdown in the first minute of the contest. No. 13 is Justice and No. 31 Johnston, both of Washington.

Times Wide World and Associated Press

PRO FOOTBALL SET ATTENDANCE MARK

55 National League Contests Drew 1,295,217 This Year, Bettering 1939 Total

Despite a severe slump by two clubs, the National Football League set an attendance record during the 1940 season, a survey by The United Press showed yesterday.

An unofficial total of 1,295,217 fans saw fifty-five games this year. The official figure for 1939 was 1,280,332, the previous record high.

The Detroit Lions, whose home attendance in the early games was kept down because of the city's interest in the world series, suffered the worst slump in the league, dropping from 185,061 spectators for six home games in 1939 to 122,282 for six this year.

The Philadelphia Eagles, who won only one game of eleven, played to only 73,841 fans at five home games, compared with 110,334 for the same number a year ago.

The Giants led the league in attendance, though they finished third in the Eastern division. They played to 247,642 spectators in seven games against 233,440 for six a year ago. Pittsburgh, Washington and Brooklyn made the most sensational gains of the year.

The best attractions on the road were the Chicago Bears, who drew 165,921 persons to six games away from home.

DRAFT PLAN ADOPTED BY AMERICAN LEAGUE

Pro Football Circuit Will Seek Fifty College Stars

Directors of the American Professional Football League, in closing their two-day meeting at the Hotel New Yorker yesterday, voted to draft fifty outstanding 1940 college stars.

Deeming it advisable to seek new talent in the name of the league rather than give each of the six clubs exclusive rights to dicker with certain players, the executives empowered President W. D. Griffith to send questionnaires to the selected men. The players thus will have an opportunity to state which teams they prefer to join if they desire to enter the league.

Tommy Harmon, Michigan's backfield ace, is among the topnotchers who will be approached by American League representatives. Other backs include Johnny Kimbrough, Texas Aggies; George Franck, Minnesota, and Len Eshmont, Fordham. Among the linemen listed are Paul Severin, North Carolina; Erwin (Buddy) Elrod, Mississippi State, and Hugh Barber, Columbia, ends; Nick Drahos, Cornell, and Johnny Kuzman, Fordham, tackles; Bob Suffridge, Tennessee, and Tom Gallagher, Columbia, guards, and Chet Gladchuk, Boston College, center.

RICHMOND ARROWS ON TOP

Down Chicago Indians, 21-20, on Bomba's Kick—Hutson Stars

MEMPHIS, Tenn., Dec. 8 (AP)—Don Bomba's unerring toe, which has not missed a try for point after touchdown all season, gave the Richmond Arrows a 21-to-20 victory over the Chicago Indians before 7,000 fans today.

Don Hutson, Green Bay Packer end, scored two Indian touchdowns, one 80 yards on a pass from Parker Hall of the Cleveland Rams, with the game less than a minute old, and the other on a 32-yard pass in the second half from Gaylon Smith, former Southwestern back loaned by the Rams for a home-town appearance. The former Alabama end also kicked two extra points.

Hall passed to Smith for a 33-yard touchdown in the third period, but Smith muffed the kick for the extra point.

Bears-Redskins Game Statistics

	1ST HALF		2D HALF		TOTAL	
	Bears.	Redskins.	Bears.	Redskins.	Bears.	Redskins.
First downs	11	9	6	9	17	18
Yards gained rushing	241	31	131	—28	372	3
Forward passes	4	27	4	22	8	49
Forwards completed	3	10	3	11	6	21
Yards gained, forwards	89	162	31	67	120	229
Forwards intercepted by	3	0	5	0	8	0
Number of punts	1	2	1	1	2	3
*Aver. dist. of punts, yards	53	81	51	67	52	49
Runback of punts, yards	18	6	9	0	27	6
Fumbles	4	1	0	4	4	5
Own fumbles recovered	3	1	0	3	3	4
Penalties	0	2	3	5	3	7
Yards lost, penalties	0	10	35	55	35	65

*From point where ball was kicked.

Section 5 SPORTS **The New York Times.** SPORTS Section 5

S Copyright, 1941, by The New York Times Company. SUNDAY, JUNE 8, 1941. L+ S

WHIRLAWAY, 1 TO 4, WINS BELMONT STAKES BY 3 LENGTHS; WOOD TAKES U. S. OPEN TITLE WITH 284; DODGERS BOW, 8-3

VICTOR BY 3 SHOTS

Wood Closes With a 70, Birdie 3 on Last Hole, to Win Links Title

SHUTE, 287, IS RUNNER-UP

Bulla and Hogan Tie for Third at 289 in U.S. Open—10,000 See Finish at Fort Worth

By WILLIAM D. RICHARDSON

Special to THE NEW YORK TIMES.

FORT WORTH, Texas, June 7—The gods of golf, so unkind to Craig Wood in the past, are now killing him with kindness.

Rebuffed more times than almost any other player in the game's history, losing both the British and American opens in play-offs and the P. G. A. in extra holes, the big, affable, 39-year-old Blond Bomber from the Winged Foot Club today had his vengeance as well as his just reward.

In a blistering drive down the final stretches of the still soggy fairways of the Colonial Club, trailed by a large portion of the 10,000 spectators who wilted in the sweltering heat, Wood won the coveted national open championship cup to bid farewell to the "always a bridesmaid, but never a bride" adage that has been tagged on him.

Coming down the last mile of the long, hard tortuous journey—one that crushes hopes and kills aspirations—with his goal in sight unless evil luck happened to overtake him, as it has so often in the past, Wood hewed straight and true to the line to finish with a par 70 that made his 72-hole total 284.

Only One Man to Beat

Wood had only one man to beat as he came closer and closer to the finish of his round and it happened to be the man who defeated him in the play-off of the 1933 British open—modest Denny Shute who, like Wood, began as an amateur. Shute was already in with a score of 287, best up to that point.

By overcoming a few moments of shakiness that hit him on the first nine of the last round, Wood virtually had the championship won when he teed off to play the last hole. Even a 6 there would have given him a tie, but after placing his drive in the middle of the fairway, Craig pitched his second shot twenty feet or so from the pin, practically hole high, and then, with a tremendous crowd looking on, thrilled the gallery with a champion's finish, rolling the putt into the cup for a birdie 3 that won the title by three strokes.

Big Johnny Bulla, North Carolina product who wings his way around the country promoting golf ball sales for a big drug store chain, had 289 to tie for third with Ben Hogan. Bulla was one of the "bad" boys of last year's championship—one of those who had the wrath of the United States Golf Association brought down on them for "beating the starter's gun" in the last round.

Runyan and Barron Tied

Two strokes behind them came two more Westchester district pros, Paul Runyan, clever little Metropolis Club artist who violates many of the game's tenets and yet gets there in the end, and sturdy Herman Barron of Fenway.

They, in turn, were trailed by a trio consisting of Gene Sarazen, E. J. (Dutch) Harrison and Harold (Jug) McSpaden. Their count was 294. Then came Dick Metz, one of Wood's playing partners; Ed Dudley and Lloyd Mangrum, with 295; Horton Smith, Henry Ransom, a local pro, Sam Snead, and Harry Todd, Dallas amateur, bracketed at 296; Lawson Little, the dethroned champion, and Byron Nelson, his predecessor, with 297; Vic Ghezzi, Deal (N. J.) ace, with 298, and Gene Kunes, one-time Canadian open champion, with 299.

By the time the final round got under way this typical Texas June afternoon when the thermometer stood at 95 and the heat was tempered by only a breath of wind, the field had narrowed down to four players, with a few others having outside chances.

First was Wood, who had shaken the dust off his heels in the faces of his rivals with his 70 in the morning. He was 214 after fifty-four holes.

Runyan and Shute came next, tied at 216; Bulla was 218 and Sarazen, Mangrum and Hogan were grouped at 219, the last mentioned having played the course in 68, best score of the tourney, to redeem himself. With the exception of Runyan and Shute and perhaps Bulla, the chances of none of these to overtake Wood were good.

Runyan remained a candidate for nine holes, but then dropped back, but Shute, a resolute golfer who

Continued on Page Six

NEW GOLF CHAMPION

Craig Wood

Times Wide World

YANKS' 5 IN NINTH HALT BROWNS, 11-7

Victors Withstand St. Louis Rally for 3 in the Eighth—Keller Hits 4-Run Homer

By JAMES P. DAWSON

Special to THE NEW YORK TIMES.

ST. LOUIS, June 7—It took severe measures, along with a fifteen-hit blistering of five hurlers and two hours and forty-one minutes for the Yankees to conquer the lowly Browns at Sportsman's Park today and escape a headlong dive into the second division.

Propelled into a five-run lead by Charley Keller's home run with the bases full in the third inning, the McCarthymen saw this margin whittled away as Luke Sewell's new charges drove Lefty Vernon Gomez and Spud Chandler to shelter. The Browns dashed to the front with a three-run assault in the eighth, but the Yanks came through with a five-run rally in the ninth before they snapped a three-game losing streak. The score was 11 to 7.

The only difference between the Yankee pitching and that of the Browns was that Joe McCarthy used fewer hurlers. The Yankee skipper found a stop-gap in Charley Stanceu, who gained the victory. The balance of power, as generally happens in such exhibitions of mediocrity, swung on the New York attack, as Bob Muncrief, Jack Kramer, George Caster, Johnny Allen and Bill Trotter discovered to their chagrin.

Gomez Routed in Fifth

Gomez lasted until the fifth, when he was removed because he was wild. He departed while the Browns were threatening to nullify the five-run salvo featured by Keller's eighth homer of the season, which shoved Muncrief out of the box in the third.

Chandler saved the day until the eighth, when the Browns charged to the front by one run. Walter Judnich hit a pinch homer with one aboard, tying the score, and another run came in as bunts refused to roll foul, St. Louis runners slid safely under infield throws and ran the bases under protection of an outfield fly.

Kramer checked the Yanks until removed for a pinch hitter in the fifth, and Caster turned them back through three more innings. Allen came out of the bull-pen after Judnich swung, with such damaging effect, for Caster in the eighth, and the fun began all over again. Only this time the Yanks had exclusive rights.

Red Rolfe's greeting to Allen, a former team-mate, was a single. Tommy Henrich doubled and raced

Continued on Page Four

REDS TOP BROOKLYN

6 Unearned Runs in 8th Follow Reese's Error, 3 on Lombardi Homer

WALTERS SENDS 2 ACROSS

Ripple, Reiser Hit for Circuit—Dodgers Fall to Second, Trail Cards Half Game

By ROSCOE McGOWEN

Developing knocks at crucial moments yesterday, the Dodger pennant machine fell apart at Ebbets Field and Brooklyn lost to the Reds, 8—3, tumbling again into second place in the National League, one-half game behind the Cardinals.

Dozens of the 17,037 Flatbush fans greeted Peewee Reese with a chorus of Bronx cheers when he came to bat in the ninth inning, which gives you a hint of what happened.

An error by the brilliant young shortstop in the eighth inning on what should have proved the third out opened the gates for the world champions to score six unearned runs off Luke (Hot Potato) Hamlin. The big blow of the frame, after the misplay, was Cyrano Lombardi's sixth home run of the campaign with two mates aboard, a wallop deep into the lower left-field stands.

Cincinnati counted only one earned run. That came in the third inning on Jimmy Ripple's first round-tripper of the year, across Bedford Avenue.

Bucky Walters, who socked a two-run double off Newell Kimball in the devastating eighth, hung up his sixth pitching victory against four setbacks, while Hamlin was debited with his second loss against three successes.

"Terrible" to Rival Chiefs

It was generally, as the two big bosses of the Reds and Dodgers, Warren Giles and Larry MacPhail, agreed afterward, a "terrible ball game" (although Giles said it with a pleased smile).

Pete Reiser sent the Dodgers out front in the first inning when he walloped his fifth homer of the season past Bedford Avenue after two were out. The ball bounced into a parking lot and a small boy was observed beating an attendant to it.

In the second the Reds tied the score because of an error by the ailing Cookie Lavagetto. With two away, Cookie fumbled a grounder by Lombardi, who got all the way around on singles by Jimmy Gleeson and Eddie Joost.

Ripple's homer put the Reds one up, but the Dodgers came back in the fourth to tie matters on Reiser's double to left center and Dolph Camilli's line single to right.

The deadlock held until the seventh, when the Reds' defense went haywire, with the exception of Ripple, who robbed Lew Riggs of a hit with a diving, rolling catch of the former Red's low liner.

Lombardi Drops Ball

Jimmy Wasdell, playing in place of Muscles Medwick, who was ill, singled to center and Lonnie Frey booted a double-play ball hit by Dixie Walker. Mickey Owen walked and Hamlin topped a ball to the right of the mound for what looked like a double-play via the plate.

However, Lombardi, taking Walters's throw, dropped the ball, permitting Wasdell to score and put the Dodgers 1 up. However, this golden opportunity was wasted when Reese looked at a third strike and Billy Herman fouled to Lombardi.

The Reds' eighth was a nightmare for Manager Leo Durocher and the

Continued on Page Four

Major League Baseball

National League

YESTERDAY'S RESULTS

St. Louis 11, New York 3.
Cincinnati 8, Brooklyn 3.
Philadelphia 2, Pittsburgh 0.
Chicago 5, Boston 1.

STANDING OF THE CLUBS

	St. Louis	Brooklyn	New York	Cincinnati	Chicago	Pittsburgh	Boston	Phila'phia	Won	Lost	Percentage	Games Behind
St. L.	—	3	5	6	5	8	4	3	34	14	.708	—
Bklyn	4	—	6	5	3	1	5	9	33	14	.702	½
N. Y.	0	4	—	3	5	1	6	3	22	22	.500	10
Cincin.	3	2	4	—	5	5	3	1	23	25	.479	11
Chic	2	3	0	4	—	3	3	5	20	24	.455	12
Pitts.	0	2	5	2	3	—	2	3	17	23	.425	13
Boston	4	0	1	1	1	2	—	6	15	27	.357	16
Phila	1	0	1	4	2	3	4	—	15	30	.333	17½
Lost	14	14	22	25	24	23	27	30	—	—		

GAMES TODAY

St. Louis at New York (2, 2 P. M.).
Cincinnati at Brooklyn (2:30 P. M.).
Chicago at Boston (2).
Pittsburgh at Philadelphia (2).

American League

YESTERDAY'S RESULTS

New York 11, St. Louis 7.
Cleveland 6, Philadelphia 2.
Chicago 5, Boston 4.
Detroit 10, Washington 6.

STANDING OF THE CLUBS

	Cleveland	Chicago	Boston	New York	Detroit	Phila'phia	St. Louis	Wash'gton	Won	Lost	Percentage	Games Behind
Cleve.	—	3	5	3	6	5	6	4	32	20	.615	—
Chic	4	—	2	3	5	2	6	6	28	20	.583	2
Boston	1	3	—	4	5	6	2	3	24	20	.545	4
N. Y.	4	2	4	—	2	3	5	6	26	22	.542	4
Detroit	4	3	4	5	—	5	4	2	27	23	.540	4
Phila.	3	4	2	3	0	—	4	8	24	24	.500	6
St. L.	3	2	1	2	1	2	—	5	16	30	.348	13
Wash.	1	3	2	2	4	1	3	—	16	34	.320	15
Lost	20	20	20	22	23	24	30	34	—	—		

GAMES TODAY

New York at St. Louis (2).
Philadelphia at Cleveland (2).
Boston at Chicago (2).
Washington at Detroit.

Odds-On Favorite on His Way to Victory in the Rich Belmont Stakes

Whirlaway (right) leading Robert Morris (center) and Itabo around the final turn in mile-and-a-half event. Associated Press

Trainer Ben Jones holding the chestnut colt after the race yesterday. Eddie Arcaro is the jockey

Times Wide World

19 HITS BY ST. LOUIS CRUSH GIANTS, 11-3

Cards Regain League Lead—Brown, Triplett and Terry Moore Get 4 Blows Each

By JOHN DREBINGER

The Giants made a noble effort at the Polo Grounds yesterday to cut some sort of a figure in the National League's currently eye-dazzling pennant race, but unhappily they made about as much impression as a man sticking his head into a high-powered electric fan.

In fact, the Cardinals virtually slashed Colonel Bill Terry's intrepid though inept troops to ribbons as they thrashed the New Yorkers, 11 to 3, in the opening clash of a four-game series before 8,507 equally helpless onlookers.

The victory, coupled with the Dodgers' defeat at the hands of the Reds in Brooklyn, sent Billy Southworth's amazingly fast-moving St. Louisans back into the pennant lead again by half a length.

Crespi Slams Homer

Nineteen hits off four pitchers, plus three stumbling errors afield, had the fleet footed Cardinals streaking around the bases as if they were competing in a college relay carnival. Frank (Creepy) Crespi, who really doesn't creep, but spends most of his time flying over the ground, touched off the explosion with a second inning home run.

But that was as nothing compared to what some of the others did. Jimmy Brown, Coaker Triplett and Terry Moore each raked the New York hurling for four singles, while Enos Slaughter contributed a triple and a single and stolid Gus Mancuso weighed in with two singles.

Cliff Melton stood it for two rounds, retiring without protest after the Cards had clubbed him for a cluster of four runs. The opening shot of this outburst was the Crespi homer into the upper left tier.

Adams Also Pounded

Long Cliff was followed by Ace Adams, who went down for three more in the fourth, a round which seemed to see Ace attacked from all sides, what with the Cards smacking him for four singles, while two of his colleagues, Burgess Whitehead and Morris Aronovich, made his lot no easier with errors.

John Wittig was flattened for three more runs in the sixth, the Slaughter triple providing the high spot of this attack, and in the ninth Walter Brown went down for one more.

About the only consolation the Giants drew from the entire afternoon was the fact that Southworth's starting pitcher did not survive the day either. In fact, Sam Nahem, the Brooklyn barrister, was chased back to his law books in less than two rounds. A towering triple to the Giants' bull-pen by Babe Young gave the Terrymen their first tally in the first inning, and when three singles greeted Nahem in the second the fellow was out.

Though the Giants gathered two more runs from this inviting start, Ernie White stopped them dead the remainder of the afternoon. They picked up only four scattered singles off the young lefthander, who thus received credit for his second victory. The defeat, charged to Melton, was Cliff's fourth to match his four victories.

Thus the Giants settled down to the .500 mark, though nightfall still

Continued on Page Four

Bogrow Triumphs in N.Y.A.C. 440; Campbell Is Spiked on Last Turn

N. Y. U. Star Wins by Three Yards at Club's 146th Games—Burrowes Is Beaten in Comeback Effort—Branch Scores

By ARTHUR DALEY

Experience counts even in a handicap race. Harold Bogrow of N. Y. U., steering clear of traffic jams, ran a carefully judged race to win the 440-yard test that featured the 146th track and field games of the New York A. C. before a gathering of 5,000 at picturesque Travers Island yesterday.

This was an event that was rich in promise after both Bogrow and Jack Campbell of Fordham had survived the preliminary heats. But in the final Campbell made his bid in the back stretch and tried to cut it too fine.

He stuck as close to the pole as he could and just as the field of eight hit the final turn they crowded in together, and Campbell was in the middle of the pack.

Campbell Is Spiked

The Ram sophomore, winner of the intercollegiate 440-yard championship just a week ago yesterday, was hit by one runner on his left and by another on his right, pinched between the pair of them. He was spiked on a knee, of all places, and forced to break stride.

The race was over then. Bogrow, moving up steadily, took command at the head of the home stretch and won by three yards in 0:49.4 from a couple of N. Y. U. teammates, Frank Cotter, off 14 yards, and Walter Welsch, off 16. Campbell was fifth in 0:50.9.

The unveiling of Ed Burrowes, Princeton's hard-luck half-miler, was not too great a success. The brilliant junior, successively crippled by shin splints and a punctured lung, made his first competitive appearance in six weeks and finished seventh in the 880-yard handicap.

He was obviously short of work as he came on from scratch in a twenty-eight-man field to sixth in the back stretch. But he could climb no further. The better-conditioned Frank Leary of Fordham, just ahead of Burrowes before the final turn, was able to pull up to third. However, before the son of Old Nassau dons his New York A. C. uniform for the national A. A. U. championships at Philadelphia on June 28 and 29 he should be back in the points.

Fordham Freshman Wins

The winner of this race was Joe Nowicki, Fordham freshman, who caught the handicapper unaware by doing a very sound 1:54 off thirty yards. Lou Cantor of City College,

Continued on Page Two

BUDGE VANQUISHES TILDEN, 7-5, 6-2, 6-0

Perry Tops Skeen in 4 Sets—Victors Meet for World Pro Title Today

By ALLISON DANZIG

Five years ago J. Donald Budge and Frederick J. Perry met in the final of the national amateur tennis championship at Forest Hills, with victory going to the Briton after he had trailed at 3—5 in the fifth set.

This afternoon these two former world amateur champions, now rivals for supremacy in the professional ranks, will face each other again in the stadium of the West Side Tennis Club. To the winner will be awarded the premier honors of

Continued on Page Five

Mrs. Leichner's Rally Beats Mrs. Whitehead By 4 and 3 in Metropolitan Links Final

By LINCOLN A. WERDEN

Special to THE NEW YORK TIMES.

MAMARONECK, N. Y., June 7—A remarkable rally by Mrs. Charles Leichner, the former Sylva Annenberg of Fresh Meadow, brought her the women's metropolitan golf championship at the Quaker Ridge club today.

Mrs. Leichner, 4 down at the end of the initial eighteen holes this morning, proceeded to win eight of the fifteen that the match required in the afternoon and beat Mrs. Charles Whitehead, New Jersey champion, by 4 and 3.

In some ways this final was one of the most unusual in this tourney. Although Mrs. Leichner had eliminated Miss Maureen Orcutt, the defending champion, yesterday, her chances were not considered good when the morning half was completed.

Being 4 down to the former Laddie Irwin, one of the long hitters of the younger players, was a mean handicap, particularly on this testing course in the hot sun. But one of Mrs. Leichner's adages in her fine match play career has been, "never consider a match over until the final putt is holed."

She certainly proved the wisdom of that today. A remarkable putting touch—she had four one-putt greens—won for her, in the final analysis. But it took more than the mechanical hitting a golf ball to overcome a lead of four holes, especially since Mrs. Leichner's game was none too steady in the early round. She had a 90 this morning.

Mrs. Whitehead did not win a hole during her rival's afternoon spurt; in fact, the last hole she won was the fifteenth this morning.

Mrs. Leichner won four of the

Continued on Page Six

ROBERT MORRIS 2D

30,801 See Whirlaway Gain Triple Crown in $52,270 Belmont

YANKEE CHANCE IS THIRD

Calumet Scores Stake Double as Some Chance Captures National Stallion

By BRYAN FIELD

Whirlaway yesterday did the expected in his own proud manner when he won the seventy-third Belmont Stakes before 30,801 persons on the final afternoon of a record-breaking Belmont Park meeting. The chestnut colt from the Calumet Farm raced through the stretch so easily that he had his ears pricking, and he also had that mightiest triple crown tilted jauntily on his handsome forelock.

When he finished the historic mile and a half run that grossed $52,270 in 2:31 flat over a fast track, the son of Blenheim II and Dustwhirl became the fifth horse in American racing history to capture the Kentucky Derby, Preakness and Belmont Stakes.

Warren Wright, owner of Whirlaway and the Calumet Farm, had to choose between seeing his son or his horse, and of course he chose to go to his boy's graduation in the West. Yet he heard by radio about one of Calumet's most successful days at any track, since his juvenile colt, Some Chance, captured the $15,640 National Stallion Stakes, which had its twenty-ninth running.

Whirlaway Earns $39,770

Thus the Calumet winning streak at Belmont zoomed to its climax, Mr. Wright's colors having earlier been first in the Juvenile and Acorn Stakes as well as in many lesser races. Whirlaway added $39,770 to his previous earnings of $196,341 and Some Chance's score was worth $12,140. Calumet was far and away the leading money-winning establishment of the meeting, but even such formidable figures are modest in comparison to the astronomical betting totals.

The betting on eight races and the daily double totaled $1,482,116, bringing the total for the twenty-four days to $22,311,349, for an average of more than $900,000 daily to smash all American records. Fred Buck of the State Tax Commission believes this per diem average higher than anywhere else in the world, but complete statistics are not available.

As for Whirlaway, he just was so good that he made ducks and drakes of his opposition. Robert Morris was second, beaten three lengths, and five lengths before Yankee Chance. Itabo trailed. The winner was a standout 1-to-4 favorite and returned only $2.50 and $2.10, there being no show betting.

Perhaps the best way to describe the manner in which Whirlaway dominated the field is to tell what Eddie Arcaro, the winning jockey, did in the race, and what he said about it. Before a half mile had been run Arcaro startled thousands by suddenly sending Whirlaway dashing to the front, a reversal of riding tactics from all of Whirlaway's previous races. It looked revolutionary from the stands, and indeed it was, for subsequently it was learned that the boy had had waiting orders from Trainer Ben Jones.

Pace Too Slow for Arcaro

But this is what happened, as Arcaro tells it: "I was last with Whirlaway going away and I was going to stay last for awhile. But at the mile post (a mile to go), there was no pace. It was very slow. So I yelled to those other jocks: 'I'm leaving.'"

It was then that the watchers in the stand saw Whirlaway shoot to the front. He dashed far ahead in a twinkling.

Through the backstretch Whirlaway opened six or eight lengths. Robert Morris, Itabo and Yankee Chance followed in Indian file.

"Would Whirlaway shoot his bolt? Had he got away from Arcaro? Was his headstrong trait coming out in a different way?" All of these questions were asked and unanswered as the race went on.

The big challenge, and the only one of the race, came from the far turn to the head of the stretch. There Alfred Robertson moved forward with Robert Morris. Robert Morris cut that big lead, but he never made Arcaro go to a drive nor did Eddie ever make use of the whip.

Here's just what that challenge amounted to, in Robertson's words after the finish: "I though we had a chance when I moved, but it was no use." That "no use," just about describes it. Coming into the

Continued on Page Eight

WHIRLAWAY FIRST IN $52,270 BELMONT

Continued From Page One

stretch Whirlaway went a little wide. Arcaro said later that he permitted this, having no apprehension of any kind.

Robert Morris went just about as wide and it was the same story, a chase through the stretch with Whirlaway winning easily. The only change in the last quarter was that Yankee Chance went past Itabo and landed third money.

Meanwhile Whirlaway was safely home with the triple crown safely his. Before him only Sir Barton, Gallant Fox, Omaha and War Admiral completed the sweep of Derby, Preakness and Belmont.

Following the finish, there was the usual presentation, but the flowers were gardenias. Apparently it is getting to be the custom for many to rush to snatch a flower from the blanket. There was a touch of irony in that one of the group that rushed forward appeared to be Wendell Eads, the Calumet Farm's regular jockey.

In the National Stallion, Arcaro was up on Some Chance, so that the lad who hails from Covington, Ky., got a double that assured him of third place in the Belmont jockey standing with sixteen winners. The leader was Conn McCreary, who scored aboard Nearsight to boost his total to twenty. Alfred Robertson, who triumphed on Smiles, was right behind with nineteen.

$60,952 Bet on Double

The record Memorial Day figures were not expected to be surpassed and the daily double wagering confirmed this. The double handle was $60,952 for a pay-off of $34.30. There were 1,596 winning tickets, Chuckatuck and Kingfisher being the two winners.

The jumping event, which went to Chuckatuck, saw one of the closest finishes of the meeting, the Log Cabin Stud representative just making it by a head. J. Penrod was the winning rider and he and his horse seemed overtaken by the favorite a furlong out, but the final drive saw Chuckatuck and Penrod prevail at $8.50.

When Naruna, the choice, ran second in Thomas Hitchcock's famous green colors it marked just about the leanest Belmont season in years for the establishment which frequently has led the list. Mr. Hitchcock expects to recoup at Delaware Park, where the jumping will begin on Wednesday.

Mr. and Mrs. Chester Dane were among the many who entertained, Mrs. Dane being the former Eunice Howard. Her father, Colonel Maxwell Howard, saw the race from his car parked on the lawn.

Kingfisher Shows Way

Several members of the Jockey Club battled things out in the second, where Kingfisher eventually won. C. V. Whitney, owner of Kingfisher, is a member, and so are Arnold Hanger, whose Big Stakes ran second; Joseph E. Widener, whose Grasshopper II ran third, and Mr. Wright, whose Blenweed got fourth. Kingfisher returned $9.20 when he made the grade in 1:12 3-5.

Aqueduct's jumping course was cut up in the reconstruction. It has only lately been reseeded, and the sod may be solid enough for use in the Fall. For the present there will be only seven races, as is the case at Empire City and Jamaica, which do not have steeplechase courses.

Winning Belmont Park tickets not already cashed will be redeemed at Window 63 tomorrow and Tuesday at Aqueduct. Otherwise holders of winning tickets will have to go to Belmont's city office to get them cashed.

The Belmont Cup, which now is the trophy presented annually for the Belmont Stakes, first came into the Belmont family in 1869. That year it was won by Fenian, colorbearer for the first August Belmont. After the death of Major August Belmont, long the chairman of the Jockey Club, the cup was given to the Westchester Racing Association to be a perpetual trophy.

A DRIVING FINISH IN THE NATIONAL STALLION STAKES

Some Chance (nearer camera) beating Eternal Bull in juvenile feature at Belmont Park yesterday

Times Wide World

Sports of the Times

Reg. U. S. Pat. Off.

By JOHN KIERAN

A Big Day at Belmont

It was hot, sweltering. Outside the gates at Belmont the customary philanthropists were hawking their tip sheets, offering a future fortune for fifty cents in hand, or even a quarter in hand. Just buy their marked cards and a fortune was as good as ready for collection inside the gates, or so the philanthropic hawkers insisted, but the hurrying thousands scurried by, paying little attention to the loud-voiced philanthropists. Maybe the racegoers were not interested in making money.

Watching the Big Board

While most of the visitors at Belmont were studying form charts, looking over the horses in the paddock or investing at the mutuel windows, this innocent bystander was gazing in awe at the big tote board in the infield. How those figures do mount up!

It was somewhat startling to see $31,000 bet on one horse in a minor race, practically all of it wagered by persons who wouldn't know that horse from a hundred others except for the number it wore. And there isn't always safety in numbers. Over $70,000 was wagered on Mioland in the Suburban and Mioland didn't bring back a nickel of it. He finished out of the money.

What else is happening in Sweden just now this observer wouldn't know, but a visitor at Belmont yesterday was Rolf Lamborn of Stockholm, recently arrived, who said that racing was going strong in Sweden and new records for mutuel handles were being made week after week. The Swedish visitor said he was over here to pick the best of the photo-finish cameras and take it back with him through the war zone for use on the Swedish turf.

There were five horses in the National Stallion Stakes, but two ran as an entry and thus there was no show betting allowed. With the Belmont, that made two races without show betting, and the biggest races on the card, one of them the big race of the meeting. This cut down the mutuel handle on the day. However, that isn't going to put the Belmont Park stockholders on the bread line. They're still doing all right.

Another explanation offered for the comparatively modest mutuel handle at Belmont yesterday was that the crowd was not entirely an aggregation of brisk bettors. One veteran estimated that some thousands came out just to see Whirlaway run and didn't expect or intend to make any money out of it.

Roughly $22,000,000 went through the mutuel windows during the Belmont meeting. This is a hint to the worried officials in Washington, D. C., just in case they are wondering where there is loose money that might be raked in to build battleships and airplanes.

The Big Race

There was a stir through the crowd as the starting gate was pulled across the track near the lower end of the grandstand. It meant that the big race was coming up. Whirlaway was going to rush off and come back with high honors, winner of the triple crown of the turf, the Derby, the Preakness and the Belmont. Or could he fail and fall short? That was what many in the crowd came out to see.

Whirlaway was escorted by his own lead pony, a stylish-stout gray. That cost Warren Wright $10, extra, but, on what Whirlaway won at Churchill Downs and Pimlico, he could well afford it.

The lead pony took Whirlaway right up to the rear of the stall gate and there they had to part. Whirlaway was on his own to try conclusions with Itabo, Yankee Chance and Robert Morris.

Strange to say, Whirlaway wasn't last from the starting gate. Robert Morris had that doubtful honor. He seemed confused and looked as if he didn't know which way to run. Whirlaway went off in third position for a change. Robert Morris finally straightened out and went in pursuit of the hurrying trio up ahead.

But there really was nothing to it but a victory parade for Whirlaway. The Calumet colt took the lead after rounding the lower turn, went away out ahead, coasted most of the way and romped in a winner, the fifth horse in turf history to win the triple crown. In adding the Belmont to the Derby and Preakness, Whirlaway won $39,770 and a blanket of flowers. The flowers were distributed among Whirlaway rooters in the crowd, but the money was kept intact.

MY PLAY BOY GAINS HONORS AT TUXEDO

Totals 11 Points to Defeat Lew Dunbar by Two as Show Comes to Close

LUCKY NIRA TAKES TITLE

Leads 3-Gaited Field, While Radiant Rhythm Triumphs in 5-Gaited Division

By KINGSLEY CHILDS

Special to THE NEW YORK TIMES.

TUXEDO PARK, N. Y., June 7—Before one of the largest final-day spectator delegations in years, the annual Tuxedo Horse Show was successfully concluded near sundown this evening with six championship awards serving as the final session's chief highlights.

The splendid hunter and jumper divisions, attracting many metropolitan district topnotchers and several formidable performers as far south as Virginia and as far west as Ohio, supplied many thrills for the grandstand occupants throughout the morning and afternoon.

Victory in the $250 stake, wind-up test for the jumpers, clinched the timber-topping crown for the bay gelding, My Play Boy, ridden by his owner, 14-year-old Russell Stewart of Albany. By earning seven points for this triumph, My Play Boy took the title rosette with a total of eleven tallies.

Lew Dunbar Runner-Up

Mrs. Elizabeth Correll's thoroughbred gelding, Lew Dunbar, captured the reserve rosette with nine.

A couple of jump-offs were necessary to decide the first four places in the stake. Besides My Play Boy and Lew Dunbar, the May Top Stable's famed chestnut gelding, Bartender, and Mrs. A. G. Homewood's black gelding, R. A. F., flawlessly cleared the six barriers on two rounds before a third tour settled the issue.

On the latter circuit, My Play Boy was charged with merely one fault, while two were chalked against Bartender, four against R. A. F. and six against Lew Dunbar. They placed in that order, with fifth and sixth positions going to Kildare Sorcerer and Brookside, both belonging to Dudley Brothwell.

Premier laurels among the working hunters were annexed by Morton W. Smith of Southport, Conn., with his chestnut gelding, Ballela. By a one-point margin, Ballela shaded Mrs. Correll's Imp. Dalchoolin, ridden by Gordon Wright. They were ranked first and fourth, respectively, in the championship preliminary event.

The other eligibles for the preliminary, Mrs. Norman K. Toerge's Camp and Martin Vogel Jr.'s Imp. Demas, placed second and third, respectively, behind Ballela in the division's climax contest. Ballela bagged the title with fifteen counters, while Dalchoolin was credited with fourteen, Camp and Demas had eleven apiece.

Cornish Hills, chestnut gelding owned by Mr. and Mrs. W. Haggin Perry of Cobham, Va., and piloted by Mrs. Perry, terminated two banner days of campaigning by taking the conformation hunter crown. Miss Blanche Clark of Bronxville gained the reserve award with her Lord Britain.

Rated one-two in the conformation hunter championship preliminary event, Cornish Hills and Lord Britain finished with 25½ and 18 tallies, respectively. Demas and Camp, qualifiers for the conformation preliminary too, took third and fourth in that order, making their point totals 16 and 11.

Luckenbach Horses Prevail

Saddle horses owned by Edgar F. Luckenbach of Sands Point, N. Y., and by Mr. and Mrs. Samuel Schiffer's Kilkare Farm of Elberon, N. J., divided honors in that division's principal events. Mr. Luckenbach's black mare Lucky Nira, ridden by Oscar Gibbs, won the three-gaited championship stake, with Kilkare's chestnut gelding Valedictorian, shown by Mrs. Schiffer, gaining the reserve rosette.

"All the News That's Fit to Print."

The New York Times.

LATE CITY EDITION
Fair and warm today. Tomorrow mostly cloudy and continued warm.
Temperatures Yesterday—Max., 78; Min., 61

Copyright, 1941, by The New York Times Company.

VOL. XC...No. 30,462. Entered as Second-Class Matter, Postoffice, New York, N. Y. NEW YORK, THURSDAY, JUNE 19, 1941. THREE CENTS NEW YORK CITY and Vicinity

TURKS AND NAZIS SIGN AMITY PACT; GERMAN-SOVIET SHOWDOWN NEAR; ALLIES OPEN ATTACK ON DAMASCUS

LOUIS, NEAR DEFEAT, STOPS CONN IN 13TH AND RETAINS CROWN

Bomber Suddenly Turns Tide, Hammering Foe to Floor With Furious Attack

CONTEST THRILLS 54,487

Polo Grounds Bout Marks 18th Successful Defense of His Title by Champion

By JAMES P. DAWSON

Joe Louis still is world heavyweight champion, after his eighteenth defense of the title he won four years ago from Jim Braddock in Chicago.

The famed Brown Bomber sank Billy Conn, former world light-heavyweight champion, with a depth-bomb in the thirteenth round of their scheduled fifteen-round battle before a crowd of 54,487 wildly excited fight fans, who paid $450,000, in the Polo Grounds last night.

But the Bomber will never come closer to being toppled from his throne than he did before Conn collapsed under the paralyzing power of nerve-deadening blows. Thus Joe escaped crashing into the category of the ring's ex-champions.

In a battle that was thrilling and highly spectacular to a degree not generally anticipated, Conn came within the proverbial eyelash of upsetting predictions as he stirred the emotions of the great crowd with a brand of battle few had dared expect, Louis least of all.

Frail in Comparison

The doughty Pittsburgher, 25½ pounds lighter than Louis, frail in comparison and with none of the heavyweight fighting experience the champion boasts, held his rival even in action and on rounds, through twelve sessions while men and women, envisioning a transfer of the title, yelled themselves hoarse, encouraging the challenger as he seemed about to succeed where few had given him a chance.

Then the fight ended, as it had been predicted it would end. Conn left himself open for one dangerous blow to a vital point. A desperate, harried Louis, fighting with savage fury, whipped home through the opening with a right to the jaw.

The blow landed high, but it was a powerful one. Conn, a few seconds before on the high road to fame and fortune, tottered backward. His knees buckled. The Brown Bomber was the Alabama Assassin. He leaped in savagely, thudding home with both hands with a crushing fire. Conn fell under the barrage, a right to the jaw, as a final thrust, sending the brave challenger careening and crumpling.

The challenger, who gave promise of becoming the champion, was counted out by Referee Eddie Joseph in 2 minutes 58 seconds of the thirteenth round, amid a scene that was veritable bedlam.

That is the way of the ring. One second you are on top. The next you are down in despair. Conn came to the realization of this painfully.

Only Six Minutes More

Billy was within two rounds of what appeared a victory. Actually, the battle had only six minutes and two seconds more to go. And the way Conn had performed there was every reason to believe a new champion would be crowned.

Perhaps it was his own contempt for the punching prowess of the champion that led Conn into the fatal error. He had felt the Louis blow and survived. More, he had outboxed and, at times, outslugged the devastating puncher who has established himself as one of the greatest heavyweight champions of all time and without a peer as defender of the throne.

Perhaps Conn had come to the end of his endurance. His energy may have been burned up with the slashing battle he gave Louis through the eighth and up to and including the twelfth round, when the challenger treated the amazed onlookers to the spectacle of Louis being pounded steadily about the ring by a lighter, fearless foeman.

Whatever it was, the battle started as it had been predicted it would start, and it ended as it had been predicted it would end. Because, in advance, it had been said that Conn must rely on his speed if he were to survive and defeat Louis. It also had been told that Conn would drop the first time Louis hit him with a powerful punch to a vital spot.

Avoids Bomber's Punches

The surprise, in addition to the wonderful battle Conn made, came in the delay before Louis connected. This was a tribute to the ability of Conn, not only to avoid the Bomber's wallops, but his ability to withstand those that Louis landed. More, it was a testimonial to the surprising manner in which Conn fought in retaliation and sometimes

Continued on Page Twenty-seven

Rise in Living Cost Parallels Last War

The cost of living in the United States and Great Britain is following much the same course in this war as it did in the early years of the World War, according to a study made public yesterday by the National Industrial Conference Board.

In the early parts of both war periods, the board said, increases were relatively great in the United Kingdom and small in the United States. By July, 1915, British living costs had advanced 25 per cent, as compared with 21 per cent by September, 1940, in the present conflict. In this country living costs were practically stationary in the first year of the World War, whereas they went up 2 per cent in the first year of this war.

Between August, 1939, and May, 1941, the rise in costs here was 4 per cent, as against 7 per cent in the first two years of the World War. During the first war costs continued to mount until June, 1920, when they reached a ceiling 101 per cent above the level for July, 1914.

TEN FOUND GUILTY IN SHIP SABOTAGE

Captain, 9 Seamen of Italian Vessel Convicted in Jersey—Scene in Courtroom

Special to THE NEW YORK TIMES.

NEWARK, N. J., June 18—A jury in Federal Court tonight returned a verdict of guilty against ten Italian seamen accused of putting their vessel, the Aussa, out of commission while it was moored at Port Newark.

The jury of ten men and two women received the case at 3:20 P. M. and brought in the verdict at 9:25 o'clock, during which time dinner was served them in the jury room.

Only a few spectators were in the courtroom and the defendants showed no emotion when the verdict was announced by Edmund Van Duhn, foreman of the jury. But a few minutes later, after Judge William F. Smith had retired to his chamber and the defendants were being led out of the courtroom by deputy marshals, Italo Verrando, general manager of the Italian Line, owner of the ship, provoked a patriotic demonstration from the defendants by raising his hand in the Fascist salute. Mr. Verrando was a spectator at the trial.

All the defendants save Arminio Scalegerri, captain of the ship, responded with upraised hands and shouted words in Italian.

Chief Deputy Marshal William Brady protested against these gestures to Mr. Verrando. The latter ignored the marshal's protests and then Homer Loomis, attorney to the defendants, assailed the marshal for attempting "to give orders."

"You can't tell this man what to do," he said, his voice rising. "What are you, a dictator?"

Attorney Raises His Hand

Then, raising his own hand in a sort of Fascist salute, Mr. Loomis declared: "I can do that as much as I want to."

Brady retorted: "You can't do that in this court room."

The attorney and the marshal argued hotly as they walked out of the room, but a few moments later they were seen shaking hands. No date was set for the sentencing of the seamen, who face a maximum penalty of twenty years. They were taken to the Hudson County jail to await sentence.

The defendants, comprising besides the ship's captain, ten "below deck" officers and hands, were specifically charged with violating Section 502, Title 18 of the Federal Statutes, prohibiting "tampering with the motive power of instrumentalities of navigation" of a vessel of foreign registry within the jurisdiction of the United States.

Earlier in today's session an indictment against Rinaldo Negri, marine superintendent of the Italian Line, was dismissed on motion of B. Thorne Lord, first assistant United States attorney. Mr. Lord later explained to reporters that it would have been necessary to call fifteen witnesses to prove Mr. Negri's alleged connection with the damage on the Aussa. Since he did not want to delay the proceedings, Mr. Lord added, he thought it would be wiser to produce the witnesses in connection with the trials of four other indictments pending against the marine superintendent.

Statements Are Read

The session, the second of the trial, began with the government's introduction of sworn statements taken from the Aussa's crew and officers while they were detained at Ellis Island in April after the vessel's seizure. The statement of Captain Scalegerri declared, in effect, that on March 28 he received a telephone call from Admiral Alberto Lais, former naval attaché at the Italian Embassy in Washington, and was told that he and the chief

Continued on Page Ten

U. S. RULING CUTS OFF MEANS OF ESCAPE FOR MANY IN REICH

Curb on Refugees Who Might Be Spies Here to Save Kin Drastically Interpreted

MANY VISAS TO BE VOIDED

Thousands Who Have Booked Passage From Lisbon Now Face Rejection

The new Department of State regulations barring immigration visas to alien refugees who would leave behind close relatives subject to pressure on the part of "certain" governments will cut off the last avenue of escape for hundreds of refugees now waiting for permission to enter the United States, shipping officials said yesterday.

Steamship companies engaged in the passenger trade between New York and Lisbon, the last western outlet through which the European refugee tide has funneled since the spread of totalitarianism, said they had been informed by agents in Europe that United States consulates were construing the State Department rulings so as to reject visas to any aliens who are now residents of Germany or any nation under Reich domination.

The State Department regulations, promulgated on June 5 and made public on Tuesday, said that visas would not be given hereafter to aliens having close relatives still residing in Germany or lands overrun by the Nazis.

Forced Into Espionage Service

The ruling was made because of the Nazi practice of forcing emigrating aliens into espionage service by threatening those the aliens left behind.

Germany was not mentioned by name in the instructions cabled to foreign representatives, but there was no mistaking the reference.

For some months the various Federal agencies engaged in protecting the country against sabotage and subversive influences have been aware that the flood of refugee aliens to this country offered an ideal mode of transmission for spies and saboteurs.

Coming in by the tens of thousands, the refugees could easily mask, however unwittingly, the importation of foreign agents traveling as refugees fleeing oppression, officials felt.

The State Department did not comment yesterday on the reports from Europe concerning interpretation of the new instructions.

It is known, however, that shipping concerns engaged in the Lisbon trade received definite explana-

Continued on Page Thirteen

Strikes in Canada Cost Only Ten Seconds a Day

Special to THE NEW YORK TIMES

OTTAWA, June 18—Only ten seconds a day were lost by strikes of all kinds in Canada in the last year and only a quarter of that time in war industries, Labor Minister Norman McLarty said today.

"It is one of our difficulties," he said, "that it is not news that 3,000,000 people go to work every day, but it is news if a hundred fail to do so."

The figures of the last five months, especially, proved conclusively that an enormous majority of those engaged in industry and labor fully realized the importance of the work on which they were engaged and were determined to go on delivering the tools, he declared.

BRITISH WITHDRAW FROM LIBYAN FIGHT

Forced Back Past Halfaya—Axis Claims Victory—Says Foe Lost Many Tanks

Special Cable to THE NEW YORK TIMES.

CAIRO, Egypt, June 18—After three days of heavy and effective assault by British tanks and Indian infantry west of Solum and near Fort Capuzzo, in Libya, heavy German reinforcements were thrown into the battle in an encircling movement and yesterday they forced the attackers to withdraw to the old British positions just east of Halfaya Pass, in Egypt's Western Desert.

Today's British communiqué said that the attack had disclosed the German strength and had inflicted heavy casualties on the Germans. However, the withdrawal naturally was a blow to the hopes of many observers who had seen the possibilities of a British drive through to Bardia or Tobruk and the clearing out of the troublesome German salient in Egypt.

[The Germans announced a "complete victory" over the British in the desert and said that the British had lost heavily in fierce tank battles. In Rome it was stated unofficially that the British had lost approximately 200 tanks.]

Although they gained no ground

Continued on Page Six

The International Situation

THURSDAY, JUNE 19, 1941

A treaty of friendship and consultation between Germany and Turkey was signed in Ankara last night. It provides that each country will respect the territorial integrity of the other and take no measures aimed at the other signatory. There is to be amicable consultation on all questions of mutual interest. Turkey emphasized that the treaty did not alter her national policy and noted the preamble, which provides that previous agreements—such as the Turkish alliance with Britain—are not affected. Berlin, announcing the pact, hailed it as a diplomatic defeat for Britain. [Page 1 Column 8.]

Disappointment, but not surprise, was expressed in Britain, where the pressure to which Turkey had been subjected was realized. [Page 4, Column 2.] Washington, while aware of the propaganda value of the treaty to the Nazis in the Middle East, indicated that its greatest significance might lie in its relation to the reported Soviet-German crisis. [Page 5, Column 5.]

This view was also held in some quarters in Turkey. Ankara had reports of the gravest Nazi-Soviet tension, of demands by Germany of an ultimative character, of further massing of troops and even of the actual outbreak of hostilities. This last was not confirmed, but it was felt that the new treaty might be a device to guard the German right flank. [Page 1, Columns 6 and 7.]

Britain was apparently considering Finland's possible position on the left flank of such a battle line. Three Finnish ships en route to Petsamo were held by the British on the ground that excessive German troop concentrations in Finland had altered the Finns' neutral status. [Page 5, Column 1.]

In Syria, where a great battle seemed to be developing, the British this morning opened an attack on Damascus after the Vichy garrison had refused to surrender the city. British reports said that French counter-attacks had been stopped and the advance resumed at all points. Vichy, however, said the counter-attacks had been successful. [Page 1, Column 5; Map, Page 2.]

On the Libyan front the British announced a withdrawal to their original positions after a three-day battle. They stated that their objectives had been attained, much enemy equipment destroyed and an encircling movement by the Nazis thwarted. [Page 1, Column 4.] Berlin and Rome called the same action an overwhelming defeat for the British and reported the destruction of 200 tanks. [Page 6, Column 3.]

For the eighth successive night British planes hammered the Continent. In a daylight raid on Northern France, London announced, nine German planes were shot down at a cost of four British ones. [Page 3, Column 1.]

In the air war to defend Britain the call went out yesterday for American volunteers. They will form the Civilian Technical Corps to assist in manning the radio plane locators. A recruiting office will be opened in New York for skilled technicians. The British air attaché indicated that more than 25,000 men could be used. Washington indicated that neither the Selective Service Act nor the Neutrality Act would be impaired. [Page 1, Column 7.]

Washington received Germany's protest on the closing of the Reich consulates in this country and it was assumed that it would be rejected. [Page 1, Column 6.]

DEFIANCE IN SYRIA

Assault on Old Capital Follows Refusal to Yield to Invaders

WAVELL REPORTED IN IRAQ

Heavier Allied Action to Clean Up Levant Foreshadowed as French Stiffen Defense

By The Associated Press.

LONDON, Thursday, June 19—The British news agency Reuters reported today from Palestine that Allied troops were attacking Damascus. A military spokesman in Jerusalem made the announcement.

Allied troops had been reported steadily surrounding the Syrian capital amid fierce fighting. An earlier report from Ankara, Turkey, said the Free French troops fighting beside the British had served an ultimatum on the French defenders, demanding the capital's capitulation by 5:30 A. M. [10:30 P. M. Wednesday, New York time.]

The indications were that the ultimatum had expired and that the Allies had thereupon attacked. The attack was launched following the occupation of Mezze, an airfield four miles west of the city.

The Allies were meeting with a "good deal of opposition," a spokesman said, but this had been expected.

Major War Developing

By RAY BROCK

Special Broadcast to THE NEW YORK TIMES.

ANKARA, Turkey, June 18—A major Middle Eastern war appeared to be developing rapidly tonight as both the British and the French rushed heavy reinforcements to Syria; the new chief of the French Air Command arrived in Beirut and Beirut reported the arrival in Baghdad of General Sir Archibald P. Wavell, Commander in Chief of the British Imperial Middle East Army, from Africa.

General Sir Henry Maitland Wilson, Commander in Chief of the British forces in Palestine and Trans-Jordan, in a broadcast tonight from Palestine, warned General Henri Fernand Dentz, French High Commissioner to the mandated territories, that the British forces would occupy Damascus at 5:30 o'clock tomorrow morning and called upon him to capitulate before the zero hour.

General Wilson declared the Vichy garrisons must wave white flags before 5:30 A. M. and that otherwise General Dentz must bear the responsibility for the slaughter of the defending garrisons.

Fears arose in both diplomatic and military pro-Allied circles that the Germans might be considering the dispatching of German troops and new air reinforcements to Syria or, at the best, were extending guarantees to the French in North Africa, thus releasing troops and matériel to the Vichy command in Syria. Air reinforcements from North Africa already are arriving.

French Enlarge Pocket

Late Ankara radio reports said the French were counter-attacking at Damascus and Saida and that the pocket, originally opened by the French counter-offensives behind the Allied lines, had been greatly enlarged and constituted a serious danger to British and Allied positions south of Damascus.

British military sources, while admitting the initial success of the sudden French counter-offensive aimed at Merdjayoun and El Kuneitra and the Free French communication lines, insisted that the back of this attack had been broken and that the Allied advances had been resumed in all sectors.

No British source could or would confirm the Beirut report of the arrival of General Wavell in Iraq, where he might be expected to assume command of the northern columns aimed at Aleppo and the severance of Vichy communications with the Turkish frontier.

Strong new British reinforcements arriving in Syria, however, envisaged as apparent intention to fight it out at all costs, lent strength to this report. The Beirut radio confirmed the arrival in Beirut of General Jean Bergeret, new chief of the French Syrian Air Command.

German sources in Ankara reported that General Dentz, in a speech last night, called for continued and intensified resistance with the declaration that "the fight for Syria is a fight for France" and that the Syrian battle against the British and Allied troops was "the first step

Continued on Page Two

Reich Ultimatum to Soviet Reported in Turkish Capital

Said to Demand the Return of Bessarabia to Rumania and Access to Russia—Helsinki Is Evacuating Women and Children

Special Broadcast to THE NEW YORK TIMES

ANKARA, Turkey, June 18—This city was full of rather convincing reports tonight that a German note of the nature of an ultimatum had already been sent to the Soviet Government and was due to expire very shortly, although wild rumors that hostilities had actually started were discountenanced.

According to information received by diplomats, the Germans are demanding that Russian representatives meet with Rumanian delegates to discuss the question of returning Bessarabia; that Russia guarantee enormous deliveries of food and raw materials to the Reich and that Russia admit German technicians and experts to the Ukraine and Caucasus. These are unconfirmed reports, but the impression here is that Moscow will in the end accept.

In diplomatic circles it is thought that the actuality of the new German-Turkish accord may clear the way for a German-Russian war by once more reassuring the right flank of the German position in the Balkans.

LONDON, Thursday, June 19 (AP)—Reuters, British news agency, relayed reports from Ankara today that German armies had launched an attack against Soviet Russia, but other sources in London said the reports had been in circulation for seventeen hours without confirmation.

Reuters said its reports came from Columbia Broadcasting System's Ankara correspondent, who heard the Nazis had attacked the Soviet border at fifteen places. The agency said it was informed from the same source of other unconfirmed reports that Rumania had served an ultimatum on Russia demanding return of the lost Province of Bessarabia.

[In New York, Columbia Broadcasting System said the report carried by Reuters was read from Ankara by the C. B. S. correspondent, Winston Burdett, after his regular broadcast had been made. It gave this version of Mr. Burdett's report:

[Various commercial radios here in Turkey today picked up unspecified and uncredited reports to the effect that Rumania had dispatched an ultimatum to Soviet Russia demanding the return of Bessarabia and that the German Army had actually launched the attack against Russia at fifteen points from the Eastern frontier. As far as any one in Turkey knows, these reports are not true, but the interesting fact is that they are being spread.]

Other German demands were reported to include free admission of Nazi technicians to the administration of Russian transport and industry.

The National Broadcasting Company's representative was quoted as saying he understood the ultimatum was under consideration now in Moscow, while Nazi and So-

Continued on Page Seven

U. S. TO REJECT NOTE ON REICH'S CONSULS

Berlin's Protest Is Received—Details of Departure Soon to Be Arranged

By BERTRAM D. HULEN

Special to THE NEW YORK TIMES.

WASHINGTON, June 18—The German note of protest against the order closing Nazi consulates in this country on account of what President Roosevelt has described as subversive activities was delivered today to Sumner Welles, Under-Secretary of State, by Dr. Hans Thomsen, the German Chargé d'Affaires, who had received it overnight from Berlin.

Mr. Welles told Dr. Thomsen that consideration would be given the note. He would not indicate later at his press conference what response would be made to it, nor would he say what it contained, other than to describe it as merely a protest, a communication that made no suggestion of possible retaliation. It is taken for granted that the protest will be rejected.

Except for its formal and customary repetition in paraphrase at the outset of the American communication of June 16 to Dr. Thomsen announcing the closing order, the note, it was learned, was brief. It was vigorous but not detailed. It charged that the closing was in violation of the German-American treaty of friendship and commerce, which grants consular rights and regulates them. It did not refer to the freezing of German funds in this country or other questions.

Assume Berlin Will Wait

Diplomats assumed that Berlin was waiting to see how the order was carried out, for it is not to become effective until July 10, and what other measures the United States may adopt before deciding upon any steps in retaliation or along parallel lines.

Mr. Welles indicated, in response to questions, that the consuls would be permitted to return to Germany under safe conduct guarantees, but that they would not be allowed to go to Latin America or other countries. As officials of a foreign government they are entitled to safe passage.

Arrangements will be made for their return, Mr. Welles said, and these arrangements will be determined along at least general lines in the next few days. Under present conditions, he explained, the procedure would be to request the belligerent governments for safe conduct and make all arrangements that are suitable and correct for their return.

In response to questions concern-

Continued on Page Ten

BRITISH TO RECRUIT U. S. RADIO EXPERTS

Thousands Sought to Work as Civilians on Device That Detects Airplanes

By CHARLES HURD

Special to THE NEW YORK TIMES.

WASHINGTON, June 18—The British Government started today its first wholesale recruiting campaign for noncombatant civilian Americans with an offer of employment to an unlimited number of radio technicians and other types of mechanics needed to service its secret weapon for detecting invading aircraft. The device has been made available to the United States.

Air Commodore George C. Pirie, Air Attache to the British Embassy, announced the opening of offices in New York to conduct the recruiting campaign for a Civilian Technical Corps. He asked to be addressed at the British Consulate General, 25 Broadway, New York.

The new program offers wages ranging from $24.12 a week to $38.65 a week plus board and lodging and a uniform to be designed for the American Civilian Corps. All of the Americans to be hired will have contracts for three-year terms, or for the duration of the war, whichever period is shorter, with two-way transportation by ship across the Atlantic.

No Military Discipline

Except for the wearing of a uniform, the Americans will be exempt from military discipline or other stipulated requirements except that they must work where they are sent in the United Kingdom. If they become subject to discipline, they will have the right of appeal to an American commandant to be chosen.

Commodore Pirie said that the British Government hoped to find a commandant for the Corps who has had experience in the British and American armies, but now has civilian status.

The entire program, which was hinted at last night in an international broadcast by Lord Beaverbrook from London, arose from the fact that British production of radiolocators for enemy aircraft is running far ahead of ability to train maintenance men for the locators. It represents a compromise reached after the State Department declined to approve direct recruiting of Americans to do this work as enlisted members of the British armed forces.

As a result, the British Government offers rates of pay that are believed to be considerably above the British civilian level, together with disability and death benefits exactly the same as those given to

Continued on Page Five

A TEN-YEAR TREATY

Ankara Agrees Not to Fight Nazis—Troop Passage Not Given

HOLDS TO BRITISH PACT

Undertakes to Increase Trade With Germany and to Control Press, Radio in Friendship

By C. BROOKS PETERS

By Telephone to THE NEW YORK TIMES.

BERLIN, June 18—Following weeks during which a sphynx-like silence had been maintained in authoritative German quarters in regard to the next developments to be expected in this ever-expanding war, the German Government tonight emerged from the smoke screen behind which political negotiations had been in progress and announced the conclusion of an amity and consultation pact with Turkey.

The immediate bearing of this newest German diplomatic bombshell on the situation in the Near East is, for the present, as unclear as the repercussions that it may have in London, Moscow and Washington. The pact, signed in Ankara at 9 o'clock tonight, specifically provides that previous commitments entered into by the Turkish and German Governments are not thereby affected.

There can be no doubt, however, that the newest agreement that the diplomacy of the Third Reich has succeeded in negotiating represents, regardless of the phraseology in which it is couched, a serious blow to British prestige, at least in the Near East, in the German point of view.

Russia Still a Question

What, if any, effect it will have on German-Russian relations, about which the most diametrically opposite rumors have been abroad in Berlin for weeks, has not yet been disclosed. Interestingly, moreover, unlike the treaty that Turkey concluded with Britain, the pact signed today makes no mention whatever of the Soviet Union.

Authoritative quarters declared, coincident with the announcement here of the signing of the pact, that it was not known whether the Russian Government had previously been informed that a Turkish-German agreement was in the offing or had been concluded. It is reported, although not officially confirmed, that the Russian Ambassador called at the Foreign Office in the Wilhelmstrasse in the early hours of the evening.

The general mystery was further intensified when authoritative quarters asserted that communications with foreign countries that had been cut off at 7 P. M. would be opened from 9 P. M. until 1 o'clock tomorrow morning—but apparently no later.

The German-Turkish pact is specifically designated a friendship pact. It was signed by Franz von Papen, the German Ambassador in Ankara, for Adolf Hitler, and by Shukru Saracoglu, Turkish Foreign Minister, for President Ismet Inonu. It contained three articles.

The first provides for respect on the part of both countries of the integrity and inviolability of each other's territory. Under Article I, moreover, both nations agree to take no measures aimed directly or indirectly against the other contracting party.

Article II provides that in the future Turkey and Germany will amicably consult with each other on all questions affecting their mutual interests "in order to arrive at an agreement regarding the treatment of such questions."

Article III concerns itself merely with protocol. It asserts that the ratification of the treaty, which became effective immediately upon signing, will take place in Berlin in the immediate future. Although concluded for ten years, both parties, it is said, will agree at the opportune time regarding extension of the treaty.

Agree to Extend Trade

At the same time, the German and Turkish governments exchanged notes in which mutual desire was expressed to increase economic relations between both countries. Both governments affirmed the wish to increase trade with each other to the fullest extent possible on the basis of the experiences that they have had with each other in war. Both countries pledge themselves to begin trade negotiations in

Continued on Page Four

LOUIS STOPS CONN IN THE 13TH ROUND

Continued From Page One

on the attack, against the man every one else has feared since he ascended the throne.

One of the greatest heavyweight battles of recent years, the struggle was waged in an atmosphere reminiscent of older and better times in boxing. In the double-decked concrete and steel stand, in the temporary wooden chairs that had been placed on what is ordinarily the Giants' baseball playing field, men and women sat, in rows extending back as far as the eye could reach in the darkness.

They came from all sections of the country and from every walk of life. They came early and stayed late to thrill to a really great battle for the championship, one that will take its place alongside the best in ring history, from the standpoint of surprise, excitement and competitive appeal.

A sportsmanlike battle, it was cleanly fought, bitterly and cagily waged. It was tense with the element of the unexpected to a high degree.

Governors of near-by States were in the gathering. There were Mayors of cities, national leaders in politics, Representatives, Senators, State lawmakers, bankers, merchants, leaders of the country's commercial and industrial life, members of the clergy, stars of the stage and screen. They were drawn by the championship magnet and that uncertainty about whether the title would change hands, the majority, wishing it would, but feeling that it couldn't.

Fights True to Style

This great gathering saw Conn fight a battle that was true to his style, of necessity, but better than usual, though it proved inadequate. And the crowd saw Louis fight as a champion should, a champion who refused to become discouraged though he was buffeted about outlandishly at times.

Naturally, the greatest thrill came from Conn. The finish by Louis was an anti-climax. Most of those in the vast throng expected Joe to knock out the challenger, as he had done to challengers in fifteen previous defenses of the title. Few, however, expected of the frail-looking Conn the battle he flashed—least of all Louis, if the truth is known.

Unmistakably Louis has slipped. Even making allowances for style—the contrast in styles was inescapable—the champion is not the champion of old. He was not sure of himself last night, a fact which might be explained by the circumstance which found him in the ring with a veritable wraith for speed. But the speed that Louis once boasted himself is gone, the accuracy behind his punch is slipping. He is becoming heavy-footed and heavy-armed, weaknesses which were reflected as he floundered at times in his quest of the target that was Conn.

One thing remains undiminished with Louis and that cannot be denied. He still is an annihilating puncher. His right hand claims a victim when it lands. His left hook jars a foe to the heels and props him for the finishing potion that is in the right hand.

Surprises Most Onlookers

Conn, almost exclusively, boxed Louis through the first seven rounds. Having gone so far, Billy became confident. He became overconfident in the eighth and surprising most onlookers, was hammering his way past Louis in grand style.

The challenger started the fight on treacherous feet. He slipped coming out of his corner soon after the opening gong and, before the first round ended, he went down while pivoting to escape Louis's rush. Neither time was Conn struck a blow.

Through the first three rounds Conn sparred cautiously and skillfully, dancing before the shuffling, plodding Louis who moved steadily, stealthily in on the attack. Billy's plan was to stay away; Louis's was to get close and strike home with short jolts to the body and head.

Louis struck a number of these blows in the first three rounds, picking most of Conn's left hooks off in midair the meanwhile. The champion's blows, however, had no deterring effect on the sprightly Conn, who only once, in the third round, resorted to a covering stance as a defensive move. But the challenger ended the third with a flurry in which he drove Louis to the ropes under a fiery volley of lefts and rights to the head and body, amid the roars of the crowd.

Conn outdid himself in the fourth when he started making the champion's jaw the target for a succession of rights. They were blows driven home at long range, but, reflecting the lack of power in Conn's fighting armor, they only made Joe blink.

Shoots Home Left Hook

The challenger was proceeding with a daring attack in the fifth, when Louis suddenly shot home a left hook to the jaw. Conn staggered under the blow and sought retreat. But Louis was upon him, drilling lefts and rights to the head and face of Billy, lurching and staggering, covered against attack. The blows opened a cut over Conn's right eye. Another cut appeared on the bridge of his nose.

But Billy survived the storm and managed to keep out of harm's way in the sixth and in the seventh. Then, with the eighth, Conn launched a thrilling attack of his own. He parried most of Louis' lunges early in the round and began making a target of Joe's jaw for right-hand smashes that went home straight and often. The blows lacked steam and merely flustered the titleholder. More important, however, is the fact that the success of his offensive lifted Conn's confidence.

This was reflected as the ninth started and Billy added a verbal assault to his fistic fire. "You got a tough fight tonight," it developed later, was what Conn said, although the words were indistinguishable at the time above the roar of the crowd. "That's right," replied Louis, who continued shuffling into a rival who was banging him around scandalously.

Trades Blows Willingly

Repeatedly Conn drilled home with his right to the jaw in the ninth. He ripped full-arm rights to the body. Left jabs brought blood from Louis's nose. A left hook to the body hurt Joe before the bell. All the time Louis was helpless to counter the fire.

Infuriated in the tenth, Louis pressed his foe hard. Once Conn slipped on the wet canvas in his own corner in escaping a fierce lunge. Billy traded blows with the champion, giving as good as he received and sometimes better.

Through the eleventh Conn fought gallantly as he hammered the titleholder from all angles, beating Louis about the face and jaw with rights at long range and about the heart and body at close quarters. Louis winced under some of these blows. He was infuriated under others. But he could do nothing about them.

In the twelfth Conn, after an exchange in which one of Louis's lefts cut him under the left eye, suddenly rocked Louis on his heels with a full-arm left hook to the jaw. Staggering, Louis dived into a clinch to keep from falling while Conn fought furiously in a bid for a knockout.

Maybe this shot that went true and staggered the champion made Conn overconfident. At any rate, he was the pursuer instead of the pursued as the thirteenth started and he made the mistake of going too close to Louis too often.

Battered by the desperate champion's powerful lefts and rights about the head, Conn suddenly emerged from close quarters flailing furiously for Louis's jaw with lefts and rights in an outburst that electrified the crowd.

Lands Flush on Jaw

Suddenly Louis's right shot out on an opening with a blow that landed flush on Conn's jaw. The challenger's knees buckled. He swayed backward. He was hurt, and Louis knew it. And Joe thundered in with that savagery that is his characteristic when he has a foe in distress.

About the head and face Louis fired countless rights and lefts while Conn sought to cover and retreat. Some of the blows missed, but many of them landed, carrying force even against Billy's defense of raised gloves. The Bomber shifted his fire to the body. Blows there hurt Conn, sapped the speed from his legs, took the last ounce of his endurance. Billy was slipping about uncertainly when Louis drove over the right-hand blow to the jaw that toppled him in defeat within two seconds of the end of the round, and shattered a dream of a championship.

The police detail was the largest ever assigned to a boxing event in this city. A total of 2,250 of New York's finest patrolled the Polo Grounds, inside and out, and the streets of Harlem.

Chief Inspector Edward M. Butler was in charge of the detail inside the park. Deputy Chief Inspector John J. DeMartino was in charge of the outside detail.

Seven hundred police, some of them carrying the old-fashioned night sticks, patrolled Harlem streets from 8 P. M. on. More than 300 others were on reserve duty between the East 126th Street and the West 135th Street stations. There were 200 detectives, sixty-six mounted police, thirty-three motorcycle men and two emergency squads on the job.

Trouble was not expected. It has been characteristic of Louis battles hereabouts that they have been taken in stride, with a minimum of disorder in the Harlem district, regardless of whether he won or lost. But the Police Department, at the same time, wanted to take no chances.

Plenty of Betting

Betting on the fight was active, with no change in the odds. Louis was the favorite at 1 to 4 to win and the price on him to score a knockout was 5 to 11. Trick bets on the number of rounds were numerous but inconsequential. The volume was reported on decision. The 1-to-4 odds appealed to many Conn supporters and others who inevitably "invest" whenever odds are better than 1 to 2 or 3.

Among those seen at the ringside were James A. Farley, John F. Curry, former Mayor John O'Brien, Mayor Frank Hague of Jersey City, J. Edgar Hoover, George Ruppert, Edward G. Barrow, Leo Bondy, Bob Hope, ex-Governor James Cox of Ohio, William F. Carey and George Weiss.

Lending a note that was in keeping with the time was the presence of many soldiers and sailors in their olive drab and their navy blue. They were sprinkled through all sections of the arena.

The first preliminary entered the ring promptly on time. The principals were José Basora, Puerto Rican, and Jerry Fiorello, Brooklynite. It was a four-round battle between middleweights and at the conclusion of twelve minutes of slugging the decision was rendered in Basora's favor without criticism from the crowd. He was the cleaner hitter and was entitled to the award.

Basora weighed 154 pounds and Fiorello 152.

Fontana Is Winner

Larry Fontana, Brooklyn welterweight, hammered his way to the decision over Johnny Cregan, Pittsburgh boxer who acted as one of Conn's sparring partners, in the first of the six-round bouts. This was a hard-fought struggle, with plenty of head-to-head fighting that held the interest of the crowd. Fontana weighed 152¾ pounds and Cregan 146¼.

Holman Williams of Detroit, a stable-mate of Louis, won the award over Antonio Fernandez, Chilian boxer, in their six-round bout. The shifty style of attack by Williams more than balanced the scales against Fernandez's fiery bursts of fighting. The decision, however, was not popular. The victor weighed 152¼ pounds and Fernandez 149.

In the semi-final of six rounds Tommy Tucker, fighting Jack Tar from Uncle Sam's Navy, hammered his way to the decision over Charlie Harvey, West Side heavyweight. Harvey was taller and heavier than Tucker, but these were handicaps rather than advantages for the West Sider. Tucker was faster and shiftier with his fire.

Tucker's right-hand drives opened a cut over Harvey's left eye which bothered the West Sider through the closing two rounds.

Tucker weighed 174 pounds, and Harvey 184½.

Herbie Katz, Brooklyn, 175¾, outpointed Henry Cooper, Brooklyn, 190¼, in the final six-round preliminary after the main bout.

KNOCKOUT IN THE CHAMPIONSHIP BOUT

Conn doubled up on the canvas and Louis standing over him at the end of the fight

BOMBER REALIZED CONN WAS WINNING

Impatience Cost Billy Chance for Title, Louis Declares in His Dressing Room

'TRIED HARD,' LOSER SAYS

Soon Recovers After Outburst of Tears and Asks for a Return Match

"I couldn't get started against that fast Conn," said Joe Louis in his dressing room after the fight last night. Explaining his relatively poor showing against the Pittsburgh fighter, Louis declared that Conn was much too speedy for him.

"I knew I was losing the fight when the thirteenth round started. My handlers let me know it, even if I didn't know it myself," the champion went on.

"He hurt me pretty much in the twelfth, and I was hoping that he'd lose his head pretty quick, because I knew I was losing the title."

Joe said that his fight strategy included the probability of Conn's becoming impatient, or cocksure. And he added that it certainly was about time that happened.

Louis revealed that he had hurt his right wrist striking down at Conn's head in the seventh. It hurt for the next three rounds, but the pain subsided after that.

Joe Grasps His Chance

"I was studying Conn all through the fight, and finally figured I'd nail him when he started to throw a long left hook. The chance came in the thirteenth, and I put all I had in the knockout punches," the Brown Bomber stated.

Commenting on Conn's fighting ability, Louis said that the Pittsburgh warrior was not particularly tough, but he certainly was an excellent ring general.

"He knows what it's all about in there," Joe went on, "and if he only could have kept his temper down he might have been the champion. I'd like to fight him again."

Conn, in his dressing room, made it clear to a mass of interviewers that he realized that his anxiety to trade punches with Louis had cost him his chance for the heavyweight championship of the world.

Billy's chief concern for a few minutes after he had entered his quarters appeared to be whether it had been a good fight.

"I tried awfully hard," he said, shaking his head. "Louis didn't hurt me," he continued, "but he certainly throws a hard punch, doesn't he?"

Soon Is Smiling Again

Not until he had taken his shower and the room had begun to clear did Conn allow his emotions to overcome him. Seated on a table, Billy bowed his head and cried softly.

"That's all right," said Manager Johnny Ray, "go ahead and cry if you want to, it'll do you good." So the young gladiator let the tears fall for a few seconds. However, he was himself almost immediately and soon was smiling.

For a man who had, only a few minutes before, absorbed so much punishment, Conn was hardly marked. There was a cut over his right eye, another under it and one across the bridge of his nose. None was serious, though.

Neither Conn nor Ray had anything to say about the immediate future. The beaten challenger said he'd like to meet the champion again. And even as he was saying that, Promoter Mike Jacobs strode into the room, grasped Billy's hand and kissed him on the cheek.

"That's for a well-done job," said Jacobs. Then he leaned over and whispered something into Conn's ears. That was a secret, but it must have been a good one, because Billy's eyes lighted up and his face beamed.

There were many other well-wishers in the room and Billy accepted all the compliments and congratulations for his great showing graciously.

"Thank you," he repeated time and again. "I tried awfully hard."

American League's 4-Run Rally in Ninth Tops National in All-Star Contest

WILLIAMS'S HOMER DECIDES 7-5 GAME

Ted's Hit With Two On, Two Out in Last of Ninth Wins for American League

VAUGHAN NATIONAL'S HERO

His Two 4-Baggers, All-Star Contest Mark, Tally 4 Runs —54,674 at Detroit

By JOHN DREBINGER

Special to THE NEW YORK TIMES.

DETROIT, July 8—Coming up with a last-minute electrifying charge that floored a foe at the very moment he appeared to have a signal triumph within his grasp, the American League snatched victory from defeat today. Scoring four runs in the last half of the ninth inning, the Harridge forces overcame the National League, 7 to 5, in the ninth annual All-Star game.

A blistering home-run smash by Ted Williams, lanky outfielder of the Red Sox, with two colleagues on base sent the final three tallies hurtling over the plate, while a crowd of 54,674, predominantly American League in its sympathies, acclaimed the shot with a thunderous roar.

Only a few moments before this blow landed with stunning and devastating force, the National League cohorts, led by Deacon Bill McKechnie, Reds' manager, appeared to have the battle tucked away.

Conflict Appears Ended

They had entered the final round leading by two runs, thanks to a pair of circuit blows by Arky Vaughan. When, with one out and the bases full, Claude Passeau, Chicago Cubs' pitcher, appeared to have induced the mighty Joe DiMaggio to slam vigorously into a double play, the contest, played for the benefit of the United Service Organizations, looked to be over.

But a rather hurried peg to first base by Billy Herman, Dodger second sacker, went a trifle wide of its mark and Jolting Joe escaped by a stride. It left Passeau still striving for one more out to clinch the struggle, but Claude never caught up with it. For a few seconds later Williams, leading batsman of the American League, bashed the ball almost on a line against the upper parapet of the right-field stands of Briggs Stadium.

Thus the squad directed by Del Baker, Tiger pilot, brought to the American League its sixth triumph in the nine All-Star games played since 1933.

Up to the time of this culminating assault, however, the National Leaguers certainly looked to be riding high, wide and handsome. Joe DiMaggio, though his current forty-eight-game hitting streak was not at stake, nevertheless had to wait until the eighth inning before he lashed out with a double to save, at least, his prestige.

Employs 1940 Tactics

Resorting to much the same tactics that he employed at St. Louis a year ago when he fired the National League's vaunted pitching talent into the foe with bewildering rapidity for a shut-out victory, McKechnie, for the first six innings, again hurled three crack moundsmen—Whitlow Wyatt, Paul Derringer and Bucky Walters—at the foe, each working only two innings apiece.

But in the home stretch, McKechnie veered from his course.

Williams of Red Sox crossing plate on ninth-inning homer that gave American League three runs. DiMaggio of Yankees (5) and Coach Shea (30) of Tigers are the first to congratulate him.

Ted Williams, whose circuit blow with two on won the game.

Perhaps the two homers which Vaughan, the Pirate shortstop, had unleashed in the seventh and eighth innings, each with a man on base, lulled the National League skipper into a feeling of false security.

Bill permitted Passeau, who had entered the fray in the seventh, to remain on the mound through the ninth, and with this, by the margin of Williams's staggering clout, the wily Cincinnati leader overreached himself.

Passeau had seen one run shot away from him in the eighth when Joe DiMaggio unfurled his double for his first and only hit and presently scored when brother Dominic DiMaggio, who had entered the battle in its later stages, whistled a single to right.

This still left Passeau with a two-run margin. When Claude concluded the eighth by fanning the renowned Jimmy Foxx with two aboard the bases, McKechnie apparently saw no reason why the Chicago right-hander could not safely navigate through the ninth as well.

As the last of the ninth opened with Frank Hayes popping out, there still seemed no danger lurking around in the last few strides to the wire.

Pass Fills the Bases

But Ken Keltner, batting for Edgar Smith, the fourth and last American League hurler, bounced a single off Eddie Miller, the Braves' shortstop who had just replaced Vaughan in the field. Joe Gordon of the Yankees singled to right, and when Cecil Travis drew a pass, filling the bases, a feeling that something dramatic was about to come to pass gripped the crowd.

Joe DiMaggio stepped to the plate. But Joe's best was a grounder at Miller that just missed ending the struggle, but Herman's wide peg, though not an error, let in one tally and missed DiMaggio at first for what would have been the final out, and Williams did the rest.

Despite the early fine pitching efforts of Wyatt, Walters and Derringer, the National Leaguers also had to wait until the struggle moved well on its way before they assumed what promised to be a commanding lead. For during the first six rounds the American Leaguers likewise flashed some brilliant hurling.

Bobby Feller, youthful Cleveland ace and ranked as the foremost pitcher of his time, blazed through the first three rounds to face only nine men. He allowed one single and that was all. The hitter was trapped off first.

Then came the left-handed Thornton Lee of the White Sox to hurl the next three rounds and it was not until the sixth that the National Leaguers managed to break through with their first tally.

Walters sparked this one by banging a double to left, advancing to third on Stanley Hack's sacrifice and then skipping home on Terry Moore's long fly to Williams in left.

That matched the run which the American Leaguers had marked up in the fourth off Derringer, although the tally was scarcely big Paul's fault. Travis, crack third sacker of the Senators, had doubled with one out and moved to third on Joe DiMaggio's fly to deep right.

Williams then followed with a sharp liner toward right that seemed to be moving straight for where Bob Elliott, Pirate outfielder, was standing, for the third out. But Elliott momentarily misjudged the ball, rushed in a few steps, caught his spikes in the turf as he tried to back-track and wound up rather inelegantly sprawled on the grass. The ball shot over his head against the stand for a double and Travis scored.

However, though Walters managed to erase this run in the sixth, the American League went ahead again in the same inning by clipping Bucky for a tally. The Cincinnati ace right-hander paved the way for his own difficulties here by walking Joe DiMaggio and Jeff Heath, and then Lou Boudreau smacked a single to center, scoring DiMaggio.

In the seventh the tide veered sharply toward the National League legions. Sid Hudson, youthful right-hander of the Senators, came on to pitch for the American Leaguers and for a few minutes threatened to have himself annihilated.

Enos Slaughter, who had replaced the hapless Elliott in the McKechnie outfield, singled to left and grabbed an extra base when Williams stumbled over the ball for an error. The misplay, however, had no bearing on what followed, for Vaughan arched his first homer into the upper right tier of the grand stand.

Herman followed with a double and it promised another tally when Al Lopez deftly sacrificed Billy to third and Joe Medwick came up to bat for Walters. Just to show that seven long years scarcely tax the memory of a baseball fan, there was again a fine round of boos for Muscles Joe, who, as a Cardinal on this same field in the 1934 world series, had seen himself shelled from the arena with a barrage of vegetables.

But though Medwick tried hard to add a little more to the general discomfiture of his old friends, he grounded to the infield and Hudson luckily escaped without any further scoring being charged against him.

However, with the eighth, the National Leaguers jacked up their lead with another pair of runs and again it was the booming bat of Vaughan that jarred the opposition.

The southpaw Smith had supplanted Hudson on the mound as this round opened and fanned Pete Reiser for a starter. But Johnny Mize, silenced up to now, rifled a two-bagger to right. His Cardinal team-mate, Slaughter, struck out, but Vaughan again belted the ball into that inviting target offered by the upper right stand and the National lead was now 5 to 2.

Hero of the Hour

It marked the first time a player ever had managed to belt two homers in an All-Star game and Vaughan decidedly was the hero of the hour.

And he still was all of that until the DiMaggio brothers whittled one tally away from Passeau's lead in the last of the eighth and Williams swept away the rest with his closing smash in the ninth.

Wyatt's pitching in the first two innings was practically as flawless as was Feller's work in the first three. The slim Brooklyn right-hander faced only six batters and, though he gave one a pass, he immediately snuffed this fellow off the base line by inducing the next man to slap into a double play.

Feller, fanning four during his three scoreless rounds, was equally invincible. Lonnie Frey opened the third with a single, but almost immediately got himself trapped off first base because somebody apparently had failed to tell Lonnie that Rapid Robert no longer is the easy mark for base runners that he used to be.

11 ALL-STAR RECORDS ARE SET AT DETROIT

Vaughan Figures in Five New Marks for the Classic

DETROIT, July 8 (AP)—Eleven All-Star records were set in today's classic at Briggs Stadium with Arky Vaughan, shortstop of the Nationals, figuring in five of them.

The records:

Most runs batted in for one game—Ted Williams, Americans, and Vaughan, Nationals, four each.

Most homers in one game—Vaughan, two.

Homers consecutive innings and times at bat—Vaughan in seventh (off Sid Hudson) and in eighth (off Edgar Smith).

Most successive hits—Vaughan, three (single in fifth and homers in seventh and eighth).

Most errors by an outfielder in one game—Pete Reiser, Nationals, two.

Most outfield errors in one game—Four; Nationals, two (both by Reiser) and Americans, two (Williams and Jeff Heath).

Most errors both teams one game—Five (Americans three, Nationals two).

Most All-Star games played—Mel Ott, Joe Medwick and Billy Herman, all of Nationals, eight each.

Most games won on home diamond—Five by American League.

Total All-Star hits—Herman, Nationals, eleven in eight games.

A New DiMaggio Feat

Special to THE NEW YORK TIMES.

DETROIT, July 8—The Dimaggio brother act supplied a new one today. When big brother Joe doubled in the eighth and younger Dom singled him home it was the first time one DiMaggio had driven another home with a run in organized baseball.

DiMaggio's Streak Ended at 56 Games, but Yanks Down Indians Before 67,468

SMITH AND BAGBY STOP YANKEE STAR

DiMaggio, Up for Last Time in Eighth, Hits Into a Double Play With Bases Full

M'CARTHYMEN WIN BY 4-3

Stretch Lead Over Indians to 7 Lengths Before Biggest Crowd for Night Game

By JOHN DREBINGER

Special to THE NEW YORK TIMES.

CLEVELAND, July 17 — In a brilliant setting of lights and before 67,468 fans, the largest crowd ever to see a game of night baseball in the major leagues, the Yankees tonight vanquished the Indians, 4 to 3, but the famous hitting streak of Joe DiMaggio finally came to an end.

Officially it will go into the records as fifty-six consecutive games, the total he reached yesterday. Tonight in Cleveland's municipal stadium the great DiMag was held hitless for the first time in more than two months.

Al Smith, veteran Cleveland left-hander and a Giant cast-off, and Jim Bagby, a young right-hander, collaborated in bringing the DiMaggio string to a close.

Jolting Joe faced Smith three times. Twice he smashed the ball down the third-base line, but each time Ken Keltner, Tribe third sacker, collared the ball and hurled it across the diamond for a put-out at first. In between these two tries, DiMaggio drew a pass from Smith.

Then, in the eighth, amid a deafening uproar, the streak dramatically ended, though the Yanks routed Smith with a flurry of four hits and two runs that eventually won the game.

Double Play Seals Record

With the bases full and only one out Bagby faced DiMaggio and, with the count at one ball and one strike, induced the renowned slugger to crash into a double play. It was a grounder to the shortstop, and as the ball flitted from Lou Boudreau to Ray Mack to Oscar Grimes, who played first base for the Tribe, the crowd knew the streak was over.

However, there were still a few thrills to come, for in the ninth, with the Yanks leading, 4 to 1, the Indians suddenly broke loose with an attack that for a few moments threatened to send the game into extra innings and thus give DiMaggio another chance.

Gerald Walker and Grimes singled, and, though Johnny Murphy here replaced Gomez, Larry Rosenthal tripled to score his two colleagues. But with the tying run on third and nobody out the Cleveland attack bogged down in a mess of bad base-running and the Yanks' remaining one-run lead held, though it meant the end of the streak for DiMaggio, who might have come up fourth had there been a tenth inning.

Started May 15

It was on May 15 against the White Sox at the Yankee Stadium that DiMaggio began his string, which in time was to gain nation-wide attention. As the great DiMag kept clicking in game after game, going into the twenties, then the thirties, he became the central figure of the baseball world.

On June 29, in a double-header with the Senators in Washington, he tied, then surpassed the American League and modern record of forty-one games set by George Sisler of the Browns in 1922. The next target was the all-time major league high of forty-four contests set by Willie Keeler, famous Oriole star, forty-four years ago under conditions much easier then for a batsman than they are today. Then there was no foul-strike rule hampering the batter.

But nothing hampered DiMaggio as he kept getting his daily hits, and on July 1 he tied the Keeler mark. The following day he soared past it for game No. 45, and he kept on soaring until tonight. In seeking his fifty-seventh game, he finally was brought to a halt.

Actually, DiMaggio hit in fifty-seven consecutive games, for on July 8 he connected safely in the All-Star game in Detroit. But that contest did not count in the official league records.

Did Better on Coast

DiMaggio's mark ends five short of his own Pacific Coast League record of sixty-one consecutive games, which he set while with San Francisco in 1933. The all-time minor league high is sixty-seven, set by Joe Wilhoit of Wichita in the Western League in 1919.

The contest tonight was a blistering left-handed mound duel between Gomez and Smith, with Gomez going ahead one run in the first on Red Rolfe's single and Tommy Henrich's double.

A tremendous home run inside the park, which Walker outgalloped, tied the score in the fourth and the battle remained deadlocked until Joe Gordon untied it with his fifteenth homer of the year into the left-field stand in the seventh.

In the eighth the Yanks seemingly clinched victory when Charlie Keller rifled a triple to center past Roy Weatherly, who played the ball badly, needlessly charging in when he might just as well have played it safe for a single.

In its wake came singles by Gomez and Johnny Sturm. A double by Rolfe and two runs were in. Smith walked Henrich to fill the bases, and in this setting, with one out, the result of a harmless grounder by Phil Rizzuto, Bagby stepped in to face the great DiMag. A moment later the streak was over.

Traffic Snarl on Bases

The Indians were guilty of atrocious work on the bases in the ninth after Rosenthal had cracked Murphy for a triple to drive in two. Hal Trosky, pinch hitting, grounded out to first. Then Soup Campbell, batting for Bagby, splashed a grounder to Murphy. Rosenthal tried to score, was run down between third and home.

To make matters worse, Campbell, dashing past first base, never looked to see what was going on and so made no attempt to grab second during the run-up. Weatherly, amid no end of hoots and jeers, grounded out for the final play.

The victory was Gomez's eighth, his sixth in a row. It was the Yanks' seventeenth in their last eighteen games and thirty-first in their last thirty-six contests. Their lead over the thoroughly demoralized Tribe was stretched to seven games.

With 40,000 reserved-seat tickets disposed of in the advance sale, a banner crowd was assured before a fan showed up, and with ideal weather conditions prevailing, the unreserved sections lost no time clinching the matter.

A swing band, barricaded behind a wire screening just to the rear of home plate, provided entertainment for the early arrivals. And just to match the southpaw efforts of Gomez and Smith the band leader also was left handed.

Although Bill Dickey has fully recovered from the charley horse which has kept him on the sidelines the past few days, Manager McCarthy decided to give his veteran backstop an additional day of rest inasmuch as Rosar has been thumping the ball at a merry clip.

Just before the game, Manager Peckinpaugh received an electric refrigerator, a gift from his admirers.

PITCHERS WHO HALTED YANKEE SLUGGER

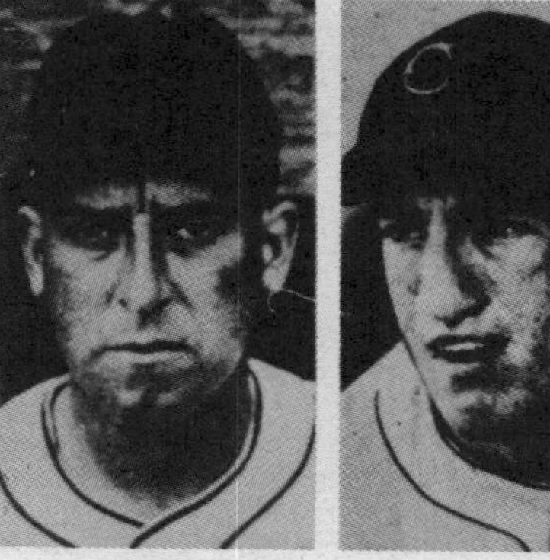

Al Smith — Jim Bagby Jr.

Times Wide World

DiMaggio's Record Streak

Date	Opponent	ab.	r.	h.	2b.	3b.	hr.
May 15	White Sox	4	0	1	0	0	0
May 16	White Sox	4	2	2	0	1	1
May 17	White Sox	3	1	1	0	0	0
May 18	Browns	3	3	3	1	0	0
May 19	Browns	3	0	1	1	0	0
May 20	Browns	5	1	1	0	0	0
May 21	Tigers	5	0	2	0	0	0
May 22	Tigers	4	0	1	0	0	0
May 23	Red Sox	5	0	1	0	0	0
May 24	Red Sox	4	2	1	0	0	0
May 25	Red Sox	4	0	1	0	0	0
May 27	Senators	5	3	4	0	0	1
May 28	Senators	4	1	1	0	1	0
May 29	Senators	3	1	1	0	0	0
May 30	Red Sox	2	1	1	0	0	0
May 30	Red Sox	3	0	1	1	0	0
June 1	Indians	4	1	1	0	0	0
June 1	Indians	4	0	1	0	0	0
June 2	Indians	4	2	2	1	0	0
June 3	Tigers	4	1	1	0	0	1
June 5	Tigers	5	1	1	0	1	0
June 7	Browns	5	2	3	0	0	0
June 8	Browns	4	3	2	0	0	2
June 8	Browns	4	1	2	1	0	1
June 10	White Sox	5	1	1	0	0	0
June 12	White Sox	4	1	2	0	0	1
June 14	Indians	2	0	1	1	0	0
June 15	Indians	3	1	1	0	0	1
June 16	Indians	5	0	1	1	0	0
June 17	White Sox	4	1	1	0	0	0
June 18	White Sox	3	0	1	0	0	0
June 19	White Sox	3	2	3	0	0	1
June 20	Tigers	5	3	4	1	0	0
June 21	Tigers	4	0	1	0	0	0
June 22	Tigers	5	1	2	1	0	1
June 24	Browns	4	1	1	0	0	0
June 25	Browns	4	1	1	0	0	1
June 26	Browns	4	0	1	1	0	0
June 27	Athletics	3	1	2	0	0	1
June 28	Athletics	5	1	2	1	0	0
June 29	Senators	4	1	1	1	0	0
June 29	Senators	5	1	1	0	0	0
July 1	Red Sox	4	0	2	0	0	0
July 1	Red Sox	3	1	1	0	0	0
July 2	Red Sox	5	1	1	0	0	1
July 5	Athletics	4	2	1	0	0	1
July 6	Athletics	5	2	4	1	0	0
July 6	Athletics	4	0	2	0	1	0
July 10	Browns	2	0	1	0	0	0
July 11	Browns	5	1	4	0	0	1
July 12	Browns	5	1	2	1	0	0
July 13	White Sox	4	2	3	0	0	0
July 13	White Sox	4	0	1	0	0	0
July 14	White Sox	3	0	1	0	0	0
July 15	White Sox	4	1	2	1	0	0
July 16	Indians	4	3	3	1	0	0
Total		223	56	91	16	4	15

Yankee Box Score

NEW YORK (A.)	ab.	r.	h.	po.	a.	e.
Sturm, 1b	4	0	1	10	2	0
Rolfe, 3b	4	1	2	2	3	0
Henrich, rf	3	0	1	4	0	0
DiMaggio, cf	3	0	0	2	0	0
Gordon, 2b	4	1	2	0	1	0
Rosar, c	4	0	0	5	1	0
Keller, lf	3	1	1	0	0	0
Rizzuto, ss	4	0	0	2	1	0
Gomez, p	4	1	1	2	1	0
Murphy, p	0	0	0	0	1	0
Total	33	4	8	27	10	0

CLEVELAND (A.)	ab.	r.	h.	po.	a.	e.
Weatherly, cf	5	0	1	4	0	0
Keltner, 3b	3	0	1	1	4	0
Boudreau, ss	3	0	0	0	2	0
Heath, rf	4	0	0	0	0	0
Walker, lf	3	2	2	1	0	0
Grimes, 1b	3	1	1	12	0	0
Mack, 2b	3	0	0	4	7	0
aRosenthal	1	0	1	0	0	0
Hemsley, c	3	0	1	5	1	0
bTrosky	1	0	0	0	0	0
Smith, p	3	0	0	0	0	0
Bagby, p	0	0	0	0	0	0
cCampbell	1	0	0	0	0	0
Total	33	3	7	27	14	0

aBatted for Mack in ninth.
bBatted for Hemsley in ninth.
cBatted for Bagby in ninth.

New York .... 1 0 0 0 0 0 1 2 0—4
Cleveland .... 0 0 0 1 0 0 0 0 2—3

Runs batted in—Henrich, Walker, Gomez, Gordon, Rolfe, Rosenthal 2.

Two-base hits—Henrich, Rolfe. Three-base hits—Keller, Rosenthal. Home runs—Walker, Gordon. Sacrifice—Boudreau. Double play—Boudreau, Mack and Grimes. Left on bases—New York 5, Cleveland 7. Bases on balls—Off Smith 2, Bagby 1, Gomez 3. Struck out—By Gomez 5, Smith 4, Bagby 1. Hits—Off Smith 7 in 7 1-3 innings, Bagby 1 in 1 2-3, Gomez 6 in 8 (none out in ninth), Murphy 1 in 1. Passed ball—Hemsley. Winning pitcher—Gomez. Losing pitcher—Smith. Umpires—Summers, Rue and Stewart. Time of game—2:03. Attendance—67,468.

D'MAGGIO SORRY IT'S OVER

Wanted to Go On Improving His Streak as Long as He Could

CLEVELAND, July 17 (AP)—Joe DiMaggio, whose hitting streak of fifty-six games was ended tonight, expressed regret that he had failed to extend the record.

After the game DiMaggio said:

"I can't say that I'm glad it's over. Of course, I wanted to go on as long as I could.

"Now that the streak is over, I just want to get out there and keep helping to win ball games."

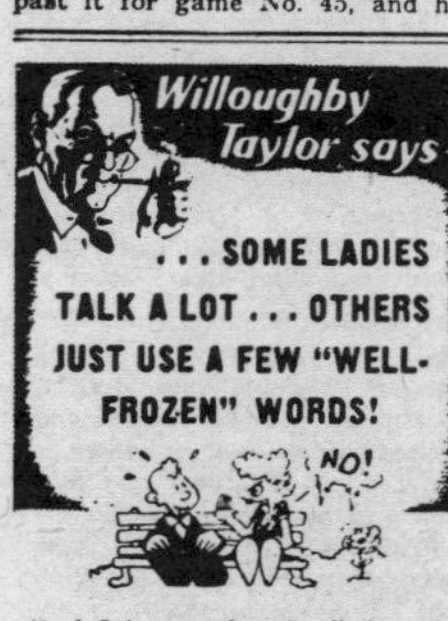

Major League Baseball

National League

YESTERDAY'S RESULTS

Cincinnati 5, New York 4 (night).
Chicago 2, Philadelphia 2 (six innings, rain).
Pittsburgh at Boston, rain.
Other clubs not scheduled.

STANDING OF THE CLUBS

	Brooklyn	St. Louis	New York	Cincinnati	Pittsburgh	Chicago	Boston	Phila'phia	Won	Lost	Percentage	Games Behind
Bklyn	—	6	8	10	5	9	9	11	56	27	.675	—
St. L	6	—	8	8	9	5	6	11	53	30	.639	3
N. Y.	4	6	—	5	5	9	8	6	43	36	.544	11
Cincin.	6	6	7	—	6	6	9	4	44	39	.530	12
Pitts.	3	1	7	4	—	9	4	10	38	38	.500	14½
Chic.	5	5	3	[illegible]	4	—	7	9	37	47	.440	19½
Boston	2	4	3	4	4	6	—	9	32	47	.405	22
Phila.	1	2	2	4	5	3	4	—	21	60	.259	34
Lost	27	30	36	39	38	47	47	60				

GAMES TODAY

St. Louis at Brooklyn (3 P. M.).
Pittsburgh at Boston (2).
Other clubs not scheduled.

American League

YESTERDAY'S RESULTS

New York 4, Cleveland 3 (night).
Detroit 7, Washington 1.
Boston 7, Chicago 4 (night).
St. Louis 4, Philadelphia 3 (night).

STANDING OF THE CLUBS

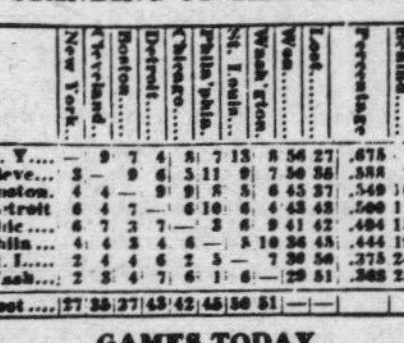

	New York	Cleveland	Boston	Detroit	Chicago	Phila'phia	St. Louis	Wash'ton	Won	Lost	Percentage	Games Behind
N. Y.	—	9	7	4	8	7	13	8	56	27	.675	—
Cleve.	8	—	9	6	5	11	9	7	50	38	.568	7
Boston	4	4	—	9	9	8	5	6	45	37	.549	10½
Detroit	6	4	7	—	6	10	6	4	43	43	.500	14½
Chic.	6	7	3	7	—	3	6	9	41	42	.494	15
Phila.	4	4	3	4	6	—	5	10	36	45	.444	19
St. L.	2	4	4	6	2	5	—	7	30	50	.375	24½
Wash.	2	3	4	7	6	1	6	—	29	51	.363	25½
Lost	27	38	37	43	42	45	50	51				

GAMES TODAY

New York at Cleveland.
Washington at Detroit.
Boston at Chicago.
Philadelphia at St. Louis.

UNBEATEN RIDDLE TRIPS GIANTS, 5-4

Reds' Pitcher Is Touched for Ten Hits in Hurling 11th Straight Triumph

3 RUNS IN FIRST INNING

Drive Sends Visitors Off to Thrilling Victory in Night Game at Polo Grounds

By JAMES P. DAWSON

What appeared to be an easy double-play ball in the first inning became the rock on which the Giants perished last night in their nocturnal strife with the champion Reds before a gathering of 20,289 at the Polo Grounds.

The scrambled play sent the Reds charging off on a three-run foray, engulfed Bill Lohrman in the painful humiliation of a quick rout, and made useless a heroic bit of relief hurling by Fiddler Bill McGee. The drive led unbeaten Elmer Riddle to his eleventh straight triumph as the Reds marched to victory, 5 to 4.

Lohrman can blame himself for what happened and Riddle can count himself lucky he survived a blistering ten-hit cuffing that carried right up to the finish where, with the tying run on third, Gabby Hartnett, swinging for Burgess Whitehead, looked at a third strike.

Giants Miss Many Chances

Johnny Rucker did yeoman's duty with his bludgeon, starting three promising outbursts with as many singles. Billy Jurges did likewise. But that three-run deficit with which Colonel Bill Terry's boys started proved an insurmountable hurdle.

It happened this way. Lloyd Waner was out as the game started on a disputed topped roller toward first. Mike McCormick singled and raced to third when Lonnie Frey poked a single to right.

In this situation Frank McCormick rapped one at Lohrman which Bill handled easily. He wheeled deliberately for the peg to second, but let fly with a wide toss to Whitehead, as Mike McCormick scored and Frey pulled up safe at second.

In rapid succession then, Bill Werber singled Frey home and, after Dick West had flied out, Harry Craft's single chased Frank McCormick in from second.

West Connects for Triple

This handicap was reduced when the Giants rapped Riddle for a run in their half of the first, but it widened again in the third when Dick Bartell's error was followed by West's triple over the head of racing Mel Ott. A single by Eddie Joost, that chased Lohrman, then sealed the doom of the Giants.

The Terrymen had Riddle on the run in the third when three singles and a force-out fashioned two runs, and in the fourth a pass to Bartell, Jurges's single and McGee's long fly brought anxious moments to mild Bill McKechnie.

Riddle made a fortunate stab on Young's blazing rap to end the fifth after Harry Danning singled. In the sixth Bill Werber launched a sparkling double play that offset Jurges's second single. And the rest was easy for Riddle.

McGee gave up a pass and two singles in his relief role, but it all added up to so much wasted effort.

Hubbell's Streak Recalled

The game marked a Carl Hubbell anniversary. It was five years ago yesterday that Old Hub, in Pittsburgh, scored his twenty-fourth straight victory in that overlapping two-year string at a time when the Giants were ten and a half games off the pace.

Rockland County admirers of Chuck Aleno, Nanuet, N. Y., flychaser for the Reds, presented a gift to their hero in a ceremony at the plate before the game.

Jack Schwartz, secretary to Colonel Terry, missed the fray. He was celebrating the birth of an eight-pound son yesterday.

The box score:

CINCINNATI (N.)	ab.	r.	h.	po.	a.	e.
Waner, rf	4	0	0	1	0	0
M. M'C'k, lf	5	1	2	3	0	0
Frey, 2b	4	1	1	4	4	0
F. McC'k, 1b	4	1	0	10	1	0
Werber, 3b	4	1	1	1	5	0
West, c	4	1	1	1	1	0
Craft, cf	4	0	1	4	0	0
Joost, ss	3	0	1	3	1	0
E. Riddle, p	2	0	1	0	3	0
Total	34	5	9	27	15	0

NEW YORK (N.)	ab.	r.	h.	po.	a.	e.
Rucker, cf	5	2	3	4	0	0
Whiteh'd, 2b	3	1	1	8	2	0
bHartnett	1	0	0	0	0	0
Moore, lf	4	0	1	2	0	0
Ott, rf	4	0	1	2	0	0
Danning, c	4	0	1	1	2	0
Young, 1b	4	0	0	10	0	0
Bartell, 3b	2	1	0	0	1	1
Jurges, ss	4	1	3	0	3	1
Lohrman, p	1	0	0	0	0	1
McGee, p	2	0	0	0	3	0
aHale	1	0	0	0	0	0
Total	34	4	10	27	12	2

aBatted for McGee in ninth.
bBatted for Whitehead in ninth.

Cincinnati .... 3 0 2 0 0 0 0 0 0—5
New York .... 1 0 2 1 0 0 0 0 0—4

Runs batted in—F. McCormick, Werber, Craft, Ott, West, Joost, Moore, Danning, McGee.

Three-base hit—West. Sacrifices—Riddle 2, Whitehead, Waner, Hale. Double play—Werber, Frey and F. McCormick. Left on bases—New York 7, Cincinnati 7. Bases on balls—Off Riddle 2, Lohrman 1, McGee 1. Struck out—By Lohrman 1, Riddle 1. Hits—Off Lohrman 7 in 2 1-3 innings, off McGee 2 in 6 2-3. Losing pitcher—Lohrman. Umpires—Barr, Sears and Jorda. Time of game—2:06. Attendance—20,289.

Major League Leaders

BATSMEN

NATIONAL LEAGUE

	G.	AB.	R.	H.	PC.
Reiser, Brooklyn	71	275	63	97	.353
Mize, St. Louis	64	239	34	80	.335
Etten, Philadelphia	78	271	38	88	.325
Slaughter, St. Louis	83	324	54	105	.324
Cooney, Boston	67	252	27	81	.321

AMERICAN LEAGUE

	G.	AB.	R.	H.	PC.
Williams, Boston	73	243	74	96	.395
DiMaggio, New York	85	334	80	124	.371
Travis, Washington	77	311	53	115	.370
Heath, Cleveland	82	313	52	114	.365
Cullenbine, St. Louis	76	247	45	89	.360

HOME-RUN HITTERS

NATIONAL LEAGUE

Ott, New York....18 | Nicholson, Chic....16
Camilli, B'klyn....16

AMERICAN LEAGUE

DiMaggio, N. Y.....20 | Johnson, Phila....17
Keller, N. Y.....20 | York, Detroit....17

RUNS BATTED IN

NATIONAL LEAGUE

Nicholson, Chic....64 | Mize, St. Louis....57
Camilli, B'klyn....60

AMERICAN LEAGUE

DiMaggio, N. Y.....76 | York, Detroit....67
Keller, N. Y.....74

THE BIG THREE OF THE DODGER MOUND STAFF

Kirby Higbe, Hugh Casey and Whitlow Wyatt, who have won a total of thirty-five games thus far this season for the leaders in the National League pennant race.

Associated Press

TIGERS, WITH TROUT, HALT SENATORS, 7-1

Washington Limited to Four Singles—Travis's 24-Game Hitting Streak Stopped

DETROIT, July 17 (AP)—Young Sid Hudson, hit hard by the National League All-Stars in his last appearance at Briggs Stadium, had little more success today as the Tigers belted fourteen hits to defeat the Senators, 7 to 1.

Paul (Dizzy) Trout limited Washington to four singles for his seventh victory of the season against five defeats. He missed a shut-out when Rudy York's error between singles by George Archie and George Case produced a run in the ninth inning.

Trout's brilliant pitching halted the batting streak of Shortstop Cecil Travis, who until today had hit safely in twenty-four consecutive games.

Hudson was chased in the two-run sixth inning, and Vernon Kennedy finished the game. Billy Sullivan and Pinky Higgins each had three hits. Frankie Croucher singled Sullivan home in the second with what proved to be the winning run.

Trout walked six batters and fanned five but left ten Senators stranded. It was Detroit's third straight victory.

The box score:

WASHINGTON (A.)	ab.	r.	h.	po.	a.	e.
Case, lf	4	0	1	1	0	0
Cramer, cf	3	0	1	2	0	0
Lewis, rf	3	0	1	0	0	0
Travis, ss	4	0	0	2	3	0
Vernon, 1b	4	0	0	10	0	0
Archie, 3b	3	1	1	0	1	0
Early, c	3	0	0	5	1	0
Bloodw'th, 2b	4	0	0	3	3	0
Hudson, p	2	0	0	0	2	0
Kennedy, p	1	0	0	0	2	0
aMyer	1	0	0	0	0	0
Total	32	1	4	24	11	0

DETROIT (A.)	ab.	r.	h.	po.	a.	e.
McCosky, cf	3	1	2	6	0	0
Radcliff, lf	4	1	2	2	0	0
Stainback, lf	0	0	0	1	0	0
Higgins, 3b	4	1	3	0	6	0
Campbell, rf	1	0	0	0	0	0
York, 1b	4	0	1	8	0	1
Meyer, 2b	4	1	1	3	3	0
Sullivan, c	4	2	3	5	0	0
Croucher, ss	4	0	2	2	3	0
Trout, p	4	0	1	0	0	0
Total	35	7	14	27	12	1

aBatted for Kennedy in ninth.

Washington .... 0 0 0 0 0 0 0 0 1—1
Detroit .... 1 1 0 0 2 2 1 0 .—7

Runs batted in—Croucher 2, Campbell 2, Higgins, Sullivan, York, Case.

Two-base hits—Sullivan 3, Higgins, Croucher. Sacrifice—McCosky. Double play—Travis and Vernon. Left on bases—Washington 10, Detroit 6. Bases on balls—Off Hudson 1, Trout 6. Struck out—By Trout 5, Hudson 4, Kennedy 1. Hits—Off Hudson 10 in 5 innings (none out in sixth), Kennedy 4 in 3. Passed ball—Sullivan. Losing pitcher—Hudson. Umpires—Geisel, Basil and Rommel. Time of game—1:58. Attendance—4,092.

BROWNS BEAT ATHLETICS

Clift's Single in Ninth With Bases Loaded Decides, 4-3

ST. LOUIS, July 17 (AP)—Harlond Clift's single with the bases full and one out in the ninth inning gave the Browns a 4-to-3 victory over the Athletics tonight.

Although outhit, 10 to 8, the Browns reached Lester McCrabb for four timely extra-base blows, including Roy Cullenbine's triple, which drove in two runs in the fifth after two were out.

Philadelphia got four hits in the eighth frame but only one run. Wally Moses and Benny McCoy singled, but Benny was out trying for second. Bob Johnson's one-baser scored Moses, and Sam Chapman singled before Frank Hayes flied out, ending the threat.

Bob Harris, on the mound for St. Louis, went the full distance for his sixth victory against eight losses. McCrabb suffered his seventh loss against an equal number of triumphs.

The box score:

PHILADELPHIA (A.)	ab.	r.	h.	po.	a.	e.
Brancato, ss	5	0	1	4	1	1
Moses, rf	4	1	1	4	0	0
McCoy, 2b	4	1	2	1	3	1
Johnson, lf	3	1	1	1	0	0
Siebert, 1b	3	0	1	10	2	0
S. Chapman, cf	4	0	2	3	0	0
Hayes, c	4	0	0	0	0	0
Suder, 3b	4	0	1	0	3	0
McCrabb, p	4	0	1	2	2	0
Total	35	3	10	*25	14	2

ST. LOUIS (A.)	ab.	r.	h.	po.	a.	e.
Heffner, 2b	4	1	1	3	3	0
Clift, 3b	5	0	1	0	2	0
McQuinn, 1b	4	1	[illegible]	10	0	0
Judnich, cf	2	1	0	4	1	0
Cul'nbine, lf	4	0	1	4	0	0
Grace, rf	4	0	1	1	1	0
Strange, ss	4	0	1	2	3	0
aLaabs	0	1	0	0	0	0
Ferrell, c	3	0	0	3	0	0
B. Harris, p	3	0	0	0	1	0
Total	33	4	8	27	11	0

*One out when winning run was scored.
aRan for Strange in ninth.

Philadelphia .... 2 0 0 0 0 0 0 1 0—3
St. Louis .... 0 0 1 0 2 0 0 0 1—4

Runs batted in—Siebert, S. Chapman, Clift 2, Cullenbine 2, Johnson.

Two-base hits—McQuinn, Grace, McCrabb. Three-base hits—McCoy, Heffner, Cullenbine. Sacrifices—Ferrell, B. Harris. Left on bases—Philadelphia 7, St. Louis 9. Bases on balls—Off McCrabb 3, B. Harris 2. Struck out—By B. Harris 2. Wild pitch—B. Harris. Umpires—Pasarella, Ormsby and Pipgras. Time of game—1:47. Attendance—1,511.

Boxer Trains at Army Base

Larry Anzalone, welterweight who boxes Pete Muscarnera in one of the four eight-rounders at Dexter Park on Monday, is a draftee stationed at Fort Dix. He is training for the fight by working out at the recreation hall.

Four Cornell Stars Annex Posts On League Nine Picked by Coaches

Sickles Tops Voting by 7 Mentors of Eastern Circuit—Bufalino, Stillman and Scholl Named—Princeton Places Two

Cornell players dominate the all-league team for the second year in a row, even though they were dethroned as the Eastern intercollegiate baseball champions during the 1941 season, according to the selections announced yesterday by Asa S. Bushnell, secretary-treasurer of the circuit.

The choices made by coaches of the seven teams in the league placed four of the Ithacans on the all-league first squad. Heading the Cornell quartet is Walt Sickles, the most efficient pitcher during the recent campaign.

Fine Three-Year Record

Sickles, credited with a three-year record of seventeen victories and only three setbacks, received thirteen out of a possible fourteen points. The points were allotted on a basis of two for a first-team selection and one for a second-team vote.

Three of Sickles's team-mates are in the first-string infield. They are Lou Bufalino, first baseman; Walt Scholl, third baseman, and Ronnie Stillman, shortstop. The choice for second base is Stan Pearson, the Princeton leader.

Another Princetonian on the first team is Roy Talcott, sophomore pitcher. Pennsylvania likewise has two representatives, Captain Frank Reagan, catcher, and Arnold Beinstein, outfielder. Completing the first squad are Captain Ken Pill of Columbia and Howie Kaye of Yale, both outfielders.

Most Runs for Pill

Sickles and Talcott were the league's top hurlers. The former was credited with the lowest earned-run average, while Talcott attained the most victories. Reagan led in total bases, made the most hits and was the outstanding base stealer. Pill scored the most runs. Scholl, Bufalino and Beinstein distinguished themselves as extra-base hitters.

Five colleges have men on the second team, for which there were two ties in the balloting. Dartmouth has four, Princeton three, Pennsylvania and Yale two each and Columbia one.

Coaches making the selections were Bill Clarke, Princeton; Mose Quinn, Cornell; Jeff Tesreau, Dartmouth; Joe Wood, Yale; Dr. Walter Cariss, Pennsylvania; Floyd Stahl, Harvard, and Andy Coakley, Columbia. Their teams finished in that order.

The Selections

FIRST TEAM		SECOND TEAM
Sickles, Cornell (13)	P.	Harrison, Yale (9)
Talcott, Princeton (10)	P.	Sexton, Dart. (3)
Reagan, Penn. (12)	C.	MacCoy, Princet. (5)
Bufalino, Cornell (8)	1B.	Jones, Dartm. (3)
		Stackhouse, Penn. (3)
Pearson, Prince. (12)	2B.	Orr, Dartm. (7)
Scholl, Cornell (10)	3B.	Plumer, Prince. (6)
Stillman, Cornell (8)	SS.	Lendo, Dart. (4)
Pill, Colum. (12)	OF.	Cosby, Prince. (4)
Kaye, Yale (8)	OF.	Governali, Colum. (4)
Beinstein, Penn. (5)	OF.	Kuczynski, Pe. (3)
		Wood, Yale (3)

OTHER VOTES

Pitchers—Ames, Yale (2); Gray, Dartmouth (1).
Catchers—Koslowski, Dartmouth (1).
First basemen—Tulley, Harvard (2); Whelan, Yale (2); Hasslinger, Columbia (2).
Third basemen—Hain, Pennsylvania (3).
Shortstops—Perina, Princeton (3); Hain, Pennsylvania (2); Carton, Yale (1); Keyes, Harvard (1).
Outfielders—Orr, Dartmouth (2); Lambert, Columbia (2); MacCoy, Princeton (2); Reagan, Pennsylvania (2); Clay, Harvard (2); Talcott, Princeton (2); Ruddy, Cornell (2); Matusczak, Cornell (1); Kelley, Cornell (1); Buckley, Harvard (1); Broberg, Dartmouth (1).

(Votes in parentheses.)

Minor League Baseball

By The Associated Press

INTERNATIONAL LEAGUE

Baltimore at Jersey City, rain.
(Night Games)
Syracuse 4, Newark 0.

AT BUFFALO

		R.	H.	E.
Rochester	0 1 0 1 0 0 0 0 0	2	8	1
Buffalo	3 4 1 0 0 0 1 1 .	10	13	0

Batteries—Lyons, Dreisewerd (2) and Robinson; Hutchinson and Parsons.

AT TORONTO

		R.	H.	E.
Montreal	2 1 0 0 0 6 2 0 1	12	13	3
Toronto	0 1 0 2 0 1 2 3 4	13	11	2

Batteries—Head, Rachunok (8), Carleton (9), Flowers (9) and Walters; Vaughan, Lanfranconi (6), Fowler (7), Piechota (9) and Garbark.

STANDING OF THE CLUBS

	W.	L.	PC.		W.	L.	PC.
Newark	60	32	.652	Jersey City	45	44	.506
Buffalo	56	38	.596	Syracuse	40	47	.460
Montreal	51	40	.560	Baltimore	35	50	.412
Rochester	50	44	.532	Toronto	25	67	.272

GAMES TODAY

(All Clubs Play Night Games)
Baltimore at Jersey City (2, 7 P. M.)
Newark at Syracuse.
Rochester at Buffalo.
Other clubs not scheduled.

EASTERN LEAGUE

(Night Games)

AT SCRANTON

(First Game)

		R.	H.	E.
Hartford	0 0 0 0 0 0 0	0	5	3
Scranton	0 1 0 0 1 2 .	4	7	0

Batteries—Barnicle and Steiner; Wood and Savino.

(Second Game)

		R.	H.	E.
Hartford	1 0 1 2 0 2 0 0 2	8	10	4
Scranton	0 0 0 9 0 0 1 0 .	10	9	4

Batteries—Williams, Dagenhard (4) and Andrews; Krausse and Colgan.

AT BINGHAMTON

		R.	H.	E.
Williamsport	0 0 0 0 0 0 0 3 0	3	6	1
Binghamton	0 0 0 4 0 0 1 0 .	5	6	1

Batteries—Arntzen and Chozen; DeBiasi and Bartola.

AT ALBANY

		R.	H.	E.
Elmira	0 0 0 0 0 0 0 0 0	0	3	4
Albany	0 4 0 0 0 2 0 2 .	8	8	0

Batteries—Maglie, Pickrel and Holbrook; Rescigno and Camelli.

AT WILKES-BARRE

		R.	H.	E.
Springfield	0 0 0 0 0 0 0 0 0	0	4	0
Wilkes-Barre	0 0 0 0 0 2 1 0 .	3	11	0

Batteries—Montero, Sivess (6) and Richards; Embree and Madjeski.

STANDING OF THE CLUBS

	W.	L.	PC.		W.	L.	PC.
Will'msp't	50	31	.617	Bingh'mton	41	42	.494
Wilkes-B.	48	34	.585	Springfield	35	46	.432
Elmira	47	39	.547	Albany	37	49	.430
Scranton	43	41	.512	Hartford	28	47	.373

TEXAS LEAGUE

Beaumont 5, Fort Worth 4 (ten innings).
(Night Games)
Shreveport 5, Dallas 1 (1st).
Dallas 6, Shreveport 5 (2d).
Oklahoma City 5, San Antonio 1.
Houston 6, Tulsa 1 (5 innings, rain).

STANDING OF THE CLUBS

	W.	L.	PC.		W.	L.	PC.
Houston	64	27	.703	Beaumont	44	48	.478
Tulsa	48	43	.527	Okla. City	44	52	.458
Shreveport	48	45	.516	Fort Worth	42	52	.447
Dallas	45	49	.479	S. Antonio	40	59	.404

AMERICAN ASSOCIATION

(Night Games)

AT KANSAS CITY

		R.	H.	E.
Louisville	0 0 0 0 0 0 0 7 0	7	12	0
Kansas City	0 0 1 0 0 0 0 0 0	1	7	3

Batteries—Dickman, Scheetz (8) and Lacy, Glenn (8); Candini, Carnett (8), Hendrickson (8) and Robinson.

AT MILWAUKEE

		R.	H.	E.
Indianapolis	1 5 0 2 0 1 1 0 0	10	16	0
Milwaukee	0 0 0 0 0 0 0 0 0	0	4	2

Batteries—Starr and Lakeman; Eaves, Schmitz (2), Blaeholder (2), Dobernic (7) and Todd.

Other games postponed, rain.

STANDING OF THE CLUBS

	W.	L.	PC.		W.	L.	PC.
Louisville	54	36	.600	Toledo	45	44	.506
Columbus	50	35	.588	Ind'napolis	42	48	.467
Minn'apolis	51	36	.586	St. Paul	37	50	.425
Kansas C.	46	38	.548	Milwaukee	25	63	.284

PACIFIC COAST LEAGUE

(Wednesday Night Games)

AT PORTLAND

		R.	H.	E.
San Diego	0 2 0 0 0 1 2 1 0	6	14	0
Portland	0 0 0 0 0 0 0 0 5	5	9	1

Batteries—Olsen, Terry (9), Dilbeck (9), Rich (9) and Salkeld; Liska and Annunzio.

AT SAN FRANCISCO

		R.	H.	E.
Los Angeles	0 0 2 0 0 1 1 0 3	7	13	0
San Francisco	0 2 0 0 0 0 0 0 0	2	8	3

Batteries—Weiland and Campbell; Joyce, Epperly (8) and Ogrodowski.

AT SEATTLE

		R.	H.	E.
Sacramento	4 0 0 0 0 2 0 0 0	6	10	1
Seattle	0 0 1 3 2 4 0 2 .	12	13	1

Batteries—Kleinke, Caplinger (6), Turbeyville (6) and Kluttz; Scribner, Brown (1) and Fallon.

AT HOLLYWOOD

		R.	H.	E.
Oakland	0 0 0 2 1 0 0 2 2	7	11	1
Hollywood	1 3 1 0 0 3 1 0 .	9	13	0

Batteries—Salveson, Mulligan (3), Ananicz (7) and Raimondi; Osborne, Tost (9) and Dapper.

STANDING OF THE CLUBS

	W.	L.	PC.		W.	L.	PC.
Sacramento	66	36	.647	L. Angeles	47	53	.470
San Diego	57	45	.559	San Fran.	47	54	.456
Seattle	55	44	.556	Oakland	44	57	.436
Hollywood	48	50	.490	Portland	38	61	.384

SOUTHERN ASSOCIATION

AT KNOXVILLE

		R.	H.	E.
Nashville	0 0 0 0 1 0 0 2 1	4	4	4
Knoxville	0 1 0 1 0 0 0 2 .	5	11	3

Batteries—Twardy, Sain (8), Dorsett (8) and Felderman; Manders and Jackson.

(Night Games)

AT MEMPHIS

		R.	H.	E.
Little Rock	0 0 0 0 1 0 0 0 0	1	7	1
Memphis	0 0 0 0 0 0 0 0 0	0	5	0

Batteries—Gumpert, Intlekofer and Rensa; Johnson and Gautreaux.

AT NEW ORLEANS

		R.	H.	E.
Birmingham	3 4 0 0 0 0 0 3 0	10	17	1
New Orleans	0 1 0 0 5 3 0 0 0	9	15	2

Batteries—Matuzak, Naktenis, Barrett, Guise and LaManno; Beazley, Seinsoth, Coffman, Jarusich and Kerr.

Other clubs not scheduled.

STANDING OF THE CLUBS

	W.	L.	PC.		W.	L.	PC.
Atlanta	66	31	.677	Chat'nooga	42	46	.462
Nashville	52	38	.578	Birm'gham	42	51	.452
Knoxville	47	47	.500	Memphis	41	50	.451
N. Orleans	46	50	.479	Little Rock	34	53	.391

RED SOX VANQUISH WHITE SOX, 7 TO 4

Dominic DiMaggio Drives In Three Boston Runs With Homer and Triple

LEE FAILS FOR FIRST TIME

Had Gone Nine Innings in All 16 Previous Starts—Victory Is Tenth for Newsome

CHICAGO, July 17 (AP)—Dominic DiMaggio, driving in three runs with a homer and triple, led the Red Sox to a 7-to-4 victory over the White Sox tonight before 27,437 spectators. Thornton Lee, big Chicago southpaw, failed to go nine innings for the first time in seventeen starts this season.

Lee was removed for a pinch hitter after the Red Sox had combed him for nine hits, six of them for extra bases in eight innings.

He had gone the route in fifteen of his sixteen previous starts and in the other, against the Yankees in early May, he pitched nine complete innings before giving way to a pinch batter. Tonight's defeat was his seventh against ten victories.

Herbert Newsome pitched seven-hit ball for his season's tenth victory, three of which have been over the Chicagoans.

The defeat, their sixth in seven games, dropped the White Sox below the .500 mark and into the second division for the first time since the early days of the season. They are now fifth.

The box score:

BOSTON (A.)	ab.	r.	h.	po.	a.	e.
L. N'some, ss	5	2	2	1	3	0
Finney, rf	4	0	0	2	0	0
Spence, lf	4	2	3	[illegible]	0	0
Cronin, 3b	4	2	2	0	1	0
Foxx, 1b	4	1	1	13	0	0
Doerr, 2b	4	1	1	1	3	0
DiMaggio, cf	3	1	2	2	0	0
Pytlak, c	4	0	0	3	0	0
H. N'some, p	4	1	1	0	5	0
Total	37	7	11	27	14	0

CHICAGO (A.)	ab.	r.	h.	po.	a.	e.
Kn'bocker, 2b	4	0	0	2	3	0
Appling, ss	4	1	1	3	3	0
Kuhel, 1b	4	1	1	10	0	0
Wright, rf	4	1	2	2	0	0
Solters, lf	4	[illegible]	[illegible]	[illegible]	[illegible]	[illegible]
Kreevich, cf	4	1	1	0	0	0
Kennedy, 3b	2	0	1	1	2	1
Webb, 3b	1	0	0	0	0	0
Tresh, c	4	0	1	7	1	0
Lee, p	2	0	1	0	1	0
aHoag	1	0	0	0	0	0
Haynes, p	0	0	0	0	0	0
Total	32	4	7	27	10	1

aBatted for Lee in eighth.

Boston .... 0 1 1 0 0 1 1 2 1—7
Chicago .... 0 2 0 0 0 0 0 2 0—4

Runs batted in—Spence 2, Cronin, Foxx, DiMaggio 3, Wright 2, Kreevich, Tresh.

Two-base hits—L. Newsome, Spence, Doerr, Wright. Three-base hits—Foxx, DiMaggio, Kreevich. Home run—DiMaggio. Sacrifice—Finney. Double plays—H. Newsome, L. Newsome and Foxx; L. Newsome, Doerr and Foxx; Knickerbocker, Appling and Kuhel. Left on bases—Boston 7, Chicago 4. Bases on balls—Off H. Newsome 3, Lee 2, Haynes 1. Struck out—By H. Newsome 3, Lee 6. Hits—Off Lee 9 in 8 innings, Haynes 2 in 1. Losing pitcher—Lee. Umpires—McGowan, Quinn and Grieve. Time of game—2:00. Attendance—27,437.

NEWARK IS BLANKED BY SYRACUSE, 4 TO 0

Burkhart Allows Three Hits in Ending Bears' Streak

SYRACUSE, N. Y., July 17 (AP)—Ken Burkhart pitched three-hit ball to blank Newark tonight and end a seven-game winning streak for the league leaders as Syracuse gained a 4-to-0 triumph in the series opener.

Only two men reached second base against the young right-hander, and both runners got there on passed balls. Burkhart struck out four and walked one man in achieving his victory.

Gene Hasson paced Syracuse's 10-hit attack against Russ Christopher and Tommy Byrne, getting three hits, one a double. An error by Shortstop Scharein, with the bases full and two out in the seventh, let in two of the Syracuse runs.

The box score:

NEWARK (I.)	ab.	r.	h.	po.	a.	e.
Holmes, cf	4	0	0	0	0	0
Non'k'mp, rf	4	0	1	0	0	0
Majeski, 3b	4	0	0	0	5	0
Sears, c	4	0	1	3	1	0
Kelleher, lf	4	0	0	2	0	0
Collins, 1b	3	0	0	10	1	0
St'weiss, 2b	2	0	0	4	3	0
Scharein, ss	2	0	0	3	5	1
aWashburn	1	0	0	0	0	0
Lang, ss	0	0	0	1	0	0
Ch'topher, p	2	0	0	1	2	0
bBrack	1	0	1	0	0	0
Byrne, p	0	0	0	0	0	0
Total	31	0	3	24	17	1

SYRACUSE (I.)	ab.	r.	h.	po.	a.	e.
Rosen, cf	3	0	1	0	0	1
Sherlock, 2b	3	0	1	2	4	0
Longacre, lf	4	0	1	6	0	0
Nagel, 3b	4	0	1	1	2	1
Hasson, 1b	4	1	3	8	0	0
Bottarini, c	4	1	1	5	1	0
B'g'vanni, rf	3	0	2	2	0	0
Williams, ss	4	1	0	3	2	0
Burkhart, p	4	1	0	0	2	0
Total	33	4	10	27	11	2

aBatted for Scharein in eighth.
bBatted for Christopher in eighth.

Newark .... 0 0 0 0 0 0 0 0 0—0
Syracuse .... 0 0 0 1 0 0 2 1 .—4

Runs batted in—Bottarini, Williams.

Two-base hits—Hasson, Rosen. Double play—Christopher, Scharein and Collins. Left on bases—Newark 5, Syracuse 8. Bases on balls—Off Christopher 2, Byrne 1, Burkhart 1. Struck out—By Burkhart 4, Christopher 2, Byrne 1. Hits—Off Christopher 8 in 7 innings, Byrne 2 in 1. Passed balls—Bottarini 2, Sears 1. Losing pitcher—Christopher. Umpires—Tobin and Solodare. Time of game—2:00.

Today's Probable Pitchers

By The Associated Press.

National League

St. Louis at Brooklyn—White (6-3) vs. Higbe (13-6.)
Pittsburgh at Boston (2)—Heintzelman (5-6) and Sullivan (3-3) vs. Errickson (4-9) and Johnson (4-6).
Other clubs not scheduled.

American League

New York at Cleveland—Russo (8-5) vs. Feller (18-4).
Boston at Chicago—Grove (6-3) vs. Rigney (7-6).
Washington at Detroit—Leonard (7-11) vs. Gorsica (5-5).
Philadelphia at St. Louis—Knott (7-7) vs. Auker (6-11).

(Figures in parentheses indicate season's won-and-lost records.)

Spoldi to Box South American

The Coliseum Outdoor Stadium feature bout on Monday will have an international flavor. Aldo Spoldi, European lightweight champion, will meet Guillermo Puentes, South American titleholder, in the eight-round main event.

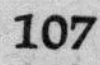

"All the News That's Fit to Print."

The New York Times.

Copyright, 1941, by The New York Times Company.

LATE CITY EDITION
Partly cloudy, continued warm today followed by much cooler this afternoon. Tomorrow fair, cooler.
Temperatures Yesterday—Max., 90; Min., 72

VOL. XCI..No. 30,571. Entered as Second-Class Matter, Postoffice, New York, N. Y. NEW YORK, MONDAY, OCTOBER 6, 1941. THREE CENTS NEW YORK CITY and Vicinity

YANKS WIN IN 9TH, FINAL 'OUT' TURNS INTO 4-RUN RALLY

Game-Ending Third Strike Gets Away From Dodger Catcher, Leading to 7-4 Victory

KELLER IS BATTING HERO

Double, His Fourth Safety, Puts New York in Front—Victors Now Lead in Series, 3-1

By JOHN DREBINGER

It couldn't, perhaps, have happened anywhere else on earth. But it did happen yesterday in Brooklyn, where in the short space of twenty-one minutes a dazed gathering of 33,813 at Ebbets Field saw a world series game miraculously flash two finishes before its eyes.

The first came at 4:35 of a sweltering afternoon, when, with two out and nobody aboard the bases in the top half of the ninth inning, Hugh Casey saw Tommy Henrich miss a sharp-breaking curve for a third strike that for a fleeting moment had the Dodgers defeating the Yankees, 4 to 3, in the fourth game of the current classic.

But before the first full-throated roar had a chance to acclaim this brilliant achievement there occurred one of those harrowing events that doubtless will live through all the ages of baseball like the Fred Snodgrass muff and the failure of Fred Merkle to touch second.

Makes Frantic Dash

Mickey Owen, topflight catcher of the Dodgers, let the ball slip away from him and, before he could retrieve it in a frantic dash in front of his own dugout, Henrich had safely crossed first base.

It was all the opening Joe McCarthy's mighty Bronx Bombers, shackled by this same Casey ever since the fifth inning, needed to turn defeat for themselves into an amazing victory which left a stunned foe crushed.

For in the wake of that excruciating error came a blazing single by Joe DiMaggio, a two-base smash against the right-field barrier by Charley Keller, a pass to Bill Dickey by the now thoroughly befuddled Casey and another two-base clout by the irrepressible Joe Gordon.

Flatbush's Darkest Hour

Four runs hurtled over the plate and, though the meteorological records may still contend that this was the brightest, sunniest and warmest day in world series history, it was easily the darkest hour that Flatbush ever has known.

For this astounding outburst gave the Yankees the game, 7 to 4, and with this victory McCarthy's miraculous maulers moved to within a single stride of another world championship. Their lead, as the series enters the fifth encounter at Ebbets Field today, now stands at three games to one, and the Bombers need to touch off only one more explosion to bring this epic interborough struggle to a close.

Almost from the moment Mayor La Guardia threw out the first ball this battle was one that had the crowd seething and sizzling under an emotional strain that at times threatened to burst out the sides of the arena in the heart of Flatbush.

Higbe First to Go

Neither of the starting pitchers, Kirby Higbe for the Dodgers and Atley Donald, survived the fierce fighting under the blistering midsummer sun. Kirby, twenty-two-game winner of the National League champions, making his delayed first appearance in the series, was the first to go. He was driven to cover in the fourth inning, by which time the Yanks had run up a lead of 3 to 0.

But this merely provided the setting for the making of a couple of Brooklyn heroes who last night would have been the toast of the borough had victory remained where it momentarily perched at 4:35 o'clock.

One was Jimmy Wasdell, who hit a pinch double in the last of the fourth to drive in two runs. The other was Pete Reiser, freshman star of the Dodgers, who, finally coming into his own, whacked a homer over the rightfield wall with Dixie Walker on base in the fifth inning to give the Brooklyn host its 4-to-3 lead.

That blow finished Donald and,

Continued on Page Twenty-one

Hurricane Pounds Bahamas, Roars On to Florida Coast

102-Mile-an-Hour Wind Hurls Boats on Shore and Darkens Nassau as Southern Resorts Put Up Boards in Preparation

By The United Press.

NASSAU, The Bahamas, Oct. 5—A 102-mile-an-hour hurricane swept past Nassau early tonight, leaving the town littered with the wreckage of boats blown out of the harbor, uprooted trees and disabled electric wires.

Buildings stood fast through the storm and no loss of life was reported.

One schooner, four sloops and a dozen smaller craft were lifted out of the water and dashed into Bay Street, Nassau's main thoroughfare. Two shipyard docks and one private dock were demolished.

A survey after the storm had passed showed considerable general damage, but there was no material damage to buildings in which the populace had taken refuge.

Waves smashed into Bay Street at the height of the storm and the street was littered with small debris. It was under a foot and a half of water two miles east of the town.

Uprooted trees littered roads in each direction from Nassau for at least three or four miles.

Government House, official residence of the Duke of Windsor, Governor of the Bahamas, was unharmed. It had been strongly boarded up. The Duke and Duchess are at his Canadian ranch.

The 102-mile-an-hour velocity

Continued on Page Ten

Record 90° Heat Drives Throngs to Beaches and Parks Here—Slow-Moving Cars Jam Roads —100,000 Visit Coney Island

Summer continued its last-ditch stand against Autumn yesterday as the temperature reached 90 degrees, setting a new record for the date, and hundreds of thousands of New Yorkers piled into cars and fled to beaches and woodlands, giving traffic policemen another dose of Sunday blues.

Yesterday was the first time since Sept. 23 that the temperature had touched 90. The low for the day was 72 degrees, which made the mean temperature 81 degrees, twenty more than normal for the date. The previous record for an Oct. 5 was 87 degrees, set in 1922.

The humidity started out at 6 A. M. with an 85, a good deal over par; fell off considerably as the temperature rose—a customary procedure—and was at 47 at sundown.

Today, the Weather Man said, will be partly cloudy and warm, growing much cooler this afternoon, and tomorrow will be fair and cooler.

Automobile traffic was particularly heavy yesterday along the Henry Hudson and West Side Highways, many of the arteries in Westchester, and in the vicinity of Coney Island and the Rockaways. At the latter resort automobiles formed solid lines along the Beach Channel Drive, Cross Bay Boule-

Continued on Page Ten

LABOR IS UNITING IN LA GUARDIA AID

Lyons Names an A. F. L. Group to Support Mayor — C. I. O. Left Wing to Act Wednesday

Mayor La Guardia seemed yesterday to be well on his way to obtaining support from both wings of organized labor in addition to that he derives as the nominee of the American Labor party.

Thomas J. Lyons, president of the New York State Federation of Labor, announced the opening of headquarters of the American Federation of Labor Non-Partisan Committee on the ninth floor of the County Trust Building, 265 West Fourteenth Street. As chairman of the committee, he said it intended to make the most intensive campaign among trade union voters in the city's history for the re-election of Mayor La Guardia.

The position of C. I. O. unions, exclusive of the Amalgamated Clothing Workers and other right-wing units that already have endorsed the Mayor, will be determined at a special meeting Wednesday night at the Fraternal Clubhouse, 110 West Forty-eighth Street.

Citizen Committee Heads

Appointment of the executive committee of the Citizens Committee for the Re-election of La Guardia, McGoldrick and Morris, composed of 550 members, including many prominent in the civic and business life of the city, was announced yesterday by William M. Chadbourne, campaign manager. Mr. Chadbourne said the membership of the general committee was more than 5,000 with many being added daily, and predicted that the people of the city would re-elect Mayor La Guardia and his running mates by a large majority.

Among the members of the executive committee are Winthrop W. Aldrich, A. A. Ballantine, James G. Blaine, Mrs. Sidney C. Borg, Henry Bruere, Dr. and Mrs. Nicholas Murray Butler, Eddie Cantor, Alfred A. Cook, Dr. Harry Woodburn Chase, David Dubinsky, Sidney Hillman, Frank L. Polk, Victor Ridder, Mrs. Kermit Roosevelt, Thomas D. Thacher, Charles H. Tuttle, Mr. and Mrs. Charles Evans Hughes Jr., Isidore Nagler, Attilio Picarelli, William M. Calder, Mrs. Alvah W. Burlingame, Mrs. Reuben L. Haskell, John Haynes Holmes, Mrs. Raymond V. Ingersoll, Duncan MacInnes, Lewis H. Pounds, Mrs. Jessie O'Brien, Manuel J. Johnson and Ernest C. Smith.

Mr. Lyons announced the appointment of Charles E. Sinnigen, secretary of the Central Union Label Council of Greater New York,

Continued on Page Twenty-five

FREEDOM RALLY THRILLS 17,000

Knudsen Pleads for Speed-Up in Defense Work — Willkie Scores Appeals to Bigotry

Bill Robinson, no Aryan, tap-danced on Adolf Hitler's coffin in Madison Square Garden last night before 17,000 persons, as the band played "When That Man Is Dead and Gone."

Bojangles, wearing gold pants, grinned happily through his tap-tap-tap a few minutes after the 17,000 onlookers had come close to having the wits scared out of them by a bombing and parachutist attack on the Garden, in the course of which thousands of soldiers descended from the vast ceiling. The Garden was in darkness for that stunt, but the darkness was broken by crisscrossing searchlights. A sound track provided real bombing raid racket.

It was a wholly realistic business—until the parachutes got within a few feet of the audience on the floor. They turned out to be about eight inches in diameter, and the soldiers they bore were of cardboard, five inches high.

Dramatization of Viewpoint

All this was part of the "Fun to Be Free" rally staged by Fight For Freedom, Inc., to dramatize its view that the United States already and necessarily is involved in the war and that the country immediately should take an active shooting part in it.

There were speakers for the occasion, among them being William S. Knudsen, director general of the Office of Production Management, who urgently called for a speed-up in the national defense program, and Wendell L. Willkie, who declared, referring to the recent speeches of Charles A. Lindbergh, that interjection of the racial issue into the American war debate had proved that the "opposition is becoming bankrupt of argument" and that the only chance of the 1942 Congressional elections being called off would result from national acceptance of the isolationist policy.

In addition to comedy, terror and oratory, the rally had considerable emotional appeal, notably when Ethel Merman called to the stage microphones a 10-year-old girl, dressed in white, her ash-blond hair caught by a bright red ribbon, and a 5-year-old boy, notable for an eager and wanting-to-be-helpful smile and for an expertly starched blue and white sailor suit.

"Where's your Mommie?" Miss Merman asked the girl.

"In London," she replied.

"Where's your Daddie?" Miss Merman asked the boy.

"In London," he said.

Continued on Page Seven

LOUIS D. BRANDEIS, RETIRED JUSTICE, DIES AT CAPITAL

Member of the Supreme Court for 23 Years Succumbs to Heart Attack at 84

LONG FAMOUS AS LIBERAL

Held People's Rule Should Mean Industrial Democracy as Well as Political

Special to THE NEW YORK TIMES.

WASHINGTON, Oct. 5 — Louis Dembitz Brandeis, retired Associate Justice of the Supreme Court and one of the greatest liberals in the history of that tribunal, died at his residence here at 7:15 o'clock this evening.

Justice Brandeis, whose name was often linked in dissents with that of the late Justice Oliver Wendell Holmes, would have been 85 years old on Nov. 13. He had a heart attack on Wednesday and had been in a coma for several hours before the end.

At his bedside were Mrs. Brandeis and their two daughters, Mrs. Elizabeth Brandeis Rauschenbusch of the faculty of the University of Wisconsin and Mrs. Susan Brandeis Gilbert, a judge in New York City.

Mrs. Brandeis received from President Roosevelt a message of condolence, which was not made public. It was stated for the family that the funeral would be private and that a memorial service would be held later.

Keen Despite Frail Health

In frail health even before his retirement, Justice Brandeis had been little heard of during the last two years, but his close friends in public and private life kept in touch with him constantly. Remaining almost all the time at his residence, he devoted himself largely to consideration of the problems of Jews, whose plight during the European war and under the Nazi persecutions affected him intensely.

More than 82 years old at the time of his retirement, Justice Brandeis was nevertheless marked for his logic, surprising intellectual energy, and extraordinary ability to obtain the basic facts in legal controversies. But his physical strength was decreasing, and after a siege of grippe in January, 1939, he decided to leave the bench where he had sat so long.

Three other former members of the Supreme Court survive Justice Brandeis, former Chief Justice Charles Evans Hughes, who retired July 1 of this year; Asso-

Continued on Page Nine

NEUTRALITY MOVE MAY BE LIMITED TO ARMING SHIPS

Roosevelt's Legal Aides Are Said to Hold He Has Power to Void Combat Zones

AND OPEN WAY TO SHIPPING

Congress Opponents Talk of Debating Change in Act as a Declaration of War

By FRANK L. KLUCKHOHN

Special to THE NEW YORK TIMES.

HYDE PARK, N. Y., Oct. 5—All indications today were that Mr. Roosevelt was preparing for one of the busiest weeks Washington has seen for some time. At a bipartisan meeting with Senate leaders Tuesday morning at the White House, the Executive is expected to make a final decision as to whether repeal or modification of the Neutrality Act is to be asked of Congress. Later in the week he may send his message on modification of the Social Security Act to Capitol Hill.

The President will return to Washington with his hand strengthened by the knowledge that the persistent sinkings in the Atlantic of American-owned ships or ships traveling in the Pan-American "safety" belt have aroused the American public. The sinking of the American-owned tanker I. C. White within the neutrality zone, which Secretary Hull yesterday termed another "act of piracy," is expected to give another fillip to American opinion, which was reported in a Gallup survey published today to be 70 per cent convinced that it is more important to defeat Hitler than to keep the United States out of war.

May Merely Ask Arms for Ships

On the other hand, Mr. Roosevelt is reported to be anxious to avoid a two-months debate in Congress on the Neutrality Act, and that is why modification, rather than repeal, may be decided upon Tuesday, according to some informed sources.

Modification may even be restricted to removing the ban on arming American ships, according to reports in a few quarters. In this case, these reports say, the President, acting under his executive powers, would eliminate by proclamation those of the declared combat zones whose existence has most hampered shipment of war supplies to Britain and her Allies. Some of his legal aides are advising the Executive that he has the power to do the latter under

Continued on Page Four

The International Situation

MONDAY, OCTOBER 6, 1941

Russian troops are still on the offensive all along the line, Moscow declared yesterday. Counter-attacks in the Ukraine were said to have made substantial gains and the Leningrad defenders were declared to be driving the Nazis back. Ridiculing Adolf Hitler's claim of Soviet losses, a Soviet spokesman put total Russian losses at 1,128,000 and those of the Germans at 3,000,000. [Page 1, Column 8.]

Berlin's reports confirmed the hard fighting of the Russians, particularly at the approach to the Crimean Peninsula. Minor successes and extensive air activity by the Nazis were reported. [Page 2, Column 2.] Stockholm heard a report that the Germans would abandon their attempt to reduce Leningrad as not worth the cost and would concentrate on other operations, possibly a drive on Moscow. [Follows the above.]

A Moscow broadcast declared that Russian planes had arrived in Yugoslavia to aid rebellious elements there. The Germans were said to be bombing centers of unrest with little effect. Guerrillas have taken more German hostages, it was reported, and have cut the Vienna-Trieste railway in fourteen places. [Page 1, Column 7.]

Moscow's reiteration of the Constitutional provisions in respect to freedom of worship and freedom of anti-religious activity appeared to have brought disappointment to United States Government quarters, where it was felt that an opportunity for real progress by the Soviet had been lost. [Page 1, Columns 6 and 7.]

A survey of British industries revealed that lease-lend materials—finished goods, raw materials and food—were now beginning to arrive in Britain. Misuse of them was vigorously denied. Schools for mechanics have been set up to improve the servicing of American planes. [Page 5, Column 1.]

Lack of a satisfactory reply from Germany continued to delay the exchange of British and German prisoners, but negotiations were continuing and the British believed that the exchange would be consummated shortly. [Page 2, Column 6.]

In Washington, President Roosevelt was expected to take up some move in respect to the Neutrality Act with Congressional leaders tomorrow. Modification rather than repeal was thought to be the likely Administration ground and there were signs that the Congressional opposition was preparing for a fight. [Page 1, Column 5.]

Reports of a naval engagement off the coast of Brazil persisted. Residents of the town of Maragogy said they had heard many shots and had seen one vessel move away under a smoke screen. No details were available in official quarters. [Page 1, Column 6.]

On the Far Eastern scene, conversations were concluded in Manila between Sir Robert Brooke-Popham, Britain's commander in the Orient, and United States defense officers there. A clarification of the United States and Philippine position was believed to have resulted. [Page 3, Column 1.]

RUSSIANS KEEP UP PRESSURE; PUT NAZI LOSSES AT 3,000,000 AND THEIR OWN AT 1,128,000

Moscow Statement on Religion Disappoints White House Circles

President Sees Taylor Tomorrow on Vatican Mission, Now Linked to Issue—Soviet's Stand 'Mockery,' Father Walsh Says

From a Staff Correspondent

HYDE PARK, N. Y., Oct. 5—President Roosevelt talked by telephone today with Myron C. Taylor, his personal representative to the Vatican, who arrived in New York by transatlantic clipper yesterday.

The President arranged to get a comprehensive report on Mr. Taylor's recent conferences with Pope Pius XII in a personal conversation at the White House in Washington Tuesday afternoon, soon after Mr. Roosevelt returns to the capital.

Mr. Taylor is expected on Tuesday to give the President full news on the Pope's attitude toward a diplomatic move seeking to induce Italy to declare a separate peace, and toward the world situation in general.

Mr. Taylor said yesterday in New York that he had information of "the utmost value" to give the President from the persons he talked with in Europe. He telephoned to Mr. Roosevelt this morning from his home at Locust Valley, L. I.

[Little doubt existed around the temporary White House, The Associated Press reported from Hyde Park, that the President wanted to consult Mr. Taylor on the latter's two audiences with Pope Pius, as well as on the animated controversy over freedom of religion in Russia.

[At a press conference in Washington on Friday Mr. Roosevelt left it an open question, pending Mr. Taylor's arrival home, whether he had asked his envoy to take up with the Pope the problem of freedom of worship in the Soviet Union.]

There was little question but that disappointment existed here today over the statement issued in Moscow yesterday by the official spokesman, S. A. Lozovsky, reiterating the guarantees of reli-

Continued on Page Four

HITLER IS DISPUTED

His Claims Cut in Half—Russians Report Gain Near Leningrad

GO 20 MILES IN UKRAINE

Counter-Offensive to Relieve Army in Crimea Is Said to Have Isolated Nazis

By C. L. SULZBERGER

Wireless to THE NEW YORK TIMES.

MOSCOW, Oct. 5—The Red Army is continuing strong counterattacks in the Ukraine and in the vicinity of Leningrad. It was reported today that Soviet troops had advanced as much as twenty miles in the former region, reoccupying a strategically important enemy stronghold, and that Major Gen. Knokoff's army in the north had forced another river passage, capturing a strongly defended village and pushing on three more miles.

These fierce sallies on the part of the Russian forces are, perhaps, the best possible answer to Reichsfuehrer Hitler's claims as the sixteenth week of this slowed-up Blitzkrieg begins. However, Alexander Scherbakoff, director of the Soviet Information Bureau, published a lengthy rebuttal to Herr Hitler's boasts of two days ago. Mr. Scherbakoff not only denied the predictions of the Nazi leader, but also gave new estimates of the casualties suffered by the contending armies thus far.

According to these latest official statistics, Russia has lost 1,128,000 men—230,000 killed, 720,000 wounded and 178,000 missing—as well as 7,000 tanks, 8,900 cannon and 5,316 aircraft. The Nazi estimates of Soviet losses were about twice as high as these.

Estimate of Nazi Loss

On the other hand, Mr. Scherbakoff said, the Germans have now lost 3,000,000 men—killed, wounded or prisoners—and 11,000 tanks, 13,000 cannon and 9,000 aircraft.

[The Nazi High Command announced the capture of 12,000 Russians in recent actions in the Southern Ukraine. Extensive Nazi operations on the approaches to Crimea were reported, but it was indicated that the Russians were fighting hard.]

Mr. Scherbakoff's statement indicated not only that the drain on German reserves of man power and matériel was far greater than the drain on those of the U.S.S.R., but also that the disparity between the two was widening and that the Nazis had been losing in increasing proportions during the last two months of fighting. That is quite contrary to Herr Hitler's predictions. The Soviet not only is far from being defeated but is handing back blow for blow and recapturing territory on many salients, according to reports received in the last forty-eight hours.

The recapture of thirty villages in the Ukraine was reported yesterday, and it was asserted today that the Axis lines had been penetrated at several points and that the Russians, in one thrust, had driven nine miles to reoccupy the small town of "B," from which the Germans and Rumanians were driven after sharp street fighting.

Russians Report Pursuit

In two days of fighting for the town the Russians captured fifty-five field pieces and nine tanks and inflicted thousands of casualties, it was reported. The town was said to have been a key point in the enemy defensive system on that salient, as well as a concentration point for forces scheduled to advance. The Russians declared that their tanks were pursuing the retreating Axis units northward.

It is increasingly evident that the extreme length of the front is too much even for the enormous German Army, and more and more advices tell of the extensive use of Hungarian and Rumanian troops. Two Hungarian companies were reported to have been wiped out

Continued on Page Two

BATTLE REPORTED OFF TIP OF BRAZIL

Townspeople Tell of Gunfire by 2 Ships Friday and New Cannonading Saturday

By The Associated Press.

MARAGOGY, Alagoas State, Brazil, Oct. 5 — Cannonading at sea accompanied by a display of searchlights last night was reported today by fishermen near Maceio, about sixty miles south of here, indicating possible continuation of a battle believed to have started between unidentified ships late Friday.

Fishermen at Pajussara Beach, near Maceio, said that the rolling thunder of what sounded like big guns came in from far out in the Atlantic.

The people of this coastal town seem firmly convinced that two unidentified ships engaged in a thirty-minute battle, exchanging thirty cannon shots, about twenty miles southeast of here last Friday evening.

Among the townspeople are many who say they saw the action. Almost every one heard the sounds that rumbled in from the sea, along the easternmost coast of Brazil.

"I haven't the slightest doubt that this was naval combat, as shots, characteristic of a cannonade, were heard clearly by all the populace," said Former Mayor Ayres Costa.

This correspondent arrived at Maragogy today to investigate rumors of the battle, which had been circulating widely in Rio de Janeiro since Saturday morning.

Among the first residents he talked with was José Bispo, a fisherman, who said that "after hearing the shots for some time I climbed a hill of about eighty meters (more than eighty yards), from where I saw a ship about twenty miles southeast, but I was unable to identify her as a warship or armored vessel."

"Another ship was more distant and I was able to see only the column of her smoke," he added.

Accounts agree that the sounds like cannonading started at 4:45 P. M. (2:45 P. M., Eastern standard time). About one detonation a minute for the succeeding half-hour was noted.

Mr. Bispo continued:

"When I reached the top of the hill the shooting ended. The nearest vessel was steaming southward and the other was visible only by her small column of smoke, and I was unable to determine if this one was fleeing or had halted to attack. Afterward the nearest ship disappeared over the horizon.

"It is not true, as reported, that lifeboats or wreckage were found on the beaches here or in the vicinity. The only thing seen was

Continued on Page Six

SOVIET FLIERS AID YUGOSLAV REBELS

Moscow Says Russian Planes Are Taking Part in Growing Guerrilla Warfare

By Telephone to THE NEW YORK TIMES.

BERNE, Switzerland, Oct. 5—The Moscow radio announced today that "a certain number" of modern Russian bombers had arrived in Yugoslavia to aid the insurgents. Heavy German aerial attacks against several important centers in Hercegovina Province were said to have failed to do more than slight material damage.

The Moscow broadcast also said there had been heavy German troop movements on the eastern frontier of Yugoslavia as large forces were rushed from their Rumanian bases to cope with outbreaks. A battle, reported to have been under way on the Belgrade-Nish railroad during the last four days, was said to have made "considerable progress."

Reports to neutral foreign diplomatic quarters in Berne — mentioned also in the late Moscow radio bulletins but unconfirmed otherwise—indicate guerrilla warfare is widespread in Yugoslavia.

Last night's report that 650 German hostages were held by the Yugoslav guerrillas was amplified this evening by the statement that these hostages included German officers and soldiers.

Reports from Belgrade state that so far the Germans appear not to have carried out their threat to shell the capital "unless guerrilla resistance ceased immediately," presumably, according to a clandestine Yugoslav radio station, "because we hold so many hostages."

Serb Rebel Regime Active

By Telephone to THE NEW YORK TIMES.

STOCKHOLM, Sweden, Oct. 5—The Berlin correspondent of the Aftonbladet reports today that an insurrectional Radical Socialist government has been established by Serbian patriots in the mountains of Montenegro and that the Germans are compelled to use dive-bombers to subdue the rebels.

The correspondent said:

"According to a Fascist newspaper, Our Fight, appearing in Belgrade, a Radical Socialist government had been built up in Montenegro under the presidency of a university professor. This government feels itself so firmly in the saddle that it issues passports and visas for those wanting to visit the inaccessible mountains of Montenegro."

The correspondent adds that the general headquarters of the rebels are established in Uzice and that officers of the former Yugoslav Army are commanding more than 10,000 men there.

"A few days ago the occupa-

Continued on Page Five

YANKEES TRIUMPH WITH 4 IN 9TH, 7-4

Continued From Page One

though Relief Pitchers Marvin Breuer and Johnny Murphy gave the Dodgers no more runs, they appeared to need no more to clinch this victory that would have squared the series at two games apiece. For Casey, the same round-faced Hugh whose brief relief turn had opened the floodgates for a Yankee triumph in Saturday's third game, looked this time to have the Bombers firmly in hand.

Casey replaced a wavering Johnny Allen in the fifth inning to repulse the Yanks with the bases full and he kept repelling them right on and up through the ninth until Owen's crowning misfortune turned the battle and the arena upside down.

Johnny Sturm, Yankee lead-off man, had opened that last-ditch stand in the ninth by grounding out to Pete Coscarart, who again was at second base for Brooklyn in place of the injured Billy Herman. Red Rolfe proved an even easier out. He bounced the ball squarely into Casey's hands and was tossed out at first with yards to spare.

Two were out, nobody was on, the Yanks looked throttled for the second time in the series and the Brooklyn horde scarcely could contain itself as it prepared to hail the feat with a tumultuous outburst of pent-up enthusiasm.

A Swing and a Miss

Casey worked carefully on Henrich and ran the count to three balls and two strikes. Then he snapped over a low, sharp-breaking curve. Henrich swung and missed. A great Flatbush triumph appeared clinched. But in the twinkling of an eye the victory was to become an even greater illusion.

As the ball skidded out of Owen's mitt and rolled toward the Dodger bench with Mickey in mad pursuit, police guards also came rushing out of the dugout to hold back the crowd which at the same moment was preparing to dash madly out on the field.

Owen retrieved the ball just in front of the steps, but Henrich, who the moment before had been at the point of throwing his bat away in great disgust, now was tearing like wild for first and he made the bag without a play.

The Yanks, of course, had not yet won the game. They were still a run behind and, though they had a man on first, Casey needed to collect only one more out to retain his margin.

But there was an ominous ring to the manner in which DiMaggio bashed a line-drive single to left that sent Henrich to second. A moment later Keller belted the ball high against the screening on top of the right-field fence. It just missed being a home run.

It was recovered in time to hold the doughty King Kong on second for a double, but both Henrich and DiMaggio streaked around the bases and over the plate. The dreaded Yanks were ahead, 5—4. To make matters even more excruciating, Casey had had a count of two strikes and no balls on Keller when King Kong pasted that one.

Down in the Brooklyn bullpen Curt Davis was warming up with great fury, but the Dodger board of strategy appeared paralyzed by the cataclysm and Manager Leo Durocher did nothing.

Casey pitched to Dickey and walked him. Again the Yanks had two on base. Casey stuck two strikes over on Gordon, then again grooved the next one. Ironically, Joe the Flash smacked the ball into left field, where Wasdell, who might have been one of the heroes, was left to chase it while Keller and Dickey raced for home with two more runs to make it four for the round.

This was enough, more than enough. Few clubs in major league history have ever had an almost certain victory snatched from them under more harrowing circumstances.

SCORING THE WINNING RUN IN THE FOURTH GAME OF THE WORLD SERIES

DiMaggio sliding home on Keller's ninth-inning double for fifth Yankee tally. Dickey, Umpire Goetz and Catcher Owen also are seen.
New York Times

Snuffing out the final three Dodgers in the last half of the ninth was almost child's play for the relief hurler whom the Yanks affectionately call Grandma Murphy. Indeed, the kindly Grandma appeared motivated by only the most humane feelings as he put those battered Dodgers out of their misery.

Like Casey in the top half of that ninth, Murphy had to face the head of the batting order. But at that moment the Dodgers didn't know whether they were standing on their heads or their heels. Peewee Reese fouled out to Dickey and Walker and Reiser ended the game by never getting the ball out of the infield.

At the outset of the conflict, as Donald and Higbe squared away on the mound, evidence came early as to why Durocher had deferred starting his so-called second ace as long as he had. Higbe went down a run in the very first inning on a single by Rolfe, a pass to DiMaggio and another sharp single to right by Keller.

Slaps Into Force Play

Keller, by far the batting star of the day with four hits, two of them doubles, started Higbe on his final downfall in the fourth by polling his first two-bagger against the right-field barrier. A walk to Dickey and a Gordon single filled the bases with none out. For a moment Higbe promised to squirm out of the difficulty by inducing Phil Rizzuto to slap into a force play at the plate and striking out Donald.

But Sturm, one of those lesser lights in the Yankee attack who occasionally strike damaging blows, struck one now. He drove a sharp single to center, Dickey and Gordon scored and Higbe gave way to Larry French who, in facing only one batter, had checked the Yanks' eighth-inning victory rally on Saturday.

This time the veteran left-hander of the National League did even better. He delivered only one ball to Rolfe. It was almost a wild pitch, Owen blocking it with considerable difficulty, but it ended the inning, for the two Yanks on the bases cut loose from their moorings and Rizzuto was trapped and run down between second and third.

However, the Yanks were ahead, 3 to 0, and with Donald working smoothly, the rest of the blistering afternoon held little excitement in prospect.

But in the last of the fourth came the first jolt when Donald, after retiring two batters, walked Owen and Coscarart. Wasdell was sent in to pinch hit for French. He caught an outside pitch on the end of his bat and the ball soared high down the left-field foul line. It fell safely in the extreme left-hand corner of the playing field, just out of Keller's desperate reach, and the stands swayed as Owen and Coscarart dashed around the bases and scored. The Yanks were now leading by only 3 to 2.

Nor was this a patch to the uproar that went up in the Dodger fifth when the aroused Flatbush Flock routed Donald before he had retired a man. Walker banged a double to left and the next instant the arena became an outdoor madhouse as Reiser, batting champion of the National League in his freshman campaign, rammed the ball over the right-field wall. It was the first Dodger home run hit in a world series in Brooklyn since 1916, when Hy Myers clouted one for the late Wilbert Robinson, and the folks really went to town on this shot.

At the same time Donald went to the clubhouse and Breuer took the mound for the McCarthy forces. He put a quietus on the show in short order and kept things quiet until he vacated for a futile pinch hitter, George Selkirk, in the eighth.

Casey Does His Share

In the meantime, Casey, who had replaced Allen in the upper half of the fifth with the bases full and then retired Gordon on an easy fly for the third out, was doing his share to keep the Yankees quiet.

But this game apparently was never meant to remain quiet and the uproar and events in that bizarre ninth will doubtless remain a nightmare in Flatbush in all the years to come.

And so the Yanks once again stand poised as they have stood in every world series they have played since 1927—seven in all. They have three victories in the bag, their opponents on the ropes and only one more encounter is needed to haul down the lion's share of the spoils.

As usual, McCarthy can continue to gamble with his inexhaustible supply of mound talent. He used three hurlers yesterday, with Murphy the winner. In the first three games he started Charley Ruffing, Spud Chandler and Marius Russo. Today, at Ebbets Field, still a fifth starter will make his debut, the husky Tiny Bonham, a strapping right-hander with a tantalizing fork ball.

Tiny came up from the farm system in August of 1940. He has never pitched a world series game before. But then neither had Russo, who spun a masterful four-hitter to win on Saturday.

In contrast with this, Durocher is strictly up against it. He must call on the veteran Whit Wyatt to keep the fading Dodgers in the struggle. And though Whit scored the only Brooklyn victory to date when he won the second game on Thursday, he has had, even with a day of postponement, only three full days of rest since.

The Flock, then, indeed is in a mighty tight spot, and all because it had a pitcher yesterday who threw such a curve it not only fooled the batter but his catcher as well.

DODGERS STRESS LUCK OF RIVALS

Yanks Could 'Catch Lightning in a Bottle,' Durocher Remarks After Game

M'PHAIL IN TEARFUL MOOD

Breathes Defiance Through the Mist—Wyatt Will Pitch Against Bonham Today

By ROSCOE McGOWEN

Nomination for the candor prize in the 1941 world series: Arnold (Mickey) Owen, the young Missouri farmer who is first-string catcher for the Dodgers.

Owen is a fellow without alibis, a chap without adverse comment on his opponents, a clear-eyed youth who will look directly at interviewers and say:

"It was all my fault."

Owen, sitting on the rubbing table in the Brooklyn clubhouse yesterday after the heart-breaking defeat by the Yankees, while his battle-scarred legs were being freshly bandaged, said just that about Hugh Casey's strike-out pitch to Tommy Henrich in the ninth inning.

"It wasn't a strike," said Mickey. "It was a great, breaking curve that I should have had. But I guess the ball hit the side of my glove. It got away from me, and by the time I got hold of it, near the corner of the Brooklyn dugout, I couldn't have thrown anybody out at first."

When told that the official scorers had given him an error on the pitch, Mickey, without hesitation, and, looking directly at his interviewer, said:

"That's right. I should have had an error on it. I should have had the ball."

Differs With Yankee Pilot

Casey, when asked about the pitch, said the ball had not hit the dirt, as Manager Joe McCarthy of the victorious Yankees is reported to have said.

"With the count three and two on Henrich," said Casey, "I figured I'd throw him a curve and put everything I had on the pitch. The ball really had a great break on it, but it didn't hit the dirt."

Manager Leo Durocher, perhaps calmer than he was the day before, when the loss of Freddy Fitzsimmons probably cost the Dodgers a victory, had implied that the police who rushed on the field when Henrich apparently struck out had interfered with Owen's recovery of the elusive ball. But Owen blamed no one but himself.

Oddly, there was by no means the atmosphere of gloom in the clubhouse that permeated it the day before.

"My boys have played all right for me," said Durocher. "You can say that."

He had a word of praise for Peewee Reese, considered in some quarters a doubtful quantity when the pressure was on. "He has played great ball," said Leo. "Great!"

One of Durocher's pet expressions for someone who expects miracles is:

"What're you tryin' to do—catch lightning in a bottle?"

Bottle Tells the Story

He had this in mind when, just before he walked out of the clubhouse yesterday he turned to a group of reporters and, pointing to an empty beer bottle near his locker, said:

"You know what that game today was, don't you?"

That remark reflected the attitude of many of the Dodgers. Said Dixie Walker:

"I tell you, those fellows have got all the luck on their side. Never saw a team get so many breaks as they have. That ball Charley Keller hit, for instance, instead of coming down off the screen, as such balls usually do, hit the top of the concrete shelf and bounced away up again. And Coscarart, who had come out (as he should) to play the ball off the wall, was in no position to take a relay after I caught up with it."

Jimmy Wasdell commented, "there are angels flying around those Yankees, I tell you."

President Larry MacPhail was moving about the clubhouse with tears in his eyes. He approached a group just as Walker was describing Keller's disastrous hit.

"Never mind that," he shouted. "Those guys haven't beat you a blasted game yet. Wait'll they really beat you. They haven't beaten you fellows a game and they haven't beaten you in the series, yet either!"

Whitlow Wyatt was asked if he was "the big man tomorrow."

"Yes, I guess I'm appointed," he responded with a cheerful grin. "I didn't know, but when I saw Curtis Davis go to the bullpen today I figured I was appointed."

33,813 Pay $161,397 At Fourth Series Game

Standing of the Teams

	W.	L.	P.C.
Yankees	3	1	.750
Dodgers	1	3	.250

Fourth-Game Statistics

Attendance (paid)	33,813
Total receipts	$161,397
Advisory council's share	24,209.55
Players' share	82,312.27
Each club's share	13,718.75
Each league's share	13,718.75

Statistics for Four Games

Attendance (paid)	201,701
Total receipts	$845,841
Advisory council's share	126,877.45
Players' share*	431,378.91
Each club's share	71,897.73
Each league's share	71,897.73

*Players on the winning club will divide $181,179.14 and those on the losing club will split $120,786.10, while $129,413.67 will be divided among the second, third and fourth place clubs of both leagues. These figures do not include radio rights.

COUNT FLEET FIRST BY THIRTY LENGTHS IN $50,090 BELMONT

1-20 Favorite Clips Record for Race as He Earns $35,340 for $250,300 Total

SWEEPS 5 SPRING STAKES

Fairy Manhurst Next in Field of 3—Mrs. Ames Beats Stir Up in National Stallion

Mrs. John D. Hertz leading Count Fleet to the winner's circle after the colt made a runaway of the seventy-fifth Belmont Stakes. By his triumph he wrote a new chapter into turf history, becoming the first horse ever to win all five of the big Spring races—Wood Memorial, Derby, Preakness, Withers and Belmont.

The New York Times

By BRYAN FIELD

Count Fleet achieved 21 yesterday—twenty-one races, the number run by Man o' War in his entire career, but a figure which only seems to be a milestone for Count Fleet on his way to further greatness.

Leading from end to end of the mile and a half of the seventy-fifth Belmont Stakes, Mrs. John D. Hertz's son of her own Reigh Count scored by thirty lengths, hard held, in 2:28 1-5, three-fifths of a second faster than the superhorse had run the same twelve furlongs in the Jockey Club Gold Cup back in 1920.

One need not compare Man o' War and Count Fleet from the standpoint of greatness, for it is a question which never can be settled. But there was a disposition among some in Belmont Park's crowd of 19,290 to take notice of the fact that this country could and did produce a champion for each World War and that the links binding the interest of men and women in thoroughbreds and patriotism were as strong as a generation ago.

Silks Sell $50,000 in Bonds

The sale for war bonds of the silks of Count Fleet in the unsaddling enclosure before Mrs. Hertz led in her champion brought $50,000. The sale for the day was estimated by Stanley Gould of the War Activities Committee to exceed $100,000, and the sale during the meeting to be beyond $500,000. Mr. Gould, congratulated for his auctions, in turn congratulated the officials of Belmont Park for having made them possible.

The victory was Count Fleet's sixteenth to raise his total earnings to $250,300, slightly more than Man o' War garnered when purses were so much smaller. Man o' War was defeated only once, and then a story went with it. Count Fleet has been second four times and third once, but never out of the money.

The way he ran to earn $35,340 of the Belmont's gross purse of $50,090 made one think that he never was going to be out of the money. There was nothing to the race, the riders of Fairy Manhurst and Deseronto giving up so far as winning was concerned after about six furlongs, even though they battled tooth and nail for the place money of $5,000. Fairy Manhurst, a son of Man o' War, got that by a length.

The track record at Belmont is Bolingbroke's 2:27 3-5, made on the teletimer. That time smashed Sorteado's mark of 2:28 2-5, which in turn had bettered Man o' War's record of 2:28 4-5.

War Admiral's Mark Broken

However, Count Fleet's clocking did break by two-fifths of a second the record for the Belmont Stakes. The previous best time for this classic since the distance was increased to a mile and a half was 2:28 3-5, set by War Admiral, a son of Man o' War, in 1937.

After the finish some one asked Jockey Johnny Longden how it was Count Fleet hadn't broken Bolingbroke's record. The lad replied: "It's a long Summer. We're trying to beat horses. Why run against the clock and risk injury, when the colt can breeze and sweep all before him?"

That's about all Count Fleet had to do—breeze. It was his sixth start of 1943 and his sixth victory, making the brown colt the first horse in history to win the five Spring specials of Wood Memorial, Kentucky Derby, Preakness Stakes, Withers Mile and Belmont.

The triple crown of Derby, Preakness and Belmont has become commonplace, half a dozen horses having brought that off since Sir Barton did it first back in Man o' War's day. It doubtless will be a long time, though, before another 3-year-old will take all five of the big Spring stakes that now feature American Spring racing.

Count Fleet bounded off at the start and his margin grew wider and wider until he reached the finish line with a sixteenth of a mile to spare. **The betting produced the legal minimum pay-off of 1 to 20, as had been expected.**

Of $261,787 wagered on the race, $249,516 went in on Count Fleet. This made for a minus pool.

The betting for the day was $1,731,155. This made the grand total at the twenty-four-day meeting $29,175,430 for a per diem average of $1,215,643, a new high for Belmont Park, but not for the State, as Jamaica's was $1,238,262.

Because of transportation difficulties, the attendance fell to a grand total of 362,617 for a per diem average of 15,109.

Longden got a consecutive double when he brought in With Regards in the seventh race, from which Whirlaway was scratched. Longden had no mount in the secondary feature, the National Stallion Stakes, which went to Mrs. Ames, a 16-5 shot.

The victory of Mrs. Ames in the National Stallion was the first Longchamps Farms score in the old stake, run for the thirty-first time. Driven to the utmost by Ted Atkinson, the daughter of Johnstown was well deserving of the victory. She finished the five furlongs down the Widener chute in 0:58 4-5, and outdid her dam, Catalysis, who had run second in the same event in 1937.

Where Mrs. Ames was a head or a nose in front of Stir Up, Catalysis had been a nose or a head behind The Chief, then owned by C. V. Whitney and now belonging to Colonel Maxwell Howard. Stir Up, one of the big string owned by Mrs. Payne Whitney, went to the post a heavy favorite.

Mrs. Ames, in with 114, was in receipt of eight pounds from Stir Up and the victory was worth $12,320 of the gross amount of $15,820.

WORLD RECORD SET FOR DISCUS THROW BY U. S. N. ENSIGN

Cannon Tops Listed Standards With 174 Feet 10⅛ Inches at Metropolitan Games

N. Y. A. C. AGAIN TRIUMPHS

Nowicki's 1:53.6 Clips 880 Time for Meet—Halliburton, Thompson, Dreyer Star

By ROBERT F. KELLEY

In the almost complete privacy of a field behind the Triborough Stadium on Randalls Island yesterday, a young ensign in the United States Navy wrote his name indelibly into the track and field records of the country with a world-record throw in the discus.

While the sparse gathering sat in the sunbaked seats, cheering the closing track events, officials came running in with the information that Ensign Hugh S. Cannon had flipped the steel plate 174 feet 10⅛ inches, defeating his nearest competitor by more than 25 feet and smashing the Metropolitan A. A. U. senior track and field championships mark, set at this meet a year ago by Al Blozis of the New York A. C.—164 feet 5 inches.

The metropolitan championships, held a year ago at Travers Island, now turned over to the Navy, were moved down to the Triborough Stadium yesterday and produced some excellent competition and one other new meet record. But the feat of Ensign Cannon dwarfed the rest of the long afternoon of competition as the New York Athletic Club, with 75½ points, won the title again, a habit with the Winged Foot athletes since the last World War.

Eclipses Harris's Feat

The accepted world record for the discus was made by Willi Schröder in Germany in 1935 at 174 feet 2½ inches. Ensign Cannon's throw also broke the American record of 174 feet 8¾ inches made by Archie Harris at Palo Alto, Calif., in 1941.

There is an unofficial mark claimed for Ernst Lampert in Germany two years ago of 175 feet 7/64 inches. But Cannon's toss broke the listed world and American records.

The new record holder has never won a national senior title, though he has been competing steadily since his graduation from Brigham Young University in 1936, in which year he took the National A. A. U. junior title.

Now serving at the Naval Station at Tompkinsville, S. I., Cannon said he felt "hot" yesterday and he continued to improve, making his record with his last throw. Bothered in the past by a tendon injured in basketball, it did not trouble him yesterday and he was well ahead of the field all the way. Harry Schneider, a football center under Chick Meehan at New York University, now competing for the Pioneer Club, was the nearest to the winner with a mark of 146 feet 11½ inches.

Victor by Ten Yards

The other meet record of the day belonged to Joe Nowicki of Fordham, who turned on a great punch in the drive to the finish of the half-mile to defeat Bill Hulse by ten yards and set the new mark at 1:53.6. The old record, made by Fred Sickinger of the New York Sporting Club a year ago, was 1:53.7. Hulse, in this event, was trying for a double, the New York A. C. runner having taken the mile a few minutes earlier.

MISS DOGWOOD, 3-2, HAWTHORNE VICTOR

Favorite Scores by Almost a Length in Steger Handicap —Daily Trouble Next

BURNT CORK GAINS SHOW

Occupy, Juvenile Full Brother to Occupation, Wins Debut Easily in Fast Time

CHICAGO, June 5 (AP)—**Brownell Combs' Miss Dogwood, one of the best 4-year-old fillies in training, turned back a strong field in today's $5,000 added Steger Handicap at Hawthorne.**

The daughter of Bull Dog-Myrtlewood, 3-2 choice with the crowd of 15,000, matched early speed with Eddie Anderson's Burnt Cork and then repulsed the late bid of David Straus' Daily Trouble to win by three quarters of a length. Daily Trouble was second and Burnt Cork third.

Mrs. A. M. Creech's Sales Talk took fourth, but the Woolford Farm's Signator, 2-1 second choice, tired under his top impost of 121 pounds and finished seventh.

The prices on Miss Dogwood, ridden by Freddie Smith, were $5, $3.40 and $3.20. Daily Trouble coupled in the betting with the Walmac Farm's Bushwhacker, returned $6.40 and $4.20, while Burnt Cork paid $4.80.

The time for the six and a half furlongs over a slow track was 1:20 3-5, best of the meeting. It was Miss Dogwood's second start of the year and her second victory. She earned $4,360.

FORDHAM NINE ON TOP, 4-1

Magee Yields 6 Hits, Fans 11 in Beating Fort Hancock

Special to THE NEW YORK TIMES.

FORT HANCOCK, N. J., June 5—Fordham University closed its baseball season by defeating Fort Hancock, 4—1, today behind the airtight pitching of Harry Magee. The Ram southpaw held the soldiers in check by yielding six scattered hits, striking out eleven and issuing three walks. The collegians finished the campaign with eleven victories and seven losses.

A two-run attack in the seventh clinched victory for the visitors. Lynk's single drove home Avallone and Szajna. The home unit avoided a shutout in its last trip to the plate. Oskroba went to first when he was hit by a wild pitch, stole second and raced home on Bielecky's single.

The score by innings:

										R.	H.	E.
Fordham	0	0	0	1	0	0	2	1	0	4	8	4
Fort Hancock	0	0	0	0	0	0	0	0	1	1	6	0

Bateries—Magee and Bach; Oldak and Moran, Cavazos.

GIANTS CONQUERED BY REDSKINS, 17-0

Akins Ground-Gaining Star as Washington Wins East Title Before 34,788

BAUGH AND DYE CONNECT

Sammy Tosses 1 Touchdown Pass After 52-Yard Drive—Field Goal by Aguirre

STATISTICS OF THE GAME

	Redskins.	Giants.
First downs	19	4
Yards gained, rushing	296	27
Forward passes	20	20
Forwards completed	11	5
Yards gained forwards	150	35
Forwards intercepted by	1	0
Number of punts	3	8
*Av. dist. punts, yds	41.3	40
Run back of punts, yds.	53	0
Fumbles	5	2
Own fumbles recovered.	3	1
Penalties	7	6
Yards lost penalties	75	39

*From line of scrimmage.

By WILLIAM D. RICHARDSON

Special to THE NEW YORK TIMES

WASHINGTON, Dec. 9—The Washington Redskins gained their fifth Eastern championship in the National Football League today when they defeated the New York Giants, 17—0, but failed to cover themselves with glory doing it.

For one thing, they were up against a Giant team weakened by the last-minute loss of Captain Frank Cope as a result of the flu and also the absence of their sturdy center, Mel Hein, who was out the entire second half due to an injury received in the second period.

Despite those losses the Giants put up a gallant defensive fight before a capacity crowd of 34,788 that limited the Redskins to only three points in the opening half and to one touchdown each in the last two periods.

New Luminary for Redskins

Chief factor in the Redskins triumph, which puts them in the play-off against the Cleveland Rams, Western winners, at Cleveland next Sunday, was not Sammy Baugh, the 'Skins great passer, nor Steve Bagarus, their rookie star from Notre Dame, who was such a surprise to the Giants in their last meeting.

This time it was their pile-driving fullback, Frank Akins, 215-pound bruiser from Washington State, Hein's old alma mater. It was Akins, one of the league's leading ground gainers, who ripped the weakened Giant line to shreds with his bull-like rushes.

The Giants, on the other hand, could do nothing against the Washington bulwarks up front, their ground-gaining being almost negligible. Neither was Arnie Herber, hero of the Giant triumph over the Eagles last Sunday, able to do much of anything to aid the Giants. His able receiver, Frank Liebel, who caught three for touchdowns against the Eagles, was seldom able to shake himself loose, so well was he looked after by the Washington defenders.

Outside of Joe Aguirre's field goal, only seven of the Redskins' seventeen points were duly earned. They came when Baugh made a twenty-five-yard toss to Les Dye, Redskin end, to wind up a fifty-two-yard drive.

Gift Score Follows Fumble

The other came in the nature of a gift when Herber fumbled on the Giants' 22 and Al Piasecky, Washington end, recovered on the 16. It didn't take the Redskins much time to capitalize on that last-quarter break, Akins busting across from the 2 to bring the total up to 16—0. The remaining point came when Baugh picked up Aguirre's attempted placement when the ball bounced off the goal posts and ran it across for the marker.

The one-sidedness of the contest is revealed by the statistics which show the Redskins making 19 first downs against 4 for the Giants and gaining 446 yards by rushing and passing to 62 for the crippled New Yorkers. Most of this Redskin yardage was by rushing, their total gains along the ground being 296 yards, whereas the Giants were limited to 27.

So stouthearted was the Giant defense down near their own goal-line that on four occasions Aguirre was forced to try for field-goals, only one of which, his first, was successful.

This one came after 12:52 of battling, the 'Skins taking Ken Strong's opening kick-off from the end zone and marching steadily to beyond midfield only to lose the ball on the 40 when Akins fumbled and DeFilippo recovered. Finding themselves unable to advance either on the ground or through the air, the Giants had to kick and this time the Redskins refused to be denied, marching all the way from their own 30 to well within the Giants' 20, where they were stopped. With fourth down coming up and eight to go, Aguirre dropped back to the 23 and split the uprights.

About the only threat the Giants made followed, but floundered when Dick Todd, one of the plethora of Redskin backs, intercepted a Herber toss on the 40. The 'Skins took up from there and moved the ball to a first down on the 15, where they were stopped by a holding penalty which forced Aguirre to try another placement, this one from the 33. It was in the third period and another from the 39 came late in the game.

One of the best Giant stands of the afternoon came near the end of the second period when they took over on downs on the 2, after the Redskins had recovered with the aid of a penalty that gave them a first down on the 8.

A 37-yard run by Akins after breaking through the Giant line set the stage for another Redskin threat early in the third. This got them to the Giant 28, but a fumble by Bob Defruiter saved the visitors, Frank Umont recovering on the 6.

The next time the 'Skins got their hands on the ball they went all the way. This followed George Franck's punt to the Skins' 40, which Bagarus ran back nine yards. Again it was Akins who was the leading factor. After a Baugh pass to Wayne Millner had given the Redskins a first down on the 40, Akins broke through for a gain that lacked inches of producing a first down on the 24, but Merlyn Condit, former Brooklyn star, made up the deficit immediately afterward and then Baugh rifled a toss that Dye caught and turned into the first touchdown of the day. It came after 9:26 in the third quarter.

Early in the final period the Giants got the ball on their own 20 after Baugh had punted over the goal line. It was shortly afterward that Herber made the fumble that gave the 'Skins their second touchdown. It took only four plays before Akins, who had bulled his way nine yards through the sagging Giant line for a first down on the 2, went the rest of the way, making the score Washington 16, Giants 0. Then it was that Baugh picked up the loose ball and ran for the extra point.

Between there and the end of the contest, which lacked luster throughout, the 'Skins threatened again, but after Baugh's pass to Bill DeCorrevont covered 27 yards and brought up a first down on the Giant 27, the Redskins were thrown back to a point where it was again put up to Aguirre, who failed from the 39.

In 1936, when they represented Boston, the Redskins also won the Eastern title.

Giants' Line-Up

REDSKINS (17)		GIANTS (0)
Aguirre	L.E.	Fox
Audet	L.T.	Tomaini
Whited	L.G.	Grate
Aldrich	C.	Hein
Stralka	R.G.	Adams
Koniszewski	R.T.	Ragazzo
Turley	R.E.	Weiss
Todd	Q.B.	Sulaitis
Bagarus	L.H.	Hovious
De Correvont	R.H.	Cuff
Baugh	F.B.	Paschal

SCORE BY PERIODS

Redskins	3	0	7	7—17
Giants	0	0	0	0— 0

Touchdowns—Dye, Akins. Points after touchdowns—Aguirre (placement), Baugh (run). Field goal—Aguirre (placement).

EASTERN TITLE DECIDED: REDSKINS 'WHOOP IT UP'

Members of the Washington team gather around their coaches in the clubhouse after their victory over the Giants. Dudley DeGroot is at the left and Turk Edwards on the right.

Sports of the Times

Reg. U. S. Pat. Off.

By ARTHUR DALEY

Scalped by the Redskins

WASHINGTON, D. C., Dec. 9—Whatever goes up must come down, and the Giants, who climbed the heights against the Eagles for last week's upset victory, made a most giddy descent against the Redskins. Stout Steve Owen would have liked to oblige his boon companion, Greasy Neale, by polishing off the Capital Braves. But his operatives, perhaps through no fault of their own, fell apart on him, and hence the minions of George Preston Marshall won the Eastern championship of the National Football League for the sixth time.

The large Mr. Owen has performed so many miracles in this series that not a soul in the stands trusted him one moment. For more than half of the game the obviously superior Redskins seemed able to do practically everything except score a touchdown. It was positively uncanny.

During the half-time intermission, however, Marshall put on a floor show with his band dressed in Santa Claus outfits, even to the long white beards. After that the New Yorkers seemed to catch a bit of the Christmas spirit and were not quite as tough. Or maybe it was that the rampaging Redskins just wore them down.

That the lads from the sidewalks of New York just didn't have it was demonstrated when Joe Aguirre's try for the extra point was blocked and Slingin' Sammy Baugh picked up the loose ball and ambled for the extra point with it. That was the crowning touch.

High Temperatures

The weather was lovely and the temperature abnormally high for December. But that didn't bother the Giants a fraction as much as Frank Cope's temperature, which soared to 103 degrees this morning. Since the huge Giant captain plays virtually the entire left side of the New York line it was like trying to halt the Redskin offense with ten men instead of eleven. The Skins tore through that makeshift forward wall as though it were made of papier-mâché.

The Capital Braves were afire anyway. Perhaps they scented a share of the play-off receipts. Or maybe George Preston Marshall is responsible. Shortly before the Washingtonians left the dressing room on their scalping expedition the Magnificent One turned to Dud DeGroot and declared modestly, "I'd like to say a few words to the boys, Dud." "Go right ahead, George," offered Dud. George thereupon went up ahead.

However, there must have been some flaw in the pep talk of Washington's most luxurious laundryman. He must not have used his super-duper special. He was able to get the Skins stampeding nicely toward the goal-line in the first half—four drives in all—but he couldn't get them across. Maybe he should have prodded the laggards with his cane.

That was the most amazing part about the early phases of hostilities. The Giants were battered from pillar to post (except the goal post) and wound up only three points in arrears. The Redskin team and the Redskin spectators were beginning to get highly nervous at such scoring futility until Slingin' Sammy Baugh pitched a strike to Les Dye in the end zone. That broke the tension—and the game wide apart.

Hein Bows Out

As quietly as he arrived on the scene fifteen long years ago, Mel Hein departed unobtrusively from professional football with an injury before the first half even was completed, a gallant and a brilliant performer to the very end. Thus did the finest center in the history of the sport bring a magnificent career to a close. He was a great player and a great fellow, an athlete, a gentleman and an admired friend. Good luck, Mel.

Two other all-time stars of the play-for-pay game to sing their swan songs were Ken Strong and Arnie Herber. There just will be no place for them in the reconversion job that Steve Owen plans for next year. That's one reconversion task that won't be hindered by union troubles.

There were a couple of comic opera touches as the game got away from the officials and rough play predominated. One such was the field judge shooting off his gun fifty seconds before the first half actually ended. There were all sorts of mysterious penalties and strange happenings. The most peculiar of these was a deft pass completion by the Giants for a long gain to the Skin 21-yard line. The fly in the ointment, however, was that Carl Grate, a guard and an ineligible receiver, made the catch. The officials ran around in circles for a while and finally awarded the ball to Washington at midfield.

Not until the Skins had the game safely in the satchel did Gen. Dwight D. Eisenhower decide to call it a day. He departed with six minutes to go. It wasn't a bad idea, although the majority of the home-town crowd, totally unused to seeing their heroes wallop the Giants so soundly, remained to enjoy it to the final gun. The Chief of Staff was seated on the New York side of the field, the first time he's ever been on the wrong side.

There hasn't been such a lopsided game here since the mighty Chicago Bears walloped the Skins by that classic 73-0 count. The main difference, however, was that this one didn't show on the score board.

But, as they say in Brooklyn, "Leave us wait until next year."

Sections 3 AND 5

SPORTS
BUYERS' WANTS
OFFERINGS TO BUYERS

The New York Times.

FINANCIAL—BUSINESS
BUSINESS OPPORTUNITIES

Sections 3 AND 5

S | SUNDAY, JUNE 2, 1946. | L + | S

ASSAULT, 7-5, WINS BELMONT STAKES FOR TRIPLE CROWN; BROWNS TRIP YANKS, 4-3; REDS TOP DODGERS IN 10TH, 5-4

HILLER IS CHASED

Loses Control and Zarilla Singles Off Wade to Win at Stadium

HOMER BY KELLER WASTED

All Yank Runs Are Scored in the Fifth—Kramer Gives Only Five Blows

By JOHN DREBINGER

Cooling out even quicker than the weather, the Yankees suffered an annoying drop in their persistent pursuit of the front-running Red Sox by dropping the opener of their four-game series with Luke Sewell's Browns at the Stadium yesterday. A gathering of 22,375 onlookers suffered and shivered along with the stalled Bombers.

They lost it by a score of 4 to 3, despite another gaudy home-run blast by Charlie Keller, and so blew an admirable opportunity of gaining another half-game on the Red Sox, who were held idle in Boston on account of rain. Instead, Bill Dickey's men are back to six and a half lengths behind the leaders, and gone too is their four-game winning streak.

For just one brief moment in the chilled performance it did look as though the Yanks would make it in their accustomed superior manner. That was in the fifth, when they sent three runs skimming over the plate, two winging home on Keller's No. 9 of the campaign, to give their young rookie right-hander, Frank Hiller, who was making his first mound start of the season, a 3-1 lead over Jack Kramer.

Hiller Loses Control

But scarcely had the hubbub attending this impressive shot subsided than the Brownies suddenly flared to life in the sixth. Johnny Berardino and Wally Judnich fired a pair of homers into the stands in rapid-fire order to tie the score and in the seventh the St. Louisans just as quickly untied it when Hiller suddenly lost control. He walked two batters, and Al Zarilla greeted Relief Pitcher Jake Wade with a single that drove home the deciding tally of the battle.

Given the lead for the second time in the game, Kramer made no more mistakes in notching his fourth pitching triumph of the season. In fact, with the exception of the fifth, he held the Yanks in a tight grip. He yielded, all told, only five blows and aside from Keller's robust wallop, kept the Yanks' long range clouters pretty well bottled up for the day. Joe DiMaggio, hitless in four tries, got the ball out of the infield just once to lift a harmless fly to Zarilla in right.

At that it was a bit of over-zealousness on the part of the usually brilliant Joe Gordon that enabled the Browns to make off with their first run, a tally that was to play as prominent a part in the defeat as the succeeding three.

Stirnweiss Gets Ball

This came in the second inning when Berardino walked and Babe Dahlgren, with one down, slammed a bounder at George Stirnweiss. Snuffy got the ball in time for a force play on Berardino at second and had Gordon, who made the put out, let well enough alone, a lot of ensuing woe might have been averted.

But the Flash, ignoring Berar-

Continued on Page 3, Column 2

McCarthy Is Sought By Mexican League

By The United Press.

MEXICO CITY, June 1—President Jorge Pasquel of the Mexican Baseball League, unsuccessful in his attempts to hire Babe Ruth, said today that he was interested in another famed New York Yankee, Joe McCarthy, for "some job with my league."

Pasquel said he had not talked with McCarthy, who recently resigned as Yankee manager, but added that "I believe he would be a good man to have around." Pasquel indicated he planned to communicate with McCarthy, possibly to offer him the permanent job as league president.

Ruth, former Yankee home run king, left here yesterday after a two-week vacation as Pasquel's guest

Two 'Single' Games For Giants Aug. 28

By The Associated Press.

ST. LOUIS, June 1 — The Cardinals and the Giants will play two games at Sportsman's Park on Aug. 28—but they're not listed as a double-header and the cash patrons will have to shell out twice to see both contests.

The game scheduled for today, postponed because of rain, was reset for 2:30 P.M. on that date, and the teams already were scheduled for a contest starting at 8:30 P.M. the same day.

Cardinal owner Sam Breadon said it was necessary to schedule the two "single" games on the same date because two other Cards - Giants games here had been postponed earlier in the season and a National League rule prohibits twilight double-headers.

TWO ERRORS LEAD TO DODGER DEFEAT

Stevens, Hero With Homer in Sixth, Makes Misplays That Set Up Reds' Run in 10th

By ROSCOE McGOWEN

Special to THE NEW YORK TIMES.

CINCINNATI, June 1—Two errors on one bunted ball by Eddie Stevens today broke up an overtime battle between Ed Head and Joe Beggs and gave Bill McKechnie's Reds an unearned but perfectly legal triumph over the Dodgers, 5-4, in the tenth inning. The defeat cut the Brooklyn first-place lead over the idle Cards to a game and a half.

A ladies day crowd of 9,063, braving rain and chill winds, saw a pinch runner for a pinch runner carry the winning tally across the plate after Lonnie Frey, a pinch hitter, had sent a fly to Dixie Walker too far out for Dixie to make the throw to the plate.

Al Libke led off the final frame with a line single just over the tip of the leaping Pee Wee Reese's glove and when Ray Lamanno laid down a nice bunt toward first base Stevens committed his double crime.

Wild Toss Follows Fumble

First he fumbled the ball, then recovered it and threw wildly to Eddie Stanky, covering first. Bob Usher, sent in to run for Libke, wound up at third base with a sprained ankle, Lamanno going to second. Mike McCormick then was inserted to run for Usher and was temporarily anchored at third while Bert Haas was purposely passed and Max West lined to Walker in short right.

Each team counted three earned runs but the Reds got the edge in tainted tallies and, fortunately for them, got the second one when it counted most.

Stevens came across with his fifth homer of the season in the sixth inning, whacking Beggs' first pitch into the right field seats, a blow that tied the score at the moment. But West assailed Head for his second homer of the campaign to the same sector to tie it again in the Reds' half of the frame.

Durocher's boys got off to an early lead by pushing two across in the first inning, which was fewer than it appeared they might

Continued on Page 3, Column 6

Major League Baseball

Sunday, June 2, 1946

American League

YESTERDAY'S RESULTS

St. Louis 4, New York 3.
Philadelphia 10, Cleveland 4.
Washington 5, Detroit 3.
Chicago at Boston, rain.

STANDING OF THE CLUBS

	Boston	New York	Washington	Detroit	St. Louis	Chicago	Cleveland	Phil'delphia	Won	Lost	Percentage	Games Behind
Boston	—	5	6	5	4	3	3	6	32	9	.780	—
New York	3	—	5	4	2	2	4	7	27	17	.614	6½
Washington	1	3	—	3	0	4	4	6	21	17	.553	9½
Detroit	1	0	2	—	4	5	5	5	22	20	.524	10½
St. Louis	1	3	2	3	—	4	3	2	18	23	.439	14
Chicago	1	2	0	3	4	—	3	2	15	21	.417	14½
Cleveland	1	3	1	1	5	3	—	3	17	24	.415	15
Philad'lphia	1	1	1	1	4	0	2	—	10	31	.244	22
Lost	9	17	17	20	23	21	24	31	—	—		

GAMES TODAY

St. Louis at New York (2, 2 P.M.).
Chicago at Boston (2).
Cleveland at Philadelphia (2).
Detroit at Washington.

National League

YESTERDAY'S RESULTS

New York at St. Louis, rain.
Cincinnati 5, Brooklyn 4 (10 in'gs).
Chicago 6, Boston 3.
Philadelphia at Pittsburgh, rain.

STANDING OF THE CLUBS

	Brooklyn	St. Louis	Cincinnati	Chicago	Boston	Pittsburgh	New York	Phil'delphia	Won	Lost	Percentage	Games Behind
Brooklyn	—	0	2	4	5	1	5	8	25	13	.658	—
St. Louis	2	—	4	5	3	4	2	3	23	14	.622	1½
Cincinnati	3	4	—	2	0	5	3	1	18	16	.529	5
Chicago	1	3	4	—	4	2	2	2	18	18	.500	6
Boston	2	2	1	2	—	1	5	4	17	20	.459	7½
Pittsburgh	2	3	2	3	1	—	1	3	15	18	.455	7½
New York	3	1	1	1	5	3	—	3	17	21	.447	8
Philad'lphia	0	1	2	1	2	2	3	—	11	24	.314	12½
Lost	13	14	16	18	20	18	21	24	—	—		

GAMES TODAY

(All clubs play two games.)
New York at St. Louis.
Brooklyn at Cincinnati.
Boston at Chicago.
Philadelphia at Pittsburgh.

The Season's Leading 3-Year-Old Scoring an Easy Victory in Belmont Stakes

King Ranch's Assault crossing the finish line three lengths ahead of Natchez in the seventy-eighth running of the feature

WISCONSIN'S EIGHT VICTOR AT ITHACA

Beats Cornell, Pennsylvania and Princeton in Sprints—Tiger Jayvees Triumph

By ALLISON DANZIG

Special to THE NEW YORK TIMES.

ITHACA, N. Y., June 1—Wisconsin's oarsmen completed their sweep of the waters of the East today and head for the Pacific Coast with high hopes of establishing national collegiate rowing supremacy in the regatta at Seattle on June 22.

The heavy, beautifully synchronized crew from the Middle West showed the way to Cornell, Pennsylvania and Princeton, which placed in that order behind Allen Walz's Badgers over the mile course on the inlet here as the Eastern rowing season came to an end.

Previously Wisconsin had won the Eastern sprint championship regatta at Annapolis, with nine crews competing, and a week ago defeated Pennsylvania on the Schuylkill in Philadelphia.

Today's regatta for varsity and junior varsity eight-oared crews was to have been rowed over a two-mile course on Lake Cayuga. Conditions on the lake, however, made it impossible for the shells to venture forth, and it was necessary to transfer the races to the sheltered inlet and reduce the distance to a mile. Because of the narrowness of the canal, the four competing crews could not become engaged at the same time, and so Referee Ned Ten Eyck of Syracuse held a drawing for two preliminary heats, with the winners meeting in the final.

Wisconsin was drawn against Pennsylvania and won its heat by two-thirds of a length in 5:01, to 5:02 2/5 for the Red and Blue. Cornell led Princeton home in the second heat by almost a full length in 5:03, as against 5:06½ for the Tigers.

In the final, the Badgers won going away from Cornell by a length and a half. The time was

Continued on Page 4, Column 5

The August Belmont Memorial Cup, which is awarded to the owner of the winner, was presented to R. J. Kleberg (left) by Admiral Marc A. Mitscher, commander of the Eighth Fleet, with Mayor O'Dwyer, Jockey Warren Mehrtens, who rode the victor, and Miss Helenita Kleberg, daughter of owner, looking on.

The New York Times

Harvard Sweeps Yale Crew Races; Varsity's 8th Straight Over Blue

By JOHN RENDEL

Special to THE NEW YORK TIMES.

CAMBRIDGE, Mass., June 1—Harvard and Yale resumed their rowing rivalry this afternoon with the same result that had become monotonous in the late pre-war years—a sweep for Harvard. But it was under circumstances somewhat different from those of the palmy days. The Crimson took the varsity and the junior varsity races, both over the same mile and three-quarters course on the Charles and by almost identical margins, four lengths and a deck in the case of the first shell and four and a half by the jayvees.

When Harvard's lads swept over the line off the M. I. T. boathouse in the major race it made the eighth straight varsity victory for the Crimson and the twenty-second altogether, counting freshman, jayvee and combination crew regattas since Tom Bolles took over as coach in the fall of 1936.

This one wasn't like some of the others at New London, though. The Roman holiday afloat and ashore that made the Yale-Harvard boat race on the Thames one of America's great sports events was conspicuously dimmed.

The expensive yacht flotilla was down to four power boats. There were a couple of thousand spectators on each side of the river. The deep-throated roars from yachts' horns was reduced to a single blast from a motor boat's whistle as they skimmed over the line. There was no observation train, only a line of parked automobiles down the final half mile.

Juniors Are Faster

The junior varsity eights stole the limelight for a change by turning in the better performances. Both Harvard and Yale's second shells covered the course faster than their presumably superior mates. The Crimson was caught in 9:12 in the jayvee test and Yale in 9:31, while in the climax the times were 9:18 and 9:36.

Yale's failure in both tests undoubtedly could be attributed to lack of action. The boys had been working hard under their new coach, Dick Pocock, but they missed the testing fire of compe-

Continued on Page 2, Column 4

RUTH TURNED DOWN AS NEWARK'S PILOT

Babe, Back From Mexican Trip, Tells of His Attempts to Get Job From MacPhail

Scorched by the sun to a deep bronze, Babe Ruth returned early yesterday from his fortnight's "vacation trip" in Mexico as guest of the Pasquel brothers and with scarcely a preliminary warm-up proceeded to take two blasts at organized baseball.

Prefacing his remarks with an insistence that he does want to return to baseball and is not above accepting a minor league portfolio, the 53-year-old retired home run monarch disclosed that early this year he tried several times to get the job as manager of the Yankee farm club in Newark and that he had been turned down by Larry MacPhail after "getting pushed around for more than a month."

Then, harking back a matter of 32 years, the Babe revealed that as a "$600-a-year rookie" with the Baltimore Orioles of the International League, he had turned down an offer to jump to the then "outlaw" Federal League because of threats that he would be barred for life from organized baseball—a threat that organized baseball never made good—and thus was "jobbed out of $20,000," for which baseball never thanked him.

"Certainly I would like to get back in baseball," said the Bambino as he discussed his efforts to land with Newark.

"Last January, after Bill Dickey signed his player's contract with

Continued on Page 3, Column 3

BRUEN TAKES FINAL IN BRITISH AMATEUR

First Irish Golfer to Capture Title Beats American-Born Bob Sweeny, 4 and 3

By Wireless to THE NEW YORK TIMES.

LONDON, June 1—James Bruen, 26-year-old insurance broker from Cork, became today the first Irishman to win the British amateur golf championship by beating Bob Sweeny, American-born London business man, 4 and 3, in the thirty-six-hole final over the Birkdale course in Lancashire.

The burly Irishman, who was the pre-tournament favorite, was behind only once against the smooth-stroking Sweeny, a native of Pasadena, Calif., but a resident of England for the last eighteen years. More than anything it was Bruen's amazing accuracy with his irons that enabled him to defeat Sweeny, who paid tribute to the

Continued on Page 5, Column 4

HOGAN KEEPS LEAD IN GOODALL EVENT

Total Is Plus 36, Five Better Than Record—McSpaden's 65 Sets Winged Foot Mark

By WILLIAM D. RICHARDSON

Special to THE NEW YORK TIMES.

MAMARONECK, N. Y., June 1—After a day featured by a sensational record-making round by Harold (Jug) McSpaden of Sanford, Me., little Ben Hogan, golf's mighty atom from Texas, continues to be the pacemaker in the fifth $10,000 Goodall round-robin tournament at the Winged Foot Golf Club.

With only two more rounds left to play, Hogan's total now stands at plus 36, five points more than the tournament's record-winning score, plus 31, made by Lighthorse Harry Cooper, the winner in 1939, the second year of the adding machine tournament.

It was during the fourth round this morning that McSpaden went on his rampage, tearing the West course apart with a 65, seven under par, that sent all previous marks into the discard.

Round of 69 by Jones

No one seemed to know exactly what the previous record was, nor who made it, but the best Bobby Jones was able to do when he won the open here in 1929 was a 69, made up of a 38 on the first nine and 31 on the second. McSpaden went out in 33 and came back in 32 today.

Great though McSpaden's score was, there was one other performance that merited mention. That was the 70 that his "Gold Dust" twin, Byron (Lord) Nelson, made during a driving rainstorm that drenched the course this afternoon.

With rain coming down in buckets and in temperatures not exactly conducive to good golf, the present United States P.G.A. king continued to keep within striking distance of the leaders when he wrested six points from Bob Hamilton and Sam Snead.

Nelson's 70 came on top of a 68 that he made in the fourth round in the morning to hold McSpaden

Continued on Page 5, Column 2

Belmont Stakes Chart

By The Associated Press.

SIXTH RACE—The Belmont (seventy-eighth running); purse $100,000 added; 3-year-olds; one mile and a half. Start good; won easily; place driving. Went to post 4:40, off at once. Winner, Ch. C., by Bold Venture-Igual by Equipoise. Trainer, M. Hirsch. Value to winner, $75,400; second, $20,000; third, $10,000; fourth, $5,000. Time: 0:24 4/5, 0:49 3/5, 1:14 1/5, 1:39 2/5, 2:30 4/5.

Starters.	Wt.	P.P.	St.	½	M.	1¼	Str.	Fin.	Jockeys.	Mutuels St.	Mutuels Pl.	Mutuels Sh.	Dollar Odds.
Assault	126	1	6	4[4]	4½	3[1½]	1½	1[3]	Mehrtens	4.80	3.10	2.70	1.40
aNatchez	126	6	2	2[3]	2[2]	2[8]	2[3]	2[1½]	McCreary	....	5.70	4.10	8.60
Cable	126	2	1	7	7	4[hd]	4½	3[hd]	Atkinson	....	....	6.50	45.50
Hampden	126	7	5	1½	1[4]	1[2]	3[1]	4[hd]	Arcaro	....	....	....	3.75
Lord Boswell	126	5	4	5½	5[2]	5[2]	5[6]	5[6]	Guerin	....	....	....	1.35
aMahout	126	4	3	6½	6[hd]	7	6[3]	6½	Longden	....	....	....	8.60
War Watch	126	3	7	3[1]	3[4]	6[hd]	7	7	Scotti	....	....	....	92.80

Scratched—Manor Lad, Windfields, Cedar Creek. aMrs. W. M. Jeffords entry.

Assault, in great form, was allowed to rate along for a mile. Then he was sent along and responded with a good burst of speed, quickly ran into lead entering stretch and drew away at end to win in a romp. Natchez followed early pace, took lead around turn, but was no match for winner. Cable was hustled along in early part and made a game effort. Hampden was sent to the front with a rush, opened a good lead, but tired badly. Lord Boswell was never able to improve his position and was a tired horse at the finish. Mahout never was a factor. War Watch had good early speed.

Owners—1, King Ranch; 2, Mrs. W. M. Jeffords; 3, Mrs. A. Wichfeld; 4, Foxcatcher Farms; 5, Maine Chance Farm; 6, Mrs. W. M. Jeffords; 7, Mrs. A. Roberts.

LORD BOSWELL 5TH

Choice Never Threatens Assault in 3-Length Belmont Victory

NATCHEZ 2D AND CABLE 3D

Kleberg's Colt Wins $77,400 for $316,270 Total—43,599 Watch Jet Pilot Triumph

By JAMES ROACH

Completing brilliantly a job started in the Kentucky Derby and continued in the Preakness, Assault yesterday slammed down the stretch to win the seventy-eighth and richest Belmont Stakes, convince the last remaining doubters of his greatness and take his place with the six other big ones of the turf who have captured the mythical triple crown.

It was a magnificent performance and a crowd of 43,599 at old—and surprisingly chilly—Belmont Park cheered lustily as the King Ranch's chocolate-colored prize package poked his nose in front just before the eighth pole and drew away from the pack. He was three lengths to the good by the time he coasted under the wire at the end of the mile-and-a-half run.

There were still many doubters when the Texas-bred colt went to the post with six others. Despite his triumphs at Churchill Downs and Pimlico, the customers made him the 7-5 second choice—by a few hundred dollars in a $640,495 mutuel pool—to Lord Boswell, but at the end Lord B. was no better than fifth, and the gold and the glory were all Assault's.

Pacemaking Hampden Fourth

Second was Mrs. Walter M. Jeffords' Natchez, in that spot most of the way and in front early in the stretch. Third was Mrs. Aksel Wichfeld's 45-1 shot Cable, and fourth was the Foxcatcher Farms' Hampden, a gallant pace-setter as far as he went, who found twelve furlongs about two too many.

Natchez had a length and a half advantage over Cable, whose margin was a head over Hampden. Another equine head separated Hampden and the Maine Chance Farm's thoroughly beaten Lord B., and then came Mrs. Jeffords' Mahout and Mrs. Alfred Roberts' War Watch to complete the parade.

At the end of the line was $77,400 in prize money for Assault, including a $2,000 nominating award for Robert J. Kleberg, owner of the vast King Ranch. This pay-off raised to $316,270 the earnings of Assault, who has taken five out of six for a 1946 total of $299,020 and hasn't far to go to surpass Gallant Fox's single-season mark of $308,275.

It was a joyous day for Owner Kleberg, for Trainer Max Hirsch and particularly for Jockey Warren Mehrtens, the youngster from Jamaica High School, who has ridden Assault to every one of his victories.

Mitscher Presents Trophy

Admiral Marc A. Mitscher, veteran of the Pacific War and commander of the Eighth Fleet, and Mayor William O'Dwyer were among those present for the handshaking and back-slapping in the winner's circle after the race. The Admiral presented the August Belmont Memorial Cup to Kleberg and the Mayor had a big handshake for pint-sized Mehrtens.

Mehrtens was beaming. Said he: "The only time I was worried was coming out of the gate when Assault stumbled. He recovered at once and we were never in difficulty again. I had more confidence this time than in either the Derby or Preakness but I still can't believe we've won the triple crown."

Said Kleberg: "We're deeply happy and we feel others will agree with us now that Assault is a great horse. I want particularly to compliment Max Hirsch on a great training job."

In the jockeys' quarters the others weren't so gay. Eric Guerin, who had ridden Lord Boswell, summed up best what had happened to the favorite when he remarked: "He didn't have it when I asked for it."

Eddie Arcaro, who had been hoping for his fourth Belmont Stakes success aboard Hampden, said: "The winner bumped us in the stretch, but Hampden was a tired horse and it made no difference in the result."

Getting his name on the triple-crown list along with those of Sir

Continued on Page 2, Column 4

Assault, 7-5, Wins Belmont Stakes By 3 Lengths to Gain Triple Crown

Continued From Page 1

Barton, Gallant Fox, Omaha, War Admiral, Whirlaway and Count Fleet—and hopping up to twelfth position on the roster of leading American money-winners—Assault was rated smartly by Master Mehrtens.

After that stumble at the start, which brought a gasp from the crowd, Assault got going in a hurry and was third behind Natchez and Hampden, the two that had been expected to set the pace, at the first turn. Then he went to fourth and he held that spot behind Hampden, Natchez and War Watch down the backstretch.

On the turn for home Assault, in his best Derby and Preakness style, was moving in high. Mehrtens had taken his time; he knew he had plenty of horse under him. Hampden and Natchez, and then Natchez alone, were still out there, but Assault was fairly flying—and the rest was easy. Just short of the eighth pole every last customer knew he had the race won, and it was a triumphal charge the rest of the way.

Natchez held on to the second position—it was worth $20,000—without too much trouble, but the next three had considerable of a fight for third before Cable, Hampden and Lord B. finished in that order.

Sound Time and Pay-off

The time didn't threaten Count Fleet's 2:28 1-5, but it was a sound 2:30 4-5 after fractions of 0:24 4-5, 0:49 3-5, 1:14 1-5 and 1:39 2-5. Those who had backed Assault thought that the pay-off of $4.80 for $2 was pretty sound, too.

Assault was at even money on the opening line, with Lord Boswell 7 to 5, but the bettors couldn't see it that way. At the end the two were almost joint choices, with $147,409 having gone in on His Lordship and $146,587 on Assault. Hampden was the third choice at close to 4 to 1, and after that came Mrs. Jeffords' Natchez-Mahout entry at better than 8½ to 1.

Betting during this day, when the pickets were no longer outside the gates, reached $3,569,281 for a total of $62,248,000 during the twenty-four-day meeting. The total attendance during the Westchester Racing Association's session was 709,523.

Jet Pilot, Maine Chance Farm whizzbang that had run off with the opener at Churchill Downs on Derby Day, led all the way to finish five furlongs of the Widener course in 0:56 3/5—only three-fifths of a second behind Distraction's record—and take the thirty-fourth National Stallion Stakes by a length and a half. Strung out behind the Blenheim II Black Wave colt were nine other top-flight youngsters, the closest being Peace Harbor, who made up half of the Brookmeade Stable's favored entry.

Second choice in the wagering—the pay-off was $6.50—Jet Pilot never left much doubt about his superiority as he won top money of $15,690 and made his record three for three. Between his Derby Day and Belmont Day outings he had beaten Shaffie at Pimlico.

Third, beaten two lengths by Peace Harbor, was the Cain Hoy Stable's Noble Creek, who had a head advantage over C. V. Whitney's Bastogne.

There were some high-priced steeds in this one, but the costliest of all, C. C. Tanner's Sir Gallascene—he went for $46,000 at the 1945 yearling sales—finished last. Jet Pilot cost $41,000 and Peace Harbor $22,500.

Picketing of the horse park, which had begun May 22, and the return to the job of an assortment of employes ended with a minimum of official word as to what had gone on behind the scenes. A track spokesman simply reported that the men were back at work—or would be as soon as they got the word.

Teamsters' representatives, according to track officials, had demanded that the track direct all workers not affiliated with the American Federation of Labor to join that organization. Refusal on the ground that such a move would be illegal resulted in picketing, and among those who became nonworkers in addition to van drivers were bartenders, admission-ticket sellers, electricians, carpenters, movie camera operators and, on Thursday and Friday, program printers.

First indication that all was serene again at beautiful Belmont came when the programs went on sale at the entrances. After the mimeographed sheets of the previous two days, racegoers gladly got up their dimes for the neat, pocket-sized jobs.

Cool Breeze Springs Up

It was steamy and sticky en route to the theatre of operations, but a cool breeze, coupled with an overcast sky, put a decided chill on the proceedings early in the afternoon. By post time for the main event thousands of shirt-sleeved gentry were wishing that they'd brought their topcoats. Many who had taken their positions early in the day atop the stands went below deck to get out of the wind.

The Belmont Stakes and the National Stallion Stakes annually attract prominent figures in the sport from far and near. Among those spotted were A. B. Hancock, Leslie Combs 2d, A. B. Gay, Del Holman, J. C. Stone, R. A. Fairbairn, Walter J. Salmon, Alfred G. Vanderbilt, Stephen Sanford, John Hay Whitney, C. V. Whitney, Robert J. Kleberg, B. F. Whitaker, George D. Widener, Major Louie A. Beard, Walter P. Chrysler, A. J. Sackett, Mrs. Dodge Sloane and Mr. and Mrs. Henry C. Phipps.

Gene Tunney, Don Ameche and Fred Astaire were among the onlookers.

A much larger crowd had been expected, but the management took comfort from the three-day holiday total of 137,038, topped by the Belmont record of 60,905 on Memorial Day.

Trainer W. O. Hicks and Jockey Lawrence Hansman, who have been having more than a bit of success with 2-year-olds, combined their talents with those of Emil Schwarzhaupt's filly, Dancing Margot, to grab the opener without too much difficulty. Dancing Margot, a $25,000 yearling bred at Idle Hour Farm in the julep belt, was running as a field horse with four others, and the quintet went off favored. Another "fielder," Conniver, was third.

The Jockey Mehrtens-Trainer Hirsch combination provided a hint of things to come by putting over the River Edge Farm's Salerno third choice, in the second race.

The New York Times

Warren Mehrtens in the winners' circle after the Belmont Stakes.

HARVARD OARSMEN BEAT YALE CREWS

Continued From Page 1

tition since this was both the start and finish of their season. Harvard's lighter crew was making its fourth start and had its first taste of victory. Neither university had boated a formal crew since 1942, so green hands were the rulers.

There was a striking similarity in the contests, not only in the way they finished but in the way they were rowed. In each, Harvard's oarsmen stepped out to half length leads right at the outset in the cold and rain. And in each case the Crimson had little to do but coast by the time three-quarters of a mile had been rowed.

In the Varsity event, the Crimson got going at 32 strokes under Sylvester Gardiner's pace-setting and Yale at 34, but with the ultimate winners showing more power and drawing out so that with the Henley distance of a mile and three-sixteenths left, the shell was a length out front.

Yale's Henry Williams held 34 for half a mile, then dropped to 32, while Gardiner lowered his beat to 30. That's the way they were to row until the finish was in sight, the difference being that Harvard always kept gaining, bearing to port though it was. At Harvard Bridge the shell had three lengths and that grew to four soon thereafter.

Crimson Rows Smoothly

Actually, Coach Bolles sent his unbeaten 150-pound crew to race as the junior varsity. The boys showed they had lots of class. Where the sons of Eli were on the ragged side, Harvard's lightweights rowed smoothly and steadily, so steadily that they never raised or lowered the beat from the 30 they started with through the entire race.

Yale was off at 34, dropped to 32 and then 30, went up to 32 again at a mile and finally to 34 for the futile chase to the line. By a mile Harvard was four lengths to the good and that was that.

GRAND ILLUSION WINNER

Hydraulic and Mont Also Gain Devon Horse Show Awards

Special to THE NEW YORK TIMES.

DEVON, Pa., June 1—A crowd of 7,500 turned out for today's judging in the fiftieth anniversary Devon horse show.

Grand Illusion, owned by Mrs. Royal Furman of Mentor, Ohio, annexed the $1,000 John Wanamaker hunter stake class which was combined with the Cassilis challenge trophy donated by Mr. and Mrs. J. Macy Willets.

The combination of the W. Newbold Ely Jr. challenge trophy and the $1,000 Arthur E. Pew Jr. stake prize was captured by Donald W. Moore's Hydraulic.

Mont, owned by Mrs. Elizabeth Perry, Orange, Va., placed first in the working hunter championship final on points gained throughout the show. Reserve went to Mrs. George P. Greenhalgh's My Venture.

OLD WESTBURY TOPS TEXAS POLOISTS, 6-5

Silvero's 3 Goals Pace Victors in Return to Long Island of High-Goal Play

SMITH LEADS LOSING SIDE

Held to One Marker for Four Chukkers. He Hits in Pair in Final Two Periods

By WILLIAM J. BRIORDY

Special to THE NEW YORK TIMES.

WESTBURY, L. I., June 1—Old Westbury, led by Alan L. Corey Jr., staved off a late bid by Cecil Smith's Texas side to score a 6-5 triumph on the Meadow Brook Club's Belmont Field today as high-goal polo returned to Long Island after a war intermission of four years.

Pedro Silvero, riding at No. 2, filled in for nine-goal Mike Phipps and paced Old Westbury with three goals. Cecil Smith, nine-goal Texan, held to one goal for four periods, rapped in two sizzling drives in the last two chukkers to keep his side in the fight.

Old Westbury, showing more strength up front than Smith's four, had Frank Fox at No. 1, Silvero, Corey, a seven-goaler, at No. 3, and R. H. (Bob) Lightfoot at back. Smith rode with Walter Reisinger, No. 1, Sidney Culver, No. 2, and George E. Kent Jr., back.

Football Weather Prevails

The weather, which took a sudden change at mid-afternoon, was more suitable for football than polo, with the result that only a small gathering watched the match. Silvero, five-goal man from the Argentine, did a superb job at No. 2 for Old Westbury. Mounted strongly, Silvero proved a fine substitute for Phipps, getting off some great hits and displaying a strong defensive game.

As for the game itself, the hitting and team play were not so crisp as they should have been, but as the season continues the action undoubtedly will take a turn for the better. The cold weather was no help, either. As a matter of fact, the teams passed up time out at the end of the third period and kept the play going.

Old Westbury wasted little time riding to the front. After Culver had tapped in a short shot in the first period, Silvero knotted the count. Then Fox put Old Westbury ahead with a goal after Kent had saved on a deft stroke by Silvero in the second chukker.

Culver's Goal Ties Score

Texas got moving in the third period, with Culver stroking a 40-yarder after carrying the ball from midfield and Smith blasting one through from just outside the coal mouth to make it 3-all. Then the agile Silvero split the goal posts on a three-stroke run to return the advantage to Old Westbury as the chapter closed.

With Texas going scoreless in the fourth, Silvero made it 5—3 by counting after Kent had made a neat save. Smith, snowing his old drive and hitting up beautifully, connected on a 75-yarder, but Corey took a neat hit-up by Silvero to score 6—4 at the end of the fifth period.

Smith ended a long run with a 50-yard poke in the sixth period for the final goal of the game. Smith's goal came late in the period, and gave his side little time to get the tying marker.

BURRA SAHIB WINS STAKE

Whitney Duo Runs One, Two With Enfilade Second on Coast

INGLEWOOD, Calif., June 1 (AP)—The C. V. Whitney entry, backed down to 9-10, ran one, two today as Burra Sahib won the $25,000 added seven-furlong Will Rogers Handicap by one length and a quarter and the filly, Enfilade, finished second at Hollywood Park. H. M. Isenberg's Going With Me was third. The time was 1:24 2/5.

"All the News That's Fit to Print"

The New York Times.

LATE CITY EDITION
Sunny and warm today. Fair and warm tomorrow.
Temperatures Yesterday—Max., 72; Min., 48
Sunrise today, 5:54 A. M.; Sunset, 5:35 P. M.
Full U. S. Weather Bureau Report, Page 39

VOL. XCVI...No. 32,395. Entered as Second-Class Matter, Postoffice, New York, N. Y. NEW YORK, FRIDAY, OCTOBER 4, 1946. THREE CENTS IN NEW YORK CITY

TRUMAN URGES PRICE CURBS, INDUSTRIAL PEACE AND RISE IN OUTPUT TO AVERT CRASH

AID OF ALL ASKED

Recovery Gains Made, He Says, but Calls Peril of Inflation Great

STEELMAN GIVES REPORT

Asserts Nation Is at Crossroads of Prosperity, Depression—Opposes Big Pay Increases

Text of President's statement on nation's economy, Page 9.

By WALTER H. WAGGONER
Special to The New York Times.

WASHINGTON, Oct. 3—Supported by a report of the Office of War Mobilization and Reconversion warning of an "early and severe" economic crash if prices continued to rise, President Truman called on the country today to do its "utmost" to preserve industrial peace, keep production high where it was booming and push levels higher where output was lagging.

The President, in a statement on the OWMR eighth quarterly report, prepared by Director John R. Steelman, said that the document "shows that we are driving steadily toward peacetime prosperity."

It allows, however, no time out for self-congratulation because "a difficult struggle lies before us," Mr. Truman asserted, adding:

"I hope every business man, worker, farmer, and consumer will take to heart this sentence from Mr. Steelman's report: 'An all-out emphasis on production of finished goods and on preventing a further increase in prices is the task immediately before us.'"

Reading his statement at a news conference, the President summarized the "milestones" of the country's progress toward post-war recovery contained in the Steelman report. These are the facts, he asserted and urged reporters to stick to them in commenting on the situation.

"Great Promise, Great Danger"

In his report entitled, "The Second Year of Peace," Mr. Steelman also emphasized the position in which the national economy was now situated, "a position," he stated, "of great promise and of great danger."

"Our position is one of promise," he added, "because we have an opportunity to move forward to higher levels of real income than any nation has ever achieved.

"We have a chance to maintain high levels of employment for extended periods, and to progress toward higher levels of production and a steadily rising living standard.

"But we do face an acute threat—the danger that we will be unable to shift from the present situation where demand exceeds supply to one where demand and supply are in approximate balance, without falling to a point of equilibrium on a far lower level of income and production than we now have."

This transition will be difficult even under stable conditions, Mr. Steelman stated, but the obstacles will be heightened if there is a "further rapid increase in prices."

"Prices have already risen further in the three months since the original price control act expired than they did in the previous thirty-eight months," he said, adding:

"A further rapid price rise might choke off demand, upset business stability and precipitate an early and severe price collapse, with serious economic and social consequences."

The OWMR chief asserted that if stable prosperity were to be accomplished, not only would "wise action by the Congress and the executive branch" be required but also "statesmanship of a very high order by management, labor and farmers and self restraint on the part of the consuming public."

With the economy at this crossroads, one lane of which leads to collapse and the other to prosperity, the country faces two "great" problems, Mr. Steelman stated.

The first and longer-range problem requires the maintenance of full production and full employment, he said, while the second

Continued on Page 9, Column 2

39 DIE IN AIR CRASH, WORST IN HISTORY OF U. S. CIVIL LINES

American Transport Smashes Against Hill and Explodes in Newfoundland Wilds

ARMY WIVES ARE VICTIMS

Six Children on Way to Join Fathers Killed—Tragedy Under Investigation

By The United Press.

STEPHENVILLE, Nfld., Oct. 3—An American transatlantic air liner exploded against a 1,900-foot hill early today and all on board, thirty-nine men, women and children, were killed.

It was the worst airplane disaster in the history of commercial aviation. Less than a month ago, and less than 200 miles away, the crash of another transatlantic plane at Gander, Nfld., took the lives of twenty-seven.

Today's tragedy occurred in a wilderness twelve miles east of this transatlantic airport town. "Mechanical failure" was the conjectural cause, but investigators of the Civil Aeronautics Board and of the American Overseas Airliners, owner of the huge four-motored Berlin-bound Douglas flagship, Erie, were en route to the scene for a detailed analysis of the charred bits of wreckage.

The victims included three babes-in-arms and three children ranging in age from 3 to 11—all children of United States soldiers or War Department civilian employes in Germany. Their mothers all died with them—all war brides, the youngest only 21.

Eleven Wives Among Victims

In all, eleven wives en route to long-separated husbands were among the thirty-one passenger dead. The other victims were the seven-man, one-woman crew, headed by Capt. William Westerfield of Long Island, veteran ocean flier.

The Erie took off from La Guardia Airport, New York, yesterday and landed at the alternative Newfoundland transatlantic airport here, Harmon Field, last night as it could not land at the regular airport in Gander because of bad weather. After the plane had been refueled, it took off for the ocean hop just before 3:30 A. M.

There was a "safe" ceiling of 5,000 feet and the take-off was normal. The plane had been inspected here and all four of its engines apparently were functioning perfectly. Yet a few minutes later, observers in the control tower heard an explosion and saw a flash of light, then flames, off to the east.

At dawn another plane flew over the rocky hills twelve miles from here and saw the charred, fragmented wreckage 100 feet from the crest of a 1,900 elevation. The plane had been so torn apart and burned that one man in the other plane said the pieces did not "even resemble" the parts of a plane.

Rescue Party Reaches Scene

Simultaneously a rescue party had set out afoot from the airport but so rugged was the terrain it did not reach the scene until six hours later. There had existed the faintest of faint chances that some had survived until the party reported back by walkie-talkie radio that all aboard had been killed.

The rescue party reported that the huge gasoline tanks, filled for the long flight across the North Atlantic, had exploded when the plane crashed into the wooded hillside. The bits of wreckage and the scrub forest burned for hours.

American Overseas Airlines technicians stationed here were at a

Continued on Page 2, Column 3

Cards Win Pennant, Beat Dodgers, 8-4

The Cardinals won the National League championship yesterday, completing a two-game sweep of the first pennant play-off in major league baseball history by defeating the Dodgers, 8-4, before 31,437 spectators at Ebbets Field.

Murry Dickson held Brooklyn to two hits for eight innings, but was routed by a three-run rally in the ninth. Harry Brecheen struck out the last two Dodgers with the bases filled.

Six pitchers tried vainly to stop the Cards, who earned the right to oppose the American League's champion Boston Red Sox in the world series starting at St. Louis Sunday.

(Complete details on Sports Pages)

Wallace Charges Baruch With 'Impasse' Over Atom

Ex-Secretary Says American Delegate Sought to Pin 'Fantastic' Statement on Him—Holds U. S. Position 'Inflexible'

By LEWIS WOOD
Special to The New York Times.

WASHINGTON, Oct. 3—Henry A. Wallace accused Bernard M. Baruch today of trying to "intimidate" him into giving a "full blank check endorsement" of Mr. Baruch's policies on atomic energy control. This he refused to do, the ousted Secretary of Commerce said.

In a lengthy statement containing caustic charges, Mr. Wallace attacked Mr. Baruch as "increasing public confusion" over the atom force and maintaining a "stern and inflexible" position concerning its disposition.

It is actually Mr. Baruch, American delegate to the United Nations Atomic Energy Commission, who has "created the impasse" on negotiations about the bomb, Mr. Wallace insisted.

The American delegate was assailed by the Iowan as proposing a "fantastic" statement for Mr. Wallace to sign, in which the former Secretary's remark that he was not "fully posted" on a certain point would be translated into an "admission of inaccuracy and a full endorsement" of the Baruch program.

Mr. Baruch, so Mr. Wallace charged, has refused to discuss the "basic issues" concerning the atomic bomb, which the Iowan outlined in his letter of July 23 to President Truman. But, added Mr. Wallace in defiant words:

"Nothing in the recent statement of Mr. Baruch would cause me to revise the basic tenets in my letter to President Truman concerning the way to peace and atomic energy controls."

In his argument that Mr. Baruch ignored the central issue of the controversy, Mr. Wallace said:

"Neither in his memorandum of Sept. 24 to the President nor in his personal blast at me do I find any indication that the United States

Continued on Page 6, Column 3

The text of the Wallace statement is on Page 6.

BYRNES URGES END OF SOVIET CHARGES ON ATOMIC THREAT

Deploring 'Conflict' of Views, He Bids Stalin Silence Fears and Join in European Pact

CITES SETTLED U. S. POLICY

In Paris Speech He Reaffirms Our Guarantee to France in Ban on German Arming

Address of Byrnes in Paris on peace outlook, Page 4.

By HAROLD CALLENDER
Special to The New York Times.

PARIS, Oct. 3—While agreeing with Premier Stalin that there is no immediate danger of war, Secretary of State Byrnes said today that he hoped the Soviet leader's statement would "put an end to the unwarranted charge that the United States is seeking to use its possession of the atomic bomb as a threat against the Soviet Union."

On Oct. 1, nine days after Premier Stalin's statement, the Russian magazine New Times accused the United States of planning an atomic war.

In a speech before the American Club of Paris, Mr. Byrnes declared he hoped Premier Stalin's words would prevent a repetition of the charge that "any nation or group of nations" sought to encircle the Soviet Union or that "the responsible leaders of the Soviet Union so believe."

Makes New Plea to Moscow

In this first comment he had made on Premier Stalin's statement, Mr. Byrnes went on to say that "it would be folly to deny the seriousness of the conflict in viewpoints among the Allies." Nor would it serve the cause of peace to exaggerate it, he added.

Though not directly linking this with his reply to Premier Stalin, Mr. Byrnes later in his speech made a new plea for his proposed forty-year treaty among the Big Four for the disarmament of Germany and expressed the hope that the Soviet Union might reconsider its view that such a treaty was unacceptable.

Mr. Byrnes thus clearly indicated that the test of Premier Stalin's words would be his willingness or unwillingness to modify Soviet propaganda against the Western Powers and to adopt a positive attitude toward the United

Continued on Page 4, Column 3

SHORTAGES IN U. S. CHARGED BY DEWEY TO TRUMAN LAXITY

Crises in Meat and Goods Due to 'Supreme Incompetence,' Governor Tells GOP Rally

HE POINTS CAMPAIGN ISSUE

Tax Cuts, War Savings, Housing for GI's, Hospital Aid Listed Among His 'Team's' Deeds

Gov. Dewey's speech opening his campaign, Page 13.

By LEO EGAN
Special to The New York Times.

ALBANY, Oct. 3—Governor Dewey formally opened his campaign for re-election tonight at a Republican rally here with a charge that post-war shortages of meat, sugar, housing, automobiles and other commodities were the result of the "supreme incompetence" of the Democratic National Administration, headed by President Truman.

"The basic question before the people of our State on election day," he declared, "will be this: do you want to bring to Albany the kind of government we have in Washington right now? Or do you want to maintain the kind of government we have had in New York State during the past four years?"

Tonight's speech, broadcast over a State-wide radio network, was Mr. Dewey's first major political address since he accepted renomination on the Republican ticket at Saratoga Springs a month ago, and apparently was designed to set a pattern for the campaigning to follow.

"Happy to Stand on Record"

Governor Dewey's criticism of the national administration was echoed at tonight's rally by Assemblyman Irving M. Ives, Republican candidate for the United States Senate, who charged that "senseless controls" kept in force by Washington edict not only were keeping the American people from the benefits of the country's natural free economy, but "rob them of even the necessities of life."

Other speakers at tonight's rally in the Hotel Ten Eyck under the sponsorship of the Albany County Republican organization were Lieutenant Governor Joe R. Hanley, Controller Frank C. Moore and Attorney General Nathaniel L.

Continued on Page 13, Column 2

Meat Pinch Will Be Worse In Winter, Says Steelman

Reconversion Director Is Probably Correct, Observes the President, Denying Conflict With View He Gave

By BESS FURMAN
Special to The New York Times.

WASHINGTON, Oct. 3—President Truman said he thought that John R. Steelman, Reconversion Director, was probably correct in his statement in today's report, "The Second Year of Peace," that the meat shortage would become worse this winter.

The President said he saw no discrepancy between this statement and his own prediction of last week when he said that the normal run of grass-fed cattle of early fall soon would appear on the market and improve supply. The President reminded reporters that he did not say that there would not be a shortage, but he said there would be no meat famine.

Mr. Truman remarked that he was having a meat survey made to find out if he agreed with Mr. Steelman that the shortage would worsen, but that it was probably true. He said that all Government departments concerned with meat were in constant touch with the situation, and that if it was necessary to take any further action he would do it.

Mr. Steelman's office was equally insistent that there was no divergence in opinion regarding the meat shortage between the West Wing of the White House, where the President has his office, and the East Wing, where Mr. Steelman has his.

The explanation there was that Mr. Truman had been talking of a short-term emergency, and what he was saying was that more meat would be coming to the counters than the extremely scarce supply there now. Mr. Steelman, however, was reporting the long-range view when he included in today's eighth

Continued on Page 9, Column 3

U. S. TO STRENGTHEN KEY PACIFIC BASES

Admiral Towers, Returning to Honolulu, Tells of Plans for Guam and Alaska

Special to The New York Times.

HONOLULU, Oct. 3 — A strengthening of the Navy's Pacific bases is due in the near future, Admiral John H. Towers, Pacific Fleet commander, revealed here today.

Just returned from conferences with top Navy officers in Washington, he said that there would be an immediate strengthening of our bases in Alaska and the Aleutians because these two key Arctic installations were vitally necessary to our national defense.

He declared that Kodiak would be further strengthened as the Navy's primary Alaskan base and that he had also advised the rebuilding of the Aleutian installation into a fully operational naval base. While he did not disclose the latter's site, it is believed that it would be either Attu or Dutch Harbor. Both these are capable of handling aircraft and surface ships.

In a few years Guam will be the "Pearl Harbor of the Western Pacific," the admiral forecast.

"We have already spent several million dollars on the breakwater and harbor at Guam and it can now accommodate four hundred ships," he said. "Eventually our installation in the Guam-Saipan area will be our key Pacific base."

Alaska and the Aleutian bases, plus Pearl Harbor in the middle Pacific, and the Marianas installation will provide a fulcrum for a Pacific defense set-up. It will have approximately 250,000 men under the Pacific command, he said.

The United States is also negotiating with the Philippine Government for bases, and Admiral Towers indicated that the Subic Bay and Cavite installations might be utilized.

PEARL HARBOR, Oct. 3 (AP)—Admiral Towers said today that he had talked with Admiral Chester

Continued on Page 7, Column 7

BIG FOUR ASK CURB ON TREATY DEBATE

Propose Limit of 30 Minutes in Discussions at Plenary Peace Conference Session

Special to The New York Times.

PARIS, Oct. 3—At the initiative of Secretary of State Byrnes the Big Four Foreign Ministers met tonight and agreed to suggest to the plenary session of the Conference of Paris a set of rules to prevent delay when it meets Monday to pass on the five peace treaties.

These rules were devised by Paul-Henri Spaak of Belgium, chairman of the rules committee, at Mr. Byrnes' suggestion after the Secretary had discussed the subject with French Premier-President Georges Bidault, Soviet Foreign Minister Molotov and British Foreign Secretary Bevin at separate meetings.

The Foreign Ministers sent the rules to the secretary general of the conference, who was asked to summon a plenary meeting of the conference Sunday afternoon at 4 o'clock to consider them. The suggested rules are:

(1) Reports from the commissions will not be read at the plenary session, since they will have been distributed to all delegations.

(2) Each delegation will have 30 minutes only to talk on each treaty in the form of one or more statements, which are to include general observations and observations on any articles. No discussion on separate articles is to be allowed.

(3) It is suggested that these statements by the delegations be mimeographed in three languages and distributed in advance so as to reduce oral translation during the meetings.

(4) No amendments to the treaties are to be presented other than those contained in the reports of the commissions. Amendments can be put to vote but not discussed separately.

(5) Each article in each treaty is to be voted on in the plenary session. Any delegate may re-

Continued on Page 3, Column 2

Stelle Supported by Legion In His Clash With Bradley

By CHARLES HURD
Special to The New York Times.

SAN FRANCISCO, Oct. 3—The American Legion convention presented a united front today behind John Stelle, the retiring National Commander, in his dispute with Gen. Omar N. Bradley, Veterans Administrator, over the question of limiting benefits to veterans. The delegates unanimously adopted a resolution which requested a special session of Congress to restore one cut it voted before adjourning.

The immediate issue over the propriety of putting a legislative ceiling of $200 on income of veterans taking on-the-job training and receiving rehabilitation subsistence grants appeared to be smothered for the time being, however, by a broader dispute over the place of the veteran in the country as a whole.

General Bradley accused Mr. Stelle yesterday of obstructing and misrepresenting the work of the Veterans Administration, then said that the VA must consider former service men as citizens first and veterans second.

Mr. Stelle repeated his charges today that General Bradley had "betrayed" veterans on the basis of the Legion definition that these men and women must be considered as veterans first and afterwards as citizens.

After he delivered his reply to General Bradley's accusations, more than 3,000 delegates gave him a rising ovation and adopted without audible dissent a resolution calling on Congress to reconvene so as to repeal the $200 maximum for veteran trainees, the first cut in benefits affecting veterans of World War II.

While it appeared that a chasm separated the governmental agency

Continued on Page 20, Column 7

CONFUSION MARKS MARITIME STRIKE

Negotiations Go On Haltingly as Shipping Men Express Fears of Long Tie-Up

By GEORGE HORNE

Maritime strike negotiations continued haltingly yesterday without any real prospect of solution and shipping men, losing hope of an early settlement, expressed fears that the nation-wide walk-out of officers might extend indefinitely.

Despite a late report from Washington that West Coast deck officers had agreed to a Government formula on which some settlement hope was based, there was still widespread doubt that an agreement was near. The Government formula would provide separate agreements with the striking deck and engine room officers with East Coast operators, and would also call for a Maritime Commission order accepting East Coast terms for Government-owned ships manned by the West Coast operators.

Washington negotiators said the talks would be resumed today at 10 A. M. That meeting will dis-

Continued on Page 12, Column 4

World News Summarized

FRIDAY, OCTOBER 4, 1946

Industrial peace and high production are essential in the "difficult struggle" ahead to avoid an economic collapse, President Truman said yesterday in releasing the quarterly report of Mobilization Director Steelman. Prices have risen more since the original OPA law died than in the previous thirty-eight months, Mr. Steelman said, and business should cut prices without raising wages. [1:8.]

Mr. Truman emphatically declared that the Federal budget would be balanced despite a deficit now estimated at $1,900,000,000. [1:6-7.] The President, disclosing that he had ordered a national meat survey, agreed that the shortage might grow worse this winter. [1:6-7.] The Price Decontrol Board recessed without acting on restoring ceilings on dairy products. [9:6-7.]

After listening to its retiring national commander, John Stelle, answer General Bradley's attack upon him, the American Legion convention adopted resolutions assailing some policies of the Veterans Administration headed by the general. [1:6-7.]

Hugh Dalton, British Chancellor of the Exchequer, was elected to succeed Treasury Secretary Snyder as board chairman of both the International Monetary Fund and the World Bank. [12:3.]

A world-wide radio system, the "Voice of America," to be operated by the Government in cooperation with the radio industry to keep the world informed on American policies, was proposed by David Sarnoff. [25:1.]

Secretary Byrnes, speaking in Paris, restated America's abandonment of isolationism and her continuing interest in Europe. He renewed his plea to Moscow to accept his plan for a four-power forty-year treaty to assure Germany's disarmament and expressed the hope that Premier Stalin's lack of fear of an imminent war would dispel "the unwarranted charges that the United States is seeking to use its possession of the atomic bomb as a threat of force against the Soviet Union." [1:4.]

Former Secretary Wallace replied to the attack made upon him by Bernard M. Baruch by saying that it was not he, but the American representative on the United Nations Atomic Energy Commission who was confusing the public by ignoring the central issue of the controversy. Mr. Wallace said that Mr. Baruch had tried to "intimidate" him into giving a "full blank-check endorsement" to the American control plan. [1:2-3.]

The Economic and Social Council ended its sitting after having adopted by a narrow margin over Slavic bloc opposition the American proposal for an international conference in Vienna on restoring freedom of navigation along the Danube. [4:2.] Russia broke the impasse in the Military Staff Committee of the Security Council: she has made suggestions on organizing the United Nations forces. [4:7.]

An American proposal to lighten Hungary's reparations was defeated in a commission of the Conference of Paris. [3:1.] To Czechoslovakia was awarded a reduced bridgehead into Hungary, but the right to expel 200,000 Hungarians was denied her. [3:8, with map.] The Foreign Ministers Council plan for speeding plenary sessions forbids new amendments and limits any delegation's remarks on any treaty to thirty minutes. [1:3.]

Admiral Towers disclosed that American bases in Alaska and the Aleutians would be strengthened immediately. [1:2.]

Chinese Communists were said to have encircled Paoting, capital of Hopeh Province, and to have sent guerrillas within four miles of Peiping. [7:5, with map.]

All thirty-nine persons on an American airliner to Berlin died in Newfoundland in commercial aviation's worst accident. [1:1; map P. 2.]

Explosions Rip Gasoline Plant; Two Dead, 200 Injured at Sun Oil

Special to The New York Times.

MARCUS HOOK, Pa., Oct. 3—Two persons were killed and 200 were injured tonight when the Sun Oil Company's $13,000,000 aviation gasoline refinery, said to be the world's largest alkylation plant, blew up with two tremendous explosions and a series of lesser blasts.

The victims were James Woodburn, 29 years old, of Claymont, Del., and Leland Bailey, 49, of Laurel, Md., an employe of the Graham Tugboat Company, who was blown from a tugboat in the near-by Delaware River and drowned.

The first explosion occurred at 6:10 P. M. and hundreds of firemen poured tons of a chemical on the blazing wreckage for four hours. At 10:15, however, they were forced to withdraw all apparatus when the flames encircled a big acid vat which was expected to explode.

The cause of the blast was not immediately determined, but one of the workers who was injured said that the packing on an equalization pump blew out. Friction ignited high-octane fumes and the blast followed. Several hundred workers were reported to have been in the plant at the time.

Nelson King of Wilmington, Del., general foreman of the plant, who was injured in the blast, said that he had no idea what happened.

"When the explosion occurred, the cracking tower simply disintegrated," he said. "That blew apart the small building I was in. A huge ball of fire seemed to roll around, hit and ignite every building."

At Chester Hospital, where 135 injured persons were treated, Dr. A. H. Bleier, the medical director, requested city officials to open the 111th Infantry armory at Chester as an emergency dispensary.

"We cannot get any more peo-

Continued on Page 10, Column 3

Truman Pledges Balanced Budget But Experts See Cuts Needed

Special to The New York Times.

WASHINGTON, Oct. 3—President Truman predicted today that the end of the current fiscal year on June 30, 1947, would find the national budget in the black.

The President's forecast, however, immediately plunged observers into speculation as to whether he might not have a further sizable reduction in Federal expenditures in mind. The last estimate, as well as the forecast of the eighth quarterly report of the Office of War Mobilization and Reconversion made public today, estimated the deficit at the end of the present fiscal year at $1,900,000,000.

The matter of the balanced budget arose at the President's press conference, when he was asked if, in the light of the latest Treasury report showing that the Government was out of the red at the end of the first quarter, there was any hope for finishing the fiscal year in the same position.

There was not only hope, said the President, but the Government was going to achieve it.

When it was suggested that a deficit of about $2,000,000,000 had been predicted, Mr. Truman said it would be cutting expenses by $2,100,000,000.

The view was expressed later by Government fiscal experts, however, that estimates of the $1,900,000,000 deficit had already been based on the prospect of a reduction in expenditures by $2,100,000,000. It was agreed, however, that the President might be considering a substantial reduction which had not yet been taken into account in figuring the budget position at the end of the year.

Questioned by reporters after a visit with the President, James E. Webb, Director of the Budget, said the President was doing his best to cut expenses.

Cards Win Pennant, Defeating Dodgers Again for Two-Game Play-Off Sweep

BROOKS LOSE, 8-4, DESPITE 3-RUN 9TH

Dickson Pitches 2-Hitter Till Last Inning, When Brecheen Saves Game for Cards

LONG BLOWS ROUT HATTEN

Redbirds, Taking 9th Flag in 20 Years, Meet Red Sox in Series Opener Sunday

By JOHN DREBINGER

Incredible as it may sound, the National League's pennant race finally has ended.

It drew to a close about 15 minutes after 4 o'clock yesterday afternoon at Ebbets Field when the Cardinals, after battering their foe with a bruising thirteen-hit attack, smothered a last-ditch demonstration by a desperate band of Dodgers to finish on top, 8 to 4.

That gave the Redbirds from St. Louis the first pennant play-off series in major league history in two straight victories and the right to engage the American League's champion Red Sox in the long deferred and almost forgotten World Series, which will get under way in St. Louis next Sunday.

Remaining in character to the end, the Flatbush Flock went down swinging with one last despairing, electrifying flourish. Held to one run and two hits by Murry Dickson, crack right-hander, for eight innings—with both the run and the hits coming in the first—Brooklyn's Beloved Bums thrilled what was left of a gathering of 31,437 of the faithful in the ninth inning by routing Dickson and continuing their attack against Harry Brecheen until they had three tallies in and the bases full.

Two Strike-Outs End Game

With the tying run at the plate and only one out, Brecheen hung up two searing strike-outs that doubtless will leave their scars for years to come. Then it was that the Bums, who had escaped seemingly inevitable extinction so many times this year, finally breathed their last.

Starting with left-handed Joe Hatten, who was blasted out inside of five rounds, by which time he had given as many runs, Leo Durocher hurled six pitchers into the struggle, but all to no avail.

So the Cardinals bagged their ninth National League pennant over a span of twenty years and for the sixth time under a different manager. Rogers Hornsby was the first one for the Redbirds in 1926. Two years later Bill McKechnie piloted them home in front. In 1930 and 1931, Gabby Street, who came all the way from St. Louis to see yesterday's encounter, was the winning skipper. Frankie Frisch led the famed Gashouse Gang in 1934 and then came Billy Southworth's three straight winning campaigns from 1942 to 1944.

Now quiet, soft-spoken Eddie Dyer, who used to operate the Cardinal farm system, retired a few years ago and returned when Southworth left for Boston, has guided St. Louis home in front in his first year as a major league manager and after one of the most thrilling campaigns in history.

Good World Series Record

Five of eight previous Cardinal pennant winners went on to take world championships, if that is of any encouragement to the present Redbirds as they prepare for the redoubtable Red Sox, who for weeks and weeks have been waiting for this big moment.

St. Louis Manager Eddie Dyer flashes his victory smile after leading his team to a pennant in his first season as a major league pilot.
The New York Times

The St. Louis Cardinals
Stan Musial

As yesterday's battle got under way under a cloudless sky, the crowd, doomed to spend most of the afternoon in stony silence, got an early chance to whoop it up a bit when the Dodgers in a surprise foray after their first two batters had been retired tore into Dickson for a run.

Augie Galan, who in a last-minute switch was moved to third while Dick Whitman started in left, outgalloped an infield hit to Red Schoendienst. On the heels of this came a pass to Dixie Walker and when Ed Stevens lashed a single through the mound and into center field Galan romped home amid considerable noise.

At that, it didn't sound quite like a genuine Flatbush roar, giving rise to the suspicion that in the general shuffle for reserved seats most of the faithful must have suffered a complete shut-out. It seemed more like a sedate world series gathering than the boisterous Flatbush host one might have expected for the occasion.

Marion Drives in Dusak

Then the Dodger lead vanished almost as quickly as the cheers in that first inning had subsided. With one out in the second, Erv (four-sack) Dusak smacked one against the left-field wall and while he didn't get all four sacks on that shot he did get three. Came a fly by Marty Marion to Carl Furillo in center and Dusak scored.

A moment later two surprise blows snapped the tie almost in the twinkling of an eye. Clyde Kluttz, whom the Giants had tossed away last May for something less than a song, considering the fact that Vince DiMaggio never could sing, slammed a single into center. That, of course, didn't seem so damaging, as the next batter was Dickson.

But the slim right-hander has a habit of producing a damaging blow when least expected. He won one of those important Cub games in the West with a single and this time he did infinitely better. He belted a line triple into right center. It fetched home Kluttz and the Cards were in front to remain there.

To be sure, the margin at that point was only 2 to 1, but somehow the folks seemed to feel it was all over and when the Redbirds went on another rampage in the fifth, routing Hatten with a three-run blast, even the last die-hard on the premises realized the Bums had run out their string of miraculous achievements. They were just in there to take a beating and they absorbed it, one must say, with exceptionally good grace.

It was quite an unexpected blow that leveled the flock in the fifth round, for there were two out and the bases were empty when Stan Musial, batting champion of the league, banged a double over Dixie Walker's head in right. Hatten then was instructed to pass Whitey Kurowski, but this was to prove a sad day for Durocher's usually successful strategems.

Enos Slaughter, who isn't a fellow to take lightly the imputation that he can't hit a left-hander as well as any right-handed batsman, smashed a terrific drive into deep right center and by the time the ball had been retrieved Slaughter was on third for another Redbird triple while Musial and Kurowski were over the plate.

Next came a single to center by Dusak, Slaughter raced in with the third tally of the inning and Hatten went out to be replaced by Hank Behrman, who finally brought the round to a close without further damage.

There was no checking those Redbirds for long, though. With Behrman passing out almost immediately for the first of four pinch-hitters Durocher tossed into the battle, little Vic Lombardi appeared in the sixth.

Lombardi Loses Control

The diminutive southpaw got by well enough in that inning, but he walked Kurowski and Slaughter to open the seventh. After a sacrifice by Dusak, Durocher made another frantic wave to the Dodger bull pen.

It called out the indefatigable Kirby Higbe and his familiar "13," but the numeral brought no particular luck on this momentous occasion. Marion executed a deft sacrifice squeeze bunt that sent Kurowski streaking home from third and while this was the only tally the Redbirds got in this round, they smacked Higbe lustily in the eighth, routing him with a three-hit splurge that accounted for their final pair of tallies.

Many Fans Leave Before Rally

Schoendienst opened this brisk assault with a single and a moment later swept around to third on a double to left by Terry Moore. Again came an intentional pass, this time to Musial, and again the move failed to meet requirements.

Kurowski, walked three times in a row, slammed a single into right and Schoendienst and Moore counted. The Redbirds now had eight runs, while the Dodgers, though still on their feet, appeared hopelessly out.

After their brief first inning demonstration against Dickson, they had been utterly unable to do a thing for seven tortuous rounds. In fact, in that stretch they got only one ball beyond the confines of the infield, a fly to left by Stevens in the fourth. They never were close to a hit, drew three passes and not a Dodger advanced to second.

It was too much for even the hardiest of Flatbush habitues and so it was that when the Dodgers, with an effort born of despair, launched their belated ninth-inning rally the stands were almost one-quarter empty.

The attack began with Galan ramming a double into right, but when the beloved Dixie Walker, hitless throughout this play-off series, flied harmlessly to centre, the folks just knew this was the bitter end. Even when Stevens followed with a three-base smash to center, scoring Galan, it caused only a feeble cheer, but soon it became evident that both the Dodgers and the noise were not to be shut down with this for a final gesture.

Furillo plunked a single in centre driving in Stevens. Then Dickson unfurled a wild pitch and walked Peewee Reese and the folks plucky enough to remain let out a full-throated roar.

Ideal Setting for Homer

Dyer, unable to stand the suspense any longer, bustled out of his dugout for the second time in the inning and called in Brecheen, a left-hander, but the Cat wasn't to solve the problem at once. Bruce Edwards greeted Brecheen with a single to left, driving in Furillo with the third run of the inning, and when Cookie Lavagetto, batting for Harry Taylor, walked, filling the bases, Flatbush could not have asked for a better setting.

There was the tying run at the plate and a homer into the stands really would have turned things upside down, but at that point the fates must have decided that Brooklyn's hour of miraculous deeds had run far enough. Either that, or Brecheen decided he had better put a little more stuff on the ball.

Stanky fanned, taking the third strike and then tall Howie Schultz, who had hit a homer in that first play-off game on Tuesday in St. Louis, batted for Dick Whitman. He swung with tremendous fervor but disturbed nothing save the atmosphere, for his strike-out ended the struggle. The Flock, at least, went down swinging to provide some measure of comfort for those who remained to the last.

With this triumph the Cards closed the season's book against their most determined foes with a record of sixteen triumphs against eight for the Flock. Never conceded the barest pennant chance at the outset of the race last April, Brooklyn remained in the running until battered down in this unprecedented play-off series.

The victory was Dickson's fifteenth against only six setbacks. It was also his fourth over the Brooks, who beat him once. Hatten, going into the battle seeking his fifteen triumph and with a six-game winning streak, went down for his eleventh reverse and fourth at the hands of the Redbirds.

DUROCHER TO STAY AS DODGERS' PILOT

Manager Expects to Remain With Brooklyn Club as Long as Rickey Is There

Leo Ernest Durocher will manage the Dodgers next year and for several years thereafter.

The Brooklyn pilot made his first unequivocal statement on that in the clubhouse after yesterday's game with the Cardinals when he was asked if he intended to see President Larry MacPhail of the Yankees.

"No doubt I will see MacPhail," replied Leo seriously. "He is my friend, the man who gave me my first chance to manage a ball club. He was a great guy to work for and gave me everything I asked.

"But Branch Rickey has been like a father to me since 1930. He has been the finest person I ever worked for anywhere, and I probably will be right here until I die, or as long as Mr. Rickey is here."

That ought to settle all the persistent rumors that Durocher will manage the Yankees next year.

One of the most interested spectators was Mrs. Ewart Walker, who had two sons in the ball game, but not on the same team. Asked afterward how she felt about the whole thing, the mother of the Dodgers' Dixie and the Cards' Harry replied:

"Well, I had to cry a little, but I suppose I would have cried a little if it had turned out the other way."

Dizzy Dean, who had the time of his life before, during and after the game, was the happiest guy in the ball park. Wearing a big, white cowboy hat Diz worked out with the Cards before the game, broadcast a play-by-play description and then went on the air for a post-game cheering session. He had been insisting all along that the Cards were much the better team and now nobody can argue with him. Possibly with some reluctance, Diz went on record as picking the Cards to beat the Red Sox in the World Series.

Joe Hatten and Murry Dickson were about even on their pitching in the first inning. Joe made fourteen pitches to get the Cards out and Dickson tossed thirteen to dispose of the Dodgers in the first inning, but the Brooks got one run and the Cards none.

The New York Times.

SUNDAY, NOVEMBER 10, 1946. L-- S

ARMY AND NOTRE DAME BATTLE TO 0-0 TIE BEFORE 74,000; PENN TOPS COLUMBIA; PRINCETON BOWS; HARVARD VICTOR

QUAKERS WIN, 41-6

Fullback Allen Leader of Penn Attack With Three Touchdowns

ELLIS DASHES 78 YARDS

Steals Pass for First Score of Game—Rossides Gallops 70 for Columbia Tally

By WILLIAM D. RICHARDSON

Columbia yesterday found itself in the position of the innocent bystander who gets mixed up in a brawl that he didn't start. Although the Lions had nothing to do with Pennsylvania's unexpected downfall at the hands of Princeton last week, they had to pay the penalty for it and the Red and Blue compounded the interest.

Stung to the quick by the Tiger defeat, Pennsylvania took revenge on the poor Lions, submitting them to a 41-6 drubbing before a capacity crowd of 35,000 in the wind-swept Baker Field stands.

Dominating the game, the twenty-ninth between the two Ivy institutions, from start to finish, the powerful Pennsylvanians ground out six touchdowns and one that was called back and didn't count.

The Red and Blue powerhouse that would be riding on football's high seas along with Army and Notre Dame had it not been for the Princeton debacle, scored in every period, twice in the first, twice in the second and once in each of the last two. It was all so easy that there was not much even that Penn's head coach, George Munger, could do about it. He gave practically every man on his well-stocked bench a chance, but all that happened was to slow down the pace to a point where things didn't get too far out of bounds.

Seventh Victory in Row

It was the biggest margin the Red and Blue has ever rolled up against Columbia, the highest total up to yesterday being 42 to 12 in 1942. It also marked the seventh consecutive year that the Red and Blue has triumphed over the Lions, and the series that started off in 1878 now stands at twenty-three victories for Pennsylvania against five for Columbia, the initial encounter back in football's prehistoric days winding up in a 0-to-0 tie.

Although almost every player on the visiting team was a thorn in the Lions' side yesterday, there was one who was particularly obnoxious. That was Ed Allen, six-foot one-inch fullback from Batavia, N. Y. While in the Army Allen broke all strength test records. He must still be filled with youth and vigor, for he alone scored three of the markers, one in the first period, one in the second and the final one at the beginning of the fourth.

Grant Ellis, 190-pound guard who prepped at Hill School, ran 78 yards for a touchdown after he had intercepted one of Don Kasprzak's passes when the game was less than four minutes old.

Up to the time of that piece of larceny the Lions were doing all right against the highly touted Philadelphians. Thanks to a 55-yard run around the Pennsylvania right end, the Lions were down inside their opponent's twenty, knocking on the door for a touchdown, but Ellis' interception took care of that threat.

Stage 78-Yard March

Inspired by that feat on the part of a lowly guard, the Red and Blue backs took a hand in the proceedings and before the period was ended Strong Man Allen had butted his way over from three yards out to end a 78-yard march. A sensational 28-yard sortie by Bob Deuber had given the Pennsylvanians a first down on the Columbia 14.

That ended the first period scoring, making it 13 to 0 in Penn's favor, Bob Evans, the point converter, having failed to connect on his second attempt.

Two more Pennsylvania touchdowns followed in the next period, one by Allen from less than a yard out and another by Bill Luongo from the one-foot mark, where Dan Schneider had plumped it down after one of the most sensational broken field runs of the day, covering approximately fifty yards. Starting around his own right end, Schneider, who proved himself a handy back to have around, cut up the middle and finally wound up in

Continued on Page 2, Column 2

An Army Flanking Thrust That Accounted for Some Yardage Against Notre Dame in the Stadium

Davis sweeping around end for what resulted in a seven-yard gain. Players whose numbers can be seen are Rowan (24) and Blanchard (35) of the Cadets and Mello (65) and Mastrangelo (75) of the Irish

The New York Times

IRISH STAGE MARCH

Move 85 Yards but Are Halted on the Army 3 in Second Period

CADETS HAVE SIX CHANCES

Unable to Capitalize on Them, Failing to Triumph After 25 Victories in a Row

By ALLISON DANZIG

Army, the scourge of the gridiron for three years, remained undefeated and unbowed but was still looking for its first point in four meetings with a Notre Dame team coached by Frank Leahy as the intersectional rivals fought to a scoreless tie at the Yankee Stadium yesterday.

The football game of the year between the nation's two top-ranking elevens resolved itself into a crunching battle of powerful lines. In vain 74,000 onlookers waited for an eruption of the explosive punch that each was expected to turn loose upon the other in a high-scoring duel dominated by the offense.

For the first time in three seasons of uninterrupted and overpowering success against twenty-five opponents, Doc Blanchard and Glenn Davis, the celebrated Mr. Inside and Mr. Outside, found themselves shackled and crushed to earth like ordinary mortals through their full sixty minutes of devotion to duty.

Stopped Time and Again

The Army attack that had rolled up 107 points in the two previous meetings of the teams—the most humiliating disasters suffered by Notre Dame in modern times—was stopped time and again deep in the opponent's territory by the powerful Fighting Irish line.

Johnny Lujack, an equally tireless worker who, without any sign of lameness in his ankle, directed the Notre Dame attack, passed, picked, ran and did defensive duty throughout the entire bruising game, except for two plays, was accorded the same lack of respect and rough treatment.

The horde of hard-running backs that were expected to pour through the Army line, as the cadets weakened and crumbled before the far greater replacement strength of their rival, never brought the ball into scoring territory except on two occasions.

Army Fails to Sag

All of the pre-conceived notions and theories went out the window. Notre Dame did not flood the field with substitutes, using the same number of linemen as Army and only four more backs. The West Pointers did not sag in the fourth quarter, holding the Fighting Irish to one first down in that period while getting one themselves, and the greater individual brilliancy and threat of Blanchard and Davis did not materialize.

So furiously did the Kelly Green line swarm upon the renowned B. & D. and also upon Quarterback Arnold Tucker and Davis when they passed that never once was Army able to break a man loose from scrimmage for any great distance. The Notre Dame carriers and receivers likewise were stopped abruptly.

Blanchard made a run of twenty-one yards, and Davis never went that far from scrimmage. Tucker got away for thirty yards and that was the longest gain of the day. Terry Brennan's run of twenty-two yards was the only one of any length made by Notre Dame. Only two passes carried for any distance, one tossed by Lujack to Bob Skoglund netting twenty-five yards, and Davis throwing to Blanchard for twenty-three.

Ends on Same Note

It was not the thrilling offensive spectacle that had been looked for. Nevertheless, the battle was so fiercely waged and the lines and the backers-up rose up so nobly when their goal lines were endangered that the crowd never found the play lacking in excitement, particularly when Army stopped a Notre Dame advance of eighty-five yards three yards short of a touchdown—the only sustained march put on by either side all afternoon.

So the resumption of the rivalry between Earl Blaik and Frank Leahy, back from two years' service in the Navy, ended on the same low note that it began in 1941. That year, too, when Leahy went

Continued on Page 3, Column 3

ASSAULT IS VICTOR OVER LUCKY DRAW

1946 Earnings Top $400,000 as He Takes Westchester Handicap at Jamaica

By JAMES ROACH

Making his final appearance of the 1946 season, the King Ranch's great 3-year-old colt Assault gave 'em something to remember him by at Empire City-at-Jamaica yesterday.

He won the $50,000 added Westchester Handicap, beating George D. Widener's Lucky Draw by more than two lengths. He added $38,600 to his earnings to become the first horse in turf history to pass the $400,000 mark in one campaign and he entered a strong claim for the title of "horse of the year."

Winning this one was easy. The little powerhouse turned on the steam going to the far turn, took command on the outside half-way around the bend and was never threatened for the rest of the way.

Lets Dance, 39-1, Third

Lucky Draw was an even easier second by four or five lengths over the Sunshine Stable's surprising Lets Dance, a 39-to-1 shot. Fourth was Mrs. Ed Mulrenan's gray First Fiddle, fifth was Bob Howard's Man O' Glory and last was William L. Brann's Gallorette, lone filly in the field.

This was a run of a mile and three-sixteenths (the distance at which Assault won the Preakness in May and the Pimlico Special on the first of the month), and all the opponents of the triple crown champion were older campaigners. None was able to withstand his challenge or stay with him when it came time to strike for victory.

The crowd of 38,783 made Lucky

Continued on Page 6, Column 5

Mexicans Beat U. S. Riders In Jump-Off at Horse Show

By JOHN RENDEL

Gallant riders of the Mexican Army team won the crowning event of the National Horse Show, the International Military Perpetual Challenge Trophy, in Madison Square Garden last night.

Major Humberto Mariles and Lieutenants Victor M. Saucedo, Raul Campero and Alberto Valdez thus broke the three-victory string of United States Army teams extending through the years 1939 to 1941, and inscribed the name of their country on the coveted trophy for team competition for the first time.

It took a jump-off with the United States officers to establish the triumph. Peru's riders, running in terrible luck through the six days of the show, finished third, eliminated in the opening round. Jump-off faults were 4 for Mexico and 15 for the United States.

When the competition was over, the 14,000 spectators, including Secretary of State and Mrs. James Byrnes, stood up as the stirring pageantry of the opening night was re-enacted. This time the salute of the international jumping teams was taken by Lieut. Gen. Hugh Drum.

The competition called for the aggregate score of the best three or four team members. Mexico and the United States had identical performances the first time around the ten-jump course—four faults for one officer and perfect rides by the others.

That sent six riders back into the ring for the jump-off and the United States Army men failed, for once, in a pinch. Col. W. H. S. Wright piled up seven faults with

Continued on Page 6, Column 2

HARVARD SUBDUES DARTMOUTH, 21 TO 7

Gannon Sprints 57 Yards for One Crimson Touchdown and Passes for Another

By JOSEPH M. SHEEHAN

Special to THE NEW YORK TIMES.

HANOVER, N. H., Nov. 9—Harvard's first football visit to this picturesque little hamlet in the foothills of the White Mountains since 1884 resulted in a 21-to-7 triumph for the Crimson eleven today.

Dick Harlow's quick-striking charges pushed across two touchdowns in the first nine minutes of the contest and added another in the final period to gain the edge over Dartmouth in the fiftieth game of this classic New England series before an overflow crowd of 16,000 at Memorial Field.

Tom (Chip) Gannon, fleet-footed right halfback from Westbury, L. I., and Vinc Moravec, battering fullback fro Bridgewater, Pa., were the boys who did the business for Harvard. Without this pair, the heavily-favored Crimson might well have succumbed to the gallant bid of the ill-starred Indians.

57-Yard Run First Pay-off

On Harvard's second scrimmage play of the game, Gannon whirled fifty-seven yards off his own left tackle for a touchdown. He whipped a seven-yard southpaw pass to Wally Flynn for the final crimson tally and generally plagued the home team with his running, passing and defensive play.

A pile-driving runner who supplies his own interference, Moravec bulled and charged his way to Harvard's second touchdown on a two-yard buck at the end of a personal

Continued on Page 4, Column 3

Virginia's Fast Start Trips Favored Princeton, 20 to 6

By JOSEPH C. NICHOLS

Special to THE NEW YORK TIMES.

PRINCETON, N. J., Nov. 9—The University of Virginia inserted itself into the upset scheme that has motivated Princeton's football fortunes the past couple of weeks. Considered a none too formidable visitor for the Orange and Black team that stunned the football world by its defeat of Pennsylvania last week, the Cavaliers from the Old Dominion contributed a reversal of their own today. They beat the well-regarded Princeton eleven by the score of 20 to 6.

It was a happy bunch of players who carried Virginia's coach, Art Guepe, from the field on their shoulders at the conclusion of the game. For these athletes were members of a team that has established itself as another famous first of Virginia. Not only did the visitors defeat Princeton, but they were the first Virginia eleven ever to score on a Princeton team in a series that began in 1890 and which now encompasses ten games.

It was an early jump that enabled the Virginians to walk off with the victory. They made all three of their touchdowns in the first half, and this margin proved more than enough to offset the sole Princeton tally, registered in the third period.

The Spark plug in the Virginia attack was quarterback George Neff. Although he did not figure directly in the scoring, Neff proved himself a veritable master of the ball handling assignment in the Cavaliers' intricately patterned maneuvers from the T-formation He had all confidence and coo ness

Continued on Page 2, Column 5

RANGERS SET BACK BY TORONTO, 4 TO 2

Three Goals by Apps Enable Leafs to Gain Undisputed Lead in Hockey Race

By The Associated Press.

TORONTO, Nov. 9—Veteran Syl Apps scored three goals tonight as the Toronto Maple Leafs downed the New York Rangers, 4 to 2, before 14,078 fans, and took over sole possession of first place in the National Hockey League race.

Apps, back in action after an injury had kept him out of action since the opening game of the sea-

Continued on Page 7, Column 2

GEORGIA TECH WINS FROM NAVY, 28 TO 20

Mathews' 95-Yard Run Turns Tide as Yellow Jackets Gain Sixth in Row

By The Associated Press.

ATLANTA, Ga., Nov. 9—A 95-yard gallop by Co-Capt. George Mathews snatched Georgia Tech from the brink of defeat today as the Yellow Jackets ran their victory streak to six straight with a 28-20 triumph over the Navy.

Ahead 20—14 with less than three minutes to play, the Middies, who had come from behind early in the period, were down at the Tech 7-yard line rolling almost at will. Billy Hawkins plowed into the Tech line but the ball squirted from his arms and Mathews snared it. He hauled it down the sideline nearly the length of the field with a half-dozen team-mates protecting him.

Another Pass Intercepted

A minute later, with Navy trying desperate passes, Pat McHugh snagged Reaves Baysinger's toss and loped 61 yards to the 6. Frank Broyles threw to George Brodnax for a clincher score. Allen Bowen, whose third straight placement had apparently resulted in the Navy's sixth straight loss, 21—20, again converted.

Completely outmaneuvered all day, Tech had managed a 14-13 lead at intermission, but the visitors wouldn't stay down and finally drove 45 yards with Hawkins going over for his second score of the day and what eventually looked like the winning points.

Then they started the fatal

Continued on Page 4, Column 2

ANDOVER ACADEMY HALTS EXETER, 7-6

Clayton's 90-Yard Touchdown on Kick-Off and Horne's Conversion Win Game

Special to THE NEW YORK TIMES.

ANDOVER, Mass., Nov. 9—Capt. John Clayton's ninety-yard touchdown runback of Exeter's opening kick-off and Horne's successful conversion gave Phillips Andover Academy its thirty-third victory over Exeter, 7—6, in the sixty-fifth contest between the two schools today.

Exeter's second-period tally put

Continued on Page 4, Column 2

YALE OVERWHELMS BROWN BY 49 TO 0

Jackson and Furse, Freshman Backs, Spark Elis—Booe Kicks 7 Extra Points

By MICHAEL STRAUSS

Special to THE NEW YORK TIMES.

NEW HAVEN, Conn., Nov. 9—Brown University suffered its worst defeat at the hands of a Yale team since the series between the schools started in 1880 when a hard-running, sharp-passing Eli eleven swept to a 49 to 0 triumph over the Bruins before 40,000 at the Yale Bowl today.

It was a banner afternoon for Yale's two scintillating freshmen backs, Levi Jackson, a New Haven lad, and Bob Furse, a transplanted Texan who learned his fundamentals at Andover. Both stars excelled at their specialties, Jackson running the opposition dizzy all afternoon and Furse clicking repeatedly on the throwing end of passes.

Brown Threatens Twice

Not since 1921, when the New Haven team subjected its rivals from Providence to a 45 to 7 reversal, has a Brown unit received such free-handed treatment from the Bulldog. Close to scoring in the opening minutes, the Bruins were able to make only two more such gestures. As for Yale, every time it gained possession of the ball, it spelled trouble for the visitors.

Jackson, whose hipper-dipper running was something to see, accounted for three of the game's touchdowns. His best effort came in the early moments of the third quarter when he broke through the

Continued on Page 9, Column 3

Football Scores

COLLEGES

East		East	
Army 0	Notre Dame 0	Montclair T. 20	Trenton T. 0
Bethany 19	Clarion T. 7	Morgan State 15	Bluefield State 6
Boston College 20	Georgetown 13	Mount Union 25	Allegheny 0
Bloomsburg T. 7	E. Stroudsburg T. 6	Muhlenberg 13	Gettysburg 7
Buffalo 20	Alfred 12	National Farm 20	New York Aggies 6
California T. 21	Potomac State 6	Navy (150-lb.) 20	Villanova 6
Case [illegible]	Carnegie Tech 0	Navy Plebes 47	Bucknell J. V. 7
Connecticut 33	R. I. State 6	New Hampshire 13	Boston U. 7
Cortland T. 28	Hartwick 0	N. Y. U. 13	Lehigh 2
Davis-Elkins 0	Glenville State 0	Niagara 25	Hobart 0
Delaware 27	Bucknell 14	Panzer 6	Lowell Textile 6
F. & M. 12	Albright 0	Penn 41	Columbia 6
Fairmont 23	Shepherd 7	Penn State 26	Temple 0
Geneva 13	Slippery Rock T. 3	Princeton (150-lb.) 6	Penn 0
Harvard 21	Dartmouth 7	R. P. I. 13	Amherst 0
Haverford 40	Hamilton 14	Rutgers 41	Lafayette 2
Hofstra 18	Bergen J. C. 0	St. Bonaventure 13	Bowling Green 9
Holy Cross 21	Colgate 6	So. Carolina 21	Maryland 17
Kings Point 41	Brooklyn Coll. 7	Springfield 24	St. Lawrence 0
Kutztown T. 6	Millersville T. 0	Springfield J. V. 22	Romford School 0
Lebanon Valley 19	Juniata 0	Susquehanna 27	Wagner 6
Lincoln [illegible]	Cheney State T. 13	Swarthmore 6	Johns Hopkins 0
Lock Haven T. 7	Shippensburg T. 7	Syracuse 14	Cornell 7
Maine 27	Bowdoin 7	Thiel 12	Grove City 7
Mansfield T. 25	Indiana T. 13	Trinity 26	Norwich 0
Mass. State 39	C. C. N. Y. 0	Tufts 18	Coast Guard Ac. 13
Middlebury 18	Union 13	Vermont 19	Rochester 6
Middlebury J. V. 19	Vermont J. V. 0	Virginia 20	Princeton 6

Continued on Page 2, Column 3

Syracuse Upsets Cornell, 14-7, With Two Touchdowns by Watt

By ROSCOE McGOWEN

Special to THE NEW YORK TIMES.

ITHACA, N. Y., Nov. 9—Erasmus Hall High School had its day by proxy on Schoellkopf Field today as Syracuse upset Cornell's Big Red team, 14—7, before a crowd of 29,000.

Joe Watt, 26-year-old graduate of that Brooklyn school, scored both the touchdowns for the Orange, the first one in the second period on a pass interception and an electrifying 80-yard run down the right side of the field.

The 182-pound back counted his second touchdown early in the third quarter by snaring a pass, which was pitched to him by Walt Slovenski, in the Cornell end zone.

George Brown, formerly of Scarsdale (N. Y.) High, place-kicked both extra points, thereby running his total of consecutive conversions to sixteen. George has missed but one all season, his first attempt, which was blocked.

The Cornell touchdown came four seconds after the start of the final period, the assault starting from the Big Red 40 as the result of Lou Daukas' recovery of a fumble by Ed Dolan late in the third quarter.

Walt Kretz, the best running back of the afternoon, then broke loose for a 40-yard scamper through the right side, aided by good blocking from Matt Bolger and Hillary Chollet.

Chollet ferried the ball to the Syracuse 8 on two rushes and an

Continued on Page 4, Column 5

Army and Notre Dame Show Keen Disappointment Over Result of Their Game

ARMY, NOTRE DAME PLAY TO 0-0 DRAW

Continued From Page 1

o South Bend from Boston College and Blaik was called to West Point from Dartmouth by General Robert Eichelberger to revive Army's sunken fortunes on the gridiron, their teams played to a scoreless deadlock.

In 1942, Notre Dame won by 13—0. In 1943, one of the great teams of all time, Leahy's last before he went into the service, smashed Army by 26—0 and was established the national champion. So four times Blaik has sent an Army team out against a Leahy eleven without a single point accruing to the West Pointers.

It was a bitter disappointment to the Army coach, in view of the many chances his team had to score yesterday. Six times the cadets had the ball inside Notre Dame's 33-yard mark, once on the 15, again on the 20 and also on the 23. But never could Blanchard or Davis carry it over or Tucker or Davis pass it across to capitalize the numerous breaks gained through interception and the recovery of fumbles.

Notre Dame, aside from its eighty-five-yard march to Army's 3-yard mark in the second quarter, on which Gerry Cowhig was the big gun and Lujack passed twenty-five yards to Skoglund, never approached the West Point goal line again except on one occasion.

The recovery of the ball on an Army fumble gave the Fighting Irish possession on the 34 in the third period, but they could get only two yards. Then Tucker, a worthy rival for Lujack for All-America honors and one of the most brilliant figures on the field, ended the threat with one of his three interceptions of the afternoon.

Teams Expertly Scouted

The defense was simply too strong for the offense on each side, and both teams had been scouted so expertly and thoroughly that neither was able to surprise the other with its operations from the T formation.

Leahy did not appear to take the tie quite as much to heart as did Blaik. Considering the many times that Army threatened, probably he had no cause to feel sad over the outcome, though it must have been a keen disappointment to him when his team put on its long march, only to fail of a first down at the 3 by a yard. Also considering what Army had done to the Fighting Irish the past two years, as well as to all others, the scoreless tie might be regarded as a moral victory for Notre Dame.

On the basis of the statistics, which are remarkably even and show a difference of only thirty yards—in Notre Dame's favor—in total gains from scrimmage between the contesting forces, a draw was the logical verdict.

The big crowd that filled the Stadium to the last seat included an impressive assemblage of distinguished guests. Seated in the Superintendent's section with Maj. Gen. Maxwell D. Taylor of the United States Military Academy were Secretary of War Robert P. Patterson, Secretary of the Navy James Forrestal and Attorney General Tom Clark, who received an urgent summons and made his departure during the game.

Also seated in the Superintendent's boxes were General of the Army Dwight D. Eisenhower, Army Chief of Staff; Generals Jacob L. Devers, Carl Spaatz, Omar Bradley and Courtney Hodges, Maj. Gen. Anthony McAullife, Admiral Thomas C. Kinkaid and a host of officers of lesser rank, from both branches of the services.

Statistics of the Game

	Army.	N.D.
First downs	9	11
Yards gained, rushing	138	173
Forward passes	16	17
Forwards completed	5	6
Yards gained, forwards	57	52
Forwards intercepted by	3	2
Number of punts	7	8
*Av. dist. of punts, yds.	40	40
Run-back of punts, yds.	86	46
Fumbles	3	5
Own fumbles recovered	1	2
Penalties	2	1
Yards lost, penalties	30	5

*From line of scrimmage.

O'Donnell at Contest

Brig. Gen. Rosy O'Donnell, Col. Red Reeder and Edgar Garbisch, Army football heroes of other days, were present.

A hundred wearers of the Purple Heart from the New York area attended the game as guests of the United States Military Academy. Col. Lawrence M. (Biff) Jones, graduate manager of athletics at West Point, sent the tickets to Col. B. B. Millenthal, officer of the First Army Special Services Division at Governors Island.

The weather was just about made to order for the game to which the whole football world had looked forward all season. The threat of rain which caused a good part of the crowd to delay its arrival at the Stadium was dissipated as the sun broke through the clouds just as Captain Blanchard and Co-Captains Lujack and Cowhig met in the center of the field for the toss of the coin.

Before the play got under way and during the intermission between the halves, the gathering was entertained by the United States Military Academy band and the Notre Dame band and by the circus acts put on by the latter organization with clowns and simulated wild animals going through stunts.

The West Point corps of 2,100 cadets entered the Stadium exactly on the dot as scheduled at 12:40. Their faultless files on parade and maneuvers on the field, with all 2,100 moving as one in absolute precision, won the usual rounds of applause. The Army mules, Mr. Jackson and Skippy, the diminutive gift of the Ecuadorean Ambassador some years ago, went galloping around the sidelines under the expert bareback riding of cadets.

Contrary to Practice

Captain Blanchard won the toss and, contrary to Army's usual practice, elected to receive the kick-off. Heretofore, Army has kicked off when it had the honor. **Yesterday, it had too much fear of Notre Dame's offensive power to give it the first crack at the ball.**

Not only in this departure from its usual custom did Army show its respect for its rival's attack but also in its willingness to gamble by rushing the ball on fourth down even in its own territory, rather than to kick. Notre Dame did likewise but only on one or two occasions.

Army had its first chance to score early in the opening quarter Steve Sitko fumbled and Tackle Goble Bryant recovered for West Point on Notre Dame's 24. A pass from Tucker to Davis, who had gone in motion, netted eight yards, but Blanchard was stopped just short of a first down on the 15 and the ball changed hands.

Notre Dame then put together two first downs, with Sitko and Brennan hitting the left side of the Army line. Army braced and got two first downs with Blanchard and Davis carrying for short gains and Davis passing for five to Barney Poole, who, with Hank Foldberg, **were tremendous in guarding Army's flanks. Joe Steffy and Art Gerometta did yeoman work in stopping plays to the inside. Notre Dame's defense stiffened at midfield and there was no further threat of a score in the first period.**

The action picked up violently in the second quarter and the Stadium roared with cheers from both sides as first Army drew near a score, then Notre Dame and then Army again.

A reverse pass from Davis to Blanchard, who went tearing down the field alone to the left, netted twenty-three yards and a first down on the Notre Dame 23. The cadet corps was standing to a man and roaring for a touchdown, but the Fighting Irish rose up and treated Davis scandalously.

On an attempt to turn Notre Dame's left flank, the Army halfback was smothered for a 5-yard loss. His pass to Blanchard failed and then he sought to get off a lateral to Blanchard as he was hemmed in. A half dozen opponents buried him on the 37-yard line, a further loss of 9 yards. Davis then kicked and Cowhig returned the punt 7 yards to his 12. It was there that Notre Dame started on its 85-yard march.

With Cowhig making most of the gains, Lujack passing to Skoglund for 25, and Bill Gompers contributing, Notre Dame looked unstoppable on the attack. Army's defense was being ripped asunder.

After Cowhig had smashed twenty yards through tackle, with a cordon of blockers clearing the way, Blaik rushed in Harvey Livesay in place of Rip Rowan to give Army a second center in backing up the line. Rowan was playing in the injured Ug Fuson's place at fullback, while Blanchard played the entire game at right half.

Lujack passed to Cowhig for two yards. Gompers got five. Then Lujack, on a quarterback sneak, got one. The place was in an uproar. The ball was on Army's 4, and it was fourth down and two to go for a first down.

On a fake at the middle, Gompers sped around Army's right end and for a moment it seemed he would make it, but he was hauled down after his long lateral run on the 3, a yard short of a first down. Army was saved and the finest offensive effort of the day had gone for nought.

Bill West, the only backfield substitute Army used except for a two-minute period of relief of Tucker by Bob Gustafson, and whose kicking was so valuable to his team, booted the ball out to midfield. After that, Army was in no danger again in the half and had the chance again to score when Tom Hayes recovered a fumble on Notre Dame's 35.

Passes Knocked Down

Blanchard got two yards and then Tucker's three passes were knocked down. Just before the end of the half, Tucker intercepted a pass, and on the last play before the intermission, ran thirty yards to Notre Dame's 30.

Blanchard turned in some magnificent defensive work in the third period, tackling with terrific impact. The play was mostly in Notre Dame territory, although the Fighting Irish were making most of the gains.

Then came Notre Dame's first and only break of the game. John Mastrangelo recovered an Army fumble on the Cadets' 34. Two plays netted only two yards and then Lujack fired a pass. The ever-vigilant Tucker snared the ball and went snaking up the field thirty-two yards to his own 42. On the next play Blanchard made his longest run of the day for twenty-one yards, and a first down on the 37. The Cadet corps was in an uproar. Davis and Blanchard got four yards and then Tucker passed over the middle to Foldberg for thirteen and a first down on the Irish 20.

Surely the deadlock was to be broken now. Army seemed definitely on its way, on its longest march of the day. Then came frustration once more. Terry Brennan gathered in Davis' pass on his 8, to end the threat, and on the next play sped twenty-two yards around end as the third quarter ended.

Early in the fourth quarter Army failed of a first down by inches on Notre Dame's 33. Shortly after Sitko intercepted a pass on his 10, fumbled and Lujack recovered on his 5. From behind his own goal line the Notre Dame quarterback got off a superb kick of fifty-five yards.

Davis brought the ball back to Notre Dame's 39 and there Martin grabbed the ball out of the air as Tucker's pass was partially blocked at midfield. A minute before the end of the game Tucker made his third interception of the day near midfield.

With forty-eight seconds left, Davis fired a long pass to Blanchard, who made a spectacular catch at the 20, with two defenders on top of him. The place was in an uproar again, but Blanchard had stepped out of bounds in catching the ball and it was brought back. That was all.

Despite the overheated rivalry that was looked for, the game was one of the most cleanly played of the year. So far as known, there were no injuries of consequence and only three penalties were inflicted.

Indicative of the strength of the defense, Davis gained a total of 30 yards in seventeen tries, Blanchard 50 yards in eighteen, Tucker 37 in nine. Brennan gained 69 yards in fourteen attempts, Cowhig 37 in seven, Sitko 24 in five and Lujack made 9 yards in carrying the ball eight times. Six of his seventeen passes were completed for 52 yards, all going to different receivers, and three were intercepted.

DEFENSIVE POWER FEATURES CONTEST

Rival Coaches Agree Brilliant Work in Stopping Attacks Overshadowed All Else

Backs Played Well for Army, Mentor Says—Injury Slowed Lujack, Leahy Declares

By LOUIS EFFRAT

There being nothing as pointless as a scoreless tie, particularly when Army and Notre Dame are the principals involved, the dressing-room scenes immediately after the contest at the Yankee Stadium yesterday best told the reaction of both sides. The picture of despair was, however, more pronounced in the West Point quarters.

No one connected with Army, the team which failed to finish on top for the first time in twenty-six games, attempted to disguise his disappointment. The manner in which the players filed into the room was evidence that the hither-to all-conquering cadets were dissatisfied. There wasn't a smiling face among the more than half-hundred persons, players, coaches, trainers, managers, etc.

Least happy of all was Army's head coach, Earl (Red) Blaik. Obviously downcast, Blaik told interviewers that he was greatly disappointed.

"There is no jubilation in this dressing room," was the first statement from the mentor. "It was a vigorously fought, terrific defensive game. Both teams played beautifully on the defense and that affected both team's attacks."

Conceding that the Fighting Irish had the cadets "well scouted" and applying the same words to Army's watchdogs, Blaik said he felt let down. "Not that I can criticize our men," he declared, "but our offense never really got rolling. Glenn Davis, Doc Blanchard and Arnold Tucker played very well, but the protection they had been receiving throughout the season was not in evidence in the game. We were not as smooth as in the past."

"You know," the colonel went on, "I had a feeling something like this scoreless tie would happen. Too much stress had been laid on these two great offensive clubs. Both sides were thinking so much about stopping the other side, that the attack suffered."

The coach praised Tucker, Davis and Blanchard, Joe Steffy and the ends, Hank Foldberg and Barney Poole. He also thought Jim Martin, Notre Dame freshman end, and George Strohmeyer, the injured South Bend center, did some good work. As a parting shot, Blaik stated: "I think that Army never will beat Notre Dame. The material is great."

Cast Vote for Tucker

Andy Gustafson, Herman Hickman and the other assistant Army coaches spoke glowingly of the West Point line. They also, as did Blaik, cast a vote for Tucker as an All-America quarterback. Maj. Paul Amen, who had scouted Notre Dame all year, wanted to know how anyone could choose Notre Dame's Johnny Lujack over Tucker.

Maj. Gen. Maxwell D. Taylor, Superintendent of the United States Military Academy's comment was: "It was a very fine game. I'm proud of both teams."

Over in the Notre Dame dressing room, the palatial quarters of the Yankees, Frank Leahy and his lads were almost, but not quite, as downhearted as were Blaik and the cadets.

"I suppose I should be elated over the tie. After all, we didn't lose, but I'm not. You know, of course, that I had expected to lose this game, but five minutes after the start, after we had stopped Army in the first period, I had a feeling that we might win," he said. Leahy, it will be recalled, predicted during the week that Army would score a 27-14 victory.

Agreeing with Blaik that the game was overshadowed by the brilliant defensive work of both teams, Leahy paid tribute to Army. Of course, the West Pointers had similar kind words about Notre Dame. "Lujack's injury slowed him down," Leahy said. "He couldn't go back fast enough to get off his passes. Martin played an outstanding game for a freshman and George Sullivan was great at right tackle."

A Simple Offense

Notre Dame, Leahy was told, did not attempt too many tricky plays. Why? "We did try a couple of new things, like a screen pass and a double reverse, which we did not use in other games, but our offense is a simple one."

Leahy was mildly surprised that Army was so strong in the second half. While he did not quite see eye to eye with Blaik's assertion that the cadets "owned the second half," Frank was disappointed that Notre Dame's greater depth in reserve strength did not permit the Fighting Irish to storm the cadets toward the finish.

For so grueling a struggle between great lines—this was definitely a contest dominated by the forward walls—it was surprising that the injuries were so few. No one on Army was seriously hurt. For Notre Dame, Strohmeyer limped off during the game and Martin required medical aid. On the whole, though, both sides emerged in fairly good physical condition.

U. C. L. A. TRIUMPHS, 14-0

Bottled Up Until Last Half by Leicht, Oregon Halfback

PORTLAND, Ore., Nov. 9 (AP)—A slender halfback named Jake Leicht staved off mighty U.C.L.A. almost single-handed for 41 minutes today, but Bruin power told in the waning minutes for a 14-0 victory over the Oregon Ducks. Leicht's quick kicks and darting forays into U.C.L.A. territory kept the Californians bottled up through the first half.

Late in the third period the Bruins got back on the Rose Bowl track, marching 52 yards for their first touchdown. Quarterback Ernie Case teamed with end Burr Baldwin to set up the score, tossing a long pass to Baldwin on Oregon's 18—a 30-yard gain. Gene Rowland went 14 yards for the score. Case converted.

The second touchdown came in the fourth quarter after the eighth fumble of the game. Halfback John Johnson recovered for U.C.L.A. on the Oregon 24. After two line plays Rowland went to the Oregon eight and halfback Jack Brown needed only two cracks at the line to score. Case again converted.

Section 5 | SPORTS SHIPPING AND WEATHER

The New York Times.

SPORTS BUSINESS OPPORTUNITIES | Section 5

S Copyright, 1946, by The New York Times Company. SUNDAY, DECEMBER 1, 1946. L+ S

ARMY CHECKS LATE NAVY RALLY TO WIN THRILLER, 21-18; NOTRE DAME TOPS SO. CALIFORNIA; BOSTON COLLEGE BOWS

IRISH VICTORS, 26-6

McGee Notre Dame Ace, Tallying on a 77-Yard Dash, Short Sprint

LEAHY, ILL, MISSES GAME

Krause Is in Charge as Squad Defeats So. California to Finish Season Unbeaten

By LOUIS EFFRAT
Special to THE NEW YORK TIMES.

SOUTH BEND, Ind., Nov. 30—A glorious gridiron campaign ended today for Notre Dame as the Fighting Irish, smothering the opposition under a relentless ground attack, recorded a 26 - 6 victory over Southern California. With this conquest, Frank Leahy's team achieved an unbeaten season, the fourteenth in Notre Dame history, and general acknowledgement as co-holder — with Army — of the mythical national championship.

If there was a sorry note connected with this triumph, it was the absence of Leahy. The head coach was at his Michigan City home, some thirty miles removed from the scene. A heavy cold, nervous exhaustion and the recurrence of an old back injury forced the mentor to pass up the finale. Today this truly great Notre Dame aggregation was in the capable hands of big Moose Krause, one of Leahy's aides.

But Leahy, listening, undoubtedly, to a broadcast of the contest, must have felt fine about the outcome. True, he may have suffered through some trying minutes of a fruitless and scoreles opening period. Also, when the Trojans, a well-coached outfit that brought credit to Jeff Cravath, its tutor, fought back for a third-period touchdown that brought them within tying distance of the home team. Leahy may have done a bit of fretting.

No Cause for Regret

In the end, however, Leahy had no cause for regret. Johnny Lujack and company had depth, an abundance of speed and deception and other weapons with which to beat a good Pacific Coast eleven. But good as were the Trojans, their best was not good enough to cope with the superior forces that Krause had under his temporary command.

The Fighting Irish wrecked the visitors on the ground, grinding out the incredible total of 517 yards on running plays, spiced with numerous laterals. Lujack and George Ratterman, his understudy at quarterback, attempted only enough aerials to keep the Trojans off balance. At that, nine of fourteen overhead thrusts netted 106 yards, so that Notre Dame amassed 623 yards offensively.

A fair idea of the Irish power may be gained from the statistics, which show the home side outdowning Southern California, 26 to 9. Only once did the victors have to punt.

This eighth victory in a season that was marred (?) only by the scoreless deadlock with Army was as convincing as it could be. Notre Dame unveiled a spectacular runner in the person of Coy McGee, 22-year-old sophomore, who stole the spotlight from Lujack, Ratterman, George Connor, George Strohmeyer and the other, more-celebrated Notre Damers. McGee was the spark that supplied the lift the Fighting Irish seemed to need after the first quarter.

Little known, the young man

Continued on Page 2, Column 5

Football Scores

COLLEGES

East

Army 21	Navy 18
Holy Cross 13	Boston College 6

South

Alabama 24	Mississippi State 7
Auburn 47	Florida 12
Georgia 35	Georgia Tech 7
Hardin-Simmons 21	Texas Tech 6
Louisiana State 41	Tulane 27
N. W. Louisiana 27	S. F. Austin 6
Tennessee 7	Vanderbilt 6
North Carolina 49	Virginia 14
No. Carolina State 28	Maryland 7
Rice 38	Baylor 6
Sewanee 13	Kenyon 6
So. Methodist 30	Texas Christian 13
Wofford 41	Erskine 6

West

Michigan State 26	Washington State 20
Notre Dame 26	So. California 6
Oklahoma 73	Oklahoma A. & M. 12

Far West

Coll. of Idaho 21	Lewis and Clark 0
Coll. of Pacific 19	San Diego State 13
Oregon State 21	Washington 12
U. C. L. A. 18	Nebraska 0

The Start of Service Classic at Philadelphia Yesterday and the No. 1 Fan at Game

Bob Schwoefferman of Navy running back the opening kick-off at Municipal Stadium. He returned twenty-one yards to the 31-yard marker.

President and Mrs. Truman, who were among the spectators

The New York Times

HOLY CROSS BEATS BOSTON COLLEGE

Crusaders Score 13-6 Upset Before 43,000 on 34-Yard Pass in Third Period

By WILLIAM D. RICHARDSON
Special to THE NEW YORK TIMES.

BOSTON, Nov. 30—It's becoming quite a habit for Holy Cross to upset Boston College in their annual gridiron feud.

It started back in 1942, when the Eagles had one of the country's outstanding teams, with a bid to the Sugar Bowl nestling in their hip pockets.

That year the Crusaders from Pakachoag Hill pulled one of the biggest upsets in history when they up-ended the high-soaring Eagles, 52 to 12, forcing them to settle for an Orange Bowl invitation.

Almost the same thing happened today when a rugged, hard-fighting Holy Cross team rebounded from a somewhat disappointing season (they lost four out of eight up to today) to upset a highly touted Boston College team, 13 to 6, and chalk up their fourth straight defeat of their Jesuit rivals.

Eagles Score First

A capacity crowd of better than 43,000 crammed its way into Braves Field to see the Purple squad from Worcester come from behind and administer a sound, thoroughgoing defeat to their Boston rivals.

After the Eagles had broken the ice in the second period on an 85-yard runback of a punt by Tony Cannava, fleet-footed freshman tailback from Medford, Mass., the Crusaders marched straightway to a touchdown that left the two teams deadlocked at 6-all at half-time.

Then, after a little more than fourteen minutes of the third period, the Crusaders put across their winning marker on a sensational pass play in which Leo Troy, substitute end, caught Walt Sheridan's diagonal toss in the Eagle's end zone. The play covered 34 yards.

Thus the Crusaders turned back against the Eagles what was supposed to be Boston's best scoring weapon. The first Holy Cross touchdown also came on a pass, with Sheridan again being the thorn in the Eagles' side.

Drive 63 Yards to Tally

This time th Crusaders started their march on their own 37 after Sheridan returned Don Panciera's kick-off, following Cannava's touchdown, for a distance of eighteen yards.

Then it was that the infuriated Crusaders started grinding out yardage as they registered four consecutive first downs, the last of which came on a 20-yard dash by Sheridan around the Eagle's left side.

Cornered as he was attempting to pass, the 172-pound speedster lit out for the sidelines and galloped to the 3 before he was thrown out of bounds. On the very

Continued on Page 4, Column 1

Schroeder, Mulloy Gain in Australia

By The United Press.

MELBOURNE, Australia, Nov. 30.—United States Davis Cuppers Ted Schroeder and Gardnar Mulloy continued their mastery over Australian tennis opponents by scoring impressive victories today in the second round of the Victoria championships on rain-soaked Kooyong Stadium courts.

With all players wearing spiked tennis shoes because of the insecure footing on the wet grass, Schroeder kept his powerful overhead ground strokes well under control to beat Jim Gilchrist, 6-3, 6-2, 6-4.

Mulloy, similarly less hampered by the rain than his Aussie opponent, Lionel Brodie, a confirmed baseliner served accurately and volleyed consistently to win, 5-7, 7-5, 7-5, 6-2.

A match involving Frank Parker and Long, Australian Davis Cupper, was postponed until Monday.

TENNESSEE DOWNS VANDERBILT, 7 TO 6

Both Score in First Period—Volunteers Will Meet Rice in Orange Bowl Jan. 1

By The Associated Press.

NASHVILLE, Tenn., Nov. 30—Tennessee's Volunteers, sniffing more at Miami's orange blossoms than tending to the business at hand, muddled through to a 7-to-6 victory over Vanderbilt today in the fortieth gridiron clash between the State's two major institutions, before a capacity crowd of 21,000 which witnessed the renewal of the ancient rivalry.

The Vols were tapped last week to meet Rice in the New Year's Day Orange Bowl classic and for awhile it looked as if they would go South with two defeats instead

Continued on Page 2, Column 5

BUTLER, AT $67.40, TRIUMPHS AT BOWIE

Beats Respingo by Length in Bryan and O'Hara Handicap as Maryland Season Ends

By JAMES ROACH
Special to THE NEW YORK TIMES.

BOWIE, Md., Nov. 30—Up on the mutuel board at old Bowie today flashed the fancy figures of $67.40 after a 4-year-old gelding named Butler, seventh choice in the field of nine, charged home in front in the twenty-fourth running of the $15,000-added Bryan and O'Hara Memorial Handicap.

This was the big event of the final day of racing at Prince George's Park—it also marked the close of the Maryland turf campaign—and the result was a stunner for most of the crowd of 18,000.

Even the owner of the winner was astounded. He's Herbert Hammond of Baltimore, who races a two-horse stable and claimed Butler last spring here for only $3,500. Today's triumph, greatest of the gelding's career, was worth $10,800. Hammond was so overcome with emotion that he had tears in his eyes when he went to the winner's enclosure.

Makes Move on Outside

Butler won by a length—and he won in the last seventy yards. D. L. West, an apprentice, was his rider, and West urged his mount up on the outside through the final yards to get the decision.

Second money went to Gustave Ring's Respingo, the Argentine-bred horse that won the Lynch Handicap here on opening day. This one finished a neck in front of Black Swan, who races in the name of Jay D. Acres and was the pace-setter into the stretch. Then, after another three or four lengths, came P. R. Hinton's Boy-Plin for the smallest part of the purse.

Out of the money were the first, second and third choices, these being H. G. Bedwell's Prognosis, Brookmeade Stable's Boss and

Continued on Page 7, Column 2

Georgia Halts Tech, 35-7; Will Play in Sugar Bowl

By The Associated Press.

ATHENS, Georgia, Nov. 30—Charlie Trippi defeated Georgia Tech today, 35—7, with some occasional help from his Georgia team-mates to earn the Bulldogs an invitation to the Sugar Bowl classic. They will play North Carolina. Trippi thrilled the capacity crowd of 55,000 with three touchdowns, one on a 66-yard dash after Tech's lone score, and with a touchdown toss to Johnny Rauch. The victory gave the Bulldogs their first perfect season since 1896, when the famed Pop Warner steered them through four games.

Between them, Trippi and Rauch completed fifteen of twenty-one passes, two of Rauch's being for

Continued on Page 4, Column 3

L. S. U. SETS BACK TULANE BY 41-27

45,000 See Thrilling Battle at Baton Rouge—Victors to Play in Cotton Bowl

By The Associated Press.

BATON ROUGE, La., Nov. 30—Louisiana State staved off a brilliant last-half rally to down a surprising Tulane football team, 41 to 27, today. After the victory Jimmy Stewart, executive secretary of the Southwest Conference, announced in Dallas that L. S. U. and the University of Arkansas would meet in the Cotton Bowl there on New Year's Day.

Forty-five thousand spectators, attracted by the renewal of the bitter State rivalry, experienced a great thrill when Don Fortier, 24-year-old Tulane freshman, threatened to pull the game out of the fire with a skillful blend of passing and running.

Explode in Second Period

The powerful L. S. U. machine, sparked by Y. A. Tittle and Ray Coates, exploded for three touchdowns in a wild second period to gain the winning margin.

Tittle threw three touchdown passes and Coates connected for

Continued on Page 3, Column 1

MILITARY PAGEANT PRECEDES CONTEST

Truman Sees Colorful Parade of Service Corps—Mule and Goat Amuse Vast Crowd

By JOSEPH M. SHEEHAN
Special to THE NEW YORK TIMES.

PHILADELPHIA, Nov. 30—That the football game is only part of the show when Army and Navy come together never was more clearly demonstrated than in the forty-seventh meeting of the service academies today. Long before the kick-off the towering horseshoe stands of Philadelphia's Municipal Stadium were teeming with fans.

Not many of the vast throng of

Continued on Page 2, Column 2

Black of Rhode Island State First In National A. A. U. Cross-Country

By JOHN RENDEL

The stamina in the long, lank frame of Robert Black produced his greatest triumph in the best race of his career in the National A. A. U. senior cross-country championship run at Van Cortlandt Park yesterday. Black, 24-year-old Rhode Island State freshman, added the bigger title to the national junior championship he had taken a week ago.

The New York A. C. sponsored the meet and kept the team title by a four-point margin over New York University, I. C. A. A. A. A. titleholder, 34 to 38. Tommy Quinn, whose victory in Buffalo led the Winged Foot athletes to the team title a year ago, did it again, but this time he was only sixth. The five ahead of him were all individual competitors.

It was a repetition of last week's junior national in two respects. The course was the same, 10,000 meters, or about six miles and a quarter, and the two who finished first and second were identical. James O'Leary of Holy Cross again was second, this time more than 200 yards back.

Before O'Leary crossed the line, Black had been photographed and was answering a lot of questions about himself. These included that he was running in his first college season, and that he was runner-up in the I. C. A. A. A. A. title quest a

Continued on Page 5, Column 2

Gilmer's Tossing for Alabama Upsets Mississippi State, 24-7

By The Associated Press.

TUSCALOOSA, Ala., Nov. 30—Harry Gilmer and his Alabama team-mates wrecked a highly favored Mississippi State eleven here today, 24 to 7, before a home-coming day crowd of 25,000.

The Crimson Tide, beaten four times previously, was in command throughout the contest, and had a wide margin all the way.

After a scoreless first period, Gilmer connected with End Ted Cook for a 44-yard gain to take the ball to the State 6. An offside penalty nullified a Tide touchdown, but Sub Quarterback Hugh Morrow kicked a field goal from placement, and Alabama was never headed.

The first touchdown followed shortly, with Gilmer passing first to Cook and then to Morrow and Billy Cadenhead to cover most of the distance in a 69-yard drive. Red Noonan, freshman fullback, made the final yard for the score.

Johnny Wozniak, junior guard, made the second touchdown after blocking Billy Murphy's punt on the State 38. He grabbed the ball on the State 20 and ran unmolested to the goal.

Gilmer shot another pass, this time for 42 yards to Cook, to set up the final Tide marker. Gilmer lugged it from over the three on second down. Gilmer netted 65 yards rushing in nineteen carries

Continued on Page 3, Column 6

MIDDIES JUST MISS

Drive to 3-Yard Line in Dying Minutes of Game Before 100,000

ARMY LEADS AT HALF, 21-6

But Navy Surges Back With Two Tallies—Davis and Blanchard Shine

By ALLISON DANZIG
Special to THE NEW YORK TIMES.

PHILADELPHIA, Nov. 30—The clock ran out on Navy. By the margin of a few precious yards the greatest record in Army football history was saved in the Municipal Stadium today.

Three yards stood between Navy and the upset of the ages over the team that had stood invincible for three years. One hundred thousand spectators, President Harry S. Truman among them, were making a bedlam in the huge horseshoe enclosure as the fighting midshipmen ripped and passed their way 64 yards down the field.

The great Army eleven was the overwhelming favorite by 28 points over an opponent that had lost seven successive games. And Army was being swept off its feet in a desperate fight to stem the tide of defeat that had set in after the cadets had led by 21—6 at the half.

Close to Defeat

The team that had conquered twenty-six foes and tied Notre Dame over a three-year period was hanging on the ropes. Nothing it seemed, could save it against the surging power and clever resourcefulness of its rampant rival from the Severn.

From their 33-yard line the amazing midshipmen, who had swept 78 yards and then 35 in the third period to make the score 21—18 at the start of the final quarter, stormed 64 yards to Army's 3-yard line. It was first down and goal to go, with a minute and a half remaining to play.

Throughout the tremendous enclosure, to its farthest reaches, the multitude was standing in a turmoil of mad excitement, cheering, pleading, urging its heroes on, or to stand and hold that line. It was drama as nerve-wracking and pulsating as anything within memory in the long history of this bitter rivalry between the service academies.

Hope Seemed Gone

All hope seemed gone for Army. The team that had scored on three of the first four times it had the ball and apparently was going to win in a rout was being hammered into helplessness.

The renowned Doc Blanchard and Glenn Davis, who had scored Army's three touchdowns and turned in one of their most dazzling twin performances in this last appearance of their college careers, were completely forgotten. There were new idols holding the stage and sending the crowd into convulsions of happiness or chilling its heart with fear—Reaves Baysinger, Pistol Pete Williams, Leon Bramlett, Lynn Chewning, Al McCully, Bill Hawkins and Bill Earl.

First down and 3 yards to go. Nine feet to go for the touchdown that would make history and send Army toppling from the lofty pedestal it has occupied for three years in the finale for Earl Blaik's invincible Black Knights of the Hudson.

The teams lined up and 193-pound Chewning, who had been held in reserve until the last quarter by Capt. Tom Hamilton, was called on by Quarterback Baysinger to carry the ball on first down. It was Chewning who had just brought the ball down to the 3 with a 20-yard end run on fourth down.

Stopped at the Line

The powerful fullback from Richmond hurled himself at the sagging Army line as the crowd screamed with what voice it had left. Goble Bryant and Hank Foldberg tore through and nailed him at the line of scrimmage. Again Chewning carried, and this time big Barney Poole smashed him down in his tracks.

The suspense was almost unbearable. The clock showed less than a minute left to play. It still didn't seem possible that Navy could be stopped.

At this critical juncture Referee Bill Halloran stepped in, picked up the ball and carried it back five

Continued on Page 3, Column 3

Blaik Says the Middies Had 'the Most Inspired Navy Team' He Ever Has Seen

ARMY SCORES, 21-18, AFTER CLOSE CALL

Continued From Page 1

yards. The midshipmen had been penalized five yards for delaying the game. A groan went up from the Navy stands, but there was still time to do it, so it seemed.

Tosses to Williams

On third down, Navy went into single wing formation, into which it had been shifting from time to time from the T. Hawkins took the snap from Dick Scott, Navy's superb center, and took two steps toward the line, then flipped the ball out to Williams.

The Army line was not fooled this time, as it had been on other buck laterals. It surged in on the fast halfback and nailed him on the five-yard line. Before another play could be run, a pistol barked, sounding the end of the game.

Army's great goal-line defense, one of its noblest efforts of the year, had saved the day. West Point was the winner by 21—18, by the margin of Navy's failure to kick a single one of its three tries for the extra point following its touchdowns.

Such was the tremendously dramatic ending of the forty-seventh meeting between the midshipmen and the cadets. Thus did Army wind up the three most glorious years it has known on the gridiron, with a record of twenty-seven victories and one tie.

Finale for Great Stars

So did Blanchard and Davis and Arnold Tucker, probably the greatest backfield triumvirate in modern times, if not of all time, conclude their glamorous record of triumph.

And so did Navy redeem itself for all the misfortune that had dogged it from the second day of the season in September. This was one of the poorest of all Annapolis teams, on the record, but the midshipmen of 1946 will long be remembered and honored for the spirit that scorned odds and came within an inch of bringing down the scourge of the gridiron—closer than even Notre Dame came in its scoreless tie with Army.

And a salute is in order to Captain Hamilton, a brilliant war leader whose fighting spirit matched his men's, whose faith in them never dimmed at any time during the campaign and who sent them into battle with expressions of confidence in their ability to win.

Army and Navy furnished the perfect ending to the football season with their enthralling rivalry. The weather was perfect for both the players and for the year's record gathering. The sun shone in a clear sky, the temperature was in the forties and the crowd, warmly clad, enjoyed the spectacle in complete comfort.

Spectacle for Crowd

The spectacle included not only the rousing fight but all of the side show that goes with an Army-Navy game. The gathering thrilled to the sight of the corps of 2,100 cadets and the brigade of 2,700 midshipmen swinging along on the field in faultless files.

It revelled in their unrivaled lung power in keeping up a constant roar of songs and cheers and was entertained by the parade of an Army tank and a Navy battleship. Bill X, the Navy goat, and Mr. Jackson and Poncho, the Army mules, emerged from the ship and tank as the tank fired blank salutes and the battleship belched forth smoke.

The gathering was not only the year's largest but one of the most distinguished to attend an Army-Navy game. Surrounding President Truman were members of his Cabinet, the highest ranking flag officers of the Army and the Navy, Senators, Congressmen, Governors and members of the diplomatic corps.

The President, arriving shortly before the West Point corps paraded into the stadium, was escorted with Mrs. Truman and the members of his party to his box, roped off by a square cordon of Pinkertons and Secret Service men. Mr. Truman sat on the Navy side for the first half of the game.

During the intermission, he was escorted by Vice Admiral Aubrey V. Fitch, Superintendent of the Naval Academy, and Rear Admiral Stuart H. Ingersoll, commandant of midshipmen, to the center of the field. There he was met by Maj. Gen. Maxwell D. Taylor, Superintendent of the Military Academy, and Brig. Gen. Gerald J. Higgins, commandant of the corps of cadets.

The President then was convoyed to his box on Army's side for the second half. As it turned out, the President was sitting on the wrong side each half. While he was on the Navy side Army was squarely in command of the play, and once he joined the cadets, Navy took over control of the game.

The turn in the tide came shortly after the second half got under way. Army took the opening kick-off after the intermission and went down to Navy's 31-yard [illegible] It seemed that the cadets were going to increase their 21-6 lead by another touchdown. But on fourth down, with 2 yards to go for a first down, Army elected to kick.

That decision, and another that came just before the end of the third period, had a vital bearing on the transformation that took place in the play.

Might Have Gone On

Had Army chosen to gamble for a first down, and it would not have been much of a gamble with the ball well in Navy territory, it might have continued on to score. It was after Davis had kicked out of bounds for only ten yards that Navy started on its 78-yard touchdown march.

The decision that came later was a real gamble, and it turned out badly. Probably influenced by the great offensive strength that Navy had shown on its touchdown march, Army elected to try for a first down deep in its own territory. Less than a yard was needed on the fourth down and Blanchard was sent into the line.

The midshipmen stopped him like a stone wall, and as a result the cadets gave up possession on their own 35. It was from there that the middies went on to their third touchdown, which came on the third play of the final quarter.

The touchdown play was one of the cleverest of the day and was typical of the resourcefulness and enterprise of Captain Hamilton's team. On fourth down, with the ball on the three, Earl took a lateral and fired the ball straight into the arms of Bramlett in the end zone for the score.

To start at the beginning, Navy took the opening kick-off, after Captain Bramlett had won the toss, and went down to Army's 45. Baysinger kicked into the end zone and Army started on its 20. Blanchard made a first down and then Davis fumbled, Newbold Smith recovering for Navy on Army's 32. The middies got to the 26 and then Baysinger fumbled as he was tackled by Poole, and Art Gerometta recovered for Army on his 37. Now Army was on its way.

In four plays the cadets went sixty-two yards for their first touchdown. After a buck had gained two yards, Tucker fired a pass to Davis, who had gone in motion from the T-formation. The rapid halfback streaked down the sideline 46 yards. Blanchard got a yard and then Davis took a pitch-out pass from Tucker, shook off three tacklers and went the 13 yards to the goal line.

Navy's answer to this characteristic example of Army striking power was to take the next kick-off and go all the way, 81 yards. Baysinger, who was an unknown until the Notre Dame game and who covered himself with glory with his passing, running of the team and kicking today, engineered the touchdown drive with the skill and poise of a veteran.

Williams and Myron Gerber did most of the carrying. Baysinger fired a pass to Art Markel for 11 and another to Bramlett for 32, putting the ball on the 2. Baysinger then made the touchdown on a quarterback sneak from a foot out. Bob Van Summern's try for the extra point was blocked, and Army led by the conversion of Jack Ray.

Ray was to kick the extra point after all three of Army's touchdowns to furnish the margin of victory. So he stood as one of Army's heroes of the day.

Army now proceeded to answer Navy in kind. And it went exactly the same distance that the Middies had gone, 81 yards, and took fewer plays. After Blanchard and Davis had carried to the 40, Tucker pitched out to Davis for 11. The scoring play was a 52-yard gallop by Blanchard. The Army fullback burst through the line and sprinted almost with the speed of Davis in outdistancing his Navy pursuers.

A break set up Army's third touchdown, which followed in this second quarter. Bill Yeomans intercepted Baysinger's pass. Army started on Navy's 38-yard mark. In just three plays the ball was across.

Davis Fires to Blanchard

Davis passed to Poole for 8 and then ran for 4. On the next scrimmage, Davis, taking a direct pass from center, fired like a flash to Blanchard, who had gone in motion to the left. The big fullback went 26 yards, and Army led, 21—6, after Ray had booted the extra point.

Before the half ended, the ball changed hands rapidly on an amazing one-hand interception by Davis, Jim Carrington's recovery of an Army fumble, and Rip Rowan's interception of another pass.

The second half started with Army going to the Navy 32 and then kicking. Navy, taking the ball on its 22, went 78 yards, with Williams, Gerber and Hawkins carrying. An interference penalty against Army kept the march alive.

Baysinger passed 18 yards to Markel over center. Williams got down to the 4 on a shovel pass, and Hawkins scored from the 2-yard mark. Hawkins failed on the try for the extra point and the score was 21—12.

On the next kick-off, Blanchard ran the ball back to his 25 and then he and Davis carried to within inches of a first down. Army decided to gamble on a first down and Blanchard was stopped without gain. Navy took over on Army's 35 and went on to its third touchdown.

Earl passed to Bramlett for 14 and Hawkins, who was wearing a brace on his knee but was surprisingly fast, broke through the middle for 16, putting the ball on the 5. A play failed to gain as the quarter ended.

Hawkins made two yards to start the final period, and then Bramlett took the pass from Earl for the touchdown. Again Hawkins' try for the extra point failed and the score was 21—18.

Crowd Is Stirred

The crowd was in a state of high excitement now. Navy had completely taken the play away from Army, and it was a question whether the middies could be held in check.

Army now started as though it would put an end to the middies' uprising. After Rowan had brought the kick-off back to his 32, Davis broke loose around left end, streaking along sideline 29 yards to Navy's 39. Now it was the cadet corps' turn to do some whole-hearted cheering for the first time in a long spell.

Apparently Army was on the way again. But on the next play Davis fired a long pass and Pete Williams intercepted. That was the last time Army made any kind of offensive gesture. The first down that Davis had made on his long run was the Army's first and last of the quarter. It had made only one in the third period, while Navy was to roll up eleven in the second half.

Navy started its final thrilling march after Davis had kicked and Williams had returned the punt to Navy's 33. Captain Hamilton, who made clever use of his substitutes, sent in Chewning, who was fresh and eager for heavy duty.

A pass from Williams to Phil Ryan, substitute end, netted 17. Williams and McCully, who also had been on the injured list, carried the ball to the 23. Army held here, but on fourth down Chewning broke away for 20 yards to the 3, as previously related.

Then came the maddest ninety seconds any ball game could possibly know, ending with the ball on Army's 5 and Earl Blaik's badly expended but dead game team the winner by 21—18.

With their handful of reserves, the cadets just barely made it, to save their great record. Blanchard and Davis played the entire sixty minutes in their farewell to college football, and Tucker was in for all but a minute or two. Baysinger, the find of the year at Navy, played almost the entire game and turned in a job to swell the heart of his father, Syracuse's famous Ribs Baysinger.

The whole Navy team did a tremendous job, and there was nothing wrong with an Army team that fought under fearful pressure all year with few replacements and still had enough to stand off the terrific challenge of the midshipmen. It was only by an eyelash that the cadets prevented repetition of the stunning upset the midshipmen sprang at Annapolis in 1942.

The line-up:

ARMY (21)		NAVY (18)
Poole	L.E.	Markel
Biles	L.T.	E. N. Smith
Steffy	L.G.	Emerson
Enos	C.	Scott
Gerometta	R.G.	Carrington
Bryant	R.T.	Shimshak
Foldberg	R.E.	Bramlett
Tucker	Q.B.	Baysinger
Davis	L.H.	Williams
Rowan	R.H.	Schwoeffermann
Blanchard	F.B.	Gerber

Truman Is a Typical Fan With Hot Dog and Apple

Special to THE NEW YORK TIMES.

PHILADELPHIA, Nov. 30—President Truman made the most of the recess today from his tasks as Chief Executive of the nation and became a typical football fan at the Army-Navy game, eating a hot dog, drinking a paper cup of hot chocolate and finishing off his half-time snack with an apple.

The President left the stadium five minutes before the end of the contest, but he did it reluctantly. With Navy in possession of the ball deep in Army territory, Mr. Truman wanted to see that final push.

"This is the best part of the game," he exclaimed. But he was hustled off before the stands unloaded and blocked his route to the train.

Statistics of the Game

	Army.	Navy.
First downs	8	20
Yards gained, rushing	185	163
Forward passes	10	19
Forwards completed	6	11
Yards gained, forwards	106	136
Forwards intercepted by	3	1
Number of punts	3	3
*Av. dist. of punts, yds	30	32
Run-back of punts, yds.	0	12
Fumbles	3	3
Own fumbles recovered	1	2
Penalties	5	5
Yards lost, penalties	29	25

*From line of scrimmage.

ALABAMA UPSETS MISS. STATE, 24-7

Continued From Page 1

and connected with eight of seventeen passes for 162 yards.

State's touchdown, which followed the final Alabama score, was engineered by Lawrence Matulich, sub tailback, and followed a 67-yard run-back of the kick-off by Graham Bramlett. Matulich connected with three passes to Kermit Davis, Kenneth Davis and Harper Davis in turn, then slammed through the line for the final 5 yards in two tries.

Expected Battle Missing

The heralded battle between Gilmer and State's all-southeastern back, Tom (Shorty) McWilliams, failed to develop because the Tide line stopped McWilliams cold most of the time. McWilliams netted 31 yards rushing in eight carriers, and his only pass attempt was incomplete.

State's line held its own in the opening period but was badly outplayed the rest of the way. Alabama had 112 yards rushing to 72 for State, and netted 162 passing to sixty-four for the losers.

The line-up:

ALABAMA (24)		MISS STATE (7)
Cook	L.E.	Hildebrand
Whitley	L.T.	Sidorik
Wozniak	L.G.	Mihalic
Mancha	C.	Corley
Filippini	R.G.	Harris
Flowers	R.T.	Garrett
Cain	R.E.	Howard
Self	Q.B.	Moates
Gilmer	L.H.	McWilliams
Tew	R.H.	H. Davis
Hodges	F.B.	Bailey

L. S. U. SETS BACK TULANE BY 41-27

Continued From Page 1

two, but it was a pair of long runs by Slim Jim Cason, neither of which went for a score, which highlighted the Louisiana attack.

Far and away the best individual performance of the day was Fortier's amazing exhibition. He passed for three touchdowns and scored another on an eighteen-yard jaunt.

L.S.U. led, 35 to 7, with the third period less than two minutes old, when the battling Greenies, spearheaded by Fortier, took over with a vengeance.

Fortier had engineered a Tulane touchdown in the second period by running back a kick-off 50 yards and throwing passes of 37 and 9 yards, the latter to Ed Heider for the score.

The line-up:

L. S. U. (41)		TULANE (27)
Lindsey	L.E.	Tarzetti
Champagne	L.T.	Tessier
Hall	L.G.	Deramee
Ballard	C.	Rice
Worley	R.G.	Bourgeois
Land	R.T.	Rowland
Richmond	R.E.	Heider
Tittle	Q.B.	Nutt
Coates	L.H.	Van Meter
Sandifer	R.H.	Waller
Knight	F.B.	Price

OREGON STATE IN FRONT

Intercepts Washington Aerials for 21-to-12 Triumph

PORTLAND, Ore., Nov. 30 (AP)—Oregon State's Beaver backfield turned Washington Husky passes into a 21-to-12 victory on a soggy gridiron today to capture second place in the Pacific Coast Conference before more than 26,800 fans.

A ground attack, with Halfback Don Samuel carrying, moved the Beavers from their own 39 to Washington's 28. Samuel tossed 18 yards to Fullback Ken Carpenter, who raced across untouched. Reserve Quarterback Warren Simas made the first of three conversion kicks.

"All the News That's Fit to Print"

The New York Times.

LATE CITY EDITION
Fair and mild today and tomorrow.
Temperature Range Today—Max.,76; Min.,57
Temperatures Yesterday—Max.,71; Min.,49
Full U. S. Weather Bureau Report, Page ...

Copyright, 1947, by The New York Times Company.

VOL. XCVII...No. 32,760. Entered as Second-Class Matter. Postoffice, New York, N. Y. NEW YORK, SATURDAY, OCTOBER 4, 1947. THREE CENTS IN NEW YORK CITY

DODGERS' ONLY HIT BEATS YANKEES, 3-2, WITH 2 OUT IN NINTH

Lavagetto's Pinch Double Bats in 2 Runs, Evens Series and Spoils Bevens' No-Hitter

10 WALKS HELP BROOKLYN

Casey Wins in Relief Second Day in Row With Lone Pitch Resulting in Double Play

By JOHN DREBINGER

With the first no-hitter in world series history in the making at Ebbets Field yesterday, Cookie Lavagetto rewrote the script with two out in the ninth inning to establish the Dodgers as the first club in baseball's autumnal classic ever to win a game on just one hit.

In his familiar role of pinch hitter, the veteran Lavagetto slammed a two-bagger off the right-field wall against Floyd (Bill) Bevens that drove in two runners put on by walks. That floored the Yankees on the spot for a 3-to-2 Brooklyn triumph, tied the series at two victories apiece, stunned about half the crowd of 33,443 and sent the other half—the faithful of Flatbush—screaming hysterically on to the field in an endeavor to lay fond hands on their hero.

Bevens, stalwart right-hander, was within one short stride of baseball immortality until he lost all in the twinkling of an eye to Burt Shotton's unpredictable Dodgers.

For eight and two-thirds innings of this nerve-tingling fourth game Bevens, a strong, silent man from Salem, Ore., held the bats of Brooklyn's Bums even more silent than a tomb. No series pitcher ever had gone that far without allowing a hit.

An Unenviable Record

On the way, Bevens established another world series mark, though he will never reflect upon that one in his later years with any feeling of gratification. He gave ten bases on balls, one more than Colby Jack Coombs of the Athletics permitted in 1910.

Two of those passes helped the Dodgers to their first run in the fifth inning to whittle away one of two tallies the Yanks had counted earlier. And the final two were indirectly to cause his defeat, though the last one was not wholly of his choosing. It was ordered by Manager Bucky Harris, who by that decision left himself open to sharp criticism. Most observers seemed to feel the usually astute Yankee skipper had pulled something of a strategic "rock."

As the final half of the ninth opened, with the Bombers leading, 2 to 1, Bruce Edwards went out when Johnny Lindell hauled down his lofty shot in front of the left-field stand with a leaping catch. But Carl Furillo walked for Bevens' ninth pass before Shotton fairly sprayed the summery afternoon with a maze of masterminding.

Jorgensen Fouls Out

After Spider Jorgensen had fouled out to George McQuinn back of first, Shotton sent Al Gionfriddo, rookie outfielder, to run for Furillo. Only one more batter need be retired then to clinch the victory for Bevens as well as that world series no-hit goal which has eluded some of baseball's greatest hurlers since 1903.

The batter was Pete Reiser, whom Shotton sent up for Hugh Casey, relief ace who had entered the contest in the top half of the ninth with the bases full and one out to end the inning on one pitch. Pistol Pete, limping painfully on a swollen ankle which he had sprained the previous day, had sat this one out up to that moment.

Shotton's strategy flashed again with one strike and two balls on Reiser as Gionfriddo streaked for second and stole the bag on an eyelash play. That pitch, too, was wide, making the count three and one.

There Harris made his questionable move. He ordered Bevens to toss the next one wide, thereby walking the lame Reiser. It seemed a direct violation of one of baseball's fundamental precepts which dictates against putting the "winning run" on base in such a situation.

Shotton followed with two more moves on the field, which seemed suddenly converted into a chessboard. He sent Eddie Miksis in to run for Reiser, an obvious shift, and then called on Lavagetto to bat for Ed Stanky.

The swarthy-complexioned veteran, a right-handed batter, swung viciously at the first pitch and

Continued on Page 11, Column 2

CHANGE IN HOLLAND

Queen Wilhelmina

Princess Juliana
The New York Times (Netherlands Information)

WILHELMINA ENDING RULE FOR A TIME

Dutch Queen Ill From Labors of 49-Year Reign—Juliana to Be Temporary Regent

By The Associated Press.

AMSTERDAM, The Netherlands, Oct. 3—Queen Wilhelmina, whose golden jubilee as the Netherlands' sovereign is less than a year away, soon will relinquish temporarily her royal power to Princess Juliana for reasons of health, the Netherlands Government announced today.

The 67-year-old Queen, who has been reported suffering from fatigue, plans to stay at her summer palace, Het Loo, for a rest, her secretariat said.

A communiqué, issued after Premier L. J. M. Beel told newsmen of the Queen's decision, said Wilhelmina had requested that it be made clear there was no reason for alarm over her condition.

"Nevertheless, it is not surprising that the heavy burdens which weighed and still are weighing on her did not leave her health unaffected," the bulletin added.

Legislation appointing Princess Juliana as regent will be introduced soon at a joint session of the two chambers of the Dutch Parliament, it was announced.

Although Netherlanders knew of the Queen's need for rest, the announcement that she would retire temporarily came as a shock. But newspapers stressed in their editorials that there was no cause for alarm.

One source said Princess Juliana's period of regency might last "from six weeks up to a few

Continued on Page 6, Column 4

BELGIUM BACKS U. S. ON BALKANS WATCH; WOULD FORGET PAST

Spaak Is Vigorous in U. N. in Defense of Move for a Permanent Inquiry

APPEALS TO SLAV STATES

Tito Delegate Cries 'Slander' —Interrupts 3 Times—New Zealand Supports Plan

By A. M. ROSENTHAL
Special to The New York Times.

LAKE SUCCESS, N. Y., Oct. 3—Premier Paul-Henri Spaak of Belgium stepped into the Balkan controversy today with a defense of the United States' aid-to-Greece policy and a direct appeal to the Slav states to accept a new United Nations commission of investigation.

The former President of the General Assembly spoke for an hour before the Political and Security Committee. He said that, if the Slav group agreed to the United States' resolution for a border watch, he would favor dropping the paragraphs that pinned direct blame for the Balkan dispute on Yugoslavia, Bulgaria and Albania. The key to peace in the Balkans, he said, is Slav acceptance of the will of the majority.

It was the first major speech by an "outsider" in the dispute, now in its second week of hearings before the committee. And it was the first point-by-point reply to repeated Slav charges of Anglo-American imperialism in the Balkans.

Yugoslav Delegate Interrupts

M. Spaak spoke harshly of Yugoslavia's refusal to cooperate with a United Nations subsidiary inquiry group that had been operating in the Balkans and called the action a "mockery" of the Security Council, which had authorized the investigation. Three times during his speech, which rose steadily in emotional intensity, M. Spaak was interrupted by Dr. Ales Bebler of Yugoslavia, and three times the delegate from Belgrade was silenced by the chairman's gavel.

Aside from his support of the United States motion to set up another Balkan commission, most of the Belgian Premier's speech was a plea for an end of the name-calling that has punctuated the long debate on Greece's quarrel with her northern neighbors. M. Spaak said repeatedly that the character of the Greek Government—and he made it plain that he was no enthusiastic supporter of the Athens regime in all its actions—was purely an internal affair of Greece and not a fit subject for United Nations debate.

"Statements on the Greek Government are out of order," he insisted. "That kind of talk will poison the debate and ruin things."

Before the Belgian delegate spoke, the committee heard the fourth attack this week on United States policy in Greece by a member of the Soviet bloc. This time the accusations came from Dimitri Z. Manuilsky, Foreign Minister of the Ukraine, who said United States "intervention" in Greece was growing more and more blatant and that Greek governments were puppet governments, made in the United States Embassy in Athens.

But until M. Spaak took the floor, most of the charges and counter-charges had come from

Continued on Page 4, Column 3

Elizabeth's Fiance Now an Anglican

Special to The New York Times.

LONDON, Oct. 3—Lieut. Philip Mountbatten, Princess Elizabeth's fiancé, was recently received into the Church of England by the Archbishop of Canterbury. The ceremony took place in the chapel at Lambeth Palace court, it was announced today.

Lieutenant Mountbatten had been baptized in the Greek Orthodox Church. During his war service in the British Navy he attended Church of England services.

SPLIT OF PALESTINE LIKENED TO MUNICH

Lebanese Calls Inquiry's Plan a 'Solution of Expediency'—Enforcement Worries Czech

By MARSHALL E. NEWTON
Special to The New York Times.

LAKE SUCCESS, N. Y., Oct. 3—The recommendations by the majority of the United Nations Special Committee on Palestine are a "solution of expediency" recalling the Munich decision of 1938, Camille Chamoun, delegate from Lebanon, told the General Assembly's Committee on Palestine today. His address was the opening gun in the Arab states' battle against the majority and minority reports.

The only other speaker at the committee session was Karel Lisicky of Czechoslovakia. He declared that a new factor had been introduced into the situation by the United Kingdom's statement that Britain could not undertake to enforce a Palestine decision that was not accepted by the Arabs and the Jews of Palestine. The majority report, he said, is based on the premise that Britain, as the mandatory power, would be willing to undertake enforcement.

Mr. Lisicky asked whether the committee could consider the report of the inquiry group, in view of the United Kingdom's position, without first determining whether some other power or group of powers could be persuaded to enforce any decision taken by the General Assembly.

Mr. Chamoun delved into the history of Palestine, discussed the background of the British mandate and appealed to principles of right and justice of the United Nations Charter.

Three principles must be observed in any solution of the Palestine problem, he said. These were the right of peoples freely to decide their own future, the need

Continued on Page 5, Column 3

GEN. LEE CLEARED OF ABUSE IN ITALY; INFRACTIONS 'MINOR'

Eisenhower and Royall Say Charges by Newsman Gave 'an Out-of-Focus Picture'

CORRECTIVE STEPS TAKEN

Wyche's Report on Inquiry Is Accepted—Columnist Claims a 'Whitewash'

By ANTHONY LEVIERO
Special to The New York Times.

WASHINGTON, Oct. 3—Secretary of the Army Kenneth C. Royall and Gen. Dwight D. Eisenhower, Chief of Staff, announced today they had found no cause of action against Lieut. Gen. C. H. Lee for alleged maladministration of his command in Italy.

Releasing their decisions in an inquiry inspired by a series of articles written by Robert C. Ruark, Scripps-Howard columnist, the Army officials said they had found only incidental abuses and infractions of regulations. They stated that corrective measures had been taken. General Lee recently returned to the United States, and General Eisenhower said today he would retire soon.

In his stories Mr. Ruark contended that General Lee lived regally and his officers and their families lived in luxury, while enlisted men were ill-fed and ill-housed and were otherwise degraded and compelled to indulge excessively in saluting.

General Eisenhower asserted in a memorandum to Secretary Royall that Mr. Ruark had presented "an out-of-focus picture" of what he had seen in Italy. He paid a high tribute to General Lee, who had fought the battle of supply for him throughout the European war. Secretary Royall concurred in every respect.

Secretary Royall and General Eisenhower endorsed the detailed findings of Maj. Gen. Ira T. Wyche, the Inspector General of the Army, who presented a report of about 12,000 words. The latter recommended that no further action be taken as he had started corrective measures.

General Wyche personally investigated the charges at the direction of General Eisenhower. He spent three weeks in Italy. Other officers questioned more than 200 persons returning from that country.

"I am impelled to remark," Gen-

Continued on Page 6, Column 3

Dewey Creates Food Board To Safeguard State's Health

Dr. Hilleboe Is Made Head of Commission Which Will Work for Nutritious Diet for All While Helping to Conserve Grain

By LEO EGAN
Special to The New York Times.

ALBANY, Oct. 3 — Governor Thomas E. Dewey established today a State Food Commisison with an initial appropriation of $100,000 to help meet the food crisis caused by shortages, high prices and the need for large shipments to Europe to prevent famine there. He gave assurances that more funds would be provided if needed.

The new commission, similar to the Emergency Food Commission which operated in the State during the war years, will be headed by Dr. Herman E. Hilleboe, State Health Commisisoner. The earlier board went out of existence with the expiration of war emergency legislation.

In announcing his program this morning following a conference with Republican legislative leaders, Mr. Dewey made it clear that the new commission would have a two-fold task: to undertake an educational program to assure residents of the State of a balanced and nutritious diet even though they should eat less in accordance with the national conservation program, and to encourage farmers to cull their dairy herds and poultry flocks of the less productive stock so as to reduce their need for feed grains.

Dr. Hilleboe's appointment as chairman of the commission appeared designed to show that its main emphasis would be on the means for maintaining a balanced diet despite high prices and shortages. The earlier commissions were headed by representatives of agriculture since their main purpose was to increase production and to make certain of the proper distribution of what was produced.

Ten or eleven others are expected to serve on the commission with Dr. Hilleboe. Most of them will be State officials. Their names will be announced tomorrow.

In disclosing his plan, Governor Dewey took occasion to endorse the voluntary food conservation

Continued on Page 2, Column 4

GOVERNMENT MAPS SHOWDOWN TO CUT GRAIN SPECULATION

Report to Truman Insists This Is Big Factor in Food Costs and Hampers Foreign Aid

DISTILLERS OFFER TO HELP

Citizens' Board Reports That 60% of Industry Has Agreed to Halve Supplies It Uses

By FELIX BELAIR Jr.
Special to The New York Times.

WASHINGTON, Oct. 3—The Administration moved toward a showdown with the country's grain exchanges today armed with a report of the President's Council of Economic Advisers that speculation in commodities had contributed heavily to rising food costs to the detriment of the domestic economy and foreign-aid plans.

At a Cabinet meeting, President Truman directed discussion to this and other findings in the report that the Administration should begin now to prepare its case for revival of some wartime controls in the event the voluntary food-conservation program proved inadequate in the European food emergency. It was decided that the report should not be made public.

The Government is powerless, officials say, to force an increase in credit margins to curb speculation in grain and other commodities, and the grain exchanges recently rejected an appeal by Secretary of Agriculture Clinton P. Anderson that grain margins be increased to 33 1/3 per cent. The report suggested the advisability of legislation to vest discretionary authority in the Commodity Exchange Authority.

Recommendations on Controls

The report of the economic advisers made no flat recommendations as such but pointed to possible revival or extension of these wartime controls:

Allocation of food supplies at the source to assure adequate shipments for relief and to guard against diversion of short supplies for distilling and excessive feeding of livestock.

Restriction of wheat and flour use and an increase in the flour extraction rate to 80 per cent.

Extension of export controls beyond the February termination date, with broader authority in the Secretary of Commerce to grant export licenses and priorities.

Maintenance of Federal revenues and income tax rates at present levels as an essential safeguard against inflation.

The economic report endorsed the voluntary conservation program, saying in substance that it was essential for purposes of "public education" on the seriousness of the foreign-relief problem. But it indicated that while the program was a laudable undertaking it might prove inadequate to the tremendous task at hand.

Other developments in the foreign-aid program included:

(1) A resolution by the President's Committee on Foreign Aid, of which Secretary of Commerce W. Averell Harriman is chairman, endorsing the stand of Secretary Anderson against the grain exchanges and urging him to apply "further pressure" for an increase in credit margins to 33 1/3 per cent or as high as necessary to curb speculative trading.

Agreement by Distillers Told

(2) Announcement by the Citizens Food Committee that 60 per cent of the liquor-distilling industry had agreed to use no more wheat and to reduce use of other grains by 50 per cent during the food emergency.

Charles Luckman, head of the citizens' group, said the action of the distillers would save 2,500,000 bushels of grain a month. They are now using double that amount of grain other than wheat each month but very little wheat. Mr. Luckman said the details of "this first major development" in the conservation drive would be worked out with distillers at a conference next week.

Secretary Anderson said after the Cabinet meeting that the Department of Agriculture was considering by-passing the grain exchanges and buying wheat direct from farmers. He later modified the statement, however, saying he doubted whether direct buying methods would be necessary at this time.

"I prefer to go through the grain trade and thus far have been able

Continued on Page 2, Column 4

Taft Law Writ Halts Strike Of Longshoremen in Albany

Special to The New York Times.

ALBANY, Oct. 3—Several hundred longshoremen at the port of Albany, on strike since September 23, returned to work today, less than twenty-four hours after a Federal court judge issued an order directing that the strike cease. It was the first such order issued under the provision of the Taft-Hartley law prohibiting secondary boycotts.

Judge Stephen Brennan signed the order in New York City last night and the men were directed to return to their jobs by Joseph P. Ryan, president of the International Longshoremen's Association, American Federation of Labor. The strikers were members of the Albany local of the ILA.

The order directed the union to appear in Federal Court at Syracuse next Tuesday to show cause why the injunction should not be made permanent.

Test of Act Hinted

Although union officials bowed to the Brennan order, there was a possibility that labor leaders would utilize the case to make a test of the act. This was hinted by Louis Waldman, union attorney, who asserted that the court action was "government by injunction."

Judge Brennan acted on an application by the National Labor Relations Board, which contended that the strike constituted a secondary boycott.

The strike involved 240 longshoremen at the Albany port. It developed from a dispute between Albany Local 294, International Brotherhood of Teamsters, and the newly organized Trailerships, Inc., which planned to transport truck trailers by water between Albany and New York City.

The NLRB claimed that the teamsters insisted that they be paid for an Albany-New York haul for delivering trailers from Albany warehouses to the Trailership dock here, as a result of which teamsters did not do business with Trailerships.

The longshoremen said the action of the teamsters deprived

Continued on Page 8, Column 4

MAYOR INTERVENES IN SAFEWAY ROW

His Citizens' Mediation Panel Confers Six Hours on Strike —Progress Is Reported

By LAWRENCE RESNER

After a six-hour conference at City Hall, a special citizen's mediation panel appointed by Mayor O'Dwyer said last night that some progress had been made toward a settlement of the two-day-old tie-up of 150 Safeway Store retail grocery outlets.

Acting promptly, in view of the gravity of the food price situation, the Mayor had announced the appointment of the committee yesterday morning.

Mayor O'Dwyer had urged that the stores, which were closed by Safeway's management in the face of a union strike threat, reopen and that "the differences between the parties be resolved amicably without any further interruption of work."

Named to the mediation panel were Terrence J. McManus, secretary of the New York County Lawyers Association, public member and chairman; Louis Broido, executive vice president of Gimbel Brothers, employer representative, and John P. Grogan, international vice president of the Industrial Union of Marine and Shipbuilding Workers of America, CIO.

This committee, which was called on one day's notice, met at City Hall at 2:30 yesterday afternoon with Clarence Dale, labor relations executive of Safeway, and Patrick Reape, business manager of Local

Continued on Page 7, Column 2

World News Summarized

SATURDAY, OCTOBER 4, 1947

The Truman Administration, having received a report from the President's Council of Economic Advisers charging that speculation in commodities had been a major factor in rising food costs, moved toward a showdown with the nation's grain exchanges, which have rejected an appeal that grain margins be increased. [1:8.]

Governor Dewey created a State Food Commission, similar to the wartime Emergency Food Commission, to study the critical food situation caused by high prices and shortages. The group will be headed by the State Health Commissioner, Dr. Herman E. Hilleboe. [1:6-7.]

After issuance of a Federal court order under the provision of the Taft-Hartley law prohibiting secondary boycotts, several hundred longshoremen who had been on strike in Albany returned to work. [1:6-7.]

A plea to the Slav states to accept a new United Nations commission of investigation in the Balkans was made by Premier Paul-Henri Spaak of Belgium before the Political and Security Committee of the General Assembly. He said he would favor omission of paragraphs placing blame for the Balkan dispute on Yugoslavia, Bulgaria and Albania if the Slav states agreed to the rest of the United States resolution calling for a border watch along the Greek frontier. [1:3.]

The Security Council took up the Indonesian case anew after an interim report from the six-nation consular commission in Batavia that, despite the Council's cease-fire order, fighting was continuing. [5:1.]

The majority report of the United Nations Special Committee on Palestine represents a "solution of expediency" like that taken in 1938 at Munich, the Lebanese delegate charged in an address to the Assembly's Committee on Palestine. [1:4.] Arabs in the Holy Land staged a dawn-to-dusk general strike as part of their campaign for the independence and unity of Palestine. [5:4.]

The deputies of the Council of Foreign Ministers met in London to discuss disposition of the Italian colonies and sped through the preliminary stages of their conference. [6:5.]

Prime Minister Attlee is expected to make sweeping changes in the British Cabinet soon. Some Ministers will receive new assignments, it is reported, while others will be dropped. [3:3-4.]

The issue of anti-Semitism arose at the annual conference of the British Conservative party. Party leaders, embarrassed by the issue, were expected to call up for debate today a resolution condemning fascism and communism. [3:6.]

The Netherland Government announced that because of ill health Queen Wilhelmina would temporarily relinquish her royal power to Princess Juliana. [1:2.]

An inquiry into charges against Lieut. Gen. John C. H. Lee of alleged maladministration in his command in Italy has shown no cause for action, according to Secretary of the Army Kenneth C. Royall and General Eisenhower. [1:5.]

A Yugoslav court sentenced two Catholic priests, one to a month and the other to six years. They had been arrested after a riot at a church. [1:2-3.]

The long-heralded Chinese Communist offensive in Manchuria appeared to be under way, with reports of renewed fighting near Kungchuling, forty miles southwest of the Manchurian capital of Changchun. The Communists were said to have cut the Szepingkai-Changchun railway in three places. [6:2; with map.]

Yugoslavia Sentences Two Priests, Victims of Attack, One to 6 Years

Special to The New York Times.

BELGRADE, Yugoslavia, Oct. 3—Two Catholic priests who were tried in Istria for their alleged part in a riot Aug. 24 that resulted in the death of a priest received prison sentences today.

The Rev. Stepan Cek, parish priest, was sentenced to six years at hard labor and Msgr. Jakob Ukmar, representative of Bishop Santini of Trieste, was sentenced to one month. Msgr. Ukmar had been held since Sept. 24, so it is believed he has been released.

[Tanjug the Yugoslav news agency, said Msgr. Ukmar's sentence was considered served, according to The Associated Press. Ansa, the Italian news agency, said Msgr. Ukmar would remain in Fiume Hospital until he was able to travel.]

Among twelve others implicated in the riot, in which the Rev. Milo Bulesitch was killed and Msgr. Ukmar was wounded, four admitted breaking into Dr. Bulesitch's home in Lanische. They received prison sentences ranging from three to eight months.

An affidavit to support an allegation connecting Dragolyub Yovanovitch, Yugoslav Peasant party leader, with Dr. Vladimir Matchek, Croat Peasant party leader, now in the United States, was introduced today as the Yovanovitch trial entered its second day.

Yesterday the prosecution brought out testimony that the defendant had a message from Dr. Matchek through a person who had visited him in Paris. M. Yovanovitch, who said the message had been in a letter, refused to divulge the name of the friend. According to M. Yovanovitch the letter criticized his cooperation with Communists.

The prosecution introduced to-

Continued on Page 6, Column 3

Judge Orders Santo to Testify; Appeal to Circuit Court Planned

John Santo, international organizer of the Transport Workers Union, CIO, was ordered to testify at his deportation hearing in accordance with the Government's demand in a ruling handed down yesterday in Federal Court by United States District Court Judge Alfred C. Coxe.

After hearing argument on a motion directing Mr. Santo to show cause why he should not be called as a witness, Judge Coxe found that the Santo hearings were being conducted by a qualified examiner, that it was not for him to determine the tactics or strategy of the Department of Justice and that the law sanctioned the calling of Mr. Santo as a witness by the Government.

The order requiring Mr. Santo to be sworn will be presented for Judge Coxe's signature on Monday. Directly after the affixing of the judge's signature a move will be made by Harry Sacher, Mr. Santo's lawyer and counsel for the TWU, to appeal his decision to the United States Circuit Court of Appeals despite the opinion expressed yesterday by Judge Coxe his ruling was not appealable.

Pending this next legal maneuver, Arthur J. Phelan, the presiding inspector, set Thursday, at 9:30 A. M., as the date when hearings will be resumed at the office of the Department of Immigration and Naturalization, 70 Columbus Avenue. They were adjourned on Wednesday when Mr. Sacher refused to permit Mr. Santo to take the stand and the Government brought legal action to force him to testify.

Mr. Sacher at the court argument on the motion yesterday made four points: 1—that Mr. Phelan was not now an immigration inspector empowered to conduct the deportation hearings un-

Continued on Page 7, Column 4

DODGERS' ONLY HIT BEATS YANKEES, 3-2

Continued From Page 1

missed. Then he swung again and connected, the ball sailing toward the right-field wall.

Over raced Tommy Henrich. The previous inning the brilliant Yankee gardener had made a glittering leaping catch of a similar fly ball to rob Gene Hermanski of a blow and keep the no-hitter alive.

There was nothing Tommy could do about this one, though it soared over his head and struck the wall. Desperately he tried to clutch the ball as it caromed off the boards in order to get it home as quickly as possible, but that sloping wall is a tricky barrier and as the ball bounced to the ground more precious moments were lost.

Finally Henrich hurried the ball on its way. McQuinn caught it and relayed it to the plate, but all too late. Gionfriddo and Miksis already were over the plate while in the center of the diamond Dodger players and fans were all but mobbing Lavagetto in their elation.

First to Lose One-Hitter

While that was going on Bevens, the silent man from the northwest, was walking silently from the field. In a matter of seconds a priceless no-hit victory had been wrenched from his grasp and converted into a galling one-hit defeat. Only two other pitchers had tossed world series one-hitters before with both, of course, winning. They were Ed Reulbach of the Cubs in 1906 and Claude Passeau, a later day Cub, in 1945.

Big Casey, relief pitcher who had won for the Flock in that stirring 9-8 game the previous day, also was returned the winner of this one, though he pitched only one ball. The Flock was still behind when he went in and under the rules he automatically became the victor, the first pitcher in world series history to take two games on successive days.

Huge Hughey entered the struggle when Hank Behrman, third of Shotton's hurlers in this extraordinary conflict, got into trouble. A single by Lindell, a belated throw to second by Edwards on Bevens' sacrifice and a single by George Stirnweiss filled the bases with one out in the ninth.

Casey Replaces Behrman

Casey replaced Behrman. Henrich slapped his first pitch right back into Casey's hands. Hughey fired to Catcher Edwards at th plate for one out and Edwards winged to Jackie Robinson at first for the double play.

That inning, too, was typical of the Yanks' play throughout. Actually they lost by wasting myriad chances to sew it up decisively. In the opening round, Harry Taylor, an experimental starter for the Dodgers, offered to roll up the series on the spot for the Bombers when he faced only four batters and forced in a run with a walk.

That tally was all the Yanks made out of their flying start. They didn't get another until the fourth when Bill Johnson cracked Hal Gregg for a triple to open the inning and Lindell followed with a double. They never did get another with Gregg pitching brilliantly from the first through the seventh and though they totaled eight blows they lost when their hurler allowed only one.

The Yanks started as if they meant to annihilate the Dodgers piecemeal and mesh the parts into the Gowanus. The opportunity lay before them to tear the game wide open as the youthful Taylor, carrying for the moment Shotton's despairing hopes, faced four batters and got none out, although he would have retired one except for a misplay.

Rookie Sensation Fails

Taylor had been one of the rookie sensations of the National League, winning ten and losing five until he tore a tendon in his right elbow in the process of beating the Cardinals. Handsome Harry, however, simply had nothing to carry into this combat beyond the best wishes of the Flatbush faithful and about the only mystifying feature was the fact that the Brooks' board of strategy never became aware of that until he started laboring on the mound.

Miksis, who went into the game as a runner for Reiser, sliding home in the ninth inning with the run that gave the Dodgers victory. Waiting for the ball is the Yankee catcher, Berra, while Umpire Goetz, Hermanksi (22) and Reese (1) look on.

Stirnweiss greeted Taylor's first pitch with a sharp single into left field. Henrich allowed the count to reach two and two before he smacked a single into center, Snuffy holding up at second.

Then followed a play that might have helped Taylor over the rough spot but instead put him deeper in the hole. Larry Berra, back behind the plate as the Yanks' starting catcher, slapped a grounder to Robinson. Jackie fired the ball to Reese for a force play on Henrich, but Peewee dropped the throw.

The error filled the bases so that Taylor, within a few minutes of the start, was up to his elbows in trouble. Moreover, he was confronted by the wholly uninviting situation of facing Joe DiMaggio with the bases full and nobody out.

At that, it is quite possible he did about the best circumstances would permit. He tossed four wide pitches for a base on balls and while that forced in a run it could have been a lot worse.

With that walk Taylor was asked to walk out himself under orders from the bench, and Gregg, who had started warming up on Taylor's third pitch, took over. McQuinn popped to Reese for the first out and a moment later Johnson slapped a grounder at Reese. In a flash, Peewee, Stanky and Robinson completed one of their gilt-edged double plays.

One run was all the vaunted Bombers extracted from that wide open position and in the third they blew another opportunity. With two down, DiMaggio drew his second pass and McQuinn tapped a ball in front of the plate. Edwards grabbed it and when his fast peg shot wide of first to bounce off the temporary boxes running down the right-field side, DiMaggio and McQuinn tore around the bases.

Rounding third, DiMaggio was waved on by the usually coldly calculating Coach Chuck Dressen, who miscued this time. Out in right Dixie Walker, who otherwise played an inconspicuous role, collared the ball and fired it to the plate in ample time for the third out.

Behrman Gives Two Hits

After the extra-base blows by Johnson and Lindell in the fourth, **the Yanks got no more hits until the ninth. Then Behrman, who had started pitching in the eighth, gave up two.**

In the meantime Bevens was weaving in and out of trouble, but only because of the endless walks he kept serving up. Only a few fine plays were needed to help him, so invincible was his stuff. Lindell made a miraculous diving catch of a foul fly off Robinson in the third and DiMaggio faded way back to haul down a shot in dead center by Hermanski in the fourth.

Bevens walked two in the first, one in the second and another in the third, to which he added a wild pitch. When he passed two in the fifth, they led to the Dodgers' first tally.

Jorgensen received the first of those to open the round and Gregg followed with the next. Stanky sacrificed the runners to second and third and on Reese's grounder to Phil Rizzuto, which resulted in Gregg being tossed out at third on a fielder's choice, Jorgensen counted.

Bevens walked one in the sixth and one in the seventh. Not until the eighth, which Henrich ended with his great catch off Hermanski, did big Bill pitch a perfect inning. Then he walked two more in the ninth, inviting disaster just once too often. He opened four of the nine innings with passes.

So this most amazing series, starting as a gay jaunt for the Yanks, threatens to develop into a real dog fight that must return to the Yankee Stadium for final decision after today's fifth game at Ebbets Field. Frank Shea, who won the opener for the Bombers, though he tossed only five innings, is slated to make his second start today. Viv Lombardi, mite southpaw whom the American Leaguers belted out in the second game, is Shotton's mound choice.

WILD CELEBRATION IN DRESSING ROOM

Flock Mobs Lavagetto, Hero of Merriwell Finish, but Had Expected Him to Hit

CASEY AND GREGG LAUDED

By ROSCOE McGOWEN

If Harry (Cookie) Lavagetto, 32-year-old veteran of the 1941 world series, lives to reach the century mark, he never will experience a thrill compared with the one he got yesterday in that story-book ninth inning finish at Ebbets Field.

Even the creator of Frank and Dick Merriwell couldn't have written the script for that one.

"You can throw everything else out," said Cookie, when he got a chance to catch his breath after a dozen of his teammates had carried him into the clubhouse, and Judge Sam Liebowitz had hugged and kissed him.

"That's the top thrill of my life, without a doubt," said Harry. "Nothing else can happen."

The word commonly used for the scene in the Dodger clubhouse after Lavagetto's double off the right field wall for the lone hit off Floyd (Bill) Bevens had sent little Al Gionfriddo and Eddie Miksis's racing across the plate with the tying and winning runs that evened the series at two-all is "pandemonium."

Not Too Surprised

But that wasn't precisely the word, despite the delighted yells and back-slappings that all the Dodgers let loose.

Oddly enough, they didn't seem to be too much surprised by the extraordinary result. You see, these boys have seen Lavagetto come through before during the season, both as a pinch hitter and a pinch player.

They remember that he hit for Spider Jorgensen when that youngster wasn't going so well and stayed in the game to play an entirely competent third base. They recall, too, when Cookie took over for Jackie Robinson, the Negro star, when Jackie came up with a lame back. Cookie played first base in two games at the Polo Grounds — and the Dodgers kept rolling along.

Some of them had the thought that Bucky Harris, Yankee boss, had not considered the possibility that Eddie Stanky would be removed for a pinch hitter and that was why he gambled on finally giving Pistol Pete Reiser an intentional pass, a bit of managerial strategy about which Bucky will hear for years to come.

"Ya know," said Peewee Reese, "I was sorry for that guy." (Meaning Bevens.) And it is conceivable that the kindly Reese really meant it as first. Then he added, with his impish face wearing a mock solemn expression:

Broke His Heart in Two

"It just broke my heart right square in two when I saw those two runs crossing the plate. I just couldn't stand it."

Manager Burt Shotton tried to be casual about the whole thing and, when asked how he felt, replied with forced calmness:

"I feel pretty good—just the same way I've felt right along."

Burt was mobbed by photographers and newsmen, posed with Lavagetto and with Hugh Casey, the round man who made some world series history by winning his second consecutive series game by making only one pitch.

"There's a hero of this game, too, if you're looking for one," shouted one of Hughey's teammates. "That pitch he made to Tommy Henrich in the ninth was the pay-off."

Casey himself presented the same calm, judicial mien he always bears.

"It was a low curve ball," he answered in reply to the usual query about what he had thrown to Tommy. "It was a perfect pitch—went right where I wanted it to go, and it was a strike. What the heck," he grinned, "you throw it and you hope it works the way you intended it to work. That one did."

"I've got quite a record," grinned Eddie Stanky, a few minutes later after he trotted into Shotton's office and reminded Barney that "you always take me out at the right time."

Stanky was referring to the fact that only once during the regular season had he been removed for a pinch-hitter—and that removal had won a ball game.

Against the Chicago Cubs in Brooklyn about mid-season Shotton sent Arky Vaughan up for Stanky to bat against Hank Borowy and Arky delivered a line single to right that brought the triumph.

Yesterday was the second time Stanky had been taken out for a pinch hitter—and the result of that move was buzzing in thousands of fan conversations last night.

"That's a hundred per cent for me," chortled Eddie. "You can't beat that."

DODGERS WILL PAY DUROCHER IN FULL

Suspended Manager Will Get $50,000 Season Salary but Chandler Bars Series Cut

Leo Durocher, suspended manager of the Dodgers, will not be permitted to accept the world series snare voted to him by the Brooklyn players, but the Lip will draw his full salary for the 1947 season. That was revealed yesterday by sources unquestionably authentic, but which may not be quoted.

Durocher already has received $20,000 of the salary he would have earned if Baseball Commissioner Albert B. (Happy) Chandler had not suspended him for the entire season just before opening day last spring. Leo will receive the balance of his pay after the series.

Chandler was asked, while sitting in his box near the Brooklyn dugout, whether he would answer the question: "Since the Brooklyn players have voted a full share to Durocher will you say whether you have any disapproval of that action?"

The commissioner was silent for a moment, with his lips tightly pressed together. Then he replied: "Not now."

The Brooklyn players already know that Chandler has disapproved of their voting a share to Durocher, but they have taken no action as yet to remove their former manager's name from the share list. The Lip's salary is thought to have been around $50,000, so even if he doesn't get his slice of the series melon Leo will derive a fair income from the Brooklyn club.

Whether Durocher will return as Dodger manager in 1948 now seems anybody's guess. There was plenty of evidence no longer than two weeks ago that he would be back.

However, Chandler's attitude about the world series share poses a new question about Leo's acceptability, despite the commissioner's statement last summer when he was asked in Cincinnati whether there would be anything more against Durocher after his suspension ended this fall. At that time the commissioner put it this way: "If a man is convicted, sent to prison for a year and serves his allotted sentence, that's the end of it, isn't it?"

That naturally was interpreted to mean that, so far as baseball's head man was concerned, Durocher would be free to return to his job and that President Branch Rickey of the Dodgers would be free to take him back. If it means anything else, the new interpretation will have to be supplied by Chandler himself.

The New York Times.

SUNDAY, OCTOBER 26, 1947. L+ S

COLUMBIA TOPS ARMY, 21-20, ENDING CADET STREAK AT 32; PENN DOWNS NAVY, 21-0; CORNELL AND DARTMOUTH WIN

QUAKERS HIT HARD

Flash Full Power to Score Twice in Last Quarter Against Navy

PENN IN LONG MARCHES

Goes 42, 55 and 50 Yards Before 78,205 Spectators in Franklin Field

By ALLISON DANZIG
Special to THE NEW YORK TIMES.

PHILADELPHIA, Oct. 25—Amid the crash of Army and Illinois, Pennsylvania maintained its place among the football elect with a convincing demonstration of its superiority over Navy today. The final score was 21 to 0.

Held to seven points going into the final quarter, the big, powerful Red and Blue eleven broke the shackles of the Midshipmen's stubborn defense as 78,205 spectators looked on at Franklin Field in summer heat.

In seven plays Penn went fifty-five yards to end the tension of a tight game at the start of the fourth period. Then, for good measure, it struck fifty yards through the air in seven more plays for a third touchdown, with the clock showing eight seconds left to play.

Penn Proves Supreme

From start to finish this was Penn's ball game, and again it was Skippy Minisi who was chief artisan of the victory, as a year ago, although he did not have a hand in any of the scoring plays.

It was Fullback Bill Luongo who registered the first touchdown, in the opening quarter, on an 11-yard burst through left tackle to cap a 42-yard march.

Ray Dooney, a substitute fullback who was unheard of at the start of the season, went 7 yards through the hole opened by huge George Savitzky at the end of the 55-yard drive, and Wayne Hellman, a third-string wing, who had just come into the game for the first time, caught a 9-yard pass from Bob Evans for the last score.

Evans threw six aerials in that closing 50-yard advance and five of them were completed for 47 yards.

But Minisi, though he failed to break into the scoring column, personally, was the big fly in the ointment for a Navy team that made a remarkably close game of it for three quarters after it had recovered from the shock of Penn's thundering opening charge to the 5 yard line.

Is Constant Threat

Every time Minisi got his hands on the ball he was a scoring threat with his running and passing from scrimmage and his returns of kicks. The first pass he launched went to Jerry McCarthy for 20 yards on Penn's advance of 63 yards to the 5 from the opening kick-off. His next one, on that same advance, was good for 16.

He threw to McCarthy for 11 on the 32-yard touchdown assault. He broke loose for 11 yards on another advance of 55 yards that stalled on Navy's 17 as Penn fumbled, and he threw to Ed Lawless for 13 on the 55 yard march for the second score.

He carried eleven times for 57 yards, eight of the ten passes he launched were completed for 67 yards, and he was a valuable man on defense against the pass. Navy is glad that it is through with Skippy for goc after today.

But as brilliant as was Minisi, it was the powerful line in front of him that gave Penn command of the ball game. The Navy forwards did a thorough job on Cornell a week ago, but today they were up against a little more than they were able to handle and could not open the holes for their own backs or stop Minisi, the swift Bob Deuber, Snaky Graham, Dooney and Luongo.

Give Ball to Bednarik

The key man in the Penn line was missing from the action. Chuck Bednarik, one of the best backers-up in college football, sat out the game on the bench, incapacited with an injury suffered against Columbia. His mates, to show how they felt toward him, presented the winning ball to him, autographed with the name of every player.

Even without Bednarik, who was ably replaced by Charley Hassler, the Penn line did so thorough a

Continued on Page 2, Column 4

As Unbeaten Army Finally Bowed to Columbia at Baker Field Yesterday

Kusserow of the Lions maneuvering to get away a pass in the second quarter of the game. In the play are his teammates Rossides (21) and Swiacki, who is blocking Kellum (85) of the Cadets.
The New York Times (by Sisto)

LIONS SCORE UPSET

Army Has 20-7 Lead at Half-Time, but Bows to Columbia Rally

AERIALS SINK THE CADETS

Swiacki Brilliant as Receiver—Yablonski's Kick Decides—Kusserow Counts Twice

By LOUIS EFFRAT

Columbia 21, Army 20!

A typographical error? No—a thousand times no—and the 35,000 fans at Baker Field yesterday will attest to the authenticity of Columbia's greatest gridiron achievement: a totally unexpected victory that overshadowed even the magnificent Rose Bowl conquest of Jan. 1, 1934, when the Lions beat Stanford.

After thirty-two straight games in which Army had not known defeat, Earl Blaik's cadets appeared to be en route to another triumph yesterday. They battered Columbia almost at will throughout a lop-sided first half and enjoyed a 20-7 margin at the intermission. Up to that point the Lions had had no ground attack to speak of and most of their gains overhead were made possible because of spectacular catches rather than by the passing of Gene Rossides.

True, the West Point offense, overpowering though it was, lacked smoothness, but it still was potent enough to grind out the yardage. Army's speedy backs, operating behind so rugged a line, had, it seemed, a comfortable lead that was likely to be widened later. Apparently Columbia once again had been overmatched.

Dominates Third Period

However, a half is only 50 per cent of the whole, and Columbia proceeded to prove this truism after the rest period. Except for one drive that brought Army to the Lions' 15-yard line, where the defense tightened and took over, the Light Blue dominated the scoreless third period. Lou Little's men then took charge of the last quarter and won going away, after having fashioned two touchdowns and conversions.

When the game ended with Columbia deep in Army territory, but more concerned over clinging to its 1-point margin than increasing it, the victors hoisted one of their mates on their shoulders and carried him from the field. He was Bill Swiacki, a pass-catching end who, more than any individual, was responsible for one of the biggest upsets of this, or any, campaign.

Swiacki caught eight passes. Half of these were the result of his own individual brilliance, and the one he snared in the end zone, the one that brought the Lions into contention at 3:32 of the final period, will have to rank with the great catches of all time. Nothing like it has been seen here since Al Gionfriddo robbed Joe DiMaggio in the sixth game of the 1947 world series.

Set All-Time Mark

It was Swiacki, who hails from Southbridge, Mass., and is playing his last season at Morningside Heights, who helped make possible an all-time Columbia passing record. Rossides and Lou Kusserow, who were on the firing end, completed twenty aerials. Eighteen of them were by Rossides. The old mark of eighteen completions was set by Sid Luckman against Army in 1937 and tied by Paul Governali against Michigan in 1941 and Colgate next season.

Swiacki it was, too, who paved the way for the deciding tally when he made another great catch of a twenty-six-yard pass by Rossides, good for a first down on the Army 3-yard line, midway in the closing chapter. Two plays later Kusserow went over. Ventan Yablonski, who hadn't failed on his first two conversion attempts, booted the vital extra point and Columbia was on top, 21—20.

This was a sad moment in Army football history. It was the first time since Oct. 12, 1946 that the cadets had fallen behind. About six and a half minutes later, when the gun barked, they still were in the red and one of the most amazing "defeatless" strings had been snapped.

The poise that had been so characteristic of Blaik's teams through the four-season span of the streak was missing yesterday, even when

Continued on Page 3, Column 2

Stymie Triumphs to Regain World Money-Winning Lead

By JAMES ROACH

"There he goes! He's sixth! He's fifth! He's fourth! He's going to win it! "The shouts went up at Jamaica yesterday in the ninth running of the $75,000 added Gallant Fox Handicap, and the horse that had the 44,735 customers in a dither was Mrs. Ethel D. Jacobs' old Stymie.

For the second successive year he took the mile-and-five-furlong run. Starting his move midway along the backstretch, he passed horse after horse en route to a smashing two-length triumph, and for the third time he became Mr. Moneybags of the turf.

With the victory went a jackpot of $56,350, boosting Stymie's earnings to $816,060 in his 114 trips to the post and dropping Armed ($761,500) to second position on the world money roster. Stymie first gained the money crown on July 5 at Delaware Park, lost it to Assault a week later, regained it July 19 in the Empire Gold Cup race at Belmont Park and lost it again to Armed earlier this month.

On Friday trainer Hirsch Jacobs was pessimistic about the chances of the blaze-faced 6-year-old chestnut horse who had made Jacobs an upper-bracket pal of the Collector of Internal Revenue. Stymie had been reluctant to train; he had acted as if fed up with the whole business of running around tracks.

Said Jacobs: "He's only a shadow of the old Stymie." But the trainer—and those who bet on the one in the salmon pink silks as the second choice at 5 to 2—were pleasantly surprised. Stymie was half a ton of chock-full-of-run horse as

Continued on Page 9, Column 2

MICHIGAN TOPPLES MINNESOTA, 13 TO 6

Wolverines, Outrushed by the Gophers, Take Advantage of Breaks Before 85,000

By WALTER W. RUCH
Special to THE NEW YORK TIMES.

ANN ARBOR, Mich., Oct. 25—The myth of Michigan was exploded today by the Golden Gophers of Minnesota. They outplayed the Wolverines and but for a series of bad breaks could have come up with the greatest reversal of the season instead of going down to a heart-breaking 13-to-6 defeat before more than 85,000 fans at the Ann Arbor homecoming.

It was a perfect setting in Indian summer weather, but the Wolverines, after running rough shod over Michigan State, Stanford, Pitt and Northwestern, didn't live up to their advance notices. It was obvious that Minnesota, too, hadn't bothered to read about H. O. (Fritz) Crisler's wonder team.

After a scoreless first quarter, both teams notched a touchdown in the second period, and the elevens went to their dressing rooms at the half with Michigan ahead, 7 to 6, on the scoreboard but trailing dismally in the statistics.

Early in the fourth quarter, Michigan scored again, but this time Jim Brieske failed in his attempted conversion, his third miss in thirty-four attempts.

The Michigan line was about as effective as a sieve against the Gophers. The Little Brown Jug remained in Michigan's hands, but it was certainly not running over.

Minnesota ran up thirteen first downs against nine for the Wolver-

Continued on Page 5, Column 2

Cornell's Rally Subdues Princeton by 28 to 21

By JOSEPH M. SHEEHAN
Special to THE NEW YORK TIMES.

PRINCETON, N. J., Oct. 25—A dazzling exhibition of passing by an unheralded substitute quarterback named Lynn Dorset carried Cornell from a two-touchdown deficit to a thrilling 28-21 triumph over Princeton today.

It was a wide-open offensive battle and was witnessed by a crowd of 34,000 at Palmer Stadium.

Entering the game in the second quarter, after the Tigers had scored twice on power marches, Dorset promptly took charge. Six times in this period and four times more in the third, he cocked his right arm and hit his receiver between the eyes on each occasion.

In the course of completing ten straight tosses—all he threw—the 5-foot 8½-inch, 165-pound sophomore from Miami, Fla., hit Bernie Babula with scoring pitches of 36 and 30 yards in the second period and Norman Dawson with an end zone peg of 30 yards in the third quarter.

Dorset's golden touch also figured in the third Cornell touchdown, made by the fleet Babula on a 5-yard sweep. Three of his passes figured in this Big Red march of 77 yards and it was he, from the close-up spot in the T, who flipped the pitchout that gave Babula a winging start around the Tigers' right flank.

Princeton, though baffled when Cornell, or more specifically Dorset, had the ball, remained potent to the end. When in possession, the men of Nassau gallantly tried to pull the game out of the fire. They shook the mercurial

Continued on Page 6, Column 1

DARTMOUTH STOPS HARVARD, 14 TO 13

Armstrong of Green Blocks Kick for Extra Point to Provide Margin of Victory

By ROSCOE McGOWEN
Special to THE NEW YORK TIMES.

BOSTON, Oct. 25—In an atmosphere that carried no chill and before a crowd of 35,000 the Big Green team from Hanover emerged from its fifty-first meeting with Harvard with a 14-13 triumph at Harvard Stadium today. And coach Tuss McLaughry doubtless was shaking the hand of big Dale Armstrong tonight.

It was the big end from Pittsburgh who made the victory safe for Dartmouth by plunging in to block an attempted placement by Bill Harrison late in the third period after the Crimson had come storming back from a first half 14-0 deficit to score the first of two touchdowns it was to register before the end.

That single missed point was the Big Green's margin, since Herb Carey, the kicker from Marblehead, didn't fail in the two conversions entrusted to him in the first and second periods.

Harvard Hopes Fade

Dick Harlow's boys seemed on their way to the winning touchdown near the end of the game, but the second of two pass interceptions by Joe Sullivan, the highly capable T-quarterback of Dartmouth, dashed the last hope of the Harvard rooters.

Jimmy Noonan, with time rapidly running out, heaved the pass from the Green 45, only to find that the only available receiver was Sullivan, who cuddled the ball to his chest on the 18 and dashed back to

Continued on Page 4, Column 2

COLGATE BATTLES BROWN TO 13-13 TIE

Raiders Score in Final Period but Late Bid to Break Deadlock Fails

By LINCOLN A. WERDEN
Special to THE NEW YORK TIMES.

HAMILTON, N. Y., Oct. 25—A touchdown in the final quarter enabled Colgate to tie Brown at 13—13 today and the traditional game ended in a deadlock as the Raiders failed to complete two subsequent drives.

This was only the third time that the team from Providence has visited this town in the Chenango Valley, coming first in 1919 to participate in the Colgate Centennial and then in 1939 to dedicate the field on which the game was played. There were no special ceremonies to mark today's meeting and the Bruins apparently were here for the sole purpose of reducing Colgate's list of victories in this series.

For three periods it appeared that Brown might do just that for after Colgate went ahead 6—0 in the second, the Providence eleven returned after the half to go 62 yards twice to score its two touchdowns.

Bill Gresh, understudy for the regular right half, Charlie Nelson, culminated the first march by going over from the five. Joe Condon's place-kick was good for the extra point to send Brown to the front at 7—6. After shifty Fred Kozak raced 61 yards, to be hauled down with a yard to go, Arnold Green plunged over for the second Brown touchdown.

Condon missed his try for the

Continued on Page 5, Column 2

TROJANS CONQUER CALIFORNIA, 39-14

Doll Runs Kick-Off 95 Yards to Score for Bowl-Bound Southern California

By The Associated Press.

BERKELEY, Calif., Oct. 25—Crashing, whirling giants from Southern California charged a long and important lap toward the Rose Bowl today by battering California's hitherto unbeaten Bears, 39 to 14, in a thrilling football classic before a capacity crowd of 80,000 in Memorial Stadium. The

Continued on Page 6, Column 5

Football Scores

COLLEGES

East

Winner	Loser
Alfred 20	Brooklyn Coll. 19
American International 28	Bergen 7
Brown 13	Colgate 13
California (Pa.) T. 28	Clarion T. 7
C. C. N. Y. 12	Wagner 6
Columbia 21	Army 20
Connecticut 27	Champlain 6
Cornell 28	Princeton 21
Cornell J. V. 13	Princeton J. V. 0
Cortland T. 10	Hartwick 0
Cushing Acad. 20	Tufts J. V. 0
Dartmouth 14	Harvard 13
Delaware 26	Gettysburg 0
Eastern M. A. 13	Arnold J. V. 0
Fairmont T. 0	Slippery Rock T. 0
F. and M. 21	Dickinson 7
Fordham 12	Kings Point 0
Geneva 40	Carnegie Tech 12
Glenville 13	Shepherd 9
Grove City 13	Allegheny 7
Hobart 6	Union 0
Holy Cross 26	Syracuse 0
Howard 14	J. C. Smith 0
Indiana (Pa.) T. 7	Lock Haven T. 7
Johns Hopkins 47	Catholic U. 0
Kimball Union Ac. 6	Middlebury J. V. 0
Kutztown State T. 33	Trenton T. 6
Lafayette 20	W. and J. 12
Looms School 13	Springfield J. V. B. 7
Mansfield T. 48	Brockport T. 0
Marshall 33	Indiana State 0
Massachusetts 39	Norwich 0
Middlebury 13	St. Lawrence 7
Montclair T. 13	Panzer 0
Morris-Harvey 14	West Va. Tech 13
Muhlenberg 40	Upsala 0
National Farm 6	New York Aggies 0
Navy 150-lb. 25	Princeton 150-lb. 13
New Hampshire 28	Vermont 6
Nichols J. C. 13	Springfield J. V. 7
Penn 21	Navy 0
Penn State 21	West Virginia 14
Pittsburgh 12	Ohio State 0
P. M. C. 25	Drexel 0
R. I. State 27	Coast Guard Acad. 0
Rochester 48	Hamilton 7
R. P. I. 12	Worcester Tech 0
Rutgers 46	Lehigh 13
Shippensburg T. 19	Bloomsburg T. 12
Storer 7	Cheyney 0
Susquehanna 20	Juniata 7
Swarthmore 7	Ursinus 0
Temple 21	Bucknell 0
Thiel 26	Edinboro T. 0
Trinity 33	Williams 0
Tufts 13	Northeastern 0
W. and M. 47	Boston U. 13
Washington Coll. 14	Mt. St. Mary's 0
Wesleyan 20	Amherst 0
Westminster 26	Bethany 13
West Va. Wesleyan 9	Waynesburg 0
Villanova 150-lb. 6	Cornell 150-lb 0
Yale 49	Springfield 0

Continued on Page 2, Column 6

ILLINOIS CHECKED BY PURDUE, 14 TO 7

DeMoss' Passes Chief Factor in Snapping String of Ten Games Without Defeat

By The Associated Press.

LAFAYETTE, Ind., Oct. 25—Alert Purdue never made a mistake today and knocked down an Illinois football machine that had gone ten games without defeat, 14 to 7, before an alumni-packed crowd of 42,000 home-coming fans.

Illinois, tied by Army but unbeaten since midseason of 1946, made 17 first downs to Purdue's 6, but the Boilermakers made the Illini do most of their running on the wrong side of the center stripe. Purdue's five-man backfield on defense was calculated to stop Illinois' top passer, Perry Moss, and while it didn't keep him from passing for the one touchdown, it knocked down most of his other tosses that might have mattered.

Moss reached receivers with 12 of 23 passes, but the net gain was only 133 yards. Bob DeMoss of Purdue completed four of five for 58 yards and set up both of his team's touchdowns.

Ground Plays Set Up Passes

Apart from DeMoss' timely passes, more effective because he called ground plays most of the afternoon, Purdue's activities were pretty much starless. Halfbacks Harry Szulborski and Norbert Adams picked up badly needed yardage on several occasions, but so did Fullback Jack Milito, who had been a doubtful starter, Quarterback Kenny Gorgal and Halfback Dick Bushnell.

The Purdue line, especially left

Continued on Page 5, Column 4

NOTRE DAME TRIPS IOWA ELEVEN, 21-0

Scatback Scampers by Sitko and Brennan Highlight Game at South Bend

By The Associated Press.

SOUTH BEND, Ind., Oct. 25—Out of a line-up including such worthy gladiators as Czarobski, Swistowicz, Kosikowski and others, rose Irishman Terry Brennan today to score a pair of touchdowns which gave unconquered Notre Dame a 21-0 triumph over Iowa. Notre Dame's fourth straight football success, which delighted a

Continued on Page 4, Column 4

Pitt Upsets Ohio State by 12-0; Fumbles Ruin Buckeyes' Chances

By The Associated Press

PITTSBURGH, Oct. 25—The Pitt Panthers, thumped by four rivals this season, burst the shackles of defeat today and gave old grads in a crowd of 55,217 a flashback to past football glories by upsetting favored Ohio State, 12—0, in a stirring climax to homecoming festivities.

The well-earned victory not only broke a string of losses this year but also ended a record of Big Nine supremacy over the Panthers which had extended nine years through twenty-four games. It was fitting that Pitt chose the team which started the Big Nine string in 1940 to repay some of the indignities suffered by the Panthers on the gridiron. Pitt last won over a Big Nine foe in 1938.

Ohio State, owning a mediocre record of one victory, a tie and two defeats before today, literally let the game slip through its fingers. Fumbles ended one serious scoring threat and put the Buckeyes constantly in the hole through the first half until Pitt negotiated its first—and winning—touchdown.

That honor fell to a substitute left halfback, Tony Dimatteo, a local product, who plunged three yards with two seconds of the half left. A poor punt that rolled out on the Ohio State 29 set the touchdown drive in motion.

A four-yard pass from Carl Depasqua of Williamsport, Pa., to Louis (Bimbo) Cecconi of Donora, Pa., accounted for the second Pitt touchdown with 10:50 of the fourth quarter gone. The score climaxed

Continued on Page 4, Column 1

COLUMBIA VICTOR OVER ARMY, 21-20

Continued From Page 1

the West Pointers were showing the way. Rip Rowan, Arnie Galiffa and Bill Gustafson showed sporadic speed and power, especially Rowan.

When it came to filling the shoes of the departed Doc Blanchard, Arnold Tucker and Glenn Davis, however, they were dwarfed. The yardage was amassed and at times a cadet got off a long run but virtually all of Army's destructive offense was crowded into the first thirty minutes.

Columbia, of course, must have had something to do with the eclipse of the visitors' attack—and the collapse of the heretofore perfect defense.

Rossides, after a wobbly start, improved his pitching and, with Swiacki and Bruce Gehrke contributing handsomely on the receiving end, Columbia was the aggressor—determined, confident, irrepressible.

That the Lions were confident was evident in the closing minute of the first half. At that stage, though trailing by 14—7, they elected to try for a field goal by Yablonski from the 13-yard line. It failed, but this was the tip-off that the Light Blue felt certain it would score later. It did—more than once.

Rowan, Blanchard's understudy last year, did some excellent running for a futile cause. The second-half let-down by the Black Knights nullified all his good work. Rowan, who must rate alongside the fleetest fullbacks in the nation, scored two touchdowns. Galiffa accounted for the other, the first in the contest.

The game was less than five minutes old when Army tallied, going all the way the first time it had the ball. A 55-yard advance, sparked by Rowan, was climaxed on the ninth play when Galiffa went over from the 2-foot line on a quarterback sneak. Jack Mackmull added the point.

Gustafson Intercepts Pass

It continued to be all Army in the opening period. After Gustafson's interception of a Columbia aerial, Win Scott and Bobby Jack Stuart went to a first down on the Columbia 15. Two plunges by Rowan brought the cadets to the 9. There, Charley Gabriel's pass was thefted by Al Kachadurian on the goal line to frustrate the visitors.

Amos Gillette, Gustafson and Rowan sparkplugged an Army drive that was good for 61 yards and a touchdown in the second quarter. After Gustafson gained 28 yards to the 1, Rowan bulled his way over his own right guard and Mackmull place-kicked the point for a 14-0 margin.

Stymied by the hard-rushing Army line, the Lions had been accomplishing next to nothing until Rossides completed three successive aerials, the first to Gehrke and the next two to Swiacki. Every catch was sensational. In less than two minutes, the Lions gained 53 yards overhead before Kusserow, taking a hand-off from Rossides, crashed over the right side for 6 yards and a tally. Yablonski's kick was perfect.

The remaining minutes of the half produced a series of thrills as George Kisiday recovered a Galiffa fumble on the Army 4-yard line. Kusserow bucked to the 1, but the referee ruled that it was no go because he had not put the ball in play. Columbia did not get that close in three tries and Yablonski unsuccessfully attempted to get three points via a field goal.

Longest Run of Day

Army took over at the 20, Gabriel made a yard, but on the next efforts the Cadets were penalized to their 16 for illegal backfield motion. Then came the day's longest and best run, an 84-yard touchdown dash along the sideline by Rowan. It started as a routine off-tackle slant, but Rip switched to the outside and he was off. On the way Rowan shook off at least three would-be tacklers.

Army's bad break, though it didn't strike home at the moment, was Mackmull's failure to add the point.

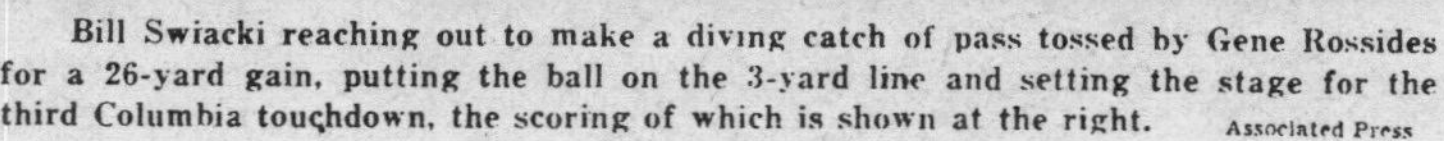
Bill Swiacki reaching out to make a diving catch of pass tossed by Gene Rossides for a 26-yard gain, putting the ball on the 3-yard line and setting the stage for the third Columbia touchdown, the scoring of which is shown at the right. Associated Press

Lou Kusserow evading Bill Gustafson (15) and Charlie Gabriel (25) as he dives over the goal-line from the 2-yard marker to tie the score at 20—20. The play climaxed a 66-yard drive. Associated Press

Statistics of the Game

	Colum.	Army.
First downs	18	12
Yards gained, rushing	100	302
Forward passes	30	10
Forwards completed	20	4
Yards gained, forwards	263	42
Forwards intercepted, by	2	1
Number of punts	6	5
*Av. dist. of punts, yds.	39.7	31.8
Run-back of punts, yds.	23	71
Fumbles	2	2
Own fumbles, recovered	1	1
Penalties	4	11
Yards lost, penalties	30	74

*From line of scrimmage.

The third chapter was scoreless, but Rossides completed eight passes and Kusserow one, an omen of what was in the offing.

Early in the fourth period Rossides passed twice to Bill Olson for 16 and 11 yards. Rossides picked up 5 on a sneak and then Swiacki came through with his acrobatic catch in the end zone. It was a diving, sliding execution that won the admiration of all except Army followers. Yablonski's boot was good and now only six points separated the teams.

Stuart ran the kick-off from his end zone 32 yards to the Army 27. Rowan added 18, Stuart 7 and a Galiffa-to-John Trent pass made it first down on Columbia's 34. When Stuart gained 6 it appeared as if Army was headed in the right direction. There, however, the Lions stopped the cadets cold and took over.

With eight and a half minutes left, the home team was confronted with the problem of negotiating sixty-six yards. It did, in six plays and in exactly 1 minute and 27 seconds. The quarterbacking of Rossides in this drive was flawless, clever.

Spotting Army spread out in a 5-man-line defense, Rossides sent Yablonski off tackle for a first down on the Lion 45. Then he sneaked twenty-two yards himself to the Army 33 and Kusserow went to the 29. Now the cadets were back in a 6-man line, so Rossides fired a pass to Swiacki and it was first down on the 3.

Rossides gained a yard, and then handed the ball to Kusserow for the touchdown. The roar that greeted Yablonski's conversion—the winning point—was deafening.

Army desperately went aloft then, and Galiffa hit Rowan with a thirty-yard pass, but that one was recalled for offside. Galiffa then fired to Trent for eight yards, but when he tried to click with another aerial Kusserow intercepted and that was the end of the streak.

The line-up:

COLUMBIA (21)		ARMY (20)
Swiacki	L.E.	Rawers
Briggs	L.T.	Galloway
Karas	L.G.	Steffy
Hampton	C.	Yeoman
Klemovich	R.G.	Henry
O'Shaughnessy	R.T.	Bryant
Gehrke	R.E.	Trent
Rossides	Q.B.	Galiffa
Kusserow	L.H.	Stuart
Olson	R.H.	Shelley
Yablonski	F.B.	Mackmull

Army's Long Football Streak

1944

Army...46	North Carolina	0
Army...59	Brown	7
Army...69	Pittsburgh	7
Army...76	U. S. Coast G. Acad.	0
Army...27	Duke	7
Army...83	Villanova	0
Army...59	Notre Dame	0
Army...62	Pennsylvania	7
Army...23	Navy	7

Totals—Army nine victories, no defeats. Army points 504, opponents 35.

1945

Army...32	Pers'nel Dist. Comd.	0
Army...54	Wake Forest	0
Army...28	Michigan	7
Army...55	Melville (R. I.) Pt. Boat School	13
Army...48	Duke	13
Army...54	Villanova	0
Army...48	Notre Dame	0
Army...61	Pennsylvania	0
Army...32	Navy	13

Totals—Army nine victories, no defeats. Army points 412, opponents 46.

1946

Army...35	Villavona	0
Army...21	Oklahoma	7
Army...46	Cornell	21
Army...20	Michigan	13
Army...48	Columbia	14
Army...19	Duke	0
Army...19	West Virginia	0
Army... 0	Notre Dame (tie)	0
Army...34	Pennsylvania	7
Army...21	Navy	18

Totals—Army nine victories, one tie. Army points 263, opponents 80.

1947

Army...13	Villanova	0
Army...40	Colorado	0
Army... 0	Illinois (tie)	0
Army...40	Virginia Tech	0
Army...20	Columbia	21

Totals—Army three victories, one tie, one defeat. Army points 113, opponents 21.

Grand totals—Army 30 victories, 2 ties, 1 defeat. Army points 1,292, opponents 182.

ENGINEERS BEATEN BY SCARLET, 46-13

Burns Paces Rutgers Victory Over Lehigh, Completing Six of Eight Tosses

HATCHETT COUNTS TWICE

STATISTICS OF THE GAME

	Rutgers.	Lehigh.
First downs	20	6
Yards gained rushing	295	105
Forward passes	10	11
Forwards completed	6	7
Yards gained, forwards	90	132
Passes intercepted by	0	1
Number of punts	1	7
*Av. dist. of punts, yds.	37	36
Fumbles	5	6
Own fumbles recovered	3	4
Penalties	5	4
Yards lost, penalties	35	20

*From point where ball was kicked.

By JOSEPH C. NICHOLS
Special to THE NEW YORK TIMES.

NEW BRUNSWICK, N. J., Oct. 25—Rutgers showed too much for Lehigh today. The Scarlet warriers from the banks of the Raritan had things their own way as they ran through to a 46—13 triumph over the Engineers before a crowd of 12,000 fans.

Lehigh gained some solace from the meeting, though, in contributing the outstanding thrill of the afternoon, an 82-yard run by Bill Heck that resulted in the Engineers' first touchdown. The score came late in the second period, at a time when the Lehigh hopes were slim, indeed, the count then being 34-to-0 against them.

It was one big period that enabled Rutgers to seal the verdict. The favored home team could score only one touchdown in the first period, but the second session had hardly begun before the Rutgers athletes pushed across three more scores, going over at the rate of a touchdown a minute—for the first three minutes. Lehigh braced somewhat after this collapse, but matters had gone too far to permit of any even-up spectacle.

Rutgers was sparked by its quarterback, Frank Burns, who did a fine job of piloting the team. Burns also held down the forward pass assignment, and he pitched ably, completing six out of eight tosses.

Rutgers Backfield Excels

The passing star had plenty of support in the backfield, his greatest aides being Herman Hering, Harvey Grimsley and Irwin Winkelreid, all of whom contributed sparkling running gains. Able in the pass receiving department was Bill Hatchett, whose catches of Burns' precise throws resulted in the first two Rutgers touchdowns.

Lehigh, unable to show much in the early stages, opened up toward the close and revealed a better than fair player in Heck, whose running set the stage for the Engineers' second touchdown which climaxed an advance of 80 yards.

When the teams swung into action Rutgers marched along smoothly to reach Lehigh's 10, after several good runs by Hering and Wiinkelreid. From the 10 Burns got off a pass to Hatchett, who scored in the end zone.

Lehigh kept the Scarlet off for the rest of the session, but Rutgers struck quickly in the second chapter. A march that began at midfield progressed to Lehigh's 15, from which point Burns hurled another scoring pass to Hatchett.

Lehigh fumbled on its own 27 following the next kickoff, and on the very next play Grimsley scooted to the Engineers' goal. Rutgers kicked and Lehigh downed the ball on its own 16. From there the visitors tried to run, but linesman Bob Ochs recovered Joe Scannella's fumble in mid-air, and ran to a score.

Grimsley Plunges Over

The Scarlet let a few minutes go by before scoring again. Then they counted on a short plunge by Grimsley, after Jim Taigia recovered a Lehigh fumble on the latter's 4.

The Engineers retrieved this score quickly and dramatically. Putting the ball in play on its own 18 after taking the kickoff, Lehigh elected to try a lateral, Scannella to Heck. The play worked neatly, and Heck ran the distance to the goal line behind excellent interference.

Rutgers counted again in the third quarter on a 9-yard run by John Sabo. Lehigh responded with another threat that saw the visitors reach the home team's 5-yard line before yielding the ball on downs. There Rutgers took over and moved forward relentlessly, to register another score. This long march was climaxed by Dick Cramer's 3-yard plunge for the tally.

Lehigh struck through the air for its second score. The Engineers came into possession on their own 20, and scored in three aerial thrusts, Scannella to Heck for 30, Scannella to Heck for 20, and Freund to Marano for the touchdown.

HOBART TRIPS UNION, 6-0

Remilen's Fine Punts Protect Early Lead on Aerial

SCHENECTADY, N. Y., Oct. 25 (AP)—Hobart defeated Union, 6—0, today after gaining an early lead which Fullback Charley Remilen of Rochester protected with fine punting.

A Union homecoming crowd of 4,000 watched Remilen keep the home team in its own territory throughout the second half with dazzling boots that included three kick-outs on Union's 2-yard line.

Hobart scored in the second period on a 12-yard pass from Halfback Jim Newman to Andy Stertzer, end, after Union had dominated play in the first quarter.

DiMaggio's 5 Blows Highlight Yank Victory

BOMBERS CONQUER WHITE SOX BY 13-2

DiMaggio Smashes 2 Homers, Triple, Double and Single to Top 22-Hit Attack

LINDELL ALSO CONNECTS

Drives 4-Bagger, Two Singles for Yanks—Raschi Coasts to His Third Victory

By JAMES P. DAWSON
Special to THE NEW YORK TIMES.

CHICAGO, May 20—Inspired by the greatest batting day Joe DiMaggio has enjoyed since pre-war times, the Yankees touched record heights in the vital statistics department at Comiskey Field today when they overwhelmed the hapless White Sox, 13 to 2.

The Bombers from the Bronx slugged four of Ted Lyons' throwers for twenty-two hits, good for thirty-eight bases, exceeding their previous high in hits by six and their best previous accumulation of total bases by twelve. Their thirteen runs bettered by one the dozen accumulated in the season's opener April 19 against Washington, when they banged out sixteen hits, good for twenty-six bases.

In today's slugging orgy DiMaggio hammered out two homers, a triple, a double and a single. He pounded in six runs and was deprived of a "6 for 6" day when Ralph Hodgin backed to the left-field wall in the eighth to pull down what would have been another extra-base blow.

Big John Lindell exploded a homer and contributed two singles to the cannonade that rang about the ears of the futile Sox hurlers. Billy Johnson had a three-hit day, with one double. Bobby Brown stroked three singles. All told the Yanks got three homers, one triple, five doubles and thirteen singles in the explosion that entertained a meager 5,001 cash customers and brought immeasurable pain to Ted Lyons.

Stirnweiss Is Hitless

Only George Stirnweiss failed to get a hit in this slugfest, and Ike Pearson was the only one of the five hurlers Lyons tossed into the fray to escape the barrage. The veteran right-hander got the call with two out in the four-run ninth, just in time to make Stirnweiss bang into a force play that dropped the curtain on the worst beating the Sox have absorbed this campaign.

Vic Raschi picked up his third straight triumph, though his performance held room for improvement. He walked in a run on four passes in the fourth. He was clubbed for three hits by Taft Wright, one a home run in the eighth, and allowed seven hits in all.

Lyons started Orval Grove, who got into trouble by messing up an easy double play in the first and finished in the fifth after being clubbed for nine hits and five runs. Fred Bradley appeared with the sixth, but was hammered to shelter with one man away and four runs in. Earl Harrist checked the scoring without interfering with the hitting. And in the ninth the aging Earl Caldwell was moved out of the contest under a six-hit salvo that included Lindell's homer and produced four more runs.

Both Wallops Off Grove

Grove was the victim of DiMaggio's two homers. Walloping Joie exploded the first with two aboard in the first inning. After the Yanks had added another run in the second on three hits, DiMaggio opened the fifth with his second homer, his sixth of the campaign. Singles by Raschi and Lindell with DiMaggio's triple finished Bradley quickly in the sixth, and a double by Yogi Berra greeted Harrist as the Yanks collected four more.

That was all until the ninth, when Bobby Brown singled, Cliff Mapes doubled, Lindell hit his homer with one on, DiMaggio doubled, Berra walked, Johnson doubled and George McQuinn singled; all for four more before Pearson came on to end the slaughter.

The home-run production boosted the Yankee total to thirty. Sox pitchers have now been clubbed for thirty-one this season.

Illustrating the sorry condition of Lyons' pitching squad is the fact that in twenty-four games, including a tie, the Southsiders have had sixty-nine in action.

Until today Grove enjoyed the distinction of being the only Sox hurler to go the route, in spring exhibitions and regular play.

The Yanks could do nothing wrong today. Contrarily, nothing went right for the Sox.

Johnson tripped and fell under Luke Appling's pop in the seventh but stuck out his glove to make the catch while lying on the ground.

The box score:

NEW YORK (A.)	ab.	r.	h.	po.	a.	e.
Brown, ss	5	0	3	2	3	0
Keller, lf	4	2	1	1	0	0
Mapes, lf	1	1	1	1	0	0
Lindell, rf	6	3	3	1	0	0
DiMaggio, cf	6	4	5	3	0	0
Berra, c	5	1	2	2	0	0
Johnson, 3b	6	0	3	1	1	0
M'Qu'n, 1b	4	0	2	10	1	0
Stirn'ss, 2b	6	0	0	2	5	0
Raschi, p	5	2	2	1	1	0
Total	48	13	22	27	11	0

CHICAGO (A.)	ab.	r.	h.	po.	a.	e.
Baker, 2b	[illegible]	[illegible]	0	[illegible]	[illegible]	0
Lupien, 1b	5	0	2	6	1	0
Appling, 3b	4	1	0	5	2	0
Hodgin, lf	3	0	1	3	2	0
Wright, rf	4	1	3	1	0	0
Robinson, c	3	0	1	3	1	0
Philley, cf	3	0	0	3	0	0
Michaels, ss	3	0	0	2	7	0
Grove, p	1	0	0	0	0	1
aKolloway	1	0	0	0	0	0
Bradley, p	0	0	0	0	0	0
Harrist, p	0	0	0	0	0	0
bWallaesa	1	0	0	0	0	0
Caldwell, p	0	0	0	0	0	0
Pearson, p	0	0	0	0	0	0
cWeigel	1	0	0	0	0	0
Total	32	2	7	27	11	1

aPopped out for Grove in fifth.
bFlied out for Harrist in seventh.
cGrounded out for Pearson in ninth.

New York	3	1	0	0	1	4	0	0	4	—13
Chicago	0	0	0	1	0	0	0	1	0	— 2

Runs batted in—DiMaggio 6, Keller, Lindell 3, Philley, Berra, Wright, Johnson, McQuinn.

Two-base hits—McQuinn, Berra, Mapes, DiMaggio, Johnson. Three-base hit—DiMaggio. Home runs—DiMaggio 2, Wright, Lindell. Double plays—Johnson, Stirnweiss and McQuinn; Stirnweiss, Brown and McQuinn. Left on bases—New York 13, Chicago 10. Bases on balls—Off Grove 1, Bradley 1, Harrist 1, Caldwell 2, Raschi 7. Struck out—By Raschi 2, Harrist 1. Hits—Off Grove 9 in 5 innings, Bradley 3 in 1-3, Harrist 2 in 1 2-3, Caldwell 6 in 1 2-3, Pearson 0 in 1-3. Wild pitch—Grove. Losing pitcher—Grove. Umpires—Rommel, Passarella and Boyer. Time of game—2:26. Attendance—5,001.

DiMaggio scoring

The New York Times

The St. Louis Cardinals

Stan Musial

CARDS TRIM BROOKS FOR 6TH IN ROW, 13-4

Pollet Coasts Behind 15-Hit Attack—Dodgers Drop Fifth Straight at Ebbets Field

By JOSEPH M. SHEEHAN

If the Dodgers ever again see the Cardinals, with emphasis on Stan Musial and Enos Slaughter, it will be too soon. In a manner that severely shook the faith of 11,953 Ebbets Field loyalists, Eddie Dyer's wrecking crew yesterday completed the deflation of Flatbush's erstwhile favorites.

Behind a smooth pitching performance by Howie Pollet, St. Louis blasted Joe Hatten, Hugh Casey and Clyde King for fourteen hits. Combined with ten walks, two hit batsmen and two errors, they added up to a 13-4 defeat for Brooklyn, which has dropped five straight games, all at home.

Traveling at a blistering pace, the league-leading Cardinals have won six games in a row and thirteen of their last sixteen. As groggy Dodger pitchers can attest, the Redbirds will continue to fly high until someone clips the wings of Musial and Slaughter.

Musial Bats .733 for Series

This slugging duo again went berserk. Musial had a four-for-six day, with a single, two doubles and a homer, to run his batting average for the series up to an incredible .733. Slaughter settled for a series mark of .500 on the strength of two singles and a double in five official trips to the plate.

Del Rice, with a brace of doubles that drove in four runs; Nippy Jones, with two singles that produced three tallies, and Ernie Dusak, who also singled twice, joined the fun at the expense of a Dodger staff so destitute that Manager Leo Durocher felt obliged to let Hatten stay through to the bitter end of the six-run Cardinal fifth inning.

Until that stanza, the Brooklyn southpaw matched the pace set by his St. Louis counterpart. Each team had scored once, the Cardinals in the third on a single by Dusak and Musial's double, the Dodgers in the fourth on a walk to Bruce Edwards, two infield outs and Dick Whitman's single.

Twelve Cards Bat in Fifth

However, Lefty Joe fell all to pieces in the fifth. Before he ended the horrendous frame by surprisingly fanning Musial with the bases full, twelve Cardinals batted. Half of them scored as the net result of three hits, six walks, two wild pitches and an error. Musial, Slaughter and Rice were the hitters.

A pinch-hitter paved the way for the entrance of Casey in the sixth. The suddenly ineffective relief ace was shelled for three hits and three runs in that inning and, with the bases empty in the seventh, served Musial a fat pitch that Stan propelled across Bedford Avenue for his fifth home run. King worked the ninth and gave two runs on two hits and a walk.

With the heat off, Pollet eased up a bit, but the Dodgers got to him too late with too little. Three Brooklyn runs on three solid hits in the eighth failed to ruffle the Redbird star, who proceeded smoothly to his third triumph against no defeats. The setback was Hatten's second in four starts.

Durocher Coach at First

Perhaps with the idea of rallying his skidding charges, Durocher appeared on the coaching lines for the first time since April 26, at first base. With commendable courage, Leo stuck it out, although his ears undoubtedly were burning by the disastrous finish.

An errant fast ball thrown by Casey skulled Rice in the eighth. However, the Cardinal catcher took the main force of the blow on his protective helmet and was able to leave the field under his own power. It was reported in the dressing room afterward that he was not seriously hurt.

Perturbed by the incident, particularly since Casey earlier had plunked Whitey Kurowski in the back, Dyer kicked up such a fuss that he was waved to the showers by Umpire Art Gore.

Brooklyn fans will pay tribute to Dixie Walker today when he makes his first appearance at Ebbets Field in a strange uniform, with the Pirates.

The box score:

ST. LOUIS (N.)	ab.	r.	h.	po.	a.	e.
Lapointe, 2b	4	1	0	4	1	0
Dusak, cf	5	1	2	0	0	0
Musial, lf	6	3	4	2	0	0
Kurowski, 3b	3	2	0	0	0	0
Lang, 3b	0	1	0	0	1	0
Slaughter, rf	5	2	3	5	0	0
Jones, 1b	4	2	2	7	0	0
Marion, ss	5	1	1	3	2	1
Rice, c	4	0	2	4	1	0
aSchoendienst	0	0	0	0	0	0
Garagiola, c	0	0	0	2	0	0
Pollet, p	4	0	0	0	1	0
Total	40	13	14	27	6	1

BROOKLYN (N.)	ab.	r.	h.	po.	a.	e.
Miksis, 2b	5	0	1	1	2	0
Robinson, 1b	4	0	1	10	1	1
Lund, lf	5	1	2	2	0	0
Furillo, cf	3	1	0	4	1	0
Edwards, c	5	1	0	4	0	0
Reese, ss	4	0	1	2	5	0
Brown, 3b	4	1	1	3	1	1
Whitman, rf	4	0	2	0	0	0
Hatten, p	1	0	1	1	3	0
bMauch	1	0	0	0	0	0
Casey, p	1	0	0	0	0	0
cHodges	1	0	0	0	0	0
King, p	0	0	0	0	2	0
Total	36	4	9	27	15	2

aRan for Rice in eighth.
bFanned for Hatten in fifth.
cFanned for Casey in eighth.

St. Louis	0	0	1	0	6	3	1	0	2	—13
Brooklyn	0	0	0	1	0	0	0	3	0	— 4

Runs batted in—Musial 2, Whitman 3, Slaughter 3, Rice 4, Jones 3, Brown.

Two-base hits—Musial 2, Rice 2, Robinson, Slaughter, Reese, Lund 2, Whitman. Home run—Musial. Double play—Miksis, Reese and Robinson. Left on bases—St. Louis 12, Brooklyn 9. Bases on balls—Off Pollet 4, Hatten 8, Casey 1, King 1. Struck out—By Pollet 5, Hatten 3. Hits—Off Hatten 8 in 5 innings, Casey 4 in 3, King 2 in 1. Hit by pitcher—By Casey (Kurowski, Rice). Wild pitches—Hatten 2. Losing pitcher—Hatten. Umpires—Gore, Robb and Pinelli. Time of game—2:53. Attendance—11,953.

CUBS, WITH 14 HITS, DOWN PHILLIES, 5-3

PHILADELPHIA, May 20 (AP)—The Cubs rapped three pitchers for 14 hits today to score a 5—3 victory over the Phillies and capture the series, two games to one.

Chicago jumped on Walt Dubiel for three runs in the first inning. Eddie Waitkus and Andy Pafko singled and both rode home when Eddie Miller and Johnny Blatnik collided chasing Bill Nicholson's short fly to left. The ball dropped for a triple and Nicholson counted on Bob Scheffing's single.

Shortstop Roy Smalley's first major league homer and a double-single combination by Nicholson and Scheffing gave Russ Meyer a five-run advantage.

Zale Regains Middleweight Title by Knocking Out Graziano in Third Round

VETERAN PUMMELS RIVAL FROM START

Zale Drops Graziano for 3 in First and 7 in Third Before a Left Ends Bout at 1:08

UPSET STIRS 21,497 FANS

Savage Fight Culminates With East Sider Unconscious on Floor of Newark Ring

By JAMES P. DAWSON
Special to THE NEW YORK TIMES.

NEWARK, N. J., June 10—Tony Zale, sturdy Gary, Ind., ring veteran, regained the world middleweight title tonight.

He knocked out Rocky Graziano, doughty warrior from New York's East Side, in three blazing rounds of what was to have been a fifteen-round bout at Ruppert Stadium, before a crowd of 21,497 yelling fight fans who paid gross receipts of $335,646 to see another primitive installment of this ring feud.

Under the paralyzing punches of the 34-year-old Hoosier, fighting a grim battle to regain the title he lost last July 16, Graziano sank unconscious after 1 minute 8 seconds of the third round, to be counted out, flat on his back, by Referee Paul Cavalier.

The flamboyant Graziano, fighting here because he is ineligible in his native New York, favorite to win entering the ring at odds of 5 to 12, was an easy victim of the remarkable Zale. The East Sider was floored for a count of three in the first round, he was rocked and staggered in a stanza in which the action became so torrid neither heard the bell ending the round.

Graziano Hits Canvas

Shortly after the third round opened, Graziano sank for a count of seven, arising game, instinctively, his face to the foe, his scattered senses dictating he must fight to defend himself, not cover up. Rocky tried to fight. But he was incapable of the effort and with a left hook to the jaw and a volley of vicious, sense-deadening rights and lefts to the body and head, the final poke a smashing left which stiffened Rocky on his heels and sent him toppling like a falling tree, Zale finished his foe.

Scoring this sensational victory, Zale went back forty years to rip a glittering page from ring history. He became the second middleweight champion to regain the crown, and he had something of the slashing, destructive, battering style of his predecessor in this respect to carry him to victory. For only Stanley Ketchel, who retrieved the title by knocking out Billy Papke in 1908, ever came back to win the middleweight crown and Ketchel is one of the ring's immortals.

Scoring one of the biggest upsets of recent years, Zale pounded out his second knockout victory over Graziano in half the time it took him to score the first and lose the title in the second. Zale knocked out Graziano in six terrific rounds at the Yankee Stadium in New York, in 1946, and was knocked out in six rounds himself in Chicago last July, when Graziano ascended the throne. In this first defense of the title he held so short a time, Graziano never had a chance.

Victor Is Unmarked

Zale was unmarked leaving the ring, conquering hero in a battle on which many of his friends and admirers looked with apprehension. Graziano was bleeding from nose and mouth and from a slight cut over the left eye, and he left the ring on shaky legs. He looked the beaten fighter.

It may be maintained, and not without justification, too, that illegal blows helped Zale on the road to his marvelous triumph. One of the most effective punches of the battle was a murderous right to the heart that Zale drove sharp and true to the target after the bell ending the first round.

This was but one of a fusillade Zale drove to the head and face and body in a tornadic outburst of punching after a left hook to the jaw sent Rocky staggering backward to sag against the ropes, just before the bell clanged the end of the round. Referee Cavalier didn't hear the bell, or was slow in his reaction. For in a brief, fiery assault, which ended with that damaging right to the heart, Zale rendered Graziano helpless before they were separated.

That this extracurricular punching had an effect on Graziano is unquestionable. It is likewise unquestionable, it was accidental, and not deliberate. Neither fighter heard the bell. Some at the ringside didn't hear it for the roars of the crowd urging Zale on, pleading with Graziano to counter.

Graziano tried to fight back but couldn't. He was being battered helpless as Zale pressed his advantage. But, even without this overtime onslaught, Zale must have won tonight. He was the master. There was no escaping that at any stage of the battle.

Rocky Tries "Weaving"

A shouted instruction, an earsplitting tempo, to "weave," sent Graziano out to battle—and to his doom. Rocky tried "weaving" as they exchanged long left hooks to the head before the bell's echo died away.

But, in a jiffy, Graziano was rushed to the ropes under a left to the body and to the head, and, backed to the ropes, Graziano had to withstand a two-fisted battering to which Zale, who seemed like a man possessed, subjected him.

Coming away from this situation, Graziano was pressed across the ring under a fire of stinging left jabs to the face and head. Trying to counter this assault, Rocky left himself open for a solid left hook to the jaw and a right which dropped him in his tracks.

He started up at the count of "two," but the count of knockdown timekeeper Nat Fleischer went to three before the defending champion was erect and the battle resumed on signal of Referee Cavalier.

Rocky was through then and there. Zale knew it would be only a question of time. Rocky must have known it, in his heart, too. For through the rest of the session Zale battered Graziano with a pitiless, two-fisted fire that raked the East Sider about the body and head alternately.

Sags in Own Corner

Near the end of the round, a smashing left hook to the jaw made Graziano sag against the ropes in his own corner. Quick as a flash, Zale leaped in with paralyzing rights and lefts to the head and body as Rocky tried to fight back. The bell clanged, but neither heard it. Zale ripped and slashed with both hands, driving at any opening that presented, seeking to batter Graziano helpless, intent only on that as the crowd roared.

Graziano's head rolled under a left hook and a sharp right and his knees sagged as his arms went up protectively. And, when the covering from the body was lifted, Zale sent a crushing right to the heart, cleanly, powerfully, with all the weight and strength of his body behind it, before Referee Cavalier belatedly stepped between the combatants. Rocky's body sagged under the impact. His handlers leaped through the ropes and propped him on his corner stool.

Through the second round Zale sparred cautiously for perhaps a minute, sticking and stabbing Rocky with unerring, snappy left jabs to the face and head, and upsetting Graziano's attempts to return the fire. Rocky lunged wildly, viciously at his foe, lashing out with both arms, flailing rights and lefts for the jaw which, for the most part were wide of the mark. When Rocky did land, it was in glancing fashion because Zale was either going away from or leading in under the blows.

Zale Parries Lunges

A right to the jaw staggered Graziano midway of the round and he sank back to the ropes, to rebound like an infuriated bull and, with a blazing, ill-directed fire of lefts and rights, forced Zale about the ring.

Several times Rocky crashed his right to the head. A long left banged against Zale's right eye and the crowd roared when Graziano grazed the jaw with a powerful, full-arm right. But, Zale, stepping nimbly back to a neutral corner, parried Graziano's lunges, picked off Rocky's desperate blows, and, smilingly, danced out to ring center and proceeded to batter Graziano through the rest of the round.

Zale was on the attack as soon as the third round opened, sticking and stabbing and pur[illegible]ng with his powerful, straight, accurate left to the head, hooking his left to the head and driving Graziano to the ropes under a withering body-fire for which Rocky had no defense and less of counter-fire.

A left hook to the jaw rocked Rocky to his heels. A right and left to the head followed. Rocky staggered backward drunkenly. Zale was after him cat-like. A right to the heart, a left hook to the body and Rocky cringed. A left hook that landed solidly on the jaw sent Rocky down to be counted out after the third round had gone 1 minute 8 seconds.

ON WAY DOWN FOR NEXT TO THE LAST TRIP

Rocky Graziano falling to the floor for a count of seven after Tony Zale landed a left hook followed by a right cross in the third round at Newark last night. The New York Times

Story of Bout Blow by Blow

From a Staff Correspondent

NEWARK, June 10—Rocky Graziano weighed 158½ pounds and Tony Zale 158¾ for the scheduled fifteen-round title bout tonight.

These were the official figures as of yesterday. There was no weigh-in today.

The referee was Paul Cavalier. No judges are employed in this state.

The round-by-round description follows:

First Round

Graziano threw a left hook which missed. Zale jabbed lightly and Rocky missed a left. Zale rushed in and punished the champion at close quarters. Zale crossed a right and left to the body.

Then Zale fired two left hooks, flooring Graziano for a count of three. Rocky missed a wild right and then was short with a left hook. Zale boxed cautiously then landed a right to the body. Zale scored with two left hooks and they clinched.

Graziano landed a left hook to the chin and crossed a right to the side of the jaw. Zale landed a left jab but took a right cross to the head. A wild melee followed with both throwing punches freely. They continued to fight after the bell and had to be separated.

Second Round

Two left hooks by Zale found the target, as did a left hook to the body by Graziano. They exchanged rights to the body. Zale worked effectively with his left, jabbing repeatedly.

Rocky crossed a hard right to the face, but Zale countered with a left. Graziano's left hook bothered the challenger. Zale crossed a solid right that rocked Graziano. Again Zale landed his right to Graziano's head, but the champion rallied. Rocky had Zale in straits with a series of lefts and rights to the head.

Third Round

Graziano sent a right to the ribs but took a left on the chin. Another left hook to the jaw staggered the champion. Graziano was in bad shape and he was floored for a count of seven by a vicious left hook followed by a right cross.

Graziano was knocked down by a left hook and was counted out in 1:08.

ZALE TO FIGHT AGAIN, BUT HE BARS GRAZIANO

From a Staff Correspondent

NEWARK, N. J., June 10—Tony Zale, unmarked and certainly unharmed by Rocky Graziano, will defend the middleweight championship he regained tonight against any man selected by the promoters—with one exception. There will be no more meetings with Graziano.

In his dressing room, immediately following his spectacular three-round knockout victory, Zale scoffed at the report that the Gary, Ind., veteran would retire after this bout—win or lose. "I'll fight again," he said straightforwardly. "I'll fight anyone."

The latter part of the new champion's statement was amended quickly by Art Winch, one of his managers. "No more Graziano—anyone except Rocky," he declared.

Zale, in need of a shave, but no other attention, was all smiles. "I sensed I had him in the first round," Tony said. He added that Graziano had not hurt him at all, but that he had regarded Rocky as dangerous until the finish.

The scene in the loser's quarters was decidedly gloomy. Interviewers were barred for some time, but when they finally were admitted Rocky still was in a sorry state.

Groggy, disillusioned and bearing a cut on his forehead, the dethroned titleholder said he could not get started and added he wanted another meeting with Zale. Of course, Graziano was unaware that Zale's pilot already had declared against a fourth such bout.

The New York Times.

SUNDAY, JUNE 13, 1948. L+ S

HOGAN TAKES U. S. OPEN WITH 276; CITATION, 1-5, VICTOR; INDIANS TOP YANKS, 7-5, 9-4; GIANTS WIN, GAIN 1ST PLACE

68,586 AT STADIUM

Gordon Belts Key 2-Run Homer in Opener and Hits 2 in Nightcap

REYNOLDS AND SHEA LOSE

Yankee Rallies Fall Short in 9th of Both Games—Indians Lead by 3½ Lengths

By LOUIS EFFRAT

The slumping Yankees suffered the embarrassment of a double defeat at the hands of the Indians yesterday before 68,586 persons at the Stadium. With Joe Gordon, the former New Yorker, poling one homer in the curtain-raiser and two in the afterpiece, Cleveland made it look easy en route to 7-5 and 9-4 victories.

Lou Boudreau's league leaders, growing more confident with each passing day, hammered Allie Reynolds and Spec Shea, the two starters, heavily. Though their own starters failed to last, the Indians counted enough runs to annex their third straight over the Yankees.

The Indians increased their lead to three and one-half games over the runner-up Athletics. In third place, the Bombers fell six lengths behind the pace.

Gordon's round-tripper in the fourth of the nightcap followed a pass to Walt Judnich for a 2-0 Cleveland lead. None was aboard when Gordon propelled his third of the afternoon in the sixth. The next time Joe strode to the plate Randy Gumpert was on the mound and Gordon contributed a run-scoring single.

Six Runs Cross in Seventh

That was in the seventh, when eleven Indians batted eight hits safely and six trotted over the plate. It was an horrendous stanza that the Yankees and their followers had to endure.

Dale Mitchell started the frame with a single. Hank Edwards tripled, Boudreau doubled and Shea was lifted. Gumpert retired Ed Robinson on a pop-up, but Judnich doubled and Gordon singled before Ken Keltner hoisted to second.

Joe Tipton and Steve Gromek singled and Mitchell, up for the second time, doubled. All that added up to six runs before Karl Drews went in and coaxed a grounder to short from Edwards.

Things came to an unpretty pass when the Yankees notched their first run on three walks and a scratch single by Johnny Lindell in their half. The Yankees added three in the ninth, but not with any awe-inspiring display of power.

Phil Rizzuto walked and Cliff Mapes hit a pinch double. Don Black replaced Gromek after the latter had pitched two balls and a strike to Snuffy Stirnweiss. Black walked George and also passed Tommy Henrich to force home Rizzuto. Russ Christopher took over and walked Lindell, Mapes counting.

DiMaggio Flies Out

Joe DiMaggio flied out, no one advancing, but Stirnweiss went over on Yogi Berra's infield out. The Yankees, however, got no farther.

The Yankees still were within reach of the Indians in the ninth inning of the opener, but Reynolds cracked right then and there, the visitors added two runs to their 5-4 margin and sealed Allie's third setback. Previously, Reynolds had made one big mistake, the Indians taking advantage of his chief weakness, the "gopher" pitch.

With two out in the seventh, Judnich on first and the Yankees on top, 4—3, Reynolds tossed a home-run ball to Gordon. The former New Yorker's sixth round-tripper of the year handed Cleveland the lead, which never was regained by the Harrismen. It was the seventh four-bagger against Reynolds, who led the club in that department last season and holds the same dubious honor currently.

It was difficult enough for Harris to forgive Gordon's wallop into the left-field pavilion, but Bucky and his charges felt completely let down when Reynolds collapsed in the ninth. It started with Edwards singling to left and Boudreau drawing a pass. Robinson's bunt was turned into a force-out of Edwards at third, Reynolds to Billy Johnson, and when Judnick bounced to McQuinn, both both runners advanced.

There was no reason for extra

Continued on Page 3, Column 2

Sedgman, Australia, Wins Kent Net Title

By The Associated Press

LONDON, June 12—Frank Sedgman, 21-year-old Australian who is ranked No. 2 in his country, won the Kent tennis championship today by defeating Jack Harper, also of Australia, in the final, 6—4, 6—4.

Later Sedgman combined with John Bromwich, veteran Australian internationalist, to take the doubles crown. They defeated Enrique Morea and A. D. Russell of the Argentine, 6—4, 6—4.

Mrs. Heraldo Weiss of the Argentine defeated Miss Patsy Rodgers, young British player, 7—5, 6—1, for women's singles honors.

M'KENLEY IS FIRST IN 400-METER RUN

Sets Track Mark at Triborough Stadium—Rucks Next and McFarlane Is Third

By JOSEPH M. SHEEHAN

Herbert McKenley failed in his attempt to break the world record for 400 meters yesterday. But the tall, slender Jamaican re-emphasized his rating as Olympic favorite by running away from a distinguished field in the fastest time ever registered in these parts.

Free-wheeling Herb whippeted around one turn of the fast Triborough Stadium track on Randalls Island in 0:46.4 to snap the tape seven yards in front of the South Carolina's Norman (Scooter) Rucks, the No. 1 native American quarter-miler on his 1948 record, and Bob McFarlane, Canada's champion.

This performance, clipping three-tenths of a second off the track record of 0:46.7, set by Cliff Bourland of Southern California in the National A.A.U. 1942 championships, provided the highlight for the 2,500 clock-conscious fans who turned out for the Sydenham Hospital benefit meet.

Race Run in Lanes

It was purely a stop-watch thrill, however. The race was run in lanes. McKenley, second from the outside, started in front of four of his five rivals and it was obvious, even with their staggered placing, that he was going away from the field.

This was confirmed when the runners came off the turn into the straightaway. Herb had almost ten yards on Rucks. The 25-year-old ex-GI from Malverne, L. I., a late-blooming sensation previously unheard of hereabouts, held his form a bit better down the stretch and closed in a yard or two as McKenley tightened up under the strain of his blazing pace.

The huge McFarlane, a 20-year-old student at Western Ontario University who may well turn out to be a dark-horse at London, came with a tremendous rush up the final straightaway and finished just a stride behind Rucks.

The clockers caught Rucks in a sparkling 0:47.2 and credited McFarlane with 0:47.5. Jim Gilhooley of New York University was fourth in 0:48.5, time that Jim McKenna of the New York A. C. equaled in the second heat of the race, in which placings were decided on time.

Slim Herb Barten of Michig returned this country's fastest 1,500-meter time to date, 3:53.5, in taking that event with a last-lap sprint that carried him across the finish line twelve yards in front of the New York A. C.'s improving

Continued on Page 2, Column 6

COLT TIES RECORD

Citation Wins 1½-Mile Belmont in 2:28⅕ for Triple Crown

FAVORITE EARNS $77,700

Better Self Next, Six Lengths Back, With Escadru Third—Mr. Busher, 7-10, First

By JAMES ROACH

In a gallop, with his ears pricked and with apparently about as much expenditure of energy as in a midweek workout, Calumet Farm's magnificent Citation completed the business of winning American racing's triple crown in an astounding performance at Belmont Park yesterday.

It was astounding because Citation, despite the ease with which he took the eightieth running of the $117,300 Belmont Stakes by more than half a dozen lengths, equaled the stake record for the mile and a half classic.

Horsemen blinked a couple of times when 2:28 1/5 flashed on the teletimer board in the infield, the same figures that had gone up after Count Fleet's triumph in 1943.

For about half the way it looked like a contest. Then Citation began to open up on the other seven.

First he had three-quarters of a length advantage. Then it was one and a half at the far turn. In practically nothing flat on the final bend he was three or four to the good. Then it was a solo flight through the straightaway.

So it was that the Belmont, sternest of the tests for 3-year-olds, proved an even easier proposition for the Calumet colt than the Kentucky Derby and Preakness had been.

Arcaro Rides Citation

And so it was that he made his record eighteen victories in twenty starts, added $77,700 to his earnings, boosted them past the half-million mark and gave Jockey Eddie Arcaro and Warren Wright's Calumet Farm their second winner among the eight that have taken the three-deck crown. Calumet's first was Whirlaway in 1941.

Closest pursuer of the champion at the end of the line was King Ranch's Better Self, who closed in along the rail in the final furlong to take the $20,000 place money by half a length from William L. Brann's Escadru.

Fourth, after a gap of some five lengths, was C. V. Whitney's Vulcan's Forge. Then followed A. J. Sackett's Gasparilla, William Helis' Salmagundi, Belair Stud's Golden Light and Glen Riddle Farm's Faraway.

For the fourteenth time in his racing career Citation was an odds-on choice. Price makers had predicted that he would be 1 to 5, and 1 to 5 he was—despite the fact that his stable-mate Coaltown was a late scratch—after the 43,046 customers had completed their scrimmaging at the mutuel windows. Citation was 3 to 20 to place and the legal minimum of 1 to 20 to show, the track having to put $3,041.80 into the show pool to make good on those nickel-on-the-dollar pay-offs to the "sure thing" gentry.

Favorite Stumbles at Start

Faraway, 28 to 1 shot ridden by Ted Atkinson, thrilled the onlookers in the early stages. He went up to run with Citation, who stumbled a bit breaking out of the gate from the inside slot but nevertheless charged almost at once into the lead. They went head and head to

Continued on Page 4, Column 4

The P. G. A. Titleholder on His Way to National Open Championship

Ben Hogan (left) sinking a 30-foot putt on the second green for a birdie at the Riviera Country Club during his second round at Los Angeles
Associated Press Wirephoto

KRAMER CONQUERS GORNTO IN 3 SETS

Triumphs by 6-2, 6-1, 6-2 as Pro Title Tennis Starts—Van Horn, Kovacs Gain

By ALLISON DANZIG

John Kramer returned yesterday to the Forest Hills Stadium where he won the National amateur tennis crown last September, to launch his first bid for the professional championship.

The authority of the high-powered strokes that carried all before him in 1947 was briefly challenged to 2—all in the opening set. Then the big, sandy-haired Californian sprayed the lines with the rifle-fire of his service, drive and smash, took nine successive games and defeated Mickey Gornto of Fort Lauderdale, Fla., 6—2, 6—1, 6—2.

A newcomer to Forest Hills, Gornto stood up to his hopeless assignment with poise and a bearing that were all to his credit. He showed a fast first service that often scored for him and a continental backhand that was good to look upon. He used the drop shot and came through occasionally with a well-turned volley.

Attack Never Abates

But the pace, depth and accuracy of Kramer's strokes in an attack that never abated allowed little redress and brought the play to a speedy conclusion. Considering that this was his first match on grass since last September, Big John's performance was a warning to defending Champion Robert Riggs, Donald Budge, Frank Kovacs, et al.

The opening round in the twenty-first tournament for the national championship was devoid of anything approaching the unusual. In only two matches did the play go beyond three sets. Al Doyle of New York furnished the nearest thing to a surprise in carrying Welby Van Horn of the Germantown Cricket Club to 6—4, 7—5, 4—6, 6—3.

Van Horn, a big Californian who won the professional title in 1945 and was runner-up for the amateur crown in 1939, was not in his best form. He was over-hitting throughout and his power was nullified in large part by his errors and lagging footwork.

Doyle made the most of his opportunity and won as much applause as any man who appeared in the stadium with his clever play. He has an easy style, with a strong wrist doing most of the work on his fine back-hand, and a litheness of movement. With a little more power and more opportunity to play the big fellows, he could be a real challenge.

Kovacs, playing the opening match in the stadium, defeated George Richey of Houston, Texas, 6—2, 6—3, 6—2. The tall Californian held nothing back and it was to Richey's credit that he took as many games as he did, with his back-hand accounting for most of his winners. Kovacs' back-hand

Continued on Page 2, Column 4

Giants Score 5 in Seventh To Overcome Cards, 7 to 5

By JOHN DREBINGER
Special to THE NEW YORK TIMES.

ST. LOUIS, June 12—The cannon-cracker bludgeon of Big Jawn Mize, which has been spluttering fitfully for some time, boomed on the west bank of the Mississippi today.

It exploded a homer, double and single and by these means so inspired the Giants that they forgot all about their troubles in the topsy-turvy National League flag race.

Instead, they piled most of them onto the mounting woes of the Cardinals as they touched off a five-run demonstration in the seventh which, coupled with another brilliant turn of relief hurling by the inexhaustible Sheldon Jones, gave Mel Ott's Polo Grounders the opener of the three-game series, 7 to 5.

The victory sent the Giants skipping back to the top rung of the league ladder, while Eddie Dyer's bewildered Redbirds sank back to fourth on their fourth straight defeat.

Winning this one, however, was no soft touch, for the Cards, in routing Larry Jansen inside of five rounds, piled up a total of thirteen blows, including a homer for Ron Northey. But once the youthful Jones took over with none out in the fifth, the St. Louis attack faded off to a whisper. The Nebraskan gave up only three scattered singles in his five full innings on the mound to notch his sixth victory, the fourth in relief, against three setbacks. It was

Continued on Page 3, Column 7

YALE NINE DOWNS PRINCETON BY 7-5

Elis Win Before Tiger Alumni Crowd of 10,000 as Quinn Stifles Rivals in Ninth

Special to THE NEW YORK TIMES.

PRINCETON, N. J., June 12—Yale failed to get an extra-base blow against two Princeton hurlers on University Field today, but the Eli nine capitalized on singles and loose Tiger fielding to gain a 7-5 victory before a crowd of 10,000 Princeton alumni here for reunion.

The home team, meanwhile, provided plenty of fireworks for the big crowd, with two doubles and two triples among its nine hits. But the Tigers never could overcome the lead which Yale built up along the route. Frank Quinn, the Eli fast-ball king, was called in to stop the Tigers in the ninth and made short work of the three batters who faced him in the first appearance of his career on University Field.

Bob Wolcott, the Princeton hurler who has vision in only one eye, started on the mound and allowed only six hits in his seven-inning stint. Two errors by Second Baseman Don West in the third frame, however, paved the way for a three-run rally and Wolcott was charged with the loss.

Walks to Open Third

Delos Smith walked to start the Blue third and was safe at second when West dropped the forcing throw on Bob Goodyear's smash to third. Art Moher singled to right and Smith held third as West took the relay. Goodyear, however, rounded second and slid into third, and as Smith broke for home West threw wild to the plate, allowing both runners to score. Jerry Breen's single over second brought Moher home.

The Elis fashioned a lone run in

Continued on Page 2, Column 2

N. Y. Y. C. FLEET LED BY BISSELL'S YAWL

Burma Away First in Run to Newport, With Temple's Stormy Weather Next

By JAMES ROBBINS
Special to THE NEW YORK TIMES.

GLEN COVE, L. I., June 12—Almost completely enshrouded in a combination of easterly breeze and heat haze, the racing craft in the

Continued on Page 6, Column 2

U. S. WOMEN RETAIN WIGHTMAN CUP, 6-1

Miss Brough Beats Britain's Mrs. Bostock in Deciding Match, 6-2, 4-6, 7-5

By The Associated Press.

LONDON, June 12 — America's strongly balanced Wightman Cup tennis team swept the final four matches on today's program at Wimbledon to complete a 6-to-1 conquest of Great Britain's game but out-gunned lassies.

The only excitement of the second day's play was supplied by Mrs. Jean Nicoll Bostock of the British side when she carried Miss Louise Brough of Beverly Hills, Calif., the United States champion, through three furiously fought sets only to lose, 6—2, 4—6, 7—5.

The British star, fighting for every point in what proved the deciding match of the series, led at 5—4 in the third set. Then suddenly she ran out of gas and won only one more point as blonde Louise powered through three straight games.

Mrs. du Pont Wins

The Americans led by two matches to one at the start of the day's play. Mrs. Margaret Osborne du Pont of Wilmington, Del., quickly extended the margin to 3—1 by trouncing Mrs. Betty Hilton, 6—3, 6—4. Miss Brough's victory, which followed, thus supplied the clincher and made mere exhibitions of the concluding two tussles.

Under no pressure, Miss Doris Hart of Miami then scored easily over Miss Joy Gannon, one of Brit-

Continued on Page 2, Column 1

LINKS MARK IS SET

Hogan, With 276, Clips Record for National Open by 5 Strokes

DEMARET SECOND ON 278

Jim Turnesa Has 280 to Take Third—Locke, 282, Is Next in Los Angeles Event

By LINCOLN A. WERDEN
Special to THE NEW YORK TIMES.

LOS ANGELES, June 12—In one of the most colorful settings in which the forty-eight-year old United States open championship has ever been staged, Ben Hogan, 35-year-old Texas-born golf professional, today won the title with a record-breaking score for the seventy-two holes of 276.

The 135-pound star who annexed the P. G. A. crown last month finally climbed the heights of which he fondly dreamed since his caddie days and played the Riviera Country Club course in 68 and 69 today to annex golf's biggest honor by a margin of two strokes.

Out here in a land where superlatives are in order, Hogan not only smashed the scoring mark for the open set by Ralph Guldahl in 1937 by five strokes but he also became the first golfer to take both the open and P. G. A. titles in the same year since Gene Sarazen accomplished the feat in 1922.

15,000 in the Gallery

With some 15,000, including many motion picture stars, on hand to witness the final phase of the three-day tournament, Hogan played almost unerring golf on the trying last rounds over the 7,020-yard layout. He clipped par by three strokes this morning and by two this afternoon.

Long before Hogan, whose club is at Hershey, Pa., tossed away the ball to an admiring youngster after the finish, the race had narrowed down to him and a fellow Texan, Jimmy Demaret, Houston-born, who registers from Ojai, Calif.

It was Demaret, the ever-colorful, arrayed in scarlet trousers, green cap and white shirt, who came within hailing distance of Hogan with a 68 and a 69 himself for 278 that earned second place.

It was also the smiling Demaret, who skipped about the greens when he missed important putts, who had a big portion of the crowd laughing and wondering whether his thrilling play would result in the more serious result of capturing the championship.

Misses Four-Footer

Demaret, with three birdies out of four holes in the final stages, contributed the real excitement. But he failed to get a four-foot putt down for a fourth birdie in a row and that proved to be the end of his brilliant streak with five holes left to play.

Demaret and Jim Turnesa of Elmsford, N. Y., who finished third with 280, were also under the previous scoring record. Turnesa, member of one of the leading golfing clans of the nation, came in with a 70 both in the morning and afternoon sessions.

Then came Bobby Locke, the South African, who was making his second bid to take the honors back to Johannesburg. He had 72 and 70 over the course that sets down in the Santa Monica Canyon to total 282, which was one stroke ahead of Sam Snead of White Sulphur Springs, W. Va.

The old three-putt hoodoo trailed Snead in the haze that hung over the course this morning and Slammin' Sam never did get entirely clear of it, as he had a 73 and a 72 for his last two rounds. It was Snead who had a record of 138 for the first two days with 69 each time he played the course, but one of the most popular golfers, who has won both the P. G. A. as well as the British Open, failed once more to win.

Worsham's Total 285

Lew Worsham of Oakmont, Pa., who beat Snead in the play-off of last year's championshhip at St. Louis, put together a 71 and a 78 for a concluding aggregate of 285, two back of Sam. Then came Herman Barron of White Plains, winner of the Goodall tourney, with a 71 and 72 for 286, while Johnny Bulla of Phoenix, accounting for the low round of 67 today, moved into the 287 bracket.

Along with Bulla at that figure were Smiley Quick of Culver City, Calif., national public links cham-

Continued on Page 5, Column 3

Belmont Stakes Chart

By The Associated Press.

SIXTH RACE—The Belmont Stakes (eightieth running); $100,000 added; 3-year-olds; one mile and a half. Start good; won easily; place driving. Went to post 4:45 off 4:46. Winner, b. c., by Bull Lea-Hydroplane II, by Hyperion. Trainer, H. A. Jones. Value to winner, $77,700; second, $20,000; third, $10,000; fourth, $5,000. Fractional times—0:24 1-5, 0:48 2-5, 1:12 3-5, 1:37, 2:28 1-5. Weather cloudy; track fast.

Starters.	Wt.	P.P.	St.	½	M.	1¼	Str.	Fin.	Jockeys.	Mutuels St.	Mutuels Pl.	Mutuels Sh.	Dollar Odds.
Citation	126	1	1	2^{4}	1^{1}	1^{4}	1^{6}	1^{6}	Arcaro	2.40	2.30	2.10	.20
aBetter Self	126	8	2	$5^{1/2}$	$5^{1/2}$	4^{hd}	3^{8}	$2^{1/2}$	Mehrtens	....	3.70	2.10	12.50
Escadru	126	3	4	6^{10}	4^{1}	2^{5}	2^{4}	3^{5}	Kirkland	....	....	2.10	6.85
Vulcan's Forge	126	5	5	7^{6}	7^{5}	7^{4}	$4^{1\frac{1}{2}}$	4^{4}	Dodson	....	....	....	15.10
aGasparilla	126	7	7	3^{hd}	3^{1}	$3^{1/2}$	5^{3}	5^{3}	Donoso	....	....	....	12.50
Salmagundi	126	6	6	$4^{1\frac{1}{2}}$	6^{10}	6^{1}	6^{2}	6^{2}	Guerin	....	....	....	22.45
Golden Light	126	4	8	8	8	8	8	7^{8}	Combest	....	....	....	82.50
Faraway	126	2	3	1^{hd}	2^{hd}	5^{8}	$7^{1/2}$	8	Atkinson	....	....	....	28.10

Scratched—Coaltown. aA. J. Sackett-King Ranch entry.

Citation stumbled coming out of the gate, but Arcaro picked him up quickly and then sent him to the front. The boy then eased him back going into the half-mile pole. He raced along with Faraway for the next quarter mile, where he jumped away to a long lead and kept increasing his advantage to the end. Better Self was kept in a contending position to the stretch, where he closed with a rush on the inside and was second in the last few strides. Escadru made his bid around the turn, moved up very fast but weakened at the end. Vulcan's Forge, out-run in the early part, closed fast. Faraway had speed for seven furlongs then quit. Gasparilla, well up for a mile, tired.

Owners—1, Calumet Farm; 2, King Ranch; 3, W. L. Brann; 4, C. V. Whitney; 5, A. J. Sackett; 6, W. Helis; 7, Belair Stud; 8, Glen Riddle Farms.

Major League Baseball

Sunday, June 13, 1948

American League

YESTERDAY'S RESULTS

Cleveland 7, New York 5 (1st).
Cleveland 9, New York 4 (2d).
Chicago 5, Boston 3.
Philadelphia 3, St. Louis 2.
Detroit 4, Washington 1.

STANDING OF THE CLUBS

	Cleveland	Phila'phia	New York	Detroit	Washington	Boston	St. Louis	Chicago	Won	Lost	Percentage	Games Behind
Cleveland..	—	5	4	3	4	6	3	6	31	13	.705	—
Philadel ...	2	—	5	4	5	4	6	4	30	19	.612	3½
New York..	2	3	—	4	4	3	6	5	27	21	.563	6
Detroit.....	2	4	3	—	5	3	3	4	24	25	.490	9½
Washgton..	2	3	3	1	—	4	5	6	24	26	.480	10
Boston......	2	3	3	4	3	—	4	3	22	26	.458	11
St. Louis..	1	0	2	6	3	3	—	3	18	28	.391	14
Chicago....	2	1	1	3	2	3	1	—	13	31	.295	18
Lost.........	13	19	21	25	26	26	28	31	—	—		

TODAY'S PROBABLE PITCHERS

Cleveland at New York (2 P. M.)—Feller (5-5) vs. Lopat (2-5).

Chicago at Boston (2) — Haynes (4-6) and Wight (2-5) vs. Parnell (1-4) and Galehouse (1-3).

St. Louis at Philadelphia (2)—Stephens (1-2) and Shore (0-0) vs. Scheib (3-2) and Brissie (5-5).

Detroit at Washington (2)—Trout (6-5) and Trucks (3-3) or Houtteman (1-8) vs. Wynn (6-5) and Hudson (2-5).

National League

YESTERDAY'S RESULTS

New York 7, St. Louis 5.
Brooklyn at Chicago, rain.
Cincinnati 3, Boston 2 (1st).
Cincinnati 11, Boston 9 (2d).
Philadelphia at Pittsburgh, rain.

STANDING OF THE CLUBS

	New York	Boston	Pittsburgh	St. Louis	Phil'delphia	Cincinnati	Brooklyn	Chicago	Won	Lost	Percentage	Games Behind
New York..	—	5	5	3	4	5	2	2	26	20	.565	—
Boston......	2	—	3	5	3	2	4	6	25	21	.543	1
Pittsbgh...	1	5	—	3	1	4	6	5	25	21	.543	1
St. Louis..	1	2	3	—	7	3	6	3	25	22	.532	1½
Philadel ...	3	4	3	2	—	4	3	6	25	24	.510	2½
Cincinnati.	4	3	3	4	2	—	1	6	23	26	.469	4½
Brooklyn...	4	2	2	2	4	5	—	2	21	24	.467	4½
Chicago....	5	0	2	3	3	3	2	—	18	30	.375	9
Lost.........	20	21	21	22	24	26	24	30	—	—		

TODAY'S PROBABLE PITCHERS

New York at St. Louis (2)—Poat (5-1) and Koslo (3-2) vs. Brecheen (6-1) and Munger (2-5).

Brooklyn at Chicago—Hatten (5-2) vs. Schmitz (5-7).

Philadelphia at Pittsburgh (2)—Rowe (2-2) and Dubiel (3-3) vs. Higbe (4-3) and Riddle (6-2).

Boston at Cincinnati (2)—Spahn (5-3) and Prendergast (0-1) vs. Blackwell (3-4) and Peterson (2-5).

Figures in parentheses indicate season's won-and-lost records.

New York Racing Association

Citation, shown crossing the finish line eight lengths ahead of Better Self and Escadru.

CITATION, 1-5, TIES RECORD IN BELMONT

Continued From Page 1

the first curve, head and head around it and down the back-stretch.

At about the seven-furlong pole there was a yell from the crowd as Arcaro let out half a wrap and jumped clearly ahead at once. Faraway stayed in the hunt for a while, then faded on the turn for home, a fade that dropped him all the way to last place.

On the bend Arnold Kirkland began his bid with Escadru, the pride of Maryland, and Warren Mehrtens cut loose from the middle of the pack with Better Self. They were second and third in that order to the stretch, but they hadn't the slightest chance of catching the flier up ahead. The fight for second place and the move-up to fourth of the late-running Vulcan's Forge provided the only excitement through the final yards. Arcaro's whip was excess baggage.

Arcaro, winning a Belmont for a fourth time—the only jockey still active to have accomplished that feat—sent the Bull Lea-Hydroplane II colt along at an even pace. The quarters were clicked off in 0:24 1-5, 0:24 1-5, 0:24 1-5, 0:24 2-5, 0:25 3-5 and 0:25 3-5. Times were 0:48 2-5 at the half, 1:12 3-5 after six furlongs, 1:3 at the mile and 2:02 3-5 after a mile and a quarter.

Said Arcaro: "He's the greatest horse I've ever seen. Maybe I shouldn't have let him win by so much, but I couldn't take any chances for that kind of money. I think he can run an eighth in 0:11 flat in any part of any race."

Said Trainer Horace Allyn (Jimmy) Jones: "Nice ride, Eddie." Jimmy's father, B. A., saddled Whirlaway in 1941 for the Derby-Preakness-Belmont three-bagger.

Owner Wright, the Chicagoan whose Calumet Farm is located at Lexington, Ky., did a job of back-patting on Master Eddie just prior to the presentation of August Belmont Memorial Cup and a permanent trophy in the winner's enclosure.

Assault's Mark Imperiled

With a dozen stakes and $544,700 to his credit in two seasons, Citation has won $389,020 this year with nine victories in ten starts. He needs only one more big stake —and the Arlington Classic is his next major objective—to eclipse Assault's record of $424,195 for earnings during one year.

The customers—some 7,000 more of them had been expected—had a warm day at the horse park. For the first time this season there was a shirt-sleeved gathering.

Two races before the Belmont, the thirty-sixth National Stallion Stakes (colt division) was presented. As expected, it went to Maine Chance Farm's Mr. Busher in another grand display of running by the 2-year-old colt, for whom Mrs. Elizabeth N. Graham paid a record $50,000 as a weanling.

It looked like a close race to the eighth pole, where Ferril Zufelt let Mr. Busher look at the whip. That did it. Mr. Busher lengthened stride instantly, moved easily and powerfully to the front and finished off by himself. William Helis' Emulate gained the photo decision for the place, with Circle M Farm's Foray Vina third and E. P. Taylor's Illuminable fourth.

Two in Row for Mr. Busher

For Mr. Busher, full brother of the great mare Busher, it was the second start and second success of what promises to be quite a career. The previous Saturday he had started for the first time and marked up 0:57 1/5, fastest five-furlong Widener Chute time of the meeting. On this occasion, carrying three additional pounds for a total of 119, he did 0:57 2/5, third best clocking in the history of the stake.

In 1946 Maine Chance's Jet Pilot, who went on to take the Kentucky Derby the following year, did 0:56 3-5 in the National Stallion, the record for the stake.

Said Zufelt of Mr. Busher: "He's the best colt I ever rode."

Mr. Busher's talents were recognized by the crowd. He was 7 to 10 in the wagering, and a total of $194,456 rode safely with him. First money of $18,550 lifted his earnings to $21,150. He also won awards for his nominator (Maine Chance Farm) and the nominator of his sire, War Admiral (Glen Riddle Farm). The stake was for the progeny of stallions nominated by Aug. 15, 1946.

New York Racing Association

With smashing eight-length victory, Citation pounds across finish line with jockey Eddie Arcaro in Belmont Stakes and becomes eighth champion to capture Triple Crown.

WOODVALE RACER WINS KENT STAKES

Page Boots Leads Soon After Start in Defeating Loser Weeper at Delaware

STANTON, Del., June 12 (AP)—Page Boots, no better than econd in four previous starts this year, showed a clean pair of heels to twelve other 3-yeaer-olds in the 11th running of the $25,000 added Kent Stakes at Delaware Park today.

The chestnut son of Our Boots from Royce G. Martin's Woodvale Farm of Toledo, Ohio, stuck his nose in front rounding the first turn and never was headed. He crossed the finish line two and one-half lengths in front of Alfred G. Vanderbilt's lightly regarded Loser Weeper to pick up the purse of $23,700.

Task, carrying the colors of Robert Kleberg's King Ranch, was another two lengths to the rear in nosing C. V. Whitney's Dinner Gong out of the money.

McCreary Rides Winner

Page Boots, ridden by Conn McCreary, was none too well liked in the betting, paying $15.20, $8.40 and $6.60 across the board. Loser Weeper returned $28 and $17.20 while Task paid $13.40 to show.

The Woodvale colt covered the mile and one-sixteenth in 1:44 4/5 over a track still fast although a light rain fell during the running of the race.

Although Page Boots took command soon after the start it was a horse race until the final eighth of a mile. Dinner Gong, Alphara and Loser Weeper were within a length or so of the Woodvale chestnut all through the run down th ack stretch.

They had enough, however, rounding the fina l turn, as McCreary used his bat twice and Page Boots pulled away to a comfortable lead. Loser Weeper also let out a notch, and while no match for the winner he easily was best of the others.

Bovard, only member of the field to clash with triple crown winner, Citation, this year, went off the favorite but never was a factor. He finished tenth.

GIBBONS IS VICTOR IN MIDGET FEATURE

Bonadies Second, Toran Third in 25-Lap Race at the Polo Grounds

Chet Gibbons of Paterson, N. J., won the twenty-five-lap feature race on the midget auto racing program at the Polo Grounds last night. A crowd of 13,146 saw the Jersey driver make a front-running performance of it almost all the way to score by a margin of 15 yards over Tony Bonadies of the Bronx.

No time was taken for the grind because of an interruption that had to be called after the twelfth lap.

At this point the car driven by Len Duncan of Brooklyn bogged down with a broken wheel, and the vehicles' presence on the track was so great a hazard to the thirteen other competitors that time had to be called while Duncan's car was towed away.

Gibbons went into the van at the third lap, supplanting the early pace-maker, Henry Renard of Baldwin, L. I. As Gibbons took over the lead position, Bonadies moved along to a point right behind him. Third was Duncan, who waged a hard fight in his attempt to go ahead until his accident forced him to quit.

The duel between Gibbons and Bonadies held the crowd's interest through every circuit. The Bronx driver made several daring attempts to pass his rival on the inside but Gibbons maneuvered skillfully and refused to budge from his position.

Dee Toran of Paterson, who finished third, rolled around in that position fairly consistently, moving into the spot when Duncan retired, and holding it to the end.

Yankees Rout Feller and Conquer Indians in Silver Anniversary Contest

BOMBERS SET BACK CLEVELAND BY 5-3

DiMaggio's 2 Triples, Homers by Berra and Rizzuto, Win as 49,641 Watch

LOPAT VICTOR ON MOUND

Annexes Third of Season With Page's Help After Yielding Two Runs in the Ninth

By LOUIS EFFRAT

For obvious reasons, it was vital for the Yankees to beat the Indians yesterday at the Stadium. They could ill afford a fourth-straight setback at the hands of the league leaders. Moreover, they needed a quick morale-lifter and could not disappoint the old-line Yankees on hand for "Silver Anniversary Day" before 49,641 fans.

It was not easy. Lou Boudreau went all out in his efforts to sweep the crucial series by nominating Bob Feller, but the Yankees did not fail this time. Joe DiMaggio, Yogi Berra and Phil Rizzuto came through with timely knocks and the memorable afternoon terminated with a 5-3 victory for the Bombers.

With this important triumph, the New Yorkers found themselves still in third place, but only five lengths out of first. It would have been worse, seven behind, if the Indians had not been stopped in their tracks by Lefty Joe Page, who relieved Ed Lopat with two on and two out in the ninth, killing a last-minute Cleveland uprising.

Berra, who had blasted a homer in the sixth behind DiMaggio's first of two triples, giving his mates a 2-1 advantage, dropped Walt Judnick's foul pop to start the ninth and Judnich subsequently walked. Then Jim Hegan propelled a four-bagger into the left-field pavilion.

A Dangerous Situation

Only two behind now, the visitors were dangerous. Lopat retired the next two, but Allie Clark singled and Boudreau walked. As the Cleveland manager inserted a pinch-runner for himself, Bucky Harris deemed it wise to remove the left-handed Lopat for the left-handed Page to pitch against Ed Robinson.

It proved a wise move by Harris, for Page proceeded to strike out Robinson and protect Lopat's third conquest of the campaign. Feller, who twirled six innings before going out for a pinch-hitter—Gene Bearden finished—was charged with his sixth setback. He has not won since May 19.

Joe Gordon, ex-Yankee, who virtually wrecked his erstwhile mates on Saturday, set the stage for Cleveland's first run when he doubled in the fourth and crossed the plate on Judnich's single. That edge lasted until DiMaggio, banging his way out of a slump, slammed his first of two triples and trotted home ahead of Berra's sixth homer of the year in the sixth.

In the eighth, DiMaggio tripled again to start a rally, which appeared destined to fade as Berra and Billy Johnson went out. However, Gordon booted George McQuinn's grounder, DiMaggio scoring and Rizzuto followed with his third homer of the season for a 5-1 lead.

No. 13 Over the Indians

Lopat, who yielded eight hits, now has a lifetime record of 13 and 3 over the Indians.

Stirnweiss (1) of New York forced at second when Manager Boudreau (lying prone) of the Indians, after making a sensational stop of Lindell's hard-hit grounder and while on the ground, tossed to Gordon (4) for the put-out. The New York Times (by Burns)

Boudreau made the outstanding play of the game when he dove to his left for Johnny Lindell's grounder, came up with the ball and forced George Stirnweiss at second in the seventh.

Feller's six-inning tenure saw the Yankees, who walloped him once earlier in the year, fashion six hits and two runs.

The Yankees will play an exhibition game at Binghamton tonight prior to opening at Chicago tomorrow night. . . . Although rain held the crowd down, the series attracted 181,151, said to be a record for a series of four games.

"What am I doing wrong?" DiMaggio asked before the game, puzzled over his recent inability to hit consistently. Following his two eye-opening three-baggers, the answer has to be "nothing."

The box score:

CLEVELAND (A.)	ab.	r.	h.	po.	a.	e.
Kennedy, rf.	5	0	0	2	0	0
Clark, lf.	5	0	2	2	0	0
B'dreau, ss.	4	0	1	2	2	0
cTucker	0	0	0	0	0	0
Rob'son, 1b.	5	0	1	5	1	0
Gordon, 2b.	3	1	2	5	2	1
Keltner, 3b.	4	0	1	1	1	0
Judnich, cf.	3	1	1	0	0	0
Hegan, c.	4	1	2	7	0	0
Feller, p.	2	0	0	0	0	0
aBerardino	1	0	0	0	0	0
Bearden, p.	0	0	0	0	0	0
bTipton	1	0	0	0	0	0
Total	37	3	10	24	6	1

NEW YORK (A.)	ab.	r.	h.	po.	a.	e.
St'weiss, 2b.	3	0	1	5	2	0
Henrich, rf.	3	0	0	2	0	0
Lindell, lf.	4	0	1	5	1	0
DiM'gio, cf.	4	2	2	3	0	0
Berra, c.	4	1	1	2	0	1
Johnson, 3b.	4	0	0	1	1	1
McQuinn, 1b	4	1	1	7	0	0
Rizzuto, ss.	4	1	2	2	4	0
Lopat, p.	3	0	0	0	0	0
Page, p.	0	0	0	0	0	0
Total	33	5	8	27	8	2

aFlied out for Feller in seventh.
bGrounded out for Bearden in ninth.
cRan for Boudreau in ninth.

Cleveland ....000 100 002—3
New York ....000 002 03.—5

Runs batted in—Judnich, Berra 2, Rizzuto 2, Hegan 2.

Two-base hits—Robinson, Gordon. Three-base hits—DiMaggio 2. Home runs—Berra, Rizzuto, Hegan. Left on bases—Cleveland 10, New York 7. Bases on balls—Off Lopat 3, Feller 2, Bearden 1. Struck out—By Feller 4, Lopat 1, Bearden 1, Page 1. Hits—Off Feller 6 in 6 innings, Bearden 2 in 2, Lopat 10 in 8 2-3, Page 0 in 1-3. Winning pitcher—Lopat. Losing pitcher—Feller. Umpires—Hubbard, Paparella and McGowan. Time of game—2:21. Attendance—49,641 paid.

RESUME PRO TENNIS PLAY

All Seeded Stars to See Action Today at Forest Hills

Play will resume in the national professional tennis championship at Forest Hills today after the interruption of yesterday's rain.

To make up for the loss of time, an extra heavy program has been arranged for this afternoon. Unless more bad weather is encountered, the championships will end Sunday, as scheduled.

Every one of the seeded players will be seen in action today on the revised card. They include defending champion Robert Riggs, John Kramer, Donald Budge, Frank Kovacs, Welby Van Horn, Dinny Pails of Australia, Francisco Segurae of Ecuador, Pierre Pellizza of France, Carl Earn, Wayne Sabin, Elwood Cooke, John Nogrady, Robert Stubbs, Robert Harman, Jack March and Jerry Adler.

Sports of the Times

By ARTHUR DALEY

Yankee Stadium Jubilee

NOSTALGIA dripped all over the Yankee Stadium yesterday in the wake of weeping skies as an amazing crowd of 49,641 turned out to celebrate the twenty-fifth anniversary of the opening of the House That Ruth Built and to welcome back the heroes of the 1923 team which brought the first world championship to the Bronx Bombers. In impressively sentimental ceremonies Babe Ruth's famed No. 3 was permanently retired and his uniform formally presented to the baseball shrine at Cooperstown as eyes grew moist and fans choked up at the touching scene.

But all was not pathos. The affair was like the weather, slightly dampish in the beginning and then drier and brighter. The game between the '23 heroes and later day stars, a rugged two-inning affair, was delightfully hilarious despite creaking bones and faltering limbs. It had Abner Doubleday spinning in his grave, the major spin coming when the Old-Timers were generously given four outs in the second frame. They didn't need any of them, either, because they already had won, 2 to 0, the perfect touch.

The Return of Burlesque

They won because the still lean Bob Meusel, who used to hit line drives in the old days, lofted a simple blooper to right center which bounced off Red Rolfe's glove for a hit. At least that's what the official scorer called it, after succumbing to his most generous and gentlemanly instincts.

Despite the presence of Mayor Bill O'Dwyer, burlesque returned to town. Bullet Joe Bush, a first baseman no less, actually caught George Selkirk's bounder and outraced—that's what it says here—Twink to the bag. He promptly bowled over Umpire Bill McGowan, somersaulted most inelegantly and landed kerplunk in a pool of casual water on the seat of his pants.

Believe it or not there was a force play at second when Oscar Roettger dribbled one at Mark Koenig, who fumbled it, recovered and threw to Rolfe at second. Thereupon the Redhead also fumbled, recovered and stepped on the bag. Later on Rolfe, the cad, pulled the hidden ball play on Waite Hoyt. But it was fun while it lasted and the crowd enjoyed it hugely.

A Sockdolager

However, the big kick of the pre-game proceedings was the sock wallop the spectators received from seeing in the flesh the almost legendary figures of yesteryear. They cheered vociferously as each was introduced, most of them grayer or rounder, or both, than they used to be. But the real climax came when the two men who made the Yankees what they are today, Ed Barrow and Babe Ruth, came ambling from opposite dugouts to embrace unashamedly at home plate.

That was a thrill which made the fans forget the rain, the lowering skies and the damp discomfort of a raw, unpleasant day. They had to swallow hard then, engulfed as they were in a wave of emotion. Thrilling, too, was the tender message the band played, "Auld Lang Syne." Should old acquaintance be forgot? Never. Not when they are such stalwarts as these. The twenty pennants which bedecked the Stadium facade eloquently bespoke the dynasty they created.

There was a reverent hush when the Bambino, no longer the hulking, dynamic and domineering figure he once was, strode hesitatingly to the microphone and spoke in his muted and strangely croaking voice. He told the fans in sincere and simple words how wonderful the occasion was for him and of his pride in having hit the first home run ever struck at the Stadium.

Central Figure

It had been a tiring day for the ailing Sultan of Swat. First of all, it was an emotional drain on him to greet his old buddies in the dressing room. To them he still was the king. Obsequiously they approached him for his autograph. That was something to see, these case-hardened old companions getting the signature of their pal and idol. But he was the central figure of the day. Without him it would have been empty.

It was a physical drain on him, too. He sat in the dank, chilling runway behind the dugout for a quarter of an hour, waiting for the drizzle to halt. A topcoat was thrown across his once sweeping shoulders and buttoned around his tender throat. He smiled wanly as the merry Hoyt entertained Bob Meusel, Wally Pipp and some of the other Old-Timers with his reminiscences.

"They took a good many years to retire your number, Babe," he remarked with a chuckle. "They retired mine in 1930—damn quick, too. And without notice, too."

The Babe grinned. He had grinned earlier in the dressing room at the irrepressible Lefty Gomez, who was going around searching for Johnny Murphy, his old relief partner. "I'm gonna be the starting pitcher," he was moaning. "Where's Murphy?" he rushed around frantically, always the clown.

Lou Boudreau sneaked in, boy-like, to greet the Babe. But his eyes popped as they lit on Joe Gordon in a Yankee uniform once more. "Hey, Gordon," he howled in mock dismay. "How did you get away from us?"

The Gomez Secret

Gordon laughed at him. But he seemed suspiciously happy to be wearing a Yankee uniform again as Hoyt remarked from the very bottom of his heart: "Once a Yankee always a Yankee." He said it proudly, too.

It often has been said that there is no place in baseball for sentiment. But it poured into the Stadium yesterday with flood force and it swept everyone before its path. The spectators loved every minute of it, too. At least the Yankees proved that there is a place for sentiment and it's a cinch that they have no copyright on the idea.

As Stars of Yesteryear and Present Gathered to Observe Silver Anniversary of the Yankee Stadium

Members of 1923 Yankees. Left to right: Front—Sam Jones, Wally Schang, Carl Mays, Whitey Witt, Fred Hofmann, Mike McNally. Rear: Hinkey Haines, Waite Hoyt, George Pipgras, Joe Bush, Oscar Roettger, Babe Ruth, Joe Dugan, Bob Meusel, Wally Pipp, Elmer Smith.

DIETRICH SEEKS RELEASE

Athletics Agree to Request of Veteran Moundsman

PHILADELPHIA, June 13 (AP)—Bill Dietrich, 38-year-old dean of active American League pitchers, demanded his unconditional releas from the Athletics today, and Connie Mack agreed to give it to him as soon as other clubs have had a chance to waive.

"He was very nice about it," said Dietrich, who was not in uniform as the Athletics concluded a four-game series with the St. Louis Browns.

"I am heart-broken at leaving the A's, the best club I was ever with," Dietrich said. "I felt that I could help the club, but I have pitched only 15 1/3 innings this year, and have started only two games, one against Cleveland and the other against the White Sox.

Dietrich spent more than ten seasons with Chicago. Prior to that he pitched for Washington and the Athletics.

The Athletics signed him again as a free agent last year after he was released by the White Sox.

DRIVER INJURED FATALLY

Shackleford Crashes in Auto Race on Dayton Speedway

DAYTON, Ohio, June 13 (AP)—John Shackleford Jr., 34, of Dayton, was injured fatally today in the 20-lap A. A. A.-sanctioned big car race at Dayton Speedway.

Shackleford, a 12-year racing veteran, was running second behind the national champion, Ted Horn, Paterson, N. J., on the third lap when his car skidded on the south turn, tore out 30 feet of the retaining fence, flipped over the wall and rolled down an embankment. He died four hours later in St. Elizabeth Hospital.

25 Years of Glorious Deeds in Stadium Revived By Babe Ruth and Host of Other Yankee Stars

Team of 1923 Players Downs Aces of Later Years, 2-0, in Two-Inning Exhibition

They rolled back the years yesterday at the Stadium and in the all-too-brief period of ninety minutes revived diamond glories of a quarter-century.

Babe Ruth and his Yankee mates who opened the park in 1923, many who joined the club later and the fans—then and now—who helped support it, all took part in the celebration that was designated "Silver Anniversary Day."

From California, Oregon, Missouri, Arkansas, Oklahoma, Michigan and other sections of the country they came to make this one of the most memorable afternoons in New York baseball history. Bob Shawkey, who pitched and won the first contest ever played at the Stadium; Sad Sam Jones, Carl Mays, Whitey Witt, Jumping Joe Dugan, Elmer Smith, Bob Meusel—never-to-be-forgotten names—were presented to the fans.

Host of Old-Time Aces

There were others. Wally Schang, Mike McNally, Fred Hofmann, Bullet Joe Bush, Wally Pipp, Oscar Roettger, Hinkey Haines and George Pipgras. Add to these the Yankees of later years—Tom Zachary, Mark Koenig, Sammy Byrd, Bill Dickey, Lefty Gomez, George Selkirk, Pat Collins, Joey Sewell, Jake Powell, Red Rolfe, Bump Hadley, Myril Hoag, Johnny Allen, Bud Metheny, Wilcy Moore and Spud Chandler, along with the still active Hank Borowy, Ernie Bonham, Joe Gordon and Joe DiMaggio.

Millions of dollars—a rough estimate would be $10,000,000—couldn't have purchased all these great athletes at their peaks. And as Mel Allen, the master of ceremonies, recounted the deeds of each, "the House that Ruth Built" rang with the cheers of 49,641 men, women and children who, undaunted by the wretched weather, turned out to welcome them to riches and glory.

Ed Barrow, the executive genius who guided the club, now an octogenarian, was accorded an ovation, as was every one introduced by Allen. However, the most vociferous applause was, as expected, reserved for the immortal Ruth. He was the man whose prowess, personality and reputation built the Yankee Stadium, the man who revolutionized the national pastime with his mighty home runs, the man whom everyone loved—then and now.

Misty-eyed, the fans stood and cheered for many minutes as the one-time Sultan of Swat came on the field carrying a bat. He was wearing his old Yankee uniform with No. 3 on the back. He was wearing it for the last time, because it was formally and permanently retired in a ceremony at home-plate before the 1923 Yankees met and defeated, 2—0, the later Yankees in a two-inning game that preceded the regular New York-Cleveland encounter.

Going to Cooperstown

Never again will No. 3 adorn the back of a Yankee. The Babe's uniform was retired officially by Will Harridge, president of the American League, and accepted by Paul S. Kerr, secretary of Baseball Hall of Fame and Museum at Cooperstown, N. Y. Hereafter, that uniform will be on display at the diamond shrine, along with other Ruth mementos.

There were speeches by Harridge, Kerr, Mayor O'Dwyer, who tossed out the same ball that the late Gov. Al Smith used when he did the honors at the 1923 opening, and Owner Dan Topping, who handed commemorative watches to Ruth and Barrow. Wreaths were placed on the Lou Gehrig, Jacob Ruppert and Miller Huggins memorials in center field, and Miss Lucille Manners led the crowd in singing Auld Lang Syne.

But the speech that tugged at the hearts of everyone was the one delivered by the Babe. In a raspy voice Ruth told the assemblage how happy he was to be present, how proud he is to have been the first man to have hit a homer in the Stadium and how glad he was to be with his old pals again.

Babe's No. 3 Is Retired for All Time—Uniform Will Go to Cooperstown

Even as you and I, the veteran ball players, whom the years have treated lightly, wanted and got Ruth's autograph. Baseballs, programs, scraps of paper and other items were handed to the Babe and he obliged everyone. Banners proclaiming every championship annexed by the Yankees—fifteen pennants and eleven world series—were draped around the Stadium. Every major newsreel company recorded the events, which also were broadcast and televised. It was indeed a gala occasion, with Mrs. Eleanor Gehrig, Mrs. Ruth, Mrs. Barrow, Mrs. John McGraw and Arthur Huggins, Miller's brother, in attendance.

The abbreviated contest went to the '23 Yankees, managed by Ruth, who was assisted by Chuck Dressen, when Meusel drove home Dugan and Pipp with a single. It wasn't much of a hit, a blooper that Rolfe, playing second base, failed to hold, but the fans, rooting for Ruth and the old, old-timers, greeted it with tremendous applause.

Surprisingly agile for their ages, the "old" fellows did not do badly at all, even if the rules were slightly disregarded when the victors sneaked by with four outs and a jumbled batting order in the second. There were laughs for all, such as when Bush, fielding Selkirk's grounder to first, fumbled, recovered and then beat the runner to the bag, dumping Umpire Bill McGowan in the mud. Dickey, hit by a pitched ball, was forced to bat again and he hoisted a fly to center.

A great day it was, all around. Even old Jupiter Pluvius relented and the rain stopped. The Yankee front-office, at an expense of approximately $25,000, spared nothing to assure its success.

And when it was all over, the Yankees of yesteryear saw the Yankees of today beat Bob Feller, 5—3, in a thriller. Nothing else would have sufficed.

The New York Times

Babe Ruth

YANK ALL STARS

	ab.	r.	h.	po.	a.	e.
Sewell, 3b	1	0	0	0	0	0
Borowy, 3b	0	0	0	0	0	0
Bonham, 3b	0	0	0	0	0	0
Rolfe, 2b	1	0	0	2	0	0
Hoag, rf	1	0	0	1	0	0
Selkirk, 1b	1	0	0	2	0	0
Byrd, cf	1	0	0	0	0	0
Dickey, c	1	0	0	2	0	0
Koenig, ss	0	0	0	0	1	1
Powell, lf	0	0	0	0	0	0
Gomez, p	0	0	0	0	0	0
Zachary, p	0	0	0	0	0	0
Moore, p	0	0	0	0	0	0
Allen, p	0	0	0	0	0	0
Hadley, p	0	0	0	0	0	0
Chandler, p	0	0	0	0	0	0
Total	6	0	0	*7	1	1

1923 YANK CHAMPS

	ab.	r.	h.	po.	a.	e.
Witt, cf	1	0	0	0	0	0
Haines, cf	0	0	0	1	0	0
Dugan, 3b	0	1	0	0	0	0
Jones, 3b	0	0	0	0	0	0
Pipp, 1b	0	1	0	2	0	0
Bush, 1b	0	0	0	1	0	0
Smith, rf	1	0	0	0	0	0
Pipgras, rf	0	0	0	0	0	0
Meusel, lf	1	0	1	0	0	0
Roettger, ss	1	0	0	0	0	0
Mays, p	0	0	0	0	0	0
McN'y, 2b.-s	1	0	0	0	0	0
aSchang, c	1	0	0	1	0	0
Hoyt, 2b	1	0	0	0	0	0
Shawkey, p	0	0	0	0	1	0
Hofmann, c	1	0	0	1	0	0
Total	8	2	1	6	1	0

*Four outs allowed in 1923 team's second inning.
aCourtesy batter for Haines in second.

Yankee All Stars	0	0—0
1923 Champions	2	0—2

(Called by agreement)

Runs batted in—Meusel 2.

Left on bases—Yankee All Stars 0, 1923 Champions 1. Bases on balls—Off Zachary 1, Moore 1. Struck out—By Shawkey 1, Gomez 1, Mays 1, Hadley 1. Hits—Off Shawkey 0 in 1 inning, Mays 0 in 1, Gomez 0 in 1-3, Zachary 0 in 0 (one batter), Moore 0 in 0 (one batter), Allen 1 in 2, Hadley 0 in 1-3, Chandler 0 in 1. Winning pitcher—Shawkey. Losing pitcher—Zachary.

TUERO GAINS NET HONORS

Beats Larned After Five Sets for Southern Crown

MEMPHIS, Tenn., June 13 (AP)—Tulane's Jack Tuero took the Southern amateur tennis title today by defeating National Intercollegiate Champion Gardner Larned of Chicago, 5—7, 6—3, 3—6, 6—3, 6—2.

Top-seeded Tuero's brilliant defense won the championship he missed last year by losing to Frankie Parker in the final at New Orleans. He won the fifth set from Larned with five straight close games.

"All the News That's Fit to Print"

The New York Times.

LATE CITY EDITION
Sunny and cooler today. Mild followed by showers tomorrow.
Temperature Range Today—Max.,80; Min.,70
Temperature Yesterday—Max.,87; Min.,69

Copyright, 1948, by The New York Times Company.

VOL. XCVII..No. 33,026. Entered as Second-Class Matter, Postoffice, New York, N. Y. NEW YORK, SATURDAY, JUNE 26, 1948. Times Square, New York 18, N. Y. Telephone LAckawanna 4-1000 THREE CENTS

WARREN WINS 2D PLACE ON TICKET; PLEDGES A 'CRUSADE' WITH DEWEY; SLATED TO RECAST U. S. BUREAUS

UNANIMOUS CHOICE

Californian Nominated by Acclamation After Dewey Selects Him

GETS CONVENTION OVATION

A Role in Cabinet and 'Full Partnership' in Work of Administration Pledged

By WILLIAM S. WHITE
Special to The New York Times.

PHILADELPHIA, June 25—Gov. Earl Warren of California was nominated by acclamation today as the Republican candidate for Vice President of the United States.

He will stand with Gov. Thomas E. Dewey of New York, the Presidential nominee, in the November election.

Mr. Warren was chosen without contest and without a roll-call after the name of Harold E. Stassen of Minnesota had been provisionally offered by Arizona and then withdrawn.

The Republican party thus closed its twenty-fourth national convention here with a ticket of two Governors—the one from the Atlantic and the other from the Pacific—neither of whom has had any connection with the controversial record of the Eightieth Congress.

Mr. Warren's nomination by the weary convention required precisely thirty-two minutes. He appeared soon afterward in the hall, where the Far Western delegations led all the others in giving him a lusty, neighborly sort of greeting. He delivered a short, impromptu speech.

"I accept the nomination," he told the delegates with a smile, "before you change your mind."

Pledges 'A Great Crusade'

Gravely then he pledged himself "in all humility" to give to Mr. Dewey "the very best that I have and every bit of loyalty that is in my make-up."

The campaign in the fall, he declared, would be "a great crusade for the return of our Government to Republican principles."

Governor Warren was the first choice of Governor Dewey for the Vice-Presidential designation, and his nomination pleased the internationalist wing of the party, whose leaders had been strongly opposed to Representative Charles A. Halleck of Indiana.

The acceptance of the nomination by Governor Warren was made, it was learned, with reservations. Reports of an early morning talk between the Californian and Mr. Dewey varied, but on one point there was agreement. Governor Warren was represented as saying he would take the nomination if, in the event of his election, he would not be only "a gavel-pounder in the Senate."

Governor Dewey took cognizance of this later as he discussed the Vice-Presidency with reporters.

"There is a story," he said, "that I intend to make an historical change in the position of Vice President and transform it into a working job.

Senate Duties Would Be Eased

"I should most earnestly hope that it would be possible, and I believe it will be entirely feasible, to take advantage of Governor Warren's superb talents in the colossal job of reorganizing the national Government and bringing some order out of the chaos.

"I should hope that he could be relieved substantially of his duties of presiding over the Senate in which the members could help and that Governor Warren would be able to give a large amount of time to administrative work of the Government and accept a full partnership in this tremendous task in these difficult times."

Mr. Dewey added that he "definitely" would want the Vice President to participate in Cabinet deliberations.

Mr. Halleck, the Republican floor leader of the House of Representatives, was reported to have been "plenty" because he had led the Indiana delegation into the Dewey camp when Governor Dewey was set to win his own great victory

Continued on Page 2, Column 7

THE REPUBLICAN TICKET FOR '48

Gov. Earl Warren and Gov. Thomas E. Dewey
The New York Times (by Tenney)

BERLIN SIEGE ON AS SOVIET BLOCKS FOOD

CITY SUPPLY SHORT

British Report Stocks In West Lower Than Previous Estimates

RUSSIANS HALT BARGES

Clay Declares Three-Zone Regime Is Near—London Cabinet Discusses Issue

By DREW MIDDLETON
Special to The New York Times.

BERLIN, June 25—About 2,250,000 Germans in the Western sectors of Berlin came face to face with the grim specter of starvation today as the siege of those sectors began in earnest.

The Soviet Military Administration banned all food shipments from the Soviet-controlled areas into Berlin as part of its calculated policy of starving the people of the Western sectors into the acceptance of the Communist demand for the withdrawal of the Western powers.

[In Frankfort on the Main, Gen. Lucius D. Clay, United States Military Governor, said the establishment of a Western tripartite military administration to supervise the establishment of a Western German Government was imminent. In London the British Cabinet considered moves to offset the Soviet curbs on supplies to Western Berlin.]

Although they see dark days ahead, the Berliners remained calm. Those in the Western sectors changed their marks for the new Deutsche mark of the Western powers with a minimum of disturbance.

Straightaway a brisk black Bourse developed in which one Deutsche mark was sold for up to thirty of the new Russian-sponsored marks, which the Germans call "tapetengeld," or wall paper money.

Clay and Robertson Meet

Although Generals Clay and Sir Brian Robertson, British Military Governor, conferred this afternoon, no announcement of policy toward the Russian siege was made after their conference.

The desperate situation in which the strategy of starvation is being exerted ruthlessly by the Russians for political ends, has been lifted out of the hands of the Military Governors to Washington, London and Paris.

According to official figures sent to London yesterday the present food situation in the Western sectors is more serious than has been admitted.

These figures were based on the food supplies available for all of Berlin June 15. Since then there has been very little addition to the existing stocks because of the increasing severity of the Soviet blockade and, of course, constant consumption.

It is estimated that the following food stocks are on hand today for all Berlin, including the Soviet sector: Seventeen days' supply of bread grains and flour, thirty-two days' supply of cereals, forty-eight days' supply of fats, twenty-five days' supply of meat and fish, forty-two days' supply of potatoes and twenty-six days' supply of skimmed and dried milk.

Foodstuff Stores Scattered

These foodstuffs are scattered throughout the city in warehouses. Most of those containing bread grains and flour stocks are in the Soviet sector and henceforth the stocks will not be available to the Western sectors.

The commandants of the three Western sectors have replied to the Soviet ban by forbidding the shipment of any food from their sectors into the Russian sector. Since the people of the Soviet sector can be supplied by the entire Soviet zone, the order, although impressive in tone, means little.

A more telling blow at the economy of the Soviet zone was leveled by the bipartite Economic Commission of the United States and British zones in Frankfort on the Main, which suspended "indefinitely" the shipment of all classes of goods from coal to fountain pens into the Soviet zone. This embargo was added to that

Continued on Page 6, Column 2

JOE LOUIS RALLIES TO STOP WALCOTT IN ELEVENTH ROUND

Trailing on Points, Champion Turns Tide With a Right to Jaw and Keeps Crown

42,667 AT THE STADIUM

Jeer Early in Bout Because of Lack of Action—Bomber Says He Is Retiring

By JAMES P. DAWSON

Because he has the punch that has made him one of the greatest heavyweights ever to hold the title, Joe Louis, the ring's Brown Bomber, still is the world champion.

He knocked out Jersey Joe Walcott of Camden, the challenger for the title, in the eleventh round of an ordinary championship battle last night in the Yankee Stadium, and plucked glorious, spectacular victory from threatened defeat.

Trailing the 34-year-old challenger through ten rounds of fighting which more than once drew jeers from the crowd of 42,667, Louis turned the tide of battle with one punch. It was a right to the jaw which shook Walcott to his toes. It was delivered as the shifty challenger was boxing in the confusing style that had baffled Louis last December and was baffling him again before a great crowd which paid $841,739 for the spectacle.

The blow provided the opening which Louis had sought from the start. The champion lost no time pressing his advantage. A savage, furious flurry of short-arm lefts and rights drilled against the head of Walcott as the challenger backed to the ropes and sought to throw up a defense of crossed arms.

One Right—and It's All Over

Louis' punches drilled home to the head, however, and they jarred. A right to the jaw shot through a brief opening, and the fight was over.

Walcott pitched forward on his face, rolled over on his back, lay with arms outstretched as the count was tolled over him by Referee Frank Fullam. He struggled to his knees at "seven," but was bewildered, befuddled. He knelt there apparently listening to the count, but probably hearing it not at all.

At "ten" he was struggling to get erect. But he was beyond the effort. He didn't know where he was, though he made as if he would resume fighting.

Referee Fullam clasped the beaten Walcott in his arms and guided him to his corner, knocked out after 2 minutes 56 seconds of the eleventh round.

Doctor Leaps Into Ring

Dr. Vincent A. Nardiello jumped through the ropes to examine the beaten veteran. His examination apparently showed Walcott had suffered no ill effects from the brief ordeal which brought about his downfall just when it appeared he was on the road to the heavyweight championship of the world.

Walcott was able to step to ring-center and clasp the hand of his conqueror and pose with Louis in wordless acknowledgment of the master's superiority. He was able, too, to talk into a radio microphone, and it was Walcott who led the procession from the ring when the excitement had subsided.

After the battle Walcott was critical of Referee Fullam. He

Continued on Page 11, Column 1

Two U. S. Educators Detained by Soviet

By the Associated Press.

BERLIN, June 25—Dr. Lester K. Ade, former State Superintendent of Education in Pennsylvania, was arrested by the Russians today and held five hours before being released.

He said his companion, Dr. Lucile Allard, Coordinator of Elementary Education in Garden City, L. I. also had been detained.

Dr. Ade said the Russians had asked them "dozens and dozens" of questions, including one about Henry A. Wallace's chances for election.

Five other Americans, including members of a constabulary patrol, also were detained. United States officials reported.

PRESIDENT SCORES DP BILL, BUT SIGNS

Calls It Anti-Semitic Mockery and Says He Approves Only for Sake of Those Aided

Text of President Truman's statement is on Page 7.

By ANTHONY LEVIERO
Special to The New York Times.

WASHINGTON, June 25—The displaced persons bill to admit 205,000 refugees into this country became law this afternoon, but in signing it President Truman denounced the measure as a mockery.

In a long statement filled with scathing denunciations of the compromise measure, passed in the hectic closing hours of the session, the Chief Executive declared he would have vetoed the bill if Congress had not adjourned.

Mr. Truman said the bill was anti-Semitic and he also asserted that it would exclude some Catholics who had fled into the American zone of Germany as anti-Communist refugees.

In explanation of why he had signed the bill so reluctantly, Mr. Truman said he did not wish to penalize its beneficiaries and that he did so with the hope that Congress would rectify its "injustices" as soon as possible.

Whether the bill was "worse than no bill at all" was a hairline question which Mr. Truman said he had decided in favor of the 200,000 persons who would be admitted in the next two years, along with 3,000 orphans and 2,000 recent refugees from the Communist coup in Czechoslovakia.

Against these three points of merit, the only ones he conceded in the bill, Mr. Truman listed "numerous" defects which he said had resulted from a compromise that combined "the worst features of both the Senate and House bills."

"If the Congress were still in session," Mr. Truman said, "I would return this bill without my approval and urge that a fairer,

Continued on Page 7, Column 3

$250,000 Is Hunted In Wreck of Plane

By The United Press.

MT. CARMEL, Pa., June 25—Authorities were searching today for an air-express package containing a reported $250,000 in small-denomination currency believed jettisoned before the crash of the United Airlines DC-6 near here June 17 in which forty-three persons were killed.

An Army helicopter being used in the search made a forced landing in an open field four miles north of here this morning. The occupants were not injured.

Discovery of a parcel of spun glass intact some distance from the crash scene gave strength to the theory that part of the cargo was dropped from the four-engined mainliner to reduce its weight.

A postal authority said the parcel weighed 240 pounds and contained bills in one, five and ten dollar denominations.

DEWEY GIVES PLANS

A Major Goal Will Be to Help China Fight Communists, He Says

SCORES 'NIGGARDLY' AID

He Says 'Conference' Plan, Used to Pick Warren, Would Be Employed With Congress

By LEO EGAN
Special to The New York Times.

PHILADELPHIA, June 25—In his first press interview since his nomination, Gov. Thomas E. Dewey said today that one of the cardinal principles of his administration, if elected, would be to help China combat Communist influences within its borders.

Mr. Dewey declared his complete approval of the platform adopted at the Republican National Convention, which ended today, and he described the procedure by which Gov. Earl Warren of California had been chosen as the candidate for Vice President.

Discussing China, Mr. Dewey renewed an accusation he made last year that the Truman Administration had been niggardly in financial aid for China. To preserve a free China against the Communists, the United States, he said, should provide "military advisers, the kind of material the Chinese need and far greater financial assistance."

He added that his general attitude toward China today was the same as it was last December, when he made a public appeal for Marshall Plan assistance to help it achieve stability and peace.

Opposes Personal Diplomacy

One reporter asked the Presidential candidate if he could handle Stalin. His answer was that he thought Russo-American relations would improve if handled through regular diplomatic channels.

"I am opposed to personal diplomacy, which always fails," he added. This did not mean, he has-

Continued on Page 3, Column 6

LEWIS AND OWNERS SIGN NEW CONTRACT

UMW Victory Preserves the Union-Shop Clause, Causing Bolt by 'Captive' Companies

By LOUIS STARK
Special to The New York Times.

WASHINGTON, June 25—John L. Lewis and the Commercial Coal Operators today signed a one-year agreement on the last effective working day of the 1947 contract. While the contract technically expires on June 30, the ten-day vacation period at midnight tonight ushered in a cessation of coal digging until July 5.

When the terms of the contract were made public shortly after 2 P. M. today, it was apparent that the magnitude of the United Mine Workers' victory was even greater than had appeared yesterday when the chief terms leaked out.

Despite a last-minute bolt by the spokesman for the "captive" mine operators, Mr. Lewis won the general operators to a renewal of

Continued on Page 8, Column 6

Truman Reported Confident His Chances Are Improved

By JOHN D. MORRIS
Special to The New York Times.

WASHINGTON, June 25—President Truman believes the Republicans' nomination of Gov. Thomas E. Dewey improved Democratic chances of retaining the Presidency in the November elections, White House callers reported today. He was represented as being "definitely encouraged about the whole political situation."

His feeling, the visitors indicated, stemmed partly from the opinion that Mr. Dewey was very much of a conservative and consequently would provide an excellent target for one of the President's favorite gibes at the Republicans—that they represented special interests while the Democrats were more solicitous of the common man.

Another consideration in Mr. Truman's appraisal of the nomination was said to be the convention's failure to choose Senator Arthur H. Vandenberg of Michigan. Many Democratic strategists feel he would have been the most dangerous opponent because of his leadership in the bipartisan foreign policy.

Reports of President Truman's reaction to Mr. Dewey's nomination came principally from Senator James E. Murray of Montana and Representative Laurie C. Battle of Alabama, Democrats, after White House visits. The Senator said Mr. Truman felt that the 1948 Republican platform was "nothing but the reiteration of promises they have failed to keep in the past."

Word that the President was "definitely encouraged" was given to reporters by Representative Battle. He also hinted at the possibility of healing the split between the President and Southern Democrats over Mr. Truman's espousal

Continued on Page 2, Column 5

WARREN EXPLAINS HIS CHANGE OF MIND

Says Dewey's Request, Status in Cabinet Swayed Him to Seek the Nomination

Governor Warren's speech of acceptance appears on Page 3.

By CLAYTON KNOWLES
Special to The New York Times.

PHILADELPHIA, June 25—Gov. Earl Warren of California declared today that Gov. Thomas E. Dewey's proposal to have the Vice President act as an assistant President with Cabinet status was a major factor in his decision to accept second place on the Republican ticket.

The Californian had stated emphatically as late as a few days before the convention started that he would not run for the Vice Presidency and his sudden change of plan baffled many, even within the convention itself.

Public bewilderment on the point was the greater because Mr. Warren had turned down the Vice Presidential nomination in 1944 when he would have had the same running mate.

Peppered with questions on this

Continued on Page 3, Column 2

World News Summarized

SATURDAY, JUNE 26, 1948

Governor Earl Warren of California will be the Republican candidate for Vice President. He was nominated by acclamation to be Governor Dewey's running mate at the closing session of the Republican National Convention yesterday. Mr. Warren pledged a campaign that would be "a great crusade for the return of our Government to Republican principles." [1:8.] An offer by Governor Dewey to have the Vice President as an assistant President with Cabinet status was cited as a major factor in persuading Mr. Warren to accept the nomination. [1:7.]

Mr. Dewey voiced approval of the Republican party platform and declared that, if elected, he would give more ample support to China to combat communism within its borders. [1:5.]

President Truman was pictured by White House callers as "definitely encouraged about the whole political situation" and convinced that Governor Dewey's nomination had increased Democratic chances of retaining control of the White House. [1:6.]

The Chief Executive reluctantly signed the compromise bill to admit 205,000 refugees into this country. He criticized the measure as anti-Semitic and anti-Catholic. [1:2.]

A new one-year agreement signed by John L. Lewis and soft-coal operators gave the miners a $1-a-day wage increase and an additional 10 cents a ton, or about $30,000,000 annually, for their welfare fund. [1:4.]

The 2,250,000 inhabitants of the Berlin zones occupied by the Western powers remained calm despite the prospect of a sharp curtailment of their food supplies as Soviet authorities halted all food shipments into the areas. [1:1.] General Clay announced the imminent organization of a tripartite military government group to serve as a control agency over the projected Western German Government. [6:6.]

The proposals for the unification of Germany advanced at the Warsaw conference of eight Eastern European Foreign Ministers provided no basis for renewed talks by the major powers, in the opinion of diplomatic representatives of the Western powers in the Polish capital. These diplomats believed Moscow would form an East Germany Government after these proposals had been rejected by the Western powers. Washington received the Warsaw program with reserve. [7:1.]

The return of Italian Communist leaders from the Warsaw meeting to Rome coincided with a new outbreak of strikes in northern Italy. [8:3.]

The United Nations withdrew its representatives from Egyptian-controlled territory in Palestine after two violations of the truce agreement. The Egyptians strafed a United Nations plane and used force to bar the passage of an Israeli food convoy through their positions in the Negeb. A United Nations spokesman indicated that the convoy was free to fight its way through if it so chose. [1:2-3.]

Count Bernadotte, United Nations Mediator, reported the two Egyptian infractions to the Security Council. [5:1.]

The Security Council ignored Soviet protests as it refused to reopen debate on Generalissimo Franco's regime in Spain. [4:6-7.]

A new sharp slump in the value of Chinese currency has followed reverses suffered by the Nanking Government in its civil war with the Communists. [7:5.]

Joe Louis retained his world heavyweight championship when he knocked out Joe Walcott in the eleventh round. [1:3.]

Egyptians Strafe U. N. Aircraft, Block Israeli Convoy to Colonies

By GENE CURRIVAN
Special to The New York Times.

TEL AVIV, Israel, June 25—The Egyptians violated the truce on two counts today by strafing a United Nations plane and refusing by force to permit an Israeli convoy to pass through their positions to colonies in the Negeb as agreed under the truce terms. The plane incident was said to have occurred in the vicinity of Negba.

As a result of these alleged infractions the United Nations has withdrawn all its representatives from Egyptian-controlled territory in Palestine and has informed the Egyptian Government that the truce was violated.

[In Cairo the Egyptian Prime Minister said the pilot of the Egyptian plane had opened fire on the United Nations craft because "he suspected that it was an enemy plane." The Associated Press reported.

[Count Folke Bernadotte, the United Nations mediator, reported to Lake Success that he had "protested vigorously" to the Egyptian Government and demanded an explanation.]

Meanwhile, according to Alexis Ladas, United Nations spokesman, the convoy was free to do as it pleased. United Nations control has been withdrawn and if the Israeli authorities decide that it should fight its way through, there are no legal ties to bind them. He pointed out that there was no general truce break, however.

The Israeli Government announced tonight that it had received the following communication from Col. Paul Bonde of the United Nations:

"The Egyptians have prevented a convoy. By decision of mediator they have therefore broken truce. Israeli forces are free to act against Egyptian forces."

The communiqué added:

"The Provisional Government desires it to be known that the defense army of Israel will exercise

Continued on Page 5, Column 2

Vote-Buying for Valente Charged; Hogan Plans Inquiry in Tammany

By JAMES P. McCAFFREY

District Attorney Frank S. Hogan announced yesterday afternoon that he would investigate reports that three Tammany district leaders had received $1,000 each to vote for Judge Francis L. Valente of General Sessions as the Democratic designee for Surrogate of New York County.

The Criminal Court jurist was designated at a meeting of Tammany Hall's executive committee last Wednesday. He defeated Vincent R. Impellitteri, president of the City Council, who was the choice of Mayor O'Dwyer and Frank J. Sampson, Tammany leader. Judge Valente was a last-minute substitution for his uncle, Justice Louis A. Valente of the Supreme Court, who had drawn the opposition of the Association of the Bar of the City of New York.

Mr. Hogan interrupted a trip to Lake George, N. Y., to make his announcement. The District Attorney was on his way to the annual convention of the New York State District Attorneys convention when he was informed of the reports. He returned to his Manhattan office immediately.

"I have read the account of the alleged bribes and it will be unsparingly investigated up to the hilt," Mr. Hogan said. "I will call anybody and everybody who may have any information with respect to the alleged bribes."

The New York County prosecutor said that the inquiry would be started Monday morning. At that time, he added, a new grand jury would be sworn in.

Judge Valente said last night: "This is Mr. Hogan's job. If he thinks there is anything to investigate, I'm sure he should bring out all the facts."

Meanwhile, the American Labor party, through its New York County secretary, Councilman Eugene P. Connolly, announced that its organization had designated Nathan Dambrot as its candidate

Continued on Page 32, Column 2

Louis, Floored in Third, Rallies to Knock Out Walcott

HARD RIGHT TO JAW TURNS TIDE IN BOUT

Continued From Page 1

arbiter had found it necessary several times to step to the corners of the rivals and urge them to greater action. The crowd more or less demanded this official move by booing and jeering at the lack of excitement.

It was this with which Walcott found fault in his dressing room. He claimed that Referee Fullam's repeated exhortations had veered him from a planned style of fighting and indirectly, at least, brought about his downfall.

The fact remains, however, that Fullam was within his rights in moving as he did. He not only urged Walcott, but he demanded greater action of Louis.

It is not for a referee to concern himself about a fighter's style. His responsibility is to see that the boxers, whether they be champion or run-of-the-mill fighters, provide a clean, honest, interesting contest in accordance with the law and it was in discharge of this responsibility that Referee Fullam acted as he did.

Perhaps the warning did disconcert Walcott, although there was nothing in his actions to support this conclusion. Rather, the inescapable fact was that Louis hit his foe just once with a good right-hand punch and it was the beginning of the end for the veteran Walcott. He was thoroughly knocked out. He was far from disgraced.

He must have known entering the ring that it was a question whether Louis could "tag" him. Every experienced follower of boxing knew or felt this, even those who had picked Walcott to win off his battle of last December.

Bomber Says He's Through

Louis repeated his previously announced intention of retiring from the ring.

"I will definitely retire from boxing," were his words. If he sticks to his determination, and there is no reason at the moment to believe he will not, Louis will join Gene Tunney as a retired undefeated world heavyweight title-holder.

That Louis was on the verge of losing his title was disclosed after the bout, when the official ballots of the referee and the two judges were disclosed.

Two of the officials had Walcott in front. Referee Fullam had Louis in the lead. The arbiter's card showed five rounds for Louis, with only two for Walcott and three even.

Jack O'Sullivan had the bout five rounds for Walcott, four for Louis and one even. Harold Barnes, the other judge, had Walcott in front, six rounds to three, with one even. Of course, on all ballots the voting involved only the ten rounds preceding the eleventh.

The writer had Walcott in front by a margin of six rounds to two, with two even. The first two rounds were adjudged even because there was no action to consider, no points to distribute. There just wasn't any fighting.

Louis won only the eighth and ninth in a brief outburst of determined offensive work when his left jab was his best weapon. All the other rounds went to Walcott.

Louis Down in the Third

Louis had to come off the floor to win this one, as he did last December. He was knocked down in the third round with a right that landed on his cheek-bone, for a count of one. The knockdown was significant only in that it reflected Walcott's power to upset the Bomber with a well-driven punch. Louis was unhurt by the blow, unless his pride suffered further damage for this indignity, which followed the two knockdowns he suffered in the battle of last December.

The champion bounced up from the experience without difficulty, but his sullen, expressionless face was a bit darker, indicating a seething fury.

Louis' rage grew in the fifth when his knees sagged under a right to the jaw in a brief exchange that interrupted a slow process of thinking which seemed to stymie the champion when he appeared to have Walcott propped for a telling blow.

His success with rights emboldened Walcott as the bout progressed and, more frequently than he had done last December, the challenger discarded his retreat to let fly with occasional rights for the jaw. No more landed, however.

Trainer Seamon Protests

Indeed, the action became so annoying to Louis, as Walcott kept out of range and bedeviled the champion with stabbing lefts and body and arm-feinting, that Trainer Mannie Seamon rushed excitedly across the ring at the end of the eighth round to protest to Referee Fullam that Walcott was striking with an open left glove. The referee brusquely ordered Seamon to Louis' corner, ignoring the protest.

As a championship battle it was not much to view. But for the suspense, it must have been taxing on the patience of the onlookers to sit through the ten rounds that preceded the knockout.

It is a testimonial to the drawing power of Louis that the crowd and the gate were so large. Two postponements had put the million-dollar goal beyond reach. It had been set last December when Walcott survived fifteen rounds with Louis, knocked the champion down twice and furnished such a surprising showing many thought him the victim of an injustice in the decision that went, rightfully, to Louis.

In representation, the crowd lived up to heavyweight title tradition. Men and women of prominence were to be seen clustered about the ringside in serried rows that extended back almost to the concrete and steel stands.

Stanton K. Griffis, Ambassador to Poland, headed a list of distinguished guests. Even royalty had been invited to this fistic spectacle, for the Count and Countess Hohenlohe were on the list.

Present, too, were college professors, newspaper and magazine publishers, Senators and Representatives, merchant princes and kings of finance, leaders of the industrial, commercial and professional worlds, stars of the stage, screen and radio, and members of the clergy.

But for the fact that a flood of refunds had followed the second postponement on Thursday night, the receipts would have exceeded the million-dollar goal. More than $100,000 was refunded to disappointed fans yesterday, when tickets were offered also at cut rates in private sales by those who could not adjust their schedules to the two delays the battle suffered.

Louis Provides the Answer

The magnet, of course, was Louis. The curiosity was about whether Walcott could repeat—more impressively—the showing he had made last December. Louis supplied the answer, in typical manner, as he scored his twenty-second knockout triumph in his twenty-fifth defense of the crown he lifted eleven years ago from James J. Braddock in Chicago.

It was unfortunate that the curtain fell on Louis' unparalleled record in a dismal battle. By the same token, it would be unreasonable to expect the 34-year-old Louis, after eleven years of championship activity, to have the verve and fire, the snap and dash, that shone through his earlier career. His reflexes are not what they used to be. The fact that Walcott went as far as he did demonstrated this.

Louis reached a stage where he could not afford the luxury of a careless moment. He had a shifty, elusive target at which to toss punches and a hitter of established ability as well. The Bomber, despite his paralyzing punching power, could not afford to take unnecessary chances.

A Matter of Style

Nor could Walcott expose himself unnecessarily, aware as he was of the punching strength of the champion. Walcott could have regarded Louis as on the wane, as indeed he is. The challenger was confident of his own ability to avoid this punching strength long enough to out-skip Louis in fifteen rounds. He had the style he thought would accomplish this end and therein lay the explanation for the desultory firing of the night: style! Walcott couldn't, and Louis wouldn't—until he was reasonably certain of success.

When the moment came, Louis, with the neatness and dispatch that have always been among his greatest characteristics, with that master's stroke of authority that had made him supreme, demonstrated his reflexes are still in good working order.

Louis looked trim as he stripped for action, contradicting the suspicion that the forty-eight-hour delay would result in excess poundage. He was trained to the minute.

It had been more or less expected that Louis would come charging out of his corner in raging fury, intent only upon avenging the wound to his pride suffered last December. He had followed this course in the return match with Max Schmeling, battering into defeat the German who knocked him out in twelve rounds for the only defeat Louis has suffered.

"I'll finish him quick," was Louis' oft-repeated promise when queried on his battle plans.

Champion Stalks His Man

But there was no blazing opening charge by the champion, no reckless, headlong, do-or-die bid for quick victory.

Instead, Louis stalked his man from the first bell until the opening presented itself for that right-hand punch which turned, and quickly finished, the battle.

He stalked Walcott through rounds in which hardly a blow was struck by either, through periods when the jeers of the crowd must have made him wonder why the people were yelling at him and at Walcott, when they were up there fighting for boxing's richest prize, fighting as best as they could under the circumstances.

Two rounds of wasted effort opened the battle. Hardly a blow was struck as Louis plodded onward and in with his shuffling gait and Walcott retreated, decorously, boxing and feinting and shifting and swaying and sparring—doing everything calculated to befuddle the champion.

Not until the third round did Louis bestir himself. Then he started reaching for Walcott with wicked rights for the jaw. He missed one by almost a foot and another by a scant margin, as Walcott retreated, boxing coolly and cleverly.

It was after missing the second that Louis exposed himself to the right-hand punch that bounced him off the ring canvas. It crashed against his left cheekbone, leaving a pink mark, and Louis went down in his tracks, to arise almost with the same motion.

Walcott displayed an offensive flurry as Louis came erect at "one." The challenger rushed close and sought to land with a more vital punch. But a clinch followed, and in this Walcott had no time to throw punches. He had to protect himself.

Walcott Gets Bolder

Emboldened, Walcott shot a right for the head after sparring for a while in the fourth. He regretted the blow almost immediately. Louis cut loose in a flurry with which he rushed Walcott to the ropes and about the ring, volleying lefts and rights furiously, trying to make an opening for a shot to the jaw. The opening never presented itself, and Louis missed most of his blows.

The lack of coordination which handicaps Louis was manifest in the fifth when, after absorbing Walcott's right to the head in an exchange, and tolerating a succession of light left jabs from the challenger in retreat, Louis pressed in swinging short-arm blows for the head which backed Walcott into a neutral corner.

There, while Louis was contemplating a move, Walcott curled over a right to the jaw and Louis' knees buckled under him. He fell back against the ropes, but before Walcott could follow the advantage the bell ended the round.

More cautious in the sixth, Louis pressed the action carefully in this round and the seventh.

Left jabs earned Louis the eighth and ninth, and what seemed like smiling acknowledgement from Walcott of his foe's marksmanship. Near the end of the ninth, however, Walcott shook the champion with a right to the head and in the tenth Walcott made so bold as to launch four rights for Louis' jaw while the champion stood flustered. Three landed on the head.

But they were the last fearless moves undertaken by Walcott. The challenger was boxing defensively in the eleventh, when Louis shot through a right to the jaw which made Walcott's knees buckle. It was the beginning of the end.

Walcott tried to back to the ropes and sagged as Louis ripped into him, firing solidly with both hands, against Walcott's desperate attempts to throw up a protective curtain of crossed arms. Lefts and rights to the head drilled home and Walcott almost went through the ropes. A right to the jaw toppled Jersey Joe, and from that there was no coming back.

Louis left the ring the conqueror, the champion, looking forward to retirement.

The weights announced for the championship were what the boxers scaled last Wednesday, Louis at 213½ pounds and Walcott at 194¾ pounds.

The Champion Successfully Defending His Title

Walcott on the floor when he was counted out in the eleventh round after Louis scored with a right to the jaw. Fullam is the referee.

LOUIS TELLS WHY HE IS RETIRING

Says That He Has Been 'Around a Long Time, and It's About Time I Quit'

Joe Louis has had his last fight. That is what the Brown Bomber declared in his dressing room immediately after his conquest of Jersey Joe Walcott.

Surrounded almost to the point of suffocation by the customary throng that visits the winner's quarters after an important bout, Louis made his farewell statement several times, and each time with conviction, despite the fact that a good many skeptics in his presence positively refused to believe the news.

"That was my last fight," was Joe's declaration. "I've been around a long time and I think that it's about time I quit. And I'm glad to quit with the title still mine."

In announcing his withdrawal from competition the Brown Bomber took occasion to thank all concerned with the boxing game for the treatment accorded him. The public, officials, opponents and promoters all came in for a word of gratitude from the fighter who ruled the heavyweight division since June 22, 1937, when he stopped Jimmy Braddock in Chicago.

Champion Queried Often

The champion was not allowed to make his farewell announcement without interruption. He was asked often whether he would not extend his career until September, to box either Gus Lesnevich, holder of the world light heavyweight championship, or Ezzard Charles, Cincinnati boxer whom Louis himself has called the most dangerous heavyweight extant.

To all these questions, though, Joe had but one answer, "I'm retiring. Tonight's fight was my last fight."

"All the News That's Fit to Print"

The New York Times.

LATE CITY EDITION
Increasing cloudiness today. Intermittent rain tomorrow.
Temperature Range Today—Max.,63; Min.,48
Temperatures Yesterday—Max.,63; Min.,45
Full U. S. Weather Bureau Report, Page 31

VOL. XCVIII..No. 33,127. Entered as Second-Class Matter, Postoffice, New York, N. Y. NEW YORK, TUESDAY, OCTOBER 5, 1948. Times Square, New York 18, N. Y. Telephone Lackawanna 4-1000 THREE CENTS IN NEW YORK CITY

WEST BARS 4-POWER TALK ON GERMANY; PRESSES U. N. TO STUDY 'PEACE THREAT'; VISHINSKY SAYS RUSSIA WON'T BE 'PARTY'

U. S. PRESENTS CASE

Soviet Plan for Meeting of Foreign Ministers Called 'Maneuver'

BERLIN HELD SOLE ISSUE

Soviet Delegate Evasive as He Is Questioned on Hint of Walkout From Council

Texts of Vishinsky, Jessup, Cadogan talks, Pages 6 and 7.

By THOMAS J. HAMILTON
Special to The New York Times.

PARIS, Oct. 4—The United States, Britain and France brushed aside today a last-minute Soviet proposal that the Council of Foreign Ministers be convened to take up the entire German question.

Dr. Philip C. Jessup, United States representative, was adamant in insisting that this proposal was merely a Soviet "maneuver" and that the United Nations Security Council must take up the question of the Berlin blockade, without going into the German question as a whole, as a "threat to international peace and security."

The opening debate on the Berlin question brought what some delegates interpreted as a threat of a walkout from Andrei Y. Vishinsky of the Soviet Union. The Soviet representative, contending that there was no blockade or threat to peace in Berlin, said that the Sovi.. Union would not "be a party" to the Security Council proceedings.

As he left the chamber Mr. Vishinsky evaded questions by correspondents about the meaning of this statement. His words to the Council today otherwise were moderate in tone as well as brief, and the prevailing belief tonight was that the Soviet Union would stay in the Security Council and fight.

First of Many Meetings

In any case, today's was merely the first of many meetings that the Security Council was scheduled to hold on the German question. Except for the Soviet proposal that the question be referred to the Council of Foreign Ministers, the arguments on each side on the question of placing the Western powers' complaint on the Council's agenda centered, as expected, on Article 107 of the United Nations Charter. The Council adjourned without coming to a vote, and debate is to be resumed at 3 P. M. tomorrow.

[Article 107 states: "Nothing in the present Charter shall invalidate or preclude action, in relation to any state which during the Second World War has been an enemy of any signatory to the present Charter, taken or authorized as a result of that war by the Governments having responsibility for such action."]

The afternoon meeting of the General Assembly's Political Committee was canceled out of deference to the Council meeting. Both Dr. Herbert V. Evatt, president of the Assembly, and Paul-Henri Spaak, head of the Political Committee, were on the stage of the assembly hall when the Council convened at 3:15 P. M., a quarter of an hour late.

Nearly an hour was consumed in a confused discussion of what system or systems of translation should be used, and the Council gave barely two and a quarter hours to the opening discussion of what is expected to prove to be the crucial test of the United Nations.

Austin Disqualifies Self

Warren H. Austin of the United States, who is chairman of the Council for October, called the meeting to order. Without waiting to read the proposed agenda, he disqualified himself by pointing out that under the Council's rules of procedure, the chairman shall decide whenever "for the proper fulfillment of his duties" he deems it necessary that he should not preside during the consideration of a question in which the country he represents "is directly connected."

Mr. Austin then called on Dr. Juan A. Bramuglia, Foreign Minister of Argentina, who is to take over the chairmanship in Novem-

Continued on Page 5, Column 3

THEY DID NOT SEE EYE TO EYE IN U. N. COUNCIL

This photograph is by chance symbolical of events in Paris yesterday as Soviet Deputy Foreign Minister Andrei Y. Vishinsky (left) and Sir Alexander Cadogan of Britain took opposite sides on the Berlin question.

Associated Press Radiophoto

RAILROADS GRANT 10¢ RISE TO 175,000 IN 2 BROTHERHOODS

Carriers, Conductor and Trainmen Unions Settle '3d-Round' Demand Without Mediation

INCREASE MAY SET TREND

Firemen, Engineers, Switchmen Continue Talks—16 Groups Take Strike Vote

Special to The New York Times.

CHICAGO, Oct. 4—The country's railroads and two operating unions agreed today on a pay increase of 10 cents an hour for 175,-000 employes. The rise, effective Oct. 16, will add about $4.80 weekly to the workers' pay checks and will cost the railroads an estimated $55,665,000 annually.

The settlement was reached here by union and railroad representatives without outside intervention. The negotiations were started on Sept. 14.

The signed agreement affects conductors, trainmen, yardmen, yardmasters and dining car employes who are represented by the Order of Railway Conductors and the Brotherhood of Railroad Trainmen.

The settlement was the first in railroad labor's "third round" wage movement and may establish a pattern for 1,175,000 other rail workers represented by three other operating unions and sixteen non-operating groups, the wage cases of which are pending.

The agreement represented a compromise, since the conductors and trainmen started out with a demand for a 25 per cent increase.

The 10-cent-an-hour rise applies to Eastern, Western and Southeastern roads. Under the old scale, which became effective Nov. 1 last year, the rail workers' pay on the Western lines was 5 cents a day lower than those on the Eastern railroads. Under the new scale the Eastern road workers will still earn 5 cents a day more than union members in the West.

Daily Scales Are Listed

The old and new daily wage scales for union classifications of employes on the Eastern trains are as follows:

Conductors — passenger, $11.84 to $12.64; passenger handling express and mail, from $12.52 to $13.32; passenger handling express or mail, $12.18 to $12.98; through freight, $11.26 to $12.06; local freight, $11.82 to $12.62; mine run, $11.82 to $12.62.

Assistant conductors — passenger, $10.55 to $11.35; passenger handling express and mail, $11.23 to $12.03; passenger handling express or mail, $10.89 to $11.69.

Baggagemen — passenger, $9.86 to $10.66; passenger handling express and mail, $10.54 to $11.34; passenger handling express or mail, $10.20 to $11.

Flagmen and brakemen—passenger, $9.69 to $10.49; passenger handling express and mail, $10.37 to $11.17; passenger handling express or mail, $10.03 to $10.83; through freight, $9.84 to $10.64; local freight, $10.27 to $11.07; mine run, $10.27 to $11.07.

Yard service—car retarder operators, $12.58 to $13.38; conductors (foremen), $12.11 to $12.91; brakemen (helpers), $11.26 to $12.06; switchtenders, $9.71 to $10.51.

Dining car employes, whose rates of pay are not uniform, will have twenty-four dollars a month added to their present scales.

Suggesting the possibility that the other unions might settle for the same increase as the conductors and trainmen, Daniel P. Loomis, chairman of the Western Railroads Wage Committee, estimated that, if the ten-cent rise were applied to all railworkers, the added cost to the carriers would be $281,170,000 annually. In the two previous wage rounds the pay settlement has been the same for all operating unions, though some held out and obtained concessions in working rules.

CHICAGO, Oct. 4 (AP)—Announcement of the settlement was made by H. W. Fraser, president

Continued on Page 44, Column 2

Because of the dispute between the Union News Company and its employes, newsstands in a number of railway stations and midtown hotels have been closed. While the dispute continues, it may therefore be impossible to buy THE NEW YORK TIMES *at certain stands. Copies of* THE TIMES *may be obtained, however, at other newsstands near those affected by the disagreement.*

Giannini Bank Chain Facing Hearings in Anti-Trust Case

Reserve Board Alleges Credit Monopoly by the Transamerica Corporation of San Francisco—Sessions to Be Public

By H. WALTON CLOKE
Special to The New York Times.

WASHINGTON, Oct. 4—After more than two years of investigation, the Federal Reserve Board announced today that it would begin public hearings here on Oct. 12 to consider anti-trust charges against the huge Transamerica Corporation of San Francisco.

The FRB's announcement was the first official disclosure that operations of the country's largest bank-holding company would be examined. Filed under the Clayton Anti-Trust Act, the Reserve Board's complaint charges that Transamerica built up a "credit monopoly" by placing directors on the boards of banks in the huge chain owned by the Bank of America National Trust and Savings Association in California and in other banks in Western states.

Transamerica, headed by Amadeo P. Giannini, West Coast financier, controls the Bank of America, which has 516 branches in seven Western states and resources of more than $5,000,000,000.

Although the complaint was filed against the company last June 25, it was not made public until today. The explanation offered for this was that hearings were to be conducted privately, and that in the event such hearings cleared the company there would be no public disclosure of the complaint.

But, according to the board, Transamerica asked that the public be admitted to the hearings so announcement of the complaint became necessary.

Filing of the complaint marked the first time in the history of the Federal Reserve that it used powers granted to it under the Clayton act. Those powers enable it to enforce the law's anti-trust provisions in so far as they affect banks and banking institutions. Like other Government agencies, the Reserve Board, in cases of this kind, serves as complainant, judge, prosecutor and jury.

If the FRB's decision is against

Continued on Page 42, Column 1

Contempt, Perjury Charges Ordered in Spy Investigation

By WILLIAM S. WHITE
Special to The New York Times.

WASHINGTON, Oct. 4—The House Committee on Un-American activities began drawing up today two citations for perjury and four for contempt against witnesses in its investigation of alleged wartime atomic espionage.

At almost the same hour, the committee's right to require replies to the most basic and frequent of all its questions—"Are you a Communist?"—was directly challenged for the first time in the United States Supreme Court.

John Howard Lawson, a motion picture writer, appealed to the Court from a $1,000 fine and a sentence of one year in jail which he was given for refusing to respond "yes" or "no" to such an inquiry.

The committee's decision to seek new prosecutions for contempt, and also for perjury, was announced by Chairman J. Parnell Thomas, Republican, of New Jersey. He set his staff to work upon the six complaints with instructions to bring them forward within a week.

They would then be sent through "proper channels" to the Department of Justice, Mr. Thomas said, with recommendations that indictments be sought at once.

He identified but two of the accused persons, Steve Nelson and J. Peters. Both, he said, would be charged only with contempt of Congress.

There was no suggestion of the identities of the others on the committee's list. Representative Thomas would say only that "altogether there will be four contempt and two perjury cases."

Mr. Peters has been denounced by the committee as the chief of Communist underground activities in the United States; Mr. Nelson is a Communist party organizer in western Pennsylvania. Just what questions they had declined to answer was not disclosed.

Mr. Lawson for his part has not been involved in the current in-

Continued on Page 15, Column 2

PSC DEMANDS DATA ON BUS LINE DEALS

Calls for Notice of Parleys on Sales to the City—Service in Bronx Evokes Warning

The Public Service Commission made public yesterday letters sent to the city's privately operated bus lines requesting them to notify the commission in advance of any negotiations that might be under way for sale of the bus lines to the city.

Not only did the commission seek details of pending negotiations in these unusual letters, but it also informed each of the bus companies that the details of any future negotiations of this nature should be forwarded promptly to the commission.

The commission explained that it wished to keep abreast of negotiations for sale of bus lines to the city "to obviate delay and unnecessary expenditures" in connection with hearings for fare increases. Eleven privately owned bus lines in the city have placed before the commission petitions for fare increases.

The letters were believed to have been prompted by the sale to the city of two bus companies without notice to the commission of these transactions. The lines were the East Side Omnibus Corporation and the Comprehensive Omnibus Corporation.

Since those sales there have been recurrent reports that other bus lines were dickering for sale terms.

Continued on Page 36, Column 5

Indians Win American League Flag, Beating Red Sox in Play-Off, 8-3

By JOHN DREBINGER
Special to The New York Times.

BOSTON, Oct. 4—Cleveland is to have its first world series in twenty-eight years.

This became an actuality today as the Indians, fired by the inspirational leadership of their talented skipper, Lou Boudreau, crushed Joe McCarthy's Red Sox in the single game that had been found necessary to break the deadlock in the American League 1948 pennant scramble.

The play-off, first in the history of the junior circuit and witnessed by a crowd of 33,957 shivering fans, most of whom watched it in glum silence, was decided by an 8-to-3 score, and as a consequence the Indians will oppose the National League champion Braves when the world series opens here Wednesday.

It marked only the second American League flag to be won by Cleveland and the first since 1920, when Tris Speaker, the famed Grey Eagle, led another band of Indians to a pennant as well as a subsequent world championship.

There never was much doubt of the outcome on this crisp autumnal afternoon. For the Tribe, which in the last few days of one of the most thrilling pennant races in major league history, had fubbed a couple of chances to win the flag outright over the regular 154-game schedule, this time shot straight for the mark.

Behind the stout-hearted five-hit hurling of Gene Bearden, 27-year-old southpaw freshman who last year was toiling on the Pacific Coast, Manager Boudreau blazed the trail with two home runs. Ken Keltner blasted another with two comrades aboard to spark a bruising four-run fourth inning, and that about tells the story.

Boudreau's play throughout was truly phenomenal. The personable graduate of the University of Illinois who in 1942 at the age of

Continued on Page 32, Column 1

VANDENBERG LINKS OUR UNITY ABROAD TO POLICIES OF GOP

Senator, on Radio for Dewey, Says Stand Is Unchanged by a Shift in Leadership

CONGRESS RECORD HAILED

Calls It 'First Best,' Replying to Attacks, and Declares Course Will Be Kept

Text of the broadcast by Senator Vandenberg, Page 21.

By CLAYTON KNOWLES
Special to The New York Times.

WASHINGTON, Oct. 4—Senator Arthur H. Vandenberg assured the nation tonight that this country's bipartisan approach to world affairs permitted a change in the national administration "without affecting the continuity of our foreign policy."

Making his first talk on behalf of the Dewey-Warren ticket in a nationwide broadcast, the chairman of the Senate Foreign Relations Committee said this was one of "the two vivid advantages" of the bipartisan foreign policy "at this hour."

The other obvious advantage, he said, was that this policy "permits our democracy to speak with a great degree of unity at critical moments when swift decision is vital, when we face totalitarian opponents who can command their own instant unity by police decree."

Party's Advances Cited

In a speech that may be unique in the campaign for its lack of strong partisan flavor, Senator Vandenberg stressed the concrete contributions of the Republican party to the bipartisan foreign policy and the determination of the party and its national candidates to continue it.

Listing some of the contributions of the Republican-controlled Eightieth Congress, the Senator made an oblique answer to President Truman's repeated attacks upon it.

"When history is written," he said "the Eightieth Congress will be remembered for this record in foreign relations long after other relatively transient issues have been forgotten. I respectfully suggest that this record makes the Eightieth Congress, in all that it relates to our foreign affairs, not 'the second worst in history,' as we sometimes hear in general attack, but the first best."

Mr. Vandenberg declared, however, that he wished to "make it plain that I claim no monopoly of Republican credit as the amazingly

Continued on Page 20, Column 5

WILBUR L. CROSS, 86, DIES IN NEW HAVEN

Former Yale Dean Had Four Terms as the Governor of Connecticut After 1930

By The Associated Press.

NEW HAVEN, Conn., Tuesday, Oct. 5—Wilbur L. Cross, former four-term Governor of Connecticut, died early today at his home here. His age was 86.

Dr. Cross, who had a distinguished career as an educator before entering politics with his election as Governor in 1930, had been ill for several weeks.

A few days ago his physician announced that he was critically ill with pneumonia and a weakened heart.

Until last winter Dr. Cross had maintained robust good health, but a respiratory infection which developed into pneumonia kept

Continued on Page 19, Column 2

Soviet Curb Restricts Aliens To Immediate Moscow Area

By W. H. LAWRENCE
Special to The New York Times.

WASHINGTON, Oct. 4—The Soviet Government has placed new restrictions upon the movement of foreign diplomatic personnel that, to all intents, limit their travel to within the city of Moscow, the State Department said today.

There was no comment as to whether this Government might consider similar restrictions upon Soviet officials here, but it was considered most unlikely because this Government has no system of road blocks and internal passport regulations by which such a measure could be made effective.

The Russians imposed the new ban on travel last week, and Soviet censors have suppressed since Friday stories by American correspondents reporting this development.

The restrictions are even more severe than those that the Russians employed during the war when the German armies were only a few miles from Moscow, according to the Department.

At the same time, the Department announced that the Vladivostok consulate had been closed on Sept. 30, and that the staff of three, headed by Consul Scott Lyon, had entrained for Moscow on Friday. That office was ordered closed by the Russians in retaliation for the expulsion by the United States of Jacob Lomakin, Soviet Consul General in New York, for his part in the "abduction" of Mrs. Oksana Kasenkina, the Soviet teacher who leaped from the consulate to escape detention and return to Russia.

TEXT OF ANNOUNCEMENT

The text of the Department

Continued on Page 3, Column 4

RUSSIAN ATOM PLAN QUESTIONED BY U. S.

Austin Says Talks Can Go On Only if Majority Report Is Accepted as Basis

Excerpts from Mr. Austin's address are on Page 14.

By A. M. ROSENTHAL
Special to The New York Times.

PARIS, Oct. 4—The United States warned the world today that no security could result from Russian proposals for the simultaneous signing of treaties outlawing the atomic bomb and setting up international atomic control.

Warren R. Austin, United States representative on the General Assembly's Political and Security Committee, served notice that the United States delegation was willing" to continue the atomic talks only on a basis of the control plan worked out by the majority of the United Nations Atomic Energy Commission and rejected by the Soviet Union.

The speech of the United States delegate was the first formal re-

Continued on Page 15, Column 4

World News Summarized

TUESDAY, OCTOBER 5, 1948

The Western powers presented the Berlin blockade to the United Nations Security Council yesterday as a threat to peace despite Moscow's last-minute attempt to bring the whole German question before the Council of Foreign Ministers. Deputy Foreign Minister Vishinsky strongly opposed consideration of the matter by the Council, and when he said Russia would not "be a party" to the proceedings, some delegates interpreted it as a threat to walk out. [1:8.]

In the Political Committee of the General Assembly the United States rejected the Soviet proposal for simultaneously outlawing the atomic bomb and setting up an international control agency. The United States insisted on a veto-less control agency first. [1:7.]

Russia came under attack in other United Nations committees. A Briton said the Communists had set up in Eastern Europe the most ruthless dictatorships in history. [15:1.] An American assailed Communist opposition to the European Recovery Program. [13:4.]

The Economic Cooperation Administration reported to Congress that the program was making notable progress. [13:2-3.] Britain asked the ECA to permit direct use of her Marshall Plan counterpart fund. [13:1.]

Formation of a committee to promote East-West trade was approved in Geneva. [16:6.]

Coal mining in France halted when the men went out on strike. [1:6-7.] Exiles representing unions suppressed in Soviet satellite states organized in Paris to try to pierce the Iron Curtain. [3:4.]

Movement of foreign diplomats in Russia has been restricted to the Moscow area, Washington disclosed. [1:6-7.]

The appointment of Field Marshal Viscount Montgomery to head the defense council of the Western European Union has been confirmed. French General mand ground forces. [3:2-3.]

This country's bipartisan foreign policy not only assures a "unity as important as our atom bombs" but also permits a change in National Administration "without affecting the continuity of our foreign policy," Senator Vandenberg declared in a speech on behalf of Governor Dewey. [1:4.]

John Foster Dulles, who flew back from Paris, will confer with Governor Dewey today. The Republicans decided to defer a statement on Palestine. [19:1.]

President Truman starts tomorrow on a campaign tour through nine states. [19:4.]

Two citations for perjury and four for contempt were being drawn by the House Committee on Un-American Activities against witnesses in the hearings into alleged wartime atomic espionage. [1:2-3.]

The nation's railroads and two operating unions signed an agreement for a 10-cent-an-hour wage increase. [1:1.]

Wilbur L. Cross, four times Governor of Connecticut, died at 86. [1:5.]

Cleveland won the American League baseball championship, defeating Boston in a play-off, 8 to 3. [1:2-3.]

French Coal Production Ceases As 300,000 Miners Go on Strike

By LANSING WARREN
Special to The New York Times.

PARIS, Oct. 4—Coal production ceased throughout France today as the miners' strike called by Communist unions was reported to have been generally effective in all mining districts. The loss to French industry was estimated at 150,000 tons of coal a day.

Reporting to a Cabinet meeting late this evening, Paul Devinat, Secretary of State assisting Premier Henri Queuille, said that negotiations were continuing with the miners' unions. It was still uncertain whether the Catholic workers would continue the strike beyond the forty-eight-hour period that they had set. Robert Lacoste, Minister of Industry and Commerce, was scheduled to confer with miners' delegates tomorrow.

The first day of the strike went off without any violent incidents, but the Communist-led General Confederation of Labor in a statement issued tonight protested against the presence of police in some of the mines in Lorraine. It threatened that security measures taken by the miners for protection throughout France would be annulled unless the police were withdrawn.

About 300,000 miners were idle today, most of them strikers and pickets. In addition to the coal miners, 100 workers in uranium mines at Saint Symphorien de Marmagne and 1,300 workers in Wolfram mines at Saint Leonard in the Haute-Vienne stopped work, as well as most of the workers in the French iron and bauxite industries.

Government circles professed optimism today as they declared that public establishments have coal stocks for one month and that the principal private industries have supplies for almost two months. It was felt also that the benefits granted to the workers today would go far toward appeasing

Continued on Page 12, Column 5

Indians Beat Red Sox and Win Pennant; Boudreau Gets 2 Homers, 2 Singles

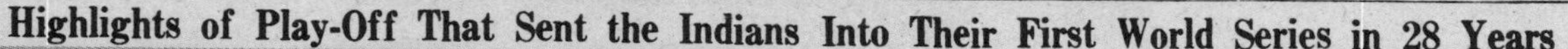

Highlights of Play-Off That Sent the Indians Into Their First World Series in 28 Years

BEARDEN 5-HITTER DOWNS BOSTON, 8-3

Continued From Page 1

25 became the youngest manager ever to direct a major league club, gave a performance seldom matched by any player in a struggle of such vast importance.

Playing his own position at shortstop flawlessly, maneuvering his men hither and yon with rare judgment and watching like a hawk every pitch of his youthful moundsman, Lou still found time not only to larrup two homers over the left field barrier, but added two singles, each of which figured in further scores.

Against this demonstration Joe McCarthy, completing his first year as manager of the Red Sox, and winner of eight American League pennants as field general of the Yankees, suddenly found himself completely out of ammunition.

For the battering Bosox, whose electrifying spurt in the last two days of the regular campaign had overcome a two-game deficit, failed Marse Joe rather badly.

Denny Routed In Fourth

In a surprise move McCarthy started his veteran righthander, Dennis Galehouse, and lived to regret it within four innings, for Denny was put to rout with the Keltner three-run homer. Then he followed with Ellis Kinder, who fell victim of the final fourth-inning tally, gave up three more in the fifth, eighth and ninth.

Even the renowned Ted Williams cast a rather sorry figure in this sudden-death struggle which the pleading Hub fans had hoped would produce the first All-Boston world series in history.

The Kid's mighty bat, which the two previous days had helped blast the Yankees out of the race, connected for only one single in four tries today. To add further to the woes of the disconsolate Boston fans, Williams capped his day by muffing a fly ball that gave the Clevelanders their tally in the eighth.

Of all the Sox, Bobby Doerr alone remained about the only "hero in defeat." With Williams on base, the result of the Indians' only misplay of the day, Doerr whacked his twenty-seventh homer of the year in the sixth.

But after this slip, Bearden kept the Sox tightly bottled the rest of the way.

Seventh Victory in Row

Inasmuch as all records compiled today go into the season's final statistics, this also marked the twentieth mound victory for the tall Coast southpaw against only seven defeats, and his seventh triumph in row.

Amid a world series setting which saw Commissioner A. B. Chandler in a "ringside" box and correspondents on hand from virtually all major league towns, the conflict had progressed only a few minutes when the indomitable Boudreau fired his first shot.

On his arrival this morning with his team from Cleveland, where the Indians had suffered an excruciating Sunday defeat at the hands of the Tigers to plunge the race into a last-day tie, Boudreau appeared a bit drawn and tired.

But there was nothing wrong with his flashing, clear eyes as he whipped into a Galehouse pitch and sent it sailing over the left-field barrier for his seventeenth homer of the year. It came with two out and nobody on and gave the Indians a one-run lead.

The margin was wiped out almost immediately when Johnny Pesky doubled in the lower half of the first and galloped home on Vern Stephens' single just inside the third-base line.

For the next two rounds Bearden and Galehouse kept the one-all deadlock intact. But in the fourth the Indians struck again and once more it was Boudreau who showed the way. This time the Cleveland pilot plunked a single into left. Joe Gordon followed with another into the same sector and a feeling of uneasiness swept through the crowd.

A moment later Keltner exploded a towering shot and as the ball streaked against the clear blue sky the Hub fans, who so often have seen enemy hopes dashed against the perilous left-field wall of historic Fenway Park, knew on the spot the worst was about to happen.

No. 31 Over the Wall

The ball soared over the wall for Keltner's thirty-first homer of the campaign and three Tribal runs scored. That was all for Galehouse and Kinder, one of the lesser lights on the Bosox staff, acquired from the St. Louis Browns last winter, emerged from the bullpen.

The former Brownie righthander didn't quell the uprising at once. Lary Doby, the Negro star, rifled a double off the wall in left center, the first of two two-baggers he was to hit during the afternoon.

A ascrifice bunt by Bob Kennedy advanced Doby to third and he streaked over the plate while Stephens was tossing out Jim Hegan at first.

The Indians were four tallies in front and the stunned gathering, now looking on in stony silence, seemed to sense that final disaster was not far away.

The fifth was almost a repetition of the first. Kinder had just retired the top two batters of the Cleveland line-up when Boudreau unfurled his second circuit smack of the afternoon and eighteenth of the campaign. That made it 6—1.

Gordon Muffs Ted's Fly

In the last of the sixth, however, came a faint flurry of Boston hope. With one out, Williams, who had grounded out in the first and fouled out in the third, lifted a towering fly back of second base.

The crowd groaned but cheered a moment later as Gordon, staggering under the ball as he tried to sight it against a blinding sun, momentarily caught it, then dropped it for an error.

Unruffled, Bearden fanned Stephens for the second out, but Doerr was not to be disposed of so easily. He, too, sent the ball winging over the left field wall and as the two runners jogged around the basepaths, Boston spirits flared again. The score was now 6 to 3.

But the Bosox were never to get any closer. Bearden quickly brought the sixth to a close by fanning Stan Spence and in the seventh the chilled spectators were to put in another harrowing period as a pair of singles by Bearden and Dale Mitchell, a sacrifice and an intentional pass to Boudreau filled the bases for Cleveland with only one out.

More Trouble in Eighth

But Kinder revived hopes by retiring Gordon on the end of an infield pop-up and holding Keltner to a fly that Williams caught in left. The folks breathed again, but not for long. For there was more trouble in the eighth. Doby lashed another double into left center. Kennedy sacrificed him to third and Hegan drew a pass.

For an instant it looked as though Kinder would again effect a miraculous escape when Doby got himself picked off third for the second out, Hegan taking second during the run-up.

But on the heels of that Bearden lifted a high fly to left center which Williams, verging on the ball with Dom DiMaggio, elected to take. Ted, however, dropped it and Hegan scored easily.

In the ninth came the Tribe's final thrust. Ed Robinson singled and so did Boudreau for his fourth hit in four official times at bat. Came a wild pitch that advanced the runners to second and third and this forced an intentional pass to Gordon.

At that, only one run scored, Robinson skipping home while Keltner was pounding into a double play. But the Indians needed no more.

There was nothing the Sox could do with Bearden's baffling slider and knuckler. Bill Goodman drew a pass in the seventh only to see Birdie Tebbetts ground into a twin killing.

Williams Hits to Left

After Dom DiMaggio, hitless all day, had grounded out in the eighth and Pesky had fanned, Williams connected with a well-placed single into left. But Stephens ended this threat by forcing Ted at second.

In the ninth came one more pass, the fifth to be given up by Bearden. But the tall lefty made Goodman his sixth strike-out victim. Then Tebbetts grounded to Keltner and the American League's thrilling flag race, which early in August had seen four entries virtually locked in a tie and which still had three in the running up to the next to the last day of the regular season, finally had come to an end.

And so the Indians, after nearly three decades of bitter disappointments and in the third year of Bill Veeck's spectacular tenure as club president, at long last brought a second pennant to Cleveland.

Veeck, whose glamorous feats of showmanship produced attendance figures in the lakefront city which surpassed even the fabulous record of the Yankees, had once threatened this summer to jump off the "highest bridge in Cleveland" if the Indians failed to win the flag. Tonight he was all smiles as jubilant American Leaguers showered him with congratulations and best wishes for success in the forthcoming world series.

Play-off Box Score

CLEVELAND INDIANS

	AB.	R.	H.	PO.	A.	E.
Mitchell, lf	5	0	1	1	0	0
Clark, 1b	2	0	0	5	0	0
Robinson, 1b	2	1	1	9	0	0
Boudreau, ss	4	3	4	3	5	0
Gordon, 2b	4	1	1	2	3	1
Keltner, 3b	5	1	3	0	6	0
Doby, cf	5	1	2	1	0	0
Kennedy, rf	2	0	0	0	0	0
Hegan, c	3	1	0	6	1	0
Bearden, p	3	0	1	0	2	0
Total	35	8	13	27	17	1

BOSTON RED SOX

	AB.	R.	H.	PO.	A.	E.
D. DiMaggio, cf	4	0	0	3	0	0
Pesky, 3b	4	1	1	3	1	0
Williams, lf	4	1	1	3	0	1
Stephens, ss	4	0	1	2	4	0
Doerr, 2b	4	1	1	5	2	0
Spence, rf	1	0	0	1	0	0
aHitchcock	0	0	0	0	0	0
bWright	0	0	0	0	0	0
Goodman, 1b	3	0	0	7	1	0
Tebbetts, c	4	0	1	3	1	0
Galehouse, p	0	0	0	0	1	0
Kinder, p	2	0	0	0	1	0
Total	30	3	5	27	14	1

aHitchcock walked for Spence in ninth.

bWright ran for Hitchcock in ninth.

Cleveland .1 0 0 4 1 0 0 1 1—8
Boston ...1 0 0 0 0 2 0 0 0—3

Runs batted in—Boudreau 2, Keltner 3, Hegan, Stephens, Doerr 2.

Two-base hits—Doby 2, Keltner, Pesky. Home runs—Boudreau 2, Keltner, Doerr. Sacrifices—Kennedy 2, Robinson. Double plays—Hegan and Boudreau; Gordon, Boudreau and Robinson; Bearden, Gordon and Robinson; Stephens, Doerr and Goodman 2. Left on bases—Cleveland 7, Boston 5.

Bases on balls—Off Bearden 5 (Spence 2, Galehouse, Goodman, Hitchcock); Galehouse 1 (Bearden); Kinder 3 (Boudreau, Hegan, Gordon). Struck out—By Bearden 5 (Goodman, Doerr, Stephens, Spence, Pesky); Galehouse 1 (Hegan); Kinder 2 (Hegan, Doby).

Hits—Off Galehouse 5 in 3 innings (none out in fourth); Kinder 8 in 6. Wild pitch—Kinder. Losing pitcher—Galehouse.

Umpires — McGowan (plate); Summers (first base); Rommel (second base); Berry (third base). Time of game—2:24. Attendance—33,957.

American League

YESTERDAY'S RESULT

Cleveland 8, Boston 3.

FINAL STANDING OF CLUBS

	Cleveland	Boston	New York	Phila'phia	Detroit	St. Louis	Washington	Chicago	Won	Lost	Percentage	Games Behind
Cleve	—	12	10	16	13	14	16	16	97	58	.626	—
Boston	11	—	14	12	15	15	15	14	96	59	.619	1
N. Y.	12	8	—	12	13	16	17	16	94	60	.610	2½
Phila	6	10	10	—	10	18	14	16	84	70	.545	12½
Detroit	9	7	9	12	—	11	16	14	78	76	.506	18½
St. L.	8	7	6	4	11	—	10	13	59	94	.386	37
Washgtn	6	7	5	8	6	12	—	12	56	97	.366	40
Chicago	6	8	6	6	8	8	9	—	51	101	.336	44½
Lost	58	59	60	70	76	94	97	101	—	—		

Boudreau is hailed by his players as he returns to the dugout after his fifth-inning circuit blow, the second he hit in the contest.

INDIANS FAVORED, 7 TO 20

St. Louis Book Quotes Braves as 11 to 5 for Series

ST. LOUIS, Oct. 4 (AP)—In betting commissioner James J. Carroll's book the Cleveland Indians look more than twice as good as the Boston Braves to win the world series.

Carroll posted odds of 11 to 5 on Boston and 7 to 20 on Cleveland. That means you could win $11 for your $5 on Boston, and would have to put up $20 on Cleveland to win $7.

For the first game he issued these odds: Sain vs. Feller, 7 to 5 on Boston; 3 to 5 on Cleveland. Sain vs. Lemon, 13 to 10 on Boston; 13 to 20 on Cleveland.

None Left in Boston Jail

BOSTON, Oct. 4 (AP)—From 2:40 A. M. Sunday until mid-forenoon today there were no hits, no runs and none left on base at the South Boston Police Station. Unable to account for such an extended period without a single arrest, Captain Robert Lynch scratched his head and suggested that maybe intense interest in baseball had smothered all interest in crime.

M'Carthy Sorry for Players' Sake; DiMaggio Lauds Bearden's Work

By ROSCOE McGOWEN
Special to THE NEW YORK TIMES.

BOSTON, Oct. 4—"I've been licked before and I can be licked again. I'm sorry for the boys, that's all. And that's all I have to say, gentlemen."

With this brief statement, Joe McCarthy, winner of eight American League pennants and one National League flag, dismissed a crowd of newspapermen from his cubicle in the Fenway Park clubhouse after his Red Sox had been soundly beaten by the Cleveland Indians in today's historic play-off game.

A few minutes later, when McCarthy had come out of his office, shooing the scribes ahead of him, Eddie Collins, vice president of the Red Sox, came in.

Hurrying towards McCarthy, Collins shook hands warmly and said: "You're still the tops in my books. I want you to know that."

Despite the rumors that McCarthy, too, might be out in so-called "housecleaning" that President Tom Yawkey started by letting out Phil Troy, assistant general manager, and George (Specs) Torporcer, farm director, there was no indication that Marse Joe would be leaving.

Decision Up to Joe

He didn't sound like a fellow who was about to quit his job, and the best information is that "it's up to McCarthy. If he wants to quit or remain the decision will be strictly his own."

There was no great gloom in the Red Sox locker room. The impression gained was that the boys felt that they had been given a reprieve by getting one more chance after the Indians seemed almost to have the flag folded away; that it would have been great to have won it but—"they beat us good," said Dom DiMaggio.

"It would have been different if we had kicked it away, but we just got beat, so what the heck!" The Little Professor said that Gene Bearden pitched a great game "and we couldn't do much about that."

"He never gives you a fast ball," said Dom. "Just keeps sending in those knucklers, sliders and curves."

Bobby Doerr, who hit the only fast ball Bearden served for a home run, was disappointed but philosophical about the whole thing.

"Another year," he said, then added, wryly: "But it was a lousy way to finish, wasn't it?"

Superstition the Bunk

Johnny Pesky, who had attended a friend's wedding yesterday and wore his naval uniform of a lieutenant, junior grade, was compelled by his teammates to wear the uniform to the ball park today because they thought it would bring 'em luck.

"And now look at it," exploded Johnny. "They said if I wore it we'd be lucky. I'm about convinced these superstitions are the bunk!"

Doerr is heading for his Far West home in the morning by auto and a lot of other Red Sox also are checking out. But six of them, in addition to Coach Earle Combs, are staying for the Indians' battle with the Braves.

The six are Jack Kramer, Pesky, Mickey Harris, Earl Caldwell, DiMaggio and Vern Stephens.

Joe Cronin's parting words to Bobby Feller after coming into the Indians' clubhouse to congratulate the winners was, "Now go out and beat the Braves."

"You weren't rooting for the Indians half an hour ago," Cronin was reminded. Joe merely grinned.

Jeff Heath, his leg in a cast and moving with difficulty on crutches, came into the Indians' locker room to congratulate his former teammates. Jeff watched the game from the lower stands and submitted his encased leg to fans who wanted to autograph it.

"Darn tootin' I'm going to Cleveland," replied Heath to a query. "It's bad enough as it is—not to play—but I'm going to see the whole series."

EXTRA GAME NETS $42,000

Indians and Red Sox to Divide Receipts on Regular Plan

BOSTON, Oct. 4 (AP)—The owners of the Indians and Red Sox will divide 97 per cent of the approximately $42,000 receipts of today's play-off game to add to what they already have made in a profitable season.

In contrast to the world series, where the players collect the largest part of the money in the first four games and the clubs don't share until later, today's game was entirely between the two clubs.

Tom Dowd, Red Sox secretary, explained that regular season arrangements were in effect for the play-off. This called for the American League to take 3 per cent of the net receipts and the two clubs to split the rest evenly.

The players do not share in the play-off receipts beyond receiving one day's pay and any added amounts that the owners care to give them.

O'Hara in Ring Tonight

Six-rounders pairing Paul O'Hara, Bronx welterweight, and Eddie White of New Jersey and Lou Russo, Astoria lightweight, and Len Holton of St. Louis feature the boxing show tonight at the Park Arena, the Bronx. Two other sixes and a brace of fours complete the card.

Gene Bearden (left), Boudreau (center) and Ken Keltner, who played leading roles in the triumph, in dressing room after the game.

Associated Press Wirephotos

SERIES SCORES ON PHONE

Telephone Company Again Will Provide Data on Classic

Continuing a service that was introduced in 1941, the New York Telephone Company will again give end-of-inning scores on the world series from its time bureau, MEridian 7-1212. Four times a minute—240 times pe rhour—during each game, score announcements will be given, the report following immediately after the time signal.

The final score of each contest will be continued in time reports until 6:30 P. M. Announcements of a postponement due to weather will be made by the same method before and after game time. Scores are received by direct press wire to the time bureau.

Please do not call THE NEW YORK TIMES for information relative to the series. This request is made to prevent impairment of other services in THE NEW YORK TIMES offices.

World Series Comparison

FIRST BASEMEN

	Bats	G	AB	R	H	2B	3B	HR	RBI	SB	PC	PO	A	E	DP	PC
Robinson, Indians	L	133	488	53	123	19	3	16	83	1	.252	1218	84	6	120	.995
Torgeson, Braves	L	133	438	71	110	22	5	10	67	19	.251	1075	81	8	86	.993
Sanders, Braves	L	5	4	0	1	0	0	0	..	0	.250					
F. McCormick, Braves	R	75	181	11	[illegible]	9	2	[illegible]	34	0	.249	338	28	5	30	.987

SECOND BASEMEN

	Bats	G	AB	R	H	2B	3B	HR	RBI	SB	PC	PO	A	E	DP	PC
Stanky, Braves	R	67	248	50	78	13	[illegible]	[illegible]	[illegible]	[illegible]	.315	[illegible]	[illegible]	7	[illegible]	[illegible]
Gordon, Indians	R	144	550	95	154	19	4	32	124	5	.279	337	444	25	95	.949
Sisti, Braves	R	83	222	29	54	[illegible]	2	0	22	0	.243	100	101	6	17	.971

THIRD BASEMEN

	Bats	G	AB	R	H	2B	3B	HR	RBI	SB	PC	PO	A	E	DP	PC
Keltner, Indians	R	153	558	91	166	24	4	31	119	2	.298	119	302	15	67	.966
Elliott, Braves	R	151	540	98	153	24	5	23	100	6	.283	145	297	26	30	.944

SHORTSTOPS

	Bats	G	AB	R	H	2B	3B	HR	RBI	SB	PC	PO	A	E	DP	PC
Boudreau, Indians	R	152	560	116	199	33	6	18	107	4	.355	292	471	21	117	.973
Dark, Braves	R	137	543	85	175	39	6	3	48	4	.322	253	392	25	66	.963

OUTFIELDERS

	Bats	G	AB	R	H	2B	3B	HR	RBI	SB	PC	PO	A	E	DP	PC
Mitchell, Indians	L	141	608	84	204	30	8	4	56	12	.336	303	12	[illegible]	3	.991
Holmes, Braves	L	139	585	81	190	35	7	6	60	1	.325	284	8	5	4	.983
Clark, Indians	R	81	271	42	84	6	1	9	37	0	.310	103	4	2	1	.982
Doby, Indians	L	121	438	80	132	24	9	14	64	9	.301	285	12	13	3	.958
M. McCormick, Braves	R	115	343	47	103	20	7	1	37	1	.299	191	7	5	3	.975
Peck, Indians	L	45	63	12	18	3	0	0	8	1	.286	11	0	0	0	1.000
Conatser, Braves	R	90	223	30	62	9	4	3	23	1	.278	147	3	4	1	.973
Edwards, Indians	L	54	155	27	43	9	2	3	18	1	.277	73	1	1	0	.987
Kennedy, Indians	R	95	185	14	50	11	3	0	19	0	.270	95	5	2	1	.980
Russell, Braves	Both	89	322	44	85	18	1	9	54	3	.264	241	3	2	0	.992
Tucker, Indians	L	83	242	52	63	13	2	1	20	11	.260	170	5	0	2	1.000
Rickert, Braves	L	11	19	1	4	0	1	0	2	0	.211	9	1	0	0	1.000

CATCHERS

	Bats	G	AB	R	H	2B	3B	HR	RBI	SB	PC	PO	A	E	DP	PC
Tipton, Indians	R	47	90	11	26	3	0	1	13	0	.289	83	17	3	1	.971
Masi, Braves	R	113	376	43	95	19	0	5	43	2	.253	153	40	6	5	.988
Hegan, Indians		144	472	60	117	21	6	11	60	5	.248	635	76	7	16	.990
Salkeld, Braves	L	78	197	26	48	8	1	8	28	1	.244	252	30	3	5	.989

PITCHING RECORDS

	Thr.	G.	IP.	H.	BB.	SO.	Comp. Gms.	Shut Outs.	W.	L.	PC.	WP.	HB.	BK.
Lyons, Braves	R	7	13	17	8	5			1		1.000			
Paige, Indians	R	21	73	61	22	43	3	2	6	1	.857	1	1	2
Shoun, Braves	L	36	75	77	20	26	1		5	1	.833	2		
Hogue, Braves	R	40	87	88	20	42			8	2	.800		2	
Gromek, Indians	R	38	130	110	51	44	4	1	9	3	.750	1	6	
Klieman, Indians	R	43	84	62	47	16			3	1	.750	1	1	
Bearden, Indians	L	37	230	187	106	[illegible]	15	6	20	7	.741	[illegible]	[illegible]	[illegible]
Potter, Braves	[illegible]	[illegible]	[illegible]	[illegible]	[illegible]	[illegible]	[illegible]	[illegible]	[illegible]	[illegible]	[illegible]	[illegible]	[illegible]	[illegible]
Bickford, Braves	[illegible]	[illegible]	[illegible]	[illegible]	[illegible]	[illegible]	[illegible]	[illegible]	[illegible]	[illegible]	[illegible]	[illegible]	[illegible]	[illegible]
Sain, Braves	[illegible]	[illegible]	[illegible]	[illegible]	[illegible]	[illegible]	[illegible]	[illegible]	[illegible]	[illegible]	[illegible]	[illegible]	[illegible]	[illegible]
Christopher, Indians	[illegible]	[illegible]	[illegible]	[illegible]	[illegible]	[illegible]	[illegible]	[illegible]	[illegible]	[illegible]	[illegible]	[illegible]	[illegible]	[illegible]
Lemon, Indians	[illegible]	[illegible]	[illegible]	[illegible]	[illegible]	[illegible]	[illegible]	[illegible]	[illegible]	[illegible]	[illegible]	[illegible]	[illegible]	[illegible]
Feller, Indians	[illegible]	[illegible]	[illegible]	[illegible]	[illegible]	[illegible]	[illegible]	[illegible]	[illegible]	[illegible]	[illegible]	[illegible]	[illegible]	[illegible]
Spahn, Braves	[illegible]	[illegible]	[illegible]	[illegible]	[illegible]	[illegible]	[illegible]	[illegible]	[illegible]	[illegible]	[illegible]	[illegible]	[illegible]	[illegible]
Muncrief, Indians	[illegible]	[illegible]	[illegible]	[illegible]	[illegible]	[illegible]	[illegible]	[illegible]	[illegible]	[illegible]	[illegible]	[illegible]	[illegible]	[illegible]
Zoldak, Indians	[illegible]	[illegible]	[illegible]	[illegible]	[illegible]	[illegible]	[illegible]	[illegible]	[illegible]	[illegible]	[illegible]	[illegible]	[illegible]	[illegible]
Voiselle, Braves	[illegible]	[illegible]	[illegible]	[illegible]	[illegible]	[illegible]	[illegible]	[illegible]	[illegible]	[illegible]	[illegible]	[illegible]	[illegible]	[illegible]
Black, Indians	[illegible]	[illegible]	[illegible]	[illegible]	[illegible]	[illegible]	[illegible]	[illegible]	[illegible]	[illegible]	[illegible]	[illegible]	[illegible]	[illegible]
Barrett, Braves	[illegible]	[illegible]	[illegible]	[illegible]	[illegible]	[illegible]	[illegible]	[illegible]	[illegible]	[illegible]	[illegible]	[illegible]	[illegible]	[illegible]
White, Braves	[illegible]	[illegible]	[illegible]	[illegible]	[illegible]	[illegible]	[illegible]	[illegible]	[illegible]	[illegible]	[illegible]	[illegible]	[illegible]	[illegible]

CLUB BATTING

Club	[illegible]
Indians	[illegible]
Braves	[illegible]

CLUB FIELDING

Club	G.	PO.	A.	E.	DP.	TP.	PB.	PC.
Indians	[illegible]	[illegible]	[illegible]	[illegible]	[illegible]	[illegible]	[illegible]	[illegible]
Braves	[illegible]	[illegible]	[illegible]	[illegible]	[illegible]	[illegible]	[illegible]	[illegible]

Records include yesterday's play-off game.

WILD CELEBRATION BY WINNING TEAM

Bearden and Boudreau Mobbed by Players, Officials After Triumph at Boston

By JAMES P. DAWSON
Special to THE NEW YORK TIMES.

BOSTON, Oct. 4—Gene Bearden, on the shoulders of admiring teammates, was carried off the field at Fenway Park this afternoon, setting off the greatest celebration any Cleveland club has known in baseball history, a fitting climax to the most exciting flag struggle in the history of the junior circuit.

An idolized survivor of another Cleveland baseball era was there to participate. His name is Tris Speaker. He used to chase a lot of flies in the outfield and do a tremendous lot of hitting for the city on the lake, and as manager he had led the Indians of 1920 to a pennant and a world championship.

Spoke, as he is called by old-timers, had to admit there was nothing to parallel what happened in the Cleveland quarters after today's 8-to-3 triumph over Joe McCarthy's Red Sox.

Cleveland players actually tore the clothes off Bearden. "Old Bag of Bones," was the cry, as first one and then another came up to pull his hair, squeeze his priceless pitching arm, tweak his nose, slam him on the back, toss him hither and yon.

No Time for Talk

Bearden had no time then for conversation, although reporters tried, in the modified bedlam, to get him to say something. Photographers, movies and stills, were clustered about him, perched on trunks, tables, benches and even atop the lockers, "shooting" the 27-year-old lefthander from all angles. He had to pose with Manager Lou Boudreau and with battering Ken Keltner and President Bill Veeck.

Somehow or other, President Will Harridge of the American League got into the clubhouse to extend his congratulations. And nobody will ever know how Jeff Heath, stricken Boston Braves' flychaser, managed to worm through the noisy mass on his crutches and his "autographed" broken left leg in a plaster cast. But he was there, greeting his old mates and posing for pictures in fond embraces with Bearden.

While all this was going on, Keltner had to defend himself against a good-natured assault. Larry Doby and old Satch Paige were trampled in a mutual exchange of felicitations. Coaches Muddy Ruel and Deacon Bill McKechnie were slapped and tossed about, and wound up kissing Bearden.

Finally, Boudreau, puffing, white-faced, smiling, yelled above the din, "Give me the clubhouse for a meeting. I have to have a meeting with my players." Then a swarm of special police swung into action and some semblance of order was restored.

Threw One Fast Ball

Bearden, spirited away to the comparative quiet of the "rubbin' room" where the graying trainer Lefty Weisman holds forth, said:

"I was throwing only sliders and knucklers all afternoon. No, I never tired. I never felt weak. I wasn't nervous. I never lost my stuff. When I might have seemed wild I was missing with my slider. I wasn't pitching to spots, so I wasn't missing corners. Doerr hit the one and only fast ball I threw all afternoon for that homer. Williams hit a knuckler I let up on.

"Am I happy? What a game to win, what a way to win it; what a spot to come through; what a gang of fellows to have behind you with their bats."

Manager Boudreau, of course, was lavish in his praise of Bearden. Suffering from a bad cold contracted in the last windy, cold day in Cleveland, the Tribe skipper really was beside himself, as well he might be, in this realization of a dream, this attainment of every ball player's goal. But he minimized his own importance, with a modesty that is one of his greatest attributes, although the word in the stands and in the press box and wherever baseball was discussed tonight was extravagant acclaim of the quiet-spoken team leader whose bludgeoning bat inspired his team to victory.

President Veeck was happy. "I think Boudreau's the greatest competitor in any sport," he said.

Vice president Hank Greenberg fought his way through the human swarm to felicitate the triumphant skipper. Manager Joe McCarthy came in before the excitement ran its course to congratulate Boudreau. "You did a great job, Lou," said Joe, with a smile. President Harridge's admonition was: "Bring home the bacon."

Major League Leaders

FINAL STANDINGS

BATSMEN

AMERICAN LEAGUE

	G.	AB.	R.	H.	PC.
Williams, Boston	137	509	124	188	.369
Boudreau, Cleveland	152	560	116	199	.355
Mitchell, Cleveland	141	608	84	204	.336
Zarilla, St. Louis	144	529	77	174	.329
McCosky, Phila	135	514	95	168	.327
Dillinger, St. Louis	153	644	110	207	.321
[illegible]	[illegible]	[illegible]	[illegible]	[illegible]	[illegible]

NATIONAL LEAGUE

	G.	AB.	R.	H.	PC.
[illegible]	[illegible]	[illegible]	[illegible]	[illegible]	[illegible]

RUNS BATTED IN

AMERICAN LEAGUE

[illegible]

NATIONAL LEAGUE

[illegible]

HOME-RUN HITTERS

AMERICAN LEAGUE

[illegible]

NATIONAL LEAGUE

[illegible]

Pep Outpoints Saddler at Garden and Regains World Featherweight Crown

HARTFORD FIGHTER SCORES DECISIVELY

Pep Takes Unanimous Decision Over Saddler in 15-Round Contest Before 19,097

BATTLE SAVAGELY WAGED

Crowd Is Thrilled as Willie Avenges 4-Round Knockout by Negro Ace in October

By JAMES P. DAWSON

A precedent was set in the featherweight ranks last night when Willie Pep, the redoubtable little battler from Hartford, Conn., became the first boxer in the history of the 126-pound class to regain a lost world championship.

Pep swept tradition aside as he battered Sandy Saddler, Harlem Negro star into defeat in fifteen rounds of savage fighting at Madison Square Garden.

Another record was set as 19,097 fans paid $87,563 to see the struggle, the first defense by Saddler of the crown he lifted from Pep by a four-round knockout last October and they witnessed one of the most startling upsets in boxing annals. The previous indoor record for a featherweight title scrap was the $71,869 established here by Pep and Chalky Wright back in 1942.

Pep regained the title on the unanimous ballot of the three State Athletic Commission officials, and by a margin which could only have been improved upon with a knockout. The referee, Eddie Joseph, who more than once had to warn one or the other of the principals against roughness, voted ten rounds to Pep and five to Saddler. Frank Forbes, one of the judges, gave Pep nine rounds, Saddler five and called one even. The other judge, Jack O'Sullivan, gave Pep nine rounds and Saddler six. The writer gave Pep the decision by a margin of twelve rounds to three, voted Saddler only the fourth, tenth and fourteenth sessions.

Finest Fight of Career

To regain the title to which he first laid claim after beating Wright in 1942, but which he did not win outright until he conquered Sal Bartolo four years later, Pep put up the greatest battle of his career. He called on every ounce of strength within his compact little body, and all the guile he has accumulated through eleven years as amateur and professional fighter to gain the triumph.

First, he had to avoid the smashing blows to which he fell victim less than five months ago, then he had to force the attack and keep forcing. How well he succeeded is reflected in the tabulation of the officials. And in riding to victory he proved to be one of the greatest featherweight champions the ring has known.

The fans who wager on boxing had installed Saddler a favorite at 5 to 7 when the rivals entered the ring. The odds had fluctuated through the day, with Pep the choice for a time at 5 to 7 shortly after the weighing at noon. The consensus before the battle was that Saddler would win again, and again by a knockout, on the generally accepted boxing theory that what has been done once will be done again.

But Pep is no believer in theory or tradition. He is a fighter of wind-mill style, tireless and with resourcefulness and baffling speed. He is champion again today because he has all these ring essentials, with unflagging courage as well.

Cuts About Both Eyes

He didn't look like a champion as he left the ring. He had nasty cuts above and below the right eye and under the left eye. He was weary. He had just enough strength left to gallop through a terrific fifteenth round, fending off the desperate bid of his rival for a knockout that would turn impending defeat into glorious victory. He had enough to do this and his rival, too.

He had the championship and that made amends for all the bruises and pain.

None disagreed with the award at the final bell. None could. There was no disputing the decision, so well had Pep baffled and bewildered and beaten the man who a few short months ago had inflicted the only knockout in a long and glorious career.

Saddler had his greatest chance for victory in the tenth and fourteenth rounds. He almost finished Pep with a terrific right to the jaw in the tenth. This blow had Pep teetering as if to fall.

In the fourteenth a right to the jaw rocked Pep, and a left hook to the jaw shook the Hartford gladiator to his toes. But he rallied quickly from these punches and was alert and strong. The blows served only to arouse his fury.

Stung by Straight Left

A straight left to the face by Saddler was his best punch in the fourth round and he cracked a right to the jaw solidly in the ninth that stung Pep. But the lad from Hartford was in top condition; he was out to win and there was no stopping him.

The fight was sensational because it was so unexpected; few in the gathering thought the Pep who crumpled last October could come back from that harrowing experience.

But Pep fooled them and he fooled the confident Saddler camp with an exhibition that was little short of amazing. In the first round he actually jabbed Saddler thirty-seven successive times in a demonstration of blinding speed that had Sandy looking like a novice. He neither gave quarter nor asked for it.

Pep was warned for wrestling in the first round and for "heeling," in the third. He prevented Sandy from landing his heavy punches at close quarters.

Giving Saddler a boxing lesson through the first three rounds, Pep appeared to weaken in the fourth, when Sammy plastered him with savage digs to the body and grazed the head with dangerous swings, almost upsetting Pep once with a left jab.

Punches From All Angles

A right opened a cut under Pep's left eye in the fifth, but the Hartford lad ignored the wound and out-boxed his foe through this session and those that followed up to the tenth. In fitful bursts Pep hammered Saddler with lefts and rights from all angles and in tireless fashion, while Saddler missed most of his blows.

Pep electrified the crowd with his boxing and fighting through the eleventh, twelfth and thirteenth rounds. He pelted Saddler with every blow known to boxing. But he gave his greatest thrill in the fifteenth when, after weathering the jarring fire of the fourteenth, he came back to fight Saddler all over the ring with a strength that few, if any thought he possessed.

Pep weighed 126 pounds, Saddler 124.

VETERAN WHO REGAINED TITLE SCORING IN GARDEN BATTLE

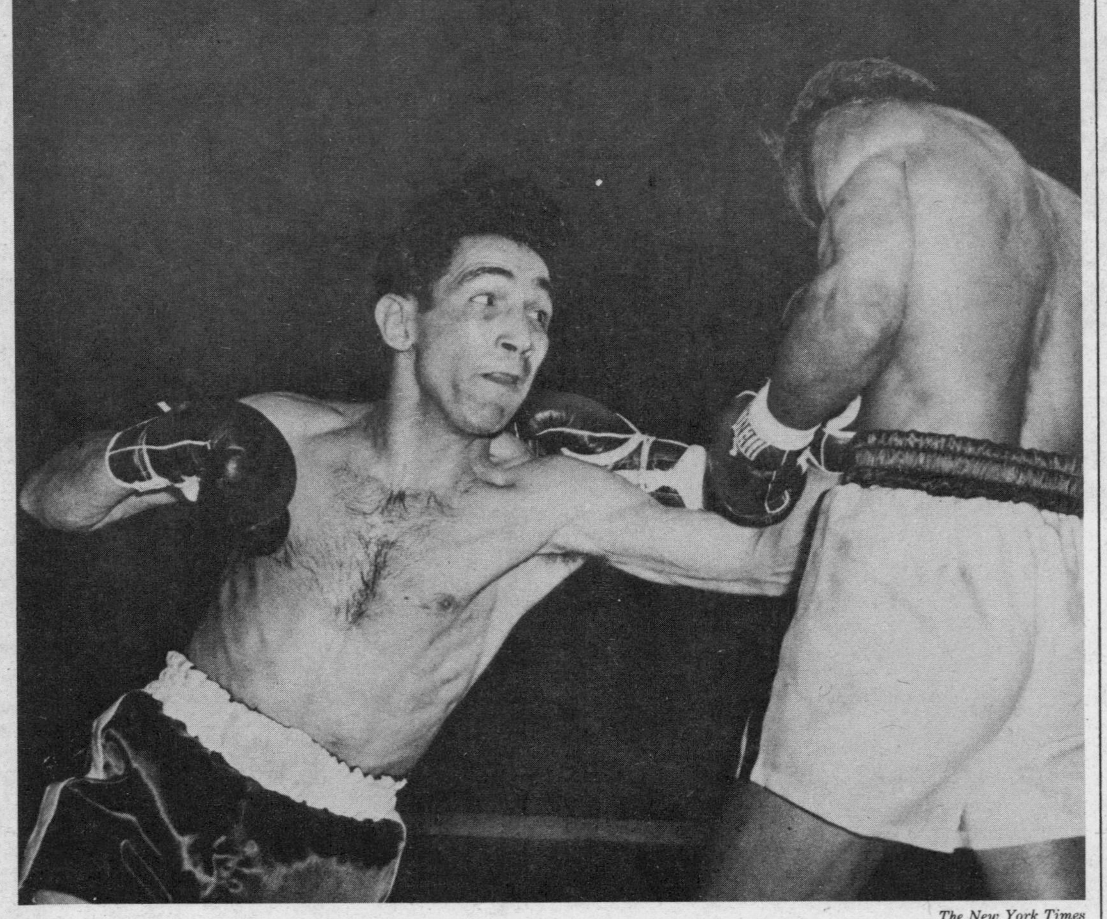

The New York Times

Willie Pep smashing a hook to Sandy Saddler's body in the first round of championship fight.

TANENBAUM GOES TO BALTIMORE FIVE

Bullets Get Ex-N. Y. U. Star From Knicks, Who Oppose Ft. Wayne Quintet Today

By LOUIS EFFRAT

What had been, more or less, an unhappy relationship between the New York Knickerbockers and Sid Tanenbaum was terminated yesterday with the announcement that the former N. Y. U. ace had been dealt away to the Baltimore Bullets. Thus, Tanenbaum will not be around this afternoon when the Knicks oppose the Fort Wayne Pistons in a Basketball Association of America encounter at Madison Square Garden.

To acquire the stylish ex-Violet, the Baltimore club had to give the Knicks first call next season on any Bullet currently on the active Baltimore roster, with only one exception. Buddy Jeannette, playing manager of the Bullets, is the only man the Knicks will not be permitted to take.

Set Record at N. Y. U.

Tanenbaum, who amassed 1,074 points in his four-year career at N. Y. U., highest in Violet history, twice won the Haggerty Memorial Award and is the only player ever to have been named on All-Metropolitan teams four straight years. He is 23 years old, and in his thirty-two games with the Knicks this campaign tallied 257 points. He was the sixth highest scorer on the club.

Thus, the Knicks, second in the Eastern Division, will have to struggle along one man short until Gene James, Marshall (W. Va.) star, who was signed Thursday, reports to the New Yorkers next week.

TRADED TO THE BALTIMORE BULLETS

Sid Tanenbaum The New York Times

WELCOME AWAITS EXILES

Cards Hope Chandler Forgives Three Men Who 'Jumped'

ST. LOUIS, Feb. 11 (AP)—The three St. Louis Cardinals who jumped to the Mexican Baseball League would be welcomed back if Commissioner A. B. Chandler lifts the five-year suspension on players who went south of the border.

"We'd be glad to have the boys back," said Cardinal Owner Fred M. Saigh Jr. "In fact, last summer, when it first was reported they might be reinstated, we put the question to the Cardinals. All our players had the same idea—that the three had been punished enough."

The three Cardinals who jumped to Mexico in May, 1946, are Pitchers Max Lanier and Fred Martin and Infielder Lou Klein. At that time, they were valued at about $200,000.

CHAMPION RALLIES TO SCORE IN 5 SETS

Gonzales Drops Record First Tilt, 18-16, Second at 6-2, Then Rises to Triumph

MISS HART BOWS, 6-4, 6-1

Florida Girl Beaten in Final by Mrs. du Pont—Hall Wins Veteran Title 6th Time

By ALLISON DANZIG

Richard (Pancho) Gonzales' reign as national amateur tennis champion was extended for a second year yesterday and no holder of the crown has shown more perseverance in enduring and surmounting the barbs of adversity than did the 21-year-old six-footer from Los Angeles to defeat Frederick R. (Ted) Schroeder of La Crescenta, Calif., in the Forest Hills stadium yesterday.

Beaten in a record-breaking 34-game opening set—the longest ever played in a championship final—after five times requiring only a point to win it, and outplayed by a wide margin in the second as the inevitable reaction brought on the blight of apathy, Gonzales took the gallery of 13,000 and his tiring older opponent by storm as he came back to win at 16—18, 2—6, 6—1, 6—2, 6—4.

The women's title also was carried off for the second successive year by Mrs. William du Pont, the former Margaret Osborne, of Wilmington, Del., in a one-sided final that contrasted with last year's epochal marathon. She defeated Miss Doris Hart of Jacksonville, Fla., 6—4, 6—1.

Scores in Straight Sets

The veterans' championship was won for the sixth successive year by J. Gilbert Hall of New York. In the concluding round on the grandstand court he won from Wilmer Allison of Austin, Tex., former men's national titleholder, 6—3, 6—2, and maintained his record of never losing a set in all the years he has held the crown.

The mixed doubles tournament will be brought to a conclusion today. The final will be held at 1 P. M. between Miss Louise Brough and Eric Sturgess of South Africa and Mrs. du Pont and William Talbert. Darkness set in at the end of the semi-finals making it impossible to continue play.

Gonzales, the victim of repeated setbacks during the year both at home and abroad, showed his characteristic genius for bringing his game to its peak in the big match that counts. He did that in the Davis Cup challenge round and he did it again in the championship.

One can hardly give the champion too much praise for his moral fiber. Almost invariably the loser of an opening set of anything like the length of yesterday's, which broke the 16—14 record set by John Doeg and Frank Shields in the 1930 final, loses heart as well and never is able to overcome the discouragement of the setback. So it seemed would be the case yesterday, as Gonzales slumped badly in the second set and appeared to be resigned to his fate.

Hits 17 Service Aces

For an hour and thirteen minutes through that thirty-four-game opener the champion had fought his rival in a tremendous duel of service and volley. Seventeen times he had scored on unquestionable service aces, which must have set a record for one set, and he had matched Schroeder in winning one love game after another.

So devastating was Gonzales' service that never until the twenty-fifth game was Schroeder able to get to "deuce" against it. The only other time he got that far was the thirty-first game until the lone break of the set was effected in the thirty-third.

Gonzales holding the trophy after he defeated Schroeder

In the thirtieth game came the most painful experience of all for the champion. Schroeder was behind at 0—40 as the champion threw two perfect lobs over his head, and the big crowd was ready to let loose with a thundering roar. Instead it cheered the Wimbledon titleholder for the great fight he made to pull out of that seemingly hopeless situation, twice as Gonzales' backhand failed on the return of service, as it did so often in the match, and the third time with one of Schroeder's overhead smashes.

Gonzales refused to become discouraged after missing that golden opportunity and won his next service. Then came the bitter blow. Behind at 0—40 in the thirty-third game, he emulated his rival in pulling up to deuce, to the thunderous applause of the crowd, and after Schroeder had gained advantage point on a net-cord shot, one of several by which he benefited, the champion brought the house down again with a searing service ace.

Then came a particularly bitter pill for the titleholder. In the next rally, an exciting exchange of lightning strokes, he executed one of his adroit drop volleys. The side linesman cried "out" and immediately an outburst of protests came from the stands.

Gonzales cried out too, then immediately accepted the decision with the fine sportsmanship Schroeder was to exhibit on the final point of the match and which both men shared throughout. In the next rally, the last of the set, the champion slipped as he made his volley and a gasp went up from the crowd as the ball fell into the net.

It seemed that the fates were against Gonzales. All the luck in the match had been with Schroeder, though it had not amounted to much, and that fact and the memory of the great opportunity he had missed at 40—0 were enough to have broken the spirit of most players after making so great a fight for seventy-three minutes—as long as many entire matches last.

To all appearances Gonzales was a beaten champion as the second set ended. But with the start of the third the big fellow lost no time in reassuring his admirers that he was in the fight again for all he was worth. It was the Gonzales of the first set with whom Schroeder had to reckon now, with his mighty service going full blast, his footwork speeded up and his volley doing deadly execution.

Four games in a row went to Gonzales without deuce being called once. Rifled service aces and blazing passing shots and volleys were speeding from his racquet in a barrage of winning shots that had his rival helpless.

The ten-minute rest period did not serve to restore the vigor of Schroeder's game. He was offering more resistance, but his play lacked the vitality of his rival's. He could not return service nor was he attacking at the net as often or making the dazzling volleys for which he is feared.

Mrs. William du Pont with prize
The New York Times (by George Alexanderson)

With the final set, Schroeder dug in and made so strong a fight that the crowd was kept on tenterhooks almost to the very end. This was the famous fifth set, and no one had beaten him down the wire in four long matches at Wimbledon or in two in the championship against Frank Sedgman and Talbert.

Schroeder saved the first game from 0—30 and then had the crowd holding its breath as he got to 30—0 against Gonzales' service in the fourth. This was his chance, and, as it proved, his last one. His backhand failed him in trying to pass on an easy volley, and he never threatened to break through again. Nevertheless, he held his own service to 4-all even though Gonzales was both serving and returning service the better of the two.

As the play went on, the crowd could sense Schroeder's weakening in the opportunities he wasted with errors unworthy of him when he is fresh. Gonzales was missing chances, too, but not because of fatigue so much as from the nervous tension as he sighted victory.

Then came the break that decided the match. Against a clearly tiring Schroeder, Gonzales went on the attack. The return of service which had been so recalcitrant for most of the match now was functioning beautifully, to keep the ball at Schroeder's feet to extract the error or elicit a half-volley that enabled the champion to take the net position away from his opponent.

Every point in this final game brought cheers or groans, so worked up was the crowd. When Gonzales double-faulted to make the score 15—all, his first in three sets, they groaned. When he fell behind, 30—40, as he reached high up and hit a ball that was going out, they groaned again in extreme anguish.

A sigh of relief went through the crowd as the score reached deuce on Schroeder's backhand drive beyond the line. Then came a smash from Gonzales' racquet that set the crowd wild with delight. Now came the final rally and Schroeder whipped a forehand down the line past Gonzales at the net. A gasp went up and then the place turned into bedlam as the linesman signaled it was out.

Schroeder, stunned by the call, cried out, and there were outcries from the stand. But the Wimbledon champion accepted the decision which meant failure to his great fight. Breaking into a grin, he pretended he was going to throw his racquet at the official and then ran forward to offer his congratulations to the happy Gonzales as the crowd cheered.

In the mixed doubles semi-finals, Miss Brough and Sturgess defeated Miss Gertrude Moran and Gonzales, 6—8, 6—3, 15—13, and Mrs. du Pont and Talbert won from Mrs. Patricia Todd and Jaroslav Drobny, 6—0, 6—2.

TWIN PONDS BELLE MID-HUDSON BEST

Alker Welsh Terrier Annexes 27th Top Award Among 582 Dogs in Pawling Show

PAWLING, N. Y., Sept. 5 — Champion Twin Ponds Belle, the Welsh terrier that is already loaded down with ring honors, tacked one more to her string today in the seventh annual Mid-Hudson Kennel Club fixture high on breezy Quaker Hill. The best-in-show award was the twenty-seventh for the dog, owned by Mrs. Edward P. Alker of Great Neck, L. I.

There were 582 dogs in the event. While the list contained lots of quality, none exceeded Belle in national stature, and the choice for best, made by Edwin L. Pickhardt, was not unexpected. John Goudie was handler for the Alker terrier as usual.

Belle was the terrier that went to best American-bred at Morris and Essex last spring and the way she showed today indicated she had lost none of her fine edge.

Disputing the winner's supremacy in the final were a Pembroke Welsh corgi, the Greencorg Kennels' ch. Formakin Orangeman; a greyhound, Mrs. Harding T. Mason's ch. Little Andely's Frabgous Day; a red cocker spaniel, Gloria Brunner's ch. Glo's Gay Pete's Repete; a bulldog, the Milsande Kennels' ch. Milsande's Lady Luck, and a white toy poodle, the Cartlane Kennels' ch. Cartlane Once.

Hurricanes Beat Bostwick Field By 12-6 to Gain Open Polo Final

Smith Scores Six Goals, Cavanagh Three to Pace Winners in U.S. Tourney—Bostwick Registers Three Tallies for the Losers

By WILLIAM J. BRIORDY
Special to THE NEW YORK TIMES.

WESTBURY, L. I., Sept. 5—Never letting the opposition get set, Laddie Sanford's Hurricanes rode into the final round of the National Open polo championship tournament today by routing Pete Bostwick's Bostwick Field four, 12 to 6, on International Field of the Meadow Brook Club.

More strongly mounted, the Hurricanes once again unloosed the power which crushed Detroit-Templeton [illegible] Sunday. And once again it was the terrific hitting of Roberto Cavanagh, nine-goal Argentine star, and the ten-goal Cecil Smith that carried the day.

Smith is still rated at ten goals—and probably worth more on any man's polo field. He directed the Hurricanes' attack beautifully. Cavanagh, although he got only three goals to Smith's six, was equally effective from the No. 2 position.

Sheerin Gets Two Goals

Young Larry Sheerin stroked two goals from the No. 1 spot, while Sanford hit one from the back post. The Hurricanes, who have won four Open titles, now have scored a total of twenty-seven goals against ten for the opposition in two matches in this Open, the thirty-third.

The Hurricanes, who won the lion's share of high-goal honors last year, will face the winner of the semi-final, between Argentina's El Trebol poloists and Mexico's Gracida Brothers. El Trebol and Mexico meet next Sunday on International Field, with the victor tackling the Hurricanes on Sept. 18.

Bostwick, who notched three of his side's goals; Peter Perkins, eight-goal internationalist, who filled in for the injured Buddy Combs; Alan Corey, eight-goaler, and Devereaux Milburn Jr. rode for the losers, in that order.

The Line-Up

HURRICANES (12)	BOSTWICK FIELD (6)
1—Larry Sheerin	1—G. H. Bostwick
2—Roberto Cavanagh	2—Peter Perkins
3—Cecil Smith	3—A. L. Corey Jr.
Back—Stephen Sanford	Back—D. Milburn Jr.

SCORE BY PERIODS

Hurricanes	2	2	3	0	4	1—12
Bostwick Field	1	2	1	0	1	1— 6

Goals—Hurricanes: Sheerin 2, Cavanagh 3, Smith 6, Sanford. Bostwick Field: Bostwick 3, Perkins, Corey 2.

Referee—W. F. C. Guest. Umpires—W. H. Gaylord and Terence Preece. Time of periods—7½ minutes.

The outmounted Bostwick Field quartet could do nothing to stop the powerful Cavanagh-Smith duo. The Hurricanes jumped to a 2-0 leeway early in the first period as Smith ripped home a penalty shot and then clicked on a four-stroke run. Corey drove one in late in the opening period to make it 2-1.

After Smith made it 3-1 in the second period on a follow-up of a drive by Sanford, Bostwick rapped in a three-stroker and took a pass from Perkins to knot the count at 3-all, the only time during the game that the score was tied. Smith connected on a three-stroke foray to break the deadlock in the second chukker.

Sheerin, Cavanagh and Smith each counted in the third to hand the Hurricanes a 7-4 lead at the intermission. Sanford's side was never in danger after that, a four-goal surge in the fifth clinching the game.

Sanford played a fine game at back despite the fact that he was nursing a sore right leg. Laddie was forced to dismount in the second period when Perkins' pony rammed into Sanford's horse. Sanford, who was hit in the back by Perkins' mount, returned to play after a short rest.

The best shot of the game was one uncorked by Cavanagh in the sixth chukker. The goal, on a difficult near-side back-handed drive, was disallowed because the whistle had been blown for a penalty before the ball went between the posts.

"All the News That's Fit to Print"

The New York Times.

LATE CITY EDITION
Sunny with pleasant temperatures today; fair tonight and tomorrow.
Temperature Range Today—Max., 75; Min., 56
Temperatures Yesterday—Max., 73; Min., 62
Full U. S. Weather Bureau Report, Page 41

VOL. XCIX..No. 33,742. Entered as Second-Class Matter, Post Office, New York, N. Y. NEW YORK, MONDAY, JUNE 12, 1950. Times Square, New York 18, N. Y. Telephone LAckawanna 4-1000 RAG PAPER EDITION SEVENTY-FIVE CENTS

U. S. COURSE IS HELD KEY TO RUSSIAN BID ON WEST GRAIN PACT

Europeans Weigh Propaganda Gain to Moscow if Americans Oppose an Agreement

THEME USED BY U. S. S. R.

Predictions Already Made That Washington Will Block Deal —Soviet Demands Seen

By MICHAEL L. HOFFMAN

Special to THE NEW YORK TIMES.

GENEVA, June 11—Some of the Western European countries are seriously concerned that the United States is going to make an important Communist propaganda theme come true.

The impression has grown among Western officials attending the United Nations Economic Commission for Europe that the Russians are really eager to sell several million tons of grain to the West this year. The Russians have proposed a European grain agreement to the secretariat of the economic commission.

Every time the Russians have mentioned their desire to cooperate in improving East-West trade they have said in effect: "But of course we do not expect the United States to permit you Westerners to trade with us because the United States wants to dump its surpluses on your poor people."

Western Europeans for their part know—presumably so do the Russians—that the United States Department of Agriculture and Department of State do not always agree on such matters.

State Department Criticized

The State Department has been under embarrassing criticism from the French for having supported or at least acquiesced in the Department of Agriculture's insistence, backed by the British, that the Germans buy mainly dollar wheat under the International Wheat Agreement.

The Economic Cooperation Administration started two years ago to tell the French to increase wheat acreage and improve output.

This year, André Philip, French delegate to the economic agency for Europe, said the other day, France was likely to have as much as 3,000,000 tons for export. But Germany, right next door, cannot buy more than 80,000 tons of French wheat until she has imported from the United States her full quota under the agreement.

This is the background of some questions being asked by Westerners here, not yet openly or directly, as to whether in fact the United States would agree to a Russian-Western European grain agreement.

American Policy Not "Cleared"

Of course, such an agreement would concern primarily coarse grains not wheat, according to European commodity experts. Nevertheless, some wheat might be included.

The United States delegation has not said anything during this E. C. E. meeting to suggest that the United States would oppose such an agreement.

On the other hand, the United States delegation here knows the issue over American policy has not been really "cleared" in Washington, notably at the Department of Agriculture.

It is inconceivable to Western European officials that the Soviet Union would make a serious offer of a grain agreement if it did not expect to derive some powerful propaganda value from it.

Merely for the Russians to say they can supply the West with grain seems scarcely enough to observers of the European scene. This is no more than normal in European trade arrangements.

Some observers believe the Russians will never make an agreement unless they get public concessions on strategic commodity lists that the United States and Western countries maintain to prevent exports of certain war potential goods to Communist countries. British sources here say the Russians roam all over British industry but seem unable to find anything that they desire with the exception of items on the lists of goods that are barred to them.

On the other hand, the Russians may be banking on a refusal by the United States to agree to a European grain agreement. In that case, they would have superb propaganda, which they are already anticipating by predicting that the United States will say no to their offer to the commission.

Formosa Executes 2 Generals in Plot

By The Associated Press.

TAIPEI, Formosa, June 11—Two generals once high in Nationalist circles were executed Saturday on charges of plotting to deliver Formosa to the Chinese Communists by staging a revolt. With them died a colonel and a woman. These were the first announced executions arising from a big round-up of Communist agents on Formosa in February and March.

Chief among them was Lieut. Gen. Wu Shih, Vice Minister of Defense when arrested March 2. A secret radio transmitter was found in the Defense Ministry. The others executed were Lieut. Gen. Chen Pao-chong, in charge of conscription when he was arrested; Col. Nyi Shih and Miss Tsu Kan-tse.

All four were forced to kneel with their hands tied behind them. Each was shot in the back of the head.

BROTHERHOOD GOAL OF NEW MOVEMENT

Conference in Paris Endorses Charter of World Organization to Spur Amity of Peoples

Special to THE NEW YORK TIMES.

PARIS, June 11—The creation of a World Brotherhood organization to promote "amity, understanding and cooperation between peoples of varying races, religions, nationalities and cultures" was unanimously approved today at the close of a conference here attended by 155 men and women delegates from twelve nations.

The conference endorsed the constitution of the organization and approved a charter for chapters to be formed throughout the world, except in Communist-governed countries. A committee of educators within the conference did, however, pass a resolution to the effect that no restrictions should be made against persons in those countries who may sympathize with and share brotherhood ideals.

World Brotherhood, now supported by Protestants, Roman Catholics and Jews, is an outgrowth of the National Conference of Christians and Jews in the United States. The final act of the meeting here was to ask that organization to take the first steps toward formation of a world organization among persons pledged to work for tolerance and brotherly harmony.

Interim Group Named

Notable persons of many countries attended the meeting, presided over by Arthur H. Compton, United States educator and pioneer in atomic energy research, and were appointed to the interim committee that will cooperate in the foundation's work.

"It has been my privilege to share in bringing great new powers of nature to the service of man," said Dr. Compton. "I am impressed by the fact that these powers make possible a great era of prosperity. In order that this goal shall be realized, however, it is necessary that we agree upon common human goals. It is to this end that we today have established World Brotherhood."

Dr. Compton said that men and women throughout the world were seeking a common basis for working in harmony. This basis is afforded by agreement on the importance of the individual and his free growth, he declared, adding:

"This is the meaning of brother-

Continued on Page 10, Column 6

CHINESE REDS GIVE SPECIAL ATTENTION TO INDIA; SNUB TITO

Nehru's Envoy Gets Favored Courtesies — Communists Stress Common Frontier

LIST OMITS YUGOSLAVIA

Belgrade Not Included Among Capitals Seeking Relations—British Bid Also Waits

By WALTER SULLIVAN

Special to THE NEW YORK TIMES.

HONG KONG, June 11—The People's Republic of China has for eight months ignored a bid for recognition by the Yugoslav Government but in recent weeks has accorded special courtesies to India.

This situation throws light on the emerging foreign policy of the Peiping Government. Yugoslavia's offer to establish diplomatic relations was, according to Belgrade press reports, sent to Peiping Oct. 5. So far as the public record is concerned it has been completely ignored by China's Communists.

A striking example received here a few days ago was a list of countries which the Chinese say have established relations or have offered to do so. It was printed in the Liberation Daily, official Communist party organ in Shanghai, on May 19. Listed were twenty-four governments, ranging from the Soviet Union to Ceylon. Yugoslavia was not included.

Last year there was much talk about a possible rise of Titoism within the Chinese Communist party. This has been countered by a continuous series of attacks by Peiping on Yugoslav leaders, by affirmations of loyalty to the Soviet Union and by theoretical dissertations on internationalism.

Government Hailed

In its note to Chou En-lai last October the Yugoslav Foreign Ministry hailed the formation of the new government and said, perhaps with special intent, that "it means the realization of a true democratic and independent China."

On the other hand, India appears to have received special treatment. The official news report describing the massive May Day parade in Peiping listed India as the only country except the Soviet Union and the "People's Democracies" represented on the reviewing platform.

Last November Mao Tze-tung, as chairman of the Chinese Communist party, wired the Indian Communist party: "India will certainly not remain long under the yoke of imperialism and its collaborators." The message was in acknowledgment of the greeting of Indian Communists on the occasion of the formation of the new Government in Peiping.

"Her fate in the past and her path to the future are similar to those of China in many points," Mr. Mao said. "Like free China, a free India will one day emerge in the Socialist and People's Democratic family. That day will end the imperialist reactionary era in the history of mankind."

However, Peiping has been far more friendly with the Government of Prime Minister Jawaharlal Nehru than with any other large nation of the non-Communist world. Early this year Mr. Mao sent a special greeting on the inauguration of the Republic of India. When K. M. Panikkar arrived

Continued on Page 14, Column 6

Neighbor Is Slain, Policeman Shot As House-Wrecker Runs Amuck

A 56-year-old house-wrecker, apparently suffering from hallucinations, started shooting up his neighborhood early yesterday morning. He began with the walls of his own three-room apartment and wound up killing a neighbor, wounding a policeman and suffering two bullet wounds from the pistol of another policeman. He was sent to Bellevue Hospital in a critical condition.

The man threw into a turmoil the whole block of the lower East Side on which he lived, East Second Street between Avenues A and B. He was subdued only after a policeman with eight previous citations for meritorious service had decided the man was out of ammunition and, with two other policemen, rushed in and overpowered him.

The man who ran amuck was Mike Shramok of 169 East Second Street. His victim was the janitor of the house next door, Harry Polochena, 56. Quiet-spoken Mr. Polochena did not even know Shramok, although they had lived next door to each other for four years and Mr. Polochena had done spare jobs in the house-wrecking business.

The policeman who ended the rampage was Patrolman Isaac Gillman, 42, of the East Fifth Street Station, who lives at 518 Pennsylvania Avenue, Brooklyn. Mr. Gillman exchanged shots with Shramok while the latter had cover, and hit him twice before he rushed him.

The wounded policeman was William F. Tekverk, also of the East Fifth Street Station. Mr. Tekverk was peppered with shot from Shramok's weapon, though he didn't realize it until the shooting was over.

Shramok used a Browning repeating .12 gauge shotgun, loaded with seven shells of .00 shot, used for large game. Neighbors first heard gunfire at 4 o'clock yesterday morning, and again at 10

Continued on Page 3, Column 6

Hogan Wins U. S. Open Golf In a Remarkable Comeback

Ben Hogan with the championship trophy

Associated Press Wirephoto

By LINCOLN A. WERDEN

Special to THE NEW YORK TIMES.

ARDMORE, Pa., June 11—The man they said never would be able to play again regained the United States open golf championship today at the Merion Golf Club.

Ben Hogan, who miraculously survived an automobile smash-up in February, 1949, and returned to tournament competition last January, defeated Lloyd Mangrum and George Fazio in an eighteen-hole play-off for the game's biggest honor by scoring a 69, four less than Mangrum and six below Fazio.

In a dramatic finish, Hogan completed one of the outstanding feats in the annals of sports to win the trophy he captured for the first time at the Riviera Country Club, Santa Monica, Calif., in 1948.

A year ago he sent the trophy back to the United States Golf Association because a blood clot in

Continued on Page 22, Column 1

RUSSIAN DIAMONDS APPEAR IN BELGIUM

Antwerp Dealers Report Sales by Soviet of $1,000,000 Worth of Pre-Revolutionary Gems

Special to THE NEW YORK TIMES.

ANTWERP, Belgium, June 11—The Soviet Union is selling polished diamonds from the pre-Revolution era in the Antwerp market.

In May, 7,500,000 Belgian francs worth ($150,000) were sold for the Russians and in April 5,000,000 Belgian francs worth.

Experts say most of these diamonds are "old-cuts," that is, polished at least fifty years ago, but some are "modern-cuts."

Belgian selling brokers have already been advised that for June, 6,000,000 Belgian francs worth will be put on the market. The diamonds are imported by the Soviet Embassy in Brussels and are sold through an Antwerp broker.

It is reported that the Russians started selling sporadically in the Antwerp market eighteen months ago. The total value of these transactions up to now is estimat-

Continued on Page 11, Column 4

EWING IS REPORTED UNWILLING TO RUN

Said to Prefer Try for Cabinet Post to the Governorship—Roosevelt Chances Gain

By JAMES A. HAGERTY

Oscar R. Ewing, Federal Security Administrator, was reported yesterday to have told labor leaders who were supporting him for the Democratic nomination for Governor that he was no longer a candidate but preferred to continue in his present post. It is understood that Mr. Ewing hopes he may be in line for Cabinet rank by establishment of a Federal Department of Health or Welfare.

Mr. Ewing has been the first choice of a group of influential labor leaders for the Democratic nomination for Governor. His retirement from the race is believed to increase the chance of the nomination of Representative Franklin D. Roosevelt Jr., as most if not all of the labor leaders who have been supporting Mr. Ewing are ready to shift to Mr. Roosevelt.

Mr. Ewing's support has been

Continued on Page 19, Column 5

World News Summarized

MONDAY, JUNE 12, 1950

The House committee that asked 166 corporations to list money spent to shape public opinion on national issues is considering if such activities would require reports to Congress under Federal lobbying regulations, Chairman Buchanan said yesterday. [1:8.]

Philip Jaffe, editor of the defunct magazine Amerasia in 1945 when Federal agents found secret Government papers in its offices, will testify today before the Senate group investigating the revived case. [1:7.]

The Senate votes today on a motion to send back to committee the bill extending Federal rent controls beyond June 30. The Administration expects to defeat the motion and then pass the measure. [2:2.] In this state, Rent Administrator McGoldrick ruled out past secrecy and will make available to landlords and tenants inter-office opinions and instructions defining rights and procedures [23:2.]

Personal income rose in April to an annual rate of $212,800,000,000, the Commerce Department reported. Wages and salaries were at a rate of $136,700,000,000. [32:1.]

Western Europe was uncertain of the attitude of the United States on Moscow's offer to sell grain to the West. Dollar restrictions and curbs on trade with the Soviet area were seen as possible checks to East-West wheat deals. [1:1.] The Soviet Union has sold more than $1,000,000 worth of cut diamonds antedating the 1917 revolution in the Belgian market. The stones are sent to the Soviet Embassy in Brussels and some of the proceeds are used to buy Belgian electrical equipment. [1:4.]

Strong language and threats marked East German comments on the Western democracies. An official Soviet paper said any effort to annul Poland's annexation of German territory "would provoke a new war." [10:4-5.] Gerhart Eisler told a Berlin meeting "the time may come soon when the Americans will have to leave not leisurely but in a hurry." [11:2.] In Vienna, an Austrian scientist upset a Communist peace congress by urging deeds that would implement their words for peace. [9:2.]

Delegates from twelve nations formed a World Brotherhood Organization for racial, religious and national understanding open to all but Communist countries. [1:2.] Prominent scientists, educators and clergymen in this country signed a new disarmament plea. [8:3.]

Tokyo police raided Waseda University, seized Communist literature and banned student meetings for one week. [15:3.]

Index to other news appears on Page 28.

CITIZENS CHAMPION SCHOOLS OF NATION IN MEETING NEEDS

300 Cross-Section Community Groups Press for Solutions in Housing and Curricula

IMPELLED BY COMMISSION

Year's Spread and Progress Reflect Surge of Concern Over Rising Enrollments

By BENJAMIN FINE

More than ever before in the nation's history, the public is taking an active interest in public school education. About 300 citizens' groups, dedicated to the improvement of the schools in their communities, are now in operation. Half of these were organized within the last year.

As a result of this significant movement the public schools are beginning to solve some of the serious problems that have vexed them since the end of World War II. An increased birth rate will flood the schools in the next ten years with 10,000,000 additional elementary and high school pupils. This 40 per cent increase will bring a host of problems to almost every village, town and city in the land.

Partly because of enrollment pressure and partly because many school plants have been allowed to deteriorate as a result of the depression and the recent war, the average citizen has become aware of the school system in his community. In the sound democratic tradition, he is now saying: "What can I do to get better schools?" instead of the often expressed: "Let George do it."

Broad Base of Movement

The citizens' groups, for the most part, are supported by all segments of the community — housewives, bankers, farmers, factory workers and professional men. In the truest sense, this is a grass-roots movement springing from an honest desire of the responsible members of the community to give their children a decent schooling.

These conclusions are reached as a result of an extensive study, conducted by THE NEW YORK TIMES, in which key educators, representative citizens and school administrators were interviewed.

To get first-hand data on how the community groups for better schools are organized and how they operate, this writer visited typical cities in the Middle Atlantic area, New England, the South and the Midwest.

In addition, detailed questionnaires were received from more than 200 citizens' school groups, describing the tangible or intangible results obtained in their campaigns to get better schools.

A definite pattern emerges. The public schools appear to be in better condition in those communities where the citizens are taking a constructive part. In some instances it was found that the schools were improved when the man on the street "pitched in" and showed the school officials that the interest was genuine. Again, it was noted that some communities literally lifted themselves up by their bootstraps.

"We were waiting for Washington to come to our rescue," one community spokesman commented. "But, when we jumped in and supported the schools ourselves, we found that we really didn't need outside help."

The impetus for the upsurge in

Continued on Page 16, Column 2

'Twas a Grand Day, Thanks to Canada

New York had a pleasant Sunday yesterday, with throngs at the beaches reaching a seasonal high, but Canada received the meteorological credit.

A mass of cool, relatively dry air, moving down from the north, reached the metropolitan area in time to reduce the high temperatures of recent days—yesterday's high was 73.4 degrees—and to cut humidity sharply. Residents responded in such numbers that Coney Island reported 750,000 visitors, the largest Sunday crowd this year.

The Rockaways, including Jacob Riis Park and near-by Atlantic Beach in Nassau County, had 500,000 visitors, and Orchard Beach in the Bronx, 40,000.

Motor traffic was reported heavy at all resorts. Nassau County's highways were unusually busy, with many minor accidents.

SENATORS TO HEAR JAFFE IN SECRECY

Ex-Editor of Amerasia Likely to Be Questioned Today on Delays in Prosecution

By JAY WALZ

Special to THE NEW YORK TIMES.

WASHINGTON, June 11—The Senate subcommittee investigating the five-year-old Amerasia case will question one of its principal figures tomorrow.

Philip Jaffe, who was editor of the now defunct magazine when, in 1945, Federal agents found hundreds of secret Government documents in its New York offices, will come before the Senators at a closed meeting at 2:30 P. M.

Mr. Jaffe, one of six persons arrested in connection with the discovery of papers, pleaded guilty when his case was prosecuted and was fined $2,500. But the whole case was revived recently in Congress on charges, first, that the arrests were held up by authorities at the highest Administration level, and, second, that prosecution was not pushed vigorously.

Presumably, Mr. Jaffe will be closely examined tomorrow on any information he may have relative to these two points. He will testify in response to a committee subpoena.

Senators to Examine Diary

The Senate investigators, headed by Senator Millard E. Tydings of Maryland, also are expected to take their first look at that part of the diary of the late James Forrestal dealing with the Amerasia arrests.

The Department of Justice confirmed yesterday that Mr. Forrestal's diary indicated that he intervened just before the Amerasia arrests were made. Mr. Forrestal was then Secretary of the Navy, and his purpose is said to have been to make certain that President Truman knew the details and was aware of the international significance of the case.

The six arrests were scheduled at the approximate time of the Charter meeting of the United Nations in San Francisco. According to the Justice Department, the Forrestal notes showed the Cabinet official's concern that the Amerasia case, breaking at that time, might "greatly embarrass" relations of the United States with Russia at San Francisco. He wanted the President to have all the facts before the arrests were ordered.

When President Truman was informed of the facts, he urged

Continued on Page 6, Column 3

Yacht Leaps Bow-First Over Dam, 4 Clinging to Hull See 4 Others Die

Special to THE NEW YORK TIMES.

PITTSBURGH, June 11—Four horror-stricken men clung to a luxurious cabin cruiser in the churning spillway of an Allegheny River dam through the night while, one by one, four others, two of them women, were swept to their deaths.

At dawn today, while 2,000 watched from the shore, boatmen rescued the four survivors of a gay cruise that ended in death and destruction of the vessel and two rescue boats.

The twenty-seven-foot cabin cruiser plunged bow-first over the eleven-foot dam into a maelstrom during the night about fifteen miles northeast of this city.

Hull Wright, a tender at Lock No. 3, where the tragedy occurred, and another lock tender put out in a skiff to aid those who clung to the whirling, bobbing larger boat. The skiff was splintered against the dam by the raging backwash of the spillway and its occupants hung onto the disabled cruiser.

In the hours that followed, Mr. Wright and three members of the pleasure party were swept to their deaths as other rescue attempts failed.

At 7 A. M. today a 30-foot sternwheeler managed, after several tries, to wedge itself against the face of the dam, permitting rescuers to pluck the survivors from the doomed cruiser. Survivors and rescuers went up ladders to the top of the lock, abandoning the riverboat, which was pounded to pieces.

The others lost were Mrs. Carol Kreig, wife of one of the survivors; Mrs. William Fisher and William Leahy Jr. of Chicago, a civil engineer. Mrs. Fisher and the Kreigs were residents of Oakmont, near here.

The pleasure boat was owned by James McHugh Jr., 24-year-old son of the head of a Chicago construction company. Young Mr.

Continued on Page 3, Column 2

HOUSE LOBBY UNIT WEIGHS PLAN TO PUT CURBS ON INDUSTRY

Buchanan Gives This Reason for Call on 166 Corporations to Submit Data on Costs

CITES PAMPHLETS AND ADS

He Says the Firms Contribute to Propaganda Groups—Utility Leader Protests

By JOHN D. MORRIS

Special to THE NEW YORK TIMES.

WASHINGTON, June 11—The special committee of the House of Representatives investigating lobbying activities wants to determine whether corporations should be brought under Federal lobbying regulations if they make a practice of spending money to sway public opinion on national issues.

That was the explanation given today by the committee chairman, Representative Frank Buchanan, Democrat of Pennsylvania, for his recent request to 166 large corporations for detailed reports on any such expenditures since Jan. 1, 1947.

Pamphleteering, contributions to lobbying organizations and newspaper advertisements possibly could be classified as indirect lobbying, he said.

The question that consequently arose, he observed, was whether business concerns engaging in such activities should report them to Congress periodically under the Regulation of Lobbying Act.

Whether the present act covers the business concerns is a question for the courts to decide, but the special committee will consider recommending amendments to the statute to bring them explicitly under the regulations applicable to lobbying groups, according to Mr. Buchanan.

Contribution Data Reported

The committee, he said, had evidence that all of the 166 corporations questioned had made contributions, to avowed lobbying organizations or to groups that had engaged in lobbying, without formally reporting their activities under the lobbying act. The corporations' names were listed as contributors in the recipient organizations' records obtained by committee investigators, he said.

Mr. Buchanan reported that about 100 of the corporations questioned had replied by the end of last week. He said that only one of them, the Southern California Edison Company of Los Angeles, had protested over the request for information.

This complaint was made by William C. Mullendorf, president of the utility, who sent a 600-word wire to Representative Buchanan on June 5.

Mr. Mullendorf described the request as "an obvious attempt to use intimidation in limiting exercise of the rights of free speech by millions of citizens in opposing or supporting proposed legislation."

Mr. Mullendorf added:

"You have demanded an entirely unreasonable volume of information to be furnished within a ten-day period.

"This telegram is to express deepest resentment and indignation at this brazen attempt at thought control on behalf of the citizens of whom you are the servant and not the master."

About half of the replies were simple acknowledgments. Of the rest, committee aides said, four provided data, twenty-five agreed to do so and fifteen said the companies would be unable to meet the June 15 deadline.

Supplementary Letter Sent

In a supplementary letter to the corporations yesterday, Mr. Buchanan said he realized that some of them would be unable to assemble the information by June 15 and asked for compliance by June 30.

The 166 corporations receiving the committee's original questionnaire read like a cross-section of big business. Covered were well-known companies in practically all industries, including aluminum, automobile, chemical, insurance, liquor, oil, rubber, railway, steel and many others.

Much of the requested information does not have to be reported to Congress under the Regulation of Lobbying Act. The committee asks for detailed information including outlays, dates, names and purposes with respect to travel of agents to and from Washington.

Yesterday's supplementary letter from Mr. Buchanan made it clear that the reports requested were not intended to cover expenditures, etc., for conducting sales or other

Continued on Page 4, Column 2

Hogan Defeats Mangrum and Fazio in Play-Off for National Open Golf Title

TEXAN'S 69 TAKES HONORS AT MERION

Continued From Page 1

one of his legs threatened his life. He told the U. S. G. A. he regretted his inability to defend his laurels. He was convalescing when the 1949 open championship was played at the Medinah Country Club outside Chicago, being content with putting on the rug in his Fort Worth, Tex., home while listening to radio reports of the tourney.

When he returned to tournament golf in the Los Angeles open in January over the same Riviera course that is now known as "Hogan's Alley" because of his numerous victories there, he stunned the followers of the royal and ancient game as well as sports adherents everywhere by finishing in a tie in his first test of the comeback trail. Sam Snead overtook him and then beat him in a play-off.

Starts The Road Back

But Hogan was not discouraged. His customary determination was in evidence as he slowly rebuilt his health, aided by his wife, Valerie, who had escaped serious injury in the automobile crash with him. Then came his decision to recreate the mechanical perfection of his great golf game. It was one thing, colleagues admitted, to regain health, quite another to regain the timing and coordination of a super-expert after a long lay-off and a nerve-testing ordeal.

Yesterday his challenge to the disbelievers was on the line. He had a chance to take the title outright with a finish of pars on the last four holes. But he went over regulation figures at two of these and posted a 72-hole aggregate of 287, the same as Mangrum, champion in 1946, and Fazio, the Norristown, Pa., born pro.

Today, in a duel that approached the bizarre with an incident at the sixteenth green, Hogan came on to win. Perhaps a bit tired at the conclusion of his first thirty-six holes of play in one day yesterday since he resumed his tournament schedule, he warded off those who proffered words of encouragement.

"I feel fine," Hogan insisted, with a trace of annoyance that anyone would dare suggest his legs might be bothering him during the championship grind.

He reiterated this statement as he sat in the locker room before starting out in this crucial three-way play-off in golf's golden jubilee championship today. But at the fifteenth hole this afternoon, almost four hours after the three professionals, followed by some 10,000 wildly enthusiastic spectators, had started, Hogan had a lead of one stroke over Mangrum and three over Fazio.

Down In the Quarry

Then came the play at a hole that is perhaps without equal in the fifty years that golfers have been battling for the cup. Mangrum drove into the heavy rough and his rivals were out in the fairway with their drives. This is the famed quarry hole that has since been "softened," but still has a series of bunkers below the green amidst trees and sand. Mangrum realized that he had almost an impossible second shot to the elevated green. Trees blocked his way. He played a safety shot to the fairway for his second.

Mangrum pitched his third to within fifteen feet of the pin. Fazio's second was at the back edge and Hogan hit a perfect iron to within six feet of the pin. Fazio played up for a certain 5. Mangrum replaced the ball on the spot from which he had lifted while Fazio was playing.

Then a strange thing happened. After sighting the line of the putt, he picked up the ball, blew on it and replaced it on the green, rolled it in for what would have been a 4. Hogan putted, missed his chance for a birdie and sank the par 4. Most of those huddled about

Par for the Course

Hole.	Yards.	Par.	Hole.	Yards.	Par
1	360	4	10	335	4
2	555	5	11	378	4
3	195	3	12	400	4
4	595	5	13	133	3
5	425	4	14	443	4
6	435	4	15	395	4
7	360	4	16	445	4
8	367	4	17	230	3
9	185	3	18	458	4
Total	3,477	36	Total	3,217	34

Grand totals—6,694 yards; par 70.

the green, still thought Hogan had only one stroke advantage over Mangrum.

But soon the signboard carried by an attendant to indicate the progress of the play-off indicated that something was amiss. Mangrum had a 6 there instead of a 4. Isaac Grainger, chairman of the United States Golf Association rules of golf committee, along with three other executives, had been sitting back of the green, as interested as any of the fans who had been following the stroke by stroke battle.

Mangrum had broken a rule, in fact two, since competitors are not permitted to lift a ball that is in play under penalty of two strokes. Neither are they permitted to "clean" a ball, without suffering a penalty. Mangrum had inadvertently done just that by blowing a bug off the ball.

Not Familiar With Rule

Questioned later, Mangrum said he did not realize that his action had been an infraction and that he was not familiar with the ruling. Coming as it did at a crucial stage in the match, it caused a stir in the crowd surrounding the seventeenth tee as the players started down the hill to the green. Few realized what had happened and on all sides questions were being asked.

Would Hogan coast in because of a rule infraction?

His lead was now three strokes over Mangrum, but there was still uncertainty among the gallery. Hogan dispelled all that soon after. His shot to the seventeenth green stopped on the lower level of the putting surface. He sighted it carefully and hit it well, the ball running up and over a ridge and on into the cup for a deuce.

"That's the way to win," shouted an overjoyed bystander.

Fazio and Mangrum had par 3s there and now Hogan was four strokes in front, or two without the penalty.

The long eighteenth was lined with spectators sensing the tenseness of the finish. Another incident might change the picture. All three players hit the green on their second shots, but they did not hold the green.

Fazio chipped up for a 5 after Mangrum and Hogan approached well, Hogan having less than a six-footer for his par. Mangrum sank his 4 and then Hogan's putt curled in for the championship. There was a mad crush and several persons were knocked down in the melee. A cordon of police saved Hogan from the happy jam of well-wishers.

Fazio Putting Brilliant

Over the outgoing nine Fazio had proved the better putter. He was constantly bringing cheers by his recoveries, and, at the turn, Hogan and Mangrum were deadlocked at 36 to the former Canadian open champion's 37. Fazio had used only thirteen putts during that stretch, Hogan sixteen and Mangrum seventeen.

Before starting out Hogan had joshed with Dick Chapman, former National Amateur champion and recent finalist in the British amateur. "No, Dick," he said, "I'm not a good putter. I've had thirty-six on every round of the championship so far." "Don't tell me that, Ben," replied Chapman. "You're one of the best in the game."

For a long while, though, it seemed that Hogan was allowing opportunity to slip by. He was putting short. Only once on the outgoing half did he snare a birdie and that was when he sank a four-footer at the seventh for a 3. He had seven pars, and the only one over par was at the eighth, where he drove into a bunker and took a 5. Mangrum had a birdie 4 at the second, where his fine second stopped three feet from the pin. He got a 4 at the short third after chipping from the back edge and having his putt for the par rim the cup. Fazio one-putted the second, fourth, fifth, eighth and ninth greens.

On the tenth Mangrum drove into a bunker at the right, standing in the hazard below the ball to make his recovery shot. But after the 5 there he birdied the eleventh when he ran in a seven footer.

At the twelfth Mangrum hit a No. 5 iron too strongly as the breeze faded and the ball flew over the crowd, going out of bounds to the road back of the green. Hogan then led Mangrum by a stroke. Hogan was 2 ahead with a 4 at the fourteenth, where Mangrum was bunkered and took a 5. At the next hole Mangrum sank a fifteen-footer for a birdie 3, and Hogan had to be content with a 4.

Then the bug alighted on Mangrum's ball at the sixteenth, and the penalty for handling the ball sealed the victory for Little Ben.

THE CARDS

Out—										
Hogan	4	5	3	5	4	4	3	5	3—36	
Mangrum	4	4	4	5	4	4	4	4	3—36	
Fazio	5	4	3	5	4	5	5	3	3—37	
In—										
Hogan	4	4	4	3	4	4	4	2	4—33—69	
Mangrum	5	3	5	3	5	3	6	3	4—37—73	
Fazio	4	4	4	3	5	5	5	3	5—38—75	

FOOTBALL SHRINE NAMES 11 OFFICIALS

Athletic Leaders Chosen for Building Committee by New Brunswick Group

NEW BRUNSWICK, N. J., June 11 (AP)—Eleven leading athletic officials from various sections of the United States were chosen today as members of the building committee of the new national football shrine and hall of fame.

The announcement was made by Arthur L. Evans, executive secretary of the National Football Shrine Organization.

Rutgers was selected last fall as the location for the gridiron shrine. College Field, on the Rutgers campus, was used for the first intercollegiate football game, played between Rutgers and Princeton, Nov. 6, 1869.

SQUADRON A IN FRONT, 11-5

Beats Blind Brook Quartet as Glynn's 4 Goals Pace Attack

Special to THE NEW YORK TIMES.

PURCHASE, N. Y., June 11—Scoring at least twice in every period except the fifth, the Squadron A foursome, led by Tommy Glynn, defeated Captain Al Parsells' Blind Brook quartet, 11 to 5, as the two "home" teams clashed in the inaugural game of the Polo season at the Blind Brook Turf and Polo Club today.

The Brooks matched their clubmates for only a little more than one chukker, then fell back permanently, Squadron A rolling to a 7-3 half-time lead. Glynn, at No. 3, topped the point scorers with four goals.

The line-up:

SQUADRON A (11)	BLIND BROOK (5)
1—Paul Miller	1—Walt Devereux
2—Walter Phillips	2—Maj. Arthur Surkamp
3—Tommy Glynn	3—Al. Parsells
Back—Tommy Long	Back—Fred Zeller

SCORE BY PERIODS

Squadron A	2	3	2	2	0	2—11
Blind Brook	2	1	0	0	1	1—5

Goals—Squadron A: Miller 3, Phillips 3, Glynn 4, Long. Blind Brook: Devereux 3, Parsells 2.

Sports of the Times

BY ARTHUR DALEY

An Anti-Climax of Sports

ARDMORE, Pa., June 11—It was inevitable, of course, that there would be something of an anti-climax to the open championship in today's play-off. There usually is to every play-off. But what set this one apart from all the others was that, in some respects, it was reminiscent of the Los Angeles Open of last January. You remember that, don't you?

Little Ben Hogan at that time was meeting his first test in his long uphill climb from the valley of death. Learned doctors had said after his terrifying auto smash-up that he would be lucky to live. Never again would his torn body be able to carry him around a golf course. Of that they were sure. The chances were that he would be unable to play even for fun. Working at his trade once more was much too insane a thought for serious consideration.

But Blazin' Ben made his return in the Los Angeles Open, and the gallant mite finished in a tie with Sammy Snead. He lost that play-off, which was not particularly important. The electrifying news was that Hogan was back in the thick of the fight, getting there on sheer grit and determination.

The experts, who can be just as wide of the mark as anybody, were pretty well agreed before this tournament started that the tenacious Texan might score well in the first two rounds, but they were equally certain that the marathon finish of 36 holes in a day would buckle his tortured legs and have him popping osselets all over the course.

The Pace That Kills

"Ben just can't do it," said the outspoken Gene Sarazen with a sympathetic shake of his head. "Thirty-six holes in one day will kill him." It was a reasonable assumption. This was only Hogan's seventh tournament since his brush with death, and in none of the others had he been forced to jam in two rounds in the one day. Yet the healthy stars faltered in the homestretch yesterday and the iron-willed, square-jawed scrapper from Texas finished in a tie.

Ben was chatting in the hotel lobby this morning. It was idle chatter. But in the course of it he dropped a couple of sentences which were highly significant.

"The trouble with Merion," he drawled, "is that it always has you on the defensive. There's no way you can take the offensive against it."

His jaw jutted grimly. It was obvious that he favors attack, even against something as inanimate as a golf links.

Appearances Are Deceiving

After studying Merion's treachery for four days, however, one can't help but wonder if this fiendish device for playing pasture pool is as inanimate as it looks. It has a par of 70 and measures only 6,694 yards, both sets of statistics being slightly on the skimpy side. Yet there is no getting around the fact that there were only fourteen sub-par rounds out of the first 434 completed.

The opening day fooled a lot of people. When an unknown like Lee Mackey tears Merion apart with a record 64, no one could be blamed for snorting, "Huh, that can't be so tough." Everyone more or less expected that par of 280 for the 72 holes would be shattered. But Mackey soared up to 81 on the second round. Non-golfers have since asked, "Why did everyone immediately disregard Mackey as a contender in spite of his record 64?"

It's a good question. The answer is simple. Some unknown rookie can hit a longer home run than Babe Ruth ever hit. But it's consistency over the long pull which marks the true champion. That rookie still hasn't hammered out sixty homers in a full season of play. That's why the kid from Alabama had no chance of ever being more than a one-day sensation.

Much Too Defiant

Merion can be licked once, but it has the resiliency of a rubber-ball or the recuperative powers of the champion who can bounce back off the floor after being knocked down and belt the other guy's block off. Unlike an ordinary golf course, it does all of the attacking.

Cary Middlecoff, for instance, was in a fine spot just before the final round to repeat as champion. He had three rounds of 71, and, as later events were to prove, only needed an ordinary 73 to win. But his luck was inordinately atrocious. Whenever his playing partner, Hogan, hit a spectator with a drive or approach, the victim helped him by keeping the ball from heading for impending disaster.

But whenever the young dentist from Memphis hit a spectator, it meant a major extraction. The ball invariably caromed in the wrong direction. Toward the end he just ceased to care and performed mechanically. That, naturally, led him into further difficulties and an eventual score of 79.

It was on the sixteenth, though, that Merion gave him a ghoulish horse-laugh—and the business. Just before the green and in a deep gully in front of it is an abandoned rock quarry, now covered with jungle growth. The second shot is across the rock quarry.

Middlecoff's second fell into the gully behind a twenty-foot rock-faced cliff. He had to play safe and, as its last ironic jest, Merion forced him to chip into a sand trap, the only spot in the gully from which he could reach the green. When safety play requires a fellow to shoot into sand traps—well, that gives you an idea of what this course is like.

Perfect Ending

If Battling Ben had lost this play-off, no one could have blamed him. After all, he had done miraculously well in dragging his wearied legs this far. Yet this was such a gushily romantic setting, and he was such an overwhelmingly sentimental favorite, that it would have been cruel indeed for him to have wavered. So the little Texas bulldog, who had defied the doctors, took it upon himself to defy the laws of probabilities and to defy Merion's constantly outrageous challenge.

He beat Lloyd Mangrum. He beat George Fazio. And as a final flourish he also beat Merion's par. A fifty-foot uphill putt of incredible accuracy on the seventeenth brought the birdie that did it. This was the cushion which handed him outright victory beyond question, one untainted by Mangrum's two-stroke penalty on the sixteenth. He was to win by a margin of four strokes.

This is a sport success story without parallel. All hail Ben Hogan, a champion among champions!

"All the News That's Fit to Print"

The New York Times

LATE CITY EDITION
Mostly sunny today, fair tomorrow and unseasonably warm in both days.
Temperature Range Today—Max., 86; Min., 67
Temperatures Yesterday—Max., 88; Min., 62
Full U. S. Weather Bureau Report, Page 41

Copyright, 1950, by The New York Times Company.

VOL. C..No. 33,854. Entered as Second-Class Matter, Post Office, New York, N. Y. NEW YORK, MONDAY, OCTOBER 2, 1950. Times Square, New York 18, N. Y. Telephone LAckawanna 4-1000 RAG PAPER EDITION SEVENTY-FIVE CENTS

SOUTH KOREANS CROSS 38TH PARALLEL ON 8TH ARMY'S ORDER, MOVE 7 MILES; REDS IGNORE M'ARTHUR ON SURRENDER

SCHOOL PURCHASES TOTALING MILLIONS MADE WITHOUT BIDS

Evidence of Wide Irregularity Sent to Three Prosecutors After Year's Investigation

INSPECTORS ARE ACCUSED

Oral Orders, Device Employed to Evade Law, Show Big Drop Since the Inquiry Began

By RICHARD H. PARKE

Evidence that millions of dollars worth of paint, glass, hardware, lumber and other materials had been purchased for the city's schools from favored contractors without competitive bidding has been submitted to the District Attorneys of New York, Kings and Queens Counties.

The evidence, which also disclosed that inspectors had approved materials delivered and work performed that failed to meet specifications, was contained in a report made public yesterday by James H. Sheils, Commissioner of Investigation, and Maximilian Moss, president of the Board of Education.

Commenting on the report, Mr. Moss hinted that the investigation had proceeded to the point where criminal prosecution and departmental trials were imminent. He said he had conferred with District Attorney Miles McDonald of Brooklyn on one phase of the inquiry, and that he was confident that the Superintendent of Schools would be "equally diligent" in preferring charges in departmental trials where the evidence so warranted.

Long Inquiry Summed Up

The joint report, addressed to Acting Mayor Impellitteri, summed up a year-long investigation by Mr. Sheils and Charles Gilman, board auditor, into the operation of the Board of Education's Bureau of Plant Operation and Maintenance. The inquiry was initiated last October after James Marshall, Manhattan board member, had accused the school system's repair and maintenance unit of "malpractices."

In a statement issued over the week-end before the report was made public, Mr. Marshall charged that the results of the inquiry had been suppressed to "let things blow over."

The report pointed out that the findings represented a general "pattern of conditions" in existence since 1931, recalled past investigations of the repair and maintenance bureau, and observed that "although some progress had been made in correcting" the irregularities "considerable corrective measures must yet be taken."

The inquiry found that over a period of years the bureau had disregarded instructions that "oral orders" for supplies or work performed must be submitted to the Committee of Building and Sites for approval if the cost exceeded $200 an order.

Purchases "Broken Up"

The report charged that bureau employes and "certain contractors" had "deliberately broken up" purchases into units of less than $200 to circumvent the regulations.

It cited as an example the issuance, on the same day and to the same contractor, of five separate "oral orders" in the amount of $138 each for five diving boards to be delivered to five different schools. It gave as another example the issuance of four separate "oral orders" on the same day for seventy-five gallons of the same kind of paint, each in the sum of $198.75, to the same paint company.

"Analysis of a total of over 25,000 oral orders issued from 1940 up to recent months," the report continued, "and examination of employes of the bureau reveal many instances of deficiencies common to all variations of oral orders, as follows:

"(A) No reasons for issuance were set forth.

"(B) The reasons given were not based upon the personal knowledge of the inspector.

"(C) Approvals by general inspectors, borough heads and the chief general inspector were merely perfunctory.

"(D) Orders were issued and work performed prior to approval by superiors.

"(E) Incomplete records or tabulations of oral orders were maintained.

"(F) The writing on orders was illegible."

The analysis also showed, the report said, that the bureau had awarded "substantial amounts" of business by "oral orders" to "cer-

Continued on Page 13, Column 3

Phils Beat Dodgers for Flag; Win 4-1 on Homer in Tenth

HAILING A HERO: Sisler (8) is joyously greeted after game-winning homer. Philadelphia regulars are Miller (center, wearing windbreaker), Heintzelman (third from left) and Goliat (hatless, rear). At left is Coach Bengough. Associated Press

By ROSCOE McGOWEN

The Philadelphia Whiz Kids, who came so close to winning the ignominious title of the Fizz Kids, captured the first National League pennant for the Quaker City in thirty-five years when they beat the Dodgers, 4—1, yesterday at Ebbets Field before the greatest outpouring of Flatbush fans—35,073—of the 1950 season.

The Brooklyn pennant bubble exploded in the top of the tenth inning when Dick Sisler, son of the Hall of Fame fellow who had been a Branch Rickey employe for years, swung with a mixture of power and desperation and drove a three-run homer into the lower left field stands.

Don Newcombe, who pitched and lost the first game of the 1950 campaign in Philadelphia, was the victim of Sisler's flag-winning wallop and Robin Roberts, the same chap who bested Newk in the season's opener, was the winning pitcher.

Roberts gained his twentieth triumph—the most important No. 20 he'll ever win — and became the first Phil hurler to win that many since the great Grover Cleveland Alexander turned in his third straight thirty-game season in 1917.

The courageous young righthander, who had failed in six previous starts to nail down No. 20, although pitching some fine games, deserved this big triumph, for he held the Brooks to five hits and would have had a shut-out but for a freakish home run by Pee-wee Reese, the gallant Brooklyn captain and shortstop.

In the sixth inning, with two out and the Phils leading, 1—0, Reese hit a towering fly to right field and the ball came down to the top of the wall and lodged in the screen.

Reese, assuming the ball had bounced off the screen or wall, raced around to third before he learned that the ball was out of play, while the crowd screamed its delight. That, they thought, would send the Brooks on to victory—and they were wrong only by a little bit, at that.

In the ninth inning the Dodgers appeared certain to push over the winning tally, but it was thrown

Continued on Page 27, Column 2

'KEY FIGURE' FOUND IN GAMING INQUIRY

James Reardon, Ex-Policeman Living in Westport, Conn., Denies He Is a Fugitive

By ALEXANDER FEINBERG

A key witness in the operations of Harry Gross, reputed head of a $20,000,000-a-year bookmaking syndicate who has admitted that police were "associates" in his enterprise, turned up yesterday at his home in Westport, Conn., apparently surprised to learn that he has been the object of a wide search.

He was James E. Reardon, who joined the Police Department in March, 1942, and seven months later was made a plainclothesman operating out of the Chief Inspector's Office. He remained in the department until Sept. 19, 1947, resigning a month after he was transferred to patrol duty in the Borough Park, Brooklyn, precinct, a transfer regarded as a demotion.

With a jail sentence on a possible contempt citation hanging over his brother, Michael Reardon Jr., who is still a member of the New York City force, James Reardon denied that he has been "hiding." He referred to his attorney queries as to whether he would willingly go before the hold-over Brooklyn grand jury investigating police-bookmaker tie-ups.

The lawyer, John H. Mountain, a former Town Prosecutor of Westport, insisted that the question was "academic" in that Miles F. McDonald, Kings County District Attorney, "has made no attempt to get in touch with him."

Mr. McDonald would say only that he was "looking into the mat-

Continued on Page 15, Column 3

MILITARY WILL GET INDUSTRY PRIORITY BY U.S. ORDER TODAY

National Production Authority to Give Defense First Call on Materials and Plants

STEEL OUTPUT TO EXPAND

Sawyer Says Companies Agree to Raise Output 9,400,000 Net Tons by the End of 1952

By CLAYTON KNOWLES

Special to THE NEW YORK TIMES.

WASHINGTON, Oct. 1—The Government prepared today to order that industries give priority on materials and plant capacity to the military.

Meanwhile, Charles Sawyer, Secretary of Commerce, announced that the steel industry planned to increase its annual productive capacity by 9,400,000 net tons within the next two years in view of increased military needs.

By the end of 1952, he said the capacity of the industry would be raised to 109,963,000 tons. This is 16,000,000 tons above capacity in 1944 when the World War II peak was reached.

Still further, the Secretary reported that the steel industry planned to increase annual blast furnace capacity by 1,734,000 net tons before Dec. 31, 1952. This would raise the nation's pig iron potential to 73,378,000 tons.

Mr. Sawyer said the programs of twenty major companies, conveyed to him by the American Iron and Steel Institute, constituted "an encouraging indication of the willingness of industry to forge ahead."

Regulation Is Prepared

The Secretary's announcement came as new controls were being prepared to help gear the national economy to the defense mobilization effort. These moves bespoke the Administration's determination to prevent a letdown following victory in Korea.

The National Production Authority in Mr. Sawyer's own department is prepared to issue tomorrow the regulation giving industrial priority to the military.

The Federal Reserve Board has meetings scheduled for tomorrow and Tuesday from which, it is expected, will come controls over private real estate credit.

[A high Government economist said that price increases were "moving" the nation toward wage and price controls, The United Press reported.]

The priority regulation is designed to assure that military requirements receive preference on the production lines. The real estate credit control move is but another in the steps being taken

Continued on Page 24, Column 4

U. N. FORCES DRIVE OVER BORDER INTO NORTH KOREA

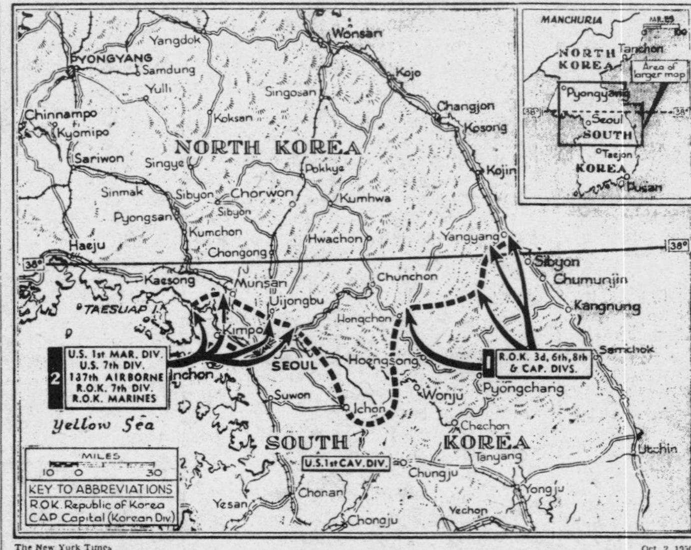

The New York Times Oct. 2, 1950

The Thirty-eighth Parallel was crossed by South Korean troops on the east coast (1). In the west (2) United States units near Munsan, above Seoul, were ten miles from the border.

2 DIVISIONS LINK UP

U. S. Marines at Same Time Move Within 10 Miles of Border

FIGHT IN NORTH EXPECTED

U. N. Pilots Say Anti-Aircraft Fire Is the Heaviest Since War in Korea Started

By LINDESAY PARROTT

Special to THE NEW YORK TIMES.

TOKYO, Monday, Oct. 2—South Korean troops yesterday crossed the Thirty-eighth Parallel, the boundary line between the Korean Republic and the Communist state to the north. Meanwhile United States Marines moved up to within ten miles of the border, near the city of Munsan, north of liberated Seoul.

Korean Republican troops, under orders of the United States Eighth Army, penetrated the border on the east coast Sunday at 11:45 A. M., just fifteen minutes before Gen. Douglas MacArthur, in a public statement broadcast in translation to North Korea throughout the day, called for the surrender of the Communist People's Army. This morning the demand was still unanswered by the North Korean Government.

By yesterday afternoon, progress of more than a mile had been made across the Parallel, with patrols pushing farther ahead. Some reports said that they had made a seven-mile advance into North Korea before pulling back for the night.

Other Divisions Closing In

The Eighth Army in Korea this morning announced that two other Republican divisions were closing in on the Parallel. Troops of the Capital Division were thirty miles north of Pyongchang and about thirteen miles south of the boundary yesterday morning, the Army's communiqué said, and leading elements of the Sixth Division at noon had reached the vicinity of Hongchon, which is twenty-one miles from the North Korean line.

[Regiments of the South Korean Third and Capital Divisions linked up Monday morning at Yangyang, six miles north of the Thirty-eighth Parallel, which was taken without a shot. The United Press reported.]

Meanwhile, south of the Parallel, the enemy's Korean front had disappeared, and only isolated groups held out in hill positions as United States and South Korean columns moved more or less at will. With few exceptions, all important South Korean cities and most of the smaller towns had been freed of the invaders.

Two North Korean regiments were still reported to be retreating near Chechon, far to the rear, with forces of the Republican Eighth Division deploying to destroy them, the Eighth Army announcement said.

Organized Resistance Offered

Organized resistance was also being offered where the Marines pushed northward from Seoul toward the strongest sector of the defense line that the Communists had built along the Thirty-eighth Parallel between 1945 and their invasion of June of this year.

Despite General MacArthur's surrender demand and the general disintegration of the enemy forces in South Korea, headquarters intelligence sources expected that the enemy would fight for his homeland at least in considerable numbers. There were no signs of construction of additional fortifications along the border, the spokesman said.

But it was always anticipated, he added, that the enemy would make a stand on the Thirty-eighth Parallel, particularly from the coast of the Yellow Sea to the central mountain spine of Korea, the closest and easiest avenue of approach to the North Korean capital at Pyongyang.

There were indications also that the enemy was stepping up the air defenses of North Korea, hitherto almost nonexistent under the tremendous pounding of United Nations planes. Saturday, an Air Force spokesman said, anti-air-

Continued on Page 4, Column 2

RED RALLY BALKED BY GERMAN POLICE

1,500 Arrests in Western Zone Upset Communist Plans for Day of 'Resistance'

By JACK RAYMOND

Special to THE NEW YORK TIMES.

BERLIN, Oct. 1—About 1,500 arrests were reported in Western Germany today, many of them "preventive" arrests, as Communist demonstrators had limited success in causing the disturbances they had threatened in the name of peace.

In Hamburg, 2,000 singing Communists assembled to march on the home of Mayor Max Brauer. The police, seeking to disperse them, were stoned and slugged by the Communists. Sixteen policemen were injured and 130 persons were arrested.

Then, about 800 tried again to march on Herr Brauer's residence.

Continued on Page 8, Column 5

Orders to Cross the Parallel Dropped to Troops by Plane

By W. H. LAWRENCE

Special to THE NEW YORK TIMES.

EIGHTH ARMY HEADQUARTERS, Korea, Oct. 1—Meeting no enemy resistance, South Korean troops crossed the Thirty-eighth Parallel this morning and by mid-afternoon had moved more than a mile into territory that was under Communist rule before the war began on June 25.

[A later front-line dispatch from the United Press said South Korean patrols had been fired on after they had advanced 2,000 yards across the parallel.]

The crossing, representing a decision to pursue the enemy into his lair and destroy his forces unless he surrendered, was made at 11:45 A. M., just fifteen minutes before Gen. Douglas MacArthur's ultimatum was broadcast.

Elements of the Korean Third Division, which had moved up along the eastern coastal road from the Pohang Airfield received the honor of being the first to enter enemy territory. They received the order from the Eighth Army to make the crossing late Saturday afternoon. It was dropped from a small observation plane by a United States major who had been unable to make a scheduled landing when he flew from the Eighth Army's advance headquarters. His plane had only three gallons of gasoline remaining when he made an emergency landing at Pohang field.

A small group of correspondents flew over the border area late Sunday afternoon to observe the historic crossing. Briefed in advance that the enemy was not resisting and that there were no indications of aerial activity or artillery fire to the north, we flew in low over burning Yangyang, about five miles north of the Thirty-eighth

Continued on Page 4, Column 5

FOE SAID TO PLAN GUERRILLA STAND

Asiatic Communists Say the Defense of North Korea Was Set Three Months Ago

By WALTER SULLIVAN

Reports from several Asiatic Communist sources indicate that preparations for prolonged guerrilla warfare against United Nations forces have been under way in Korea for more than three months. These reports would make it appear that surrender of the North Korean regime is unlikely either now or when its military fortunes decline even further.

The Korean Reds appear to have been following the formula employed by the Chinese Communists when faced with overwhelming force. They have reportedly been distributing rice lard to the landless peasants and then arming and training them to defend their new property.

Many of the Korean Communist leaders received their training with the Chinese at Yenan. They remember that by radical land distribution the Chinese Reds built up an army that followed them on the

Continued on Page 6, Column 3

World News Summarized

MONDAY, OCTOBER 2, 1950

Units of Republic of Korea divisions pushed across the Thirty-eighth Parallel and took the center of Yangyang on the east coast, six air miles north of the line. United States Marines met organized resistance near the line northwest of Seoul. The Communists had given no reply to General MacArthur's demand for surrender. [1:8.]

The first crossing of the Parallel, to carry out the United Nations military action, was made fifteen minutes before General MacArthur's demand was broadcast to North Korea. [1:6-7.]

Chinese Communist Premier Chou declared his regime would "not stand aside" if "its neighbor" were invaded. [3:1.] Reports indicated that Peiping was more likely to send arms than men across the border into North Korea to maintain a guerrilla war until time could work a Communist success there as it had done in China. [1:7.] At the United Nations, where a Soviet attack on the eight-nation plan to unify and rehabilitate Korea is scheduled, doubt was expressed that the Chinese Communists would enter the conflict. [6:3.]

"Peace rallies" called by the Communists in West Germany failed to develop serious disturbances. The crowds were smaller than had been forecast and the police, in most cases, easily dispersed them. In Hamburg sixteen policemen were hurt. A total of 1,500 demonstrators was arrested. [1:5.] President Truman and British Foreign Secretary Bevin promised Berlin full protection on the occasion of the dedication of the West sector's new constitution and the opening of the city's Industries Fair. [9:2.]

Britain and West Germany put a new $1,000,000,000 trade treaty into effect under terms placing the Germans on a par with the rest of Western Europe. [8:2.]

Marshall Plan countries were urged by the E. C. A. to raise production as the best way to keep the enlarged arms program from lowering the people's living standards. [11:2.]

The steel industry has agreed to expand steel production and to enlarge pig-iron capacity, Commerce Secretary Sawyer announced. Orders giving the military priority on production items will be issued today. [1:4.] Unjustified price increases "are moving us to controls," a Federal economist said. [10:2.]

Middle-income families are being forced off Manhattan Island for lack of housing, a survey disclosed. Post-war building has been largely of the "luxury" type and subsidized projects for low-income groups. Moderately priced older apartments under rent control are fully occupied. [1:2-3.]

Favored contractors have received millions of dollars of work in this city's schools without competitive bidding, a report to Acting Mayor Impellitteri charged. Faulty work, the report added, has been approved by inspectors. Criminal action was forecast. [1:1.]

NEWS BULLETINS FROM THE TIMES
Every hour on the hour
7 A.M. through Midnight
WQXR AM 1560
WQXR FM 96.3

Index to other news appears on Page 24.

Population Upset in Housing Seen, With Manhattan Middle Class Out

By ROBERT C. DOTY

Manhattan rapidly is being transformed into forbidden ground for middle-income families who neither can afford today's high rents in the free market nor qualify for admission to subsidized public housing.

Post-war residential construction in the city's geographic and traditional heart has set a pattern that threatens to expedite the migration of middle-class families to other boroughs and suburbs and, ultimately, to complete the upset of Manhattan's population balance.

New building has been predominantly of high rental, luxury apartments or of subsidized public housing for low-income groups. Mushrooming acres of garden-type apartments at moderate rentals, and one-family dwellings with federally financed mortgages have found no vertical counterparts in crowded Gotham.

As a result, according to urban planners and real-estate men questioned in a study of rental conditions, the flight of middle-income families that began many years ago now has reached an abnormal rate. If unchecked, it might turn Manhattan into the exclusive province of the rich and subsidized lower income families.

Decentralization of big-city populations has been proceeding for many years, prompted by many factors in addition to high rents, these experts point out. Many middle-income families move to the suburbs in search of greener fields and bluer skies than Manhattan offers, or of newer, less-crowded schools.

But there also is evidence that many families that would prefer the conveniences and cultural advantages of urban living are being forced to leave Manhattan because they can find no suitable living space. As evidence of this, more than 200,000 applications were received by the Metropolitan Life Insurance Company for the 8,755 apartment units in Stuyvesant Town, largest middle-income hous-

Continued on Page 26, Column 3

Encore of Summer Surprises City With Mercury at 88.4 Record High

Summer gave New York a repeat performance yesterday. In a form reversal as unexpected as the Dodgers' short-lived bid for the National League pennant, the temperature soared to 88.4 degrees at 3:45 P. M., a record high for the date. The previous record of 83.3 for Oct. 1 was recorded in 1881.

The mild weather caught the city flat-footed. Heavy coats and woolens brought out by last Sunday's near-record low of 43.2 degrees went back into closets and summer apparel was hastily retrieved from bureau drawers and moth bags. Some suburban visitors said buds were popping again in the country.

The afternoon sun sank like a huge orange disk in the West, presaging another spell of St. Luke's Summer for today. The Weather Bureau predicted a high in the middle 80's.

An estimated 300,000 persons visited Coney Island and paraded coatless on the Boardwalk. Several thousand younger folk donned bathing suits, but only a handful ventured into the surf. The water was seasonably cold.

Another 60,000 Sunday excursionists visited the Rockaways. There, too, the Boardwalk was crowded with girls in summer dresses and men in shirt sleeves. The police reported heavy automobile traffic over the Marine Park and Cross Bay Boulevard bridges.

The New Jersey seashore had an unusually large influx of visitors, sizable crowds on the Boardwalk, but few bathers. State Highways 25 and 29, which lead from the Hudson Tunnel to the New Jersey and Pennsylvania resorts, doubled last week's traffic. Early last night cars were jammed fender to fender coming through Elizabeth and Rahway to New York.

Undaunted by the heat, 500 persons, following earlier plans, went ice skating on the outdoor rink at Rockefeller Center. The rink had been opened on Tuesday.

While it was hot here yesterday,

Continued on Page 24, Column 3

Philadelphia's Victorious Whiz Kids 'Whoop It Up'

PHILLIES SET BACK DODGERS, WIN FLAG

Continued From Page 1

out at the plate, and from now on through the winter it will be hard to convince a lot of Flatbush fanatics that Coach Milt Stock didn't make a bad decision.

That momentous inning started with Cal Abrams, the lead-off man, drawing his second pass from Roberts on a three-and-two pitch. Reese tried twice to bunt and, with two strikes against him, lined a clean single into left center field, Abrams stopping at second.

Naturally, the Phils had to look for a bunt from Duke Snider, and were playing fairly close, but Duke rifled the first pitch into center—and the stands exploded in a vast roar. This was it.

But Richie Ashburn, coming in fast, fielded the hit cleanly and fired it with deadly accuracy to Stan Lopata at the plate. Meanwhile, Stock was waving Abrams around third, with the disappointing, but certainly not unexpected result that Lopata was waiting with the ball when Cal arrived.

Robinson Purposely Passed

Even then, since Reese and Snider had advanced on the throw, the Dodgers had a big chance for the victory that would have sent them into a play-off today.

Jackie Robinson, of course, was purposely passed to fill the bases. Then Carl Furillo swung at the first pitch and the fans groaned as Eddie Waitkus camped under the feeble foul near first base.

The last hope faded when Gil Hodges, the Brooks' leading home run hitter, drove a high fly to right that Del Ennis took near the center field side of the scoreboard.

Then came the Phils' tenth and one could almost sense the feeling in the stands that this was all for the Dodgers. This feeling became more pronounced when Roberts started the winning frame with a single through the middle.

Waitkus, making one attempt to bunt, then swung and dropped a pop-fly single into short center out of everybody's reach, Roberts stopping at second. The bunt was on again but Ashburn, a good bunter and a fast runner, bunted into a force out at third, Newcombe making a good play on the attempted sacrifice.

Up came the extremely dangerous Sisler, who already had driven three consecutive singles into right field off Newcombe's slants. Dick swung at the first two pitches, missing one and fouling one, then looked at a wide one.

Biggest and Shortest

When he let go at the next one and the ball arched high toward left field, Abrams stood for a split second, then ran madly toward the wall. But it was no use. The biggest home run—and possibly one of the shortest—the stands are only 348 feet from home plate—that young Sisler ever hit, was on the records and the Whiz Kids had won the pennant that had been eluding them so exasperatingly for the longest week of their lives.

What followed was anticlimax, Newcombe striking out Ennis and getting Puddin' Head Jones on a simple grounder to Reese.

The Dodger tenth was a breeze for Roberts. Roy Campanella hit a solid liner to deep left but it was caught easily by Jack Mayo, who had just been sent into left field in place of Sisler as a defensive move—one which Manager Eddie Sawyer frequently has made this year.

Then Jim Russell, pinch-hitting for Billy Cox, struck out and Tommy Brown, taking Newcombe's place at bat, lifted a high one to Waitkus at first.

The first break for the Phils came in the fifth inning, when they scored their first and all-important run, which might have been averted.

Waitkus and Ashburn had been retired on a couple of fine plays by Hodges, with Newcombe covering first base in each instance, when the tough young Sisler slashed his second single just out of Gil's reach.

Here Ennis lifted a high fly to right center and it appeared it could be caught. But Snider, playing deep for the Phil slugger in left center, couldn't race in fast enough, and Jackie Robinson didn't get out under the ball.

Whether Jackie could have made the catch is something that won't be known. Certainly Robby must have thought Snider would get under it, because Duke was running at top speed all the way.

Anyway, immediately following that, Sisler, having moved around to third, Jones swung at Newcombe's first pitch and rifled the ball through to Reese's left for the single that brought in the run.

Reese delivered three of the five Brooklyn hits, opening the fourth inning with a line double to left that bounced around in the densely populated Phil bullpen. But here the Dodgers got a bad break when Snider tapped a ball toward first that he probably would have beaten out for a hit.

Marooned at Second

That would have put men on first and third with none out, but the ball just brushed Duke's leg as he dashed for first and the alert Larry Goetz, calling balls and strikes for the second straight day, promptly called Duke out and Reese had to return to second.

That's where the Little Colonel stayed, for Robinson bounced out to Roberts and Furillo lifted one of the few flies to the outfield hit by the Brooks, Ashburn taking it in right center.

As an indication of the caliber of Roberts' pitching, the big bonus boy had six assists and one putout, while his first baseman had seventeen putouts.

Newcombe, on the other hand, was rather soundly smacked, even when he got his man out. A double play following Ennis' single to open the second frame, started by Reese, got Don out of trouble then, and at the start of the Phils' ninth Abrams made a spectacular leaping catch of Gran Hamner's drive against the left-field wall.

When Andy Seminick followed with a single and the fleet Ralph Caballero ran for him, Newcombe was helped out again by the fine collaboration of Campanella and Robinson, who nailed Ralph trying to steal.

Altogether the Phils made eleven hits, which helps to indicate that, on one important day, at least, the better pitcher and the better team won.

Thirteenth for Dick

A touch of irony may be noted in the fact that Sisler's homer was his thirteenth of the year, his third off Brooklyn pitching, and that all three were struck at Ebbets Field.

Seminick came into second with considerable vigor in the seventh when Mike Goliat bunted into a force play, Campanella to Reese, and Pee Wee had his right foot spiked slightly. Robinson was observed making a few comments to the big Phil catcher as Andy was heading for the dugout.

The box score:

PHILADELPHIA (N.)	ab.	r.	h.	po.	a.	e.
Waitkus, 1b.	5	1	1	18	0	0
Ashburn, cf.	5	1	0	2	1	0
Sisler, lf.	5	2	4	0	0	0
Mayo, lf.	0	0	0	1	0	0
Ennis, rf.	5	0	2	2	0	0
Jones, 3b.	5	0	1	0	3	0
Hamner, ss.	4	0	0	1	2	0
Seminick, c.	3	0	1	3	1	0
aCaballero	0	0	0	0	0	0
Lopata, c.	0	0	0	1	0	0
Goliat, 2b.	4	0	1	1	3	0
Roberts, p.	2	0	1	1	6	0
Total	38	4	11	30	16	0

BROOKLYN (N.)	ab.	r.	h.	po.	a.	e.
Abrams, lf.	2	0	0	2	0	0
Reese, ss.	4	1	3	3	3	0
Snider, cf.	4	0	1	3	0	0
Rob'son, 2b.	3	0	0	4	3	0
Furillo, rf.	4	0	0	3	0	0
Hodges, 1b.	4	0	0	9	3	0
Camp'lla, c.	4	0	1	2	4	0
Cox, 3b.	3	0	0	1	2	0
bRussell	1	0	0	0	0	0
N'combe, p.	3	0	0	3	2	0
cBrown	1	0	0	0	0	0
Total	33	1	5	30	17	0

aRan for Seminick in ninth.
bStruck out for Cox in tenth.
cFouled out for Newcombe in tenth.

Philadelphia	000	001	000	3—4
Brooklyn	000	001	000	0—1

Runs batted in—Jones, Reese, Sisler 3.

Two-base hit—Reese. Home runs—Reese, Sisler. Sacrifice—Roberts. Double plays—Reese, Robinson and Hodges; Roberts and Waitkus. Left on bases—Philadelphia 7, Brooklyn 5. Bases on balls—Off Roberts 3, Newcombe 2. Struck out—By Roberts 2, Newcombe 3. Winning pitcher—Roberts (20—12). Losing pitcher—Newcombe (19—11). Umpires—Goetz, Dascoli, Jorda and Donatelli. Time of game—2:35. Attendance—35,073.

Robin Roberts (left) and Dick Sisler in the dressing room after the contest. The New York Times

HEROES OF BATTLE MOBBED BY MATES

Roberts, Sisler and Ashburn Draw Highest Praise for Brilliant Performances

JOYOUS DAY FOR SAWYER

Phils' Pilot 'Glad We Won It This Way'—Shotton Says 'Great Team Beat Us'

By JOSEPH M. SHEEHAN

The long and harrowing wait the Phillies had before they wrapped up their first National League pennant since 1915 made the taste of victory all the sweeter when, at long last, it came.

Historians of such matters unanimously agreed that the spontaneous celebration staged by the Whiz Kids in their dressing room yesterday after they had killed off the Dodgers was one of the most uproarious of all time.

A full hour after Robin Roberts had retired the last Brooklyn batter in the tenth, the Phillies, in various stages of undress, were still whooping out their joy and reiterating mutual felicitations in a happy daze.

Manager Eddie Sawyer, who never lost his professional calm or wavered in his confidence in his team through the heart-rending developments of the past few weeks, sounded the keynote of the demonstration.

"It's great to win this way," said Eddie. "We did it on our own."

Heroes Ask for Quarter

His cry was picked up and echoed around the crowded, steamy room as the jubilant Phillies traded bear hugs and pounded Dick Sisler, Roberts and Richie Ashburn, chief heroes of the occasion, until those worthies were forced to call for quarter.

"How I love this park!" exclaimed the grinning Sisler, who made four straight hits, including the three-run homer that broke up the tense contest in the tenth.

"It was a fast ball, high and outside," he said of the pitch he slammed into the left field stands.

"Do you know, I almost did not have the chance to hit it," Sisler divulged. "I nearly sprained my right wrist again sliding into second in the fourth inning." A wrist sprain had kept him out of action for three weeks recently and he still sported a heavy protective bandage.

"No, I felt strong all the way," said Roberts, Philadelphia's first twenty-game winner since the great Grover Cleveland Alexander, in answer to a reporter who remarked that he certainly must have been tired after starting four games within a week.

Lime in Pitcher's Eyes

The husky 24-year-old pitcher's eyes were red-rimmed and inflamed, from some flecks of lime from the foul line that got into them when he slid into third in the tenth. Jocko Thompson, a team-mate standing by, said "That didn't bother Robby. He'd keep pitching if he were blind."

"Maybe it wasn't the best throw I made all year," said Ashburn of his peg to home that cut down Cal Abrams, who represented the winning Dodger run, in the ninth. "But I don't know of one that came at a better time."

Among the early arrivals in the Philly dressing room, jam-packed by photographers, newsmen, roving radio reporters and assorted well-wishers, was Burt Shotton, who immediately sought out Sawyer.

"Congratulations, Eddie!" the Brooklyn manager boomed as he clasped his rival's hand. "You did a great job. If we had to lose, I'm sure glad it was to you." Later, the Dodger players filed through the connecting door from their dressing room to add their congratulations and the exhortation "Go get those Yankees now!"

Writer Loses Mustache

All manner of high jinks marked the Phillies' blow-off, as Bob Carpenter, their young owner, and Ford C. Frick, National League president, looked on with tolerant and beaming approval. Granny Hamner and Bubba Church grabbed Frank Yeutter of The Philadelphia Bulletin as soon as he appeared and clipped off the handsome mustache that has been that veteran baseball writer's pride and joy for more than ten years.

"I told Frank a couple of years ago that if we ever won the pennant, I'd shave him clean and this sure is it." explained the exultant Hamner. Yeutter didn't lift a hand in protest.

Andy Seminick went wandering about shouting in his brassy voice, "We're the champs! Wow-w-ow!" Then the burly catcher, with the willing assistance of others, poured a cascade of beer over the shining pate of Coach Benny Bengough.

Russ Meyer did a veil dance with a towel for his prop, as half a dozen team-mates beat time, and the general tumult increased, rather than subsided, as time wore on.

No Regrets, Say Brooks

In the Brooklyn dressing room, funereal quiet prevailed. Knowing they had given it the good fight, the Dodger players weren't as dejected as might have been imagined. They just had little to say.

"We have no regrets," said Shotton. "We didn't cry all season and we won't cry now. It took a great team to beat us. It had to be a great team to beat us."

Except to ask "How did Ashburn dare to play Duke Snider so short?" and point out "We've run for extra bases on Ashburn all year" no one was inclined to discuss the play on which Abrams was caught at the plate.

"You can sum up the season in one sentence," said club secretary Harold Parrott, "We were short one fly ball."

BOMBERS LOSE, 7-3, AS WILLIAMS STARS

Ted Explodes Four Hits, One a Double, and Bats In 3 Runs to Pace Red Sox Drive

2D VICTORY FOR TAYLOR

By JOHN DREBINGER

Special to THE NEW YORK TIMES.

BOSTON, Oct. 1—With all four positions in the first division of the American League indelibly set for the records before even a ball was tossed, the Yankees finally got around to relaxing on this closing day of the campaign and, as with most everything else they do, they made a thorough job of it.

In fact, Casey Stengel's 1950 champions relaxed to such an extent that the Red Sox, plodding home in third place, experienced no great difficulty winning this concluding engagement, 7 to 3, by way of providing some measure of comfort for a gathering of 27,729 mourners.

It was, of course, a pretty hollow triumph since the big prize already had been safely stowed away and with even the season's series going to the Bombers by a margin of thirteen games to eight.

However, it was something at that to see the champs get cuffed around, Ted Williams alone exploding four hits, one a double. The Kid, indeed, was in fine fettle and drove in three runs to wind up the year with a 97 R. B. I. total for his eighty-nine games.

With quite a few of the Yankee regulars sitting this one out, Stengel opened with two of his rookie hurlers, Ernie Nevel, twenty-one-game winner from Beaumont, and Lou Burdette.

Nevel was tagged for four of the Sox runs and seven hits in his three innings on the mound and Burdette gave up one more tally on three singles in the fourth.

Then Eddie Lopat came on for his final World Series tune-up, the lefty blanking the Sox in two innings. Eddie Ford gave up the final Boston tallies in the seventh on a two-run homer by Buddy Rosar.

Harry Taylor, the Flatbush refugee, went the entire distance for the Sox to hang up his second victory of the year against no defeats—his first triumph had been a two-hitter against the Athletics last Monday at a time Steve O'Neill's men were still in the race.

This time the slim righthander allowed ten blows, but confined the Yanks' scoring to one inning. That was in the sixth when a single by Hank Workman, who played the entire game at first for the Bombers, a triple by Bobby Brown and pair of singles by Jackie Jensen and Lopat accounted for all three Yankee tallies.

Stengel today scouted the report that he already had received a two-year contract calling for an annual stipend of $75,000. Not only has he signed no new contract, declared Casey, but he hasn't even discussed the proposition with either of the Yankee co-owners, Dan Topping or Del Webb.

"Been altogether too busy winning the pennant to give it even a thought," said Stengel, "and now I've still got a world series to win. It'll be time enough to talk over a new contract when all this is over."

The New York Times.

SUNDAY, DECEMBER 3, 1950. L+ S

NAVY UPSETS ARMY, 14-2, ENDING CADET 28-GAME STREAK; FORDHAM TOPS SYRACUSE; OKLAHOMA AND TENNESSEE WIN

RAMS VICTORS, 13-6

Hyatt Scores on Doheny Pass in First Period, Runs to Goal in 4th

8TH TRIUMPH FOR MAROON

Keen Fordham Defense Halts Syracuse Except for Tally by Young in the Second

By LINCOLN A. WERDEN

Fordham celebrated Ed Danowski Day at the Polo Grounds in appropriate fashion yesterday. Members of the alumni and coaching staff presented the football coach with an automobile and other suitable gifts before the game, but most pleasing to the Maroon mentor was the subsequent performance of his pupils, who defeated Syracuse, 13 to 6.

The triumph was the eighth in nine games for the Rose Hill athletes, who closed their most successful campaign since 1937, when the famed "seven blocks of granite" helped to sweep through a schedule unbeaten, with one tie and seven victories.

Played partially in the rain and over a muddy field that hindered both teams, the game was witnessed by 13,282. Until the fourth period most of the spectators envisaged a deadlock, with a 6-6 score carried over from the second quarter.

Then a combination of running and passing in twelve plays produced a 56-yard drive for the decisive score. It was Jack Hyatt, sophomore left halfback, who had snared a pass from Dick Doheny for the initial Fordham touchdown, who went over the second time also.

Last Game for 25 Rams

The fast moving Hyatt, hobbled with injuries for the greater part of the season, was an impressive ball carrier in this last game for twenty-five Fordham players, including Doheny. Racing around his right end, Hyatt tallied from the 7. Then Jim Ericksen's placement kick sailed over for the extra point.

With Syracuse apparently primed for the Doheny-to-Alan Pfeifer combination, Fordham deployed other receivers instead of their stellar end to grab Doheny passes. This became evident when Hyatt raced twenty-five yards with a Doheny aerial to complete a 45-yard gain for the first touchdown.

In the march downfield in the crucial fourth period, Doheny completed an important one to Captain Andy Lukac for a 25-yard gain. Then Mike Renaldo, reserve end, snared another on the 18.

Doheny completed seven of thirteen, including the touchdown pass, for 115 yards. Thus he ended a career as the outstanding passer in Fordham's history, topping the East with a mark this season of 79 completions in 143 tries for a total of 1,344 yards.

Custis Ends College Career

Bernie Custis, Syracuse Negro quarterback and co-captain who also was bowing out of collegiate football, thrilled the onlookers in the closing minutes as he attempted to overhaul Fordham with passes. From its 28, the Orange reeled off gains in the fleeting minutes to reach the Fordham 26 as Ed Yaple caught a Custis toss.

That was the last bit of success. The Orange had a first down there, but two more Custis passes were knocked down and a third was intercepted by Mario Demarzo on the Ram 10 with less than two minutes to play.

Feeling was running high at this point and after the interception several fights broke out on the field. The announcer said: "We are now having fisticuffs."

After the melee the game proceeded without any penalties, evidently nothing amiss having occurred during the actual play, and Fordham had possession with 1 minute 20 seconds remaining. Lukac was forced back to his 5, but a subsequent Syracuse offside hurt the Orange hopes. The game ended with Fordham hanging on to the ball on its 7.

Custis completed 10 of 22 passes for 78 yards, but the Syracuse quarterback was stopped at important junctures. In fact, Syracuse lost the ball four times on downs in the opening half.

It had to relinquish possession on the Ram 31 and from there

Continued on Page 2, Column 4

Pacific Turns Back Le Baron's Marines

By The Associated Press.

STOCKTON, Calif., Dec. 2—The College of Pacific Tigers spoiled quarterback Eddie Le Baron's homecoming today by defeating their little All-America star of 1949 and his Quantico Marines, 37—14, before a crowd of 16,000.

The game, played in cold weather, under overcast skies and in intermittent rain, saw the Leathernecks in front, 14—9, at half-time. The Tigers roared back with three touchdowns in the third period and one in the fourth. It became so dark in the final period that the lights were turned on.

Left half Eddie Macon led the Cop scoring with two touchdowns.

Le Baron completed eight of nineteen passes and had four intercepted. Pacific completed 10 of 19 with one interception.

NOTRE DAME LOSES TO TROJANS BY 9-7

Sears' 94-Yard Runback of Kick-Off, Safety Win for Southern California

By The United Press.

LOS ANGELES, Dec. 2—Halfback Jim Sears' 94-yard return of a kick-off and a safety gave Southern California an upset 9-7 victory today over Notre Dame before 70,177 fans in Memorial Coliseum.

This was only the fourth time that an Irish football team lost four games in one season. Notre Dame's coach, Frank Leahy, was in South Bend, Ind., ill with influenza when 1950's humiliation was completed. Notre Dame previously lost to Purdue, Michigan State and Indiana. The Irish won four games this year and tied one.

Southern California couldn't gain an inch most of the time against the stubborn Irish line and made but one first down in the game. When it counted, the Trojans had the ability to dig in and stop the Irish time after time.

Sears was not the only hero for Southern California in its second victory of the season. The brilliant punting of end Bill Jessup in the second half put Notre Dame deep in the hole, and guard Paul McMurtry got credit for blocking Bob Williams' punt for the safety that gave the Trojans their margin of victory.

The Irish played their hearts out in the savagely fought game, but they never could mount an offense in the second half. As the game progressed, the safety scored against Williams loomed larger and larger.

Southern California's lack of offense, however, was more than made up for by the brilliance of the Trojan defense. In addition to McMurtry and Jessup, End Winston Goller and line-backer Pat Cannamela stood out in the upset of the Irish.

Neither team could get rolling in the first period. Southern California fumbling away several opportunities and Notre Dame losing the ball on interceptions and bobbles. But the Irish started driving in the second period sparked by the running of John Pettibon and two quarterback sneaks on fourth down by Williams to make the required yardage.

The Irish score was set up by

Continued on Page 4, Column 3

Navy Back Racing for the First Touchdown in Major Upset at Philadelphia

Bob Zastrow going through huge hole in the Army forward wall. Providing interference are Tom Bakke, left, and Dave Bannerman. Associated Press Wirephoto

ZASTROW IS STAR

Crosses First, Then His Pass to Baldinger Clicks for Navy

ARMY'S BACKS SHACKLED

Victorious Defenders Tackle Fiercely—101,000 Fans See Cadets Tally on Safety

By ALLISON DANZIG

Special to The New York Times.

PHILADELPHIA, Dec. 2—The lightning of an infuriated band of Navy demons struck an overwhelmingly favored Army eleven, not a second but a third time, in the same place at the Municipal Stadium today. Thus the team that had bowed to no foe since 1947 finally met its master in possibly the most shocking verdict of a season of bewildering reversals.

Battered and outplayed in almost every category by an opponent it was expected to humble by three touchdowns, Army came to the end of its twenty-eight-game sequence without defeat in a stunning 14-2 setback that marked Navy's first victory over the cadets since 1943.

A gathering of 101,000 spectators, among whom were President Truman, members of his Cabinet and generals and admirals galore, watched in amazement as the oft-beaten sailors from Crabtown tore into the second-ranking team of the country to give it a thumping physical beating from which it will not soon recover.

Like so many wildcats, the gang-tackling midshipmen hurled themselves upon the big-name Army backs, to smother their running operations, and knock down and intercept their passes while their own fiery ball carriers were tearing loose and scoring through the air with their cleverly executed flanker T-formation attack.

The Clock Runs Out

It was 1946 and 1948 all over again. Four years ago a despised Navy team went on the rampage against the great Blanchard-Davis outfit, only to lose by 21—18 as the clock ran out with the middies inside the cadets' 5-yard line. In 1948 a West Point eleven that had won eight games, while Navy was losing eight, could do no better than hold the rampant tars to a tie.

This time the long-suffering eleven from the Severn, playing under the direction of a new head coach, Eddie Erdelatz, finally broke the back of Army's resistance and won a glorious victory that was earned on merit beyond any question of doubt.

President Truman was a winner with Navy today and Truman "luck" came through for the third successive time. The Commander in Chief initiated the practice of remaining seated on the side of the host team in 1948, instead of crossing to the other side of the field at halftime, and that year he rejoiced with the midshipmen around him as the sailors gained a moral victory with their 21-21 tie. Last year Mr. Truman sat with Army as Earl Blaik's Black Knights gave Navy the worst beating in the fifty-one game history of the rivalry, a 38-0 decision.

Today, heavily guarded by an extra-large detail of Secret Service men, as well as by F-51 Mustangs patroling the skyway because of the attempt made on his life a month ago in Washington, the

Continued on Page 3, Column 1

Oklahoma Takes 31st in Row, Downing A. and M., 41-14

By The United Press.

STILLWATER, Okla., Dec. 2—The top-ranking Oklahoma Sooners, prepping for the Sugar Bowl, relied on the superb passing of Quarterback Claude Arnold today to defeat Oklahoma A. & M., 41—14, for their thirty-first straight victory.

Arnold pegged four touchdown passes, with Jack Lockett on the receiving end of three of them, in a dazzling second-quarter exhibition.

A crowd of 33,000 saw the forty-fifth renewal of the intrastate rivalry.

One of the spectators was Kentucky Coach Paul (Bear) Bryant, whose team goes against the Sooners in the Sugar Bowl Jan. 1. Bryant said he suspected Oklahoma Coach Bud Wilkinson was keeping some of his power and secrets in reserve in winding up his second straight undefeated, untied regular season against the outclassed Aggies.

Whether or not Wilkinson was intentionally holding back, the Aggies made it a close ball game during most of three quarters. But the sudden-death Sooner attack needed only one period to uproot any Aggie notions of an upset.

Oklahoma scored first when Arnold shot a 21-yard pass to End John Reddell with ten minutes of the first period gone. The Aggies evened the count four minutes

Continued on Page 4, Column 3

TENNESSEE ROUTS VANDERBILT, 43-0

Volunteers Play Carefully in Opening Half, Break Loose in Second for 33 Points

By The Associated Press.

NASHVILLE, Tenn., Dec. 2—The Tennessee Volunteers made their game with Vanderbilt just a whistle stop on the road to the Cotton Bowl today with a 43-0 victory over their ancient rivals.

Tennessee, ranked fourth in the final Associated Press poll, drove to a 10-0 lead in the first half, then scored almost at will in the final periods. A crowd of 28,000 watched Tennessee give Vanderbilt the worst thrashing it had suffered since 1945.

It was the tenth victory in eleven starts for Tennessee and the loss was Vanderbilt's fourth in eleven. But Tennessee was the first team to hold Coach Bill Edwards' T-formation scoreless.

Several scouts from Texas, the Vols' Cotton Bowl opponent, got an eyeful as they watched Gen. Bob Neyland's power-studded single wing eleven score two touchdowns through the air, four on the ground and add a field goal for good measure.

Sophomore Pat Shires kicked four conversions. He missed one and so did Harold Johnson.

Halfback Harold Payne got two touchdowns for Tennessee and Basil Drake two. Their scores were made by rushing. End Vince Kaseta and Quarterback Bernie Sizemore grabbed touchdown passes, one hurled by Hank Lauricella and the other by Payne.

Vanderbilt managed to make a game of it in the first half but faded badly in the fourth period when Tennessee racked up 20 points.

The Commodores threatened only

Continued on Page 2, Column 5

Big Show, Whale of a Game Thrill Truman, Top Brass

By JOSEPH M. SHEEHAN

Special to The New York Times.

PHILADELPHIA, Dec. 2—Hardy souls who retained their love for football after last Saturday's drenching, reveled in conditions that were just moderately disagreeable, rather than completely intolerable, at the Army-Navy game today.

But weather, or not, the fifty-first service classic lived up to its long-standing reputation as the nation's most colorful sports spectacle, and the 101,000 spectators who jammed Municipal Stadium were altogether oblivious to the near-freezing temperature and the occasional light spatters of rain that fell early in the proceedings. They saw a great show and a whale of a football game and not only had occasional glimpses of the sun but a good look at many of those who live in it.

Despite the tense international situation, President Truman and most of his Cabinet attended, along with other high Government officials and, of course, the top brass of all the armed services.

This was Navy's home game, so the President sat on the Annapolis side of the field. His party, guests of Vice Admiral H. W. Hill, Naval Academy superintendent, included Gen. Omar Bradley, chairman of

Continued on Page 3, Column 2

SEAWARD, 3-2, FIRST IN BOWIE FEATURE

Choice Beats Arcave in Bryan and O'Hara as Maryland Turf Season Closes

By The Associated Press.

BOWIE, Md., Dec. 2—Leading from gate to wire, Hasty House Farms' Seaward captured the $20,000 added Bryan and O'Hara Memorial Handicap by three-quarters of a length in a driving finish as the Maryland turf season closed here today.

Valiantly striving to overhaul the pacesetter at the wire was Sylvester W. Labrot Jr.'s Arcave, an outsider, who beat L. J. Shaw's Abstract by three lengths for the place. Fourth money went to Brookmeade Stable's Dart By.

Continued on Page 6, Column 2

L. I. U. FIVE DEFEATS KANSAS STATE, 60-59

Checks Wildcats' Late Drive in Garden—St. John's Tops William and Mary, 63-47

By LOUIS EFFRAT

St. John's comfortably and Long Island University by the narrowest margin possible were the victors in last night's college basketball double-header at Madison Square Garden. The former, finishing fast, conquered William and Mary, 63—47, after which L. I. U. just lasted for a thrill-packed 60-59 decision over Kansas State.

Not nearly as exciting or as well played as the afterpiece was the curtain-raiser. Clair Bee's talented Blackbirds twice enjoyed 11-point spreads, the second time so late as the 13-minute mark in the second half, when Long Island enjoyed a 52-41 lead.

A team with less fortitude might have folded then and there, but Jack Gardner's soundly coached Wildcats did not and thereafter every minute of the contest have seemed like an hour.

Obviously rattled by the full-court press of the visitors, the Long Island players forfeited much of the poise that earlier had made them look so good. For, in this, their season's inaugural, the 'Birds flashed like a quintet that might go places nationally this season. Endowed with height, speed and experience, L. I. U. threatened to win going away.

Instead, the Kansans, forcing the home side into errors throughout the closing three minutes, threw a tremendous scare into the Blackbirds. With less than a minute remaining, baskets by Don Upson, Jim Iverson and Iverson again brought the Wildcats to within a single point of the leaders. Then, however, time was on Long Island's side and the now-jittery favorites

Continued on Page 5, Column 4

RANGERS TRIUMPH ON BOSTON RINK, 3-2

New Yorkers Gain Fifth Place Undisputed as Toppazzini, Leswick, O'Connor Tally

By The Associated Press.

BOSTON, Dec. 2—New York's Rangers grabbed a 3—2 National Hockey League victory over Boston before 8,303 persons tonight, moving into fifth place undisputed, two points ahead of the faltering Bruins.

It was the first Ranger victory over Boston of the season. Previously the clubs had played three ties and Boston had fashioned a 4-3 decision. The same teams oppose each other tomorrow night in New York's Madison Square Garden.

The Bruins even pulled Jack

Continued on Page 4, Column 7

HOLY CROSS RALLY TRIPS EAGLES, 32-14

Turco Gets 4 Touchdowns, One a 97-Yard Kick-Off Return, Against Boston College

By MICHAEL STRAUSS

Special to The New York Times.

BOSTON, Dec. 2—Unable to post a victory all season, Boston College's eleven started well this afternoon, jumping into a two-touchdown lead over its arch rival, Holy Cross, but the Crusaders changed the complexion of things in short order and emerged with a 32-to-14 triumph.

Leading man in the Purple's sudden shift of fortunes was Johnny Turco, 160-pound halfback from near-by Walpole, who ignited the spark that sent Holy Cross soaring to victory as he turned in a 97-yard runback of a kick-off for a touchdown in the second period.

The tally, coming at a time when the Crusaders were trailing, 14—0, looked rather important, since the Purple seemed in for a rough afternoon.

Eagles' Attack Stalls

But Turco's sensational dash was only the beginning of his contributions to his team's cause. Aided by the fine tossing of Charlie Maloy, one of the East's top aerialists, and some superb blocking by the Holy Cross line, Turco reeled off the winners' next three touchdowns, scoring two more in the second session and the other in the third.

Thus it was that the remaining tally made by the Purple's Mel Massucco later in the third quarter left the thoroughly chilled crowd that sat in on the procedings at Braves Field absolutely unmoved. By that time the winners' defense was clicking on all fours, while the Eagles' attack stalled as they were held scoreless in the second half.

The outcome proved discourag-

Continued on Page 2, Column 6

Snead and Burke Deadlock at 201 After 3 Rounds in Miami Open Golf

By The Associated Press.

MIAMI, Fla., Dec. 2—Sammy Snead and Jack Burke Jr. tied for the lead at the end of the third round of the $10,000 Miami open golf tournament today with nine-under-par 201s.

Snead, of White Sulphur Springs, W. Va., who has won the 72-hole tournament three times, dropped a 12-foot putt on the eighteenth green for a birdie 3 to card his second straight four-under-par 66. He started with a 69 and yesterday fired a 66 to trail the leaders by three strokes at 135. Burke, 27-year-old professional who is sixth ranking money winner this year, turned in a two-under-par 68 on the third round to couple with his 67 and 66 of the first two rounds.

A stroke behind the leaders were Dick Mayer, Old Greenwich, Conn., and part time movie actor Joe Kirkwood Jr., Daytona Beach, Fla. Mayer shared the lead with amateur Frank Stranahan at the end of 36 holes with 132. He dropped an 18-footer on the last green to salvage an even par 70. Kirkwood, whose 66 led the field on the first day, carded a 68 in his most erratic round of the tournament.

Jim Turnesa, Briarcliff, N. Y., youngest of the six Turnesa brothers, and Jim Ferrier, San Francisco, Calif., were two strokes off the pace at 203.

Turnesa had an even par 35, 35—70 for the 7,000-yard Miami Springs course to add to 66 and 67 rounds.

Still using a borrowed set of

Continued on Page 4, Column 1

Penn State Topples Pitt by 21-20 In Muddy Battle on Forbes Field

By The Associated Press.

PITTSBURGH, Dec. 2—Penn State slipped and slid through mud today to eke out an upset 21-20 victory over a University of Pittsburgh football team that made a thrilling but futile second-half comeback.

It was Penn State's fourth straight victory of the season and its first over Pitt since 1947. A meager crowd of only 7,000 rode trolleys to the Forbes Field battle where parking lots were still blanketed with the city's record snow.

It was all Penn State in the first half but Pitt showed a threat with consistent gains by Fullback Joe Capp and potent passing of Quarterback Bobby Bestwick.

State sophomore End Bill Leonard intercepted a Bestwick pass on the 35 and raced 65 yards for the first Nittany Lion tally.

Sophomore Paul Anders plunged through the Pitt line from the five for the second score. State got its final marker in the second quarter as Anders ripped through tackle from the 15.

Pitt put over a touchdown in each of the last three quarters to get back into the ball game. Nick Bolkovac's failure to make his final conversion kick prevented the Panthers from emerging with a tie.

Pitt started making it look like a ball game in the second quarter. Bestwick tossed 24 yards to End Chris Warriner, who slid over the goal line with two State players hanging on his back.

The favored Panthers got their second touchdown the hard way. They started driving shortly after

Continued on Page 4, Column 4

Football Scores

COLLEGES

East

Fordham 13	Syracuse 6
Holy Cross 32	Boston College 14
Maryland 63	Virginia Tech 7
Navy 14	Army 2
Penn State 21	Pittsburgh 20

South

Alabama 34	Auburn 0
Allen 47	South Carolina A. & M. 13
Baylor 33	Rice 7
Georgia Tech 7	Georgia 0
Hardin-Simmons 28	Texas Tech 13
Louisiana State 14	Tulane 14
Mississippi 27	Mississippi State 20
Sul Ross 7	East Texas State 7
Tennessee 43	Vanderbilt 0
Texas Christian 27	Southern Methodist 13
Tulsa 28	Houston 21
Virginia 44	North Carolina 13
Wilberforce 13	Florida A. & M. 7
William & Mary 40	Richmond 6

West

Abilene Christian 13	Gustavus Adolphus 7
Central State (Mo.) 32	Pittsburgh State 21
Kansas State 6	Wichita 6
Oklahoma 41	Oklahoma A. & M. 14

Far West

College of Pacific 37	Quantico Marines 14
So. California 9	Notre Dame 7

101,000 See Navy Upset Army as Zastrow Scores Once and Passes for a Tally

MIDDIES TRIUMPH IN CLASSIC BY 14-2

Continued From Page 1

President was the guest of Vice Admiral Harry W. Hill, Superintendent of the Naval Academy. He had a royal good time again, even though the Commander in Chief is theoretically supposed to be neutral when the cadets do battle with the midshipmen.

It was Navy's day this drab, overcast but dry afternoon, from the time the captains of the teams, Tom Bakke of Annapolis and Dan Foldberg of West Point, assembled at the Presidential box with the coaches and Referee Paul N. Swaffield, for the spin of the coin. The toss was won by Captain Bakke, who received, as did Foldberg, a silver dollar from Mr. Truman, and that was an omen of what was to come, though there was no way of knowing it at the time.

It was not until the second quarter began that anyone had a real inkling of the disaster that was in store for an Army team that was seeking to complete its third successive season and its sixth in seven years without defeat and that was bent on demonstrating, at Navy's expense, that it had as much right as Oklahoma to rank as the No. 1 eleven of the country.

There was indication enough in the first quarter that the cadets were mixing with a lot of furies as they were stopped dead four times, once at the Annapolis 15 after taking possession on Navy's 22 as Quarterback Bob Cameron, who kicked so superbly all afternoon, was unable to get off a fourth-down punt and fumbled the ball. But even though Army could not move the ball and failed to make a first down in the quarter, Navy was not making any offensive threats, with the ball deep in its territory.

Early in the second period, after Halfback Frank Hauff, one of Navy's numerous heroes, had intercepted the first of five passes by Bob Blaik that went into enemy hands, the midshipman attack began to get up a full head of steam, and now it was that the vast crowd came to a realization of the fate that was in store for the team that was supposed to win by a lopsided score.

Day of His Life

From then on it was Navy's game, the game of Hauff, Fullback Dave Bannerman, Quarterback Bob Zastrow, who had the day of his life with his running and passing and scored the first touchdown on a 7-yard buck; End Jim Baldinger, who made a great catch in the end zone of Zastrow's 30-yard pass for the second score twenty seconds before the end of the half; End John Gurski, who intercepted two passes in the fourth quarter and the game of those embattled sailors in the line and secondary who swarmed in and all but tore the cadet backs limb from limb with the ferocity of their tackling.

The 3,700 midshipmen in the stands were in a delirium of happiness over the seeming miracle they beheld until they stormed down from the stands on the final play to raise Coach Erdelatz. Captain Bakke and their other heroes to their shoulders.

They had waited seven long years—almost two undergraduate generations—for this day of retribution, which wiped out the mortification of the adversity they had suffered season after season.

They saw their line, in which some of the men were playing on both offense and defense against the Army platoons, knock the Army backs loose from the ball with their savage tackling, harry Blaik in his attempts to pass as he has never been harried before and stop such feared carriers as Al Pollard, Vic Pollock, Gil Stephenson, Jim Cain, Frank Fischl, Jack Martin and Gene Filipski stone dead in their tracks, limiting them to 77 yards, to Navy's 200.

They also saw their secondaries back up the line violently and cover Foldberg, a great pass catcher, and the other receivers with amazing thoroughness, and their interferers open the way for their carriers with berserk blocking that even as fine an end as Hal Loehlein could not resist.

Another Pass Interception

Army, able to make only one first down and 3 yards by running in the opening half, while Navy was going 32 yards and then 63 in five plays for its two scores and a 14-0 lead, was expected to do something drastic about the situation after the intermission. But right off the bat another Blaik pass was intercepted and Navy, reaching the cadet 21-yard line, threatened to score again, only to fail as Roger Drew's attempted field goal from the 30 fell short.

A Navy fumble, which Herb Johnson recovered near mid-field, contributed to Army breaking into the scoring column on a safety in this third period, Zastrow being hurled back 14 yards into his end zone for the two points after Blaik had punted out on the 12, one of his numerous good spot kicks.

At the very end of the quarter the cadet attack started to roll for the first time as Pollard went 24 yards for a first down, the second one Army had made up to this point. The attack carried to the Navy 21 as the final period opened and the 2,400 cadets in the stands were roaring in the hope that their team had finally set sail. There was still time to save the day, and the way the West Pointers were battling it seemed that they might possibly do it.

Then came one of the wildest final quarters any football game has produced. In those last fifteen minutes three Army passes were intercepted, each team lost the ball twice on fumbles, a Navy kick was blocked by Charley Shira and Elmer Stout, the middies were penalized time and again. On the very last play, with Army three yards from a touchdown, Gurski intercepted, ran the ball back nearly to midfield and fumbled for the fifth bobble of the period.

Army, in this last quarter, was on Navy's 21, 15, 6 and 3-yard marks and it could not get across once, marking the first time the cadets have failed to register a touchdown since 1947.

Gurski's first interception stopped them at the 21. After getting the ball on the 20 on a Navy bobble, they gave up the ball on downs on the 22. They got the ball again on the 29 on Gerald Hart's recovery of a fumble, after Pollard and Pollock's march had been stopped by Martin's fumble, and went to the Navy 6, where Cain lost the ball on a bobble.

The blocked kick gave the cadets their last chance, with less than a minute remaining, Army taking possession on the 9. But, after Cain had carried to the 3 and two plays had failed, Gurski made his second interception of the quarter on the final scrimmage.

Navy's special defense was partly responsible for Army's utter frustration on the attack. The middies were looping and charging on a slant in the line and shooting in the backers-up in the 6-2, 2-1 alignment. The cadets attacked from their usual straight T formation and did not appear to have any new devices. At any rate, Navy seemed to be ready for anything sent at them—rough and ready, that is.

On the offense, the sailors confined themselves to the T formation, abjuring the single wing, of which there had been talk and which they have used briefly during the season. Most of the time they had one or two flankers, either a halfback alone or paired with an end.

From this alignment they had a wide variety of plays, hitting both through the middle and sweeping off the tackles or outside, and passing. Zastrow has never been more effective than he was on quarterback sneaks and all of the backs, particularly Bannerman and Hauff, ran with a drive and determination that carried them on after they appeared to have been stopped.

Zastrow scored from the 7 in the second period after he had apparently been stopped at the 5, digging and churning to get across. His touchdown was set up by two passes he threw to Art Sundry for 18 and to Hauff for 5.

Makes Spectacular Catch

On the second march of 63 yards Zastrow went 11 yards and Bill Powers, a yeoman worker on both offense and defense, reversed around right end for 22. Then Zastrow passed 30 yards into the end zone to Baldinger. The Navy end was covered by Gene Gribble, but he leaped high into the air and snatched the ball in a spectacular catch.

That score, making the count 14—0 after Drew's second extra-point kick, almost broke the heart of Army. It had been trying desperately to make a tying touchdown and seemed to be on the way when Blaik passed 26 yards to Foldberg, but that effort went for naught. Thereafter, until the mad last quarter, Navy had possession of the ball and gave the cadets few chances to go on the attack.

The 14 points that Navy scored were the most made against Army by any team all season. The victory, in all probability, marks the dawn of a new era for football at Annapolis.

After all their years of adversity, the midshipmen should now be on their way to regaining the stature they enjoyed prior to 1944. Nothing could be a greater tonic for them than a triumph over Army, which has stood for the best in Eastern football, if not in the country, for most of that period.

The line-up:

NAVY (14)

Left Ends—Treadwell, McDonald.
Left Tackles—Tetrault, Davis
Left Guards—Fischer, Denfeld, McCowan.
Centers—Bryson, Sieber, Kukowski.
Right Guards—Steele Parker, Pertel, Lowell.
Right Tackles—Hunt, Gragg Dumont.
Right Ends—Bakke, Gurski, Baldinger.
Quarterbacks—Zastrow, Cameron.
Left Halfbacks—Hauff.
Right Halfbacks—Powers, Brady, Sundry Etchison.
Fullbacks—Bannerman, Botula Drew, Franco, Owens.

ARMY (2)

Left Ends—Foldberg Loehlein, McShulskis, Denman.
Left Tackles—Zeigler, Shira.
Left Guards—Elmblad, Bara, Brian Hart, Volonnino.
Centers—Haas, Stout, Bretzke, Guess.
Right Guards—Roberts, Malavasi, Cox.
Right Tackles—Ackerson, Kimmel.
Right Ends—Weaver, Rowekamp Krobock, Conway.
Quarterbacks—Blaik, Reich.
Left Halfbacks—Pollock, Schultz, Cain, Gribble.
Right Halfbacks—Fischl, Johnson, Martin, Filipski.
Fullbacks—Pollard, Beck, Stephenson.

SCORE BY PERIODS

Navy	0	14	0	0—14
Army	0	0	2	0—2

Touchdowns—Zastrow, Baldinger. Points after touchdown—Drew 2 (placements). Safety—Army.

Referee—Paul N. Swaffield, Brown. Umpire—Leonard Dobbins Fordham. Linesman—William J McConnel, Middlebury. Field judge—Clifford Montgomery, Columbia. Electric clock operator—Charles G. Eckles

The President and Mrs. Truman in the stands
Associated Press Wirephotos

Statistics of the Game

	Navy.	Army.
First downs	13	5
Yards gained, rushing	200	77
Forward passes	10	24
Forwards completed	5	6
Yards gained, forwards	68	60
Forwards intercepted by	5	1
Number of punts	8	8
*Av. dist. of punts, yds.	40	40
Run-back of punts, yds.	23	65
Rival fumbles recovered	3	4
Penalties	9	3
Yards lost, penalties	65	35

*From line of scrimmage

BIG SHOW THRILLS TRUMAN, TOP BRASS

Continued From Page 1

the Joint Chiefs of Staff; Secretary of Navy Francis P. Matthews, Admiral Forrest C. Sherman, Chief of Naval Operations; Secretary of Commerce Charles Sawyer, Secretary of Labor Maurice Tobin and Secretary of the Treasury John W. Snyder.

On the Army side of the field, Maj. Gen. Bryant E. Moore, superintendent of the Military Academy, had among his guests Gen. George C. Marshall, Secretary of Defense; Frank Pace Jr., Secretary of Army; Thomas Finletter, Secretary of Air Force, and Gen. Hoyt S. Vandenberg, Air Force Chief of Staff.

Also on hand were Postmaster General Jesse L. Donaldson, Attorney General J. Howard McGrath and Secretary of the Interior Oscar L. Chapman.

President Truman took his seat a few minutes before noon. Just before the corps of cadets, 2,400 strong and led by Wiliam J. Ryan of Paducah, Ky., marched into the stadium, swinging along in faultless cadence.

After the cadets had taken their seats, the blue-garbed midshipmen entered the arena. The 3,700-man Annapolis brigade was led by William Lawrence of Nashville, Tenn.

Then the rival cheerleaders took over for the customary exchange of elaborately stage-managed taunts.

Navy's band played "The Thing," the novelty song that has taken the airwaves by storm, as a truck bearing a huge box carrying the legend "Who Wants It?" circled the stadium. Finally, the box was opened and out trotted a small and very obstreperous burro.

EXULTANT MIDDIES TOUCH OFF BEDLAM

Tears of Joy Flow in Navy's Dressing Room—Coach Says Spirit Brought Victory

PHILADELPHIA, Dec. 2 (AP)—Tears of delirious joy streaming down his cherubic face, Navy Coach Eddie Erdelatz declared "it was one of the greatest team efforts I've seen."

He had to struggle to talk sense in the uproar of the middie dressing room today after the sailors upset mighty Army. The place was an uproar, with bruised stalwarts screaming, kissing and hugging everybody in sight.

Navy admirals, captains and on down the line were just other guys in seventh heaven.

"I've said all along, and still say, that the big thing is spirit and we've got it," Erdelatz declared. "The Brigade of Midshipmen, with their rooting all the time and Admiral Harry Hill, the superintendent, had as much to do with winning as the players."

"Everybody's Best Game"

Coach Erdelatz refused to single out any one player for praise.

"To me, that was everybody's best game. It had to be to beat Army."

He explained, over the "we won, we won" chant of the players, that defensive maneuvers played a major part in the triumph.

"We knew Army had a fast-pacing team, starting fast when they came out of the huddle. So we got in position while they huddled and we were ready before they got over the ball."

In that way, the Navy line got the jump and stopped Army's vaunted running game cold.

When he saw "that their running game wasn't hurting us," Coach Erdelatz said he changed his defense from a six to a five-man line. "That gave us three line-backers who could drop back to protect against passes."

He figured Army would have to "play differently in the second half because they were 14 points behind, so we changed our defense accordingly."

Two-Week Rest Helped

The big, curly-haired coach also credited the two-week respite from competition with helping. "It gave us a chance to get well."

It was a bruising battle and an old Navy hand chortled—"we beat Army at its own game—physically."

While there was plenty of blood and bruises on the Navy squad, the team physician reported: "If we had to play next week everybody would be ready."

Quarterback Bob Zastrow, who had a big hand in both Navy touchdowns, was enjoying the post-game festivities so much he was still in game uniform after most of his mates had showered and dressed.

"It was the greatest thrill of my life," said the big junior. "Particularly since my girl, Junette Pfuehler, was here to see it." Zastrow said they lived two blocks apart in Algoma, Wis., but aren't engaged—"yet."

Center Ted Kukowski from Clifton, N. J., broke up Zastrow's press conference by telling him "you were impeccable, absolutely impeccable, today."

Paul Tetreault, big tackle from Greenfield, Mass., summed up the whole affair and season. He said simply to Coach Erdelatz, "We owed it to you."

Room Made for Band

Apparently something went wrong with the seating arrangements on the midshipman side for there was no space for the band. Finally a group of middies moved down to empty seats in front of the President's box and everything was okay.

Browns Win Pro Football Title in Final 20 Seconds

CLEVELAND DOWNS LOS ANGELES, 30-28

16-Yard Place-Kick by Groza Decides Thrilling Uphill Battle for the Browns

WATERFIELD, DAVIS EXCEL

They Start Rams in Front With Spectacular 82-Yard Play —Graham Aerial Wizard

STATISTICS OF THE GAME

	Browns	Rams
First downs.............	22	22
Yards gained, rushing..	73	95
Forward passes	33	32
Forwards completed	22	18
Yards gained, forwards.	298	312
Forwards interceptea by	5	1
Number of punts.......	5	4
*Av. dist. of punts, yds.	38.2	50¾
Run-back of punts, yds.	22	14
Fumbles	3	0
Own fumbles recovered.	0	0
Penalties	3	4
Yards lost, penalties....	25	48

*From line of scrimmage.

By LOUIS EFFRAT

Special to THE NEW YORK TIMES.

CLEVELAND, Dec. 24—It was the day before Christmas and all through the house 29,751 rabid rooters hoping for a miracle, while gazing gloomily at the clock, all but gave up on the 'Cleveland Browns in their National Football League championship play-off against the Los Angeles Rams today.

But the Browns, who never have lost a play-off, did not give up on themselves and with a successful last-gasp effort became monarchs of all they survey in the gridiron world.

The seemingly impossible—impossible because of the time element—came to pass when, with only twenty seconds remaining in a spectacularly fought contest over Municipal Stadium's frozen turf, Lou Groza booted a perfect 16-yard field goal. Groza's specialty—he did it twice against the Giants last week—turned an almost certain 28—27 setback into a glorious 30—28 victory for the Browns.

All of a sudden it was a "joyeux noel" for Paul Brown's charges, who despite the herculean efforts of Otto Graham, spent most of the cold afternoon trailing Joe Stydahar's Pacific Coast representatives. In the end, it was somewhat ironic that so flashy an aerial duel between Graham and Bob Waterfield should be decided by a placement kick from the very same distance at which Waterfield had barely missed a 3-pointer in the second period.

Passes Gain 298 Yards

Between intermittent snow flurries, a 28-mile-an-hour wind that blew in from Lake Erie and the 29-degree temperature, Graham completed 22 of 32 passes, four for touchdowns and an over-all 298 yards. Waterfield fired only one 6-pointer, but his 18 completions in 31 attempts gained 312 yards. Four of Waterfield's thrusts were intercepted by the victors.

It will be recalled that before peace came to professional football, the Browns, under the guidance of their canny coach, annexed every All-American Conference crown.

There were some who attempted to discredit Brown's accomplishments on the basis of a weak league. "Just wait until he gets into the National League," they said.

After four years of monotonous winning in the A. A. C., Brown and his Browns joined the National. This, the first season, was a rough one, but aside from two defeats by Steve Owen's Giants, whom they conquered, 8—3, in the American Conference play-off a week ago, it was not rough enough to make a difference. Nor was it

The Cleveland Browns

Otto Graham

tough enough to stymie them today.

That the Rams, with Waterfield a threat every inch of the way, almost turned the trick, was a credit to themselves and their coach. Disdaining rubber sneakers—only four Rams wore them, while every Brownie was so equipped for better footing—the Californians scored on their very first offensive maneuver. This was an electrifying 82-yard-pass play from Waterfield to Glenn Davis. Waterfield's toss went 30 yards and Davis galloped 52 for the score. The contest was only 27 seconds old when Waterfield kicked the extra point and Los Angeles had a 7-0 lead.

Rugged and Well-Played

Between this and Groza's field-goal at 14:40 in the fourth quarter, it was, in spite of discouraging weather conditions, one of the best-played and most rugged clashes of the campaign, as six play-off records were surpassed and three tied.

As the minutes passed, every indication was that the Rams, who, as the Cleveland Rams in 1945 took the championship in the play-off that year, would be crowned in Bert Bell's circuit. Trailing, 28—20, the Browns appeared to be out of the running when the final period started. There was a slight chance when Graham's running and passing brought the home club to the Los Angeles 14-yard line.

Then Graham flipped a 14-yard aerial to Rex Bumgardner in the end zone and Groza converted. Now only one point separated the teams, and time was running out.

Twice they exchanged punts and when with five minutes to go, Tom Thompson intercepted a Waterfield pass at midfield and Graham hit Dub Jones with a 22-yard toss, the Cleveland fans went wild. Then Graham bootlegged to the 21, but he fumbled and Milan Lazetich made a timely recovery for the Rams.

It looked bad for Cleveland, even if the visitors were held to a minor gain and Waterfield was forced to punt. Bob got off a long one which Cliff Lewis caught on his own 14 and returned to the 32. This meant the Browns, in possession 68 yards away from the goal-line, had exactly 1 minute 48 seconds in which to produce a tally.

Plays Against the Clock

Graham, trying to spot a receiver, found none and ran for 14, stepping out of bounds to stop the clock. On the next play Otto clicked with a 15-yarder to Bumgardner in the left flat, the latter running outside and again stopping the clock. The tension mounted when Graham found Jones in the right flat and the Browns had a first down on the 22. Again Graham reversed the pattern, passing to the left flat, where Bumgardner made the catch on the 11 and stepped out. Everything that was being done by the Browns was being dictated by time.

Thus, when Graham looked up and saw 40 seconds remaining, he tried a quarterback sneak. Unmindful of gaining, Otto's plan was to run diagonally in order to put the ball nearer to the center. He gained only a yard, but his principal purpose had been served.

It was only second down, but Graham refused to gamble on another pass. He was confident that Groza's talented toe, which had kicked fifteen field goals this year, would do it again. A hush fell over the stadium as the teams lined up for the most important play of the game. Earlier, Tom James, the holder for Groza's placements, had been unable to handle a low pass from center following the second Cleveland touchdown. A similar occurrence would be ruinous.

This time, however, everything went smoothly. James took the perfect pass from center, spotted it perfectly on the 16 and Groza booted it perfectly between the uprights. There was little that the Rams could do in the twenty seconds that remained and their dying gesture, a 55-yard pass by Norm Van Brocklin, was intercepted by Warren Lahr as the game and season ended.

The story-book finish dwarfed all that had happened earlier. Off winging on Waterfield's record-breaking pass, the Rams were tied at 3:10 in the first when Graham fired 31 yards to Jones for a touchdown and Groza converted. At 7:05, the Rams, after an 80-yard advance on eight plays, scored again as Dick Hoerner plunged over from the 3 and Waterfield kicked the point.

A 35-yard aerial from Graham to Dante Lavelli produced the next Cleveland touchdown at 2:20 in the second. Then it was that James was unable to put down the ball for the attempted placement by Groza. James recovered and tried to pass to Tony Adamle in the end zone, but the latter dropped the ball and Los Angeles was ahead 14—13.

It became Cleveland's turn to lead at 4:00 in the third when Lavelli snared his second touchdown pass, a 39-yarder from Graham, and Groza made it 20—14, but the Rams rebounded quickly and scored twice within twenty-one seconds. They drove 71 yards in eleven plays, Hoerner going over for his second tally from the 1 and Waterfield converting. Then a fumble by Marion Motley was recovered by Larry Brink of the Rams and he ran seven yards into end zone. Again Waterfield made the point and the picture was black, despite the white background, for the Browns.

Then it was that the Browns, overcoming every obstacle, including the clock, marched to victory.

The line-up:

CLEVELAND BROWNS (30)

Left Ends—Young, Speedie, Gillom.
Left Tackles—Palmer, Groza, Kissell.
Left Guards—Agase, Humble, Gibron.
Centers—Herring, Gatski, T. Thompson.
Right Guards—Willis, Houston.
Right Tackles—Grigg, Rymkus, Sandusky.
Right Ends—Martin, Lavelli, Ford.
Quarterbacks—Gorgal, Graham, C. Lewis.
Left Halfbacks—Lahr, Baumgardner, Carpenter, Moselle.
Right Halfbacks—James, Jones, Phelps.
Fullbacks—Adamle, Motley, Cole.

LOS ANGELES RAMS (28)

Left Ends—Fears, Brink, Keane.
Left Tackles—Huffman, Champagne.
Left Guards—Finlay, Vasicek.
Centers—Statuto, Naumetz, Paul.
Right Guards—West, H. Thompson, Stephenson, Lazetich.
Right Tackles—Reinhard, Bouley.
Right Ends—Hirsch, Zilly, Boyd, Smyth.
Quarterbacks—Waterfield, Van Brocklin.
Left Halfbacks—Davis, Williams.
Right Halfbacks—Smith, Kalmanir, Barry, W. Lewis.
Fullbacks—Hoerner, Towler, Younger, Pasquariello.

SCORE BY PERIODS

Cleveland Browns	7	6	7	10—30
Los Angeles Rams	14	0	14	0—28

Touchdowns—Davis, Jones, Hoerner 2, Lavelli 2, Brink, Baumgardner. Points after touchdown—Waterfield 4, Groza 3 (placements). Field goal—Groza (placement).

Referee—Ronnie Gibbs. Umpire—Sam Wilson. Linesman—Charlie Berry. Back judge—Norman Duncan. Field judge—Lloyd Brazill.

NORTH-SOUTH TEST TO ATTRACT 40,000

Teams Rated Evenly Matched for Mahi Shrine Charity Game in Miami Tonight

MIAMI, Fla., Dec. 24 (AP)—Hand-picked college football players from the North and South will meet tomorrow night in Mahi Shrine Temple's third annual All-Star charity game in the Orange Bowl Stadium.

A crowd of 40,000 or more is expected, with proceeds going to the Shrine's crippled children fund.

The rival 30-man squads will be seeking the edge in games. Miami coach Andy Gustafson's South eleven won the opener, 24—14, and Yale coach Herman Hickman's North squad won last year, 20—14. This game is rated a toss-up.

The South will count on the passing of John (Model T) Ford of Hardin-Simmons, the running of John Dottley of Ole Miss and the receiving of C. P. Youmans of Duke.

Georgia Tech's Bobby Dodd, who has handled the South squad while Gustafson was busy preparing his University of Miami team for its New Year's Day Orange Bowl game with Clemson, has a wealth of other material, in the backfield and on the line.

Lucia in the Backfield

The South's backs include Tom Lucia of Louisville, Wade Stinson of Kansas, Darrell Meisenheimer of Oklahoma A. & M., Bobby North of Georgia Tech, Angus Williams of Florida, Bishop Strickland of South Carolina, Dean Davidson of Vanderbilt, John Idzik of Maryland, Ebert Van Buren of Louisiana State and Pat Field of Georgia.

Hickman's starting backfield is expected to be made up of John Miller of Northwestern, Reds Bagnell of Pennsylvania, Stu Tisdale of Yale and Jeff Fleischmann of Cornell.

Others in the North backfield squad include Frank Miller of Cornell, Jack Martin of Army, Dick Gabriel of Lehigh, James Cain of Army, Carl Taseff of John Carroll, Bill Dechard of Holy Cross, Bill Roberts of Dartmouth, Gil Stephenson of Army, Bob Radcliffe of Wisconsin and Dick Doheny of Fordham.

Hero of Gridiron Thriller Kisses Shoe That Booted Winning Points

Groza Mobbed by Brown Team-mates After Game at Cleveland—Graham Also Gets High Praise—Coach Lauds Losers

CLEVELAND, Dec. 24 (UP)—Lou (The Toe) Groza, Cleveland's kicker de luxe, kissed his shoe today in mute thanks for a tight-squeeze championship victory.

Pushed and happily pummeled from one side of the dressing room to the other, the perspiring, 235-pound Groza, whose field goal in the final twenty seconds gave the Browns a 30-to-28 triumph over the Los Angeles Rams along with the National Football League title, wearily accepted all congratulations.

He grinned weakly, sighed heavily several times and then kissed his shoe as teammates yelled approval.

Said One Hero to Another

"You were great, Groza, just great," thundered passing star Otto Graham.

"You were all right yourself," Lou reminded the tuckered out Graham.

Coach Paul Brown, on the receiving end of his fifth straight professional gridiron title, still showing the numbing effects from the freezing temperature, shouted: "What the heck was the final score?"

Standing in the middle of a pile of equipment, Brown piped up: "Did you ever see one as rugged as that?"

Then Brown, whose teams had swept to four previous titles in the defunct All-America Conference, said:

"Maybe it's better to be lucky than good. I've got the gamest bunch of ball players in the business."

No one challenged his statement as the carefree Browns celebrated.

Praise for the Losers

Coach Brown didn't overlook the valiant battle put up by the defeated Rams.

"We played a magnificent team," he said.

In the Rams' dressing room no one said much and Head Coach Joe Stydahar, mumbling through stiff lips and blurred eyes, said:

"The Browns are a great team."

Quarterback Bob Waterfield stared emptily into space. Nearby, End Tom Fears slumped on a bench and kicked idly at the floor.

Everywhere in the room, defeat stuck hard in everyone's throat.

It was a tough one to lose.

Yanks Top Red Sox and Lead League; Feller Hurls Third No-Hitter for Indians

LOPAT WINS NO. 11 FOR BOMBERS, 5-2

He Limits Red Sox to 6 Blows as Yanks Take League Lead by 4 Percentage Points

COLEMAN, PESKY CONNECT

Doerr Gets His 2,000th Hit of Major Career at Stadium—Parnell Loses in Box

By JOHN DREBINGER

The Red Sox, it seems, cannot nail down the one they must win. Inversely, on such occasions, the Yankees seldom miss.

Certain it is the Bombers never even came close to missing at the Stadium yesterday when, before a cheering crowd of 58,815, they toppled Steve O'Neill's Bosox, 5 to 2, in the deciding encounter of the three-game series.

With the victory, the Yankees rose to first place by four percentage points over the White Sox. The teams are tied in games, however.

Slick pitching by Southpaw Eddie Lopat, a robust nine-hit attack that included a Jerry Coleman homer off Mel Parnell and the usual mystifying managerial moves by Prof. Casey Stengel combined to trip the Sox in this encounter which meant so much to the Boston entry. For had they won it, the Sox would have pulled themselves right up on the necks of the Bombers. Instead, they now trail the Yanks by three and a half lengths.

Pesky Connects in Sixth

Lopat, in ringing up his eleventh victory against only three defeats, allowed only six hits. One of these was a sixth-inning homer by Johnny Pesky, while another, a ninth-inning single by Bobby Doerr, not only paved the way for Boston's second and concluding tally, but gave the veteran second sacker the 2000th hit of his major league career.

Perhaps most baffling of all, however, were the mystic maneuverings of Prof. Casey. In open defiance of one of baseball's fundamental precepts, Stengel started three of his alternating left-handed hitters—Gene Woodling, Cliff Mapes and Bobby Brown—even though the opposition was tossing its ace southpaw.

To be sure, the three batsmen didn't contribute much. Mapes got a single, Woodling a pass, and both got themselves picked off first. But it's a cinch it did puzzle the Bosox and by the time they thought they had it all solved Casey had a few more left in the eighth that helped fetch home the final pair of Yankee tallies.

Luck rode with the Yanks in the first when, with Phil Rizzuto on third and Yogi Berra on first, the result of a pair of singles, Joe DiMaggio slapped the ball back to Parnell for a simple double play to end the inning. But Doerr's throw from second to first went wide and Rizzuto scored the first Yankee run.

Ball Skids Off Mapes' Glove

The second came in the fifth when Coleman larruped his No. 3 of the year into the left field seats, an admirable piece of foresight since in the top of the sixth the Sox broke in with their first run on Pesky's homer which skidded off Mapes' glove in right as Cliff's arm crashed into the front railing.

In the same round the Yanks picked up another on Rizzuto's second single, a pass to DiMaggio and a single by Johnny Mize. That inning ended Parnell and Bill Wight came on to get cuffed for two more in the eighth which Ellis Kinder had to finish. With two out and two on, the result of a pass to Rizzuto and an intentional walk to DiMaggio, Casey now made another notable shift.

He called upon Hank Bauer to bat for Joe Collins who had gone in to run for Mize in the sixth and the ex-Marine blasted a single to right to score Li'l Phil. On came Kinder only to be greeted by a single by Gil McDougald who now had replaced Brown at third and that produced the second marker and fifth for the day.

All this reduced the Sox ninth inning demonstration to a mere flurry when they counted their final tally with the help of a pinch double by Lou Boudreau.

The big stickers of the Boston battlefront, Ted Williams, Dom DiMaggio and Vern Stephens were all held hitless.

Stengel weakened a bit on his hunch of shooting left-handed swingers against southpaw pitching when he called on McDougald to bat for Bobby Brown in the sixth, but that one didn't pan out so well. Neither did the move that sent Collins in to run for Mize after Big Jawn singled in this inning. For McDougald's grounder to Stephens got DiMaggio trapped between third and home and Collins got doubled up rounding second too far.

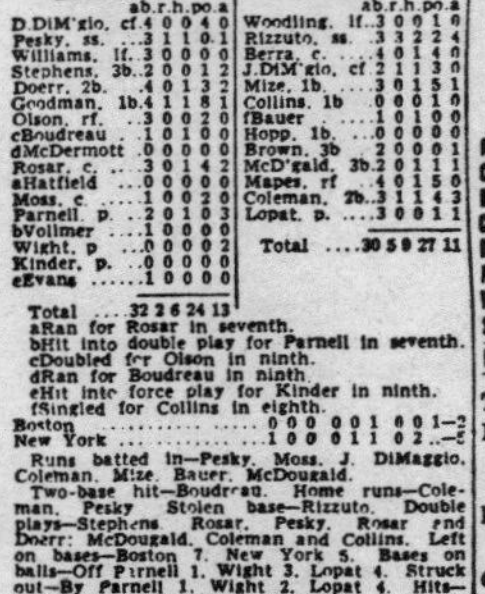

The box score:

BOSTON (A.)	ab.	r.	h.	po.	a.
D.DiM'gio, cf	4	0	0	4	0
Pesky, ss	3	1	1	0	1
Williams, lf	3	0	0	0	0
Stephens, 3b	2	0	0	1	2
Doerr, 2b	4	0	1	3	2
Goodman, 1b	4	1	1	8	1
Olson, rf	3	0	0	2	0
cBoudreau	1	0	1	0	0
dMcDermott	0	0	0	0	0
Rosar, c	3	0	1	4	2
aHatfield	0	0	0	0	0
Moss, c	1	0	0	2	0
Parnell, p	2	0	1	0	3
bVollmer	1	0	0	0	0
Wight, p	0	0	0	0	2
Kinder, p	0	0	0	0	0
eEvans	1	0	0	0	0
Total	32	2	6	24	13

NEW YORK (A.)	ab.	r.	h.	po.	a.
Woodling, lf	3	0	0	1	0
Rizzuto, ss	3	3	2	2	4
Berra, c	4	0	1	4	0
J.DiM'gio, cf	2	1	1	3	0
Mize, 1b	3	0	1	5	1
Collins, 1b	0	0	0	1	0
fBauer	1	0	1	0	0
Hopp, 1b	0	0	0	0	0
Brown, 3b	2	0	0	0	1
McD'gald, 3b	2	0	1	1	1
Mapes, rf	4	0	1	5	0
Coleman, 2b	3	1	1	4	3
Lopat, p	3	0	0	1	1
Total	30	5	9	27	11

aRan for Rosar in seventh.
bHit into double play for Parnell in seventh.
cDoubled for Olson in ninth.
dRan for Boudreau in ninth.
eHit into force play for Kinder in ninth.
fSingled for Collins in eighth.

Boston .... 000 001 001—2
New York .... 100 011 02 . —5

Runs batted in—Pesky, Moss, J. DiMaggio, Coleman, Mize, Bauer, McDougald.

Two-base hit—Boudreau. Home runs—Coleman, Pesky. Stolen base—Rizzuto. Double plays—Stephens, Rosar, Pesky, Rosar and Doerr; McDougald, Coleman and Collins. Left on bases—Boston 7, New York 5. Bases on balls—Off Parnell 1, Wight 3, Lopat 4. Struck out—By Parnell 1, Wight 2, Lopat 4. Hits—Off Parnell 7 in 6 innings, Wight 1 in 1 2-3, Kinder 1 in 1-3. Winning pitcher — Lopat (11—3). Losing pitcher—Parnell (9—5). Umpires—Stevens, Paparella, Hubbard and Rommel. Time of game—2:14. Attendance—58,815.

A MIGHTY BUT FUTILE EFFORT TO NAB HOME-RUN DRIVE

Cliff Mapes, in an all-out try, just missed catching ball hit by Johnny Pesky in sixth inning. Ball was knocked from Mapes' glove as he came down and his arm hit top of railing. Associated Press

ROBINSON HALTS DELANNOIT IN 3D

Belgian Quits at 2:53 After Being Floored for Eight in Non-Title Bout at Turin

TURIN, Italy, July 1 (AP)—Ray (Sugar) Robinson, world middleweight champion, stopped Cyril Delannoit of Belgium in 2:53 of the third round of a scheduled ten-round non-title fight today.

Robinson swarmed all over the Belgian, raining blows upon him until Delannoit suddenly threw up his arms and quit just before the end of the third round. The bout was scored as a technical knockout.

It was the fifth victory for Robinson in six bouts on his European tour. The fight was held without any of the bottle-throwing demonstrations which accompanied Robinson's "no decision" bout with Gerhard Hecht, German light heavyweight, in Berlin last Sunday.

Robinson received a wild ovation from the crowd of about 25,000 as Delannoit staggered to his corner after arising from taking an eight count. He went down when Robinson slashed him with a vicious left hook followed by a right hook.

The champion opened a cut over Delannoit's left eye with the first punch he threw — a stinging straight right.

Forcing the former European middleweight champion against the ropes continually, Robinson raked him with bolo punches, jabs, hooks and right crosses.

Delannoit was down once earlier in the third round, slipping to one knee after Robinson pinned him against the ropes and slammed him in the stomach. Delannoit bounced up right away, however.

Once in the second round and again at the beginning of the third the Belgian gestured to the referee that he thought Robinson struck low blows. The referee ordered the fighters to continue both times, however.

Danny Womber, 149, New York, stopped Luigi Male, 150¾, Italy, in a preliminary.

White Sox Lose by 3-1 to Garver After Beating Browns in 11th, 2-1

Minoso's 400-Foot Blow Decides Opener—Chicago, Dropping From League Lead, Is Held to 2 Hits in Second Game

CHICAGO, July 1 (AP)—Ned Garver's two-hit masterpiece gave the Browns a 3-1 victory today after the White Sox had won the opener, 2—1, on Minnie Minoso's eleventh-inning home run. By splitting the double-header, Chicago dropped from the league lead for the first time since May 28.

Comiskey Park's 27,572 fans went home disappointed as the Sox fell before the wizardry of Garver, who bagged his tenth triumph against four losses.

Garver fanned three and issued four walks, two of them in the second inning when the Sox got their only run. He walked Al Zarilla. Al was sacrificed to second by Jim Busby and driven home by Chico Carrasquel.

Sox Baffled After Second

Garver faced only twenty-two batters in the last seven frames and set the Sox down in order the final four.

The Browns gave their ace a 2-1 lead in the fourth. Lou Kretlow walked Max Batts and then served a double to Dale Long that parked Batts on third. Ken Wood's long fly brought home Batts and Fred Marsh's fluke hit scored Long. Marsh grounded hard to Second Baseman Nellie Fox who lost a cleat in his shoe when pivoting for the throw to first and tossed wide while on his knees.

The Browns picked up their third run in the sixth when Batts clouted his No. 3 homer into the left field stands.

Kretlow, striving for his third decision after two losses, was nicked for only six hits in eight innings before being lifted for a pinch hitter. He struck out seven.

Holcombe Victor in Duel

In the first game, Minoso's 400-foot homer into the left center stands broke up a pitching duel between loser Duane Pillette and Ken Holcombe, who gained his sixth victory against four defeats. Each yielded eight hits.

The Browns took a 1-0 edge in the third inning when Bob Young tripled and scored on a fielder's choice. The Sox tied it in the same inning. Phil Masi scratched a single and Holcombe sacrificed him to second. Bob Dillinger tripled Masi home.

The Sox blew their best chance in the tenth. They loaded the bases with one out. Then Fox lined out to Bob Young. Holcombe, on second, apparently thought Young had scooped the ball instead of catching it and started for third. Catcher Sherm Lollar eventually rifled to third baseman Fred Marsh, who tagged Holcombe between bases to complete the double play.

The Box Scores

FIRST GAME

ST. LOUIS (A.)	ab.	r.	h.	po.	a.
Young, 2b	5	1	2	4	5
Coleman, lf	5	0	1	5	0
Lollar, c	4	0	0	3	1
Arft, 1b	4	0	2	10	1
Bero, ss	0	0	0	1	0
Wood, rf	5	0	0	2	0
Lehner, cf	5	0	1	2	0
Marsh, 3b	5	0	1	1	2
Upton, ss	3	0	1	0	5
aSleater	1	0	0	0	0
Long, 1b	0	0	0	1	1
Pillette, p	3	0	0	1	0
Total	40	1	8	*30	15

CHICAGO (A.)	ab.	r.	h.	po.	a.
Dillinger, 3b	5	0	2	6	1
Fox, 2b	5	0	0	3	3
Minoso, lf	4	1	1	2	0
Robinson, 1b	4	0	1	9	1
Zarilla, rf	3	0	0	1	0
Busby, cf	4	0	0	6	0
Carr'squel, ss	3	0	0	1	5
Masi, c	4	1	2	5	0
Holcombe, p	3	0	2	0	2
Total	35	2	8	33	12

*None out when winning run scored.
aGrounded out for Upton in ninth.

St. Louis .... 001 000 000 00—1
Chicago .... 001 000 000 01—2

Runs batted in—Coleman, Dillinger, Minoso.

Two-base hit—Lehner. Three-base hits—Young, Dillinger. Home run—Minoso. Sacrifices—Holcombe, Pillette. Double plays—Upton, Young and Arft; Carrasquel, Fox and Robinson. Left on bases—St. Louis 9, Chicago 7. Bases on balls—Off Pillette 3, Holcombe 2. Struck out—By Pillette 3, Holcombe 3. Winning pitcher—Holcombe (6—4). Losing pitcher—Pillette (3—6). Umpires—McGowan, Honochick, McKinley and Soar. Time of game—2:40.

SECOND GAME

ST. LOUIS (A.)	ab.	r.	h.	po.	a.
Young, 2b	4	0	1	6	3
Coleman, lf	4	0	1	2	1
Batts, c	3	2	1	3	1
Long, 1b	3	1	1	3	1
Wood, rf	4	0	0	4	0
Lehner, cf	4	0	1	1	0
Marsh, 3b	4	0	1	0	4
Upton, ss	4	0	1	1	2
Garver, p	3	0	0	0	2
Total	33	3	7	27	14

CHICAGO (A.)	ab.	r.	h.	po.	a.
Dillinger, 3b	4	0	0	0	3
Fox, 2b	3	0	1	4	1
Minoso, lf	4	0	0	4	0
Robinson, 1b	4	0	0	8	0
Zarilla, rf	2	1	0	1	0
Busby, cf	2	0	0	0	0
C'rasquel, ss	3	0	1	2	1
Niarhos, c	1	0	0	8	1
Kretlow, p	2	0	0	0	1
aBaker	1	0	0	0	0
Aloma, p	0	0	0	0	0
Total	26	1	2	27	7

aGrounded out for Kretlow in eighth.

St. Louis .... 000 201 000—3
Chicago .... 010 000 000—1

Runs batted in—Carrasquel, Wood, Marsh, Batts.

Two-base hits—Long, Lehner. Home run—Batts. Stolen base—Marsh. Sacrifice—Busby. Double play—Dillinger, Fox and Robinson. Left on bases—St. Louis 5, Chicago 3. Bases on balls—Off Kretlow 2, Garver 4. Struck out—By Kretlow 7, Garver 3, Aloma 1. Hits—Off Kretlow 6 in 8 innings, Aloma 1 in 1. Wild pitch—Garver. Winning pitcher—Garver (10—4). Losing pitcher—Kretlow (2—3). Umpires—Honochick, McKinley, Soar and McGowan. Time of game—2:15. Attendance (actual)—27,572.

ACE HELPS TRIBE TAKE TWO, 2-1, 2-0

Errors Enable Tigers to Tally in Feller's No-Hitter That Makes Baseball History

CLEVELAND, July 1 (AP) — Bobby Feller, who had to talk a coach into letting him stay in the game, pitched the third no-hitter of his career — and became the first pitcher in modern times to do so — as the Indians beat the Tigers, 2—1, today. The Indians also won the second game of the double-header, 2—0, on Bob Chakales' four-hitter.

The venerable fireballer, who was tossed aside as "through" only a few months ago and left off the American League All-Star team, said he was never better than when he set down the Tigers this afternoon. The one run he gave up was the result of two errors, one of them Feller's.

In the third inning Coach Mel Harder went out to the mound and asked Feller, "Do you feel okay? You don't look too good."

But Feller insisted that he was good enough to stay in — and then he proved it in historic fashion. Only four men reached base — three on walks, one on an error.

Throws Sliders, Curves

"I didn't even have a very good fast ball," Feller mused after the game. "I threw mostly sliders and curves. It was a wonderful thrill, but I still think my second no-hitter — against the Yankees — was better."

He is the first modern pitcher in history to throw three no-hitters. The legendary Cy Young pitched one in 1897, another in 1904 and the third in 1908.

Feller pitched his first no-hitter against the White Sox on opening day in 1940, his second against the Yankees on April 30, 1946, and then today he did it again before 42,891 nearly hysterical fans.

The Tigers got their run in the fourth inning. It came as the result of Ray Boone's error, a stolen base, a wild pick-off throw and a fly ball.

It's all part of a monumental comeback for the Iowa farm boy who broke into the majors in 1936 at the age of 17. He had a 16-11 record last season and that—for him—was dismal.

His No. 219 in Majors

But he started like a whirlwind this season, winning four straight, losing a game, then winning six straight. The triumph today was his eleventh of the season against two losses, and the 219th of his career—more than any other active major league pitcher. Both of his previous no-hitters were by 1—0 scores.

The crowd rocked huge Cleveland Stadium as Feller slipped a third strike past Vic Wertz with the count 3—2 for the last out of the game.

Feller was forced to go at top form all of the way against Bob Cain, who threw a six-hitter, and the Indians did not win until the eighth when Sam Chapman tripled and Luke Easter slashed a single off Dick Kryhoski's glove to score Milt Nielsen who ran for Chapman.

The Tigers hit only five flies to the outfield and Feller struck out five. He walked only three men and retired the first nine batters in order.

Cain allowed a run in the first inning on singles by Dale Mitchell and Bob Avila and Easter's infield out. The last time Cain pitched against Cleveland Bob Lemon beat him with a one-hitter.

Second No-Hitter of Year

Feller's no-hitter was the second of the year in the majors. Cliff Chambers pitched one for the Pirates against the Boston Braves on May 6. The last no-hitter by an American League pitcher was turned in by Lemon on June 30, 1948, and the victims were the same Tigers.

The Indians completed the humiliation of the Tigers in the second game as they made it ten victories in a row for the season. In the ten games, the Tigers have scored a total of eight runs against Cleveland pitching. They were shut out three times, scored one run in seven games and two runs in one game.

The Indians collected seven hits off Ted Gray and Virgil Trucks and scored their runs in the sixth on a walk to Avila, singles by Chapman and Easter and a double by Bob Kennedy.

In New York, Yankee Manager Casey Stengel, who will pilot the American League All-Stars in the annual dream game with the National League, said he left Feller off the team "because I think Lemon would relieve better."

Casey shook his head and added: "That cooks me. How could I know the guy was gonna pitch a no-hitter?" The box scores:

FIRST GAME

DETROIT (A.)	ab.	r.	h.	po.	a.
Lipon, ss	3	1	0	1	3
aHutchinson	1	0	0	0	0
Berry, ss	0	0	0	0	0
Priddy, 2b	3	0	0	2	1
bKeller	1	0	0	0	0
Kell, 3b	4	0	0	1	1
Wertz, rf	3	0	0	1	0
Evers, lf	3	0	0	5	0
Kryhoski, 1b	3	0	0	8	1
Ginsberg, c	3	0	0	3	1
Groth, cf	2	0	0	2	0
Cain, p	2	0	0	1	1
Total	28	1	0	24	8

CLEVELAND (A.)	ab.	r.	h.	po.	a.
Mitchell, lf	3	1	1	3	0
Avila, 2b	4	0	1	0	3
Chapman, cf	4	0	1	1	0
cNeilsen	0	1	0	0	0
Doby, cf	0	0	0	0	0
Easter, 1b	4	0	1	13	0
Simpson, 1b	0	0	0	0	0
Rosen, 3b	4	0	0	0	4
Kennedy, rf	4	0	0	3	0
Boone, ss	2	0	0	2	5
Hegan, c	3	0	2	5	0
Feller, p	2	0	0	0	0
Total	30	2	6	27	12

aFlied out for Lipon in eighth.
bFlied out for Priddy in ninth.
cRan for Chapman in eighth.

Detroit .... 000 100 000—1
Cleveland .... 100 000 01 . —2

Errors—Boone, Feller. Runs batted in—Easter, Kell.

Three-base hit—Chapman. Stolen base—Lipon. Left on bases—Detroit 3, Cleveland 7. Bases on balls—Off Cain 3, Feller 3. Struck out—By Cain 3, Feller 5. Winning pitcher—Feller (11-2). Losing pitcher—Cain (6-6). Umpires—Berry, Napp, Hurley and Passarella. Time of game—2:05.

SECOND GAME

DETROIT (A.)	ab.	r.	h.	po.	a.
Lipon, ss	4	0	0	1	4
Priddy, 2b	4	0	1	5	5
Kell, 3b	4	0	0	1	2
Wertz, rf	3	0	0	1	1
Evers, lf	4	0	1	0	1
Kryhoski, 1b	3	0	0	10	0
Groth, cf	2	0	0	2	0
Robinson, c	2	0	0	3	0
Gray, p	2	0	1	1	2
aGinsberg	1	0	1	0	0
Trucks, p	0	0	0	0	1
Total	29	0	4	24	16

CLEVELAND (A.)	ab.	r.	h.	po.	a.
Mitchell, lf	4	0	2	1	0
Avila, 2b	2	1	0	1	4
Chapman, cf	4	1	2	1	0
Easter, 1b	3	0	2	8	0
Simpson, 1b	0	0	0	0	0
Rosen, 3b	3	0	0	2	1
Kennedy, rf	2	0	1	3	0
Boone, ss	3	0	0	6	2
Tebbetts, c	2	0	0	5	0
Chakales, p	3	0	0	0	1
Total	26	2	7	27	8

aSingled for Gray in eighth.

Detroit .... 000 000 000—0
Cleveland .... 000 002 00 . —2

Runs batted in—Easter, Kennedy.

Two-base hit—Kennedy. Sacrifices—Kennedy, Avila. Double plays—Gray and Kryhoski; Avila, Boone and Easter 2. Left on bases—Detroit 5, Cleveland 6. Bases on balls—Off Gray 3, Trucks 1, Chakales 3. Struck out—By Gray 1, Trucks 1, Chakales 4. Hits—Off Gray 6 in 7 innings, Trucks 1 in 1. Winning pitcher—Chakales (3—2). Losing pitcher—Gray (3—8). Umpires—Napp, Hurley, Passarella and Berry. Time of game—1:41. Attendance—42,891.

Sports of The Times

By ARTHUR DALEY

Overheard at the Stadium

PHIL RIZZUTO came bouncing up the dugout steps at the Yankee Stadium yesterday, glanced at the line-up card on the wall and whistled in wonderment.

"Gee!" he gasped. "A left-hander is pitching for them and we got seven left-handed hitters in the line-up!"

"Eight," said Frank Shea.

"No, seven," gushed The Scooter. "Me and Joe bat rightie."

"I guess I forgot DiMaggio," said Shea. "I musta thought he was a switch hitter."

"How do you like it, boys?" asked Casey Stengel, looking like the cat that had just swallowed the canary. "But I have only six. You forgot Gerry Coleman. But here's the way I figger it. Is Parnell as hard to hit as that guy the other day? What's his name? McDermott, I mean."

"He should be easier than that first guy," commented Big Jawn Mize.

"Lookit here," cackled the delighted Stengel, "our lefties always have hit Parnell, but he breaks his curve in on the hands of our righties and they can't hit him nohow. Sometimes it happens that way, you know."

Hubbell and Dean

"It sure does," drawled Dizzy Dean in agreement. "Lefties could hit Carl Hubbell better'n righties."

"Yeah," chortled the Ol' Perfesser. "I could always beat him at Brooklyn by using Johnny Fredericks, who would always belt him for a home run. McDermott is rough 'cause he throws curves around a corner. But Parnell? I dunno."

"Our lefties on the Cards usually hit Hub best," said Dean. "Let's see. We had three right-handed hitters—Medwick, Martin and Durocher. I reckon Leo will feel flattered that I mention him in the same breath with Medwick and Martin."

"Hey, Case," said Yogi Berra, "ever see him pitch?" He nodded in the direction of Marius Russo, Yankee world series hero of a decade ago, who was back in uniform for a workout.

"Only on the Coast," said Stengel regretfully. "His arm was so shot then that he could only float the ball up. But he still win three games."

Prophetic Dream

"Funny thing about Russo," said Rizzuto musingly. "I haven't seen him in years. But last night I had the most vivid dream about him. It was as sharp and as clear as if we were on the field today. He was pitching for us and I was playing shortstop behind him. And now I see him in the flesh. I can hardly believe it."

"There was a pitcher who could field his position," said Ed Lopat, admiringly. "You've seen Lemon and Shantz, who are awfully good. But this guy was better than both combined. He was a fine base runner, too."

Phil Rizzuto

"Better'n Dean?" asked Stengel, giving Diz the needle. "I'll bet he never got hit on the head by no thrown ball the way Diz did."

"Know what?" chuckled the grinning Diz. "When I was conked on the noggin in the '34 world serious, they done took an X-ray of my haid. The next day the papers come out with the news, 'X-rays show nuthin.'"

The Yankee regulars moved out to the batting cage and took over from the junior varsity hitters. Coleman was taking his cuts.

"Step in the bucket more, Gerry," advised Yogi, a friendly soul.

"Leave him alone, Yog," said Rizzuto. "He had a pretty good year last season hitting the way he is. If he wants to change, he can do it himself. I did the last time against Parnell. I opened up my stance."

The Watchful Pitchers

"That's what I mean," insisted the Yogi man. "But the pitchers watch the way you place your feet," said Ed Lopat.

"They don't learn nuthin' from me," said the grinning Berra. "I move my dogs around all the time and mess 'em up real good."

"Mind if I take a cut, fellers," softly asked Joe DiMaggio as he joined the party, "or do I have to bat left-handed today?" he smiled.

"Only left-handers allowed," growled Yogi. "Gerroota here."

The Jolter ignored him and took his cuts.

Over on the other side of the field the Red Sox dugout was abuzz with the news that Stengel was starting six left-handed hitters against Parnell.

"If Casey gets away with it," said the obviously surprised Steve O'Neill, "he's seen something none of the rest of us have seen. Gosh, he's benching two right-handed power hitters like Bauer and Jensen, guys who actually scare you when they come up to the plate. I'm curious about that move. I wonder if he'll get away with it."

He got away with it.

ATHLETICS TOPPLE SENATORS, 10-7, 3-2

Valo's 3 Homers, Two in First Game, Help Philadelphians Rise to Sixth Place

PHILADELPHIA, July 1 (AP)—Philadelphia's Athletics stretched their home-winning streak to eight games and rose to sixth place by a double victory over the Washington Senators today, gaining a 3-2 triumph after winning the opener, 10—7, with a six-run rally in the seventh inning.

Elmer Valo had three home runs, two in the first game. Irv Noren hit for the circuit, and Gus Zernial walloped his eighteenth round-tripper in the opener.

The box scores:

FIRST GAME

WASHINGTON (A.)	ab.	r.	h.	po.	a.
Yost, lf	3	0	1	1	0
Coan, lf	1	0	1	0	0
Michaels, 2b	5	1	1	1	1
Noren, cf	5	2	3	5	0
Mele, rf	3	0	2	1	0
Vernon, 1b	5	0	1	9	0
Runnels, ss	4	2	1	4	2
Kluttz, c	5	1	3	3	0
Dente, 3b	4	1	2	0	2
Johnson, p	1	0	0	0	2
Ferrick, p	0	0	0	0	1
aRobertson	1	0	0	0	0
Consuegra, p	0	0	0	0	0
Total	39	7	15	24	8

PHILADELPHIA (A.)	ab.	r.	h.	po.	a.
Joost, ss	2	3	0	2	1
Valo, cf	3	3	3	3	0
Moses, rf	4	1	1	5	0
Zernial, lf	4	1	2	3	0
Fain, 1b	4	0	1	8	1
Majeski, 3b	4	0	0	1	4
Klein, 2b	4	1	1	2	2
Suder, 2b	0	0	0	1	1
Murray, c	4	0	0	2	1
Fowler, p	2	0	0	0	1
Kucab, p	1	1	0	0	0
Total	32	10	8	27	11

aStruck out for Ferrick in eighth.

Washington .... 010 211 101—7
Philadelphia .... 002 020 60 . —10

Errors—Moses, Runnels 2.

Runs batted in—Dente 2, Vernon, Yost, Noren, Mele, Valo 5, Moses, Zernial 2.

Two-base hits—Noren 2, Yost, Coan. Home runs—Valo 2, Noren, Zernial. Sacrifices—Johnson 2. Double plays—Majeski, Klein and Fain; Michaels, Runnels and Vernon. Left on bases—Washington 10, Philadelphia 3. Bases on balls—Off Fowler 3, Johnson 4, Ferrick 1. Struck out—By Johnson 2, Fowler 1, Kucab 1. Hits—Off Johnson 6 in 6 1-3 innings, Ferrick 2 in 2-3, Consuegra 0 in 1, Fowler 9 in 6, Kucab 6 in 3. Winning pitcher—Kucab (2—3). Losing pitcher — Johnson (3—4). Umpires — Grieve, Duffy and Summers. Time of game—2:25.

SECOND GAME

WASHINGTON (A.)	ab.	r.	h.	po.	a.
Yost, 3b	3	1	0	3	1
Coan, lf	4	0	1	3	0
Noren, cf	4	0	3	2	0
Mele, rf	4	0	0	2	1
Vernon, 1b	4	0	0	4	2
Runnels, ss	4	0	1	0	0
Michaels, 2b	4	0	1	1	3
Guerra, c	4	0	0	7	0
Moreno, p	2	0	0	2	1
aKluttz	0	0	0	0	0
bRobertson	0	1	0	0	0
Consuegra, p	0	0	0	0	0
Total	33	2	6	24	8

PHILADELPHIA (A.)	ab.	r.	h.	po.	a.
Joost, ss	1	1	0	2	2
Valo, cf	4	1	1	5	0
Moses, rf	4	1	1	1	0
Zernial, lf	4	0	1	3	0
Fain, 1b	4	0	2	9	1
Majeski, 3b	3	0	0	2	3
Suder, 2b	3	0	0	0	1
Astroth, c	3	0	0	4	0
Hooper, p	3	0	1	1	2
Scheib, p	0	0	0	0	0
Total	29	3	6	27	9

aWalked for Moreno in seventh.
bRan for Kluttz in seventh.

Washington .... 000 000 020—2
Philadelphia .... 201 000 00 . —3

Runs batted in—Valo 2, Fain, Noren, Mele.

Two-base hits—Hooper, Coan, Runnels, Fain, Michaels, Noren. Three-base hit—Fain. Home run—Valo. Stolen base—Joost. Left on bases—Washington 6, Philadelphia 5. Bases on balls—Off Moreno 3, Hooper 2. Struck out—By Hooper 4, Moreno 6. Hits—Off Moreno 6 in 7 innings, Consuegra 0 in 1, Hooper 6 in 7 1-3, Scheib 0 in 1 2-3. Winning pitcher—Hooper (3—6). Losing pitcher—Moreno (2—5). Umpires—Duffy, Summers and Grieve. Time of game—2:05. Attendance—6,364.

Columbia Nine Wins, 6-1, 18-1

SAO PAULO, Brazil, July 1 (AP)—Columbia University's touring baseball team won a double-header from the Sao Paulo All-Stars today, 6—1 and 18—1.

EXHIBITION SOCCER

Necaxa (Mexico) 5, Stuttgart 1.

Joe DiMaggio Named 13th Time On Squad for All-Star Fixture

CHICAGO, July 1 (AP) — The American League today announced its complete player roster for the all-star game in Detroit, July 10.

With the exception of the eight starting players chosen by the vote of fans, the squad was selected by Casey Stengel, manager of the Yankees. Stengel will pilot the American League entry.

The National League's complete roster for the game will be announced in New York on Tuesday.

Stengel selected one pitcher from each of the eight clubs in the league, as previously agreed on by the club owners. The starting pitcher, as well as the batting order, will not be announced until the day before the game.

Only repeater from last year's American League pitching staff will be Cleveland's Bob Lemon. The others picked by Stengel were: Ned Garver of St. Louis, Randy Gumpert of Chicago, Fred Hutchinson of Detroit, Ed Lopat of New York, Conrad Marrero of Washington, Mel Parnell of Boston and Bob Shantz of Philadelphia.

More players from Chicago's White Sox will be on the team than from any other club. Chicago is represented by six players, Boston's Red Sox by five and Stengel's own New York Yankees by four.

Among the Yankee entries will be Joe DiMaggio, picked by Stengel although not selected in the fans' poll. This is the thirteenth time DiMaggio has been named. Joe has played in eleven all-star games, a knee injury keeping him out of action in 1946.

Another old hand at the all-star game will be Boston's slugging Ted Williams. He has played in eight games, holding a batting average of .417. Boston's second baseman Bobby Doerr, also named to the squad, has played in seven of the inter-league matches.

Infielders on the squad will be Al Carrasquel (Chicago), Bobby Doerr (Boston), Ferris Fain (Philadelphia), Nelson Fox (Chicago), George Kell (Detroit), Phil Rizzuto (New York), Ed Robinson (Chicago), and Vern Stephens (Boston).

Outfielders named were James Busby (Chicago), Larry Doby (Cleveland), Vic Wertz (Detroit), Orestes Minoso (Chicago), Joe DiMaggio and Williams.

Yogi Berra, New York, and James Hegan, Cleveland, will be the catchers.

Under the game's rules, no pitcher can remain in the box for longer than three innings. However, if the game goes more than nine innings, the pitcher who is in the game at the close of the ninth inning may continue to pitch at the discretion of the manager. If a pitcher enters the game after commencement of an inning, that part inning will not be included in his three innings of pitching.

The eight players—all but the pitcher—picked by the newspaper, magazine and radio station vote of fans must start the game and play a minimum of three innings, barring injury or illness. These eight players are:

Fain, first base; Fox, second base; Kell, third base; Carrasquel, shortstop; Wertz, right field; Dom DiMaggio, center field; Williams, left field; and Berra, catcher.

This will be the eighteenth all-star game. The American League has won twelve and the national league five. The American League will be the home team and each player will wear his home uniform bearing his club number.

Major League Baseball

Monday, July 2, 1951

American League

YESTERDAY'S GAMES

New York 5, Boston 2.
Chicago 2, St. Louis 1 (1st, 11 innings).
St. Louis 3, Chicago 1 (2d).
Cleveland 2, Detroit 1 (1st).
Cleveland 2, Detroit 0 (2d).
Philadelphia 10, Washington 7 (1st).
Philadelphia 3, Washington 2 (2d).

STANDING OF THE CLUBS

	New York	Chicago	Boston	Cleveland	Detroit	Philadel.	Wash'gtn	St. Louis	Won	Lost	Perc'tage	Games Behind
N. Y.	—	7	4	8	5	7	5	7	43	24	.642	—
Chic.	4	—	7	6	4	5	10	8	44	25	.638	—
Bost.	6	4	—	5	5	7	6	7	40	28	.588	3½
Cleve.	3	2	7	—	10	6	4	6	38	30	.559	5½
Det.	3	3	5	6	—	7	8	5	31	34	.477	11
Phila.	3	5	1	3	3	—	5	8	28	41	.406	16
Wash.	3	1	2	5	3	5	—	6	25	41	.379	17½
St. L.	2	3	2	3	4	4	3	—	21	47	.309	22½
Lost	24	25	28	30	34	41	41	47	—	—		

TODAY'S PROBABLE PITCHERS

New York at Philadelphia (night)—Reynolds (8-4) vs. Shantz (7-4).
Boston at Washington (night) Kiely (0-0) vs. Marrero (7-4).
Cleveland at Chicago (night)—Garcia (7-6) vs. Rogovin (4-3).
Other clubs not scheduled.

National League

YESTERDAY'S GAMES

New York 4, Boston 1.
Brooklyn 2, Philadelphia 0.
Chicago 7, Cincinnati 0 (1st).
Chicago 7, Cincinnati 5 (2d, 11 innings).
St. Louis 5, Pittsburgh 4 (12 innings).

STANDING OF THE CLUBS

	Brooklyn	New York	St. Louis	Philadel.	Cincinnati	Chicago	Boston	Pittsb'gh	Won	Lost	Perc'tage	Games Behind
Bklyn	—	8	8	7	7	7	3	5	43	25	.632	—
N. Y.	3	—	6	5	7	7	4	7	39	32	.549	5½
St. L.	2	6	—	7	5	4	5	6	35	32	.522	7½
Phila.	4	4	4	—	2	7	4	8	33	35	.485	10
Cinc.	3	3	5	6	—	2	9	4	32	35	.478	10½
Chic.	4	2	4	3	5	—	7	5	30	33	.476	10½
Bost.	3	7	4	4	4	3	—	6	31	35	.470	11
Pitts.	6	4	1	3	5	3	3	—	25	41	.379	17
Lost	25	32	32	35	35	33	35	41	—	—		

TODAY'S PROBABLE PITCHERS

Philadelphia at New York (8:30 P. M.)—Heintzelman (3-7) vs. Hearn (6-5).
Brooklyn at Boston (night)—Roe (10-1) vs. Sain (4-8).
Chicago at Pittsburgh (night)—Hiller (5-5) vs. Dickson (9-7).
St. Louis at Cincinnati (night)—Lanier (4-5) vs. Perkowski (2-2).

(Figures in parentheses indicate season's won-and-lost records.)

Batting Averages

YANKEES

	AB.	H.	PC.		AB.	H.	PC.
Collins	81	26	.321	Lopat	43	10	.233
Berra	246	74	.301	Silvera	13	3	.231
Mize	137	41	.299	Mapes	35	8	.229
McDougald	114	34	.298	Shea	23	5	.217
Rizzuto	255	74	.290	Hopp	43	9	.209
Bauer	134	38	.284	Martin	25	5	.200
Woodling	134	38	.284	Houk	5	1	.200
DiMaggio	153	43	.281	Morgan	12	2	.167
Jensen	123	34	.276	Kuzava	19	3	.158
Coleman	204	54	.265	Raschi	42	6	.143
Mantle	233	61	.262	Reynolds	34	3	.088
Kramer	4	1	.250	Overmire	15	1	.067
Brown	112	27	.241	Ostrowski	11	0	.000

Team batting—2,274, 612, .269

GIANTS

	AB.	H.	PC.		AB.	H.	PC.
Dark	281	94	.335	Hartung	34	8	.235
Mueller	137	42	.307	Lohrke	36	8	.222
Mays	136	39	.287	Thomson	236	52	.220
Lockman	300	84	.280	Kennedy	10	2	.200
Irvin	231	64	.277	Maglie	50	8	.160
Stanky	262	69	.263	Rigney	29	4	.138
Westrum	168	44	.262	Gettel	10	1	.100
Hearn	31	8	.258	Jansen	46	4	.087
Yvars	4	1	.250	Koslo	14	1	.071
Noble	90	22	.244	Spencer	18	1	.056
Thompson	219	53	.242	Hardy	0	0	.000
Jorgensen	51	12	.235	Jones	10	0	.000

Team batting—2,351, 631, .268.

DODGERS

	AB.	H.	PC.		AB.	H.	PC.
Robinson	245	86	.351	Walker	111	26	.234
Schmitz	9	3	.333	Newcombe	46	10	.217
Campanella	229	74	.323	Edwards	23	5	.217
Abrams	124	38	.306	Terwilliger	195	41	.210
Erskine	23	7	.304	Thompson	44	9	.205
Reese	255	76	.298	Podbielan	5	1	.200
Furillo	283	83	.294	Roe	45	5	.111
Snider	270	77	.285	Branca	22	1	.045
Hodges	258	70	.271	King	20	1	.050
Bridges	104	27	.260	Branca	22	1	.040
Williams	27	7	.259	Bankhead	0	0	.000
Pafko	213	54	.254	Haugstad	0	0	.000
Cox	147	37	.252				

Team batting—2,397, 665, .277.

Major League Leaders

BATTERS

(Based on 150 times at bat)

AMERICAN LEAGUE

	G.	AB.	R.	H.	PC.
Minoso, Chicago	67	231	62	82	.355
Fain, Philadelphia	69	250	31	88	.352
Fox, Chicago	71	274	53	92	.336
Williams, Boston	68	240	62	80	.333
DiMaggio, Boston	64	284	52	94	.331

NATIONAL LEAGUE

	G.	AB.	R.	H.	PC.
Musial, St. Louis	66	246	54	90	.366
Ashburn, Phila.	68	279	43	98	.351
Robinson, Brooklyn	68	245	51	86	.351
Elliott, Boston	63	232	38	80	.345
Dark, N. Y.	71	281	53	94	.335

RUNS BATTED IN

AMERICAN LEAGUE

Williams, Boston ..70 | Stephens, Boston ..56
Robinson, Chicago. 66

NATIONAL LEAGUE

Westlake, St. Louis 55 | Musial, St. Louis...51
Snider, Brooklyn . 54

HOME-RUN HITTERS

AMERICAN LEAGUE

Zernial, Phila. ....18 | Wertz, Detroit 14
Robinson, Chicago 16 | Williams, Boston ..14

NATIONAL LEAGUE

Hodges, Brooklyn . 24 | Kiner, Pittsburgh ..17
Snider, Brooklyn ..17 | Westlake, St. Louis.17

Feller's Pitching Masterpieces

NO-HIT GAMES

Date.	Opponent.	Score.	Strikeouts.	Walks.	*Spoiler.
April 16, 1940	Chicago	1—0	8	5	——
April 30, 1946	New York	1—0	11	5	——
July 1, 1951	Detroit	2—1	5	3	——

ONE-HIT GAMES

Date.	Opponent.	Score.	Strikeouts.	Walks.	*Spoiler.
April 20, 1938	St. Louis	9—0	6	6	Sullivan
May 25, 1939	Boston	11—0	10	5	Doerr
June 27, 1939	Detroit	5—0	13	6	Averill
July 12, 1940	Philadelphia	1—0	13	2	Siebert
Sept. 26, 1941	St. Louis	3—2	6	7	Ferrell
Sept. 19, 1945	Detroit	2—0	7	4	Outlaw
July 31, 1946	Boston	4—1	9	9	Doerr
Aug. 8, 1946	Chicago	5—0	5	3	Hayes
April 22, 1947	St. Louis	5—0	10	1	Zarilla
May 2, 1947	Boston	2—0	10	4	Pesky

*All hits were singles.

100TH ANNIVERSARY
"All the News That's Fit to Print"
1851 1951

The New York Times.

LATE CITY EDITION
Cloudy today and tonight. Showers early tomorrow, clearing later.
Temperature Range Today—Max., 83; Min., 67
Temperatures Yesterday—Max., 83; Min., 68
Full U. S. Weather Bureau Report, Page 63

VOL. C..No. 34,200. Entered as Second-Class Matter, Post Office, New York, N. Y. NEW YORK, THURSDAY, SEPTEMBER 13, 1951. Times Square, New York 18, N. Y. Telephone LAckawanna 4-1000 RAG PAPER EDITION SEVENTY-FIVE CENTS

GENERAL MARSHALL RETIRES; TRUMAN PRAISES HIS WORK; LOVETT NAMED SUCCESSOR

LONG SERVICE ENDS

Defense Head Also Was Secretary of State and Army Chief of Staff

CONGRESS PAYS TRIBUTE

A Few Republicans Cite Dislike of His China Role—Bissell Acting Head of E. C. A.

Text of Marshall letter and Truman reply, Page 6.

By W. H. LAWRENCE
Special to THE NEW YORK TIMES.

WASHINGTON, Sept. 12—General of the Army George Catlett Marshall, 70-year-old soldier-statesman who played a monumental role in waging both hot and cold wars, retired today as Secretary of Defense and his deputy, Robert A. Lovett, was nominated to succeed him.

President Truman acceded to General Marshall's "personal reasons" for leaving the Defense Department "with very great reluctance," noting that "no man ever has given his country more distinguished and patriotic service."

The career of General Marshall, commissioned a second lieutenant in the Army forty-nine years ago last February, was unique in that he was the only man ever to serve successively as Army Chief of Staff for six years, Secretary of State for two years and Secretary of Defense for one year.

Helped Buttress Free World

As Chief of Staff he organized the largest and most powerful American Army in history and guided its efforts to victory in World War II. In the post-war era his plan for American economic aid to buttress the free world against Communist encroachment was better known as the Marshall Plan than by its formal title, the European Recovery Program.

Mr. Lovett, the new defense chief, is a 56-year-old New York investment banker who served as General Marshall's Under Secretary of State for eighteen months from July, 1947, to January, 1949, and as his Defense Department Deputy for the last year. A Yale graduate and naval aviator in World War I, Mr. Lovett has been a partner in the banking firm of Brown Brothers, Harriman & Co., in New York City.

Mr. Truman, at the same time, nominated William C. Foster, 54, of Scarsdale, N. Y., now administrator of the Economic Cooperation Administration, which administers the Marshall Plan, to succeed Mr. Lovett as Deputy Defense Secretary. Mr. Foster in private life headed the Pressed and Welded Steel Products Co., Inc., and served as Under Secretary of Commerce from 1946 to 1948.

Richard M. Bissell Jr. was named Acting E. C. A. Administrator to succeed Mr. Foster. He now is Deputy Administrator.

Expressions of Regret

Congress generally heard the news of General Marshall's retirement with expressions of tribute and regret, but a few Republicans, led by Senator Kenneth S. Wherry of Nebraska, Senate minority leader, recalled their dissatisfaction with his efforts to mediate the dispute between the Chinese Nationalist and Communist governments to produce a coalition.

There was no comment from Senator Joseph R. McCarthy, Republican of Wisconsin, who on June 14 delivered a 60,000-word Senate speech charging that General Marshall was associated in a conspiracy to weaken the United States for its eventual conquest by the Soviet Union.

Most Senators, both Republicans and Democrats, indicated immediate approval of the nomination of Messrs. Lovett and Foster as a younger, more vigorous defense team. Little, if any, opposition to their confirmation was expected.

By coincidence, General Marshall's retirement was announced one year to the day from the ouster of Louis A. Johnson as Secretary of Defense. Mr. Truman had persuaded the general, whom he frequently referred to as "the greatest living American," to take the

Continued on Page 6, Column 2

Senate Votes 500,000 Limit On Civilian Military Workers

Curb Would Reduce Jobs 40,000 Below Defense Department Request—5% Cut in Pentagon Personnel Also Adopted

By C. P. TRUSSELL
Special to THE NEW YORK TIMES.

WASHINGTON, Sept. 12—The Senate voted today to reduce by 30,000 the number of civilian employes that its Appropriations Committee approved for the armed services during the present fiscal year.

The Department of Defense had asked for 540,000. The House of Representatives approved 514,000. The Senate committee recommended 530,000, and the Senate settled for an even 500,000 after Senator Everett M. Dirksen, Republican of Illinois, had proposed a cut to 491,000.

Under another amendment adopted, the 500,000 limit would include part-time employes and consultants as well as permanent workers. Senator Harry F. Byrd, Democrat of Virginia, sponsor of the amendment, argued that without this provision the payrolls might be built up to any proportions.

The potential saving under the 500,000 compromise was estimated at $112,000,000, unless this money were transferred to other than payroll uses. Senator Joseph C. O'Mahoney, Democrat of Wyoming, who is in charge of the pending $61,104,856,000 Defense Department appropriation bill, accepted the compromise. But it was against his "better judgment," he said.

In a more direct attack on openly suspected overstaffing of the civilian phase of the defense program, Senator Paul H. Douglas, Democrat of Illinois, won acceptance of a 5 per cent reduction in the civilian payrolls at the Penta-

Continued on Page 24, Column 3

Bowles Ambassador to India; Henderson Gets Post in Iran

Special to THE NEW YORK TIMES.

WASHINGTON, Sept. 12—Chester Bowles, former Governor of Connecticut and wartime Price Administrator, was nominated today to be Ambassador to India and Nepal, replacing Loy W. Henderson, who was named Ambassador to Iran.

President Truman asked the Senate to confirm both men as he accepted formally the resignation of Dr. Henry F. Grady as Ambassador to Iran.

Mr. Bowles, a left-of-center Democrat, inherits the difficult task of attempting to bring greater accord between the West and India, which refused to participate in the Japanese peace treaty conference and has been critical of the United Nations strategy in Korea. This is Mr. Bowles' first diplomatic assignment.

Mr. Henderson, a career diplomat and former director of the State Department's Office of Near Eastern and African Affairs, will step directly into the bitter dispute between Iran and Britain over nationalization of the Iranian oil.

None of the diplomatic changes came as a surprise. Dr. Grady's desire to retire had been known for some time, and there had been rumors for months that Mr. Bowles would get the Indian post if and when Mr. Henderson was shifted to Iran.

Dr. Grady had submitted a brief resignation effective at the President's pleasure in which he declared that "it has been a great honor for me to serve under you, our Commander in Chief, in the cold war in this critical zone."

The White House made public a letter from the President, accepting the resignation "with the greatest reluctance," and in which

Continued on Page 9, Column 1

UNITY IS ADVANCED AT 3-POWER TALKS

U. S., Britain and France View Ways to Contain Soviet—Outlook Held Favorable

By WALTER H. WAGGONER
Special to THE NEW YORK TIMES.

WASHINGTON, Sept. 12—The Foreign Ministers of the United States, Britain and France concluded today the first two sessions of a scheduled two-day conference on ways for the free world to check the spread of Soviet communism.

The Western Big Three will take the results of these talks, expected to end tomorrow, to a meeting of the North Atlantic Council, opening in Ottawa, Saturday.

Spokesmen for the three Governments insisted that no conclusions had been reached, but at least one official said that the views of the three Foreign Ministers "seemed to be in line."

Participants in the talks also said that the factors for optimism on attaining the Western goal probably outweighed those for pessimism, and that the continued unity of the three allies was one of the favorable factors.

The attention of the trio, supported by eight or ten advisers

Continued on Page 19, Column 2

Soviet Bids U.S. Pay Half U.N. Cost On Ground Economy Can Bear It

Special to THE NEW YORK TIMES.

UNITED NATIONS, N. Y., Sept. 12—The Soviet Union has demanded that the United States pay half of the yearly operating costs of the United Nations—arguing that the American economy appears capable of bearing the increased burden.

The proposal for increasing the United States' present 38.92 per cent share in the annual budget came from A. A. Soldatov, Soviet representative, who along with other Russian diplomats has repeatedly blasted the United States capitalist system as "unworkable."

Mr. Soldatov made his proposal to a ten-member committee that calculates the yearly dues of the sixty member states in the world organization.

The committee did not accept Mr. Soldatov's views and favored instead a cut of 2.02 per cent in the United States share of the $46,568,300 budget for 1952 and an increase of almost 4 per cent in the combined contributions of the Soviet Union and its satellites.

The committee's recommendations, however, must be approved by the General Assembly, which opens its next session in Paris on Nov. 6, at which time Soviet bloc members are virtually certain to assail the committee's decisions and to attempt once more to increase the United States share of the United Nations' running expenses.

The United States, Mr. Soldatov reasoned, was better equipped to pay these expenses than countries still recovering from war devastation. He maintained also that the committee's examination of comparative incomes indicated the United States should contribute 50 per cent of the operating costs.

Unlike other members, Mr. Soldatov insisted, the United States has no dollar shortage to hamper its payment of dues and the coun-

Continued on Page 14, Column 5

Robinson Knocks Out Turpin In Tenth Round of Title Bout

American Boxer Regains Middleweight Crown When Referee Halts Action Before 61,370 at Polo Grounds

By JAMES P. DAWSON

Ray Robinson brought the world middleweight championship back to America last night.

With a savage attack in the tenth round, he knocked out Randy Turpin, gallant British fighter to whom he had lost the title in London two months ago.

Amid the roars of a crowd of 61,370 fans who had paid record receipts of $767,630 to see the spectacle at the olo Grounds, Robinson battered Turpin into such a helpless state that the referee, Ruby Goldstein, stopped the battle after the tenth round had gone 2 minutes and 52 seconds.

At that time, Turpin was an open target, unable to defend himself from the blazing drives of a merciless foe who was smarting under the terrific blows the Englishman had landed in two previous rounds.

The British defender had been floored early in the round by a right to the jaw for a count of nine. When he arose, Robinson, going all out for victory, battered his rival to the ropes, ignoring blood which streamed from an old cut above his own left eye, intent only upon the complete destruction of the man who had dethroned him last July 10.

Loosing a barrage of rights and lefts, Robinson raked his foe about the head, face and body.

Randy tried to cover against the blows. He crouched behind upraised arms and gloved fists in an attempt to ward off the stunning punches to the head and jaw. Robinson then shifted his attack to the body and with wicked smashes of the right to the ribs, brought down his rival's guard. Then he pounded his head again.

It seemed that Robinson would fight himself out in this frenzied outburst. But he got home clean with a right to the jaw, and then another. Randy sagged. It seemed

Continued on Page 40, Column 1

PEIPING INDICATES REDS WILL REJECT STRAFING APOLOGY

Broadcast Calls Explanation of Kaesong Incident 'Absurd'—Leaders Remain Silent

By LINDESAY PARROTT
Special to THE NEW YORK TIMES.

TOKYO, Thursday, Sept. 13—The Peiping radio indicated this morning that the Communist command would reject the explanation yesterday by Vice Admiral Charles Turner Joy that an allied plane, by accident, strafed the neutral zone around Kaesong. Conferences looking to an armistice in the Korean war were held at Kaesong before their suspension by the Chinese and North Korean delegation last month.

Peiping's Government-controlled radio broadcast dispatches from Communist correspondents asserting that Admiral Joy's statement that the attack was a mistake due to faulty navigation was "absurd." While such reports from Kaesong were not official utterances, enemy correspondents frequently have been able to forecast accurately the line their command would take.

The Peiping radio also put on

Continued on Page 3, Column 2

U. S., BRITAIN REACH IMPASSE ON LIFTING TRADE RESTRAINTS

London Informs World Fund Meeting Curbs May Have to Remain for Two Years

By FELIX BELAIR Jr.
Special to THE NEW YORK TIMES.

WASHINGTON, Sept. 12—The whole future of the $8,000,000,000 International Monetary Fund was placed in doubt today when the United States and Britain parted company over the policy controlling access to the agency's resources in the period immediately ahead.

The issue arose over the United States position, written into official policy of the fund, that the time had come to remove or substantially modify exchange restrictions and other discriminations in trade and payments practices as provided by the articles of agreement adopted at Bretton Woods, N. H., in 1944.

At a meeting behind closed doors, spokesmen for the United States insisted there could be no retreat from these objectives, that any "alternative program" was out of the question and that, unless they were pursued now, the Inter-

Continued on Page 20, Column 3

World News Summarized

THURSDAY, SEPTEMBER 13, 1951

The head of a former $20,000,000-a-year bookmaking enterprise, 35-year-old Harry Gross, who disappeared from his home here Tuesday night, was arrested yesterday at the racetrack in Atlantic City. The former bookmaker, the key witness in the graft conspiracy trial of eighteen present or former members of the Police Department, said he had gone to the racetrack for a good time, not to "hide." He was being brought back to New York. [1:8.]

The Senate amended the pending $61,000,000,000 appropriation bill for the armed forces to limit to 500,000 the number of civilian employes of the Defense Department. [1:2-3.]

The Army announced that early next year two more National Guard infantry divisions, the Thirty-seventh from Ohio and the Fourty-fourth from Illinois, would be called into Federal service. [23:1.]

General Marshall retired as Secretary of Defense for "personal reasons" and President Truman, accepting his retirement "with very great reluctance," said no one had "given his country more distinguished and patriotic service." Mr. Truman nominated Robert A. Lovett, the Deputy Secretary, to succeed General Marshall. [1:1.]

The Chief Executive also nominated Chester Bowles to be Ambassador to India, succeeding Loy W. Henderson, who was nominated to the post of Ambassador to Iran. [1:2-3.]

The explanation of the United Nations Command that one of its planes mistakenly had strafed the neutral zone at Kaesong was termed "absurd" by the Peiping radio, which indicated the explanation and the accompanying apology might be rejected. [1:4.]

On the battlefront United Nations forces seized two more hills above Kumhwa in the central sector. [3:1.]

Early Senate ratification of the Japanese peace treaty was urged by Republican Senator Knowland, who has appealed to the State Department to reverse its decision not to press for ratification at the current session of Congress. [4:3.]

The Washington meetings of the foreign ministers of the Western Big Three, due to end today in time to permit the three leaders to journey to Ottawa for the conference of the North Atlantic Council, appeared to have achieved considerable harmony in views. [1:2.]

Britain told the International Monetary Fund that her rearmament efforts would not allow relaxation of restrictions on trade and payments as advocated by the United States, and indicated that such restrictions might have to be intensified. [1:5.]

A Papal encyclical appealed to all Christians to "unite and fight under a single banner" against communism. [10:1.]

The United States, which now pays 38.92 per cent of the annual costs, should pay half of the United Nations budget, the Soviet Union maintained. [1:2-3.]

Index to other news appears on last page of this section.

GROSS SEIZED AT RACE TRACK; KEY POLICE GRAFT WITNESS DENIES HIDING, JOKES AT HUNT

LOST AND FOUND: ONE BOOKMAKER

Harry Gross being questioned by Capt. Robert J. Ryder of the Atlantic City race track police after his arrest yesterday.
Associated Press Wirephoto

HE JUST 'DROVE OFF'

Bookie Planned to 'Take a Walk for Few Days,' He Tells Captors

F. B. I. ASSUMES CUSTODY

Tie Clasp Clinches Suspicion of Atlantic City Track Police—McDonald Criticizes Guards

By WILLIAM R. CONKLIN

Harry Gross, fugitive Brooklyn ex-bookmaker whose disappearance on Tuesday night had threatened the collapse of the state's graft-conspiracy case against eighteen present or former policemen, was recaptured at 5:45 P. M. yesterday at the Atlantic City Race Track.

The most important witness in the most important criminal case pending in the East, the 35-year-old Gross is believed to hold the key to the successful prosecution of the eighteen defendants. Their trial on an indictment charging conspiracy to obstruct justice by protecting the $20,000,000-a-year Gross bookmaking empire in return for an estimated $1,000,000 in yearly graft began on Monday in Kings County Court.

Early today Gross was taken from Hammonton, N. J., to Atlantic City before United States Commissioner Herman J. Finn where he signed a waiver of extradition. He was due back in New York early today. Soon after his capture at Atlantic City, the Federal Bureau of Investigation took him into custody on a charge of "interstate flight to avoid giving testimony."

McDonald Talks to Gross

After his capture the former bookmaker was transferred to the New Jersey state police barracks at Hammonton. Kings County District Attorney Miles F. McDonald traveled by car last night from Brooklyn to the barracks and talked with the prisoner alone in the kitchen there. Gross was observed to wipe his forehead repeatedly with a tissue while the District Attorney paced the floor.

Later, after an hour-long conference with state police and F. B. I. agents, Mr. McDonald announced that Gross would be returned to New York in a motorcade. The plans were changed, however, after a telephone conference with United States Attorney General J. Howard McGrath in Washington.

The motorcade left Hammonton at 1 A. M. today for Atlantic City. Traveling with the prisoner in the same car were Leo Clarke and Harry Welsh, F. B. I. agents from New Jersey, and Elliot Gross, an assistant to Mr. McDonald. The District Attorney rode in another automobile.

The prisoner was scheduled to be returned by automobile to New York after appearing before the Commissioner in New Jersey. Gross will be arraigned this morning before United States Commissioner Martin Epstein in Brooklyn, who yesterday afternoon signed a Federal warrant to bring him back to this state.

McDonald in Vigil

After Gross had escaped police custody on Tuesday at 6:15 P. M. from his home at 13 Putnam Boulevard, Atlantic Beach, L. I., District Attorney McDonald of Brooklyn and his chief aides passed a sleepless night.

Police Commissioner George P. Monaghan said the Police Telegraph Bureau had received word of the disappearance at 12:24 A. M. Wednesday. An alarm was broadcast over the thirteen-state police teletype at 12:32 A. M. Early yesterday the search was extended on a nation-wide basis, and Gross was reported in Chicago and in an airplane over Arizona.

When he was apprehended, the happy-go-lucky Gross was said to be completely unaware of the furor his departure had caused. Capt. Robert Ryder, head of the private track police at the Atlantic City race track, saw a man he was sure was Gross in the lower clubhouse just before the start of the day's

Continued on Page 26, Column 1

3d Lincoln Tube Opposed By City's Planning Board

By CHARLES G. BENNETT

The Port of New York Authority's plan for the construction of the proposed $80,000,000 third tube for the Lincoln Tunnel, including an expansion and enlargement of existing mid-Manhattan street connections, was rejected yesterday as "fundamentally deficient" by the City Planning Commission.

Lining up with City Construction Coordinator Robert Moses against a project ardently advocated by Howard S. Cullman, chairman of the Port Authority, the commission held that to add 8,500,000 vehicles a year to the Thirty-eighth Street and Tenth Avenue area of "supersaturated" Manhattan would be "neither logical nor warranted."

Conceding the need for a third tube for the Lincoln Tunnel, the commission concentrated its fire on what it termed the inadequacy of the Port Authority's companion $20,000,000 proposal for extending and enlarging the existing connections between the tunnel and the street system.

The commission flatly rejected the "elaborate statistics" furnished by the authority "purporting to prove that the traffic that will flow through the existing and proposed tubes of the Lincoln Tunnel can safely be discharged into the local street system."

The only satisfactory handling that the authority could propose for the "enlarged streams" of traffic seeking to enter the tunnel or to leave it from or to the east, north and south, the commission stipulated, would be "by direct off-street connections with adequate express highways, either existing or to be constructed, including a cross-Manhattan Expressway and the Miller [West Side] Highway."

Despite this allusion to a cross-Manhattan Expressway, Commis-

Continued on Page 29, Column 7

PRINTING SALESMAN CONTRADICTS OLSON

Says Tax Unit Ex-Chief Gave List of Prospects, Not Just 2, and Was Eager for Fees

By ROBERT C. DOTY

New evidence on the active interest of James B. E. Olson, former supervisor of the Federal Alcohol Tax Unit here, in obtaining printing contracts from liquor companies under his jurisdiction was presented yesterday.

The testimony ended three days of hearings here by a subcommittee of the House Ways and Means Committee investigating administration of the Internal Revenue laws.

A salesman for the American Lithofold Company of St. Louis contradicted the version given earlier by Mr. Olson of his relations with that concern. The salesman testified about receiving frequent telephone calls from Mr. Olson in which the latter inquired about the progress of negotiations and once protested that he had failed to receive commissions due him.

At the close of yesterday's session in the Federal Court House, Foley Square, Representative Cecil R. King, Democrat of California,

Continued on Page 26, Column 8

Atomic Testing Scene a Wasteland With Few Scars of Historic Blasts

By GLADWIN HILL
Special to THE NEW YORK TIMES.

FRENCHMAN'S FLAT, Nev., Sept. 12—The mountain-rimmed desert basin that was rocked by explosions last winter in the United States drive for supremacy in atomic weapons was shown to lay observers for the first time today, with massive new installations for future tests.

Gingerly lifting the secrecy that has shrouded the area since it was selected as the testing ground, the Atomic Energy Commission admitted a group of twenty-six newsmen for a carefully chaperoned three-hour visit. Violations of the secrecy rules carry a possible death penalty.

The expanse of sagebrush where the five nuclear explosions heard and seen for more than 300 miles were staged bears no visible evidence today of the historic blasts.

Traversed now by an asphalt highway built for the atomic project, the erstwhile domain of grazing cattle, grizzled prospectors and gila monsters exhibits little but parched Joshua-tree cacti to break the monotony of the wasteland.

An area of hundreds of square miles, closed from outside view by interlaced ranges of low jagged mountains, was pointed out by a guide's wave, and the visitors were told: "This is where it took place."

Visible from the road at a few points were barren circles of ground denuded even of sagebrush, or speckled with conspicuously young sagebrush plants, which might have been seared by one or more blasts. The absence of positive signs of destruction, however, tended to support the inference that the explosions had been set off in the air by towers, airplane drops or missiles projected upward so that their force was expended outward. It has been conjectured

Continued on Page 22, Column 4

Robinson Knocks Out Turpin, Regains Championship

61,370 SEE FIGHT AT POLO GROUNDS

Continued From Page 1

he would fall. Then Referee Goldstein stepped between them and Turpin was knocked out for the second time in a career that goes back to 1946 and through forty-five engagements.

Because he wasn't actually counted out this bout will probably go into the records as a "technical knockout," but that will be misleading. Actual counting over Turpin would have been a mere formality had Robinson withheld his fire long enough to let the defending champion fall. And Turpin would have gone down but for the fusillade of blows that pinioned him to the ropes, rendered him helpless and brought a dramatic finish to a bout that had attracted more international attention than any ring battle since Joe Louis polished off Max Schmeling in a brief round back in 1938.

Turpin was collapsing like a deflated balloon in the arms of Referee Goldstein, but he tried, instinctively, to protest the interference and fight his way clear. His legs buckled. Goldstein took a firmer grasp on the helpless fighter, holding him as he would a child until Turpin's handlers scrambled through the ropes to lead the beaten warrior away.

A squad of police moved quickly into the ring under Inspector Cornelius Lyons. They blocked the four sides of the ring against the possibility of intrusion by excited fans.

Turpin was soon restored to his senses and walked to the center of the ring where Robinson was acknowledging the thunderous roar of acclaim which rang out over the scene. Smilingly, gripping the hand of his conqueror, the hand that had battered him from under the valuable ring title he held so short a time, Turpin posed for pictures. This over, he was led out of the ring amid an ear-splitting cheer from a crowd which was paying its tribute to a fighter who went down giving his best.

The cheers for Turpin were followed by a mighty roar for Robinson, who had dissipated the idea that he was no longer the sparkling, capable boxer of yore with this thrilling, highly dramatic return to the heights.

Referee Goldstein said after the battle that when he stopped the bout he was certain that Turpin was a beaten fighter.

"He couldn't go on. The punches were coming fast and furious. He might have been seriously hurt had I let it go further."

Tribute to the Winner

George Middleton, Turpin's manager, was stunned by the knockout.

"I think it was a great fight," he said. "I'm disappointed at the result, of course. But I think Robinson showed he has the punch many people thought he'd lost. I don't want to make excuses. But, perhaps the humidity hurt Randy. It was kind of close after the mountain air we've been used to, you know. But that is not offered as an excuse. Randy lost in a great fight. Robinson is a great fighter. He beat a great fighter tonight."

All middleweight attendance and receipts records were shattered by this battle which finds Robinson the third man in the long history of the 160-pound division to regain the title. The crowd of 61,370 exceeded the 60,071 which turned out for the last heavily attended battle here, the first Joe Louis-Billy Conn heavyweight championship in 1941. It dwarfed the 44,266 which saw the second Louis-Conn clash in 1946, without, however, threatening the receipts for that match, which drew $1,925,564 at a $100 "top" ticket price.

The receipts, amounting to $767,630, gross will send this fight into the $1,000,000 class, the ninth in ring history. To this box-office figure $250,000 will be added from the sale of motion picture and theatre-television rights. There will be the added income from a percentage of the picture which will accrue to the International Boxing Club, Inc.

Randy Turpin, dethroned middleweight champion, landing a punch to the face of Ray Robinson in the fourth round Associated Press

Robinson will collect 30 per cent of all the net receipts for his victory. Turpin's wounds in defeat will be assuaged by 25 per cent of the net. In each case the boxers will receive the largest purses of their careers.

From all corners of this country, from Canada and England, boxing followers and sport adherents came to this battle, attracted by a struggle that captured the public fancy as had no international ring event since Jack Dempsey engaged in Tex Rickard's first $1,000,000 fight in the 1921 clash against Georges Carpentier in Jersey City's Boyles' Thirty Acres.

Turpin gave his best last night but it was not good enough. He faced a different Robinson than the shopworn tourist who went down to defeat in London. The Robinson who battered his way back to the heights was the Robinson of old, sharp as a razor's edge, master of boxing finesse, alert, and conditioned for the test of his life.

The great crowd left the arena convinced of the Harlem Negro boy's ring greatness. In the crowd were figures of international prominence, led by General of the Army Douglas MacArthur, innumerable stars of the entertainment world, leaders in finance, industry, the arts and professions, political leaders and society folk.

Champions, past and present, in many sports fields were among the onlookers. Gene Tunney, Joe Louis and Ezzard Charles were three former holders of the heavyweight title present, along with the current titleholder, Jersey Joe Walcott; Sandy Saddler, world featherweight champion, was there, as was Jake LaMotta, former world middleweight titleholder.

This gathering set attendance and receipts records for a ring championship below the heavyweight class. Until last night the mark was the 49,186 who paid $461,789 to see the light heavyweight championship bout between Jack Delaney and Paul Berlenbach back in 1926.

Only two other middleweight champions have lost and regained the title. Stanley Ketchel, the "Michigan Assassin," regained the crown from Billy Parke in 1908. Tony Zale did it in 1948 when he stopped Rocky Graziano.

There was some confusion outside and inside the arena before the fight. Fans arriving late had to fight a way through the struggling masses that blocked the entrance gates on two sides. Eighth Avenue on the east end of the ball park was almost impassable. The ramp leading from the speedway entrance on the west side of the plant was blocked so thoroughly that mounted police were sent there to straighten things out.

There were several thousand fans trying to buy the last 200 tickets an hour before the title bout entered the ring and that added to the mix-up.

Inside everything was all right until the late-comers were jammed trying to get to the field, where there were 15,000 seats which sold at $30 per copy at the box-office and $130 per copy at the speculators.

Leap From Dugout Roof

Leaping upon the roof of one of the baseball dugouts, these fans started jumping down on the field in waves. This encouraged similar leaping by ticket-holders whose seats were in the stands. It was strenuous work for a hastily summoned group of special police to restore order.

But, when the main fight started, every seat in the place was occupied and the overflow was standing back of the ringside rows on the field and in the rear of the lower stands. Many were turned away for the first time since Jack Dempsey knocked out Luis Angel Firpo, the Wild Bull of the Pampas, twenty-eight years ago, in the same arena.

The ring battle was a thriller, as had been expected. It ended as the majority predicted it would. Robinson was the favorite at odds of 5 to 11.

Younger Man Beaten

Before the battle there was a disposition in some quarters to regard Robinson as past his peak and that he would be unable to withstand the attack of the 23-year-old Englishman, a warrior less used up in a five-year career than Robinson in eleven years of campaigning. Robinson is 31 years old.

True, Turpin had battered Robinson into defeat in fifteen rounds in London. But many thought that Robinson had taken the London assignment lightly and that his preparations for that bout were inadequate. They recalled, too his tour of the Continent, which was more or less a lark.

Before that London fight Robinson had been regarded as "the greatest fighter, pound by pound, the ring has ever known."

To all this, Robinson gave the answer last night. He was the old Robinson, trained to the minute, determined to prove that the things they used to say about him were true.

He boxed skillfully. He was careful not to let Turpin swarm all over him, not to let the defending champion take the lead at any stage of the battle.

On this writer's score Robinson swept the first seven rounds. He seemed to tire after the seventh, however. In the eighth and ninth Turpin repeatedly beat Robinson to stiff, powerful left jabs, crashed right-hand drives to the head, hammered the body with solid rights.

Early in the tenth a head-on collision re-opened the wound Robinson suffered in the London battle. Like a wounded stag, Robinson ripped into his foe. Two minutes later he was champion again.

Official score cards on the bout varied. Referee Goldstein had the bout even on rounds at four, four and one even. Joe Agnello, a judge, had Robinson in front, five rounds to four, and the other judge, Harold Barnes, had Robinson leading, five rounds to three, with one even.

Elkins Brothers, Washington, D. C., heavyweight, and Aaron Wilson, Knoxville, Tenn., were the principals in the eight-round semi-final, in which Ray Miller was the referee. Brothers weighed 191½ pounds and Wilson 192.

A slugging match from the outset, the bout ended dramatically in 2 minutes 31 seconds of the eighth round when Wilson knocked out Brothers with a left hook to the jaw. The left hook pulled victory out of defeat for the Tennesseean, for at the time he was staggering from the effects of a left hook to the jaw which Brothers had landed.

Mike Spataro, Bronx featherweight, knocked out Johnny Caro, a borough rival, in 1 minute 42 seconds of the first round, in the opener. Caro went down and out under a left hook to the jaw. Spataro weighed 123½ pounds and Caro 128½.

In the second bout Billy Hazel, Harlem lightweight, disposed of Jay Parlin, Philadelphian, in 2 minutes 49 seconds of the third. Parlin sank several left hooks to the body and was through for the night when Referee Ray Kazak stepped in. Hazel weighed 137¾ pounds and Parlin 135¼.

ROBINSON ASSERTS GRAZIANO IS NEXT

Tired Ray Requires 8 Stitches in Cut—Turpin Handlers Dispute Referee's Action

By JOSEPH C. NICHOLS

Ray Robinson was a tired fighter as he sat on a rubbing table accepting congratulations from a crowd that occupied every available bit of space in the Giants' dressing room after his fight with Randy Turpin at the Polo Grounds last night. Mayor Impellitteri greeted him, but more important to the newly crowned champion was the solicitude of Dr. Vincent A. Nardiello, who inspected Ray's cut left eyebrow and who decided eight stitches would have to be taken in the wound.

The operation was deferred until Ray answered the usual barrage of questions, while a handler held a compress to his cut eye.

"Turpin wasn't any worse than he was in London," explained Ray. "But I felt that I was better than in our first fight."

The Englishman hurt Ray a couple of times in the fight, but Robinson couldn't remember exactly when, or what the specific punches were.

Regarding his style of fighting, Ray said that his plan was to try for an early knockout and, failing that, to conserve his strength for the long pull of fifteen rounds.

Revenge for Cut

"I paced myself slowly in the seventh, eighth and ninth, but when I was cut I went out after him with all I had. He would have fallen at the end, but he was on the ropes."

Robinson said that his next fight would be against Rocky Graziano, probably in Chicago in February. "I think an American should have a chance at my title this time," he explained.

The scene in Turpin's dressing room was a matter-of-fact one, with the defeated boxer articulate but extremely soft-spoken.

Turpin did not agree that Referee Ruby Goldstein should have stopped the bout, but the British fighter conceded that if he had been the referee he might have acted similarly.

"Robinson shook me two or three times, but he did not hurt me. I had my full senses at all times and was trying to roll with the blows."

Knew Bell Was Due

Turpin said he was aware of the closeness of the bell, but that he did not wait to take a count for fear that the bout would be stopped.

Turpin's handlers were more perturbed about the stopping. They pointed to Randy's normal behavior in the dressing room, his reactions and quick, natural answers.

Turpin, remarkably calm and healthy for a man who a few minutes earlier had been subjected to so much punishment, complimented Robinson. "I lost to a good sport," he said, adding he would welcome a third meeting.

Turpin thought that the fight had been fairly even up to the finish and that Robinson "definitely was tiring."

Soft-spoken throughout the mass interview, Turpin could not be heard clearly over the din.

He plans to return home on Sept. 21—after resting and taking in the sights here.

100TH ANNIVERSARY
"All the News That's Fit to Print"
1851 1951

The New York Times.

LATE CITY EDITION
Fair, continued cool today.
Fair and cool tomorrow.
Temperature Range Today-Max., 60; Min., 48
Temperatures Yesterday—Max., 70; Min., 53
Full U. S. Weather Bureau Report, Page 33

VOL. CI..No. 34,216. Entered as Second-Class Matter. Post Office, New York, N. Y. NEW YORK, SATURDAY, SEPTEMBER 29, 1951. Times Square, New York 18, N. Y. Telephone LAckawanna 4-1000 RAG PAPER EDITION SEVENTY-FIVE CENTS

BRITAIN TO BID U. N. INTERVENE IN IRAN; SHUNS USING FORCE

Security Council Will Be Asked to Tell Teheran to Adhere to World Court Ruling

EXPULSION HALT SOUGHT

London Stresses Issue of 300 Refinery Employes — U. S. Not Surprised by Move

Text of British Foreign Office statement is on Page 5.

By RAYMOND DANIELL
Special to THE NEW YORK TIMES.

LONDON, Sept. 28—The British Government decided tonight to appeal to the Security Council of the United Nations to call upon the Iranian Government to adhere to the interim recommendation of the International Court of Justice at The Hague in the dispute with Iran over oil.

This recommendation was that neither side in the dispute take any irrevocable action pending a final decision of the merits of the case.

Sir Gladwyn Jebb, head of the British delegation to the United Nations, who has been home on holiday, will leave by air tomorrow to present the British case to the Security Council at the earliest session that can be convened.

He will ask the Council to call upon the Government of Iran not to carry out its eviction notice against the 300 or more Anglo-Iranian Oil Company employes still in Abadan, where the company's refinery has been seized by Iranian troops.

Possibilities Considered

It is still conjectural what will happen if there is no decision by the Council before the deadline for the departure of the British is reached, in the event of a Soviet veto of a decision favorable to Britain, or a refusal by the Iranians to accept a decision unfavorable to themselves. But it would appear that the Government here has decided against a resort to force.

What has restrained the Labor Government from putting troops into Iran to guard the Anglo-Iranian property — more than half owned by the British Government — has been fear of the effect on world opinion, and especially United States opinion of such action. It was the judgment of the Government that any resort to force in the dispute with Iran would arouse in the United States a new outburst against colonialism and imperialism.

What the Government did want from the United States was a public statement from the White House that President Truman supported the decision of the International Court. This has been sought for some time but has not been forthcoming.

U. S. Clarification Sought

Prime Minister Attlee's appeal to Mr. Truman the day before yesterday was for clarification of the United States position in the event of a British appeal to the Security Council. What the British Government would have liked most, of course, was for the United States to sponsor the appeal itself, but apparently that hope has fallen flat.

The big question here is what response Mr. Truman has made to Mr. Attlee's appeal. There is no evidence to show whether it was favorable or unfavorable. It might be argued that it must have been favorable or the British would not have decided to submit their case

Continued on Page 5, Column 4

Argentine Revolt Is Quelled; Only Handful of Shots Fired

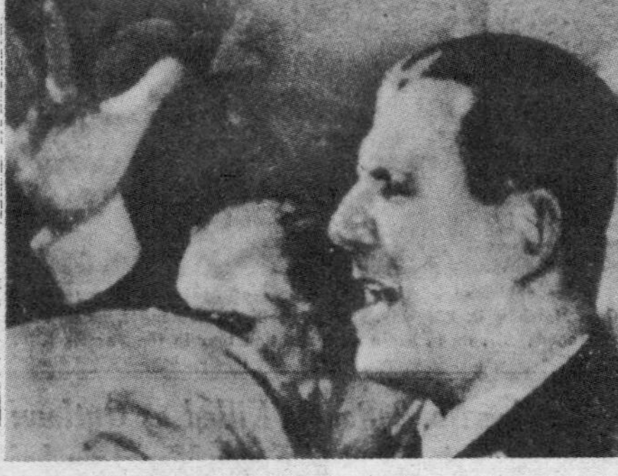

President Peron telling workers in Buenos Aires yesterday how uprising was put down. Associated Press Radiophoto

By FOSTER HAILEY
Special to THE NEW YORK TIMES

BUENOS AIRES, Sept. 28—Groups of Argentina's armed forces revolted against the Peron Government this morning. At 3:30 P. M., in a speech from the balcony of Casa Rosada, or Government House, President Juan Perón announced that the bulk of the Army, Navy and Air Force had remained loyal and that the revolt had been crushed.

That appears to be the fact. As this is written the Government is in full control of the capital, of the main military base of Campo de Mayo on the outskirts, and of the adjacent military and civilian airfields. The rest of the country was and is, so far as is known, quiet.

[The State Department has made no official comment on the revolt, but informed observers in Washington said they suspected that the abortive plot could have been conjured up by the Perón Administration to strengthen the hands of the regime.]

Fighting was reported between the forces in revolt and the loyal groups at Campo de Mayo, at two military airfields and at one Navy airfield. But there was no march on the city and there has been no plane in the sky over Buenos Aires since 2:30 P. M., when a flight of eight jet fighters flew at rooftop level in what the Government-controlled radio said would be a demonstration of Air Force loyalty to General Perón. The Government maintained control of radio stations throughout the day.

Airmen Also Implicated

An announcement issued by the Subsecretariat of Information at 2 P. M. said the revolt had been organized by two retired generals, Benjamin Menéndez and Arturo Rawson.

At 7 o'clock tonight it was officially announced that General Menéndez and several other rebellious officers had been captured.

Earlier, General Perón had issued two orders of the day to the armed forces. One ordered the summary shooting of any uniformed man attempting to take part in the revolt or refusing to obey the commands of his officers. The second, issued to commanders of all military units, ordered them to report on the conduct of all members of their command during the hours of crisis. Men who showed unusual valor and loyalty will be promoted out of turn, the order added.

Leaflets announcing the revolt dropped by planes over the city early in the morning carried the name of General Menéndez. General Rawson is the officer who led the successful revolt against the civilian government of the late President Ramón Castillo on June

Continued on Page 4, Column 3

FOE IS STILL SILENT ON RIDGWAY'S NOTE

No Propaganda Barrage Comes From the Peiping Radio — Bradley Confers in Tokyo

Special to THE NEW YORK TIMES.

TOKYO, Saturday, Sept. 29—The Communist High Command remained silent for the second day today on the proposal of Gen. Matthew B. Ridgway to shift the site of the interrupted negotiations for an armistice in the Korean war from Kaesong to the no-man's-land village of Songhyon, eight miles to the southeast.

Even the Peiping radio suspended its propaganda barrage after charging that the proposal to change the location of the truce talks was an attempt to delay their resumption and avoid United Nations "responsibility" for alleged violations of the neutral zone around the city. In an English-language broadcast this morning neither the Korean war nor the armistice conversations came in for mention.

General of the Army Omar N. Bradley, chairman of the United States Joint Chiefs of Staff, arrived by plane last night with Charles E. Bohlen, State Department expert on Soviet affairs.

[Generals Bradley and Ridgway had a forty-minute conference Saturday noon, presumably on the stalled Korean truce situation, The United Press said.]

Guest of the Ridgways

General Bradley is the guest of General and Mrs. Ridgway at the former United States Embassy building, now occupied by the United Nations Commander.

William J. Sebald, United States diplomatic representative; Lieut. Gen. Doyle O. Hickey, General Ridgway's chief of staff, and Lieut. Gen. Otto P. Weyland, commander of the Far East Air Forces, were among the welcoming group at the airport.

In the present state of the truce conferences, dragged out since early July and now deadlocked on every minor as well as major issue, the progress of the war and apparently the waning chances for an armistice seemed bound to be the most important subjects of

Continued on Page 2, Column 2

INQUIRY DEMANDS BOYLE'S BANK DATA AND MORE ON TAXES

May Recall Democratic Official — Lithofold Accusation Is Defended by Reporter

HE DOUBTS SUIT FOR LIBEL

R. F. C. Discharges Examiner, Suspends Engineer Accused of Accepting Video Sets

By C. P. TRUSSELL
Special to THE NEW YORK TIMES.

WASHINGTON, Sept. 28—Demands for the bank records of William M. Boyle Jr., chairman of the Democratic National Committee, and for more information than he had furnished concerning his income tax returns for 1949 and 1950, were made by the Senate Permanent Investigating subcommittee today.

The demands came as the group questioned Theodore C. Link, a reporter for The St. Louis Post-Dispatch who had written that Mr. Boyle had received $8,000 from the American Lithofold Corporation, a St. Louis printing concern, after the company had received a loan from the Reconstruction Finance Corporation in 1949.

It was indicated that Mr. Boyle would be recalled for more questioning.

Mr. Boyle testified yesterday that he had had nothing to do with the loan and had received nothing from Lithofold beyond $1,250 in fees as an attorney between February and April of 1949 while he was an unpaid executive vice chairman and acting chairman of the Democratic Committee. He called the charge published in The Post-Dispatch "unfounded, distorted and false," said he had been libeled and announced that the matter was in his attorney's hands.

Their Testimony Conflicts

Mr. Link testified that he had written his articles on information considered so reliable that his newspaper risked libel action to publish them. As to possible court action, he told the subcommittee:

"Of course, a libel suit would open this thing up so wide that I doubt that one will ever be filed."

Mr. Link's testimony clashed with that given by Mr. Boyle at points that committee members considered "most important." These points concerned mainly what was said during a meeting between the two several weeks before the Link articles were published. Also at issue were dates in 1949 and 1950 that differed in testimony and news articles.

Meanwhile, the R. F. C. dis-

Continued on Page 34, Column 8

$5,500,000,000 RISE IN FEDERAL TAXES VOTED BY SENATE

Ballot of 57-19 Sends Bill to Conference With House, Which Approved $7,200,000,000

TRUMAN BACKERS BEATEN

George and Millikin Defeat All Efforts to Increase Finance Group's Total

By JOHN D. MORRIS
Special to THE NEW YORK TIMES.

WASHINGTON, Sept. 28—The Senate passed the tax-increase bill tonight, after rejecting all efforts to increase its annual revenue yield over the $5,500,000,000 recommended by the Finance Committee.

The vote was 57 to 19.

The action followed nine full days of consideration in which a group of fifteen members, headed by Senator Hubert Humphrey, Democrat of Minnesota, failed in repeated attempts to stiffen the measure's terms along lines urged by President Truman.

Except for a single lapse, the bipartisan managers of the bill, Senators Walter F. George, Democrat of Georgia, and Eugene D. Millikin, Republican of Colorado, maintained full control over the Senate throughout the long fight.

Only one amendment that they opposed was approved. This was a proposal, adopted tonight on a ballot of 52 to 22, to eliminate washing machines and vacuum cleaners from a list of household appliances on which a 10 per cent manufacturers tax would be applied under terms of the bill.

Moody Offered Amendment

The amendment, sponsored by Senator Blair Moody, Democrat of Michigan, reduced the measure's prospective revenue yield by an estimated $53,000,000.

Another amendment, agreed on in the last minutes of debate, would require annual statements of net worth, to be filed with returns of income, from all individuals receiving more than $2,500 in any taxable year from an illegal enterprise.

It was offered on behalf of the Senate Crime Investigating Committee, with the idea it would supply clues to law-enforcement officers pointing to persons building up fortunes from professional gambling, racketeering and such businesses.

The bill now goes to a Senate-House conference committee for settlement of differences between its provisions and a House-approved version that would produce

Continued on Page 7, Column 5

Yanks Clinch 3d Flag in Row; Dodgers Lose, Race Is Tied

Reynolds Hurls His Second '51 No-Hitter—Giants Now Even With Brooks

Aided by Allie Reynolds' second no-hit, no-run game of the season the Yankees clinched their third straight American League pennant yesterday. In the National League, a 4-3 Dodger defeat at Philadelphia last night dropped the Brooklyn club into a tie for first place with the Giants, who were idle.

Following Reynolds' 8-0 triumph over the Red Sox in the first game at Yankee Stadium, Vic Raschi pitched an 11-3 victory, his twenty-first, to put the Bombers beyond reach of the Indians.

Striking out nine batters and walking four in the first contest, Reynolds became the second pitcher in major league history and the first in American League annals to achieve two no-hit games in one year. The first was Johnny Vander Meer, Cincinnati Reds' left-hander, who pitched two in succession in the National League in 1938.

Reynolds hurled his no-hitters at the expense of New York's most powerful rivals. His first, a 1-0 game in Cleveland the night of July 12, was against the Indians, who clinched second place as the result of third-place Boston's loss to Reynolds.

Allie Reynolds after pitching his second no-hitter. The New York Times

In the last two innings of the Dodger game the Phils rallied to win. Andy Seminick drove a homer with one on base in the eighth to even the score and in the ninth Willie Jones' single batted in Richie Ashburn, who had opened with a single, from second base to end the contest.

The Dodgers and Giants have two games each to play before the regular season closes tomorrow.

Details on Page 11

Du Pont and 3 Others Ruled Violators of Anti-Trust Law

By EDWARD RANZAL

Federal Judge Sylvester Ryan ruled yesterday that E. I. du Pont de Nemours & Co., Inc.; Imperial Chemical Industries, Ltd., of Great Britain, and the Remington Arms Company, Inc., had conspired to divide markets in munitions, chemicals and small arms in volation of the Sherman Anti-Trust Law.

The decision in the seven-year-old civil action, which upheld the Government's charge that four corporations and five officers of the corporate defendants entered into agreements in restraint of trade in a world cartel, will break du Pont's nylon monopoly unless the ruling is upset on appeal.

Leonard J. Emmerglick, special assistant to the Attorney General, who headed the Government staff, will move within the next thirty days to propose relief decrees. He said the Government would ask for the compulsory licensing of du Pont's nylon patents so that other manufacturers might use the process.

This is the first time, Mr. Emmerglick said, that a British company has been made subject to the anti-trust laws. The complaint named the three companies and Imperial Chemical Industries (New York) Ltd., a subsidiary of the British Corporation. Seven Canadian, South American and German companies were accused of engaging in the cartel, but were not named as defendants. One of these companies was Dynamit Aktiengesellschaft, affiliated with I. G. Farben Industrie, described as the most important manufacturer of explosives in Germany.

As the result of a two-month trial last year, the Government sought to have the agreements among the various companies enjoined and also asked the court to compel du Pont to dispose of its interests in Canadian, Argentine and Brazilian companies and that both du Pont and Imperial Chemi-

Continued on Page 20, Column 2

RUPPELL TO RESIGN AS G.O.P. CHAIRMAN

Statement Today Planned by Staten Island Leader Linked to Job, License Shakedowns

By DOUGLAS DALES

Edward A. Ruppell, Staten Island Republican leader accused by witnesses before the State Crime Commission of shaking down Republican officeholders and exacting cash tributes for interceding for liquor licenses, announced yesterday his intention of resigning as chairman of the Richmond County Republican Committee.

In a twelve-word telegram to William L. Pfeiffer, Republican state chairman, Mr. Ruppell said he was "arranging" his resignation and was preparing a statement for release at 10 A. M. today.

On the basis of testimony during the seven days of public hearings conducted by the Crime Commission at the West Brighton Courthouse, Mr. Pfeiffer on Thursday had "demanded" the county leader's resignation and declared that he would no longer recognize Mr. Ruppell's leadership.

Mr. Ruppell's telegram indicated no specific date when his resignation would become effective but left the implication that it would be soon.

Other leaders of the Richmond Republican Committee were not consulted by Mr. Ruppell and were

Continued on Page 34, Column 6

GROSS SAID BOOKIES HAD O'DWYER FUND; LISTED $20,000 GIFTS

Told Grand Jury of Campaign Donations in '45-'49—Moran Identified as the Collector

ANOTHER CHANCE TO TALK

Gambler Will Be Summoned as Witness in the Departmental Trial of 32 Policemen

Harry Gross told the Brooklyn grand jury of a "bookie fund" into which regular contributions were made for the election campaigns of former Mayor William O'Dwyer, both in 1945 and in 1949, it was learned last night. Gross said his own contributions totaled $20,000—$5,000 in 1945 and $15,000 in 1949.

The source of the disclosures, one privileged to have access to testimony before the panel, said Gross had testified that James J. Moran, chief clerk in Mr. O'Dwyer's office when the present Ambassador to Mexico was Kings County District Attorney, had solicited the bookmaker's contributions and identified himself as the "collector" for the fund.

Gross told the grand jury he had paid the $20,000 in cash. He volunteered the information that because his business was flourishing in 1949 he had been expected to pay a larger sum, and that he had assumed other bookies were being assessed in proportion to the business they were doing.

McDonald Withholds Comment

Without disclosing the source of the revelation of Gross' testimony, reporters sought out District Attorney Miles F. McDonald for confirmation. The Brooklyn prosecutor withheld comment, pointing out that this testimony had not been read in Special Sessions on Thursday when Gross was sentenced to twelve years in the penitentiary, and therefore was still a grand jury secret.

Mr. McDonald, it was learned, had the testimony concerning the "bookie fund" in the grand jury minutes that he read, with names of policemen and identifying data deleted at the last-minute order of Kings County Judge Samuel S. Leibowitz.

The jurist at that time said it would be unfair and "un-American" to read the names at a court session in which the persons named would have no opportunity to defend themselves. He said also it would violate every elementary rule of civil liberties and due process of law.

Although the story of the "bookie fund" was in his summary of the grand jury minutes, Mr. McDonald omitted mention of it, confining himself, it was said, to so much of the Gross story as was pertinent to his recital of graft payments.

Moran's Role Pictured

According to Gross' story of the "bookie fund," Moran, when he allegedly asked for the contribution, had said other bookies were contributing and that he was the collector. Moran, who later became a Deputy Fire Commissioner, is under sentence of five years in prison for perjuring himself as a witness before the Senate Crime Investigating Committee.

In testimony before the Kefauver Committee, John P. Crane, former president of the Uniformed Firemen's Association, said he had made similar contributions to Moran, which totaled $55,000 over a period of years.

It was learned also that other deleted portions of Gross' testimony dealt with the bookmaker's

Continued on Page 34, Column 2

Churchill Sponsors Excess Profits Tax

Special to THE NEW YORK TIMES.

LONDON, Sept. 28—Only the Conservative party can give Britain a stable government "free of doctrinal prejudices" and the "passions of class warfare," Winston Churchill declared today in an election manifesto calling for a halt in the socialization of the nation's economy.

The manifesto laid down the broad lines of policy the Conservatives would follow if returned to power on Oct. 25 but its author made it clear that he was seeking to proclaim a theme rather than to write a prospectus." He said the Conservatives would do their best to lead the country out of its present difficulties but he warned

Continued on Page 3, Column 3

Canada Offers to Build Seaway; Truman for Move as 'Second Best'

By W. H. LAWRENCE
Special to THE NEW YORK TIMES.

WASHINGTON, Sept. 28—Canada formally offered today to construct alone the $219,000,000 St. Lawrence Seaway to open the way for large ocean-going ships as far west as Detroit.

The proposal was made to President Truman by the Dominion's Prime Minister Louis St. Laurent, at a White House conference this morning.

Mr. Truman expressed strong preference for joint development of the Seaway by the United States and Canadian Governments, but said that unless Congress assured an early commencement of work, he would support action by the Dominion alone as "second best."

There was agreement between the President and the Prime Minister that if Canada went ahead on the Seaway, arrangements would be made between the two countries for simultaneous joint development of a [illegible] hydroelectric power project opposite Massena, N. Y. This would be done by agreement between the Federal Government, or the New York State Power Authority, and the Province of Ontario to share the cost and the resultant power production.

The Canadian offer is certain to generate new pressure on Congress to authorize participation by this country in the Seaway and power project, which has been in a state of deadlock on Capitol Hill since it first was formally proposed in 1934. As recently as July 26, the House Public Works Committee, after long hearings, voted 15 to 12 to table a measure authorizing both segments of the St. Lawrence project.

But United States advocates of the Seaway almost certainly will ask Congress to take a new look at the bill, either before its coming adjournment, or certainly early in

Continued on Page 10, Column 3

World News Summarized

SATURDAY, SEPTEMBER 29, 1951

Harry Gross, charged with having given the police $1,000,000 a year in graft, has informed the grand jury that he paid $5,000 in 1945 and $15,000 in 1949 into a "bookie fund" to support the election campaigns of former Mayor O'Dwyer, it was learned yesterday. Gross will be called to testify in the mass departmental trial of thirty-two active and retired policemen. There was no indication whether he would be more cooperative in furnishing names and details for the record. [1:8.] In Staten Island Edward A. Ruppell, under fire as chairman of the county Republican Committee, announced he would resign. [1:7.]

Elements of Argentina's armed forces revolted against the Perón Government, which reported that within a few hours the attempt had been snuffed out. [1:2-3; map on P. 4.] Well-informed sources in Washington suggested the incident had been engineered by President Perón. [4:7.] The records of those said to have been leading the revolt showed they had virtually no prospect for success. [4:6.]

The Communist High Command in Korea remained silent on allied proposals that the site of armistice negotiations be moved. The Peiping radio, after charging General Ridgway with maneuvering for delays, suspended propaganda broadcasts. [1:2.] United Nations forces were attacked along a sixty-mile front, yielding scattered gains to the enemy. [2:1; with map.]

In London the British Government announced that it would request the Security Council of the United Nations to call upon Iran to abide by the interim recommendations of the International Court of Justice, under which the position of British workers would be protected pending settlement of the oil dispute. It was further indicated that there would be no resort to force, probably in deference to American public opinion. The Security Council has been summoned to meet Monday. Meanwhile, a personal message from President Truman will be handed to the Shah of Iran. [1:1.]

Italian Premier De Gasperi, in a City Hall welcome, urged this country to ease present immigration laws. [3:1.] At the United Nations he asked for the admission of Italy. [3:2-3.]

Prime Minister St. Laurent of Canada informed President Truman of his country's willingness to construct the $219,000,000 St. Lawrence Seaway alone if Congress did not soon approve United States participation. This alternative was supported by the President as an acceptable "second-best" solution. [1:2-3.]

A Federal court decision ruled that E. I. du Pont de Nemours & Co., Inc., Imperial Chemical Industries, Ltd., and the Remington Arms Company, Inc., had violated anti-trust laws in conspiring to divide markets in munitions and chemicals. [1:6-7.]

Senator Joseph R. McCarthy was assailed in a 25,000-word indictment before a Senate subcommittee by Senator Benton, who demanded his expulsion on misconduct charges. [1:6-7.]

Index to other news appears on last page of this section.

Benton Gives Senate 10-Case Brief On McCarthy 'Lies' and 'Deceits'

By WILLIAM S. WHITE
Special to THE NEW YORK TIMES.

WASHINGTON, Sept. 28—Senator William Benton, Democrat of Connecticut, charged under oath today that Senator Joseph R. McCarthy, Republican of Wisconsin, had perjured himself before the Senate in his campaign against alleged Communists in the State Department.

In 25,000 words of accusation before a Senate subcommittee, Senator Benton demanded Senator McCarthy's expulsion from the Senate, or at least his public censure by that body, for ten major "cases" of misconduct.

Apart from asserting that Senator McCarthy had lied under oath to fellow Senators last year in denying that he ever had said he knew of 205 Communists in the State Department, Senator Benton challenged Senator McCarthy's personal and public honor a dozen times and more.

He called Senator McCarthy "an amoral man who used the lie as an instrument of policy"—a man of "corruptibility and mendacity" and "gross irresponsibility" who had followed "a pattern of distortion and deceit."

Senator Benton appeared as the first witness in hearings before the Subcommittee on Privileges and Elections of the Senate Rules Committee in support of his resolution demanding an investigation of Senator McCarthy's conduct to determine whether his expulsion should be recommended. The proceeding in its present form was compared by subcommittee members to the deliberations of a grand jury considering a possible indictment.

To expel a member requires a vote in the Senate itself of two-

Continued on Page 6, Column 2

"Case studies" listed by Senator Benton, Page 6.

Store Santa Leaves $156,445 to College

Special to THE NEW YORK TIMES.

BRIDGEPORT, Conn., Sept. 28—The $156,445 estate of a department store doorman-Santa Claus will go to Williams College, his alma mater, according to documents filed here today with Probate Judge John P. Flanagan. The estate includes the alumnus' final pay check—$37.41—as well as a quantity of excellent securities.

Burritt Fitch Prudden, who left the legacy, was 76 years old when he died last June 17. His home was a modest apartment at 850 Lafayette Street. He was a quiet and thrifty man, and his fellow employes at the D. M. Read Company department store knew little about him. One thing he did confide was that, in the

Continued on Page 6, Column 7

Yanks Clinch Flag, Aided by Reynolds' No-Hitter

BOMBERS CONQUER RED SOX, 8-0, 11-3

Yanks Take 3d Flag in Row, Reynolds' 2d No-Hitter of Year Winning Opener

RASCHI'S 21ST IS CLINCHER

7-Run Second Inning Decides Second Game—Joe DiMaggio Drives 3-Run Homer

By JOHN DREBINGER

In a brilliant display of all-around skill that included a nerve tingling no-hitter in one encounter and a seven-run explosion in the other, the Yankees yesterday clinched the 1951 American League pennant. It was their third flag in a row and eighteenth in thirty years.

With Allie Reynolds tossing his second no-hitter of the year—a feat previously achieved by only one other hurler in history—the Bombers vanquished the Red Sox in the opener of the double-header at the Stadium, 8 to 0.

Then, behind big Vic Raschi, the Stengeleers crushed the already eliminated Bosox, 11 to 3, to the cheers of 39,038 fans. Joe DiMaggio further embellished the triumph with a three-run homer as another flag was nailed to the Yankee masthead.

Tribe Clinches Second

Even were the Bombers to lose their three remaining games to the Steve O'Neill's Red Sox, they could not be overtaken by the last to survive. Cleveland's doleful Indians who, three and a half games out, have only two more encounters to play. The Tribe clinched second place as a result of Boston's two defeats.

Thus there remains nothing more for the Bombers to do now but await the outcome of the seething National League race between the Giants and the Dodgers to determine which club they shall meet in the world series. Unless the National's struggle ends in a deadlock tomorrow, necessitating a best-two-of-three game play-off, the big series will start at the Stadium on Wednesday.

In yesterday's smashing Yankee triumph, Reynolds' masterful performance provided most of the thrills, making even the clinching of the pennant somewhat anti-climactic.

Those who sat in on the show are not likely to forget those last tense moments when Reynolds, who had walked four batters during the game, had to collect "twenty-eight outs" before reaching his goal.

Berra Goes Sprawling

With two out in the ninth and the still fearsome Ted Williams at bat, a high foul was struck back of home plate. Yogi Berra, usually sure on these, scampered under it, but in the next agonizing moment the ball squirmed out of his glove as the Yanks chunky backstop went sprawling on his face.

It meant Williams would have to be pitched to some more. But Reynolds, an amazingly good-natured competitor under the most trying circumstances, patted Berra consolingly on the back and said. "Don't worry, Yogi, we'll get him again."

And, sure enough, up went another high, twisting foul off to the right side of the plate. It looked tougher than the first one. But Yogi meant to catch this one if it burst a girth rope and as he finally froze to the ball directly in front of the Yankee dugout, Reynolds first, and virtually all the other Yanks jubilantly piled on top of him. For a moment it looked as if Berra, not Reynolds, was the hero of the occasion.

Only one other major league hurler has ever fired two no-hitters in one season, and none ever in the American League. In 1938, Johnny Vander Meer, Cincinnati southpaw, turned in two on successive mound appearances, holding the Braves hitless on June 11 and repeating the trick on June 15 against the Dodgers in the first night game played in Ebbets Field.

This was the fourth no-hitter recorded in the majors this season. Aside from Reynolds, Bob Feller of the Indians hurled one against the Tigers on July 1, and Cliff Chambers of the Pirates posted one on May 6 against the Braves.

Reynolds' first no-hitter this year was tossed on the night of July 12 against the Indians at Cleveland. After the forthcoming world series, the Chief expects to undergo an operation on his right elbow.

Apart from the four batters who drew walks, the passes coming singly in the first, fourth, seventh and ninth innings, no other member of the Sox reached first base. No one reached second. The ace right-hander struck out nine and not one Boston batter seemed to come even close to a hit.

Behind this superlative hurling, which gave Reynolds his seventeenth triumph of the season against eight defeats, the Yanks lost no time getting the upper hand. They counted twice in the first off Mel Parnell, their conqueror in Boston last week, and added two more in the third with the help of a Dom DiMaggio error.

Then Ray Scarborough came on to be clubbed for a two-run homer by Joe Collins in the sixth and in the eighth Gene Woodling larruped his No. 15 into the right field seats off Harry Taylor.

With this victory, the Yanks were assured of at least a first-place tie. Then they went after the clincher.

Some Anxious Moments

At the start there were some anxious moments as the Sox, with Williams out of their line-up, clipped Raschi for two runs in the first and another in the second with the aid of two surprising wild pitches. Williams, it was explained, had suffered a painful bruise when hit by a foul tip on the right leg in the first game.

Trailing by three, the Bombers made their move in the last of the second. With Commissioner-elect Ford C. Frick looking on, they crushed the Bosox with a seven-run demonstration, raking Bill Wight and Walt Masterson for five blows, the last a tremendous triple by Gil McDougald.

Commissioner Frick had missed the no-hitter, but he was in at the "kill" of the flag race. It probably marked the first time since his days as a baseball scribe covering the Yankees that the man who for seventeen years has been the National League president, saw an American League pennant decided.

From the third inning on, Raschi swung into his usually flawless style and so rolled on to his twenty-first victory against ten defeats. The closing crusher for the crestfallen Bosox came in the sixth, when Joe DiMaggio, not to be denied a share in the final spotlight, belted Chuck Stobbs for his twelfth homer with two runners aboard.

And so, to this most successful organization in baseball history not only comes its eighteenth pennant but for the fourth time the Bombers have annexed three in a row. Once they stretched the string to four and the chance to repeat this feat lies before them in 1952.

Also to the astounding Charles Dillon Stengel, who never had spent a day in the American League prior to 1949, when he succeeded Bucky Harris as Yankee manager, comes the distinction of being the third pilot to win pennants in his first three years in a league. The fabulous Frank Chance did it with the Cubs in 1906-07-08. In the American League Hughey Jennings did it with the Tigers in 1907-08-09.

It was on this same corresponding Friday date that Bombers clinched their pennant last year, although on that occasion they had it much easier. The Yanks sitting idly in their hotel quarters in Boston while the runner-up Tigers were eliminated by the Indians. The most difficult victory came in 1949, when the Yanks, trailing the Red Sox by one with two games to go, vanquished the Sox in both games to win on the last day.

The span of Yankee triumphs covers only three decades. They won their first pennants under the late Miller Huggins in 1921-22-23, and with the little Miller still added three more in 1926-27-28.

After Huggins' death in 1929, the Bombers lapsed for a few years, but Joe McCarthy had them back with a flag in 1932 and then with 1936 followed the greatest sustained effort of winning in baseball history.

The Bombers, under McCarthy, won four in a row from 1936 through 1939. They were nosed out in a close finish in 1940. But in 1941 were back to reel off three more through 1943. In eight years, Marse Joe had bagged seven flags, a feat without precedent in the majors. But Professor Casey, with three victories in three tries, may give that record a terrific go.

The New York Yankees

Allie Reynolds

Yankee Pennant Winners

Year.	Manager	World Series.
1921	Huggins	Lost to Giants. 5—3
1922	Huggins	Lost to Giants. 4—0
1923	Huggins	Beat Giants .... 4—2
1926	Huggins	Lost to Cards .. 4—3
1927	Huggins	Beat Pirates ... 4—0
1928	Huggins	Beat Cards ..... 4—0
1932	McCarthy	Beat Cubs ...... 4—0
1936	McCarthy	Beat Giants .... 4—2
1937	McCarthy	Beat Giants .... 4—1
1938	McCarthy	Beat Cubs ...... 4—0
1939	McCarthy	Beat Reds ...... 4—0
1941	McCarthy	Beat Dodgers ... 4—1
1942	McCarthy	Lost to Cards .. 4—1
1943	McCarthy	Beat Cards ..... 4—1
1947	Harris	Beat Dodgers ... 4—3
1949	Stengel	Beat Dodgers ... 4—1
1950	Stengel	Beat Phillies ... 4—0
1951	Stengel	——

Stengel Heaps Praise on DiMaggio Amid Quiet Joy of Yank Clubhouse

'We Never Would Have Won' Without Joe, Says Pilot—'Becoming Monotonous,' Quips Rizzuto of 3 Flags in Row

By LOUIS EFFRAT

Indicating that the business of winning a pennant was "old hat" to them, the Yankees showed remarkable restraint yesterday at the Stadium, after they had clinched their eighteenth American League flag. A group of casual acquaintances, meeting by chance in the subway, would display more emotion than Casey Stengel's heroes did in the clubhouse after the twin bill.

The usual hand-shaking, back-slapping and other amenities that go with the wrapping up of a championship were in evidence. The "Attaboys" "Nice goings!" floated through the quarters, as did photographers, reporters, executives and just plain well-wishers.

A Magnificent Performance

Yet, one got the impression that the Yankees were taking it all in good, easy stride. Happy? Yes. Elated? Unquestionably. Hilarious? Definitely no. In fact, it would appear that the Yankees clinched pennants every day in the season, so comparatively quiet was the clubhouse.

It was with similar restraint that the Yanks had greeted Allie Reynolds' no-hitter several hours earlier. That magnificent performance on American Indian Day by the Creek from Oklahoma brought nothing resembling a celebration. Allie was congratulated warmly and the Yankees were all smiles, but little more happened.

Perhaps, those watching the proceedings after the first game felt the display of enthusiasm would come if and when the Yankees won the nightcap. But it was the same sedate story then.

Little Phil Rizzuto facetiously supplied the answer. "Three straight pennants," he said, "it's becoming monotonous."

Stengel seemed most affected by the climax. His first move, after returning to the clubhouse, was straight to Joe DiMaggio. Pumping the veteran's hand solemnly, the manager exclaimed, "I want to thank you for everything you did."

To the reporters who surrounded him, Stengel said, "I never wavered in my belief that the boys would win it, but we never would have won without DiMaggio. With the possible exception of his brother, Dom, Joe is the best outfielder in the league. He saved me from looking bad many times. There were times when I should have removed a pitcher, but a great catch by DiMaggio took us out of a hole. And don't forget his timely hits and his excellent base-running. No, sir, without DiMaggio we never would have won it."

Tired but happy, DiMaggio sat with a baseball in his hand. It was the ball that his brother had hit and Gene Woodling had caught, ending the second game and qualifying Joe for his tenth world series. "Gene gave it to me," DiMaggio explained, "and this is one I'm going to keep. It was with this ball that the Yankees clinched the pennant—my tenth pennant."

DiMaggio had right to be proud. Only the late Babe Ruth had played on ten flag-winning clubs—three with the Red Sox, seven with the Yankees—and no active player is close to matching the Jolter's record.

The homer he smashed yesterday made Joe feel good, too. This brought up the question of DiMaggio's future. He had announced last spring this might be his farewell campaign. "I honestly don't know about next year," he declared. "Right now we have some unfinished business—the world series—and I don't care particularly whether it will be against the Giants or the Dodgers."

Not Too Concerned

Reynolds was aware at all times that he had a no-hitter going in the opener. "I couldn't help knowing it," Allie said. "It was always up there on the scoreboard. However, I wasn't too concerned. After nine years, you're more concerned with winning and staying in the league."

Allie said his curve was especially good. Yogi Berra, whose failure to catch Ted Williams' first foul in the ninth might have wrecked everything (Yogi caught the second, though) thought Reynolds threw a better curve at Cleveland.

Del Webb, co-owner of the Yankees, was at Cleveland when Allie fashioned his first no-hitter. He was at the Stadium yesterday. Between these two, Webb had not seen the Yanks in action.

Webb had been present at only one other no-hitter. Thirty years ago, a tall righthander hurling for Oakland in the California State League, turned back Monterey, 10—1, yielding no safeties.

That pitcher was the same Del Webb who cheered Reynolds yesterday.

In recognition of his second no-hitter, the hotel at which Reynolds stops here announced the change of his room number from 2019 to 0002.

Williams, hit on the right foot by a foul-tip in the opener, was X-rayed at Lenox Hill Hospital. He has a bad bruise, which is likely to keep Ted out of the remaining games.

DODGER TRIO FINED FOR BOSTON 'SCENE'

The baseball dispute in Boston on Thursday had repercussions yesterday when Ford Frick, president of the National League, fined Jackie Robinson and Roy Campanella of the Dodgers $100 each and Preacher Roe $50. There were no suspensions.

Frick said he penalized the players "for the scenes they put on in the runways and in front of the umpires' dressing room in the presence of fans and opposing ball players."

The flare-up occurred after the Braves had beaten the Brooks, 4 to 3, and shaved the Dodgers' first-place lead over the Giants to a half-game. A decision against the Dodgers by Umpire Frank Dascoli started the trouble.

In the eighth inning Dascoli called Bob Addis of the Braves safe at home with what proved to be the winning run. Campanella, the catcher, and Coach Cookie Lavagetto were ruled off the field by Dascoli when they protested his decision.

Before the Braves finished their turn at bat, Dascoli cleared the Brooklyn bench. The banishment of Campanella was a serious blow because Peewee Reese opened the ninth with a double and was on third with one out when the catcher would have been due to bat.

With the tying run on third, Manager Chuck Dressen called on Wayne Terwilliger to hit for Rube Walker, who had replaced Roy behind the plate. Terwilliger grounded out and Andy Pafko fanned to end the game.

Frick, after receiving reports from the arbiters, took no action against Campanella for his conduct on the field. His announcement made no mention of the report from Boston that, after the game, Robinson had splintered a panel in the door of the umpire's room with a kick.

Robinson, when asked about the door-kicking episode, denied the charge. "I know who did it, and it wasn't me," he said. "But I won't tell who did it."

Roe, the Brooks' ace pitcher, supported Robinson's statement. "I know who did it, too, but it wasn't Jackie," said the Preacher. "I'll take an oath on that."

100TH ANNIVERSARY
"All the News That's Fit to Print"
1851 1951

The New York Times.

LATE CITY EDITION
Cloudy, windy today and tonight. Possibly clearing tomorrow.
Temperature Range Today—Max., 74; Min., 64
Temperatures Yesterday—Max., 72; Min., 64
Full U. S. Weather Bureau Report, Page 67

VOL. CI..No. 34,221. Entered as Second-Class Matter. Post Office, New York, N. Y. NEW YORK, THURSDAY, OCTOBER 4, 1951. Times Square, New York 18, N. Y. Telephone LAckawanna 4-1000 RAG PAPER EDITION SEVENTY-FIVE CENTS

GIANTS CAPTURE PENNANT, BEATING DODGERS 5-4 IN 9TH ON THOMSON'S 3-RUN HOMER

MEET YANKS TODAY

Third Baseman's Clout Sends Giants Into the World Series

BROOKLYN'S BRANCA LOSER

Yields Homer on Second Pitch After Relieving Newcombe in the Play-Off Final

By JOHN DREBINGER

In an electrifying finish to what long will be remembered as the most thrilling pennant campaign in history, Leo Durocher and his astounding never-say-die Giants wrenched victory from the jaws of defeat at the Polo Grounds yesterday, vanquishing the Dodgers, 5 to 4, with a four-run splurge in the last half of the ninth.

A three-run homer by Bobby Thomson that accounted for the final three tallies blasted the Dodgers right out of the world series picture and this afternoon at the Stadium it will be the Giants against Casey Stengel's American League champion Yankees in the opening clash of the world series.

Seemingly hopelessly beaten, 4 to 1, as the third and deciding game of the epic National League play-off moved into the last inning, the Giants lashed back with a fury that would not be denied. They routed big Don Newcombe while scoring one run.

Then, with Ralph Branca on the mound and two runners aboard the bases, came the blow of blows. Thomson crashed the ball into the left-field stand. Forgotten on the instant was the cluster of three with which the Brooks had crushed Sal Maglie in the eighth.

For a moment the crowd of 34,320, as well as all the Dodgers, appeared too stunned to realize what had happened. But as the long and lean Scot from Staten Island loped around the bases behind his two team-mates a deafening roar went up, followed by some of the wildest scenes ever witnessed in the historic arena under Coogan's Bluff.

Mobbed at Home Plate

The Giants, lined up at home plate, fairly mobbed the Hawk as he completed the last few strides to the plate. Jubilant Giant fans, fairly beside themselves, eluded guards and swarmed on the field to join the melee.

When the players finally completed their dash to the center-field clubhouse, the fans, thousands deep on the field, yelled themselves purple as Thomson repeatedly appeared in the clubhouse windows in answer to the most frenzied "curtain calls" ever accorded a ballplayer.

And so, as this extraordinary campaign moves on in a flow of diamond drama, it will be the Giants and Yankees meeting for the sixth time in world series history. They last were rivals in the classic of 1937.

The second game also will be staged in the Bronx arena that so quietly looked down on the scene yesterday from the other side of the Harlem.

On Saturday the action will shift to the Polo Grounds, where the third and fourth games will be played, as well as the fifth, if necessary. Should neither side have four victories racked up by then, the struggle will return to the Stadium for the sixth and seventh games.

A Long Uphill Battle

As soon as Durocher was able to regain his voice he announced that Dave Koslo, his lone southpaw of any account, will be the starter against the Bombers today. Casey Stengel announced, following the clinching of the American League pennant last Friday, that Allie Reynolds, hero of two no-hitters the past season, would be his mound choice for the opener.

The pennant, which the Giants so dramatically won in the second play-off series in National League history and the first to go the full three games, brought to a climax one of the most astonishing uphill struggles ever waged in the annals of the sport.

Off to an atrocious start in the spring when they lost eleven in a

Continued on Page ..., Column 2

AFTER THE GAME WAS OVER

Bobby Thomson and Manager Leo Durocher of the Giants in the clubhouse after the victory over the Dodgers. Associated Press

It's Like a Wake in Brooklyn As Fans 'Replay' Fatal 9th

All Gotham was divided yesterday into three parts. The first of these the lordly Yankees inhabit; the second is the joyful country of the Giants; the third belongs to the fiercest and most desperate of all, the Brooklyn Dodgers.

When Bobby Thomson exploded the home run that "snatched" the ball game and the National League pennant from the Dodgers in the ninth inning, it was murder in Brooklyn.

The long-faced fans rehashing the sour mess outside the Dodgers' office at Court and Montague Streets, near Borough Hall, heaped their bitterness upon Chuck Dressen, Brooklyn manager. It was the consensus of the sidewalk coaches that Dressen lost the pennant by substituting Ralph Branca for Don Newcombe in the crucial moment of the last inning.

"Thomson had hit six homers off Branca already this season," an irate lawyer in a blue suit and with a briefcase under his arm lectured the fans clustered before the Dodgers' office windows. "As soon as Branca walked out to the box, I said, 'Get the crepe.'"

"Well, I don't know about that," a stout taxi driver argued. "Newcombe looked dead on his feet to me on the television. But Branca should of walked Thomson, even if it filled the bases."

"That's right," an aproned storekeeper agreed. "He could have taken a chance on Willie Mays, and there was always the chance of a double play."

A little man with a big, black mustache seemed to speak for all of mourning Flatbush as, pacing up and down in front of the score-

Continued on Page 44, Column 1

GEN. HUGH A. DRUM DIES AT DESK AT 72

Noted Soldier Headed Empire State Building—Governor, Mayor Decree Mourning

Lieut. Gen. Hugh A. Drum, U. S. A., retired, one of the nation's most distinguished Army leaders, died of a heart attack yesterday at his desk in the Empire State Building. He had been president of the Empire State Building Corporation since 1944. He was 72 years old.

General Drum arrived at his office, on the thirty-second floor, at his usual time of 9:30 o'clock, and just before 10 o'clock pushed the button on his intercommunications system to summon his secretary, Miss Mary Carr. When she entered, she found the general slumped over his desk. A police emergency squad administered oxygen for thirty minutes, in a futile attempt to revive him. He was pronounced dead by Dr. Joseph S. Amster of 437 Fourth Avenue, summoned by members of General Drum's office staff.

The body was removed later to the Frank E. Campbell Funeral

Continued on Page 33, Column 2

Building Service Men Out in Bronx; 450 Houses Involved, Goal Is 1,300

Building service employes went on strike yesterday against 450 Bronx apartment houses, mainly along Grand Concourse, and planned to widen their walkout to involve 1,300 structures in the borough by tomorrow.

The strike, which was called by Local 32-E of the Building Service Employes International Union, A. F. L., actually caused little personal hardship to the thousands of tenants affected because most of the apartment houses are no more than six stories high and have self-service elevators.

The effect of the walkout in a few luxury-type buildings of ten stories or more was softened by the willingness of the union to honor an appeal by the Department of Health to provide emergency service for the sick and for doctors, nurses, clergymen and utility workers. However, some garbage went uncollected and hot water and other conveniences of urban living were lacking.

In mid-afternoon the Bronx Realty A... 1,300 buildings in the borough, offered to resume negotiations with the union on the condition that the strike be ended. The proposal was made by Simon R. Bregman, president of the group.

The executive board of the union, headed by Thomas Lewis, president, rejected the suggestion. Thereupon, the realty board advised members to give striking superintendents ten days' notice to get out of their rent-free apartments.

The outlook was, however, not entirely gloomy. Soon after the strike began, Julius J. Manson, supervising mediator of the State Mediation Board, sent telegrams to both sides inviting them to a peace meeting tomorrow morning at 11 o'clock in the board offices at 270 Broadway.

The union and the landlord group accepted the invitation, although the union did so with the understanding that the strike would continue. Late in the afternoon Mr. Manson said he would

Continued on Page 22, Column 1

NEW CHIEF ORDERS INQUIRY ON INCOMES OF U.S. TAX OFFICIALS

Dunlap Starts an Investigation of Returns, Including All Enforcement Officers

TRUMAN APPROVAL CITED

Examination Stems From Test Questionnaires Issued for the New York Area

By CLAYTON KNOWLES
Special to The New York Times.

WASHINGTON, Oct. 3—John B. Dunlap, Commissioner of Internal Revenue, revealed today that he had ordered a thorough examination of the income tax returns for 1948, 1949 and 1950 of all officials and front-line enforcement officers of the bureau.

In reporting the order, dated Oct. 1, the commissioner, just a month on the job, told the Ways and Means subcommittee of the House of Representatives investigating recurring irregularities in the agency, that he had received "carte blanche authority to clear things up" from both President Truman and John W. Snyder, Secretary of the Treasury.

The order stated that the examination of returns would be made "whether or not the information on the return indicates that an examination is warranted" and that returns for earlier years would be requisitioned if the current audit revealed the need.

Continuing Check Ordered

Returns for all coming years will be examined automatically. All rights reserved for any taxpayer, including the right to appeal, are preserved for affected bureau employes under the order.

For the purposes of the order, officials are defined on a basis broad enough to include everyone from a division head to the commissioner himself.

Front-line enforcement employes will be interpreted to include office and field deputy collectors, collectors' office auditors and returns examiners, revenue agents in the office and field, conferees, technical advisors, reviewers, special agents, miscellaneous tax agents, alcohol tax inspectors and investigators and storekeeper-gaugers.

The subcommittee learned of this order as it prepared to go into the activities of James P. Finnegan, who resigned while under fire early this year as Collector of In-

Continued on Page 29, Column 4

U. N. UNITS ADVANCE ON A 40-MILE FRONT; TRUCE SHIFT UPSET

U. S., British, Greek, Filipino, South Korean, Turkish Units Follow Up Heavy Barrage

ENEMY COUNTER-ATTACKS

His Artillery Also Opens Up, but Fails to Halt Push—Red Reply Bars Move From Kaesong

Reds Reject Truce Shift

By The United Press.

TOKYO, Thursday, Oct. 4—The Communist High Command today rejected Gen. Ridgway's proposal to change the site of the Korean truce negotiations.

Special to The New York Times.

TOKYO, Thursday, Oct. 4—A massive United Nations offensive jumped off at dawn yesterday in Central and Western Korea against an estimated quarter-million Communist troops.

The allied attacking force comprised elements of five divisions containing men of nine nations—Americans, Britons, Australians, New Zealanders, Canadians, Filipinos, Greeks, Turks and South Koreans. They stepped off after a heavy barrage.

The front where the battle is now raging stretches forty miles northeastward from near Korangpo, within twelve miles of Kaesong, the erstwhile truce-talk city.

[United Nations liaison officers flew to Panmunjom and received a message from the Communist High Command. Breaking a seven-day silence by the Communists, it was presumably an answer to Gen. Matthew B. Ridgway's request of Sept. 27 that cease-fire talks be resumed, but shifted from Kaesong.]

Big British Tanks in Action

The South Korean First Division troops gained their immediate objective on the extreme west of the battle line by early afternoon.

Eastward, on their right flank, the British Commonwealth Division, working under heavy artillery fire and supported by huge fifty-seven-ton Centurian tanks, apparently surprised the Reds and secured its objective west of Yonchon by 7 A. M.

Next, the Greek battalion and the United States First Cavalry Division, employing its Fifth and Seventh Regiments, struck hard at the enemy position in their sector, only to hit a solid wall of Communist resistance and a heavy rain of

Continued on Page 2, Column 3

World News Summarized

THURSDAY, OCTOBER 4, 1951

"Another atomic bomb has recently been exploded within the Soviet Union," the White House announced yesterday. By calling it "another" bomb, the White House was more precise than in its announcement of an atomic explosion in Russia two years ago. The statement said the new blast unmasked "Soviet pretensions" of peaceful atomic development [1:8.]

Western troops in Germany meanwhile opened large-scale maneuvers along routes an invading Soviet army might follow. [9:3-4.] Senator Lodge, saying North Atlantic nations were getting "little more than a trickle" of the arms they should, asked a Senate inquiry into the delay in shipping supplies. [17:1.]

The State Department barred a Swiss and a Dutch company from any part in this country's export trade for having violated controls over shipments to Soviet areas. [51:2-3.]

Britain evacuated her oil technicians from Abadan in Iran. [1:7.] She reported she had a $638,000,000 deficit in gold and dollar reserves in the third quarter of this year. [15:1.]

United Nations tanks and flame throwers pushed back stubbornly resisting Communists as much as two miles in Korea after a massive barrage had prepared the way for the troops. Details of the fighting on a forty-mile front were obscured by a partial news blackout. [1:5; map P. 2.]

A message on the truce negotiations came to General Ridgway from the Communist command. [3:1.]

Communist-led Vietminh troops opened an offensive in Indo-China. [1:6-7; map P. 5.]

Dr. Philip C. Jessup, before a Senate subcommittee considering his nomination as a member of this country's United Nations delegation, characterized as unqualifiedly "false" Senator McCarthy's charge that he had been "affiliated with six Communist fronts." Dr. Jessup presented evidence designed to refute other accusations. [1:6-7.] The State Department, in a second reply to Harold E. Stassen's testimony before another committee, admitted that military advice in 1949 to end aid to Chinese Nationalists had been rejected. [3:2-3.] Senate Republicans decided to oppose confirmation of Chester Bowles for Ambassador to India. [4:3.]

Senate-House conferees agreed on income tax provisions in the new revenue bill. [27:1.]

Inspection of income-tax returns for the last three years of all Internal Revenue officials and front-line enforcement officers has been ordered as a result of irregularities in the bureau. [1:4.] A Senate subcommittee heard charges that Democratic National Chairman Boyle had made payments to an R. F. C. employe. [25:1.]

Workers in 450 Bronx apartment houses struck for higher pay and threatened to spread the walkout. [1:2-3.]

The New York Giants, by a ninth-inning rally, beat the Brooklyn Dodgers, 5 to 4, in the third play-off game for the National League pennant. The Giants will meet the New York Yankees, American League champions, in the first world series game at the Stadium today. [1:1.]

Index to other news appears on last page of this section.

SOVIET'S SECOND ATOM BLAST IN 2 YEARS REVEALED BY U. S.; DETAILS ARE KEPT A SECRET

ANSWERING CHARGES BY M'CARTHY

Dr. Philip C. Jessup, Ambassador at Large, before a Senate Foreign Relations subcommittee yesterday. The New York Times

Jessup Denies Any Red Ties, Calls McCarthy Charge False

By WILLIAM S. WHITE
Special to The New York Times.

WASHINGTON, Oct. 3—Ambassador at Large Philip C. Jessup produced documentary evidence today to show that he followed an isolationist position in World War II long after the Communists had reversed themselves and had come out for aid to the Allies.

Under oath he denounced as false, in general and in every detail, the accusations of Senator Joseph R. McCarthy, Republican of Wisconsin, that he had been associated with six Communist fronts and had followed the Communist line in the past.

He testified before a Senate Foreign Relations subcommittee that is considering his nomination by President Truman to be a member of the United States delegation to the United Nations.

Some hours later, the State Department, after rechecking its records, acknowledged that there was a White House conference in February, 1949, at which Congressional leaders objected to a halt in United States arms aid to Nationalist China.

The department's statement was a reversal of its stand yesterday when it said that Harold E. Stassen's memory was "playing him tricks" at the time he said that such a conference had been held.

America First Links Cited

Dr. Jessup told the subcommittee that if in 1940 and thereabouts he had taken a Communist view, as had been charged to him by Senator McCarthy, then so had the isolationist organization called America First and such of its backers as Col. Robert R. McCormick of The Chicago Tribune.

He had remained active in America First, he testified, until the Japanese attack on the United

Continued on Page 3, Column 4

BRITISH EVACUATE STAFF FROM IRAN

Remaining Oil Technicians Are Withdrawn Without Incident From Abadan Refinery

Special to The New York Times.

TEHERAN, Iran, Oct. 3—The evacuation of the remaining British personnel of the Anglo-Iranian Oil Company took place today without incident in an atmosphere of stiff cordiality.

The first contingent to leave Abadan went out on a British airliner at 8:40 A. M. It included nineteen women, of whom sixteen were trained nurses.

The rest, numbering about 300, were taken aboard the British cruiser Mauritius, which was lying off Abadan on the Iraqi side of the Shatt-al-Arab River. After cursory customs formalities at the British Gymkhana Club—no cases were opened—the men were ferried out to the Mauritius in launches flying the Iranian flag. The launches, provided by the Iranian Navy, had once been Royal Air Force rescue boats.

The British staff left Iranian soil from the No. 1 jetty, the first to be built by their company forty-four years ago. The area was cordoned off by Iranian naval, military and police detachments.

At 1:40 P. M. the Mauritius

Continued on Page 11, Column 1

Vietminh Opens Indo-China Drive; Captures 2 Strong Points in North

By The Associated Press.

SAIGON, Indo-China, Oct. 3—The Communist-led Vietminh insurgent army has launched its long-awaited fall offensive with two swift tactical gains in northwest Indo-China.

The French announced tonight the loss of strong points eighty miles apart in the mountainous country west of the upper Red River.

Three battalions of rebel infantrymen struck southwestward from Laokay, a Red River stronghold on Communist China's frontier, and seized the fortress town of Binhlu as its garrison withdrew thirty miles to Laichau, capital of the Thai Federation.

About eighty miles to the southeast, a column of eight to ten battalions overran an outpost guarding the Thai country's largest town, Nghialo.

The Vietminh leader, Moscow-trained Ho Chi Minh, already has won hundreds of square miles of territory, including vital sections of the China-Indo-China frontier, with troops the French declare were trained and armed in Communist China.

The United States is helping arm the French and their Vietnam allies for the showdown battles. A shipload of United States Army Garand rifles, ammunition and 100 Army trucks was delivered here Monday for the Vietnam troops, nearing four divisions.

A French communiqué suggested Ho Chi Minh's westward push might be aimed at seizing rice crops in the Thai valleys. Control by the French of plantations along the Red River has cut into Vietminh food supplies. The rich delta country between Hanoi, the capital of North Vietnam, and its seaport of Haiphong remains in French hands.

The Thai country, though lightly defended, affords the French one of their two remaining windows on the frontier of Communist China. The other is at Monkay, on the Tongking Gulf.

United States-built Hellcat and Bearcat fighters and B-26 bombers

Continued on Page 5, Column 3

SPEED HERE URGED

White House Says Event Discounts Peace Aims Voiced by Stalin

STRESSES SECURITY ANGLE

Time and Place of Explosion Are Withheld—Capital Is Surprised by Report

By W. H. LAWRENCE
Special to The New York Times.

WASHINGTON, Oct. 3—Soviet scientists and military men succeeded recently in exploding "another atomic bomb" inside the Soviet Union, the White House announced today. All details on the location and scope of the blast were ordered withheld on the ground that disclosure of the information would affect adversely United States security interest.

News of the atomic experiment was made public by Joseph Short, White House Press Secretary, who declared that the event belied persistent Communist propaganda, led personally by Premier Stalin, that the atomic energy development of the Soviet Union was being devoted exclusively to peaceful purposes and not to the manufacture of weapons.

The White House statement said flatly that the latest explosion was "another atomic bomb" and thus was much more precise than was President Truman's announcement Sept. 23, 1949 of the first Russian blast. At that time Mr. Truman reported that "we have evidence that within recent weeks an atomic explosion occurred in the U. S. S. R."

News Not Unexpected

Today's announcement took most of Washington by surprise, but it was received much more calmly than Mr. Truman's original announcement that the Russians had solved the secret of controlling the explosion of the atom and thus had ended the monopoly enjoyed by the United States in the field of atomic warfare.

On Capitol Hill, legislators concerned with pushing the United States atomic and hydrogen bomb program ahead faster said the news was not unexpected but that it underlined the need for speed in developing both offensive and defensive weapons and in perfecting United States civil defense planning.

Mr. Short said that President Truman had directed him to emphasize "that the second explosion increased the necessity "for that effective, enforceable international control of atomic energy which the United States and a large majority of the members of the United Nations support." The Soviet Union had blocked United Nations agreement on such a program.

Keeping the People Informed

Mr. Short said that the President had directed him to make public the fact of the new Russian explosion "in accordance with the policy of the President to keep the American people informed to the fullest extent consistent with our national security." But he added that "further details cannot be given without adversely affecting our national security interests."

There was, therefore, no official information available as to when or where the latest experimental blast had occurred and no disclosure as to how the United States Government had found out about it. It is known, of course, that each atomic blast sends clouds of radioactivity through the atmosphere and these can be detected with sensitive instruments hundreds and thousands of miles from the scene of the explosion.

It was possible too that seismographs might have detected the explosion if they were operating close enough to the scene of the blast, presumably somewhere in Siberia.

But whether the news of the latest Russian bomb was detected by high-flying B-29's or by United States espionage agents was not disclosed.

Despite the White House ban on detailed information, The Associated Press quoted an unnamed source, whom it described as authoritative, as h... reported that

Continued on Page 3, Column 2

Homer Wiped Out Stigma of Play-off Hero's Boner

GIANTS ANNEX FLAG ON THOMSON HOMER

Continued From Page 1

row, the Giants plugged away grimly for weeks to make up the lost ground. But as late as Aug. 11 they were still thirteen and a half games behind the high-flying Brooks who, hailed by experts as the "wonder team" of the modern age, threatened to win by anywhere from fifteen to twenty lengths.

Then, on Aug. 12 began the great surge. Sixteen games were won in a row and from there the Polo Grounders rolled on to finish in a deadlock with the Dodgers at the close of the regular schedule. Majestically they swept ahead on Monday in the opener of the three-game play-off series in Brooklyn. Then disaster engulfed them as they came to the Polo Grounds Tuesday to be buried under a 10-0 score.

And they were still struggling to get out from under as late as the ninth inning yesterday when Thomson, whose two-run homer had won on Monday, exploded his No. 32 of the year that ended it all.

In the stretch from Aug. 12 until yesterday's pennant-clincher Durocher's minions hung up the almost incredible record of thirty-nine victories, against only eight defeats, an achievement to match that of the Miracle Braves of 1914.

The pennant is the sixteenth in the long history of the Giants, who captured their first two flags back in the late Eighties under Jim Mutrie, who also gave them their nickname. Under John J. McGraw they won ten in a span that began in 1904 and ended in 1924, when the Little Napoleon became the first manager in history to win four in a row.

In 1933 Bill Terry, a spectator at yesterday's game, piloted the Giants to the top again and repeated it in 1936 and 1937. Since then, however, the years have been lean and bleak, until the fiery Leo the Lip came through for them this year. The Giants thus tied the sixteen-pennant record of the Chicago Cubs in the National League.

The clincher was a struggle that should live long in the memory of the fans who saw it, as well as those who had it portrayed for them by radio and television in a coast-to-coast hook-up.

And many a night will Bob Thomson recall that, despite his game-winning homer, his third hit of the day, he might well have wound up the "goat" of the game by reason of some blind base running back in the second inning, when the Giants were trailing, 1—0.

Nor will Sal Maglie, the Barber, soon forget those agonizing moments he spent directly after the Giants had wrenched a run away from Newcombe in the seventh to tie the score at one-all. The Dodgers laced him for three runs in the top of the eighth, the first coming in on a wild pitch.

But the most poignant memory of all will be that which hapless Chuck Dressen, the Brooks' pilot, will carry with him for years to come. His club had blown a thirteen-and-a-half game lead. But all this would have been forgotten and forgiven had Branca held that margin in the last of the ninth.

He Follows the "Book"

But with one out and runners on second and third Dressen, as daring a gamester as Durocher, chose to follow the "book." He refused to walk Thomson because that would have represented the "winning run." Yet behind Bobby was Willie Mays, a dismal failure throughout the series and behind that the Giants had even less to offer. It's something the second guessers will hash over through many a winter evening.

For seven innings this was a bitter mound duel between Newcombe, seeking his twenty-first victory, and Maglie, gunning for his twenty-fourth. In the end neither figured in the decision. For it was Branca who was tagged with the defeat while the triumph went to Larry Jansen, who pitched for the Giants in the ninth when the cause seemed lost.

Larry retired three batters in a row and the Dodgers, three runs in front, thought absolutely nothing of it. They were certain they had this one in the bag.

The Blast That Won Pennant

Bobby Thomson following through on his home run. The catcher is Al Walker and the umpire Lou Jorda. The New York Times

But a few minutes later Jansen was jubilantly stalking off the field in possession of his twenty-third triumph, fitting tribute at that, considering that the tall right-hander from Oregon had pitched the 3-2 victory over the Braves last Sunday to send the race into the play-offs.

A momentary break in control put Maglie a run behind in the first inning when, with one out, he walked Pee Wee Reese and Duke Snider, the latter on four straight pitches. Jackie Robinson followed with a single to drive in the Dodger captain.

From then through the seventh, Maglie pitched magnificently. But not until the last of the seventh were the Giants able to match that Brooklyn run that kept taunting them on the scoreboard. With one out in the second, Whitey Lockman singled and Thomson blasted a line drive down the left field line.

Lockman had to pull up at second, but Thomson kept on running until he, too, was almost on top of second. He was promptly run down and that wrecked that rally.

In the fifth the indomitable Thomson got a double because there was no one in front of him to watch. But that availed nothing. For there was one out and Mays fanned. After Wes Westrum walked, Maglie grounded out.

Finally in the seventh the Giants made it and again it was Thomson's bat that played the decisive stroke.

Monte Irvin opened with a double. He advanced to third on Whitey Lockman's attempted sacrifice on which the Dodgers retired nobody and a moment later Thomson lifted a high fly to Snider in dead center to bring Irvin over the plate.

The Giants at long last were even, but victory was shunted far into the background when Maglie faltered in the eighth. Reese singled, went to third on Snider's single and scored on a wild pitch.

Following an intentional pass to Robinson came a scratch hit off Thomson's glove by Andy Pafko to drive in another run and then Bill Cox rifled one past Thomson to fetch in the third tally of the inning.

The Scot, converted into a third baseman by Durocher in midseason, certainly seemed to be moving in the center of everything in this great struggle.

In the last of the eighth the stunned Giants were three easy outs for Newcombe, who had a four-hitter going. In the top of the ninth hardly anyone paid attention as Jansen polished off three Dodgers in a row.

Wait for Final Outs

Through eight innings the Dodgers gave Newcombe brilliant support afield. Cox was a stone wall at third. Reese was an artist at short. Robinson made a great play on a wide throw from left by Pafko to save a run. Hodges made a leaping catch of a rifled shot over first. In the ninth of course, the Dodgers couldn't do much about it. There's no defense against home runs.

Jubilant Brooklyn fans were waiting for just "three more outs." Even the most devout of Giant diehards were preparing to slink out as quietly as possible. Their pets had waged a great uphill fight, but to win it all, perhaps, was just a trifle too much to expect.

Then Alvin Dark raised a feeble hope as he opened this last ditch stand by banging a sharp single off Gil Hodges' glove. Don Mueller, who was to wind up a casualty in the inning, slammed another single into right. To a deep groan, Monte Irvin popped out. But Whitey Lockman rammed a double into left, with Mueller racing to third. As Don slid into the bag he sprained his left ankle and the Giant outfielder had to be carried off the field on a stretcher.

At this point Dressen made his two most momentous decisions. Deciding that Newcombe, who had hurled fourteen and two-third innings to keep the flock in the race over Saturday and Sunday in Philadelphia, could go no further, he called in Branca.

Then, following a further consultation, it was decided that though first base was open, Big Ralph was to pitch to the Scot.

It was a decision that in a few more minutes was to bring to a suprising end the tremendous struggle which had been going on for 157 games.

Branca fearlessly fired the first strike past Robert.

What he tossed on the next pitch brought a varied assortment of opinion even from those most involved. But there was no doubt about where it went.

It sailed into the lower left-field stand a little beyond the 315 foot mark. The ball, well tagged, had just enough lift to clear the high wall.

And with that Leo Durocher almost leaped out of his shoes as he shrieked and danced on the coaching line.

Now Leo the Lip, who as manager of the Dodgers fought the Yankees in 1941 in a world series and lost, will try it again, and with one of the most extraordinary Giant teams in the long history of baseball on the banks of the Harlem.

GIANT FANS DANCE AS DODGERS MOURN

Continued From Page 1

board drawn on the Dodgers' window, he kept crying, "I can't believe it! I can't believe it!"

In Manhattan, the Giants' victory was signaled about 3:58 P. M. by a concerted blowing of automobile horns as fans got the news on their car radios. The taverns suddenly emptied of men who had been nursing beer for hours while watching the television screen.

The Giants rooters whooped and danced about jubilantly in the streets, while the morose Dodgermen walked away quickly and silently.

In Harlem, the loyalties of the populace were divided between the Dodgers and the Giants since each team has Negro players. Perhaps the Dodgers were a slight favorite since Brooklyn was first in the major leagues to hire a Negro player, Jackie Robinson.

Cheer Heroes on Television

The bar of the Theresa Hotel, Seventh Avenue and 125th Street, in the heart of Harlem, was jammed with intense men and women watching three television screens. When Robinson or Monte Irvin, the Giants' slugger, would come to bat, their rooters would shout affectionate encouragement to the images on the flickering screens.

The bars in the Times Square area were crowded to the doors. As usual, also, draft beer in many taverns was shut off during the game, and bottled beer, at 35 cents a bottle, substituted.

Uncountable housewives neglected their chores to sit before TV screens. Hundreds of thousands of their husbands left their work at intervals to rush back into the shipping department, where the boys had a portable radio. In some offices, the executives complained, it seemed more accurate to say that their staffs tore themselves away from the radio at intervals to make quick stabs at work.

As soon as the game ended, Borough President James J. Lyons of the Bronx, a Yankee rooter, telephoned his "condolences" to Borough President John Cashmore of Brooklyn. The Borough President of the Bronx told the Borough President of Brooklyn to go fly his flags at half-staff.

Then Mr. Lyons, in high humor, phoned Borough President Robert F. Wagner Jr. of Manhattan, who is a Giant fan, and bet him a crew haircut on the world series, starting today. If the Giants win, Mr. Lyons will have his locks shorn, whereas if the Yankees win, it will be a close shave for Mr. Wagner.

Fans Arrive Early

Eight thousand fans were lined up before the ticket windows at the Polo Grounds when the sale of unreserved seats for yesterday's game opened at 10:15 A. M. Many of them had been waiting since dawn. Thirteen eager fans were counted as early as 2 A. M., eight at the grandstand window, four at the bleacher gate and one eccentric who specializes in crashing big games.

He was Irving Aks, 21 years old, a florist, who lives at 488 New Jersey Avenue, Brooklyn. It is unnecessary to say what team Mr. Aks was rooting for. He carried a wreath labeled "Sympathy to the Giants" over the fence about 8:30 A. M. despite a patrol of more than 100 policemen, and had his picture taken by the news photographers.

The line at the unreserved grandstand seat window was led by four students from Benjamin Franklin High School, who said they had camped there since midnight, with pillows, blankets, sandwiches and a deck of cards. The fanatics at the bleachers window were headed by Robert Berman, 32, of 207 West Eighty-seventh Street, a Dodger from Manhattan, who also bivouacked on the sidewalk with a blanket from midnight on. Mr. Berman has been faithfully rooting for the Brooks from the bleachers for the last three days.

Weather Cuts Crowd

All reserved seats were sold out at 9:40 A. M. The disappointed patrons on that line rushed to join queues outside the unreserved seat windows. Nevertheless, such heroic efforts to get into the park proved unnecessary, since sizable blocks of seats in the upper left and right field stands remained empty throughout the game. Officials of the Polo Grounds attributed their failure to sell out to the dark and threatening weather.

Sales of tickets for the world series began yesterday morning at the Giants' office, 100 West Forty-second Street, long before the issue of whether the Giants were to play in the series was settled. When the office closed at 5:30 P. M., half of the 5,000 reserved seats at the Polo Grounds for the third, fourth and fifth games had been sold at $18 the set.

Some patrons refused to buy when they discovered the best locations offered were rear rows of right and left field.

RODE 'ON A CLOUD' ON TOUR OF BASES

Thomson 'Even Loves Dressen' After Wallop in Ninth—Cites Club's Spirit

By BOBBY THOMSON
As Told to The United Press

I didn't run around the bases—I rode around 'em on a cloud.

Wow, I still don't know what time it is or where I am! Frankly I don't care.

Going around those bases in the ninth inning, I just couldn't believe what was happening to me. It felt as if I was actually living one of those middle-of-the-night dreams. You know, everything was hazy.

I heard yells . . . I saw paper flying . . . I noticed people jumping in the air but through it all I just kept riding high on that cloud.

After I swung, I knew I had hit the ball well but I wasn't sure at all that it was gone. It seemed to me it was sinking as it neared the stands, but how could I be sure? I just kept riding until I came to the end of the line.

While I'm about it, I'd like to point out that this ball club never gave up . . . not even after Brooklyn got three runs in the eighth. We all felt we would still win.

But, I don't want to write in too serious a vein now. I feel too light and happy for that.

National League

YESTERDAY'S PLAY-OFF
New York 5, Brooklyn 4

FINAL STANDING OF CLUBS

	New York	Brooklyn	St. Louis	Boston	Philadel.	Cincinnati	Pittsb'gh	Chicago	Won	Lost	Perc'tage	Games Behind
N. Y.	—	11	11	14	16	17	14	15	98	59	.624	—
Bklyn.	14	—	18	12	15	14	10	14	97	60	.618	1
St. L.	11	4	—	9	13	14	17	13	81	73	.526	15½
Bost.	8	10	13	—	12	10	13	10	76	78	.494	20½
Phila.	6	7	9	10	—	11	15	15	73	81	.474	23½
Cinc.	5	8	8	12	11	—	12	12	68	86	.442	28½
Pitts.	8	12	5	9	7	10	—	13	64	90	.416	32½
Chic.	7	8	9	12	7	10	9	—	62	92	.403	34½
Lost	59	60	73	78	81	86	90	92	—	—		

Dodgers' Pennant Failure Finds Players Despondent

O'MALLEY PUTS OFF TALK ON MANAGER

Dodgers' President Says He'll Make Statement About Next Year's Pilot After Series

SKIPPER SEEMS CONFIDENT

Dressen Reviews Bad 'Breaks' —Branca and Newcombe Downcast in Clubhouse

By ROSCOE McGOWEN

Two fellows were able to summon a smile in the Dodger dressing room yesterday after the unbelievable finish of the most fantastic pennant race in major league baseball history.

One was Walter O'Malley, president and part owner of the defeated Brooks, who, incidentally, was the first visitor to get into the Giants' quarters to congratulate Leo Durocher and his team.

The other was Chuck Dressen, Dodger manager, who is even more of an extrovert than the rival manager whose story-book club beat the Brooks in a ninth-inning finale that not even the dizziest script writer would dream up.

Other Dodgers were down—deep down. Buzzie Bavasi, vice president and general manager of the Brooks, was sick at heart and looked it—plus.

Ralph Branca, who threw the fatal home-run pitch to Bobby Thomson, did manage to summon a wan smile as he slowly got into his street clothes in front of his locker.

"I guess we weren't meant to win it," he sighed. "The ball was high and inside, not a good pitch," he added, "and it only cleared the wall by that much." He spread his arms in a gesture that indicated a matter of inches.

Dressen, who followed O'Malley into the Giants' dressing room to congratulate Durocher, seemed to have seen the big pitch differently.

Pilot Calls It Belt-High

"It was about here," said Charley, indicating a spot just a little above his belt. But high, low, inside or outside didn't matter much by that time.

What may matter now is how the biggest pennant "bust" in National League annals will affect the fortunes of Dressen.

Naturally, numerous writers brought that subject up in one way or another in talking to O'Malley, and the Dodger head man's reply was frank, or cryptic, depending upon the interpretation of his various listeners.

Asked if there was "any fair reason for the undercurrent of talk that Dressen's job is in jeopardy," O'Malley replied:

"No, there is no fair reason. The manager's job did not depend upon the outcome of this game." Then O'Malley went on:

"I don't think it would be fair to encroach on the world series with anything we might have to say. Some time after the series is over I'll get all the writers together and we'll have something to say then."

"Does that mean," the writer asked O'Malley, "that what you'll have to say then will be about next year's manager?"

Still smiling—with his face, but possibly not with his eyes—O'Malley siad, "Yes, it will," and added nothing more.

In the light of Dressen's comments about the excellence of the team he took over after Burt Shotton was deposed—for instance, "they tell me this was the best team in the league last year, and if that's true I see no reason why they shouldn't win the pennant this year"—some listeners read into O'Malley's remarks a significance that perhaps wasn't there.

O'Malley, Bavasi, Fresco Thompson and all the executive Brooklyn family picked Dressen unanimously. Despite what has happened—the unexpected loss of the flag by a team that was rated a "shoo-in" even two weeks before Sept. 30—it doesn't necessarily follow that Dressen won't pilot the club again next year.

Charley himself didn't act at all like a man who had just lost his job. On the contrary, the little skipper, never lacking in self-confidence, behaved little differently than would have been the case had the Dodgers lost a mid-season game rather than a pennant.

Dark's Hit "Break"

Chuck still was willing to talk about "breaks" of the game, one of which he said was Alvin Dark's opening ninth-inning single—Dark's second hit in the three-game play-off.

"It was just a protective swing," said Dressen. "And he just got it out of Hodges' reach. If Gil could have held the ball in his glove Dark would have been out."

Asked about Don Newcombe, who, after he was taken out, came into the clubhouse with his head down and looking at nobody, Dressen said Newk had tired.

"He tired in the seventh and then came back stronger in the eighth," said the manager. "But in the ninth he couldn't do it, so I brought Branca in."

Asked whether he had considered walking Thomson purposely, Dressen said he would have "if the situation had been right."

Chuck said there were two strikes and no balls against Bobby, which wasn't correct. Actually, Branca threw one called strike, and it was the next pitch that Thomson lined into the stands.

So far as the Dodger collapse goes—and perhaps the extraordinary Giant surge should be considered more than Brooklyn's "collapse," the best answer was supplied by a Dodger regular, who was quoted anonymously in these columns before the play-off series began.

Now he may as well be identified. It was Carl Furillo, the competent right fielder of the Brooks, who said, referring to the fact that the Dodgers had reached the point where a play-off was necessary:

"When you've got something right in your hand, and then you drop it yourself, with nobody pushing you—well, that ain't good, is it?"

No, it "ain't good," and a lot of Dodgers, who won't be banking the world series share they had all but deposited, won't forget about it for a long, long time.

In the Giants' clubhouse after the game. In the front left is Don Mueller, who was injured in the ninth inning. The others, left to right, are Coach Fred Fitzsimmons, Pitcher Larry Jansen, Thomson and President Horace Stoneham. The New York Times

SCOT MAKES LIGHT OF DECIDING BLOW

'Hit a Bad Pitch Because I Had to Do Something,' Says Bobby Thomson

WILD SCENE IN CLUBHOUSE

Happy Giants Are Besieged by Well-Wishers—All Ready to Battle the Yanks

By JAMES P. DAWSON

"If I was a good hitter I'd have taken that one."

That's what Bobby Thomson said in the clubhouse yesterday after his three-run homer had ended the third play-off game and plunged the Giants into the world series against the Yankees.

Thomson was just trying to make light of the most exciting moment in his life.

He was shouting actually and even then he could hardly be heard above the din raised by the jubilant Giant team.

The dressing room was crowded with club executives, league officials, friends, admirers, newspaper men, photographers, movie operators, radio and television men.

Counted out of the pennant race a fortnight ago, the Giants really let go in celebration of this movie-script finish to one of the most spectacular pennant dashes in the league's history.

Thomson, like the other Giants, had to fight his way to the clubhouse. The public address system announcement in the ninth inning, when the Dodgers were leading, 4 to 1, said, "following the game nobody will be allowed on the field until the players have reached the clubhouse."

Crowds on the Field

But nobody paid any attention to that order. Finally, the players reached the dressing room. Dr. Anthony Palermo, who was helping the boys celebrate, had two calls to aid heart-attack victims in the emergency station under the stands.

Outside a crowd of several thousand gathered at the clubhouse steps. "We want Thomson," was the chant. "We want Stanky," it continued. "We want Maglie," on and on it went while a detail of police, under Deputy Inspector Cornelius Lyons, barred the door.

In desperation the police appealed to the players. "They won't leave until they see you," was their plea. And not until each player had appeared on top of the steps and the wild, rampant joy of the fans had run its course, did the crowd disperse.

"What a finish," said Thomson, echoing the sentiment of every player and visitor. "Imagine being lucky enough to win a ball game that way. And, it wasn't a good pitch. It was high and inside, the kind they've been getting me out on all season.

"But I had to do something. I had messed things up pretty much earlier. I don't imagine I looked too good running wild on the bases in the second after Whitey (Lockman) had singled. I really pulled a rock that time. But I thought my single was going to hit the wall and Whitey would reach third. So I just kept right on going, running with my head down, so that I didn't see Fitz (Coach Freddie Fitzsimmons) trying to flag me down. All I was thinking was that we needed a run to tie and with another run in scoring position we could go in front.

"I was to blame in that one. But maybe the homer made up for it. I know it gave me the thrill of my life. I don't ever expect to hit another just like it."

Durocher was speechless. That's a switch. He was so thoroughly overcome he couldn't say a thing when the inquisitors stormed at him. All he could do was smilingly acknowledge the congratulations which came to him from all sides.

Tears of joy were in the eyes of President Horace Stoneham, who was in the clubhouse to greet his manager. He had gone down from his office in the eighth inning to sympathize with a weary, saddened Maglie, while Larry Jansen was out there turning the Dodgers back, one-two-three in the upper half of the ninth.

"We can get some runs, too," optimistically shouted the Giant executive as he left his guests. He sat with Maglie, looking through the clubhouse screened windows as the drama unfolded—and then was overcome with joy and engulfed in the turmoil of the celebration.

Stoneham's prophecy had come true, more spectacularly than he had imagined or expected. He clutched Durocher in a fond embrace when the pilot reached the dressing quarters.

Leo folded his arms about his adopted son, Cris, five and one-half years old, who was at his knee, clad in a baby Giant uniform. "You did it, sonny, boy, you did it," Durocher exclaimed as he crushed the smiling boy to him.

"He said to me this morning, Daddy let me come out and put my suit on, we'll win. I'm good luck. And I let him come out for the first time in the play-offs and we won.

"Now we take on the Yanks. I'll pitch Dave Koslo tomorrow. Then it will be Jansen. Then Jim Hearn. Then Maglie. We're ready."

Chuck Dressen of the Dodgers forced his way through the crowd to congratulate Durocher. There was a trace of tears in Dressen's eyes as he gripped Durocher's hand and shook it in the gesture of a good loser for a good winner.

"Somebody had to win," said Charlie. "And if it couldn't be me, I'm glad it was you. Now go out and beat those Yankees four straight."

REYNOLDS OPPOSES KOSLO AT STADIUM

Yankees to Pit Double No-Hit Pitcher Against Giants in Opener of Classic Today

By LOUIS EFFRAT

It's world series time—and about time.

The delayed 1951 classic, the first between the Yankees and Giants since 1937, will get under way at 1 P. M. today at the Stadium, with the teams battling for the richest prizes in diamond history.

Excluding even the $1,185,000 for television and radio (it goes into the players' pension fund) the receipts from the best-of-seven series are likely to surpass any figures achieved in the past.

Leo Durocher, his game, fearless athletes yesterday having earned the right to oppose the American League champions, will start Dave Koslo, veteran southpaw, with a 10-won, 9-lost regular season record. Casey Stengel, whose Yankees had had to sit by three extra days to learn the identity of their National League opponent, will counter with Double No-Hit Allie Reynolds (17—8).

The consecutive schedule calls for the first two games to be played at the Stadium. The site of the struggle then will shift across the Harlem River to the Polo Grounds, home of the Giants, for the third, fourth and, if necessary, fifth contests. Should other games be needed, these will be played at the Stadium.

Warm weather has been forecast and all is in readiness for the inaugural. Stadium Superintendent Charles McManus yesterday directed all personnel through a rehearsal. Electricians, ushers and others who will strive to make everyone comfortable went through their paces, after the Yankee players, trying to remain loose, had completed their final practice session on the field. All the Bombers are in fine condition.

Button Keeps Olympic Figure-Skating Title, With U. S. Also Third and Fourth

ENGLEWOOD YOUTH DEFEATS AUSTRIAN

Button's Daring Skating Beats Seibt With Ease—Grogan Is Third and Jenkins Fourth

GERMAN 4-MAN BOB LEADS

Benham's American Sled Next After Two Heats—Sweden Halts U. S. at Hockey

By GEORGE AXELSSON

Special to THE NEW YORK TIMES.

OSLO, Feb. 21—Dick Button of Englewood, N. J., won a fourth gold medal for the United States, as generally expected, in the men's figure skating decided tonight at Bislett Stadium, but otherwise this eighth day of the sixth winter Olympics was not favorable for America.

The ice hockey team dropped back in the round-robin tournament, losing two valuable points to Sweden, and after the first two of the four heats in the four-man bob event down the Frognerseteren course, the "meat trust," as the American sled No. 1 affectionately is nicknamed because of its aggregate weight, was second to the German No. 1 driver who had downed them in the boblet event.

Sudden springlike weather, raising the mercury above 60 degrees Fahrenheit at noon, was a source of worry to officials and competitors. The thaw rendered the bobsledding course, which faces due south, soft on top, so the third heat will have to be staged one hour earlier than originally scheduled tomorrow morning before the ice starts melting.

French Youth Applauded

Button's figure-skating victory had been forecast by his magnificent showing in the compulsory figures earlier in the week, so only a small crowd showed up to watch him and thirteen other contestants from eleven nations compete for the Olympic title. As in yesterday's free skating for women, the bulk of the applause went not to the winner, but to a representative from France.

In this case it was diminutive Alain Giletti, the 12-year-old boy who skates like a true champion and can show most of the adults among the world's elite a trick or two, as he did today.

Placings after the compulsory figures were unchanged by today's performances. Austria's Hellmut Seibt was second, with an American, James David Grogan of Colorado Springs, taking third place. A third member of the United States figure-skating team, Hayes Alan Jenkins of Akron, added three points to America's over-all point score by taking fourth place.

The four-man bob situation after the first two heats is analagous to what it was at the same stage in the boblet category. The German No. 1 sled is leading America's No. 1 by a fraction of one second, but a smaller fraction than in the boblet.

Swiss Third and Fourth

The combined times for the morning's two runs were for Germany 2 minutes 31.43 seconds and for the United States 2:35.22. Switzerland's No. 1 was third with 2:36.75 and the Swiss No. 2 fourth with 2:37.20. The American bob was driven by Stanley D. Benham of Lake Placid, N. Y., who was accompanied by Patrick H. Martin of Massena, N. Y.; Howard W. Crossett of Bradford, N. H., and James N. Atkinson of Hamilton, N. Y.

The United States No. 2 bob, driven by James J. Bickford of Saranac Lake, N. Y., and manned by Hubert G. Miller of Saranac Lake, Maurice R. Severino of Saratoga Springs, N. Y., and Joe Scott of Ausable Forks, N. Y., had an unlucky day. In the first heat, a stirrup on the left front broke on the first curve. Bickford had difficulty in holding the sled on the track.

The stirrup was welded during the intermission, but broke again on the first curve in the second heat. In spite of that, Bickford was ninth among fifteen sleds with a two-heat time of 2:39.10.

The Germans, with Andreas Ostler driving, lopped valuable fractions of a second from their running time with perfect starts and expert taking of curves.

Canadians Stay Unbeaten

In the ice hockey tournament, Canada and Sweden continued undefeated and were tied for first place, each with five victories in as many games. Canada trounced Switzerland, 11 to 2, in a dull game that looked more like an exhibition than an Olympic contest.

Then the American team, which had won its first four games, skated out o nthe Jordal rink a decided favorite over the Swedes, but Sweden won, 4 to 2. The game hadn't been in progre. s many minutes before it was plain where the victory was headed.

The American boys seemed to have mislaid their passing somewhere and hence became easy prey to a Swedish defense which easily broke up most attacks. The Swedes scored their first goal—by Hans Oeberg—after 12 minutes of the first period.

While the match at no point got rough, the usual minor incidents occurred. In the first period, Sweden's Goesta Johansson and the United States' John Noah clashed and went to the penalty box for two minutes each for high sticking.

The second period was scoreless. Play was swift and the puck traveled back and forth, but mostly in United States territory. The Swedes made a goal in the seventh minute which was disallowed because a Swedish player was inside America's cage when the puck was netted. America's Gerald Kilmartin drew a 2-minute penalty for holding.

The United States team opened the third period in rapid fashion in a bid to tie the score, but Joseph Czarnota drew two minutes in the box for elbowing. Czarnota, whom the capacity crowd hadn't forgotten for his rough play in the match against the Swiss Tuesday, was booed.

The American team generally drew little applause with the stands full of Swedes rooting for their team and the few Americans among the spectators hopelessly drowned out. Despite the fury of the American attack, the Swedes opened the scoring in the last period, making it 2—0 as Goesta Johansson placed a beautiful shot right behind Donald Whiston.

Eight minutes later, Johansson again drove the puck into America's cage, but in another minute the Americans scored their first goal, Ken Yackel picking up Robert Rompre's pass and neatly evading the defense. With Aake Andersson off for hooking, the Americans were quick to take advantage of a weakened defense as Clifford Harrison quickly added the record goal, but Sweden retaliated in the twelfth minute.

Jeannette Altwegg, British brunette who won the Olympic figure-skating title last night, said she was retiring from competition and would not defend her world title in Paris next week. Jeannette does not plan to turn professional, as her predecessors, Canada's Barbara Ann Scott and Norway's Sonja Henie, did.

Miss Altwegg, from Streatham, began skating at the age of 6. She celebrated her victory by having chocolate ice cream, her favorite dish.

Button Captivates Judges

OSLO, Feb. 21 (UP)—Dick Button, America's incomparable figure skater, retained his Olympic championship tonight with one of the most glittering performances of his career.

Despite one stumble during a difficult spin, the handsome, 21-year-old Harvard senior from Englewood, N. J., captivated the stern judges with the daring of his free-skating routine.

Placed first by all nine judges, Button earned fourth United States gold medal of the games. With a total of 17 points picked up by the figure skaters, the Americans had a firm grip on second place in the unofficial team standings with 73½ points. Norway leads with 101, Austria is third with 56, Finland fourth at 41 and Germany fifth with 28.

Button was happy but not satisfied. His near fall piqued him.

"The ice is never bad," he said. "It's my own fault. Don't blame it on anything else."

But his veteran trainer, Gus Lussi, did blame the fumble on cracked ice as Button was executing one of the most difficult maneuvers on skates—three consecutive double axels.

Clad in a specially tailored white mess jacket and black trousers, Button skated with confidence to a recording of the "Rumanian Rhapsod[illegible] y Enesco.

The Sweden-U. S. hockey line-up:

SWEDEN—Goal: Flodquist; defense: Anderson, Johansson, Thunman, Almquist; forwards: Blomquist, G. Johansson, E. Johansson, S. Andersson, H. Andersson, Pettersson, Oeberg, S. Johansson, Nurmela.

UNITED STATES—Goal: Whiston; defense: Van, Czarnota, Noah, Sedin; forwards: Rompre, Kilmartin, Yackel, Ceglarski, Bjorkman, Gambucci, Harrison, Oss, Mulhern.

FIRST PERIOD—1, Sweden, Oeberg (Nurmela), 14.06.

Penalties—G. Johansson, 14:19; Noah, 14:19.

SECOND PERIOD—No scoring.

Penalties—Kilmartin, 7:01; Mulhern, 12:12.

THIRD PERIOD—2, Sweden, Goesta Johansson (unassisted) 1:47. 3, Sweden, Goesta Johansson (Erik Johannson) 7:57. 4, U. S. A., Yackel (Rompre) 8:09. 5, U. S. A., Harrison (Oss) 8:43. 6, Sweden, Nurmela (Sven Johansson) 11:31.

Penalties—Czarnota, 2:40; Andersson, 8:13; Ceglarski, 18:54.

Jaffee, Shea Score Doubles

Mrs. Andrea Mead Lawrence, who captured the women's slalom title on Wednesday at Oslo after having taken the giant slalom on Feb. 14, was not the first American ever to win twice in the same Winter Olympic Games, as was reported in THE NEW YORK TIMES yesterday. She was, however, the first woman to do so.

Doubles in speed skating were scored by both Irving Jaffee and Jack Shea in 1932. Jaffee prevailed in the 5,000 and 10,000 meter tests, while Shea won in the 500 and 1,500 meter events.

Kentucky Home Streak 110

LEXINGTON, Ky., Feb. 21 (UP)—Kentucky rolled over Vanderbilt, 75 to 45, tonight to finish its ninth straight undefeated home basketball season. The Wildcats also gained their 110th home-court victory in a row.

A FATHER CONGRATULATES HIS CHAMPION SON AT WINTER GAMES

Dick Button getting a playful nudge from George Button after the former's triumph. On the right is Gus Lussi, the figure skater's trainer.

Associated Press Radiophotos

The No. 1 United States bobsled team, composed of Stanley Benham of Lake Placid, N. Y.; Patrick H. Martin of Massena, N. Y.; Howard Crossett of Bradford, N. H., and James N. Atkinson of Hamilton, N. Y., in the competition yesterday in which they were runners-up to a German sled after the first two of four heats.

List of the Champions

OSLO, Feb. 20 (AP)—Here is a list of champions crowned in the sixth winter Olympics:

MEN

Giant Slalom Skiing—Stein Eriksen, Norway, 2:25.
Downhill Skiing—Zeno Colo, Italy, 2:30.8.
Two-Man Bobsled—Germany No. 1 (Andreas Ostler), 5:24.54.
500-Meter Speed Skating—Ken Henry, U. S. (Chicago), 0:43.2.
1,500-Meter Speek Skating—Hjalmar Andersen, Norway, 2:20.4.
*5,000-Meter Speed Skating—Hjalmar Andersen, Norway, 8:10.6.
Nordic combined (Ski Jump and Race)—Simon Slaatvik, Norway, 451.621 points.
18-Kilometer (11¼ Miles) Ski Race—Halgeir Brenden, Norway, 1:01.34.
Slalom Ski Race—Othmar Schneider, Austria, 2:00.
†10,000-Meter Speed Skating—Hjalmar Andersen, 16:45.8.
50-Kilometer Ski Race—Veikko Hakulinen, Finland, 3:33.33.
‡Figure Skating—Richard Button, U. S. (Englewood, N. J.), 192.256 points.

*Olympic record. †Olympic and world record. ‡Retained championship.

WOMEN

Giant Slalom Ski—Andrea Mead Lawrence, U. S. (Rutland, Vt.), 2:06.8.
Downhill Skiing — Trude Jochum Beiser, Austria, 1:47.1.
Slalom Ski Race—Andrea Mead Lawrence, U. S. (Rutland, Vt.), 2:10.6.
Figure Skating—Jeannette Altwegg, England, 161.760 points.

Winter Olympic Summaries

MEN'S FIGURE SKATING

By The Associated Press.

	Points.	Place Pts.
1—Richard Button, U. S.	192.256	9
2—Hellmut Seibt, Austria	180.144	23
3—Jimmy Grogan, U. S.	180.822	24
4—Hayes Jenkins, U. S.	174.589	40
5—Peter Firstbrook, Canada	173.122	43
6—Carlo Fassi, Italy	169.822	50
7—Alain Giletti, France	163.233	63
8—Xreimut Stein, Germany	155.956	72
9—Francois Pache, Switzerland	139.922	92
10—Adrian Swan, Australia	138.689	96

FOUR-MAN BOBSLED

FIRST TWO OF FOUR RUNS

	1st Run.	2d Run.	Total Time.
1—Germany No. 1	1:16.86	1:17.57	2:34.43
2—United States No. 1	1:17.44	1:17.78	2:35.22
3—Switzerland No. 1	1:18.67	1:18.08	2:36.75
4—Switzerland No. 2	1:17.75	1:19.45	2:37.20
5—Austria No. 1	1:19.34	1:18.91	2:38.25
6—Sweden No. 2	1:18.84	1:19.93	2:38.77
7—France No. 1	1:18.90	1:19.91	2:38.81
8—Sweden No. 1	1:19.11	1:19.90	2:39.01
9—United States No. 2	1:19.13	1:19.97	2:39.10
10—Austria No. 2	1:19.51	1:20.25	2:39.76

Drivers—1, Andreas Ostler; 2, Stan Benham, Lake Placid, N. Y.; 3, Feierabend; 4, Endrich; 5, Wagner; 6, Ahs; 7, Robin; 8, Holstrom; 9, Jim Bickford, Saranac Lake, N. Y.; 10, Luserth.

ICE HOCKEY

By The United Press.

Sweden 4, United States 2.
Canada 11, Switzerland 2.
Czechoslovakia 11, Finland 2.
Germany 6, Norway 2.

STANDING OF THE TEAMS

Team.	W.	L.	T.	Pts.	Goals For	Goals Ag'st
Canada	5	0	0	10	54	7
Sweden	5	0	0	10	41	10
United States	4	1	0	8	29	12
Switzerland	3	2	0	6	29	24
Switzerland	3	2	0	6	27	24
Germany	1	4	1	3	17	42
Finland	1	5	0	2	14	55
Poland	0	4	1	1	10	46
Norway	0	6	0	0	10	31

UNOFFICIAL TEAM SCORES

Based on 10 points for a first place, 5 for a second, 4 for a third, 3 for a fourth, 2 for a fifth and 1 for a sixth

Team.	Skiing.	Bobsled.	Skating.	Total Pts.
Norway	56	0	45	101
United States	26½	5	42	73½
Austria	51	0	5	56
Finland	37	0	4	41
Germany	18	10	0	28
Netherlands	0	0	24	24
Italy	23	0	1	24
Switzerland	7	7	0	14
Sweden	5½	0	8	13½
Britain	0	0	10	10
France	1	2	4	7
Canada	0	0	6½	6½
Belgium	0	1	0	1
Japan	0	0	½	½

Norway Premier Finds Criticism Of U.S. Hockey Tactics 'Ignorant'

OSLO, Feb. 21 (AP)—Prime Minister Oscar Torp of Norway, a pretty good soccer player in his day, rose to the defense of American and Canadian ice hockey tactics today, calling the blow-up over rough stuff in Tuesday night's game the result of "ignorance."

"Hockey is a new game here," Torp said. "Our big game is soccer and we don't understand the idea of these penalties in hockey."

The controversy, first serious one of the Winter Olympics, was touched off when Joe Czarnota, red-haired defenseman from Wakefield, Mass., took a couple of half-hearted swings at Switzerland's Gian Bazzi in the course of the game, won by the United States, 8—2.

As Czarnota skated to the penalty box, the Norwegian fans screamed "Chicago gangsters" and littered the ice with orange peels.

A Switzerland newspaper criticized the North Americans as "rowdies" and suggested that ice hockey probably should be dropped from the Olympic program unless such tactics were changed.

The ruling fathers of amateur hockey investigated Czarnota's case after the game and gave a clean bill of health to the American. Czarnota and Bazzi later shook hands and embraced each other, indicating no hard feelings.

"People should understand penalties make ice hockey a human game," Norway's Prime Minister added. "When the boys get so het up that they do something wrong or get too rough—give them two minutes to cool down and think it over."

Dr. Fritz Kratz of Zurich, president of the International Ice Hockey Federation, said he had seen the Canada-Czechoslovakia and United States-Swiss games and thought they weren't rowdy.

"If athletes in other Olympic sports came into bodily contact such as hockey players I'm convinced there would be plenty of so-called incidents," he declared.

Torp said he had been so busy with affairs of state so far he hadn't been able to see any of the Olympics, but he said he wouldn't miss Sunday night's game between the United States and Canada for anything.

Norwegian fans are expected to get a real load of contact work when those teams clash in the final game of the round-robin tournament.

Players of both teams will be warned to lay off the rough stuff by the International Ice Hockey Federation. But if the championship hinges on this game, some hard body-checking may be expected.

Canadians and Americans have been doing everything except bowing from the waist in "after you" fashion in games against Europeans. They may be expected to take off the gloves against each other.

Czarnota hit the Swiss player only on the arms, but it caused a wave of censure.

U. S. MATMEN BEATEN

Touring Japanese Team Scores Over All-Stars by 18-5

The touring Japanese national wrestling team, near the end of its invasion of the East, downed an American All-Star squad, 18—5, in an amatuer match staged at the New York Athletic Club.

Only man to score for the losers was Carmine Leggio of the home club who won on a forfeit from Yushu Kitano of Kero University in the 114½-pound class. The loser, who entered the match with his ribs bandaged was unable to continue.

Outstanding for the visitors was Maysayoshi Betto of Icelo Universit. Betto pinned Alan Rice, former Big Ten champion from the University of Minnesota, after fourteen minutes in a 147½-pound encounter. Rice held the advantage at the time of his fall.

Professional Basketball

NATIONAL ASSOCIATION

LAST NIGHT'S RESULT

Syracuse 88, Minneapolis 80.

STANDING OF THE TEAMS

EASTERN DIVISION

	W.	L.	PC.		W.	L.	PC.
Syracuse	34	18	.654	Philadelphia	24	28	.462
Boston	28	23	.549	Baltimore	16	37	.302
New York	29	25	.537				

WESTERN DIVISION

	W.	L.	PC.		W.	L.	PC.
Rochester	34	18	.654	Fort Wayne	24	30	.444
Minneapolis	33	22	.600	Milwaukee	15	39	.278
Indianapolis	29	26	.527				

Schedule Today

OSLO, Feb. 21 (AP)—The winter Olympic Games schedule for tomorrow (all times Eastern Standard):

3:30 A. M.—Four man bobsleds, final two heats, Frognersteren, U. S. No. 1 sled, Stan Benham, Pat Martin, Howard Crossett, Jim Atkinson; U. S. No. 2 sled, Jim Bickford, Hubert Miller, Maurice Severino, Joseph Scott.
8 A. M.—Ice hockey, Finland-Germany, Jordal Stadium.
11 A. M.—Ice hockey, Switzerland-Germany, Jordal Stadium.
1 P. M.—Ice hockey, U. S.-Poland, Daelenerga Rink; figure skating, couples, Bislett Stadium (U. S. pairs, Michael and Karol Kennedy, Seattle; John S. Nightingale, St. Paul, and Janet Gerhauser, Minneapolis).
3 P. M.—Ice hockey, Canada-Sweden, Jordal Stadium.

Bibbia Takes Bobsled Cup

ST. MORITZ, Switzerland, Feb. 21 (AP)—Nino Bibia of Italy, 1948 Olympic skeleton champion, won the Heaton Gold Cup on the cresta bobsled run here today in a field of twelve entries from six countries. Bibbia completed six runs down the one-mile course in a total of 277.9 seconds. Paul Arnold, Miami, Fla., was second in 278.1 seconds, followed by N. L. Barclay, England, in 281.9 seconds and E. G. Nelson, Honolulu in 282.9 seconds.

MANHATTAN UPSETS NEW YORK U., 74-66

Takes Overtime Thriller at Garden—St. John's Downs Cincinnati Five, 76-64

By JOSEPH M. SHEEHAN

Manhattan College upset New York University's quintet, 74—66, at Madison Square Garden last night. A five-minute overtime period decided the intracity battle, opening contest of a double-header watched by 8,128 spectators. The teams were tied, 65-all, at the end of regulation playing time.

St. John's had little difficulty in subduing the University of Cincinnati, 76—64, in the second game. It was the eleventh straight triumph for the Redmen, whose record now shows twenty victories and only two defeats.

Ed O'Connor, 6-foot 6-inch freshman center, and Andy McGowan, hard-driving junior guard, were the heroes of Manhattan's winning drive in the extra session of the thrilling opener, which saw the Jaspers score their fourth straight victory over the Violets.

O'Connor tallied three baskets and McGowan, beside quarterbacking the freezing tactics by which Manhattan kept possession of the ball for virtually the whole five minutes of the overtime period, accounted for his team's other 3 points on fouls.

A Tactical Victory

Basically, this was a tactical victory for Ken Norton's charges. Manhattan, an in-and-out team that had a 9—8 won-lost record going into action, as against N. Y. U.'s mark of 16—3, did a clever job of spiking the vaunted Violet attack, which had rolled up an average of more than 76 points a game.

With a sagging defense that almost had the effect of a zone, Manhattan slowed the driving N. Y. U. attack to a walk. And with the Jaspers keeping three men in back on offense, the Violets could not make their fast break work.

On the set shooting of Tom Carroll and Willard Doran, Manhattan clung close through the first half, which ended with N. Y. U. in front, 35—32. Down by as much as six points at one stage of the third period, the Jaspers surged back to tie the score early in the fourth quarter, then set the pace during the drive to the wire.

McGowan Ties Score

N. Y. U. caught up, at 64-all, with two minutes to go and a free toss by Dick Bunt put the Violets ahead. McGowan was fouled with just three seconds remaining and made his shot to send the game into overtime.

Bob Zawoluk and Jack McMahon paced St. John's to its easy triumph. Big Zeke tallied 29 points, one off the season's record for the Garden, and Sailor Jack got 24. Cincinnati, which had a 9-13 record going into action, was led by Jim Holstein, who had 15 points.

The line-ups:

MANHATTAN (74)	G.	F.	PF.	P.
Carroll, lf	5	4	3	14
Doran, rf	5	0	5	10
King	0	0	1	0
Kellogg, c	5	6	5	16
O'Connor	5	0	4	10
Loprete, lg	1	1	3	3
Cahill	0	0	0	0
M'Gowan, rg	6	7	3	19
Hunt	1	0	2	2
Garvey	0	0	2	0
Total	28	18	28	74

N. Y. U. (66)	G.	F.	PF.	P.
Brasco, lf	3	2	5	8
Elsberg	0	2	4	2
Doherty	0	0	1	0
Solomon, rf	7	5	3	19
Nachamkin	5	4	5	14
Dinegar	0	0	0	0
Seeman, c	0	2	5	2
Naimoli, lg	5	0	5	10
Carrillo	0	0	1	0
Bunt, rg	3	3	3	9
Weltz	1	0	0	2
Elsner	0	0	2	0
Total	24	18	34	66

Manhattan	17	15	19	14—9—74
N. Y. U.	17	18	18	12—1—66

Free throws missed—Carroll 3, Doran, Kellogg 5, Loprete 3, McGowan 3, O'Connor 2, Hunt 2, King 2, Garvey, Brasco 3, Solomon 4, Seeman, Bunt, Nachamkin 2, Elsberg.
Officials—John Nucatola and Jammy Moscowitz.

ST. JOHN'S (76)	G.	F.	PF.	P.
Davis, lf	0	2	0	2
Walker	1	1	3	3
McMorrow	0	0	1	0
Duckett, rf	3	2	5	8
Sagona	0	0	2	0
Zawoluk, c	13	3	2	29
Walsh	0	0	0	0
McMahon, lg	10	4	3	24
M'Gilvray, rg	1	4	5	6
Gioncontieri	2	0	3	4
Total	30	16	24	76

CINCINNATI (64)	G.	F.	PF.	P.
Holstein, lf	6	3	2	15
Twyman	0	0	1	0
Cassidy	0	0	1	0
Melzer, rf	4	3	5	11
Lammert	3	1	0	7
Armstrong, c	4	3	3	11
Vogele	0	0	1	0
Moeves, lg	3	4	5	10
Okruhlica	0	0	0	0
Rain, rg	3	1	4	7
Surface	1	0	4	2
Total	24	16	25	64

St. John's	15	23	19	19—76
Cincinnati	13	17	13	21—64

Free throws missed—Davis, Duckett, Zawoluk 2, McMahon 3, MacGilvray, Walker, Walsh, Holstein 2, Melzer 2, Moeves 4, Lammert 2, Surface 2, Okruhlica.
Officials—Lou Eisenstein and Julie Meyer.

Tour of Europe, Egypt Offered Duquesne Five

By The Associated Press.

PITTSBURGH, Feb. 21—Duquesne University, the nation's only major unbeaten basketball team, received an invitation today to tour Europe and Egypt.

The bid was extended by a New York booking agency. The offer calls for the Dukes to fly to Egypt April 1 and complete the junket April 21. Games will be booked in Rome, Milan, Cairo and Alexandria in addition to other cities.

The Rev. Vernon Gallagher, president of the university, said the university was interested in the proposal. He said it would offer the players an "educational opportunity."

If the Suez Canal remains a trouble spot, the agency is prepared to make a second offer—appearances in Israel.

CANADIENS' RALLY TIES BRUINS, 3-ALL

2 Goals in Last 4½ Minutes Deadlock Montreal Game—Hawks Rout Leafs, 5-1

MONTREAL, Feb. 21 (UP)—The Montreal Canadiens scored twice in the last four and a half minutes tonight to tie the Boston Bruins, 3 to 3, before a crowd of 14,301 at the Forum.

Dickie Moore scored the tying goal, his second of the night, at 16:43 when the Bruins appeared on their way to a victory which would have enabled them to tie the idle New York Rangers for fourth place in the National Hockey League. Elmer Lach set up Moore's tying goal to move within two of Bill Cowley's total points record of 548 in regular N. H. L. play.

The line-up:

MONTREAL—Goal, McNeil; defense, Harvey, St. Laurent; center, Lach; wings, Moore, Gamble. Alternates—Bouchard, Geoffrion, Johnson, Reay, Olmstead, McCormack, Mosdell, Meger, MacPherson, Davis.
BOSTON—Goal, Henry; defense, Henderson, Quackenbush; center, Schmidt; wings, Fisher, Chevrefils. Alternates—Kyle, Sandford, Laycoe, Sullivan, Creighton, McIntyre, Lund, MacKell, Kryzanowski, Peirson.
FIRST PERIOD—1, Boston, Chevrefils (Schmidt), 0:36; 2, Boston, Fisher (Schmidt, Chevrefils), 8:02; 3, Montreal, Moore (Harvey, McCormack), 9:24.
Penalties—Henderson (1:22), Laycoe (16:41).
SECOND PERIOD—4, Boston, Kryzanowski (Sullivan), 3:07.
Penalties—Moore (2:26), Creighton (17:37).
THIRD PERIOD—5, Montreal, Meger (Reay, Geoffrion), 15:31; 6, Montreal, Moore (Lach), 16:43.
Penalty—Kyle (4:24).
Referee—George Gravel. Linesmen—Frank Udvari and Bill Morrison.

Rough Game at Chicago

CHICAGO, Feb. 21 (UP)—The Chicago Black Hawks put on one of their best exhibitions of the season tonight to beat the Toronto Maple Leafs for the fifth time this season, 5 to 1, in a rough contest.

The line-up:

CHICAGO—Goal, Lumley; defense, Fogolin, Dewsbury; center, Gee; wings, Bodnar, Witiuk. Alternates—Hucul, Mosienko, Peters, McFadden, Finney, Guidolin, Horeck.
TORONTO—Goal, Rollins; defense, Juzda, Bolton; center, Gardner; wings, Watson, Meeker. Alternates—Thomson, Morrison, Bentley, Kennedy, Sloan, MacKell, Lewicki, Timgren, Smith, Armstrong, Morrison.
FIRST PERIOD—1, Chicago, Horeck (Peters) 4:58; 2, Chicago, Mosienko (Bodnar, Gee) 8:34; 3, Chicago, Hucul (McFadden, Peters) 15:19.
Penalties—Bolton (0:41).
SECOND PERIOD—4, Chicago, Dewsbury (Mosienko) 4:37; 5, Toronto, Sloan (Kennedy) 18:18.
Penalties—Guidolin (2:20), Juzda (2:20), Fogolin (10:14), Hucul (major 16:36), Bolton (major 16:36).
THIRD PERIOD—6, Chicago, Mosienko (unassisted) 14:07.
Penalties—Fogolin (major, 14:23); Juzda (major, 14:23); Raglan (15:00); Morrison (15:00); Juzda (misconduct, 15:00); Raglan (misconduct, 15:00).
Referee—Red Storey. Linesmen—Doug Young and George Hayes.

National Hockey League

Last Night's Results

Boston 3, Montreal 3.
Chicago 5, Toronto 1.

Standing of the Teams

	W.	L.	T.	Pts.	Goals For	Goals Agst.
Detroit	33	11	11	77	155	99
Montreal	27	22	8	62	156	132
Toronto	24	19	14	62	134	122
Rangers	19	25	12	50	144	165
Boston	18	25	13	49	123	145
Chicago	15	34	6	36	124	173

Tomorrow Night's Schedule

Chicago at Montreal.
Detroit at Toronto.

AMERICAN HOCKEY LEAGUE

Indianapolis 2, Syracuse 2.

M'NEILL PUT OUT BY MAIN IN 4 SETS

Ex-Champion Bows to Young Canadian in U. S. Tennis—Talbert, Mrs. Todd Gain

By ALLISON DANZIG

Donald McNeill of Searingtown, L. I., former national champion both outdoors and indoors, was eliminated from the United States indoor tennis championship last night.

A young Canadian Davis Cup player, Lorne Main, overcame the Oklahoman at the Seventh Regiment Armory, 6—4, 5—7, 6—1, 9—7.

Hard hitter though he is, McNeill was up against more pace and length than he could withstand. Main hits with two hands on the racquet on both sides, and the depth and velocity of his drives broke down the former champion's control and also made it risky for him to go into volley.

McNeill Loses Chance

McNeill had his chance to win the fourth set after his control had failed in the third. Three times he broke through in the final, but he could not hold his advantage, dissipating a 5-3 lead.

When he double-faulted and lost his service again, after leading at 6—5, he missed his last opportunity. The hammering blows of his young opponent were too much for him in spite of his gameness and his energy in retrieving all over the court.

Main gained a place in the semi-finals with his victory over the fourth seeded player. There he was joined by William Talbert of New York, the defending champion.

Talbert defeated Nils Rohlsson, veteran Swedish player, 6—3, 6—3, 6—3.

Champion's Service Strong

Rohlsson was a clever, stubborn antagonist who attacked at the net, used the lob and the drop shot effectively, and made Talbert do a great deal of running. But the champion was so strong off the ground and with his service that the older man could never gain the upper hand.

Mrs. Patricia Canning Todd of La Jolla, Calif., and Miss Pat Ward of England reached the semi-finals in the women's singles. Both scored crushing victories, Mrs. Todd winning in love sets and Miss Ward yielding only two games.

Beginning today the matches will be held in the afternoon through Sunday, when the finals are scheduled.

THE SUMMARIES

MEN'S SINGLES

Quarter-Final Round—William F. Talbert defeated Nils Rohlsson, 6—3, 6—3, 6—3; Lorne Main defeated Donald McNeill, 6—4, 5—7, 6—1, 9—7.

WOMEN'S SINGLES

Quarter-Final Round—Mrs. Patricia Canning Todd defeated Susan Bralower, 6—0, 6—0; Pat Ward defeated Harriet Stokes, 6—1, 6—1.

MEN'S DOUBLES

Quarter-Final Round—Richard Savitt and Irvin Dorfman defeated Kurt Nielsen and Rohlsson, 6—2, 6—3; Sidney Wood and Harold M. Burrows defeated Jean Borotra and Grant Golden, 6—3, 8—6; Talbert and Budge Patty defeated Main and Brendan Macken, 11—9, 6—4.

WOMEN'S DOUBLES

Quarter-Final Round—Mrs. Jean French Fallot and Mrs. Andreina Drew-Bear defeated Barbara Lee Friedmerg and Miss Bralower, 6—4, 7—5; Mrs. Nancy Chaffee Kiner and Mrs. Todd defeated Christina Morley and Helen W. Reynolds, 6—2, 6—0.

FEATURE MATCHES TODAY

1:30 P. M.—Miss Althea Gibson vs. Miss Helen Fletcher.
2:00 P. M.—Richard Savitt vs. Charles Masterson.
2:30 P. M.—Mrs. Nancy Craffee Kiner vs. Mrs. Edna Salichs.
3:00 P. M.—Budge Patty vs. Kurt Nielsen.
4:00 P. M.—Dick Savitt and Irvin Dorfman vs. Donald McNeill and Frank Guernsey.

SETON HALL ACCEPTS BID

Holy Cross, Dayton Fives Also in National Invitation Fold

Seton Hall, Holy Cross and the University of Dayton yesterday accepted bids to compete in the national invitation basketball tournament. With St. John's, St. Bonaventure and Duquesne previously in the fold, the field now is half filled for the twelve-team competition, scheduled at Madison Square Garden on March 8, 10, 11, 13 and 15.

All three new nominees have outstanding records. Seton Hall has a mark of 22—1, with four games to play; Dayton, 27—3, with two to play; Holy Cross, 18—2, with six to play.

This will be the first N. I. T. appearance of Holy Cross, but the Crusaders have qualified for the National Collegiate A. A. tournament three times. Seton Hall and Dayton were contestants in the 1951 N. I. T., Dayton surviving to the final, where it lost to Brigham Young, 62—43.

DETROIT, Feb. 21 (UP)—Lawrence Tech today agreed to play in the National Association invitation basketball tourney at Kansas City, Kan., starting March 10.

HOLY CROSS IN FRONT

Crusaders Defeat Dartmouth in Basketball Duel, 65-53

Special to THE NEW YORK TIMES.

WORCESTER, Mass., Feb. 21—The Holy Cross Quintet set back Dartmouth, 65—53, tonight. The Crusaders clinched the verdict in the last five minutes.

The line-up:

HOLY CROSS (65)	G.	F.	PF.	P.
O'Neil, lf	6	0	5	12
Dilling	1	1	1	3
Pallazzi, rf	6	4	1	16
Supronowicz	0	0	0	0
Nangle, c	2	2	2	6
Kielley	1	0	0	2
McDon'gh, lg	1	0	2	2
Perry, rg	6	4	5	16
McLarnon	3	2	4	8
Dyson	0	0	0	0
Total	26	13	20	65

DARTMOUTH (53)	G.	F.	PF.	P.
Gieg, lf	5	1	5	11
Pierce, rf	1	1	4	3
Wisdom	0	1	2	1
Parker	0	0	0	0
Nixon	0	0	0	0
Kasparson	0	0	0	0
Hedberg, c	3	3	2	9
O'Neil	1	1	1	3
Biggs, lg	7	3	0	17
Calhoun, rg	1	1	4	3
Boyges	1	3	1	5
Gelthner	0	0	0	0
Sherman	0	1	0	1
Total	19	15	17	53

Holy Cross	10	20	15	20—65
Dartmouth	13	22	11	7—53

Free throws missed—O'Neil, Dilling, Pallazzi 4, McDonough, Perry, Supronowicz, Hedberg, Biggs 3, Wisdom, Kasparson 2.

College and School Scores

BASKETBALL

Colleges

Beloit 53 ... Creighton 51
Chicago T. 93 ... Great Lakes Naval 41
DePauw 68 ... Wabash 66
Detroit Tech 72 ... Assumption 53
Duke 87 ... Wake Forest 62
Georgetown 71 ... Maryland 61
Gettysburg 62 ... Mt. St. Mary's 57
Holy Cross 65 ... Dartmouth 53
Kentucky 75 ... Vanderbilt 45
Lincoln Memorial 82 ... Bethel 68
Louisiana College 67 ... Northeast Louisiana 57
Loyola (Chi.) 74 ... Marquette 55
Manhattan 74 ... (overtime) ... N. Y. U. 66
Manhattan J. V. 66 ... N. Y. U. J. V. 60
Maryland State 85 ... Adelphi 77
Marshall 74 ... Morehead State 61
Millsaps 65 ... Mississippi College 45
Morris Harvey 65 ... Potomac (W. Va.) 63
Ohio Wesleyan 59 ... Oberlin 53
Pace 81 ... C. C. N. Y. Commerce 74
Plattsburgh T. 59 ... Potsdam T. 47
Pratt 77 ... New Bedford Textile 49
Providence 84 ... Bates 58
St. John's 76 ... Cincinnati 64
San Francisco 56 ... St. Mary's (Calif.) 46
Siena 55 ... Niagara 47
S. E. Louisiana 68 ... Loyola of South 66
Stetson 71 ... Mercer 60
Union 80 ... Middle Tennessee 56
Valparaiso 62 ... St. Joseph's (Ind.) 54
Vermont 68 ... Massachusetts 61
Virginia 74 ... Virginia Tech 59
Waynesburg 63 ... Bethany (W. Va.) 54
West Texas 75 ... Arizona State (Tempe) 62
Western Kentucky 83 ... Evansville 63

Schools

Adelphi Ac. 48 ... Riverdale 42
Amityville 56 ... Babylon 50
Baldwin 79 ... Freeport 67
Bayside 59 ... Flushing 48
Bayshore 71 ... Huntington 45
Bedford Hills 43 ... Horace Greeley 34
Bellport 66 ... East Islip 60
Belmont Hill 44 ... Milton Ac. 37
Bergenfield 81 ... Wood Ridge 27
Bernard 85 ... Englewood Sch. 52
Bishop Loughlin 62 ... Brooklyn Cathedral 33
Blessed Sacrament 57 ... Pelham Memorial 44
Bridgehampton 51 ... Sag Harbor 45
Cardinal Hayes 62 ... Stepinac 53
Chaminade 50 ... St. Augustine 46
Cleveland 72 ... Edison Vocational 54
Columbus 56 ... Evander Childs 54
Croton-Harmon 44 ... Hendrick Hudson 43
Delbarton 56 ... Montclair Ac. 34
Demerest 72 ... St. Joseph's 55
Dumont 51 ... Hasbrouck Heights 36
Dwight 48 ... New York Friends 43
East Rockaway 60 ... Lynbrook 55
Edison Tech 56 ... F. E. Bellows 47
Fort Lee 69 ... Westwood 54
Great Neck 55 ... Glen Cove 34
Greenwich 68 ... Saunders Trade 58
Haldane 60 ... St. Mary's (Katonah) 50
Harrison 53 ... Rye 41
Hicksville 55 ... Manhasset 52
Horace Mann 47 ... St. Paul's 41
Islip 72 ... Central Islip 28

BASKETBALL

Schools

James Monroe 54 ... Bronx Vocational 32
Katonah 83 ... Briar Cliff 81
Kings Park 60 ... Bayport 51
Lawrence 52 ... Sewanhaka 47
Long Island City 72 ... Forest Hills 68
Malverne 65 ... Woodmere H. S. 44
Mepham 60 ... Mattituck 45
Needle Trades 50 ... Textile 49
New Rochelle 66 ... Port Chester 56
Newtown 75 ... Bryant 59
North Tarrytown 57 ... Peekskill 54
Oyster Bay 59 ... Roslyn 33
Port Jefferson 56 ... Patchogue 53
Roosevelt (Yonkers) 72 ... A. B. Davis 54
St. Cecelia's 61 ... Ridgewood 58
St. Francis Prep 56 ... St. John's Prep 50
St. Michael's 63 ... Holy Family 47
Sea Cliff 69 ... Farmingdale 51
Seward Park 60 ... Food Trades 57
Shelter Island 56 ... Eastport 51
Smithtown 49 ... South Huntington 44
South Side 60 ... Oceanside 51
Southold 71 ... Center Moriches 41
Union Hill 50 ... Dickinson 46
Valley Stream 47 ... Hempstead 44
Wappingers Falls 39 ... Cardinal Farley M. A. 38
Washington Irving 54 ... Ossining 39
Westhampton 42 ... Southampton 41

Girls

Bishop McDonnell 38 ... St. Angela Hall 33

BOWLING

Schools

Boys High 5 ... Wilson 0
Erasmus 4 ... Manual Training 1
Lincoln 3 ... Brooklyn Auto 2
Madison 5 ... Fort Hamilton 0

HOCKEY

Colleges

Amherst 12 ... Springfield 0
Norwich 3 ... Middlebury 1

Schools

Lawrenceville 5 ... New Rochelle 2

SWIMMING

Colleges

Connecticut 44 ... Massachusetts 31
Drexel 49 ... Penn M. C. 35
Trinity (Conn.) 45 ... Boston U. 30

Schools

Horace Mann 41 ... Riverdale 34
Poly Prep 43 ... Regis 31

WRESTLING

Colleges

Iowa T. 18 ... Iowa State 10

Schools

Garden City 31 ... Manhasset 10
Huntington 21 ... Stony Brpok 21

Section 5 | SPORTS BOATS AUTOMOBILES

The New York Times.

SPORTS SHOPPING GUIDE SHIPS—WEATHER REPORTS | Section 5

S SUNDAY, JULY 27, 1952. L+ 8

MATHIAS VICTOR IN U. S. SWEEP OF OLYMPIC DECATHLON; GIANTS TRIP REDS, 7-2; CARDS TOP DODGERS, 5-3; YANKS BOW

JANSEN TAKES 11TH

He Beats Reds 12th Time in Row on Grand Slam Homer by Thompson

GIANTS ROUT WEHMEIER

Rally for Five Runs in Fifth and Move Within 4½ Games of First-Place Dodgers

By JOSEPH M. SHEEHAN

Have the Giants launched their big push? That question was buzzing around the Polo Grounds yesterday after a grand slam homer by Henry Thompson and a solid pitching job by Larry Jansen defeated the Reds, 7—2, for the New Yorkers' fifth consecutive victory.

The triumph enabled the Giants to move within 4½ games of first place as the league-leading Dodgers lost to the Cardinals.

Joining Jim Hearn and the temporarily disabled Sal Maglie as an eleven-game winner, Jansen scattered nine hits in hanging up his twelfth successive triumph over Cincinnati. The Reds last beat Larry on Aug. 29, 1948.

The lean right-hander from Oregon, going the full distance for the first time since he shut out the Braves on June 30, would have had a shut-out with better luck. Cincinnati's runs, scored in the fifth inning, both were unearned.

Giants Strike Back

In a vigorous response to the lapse that put them behind, the Giants came back to wrap up the decision in the bottom half of this same frame with a five-run rally that routed Herman Wehmeier, Cincinnati's starter.

Jansen, who had driven in his team's first run in the second inning with a single that followed similar blows by Jim Rhodes and Don Mueller, launched the winning splurge by drawing a pass.

Davey Williams flied out, but Alvin Dark and Whitey Lockman kept the rally rolling with singles that filled the bases. Thompson promptly unloaded them with a towering wallop that carried deep into the upper right field tier. It was Henry's fourteenth four-bagger.

Not content to let matters rest there, the Giants went on to score again. Bobby Thomson was nicked by a pitch, stole second as Rhodes was striking out and, after Mueller had been intentionally passed, came home on Sal Yvars' single through the middle.

This blow finished Wehmeier and Bud Podbielan brought the inning to a close by retiring Jansen, up for the second time.

Rhodes Finds Range

Against Frank Hiller, who took over for Cincinnati in the sixth, the Giants rang up another tally in the seventh. This came on a homer by Rhodes, who duplicated Thompson's wallop, but with the bases empty.

The rookie outfielder from Nashville is finding the Polo Grounds much to his liking. He has hit three homers in the four games he has played there.

A throwing error by Dark was at the bottom of Jansen's difficulties in the fifth. On a grounder by Wehmeier, the Giant captain threw into the dirt, pulling Lockman off first.

After Cal Abrams popped up, successive singles by Bobby Adams and Willard Marshall produced a run. Another came across when the Giants narrowly missed double-

Continued on Page 2, Column 8

Speed and Brawn at Helsinki: Racing to an Olympic Title and Heaving Discus in the Decathlon

Joseph Barthel of Luxembourg winning the 1,500-meter final, with Bob McMillen, United States, second; Werner Lueg (739) of Germany, third, and Roger Bannister, Great Britain, fourth.

Associated Press Radiophotos

Bob Mathias, who successfully defended his decathlon championship, tossing the platter 153 feet, 10.06 inches, to gain 838 points. He scored a total of 7,887 points in the ten events.

RALLY BY REDBIRDS SUBDUES BROOKLYN

Cardinals Again Beat Dodgers on Johnson's 2-Run Single Off Black in Eighth

By LOUIS EFFRAT

The Dodgers' lead over the second-place Giants was cut to four and a half games after they dropped their second straight to the Cardinals, 5—3, at Ebbets Field yesterday. Only five days ago the Brooks were riding high on the strength of a seven-and-a-half length spread over the runners-up.

The situation, while not yet acute, is not one to be given the once-over-lightly treatment. The Brooklyn brass is aware that what happened last fall might be repeated if the Flatbush forces do not stage an immediate rally. Vice President E. J. (Buzzie) Bavasi is on the hunt for a pitcher or two, but pitching alone is not what ails the Brooks.

Seven Hits, All Singles

The club appears sluggish and it is not hitting. Following the nine-game winning streak, it has lost four out of six at home. Jackie Robinson, employed only as a pinch-hitter yesterday, and Billy Cox are sidelined with torn muscles and, as a result, the team's offense and defense has been below par.

Against Wilmer (Vinegar Bob) Mizell and Alpha Brazle, the Dodgers collected seven hits but the power was not there. All were

Continued on Page 2, Column 2

Tigers Down Bombers, 10-6, On Souchock Homer in 11th

By JOHN DREBINGER

Special to THE NEW YORK TIMES.

DETROIT, July 26—Mickey Mantle, who, the Tigers are convinced, must be twins, because he belts them from the left as well as the right, hit the first grand-slam homer of his major league career today. But even that didn't win for the Bombers, for after blowing two leads, they had to carry the battle into extra innings and went crashing down to defeat.

With the bases full in the last of the eleventh, Steve Souchock, the same old Yankee cast-off who had tripped the world champions with a ninth-inning homer last night, clouted one in the role of pinch-hitter into the seats and that shot sank Bob Hogue and all his New York colleagues, 10 to 6.

It was the second straight victory for the tail-end Bengals, a feat wildly cheered by 13,060. Meanwhile, the Yanks plunged down to their fourth straight setback, their longest losing streak of the year. However, their luck in the flag race still ho[illegible] for with Red Sox and Indians again losing, the Bombers maintained their four-game lead.

The happiest fellow in the park was Ted Gray, Tiger southpaw, and victim of Mantle's first-inning blast. For Gray hung on to pitch the full eleven innings. When he finally did step out it was to let Souchock pinch hit for him. Steve's wallop therefore gave Ted his ninth victory of the year.

As for the Yanks, they seemed to doze off completely after Mantle had put them in front the first time. Vic Raschi, seeking his

Continued on Page 2, Column 6

Major League Baseball

Sunday, July 27, 1952

National League

YESTERDAY'S GAMES

New York 7, Cincinnati 2.
St. Louis 5, Brooklyn 3.
Philadelphia 7, Chicago 2.
Pittsburgh 6, Boston 4.

STANDING OF THE CLUBS

	Brooklyn	New York	St. Louis	Chicago	Philadel.	Boston	Cincinnati	Pittsburgh	Won	Lost	Percentage	Games Behind
Bklyn..	—	3	6	8	4	13	14	13	61	26	.701	—
N. Y....	6	—	11	7	6	7	13	7	57	31	.648	4½
St. L...	8	7	—	6	10	8	5	9	53	41	.564	11½
Chic....	4	5	6	—	6	9	8	9	47	45	.511	16½
Phila...	5	7	4	8	—	4	7	12	47	46	.505	17
Bost....	0	2	6	9	6	—	5	11	39	53	.424	24½
Cinc....	3	2	5	4	8	7	—	9	38	57	.400	27
Pitts...	0	5	3	3	6	5	5	—	27	70	.278	39
Lost....	26	31	41	45	46	53	57	70	—	—		

TODAY'S PROBABLE PITCHERS

Cincinnati at New York (2, 2 P. M.)—Perkowski (8-6) and Nuxhall (0-3) vs. Koslo (7-3) and Kennedy (2-3).

St. Louis at Brooklyn (2 P. M.)—Clark (0-0) vs. Roe (7-0).

Chicago at Philadelphia (2)—Minner (9-6) and Rush (10-7) vs. Meyer (7-12) and Drews (7-10).

Pittsburgh at Boston (2)—Main (2-8) and Friend (4-15) vs. Surkont (6-9) and Bickford (6-9).

American League

YESTERDAY'S GAMES

Detroit 10, New York 6 (11 innings).
Chicago 9, Philadelphia 3.
St. Louis 7, Boston 2.
Washington 11, Cleveland 10.

STANDING OF THE CLUBS

	New York	Boston	Wash'gton	Cleveland	Chicago	Philadel.	St. Louis	Detroit	Won	Lost	Percentage	Games Behind
N. Y....	—	4	6	10	10	8	9	9	56	38	.596	—
Bost....	6	—	6	5	11	4	7	12	51	41	.554	4
Wash...	3	7	—	9	6	6	10	10	51	42	.548	4½
Cleve...	9	9	7	—	6	7	7	7	52	43	.547	4½
Chic....	4	7	8	5	—	9	10	8	51	46	.526	6½
Phila...	5	3	3	6	7	—	10	8	42	45	.483	10½
St. L...	5	9	4	4	3	7	—	6	38	58	.396	19
Det.....	6	2	8	4	3	4	5	—	32	60	.348	23
Lost....	38	41	42	43	46	45	58	60	—	—		

TODAY'S PROBABLE PITCHERS

New York at Detroit (2)—Reynolds (12-5) and Miller (2-3) vs. Trucks (4-11) and Hoeft (1-3).

Boston at St. Louis (2)—Nixon (2-3) and Parnell (7-5) vs. Pillette (6-9) and Bearden (3-2).

Philadelphia at Chicago (2)—Shantz (17-3) and Kellner (6-8) vs. Grissom (7-5) and Dobson (9-7).

Washington at Cleveland (2)—Marrero (8-4) and Masterson (4-4) vs. Lemon (10-8) and Garcia (14-7).

(Figures in parentheses indicate season's won-and-lost records.)

U. S. Defeats Japan In Davis Cup Tennis

By The Associated Press.

CINCINNATI, July 26—The doubles combination of Billy Talbert of New York and Gardnar Mulloy of Miami, Fla., today steered the United States into the second round of 1952 Davis Cup tennis competition.

Talbert and Mulloy, appearing to be anything but the nation's No. 1 doubles team, knocked Japan out of the running with a 6—2, 3—6, 6—3, 6—2 victory over Jiro Kumamaru and Fumiteru Nakano.

The victory gave to the United States a 3-to-0 lead over the Japanese and the right to meet Cuba next week at Havana in the second round, regardless of what happens in tomorrow's final two singles matches.

Japan's none too robust hopes

Continued on Page 8, Column 2

MARRA VANQUISHES JACOBSON, 7 AND 6

Gains Final of Metropolitan Amateur Golf—Cherry Sets Back Sanok, 7 and 5

By LINCOLN A. WERDEN

Special to THE NEW YORK TIMES.

PARAMUS, N. J., July 26—A golfer who learned to play the game in Texas and another who started as a caddie in Westchester reached the final of the Metropolitan amateur championship at the Ridgewood Country Club today.

Don Cherry, a singer, from Wichita Falls of the Lone Star State who is a member of the Garden City Country Club of Long Island, downed Chet Sanok of Upper Montclair, 7 and 5. Joe Marra of Dunwoodie eliminated Bobby Jacobson of Deal, N. J., 7 and 6, in the other semi-final.

Cherry, who took part in one other district tourney this season, is playing in his first metropolitan title test. Marra has been competing in this event for the last ten years or more, but this is the first time he has advanced this far in the fifty-year-old championship. The pair will meet for the title in the 36-hole final tomorrow.

Sanok Cards 80 in Morning

Against Sanok, who finished second in the New Jersey Open last week after winning it in 1951, Cherry was by far the steadier player. Off the tee and around the greens he constantly held the edge over the big fellow who has a reputation for long-hitting.

Sanok has played some fourteen rounds of tournament golf during the last nine days, but he scoffed at the idea that he was stale and tired. "I just didn't play well," he commented, "and Cherry did."

How far Sanok was from his customary style was reflected in the 80 he had in the morning round. Going into luncheon, Cherry had a lead of 4 up, after Sanok had led 1 up at the ninth. By the twenty-seventh, there was little doubt of the outcome for at that point, Cherry was well ahead with a 37 to be 7 up. Sanok, struggling to keep his long game clear of the trees and out of the traps, was out in 40.

There was one bright spot for Sanok almost at the end of the encounter. His lone birdie came at the twenty-ninth and reduced Cherry's advantage to 6 up. They halved the next in 5's, but Cherry rolled in an 8-footer for a birdie 4 to win the thirty-first and end the match.

In the morning, Cherry, who bowed in the final of the William

Continued on Page 8, Column 2

RICH SARANAC WON BY GOLDEN GLOVES

Beats Hitex as York Protest Against Wall Backfires—Jamaica Double $882

By JAMES ROACH

With Sunny Jim Fitzsimmons peering at the proceedings from his favorite spot under a tree on the clubhouse turn, the Fitzsimmons trained Golden Gloves, bred and owned by William Woodward's Belair Stud, won the $23,-550 Saranac Handicap for 3-year-olds at the Saratoga-at-Jamaica session yesterday.

It was a tight finish in which Golden Gloves inched in front of Mrs. Ben F. Whitaker's favored Hitex in the last three or four strides and scored by a head in the role of $12.70-for-$2 third choice.

Hitex, a front-runner, was handled by Ray York. Golden Gloves was ridden by the remarkable Nick Wall, 45-year-old lightweight ace who was riding winners before York was born.

A Final Curious Twist

There was a York-vs-Wall aftermath to the mile-and-a-sixteenth contest. Juice wasn't piped into the "official" neon till the stewards had done a Bosley Crowther job. York asserted that Golden Gloves had interfered with his mount early in the race, and so the stewards went to the movie room under the stands to review the film.

The movie provided a final curious twist to the forty-fifth running of the Saranac. It showed that there had been a foul, shortly after the start—but that Hitex had caused it. Hitex, starting from the outside slot and bidding for the lead under six whacks with York's whip, cut in and bumped

Continued on Page 4, Column 2

To Market, 2-1, Captures $152,350 Arlington Race

By The Associated Press.

CHICAGO, July 26—King Ranch's To Market, a sensation on Chicago race tracks as a juvenile two years ago, returned to the scene of his earlier triumphs today, winning the $152,350 Arlington Handicap by ten lengths. Oil Capitol was second and Ruhe third on the slow track.

Owner Robert Kleberg gained $107,050 by To Market's victory.

The winner, ridden by Willie Boland, covered the distance in 1:52 1-5.

Injuries and track conditions riddled the original overnight field of fifteen starters until only ten answered the call to the post for the mile and a furlong race before an Arlington Park closing-day crowd of 28,716.

Spartan Valor, the nation's top handicap star, and Blue Man, leading money-winning thoroughbred for 1952, with three other horses were declared out of the race.

Blue Man was suffering from a swollen tendon and Spartan Valor was injured slightly when kicked in the left hind leg by his lead pony during the early morning workout.

Going to the post as a 2-1 favorite, To Market returned a mutuel of $6, $3.40 and $3.20. The place and show prices on Oil Capitol were $3, and $3.20. Oil Capitol, Ruhe and Inseparable ran as an entry for the Hasty House Farm, owned by Mr. and Mrs. A. S. Reuben.

Pet Bully, owned by Mrs. Ada L. Rice of Chicago, and piloted by Eddie Arcaro, finished fourth with Dr. Ole Nelson fifth. The Greentree Stable's One Hitter, with Ted Atkinson up, was sixth.

The balance of the field finished in this order:

Inseparable, seventh; Abbe Sting, eighth; the Argentine-bred Tio Ciro, ninth, and Royal Mustang, tenth.

To Market, winner of the Ar-

Continued on Page 4, Column 6

LAFFANGO IS FIRST IN THE TYRO STAKES

South Point Captures Other Division of Feature Race at Monmouth Park

By JOSEPH C. NICHOLS

Special to THE NEW YORK TIMES.

OCEANPORT, N. J., July 26—Laffango and South Point shared the honors in the Tyro Stakes at Monmouth Park today. The event was divided into two sections, and the crowd of 30,014 was pleased with the way things turned out because each half was won by the favorite.

The six-furlong event, for colts and geldings 2 years old, enjoyed its inaugural running, with each section carrying a value of $15,000. The winning owners were the Trio Stable for Laffango and J. M. Roebling.

Laffango's performance was better, the son of Errard being timed in 1:11 4-5 under Fred Pannell. He led from the start, with James Cox Brady's Landlocked running closest to him. Landlocked made a good bid for the victory in the stretch, but failed by a length. However, he managed to beat the highly-regarded Bradley for runner-up honors.

The weight burden on Laffango was 111, and his price was $5.60 for $2. This division of the Tyro was worth $19,775 gross, with $14,-025 going to the winner.

The race was the first stakes event for Laffango, whose previous record was two victories and a second in three starts.

Favorite Five-Length Victor

In the first division, South Point made the figures in his favor stand up by scoring a five-length victory over J. H. Miles' White Cliff. With Fernando Fernandez in the saddle, South Point was rated fourth to the turn, behind Dandolo, Belfaster and Lord Jeffrey.

When the field of nine hit the turn, South Point started to go, and he took over the lead in a few seconds. Moving with him was White Cliff, ridden by Harold Keene, the country's leading winning jockey. There was no danger, however, that White Cliff would overtake the leader. His time was 1:12 1-5, and he paid $9.60, $4.80 and $3.40.

South Point is a son of Pavot. In four previous races, he had finished second each time. His weight of 108 was the feather in his division of the Tyro, which was worth $19,975 gross and $14,225 to the winner. Belfaster, owned by Edward Potter and ridden by Jim Nichols, was the big disappointment. He was well-played, but did not show any late speed. He fin-

Continued on Page 4, Column 5

Scholes Clips Olympic Swim Mark In Semi-Finals of 100-Meter Test

By The Associated Press.

HELSINKI, Finland, July 26—Clarke Scholes of the United States churned out a new Olympic swimming record today in the 100-meter free-style semi-finals.

A Hungarian, Judith Temes, set a new Olympic record for the same distance in the women's competition.

Scholes' time was 57.1 seconds, two-tenths of a second lower than the mark set by America's Wally Ris in London in 1948. It was in the nature of a revenge comeback victory for the 21-year-old Michigan State graduate, who suffered an upset loss in the preliminary heat earlier in the day.

Miss Temes' time was 1:05.5, bettering the 1:05.9 made by Hendrika Mastenbroek of Holland in Berlin in 1936.

Another Hungarian girl, Eva Novak, shattered an Olympic record when she won her heat in the women's 200-meter breast stroke in 2:54. She broke the old record of 2:57.2 set in London in 1948 by Nel Van Vliet of Holland.

The winner of the second heat in the women's 200-meter breast stroke was Elisabeth Bonnier of Holland who did it in 3:00.6. Judy Cornell of Portland, Ore., started well but faltered before she reached the 100-meter mark and finished fifth in 3:17.7.

Gail Peters of Washington finished sixth to Eva Novak in the first heat of the women's 200-meter breast stroke.

A little Japanese girl, 19-year-old Sadako Yamashita, failed when she ran out of gas at the end of the first 50 meters.

Americans fared better in the men's competition. Dick Cleveland of Ohio State won the fourth heat in the men's 100-meter free-style, and Ronald Gora, 19-year-old Chicago schoolboy, won the fifth heat easily in 58 seconds.

Y. Hamaguchi gave Japan its first Olympic swimming thrill in sixteen years by capturing the first heat, also in 58 seconds flat. Goren Larsson of Sweden upset Scholes in the sixth with 0:57.5. Toru Goto,

Continued on Page 5, Column 6

WORLD RECORD SET

Mathias Keeps Title as Campbell and Simmons Follow in Decathlon

13TH GOLD MEDAL FOR U. S.

But Russia Retains Olympic Lead—Luxembourger Beats McMillen to Win 1,500

By ALLISON DANZIG

Special to THE NEW YORK TIMES.

HELSINKI, Finland, July 26—Bob Mathias paced an American sweep of the gruelling Olympic decathlon event tonight, shattering his own world record and raising to thirteen the number of gold medals taken by the United States in these games.

A bandage covering his painful leg injury, the Tulare Calif., giant retained the title he won in 1948 as darkness was enveloping the huge arena after twelve hours of gruelling competition. Earlier another American, Bob McMillen, had just missed taking another gold medal for the United States.

A completely overlooked outsider, Joseph Barthel, beat McMillen by less than a yard in the 1,500-meter run for Luxembourg's first track and field gold medal within memory and wept on the victory stand when his national anthem was played.

[Russia continues to lead the unofficial team scoring with 392½ points, according to The Associated Press. The United States is next with 294, followed by Hungary, 110; Sweden, 101½, and Germany, 76.]

McMillen and Barthel finished in the same time of 3 minutes 45.2 seconds. In a performance comparable to the stunning steeplechase triumph of Horace Ashenfelter, the 24-year-old Californian ran the fastest metric mile ever credited to an American only to fall short of victory despite his tremendous burst of speed down the home stretch.

Lueg Third in 1,500

McMillen must have sped the last 100 in 10 seconds as he and Barthel charged past the famed Werner Lueg of Germany. Roger Bannister of Great Britain, one of the top favorites, finished fourth as the first eight men across the line broke the Olympic record to the cheers of 60,000 spectators.

Mathias ran the 1,500 meters in the final ordeal of the two-day grind of ten events, in 4:50.8, to raise his total to 7,887 points. Milton Campbell, 18-year-old athlete from Plainfield, N. J., finished second with 6,975, and Floyd Simmons of Charlotte, N. C., was third with 6,788. Vladimir Volkov of Russia placed fourth with 6,674.

In the Olympic trials in his home town early this month, Mathias had set a new decathlon record of 7,825. He excelled that performance today by 62 points under the pressure of competition from the world's best and despite the fact that he had suffered a muscle twinge in broad jumping yesterday.

His leading European rival, Ignace Heinrich of France, had been forced to retire from competition today because of an injury that befell him yesterday. While high jumping, Heinrich hurt his Achilles tendon and it paind him so much after the first event today, sixth on the decathlon program, that he retired when in fourth place.

For a while this afternoon it

Continued on Page 3, Column 2

U. S. Trounces Czechs In Basketball, 72-47

By The Associated Press.

HELSINKI, Finland, July 26—America served up a mixed grill in the Olympic basketball arena today and the result was a tasty victory that sent the United States squad into the semi-finals of the sixteen-team tournament.

Coach Warren Womble scrapped the platoon system he had tried yesterday in favor of the conventional substitution-when-necessary method. The team looked better for it in crushing Czechoslovakia, 72—47.

After starting his Amateur Athletic Union five, Womble began clearing the bench mid-way in the first half with the United States holding an 11-10 lead. Immediately things got better.

With A. A. U. and the Univer-

Continued on Page 5, Column 6

Mathias Announces Retirement After Beating Own World Record in Decathlon

MATHIAS RETAINS DECATHLON TITLE

Continued From Page 1

seemed that Mathias might not break his record. His performances in the 100 meters, broad jump, hurdles, and discus had not been up to his efforts at Tulare and though he exceled in the shot-put and 400 meters and equaled his high jump mark, he was 99 points behind his record as he came up to the pole vault.

Mathias Excels in Vault

But this youngster from the Far West has the heart of a lion. Despite his fatigue, he vaulted 13 feet 1½ inches on his second try to beat his Tulare effort by 9⅜ inches.

Mathias made no effort to try for a higher vault, deciding to save himself for the javelin throw and 1,500-meter run. He had thrown the javelin 193 feet 10⅝ inches at Tulare and in his tired condition that distance called for exceptional effort to equal it. Not only did he do it but he beat the mark.

A tremendous cheer went up from the thousands who remained to the last, though they could hardly make out the figures in the darkness as he hurled the spear 194 feet 3⅛ inches.

With that wonderful performance, Mathias was in. He knew he could beat the 4:55.3 he did for 1,500 in the trials. In almost complete darkness, with the track lighted only by the illumination from the electric scoreboard, he traveled the distance in 4:50.8 and the thousands acclaimed a great champion who had far excelled his amazing achievement as a 17-year-old schoolboy at London four years ago.

Campbell's feat in scoring just short of 7,000 points was a notable accomplishment for an 18-year-old. The schoolboy hurt his shoulder in a fall during the pole vault, but stayed in the fight and finished almost 200 points ahead of the 29-year-old Simmons.

As he left the dressing room, Mathias turned to his coach and said, "I'm glad I didn't let you all down." He said that he felt fine and that the toughest event for him had been the pole vault because of his weight. The victory of the Tulare giant enabled the United States to surpass the total of twelve gold medals it won in the Berlin games, a record up to today for the post-World War I period.

U. S. Seeks Relay Medals

There is a good chance it will add a fourteenth tomorrow in the closing track and field program. Both its 4x100 and 4x400 quartets qualified for the finals. Dean Smith, Harrison Dillard, Lindy Remigino and Andy Stanfield comprised the first, marking the first time that three Olympic champions ever ran in a relay for the United States. Ollie Matson, Gerald Cole, Charley Moore and Mal Whitfield ran in the 4x400.

Another world record was established today as the Duke of Edinburgh and the Duke of Kent looked on from the presidential box. Galina Zybina, a big blonde Russian, not only broke the world mark with her final shot-put but excelled the Olympic figure on all of her five other tosses.

The Olympic mark was smashed no fewer than twenty-one times during the competition. Russia took first, third and fourth places and Germany second and fifth.

Another gold medal went to Australia, the third won by its women athletes. Marjorie Jackson, who had taken the 100-meter race in a time that equaled the world record, carried off the two-hundred meter title in 23.7 seconds. This broke the Olympic record on the books but was not up to her 23.4 figure in the semi-finals that lowered the world mark. Mrs. Shirley Strickland de la Hunty won Australia's other gold medal in the 80-meter hurdles.

GOOD SPORTSMANSHIP EVIDENCED AT THE OLYMPICS

Jack W. Davis (left) being congratulated by E. Bulanchik of Russia after the American star had finished second in the 110-meter high hurdles. The winner was Harrison Dillard (1002) of the United States. At right is another competitor, R. H. Weinberg of Australia.

Unofficial Team Scores

By The Associated Press.

Teams are credited with points for placing in the first six of any event on a 10—5—4—3—2—1 basis.

	Pts.		Pts.
Russia	392½	Egypt	13
United States	294	The Netherlands	12
Hungary	110	Yugoslavia	12
Sweden	101½	Poland	11
Germany	76	South Africa	10
Switzerland	62	South Korea	10
Great Britain	60	Denmark	9
Czechoslovakia	59½	Belgium	5
Australia	58	Spain	5
France	57	Uruguay	4
Japan	56	Venezuela	4
Finland	44½	Trinidad	4
Italy	44	Philippines	4
Iran	35	Austria	3
Turkey	31	Pakistan	3
Jamaica	29	Norway	2
Brazil	18	Lebanon	2
India	17	Rumania	2
New Zealand	15	Singapore	1
Canada	15	Greece	1
Argentina	14½	Bulgaria	1
Luxembourg	13		

The victory of Barthel in the 1,500 meters and McMillen's placing second caught the form fanciers completely off guard. No one except a few Europeans realized how strong a runner Luxembourg youth was and as for McMillen, even his stanchest American admirers scarcely dreamed he would finish in the forefront.

Barthel had been an 800-meter man until last year. His best clocking for the metric mile up to this year had been 3:51 and 3:48.4 was the fastest he had been timed in 1952.

McMillen Surprises in 1,500

McMillen's best previous performance was 3:49.3 in the Olympic trials and yet he ran the fastest 1,500 ever turned in by an American. The best up to today was Walter Mehl's 3:47.9 in the A. A. U. championships of 1940, in which Glenn Cunningham did 3:48.

On McMillen's past performances, how was anyone to suspect that he would come closer to winning the gold medal than any other American in forty-four years? Abel Kiviat was second in 1936 but finished three-tenths of a second behind the winner and Cunningham was three-fifths of a second off the pace. McMillen was clocked in the identical time with the winner.

The Californian ran his first good 1,500 this year in winning the N. C. A. A. championship and then came his 3:49.4 in the trials. His work as a carpenter interfered with his training and he suffered a groin injury following the trials. He did not appear to be in the best shape during training in the Olympic Village here. He had his stamina back but not his speed. It seemed that he would hardly do much better than he did in 1948, when he made the Olympic team as a steeplechaser but fell at the final water jump and was completely submerged.

McMillen was at the tail end of the field up to the last lap and Barthel was far back also until he came to the turn at the end of the back stretch on the third circuit of the track. Then the Luxembourg runner worked his way up to second place behind Lueg, who had done 3:43 this year and was a co-favorite with Bannister. The Briton had laid off the pace, like McMillen, much to the surprise of his countrymen, who thought he made a mistake in not stepping out earlier.

As the bell sounded for the final lap, Barthel was on the heels of the German and stayed there, followed by Bannister. As he headed into the first turn, McMillen began to move up. On the backstretch he was sixth, then fifth and then fourth. Lueg sprinted there and pulled away from Barthel to open a two-yard gap as they headed into the final bend.

Californian Closes Gap

As they came around into the homestretch, Lueg still had his two yards on Barthel, who was followed by Bannister and McMillen. Down the straightaway they came, with the crowd roaring. Then Barthel made his bid and came up so fast on the German that Lueg turned around to see what the situation was. In that moment, Barthel shot past him and the curly haired McMillen also put on a sprint that brought roars from the stands.

McMillen came up so fast that he made the badly winded Lueg appear as though he were standing still. More than that, the Californian was gaining swiftly on Barthel. With each stride he drew closer amid the deafening roars from the Americans in the stands and for a few moments it seemed that he was to be the winner. Had the race gone a few yards further McMillen surely would have taken the gold medal, so rapidly was he gaining, but Barthel had just enough left to beat him to the tape.

After the race, McMillen said that had he started his sprint four or five yards sooner he felt he could have won. He said that he had decided to lay off the pace so long because he almost had failed to qualify in the heats by staying with the leaders. "I decided to lay back and keep out of trouble today," the dark-haired youth said with a smile. "I had no idea I could do so well at the start of the race."

REDS CRITICAL OF JUDGES

But Officiating Is Censured in Events Soviets Dominated

HELSINKI, Finland, July 26 (AP)—Russia was critical tonight of the way some Olympic Games were judged. The criticism was particularly directed at gymnastics, in which the Soviet Union scored heavily.

N. N. Romanoff, Soviet member of the International Olympic Committee, told some 200 newsmen that "there were cases of unjust judging in gymnastics."

"It is not excluded that we will prepare for and compete in the Olympic Games in Melbourne in 1956," Romanoff said.

OLYMPIC FANS HAIL IRON MAN OF SPORTS

'My Last Decathlon,' Says Mathias, Still Weary From Grueling 1,500 Meters

COACH PRAISES CHAMPION

'He's Best That Ever Lived,' Hamilton Claims—Young Campbell Wins Plaudits

HELSINKI, Finland, July 26 (UP)—"I didn't think yesterday I could do it. But I did and now I'm finished."

Strong, square Bob Mathias, perspiration running off his face, leaned against the door from the field where he had just smashed his own world record total in the Olympic decathlon. Newsmen, team members, well-wishers and the Finnish version of pushing, clawing bobby sockers crushed in about him.

"This will be my last decathlon," said the 21-year-old wizard of strength and endurance. "You can't keep this up forever."

Shifting from foot to foot, still weary from his grueling last effort in the 1,500 meters, Mathias said he had felt before starting the event that he could better his own record.

Pulled Muscle Hurt

"After the high hurdles yesterday I didn't think I could do it. Then I pulled a muscle in the broad jump and it hurt pretty much all day today."

But he said after the pole vault today he thought again it would be possible.

"I heard some great man in the stands figuring my total points," he said. "I don't even know what his name was. But after the pole vault I went over and he said if I could keep up my usual distances in the javelin and run the 1,500 under 4.54 minutes I could beat the record. I thought for sure I could do that."

The California wonder boy ran even better.

Brutus Hamilton, coach of the American team, pushed through the crowd, congratulated his brown-haired iron man and said triumphantly:

"What do I think of Mathias? He's just the best that ever lived."

Mathias himself had something to say about others, specifically Milt Campbell, the 18-year-old who ran second in the American one-two-three sweep of the world's most arduous event.

Praise for Campbell

"He's a good boy," Mathias blurted out with a grin. "In fact, he's great."

As for Campbell, who put on a tremendous kick in the stretch of the 1,500 to finish in 5.07.2, he already was in the dressing room, but he sent two words to the crowd outside:

"I'm dead."

Floyd Simmons, the third member of the triumphant trio, stood off from the crowd around Mathias, smiling and tired, signing the inevitable autographs.

"This is my last, too," he said. "I've had two Olympics now and I get feeling sometimes I never want to see a track again. This running and jumping and throwing things can make an old man of a guy."

Hamilton later was asked about Campbell's chances of breaking Mathias' record some day:

"Maybe with three years of the kind of expert coaching Bob has had," he said. "But it takes something a little extra—a spark—and Bob has it."

"All the News That's Fit to Print"

The New York Times.

LATE CITY EDITION
Mostly fair and continued cool today, tonight and tomorrow.
Temperature Range Today—Max., 68; Min., 54
Temperature Yesterday—Max., 67; Min., 56
Full U. S. Weather Bureau Report, Page 47

Copyright, 1952, by The New York Times Company.

VOL. CII..No. 34,577. Entered as Second-Class Matter, Post Office, New York, N. Y. NEW YORK, WEDNESDAY, SEPTEMBER 24, 1952. Times Square, New York 36, N. Y. Telephone LAckawanna 4-1000 FIVE CENTS

NIXON LEAVES FATE TO G.O.P. CHIEFS; EISENHOWER CALLS HIM TO A TALK; STEVENSON MAPS INFLATION CURBS

MARCIANO ANNEXES TITLE IN 13TH BY KO OVER JOE WALCOTT

Brockton Heavyweight Ends Reign of 38-Year-Old Rival With Right to Jaw

40,379 FANS WATCH BOUT

Hundreds Besiege Philadelphia Stadium in Wild Rush to Acclaim New Champion

By JAMES P. DAWSON
Special to The New York Times.

PHILADELPHIA, Sept. 23 — Rocky Marciano, undefeated Brockton, Mass., fighter, knocked out Jersey Joe Walcott, 38-year-old ring warrior from Camden, N. J., tonight to become the world heavyweight champion.

With a devastating right to the jaw, Marciano ended the reign of the old champion after forty-three seconds of the thirteenth round. Until that moment it was a bruising battle that thrilled 40,379 fans from all over America in Philadelphia's Municipal Stadium. The receipts were $504,645.

Under the impact of that one terrific blow Walcott sank against the ropes, then slid head first to the canvas, while Referee Charley Daggert counted him out of the title he had won after much desperate effort slightly more than a year ago.

The knockout was the cue for a tremendous demonstration. Fans swarmed into the ring as the unbeaten Bay State boxer with the paralyzing punch stood in his corner, winner of the ring's richest prize after a battle that he could have lost as early as the first round. He was the first white heavyweight to hold the title since Jim Braddock was stopped by Joe Louis in Chicago in 1937. Here was the new champion and nothing could halt the crowd in its eagerness to acclaim him.

Many Trampled in Rush

From all sections of the vast arena, where Gene Tunney had lifted the title from Jack Dempsey just twenty-six long years ago, fans rushed on the ring to greet the conqueror.

Many were trampled in the rush, which started in the lower-priced seats in the permanent stands and, under increasing momentum, moved across and through the seats at the ringside.

For a time a wall of police about the working press rows checked the rush. Police climbed into the ring. A straggler broke through the cordon back of the press rows. Then another. Then it was a steady stream of humanity climbing and clambering over the backs of the writers.

Then the crush became too much for the police. They gave up and let the demonstration run its course. Several telegraph instruments and typewriters at the ringside were kicked under the ring. A movie camera was broken.

Most of the demonstrators were young fellows with the reckless abandon that only youth can boast. They risked broken and bruised limbs to get into the ring.

When Walcott had been counted out his stricken handlers leaped through the ropes to the side of their fallen idol and carried him to his corner. It was several minutes before he could be revived sufficiently to leave the ring, with the assistance of Trainer Dan Florio and his brother Nick, and his manager Felix Bocchicchio.

Marciano, on the other hand,

Continued on Page 41, Column 1

Frauds in U. S. Grain Are Put at 10 Million

By JOHN D. MORRIS
Special to The New York Times.

WASHINGTON, Sept. 23 — The Senate Agriculture Committee blamed lax administration and poor enforcement policies today for the Federal grain storage scandals brought to light in public hearings earlier this year.

In a forty-one-page report of findings and recommendations, the committee estimated that 131 private warehouse men had embezzled about $10,000,000 of Government-owned grain over the last five years. Slightly more than $2,000,000 of the losses have been recovered, and some additional recoveries are possible.

The "conversions," as such embezzlement is called in the grain trade, were of crops stored for the Agriculture Department's Commodity Credit Corporation under the Federal farm price support program.

However, the report said, "no

Continued on Page 19, Column 1

Dodgers Take Flag By Defeating Phils

The Brooklyn Dodgers clinched the National League pennant last night with a 5-4 victory over the Philadelphia Phillies in the twilight opener of a double-header at Ebbets Field. The Dodgers lost the second game, 1—0, in twelve innings.

A two-run double by Duke Snider during a three-run fifth inning enabled Brooklyn to take the opener. The Brooks now lead the second-place Giants by six games. The Giants have only six to play and the Dodgers four. New York's double-header yesterday with Boston was rained out.

Gran Hamner accounted for the Phillies' runs with a third-inning home run against Johnny Rutherford, the winning pitcher, with the bases filled.

Details on Page 42.

U. N. IN NEW DRIVE ON BATTERED HILL

Reply to 'Harassing' Jabs Hits Enemy in West—Red Probes Repulsed on Wide Front

By LINDESAY PARROTT
Special to The New York Times.

TOKYO, Wednesday, Sept. 24—United Nations troops struck back today at the Communists on the western front in Korea after the enemy, probing all along the 100-mile Allied line yesterday from Panmunjom in the west to the "Punchbowl" in the eastern Korean mountains, sought but failed to find weak spots.

Allied infantry jumped off this morning in an attack on "Kelly Hill," battered hillock in the west, which hard-fighting Chinese had captured last Thursday. Front reports said the combat still was in progress at 7:30 A. M.

For the second time United Nations infantry fought its way to the top, but resistance continued and the issue was in doubt. The Allies reached the summit Saturday, but were turned back later by an enemy counter-attack. Today's assault was the third effort to retake the hill, which is seven miles southwest of bitterly contested "Old Baldy," near Panmunjom, captured from the Chinese Sunday by a battalion from the United States Second Infantry Division.

Attacks at 20 Points

The enemy's series of local attacks yesterday were made in strength of no more than two platoons, but Eighth Army Headquarters said the jabs were delivered in twenty places along the outpost line. All were driven back.

A military spokesman said the Communist tactics probably were intended as "harassing actions" following the heavy local fighting of the last two weeks.

The enemy's apparent determination during the last fortnight to increase the scale of the ground fighting in a series of drives for outpost positions has cost the Chinese and North Koreans a considerable number of casualties, intelligence estimates said. Eighth Army Headquarters said 3,332 enemy were killed or wounded during the week of September 15-21, and 3,743 in the previous week. The total of more than 7,000 casualties is approximately the usual strength of an enemy division.

South Koreans Rewon Hill

The heaviest toll in the last few days was taken during the seesaw fighting for a hill north of the "Punchbowl," a strategic cup-shaped valley that controls the best lines of communication in the rugged eastern Korean watershed. Communist casualties there in fifteen hours of fighting Tuesday were estimated at 117 killed and 322 wounded.

The troops that stormed the hill in a tank-led attack after the heights had been seized by the enemy during darkness were identified as members of the Republic of Korea Eighth Division, one of the outfits of the retrained and re-equipped South Korean Army now holding much of the front. The R. O. K.'s recaptured the hill after Allied planes had made eighty-seven strikes against North Koreans dug in there.

Four new probes were made by the enemy yesterday on a four-mile front in the eastern sector, Eighth Army Headquarters said. In each case the Communists withdrew after engagements lasting up to a half-hour and the R. O. K.'s continued to hold the contested hill.

On the central front the enemy felt out Allied advance positions northwest of Yonchon, and in the west the Chinese Communists made five light attacks against scarred "Bunker Hill," won and lost several times in recent fighting. Contact was maintained during the night and up to 6 A. M.

Continued on Page 2, Column 6

WEST REJECTS BID FOR BIG 4 SESSION ON GERMAN TREATY

Reply to Moscow Insists That First Such Conference Deal Only With Free Elections

OCTOBER TALK SUGGESTED

Identical Notes Say Russians 'Shifted' Stand Since They First Urged Peace Moves

By WALTER H. WAGGONER
Special to The New York Times

WASHINGTON, Sept. 23—The United States, Britain and France rejected today a proposal by the Soviet Union for a Big Four conference on a German peace treaty and insisted again that such a meeting be limited to making plans for free, all-German elections. The meeting "could take place in October," the Western powers said.

In identical notes delivered by their envoys in Moscow to the Soviet Ministry of Foreign Affairs, the Western Big Three restated their conviction and determination that first things come first — that machinery must be set up for carrying out free elections throughout divided Germany, that the elections must be held, and that a unified German government must be created before a German peace treaty could be discussed.

Today's note was the Western reply to the Soviet communication of Aug. 23, in which a three-point agenda for possible Big Four talks was proposed, with the "preparation of a peace, treaty with Germany" at the top of the list.

Eighth Item in Exchanges

The reply constituted the eighth item of correspondence between the three Western capitals and the Soviet Union, with four notes issuing from each side, since Moscow first formally suggested Big Four talks on Germany last March 10.

From the beginning, the Soviet Union has proposed talks on a broader basis than the Western powers, especially the United States, have been willing to accept. Countering, Washington, London and Paris have proposed an agenda, restricted to the question of free elections, that has not been acceptable to the Kremlin.

Western diplomats have shown no enthusiasm for getting into a propaganda battle with the Soviet Government on the question of Germany, which, they feel, would be a certainty if the Russians had all of Germany's difficulties, problems and grievances to work over in a forum as important as a Big Four conference.

Today's Western note, hinting at the prospects for Soviet propaganda blasts at a meeting on Germany, called attention to the "wholly unfounded attacks" on the Atlantic pact, the European Defense Community Treaty and the Bonn peace contract with the Western Allies in the Soviet communication of Aug. 23.

Describing all those develop-

Continued on Page 9, Column 1

PRAISE BY GENERAL

He Commends Senator for 'Magnificent' Talk on His Finances

STUMPS OHIO WITH TAFT

Then Discards Cleveland Text to Laud Running Mate as a Courageous Person

Text of the Eisenhower speech in Cleveland is on Page 24.

By JAMES RESTON
Special to The New York Times.

CLEVELAND, Sept. 23—Gen. Dwight D. Eisenhower listened to Senator Richard M. Nixon's explanation of his defense fund tonight and immediately indicated that he would retain the Senator as his Vice Presidential running mate.

In an extraordinary evening that started with a defense of Senator Nixon's honesty and developed into a Hollywood-type story of the Senator's life, General Eisenhower told a roaring crowd of 15,000 in the Cleveland Public Auditorium that his personal admiration and affection for the Californian were "undiminished."

The Republican Presidential nominee, who watched the Nixon telecast while the audience in the Public Auditorium listened to it over a loudspeaker, withheld final judgment on the case, but he praised Senator Nixon's courage and left no doubt that, unless some wholly new element were introduced into the controversy, Senator Nixon would receive his endorsement. He also called the Senator to a personal meeting with him.

'Affection' Is Undiminished

General Eisenhower wired Mr. Nixon tonight as follows:

"Your presentation was magnificent. While technically no decision rests with me, yet you and I know that the realities of the situation will require a personal pronouncement, which so far as the public is concerned, will be considered decisive.

"In view of your comprehensive presentation, my personal decision is going to be based on a personal conclusion. To complete the formulation of that personal decision, I feel the need of talking to you and would be most appreciative if you could fly to see me at once. Tomorrow night I shall be at Wheeling, W. Va.

"I cannot close this telegram without saying that whatever personal admiration and affection

Continued on Page 25, Column 1

The New York Times

EXPLAINS SPECIAL EXPENSE FUND: Senator Richard M. Nixon, Republican Vice Presidential nominee, as seen on television screens here.

'I'M NOT A QUITTER'

Senator Says He'll Let Republican National Committee Decide

HE REVIEWS HIS FINANCES

Accepts Bid to Meet General—Cites Legal Opinions on Use of $18,235 Fund

Text of Nixon speech, Page 22; financial record, Page 23.

By GLADWIN HILL
Special to The New York Times.

LOS ANGELES, Sept. 23—Senator Richard M. Nixon, in a nation-wide television and radio broadcast tonight, defended his $18,235 "supplementary expenditures" fund as legally and morally beyond reproach.

He laid before the Republican National Committee and the American people the question of whether he should remain on the Republican party's November election ticket as the candidate for Vice President.

Rising, near the end of his talk, from the desk at which he had sat, Senator Nixon urged his auditors to "wire and write" the Republican National Committee whether they thought his explanation of the circumstances surrounding the fund was adequate.

"I know that you wonder whether or not I am going to stay on the Republican ticket or resign," he said. "I don't believe that I ought to quit, because I'm not a quitter * * *.

Decision 'Not Mine'

"But the decision, my friends, is not mine. I would do nothing that would harm the possibilities of Dwight Eisenhower to become President of the United States; and for that reason I am submitting to the Republican National Committee tonight, through this television broadcast, the decision which it is theirs to make. * * *.

"Wire and write the Republican National Committee whether you think I should stay or whether I should get off; and whatever their decision is, I will abide by it."

Later he accepted an invitation from General Eisenhower for a conference.

In a half-hour talk that was partly personal, including a frank exposition of his finances, and partly an appeal for support of the Republican ticket such as he has been making in his current whistle-stop tour, the Senator declared of the Southern California supporters' fund disclosed last week:

"I say that it was morally wrong if any of that $18,000 went to Senator Nixon for my personal use.

"I say that it was morally wrong if it was secretly given and secretly handled.

"And I say that it was morally wrong if any of the contributors got special favors for the contributions that they made."

But he declared that, on all three points, the factual answer was negative.

Speaks With Assurance

The candidate, clad in a gray suit and a dark tie, delivered his address in a Hollywood radio-television studio—from which the public was excluded—with composure and assurance. His wife, Patricia, was seated close to him, and he made frequent references to her in detailing his career.

His talk also was peppered with barbed references to the Democratic opposition.

Referring to an Illinois political fund with which Gov. Adlai E. Stevenson, Democratic Presidential nominee, has been linked, Senator Nixon, while stipulating that he did not "condemn" this, suggested that both Mr. Stevenson and his running mate, Senator John J. Sparkman of Alabama, should "come before the American people" and report on their incomes.

"If they don't," he said, "it will be an admission that they have something to hide."

In support of his position, he cited two independent reports he had prepared, one on his finances and one on the legal aspects of the "supplementary expenditures" fund, for the information of Gov. Sherman Adams of New Hampshire, campaign executive of Gen-

Continued on Page 23, Column 1

OUSTER A MISTAKE, CAUDLE TESTIFIES

He Says He Was Told Truman Called It 'a Great Injustice'—White House Denies This

By LUTHER A. HUSTON
Special to The New York Times.

WASHINGTON, Sept. 23—President Truman was quoted in testimony before a House of Representatives Judiciary subcommittee today as saying that he had done Theron Lamar Caudle "a great injustice" when he dismissed him as Assistant Attorney General in charge of the Tax Division of the department.

Mr. Caudle gave the testimony near the end of an emotional recital of his version of his dismissal. The President's statement, he said, had been made to Representative Frank W. Boykin, Democrat of Alabama, during a private interview at the White House last March. Mr. Boykin disclosed the conversation to Mr. Caudle and members of his family, the witness related.

When Mr. Boykin asked Mr. Truman what he was going to do to rectify the "injustice" the President answered, "What can I do?" Mr. Caudle testified.

Representative Boykin also said, according to Mr. Caudle, that Mr. Truman had told him that if Donald S. Dawson, one of the President's aides, had arrived at Key West two hours earlier "I never would have done it."

Dismissal Ordered From Florida

The President ordered Mr. Caudle's dismissal from Key West, Fla., where he was on vacation on Nov. 16 last. Mr. Dawson arrived soon after the action was taken.

The White House said that there was no truth in the statement that the President had told Representative Boykin he had done Mr. Caudle a great injustice.

At Mr. Boykin's office here it was said that he was in Alaska on a business trip and could not be reached immediately for comment.

Mr. Caudle was dismissed while a Congressional inquiry was under way into tax scandals in the Bureau of Internal Revenue and the Justice Department's handling of cases referred to it by the bureau. The only statement made at the time was that the President had acted because of "outside activities" incompatible with Mr. Caudle's responsibilities as a Government official.

Representative Frank L. Chelf, Democrat of Kentucky and chairman of the subcommittee, asked Mr. Caudle if he had ever heard "the basis upon which the President acted."

"No, sir," replied Mr. Caudle. "I never have found out."

Mr. Caudle said that Representative Boykin told him that during the White House interview "the

Continued on Page 12, Column 3

Stevenson Willing to Impose Tighter Controls if Needed

By W. H. LAWRENCE
Special to The New York Times.

BALTIMORE, Sept. 23—Gov. Adlai E. Stevenson of Illinois told a cheering capacity audience of 9,000 Maryland Democrats tonight that he would not hesitate to impose tighter wage and price controls if necessary to halt inflation.

The Democratic nominee's speech was heard also by a nation-wide radio and television audience. It was made just after Senator Richard M. Nixon of California, the Republican Vice Presidential nominee, had concluded his report about his personal finances.

[The text of the Stevenson speech is printed on Page 26.]

But the Governor did not refer in any way to Senator Nixon's speech, of which he saw about two minutes on television before he left his hotel room, nor to the question of whether the Californian should be dropped from the Republican ticket.

As he was leaving the platform Mr. Stevenson was informed by a reporter of the gist of the address by Senator Nixon, in defense of his $18,235 expense fund. Asked to comment, he replied:

"I'll have nothing to say on that tonight."

[The American Federation of Labor convention in New York adopted a resolution on Tuesday giving unanimous support to Governor Stevenson. Similar action had been taken previously by the executive committee of the Congress of Industrial Organiations.]

The Baltimore speech, delivered in the Fifth Regiment Armory, was Governor Stevenson's set speech on the inflationary problem, for the solution of which he

Continued on Page 27, Column 5

U. S. WIDENS STUDY INTO NIXON'S FUND

Aide First Affirms Then Denies That Truman Asked Inquiry—Senator Tied to Tax Case

By ANTHONY LEVIERO
Special to The New York Times.

WASHINGTON, Sept. 23 — The White House at first confirmed and later denied today that President Truman had directed James P. McGranery, Attorney General, to study the possibility of criminal prosecution of Senator Richard M. Nixon, Republican Vice Presidential candidate, and the seventy-six Californians who contributed $18,235 to his expense fund.

Before the White House had withdrawn its statement, however, a Justice Department spokesman confirmed that the study was being made. Moreover, the spokesman said that the study was wider in scope than at first indicated — wider in that he indicated an intent to assure the involvement of Senator Nixon if it was concluded that his seventy-six sponsors were liable to prosecution.

Meanwhile, The St. Louis Post-Dispatch reported that Dana C.

Continued on Page 17, Column 1

Teachers Union Witnesses Assail Senate Red Inquiry

By CHARLES GRUTZNER

Two officers of the Teachers Union testified under oath yesterday that they were not and never had been members of the Communist party, but they joined eight other witnesses who refused to tell a Senate Internal Security subcommittee whether they were Communists in denouncing the current investigation into communism in the schools as an attack upon the concept of the open mind in education.

Several of the witnesses in the Federal Court House on Foley Square charged that the "inquisition" of teachers had been inspired in church circles that were trying to "intrude" upon public education.

Charles J. Hendley, former president of the union, named George A. Timone, prominent Roman Catholic layman and chairman of the Board of Education's law committee, as a foe of the union because it "has defended the American principle of separation of church and state and has strenuously opposed clerical interference with public education."

Mr. Hendley, one of the eight who refused to say whether they were or ever had been Communists, denied that the Teachers Union was or ever had been controlled by Communists, as had been charged by Mr. Timone and Dr. Bella V. Dodd, former Communist functionary and former legislative representative of the union, in testimony two weeks ago.

Public hearings will continue today at 9 A. M. before Senator Homer Ferguson, Republican of Michigan, sitting as a one-man subcommittee, and Robert Morris, counsel to the subcommittee. After an hour of open testimony the committee will go into closed session to examine teachers in all four of the municipal colleges and several other local institutions, including Columbia, New York and Long Island Universities.

Additional officers of the Teachers Union will be questioned at the open hearings before and after the closed session. It is expected that members of the college and university faculties will be put on the stand at an open hearing tomorrow.

James Nack, the union treasurer, and Mrs. Mildred K. Garvin, vice president in charge of elementary schools, swore they never had been Communists. Mr. Nack is a mathematics teacher and director of the school honor society at Stuyvesant High School. Mrs. Garvin is a grade teacher at Public School 192, Manhattan.

Mr. Nack and Mrs. Garvin became the first, among twenty teachers or union officials questioned so far, to answer what have come to be known as the "$64

Continued on Page 4, Column 3

Truman Buys Painting for Wife, Trying His Art On First for Size

By PAUL P. KENNEDY
Special to The New York Times.

WASHINGTON, Sept. 23—President Truman took a brief recess from the affairs of state and the political turmoil this afternoon for a bit of a esthetic shopping.

After a surprise visit to a Georgetown antique shop, the President came away with a Dutch castle scene, painter unidentified, which he will present to Mrs. Truman to be hung in their Independence, Mo., home.

In the course of seventeen minutes, Mr. Truman inspected about 150 paintings in a collection bought a year ago by Charles Kohen for his shop.

Quiet Georgetown was startled at 4 P. M. when a squad of Secret Service men set up a guard around Mr. Kohen's small shop. By the time the President's limousine rolled up thirty minutes later, followed by a Secret Service car, a handful of the curious had gathered in front of the shop.

Immediately on entrance, Mr. Truman was taken to the shop's second floor by Mr. Kohen. After one look at the large room, the walls of which were lined and the floors stacked with pictures, the President, according to Mr. Kohen, exclaimed:

"You've got too damn many pictures here."

The President, Mr. Kohen said, had no clear idea about the subject matter, the school or the painter, but he knew the exact size he wanted.

"I know exactly the place I want to hang it," the President explained.

He was finally torn between the Dutch painting and a landscape by Joseph Turner. The choice went to the Dutch picture, but the President was at first insistent on knowing the painter.

"Don't ask me that, Mr. Presi-

Continued on Page 13, Column 1

Marciano Knocks Out Walcott in 13th to Win Title

RIGHT TO JAW ENDS PHILADELPHIA BOUT

Continued From Page 1

was virtually a prisoner in the ring, in more danger of injury at the hands of the crowd than he had been against Walcott through twelve bruising rounds of fighting.

It was at least fifteen minutes before the ring was cleared and order restored. Then Marciano was taken through the crowd under protection of a flying wedge of police and his handlers. Hundreds followed the conqueror to his dressing quarters, singing his praises, yelling themselves hoarse.

Marciano pulled victory from imminent defeat with that one paralyzing punch to the jaw. He didn't know it, but the three bout officials all had Walcott in front on a round basis for the twelve completed sessions.

Referee Daggert had Walcott leading, seven rounds to four, with one even. Zach Clayton, one of the judges, called it eight rounds for Walcott and four for Marciano. Pete Tomasco, the other judge, had Walcott leading, seven rounds to five. The writer had it even at six rounds apiece, giving Marciano the third, fourth, fifth, sixth and seventh, and Walcott the first, second, eighth, ninth, eleventh and twelfth.

Suffers First Knockdown

Marciano came on to win after being knocked down in the first round, the first knockdown of his career. He rallied courageously, shook off the best punches of Walcott, and gradually wore down his 38-year-old rival with blistering blows. And, finally, to the stage where Walcott exposed his jaw for the finishing wallop.

Fighting before the largest crowd of his career, Rocky proved himself every inch a fighting man. He was crude and awkward so far as ring finesse is concerned, but amazing in his resistance to punishment and altogether destructive in administering it.

A less hardy soul would have been finished in the first round. Rocky took an unmerciful beating then, and went to the canvas under a short left hook to the jaw. It was with such a punch that Walcott had knocked out Ezzard Charles in July of 1951 to win the title.

But, whereas Charles, as champion, succumbed to the blow, Marciano, as challenger, arose at the count of three, infuriated, enraged at having been floored for this first time in an undefeated record of forty-two engagements that held thirty-seven knockouts. He was determined not only to avenge the indignity, but to accomplish the complete destruction of his foe.

So Marciano plodded on, though buffeted about at times like a cork on an angry sea, until he had registered his thirty-eighth knockout. This was the big one.

Marciano was bruised and bleeding at the finish. He bled from a cut on the crown of his head, suffered in the sixth round when he accidentally bumped heads with Walcott. Joe got a severe cut over the left eye. Marciano had a puffed left eye and he bled from a cut above the right eye.

Walcott had only the cut over his left eye to show for the fifth knockout in a career that extends back over twenty-two years. His ribs must have been sore, his body must have been weary and his nervous system certainly was upset under the pounding to which he had been subjected. But he had made a gallant stand, one that came near to completely upsetting the dope.

A Crafty Old Battler

Marciano entered the ring a favorite to take the crown, at odds of 8 to 5. It was forecast in advance of the fight that he must score a knockout to win. He won just as had the majority predicted, but with greater contention than had been anticipated. It did not seem possible that the aging Walcott legs could carry Joe on the long journey he traveled before going down for the count.

Walcott surprised all but his own supporters by the crafty, perfectly paced battle he waged until Marciano broke through with the crusher.

The finishing blow was a surprise. It was the first really clean punch of the fight landed by Marciano. Bewildered and confused earlier by the strategy of his more experienced and heavier rival, Rocky floundered badly through most of the battle, while winning some of the rounds principally through his fiery offense.

It was a short punch, straight and true to the mark, delivered as Walcott backed into the ropes near a neutral corner. Walcott appeared to be taking it easy at the time, boxing superbly, retreating cagily, letting Marciano fight himself out, as he had done earlier.

In the twelfth round, Walcott had befuddled by his clever defensive fighting followed by furious slugging. In the eleventh Walcott hurt Marciano with a right under the heart and, volleying furious lefts and rights to the head, face and jaw, had Rocky sagging.

The thirteenth had opened as had many of the rounds preceding, with Marciano pressing forward on the attack, half-crouched on his toes, boring in, fist and arms poised to strike. Walcott backed away carefully, pecking and pawing with straight lefts, circling about the ring. A rush by Rocky and a wild left and right sent Walcott to the ropes.

Walcott parried a left for the head and blocked a left for the body. Walcott swayed slightly. His left arm and shoulder was down. Marciano swung with a right that didn't travel more than eighteen inches, and the fight was over. Marciano, 28 years old, weighed 184 pounds and Walcott 196.

There was an interesting preliminary program.

Rocky Jones, 178, Chester, Pa., won a six-round decision over Tommy Harrison, 171, Los Angeles. Oakland Billy Smith, 171, California, knocked out Billy Black, 178½, Philadelphia, in 33 seconds of the first round in their scheduled six-rounder. Cleveland Williams, Tampa, Fla., 201, knocked out Joe McFadden, 202, Winston Salem, N. C., in 2:09 of the fourth round of a six-round bout.

Vinnie de Carlo, 148, Philadelphia, knocked out Chick Alexander, 146½, Philadelphia, in 2:11 of the first of their six-rounder. Calvin Wilson, 197, Philadelphia, won a six-round decision over Gil Newkirk, 212, Brooklyn, N. Y., and Bert Whitehurst, 189, Baltimore, took a four-round verdict over Walter Parker, 184½, Philadelphia.

Jersey Joe Walcott falling in the thirteenth round after Rocky Marciano landed a right to the jaw to end the fight.

The Official Score Cards Of Championship Contest

By The Associated Press.

PHILADELPHIA, Sept. 23—The cards of the three officials for the first twelve rounds of tonight's Marciano-Walcott bout follow:

Referee Charley Daggert

1-W, 2-M, 3-W, 4-M, 5-M, 6-M, 7-W, 8-W, 9-W, 10-E, 11-W, 12-W.

Totals—Walcott 7, Marciano 4, one even.

Judge Pete Tomasco

1-W, 2-W, 3-M, 4-W, 5-M, 6-M, 7-W, 8-W, 9-M, 10-M, 11-W, 12-W.

Totals—Walcott 7, Marciano 5.

Judge Zach Clayton

1-W, 2-W, 3-M, 4-M, 5-M, 6-W, 7-W, 8-W, 9-M, 10-W, 11-W, 12-W.

Totals—Walcott 8, Marciano 4.

JOYOUS FANS MOB HEAVYWEIGHT KING

And Marciano Enjoys Turmoil in Dressing Room—Walcott May Give Up Boxing

By JOSEPH C. NICHOLS

Rocky Marciano had almost as tough a fight getting into his dressing room afterward as he did in the ring. After all, he had only one man to confront in Joe Walcott, while his opposition in the battle of the dressing room was a fair segment of the population of his home town plus a sizable gathering of Philadelphia fans.

The difference, though, was obvious, and Rocky enjoyed every minute of the turmoil in the dressing room. After all, in the ring Jersey Joe's aim was to knock Marciano's block off, whereas the dressing room situation was one in which every one in sight was out to shake the new champion's hand or pound his back.

The Rock enjoyed all this, for after all he was in the first hour of his reign as heavyweight ruler of the world. Only Al Weill, his manager, seemed a little beaten by the milling mob, but Al managed to smile his way through all the buffeting.

Not Hurt in First

Marciano, a naturally taciturn but literate talker, tried to analyze the progress of the battle with Walcott. He said that he was not hurt in the first round when he was knocked down, but admitted that Walcott did hurt him with some solid wallops through the middle rounds.

Rocky also said that there was something on Walcott's shoulder that stung him and made him blink after he was cut, but the new champion didn't go beyond that, even after questioning.

Marciano didn't seem certain about the punch that brought him the title. First he said it was a straight right and then he allowed that it might have been a left hook. All ringside observers were in agreement that the finishing punch was a short right to the jaw.

The new champion was too flushed to discuss his immediate plans. The same applied to Weill who, after many years of association with the ring sport, finds himself in charge of the heavyweight king. Al's former champions were Featherweight Joey Archibald, Lightweight Lew Ambers and Welterweight Marty Servo.

Marciano was cut on the scalp and about the eyes and Dr. Vincent Nardiello was prepared to sew him up when the fighter arrived at his hotel.

The defeated Walcott showed a patch over his left eye, but otherwise he was all right. He was a sad figure though, as he sat on his rubbing table, a towel draped over his bowed head and tears wetting his eyes.

In response to the question "What did he hit you with?" Joe said, "I don't know, but he certainly hit me. I just got caught, that's all."

Jersey Joe thought he was ahead as far as it went, but bemoaned the fact that he let his opponent get away in the first round.

Joe's future is dependent on the plans of his manager, Felix Bocchicchio. The latter said that Joe could retire, but Joe opposed such a move. Walcott said that should he decide to call it a career, he would go into business with his pilot.

MOTHER PRAYS FOR ROCKY

But Husband and Five Children See Battle at Philadelphia

BROCKTON, Mass., Sept. 23 (AP)—For the first time in her life the mother of Rocky Marciano prayed tonight that he would be victorious in a boxing bout.

Mrs. Lena Marchegiano, mother of the Brockton Block Buster, walked into St. Patrick's Church to pray until the fight was over.

She said that previously she had always prayed that her son—and his opponents—would escape from the ring unharmed.

She was accompanied to the church by her two sisters.

Mrs. Marchegiano has never seen her son fight, nor watched or listened to an account of his fights.

Her husband, two younger sons and three daughters, as well as Rocky's wife, were all in Philadelphia to watch the bout.

Mrs. Marchegiano said she wished her son to reap the financial rewards of holding the championship and hoped he would be as fortunate as other boxing champions.

Meanwhile crowds of loyal Rocky rooters gathered outside the Ward Memorial Club, a few yards from the Marchegiano home, and outside the Brockton Enterprise office, to hear reports of the battle.

Section 5 | SPORTS AUTOMOBILES—BOATS SALES HELP WANTED BUSINESS OPPORTUNITIES

The New York Times.

SPORTS SHOPPING GUIDE SITUATIONS WANTED HOUSEHOLD EMPLOYMENT | Section 5

S SUNDAY, MARCH 22, 1953. L+ 5

DODGERS TRIUMPH OVER RED SOX, 8-4, IN GAME AT MIAMI

Meyer, the Victor, and Mickens, Who Yields Only One Blow, Excel for the Brooks

TALLY IN SIXTH DECIDES

Williams, Campanella, Furillo Hits Bring Run After Bosox Get 3 Markers to Tie

By ROSCOE McGOWEN

Special to The New York Times.

MIAMI, March 21—Lou Boudreau's Red Sox were just another woeful group of "Saturday's Children" against the Dodgers at Miami Stadium today before 3,876 fans. The Brooks took the game, 8—4, after permitting the Sox to tie it at 4-all with a three-run surge in the sixth inning.

Russ Meyer suffered that slight indignity. None of the three runs would have scored if Dick Williams had held a double play relay from Don Zimmer. But Meyer's temper didn't even threaten to get out of control.

Williams wasn't given an error, so the runs were officially earned. The other Sox run, scored in the fifth, was definitely unearned, also because of a Williams miscue. Dick fumbled a grounder from Billy Goodman, when Jim (Showboat) Piersall, who was on first at the time, paused long enough to screen the ball from Williams' view.

Maury McDermott was Boudreau's starter, going four innings, and Mel Parnell, another southpaw, went the rest of the way.

Score Four in First

The Dodgers jumped on McDermott for four runs on as many hits in the first inning, scoring all of them after two were out. Jim (Junior) Gilliam opened with a double to left center and, after Pee Wee Reese had lined out to right field and Duke Snider had grounded to the second baseman McDermott started his downfall by walking Jackie Robinson, today's first baseman.

Roy Campanella lined a single to right center, Carl Furillo bounced another through the middle and Bobby Morgan got a two-run double when his liner to left took a sudden high hop over Al Zarilla's head.

That ended the scoring off McDermott and Parnell set the Brooks down in order in the fifth but ran into trouble in the next inning.

Williams opened it with a line single to left, moved to third on Campanella's double to right—a high drive that Gene Stephens lost in the sun—and scored when Furillo bounced another single through the middle.

This run gave the Dodgers a 5-4 lead and made Meyer the winning pitcher, but in the seventh the Brooks broke loose to score three more. Zimmer walked, Don Thompson lined a single to center and Williams beat out a bunt toward third. When Parnell threw the ball wildly past first both runners scored and Williams reached third on the error.

Final Run by Furillo

Dick was cut down at the plate trying to score on a short passed ball, Sammy White to Parnell, after Campanella had grounded out to short. But Billy Cox lined one through to the right center wall for a triple to score Furillo, who had walked, with the final run of the game.

The Red Sox sixth started with a pass to Dick Gernert, then Stephens rifled a single through the right side, Gernert stopping at second. Here Zarilla grounded sharply to Gilliam, whose quick toss to Zimmer was as quickly re-

Continued on Page 2, Column 5

Carruthers Stops Toweel in the 10th

By The United Press.

JOHANNESBURG, South Africa, March 21—Jimmy Carruthers of Australia knocked out Vic Toweel of South Africa in the tenth round tonight to retain his world bantamweight championship. Toweel lost the title to Carruthers last year.

Carruthers started like a whirlwind, shooting for an early knockout. He lashed away at the ex-champion and had him wobbly at the end of the ninth round.

In the tenth, the Aussie moved in for the kill. He drove Toweel into a corner and plastered him with lefts and rights to the head and stomach.

Toweel dropped to his hands and knee, and the referee tolled the full 10 count. There was no time during the count that the record

Continued on Page 4, Column 7

Celtics Beat Nats In Fourth Overtime

Bob Cousy, record-breaker

By The Associated Press.

BOSTON, March 21—The Boston Celtics, led by the brilliant Bob Cousy, advanced to the second round of the National Basketball Association play-offs for the first time in their seven-year history today by defeating the Syracuse Nationals, 111—105, in four overtime periods at the Boston Garden. The victory was the Celtics' second straight in the best-of-three series.

Cousy set a new N. B. A. play-off record by scoring 50 points. He tossed in 10 field goals and connected on 30 of 32 throws from the foul line.

The sensational former Holy

Continued on Page 3, Column 7

GIANTS' 16 BLOWS CRUSH SEALS, 12-0

Homers by Irvin, Mueller and Yvars Pace Attack—Maglie and Koslo Star in Box

By JOHN DREBINGER

Special to The New York Times.

SAN FRANCISCO, March 21—Two days of rest, the return of Leo Durocher to active command and, for the first time this spring, an absence of major league competition combined to have a highly beneficial effect upon the Giants today. They walloped Jeff Heath's San Francisco Seals, 12 to 0, with sixteen hits.

This ended a four-game losing streak for the New Yorkers.

Five of the Giant tallies were driven in by Monty Irvin, though Monty played only four innings. He exploded a three-run homer to cap a five-run third inning and in the fourth belted in two more with a single.

Don Mueller and Sal Yvars also hit for the circuit to give the Polo Grounders a total of twenty-three for the exhibition campaign. Another star in the attack was Daryl Spencer, who contributed two doubles and a single.

And behind this blistering assault Durocher looked upon some mighty slick pitching, first from Sal Maglie, and then from Dave Koslo. Making his fourth start this spring, the Barber breezed through five innings during which he gave up three well spaced singles and walked no one.

As if this weren't enough, Maglie also led off successive Giant rallies in the third and fourth innings with

Continued on Page 2, Column 3

SCORING FROM FIRST: Al Zarilla of the Red Sox hitting the plate after Al Richter's drive to right in sixth inning. Dodger Catcher Roy Campanella reaches out too late for the tag, while Boston's Jim Piersall watches.

Associated Press Wirephoto

YALE'S SWIMMERS SCORE NEAR-SWEEP AT EASTERN MEET

Add Four Titles for Total of Ten Out of 14 as the 13th Annual Event Closes

M'LANE AND THOMAN STAR

They Are Only Dual Victors —Latter Breaks a Record in 100-Yard Back-Stroke

By JOSEPH M. SHEEHAN

Special to The New York Times.

CAMBRIDGE, Mass., March 21—Tuning up for an all-out bid for the National Collegiate Athletic Association team title at Columbus, Ohio, a week hence, Yale's brilliant array of aquatic stars tonight completed a near clean sweep of the top honors in the Eastern Intercollegiate Swimming League's thirteenth annual invitation individual championships.

Four more victories in the final session of the three-day carnival gave the buoyant Bulldogs a total bag of ten first places out of a possible fourteen. No team tally is kept in this meet but the extent of the Eli domination is emphasized by the fact that Yale took twenty-six of the seventy medals at stake in an event that attracted entries from thirty colleges.

Dick Thoman and Jimmy McLane were the ranking Blue heroes tonight, with triumphs that established them as the meet's only double victors. Thoman, who also helped Yale's 300-yard medley relay team set a meet record, came through with the most distinguished performance of the entire carnival when he took the 100-yard backstroke in 56.6 seconds.

This clocking not only shaved three-tenths of a second from his own 1952 meet and national collegiate record (an N. C. A. A. record can be made only in the N. C. A. A. championships), but also marked the fastest time ever returned for the dorsal century in a "flat" race.

Marks Held by Taylor

By a quirk of the rules, however, Thoman cannot receive credit for a world or American standard. These marks are held by Ohio State's Jack Taylor, who achieved 56.5 seconds last year on the lead-off leg of a medley relay. Under similar circumstances this winter, Thoman posted an applied-for effort of 56.4 seconds.

It was Thoman's second meet record of the carnival. He set a 200-yard backstroke mark of 2:07.2 last night.

Another meet record fell in Yale's major disappointment of the carnival, when Milward (Dick) Martin, the New England sprint champion from Williams, turned the tables on Yale's previously unbeaten Kerry Donovan, his 50-yard conqueror of last night in meet-record time, in the 100-yard free-style.

With a tremendous surge up the last length of Harvard's pool, the tall Williams senior from Maplewood, N. J., touched out Donovan by no more than a couple of finger joints in 50.3 seconds. This clocking knocked eight-tenths of a second from the listed meet record set in 1950 by Yale's Ray Reid. In an afternoon trial, Martin had

Continued on Page 3, Column 4

FINISH OF FLORIDA DERBY: Money Broker, left, ridden by Al Popara and paying $33.80 for $2, going under the wire ahead of Blaze in the mile-and-a-furlong $133,750 race at Gulfstream Park. Jamie K and Slim ran a dead heat for show.

Associated Press Wirephoto

YANKEES TO RELY ON 1952 LINE-UP

Seeking His 5th Straight World Title, Manager Stengel Is Satisfied With Team

By LOUIS EFFRAT

Special to The New York Times.

ST. PETERSBURG, Fla., March 21—It rained here today. No matter what Al Lang may have called it, a heavy rainstorm deluged the city of sunshine and washed away the Grapefruit League game listed between the Yankees and Milwaukee Braves, giving the New York squad its first full day off since the athletes reported for spring training on Feb. 22.

This called for a press conference. The layman has no idea what a struggle goes on when Casey Stengel is surrounded by baseball writers. They bombard the manager with questions and most of the time he replies with questions of his own. Once in a while, Casey comes to the point of a direct reply, but many a young scribe has grown old, just waiting.

Today, it seemed, Casey liked everyone. All his players "look good—don't you think?" Pitchers, catchers, infielders, outfielders have been "tremendous — don't you agree?" From Vic Raschi he skipped to Mickey Mantle, then to Billy Martin, back to Hank Bauer, Yogi Berra, Gene Woodling, etc. He spoke glowingly about Jim Bridewesser, Andy Carey, Loren Babe, Bill Renna and Irv Noren.

More Questions From Casey

"No, I'm not worried about third base," the professor said. "Gil McDougald got a late start in the hitting, but after going 19-for-0, he's come through with five hits. The only question concerning Phil Rizzuto at short is how many games will he be able to play? You know, don't you, that Martin can play second base?

"What about infield reserves? Bridewesser, Carey and Babe have been doing fine, but I don't know how many reserve infielders I'll be able to keep. I'm trying to find among them one utility man who could fill in at all three positions. That would make room for an extra pitcher or an extra outfielder.

"Right now I would have to say that the team that finished the last season will be the team that opens the next one."

The last remark by Stengel was the most pertinent, but it surprised no-one. Every fan on the street has been aware that the Yankees,

Continued on Page 2, Column 6

Grand Street Boys Set Relay Record

By The Associated Press.

BUFFALO, March 21—New York City's Grand Street Boys Club mile relay team of Olympic champions set a new unofficial world indoor record tonight, winning the 174th Armory games mile in 3:14.4.

The four Olympians shattered the long-track indoor record of 3:15 set at Dartmouth in 1940 by New York University.

The anchor man was Mal Whitfield, two-time Olympic 800-meter champion. His mates were Herb McKenley, Andy Stanfield and George Rhoden.

Their only opposition was a Syracuse University quartet. Alfred and Cornell teams withdrew. It was hardly a contest.

Harrison Dillard, two-time Olympic winner, won the 70-yard

Continued on Page 5, Column 6

Bolt Ties Hawkins at 134 In Jacksonville Open Golf

By The Associated Press.

JACKSONVILLE, Fla., March 21—Tommy Bolt, refreshed by a two-week rest from the tournament tour, covered the Hyde Park municipal course in 66 strokes today and tied Fred Hawkins at the midway point in the Jacksonville open golf tournament.

Bolt, Maplewood, N. J., pro, had 68, 66 for his 134 card, 10 under par for the two rounds. Hawkins, El Paso, Tex., added a 69 to his opening round 65 for his 134.

The leaders were 2 strokes ahead of Sam Snead, White Sulphur Springs, W. Va., and Lew Worsham, Oakmont, Pa. Five players tied at 138, including Jim Turnesa, Briarcliff, N. Y., National Professional Golfers Association champion; Marty Furgol, Lemont, Ill.; Charles Harper, Fort Benning, Ga.; Jim Ferrier, San Francisco, and Jay Hebert, Erie, Pa.

Bolt carded an eagle to gain his tie. Hawkins had an eagle on his first round.

Bolt hit a No. 2 iron shot to the fourteenth green and sank an 18-foot putt for his eagle on the 466-yard par 5 hole. On the sixteenth, Bolt's ball rimmed the cup and he missed birdie putts from 10 and 7 feet on the next two holes.

"I got to gassing those last three holes," Bolt reported. "I guess I was afraid I was going to break the record."

Hawkins' 65 yesterday had tied the course record first set two years ago by Jerry Barber.

Stranahan Leads Amateurs

Hawkins had one bad break on his 3-under-par round today. On the third hole, his drive hit something in the fairway and kicked to the left, stopping squarely under the boundary fence. He managed to knock the ball a couple of yards and reached the green with his third shot, but had to take two putts for a bogey.

The El Paso player pushed his drive a bit on two other holes but came out of trouble to get pars.

"Outside of that I hit the ball well, Hawkins commented. "Maybe I was trying a little harder because I wanted those putts so bad."

Frank Stranahan, Toledo, bettered his opening round by a stroke and led the amateurs at 71, 70—141. The tournament continues with single rounds tomorrow and Monday.

Snead shot eight birdies in his

Continued on Page 8, Column 8

MRS. GRANT TAKES DOWNHILL LAURELS

Mrs. Anne Jones Runner-Up in Eastern Title Ski Event—Miss Tibbot Is Third

By FRANK ELKINS

Special to The New York Times.

WAITSFIELD, Vt., March 21—Mrs. Nancy Taylor Grant, a 20-year-old North Conway, N. H., housewife, today turned in the best performance of her skiing career in winning the Women's United States Eastern Amateur Ski Association downhill championship on sun-drenched Mad River Glen. The 110-pound blond speedster, who "never took a ski lesson," covered the mile - and - a - quarter course, which dropped 1,700 feet, in 2 minutes 16 seconds.

Four-tenths of a second back was the favorite, Mrs. Anne Jones of Rockland, Vt., three-time winner of the Gibson Trophy and the present Eastern giant slalom titleholder. Then came a local skier, Nancy Tibbot, who was clocked in 2:18.5.

Ann Shaw, University of Vermont captain, was fourth in 2:19.7. Leona Reny, 16-year-old neighbor of the winner, was fifth in 2:20.3 and Betsy Strong, Middlebury captain, was sixth in 2:20.4.

Slalom Race Slated

A field of more than forty women was on hand as bright sunshine, following a six-inch snowstorm, provided an almost ideal setting for the opener of a three championship event week-end program. Tomorrow's slalom will be used with today's downhill to determine the Eastern Alpine combined champion. The results of the meet also will be considered in selecting the team to represent the United States in the world ski championships in Sweden next winter.

The course proved a test of ability and control. The toughest phase was the first half mile of the Catamount Trail, where grades of 38 degrees called for absolute control and keen judgment of pace. Several "gates" were set at the steep pitch, full of bumps, to keep the racers from gaining excess speed on their dashes down to the valley floor.

The bright sun and spring temperature turned the previous icy base into a granular cover, just what the racers desired. From the beginning, the women tried for as much speed as possible hoping to make the controlled turns with the straightest line. At the bottom of the incline another series of flags led into a sort of S-turn where a huge bump sent many of the racers almost flying into the traverse under the chair lift line.

The early starters had the best snow of the course up to this stage as the sun began to soften the cover toward the middle of the race. Past the Midway Station, the trail led into the flats, the easiest part of the course.

It was a straight run thereafter to get quickly down to the finish. Through the shaded areas, the frozen snow was extremely fast.

Continued on Page 4, Column 4

BARBARA M'INTIRE GAINS SEMI-FINALS

Defeats Miss Romack, 2 Up—Misses Faulk, O'Sullivan, Diringer Win on Links

By The Associated Press.

PINEHURST, N. C., March 21—Eighteen-year-old Barbara McIntire of Toledo, Ohio, finished with three birdies today to eliminate the defending champion, Barbara Romack of Sacramento, Calif., 2 up, and gain the semi-finals of the North and South golf championship tournament.

The rising Midwest star, who is headed for Ohio State University in the fall, will meet Mary Lena Faulk of Thomasville, Ga., tomorrow afternoon. Miss Faulk led from the first hole to score a 4-and-3 triumph over Mae Murray of Rutland, Vt.

Medalist Pat O'Sullivan of Orange, Conn., captured the first four holes in even 4's against Mary Patton Janssen of Charlottesville, Va., for an 8-and-6 victory. Miss O'Sullivan's next opponent will be Carol Diringer of Tiffin, Ohio, her co-worker at a near-by resort hotel. Miss Diringer turned back Mrs. R. M. Torgerson of Forest Hills, N. Y., 3 and 2.

Miss McIntire, who last year lost a quarter-final Western open match to Miss Romack, had 23 putts for 18 holes in registering a medal score of 39, 34—73, one under women's par for the 6,000-yard No. 2 Pinehurst Country Club course. She never let the Pacific Coast girl take the lead.

The Ohioan took the sixth hole with a par 3 and chipped in for a winning eagle 3 on the eighth for a 2-up lead. Miss Romack's par 3 on the ninth cut the lead to one hole.

Miss McIntire's par 4 won the tenth, but the 1952 winner dropped a fifteen-footer for a birdie 3 to win the twelfth and her par 4 on No. 13 evened the match.

After Miss McIntire regained the lead with a birdie 4 on the fourteenth, a par 3 on No. 15 by Miss Romack deadlocked the match again. Both birdied the par-5 sixteenth. Then Miss McIntire sank a twenty-footer for a birdie 2 on the seventeenth and a seven-footer for a birdie 3 on the last hole to take the match.

Florida Derby Chart

HALLANDALE, Fla., March 21—The following is the chart showing how the Florida Derby was run at Gulfstream today:

SEVENTH RACE—The Florida Derby; $100,000 added; 3-year-olds; one mile and a furlong. Start good; won driving; place same. Went to post 4:51, off at once. Winner, ch. c., by Half Crown-Chartreuse II, by Poughatchey. Trainer, V. R. Wright. Value to winner, $88,000; second, $25,000; third, $9,750 each. Times—0:23 2/5; 0:47 1/5; 1:13; 1:39 4/5; 1:53 4/5. Weather clear, track fast.

Starters.	Wt.	P.P.	St.	1/4	1/2	3/4	Str.	Fin.	Jockeys.	Mutuels St.	Mutuels Pl.	Mutuels Sh.	Dollar Odds.
Money Broker	117	5	8	8^{2}	7^{1}	3^{hd}	$1^{1\frac{1}{2}}$	1^{hd}	Popara	33.80	13.70	6.60	15.90
*Blaze	111	14	3	2^{hd}	$1^{\frac{1}{2}}$	1^{hd}	2^{hd}	2^{2}	McCreary	....	5.10	3.20	6.05
†aJamie K.	117	9	14	14^{1}	11^{hd}	6^{2}	4^{2}	3	Gorman	....	....	3.80	7.40
†Slim	117	15	4	3^{2}	$2^{1\frac{1}{2}}$	$2^{1\frac{1}{2}}$	3^{4}	3^{4}	Woodhouse	....	....	3.90	13.[illegible]
*Mikeaby	111	2	16	$15^{1\frac{1}{2}}$	14^{hd}	12^{2}	9^{3}	5no	Batcheller	....	....	....	6.05
Ace Destroyer	126	3	9	6no	5^{2}	4^{8}	5^{5}	[illegible]	J. Adams	....	....	....	16.25
*Precious Stone	[illegible]	[illegible]	7	10^{hd}	[illegible]	8^{2}	6^{1}	7^{hd}	Barrow	....	....	....	
Ram o' War	123	16	11	11^{5}	9^{2}	10^{hd}	10^{1}	$8^{1\frac{1}{2}}$	Dodson	....	....	....	3.15
aDr. Stanley	117	11	12	9^{hd}	10^{hd}	$9^{\frac{1}{2}}$	$8^{\frac{1}{2}}$	9^{2}	Bauer	....	....	....	7.40
Air Pine	118	7	[illegible]	[illegible]	6^{2}	7^{hd}	7^{hd}	10^{1}	Boulmetis	....	....	....	28.95
Powhatan	117	1	10	12^{hd}	15^{2}	15^{2}	13^{5}	[illegible]	Stout	....	....	....	[illegible]
*Sickle's Sound	117	4	17	17	17	11^{1}	[illegible]	[illegible]	Brooks	....	....	....	6.05
Dark Star	[illegible]	13	5	4^{hd}	4^{hd}	$11^{\frac{1}{2}}$	11^{1}	[illegible]	Burr	....	....	....	4.15
Sir Mango	123	6	1	$1^{\frac{1}{2}}$	3^{1}	[illegible]	14^{8}	[illegible]	G. Hettinger	....	....	....	114.80
Hit the Spot	117	17	6	7^{2}	$8^{\frac{1}{2}}$	13^{hd}	16^{6}	[illegible]	Madden	....	....	....	16.30
*Gulf Stream	117	12	15	16^{2}	16^{hd}	16^{2}	15^{hd}	16^{8}	Lester	....	....	....	6.05
Matagorda	126	8	13	$13^{1\frac{1}{2}}$	$13^{1\frac{1}{2}}$	17	17	17	P. J. Bailey	....	....	....	6.25

*Field. †Dead heat for third. aSpring Hill Farm entry.

Money Broker, unhurried while well off the early leaders, reached serious contention on the final turn, attained command and drew clear when straightened into the stretch, then held on tenaciously. Blaze raced Sir Mango into defeat early, set the pace under rating and, after having been displaced, continued on gamely. Jamie K. moved from far back to attain prominence but lacked further response in the final furlong and finished in a dead-heat with Slim.

The latter held on well after being formidable from the start. Ace Destroyer enjoyed sufficient racing room but lacked a response when hard urged from midway of the final turn. Ram o' War was within striking distance to midway of the final turn where he was forced to take up sharply. Air Pine could not keep pace. Dark Star flattened out badly. Sir Mango stopped to a walk. Matagorda was always far back and was badly bothered on the final turn.

Owners—1, Grissom and Grosfield; 2, L. B. Mayer; 3, Spring Hill Farm; 4, Mrs. W. Gilroy; 5, Mrs. M. W. Huckaby; 6, Mrs. T. M. Daniel; 7, Mrs. A. Kuhn; 8, B. S. Campbell; 9, Spring Hill Farm; 10, C. A. O'Neil Jr.; 11, Greentree Stable; 12, Warbern Stables; 13, Cain Hoy Stable; 14, H. N. Eads; 15, Mrs. E. E. D. Shaffer; 16, R. A. Parachek; 17, J. W. Brown.

MONEY BROKER, 16-1, VICTOR OVER BLAZE IN $133,750 DERBY

Long Shot, Ridden by Al Popara, Holds Off Runner-Up by Head at Gulfstream Park

DEAD HEAT FOR THIRD SPOT

Jamie K. and Slim Finish Even —Favored Ram o' War Eighth in 9-Furlong Florida Race

By JOSEPH C. NICHOLS

Special to The New York Times.

HALLANDALE, Fla., March 21—Money Broker, slightly less than 16 to 1, held off a mighty stretch challenge by Louis B. Mayer's Blaze to win the $133,750 Florida Derby today. The chestnut colt, owned by Allie Grissom and Ed Grosfield of Detroit, scored by a head.

A crowd of 23,547, the largest ever to visit the Gulfstream Park Race Course, saw the mile-and-a-furlong test, in which Jockey Al Popara, on the winner, kept his horse up there just long enough to neutralize the characteristic closing burst made by Conn McCreary, who had the mount on Blaze.

A record number of seventeen 3-year-olds competed in the race. To the winner went the sum of $88,000, and of this the 10 per cent that accrued to Jockey Popara, an ex-amateur flyweight boxing champion of Michigan, constituted the biggest payday of his life.

The fight between Money Broker and Blaze was close, but the contest for third place was as even as possible, with Jamie K. of the Spring Hill Farm finishing in a dead heat with Mrs. Wallace Gilroy's Slim for this spot.

First Two Choices Trail

The favorite, Bruce Campbell's Ram o' War, had to be content with eighth, after being pocketed at the three-eighths pole, while the second choice, Dark Star of the Cain Hoy Stable, finished thirteenth.

Although he had a pretty good record, Money Broker was relatively ignored in this wide open race, and his payoff in the mutuels was $33.80, under an impost of 117 pounds. The winner was timed in 1:53 4/5.

Money Broker got away almost in the exact center of the pack, and was held off the pace until the turn. McCreary, strangely for him, was up in front early, keeping Blaze second to Sir Mango and then second to Dark Star. It was not until the three-quarters that Popara entered the fight, moving into third place behind Blaze and Slim.

In the stretch Money Broker moved 'way ahead, a length and a half in front of Blaze, and he seemed to be on his way to an easy victory. But McCreary started Blaze going again. The duel became a furious one as they approached the wire, where Money Broker held his advantage, albeit by a mere head.

Joe W. Brown's Matagorda, who beat Money Broker in winning the Louisiana Derby last Saturday, finished seventeenth and last.

Purchased for $3,300

Money Broker is a son of Half Crown and Chartreuse II, and was bought by Grissom and Grosfield partnership at the yearling sales in Keeneland, Ky., for $3,300. As a 2-year-old he earned $12,810 while compiling a record of six victories, three seconds and two thirds. This year the colt has won three of five with one second. His total earnings amount to $112,710.

Blaze ran as a member of the field, which included four others, while Jamie K., owned by the Spring Hill Farm, was an entry with his stable-mate, Dr. Stanley.

Popara, commenting on his triumph, said that he had "a lot of luck, and a good horse."

Early Show a Success

The Derby Day program was a complete success from the pageantry standpoint, what with bands, parades, water skiing and small craft sailing in the infield lagoon. The gates to the park opened at nine o'clock, and by that time until eleven a.m. the stand and clubhouse restaurants were open for breakfast.

Frank Stevens, head of the famous catering family, reported that this phase of the bill did not come up to expectations, explaining that the people down here like to sleep in the mornings.

At noon, a good many fans must have wished that they had arisen earlier and had breakfast, for the crowds at the doors were pretty thick. Oscar and Charley, the urbane headwaiters well known to New York's turf and trotting fans, handled the situation expertly.

Continued on Page 4, Column 2

CELTICS BEAT NATS IN 4TH OVERTIME

Continued From Page 1

Cross star tied the game at 99—99, with five seconds remaining in the third overtime session, with a long one-handed push shot.

In the fourth overtime period, the Nationals raced to a 104-99 lead but Cousy then sank a foul shot and two successive field goals. He connected with four more free throws as the Celtics pulled ahead to the victory.

The Celtics will meet the New York Knickerbockers in the first game of a best three-out-of-five series at New York Wednesday. The winner then will meet the survivor of the Western Division play-offs.

Cousy's performance topped the old N. B. A. play-off scoring mark of 47 set by George Mikan of Minneapolis last year.

A total of 107 fouls were called during the long game, 55 against Syracuse and 52 against the Celtics. In the end, the fouls caught up with the Nats as seven men had the limit of six, resulting in technicals every time they committed a foul.

Syracuse was handicapped further by the loss of Dolph Schayes, its top scorer, who was banished from the game with Boston's Bob Brannum for fighting at the four-minute mark of the second period.

A crowd of 11,058 watched the lead change hands often until the Celtics' final spurt in the fourth extra session.

Easy Ed McCauley scored 18 points for Boston, while teammate Bob Harris tossed in 14. Red Rocha was top man for Syracuse with 19 points, followed by George King with 16.

The line-up:

BOSTON (111)	G.	F.	PF.	P.
Donham, lf	1	0	6	2
Harris, rf	4	6	6	14
Cooper	2	5	7	9
Brannum	3	0	1	6
Mahnken	0	1	5	1
Macauley, c	4	10	6	18
Mahoney	0	0	5	0
Cousy, lg	10	30	5	50
Sharman, rg	3	3	6	9
Rollins	0	2	5	2
Total	27	57	52	111

SYRACUSE (105)	G.	F.	PF.	P.
Schayes, lf	2	4	2	8
Gabor, rf	3	3	6	9
Lochmueller	1	1	6	3
Osterkorn	1	0	6	2
Lloyd, c	4	5	5	13
Rocha	5	9	6	19
Jorgenson	2	4	6	8
King, lg	4	8	6	16
Cervi, rg	0	9	7	9
Seymour	5	8	5	18
Total	27	51	55	105

Boston	21	19	22	15	9	4	9	12—111
Syracuse	22	20	17	18	9	4	9	6—105

Free throws missed — Boston: Donham 3, Cousy 2, Mahoney, Cooper Rollins. Syracuse: Rocha 3, Lochmueller 2, Lloyd 2, Gabor 2, Cervi 2, Jorgenson, King, Seymour.

YALE'S SWIMMERS SCORE NEAR-SWEEP

Continued From Page 1

lowered the old mark to 50.5 seconds.

Ahead until the last few strokes, Donovan was timed in 50.4 seconds, as both he and Martin finished nearly a full body-length in front of Yale's Don Sheff, last year's winner.

McLane, who opened the meet by taking the 1,500-meter free-style on Thursday night, dethroned Wayne Moore, the Bulldog captain, in leading home a Yale sweep of the first four places in the 440-yard free-style.

The two-time Olympian, who won twelve national titles and one Olympic crown before entering Yale and then had to wait for his last time around in varsity competition to win another major title of any description, swam the fastest quarter-mile in his career.

On top from the start, McLane slapped the flags in 4:34.1, just a stroke ahead of Moore, who was clocked in 4:34.9. It was a reversal of their close-order finish in last night's 220. Moore also trailed McLane, but not so closely, in the 1,500.

John Marshall had his first competitive outing of the season in the 440 and placed third in 4:40.6. Yale's Australian ace, whose training has been retarded by sinus infections, swept the three Eastern titles as a sophomore two years ago and repeated in the 220 and 1,500 last year.

Martin Smith, a junior from Newark, N. J., brought up the rear of the Yale sweep with a clocking of 4:42, fast enough to have won the N. C. A. A. title in any year prior to 1951, when Marshall took that meet's mark all the way down from 4:42.6 to 4:30.2.

The other victors were Dennis O'Connor of Yale, who took the 100-yard breast-stroke in the fast time of 1:00.5; John Mayers of Springfield, who captured the 150-yard individual medley in 1:34.2, and Owen Davies of Navy, who retained his 3-meter diving title.

Yale's medley trio of Thoman, O'Connor and Sheff was clocked in 2:48.4, as against the mark of 2:50 set by the Bulldogs last year, with Stanton Smith, who missed this meet because of a cold, and Sheff swimming the breast stroke and free-style legs. The Yale splits were 57.2 seconds for Thoman, who did not hit his turns right in this race, 60.3 for O'Connor and 50.8 for Donovan.

Martin's victory gave Williams its second title of the meet, Charles Douglas of the Ephmen having edged O'Connor last night in the 200-yard breast-stroke. Douglas finished third in the butterfly century, behind Harvard's Ken Emerson. No other college won more than one event.

THE SUMMARIES

100-Yard Back-Stroke—1, Richard Thoman, Yale, 0:56.6 (meet and national collegiate record; old record, 0:56.9, by Thoman, 1952); 2, Peter Wittereid, Army, 1:00.2; 3, Donald Mulvey, Harvard, 1:00.4; 4, Gerard Curran, Fordham, 1:01.5; 5, George Kouch, Niagara, 1:02.1; 6, Richard Auwater, Columbia, 1:02.

100-Yard Breast-stroke—1, Dennis O'Connor, Yale, 1:00.5; 2, Kenneth Emerson, Harvard, 1:02.9; 3, Charles Douglas, Williams, 1:02.9; 4, Neale Bird, Navy, 1:03.9; 5, Ralph Zani, Harvard, 1:03.6; 6, Gerald Nay, Navy, 1:04.7.

100-Yard Free-style—1, Milward Martin, Williams, 0:50.3 (meet record; old record, 0:51.1, by Raymond Reid, Yale, 1950; Martin was clocked in 0:50.5 in his qualifying heat); 2, Kerry Donovan, Yale, 0:50.4; 3, Don Sheff, Yale, 0:51.2; 4, Ralph Brisco, Brown, 0:51.9; 5, John Glover, Dartmouth, 0:52.1; 6, John Stone, Princeton, 0:53.0.

440-Yard Free-style—1, James McLane, Yale, 4:34.1; 2, Wayne Moore, Yale, 4:34.9; 3, John Marshall, Yale, 4:40.6; 4, Martin Smith, Yale, 4:42; 5, William Yorzyk, Springfield, 4:45.2; 6, Philip Ware, Niagara, 5:29.9.

150-Yard Individual Medley—1, John Mayers, Springfield, 1:34.2; 2, Monroe Pray, Amherst, 1:37.2; 3, Roy Swanson, Cornell, 1:38.3; 4, Paul Slack, Navy, 1:38.5; 5, John Joslyn, Yale, 1:39.6; 6, Kenneth Abbe, Yale, 1:39.6.

300-Yard Medley Relay—1, Yale (Richard Thoman, Dennis O'Connor, Kerry Donovan), 2:48.4 (meet record; old record, 2:50, by Yale, with Thoman, Stanton Smith and Don Sheff, in 1952); 2, Harvard, 2:53.9; 3, Army, 3:00.3; 4, Columbia, 3:02.2; 5, Princeton, 3:02.7; 6, Niagara, 3:02.8.

Three-Meter Dive—1, Owen Davies, Navy, 168.27 points; 2, Paul Dillingham, Harvard, 161.55; 3, Kenneth Welch, Yale, 158.25; 4, William Davis, Navy, 137.77; 5, Cornelius Christie, Princeton, 129; 6, Robert Smalls, Harvard, 114.46.

Eastern Swim Champions

50-Yard Free-Style—Kerry Donovan, Yale.

100-Yard Free-Style—Milward Martin, Williams.

220-Yard Free-Style—Wayne Moore, Yale.

440-Yard Free-Style—James McLane, Yale.

1,500-Meter Free-Style—McLane, Yale.

100-Yard Back-Stroke—Richard Thoman, Yale.

200-Yard Back-Stroke—Thoman, Yale.

100-Yard Breast-Stroke—Dennis O'Connor, Yale.

200-Yard Breast-Stroke—Charles Douglas, Williams.

150-Yard Individual Medley—John Mayers, Springfield.

One-Meter Dive—Kenneth Welch, Yale.

Three-Meter Dive—*Owen Davies, Navy.

300-Yard Medley Relay—*Yale.

400-Yard Relay—*Yale.

*Retained title.

ELIS IN RUGBY TEST JUST FOR THE KICKS

No Cheering Crowd Nor Band as Yale Men Foot Bill and Ball in Brooklyn

By ALLISON DANZIG

The Yale varsity played a game of football here yesterday and it is a matter for the Ivy League to look into, seeing as how there's not only a ban on extramural contests but they dasn't even hold practice at this time of the year.

Without fanfare and hardly even a mention in the public prints, the Elis slipped into our town from New Haven by motorcars. Proceeding on across the bridge they managed somehow to find their way to a small stadium in the Red Hook section of Brooklyn, where no one ever dared raise his voice in rendition of Boola Boola.

Seeing as how the two-platoon system has been ruled out, the Yales brought down only fifteen men. Among them were such stalwarts of Jordan Olivar's amazing eleven of last fall as Ted Woodsum, Baird Brittingham, Charlie Coudert, Bob Parcells, Pete Radulovic, Harris Ashton, Bob Poole, Charlie Deen and Harry Baldwin.

No Band, No Crowd, No Cheers

Instead of the vast crowds of thirty to forty thousand that turn out in the Bowl, there were only a few score men, women and children on hand to greet the Elis. Some of them looked on curiously, wondering who the athletes were and what in the world had brought them to this outlying area of Brooklyn. No bands were tuning up. No cheerleaders were turning handsprings and no vendors were out with chrysanthemums, souvenirs and winning colors.

Casually the Elis filed into the modest dressing room to put on their uniforms. When they came out on the field they were wearing shirts instead of jerseys and no headguards were in sight. In place of silken knee-length pants they were garbed in shorts and stockings, and their feet were encased in cleated shoes.

The general effect of their appearance was much slimmer than when they were last seen in the Bowl. The explanation was that they were minus the shoulder harness and hip pads that add so much to the bulk of the American football player.

Then the game got under way and the mystery was cleared up. This wasn't the American game of football they were playing. It was Rugby, the English game from which the American brand of football was derived after its introduction into the United States in a contest between Harvard and McGill University of Canada at Cambridge in May, 1874. That was five years after Princeton and Rutgers met in the first intercollegiate football game under association or soccer rules.

First Game Since 1943

Yale was playing the New York Rugby Football Club in the first game of Rugby staged here since the war ended activity in 1943. The local team is comprised largely of men who played at English schools and universities and make their home here now. The captain, George Jack, led the team before the war and he is the only holdover.

Rugby and American Football have points in common. They are played on a field somewhat of the same dimensions with a prolate spheroid and there is kicking and running with the ball and tackling in both games. But they differ in so many respects that the American football fan would require a rugby expert at his side to understand what was going on in Red Hook Stadium yesterday.

There is no forward passing and no blocking in rugby, in which there are fifteen men on a side, as compared to eleven in American football. Possession of the ball means little, the spheroid changing hands constantly and often moving from one end of the field to the other and back again in the space of seconds.

Instead of the American scrimmage there is the rugby scrum, in which the eight forwards of each side lock arms around shoulders and hips in two tight opposing masses and seek to heel the ball backward to the scrum half.

The scrum half, one of seven backs, seizes the ball as it rolls out from the pack and gives it to the stand-off half. This gentleman is not really stand-offish. He is in the thick of things and is the key man who opens up all the movements of the running attack as he hands off the ball to the three-quarter halves.

These four operatives then go into the lateral passing maneuvers that are the prettiest sight of rugby, sweeping down the field together and shuttling the ball out wider and wider in evasive action against opposing tacklers. The lateral is a part of American football but only a minor phase of the offense.

One of the chief differences in the two games is the spirit in which they are played. American intercollegiate football is a thoroughly organized sport in which highly paid coaching staffs train the athletes and develop the teams. Expenses and receipts run high into six figures and attendance may reach 100,000 spectators for a single game. Rugby is conducted on an informal basis. There are no paid coaches. A purely nominal admission is charged if any and the athletes do not follow any strict training rules.

The Yale players came to New York yesterday on their own. They get no help from the university other than the loan of their shirts and shorts. They play Rutgers strictly for the fun of it and big Charlie Dean said that he personally prefers it to the strict regime of spring football practice and most of the others feel the same way about it.

Playing Rugby Again

Harvard and Princeton, like Yale, have been playing Rugby again after giving it up during the war and M. I. T. has organized a team. Cornell, Dartmouth, Long Island U., and Hofstra, which had teams before the war, have not resumed the spot as yet.

Visits of Cambridge University teams to the United States in 1931 and again in 1938 had to arouse interest in rugby in Eastern colleges, and Albert Woodley, New York advertising executive, has done much to keep the game going.

Oh yes. Yale won the game yesterday, 17—3. Deen, Brittingham, Radulovic, Albert Barclay and Ed Schmults each scored a try (touchdown) with three points and Parcells kicked a conversion for two points. Jim Philip scored on a penalty goal for the New York team.

Yale's physical fitness and the superior weight and strength of the forwards told part of the story. Barclay was a fine scrum half and the three-quarter halfbacks did an exceptionally good job in the second half of thirty minutes. New York's weakness was in the link between the scrum and the three-quarterback. At least, so the referee, Fred Cosstick, an Oxford Greyhound, saw it.

EASTERN COLLEGES LIST LOOP BASEBALL

The Eastern Intercollegiate Baseball League this year will return to a single round-robin type schedule originally adopted in 1948 but abandoned last season for two-division competition.

The forty-five game card, in which each team faces each other team once, will open April 8, with Columbia at Navy. The schedule ends on May 16.

Last season, Brown won the "northern" division title and Cornell the "southern," and no play-off was held. The current plan permits an end to the season before final college examinations.

UTE FIVE DEFEATS FLUSHING, 54 TO 52

Wins in 1:13 of Sudden-Death Overtime, 2d Extra Period, to Take City Crown

PARENTI LEADS ON ATTACK

Sinks Deciding Basket, Gets 31 Points—Jefferson Tops Commerce, 56 to 55

By WILLIAM J. BRIORDY

Mike Parenti, 6-foot 8-inch center, led New Utrecht High to its first city P. S. A. L. basketball championship yesterday afternoon.

Taking a pass from Herb Markman, Parenti counted on a short jump shot in 1:13 of the sudden-death overtime, second extra-session, to give the Utes a 54-52 triumph over Flushing High of Queens at Madison Square Garden.

The gathering of 6,500 saw Coach Irv Goldberg's unbeaten five win its twentieth game of the season. This was a thriller from start to finish. The Ute supporters mobbed their team at the conclusion of the contest.

The Markman-Parenti combination kept the Green and White in the game by teaming to tie the score at 52-all at the end of the first three-minute overtime. With fifteen seconds to go, Markman fed to Parenti, who scored from underneath to send the game into the second extra period.

Parenti was high scorer in the contest with 31 points, the result of twelve field goals and seven charity tosses. But Flushing had a star of its own in Ransom Robinson. In addition to turning in a standout defensive game, Robinson was ever-present on the attack.

After Sheldon Brodsky had put the Utes ahead at 49—48 with 1:55 of the regular game remaining on a side-set shot, Robinson knotted it at 49-all, getting a one-pointer when he was fouled by Danny Berlin. Then Robinson stole the ball, and the Red Devils appeared headed for victory, with fifty-five seconds left.

Flushing froze the ball and played for one shot. The Red Devils took time out with sixteen seconds left. Then Robinson pegged one that rimmed the hoop with two seconds remaining.

The score was tied four times in the fourth quarter and fourteen times in all.

In the first overtime, Robinson's two one-pointers gave the Red Devil charges of Jack Levitts a 51-49 leeway. Ken Clark of Flushing fouled Herb Kesten, who made one of two charity tosses. Berlin fouled Mike Musio of Flushing, who made one of two tries with forty seconds left. Then Markman and Parenti teamed to make it 52-all.

The lead changed hands three times in the first quarter, with Flushing ahead by 16—10 when the period ended. The score was knotted four times in the second quarter, and the teams left the floor at intermission on even terms, 25—25, it was 41-all when the third quarter ended. The count was knotted on five occasions in that session.

Before yesterday the Red Devils had captured their last ten contests. They last won the city crown in 1903. Robinson threw in 14 points for Flushing. Bill Hendriks, 6-9 center, topped the Red Devils with 17.

In the consolation play-off, Thomas Jefferson High of Brooklyn turned back the High School of Commerce, 56—55. This was a tense struggle, and the teams never were more than three points apart.

Commerce's Stan Hill was high man with 20 points, one more than Jefferson's Harvey Salz.

Visiting Police Man Indiana 'Ghost Town' As All 1,014 Go Off to a Basketball Game

MILAN, Ind., March 21 (UP) — Firemen and police from neighboring cities kept order in a "ghost town" today as Milan's 1,014 residents moved en masse to Indianapolis for a high school basketball tourney.

Milan's team, unheralded among Hoosierland's 755 prep squads until it won three elimination tourneys and became one of only four survivors, sought the first state title for a small town since 1915. But no miracle occurred. South Bend Central eliminated Milan in an afternoon game, 56—37.

In Indiana, world events are shunted to inside pages of newspapers during four weeks of "March madness." Nothing thrills the fans so much as a "people's choice" staying in the field while dozens of big cities are sidelined in this one-class 43-year-old championship meet.

Six firemen from Batesville and two policemen from Madison showed up at the Town Hall to substitute for their Milan counterparts.

"This town's really deserted," said a Batesville fireman during the day. "There's nobody on the streets at all."

Milan normally has its biggest crowds of the week on Saturdays, when the farmers come to town to shop and talk in stores and on street corners. Today all the stores were locked tight and signs said: "Back on Monday."

The visiting policemen hoped nothing would happen to violate the peace while Milan was in action on the Butler University fieldhouse court before 15,000 fans. "We're sitting in the firehouse listening to the radio broadcasts," said one.

Only a few old and feeble persons stayed home. The rest packed lunches in baskets and set out by auto bright and early this morning for the 75-mile trip to the state capital.

The New York Times.

 SUNDAY, JUNE 14, 1953. L++ S

HOGAN, WITH A 283, TAKES FOURTH U. S. OPEN GOLF TITLE; NATIVE DANCER WINS BELMONT; YANKS CRUSH INDIANS, 9-4

The New York Times (by Edward Hausner)

NECK FINISH IN BELMONT STAKES: Native Dancer, left, Eric Guerin aboard, beating Jamie K., with Eddie Arcaro up, in eighty-fifth running of mile-and-a-half classic at Belmont Park yesterday. Royal Bay Gem, right, is finishing third.

JAMIE K. NECK BACK

Native Dancer's Strong Finish Takes $118,600 Mile-and-Half Test

By JAMES ROACH

In what amounted to a re-run of the May 23 Preakness at Pimlico, Alfred Gwynne Vanderbilt's grand 3-year-old colt, Native Dancer, yesterday won the eighty-fifth Belmont Stakes at cold, rainy, windy Belmont Park.

The mile-and-a-half race is billed as "the test of the champion." The Dancer is a champion.

The one, two, three, four finish in the Preakness was the one, two, three, four finish in the Belmont. Again the Spring Hill Farm's Jamie K. was the runner-up, and again he was beaten by a neck after a pulsating duel through the stretch.

Third was Eugene Constantin Jr's Royal Bay Gem, ten lengths back of Jamie K., and fourth was Bruce S. Campbell's Ram o'War, an additional four-and-a-half lengths away.

In the mile-and-three-sixteenths Preakness, Royal Bay Gem finished half a dozen lengths away from the runner-up and two lengths in advance of the Campbell colt.

The Preem at 122 to 1

There were two others in the $118,600 race. They made up-the-stretch finishes. The Preem, 122-to-1 shot owned by Louis Prima, the band-leader, reached the wire thirty lengths astern of Ram o'War and twenty lengths ahead of the King Ranch's Kamehameha.

The King Ranch's jockey had trouble in the stretch. His saddle slipped. Perhaps Kamehameha could have beaten The Preem if that hadn't happened.

For the fourteenth successive time in a fifteen-race career in which he has been beaten only once (by Dark Star in the Kentucky Derby), Native Dancer was an odds-on-favorite. He was bet down to 9 to 20. Jamie K. was the second choice at a bit over 5 to 2. Royal Bay Gem, who drew an unexpectedly heavy play, was 6 to 1.

The stretch part of the race was a thriller. There, just as had been expected, the Dancer and Jamie K. hooked up. Jamie K., with Eddie Arcaro bidding for his sixth Belmont triumph, took the lead on the last turn. The Dancer, Eric Guerin in the saddle, moved with him. At the eighth pole the Dancer, on the outside, moved slightly ahead.

Arcaro rode his hardest. Guerin rode his hardest. For the rest of the way the Dancer had the situation under control. It seemed that he wasn't under quite as much pressure as he had been in the Preakness.

Near Record for Race

The clocking was an excellent 2:28 3-5. That's only two-fifths of a second away from the Belmont Stakes record set by Count Fleet in 1943 and equaled by Citation in 1948.

And the clocking was just one second away from the track record set by the 5-year-old Bolingbroke, under 115 pounds, in 1942.

Each of the Belmont Stakes contestants carried 126 pounds in this richest running of the great race for 3-year-olds.

The track was fast, despite rain that started pelting the premises with the running of the third of the eight races.

The quarters were clicked off in 0:25, 0:25 1-5, 0:24 4-5, 0:24 2-5, 0:24 4-5 and 0:24 2-5. The mile time was 1:39 2-5.

Now Native Dancer, gray son of Polynesian and Geisha, has a fourteen-for-fifteen record (twelve of the triumphs have been scored in stakes races) and earnings of $522,745. He's the ninth horse in racing history to go over the half-million mark. It took Citation, the cash-collecting champion, twenty races to get his first half-million. The Dancer had turned the cushy trick in 22½ minutes of under-silks exercise.

Well aware of the fact that the plunging on the Dancer caused a minus show pool of $46,000 in the Preakness, the Belmont management kept the show windows shut for yesterday's little number. Of the $307,036 in the win pool, $175,946 rode with the Vanderbilt colt. Of the $99,379 in the place pool, $80,885 was bet on the favorite.

There was a minus pool, after all. It didn't amount to much. In order to make the $2.10-for-$2 returns on the Dancer to place, the management had to put $134.68 into the pool.

Maybe it should be noted, among

Continued on Page 4, Column 2

CINDA, $23.80, FIRST AT MONMOUTH PARK

Only Filly in Race Defeats Indian Land by 5 Lengths in Oceanport Handicap

By JOSEPH C. NICHOLS

Special to The New York Times.

EATONTOWN, N. J., June 13—Cinda, the only filly in the race, was the winner of the Oceanport Handicap, the $19,200 event that served as the feature on the opening-day's card at Monmouth Park today.

Neglected in the betting by the crowd of 22,700, Cinda crossed the finish line more than five lengths ahead of Indian Land, and paid $23.80 straight, in the six-furlong test.

Jimmy Stout, who has made a habit of leading all other jockeys at this track for the past three years, guided the filly to the triumph, in 1:12 over a track that was fast despite a steady downpour. Cinda, a 4-year-old daughter of Occupy, is owned by Jouett Shouse.

When the final line-up for the Oceanport was made known, it revealed that fourteen would compete, with five grouped in the mutuel field. This odd set-up was necessitated by two late scratches. Squared Away, owned by Mrs. Jan Burke, was made the favorite, but finished an unimpressive third, after putting up a good battle in the early stages.

The Brookmeade Stable's Safety, holder of a victory over Jamie K., was the first one to get away from the gate, and Squared Away was right with him. Cinda was in the pack at the start, but Stout moved her into the lead before a furlong had been traversed, and the "home course" jockey proceeded to keep her there all the way.

The crowd refused to take Cinda's front-running effort seriously, and centered most of its

Continued on Page 4, Column 6

American Collegians Defeat British in Dual Track Meets

By MICHAEL STRAUSS

Special to The New York Times.

PHILADELPHIA, June 13—A combined Oxford and Cambridge track team matched its prowess against four American collegiate squads at Franklin Field today and lost both ends of the double dual meet as the United States athletes achieved fine efforts in field competition and in the shorter running events.

In contrast to past years, when the British visited two campuses to compete each time in meets against the combined representatives of two colleges, the visitors tried to achieve the same goal all at once today. Despite a damp setting, they went through their paces on schedule, but found the opposition too formidable.

Opposing the visitors was the cream of the Army and Yale track team in one instance and the top performers from Cornell and Pennsylvania in the other. While the event was run along the lines of a triangular meet in that competitors had to take part in any single test only once—separate dual meet scores were kept—the order proved too large. In both meets, the British were beaten by 9-to-6 margins.

Chataway Double Winner

The visitors gave a fine account of themselves, particularly Chris Chataway, the 22-year-old flier who represented Great Britain in the 5,000-meter event at Helsinki last summer but fell while leading around the last turn. The red-haired Englishman, a student at Oxford, was one of three double winners in the meet, taking the mile and two-mile events.

The dual victory by the British distance star enabled the losers to round out a total of five triumphs in the fifteen-event meet. It also gave Chataway a tie with Henry Thresher, Yale's great sprinter, and Stewart Thomson, the Eli's discus thrower and shot-putter, in the individual triumph department. Thresher, who won the 100 and

Continued on Page 6, Column 2

PEARMAN ANNEXES TWO A. A. U. TITLES

Bill Ashenfelter Gains Double Also as N. Y. A. C. Clinches Metropolitan Meet Crown

By WILLIAM J. BRIORDY

Picking up points in the eighteen events staged, the New York A. C.'s power-packed squad clinched the team crown in the sixty-third annual senior Metropolitan Amateur Athletic Union track and field championships at Triborough Stadium, Randalls Island, last night.

Because of the miserable conditions resulting from the heavy rains, three field events were deferred until today at 2 P. M. The track and the jumping pits were in such bad condition, it was a wonder the meet was conducted.

Portable lights were employed for the games, the first twilight-night affair in the history of the Metropolitan A. A. U. Despite the lights, it was very difficult to pick out the athletes as they sloshed around the track.

Even if the Winged Footers fail to score a point in the pole vault, the high jump and the running hop, step and jump this afternoon, they are assured of the team laurels with 102 points. The New York A. C. has won the championship for thirty-five straight years. Coach Joe Yancey's New York Pioneer Club was runner-up with 66 points and the Grand Street Boys were third with 13, after the eighteen events.

Fuchs and Keegan Dethroned

There were no records, of course, but the meet produced two double winners in Reggie Pearman of the Pioneers and Bill Ashenfelter of Coach Tommy Quinn's Winged Foot team. Six athletes retained their crowns. Nine champions were dethroned, including Jim Fuchs and Bob Keegan, both of the New York A. C., in two events each. The New York A. C. captured eight events, the Pioneers six.

Pearman, the national 800-meter champion, came through in fine style in the 880-yard event. Reggie annexed his sixth senior metropolitan half-mile crown and scored a major upset in beating George Rhoden of the Grand Street Boys, Olympic 400-meter champion, in the quarter-mile.

In the half, which attracted fourteen starters, Pearman drove to the front approaching the final turn and beat Lester Wallack, New York A. C., to the tape by two

Continued on Page 6, Column 4

U. S. TRACKMEN WIN 3 GLASGOW EVENTS

O'Brien and Mashburn Better Marks as Whitfield Also Stars Before 25,000

By The Associated Press.

GLASGOW, June 13—A touring American track and field squad won three events—setting records in two of them—before 25,000 today in the Glasgow Police Coronation games.

The Olympic champion, Parry O'Brien of Southern California, who twice this spring has bettered the world shot-put record, won his specialty with a heave of 57 feet 10 inches. This eclipsed the British all-comers record of 56-2 set by his predecessor as Olympic shot-put champion, Wilbur Thompson.

J. W. Mashburn of Oklahoma, who made the trip to Helsinki last year, too, but did not run in the 400-meter race, turned in the fastest quarter-mile ever run in Europe as he whirled around the track in 47 seconds flat. Karl Friedrich Haas of Germany, who was fourth in the Olympic 400-meter final, chased Mashburn to the wire in 47.2 seconds, losing by four feet.

The third United States winner was Mal Whitfield, two-time Olympic champion at 800 meters. The smooth-striding middle-distance ace survived a first-lap spike wound and won the 880 by four yards in 1:50.9, good time under the conditions. G. Stracke of Germany was second.

Whitfield later tested his injured leg in a heat of the open 220-yard handicap and appeared to show no ill effects. Running with the right leg taped below the knee, Whitfield was clocked in 22 seconds flat.

Fred Dwyer of Villanova, king of the United States indoor milers last winter, faded to fourth in the mile race and John O'Connell of

Continued on Page 6, Column 3

Chart of Belmont Stakes

SIXTH RACE—The Belmont Stakes; $100,000 added; colts and fillies, 3-year-olds; one mile and a half. Start good; won driving; place same. Went to post 4:46, off at once. Winner, gr. c., by Polynesian-Geisha, by Discovery. Trainer, W. C. Winfrey. Value to winner, $82,500; second, $20,000; third, $10,000; fourth, $5,000. Times—0:25; 0:50 1-5; 1:15; 1:39 2-5; 2:04 1-5; 2:28 3-5. Weather drizzling; track fast.

Starters.	Wt.	P.P.	St.	½	M.	1¼	Str.	Fin.	Jockeys	Mutuels St.	Pl.	Sh.	Dollar Odds
Native Dancer	126	5	2	4 2½	3 3½	2 2	1 hd	1 nk	Guerin	2.90	2.10	Out	.45
Jamie K.	126	4	5	3 2½	2 2	1 hd	2 7	2 10	Arcaro	....	2.30	Out	2.55
Royal Bay Gem	126	1	1	5 5	1 12	4 15	3 2½	3 1½	J. Combest	....	....	Out	5.95
Ram o'War	126	3	4	1 2	1 ½	3 1½	4 25	4 30	Gorman	....	....	....	22.25
The Preem	126	2	3	6	6	5 3½	5 [illegible]	5 20	Catalano	....	....	....	122.15
Kamehameha	126	6	6	2 hd	5 4	6	6	6	Green	....	....	....	23.95

Scratched—Bassanio, Bob o Boy.

Native Dancer, a sharp factor from the beginning, came to the outside to reach near even terms with Jamie K. when straightened for the stretch run, forged to the front at the furlong marker and gamely withstood the latter. Jamie K. raced closest to the early pacesetter during the run down the backstretch, went to the front on the final turn, gave way to the winner entering the stretch, then held on tenaciously.

Royal Bay Gem, slow to gain his best stride, moved up readily when shaken for the drive, but under stern pressure was no match for the top ones. Ram o'War, much used early, had little left. The Preem never was formidable. Kamehameha displayed brief speed and was unable to be perservered with during the late stages when his saddle slipped after he was hopelessly beaten.

Owners—1, A. G. Vanderbilt; 2, Spring Hill Farm; 3, E. Constantin Jr.; 4, B. S. Campbell; 5, L. Prima; 6, King Ranch.

Peters Sets Record In London Marathon

By The Associated Press.

LONDON, June 13—Jim Peters, Britain's 34-year-old Olympic runner, today recorded the fastest time ever for the marathon distance of 26 miles 385 yards.

Peters, who weighs only 126 pounds, was timed in 2 hours 18 minutes 40.2 seconds for the run from Windsor to Dhiswick. This was 10.8 seconds faster than the previous best performance for the distance, by Japan's Keizo Yamada in the Boston Marathon last April, and 4 minutes 23 seconds better than Emil Zatopek's winning time in the 1952 Olympics.

The gritty little foot-racer started the grind suffering from a strained thigh and a sore foot. But he finished the grueling course

Continued on Page 6, Column 1

BOMBER STREAK 16

Yanks Increase Lead to 8½ Lengths as Lopat Sets Back Indians

By LOUIS EFFRAT

Special to The New York Times.

CLEVELAND, June 13—The Yankees continued today to make a runaway of the American League race. The campaign is only one-third over and the champions, who overwhelmed the runner-up Indians, 9—4, at Municipal Stadium for their sixteenth straight triumph, are eight-and-a-half games ahead of the Cleveland club. Most of the other teams have been outdistanced.

Casey Stengel had no pity for the Tribe today. Even with a seven-run lead behind Lefty Ed Lopat, the manager continued to two-platoon the opposition. When Al Lopez switched from a right-hander to a southpaw in the sixth, Stengel replaced the portside-swinging Irv Noren with Hank Bauer.

Lopat's seventh straight was easy for the unbeaten left-hander. He was handed a 6-0 cushion before the Tribe got around to scoring on a homer by George Strickland in the fifth. The losers achieved their other runs on a round-tripper by Jim Hegan in the seventh and Harry Simpson's four-bagger with one aboard in the ninth.

Mantle Throws Out Runner

The Yankees looked good, as does any team on a long winning streak. The Indians, on the other hand, were pathetic. Flies that should have been caught dropped safely. One runner singled sharply to center, turned toward second and found himself out at first because of Mickey Mantle's throw to Joe Collins. Another runner was fooled by Lopat's motion and was picked off first.

Little wonder, then, that the Indians dropped their second straight to the New Yorkers and their third in a row. If the Indians cannot stay with the Yankees, which outfit in the league can?

Bob Feller was Lopez' starter before a Ladies' Day turnout of 37,538, of which 23,988 were paying customers. Feller was routed during the Bombers' fourth-inning attack and was charged with his fourth setback of the season. Dave Hoskins, Lou Brissie and Bob Chakales finished for the losers. The Yankees, incidentally, are the only team that enjoys a lifetime advantage over the one-time fireball artist. Through the years, their record against Feller is 37—29.

Lopat, who was rested when the home side came up in the eighth—Ray Scarborough mopped up—has a 37—9 record over the Indians.

Two of the ten hits collected by the visitors came in the second against Feller and sent the Yankees into the lead. Mantle doubled, moved to third on Yogi Berra's infield out and scored as

Continued on Page 3, Column 3

Associated Press Wirephoto

SMILE OF WINNER: Ben Hogan, the only American pro to take U. S. Open four times, tips his cap to crowd's ovation at Oakmont, Pa., yesterday.

MULLOY IS TOPPLED IN KENT NET FINAL

Worthington Upsets American Star by 6-4, 4-6, 6-3—Seixas Wins at Bristol

By The Associated Press.

BECKENHAM, England, June 13—Gardnar Mulloy of Miami, Fla., the United States top-ranking tennis player, was beaten in the final of the Kent championships today by George Worthington in a stunning upset, 6—4, 4—6, 6—3.

Maureen Connolly of San Diego, Calif., tuning up for defense of her Wimbledon title, trounced her doubles partner, Julie Sampson of San Marino, Calif., 6—2, 6—3, in the women's final. Miss Sampson gambled by rushing the net, and the strategy failed as Maureen passed her down the sidelines almost every time.

Worthington, 25-year-old former Australian Davis Cup substitute who now lives in New Zealand, outclassed Mulloy, 39, in the final set after the American had tightened his game in the second set.

Mulloy lost his service in the fifth game of the deciding set and that was all Worthington needed. The former Aussie star, making his return to big-time tennis after three years out of the game because of illness, was too strong for his older opponent.

Mulloy and Worthington later teamed to win the men's doubles title, defeating Grant Golden of Chicago and Armando Vieira, Brazil, 4—6, 6—1, 7—5.

Miss Connolly and Miss Sampson walked off with the women's doubles crown by defeating Britain's Mrs. Jean Rinkel and Helen Fletcher, 2—6, 7—5, 9—7.

BRISTOL, England, June 13 (AP)—Vic Seixas of Philadelphia, Amer-

Continued on Page 3, Column 1

Major League Baseball

Sunday, June 14, 1953

American League

YESTERDAY'S GAMES

New York 9, Cleveland 4.
Chicago 5, Boston 2.
Detroit 7, Washington 6.
Philadelphia 8, St. Louis 3.

STANDING OF THE CLUBS

	New York	Cleveland	Boston	Chicago	Wash'gton	Philadel.	St. Louis	Detroit	Won	Lost	Percentage	Games Behind
N. Y....	—	5	7	4	7	4	6	6	39	11	.780	—
Cleve...	0	—	2	3	4	7	7	7	30	19	.612	8½
Bost....	2	5	—	3	3	4	7	6	30	25	.545	11½
Chic....	4	3	3	—	3	1	7	7	28	26	.519	13
Wash....	2	2	5	4	—	7	6	2	28	26	.519	13
Phila....	2	1	5	6	3	—	3	5	25	29	.463	16
St. L....	0	2	1	3	3	3	—	7	19	36	.345	22½
Det.....	1	1	2	3	3	3	0	—	13	40	.245	27½
Lost....	11	19	25	26	26	29	36	40	—	—		

TODAY'S PROBABLE PITCHERS

New York at Cleveland (2)—Sain (7-2) and Raschi (3-3) vs. Lemon (7-5) and Garcia (7-3).

Boston at Chicago (2)—Parnell (8-3) and Grissom (2-4) vs. Pierce (6-3) and Consuegra (1-1).

Philadelphia at St. Louis (2)—Byrd (5-6) and Martin (3-4) or Scheib (1-4) vs. Larsen (1-3) and Brecheen (1-7).

Washington at Detroit—Shea (4-1) vs. Gray (0-8).

National League

YESTERDAY'S GAMES

St. Louis at New York, rain.
Chicago at Brooklyn, rain.
Milwaukee 5, Pittsburgh 4.
Cincinnati at Philadelphia, rain.

STANDING OF THE CLUBS

	Brooklyn	Milwaukee	Philadel.	St. Louis	New York	Cincinnati	Pittsburgh	Chicago	Won	Lost	Percentage	Games Behind
Bklyn....	—	4	5	4	5	7	8	2	35	17	.673	—
Milw....	3	—	5	3	7	6	4	7	35	17	.673	—
Phila....	4	2	—	4	3	1	6	8	28	19	.596	4½
St. L....	2	3	3	—	3	7	6	4	28	22	.560	6
N. Y....	4	2	1	2	—	4	6	5	24	26	.480	10
Cinc....	3	2	2	4	2	—	4	2	19	29	.396	14
Pitts....	0	1	3	2	4	2	—	6	18	37	.327	18½
Chic....	1	3	0	3	2	2	3	—	14	34	.292	19
Lost....	17	17	19	22	26	29	37	34	—	—		

TODAY'S PROBABLE PITCHERS

St. Louis at New York (2, 2 P. M.)—Mizell (5-2) and Haddix (6-3) vs. Maglie (3-3) and Gomez (1-2).

Chicago at Brooklyn (2, 2 P. M.)—Hacker (2-10) and Klippstein (4-5) vs. Loes (7-2) and Labine (2-1).

Cincinnati at Philadelphia (2)—Perkowski (1-5) and Nuxhall (3-2) vs. Drews (2-5) and Roberts (10-3).

Milwaukee at Pittsburgh (2)—Liddle (2-1) and Buhl (4-2) vs. Hall (2-1) and Bowman (0-1).

(Figures in parentheses indicate season's won-and-lost records.)

SNEAD'S 289 SECOND

He Soars to 76 in Last Round as Hogan Closes With 71 at Oakmont

By LINCOLN A. WERDEN

Special to The New York Times.

OAKMONT, Pa., June 13—Ben Hogan stepped to a new place in the history of American golf today by winning the United States open championship for the fourth time.

The 40-year-old Texan finished the seventy-two-hole tournament at the Oakmont Country Club with a brilliant closing streak that gave him a score of 283. He had a final 71 after a third-round 73.

As the cup, symbolic of victory, went to the dark-haired sun-tanned golfer, it marked the first time that a home-bred professional had carried it off on four occasions. Only two others before him, Willie Anderson, Scottish-born professional star of the early days of the game on this continent and the amateur from Atlanta, Bob Jones, had ever accomplished a feat of similar magnitude.

Anderson won in 1901, 1903, 1904 and 1905. Jones scored his victories in 1923, 1926, 1929 and 1930, the year of his grand slam.

Closes With Birdie 3

Hogan, the sturdy challenger as the tourney got under way, once more demonstrated the qualities that rank him among the world's greatest shotmakers on a golf course. Leading the indomitable Sam Snead by one stroke at the conclusion of fifty-four holes, after Snead had a similar edge over Hogan after forty-five, Hogan played the concluding nine in 33, two under par. He had a birdie 3 to finish his bid in dramatic fashion while thousands cheered in approval.

Although thrilled and smiling by his triumph here over a course that in other years proved an enigma to those who sought to smash par, Hogan said, "I'm not so sure that I will play next year to try to make it five."

He plans to leave for Scotland within ten days to begin practice for the British open championship at Carnoustie, one major golfing honor he has not tried to capture. His success here unquestionably will spur him on in a year that has been marked by achievements in four of the five tournaments in which he has competed.

Hogan won the Masters at Augusta in April and then went on to take the Pan-American in Mexico City and the Colonial at Fort Worth. He did lose in the Greenbrier open at White Sulphur Springs, West Va., where Snead was the winner.

It was Snead who took up the task of trying to stop Hogan today. Snead was making his thirteenth quest for his first open title, the one big golf plum that has eluded him. Only one stroke separated them as they went into the last round this afternoon.

Both were 38 over the next nine holes, but Snead needed another 38 in and took a 76, four over par, finishing second with a total of 289, six strokes back of Hogan.

Tourney Won 'On Greens'

Snead conceded that Hogan won this tournament "on the greens."

Others who tried to overtake the Texan were Lloyd Mangrum, who finished with 292; George Fazio, who had rounds of 77 and 76 today for 294, and Jimmy Demaret, who went four over par on the last trip, after a 71 this morning, for 294.

Pete Cooper of White Plains, N. Y., had two eagles and the low two rounds of the day with a 71 and a 70 for 294. He sank a

Continued on Page 5, Column 2

Braves Nip Pirates In 9th, Tie for Lead

By The United Press.

PITTSBURGH, June 13—The Braves scored a run in the ninth inning today to defeat the Pirates, 5—4, and tie the idle Dodgers for the league lead.

Lew Burdette, who relieved Warren Spahn in the seventh inning, was credited with his fifth straight victory without defeat. Paul LaPalme went eight innings for Pittsburgh and was charged with the loss.

LaPalme held the Braves in check on five hits going into the final inning, but he walked the lead-off man, Sid Gordon, to ignite the Braves' rally.

With Jim Pendleton running for Gordon, Andy Pakfo sacrificed but both runners were safe when La-

Continued on Page 3, Column 6

HOGAN'S 283 TAKES FOURTH OPEN TITLE

Continued From Page 1

20-footer at the first hole of the final round and then a wedge shot for a deuce at the fourteenth.

Dick Metz, 45-year-old Kansas rancher, who was Hogan's partner today, had 295, as did Ted Kroll. Jay Hebert, the young Pennsylvania pro, in his first open, posted 296, deadlocking Marty Furgol.

Julius Boros, who won at Dallas a year ago, when Hogan finished third back of Ed Oliver, had a pair of 76's for his efforts today and was down the list at 299, the same figure returned by Clarence Doser, Jim Turnesa and Bill Nary. Bill Ogden and Fred Haas were at 297, while E. J. Harrison and Jack Burke had 298's.

Frank Souchak of Oakmont, a former Pitt football star, closed with a 74 to lead the amateurs with a score of 296. Bobby Locke, British Open champion, with a final 76, had 298.

Hogan matched the triumph of Jim Barnes, who won the title in 1921, by leading all the way. Oakmont's four-round scoring record of 294, credited to Willie MacFarlane in winning the Pennsylvania open in 1934, also went by the boards.

As far as he was concerned, Hogan did not try to catalogue this victory. He was satisfied, he explained, to chalk it up along with his first United States open triumph in 1948 at the Riviera Country Club in Santa Monica, Calif.; his second at Merion, Pa., in 1950, which marked his comeback after an automobile accident, and his third in 1951 at Oakland Hills, Birmingham, Mich., where he closed with a scintilating 67.

Snead, who finished second in 1937, lost in the play-off for the title in 1947 to Lew Worsham, after missing a tiny putt, and tied for second in 1949, had a tremendous crowd with him as he started out after lunch. He and Jimmy Demaret were paired and Hogan was an hour ahead of them on the course.

"I had opportunity after opportunity," commented Snead, who three-putted at crucial junctures. This morning at the eighth green of the course he three-putted from eight feet. He had been two under par until then. This afternoon, while Hogan was pressing on, his goal in sight, Snead, after being one over par, three-putted at the twelfth green and again at the fifteenth.

There were two other chances, Snead believed, where he could have saved strokes—on the first green this afternoon and two holes later, where chip shots brought him within three feet and he could not sink the putts for important 4's.

The feature of Hogan's fourth round came over the rugged last three holes. Earlier he had said he would not envy anyone who was trying for birdies over this route. After he had taken a bogey 5 at the fifteenth, where he pulled a No. 2 iron ("too much club," he said later) into a trap, his words almost seemed prophetic. With that 5 he was one over par for fifteen holes.

Would Oakmont finally gain some sort of revenge for the sub-par rounds in his championship? The famed course had given way only in the 1927 and 1935 tournaments to four men who were below regulation figures. But since then the course has been materially changed.

Some sixty traps have been eliminated. The fairways have been widened a bit, but the greens today were almost in the traditional pattern, fast and on such undulating surfaces that the more timid putters might describe them as treacherous. Snead was having his troubles on them and here was Hogan with three more holes to go. Could he hold them with his approaches?

The answer almost came from Hogan's play thereafter. He smashed a brassie to the green, 234 yards away, at the sixteenth. Trying to select his "outstanding shot," he named this one hours afterward. But on the course those who saw him play to the center of the green, avoiding the pitfall on the right where the pin was placed, tantalizing perhaps to the player who might gamble, but acting as a signal to Hogan to beware of the trap off to the right side. They realized it was a key stroke. Hogan got down in two putts for a par 3 there.

Drives for 17th Green

After that Hogan decided to hit his drive at the 292-yard seventeenth with all his power. Usually he had driven purposely into the rough and tried for a par 4, since traps hem in the putting surface at the hole that calls for perfect placement to a green uphill. Hogan hit it and on the ball flew, rolling on and stopping thirty-five feet to the left of the pin. Two putts and he had his birdie 3—almost a 2 as the try for a deuce stopped inches away. Now all even with par for the round Hogan uncorked another long drive at the eighteenth or seventy-second hole of the round.

This was a 462-yarder and Hogan had a No. 5 iron left for his second. He hit beautifully amid almost complete silence, notwithstanding that there were thousands lined on both sides of the fairway and encircling the green. When the ball came to rest it was some eight or ten feet from the pin. After Metz had putted out, Hogan lined up his putt and stroked the ball in for a concluding birdie 3, a finish of 3, 3, 3, and a 71, his third sub-par round.

Going out Hogan had a birdie at the first and after five pars, three-putted for a 5 at the seventh. At the eighth his No. 4 wood shot from the green carried over into a trap and he had another bogey when he sank a 4 there. At the ninth hole, he was trapped in 2, recovered well and sank a par 5 to be out in 38.

Hogan had thirty-four putts on his last round and the most unusual of these was the 18-footer that ran over a ridge in the green and fell into the cup for a deuce at the thirteenth. He hit the cup with putts for birdies that rimmed but stayed out at the twelfth and fourteenth. At both these holes he had pars.

Hogan Composed at Lunch

Hogan started the final round before Snead had finished the morning session. The man from Texas was composed as he ate a light lunch of vegetables and fruit and conducted an informal press interview at the same time.

His chief comment concerning his prospects and those of the others in the field was that anyone needing a birdie on one of the last four holes would be in a dangerous spot. "That's the toughest part of the course," said Ben.

Because of his 73 this morning, Hogan was able to maintain a lead of one stroke since Snead carded par 72 and had a total of 213 to Hogan's 212. Next was Mangrum with a 74 at 217, while Fazio soared to a 77 and as a result he, Hebert and Demaret were in the 218 bracket. Demaret, who was paired with Snead, had another 71. He started with a 71 on Thursday and carded a 76 yesterday.

Metz, who returned to the golf circuit a year ago, after several years' absence during which he concentrated on ranching, finished with a 6 at the eighteenth, after a fine round, for a 74. His aggregate of 219 was the same as Haas'. Fred took a 72 after going two over par on the last four holes. Burke and Kroll were tied at 221.

Locke, the British open champion, holed a birdie 3 at the eighteenth for a 74 to score 222 the same as Souchak who had a third round of 76.

A crowd estimated at 10,000 formed early, a good share of the spectators trailing Hogan and Metz, while Snead and Demaret attracted most of the others. When word was spread that Snead was two under par at the end of four holes, thousands raced to get a glimpse of the Virginia-born star, one of the game's favorites.

"Why are you rooting for Snead?" asked one bystander of another as Sam and Demaret approached the ninth green. "He's never won, that's why I'm for him," was the reply.

Snead, however, tossed away a golden opportunity at the eighth, where he three-putted from eight feet, leaving his putt for a birdie 2 some two feet short, and then he failed to drop the ball the remaining distance on his next attempt.

He had played beautifully with a birdie 4 at the first, a birdie 3 at the next on a 14-footer and a birdie 4 at the long fourth, where he recovered from a trap and sank a 3-footer. He was trapped also at the sixth and took a bogey 4.

The long-hitting ability of Snead was in evidence at the uphill ninth, where he was home with a No. 2 iron and netted a birdie 4 after two putts to be out in 35, two under. Hogan, playing ahead, had taken a 38 there, so at that stage Snead was the leader with 176 to Hogan's 177 for forty-five holes.

Coming in, however, Snead injured his chances further by three-putting at the seventeenth. Snead laced out a drive that reached the green there which is uphill from the tee, but three-putted from within thirty feet for a bogey 4.

Snead drove into the rough and took a bogey 5 at the tenth and he was trapped to lose a stroke to par at the short thirteenth. After playing the other six holes of the nine in par he came to the eighteenth of his third round as a huge gallery formed from tee to green. To their delight he unleashed a tremendous drive. He pitched his second to the green and two-putted for an incoming 37, two over, and his 72.

Hogan's third round found him driving off the fairway at four holes. The fifth hole cost him a bogey 5, as it did yesterday, and sent him one over at that stage. He recovered well from a corner of the trap at the eighth for par 3 and he pitched from the rough at the left of the ninth for par 5 and an outgoing 38, one over par.

On the inward nine he was even with par, aided by a 20-footer he sank for a birdie 4 at the twelfth. Hogan ran into his first 6 of the tourney when he drove into the side of a bunker at the fifteenth. He recovered from there, only to knock his third into a trap before getting to the green. Where Snead later was to three-putt at the seventeenth on this round, Hogan chipped to within two inches of the pin and carded a birdie 3. At the eighteenth, Hogan had a 4 for his 73.

Boros, the defending champion, had a ruinous finish of 6, 2, 4, 6 on the last four holes this morning for a 76. He was trapped for the first 6 and overplayed on his recovery. He found his drive at the eighteenth in a small declivity and was trapped on his second, finally going over the green before holing out.

Associated Press Wirephoto

FOURTH TIME WINNER: Ben Hogan, who captured the U. S. Open yesterday at Oakmont, Pa., with a 283 score, lifts ball in a shower of sand to blast from eighth-hole trap in the homestretch round of the fifty-third edition of the tourney.

Middlecoff Withdraws, Scoring Late Open Start

OAKMONT, Pa., June 13 (AP)—Cary Middlecoff, Sam Snead and Lloyd Mangrum joined in criticizing their late starting times in the national open golf tournament today and, without mentioning names, hinted that Ben Hogan had received preferential treatment with his 9 A. M. (New York time) start.

Middlecoff, the 1949 champion, picked up in a huff on the eleventh hole of the third round. He started at 10:48 A. M.

"I got to thinking about how they'd put me late for the last four years and I said the heck with it," Middlecoff remarked. "It's unfair and I don't think it's accidental. The late starters have to play on a course that's chopped to pieces by 10,000 people."

Snead said, "They shouldn't give the leader the early schedule all the time. They ought to give everybody a fair chance."

"There are some guys behind me with good scores who ought to be twice as mad," commented Mangrum.

Description of the Course

Hole	Yds.		Par
1	493	Second shot downhill to green	5
2	355	Ditch lines fairway on left; green undulating	4
3	428	Traps flank fairway, uphill to green	4
4	544	Dogleg to right, well trapped shallow green	5
5	384	Gully in front of undulating green	4
6	183	Large traps guard narrow green	3
7	387	Blind drive from tee, rolling green	4
8	253	Trap on left for forty yards, traps on right	3
9	480	Drive and second uphill to green	5
Out	3,507		37
10	470	Downhill all the way, ditch crosses fairway	4
11	372	Deep ditch cuts fairway, green well guarded	4
12	598	Ditches parallel fairway, sloping green	5
13	161	Practically island green, severely trapped	3
14	362	Large trap left, green deep and undulating	4
15	458	Sloping fairway, green long, slanting	4
16	234	Traps along left side, difficult par	3
17	292	Uphill from tee, deep guarded traps at green	4
18	462	Ditches both sides, mound in front of green	4
In	3,409		35

Grand totals—6,916 yards; par 72.

"All the News That's Fit to Print"

The New York Times.

5:00 A.M. EXTRA
Fair today, tonight and tomorrow, little change in temperature.
Temperature Range Today-Max., 78; Min., 62
Temperatures Yesterday—Max., 78; Min., 66
Full U. S. Weather Bureau Report, Page 55

VOL. CII No. 34,926. Entered as Second-Class Matter. Post Office, New York, N. Y. NEW YORK, TUESDAY, SEPTEMBER 8, 1953. Times Square, New York 36, N. Y. Telephone Lackawanna 4-1000 FIVE CENTS

LABOR DAY TRAFFIC MOVES SMOOTHLY; GALES BY-PASS CITY

Hurricane Veers Eastward, Bringing Strong Winds to Long Island Shore

HIGH SEAS LIMIT BATHING

Near-By Beach Crowds Thin, With Peak Temperature a Comfortable 78°

Traffic flowed freely in and out of the city yesterday as the summer holiday season unofficially ended. Homeward-bound vacationists and Labor Day week-end crowds encountered no serious obstacles to smooth passage as they motored cityward, and the estimated 400,000 persons who visited New York between Friday and last night had equally uneventful return journeys.

The lack of congestion on main metropolitan area highways was attributed to two main factors. A Weather Bureau forecast of rains and high winds expected from the off-shoot of Hurricane Carol caused thousands of motorists to start ahead of schedule, with the result that the traffic load was well distributed throughout the daylight hours. Travel from the Catskill Mountain section was also lighter than normal for a holiday, as thousands of persons remained at resorts to celebrate the Rosh ha-Shanah holiday, which will start at sundown Wednesday.

A patrolman at the Lincoln Tunnel commented last night that "traffic i. so light you can race through on a bicycle."

As far as the city area was concerned, Hurricane Carol, the third of the season, might never have been reported. It veered sharply eastward long before it had come as far north as the city, but it did cause strong winds and exceedingly rough seas along the south shore of Long Island from Long Beach to Montauk. At the easterly end of Long Island in the Hamptons the heavy seas swept over sand dunes but did no damage to big houses bordering the shoreline.

Small Craft Warned Off Ocean

The ocean off Long Island was so rough that many beaches were out-of-bounds to bathers and Coast Guard picket boats patroled the waters to discourage small craft from venturing into the Atlantic. Fishermen were disappointed as owners of "party boats" decided it was safer to keep their craft moored at docks. In contrast to the turbulent ocean side, in-shore bay areas were relatively calm.

Justifying its warning of "maximum precautions" against Hurricane Carol that were sent out late Sunday and up to 7 A. M. yesterday, the Weather Bureau noted that this area was "fortunate" in that the storm moved more easterly than northerly and charted it up to the "unpredictable course of all hurricanes."

The fringe of the hurricane brought moderate to fresh winds of twenty to twenty-five miles an hour early yesterday, with strong winds up to thirty-five miles an hour sweeping the easterly part of Long Island.

The weather generally was seasonal, with the high temperature of the day 78 degrees at 12:55 P. M. and the low 66.3 at 7:25 A. M.

With the exception of New England, where high winds and rain prevailed, generally fair weather

Continued on Page 56, Column 3

Chief Justice Vinson Dies of Heart Attack in Capital

Jurist Succumbs Unexpectedly at Apartment at Age of 63—Had Been Appointed to the Highest Tribunal by Truman

By The Associated Press.

WASHINGTON, Sept. 8—Chief Justice Fred M. Vinson died unexpectedly of a heart attack at his apartment at 2:15 A. M. today.

The Chief Justice was stricken fatally early this morning.

Mrs. Vinson and their son, Fred Jr., were at the apartment.

They summoned the physician who recently had been treating Mrs. Vinson. The physician, Dr. Henry Ecker, was called at 1:30 A. M., but Justice Vinson died shortly afterward.

He had returned to Washington recently after attending meetings of the American Bar Association in Boston.

Mr. Vinson took over leadership of the Supreme Court on June 24, 1946, as an appointee of President Truman.

Justice Vinson is survived by his widow and son and another son, James R. Vinson. He had one grandchild, James R. Vinson Jr. A sister, Miss Lou Vinson, also survives. She resides in Kentucky.

In 3 Federal Branches

Fred M. Vinson enjoyed a noteworthy career in each of the three branches of the Federal government—legislative, executive and judicial. In twelve years in the House of Representative he won wide renown as a tax and fiscal expert. Then, in World War II, he served in top administrative posts, as Economic Stabilizer, Federal Loan Administrator, Assistant President, and Secretary of the Treasury. Finally, in 1946, he was appointed by President Truman as Chief Justice of the United States.

In all three fields he distinguished himself by the exercise of his most characteristic quality, his exceptional ability as a negotiator, a trouble-shooter, a reconciler of conflicting views, a man who could reduce warring factions to at least outward harmony and so get things done.

Probably his finest achievement was the application of this soothing technique to the bitter personal feuds and doctrinal disputes that had rent the Supreme Court for a long time before his appointment. Within a year after he became Chief Justice, members of

Continued on Page 18, Column 1

Rebel Dock Union Leaders To Ask A.F.L. Charter Now

Insurgent vice presidents of the International Longshoremen's Association, who represent locals outside the racket-encrusted Port of New York, disclosed yesterday that they would ask the American Federation of Labor for a new pier union charter without waiting for the A. F. L. to expel the present union.

The disclosure that a formal application for a new charter would be submitted this week was made as the two-man commission set up by New York and New Jersey to wipe out waterfront crime made preparations to put the port clean-up program into operation.

Lieut. Gen. George P. Hays, Governor Dewey's representative on the commission, and Maj. Gen. Edward C. Rose, Gov. Alfred E. Driscoll's designee, held a week-end meeting at General Rose's home in Mantoloking, about ten miles south of Asbury Park on the Jersey shore.

General Rose, chief of staff of the New Jersey Department of Defense, said the commissioners would resume their meeting today in Trenton, where their ideas will be recorded by a stenographer. They will spend the rest of the week shuttling between the Jersey capital and New York and hope to have their plans sufficiently well formulated to permit a public announcement by Friday.

The bi-state compact, under which all longshoremen will be required to register for jobs at state employment information centers, does not become fully operative until Dec. 1, but the commission intends to make a start toward

Continued on Page 22, Column 1

DEMOCRATIC RIVALS FRET OVER APATHY

Lag in Gifts and Rallies Stirs Worry Here—Sharp Speed-up in Campaigns Is Planned

By LEO EGAN

A seeming lack of interest in the outcome of next Tuesday's primary appeared yesterday to be giving serious concern to the three principal rivals for the Democratic nomination for Mayor, their running mates and supporters. Apathy was indicated by small attendance at rallies, the difficulty of getting campaign contributions and a lag in the recruitment of volunteer workers.

Mayor Impellitteri's campaign advisers demonstrated their perturbance over the situation by arranging a series of television programs that will bring the Mayor or one of his running mates for city-wide office before the public every night remaining before the primary except tomorrow. They also approved a sharp increase in the Mayor's schedule of personal appearances.

Mr. Impellitteri was greeted yesterday in Harlem and East Harlem by the largest crowds he has seen thus far in the primary campaign but they were assembled for nonpolitical occasions. Taking part with others of Italian extraction in the annual feast of St. Anthony of Padua in East Harlem, the Mayor was welcomed with greater enthusiasm than he has received in most of his political appearances. At another festive appearance in central Harlem he shared honors with Borough President Robert F. Wagner Jr. of Manhattan, his chief rival in the primary.

Concern over the seeming lethargy was evident also at the Wagner headquarters. One reason is that many of Mr. Wagner's advisers believe that his chances of winning would be increased by a large turnout on primary day.

Mr. Wagner's schedule of campaign appearances is being increased from three or four a day to six or eight. In addition his headquarters staff, starting today, is mailing personal appeals to come out to vote to 1,000,000 of the 2,100,000 enrolled Democrats in the city. Enclosed with the mailed appeals are sample ballots showing Democratic voters how to indicate their choice of the Manhattan Borough President and his running mates on the paper ballots that will be used on primary day.

Lacking the funds available to his rivals, Robert B. Blaikie, West Side Tammany district leader who is third man in the race, has arranged an intensive program of street corner rallies, starting today with a noon day meeting at Thirty-ninth Street and Seventh Avenue

Continued on Page 19, Column 4

Hurricane Strikes Coast in Northeast

By The Associated Press

BOSTON, Sept. 7 — Coast Guardsmen, battling twenty-foot waves, rescued by breeches buoy and amphibious duck today seventeen seamen of the Panamanian freighter Evgenia, which had been hurled aground seventy-five yards off a Cape Cod beach in the tail of the hurricane Carol.

Capt. Elias Sharellis and six members of his crew elected to stay aboard the freighter pending salvage operations. The Coast Guard said that they were in no danger, with the tide receding. Boston tugs are expected to reach the scene at forenoon tomorrow, and an effort will be made to pull the ship free on the noon high tide.

The 225-foot, 3,500-ton freighter went aground after washing over Peaked Hill Bar about three miles from Provincetown. A boiling surf made boat rescue impossible, although the craft was driven to within seventy-five yards of shore.

The rescue operations were

Continued on Page 56, Column 1

Trabert Takes U. S. Tennis Title By Crushing Seixas in Big Upset

Ex-Sailor Victor, 6-3, 6-2, 6-3—Miss Connolly Wins and Completes Grand Slam

By ALLISON DANZIG

An ex-sailor, less than three months out of the Navy, won the amateur tennis championship of the United States yesterday in as stunning a final-round reversal as Forest Hills has seen in many years.

With an onslaught of the leveling fire power of 16-inch rifles, Tony Trabert of Cincinnati silenced the guns of the favored champion of Wimbledon, Victor Seixas of Philadelphia, and in exactly one hour won the match, to the acclaim of 12,000 in the stadium of the West Side Tennis Club. The score was 6—3, 6—2, 6—3.

Preceding the triumph of the 23-year-old six-footer, one of the few to go through a championship without losing a set, Maureen Connelly of San Diego, Calif., carried off the women's crown for the third successive year.

In so doing she completed the first grand slam of the world's four major national tournaments scored by a woman. She, too, went through the ten days of play without yielding a set.

Miss Connolly previously had

Continued on Page 39, Column 2

The New York Times

Tony Trabert after yesterday's victory at Forest Hills.

ADENAUER VICTORY CALLED A MANDATE FOR UNITED EUROPE

German Chancellor Has Safe Majority—His Party Has 244 Seats, Socialists 150

By CLIFTON DANIEL

Special to THE NEW YORK TIMES.

BONN, Germany, Sept. 7—Chancellor Konrad Adenauer emerged today from West Germany's second post-war general election with a secure majority for another four-year term and a clear mandate to carry on with his policy of integrating Germany with the West.

In the final returns from yesterday's voting the Chancellor's party, the Christian Democratic Union, won 244 seats in the new Bundestag, the lower House of Parliament, an absolute majority of one. His partners in the present coalition Government, the Free Democrats and the German party, won forty-eight and fifteen seats respectively.

The Opposition Social Democrats who put the reunification of Germany ahead of integration, captured only 150 places.

And so the green and white flag of "European unity" was triumphantly unfurled today beside the banner of West Germany on Schaumburg Palace, Dr. Adenauer's official residence in Bonn.

"A new great impulse" has been given to the "European idea," the Chancellor declared at an afternoon news conference. He added that "the election results will certainly have a great influence on all the future negotiations on the integration of Europe."

Other Policies to Stand

The overwhelming verdict of the West German voters also means that the steady policy of the present Government will continue for four years and will strengthen the reputation of West Germany abroad and increase confidence in the country, the Chancellor continued.

There were few to challenge the 77-year-old Chancellor's assurance. He had the votes and he called on Dr. Theodor Heuss, West German President, in the morning to give formal notice that he for the first time was the leader of a party with an absolute majority in the Bundestag.

The new Bundestag is expected to meet Oct. 2 and re-elect Dr. Adenauer as Chancellor on the nomination of Dr. Heuss. Spokesmen of the two junior partners in the coalition said they were prepared to continue in the Government but Dr. Adenauer, who fought the election in alliance with them, was strangely reticent about the future composition of the coalition. He no longer needs to pay a high price for support.

Aside from the 307 seats that will be occupied by the three coalition parties and the 150 held by the Socialists, the Catholic Center party, thanks to an election agreement with Dr. Adenauer, won three. The All-German bloc, or Refugee party, contesting its first general election, got twenty-seven, becoming West Germany's fourth largest party.

If Dr. Adenauer ever needs or

Continued on Page 2, Column 3

Associated Press Wirephoto

CONFIDENTIAL ASIDE: Former President Truman and Walter P. Reuther, president of the Congress of Industrial Organizations, enjoy a private joke at Labor Day rally in Detroit.

EISENHOWER HAILS TREND IN GERMANY

Dulles Quotes Him as Saying Vote Exceeded Expectations—Rift on Remarks Denied

By ANTHONY LEVIERO

Special to THE NEW YORK TIMES.

DENVER, Colo., Sept. 7—John Foster Dulles, Secretary of State, quoted President Eisenhower as saying today that the results of the election in West Germany were far better than this country had "dared to expect" as a good augury for German and European unity.

After a long conference with the President, Secretary Dulles denied that General Eisenhower had disapproved recent remarks by him that had aroused controversy in Germany, Italy, India and Japan.

As for the stormy issue of Trieste, Secretary Dulles contended that the position he had stated in a news conference last Thursday in Washington had been the unchanged position of the United States for several years. He reiterated, however, that the United States was open-minded in seeking a solution acceptable to both Italy and Yugoslavia.

Mr. Dulles reflected the President's view of the German election in reiterating that he had not expressed displeasure with last week's press conference statements.

"On my own initiative I told him precisely what I had said," Mr. Dulles declared, "and he saw nothing out of the way with what I had said. As far as Germany is concerned, he said the answer is in the result, which is far more than we had dared to expect."

Confer for 2½ Hours

The Labor Day conference of the Secretary of State and the President lasted two and a half hours, after which President Eisenhower left for lunch and golf at the Cherry Hill Country Club and Mr. Dulles flew back to Washington. He came here last night, he said, to review foreign affairs questions that had accumulated in the three weeks since he had last seen the President in his office here at Lowry Air Force Base.

"It was a matter of satisfaction to the President and to me," said Mr. Dulles of the sweeping victory won by the pro-United States coalition parties headed by Chancellor Konrad Adenauer of West Germany.

"It showed that the German people appreciate and are responsive to the policies that have been followed by the three Western powers—Great Britain, France and the United States—in cooperation with Chancellor Adenauer over the past years and which we hope will bring about the unification of Germany and the increased unification of Europe."

Mr. Dulles held a news conference in the air base press room. Afterward, in speaking briefly before newsreel and television microphones outside, he said the election showed that the people of West Germany overwhelmingly supported the policies of the three Western powers, the prospective unification of Germany and the

Continued on Page 3, Column 2

Allies Beginning to Transfer Captives to Neutral Custody

Special to THE NEW YORK TIMES.

TOKYO, Tuesday, Sept. 8—The United Nations Command begins today the transfer to the Korean demilitarized zone North Korean and Chinese war prisoners who have refused to return to their homelands. The Allies hold an estimated 22,600 prisoners who have said they would resist their transfer to Communist authorities.

These prisoners will be handed over to the custody of a Neutral Nations Repatriation Commission for three months, during which Communist spokesmen will try to convince them to change their minds.

The Communists have said they hold more than 300 South Koreans and more than twenty non-Koreans who refused to return to United Nations authorities during Operation Big Switch, the exchange of captives, which ended Sunday.

The first group to be moved today by the Allied Prisoner-of-War Command will be about 2,000 Chinese prisoners. They will be transported by sea from Cheju Island off South Korea to the port of Inchon and then be taken by train to the demilitarized area. North Korean prisoners from Koje Island and Nonsan are expected to be handed over to Indian guards of the neutral commission on Thursday.

Thus far, there was no indication from the Communists when they would begin the transfer of Allied personnel refusing repatriation.

Official notification that the United Nations was ready to begin to move the prisoners was given to the Communists during a meeting yesterday of the Military Armistice Commission by Maj. Gen. Blackshear M. Bryan, senior Allied representative.

General Bryan said the United Nations guards handling the transfer of the prisoners to Indian custody would number eighty at first, being gradually increased to 266, with one exception. "On or about

Continued on Page 10, Column 5

LABOR SEES PERIL FROM REPUBLICANS

Meany, Reuther and Harrison Criticize G. O. P. Policies as a Threat to Prosperity

Leaders of the American Federation of Labor and the Congress of Industrial Organizations criticized the Republican Administration yesterday and warned against policies that might endanger peace and prosperity.

George Meany, president of the A. F. L., listed six "glaring weaknesses" that he said demanded correction. He asked that inflation be stopped, curbs be removed from slum clearance and housing programs, social security be expanded, health and education services improved and the Taft-Hartley Act changed to end "manifest unfairness" to labor.

In a similar vein, George M. Harrison, president of the Brotherhood of Railway Clerks and a second vice president of the A. F. L., denounced the Administration's tighter credit policies, already in effect, and cautioned against the campaign for a national sales tax.

Walter P. Reuther, C. I. O. president, charged "special interest groups" had moved in with the Eisenhower Administration "determined to reverse a twenty-year trend of Government for the people." He declared these groups planned to convert the country's national resources to quick exploitation for their private gain in-

Continued on page 24, Column 2

British Jet Pilot Sets Speed Mark, 727.6 Miles an Hour in New Plane

Special to THE NEW YORK TIMES.

LONDON, Sept. 7 — Britain claimed the world's air speed record for level flight tonight after a Hawker Hunter fighter piloted by Squadron Leader Neville Duke had flashed four times over a three-kilometer (1.7 miles) course off England's south coast for an average speed of 727.6 miles an hour.

Squadron Leader Duke, who is chief test pilot for the Hawker Aircraft Company, thus erased the disappointment of a near miss just a week ago. On that attempt over the same course he averaged 722 miles an hour, better than the claimed, but still unofficial, record of 715.7 miles an hour set by Col. William F. Barns of the United States Air Force in July in a Sabre jet, but not better by a sufficiently wide margin. The difference of six miles an hour fell barely short of the required 1 per cent.

Today's margin—a clear twelve miles an hour—is ample, and although the figures have to be accepted by the Federation Aeronautique Internationale, there is no reason to suppose there will be any difficulty about it.

In the four runs in swift succession Squadron Leader Duke clocked 716.7 miles an hour, 738.8, 716.5 and 738.6. Weather conditions were favorable except for a strong wind, which the British pilot said made his runs "rough."

The plane that smashed the Sabre jet's hold on the record is an arrow-shaped craft whose military version is just about to go into general service with the Royal Air Force Fighter Command. Its motive power is supplied by a Rolls Royce Avon engine whose performance figures are secret but one version of which has been tested at 9,500 pounds thrust. This figure may have been increased by the use of an after-burner.

Britain last won the level speed record in September, 1946, when a Gloster Meteor went 616 miles an

Continued on Page 9, Column 3

TRUMAN DENOUNCES G. O. P. DEFENSE CUTS AND DOMESTIC AIMS

In Detroit Speech, He Declares 'Big Business' Philosophy Hurts Farmer and Labor

HITS INTEREST RATE RISE

Terms Offshore Oil Land Law 'Biggest Steal' and Sees Power Project 'Giveaway'

Text of the Truman Address in Detroit is printed on page 21

By ELIE ABEL

Special to THE NEW YORK TIMES.

DETROIT, Sept. 7 — Former President Truman, a silent observer since the Eisenhower Administration took office last Jan. 20, opened fire today on the Republican successors to his regime, charging them with betrayal of the people's interests and disregard of the nation's defense needs.

Speaking at a dinner in his honor arranged jointly by American Federation of Labor and Congress of Industrial Organizations unions this evening, Mr. Truman served notice that his period of watchful waiting had ended.

"I wanted to see this Administration a success," he declared. "I advised our people in the Senate to give them a chance. We gave them their chance, and they threw it out the window. Now, let's go after them and get this thing corrected."

In his main address earlier before a Labor Day audience of 20,000, massed before the Detroit City Hall in Cadillac Square, Mr. Truman denounced "the dangerous philosophy that balancing the Federal budget is the most sacred objective of the Government"—more important than building a strong Air Force or protecting the country's industrial centers from atomic devastation.

'First Things First'

"We have to put first things first," he said. "I don't see how any one can take chances with our national defense at a time like this in the world's history.

"I should think a first-class Air Force and air-raid defense system that would protect all our great cities and industrial centers would be worth quite a lot to us now—even if it unbalanced the budget for a while and deferred a tax cut for some years to come."

In his speech, Mr. Truman warmly praised Adlai E. Stevenson, the 1952 Democratic Presidential candidate.

The former President, who appeared fit and relaxed, was warmly cheered in this Democratic party stronghold as he resumed the free-swinging style of his 1948 campaign. A voice from the crowd shouted, "Give 'em hell, Harry," as he walked to the platform. Grinning broadly, Mr. Truman replied, "Thank you. I'll try."

He then proceeded to a point-by-point criticism of Republican policies and actions, asserting that the Federal Government served the interests of big business while organized labor, the farmer and the consumer were losing ground.

"The majority of the people last fall voted for a change in the political party that controls the Government," Mr. Truman said. "That was their perfect right and privilege. But, oh, how sorry they are.

Scores Interest Rate Rise

"I don't think they voted for a change in the social and economic principles that have made us so strong and prosperous. But that is the kind of change we are getting.

"There are plenty of signs of a return of that old philosophy that the object of government is to help big business—on the theory that if big business is well off, enough of its wealth will trickle down to the rest of the population to keep the system going."

As an example of the "discredited trickle-down theory," Mr. Truman cited the recent rise in interest rates.

"That may be of benefit to the money lenders, but it surely does hurt the rest of the people," he said.

The veteran who wants to buy a house, start a business or buy a farm, the small business man who needs credit for expansion and the taxpayer who pays more interest on the public debt are harmed, the former President added.

Mr. Truman declared that public housing had been "condemned to death," funds for enforcement of the minimum wage law have been cut and the farmer has been told that he must "go it alone." He said there were signs that the Federal Government no longer was

Continued on Page 20, Column 6

TRABERT CAPTURES U. S. TENNIS TITLE

Continued From Page 1

won the Wimbledon, Australian and French grass-court titles.

The little, blonde Californian, who will shortly attain the age of 19, repeated her victory of last year's final over Doris Hart of Coral Gables, Fla., whom she also defeated in a magnificent final at Wimbledon in July.

In forty-three minutes Miss Connolly, with her devastating speed and length off the ground and showing vast improvement since last year, took the match, 6—2, 6—1.

Miss Hart, a finalist five times and a strong hitter in her own right, resorted to every device, including changes of spin, length and pace, in an effort to slow down her opponent. But Miss Connolly went implacably on to victory in one of her finest performances. She was irresistible except for a momentary wavering when she stood within a stroke of ending matters at 6—2 in the final set and yielded two more games to Miss Hart.

In the final event of the seventy-second annual tournament, Miss Hart paired with Seixas to win the mixed doubles title. They defeated Julia Sampson of San Marino, Calif., and Rex Hartwig of Australia, 6—2, 4—6, 6—4. It was the third time in a row that Miss Hart shared in the crown, which she carried off with Frank Sedgman of Australia in 1951 and 1952.

The victory of Trabert over Seixas, the player with whom he is expected to shoulder the burden of America's challenge for the Davis Cup at Melbourne, Australia, in December, was achieved with the finest tennis to come from his racquet this observer has seen.

Food for Thought

It was disturbing enough for Australia that its two 18-year-old aces, Kenneth Rosewall and Lewis Hoad, failed to win a set in the semi-finals. The performance of Trabert in crushing the Wimbledon champion by almost as decisive a margin as did Sedgman in the 1951 final should be of even more concern Down Under.

On the best day Rosewall and Hoad ever had they could hardly have stood their ground against the all-court attack Trabert turned loose against Seixas.

Two years ago the rugged ex-sailor, who has the proportions of a football player, carried Sedgman to five sets in the championship. In 1952 he laid aside his racquets to serve in the Navy and was out of major competition except for the French championship while his aircraft carrier was in the Mediterranean Sea.

Since leaving the service in June, Trabert has been laboring hours daily in practice and physical conditioning work to bring his game back to where it was in 1951 and to get his weight down and regain his speed of foot.

At the Merion Cricket Club he met Seixas in the final and was crushed after a promising start. He won the Baltimore tournament, lost to Rosewall at South Orange and then met Seixas again at Newport.

The Philadelphian, with his speed and agility and his faultless volleying, won the first two sets, 7—5, 6—0, and then injured his knee early in the third set and lost the match. Trabert got little credit for the victory, under the circumstances.

Yesterday he went on the court again against Seixas. This time the Wimbledon champion was thoroughly fit, with his knee completely healed, and primed with the confidence gained from his earlier victories over Hoad, Kurt Nielsen of Denmark and William Talbert of New York.

Seixas was favored in the final in spite of the excellence of Trabert's tennis against Rosewall. How was any one to suspect that Trabert would show the most punishing and solid ground strokes on display at Forest Hills in recent years or that they would wreak such havoc against an opponent who had made a shambles of the highly respected back court game of Talbert?

The explanation of the massacre that was perpetrated in the last two sets yesterday came down to the fact that Trabert on this day suddenly caught fire as he never had before and attained the mastery toward which he has strived over the years. On this day he measured up to a Don Budge, a Jack Kramer in the fearful toll taken by his forehand and backhand, particularly the latter.

It is premature to rank him with those two former champions, but if he can sustain the form he showed against Seixas, the time may well come when Trabert will receive that recognition. At any rate, Australia has much to worry about as it prepares for the defense of the Davis Cup.

In his powerful serving and deadly play in the forecourt and in his speed in bringing off one amazing recovery after another for spectacular winners, Trabert was a foe for the best to reckon with. But his ground strokes were what broke Seixas' resistance and turned the match into something of a rout in the second set. The Wimbledon champion was harried at every turn, driven to the far corners and tied in knots as he tried to get his racquet on the ball at the net.

In the final analysis, it was Trabert's top-spin backhand that made the match a nightmare for Seixas. The Philadelphian had beaten Hoad by putting his twist service high on the backhand preparatory to rushing in for the finishing volley. Such tactics also had worked successfully against other opponents. They did not succeed against Trabert.

In his overspin backhand Trabert had the antidote, and his return of service from the left side, falling low below the level of the tape and usually wide of Seixas' racquet, wrecked the loser's net attack.

In game after game Seixas came rushing in, only to find himself passed or unable to take the ball at his feet with a regularity that finally left him at his wits' end, discouraged and baffled, though he kept going forward to the last.

The Wimbledon champion had little alternative. From the back of the court, with his looping forehand and undercut backhand, he was not sufficiently equipped to stand up to the long, heavy strokes that stemmed from Trabert's racquet. He had to get in.

The inadequacy of his ground strokes was revealed in his inability to return Trabert's powerful service, which was usually directed to the backhand, or to make the passing shot on the run from the forehand as the Cincinnatian angled his following volley across the court. Trabert was using the tactics that his rival had employed so successfully against others.

The play turned into a rout for Seixas beginning with the fourth game of the second set, just before the players donned spikes, with a light rain falling.

In the opening set it had been an even fight until Seixas missed his chance to break through in the 18-point fifth game. Then he lost his service in the seventh as Trabert's returns forced him into volley errors. That was the margin of the difference between them in the set.

United Press International

Maureen Connolly bends for a low one during her finals match with Doris Hart.

The New York Times

TO THE VICTOR: Maureen Connolly, center, who defeated Doris Hart, left, for the women's national singles tennis title yesterday, receives trophy from Mrs. Hazel Hotchkiss Wightman.

Up to this time there had been no inkling of the beating in store for Seixas. Indeed, few of his backers had lost faith in his capacity to win. When he took the opening game of the second set at love and won the third on the strength of his service, he seemed to be strongly in the running.

Then the storm broke and the spectators forgot about the sprinkle of rain as they looked on spellbound at the whirlwind that engulfed the clean-cut and wonderfully conditioned 30-year-old as Trabert swept through seven games in a row.

Trabert's service, with its length and varying speed and spin, extracted errors or scored outright in the fourth game. In the fifth his return of service had Seixas reeling and diving for the ball, to set up scorching passing shots and volleys. His service won at love in the sixth and Seixas had got just 2 points in the last three games.

Then came a magnificently fought seventh game, with Seixas battling might and main and scoring thrice at the net but yielding finally as Trabert scored six outright winners, four with his ground strokes. When Seixas lost the eighth game also, after leading by 40—0, it was seen to be all over.

Trabert continued his string of games to seven by breaking through at love in the first of the final set, making a sensational recovery of a cross-court volley, and taking the second game with a volley and two beautiful backhand drives. Seixas had a brief reprieve as his service picked up to win a love game in the third. Then he pulled out the fifth after being down 0—40.

When the Philadelphian broke through service for the first time in the match to draw even at 3-all, a spark of hope was revived. But Trabert came back like a tiger. The Cincinnati youth broke through in the seventh at love with another of his amazing recoveries and two passing shots down the line, won the eighth with two overhand smashes and then hit two hammering forehand returns of service that Seixas could not volley and finished matters with a tremendous backhand passing shot down the line.

With a cry of joy, Trabert tossed his racquet into the air and then, after shaking hands with his opponent, turned and blew a kiss to his fiancée, Shauna Wood of Salt Lake City, Utah, who was seated in the marquee. Miss Wood, whom Trabert will marry in January, was called on the court to receive the winner's prize from Col. James H. Bishop, president of the United States Lawn Tennis Association.

"All the News That's Fit to Print"

The New York Times.

LATE CITY EDITION

Cloudy, cool with rain today. Mostly fair, cool and windy tomorrow.

Temperature Range Today—Max., 58; Min., 50

Temperatures Yesterday—Max., 66; Min., 55

Full U. S. Weather Bureau Report, Page 5

Copyright, 1953, by The New York Times Company.

VOL. CIII..No. 34,954. Entered as Second-Class Matter, Post Office, New York, N. Y. NEW YORK, TUESDAY, OCTOBER 6, 1953. Times Square, New York 36, N. Y. Telephone LAckawanna 4-1000 FIVE CENTS

U. S. COURT STAYS PIER STRIKE TO OCT. 15 PENDING HEARING; UNION ORDERS DOCKERS BACK

80-DAY BAN LIKELY

President Uses Taft Act on Board's Report That Tie-Up Is 'Serious'

Texts of report to President and his and judge's orders, Page 24.

By A. H. RASKIN

Bowing to an injunction issued under the national emergency provisions of the Taft-Hartley Act, the International Longshoremen's Association last night ordered 50,000 striking longshoremen to return to their jobs tonight or tomorrow morning in ports from Newport News, Va., to Portland, Me.

The back-to-work move came after Federal Judge Edward Weinfeld had ordered a ten-day halt in the coast-wide strike to prevent "immediate and irreparable injury" to the national welfare. The judge set next Tuesday for a formal hearing, at which he is expected to extend his no-strike order to the full eighty-day period permitted under the Taft law.

The court order was served on Patrick J. Connolly, executive vice president of the pier union, at 10:30 P. M. in his room at the Governor Clinton Hotel. He said it was too late to arrange for an orderly return in all ports this morning. He directed his men to try to be on hand for the 7 o'clock shape-up tonight, but union officials predicted that most would not answer the whistle until 8 A. M. tomorrow. At some piers, however, it was understood that plans were under way to have men work this morning and that no union objection was anticipated.

Capt. William V. Bradley, leader of the I. L. A. towboat division, which had been striking in sympathy with the dock workers, instructed his members to return to their tugs at 3 A. M. today. This will enable the sixty-two freight ships that have anchored outside this port since the tie-up began at midnight last Wednesday to start toward their docks.

Trouble Seen on Some Docks

Union officials expressed certainty that there would be no defiance of Judge Weinfeld's order, but they hinted that trouble might break out on some piers through the refusal of the I. L. A. members to work alongside members who had quit the union to join the rival group chartered by the American Federation of Labor. This might force a fresh shutdown of work in large sections of Manhattan and Brooklyn, where the A. F. L. has made its heaviest inroads.

President Eisenhower, acting through the Department of Justice, had asked the court to issue an injunction to protect "the national health and safety." It was the first time since he entered the White House last January that the President invoked the strike-ending provisions of the controversial labor law.

The injunction, if extended by Judge Weinfeld after he has heard union and employer arguments at Tuesday's hearing, would keep the ports open until Christmas Eve. If the turbulent waterfront situation has not been stabilized by then, the

Continued on page 24, Column 1

Jurist Puts Off Transit Suit, Urges Out-of-Court Accord

Justice Hart Offers Plan to End Dispute Between Union and Authority, but Refuses to Tell What It Is

By LEONARD INGALLS

The New York City Transit Authority and the Transport Workers Union, C. I. O., agreed yesterday at the behest of Justice Walter R. Hart in Supreme Court, Brooklyn, to try to settle their differences over new transit operating schedules out of court within a week.

The hearing in a suit by the union, headed by Michael J. Quill, to enjoin the authority from proceeding with the new work assignments for 14,570 transit employes was postponed until next Tuesday at 2 P. M. Meanwhile, the effort to settle the dispute on the basis of recommendations by Justice Hart is to be made.

After two conferences in his chambers with attorneys for both sides, Justice Hart told reporters that it would not be desirable or in the public interest to have prolonged litigation in the case and that it had been decided to try for a compromise without formal court proceedings.

It also became known during the conferences that the T. W. U. had accepted new schedules proposed by the Transit Authority for the B. M. T. subway and elevated lines and for the Manhattan, Queens, North Shore and Staten Island bus divisions. This leaves the I. R. T., IND and Brooklyn surface lines schedules still in dispute.

As a result of yesterday's meetings, the authority agreed to suspend until Tuesday a pick of new runs from the disputed schedules, which had been ordered to start yesterday. The schedules outline the work assignments of all motormen and conductors on the rapid transit lines and of all bus and trolley operators on the surface lines, as well as the runs of all trains and surface vehicles. They are designed to effect a $1,250,000 annual operating saving on the city-owned lines by reducing service.

The union objected to the new schedules on the ground that they would affect unfavorably transit

Continued on Page 59, Column 2

CLARK LETTER ASKS P.O.W. UNIT TO SEEK VIEWS OF CAPTIVES

Says Queries Would Dispel 'Assumption' Men Desire to Return to Communism

NEW RULING IS PROTESTED

U. N. Commander Bids Neutrals Open Talks With Prisoners Who Change Their Minds

By WILLIAM J. JORDEN
Special to THE NEW YORK TIMES.

TOKYO, Tuesday, Oct. 6—Gen. Mark W. Clark urged the Neutral Nations Commission today to seek the views of anti-Communist prisoners concerning repatriation to dispel the commission's apparent "assumption" that the Chinese and North Korean captives actually desired to return to communism.

The United Nations commander said it appeared that the repatriation commission's decisions and activities to date were based on the assumption that the prisoners in Korea wanted to return home. He said it was difficult to understand that attitude, in view of the "strong opposition the Korean and Chinese anti-Communist prisoners have demonstrated, individually and collectively, even to the physical presence of Communist representatives."

In order to remove the commission's seeming doubts about the sincerity with which the captives oppose their return to communism, General Clark proposed that the neutral group take advantage of its terms of reference in the armistice agreement and that the prisoners "be encouraged to state their views directly to the Neutral Nations Repatriation Commission and its subordinate bodies, on the situation as they see it."

'Conclusive Evidence' Sought

"This should provide conclusive evidence of their personal feelings and desires," the general said.

The United Nations commander's views were contained in a letter to the chairman of the neutral commission, Lieut. Gen. K. S. Thimayya of India. It was delivered to General Thimayya at his Panmunjom headquarters this morning.

[The Associated Press said that thousands of South Koreans jammed the streets of downtown Seoul Tuesday in a demonstration against Indian custody of anti-Communist war prisoners. The demonstrators demanded the immediate release of the prisoners and the withdrawal of the Indian forces from Korea.]

General Clark attacked strongly the commission's decision not to permit United Nations representatives to witness meetings between neutral delegates and prisoners who reportedly change their minds about returning home. At such meetings the prisoners declare their desire to return to the Communist side and the commission validates their requests.

The decision not to allow United Nations witnesses at such meetings, General Clark said, was "surprising and disappointing." He reminded the commission of its decision to allow Communist observers to watch the transfer of anti-Communist prisoners to the neutral camp.

General Clark also urged that the validations should be witnessed by the press.

Thus far 111 North Koreans and Chinese have appealed to the neutrals for repatriation and have been returned to the Communists. Three more North Koreans were scheduled to appear before neutral

Continued on Page 2, Column 5

Yanks Take 5th Series in Row, a Record; Martin's Hit in 9th Beats Dodgers, 4 to 3

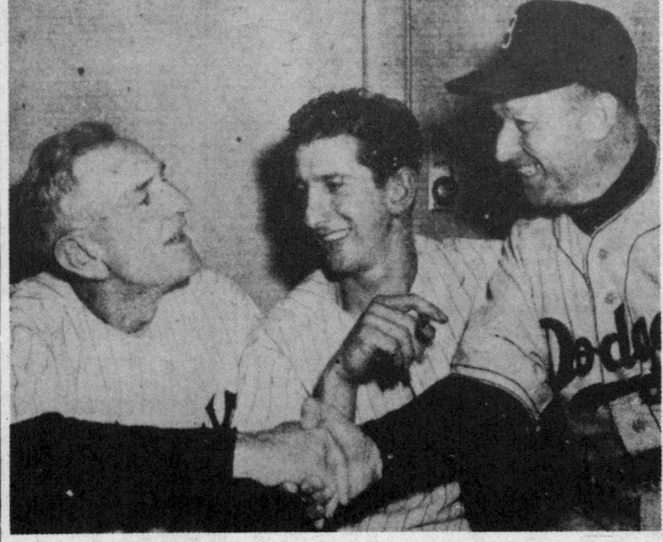

The New York Times

With a brave smile, Chuck Dressen congratulates Casey Stengel on the Yankees' fifth straight world series victory. In center is Billy Martin, who won last game with ninth-inning hit.

Furillo's Last-Inning Homer Ties Score, Then Bomber Star Gets 12th Safety

By JOHN DREBINGER

In a whirlwind, breath-taking finish that doubtless will be remembered as long as baseball is played, Casey Stengel's Yankees yesterday became the first club in history to win five world series championships in a row.

The extraordinary feat was achieved at the Stadium before a crowd of 62,370 roaring fans. They saw the American League's amazing Bombers vanquish a fighting band of Dodgers, 4 to 3, to clinch the 1953 classic by a margin of four games to two.

For one throbbing moment in a thrill-packed ninth inning, Chuck Dressen's Flatbush Flock stood even. This came when Carl Furillo blasted a two-run homer off Allie Reynolds. It deadlocked the score at 3-all.

Minutes later, in the last half of the ninth, amazing Bill Martin, doubtless cast from the start to fill the hero's role, slammed a single into center field off relief hurler Clem Labine. That shot, which gave Billy a series record of twelve hits, sent Hank Bauer racing over the plate with the decisive tally.

Sixteen in Thirty Years

And so to 63-year-old Charles Dillon Stengel, who in some forty-odd years has just about touched all the bases in an astounding career, now goes the distinction of becoming the first manager to match five straight pennants with five successive world titles. He did it, too, in his first five years in the American League. For prior to 1949 the Ol' Perfessor, as the gravel-voiced philosopher, sage and wit of the diamond is fondly known, had never so much as played, coached or managed a single inning in the junior circuit.

As a fitting climax to the classic's fiftieth anniversary, the Yankees chalked up their sixteenth world championship against only four defeats. This achievement is all the more remarkable in that all sixteen triumphs were gained in a span of thirty years. Also, it boosted the American League's lead over the rival loop to a margin of thirty-three series victories to seventeen.

On the other hand, Brooklyn's

Continued on Page 35, Column 2

U. N. NAMES TURKEY TO SEAT ON COUNCIL

Vishinsky Protests as Choice of U. S. Defeats Poland, Soviet Candidate, on 8th Ballot

By THOMAS J. HAMILTON
Special to THE NEW YORK TIMES.

UNITED NATIONS, N. Y., Oct. 5—The United Nations General Assembly today elected Turkey, the United States candidate, to the Eastern European seat on the Security Council, now held by Greece. Eight ballots were required before Turkey obtained forty votes, the exact two-thirds majority required, over Poland, the candidate of the Soviet bloc.

Andrei Y. Vishinsky, Soviet representative, protested before the vote against what he said was discrimination against the Eastern European countries.

Mr. Vishinsky was called to order by Mme. Vijaya Lakshmi Pandit of India, President of the Assembly, who asserted that Assembly rules of procedure forbade any nominating speeches. When Mr. Vishinsky continued to speak, the Assembly translators, on orders from the President, stopped translating his protest.

2 Other Countries Named

The Security Council seat assigned to the British Commonwealth, and one of the two seats assigned to Latin America, like that held by Greece, will become vacant at the end of the year. However, the British Commonwealth countries had agreed on New Zealand to replace Pakistan, and the Latin-American countries on Brazil to replace Chile. Both were elected without opposition on the first ballot.

Since the start of the United Nations in 1946 the six seats on the council assigned to non-permanent members—the small and medium powers—have been informally allocated to the various geographic regions. In the case of all except the seat from Eastern Europe, the Assembly has accepted the choice of the delegates from the region involved. Non-permanent seats are for two-year terms, while the five great powers have permanent seats.

However, in 1949 the United States successfully challenged the practice of accepting the Soviet bloc's nominee for the Eastern European seat. In that year the United States backed Yugoslavia, whose Communist government had broken with the Soviet regime, against the Soviet candidate, Czechoslovakia.

More Opposition in 1951

The United States did so again in 1951, when it backed Greece against Byelorussia. That time more opposition was encountered, and the Assembly had to take nineteen ballots before electing Greece.

Members of the Security Council are not eligible for immediate re-election, and this year the United States decided to support Turkey, the only other non-Communist member from Eastern Europe, to succeed Greece. However, Turkey's candidacy was complicated by the fact that while Istanbul, her principal city, is on the European side of the Bosporus, Ankara, the capital, and the larger part of Turkish territory are in Asia Minor.

Mr. Vishinsky charged today

Continued on Page 3, Column 5

WARREN SWORN IN; PRESIDENT ATTENDS

Mrs. Eisenhower Also Is Among Notables at Brief Ceremony for New Chief Justice

By LUTHER A. HUSTON
Special to THE NEW YORK TIMES.

WASHINGTON, Oct. 5—Earl Warren, a smiling, broad-shouldered Californian, was sworn in today as the fourteenth Chief Justice of the United States. He succeeded Fred M. Vinson, who died on Sept. 8.

President and Mrs. Eisenhower and Vice President Richard M. Nixon, himself a Californian, witnessed the brief ceremonies in the Supreme Court chamber. Mrs. Warren, the only member of the new Chief Justice's family who was present, sat between Mrs. Nixon and the Vice President and smiled as her husband took his seat on the high bench. She wore a red hat and an orchid.

Mr. Warren, who left his resignation as Governor of California on his desk when he closed his office in Sacramento last Saturday, holds a commission from President Eisenhower to serve as Chief Justice "until the end of the next session of the Senate of the United States and no longer, subject to the provision of the law."

This means he must be confirmed by the Senate during its next session. No major opposition to his confirmation has been raised since the President announced that he would name the Californian to the Chief Justiceship.

Mr. Warren took two oaths before he became Chief Justice. The first, in which he swore to defend the Constitution and "bear true faith and allegiance" to it, was administered in the justices' conference room by Associate Justice Hugo L. Black, as senior justice

Continued on Page 21, Column 2

WICKS CHALLENGES DEMOCRATS ON FAY; REFUSES TO RESIGN

Charges New Deal 'Coddled' Racketeers—Action Viewed as Bid for G.O.P. Backing

By WARREN WEAVER Jr.
Special to THE NEW YORK TIMES.

ALBANY, Oct. 5—Senator Arthur H. Wicks, Acting Lieutenant Governor, today vigorously rejected demands that he resign because of his visits to Joseph S. (Joey) Fay, a convicted labor extortionist, at Sing Sing.

"I shall not resign from any position I now hold," the Republican legislator and Senate majority leader declared flatly in a telegram to Robert F. Wagner Jr., Borough President of Manhattan and Democratic candidate for Mayor of New York. Mr. Wicks' office made the message public this afternoon.

[In New York, Mr. Wagner urged Governor Dewey to call a special session of the Legislature to impeach Mr. Wicks.]

Last Friday, when Mr. Wicks' association with the imprisoned racketeer, since transferred to Dannemora, came to light, the Senator said only that he felt he had done nothing wrong. His action today amounted, in the eyes of many capital observers, to a showdown call to his Republican colleagues either to support or to repudiate him.

Fay's Transfer Urged Earlier

At Ossining, N. Y., it was revealed that Sing Sing officials had recommended nearly three years ago that Fay be transferred to an upstate prison, but the suggestion had gone unheeded. Prison officials said the proposal had been made shortly after Wilfred L. Denno had become warden and while the late John Lyons had been State Commissioner of Correction, a post now held by Edward J. Donovan.

In replying to Mr. Wagner's demand Saturday for his resignation, Mr. Wicks made it clear he felt that the evil in the situation lay not in his actions but in the degree of influence that Fay apparently was able to wield over labor matters from his prison cell.

"I did not create the deplorable condition that permits a convict to continue to be a power in labor circles even though he is serving a prison term," Mr. Wicks declared. "The coddling of labor racketeers by the New Deal and the Fair Deal created that condition and permitted convicts and thugs to gain and keep control of many labor unions, to the detriment of the honest working man."

Wicks Replies To Balch

From his home in Kingston Mr. Wicks also countered to a request for his resignation made yesterday by Richard H. Balch, Democratic State Chairman, in Utica. Repeating his stand against Mr. Wagner, the Senator said:

"I have done nothing to require my resignation. If Mr. Balch thinks I have shaken the faith of my people he ought to come into my district and see how the people feel about me. If I were a racketeer or associated with racketeers, I would not enjoy the enviable reputation that I do."

On Friday Mr. Wicks declared his only purpose in visiting Fay had been to aid in settling labor

Continued on Page 40, Column 4

VOTE REGISTRATION LIGHT ON FIRST DAY

259,630 Total Here 10% Less Than Count for Same Period in Last City-Wide Election

Registration in the city was extremely light yesterday, the first day to enroll for the election on Nov. 3. Only 259,630 men and women qualified, 10 per cent fewer than in the last comparable year of 1949 when the previous city-wide election took place. First day registration in 1949 was 288,166.

The slow pace yesterday was attributed to a combination of world series "hangover," the threat of rain and general apathy toward the political situation. The only boroughs to show a gain were Queens and Richmond, which reflected the population growth there in the last four years rather than any deep interest in the campaign.

Compared with last year's huge first-day enrollment of 550,273, a Presidential year, potential voters made a dismal showing for this year's Mayoralty contest and other city offices. The enrollment also lagged behind 1950 when a Governor, Senator and Mayor were elected and 294,639 persons qualified on the first day.

Registration was particularly weak in Manhattan, where only

Continued on Page 22, Column 3

$490,000 CITY SUIT BY GEROSA BARED

Construction Company Run by Democratic Candidate for Controller Seeks Payment

A construction company controlled by Lawrence E. Gerosa, Democratic candidate for Controller, is suing New York City for $490,000 in connection with excavation work, Vito Marcantonio, state chairman of the American Labor party, noted yesterday at an interview in his office at 11 Park Place.

Mr. Marcantonio said the City Charter made it a misdemeanor for a city official to be "interested" in any litigation against the city and added: "People engaged in contracting for the city should either get out of that business or not run for office."

After learning of Mr. Marcantonio's remarks, Mr. Gerosa issued a statement in which he called Mr. Marcantonio a "disgruntled fellow traveler" whose statements had indicated "either his complete ignorance of city government or else his spite."

"In 1946 the Gerosa Construction Company built a Queens subway extension," Mr. Gerosa explained. "Unanticipated underground water conditions were encountered which naturally increased the cost of the

Continued on Page 20, Column 8

Red Army Deserter Asking Refuge Here

An 18-year-old Russian youth who said he had deserted from the Soviet Army in East Germany and stowed away on a ship to reach this country surrendered voluntarily to immigration authorities here yesterday and asked for asylum.

The blond, blue-eyed youth, who spoke only German and Russian, said he had been befriended by three French sailors after his escape last month from East Germany. The sailors, he said, gave him old clothes to replace the Russian Army uniform he was wearing, smuggled him aboard their ship and, when it arrived in this country last Thursday, managed to slip him past immigration officers and into the city.

They had given him $5, he said, and told him to get in touch with Russian emigrés in this country who would help him out. For two

Continued on Page 15, Column 4

Revered Peru Image Is Reported Missing

By SAM POPE BREWER
Special to THE NEW YORK TIMES.

LIMA, Peru, Oct. 5—Church and civil authorities have opened separate investigations of a sensational charge that Peru's most venerated religious image has disappeared and been replaced by a modern imitation.

A priest of the Mercedarian Order, which has custody of the image of Our Lady of Mercy, patroness of Peru's armed forces and looked on as the country's principal religious protector for four centuries, has admitted that he retouched the face of the image but denies that the statue has been replaced by another.

The priest said he found its facial features "too masculine" and worked five months to give them a "more tender expression."

That in itself, according to some

Continued on Page 15, Column 3

Associated Press Wirephoto

REPORT ON DOCK STRIKE: President Eisenhower receiving yesterday at the White House the report of the fact-finding board he had appointed in the longshoremen's strike, the final step required before the Government could apply for injunction. Left to right, the Rev. Dennis J. Comey, the President, David Cole, board chairman, and Dr. Harry Carman.

Stockholder in Track Loses Post in Nassau

By ALEXANDER FEINBERG

The Nassau County Board of Supervisors yesterday failed to reappoint Irving T. Bergman as special counsel for the county in labor matters following the disclosure that he owned 8,060 shares of stock in the Nassau Trotting Association. The association, together with the Old Country Trotting Association, operates the meets at Roosevelt Raceway, Westbury, L. I.

Mr. Bergman is a son-in-law of Benjamin F. Feinberg, former majority leader of the State Senate and now chairman of the Public Service Commission. Mr. Bergman, a lawyer, of Oceanside, L. I., also is chairman of the Nassau-Suffolk Commuters Committee, Inc., the leading commuter organization in the two counties.

Other developments in investiga-

Continued on Page 30, Column 3

Stengel Talks of 'Good Chance' for Bombers in 1954

YANKEES CAPTURE 5TH SERIES IN ROW

Continued From Page 1

record of gloom took on an even darker hue. For this was the seventh time that a Dodger team had tried and failed to bring to that hotbed of diamond fanaticism its first world series crown. But even the most sorely disappointed Flatbush fan could not complain about the way Dressen's National Leaguers, on this occasion, fought off defeat until the last gasp.

Chuck had started Carl Erskine, the trim righthander who on Friday had set a world series record with fourteen strikeouts to win the third game in Ebbets Field. But Carl had only two days of rest and the Bombers got a three-run lead in the first two rounds behind their own Whitey Ford.

If there were any mistakes up to now it was the Yanks who made them. They tossed away an extra tally in the second inning when Ford, in an astounding mental lapse, failed to score on a fly ball that traveled almost 400 feet.

Though Dressen was later to get superb relief hurling from Bob Milliken and Labine until Clem's final cave-in in the last of the ninth, overhauling that three-run deficit proved a herculean effort. Off Ford the Dodgers never did make it.

One Tally In the Sixth

They knicked the young southpaw from Astoria for one tally in the sixth which Jackie Robinson personally conducted around the paths by stroking a two-bagger, stealing third and scoring on an infield out. But the pair that tied it in the ninth on Furrillo's homer was not made off Ford at all.

Actually, all that final drama began with the eighth inning. It was then that Stengel, in a move as startling as any in his brilliant managerial career, withdrew Ford. The bull-pen gates opened to reveal the confidently striding figure of Reynolds. The redoubtable Chief, who had started the opener for the Yanks, had strained a muscle in his back in that game. He came back to stop the Flock in its tracks in the ninth inning of the fifth game in Brooklyn Sunday. Now he was being called upon to lock up the clincher.

Ford, in his seven innings, had given up only six hits. He was leading 3 to 1, and there seemed to be no particular reason for making a change. Still, the Ol' Perfessor often makes alterations that defy analysis by baseball's outstanding academic minds.

Ford had made a spectacular comeback after his ill-starred one-inning effort which had cost the Bombers the fourth game. Perhaps the shot which pinch hitter Bob Morgan had streaked toward the right field stands in the seventh with a runner aboard helped Casey to make up his mind.

Bauer had caught that one off Morgan's bat as it was about to fall into the seats. Anyway, little did anyone suspect that Reynolds, now entering the game simply to save it for the youthful Ford, would wind up the winner himself, for it was his seventh world series mound triumph, tying the record of another Yankee stalwart of another period, Red Ruffing.

Robinson singled in the eighth, but there were two out and Roy Campanella, striving desperately to answer the prayers of the Flatbush faithful, went down swinging on a third strike.

Big Jawn Called to Bat

In the last of the eighth Stengel made another move, startling, yet withal a nice gesture. Phil Rizzuto and Reynolds had singled with one out. A close play at the plate had rubbed out Rizzuto when he tried to score on Gene Woodling's grounder, but there were still two on base.

So the Ol' Perfessor called in Johnny Mize to pinch hit. A year ago the big Georgian had been the hero. This year there had not been much occasion to call on him and at the age of 41 this easily could prove his farewell as an active player. His best was a grounder down the first base line that ended the round.

Hank Bauer scoring from second with the winning Yankee run on Martin's drive. Gil McDougald yells with glee and Coach Frank Crosetti rushes in from 3d base for some back-patting.

But the Yanks were still two in front and they were still that way when Gil Hodges, first Dodger up in the ninth, flied out. But Duke Snider, whom Ford had fanned three times earlier in the battle, now worked Reynolds for a pass after running the count to three and two.

Then came Furillo. He, too, worked it to three and two. Then he lashed one on a line into the lower right field stand and the Flatbush host was beside itself. The score was deadlocked and one could see Reynolds felt keenly disappointed.

The Chief fairly burned the ball across the plate as he next struck out Billy Cox and Labine to end the inning. But the score was tied.

Now the grand finale. Bauer, first up in the last of the ninth, walked. Yogi Berra flied out but Mickey Mantle topped a ball to the left of the diamond which skipped off Cox's glove and went for a hit. This set up the break in the game.

For up came that incredible 25-year-old star, Martin, a .257 hitter through the regular season who was now emerging as the grand hero. His base clearing first inning triple had sent the Yanks off to a flying start at the outset of the series. He later was to hit two homers and up to this moment he had made eleven hits, tops for the series.

One Smack to Glory

Labine worked carefully, got the count to one and one. Then Billy smacked it. Right over second base it went and that was all.

It was the twelfth hit of the series for the peppery Californian who once played for Stengel when the latter managed Oakland in the Coast League before coming to the Yanks. In fact, it was largely on the insistance of Casey that Martin came to the Yanks at all. They never did think too much of him. Now he can name his own price. Those twelve hits gave Martin the record for a six-game series and tied the mark of a dozen blows made in a seven-game classic.

For the first time since the series began, the weatherman, who so obligingly had provided a midsummer setting for the first five games, walked out on the show. A gray sky that threatened rain almost from the first, blotted out every trace of the sun, so that the fielders had nothing to worry about on that score. Shirt sleeves also went out of fashion overnight for the fans. It was, in fact, more than a trifle chilly.

However, though the weather slumped, not so those toughened pioneers of that first world series fifty years ago who have been rotating in tossing out the first ball. Yesterday it was Fred Parent, 1903 Red Sox shortstop, who took his turn. Fred really put something on it as he fired into Berra's big mitt. Then the stars of today took over.

It soon became evident that Erskine wasn't the pitcher of the third game of last Friday and that the two intervening days had not given him sufficient rest.

In Trouble From the Start

He was in trouble right from the start and but for some blundering by the Bombers on the basepaths in the second inning, the handsome Hoosier righthander would have plunged deeper in the hole.

He walked Woodling, who again was leading off in the Stengel batting order. He fanned Joe Collins, one of his four-time victims last Friday at Ebbets Field, but Bauer lined a single to left and Berra hammered a drive down the right field line that hopped by Furillo and bounced into the stand for an automatic two-bagger.

In a way that helped the Dodgers since Bauer, who almost certainly would have scored had the ball remained in play, had to hold up at third, while only Woodling was permitted to count. The break didn't help much, however.

Erskine, who also fanned Mantle four times the last time he faced him, was not permitted to embellish that record. He was instructed to pass the Oklahoma Kid intentionally and that filled the bases.

This strategy might have paid off. Martin sent a blistering one hopper to the right of second base. Junior Gilliam momentarily collared the ball only to let it get away. Had he held it, it most likely would have resulted in an inning-ending double play.

Instead, it was scored an error, although this verdict did not meet with the general approval of the press box occupants. Quite a few of the experts were of the opinion it should have been called a hit, since it looked to have Gilliam handcuffed all the way.

Be that as it may, it allowed Bauer to come home with the second tally and though Gil McDougald here slapped into a double play, the Bombers for the fourth time in the series had skipped off to a first-inning lead.

And in the second they got with another run. They should have had two, but lost one on an incredible bit of base running—or lack of it—on the part of Master Ford.

Rizzuto opened the inning with a single to center and Whitey lined one into right that swept Li'l Phil around to third. Woodling followed with a long fly to Jackie Robinson in left and Rizzuto scampered over the plate with one run.

Now came some harrowing moments for the Dodgers. They seemed about to blow sky high. But the Bombers themselves bungled it. Collins, in backing away from a pitch, accidentally bunted one down the third-base line that could not have been more scientifically placed.

Erskine tracked it down and fired the ball to first, but too late and too wide. In fact, Carl threw the ball right over Hodges' head and it went for a hit and an error, the play winding up with Ford on third, Collins on second and still only one out.

Pitching cautiously to Bauer, Erskine walked him to fill the bases. Then Berra lifted a towering fly that Snider caught in deep right center. It was so deep that no one even thought Ford would fail to score from third. All eyes were focused on Collins as he tagged up at second and lit out for third the moment the ball landed in Duke's glove.

But as Gilliam received Snider's throw-in someone in the infield yelled, "Home, home, throw it home." Gilliam whirled around, fired the ball to Campanella at the plate and there, lo and behold, was Ford, still leisurely jogging home and never making it. For Campy tagged him with the ball for the third out. That "lost" run was almost to come up and haunt the Bombers in the end.

From Force of Habit

It probably was destined right from the beginning that the Yanks should win this series if only in response to an overwhelming force of habit.

It was in 1923 that the Yanks won their first world title under the late Miller Huggins. They had won their first league pennants in 1921 and 1922, but had been turned back by the Giants in the series. Since 1923 they have been stopped only twice, by the Cardinals in 1926 and again by the Redbirds in 1942.

After '23 they triumphed again under Huggins in 1927 and 1928. They won next in 1932 under Joe McCarthy, who then led them through four successive series triumphs from 1936 to 1939, a mark that stood until Stengel tied it last year and surpassed it this year.

Two more titles went to the Yanks under McCarthy in 1941 and 1943. Then Marse Joe stepped out, but in 1947 the Yanks were back with another world crown under Bucky Harris and in 1949 there began the present act of five in a row under Stengel.

HURLING STRENGTH NEEDED, PILOT SAYS

By LOUIS EFFRAT

The tumult in the clubhouse of the champions had subsided to a degree that permitted Casey Stengel to express himself in a tone slightly under a shout. For a half-hour or so, following his Yankees' wrap-up of their fifth straight world series yesterday at the Stadium, the dressing room scene was the familiar picture of happy confusion, boisterous backslapping and vigorous handshaking.

However, when Stengel, seated in his private cubicle—no privacy on such an occasion—had relaxed a bit, it was about the future that he spoke. "The Yankees, as they are now constituted, have a good chance to win the pennant in 1954," he said. Then the most successful manager in diamond history added, "unless the other clubs get stronger."

Something will have to be done to strengthen the Yankee pitching, Stengel conceded. But he reviewed his line-up and could not find a weak link.

"Mickey Mantle should be better," he stated. "Gene Woodling is an outstanding player and Hank Bauer had a great year. In Irv Noren we have the best fourth outfielder in the league. He'd be playing regularly on another club. The infield and the catching are excellent."

Here was a man, flushed with pride over a job well done. Some thirty minutes earlier his charges had eliminated an ever-dangerous enemy and already he was talking about next year. And, while on the subject of next season, Casey said that unless his health dictated against it or the owners of the Yankees did not want him, he would be back to guide the Bombers in 1954. Stengel's contract has one more year to run.

Stengel was the first man in the room, immediately after Billy Martin's hit had clinched the decision and the series. There Casey was greeted by Dan Topping and Del Webb, the co-owners, who almost crushed the manager with hugs and embraces. Bill Dickey, Ed Lopat, Allie Reynolds, Vic Raschi and Mickey Mantle followed and by that time—pandemonium. Writers, photographers, newsreel and television men jammed the room.

Martin, easily the outstanding individual in the six-game classic, found himself everwhelmed. Stengel, Reynolds, Whitey Ford and others did not lack for attention. And in a moment, there was Chuck Dressen, the losing pilot, alongside Stengel shaking his hand and offering congratulations. Walter O'Malley, the Brooklyn president, also dropped in to pay his respects, as did Commissioner Ford Frick, Will Harridge, the president of the American League, Horace Stoneham of the Giants and numerous former ballplayers.

Stengel took it all gracefully. He told everyone "the Dodgers are the best ball club we played in the past five seasons." He extolled Martin, who, incidentally, was termed by Dressen "a .250 hitter, who is the best man the Yankees have." Then the pilot proceeded to explain why he had removed Ford at the end of the seventh inning.

"Whitey pitched well," Casey said, "but that Bobby Morgan's fly at the end of the seventh was hit real hard. I didn't want to take any chances against those good hitters the Dodgers would have coming up in the eighth. I figured Reynolds with a two-run lead would hold it for two innings."

Casey said he did not know whether Ford was tiring, but the left-hander averred that he could have finished. "I was not tired," Whitey stated. "At the moment, when Casey removed me, I was somewhat on the angry side, but the manager knew what he was doing. He was right, as he has been the last five years. Anyway, we won and that's most important."

Ford's explanation for his failure to score after Yogi Berra's long fly in the second was that he had left third base too soon. "I was unable to see Duke Snider complete the catch and left early. Frankie Crosetti told me to return and tag up. I did and was an easy out at the plate.

"On Jackie Robinson's steal of third in the sixth, I looked back while taking the stretch and saw Jackie with a big lead. 'Gosh,' I said to myself, 'he's got a tremendous jump. I'll pick him off on the next pitch.' Before I knew it, though, Robinson was on third."

Martin had an explanation, too. He said the reason for his consistent hitting was that he had made up his mind to swing only at strikes.

Never Started a Fight

Billy the Kid also had something to say about his reputation for being a fighter. "I'd like to straighten that out," he said. "I've made this statement before and now I repeat it. I've never started a fight in my life."

Dodgers Once Again Hear 'Wait 'Til Next Year'

VANQUISHED PRAISE MARTIN OF VICTORS

O'Malley Commends Dodgers —Erskine Points to Faulty Control in Final Game

By ROSCOE McGOWEN

Three or four minutes after Billy Martin's bat had killed for the seventh time the Dodgers' hopes of winning a world series, the mourners' procession came marching, heavy-footed, into the Brooklyn dressing room yesterday at Yankee Stadium.

Close to the front was Walter O'Malley, Brooklyn president, with an arm around the shoulders of Carl Erskine, the little Hoosier righthander, who tried valiantly but vainly to keep the Brooks alive.

Then followed Buzzie Bavasi, a Dodger vice president and saddest looking of all the mourners for the failure of "the best team Brooklyn ever had."

"You all had a good season. You did well and there are no regrets," O'Malley told Manager Chuck Dressen. "Once more," O'Malley added—and he may have winced a little as he repeated the old line —"we'll have to wait 'til next year."

Sees Yanks as Good Club

Erskine, sad at his failure, still wouldn't go for one sympathetic remark that the Yankees were lucky.

"I'm afraid nobody can sell me on their being lucky," said Carl. "A team that wins as often as they do has to have something more than luck. They're a good ball club."

Erskine said he had not had as good stuff as in the third game in Brooklyn last Friday when he broke the world series strike-out record.

"But I thought I had pretty good stuff—the kind I've won with at times during the season. My control wasn't too good, though, and brought trouble."

Bases on balls, indeed, were ruinous to the Brooks. The first and last Yankees to walk scored—Gene Woodling in the first inning and Hank Bauer, passed by Clem Labine, in the ninth with the winning run.

Labine, nicked for the Martin single that gave Billy a tie for the most hits in one series—twelve—said he had made "another bad pitch—and I said I wouldn't do it again."

"That Martin must be the best .250 hitter in the world," said Clem, when told that Billy had batted .257 during the season.

Dressen had a similar comment about Martin, who used to play for him at Oakland.

Dressen Lauds Martin

"Martin's the best on the club," declared Dressen. "He don't try to hit home runs—he just tries to get base hits, and he got 'em in this series."

Labine said Martin hit "what I thought was a good sinker, but I guess it wasn't so good—at least you can't say it was good now, can you?"

Peewee Reese, captain and shortstop and only active player who was in the 1941 series, was asked if he could say anything about why the Dodgers were beaten.

"I wish I could think of something real brilliant," grinned Peewee, "but I'm afraid I'm not up to it.

"I think, yes," he replied to another query, "that we didn't play as good ball as we're capable of playing. In fact, we played lousy at times."

Billy Herman, a Dodger coach, was a bit more outspoken.

"We played our worst and they played their best," declared Billy. Then he added a few comments that, from anybody else, might have been considered "sour grapes," but, so far as Herman was concerned, were merely statements of fact.

Gil Hodges, Dodger first baseman, making leap in attempt to get Carl Erskine's second-inning throw. The throw was too high and Joe Collins was able to continue to second base on error.

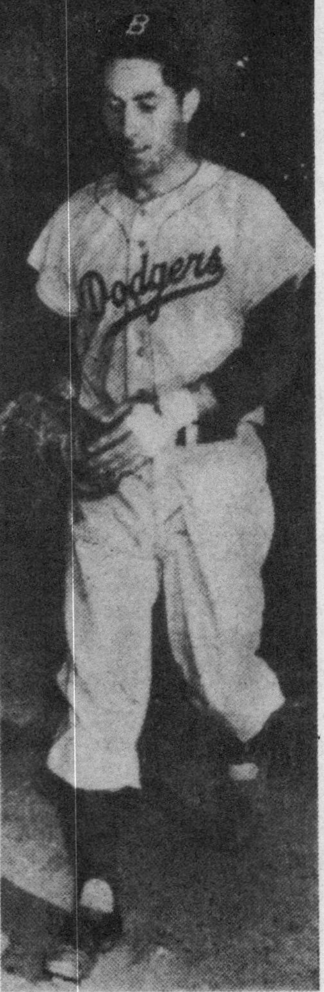

The New York Times

Furillo, leading hitter in the National League, whose dramatic home run gave Dodgers a lease on life in the ninth, walks slowly back to Brooklyn dressing room after the game.

"I don't think there is a man on this Yankee team who could have made the one that beat the Cubs four straight in 1932 when I was with Chicago. You think I'm kidding? Well, look back at that outfit.

1932 Stars Cited

"There was a fellow named Ruth and another named Gehrig. Pretty good, weren't they? A guy named Lazzeri—he wasn't so bad. A fellow named Combs, who did all right in center field and at bat. And Yogi Berra is maybe their best man, isn't he? You think he would have been catching ahead of Bill Dickey?

"I'll give these Yankees this much," concluded Billy. "Phil Rizzuto in his prime could have made that club."

Junior Gilliam, who was charged with an error on a hot shot from Martin in the first inning—which, had it been called a hit, would have given Martin the record for most hits in one series—said he thought he should have fielded the ball.

"I've fielded others like that—and I've missed 'em, too," said Junior.

"But I expected to get the ball. It was a low liner that came on a short hop. It hit my glove but it didn't stick. Guess I'd have had the double play if I came up with the ball."

The Dodger who could have been the happiest man yesterday was perhaps the unhappiest.

That was Carl Furillo, the ace right fielder who belted the home run off Allie Reynolds to tie the score at 3-all in the ninth.

"Tough to get even and then not be able to hold it and go on to win," said Carl, as he sat in front of his locker, rubbing his swollen hand.

Jackie Robinson, who did his share with a double and single and with his theft of third base, which brought a run the Brooks otherwise would not have scored, brushed off any congratulations.

"Fine, if we had won," said Jack. "But what good when we lost?"

What good, indeed? as disconsolate fans throughout all Brooklyn probably were asking last night.

23 MARKS ARE SET, 17 TIED IN CLASSIC

Yanks Establish 3 Cumulative Marks—Reynolds Has Most Series Strike-Outs, 62

Twenty-three world series marks were broken and seventeen were tied during the six-game 1953 classic between the Yankees and Dodgers that ended yesterday, The Associated Press reported.

Seven of the records were cumulative ones, with the Yankees' fifth straight world championship the top mark established. The Yankees have also played in the most series, twenty; have won the most series, sixteen, and have won the most series games, seventy-one.

Allie Reynolds, the star pitcher of the Yanks, monopolized the cumulative individual records. Allie has the most strike-outs by a pitcher in total series, sixty-two, and shares two other marks.

Reynolds has posted seven series victories and has issued thirty-two bases on balls to match records for the classic.

Other records set (based on a six-game series):

INDIVIDUAL RECORDS

Most base hits, one series—Billy Martin, Yankees, 12.

Most total bases, one series—Billy Martin, Yankees, 23.

Most strike-outs, one pitcher, game—Carl Erskine, Dodgers 14 (third game).

Most chances accepted, catcher, one series—Roy Campanella, Dodgers, 56.

TEAM RECORDS

Most base hits, both clubs, one series—120 (Dodgers 64, Yankees 56).

Most home runs, one club, one series—Yankees 9.

Most home runs, both clubs, one series—17 (Yankees 9, Dodgers 8).

Most total bases, one club, one series—Dodgers 103.

Most total bases, both clubs, one series—200 (Dodgers 103, Yankees 97).

Most total bases, both clubs, game—47 (Yankees 27, Dodgers 20), fifth game.

Most extra-base hits, one club, one series—Dodgers 22.

Most extra bases on long hits, one club, one series—Yankees 41.

Most extra bases on long hits, both clubs, one series—80 (Yankees 41, Dodgers 39).

Most left on bases, both clubs, one series—96 (Dodgers 49, Yankees 47).

Highest batting percentage of club losing series—Dodgers .300.

Most runs, losing club, one series—Dodgers 27.

MARTIN SENT BALL TO PROMISED LAND

Hero on High-Altitude Cloud Following Series—Winning Drive Against Labine

By BILLY MARTIN
As told to The United Press.

The ball I hit in the ninth inning went out into center field, they tell me, but I'll always believe it rolled into the Promised Land.

When I crossed first base and realized that we had won, a thousand sensations seemed to pass through my body all at once. It was just like stepping under a needle shower on a hot day. "You did it, kid!" That's what I kept telling myself over and over again. But I just couldn't believe it.

Thomson's Feat Recalled

It seemed to me as if it was happening to somebody else, not me. Now I know how Bobby Thomson of the Giants felt when he hit that pennant-winning homer against Brooklyn in 1951. He said he didn't run around the bases that day, but that he rode around them on a cloud. Believe me, the cloud I was on after that hit was higher than Thomson's.

If what I am saying now isn't making too much sense, you'll have to excuse me. I'm still so excited that I can't keep my thoughts from colliding with one another.

All I know is that when I came up to face Clem Labine in the ninth I thought to myself how nice it would be if I could come through with a hit. I saw Hank Bauer dancing off second base and I figured how great it would be if I could wind up the year with just one more R. B. I.

Labine Pitches Fast Ball

Labine came with a fast ball and I followed it from the moment it left his hand. When I hit the ball I wasn't sure it would go through the box but I got a glimpse of it as I started down the baseline and I think I said, "Hot dog!"

Actually, the ball I hit in the first inning—the one on which they charged Junior Gilliam with an error—was the hardest ball I hit all day. I kind of felt cheated when they ruled it an error but after that ninth-inning hit I don't feel short-changed in the least.

Now, I'm just going some place quiet and relax for a long time. Any minute I expect someone to jab me in the ribs and say:

"Hey, Martin, wake up! You're dreaming."

Musial Sets Record With 5 Homers as Cards Split With Giants; Yanks Divide

ST. LOUIS SLUGGER PACES 10-6 VICTORY

Musial Belts 3 Homers, Then Adds 2 for Twin-Bill Mark as Giants Triumph, 9-7

By JOHN DREBINGER
Special to The New York Times.

ST. LOUIS, May 2—Stan Musial set one major league record and tied another today as he walloped five home runs in the course of a double-header. But all it got the Cardinals was an even break with the Giants in a bruising twin bill that kept 26,662 roaring fans in a dither for the better part of seven hours.

In the opener the Redbirds downed the Polo Grounders, 10 to 6, with an outburst of five circuit drives to three for the New Yorkers. Stan the Man hit three in this game, his final blast, off Jim Hearn, coming with two aboard in the last of the eighth to break a 6-all tie.

Then, in the nightcap, practically all of it played under lights, Musial hit two more. But Leo Durocher's minions, erupting for eight runs in the fourth inning, managed to hang on to win this one, 9 to 7.

Cards Get 12 Homers

In all the Cards hit three homers in the second encounter to one for the Giants, making a grand total of twelve round trippers for the day.

Musial set a new mark with his five for the twin bill, the previous high for most homers in a double-header being four.

Musial also tied the major league record of five homers for two consecutive games.

The second game was, indeed, a bruising affair. When it wound up, Musial had a season's total of eight home runs.

At the outset it looked as though the Giants were headed for another drubbing when Tom Alston clubbed Don Liddle for a base-clearing double in the first inning. But in the fourth, the Polo Grounders came back with their cluster of eight as they battered Joe Presko, Royce Lint and Mel Wright for eight hits.

Mueller, who came up with five blows in this game, got two in this inning, one a triple, while Bobby Hofman contributed a three-run homer. But Hoyt Wilhelm, who replaced Liddle, ran into a three-run squall in the fifth on homers by Musial and Ray Jablonski and in the seventh Musial whacked him for another.

Both of the shots by Stan were tremendous wallops clear out of the park into Grand Avenue. They drove in three runs which, along with six in the first game, gave Musial a total of nine runs-batted-in for the day.

But at this point, Larry Jansen came on to stop the Redbirds cold. He blanked them through the eighth and ninth, and for good measure drove in an extra run for the Giants in the top of the ninth with a single.

Brazle Gains Victory

Stan the Man was pretty much the whole show in the opener, which saw Alpha Brazle, the ancient southpaw replace Starter Gerry Staley in the sixth inning to notch his first victory of the season.

Warming up on a base on balls off Johnny Antonelli in the first inning, Musial then proceeded to ring up a perfect game at bat for himself.

He hit homers in successive times at bat off Antonelli in the third and fifth, the first of these shots coming with the bases empty, the second with one on. He singled off Hearn in the sixth and in the eighth whacked the big right-hander for his game-clinching clout with two runners aboard.

It was, in fact, pretty much a home-run or no count affair most of the way, with eight of the ten tallies by the Cards coming as the result of circuit clouts.

Antonelli was slapped for six runs and four homers before being belted out in the fifth. In addition to Musial's first two, the former Brave lefty saw Wally Moon hit his third four-bagger of the season in the first and Tom Alston his third in the fourth.

The Giants, however, weren't exactly standing still. They reached Staley for three runs in the fourth with the aid of a couple of doubles by Henry Thompson and Irvin. Successive homers by Lockman and Westrum produced two more tallies in the fifth and in the sixth Irvin's No. 4 off Brazle deadlocked the score at 6-all.

From here on Brazle held firm while Hearn blew wide open in the eighth and went down to his second setback of the year.

GIL McDOUGALD CHECKED: The Yankee infielder is tagged out by Catcher Matt Batts of Detroit in eighth inning of yesterday's first game at Stadium. Umpire is Jim Honochick.

Giants' Box Scores

FIRST GAME

NEW YORK (N.)	ab	r	h	po	a
Williams, 2b	4	1	1	2	1
Dark, ss	4	0	1	0	2
Tho'son, 3b	4	1	1	1	4
Irvin, lf	3	2	2	2	0
Mueller, rf	4	0	1	0	0
Mays, cf	3	0	0	2	0
Lockm'n, 1b	4	1	1	9	1
Westrum, c	4	1	2	7	2
An'nelli, p	2	0	0	1	1
Hearn, p	0	0	0	0	0
Picone, p	0	0	0	0	0
cHofman	1	0	0	0	0
Total	33	6	9	24	11

ST. LOUIS (N.)	ab	r	h	po	a
Moon, cf	5	2	2	2	0
S'dienst, 2b	3	3	0	3	3
Musial, rf	4	3	4	4	0
Jab'ski, 3b	5	0	1	0	2
Repulski, lf	5	1	2	2	0
Alston, 1b	4	1	4	8	1
Gram'as, ss	2	0	0	1	1
aHemus, ss	3	0	1	0	0
Rice, c	3	0	0	6	1
Staley, p	1	0	0	1	2
bLowrey	1	0	0	0	0
Brazle, p	1	0	0	0	0
Total	37	10	14	27	10

aHit into force out for Grammas in fifth.
bStruck out for Staley in fifth.
cStruck out for Picone in ninth.

New York ......0 0 0 3 2 1 0 0 0—6
St. Louis ......2 0 1 1 2 0 0 4 .—10

Errors—Thompson, Dark. Runs batted in—Moon, Alston 2, Musial 6, Hemus, Thompson, Irvin 2, Mueller, Lockman, Westrum. Two-base hits—Thompson, Irvin, Repulski. Home runs—Moon, Musial 3, Alston, Lockman, Westrum, Irvin. Sacrifices—Staley, Hearn. Double plays—Schoendienst, Grammas and Alston; Jablonski, Schoendienst and Alston. Left on bases—New York 3, St. Louis 9. Bases on balls—Antonelli 3, Hearn 2, Brazle 2. Struck out—By Antonelli 4, Hearn 2, Staley 3, Brazle 3. Hits—Off Antonelli 6 in 4 innings (faced three men in fifth), Hearn 8 in 3 1-3, Picone 0 in 2-3, Staley 7 in 5, Brazle 2 in 4. Runs and earned runs—Off Antonelli 6 and 5, Hearn 4 and 4, Staley 5 and 5, Brazle 1 and 1. Winning pitcher—Brazle (1-0). Losing pitcher—Hearn (0-2). Umpires—Donatelli, Ballanfant, Barlick and Warneke. Time of game—2:48.

SECOND GAME

NEW YORK (N.)	ab	r	h	po	a
Lockman, 1b	2	1	0	10	1
Dark, ss	5	0	0	3	1
Thompson, 3b	4	1	1	0	2
Irvin, lf	4	1	1	1	0
Mueller, rf	5	3	5	2	0
Mays, cf	4	0	1	6	0
St. Claire, c	4	1	2	3	1
bAmalsitano	0	0	0	0	0
Westrum, c	0	0	0	0	0
Samford, 2b	1	0	0	0	0
aRhodes	1	1	1	0	0
Wilhelm	1	0	0	0	1
Jansen, p	2	0	1	0	2
Liddle, p	1	0	0	1	0
fTaylor	1	1	1	0	0
cHofman, 2b	4	1	1	2	3
Total	38	9	13	27	12

ST. LOUIS (N.)	ab	r	h	po	a
Moon, cf	4	0	1	2	0
Sch'ienst, 2b	5	2	2	2	2
Musial, rf	4	3	2	4	1
Jablonski, 3b	5	1	3	1	0
Repulski, lf	4	1	0	3	0
Alston, 1b	4	0	1	7	0
Grammas, ss	3	0	0	2	3
Poholsky, p	0	0	0	0	1
gLowrey	0	0	0	0	0
Deal, p	0	0	0	0	0
Sarni, c	2	0	0	2	0
dHemus, ss	2	0	0	0	0
Presko, p	0	0	0	0	1
Lint, p	0	0	0	0	0
Wright, p	1	0	0	0	0
eFrazier	1	0	1	0	0
fMiller	0	0	0	0	0
Rice, c	1	0	0	4	0
Total	35	7	10	27	8

aSingled for Samford in fourth.
bWalked for Liddle in fourth.
cHit home run for Taylor in fourth.
dFiled out for Sarni in sixth.
eDoubled for Wright in sixth.
fRan for Frazier in sixth.
gWalked for Poholsky in seventh.
hRan for St. Claire in ninth.

New York ......0 0 0 8 0 0 0 0 1—9
St. Louis ......3 0 0 0 3 0 1 0 0—7

Errors—None. Runs batted in—Alston 3, Musial 3, Jablonski, Mays 3, Hofman 3, Mueller 2, Jansen. Two-base hits—Schoendienst, Alston, Mueller, Thompson. Three-base hits—Mueller. Home runs—Hofman, Musial 2, Jablonski. Stolen base—Jablonski. Sacrifice fly—Mays. Double plays—Thompson, Hofman and Lockman; Jansen, Dark and Lockman. Left on bases—New York 9, St. Louis 7. Bases on balls—Off Liddle 3, Jansen 2, Presko 3, Lint 2. Struck out—By Wilhelm 3, Jansen 1, Wright 1. Hits—Off Liddle 3 in 3 innings, Wilhelm 6 in 3 (none out in seventh), Jansen 1 in 3, Presko 4 in 3 1-3, Lint 3 in 1-3, Wright 4 in 2 1-3, Poholsky 0 in 1, Deal 2 in 2. Runs and earned runs—Off Liddle 3 and 3, Wilhelm 4 and 4, Presko 3 and 3, Lint 5 and 5, Deal 1 and 1. Hit by pitcher—By Moon (Liddle); St. Claire (Deal). Winning pitcher—Jansen (1-0). Losing pitcher—Lint (1-1). Umpires—Ballanfant, Barlick, Warneke and Donatelli. Time of game—2:58. Attendance—26,662.

Story of Stan Musial: His Big Day With Bat

ST. LOUIS, May 2 (AP)—The Stan Musial story of Sunday, May 2, 1954:

FIRST GAME

First Inning — Walked by Johnny Antonelli.

Third Inning—Hit home run on roof of right-field pavilion off Antonelli with nobody on base.

Fifth Inning—Hit home run on roof of right-field pavilion off Antonelli with Red Schoendienst on base.

Sixth Inning—Singled to right off Jim Hearn.

Eighth Inning—Hit home run on roof of right-field pavilion off Hearn with Wally Moon and Schoendienst on the bases.

SECOND GAME

First Inning — Walked by Johnny Liddle, later scoring.

Third Inning — Flied out to Willie Mays in deep center off Liddle.

Fifth Inning—Hit home run over pavilion roof in right off Hoyt Wilhelm with Schoendienst on base.

Seventh Inning — Hit home run over pavilion roof in right off Wilhelm with nobody on.

Ninth Inning — Popped to Whitey Lockman against Larry Jansen.

SUMMARY

Eight Official Trips — Five home runs, one single; nine runs batted in; 21 total bases; two bases on balls.

Associated Press Wirephoto

STAN THE (HOMER) MAN: Stan Musial holds bat he used to blast five homers in a double-header against the New York Giants and ball that was knocked out of the park for No. 5.

White Sox Subdue Athletics, 4-0, Before Dropping 2-to-1 Decision

Johnson Triumphs in Opener With 2-Hitter—Valo Blow Decides 2d Game in 9th

PHILADELPHIA, May 2 (UP)—Elmer Valo's pinch-hit single with one out in the ninth inning drove home Bill Renna with the winning run today as the Philadelphia Athletics scored a 2-1 victory over the Chicago White Sox after dropping the first game of the double-header, 4—0.

Don Johnson hurled a two-hitter for the Sox in the opener.

Valo, batting for Catcher Jim Robertson, smashed the winning blow off Relief Pitcher Harry Dorish after Renna had opened the Philadelphia ninth with an infield single. Renna advanced to second on Jim Finigan's sacrifice bunt.

Fricano's Hurling Excels

Brilliant relief pitching by Marion Fricano thwarted Chicago in the ninth. Fricano was called in by Manager Eddie Joost after Starter Arnold Portocarrero had walked Minnie Minoso on four pitches.

Ferris Fain greeted Fricano with a line smash that bounced off Shortstop Joe DeMaestri's knee for a hit. Minoso stopped at second. Jim Rivera then popped to DeMaestri and Grady Hatton lined a single to right, but Renna's great throw to the plate forced Minoso to hold at third. Fricano then made Johnny Groth and Pinch-hitter Sherman Lollar pop out.

Chicago's only tally of the second game scored on a third-inning home run by Catcher Bill (Red) Wilson. It was Wilson's first major league homer.

The Athletics scored a run off Starter Mike Fornieles on successive singles by Gus Zernial, Don Bollweg and Renna with two out in the sixth. The run was the first off Chicago pitching in thirty-five innings.

Wilson Clouts Homer

In the first game, Right-hander Johnson's pitching was backed by home runs by Wilson and Chico Carrasquel. Wilson's four-bagger came after Groth had walked in the seventh. Carrasquel clouted for the circuit in the same inning with the bases empty.

Chicago's final tally was registered in the ninth when Nelson Fox reached first on a force-out and Relief Pitcher Ed Burtschy made a double error on a Minoso grounder. Fox took third on the miscues and scored on Fain's sacrifice fly.

No Philadelphia runner got past second base against Johnson. The only hits were Joost's single in the fifth and Pitcher Morrie Martin's double in the sixth.

The Box Scores

FIRST GAME

CHICAGO (A.)	ab	r	h	po	a
Car'quel, ss	5	1	3	1	3
Fox, 2b	4	1	0	3	3
Minoso, rf	5	0	0	1	0
Fain, 1b	4	0	1	10	0
Lollar, c	5	0	1	4	0
Michaels, 3b	3	0	1	1	1
Groth, cf	3	1	2	4	0
W Wilson, lf	2	1	2	3	0
Johnson, p	4	0	0	0	3
Total	35	4	10	27	10

PHILADELPHIA (A.)	ab	r	h	po	a
Joost, ss	4	0	1	5	2
Jacobs, 2b	4	0	0	4	2
Power, cf	3	0	0	1	0
Zernial, lf	3	0	0	3	0
Bollweg, 1b	3	0	0	6	0
Renna, rf	3	0	0	3	0
Finigan, 3b	3	0	0	0	1
Astroth, c	3	0	0	3	3
Martin, p	2	0	1	0	1
Burtschy, p	0	0	0	0	0
aValo	1	0	0	0	0
Total	29	0	2	27	9

aPopped out for Burtschy in ninth.

Chicago ......0 0 0 0 0 0 3 0 1—4
Philadelphia ......0 0 0 0 0 0 0 0 0—0

Errors—Burtschy 2. Runs batted in—W. Wilson 2, Carrasquel, Fain. Two-base hits—Michaels, Martin, Groth. Home runs—W. Wilson, Carrasquel. Stolen base—Minoso. Sacrifice fly—Fain. Double play—Martin, Joost and Bollweg. Left on bases—Chicago 10, Philadelphia 2. Bases on balls—Off Martin 4, Burtschy 1. Struck out—By Johnson 4, Martin 2, Burtschy 1. Hits—Off Martin 7 in 6 1-3 innings, Burtschy 3 in 2 2-3, Johnson 2 in 9. Runs and earned runs—Off Martin 3 and 3, Burtschy 0 and 1. Winning pitcher—Johnson (2-0). Losing pitcher—Martin (1-1). Umpires—Stevens, Rommel, Napp and Flaherty. Time of game—2:25.

SECOND GAME

CHICAGO (A.)	ab	r	h	po	a
Carasquel, ss	4	0	0	0	4
Fox, 2b	4	0	0	4	2
Minoso, rf	3	0	0	1	0
Fain, 1b	3	0	2	11	0
bNicholas	0	0	0	0	0
Michaels, 3b	3	0	0	0	0
Boyd, lf	3	0	0	0	0
Rivera, lf	1	0	0	1	0
Hatton, 3b, 1b	4	0	1	1	2
Groth, cf	4	0	1	1	0
Wilson, c	3	1	1	6	0
cLollar, c	1	0	0	0	0
Fornieles, p	2	0	1	0	2
aStewart	1	0	0	0	0
Dorish, p	0	0	0	0	1
Total	33	1	6	*25	11

PHILADELPHIA (A.)	ab	r	h	po	a
DeMaestri, ss	4	0	0	6	2
Jacobs, 2b	3	0	0	1	3
Power, cf	4	0	1	1	0
Zernial, lf	3	1	1	1	0
Bollweg, 1b	3	0	1	8	1
Renna, rf	4	1	2	2	0
Finigan, 3b	3	0	0	0	3
Robertson, c	3	0	1	6	0
dValo	1	0	1	0	0
Portocar'o, p	3	0	0	2	0
Fricano, p	0	0	0	0	0
Total	31	2	7	27	9

*One out when winning run scored.
aStruck out for Fornieles in eighth.
bRan for Fain in ninth.
cPopped out for Wilson in ninth.
dSingled for Robertson in ninth.

Chicago ......0 0 1 0 0 0 0 0 0—1
Philadelphia ......0 0 0 0 0 1 0 0 1—2

Errors—None. Runs batted in—Wilson, Renna, Valo. Two-base hits—Fain, Power. Home run—Wilson. Stolen base—Fornieles. Sacrifice—Finigan. Left on bases—Chicago 7, Philadelphia 8. Bases on balls—Off Fornieles 2, Portocarrero 2, Dorish 1. Struck out—By Portocarrero 5, Fornieles 5, Dorish 1. Hits—Off Fornieles 5 in 7 innings, Portocarrero 4 in 8 (none out in 9th), Fricano 2 in 1, Dorish 2 in 1 1-3. Runs and earned runs—Off Fornieles 1 and 1, Portocarrero 1 and 1, Dorish 1 and 1. Winning pitcher — Fricano (1-1). Losing pitcher—Dorish (1-1). Umpires—Rommel, Napp, Flaherty and Stevens. Time of game—2:46. Attendance—12,690.

BEADLING CAPTURES CUP

Beats the St. Louis Simpkins in National Amateur Soccer

PITTSBURGH, May 2 (AP)—Beadling (Pa.) won the national amateur soccer cup today by scoring an upset 5-1 victory over the St. Louis Simpkins.

Albert Lorenzato, Beadling's outside right, tallied three goals to pace the triumph. John Bressanelli, center forward, accounted for Beadling's other points. G. Parloni scored St. Louis' goal.

The championship was decided on the basis of most goals scored in a two-game play-off. The Simpkins team whipped Beadling, 5—2, in St. Louis last Sunday.

Batting Averages

YANKEES

	AB.	H.	PC.		AB.	H.	PC.
Carey	7	3	.429	Lopat	8	1	.125
Reynolds	3	1	.333	Cerv	20	1	.050
McDonald	7	2	.286	Gorman	0	0	.000
Bauer	57	16	.281	Miranda	0	0	.000
Robinson	15	4	.267	Sain	0	0	.000
Berra	62	16	.258	Schallock	0	0	.000
Rizzuto	43	11	.256	Houk	1	0	.000
Skowron	36	9	.250	Kuzava	1	0	.000
Slaughter	16	4	.250	Leja	1	0	.000
Woodling	33	8	.242	Miller	1	0	.000
Noren	13	3	.231	Silvera	1	0	.000
Coleman	49	11	.224	Morgan	3	0	.000
Mantle	49	10	.204	Byrd	4	0	.000
McDougald	57	11	.193	Ford	4	0	.000
Collins	16	2	.125	Grim	4	0	.000

Team batting—511, 113, .221. Home runs—14.

DODGERS

	AB.	H.	PC.		AB.	H.	PC.
Belardi	1	1	1.000	Shuba	6	1	.167
Palica	3	2	.667	Amoros	20	3	.150
Podres	10	5	.500	Loes	7	1	.143
Hoak	12	5	.417	Williams	8	1	.125
Snider	65	25	.385	D.Th'pson	10	1	.100
Hodges	58	21	.362	Black	0	0	.000
Gilliam	72	26	.361	Hughes	0	0	.000
Robinson	39	14	.359	Labine	0	0	.000
Furillo	62	17	.274	Wade	0	0	.000
Reese	68	18	.265	Milliken	1	0	.000
Cox	40	9	.225	C.Th'pson	1	0	.000
Newcombe	9	2	.222	Walker	1	0	.000
Erskine	11	2	.182	Roe	3	0	.000
Camp'ella	67	10	.167	Meyer	4	0	.000

Team batting—571, 164, .287. Home runs—23.

GIANTS

	AB.	H.	PC.		AB.	H.	PC.
Gardner	1	1	1.000	Jansen	5	1	.200
Rhodes	6	3	.500	Williams	55	8	.145
Mueller	63	25	.381	Westrum	21	3	.143
Antonelli	13	4	.308	Hofman	13	1	.077
Taylor	7	2	.286	Maglie	14	1	.071
St. Claire	18	5	.278	Amalfitano	0	0	.000
Katt	11	3	.273	McCall	0	0	.000
Irvin	61	16	.262	Picone	0	0	.000
Dark	73	19	.260	Hearn	1	0	.000
Gomez	4	1	.250	Liddle	1	0	.000
Mays	70	16	.229	Wilhelm	3	0	.000
Thompson	53	12	.226	Samford	4	0	.000
Lockman	62	13	.210	Grissom	5	0	.000

Team batting—568, 134, .236. Home runs—17.

DETROIT WINS, 4-0, AFTER 12-4 DEFEAT

Yankees Take Opener With 6 Runs in 3d—Hoeft Victor in 5-Inning 2d Contest

By LOUIS EFFRAT

Harry Byrd is not complaining, but the side-arming right-hander of the Yankees must be wondering whatever happened to the Yankee power he used to hear about when he was pitching for the Athletics. Yesterday at the Stadium Byrd made his third start for the Bombers and suffered his third defeat, a 4-0 setback by the Tigers in a dramatic five-inning contest that was called on account of darkness.

Since the Yankees, behind Jim McDonald and Allie Reynolds—the latter hurled six innings in relief and was the winner—had taken the opener, 12—4, the split before 24,416 chilled fans kept the champions below the .500 mark for the season. The Yankees are 7—9 for the campaign.

In his three outings for the Yankees, Byrd has gotten only one run from his new mates. That was in a losing, 2—1, encounter at Boston. Then he was the victim in a 1-0 game at Philadelphia and yesterday Byrd opposed Southpaw Billy Hoeft, who came within one out of achieving an abbreviated no-hitter.

Carey Belts Double

Only a fifth-inning, two-out double by Andy Carey spoiled Hoeft's bid. Of course, there would have been no official recognition of Hoeft's no-hitter—only full-length ones are listed in the record book—but it would have been nice for the 22-year-old left-hander to have accomplished it, nevertheless.

Hoeft retired the first eleven Yankees. With two out in the fourth, Mickey Mantle walked and Yogi Berra was safe on an error by Frank Bolling. Here Bill Skowron was robbed by a spectacular catch by Al Kaline.

In the fifth, when it was obvious that the game could not continue more than a few minutes, Hoeft got the first two outs, but Carey lined his spoiler to left center. The final out came on Enos Slaughter's pinch-hit fly to center.

While Hoeft was puzzling the champions, the Tigers were cuffing Byrd for six hits, but only one of their runs was earned. That was on Ray Boone's homer in the second. Two singles and throwing errors by Mantle figured in the scoring of the second run in that round. Two hits and three errors in the fifth gave the Tigers their final pair.

Of course, the five misplays made it the worst Yankee performance of the season. It was different in the opener, when they collected thirteen hits and a dozen runs against Ted Gray, Ray Herbert, Dick Donovan and Dick Marlowe. These were the most hits and runs by the Bombers in a contest this year.

McDonald Walks Six

McDonald's wildness—he walked six—caused Casey Stengel to remove him after he had passed the first three Tigers in the fourth. The Yankees, who had scored six runs in the third, had a 6-2 spread at the time. Reynolds got the visitors out after a single and a fly had accounted for two runs.

Thereafter, Reynolds checked the Tigers. They got only two singles against him and the Chief earned his first triumph of the campaign. It was Allie's longest relief chore in three years.

The big Yankee third saw twelve Bombers come to bat. Carey started with a lead-off single and McDonald walked. Phil Rizzuto sacrificed and when Gray threw wildly past first, Carey scored and the other two were safe.

Hank Bauer lined a single to right, filling the bases whereupon Mantle slashed a two-run single to center. Gray departed and Berra greeted Herbert with a double. By the time the reliever could stop the Yankees they had enough to win.

A 2 o'clock announcement revealed that Bobby Brown, just back from Japan, had requested reinstatement, which had been granted. A half-hour later came the disclosure that Brown was believed to be in town. In the fourth inning, Bobby appeared in the Yankee dugout, wearing a New York uniform. He was introduced to the crowd and received a big hand.

Dr. Brown, who is on record that he is desirous of pursuing his medical career, is due to report to the City and County Hospital at San Francisco on July 1. In the meantime, Bobby would like to remain with the Yankees. That matter must be discussed with the front office. In the meantime, the physician-infielder plans to work out with the Bombers for the next few days.

Yanks' Box Scores

FIRST GAME

DETROIT (A.)	ab	r	h	po	a
Bolling, 2b	4	0	0	4	5
eHatfield	1	0	0	0	0
Kuenn, ss	4	1	1	2	3
Nieman, lf	3	1	0	4	0
Boone, 3b	3	0	0	0	5
Dropo, 1b	4	0	2	8	0
Kaline, rf	2	1	0	1	0
Tuttle, cf	3	1	0	1	0
Batts, c	3	0	0	4	0
Gray, p	1	0	0	0	0
Herbert, p	0	0	0	0	0
bKress	1	0	1	0	0
Donovan, p	1	0	0	0	0
Marlowe, p	0	0	0	0	0
dPesky	1	0	0	0	0
Total	31	4	4	24	13

NEW YORK (A.)	ab	r	h	po	a
Rizzuto, ss	5	1	0	3	4
Miranda, ss	0	0	0	1	1
Bauer, rf-lf	3	2	1	1	0
Mantle, cf	4	2	2	4	0
Noren, cf	1	0	1	1	0
Berra, c	5	2	2	3	0
Skowron, 1b	2	0	1	4	0
cCollins, 1b	1	1	0	6	0
M'D'g'ld, 2b	4	1	2	2	6
Cerv, lf	1	0	0	0	0
aSl'ghter, rf	3	1	1	1	0
Carey, 3b	5	1	2	1	1
McDonald, p	0	1	0	0	0
Reynolds, p	3	0	1	0	1
Total	37	12	13	27	13

aHit into a force-out for Cerv in third.
bSingled for Herbert in fourth.
cWalked for Skowron in fourth.
dGrounded out for Marlowe in ninth.
eGrounded out for Bolling in ninth.

Detroit ......2 0 0 2 0 0 0 0 0—4
New York ......0 0 6 1 0 4 1 0 .—12

Error—Gray. Runs batted in—Dropo 2, Kress, Kuenn, Mantle 2, Berra, Slaughter 3, Carey 2, McDougald 2, Noren. Two-base hits—Dropo, Skowron, Berra. Three-base hit—Slaughter. Sacrifice flies—Kuenn, McDougald, Carey. Double play—Kuenn, Bolling and Dropo. Left on bases—Detroit 6, New York 11. Bases on balls—Off McDonald 6, Gray 2, Herbert 2, Donovan 5, Marlowe 1. Struck out—By Reynolds 3, Herbert 1, Donovan 1, Marlowe 1. Hits—Off Gray 4 in 2 innings (pitched to five batters in third), Herbert 2 in 1, Donovan 7 in 4 (pitched to two batters in eighth), Marlowe 0 in 1, McDonald 2 in 3 (pitched to three batters in fourth), Reynolds 2 in 6. Runs and earned runs—Off Gray 5 and 2, Herbert 1 and 1, Donovan 6 and 6, McDonald 4 and 4. Winning pitcher—Reynolds (1-1). Losing pitcher—Gray (0-2). Umpires—Honochick, McGowan, Paparella and Chylak. Time of game—2:44.

SECOND GAME

DETROIT (A.)	ab	r	h	po	a
Bolling, 2b	3	0	1	0	0
Kuenn, ss	3	0	1	0	1
Nieman, lf	3	0	1	0	0
Lund, rf	0	0	0	0	0
Boone, 3b	2	1	1	0	3
Dropo, 1b	3	0	0	4	0
Kaline, rf	1	0	0	2	0
Tuttle, cf	2	1	1	2	0
House, c	2	1	1	7	0
Hoeft, p	2	1	0	0	0
Total	22	4	5	15	4

NEW YORK (A.)	ab	r	h	po	a
Rizzuto, ss	1	0	0	1	3
aRobinson	1	0	0	0	0
Miranda, ss	0	0	0	0	1
Bauer, rf	2	0	0	1	0
Mantle, cf	1	0	0	1	0
Berra, c	2	0	0	2	0
Skowron, 1b	2	0	0	6	0
McDo'ld, 2b	2	0	0	2	1
Cerv, lf	2	0	0	1	0
Carey, 3b	2	0	1	1	2
Byrd, p	1	0	0	0	1
bSlaughter	1	0	0	0	0
Total	17	0	1	15	8

aStruck out for Rizzuto in fourth.
bFlied out for Byrd in fifth.

Detroit ......0 2 0 0 2—4
New York ......0 0 0 0 0—0

Errors—Bolling, Miranda, Mantle 2, McDougald, Skowron. Runs batted in—Boone, House, Nieman. Two-base hit—Carey. Home run—Boone. Stolen base—Kaline. Double play—McDougald, Rizzuto and Skowron. Left on bases—Detroit 4, New York 3. Bases on balls—Off Hoeft 1, Byrd 1. Struck out—By Hoeft 6, Byrd 2. Runs and earned run—Off Byrd 4 and 1. Wild pitch—Byrd. Winning pitcher—Hoeft (1-1). Losing pitcher—Byrd (0-3). Umpires—McGowan, Paparella, Chylak and Honochick. Time of game—1:21. Attendance—24,416.

Indians Beat Senators, 6-4, 6-3, Extending Streak to Six in a Row

Westlake's 2-Out Blow in 10th Decides 2d Game as Relief Hurlers Star in Opener

WASHINGTON, May 2 (AP)—Cleveland rallied with two out in the ninth inning to score the tying run, then made three runs with two out in the tenth to defeat Washington, 6—3, in the second game of a double-header today. Cleveland also beat the Senators, 6—4, in the opener.

Wally Westlake's bases-loaded double in the tenth off Johnny Schmitz carried the Indians to their sixth straight victory. Larry Doby scored Bobby Avila from third base in the ninth inning to tie the score.

The Senators, who have lost five in a row, were restricted to six hits by Art Houttemann, who registered his first victory. Westlake led the thirteen-hit attack on Schmitz with three singles in addition to his decisive blow.

Fine relief pitching by Ray Narleski and Hal Newhouser checked the Senators in the first game after Bob Feller allowed a 5-1 lead to be whittled. Narleski got the decision as the Indians pounded Chuck Stobbs for seven of their eight hits in the five innings he worked.

The Senators came up with three double plays in the second game to the Indians' one. Pete Runnels was involved in each.

Schmitz walked six to Houtteman's one and struck out two to the Cleveland pitcher's three.

The Indians stranded thirteen men while Washington left six on the bases.

The Box Scores

FIRST GAME

CLEVELAND (A.)	ab	r	h	po	a
Avila, 2b	4	1	2	2	3
Smith, 3b	4	1	1	0	0
W'lake, lf	3	0	0	2	0
Rosen, 1b	2	2	2	8	0
Doby, cf	4	1	1	3	0
Philley, rf	3	0	1	2	0
St'land, ss	4	0	1	1	3
Hegan, c	4	0	0	9	0
Feller, p	1	0	0	0	1
Narleski, p	1	0	0	0	0
N'houser, p	1	0	0	0	0
Total	31	6	8	27	7

WASHINGTON (A.)	ab	r	h	po	a
Yost, 3b	3	1	0	1	2
Busby, cf	5	1	2	3	0
Vernon, 1b	4	1	2	12	0
Sievers, lf	4	0	2	3	0
Wright, rf	4	1	2	0	0
Runnels, ss	1	0	1	1	6
bUmphlett	1	0	0	0	0
F'gerald, c	4	0	0	1	0
Ter'liger, 2b	5	0	0	4	4
Stobbs, p	2	0	0	0	1
aMcD'mott	1	0	0	0	0
Dixon, p	1	0	0	0	1
Total	35	4	9	27	14

aStruck out for Stobbs in fifth.
bFlied out for Runnels in ninth.

Cleveland ......0 2 1 0 2 0 0 1 0—6
Washington ......1 0 0 0 3 0 0 0 0—4

Errors—Sievers, Runnels, Terwilliger. Runs batted in—Sievers, Strickland 2, Rosen, Smith, Westlake, Vernon, Runnels, Terwilliger, Philley. Two-base hits—Sievers 2, Smith, Wright. Three-base hit—Vernon. Sacrifice flies—Sievers, Rosen, Westlake, Philley. Double plays—Runnels, Terwilliger and Vernon 2. Left on bases—Cleveland 5, Washington 13. Bases on balls—Off Feller 4, Stobbs 3, Narleski 3, Dixon 1. Struck out—By Stobbs 1, Feller 3, Narleski 4, Newhouser 1. Hits—Off Feller 6 in 4 1-3 innings, Narleski 3 in 3 1-3, Newhouser 0 in 1 1-3, Stobbs 7 in 5, Dixon 1 in 4. Runs and earned runs—Off Feller 4 and 4, Stobbs 5 and 5, Dixon 1 and 0. Hit by pitcher—By Feller (Wright). Winning pitcher—Narleski (1-0). Losing pitcher—Stobbs (1-2). Umpires—Berry, Hurley, Grieve and Umont. Time of game—2:42.

SECOND GAME

CLEVELAND (A.)	ab	r	h	po	a
Avila, 2b	6	2	2	3	3
Smith, 3b	3	2	0	3	1
Westlake, lf	6	0	4	2	0
Rosen, 1b	3	0	0	10	0
aPope	0	0	0	0	0
Glynn, 1b	1	0	0	0	0
Doby, cf	5	0	1	4	0
Philley, rf	5	1	1	2	0
Strick'd, ss	4	0	2	3	2
Naragon, c	5	0	2	3	1
H'tteman, p	4	1	1	0	5
Total	42	6	13	30	12

WASHINGTON (A.)	ab	r	h	po	a
Yost, 3b	5	0	0	2	3
Busby, cf	5	0	2	4	0
Vernon, 1b	5	0	0	11	1
Sievers, lf	3	0	0	1	0
Wright, rf	2	1	0	1	0
Umphlett, rf	2	0	0	1	0
Runnels, ss	4	1	1	4	5
Tipton, c	4	0	2	4	1
Terwill'r, 2b	3	1	0	1	2
bMcDermott	1	0	0	0	0
Schmitz, p	3	0	0	1	1
cVollmer	1	0	1	0	0
Total	36	3	6	30	13

aRan for Rosen in ninth.
bFlied out for Terwilliger in tenth.
cSingled for Schmitz in tenth.

Cleveland ......0 0 1 0 0 1 0 0 1 3—6
Washington ......0 2 0 0 1 0 0 0 0 0—3

Errors—Schmitz, Avila 2, Terwilliger, Runnels, Smith 2. Runs batted in—Tipton, Terwilliger, Doby 2, Naragon, Westlake 3. Two-base hit—Westlake. Sacrifice—Smith. Double plays—Schmitz, Runnels and Vernon; Runnels, Terwilliger and Vernon; Yost, Tipton and Vernon. Left on bases—Cleveland 13, Washington 6. Bases on balls—Off Schmitz 6, Houtteman 1. Struck out—By Houtteman 3, Schmitz 2. Runs and earned runs—Off Houtteman 3 and 0, Schmitz 6 and 5. Winning pitcher—Houtteman (1-1). Losing pitcher—Schmitz (0-2). Umpires—Hurley, Grieve, Umont and Berry. Time of game—2:53. Attendance—19,432.

DODGERS' HODGES ON CASUALTY LIST

First Baseman Likely to Miss Milwaukee Game Today—Newcombe Also Ailing

Special to The New York Times.

MILWAUKEE, May 2—Gil Hodges and Don Newcombe were added to the list of ailing and injured Dodgers today. Hodges, the Brooks' star first baseman, is not expected to play against the Braves tomorrow.

Both visited the Milwaukee Hospital shortly after the Brooks arrived in a rainstorm that washed out today's scheduled contest—Hodges for a check-up for a colonic disorder and Newcombe, a right-handed pitcher, for X-rays of his left elbow.

The pictures of Newk's elbow, which he injured sliding into third base in the second inning last Friday night at Cincinnati, proved negative. Don is expected to take his next turn against the Cubs in Chicago.

Manager Walter Alston plans to keep Roy Campanella out of tomorrow's game. Rube Walker will take his place behind the plate.

"I don't know that Campy's left hand is hampering his hitting," said Smokey. "Maybe it is, although until yesterday he has been swinging as hard as ever. I think a rest may help him."

Campy has made only one infield single in his last fourteen times at bat and his average has dwindled to .167.

Today's washout was a heavy financial blow to both clubs. A record attendance of 40,000 or more was expected with good weather. But the downpour was so heavy and lasted so long that there was no chance to play. It was uncomfortably chilly, too. No date for the postponed game has been set.

Russ Meyer, who pitched five complete games against the Braves last year, beat them four times and lost twice, will pitch tomorrow. Lew Burdette probably will be Meyer's opponent.

GONZALES TOPS SEDGMAN

Takes Cleveland Pro Tennis Honors in Four Sets

CLEVELAND, May 2 (AP)—Pancho Gonzales overpowered Australia's Frank Sedgman today and retained his singles honors in Cleveland's annual world professional tennis tournament. The score was 6—3, 9—7, 3—6, 6—1.

After winning the singles title, Gonzales teamed with Pancho Segura to win the doubles championship from Don Budge and Sedgman, 11—9, 3—6, 6—3.

Major League Leaders

By The Associated Press.

BATTERS
(Based on 25 or more times at bat)

AMERICAN LEAGUE

	G.	AB.	R.	H.	PC.
Glynn, Cleveland	10	32	3	13	.406
Tuttle, Detroit	14	52	8	21	.404
Goodman, Boston	13	54	5	20	.370
Avila, Cleveland	15	62	12	22	.355
Jensen, Boston	13	48	8	17	.354
Westlake, Cleveland	12	46	5	16	.348
Rosen, Cleveland	15	55	10	19	.345
Groth, Chicago	17	61	6	21	.344
Fain, Chicago	17	64	9	21	.328
Courtney, Baltimore	11	34	1	11	.324

NATIONAL LEAGUE

	G.	AB.	R.	H.	PC.
Jackson, Chicago	13	54	15	23	.426
Sauer, Chicago	13	51	21	21	.412
Musial, St. Louis	16	60	16	24	.400
Snider, Brooklyn	15	65	10	25	.385
Mueller, New York	16	63	11	24	.381
Jablonski, St. Louis	16	71	8	27	.380
Baker, Chicago	13	46	11	17	.370
Temple, Cincinnati	[illegible]	[illegible]	[illegible]	[illegible]	[illegible]
Hodges, Brooklyn	16	58	11	21	.362
Gilliam, Brooklyn	16	72	16	26	.361

RUNS BATTED IN

AMERICAN LEAGUE

Fain, Chicago ....14 | Doby, Cleveland ..13
Westlake, Clev. ..14 | Dropo, Detroit 13
Rosen, Cleveland ..13

NATIONAL LEAGUE

Musial, St. Louis ..21 | Greengrass, Cin. ..16
Sauer, Chicago ...19 | Jablonski, St. L...15
Bell, Cincinnati ..18

HOME-RUN HITTERS

AMERICAN LEAGUE

Jensen, Boston ... 4 | Vernon, Wash. 4
Westlake, Cleve. .. 4
Six players tied with three each.

NATIONAL LEAGUE

Sauer, Chicago ... 8 | Jackson, Chicago .. 5
Musial, St. Louis .. 8 | Kluszewski, Cin. .. 5
Hodges, Brooklyn .. 5

CUBS BREAK EVEN WITH THE PIRATES

Pittsburgh Gets 18 Safeties to Win Finale, 18 to 10, After 5-3 Setback

CHICAGO, May 2 (AP)—The Pittsburgh Pirates exploded for eighteen hits to rout the Chicago Cubs, 18—10, in the second game of a double-header before 7,636 today, after a 5-3 loss in the opener.

The Pirates pounded seven pitchers for seven doubles, a triple, and two home runs as Bob Friend, although replaced in the eighth by John Hetki, received credit for his first 1954 triumph.

The Cubs were also in a hitting mood, getting two doubles and four homers, two by Hank Sauer, who also hit a round-tripper in the opener, as Starter Bubba Church suffered his first loss.

Pittsburgh pounded Church and Lefty Jim Davis, the first of six relievers, for eight runs in the first inning to turn the game into a rout.

The Pirates scored a run in the second, five in the third, and another in the fourth as Outfielder Frank Thomas smashed three straight doubles before driving his fourth home run into the left-field seats in the fourth.

Before Jim Brosnan fanned Thomas in the sixth, the Pittsburgh star had a string of seven straight hits—two singles and a double to conclude the opener which was delayed at the start fifteen minutes due to rain and fog.

The box scores:

FIRST GAME

PITTSBURGH (N.)	ab	r	h	po	a
Abrams, lf	2	0	0	2	1
Cole, 3b	4	0	0	2	5
Skinner, 1b	4	0	1	9	1
Thomas, cf	4	2	3	2	0
Lynch, rf	3	1	1	1	0
Shepard, c	4	0	1	4	0
Roberts, 2b	4	0	1	2	1
Allie, ss	3	0	2	2	0
Law, p	[illegible]	[illegible]	[illegible]	[illegible]	[illegible]
aPellagrini	1	0	0	0	0
King, p	0	0	0	0	2
bR. Smith	1	0	0	0	0
Thies, p	0	0	0	0	1
Total	31	3	9	24	11

CHICAGO (N.)	ab	r	h	po	a
Talbot, cf	4	1	2	1	0
Fondy, 1b	4	0	1	12	1
Kiner, lf	3	1	1	4	0
Marquez, lf	0	0	0	0	0
Sauer, rf	4	1	2	0	0
Robertson, rf	0	0	0	0	0
Jackson, 3b	3	0	0	0	2
Banks, ss	4	0	0	2	5
Baker, 2b	4	1	3	3	3
Tappe, c	3	1	1	5	2
Minner, p	2	0	0	0	3
Total	31	5	10	27	16

aStruck out for Law in fifth.
bStruck out for King in seventh.

Pittsburgh ......0 0 0 0 0 0 1 0 2—3
Chicago ......1 0 2 2 0 0 0 0 .—5

Errors—None. Runs batted in—Sauer 3, Minner, Talbot, Roberts, Lynch 2. Two-base hits—Fondy, Talbot, Thomas. Home runs—Sauer, Lynch. Sacrifices—Tappe, Lynch. Sacrifice fly—Minner. Double plays—Minner, Banks and Fondy; Baker and Fondy; Baker, Banks and Fondy; Banks, Baker and Fondy. Left on bases—Pittsburgh 5, Chicago 6. Bases on balls—Off Minner 3, Law 2. Struck out—By Law 1, Minner 3, King 3. Hits—Off Law 8 in 4 innings, King 1 in 3, Thies 1 in 1. Runs and earned runs—Off Law 5 and 5. Wild pitch—Law. Winning pitcher—Minner (2-0). Losing pitcher—Law (2-2). Umpires—Jackowski, Conlan and Secory. Time of game—2:10.

SECOND GAME

PITTSBURGH (N.)	ab	r	h	po	a
Abrams, lf	5	4	4	2	0
Cole, 3b	4	2	3	0	1
Skinner, 1b	6	2	3	7	1
Thomas, cf	5	4	4	4	0
Lynch, rf	4	1	1	1	0
Atwell, c	5	0	1	7	0
Roberts, 2b	4	1	1	3	2
Allie, ss	3	1	0	1	3
Friend, p	4	2	1	0	3
Hetki, p	0	0	0	0	0
Total	39	18	18	*24	9

CHICAGO (N.)	ab	r	h	po	a
Talbot, cf	5	1	2	1	0
Fondy, 1b	5	0	0	4	1
Kiner, lf	5	1	2	1	0
Sauer, rf	4	4	1	1	0
Jackson, 3b	4	1	1	0	1
Banks, ss	4	1	1	0	3
Baker, 2b	3	0	1	3	3
Garagiola, c	3	1	0	8	1
Church, p	0	0	0	0	0
Willis, p	0	0	0	0	0
aBaumhol	1	0	0	0	0
Jeffcoat, p	0	0	0	0	0
bRobertson	1	0	0	0	0
Brosnan, p	0	0	0	0	0
cSerena	1	0	0	0	0
Lown, p	0	0	0	0	0
dBilko	1	0	0	0	0
Zick, p	1	0	0	0	0
Total	38	10	14	24	14

*Game called in eighth, darkness.
aHit into force play for Willis in second.
bFlied out for Jeffcoat in fourth.
cStruck out for Brosnan in sixth.
dGrounded out for Lown in seventh.

Pittsburgh ......8 1 5 1 0 3 0 0—18
Chicago ......0 2 0 0 4 0 2 2—10

Errors—Banks. Runs batted in—Skinner 5, Roberts 3, Allie, Friend 3, Abrams, Cole, Sauer 3, Baumholtz, Thomas 3, Banks 3, Garagiola 2, Talbot. Two-base hits—Thomas 3, Cole, Roberts, Kiner, Abrams, Sauer. Three-base hit—Abrams. Home runs—Sauer 2, Thomas, Banks, Skinner, Talbot. Stolen bases—Lynch, Atwell. Sacrifice—Cole. Sacrifice fly—Roberts. Left on bases—Pittsburgh 6, Chicago 8. Bases on balls—Off Church 4, Jeffcoat 3, Friend 1. Struck out—By Church 1, Willis 1, Brosnan 3, Lown 2, Friend 6, Hetki 1. Hits—Off Church 3 in 2-3 inning, Davis 5 in 1, Willis 0 in 1 1-3, Jeffcoat 6 in 2, Brosnan 1 in 2, Lown 0 in 1, Zick 1 in 1, Friend 14 in 7 2-3, Hetki 0 in 1-3. Runs and earned runs—Off Church 6 and 6, Davis 3 and 3, Jeffcoat 6 and 6, Brosnan 3 and 3, Friend 10 and 10. Winning pitcher—Friend (1-2). Losing pitcher—Church (1-1). Umpires—Conlan, Secory and Jackowski. Time of game—2:48. Attendance—7,636.

Major League Baseball

Monday, May 3, 1954

National League

YESTERDAY'S GAMES

St. Louis 10, New York 6 (1st).
New York 9, St. Louis 7 (2d).
Brooklyn at Milwaukee, rain.
Chicago 5, Pittsburgh 3 (1st).
Pittsburgh 18, Chicago 10 (2d, 8 innings), darkness.
Philadelphia 4, Cincinnati 3 (1st).
Philadelphia at Cincinnati (2d), wet grounds.

STANDING OF THE CLUBS

	Philadel.	Brooklyn	St. Louis	Cincinnati	New York	Chicago	Pittsburgh	Milwaukee	Won	Lost	Percentage	Games Behind
Phila	—	1	0	1	1	0	3	3	9	6	.600	—
Bklyn	2	—	0	2	1	0	4	0	9	7	.563	½
St. L.	0	2	—	2	1	1	1	2	9	7	.563	½
Cinc.	0	1	1	—	0	3	2	3	10	8	.556	½
N. Y.	3	2	1	0	—	1	1	1	9	8	.529	1
Chic.	0	0	2	2	1	—	1	0	6	7	.462	2
Pitts.	1	1	1	0	3	1	—	0	7	12	.368	4
Milw.	0	0	2	1	1	1	0	—	5	9	.357	3½
Lost.	6	7	7	8	8	7	12	9	—	—		

PROBABLE PITCHERS TODAY

New York at St. Louis (night)—Gomez (1-2) vs. Raschi (1-0).

Brooklyn at Milwaukee—Meyer (1-0) vs. Burdette (1-2).

Other clubs not scheduled.

American League

YESTERDAY'S GAMES

New York 12, Detroit 4 (1st).
Detroit 4, New York 0 (2d, 5 innings), darkness.
Chicago 4, Philadelphia 0 (1st).
Philadelphia 2, Chicago 1 (2d).
Cleveland 6, Washington 4 (1st).
Cleveland 6, Washington 3 (2d, 10 innings).
Baltimore at Boston (2), rain.

STANDING OF THE CLUBS

	Chicago	Detroit	Cleveland	Philadel.	New York	Wash'gton	Baltimore	Boston	Won	Lost	Percentage	Games Behind
Chic.	—	2	2	1	1	0	3	2	11	6	.647	—
Det.	0	—	3	0	1	2	3	0	9	5	.643	½
Cleve	2	1	—	0	2	2	1	1	9	6	.600	1
Phila	1	0	0	—	2	1	2	2	8	6	.571	1½
N. Y.	1	1	0	2	—	1	0	2	7	9	.438	3½
Wash	0	0	0	2	2	—	0	2	6	9	.400	4
Balt.	2	1	1	0	0	1	—	0	5	9	.357	4½
Bost.	0	0	0	1	1	2	0	—	4	9	.308	5
Lost.	6	5	6	6	9	9	9	9	—	—		

PROBABLE PITCHERS TODAY

Chicago at Philadelphia—Consuegra (1-0) vs. Scheib (0-0).

Cleveland at Washington (night)—Garcia (1-2) vs. Marrero (1-0).

Other clubs not scheduled.

(Figures in parentheses indicate season's won-and-lost records.)

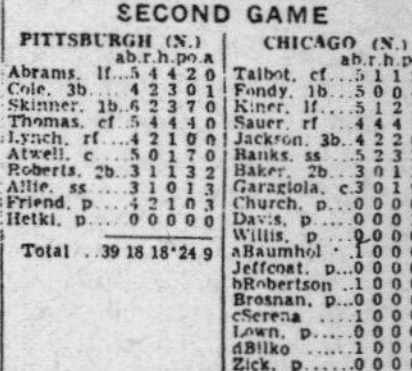

"All the News That's Fit to Print"

The New York Times.

LATE CITY EDITION
Fair, moderate temperatures today. Partly cloudy tomorrow.
Temperature Range Today-Max., 63; Min., 45
Temperatures Yesterday—Max., 59; Min., 47
Full U. S. Weather Bureau Report, Page 47

VOL. CIII..No. 35,167. Entered as Second-Class Matter. Post Office, New York, N. Y. NEW YORK, FRIDAY, MAY 7, 1954. Times Square, New York 36, N. Y. Telephone LAckawanna 4-1000 FIVE CENTS

WESTERN BIG THREE AGREE ON INDO-CHINA COMPROMISE FOR 'PROTECTED ARMISTICE'

U.S. FOR PARIS PLAN

Allies Will Suggest Reds Retire in Vietnam, Quit Laos and Cambodia

By JAMES RESTON
Special to The New York Times.

WASHINGTON, May 6—The United States, Britain and France are now in substantial agreement on a compromise plan for a "protected armistice" in Indo-China.

It is understood that the Laniel Government in Paris has told Washington that it is prepared to fight on in Indo-China unless the Communists agree to evacuate Laos and Cambodia and withdraw to certain "fixed areas" in the third independent state of Vietnam.

The Eisenhower Administration, determined to block the Communist conquest of the whole peninsula, but unwilling to intervene at this time in the war with United States military power, is prepared to go along with Paris in its attempt to negotiate this compromise in Geneva.

The Secretary of State was reported tonight to have discussed this compromise arrangement with representatives of the Senate and the House of Representatives at the State Department last evening. He also outlined to them his own plans for the negotiation of an "extended" Southeast Asia security arrangement that would b[illegible]ned to guarantee the ter[illegible] any honorable armistice that could be arranged.

Briefing by Dulles Reported

Washington tonight was full of gloomy reports that the Eisenhower Government had virtually abandoned hope of any "collective action" to save the major Indo-Chinese state of Vietnam, but as a matter of fact the Administration was actually a little more hopeful tonight that a "bearable compromise" could be negotiated.

President Eisenhower went over the Indo-China situation with the National Security Council today. John Foster Dulles, the Secretary of State, was represented by his associates in that body as having taken a solemn but not unhopeful view of the situation.

At the end of the meeting it was understood that the position of the United States was about as follows:

¶There was no question of direct United States intervention in the war in the foreseeable future, even though it was assumed that the French garrison of Dienbienphu would probably fall.

¶The United States should do what it could to negotiate a security pact for the defense of Southeast Asia, but there was no hope of doing so without a French promise of "unequivocal independence" to the three associated Indo-Chinese states of Vietman, Laos, and Cambodia.

¶Meanwhile, the United States and Britain should go along with the French on trying to negotiate a "protected armistice" on the following terms: The Communists should withdraw from Southern Vietnam, Cambodia and Laos; there should be a "neutral zone"

Continued on Page 2, Column 2

Democrats Launch Attack On Dulles' Foreign Policy

Truman and Johnson Lead Assault — Latter Fears U.S. 'Naked and Alone'

By WILLIAM S. WHITE
Special to The New York Times.

WASHINGTON, May 6 — An all-out Democratic attack on the Eisenhower Administration's foreign policy, the first such attack since the President took office, was opened tonight.

The effect was to put the Administration on dual notice (1) that the bipartisanship of the last sixteen months was breaking up and (2) that the Congressional Democrats could not be counted upon for unquestioning general support in the field of world affairs.

Senator Lyndon B. Johnson of Texas, Democratic leader of the Senate, and former President Harry S. Truman both took the occasion to declare that the Administration was alienating allies of the United States.

Senator Johnson said that the

Harris & Ewing

Senator Lyndon B. Johnson

Administration had put the United States "in clear danger of being left naked and alone in a hostile world."

The results thus far of the

Continued on Page 14, Column 4

LANIEL IS UPHELD IN INDO-CHINA TEST

French Chamber, 311 to 262, Gives Him Confidence Vote —Deputies Avert Crisis

By LANSING WARREN
Special to The New York Times.

PARIS, May 6—Premier Joseph Laniel won a vote of confidence today on his refusal to hold a debate on the Indo-China war. The vote was 311 to 262.

By reason of abstentions the vote fell short by three of a majority of the Assembly members and it gave an indication of a deep uneasiness in France about the Government policies in the Indo-China conference at Geneva.

Premier Laniel, nevertheless, avoided the necessity of giving information that might hamper Foreign Minister Georges Bidault in the Geneva negotiations and gained time for him to get some limited achievement through that conference before the Assembly's restiveness returns.

Discussions by the Deputies gave an indication that this might be soon in case of adverse events, such as the fall of Dienbienphu or of rebuffs to France by the delegations of Ho Chi Minh of Vietminh or the Chinese Communists.

Most of the speeches made in the debate today gave the impression of the strong desire of the French to get a cease-fire in the Indo-China war at once if only long enough to save the heroic garrison at Dienbienphu.

It was understood that one reason the Deputies avoided a crisis was the news that there was progress in the negotiations at Geneva and on the spot to get a truce at Dienbienphu for the evacuation of the wounded.

It was also obvious that the

Continued on Page 3, Column 5

PEACE PRESSURES ON BIDAULT MOUNT

Geneva Observers Consider French Vote as Move for Indo-China Settlement

By TILLMAN DURDIN
Special to The New York Times.

GENEVA, May 6—Georges Bidault, French Foreign Minister, is believed in some quarters to be under increased pressure from Paris to agree to a settlement in Indo-China as a result of today's challenge to the French Government.

Although the Laniel Cabinet won today's Assembly confidence vote, informed French political sources here say that new moves against the Government can be expected shortly if M. Bidault does not achieve an early solution in Indo-China at the forthcoming Geneva conference sessions on the Indo-China problem.

Marc Jacquet, French Undersecretary of State for the Associated States of Indo-China, arrived here late today from Paris to report to M. Bidault on the result of the day's political activity in the French capital. It was reported that he brought new instructions on Indo-China for the Foreign Minister. He refused to give correspondents any indication of what they might be but the surmise in French quarters was that M. Bidault would be asked to reinforce his efforts to get an Indo-China settlement.

Start Remains Uncertain

However, the French Assembly vote at least gave M. Bidault assurance that he could look forward to continued participation in the Indo-China talks and plan accordingly. He dined tonight with M. Jacquet and representatives of the Associated States of Vietnam, Cambodia and Laos and there was a general discussion of prospects and policies for the talks.

Just when the Indo-China sessions will get under way remained uncertain tonight. Because a formal conference session on Korea has been arranged for tomorrow afternoon, and because the delegations for the Indo-China states are still incomplete, it was considered certain that there could be no Indo-China meeting tomorrow.

A French spokesman said it was possible that the Indo-China talks would start Saturday, but the Vietnamese representatives here doubt if the delegation will be ready by then. The chiefs for the Laotian and Cambodian delegations have not yet arrived in Geneva and these two delegations may also not be prepared to participate Saturday.

Nguyen Trung Vinh, chief of the Bao Dai delegation, arrived with a number of ranking delegation members this morning.

A Vietnamese spokesman said that Chief of State Bao Dai

Continued on Page 3, Column 2

Junta Reported Ruling Paraguay After Army Ousting of President

By The United Press.

ASUNCION, Paraguay, May 6—A junta took over the government today following an uprising by army cavalry forces that deposed President Federico Chaves yesterday.

In a statement signed by its leader, a civil engineer, Tomas Romero Pereira, the junta said the "present political situation in the country remains under the control of the Colorado party."

Dr. Chaves had been a leader of the Colorado party. There was no word on his fate.

The statement from the junta said order prevailed throughout the country.

The junta met here all afternoon to consider steps toward full restoration of political normalcy.

Gen. Alfredo Stroener, Commander in Chief of the Paraguayan Army, broadcasting over a nation-wide hook-up, assured the people that "order has been re-established in units of the First Cavalry Division, all garrisons are still obeying the orders of the Commander in Chief and of the Government Junta, and calm reigns in the republic."

The First Cavalry Division was the main factor in the rise against the Chaves Government and earlier reports indicated Dr. Chaves was a virtual prisoner of the armed forces.

[Buenos Aires reported indications of a severe censorship in effect in Paraguay. Communications were generally open, but subject to delays.]

Lieut. Col. Mario B. Ortega, new police chief in Asunción, also assured the country that order had been restored and that the Army supported the Junta.

Colonel Ortega succeeded Police Chief Robert L. Petit, who was killed yesterday when re-

Continued on Page 8, Column 5

SEAWAY IS VOTED BY HOUSE, 241-158; LONG BATTLE ENDS

Bill to Join Canada in Project Goes Back to the Senate for Approval of Minor Changes

By CLAYTON KNOWLES
Special to The New York Times.

WASHINGTON, May 6—The House of Representatives voted today, 241 to 158, to authorize the United States to join Canada in constructing the St. Lawrence Seaway.

The vote gave President Eisenhower his biggest legislative victory in his seventeen months in office. Since World War I every President has urged passage of legislation to accomplish the Seaway project.

Approved Jan. 20 by the Senate in slightly different form, the measure now must go back to the upper chamber for concurrence in minor changes voted by the House. The Senate passed the bill by 51 to 33.

As was the case in the Senate, Democratic help was needed in the House to pass the Administration bill. On final passage, 144 Republicans, ninety-six Democrats and the one independent voted with the President. Ninety-four Democrats and sixty-four Republicans voted in opposition.

Strong Administration pressure was exerted for passage of the bill without change. The word was passed that the President "wanted the bill as it passed the Senate."

President Cites Satisfaction

Informed of the final vote, the President noted that it "marks the end of a long and historic effort." He said:

"It is a source of tremendous personal satisfaction to me that this Eighty-third Congress has made it possible for the United States to join hands with its close neighbor, Canada, in building this Seaway and by this means to contribute materially to the economic well-being and security of both our countries.

"The sponsors of the legislation are to be congratulated for developing a new approach to the St. Lawrence project which eliminated objectionable features responsible for the defeat of similar proposals in the past."

Before final passage, Representative Charles A. Halleck of Indiana, the House Republican leader, led Administration forces in beating down a move that, it was contended, would "kill the bill."

The test came on an amend-

Continued on Page 18, Column 2

WIDER SALES TAX SEEMS INEVITABLE, MAYOR DECLARES

In Reply to Business Group's Protest, He Asks Its Help in Getting Action by State

Wagner and McGraw messages are printed on Page 34.

By PAUL CROWELL

Mayor Wagner declared yesterday that extension of the 3 per cent sales tax to commercial services was "seemingly" inevitable. Nothing else can be done, he said, unless a "practical" substitute source of revenue is made possible at a special session of the Legislature.

"We have an obligation to keep the government of the City of New York in first-class running order," the Mayor said. "To do this we need $30,000,000 more in funds than the state allows us to retain or collect except through the imposition of taxes like the 3 per cent service tax and others equally onerous. I regret to state that no practical substitute for that tax has yet appeared and that, barring an agreement on a special session and a program for that session, its imposition is seemingly our only present course of action."

Aid Asked for Special Session

The Mayor called upon business and financial interests opposing the extended sales tax to cooperate with the city in persuading Governor Dewey to call a special session.

The bill to impose the extended sales tax, estimated to yield an annual revenue of $30,000,000, is now in the hands of the Finance Committee of the City Council, which held a public hearing on the measure on April 20.

The Mayor's declaration of policy was made in a letter to Harold W. McGraw, chairman of the Joint Conference for Better Government, representing sixty-seven business, trade and taxpayer associations. The letter was in reply to a telegram sent to the Mayor by Mr. McGraw last Monday. The telegram urged the Mayor to drop the proposed extended sales tax and quit his "efforts to brush responsibility for this vicious tax to Albany."

A spokesman for the Dewey Administration, commenting in Albany on the Mayor's letter, hinted broadly that the special session sought by the city with the aid of pressure from business and financial groups affected by

Continued on Page 34, Column 2

4-Minute Mile Is Achieved By Bannister of England

Associated Press Wirephoto

Roger Bannister hits the tape in 3 minutes 59.4 seconds

By DREW MIDDLETON
Special to The New York Times.

LONDON, May 6—Roger Gilbert Bannister ran a mile in 3 minutes 59.4 seconds tonight to reach one of man's hitherto unattainable goals.

The 4-minute time sought by every great miler for twenty years was beaten by the slim, sandy-haired medical student in a dual meet at Oxford University.

Running on the four-lap Iffley Road track, Bannister swept through the first quarter in 57.5 seconds. The middle quarters of the race were run in 0:60.7 and 0:62.3. Then with a final explosive burst, Bannister raced to the record with 0:58.9 for the last quarter.

The 25-year-old miler ran under exceedingly unfavorable con-

Continued on Page 29, Column 1

M'CARTHY DEMANDS A TEST OF EXECUTIVE RIGHT TO BAR SECRET DATA TO CONGRESS

McClellan Suggests 'Crime' By McCarthy on Security

Says Receiver of Secret May Be Just as Guilty as Person Who Passed It

By ELIE ABEL
Special to The New York Times.

WASHINGTON, May 6—A suggestion that Senator Joseph R. McCarthy may have violated the law in accepting material officially classified as confidential was put up to the Department of Justice today.

Mr. McCarthy has testified under oath that he received an altered and abbreviated version of a confidential Federal Bureau of Investigation document from a young Army Intelligence officer whom he refused to identify.

Senator John L. McClellan called on Herbert Brownell Jr., the Attorney General, to determine whether "a crime was committed" by the receiver of the paper, as well as the man who passed it to him.

He said it was for this purpose that he had proposed that the Attorney General examine the record

The New York Times

Senator John L. McClellan

of the Army-McCarthy dispute "for such attention and consideration as it may merit."

It was not until after today's hearing that the Arkansas mem-

Continued on Page 13, Column 6

CHALLENGES RULE

Asks Colleagues to Join After Brownell Rules Against Publicity

Excerpts from transcript of the hearing, Pages 12 and 13.

By W. H. LAWRENCE
Special to The New York Times.

WASHINGTON, May 6—Senator Joseph R. McCarthy threw down the gauntlet today to President Eisenhower and the entire Executive Branch of Government.

The Wisconsin Republican served notice that he would not be bound by any secrecy decisions by anyone in the Executive Department. He called on the Legislative Branch to join him in a clear-cut test of Presidential authority.

He demanded a closed session of the Senate Permanent Subcommittee on Investigations to decide "once and for all * * * this question of whether or not we are the lackeys to obey and afraid to overrule a decision made by someone in the Executive Department."

The oratory of Senator McCarthy highlighted a day in which there were these developments:

¶Herbert Brownell Jr., Attorney General, ruled that the Senator was not authorized to have possession of information from a confidential report of the Federal Bureau of Investigation. The Attorney General said it would not be in the public interest to make this information public. The Senator threatened to make it public anyway.

Senator McCarthy testified under oath yesterday that he had received an altered, condensed version of a classified F. B. I. report from a young Army Intelligence officer who realized he was violating a Presidential directive. He refused to name the informer, and was not required to do so.

¶Senator McCarthy, on his side, suggested possible perjury actions against Robert T. Stevens, Secretary of the Army, and Maj. Gen. Ralph W. Zwicker, Commanding General of Camp Kilmer, N. J., but was rebuked by the committee for improperly suggesting legal conclusions in the guise of questions.

¶The Army presented a legal opinion by the Attorney General supporting its contention, challenged by Senator McCarthy, that it is not required to honor subpoenas for members of loyalty-security boards when it is aware the questions deal with activities kept secret by Presidential directive.

¶There was a long but indecisive wrangle about "Mr. X," a former member of the Army's loyalty-security "screening board." It was alleged by Senator McCarthy and his associates that Mr. X had a record of Communist-front activities.

Secretary Stevens was succeeded on the stand by Mr. Adams, who developed testimony that the charges against Mr. X

Continued on Page 11, Column 1

NEW HAVEN DROPS COMMUTATION RISE

New President Wants Study of Railroad's Role—Dewey 'Discouraged' Over L.I.R.R.

The New York, New Haven and Hartford Railroad's new management withdrew yesterday a proposal its predecessor had made for a 24 to 30 per cent commutation fare increase.

Patrick B. McGinnis, newly elected president, said he first wished to study the various methods of travel used by commuters and to confer with governmental agencies on what part the railroad was to play in the future of mass transport.

Meanwhile, Governor Dewey in Albany termed "discouraging" the action by the Interstate Commerce Commission Wednesday, which he said in effect sought to force a 25 per cent increase in Long Island Rail Road commutation fares in sixty days by the State Public Service Commission.

Governor Dewey summoned members of the Long Island Transit Authority to meet with him "at their earliest"—probably late next week—to discuss that line's problems. If some kind of plan for private rehabilitation of the bankrupt Long Island can be worked out, Mr. Dewey plans to call a special session of the Legislature in June.

New Haven Filed Dec. 30

The New Haven's former management had filed a Dec. 30 petition with the Interstate Commerce Commission to raise commutation fares both interstate and within New York State. Plans were to ask the Connecticut, Rhode Island and Massachusetts Public Service Commissions for similar increases in their areas.

But Mr. McGinnis, who won control of the $500,000,000 New Haven in a management fight last April 16, asserted that "entirely new thinking must be introduced by railroad management to change the general trend from rails to rubber."

Asserting that rate increases are "attended by decreases in the number of commuters," Mr. McGinnis contended that the answer to problems of commutation trains rested in convincing more riders that it was as cheap and convenient to use trains as to use buses and automobiles.

The New Haven's new chief argued that the problem of mass transportation should be studied as a whole, rather than "merely as a railroad problem." He bid for conferences with the Port of New York Authority, the Triborough Bridge and Tunnel Authority and officials of New York State, New York City and Westchester County.

"Thus far," he said, "the tendency has been for these other agencies to avoid even discussing the problem with the rail-

Continued on Page 17, Column 2

AUTHORITY SPURNS TRANSIT PLANT BID

Terms Edison Offer So Low as to Make Modernizing of Power Facility Feasible

By LEONARD INGALLS

The Transit Authority rejected yesterday an offer by the Consolidated Edison Company to buy one of the three city-owned subway power plants.

Acting on a recommendation by Sidney H. Bingham, executive director and general manager of the transit system, the authority decided that it would be cheaper to rehabilitate the plant and continue to generate its own power rather than buy it from the utility.

The authority's decision was basic. Up to yesterday the question of whether to sell the power plants and buy electricity or to retain and modernize them had been unresolved.

By rejecting the Consolidated Edison proposal, the authority placed itself on record as favoring the latter course which would cost an estimated $176,500,000 in city capital funds.

Consolidated Edison, the authority reported, submitted a bid of $8,000,000 on Feb. 5 for the plant at Kent and Division Avenues, Brooklyn, which supplies power for the B. M. T. division. The land, structure and equipment are valued by the city's real estate assessors at $18,000,000.

Two power plants serving the I. R. T. are operated by the Transit Authority in Manhattan—one at West Fifty-ninth Street and the Hudson River and the other at East Seventy-fourth Street and the East River. Power for the IND subway division is

Continued on Page 17, Column 1

Crippled Airliner With 62 Aboard Jettisons 'Gas,' Lands Safely Here

In a superb show of airmanship, a Pan American World Airways pilot brought a Boeing Stratocruiser—the world's largest and heaviest commercial transport—in to a safe landing here yesterday in spite of a damaged nosewheel.

None of the fifty-three passengers or crew of nine was even jarred.

The plane, bound for London, had taken off from the New York International Airport, Idlewild, Queens, at 4:23 P. M. Shortly after the takeoff the pilot, Capt. Cameron Walker of 115 Fox Boulevard, Massapequa, L. I., radioed back that the nosewheel was twisted to a 65-degree angle and would not retract.

Deciding to return, the former Marine Corps combat pilot took his two-deck aircraft out over the Atlantic and dumped 2,500 gallons of the 4,000 gallons of gasoline aboard. Normally Stratocruisers carry nearly 8,000 gallons, but because of bad weather in the North Atlantic the plane had been routed via Bermuda and the Azores, and could have been refueled there.

When Idlewild learned of the plane's plight and Captain Walker's decision to return for an emergency landing, all measures were taken to handle what might well turn out to be a disaster. Five police cars, four ambulances, four Port of New York Authority fire trucks, two buses, a small derrick and two jeeps were called out to the end of Runway 31—a 9,500-foot strip.

Meanwhile, the passengers had been informed that the plane was returning because of mechanical difficulties. In the control cabin Captain Walker and his co-pilot, John H. Brink of Westbury, L. I., were confronted with a number of decisions.

The Stratocruiser, which weighs

Continued on Page 33, Column 7

Bannister Runs Mile in Record Time of 3:59.4

BRITON FIRST MAN UNDER 4 MINUTES

Continued From Page 1

ditions. There was a fifteen-mile-an-hour cross wind during the race and gusts touched twenty-five miles an hour just before the event began.

Track authorities said they thought Bannister would have come close to 3:58 had there been no wind.

Experienced With Weather

But out of long experience with English weather, Bannister said later, there "comes a moment when you have to accept the weather and have an all-out effort and I decided today was the day."

Bannister's mile smashed the world record of Gunder Haegg of Sweden, who ran the distance in 4:01.4 at Malmo, Sweden, on July 17, 1945.

The English runner's time at 1,500 meters, taken unofficially, was 3:43, equaling the world record held jointly by Haegg, Lennart Strand of Sweden and Werner Lueg of Germany.

Bannister was running in a meet between Oxford University and a British Amateur Athletic Association team of which he is member. Bannister had trained intensively for the event in an effort to better 4 minutes before Wes Santee of the United States and John Landy of Australia could do it.

Pace-Setters Praised

After the race, Bannister praised Chris Brasher and Chris Chataway, his team-mates who set the pace for most of the with Brasher doing the first quaretr in just under 60 seconds.

"We were under evens, so to speak, at the half-mile," Bannister said, "and then Chataway took over for the third lap and we reached the three-quarters in just a shade over three minutes.

"So I had to take over then and try to do the last lap in about 59 seconds," the record-breaker added.

Bannister seemed particularly pleased to have set the record at Oxford. He recalled he had run his first race here as an Oxford freshman and that his time then was over 5 minutes.

Bannister said casually he thought that "the 4-minute mile has been overestimated.

"Naturally, we wanted to achieve the honor of doing it first, but the main essence of sport is a race against opponents rather than against clocks," he added.

Chataway, who ran for Cambridge in the past, was just ahead of Bannister after three-quarters of a mile and he continued to hold the lead until the two runners were about 300 yards from the finish.

Speeds Down Final Stretch

Then Bannister, who runs with a conventional style, effortlessly went ahead and sped down the final stretch.

"I felt pretty tired at the end," Bannister remarked, "but I knew that I would just about make it."

Bannister's fastest previous time for a mile was 4:02 in a specially paced race. This time was not recognized by the British Amateur Athletic Board.

Bannister's feat made up for his showing in the 1952 Olympic Games at Helsinki, Finland, where he finished fourth in the 1,500-meter race.

The record-breaker is a medical student at St. Mary's Hospital in London. He has been taking final examinations the last three weeks and hopes to get his degree this summer.

Bannister always had been convinced that a mile in better than 4 minutes was possible. With that in mind, he carefully studied the mechanics of running.

Associated Press Radiophoto

RECORD-BREAKER CONGRATULATED BY RIVAL: Roger Bannister, left, who ran the mile in 3:59.4 at Oxford, England, is felicitated by Chris Chataway, his nearest competitor.

Bannister's Record Feat Is Another Milestone In Eternal Quest for Improvement by Athletes

Running, Jumping, Throwing Began as Means of Self-Preservation by Man

By JOSEPH M. SHEEHAN

Roger Bannister's feat of cracking the 4-minute barrier for the mile run is more than just an epic sports achievement. It dramatizes man's eternal efforts to run longer distances in faster times, to leap higher and to throw farther.

These basic physical activities have been subject of keen proprietary interest to humanity through all recorded history—and before that. It does not require much imagination to appreciate why.

Running, jumping and throwing are largely proscribed within the field of sports today. In the pre-dawn of civilization, and well into the era of enlightenment, they were prime means of self-preservation.

Physical Prowess Important

In early society physical prowess also was an important instrument of personal power. The swift, the nimble and the strong became the tribal leaders.

Even after civilization had advanced to an extent where intellect carried greater weight than muscle, running, jumping and throwing were the vehicles to high prestige.

Ancient Greece glorified its athletes and, in so doing, left to posterity the great heritage of the Olympic Games.

Before its healthy interest became perverted with the blood lust of decadence, competitive athletics also flourished in ancient Rome.

The jousts and tournaments of medieval Europe reflect the fundamental appeal that contests of speed, strength and skill hold to all peoples.

Aside from their competitive aspects, human speed and endurance have played a key role in communication.

Fabled in history is the famous runner, Pheidippides. It was he who carried to Athens the tidings of the great Greek victory at Marathon over the Persian hosts of Darius in 490 B. C.

Although exhausted after having fought through the battle, on orders from Miltiades, the Greek commander, he doggedly set forth on the grueling eight-league journey to the city.

Pheideppides paid for his great effort with his life. But before he dropped, he had reached his goal and gasped his stirring message: "Rejoice; we conquer!"

Held Empire Together

The modern marathon run of 26 miles 385 yards, showpiece of the Olympic Games, is a commemorative event in honor of Pheidippides.

Only a few months ago a scientific expedition to the Peruvian Andes uncovered irrefutable evidence of an Inca courier service that spanned vast distances in incredibly short times.

Early Spanish chronicles had reported with wonder how the Incas bound their vast empire by communication systems that allowed them to know in a matter of hours everything that occurred in the realm. No uprising, no invasion occurred without the Inca rulers knowing it and taking counter-action.

The chroniclers wrote that the Incas could get word from their capital at Cuzco to Quito—1,400 miles away—in five days. Such speed of transmission was regarded with skepticism back in Spain.

The recent expedition discovered how the Incas achieved those "impossible" results. They used relays of trained carriers, each of whom would cover a couple of miles. Test runs by the scientists with local Indians proved the feasibility of the system.

15 M. P. H. Pace Set

The Inca courier pace of 280 miles a day was approximately eleven and one-half miles per hour. Bannister ripped along at fifteen miles per hour yesterday in his record mile.

Belgium's Gaston Reiff would have made another ideal courier. He covered the approximate Inca relay stint at a rate of nearly fourteen miles per hour in setting his world two-mile record of 8:40.4 in 1952.

Emil Zatopek, the great Czechoslovak distance star, has run six miles in 28:08.4 (about twelve and three-quarters miles per hour) and has covered twelve miles 810 yards in an hour.

The dedicated athletes who bend their efforts to setting records in an era when "shank's mare" is in general disrepute deserve more than the plaudits of the sport-loving coterie. They are running in the footsteps of precursors who left deep tracks in history.

Evolution of Mile Record

Here is the evolution of the world record in the mile run, as listed in Frank G. Menke's The Encyclopedia of Sports:

Time.	Runner and Country.	Year.
4:36	Charles Lawes, Britain	1864
4:36.5	Richard Webster, Britain	1865
4:29	William Chinnery, Britain	1868
4:28.8	W. C. Gibbs, Britain	1868
4:26	Walter Slade, Britain	1874
4:24.5	Walter Slade, Britain	1875
4:23.2	Walter George, Britain	1880
4:21.4	Walter George, Britain	1882
4:19.4	Walter George, Britain	1882
4:18.4	Walter George, Britain	1884
4:18.2	Fred Bacon, Scotland	1894
4:17	Fred Bacon, Scotland	1895
4:15.6	Thomas Conneff, United States	1895
4:15.4	John Paul Jones, United States	1911
4:14.4	John Paul Jones, United States	1913
4:12.6	Norman Taber, United States	1915
4:10.4	Paavo Nurmi, Finland	1923
4:09.2	Jules Ladoumegue, France	1931
4:07.6	Jack Lovelock, New Zealand	1933
4:06.8	G. Cunningham, United States	1934
4:06.4	Sydney Wooderson, Britain	1937
4:06.2	Gunder Haegg, Sweden	1942
4:06.2	Arne Andersson, Sweden	1942
4:06.2	Gunder Haegg, Sweden	1942
4:02.6	Arne Andersson, Sweden	1943
4:01.6	Arne Andersson, Sweden	1944
4:01.4	Gunder Haegg, Sweden	1945
3:59.4	Roger Bannister, Britain	1954

Pheidippides' Endurance and Speed of the Inca Couriers Played Historic Roles

TRACK STARS PAY TRIBUTE TO MILER

Santee Will Make an Attempt to Break Bannister's New Mark on Coast June 2

By The United Press.

The world's track stars paid tribute to Roger Bannister last night and said they hoped to follow soon in his footsteps.

Wes Santee, the United States No. 1 mile runner, called Bannister's 3:59.4 mile clocking "a great performance and a great challenge."

"Of the ones capable of running a 4-minute mile, Bannister was the one I would just as soon see run it," said the University of Kansas ace, who holds the American record of 4:02.4. Santee said he was not "exceptionally disappointed" that he himself was not the first man to crack the time barrier.

Santee said he would make his first attempt at the new mark in the Compton (Calif.) Relays on June 2 and had high hopes "if the weather and the track conditions are right and the competition is good enough."

Whitfield Not Surprised

Mal Whitfield of the United States, the world's premier half-miler who had joined the competition for the mile mark, said he "wasn't at all surprised" when he heard of Bannister's feat.

"I had heard he was training hard to become the first man to run the four-minute mile, so I'm not surprised," said Whitfield in New York. The former Ohio State star pointed out he had predicted recently that the mile soon would be run in 3:59.5—a tenth of a second slower than Bannister's time.

John Landy of Australia, who ran 4:02 last year, said Bannister "is a great runner" and called his race "great, great."

"I want to congratulate Bannister for this brilliant achievement," said Landy, in Turku, Finland. "It will be remembered all over the world, and I am sure this is not the best result he can do."

Denis Johansson of Finland, who has clocked 4:04, called Bannister's time "unbelievable."

News Cheers Pirie

In Freiburg, Germany, Gordon Pirie, who was Bannister's most formidable British rival for the honor, said he was glad that a fellow Briton had been the one to turn the trick.

In Milwaukee, Don Gerhmann, a former star miler, said that he had predicted the 4-minute mile was possible but was somewhat surprised that Bannister was the first to do it.

"I know that Roger is a strong runner," Gerhmann said, "but I was surprised that he was the first one. My congratulations go out to him."

Gerhmann predicted now that the "psychological barrier" was broken, more runners would break the 4-minute mark.

Josey Barthel of Luxembourg said at Cambridge, Mass., that Bannister "merits" the honor "because he works hard and loves running, not for the glory, but for the satisfaction it gives him."

"He is an amateur in a real and true sense—in the best English tradition," he said.

Barthel, the 1,500-meter Olympic champion, lost to Bannister in 1950.

A graduate student at Harvard University, Barthel indicated he might try to crack the 4-minute mark after he gets his master's degree in chemistry this summer.

"All the News That's Fit to Print"

The New York Times.

LATE CITY EDITION

Fair and pleasant today; increasing cloudiness tomorrow.

Temperature Range Today—Max., 73; Min., 57
Temperatures Yesterday—Max., 70; Min., 56

VOL. CIII..No. 35,209. Entered as Second Class Matter, Post Office, New York, N. Y. NEW YORK, FRIDAY, JUNE 18, 1954. FIVE CENTS

PREMIERSHIP WON BY MENDES-FRANCE ON PEACE PLEDGE

REDS' AID SPURNED

Leader Gets a 419-47 Vote—Sets July 20 to Achieve Goal

Excerpts from Mendès-France speech appear on Page 2.

By HAROLD CALLENDER

Special to The New York Times.

PARIS, Friday, June 18—Pierre Mendès-France, 47-year-old Radical intellectual, was chosen Premier early today, contrary to all expectations. He won by the extraordinary vote of 419 to 47 because of the appeal to nearly all parties of his proposal to negotiate a cease-fire in Indochina by July 20.

He also proposed to seek by that date a compromise on the European army treaty to break the deadlock over it in France. This seemed likely to entail new negotiations with the five other signatory states, West Germany, Italy, Belgium, The Netherlands and Luxembourg.

A dramatic aspect of yesterday's debate was M. Mendès-France's rejection of the ninety-five Communist votes, which were formally offered to him and finally cast for him on the professed ground that the Communists approved his quest for peace in Indochina. M. Mendès-France said no Government having Communist support could negotiate with the enemy whose cause the Communists had espoused, and he warned the Assembly that his majority must consist of non-Communist votes to be acceptable to him.

324 Votes Without Reds'

He received such a majority, for subtraction of the Communist ballots left him with 324 votes, ten more than the required majority of 314.

[There was an indication at Geneva Thursday that the talks on Indochina were likely to continue for an indefinite time. The indication appeared as the Western delegations considered the prospectives opened up by seeming concessions offered Wednesday by Communist spokesmen.]

The new Premier is committed to seek to end the fighting in Indochina within about a month. At the same time he promised to prepare the French forces there to meet exigencies that might arise if these negotiations failed or if there were meanwhile a mass attack against the northern delta. He said he would seek

Continued on Page 2, Column 6

Marciano Outpoints Charles, Keeps Title

The New York Times

Rocky Marciano

Rocky Marciano retained the world heavyweight championship last night by outpointing Ezzard Charles in fifteen rounds at Yankee Stadium. The favored titleholder gained a unanimous decision in a savagely fought bout.

A crowd of 47,585 saw the undefeated champion register his forty-sixth straight victory. For Charles, it was his second unsuccessful attempt to become the first man to regain the crown.

(Details on Page 27.)

INDOCHINA POSES DEFENSE DILEMMA

Military Conferees Say That Weapons and Men Available Are Far Short of Needs

By ANTHONY LEVIERO

Special to The New York Times.

WASHINGTON, June 17—When President Eisenhower and Sir Winston Churchill reach the Southeast Asia question in their forthcoming talks they will be confronted by the military realties of the Indochina situation as focused in the recently ended five-power military staff talks.

The military chiefs of the United States, Great Britain, Australia, France and New Zealand considered the how, when and wherewithal of possible intervention in the Indochina war, assuming a satisfactory united front could be arranged.

The military leaders made it plain that the military means were far short of the minimum requirements. In other words, the dilemma at the military level was fully as thorny as at the political.

The considered United States view is that intervention in Indochina would require an effort greater than the United States forces made in Korea. That would be approximately eight divisions as a minimum, and these would be in addition to the forces now at the disposal of France in her eight-year-old war against the Vietminh Communist forces.

Outside Forces Required

These would be the outside forces needed for the effort on the ground. They would have to be balanced by commensurate naval forces and air power.

Moreover, the United States believes it would be a serious mistake to employ white ground troops of a force approximating eight divisions in Indochina. Yet there are not that many indigenous troops in the Southeast Asia area, even if the countries there were willing to participate.

The conviction is firmly held here that in Indochina, as in the later stages of the Korean conflict, the native peoples will have to assume a major burden of the ground fighting if their yearning for freedom and sovereignty is to make any headway against the Communist ideology. Furthermore, Washington is convinced that this kind of participation is essential if the Asian hatred of colonialism is to be dispelled.

In assessing the ground force requirements for intervention United States military leaders have considered the Indochina terrain and the tactics the French

Continued on Page 3, Column 3

RED CHINA TO SEEK FULL BRITISH TIES

Will Send Charge d'Affaires to Launch Diplomatic Links

By DREW MIDDLETON

Special to The New York Times.

LONDON, June 17—Communist China has agreed to send a chargé d'affaires to Britain to negotiate the establishment of full diplomatic relations. In addition, arrangements for the visit of a party of Chinese trade experts to Britain are almost complete.

These developments toward the elimination of diplomatic and economic barriers between the two nations were accompanied by an announcement that the Labor party delegation, headed by former Prime Minister Clement R. Attlee, would leave London for Peiping and a tour of China by air Aug. 9. The tour was announced earlier.

Sir Winston Churchill's announcement in the House of Commons that after a four-year delay the Communist Chinese had agreed to send a small diplomatic mission to London produced a mixed response.

Labor members cheered it heartily. But some Conservative members of Parliament and diplomats are concerned about the effect of this and other developments upon the Prime Minister's coming discussions in Washington with President Eisenhower.

Authoritative Foreign Office sources emphasized, however,

Continued on Page 3, Column 6

U.S. SEEKING RIGHT TO SEARCH SHIPS IN GUATEMALA BAN

Bid to Allies Tied to Plea for Free World Arms Embargo—Resistance Army Gathers

By WALTER H. WAGGONER

Special to The New York Times.

WASHINGTON, June 17—The United States has asked for a complete embargo by the free world on arms sought by Guatemala. The right to search and seize Allied vessels suspected of violating it is included in the request.

The request, made in recent consultations with many of this Government's allies, would put the Central American republic in virtually the same category as the Soviet bloc in Eastern Europe and Communist China.

[Reports from Tegucigalpa, capital of Honduras, said that Guatemalan exiles were being flown to points near the Guatemalan border.]

Linking "the threat of Communist aggression in Europe and the open aggression of the Communists in the Far East" to the situation in Guatemala, the State Department said in a statement: "We have had informal discussions with the important non-Communist maritime nations with a view of obtaining their cooperation in preventing the shipment of arms to that country."

Aid Boycott Posed

Shortly after the State Department had said that the "attitude of these countries has been favorable," the Foreign Operations Administration disclosed that the withdrawal of United States Technical Cooperation Assistance to Guatemala was under "serious consideration."

The United States is spending about $188,000 in Guatemala during the current fiscal year on the design and management of a hospital, rubber development and agricultural research. Nine technicians are involved. There were indications the economic squeeze might be tightened in other respects.

Harold E. Stassen, director of the Foreign Operations Administration, said at a news conference that the question of classifying Guatemala as a Communist country under the terms of the Battle Act "is under serious consideration" in the Executive branch of the Government.

The Battle Act bars United States aid to any country sending arms or strategic materials to any of the Communist countries in Europe or the Far East.

Denmark Is Approached

Denmark disclosed Washington's suggestion that United States warships be allowed to "visit and search" her merchant vessels as a further step to cutting off arms shipments to Guatemala.

The State Department did not officially confirm the Danish report, and answered inquiries about it only by referring to the "informal discussions" aimed at "preventing the shipment of arms to Guatemala."

Other authorities, however, acknowledged that "search and seizure" on the high seas would be resorted to only as a "last ditch" measure, should a cargo of arms escape the other barriers and restrictions on which the United States seeks agreement with its allies.

Lincoln White, State Department press officer, said that "through the cooperation of friendly countries, shipment of

Continued on Page 6, Column 4

PRESIDENT REVIVES T.V.A. POWER ISSUE BY ORDER TO A.E.C.

Directs Atomic Board to Make Contract With Private Utility Involving New Steam Plant

By WILLIAM M. BLAIR

Special to The New York Times.

WASHINGTON, June 17—President Eisenhower touched off today another fight over public versus private power.

He directed the Atomic Energy Commission to negotiate a twenty-five-year contract with a private utility group to supply power to the Tennessee Valley Authority. This would involve the private construction under A. E. C. contract of a $107,250,000 steam plant at West Memphis, Ark.

Power from this plant would feed 600,000 kilowatts into the T. V. A. System to replace an equal amount of power the T. V. A. is delivering to the atomic plant at Paducah, Ky.

Disclosure of the President's directive, conveyed to the A. E. C. by Rowland R. Hughes, Director of the Bureau of Budget, was made at a hearing of the Joint Congressional Committee on Atomic Energy.

The testimony included evidence of a continuing 3-to-2 split in the A. E. C.

Attitudes in the A. E. C.

It was testified that Dr. Henry DeWolf Smyth, Thomas E. Murray and Eugene M. Zuckert doubted the wisdom of the contract on the ground that it was not essential to the commission's atomic mission. They would, however, accept the responsibility, if directed by the President or Congress.

Rear Admiral Lewis L. Strauss, who was appointed by President Eisenhower, favored the proposal, if directed by the President, as did Joseph Campbell, also an Eisenhower appointee, the hearing was told.

Senator Albert Gore, Democrat of Tennessee, demanded that the committee stop the negotiations until the "fundamental issue" of the independence of such agencies as the A. E. C. and the T. V. A. had been established.

Representative Chet Holifield, Democrat of California, a member of the committee, challenged the legality of the proposal and charged it would cost the Government "at least $90,000,000 more than the cost of equivalent power" supplied by the T. V. A. The proposal, he declared, was "dishonest and costly."

Cost Views at Variance

Several Democrats, including Senators Gore and John J. Sparkman of Alabama, accused the Administration of an effort to block further T. V. A. development by using the A. E. C. as a vehicle for promoting power combines.

There was indication that a fight to keep the A. E. C. from signing the contract would be carried to the floor of Congress.

T. V. A. officials testified that the proposed plant would cost $5,567,000 more a year to operate than steam plants the T. V. A. has proposed but for which it has been unable to get appropriations

The additional annual cost was estimated by the A. E. C. at $3,685,000, this figure including the need of the A. E. C. to pay state and local taxes and meet the higher cost of borrowing that falls on a private enterprise.

The joint committee's public hearing was forced by Mr. Holifield and Representative Melvin

Continued on Page 12, Column 3

Transit Election Put in Jeopardy; Authority Split on Plans for Vote

By LEONARD INGALLS

Efforts to cement friendly relations between the Transit Authority and the Transport Workers Union, C. I. O., struck a snag yesterday.

Two members of the authority balked at approving arrangements for a union representation election that had been worked out by negotiators for both sides with Joseph E. O'Grady, City Commissioner of Labor.

Union and authority representatives had agreed Wednesday, presumably with the full backing of the transit agency and the T. W. U. membership, to a vote next Friday by 37,000 hourly paid authority employes on the union or organization to represent them in grievance proceedings.

It was the first step toward agreement on wages, working conditions and union recognition since the T. W. U. canceled a strike threat last Friday and negotiations were resumed. A dispute over these issues has raged between the T. W. U. and the authority since last fall.

An element of tension returned to the delicate situation yesterday. Officials of the T. W. U. were reported to be "concerned" by the development, and Michael J. Quill, union president, said:

"To meet this unusual situation, we are calling an emergency meeting of the executive board of Local 100 at 11 A. M. [today] at the Piccadilly Hotel."

The authority members who blocked action yesterday on a resolution that would have authorized the election were Maj. Gen. Hugh J. Casey, chairman, and Douglas M. Moffat.

Only two other members of the five-member agency were present at the meeting at 370 Jay Street, Brooklyn. Harris J. Klein and

Continued on Page 24, Column 6

M'CARTHY HEARINGS END ON 36TH DAY AS POTTER SUGGESTS PERJURY ACTION, REMOVAL OF TOP AIDES ON BOTH SIDES

MOVE A SURPRISE

Wisconsin Senator Is Stunned—Wrangling Marks the Close

Excerpts from transcript of the hearings are on Page 10.

By W. H. LAWRENCE

Special to The New York Times.

WASHINGTON, June 17—The Army-McCarthy hearings ended late today with a suggestion by Senator Charles E. Potter for perjury prosecutions and the dismissal of employes on both sides who played top roles in the controversy.

The Michigan Republican declared in a formal statement that he was "convinced that the principal accusation of each side in this controversy was borne out by the testimony," even though that testimony "was saturated with statements which were not truthful and which might constitute perjury in a legal sense."

"I believe there may have been subornation of perjury," Senator Potter said. "* * * I believe a criminal case against some of the principals might be developed if the case were taken to a grand jury room where the testimony would have to be repeated without others being present."

The Strongest Statement

His was the strongest statement as the curtain fell on the stormy drama involving Senator Joseph R. McCarthy and his chief assistants on the one side, and Robert T. Stevens, Secretary of the Army, and his legal counselor, John G. Adams, on the other.

Senator Potter's statement appeared to shock Senator McCarthy.

The hearings began eight weeks ago today and continued through thirty-six days. Thirty-two witnesses were heard and about 2,000,000 words of questions, answers and arguments were recorded.

The hearings were recorded on 7,424 pages of transcript and the television time on the air totaled 187 hours, according to the DuMont network.

To the end, the Army held to its contention that Senator McCarthy, a Wisconsin Republican, and his chief counsel, Roy M. Cohn, had sought by improper means to obtain special and preferential treatment for Pvt. G. David Schine, who was an unpaid committee consultant before he was drafted.

Senator McCarthy and Mr. Cohn countercharged that the

Continued on Page 11, Column 2

HIS LAST OFFICIAL ACT: Ray H. Jenkins, left, at close of hearing, hands Acting Chairman Karl E. Mundt a sealed and confidential Army document that he has been carrying around for weeks. It contains names of Army personnel having a part in honorable discharge of Maj. Irving Peress, named by Senator McCarthy a "Fifth Amendment Communist."

EISENHOWER WINS ON ARMS BUDGET

Senate Approves 29 Billion Outlay—Democrats Unable to Prevent Army Cut

By The United Press.

WASHINGTON, June 17—The Senate passed today the Administration's $29,000,000,000 "new look" military budget for the 1955 fiscal year beginning July 1. Democratic efforts to block a planned reduction in Army strength were defeated.

Passage of the bill, which places increased emphasis on atomic air power and less on ground forces, came on a voice vote with about fifteen Senators on the floor. It now goes to a joint conference committee to thresh out differences with the House version.

Earlier, the Senate rejected by 50—38 an amendment by Senator John F. Kennedy, Democrat of Massachusetts, and six other Democrats, to maintain a nineteen-division Army in the twelve months starting July 1.

The Administration plans to cut Army strength from twenty to seventeen divisions between now and June 30, 1955. Mr. Kennedy's amendment would have added $350,466,000 to the bill.

Objective Trimmed

The Senate measure provides $29,211,584,486 in new military funds. The Administration originally requested $29,887,055,000, but trimmed its sights when the House approved a $28,681,250,486 outlay. The Senate version is about $5,500,000,000 less than the military appropriation approved by Congress for the present fiscal year.

Hardest hit by the cut would be the Army, which is slated to receive $7,619,066,986, a slash of about $5,300,000,000 from its current appropriation.

The Navy would get $9,719,102,500, or slightly more than it got this year. The Air Force would get $10,982,860,000, about a $185,000,000 reduction.

The bill also carries funds for two new atomic submarines in addition to the two in construction.

The only contest developed over Mr. Kennedy's amendment, which was defeated by forty Republicans and ten Democrats. Voting for the amendment were thirty-seven Democrats and Senator John Sherman Cooper, Republican of Kentucky.

Mr. Kennedy was joined in the amendment by Democratic Senators Albert Gore of Tennessee, Mike Mansfield of Montana, A. S. (Mike) Monroney of Oklahoma, Stuart Symington of Missouri, Herbert H. Lehman of New York and Hubert H. Humphrey of Minnesota.

They charged during the two days of debate that the Administration was gambling with the national security by cutting Army strength in the present

Continued on Page 15, Column 6

Brownell Says McCarthy Asks Rule by 'Individual'

By The United Press.

BALTIMORE, June 17—Herbert Brownell Jr., Attorney General, today accused Senator Joseph R. McCarthy of actions that "would substitute government by an individual for government by law." Mr. Brownell did not mention the Wisconsin Republican by name.

He referred merely to the Senator who recently had invited Federal employes to give his committee "any information which they have" on communism. Mr. Brownell said:

"This open invitation to violate the laws of the United States would substitute government by an individual for government by law."

Addressing the convention of the National Editorial Association, Mr. Brownell also denounced Senator McCarthy's proposal to call members of the Army Loyalty Board before the Senate Permanent Subcommittee on Investigations, of which he is chairman.

Mr. Brownell said that Mr. McCarthy's invitation to Federal employes to give him information would destroy the effectiveness of the Federal Bureau of Investigation and seriously cripple the Justice Department's effectiveness as a prosecuting agency.

He said Mr. McCarthy's proposal to examine loyalty board hearing officers, renewed just before today's close of the Army-McCarthy hearings, would destroy any employe security program.

Mr. Brownell condemned "those who, regardless of motive, break down our system of government by law in an effort to investigate communism."

"Anyone who attempts to put himself above the law and invite Government employes to turn over classified information relating to our national security, in violation of statute and Presiden-

Continued on Page 8, Column 2

U. S. HOUSING BILL GOES TO CONFEREES

House Votes Down Attempt to Ban Public Projects in Measure, 360-19

Special to The New York Times.

WASHINGTON, June 17—The House of Representatives voted today, 360 to 19, to send the Administration's housing bill to conference without any strings attached.

A stand by Representative Charles A. Halleck of Indiana, Republican floor leader, killed off a move to instruct the House members of the Senate-House conference committee to vote against any provision in a compromise bill to continue public housing.

Mr. Halleck told the House that he had never before seen a move made to tie the hands of House conferees on a bill before they even went into conference. He asked the defeat of such a motion on the grounds that it violated orderly legislative procedure.

Opposition Draws Back

The emphasis Mr. Halleck placed upon orderly procedure frightened foes of public housing who had hoped to deliver the coup de grace on even the modest program advocated by the President.

Fearful that some in Congress, not too strongly against the program, might be swayed, the opposition withdrew a motion to instruct conferees on this issue within a matter of minutes after it was offered.

The motion had been put by Representative Howard W. Smith, Democrat of Virginia, but he pulled it back after receiving assurance from Mr. Halleck that the House would have an opportunity for a "yes or no vote" on any public housing provision contained in the compromise bill emerging from conference.

This retreat by the opposition was a victory for the Administration because three times within the last two years the House has voted against public housing. In each instance a Republican-Southern Democratic coalition has prevailed on the issue.

In the most recent action on the matter, the House voted, 211 to 176, on April 2 against the public housing the President wanted in his bill, which encompasses scores of separate Federal aids for home construction.

The President specifically had sought authority for construction

Continued on Page 14, Column 7

Monaghan Defender Ends Congress Fight

By CLAYTON KNOWLES

Special to The New York Times.

WASHINGTON, June 17—Representative Sidney A. Fine, Democrat of the Bronx, abandoned today an eleven-month effort to stop publication of a report critical of George P. Monaghan, former New York City Police Commissioner.

The criticism concerned an arrangement, said to have been made with the Justice Department, exempting the New York City police from questioning by the Federal Bureau of Investigation in complaints of police brutality violating Federal civil rights laws.

Mr. Monaghan, now harness-racing commissioner in New York State, denied before a special House Judiciary subcommittee last year that there was such an arrangement. The denial came after Daniel H. Greenberg, as-

Continued on Page 26, Column 3

FORGERIES HUNTED IN HOFFMAN CASE

Expert Studies Handwriting in Search for $300,000

By GEORGE CABLE WRIGHT

Special to The New York Times.

TRENTON, June 17—Gov. Robert B. Meyner took steps here today to effect a drastic and swift reorganization of the State Division of Employment Security.

This agency was headed by former Gov. Harold G. Hoffman until his suspension March 18. It handles tens of millions of dollars a year in Federal and state funds.

The move was said to have been taken to increase efficiency and effect economies and also to determine the extent of malpractices in the division. A study of the duties and qualifications of each of the 2,000 employes of the agency is planned. Many jobs are to be reclassified and some are expected to be abolished.

State and Federal officials continued today their efforts to unravel the maze of alleged frauds and juggling of public and bank funds by Mr. Hoffman and other state employes. Albert D. Osborn, the handwriting expert, examined and photographed signatures on bank certifications that are alleged to have been forged.

The name of George A. Kress recurs on the certifications that were submitted to the examining officials by the South Amboy Trust Company of which Mr. Hoffman was president at his

Continued on Page 24, Column 3

47,585 SEE RALLY BY CHAMPION WIN

Marciano Takes Command in Savage Bout at Stadium After a Slow Start

By JOSEPH C. NICHOLS

Rocky Marciano successfully defended the heavyweight championship of the world against Ezzard Charles at the Yankee Stadium last night. The favored titleholder from Brockton, Mass., gained the unanimous decision over his Cincinnati opponent, who once was the ruler of the division.

The contest was a savagely waged one in which Marciano's greater strength and punching power enabled him to gain the award. Referee Ruby Goldstein had it eight rounds to five, with two even. Judge Artie Aidala scored it nine, five and one, and Judge Harold Barnes had it eight, six and one. This observer favored Rocky by nine rounds to six.

A crowd of 47,585 fans witnessed the fight, and the onlookers were pleased with both the action and the decision. Although he was plainly defeated, Charles made one of the best showings of his career. He gamely mixed with the ponderous-punching Rocky, and dealt out considerable punishment with his left hook through the first half of the proceedings.

Marciano's strong point was his right hand, and he landed the weapon quite often. Strong as it was though, it failed to knock down the challenger. This circumstance was in the nature of a surprise in that while Rocky was the betting favorite to win, at odds of 7 to 2, his supporters expected him to score by a knockout.

Marciano Absorbs Blows

It really was not through boxing that Marciano gained the award. It was more through his ability to take great punishment, to absorb everything that came his way until his opponent became tired of punching.

When Charles showed that he had little left, after tagging the champion, Rocky moved in and slammed away almost without let up. Only the fact that he was in the best of condition permitted Ezzard to go through the grueling fifteen rounds without hitting the canvas.

For Marciano, the victory extended a string that is without equal in the history of modern boxing. It was his forty-sixth professional contest and his forty-sixth victory.

Nobody before him in the ranks of the heavyweight champions reached the top of the class with a perfect record. Only in the matter of knockouts did Marciano's average fall off against Charles. The champion has stopped forty of his rivals.

Charles Best Boxer in Division

Despite the decisive count in his favor on the ballots, Marciano did not have an easy time of it at all, particularly at the start. For Charles, probably the best boxer now in the heavyweight division, caused Rocky to make many mistakes and at the same time succeeded in scoring with excellently timed left hooks to the body and right counters to the head.

For the first four rounds Rocky could do little but lunge and seek to grab Charles, to make him stand still and serve as a target for his pile-driving right. Of course, Charles would have none of that. He moved in fearlessly on the champion, whipped away at the head and body until he felt that he had delivered enough punishment, and then stepped back to avoid Marciano's eager rushes.

This pattern gave the Charles followers much hope, especially when a cut appeared over Marciano's left eye after a clinch that was followed by a Charles right to the head.

The slow-starting Marciano probably needed this blood-letting to urge him into formidable action. At any rate, he took command in the fifth round when, after sampling some of Ezzard's right-hand punches to the head, he bethought himself of his own right, and applied it to Charles steadily.

Champion Hits After Bell

So eager was the champion to employ the weapon that he even landed after the bell. Charles, of course, hit him right back.

In the sixth Marciano dared everything in the hope of bringing about a sudden termination. Making little effort to avoid Charles' blows, the champion moved forward firing right-hand punches.

A good number of these wallops bounced off Ezzard's jaw, but the latter took them well and he thrilled the crowd by springing back at the close of the session to hurt Rocky with a well-placed left hook to the jaw.

Carrying over his attack to the seventh, Marciano found that Charles was willing enough to mix with him, so much so that the challenger had the better of the several exchanges, in which the left hook was the key drive. These blows made Rocky stop his attack several times, but beyond that they did not seem to carry enough force to spill him.

The great strength that Rocky possesses began to manifest itself at this point. He seemed to retain his freshness after every bitter exchange, whereas Ezzard, for all his courage, seemed slower and slower getting his punches across.

Marciano punched away with little concern for any return in the eighth. He evened the matter of cuts then by opening a small one beside Charles' right eye.

The ninth showed the tide strongly in Marciano's favor and he bounced right after right off Ezzard's chin. The latter seemed on the verge of "going" several times, but he thrilled the crowd by rallying toward the close and shaking Rocky with his left hook.

An exchange in the tenth round was one of the highlights. The pair waded willingly toward each other, Rocky matching his right against Ezzard's left, to the latter's advantage.

Officials' Score Cards For Heavyweight Fight

Referee Ruby Goldstein

1	2	3	4	5	6	7	8	9	10	11	12	13	14	15
C2	M1	E	C2	M2	M2	C1	C1	M1	M1	M2	E	M2	C1	M2

Rounds: 8—5—2. Points: M13—C7.

Judge Harold Barnes

1	2	3	4	5	6	7	8	9	10	11	12	13	14	15
C1	C1	M1	C2	E	M2	C1	M1	M2	M3	M2	C1	M2	C1	M3

Rounds: 8—6—1. Points: M16—C7.

Judge Arthur Aidala

1	2	3	4	5	6	7	8	9	10	11	12	13	14	15
C1	C1	C1	C2	M1	M2	E	C1	M1	M2	M2	M1	M2	M1	M2

Rounds: 9—5—1. Points: M14—C6.

In the eleventh, the champion hit Charles with "everything." These punches shook the challenger often, but Ezzard took them and fought back. So well did he react, in fact, that he outsmarted Rocky in the twelfth with his left hook delivery.

From there on, though, the champion was in command. He had the better of every trade in the thirteenth and fourteenth, and in the fifteenth he swarmed over Ezzard in an effort to floor him.

The latter took many punches, but he showed that he was still in a fighting mood by tagging Rocky with two solid left hooks just before the end.

Charles' Weight Surprises

Marciano weighed 187½ pounds and Charles 185½. The latter figure was a surprise since Ez was expected to weigh 190, but there was no fault to find with his condition.

The gross receipts were $543,092 and the net $469,653. Marciano gets 40 per cent and Charles 20 per cent of "everything," including some $200,000 theatre-TV money and $35,000 from the radio. The same split will be made on money received from movie rights.

Marciano was born in Brockton on Sept. 1, 1924. His right name is Rocco Marchegiano, and he is the oldest of six children born to Piecino and Pasqualina Marchegiano.

The father, an Italian immigrant, supported his family as a cobbler, and Rocky had the typical American town upbringing. Baseball and football were his main sports pursuits in the two years that he went to high school. It was not until 1943, when he entered the Army, that he took boxing seriously. He was a full-fledged heavyweight then.

In the service Rocky took part in camp tournaments and built up a fine record.

After the service Marciano, who had been a good enough baseball player to get a trial with the Chicago Cubs, decided to take up boxing in earnest and turned professional in 1947.

He gradually gained renown in New England, and presently came under the management of Al Weill. Charley Goldman became Rocky's trainer and Marciano made rapid progress.

His first "big" fight occurred in New York on March 24, 1950. He met Roland LaStarza, also previously undefeated and considered an exceptionally good boxer for a heavyweight. Marciano gained a split decision and became a top star. He continued to topple all opposition and was matched with Joe Louis, the erstwhile champion of the world.

Rocky knocked out Louis in eight rounds on Oct. 26, 1951. He stopped four subsequent rivals before getting into the ring with Jersey Joe Walcott for the championship, in Philadelphia, on Sept. 23, 1952.

Marciano knocked out Jersey Joe in thirteen rounds to become the titleholder. In his defenses previous to last night Rocky knocked out Walcott again and LaStarza.

'I THOUGHT I WON,' EZZARD DECLARES

Never in Knockout Danger, Charles Says—Marciano Calls Fight His Toughest

By JOSEPH M. SHEEHAN

"It was my toughest fight," said Rocky Marciano.

"I never was in danger of being knocked out and I thought I won," said Ezzard Charles.

Those were the key quotes from the rival dressing rooms following last night's heavyweight championship fight.

Sporting an inch-and-a-half cut that will require stitching just below his left eyebrow and a sizable mouse beneath the same eye, Marciano paid tribute to his beaten challenger as "a tough, game guy."

"He hit me with some good right hands and hurt me in three or four different rounds," said Rocky. "But I never was in any real trouble, except from the cut, which hindered me when he opened it early in a round.

"I felt it was a close fight until about the tenth round. After that I was sure I had it. His punches were beginning to lose their early steam and I thought I had a good chance to get him," the champion continued.

Charles Clever Opponent

"I was sure I had him on the way several times, especially at the end, but he was clever at slipping punches and I never could quite nail him clean," said Marciano.

"I was surprised that he mixed it as much as he did and I must admit I didn't expect to have such a hard time. This was a real tough fight—tougher than my first one with Walcott."

Reporters who had run the gauntlet into Marciano's dressing room were through with questioning Rocky before Charles opened the doors of his quarters to the press. Whereas Rocky received visitors in his ring togs, Ezzard had showered and was half-dressed when he faced the questioners.

While his face was lumped from the pounding he took about the head and there was a sizable swelling around the cut at the corner of his right eye, his chief concern was his voice.

Supplementing his sparing words with sign language, Charles croakingly explained that he had been struck in the "Adam's apple" by a punch in the eighth round.

"It bothered him a lot," Tom Tannas interpolated.

"I thought I won," Charles repeated. "And there wouldn't have been any doubt of it if it hadn't been for that punch. I was ahead when he hit me with it and it slowed me down."

The former champion did not seem overly impressed with Marciano's punching power, apart from that misdirected blow. He rated Jersey Joe Walcott a better hitter and said that all three of his battles with Walcott had been "tougher fights."

Champion Rocky Marciano, blood streaming from left eye, jars Ezzard Charles, challenger, in thirteenth round of title bout.

Drobny Tops Rosewall in 4 Sets to Gain Wimbledon Title in 11th Attempt

SOUTHPAW, 32, CAPS QUEST OF 16 YEARS

Drobny Captures Wimbledon Singles, Beating Rosewall by 13-11, 4-6, 6-2, 9-7

By FRED TUPPER

Special to The New York Times.

WIMBLEDON, England, July 2—Jaroslav Drobny of Egypt defeated Ken Rosewall of Australia, 13—11, 4—6, 6—2, 9—7, today for the men's singles title in the all-England lawn tennis championships. And the thunderous applause that rang down the crowded center court at Wimbledon must have echoed wherever tennis is played.

For "Old Drob" had finally made it. He had been eleven times trying, first in 1938 as a 16-year-old ball boy from Prague. He had reached the semi-finals six times, the finals thrice, and at long last his dream had come true.

King Gustav of Sweden, Princess Margaret of Britain and the Duchess of Kent saw him achieve his goal.

"I was holding thumbs for you all the way," said the Duchess as she presented the huge silver loving cup to the left-handed Drobny. "The finest tennis I've ever seen," she added.

The finalists went on the court in the early afternoon. Drobny, 33 next month, faced Rosewall, 19—the aging tactician with the all-court game against the subtle, young genius with the delicate lob and the best backhand in tennis.

Drobny Loses Two Games

Two rapier backhands knifed down the line meant the service break and a 2-0 lead for Rosewall as Drobny started shakily. But, cross-courting brilliantly off his own backhand, he was quickly even and then had four games running as Ken seemed tense and stiff under increasing pressure. Drobny was 5 to 4, with his own big serve to hold for the set.

But Rosewall came alive, as he was to do all afternoon in the crises. A gorgeous forehand passing shot down the line meant the game.

Drobny broke through again at 7—6; again Rosewall smashed him back, always forcing him on the backhand. Ken suddenly had a set point at 11—10, but Drobny just saved with a lunging smash return that clicked off the baseline.

Drobny was staying in the backcourt now, chopping deeply to either side, but concentrating chiefly on Ken's backhand in defiance of its reputation. His own strokes grew sharper and two forehands down the ribbon gave him the break and then the set at 13—11.

Pattern Becomes Clearer

They were 4—3 in the second when Drobny lost his concentration briefly. A missed volley off his shoestrings and a flubbed drop shot had him in trouble. Then Ken whipped a flashing backhand across court to lead at 5—3. The pattern was becoming clearer.

It is axiomatic in big-time tennis that a server should follow his delivery to the net. But Rosewall's service has not the power of Drobny's and Ken went up only on service return.

Twice Drobny saved, once with an incredible return of a Rosewall smash, but the Australian made sure of his next volley and the set.

With the tide running against him, Drob abruptly shifted his whole game. He had been staying in backcourt; now he followed up his return of service.

Ken tried to pass him, but Jaroslav cut off his volleys dead to the corners. Then Rosewall pushed up a series of lobs but Drobny was simply lethal overhead. Quickly, the former Czech had the third set at 6—2.

This was beautiful tennis as each contrived for the narrow opening, the single shot that would pull the other off balance for the thrust and kill.

Scores With Forehand

They were 3-all in the fourth set when a pair of searing forehands into the corner gave Drob the advantage. Three times he had it before Ken stumbled and his volley just drifted beyond the baseline.

At last Drobny was at 5—4 with his service, just where he wanted to be. There was hardly a sound in the huge crater as he toed the line.

He was 15—love. Then, as they had been all this long fortnight, the gods were with Rosewall. A backhand nipped the cord and popped in. Another backhand straight down the line and an overhead smash on the gallop broke Drobny's service. It was 5—5.

So near had Drobny come. He hadn't failed under the tremendous tension; he had been outgunned by a man who dared to fire all when he had to.

Still scrambling desperately, Drobny had an advantage in the fifteenth game, one more chance to break through. They traded drives and Drob hammered at the top of the net. The ball stuck there for a tantalizing split-second, then dropped over. Luck had evened up. Again he was ahead, again he had service to come.

Rosewall seemed exhausted now—a limp, little figure bent almost double over the baseline as he waited for service. Once more Drobny was 15—love. Then Rosewall fired a backhand down the side and produced a roaring forehand across court, falling as he swung, to leave Drobny bewildered at the net.

Another point and it was 15—40. Drobny seemed about to fail again. Then it was level and a service ace that popped off the wood made it match point. Drobny smashed to the backhand. Ken netted.

For fully five minutes the 15,000 spectators cheered and waved. Some of them had queued all night to root for their favorite.

Tickets sold as high as $30 apiece.

[A ticket speculator tried to sell Drobny a seat when the athlete showed up for the match, The United Press reported. "Sorry, I shall have to stand during the match," Drobny said.]

After the match, Drobny said, with a smile, "That's it and that's all. From here in it will be fun."

Misses Hart-Fry Win

The two best doubles teams in women's tennis will meet in the final tomorrow.

In today's semi-finals, Doris Hart of Coral Gables, Fla., and Shirley Fry of Akron, Ohio, defeated Angela Mortimer and Ann Shilcock of Great Britain, 6—2, 6—1, and Louise Brough of Beverly Hills, Calif., and Mrs. Margaret Osborne du Pont of Wilmington, Del., won from Kay Hubbell of Boston and Mrs. Heather Brewer of Bermuda, 6—1, 6—1.

Miss Hart and Miss Fry have won at Wimbledon three times running; Miss Brough and Mrs. du Pont have scored four times previously.

In some spirited mixed doubles, Mrs. du Pont and Rosewall won from Maureen Connolly of San Diego, Calif., and Lew Hoad of Australia, 6—8, 6—4, 6—4. They will meet the defenders, Miss Hart and Vic Seixas of Philadelphia, who had easier passage through Judy Burke and Mark Otway of New Zealand, 6—4, 6—1.

The women's singles final also will be played tomorrow. Miss Connolly, seeking her third title in a row here, will meet Miss Brough.

THE SUMMARIES

MEN'S SINGLES

Final Round—Jaroslav Drobny, Egypt, defeated Ken Rosewall, Australia, 13—11, 4—6, 6—2, 9—7.

WOMEN'S DOUBLES

Semi-Final Round—Louise Brough, Beverly Hills, Calif., and Mrs. Margaret du Pont, Wilmington, Del., defeated Mrs. Heather Brewer, Bermuda, and Katherine Hubbell, Boston, 6—1, 6—1; Shirley Fry, Akron, Ohio, and Doris Hart, Coral Gables, Fla., defeated Angela Mortimer and Ann Shilcock, Britain, 6—2, 6—1.

MIXED DOUBLES

Quarter-Final Round—Mark Otway and Judy Burke, New Zealand, defeated Rex Hartwig, Australia, and Mrs. Betty Rosenquest, South Orange, N. J., 7—5, 6—3.

Semi-Final Round—Vic Seixas, Philadelphia, and Miss Hart, defeated Otway and Miss Burke, 6—4, 6—1; Rosewall and Mrs. du Pont defeated Lew Hoad, Australia and Maureen Connolly, San Diego, Calif., 6—8, 6—4, 6—4.

Became Egyptian Citizen

WIMBLEDON, England, July 2 (AP)—Jaroslav Drobny became an Egyptian citizen in 1949 when he refused to return to his Communist homeland. In his previous Wimbledon finals, he lost to Ted Schroeder in 1949 and Frank Sedgman in 1952.

Drobny said after winning today that he would "not be turning professional."

When he lost to Schroeder five years ago Drobny was on the verge of becoming a professional. But now he has a good export business, spends much time at tennis, or in the London home of his wife's family. He expects to become a father in September.

The new champion said this would be his last serious competition at Wimbledon.

WIMBLEDON, England, July 2 (AP)—Jaroslav Drobny was the first southpaw to win the title since Sir Norman Brookes of Australia triumphed forty years ago. Drobny today also became the first bespectacled champion in Wimbledon history.

Self-Exiled Czech Captures Top Prize in Tennis

Jaroslav Drobny receiving the huge silver trophy from the Duchess of Kent after winning the men's singles championship at Wimbledon. Drobny defeated Ken Rosewall of Australia.

Associated Press Radiophotos

Drobny moves in for a shot in his match against Rosewall

ARNOLD IS JUNIOR VICTOR

Scores in Jersey Tennis Final—Silverman Boys' Winner

MAPLEWOOD, N. J., July 2 (AP)—Jeff Arnold of Coral Gables, Fla., won the junior title and Alan Silverman of Brooklyn the boys' crown today in the New Jersey State junior and boys' tennis tournament.

Arnold trounced Carl Norgauer of Yonkers, 6—1, 6—2, 6—1. Silverman also won with ease, downing James Ellenberg of Harrison, N. Y., 6—1, 6—0.

Norgauer gained a consolation prize by winning the junior doubles title in combination with George Mandel of Astoria, Queens, against Arnold and Bob Macy of Coral Gables, Fla., 6—3, 0—6, 0—6, 13—11, 6—2.

Silverman and Ogden Phipps of Roslyn, L. I., won the boys' tandem crown by defeating Norgauer and Don Rubell of Brooklyn, 6—3, 6—4.

MOYLAN, DEWITTS SCORE

Reach Semi-Finals in Singles of Eastern Clay Court Tennis

Special to The New York Times.

HACKENSACK, N. J., July 2—Ed Moylan of Trenton and Jerry DeWitts of Oakland, Calif., scored victories today in the quarter-final round of the Eastern clay court tennis championships at the Oritani Field Club.

Moylan, seeded No. 1, turned back Ronnie Kerdasha of North Bergen, N. J., 6—2, 6—4, and DeWitts, No. 3, defeated William Lurie of Brooklyn, 6—2, 6—2.

Moylan and DeWitts qualified for the doubles semi-final by defeating Berkeley Bell of Cresskill, N. J., and Robert Kerdasha Sr. of New York, 6—3, 7—5.

Cash Quits at Tennessee State

NASHVILLE, July 2 (AP)—Clarence B. Cash resigned today as basketball coach at Tennessee State University, first Negro school to play in the National Association of Intercollegiate Athletics tourney. Cash's teams won sixty-eight games and lost three during his three seasons at Tennessee State.

M. I. T. EIGHT GAINS SEMI-FINAL ROUND

Americans Victors by Length in Cup Event at Henley—Russians in 3 Finals

HENLEY-ON-THAMES, England, July 2 (UP)—The Massachusetts Institute of Technology eight, the only remaining American crew in the Henley Royal Regatta, reached the Thames Challenge Cup semi-finals today, while Britain and Russia headed for a showdown in the Grand Challenge Cup.

The competition ends tomorrow in all events. Britain's Leander crew is expected to meet the Volga boatmen of Russia's Krylia Sovetov Club in the final of the Grand Challenge Cup for eight-oared shells, premier event in the classic.

M. I. T. advanced by defeating the London Rowing Club "B" crew by one length. The Americans were timed in 7 minutes 17 seconds over the Henley distance of one mile 550 yards.

In tomorrow's semi-finals the Cambridge, Mass., oarsmen will face the Thames Rowing Club "B" shell. The final will be held in the afternoon.

Americans Take Early Lead

In today's race the Americans, bolting from the start at a 41 beat, took an early lead and were a half-length in front at the three-quarter-mile mark. The Britons made a strong effort near the mile post and closed the gap to a few feet, but M. I. T. spurted again in the final 200 yards.

Meanwhile, the Russians, dipping their red-tipped oars into the water like a well-oiled machine, qualified for a final showdown with Leander Club tomorrow by winning their semi-final of the Grand Challenge Cup in 6 minutes 54 seconds.

Leander, with a boatload of Oxford and Cambridge Blues and six members of Britain's 1952 Olympic eight, won the other semi-final in a nip-and-tuck encounter with the Lady Margaret Boat Club of Cambridge.

The Russians, who have drawn unprecedented crowds to this tree-filled river town in their first appearance on British water, showed they had plenty in reserve when they came from behind to beat the Thames Rowing Club.

Russians Hold off Challenge

Cheers resounded across the river when word came that the Thames sweepswingers were leading at the quarter-mile post. But the Russians got in their stride and whipped up the stroke to a piston-like 37 to forge ahead and then hold off a challenge from the game Britons to triumph handily.

Experts predicted their time—almost two seconds faster than that of Leander—was an indication of things to come and said the Iron Curtain crew would easily take the cup.

The Russians are in two other finals tomorrow. In the semi-final of the Stewards Cup for fours today, they gained the lead in the first two minutes and scored handily, dropping their stroke to 30 at the end. They will meet the Royal Air Force quartet tomorrow.

In the Silver Goblets for pairs, Russia's O. Buldakov and V. Ivanov beat the Royal Navy's N. Clack and T. Cristie to insure an all-European final tomorrow. Their opponents will be S. I. Blom and R. Gitz of the Netherlands.

Ford Wins Empire Boxing Title

MELBOURNE, July 2 (AP)—Pat Ford of West Melbourne won the British Empire lightweight title tonight on a decision in fifteen rounds over a West Indian, Ivor Germaine, the defending champion. Ford was down twice but piled up points with his left when Germaine bulled in recklessly, trying for a knockout. Ford weighed 134¼ pounds and Germaine 134¾.

Canadiens Trade 3 for Leclair

MONTREAL, July 2 (AP)—The Montreal Canadiens of the National Hockey League today traded Gaye Stewart, Ed Slowinski and Pete Babando to the Buffalo Bisons of the American League for Jackie Leclair and an undisclosed amount of cash.

PODOLEY LEADER IN U. S. DECATHLON

Ahead by 177 Points, With Lewis Next and Richards Third After 5 Events

By MICHAEL STRAUSS

Special to The New York Times

ATLANTIC CITY, July 2—Jim Podoley, Central Michigan College sophomore, gained the jump over the twenty-three-man field in the thirty-sixth annual national decathlon championship tonight.

The 20-year-old 170-pounder from the Midwest had a 177-point lead over the second-place Aubrey Lewis of Montclair, N. J., at the completion of the first half of the program. Podoley had a total of 3,831 points.

The Rev. Bob Richards, the high-flying parson from the Los Angeles A. C., who is favored to win the title, was well established in third place. Richards, the winner in 1951, had 3,542 points. Rafer Johnson of Kingsburg, Calif., competing unattached, followed with 3,511.

The "so-so" position of Richards after five events was no surprise. The coast star's strongest events, such as the pole vault, javelin and discus, are scheduled tomorrow. Then the 28-year-old Olympic pole vault king is expected to make things really rough for the opposition.

Podoley Wins Two Events

Podoley, who gained attention earlier this season by capturing the decathlon honors at the Kansas Relays, was in fine fettle tonight. He won the broad jump and the high jump with respective performances of 22 feet 3 inches and 6 feet 1¾ inches. He also placed high in both running events, the 100 and 400-meter tests.

The pace-setter's only poor showing took place in the shot-put, in which he was eleventh. It was an event with an important bearing on the chances of the Central Michigan collegian, who is not expected to do too well in the field events tomorrow.

Lewis, who placed sixth in the National held at Plainfield, N. J., last summer, turned in his usual strong showing in the running events.

He triumphed in the 100-meter dash—the curtain raiser—in 11 seconds flat and came up with a fine performance in the 400-meter test with an 0:49.1 effort.

As for Richards, he went through his paces in his usual colorful manner. He won the approbation of the crowd early and, by the time the first half of the program was completed, had the spectators applauding his efforts regardless of their merit.

Easier Task for Richards

One thing appeared certain and that was that the traveling parson from California was facing an easier task than confronted him last year, when the decathlon crown was won by Milton Campbell.

The husky Plainfield star, who scored 7,235 points in 1953, to 6,456 for the runner-up Richards, is out of competition with an injured elbow.

THE SUMMARIES

100-METER DASH

1. Aubrey Lewis, Kearny (N. J.) A. C., 0:11, 945 points; 2. Rafer Johnson, unattached, Kingsburg, Calif., and Jim Podoley, Central Michigan College, 0:11.1 and 871 points each; 4. Joel Shankle, Duke, 0:11.2, 835; 5. Robert Richards, Los Angeles A. C. and Tony Conkle, East Palestine (Ohio) A. C., 0:11.3 and 800 each; 7. James Brown, Syracuse U., and Clarence Smith, Shanahan Catholic Club, Philadelphia, 0:11.4 and 767 each; 9. Jack Kuhn, Kearny A. C., Perry Moore, U. S. Navy, and Tom Bowman, unattached, Auburndale, Fla., 0:11.5 and 736 each; 12. Carl Pescosolido, Governor Drummer Academy, Don Luke, Central Connecticut A. A., and Arthur Battles, Kearny A. C., 0:11.6 and 706 each; 15. Stan Huntsman, unattached, Crawfordsville, Ind., 0:12, 598; 16. Rev Franse, Portales, N. M.; Wesley Hall, Bishop College, and Dale Saxton, Sertoma Club, Clovis, N. M., 0:12.1 and 574 each; 19. David Gately, Phillips Exeter, and John Blakesley, Lakewood, Ohio, 0:12.2 and 550 each; 21. Allen Norris, Portales, N. M., and James Harrington, Mountainside, N. J., 0:12.3 and 527 each; 23. Terry Anderson, Kearny A. C., 0:13, 386.

BROAD JUMP

1. Podoley, 22 feet 3 inches, 719 points; 2. Shankle, 22 feet 1 inch, 704; 3. Battles, 22 feet ½ inch, 698; 4. Smith, 21 feet 6 inches, 640; 5. Lewis, 21 feet 1 inch, 618; 6. Johnson, 20 feet 7 inches, 590; 7. tie between Moore and Richards, 20 feet ¾ inch and 540 points each; 9. Huntsman, 19 feet 11½ inches, 532; 10. Brown, 19 feet 8¾ inches, 515; 11. Luke, 19 feet 5¾ inches, 497; 12. Hall, 19 feet 4¾ inches, 490; 13. Bowman, 19 feet 4½ inches, 490; 14. Conkle, 19 feet 3 inches, 481; 15. Gately, 19 feet 2¾ inches, 479; 16. Saxton, 18 feet 10¾ inches, 457; 17. Franse, 18 feet 10¾ inches, 455; 18. Pescosolido, 18 feet 7 inches, 435; 19. Blakesley, 18 feet ¾ inch, 400; 20. Harrington, 17 feet 3 inches, 347; 21. Kuhn, 16 feet 2½ inches, 282; 22. Anderson, 16 feet 2 inches, 282; 23. Norris, 15 feet 9 inches, 236.

SHOT-PUT

1. Huntsman, 46 feet, 771 points; 2. Conkle, 45 feet 11 inches, 770; 3. Richards, 43 feet 11½ inches, 709; 4. Moore, 41 feet 1 inch, 627; 5. Bowman, 40 feet 1 inches, 609; 6. tie between Brown and Johnson, 39 feet 7½ inches, 589 each; 8. Lewis, 39 feet 7 inches, 587; 9. Pescosolido, 39 feet 6 inches, 584; 10. Gately, 39 feet 4 inches, 581; 11. Podoley, 38 feet 8 inches, 562; 12. Harrington [illegible]

400-METER RUN

[illegible]

HIGH JUMP

[illegible]

POINT SCORES

Podoley, Lewis, Richards, Johnson, Smith, Shankle, Moore, Conkle, Bowman, Brown, Pescosolido, Huntsman [illegible]

Wood, Field and Stream

Special Fall Deer Hunting Season Is S in Adirondack Park Wilderness Areas

By RAYMOND R. CAMP

THE New York hunters who like to "rough it," and enjoy scoffing at the Sybarites who scour the farm-fringe jungles for their deer, have an opportunity to get in some wilderness hunting and two deer by packing in to some sections of the Adirondack Park this fall.

The over-population of deer in several portions of the park, which has resulted in over-browsing and excessive winter losses, has caused the Conservation Department to set aside some areas, remote from highways, where one antlerless deer as well as a buck may be taken. The hunter, however, must back-pack his camping equipment in and his deer—if any—out.

The department has now defined the boundaries of two of the six areas to be included in the program. In all of the areas, the boundaries are three miles or more from the nearest highway, and "highway" is defined loosely enough to take in anything remotely resembling a track passable by a wheeled vehicle.

Whether any of the areas are accessible by canoe, and whether this means of transportation will be permitted, is not known at this time. Admittedly, a more comfortable camp could be established by using a canoe, and transportation in and out would be easier.

The necessity of a special buck-and-doe season in this area can, in a sense, be attributed to the tendency of the average deer hunter to do his hunting the easy way. The wilderness area is hunted, but seldom does a hunter move in more than a mile from the nearest road. Consequently, the interior herds have built up to a point where the winter losses are excessive.

As deer often tend to remain on their range and face starvation rather than move, the department wisely decided it was better to provide sport and meat for hunters rather than accept the starvation losses.

To participate, the hunter must obtain a special license, costing $1.50, in addition to his regular deer license, and must have a camping permit if he plans to spend three days or longer. The special antlerless license applications will be available by writing the Department after Sept. 15, and applications will be accepted in order of receipt until the quota is exhausted.

The hunter must check in at one of the check stations upon entering the area, and contact the station upon departing. While hunting in the area he may take one buck and one antlerless deer, and in the event he has taken an antlered deer in another area, he may still enter for the purpose of taking an antlerless deer. The department explains that those participating will be doing a good "conservation" act.

Table for High Tide for Waters Adjacent to New York

Hours are given in Eastern Standard Time

July 3—Sun rises at 4:29 A.M., sets at 7:31 P.M.; moon rises at 7:52 A.M., sets at 9:32 P.M.

	Sandy Hook A.M.	Sandy Hook P.M.	Willets Point A.M.	Willets Point P.M.	Peconic Bay (Cutchogue) A.M.	Peconic Bay (Cutchogue) P.M.	Fire Island Inlet A.M.	Fire Island Inlet P.M.	Barnegat Bay Inlet A.M.	Barnegat Bay Inlet P.M.	New London A.M.	New London P.M.
Saturday, July 3	9:46	9:53	0:38	1:31	1:01	1:36	9:11	9:18	9:26	9:53	11:16	11:29
Sunday, July 4	10:35	10:59	1:42	2:18	1:49	2:26	10:00	10:04	10:15	10:19		12:16
Monday, July 5	11:22	11:24	2:23	3:0[illegible]	2:38	3:18	10:47	10:49	11:02	11:04	0:18	12:58
Tuesday, July 6		12:08	3:05	3:44	3:28	4:1[illegible]	11:33	11:33	11:48	11:18	1:08	1:52
Wednesday, July 7	0:08	12:52	3:51	4:31	4:23	5:05		12:17		12:32	2:03	2:15
Thursday, July 8	0:52	1:39	4:43	5:23	5:18	5:59	0:17	1:04	0:32	1:19	2:58	3:39
Friday, July 9	1:40	2:29	5:50	6:19	6:17	6:50	1:05	1:54	1:20	2:09	3:57	4:40

For high tide at Asbury Park and Belmar, N. J. deduct 40 minutes from Sandy Hook time.
For high tide at Atlantic City, N. J. (Steel Pier), deduct 35 minutes from Sandy Hook time.
(Supplied by the United States Coast and Geodetic Survey)

CRICKET STAR HITS 278

Compton's Score for England Post-War Test-Play Record

LONDON, July 2 (Reuters)—Denis Compton, in a brilliant batting display, today registered 278 in four hours 50 minutes on the second day of the second test cricket match between England and Pakistan at Nottingham.

It was the highest score in post-war tests throughout the world. The previous best was the 261 racked up by Frank Worrell, West Indies batsman, against England in 1950, on the Nottingham ground.

The outplayed Pakistan team fought back creditably after David Sheppard, England's captain, declared at 558 for six wickets.

Facing a deficit of 401, the touring team made 59 without loss in its second innings and will resume in the morning needing 342 to avoid an innings defeat.

The scores in first class cricket:

Pakistan 157 and 59 for no wicket, England 558 for six declared.

Hampshire 159 and 224, Nottinghamshire 324 for nine declared and 63 for no wicket. Nottinghamshire won by ten wickets.

Somerset 146 and 231 for nine declared, Royal Air Force 170 and 211 for eight. Royal Air Force won by two wickets.

Yorkshire 262 and 265, Northamptonshire 257 and 108. Yorkshire won by 162 runs.

Glamorgan 259 and 213, Essex 354 for nine declared and one run for no wicket. Match drawn.

Warwickshire 358 and 208 for three, Middlesex 339 for eight declared. Match drawn.

Leicestershire 232 and 104 for four declared, Lancashire 156 and 112 for four. Match drawn.

Sussex 322 for five declared, Cambridge University 126 and 353 for six. Match drawn.

Delaware Park Results

STANTON, DEL.

By The Associated Press.

SPECIAL EVENT—The Indian River Steeplechase Handicap; $10,000 added; 4-year-olds and up; about two and a half miles (no wagering).

Sun Shower, 159 (Smithwick) Out Out Out
Goose Bay, 135 (R. McDon'd) Out Out
Tourist List, 134 (K. Field) Out

Time—4:46 2-5. Monkey Wrench and Banner Waves also ran.

FIRST RACE—Purse $3,000; claiming; 3-year-olds; six furlongs.

Henryi, 117 (Cox) 5.60 3.80 2.60
Beauty Miss, 106 (Conlon) 6.00 3.00
A. Wanda, 113 (Vasil) 2.60

Time—1:12 1-5. The Tormentil, Sir Country, Keno Hill, Naval Affaire and Exorbitant also ran.

SECOND RACE—Purse $3,000; claiming; 3-year-olds; six furlongs.

Happy Rhythm, 119 (Cutshaw) 4.40 2.80 2.40
Shore Line, 108 (W. Passm're) 7.20 4.60
Cedar Lane, 116 (J. Regalb'o) 7.40

Time—1:12 3-5. Milady Mowlee, Nobel, Confuser, Golden Vale, Joan of Arc and J. P. Marquand also ran.

Daily double (Henryi and Happy Rhythm) paid $15.60.

THIRD RACE—Purse $3,000; claiming; 4-year-olds and up; six furlongs.

Challa Rock, 116 (J. Regalb'o) 35.20 10.00 7.20
Count Breeze, 116 (Westrope) 3.80 3.20
Mr. Lucille, 108 (Small) 8.40

Time—1:11 3-5. Race Tandem, Dream Paises, Moneeavay, Jeepersereeper, Nona Belle, Peconic and Puppet also ran.

FOURTH RACE—Purse $3,000; maiden 2-year-olds; five and a half furlongs.

Lady Browne, 117 (J. Regalb'o) 11.60 6.00 3.80
Coimbra, 117 (Lester) 10.20 5.80
Fine Lady, 117 (Vasil) 7.40

Time—1:06 4-5. Gau, Cumulus, Marga, Reta Run and Short Bit also ran.

FIFTH RACE—Purse $3,500; claiming; 2-year-olds; five and a half furlongs.

Chuck Thompson, 113 (W. Passm're) 5.60 2.60 2.40
Royal Punch, 113 (Cutshaw) 2.60 2.40
Williamsport, 115 (Cox) 3.40

Time—1:07. aStail's Pride, Tee Shirt, Picot and Thane of Fife also ran.
aSagey Farm-Cohen entry.

SIXTH RACE—Purse $4,000; optional claiming; 3-year-olds; six furlongs.

Helianthus, 111 (W. Passm're) 6.80 4.20 2.80
Ladies Nishil, 105 (Stovall) 7.40 4.00
Bones, 121 (Vasil) 3.00

Time—1:11 4-5. Turf Pic, Mike O'Hercon, Nick Zimmare, Border Son, Gosh and Capt Tim also ran.

SEVENTH RACE—Purse $3,500; claiming; 4-year-olds and up; 1½ miles.

[illegible]

Time—1:[illegible]. Hearth, Mouse, Privilege and Yellow Dot also ran.

EIGHTH RACE—Purse $3,500; claiming; maiden 3-year-olds and up; 1⅛ miles.

Tenn. Boy, 110 (J. Regalbuto) 18.00 7.60 4.80
Cedarscope, 105 (Stovall) 4.60 3.00
Flower Queen, 116 (Lester) 2.80

Time—1:56 3-5. Charity Ball, Bletto, Bow and Crown, Seeonee, Terry B., York Bill, Ruffler, Collision and General Fang also ran.

Attendance, 12,253. Pari-mutuel handle, $1,003,720.

Weather clear; track fast.

Miss Schneider Tennis Victor

Special to The New York Times.

BRONXVILLE, N. Y., July 2—Lorraine Schneider of Fort Pierce, Fla., beat Mary Pigott of Northford, Conn., 6—8, 6—1, 6—3, in the State junior girls' tennis final at the Field Club today. In the doubles final, Norma Harris of Brooklyn and Lorie Lewis of Yonkers defeated Miss Pigott and Nancy Niering of Newburgh, N. Y., 6—1, 6—2.

Sports Today

BASEBALL

Yankees vs. Washington Senators, at Yankee Stadium, River Avenue and 161st Street, the Bronx, 8:30 P. M. (Television—Channel 11, 8:25 P. M.).

BOXING

Hoacine Khalfi vs. Arthur Persley, at Atlantic City, N. J. (Television—Channel 7, 9 P. M.).

HARNESS RACING

Grand Circuit meeting, at Roosevelt Raceway, Westbury, L. I., 8:40 P. M.

HORSE RACING

Queens County Jockey Club meeting, at Aqueduct (Queens) race track, 1:15 P. M. (Television—Channel 2, 4 P. M.).

Monmouth Park, Oceanport, N. J., 2:30 P. M.

SHELTON MISSES MARK

High Jumper's Try Foiled by His Knee—Lea Takes Dash

GOTHENBURG, Sweden, July 2 (AP)—Ernie Shelton of the University of Southern California inspired Sweden's Bengt Nilsson to a Swedish high-jump record tonight but the American failed in his attempt to break the world record at an international track meet.

Shelton, in his first try, reached 6 feet 10½ inches and had three good attempts at 6 feet 11⅞ inches, a fraction of an inch over Walter Davis' world record set in 1953. Shelton was over the bar in his last leap, but touched it with his left knee on his way down and saw it fall.

Inspired by Shelton, Nilsson jumped 6 feet 7⅞ inches, a half-inch over the Swedish mark.

Jim Lea, also of the University of Southern California, won the 200-meter dash in 21.7 seconds.

The 1,000-meter event was taken by Harry Bright of New York in 2:27.8, followed by Lou Spurrier of Berkeley, Calif., in 2:28.2.

RATSEY SAILING WINNER

Scores as U. S. Crews Share Honors With Canadians

TORONTO, July 2 (AP)—United States and Canadian crews split the honors today in the first two of six international races in the Lake Sailing Skiffs Association regatta.

Canada took the first of three races for the Douglas Trophy in the 14-foot dinghy class, with Paul McLaughlin, Toronto, finishing in one hour five minutes 33 seconds. George O'Day of Boston was second with a time of 1:09.55.

In the first of three races for the Emerson Trophy, two-boat teams, Colin Ratsey of Essex, Conn., posted a first for the United States with a time of 1:08.27.

Crystal Blue First on Coast

INGLEWOOD, July 2 (AP)—J. Ross Clark's Crystal Blue scored a three-length victory in the $10,000 Miss Firecracker Handicap for 3-year-old fillies at Hollywood Park today. Frosty Dawn was second, while Satin Queen was third.

ISABEL TROCCOLE WINS, 2-6, 6-4, 10-8

Defeats Jane Breed to Gain Eastern Clay Court Final—Mrs. Kagan Triumphs

In a match lasting three and a quarter hours, Isabel Troccole of New York defeated Jane Breed of New Canaan, Conn., in the women's Eastern clay court tennis championship yesterday at the Bayside Tennis and Racquets Club. The score was 2—6, 6—4, 10—8.

Mrs. Nellie Sheer Kagan of New York, seeded first, won the other semi-final from Betty Coumbe of Westfield, N. J., 6—4, 6—3. She will play Miss Troccole, last year's winner of the title, at 11 o'clock this morning.

The final of the doubles will follow the singles. Miss Troccole and Mrs. Norma Laidlaw won their semi-final by default from Miss Breed and Joan Kock. Miss Breed was so spent after her singles match that she was unable to go on in the doubles. Miss Troccole and Mrs. Laidlaw will face Mrs. Elfie Carroll and Mrs. Louise Ganzenmuller of Sea Cliff for the title.

Miss Breed, a Vassar student, and Miss Troccole met in the final last year. Yesterday's match was much more of a fight. Both played beautifully at the net as well as from the back court.

In the final set Miss Troccole led, 3—1. Miss Breed went ahead at 4—3. After that it was even to 8-all. Miss Breed saved three match points before the end.

BILLY TALBERT IS UPSET

Beaten by Rubinoff in Tri-State Tennis—Miss Stewart Loses

CINCINNATI, July 2 (AP)—Billy Talbert of New York, a former national doubles champion, was eliminated today from the Tri-State tennis tournament by E. Rubinoff, 19, of Miami Beach. Talbert lost in the third round, 6—3, 3—6, 6—1. Earlier in the day he had scored a 6—4, 6—2 victory over Rawdon Mysters of Cincinnati.

The top ranked woman in the tourney, Pat Stewart of Indianapolis, also was ousted. Miss Stewart was defeated, 6—3, 7—5, by June Kroeger of Louisville.

Another Miami Beach player, 18-year-old Jerry Moss, surprised Fred Hagist of Berkley, Calif., 6—8, 6—0, 6—3. Hagis was the finalist in the 1952 Tri-State event.

Lois Felix of Meriden, Conn., second seeded; Ethel Norton of San Antonio, third seedet, and Karol Fageros of Miami, moved into the semi-finals with Miss Kroeger.

"All the News That's Fit to Print"

The New York Times.

LATE CITY EDITION
Partly cloudy today; chance of showers tonight and tomorrow.
Temperature Range Today—Max., 76; Min., 66
Temperature Yesterday—Max., 79; Min., 64
Full U. S. Weather Bureau Report, Page 4.

Copyright, 1954, by The New York Times Company.

VOL. CIV..No. 35,313. Entered as Second-Class Matter, Post Office, New York, N. Y. NEW YORK, THURSDAY, SEPTEMBER 30, 1954. FIVE CENTS

GIANTS WIN IN 10TH FROM INDIANS, 5-2, ON RHODES' HOMER

Pinch-Hitter Decides World Series Opener With 3-Run Wallop at Polo Grounds

52,751 SEE LEMON LOSE

Grissom Is Victor in Relief—Mays' Catch Saves Triumph—Wertz Gets 4 Hits

By JOHN DREBINGER

At precisely 4:12 o'clock by the huge clock atop the center-field clubhouse at the Polo Grounds yesterday afternoon, Leo Durocher peered intently at his hand and decided it was time to play his trump card.

It was the last half of the tenth inning in the opening game of the 1954 world series. The tense and dramatic struggle had a gathering of 52,751, a record series crowd for the arena, hanging breathlessly on every pitch.

The score was deadlocked at 2-all. Two Giants were on the base paths and on the mound was Bob Lemon, twenty-three-game winner of the American League, who had gone all the way and was making a heroic bid to continue the struggle a little further. Then Leo made his move.

He called on his pinch-hitter extraordinary, James (Dusty) Rhodes from Rock Hill, S. C., to bat for Monte Irvin. Lemon served one pitch. Rhodes, a left-handed batsman, swung and a lazy pop fly sailed down the right-field foul line.

Ball Just Clears Wall

The ball had just enough carry to clear the wall barely 270 feet away. But it was enough to produce an electrifying three-run homer that enabled the Giants to bring down Al Lopez' Indians, 5 to 2.

It was a breath-taking finish to as nerve-tingling a struggle as any world series had ever seen. The game had started as a stirring mound duel between 37-year-old Sal Maglie and the Tribe's brilliant Lemon.

It saw Vic Wertz, sturdy first sacker, rake Giant pitching for four of the Indians' eight hits. His first one was a triple that drove in two first-inning runs off Maglie. In the third the Polo Grounders wrenched those two tallies back from Lemon.

Then, in the eighth, Maglie faltered and Don Liddle, a mite of a southpaw, went in, almost to lose the game on the spot. With two runners on base, Wertz connected for another tremendous drive that went down the center of the field 450 feet, only to have Willie Mays make one of his most amazing catches.

Traveling on the wings of the wind, Willie caught the ball directly in front of the green boarding facing the right-center bleachers and with his back still to the diamond.

That brought on Marvin Grissom, another Giant relief ace, who was to go the rest of the way fending off one Cleveland threat after another. And in the tenth it was Willie the Wonder who again moved into the picture.

Mays Gets a Walk

For though Mays was to go hitless throughout the afternoon, here he made an offensive maneuver that presently was to set the stage for Rhodes' game-winning homer. With one out, Mays drew a pass, his second walk of the day.

Then, with Lemon pitching carefully to Henry Thompson, Willie stole second. That immediately changed Cleveland's strategy. Thompson received an intentional pass, doubtless in the hope that Irvin, whom Durocher had insisted on playing in left field and who had been ineffective, would obligingly slap into a double play. But Monte never went to bat.

Instead, up went Dusty. An instant later he leaned into the first pitch and produced a shot that doubtless was heard around the world, though for distance it likely could go as one of the shortest homers in world series history.

The ball hit the chest of a fan in the front row about seven feet from the foul line and bounced back on the playing field. It would have made no difference if the ball had been ruled in play, for Mays undoubtedly would have scored the winning run on the blow.

At any rate, the clout, which was only the fourth pinch homer

Continued on Page 40, Column 2

The New York Times (by Ernest Sisto)

PAY-OFF DRIVE: Dave Pope, Cleveland right fielder, goes high against the wall, about seven feet from foul line, in futile effort to grab home-run ball off the bat of Dusty Rhodes.

Registration Starts Today; Harriman Urges Big Vote

Registration in New York City and Westchester for this year's state election starts today and will continue, with two breaks, until a week from Saturday. In all, the registry books will be open for six days.

Today and tomorrow they will be open from 3:30 P. M. until 10:30 P. M. They will be closed Saturday and Sunday and will be open Monday, Tuesday and Friday of next week during the same hours. On the final day, Saturday, Oct. 9, they will be open from 7 A. M. to 10:30 P. M.

Outside of New York City and Westchester, registry books will be open in cities and in incorporated villages of 5,000 or more population, where personal registration is required, tomorrow, Saturday and the following Friday from 10 A. M. to 10 P. M. On Saturday, Oct. 9, they will be open from 7 A. M. to 10 P. M. Elsewhere personal registration is not required.

To qualify as a voter, a resident of New York must be a citizen, must be able to read and write English, must have reached his twenty-first birthday by Election Day, must have lived in the state for a year, in the county—or in the City of New York—for four months and in his election district for thirty days.

Because of the two breaks, many Democrats, including those heading this year's state ticket, are concerned lest the total number who qualify to vote by registering falls below previous years' figures. If it does, they fear their chances of winning will be impaired.

Averell Harriman, Democratic-Liberal candidate for Governor, voiced his concern openly last night in a radio address over Station WOR and warned potential voters that they would be unable to cast a ballot this year

Continued on Page 22, Column 4

NIXON EMPHASIZES 'AN UPHILL FIGHT'

Vice President Visits Upstate —Lauds Dewey and Javits and Attacks Stevenson

By PETER KIHSS

Special to The New York Times.

ALBANY, Sept. 29—Vice President Richard M. Nixon predicted today that the Republicans would pick up Senate seats in Illinois and Ohio at the November election, but "have an uphill fight" to retain control of the House of Representatives.

The Illinois gain would mean electing Joseph Meek in place of Democratic Senator Paul H. Douglas. An Ohio victory would have Representative George H. Bender ousting Senator Thomas Burke, a Democrat appointed to succeed the late Republican leader, Robert A. Taft.

Winding up the second day of his northeastern campaigning, Mr. Nixon told a Rensselaer County Republican field-day audience at Averill Park that the signals in a Democratic Congress would be called by "Americans for Democratic Action-Left Wing elements." These elements, he said, "ruthlessly ran the Chicago Convention [in 1952] and from whose ranks most of the gains the Democrats make in the House and Senate will inevitably come."

Questioned here on the basis of

Continued on Page 19, Column 4

CHRYSLER IS GIVEN A TANK CONTRACT

Company to Replace General Motors as the Sole Supplier of Patton M-48 Model

Special to The New York Times.

WASHINGTON, Sept. 29—The Army awarded today to the Chrysler Corporation a $160,601,200 contract for Patton M-48 medium tanks, now built solely by the General Motors Corporation.

Frank Higgins, Assistant Secretary of the Army, said Chrysler had underbid the Fisher Body division of General Motors, whose existing order for the Patton M-48 runs through next June, by $7,600,000.

Mr. Higgins and Robert T. Stevens, Secretary of Army, denied at a news conference that the award to Chrysler had been influenced by the complaint last week-end of Senator Henry M. Jackson, Democrat of Washington, that General Motors was getting the lion's share of defense contracts among the automobile companies.

"We couldn't run a railroad that way," Mr. Higgins said, meaning that the Army could not allow public criticism to dictate its placing of defense orders.

Kefauver Hails Award

Mr. Stevens said the competitive bids had been submitted two or three weeks ago, before Senator Jackson issued his statement. The Army's exclusive reliance on General Motors for light as well as medium tanks also had been criticized last winter by Senator Estes Kefauver, Democrat of Tennessee.

Senator Kefauver hailed the Chrysler award today, saying he was happy to learn that the corporation's Newark, Del., tank plant would be getting back into production.

"I have fought this fight from the beginning on the basis that it was uneconomic and dangerous for the Government to depend on one supplier—General Motors—in its tank production," he said.

The effect of the change, however, will be the replacement of General Motors by Chrysler as the only supplier of the Patton tank, once General Motors' present contract at Grand Blanc, Mich., has run out.

General Motors will continue to produce the M-41 Walker Bulldog light tank and the M-42 self-propelled gun at a Government-owned plant in Cleveland.

Chrysler, the Ford Motor Company and General Motors all built the M-48 tank when the post-Korean defense program was running at full tilt. Ford dropped out of the tank program almost a year ago and Chrysler halted M-48 production last summer.

The Army said Chrysler was scheduled to resume production at Newark next June, but reports from Detroit were that the company might get under way several months earlier. Continental

Continued on Page 14, Column 3

McCarran's Death Stirs Dispute; Ruling Is Awaited on a Successor

Special to The New York Times.

RENO, Nev., Sept. 29—Political leaders were awaiting a ruling today on procedure to be followed in choosing a successor to Democratic Senator Pat McCarran, who died unexpectedly last night.

William T. Mathews, Nevada's Attorney General, was to make the decision. He said he would not make his ruling until tomorrow, "at the earliest."

Keith Lee of Reno, Democratic State Chairman, cited a provision in the state law that authorizes party committees to nominate candidates for a general election when a vacancy occurs after the primary balloting.

Following this line, Mr. Lee called a meeting of the Democratic State Committee for the purpose of nominating a candidate for United States Senator. The committee will convene here at 1 P. M. Friday.

Gov. Charles H. Russell, a Republican candidate for re-election, interrupted a state-wide political tour to fly to Reno for conferences with leaders of his party.

Although some Republicans contended the state law cited by the Democrats applied only to cases where a candidate had been nominated for the general election, and Mr. McCarran's term does not expire until 1956, Governor Russell would not comment on the Democrats' stand. The Governor said only that if he was to appoint a successor to Mr. McCarran, he would name a Republican.

The State Republican Chairman, Tom Smith of Ely, called a meeting of his central committee for tomorrow night. Pending the Attorney General's ruling, the Republicans were not planning to nominate a candidate.

Prominently mentioned as a

Continued on Page 21, Column 1

JENNER REQUESTS WATKINS TESTIFY ON RULES CHANGES

Points to 'One-Man Hearing' Held by the Chairman of McCarthy Censure Group

By ANTHONY LEVIERO

Special to The New York Times.

WASHINGTON, Sept. 29—Senator William E. Jenner today invited Senator Arthur V. Watkins, chairman of the committee that recommended censure of Senator Joseph R. McCarthy, to testify on his proposals for Senate rules changes.

Mr. Jenner, an Indiana Republican, and an adherent of the Wisconsin Republican, is chairman of the Senate Rules Committee.

Earlier in the day, he expressed curiosity about the fact that Senator Watkins, a Utah Republican, had held a "one-man hearing," although the censure report urged the Senate to prohibit such hearings.

Senator Jenner referred to questioning of Charles L. Watkins, the Senate parliamentarian, who is no relation to Senator Watkins.

"I'm sure there may have been circumstances that justified it," Senator Jenner said, "but I will be interested to hear the testimony of Senator Watkins on this subject."

Situation Outlined

The situation with respect to the parliamentarian was this:

Senator McCarthy, in his defense against the censure charges, contended that he had refused to appear before a Senate Elections subcommittee that investigated him in 1952 because, among other reasons, he believed that it was not a legal group.

Senator Carl Hayden, Democrat of Arizona and 1952 chairman of the Rules Committee, testified that the Elections subcommittee was legal and produced a supporting memorandum that his secretary had obtained from the parliamentarian. Senator Watkins ruled the memorandum was hearsay evidence and decided to seek the testimony of the parliamentarian himself.

The parliamentarian was convalescing from a serious operation, however, and it was decided that he would be questioned by means of joint interrogatories of the Watkins committee and of Edward Bennett Williams, counsel for Senator McCarthy. The interrogatories were to be sent to the parliamentarian's home.

But Mr. Watkins managed to appear in person and was questioned by the Watkins committee, and testified the subcommittee was valid. Mr. Williams, who was not present, protested that the questioning had gone beyond the interrogatories.

The committee felt it had merely added some clarifying questions as Mr. Watkins talked. But the chairman recalled the parliamentarian, and on the second occasion, Senator Watkins interrogated him while other members of the committee were in an adjoining room, the door open.

Continued on Page 18, Column 1

U. S.-BRITISH MILITARY AID PLEDGED TO UNITED EUROPE; SWIFT PACT ON BONN LIKELY

PARIS HELD VICTOR

Premier Said to Have Won British Promise Bidault Asked in Vain

By HAROLD CALLENDER

Special to The New York Times.

PARIS, Sept. 29—Premier Pierre Mendès-France appears to have obtained from Britain today a commitment similar to that the French tried in vain to get at the Bermuda conference last December.

At that time his predecessor as Foreign Minister, Georges Bidault, asked that Britain and the United States agree to station their troops on the Continent of Europe without reduction until the French Government consented to a change in that policy. Now Britain seems ready to agree to keep contingents of the size of her present ones in Germany as long as a majority of the Brussels treaty nations consider their presence necessary.

These nations, under the planned revisions of the treaty, will be Britain, France, West Germany, Italy, Belgium, the Netherlands and Luxembourg.

Thus there would be a British commitment as to the time and as to the number of troops that would be dependent on the judgment of other nations, except in the emergencies mentioned by Anthony Eden, British Foreign Secretary.

British Pledge Is Broad

Never has Britain or probably any other nation made such a commitment. The United States cannot constitutionally make any similar one, as John Foster Dulles, Secretary of State, explained today.

In agreeing that other nations might determine Britain's policy regarding troops on the Continent, the British Government in effect accepted a form of supranational authority such as the French National Assembly had rejected in turning down the European Defense Community.

This British action should go a long way to reassure the French and to enable M. Mendès-France to get his parliament to accept West Germany's entry into the North Atlantic Treaty Organization.

For one of the main conditions attached to the European Defense Community project by the French National Assembly was that there should be assurance of the presence of British and United States troops on the Continent.

The dominant French aim at the London conference has been to tie the British as tightly as possible in a new kind of French-British alliance.

With a solid British tie, the

Continued on Page 6, Column 4

The New York Times

Gen. Alfred M. Gruenther as he spoke here last night.

GRUENTHER HAILS GAINS IN DEFENSE

Says Bonn Arming and Atom Bomb Could Bar a Soviet Sweep 3 to 4 Years Hence

By RUSSELL PORTER

Gen. Alfred M. Gruenther, Supreme Allied Commander in Europe, predicted last night that West German armament and the tactical use of the atomic bomb could produce in three or four years a reasonably good chance of preventing the Soviet Union from overrunning Europe.

He said further that, although the North Atlantic Treaty Organization was making progress, "we still do not have enough to meet an all-out attack of Soviet aggression successfully."

General Gruenther spoke before 1,800 persons at the eleventh annual dinner of the National Security Industrial Association at the Waldorf-Astoria Hotel. His topic was "The Defense of Western Europe—a Progress Report."

He flew here from Paris yesterday for a short visit. Tomorrow he will fly to St. Paul, Minn., to receive an honorary degree from the College of St. Thomas. He will then go to Washington before flying back to Europe.

Military Progress Noted

In an interview at La Guardia Field he said the integration of West Germany into the North Atlantic Treaty Organization would be helpful. Last night in his speech he said he felt there were good chances of reaching a solution of the German problem at the London conference.

The general said he was sure that Pierre Mendès-France, the French Premier, was determined to solve the problem of West Germany at the London nine-power conference and to find an arrangement for "bringing the Germans into an organization where they will be able to contribute to the defense of Europe."

While the political crisis of arming West Germany has been developing, steady progress has been made on the military side, General Gruenther added.

He said he had just returned from this year's European maneuvers of Atlantic alliance forces. He declared these military exercises had demonstrated an improvement in effectiveness that was not dreamed of when President Eisenhower went to Europe in 1951 as General Gruenther's predecessor.

While there were deficiencies that need correction, the state of

Continued on Page 8, Column 4

9 POWERS CHEERED

Offer by Dulles and Eden Disperses Squabbles on German Arming

Texts of statements by Eden and Dulles, Page 4.

By DREW MIDDLETON

Special to The New York Times.

LONDON, Sept. 29—The United States and Britain pledged full military support for a united Europe today. Thus they broke the back of French resistance to the restoration of West Germany's military and political independence.

John Foster Dulles, United States Secretary of State, and Anthony Eden, British Foreign Secretary, dispersed squabbles over controls and restrictions on Germany by statements to the nine-power conference this afternoon that convinced Pierre Mendès-France, French Premier and Foreign Minister, "a solution now is in sight."

This transformation was accomplished by the bold use of the diplomatic initiative.

It is not discounting the value of the United States pledge to say that from the French standpoint the British guarantee of continued military commitments on the Continent is the more important.

Jettisoning its traditional military insularity, the British Government promised to maintain on the mainland of Europe four divisions and a tactical air force. In the eyes of the French, this force, with that contributed by France to the defense of the Continent, will balance the power of a rearmed Germany.

Both Pledges Conditional

Both pledges are conditional on the establishment of a united Europe under the Brussels Treaty Organization and the North Atlantic Treaty Organization. But the guarantees are such that this outcome is now considered assured.

The conference had been stumbling over familiar obstacles such as the future of the Saar, controls on the size of forces and the location of armaments industries when Mr. Dulles intervened.

The essence of Mr. Dulles' statement was that if the conference, using the Brussels treaty as a nucleus, was able to create a system of European unity embodying the great aspirations of the European Defense Community, he would recommend to President Eisenhower that the United States renew a pledge comparable to that offered to the defense community.

This pledge was given by President Eisenhower to the premiers of six signatory powers to the defense community treaty April 16 this year. Its principal undertaking is:

"The United States of America will continue to maintain in Europe, including Germany, such units of its armed forces as may be necessary and appropriate to contribute its fair share of the forces needed for the joint defense of the North Atlantic area

Continued on Page 4, Column 4

U. S. Would Link Atom Unit To U. N. as Special Agency

By THOMAS J. HAMILTON

Special to The New York Times.

UNITED NATIONS, N. Y., Sept. 29—The United States wants the proposed new agency for developing peaceful uses of atomic energy to be on a basis corresponding to that of a specialized agency of the United Nations.

The new agency thus would not be a part of the United Nations itself, but would be connected with it on a basis similar to that of the World Health Organization, the United Nations Educational, Scientific and Cultural Organization and other agencies.

These agencies, most of which were established concurrently with the United Nations itself, are intended to further United Nations aims in particular fields. However, each has its separate budget and secretariat and all of them have established headquarters away from United Nations headquarters. Most of them have settled in Europe.

The exact form of the proposed atomic agency is being worked out in Washington and in discussions with the five original countries—Britain, France, Canada, Australia and South Africa—that this month to take part in setting it up. According to tentative plans, the headquarters would be in Washington.

Under legislation approved by Congress last summer, the rigid security regulations on all information connected with atomic energy were relaxed somewhat to permit the United States to share with friendly countries certain information about peaceful uses.

However, these changes did not authorize the United States to allocate nuclear fuel or divulge information to the proposed agency. Once its form was determined, the Eisenhower Administration would have to ask Congress for enabling legislation for these purposes.

Last week, at the start of the current session of the General Assembly, Secretary of State John Foster Dulles announced the four-point atomic program of the United States, including an international scientific conference to be held next spring under the auspices of the United Nations.

Mr. Dulles did not say what connection the proposed agency would have with the United Nations. He merely asked the Assembly to put the program on its agenda for a "report" by the United States on its efforts

Continued on Page 10, Column 5

Russia Re-Viewed

Today's installment of the series by Harrison E. Salisbury, a correspondent of The New York Times who has just returned to this country after five years in the Soviet Union, will be found on Page 33.

Pole Now Suggests Noel Field, Wife Dead

By WALTER H. WAGGONER

Special to The New York Times.

WASHINGTON, Sept. 29—Jozef Swiatlo, former Polish secret police official, said today he believed Noel Field and his wife Herta, United States citizens seized by Hungary five years ago, were dead.

Mr. Swiatlo also related that Hermann Field, Noel's brother jailed in Poland, had twice gone on a hunger strike, had attempted suicide by hanging, and now faced almost certain death in his prison cell.

After his suicide attempt, Hermann Field tried to send a letter to the United States Embassy in Warsaw, according to Mr. Swiatlo. The note was intercepted, however, and he never received his destination, he said.

The former Polish internal security officer broke with Warsaw last December and has been

Continued on Page 13, Column 1

Heroics of Mays, Rhodes, Grissom Regarded as Routine by Happy Giants

Wide World Photos

Willie Mays making sensational catch of Vic Wertz' 450-foot drive in the eighth inning. After taking the ball on the dead run, Mays wheels around and throws back to the infield.

GIANTS WIN IN 10TH FROM INDIANS, 5-2

Continued From Page 1

hit in a modern fall classic, served its purpose. It sent the National Leaguers roaring out of the arena.

It was a steaming, summery afternoon right out of a July calendar. As Perry Como, accompanied by Artie White's orchestra, led the crowd in the singing of the national anthem, white shirts were the fashion in the sun-bathed seats along the left side of the park. Then the spotlight turned on 12-year-old Jimmy Barbieri, captain of Schenectady's champion team of Little Leaguers, who at this moment doubtless was the proudest youngster in all the land.

Youngster Tosses First Ball

They had conferred the honor of tossing out the first ball upon Jimmy and there were lusty cheers as he fired it with a thud into the big mitt of Wes Westrum, the Giants' catcher. A moment later the fifty-first modern world series was on its way and in no time at all it became evident that not all in the packed stands were Giant partisans.

The American League had its representation, too, including disgruntled Yankee fans, not to mention a few disguised National Leaguers from Brooklyn.

And they made their presence known in no mistaken tones as Maglie got off to a shaky start that sent the Indians off to a two-run lead.

The Barber, whose control is his chief stock in trade and is usually razor sharp, confounded nearly everyone by serving three wide pitches to Al Smith, Cleveland's lead-off batter.

The fourth pitch was even wider, hitting Smith in the side, and the first man up was on. Bobby Avila, the American League's batting champion, followed. Maglie served another ball, making it five in a row that missed the plate. A feeling of uneasiness swept through the stands.

Finally Maglie sent over a strike. It brought a cheer, but the applause was short-lived. For Avila stroked the next one into right field for a single and when Don Mueller, charging the ball, fumbled it, Smith raced to third. The Indians had runners on first and third with nobody out.

Here, the Barber of old asserted himself. He snuffed out Larry Doby, the American League's top home-run clouter, on the end of a pop foul that Thompson gobbled up back of third, and the slugging Al Rosen went out on an infield pop-up to Whitey Lockman.

But Maglie's opening-round troubles weren't over yet and a moment later the situation became serious as Wertz lined a powerful drive over Mueller's head in deep right-center. The ball caromed off the wall and bounded gaily past the Giant bullpen before the fleet-footed Mays collared it and started it on its way toward the infield.

Liddle Warms Up

When order was restored, Wertz was on third with a triple, Smith and Avila had crossed the plate to put the Tribe two in front and Liddle started warming up with feverish haste in the Giant bullpen. But Maglie wasn't needing any help yet. He got Dave Philley to line the ball to Mueller for the third out, and Giant fans breathed again.

In fact, in a few more minutes the New York fans were setting up quite a din of their own as, in the lower half of the first, the Polo Grounders launched their first threat against Lemon. With one down, Alvin Dark drew a pass and Mueller punched a single to right, sweeping Dark around to third.

But Lemon quickly quelled the uprising. With the crowd imploring Mays to square matters, Willie went out on a pop fly to George Strickland, Cleveland shortstop, and Thompson ended it by grounding to Wertz down the first-base line.

With the third, however, the Giants did draw even as they lashed into Lemon for three singles which, along with a pass, gave them two tallies. Lockman, the blond North Carolinian, opened the assault on the Cleveland right-hander with a single to right and a moment later was on his way to third as Dark blasted a single through the mound and into center field.

Mueller folowed with a grounder to Avila that resulted in a force play at second, but it permitted Lockman to score. Mays walked and Thompson singled to right to drive in Mueller, and the contest was tied at 2—all.

What is more, the Giants had runners on first and third, there was only one out and it was now Cleveland's turn to show uneasiness in the dugout. In the Tribe bullpen Art Houtteman started warming up.

But Lemon stopped the assault himself. He fanned Irvin, who patrolled left field in place of Rhodes, and Davey Williams ended matters with a grounder to short.

But the Giant fans were happy. Maglie was back on an even footing with the American League's top winning pitcher and from here on it was touch and go.

Westrum Gets Two Hits

For a time both hurlers steadied. There were two Giant singles in the fourth. One was by Westrum, the Polo Grounders' supposedly weak-hitting receiver, who contributed two blows to the New York final total of nine. But the second safety of the inning by Dark fell with two out, and Lemon got out of that spot.

Meanwhile, Maglie was staging a fine recovery, even though Wertz clipped him for a single to left in the fourth, and it wasn't until the sixth that the Barber seemed headed for more trouble.

Again his tormentor was Wertz, who this time singled to right, with Mueller adding another error. Don tried to nip the runner off first, but his throw shot by Lockman and Vic wound up on second. An infield out put him on third with one down.

But Maglie got Strickland to pop up and then was saved when Thompson came up with the first of several sparkling plays he made at third. Knocking down Jim Hegan's hard smash over the bag, Henry had to recover the ball in foul territory. Yet he fired it to first in time to make the third out, and in the seventh Thompson again made a fine stop. Henry was really playing a great defensive game at the hot corner.

In the eighth, however, Maglie faltered again. He walked Doby, and Rosen, hitless to this point, banged a scorching single off Dark's bare hand. That brought in Liddle, who saw Wertz almost wreck everything with his tremendous bid for a fourth straight hit. Mays alone saved Don with his miraculous catch in center.

Grissom went in immediately as both managers now surcharged the air with masterminding maneuvers. Lopez already had sent up Hank Majeski to pinch-hit for Philley, but when Leo switched to the right-handed Grissom, Lopez countered with Dale Mitchell, a left-handed batter. This duel of wits ended with Mitchell drawing a pass, filling the bases with one out.

The Indians were poised for a big killing, and as another lefty swinger, Dave Pope, capable of hitting a long ball, stepped up to bat for Strickland, the National League enthusiasts scarcely were able to breathe.

Grissom Fans Pope

But Grissom slipped a third strike over on an astonished Indian and that doubtless was the turning point of the battle. A moment later the inning and big threat ended with Hegan flying out.

In the last of the eighth the Giants crowded Lemon for the first time since the third. Thompson walked and presently got around to third on a sacrifice and a wild pitch. But Westrum ended this threat with a long fly to Doby in center.

In the ninth Giant hearts stopped beating when, with two out, Irvin, dropped Avila's pop fly for a two-base error. That put Grissom in a jam again, but he got out of it by giving Doby an intentional pass and rubbing out Rosen on another fly to left, which Irvin this time froze to with a great sigh of relief.

In the top of the tenth the desperately straining Clevelanders made another bid and once more Wertz started it. Vic blasted a double into left-center that even Mays couldn't track down. As Wertz jogged off the field after being replaced by a pinch-runner, Rudy Regalado, the crowd generously gave him an ovation.

Sam Dente's sacrifice put Regalado on third with only one out. But Grissom fanned Glynn after Pope walked, and Lemon, striving to win his own game, lined the ball squarely into Lockman's glove inches off the ground.

That was to prove the Indians' last threat, for in the last of the tenth it all vanished on the end of Rhodes' poke.

The pinch home run, which so spectacularly had won for the Giants all summer, had paid off again. During the regular season the Polo Grounders had set a major league record with ten pinch home runs. Rhodes contributed two of these.

In world series play the only previous pinch homers ever hit were those by Yogi Berra of the Yanks in 1947, Johnny Mize, another Yank, in 1952 and George Shuba of the Dodgers last year. And yesterday's game was the first extra-inning affair since Oct. 5, 1952, when the Dodgers beat the Yankees, 6—5, in eleven innings.

And so Leo the Lip considered himself sitting pretty last night as he prepared to fire his south-paw ace, Johnny Antonelli, against the Clevelanders in the second game at the Polo Grounds this afternoon.

There were, to be sure, some critics unkind enough to remark that had Leo played Rhodes in left field from the beginning, victory might have come easier. Perhaps so, but then just look at the tremendous thrill the crowd, which had to pay a net sum of $316,957 into the till, would have missed.

As for Lopez, the Cleveland skipper's big hope was that his other twenty-three-game winner Early Wynn, would fare better than Lemon and square the series before it moves to Cleveland tomorrow.

MAYS' CATCH APPRAISED

Although Willie Mays had no answer when asked if his catch of Vic Wertz' terrific drive yesterday was his greatest or not, his chief admirer—and an expert observer—had one.

Tom Sheehan, the chief scout for the Giants, said, "His greatest catch, and the greatest I ever saw anybody make, was in Ebbets Field. He caught a ball 'way down here (Sheehan indicated a point a few inches from the ground) on the cinder track in left center, rolled over against the wall and came up with the ball.

"His catch on a ball hit by Bob Skinner of the Pirates was better than the one against Wertz, and I think one he caught off Bill Bruton of the Milwaukee Braves was better."

REMINDER OF GIONFRIDDO

DiMaggio Calls Dodger's Catch Better Than Mays' Play

Joe DiMaggio offered his divergent opinion about Willie Mays' spectacular catch of Vic Wertz' drive in yesterday's opening game.

"I think that the catch Al Gionfriddo made on the ball I hit in the sixth game of the 1947 series with the Dodgers was greater than Mays' catch."

The catch the former Yankee referred to was a tremendously high drive that the little outfielder caught leaning against the exit gate in left field at Yankee Stadium.

The play by Gionfriddo was, in the opinion of most observers, easier than Willie's catch—but DiMaggio hit the ball and sticks to his opinion.

Cleveland Contends Wind Contributed to Downfall

BREEZE IS BLAMED FOR AIDING HOMER

Indians Say Wind Sent Rhodes Drive Into Stands, Allowed Hegan Blow to Be Caught

By LOUIS EFFRAT

An ill wind, the Indians said, blew them out of the ball game at the Polo Grounds yesterday. The same left-to-right air current that prevented Jim Hegan's long drive to left from going into the stands in the eighth inning pushed Dusty Rhodes' game-winning homer into the stands in the tenth, they insisted.

In the dressing room, five minutes after the dramatic wind-up, the beaten Indians reviewed numerous incidents in the contest but, with one exception, the spectacular catch by Willie Mays, the wind dominated each discussion. Al Lopez, Al Rosen, Hegan, Wally Westlake, Bobby Avila, Dave Pope, almost everyone had something to say on the same subject.

Lopez said it most articulately and with the least emotion. "Yes, the wind hurt us," he declared. "I thought Bob Lemon pitched well enough to win and we played well enough behind him to have beaten a good Giant ball club.

"Hegan hit a ball nearly 400 feet to left with the bases filled and two out in the eighth. It looked like a homer, but the wind, blowing toward the right, pulled the ball in so that Monte Irvin was able to make the catch.

Ball Thought to Be Foul

"But the same wind didn't do right by us when Rhodes came up with two on in the tenth. Dusty didn't hit that ball too well and we all thought it was going to twist foul, but the wind held it in fair territory and pushed it into the stands. I realized it was going to be fair, but I didn't think it would reach the wall."

At this point Rosen remarked that it was "a 257½-foot homer." Others joined in. Avila said he raced back confident that he or Pope, the right-fielder at the time, would be able to capture the pop fly.

Lemon took the defeat gracefully. "I threw Rhodes a curve, a good curve," he said, "and Dusty hit it. That was his job—to hit it and I give him all the credit in the world. Never mind what kind of hit it was, he hit it."

Did the right-hander think the ball was going to travel so far?

"I didn't know what to think," Lemon replied. "After all, I'm a stranger here. They tell me everything that is hit in this park goes 500 feet on paper. I do know that he hit a good curve, one that I wouldn't hesitate to throw to him again. I'd like another chance to try it, anyway."

Unanimously the Indians agreed that the catch by Mays, robbing Vic Wertz in the eighth, was the turning point in the encounter. Willie's amazing, almost incredible back-to-the-plate snare with Larry Doby at second and Rosen at first and none out took the Tribe out of a most promising inning. "It was one of the greatest catches I ever have seen," Lopez averred. Doby, a centerfielder, echoed his manager's praise of Mays.

Wertz, the batting star of the first world series game, with a triple, two singles and a double, said, "I never hit a ball so hard in my career as the one Willie caught."

Wertz Failed to Take Third

Vic then explained his failure to go to third, following his lead-off single to right in the sixth. On that play Don Mueller, the local right-fielder, fired to first as Wertz made a turn toward second.

The ball flew over the head of Whitey Lockman, the first-sacker, and bounced past Wes Westrum, the catcher. Wertz, after returning to first, ran to second, then, despite frantic waves by Tony Cuccinello, the third base coach for Cleveland, Vic made no effort to continue.

Since 1952, when he was injured by his own foul-tip, Vic has been wearing a fiber shin guard when batting. When he returned to first and kicked the bag, he inadvertently opened the clasp of the guard. This flapping fiber, which weighs approximately a pound, hampered his running and he elected to remain at second.

In the tenth Mays walked and stole second, getting a big jump on the pitcher. Mickey Grasso, the catcher at the time, had to hurry his throw, which reached second on a bounce, and Mays was credited with an easy steal. Grasso insisted on taking the full blame. "I just made a bad throw," he said.

Lopez refused to disclose what he said to Lemon on the mound, before he pitched to Mays in the third. The pilot also declined to reveal what he said to the plate umpire, Al Barlick, a minute later. However, Lemon supplied the answers.

"Oh, that," he said. "Barlick had told Hegan to tell me that I was not coming to a halt on my wind-up. Lopez came out and told me not to let it bother me. I didn't.

"I just made sure of stopping and it helped me rather than bothered me. I wasn't too sharp in the early innings, but later my control was better."

Rosen's injured thigh and Doby's wrenched shoulder slowed both Cleveland aces, but they will continue to play. The only change in the line-up might be Westlake for Dave Philley in right field.

STARS' PLAY FAILS TO SURPRISE PILOT

Durocher Declares Heroes of Opener Have Turned in Top Performances All Year

By ROSCOE McGOWEN

It was difficult to find the No. 1 hero in the Giants' clubhouse yesterday. Of course, Dusty Rhodes, who popped Bob Lemon's first pitch into the right field stands to win the ball game, was a big man.

But so was Marv Grissom, with his great relief pitching, especially in the eighth when the Indians threatened to break the game wide open.

And how about Willie Mays? The catch Willie made on Vic Wertz' more than 450-foot drive in that same eighth inning was another one of those "out-of-this-world" plays—but not for Mays.

"I've been watching him make catches like that so long," said a tired but happy Leo Durocher, as he sat before his locker, "that I couldn't say it was the greatest."

Willie Had Ball All the Way

Willie, his usual happy self, couldn't say about that, either.

"I don't know whether I made a greater catch any time," said Willie. "I just try to get a jump on the ball and go get it. I thought I had that one all the way," he grinned.

When Rhodes' homer was deprecated slightly, Durocher grinned broadly and retorted:

"Look, he's been doing that for me all year. I don't care where they go when he hits 'em. All I know about that one is that they had to have a ticket to catch it."

Rhodes had a rather funny observation to make about his homer.

"The minute I hit it I knew it was going in—or he'd catch it."

Al Dark, asked just how far the ball went in and where, said, "I'd say it was five or ten feet fair and it just dropped over the top of the wall."

Sal Maglie, who was lifted in the eighth inning, was asked about Wertz, who had smacked the Barber for a triple and two singles. Did Sal find Wertz a tough guy to pitch to?

Distance Not Sole Factor

"He was tough all right," replied Maglie. Then he grinned and added: "he was good enough to hit a 420-foot triple and a 450-foot out but Vic should have done what Rhodes did—just hit a 270-foot home run."

Grissom's pitching brought praise from Durocher, but also with the familiar line that "he's been doing it all year."

"Marv did a magnificent job," said Leo. "Just the sort of thing he has done right along. He gives you all he's got all the time."

Maglie also added something on Grissom. "He's got it in here," said Sal, pointing to his heart. "He's always in there with that old will to win, and that," added the Barber, with emphasis, "helps a lot."

Grissom said he threw a high screwball to Dave Pope when the Cleveland pinchhitter looked at a third strike for the second out in the eighth with the bases filled.

"What fooled Pope," interposed Freddy Fitzsimmons, the Giants' coach, "was that the ball came in high and he may have thought it was a fast ball, because Grissom's screwball is pretty fast.

"When the ball broke down, it had him fooled and it was too late for him to swing."

The New York Times

Dusty Rhodes waves his big bat in dressing room after winning game with dramatic homer with two on in tenth inning.

Sports of The Times

By ARTHUR DALEY

The Psychic Durocher Clicks

THE Merriwell boys are still in business. In another of their frantic and fictional finishes, the Giants wrenched the opening game of the world series from the Indians at the Polo Grounds yesterday. They did it in the same implausible fashion they had used for winning the big ones all year long—with a pinch-hit home run.

For the better part of ten innings Leo Durocher had been writhing in envy while the usually unobtrusive Al Lopez was encroaching on his preserves. The Señor had juggled his line-up with sure-handed dispatch. He tossed in pinch-hitters, a pinch-runner and even a pinch-hitter for a pinch-hitter. Except for two pitching changes, poor Leo was out of it, a victim of his own self restraint.

But the Dandy Little Manager pounced on his ouija board in the tenth and began communing with the spirit world. The answer came. "Use Dusty Rhodes," whispered the spectral voices. The ouija board jerked furiously to "yes." So Leo used Dusty, and Dusty hit a home run.

Nothing Fancy

When Babe Ruth played at the Polo Grounds, he was in the habit of belting majestic wallops out of sight. Shoeless Joe Jackson, they say, once hit one out of the ball park and onto Eighth Avenue. Dusty's homer was not precisely that type. It was a mite shorter. In fact, that's the understatement of the century.

It was a harmless little pop-up that peeked timidly above the roof of the grandstand and then was wafted gently closer and closer to the front row of the seats near the foul-line. Dave Pope, the Cleveland right fielder, was so sure he could get it that he leaped high with glove outstretched. But another gust prankishly brushed it a couple of inches more and it was a home run.

You have heard the expression, "Chinese home run." This hit was more Chinese than chow mein and just as Chinese as Shanghai and Peiping. But the homer will go in the record book with no more fanfare than the dramatic one Ruth hit off Charlie Root after calling his shot in the 1932 series. It will merely read: Home run—Rhodes. The measurement will not be given.

But Leo did set the stage for it with a slick managerial move that lots of folks didn't notice. With one out in the tenth Willie Mays had walked. Willie the Wonder is swift, but not a clever base stealer. He would never have dared to run on the cat-like, rifle-armed Jim Hegan, the Cleveland catcher. But Hegan had departed for a pinch-hitter in the tenth and Mickey Grasso was behind the plate. Mickey is a noble character, but he would have difficulty throwing out his grandmother, if that kindly lady had elected to attempt to purloin a base.

So the Little Shepherd of Coogan's Bluff flashed the steal sign to Willie. Grasso's throw was a one-bouncer. Willie slid under it. So there was nothing for the Indians to do but give Henry Thompson an intentional walk, which was what the Machiavellian Durocher had been plotting all along. It gave him a chance to use Rhodes. Well, Dusty hit a titanic smash—or at least a smash—or at least he hit something. Feeble though it was, the shot won the ball game.

The amusing part about this Chinese effort is that both base runners, Mays and Thompson, had to hold up for fear that the ball would be caught. Willie the Wonder, an incredulous look on his smiling face, was just a few feet beyond second base and Henry not far from the bag. Henry started to run. Willie was transfixed, rooted to the ground in admiration.

Imperiously he raised his hand to Thompson. "Slow down, man," he piped in his shrill voice. "Don't you go passin' me on the base paths." And Willie directed traffic the rest of the way home. He touched third base firmly and then pointed back to it so that Henry wouldn't forget to implant a brogan on it. He looked back to make sure Rhodes did the same. Then the three of them crossed home plate as tightly packed as three subway riders whisking through the same turnstile.

Grand Larceny

Willie the Wonder dominated this game in many respects. He made a catch in the eighth inning that had to be seen to be believed and even then you couldn't quite believe it. This was akin to an optical illusion. With two men on base, Vic Wertz belted a shot to center that must have gone almost twice as far as Rhodes' homer.

It roared over the head of the 'Mazing Mays, with Willie the Wonder in hot pursuit. Catching the ball appeared a sheer impossibility. But Willie, running like a frightened gazelle for the bleacher wall and with his back to the plate, speared it over his shoulder with gloved hand. It was one of the great catches in world series history.

In the tenth Willie held the pesky Wertz to a double on a blast to left center, a shot that might have been a triple. He made a throw to third base from against the bleacher wall that looked as if it had come from a howitzer. As a matter of fact, the Giants were walking a tightrope for the last three innings, teetering perilously but never losing balance.

Then came Leo the Magnificent with his magic act in the last of the tenth. It was a sure-fire sensation. It always is.

Section 5 | SPORTS | BOATS—AUTOMOBILES

The New York Times.

SPORTS | SHOPPING GUIDE | Section 5

S Copyright, 1955, by The New York Times Company. SUNDAY, MAY 8, 1955. L+++ S

SWAPS BEATS NASHUA IN DERBY; NAVY CREW LOSES; DODGERS DEFEAT PHILS, 6-3; GIANTS AND YANKEES WIN

NO. 5 FOR ERSKINE

Brooks Win 20th Game in 22—Fans Toss Cans at Umpires in 7th

By ROSCOE McGOWEN

Special to The New York Times.

PHILADELPHIA, May 7—Still rolling in high gear, the Dodgers and Carl Erskine beat the Phils and Robin Roberts, 6—3, tonight for the Brooks' ninth straight triumph. The Brooks have won twenty of their twenty-two games.

Three of the Dodger runs were unearned. The defeat was the eighth in a row for the Phils, who tumbled into the National League cellar.

In the seventh inning, after Art Gore, plate umpire, had chased Earl Torgeson, Roberts and Jack Meyer from the Phillies' bench, there loomed the possibility that the game would be forfeited to the Brooks.

Dozens of fans in the Connie Mack Stadium crowd of 27,922 showed their anger by throwing empty beer cans on the field near Gore and Jocko Conlan, the third-base arbiter.

Conlan Threatens Forfeit

The game was held up for ten minutes. Conlan finally rushed to the park announcer and ordered the announcement made that the game would be forfeited if the can-throwing didn't cease.

A few more cans were tossed, but the game finally was resumed. The Phils at the moment had a mild threat going, Bobby Morgan having opened with a single. But Erskine not only retired the next three men but continued that procedure to the end of the game.

Erskine now has won five games without a loss. The unfortunate Roberts has broken even in six games. Two of his losses were to Brooklyn.

All the Philadelphia runs were scored on homers. Willie Jones whacked two of them and Del Ennis the other.

Ennis opened the fourth with a drive into the lower left field stands just inside the foul pole. Jones followed by walloping a first pitch off the upper left field stands. It was No. 5 for each man.

The Dodgers scored their three unearned runs off Roberts in the third inning. At the start, Carl Furillo was safe on Gran Hamner's wild throw. Then Erskine lifted a simple fly ball to left center field. Ennis and Richie Ashburn converged on the ball at an easy trot.

Gilliam Beats Out Bunt

Apparently each thought the other would catch the ball. Ashburn made a final grab, but muffed it for an error. Then Junior Gilliam beat out an unplayable bunt toward third base to fill the bases.

Pee Wee Reese scored Furillo with a long sacrifice drive to Ennis and Duke Snider rammed a hot single through the middle to score Erskine. Roberts got one break when Gilliam hesitated around second, then tried to make third base. Ashburn threw Junior out.

Roy Campanella then scored Snider with a drive high off the right field wall for the second of his three doubles.

A single by Robinson and Furillo's long double into the left-field corner brought the fourth run in the fourth inning.

When Reese and Snider opened on Roberts with singles to center in the fifth, Robin was taken

Continued on Page 3, Column 4

Indians, With Wynn, Rout Athletics, 9-3

By The United Press.

CLEVELAND, May 7—The Cleveland Indians defeated Kansas City, 9—3, today to gain their second straight victory over the Athletics.

Bobby Shantz, who shut out the Yankees with three hits in his previous start, lasted only until the fourth inning today. He was rapped for seven runs on nine safeties and dropped his third decision of the season.

Early Wynn, ill at the start of the season, scored his second victory and made himself eligible for the Yankee series in New York next week. Al Lopez lifted Wynn in the ninth, but only to rest him.

After Shantz had slipped through the first inning today, the Indians went to work in the second. They got four runs and it all started with Ralph

Continued on Page 2, Column 1

HEARN SETS BACK PITTSBURGH, 11-3

Giants' Pitcher Gains Fourth Victory, Drives Homer—Mueller Gets 4 Hits

By JOSEPH M. SHEEHAN

Midnight struck for the Pirates at the Polo Grounds yesterday. After masquerading as bold, bad buccaneers through a six-game winning streak, the Pittsburghers were exposed for the callow youths that they really are by an aroused Giant team.

Miffed at having let a victory slip away in the ninth inning of the series opener the night before, the New Yorkers left nothing to chance this time. In command from the outset, the Giants kept the pressure on all the way to win by 11—3.

Jim Hearn and Don Mueller shared top honors in a triumph that returned the Giants to the .500 mark. Hearn, all of a sudden the right-hand bellwether of Leo Durocher's staff, turned in a powerful seven-hit pitching performance to post his fourth victory. Jim also contributed a homer to the cause.

Mueller endeared himself to the Ladies Day crowd of 11,236 by slashing four hits through the baffled Pittsburgh defense with the magic wand he uses for a bat.

Pirates Made Five Errors

In their most satisfactory over-all offensive display in too long, the Giants hammered five Pirate pitchers for fourteen hits. With the added benefit of eight walks and four Pittsburgh errors they scored in five different innings.

They swung into action with two runs in the first inning. Al

Continued on Page 3, Column 2

The Victor in Louisville Classic Races to His Reward—Roses in the Winner's Circle

Swaps reaching the finish line ahead of the favored Nashua yesterday to capture eighty-first running of the Kentucky Derby at Churchill Downs course

Penn Eight's Victory Ends Middie Rowing Skein at 31

By ALLISON DANZIG

Special to The New York Times.

CAMBRIDGE, Mass., May 7—After three years of invincibility, Navy met its master on the water today. By the margin of a length and a half, the University of Pennsylvania eight defeated Rusty Callow's midshipmen over the course of a mile and three quarters on the Charles.

It was a crew coached by one of Callow's former oarsmen at Penn, Joe Burk, a winner of the Diamond Sculls, that brought about Navy's defeat. In winning, Penn turned in the fastest time ever made on the Charles in an Adams Cup regatta.

Penn, the winner of the cup for the first time since 1935, and also of the Childs and Blackwell Cups, was clocked in 8:47.7. The former record, set by Harvard in 1949, was 8:48.4. Navy's time today was 8:53.8. Harvard finished in 9:08.7, five lengths to the rear of Pennsylvania.

So ended the longest winning streak in the history of intercollegiate rowing. No one could challenge that Penn was the superior crew at the finish of the race, in which it led throughout.

The Navy eight had triumphed in thirty-one successive races from Meilahti Gulf in Finland to Newport Beach, Calif. The middies had won the Olympic gold medal at Helsinki in 1952 and led the procession in three intercollegiate championships. Navy had not taken the wash of a rival since its shells were ruined in the swollen, debris-strewn Ohio River at Marietta in 1951, the blackest day in Navy rowing.

Navy Victor Over Princeton

The all-victorious crew was not the same combination that was beaten today. Six members of the 1954 eight who had rowed at Helsinki became ensigns last June. Along with the six oarsmen departed the coxswain who was found to have been ineligible to row all season. As a result of this finding, Navy turned back its championship trophies.

Though it was largely a rebuilt crew, Navy defeated Princeton in its first test of 1955 by a comfortable margin. Last week it led home the Cornell eight that was expected to prove its most dangerous rival this season.

It was by only six feet that Navy beat Cornell on the Severn. That was indication enough that it was in danger. For Cornell, held up in its development by the late winter at Ithaca, was not yet ready to measure up to its full potential in spite of its crack 1954 freshman crew.

Penn figured to be the crew that might finally beat Navy. Penn entered this race with victories in the Childs and Blackwell Cup regattas. More important, it had more mileage behind it than any Eastern crew in recent years, thanks to the good weather and the improved conditions on the Schuylkill in Philadelphia.

So victory was gained by a

Continued on Page 6, Column 5

BOMBERS' 3 IN 9TH DOWN RED SOX, 9-6

Double by Berra Caps Rally After Yankees Erase Early Boston Margin of 5-0

By LOUIS EFFRAT

Special to The New York Times.

BOSTON, May 7—The Red Sox took an early lead at Fenway Park today, but they were unable to remain ahead. The Yankees, noted for their strong finishes, erased a 5-0 deficit and won, 9—6, with a three-run uprising in the ninth.

It was neck-and-neck going into the homestretch. The 29,925 fans settled back in anticipation of extra innings. With one out in the ninth, though, Tom Morgan, the sixth pitcher employed today by Casey Stengel, launched the victorious rally with a solid single to center against Ike

Continued on Page 2, Column 5

ROSEBEN IS TAKEN BY RED HANNIGAN

7-to-1 Shot Beats Artismo in $31,050 Belmont Race—Favored First Aid 3d

By JOSEPH C. NICHOLS

Red Hannigan of the Woodley Lane Farm made a game finish to win the $31,050 Roseben Handicap at Belmont Park yesterday. The 4-year-old son of Heliopolis beat the fleet Artismo by a head in the seven furlong dash under a persistent ride by Paul Bailey.

There were thirteen sprinters in the test, which was run for the sixteenth time.

The crowd of 35,883 installed the Brookmeade Stable's First Aid the favorite. First Aid, with Augie Catalano in the saddle, finished a half-length in back of Artismo, who was ridden by Teddy Atkinson.

Bailey, a 31-year-old rider from Kentucky, kept Red Hannigan in a favorable spot after getting away in seventh place. While the speedy Duc de Fer set the early pace, Red Hannigan moved along comfortably in the fourth spot, behind Bobby Brocato and Artismo.

It was when the field straightened out for the rush to the wire that Red Hannigan showed his speed. Bobby Brocato was going nicely and appeared to have enough power to win, but Artismo ran "at him" and put him away. While Artismo moved along, Red Hannigan moved with him, and in the final seventy yards the pair put up a tense duel, Atkinson on the inside and Bailey on the outside.

As the pair crossed the line, there was no certainty as to the winner, although most of the fans were of a mind to call No. 10, which was the identification borne by Red Hannigan. These

Continued on Page 7, Column 2

Associated Press Wirephotos

Willie Shoemaker waves aboard the rose-bedecked winner

Manhattan's Track Squad Gains Sixth Metropolitan Title in Row

By WILLIAM J. BRIORDY

Record-breaking performances by Charley Pratt, Len Moore and Jim Doulin sparked Manhattan College to its sixth straight team title in the twenty-second annual Metropolitan intercollegiate track and field championships yesterday.

Five varsity meet records were set as Manhattan established a mark with 114 points. The Jaspers eclipsed the previous high of 112 made by New York University in 1947.

St. John's was runner-up in the varsity point scoring with 49½ markers. Third spot went to N. Y. U. with 34 tallies. Fordham was fourth, with 16.

Pratt's superb 0:14.1 clocking in the 120-yard high hurdles was easily the top showing at John J. Downing Stadium on Randalls Island. Coach George Eastment's Jaspers showed their full strength outdoors for the first time this season.

The meet was a most satisfactory dress rehearsal by Manhattan for the Intercollegiate Amateur Athletic Association of America games at Downing Stadium on May 27 and 28. Eastment's squad will be a strong contender for Penn State's crown in that meet.

In keeping his high hurdles laurels, Pratt broke his own standard of 0:14.8 made last year. The swift senior led throughout in beating Lou Knight, a team-mate, by 10 yards.

Pratt's time tied a Stadium mark made in 1911 by Ed Dugger, Tufts, and matched the following year by Bill Cummings, Rice. Pratt also did 0:14.5 in taking the first heat, but the time was disallowed because of a following wind.

A leading scorer for Manhattan was Ken Bantum. He was a triple winner. Bantum, who took the hammer and discus events on Friday at Baker Field, added the 16-pound shot-put title to his list. Bantum won the shot with a toss of 52 feet 4½ inches.

Moore also scored a triple. After leaping 21 feet 4 inches for a record in the broad jump, Moore retained his 220-yard-

Continued on Page 6, Column 2

SUMMER TAN IS 3D

Swaps, 14-5, Outruns Favored Nashua by Length and Half

By JAMES ROACH

Special to The New York Times.

LOUISVILLE, May 7—Californians did some high-decibel whooping today at the Kentucky Derby. And they were joined in their celebrating by those in a crowd of 100,000 at Churchill Downs who had backed Rex C. Ellsworth's Swaps.

For Swaps, California-bred and California-owned, won the eighty-first Derby. He won it by taking the lead shortly after the start of the mile-and-a-quarter run—and by holding onto the lead for the rest of the way.

Swaps was the $7.60-for-$2, or 14-to-5, second choice. The favorite was the Belair Stud's Nashua, the winner of three $100,000 added races this year. Nashua went into the Derby with a record of six straight triumphs since September of last year.

But Nashua took a licking today. He charged up to challenge the front-runner at the top of the stretch. They were lapped on each other for a while, with Nashua on the outside. Then Swaps, under the urging of wondrous Willie Shoemaker, opened up on the Belair colt in the final yards.

The margin between them went from half a length to a length—and then, at the wire, to a length and a half.

Two-Horse Race in Stretch

As far as first and second money were concerned, it was a two-horse race in the last 440 yards—from the top of the stretch to the finish mark. The other eight 3-year-olds in the line-up were out of the big-money hunt by that time.

Third money went to Mrs. John W. Galbreath's Summer Tan, who has been Nashua's arch-rival in Eastern racing. Two Saturdays ago, in a sensational race at Jamaica, Nashua beat Summer Tan by only a neck in the Wood Memorial.

At pay-off time on this gray afternoon Summer Tan was in third place—six and a half lengths back of the runner-up.

Summer Tan made his pitch on the second turn. He wasn't able to keep pitching.

Fourth money went to a member of the Cain Hoy Stable team—Racing Fool. There were four lengths between him and Summer Tan at the end of the $152,500 run.

The others, in order, were the Murgain Stable's Jean's Joe, Cain Hoy's Flying Fury, W-L Ranch's Honeys Alibi, Harvey C. Fruehauf's Blue Lem, Clifford Mooers' Nabesna and G. Rollie White's Trim Destiny.

Second California-Bred Winner

How many times have Californians had a chance to whoop it up over a Kentucky Derby victory? Just twice, sir, just twice. Swaps is only the second California-foaled winner in the history of the race. The first one was Morvich in 1922.

Comparatively few California-bred horses have tried to win Kentucky's No. 1 horse race. But there'll be more in the future. For the breeding stock in California is improving, more and more expensive importations are being made, and the score by Swaps will give owners in the sunkist state hope for the future.

Eddie Arcaro rode Nashua. He

Continued on Page 4, Column 2

Major League Baseball

Sunday, May 8, 1955

National League

YESTERDAY'S GAMES

New York 11, Pittsburgh 3.
Brooklyn 6, Philadelphia 3 (night).
Cincinnati 8, Chicago 7.
Milwaukee 9, St. Louis 7 (night).

STANDING OF THE CLUBS

	Brooklyn	New York	Milwaukee	Chicago	Pittsburgh	St. Louis	Cincinnati	Philadel.	Won	Lost	Percentage	Games Behind
Bklyn	—	3	2	2	4	2	1	6	20	2	.909	—
N. Y.	2	—	1	2	2	1	1	1	10	10	.500	9
Milw.	0	1	—	3	0	3	3	1	11	11	.500	9
Chic.	0	1	0	—	0	2	5	3	11	12	.478	9½
Pitts.	0	1	3	1	—	2	1	1	9	12	.429	10½
St. L.	0	1	2	2	1	—	2	0	8	11	.421	10½
Cinc.	0	0	1	2	2	1	—	2	8	13	.381	11½
Phila	0	3	2	0	3	0	0	—	8	14	.364	12
Lost	2	10	11	12	12	11	13	14	—	—		

American League

YESTERDAY'S GAMES

New York 9, Boston 6.
Cleveland 9, Kansas City 3.
Detroit 7, Chicago 1.
Baltimore 5, Washington 1 (night).

STANDING OF THE CLUBS

	Cleveland	Detroit	New York	Chicago	Kan. City	Wash'gton	Boston	Baltimore	Won	Lost	Percentage	Games Behind
Cleve	—	3	1	2	3	2	3	1	15	7	.682	—
Det.	2	—	1	1	3	3	2	2	14	8	.636	1
N. Y.	1	1	—	1	1	2	5	2	13	8	.619	1½
Chic.	2	2	1	—	3	1	2	1	12	8	.600	2
K. C.	1	1	1	1	—	1	2	2	9	11	.450	5
Wash	0	0	1	1	1	—	1	4	8	13	.381	6½
Bost.	0	1	2	1	0	1	—	4	9	15	.375	7
Balt.	1	0	1	1	0	3	0	—	6	16	.273	9
Lost	7	8	8	8	11	13	15	16	—	—		

TODAY'S PROBABLE PITCHERS

Pittsburgh at New York (2, 2 P. M.)—Littlefield (1-2) and Law (0-0) vs. Gomez (1-2) and Maglie (1-3) or Liddle (1-1).

Brooklyn at Philadelphia—Podres (2-1) vs. Wehmeier (2-1).

Chicago at Cincinnati (2)—Rush (1-2) and Jones (2-4) vs. Ridzik (0-1) and Staley (3-2).

Milwaukee at St. Louis—Spahn (2-3) vs. Haddix (1-3).

New York at Boston—Grim (0-2) vs. Nixon (4-1).

Baltimore at Washington (2)—Palica (1-3) and Miller (0-0) vs. Stobbs (0-2) and Pascual (0-1).

Detroit at Chicago (2)—Hoeft (3-1) and Lary (2-2) vs. Donovan (2-1) and Consuegra (2-0).

Kansas City at Cleveland (2)—Boyer (1-1) and Ceccarelli (0-0) vs. Feller (1-1) and Garcia (2-3).

(Figures in parentheses indicate season's won-and-lost records.)

Kentucky Derby Chart

LOUISVILLE, Ky., May 7—The following is the chart showing how the Kentucky Derby was run at Churchill Downs today:

SEVENTH RACE—The Kentucky Derby; $125,000 added; 3-year-olds; one mile and a quarter. Start good; won driving; place same. Went to post 5:31, off 5:31½ (New York time). Winner, ch. c., by Khaled—Iron Reward, by Beau Pere. Trainer, M. A. Tenney. Value to winner, $108,400; second, $25,000; third, $12,500; fourth, $5,000. Times—0:23 3-5; 0:47 2-5; 1:12 2-5; 1:37; 2.01 4-5. Weather cloudy; track fast.

Starters.	Wt.	P.P.	St.	½	¾	M.	Str.	Fin.	Jockeys.	Mutuels St.	Mutuels Pl.	Mutuels Sh.	Dollar Odds.
Swaps	126	8	4	1^{1}	1^{1}	$1^{1\frac{1}{2}}$	$1^{1\frac{1}{2}}$	$1^{1\frac{1}{2}}$	Shoemaker	7.60	3.40	2.60	[illegible]
Nashua	126	5	1	3^{1}	3^{1}	2^{1}	2^{3}	$2^{1\frac{1}{2}}$	Arcaro	....	3.00	[illegible]	1.30
Summer Tan	126	10	6	4^{8}	[illegible]	3^{4}	3^{2}	3^{1}	Guerin	....	....	3.00	4.90
Racing Fool	126	7	5	5^{1}	5^{1}	5^{1}	4^{3}	$4^{\frac{1}{2}}$	H. Moreno	....	....	....	3.70
Jean's Joe	126	9	9	10	8^{3}	$6^{\frac{1}{2}}$	5^{2}	$5^{1\frac{1}{2}}$	Brooks	....	....	....	13.20
Flying Fury	126	2	10	8^{3}	9^{1}	9^{2}	$6^{\frac{1}{2}}$	$6^{\frac{3}{4}}$	McCreary	....	....	....	5.70
Honeys Alibi	126	4	2	6^{3}	6^{3}	7^{1}	$7^{1\frac{1}{2}}$	[illegible]	Harmatz	....	....	....	[illegible]
Blue Lem	126	1	7	$9^{1\frac{1}{2}}$	10	10	9^{4}	$8^{1\frac{1}{2}}$	Rogers	....	....	....	[illegible]
Nabesna	126	3	8	7^{3}	$7^{1\frac{1}{2}}$	8^{1}	8^{1}	9^{10}	J. Adams	....	....	....	[illegible]
Trim Destiny	126	6	3	$2^{1\frac{1}{2}}$	2^{hd}	4^{hd}	10	10	L. C. Cook	....	....	....	50.90

aCain Hoy Stable entry.

Swaps took command soon after the start, raced Trim Destiny into defeat before reaching the upper turn, responded readily when challenged by Nashua during the stretch run and drew clear in the last sixteenth mile. Nashua, well placed from the outset, was kept in hand to the last three-eighths, then moved up boldly on the outside of Swaps for the stretch run but was not good enough.

Summer Tan, never far back and reserved to the last half mile, made a bid approaching the stretch, then faltered. Racing Fool, in hand to the stretch, was unable to threaten the leaders when set down in the drive. Jean's Joe lacked early foot and was never dangerous.

Flying Fury began sluggishly and was never prominent. Honeys Alibi was outrun and had no mishap. Blue Lem raced far back the entire trip. Nabesna was through early. Trim Destiny raced nearest Swaps for three-quarters, then gave way.

Owners—1, R. C. Ellsworth; 2, Belair Stud; 3, Mrs. J. W. Galbreath; 4, Cain Hoy Stable; 5, Murcain Stable; 6, Cain Hoy Stable; 7, W-L Ranch Co.; 8, H. C. Fruehauf; 9, C. Mooers; 10, G. R. White.

Boxer Not Drugged, One Report States

By The Associated Press.

PHILADELPHIA, May 7—A well-posted source said today that Boxer Harold Johnson had not been drugged but that he might have become dizzy from nose drops he used shortly before last night's fight. The source declined to be named.

Johnson collapsed after the second round and a technical knockout victory was awarded to Julio Mederos, a Cuban heavyweight.

As Johnson was carried out on a stretcher and taken to Hahnemann Hospital—where he is under twenty-four-hour police guard—investigations were begun by the Pennsylvania State Athletic Commission and the police. The source disclosed

Continued on Page 7, Column 5

Sowell of Pitt Runs 440 Yards in 0:45.4

By The Associated Press.

PITTSBURGH, May 7—Arnie Sowell, University of Pittsburgh track star, ran one of the fastest quarter miles in the history of foot racing today.

The 20-year-old junior ran his anchor 440 yards in the mile relay in 0:45.4.

The world record for 440 yards is Herb McKenley's 46 seconds flat set at Berkeley, Calif., in 1948.

Sowell's performance will not replace McKenley's because split times in relays are unofficial. One reason for this is that relay runners have the benefit of a flying start.

The brilliant quarter not only enabled Pitt to make up almost

Continued on Page 5, Column 2

SWAPS OUTRACES NASHUA IN DERBY

Continued From Page 1

was seeking his sixth Derby success. He has ridden more Derby winners than any other jockey. And he was seeking to give Belair and the stable's trainer, 80-year-old Sunny Jim Fitzsimmons, a fourth score.

Arcaro did his best. Nashua did his best. Swaps was a bit too good for them.

"No excuses," said Arcaro. He said his horse had been lapped on the front-runner, and then "swoosh went Swaps."

Shoemaker, the nation's leading winner-rider for the past three years, won his first Derby in his fourth try.

He said Swaps had plenty left at the finish, and that he had no doubt of the identity of the winner after he had straightened out for the stretch run.

Swaps, according to Willie the Shoe, veered out slightly at the turn into the stretch just as Nashua made his challenge. Shoemaker said that the sight of the crowd or the starting gate startled the colt.

Shoemaker made his first use of his whip at that point in the high-octane proceedings. Swaps was whacked a couple of times after that.

Guerin Has No Excuses

Eric Guerin, rider of Summer Tan, said his colt had no excuses.

Quote from Guerin: "When we tried to run with Nashua, Summer Tan died."

Johnny Adams, rider of the ninth-place Nabesna, was asked for some remarks about the race. "I didn't see much of it," said Johnny.

Here's the way the richest Derby in history was run:

Swaps went quickly to the lead. At the wire the first time, with a mile to go, Swaps was a head in front of the 50-to-1 Trim Destiny, the 13-to-10 Nashua was third and Cain Hoy's Racing Fool was next.

On the first turn Swaps opened a length on Trim Destiny, and the long shot opened two lengths on the favorite. Summer Tan was running fourth by that time.

In the run down the backstretch Arcaro sent Nashua to second place. The advance to second was completed at the half-mile pole. There Summer Tan went to third, and Trim Destiny started to fade. It will be recalled that the fade resulted in a last-place finish.

Midway on the second turn the first three—Swaps, Nashua and Summer Tan—were a length apart. Then Nashua made his bid. Summer Tan tried to keep pace—and Swaps scooted home for first money of $108,400.

Time of Race 2:01 4-5

The clocking, over a hard, fast track, was a frisky 2:01 4-5. Swaps was only a couple of watch-ticks away from Whirlaway's track record of 2:01 2-5, set in 1941.

The way-station clockings were 0:23 3-5 for the quarter, 0:47 2-5 for the half, 1:12 2-5 for six furlongs and 1:37 for the mile. The last quarter was run in 0:24 4-5.

As a betting race, it was a whopper. In fact, it was the whoppingest betting race in the history of old Churchill Downs, which dates back to 1875. In on the Derby went $1,677,178.

It had been expected that Nashua would be the odds-on favorite, that Summer Tan would be the close second choice and that Swaps would be the third choice at 5 or 6 to 1.

But there were so many backers of Swaps on the premises that he went to the post at 14 to 5. He had impressed many persons—more than the price-makers had figured — with an eight-and-a-half-length score in a sprint here last Saturday.

In his other 1955 starts he had won the San Vicente Stakes and the Santa Anita Derby at Santa Anita Park. So now he has a four-for-four record for 1955. He has earned $215,700 this year.

He hasn't been nominated for the Preakness and Belmont Stakes. So there'll be no triple-crowner among the 3-year-olds this year.

Nashua is still the top money-winner among the 3-year-olds. Second money of $25,000 today increased his 1955 earnings to $309,575.

The total mutuel turnover on the program was $4,280,287. Last year $4,234,231 was set. The record Derby Day handle was $4,306,065 in 1953.

It was a hot day in the Julep Belt but it ceased to be sunny in mid-afternoon. The sky became grayish then, and the customers in the infield and on the first turn and in the uncovered seats began to wonder aloud whether they were in for a dousing.

There was thunder in the distance, and a light rain began to fall, as an Army band played "The Star Spangled Banner" eighteen minutes before off-time for the Derby.

As the horses were ridden onto the track for the ten-minute post parade, the rain increased in intensity. There was more thunder. There was some lightning. But the rain slackened, and there was not much more than a pitter-patter during the ten-furlong run.

There were surprises for all hands when the results of the "blind betting" on the Derby were flashed on the tote boards about fifty minutes before the big race.

On Derby Day, tickets on the big race are sold from racks for several hours. During that time there is no totalisator check on odds fluctuations. The out-of-the-racks betting continues until an hour and fifty minutes before post time before the Derby.

After the sixth race, machine betting on the Derby begins. And the results of the "blind betting" go onto the boards.

Swaps Early Favorite

The preliminary-hours betting amounted to $653,833, and at its conclusion Swaps was the 9-to-5 favorite, Nashua was the 2-to-1 second choice, the Cain Hoy entry was 7 to 2, Summer Tan was 7 to 1, Jean's Joe was 14 to 1, Blue Lem was 24 to 1, Trim Destiny was 35 to 1, Nabesna was 45 to 1, and Honeys Alibi was 50 to 1.

On the "morning line" Nashua had been 4 to 5, Summer Tan 2 to 1, Swaps 5 to 1 and the Cain Hoy entry 10 to 1.

Swaps wasn't the favorite for long. By the time the Derby horses were being led around the first turn, from the barns across the track, with half an hour to go to post time, Nashua was officially the people's choice. But he was 8 to 5, instead of the expected 4 to 5, with half an hour of betting remaining.

As the horses were led down the track, on the way to the back - of - the - stands saddling ring, a couple of bands prepared to play the National Anthem and the Derby theme song — "My Old Kentucky Home."

And the customers became more tense as they awaited what some persons think is the most electric moment in sports —the moment when the starter sends the field away in the Derby.

The Derby was the seventh event on a nine-race program. The Debutante Stakes, for 2-year-old fillies, was run in the No. 5 spot. The Debutante winner, who gained the lead in the last few yards, was Cherry, bred and owned by Clifford Mooers. She and her fourth-place running mate, Birch, were $8.20-for-$2 items.

James Paddock's Babcha finished second, beaten by half a length, after having led till near the wire. There Cherry, under the urging of John Heckmann, edged ahead.

William Faulkner, winner of the Nobel and Pulitzer prizes for his writing, has been a pressboxer this week. He's doing a magazine story on the Derby. He has been doing diligent horseplaying. Early in the week he was $60 ahead of the game. But, like many another horseplayer, he didn't quit while he was ahead. At the start of today's proceedings he was $3.20 in arrears.

A small white card hung from the rail of a clubhouse box. On it was printed "M. J. W." Also on the rail of the box was a bronze plaque, with the inscription "In Memory of M. J. Winn." The late Col. Matt Winn, a promotional genius, made the Derby the nation's No. 1 horse race.

The second, third and fourth finishers in the Derby, Nashua, Summer Tan and Racing Fool, were foaled at Claiborne Farm, Paris, Ky.

The summaries (AP):

FIRST RACE—Purse $2,500; claiming; maiden 3 and 4-year-olds; one mile.

Suduese, 113	(Erb)	7.60	4.40	3.40
Bobs Pamela, 109	(J.R.Ad'ms)	....	10.20	5.00
Rebelled, 114	(Heckmann)	....	....	3.80

Time—1:39 2-5. Shillelah Mike, Besmark, Springback, Carlo C and Hard Top also ran.

SECOND RACE—Purse $2,500; claiming; 3-year-olds; six furlongs.

Maid of C'ton, 109	(Popara)	12.00	6.20	4.00
Mahm'd Relic, 108	(L.C.Cook)	....	7.20	4.00
My Thesis, 120	(Brooks)	....	....	2.80

Time—1:12 3-5. Goat's Bel, aTricky Homer, Gay Joy, aBlue Reno and Fem Fox also ran. aForrest and Mundy entry.

THIRD RACE—Purse $2,500; claiming; 3-year-olds; six furlongs

Calabash, 112	(Dever)	7.40	4.40	3.20
Mighty Warrior, 113	(Swain)	....	8.00	4.60
Bumpsy Up, 115	(J.Adams)	....	....	3.20

Time—1:12 1-5. Open Lake, Dibba Dee,

OWNER OF SWAPS INVESTED WISELY

From Developing Cow Ponies to Derby Winner Story of Ellsworth Success

Special to The New York Times.

LOUISVILLE, May 7—Swaps raced to victory in the Kentucky Derby today flying the red and black silks of Rex C. Ellsworth. But the 3-year-old chestnut colt has a couple of other owners: Mrs. Ellsworth and the trainer of Swaps, Mesach Adams Tenney.

The Ellsworths own 75 per cent of the stable and Tenney owns the rest.

Ellsworth and Tenney are ex-cowhands. They have been close friends since they were boys. Their first experience with thoroughbreds was when they bought a stallion to cross with their mares to develop better cow ponies.

Ellsworth today hit the peak in a racing career that started with a $600 investment. In the fall of 1933 he went to the Lexington (Ky.) horse sales with a rented truck and a $600 capital. He bought broodmares. In time, he prospered.

In 1947 Ellsworth had attained sufficient property to buy a farm near Ontario, Calif. It was named Ellsworth Ranch. It was bought primarily so that horses foaled there might be eligible for rich California-bred races.

In 1953 a 220-acre tract, near Chino, Calif., was bought. The 80-acre ranch near Ontario and the place near Chino are known as the Ellsworth Ranches.

In 1946 Ellsworth went to Europe seeking a stallion. The story is told that he wanted to buy Nasrullah, sire of Nashua, the Derby favorite beaten by Swaps today.

But—so the story goes—he got an unpromising report on Nasrullah and decided instead to buy Khaled, a brown horse foaled in 1943. Khaled was raced in England at 2 and 3, and won five times in eight races. Khaled was bought from the Aga Kahn.

Khaled is the sire of Swaps. And Swaps was foaled at the Ellsworth Ranch near Ontario on March 1, 1952. Also foaled at the ranch was Correspondent, who finished fifth in the 1953 Derby, under the silks of Mrs. Gordon Guiberson.

Ellsworth bred Correspondent. But Swaps was the first Ellsworth-owned horse to go after the Derby.

The dam of Swaps is Iron Reward, who was bred in California by W. W. Naylor. She raced unplaced at 2 and 3. She is a daughter of Beau Pere, who was imported from Australia by Louis B. Mayer.

Swaps Unbeaten This Year

So there's a horse-across-the-seas angle to the winning of the eighty-first Derby today.

Swaps had a three-for six record last year. He won one stakes event—the June Juvenile Stakes at Hollywood Park, with John Burton up.

This year he has raced four times—and has won four times. On Jan. 19 he won the San Vicente Stakes at Santa Anita and on Feb. 19 he won the Santa Anita Derby. Willie Shoemaker has ridden him in four of his last five starts.

Tenney, who is 47 years old, has been a horse-trainer since 1935. He does all the shoeing of his horses. Swaps was his first Derby starter.

While Swaps was nibbling grass on the backstretch here earlier in the week, Tenney told how the colt was named.

"We sent in several names to the Jockey Club," he said, "and they were rejected. So finally I said, 'Let's stop swapping names and call him Swaps'."

Wide World Photos

Swaps, ridden by Jockey Willie Shoemaker, pounds down the final yards of the home-stretch to beat Nashua (left) in the 81st running of the Kentucky Derby.

"All the News That's Fit to Print"

The New York Times.

LATE CITY EDITION
Fair and cooler today. Partly cloudy tomorrow.
Temperature Range Today-Max., 78; Min., 63
Temperatures Yesterday-Max., 81.6; Min., 70
Full U. S. Weather Bureau Report, Page 52

VOL. CIV..No. 35,599. Entered as Second-Class Matter, Post Office, New York, N. Y. NEW YORK, WEDNESDAY, JULY 13, 1955. Times Square, New York 36, N. Y. Telephone LAckawanna 4-1000 FIVE CENTS

S. E. C. HEAD BALKS AT POWER QUERIES DESPITE WARNING

Refuses to Tell Inquiry if White House Intervened in a Dixon-Yates Hearing

CONTEMPT ACTION SEEN

Senate Unit Summons Others on Commission—Terms of Pact Termination Studied

By RUSSELL BAKER

Special to The New York Times.

WASHINGTON, July 12—The Dixon-Yates power controversy struck the Securities and Exchange Commission today. It involved all its commissioners in a threatened contempt action.

The four Commissioners were called to appear before the Senate Antimonopoly Subcommittee tomorrow morning.

Senators asked to question the entire group after J. Sinclair Armstrong, S. E. C. chairman, refused to tell whether the White House had intervened for political reasons in a Dixon-Yates hearing before an S. E. C. examiner.

Angered by Mr. Armstrong's refusal, the Senators warned him that he was risking "possible contempt of the Senate."

With great meekness, Mr. Armstrong persisted in his refusal. He said his decision not to say whether the White House had intervened was based on Presidential authority and had been discussed with all the Commissioners.

The subcommittee then called for the full commission to appear tomorrow. Each Commissioner will be asked whether he supports Mr. Armstrong's refusal to testify about White House involvement.

The S. E. C. commissioners are Mr. Armstrong, Clarence H. Adams, A. Jackson Goodwin and Andrew Downey Orrick.

Controversy Still Rages

Though President Eisenhower yesterday ordered the Dixon-Yates contract canceled, the bitter controversy over it still reverberated through Washington today. There were these other developments:

¶In the face of Democratic hosannas over the contract's imminent death, President Eisenhower again defended it as "a good, fair agreement."

¶Preliminary discussions of the negotiations in which the Government's termination costs will be decided, took place at Atomic Energy Commission headquarters.

¶On Capitol Hill, Democrats were preparing to fight any liberal cancellation settlement with the Dixon-Yates group. There was some sentiment against any fee payment.

The Dixon-Yates contract called for construction of a power plant at West Memphis, Ark., at a cost of $107,000,000, to supply an anticipated power shortage in the Memphis, Tenn., area. Under it Memphis would have been supplied without expansion of the Tennessee Valley Authority Power System. The power would have "replaced" that supplied to atomic installations by the T. V. A.

The decision of Memphis au-

Continued on Page 17, Column 3

Associated Press Wirephoto

ADVICE OF COUNSEL: J. Sinclair Armstrong, right, chairman of the Securities and Exchange Commission, as he received advice from William Timbers, S. E. C. general counsel, at yesterday's Senate inquiry in Washington on the Dixon-Yates contract.

Treasury Agrees to 1c Rise In 'Gas' Tax to Build Roads

By JOHN D. MORRIS

Special to The New York Times.

WASHINGTON, July 12—George M. Humphrey, Secretary of the Treasury, accepted today a use-tax increase sponsored by Democrats as a second-best but satisfactory way to finance a highway construction program.

Mr. Humphrey told the Public Works Committee of the House of Representatives that he was "perfectly willing" for Congress to impose higher gasoline and other highway use taxes.

While President Eisenhower's proposal for issuance of $21,000,000,000 in special bonds "still offers the best method," he testified, "the determination of policy is in your hands, not in ours."

"A treasurer never objects to paying as you go," he added.

The Secretary's testimony improved the prospects of favorable Congressional action on a vast road-building program acceptable to the Administration.

The financing plan under consideration, as approved by a subcommittee, calls for a 1-cent increase in the Federal gasoline tax of 2 cents a gallon, with rises in Federal levies on Diesel fuel, heavy tires and tubes and trucks, buses and trailers.

Secretary Humphrey estimated that they would raise the yield from such revenue sources by $12,500,000,000 to a total of $33,000,000,000 over the fourteen years that they would remain in effect.

Within 10 Per Cent of Goal

He noted that this would be within 10 per cent of the $37,000,000,000 that the Federal Government would spend in the ten-year highway program recommended by President Eisenhower and added:

"I couldn't quarrel with that."

The pending bill is sponsored by Representative George H. Fallon, Democrat of Maryland, with the backing of House Democratic leaders. It calls for $35,500,000,000 of Federal outlays over twelve years.

The Senate has passed a bill by Senator Albert Gore, Democrat of Tennessee, for $12,600,000,000 of Federal road expenditures in five years out of general revenues. It rejected the Eisenhower bond plan, 60 to 31.

Secretary Humphrey was emphatic in his opposition to any program, such as the Senate's, that failed to provide for financing the outlays.

"I think it would be about as irresponsible a thing as you could do," he asserted.

He was asked about a possible combination of "a little bit of bonds and a little bit of taxation."

"It could be done wholly either way or by any combination you wished to adopt," he replied.

In response to other questions, the Secretary said he thought the Democratic bill provided "a pretty good spread of the taxes among the people who would benefit from a substantially improved highway system."

He said the President's bond proposal would have a greater inflationary potential than the higher taxes "if taken all by itself." He suggested, however, that the inflationary impact would be offset by reductions in other Federal expenditures.

He did not take a definite stand on possible exemptions

Continued on Page 15, Column 5

MRS. HOBBY SLATED TO QUIT POST TODAY

Special to The New York Times.

WASHINGTON, July 12—The resignation of Mrs. Oveta Culp Hobby as Secretary of Health, Education and Welfare will be announced tomorrow, barring some quite unexpected overnight changes in White House plans.

President Eisenhower's appointment of Marion B. Folsom to succeed her probably will be announced at the same time. Mr. Folsom, of Rochester, N. Y., is now Under Secretary of the Treasury.

This change in the Cabinet was made possible today by Senator Irving M. Ives, Republican of New York.

Mr. Ives reluctantly agreed not to oppose Senate confirmation of the Folsom appointment, about which he was not consulted in advance.

The Constitution requires Senate approval of such appointments by a simple majority of those voting.

BOAT SPEEDS 185 M. P. H.

Don Campbell Surpasses World Record in England

AMBLESIDE, England, July 12 (Reuters)—Donald Campbell tonight traveled at the rate of more than three miles a minute in a trial run of his turbo-jet speedboat Bluebird on Lake Ullswater.

His unofficial run of 185 miles an hour bettered the present world speed boat record of 178.49 miles set in 1950 by Stanley Sayres of the United States.

Campbell, 34-year-old son of the late famous British racing car driver, Sir Malcolm Campbell, reached the speed on an outward run over the course. He is preparing to attempt an official record.

WHOOPING CRANE GAINS

Nearly Extinct Species Brings Its Population Up to 25

OTTAWA, July 12 (AP)—The nearly extinct whooping crane is staging another comeback. Four young were hatched in Canada this spring, increasing the known number of the rare bird to at least twenty-five.

The world population of the white cranes, which have a seven-foot wingspread, sank to fifteen, its lowest point, in 1941, but rose to twenty-four in 1953. Their numbers started dropping again until last year there were only twenty-one.

Super Carrier Trials Set

WASHINGTON, July 12 (UP)—The new super aircraft carrier Forrestal will start her sea trials in mid-August and join the Atlantic Fleet on Oct. 1, the Navy announced today. The 60,000-ton warship, the world's largest, will undergo builder's sea trials Aug. 16 and 17. She will undergo further trials with Navy inspectors aboard on Aug. 29 and Sept. 1.

National All-Stars Win in Twelfth, 6-5

By JOHN DREBINGER

Special to The New York Times.

MILWAUKEE, July 12—Short of winning a world championship, which it some day hopes to achieve, this seething baseball metropolis of the Midwest experienced its greatest baseball thrill today.

A gathering of 45,314 roaring fans watched a grimly fighting band of National Leaguers rally to draw even with the American League and carry the 1955 All-Star game into extra innings.

The fans saw, in the top half of the twelfth, their own Gene Conley, the beanpole right-hander of the Braves, step to the mound to fan three batters in a row.

In the last half of the inning they saw Stan Musial of the St. Louis Cardinals blast a home run into the right field bleachers.

The blow gave the Nationals the game, 6 to 5. It also gave

Continued on Page 29, Column 1

GANG EFFORT SEEN TO RULE TRUCKING

Braden Crime Report Calls on Beck, Teamster Head, to Curb Racketeers

By RUSSELL PORTER

New York was warned yesterday that racketeers were trying to take over its trucking industry.

Spruille Braden, chairman of the New York City Anti-Crime Committee, gave the warning. He criticized Dave Beck, president of the International Brotherhood of Teamsters, A. F. L., as failing to curb the racketeers.

Mr. Braden, in his annual report, urged Mr. Beck to take "vigorous and forthright" action against James R. Hoffa of Detroit, the teamsters' vice president. Mr. Hoffa recently installed as spokesman for New York trucking unions a man who, Mr. Braden said without identifying him, has been a "lifelong associate of the worst gangsters in this city."

According to Mr. Braden, Mr. Hoffa also has been "a friend and associate of several major figures in the ranks of gangsterdom."

Mr. Braden recalled that Mr. Hoffa's activities in the field of union welfare funds had been the subject of congressional investigation. Last year a Congressional committee termed Mr. Hoffa the boss in a Detroit situation characterized by racketering, extortion and gangsterism.

Mr. Braden said New York

Continued on Page 22, Column 2

TRANSIT AGENCY FACES BIG DEFICIT AS IT MEETS QUILL

But Members Are Undaunted by Their Tasks—Talk With Union Chief Is Amiable

By A. H. RASKIN

Budget estimates awaiting action by the new Transit Authority indicate that the city-owned subway and bus lines may slip back into the red this year.

If the estimates prepared by the authority's operating and fiscal experts hold true, most of the $10,715,000 cushion the agency inherited from its predecessor will have to be spent to offset losses under the 15-cent fare.

The gloomy financial outlook cast no outward cloud over the first meeting yesterday between the authority and Michael J. Quill, whose wage demands have accounted for much of the transit system's troubles.

Smiles and good feeling were the order of the day on both sides of the bargaining table at the authority's headquarters, 370 Jay Street, Brooklyn. The president of the Transport Workers Union, C. I. O., asked for a pay increase that would add $15,895,000 a year to the subway labor bill. He raised no objection when the three-man board asked for two weeks to think it over.

Authority Not Discouraged

The authority, under the chairmanship of Charles L. Patterson, Pittsburgh railroad executive, takes no defeatist view of the proposed budget. It is convinced that ways can be found to bolster the system's income by checking the decline in riders that began when the nickel fare was abandoned seven years ago.

However, the dimensions of the task confronting the new board were made clear in the estimates officially submitted by James A. Dearie, the authority's budget director. O. the basis of present trends, he predicted that the number of riders would drop 3 per cent in the next twelve months.

This would mean an $8,000,000 fall-off in fare collections. New Yorkers dropped $262,475,000 into turnstiles and fare boxes in the fiscal year ended June 30. The budget forecasts a drop to $254,400,000 this year.

Revenue from advertising, concessions and rentals is expected to remain steady at $5,900,000, bringing the total anticipated income to $260,300,000. Against this figure, the budget lists $251,212,100 in prospective expenditures without any allowance for deferred maintenance or higher wages.

The sum required for maintenance projects, many of which have gone undone since pre-war years, is estimated at $12,000,000. The report emphasizes the

Continued on Page 18, Column 3

WHITE HOUSE TALK ON GENEVA WELDS BIPARTISAN UNITY

President Promises to Keep Congress' Leaders Advised on Progress of Parley

By WILLIAM S. WHITE

Special to The New York Times.

WASHINGTON, July 12—President Eisenhower and Congressional leaders agreed today that firm national unity in support of his position was a necessity for the coming Big Four conference at Geneva.

Any remotely partisan approach was cast aside at a White House breakfast consultation between the President, Secretary of State Dulles and twenty-five of the highest figures from both parties.

Later, in an informal talk to a student group in the White House Rose Garden, General Eisenhower indicated his basic attitude by saying that the world's people did not want conflict and that it was their "mistaken leaders that grow too belligerent."

The President promised his Congressional callers that he would have them kept fully informed of the progress of his meeting with the heads of government of Britain, France and the Soviet Union. Confidential reports will be sent back on a running basis to the leaders of Congress.

He left the firm impression, moreover, that though he would agree to a wide range of discussion at Geneva, he would specifically exclude the affairs of the Far East.

Agenda to Exclude China

The understanding of Senators present was that the President would take the position that he would not discuss, for example, the issues between Communist and Nationalist China in the absence of the Nationalist Chinese.

This view was highly popular with a large Congressional group, mainly Republican in composition, that has feared some sort of conclusion at Geneva that would set back the anti-Communists in Asia.

Whether the President's policy in this regard would appeal to the British and the French—and many questioned that it would—there was no doubt that any other attitude would have provoked hostility at the Capitol.

The Democrats who met with the President did not offer any qualification of their support for the Geneva conference. They recognized that they were now unalterably committed to the meeting, whatever its results might be.

Thus, it was said tonight by senior Senators that the country rarely, if ever, had approached a great diplomatic test with so intimate a liaison between the executive and the legislative branches of the Government.

In promising regular reports

Continued on Page 3, Column 2

Transit Chief 'Lost' on I.R.T. Tour

He Declares Subway Is in Good Shape but Could Be Better

By LAWRENCE O'KANE

Charles L. Patterson, the city's new Transit Authority chairman, went on a tour of the I. R. T. yesterday with some of his subordinates. Like other underground travelers before them, the subway officials felt the heat, and even lost their way briefly at Grand Central.

Mr. Patterson, a Pittsburgher and a railroad man for thirty-two years, was sworn in a week ago. He had lived for several years in the New York area, but not for four years had he ridden the I. R. T. Tours of the other subway lines are planned for the future.

Accompanied by Edward T. McNally, the authority's general superintendent, and John Ford, superintendent of the I. R. T. division, Mr. Patterson left his Brooklyn offices at 370 Jay Street at 12:30 P. M. His announced intention was a "no punches pulled" picture of the authority's oldest property, the I. R. T.

Three and a half hot hours and nineteen underground miles later he was able to declare that he found the line "better" than he had anticipated.

"I see signs of new thinking among the operators," he said. "The state of the subway is

Continued on Page 18, Column 6

The New York Times

Charles L. Patterson, standing, new chairman of the Transit Authority, looks over car during a subway tour yesterday.

SOVIET PROPOSES UNITING GERMANY A STEP AT A TIME

Canadian Avalanche Kills 7 U. S. Boys

The New York Times July 13, 1955

Scene of accident (cross)

By The United Press.

BANFF, Alta., July 12—Seven American teen-agers were killed yesterday by an avalanche on the slopes of Mount Temple in the Canadian Rockies. Two others were injured and only two escaped unharmed.

The victims were members of Camp Wilderness of Philadelphia. They were among twenty-four boys who had

Continued on Page 6, Column 6

ASKS EUROPE PACT

Moscow Bars NATO Tie —Says Bonn Arming Is Decisive Issue

The text of Soviet statement on Germany is on Page 2.

By WELLES HANGEN

Special to The New York Times.

MOSCOW, July 12—The Soviet Union called tonight for step-by-step reunification of Germany within the framework of an all-European collective agreement.

Moscow issued a statement outlining its position six days before the Big Four conference in Geneva. The statement declared such a course would be necessary "if under present conditions it should be impossible to achieve an immediate agreement on uniting Germany on peace-loving and democratic foundations."

The creation of a general European security system, including both Communist East Germany and West Germany, would ease international tension and prepare the way for the eventual restoration of German unity, the Moscow statement declared.

The Soviet statement also urged a reconciliation between the two German states as necessary to accelerate reunification.

The statement, distributed by Tass, official Soviet news agency, again made it clear that the Soviet leaders would not consider Western proposals for all-German elections so long as the Western part of the country was integrated in the North Atlantic Treaty Organization.

Bonn Arming Called Decisive

The question "whether West Germany is turned into a militarist state included in a military group, or whether measures are taken to prevent such development, is of decisive importance," the Soviet statement declared.

The statement said this problem could never be supplanted by the "subordinate problem of the way in which elections are held." It added that the "so-called Eden plan" proposed at the Berlin conference of foreign ministers last year had "a certain significance" but could not be considered an acceptable approach to the German problem.

[The Eden plan proposed free elections as early as possible in both parts of Germany to choose a national assembly to draft a constitution for the whole of Germany.]

A new war would be "of greatest danger" to Germany, the statement said, "because Germany would be in the center of military operations with all the ensuing disasters for the German people."

In this situation, and in view of the West's insistence on binding Germany to "military blocs," the solution for the Germans depends on "establishing and strengthening confidence among

Continued on Page 2, Column 3

NEHRU AND NASSER SCORE ALLIANCES

In Joint Statement They Say Peace Is Not Strengthened by Military Pacts

By A. M. ROSENTHAL

Special to The New York Times.

NEW DELHI, July 12—The Prime Ministers of India and Egypt joined today in denouncing military alliances as hindrances to peace.

Jawaharlal Nehru for India and Gamal Abdel Nasser for Egypt issued a statement saying peace could not be strengthened by any step "which causes apprehension to any other country."

In the past Mr. Nehru has expressed a great many apprehensions about United States military aid to Pakistan, and Egypt has reacted strongly against the Turkish-Iraqi pact. It seemed clear that in part at least the statement was directed against those two agreements.

The joint communiqué was issued simultaneously in New Delhi and Cairo. The Indian leader left the Egyptian capital this morning, after a day's visit with Premier Nasser, and arrived in Bombay tonight.

Mr. Nehru returned to India after a trip of thirty-seven days. His journey took him to seven countries for official visits. Mr. Nehru will return to this capital tomorrow and early next month is expected to give the Indian Parliament a report on his trip.

Stresses Their Friendship

Mr. Nehru and Colonel Nasser have gone out of their way in the last few months to emphasize the warmth of relations between the two countries and the identity of the two men's views on international affairs. One reason has been the tendency of countries "noncommitted" in the "cold war" to seek each other out and pool their influence informally.

For her part India is also apparently interested in showing that her quarrels with Pakistan are not based on religion and that the Indians can get along well with an important Islamic power.

Mr. Nehru and Colonel Nasser also share a strong distaste for military alliances and their communiqué today reflected it. Aside from any ideological opposition to pacts, the Indians feel their own national interests have been hurt by the United States military aid agreement with Pakistan. And the Egyptians are angered at the alliance between Turkey and Iraq, which Pakistan recently joined.

The sentences in the communiqué attacking military alliances seemed to have been intended as an especially important part of the statement. At any rate the Indian Government's Press In-

Continued on Page 8, Column 4

Muscovite Shoppers Hail Ho Chi Minh

By CLIFTON DANIEL

Special to The New York Times.

MOSCOW, July 12—"He" arrived in Moscow today.

People lined the streets to see him but there were not nearly so many as when "the other one" came five weeks ago.

"He" was Ho Chi Minh, President of North Vietnam, Communist republic in northern Indochina. "The other one" was Prime Minister Jawaharlal Nehru of India, whose tour of this country brought out the biggest crowds that any foreign visitor to the Soviet Union has ever seen.

Today it seemed that no one had been specially notified to go out on the streets. There were no bouquets in the hands of those who waited. Most of the persons who stood one or two deep along the curbstones of Gorki Street seemed to be either out shopping or on their way home from work. Near-

Continued on Page 10, Column 3

National League Beats American in All-Star Game

MUSIAL'S WALLOP GAINS 6-5 VICTORY

Continued From Page 1

Leo Durocher, who directed the National League forces, another signal triumph over Cleveland's skipper, Al Lopez, who led the American Leaguers and who last October bowed to Leo in the world series.

Lopez, during the early stages of the battle, had directed his forces well. But then he seemed to lose command in the closing rounds as the Nationals closed with a rush.

The Americans had ripped into Robin Roberts for four runs in the opening round. Three tallies rode in on a homer by the Yankees' Mickey Mantle. By the sixth the Americans had increased the advantage to 5—0.

But as the game progressed, Durocher, who hadn't been doing so well with the starting line-up the fans had voted him in the nationwide poll, began making changes of his own. The Giant manager inserted his own Willie Mays, who in the seventh inning made an electrifying catch that robbed Ted Williams of a homer, which would have given the Americans two additional runs.

On the heels of that, the Say Hey Kid, with a pair of singles, helped ignite two rallies that enabled the Nationals to draw even. They counted twice in the seventh and three times in the eighth to make it 5-all.

Meanwhile, Don Newcombe blanked the Americans in the seventh. In the eighth, the Cubs' Sam Jones got into difficulties and filled the bases with two out. But here Cincinnati's left-hander, Joe Nuxhall, entered the struggle to turn in some of the day's best pitching.

The Redlegs' hurler struck out Whitey Ford of the Yanks, a development that later was to cause some more second guessing on Lopez. Most experts seemed to feel Lopez, even though still three runs ahead, should have called on a pinch hitter, since he had ample pitching strength in Bob Turley, Herb Score and Dick Donovan.

Nuxhall held the Americans scoreless through the ninth, tenth and eleventh. Then Conley put on his magnificent performance in the twelfth as he fanned Kaline, Mickey Vernon and Al Rosen to become the eventual winner.

Sullivan Yields Homer

In gaining their winning tally, which Musial hammered out of bounds, the Nationals had to overcome an equally rugged foeman. Frank Sullivan, the Red Sox right-hander, after relieving Ford in the eighth, had held the Nationals at bay through three and one-third innings before Musial's blow laid him low.

It was the fourth All-Star home run of his career for Stan the Man, a record for the competition. Like Mays, Musial was a late starter in the game, since he was not one of the originals chosen by the fans. Although a first sacker all this season, Stan replaced the Phils' Del Ennis in left field to allow Cincinnati's mighty Ted Kluszewski to play the entire game at first.

Musial's appearance also made him the dean of all present-day active players in All-Star competition. This was his twelfth classic, one more than Williams, who today played in his eleventh.

Williams, however, did not finish and the move doubtless was one that Lopez long will regret. He permitted the Red Sox slugger, who had singled earlier in the day, to retire after Mays made his spectacular catch to end the Americans' seventh. The Americans were still leading by five and the victory seemed safe.

Just before the battle got under way the crowd, which had tossed $179,545.50 into the till, stood in silent tribute to the memory of Arch Ward, the Chicago Tribune sports editor, who had founded the All-Star game in 1933. Funeral services for Ward were held in Chicago this morning.

Then, scarcely had the fans settled back in their seats after the singing of the National Anthem, than the American Leaguers opened fire on Roberts. The right-handed ace of the Phillies was starting his fifth mid-summer classic.

Harvey Keunn singled to left. Nellie Fox singled to right and runners were on first and third. Next occurred a wild pitch as Roberts worked on Williams. Kuenn scored on the slip.

Williams Draws Walk

Roberts, who seemed to be having unusual trouble with his control, wound up walking Williams. A moment later, Mantle sent a tremendous smash straight down the middle. It cleared the barrier between the bleachers and bullpens, more than 400 feet away. It also gave the American Leaguers a 4-0 lead.

For all of five innings after that, the game became one of the most silent All-Star struggles in history. The crowd, predominantly National League in its sympathies, watched the futile efforts of its favorites to cut down the margin.

Billy Pierce, the crack southpaw of the White Sox, blanked the Nationals and allowed only one hit in the first three innings. In fact, he faced only nine batters.

Red Schoendienst, leading off the Durocher batting order, singled in the first. But the Cardinal second sacker was then rubbed out trying to steal second on a pitch that bounced out of Catcher Yogi Berra's glove.

Early Wynn, the star right-hander of Lopez' Indians, then blanked the Nationals for three more innings. He gave up three blows. In the fifth, Kluszewski doubled and Don Mueller singled to left. But Kluszewski couldn't score on the hit and Wynn worked his way out of the jam.

In the sixth, the gloom of the Milwaukee fans went even a shade deeper. Harvey Haddix, a Cardinal left-hander, yielded a tally after blanking the American Leaguers in the fourth and fifth.

Berra singled and Al Kaline banged a double off Ed Mathews' wrist. The injury later sent the Braves' third sacker to the hospital for X-rays. The examination showed no fracture.

Berra went to third on Kaline's blow. Vernon bounced a grounder to Kluszewski and Yogi scooted home. The Americans were ahead, 5 to 0.

Mays Takes Over

With the seventh, however, the Nationals began to bestir themselves. The Dodgers' Duke Snider had not overly distinguished himself when he gave way in center field to Mays. Willie made his presence felt almost immediately.

Two were out and Chico Carrasquel was on first in the American's seventh when Williams stroked a powerful smash toward right center. But Willie gave chase and just as the ball appeared to clear the wire railing, the Say Hey Kid leaped up to snare the ball in his glove.

First up in the last of the seventh, Mays greeted Ford with a single to left. The Yankee southpaw had just taken the mound. He got the next two, but Hank Aaron of the Braves, in as the result of another belated, though popular, move by Durocher, drew a pass.

A moment later, the Braves' Johnny Logan singled to right and one run scored. Then Stan Lopata grounded to Carrasquel, who had just taken over at short for the Americans. Chico booted the ball, threw wide to second and a second run scored on the error.

Two were out in the eighth when the Nationals launched another offensive against Ford. Again it was Mays who started it with a single. Kluszewski and Randy Jackson, who had replaced Mathews, also singled. That scored Willie and Ford went out for Sullivan.

Before the Red Sox right-hander got matters under control, Lopez was to receive another jolt as two runs tallied to tie the score.

Aaron blasted a single to right and when Kaline's throw toward third got away from Rosen for an error, both Kluszewski and Jackson tallied. The Indians' Rosen had been another delayed entry by Lopez that did not pan out so well.

The aroused Nationals appeared set for a killing in the ninth when, with two down, Schoendienst singled and Musial walked. But Sullivan this time mastered Mays and got him on a third strike.

Nuxhall drew thunderous cheers when, after walking Kaline in the tenth, he fanned three in a row, but he had a close call in the eleventh. A pass to Avila and a single by Mantle had two on with two out when Berra bounced a grounder over second.

Schoendienst made a miraculous stop and fired the ball over his shoulder toward first. A mighty close play followed and when Yogi was called out, he protested vehemently. That, too, was to prove the American Leaguers' last gasp.

The cheering for Conley in the twelfth had barely subsided when Musial hit Sullivan's first pitch in the lower half. With that, another stirring interleague classic had gone into the records. The Americans still lead in the series, thirteen games to nine, but the Nationals have won five of the last six contests.

For the vanquished, Berra set a record by becoming the first catcher to work five complete All-Star games. He had previously been tied with Roy Campanella at four. Three other American Leaguers went all the way today, Mantle, Kaline and Vernon. Kluszewski and Schoendienst were the two "iron men" for the triumphant National League 3.

Stan the Man Breaks Up a Ball Game After Some Tense Moments

Stan Musial, who hit the game-winning homer for the National League All-Stars, is congratulated by Pitcher Robin Roberts, wearing jacket, after climactic drive against the American Leaguers in the twelfth inning of Milwaukee game.

Box Score of All-Star Game

AMERICAN LEAGUE

	ab.	r.	h.	po.	a.	e.
Kuenn, ss	3	1	1	1	0	0
Carrasquel, ss	3	0	2	1	3	1
Fox, 2b	3	1	1	2	0	0
Avila, 2b	1	0	0	1	2	0
Williams, lf	3	1	1	1	0	0
Smith, lf	1	0	0	0	0	0
Mantle, cf	6	1	2	3	0	0
Berra, c	6	1	1	8	2	0
Kaline, rf	4	0	1	6	0	0
Vernon, 1b	5	0	1	8	0	0
Finigan, 3b	3	0	0	2	0	0
Rosen, 3b	2	0	0	0	0	1
Pierce, p	0	0	0	0	0	0
bJensen	1	0	0	0	0	0
Wynn, p	0	0	0	0	1	0
gPower	1	0	0	0	0	0
Ford, p	1	0	0	0	1	0
Sullivan, p	1	0	0	0	0	0
Total	44	5	10	*33	9	2

NATIONAL LEAGUE

	ab.	r.	h.	po.	a.	e.
Schoendienst, 2b	6	0	2	3	2	0
Ennis, lf	1	0	0	1	0	0
cMusial, lf	4	1	1	0	0	0
Snider, cf	2	0	0	3	0	0
Mays, cf	3	2	2	3	0	0
Kluszewski, 1b	5	1	2	9	1	0
Mathews, 3b	2	0	0	0	3	1
Jackson, 3b	3	1	1	0	0	0
Mueller, rf	2	0	1	0	0	0
dAaron, rf	2	1	2	0	0	0
Banks, ss	2	0	0	2	1	0
Logan, ss	3	0	1	1	1	0
Crandall, c	1	0	0	1	0	0
eBurgess, c	1	0	0	2	0	0
hLopata, c	3	0	0	10	0	0
Roberts, p	0	0	0	1	1	0
aThomas	1	0	0	0	0	0
Haddix, p	0	0	0	0	2	0
fHodges	1	0	1	0	0	0
Newcombe, p	0	0	0	0	0	0
iBaker	1	0	0	0	0	0
Jones, p	0	0	0	0	0	0
Nuxhall, p	2	0	0	0	1	0
Conley, p	0	0	0	0	0	0
Total	45	6	13	36	12	1

*None out when winning run was scored.
aPopped out for Roberts in third.
bPopped out for Pierce in fourth.
cStruck out for Ennis in fourth.
dRan for Mueller in fifth.
eHit into force out for Crandall in fifth.
fSingled for Haddix in sixth.
gPopped out for Wynn in seventh.
hSafe on error for Burgess in seventh.
iFlied out for Newcombe in seventh.

American	4 0 0	0 0 1	0 0 0	0 0 0	—5
National	0 0 0	0 0 0	2 3 0	0 0 1	—6

Runs batted in—Mantle 3, Vernon, Logan, Jackson, Aaron, Musial.

Two-base hits—Kluszewski, Kaline.

Home runs—Mantle, Musial. Sacrifices—Pierce, Avila. Double plays—Kluszewski, Banks and Roberts; Wynn, Carrasquel and Vernon. Left on bases—American 12, National 8. Bases on balls—Roberts 1 (Williams), Ford 1 (Aaron), Jones 2 (Vernon, Rosen), Nuxhall 3 (Smith, Kaline, Avila), Sullivan 1 (Musial). Strike outs—Pierce 3 (Ennis, Snider, Banks), Haddix 2 (Kaline, Finnigan), Wynn 1 (Musial), Newcombe 1 (Avila), Jones 1 (Mantle), Nuxhall 5 (Ford, Vernon, Rosen, Sullivan, Smith), Sullivan 4 (Mays, Jackson, Logan, Lopata), Conley 3 (Kaline, Vernon, Rosen).

Hits—Off Roberts 4 in 3 innings, Pierce 1 in 3, Haddix 3 in 3, Wynn 3 in 3, Newcombe 1 in 1, Jones 0 in 2-3, Ford 5 in 1 2-3, Nuxhall 2 in 3 1-3, Sullivan 4 in 3 1-3 (faced one batter in twelfth), Conley 0 in 1. Runs, earned runs—Roberts 4 and 4, Haddix 1 and 1, Ford 5 and 5, Sullivan 1 and 1. Hit by pitcher—By Jones (Kaline). Wild pitch—Roberts. Passed ball—Crandall. Winning pitcher—Conley. Losing pitcher—Sullivan. Umpire—Barlick (N.), Soar (A.), Boggess (N.), Summers (A.), Secory (N.), Runge (A.). Time—3:17. Attendance—45,314. Receipts (gross)—$179,545.50.

"All the News That's Fit to Print"

The New York Times.

LATE CITY EDITION
Partly cloudy and seasonable today. Mostly fair tomorrow.
Temperature Range Today-Max., 68; Min., 58
Temperatures Yesterday—Max., 69; Min., 59
Full U. S. Weather Bureau Report, Page 69

© 1955, by The New York Times Company.

VOL. CV..No. 35,683. Entered as Second-Class Matter, Post Office, New York, N. Y. NEW YORK, WEDNESDAY, OCTOBER 5, 1955. Times Square, New York 36, N. Y. Telephone LAckawanna 4-1000 FIVE CENTS

DODGERS CAPTURE 1ST WORLD SERIES; PODRES WINS, 2-0

He Beats Yanks Second Time as Team Takes Classic in 8th Try, 4 Games to 3

HODGES DRIVES IN 2 RUNS

Single in 4th and Sacrifice Fly in 6th Decide—Amoros Catch Thwarts Bombers

By JOHN DREBINGER

Brooklyn's long cherished dream finally has come true. The Dodgers have won their first world series championship.

The end of the trail came at the Stadium yesterday. Smokey Alston's Brooks, with Johnny Podres tossing a brilliant shutout, turned back Casey Stengel's Yankees, 2 to 0, in the seventh and deciding game of the 1955 baseball classic.

This gave the National League champions the series, 4 games to 3. As the jubilant victors almost smothered their 23-year-old left-handed pitcher from Witherbee, N. Y., a roaring crowd of 62,465 joined in sounding off a thunderous ovation. Not even the stanchest American League die-hard could begrudge Brooklyn its finest hour.

Seven times in the past had the Dodgers been thwarted in their efforts to capture baseball's most sought prize—the last five times by these same Bombers.

When the goal finally was achieved the lid blew off in Brooklyn, while experts, poring into the records, agreed nothing quite so spectacular had been accomplished before. For this was the first time a team had won a seven-game world series after losing the first two games.

Victor in Third Game

And Podres, who had vanquished the Yankees in the third game as the series moved to Ebbets Field last Friday, became the first Brooklyn pitcher to win two games in one series.

Tommy Byrne, a seasoned campaigner who was the Yanks' "comeback hero of the year," carried the Bombers' hopes in this dramatic struggle in which victory would have given them their seventeenth series title. But Byrne, whose southpaw slants had turned back the Dodgers in the second encounter, could not quite cope with the youngster pitted against him.

In the fourth inning a two-bagger by Roy Campanella and a single by Gil Hodges gave the Brooks their first run.

In the sixth a costly Yankee error helped fill the bases. It forced the withdrawal of Byrne, though in all he had given only three hits.

Stengel called on his right-handed relief hurler, Bob Grim.

Bob did well enough. But he couldn't prevent Hodges from lifting a long sacrifice fly to center that drove in Pee Wee Reese with the Brooks' second run of the day.

Fortified with this additional tally, Podres then blazed the way through a succession of thrills while a grim band of Dodgers fought with the tenacity of inspired men to hold the advantage to the end.

Fittingly, the final out was a grounder by Elston Howard to Reese, the 36-year-old shortstop and captain of the Flock. Ever since 1941 had the Little Colonel

Continued on Page 42, Column 1

The New York Times

BATTERY IS CHARGED WITH VICTORY: Johnny Podres is hoisted aloft by Catcher Roy Campanella after pitching the Dodgers to triumph over Yankees yesterday in seventh game of the world series. Don Hoak, third baseman, rushes over to join the festivities.

Capital Budget, No Record, Is $799,876,189 for 1956

By CHARLES G. BENNETT

New York City would spend $799,876,189 for its major public improvements next year under a capital budget brought out yesterday by the City Planning Commission. The budget, as prepared for public hearings, included $468,663,938 within the city's constitutional debt limit and $331,212,251 exempt from the debt limit.

Public hearings will be held by the commission at City Hall next Tuesday, Thursday and Friday.

The proposed budget would not be a record. The 1955 budget as proposed a year ago was $814,587,730.

As finally adopted, the 1955 budget was $670,806,313. Because of the probable expenditure this year of some funds earmarked for renewal next year, if still unspent by next Jan. 1, the 1956 budget is expected to show similar shrinkage.

175 Million in New Funds

Of the $468,663,938 proposed to be spent within the debt limit, $225,349,710 would be a renewal of unspent allocations within the 1955 capital budget, $68,327,190 includes renewals of sums shifted from 1955 proposals to different projects in 1956, and $174,987,038 would be new funds.

The commission noted that the $174,987,038 figure was within the $175,000,000 certified by Mayor Wagner on Sept. 15 as being available in new funds for the 1956 capital budget.

On Aug. 10 twenty-eight city agencies submitted 1956 capital budget requests totaling $1,112,423,020. Therefore in the proposed allocations the departments have been cut by $312,546,831. The agencies asked for $426,000,000 in new money, both inside and outside the debt limit, and got $243,000,000.

In new funds, both inside and outside the debt limit, the commission allocated $133,565,000 to transit improvements — largely exempt from the debt limit—$93,226,215 for schools, $13,581,822 for marine and aviation waterfront improvements, and $43,000,000 for pollution control projects.

Mayor Ordered Preference

Mayor Wagner directed the commission, which prepares the capital budget, to give generous allocations to these four areas.

The $93,226,215 earmarked for the Board of Education would be spent for two new high schools, eight junior high schools and ten elementary schools, in addition to equipping and modernizing existing schools.

The new money allocated for rapid transit improvements would include another bite of $104,000,000 from the $500,000,000 bond issue voted for rapid transit outside the debt limit. The commission disclosed that $118,000,000 would remain in this fund above the amounts spent and earmarked through 1956.

At the time the fund was voted, the city planned to use it

Continued on Page 29, Column 2

AUTO INSURANCE TO ADD BENEFITS

Owners Will Be Indemnified for Personal Injuries Laid to Uninsured Drivers

By LEO EGAN

A new automobile liability insurance coverage was announced yesterday. It will indemnify owners of insured cars for personal injuries caused by uninsured drivers.

Leffert Holz, State Superintendent of Insurance, made the announcement. The companies offering the new coverage, he said, will add it free to all their existing policies. But they will charge an extra premium, ranging from $2.50 to $4, for continuing the coverage when renewing outstanding policies.

Governor Harriman commended the insurance companies for their action. He said in Albany that it represented "a major step" in meeting the problem of injuries caused by financially irresponsible drivers.

"This is not, of course," he added, "the complete answer to the problem of the financially irresponsible motorist but it represents an important gain."

The broadened coverage will apply not only to the owner of an insured car but to his spouse and to relatives of either if they live in his household. It will cover them while they are riding in the insured vehicle or any other

Continued on Page 70, Column 4

FINANCIER SOUGHT IN FRAUD INQUIRY

Robert Morman of Lawyers Mortgage and Title Hunted by Hogan for Questioning

By JACK ROTH

District Attorney Frank S. Hogan said yesterday he was seeking to question a prominent business man concerning a swindle that "may run into hundreds of thousands of dollars."

The man sought is Robert Morman, a vice president and a member of the board of directors of the Lawyers Mortgage and Title Company, 115 Broadway. Mr. Morman also heads New York Investors Mutual Group, Inc., a real estate company, and seven smaller concerns, all with offices at 271 Fifth Avenue, near Twenty-ninth Street.

There are three specific subjects the District Attorney would like to question Mr. Morman on: a shortage of $130,000 in the funds of Lawyers Mortgage and Title Company, the issuance of fraudulent stock certificates of an unknown amount in behalf of the company, and the possibility that "hundreds of thousands of dollars" worth of stock issued by the New York Investors Mutual Group is "tainted with fraud."

The District Attorney's office said New York Investors had sold $1,000,000 worth of stock.

Mr. Morman, who is said to be in his middle 50s, has been missing from his home at 521 Park Avenue, near Sixtieth Street, at least since the matter was turned over to Mr. Hogan's office two weeks ago.

The investigation is being conducted by Jerome Kidder, assistant District Attorney in charge of the Frauds Bureau.

Mr. Hogan said friends and associates of Mr. Morman had been questioned, but that none

Continued on Page 28, Column 3

PRESIDENT SHOWS STEADY PROGRESS; MOOD IS CHEERFUL

Eisenhower Signs 6 Papers and Confers With Adams—Rests for Long Periods

By RUSSELL BAKER
Special to The New York Times.

DENVER, Wednesday, Oct. 5—President Eisenhower is continuing his steady progress toward recovery.

Midway in his second week in the hospital, he again was reported comfortable, cheerful, relaxed and making satisfactory progress without complications. The end of the week will mark the conclusion of the fourteen-day critical period.

There was no evidence of a recurrence of the depression and fatigue that on Sunday night had given the President his only minor setback since he entered the hospital Sept. 24 after an attack of coronary thrombosis. This is the formation of a clot in the heart or near-by blood vessels.

Yesterday's last scheduled medical bulletin was issued at 8:45 P. M. It said:

"The President had another good day. His condition continues to be satisfactory without complications."

The hospital had issued no further report by 2 A. M. today (5 A. M., New York time).

For the second consecutive day General Eisenhower conferred briefly on official business with Sherman Adams, The Assistant to the President, who is in charge of the White House.

In the ten minutes that Mr. Adams was at his bedside, the President signed six routine official papers. These included a letter accepting the resignation of an ambassador because of a "heart condition."

Approves Choice of Lodge

General Eisenhower also approved the designation of Henry Cabot Lodge Jr., United States representative to the United Nations, as his personal representative at the funeral of Maj. Gen. Julius Ochs Adler, retired, first vice president and general manager of The New York Times.

Mrs. Eisenhower visited with the President during breakfast and luncheon. The President listened to soft music in his room and napped or rested for long periods in mid-morning and mid-afternoon.

It was a completely routine and reassuring day, both at Fitzsimons Army Hospital and at the White House offices at Lowry Air Force Base.

The bulletins from the hospital contained such words as "refreshed," "rested," "comfortable," "relaxed" and "cheerful."

One document the President signed appointed Mansfield D. Sprague, 45-year-old Bridgeport, Conn., attorney, as general counsel of the Department of Defense. Mr. Sprague, a Republican, will succeed Wilber M. Brucker, who was appointed Secretary of the Army.

The President also named

Continued on Page 26, Column 2

Dulles Indicates Deferring Of Foreign Policy Decisions

Foresees No Emergency and Implies All Non-Urgent Items Await President—Sees Pattern Set for Many Actions

By JAMES RESTON
Special to The New York Times.

WASHINGTON, Oct. 4—Secretary of State Dulles indicated today that, except in urgent matters, important foreign policy decisions would be postponed until President Eisenhower was well enough to give them his personal attention.

The Secretary told his news conference this morning that he did not anticipate any emergency in this field that could not be dealt with on the basis of established policies.

He added that "there is every reason to anticipate that before long it will be possible to talk to the President about any of these matters that become urgent."

Thus the ranking member of the Cabinet supported the thesis that no formal delegation of Presidential powers was expected, but in the process he described certain procedures that were still a subject of controversy in the capital.

These were as follows:

¶First, most foreign policy decisions could be taken on the basis of policies already debated in the National Security Council and approved by the President. There is general agreement on this.

¶Second, Cabinet members would continue to run their departments on the basis of precedents followed in the past with the President's knowledge.

For example, Mr. Dulles sent George V. Allen, Assistant Secretary of State, to Cairo to try to block the purchase of arms by Egypt from Czechoslovakia. He explained today that the movement of his assistant secretaries of state in the past had been his personal responsibility

Continued on Page 26, Column 6

INDIA URGES BAN ON NUCLEAR ARMS

Krishna Menon Warns U. N. Nothing but Prohibition of Use Will Suffice

By THOMAS J. HAMILTON
Special to The New York Times.

UNITED NATIONS, N. Y., Oct. 4—V. K. Krishna Menon of India urged the United Nations today to accept nothing less than the total prohibition of nuclear weapons, regardless of the positions taken by the United States and the Soviet Union.

"Without meaning any offense," he told the General Assembly, "I would say, representing a country that is not an atomic power, that does not believe in the balaance-of-power doctrine, that does not believe that preparation for war creates peace or that war creates peace, that even if the Soviet Union and the United States were to agree that they should have atomic weapons, we would not think that that would be good for the world."

He added: "We do not believe that there is more safety in two hydrogen bombs than there is in one."

"Therefore, there is only one thing to do with the atomic weapon, and that is to throw it away," Mr. Krishna Menon said.

Mr. Krishna Menon expressed opposition also to the "idea" that nuclear weapons could be used to establish peace in the case of "so-called aggression." This proposal is under study in the United Nations Disarmament Commission's subcommittee, which includes the United

Continued on Page 14, Column 3

FAURE FACES TEST ON AFRICA POLICY

Reconvened Assembly Wants to Challenge Him on Crisis in Algeria and Morocco

By ROBERT C. DOTY
Special to The New York Times.

PARIS, Oct. 4—Parliament reconvened today in a fever of impatience to call Premier Edgar Faure's Government to account for the troubled state of France's North African empire.

The most recent news from across the Mediterranean did little to help M. Faure's chances of weathering the expected storm of parliamentary criticism.

The long and eagerly awaited "settlement" in the protectorate of Morocco, as it was interpreted there by the Government's executive agents, has produced not peace but new outbreaks of tribal violence in the Riff area.

The plan of reforms for France's three Algerian departments that was to consecrate the policy of "integrating" them with the homeland has met with open opposition from Moslem leaders and apathy on the part of the European population of Algeria.

Finally, the fellagha (outlaw) revolt, until recently concentrated in two areas of the Constantine Department and a corner of the Department of Algiers, has broken out in the Department of Oran, adjoining the newly troubled areas of Morocco.

The only action of recent weeks that is likely to appease a part of the potential opposition is the Government's order to withdraw France's delegation to the United Nations General As-

Continued on Page 9, Column 5

U. S. TELLS SOVIET ARAB ARMS DEAL IS HURTING AMITY

Dulles Says He Gave Molotov Views on the Middle East at Recent Parley Here

REPORTS ON CAIRO TALK

Details of Czech-Egyptian Pact Not Entirely Settled, Secretary Declares

The transcript of Dulles news conference is on Page 8.

By DANA ADAMS SCHMIDT
Special to The New York Times.

WASHINGTON, Oct. 4—Secretary of State Dulles has told Soviet Foreign Minister Vyacheslav M. Molotov that delivery of arms from the Soviet bloc to Egypt would not help relax tensions between the United States and the Soviet Union.

Mr. Dulles said at his news conference today that he had followed this line in talks with Mr. Molotov in New York two weeks ago, and again a week ago today when he dined with the Soviet, British and French foreign ministers.

"It is not easy or pleasant to speculate on the probable motives of the Soviet bloc leaders" in authorizing such deliveries, Mr. Dulles added today.

This aspect of the Egyptian-Czechoslovak arms deal, with its implications for general East-West relations and the foreign ministers' conference in Geneva later this month, is giving United States officials even more concern than Egypt's acceptance of the arms.

Nevertheless, Mr. Dulles said he looked for "positive progress" toward unification of Germany at the October conference and would be "greatly disappointed" if this were not achieved.

Comments on Peiping Talk

Observing that he was aware of no slowdown in United States talks with Communist China, Mr. Dulles said he had no clear evidence that Peiping would renege on its promise to release the United States citizens it still detained.

United States officials see in the Soviet bloc's effort to supply arms to Arab countries a major test of Soviet intentions. If, as seems to be the case, the Soviet bloc is out to stir up trouble in the Middle East, the officials observed, it will be difficult to believe its protestations of a desire to seek settlements of East-West issues.

Mr. Dulles said he had "no reason to believe" that the Egyptians would not carry through their arms deal with Czechoslovakia. But he added that the United States still had no detailed information about the arrangement.

In two "rather full" talks with Premier Gamal Abdel Nasser of Egypt on the subject, Assistant Secretary George V. Allen got the impression, Mr. Dulles said, that most of the details had not been finally settled.

Asked whether Egypt was making the deal with Czechoslovakia or the Soviet Union, or with both, Mr. Dulles replied that "for this purpose it is hard to draw much distinction between the Soviet Union and Czechoslovakia."

Mr. Dulles said he "could not say" whether it was likely the

Continued on Page 8, Column 4

About New York—And Brooklyn: Dodger Fans Have Their Innings

By MEYER BERGER

Dodger hysteria manifested itself in curious ways yesterday after the last out at Yankee Stadium saw the Brooklyns lifted to their first modern baseball championship.

Calls into Brooklyn and Long Island from Manhattan—mostly from the lower and upper East Side, for some unfathomed reason—overloaded all dial relays in the Murray Hill, Oregon, Lexington, Plaza, Templeton and Eldorado exchanges, so that anyone trying to put through a business call from 3:44 to 4:01 P. M. got no dial repsonse.

Telephone Company officials said the flood was the greatest since V-J Day. They figure many of the calls had to do with bet collections or arrangements for victory dinners, but that most were just floods of plain hosannas.

* * *

There was a sad autumnal touch after the game in the clusters of dazed Yankee fans still in the stands, with the tall sun slanting across them in the sudden twilight that had overtaken their invincibles.

* * *

A Western-hatted gentleman in the lower grandstand, explaining his presence there yesterday to a neighbor fan, said: "I just got tired of seeing the series in black and white. I thought I'd come out and see it in color."

* * *

After the last Yankee out, Wall Street skyscrapers opened their windows and released millions of bits of homemade confetti to turn in glinting beauty in the sun. A foreign gentleman stared in astonishment at the display in Maiden Lane.

"Pardon me, sir," he said to a passing artist. "Why do the

Continued on Page 44, Column 3

3 Figurines Found; Theft Laid to 2 Boys

Two 14-year-old Brooklyn boys suddenly got a "bright idea" while in the Brooklyn Museum Saturday afternoon and took eight silver figurines on exhibition. The police said the boys told them this last night and turned over two of the eight pieces of sculpture, Panther and Statuette of the Virgin.

A third figure, Box in the Form of a Ram, was thrown down a sewer because "it didn't look nice." They said the others had been hidden in the grass and under benches of the eight-square-block Red Hook Housing Development. A woman found one of these, Man Riding the Llama, and turned it over to the police last night.

Detectives and others were making an intensive search of the area for the four pieces unaccounted for. If all have

Continued on Page 28, Column 7

Sunlight Powers a Telephone Call for First Time

Telephone employe in Americus, Ga., adjusts device to capture sun's rays for rural line

By ROBERT K. PLUMB
Special to The New York Times.

AMERICUS, Ga., Oct. 4—The light of the sun was harnessed to power a rural telephone circuit near here this morning. At 10 A. M. a Bell Telephone Company engineer threw a switch to shift a rural circuit from usual battery power to operation on electricity made from solar energy.

In a sense, all energy used on earth (excepting atomic energy) comes from the sun. For sunlight lays down fossil fuels, draws water to the mountain tops, and in other ways provides the energy from which man gets electricity. But here this morning, the power of sunlight was trapped

Continued on Page 39, Column 1

Peron Still Insists He Is the President

By The United Press.

ASUNCION, Paraguay, Oct. 4—Gen. Juan D. Perón said today he still was the "constitutional President" of Argentina.

He denied that he had ever resigned. He said, "I would have remained in my country if a minimum of guarantees existed there because I have nothing to reproach myself for."

He did not rule out the possibility that some day it would occur to him to return to Argentine politics, but he said that, for now, he intended to remain in Paraguay.

"Despite the wealth attributed to me by my occasional detractors," he added, he does not have the money to go to Europe and "play the tourist."

The ousted dictator's statements were made in reply to a questionnaire. In addition, he talked with a United Press cor-

Continued on Page 16, Column 3

Dodgers Win First World Series Title in 8th Try

SOUTHPAW TAKES 7TH CONTEST, 2-0

Continued From Page 1

from Kentucky been fighting these Yankees. Five times had he been forced to accept the loser's share.

Many a heart in the vast arena doubtless skipped a beat as Pee Wee scooped up the ball and fired it to first. It was a bit low and wide. But Hodges, the first sacker, reached out and grabbed it inches off the ground. Gil would have stretched halfway across the Bronx for that one.

Thus to the 43-year-old Walter E. Alston of Darrtown, Ohio, goes the distinction of piloting a Dodger team to its first world title. As a player, Smokey had appeared in the majors only long enough to receive one time at bat with the Cardinals. What is more, he ruefully recalls, he struck out.

Dropped back to the minors soon after that, Alston didn't appear in the majors again until he was named manager of the Brooks in 1954.

Yet, in his second year he not only led the Dodgers to an overwhelming triumph for the National League pennant but also attained a prize that had eluded such managerial greats as the late Uncle Wilbert Robinson, Leo Durocher, Burt Shotton and Chuck Dressen.

The Dodgers made their first world series appearance in 1916. They lost to the Boston Red Sox. In 1920 they bowed to the Cleveland Indians. Then in 1941, '47, '49, '52 and '53 they went down before the mighty Bombers.

As for the Yanks, the defeat brought to an end a string of world series successes without parallel. Victors in sixteen classics, they suffered only their fifth setback. It was their first defeat under Charles Dillon Stengel, who bagged five in a row from 1949 through 1953.

Giants, Cards Did Trick

Back in 1921 and 1922 the Bombers lost to John McGraw's Giants. Until yesterday the Cardinals had been the only other National League champions to stop them. St. Louis won in 1926 and again in 1942. Since then the Yankees had bagged seven classics until the Brooks broke their spell.

Perfect baseball weather again greeted the belligerents as the battle lines were drawn for this final conflict.

The crowd, though smaller than for the three previous Stadium games, contributed $407,-549 to the series pool, to help set a world series "gate" total of $2,337,515. This, of course, is apart from the addition revenues derived from radio and television.

As the players took the field there was a final check on the invalids, of whom both sides provided more than a fair share.

Duke Snider was back in the Dodger line-up. Duke had gone out of the sixth game on Monday with a twisted knee when he stepped in a small hole fielding a pop fly in center field.

But Jackie Robinson, who had fought so valiantly for the Brooks in the three straight games they won in Ebbets Field, had to remain on the sidelines. He was suffering from a strained Achilles tendon in his right leg. So Don Hoak played third.

Bauer in Right Field

In the Yankee camp, Hank Bauer, the ex-marine, was in right field again despite a pulled thigh muscle. But Mickey Mantle, a serious loss to the Bombers throughout the series, was still out with his painfully torn leg muscle. He did manage to get into the game for one pinch-hit performance. His best was a towering, though harmless, pop fly.

Since the Yanks, who on Monday had squared the series by crushing the left-handed Karl Spooner with a five-run first-inning blast, were again being confronted by a southpaw, Stengel strung along with his right-handed batting power. But defensively this was to prove costly. For it was Bill Skowron, his first-sacker, who made the damaging fielding slip in the sixth.

For three innings Podres and Byrne maintained a scoreless deadlock. Skowron, a right-handed hitter who had stunned the Brooks with his three-run homer into the right-field stands Monday, gave them another mild jolt in the second.

This time he bounced a ground-rule double into the same stands. But there already were two out and Podres quickly checked this scoring bid.

There again were two out when the Yanks strove to break through in the third with a threat that had a freakish end. Phil Rizzuto walked. Incidentally, this was Li'l Phil's fifty-second world series game, topping by one the record held by Joe DiMaggio.

Behind that pass Billy Martin singled to right, Rizzuto pulling up at second. Gil McDougald then chopped a bounding ball down the third-base line. Had Hoak fielded it he doubtless would have been unable to make a play anywhere.

But Don didn't get his hands on it. The ball struck Rizzuto at the moment Li'l Phil was sliding into third base. McDougald, of course, received credit for a hit. But Rizzuto was declared out for getting hit by a batted ball and the inning was over.

In the fourth the Dodgers broke through for the first run and they did it with their first two hits off Byrne.

The 35-year-old lefty from Wake Forest, N. C., had just fanned Snider for the first out when Campanella slammed a double into left. Roy moved to third on Carl Furillo's infield out and a moment later Campy was over the plate on Hodges' solid single into left.

In the last of this round Podres had to turn back a serious Yankee threat. A mix-up of signals in the usually smooth operating Dodger outfield had Johnny in a hole.

Yogi Berra lifted an easy fly slightly to the left of center. It appeared to be a simple catch for Snider. But Junior Gilliam, who had started the game in left, also dashed for the ball. As a result the Duke at the last second shied away from the ball and it fell to the ground for a flukey two-bagger.

Work Cut Out for Podres

Since this happened on the first play of the Yankee inning, Podres had his work cut out for him. But he got Bauer on a fly to right. Skowron grounded to Zimmer and Bob Cerv ended it with a pop to Reese.

A single by Reese started the drive against Byrne in the sixth. Ill fortune then overtook Tommy in a hurry. Snider laid down a sacrifice bunt. Byrne fielded it and flipped it to Skowron, who had an easy out at first. But Moose, who had been the big hero on Monday, now became the goat.

Seeking to make the out on Snider by way of a tag, Skowron had the ball knocked out of his hand and the Dodgers had two aboard. Campanella then sacrificed and the runners were on second and third.

Byrne was allowed to remain long enough to give Furillo an intentional pass. Then Tommy gave way to Grim. Bob couldn't keep Hodges from hitting a long fly to center that scored Reese with the second run of the game.

For a moment it looked as if the Dodgers would pile up more since Grim, before steadying, unfurled a wild pitch and gave a pass to Hoak to fill the bases a second time.

But here Alston called on Shotgun George Shuba to pinch-hit for Zimmer. George grounded to Skowron to end the round.

However, this maneuver indirectly was to play a prominent part in what followed. For, just as on Monday Stengel's move to replace Skowron by the better-fielding Joe Collins at first had resulted in the nipping of a Dodger threat, something of the sort now worked for Alston.

For with Zimmer out, Gilliam was switched to second base and Sandy Amoros went in as the left fielder. Minutes later Sandy was to make a glittering catch and throw that were to save the Brooks some mighty bad moments.

Martin walked in the last of the sixth and McDougald outgalloped a bunt for a hit to put two on with nobody out. Berra then stroked an outside pitch, the ball sailing down the left-field foul line.

It appeared to be a certain hit. But Amoros, racing at top speed, stuck out his glove and caught the ball in front of the stand. Martin, meanwhile had played it fairly safe and was only a few feet up from second.

But McDougald had gone well down from first, with the result that when Sandy fired the ball to Reese, who in turn relayed it to Hodges at first, McDougald was doubled off the bag by inches. It was a killing play for the Yanks.

Then in the eighth the Bombers made their last bid. Rizzuto, fighting heroically to the last, singled to left. Martin flied out. But McDougald slashed a fierce hopper down the third-base line that struck Hoak on the shoulder and bounded away for a single.

The Yanks again had two on and with the still dangerous Berra and Bauer the next two batters. Podres now turned on his finest pitching of the afternoon. He got Berra on a short pop-up that Furillo snared in right. He then fanned Bauer amid a deafening salvo of cheers.

That about clinched it. For even though Bob Turley tossed two scoreless rounds for the Yanks in the eighth and ninth, Stengel's best stretch of relief pitching in the entire series had come too late and to no purpose.

PLAY THAT HURT YANKS: Phil Rizzuto races toward third base on Gil McDougald's grounder for the Yanks with two on and two out in third inning of yesterday's game . . .

. . . but the ball hits Rizzuto as he slides for the bag, resulting in an automatic out. . . .

The New York Times

. . . and Umpire Lee Ballanfant signals that Rizzuto is out. Third baseman is Don Hoak.

PITCHER IS HAILED IN HIS FINEST HOUR

Podres Center of Dodgers' Celebration—Amoros Is Happy in 3 Languages

By ROSCOE McGOWEN

The millennium and pandemonium arrived at approximately the same time in the Brooklyn Dodgers' clubhouse at the Yankee Stadium yesterday.

The millennium arrived when Brooklyn won its first world series in modern times after seven failures. Pandemonium followed as a matter of course.

Johnny Podres, the 23-year-old southpaw, was mauled, slapped, hugged and kissed by his team-mates. Before the boy was through this happy ordeal, he was more tired than he had been made by the courageous game he pitched and won.

Johnny's father, Joseph, an iron miner in the Podres home town of Witherbee, N. Y., was completely overcome. He wouldn't enter the clubhouse and he couldn't be found outside.

"He's crying," said Johnny, in one lull in the wild celebration when a friend could get his ear. "He doesn't want anybody to see him."

Tears Shed in Victory

There were other tears in the clubhouse, too. Clem Labine, the handsome young right-hander, who had been "heating up" in the bullpen in momentary expectation of being called into the game, moved back in the shadows of his locker and sat with bowed head.

He looked up and smiled through the tears running down his cheeks.

"Imagine," he said sheepishly, "a grown man crying."

Manager Smokey Alston was interviewed again and again by hordes of writers who went after the job in group relays.

"Podres pitched a brilliant game," he said. "In the sixth inning, I would have brought in Labine if Johnny hadn't got Yogi Berra out."

Getting Berra out was the play that made a hero of Sandy Amoros. The Cuban speedster raced almost to the foul line to pull down Berra's long high fly. Sandy not only got Yogi out, but also nailed Gil McDougald off first base on Pee Wee Reese's relay to Gil Hodges.

Sandy was having the time of his life. He was waving a can of beer and a big cigar. He was shouting more English than he has used all year—mixed with Spanish and, when he was addressing Carl Furillo, a bit of Italian.

Don Newcombe, who had become incensed when beer was poured over him in Milwaukee when the Brooks clinched the pennant, was in a different mood. He poured beer on himself and also drank beer out of his hat.

He posed with an arm around Duke Snider, the fellow who had filled the Newcombe hat with beer in Milwaukee. The Duke wore a battered derby that also had been used as a beverage container.

Reese Quietly Happy

Reese was the most quietly happy fellow in the room. Five times he had been on Brooklyn teams that were beaten by the Yankees in world series play. Now that he had finally made it, he was too happy to be wildly demonstrative.

His friendly enemy, Berra, visited Pee Wee and other friends on the club. Yogi spent more than half an hour there. Asked if he thought Amoros was a nice fellow, Yogi grinned and pretended to snarl—a hard thing for Berra to do.

"No, I think he's a little so-and-so," said Berra.

A moment later, he got hold of Amoros and pretended to rough him up. Sandy grinned in sheer delight and spouted Spanish at Yogi.

THE JOY OF TRIUMPH: Gil Hodges, left, who drove in both runs, and Carl Furillo show their affection for Johnny Podres in Dodgers' dressing room. Podres pitched entire game.

WELL-EARNED: Sandy Amoros enjoys victory cigar.

A mix-up occurred at the narrow door to the clubhouse when policemen and some of the executives got their orders mixed.

The policemen understood they were to let the players in first, but Brooklyn officials—Walter O'Malley, Arthur (Red) Patterson, Buzzie Bavasi and Fresco Thompson—wanted the writers let in along with the players. This, they felt, was a different occasion and nobody should be barred.

Warren Giles, the National League president; Eddie Brannick of the Giants and other National League figures crowded in to offer their felicitations to everybody on the Brooklyn club.

Stengel Visits Alston

Casey Stengel, a manager who is not accustomed to losing world series, dropped in to see Alston and his first words were an apology.

"I'd have been in sooner," he told Smokey, "but they wanted a couple of pictures and held me up. I wanta congratulate you. You did a fine job and so did your boy (meaning Podres)."

Ford Frick, baseball's commissioner, was an early visitor, and shook hands with Alston, O'Malley and several of the players.

Jake Pitler, the old Dodger first base coach, reached an emotional pitch he could not control. He embraced practically everybody and his praise of the Dodgers took in every player on the squad.

"They did great," he said. "You shoulda heard our bench. Never saw them that way all season. They were hollerin' on every pitch—and that kid Podres."

Jake shook his head almost in awe.

"What a lotta moxie he's got. He pitched his heart out and was ready to keep on pitching it out. Never saw a kid so determined as he was."

Snider took all the blame for letting Berra's high fly ball fall safely between the Duke and Junior Gilliam for a double in the Yankee's fourth inning.

Since the Dodgers had only a 1-0 lead at the moment, this play put Podres in a precarious situation—with the tying run on second base and none out.

"It didn't hurt any, thank the Lord," said Snider, "but it was all my fault. I saw Gilliam out of the corner of my eye as we were converging on the ball. Then I heard him say 'take it.' But I couldn't make it then."

About New York—And Brooklyn: Dodger Fans Have Their Innings

Continued From Page 1

fragments fly? Why is there shouting?"

The artist told him:

"It's over the Dodgers. They just beat the Yanks."

The foreign gentleman did not understand.

"Dodgers?" he asked. "Yankees?"

He shrugged and plodded on through the confetti blizzard.

The stock market, incidentally, had a busy morning, but trading fell to a mere trickle as game time neared. It stayed that way throughout the afternoon.

* * *

Up to 4 o'clock yesterday afternoon, few Dodger fans could, with safety, have spoken their allegiance anywhere north of the Harlem River. When Brooklyn finally won the championship, though, hundreds, in a sudden fit of baseball madness, worked their way from bar to bar into the darkest Bronx. They flaunted their banners and their victory buttons, even on the Bronx Courthouse lawn. So crushed were the ordinarily voluble folk up that way that none spoke out against them; in fact, none even so much as passed the natives' embittered labial salute.

* * *

Sandy Amoros, who endeared himself to all Brooklyn and to Dodger fans everywhere by his astonishing catch in the sixth inning, understands little English. He is a Cuban. When the contest was over, a great knot of Latin Americans excitedly bore down on Sandy at the players' gate and, in high-pitched Spanish, let them know their pride in his achievement. City police had to form a flying wedge to get Sandy out of the hands of his fans.

* * *

In theory, the City of New York officially took no sides in the world series. When the Dodgers won the championship, though, there was a definite, if mute, expression of opinion. It took the form of confetti fashioned of used desk pads, vouchers and city forms of one kind or another. The paper twisted and turned from the upper floors of the Municipal Building on all sides. One flurry, like a flock of pale miniature birds, floated out toward the East River—and Brooklyn.

In Brooklyn, there was wholesale delirium. It rose hoarsely in bars and in pool rooms and even passed contagiously to lady shoppers downtown. Horns screamed in chorus along Flatbush Avenue Extension, on Kings Highway and on marginal roads.

Motorcades raced up and down Eighty-sixth Street, Fourth and Flatbush Avenues, Ocean Parkway and other main thoroughfares, ringing the welkin with the clang of cowbells, the tootle of horns and the pop-off of toy cannons. Firecrackers were exploded and people stood on front doorsteps banging cutlery against pots and pans. At the same time, stuffed pillows and bolsters, hastily molded into the form of human effigies, were strung from lampposts bearing crude signs, "Yankees!"

* * *

Borough President John Cashmore was moved to florid utterance about the Dodgers. He promised in an official statement (after municipal working hours) to order a survey for a new Dodger stadium at Atlantic and Flatbush Avenues. He orally challenged upstart communities outside the city that have tentatively offered a new playing field for the team.

"They must never leave Brooklyn," he said.

And the sunset over the Narrows in Bay Ridge yesterday was extraordinarily warm and rosy for a fall. It seemed to have caught additional glow from a delirious populace.

* * *

There also was a "Greater love hath no man" angle in the Brooklyn celebration. Joseph Saden, who owns Joe's Delicatessen at 324 Utica Avenue, deep in the borough, was so utterly overcome by the Dodgers' first hold on the series flag that he set up a sidewalk stand and gave away hot dogs to passing celebrators. This, for a Brooklyn merchant, is but one step from total numbness.

206,298 Calls Made Monday

The New York Telephone Company reported that 206,298 calls had been made to its time bureau for the sixth game world series scores on Monday. A total of 848,981 calls were received the first six days of the classic.

The Box Score

SEVENTH GAME

BROOKLYN DODGERS

	AB.	R.	H.	PO.	A.
Gilliam, lf., 2b	4	0	1	2	0
Reese, ss	4	1	1	2	6
Snider, cf	3	0	0	2	0
Campanella, c	3	1	1	5	0
Furillo, rf	3	0	0	3	0
Hodges, 1b	2	0	1	10	0
Hoak, 3b	3	0	1	1	1
Zimmer, 2b	2	0	0	0	2
aShuba	1	0	0	0	0
Amoros, lf	0	0	0	2	1
Podres, p	4	0	0	0	1
Total	29	2	5	27	11

NEW YORK YANKEES

	AB.	R.	H.	PO.	A.
Rizzuto, ss	3	0	1	1	3
Martin, 2b	3	0	1	1	6
McDougald, 3b	4	0	3	1	1
Berra, c	4	0	1	4	1
Bauer, rf	4	0	0	1	0
Skowron, 1b	4	0	1	11	1
Cerv, cf	4	0	0	5	0
Howard, lf	4	0	1	2	0
Byrne, p	2	0	0	0	2
Grim, p	0	0	0	1	0
bMantle	1	0	0	0	0
Turley, p	0	0	0	0	0
Total	33	0	8	27	14

aGrounded out for Zimmer in sixth.

bPopped out for Grim in seventh.

Brooklyn	0 0 0	1 0 1	0 0 0	—2
New York	0 0 0	0 0 0	0 0 0	—0

Error—Skowron.

Runs batted in—Hodges 2.

Two-base hits—Skowron, Campanella, Berra. Sacrifices—Snider, Campanella. Sacrifice fly—Hodges. Double play—Amoros, Reese and Hodges. Left on bases—Brooklyn 8, New York 8. Bases on balls—Off Byrne 3 (Hodges, Gilliam, Furillo), Grim 1 (Hoak), Turley 1 (Amoros), Podres 2 (Rizzuto, Martin). Struck out—By Byrne (2 (Snider, Zimmer), Grim 1 (Reese), Turley 1 (Snider), Podres 4 (McDougald), Byrne 2, Bauer). Hits—Off Byrne 3 in 5 1/3 innings, Grim 1 in 1 2/3, Turley 1 in 2. Runs and earned runs—Off Byrne 2 and 1. Wild pitch—Grim. Losing pitcher—Byrne.

Umpires—Honochick (A.), plate; Dascoli (N.), first base; Summers (A.), second base; Ballanfant (N.), third base; Flaherty (A.), left field; Donatelli (N.), right field. Time of game—2:44. Paid attendance—62,465.

Final Standing and Figures

	W.	L.	P.C.
Dodgers	4	3	.571
Yanks	3	4	.429

Seventh-Game Statistics

Paid attendance—62,465.
Net receipts—$407,549.81.
Commissioner's share—$61,132.47.
Clubs' and leagues' share—$346,417.34.

Seven-Game Statistics

Paid attendance—362,310.
Net receipts—$2,337,515.34.
Commissioner's share—$350,627.30.
Players' share (first four games only)—$654,853.59.
Clubs' and leagues share—$1,332,034.45.

SOONERS CAPTURE 30TH IN ROW, 20-6

Record 76,561 See Speedy Oklahoma Tally 3 Times After Maryland Scores

By LINCOLN A. WERDEN

Special to The New York Times.

MIAMI, Jan. 2 — Oklahoma was a football team "in a hurry" as it beat Maryland, 20 to 6, today in the balmy atmosphere of the Orange Bowl.

Running off plays so speedily that often the Terrapins were unable to set their defenses, the Sooners strengthened their claim to the mythical national championship.

Before a record crowd of 76,561 in this twenty-second annual post-season game, Oklahoma continued its winning streak through thirty games.

National leaders in scoring during the regular season, which they completed undefeated, as did Maryland, the Sooners produced all their points in the second half.

Maryland scored a touchdown shortly before the intermission. Ed Vereb, a speedy left halfback, crossed the goal line after a 15-yard dash. Vereb also accounted for a 66-yard run and gained 96 yards during the two opening periods. The score put Oklahoma in a spot.

But the fast-moving Sooners exploded in the second half. They scored 14 points in the third period and 6 on a spectacular touchdown run in the fourth.

Dodd Races 82 Yards

Carl Dodd, a sophomore from Norman, Okla., dashed 82 yards with an intercepted pass with a little more than five minutes to go in the closing chapter. It was the game's longest run.

After that, Bud Wilkinson, in shirt sleeves, was a smiling figure along the Oklahoma sideline. Wilkinson, whose Sooners beat Jim Tatum's Maryland eleven, 7—0, in the 1954 edition of this series, forgot his pre-game worries and appeared to enjoy the dazzling setting.

Even a last-minute drive that failed when Maryland intercepted a Sooner pass on the Terrapins' 11-yard line did not perturb Wilkinson. When it was all over Wilkinson's players swooped down on him, lifted him in the air and carried him off on their shoulders.

The pre-game ceremonies had the color and glamour that are generally associated with the highlight of the annual Orange Bowl festival. The crowd at the stadium prayed for peace and eight bands joined in playing the national anthem.

Then the contest between Oklahoma, representing the Big Seven Conference, and Maryland, the Atlantic Coast Conference champion, began.

It was a team triumph for Oklahoma. There were individual stars to be sure. Dodd, who went in for the injured right half, Bob Burris, early in the fourth, was one. So was Tom McDonald, a rapid right half, who took a pitchout from Burris and circled right end at 5 minutes 49 seconds of the third period for the tying touchdown.

Pricer Stands Out

Then there was Billy Pricer. The fullback was a standout as a backer-up on defense and he place-kicked the point after touchdown that sent Oklahoma ahead at 7—6. He converted again after the Sooners had gone 52 yards in sixteen plays for their second touchdown.

Jerry Tubbs, at center, who came through with an important interception in the fourth period, and his team-mates in the line did fine work as Oklahoma ground out its thirtieth straight triumph since bowing to Notre Dame in the 1953 season opener.

After the game, Wilkinson admitted he had instructed his team "to get off as fast as possible. We have been trying to do it all season and we clicked today."

Tatum said, "All the Oklahoma backs were fast. They kept the pressure on us constantly. They certainly outhustled us in every department. Oklahoma is definitely the best football team in the country."

A pitchout during Oklahoma's first touchdown march was cited as the turning point of the game by Wilkinson.

McDonald received a Maryland kick on his 21 and dashed along the left sideline to the Maryland 46. Pricer, Burris on two carries and McDonald advanced the ball to the Terrapins' 26.

Pitchout Sets Up Score

Then came the pitchout, Harris to McDonald, who passed to Burris. The play gained 19 yards. Maryland's crack center, Bob Pellegrini, brought Burris down. McDonald made 3 yards through left tackle. Then Harris pitched out to McDonald, who went around his right end to score.

Oklahoma, with its second backfield in action, chopped out short gains during its subsequent march to the goal. Jay O'Neal, at quarterback in the split-T attack, was effective on "keep" plays and kept the rapid-fire action going.

This bit-by-bit advance ended when O'Neal knifed through from the half-yard stripe.

The fourth period opened with Maryland's second quarterback, Lynn Beightol, unleashing a kick good for 76 yards. The record for an Orange Bowl game is 82 yards, credited to Ike Pickle of Mississippi State against Duquesne in 1941.

Oklahoma returned the kick to its 8. The Sooners' advance fizzled after Burris suffered a sprained knee and had to be removed from the field on a stretcher.

Maryland then threatened and penetrated to Oklahoma's 34. But Beightol, hoping to overcome the stalwart Oklahoma forwards and alert 6-3-2 defense, attempted to pass and Tubbs intercepted the toss intended for Phil Perlo.

Oklahoma now had the ball on its 26. Once more the offense made no headway and Oklahoma punted. Beightol moved the ball to the Oklahoma 30 for a first down. Then as he tried to pass to Vereb, Dodd went in fast and intercepted without a Maryland player near him. Dodd went down the right side of the field for 82 yards and a touchdown.

The longest run on an intercepted pass in Orange Bowl history is one of 89 yards by Al Hudson of Miami against Holy Cross in 1946.

Placement Attempt Wide

The time of Dodd's score was 9:58 of the period. Pricer's placement was wide.

After the next kick-off, Maryland lost the ball on a fumble by Beightol. Pricer recovered for the Sooners on Maryland's 38. They went to the 7 before McDonald's pass was intercepted by Pellegrini. Two plays later and another Bowl game was a part of the history of this series.

Vereb gained 108 yards rushing for Maryland. He averaged 13.5 on eight carries.

Oklahoma went 32 yards after taking the opening kick-off. But it was Vereb's quick-opening dash of 66 yards for Maryland that featured the initial period.

Maryland was down to the 5 as its stalwarts yelled for "an upset." But Frank Tamburello fumbled and Oklahoma recovered on its 10. Then O'Neal's decision to "keep" the ball bothered the Maryland defense. Oklahoma worked out of danger before punting.

A fumble by O'Neal stalled an Oklahoma drive in the second period. Maryland went to its rivals' 43 before punting. After the Maryland punt went into the end zone, Oklahoma had the ball on its 20.

A holding penalty was charged against the Sooners on the next play. Clendon Thomas quick-kicked and the Terrapins took over on the enemy 39.

Vereb made a first down on the 15 on a quick-opener. Then he faded to the right to pass, but seeing his receivers covered, he reversed his field and ran to the left for a touchdown.

Going into the contest, Maryland had a record of fifteen triumphs in a row. The Terrapins' last previous defeat was at the hands of the University of Miami in 1954.

Associated Press Wirephoto

INCOMPLETE OKLAHOMA PASS: John Bell, right, fails to catch pass from his quarterback, Jim Harris, during first-quarter action against Maryland at the Orange Bowl. Breaking up the play for the Terrapins is Ed Vereb.

Statistics of the Game

	Okla.	Md.
First downs	16	9
Rushing yardage	202	187
Passing yardage	53	46
Passes attempted	10	10
Passes completed	4	3
Passes intercepted by	3	1
Punts	8	7
Punting average, yds.	34.5	40.4
Fumbles lost	1	2
Yards penalized	35	61

The Line-Up

OKLAHOMA (20)

Left Ends—Mobra, Stillers, Long.
Left Tackles—Woodworth, Greenlee, Searcy, Loughridge
Left Guards—Bolinger, Oujesky, Jennings
Centers—Tubbs, Northcutt, Darnell.
Right Guards—C. Morris, Krishor, Broyles.
Right Tackles—Gray, Emerson, Ladd.
Right Ends—Bell, Timberlake, Ballard
Quarterbacks—Harris, O'Neal, Sturm.
Left Halfbacks—McDonald, Thomas, Serrod.
Right Halfbacks—Burris, Dodds, Derrick.
Fullbacks—Pricer, D. Morris, Brown.

MARYLAND (6)

Left Ends—Walker, Parsons, Waters.
Left Tackles—Heuring, Wharton.
Left Guards—Tullai, Dyson, Kolarac, Tonetti.
Centers—Pellegrini, Alderton, Weber.
Right Guards—Davis, DeCicco
Right Tackles—Sandusky, D. Healy.
Right Ends—Dennis, Cooke, Flynn.
Quarterbacks—Tamburello, Beightol.
Left Halfbacks—Vereb, Nusz, McVicker.
Right Halfbacks—J. Healy, Dare, Burgee.
Fullbacks—Hamilton, Perlo, Skarda, Laughery

Oklahoma	0	0	14	6—20
Maryland	0	6	0	0—6

Oklahoma scoring—Touchdowns: McDonald (4, run), O'Neal (½, plunge), Dodd (82, run). Conversions: Pricer 2 (placements).

Maryland scoring—Touchdown: Vereb (15, run).

Referee—John Waldorf, Big Seven Conference. Umpire—W. C. Clary, Atlantic Coast Conference. Linesman—M. B. McClenny, Atlantic Coast. Back judge—H. Lawn, Atlantic Coast. Field judge—Herman Rohrer, Big Seven. Clock operator—M. G. Voltz, Big Seven.

Rebels' Late Touchdown Upsets Horned Frogs at Dallas, 14 to 13

Mississippi Tallies With 4 Minutes 22 Seconds to Go in Cotton Bowl Game

DALLAS, Jan. 2 (AP)—Versatile Eagle Day and hammering Paige Cothren pulled Mississippi to a 14—13 upset victory over Texas Christian in the Cotton Bowl today in spite of a standout performance by the T. C. U. All-America, Jim Swink.

The Rebels, uncorking their Sunday punch when all seemed lost, scored with only 4 minutes 22 seconds to go before a crowd of 76,504 for Coach Johnny Vaught's first triumph in a major bowl.

Texas Christian played without its talented quarterback, Chuck Curtis. He was hurt on the first play of the game and was taken to a hospital with broken ribs and an injured shoulder.

Swink almost carried T. C. U. to victory, scoring both touchdowns and getting off some glittering runs that kept the Horned Frogs in front until the last minutes.

Two 66-Yard Drives

Mississippi swept 66 yards twice for touchdowns, one made on the passing of Day and the running of Cothren, and the other set up by Day's 25-yard dash.

Cothren bounced over from 3 yards out for the first Rebel score, then kicked the extra point. He also converted after the second touchdown and that was the margin of victory. A second-stringer, Billy Lott, ran around right end for 5 yards and the second Mississippi score.

Swink was the leading ground-gainer, as he had been in every game of the past season. The great Frog runner rolled up 107 yards through the hard-bitten, hard knocking Mississippi line.

Penalties figured prominently in the outcome and the one that hurt most was assessed against T. C. U., preventing the point after its second touchdown. Harold Pollard made good on the kick but T. C. U. was penalized for illegal formation. On the next try, Pollard's kick was wide.

Day was named the outstanding back of the game with 22 votes. Swink was second with 13 and Cothren third with 5.

Buddy Alliston, the 200-pound Mississippi guard, was the top lineman. He got 20 votes while Norman Hamilton, the huge T. C. U. tackle, was second with 9 and Gene Dubuisson, the Mississippi center, next with 7.

Statistics of the Game

	Miss.	T.C.U.
First downs	12	11
Rushing yardage	92	233
Passing yardage	137	20
Passes attempted	21	5
Passes completed	10	2
Passes intercepted by	2	0
Punts	6	5
Punting average, yds.	42.7	29.0
Fumbles lost	1	1
Yards penalized	80	80

"All the News That's Fit to Print"

The New York Times.

LATE CITY EDITION

Condensation of U.S. Weather Bureau forecast: Mostly fair, windy and cool today, tonight and tomorrow. Temperature range today: 58—45. Temperature range yesterday: 66.1—47.3. Full U. S. Weather Bureau Report, Page 68.

© 1956, by The New York Times Company.

VOL. CVI.. No. 36,053. Entered as Second-Class Matter, Post Office, New York, N. Y. NEW YORK, TUESDAY, OCTOBER 9, 1956. Times Square, New York 36, N. Y. Telephone LAckawanna 4-1000 FIVE CENTS

Larsen Beats Dodgers in Perfect Game; Yanks Lead, 3-2, on First Series No-Hitter

END OF A PERFECT DAY: Yogi Berra leaps into arms of Pitcher Don Larsen.

WHERE'S EVERYBODY? Coach Jake Pitler, the only Dodger to reach first base.

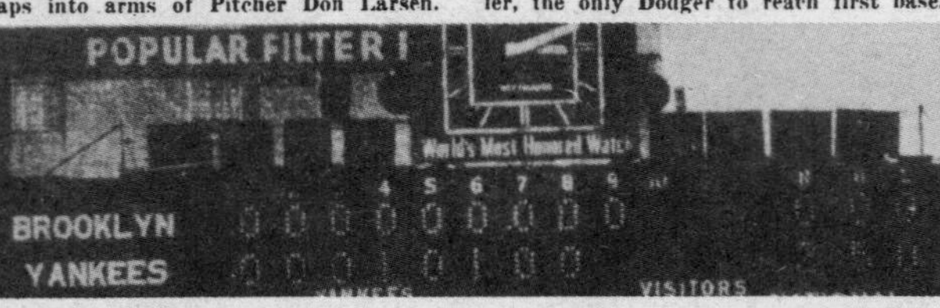

The New York Times

NO HITS, NO RUNS, NO NOTHING: Scoreboard at Stadium after yesterday's game

BILLION IN DECADE DEMANDED OF CITY FOR NEW SCHOOLS

$350,000,000 Bond Issue to Replace Old Units Also Is Asked by Bensley

BUDGET HEARINGS OPEN

Dock Commissioner Assails Renewed Effort to Let Port Agency Take Over Piers

By CHARLES G. BENNETT

A ten-year $1,000,000,000 program for building new schools and a $350,000,000 bond issue for replacing obsolete schools were demanded yesterday by a member of the Board of Education.

Charles J. Bensley, chairman of the buildings and sites committee of the board, told the City Planning Commission that the $95,014,340 in new money tentatively allocated by the commission for school construction next year was "not enough."

School construction costing $104,000,000 is the "irreducible minimum" the Board of Education can accept for 1957, Mr. Bensley declared.

Mayor Wagner and other officials have certified $180,300,000 as the total in new capital funds available for all construction planned by thirty city agencies next year.

Mr. Bensley was one of the first speakers as three days of public hearings opened before the City Planning Commission at City Hall on the tentative 1957 capital budget of $710,037,433.

Budget Is for Next Year

The capital budget is a set of allocations for all proposed city construction of public improvements for the calendar year. The improvements still require individual appropriations for their authorization.

The needs of the city's schools were discussed by most of the speakers at the first day of hearings.

Mr. Bensley criticized the White House Conference on Education last year as having produced little more than "a cascade of words." He proposed that tangible Federal aid for school construction be set up. Under his plan, he said, much of the $350,000,000 debt incurred for replacing obsolete school buildings here would be met with Federal aid.

The proposed $100,000,000 a year for ten years for school construction could "only nibble" at the essential replacement of existing schools more than fifty years old, Mr. Bensley said. His proposal was an amplification of a suggestion he made at a departmental hearing last month.

He called it a "sad fact" that the city must continue to maintain such obsolete schools, some dating as far back as 1847. These schools are too old to modernize

Continued on Page 44, Column 6

RED CASES LEAD HIGH COURT'S LIST

Nelson and Watkins Among Seven Who Win Hearings

By LUTHER A. HUSTON
Special to The New York Times

WASHINGTON, Oct. 8—Cases involving communism and subversion dominated the list of orders issued by the Supreme Court today.

The orders affected 360 cases out of more than 800 on the docket. They were the first issued in the current term, which began a week ago. Most appeals were rejected.

Appellants seeking a review of lower court rulings in so-called Communist cases, or rulings in cases already accepted, fared well. Hearings were granted in seven cases and denied in three.

Immediately after issuing the orders, the court began two weeks of hearings in which Communist cases predominate. For the most part these involve challenges to the Smith Act, the Federal statute that makes it a crime to teach or advocate revolutionary overthrow of the Government.

One of these is known as the Steve Nelson case. Nelson, a Pennsylvania Communist leader, and three co-defendants have appealed their conviction under the Smith Act.

Several days ago the Govern-

Continued on Page 16, Column 5

CITY REGISTRATION HAS RECORD START

559,659 Turn Out at 4,601 Polling Places—Late Lines Reverse Earlier Lag

By JOSEPH C. INGRAHAM

Registration set a new first-day record yesterday when 559,659 persons thronged the city's 4,601 polling places to qualify for the election on Nov. 6.

The registration was 9,386 higher than the mark of 550,273 established on the first registration day of 1952, the last Presidential year.

The rise was made possible mainly by a very late turnout that found hundreds of polling places with long lines at the closing hour of 10:30 P. M. Earlier, local boards had reported registration lagging, compared with four years ago. They attributed this to a combination of world series fever and confusion on the part of many persons who bother to vote only in Presidential elections.

The once-in-four-year voters faced the problem in many cases of going to polling places relocated since 1952. Because of population shifts, Assembly district lines were redrawn in 1954. As a result, election districts, the controlling units for voters, also were readjusted.

Queens Leads in Gains

As expected, Queens, where the population has been rising steadily, reported the biggest first-day gain over 1952. The registration there yesterday was 128,285, up 12,218 since four years ago.

The Bronx and Brooklyn showed minor declines of 4,118 and 3,845 respectively, compared with 1952.

But the major surprise was in Manhattan, where, because of the trend to the suburbs, registration was expected to be off substantially. Instead, Manhattan recorded a first-day gain over 1952 of 5,989 persons, with the total at 132,927.

In Richmond registration was 13,073, only 528 fewer than in 1952.

The relatively heavy vote in Manhattan was seen as a good augury for the Democrats. The rise in registration in Queens was subject to two interpretations: a Republican trend, as the borough has gone Republican in national elections for the last twelve years; or a shift to the Democratic side resulting from the appeal of Mayor Wagner's candidacy for the United States Senate.

The heavy registration indicated that a new city-wide mark might be in the making and that

Continued on Page 18, Column 3

Mantle's Home Run and Bauer's Single Send Maglie to 2-0 Loss

JOHN DREBINGER

Don Larsen is a footloose fellow of whom Casey Stengel once said, "He can be one of baseball's great pitchers any time he puts his mind to it." Larsen had his mind on his work yesterday.

He pitched the first no-hit game in world series history. Not only that, but he also fired the first perfect game no batter reaching first base to be posted in the major leagues in thirty-four years.

This nerve-tingling performance, embellished with a Mickey Mantle home run, gained a 2-0 triumph for the Yankees over the Dodgers and Sal Maglie at the Stadium. It enabled Casey Stengel's Bombers to post their third straight victory for a 3-2 lead in the series. The Bombers are within one game of clinching the series as it moves back to Ebbets Field today.

Crowd Roars Tribute

With every fan in a gathering of 64,519 hanging breathlessly on every pitch, Larsen, a 27-year-old right-hander, slipped over a third strike on Dale Mitchell to end the game.

Dale, a pinch hitter, was the twenty-seventh batter to face Larsen. As he went down for the final out, the gathering set up a deafening roar, while jubilant Yankees fairly mobbed the big pitcher as he struggled to make his way to the dugout.

The unpredictable Larsen had triumphed at a time when the Bombers needed it most with one of the most spectacular achievements in diamond history. Last

Continued on Page 38, Column 2

2 Shot in Bank Here; Guards Beat Gunman

By MILTON BRACKER

A man with a loaded .45-caliber pistol tried to cash a $7,000 check with a forged signature in an East Forty-second Street bank yesterday. He touched off a wild scuffle in which his bullets wounded two bank employes in the leg.

But neither was in as poor condition at Bellevue Hospital last night as the suspect himself. Overpowered by four members of the bank staff, he suffered head injuries and his condition was listed as critical.

Meanwhile, the police charged him with forgery, felonious assault and violation of the Sullivan Law.

The shooting drew a large crowd that cluttered crosstown traffic on Forty-second Street between 10:30 A. M. and noon. The site was the Industrial Bank of Commerce

Continued on Page 29, Column 5

DEMOCRATS LEAD IN WEST VIRGINIA

Depression of Thirties Still Sways Vote, Survey Finds —G.O.P. Pressing Drive

A Times Team Report

Here is another in the daily series of reports from four teams of New York Times reporters who have been surveying political sentiment in closely contested states. This one is from a team composed of John C. Devlin, Leo Egan, Stanley Levey, Layhmond Robinson Jr. and George Cable Wright, with Mr. Egan writing the team's report.

By LEO EGAN
Special to The New York Times.

CHARLESTON, W. Va. Oct. 7—In West Virginia, time has moved more slowly than in other states. The great depression of the Nineteen Thirties is still a fresh memory in the southern coal fields. Its ravages are still the most important single influence on the political thinking of the region.

In the southern coal counties it would be hard to forget the miseries of the depression even if one wanted to. On the streets and in the shops the effects of the past can be seen in the disproportionate number of older people.

"Any miner who lived through the depression will never vote anything but Democratic," one old miner declares with profound conviction. "The Republicans never did anything for us."

50,000 Leave the State

During the last five years some 50,000 persons have migrated from West Virginia to other states in search of better economic opportunities. The bulk of this migration was made up of younger people from the southern coal region. Some went also from the mountain farms in the central part of the state and from the northern coal fields near the Pennsylvania border.

Vivid recollections of the great depression were primarily responsible for keeping West Virginia in the Democratic column in the Presidential election of 1952 when so many other states went Republican. In the opinion of most political leaders and commentators those memories are likely to keep West Virginia in the Democratic column again this year.

Democrats hold a 250,000 lead over Republicans among approximately 1,100,000 voters registered in the state. But the difference is not as significant as it seems because there are so

Continued on Page 28, Column 8

STEVENSON URGES WIDER INSURANCE TO HELP THE SICK

Asks U. S. Grants and Loans in National Plan—Opposes Socialized Medicine

Stevenson statement and text of telephone talk, Page 24.

By HARRISON E. SALISBURY
Special to The New York Times.

CHICAGO, Oct. 8—Adlai E. Stevenson proposed tonight that the Federal Government subsidize with grants and loans a national health insurance program.

The Democratic Presidential candidate also declared his opposition to socialized medicine. In addition to aid for health insurance he urged more funds for medical research, the training of more medical personnel and construction of more hospitals.

Mr. Stevenson's declaration was contained in the third major statement of his policy issued since the formal start of his Presidential campaign.

The statements set forth the characteristics of Mr. Stevenson's New America program. The program consists of the recommendations that he plans to make to Congress if elected President.

Stevenson Is Confident

Mr. Stevenson was in a confident mood as he presented his national health program and prepared for his third big campaign swing—a strike into the West. He told Democratic campaign workers in a national telephone conference from his Libertyville, Ill., home that "we are winning the campaign." At the same time he appealed for campaign contributions.

Mr. Stevenson will leave by plane tomorrow on a four-day trip to Montana, Idaho, Washington, Oregon and California.

He will spend most of his time in the Pacific Coast States, which have forty-seven electoral votes. Two of the hottest Senatorial races of the year are under way in Washington and Oregon. In Washington Senator Warren G. Magnuson, Democrat, faces Gov. Arthur Langlie and in Oregon Senator Wayne Morse, Democrat, opposes Douglas McKay, General Eisenhower's former Secretary of Interior.

The Stevenson campaign is expected to hit a higher tempo when it reaches the Pacific Coast. Mr. Stevenson's advisers hope to open up several new lines of assault.

Their reports indicate that California's voters have not made a firm choice between the nominees. Mr. Stevenson hopes to give momentum to a trend in his direction this week.

Reports from Mr. Stevenson's tour last week of New Jersey, Pennsylvania, West Virginia, New England and New York City, indicate that only West Virginia can be counted as firmly in his column.

However, his swing into Penn-

Continued on Page 24, Column 3

Poles Expected to Restore Purged Aide Next Week

Gomulka, Foe of Stalin, May Regain His Seat in Party Politburo

By SYDNEY GRUSON
Special to The New York Times.

POZNAN, Poland, Oct. 8—Wladyslaw Gomulka is expected to be restored to a leading post in the Polish United Workers (Communist) party next week.

It was learned tonight that the party's Central Committee had been called to meet next Monday to act on the Gomulka case and to consider an electoral law for the Dec. 16 elections. The meeting was originally scheduled to be held next month.

The present plan is for M. Gomulka to be reinstated to the Central Committee on the ground that his expulsion in 1948 was illegal because it was ordered without the approval of a party congress. He is expected to be elected to the party's Politburo immediately after his reinstatement to the Central Committee.

Advancing the date of the Central Committee meeting reflects a growing crisis within the leadership of the party. M.

Associated Press
Wladyslaw Gomulka

Gomulka's presence, it is hoped, will do something to restore the situation. Support for the leadership, even among the mass of Communists, has been draining away steadily and is continuing

Continued on Page 6, Column 3

Knowland Informs President His Trips Offset Foe's Gains

By RUSSELL BAKER
Special to The New York Times.

WASHINGTON, Oct. 8—President Eisenhower was told today that his recent campaigning had helped offset a fast Democratic start and given a definite lift to Republican victory chances within the last ten days.

This report came from William F. Knowland, Senate Republican leader who talked to the President this morning about his 10,000 mile tour in ten states.

Senator Knowland noted a "definite upturn" in the G. O. P. campaign during the last ten days. He conceded that the Democrats had gotten "a little drop" on the Republicans because of their early start.

Slugging Campaign Factor

But this, he said, had now been offset largely by the "very fine impact" the President's appearances have made. He asserted that President Eisenhower's switch to a tougher, slugging campaign had "undoubtedly played a part" in the Republican gains throughout the country.

As a result, Senator Knowland continued, he thought that prospects for winning a Republican-controlled Senate and House of Representatives had "greatly improved." G. O. P. victory in the Senate, however, would be won by "a very close margin," he predicted.

Senator Knowland also took the occasion of his White House visit to attack Adlai E. Stevenson's proposal for eventual abolition of the draft and hydrogen-bomb tests.

These proposals, he said, sug-

Continued on Page 21, Column 2

Presidential Nominees on Tour: Rocky Road vs. a Magic Carpet

Stevenson Finds Shaving Twice a Day Is a Chore —Laundry a Problem

Special to The New York Times.

CHICAGO, Oct. 8—At least once a week Adlai E. Stevenson remarks to an audience that one of the great tribulations of political campaigning is that a man has to shave twice a day.

Electronic marvels carry Mr. Stevenson's picture and his voice to the most remote farmhouses in the land. Airplanes whisk him from the Atlantic Coast to the Pacific in a twinkling.

But the national genius that has mastered the atom and is beginning to probe into outer space has not yet conquered the beard.

Mr. Stevenson's whiskers are fast growing and rather dark. He shaves himself regularly in the morning and again before an evening appearance, using an ordinary 75-cent safety razor, brush and lather.

The twice-a-day shave is but one of the trials of campaigning.

Take laundry for instance. Mr. Stevenson does not like modern, quick-drying, self-pressing synthetic fabrics. He carries with him half a dozen broadcloth shirts. Not every hotel has overnight laundry service. Where

Continued on Page 25, Column 6

Eisenhower's Staff Eases Every Inch of the Way— Local Police Guard Path

Special to The New York Times.

WASHINGTON, Oct. 8—Compared with the agonies other candidates must endure at election time, campaign travel for the President of the United States is a ride on a magic carpet.

At his command is the well-oiled machinery behind the most powerful office on earth to propel him from place to place, convey his image through time and space, to keep him well fed, neatly pressed, comfortably rested and protected from crackpot and well-wisher.

Consider a typical trip by President Eisenhower in this campaign. His personal plane, the super-Constellation Columbine III, under constant guard at Washington National Airport, is rolled out, every spark plug freshly checked, every inch of its metal skin polished to dazzling silver.

It is surrounded by armed soldiers until the President's arrival. Meanwhile, back at the White House, bales of advance texts on the President's speech, or speeches, are en route to the airport for deposit aboard the press plane.

These are the brain children

Continued on Page 25, Column 2

SENTENCES LIGHT IN POZNAN TRIAL

First Verdict in Major Case Sets Prison Terms for 3 in Slaying of Policeman

Special to The New York Times.

POZNAN, Poland, Oct. 8—Lenient sentences were pronounced today in the first verdict to come out of the major Poznan riot trials.

Tensed for the worst, a packed courtroom relaxed perceptibly as Judge Wieslaw Celinski sentenced Jozef Foltynowicz, 20 years old, and Jerzy Sroka, 18, to four and a half years in prison, and Kazimierz Zurek, also 18, to four years.

The youths were accused of having murdered a member of the secret police during last June's rioting.

The prosecution had demanded judgment under the emergency criminal code passed in 1946 when conflict near to civil war raged in Poland between the Communist Government and the anti-Communist underground. Under this code the defendants could have been sentenced to death. A minimum imprisonment of ten years would have been mandatory.

Use of Code Barred

But Judge Celinski, in a lengthy explanation of the sentences, found that use of the emergency code was unwarranted.

The judge ruled that the prosecution had not proved that the accused men had caused the death of the police officer, Cpl. Zygmunt Izdebny. But, the judge said, the defendants had participated in the brutal beating of the corporal, and for this participation they must take the consequences.

The same fairness and impartiality that had marked Judge Celinski's conduct of the trial was evident in his verdict. The court, he said, had considered only the statements made in the courtroom where "the accused could talk freely" and had thrown out pretrial interrogation, at which the police allegedly had resorted to brutality. The defendants showed no emotion as they heard the verdict.

But afterward, in the corridor, the parents of Sroka and Zurek and two brothers of Foltynowicz expressed relief. They said they had feared the sentences would be much heavier.

Appeals Are Considered

Dr. Stanislaw Hejmowski, the chief defense counsel for Sroka, described both the verdict and the sentences as "very fair" and said he would not appeal them.

However, counsel for Foltynowicz indicated that he would ask the Supreme Court to reduce the sentence of his client. Counsel for Zurek made no comment.

The prosecutor told reporters he still thought the emergency code should have been applied. He said he would decide on whether to appeal for heavier sentences only after a thorough re-examination of the judge's explanation and the record of the case.

Judge Celinski's explanation was mainly legalistic, but he said that the ages of the accused men, their retarded mental development and their backgrounds of poverty and limited

Continued on Page 7, Column 3

EGYPT AND SOVIET JOIN IN U. N. FIGHT ON SUEZ PROPOSAL

They Reject Western Plan for International Control, but Keep Door to Talks Open

SECRET PARLEY TODAY

Little Hope Held for Accord on Any Terms but Cairo's —Dulles to Give View

Excerpts from debate in U. N. are printed on Page 14.

By THOMAS J. HAMILTON
Special to The New York Times.

UNITED NATIONS, N. Y., Oct. 8—International operation of the Suez Canal was rejected again today by Egypt and the Soviet Union.

Their Foreign Ministers told the Security Council that Egypt must continue to operate the canal but that there was room for negotiation on an undefined amount of international participation.

The eleven-member Security Council is scheduled to start secret negotiations with Egypt tomorrow at 4 P. M. Koca Popovic, Yugoslav Foreign Minister, and Secretary of State Dulles, the only representatives who have not made opening statements in the debate, will speak tomorrow morning in that order.

Most Western delegates remained pessimistic about the possibility of an agreement on the Suez question on anything except Egyptian terms. Although some thought that the Egyptian and Soviet statements seemed to offer possibilities for negotiation, this was counterbalanced by the harsh attacks on Britain, France and the United States by both Foreign Ministers.

Accusation by Fawzi

Dr. Mahmoud Fawzi, Egyptian Foreign Minister, charged that Britain and France were trying to "see to it that the Suez Canal be finally amputated and severed from Egypt."

In addition, he denounced Secretary of State Dulles' cancellation of a United States offer to help finance the Aswan High Dam, a Nile Valley development project.

Dmitri T. Shepilov, Soviet Foreign Minister, accused Britain and France of "playing with fire." He charged that they had brought the Suez issue before the Security Council merely to obtain an excuse for subsequent action outside the United Nations.

Mr. Shepilov accused "American monopolists" of planning to take the canal away from Britain and France as well as from Egypt.

Dr. Fawzi, who maintained that use of the canal was continuing unhindered despite British-French efforts at "sabotage" through the withdrawal of

Continued on Page 14, Column 3

AFRICA-ASIA BLOC HELD NASSER AIM

Egyptian Is Said to Urge End of Need for Western Aid

By OSGOOD CARUTHERS
Special to The New York Times

CAIRO, Oct. 8—President Gamal Abdel Nasser was reported today to have proposed an economic organization among African and Asian countries.

The Egyptian leader was quoted as having said this should be done "to foil Western conspiracies against their economies and overcome obstacles created by imperialist banks."

The proposals attributed to President Nasser were published in Al Messaa, an evening newspaper, but there was no official confirmation that this was the Egyptian leader's aim.

According to the newspaper, President Nasser suggested that the African and Asian nations that attended the conference in Bandung, Indonesia, in April, 1955, work out mutual economic arrangements that would free them from dependence on Western aid and trade.

No detailed plan was put forth. However, the Nasser regime has been actively seeking new markets outside the sterling and dollar areas ever since the Suez Canal crisis brought on economic restrictions by Britain,

Continued on Page 15, Column 3

Larsen Says His No Wind-Up Delivery Aided Control

LARSEN WINS, 2-0, ON PERFECT GAME

Continued From Page 1

spring the tall, handsome Hoosier, who now makes his home in San Diego, Calif., had caused considerable to-do in the Yankees' St. Petersburg training camp. In an early dawn escapade, Don wrapped his automobile around a telephone pole. He later explained he had fallen asleep at the wheel.

Yesterday big Don remained wide-awake through every moment of the nine innings as he wrapped his long fingers around a baseball to make it do tricks never seen before in world series play.

He did it, too, with a most revolutionary delivery, which might account for his sudden rise to fame. Don takes no wind-up at all. Each pitch is served from a standing delivery that he adopted only a little over a month ago.

In the history of baseball this was only the seventh perfect game ever hurled in the major leagues and only the fifth in baseball's modern era, which dates back to the beginning of the present century. A perfect game is one in which a pitcher faces exactly twenty-seven men with not one reaching first base through a hit, base on balls, error or any other means.

The last perfect game in the majors was achieved by Charlie Robertson of the Chicago White Sox on April 30, 1922, when he vanquished the Detroit Tigers, 2—0.

No-hitters during the season, of course, have been common enough. In fact, Maglie, beaten yesterday despite a commendable five-hitter, tossed one earlier this year for the Dodgers.

In modern world series play, which started in 1903, three pitchers missed no-hitters by one blow. Ed Reulbach of the Cubs fired a one-hitter against the White Sox on Oct. 10, 1906. Jiggs Donohue, the White Sox first baseman, wrecked that no-hit bid.

Rudy York of the Tigers made the only hit off Claude Passeau of the Cubs on Oct. 5, 1945. In that game Passeau allowed only one other Tiger to reach first base, that one on a pass.

Bevens' Bid Fails

On Oct. 3, 1947, Floyd Bevens, a Yankee right-hander, got closest of all to the no-hit goal, when, against the Dodgers at Ebbets Field, he moved within one out of his objective. Then Cookie Lavagetto rattled a pinch two-bagger off the right-field wall that not only broke the no-hit spell but also defeated the Yankees.

So amazing was Larsen's feat that only four batted balls had a chance of being rated hits. One was a foul by inches. Three drives were converted into outs by miraculous Yankee fielding plays.

In the second inning, Jackie Robinson banged a vicious grounder off Andy Carey's glove at third base for what momentarily appeared a certain hit. But Gil McDougald, the alert Yankee shortstop, recovered the ball in time to fire it for the put-out on Jackie at first base.

In the fifth, minutes after Mantle had put the Yanks ahead, 1—0, with his blast into the right field stand, Gil Hodges tagged a ball that streaked into deep left center, seemingly headed for extra bases.

But Mantle, whose fielding in the series has at times been a trifle spotty, more than made amends. He tore across the turf to make an extraordinary glove-fanned seven.

On the next play, Sandy Amoros leaned into a pitch and rocketed a towering drive toward the right field stand. This drive promised to tie the score, but at the last moment the ball curved foul.

CASTING HIS SPELL: Don Larsen of the Yankees with only two outs to go in ninth

And then, in the eighth, Hodges once again was victimized by a thrilling Yankee fielding play. Gil drove a tricky, low liner to the left of Carey. The Yankee third sacker lunged for the ball and caught it inches off the ground.

For a moment it was hard to say whether he had caught the ball or scooped it up. Andy, just to make certain, fired the ball to first in time to make the putout doubly sure. Officially, it was scored as a caught ball.

So accurate was Larsen's control that of the twenty-seven batters to face him, only one managed to run the count to three balls. That was Pee Wee Reese, the doughty Dodger captain and shortstop, in the first inning. Pee Wee then took a third strike. In all, Larsen fanned six.

For Maglie, the performance by his youthful rival was a heartbreaker. The 39-year-old Barber, whose astounding comeback this year had reached its peak when he hurled the Dodgers to victory in the series opener last Wednesday, did a pretty good job of pitching, too.

For three and two-third innings the one-time Giant star right-hander matched Larsen batter for batter, turning back the first eleven Yankee batters. But with two out in the fourth and the bases empty, Mantle blazed his homer into the lower right stand.

A moment later Yogi Berra appeared to have connected for another hit as he stroked a powerful low drive toward left center. However, Duke Snider tore over from center field and snared the ball with a headlong dive.

In the sixth, the Yanks tallied their second run when they ganged up on the Barber for three singles, although they needed only two of them to produce the tally. Larsen had a hand in the scoring.

Carey had opened the inning with a single over second for only the second blow off Maglie. Then Larsen, one of several accomplished batsmen Stengel lists among his pitchers, laid down a perfect bunt sacrifice.

That sent Carey to second. On the heels of the sacrifice, Hank Bauer drove another single to center to send Carey scampering over the plate. For a moment it looked as though the Yanks would pile up some more runs as Joe Collins followed with a single into right that swept Bauer around to third.

A rather freakish double play put a quick finish to this rally. Mantle crashed a sharp grounder down the first base line. Hodges scooped up the ball and stepped on the bag almost in the same instant to retire Mantle. Then, seeing Bauer heading for home, Hodges got the ball to the plate in time to head off Hank, who was tagged in a rundown between third and home.

Another double play had saved the Barber in the fifth. Enos Slaughter had opened with a pass only to be forced at second on Billy Martin's sacrifice attempt. Then McDougald followed with a drive that appeared headed for left center.

But the ball never cleared Reese, who leaped in the air, deflected the ball with his glove, then caught it. Martin, certain the drive was a hit, had gone too far off first to get back and was doubled off the bag.

With two out in the seventh, the irrepressible Martin singled to left and McDougald walked to receive the second and last pass given up by Maglie. But the Barber ended this threat by inducing Carey to slap into a force play at second.

Just to show he still had plenty left, the ancient Barber swept through the eighth by fanning three Yanks in a row. Maglie got Larsen, Bauer and Collins and as he walked off the mound toward the Dodger dugout he received a rousing ovation.

Nevertheless, the noise then was barely a whisper compared with the din set up minutes later when Larsen finished his perfect game.

One could have heard a dollar bill drop in the huge arena as Carl Furillo got up as the first Dodger batter in the ninth. Carl lifted a fly to Bauer in right and one roar went up. Roy Campanella slapped a grounder at Martin for out No. 2 and the second roar followed.

Then only Mitchell, batting for Maglie, remained between Larsen and everlasting diamond fame. The former American League outfielder, for years a sure-fire pinch hitter with the Cleveland Indians, ran the count to one ball and two strikes.

Mitchell fouled off the next pitch and as the following one zoomed over the plate Umpire Babe Pinelli called it strike three. At this point the Stadium was in an uproar.

Mitchell whirled around to protest the call and later he said it was a fast ball that was outside the strike zone. But Dale was in no spot to gain any listener. The Yanks were pummeling Larsen and the umpires were hustling off the field.

Doubtless for Pinelli, this, too, could have provided his greatest thrill in his long career as an arbiter. For after this series, Babe, as the dean of the National League staff of umpires, is to retire.

And so, with this most spectacular of all world series spectaculars, the pattern, in reverse of last October's series between these two rivals continues to hold. Last fall the Dodgers blew the first two games at the Stadium, then swept the next three in Ebbets Field. Returning to the Stadium, they lost the sixth game to tie it at three-all, but then bagged the seventh to gain Brooklyn's first world championship.

This time the Yanks hold the 3-2 advantage. They need only one more victory to clinch it. But that victory will have to be gained either today or tomorrow in the lair of the Dodgers and the Yanks haven't won a world series game at Ebbets Field since Oct. 4, 1953.

Even Larsen, yesterday's no-hit hero, couldn't win there when he pitched the second game of the series last Friday. In fact, Don started that game, which wound up with the Yanks going down to a 13-8 defeat. He went out in the second inning after the Bombers had got him off to a 6-0 lead.

However, with two out, the Dodgers had scored only one run when Stengel removed Larsen with the bases filled. What followed was the doing of others and some experts had hinted Casey had been a bit hasty in hauling Don out so soon.

All's Well That Ends Well

Stengel later admitted this could have been the case. "However," added the philosophical skipper of the Bombers, "it might also help to get him really on his toes the next time he starts." And that it most certainly did yesterday.

At a late hour last night Stengel was still undecided whether in today's encounter, which could win it all for him, he would start Johnny Kucks or Bob Turley.

Johnny, a 23-year-old sophomore right-hander and an eighteen-game winner the past season, also appeared briefly in that Friday rout in Flatbush. He followed Larsen and gave up the bases-filled single to Reese that drove in two runs. He then gave way to Tommy Byrne, who was tagged for Snider's three-run homer.

Turley is the right-hander who also joined the Yanks along with Larsen in the Baltimore eighteen-player deal.

Walter Alston of the Dodgers, now fighting desperately to remain alive in the series, will stake all on his prize relief specialist, Clem Labine. Clem has been used only sparingly as a starter this year, but in this trying hour Alston suddenly seems to have no other choice.

YANKEE IS PRAISED FOR BRILLIANT JOB

Larsen Success May Prompt Other Hurlers to Discard Wind-Up Technique

By LOUIS EFFRAT

Since nothing succeeds like success, Don Larsen's history-making performance at the Stadium yesterday may start a trend that could revolutionize the entire pitching industry. The big right-hander, overnight a man of distinction, is likely to find innumerable imitators before another season runs its course.

Already two of Larsen's Yankee team-mates have endorsed Don's unorthodox delivery. Bob Turley and Mickey McDermott, like Larsen, have switched to the no-wind up technique. The prediction in the victorious team's dressing room following Larsen's perfect exhibition in the firth game of the World Series was that other pitchers will follow suit next year.

Pitching from a so-called standing start is not entirely new. Some hurlers experimented with such a stance many years ago. Hollis Thurston of the Chicago White Sox was one. No one, however, even approached the effectiveness that was Larsen's yesterday.

The credit—or the blame, if one is a Dodger rooter—belongs to a man who was some 2,000 miles away from the Stadium yesterday. For, it was Del Baker, the coach of the Boston Red Sox, who prompted Larsen to change his delivery. It happened at Fenway Park during the waning days of the 1956 American League season.

Pounded Harder by Mates

Larsen, who was pounded harder by his team-mates after the game than he was by the Brooks during it, told how he happened to discard the wind-up.

"All the time I was using the wind-up I was tipping off my pitches," he said. "No matter what I threw, Baker knew in advance what was coming. So I went to Jim Turner (Yankee pitching coach) and asked his permission to drop the wind-up. He gave me the okay and I've pitched without a wind-up ever since. I like it, too."

Larsen was asked what a standing start does for him.

"It gives me better control," he replied. "It takes nothing off my fast ball and it keeps the batters tense. They have to be ready every second. And don't forget, no coach can "read" the pitch in advance."

The idol of every man in the clubhouse, Larsen was lionized for an hour. Mickey Mantle, whose homer provided the original edge in the contest, was quite willing to let Larsen have the center of the stage. "This will be the first time a home run by me will not make the headlines," he said.

To get to Larsen in the clubhouse after the game was next to impossible. He was besieged by photographers, team-mates, opponents, officials and interviewers. Sal Maglie, Jackie Robinson, Walter F. O'Malley, the president of the Dodgers, and Ralph Branca made their way close enough to Don to congratulate him.

Ford Frick, the commissioner of baseball, tried to do likewise, but he had no chance. He relayed the message through Casey Stengel.

Terrific! Says Stengel

"Terrific! Terrific!" was Stengel's reaction to Larsen's masterpiece.

It was easier, much easier, to reach any Yankee. That is, if you were willing to settle for anyone aside from Larsen. Incidentally the day's hero said he had thought nothing about a no-hitter—and no one suggested it to him—until the sixth or seventh inning.

Yogi Berra, who had caught both the no-hitters by Allie Reynolds in 1951, raved about the "fast balls, slider and slow curves" Larsen threw. "He only shook me off twice, but each time he finally signaled for the original pitch. He was great. In fact, I've never caught a greater pitcher than Don was today."

One of three hard-hit balls off Larsen was the foul-homer by Sandy Amoros in the fifth. "When I saw that ball heading for the right-field seats I was ready to concede the homer," Hank Bauer said. "But when it hooked foul by this much (he indicated three inches) I was the happiest guy in the park."

The 1922 Perfect Game

By The Associated Press.

Here is the box score of the perfect game pitched by Charlie Robertson of the Chicago White Sox against the Detroit Tigers on April 30, 1922:

CHICAGO (A.)	ab	r	h	po	a
Mul'gan, ss	4	0	1	0	0
McL'lan, 3b	3	0	1	1	3
Collins, 2b	3	0	1	4	3
Hooper, rf	3	1	0	3	0
Mostil, lf	4	1	1	3	0
Strunk, cf	3	0	0	0	0
Sheely, 1b	4	0	2	9	0
Schalk, c	4	0	1	7	1
Rob'son, p	4	0	0	0	1
Total	32	2	7	27	8

DETROIT (A.)	ab	r	h	po	a
Blue, 1b	3	0	0	11	3
Cutshaw, 2b	3	0	0	2	3
Cobb, cf	3	0	0	1	0
Veach, lf	3	0	0	2	0
Heilman, rf	3	0	0	1	0
Jones, 3b	3	0	0	1	5
Rigney, ss	2	0	0	2	1
Mannion, c	3	0	0	7	1
Pillette, p	2	0	0	0	3
aClark	1	0	0	0	0
bBassler	1	0	0	0	0
Total	27	0	0	27	16

aStruck out for Rigney in ninth.
bFlied out for Pillette in ninth.

Chicago	0 2 0	0 0 0	0 0 0	—2
Detroit	0 0 0	0 0 0	0 0 0	—0

Error—Blue.
Two-base hits—Sheely, Mulligan. Sacrifices—McLellan, Collins, Strunk. Left on bases—Chicago 8, Detroit 0. Bases on balls—Off Pillette 2. Struck out—By Pillette 5, Robertson 6. Umpires—Nallin and Evans. Time of game—1:55.

Section 5 | SPORTS BOATS—AUTOMOBILES BUSINESS OPPORTUNITIES

The New York Times.

SPORTS SHIPPING NEWS SHOPPING GUIDE | Section 5

S © 1956, by The New York Times Company. SUNDAY, NOVEMBER 18, 1956. L++ S

YALE BEATS PRINCETON, 42-20; PITT TRIPS ARMY, 20-7; SYRACUSE ROUTS COLGATE, 61-7; PENN TOPS COLUMBIA

OFF ON 33-YARD TOUCHDOWN: Dennis McGill of Yale eluding Princeton's Ron Nelson after receiving Dean Loucks' pass in first period yesterday

The New York Times

PANTHERS WIN 6TH

Salvaterra Paces Pitt in Rally Wiping Out Cadets' 7-0 Lead

By LOUIS EFFRAT
Special to The New York Times.

PITTSBURGH, Nov. 17—Jungle Cats—that's what the University of Pittsburgh football players are called and that's what they were in the second half of their game with Army today. More or less docile in the first half, the Panthers clawed and battered the cadets after the intermission and the result was a 20-7 victory for Johnny Michelosen's powerhouse.

Pitt's reputation as a comeback team, built by winning rallies over West Virginia, Duke and Syracuse, was upheld before a near-capacity turnout of 55,639 spectators in Pitt Stadium. Again the Panthers had to come from behind, this time after they had trailed, 7—0, early in the second quarter.

In a brisk encounter, marred occasionally by fumbles, Pitt got going after changing its offensive tactics in the second half. During the first half the home-side quarterback, Cornelius (Corny) Salvaterra had been content to use straight, undisguised hand-offs on the power plays. Then he made a complete switch.

Salvaterra had scored Pitt's first touchdown, in the second quarter. With the start of the third period, he began faking like a Houdini from Pitt's split-T attack. He made the most of his options and his keeps and had the West Pointers guessing wildly. The 6-foot 198-pound star from Wilkes-Barre, Pa., fashioned the game's longest run, a 51-yard dash on a third-period keep.

Cadets Worn Down

Army, despite the giant efforts of Bob Kyasky, Dave Bourland, Dick Murtland and Mike Morales on offense, was unable to stave off its third setback. The defense, superb in the opening half while Jim Kernan, Stan Slater, Dick Fadel and Flay Goodwin still had their strength, appeared to have been worn down by the big, bruising Panthers in the second half.

The king-sized group Michelosen has in his charge recorded its sixth triumph. Beaten only by California and Minnesota, the Jungle Cats are in the running for Eastern collegiate honors. Perhaps the Pitt passing attack is on the meager side, but there is no faulting the ground offensive when Salvaterra becomes imaginative, as he did today.

This was Army's first visit here since 1935. The last time the Black Knights played here, Michelosen quarterbacked the late Jock Sutherland's outfit to a 29-6 conquest. Today it was Michelosen's outfit and it was a quarterback who again made the difference.

Pitt did no scoring in the first quarter, but that surprised no one. The Panthers have not tallied in any first period this season. The best thing Pitt did in the first fifteen minutes was to stop Army on the goal line as the quarter ended.

A Pitt fumble, recovered for Army by Lowern Reid, had given possession to the cadets at midfield. The running of Murtland and Bourland, and a spinning jump pass from Bourland to Art Johnson, figured in the advance that brought Army a

Continued on Page 3, Column 2

Rangers Tied, 4-4, By Late Bruin Goal

By JOSEPH C. NICHOLS

The best the Boston Bruins could do against the New York Rangers at Madison Square Garden last night was a 4-to-4 tie. But the way they tied it certainly gave evidence of the strength and aggressiveness possessed by the Beantown sextet.

With less than ten seconds to go, and with the Broadway Blues enjoying the advantage of a goal, Coach Milt Schmidt pulled Terry Sawchuck out of the Boston net. He sent six skaters into the New York Zone.

This strategy, which so rarely works, brought results for the visitors. They swarmed

Continued on Page 12, Column 3

Tennessee Subdues Mississippi, 27 to 7

By The Associated Press.

KNOXVILLE, Tenn., Nov. 17—Tennessee players grabbed a fumble and intercepted a pass today to rally to a 27-7 victory over Mississippi before a crowd of 42,000.

A pair of second-stringers Bobby Gordon and Carl Smith, put on an offensive show late in the game to roll up the score and help the Volunteers in their bid to become the nation's No. 1 team. Smith, a sophomore, scored three touchdowns.

Mississippi, striving for an upset, had only one big weapon—Ray Brown's passing—and it was a double-edged sword.

Brown's arm put Mississippi ahead right after the kick-off. The Vols tied the score before the half, however, and when Brown had an aerial intercepted early in the third period, Tennessee was off. Tommy

Continued on Page 3, Column 5

IOWA TURNS BACK OHIO STATE BY 6-0

Hawks Win Rose Bowl Berth on Ploen's Third-Period Aerial to Gibbons

By The Associated Press.

IOWA CITY, Nov. 17—Iowa's Hawks scored a 6-0 victory today over Ohio State and gained at least a share of the Big Ten football title and a Rose Bowl appearance.

Not since 1922 had an Iowa team shared the title and never has Iowa been in a bowl game.

The victory, which thrilled a crowd of 57,732, gave a 5-1 Big Ten record to Iowa. The Hawks would get an undisputed championship if Michigan defeated Ohio State next Saturday.

Ohio State went into the contest with a 4-0 season mark and a record-breaking seventeeen conference victories. The defending conference champions were shooting for an unprecedented third straight undisputed title.

A 17-yard touchdown pass in the third period from Kenny Ploen to Jim Gibbons just inside the end zone capped an Iowa spurt from its 37 after the kick-off.

Iowa got a big lift on a pass interference ruling against Halfback Don Clark that landed Iowa on the Ohio State 20. The Hawks made the most of it two plays later on Ploen's arrow-straight throw to Gibbons, the big end.

The Iowa defense confined the normally hard-punching Ohio backs, who had rolled up an average of 308 yards a game, to three first downs in the last half after getting six in the first half.

The Buckeyes had only 147 yards by rushing at the finish.

Iowa fans by the hundreds poured on to the field in a confusing ending in which Iowa had driven the desperate Buckeyes back to their 3 yard line.

The excited Iowans, thinking

Continued on Page 3, Column 3

Riepl of Quakers Excels In 20-6 Victory Over Lions

By ROSCOE McGOWEN
Special to The New York Times.

PHILADELPHIA, Nov. 17—Lou Little lost another to his alma mater, the University of Pennsylvania. In a rain-soaked game at Franklin Field, Penn beat Columbia, 20—6, today. Thus Little will go into retirement with a losing streak of fourteen straight against the Red and Blue.

Since Little began coaching at Morningside Heights his Lions have outscored Penn only twice—the most recent time in 1937, when the Lions won, 26—6.

This marked the thirty-sixth meeting between the two Ivy League schools, with Penn holding the decided edge of thirty victories, five losses and one tie.

Benham Prevents Shut-Out

Claude Benham, recovered sufficiently from his injury to play all but a few minutes of the second quarter, was able to engineer a touchdown that saved his team from a shut-out.

That touchdown was a dandy—a forward pass play that covered 65 yards and came at 9:06 of the fourth period. The play came immediately after Hal Musick had punted out of bounds on the 35-yard line.

Benham faded back and fired a long pass down the left side to Bruce Howard, a substitute left end. Bruce caught the ball on the 40 and went the rest of the way down the sidelines to score. Bob Ott's try for the extra point went wide.

The outstanding back on the field, though, was Penn's Frank Riepl. He became the first Red and Blue ball-carrier to tote the pigskin at least 100 yards in a

Continued on Page 5, Column 2

BROWN SETS BACK HARVARD, 21 TO 12

McTigue Scores Twice and Finney Aids Bruins With Aerials and End Run

By WILLIAM J. BRIORDY
Special to The New York Times.

CAMBRIDGE, Mass., Nov. 17—John McTigue and Frank Finney, two sophomore backs, spearheaded Brown's football team to a 21-to-12 success over Harvard today at Harvard Stadium.

McTigue, a shifty left halfback from Wellesley, Mass., and Finney, a standout passing quarterback from Royal Oak, Mich., did yeoman work as the Bruins registered a mild upset over their Ivy League foes.

A crowd of 13,500 saw Coach Al Kelley's eleven rebound in strong fashion to score once in each of the second, third and fourth quarters after Harvard had clicked on a 49-yard drive to get its first touchdown in the second period.

John Simourian, a senior quarterback from near-by Newton, turned in a whale of a job for

Continued on Page 11, Column 2

DAVIS SURPASSES MARK IN HURDLES

U.S. Athlete Timed in 0:13.3 for 120-Yard Event During Pre-Olympic Meet

By ALLISON DANZIG
Special to The New York Times.

MELBOURNE, Australia, Nov. 17—Jack Davis of Glendale, Calif., set a world record of 13.3 seconds for the 120-yard high hurdles today as the United States track and field team engaged in a final tune-up for the Olympics, which start on Thursday and run through Dec. 8.

The mark was established on a grass track at Bendigo, 100 miles northwest of Melbourne. Another world mark was equaled and several Australian standards lowered before 10,000 fans.

The showing of the Americans in competition with athletes of thirteen other nations, mostly from Asia and Africa, proved satisfying to Coach James Kelly. His fears in a number of instances were relieved.

However, there was one keen disappointment. Lieut. Jim Lea of the Air Force finished in third place, behind Nil Milkha Singh of India, in a 440-yard heat in the slow time of 0:49.2. Charley Jenkins of Villanova won the heat in 0:48.

Lea Set World Mark

Lea, a Southern California graduate, set the world record of 0:45.8 this year, He has been troubled with a weak Achilles tendon and of recent days has been discouraged about it.

From the way he ran tonight it appears Lea can hardly be counted on to finish in the first two in the Olympics 400-meter race. Lou Jones of New Rochelle and Jenkins will have to carry the hopes of the United States.

Jones was defeated in his heat today, placing second to Jesse Mashburn of Oklahoma City.

Continued on Page 12, Column 1

Lehigh Power Halts Lafayette, 27 to 10

By GORDON S. WHITE Jr.
Special to The New York Times.

EASTON, Pa., Nov. 17—Lehigh University packed its big scoring punch into the second period and rolled up a 27-10 triumph over Lafayette before 19,000 fans at Fisher Field today.

Dan Nolan, a quarterback known for his passing, stuck to running to lead the Engineers in this ninety-second contest of the series between the institutions. Lehigh, which has entered this clash favored ever since 1953, gained its first victory over Lafayette since 1952.

The series began in 1884. It has resulted in more games than any other football series.

Continued on Page 3, Column 4

WITH THE GREATEST OF EASE: The Rev. Bob Richards, U. S. pole vaulter, warming up on low hurdle in preparation for opening of Olympics Thursday at Melbourne, Australia.

Associated Press

Brown Scores 43 Points In Last Game for Orange

By LINCOLN A. WERDEN
Special to The New York Times.

SYRACUSE, Nov. 17—As far as the Colgate football team was concerned, there was just too much Jimmy Brown in the game today. The crushing Syracuse left halfback from Manhasset, L. I., in an individual performance of All-America proportions, led his team to a 61-7 triumph before a sellout crowd of 39,701.

In his final game for the Orange, Brown accounted for 43 points, scoring six touchdowns and kicking 7 extra-point placements. No other team in this fifty-seven-year-old series had tallied as many points as the Syracuse aggregation did in Archbold Stadium this cold gray afternoon.

The highest total credited to any previous Syracuse squad came in 1944. That was 43 points, the total that Brown amassed by the time he made his final exit early in the fourth period.

In 1898, Colgate defeated Syracuse, 58 to 0, and that was the scoring mark shattered by Brown and this alert, fast-moving squad that rolled on to accumulate 511 yards by rushing.

Davis' Record Broken

Brown's share of this figure was 197 yards on twenty-two carriers. As a result, the senior left half sent his season's ground-gaining yardage to 986 yards. This erased the previous best by any Syracuse player, which was the 805 yards compiled by George Davis in 1949.

Syracuse was on the way to a touchdown after taking the op-

Continued on Page 6, Column 2

DARTMOUTH TRIMS CORNELL, 27 TO 14

Rovero and Pratt Pace Big Green to First Victory at Ithaca in 20 Years

By MICHAEL STRAUSS
Special to The New York Times.

ITHACA, N. Y., Nov. 17—The football picture remains a bleak one far above Cayuga's waters. Today, the victory-starved Cornell eleven added another chapter to its disastrous season by bowing to Dartmouth, 27—14.

The setback was the first in twenty years for the Ithacans at the hands of the Hanoverians on Schoellkopf Field.

Now, the Big Red has only its Thanksgiving Day date with Pennsylvania left on which to win one. But, no matter what happens, the 1956 season will go down as the one in which Cornell dropped at least eight games for the first time since it began the sport in 1887.

Filling the roles of chief villains in the Ithacans' debacle were Lou Rovero and Dave Pratt. Rovero, a 161-pound halfback

Continued on Page 2, Column 2

Football Scores

COLLEGES

East		South	
Albright 13	Scranton 7	Alcorn 51	Tougaloo 0
Allegheny 24	Dickinson 19	Allen 19	Bethune-Cookman 0
American Int'l 21	New Britain T. 7	Arkansas 27	Southern Methodist 13
Bethany (W. Va.) 40	Grove City (Pa.) 34	Arkansas State 27	Austin Peay 13
Boston College 13	Boston University 0	Auburn 20	Georgia 0
Brown 21	Harvard 12	Butler 25	Leland 7
Connecticut 51	Rhode Island 6	Carson-Newman 27	Maryville (Tenn.) 14
Dartmouth 27	Cornell 14	Coll. of Ozarks 21	Arkansas St. T. 12
Delaware 14	Temple 7	Delaware State 13	St. Augustine 13
D. C. Teachers 36	Montclair State T. 13	Duke 26	Wake Forest 0
Drexel Tech 20	Coast Guard 7	Elizabeth City T. 14	Norfolk State 8
E. Stroudsburg 21	Kutztown T. (Pa.) 0	Elon 20	Guilford 0
Edinboro T. (Pa.) 19	California T. (Pa.) 6	Emory & Henry 50	Randolph-Macon 0
Gettysburg 21	F. and M. 0	Fayetteville 25	J. C. Smith 8
Haverford 0	Swarthmore 0	Fisk 26	Morehouse 9
Hobart 33	Buffalo 12	Florida State 20	Mississippi Southern 19
Johns Hopkins 7	Western Maryland 0	Florida A. & M. 34	Southern 6
Juniata 33	Ursinus 6	Florence St. (Ala.) 61	Southeast (Mo.) 13
King's College 24	Kings Point 0	George Washington 20	The Citadel 0
Lehigh 27	Lafayette 10	Georgia Tech 27	Alabama 0
Lock Haven T. 33	Mansfield 7	Hampden-Sydney 12	Washington & Lee 0
Lycoming 33	Geneva 19	Houston 26	Villanova 13
Moravian 45	Wilkes 13	Howard (Ala.) 24	Livingston St. (Ala.) 6
Navy 34	Virginia 7	Jackson 20	Wiley 20
New Hampshire 28	Massachusetts 7	Kentucky 33	Xavier (Ohio) 0
New Haven T. 33	Bridgeport 12	Knoxville 27	Alabama A. & M. 20
Penn M. C. 40	Lebanon Valley 25	Lamar Tech 34	Sul Ross 7
Penn State 14	North Carolina State 7	Louisville 14	Eastern (Ky.) St. 6
Pennsylvania 20	Columbia 6	Louisiana College 73	Henderson T. 0
Pittsburgh 20	Army 7	Maryland State 7	Shaw 0
Rochester 13	Washington & Jefferson 0	Miss. State 32	L. S. U. 13
Rutgers 20	William & Mary 6	Murray State 34	W. Kentucky State 13
Springfield 27	Hofstra 9	New Mexico Western 20	Adams St. 14
Syracuse 61	Colgate 7	Winston-Salem 28	St. Paul Poly 12
Trinity (Conn.) 14	Wesleyan 7	Prairie View 12	Langston 0
Tufts 53	Upsala 19	Richmond 45	Eastern Carolina 7
Union (N. Y.) 14	Hamilton 13	Rust 0	Okolona 0
West Liberty T. 13	Slippery Rock 6	Sam Houston St. 31	Stephen F. Austin 0
West Virginia 7	Furman 0	Savannah State 13	Claflin 6
Westminster (Pa.) 48	Carnegie Tech 0	South Carolina 13	Maryland 0
Williams 27	Amherst 12	Southeastern (La.) 20	Northwestern (La.) 15
Yale 42	Princeton 20	S. W. Texas State 14	East Texas State 0

Continued on Page 4, Column 3

ELI REACHES PEAK

68,000 Fans See Yale Topple Tiger From Unbeaten Ranks

By JOSEPH M. SHEEHAN
Special to The New York Times.

NEW HAVEN, Conn., Nov. 17—Yale's senior-dominated football team, frustrated in ventures against Princeton the past two seasons, rose to the heights today to bury the previously unbeaten Tigers, 42—20, under a six-touchdown avalanche.

The victory clinched at least a tie for the Ivy League title for Yale. The once-beaten Bulldogs, with the Harvard game to go next Saturday, have won all six of their Ivy tests. Princeton's record now is 5—1 in the circuit.

The historic Bowl, populated by a near-capacity crowd of 68,000 on a cold and dripping afternoon, has seen no more devastating exhibition of offensive play than the Bulldogs staged in the first half.

Coach Jordan Olivar's superbly-drilled all-senior backfield of Dean Loucks, Al Ward, Dennis McGill and Steve Ackerman, operating behind an explosive line led by Mike Owseichik and Paul Lopata, levelled Princeton's defenses almost at will in the first two periods.

Beginning with a sustained drive back from the opening kick-off, the Bulldogs scored on long marches on five of the six times they came into possession of the ball. They were all but unstoppable, on the ground and in the air.

McGill Scores for Yale

Their first touchdown came at 4:10 of the first period on a 33-yard pass play from Loucks to McGill that completed a thirteen-play drive covering 91 yards. Ward plunged across from short range for the second at 10:41 of the first quarter. This came on the third play of an 83-yard movement.

It was Ward again, from 2 yards out, at 1:59 of the second quarter to culminate a five-play march of 40 yards. At 7:46 of the second period, McGill took a 24-yard pass from Loucks to bring an eight-play drive of 55 yards to a successful culmination.

Then, fifty-one seconds before the intermission, McGill, who had not thrown a pass previously this season, flipped an 8-yard strike into the end zone to John Pendexter at the end of a six-play movement good for 37 yards.

This surprise play completed Yale's productive offensive activity but the Bulldogs made still another touchdown. It came at 4:10 of the third period when Ackerman scooped up a Princeton kick that had been blocked by Charles Griffith and raced 48 yards to a score.

To round out an almost perfect game for the Elis, Vern Loucks made good on all five of his conversion tries and Bob Corry found the target on the single occasion he was called on.

Morris Goes 71 Yards

Princeton was by no means disgraced. Led by Tom Morris, Coach Charley Caldwell's Tigers moved the ball well at times from their baffling single-wing sequences, traveling long distances for their three touchdowns.

On the second play following the kick-off after Yale's first touchdown, Princeton shook Morris loose for a 71-yard scoring

Continued on Page 8, Column 3

Penn State Downs N. C. State, 14 to 7

By The United Press.

UNIVERSITY PARK, Pa., Nov. 17—Penn State defeated North Carolina State, 14—7, today in a bruising ground game that had been scoreless with less than four minutes left in the game.

Penn State's Nittany Lions counted first with three minutes and fifteen seconds remaining. Taking a punt on their 43 they moved 57 yards in nine plays, Bill Kane pushing over from the 2.

The Wolfpack from North Carolina State came roaring back. Less than two minutes later Bill Franklin passed 9 yards to Bob Pepe in the end zone. Dick Hunter added the extra point to make it a 7-7

Continued on Page 4, Column 3

SYRACUSE DOWNS COLGATE, 61 TO 7

Continued From Page 1

ening kick-off. During the first half, Syracuse scored four of the five times it had the ball. On the other occasion, a fumble on the 2-yard line enabled Colgate to gain possession. But the Orange attack was soon rumbling goalward again.

In the second half, Syracuse scored five of the six times it had possession. An intercepted pass momentarily stalled Syracuse on the Red Raiders' 20. But then, as in the second quarter, the Orange recovered quickly from this error and pounded out a touchdown.

Jamison Scores on Pass

On the Colgate side, Guy Martin, the team's top quarterback and passing ace, tried mightily to overcome the Syracuse line and hit his receivers. He completed four out of four in the initial quarter and hit his left end, Al Jamison for the Raider touchdown in 14:00 of the opening period. Martin converted with a placement.

Martin fought doggedly on defense. Although pressed as the game wore on, he completed sixteen of thirty-five for 195 yards.

With Governor Harriman among the spectators, the Syracuse fans enjoyed this concluding game of one of the Orange's successful football seasons. There are rumors on the campus that their team may be selected for a post-season bowl game.

Colgate, victor over Yale earlier in the season, had been beaten thrice before this contest. Syracuse was the pre-game favorite, having lost only once, by 14-7, to Pitt. But no one anticipated the stunning show that Brown was to put on.

This victory put Syracuse's string at six over the Raiders, a record. At half-time, the press box announcer jocularly said: "The score is now Brown 27, Colgate 7." Brown was responsible for scoring all of his team's points in the first half.

In the first period Brown scored at the end of Syracuse's initial 75-yard drive from the 1-yard line. A 43-yard running pass, Jim Ridlon to Dick Lasse, right end, surprised Colgate and was the highlight of this march. Brown converted to make it 7—0 in 4:54.

Syracuse kicked off but Colgate was soon forced to punt. Moving from its 29, Syracuse went 71 yards in ten plays. Brown went the concluding 15 yards around his left end for the touchdown. His conversion made it 14—0. The time was 11:14.

It was Colgate's turn to score as Martin began firing with extreme accuracy. Colgate moved 76 yards in six plays, the biggest chunk being a 33-yard gain on an aerial to Dick Randall.

The Syracuse alternate team was in on defense during this Colgate attack. The starting line-up returned to the game and Syracuse had the ball at midfield after two Colgate kick-offs went out of bounds. Taking a pitch-out from Quarterback Chuck Zimmerman, Brown raced down his right sideline 50 yards for the touchdown. It was 20—7 and Brown's try for the extra point was wide.

After the three touchdowns in the first quarter, Syracuse bagged one in the second. Colgate penetrated to its rival's 19, only to have Zimmerman intercept a Martin pass to give Syracuse the ball on the Orange 13.

Alan Cann, Syracuse fullback, carried twelve times in the first half for 91 yards and was a constant threat before he hobbled off with a knee injury in the third chapter. Brown gained a first down on the Colgate 3. Here Ridlon fumbled as he appeared to be going for the touchdown.

Martin of Colgate recovered and Syracuse was momentarily thwarted. Martin tried to connect with a receiver and after failing twice, punted to Brown on fourth down.

Syracuse University

Jim Brown

Statistics of the Game

	Syr.	Col.
First downs	31	14
Rushing yardage	511	95
Passing yardage	99	195
Passes attempted	7	35
Passes completed	4	16
Passes intercepted by	5	0
Fumbles lost	1	2
Number of punts	0	4
Av. dist. of punts, yds.	0	33.7
Yards penalized	44	16

From the Colgate 29, Syracuse went on to score by 11:27. Brown went to his right for the last 8 yards. His conversion made it 27—7.

Pass by Martin Fails

John Call, Colgate right half, went 45 yards on a big bid by the Raiders before the half ended. Colgate was down to the Syracuse 4 as Martin tried to pass for a touchdown in the last fifteen seconds, but failed.

Brown had carried thirteen times for 127 yards in the first half.

In the third period Syracuse added 21 points.

Syracuse went 74 yards on fourteen plays, with Zimmerman keeping the ball on a quarterback sneak for the fifth touchdown. Brown converted again. The time was 8:21 and the score 34—7.

When Syracuse had the ball a little later Brown went 19 yards to his left and then 19 yards to his right for the touchdown on the last two of four plays that were required for this score.

Brown avoided all tacklers on this touchdown sprint. He then kicked the placement to make it 41—7 at 10:50.

Before the third period was over, Syracuse went 46 yards on six plays, with Fred Kuczala, a reserve quarterback, going over from the one-foot line.

Dean Danigelis attempted to convert and Colgate was charged with roughing the kicker. Brown came in to replace Danigelis and kicked the placement for a 48-7 margin at 14:56.

Syracuse recovered a Colgate fumble at the outset of the final quarter. From the Raiders' 20, Syracuse went for its eighth touchdown in 1:54 after Brown had charged through from the 1-yard line. Brown's placement was good and the score was 55—7.

The Orange began from their 24 in a drive midway through the fourth session, but Martin's interception gave the ball to Colgate on the Syracuse 20. With reserves in the line-up for most of this period, Syracuse headed goalward immediately after the Martin interception.

Ed Coffin, Syracuse fullback, grabbed a subsequent Martin toss and Syracuse had the ball on the Colgate 9. Three plays later and Dan Ciervo, one of Brown's replacements at left half, knifed through from the 2 yard line. Dan Fogarty's placement was wide and the score was 61—7. Colgate went all the way to the Orange 9 before the game closed, but Syracuse was moving again after Danigelis interecepted a pass on his goal line and raced back 45 yards.

The Line-Up

SYRACUSE (61)

Left Ends—Baccile, Althouse, Stephens, Aloise, Taylor.
Left Tackles—Strid, Hersney, Podraza, Stock.
Left Guards—Farmer, Warholak, Anderson.
Centers—C. Brown, Ringo, Krivak.
Right Guards—Bailey, Bill, Stock, Kiviat.
Right Tackles—Cashman, Benecick.
Right Ends—Lasse, Preising, Aloise, Youmans.
Quarterbacks—Zimmerman, Kuczala, Fogarty.
Left Halfbacks—J. Brown, Ackley, Ciervo.
Right Halfbacks—Ridlon, Jackson, Danigells.
Fullbacks—Cann, Coffin, Zazo, Williamson.

COLGATE (7)

Left Ends—Jamison, Nastonovich, Van Cleave.
Left Tackles—Antone, Morog, Vitko.
Left Guards—Yurak, Paratore.
Centers—Solana, Lockwood.
Right Guards—Mascellino, Cinklin.
Right Tackles—Usinger, Garn, Thomas.
Right Ends—Conwicke, Randall, Walker.
Quarterback—Martin.
Left Halfbacks—Garivaltis, Betts.
Right Halfbacks—Call, Boccazzi, Ammon.
Fullbacks—Conklin Whitehair, Deming.

Syracuse	20	7	21	13—61
Colgate	7	0	0	0—7

Syracuse scoring—Touchdowns: J. Brown (6 inch, line: 15, run: 50, run: 8, run: 19, run: 1, plunge). Zimmerman (1 foot, plunge). Kuczala (1, run). Ciervo (2, line). Conversions: Brown 7 (placements).

Colgate scoring—Touchdown: Jamison (10, pass from Martin). Conversion: Martin (placement).

Referee—Albert J. Booth Jr., Yale. Umpire—Lewis V. Kost, Gettysburg. Linesman—August P. Cervini, Holy Cross. Field judge—Henry D. Hormel, N. Y. U. Electric clock—Francis J. Nicholson, Niagara.

TAYLOR SETS PACE IN 21-TO-7 VICTORY

He Sets Up 2 Touchdowns, Scores Other in Texas Aggies' Early Offense

STATISTICS OF THE GAME

	A & M	Rice
First downs	13	14
Rushing yardage	254	127
Passing yardage	9	147
Passes attempted	3	19
Passes completed	1	12
Passes intercepted by	1	0
Punts	7	7
Av. dist. of punts, yds.	31.4	38.7
Fumbles lost	1	2
Yards penalized	59	40

COLLEGE STATION, Tex., Nov. 17 (AP)—Loyd Taylor led the Texas Aggies to a 21-7 victory over Rice today to clinch at least a tie for the Southwest Conference championship for the victors.

Taylor, the unsung member of the Aggie quartet that has rumbled unbeaten through nine games, set up two of the touchdowns and scored the other. The Aggies made all their points in the first half, then looked like a group that was tired of it all in the last half.

Taylor Gains 86 Yards

Taylor, the 165-pound speedster from Roswell, N. M., led the ground-gainers with 86 yards, getting 71 in the first half.

The Aggies punched out 254 yards on the ground to 127 for the Owls. But Rice got 147 yards in the air to only 9 for the Aggies.

Rice, obviously outclassed in everything except effort, outplayed the Aggies in the final two periods but only once could puncture the A. & M. defense for a score.

Victor Ineligible for Bowl

A crowd of 36,000 watched the Aggies get their first share of the championship in fifteen years. They close the season on Thanksgiving Day against Texas and are favored to win and take the title undisputed. But that will wind up things for A. & M. It is on National Collegiate Athletic Association probation and can't play in a bowl game.

At the end of the game four Aggie cheer leaders carried a black coffin around the field. It was labeled "N. C. A. A." in big white letters. Yesterday a dummy tagged "N. C. A. A." was strung to a tree on the campus.

Texas A. & M.	7	14	0	0—21
Rice	0	0	7	0—7

Texas A. & M. scoring—Touchdowns: Pardee 2 (4, run: 1 foot, plunge). Taylor (23, run). Conversions: Taylor 3.

Rice scoring—Touchdown: Hill (1, plunge). Conversion: Hall.

BOSTON COLLEGE TRIUMPHS BY 13-0

Eagles Strike in 2d Period to Turn Back Boston U.—Allard Runs 75 Yards

BOSTON, Nov. 17 (UP)—Boston College parlayed a trio of talented backs and a charging line into a 13-0 victory over Boston University today in 40-degree weather at Fenway Park.

The Eagles struck for two second-period touchdowns to bring their season's record to four victories and three losses. Boston University, held to a net gain of 142 yards in the air and on the ground, ended its season with a 1-5-2 slate, its only triumph being a season-opening victory over Massachusetts.

The Boston College fullback, Bernie Teliszewski, opened the scoring early in the second quarter to cap an 80-yard march. Teliszewski, who gained 28 of the Eagle's last 31 yards of the drive in six carries, dove over from the one-yard line. End Jim Cotter's try for the point after was wide.

Statistics of the Game

	B. C.	B. U.
First downs	18	10
Rushing yardage	218	77
Passing yardage	59	65
Passes attempted	11	18
Passes completed	4	8
Passes intercepted by	0	1
Punts	4	5
Av. dist. of punts, yds.	30	32
Fumbles lost	4	3
Yards penalized	20	25

Don Allard, sophomore quarterback from Somerville, turned in the game's most spectacular play to set up the second score 90 seconds before the half ended.

Allard took a Terrier punt on his own 22, came back up the middle, cut to the left sideline at midfield and raced 75 yards before tripping on the Boston University three.

Halfback Alan Miller tallied two plays later from the 2. Capt. Henry Sullivan, hobbled with a leg injury, came in to convert.

Boston University's best scoring chance came in the third period when it went 50 yards to the Eagle 4 before being stopped. The Terriers took a Boston College fumble late in the game to take possession on the Eagle 19.

Check Terrier Bids

Boston University, with Charlie Fiorino and Len Hill pitching, completed eight of eighteen passes for 65 yards but the Boston College line, led by Tony Quintiliani, Tino Bertolini and Tony Folcarelli, repeatedly drove back Terrier ground thrusts.

There were seven fumbles lost in the game, Boston College the victim of four, but none of the miscues figured in the scoring, or in scoring opportunities.

GA. TECH SUBDUES ALABAMA, 27 TO 0

Vann and Thompson, Reserve Backs, Spark Attack for Engineers at Atlanta

STATISTICS OF THE GAME

	Tech	Ala.
First downs	21	12
Rushing yardage	225	160
Passing yardage	167	45
Passes attempted	20	13
Passes completed	14	3
Passes intercepted by	2	0
Punts	4	6
Av. dist. of punts, yds.	24.3	36.7
Fumbles lost	2	2
Yards penalized	84	59

ATLANTA, Nov. 17 (AP)—Toppy Vann and Jimmy Thompson sparked Georgia Tech to a 27-0 football victory over Alabama today.

Vann, filling in for the ailing Wade Mitchell, and 148-pound Thompson, replacing injured George Volkert, scored a touchdown apiece as Tech gained its fifth Southeastern Conference victory and its seventh triumph in eight games.

A crowd of 38,888 saw Vann engineer a 30-yard scoring drive in the waning seconds of the first quarter against a sturdy Crimson Tide defense.

The score came on an 8-yard pass from Stan Flowers to Johnny Menger. Thompson, from Bessemer, Ala., got the second on a 48-yard scamper.

Paul Rotenberry fumbled a hand-off from Vann, picked it up and gave it to Thompson who followed superb blocking for the score with one second left in the third quarter.

Vann, turning the quarterback sneak into a potent attack weapon, sent Tech 61 yards in ten plays for the third score. He tore off the last 12 on a quarterback option.

Texas Western 16-13 Victor

CANYON, Tex., Nov. 17 (AP)—Truman Hobbs kicked a 38-yard field goal with two seconds left to give a 16-13 victory to Texas Western in a Border Conference football game against West Texas State today. A homecoming crowd of 7,000 saw Hobbs' kick that meant a clean sweep of the conference for the winners.

The New York Times.

S SUNDAY, MARCH 24, 1957. L+++ S

DODGERS SET BACK YANKS IN 9TH, 3-2 ON GILLIAM'S HIT

Single Decides for Kipp of Brooks Before 11,047 at Night Game in Miami

BOMBERS TALLY IN FIFTH

Kubek's Triple Bats in Two Markers Against Maglie—Grim Is Losing Pitcher

By JOHN DREBINGER

Special to The New York Times.

MIAMI, March 23—The Dodgers, who have been doing a deal of brooding since last October when they blew the seventh game of the 1956 world series to the Yankees, got a measure of a revenge tonight.

Cheered by a gathering of 11,047, Walter Alston's Brooks tripped the Bombers, 3 to 2, in the opening clash of this spring's six-game exhibition series.

With the bases filled, the score tied at 2-all and none out in the last half of the ninth inning, Jim Gilliam cracked Bob Grim for a single over the drawn in Yankee infield to break up the battle.

For Alston, the victory provided a fillip. For in the top half of the ninth the Brooklyn skipper had deftly out-slickered Casey Stengel, which is no simple trick in or out of season.

Kipp Commits Balk

In this inning, the Yanks worked a runner around to third with two out. Joe Collins walked, advanced to second on a balk by Fred Kipp, a young left-hander, and went to third on a sacrifice.

After an infield out left the position unchanged, Stengel sent Mickey Mantle up to bat for Bob Martyn. But Alston, noting that Grim was the next batter and that Stengel had no other pitcher warmed up, directed Kipp to walk Mantle intentionally.

Grim then ended the threat, as expected, by grounding into a force play at second base.

A single by Randy Jackson launched the Dodgers' winning drive in the last of the ninth. Incidentally, it was Randy's first hit of the exhibition season.

Collins, playing first base, then threw wide to second on Don Demeter's attempted sacrifice bunt and when Sandy Amoros, batting for Kipp, got hit by a pitched ball, the bases were filled. Gilliam followed with the single to left center to end the struggle.

Ford, Maglie Start

Whitey Ford and Sal Maglie were the starting hurlers and the left-hander made out slightly the better. Whitey went six innings and not until the sixth did he give up a tally. The Dodgers scored on a single by Roy Campanella and a two-bagger by Don Zimmer.

But that still left the Brooks one behind, for Maglie, after blanking the Yanks for four innings, was tagged for two tallies in the fifth. After Andy Carey walked and Ford singled, Tony Kubek drove in both with a triple.

That, however, ended the scoring for the world champions. Roger Craig blanked the Yanks in the sixth and seventh and Kipp did the same in the final two innings.

Successive singles by Gilliam and Chico Fernandez off Grim scored the Dodgers' second run to tie the score in the seventh.

Alston almost upended a delegation of Yankee scribes when

Continued on Page 2, Column 4

START OF GRAND PRIX: Drivers running to their sports cars to begin yesterday's endurance test of men and machines at Sebring, Fla., air terminal

Associated Press Wirephotos

FATAL ACCIDENT: Bob Goldich of Chicago is lifted from his overturned Arnolt Bristol after it crashed on the 5.2-mile course. Goldich was killed instantly.

Fangio Takes Auto Race; Chicago Driver Is Killed

By FRANK M. BLUNK

Special to The New York Times.

SEBRING, Fla., March 23—Juan Manuel Fangio of Argentina and Jean Behra of France drove a 4.5-liter Maserati to an easy victory in the Sebring twelve-hour Grand Prix of Endurance today. In doing so they set records in all the main categories.

Another Maserati, this one with a 3-liter engine, finished second with two other world-famous drivers, Stirling Moss of England and Harry Schell of Paris and New York, but they were close to two laps behind at the stirring finish witnessed by a crowd exceeding 25,000.

In the first hour an accident on the Double S turn took the life of Bob Goldich, a Chicago driver. Goldich drove his Arnolt-Bristol into the twisting segment too fast, went into a four-wheel drift or slide and rolled over in the dirt.

Goldich, 33 years old, was a manufacturers' representative and had been an auto racing enthusiast and driver since his teens. He started in midget racing cars and made a switch to sports cars in 1954 as the pilot of an Excalibur owned by Brooks Stevens.

The 1954 race was Goldich's first at Sebring. Since then he had been a member of the Arnolt-Bristol teams owned by S. H. Arnolt, a Warsaw (Ind.) manufacturer.

Following the fatal crash, Arnolt withdrew his other two cars from the race and closed his pits. Goldich was married and had two sons, aged 5 and 1.

The crowd, which had been

Continued on Page 5, Column 2

N.Y.U. GAINS TITLE IN N.C.A.A. FENCING

Rosenberg's Epee Victories Help Violets Outscore Columbia, 65 to 64

By The Associated Press.

DETROIT, March 23—N. Y. U. won the thirteenth annual National Collegiate fencing championship today by piling up 65 points to beat the runner-up, Columbia, by a point.

The Violets, who dethroned Illinois as champions, were in third place after yesterday's opening session. They didn't move into first place until their Paul Rosenberg upset Jim Woods of Navy in one of the last épée matches of the meet.

Columbia had been leading N. Y. U. by 3 points after yesterday's competition. But Bernie Balaban won the sabre. Rosenberg added points in the épée. Al Peredo did the same in the foils and the Violets came on to take their third N. C. A. A. championship in fencing.

Wisconsin and Navy tied for third with 60 points each. Then

Continued on Page 3, Column 7

GIANTS TRIUMPH OVER INDIANS, 9-3

Mays Clouts Two Home Runs—Thompson Fined $150 as Rigney Discipline Move

Special to The New York Times.

LOS ANGELES, March 23—As if he were putting on a special show for his former boss—Leo Durocher was on the scene—Willie Mays belted a pair of 350-foot homers as the Giants walloped the Cleveland Indians, 9—3, today at Wrigley Field.

The Say Hey Kid, the acknowledged pet of Durocher when the Lip managed the New Yorkers, now has slammed five round-trippers this spring. He is tied with Gail Harris, who, along with Ossie Virgil, also hit a homer today.

This Cactus League exhibition between major league outfits attracted a gathering of 7,637 spectators. More had been anticipated, so that the turnout was on the disappointing side, bearing in mind that this town is anxious to house a major league club—the Brooklyn Dodgers—next year or shortly afterward. The big Sunday test, however, will come tomorrow when the Giants and the Indians meet here again.

One Giant Unhappy

For one Giant, in particular, the day was especially sorry. Henry Thompson, the 31-year-old outfielder, was the target of the most drastic action taken by Bill Rigney since Rigney became a manager. The pilot imposed a fine of $150 upon Thompson for disciplinary reasons.

Hank was penalized for failing to appear last night at San Diego, where the Giants defeated the Indians, 8—4, before 10,089 spectators.

It developed that Thompson was here all the while his teammates were playing in San Diego. Henry was one of three men who took the train from Phoenix Thursday night. He, Whitey Lockman and Bucky Walters were aboard—the others flew to San Diego. Not until Lockman and Walters arrived at San Diego was anyone aware that Thompson had left the train at Los Angeles.

Nothing was said about the

Continued on Page 2, Column 2

Bardstown, Fabius Of Calumet One, Two In $126,600 Stakes

By The Associated Press.

HALLANDALE, Fla., March 23—The Calumet Farm's Bardstown clinched the winter handicap honors today by speeding to a half-length victory in the $126,600 Gulfstream Park Handicap before 24,851 racing fans.

Bardstown carried high weight of 130 pounds and ran a mile and a quarter in the excellent time of 2:00 2/5. His stablemate, Fabius, was second and Florida-born Needles finished third in the field of seven.

The time of the race, over a lightning fast track, was only three-fifths of a second slower than the track record set by another Calumet horse, Coaltown. Carrying 128 pounds, Coaltown was timed in 1:59 4/5 on March 19, 1949.

Willie Hartack, the nation's leading jockey last year, kept Bardstown well off the pace set by the Keystone Stable's Pieces-ofeight. Fabius, ridden by Eddie Arcaro, was alongside the leader for the first mile.

Needles, winner of the Kentucky Derby and other rich stakes last year, trailed, as expected, in the early running. He had passed only one horse at the end of a mile.

When they reached the far

Continued on Page 4, Column 2

LINCOLN CAPTURES MILE RACE IN 3:59

He Is Third Australian and Eleventh Runner to Break Four-Minute Barrier

By The United Press.

MELBOURNE, Australia, March 23—Mervyn Lincoln of Australia became today the eleventh runner to race a mile in less than four minutes. He pounded over the Olympic Games training track in 3 minutes 59 seconds.

En route to his spectacular mile clocking, Lincoln equaled the Australian national 1,500-meter record of 3:42 set by the now retired John Landy.

Three timers caught the 24-year-old school teacher in 3:58.9, but three others made it 3:59 and that was posted as the official time. It was a second slower than the world record of 3:58 set by Landy at Turku, Finland, on June 21, 1954.

Lincoln's clocking was the third under-4-minute mile run on Australian soil, Landy accounting for the other two. Lincoln also became the third Aussie among the eleven who have succeeded in breaking the 4-minute barrier. Jim Bailey, running for the University of Oregon, did it

Continued on Page 7, Column 1

Promised Land Wins $35,750 Bowie Test

By The Associated Press.

BOWIE, Md., March 23—Promised Land let his stablemate Pertshire take the lead and wear out the pack in the $35,750-added Governor's Gold Cup race at Bowie today. Then the Kentucky Derby hopeful moved up to win.

The colt, one of three entries of Mrs. Ethel D. Jacobs, raced between horses in the pack to finish a neck in front of John L. Applebaum's Mister Jive. Mrs. Jules Schwartz' Nah Hiss was third more than two lengths back. The Brandywine Stable's Cannon Fire was fourth.

Pertshire set a fast pace at the start of the seven-furlong test and succeeded in burning out such front-runners as Olive

Continued on Page 4, Column 5

Rangers Vanquish Bruins, 4-2; Canadiens Score, Finish Second

By The United Press

BOSTON, March 23—The fourth-place New York Rangers, Boston's jinx team all season, defeated the Bruins, 4—2, tonight. The Rangers will meet the Montreal Canadiens and the Bruins will play the National Hockey League's champion Detroit Red Wings in the semi-final Stanley Cup post-season play-offs.

Danny Lewicki was the big gun in the New York attack. He scored in the second and third periods, with Boston short-handed both times. Andy Hebenton got his twenty-first tally early in the first period. Andy Bathgate, the Rangers' leading scorer, registered his twenty-seventh goal later in the period.

Continued on Page 10, Column 2

By The United Press

MONTREAL, March 23—The Montreal Canadiens clinched second place in the National Hockey League and their goalie, Jacques Plante, won his second straight Vezina Trophy tonight by blanking the Chicago Black Hawks, 3—0.

As the final buzzer sounded, Plante threw up his arms in joy at coming from behind to beat out Detroit's Glenn Hall for the Vezina Trophy. The trophy is awarded to the goalie playing the most games for the team allowing the fewest goals. The Canadiens finished the season with 155 goals scored against them, while Detroit has 156 with one more game to play.

The crowd of 14,280 saw the

Continued on Page 10, Column 1

Celtic Five Downs Syracuse, 120-105

By The Associated Press.

SYRACUSE, March 23—The Boston Celtics defeated the Syracuse Nationals, 120—105, today for their second straight victory in the play-off for the Eastern Division championship of the National Basketball Association.

The Celtics need one more triumph in the three-out-of-five-game series to eliminate Syracuse and qualify to meet the Western Division winner.

The Celtics were never behind after the first minute. They led by as many as 13 points before the Nats scrambled back into a pair of third-period ties. After a 66-all deadlock, the division's regular-season leaders spurted ahead again and stayed in front the rest of the way.

Tom Heinsohn paced the

Continued on Page 12, Column 2

BRADLEY QUINTET IS VICTOR, 84 TO 83

Sets Back Memphis State in Tourney Final at Garden on McMillon's Score

By WILLIAM J. BRIORDY

Bradley University's basketball team made its sixth National Invitation Tournament showing a victorious one yesterday afternoon. In one of the most thrilling finals in the history of the competition, the big Braves from Peoria, Ill., checked Memphis State's gamesters, 84 to 83, at Madison Square Garden.

A crowd of 11,327 saw Shellie McMillon, the Bradley center, crush the hopes of the hustling Tigers from Tennessee by completing a 3-point play with thirty seconds remaining.

Coach Bob Vanatta of the Tigers, who formerly coached Bradley, saw Memphis State move ahead with 1:06 of the rugged game remaining when Jack Butcher hit on a driving lay-up. That shot appeared to place Vanatta's lads in command.

Braves Capitalize on Height

But the Braves, using their greater height and rebounding strength to the fullest, stormed back to draw even as McMillon tallied on a rebound. When Shellie was fouled by Bob Swander, the Bradley center converted to sew it up.

After Butcher's shot, there ensued a session of wild and wooly play as each team pressed mightily. It was after Memphis State's Orby Arnold lost the ball at mid-court that Bradley hustled for the winning points. The play was so feverish that both outfits took turns losing the ball in the final fifty-four seconds.

When Swander missed a long one-hander with five seconds left, Coach Chuck Orsborn's Braves

Continued on Page 3, Column 2

The New York Times (by Ernest Sisto)

IT NETTED HIM NOTHING: Win Wilfong, right, of Memphis State trying for a basket yesterday at the Garden. Blocking him is Dick Dhabalt of victorious Bradley quintet.

NO. CAROLINA FIVE NIPS KANSAS, 54-53, IN THIRD OVERTIME

Undefeated Tar Heels Extend Streak to 32 in Final of National College Play

QUIGG'S 2 FOULS DECIDE

Winning Tallies Made With Six Seconds Remaining—San Francisco Victor

By The United Press.

KANSAS CITY, March 23—North Carolina defeated Kansas, 54—53, in three overtime periods tonight to win the National Collegiate basketball tournament. Joe Quigg won the game for the unbeaten Tar Heels with two foul shots in the final six seconds and then blocked a pass to Wilt Chamberlain to foil a Jayhawk scoring bid.

Quigg's jumping one-hand block kept Chamberlain from attempting one desperate shot in the last five seconds of the third extra period.

It was the first time a national championship game went into overtime. The Tar Heels' victory extended their unbeaten streak to thirty-two games.

The final, frantic fifteen minutes of play produced two heated incidents on the court. In the first one Pete Brennan of North Carolina clamped his arms around Chamberlain's waist and began to wrestle. The second occurred when Tommy Kearns of North Carolina swung aside Gene Elstun of Kansas.

Michigan State Bows

Third place in the championship went to San Francisco, the defending champion. The Dons defeated Michigan State, 68—60.

The dramatic finish of the title game occurred after a tight battle that was close except for the opening ten minutes, when North Carolina racked up a 19-7 margin.

It was North Carolina by 29—22 at the half. The score was 46—46 at the end of regulation play.

The two teams scored only 2 points each in the first overtime. Chamberlain hit for Kansas and Bob Young, a substitute, tallied for North Carolina. The second overtime was scoreless.

Chamberlain was the top scorer with 23 points. North Carolina's All-America, Lennie Rosenbluth, had 20. Rosenbluth fouled out with 1:45 remaining in standard playing time and did not play in the extra periods, which were mostly displays of stalling and ball control.

Kearns and Quigg won the game for North Carolina, hitting for all the Tar Heels' points in the third extra session. Kearns had a field goal and two free throws to match Chamberlain's overtime production.

Kansas Takes Time Out

Gene Elstun added another free throw to send Kansas ahead, 53—52, with twenty seconds left. Chamberlain blocked Kearns' shot, but fouled Quigg and Quigg hit for the 2 winning points.

Kansas took time out with five seconds left and tried to feed the ball to Chamberlain, but Quigg made the game-saving block.

North Carolina led the entire first half and Kansas did not catch up until it took the lead at 36—35 with 16:40 left

Kansas was on top, 40—37, with ten minutes left. The score was twice tied and the lead

Continued on Page 3, Column 3

Boys Tops Jefferson For City Title, 53-44

By MICHAEL STRAUSS

Boys High's quintet checked a second-half rally by Jefferson High last night to defeat the Orange an Blue in the city Public Sch ls Athletic League championship final, at Madison Square Garden, 53—44.

Trailing by 28—15, at the intermission, the losers staged a comeback in the third quarter. They came within 4 points of their opponents at 36—32 late in the period. But they could come no closer.

As a result, Boys was able to end its campaign with an unbeaten record in twenty games. Its decision over Jefferson, which entered the game with a slate of 18 and 3, was its third of the campaign. Both

Continued on Page 3, Column 5

NO. CAROLINA NIPS KANSAS FIVE, 54-53

Continued From Page 1

changed twice before the 46-46 deadlock.

The pattern of stalling began as soon as Kansas got its 3-point lead. North Carolina started slowing it down and Kansas followed suit.

From ten minutes left to five minutes, not a shot was fired. Both teams continued the stalling in the first two overtimes.

In the first overtime, Young broke through [illegible] a lay-up for North Carolina. During the stall, which succeeded in pulling the Kansans out of position, Chamberlain retaliated with a two-handed push off the post to tie it at 48—48.

M'GUIRE SAYS HE GOT HIT

North Carolina Five's Coach Accuses Kansas Assistant

KANSAS CITY, March 23 (UP) -- Coach Frank McGuire of North Carolina said that Kansas' coach, Dick Harp, told him to "shut up" and that an assistant Kansas coach punched him in the stomach during a "rhubarb" at the National Collegiate championship basketball game tonight.

"I moved up to see what was happening on the floor," McGuire said. "Then I heard Harp yell at me to shut up. I told Dick I hadn't said anything. Then a big fellow on the Kansas bench — I don't know his name —hit me in the stomach.

"Then everything calmed down. I have no argument with Harp but that big fellow on his bench had no right to punch me in the stomach."

Jack Eskridge, a 6-footer, who is Harp's assistant, said McGuire went over to the Kansas bench, but "nothing happened."

N.C.A.A. Line-Ups

N. CAROLINA (54)	G.	F.	PF.	P.	KANSAS (53)	G.	F.	PF.	P.
R'bluth, lf	8	4	5	20	Elstun lf	4	3	2	11
Lotz	0	0	0	0	Loneski, rf	0	2	2	2
Brennan, rf	4	3	3	11	L. Johnson	0	2	1	2
Young	1	0	1	2	Ch'berlain, c	6	11	3	23
Quigg, c	4	2	4	10	King, lg	3	5	4	11
C'ngham, lg	0	0	4	0	Parker, rg	2	0	0	4
Kearns, rg	4	3	4	11	Billings	0	0	2	0
Total	21	12	21	54	Total	15	23	14	53

Half-time score—North Carolina 29, Kansas 22. Regulation-time score—North Carolina 46, Kansas 46. First overtime score—North Carolina 48, Kansas 48. Second overtime score—North Carolina 48, Kansas 48.

Free throws missed—Brennan 4, Quigg, Cunningham, Kearns 4, Elstun 3, Loneski, Chamberlain 5, King.

S. FRANCISCO (67)	G.	F.	PF.	P.	MICHIGAN ST. (60)	G.	F.	PF.	P.
Day lf	6	0	3	12	Lux, lf	2	1	2	5
Lillevand	0	0	0	0	Scott	2	0	1	4
J. King	0	0	2	0	Green, rf	4	1	5	9
Dunbar, rf	4	1	4	9	Quiggle	2	2	1	6
Brown, c	8	6	3	22	Ferguson, c	4	6	2	14
Farmer, lg	4	8	1	16	Hedden, lg	4	1	5	9
Preaseau, rg	2	4	4	8	Bencie	0	0	1	0
Malien	0	0	0	0	Wilson, rg	3	0	1	6
					Anderegg	2	3	5	7
Total	24	19	17	67	Total	23	14	23	60

Half-time score—San Francisco 33, Michigan State 30.

Free throws missed—Day 3, Dunbar 3, Brown 5, Farmer, Scott, Ferguson 3, Hedden, Wilson, Anderegg.

BRADLEY QUINTET IS VICTOR, 84 TO 83

Continued From Page 1

had the victory and their first N. I. T. title.

The setback was a bitter one for the Tigers, who made their debut in the N. I. T. this year. They trailed by 51—43 at the intermission before setting the taller Braves on their heels with a 15-point spree as the second half opened. Win Wilfong, a jump-shot specialist who headed the scorers with 31 points; Swander, Butcher and Arnold figured in that spurt.

When Arnold converted twice from the foul line and then Butcher got two 1-pointers at 6:00, Memphis State had a 10-point bulge. But the hustling Tigers, essentially a six-man squad, fought their hearts out only to run out of gas against depth-laden Bradley.

Bradley, with Bobby Joe Mason and the 6-foot 7-inch Barney Cable supplying the spark, quickly put a halter on the Tigers' ambitions. Cable pegged three straight one-handers. Bobby Joe got a free throw and then tossed a one-hander from the side for a 74—73 lead at 12:15.

But the gamesters from Tennessee were not through by any means. Wilfong hooked one at 12:25 to return the lead to Memphis State. Then McMillon clicked with a hook shot. Wilfong drove for a lay-up at 13:35, but McMillon tied the score at 77-all with a free throw.

Bradley's Dick Dhabalt put the Indians ahead again with 4:50 remaining on a one-hander. Then Wilfong charged Dhabalt and the Bradley player converted two free throws. That was Wilfong's fifth personal, putting him out of the game with 3:55 to go.

Then the plucky Butcher hit with a one-hander and fed to Ragan underneath to tie it at 81-all with 3:20 left. When Butcher drove in for his lay-up with 1:06 to go, the Memphis State supporters went wild. Then followed the feverish action and McMillon's 3-pointer.

Bobby Joe Mason paced the Braves with 22 points. McMillon had 18 markers, 1 more than Cable. Butcher hit for 21 points. McMillon topped the rebounders with twelve. The last time Bradley appeared in the N. I. T. was in 1950, when the Braves bowed to City College.

Wilfong received a trophy as the most valuable player of the twentieth annual tournament.

Orsborn received the Edward A. Kelleher Memorial Trophy from Walter T. McLaughlin of St. John's, the president of the Metropolitan Intercollegiate Basketball Association, at the end of the game. The M. I. B. A. is the sponsor of the N. I. T. The team members of the finalists also received awards from McLaughlin.

Temple's team gained third place in the tournament when it defeated St. Bonaventure, 67 to 50, in the consolation play-off.

The final, which was played first, was nationally televised by the Columbia Broadcasting System.

BRADLEY (84)	G.	F.	PF.	P.	MEMPHIS ST. (83)	G.	F.	PF.	P.
Cable, lf	8	1	4	17	Wilfong, lf	10	11	5	31
McDade	1	3	3	5	Ragan, rf	3	4	3	10
B. Mason, rf	5	12	2	22	Hockaday	0	2	1	2
Johnson	0	0	2	0	Arnold, c	5	4	4	14
McMillon, c	8	2	4	18	Butcher, lg	7	7	4	21
Emerson	0	1	1	1	Swander, rg	2	1	4	5
Sedgwick, lg	0	0	2	0	Hays	0	0	1	0
Myers	1	2	2	4					
Morse, rg	4	1	0	9	Total	27	29	22	83
Dhabalt	3	2	3	8					
Total	30	24	23	84					

Half-time score—Bradley 51, Memphis State 43.

Free throws missed—Cable 2, B. Mason 2, McMillon 2, Sedgwick, Morse, Dhabalt, McDade, Meyers, Emerson, Filfong, Ragan, Arnold 3, Butcher 3, Swander 2, Hays 2, Hockaday.

Officials—John Nucatola and John Stevens.

TEMPLE (67)	G.	F.	PF.	P.	ST BONAV'E (50)	G.	F.	PF.	P.
Norman, lf	2	7	3	11	McCann, lf	5	0	3	10
Fleming, rf	0	4	2	4	Durr	0	0	0	0
Smith	1	0	3	2	Fairf'd, rf	4	4	2	12
Frank'n, c	6	3	3	15	Fitzpatrick	0	0	2	0
Rodgers, lg	8	5	4	21	Olshefsky c	4	3	2	11
Goldstein	0	3	0	3	Caval'e, lg	2	5	2	9
Brodsky, rg	4	3	0	11	Connors	1	2	3	4
					Weise, rg	2	0	4	4
Total	21	25	15	67	Odell	0	0	1	0
					Total	18	14	19	50

Half-time score—Temple 34, St. Bonaventure 29.

Free throws missed—Norman 2, Franklin, Rodgers, Brodsky 3, Goldstein, McCann 2, Fairfield, Olshefsky 2, Cavaliere 3.

Officials—Ed Stricker and Dallas Shirley.

BOYS HIGH DOWNS JEFFERSON, 53-44

Continued From Page 1

schools are in Brooklyn. Neville Smith, Ed Simmons and John Jasiel were the chief guns for the winners. It was Smith who continually came through when it counted most. His scoring was done when it seemed as if Jefferson might catch the pace-setters.

The 5-foot 9-inch Red and Black star tallied fourteen points, all on floor tallies. Simmons, the team's sparkplug registered thirteen, while Jasiel came through with a dozen.

For the losers, the 6-foot 8-inch Leroy Ellis starred with 23 markers.

A crowd of 8,000 witnessed the contest.

The winners held a clear edge for most of the first half. Then, in the final quarter, with the heat still on, the Red and Black clinched matters with some heads-up play.

Leading by 45—40, with four minutes to go, the victors began a freeze which settled matters. Jefferson appeared unable to cope with these tactics and Boys coasted out of danger.

On defense, Al Barden, a 6-foot 4-inch forward, and Bill Burwell, a 6-8 sophomore, excelled for the winners.

Barden held high-scoring Charlie Jackson to one field goal throughout the game while Burwell did a fine all-around job around the boards.

The inability by Jackson to score from the field did much to damage Jefferson's cause. He had hit in the three preceding play-off games with remarkable consistency averaging 42 points.

Last night his total output was only 11. The performance gave him a total of 139 points for the four extra-curricular games. It easily topped the tournament mark of 131 set by Jackson in five play-off games last season.

In the third-place consolation game, which preceded the final, James Madison defeated Commerce, 58—44. The losers, 1956 city champions, trailed at half-time, 26—22.

BOYS (53)	G.	F.	PF.	P.	JEFFERSON (44)	G.	F.	PF.	P.
Jasiel, lf	5	2	3	12	Kaza'kas, lf	3	2	2	8
Barden, rf	3	1	3	7	Hassenbein	0	0	0	0
Burwell, c	1	5	4	7	Jackson, rf	1	9	4	11
Thomas	0	0	2	0	Ellis, c	9	5	2	23
Smith, lg	7	0	1	14	Sherman, lg	1	0	2	2
Simmons, rg	3	7	1	13	Slugh, rg	0	0	5	0
					Wilkins	0	0	0	0
Total	19	15	14	53	Total	14	16	15	44

Half-time score—Boys High 28, Thomas Jefferson 15.

Free throws missed—Jasiel 3, Barden, Buwell 3, Smith, Simmons 4, Kazaluskas, Hassenbein 2, Jackson 3, Ellis 2, Slugh.

Officials—Artie Meinhold and Ed Russell.

MADISON (58)	G.	F.	PF.	P.	COMMERCE (44)	G.	F.	PF.	P.
Carner, lf	3	2	1	8	Simon, lf	3	1	4	7
Berkowitz	0	0	0	0	Gomez	1	0	1	2
L. Gecker, rf	5	4	3	14	Priester	0	0	0	0
H. Gecker	1	0	0	2	Wiggins, rf	4	3	1	11
Besserman	0	0	0	0	Caton	0	0	0	0
Marks, c	5	1	3	11	Morales, c	1	0	4	2
Ryan	0	0	0	0	Harris, lg	4	2	3	10
Lesser	0	0	0	0	Richardson	2	0	0	4
Multer, lg	3	2	2	8	W'liams, rg	3	2	1	8
Miller	0	0	0	0	Padilla	0	0	0	0
Goldberg, rg	5	1	4	11					
Lynn	0	2	1	2	Total	18	8	14	44
Budin	1	0	0	2					
Total	23	12	14	58					

Half-time score—Madison 26, Commerce 22.

Free throws missed—Carner 5, L. Gecker, Multer, Goldberg, Morales 4, Harris 3, Richardson, Williams 5.

Officials—King and Garfinkel.

CHAMPIONS DECIDE TO SPLIT UP TEAM

Martin-Knox, Easy Winners in Court Tennis, Plan to Play Separately in '58

By ALLISON DANZIG

Alastair Martin of Glen Head, L. I., and Northrup Knox of Buffalo and Aiken, S. C., retained the national court tennis doubles championship yesterday.

In the final at the Racquet and Tennis Club they defeated J. S. (Bud) Palmer of New York and William E. Lingelbach Jr. of Philadelphia, 6—4, 6—1, 6—0.

Despite the decisiveness of the victory the match lasted an hour. The first set contained one of the most spectacular and exciting displays of sustained hard hitting the championship has produced in years.

The losing team offered a dead game fight to the most destructive hitters in the amateur ranks and was simply overpowered by the ferocity of their attack.

The 28-year-old Knox, a polo player of marked ability, recently won the national singles crown in court tennis. Martin, whom he defeated in the final at Boston, held the title from 1950 through 1956. No team received an outside chance against them and they will split up next season to make for more competition.

Former Basketball Star

Palmer, a top basketball player at Princeton, is playing in court tennis tournaments for only his second year. Lingelbach, a former national champion, is not quite the player he was. But he is a tough, skilled competitor who knows the game thoroughly and stands up unflinchingly under punishment.

The champions were expected to win almost as they pleased and they did so in the final stages. But for the first set they were challenged to the utmost and for the first four games of the second set the blazing fight continued. After that, the defenders' onslaught all but disarmed their opponents and they won the last eleven games in succession.

Palmer and Lingelbach had a good chance to take the opening set. Had they done so it is likely the outcome would have been in doubt much longer than was the case. They endeavored to mix their game—their pace and shots—to slow and confuse their opponents, rather than give the speed they relish.

These tactics served to induce the champions to play them more or less at their own game rather than bring their full hitting power to bear. So it was that Palmer and Lingelbach led at 2—1 and 30—0 and were doing surprisingly well. They appeared to be fully in the fight.

Interest Kept at High Pitch

Losing the 30—0 lead was costly, but they continued to make a strong fight to 4—3 in their favor. The violence of the play kept the gallery's interest at a high pitch. The fury of the hitting, the feats in retrieving and the length of the rallies were exciting in the extreme. The big court fairly boiled with action as the four men hurled themselves about. It was no place for boys.

Palmer, with his athletic ability, his wonderful eye and coordination for so tall a man and his unflagging spirit, gave a marvelous account of himself for one with so little experience. His return of service was uniformly good and his volleying on both sides staunch.

Lingelbach was cutting down the ball beautifully, slamming into the walls for the most difficult gets and playing his hand knowingly under the heaviest pressure.

Such effort and skill were worthy of the reward of a set even against such formidable opposition and it seemed they might achieve it. But they could not quite make it. When they failed they were engulfed, but not until they had lost a 40-15 lead in the fourth game of the second set.

Martin and Knox from 3—4 in the first set were in control. They won the last three games of the set at 15, love and 15 and the last three of the second set at love, love and 15. The force with which they were cutting the ball down on the floor, their deadly targetry in hitting for the dedans and grille and the power with which they met the hurtling ball on the volley for forcing returns or winners must have been disheartening for their opponents.

The youthful Knox was fast and strong, getting stronger as the play went on. But he was no more volatile than his 41-year-old partner. Martin showed how great a player he was in these last two sets. In the last set his volleys into the winning gallery were hard to believe.

Frederick S. Mosley Jr., president of the Racquet and Tennis Club, was referee of the match. Charles (Babe) Pearson of Philadelphia, national racquets champion, called faults. Charley Petrosky was the marker.

TURNER WILL OPPOSE LOGART HERE FRIDAY

Isaac Logart, a welterweight from Camaguey, Cuba, will face Gil Turner of Philadelphia in the feature bout at Madison Square Garden on Friday night. The fight is listed for ten rounds, and will end the boxing season at the Garden.

Logart and Turner met once before, with the Cuban gaining a unanimous decision, on Oct. 21. Although Turner has shown to excellent advantage in his recent starts, it is expected that Logart will be favored to beat him again.

BIOLOGY TEACHER KEEPS LIFT TITLE

Chasnov Raises 695 Pounds to Beat Paghense, Long-Time Foe, in A. A. U. Meet

By GORDON S. WHITE JR.

Close to 65,000 pounds of steel were raised skyward as thirty-one strong men battled for Metropolitan Amateur Athletic Union senior weightlifting championships yesterday.

Any one of the athletes could lift from 170 to 300 pounds at a time depending upon his weight class. The eight classes range from the 123-pound group to the unlimited heavyweight.

A pair of weightlifters were engaged in a struggle for the lightweight honors. One, a machinist from Yonkers, thought he had what it took to beat his rival. The man the machinist wanted to beat was a biology teacher from Levittown Memorial High School on Long Island.

Vincent Paghense, 32, who helps make machines run, could be found under 200 or more pounds of weight or just relaxing between struggles. His mind was on the competition and particularly on how Alan Chasnov, the 35-year-old teacher, was faring.

Two Friendly Rivals

These friends have been pushing to beat one another for the past four or five years and each has done fairly well. One day is Paghense's and the next belongs to Chasnov.

Chasnov was yesterday's lightweight defender during the championships at the Adonis Health Club in Brooklyn. Paghense held the mat title in 1955.

Yesterday was Chasnov's day to win as he lifted 695 pounds. Paghense came in second with 675.

Paghense had a concern that always would be to Chasnov's advantage. They both stand 5 feet 5 inches. But Paghense outweighed his rivals by a couple of pounds. They weighed in at 148 pounds and 146 pounds, respectively.

It was such a difference that gave Paul Anderson of Georgia the heavyweight Olympic title last fall in Melbourne. He tied his closest competitor in total weight, but since he was lighter he got the award.

As Chasnov said, "Vince usually weighs more than I do so that if we're near a tie he always puts five extra pounds on his bar to break the weight tie. I'd win if we lifted the same amount."

An Enthusiastic Lifter

Paghense, who didn't think much of the sport a few years ago, is now an enthusiastic competitor. He is as eager about the weightlifting as a Sunday golfer is about his favorite recreation. Paghense admitted he had always had the wrong impression of the sport before joining its ranks.

"I was on a Florida vacation when someone saw me playing on the beach and wanted to know if I'd ever done any weightlifting. I hadn't and told him I didn't want to because it was only for sissies and guys who wanted to show off muscles," Paghense said.

"He got me to try it once and now I know I was wrong. To beat Chasnov and the rest is as much fun for me as it is for a kid when he hits a homer to win the neighborhood sandlot baseball game.

"However, I'll admit the sport still has a lot to overcome. Persons think the way I used to. The fellows in the competitive weightlifting want to win at the sport, not show off any more than a football player who can and does make a touchdown."

Chasnov views the sport as one "with a lot of drudgery involved." He said, "You've got to put in a lot of work practicing to try and reach the ceiling with the weights. I don't get as much practice as I'd like to or as much as most of these fellows get. In addition to teaching, I am a Boy Scout swimming instructor and have to help my wife with our two children."

"All the News That's Fit to Print"

The New York Times.

LATE CITY EDITION
U. S. Weather Bureau Reports (Page 54) forecasts: Mostly fair and seasonably cool today, tonight and tomorrow. Temp. range: 60—50. Yesterday: 67.5—54.0.

VOL. CVII—No. 36,420. © 1957, by The New York Times Company, Times Square, New York 36, N. Y. NEW YORK, FRIDAY, OCTOBER 11, 1957. 10c beyond 100-mile zone from New York City FIVE CENTS

PRESIDENT MEETS WITH TOP EXPERTS IN MISSILE REVIEW

Impact of Soviet Advances in Rocketry Discussed by National Security Group

NO RULING ON WEAPONS

Choice of Army or Air Force Intermediate Missile Delayed by Department

By JOHN W. FINNEY
Special to The New York Times

WASHINGTON, Oct. 10—President Eisenhower met with his top military, scientific and diplomatic advisers today to discuss the impact of recent Soviet rocketry advances on the United States missile program.

The discussion was held at the first meeting of the National Security Council since the Soviet Union startled the free world on Friday by hurling a 184-pound satellite into an orbit around the earth. The council is the nation's top planning body on military and diplomatic policies.

The unusual significance of the secret meeting was indicated by the long list of Government officials attending the conference at the White House. The two dozen officials at the meeting represented all sectors of government directly or indirectly concerned with the missile program and the international race into space.

I. R. B. M. Decision Put Off

In another missile development, the Defense Department announced late in the day that it had postponed choosing between the intermediate range ballistic missiles being developed by the Army and Air Force.

Neil H. McElroy, the new Secretary of Defense, announced that testing of both missiles would be continued "until a better technical basis is established" for evaluating the two missiles. Charles E. Wilson had hoped to reach a decision on the missiles before stepping down yesterday as Defense Secretary.

Defense officials insisted that the postponement would not result in any delay in the development of an I. R. B. M. Continued testing of both missiles was described as the best possible course for development of an I. R. B. M. to go into the nation's arsenal.

Centers on Program Status

The council's early morning meeting lasted 2 hours 5 minutes, a period in which the Soviet satellite whirled around the earth one and three-tenths times.

As always, the White House declined to disclose the subject matter discussed at a National Security Council meeting. But the list of officials, extending far beyond the basic membership of the council, was an indication that the discussion centered on the status of the missile program in light of recent Soviet accomplishments.

From the list of officials it could be gathered that the discussion ranged from the problems of basic scientific search to propaganda and international control over space weapons.

Among those at the meeting were officials of the National Science Foundation, the Defense, Treasury and State Departments, Civil Defense Ad-

Continued on Page 6, Column 1

Braves Beat Yanks, 5-0, to Win Series

The New York Times

The Braves' catcher, Del Crandall, hugs Eddie Mathews, center, and Lew Burdette.

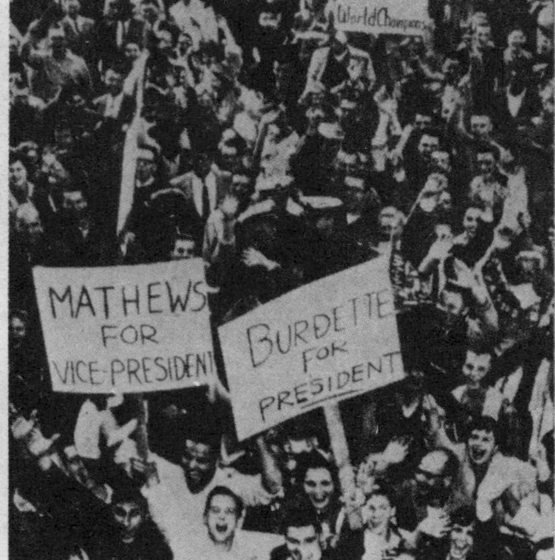

Associated Press Wirephoto

Fans at home in Milwaukee show their appreciation for Burdette, the winning pitcher, and Mathews, who starred at bat and in the field.

U. S. OFFERS PLAN FOR SPACE PEACE

Lodge Urges a U. N. Study Preceding Arms Accord—Gromyko Assails West

Excerpts from talks by Lodge and Gromyko, Page 4.

By THOMAS J. HAMILTON
Special to The New York Times

UNITED NATIONS, N. Y., Oct. 10—The United States offered today to work with other nations to assure the use of outer space "for exclusively peaceful and scientific purposes."

Henry Cabot Lodge told the General Assembly's Political Committee that, if there was "general agreement," a technical committee should start work without awaiting the conclusion of negotiations on other phases of disarmament.

Andrei A. Gromyko, Soviet Foreign Minister, replied in one of the toughest speeches that any Soviet spokesman has ever made in the United Nations.

After he accused the Western powers of not wanting a disarmament agreement, he said, "We call upon the Governments of the United States, Britain and France to accept an honest and mutually acceptable agreement."

Gromyko Speaks of Trickery

"It is time to put trickery aside in the talks and to stop making a good face when the game is lost," Mr. Gromyko added.

The Soviet Foreign Minister stood firm on the Soviet disarmament proposals submitted to the Disarmament Subcommittee in London during five and a half months of negotiation. In addition, he made a grim attack on United States policy in the Middle East and Germany.

Mr. Gromyko did not refer to the Soviet earth satellite, or repeat the boastful language used by Nikita S. Khrushchev, First Secretary of the Soviet Communist party, in his talk with James Reston of The New York Times.

'Position of Strength' Noted

Neither did he repeat Mr. Khrushchev's offer to bring the earth satellite, and all pilotless missiles, under international control as part of a general agreement between the United States and the Soviet Union.

However, the general reaction of delegates was that the Soviet Union, which also asserts it has made a successful test of an intercontinental missile, now felt that it could talk to the United States from a "position of strength."

As one example, Mr. Gromyko placed special emphasis on his statement that the Soviet disarmament plan would prohibit the manufacture of "rockets of any range with atomic and hydrogen warheads, and so forth."

In contrast with Mr. Gromyko's menacing language, Mr. Lodge abstained from attacking Soviet policy. He said, in fact, that while Valerian A. Zorin, the Soviet representative at the London disarmament talks, had rejected the Western disarmament proposal of Aug.

Continued on Page 4, Column 3

Burdette Hurls 7-Hit Shutout in 7th Game for His 3d Victory

By JOHN DREBINGER

Milwaukee, which less than five years ago didn't even boast a major league club, bestrides the baseball universe today.

Manager Fred Haney's Braves, playing inspired ball behind another brilliant pitching effort by their tireless Lew Burdette, smothered the supposedly invincible Yankees, 5 to 0, in the seventh and deciding world series game at the Stadium yesterday.

The victory, generously cheered by a gathering of 61,207 as Burdette gained his third mound triumph of the classic, gave the National Leaguers the series, 4 games to 3. It brought to Milwaukee a world championship in its first crack at the title.

Inversely, it wound up a damaging campaign for New York. In little more than a month Old Gotham had lost two ball clubs, the Dodgers and Giants. Yesterday it was shorn of the world series crown it had held, with one or another of its three entries, since 1949.

Takes It From Both Sides

One sharp, decisive four-run thrust in the third inning yesterday gave the Milwaukeans a stranglehold they never relinquished. There just wasn't a thing the inexhaustible baseball brain of Casey Stengel could do about it.

Haney, a one-time pint-sized infielder who was appearing in a world series for the first time, had Stengel licked from the start of the game.

A costly error by Tony Kubek, rookie star of the Bombers during the earlier stages of the series, opened the gates for the Braves in the third. Before the inning was over, Don Larsen, Casey's starting pitcher, had been put to rout.

The big fellow, hero of last year's epic perfect game against the Dodgers, had been carefully groomed for this one. But he couldn't weather the punishment he took from both sides.

Eddie Mathews unloaded a two-run two-bagger. Bobby Shantz replaced Larsen, but the Braves rolled on. Hank Aaron

Continued on Page 33, Column 3

Milwaukee Explodes With Joy—Greets New Champions

By RICHARD J. H. JOHNSTON
Special to The New York Times

MILWAUKEE, Oct. 10—An emotional explosion rocked this staid city, famed for beer and common sense, at precisely 1:35 P. M. (Central Standard Time) today.

A second no less hysterical outburst occurred six hours later as a crowd of about 12,000 welcomed home its world champion baseball team. The Braves' chartered United Airlines DC-7 appeared over Billy Mitchell Field, flashing its landing lights in a victory signal.

The celebration was triggered this afternoon when Eddie Mathews, the Braves' third baseman, touched third base in the Yankee Stadium 900 miles from here. That act ended the 1957 world series and the National League champion Milwaukee Braves became the baseball champions of the entire universe.

Happy Tidings Are Spread

"They did it." That was the cry that went up and Milwaukeeans poured in a flood from taverns, restaurants, office buildings, railroad stations and their homes to bring the happy news to each other.

Within minutes this town on the shores of Lake Michigan known for its clean streets and clear beer was littered with torn paper. From office buildings cascades of home-made confetti poured into the street.

On the sidewalks women wept openly. Total strangers hugged each other and danced like persons possessed.

Never in the 111-year history of Milwaukee had there been

Continued on Page 35, Column 5

M'CLELLAN SEEKS TEAMSTERS' FILES

Demands Convention Data—Describes Election of Hoffa as 'Scandalous'

By ALLEN DRURY
Special to The New York Times

WASHINGTON, Oct. 10—The Senate's rackets investigators have demanded all records on the selection of delegates to the teamsters convention at Miami Beach. All locals of the union in the United States were directed to comply.

This became known tonight after the committee had charged that James R. Hoffa could not have been elected president of the International Brotherhood of Teamsters at the convention last week without "dictatorial action" by his predecessor, Dave Beck.

This allegation was made by Senator John L. McClellan, chairman of the Senate Select Committee on Improper Activities in the Labor or Management Field. In a sharply worded statement the Arkansas Democrat asserted that the committee had found "some situations which are just plain scandalous" in the selection and seating of delegates at the teamsters Miami Beach convention that overwhelmingly elected Hoffa.

It also announced the opening of a new phase of its investigations involving New York City locals of the Amalgamated Meat Cutters, affiliated with the American Federation of Labor and Congress of Industrial Organizations.

Mr. McClellan disclosed ear-

Continued on Page 15, Column 3

PHONE RATE RISE GRANTED IN STATE AFTER LONG FIGHT

$33,000,000 Yearly Increase Authorized for Business and Home Services

By WARREN WEAVER Jr.
Special to The New York Times.

ALBANY, Oct. 10—The Public Service Commission authorized today a $33,000,000-a-year rate increase for the New York Telephone Company.

The move will mean a 35-cent monthly increase in every bill for residential telephone service and a $1 monthly increase for business telephones. A total of 4,360,000 will be affected.

It will also mean higher charges in New York City, the suburban counties and Buffalo for subscribers on a "message unit" basis who use more than the seventy-five units a month covered by the basic rate.

The telephone company had proposed monthly rate increases of 50 cents on private home phones, 65 cents on party lines and $1.50 on business phones.

[In New York, Keith S. McHugh, president of the New York Telephone Company, voiced disappointment at the amount of the rate increases.]

Under the commission ruling hotels will be permitted to increase the maximum charge for each out-going local call by a guest from 17 cents to 20 cents.

The higher rates will be effective when the company files a new schedule of charges with the commission. Because some policy decisions and computations must be made in drafting the full schedule, the process may take several days.

Dispute Lasted 4 Years

The decision brought to an end one of the longest and most controversial rate proceedings in the history of this state's regulation of utilities. It began nearly four years ago with a company application for a $68,850,000 increase and was fought through the courts and the Legislature, as well as four sets of commission hearings.

A major issue throughout the proceedings was whether the telephone company was entitled to a rate of profit based on the original value of its plant or on the amount it would cost to reproduce that plant today in inflated dollars.

The company had insisted throughout that the "reproduction cost" figure, which is substantially larger, should be used, thus justifying a higher profit and higher rates to earn it.

In the first series of commission hearings, evidence on reproduction cost was excluded over the objections of the utility. The courts later ruled that the commission should receive and consider such evidence. This was done in the last series of hearings.

However, Commissioner Spencer B. Eddy held in an

Continued on Page 16, Column 7

SOVIET IS WARNED U. S. WILL DEFEND TURKEY IN ATTACK

Moscow Softened Text of Interview

By JAMES RESTON
Special to The New York Times.

WARSAW, Oct. 10—The Soviet Government made some interesting and perhaps significant changes in the official text of the interview between Nikita S. Khrushchev and this correspondent in Moscow this week.

For example, the First Secretary of the Central Committee of the Communist party said through his interpreter, Viktor Sukhodrev, during the interview last Monday that President Gamal Abdel Nasser of Egypt was not a Communist and that he "has no hopes for Nasser."

In the official text released last night, after a two-day delay by the Foreign Ministry, Mr. Khrushchev's statement about his lack of hope

Continued on Page 3, Column 2

TREATY TIE CITED

Khrushchev's Charge Against Henderson Called Unfounded

Text of the State Department's statement is on Page 2.

By DANA ADAMS SCHMIDT
Special to The New York Times.

WASHINGTON, Oct. 10—The United States warned the Soviet Union today to be under no illusions about this country's determination to stand by Turkey and carry out its treaty obligations.

The State Department thus answered threats against Turkey and charges that the United States was fomenting war in the Middle East, made by Nikita S. Khrushchev in an interview with James Reston of The New York Times.

Noting that the First Secretary of the Soviet Communist party said that it was dangerous to assume that hostilities could be confined to any particular locality, the State Department observed:

"That truth should be prayerfully and constantly contemplated by every responsible official of every country."

Statement Is Read

A statement, read by Jameson Parker, press officer, specifically denied as "completely unfounded" two charges made by Mr. Khrushchev: That Deputy Under Secretary of State Loy W. Henderson was sent to the Middle East in August to incite "certain states," namely Jordan and Iraq, against Syria; and that the United States was then and is now still trying to push Turkey into war against Syria.

The refutation of Mr. Khrushchev's statements to The Times was formulated with particular care. It had been in preparation since this morning. State Department officials declined to say whether it had been cleared by the White House.

Mr. Henderson's visit to the Middle East was merely an effort to consult and bring back first-hand impressions, the statement said.

Suez Crisis Recalled

The charge that the United States could push Turkey or any other country into war is "an absurdity" when considered in the light of "the United States record" in the Suez crisis, it continued.

The United States last winter opposed the British-French-Israeli operation against Egypt and used its influence in the United Nations to force the three nations to withdraw from Egyptian territory.

Today's statement called Turkey "a respected member of the United Nations," "an independent nation" and a "friend and ally" of the United States. It declared that the United States would honor its obligations under the North Atlantic Treaty, of which Turkey is a member, and under the Eisen-

Continued on Page 2, Column 4

SYRIA SAYS TURKS PROVOKE TROUBLE

Protests Against Maneuvers Near Border and 'Several' Violations of Air Space

By Reuters.

DAMASCUS, Syria, Oct. 10—The Syrian Government has protested to Turkey against "holding continuous demonstrations coupled with provocative acts" near the border of northern Syria.

The text of the protest, made public today, said Syria had noticed "unusually large" concentrations of Turkish troops near her border.

"Several times Turkish aircraft have violated Syrian skies," the note charged.

It said Damascus was glad to have Turkey's assurance that she had no aggressive intentions toward Syria. But the Damascus Government felt disappointed, the note added, "that such assurances are accompanied by statements about alleged subversive activities and arms stores in Syria, which Syria considers interference in her internal affairs."

[Foreign Ministry sources in Ankara termed the complaint on troop concentrations Soviet-inspired. A formal reply, it was said, probably will be made by Saturday.]

Meanwhile, another official statement here said that a Turkish patrol crossed the

Continued on Page 2, Column 6

5th Avenue Parade Salutes Golden Jubilee

March by Torchlight Draws 150,000 to Association Fete

By MILTON BRACKER

Fifth Avenue was the host last night to a fiftieth anniversary party for the organization most closely identified with it.

The group is the Fifth Avenue Association. The party took the form of a torchlight parade combining features of the New York scene in 1907 with those of 1957. There were, according to Chief Police Inspector Thomas A. Nielson, 150,000 "guests."

The spectators lined the route between Washington Square and Fifty-ninth Street. The reviewing stand was outside the Public Library, between Fortieth and Forty-second Streets.

Wherever one watched, it was chilly. The temperature had fallen to 56 by 10 o'clock, when the last unit passed the stand. Some of the models on the fashion floats shivered but managed gallant smiles most of the way.

Mayor Wagner was chief marshal of the parade. With John C. Wood, president of the celebrating association, he first rode the route in a carriage with golden wheels, a driver in a golden topper and a pair of horses with gilded hooves.

Later, the Mayor backtracked behind a motorcycle escort. At 9:25 he joined and kissed his gold-hatted wife in the reviewing stand, remaining there until the end. Grover A. Whalen, general chairman of the jubilee, and Police Commissioner Stephen P. Kennedy shared the stage with the Wagners and Mr. Wood. The demonstration had been billed as the first major torchlight parade along Fifth Avenue in almost a century. The last one was on Oct. 13, 1860, when the Prince of Wales later King Edward VII reviewed Manhattan's husky volunteer firemen. The torches then were the garish red-toned sizzlers long associated in the city with political parades.

This time, the flares had given way to streamlined aluminum vessels, filled with kerosene and a cotton wick; and mounted on six-foot poles. They

Continued on Page 30, Column 2

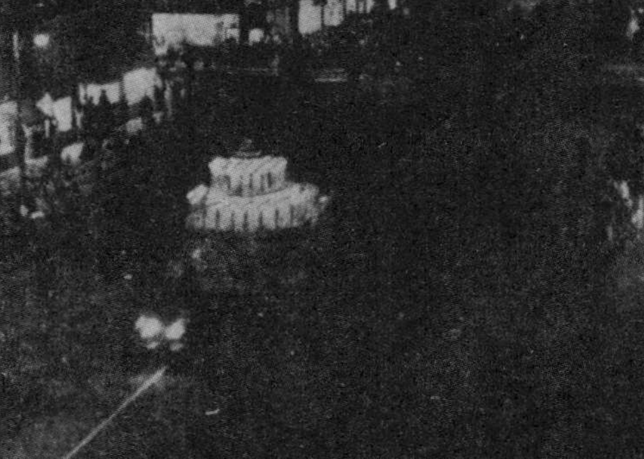

The New York Times (by Larry Morris)

A float in the form of a birthday cake approaching Thirty-eighth Street in the parade

Eastern Railroads Lose Trucking Suit

By WILLIAM G. WEART
Special to The New York Times

PHILADELPHIA, Oct. 10—The United States District Court today found twenty-six Eastern railroads, including the Pennsylvania and New York Central, guilty of violating the Sherman Antitrust Law.

The ruling was made by Judge Thomas J. Clary in the $250,000,000 treble damage suit brought against the railroads by the Pennsylvania Motor Truck Association and forty long-distance trucking concerns.

The judge also dismissed a counter-suit in which the railroads had sought $120,000,000 in treble damages. The counter-suit accused the truckers of having conspired since 1945 to restrain trade and commerce in violation of the antitrust law.

The individual trucking companies were awarded nominal

Continued on Page 16, Column 4

U. S. Teams Detect 3 Objects in Orbit

By WALTER SULLIVAN

Three objects pitched into orbits around the earth by the Soviet Union a week ago today have been detected by direct observation in this country for the first time.

Before dawn yesterday morning a team of volunteer observers atop the Connecticut State Teachers College in New Haven sighted what is believed to have been the final-stage rocket that hurled the satellite—and itself—into an orbit.

At the Stanford Research Institute in Palo Alto, Calif., a giant research radar late Wednesday detected the satellite and both its traveling companions. These consist of the rocket and a nose shield that protected the satellite as it soared through the atmosphere.

All three items separated, probably by means of small ex-

Continued on Page 5, Column 3

Fingerprint Order Is Eased for Aliens

Special to The New York Times.

WASHINGTON, Oct. 10—The United States ordered today an end to fingerprinting for almost all visitors to this country.

John Foster Dulles, Secretary of State, and Attorney General Herbert Brownell Jr. acted jointly, under authority voted by Congress on Sept. 11, to eliminate most aspects of the widely criticized requirement. It was introduced fifteen years ago.

Aside from making life easier for nearly 50,000 persons from the free world who visit the United States each year, the change will open up the possibility of larger-scale visits from the Soviet Union and other Communist countries.

Except for Poland and Yugoslavia, these nations have declined to allow their citizens to be fingerprinted, alleging that

Continued on Page 14, Column 7

Yankees Pay Tribute to Pitching Artistry of Braves

BRAVES WIN, 5-0, AND TAKE SERIES

Continued From Page 1

and Wes Covington singled. Before the little Yankee southpaw could stem the tide, four runs were in and the American Leaguers were about out on their feet.

For good measure and by way of giving his team additional security, Del Crandall, Burdette's catcher, dropped a home run into the left-field stand in the eighth. But that shot was not needed.

For by then one Selva Lewis Burdette Jr., 30-year-old right-hander and one-time farm hand in the Yankee chain, was putting the finishing touches to one of the most astounding exhibitions of sustained pitching mastery in more than a half-century of world series competition.

Burdette vanquished the Yankees in the second game, 4 to 2, last Thursday in New York. Last Monday in Milwaukee he shut them out, 1 to 0, in the fifth game to put the Braves in front. Yesterday, with his second dazzling shutout after only two days of rest, he completed a stretch of twenty-four scoreless innings. In the twenty-seven innings of his three complete games he allowed only two runs.

Only one hurler, perhaps the greatest of all, topped this. In 1905, the immortal Christy Mathewson rolled up twenty-seven innings of scoreless hurling to win three shutouts for the Giants.

Seven 3-Game Winners

Burdette yesterday became the seventh pitcher to gain three victories in a world series. The last was Harry Brecheen in 1946. But the Cardinal southpaw gained one in a relief role.

Four, besides Burdette, posted three complete-game victories. They were Mathewson, Jack Coombs of the Philadelphia Athletics in 1910, Babe Adams of the Pittsburgh Pirates in 1909 and Stanley Coveleskie of the Cleveland Indians in 1920.

The only other pitcher to win three games was Urban Faber of the Chicago White Sox in 1917. But in one of his triumphs he was removed for a relief hurler.

For Milwaukee, of course, yesterday easily was the day of days. That metropolis, home of the brew, the Braves and the finest of cheeses, doubtless will remain in a daze for some time to come.

Milwaukee entered the National League officially on March 18, 1953, when Owner Lou Perini moved his Braves from Boston. It was the first franchise shift in the senior league in more than half a century.

The transfer started a chain of upheavals. The Athletics moved from Philadelphia to Kansas City, the Browns from St. Louis to Baltimore, where they became the Orioles, and next year will see the New York Giants playing in San Francisco and the Brooklyn Dodgers in Los Angeles.

Four seasons of frustration followed the shift to Milwaukee. The Braves, despite a tremendous improvement from their sixth-place finish in Boston, were second in 1953, third in 1954, and second again the next two years. The 1956 season was the most bitter disappointment, for Haney's men let the pennant slip away in the last few days.

Sixth Yankee Setback

For New York, defeat perhaps was not too difficult to take. Seventeen times in the past have the Yankees brought the title here. This was only their sixth series setback.

For Stengel the defeat was only his second in his nine seasons as manager of the Bombers. He has been the winner six times.

Associated Press

WHO'S ON SECOND? Both Hank Bauer (9) and Enos Slaughter (17) of Yanks, but Umpire Joe Paparella's safe sign is only for Bauer, who evaded tag by Logan, left. First-inning mix-up began when Slaughter hit to Pitcher Lew Burdette, whose throw started rundown on Bauer between second and third. Felix Mantilla backs up play.

He fought hard to save this one. In desperation he even returned Mickey Mantle to action in a surprise move. The Oklahoma slugger had gone to the sidelines with a shoulder injury after the fourth game and almost everyone thought he had made his last appearance save for a possible role as pinch-hitter.

But there he was, out in center field, playing the entire game. He singled for one of the seven hits permitted by Burdette.

Even Bill Skowron, out since the first game with a lame back, got into it in the closing innings.

The Braves, on the other hand, played without their wounded. Red Schoendienst, crippled in the fifth game with a groin injury, remained on the sidelines. Warren Spahn sat it out in the bullpen. The ace lefty was to have hurled this game but had to be sidetracked because of a mild influenza attack on Wednesday.

The incredible Burdette, however, needed no help once the Yankees let the game fall apart in the third inning.

Larsen had just retired his mound adversary, Burdette, on a foul back of third for the first out in the fateful inning when Bob Hazle, a rookie outfielder, stroked a "wrong field" single to left. Then came a play that doubtless will remain seared in Stengel's amazing memory through many a wintry night.

Peg to Second Wide

For the player who gummed it up had been the apple of Casey's eye all season—the brilliant and versatile Kubek. Tony had started the series last week at third, then switched to left field and center when Mantle went out of action. With Mantle back in center, Tony was on third again and that's where all the trouble started.

Johnny Logan slammed a grounder at Kubek. It looked like a sure-fire double play. But Tony's peg to second was wide. It pulled Jerry Coleman off the bag and there was no out there.

Desperately, Jerry fired the ball to first in an effort to get at least one man. But Logan beat the throw and the Braves, instead of having been retired, had two on with one out.

It reminded one of what Uncle Wilbert Robinson of early Brooklyn baseball vintage, once described as the "phantom double play."

A moment later Mathews lined a two-bagger down the right-field foul line. Before the ball could be brought back to the infield both Hazle and Logan had scored. That was all for the crestfallen Larsen. Shantz went in.

Aaron, one of the Braves' top hitters in the series, punched a single into center and Mathews scored. **Covington singled to left, sending Hank to third. Then when the Yanks failed to complete a double play by way of second base on Frank Torre's** grounder to Coleman, Aaron streaked home with the fourth tally.

After that nothing really mattered as Burdette kept firing his bewildering assortment of screwballs, sliders and sinkers.

So perfect was his control he walked only one batter, and that was intentional. **It came after Hank Bauer had opened the Yankee first inning by belting Burdette's first pitch for a double.**

This gave Hank the distinction of having connected in fourteen consecutive games for a world series record. Bauer had hit in each of the seven games in last October's classic.

He topped by one the former mark of thirteen games held jointly by Frank Schulte of the Cubs fifty years ago and Harry Hooper of the Red Sox of 1915, 1916 and 1918. To add luster to the record was the **fact that the Yanks' ex-Marine had compiled his mark in only two series.**

However, nothing else came of this blow even though there was a slight mix-up by the Braves on the next play. Enos Slaughter grounded to Burdette. This hung up Bauer between second and third.

But the Brave inner defense didn't play well and Hank scrambled back to second. However, the situation still was saved for Milwaukee since by then Slaughter had ambled down to second and so was an easy out.

Mantle, taking his first turn at bat since the tenth inning of the fourth game, then went out on a grounder to the mound. Yogi Berra was intentionally passed and Gil McDougald ended the inning with an infield pop-up.

Following the four-run third, Art Ditmar and Tom Sturdivant held the Braves scoreless for two innings apiece and Tommy Byrne did well enough in the last two.

But in the eighth, with two out and the bases empty, Byrne was guilty of one errant pitch. Crandall lifted it into the left-field seats, the ball just going beyond Slaughter's frantic reach.

After the Yanks' brief first-inning splurge, they didn't get a man on base until Coleman singled in the fifth.

In the sixth the Bombers made another bid, which didn't get started until two were out. Here Mantle singled and Mathews fumbled Berra's grounder. But McDougald then grounded to Mathews, who this time froze to the ball.

Game to the end, the Bombers made a despairing effort to break through Burdette in the last of the ninth. With one away, McDougald singled. After Kubek flied out, Coleman outgalloped an infield tap for his second hit.

Byrne then smashed a hard grounder over second base. It threatened to ruin Burdette's shutout. But Felix Mantilla, again substituting at second for Schoendienst, threw himself headlong at the ball and blocked its path. It was a hit, but merely filled the bases. The Yanks still were looking for a run. Skowron banged a sharp one-hopper down the third-base line. Mathews scooped it up, stepped on third and the series was over.

A record attendance of 394,712 was **set for a seven-game series. This topped the former mark of 389,763 set by the Yankees and Dodgers in 1947. The total receipts, exclusive of revenues from radio and television,** reached $2,475,978, also a record.

But perhaps its greatest record was the bringing of the first world championship to what could well develop into the most fanatic baseball center in the nation. At least it has given the newcomers, Los Angeles and San Francisco, something to shoot at.

On March 15, 1953, when the prospect of Milwaukee getting the Braves' franchise was still a rumor, a crowd of 15,000, unmindful of wind and snow, gathered at Milwaukee's Municipal Stadium. They undoubtedly dreamed of the day when perhaps they might win a pennant and world series. Last night in that sizzling midwestern metropolis that dream came true.

119 Pitches Win for Burdette

It took Lew Burdette 119 pitches to defeat the Yankees for the third time yesterday. Almost always ahead of the hitters, he delivered eighty-one strikes and thirty-eight balls. **His hardest inning was the first, when he was obliged to serve twenty times. In his previous series victories, the Milwaukee right-hander made 120 and 87 pitches, respectively.**

Minneapolis Mayor Ecstatic

MINNEAPOLIS, Oct. 10 (AP)—Milwaukee's world series victory was enthusiastically described today as a feat ranking with "the discovery of America and the flight of Sputnik I." Mayor P. Kenneth Peterson of Minneapolis wired congratulations to Mayor Frank Zeidler of Milwaukee and made all Milwaukee residents "Honorary Citizens of Minneapolis."

Section 5 | SPORTS AUTOMOBILES—BOATS | **The New York Times.** | SPORTS SHIPPING NEWS SHOPPING GUIDE | Section 5

SUNDAY, NOVEMBER 17, 1957. L++ S

NOTRE DAME TOPS OKLAHOMA, 7-0; TEXAS AGGIES BOW; YALE BEATS PRINCETON, 20-13; DARTMOUTH WINS, 20-19

ELI PASSES CLICK

Cavallon Scores Three Times on Aerials to Upset Princeton

By ALLISON DANZIG

Special to The New York Times.

PRINCETON, N. J., Nov. 16—A pair of Illinois lads, forming an unstoppable passing combination for Yale, brought about favored Princeton's first defeat in the Ivy League today, 20—13.

The Tiger setback and Dartmouth's 20-19 victory over Cornell at Hanover set the stage for the game that will decide the Ivy championship here next Saturday when the Tigers meet the Hanoverians. Dartmouth, unbeaten in the league but tied by Yale, can win the title by holding Nassau to a draw.

Dick Winterbauer, a senior quarterback from Arlington Heights, Ill., and Mike Cavallon, a senior end from Winnetka, Ill., were the heroes of the Yale victory, the first scored in succession by the Elis over Princeton since they won their fourth in a row in 1946.

Fullback Gene Coker, and Capt. John Embersists also starred for Yale in the upset. Fist fights broke out between scores of undergraduates around the goal posts at the south end of the field and thousands of handkerchiefs fluttered in the Yale stands derisively. The Yale captain was carried off the field on the shoulders of his teammates.

46,000 Watch Game

But it was Winterbauer, with one of the best passing performances of his career, and Cavallon, with a great exhibition on the receiving end of the aerials, who provided most of the thrills of a typical Yale-Princeton game. From start to finish it was a game that had the 46,000 people in Palmer Stadium roaring over the excitement and fury of the action.

Cavallon, 6 feet 4 inches and 200 pounds, played the full sixty minutes. He scored all three of Yale's touchdowns on passes. Two of them were thrown by Winterbauer and the other by Coker, who took a toss from Winterbauer in the slot-T passing formation that the Elis sprang on Princeton to exploit the weakness the Tiger had shown previously against aerials.

The first touchdown pass was good for 62 yards at the end of Yale's march of 71 yards in four plays from the opening kick-off. Cavallon reached above the two Princeton backs who were on top of him, grabbed Winterbauer's toss on the 29-yard mark and continued on across the goal line as the two Tigers fell to the ground.

That put Yale ahead by 7—0. After Princeton had completed a march of 74 yards in eleven plays to tie the score at 7—7 on Tom Morris' touchdown at the start of the second quarter, Cavallon went into action again. With the ball on the Tiger 27-yard line after an advance from midfield, Coker took the ball from Winterbauer in the slot-T formation, advanced a step and fired.

Cavallon was waiting for the ball a yard from the goal line. Three defenders surrounded him, but the towering end grabbed the ball and fell across the goal

Continued on Page 3, Column 2

Williams Trounces Amherst by 39 to 14

By WILLIAM J. BRIORDY

Special to The New York Times.

WILLIAMSTOWN, Mass., Nov. 16—Williams College posted its first undefeated football season in forty years as the Ephmen kept the Little Three championship by crushing previously unbeaten Amherst, 39 to 14, today.

An overflow gathering of 8,000 at Weston Field saw Coach Len Watters' rugged outfit jolt the Lord Jeffs for four touchdowns in the first half and add two more in the second.

The once-tied Williams eleven had hard-hitting linemen and clever backs who sent the Lord Jeffs to their first defeat in eight games this year. It was the final contest for both schools.

Spearheaded by its clever left halfback, Chip Ide, the Purple had the Lord Jeffs

Continued on Page 2, Column 2

RICE TURNS BACK NO. 1 ELEVEN, 7-6

Sends Texas Aggies to First Loss as Hill's Conversion Decides Houston Game

By The Associated Press.

HOUSTON, Nov. 16—Rice's Owls combined a mighty defense with the fancy work of two senior quarterbacks, Frank Ryan and King Hill, to upset Texas A. and M., the nation's No. 1 team, 7-6, in a thrilling battle before a crowd of over 72,000 today.

The Owls, 7-point shortenders, drove 79 yards in the second period for a touchdown. Rice then stopped three Aggie threats inside the 20-yard line before yielding a score on the second play of the final period.

The difference in the score was the extra point kicked by Hill. The conversion attempt by Lloyd Taylor, an Aggie halfback, was wide and to the right.

First Loss in 15 Games

It was the first defeat for Texas A. and M. in fifteen games. The lost deprived the Aggies of at least immediate claim to the Southwest Conference championship. Rice and Texas now join the Aggies in a showdown race for the final two weeks of the title campaign. The defeat also knocked the Aggies out of an immediate invitation to be host team at the Cotton Bowl.

Hill scored the Rice touchdown from the 1 after Ryan had directed a 78-yard surge that began late in the first period.

Quarterback Roddy Osborne powered over from the 1 to cap the Aggie drive that began when the losers recovered a fumble on the Owl 14.

The entire third period was

Continued on Page 5, Column 1

Associated Press Wirephoto

THE SCORE THAT SANK THE SOONERS: Dick Lynch of Notre Dame carrying the ball over goal line yesterday. Irish beat Oklahoma by 7 to 0.

Penn Crushes Columbia, 28 to 6, as Riepl Excels

By LOUIS EFFRAT

Columbia bowed to Pennsylvania, 28—6, yesterday at Baker Field, but there was nothing new or surprising about that. Columbia football teams have been bowing to the Red and Blue with a most disturbing regularity since 1937. The latest setback was the fifteenth straight inflicted upon the Lions in the eighty-year rivalry.

Penn's multiple offense, neatly conducted by Frank Riepl, overwhelmed Columbia. Whether the Philadelphians attacked from the straight T, the winged T or the single-wing made little difference. It was Penn all the way, comfortably and convincingly.

Once Riepl had put the visitors ahead with a 66-yard touchdown dash midway in the initial quarter, Columbia's seventh defeat in a row this season was virtually sealed. Buff Donelli's Lions were no match for the favored Quakers, who made certain that Columbia would wind up in the Ivy League cellar this year.

However, it was not this year that the Donellis, pere et fils, were particularly concerned about. While the Lions were being crushed yesterday, it was evident that Buff, the coach, and Dick, the quarterback, faced a brighter gridiron future.

Throughout the current campaign — in which the Lions opened with an upset over Brown and then forgot the winning formula—everyone concerned has been attempting to convince Dick to "open up." He did precisely that yesterday, discarding the cloak of conserv-

Continued on Page 2, Column 2

PENN STATE TRIPS HOLY CROSS, 14-10

Crusaders Stopped 6 Inches From Score, Then Safety Insures Lions' Victory

By The Associated Press.

WORCESTER, Mass., Nov. 16—Penn State stopped Holy Cross six inches from its goal and took a precautionary safety in the final two minutes today to preserve a 14-10 victory.

The Nittany Lions as a result won Gator Bowl consideration.

Bill Wehmer, a left tackle, and Les Walters, a left end, dropped Tommy Greene, the nation's leading total offense player, inches from an upset with two minutes to play. Richie Lucas, Penn State quarterback, then stepped out of his end zone for an automatic safety rather than try to punt into the teeth of an onrushing Crusader line.

The twice-beaten Pennsylvanians rallied behind Dave Kasperian's 67-yard kick-off return to erase an 8-0 deficit with two quick third-period touchdowns.

The touchdowns came on a 16-yard pass from Lucas to

Continued on Page 13, Column 3

ARMY VANQUISHES TULANE BY 20-14

Anderson Tallies for Cadet Eleven in Last Quarter to Beat Green Wave

By JOSEPH M. SHEEHAN

Special to The New York Times.

WEST POINT, N. Y., Nov. 16—Trailing by one point and apparently doomed to defeat, Army's football team struck with explosive fury in the final minutes today to turn back a surprising Tulane eleven, 20—14.

Bob Anderson, again a brilliant halfback, and Pete Dawkins, an even better one today, led the Black Knights on their thunderous winning charge, which consumed 74 yards in five irresistible running plays.

The 200-pound Anderson, who gained 145 yards in twenty-four rushes to eclipse Glenn Davis' 1945 Academy rushing record, bolted 10 yards around end for the decisive score.

It was the fourteenth touchdown of the season for Bob, who leads the nation in scoring. With only the Navy game remaining two weeks hence, Anderson has run the ball for 965 yards, as against 930 yards by the great Davis in nine games twelve years ago.

With all that Anderson accomplished, he did not match the performance of Dawkins, Army's 195-pound right halfback. The junior from Royal Oak, Mich., ripped and slashed through Tulane's packed defense for 165 yards in twenty-six rushes.

Pete scored Army's second

Continued on Page 5, Column 2

Indians Set Back Cornell With 2 Late Touchdowns

By MICHAEL STRAUSS

Special to The New York Times.

HANOVER, N. H., Nov. 16—In another of those tense, comeback finishes that have marked its play this season, Dartmouth's unbeaten eleven topped Cornell, 20—19, at Memorial Field today. Two Hanoverian touchdowns in the concluding quarter turned the trick. Behind, 19-to-7, as the teams changed sides for the last time, the Big Green turned in some aerial fireworks to produce the victory.

The 6-pointer that led to the triumph was scored with only 2 minutes 45 seconds remaining. Accounting for the big tally, on a 4-yard sortie around right end was Johnny Crouthamel, a sophomore halfback from Perkasie, Pa.

Then Joe Palermo, the guard whose play has been the subject of much praise all season, contributed the finishing touches. With the score knotted at 19-all, he kicked from placement. The boot soared over the crossbar.

These late developments sent the Big Green's student body whooping through East Wheelock and Lebanon Streets, arteries that lead from the stadium, like Indians—wild ones. Adding to the jubilation was word from Princeton that the Tigers had been topped by Yale.

As a result, Dartmouth displaced the Tigers as first-place tenants in the Ivy League race.

The Hanoverians have won five loop tests and tied one. Only the encounter with Princeton in New Jersey next Saturday stands in the way of a championship.

The late display of elation on the campus provided a decided contrast to the mood of the crowd of 13,000 through most of the contest. Cornell, taking advantage of Big Green lapses, opened the game as though it was determined to make a runaway of it.

After only 5 mintues 25 seconds of play, the Ithacans boasted a 12-0 advantage. The spec-

Continued on Page 3, Column 4

OHIO STATE RALLY HALTS IOWA, 17-13

Bob White Scores in Fourth Period as Buckeye Eleven Wins Big Ten Title

By The Associated Press.

COLUMBUS, Ohio, Nov. 16—A third-string fullback, Bob White, sparked Ohio State to the Big Ten football championship and a berth in the Rose Bowl today.

The 207-pound sophomore gained 157 yards on twenty-two rushes and scored the winning touchdown as the Buckeyes rallied twice to dethrone Iowa's Hawkeyes in a 17-13 thriller.

With Iowa leading, 13—10, late in the final period, White carried the ball on seven of eight plays for 65 yards in a 68-yard drive to the final touchdown. He scored the winning marker on a 5-yard smash over tackle.

Don Clark, Ohio State's ace ball carrier and top scorer, did not see action, but White more than took up the slack as he thrilled a crowd of 82,935, the largest ever to fill Buckeye Stadium, with his tremendous smashes up the middle.

The victory was Ohio State's sixth straight in Western Con-

Continued on Page 4, Column 2

SKEIN ENDS AT 47

Oklahoma Toppled as Lynch Scores From 3 in the Final Quarter

By The Associated Press.

NORMAN, Okla., Nov. 16—Oklahoma's record streak of forty-seven football victories was ended today by a Notre Dame team that marched 80 yards in the closing minutes for a touchdown and a 7-0 triumph.

Oklahoma, ranked No. 2 in the nation and an 18-point favorite, couldn't move against the rock-wall Notre Dame line and the Sooners saw another of its streaks shattered—scoring in 123 consecutive games.

The defeat was only the ninth for the Oklahoma coach, Bud Wilkinson, since he became head coach at Oklahoma in 1947. It virtually ended any chance for the Sooners of getting a third straight national championship.

Although the partisan, sellout crowd of 62,000 came out for a Roman holiday, they were stunned into silence as the Sooners were unable to pull their usual last-quarter winning touchdowns—a Wilkinson team trademark.

Rousing Cheer for Irish

As the game ended when Oklahoma's desperation passing drive was cut off by an intercepted aerial, the crowd rose as one and suddenly gave the Notre Dame team a rousing cheer.

It was a far cry from last year when the Sooners ran over Notre Dame, 40—0. The victory gave the Irish a 3-1 edge in the five-year-old series dating back to 1952.

The smashing, rocking Notre Dame line didn't permit the Sooners to get started either on the ground or in the air.

The Sooners were able to make only 98 yards on the ground and in the air just 47. Notre Dame, paced by its brilliant, 210-pound fullback Nick Pietrosante, rolled up 169. In the air, the Irish gained 79 yards by hitting nine of twenty passes. Bob Williams did most of the passing for Notre Dame.

Notre Dame's touchdown drive, biting off short but consistent yardage against the Sooners' alternate team, carried from the 20 after an Oklahoma punt went into the end zone.

Sooners Call First Team

Time after time, Pietrosante picked up the necessary yard he needed as the Irish smashed through the Oklahoma line. Notre Dame moved to the 8 and the Sooner first team came in to try to make the third Sooner goal-line stand of the day.

Pietrosante smashed four yards through center and Dick Lynch was stopped for no gain. On the third down, Williams went a yard through center.

Then Lynch crossed up the Sooners and rolled around his right end to score standing up. Monty Stickles converted to give Notre Dame the upset and end collegiate football's longest winning streak.

The closest Oklahoma could get to Notre Dame's goal was

Continued on Page 5, Column 4

PromisedLand, 13-5, First by 3 Lengths

By JAMES ROACH

There were 37,802 horseplayers at the Jamaica track yesterday. They bet $508,937 on the main event, the $55,600 Roamer Handicap for 3-year-olds.

The win-window cash-collectors were those who had bet on the 13-to-5 second choice, Mrs. Hirsch Jacobs' Promised Land, who was named for his sire, Palestinian. Promised Land charged past the opposition in the stretch and, with the greatest of ease, made a three-length score.

The favorite, carrying eight more pounds than Promised Land, was Vertex, owned by Frank A. Piarulli and Joseph J. Burnetti. He took second money, finishing a length in front of

Continued on Page 6, Column 2

The New York Times (by Ernest Sisto)

TUMBLING TOUCHDOWN: Jack Hanlon (17) of Penn flying over Columbia line to score in the second period

Rangers Overcome Canadien Six, 4 to 2

By The United Press.

MONTREAL, Nov. 16—The New York Rangers, showing some of their best hockey of the season, defeated the Montreal Canadiens, 4—2, tonight to move to within one point of the National Hockey League's leading Canadiens.

The hustling Rangers, scoring one of their rare victories at the Forum, have now beaten the Canadiens twice and tied once in the three times they have met Montreal this year. It was New York's ninth victory of the season and, coupled with three ties, made their tally 21 points in seventeen games—one point fewer than the Habitants, who have played two fewer games.

Dave Creighton paced the

Continued on Page 6, Column 6

Football Scores

COLLEGES

East

Winner	Loser
American Internat. 35	New Britain T. 6
Army 20	Tulane 14
Army 34 (150-pound)	Rutgers 14
Baldwin-Wallace 26	New Haven T. 26
Boston College 19	Marquette 14
Brandeis 33	Bridgeport 12
Brown 33	Harvard 6
Carnegie Tech 27	Westminster 6
Central State (Ohio) 44	Waynesburg 7
C. W. Post 15	Kings Point 0
Cornell 19 (150-pound)	Pennsylvania 0
Connecticut 0	Rhode Island 0
Dartmouth 20	Cornell 19
Delaware 34	Bucknell 13
Dickinson 13	Johns Hopkins 13
Drexel Tech 6	Coast Guard 0
E. Stroudsburg 14	Kutztown T. (Pa.) 14
F. and M. 41	Muhlenberg 20
Gettysburg 42	Temple 7
Grove City 13	Hiram 7
Hamilton 21	Union (N. Y.) 7
Haverford 20	Susquehanna 2
Hobart 19	Upsala 0
Indiana T. (Pa.) 14	Clarion T. (Pa.) 7
Juniata 40	Albright 13
Lafayette 40	Western Maryland 13
Lebanon Valley 13	Ursinus 7
Lehigh 27	Buffalo 7
Lock Haven T. 13	Mansfield T. 0
Lycoming 21	Geneva 19
Massachusetts 7	New Hampshire 7
Moravian 32	Wagner 14
Morehouse 10	Howard (D. C.) 0
Navy 52	George Washington 0
Navy 27 (150 lb.)	Princeton 21
Pennsylvania 28	Columbia 6
Penn State 14	Holy Cross 10
Princeton J. V. 31	Yale J. V. 6
Rochester 25	Washington and Jefferson 12
Scranton 27	Wilkes 0
Slippery Rock T. (Pa.) 12	West Liberty 0
Springfield 19	Hofstra 7
Swarthmore 14	Penn M. C. 8
Syracuse 34	Colgate 6
Thiel 19	Allegheny 9
Trenton T. 32	Millersville T. (Pa.) 6
Trinity 20	Wesleyan 19
Tufts 39	Norwich 13
West V. Tech 6	West Va. State 6
Williams 39	Amherst 14
Yale 20	Princeton 13

South

Winner	Loser
Alabama State 20	Fisk 6
Abilene Christian 40	Trinity (Tex.) 12
Arkansas A. & M. 42	Ouachita 6
Auburn 6	Georgia 0
Benedict (S. C.) 26	Miles (Ala.) 21
Bethune-Cookman 18	Xavier (La.) 7
Bluefield St. 14	North Carolina Coll. 0
Chattanooga 34	Furman 0
Clark 40	Savannah State 8
Davidson 23	Richmond [illegible]
Dillard 19	Tuskegee 7
Duke 7	Clemson 6
E. Texas St. 32	Southwest Texas St. 13
Emory and Henry 34	Randolph-Macon 7
Elon 20	Lenoir Rhyne 7
Florence St. 40	Austin Peay 13
Florida 14	Vanderbilt 7
Florida A. & M. 42	Allen 0
Fort Valley 12	Knoxville 0
Georgia Tech 10	Alabama 7
Hampden-Sydney 32	Washington & Lee 18
Howard (Ala.) 14	Livingston 6

Continued on Page 4, Column 3

NOTRE DAME TOPS OKLAHOMA, 7 TO 0

Continued From Page 1

in the first quarter when the Sooners' alternate team moved to the 3 before being held on downs.

In the third period, brilliant punting by Clendon Thomas and David Baker kept Notre Dame back on its goal line but the Sooners couldn't capitalize.

Thomas sent punts down on the Notre Dame 15 and 4 and Baker put them down on the 3 and 7.

This time there were no breaks as Notre Dame shook off last week's jitters that saw the Irish fumble away the ball five times in losing to Michigan State, 34—6.

Pietrosante gained almost a third of Notre Dame's rushing yardage as he made 56 yards on seventeen carries. Lynch was just two yards behind with 54 in seventeen carries. The best an Oklahoma player could muster was 36 yards in ten tries. This was made by Thomas.

Williams completed eight of nineteen passes for 70 yards. In Oklahoma's last-minute desperation drive, Quarterback Bennett Watts made two of three aerials for 31 yards.

Notre Dame was the last team to beat Oklahoma, at the start of the 1953 season on the same field that it smothered the Sooners today. Then Coach Frank Leahy's Irish beat Oklahoma, 28—21. The next game, Oklahoma and Pittsburh tied at 7—7. Then the Sooners set sail through the forty-seven games until Terry Brennan's Irish stopped the string today.

Wilkinson, the nation's winningest, active coach, had amassed 101 victories in his ten years at Oklahoma. There were three ties.

Oklahoma started as if it would stretch its string. It marched the first time it got its hands on the ball from the Sooner 42 down to the Irish 13, but the big Notre Dame line stiffened on the 13.

Oklahoma continued to play in Notre Dame territory the rest of the first quarter. It had another chance when a fumble, with nine minutes gone, was recovered by Guard Dick Corbitt on the Notre Dame 34. However, the Sooners were stopped cold and finally Baker had to punt on fourth down.

In the second quarter another Sooner drive got down to the 23 but on the first play of the second quarter, Carl Dodd fumbled. The ball was punched around in the Sooner backfield and Pietrosante finally smothered it on the Notre Dame 48.

Then Williams started his passing attack to three different receivers and piloted the Irish down to the 3 with first and goal. Pietrosante picked up a yard in each of two plunges, Frank Reynolds went to the one-foot line and then Jim Just was held for no gain.

Later Notre Dame came back with its bruising ground game and moved to the 16. With fourth down Stickles came in for his fake place kick but instead Williams hit Just on the 6 for a first down. It was then on the second play that Reynolds' pass was intercepted by Baker in the end zone.

NOTRE DAME (7)

Left Ends—Royer, Prendergast.
Left Tackles—Puntillo, Geremia.
Left Guards—Schaaf, Adamson, Sabal.
Centers—Scholtz, Sullivan, Kuchta.
Right Guards—Ecuyer, Djubasak.
Right Tackles—Lawrence, Nagurski, Dolan.
Right Ends—Stickles, Wetoska, Colosimo.
Quarterbacks—Williams, Izo, White, Hebert.
Left Halfbacks—Reynolds, Doyle.
Right Halfbacks—Lynch, Just.
Fullbacks—Pietrosante, Toth, Lima.

OKLAHOMA (0)

Left Ends—Stiller, Coyle.
Left Tackles—Searcy, Thompson.
Left Guards—Northcutt, Oujesky, Gwinn.
Centers—Harrison, Davis.
Right Guards—Krisher, Corbitt.
Right Tackles — D. Jennings, Lawrence, Ladd.
Right Ends—Rector, S. Jennings.
Quarterbacks—Dodd, Baker, Watts, Sherrod.
Left Halfbacks—Sandefer, Boyd, Hobby.
Right Halfbacks—Thomas, Carpenter, Gautt, Pellow.
Fullbacks—Morris, Rolle.

Notre Dame	0	0	0	7—7
Oklahoma	0	0	0	0—0

Touchdown—Lynch (3, run). Conversion—Stickles.

ARMY VANQUISHES TULANE BY 20-14

Continued From Page 1

touchdown, his eleventh of the season, from 5 yards out. He had set up their first cadet score, for Harry Walters, by carrying 5 yards to Tulane's 1-foot line.

Both these tallies came in the second period.

To complete their bedevilment of Tulane's gallant forces, Anderson and Dawkins combined to break up a potential Green Wave scoring march with two minutes to play.

Tulane, with Carlton Sweeney passing, had moved to Army's 29 after the kick-off following Anderson's touchdown. The way things were going, it seemed quite possible that the Black Knights were to lose their hard-won lead—and the game.

Then, Anderson leaped high in the end zone to bat down a long Sweeney pass aimed at Will Ellizey and Dawkins, also covering the Tulane receiver, made a diving catch of the ball before it hit the ground for a touchback interception.

Brucker Reviews Parade

This contest, which figured in advance to be little more than an Army tune-up for the Navy game, turned out to be a whale of a show for a Michie Stadium gathering of 21,125 that included Secretary of the Army William M. Brucker. The Secretary reviewed the pre-game cadet parade with Lieut. Gen. Garrison H. Davidson, the superintendent of the academy.

Two long-range strikes accounted for the Green Wave's touchdowns. Claude (Boo) Mason raced 61 yards on a sweep for the game's first score at 7:55 of the first quarter. Then, after Army had taken a 13-7 half-time lead, the Greenies recaptured the advantage at 12:55 of the third period by converting for the second time after Dick Petitbon's 65-yard punt return.

These were not isolated thrusts. Tulane penetrated deep into Army territory on five other occasions. It took a last-ditch stand by the Black Knights to avert a touchdown early in the third period, when Tulane punched out a first down on the 8. Army finally stopped this drive on its 1.

Yardage in Short Takes

Until its last-quarter outburst, Army, which emphasizes the long-gainer, had to settle for yardage in short takes.

Tulane, using seven and eight-man fronts, continually disconcerted the cadets by shuttling its linemen laterally just before the snap. This strategy complicated Army's blocking assignments and, effective as they were, Dawkins and Anderson always were under heavy pressure from such aggressive Tulane line-men as Bill Clements and Jim Blount.

Except in its final flurry, Tulane was no more effective overhead. However, the Greenies did bother Army with a highly diversified running attack that featured a shuttle relay of talented quarterbacks.

Little Gene Newton, Tulane's starting quarterback, emphasized split-T sequences, on which he frequently kept the ball himself on sharp thrusts inside and outside of Army's end. Mason's long scoring run developed out of a pitch-out from Newton on the basic split-T quarterback option play.

Army, twice losing the ball on a fumble and an interception and hit by penalties, could not get untracked in the first quarter. So Tulane seized the initiative when it shook Mason loose for his long run. On this play, the shifty Tulane halfback shook loose from several tacklers and reversed direction twice before making it to the goal with Dawkins riding his back at 7:55. Newton kicked the extra point.

In the second quarter, the Black Knights began to make their power felt. Starting from the Army 11 on the last play of

Statistics of the Game

	Army	Tul.
First downs	21	10
Rushing yardage	344	162
Passing yardage	11	75
Passes attempted	12	11
Passes completed	1	4
Passes intercepted by	2	1
Punts	6	7
Av. dist. of punts, yds.	36	27.7
Fumbles lost	1	0
Yards penalized	65	25

the first period, they punched out 89 yards in eighteen plays. Army's single pass completion figure in this drive, with Dave Bourland hitting Bill Graf on fourth down for a first down on the 15.

From there, Dawkins slashed to the 5 and the 1-foot marks. Walters hit the middle for the score at 6:50. Jim Kennedy converted.

With a hurry-up attack worthy of Oklahoma at its quickest, Army moved the ball 52 yards in twelve running plays, launched within the span of four minutes, to send Dawkins across at 13:56. Virgil Jester blocked Maurice Hilliard' attempted conversion, which loomed as a possible decisive factor when Blount split the uprights after Petitbon's third-period punt-return score for Tulane.

Two Drives Checked

In the final period, two Army drives bogged down near midfield, on missed passes and a bobbled pitchout, before the Black Knights caught fire.

They took off from their own 26 after a short punt by Newton. Anderson raced around end for 9 yards. Then Dawkins, running on a tricky reverse from Anderson, galloped 21 yards to Tulane's 44.

On a thrust inside Tulane's trap-blocked left tackle, Anderson stampeded to the Tulane 12, running over would-be tacklers until finally borne down by the weight of numbers.

In a change of pace, Bourland sent Walters catapulting into the line for 2 yards. Then Army's quarterback quick-pitched to Anderson. Behind blocks by Bourland and Walters, Bob broke loose around end, drove through a Tulane defender inside the 5 and hurtled into the end zone for the game-winning score.

RICE TURNS BACK TEXAS AGGIES, 7-6

Continued From Page 1

played in Rice territory, with the Owls halting threats that carried to the 16 and 11. Rice threatened in the final period with a 46-yard surge that failed with a fourth down incomplete pass from the Aggie 4.

Time ran out as the Aggies made a desperate final bid. With four minutes to play, Hill punted out on the A. and M. 1. From that point Osborne and a reserve quarterback, Jimmy Wright, needed only ten plays to move the Aggies 76 yards to the Rice 23.

Matt Gorges, a 198-pound right guard, then crashed through to throw Wright for an 11-yard loss. The final gun sounded with the Aggies holding third down and needing 21 yards from the 34.

Ryan used two neat pitchouts to Sonny Searcy and Gordon Speer, a pair of reserve halfbacks, to gain key first downs in the Rice touchdown drive. Searcy gained 12 yards at left end to the Aggie 41. Two plays later Speer moved around right end for 16 yards to the 26.

Fullback Raymond Chilton powered on the draw play for 15 yards to the 11. On the final play of the third period, Ryan, fighting off Bobby Marks, Aggie left end, raced around left end to the 1. Hill then replaced Ryan and scored on the second play.

Guard Allen Goehring started the Aggie touchdown march by recovering a fumble by Howard Hoelscher, Rice fullback, on the Owl 14. Three carries by Osborne and one by Fullback Gordon Leboeuf got a first down on the 2.

The Rice line stopped Osborne for no gain, gave up 1 yard, and then stopped the 175-pound quarterback inches short of the goal line. On fourth down Osborne powered across for the touchdown.

REBELS WIN, 14-7, WITH ALERT PLAY

Mississippi's Running Game and Strong Line Decide—Vols' Carter Scores

MEMPHIS, Nov. 16 (UP)—Halfback Leroy Reed ran a punt back 41 yards to set up a Mississippi touchdown and started the Rebels to a 14-7 upset victory over Tennessee today in the battle for the Sugar Bowl bid.

A capacity crowd of 31,000, including representatives of three major bowls, watched as the once-beaten Rebels capitalized on elusive running and breaks to topple the seventh-ranked Volunteers.

Fullback Bill Hurst punched over from the one-foot line in his second stab at the line after Reed's sensational sprint put Mississippi on the Tennessee 2. A later touchdown that followed a fumble recovery gave the Rebels the victory and an almost certain invitation to the Sugar Bowl, although Cotton and 'Gator Bowl officials were watching, too.

Carter Goes 8 Yards

Mississippi's powerful line kept Tennessee's vaunted single wing bottled up until the fourth period, when tailback Al Carter, returning to the lineup after being injured in the second game of the season, raced 8 yards for the touchdown to cap an 80-yard drive. The score came with only one minute, 24 seconds to play.

Mississippi scored first early in the second period on Hurst's one-foot plunge.

Left guard Jackie Simpson set up Mississippi's second tally by recovering fullback Tommy Bronson's fumble on the Tennessee 5. Quarterback Ray Brown plunged over from the one.

Both Mississippi touchdowns came after the Rebels had driven to the Tennessee 5 only to lose the ball on downs.

Tennessee was able to gain only 92 yards through the first three periods. The Vols' deepest penetration going into the final period had been to the Mississippi 33.

March Starts From 20

Tennessee started on its own 20 after Brown had kicked into the end zone. Smith went 36 yards to the Mississippi 44 on the first play. Carter connected with passes to Tommy Potts for 10 yards and to Jim Grubb for seven to put the ball on the Rebel 22. Carter and Smith alternated in running plays to put it over after five attempts, Carter scoring from the 8.

27-14 GAME WON BY WEST VIRGINIA

Longfellow's Passing Helps Mountaineers Score Over Wake Forest Eleven

WINSTON-SALEM, N. C., Nov. 16 (UP)—Second String Quarterback Dick Longfellow personally made up for the weakness in West Virginia's crippled ground attack today by throwing three touchdown passes that led the Mountaineers to a 27-14 victory over Wake Forest.

Playing without their powerful fullback, Larry Krutko, the Mountaineers drove 74 yards for a first-period score capped by Halfback Ray Peterson's 43-yard touchdown run. Then the West Virginia ground game bogged down and Longfellow came into his own.

Midway in the second period, after West Virginia recovered a Wake Forest fumble on the Deacon 43, Longfellow completed three straight passes, the last one to End Bruce McClure for a touchdown.

After Wake Forest struck back for its first touchdown, Longfellow's passing arm spelled death to the Deacons' chances for their first win in eight starts this season.

With the ball on the West Virginia 40, Longfellow heaved a pass to Peterson, who grabbed it on the 20 and sped across untouched. Tackle Dick Guesman converted to put the Mountaineers ahead, 21—7, with twenty-five seconds left in the first half.

Longfellow's third scoring pass came with only a minute left in the game and topped a 65-yard drive. He passed seven yards to end Roger Chancey. Mikanik missed the conversion.

Wake Forest was again hampered by injuries, but put its attack into smooth motion twice.

Halfbacks Pete Barham and Roy Ledford and Fullback Pete Manning combined talents to

FLORIDA TOPPLES VANDERBILT, 14-7

Parrish Tallies on 45 and 22 Yard Sprints—King Scores for Losers

STATISTICS OF THE GAME

	Fla.	Vand.
First downs	11	17
Rushing yardage	228	148
Passing yardage	12	135
Passes attempted	6	20
Passes completed	1	11
Passes intercepted by	0	4
Punts	8	5
Av. dist. of punts, yds.	33	33
Fumbles lost	3	3
Yards penalized	29	28

GAINESVILLE, Fla., Nov. 16 (AP)—Bernie Parrish circled left end on 45-yard and 22-yard touchdown runs within five minutes today and led Florida to a 14-7 victory over Vanderbilt.

Parrish also kicked both conversions. He also intercepted a Vandy pass midway in a fourth quarter when Vanderbilt's Boyce Smith twice wheeled the Commodores deep into Florida territory and threatened to pull out a tie or victory.

Smith destroyed Florida's ranking as No. 5 in the nation on pass defense but he couldn't hit the big ones that would have given Vanderbilt its fourth straight victory and a chance at a bowl bid.

Only 28,000 turned out. Both teams were already out of contention for the Southeastern Conference title — Vandy through a loss to Mississippi and a tie with Alabama; Florida after losses to Mississippi State and Auburn.

Those who came saw a real thriller after the players got over a bad case of fumbling during a light rain in the first quarter.

Early in the second quarter Florida began a 78-yard drive and Parrish broke the scoring famine with his 45-yard romp.

Jimmy Dunn intercepted one of Smith's passes a couple of minutes later and Florida went 51 yards, capped by Parrish's 22-yard scoring caper.

Vanderbilt also got its score in the second period after Phil King ran the kickoff, following Florida's second touchdown, 88 yards to the Florida 12. He then took a 10-yard touchdown pass from Smith.

"All the News That's Fit to Print"

The New York Times.

LATE CITY EDITION
Rain and windy today and tonight. Rain ending tomorrow.

VOL. CVII..No. 36,586. NEW YORK, WEDNESDAY, MARCH 26, 1958. FIVE CENTS

DULLES DECLARES SOVIET PUTS PRICE ON TALKS TOO HIGH

U. S. Would Lose Its Shirt if It Accepted the Terms in Latest Note, He Says

WARNS OF A 'SPECTACLE'

Secretary Rejects Demand on Satellites, Germany and Wider U. N. Veto

Transcript of the Dulles news conference is on Page 10.

Special to The New York Times.

WASHINGTON, March 25—Secretary of State Dulles said today that the United States would lose its shirt if it accepted Soviet terms for a heads-of-government meeting.

The Secretary was asked at his news conference whether the conditions the Soviet Union made in its note yesterday would make such a conference a mere "spectacle," as a recent United States note to Moscow suggested it might become.

"I would say that if those terms were accepted, it would turn the summit meeting into something much worse than a 'spectacle,'" he replied. "It would mean that on the way to the summit we would have lost our shirt. Perhaps that would result in a 'spectacle.'"

Mr. Dulles dwelt on what he termed the "terribly high political price" the Soviet Union was trying to exact for a summit meeting.

Enumerates Moscow 'Tags'

He listed five Soviet "price tags":

1. The Soviet Union wants to use satellite nations such as Czechoslovakia and Rumania as members of its negotiating team as if they were the equals of Western nations such as Britain, France and Italy.

2. It demands that the West acquiesce in the partition of Germany and recognize the Soviet puppet regime in the eastern part.

3. It would have the West abandon the joint responsibility of the Big Four for the reunification of Germany, which was recognized at Yalta and Potsdam and reaffirmed at the Geneva summit conference in 1955.

4. It wants Soviet-controlled governments to be represented

Continued on Page 10, Column 3

Ray Robinson Wins Title for Fifth Time

Sugar Ray Robinson

Ray Robinson of Harlem won the world middleweight championship for the fifth time last night. He received a split decision over Carmen Basilio of Chittenango, N. Y., in a fifteen-round fight before 19,000 persons at the Chicago Stadium.

Details on Page 45.

MAYOR PROMISES HE WILL ROOT OUT ANY CORRUPTION

Invites Top Aides to Hear Stern Warning in Annual Report to the Council

The text of Wagner address appears on Page 30.

By CHARLES G. BENNETT

Mayor Wagner served notice on the City Council and his top aides yesterday that every instrument at his disposal would be used to frustrate unethical actions by city officials.

The city will act swiftly to root out corruption and inefficiency wherever found, the Mayor promised.

In an address to the City Council presenting his annual report for 1957, the Mayor declared that wrongdoing by unethical public officials or civil servants "will not be condoned or ignored."

Strong emphasis was given to the Mayor's declaration by the presence in the City Council chamber of about sixty commissioners and deputies. They had been invited by the Mayor's office to attend.

3 Borough Heads Present

Also present were three members of the Board of Estimate; Borough Presidents Hulan E. Jack of Manhattan, John Cashmore of Brooklyn and Albert V. Maniscalco of Richmond.

"As long as I am Mayor, honesty, integrity and clean government will be the guideposts upon which I insist, as they have been in every public office I have held," Mayor Wagner asserted. "We are a government that consciously seeks out bad spots, wherever they may occur, and we act vigorously to get rid of these bad spots."

The Mayor's pledge of clean government in the future was an indirect recognition of scandals that have plagued many city agencies in the last year.

Preusse's Work Cited

In his 130-page printed, profusely illustrated report, Mr. Wagner declared that studies and reports by City Administrator Charles F. Preusse had led to needed improvements in procedures of the troubled departments.

Specifically, the Mayor credited the City Administrator with having improved conditions in the City Housing Authority, leading to a plan to reorganize that agency, and with bringing about reforms in inspectional practices in the Department of Buildings.

Mr. Wagner also cited Mr. Preusse's work in studying privately owned dumps and trade waste disposal, and recommendations leading to administrative changes in the Correction Department.

Neither in his report nor his message did Mayor Wagner take cognizance of the scandals

Continued on Page 30, Column 2

The New York Times (by Patrick A. Burns)

REPORTS ON STATE OF THE CITY: Mayor Wagner addresses City Council and other officials at City Hall

EISENHOWER ASKS FUND TO PROLONG PAY FOR JOBLESS

Wants U. S. to Finance Aid 50% Beyond the Present State Maximum Periods

MESSAGE TO CONGRESS

President Also Takes Steps to Speed Procurement of 600 Million in Materials

Text of Eisenhower message will be found on Page 25.

By FELIX BELAIR Jr.

Special to The New York Times.

WASHINGTON, March 25—President Eisenhower asked Congress today to approve Federal payments to jobless workers during an extended period of state-operated unemployment compensation.

The White House estimated at $500,000,000 to $600,000,000 the immediate cost of compensating some 2,000,000 unemployed who will have exhausted their benefit rights and who would be eligible for the new payments.

These would cover a compensation period half again as long as that now provided in each state's program.

Thus, workers who have used up their benefits in states that pay benefits for twenty-six weeks could collect for thirteen additional weeks, if they were out of work that long. In states that make payments for twenty weeks, the unemployed could get the benefits for an additional ten.

Acts to Speed Procurement

At the same time, the President took steps to speed up the procurement of some $600,000,000 of materials and equipment for the nonmilitary Federal establishment during the next fifteen months.

He plans to ask Congressional authority in the next day or two to place orders for future delivery that ordinarily would not be placed until well into the next fiscal year, which begins July 1.

In a special message to Congress, the President said his recommendations were intended "to temper the hardship being experienced by workers whose unemployment has been prolonged."

He said the plan also reflected "my conviction that the need

Continued on Page 25, Column 1

BONN HOUSE BACKS NUCLEAR WEAPONS

Approves Adenauer Program After a Four-Day Debate Marked by Bitterness

By M. S. HANDLER

Special to The New York Times.

BONN, Germany, March 25—The Bundestag approved the Government's nuclear armament policy tonight after a four-day debate marred by violent scenes.

A resolution submitted by the Christian Democrats authorized Chancellor Konrad Adenauer and Franz Josef Strauss, Minister of Defense, to accept a United States offer of dual-purpose weapons such as the Matador C. The resolution was approved by a show of hands.

Most of the European defense ministers who will attend a North Atlantic Council meeting in Paris April 16 have been empowered to approve a recommendation by Gen. Lauris Norstad, Supreme Allied Commander, Europe, to strengthen the Atlantic alliance defenses with dual-purpose tactical weapons.

Heads Are Interchangeable

A dual-purpose weapon can be fitted with either a conventional or a nuclear warhead.

Final arrangements between the United States and its European allies will involve the retention of nuclear warheads by the United States armed forces. They would be released only under specific conditions.

The decision of the defense ministers will be made final at a meeting of the Atlantic pact foreign ministers in Copenhagen, Denmark, in May.

As the Bundestag debate entered its final stage late in the

Continued on Page 10, Column 4

ASSEMBLY BALKS REFORM IN COURTS

Senate Versions of Tweed Plan Rejected—Harriman Acts on Crime Unit

By LEO EGAN

Special to The New York Times

ALBANY, March 25—The Assembly rejected two revised Senate-approved versions of the Tweed court reform plan today.

In both cases the affirmative votes came from Republicans. The Democrats, despite Governor Harriman's statement that he would like to see a court reform measure approved, voted solidly in opposition.

Other legislative developments as the Senate and Assembly sped toward adjournment tomorrow included:

¶A new offer from Governor Harriman to compromise on creation of a state crime commission.

¶Senate approval over solid Democratic opposition of a bill to raise maximum weekly workmen's compensation benefits from $36 to $45 and provide a new basis for judicial review of workmen's compensation board decisions.

¶An attack on Republican plans for outlawing racketeering abuses in labor unions from a member of the Governor's committee that studied the subject.

¶A new rejection by the Assembly of a Senate-approved bill to require one year's residence within the state to qualify for relief.

¶Senate approval of a measure previously passed by the Senate to double the number of

Continued on Page 23, Column 1

'Shook' Youngsters Spring From the Housing Jungles

This is the third of seven articles on the city's school students and their backgrounds and delinquency problems.

By HARRISON E. SALISBURY

Most visitors to the Fort Greene Houses in Brooklyn prefer to walk up three or four flights instead of taking the elevator. They choose the steep, cold staircases rather than face the stench of stale urine that pervades the elevators. Nowhere this side of Moscow are you likely to find public housing so closely duplicating the squalor it was designed to supplant.

The Fort Greene project houses more than 3,400 families. It is described as the world's largest public housing project. It is also described as a $20,000,000 slum. The epithet is a fitting one.

In recent years two slayings have occurred on Fort Greene's doorstep—the "stomping" to death of an adolescent gang member and the fatal knifing of a sailor by teen-agers.

Low-rent public housing projects, the dreadful 100-year-old tenements of the lower East Side, the brownstone barrens of the upper West Side and the slum jungles of East Harlem are prime breeding places of the stresses, the strains that produce New York's "shook-up" generation.

All Society Affected

These are the areas of constant population shifts and currents.

Into these areas have poured a heavy percentage of the more than 300,000 Puerto Ricans who have emigrated here in the last seven years. Into these areas have gone many of the 300,000 Negroes who have settled in the city in the same period. Here are to be found displaced and shifting white ethnic groups.

Vast sums of public funds and enormous social energy are being mustered to combat the degenerative effects of this corrupt and rotten environment upon adolescents.

"Shook-up," or disturbed, youngsters are to be found in all strata of society. They come from well-to-do areas and middle-class homes as well as from the ragged barracks of the poor.

But the heavy concentrations are found in areas of depriva-

Continued on Page 32, Column 1

F.C.C. AIDE DENIES INQUIRY CHARGES

Testifies Broadcasters Paid Some Hotel Bills, but Sees No 'Impropriety'

By JAY WALZ

Special to The New York Times.

WASHINGTON, March 25—The senior member of the Federal Communications Commission testified today that the broadcasting industry had paid some of his hotel bills and had put color television sets in his home.

Rosel H. Hyde, the commissioner, challenged a House investigating subcommittee, however, to find any "impropriety" in this. Besides, he said, the television sets—usually big, experimental models—became "a considerable nuisance to my wife."

The commissioner said that the television equipment was installed for "study" purposes, and brought so many people into the house that Mrs. Hyde gathered the impression that "color TV was developed in our living room."

Prepared by Schwartz

The slight, gray-haired official was appointed to the commission by President Truman in 1946 after being employed in the agency or its radio predecessor since 1928. He came before the Subcommittee on Legislative Oversight to answer charges of "personal, official misconduct," including that of "over-fraternizing" with the industry regulated by the commission.

The charges were prepared by Dr. Bernard Schwartz, the subcommittee's former counsel who was discharged in February. Today's witness had the benefit of a gentler approach by Dr. Schwartz's successor, Robert W. Lishman.

Mr. Lishman, making his public debut as a subcommittee interrogator, questioned Mr. Hyde in low tones. Once he apologized for having to go into such details of official business as hotel bills and Government travel vouchers.

No 'Personal Misconduct'

"I don't know of any personal misconduct, and I have no confessions to make that you gentlemen don't know about," Mr. Hyde told the subcommittee in a preliminary statement.

He testified that on five "official" trips, four of them to industry conventions, he had accepted a total of $192 from the Government for expenses.

"If this $192 involves any possible impingement on the rightness, the correctness, of my behavior, I'm ready to pay it right now," Mr. Hyde declared.

Mr. Hyde was asked about

Continued on Page 22, Column 3

FARM BILL BACKED BY G.O.P. SENATORS

Price Support Freeze Urged on President—Action Is a Rebuff to Benson

By ALLEN DRURY

Special to The New York Times.

WASHINGTON, March 25—Senate Republicans today voted, 17—14, to urge President Eisenhower to sign the one-year farm price-support freeze now on his desk.

Their stand was echoed by George Meany, president of the American Federation of Labor and Congress of Industrial Organizations, in a telegram to the President. Mr. Meany said the President should sign the measure as a matter of "simple justice and economic wisdom."

The vote came at a stormy closed session of the G. O. P. Senate Conference. It was a rebuff to Ezra Taft Benson, Secretary of Agriculture, whose policies have been criticized by farm-state Senators of both parties.

This was the most powerful challenge to Mr. Benson yet made within his party. It arrayed against him a large segment of Republicans in the Senate and raised the possibility that his critics might form a coalition that could override an expected Presidential veto of the price-support freeze.

Would Cancel Cuts

At issue is a measure that would cancel Mr. Benson's proposed reductions in price supports for dairy products, wheat, rice, barley, rye, dry beans, flaxseed, grain sorghums and cottonseed. It would bar reductions below the 1957 levels on these and all other supported farm products, and would also bar cuts below 1958 planting levels in acreage allotments for all crops except tobacco.

The President has called the measure "a 180-degree turn in the wrong direction." An Administration source said a veto message was "being written" and would be sent to Congress "probably this week."

The Republican conference turned to the farm question at

Continued on Page 21, Column 3

HOUSE VOTES RISE IN MILITARY PAY

668 Million Added in Drive to Keep Men in Service

By C. P. TRUSSELL

Special to The New York Times.

WASHINGTON, March 25—The House approved overwhelmingly today a bill designed to add $668,397,000 a year to the pay of military men. The vote was 366 to 22.

The measure now goes to the Senate, where passage is expected.

This was a key move in a drive to stem the rising tide of departure of service men with vital skills. The objective is to give all service men a sound basis for careers in the military services, to hold them there and lessen the appeal of better earnings and opportunities outside.

Representative Paul J. Kilday, Democrat of Texas and chairman of the Armed Services subcommittee that handled the bill, conceded that this was a costly program. He contended, though, that it would pay off in a continued increasing of efficiency within the services.

A new system of proficiency pay for enlisted men showing military promise was included. It could run to extra compensation up to $150 a month.

At earlier stages today the bill ran into protests. Members complained that they could not tell from the bill and the report accompanying it just what pay rises would be made. It appeared to some that much larger increases were being given to higher officers, with enlisted personnel bringing up the rear.

This opposition disappeared as debate went on. It was brought out that skilled per-

Continued on Page 16, Column 3

NEW AID TO INDIA URGED IN SENATE

Cooper and Kennedy Ask Step to Save 5-Year Plan

By RUSSELL BAKER

Special to The New York Times.

WASHINGTON, March 25—Senators John F. Kennedy and John Sherman Cooper urged Congress today to underwrite the success of India's imperiled Five-Year Plan.

A resolution put before the Senate would, if adopted, declare "the sense of the Congress" to favor all the support needed "to assist India to complete successfully its current program for economic development."

Senator Cooper, a Kentucky Republican and former Ambassador to India, said that this would probably require United States loans of $500,000,000 by 1961, in addition to the $225,000,000 loan authorized earlier this year.

Senator Kennedy, a Massachusetts Democrat, supported his position with a treatise on international economics and politics amounting to a defense of aid to "neutrals."

If India's Five-Year Plan collapses, he said, "so may democratic India and the democratic hope in all of Asia, setting in motion forces which would erode the broad security interests of the United States and its allies."

He added:

"No thoughtful citizen can fail to see our stake in the survival of free government in India. India stands as the only effective competitor to China for the faith and following of the millions of uncommitted and restless peoples."

India's leaders, Senator Coop-

Continued on Page 3, Column 4

Russians Doubt U. N. Chief Will Sway Them on Arms

Associated Press Radiophoto

Dag Hammarskjold being greeted in Moscow on Monday by Nikita S. Khrushchev. At left is Foreign Minister Andrei A. Gromyko and behind U. N. Secretary General is interpreter.

Special to The New York Times

MOSCOW, March 25—Deputy Premier Anastas I. Mikoyan expressed doubt tonight that Dag Hammarskjold, United Nations Secretary General, could convince the Soviet Union to rejoin the disarmament negotiations in the United Nations. Chatting with Western correspondents at a reception at the Greek Embassy, Mr. Mikoyan welcomed Mr. Hammarskjold's four-day visit to Moscow. But in discussing his mission the Deputy Premier restated the Soviet position that the proposed United Nations disarmament talks would serve no useful purpose. Mr. Hammarskjold had said before his

Continued on Page 15, Column 1

Hoffa Called Ruler Of Hoodlum Empire

Special to The New York Times.

WASHINGTON, March 25—The Senate rackets committee labeled James R. Hoffa today the boss of a "hoodlum empire" surrounded by men who used union funds for the care and feeding of idle thugs.

It found him dangerous for the country at large because of the economic power lodged in him.

It also termed this tragic for the union he heads, the International Brotherhood of Teamsters, and said his associates were distinguished for their corruption.

The committee will have another look at Hoffa's record this year, it said in the second section of its first-year report. Part of the report was released yesterday.

Hoffa testified for several days last August before the

Continued on Page 29, Column 1

U. S. Is Tightening Oil Import Quotas

By JOHN D. MORRIS

Special to The New York Times

WASHINGTON, March 25—The Eisenhower Administration has agreed on a new "voluntary" program for the further restriction of oil imports.

"The decision has been made and will be released this afternoon," Sinclair Weeks, Secretary of Commerce, told the House Ways and Means Committee today.

Later, when the expected White House announcement failed to materialize, Mr. Weeks said he hoped and believed it would be forthcoming tomorrow. There was no explanation of the delay.

One theory was that the State Department may have interposed last-minute objections at the urging of the Canadian Government.

Canada has formally pro-

Continued on Page 3, Column 5

Robinson Outpoints Basilio and Wins World Middleweight Title Fifth Time

CHICAGO OFFICIALS SPLIT ON OUTCOME

Judges Vote for Robinson, but Basilio Is Named Winner by Referee

By JOSEPH C. NICHOLS

Special to The New York Times.

CHICAGO, March 25—Sugar Ray Robinson beat Carmen Basilio in a fifteen-round bout at the Chicago Stadium tonight to become the middleweight champion of the world for the fifth time.

The famed Sugar Ray of Harlem registered a split decision over his smaller rival in a contest that just about matched their first clash for grueling action and savage exchanges.

The verdict that enabled Robinson to lift the crown from his Chittenango (N.Y.) rival was based on the votes of the judges. Boxing rules in this state call for scoring on a basis of five points maximum per round, with the winner of a round getting the maximum and the loser getting a proportionate lesser number of points. Judge John Bray scored it for Sugar Ray, 71 to 64, and Judge Spike McAdams voted for Sugar, 72 to 64.

Frank Sikora, the referee, favored Basilio by 69 to 66. The ballots, announced by Ben Bently, had Sikora's vote in the middle. When it was made known, the crowd of 19,000 booed loudly. The fans quickly became quiet, though, for everything depended on the next announcement—of McAdams' vote. When it was announced, the spectators went wild.

This observer, scoring on the New York State system of rounds won, favored Robinson by a margin of eleven rounds to four. True, many of the sessions were exceedingly close, but any margin was Robinson's creation.

Throughout the bruising contest the fans showed a heavy sentiment for Basilio, as well they might. For the doughty former marine, fighting with his left eye closed almost tight from the seventh round, waded into his rangier rival with a willingness and persistence that at times threatened to discourage Robinson. At other times Carmen caused Sugar Ray to rip away with both hands in an attempt to bring matters to a sudden termination.

There was no knocking out Basilio, although for a time or two in the fifteenth round it seemed that Robinson would be able to knock him down. The Harlem flash tried with all the skill and power he possessed and he had Carmen shaky once or twice, but he couldn't send him down. The Chittenango fighter is still proud in the boast that he has never been floored.

The pattern of the fight was that of the plodding, chunky Basilio moving forward steadily in an attempt to wear Robinson down with body punches. There was a substance to this strategy, in that Robinson, at the age of 37, was not expected to be too strong around the middle for the attack of his 31-year-old foeman.

Robinson Scales 159¾

Robinson had to go without food for almost twenty hours before weighing in at noon. He scaled 159¾ pounds and Basilio, a recent welterweight champion had no trouble, weighing 153.

Basilio's board of advisers had the idea that the rigors of weight-making might also have contributed to a weakness about the stomach for Ray. And there were times when the Harlem boxer did show some fatigue under the pounding. But when things got too tough, he managed to hold until the referee stepped in.

Basilio was the first one to "rough it up" and drew a warning in the first round for hitting on the break. In this session, Robinson tried to box, but Basilio bulled his way inside and he outpunched Ray. They were so intent at their task that they slashed away at each other after the bell. This action infuriated a Robinson handler, who tried to climb into Basilio's corner, but the Stadium staff restrained him.

Robinson brought his boxing ability into play in the second round and speared Carmen with a variety of sharp punches. They didn't seem to have much effect as the Onion Farmer—as Basilio is known—moved ahead with his determined aim to strike the body. Robinson, though, succeeded in avoiding his punishment.

In the third and fourth, Robinson exhibited a willingness to trade and he landed more punches than his forward-moving rival. Robinson again boxed at long range in the fourth and his left jab began to have its effect on Carmen's eye.

In the fifth, Basilio's body punches slowed Robinson, but Sugar Ray took charge in the sixth, mainly by use of his left. This weapon banged against Carmen's eye steadily and the Chittenango boxer could not defend against it.

Basilio presented a sad picture in the seventh when his eye was shut tight. Robinson poked away at him as if a quick victory was to be his. But Carmen absorbed all the punishment and occasionally lashed out with left hooks to the head and body that indicated that he was still dangerous.

After Robinson built up a slight margin in the eighth, Basilio staged a fine rally in the ninth and tenth. He dealt but considerable damage with his crashing left hooks to the body. Robinson changed his style after that and boxed instead of trading.

Through each of the last five rounds Sugar Ray had at least one good shot at Carmen's jaw and some of these punches had enough impact to floor anyone except the iron-jawed Basilio. In the fifteenth round Basilio moved in and butted Robinson, for which he was warned by the referee. They shook hands and then Robinson tore after Basilio with a studied sharp right-hand attack, punishing Carmen quite a lot, but failing to floor him.

The odds on the fight favored Basilio at 2 to 1. When the pair met in New York on last Sept. 23 Basilio gained a split decision over Robinson. Oddly, the referee in that fight, Al Berl, also voted for the loser.

The receipts tonight amounted to $351,955 contributed by 17,976 paying fans. The gladiators received 30 per cent of this sum, as well as 30 per cent of the television, radio and motion picture receipts. The video was sent off on a closed circuit for a minimum guarantee of $275,000.

United Press International

Sugar Ray Robinson, right, lands with flurry of blows to Carmen Basilio during 11th round of middle-weight title bout.

Carmen, Eager for Return Bout, Refuses to Acknowledge Loss

CHICAGO, March 25 (AP)—Courageous Carmen Basilio sat on a dressing-room table tonight and spoke of a return bout against Sugar Ray Robinson.

Basilio, his left eye area swollen to the size of a discolored billiard ball, said he was not able to see well from the fourth round through the rest of the fight.

"We want a return match," said Basilio's co-manager, Joe Netro.

James Norris, the president of the sponsoring International Boxing Club, said he would be "very happy" to put Basilio and Robinson in the ring again. The promoter shook hands with Carmen in the dressing room.

Basilio, who lost the middleweight title to Robinson on a split decision six months and two days after he won it from Robinson, refused to acknowledge that he had lost tonight's savage brawl.

He did say, however, that Referee Frank Sikora, who voted for Basilio, did a good job.

Basilio, holding an ice bag to his bad eye and spitting blood into a bucket on the table beside him, said his vision had been impaired in the fourth round.

Newsmen at the ringside had noted that his left eye was closed when he went out for the sixth round.

"I couldn't get my distance right," Basilio said in explaining the effect of his limited sight.

"If you can't get distance, you find yourself off balance."

John De John, also a co-manager of Basilio, said there never had been any thought of stopping the fight.

Basilio and his handlers, looking forward to a third bout against Robinson, said they would talk about the site of match No. 3 later.

Physicians were summoned to examine and treat Basilio's bad eye.

That grotesque, black eye was more eloquent of Basilio's dogged courage than anyone in the dressing room.

Anyone, that is, but Basilio's trainer, Angelo Dundee.

He looked at the man who had refused to quit and who had refused to concede he had been beaten, and he said:

"He's a great——champion."

Buchman Elected at Columbia

Steve Buchman, a 19-year-old junior from West Englewood, N. J., yesterday was elected captain of the 1958-59 Columbia fencing team. Buchman, who never fenced before entering Columbia, finished second in the epee competition in the National Collegiate and Intercollegiate championships this year.

"All the News That's Fit to Print"

The New York Times.

LATE CITY EDITION

U.S. Weather Bureau Report (Page 35) forecasts: Mild, chance of rain today; partly cloudy, colder tonight and tomorrow. Temp. range: 45—38. Yesterday: 49.3—32.5.

VOL. CVIII....No. 36,864. THE NEW YORK TIMES, MONDAY, DECEMBER 29, 1958. 10c beyond 200-mile zone from New York City. Higher in air delivery cities. FIVE CENTS

DE GAULLE URGES BELT-TIGHTENING TO REVIVE NATION

Outlines in Talk to People Sacrifices Needed to Lift France to Greatness

ALTERNATIVE HELD DIRE

Tax Rise, Cut in Subsidies and Increased Prices for Imports Are in Store

By ROBERT C. DOTY
Special to The New York Times.

PARIS, Dec. 28—Premier Charles de Gaulle told the French people tonight that the price of salvation and national greatness was sacrifice.

The Premier and Finance Minister Antoine Pinay, in radio-television addresses, then outlined the degree of austerity demanded by the 17.55 per cent devalulation of the franc and other stringent financial measures announced yesterday.

At the new rate of 493.7 francs to the dollar, these included new taxes of equivalent of $626,000,000, a reduction of $345,000,000 in subsidies that kept cost-of-living items cheap and inevitable price increases for foreign products bought with devalued francs.

Great Progress Forecast

General de Gaulle said that without these sacrifices France would remain "a country in tow, swinging perpetually between drama and mediocrity."

"But, on the other hand," he added, "if we succeed in the great national enterprise of finanical and economic recovery, what great progress on the road that leads France toward the heights!"

The Premier recalled at the outset the series of electoral successes his name and program had won since he assumed power in near-chaos last June 1—the constitutional referendum, the legislative elections of November and his own election to the Presidency last Sunday.

Service Since 1940 Recalled

"The national task that has been mine for eighteen years finds itself, by this fact, confirmed," he said. This seemed to imply that the task had been his ever since he began the Free French movement in 1940 and that his twelve years out of power under the Fourth Republic had been a mere interregnum.

"Guide of France and chief of the Republican state, I will exercise the supreme power to the full extent it allows from now on and according to the new spirit that has conferred it on me," he said.

General de Gaulle said he found the state last June faced with economic perils beyond its strength, the balance of payments dangerously unbalanced and with signs of imminent recession. The new program was designed to "place the nation on a basis of truth and severity" that would unquestionably entail severe trials, he added.

The imperative need to carry out development pograms in Al-

Continued on Page 3, Column 3

Colts Beat Giants, Win in Overtime

23-17 Game Tied With 7 Seconds Left in Regulation Time

By LOUIS EFFRAT

Time and fortune finally ran out on professional football's Cinderella team, the New York Giants, yesterday at the Yankee Stadium. And so it was that the Baltimore Colts, with a 23-17 victory, won the championship of the National Football League.

With a couple of minutes to go in the fourth period, the Giants seemed to have the triumph in their grasp. But with seven seconds to go, Baltimore tied the score at 17—17 on a field goal.

Then, in a sudden-death overtime period, the Baltimore team coached by Weeb Ewbank fashioned the winning touchdown after 8 minutes 15 seconds.

The excitement generated by football's longest game left most of the 64,185 spectators limp. Aside from an experimental exhibition contest, it was the first sudden-death game (with victory going instantly to the first team to score) in the league.

Alan (The Horse) Ameche, who had plunged for a 2-yard touchdown in the second quarter, drove over from the 1 for the tally that crushed the New Yorkers.

Ameche was a hero, but he was not THE hero. The 15,000 fans who had made the trip from Baltimore could have pointed to any one of a number of outstanding Colts.

Johnny Unitas was the man who engineered the dynamic offensive that moved the visitors from the shadow of defeat to the glory of their ultimate success. Then there was Steve Myrha, who kicked a 20-yard field goal at 14:53 in the fourth quarter.

Not to be ignored was the spectacular pass-catching of Ray Berry, the end, who captured twelve of Unitas' aerials for a gain of 178 yards. The receptions and yardage were

Continued on Page 25, Column 1

Associated Press

Alan Ameche storms across the Giants' goal line for the winning touchdown as his teammates open a wide gap in the New York line during overtime period at Yankee Stadium.

U.S. MAY SPONSOR A WIDENED ROLE FOR WORLD COURT

President Is Studying a Bid in State of Union Message —Senate Action Needed

By JAMES RESTON
Special to The New York Times.

WASHINGTON, Dec. 28—The Eisenhower Administration is actively considering an appeal to all nations to widen the scope and authority of the International Court of Justice at The Hague.

It is understood that a draft of such a proposal is now before President Eisenhower for inclusion in his forthcoming State of the Union message.

This draft—not finally approved by the President—contains a recommendation to the new Congress that the United States lead the way in offering to be more liberal in accepting the jurisdiction of the World Court over international legal disputes involving the United States.

Specifically, he is being urged to ask the Senate to repeal the so-called Connally amendment, passed in August of 1945. This limited the power of the President to submit disputes to the World Court without prior authority of the Congress.

May Seek to Change Trend

The purpose of raising this question in the State of the Union Message would be to help break the present trend toward making every international dispute a political issue and to try to start a movement toward arbitration of international legal disputes.

The President himself has recently been discussing in private the need to try to make a new beginning toward giving some vitality to the World Court. When Arthur Larson, his former chief speech writer, left Washington to head a "rule of law" institute at Duke University, the President asked him to continue working with the Administration on this subject.

Since then, the Department of Justice has been requested to look into the possibility of repealing the Connally amendment, and its report on the matter, together with Mr. Larson's recommendations, are now in the White House.

The background of this is as follows:

In voting, 89—2, for ratification of the United Nations Charter and the statutes of the International Court of Justice, the Senate accepted this amendment to the ratification by Senator Tom Connally of Texas:

"Provided that this declaration shall not apply to: (a) disputes the solution of which the parties shall entrust to other tribunals; and (b) disputes with regard to matters which are essentially within the domestic jurisdiction of the United States of America as determined by the United States of America."

'Advice and Consent' Required

The State Department had originally wished to leave to the President sole authority to accept the compulsory jurisdiction of the World Court "in all legal disputes concerning: (a) the interpretation of a treaty; (b) any question of international law; the existence of any fact which, if established, would constitute a breach of an international obligation; (c) the nature or extent of the reparation to be made for the breach of an international obligation."

Opposition to this developed during the Senate debate on ratification of the Charter and World Court Statute, however, and the State Department, in a formal "brief" filed with the Senate, finally agreed that if the President decided to accept the "optional clause" (Article 36 (2)) of the Court Statute, it would submit the proposal to the Senate for "advice and consent" or follow any other procedure laid down by the Congress.

Thus, while the Senate Foreign Relations Committee had urged the Senate to support the principle of "compulsory jurisdiction" of the World Court in order to demonstrate that the United States was a "champion" of the "judicial settlement of legal disputes," the Senate itself insisted on what was widely regarded in the world as a purely "nationalistic" attitude toward the court.

Since then, Washington has

Continued on Page 13, Column 8

PAPERS RESUME AS DELIVERYMEN END 19-DAY TIE-UP

To Our Readers

The New York Times, which has been shut down for seventeen days by the strike of the Newspaper and Mail Deliverers Union, resumes publication today.

Because of the difficulty in re-establishing normal operations after a shutdown and because of the late hour at which the strike ended, the size of today's issue is smaller than normal.

To bring the news up to date, a day-by-day chronology of events during the strike period is published in this issue. In addition, with each story of a continuing nature a synopsis of what has gone before appears under the heading "Fill-In."

On Wednesday, Dec. 31, the issues missed during the strike period will be published, each in two-page form, to complete the record. These issues were prepared each day during that period.

NEW PACT IS VOTED

Union Accepts 2-Year Terms, 2,091 to 537 —Walkout Costly

The texts of statements on strike are on Page 18.

By RUSSELL PORTER

A nineteen-day deliverers' union strike that had closed nine New York newspapers ended last night.

The New York Times resumed publication today, as did The News, The Mirror and The Herald Tribune. The evening papers planned to publish this afternoon.

Newspaper deliveries on Long Island, which had been disrupted for most papers for two weeks before publication was suspended, were also to be resumed.

The strike ended shortly after 10 o'clock last night when it was announced that members of the Newspaper and Mail Deliverers Union had voted nearly 4 to 1 to ratify a new contract and return to work.

The vote was 2,091 to 537, a majority of 1,554 out of 2,628 ballots cast.

Announcement Cheered

The result was announced by George J. Abrams, executive secretary of the Honest Ballot Association, which supervised the vote at the Manhattan Center, 311 West Thirty-fourth Street. More than 1,000 deliverers and friends [illegible] the announcement at [illegible].

Sam Feldman, union president, ordered the strikers to report to their jobs without delay.

"The morning papers are open and ready to roll," he said.

Mr. Feldman said that in addition to the 2,000 strikers, 1,700 delivery workers who had been laid off by wholesale newspaper distributors because of the strike would go back to work at once.

The union president thanked the press, radio and public "for their patience with us, despite the obvious inconveniences and losses which they have suffered along with us, through no fault of theirs."

'Undermining' Charged

He said the union would try to avoid such consequences in the future "if the publishers will show the respect for our views and for our strength to which we are entitled."

Asher Schwartz, union counsel, said the publishers had failed in attempts to "undermine" the trust of the union membership in its leaders.

"Union leadership is always a difficult burden," he said. "In this independent, ultra-democratic union, it is a really imposing challenge."

Barney G. Cameron, chairman of the Publishers Association of New York City, said:

"It is estimated that the strike cost the publishing business $25,000,000 in revenue.

"The cost outside the news-

Continued on Page 18, Column 7

NEW PLAN MAPPED TO END AIR STRIKE

Mediators to Offer Proposal to Eastern Today—Pilot Reply to American Due

By A. H. RASKIN

Federal mediators plan to submit a new settlement proposal today in the five-week-old strike that has paralyzed Eastern Air Lines. The proposal will be put forward while the Government peacemakers await union action on recommendations they made last week to end the nine-day-old walkout at American Air-lines.

The two strikes have grounded a third of the country's commercial air fleet, disrupted holiday travel arrangements for thousands of students, service men and other air passengers and caused heavy losses to resort areas in Florida, Mexico and the West Indies.

The stoppages are costing each line nearly $1,000,000 a day in lost income. However, these losses are offset by reduced expenses and by payments American and Eastern are scheduled to receive under a strike-aid pact involving six major air carriers.

The pact provides that struck lines are to receive any extra profits derived by other com-

Continued on Page 19, Column 4

FREER TRADE SEEN IN CONVERTIBILITY

New European Money Policy Also May Ease Clash Over Common Market Plans

By HAROLD CALLENDER
Special to The New York Times.

PARIS, Dec. 28—The common monetary action taken yesterday on behalf of ten European nations is considered likely to facilitate freer world trade and to moderate a hot dispute over trade discrimination by the nations of the European common market.

The nations involved made their currencies convertible when held by persons, regardless of nationality, living outside the territory or the monetary area of the issuing country. That is, each currency so held may henceforth be freely changed into any other currency, including dollars.

France alone took advantage of this international action to devalue her currency, by 17.55 per cent, without which it could not have become convertible in the limited sense defined above.

Effect of the Action

The same steps toward convertibility were taken by France, Britain, West Germany, Italy, the Netherlands, Norway, Denmark, Sweden and Belgium. Belgium's action covered Luxembourg, which forms a monetary union with her.

The action means that a Frenchman, a Japanese or even a Briton owning pounds and living outside the sterling area can buy dollars with pounds at the official rate. Hitherto such nonresidents could buy dollars, but at a slightly higher rate.

The action also means that a West German holding French francs can exchange them for

Continued on Page 3, Column 5

West Hears of New Unrest Stirring in East Germany

By DREW MIDDLETON
Special to The New York Times.

LONDON, Dec. 28—The Western powers have received information that East Germany is restive, and they hope that this will induce the Soviet Union to see its long-term interest in early negotiations on German unity.

Responsible United States and British officials also have said that only 5 per cent of the population supports the Communist Government of East Germany and that tens of thousands of East Germans are seeking asylum in the West.

The rapid deterioriation of the Communist position has created a situation that cannot be "safe" for imperialist and authoritarian power, these officials said. Consequently, they believe that negotiations on Germany with the Soviet Union are still possible despite the blustering tone of Soviet statements.

The United States, British, French and West German Governments will offer such negotiations again in notes that probably will be dispatched to Moscow in the first half of January. These notes will reply to Soviet Premier Nikita S. Khrushchev's note of Nov. 27 announcing Soviet withdrawal from East Berlin and proposing a free city status for three Western sectors of the city.

United States, British, French and West German diplomats have completed the drafting of the replies. These will be sent to the permanent North Atlantic Council for discussion tomorrow and then to Moscow

Continued on Page 6, Column 1

CUBA REBELS PLAN PROVISIONAL RULE

Urrutia Is to Head a Regime in 'Free Territory' Soon— Santiago Drive Looms

By R. HART PHILLIPS
Special to The New York Times.

HAVANA, Dec. 28—The Cuban rebels will "very soon" establish a provisional government in "free Cuban territory," with Dr. Manuel Urrutia as President, the rebel radio said today.

Dr. Urrutia, former president of the Urgency Court in Santiago De Cuba, fled to the United States more than a year ago when he voted against condemning revolutionists. He arrived in the Sierra Maestra headquarters of Fidel Castro, rebel leader, several weeks ago with his wife and child.

At the same time the rebels said four insurgent columns were advancing on Santiago de Cuba, which has been blockaded by the rebels from the land side for several weeks. The rebels have long desired to set up their provisional government in Santiago de Cuba, but the big Moncada army post there has been too strong to be attacked.

Havana Sends Reinforcements

Now, however, the rebels apparently feel they have sufficient strength to attack the city. The Government has sent heavy reinfocements into Santiago during the last two weeks, including tanks, cannon and planes based on the Santiago commercial airport, which also is used by the military.

The rebel radio reported last night the capture of the Central Highway from just outside Bayamo Army Field headquarters to Santiago de Cuba.

The insurgent radio said 600 soldiers were killed, wounded or captured in the fighting on the seventy-mile stretch between Bayamo and Santiago. The town of Maffo, with 150 Government soldiers in the garrison, fell this afternoon, the radio said.

Travelers reported Giboney Beach, near Santiago de Cuba, where American troops landed in the Spanish-American War, was in the hands of the rebels. Thirty Cuban marines and an officer are said to have gone over to the rebels and the rest were evacuated by naval authorities.

The travelers also said the

Continued on Page 30, Column 5

MILDER U. S. STAND ON NASSER HINTED

New Gestures Imply a Shift in Policy as Communism Appears to Gain in Iraq

By DANA ADAMS SCHMIDT
Special to The New York Times

WASHINGTON, Dec. 28—The United States seems to be edging closer to President Gamal Abdel Nasser of the United Arab Republic while Communist infiltration seems to be gaining in Iraq.

These two political currents seemed today to be discernible beneath the surface tranquility prevailing in the Middle East. Yet the emphasis remained on "seems."

The direction of United States policy can only be inferred from recent events. It has not been publicly stated.

A number of signs that the United States was warming toward President Nasser appeared recently:

¶ The United States concluded a surplus wheat deal that will supply about half the United Arab Republic's needs in the coming year, thereby reducing Cairo's dependence on the Soviet Union.

¶ The United States Army Corps of Engineers lent the United Arab Republic the huge mobile dredge Essayons to help clear approaches to Port Said and the Suez Canal. Several private United States concerns contracted to deepen the canal.

¶ Partly as a consequence of

Continued on Page 7, Column 1

Fall-Out Increases 25% in City But Its Hazards Are Minimized

Special to The New York Times.

WASHINGTON, Dec. 28—The fall-out of radioactive strontium on New York City increased 25 per cent in the first eight months of the year.

However, the amount of strontium 90 in the city's milk remained constant. It dropped sharply in the drinking water.

These statistics are contained in the Atomic Energy Commission's latest quarterly report on radioactive contamination resulting from atomic weapon tests. Prepared by the commission's health and safety laboratory in New York, the report gives the first definitive estimates on fall-out during a period of intensive nuclear testing by the United States and the Soviet Union.

It attempts no evaluation of the hazard to health posed by the steadily increasing accumulation of radioactive strontium in New York and most places in the Northern Hemisphere. The concentration of strontium 90 in such important food products as milk, however, is still far below danger levels set by the National Committee on Radiation Protection.

As could be expected from the large number of nuclear and hydrogen bombs exploded by the Soviet Union and the United States last spring and summer, fall-out continued to show a steady upward trend.

Although the two countries have halted atomic testing, at least temporarily, fall-out levels can be expected to increase, since much long-lived radioactive debris from hydrogen-bomb tests is blasted into the stratosphere and only gradually falls back to earth over a period of several years.

How much the United States and the Soviet Union individually have contributed to the increasing amount of fall-out was not indicated in the report. Commission officials said, however, that the Soviet contribution in the last year had been far greater than that of the United States.

Dr. Willard F. Libby, commission member, described the Soviet series this year as the "biggest" held in that country. He spoke of "a considerable number of substantial shots."

Because of uncertainties in judging the magnitude of the Soviet shots, Dr. Libby noted, it is impossible to say definitely that the Soviet series created

Continued on Page 10, Column 5

Red China Faces High Hurdles But Meets '59 as Going Concern

By TILLMAN DURDIN
Special to The New York Times.

HONG KONG, Dec. 28—Most knowledgeable observers here believe that Communist China faces the coming year as very much a going concern.

However, it is recognized that Communist China, like every other country in the world, including the United States, is having difficulties.

Consolidating China's new system of communes will be a long and tough process. Keeping the Chinese people working at maximum exertion for another year of big "leap forward" production targets will be hard to accomplish without aggravating the already existing weariness and discontent.

Operating an increasingly complex and highly centralized economic machine incorporating [illegible] before will tax the country's leadership and bureaucracy to the utmost.

However, on the basis of information available here, the Peiping Government seems capable of coping with its problems and achieving in 1959 new economic, social and political objectives.

The experts here who make this assessment hasten to add that no predictions on Communist China can be solidly based, because of the secrecy of the Peiping regime.

The biggest task of 1959 on the Communist-held mainland will undoubtedly be to make the new communes work. These new units merge groups of collective farms into large organizations that combine agriculture, industry, trade, education and mili-

Continued on Page 8, Column 3

New State and City Taxes Loom As Rockefeller's Biggest Woes

Special to The New York Times

ALBANY, Dec. 28—Nelson A. Rockefeller is to be inaugurated as Governor of New York on Thursday and will immediately face several difficult problems. At the same time he will cast a long shadow over both state and national politics.

The most pressing problem confronting the new Republican Governor when he replaces Averell Harriman, a Democrat, involves state and New York City finances. He will be called upon to impose or authorize more new taxes than any Governor in history.

Advance estimates are that the state will have to raise upward of $220,000,000 more than under the present tax structure to meet its needs in the new fiscal year, which starts April [illegible] consideration are a 2-cent increase in the gasoline tax, now 4 cents a gallon, with comparable increases in the Diesel fuel tax, and a 1-cent increase in the cigarette tax, now 3 cents a package.

In addition the new Governor and Republican-controlled Legislature will be called upon to authorize Mayor Wagner's Democratic Administration in New York City to impose new taxes capable of producing at least $135,000,000 to balance the next city budget. The chief measure under consideration is a 1 per cent increase in the sales tax, now 3 per cent.

For the state a combination of gasoline and cigarette tax increases would produce nearly $[illegible]00,000, covering less than half of the deficit Mr. Rockefeller has indicated was in sight.

Continued on Page 13, Column 4

Colts Defeat Giants for Football Championship in Sudden-Death Overtime

PLUNGE BY AMECHE DECIDES, 23 TO 17

64,185 Fans at Stadium See Colts Win After Gaining Tie at 14:53 of Fourth

Continued From Page 1, Col. 5

championship play-off records. And votes would not be difficult to get for Lenny Moore, L. G. Dupre, Jim Mutscheller and members of Baltimore's defensive unit.

The Giants, too, had their share of standouts in what was easily the most dramatic, most exciting encounter witnessed on the pro circuit in many a season.

Some voiced the opinion that it was the "greatest game I've even seen." Among those who expressed that sentiment was Bert Bell, the commissioner of the N.F.L.

Each side had its ups and downs. The Giants, after it appeared that they had fumbled away their chance for the championship, stormed back from a 14-3 deficit at the half. With the 37-year-old Charley Conerly turning in a magnificent job of passing and quarterbacking the New Yorkers made an almost incredible comeback.

Triplett Goes Over.

Mel Triplett scored on a dive play from the 1 for the Giants' third-period touchdown. A 15-yard aerial from Conerly to Frank Gifford accounted for the touchdown that moved the Giants ahead early in the fourth quarter.

It was fitting that Gifford recorded the 6-pointer. Two fumbles by Gifford were recovered by the Colts and led to two Baltimore touchdowns earlier in the game.

To report that the Giants were unimpressive while the favored Colts were taking charge during the first half would be an understatement.

The outlook did not become brighter immediately after the intermission, either. The Colts, with Unitas hitting receivers with amazing regularity, moved to the 1-yard line and it seemed that Cinderella was about to be chased out of the park.

Something had to happen—fast. It did. The New Yorkers won nearly everyone's admiration with a wonderful goal-line stand. Cliff Livingston, on fourth down, dropped Ameche on the 5 and the fine effort of the defense seemed to ignite a fire under the local offensive unit.

Gifford plunged for 5 and Alex Webster for 3. Then occurred a big play. Conerly clicked with a long pass to Kyle Rote, who gained 62 yards before he fumbled on the 25. There Webster scooped up the ball and raced to the 1, where Carl Taseff forced him out of bounds. It was then that Triplett scored. Pat Summerall, who had booted a 36-yard field goal in the opening quarter, converted for the first of his two extra points.

Conerly's Passes Click.

Early in the fourth period, a pass from Conerly to Bob Schnelker was good for 46 yards. Then Conerly fired to Gifford, who carried Baltimore's Milt Davis over on his back. Summerall added the point and the Giants were on top, 17—14.

Along about this time the Colts might have been regretting their decision to pass up a virtually certain field goal, before the Giants had made their inspired goal-line stand. But there was a job to be done and Unitas went about his chores calmly and effectively. His passes carried the Colts to the 38, where Bert Rechichar's attempt for a field goal was short.

Later a fumble by Phil King allowed the Colts another opening and they advanced to the 27. There, however, Andy Robustelli and Jim Katcavage did yeoman work in throwing Unitas for successive big losses and it appeared that the Giants were home free.

But the Colt defense stopped the Giants. On third down, Gifford's run was a foot short of a first down. Don Chandler had to punt and the Colts took over on their 14-yard line.

When the visitors put the ball in play they were 86 yards from the goal. They had 1 minute 56 seconds to go the distance. Unitas missed with a toss to Dupre, losing four seconds. Then he hit Moore with an 11-yarder at the cost of twenty-two seconds.

Another aerial failed, but the next, to Berry, was good for 25 yards. Then, twice in succession, it was Unitas to Berry for 16 and 21 yards. Suddenly the Colts were on the 13-yard line.

The seconds continued to tick away. When Myhra put his toe to the ball on the 20 and sent the ball between the uprights, only seven seconds remained.

That, of course, made it 17—17 and necessitated the sudden-death finish. The Giants won the toss and elected to receive. Again the Giants were held by the defense. On third down, Conerly's option run was inches short of a first down and Chandler punted to the Colts. That was the last time the Giants handled the ball.

Starting on the 20, the Colts drove 80 yards in thirteen plays. Unitas, the quarterback no one seemed to want several years ago, hit with four of five passes. At the 1, Unitas handed off to Ameche and The Horse rammed over the right side to the championship. There was no try for the extra point.

At one stage during the campaign the Giants trailed the Cleveland Browns by two games. Coach Jim Lee Howell's squad upset the Colts and the Browns in succession and wound up tied with the Browns for the Eastern Conference crown. They beat the Browns in a play-off and took their ninth division championship a month after the Colts had wrapped up their first Western Conference title. Baltimore is "west" because of the crazy-quilt geographic set-up in the N. F. L.

Each Colt earned a record $4,718.77 share yesterday. Each Giant share was worth $3,111.33, also a record.

The New York Times

Colts and Giants at Yankee Stadium

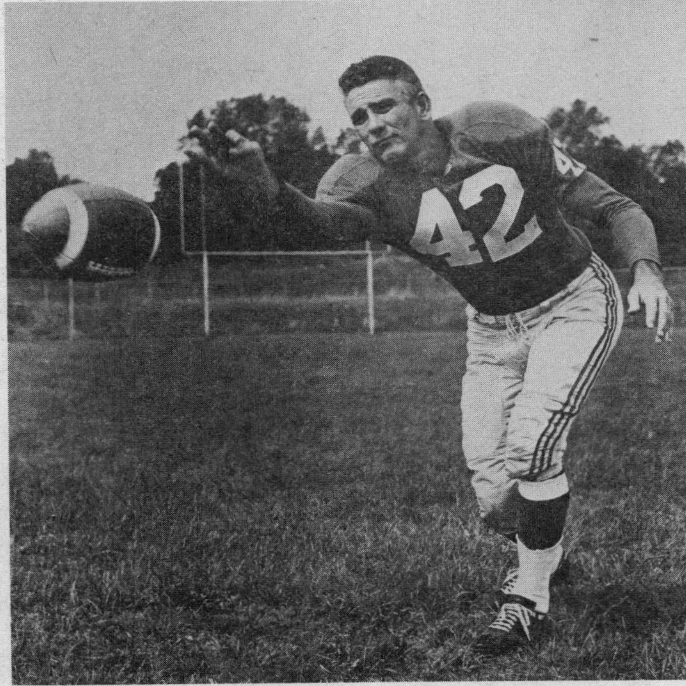

Charlie Conerly

Stadium Line-Up

BALTIMORE COLTS (23)

Left Ends—Berry, Marchetti, Braase.
Left Tackles—Parker, Donovan.
Left Guards—Spinney, Myhra, Thurston.
Centers—Nutter, Shinnick, Sanford.
Right Guards—Sandusky, Plunkett.
Right Tackles—Preas, Lipscomb, Krouse.
Right Ends—Mutscheller, Joyce.
Quarterbacks—Unitas, Shaw, Brown, Rechichar.
Left Halfbacks—Dupre, Taseff, Nelson, Simpson, Sample.
Right Halfbacks—Moore, Davis, DeCarlo, Call, Lyles.
Fullbacks—Ameche, Pellington, Pricer.

NEW YORK GIANTS (17)

Left Ends—Rote, Katcavage, Livingston, Summerall.
Left Tackles—Brown, Modzelewski.
Left Guards—Barry, Brackett.
Centers—Wietecha, Huff.
Right Guards—Mischak, Guy.
Right Tackles—Youso, Grier, Stroud.
Right Ends—Schnelker, MacAfee, Robustelli, Svare.
Quarterbacks—Heinrich, Conerly, Tunnell.
Left Halfbacks—Gifford, Maynard, Crow, Hughes, Lott.
Right Halfbacks—Webster, Patton, Karilivacz, King.
Fullbacks—Triplett, Svoboda, Chandler.

Baltimore Colts	0	14	0	3	6—23
New York Giants	3	0	7	7	0—17

Baltimore Scoring—Touchdowns: Ameche 2 (2, 1, plunges), Berry (15, pass from Unitas). Conversions: Myhra 2. Field goal: Myhra (20).

New York Scoring—Touchdowns: Triplett (1, plunge), Gifford (15, pass from Conerly). Conversions: Summerall 2. Field goal: Summerall (36).

Referee—Ronald Gibbs, St. Thomas. Umpire—Louis Palazzi, Penn State. Head Linesman—Charles F. Berry, Lafayette. Back Judge—Cleo N. Diehl, Northwestern. Field Judge—Charles Sweeney, Notre Dame.

STATISTICS OF THE GAME

	Colts	Giants
First downs	27	10
Rushing yardage	138	88
Passing yardage	322	178
Passes attempted	40	18
Passes completed	26	12
Passes intercepted by	0	1
Punts	4	6
Av. dist. of punts, yds.	51	48
Fumbles lost	2	4
Yards penalized	62	52

BALTIMORE COACH NETTLED BY HUFF

Ewbank Says Giants' Guard Set Off Sideline Scuffle by Kneeing One of Colts

By GORDON S. WHITE JR.

World champion players shouted and jumped and whooped it up in the Baltimore Colt dressing room after yesterday's victory. During the din, Coach Weeb Ewbank, who speaks only sparingly to newsmen, was trying his best to yell answers.

A few comments such as "They've always been a come-from-behind team this year so I didn't worry much," and "We changed our attack to meet the Giants' personnel and that was all," could be heard from the little man who directs the Colts.

He praised all the players, shook hands with all the visitors and frowned only when asked whether he had taken a punch at Sam Huff during a sideline squabble in the first half.

Then the frown became a smile and Ewbank said, "We all pushed him. That guy should have been thrown out of the ball game."

A Tangle and a Scuffle

Huff and a number of Baltimore players had got tangled on a play that finished out of bounds near the Colts' bench. There was a scuffle and it was apparent that Ewbank had swung at Huff.

"Huff kneed one of my men out of bounds and he should have gotten thrown out," the Baltimore coach said.

It took spunk for Ewbank to aim one at Huff. The Giant guard, at 230, outweighs Ewbank by at least 80 pounds.

Ewbank and John Unitas, the Colts' quarterback, said that neither considered a field goal attempt when the Colts were on the Giants' one with four downs to try for a score in the third period. Their failure to score at the time loomed large until the Colts tied, and then won in overtime.

The coach and quarterback said they had passed up 3 points then because only twice during the season had the Colts failed to score from inside the 10. Both failures were against the Giants in a regular league game last month.

The only upsetting note for the Colts was the injury to Gino Marchetti, an end. The Colts' physician, Dr. Erwin Mayer, said, "Marchetti probably suffered a fractured right ankle. We're taking him back to Baltimore with us and he'll be X-rayed at Baltimore Memorial Hospital tomorrow."

Marchetti was injured in the final minutes of the fourth period. He was carried off the field on a stretcher and a cast was put on the right leg.

Steve Myhra, whose field goal tied the game in the last few seconds of regulation play, said he was "really only worried about a good snap from center so I could get a fair chance at the goal."

Section 5 | SPORTS | SHOPPING GUIDE

The New York Times.

SPORTS | AUTOMOBILES—BOATS | Section 5

SUNDAY JUNE 19, 1960. L+++ S

PALMER'S 280 TAKES U. S. OPEN GOLF BY TWO STROKES; YANKS BEAT WHITE SOX, 12-5; CALIFORNIA CREW VICTOR

MARIS HITS NO. 19

Mantle, Skowron Also Connect—Yankees Go Into First Place

By LOUIS EFFRAT

Special to The New York Times.

CHICAGO, June 18 — When the Yankees left New York last Sunday night, they were determined to be alone in first place by Father's Day. With hours, runs and base-hits to spare, they achieved their objective today.

They mistreated Early Wynn, Bob Rush and other White Sox hurlers in posting a 12-5 victory before a Ladies' Day crowd of 34,640 at Comiskey Park.

Without resorting to any stunts, such as sparklers, dug-out dances or bullpen blowouts, Casey Stengel's men did it like the champions they used to be —they slugged their way to the top with a 19-hit offensive that included homers by Mickey Mantle (No. 14), Roger Maris (No. 19) and Moose Skowron (No. 8). It was the most hits collected by the Bombers in a game this year.

As a result of today's action here and at Detroit, the American League standing shows New York on top by 2 percentage points, although a half-game behind Baltimore, which has played seven more games than the Bombers.

Bob Turley started for the visitors, failed to find a quick 4-0 lead sufficient and made way for Eli Grba. The young man with an aversion for vowels worked the last six innings. He yielded three hits and was credited with the victory. It was his first outing since his recent recall from Richmond in the International League.

Two Bombers Draw Walks

Wynn had himself, Yogi Berra and Skowron to blame for dropping behind in the first inning. Tony Kubek and Hector Lopez posed no problems for the venerable hurler, but the appearance of Mantle and Maris affected Wynn's control and he lost both on passes. Then Berra worked the count to 2-and-2, and lined a single to right center.

That made it easy for Mantle to score and for Maris to race to third. Up stepped Skowron, who saw to it that the racing continued. He lashed a double to right center, and in less time than it takes to describe it, the Yankees enjoyed a 3-0 bulge.

Two fine defensive plays by Luis Aparicio and Nellie Fox helped Wynn immeasurably in the second, after Bobby Richardson had let off with a single to left. Turley's slow roller to short may have embarrassed another shortstop, but the speedy Aparicio charged in and threw out Turley, with Richardson moving to second.

When Kubek rifled a sizzling grounder to the right side, apparently headed for a hit, Fox scampered over and grabbed it.

Continued on Page 3, Column 4

Rigney Out, Sheehan Named

Giants, Under New Manager, Defeat Phillies, 7 to 4

By United Press International.

SAN FRANCISCO, June 18—Bill Rigney was released as manager of the Giants today and replaced by Tom Sheehan, who went out ninety minutes later and directed the team to a 7-4 victory over the Philadelphia Phillies.

The 66-year-old Sheehan is a former minor league manager. Horace Stoneham, the president of the San Francisco club, said that Sheehan would run the team for "two or three weeks, or possibly for the rest of the year."

The 41-year-old Rigney was in his fifth year at the helm, and Stoneham had expected him to bring home a winner this year.

"But we had to make the change now before it was too late," said Stoneham. "I was afraid that if I waited until next week, the way the team is going, we would drop back to the place where he couldn't regain first place.

"The decision was a hard one to make," the Giants' owner continued. "On the surface it looks like a criticism of Rigney, which it isn't. Either the club's not as good as we thought it was, which we don't think is true, or it's a good club that couldn't get inspired. I'm sure all the players liked Rigney."

The Giants started the campaign well, and were only one game out of first place when they opened a three-game series with Pittsburgh earlier this week. But the Pirates swept the series and increased their National League lead to four

Continued on Page 3, Column 6

United Press International Telephoto

Bill Rigney, left, deposed as manager of the Giants, offers best wishes to Tom Sheehan, named as interim manager.

NAVY EIGHT NEXT

California Scores in College Rowing by $1\frac{1}{4}$ Lengths

By MICHAEL STRAUSS

Special to The New York Times.

SYRACUSE, June 18—Starting slowly as if it wanted to see what the opposition offered, California settled down to business and scored a stirring triumph in the Intercollegiate Rowing Association regatta today.

The victory was the first by a Bear varsity in the I. R. A. since a powerful California eight won from Washington at Poughkeepsie in 1949. The famed Carroll (Ky) Ebright was the coach.

Ebright, however, retired last July after thirty-five years and one of his proteges, Jim Lemmon, replaced him. As a result, those close to the rowing scene were not sure what to expect from California this season.

This afternoon, Lemmon's charges showed he had done his job well. Boasting six victories in seven previous outings, the Bears posted their most important triumph in winning by a length and a quarter.

Navy finished second and Washington was third, only four-tenths of a second behind the middies. The rest of the twelve-boat fleet was strung out on Onondaga Lake.

Brown Crew Fourth

The race, witnessed by a crowd estimated at 15,000, was filled with unexpected developments. Brown, competing in the regatta for the first time, was fourth. Rowing is not even a recognized varsity sport at the Providence University.

Cornell and Pennsylvania, the pre-regatta favorites, were disappointments. Both eights faded badly in the closing stages and finished in a dead heat for fifth, about two lengths behnd the Bruins.

The Big Red's chances for a creditable finish went a glimmering when Bob Simpson, its sophomore stroke, stopped rowing 450 yards from home. Simpson, who apparently fainted, resumed stroking some 300 yards later, but by that time the issue had been resolved.

There was no official decision on the clockings and margins below third place in this fifty-eighth I. R. A. regatta. Because of confusion on the barge at the finish line, erroneous times were "unofficially" announced immediately after the race. These were retracted almost immediately.

However, the officials had to view films of the finish before the placings were final. Even at that, no times were given for the finishes below third place.

The finish involving Washing-

Continued on Page 7, Column 1

Associated Press Wirephotos

MOMENT OF VICTORY: Arnold Palmer jumps for joy on sinking final putt to win the U. S. Open golf championship.

NICKLAUS SECOND

Amateur Posts 282—6 Pros Tie at 283—Souchak Falters

By LINCOLN A. WERDEN

Special to The New York Times.

DENVER, June 18—Golf's man of steel won the United States Open championship today.

Refusing to concede defeat when he trailed by seven strokes going into the final round, Arnold Palmer scored an incredible closing 65 for the greatest winning finish anyone has made in the game's top tournament.

While thousands cheered him at the Cherry Hills Country Club, the 30-year-old Ligonier (Pa.) professional brought his 72-hole total to 280. He won by two strokes.

In a dramatic fourth round, Palmer played the first nine holes in 30. That equaled the Open record set by Jimmy McHale, a Philadelphia amateur, in 1947. It also turned Palmer from an also-ran into a challenger. Palmer started the round with four straight birdie 3's.

A tremendous bid by 20-year-old Jack Nicklaus, the National Amateur titleholder from Columbus, Ohio, fell just short. Nicklaus finished with a par 71 for 282 and runner-up laurels.

No amateur since Johnny Goodman in 1933 has carried off this title. But the score by Nicklaus, an Ohio State University junior, is the lowest ever by an amateur, including Bob Jones, in this championship.

Souchak Finishes at 283

Six pros tied for third place at 283. They were Mike Souchak, Dutch Harrison, Julius Boros, Dow Finsterwald, Jack Fleck and Ted Kroll. Souchak led for the first three rounds but took a 75 for the final 18-hole tour.

At 284 were Ben Hogan, Jerry Barber and Don Cherry, an amateur. Bill Casper Jr., the defender, finished at 286 with George Bayer and Paul Harney.

Nicklaus was caught in the midst of tremendous interest because his playing partner on the last two rounds was Hogan. The 47-year-old Texan made his bid when Souchak started to falter.

Hogan reached the brink of a fifth championship, a feat never achieved in this tournament. But the seventy-first and seventy-second holes smashed his fondest hopes.

Hogan was 4 under par until then. But he slipped to a 6 and 7 on these holes for a 73.

At the moat-hole seventeenth Hogan tried valiantly for a par 5. His third shot fell close to the edge of the water guarding the green. Hogan took off his right shoe and sock, stood in the water and splashed the ball to within 18 feet of the pin. He two-putted for a 6.

Hogan Drives Into Lake

With excited spectators lining the eighteenth, where the lake borders the fairway on the left, Nicklaus drove into the rough on the right. Hogan, intending to put the ball in position on a level part of the fairway, hooked it the least bit. It fell into the lake.

Hogan hit another ball. His subsequent approach fell short below the crest of the green. After he chipped 4 feet by the

Continued on Page 5, Column 1

Hansgen's Maserati First In Cup Race at Westbury

By FRANK M. BLUNK

Special to The New York Times.

WESTBURY, L. I., June 18—Walter Hansgen of Westfield, N. J., drove his birdcage Maserati to an easy victory today in the Capt. Eddie Rickenbacker Trophy race. The event was the first-day feature of a series that will be capped by tomorrow's Vanderbilt Cup race for Formula Junior cars.

A crowd of 22,000 watched the first day of racing on the new mile-and-a-half track laid out on the vast parking area adjacent to the famous Roosevelt Raceway harness racing plant. Many of the nation's top drivers competed in the program that marked the return of big-time automobile racing to Long Island.

Hansgen, a two-time American sports car champion, moved ahead in the first 200 yards of the twenty-lap Rickenbacker Trophy race. His closest pursuers for the first four laps were George Cons[illegible]ine of South-Bridge, Mass., in a Chevrolet-powered Special, and Charles Kolb of Silver Spring, Md., in a Cooper Monaco owned by Charles Kreisler of New York.

Plaisted's Car Second

John Plaisted of Lynnfield Center, Mass., moved ahead of Kolb on the fifth lap and began battling with Constantine for second place. He passed Constantine, then lost the place to him again. Finally Plaisted took the runner-up spot and held it all the way.

Constantine was forced out by a broken drive shaft on the eighteenth lap, and Kolb moved into third place to stay.

In winning from thirteen rivals, Hansgen averaged 73.6 miles an hour, the fastest speed on the day's program.

The Rickenbacker Trophy was presented to Hansgen by Dav[illegible]l Rickenbacker, son of the former

Continued on Page 8, Column 2

HOMER BY TIGERS SINKS ORIOLES, 5-3

Maxwell Connects With Two On in Sixth Inning for His Second of Game

By The Associated Press.

DETROIT, June 18—Charlie Maxwell, after twice fouling off bunts in attempting to move two runners along, belted a home run that lifted the Detroit Tigers to a 5-3 victory over the Baltimore Orioles today.

The Tigers collected only five hits, but three of them were home runs.

Maxwell hit two. His first was off Chuck Estrada in the first inning. His game-winning smash in the sixth was off Billy Hoeft.

Estrada walked the first two batters in the sixth and had a 2-0 count on Maxwell when Hoeft was summoned. Maxwell fouled off two bunt tries and worked the count to 3—2 before socking his tenth home run of

Continued on Page 3, Column 7

MOSS HURT IN SPILL AT BELGIAN TRIALS

Driving at 120 M.P.H. When Wheel Falls Off—Taylor Injured in 2d Accident

By ROBERT DALEY

Special to The New York Times.

FRANCORCHAMPS, Belgium, June 18—Stirling Moss, the fastest Grand Prix race driver in the world and the favorite for tomorrow's Grand Prix of Belgium here, lost control of his Lotus in practice today, spun off the road and crashed at about 120 miles an hour.

In another accident, Mike Taylor, a British compatriot of Moss', apparently escaped serious injury when his Lotus overturned. Moss was in the hospital tonight at Malmedy, one of the towns bordering this circuit. He has three broken ribs, a broken nose and possible internal injuries.

His father, Dr. Alfred Moss, said that Stirling also had fractured both knees.

Dr. Edmond Colette reported that the 30-year-old Moss did not appear in immediate danger, but that judgment would be reserved for forty-eight hours. Moss' pulse and blood pressure were normal and he was conscious.

The 8.3-mile circuit here,

Continued on Page 8, Column 3

Harvard Conquers Yale in Three Races For Regatta Sweep

By GORDON S. WHITE Jr.

Special to The New York Times.

NEW LONDON, Conn., June 18 — Harvard's mighty eight-oared crews swept a three-race regatta with Yale on the Thames today. The Crimson varsity scored a seven-length triumph in the classic test of four miles.

Harvard's varsity, rated the nation's best and a possible Olympic winner at the start of the season, had lost some of its sheen by suffering two late-season defeats, but the victory over the Yale eight was so convincing that Harvard is going to the Olympic trials next month.

Coach Harvey Love's charges from Cambridge, Mass., made it a winning effort from the start in Bartlett's Cove. Harvard's big crew moved slightly in front at the beginning and built a commanding lead after two miles. Yale had no chance to catch the skimming Crimson.

Harvard's junior varsity and freshmen crews also took decisions in races they led all the way.

For the Harvard heavyweight

Continued on Page 8, Column 7

AMBER MORN, 16-1, WINS AT BELMONT

Defeats Dunce by a Neck in $59,400 Bowling Green With Stretch Drive

By WILLIAM R. CONKLIN

Under an outstanding ride by Pete Anderson, the Ken-Love Farm's 16-1 shot, Amber Morn, finished on the rail at Belmont yesterday and won the $59,400 Bowling Green Handicap by a neck from Dunce.

For a turf race of a mile and a half, the finish was as tight as could be. Going around the last turn, Anderson drove Amber Mount through on the rail and held the inside to the finish. His tactic made the difference, for Larry Adams had to take Dunce to the outside.

Dunce, owned by the Claiborne Farm, had a neck on the third finisher, John S. Kroese's North Pole II. Ridden by Henry Moreno, a last-minute choice, North Pole II closed stoutly in depriving F. Ambrose Clark's Han-

Continued on Page 4, Column 2

Major League Baseball

Sunday, June 19, 1960

American League

YESTERDAY'S GAMES

New York 12, Chicago 5.
Cleveland 2, Boston 1.
Detroit 5, Baltimore 3.
Washington 7, Kansas City 2 (night).

STANDING OF THE CLUBS

	New York	Baltimore	Cleveland	Detroit	Chicago	Washington	Kan. City	Boston	Won	Lost	Percentage	Games Behind
N. Y.	—	5	3	2	5	5	6	5	31	22	.585	½
*Balt	6	—	5	2	4	5	5	8	35	25	.583	—
Cleve	3	3	—	4	4	3	6	7	30	23	.566	1½
Det.	2	6	6	—	4	5	2	4	29	25	.537	3
Chic.	4	1	4	4	—	5	8	4	30	27	.526	3½
Wash	3	4	2	3	2	—	5	5	24	30	.444	8
K. C.	1	5	2	7	4	2	—	2	23	34	.404	10½
Bost.	3	1	1	3	4	5	2	—	19	35	.352	13
Lost	22	25	23	25	27	30	34	35	—	—		

*Games behind based on Baltimore.

National League

YESTERDAY'S GAMES

Cincinnati 7, Chicago 1.
Milwaukee 5, St. Louis 0.
San Fran. 7, Philadelphia 4.
Pittsburgh 4, Los Angeles 3 (10 innings, night).

STANDING OF THE CLUBS

	Pittsburgh	San Fran.	Milwaukee	St. Louis	Cincinnati	L. Angeles	Chicago	Philadel.	Won	Lost	Percentage	Games Behind
Pitts.	—	5	7	3	7	4	4	7	37	20	.649	—
S. F.	4	—	3	6	2	5	6	8	34	25	.576	4
Milw.	2	3	—	5	6	3	4	6	29	22	.569	5
St. L.	4	5	1	—	6	5	4	3	28	29	.491	9
Cinc.	1	5	4	4	—	5	3	5	27	31	.466	10½
L. A.	4	3	3	4	2	—	6	4	26	31	.456	11
Chic.	2	4	2	4	2	5	—	4	23	29	.442	11½
Phila.	3	0	2	3	6	4	2	—	20	37	.351	17
Lost	20	25	22	29	31	31	29	37	—	—		

TODAY'S PROBABLE PITCHERS

New York at Chicago (2)—Coates (7-0) and Terry (3-2) vs. Shaw (5-5) and Baumann (3-3) or Kemmerer (3-3).

Baltimore at Detroit (2)—Wilhelm (3-4) and Pappas (4-5) vs. Mossi (3-4) and Bunning (4-3).

Boston at Cleveland (2)—Brewer (4-6) and Monbouquette (5-6) vs. Bell (6-5) and Perry (7-2).

Washington at Kansas City—Lee (2-1) vs. Kucks (1-1) or Trowbridge (1-2).

Chicago at Cincinnati (2)—Hobbie (6-7) and Ellsworth (3-3) vs. O'Toole (4-6) and McLish (2-4).

Philadelphia at San Francisco—Roberts (2-7) vs. Antonelli (3-4).

Pittsburgh at Los Angeles—Daniels (1-2) vs. Koufax (2-8).

St. Louis at Milwaukee (2)—Sadecki (1-2) and Simmons (0-0) vs. Spahn (4-3) and Willey (3-3).

(Figures in parentheses indicate season's won-and-lost records.)

Pirates Turn Back Dodgers in 10th, 4-3

By United Press International.

LOS ANGELES, June 18—The league-leading Pittsburgh Pirates rallied on the slugging of two catchers, Hal Smith and Smokey Burgess to beat the Los Angeles Dodgers, 4—3, tonight before a Coliseum turnout of 63,699.

The game-winning run came in the tenth inning after the Pirates had rallied for three runs to tie the score, 3-3, in the ninth.

Smith lined a two-out home run into the left-field seats against Danny McDevitt in the ninth inning. Then Burgess came up in a pinch-hit role against Larry Sherry and singled to left, scoring Don Hoak from second base with the tying run.

It was Smith again in the tenth who supplied the big blow. His single beyond the out-

Continued on Page 6, Column 2

Ten N. C. A. A. Track Meet Records Tumble

Kansas Team Keeps Crown as Tidwell Scores Double

By JOSEPH M. SHEEHAN

Special to The New York Times.

BERKELEY, Calif., June 18—Ten meet records were broken and another was tied today as the varsity aspirants for berths on the United States Olympic team concluded their two-day exercises in the thirty-ninth National Collegiate track and field championships.

To the surprise of local railbirds, who had expected Southern California to resume its domination, the University of Kansas retained the team crown. Coach Bill Easton's Jayhawks, who had four individual winners, piled up 50 points.

The Trojans scored 37 points.

Foreign athletes who will be competing under other banners at Rome took three titles with record performances. However, there were ample grounds for encouragement to Larry Snyder of Ohio State and his associates of the United States Olympic coaching staff.

On the track, the resident record-breakers were Ted Woods of Colorado, who ran 400 meters around two turns in 0:45.7; Dyrol Burleson of Oregon, who captured the 1,500 meters in 3:44.2 (equivalent to a 4:01.2 mile), and Charlie Clark of San Jose State, who lowered the 3,000-meter steeplechase standard to 9:01.1. All are sophomores.

In the field, John Thomas of Boston University high-jumped 7 feet and Bill Alley of Kansas improved his qualifying javelin mark of yesterday to 268 feet 9 inches. Dallas Long of Southern California set a shot-put record of 61 feet 9 inches in Friday's trials and Luther Hayes of Southern California established a hop, step and jump mark of 50 feet 11½ inches.

Associated Press Wirephoto

Jim Moreland of Brown, his knee injured on a previous hurdle, halts in pain in N.C.A.A. 400-meter semi-finals.

Burleson, Thomas, Alley Set Marks—Kerr Also Victor

In addition, Charlie Tidwell of Kansas, the meet's only double winner, tied the meet 100-meter dash record of 0:10.2, a mark equaled by Paul Winder of Morgan State in the semi-finals. Tidwell later captured the 200-meter dash in 0:20.8.

Perhaps the top performance of the day, from the Olympic point of view, was the 1:46.4 clocking of George Kerr of Illinois (and Jamaica, B. W. I.) in retaining the 800-meter title. It was the fastest time in the world this year.

Al Lawrence of Houston (and Australia) set a 5,000-meter record of 14:19.8 in a runaway from native competition. John Lawlor of Boston University (and Eire) improved his 1959 hammer-throw mark to 209 feet 2 inches.

The 800-meter run was the competitive highlight of the day to the 13,750 railbirds who looked on in bright, nearly windless 70-degree weather at the University of California's handsome Edwards Stadium, one of the few arenas specifically designed for track.

Gritty Ernie Cunliffe of Stanford set out to run the sting out of Kerr's dreaded

Continued on Page 6, Column 5

Mrs. Mason Downs Mrs. Cudone in Final

By WILLIAM J. BRIORDY

Special to The New York Times.

STONY BROOK, L. I., June 18—Mrs. Marge Mason of Ridgewood, N. J., won the Women's Metropolitan Golf Association championship today over the 5,843 yard par-71 St. George's Golf and Country Club course.

In the thirty-six-hole final, Mrs. Mason beat Mrs. Philip Cudone of Forest Hill Field Club, 3 and 2.

Mrs. Mason called upon her superior chipping and putting against her long-hitting rival to gain a prize she had long coveted. Mrs. Mason beat Maureen Orcutt, the 1959 winner, in the semi-finals.

In a reversal of form, Mrs. Mason rallied from 2-down at the end of the twenty-fifth hole and went up for the first time

Continued on Page 5, Column 5

Palmer Wins U. S. Open by Two Strokes With 65

NICKLAUS SECOND AND SIX TIE AT 283

Palmer Starts Final Round With Four Straight Birdie 3's as Souchak Falters

Continued From Page 1

pin, Hogan failed to sink his first putt. He ended with a 7.

Playing back of Nicklaus and Hogan, Palmer learned what was happening ahead and adhered to pars on the last four holes for the victory. It brought to him a first prize of $14,400.

One by one, the others among ten players who were within two strokes of each other with nine holes to go saw their chances fade. None faded quite as badly, however, as Souchak, who had a seven-stroke advantage over Palmer beginning the fourth round.

Camera Upsets Souchak

Souchak was upset this morning at the eighteenth when an amateur camera man started taking movies just as Mike was on the backswing of his drive. Startled by the noise, Souchak drove the ball out of bounds and took a 6 for a 73.

A par 4 would have made a big diference. But Souchak, who had a 68 and 67 in the earlier rounds, was still the leader by two strokes after the morning round.

"I would have had a four-stroke lead if it weren't for that 6 this morning," Souchak said. But his last round of 75 was even more disappointing to him.

Souchak was off to a bad start in the afternoon and never regained his stride of previous rounds. He used a driver instead of a No. 4 wood on the first hole and knocked the ball into the meandering creek on the right, which cost him a penalty stroke.

He had an unplayable lie at the ninth as he hooked a drive into a pine tree. This, too, resulted in a 5. At that, he was out in 36.

But the race had tightened at this stage of the championship. Souchak's score then was 244. Nicklaus had 243, Fleck 244, Hogan 245, Palmer 245, Boros 245, Finsterwald 246, Barber 246 and Cherry 246.

Souchak Drops Back

Then "everything happened," as Souchak put it later.

The ex-football end from Duke went over par when Palmer was making his bid. Souchak, who tied for third in the 1959 Open, dropped back.

The chief trouble came at the short twelfth, where Souchak dropped his tee shot into the pond for a 5. And he three-putted for a 5 at the seventy-second green.

Palmer is a determined fellow on a golf course. He is the son of a professional and grew up in a golfing atmosphere.

After winning the Masters in April, he said his goal this year would be to win here, the British Open and the Professional Golfers Association championship. Those who know him think that the task is not necessarily too big for Palmer.

Palmer was confident as he drove the first green and started his string of birdies. He had thirteen birdies in earlier rounds of 72, 71 and 72 and bagged seven more in the final eighteen holes.

'I Never Lost My Desire'

"I never lost my desire to win here. But you must have the breaks, too," Palmer said after he had won.

The turn of the tide, he said, came at the second hole. There, he chipped in from about 30 feet for a birdie.

This acted as a spur, he said, and on he went, "fired up." A putt of less than a yard went in for a 3 at the third. A 20-footer for a 3 followed at the fourth. Then came a par 5 at the fifth.

"I hit a No. 7 iron to within 25 feet of the pin at the sixth and sank it. That was sweet," Palmer said.

At the seventh hole, Palmer dropped a 6-footer for a birdie 3. He was trapped at the short eighth, blasted from the sand and took two putts for a 4. This was the only time he went over par. Palmer hit over the ninth green with a No. 6 iron, pitched to about 8 feet away and got a 4 for his 30.

A par followed at the tenth. Then, with a drive and a No. 4 iron, he reached the green at the 563-yard eleventh. Two putts there resulted in a birdie 4.

Pars the Rest of the Way

At the twelfth, where Souchak had trouble, Palmer two-putted for a par 3. He got pars the rest of the way for an incoming 35.

Palmer drove with a No. 1 iron at the eighteenth, where Hogan had met disaster earlier. Palmer was safe and with a No. 4 iron was 80 feet to the left of the pin on his second. He chipped to within a yard and ran in the putt for a 4.

The only other closing rush to the title that approached Palmer's was a 66 by Gene Sarazen as he triumphed in 1932 at Fresh Meadow.

Palmer, who attended Wake Forest College, won the National Amateur in 1954 and subsequently joined the pro ranks, a life-long ambition. This was his eighth appearance in the Open championship. He tied for fifth in his best previous performance last year at Winged Foot.

Players Seek the Elusive Open Golf Championship

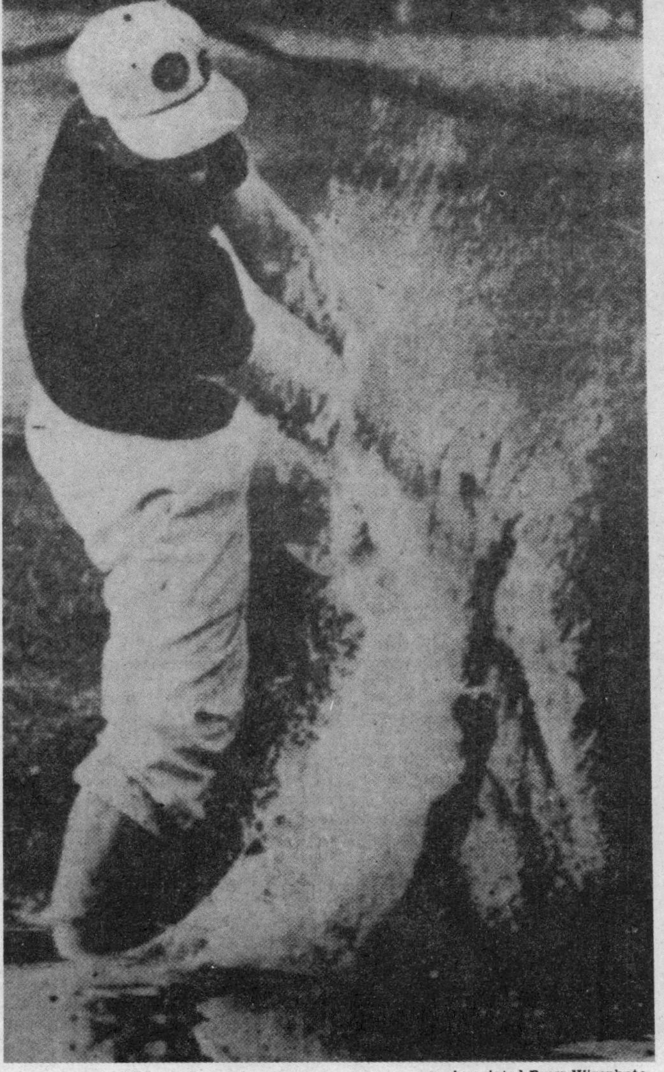

Associated Press Wirephoto

Bob Hill of Webster, N. Y., sends up a small geyser as he tries to lift ball from hazard to the seventeenth green.

United Press International Telephoto

Jack Fleck of Los Angeles is forced to shoot from the rough on fourth hole of the U. S. Open, played at Denver.

MRS. MASON WINS LAURELS IN GOLF

Continued From Page 1

in the match at the twenty-ninth.

Both played top golf during the morning round, but Mrs. Cudone had an edge. Her putter was clicking. Mrs. Cudone, who won the Eastern championship last week, played so well that she was never over par.

Mrs. Mason, hitting strongly throughout, appeared to be steadier than ever. This helped her to win the metropolitan title for the second time. She also won in 1952 at the Upper Montclair course.

By beating Mrs. Cudone, Mrs. Mason gained revenge for her defeat in the final of the New Jersey State championship last year.

Mrs. Cudone went 1 up at the fifth hole when her opponent put her second shot into a trap. The match was squared on the short downhill seventh hole when Mrs. Mason won with a one-over-par 4 after both were in traps. That was the way the match stood at the ninth, with both players scoring a four-over-par 40.

Mrs. Cudone went 1 up again on the short eleventh with a par 3, when Mrs. Mason needed three putts from the edge. She took the twelfth and par and went 2 up.

However, the victor shot a birdie 4 on the downhill par 5 thirteenth and was only 1 down.

The next three holes were halved, but Mrs. Mason squared the match again on the short seventeenth when her opponent three-putted. Both got par 5's on the eighteenth, scoring two-over-par 37's for the second nine.

Starting out after lunch all even, Mrs. Cudone won the twentieth in par when Mrs. Mason missed her third shot to the par 5 hole. The next three holes were halved in par, but Mrs. Cudone went 2 up by sinking a long putt for a birdie 4 on the twenty-fourth.

This was the last time that Mrs. Cudone held the lead. When Mrs. Mason won the twenty-sixth and twenty-seventh holes in par figures to once again square the match, Mrs. Cudone appeared to lose her touch.

The turning point came on the short eleventh or twenty-ninth of the match. Mrs. Mason won this hole to go 1 up for the first time. She took a par 3 as her opponent required three shots from the edge.

After hitting a hooked second shot into trees on the downhill thirty-first hole, Mrs. Mason saved herself with a great third shot to the green.

The match ended on the thirty-third hole when Mrs. Cudone hooked her tee shot into the rough, was short with her second and reached the green in 3.

MRS. JOHNSTONE DOWNED IN GOLF

Mlle. Varangot Triumphs in Semi-Finals of French Tourney, 5 and 4

PARIS, June 18 (UPI) — Mrs. Ann Casey Johnstone of Mason City, Iowa, America's only representative in the French women's golf championship, was eliminated today in the semi-finals by Brigitte Varangot of France, 3 and 2.

Mrs. Johnstone, a member of the United States Curtis Cup team that defeated Britain's top women amateur golfers last month, had reached the semi-finals with a 5-and-4 victory over Mme. Philippe Eloy of France in the morning.

Mrs. Johnstone didn't get a chance to play a competitive round on the 6,367-yard St. Germain course until today because she drew a first-round bye and her second-round opponent failed to show up. She had no trouble ousting Mme Eloy, but her lack of familiarity with the links, particularly with the greens, hampered her in her match with Mlle. Varangot.

CORTAZZO SCORES ON JERSEY LINKS

Special to The New York Times.

RIDGEWOOD, N. J., June 18. —Frank Cortazzo, 41 years old, of Orchard Hills and William Anderson, 31, of Raritan Valley will meet tomorrow for the New Jersey amateur golf championship at the Ridgewood Country Club.

They gained the 36-hole final by winning semi-final matches today, Cortazzo with ease and Anderson after a hard struggle.

Cortazzo scored a 9-and-7 decision over Allen Werksman, a 26-year-old lawyer from Preakness Hills. Anderson withstood a late rally by Frank O'Brien, a 42-year-old Plainfield lawyer, and won, 1 up.

Cortazzo won five of the first seven holes on the first morning nine and maintained that margin to the end of the round.

Three birdies on the first nine in the afternoon lifted his lead to 8 up and he ended the match with a winning par on the twenty-ninth.

"All the News That's Fit to Print"

The New York Times.

LATE CITY EDITION
U. S. Weather Bureau Report (Page 66) forecasts: Fair and mild today and tonight. Partly cloudy, warmer tomorrow. Temp. range: 77—60; yesterday: 75.4—64.3. Temp.-Hum. Index: low 70s; yesterday, 71.

VOL. CIX. No. 37,404. NEW YORK, TUESDAY, JUNE 21, 1960. 10 cents beyond 50-mile zone from New York City except on Long Island. Higher in air delivery cities. FIVE CENTS

SENATE APPROVES YEAR EXTENSION OF EXCISE TAXES

Johnson Leads Fight to Save the Telephone, Telegraph and Travel Levies

ROLL-CALL VOTE 84-0

Repeal of the 4% Credit on Stock Dividends Passed by 42 to 41 Ballot

By RUSSELL BAKER
Special to The New York Times.

WASHINGTON, June 20—The Senate passed today a one-year extension of excise and corporate income taxes that bring in $4,000,000,000 a year in revenue. The vote was 84—0.

In a surprisingly strong uprising against election-year tax cuts, the Senate rejected its Finance Committee's proposals for repealing the 10 per cent tax on transportation and on telephone and telegraph service.

It also adopted three new provisions to close so-called loopholes in the basic tax laws. It was considered doubtful that the House would accept all of these.

Scope of Provisions

They would do the following:

¶End the 4 per cent tax credit on dividends exceeding $50 a year.

¶Sharply limit allowable business deductions for large-scale entertaining.

¶Narrow the base for computing depletion allowances in the mining and minerals industry.

The Senate also approved a routine rise in the statutory Federal debt limit from $285,000,000,000 to $293,000,000,000 for one year. This year's temporary ceiling is $295,000,000,000.

The House has already approved the broad features of the measure, but its bill does not include the three "loophole" amendments adopted by the Senate. An agreement on whether to keep these in the bill will be worked out in a Senate-House conference.

Bid for Repeal Beaten

The attempt to repeal communication and transportation taxes, once given a fair chance of success in the Senate was easily beaten as demands for "fiscal responsibility" filled the chamber throughout the day.

Only on two major items of controversy did the Senate balk at the Democratic liberal wing's campaign to close loopholes. The annual attempt to reduce the 27½ per cent depletion allowance on oil and gas was defeated by a vote of 56 to 30.

Another proposal, to compel withholding taxes on dividends and interest, was beaten by a vote of 62 to 24.

Repeal of the dividend tax credit, sponsored by Senator Eugene J. McCarthy, Democrat of Minnesota, was adopted by a vote of 42 to 41 after the Democratic leader, Lyndon B. Johnson of Texas, switched two votes on the floor to save it from certain defeat.

Senator Johnson was also instrumental in blocking the attempt to remove the telephone and transportation taxes.

"Instead of decreasing our revenues," he declared in a rousing floor speech, "we ought

Continued on Page 14, Column 1

Patterson Knocks Out Johansson in 5th; First to Regain the Heavyweight Title

Associated Press

Floyd Patterson flings his arms wide in victory as Ingemar Johansson is counted out

By JOSEPH C. NICHOLS

Floyd Patterson last night became the first man in the history of boxing to regain the heavyweight championship of the world.

The 25-year-old fighter from Rockeville Centre, L. I., knocked out the defending titleholder, Ingemar Johansson of Goteborg, Sweden, with a left hook in 1:51 of the fifth round of their scheduled fifteen-round fight at the Polo Grounds.

Patterson was clearly the master of the man who sent him to a humiliating defeat and deprived him of his title last June 26. He outboxed the Swede at almost every turn, withstood Johansson's famed right hand, then showed power sufficient to bring him the triumph with two quick, sharp strokes.

The surprisingly large crowd of 31,892 fans thrilled to Patterson's conquest. Johansson, who weighed 194¾ pounds to Patterson's 190, had been the 8-to-5 choice to retain his crown. A year ago Patterson had been the favorite at 5 to 1.

Continued on Page 36, Column 1

Ungar Says He Aided Jack In Hope of Winning Favors

By RUSSELL PORTER

Sidney J. Ungar testified yesterday that he had agreed to pay for remodeling Hulan E. Jack's apartment because Mr. Jack was in politics and "probably could do favors for me." Mr. Ungar, a lawyer and real estate promoter, was a prosecution witness at Mr. Jack's trial before Judge Joseph A. Sarafite and a jury in the Court of General Sessions.

Mr. Jack, who is Borough President of Manhattan, has suspended himself from office pending the outcome of the case. He is charged with accepting illegal gratuities from Mr. Ungar and with conspiring with the lawyer to conceal the gratuities.

Mr. Ungar, who testified before the grand jury that indicted Mr. Jack, was named as a co-conspirator in the indictment but was not indicted.

Witness Is Hostile

The real estate man proved a hostile witness yesterday, as the prosecution had expected. He balked at so many questions that Alfred J. Scotti, chief assistant district attorney, was forced to cross-examine his own witness and to confront him frequently with his testimony before the grand jury.

On some key points Mr. Scotti finally had to hint in his questioning at possible perjury and contempt proceedings before he could get the witness to tell the trial jury what he had told the grand jury.

Mr. Ungar testified that at the time he had agreed to pay for the remodeling the Borough President had already aided him on many occasions. He said that Mr. Jack had "opened many doors" for him in connection with Mr. Ungar's efforts to sponsor a Title I slum clearance project and to get higher rent for city-occupied office space in a building at 299 Broadway.

Jack Won Aid of Moses

The witness testified that Mr. Jack had persuaded Robert Moses, chairman of the city's former Slum Clearance Committee, to switch from opposition to support of the Title I project.

He also said the Borough President had made contacts by telephone for him to see other city officials, including James Felt, chairman of the City Planning Commission; Charles H. Tenney, Corporation Counsel,

Continued on Page 21, Column 1

HIGH COURT VOIDS VOTE-INQUIRY BAR

Enables Civil Rights Board to Move in South Without Naming Negro Informants

By ANTHONY LEWIS
Special to The New York Times.

WASHINGTON, June 20—The Supreme Court cleared the way today for more hearings by the Civil Rights Commission on Negroes' voting rights in the South. The court held that the commission could subpoena voting registrars and compel them to testify without giving them the names of Negroes who had filed complaints against them. The vote was 7 to 2.

For almost a year, since last July 12, the commission had been barred by lower court injunctions from holding any hearings in western Louisiana unless it identified all the informants. The commission called off all voting hearings pending a Supreme Court review.

The lower-court injunctions were overruled by today's decisions.

This was a busy day for the Supreme Court. It disposed of eighteen argued cases, leaving sixteen to go before it can adjourn for the summer. The court said it would adjourn

Continued on Page 18, Column 3

GEROSA SUSPENDS SALT INSPECTOR

Aide Named as Receiver of $3,050 in Bribes—Inquiry to Hear Spagna Today

By PETER KIHSS

John J. Stanton, a $6,280-a-year inspector, was suspended yesterday by City Controller Lawrence E. Gerosa. This was a result of testimony last week that he had taken bribes so that rock-salt purchases that failed to meet city specifications would not be rejected.

Sidney O. Raphael, counsel for the inspector, would say only, "We will do all in our power to vindicate him."

Mr. Stanton told the State Commission of Investigation last Friday that he "never got a dime" from John F. Shea, an official of the Bulk Carriers Corporation, which supplied the rock salt. Mr. Shea had testified, after being given immunity by the commission, that $3,050 was paid to the inspector.

The state inquiry will resume public hearings at 10 A. M. today at 270 Broadway. It will hear Purchase Commissioner Joseph V. Spagna, who has announced that he will defend the procedures used in letting the rock-salt contracts. The deals have involved roughly $3,500,000 since 1955.

Mr. Spagna was suspended from his $20,000-a-year post by Mayor Wagner last Friday after he had refused to answer questions on the ground that the commission had already completed its investigation and was engaged in public exposure. The Mayor then or-

Continued on Page 22, Column 2

MAYOR SUPPORTS KENNEDY TO SPUR BANDWAGON MOVE

Wagner Plans New Attempt to Win Delegate Seats for Mrs. Roosevelt, Lehman

By LEO EGAN

Mayor Wagner announced yesterday his support of Senator John F. Kennedy for the Democratic nomination for President.

His action was taken by prearrangement with the Massachusetts Senator. Its apparent purpose was to start a bandwagon movement that would insure Mr. Kennedy of the nomination on the first ballot.

Meanwhile, Michael H. Prendergast, Democratic state chairman, made public last night a strong civil rights plank, which the New York Democratic organization will offer today to a panel of the national platform committee. It will call for Federal financial and technical aid to schools and local governments that effect school desegregation.

Place on Ticket Unlikely

Mayor Wagner, by his announcement, appeared to abandon any hope of winning the nomination for Vice President himself. Both the Senator and the Mayor are Easterners and Roman Catholics. Politically this traditionally eliminates any possibility of their being running mates.

At the same time that he declared for Senator Kennedy, Mayor Wagner said he would make a new attempt on Thursday to win places in the New York delegation to the Democratic National Convention for former Senator Herbert H. Lehman and Mrs. Franklin D. Roosevelt.

Abe Stark, President of the City Council, warmly seconded the proposal to offer a place as delegate to Mr. Lehman. He described the Democratic State Committee's failure to designate the former Senator a delegate at its meeting last week "an injustice."

'Bossism' Is Issue

Mr. Lehman apparently was turned down because of his fight to oust Carmine G. De Sapio as New York's national committeeman and Mr. Prendergast as state chairman on the ground that they symbolized political "bossism."

Mr. Prendergast said last night that he saw no reason for calling another meeting of the 300-member state committee to reconsider its selection of delegates at large. As chairman, he is the only one with the power to summon such a meeting.

Legally the committee has the sole right to designate delegates at large. The delegates themselves have no such right.

Mr. Wagner announced his support for Senator Kennedy at a press conference in City Hall when he was asked if he was ready to disclose his choice for the Presidential nomination.

"Yes," the Mayor answered

Continued on Page 20, Column 4

Rebels in Algeria Accept A Peace Parley in Paris

Abbas to Lead Delegation to Meet With de Gaulle to End Long War

By THOMAS F. BRADY
Special to The New York Times.

TUNIS, June 20—After nearly six years of war, the leaders of the Algerian National Liberation Front agreed today to go to Paris to talk peace.

The decision was announced in a communiqué read here today by Ferhat Abbas, Premier of the nationalists' Provisional Government. The communiqué was in response to a speech by President de Gaulle Tuesday that said: "We await you here to find an honorable end to the combat that still drags on."

Outside in a little Tunisian side street, about 100 Algerian exiles heard the news from a recording truck of the Tunis radio. They broke into applause. Within the building, half a dozen French newsmen also applauded.

The communiqué said:

"The Provisional Government of the Algerian Republic has decided to send a delegation headed by M. Ferhat Abbas to meet General de Gaulle. It is dispatching a responsible representative to Paris to organize a means for the voyage."

The name of the "responsible representative" had not been disclosed tonight, nor had the

Continued on Page 6, Column 5

United Press International Radiophoto

Ferhat Abbas announces forthcoming trip to Paris.

NIXON ADVOCATES A U. N. FOOD POOL

In Outlining Farm Plan He Also Backs Rockefeller Stockpile Proposal

Text of the speech by Nixon is printed on Page 16.

By WILLIAM M. BLAIR
Special to The New York Times.

MINOT, N. D., June 20—Vice President Nixon said tonight that he favored creation of a United Nations' pool of surplus food to feed the world's hungry.

Mr. Nixon backed the plan in a farm speech in this wheat state. He included it as part of his program for a new attack on the United States' own problem of surplus agriculture production and low farm income.

President Eisenhower, he said, had the proposal prepared for presentation at the May summit conference but Premier Khrushchev's actions, which led to collapse of the meeting, "ruled out" Soviet Union participation at this time.

Now the United States should move forward with the plan, he went on, and "explore with other surplus-producing nations their attitude toward joining us in such a program."

The Vice President's first major presentation on the politically explosive farm issue offered the U. N. pool proposal as one of three ideas to help bring American agriculture pro-

Continued on Page 16, Column 1

KISHI RESIGNATION IS REPORTED NEAR

He Is Said to Have Stated He Will Quit After Pact With U. S. Is Effective

By ROBERT TRUMBULL
Special to The New York Times.

TOKYO, Tuesday, June 21—Premier Nobusuke Kishi is reliably reported to have stated his willingness to announce his "intention to resign" as soon as the new United States-Japanese mutual security treaty comes into force.

The treaty could come into force this week. The actual date of Mr. Kishi's resignation it was thought, might be some time later.

The 63-year-old Premier, who has been in office nearly three and a half years, was understood to have disclosed his decision yesterday to Shojiro Kawashima, secretary-general of Mr. Kishi's Liberal Democratic party, and other close associates.

Demonstrations Continue

Mr. Kishi's action, taken in the cause of party unity, caused dissident elements in the party to abandon their attempts to prevail upon the Premier to resign before the treaty takes effect.

Demonstrations continued yesterday against Mr. Kishi's Government and the treaty. About 4,000 chanting, snake-dancing students and unionists were apparently getting ready for na-

Continued on Page 13, Column 2

EISENHOWER ENDS 9-DAY ASIAN TOUR; HAILED IN HAWAII

Received With 'Aloha' Shouts on Return From Pacific Goodwill Journey

GREETED BY GOV. QUINN

President Pays Tribute to 50th State as a Land of Racial Concord

Texts of speeches in Korea and joint communiqué, Page 12.

By HARRISON E. SALISBURY
Special to The New York Times

HONOLULU, June 20—President Eisenhower returned to the United States today from a nine-day Far Eastern journey of goodwill to hear welcome shouts of "Aloha!" from cheering Hawaiian crowds.

The President stepped from his jet transport at 12:08 P. M. after a flight from Seoul, Korea, which included a brief refueling stop at Wake Island. The Hawaiian sun was shining brightly and a fresh wind blew in from the turquoise sea as General Eisenhower stepped from the plane.

In a speech of greeting the President hailed Hawaii as a land where men of many races and creeds had demonstrated their ability to live and prosper in amity and mutual goodwill He had a special word of tribute for Hawaii's Japanese citizens, particularly those men of Japanese ancestry who fought in World War II.

Praises Study Center

General Eisenhower put in a word of praise for the East-West Center of the University of Hawaii, which has been authorized as a project for improving relations of the nations around the Pacific. The President said he hoped the center would bring about better feeling among peoples of the Pacific area.

The President was warmly greeted by Gov. William F. Quinn of Hawaii, who praised his efforts in behalf of peace and justice throughout the world.

General Eisenhower was presented with the traditional Hawaiian lei, a magnificent crimson circlet made of 150 red carnations. It was put around his neck by Mrs. Quinn, wife of the Governor, who kissed the President in the traditional Hawaiian fashion.

2,500 at Airport

The President was given a rousing cheer by about 2,500 people gathered at the airport, many of whom had United States flags and signs saying "Aloha, President Eisenhower." Several waved Japanese flags.

General Eisenhower drove to the heart of Honolulu through throngs of people, many of whom showered confetti on him and cheered as his motorcade passed.

He then drove outside the city through Pali Pass in the Koolau Mountains to the Kaneohe Marine Corps Air Station, where he will stay for a few days before returning to Washington.

Within an hour the President, his aide, Brig. Gen. Andrew

Continued on Page 13, Column 1

Navy Gives Dolphin High I. Q., Perhaps Equal to Human Being's

By JOHN W. FINNEY
Special to The New York Times.

WASHINGTON, June 20—The bottle-nosed dolphin, the playboy of the sea and the age-old friend of mariners, was said today to be at least equal, and perhaps superior, to man in some aspects of brain power.

Navy-sponsored research has established that dolphins can talk to each other, can mimic words of humans, and will come to each other's assistance in moments of distress. They apparently even have a sense of humor as far as humans are concerned.

These conclusions on the I. Q. of the dolphin were reported today at a news conference by Dr. John C. Lilly, a neurophysiologist and director of the Communications Research Institute in the Virgin Islands.

Under a research grant from the Office of Naval Research, Dr. Lilly has been conducting experiments for the last five years to determine the intellectual capabilities of the bottle-nosed dolphin.

Dr. Lilly raised the possibility that as more is learned of the dolphins' "language" it may be possible for man to converse with them

The bottle-nosed dolphin so-called for the bulbous beak protruding from its forehead is popularly known as a porpoise. It is common off the Atlantic Coast, where it travels in large schools. A small species of the whale family, it is a mammal that, several million years ago in its evolutionary development, left the land to return to the sea.

Dr. Lilly reported that the

Continued on Page 19, Column 3

NEWS INDEX

West Virginia Vault Looted of $368,000

By The Associated Press.

CHARLESTON, W. Va., June 20 A cash haul that the police estimated at $368,000 was taken by thieves who smashed through the ceiling of a vault in the State Motor Vehicles Department early today. It was the biggest robbery in West Virginia history.

Dallas Bias, the Charleston police chief, and state police investigators concurred tonight in the $368,000 cash loss figure. J. Marshall Holcomb, motor vehicles commissioner, said "That's only an estimate."

The police thought the value of the checks taken would turn out to be relatively small. Earlier in the day, Mr. Holcomb had estimated the cash loss at more than $300,000 and he said then he feared stolen checks $500,000. The stolen money consisted of receipts of the last

Continued on Page 28, Column 6

United Press International Telephoto

HAWAIIAN WELCOME: President Eisenhower is greeted by a delegation of school children on arrival in Honolulu. Standing in rear is Gov. William F. Quinn of Hawaii.

Eaton Urges U. S. Modify Arms Plan

By DANA ADAMS SCHMIDT
Special to The New York Times

WASHINGTON, June 20—The United States' delegate to the East-West disarmament talks at Geneva said today that the West needed a fresh approach to disarmament.

Fredrick M. Eaton, who for three months has headed the United States delegation to the ten-nation conference in Geneva, made the suggestion at a meeting with Secretary of State Christian A. Herter, Secretary of Defense Thomas S. Gates Jr. and the Chairman of the Atomic Energy Commission, John A. McCone.

Also participating were Douglas Dillon, Under Secretary of State; John N. Irwin 2d, Under Secretary of the Defense Department; and James H. Douglas, Secretary of the Air Force.

Mr. Eaton was reported to

Continued on Page 4, Column 3

LEFT HOOK TO JAW ENDS FIGHT IN 5TH

31,892 at Polo Grounds See Johansson Counted Out on Second Knockdown

Continued From Page 1, Col. 4

In bringing about Johansson's downfall, Patterson used a "picture-punch" left hook. He ripped the blow across to the chin early in the fifth and Johannson went down heavily. But it was plain that he was not senseless. He was certain to get up, and he did at the count of 9.

Patterson was unhurried now in the approach to his task. He stalked Johansson eagerly and even recklessly, as if aware that Johansson couldn't hurt him.

Johansson kept his eyes wide open, almost unnaturally so, as Patterson came at him. But he didn't have enough vision to pick off Patterson's next wallop.

This punch, like the earlier one, traveled in the perfect arc that makes the left hook the deadly blow it is. It hit the mark perfectly, right on the Johansson jaw, and down went the Swede.

Referee Arthur Mercante went through the motions of the full count, but Patterson knew his foe was out as soon as Johansson hit the canvas.

The new champion leaped for joy even as Mercante was tolling off 10. When the count was was completed, Patterson was mobbed by his handlers and the many fanatics climbing into the ring.

Again A Surprise

The fight was the first for both boxers since Johansson beat Patterson. As in the 1959 encounter, the results confounded the majority of the experts. The fight followers were heavily in favor of Patterson last year. Last night they were much in favor of the 27-year-old Johansson.

Johansson's setback was the first in his professional career of twenty-three fights. Fourteen of his twenty-two triumphs had been knockouts.

Patterson's record before last night had showed thirty-five victories in thirty-seven starts, with twenty-six knockouts. The only one to beat him besides Johansson was Joey Maxim, who outpointed Floyd before the latter became the heavyweight king.

There was tension throughout the fight, most of it generated by the belief that Johansson's mighty right-hand punch—last year likened to the Hammer of Thor—could end matters whenever it hit the target.

Patterson was most careful in not presenting a target, but Johansson succeeded, at least once, in crashing his right to the jaw. When it landed, Patterson surprised the excited crowd, and the eager Johansson, by remaining on his feet. This was in the second round, the only one of the four complete rounds that Johansson won.

In the first round, Patterson, aggressive and confident, moved into his rival, firing left hooks to the head. These punches were more probing than potent. It was as if Patterson was trying to ascertain how to bring the Johansson chin into the left-hook orbit.

Johansson Also Waits

Johansson did little but send light punches to the head and body in close through the first round. He, too, seemed to be waiting for the opportunity to crush once more the man whom his heavy artillery had felled so easily last year.

In the second round Johansson let go with the right hand, and his supporters were certain he was going to make it two in a row over Patterson.

Patterson had opened the round with his left hooks and jabs, and when he was short with one of these blows, Johansson countered. He fired a long right-hand punch. It landed on Patterson's jaw and Floyd was shaken.

Immediately Patterson went into reverse, releasing light, flicking jabs into the face of the steadily advancing Johansson. Johansson caught Patterson on the ropes and fired one more right. This one was a little high on the cheek and did not shake Patterson so much as the first.

In few moments the effect of these blows wore off. Patterson ceased retreating and stepped in to trade body punches.

Patterson did all the leading in the third round. He continued to pump his left to the face and, infrequently, to the body.

Patterson's boxing was excellent in the fourth. He moved in and out gracefully, peppering Johansson with lefts, holding his right out merely as a threatening weapon, and agilely stepping away from Johansson's rigid moves.

The only punch of any consequence that Johansson landed in the fourth was a right to the head that connected at the bell.

Opening the fifth round, Patterson drove several lefts to the face. Johansson sank a right to the body and Patterson responded with the first left hook, the one that was just short of being the crusher, though it floored Johansson.

The crusher was not long in coming. After a few moments of measuring his man, Patterson had his sights properly set. He released the left hook and down went the foreigner, down and out.

Johansson had been cut and bruised over the left eye in the first round. And he bled freely from his mouth after the first knockdown.

Last week at his training camp Johansson had said, "When I hit him square with my right, the referee can count to a thousand."

Instead, it was Johansson who was hit square, and by a left. He was completely out, and he remained out for several minutes after his handlers had helped him to his corner.

Man in a Fog

He was still in a daze as he was escorted down the ring stairs.

Patterson's joy was something to see. Frequently in his training campaign he had said that he was eager for this fight for two reasons: One, to even matters with Johansson and two, to become the first man in boxing history to regain the heavyweight title.

A number of the best-known heavyweights, starting with James J. Corbett, had failed in the attempt to return to the pinnacle of pugilism. After Corbett, those who missed were Bob Fitzsimmons, Jim Jeffries, Jack Dempsey, Max Schmeling, Joe Louis, Ezzard Charles and Jersey Joe Walcott.

Last night's promotion was a highly successful one. The gross gate was announced as $824,814.07. But much more important than the local gate were the receipts from the ancillary rights of television, motion pictures and radio.

With the fight televised on closed circuit into 230 locations in 160 cities in the United States and Canada, and with the motion pictures and radio bringing guarantees of a half-million dollars, the final financial figures may approximate $2,500,000.

The pay-out commitments are complicated, but the general acceptance is that each fighter will receive about 35 per cent of all this money.

Neither Patterson nor Johansson has a manager. Cus D'Amato discovered Patterson and managed him to the title, but his license was revoked by the State Athletic Commission for violation of the local rules. Johansson does his own business, but works with an adviser, Edwin Ahlquist of Goteborg.

Patterson won the title for the first time on Nov. 30, 1956, by knocking out Archie Moore, also with a left hook. He and Moore fought for the crown vacated by the retirement of the undefeated Rocky Marciano and Patterson became the youngest to win the heavyweight championship.

Associated Press

IMPACT: A left to the jaw by Floyd Patterson knocks out Ingemar Johansson in fifth

United Press International

IT'S ALL OVER: Arthur Mercante, referee, ends his count over prostrate Johansson

FALLEN CHAMPION SMILES, DEPARTS

Johansson Lauds Patterson but Puts Off Interview at Least Until Today

By FRANK M. BLUNK

The defeat of a world champion is a stunning, jarring thing. Especially to the man who has been conquered. To imagine invincibility, then suddenly to find yourself a piece of common clay, is a sad thing.

Ingemar Johansson was stunned, and afterward, despite a brave front, he was sad. How could he wave aside with a gesture or a word the devastating defeat he had just suffered at the hands of Floyd Patterson? He wouldn't even try. A gallant loser, he had only praise for his conqueror.

He sent these words by a member of his entourage, smiled in a strained, professional way and left the Polo Grounds and the scene of his humiliation surrounded by a cordon of police.

Johansson kept a group of 150 reporters and photographers waiting more than an hour while recuperating in his dressing room, part of the quarters once occupied by the New York Giants baseball teams.

"He will be out soon," was the promise repeated at ten-minute intervals.

Then, finally at midnight, he appeared, dapper in sports jacket and gray trousers, but with a blue mouse under his left eye and his lips swollen.

He wouldn't talk tonight, his manager said. He would submit to interviews tomorrow, maybe.

The defeated man had a slow and staggering trip from the ring where he had fallen to the sanctuary of his dressing room. Hundreds of spectators barred the way, some with sympathetic remarks, others with jeers. Johansson was glassy-eyed and weak-kneed. He had to be helped up the steps. Two doctors visited him and reported he was all right.

His fiancee, Birgit Lundgren, and his mother spent some time with him. None of his family wanted to talk. What was there to say?

Over in a far corner of the large dressing room, unnoticed by the group, sat another dejected figure, Andre Tessier, who had been knocked out by Clarence Floyd in a bout after the title fight.

"What's with you?" he was asked.

"The fairy tale is ended," he said, cryptically. He wasn't speaking of himself but of the man whose dressing room he shared.

"All the News That's Fit to Print"

The New York Times.

LATE CITY EDITION
U. S. Weather Bureau Report (Page 64) forecasts: Mostly fair, mild today and tonight. Some cloudiness and warm tomorrow. Temp. range: 74—54; yesterday: 71.2—52.

VOL. CX..No. 37,519. | NEW YORK, FRIDAY, OCTOBER 14, 1960. | FIVE CENTS

10 cents beyond 50-mile zone from New York City except on Long Island. Higher in air delivery cities.

KHRUSHCHEV GOES HOME AFTER A THREAT IN U.N. TO BOYCOTT ARMS TALKS

ANGRY FAREWELL

Soviet Loses Vote on U.S. 'Aggression' but Gains One Victory

By THOMAS J. HAMILTON
Special to The New York Times.

UNITED NATIONS, N. Y., Oct. 13—Premier Khrushchev bade an angry farewell to the General Assembly today after threatening to walk out on any future disarmament negotiations unless they were conducted on Soviet terms.

The Soviet leader departed for Moscow in a Soviet TU-114 turbo-prop plane that took off from New York International Airport at 11:47 P. M. In a departure statement he called anew for world disarmament and again urged changes in the structure of the United Nations.

In his final speech at the United Nations during the afternoon, Mr. Khrushchev absolved President Eisenhower of responsibility for the U-2 and RB-47 reconnaissance plane flights this year, which were the subject of a Soviet complaint to the Assembly.

Good-By From Wadsworth

He explained to the delegates that it was his belief that "the President, after all, followed on somebody else's leash," and "he himself did not want to aggravate relations with us."

"But he has not got long to stay in office," Mr. Khrushchev added, "and I'm not preparing any grounds for a meeting."

James J. Wadsworth of the United States declared in reply that after Mr. Khrushchev's departure "perhaps the thunder will go away, perhaps then the Assembly will get down to work." He said he hoped Mr. Khrushchev's next visit to the Assembly would bring "a better attitude."

Earlier in the day, Mr. Khrushchev had appeared to be in high good humor over an Assembly decision, by acclamation, to debate a Soviet "declaration" on colonialism in plenary session.

The Premier and the rest of the Soviet delegation rocked with laughter a few minutes later when a delegate of the Philippines protested against "unparliamentary and unkind remarks by Mr. Khrushchev but said he would not seek to compete with the Soviet leader in the "vocabulary of the gutter."

The Soviet Premier's mood changed during the afternoon

Continued on Page 2, Column 3

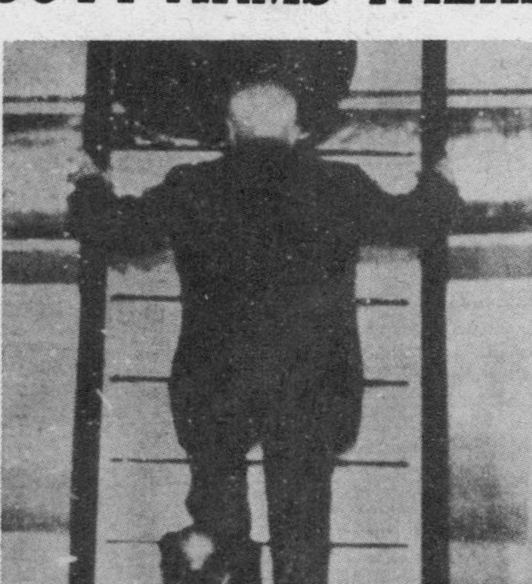

The New York Times by Robert Walker

THERE HE GOES: Premier Khrushchev ascends a ramp leading to Soviet turbojet plane at New York International Airport last night, ending his twenty-five day stay. Soviet leader called for changes in structure of the U. N.

PIRATES WIN, 10-9, CAPTURING SERIES ON HOMER IN 9TH

Mazeroski Hit Beats Yanks, Lifts Pittsburgh to First World Title in 35 Years

By JOHN DREBINGER
Special to The New York Times.

PITTSBURGH, Oct. 13—The Pirates today brought Pittsburgh its first world series baseball championship in thirty-five years when Bill Mazeroski slammed a ninth-inning home run high over the left-field wall of historic Forbes Field.

With that shot, Danny Murtaugh's astounding Bucs brought down Casey Stengel's Yankees, 10 to 9, in a titanic struggle that gave the National League champions the series, four games to three.

Minutes later a crowd of 36,683 touched off a celebration that tonight is sweeping through the city like a vast conflagration. For with this stunning victory, which also had required a five-run Pirate eighth, the dauntless Bucs avenged the four-straight rout inflicted by another Yankee team in 1927.

First Title Since 1925

The Steel City thus had its first world title since 1925, when the Corsairs of Bill McKechnie conquered the Washington Senators.

As for the 70-year-old Stengel, if this is to be his exit—his retirement has been repeatedly rumored—the Ol' Professor scarcely could have desired a more fitting setting short of a victory.

For this was a terrific, nerve-tingling struggle that saw a dazzling parade of heroes who followed on the heels of one another in bewildering profusion.

It saw the Bucs dash off to a four-run lead in the first two innings as they clobbered Bob Turley and Bill Stafford. The first two runs scored in the first inning on a homer by Rocky Nelson.

Berra Hits 3-Run Homer

But in the sixth the Bombers suddenly opened fire on their two arch tormentors of the series, Vernon Law and the Bucs' ace reliever, ElRoy Face. Law, with the help of Face, was seeking his third victory over the Bombers, but the Yanks scored four times in this round, three riding in on a homer by the incomparable Yogi Berra.

These four tallies, along with one which they had picked up in the fifth on a Bill Skowron homer, had the Yanks in front, 5 to 4. When they added two off Face in the eighth for a 7-4 lead, Stengel appeared to have his eighth world series title wrapped up, along with the Bombers' nineteenth autumn triumph.

But in the eighth the Corsairs suddenly erupted for five runs, the final three scampering across on an electrifying homer by Hal Smith. That had

Continued on Page 36, Column 5

NIXON AND KENNEDY RENEW FIGHT OVER QUEMOY IN HEATED DEBATE; ALSO CLASH ON LABOR PROGRAMS

The New York Times

AT START OF DEBATE: Vice President Nixon and Senator John F. Kennedy as they appeared on the television screen. Mr. Nixon was in Los Angeles and Mr. Kennedy here.

EXCHANGE BITTER

Vice President Takes a Softer Position on Defending Islands

Transcript of Nixon-Kennedy debate is on Pages 20-21.

By RUSSELL BAKER

Senator John F. Kennedy and Vice President Nixon bitterly accused each other before a national television audience last night of advocating policies on Quemoy and Matsu that would lead to war.

While the rhetorical temperature of the third debate was torrid, the actual policy difference between the two Presidential candidates appeared to have narrowed considerably. Mr. Nixon pulled back from the strong position he took last week.

Debate over Quemoy and Matsu, which both candidates have decided to make a major issue of the campaign, dominated the program.

It was not entirely a foreign policy fight, however. In other exchanges the candidates clashed on such domestic issues as labor legislation, farm policy, spending, the costs of their respective proposals, economic growth and the 27½ per cent depletion allowance given oil and gas producers.

Arbitration Disputed

The clash on labor arose from Mr. Nixon's assertion that Senator Kennedy favored compulsory arbitration of major disputes. Mr. Kennedy denied vehemently that this was his position.

Last week the Vice President said that defending the two islands, situated four and five miles off the Chinese mainland, was a matter of "principle" because no territory "in the area of freedom" should be surrendered.

In last night's hour-long debate he was much less categorical. He suggested that Quemoy and Matsu would be defended if an attack upon them were "a prelude to an attack on Formosa [Taiwan]." This is essentially the position taken by the Eisenhower Administration since 1954.

Senator Kennedy sought to remind the audience that this was not the position that Mr. Nixon took in their television debate last Friday. Mr. Kennedy, who favors defending

Continued on Page 21, Column 2

BRITISH TOUGHEN POLICY ON SOVIET

Stand Outlined to Meeting of Conservatives—Unity of Europe Also Supported

By DREW MIDDLETON
Special to The New York Times.

SCARBOROUGH, England, Oct. 13—British foreign policy moved today toward a tougher attitude toward the Soviet Union and more emphatic support of economic unity with Europe.

These developments were explained to the annual conference of the Conservative party by the new team directing Britain's foreign policy. The team consists of the Earl of Home, the Foreign Secretary, and Edward Heath, Lord Privy Seal.

Lord Home depicted Communist strategy as a constant effort to overthrow democracy rather than "short-term policies alternating rapidly between toughness and conciliation." Consequently, British policy, he said, must "give ground nowhere."

Unity Set as Goal

Mr. Heath, who conducts British relations with the European Economic Community and the European Free Trade Association, said that the British Government wanted "to see unity created in Europe" and wanted to be a part of that unity.

He said that Britain had been assured by France that the Commonwealth and British colonies would be included in a British agreement with the economic community.

Cabinet ministers and party officials thought the speeches marked a departure from some

Continued on Page 11, Column 1

Mobutu Disavows Any 'War' on U.N. On Lumumba Issue

By PAUL HOFMANN
Special to The New York Times.

LEOPOLDVILLE, the Congo, Oct. 13—Col. Joseph D. Mobutu denied today that his military regime intended to make "war on the United Nations."

The Congo's strongman thus disavowed statements by members of his governing commission who had warned of a military uprising if the United Nations refused to permit the arrest of Patrice Lumumba.

Colonel Mobutu said his regime's views had been "distorted" in reports of a conflict between it and the United Nations.

The colonel's statement followed a declaration attributed to Mr. Lumumba, who has been deposed as Premier by President Joseph Kasavubu. One of Mr. Lumumba's aides quoted Mr. Lumumba as having praised the United Nations for preventing his arrest.

Mr. Lumumba, who has refused to bow to his dismissal by Mr. Kasavubu, was reported today to be in "complete isolation" at his official residence. The building was surrounded by a double cordon of United Nations and Congolese troops.

Mr. Lumumba's physician, an

Continued on Page 8, Column 3

VICTIM DESCRIBES BOMBING SUSPECT

Teen-Ager Hurt in Subway Saw Man Leave Scene —Scare at 'Met'

By FOSTER HAILEY

A stockily built man in his thirties who was seen limping away from the Times Square shuttle station just before a bomb went off Wednesday was described last night by the Transit Authority police as a prime suspect.

He was observed by a teen-age girl who was injured in the explosion on Columbus Day. She gave such a detailed description that a Transit Authority artist was able to draw a sketch of the suspect.

As the Transit Police pressed their search for the subway bomber, a telephoned warning of another bomb—a hoax—brought more than 100 city policemen and firemen to the Metropolitan Opera House last night during a special performance.

A man, described as having a foreign accent, called the opera house at 9:10 P. M. and said: "Listen carefully, listen carefully. Before the evening is over a bomb will go off."

The Fire Department sent six pieces of apparatus and forty firemen, and sixty policemen and detectives were dispatched to the opera house, at Broad-

Continued on Page 43, Column 1

President Said to Agree To Role as Roving Envoy

Special to The New York Times.

LOS ANGELES, Oct. 13—President Eisenhower has expressed willingness to serve as a roving ambassador of goodwill after he leaves the White House a highly placed source said tonight. A top campaign aide for Vice President Nixon said that the President was "passionately devoted" to serving the cause of peace whether in or out of the White House.

It was indicated an announcement of the President's plans might soon be forthcoming, perhaps in a foreign-policy speech Mr. Nixon was scheduled to make tomorrow night before the World Newspaper Forum in the Beverly Hilton Hotel.

Such an announcement would be calculated to assist Mr. Nixon's campaign by linking the President to a future role in a Nixon administration.

The Nixon source questioned whether President Eisenhower might also be willing to play the same role if Senator John F. Kennedy, the Democratic nominee, were elected. He said that might depend on the world situation.

The President, it was said, would like to travel widely, capitalizing on the friendship people around the world feel and demonstrate toward him.

His trips as President have demonstrated his enormous prestige, partly because of his role as Supreme Allied Commander in World War II.

A most recent problem concerning the President, it was said, has been the weakening of the North Atlantic Treaty Organization, of which he was the first post-war supreme commander.

The Nixon source speculated that President Eisenhower would be available for overseas travel shortly after his term ends Jan. 20. He said the President would first want to take a leave to "recharge his batteries," but would then be willing to go anywhere for the cause of peace.

PLEDGE ON NEGRO DILUTED BY LODGE

Candidate, in South, Says He Would Like One in Cabinet but Can Promise Nothing

By EDWARD C. BURKS
Special to The New York Times.

WINSTON-SALEM, N. C., Oct. 13—Henry Cabot Lodge's pledge to a Harlem crowd that a new Republican Administration would name a Negro to the Cabinet was modified drastically by Mr. Lodge in the South today.

"I cannot pledge anything," the Republican Vice-Presidential candidate commented to newspaper men as he made a one-day sweep into Virginia and North Carolina.

His Harlem pledge has caused consternation and anger among some high Virginia Republican officials.

Mr. Lodge said this afternoon that his pledge about a Negro Cabinet officer had been an expression of what he thinks should be done and not a Republican commitment.

He said he thought his statement was not inconsistent with Vice President Nixon's thinking that race should not be a criterion in picking Cabinet officers.

Harlem Statement

At a Harlem street rally in New York last night Mr. Lodge stated:

"This is where my party stands, and this is where I stand. If elected, we will be guided by the following: 1. There should be a Negro in the Cabinet."

He then listed seven other planks in a strong civil rights statement.

He topped off his program by announcing:

"It is offered as a pledge—and as a pledge that will be redeemed beginning in January, 1961, if you elect Richard Nixon President."

Shortly after his arrival at midday in Norfok, Va., a high Virginia Republican told one of Mr. Lodge's advisers:

"Whoever recommended that Harlem speech ought to have

Continued on Page 24, Column 1

GOMULKA IS HOME WITH NEW U.S. AID

Polish Party Chief Reports Favored-Nation Pledge

By ARTHUR J. OLSEN
Special to The New York Times

WARSAW, Oct. 13—Wladyslaw Gomulka, Poland's Communist leader, returned from New York today with assurances that the United States would restore most-favored-nation treatment to Polish commerce within a few weeks.

This privilege, granting Polish exports preferential tariff treatment, was withdrawn in 1951. Foreign trade experts estimated that a return to a most-favored-nation status would mean a 50 per cent increase in exports to the United States next year.

Duties on Polish goods will be reduced across the board, in some cases drastically. Officials talked of increasing Polish sales from this year's total of $35,000,000 to $100,000,000 by 1965.

The next Polish objective in the area of economic cooperation with the United States will be amendment of the Battle Act. This 1953 law forbids the sale of strategic commodities to Communist countries.

It also bars United States commercial banks from doing business with Communist financial institutions, which is the point Poland is interested in.

Polish trade authorities want to establish such banking relations in the United States with

Continued on Page 4, Column 8

Three Mice Survive 700-Mile Atlas Shot

By The Associated Press.

CAPE CANAVERAL, Fla., Oct. 13—Three black mice named Sally, Amy and Moe rode a missile nose cone 700 miles into space today and survived radiation, weightlessness and a dive back through the earth's atmosphere. They were recovered alive and in good condition.

The Air Force reported that the mice appeared to have suffered no harmful effects during the jarring twenty-five-minute journey in an Atlas cone, making them the first living creatures returned alive from this distance in space.

The tiny travelers made the ride in a miniature model of a man-in-space capsule. The experiment, which took the mice into the dangerous Van Allen radiation belt at speeds up to 18,000 miles an hour, was an

Continued on Page 11, Column 6

Associated Press Wirephoto

THE HERO COMES HOME: Gleeful Pittsburgh fans and a happy coach, Frank Oceak, greet Bill Mazeroski as he rounds third in ninth on series-winning homer against Yanks.

American Among 13 Executed by Cubans

Special to The New York Times.

HAVANA, Oct. 13—Anthony Zarba, a 28-year-old American, and seven Cubans were executed today. Five other Cubans were executed last night.

Mr. Zarba, of Boston, was the first American executed in Cuba since the republic's establishment in 1902. He and seven Cubans were put to death at Santiago de Cuba. Those shot were convicted by a military court of armed revolt against the regime of Premier Fidel Castro.

The mass trial started yesterday morning and the verdict was announced at 8:40 o'clock last night. An appeal by defense attorneys was rejected. The executions were carried out on a Cuban Army firing range at Santiago.

Mr. Zarba was a member of an armed expedition that landed on the north coast of Oriente

Continued on Page 13, Column 8

NIXON IS 'SHOCKED' BY KENNEDY NOTES

Democrat Denies Violation of Rules—A.B.C. Neutral

By W. H. LAWRENCE
Special to The New York Times.

LOS ANGELES, Oct. 13—An obviously angry Vice President Nixon declared today he was "shocked" that Senator John F. Kennedy had brought "notes" to their third joint television appearance.

Mr. Nixon called the use of notes a violation of the rules as he understood them to have been agreed upon by representatives of the two Presidential candidates before the "great debate" television series began.

[In New York, Pierre Salinger, Senator Kennedy's press secretary, said "we know of no agreement on notes—or on television make-up." The Senator, he said, had a letter President Eisenhower had written, along with some other notes.

[Mr. Salinger said "the Senator feels that when he quotes the President of the United States, he wants to quote him accurately, and it may be that since these quotations disprove Mr. Nixon's position, that this led to his displeasure on the matter. He feels it would be advantageous to all candidates if they quoted the record accurately.]

The American Broadcasting Company, which originated to-

Continued on Page 22, Column 5

NEWS INDEX

Champagne Corks Pop Like Machine-Gun Fire as Pirates Celebrate Victory

PIRATES WIN, 10-9, AND TAKE SERIES

Continued From Page 1, Col. 4

the Bucs two in front, but still the conflict raged.

In the ninth the embattled Yanks counted twice as once again they routed Bob Friend. Then left-handed Harvey Haddix, winner of the pivotal fifth game, brought them to a halt.

In the last of the ninth it was the clout by Mazeroski, first up, that ended it. Ralph Terry, the fifth Yankee hurler, was the victim. It made him the losing pitcher and Haddix the winner.

So, instead of the Bombers winning the nineteenth title, they had to accept their seventh world series defeat. As for Stengel, he remains tied with Joe McCarthy, a former Yankee manager, with seven series triumphs. The setback was his third. McCarthy lost two, one with the Yanks and one with the Chicago Cubs.

Bobby Shantz, a diminutive left-hander, who had gone to the box in the third to do some brilliant relief hurling for five innings, was one victim of the Bucs' startling five-run eighth.

The assault opened with Gino Cimoli, hitting for Face, cracking a single to right. Bill Virdon followed with a vicious grounder to short that resulted in doubtless the crucial play of the entire series.

It looked like a double play until the ball took a freak hop and struck Tony Kubek in the larynx. Instead of a double play, Tony was stretched on the ground. Virdon was on first with a single and Cimoli was on second. Kubek had to leave the game and was rushed to a hospital.

Coates Slow Covering First

Meanwhile the Pirate attack rolled on. Dick Groat followed with a single to left, scoring Cimoli. That was all for Shantz and Jim Coates, a lean right-hander, took the mound.

Bob Skinner, back in the Buc line-up despite a still swollen left thumb, sacrificed the runners to second and third. Nelson flied out, leaving the position unchanged, and then came another rough break for the Stengeleers.

Bob Clemente dribbled a grounder to the right of the mound. Skowron scopped up the ball and this should have been the third out of the inning had Coates covered first base. But the tall Virginian failed to get to the bag in time. Clemente thus got an infield hit that enabled Cimoli to score the second run of the inning.

Three more followed as Smith, a one-time Yankee prospect, belted the ball high over the left-field wall. The Bucs were in front, 9—7, and the fans were in a delirium.

They cooled perceptibly in the top of the ninth. Murtaugh called on Friend, twice knocked out earlier in the series, to protect that two-run lead. But Bobby Richardson singled, as did Dale Long, a pinch-hitter, and Murtaugh lost no time hustling in his fifth-game winner, Haddix.

The little lefty retired Roger Maris on the end of a foul back of the plate, but Mickey Mantle singled to right, scoring Richardson and sending Long to third.

Skowron Ends Inning

Another bewildering play followed. Berra grounded sharply down the first-base line. Nelson grabbed the ball, stepped on the bag for one out, then made a lunge for Mantle who, seeing he had no chance to make second, darted back to first. Mickey made it with a headlong dive

. . . Bob Clemente jumps with joy as he crosses plate on Smith's homer, which also scored Dick Groat, at left.

that sent him under Rocky's tag.

Meanwhile, Gil McDougald, in as a runner for Long, crossed the plate and the score was 9-all. Haddix, getting Skowron to ground to Groat, brought the round to a close. Minutes later the game was over.

Although the weather again was warm and summery, the sun for the first time had difficulty breaking through a haze which enveloped the park with something akin to a Los Angeles smog.

However, no one was paying much attention to the weather and once the game got on the way it could have snowed without anyone paying the slightest attention.

For this was Pittsburgh's first big chance to win a world championship in three and a half decades and the fans were out to make the most of it. Nor did the Bucks keep their cohorts long in suspense.

The cheers, following the setting down of the first three Yankees in the first inning by Law, barely had subsided before they broke out afresh.

Turley, Stengel's starting choice over the youthful Stafford, got by the first two Pirates, but Skinner walked.

Next came Nelson. Before the series returned here, Murtaugh had been emphatic that, regardless of Yankee pitching, Dick Stuart would be his first baseman. Yet here was the 36-year-old Nelson in the starting line-up as the first baseman.

Rocky, a left-handed swinger who began his professional baseball career eighteen years ago and spent most of the intervening time trying to convince managers he was a major league ball player, waited for Turley to run up a count of two balls and one strike. Then he lifted one that had just enough carry to clear the thirty-foot screen in front of the lower right-field stand at a point about 350 feet from home plate.

The fans went wild with joy as Nelson rounded the bases behind Skinner. Rocky had appeared in one series before this one. That was as a Brooklyn Dodger in 1952, when he was up four times as a pinch-hitter, but got no hits.

In the second; the Bucs went to work on Turley again, but this time not for long. For after Smoky Burgess had opened with a single to right, Stengel called on Stafford, the 22-year-old right-hander who had pitched five scoreless innings in relief in a hopeless Yankee cause in the fifth game.

In fact, Stengel had to weather some rough second-guessing after that defeat because he didn't start the youngster in that game instead of Art Ditmar.

This time Stafford spared his manager further embarrassing moments so far as this game was concerned. He walked Don Hoak and allowed Mazeroski to outgallop a bunt for a hit that filled the bases.

Stafford momentarily did get a grip on the situation when he induced Law to slap a roller to the mound. Stafford converted this one into a double play via the plate.

However, the Bucs still had runners on second and third and a moment later Virdon drove both home with a single to right, to which Maris added a fumble to put Virdon on second. The error didn't matter, but the Bucs were four in front.

Meanwhile Law, making a heroic bid to pitch his third victory of the series, held the Yanks in a tight grip. Like Ford yesterday, Law was back with only three days' rest, but he certainly didn't show it in the first four innings.

A dazzling stop and throw by Hoak took a possible hit away from Berra in the second. Hector Lopez delivered a pinch single in the third and Mantle singled with two down in the fourth.

In the fifth inning, the first tinge of uneasiness swept through the stands. Skowron stroked an outside pitch into the upper right deck. It was the Moose's second homer of the series and his sixth in series competition.

An inning later almost the entire arena was enveloped in a deep and profound silence. The Yanks ripped into both Law and Face for their cluster of four to take the lead.

Richardson Gets Single

Richardson, a thorn in the side of the Bucs throughout the series, opened the assault with a single. When Kubek drew a pass Murtaugh decided the moment had arrived for Face to do his usual flawless relief work.

He had done the rescue work in the three Pirate victories preceding this game, saving Law twice and Haddix in the fifth game.

This time he encountered trouble. He retired Maris on a foul back of third, but Mantle punched a single over second which a diving Groat just missed flagging down. The hit scored Richardson and sent Kubek to third.

Up stepped Berra, who again was in left field for the Bombers while a rookie, John Blanchard, worked behind the plate in place of the injured Elston Howard. The latter had gone out with a fractured hand when hit by a stray pitch in the sixth game.

Yogi fouled off one pitch. Then he unfurled a lofty shot that sailed into the upper right-field deck close to the foul pole, which at the base measures only 300 feet from the plate. Mantle and Kubek scored ahead of Berra.

It was Yogi's eleventh homer in world series competition, tying him for third place with the Dodgers' Duke Snider. Only Babe Ruth, with fifteen, and Mantle, with fourteen, have hit more.

The Yanks were now a run in front and in the eighth they clubbed Face for two more tallies.

The trim right-handed reliever had the Yanks' two most formidable clouters, Maris and Mantle, out of the way, when Berra drew a pass. Skowron sent a bounder down the third-base line which Hoak fielded but couldn't play. It went for a single and Berra was on second.

Two sharp thrusts did the rest. Blanchard pulled a single into left, scoring Yogi. Cletis Boyer drove a two-bagger down the left-field line, sending in Skowron. Moose's single was his twelfth hit, thereby tying another world series record.

Meanwhile, with Shantz reeling off one scoreless inning after another, the game looked tucked away for the Bombers. For five innings the little lefty allowed only one hit, a single.

But in the Pittsburgh eighth the real pyrotechnics began. They never stopped until Mazeroski, with a count of one ball and no strikes in the ninth, whacked the ball over the left-field brick wall directly over the 402-foot mark.

DOUBLE-PLAY BALL CITED BY STENGEL

Five-Run Rally Follows Play —Kubek Has a Possible Fracture of Larynx

By LOUIS EFFRAT

Special to The New York Times.

PITTSBURGH, Oct. 13 — Did the better ball club win the world series?

The question was put to the Yankees in their dressing room a few minutes after the ninth-inning homer by Bill Mazeroski of the Pirates had rung down the curtain at Forbes Field today.

Some Yankees declined to comment. Some were evasive. But those who answered did so with a firm, unbending "no."

Casey Stengel, the losing manager for only the third time in a world series, with an obvious effort to detract nothing from Pittsburgh's victory, answered the question with a question of his own.

"What do you think?" Casey countered. It was his way of ducking the issue and thereby not leaving himself open to a possible charge of "sour grapes."

However, the manager, who was hardly satisfied with his pitching today, did stress the bad break of the bounce that cost the Bombers a double play and most likely the game and series. It also sent Tony Kubek to the Eye and Ear Hospital here with a possible fracture of the larynx.

'I'll Never Believe It'

What Stengel, Gil McDougald and other Yankees who might have felt but did not say, was said unhedgingly by Yogi Berra, Bill Skowron, Cletis Boyer, Dale Long and others.

All hewed to the good sportsmanship line and gave credit to the Bucs for being a "good ball club." That, though, is as far as they went.

"I can't believe it," Berra said.

"I'll never believe it," Long said.

All were convinced that the ball Bill Virdon rapped toward Kubek at short, with one on and none out in the eighth, was the turning point. The ball apparently hit a pebble, hit Kubek on the throat and sent him sprawling. What looked like a double play became a fluke single, and the gates were opened for the five-run outburst that followed.

Certainly, all the Yankees, including Stengel and Bobby Shantz, thought it would have been a double play.

"I wasn't tired," Shantz, the industrious southpaw, said. "Casey took me out because they got three straight hits off me and I guess he was right.

"But the first two hits shouldn't have been hits. Gino Cimoli got a single by hitting a ball off his fist, and the one by Virdon would have been an easy double play if it weren't for the bad hop."

After a single by Dick Groat, Jim Coates took over. Before long, a slow-rolling infield single by Roberto Clemente—another tough break for the Bombers—and Hal Smith's homer returned the lead to the Pirates.

And after the Yankees had fought back to a tie in the ninth, along came Mazeroski with the shot heard 'round the world. Here, it not only was heard, but it also provoked a seemingly endless round of noisy rallies and celebrations, which still were going strong hours after the final out.

Mazeroski said his homer was hit off a high fast ball. Verification was sought from Ralph Terry, who delivered the pitch to Mazeroski.

"I don't know what the pitch was. All I know is it was the wrong one," Terry said.

The Yankees were gloomy in their dressing room. Not even Bobby Richardson, who won the Corvette given by Sport magazine as the outstanding player of the series, could smile.

Bob Turley, the starter, said his stuff might not have been overpowering, but that it was not too bad. This even though the right-hander lasted for only twenty pitches.

Turley's fourteenth was the one on which Rocky Nelson slugged a two-run homer in the first. "Nelson hit a bad pitch," Turley said. "It was cap high and a foot wide, yet he pulled it over the fence in right field."

Stengel repeated his previous statement that he would say nothing about his future with the Yankees or in baseball until later in the month.

Elliott of Australia and Otis Davis of U. S. Run to World Marks in Olympics

DECATHLON TAKEN BY RAFER JOHNSON

American First by 58 Points —Elliott Captures 1,500— Davis Wins 400-Meter

By ALLISON DANZIG

Special to The New York Times.

ROME, Sept. 6—Herb Elliott and Otis Davis today ran the two most brilliant races probably ever seen on the same day in the Olympic Games.

Elliott, Australia's 22-year-old wonder runner, sped 1,500 meters in 3 minutes 35.6 seconds, the equivalent of a 3:52.6 mile, in winning the final.

With this almost incredible performance, in which he took the lead 500 meters from the finish, utterly crushed all opposition and won by nearly 30 yards, Elliott broke his own world record of 3:36. It was made in 1958, his year of glory, when he also set the existing world record of 3:54.5 for the mile.

The tremendously thrilling run of the lithe, hawk-faced youth from Down Under followed half an hour after Davis had electrified 60,000 spectators in Stadio Olympico with another world-record-breaking display of flawless running speed.

Gasps of astonishment went up when it was announced that the 28-year-old former University of Oregon student from Los Angeles had lowered the record by three-tenths of second in winning the 400-meter final in 0:44.9. The old record was 0:45.2, made by Lou Jones of Manhattan College in 1956.

Davis Jumps for Joy

Davis was so overcome with happiness that he jubilantly jumped up and down and waved his arms above his head to the acclaim of the cheering crowd.

The two unforgettable races with their fabulous clockings surpassed in interest even so big an event as the decathlon, traditionally a top attraction of the games.

Tonight, after more than twenty-six hours of exhausting competition, Rafer Johnson of Kingsburg, Calif., was crowned as the winner of the punishing two-day, ten-event test of versatility, speed, skill and strength.

In an excruciatingly close fight with C. K. Yang of Taiwan, the powerful world record-holder managed to finish on top by 58 points. Johnson's total was 8,392 points, an Olympic record but under the world mark of 8,683 points he set in winning the combined Amateur Athletic Union championship and United States Olympic trials in July.

Yang was second with 8,334 points and Vasily Kuznetsov of the Soviet Union, the former world record-holder, third with 7,809.

In the A. A. U. championship, Johnson defeated Yang by 258 points. The Chinese youth was handicapped by an injury in the final event—the 1,500-meter run—then, and it was thought that he might well defeat Johnson this time.

Yang Better in 7 Events

He topped Johnson in seven of the ten events here, but he could not quite overcome Johnson's superiority in the shot-put, discus throw, and javelin throw.

Yang held his head in dejection when they finished the decathlon 1,500-meter run. He finished 4 yards ahead of Johnson in a race in which both were wabbling and barely able to keep their feet under them to the last killing stride. But Yang's margin was not enough to make up his point deficit.

Johnson failed to break his world record because of his inability to equal his performances in the A. A. U. meet in seven of the ten events. It was all the more to his credit that despite this he still was able to overcome so formidable a challenger as Yang.

Johnson's courage pulled him through the final event when it seemed that he might well be beaten.

After so long and wearing an ordeal, running 1,500 meters was a heavy burden for one of his size and weight. He hung on grimly at Yang's heels, and the Chinese youth could not shake him off.

Johnson Hangs On

As they moved into the stretch, Yang, summoning his last bit of strength, drew away, but Johnson never let him get more than four or five yards ahead. Johnson's victory was assured as he kept within that distance to the tape.

The other gold medal in track and field was won by Jozef Schmidt of Poland in the hop, step and jump. He set an Olympic record and broke his listed world record by leaping 55 feet 1¾ inches.

Al Oerter of West Babylon, L. I., also set an Olympic mark by throwing the discus 191 feet 8⅜ inches in qualifying for the final. Rink Babka of Manhattan Beach, Calif., and Dick Cochran of Brookfield, Mo., also qualified.

Ira Davis of Philadelphia was leading for the silver medal in the hop, step and jump but then lost second place to Vladimir Goriaev of the Soviet Union. On the last jump, Vitola Kreer of the Soviet Union barely beat Davis for the bronze medal.

In qualifying heats for the women's 800-meter run, the winners of three of the four heats broke the Olympic record.

The United States won five gold medals during the day and clinched a sixth. The winners, in addition to Otis Davis and Johnson, were three free-style wrestlers from Oklahoma—Terry McCann, a bantamweight from Tulsa, and Shelby Wilson, a lightweight, and Doug Blubaugh, a welterweight, both from Ponca City.

George O'Day of Dover, Mass., clinched the gold medal in 5.5-Meter Class yachting. However, the regatta will end tomorrow and the results will not become official until then. The Soviet Union and Norway also have clinched gold medals.

Turkey won four gold medals and Germany one in wrestling. The Soviet Union took one in shooting and Italy one in fencing.

Not counting the yachting results, the United States took the lead over the Soviet Union in gold medals, 26 to 22. However, The Associated Press reported that the Soviet team still led in the unofficial point standing with 446½. The United States is second with 416½.

Jazy Second to Elliott

The big show of the day, of course, was track and field.

If the 1,500 and 400 were not two most sensational races ever run in one day in the Olympics, no one could recall their equal. In each, six finalists were under the winning time made in the Melbourne Games in 1956.

Michel Jazy of France was the surprising winner of the 1,500 silver medal. He was followed across the line by the more favored and celebrated Istvan Rozsavolgyi of Hungary and Dan Waern of Sweden. Then came Zoltan Vamos of Rumania and Dyrol Burleson, the 20-year-old Oregon student from Cottage Grove, Ore.

Indicative of the killing pace, the youthful Burleson ran faster than did Ron Delany of Ireland in winning the gold medal at Melbourne. Yet Burleson finished sixth. Delany did not run in the 1,500 this year.

In the 400, Carl Kaufmann of Germany was clocked in the same remarkable time as Davis, though he lost by 3 feet. In a desperate effort to match the terrific pace of the American, he went sprawling on his face at the tape.

Feared Malcolm Spence of South Africa was third in 0:45.5, and equally feared Milkha Singh, a bearded Indian, was fourth in 0:45.6.

Manfred Kinder of Germany was fifth and 19-year-old Earl Young of San Fernando, Calif., sixth, though he was eight-tenths of a second under Charlie Jenkins' winning time at Melbourne.

The stunning victory of Davis was one of the great achievements of the Games at Rome. He had barely made the team in trials as the third American because of his inexperience in running in an outside lane. Today, he was in a middle lane. He ran with authority all the way and at a pace that killed off Singh and Spence in the stretch.

Elliott, the most glamorous figure in track in 1958, was something of a question mark when he came to Rome. He had done little running since then, and though he ran a 3:59.2 mile in California this year, there was a question whether he was still the great miler who had run the distance ten times under four minutes in 1958.

He had trained long and hard enough to get back in shape. But he had become a different man since he married and gave up eating nuts, raisins, dried fruit and oats for meat and other normal fare.

His trainer, Percy Cerutty, said he was the Elliott of old and stronger than ever. He knew that the wonder runner had been working hours daily for months, running along the beach and through heavy brush in his bare feet.

In qualifying heats here, track fanciers saw enough to persuade them that Cerutty was right. The ease and power with which Elliott raced with his long, smooth stride was entirely convincing.

Elliott was on the pole as the race started. He fell back to fourth place as Michel Bernard of France, Waern and Vamos set the pace. He stayed there, followed by Jazy and Rozsavolgyi, with Burleson and Jim Grelle of Portland, Ore., further back, until 600 yards from the finish.

On the backstretch, Elliott went outside and moved into third place, close behind Bernard and Waern. Rounding the turn, he cut loose in earnest and took the lead with 500 meters to go. Rozsavolgyi went with him and from sixth place moved into second. Jazy went up to third place. Vamos was fourth and Bernard fifth.

At the start of the last lap, with 400 meters to go, Elliott went away so fast that he removed any doubts about the outcome. He was the dictator of the race now.

Elliott Pulls Away

The crowd cheered him madly as he widened the gap to 20 yards over Jazy and Rozsavologyi on the backstretch. For the rest of the way it was a triumphant procession for the great Australian miler to thunderous cheers. He sped on at his killing pace and won overwhelmingly.

Indicative of the murderous pace of the race, the time for the first 400 meters was 0:58.2 and for the first 800 was 1:58.8. When Elliott set the previous world record in 1958 he did the first 400 in 0:58 and 800 meters in 1:58.

In the 400-meter final, Singh and Spence went out in front. Going around the turn into the stretch, Otis Davis started moving up and took Kaufmann with him. Spence was third.

Kaufmann, born in New York, challenged Davis and gained on him. The murderous pace of the fight for first place was too much for Spence and Singh.

Kaufmann drew almost even with Davis but could not quite catch him. Kaufmann lost his balance and fell heavily at full length at the finish.

Associated Press Radiophoto

ELECTRIFYING FINISH: Otis Davis of the U. S. steals a look at his opponent, Carl Kaufmann of Germany, at finish of the 400-meter dash in Rome. Davis won the final in 44.9 seconds, setting a world and Olympic record. Kaufmann was clocked in same time.

Associated Press Radiophoto

FRONT VIEW of the finish of the 400-meter dash. Davis, second from the left, breasts the tape as Kaufmann, right, begins to fall. Malcolm Spence, left, of South Africa was third. Earl Young, rear, of the U. S. finished sixth.

Final of 1,500 Meter Is Fastest Race Ever

ROME, Sept. 6 (UPI)—The 1,500-meter final in the Olympics today was the fastest race ever at the distance. The first seven finishers ran the equivalent of better than a four-minute mile.

Herb Elliott of Australia won in 3 minutes 35.6 seconds, breaking his world record. He also holds the world record of 3:54.5 for the mile.

Track statisticians add seventeen seconds to a 1,500-meter clocking to get a projected time for the mile. Fifteen hundred meters equal 1,640.2 yards, or 119.58 yards less than a mile.

Here are the times in the 1,500-meter final and the projected times for a mile:

	1,500 Meters	Mile
1—Herb Elliott, Australia	3:35.6	3:52.6
2—Michel Jazy, France	3:38.4	3:55.4
3—Istvan Rozsavolgyi, Hung.	3:39.2	3:55.4
4—Dan Waern, Sweden	3:40.0	3:57.0
5—Zoltan Vamos, Rumania	3:40.8	3:57.8
6—Dyrol Burleson, Cottage Grove, Ore.	3:40.9	3:57.9
7—Michel Bernard, France	3:41.5	3:58.5
8—Jim Grelle, Portland, Ore.	3:45.3	4:02.3
9—Arne Hamarsland, Norway	3:45.3	4:02.3

Elliott Loses Dedication but Not Greatness

Aussie Relaxes His Rigorous Training but Is Still Best

BY ROBERT DALEY

Special to The New York Times.

ROME, Sept. 6—At the age of 18, Herb Elliott had given up running, liked to smoke, drink beer, keep late hours and tool around Perth, Australia, on his motor scooter.

At 20, he was the greatest and most dedicated running machine the world had ever seen. He smashed the 4-minute-mile barrier a dozen times, lowering the record finally to an incredible 3 minutes 54.5 seconds.

Then he got married, became a father, considered turning pro. He gave up the Spartan life, raced rarely, spoke lightly of his future. He said, in effect, "Having raced so fast once, I no longer have to train hard."

At 22, he came to Rome for the Olympics, winner of half a dozen unimpressive races this season. He was relaxed and airy about his running now. He was, naturally, a potential winner of today's 1,500-meter race. But his days as a record-breaker seemed over.

And yet, today, winning the 1,500 by thirty yards in 3:35.6, he ran faster than ever before in his life. He ran the equivalent of a 3:52.6 mile. He ran every other man into the ground. He destroyed the race. There was no race. There was simply Elliott, running on and on. Faster and faster. The others wilted, the gap behind him widened, and he seemed all alone on the track.

He was born in Perth on Feb. 25, 1938. His father had a home furnishings business, but had been a top cross-country cyclist and loved all sports. As a child, Herb was, says his mother, always commanding and terribly aggressive. The boy went to a Catholic high school, got good marks in mathematics and ran the mile in 4:20.4.

Then, he dropped a piano on his foot, crushing the foot. He was 17, gave up track for good and took up what he calls carousing.

But, when the 1956 Olympics came to Melbourne, the Elliott family flew up from Perth. Herb watched enthralled—not at the 1,500-meter winner, Ron Delany, but at the Soviet star, Vladimir Kuts, who won both the 5,000 and 10,000 meter runs.

It seemed to 18-year-old Elliott that Kuts knew how to suffer, and suffering appealed to him.

He wrote to the mile record-holder, John Landy, for advice. Landy answered, encouraging

Continued on Page 51, Column 3

Associated Press Radiophoto

Autograph seekers asking signature of Herb Elliott of Australia after he received gold medal as winner of Olympic 1,500-meter run. Elliott broke his own world record for event.

JOHNSON RETIRES FROM 2-DAY GRIND

Exhausted Decathlon Victor Mobbed by Well-Wishers, Including Kuznetsov

ROME, Sept. 6 (AP)—Rafer Johnson was crowned as the world's greatest amateur athlete tonight, and then announced his retirement from such competition.

"I wanted this one real bad," said the Olympic decathlon champion after a grueling two-day competition in ten track and field events in Olympic Stadium. "But I never want to go through that again—never," added the 200-pounder from Kingsburg, Calif. "I'm awfully tired."

Referring to his principal challenger, Chuan-Kwang Yang of Taiwan, Rafer said, "So's he."

"I knew I had a working margin of about ten seconds in the 1,500 meters (the last event on the program)," Johnson said when it was all over. "But I wasn't going to let Yang get away. I just wanted to stay with him and that's what I did."

Johnson told the truth. In the 1,500-meter run he stuck to Yang like a buddy in combat.

In the dressing room later the winner was mobbed by well-wishers. One of them was the third-place bronze medal winner, Vasily Kuznetsov of the Soviet Union, a former world record holder. He grabbed Johnson and kissed him on the cheek. Then they embraced and patted each other on the back.

Yang sat on a bench and wept while Johnson was being hailed. He finally struggled to his feet, a very tired man, and moved toward Johnson. Yang seized Johnson's left hand and muttered:

"Nice going, Rafe."

ITALIAN BEST IN EPEE

Delfino Beats Briton, 5 to 2, for Olympic Gold Medal

ROME, Sept. 6 (UPI). — Giuseppe Delfino of Italy, six times a world champion, tonight added the Olympic men's individual épée crown to his collection with a 5-2 victory over a Briton, Allan Jay, a less-experienced but tireless campaigner.

Delfino, 39, defeated Jay in the fence-off for the gold medal, with the silver award going to the Britisher.

Earlier, Bruno Khabarov, a Russian, won the bronze medal in a fence-off with Josef Sakovits of Hungary.

Associated Press Wirephoto

GOLD-MEDAL EFFORT: Rafer Johnson of the United States throwing the discus yesterday during the Olympic decathlon. Californian won the ten-event competition.

Summaries of Olympic Games

By The Associated Press and United Press International

Men's Track and Field

HOP, STEP AND JUMP

PRELIMINARY ROUND

[illegible] Baguley, Australia, 51—[illegible]; Adhemar da Silva, Brazil, 51—2½; Yevgeni Mikhailov, Soviet Union, 51—5¼.

Failed to Qualify—Bill Sharpe, Philadelphia, 50 feet 7¾ inches; Herman Stokes, Los Angeles, 48—5¼; David Norris, New Zealand; Federico Bisson, Italy; Ramon Lopez, Cuba; Jan Jaskolski, Poland; Koji Sakurai, Japan; Samperiz Areta, Spain; Hannu Rantala, Finland; Hiroshi Shibata, Japan; Samuel Igun, Nigeria; Emil Thierfelder, Germany; Rouhollah Rahmani, Iran; Tomio Ota, Japan; Ygiray Pagda, Turkey; Reric Battista, France; Pedro Comacho-Cotto, Puerto Rico; Constantin Sfikas, Germany; Jory Wischmeier, Germany; Muhammed Khan, Pakistan; Pierre William, France; Enzo Cavalli, Italy; Abdul Abdul-Rzzak, Iraq; Dodin Patarinski, Bulgaria, Ben Maldin Kamaruddin, Malaya, did not compete.

FINAL

1. Jozef Schmidt, Poland, 55 feet 1¾ inches (betters listed world record of 54—9¼, set by Oleg Fedoseyev, Soviet Union, 1959; Schmidt has pending world record of 55—10½, set Aug. 5, 1960; also betters Olympic record of 53—11¼, set by Schmidt in qualifying); 2. Vladimir Goriaev, Soviet Union, 54—6¾; 3. Vitold Kreer, Soviet Union, 53—10¾; 4. Ira Davis, Philadelphia, 53—10; 5. V. Einarsson, Iceland, 53—8½; 6. Ryszard Malcherczyk, Poland, 52—6¾; 7. Manfried Hinze, Germany; 8. Kari Rahkamo, Finland; 9. Ian Tomlinson, Australia; 10. Yevgeni Mikhailov, Soviet Union; 11. Sten Erickson, Sweden; 12. Frederick Alsop, Britain; 13. John Baguley, Australia; 14. Adhemar da Silva, Brazil; 15. Pierluigi Gatti, Italy.

400-METER RUN

FINAL

1. Otis Davis, Los Angeles, 0:44.9 (world and Olympic record; old world record, 0:45.2, set by Lou Jones, U. S. A., 1956; old Olympic record, 0:45.5, set by Davis in preliminaries); 2. Carl Kaufmann, Germany, 0:44.9; 3. Mal Spence, South Africa, 0:45.5; 4. Milkha Singh, India, 0:45.6; 5. Manfred Kinder, Germany, 0:45.9; 6. Earl Young, San Fernando, Calif., 0:45.9.

1,500-METER RUN

FINAL

1. Herb Elliott, Australia, 3:35.6 (world and Olympic record; old world record, 3:36, set by Elliott in 1958. Old Olympic record, 3:41.2, set by Ron Delany, Ireland, 1956); 2. Michel Jazy, France, 3:38.4; 3. Istvan Rozsavolgyi, Hungary, 3:39.2; 4. Dan Waern, Sweden, 3:40; 5. Zoltan Vamos, Rumania, 3:40.8; 6. Dyrol Burleson, Cottage Grove, Ore., 3:40.9; 7. Michel Bernard, France, 3:41.5; 8. Jim Grelle, Portland, Ore., 3:45.3; 9. Arne Hamarsland, Norway, 3:45.3.

DISCUS THROW

PRELIMINARY ROUND

(Qualifying distance 170 feet 7¼ inches) Qualifiers for Final—Al Oerter, West Babylon, L. I., 191 feet 8⅜ inches (Olympic record; old record, 184—10½, set by Oerter in Melbourne, 1956); Rink Babka, Manhattan Beach, Calif., 178—8½; Dick Cochran, Brookfield, Mo., 176—5¾; Edmund Piatkowski, Poland, 176—6¼; Viktor Komparneec, Soviet Union, 172—9¼; Antonios Kounadis, Greece, 172—2½; Warwick Selvey, Australia, 170—10; Ferenc Klics, Hungary, 175—0; S. Haugen, Norway, 173¾; Cornelius Koch, the Netherlands, 175—5¼; Zdenek Nemec, Czechoslovakia, 172—10; Carmelo Rado, Italy, 173—9⅝; Zdenek Cihak, Czechoslovakia, 175—3¼; Jozsef Szwecsenyi, Hungary, 182—1¾; Todor Todorov, Bulgaria, 174—11⅝; Pentti Repo, Finland, 179—11¼; Manfred Grieser, Germany, 171—3¾; Vladimir Trusenev, Soviet Union, 178—2¼; Zenon Begier, Poland, 173—11¾; Lothar Milde, Germany, 174¼; Kim Bukhancov, Soviet Union, 174—1¾; Adolfo Consolini, Italy, 171—10.

Failed to qualify—Fritz Kuhl, Germany; Leslie Mills, New Zealand; Pierre Falard, France; Carol Lindroos, Finland; Stephanus du Plessis, South Africa; Solcede do la Quadra, Spain; Haider Khan, Pakistan; Naif Hamid, Iraq; Erik Uddebom, Sweden; Mesulama Rakuro, Fiji Islands; Osten Edlund, Sweden; Mike Lindsay, Britain; Franco Grossi, Italy; Salem El Jsiir, Lebanon; Godeon Uriel, Israel, and Herber Egermann, Austria, did not compete.

DECATHLON

110-METER HIGH HURDLES

First Heat—1, Rafer Johnson, Kingsburg, Calif., 0:15.3, 740 points; 2, Seppo Suutari, [illegible]

[illegible] Soviet Union, 0:15.0, 813; 3, Yiry Diachkov, Soviet Union, 0:15.3, 740; 4, Joze Brodnik, Yugoslavia, 0:15.7, 652.

Sixth Heat—1, Herman Timme, the Netherlands, 0:15.7, 652; 2, Hans Muchitzch, Austria, 0:15.8, 632; 3, Manfred Bock, Germany, 0:16.1, 575; 4, Gurcaschan Randhaa, India, 0:16.3, 523.

Seventh Heat—1, Franco Sar, Italy, 0:14.7, 894; 2, Luciano Paccagnella, Italy, 0:15.7, 632; 3, Walter Meier, Germany, 0:16.0, 593; 4, Holm Bjoergvin, Iceland, 0:16.2, 537.

DISCUS THROW

1, Kuznetsov, 166 feet 3¾ inches, 972 points; 2, Sar, 162-8, 935; 3, Johnson, 159-1, 894; 4, Paccagnella, 149-10, 797; 5, Kutenko, 149-8½, 795; 6, Kahma, 147-5, 773; 7, Kamerbeek, 145-5, 753; 8, Thomas, 133-9, 648; 9, Laipenieks, 132-10, 640; 10, Grogorenz, 131-7½, 630; 11, Yang, 130-8, 622; 12, Bjorgvin, 129-7, 612; 13, Meier, 128-6¾, 603; 14, Timme, 125-2¼, 601; 15, Suutari, 124-5¾, 571; 16, Diachkov, 124-3, 569; 17, Bock, 123-7¾, 564; 18, Brodnik, 123-6¾, 563; 19, Mijares, 123-2¼, 561; 20, Stulac, 112-9½, 457; 24, Mulkey, 111-11¼, 473; 22, Epitropoulos, 113-8¼, 487; 23, Marien, 112-9½, 457½; 24, Mulkey, 111-11¼, 473. (Randahawa withdraw).

POLE VAULT

1, Yang, Taiwan, 14 feet 1¼ inches, 915 points; 2, Kutenko, Soviet Union, 13—9, 855; 3, Brodnik, Yugoslavia, 13—3¾, 795; 4, tie between Bock, Germany, and Kuznetsov, Soviet Union, 12—9¼, each, 695; 6, Tie among Sar, Italy, Diachkov, Soviet Union, Johnson, Kingsburg, Calif., Kamberbeek, The Netherlands, 12—3¼, each, 645; 10, Tie between Meier, Germany, and Grogorenz, Germany, 12—1¼, each, 596; 12, Vogelsang, Switzerland, 12—1½, 745; 13, Tie among Paccagnella, Italy, Kahma, Finland, Stulac, Canada, 11—9¾, each, 556; 16, Suutari, Finland, 11—5¾, 516; 17, Mijares, Mexico, 11—1½, 476; 18, Tie among Marien, Belgium, Bjoergvin, Iceland, Laipenieks, Chile, Timme, The Netherlands, 10—9½, each, 438; 22, Tie between Thomas-Martinez, Venezuela, and Muchitsch, Austria, 10—6 each, 400.

JAVELIN THROW

1, Kutenko, Soviet Union, 234 feet 4½ inches, 1,031 points; 2, Kuznetsov, Soviet Union, 233-7½, 1,024; 3, Johnson, Kingsburg, Calif., 229-10½, 980; 4, Yang, Taiwan, 223-9¾, 937; 5, Brodnik, Yugoslavia, 214-3¾, 856; 6, Bock, Germany, 208-9¾, 817; 7, Laipenieks, Chile, 201-7, 764; 8, Grogorenz, Germany, 199-6, 750; 9, Kahma, Finland, 198-5½, 743; 10, Suutari, Finland, 196-4¾, 729; 11, Kamerbeek, the Netherlands, 188-7¾, 677; 12, Bjoergvin, Iceland, 188-5½, 676; 13, Sar, Italy, 182-10¼, 641; 14, Vogelsang, Switzerland, 172-1¼, 578; 15, Timme, the Netherlands, 169-9, 561; 16, Thomas-Martinez, Venezuela, 167-9¼, 549; 17, Epitropoulos, Greece, 166-2½, 540; 18, Stulac, Canada, 165-4½, 536; 19, Paccagnella, Italy, 159-5¾, 503; 20, Meier, Germany, 155-3¾, 480; 21, Marien, Belgium, 146-8¼, 434; 22, Mijares, Mexico, 142-3, 411; 23, Muchitsch, Austria, 126-1½, 330.

1,500-METER RUN

First Heat—1, Kahma, Finland, 4:22.8, 582 points; 2, Muchitsch, Austria, 4:23.3, 575; 3, Mijares, Mexico, 4:49.3, 339; 4, Paccagnella, Italy, 4:55.4, 294; 5, Timme, The Netherlands, 5:21.4, 137; 6, Thomas-Martinez, Venezuela, 5:25.2, 116.

Second Heat—1, Grogorenz, Germany, 4:27.0, 536 points; 2, Bock, Germany, 4:27.6, 530; 3, Marien, Belgium, 4:40.0, 414; 4, Bjoergvin, Iceland, 4:40.6, 409; 5, Jaipenieks, Chile, 4:57.5, 279; 6, Stulac, Canada, 5:59.6, 265.

Third Heat—1, Meier, Germany, 4:30.6, 500 points; 2, Brodnik, Yugoslavia, 4:37.7, 434; 3, Kamerbeek, The Netherlands, 4:43.6, 384; 4, Kuznetsov, Soviet Union, 4:53.8, 306; 5, Epitroupolos, Greece, 4:55.0, 297.

Fourth Heat—1, Vogelsang, Switzerland, 4:27.7, 528 points; 2, Kutenko, Soviet Union, 4:44.2, 379; 3, Yang, Taiwan, 4:48.5, 345; 4, Sar, Italy, 4:49.2, 340; 5, Johnson, Kingsburg, Calif., 4:49.7, 336; 6, Suutari, Finland, 5:04.8, 231.

FINAL POINT STANDING

Johnson	8,392	Paccagnella	6,283
Yang	8,334	Bjoergvin	6,261
Kuznetsov	7,809	Timme	6,206
Kutenko	7,567	Meier	6,000
Kamerbeek	7,236	Muchitsch	5,950
Sar	7,195	Merian	5,919
Kahma	7,112	Leipenieks	5,865
Grogorenz	7,032	Thom.-Martin'z	5,783
Brodnik	6,918	Mijares	5,413
Bock	6,894	Stulac	5,198
Vogelsang	6,767	Epitropoulos	4,737
Suutari	6,751		

Continued on Page 51, Column 1

PATTERSON FACES UNYIELDING FOES

Autograph Seekers in Rome Overwhelm Boxer as He Visits U. S. Victors

ROME, Sept. 6 (AP)—Floyd Patterson, the world heavyweight champion, fought one of his toughest fights today—and barely staggered through to a draw.

His opponents were a horde of persistent autograph seekers at the Olympic Village.

"By my book, I lost," said the champion, rubbing his tired right hand.

"Not you, champ," said the Olympic light-heavyweight champion, Cassius Clay of Louisville. "You got a draw at least."

Patterson said he wasn't sure.

"Were they tougher than Ingemar Johansson?" Patterson was asked.

"Just about," he replied.

Patterson visited the Olympic Village shortly before lunch. The place was full of hungry athletes and a large group of sight-seers, most of them German. For the last two days, parties of tourists—by special permission—have been admitted to the village.

Hatless and wearing dark glasses, Patterson went unrecognized until he neared his destination—the American section of the village.

Then he was sighted by the 18-year-old Clay. It was a signal for the autograph collectors, and they can run down a subject with all the deadliness of a big-game hunter on safari.

Swarming around Patterson they all but submerged him with autograph books, pieces of paper, envelopes, old letters and pencils and pen. After a few minutes, policemen helped extricate the champion—but it was a hard struggle.

Wearily Patterson signed on and on and on. Aided by officials and athletes, he finally managed to meet and congratulate the three American boxers who won gold medals last night. They were Clay, Wilbert McClure of Toledo, Ohio, a light middleweight, and Eddie Crook, an army sergeant from Fort Campbell, Ky., a middleweight.

Clay to Turn Pro

ROME, Sept. 6 (UPI)—Professional boxing holds an attraction at the moment for only one of the three United States gold medal winners in the Olympics.

Cassius Clay plans to cash in immediately. Wilbert McClure has another year at the University of Toledo, and then "I'll see about turning pro."

Eddie Crook, 31, is an Army career man and one of the best quarterbacks in service football. The coach at Fort Campbell, Ky., is anxiously awaiting his return from Rome.

Denmark Tops Hungary, 2-0

ROME, Sept. 6 (AP)—Denmark reached the final of the Olympic soccer tournament tonight with a 2-0 upset victory over Hungary before 15,000 fans in the Flaminio Stadium. The winners will meet Yugoslavia Saturday.

Crowd Jeers Russian For an Apparent Snub

ROME, Sept. 6 (AP)—Vitola Kreer of the Soviet Union created an incident today in the Olympics when he apparently refused to accept congratulations from Ira Davis of Philadelphia after a leap that placed Davis out of the running for a medal in the hop, step and jump.

The crowd hooted and jeered when Kreer raised both arms forward and shook his head as if to hold Davis at a distance.

A Soviet official explained that Kreer had not rejected congratulations but wanted to indicate that congratulations had not been in order because three competitors had one jump apiece left.

After the event had ended and the situation had been explained to Davis, he and Kreer shook hands and put their arms around each other.

However, when Kreer stood on the victory stand to get his medal, the crowd jeered loudly. When Kreer left the stand his head was bowed, and he rubbed his eyes as if weeping.

Lakers Down Knicks as Baylor Sets League Record of 71 Points at Garden

COAST ACE EXCELS IN 123-108 GAME

Baylor, Lakers, Clips Own Mark Against Knicks—Pistons Win, 115-114

By ROBERT L. TEAGUE

Nobody wearing the livery of the New York Knickerbockers came close to keeping up with Elgin Baylor of the Los Angeles Lakers last night. The penalty was a record 71-point spree for the star forward and a 123-108 victory for the Coast quintet at Madison Square Garden.

A crowd of 10,132 gave him a standing ovation that lasted for nearly a minute when the 6-foot 5-inch athlete left the floor with his National Basketball Association mark.

His performance all but made the spectators forget the thrilling finish of the first game in the league double-header in which the Detroit Pistons erased a 20-point deficit and downed the Boston Celtics, 115—114, in overtime. The deciding basket came on a 20-foot jump shot by Gene Shue at the final buzzer.

Baylor was as unpredictable as he was unstoppable. He counted quite a few points on orthodox driving lay-ups and tap-ins, but a good number came from angles that seemed impossible. He frequently popped out of a concentration of milling players, twisted his body in mid-air and scored with a deft flick of the wrist that put a knowledgeable backspin on the ball.

Once Baylor had established the possibility of such maneuvers, the Knicks tried them. They had no success. To make matters worse, the home forces began finding it difficult to make even routine shots and fell farther and farther off the pace.

Baylor was greatly aided by the ball stealing and passing of Jerry West and by the threat that Rudy LaRusso posed with his jump shot from near the free-throw circle. Willie Naulls paced New York's attack with 35 points.

Knicks Gain Early Lead

Naulls and Ken Sears collected a total of 15 points in the first ten minutes, helping the Knicks assume a 17-10 lead. Tap-ins by Baylor and jump shots by West tied it at 21-21 but Naulls and Bob McNeill each turned in a 3-point play to stave off the threat for the time being.

High-flying rebounding by Johnny Green and his subsequent passes to Guerin and Naulls for lay-ups enabled the New Yorkers to retain a slim lead throughout most of the first half.

As half-time approached, however, LaRusso joined Baylor in the unstoppable class, connecting on one-handed jump shots while apparently off balance. A theft by West led to a lay-up by Frank Selvy, a former Knickerbocker. That tied the score at 55-all with 2:30 left in the second period.

Seconds later, West grabbed a rebound and passed to Baylor automatically. The Lakers went to the front for the first time, at 57-55, 1:35 before the intermission.

It was all Baylor and LaRusso in the closing minute of the half, which ended with Los Angeles ahead, 65-58. By connecting on fifteen of twenty shots in the first half, Baylor set a Garden record of 34 points for one half. His fifteen field goals also established a one-half mark for the Eighth Avenue arena.

Naulls was the main reason why the Knicks were in close contention at this point, having tallied 20 points in the first two quarters.

Charlie Tyra and Naulls paced an uprising that caught the Lakers at 66—66 in the first two and a half minutes of the third quarter. Almost five minutes elapsed before Coach Carl Braun's quintet picked up another point, however. Meanwhile, Los Angeles ran 11 straight points—most of them by Baylor and West—making the count 77—66.

Elgin kept hitting on his driving lay-ups and tap-ins. His team enjoyed a 90-73 cushion when the third period ended. About the only question left in the time, it seemed, was whether the former Seattle star would also shatter the N. B. A.'s one-game record of 64 points, which he set last season against the Celtics.

His team-mates fed him generously in the closing minutes and he got his record with 1:35 remaining.

In the opener Boston appeared to be headed for a runaway triumph after erasing an 11-point deficit and taking the lead for the first time late in the second quarter. Bob Cousy, Sam and K. C. Jones were the mainsprings in the Celtics' second-quarter spurt that put them into a 60-47 advantage at half-time.

A rout appeared to be in prospect as Frank Ramsey, Tom Heinsohn and Bill Russell continued the onslaught for Boston in the early minutes of the third period, increasing the margin to 67-47. But this 20-point spread seemed to act as an opiate on the defending champions. Their attack suddenly slowed to a crawl.

The Pistons steadily closed the gap on long set shots by Chuck Noble, short hooks by Walt Dukes and jump shots by Shue and Shellie McMillon.

With 3:30 remaining in the fourth period, McMillon of Detroit took a pass from Shue and sank a basket that cut the deficit to 99-91. And with ten seconds to go, Shue connected on another jump shot that evened the teams at 103-all.

Shue Connects at End

The lead changed hands three times in the five-minute overtime period, with Bill Sharman and Jim Loscutoff leading the Celtics to a 114-113 edge. Then, just when it appeared that time would overtake the Pistons, Shue connected on his pet shot in the last second.

Shue, an all-league guard, wound up as the game's high scorer with 26 points. Heinsohn led Boston with 23.

DETROIT (115)	G.	F.	PF.	P.	BOSTON (114)	G.	F.	PF.	P.
Howell, lf	8	5	3	21	Heins'n, lf	9	5	6	23
Dees	2	0	0	4	Loscut'f, rf	3	0	5	6
McMillon	3	2	0	8	Ramsey	6	2	2	14
Morel'd, rf	2	1	0	5	Russell, c	4	2	2	10
Lee	2	3	0	7	Conley	2	0	3	4
Dukes, c	5	6	3	16	Cousy, lg	6	6	4	18
Ferry	3	2	2	8	K. C. Jones	3	2	2	8
Shue, lg	9	8	2	26	Sh'man, rg	8	3	1	19
Ohl, rg	5	2	3	12	Sam Jones	6	0	3	12
Noble	2	4	4	8					
Total	41	33	17	115	Total	47	20	28	114

Detroit	27	20	24	32	12—115
Boston	23	37	24	19	11—114

Free throws missed—Howell 4, Moreland 2, Lee 2, Dukes, Shue 2, Noble 2, Russell 2, Sam Jones.
Officials—Sid Borgia and Pete D'Ambrosio.

LOS ANGELES (123)	G.	F.	PF.	P.	KNICKS (108)	G.	F.	PF.	P.
Baylor	28	15	5	71	Naulls, lf	14	7	4	35
LaRusso, rf	6	3	4	15	Budd	0	0	1	0
Felix	0	0	0	0	Sears, rf	5	7	5	17
Alcorn, c	1	0	5	2	Green	1	2	2	4
Hawkins	3	1	5	7	Tyra, c	3	3	1	9
Jolliff	1	0	0	2	Imhoff	1	0	2	2
Selvy, lg	4	1	1	9	Palmer	4	2	1	10
West	4	2	3	10	Guerin, lg	7	1	5	15
Hundley, rg	3	1	2	7	George	0	0	1	0
Leonard	0	0	0	0	G'rm'k'r, rg	1	3	2	5
					McNeill	4	3	3	11
Total	50	23	25	123	Total	40	28	27	108

Los Angeles	33	32	25	33—123
Knicks	35	23	15	35—108

Free throws missed—Naulls, Budd 2, Guerin, Garmaker 2, Baylor 3, La Russo 4, Hawkins 2, Selvy 2, West 3, Hundley 2.
Officials—Mendy Rudolph and Dick Sheldon.

Associated Press

SETS LEAGUE MARK: Elgin Baylor of the Los Angeles Lakers, who scored 71 points against the Knickerbockers last night.

Hun School Booters Win, 6-0

Special to The New York Times.

PRINCETON, N. J., Nov. 15—The Hun School beat Pennington Prep, 6 to 0, today and won the New Jersey prep school soccer championship.

Associated Press

TAKE TWO SHOTS: Bailey Howell of Detroit is fouled during first period of game against Boston at Madison Square Garden. Knocking the ball away is Bill Russell of Celtics. In foreground is Jackie Moreland of Pistons.

$3.5 Million Offer for Athletics Accepted From St. Louis Group

Formal Order of Sale of Stock Owned by Johnson's Widow Expected to Be Signed by Judge Today

CHICAGO, Nov. 15 (AP)—A St. Louis group headed by Elliot Stein bought the Kansas City Athletics' baseball club today for $3,500,000.

The formal order for the sale, which includes 52 per cent of the stock owned by the late Arnold Johnson, was expected to be signed tomorrow by Probate Judge Robert J. Dunne.

Mrs. Warren Humes, remarried widow of Johnson, and the City National Bank of Chicago, co-executors of the Johnson estate, reached an out-of-court agreement to sell the stock to pay debts and taxes of $1,500,000 owed by Johnson. He died March 10.

Arrangements also included sale of the 48 per cent of stock held by minority stockholders.

Mrs. Humes and the bank had been at odds over the sale of the 52 per cent. Mrs. Humes wanted to keep the stock, but the bank wanted to sell it.

Last week, Judge Dunne ruled that the Cook County Probate Court had jurisdiction in the dispute. Judge Dunne postponed hearings this week in hopes an agreement would be reached between Mrs. Humes and the bank. The Johnson estate will receive $1,800,000 from the sale.

Stein, who refused to comment on the sale, will be associated with Gordon Scherck, a business partner; Lester Crown, a Chicago business man, and Charles Baxter, who formerly owned 30 per cent of the Cleveland Indians.

A spokesman also refused to comment on the sale and Judge Dunne could not be reached in an attempt to learn why the club had been sold to the St. Louis group. A syndicate of Kansas City business men also were reported to have offered $3,500,000 for the team.

It was reported in Kansas City, however, that there had been no agreement for sale of the 48 per cent held by the minority stockholders. The Kansas City group said it would make strenuous efforts to buy the stock not held by Mrs. Humes.

College and School Results

BASKETBALL

Schools

Aviation 62 .... Metal Trades 34
Cleveland 72 .... Bayside 61
Dodge 58 .... Clinton 45
Eastern District 51 (o'time) Ft. Hamilton 49
Jackson 58 .... Richmond Hill 57
John Jay 52 .... Brooklyn Tech 36
Lane 48 .... Bryant 41
Madison 48 .... Midwood 47
Morris 40 .... Haaren 27
Tilden 62 .... Sheepshead Bay 52

CROSS-COUNTRY

Schools

Bogota 15 .... Bergen Catholic 40
Pascack Valley 23 .... Westwood 32
Ramsey 23 .... Paramus 32

SOCCER

Colleges

Hunter 3 .... Queens 0
Pratt 8 .... L. I. U. 0

Schools

Chatham 9 .... Madison 0
East Paterson 2 .... Ramapo 0
Fieldston 2 .... Riverdale 0
Hun School 6 .... Pennington Prep 0
Jamaica 1 .... Van Buren 1
Rudolf Steiner 3 .... Elisabeth Irwin 0
Seward Park 4 ..... (overtime) ..... Morris 1

SWIMMING

Schools

Metropolitan Vocational 48 . N.Y. Printing 20

Scudero of Steelers Retires

PITTSBURGH, Nov. 15 (AP)—Joe Scudero, a Pittsburgh steeler defensive back retired today. Scudero, 30 years old, told Coach Buddy Parker he felt he was "a little old, a little slow," to compete in the National League.

EXPANSION MOVE FACES MISGIVINGS

National League Expresses Reservations on Rival's Plan for Los Angeles

By LOUIS EFFRAT

It became more and more apparent yesterday that the American League's plans for expansion to ten teams in 1961 were not proceeding smoothly or according to schedule.

In the wake of a demand by Commissioner Ford Frick that the majors amend the rule dealing with the legality of territorial invasion, the National League disclosed it would oppose such an amendment, slated to be proposed by the American League.

Commissioner Frick had advised the leagues that although he favored expansion, he would not approve it until Rule One was amended. The rule states:

"To provide and stimulate competition for the league pennants and for the world championship, the circuit of either major league shall not be changed to include any city in the circuit of the other major league except by the unanimous consent of the clubs constituting both major leagues."

League Meets Tomorrow

The American League club owners began drifting into town yesterday for the league meeting tomorrow at the Savoy Hilton Hotel.

There the question of expansion will get a full-dress review.

When the National League met in Chicago on Oct. 17, it voted to admit New York and Houston in 1962. The American League, in session here on Oct. 26, also agreed to enlarge to ten clubs. But there was one big difference:

Where the National League had picked 1962 as the year of expansion, the American League decided to expand in 1961. The two new American League locales were announced as Los Angeles and Minneapolis-St. Paul.

It had been assumed that everything between the leagues was sugary. In fact Warren Giles, the president of the National League, had stated on Oct. 17 that his league would propose an amendment to Rule One during the joint major league meeting to be held Dec. 7 in St. Louis.

Now the National League has changed its mind. Giles disclosed that yesterday. From his office in Cincinnati, he said his league would not propose the change.

A Change of View

"We are not going to make the proposal," Giles said by telephone. "We have been advised by Commissioner Frick that the proposal will be made by the American League at our joint meeting, so it is on the agenda, anyway.

"We do expect to debate the merits of the American League proposal. I contend that the proposed entry of the American League into Los Angeles in 1961 and the relocation of the National League in 1962 are in no way analogous. The National League was invited and urged to return to New York. The American League was not urged to come to Los Angeles."

There are, Giles said, other reasons for National League reservations.

"The rapidity with which the American League is moving is one," he said. "Furthermore, all the National League owners agree with Walter O'Malley, who brought the Dodgers from Brooklyn to Los Angeles. They would like for Walter to enjoy the honeymoon before the relatives arrive."

Obviously a part of whatever "peeve" the National League may hold is the matter of reimbursement for O'Malley.

According to Frick, "O'Malley has done very little squawking," but his fellow club owners feel he is entitled to some money for permitting the American League to share California.

It is believed O'Malley's expenditures for clearing the territory, indemnifying the Pacific Coast League and fixing the playing field at the Coliseum were about $700,000.

Sideline observers feel the two leagues will get together. Joe Cronin, the president of the American League, declined to comment until after tomorrow's meeting, but Frick was not at all reluctant to discuss the situation.

"I am in favor of expansion," the Commissioner said, "but it must be done in orderly fashion. Rule One must be amended. Both leagues must get together and amend the rule. It must be done legally and it must be fair and decent, on the basis of respect for the rights of others, not only for the present but for the future.

"As I have said repeatedly, I believe in expansion. I will support it. Some time ago I declared New York and Los Angeles open territory. I believe that any city with a population of 2,000,000 or more should be open territory.

"But the two leagues must first see to it that Rule One is amended. Unless and until that is done, I will not permit a second team to go into Los Angeles or into New York for that matter."

Frick pointed out that Washington, Houston and Minneapolis-St. Paul were not involved in the question of legality, for there are no other big league teams in those cities.

WASHINGTON, Nov. 15 (AP)—Chairman Estes Kefauver of the Senate Antimonopoly Subcommittee warned Commissioner Ford Frick today against any delay in expansion.

The Tennessee Democrat's views were relayed by Rand Dixon, the subcommittee chief counsel. Dixon has conducted Senate hearings on baseball for Kefauver since 1957.

BASEBALL BID STALLED

New Yorkers Seek Control of Franchise in Washington

WASHINGTON, Nov. 15 (AP)—Plans for a joint bid for the new Washington baseball franchise in the American League appeared stalled tonight, apparently over the question of which group would have control.

Elwood R. Quesada, Federal Aviation Agency administrator, said the group headed by the New York financier, John J. Bergen, wanted complete control of the baseball team.

"We—my group and I—have a strong conviction that control of the Washington club should be in the hands of Washington people," Quesada said.

The eight American League owners will weigh all bids Thursday in New York. It will take a minimum of six votes to decide which groups will operate the proposed new franchises in Washington and Los Angeles.

Orioles Sign Richards for 3 Years

BALTIMORE, Nov. 15 (UPI)—Paul Richards, who built the Baltimore Orioles from a second-division team into a pennant contender, became the highest paid manager in baseball today.

The lean Texan signed a three-year contract at $50,000 a year. He had a year to go on his existing contract, which called for $45,000 annually plus bonuses based on the team's home attendance.

Lee MacPhail, the president and general manager, said the Orioles were "extremely happy" about the contract. MacPhail added, "I happen to think that Paul is the best manager in baseball."

Richards will receive 5 cents for every customer above the 800,000 mark during each year of the contract. The Orioles drew 1,187,849 fans at home during the 1960 season.

Casey Stengel, who was let out last month as the New York Yankee manager, had been the highest paid manager in baseball. He drew a reported $75,000 annually.

Richards astonished the baseball world this year by leading the Orioles to a second-place finish behind the Yankees, the highest in their modern history.

Paul Richards

He was named the American League manager of the year by United Press International. [He won the same honor in an Associated Press poll.]

Sports of The Times

By ARTHUR DALEY

Momentous Meeting

RAW winds knifed in from Lake Michigan and blunted themselves against the ornate coping and windows of the Grand Palace Hotel in Chicago on Nov. 21, 1900. In a third-floor room sports history was being made. In a clear and flowing hand the secretary of the group wrote out baseball's Declaration of Independence. He began it this way:

"We the undersigned, desiring to reorganize The American League of Professional Base Ball Clubs * * *."

Thus did the American League spring into being as a challenger to the National League. It was the culmination of nine years of thorough and careful planning by a reformed Cincinnati sports writer named Byron Bancroft Johnson. A dominating, domineering figure, Ban Johnson drove the Americans to a position of pre-eminence during his twenty-seven years as president.

Sixty years—less four days—later the American League will gather in another momentous meeting tomorrow. Once again reorganization will be a topic but if any raw winds knife against the conclave headquarters at the Savoy Hilton they'll be from the lake in Central Park, not from Lake Michigan. And the preparatory work has not encompassed nine years but twenty-two days.

Without Haste

The amiable and imperturbable Joe Cronin now occupies the swivel chair once filled by the dynamic Johnson. Jovial Joe is unruffled by criticism that the American League is moving too fast in its attempt to expand to ten teams for the 1961 season, contrasted with the measured pace of the Nationals in setting 1962 as a target date.

"I don't know how you can say we're hasty," he said pleasantly. "As far back as 1953 we altered our constitution to provide room for ten clubs. We even had to talk some of our more impetuous members out of voting in October of 1959 to expand to nine clubs for 1960. Then we could move up later to ten and perhaps twelve.

"But we would have needed interleague play with the Nationals to go to nine and we didn't get the cooperation. What's wrong with going to ten teams for next season? We have to get off the ground some time."

Since the Americans already have granted permission to Calvin Griffith to move his Washington franchise to the Twin Cities of Minneapolis and St. Paul, their main business in reorganizing the set-up will be to approve of new franchise holders in Los Angeles and Washington.

The Coast group will be bankrolled by C. Arnholt Smith of San Diego and run by Hank Greenberg. Washington is likely to be under the joint ownership of John Bergen, an admiral, and Pete Quesada, a general. Considering the type of ballplayers they'll have, this team may get the nickname of the Pentagon Patsies.

Diamond Socialism

Once the franchises are awarded, the American Leaguers will wrestle with the titanic problem of stocking the two new teams. They probably will use some version of the Disaster Plan—it's also known as the Ghoul Pool—for replenishing personnel in the event some team should be erased by air or other disaster. It never has been publicized or detailed. Presumably a majority of key players on each club would be set aside as untouchables and fringe players made available.

Culver Service

Ban Johnson

His reorganization plan took nine years

Although the Americans advance toward their meeting with a blind serenity, blissfully believing that expansion in 1961 is virtually a fait accompli, disqueting words were uttered elsewhere. They came from that ardent advocate of expansion, Commissioner Ford Frick.

"No one is going anywhere," he said firmly, "until Rule One is amended. I've been urging for four years that the two leagues amend it but they didn't want to do it. I'm interested in what's good for baseball and I will insist on orderly procedure in a fair and decent way."

Rule One provides that no league may enter the city of another league without unanimous consent of all clubs in both leagues. The Americans propose to barge into Los Angeles in 1961 and the Nationals into New York in 1962.

If there is a vote on changing Rule One, the commissioner can cast the deciding ballot to break a tie and he will do so for 1962. But there's no guarantee that he'll do so for 1961. And the matter cannot come to the head before the winter meetings on Dec. 5, thus eliminating the two new American League teams from participating in the minor league player draft a week earlier. Frick is not enamored with the precipitate action of the Americans in setting their target date of next season.

Panic and Pique

Someone once said that the Americans were driven to immediate expansion partly by panic and partly by pique. Their noses were knocked out of joint by the way the Nationals took the initiative from them, grabbing two prize franchises in New York and Houston without even asking for a by-your-leave. So the Americans responded in kind.

This is kid stuff, not the weighted action of multimillion dollar organizations arranging their destinies. Nor have the Americans strengthened their position by insisting on 1961 delivery of a mechanism far too intricate to be manufactured in so brief a time. Frick might do the Americans a favor by refusing to slap a rush label on their order.

ROYALS SET BACK WARRIORS, 124-115

Robertson Paces Drive With 44 Points—Chamberlain Gets 36 for Losers

CINCINNATI, Nov. 15 (AP)—Oscar Robertson poured in 44 points tonight as the Cincinnati Royals raced to a 124-115 victory over the Philadelphia Warriors, leaders of the Eastern Division of the National Basketball Association.

It was the biggest point-scoring night in Robertson's brief professional career and he outscored the Warriors' Wilt Chamberlain, who had 36.

In a brilliant second-quarter effort, the Royals outscored the Warriors, 33—13, with Robertson, Jack Twyman and Bob Boozer scoring 23 of the points. That outburst enabled Cincinnati to carry a 67-46 lead into the last half.

The Warriors quickly pared 6 points off that margin at the start of the third quarter, but the Royals rallied again and led, 91—81, going into the final quarter.

With the score at 97—89, Robertson hit the next 8 points.

Robertson connected on seventeen of thirty-four shots from the field and ten of twelve from the free-throw line. Chamberlain hit on sixteen of twenty-nine field-goal attempts, but he missed seven of his eleven free-throw attempts.

It was the first time the Royals had beaten Philadelphia since Feb. 13, 1959. They had lost thirteen straight to the Warriors.

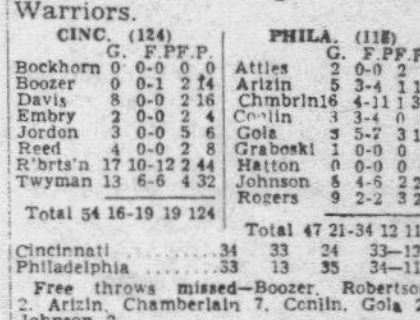

CINC. (124)	G.	F.	PF.	P.	PHILA. (115)	G.	F.	PF.	P.
Bockhorn	0	0-0	0	0	Attles	2	0-0	2	4
Boozer	0	0-1	2	14	Arizin	5	3-4	1	13
Davis	8	0-0	2	16	Chmbrln	16	4-11	1	36
Embry	2	0-0	2	4	Conlin	3	3-4	0	9
Jordon	3	0-0	5	6	Gola	3	5-7	3	11
Reed	4	0-0	2	8	Graboski	1	0-0	0	2
R'brts'n	17	10-12	2	44	Hatton	0	0-0	0	0
Twyman	13	6-6	4	32	Johnson	8	4-6	2	20
					Rogers	9	2-2	3	20
Total	54	16-19	19	124	Total	47	21-34	12	115

Cincinnati	34	33	24	33—124
Philadelphia	33	13	35	34—115

Free throws missed—Boozer, Robertson 2, Arizin, Chamberlain 7, Conlin, Gola 2, Johnson 2.
Attendance—5,279.

Nevada Cancels Plane Trip

RENO, Nov. 15 (AP)—The University of Nevada canceled today a scheduled six-hour flight for its football team to Denver and substituted a bus ride because of the Oct. 29 air crash that had killed sixteen players from California Polytechnic. The flight had been booked with Arctic-Pacific whose plane crashed with the Cal Poly team.

National Basketball Ass'n

Los Angeles 123, New York 108.
Detroit 115, Boston 114 (overtime).
Cincinnati 124, Philadelphia 115.

STANDING OF THE TEAMS

EASTERN DIV.	W.	L.	PC.	WESTERN DIV.	W.	L.	PC.
Phila.	9	2	.818	St. Louis	7	2	.778
Boston	5	3	.625	Cincinnati	7	7	.500
Syracuse	2	6	.250	Detroit	5	5	.500
New York	2	10	.167	L. A.	5	7	.417

TONIGHT'S SCHEDULE

Cincinnati at Syracuse.
Philadelphia at Detroit.
St. Louis at Boston.

The Big Game? Why, It's at Haverford Saturday

Swarthmore and Host to Play 51st Contest of Series

By JOSEPH M. SHEEHAN

This is the week of The Game (Harvard-Yale) and The Big Game (California-Stanford) in college football. At Cambridge, at Berkeley and at intervening and surrounding centers of culture, the fierce concentration on the gridiron affair at hand lowers an impenetrable screen on all events outside the pale.

College Sports Notes

It's that way also at Bethlehem (Lehigh-Lafayette), Pittsburgh (Pittsburgh-Penn State), Chapel Hill (North Carolina-Duke), Knoxville (Tennessee-Kentucky), Columbus (Ohio State-Michigan), Madison (Wisconsin-Minnesota), Bloomington (Indiana-Purdue), Columbia (Missouri-Kansas), Los Angeles (Southern California-University of California at Los Angeles), Corvallis (Oregon State-Oregon) and Pullman (Washington State-Washington).

On a lower level of competition, preparations are being pursued on the same high level of intensity for another game that is big to those who play and watch it. That's the fifty-first contest between Swarthmore College and Haverford College, to be played on Walton Field in Haverford at 1:45 P. M. Saturday.

The old rivals haven't had lustrous seasons. Haverford hasn't won a game. Swarthmore's record shows only one victory. Their joint lack of success won't dampen the occasion a bit. Alumni and friends of both institutions still will flock to the scene in force for a communal celebration that has become a treasured tradition.

As usual, the festivities will begin with a soccer game between the colleges at 10:30 A.M. Separate luncheons for the combined student and alumni bodies follow. Then the rival adherents will disperse to opposite sides of the football field to cheer their teams.

It's characteristic of the athletic philosophy at Swarthmore and Haverford that the soccer and football games carry equal weight in determining the disposition of the Hood Trophy. In fact, so do the cross-country, basketball, wrestling, track, tennis, golf and baseball contests held between the colleges at other times.

The Hood Trophy, put in competition in 1941 in memory of Albert L. Hood Jr., Swarthmore, '31, goes each year to the college winning a majority of the nine Haverford-Swarthmore sports contests. Swarthmore hasn't beaten Haverford in football since 1954 but it has won the Hood Trophy three times in a row.

Swarthmore gives much of the credit for its healthy overall sports picture to the institution in 1947 of a faculty-representative system for its athletic program. A member of the academic faculty is assigned to each sport. He attends practices and games, makes all trips and is very much a member of the team.

Professors Join Drills

It's a familiar sight at Swarthmore to see a Russian profesor scrimmaging with the soccer players, a philosophy professor shooting practice rounds with the golfers, a history profesor volleying with the team on the tennis court or an engineering professor clamping a half nelson on a varsity wrestler.

"The faculty-representative system does a lot for team morale, particularly in the more obscure sports," noted one close observer of the Swarthmore scene.

"Faculty representatives are good for the boys. Often a boy really likes sports and wants to play but feels guilty about taking the time and leaving lab classes before everyone else. It helps him to know that faculty members think sports are important enough to give their own time to them.

"Also, when the teams play away, coaches are proud to introduce a member of the faculty as part of the group. It's like saying Swarthmore College is here, not just the team."

Visitors' Team Morale Lifted by Faculty-Aide System

New Series Hinted

Is a home-and-home football series between Princeton and Stanford, to start in 1964, in the making? The Princeton Alumni News asks the question. . . . In catching twenty-eight passes during the past season, Dick Eustis Jr. joined his father in New Hampshire's football record book. The senior Eustis set the Wildcat career scoring record of twenty-six touchdowns in 1929, 1930 and 1931.

Some sideliners tab Brown's freshman football team as the strongest cub unit in the Ivy League, which may mean that things will be looking up for John McLaughry at Providence before long. . . . Amherst's fall sports teams had probably the most successful seasons in Lord Jeff annals. Six squads compiled a combined record of twenty-six victories, eight defeats and four ties. The varsity and freshman soccer teams and the freshman football team were undefeated.

"All the News That's Fit to Print."

The New York Times.

LATE CITY EDITION
U. S. Weather Bureau Report (Page 48) Forecasts
Early morning rain becoming cloudy, colder later today. Fair tomorrow.
Temp. range: 36—24; yesterday: 41.6—30.8.

VOL. CX..No. 37,593.

NEW YORK, TUESDAY, DECEMBER 27, 1960.

10 cents beyond 50-mile zone from New York City except on Long Island. Higher in air delivery cities.

FIVE CENTS

TITO SCORES WEST AS MAJOR SOURCE OF WORLD DISCORD

Tells Parliament Yugoslavia Agrees With Moscow on Main Issues of Day

BUT HE ASSAILS PEIPING

Blames Chinese for Attack on Him in Red Manifesto —Outlines 5-Year Plan

By PAUL UNDERWOOD
Special to The New York Times.

BELGRADE, Yugoslavia, Dec. 26—President Tito accused the West today of being the principal source of discord in the contemporary world.

Brushing aside attacks on Yugoslav policies contained in the communiqué issued following last month's conference in Moscow of leaders of eighty-one Communist parties, the Yugoslav chief declared that Belgrade and Moscow had identical views on "the most important issues of the day."

Marshal Tito's statement, made at a special session of the Yugoslav Parliament, was the frankest avowal yet of Yugoslavia's alignment with the Soviet Union that has been evident in Belgrade's policies for the last several months.

The present "aggravation" of the international atmosphere, Marshal Tito declared, is the fault of "certain bellicose people, especially in the West, who still adhere to the position of power policy in the settlement of international problems and are therefore against the easing of international tension."

Remarks Called Mild

Although the Yugoslav chief called the Moscow communiqué a "rotten compromise" and "interference in our internal policies," Moscow bloc sources described his remarks on this subject as "unexpectedly mild."

He contented himself largely with denials of charges at the Moscow meeting that the Yugoslav Communists had abandoned Marxism-Leninism or had sought to undermine the unity of the Communist world by their international policies. He declared that the Yugoslav party would continue its own way regardless of what others thought or said.

Only the last three pages of President Tito's statement were devoted to the Moscow communiqué. Describing the charges against Yugoslavia as "a series of the harshest untruths," he accused the Chinese Communists of responsibility for the attack.

"We know that the main initiators this time were the Chinese delegates," he declared, adding: "But do socialist morals permit that by means of false accusations a rotten compro-

Continued on Page 2, Column 4

Scientists Hear Red China Taps Vast Mineral Riches

Deposits Found by Prospectors Among World's Biggest, Parley Here Told—Advance in Atomics Also Cited

By WALTER SULLIVAN

Intensive geological prospecting on the Chinese mainland in the last decade has disclosed mineral resources so extensive that they appear to make China one of the world's chief reservoirs of raw materials.

This was reported yesterday at a symposium on China sponsored by the Government's National Science Foundation and by ten leading scientific societies. The two-day symposium at the Commodore Hotel is designed to help fill large gaps in American knowledge of scientific and technological developments in Communist China.

It forms part of the annual meeting of the American Association for the Advancement of Science, which began here yesterday. The meeting will continue until Friday, with some 7,000 scientists participating.

The symposium was told that, in the last ten years, Communist China had jumped from twentieth place, in extent of weather observations, to rival Canada for third place. The United States and Soviet Union lead in this field.

Likewise, it was reported, the Chinese have made important advances in nuclear physics. They now have four known nuclear reactors, all apparently designed for research, rather than for making atomic-bomb fuel. This report, of course, does not rule out the existence of secret fuel-producing reactors.

In this connection, one speaker noted that a number of Chinese nuclear physicists of wide repute had faded from the scientific literature. His interpretation was that they were too

Continued on Page 14, Column 5

BUSINESS IN 1960 FOUND GOOD HERE; HOPE HIGH FOR '61

Only 24% in Survey Report Less Volume Than in '59 —58.2% Cite Gains

By CHARLES GRUTZNER

This has been a good year for business in New York City and the first half of 1961 is expected to be as good or better, according to the Commerce and Industry Association.

The association said yesterday that these views were shared by about three-fourths of the 204 business and industrial executives covered in its annual survey. Ralph G. Risley, survey manager, said the sampling represented all major business classifications in the five boroughs.

Mr. Risley reported that 58.2 per cent of the participants had said their 1960 business volume was higher than in 1959 while 17.8 per cent said it was about the same. Twenty-four per cent reported a drop.

Manufacturing was the only one of the eight major classifications that showed an industry-wide drop in employment this year.

44.2% See a Gain

On the outlook for the next six months, 44.2 per cent of those surveyed saw business climbing—a third of them by 10 per cent or more—while 40.2 foresaw a static period ahead.

A falling off in their business was feared by 15.6 per cent, about a third of whom expected their volume to drop by 10 per cent or more.

Meanwhile, a report by the City Planning Commission indicated that about two-thirds of the work force here was employed in Manhattan.

The commission report, based on state Department of Labor statistics for 1958, put the number of employed here at 3,169,-300 in 1958, exclusive of government employes and the self-employed.

3,897,000 Hold Job

Figures from sources other than the commission indicated there were about 390,000 local, state and Federal Government employes and 337,000 self-employed here. This would bring the total number of jobholders in the city in 1958 to about 3,897,000.

A spokesman for the Planning Commission said this year's total of jobs might be slightly higher because 1958 had been a recession year. However, the distribution of the work force by boroughs, made available for the first time in the Department of Labor figures, is substantially the same as in 1958, he said.

On the basis of the 1958 figures, 66.5 per cent of those employed worked in Manhattan, 16 per cent in Brooklyn, 11 per cent in Queens, 5.7 per cent in

Continued on Page 20, Column 4

Associated Press Wirephoto

DISCUSS SPACE PROGRAM: President-elect Kennedy confers with Senator Robert S. Kerr, left, of Oklahoma, and Vice President-elect Lyndon B. Johnson in Palm Beach, Fla.

LANDIS CHARGES MAJOR DEFECTS IN U.S. AGENCIES

Kennedy Gets Study Calling for Reorganization and Better Appointments

'POLITICAL' JOBS SCORED

'Deterioration' in Personnel of Units Is Found Under Post-War Presidents

Excerpts from Landis report will be found on Page 16.

By ANTHONY LEWIS
Special to The New York Times.

WASHINGTON, Dec. 26—James M. Landis charged today that there were many and serious shortcomings in Federal regulatory agencies. He gave his views in a report to President-elect John F. Kennedy.

The report is severely critical of Presidents Eisenhower and Truman, although they are not named. It says that better appointments, internal reorganization and leadership by the President are the answers to the alleged failings.

Since World War II, the report says, there has been a general "deterioration" in agency personnel, both in the staff and in the commission heads. This alleged decline was attribute[d] primarily to what was said to be the making of appointments o[n] political grounds.

The report makes a numb[er] of recommendations applying [to] all the regulatory agencies [and] some proposals limited to sp[eci]fic agencies.

Major Proposals Made

These are the major rec[om]mendations for all the agenc[ies]:

¶Congress should give [the] President power to reorgan[ize] any of the administrat[ive] agencies, subject only to a ve[to] by a concurrent resolution [of] both houses.

¶Using that power, the Pre[si]dent should stipulate that [he] designate the chairmen of [the] agencies and that the chairm[en] have greater authority to hi[re] personnel and handle the agen[cy] budgets. Some Federal agenc[ies] elect their chairmen.

¶A reorganization plan shou[ld] be drafted to permit the age[n]cies to openly delegate dec[i]sions to single members, pane[ls] or staff examiners, with review by the agency heads only at their discretion.

¶There should be created within the President's Executive Office an office for the coordination and development of transportation policy and similar offices for communications and energy policies.

¶There should be established within the Executive Office an office to oversee regulatory agencies.

Mr. Kennedy requested that

Continued on Page 17, Column 1

Deaths in Traffic Increase As Families Return Home

A fresh surge of traffic deaths marred the holiday yesterday as millions hurried home in the final hours of the three-day Christmas week-end. Early hopes for a relatively low figure faded. Through Sunday night the accident rate had been lower than expected.

At 3 A. M. here, The Associated Press reported 466 traffic deaths across the country since the holiday tabulation began at 6 P. M. Friday.

There was a possibility that by the time a final count could be compiled some time today, the toll might pass the forecast of 510 highway fatalities made by the National Safety Council as the holiday began.

Five persons were killed and 686 injured in New York City between 6 P. M. Friday and last midnight, the Police Department reported. A spokesman said there had been 1,193 accidents in the period, 426 of them involving personal injuries.

Heavy Toll in 1955

Traffic deaths in New York State had reached twenty-three by last evening.

Although the national death toll this year was heavy, the three-day Christmas week-end in 1955 held the record; 609 persons were killed in traffic accidents.

A count made for comparative purposes by The Associated Press on the non-holiday week-end of Dec. 9 to 12 listed 293 traffic deaths, forty-seven in fires and 113 in other accidents. As on holidays, the period checked ran from 6 P. M. Friday to midnight Monday. In the seventy-eight hour Christmas

Continued on Page 21, Column 3

BELGIAN OFFICIALS SUPPORT STRIKERS

Governor and 102 Mayors Refuse Orders Aimed at Ending 6-Day Walkout

By The Associated Press.

BRUSSELS, Belgium, Dec. 26—An acting provincial governor and 102 Socialist mayors refused today to carry out new Government measures aimed at smashing the six-day-old strike against Belgium's proposed austerity program.

René Thone, Socialist member of the Hainaut Province Government and acting Governor, refused to accept a decree enabling governors to call out the army to maintain order.

Hainaut is one of the areas hardest hit by the strike. Officials said Jean Roland, Director General of the Interior Ministry, would replace M. Thone as acting Governor.

Refuse to List Strikers

The 102 mayors—all representing southern and eastern Belgian towns—refused to supply Brussels' officials with the names of striking municipal workers.

"We did not want to be informers," said one of the mayors.

Socialist party officials called on the Government earlier to cancel the austerity program, which includes higher taxes and reduced welfare spending. The program is designed to offset losses of revenue from the Congo after the former Belgian colony received its independence last summer.

The Communist party said the use of troops to break the strike "threatens to create serious troubles and lead the country to chaos."

The Socialist and Communist

Continued on Page 5, Column 3

EISENHOWER PLANS A FOREIGN AID CUT

Request in His Final Budget Will Be 175 Million Below Figure for This Year

By E. W. KENWORTHY
Special to The New York Times.

WASHINGTON, Dec. 26—In his final budget next month, President Eisenhower will ask less for foreign aid than last year, despite urgent State Department appeals for an increase to meet pressing needs in South Asia, Latin America and Africa.

Last year Douglas Dillon, Under Secretary of State with responsibility for foreign economic affairs, recommended that the President ask Congress for nearly $5,000,000,000 for foreign aid. In its review the Budget Bureau cut the request to $4,175,000,000.

Dillon Asked 5.5 Billion

This year Mr. Dillon, who will be Secretary of the Treasury in the Kennedy Administration, recommended a request of roughly $5,500,000,000. The Budget Bureau has trimmed this to $4,000,000,000, which is the amount that will be included in the budget to be submitted to Congress just before President Eisenhower leaves office.

The Budget Bureau normally reduces Government departments' estimates of their need, but the 27 per cent cut in the State Department recommendation is regarded as extremely sharp. Most regrettable, in the view of the State Department and the International Coopera-

Continued on Page 18, Column 5

Kennedy Confers on Plans To Spur Space Research

By W. H. LAWRENCE
Special to The New York Times.

PALM BEACH, Fla., Dec. 26—President-elect John F. Kennedy held long conferences with key advisers today on plans to expand the United States' exploration of space and to strengthen State Department representation abroad.

There was no official announcement of progress, but the sessions that began this afternoon extended into the evening and may continue tomorrow.

For the sessions, Vice President-elect Lyndon B. Johnson of Texas and Senator Robert S. Kerr, Oklahoma Democrat, flew in from their home states, arriving on Senator Johnson's privately owned Convair, the Lucy B., about 1 P. M. Representative John J. Rooney, Brooklyn Democrat, came in from New York and Douglas Dillon, the Secretary of the Treasury-designate who is now Under Secretary of State in the Eisenhower Administration, motored over from his winter home at near-by Hobe Sound, Fla.

Recess for Golf

The five men lunched together and then talked for several hours in the afternoon before recessing for a nine-hole round of golf. Mr. Dillon left at dinner time, but the other four continued their talks over dinner and into the evening.

The inclusion of Mr. Rooney in all these talks indicates the strong appeal Mr. Kennedy was making to induce those close to him to take a more liberal attitude toward State Department representation allowances. Mr. Rooney is chairman of the House Appropriation

Continued on Page 17, Column 2

JET RECORD BARES DATA ON COLLISION

Flight Unit Shows Mid-Air Crash Occurred Shortly After Last Radio Call

By RICHARD WITKIN

The flight recorder recovered from the jet airliner in the Dec. 16 mid-air collision here is understood to indicate that the accident occurred no more than one minute after the last message from the plane.

The recorder also is said to indicate that the jet was traveling well over 300 miles an hour in the last few minutes of the flight.

The evidence from the recorder is potentially of the greatest importance. But it does not yet permit firm conclusions about the genesis of the disaster.

Speculation Is Challenged

The evidence on the time of the collision would tend to support one prevalent line of speculation: that when the crew radioed it was approaching its assigned circling area, it may already have passed it.

Some observers challenge the basis of the speculation, however.

The theory is based on two prime points:

¶That the collision took place up to eleven miles from the circling area.

¶That it was only a minute or less before the collision that the jet's crew radioed that the plane was approaching the circling area. To have covered the intervening eleven miles in one minute, the plane would have had to be going 660 miles an hour, 300 to 400 miles an hour more than it would normally have been going.

Neither point has been proved incontrovertibly. Conjecture on

Continued on Page 48, Column 6

EAGLES WIN, 17-13, TO TAKE PRO TITLE

58-Yard Return of Kick-Off Helps Defeat Packers

By JOSEPH M. SHEEHAN
Special to The New York Times.

PHILADELPHIA, Dec. 26—The National Football League championship, as well as baseball's supreme crown, now reposes in the Commonwealth of Pennsylvania.

With a comeback worthy of the Pittsburgh Pirates, the Philadelphia Eagles defeated the Green Bay Packers, 17—13, in the title play-off today. A sellout crowd of 67,325 saw the game at Franklin Field.

Coach Buck Shaw's Eastern Conference champions beat the favored Packers at the Packers' game—running. The normally pass-minded Eagles went overhead only once in driving 32 yards in seven plays to score the winning touchdown at 5:21 of the final period.

Ted Dean, a fleet, powerful rookie halfback from near-by Radnor, Pa., slammed across for the deciding points from 5 yards out on a sweep around Green Bay's right end behind a crushing block by Gerry Huth.

Dean had set the winning drive in motion by sprinting 58 yards to Green Bay's 39-yard line with a kick-off. That followed the touchdown that put

Continued on Page 34, Column 1

Mobutu Seizes Two For Links to Reds

By The Associated Press.

LEOPOLDVILLE, the Congo, Dec. 26—Two Congolese Government officials are under arrest, charged with having had illegal contacts with the Soviet Union and Communist China.

They are Dominique Tchiteya, permanent director of the Foreign Trade Ministry, and Alphonse Makwambala, head of the National Statistics Office.

Gilbert Pongo, security chief of Col. Joseph D. Mobutu's pro-Western regime, announced that the two were arrested before Christmas and would be tried for "crimes against state security."

Mr. Pongo said the two officials were found to possess documents indicating they had been in regular contact with officials. All such contacts are illegal in the Congo—and par-

Continued on Page 7, Column 3

Norfolk to Get MacArthur War Collection

The New York Times

The courthouse in Norfolk, Va., which will hold memorabilia of Gen. Douglas MacArthur

General Accepts Bid for a Memorial—Hailed by City

By The Associated Press.

NORFOLK, Va., Dec. 26—General of the Army Douglas MacArthur has accepted an invitation from Norfolk to place his war mementoes, decorations and papers in a memorial to be established by the city.

General MacArthur has various ties with Norfolk. His mother was born and married here and he became the city's first honorary citizen.

General MacArthur also requested that he and his wife be buried in Norfolk.

The city said today it would renovate its 111-year-old courthouse, which is soon to be vacated, at a cost of nearly $500,000. Other tentative plans call for landscaping the courthouse block and renaming it "MacArthur Square."

Maj. Gen. Courtney Whitney, retired, General MacArthur's long-time aide, friend and biographer, is donating his services to the city in assisting with the renovation of the building and preparing the items for shipment.

General MacArthur told Norfolk officials:

"As a Virginian myself, whose mother came from a long line of Virginians and whose mother and father were married in the

Continued on Page 18, Column 3

Jersey Priest Tells His Parish to Tithe

Special to The New York Times.

WEST NEW YORK, N. J., Dec. 26—The pastor of a Roman Catholic church here has told his parishioners that henceforth they must contribute one-tenth of their income before taxes to the support of their church and to charity.

In a letter distributed at the masses on Christmas Day, the Rev. John P. Weigand, pastor of St. Joseph's Church, said this would eliminate all church fund-raising affairs—including raffles, bingo and special collections.

Roman Catholic sources said that tithing—the contribution of a tenth of a family's income to the support of the church—was at present rarely practiced in Catholic parishes in the United States. Officials of the Newark

Continued on Page 49, Column 4

CITY TO DROP RACE FROM BIRTH DATA

Information to Appear Only in Confidential Files

By LAWRENCE O'KANE

Color or race will no longer be listed on the birth certificates of persons born in New York City, starting Jan. 1.

In announcing the change yesterday, Dr. Leona Baumgartner, the Health Commissioner, said New York would be the first community in the nation to eliminate such information from birth certificates.

However, this statistical information is not being abandoned by the Health Department. Instead of appearing on the face of an individual's certificate, Dr. Baumgartner explained, it will appear on the back of the corresponding document in the department's files.

The information thus will pass behind an effective legal barrier. The back of the certificate is the Confidential Medical

Continued on Page 20, Column 2

NEWS INDEX

5-YARD END SWEEP DECIDES, 17 TO 13

67,325 See Dean's 58-Yard Return of Kick-Off Start Eagles' Winning Drive

Continued From Page 1, Col. 1

the Packers in the lead for the second time.

Dominant in the early going, Green Bay scored on field goals of 20 and 23 yards by Paul Horning in the first two periods.

On the pinpoint passing of their great Norm Van Brocklin, the Eagles struck back late in the second quarter. A 35-yard pass from Van Brocklin to Tommy McDonald moved Philadelphia ahead, 7–6, at 8:08 of the second period.

Before the half ended, Van Brocklin also had passed his team into position for a 15-yard field goal by Bobby Walston.

The Eagles' embattled defense, which checked the Packers in scoring territory five times, held firm through the third period. Then it yielded at 1:53 of the last quarter to a 7-yard touchdown pass from Bart Starr to Max McGee.

Time Runs Out on Packers

Philadelphia's offensive unit quickly recouped on Dean's touchdown. The Eagle defenders hung grimly on the rest of the way, with the clock as an ally. They stopped a last-ditch Packer drive on the Eagle 10-yard line as time ran out.

The result sent the partisan onlookers into a state of delirium. The enthused Eagle adherents leveled the goal posts in a jiffy as soon as the police had lifted their guard and still were whooping it up in the near-by streets two hours later.

The game started at noon, earlier than usual for a professional contest. This was done to allow for a sudden-death overtime, which was planned had regulation time ended with the score tied. Franklin Field has no lights.

It was Philadelphia's first National League championship since Greasy Neale's Eagles of 1949 defeated the Los Angeles Rams, 14–0, in the second of two consecutive title victories.

Coach Vince Lombardi's Packers, whose Western Conference victory was as great a surprise as that of the Eagles in the East, had all the best of the statistics. Green Bay outgained Philadelphia from scrimmage, 401 yards to 296, and piled up twenty-two first downs against thirteen.

Packers Lack Decisiveness

With their powerful running game, which accounted for 223 yards, the Packers controlled the ball for long intervals. But they lacked decisiveness when opportunity beckoned. The Eagles, who ran only forty-eight scrimmage plays to the Packers' seventy-seven, did the better job of the cashing in on the chances.

Having Van Brocklin on its side helped Philadelphia immeasurably. The 34-year-old quarterback, who confirmed his decision to retire, has had better days passing, but he called a magnificent game.

Sharing honors with Van Brocklin, Dean, McDonald and Walston, who also place-kicked 2 extra points, was Chuck Bednarik, the 35-year-old Eagle center. Doubling on offense and defense, he was on the field every scrimmage play.

Among other things, Bednarik knocked Paul Hornung, Green Bay's league scoring leader, out of action with a rib-rattling tackle early in the third pediod; recovered a fumble that stopped a promising Packer march in the fourth period and made the game-ending tackle that assured victory for the Eagles.

The weather was fine—sparkling clear and surprisingly warm, with the temperature ranging up to 48 degrees. The field was a bit treacherous, though, frozen hard underneath and soft on top, with muddy spots where icy patches had melted.

The Eagles won the toss, elected to receive and promptly put themselves in a deep hole. On their first scrimmage play, Van Brocklin flipped a lateral to Bill Barnes, who had flared to the left. The ball bounced off Barnes' reaching hands into those of Bill Quinlan, Green Bay's defensive right end.

This break set up the Packers on Philadelphia's 14. Jim Taylor, Green Bay's admirable fullback, whose line-cracking activities netted 105 yards, smashed to the 9 on the first play. But the Eagles dug in, held three more rushes to 3 yards and took the ball on downs on their 6.

Almost immediately, the Eagles gave away the ball again. On the third play, Barnes, after breaking loose for what would have been a first down, fumbled when tackled. Bill Forester recovered for Green Bay on the Philadelphia 22.

Two power thrusts by Hornung and Taylor produced a Packer first down on the 12. Then Hornung ripped through to the 8. But Green Bay went offside on its next rush, and two passes by Starr missed connections. So the Packers settled for a field goal by Hornung from the 20.

Late in the first period, Green Bay got rolling from its 37 on a march that carried to Philadelphia's 17 at the start of the second quarter. But after Taylor had reached the 12, the Packers again were guilty of an offside. Again two passes failed, and again Hornung kicked a field goal, from the 23.

On this movement, the Packers missed a glowing chance to score a touchdown on the first play of the second quarter. Hornung, on a halfback option pass, failed to get the ball to Boyd Dowler, in the clear behind the last Packer defender. The underthrown pass was knocked down.

A few minutes later, Van Brocklin had the same chance and didn't fail. The elusive McDonald broke loose from his right flanker post, and Van pitched a strike to him for a 22-yard gain. On the next play, the same combination clicked again for a 35-yard touchdown.

Pass Gains 41 Yards

The next time the Eagles had the ball, Van Brocklin hung a 41-yard pass on a handle for Pete Retzlaff. This put Philadelphia on Green Bay's 33. Dean picked up 3 yards, Van Brocklin missed once, then hit Dean for a 22-yard gain to the Packer 8.

Green Bay balked Van Brocklin's next three passes, but the Eagles were in position to take a 15-yard field goal by Walston that stretched their lead to 10–6.

From the kick-off that followed, the Packers roared 72 yards to a first down on Philadelphia's 7. But time was running out in the half. After Starr had failed to gain when trapped behind his line on an attempted pass, the Packers tried a field goal. Hornung's boot from the 12 was wide to the left.

Early in the third period, the Packers, on 15-yard runs by Hornung and Taylor, reached Philadelphia's 34. But, after yielding 5 yards to Hornung's next thrust, the Eagles clamped down and took the ball on downs just inside their 25. On this sequence Hornung's shoulder was reinjured. Except to kick the point after Green Bay's touchdown, he played no more.

Symank Intercepts Pass

From this point, the Eagles swiftly moved to Green Bay's 5, with passes by Van Brocklin to McDonald and Walston accounting for most of the yardage. But on second down, John Symank ended the threat by intercepting a pass by Van Brocklin in the end zone.

An enterprising play by McGee got Green Bay started on the touchdown drive that followed. After the interception, the Packers were stalled on their 20.

Back to punt on fourth down with 10 yards to go, McGee spotted the Eagle defense dropping back and ran instead. He raced 35 yards to Philadelphia's 45 before being hauled down.

A pass by Starr to Gary Knafelc moved the ball to the Eagle 34 as the third period ended. From there, Tom Moore, standing in for Hornung, and Taylor advanced to the 7. Then Starr switched to the air and hit McGee, who cut in sharply from the left flank, with a perfect pass on the goal line.

Philadelphia retaliated explosively. Taking the kick-off on his 3, Dean raced back to Green Bay's 39, where Willie Wood fought through two blockers to knock him out of bounds.

Green Bay was penalized 7 yards for defensive holding on Philadelphia's first play, a pass by Van Brocklin that never got airbound. From the 32, Van Brocklin crossed the Packer defense by calling running plays.

Hitting hard on off-tackle plays, Dean and Barnes punched out a first down on the 20. The Packer line then spilled Van Brocklin for a 7-yard loss. He recouped it with a couple of yards to spare on a screen pass to Barnes.

Then the cagy Philadelphia signal-caller caught the Packers off guard again. On third down with 8 to go, they were looking for a pass. He sent Barnes off tackle and the stumpy halfback slashed and squirmed to a first down on the 10.

From there, Dean hit off tackle to the 5 and then circled end for the score. Huth's crushing block got him around the corner but he still had to drive through a couple of tacklers on his own.

Green Bay moved past midfield from the following kick-off, but on-the-spot Bednarik was there to grab the ball when McGee fumbled a pass from Starr on Philadelphia's 48.

Packers Make Final Bid

Nothing was accomplished by either side in the next couple of exchanges. Then, with 1 minute 15 seconds to go, the Packers aroused themselves. From their 35, they stormed to Philadelphia's 22 on Starr's passing to various receivers.

But they couldn't break anyone completely loose and there was time for just one more play. Again Starr had no free deep receiver. So he threw short—just over the line to Taylor.

Bednarik quickly clamped the Green Bay fullback in a bear hug and, with the assistance of another tackler, wrestled him to the ground on the 10. That was the ball game.

PHILADELPHIA EAGLES (17)

Left Ends—Retzlaff, Robb.
Left Tackles—McCusker, Keys, Gossage.
Left Guards—Huth, Wittenborn, Richardson, Gunnels.
Centers—Bednarik, Lapham, Weber.
Right Guards—S. Campbell, Khayat.
Right Tackles—Smith, Wilcox, M. Campbell.
Right Ends—Walston, Reichow, Lucas, Baughan, Nocera.
Quarterbacks—Van Brocklin, Jurgensen, Freeman.
Left Halfbacks—Barnes, Brown, Carr, Jackson.
Right Halfbacks—McDonald, Brookshier.
Fullbacks—Dean, Burroughs, Sapp.

GREEN BAY PACKERS (13)

Left Ends—McGee, Currie, R. Kramer.
Left Tackles—Skoronski, Masters, Davis, Beck, Miller.
Left Guards—Thurston, Cvercko, Hanner.
Centers—Ringo, Iman, Nitschke, Bettis.
Right Guards—J. Kramer, Jordan.
Right Tackles—Gregg, Quinlan.
Right Ends—Knafelc, Meilinger, Forester.
Quarterbacks—Starr, McHan, Symank, Wood, Pesonen.
Left Halfbacks—Hornung, Moore, Winslow, Gremminger, Hackbart.
Right Halfbacks—Dowler, Carpenter, Whittenton.
Fullbacks—Taylor, Hickman, Tunnell.

Philadelphia Eagles	0	10	0	7—17
Green Bay Packers	3	3	7	0—13

G.B.-FG, Hornung, 20.
G.B.-FG, Hornung, 23.
Phil.—McDonald, 35, pass from Van Brocklin (Walston, kick).
Phil.—FG, Walston, 15.
G.B.—McGee, 7, pass from Starr (Hornung, kick).

United Press International Telephoto

GET UP AND GET SOME MORE: Tommy McDonald of the Eagles is helped by policeman after he scored touchdown and rolled into the end zone during championship game with Green Bay. Score came in the second period.

Associated Press

THE CLINCHER: Ted Dean of the Eagles takes ball into end zone for the winning score in fourth quarter against Packers.

"All the News That's Fit to Print"

The New York Times.

LATE CITY EDITION

Cloudy today, tonight and tomorrow. Cooler tomorrow.

Temp. range 74–69; yesterday 76–57.

VOL. CXI...No. 37,872.

NEW YORK, MONDAY, OCTOBER 2, 1961.

FIVE CENTS

PLAN BOARD ASKS 746 MILLION IN '62 FOR CITY PROJECTS

Proposed Capital Budget Sets Record, Comparing With 669 Million for '61

SUM HELD 'REASONABLE'

Fiscal Outlook Found Less 'Grim' Than Year Ago—Schools Get Top Priority

By PAUL CROWELL

A moderately optimistic City Planning Commission made public yesterday a proposed record capital budget of $746,624,713 for the calendar year 1962.

Last October the commission proposed a 1961 capital budget of $669,461,253. The capital budget later adopted by the Board of Estimate and approved by the City Council was $532,224,711.

Just a year ago the commission found prospects for financing needed public improvements within the city's constitutional debt limit "considerably grimmer" than in October, 1959.

Allocation Is Explained

In a message explaining its proposed 1962 budget allocations yesterday, the commission said changed conditions now made it possible to set up a "reasonable" program of public improvements for the next two years.

"Thereafter," the commission warned, "unless another increase in assessed valuations or a favorable change in the equalization rate, or both, materialize, we may be again faced with a capital budget and program which falls short of the city's needs."

The capital budget covers the acquisition of real estate and the construction of city buildings and permanent improvements. It is distinct from the much larger expense budget, which covers general operating expenses.

The Equalization Rate

The city's borrowing within the debt limit cannot exceed the average full valuation of taxable real estate for the nearest five-year period.

The equalization rate, fixed by the State Board of Equalization and Assessment, shows the percentage of market value of real estate represented by the city's assessed valuation. A reduction in the equalization rate gives the city more taxing power by increasing the average full value of realty.

This year the city's assessed valuations have risen materially, and the equalization rate has been reduced.

The main result of these changes is to increase from

Continued on Page 25, Column 5

Maris Hits 61st in Final Game

Yank First to Exceed 60 Home Runs in Major Leagues

By JOHN DREBINGER

Roger Maris yesterday became the first major league player in history to hit more than sixty home runs in a season.

The 27-year-old Yankee outfielder hit his sixty-first at the Stadium before a roaring crowd of 23,154 in the Bombers' final game of the regular campaign.

That surpassed by one the sixty that Babe Ruth hit in 1927. Ruth's mark has stood in the record book for thirty-four years.

Artistically enough, Maris' homer also produced the only run of the game as Ralph Houk's 1961 American League champions defeated the Red Sox, 1 to 0, in their final tune-up for the world series, which opens at the Stadium on Wednesday.

Maris hit his fourth-inning homer in his second time at bat. The victim of the blow was Tracy Stallard, a 24-year-old Boston rookie right-hander. Stallard's name, perhaps, will in time gain as much renown as that of Tom Zachary, who delivered the pitch that Ruth slammed into the Stadium's right-field bleachers for No. 60 on the next to the last day of the 1927 season.

The New York Times

Roger Maris hitting his sixty-first home run of the season yesterday in the fourth inning at Yankee Stadium.

Along with Stallard, still another name was bandied about at the Stadium after Maris' drive. Sal Durante, a 19-year-old truck driver from Coney Island, was the fellow who caught the ball as it dropped into the lower right-field stand, some

Continued on Page 38, Column 1

NASSER CUTS TIES TO JORDAN, TURKEY OVER SYRIAN ISSUE

U.A.R. Replies to Recognition of Rebel Regime—Report of Aleppo Strife Denied

By The Associated Press.

BEIRUT, Lebanon, Oct. 1—Cairo announced today that President Gamal Abdel Nasser was breaking diplomatic relations with Jordan and Turkey in the wake of Syria's withdrawal from the United Arab Republic.

The Jordanians and the Turks were the first to recognize the provisional Government set up by Premier Mahmoun al-Kuzbari, a conservative, in Damascus last week.

"President Nasser has issued a decision calling for the severing of diplomatic relations with Jordan and Turkey as a result of the hostile attitude adopted by them toward the United Arab Republic and Arab nationalism," the Cairo radio said.

Nasser-Hussein Feud

Mr. Nasser and King Hussein of Jordan, though partners in the Arab League, have feuded off and on for years. More staid relations have been evident between the Nasser Administration and Turkey, which is a member of the North Atlantic Treaty Organization.

Nationalist China extended recognition to the Kuzbari Administration today, as Guatemala did yesterday.

Radio dueling between the Syrians and Egyptians was marked by a roundabout report from Cairo of an uprising in Aleppo, the industrial center of the north, against Dr. Kuzbari's rebel regime. This was denied by Americans living in Aleppo. Reached by telephone from Beirut, they said there was no evidence of renewed fighting.

Conflicting Reports

Cairo attributed its Aleppo report to an intercepted broadcast from an unidentified station. It said heavy fighting was going on between the people and the police and army.

The Damascus radio countered with a declaration by the Syrian Army command that reports from all districts showed that security prevailed and life had returned to normal. This was called proof that the people had full confidence in the revolution.

The conflicting reports on fighting and the fact that Syria's borders remained closed indicated that the country still was in a state of tension. Foreign reporters were turned back at border points for the fourth day.

There also was a warning by the Syrian Army command to "foreign destructive elements" to be quiet or face expulsion. Since all the several thousand Egyptians in Syria already

Continued on Page 10, Column 4

Reds Widen Razed Strip in Berlin

Associated Press

East German workers level a fifty-yard-wide strip of land on their side of barbed-wire fence they erected to separate Soviet sector of Berlin from Western areas.

Special to The New York Times.

BERLIN, Oct. 1 -- Several thousand Communist policemen, blue-shirted members of the Communist youth organization and militia men worked under a gray sky today to widen the razed area along the barrier that cuts Berlin in two. They used picks and shovels to demolish garden plots and tear down summer homes to create an open strip of land fifty yards wide. This provides a wide field of fire for the armed East German border guards. The demolition work that has been carried on

Continued on Page 3, Column 1

LORD HOME SAYS TALKS CONVINCED SOVIET OF DANGER

Tells Britons He and Rusk Made Russians Realize War Peril Was Real

MEETINGS CONSTRUCTIVE

Gromyko to See President After Fourth Session With Secretary of State

Special to The New York Times.

LONDON, Oct. 1—Britain's Foreign Secretary declared today that the West had succeeded in making the Soviet Union realize that it had been on a "collision course" in the Berlin crisis and that if it continued, such a course could lead to war.

The Earl of Home made this point at London Airport on his return from New York, where he attended the opening sessions of the United Nations General Assembly.

He also had private talks in New York with Secretary of State Dean Rusk and Andrei A. Gromyko, the Soviet Foreign Minister.

[A White House spokesman said President Kennedy had been encouraged enough by the meetings to wish to meet with Mr. Gromyko in Washington this week.]

Treaty Holds Threat

Lord Home declared:

"We made Mr. Gromyko and the Russians understand that the Berlin situation was extremely dangerous and, if they went right ahead with their proposals to make a treaty with East Germany, it might be extremely dangerous also," Lord Home said.

Asked if he now felt more optimistic over the chances for a peaceful settlement of the Berlin problem, Lord Home replied:

"We have been preparing the way for what one hopes may be negotiations at some future date. Certainly the atmosphere of the talks that took place between Mr. Rusk and Mr. Gromyko and myself has been very friendly and good. They have also been constructive."

More Contacts Likely

Lord Home said he understood that Mr. Gromyko would go to Washington some time this week to confer with President Kennedy.

"It would be too early to say whether a heads-of-state meeting will come into the picture at this time," he said, "but I have no doubt that ways and means will be found of continuing the contacts with the Russians."

The Foreign Secretary, replying to a question on whether he thought the threat of war over

Continued on Page 2, Column 3

Wagner Charges G.O.P. Cheats City on State Aid

By LAYHMOND ROBINSON

Mayor Wagner charged yesterday that "Republican rule in Albany" had resulted in "scandalous short-changing" of the city on state aid. His charge came in what was billed as a "major statement" formally opening Mr. Wagner's drive for re-election Nov. 7.

The attack was seen as a move to make state aid to the city a central issue in the mayoral campaign and to fix the blame for shortcomings in some city services on "penny-pinching" Republicans.

The attack drew a sharp retort from State Attorney General Louis J. Lefkowitz, Mr. Wagner's Republican opponent in the mayoral race. Mr. Lefkowitz charged that the Mayor was attempting to cover up his own "feeble, incompetent leadership" and "avoid personal responsibility for the mess he's made of things."

Jab at Lefkowitz

Referring to Republican control of the Legislature and the Governor's office, the Mayor asserted that failure to return to New York City a fair share of collected taxes had "dealt crippling blows to the city in our effort to obtain decent rentals for our citizens, to properly educate our children and to halt the spread of juvenile delinquency and crime."

Mr. Lefkowitz "has never once been heard to contradict that policy," Mr. Wagner charged.

"The Republicans must be brought to account for this Albany short-changing of the city and its people," the Mayor went on. "The voters will find Republican promises cynical and empty in the light of their record of eagerly making New York City pay more and receive less."

The Mayor complained that New York City got back from the state only 39 cents on every dollar obtained from the city's

Continued on Page 44, Column 1

RACIAL CENSUS SET IN STATE SCHOOLS

Dr. Allen Says Tally Starting Next Month Will Attack De Facto Segregation

By LEONARD BUDER

Special to The New York Times.

SARANAC INN, N. Y., Oct. 1—A racial census of every public school in the state will start next month as the first step in a planned attack on segregation.

This was disclosed here tonight by Dr. James E. Allen Jr., the State Education Commissioner. He addressed the opening session of the annual meeting of the State Council of City and Village School Superintendents.

Although noting that racial discrimination was prohibited by state law, Dr. Allen asserted that in some communities residential patterns and customs had in fact created schools "which are indeed segregated."

These schools, he declared, "are detrimental, psychologically and educationally, to the students in attendance."

Amplifying his remarks at a news conference, the commissioner said that the state "will take a look at everything that stands in the way of assuring equal educational opportunities for all children."

Once the census is completed, he said, the State Education Department will examine school zoning policies to see if they are the cause of racial imbalances.

He indicated that if it were found that school zones were gerrymandered or rigged, the department would intervene to correct the situation. However, he emphasized that he hoped that such state action would not be necessary.

Dr. Allen said that the census, which would provide a count of Negro and Puerto Rican pupils in the state, would be conducted under the authority of the Education Practices Act. The act, he said, empowers the department to make studies

Continued on Page 22, Column 5

HIGH COURT OPENS NEW TERM TODAY

Reargument Is Scheduled on a Tennessee Urban Plea to Force Redistricting

By ANTHONY LEWIS

Special to The New York Times.

WASHINGTON, Oct. 1—The struggle of city dwellers to obtain their share of political power poses a critical issue for the Supreme Court in its new term beginning tomorrow.

Urban areas are asking the court to force redistricting of state legislatures so that cities would be assigned seats in fair proportion to their population. In many states city voters are now in a majority but have only a minority of the legislative seats.

The case before the court comes from Tennessee. That state's constitution requires districts of equal population and redistricting every ten years. But there has been no change since 1901, and some districts are now twenty times as populous as others.

The plaintiffs are voters in Nashville and other urban areas of Tennessee. They argue that the state is denying them the equal protection of the laws guaranteed under the Constitution. Officials of New York and other cities have joined in on

Continued on Page 20, Column 1

Ngo Says Struggle With Vietnam Reds Is Now a 'Real War'

By ROBERT TRUMBULL

Special to The New York Times.

SAIGON, Vietnam, Monday, Oct. 2 -- South Vietnam's struggle against armed Communist insurgents has grown from guerrilla action to "real war" in the last year, President Ngo Dinh Diem said today.

"It is no longer a guerrilla war we have to face but a real war waged by an enemy who attacks us with regular units fully and heavily equipped and who seeks a strategic decision in Southeast Asia in conformity with the orders of the Communist International," President Ngo declared.

The President spoke at the opening of the budget session of the National Assembly.

The conflict here has taken on a new dimension in the last twelve months, Mr. Ngo said, after the Communists failed in a program of political subversion.

He declared that the Communists had mounted new attacks in the high plateaus of the central and northeastern provinces, where the terrain is difficult, to compensate for losses in the southwest that he

Continued on Page 17, Column 1

HIGH-LEVEL TALKS ON GERMANY SEEN

U.S. Expects U.N. or Summit Parley Before Soviet Step to Curb Berlin Rights

By THOMAS J. HAMILTON

Special to The New York Times.

UNITED NATIONS, N. Y., Oct. 1—The United States believes that the West Berlin crisis will be submitted either to the United Nations or to a summit conference before the Soviet Union takes any decisive action to curb Western rights in the former German capital.

According to dependable sources, Secretary of State Dean Rusk does not foresee an appeal to the United Nations or a meeting of heads of government at this stage.

The Big Four foreign ministers are expected to meet in Europe, possibly in Geneva, in November if further talks between Mr. Rusk and Andrei A. Gromyko, Soviet Foreign Minister, reveal that the Soviet Union will agree to a framework of negotiations acceptable to the Western powers.

Three exploratory conversations in New York between the United States and Soviet officials, and two between Mr. Gromyko and the Earl of Home, British Foreign Secretary, have not yet uncovered such a basis for negotiation.

A United States spokesman said Mr. Rusk and Mr. Gromyko would resume their talks in Washington this week.

According to persons acquainted with Mr. Rusk's thinking, the Western powers would not turn to the United Nations until after a meeting of Foreign

Continued on Page 3, Column 5

PRODUCE OR QUIT, SCHOOL AIDES TOLD

Rubin Warns Staff and Asks for Backing in First Speech

By GENE CURRIVAN

Max J. Rubin, president of the Board of Education, served notice last night in his first public address that the board's top administrators must produce results or be replaced.

When the Legislature removed the old board in August, after scandals had shaken the system, it gave the new board the power to remove Dr. John J. Theobald, the Superintendent of Schools, and other high ranking personnel. Such dismissals, however, must be made before July.

Mr. Rubin, who was a member of the Heald Commission, which investigated the school system in 1959, spoke over radio station WNYC and television station WNTA. He outlined the board's plans and appealed for public support.

He pledged an end to red tape and other factors that produce delay and duplication. He promised decentralization with increased responsibility at the local level. He assured his listeners that when the board made requests of the city for funds it would not be humbly imploring.

He said the board would ask

Continued on Page 21, Column 2

NEWS INDEX

Quill Urges Labor To Readmit Hoffa

By STANLEY LEVEY

Michael J. Quill called yesterday for the readmission of James R. Hoffa's International Brotherhood of Teamsters to the merged labor movement.

He called Mr. Hoffa "the cleanest man in the United States."

"If after a Senate investigation and trial before half a dozen juries they weren't able to convict him, and if all the law-enforcement agencies have made an honest man of him, is there any need to keep Hoffa and his 1,700,000 members outside the orbit of organized labor?" the Transport Workers' president asked.

Mr. Quill made his proposals on the eve of the opening of his union's eleventh constitutional convention today at the Roosevelt Hotel. He said the 750 delegates would discuss and

Continued on Page 61, Column 6

Franco, in Power 25 Years, Seeks U. S. Pact Revision

Associated Press Radiophoto

Generalissimo Francisco Franco saluting parading troops yesterday in Burgos, Spain

By United Press International.

BURGOS, Spain, Oct. 1—Generalissimo Francisco Franco, marking the twenty-fifth anniversary of his rise to power, said tonight that "circumstances advise the revision" of the treaty between the United States and Spain. But there was no indication he intended to alter the agreement authorizing United States bases in Spain. General Franco said that Spain would maintain her relations with the United States but that a revision of the treaty might be necessary. He made the statement at a meeting here with Spanish officers who paid him tribute. Spain is not a member of the North

Continued on Page 8, Column 3

Panama Demands New Canal 'Rights'

Special to The New York Times.

PANAMA, Oct. 1 — Panama publicly revived today her demands on the United States for improved terms and fully "sovereign" rights in the Panama Canal Zone.

President Roberto F. Chiari, in his annual state of the nation address to the National Assembly (Congress), said he had submitted a formal request to Washington for revision of the treaty affecting the canal and the Canal Zone.

Two years ago, in the preceding administration of President Ernesto de la Guardia Jr., rioting flared here for Canal Zone "rights." Panama obtained assurances then that the Panama flag would be shown in the

Continued on Page 13, Column 3

STEVENSON HINTS OF SOVIET CHANGE

Expects Softening of Stand on Nuclear Test Ban

Adlai E. Stevenson said yesterday he had "some expectation" that the Soviet Union would relent in its opposition to a treaty to ban nuclear weapons tests.

Mr. Stevenson, the United States delegate to the United Nations, and Secretary of State Dean Rusk also expressed confidence that the United Nations would reject the Soviet troika plan for a three-man directorate and replace Secretary General Dag Hammarskjold with a single, strong executive.

"The troika proposal has run into the opposition of the overwhelming majority of the General Assembly," Mr. Rusk said. "If it were to get anywhere it would require a revision of the Charter, which is just not acceptable to the membership."

Mr. Stevenson agreed, saying, "It may turn out to be sort of a blessing in disguise that we'll meet this issue and be able to dispose of it." He said he had no doubt that smaller nations would recognize that a strong United Nations was vital to their security.

The Soviet troika plan calls for replacing the Secretary General with one executive each

Continued on Page 4, Column 5

Maris Hits 61st Home Run in Yankees' Final Game

RIGHT-FIELD SHOT WINS 1-TO-0 GAME

Maris Is First to Go Above 60 Homers—4th-Inning Drive Caught by Youth

Continued From Page 1, Col. 4

ten rows back and about ten feet to the right of the Yankee bull pen.

For this achievement the young man won a $5,000 award and a round trip to Sacramento, Calif., offered by a Sacramento restaurant proprietor, as well as a round trip to the 1962 World's Fair in Seattle.

Maris was fooled by Stallard on an outside pitch that he stroked to left field for an out in the first inning. He let two pitches go by when he came to bat in the fourth with one out and the bases empty. The first one was high and outside. The second one was low and appeared to be inside.

Waist-High Fast Ball

The crowd, interested in only one thing, a home run, greeted both pitches with a chorus of boos. Then came the moment for which fans from coast to coast had been waiting since last Tuesday night, when Maris hit his sixtieth.

Stallard's next pitch was a fast ball that appeared to be about waist high and right down the middle. In a flash, Roger's rhythmic swing, long the envy of left-handed pull hitters, connected with the ball.

Almost at once, the crowd sensed that this was it. An ear-splitting roar went up as Maris, standing spellbound for just an instant at the plate, started his triumphant jog around the bases. As he came down the third-base line, he shook hands joyously with a young fan who had rushed onto the field to congratulate him.

Crossing the plate and arriving at the Yankee dugout, he was met by a solid phalanx of team-mates. This time they made certain the modest country lad from Raytown, Mo., acknowledged the crowd's plaudits.

He had been reluctant to do so when he hit No. 60, but this time the Yankee players wouldn't let Roger come down the dugout steps. Smiling broadly, the usually unemotional player lifted his cap from his blond close-cropped thatch and waved it to the cheering fans. Not until he had taken four bows did his colleagues allow him to retire to the bench.

Ruth's record, of course, will not be erased. On July 17, Commissioner Ford C. Frick ruled that Ruth's record would stand unless bettered within a 154-game limit, since that was the schedule in 1927. Maris hit fifty-nine homers in the Yanks' first 154 games to a decision. He hit his sixtieth four games later.

However, Maris will go into the record book as having hit the sixty-first in a 162-game schedule.

Maris finished the season with 590 official times at bat. Ruth, in 1927, had 540 official times at bat. Their total appearances at the plate, however, were nearly identical—698 for Maris and 692 for Ruth.

According to the official baseball rules, a batter is not charged with an official time at bat when "he hits a sacrifice bunt or sacrifice fly, is awarded first base on four called balls, is hit by a pitched ball or is awarded first base because of interference or obstruction."

Though it had taken 162 games (actually, 163, since the Yankees played one tie) a player finally had risen from the ranks to pass Ruth's majestic record. Maris himself missed only two of these games, although he sat out a third without coming to bat when, after playing the first inning in the field, he was bothered by something in his eye.

For thirty-four years the greatest sluggers in baseball had striven to match Ruth's mark. Mickey Mantle fought Maris heroically through most of the season, but in the closing weeks he fell victim to a virus attack and his total stopped at fifty-four.

The two who came closest in the past were Jimmy Foxx and Hank Greenberg. In 1932, Foxx hit fifty-eight. In 1938, Greenberg matched that figure. Indeed, Greenberg had the best chance of all to crack the record. When he hit No. 58, he still had five games to play in a 154-game schedule.

When Stallard came to bat in the fifth the fans, who earlier had booed him when it seemed he might walk Maris, now generously applauded the hurler.

In the sixth, Maris, coming up for the third time, tried mightily to oblige the crowd with another home run. This time, however, Stallard struck him out on a 3-and-2 pitch.

With the Boston right-hander then stepping out for a pinch-hitter, Chet Nichols, an experienced 30-year-old left-hander, opposed Maris on his last turn at bat in the eighth. Roger ended the inning with a pop fly that the second baseman, Chuck Schilling, caught for the third out.

Apart from Maris, the Yankee hitters did not overly distinguish themselves, but Manager Ralph Houk saw enough to satisfy him. Superlative pitching made the biggest home run of 1961 stand up to the end.

Bill Stafford, who is to pitch the third game of the series against the Reds, hurled the first six innings and allowed only two hits, both by Russ Nixon. The first was a single, the second a triple. Hal Reniff then retired three Red Sox in the seventh and Luis Arroyo held them to one single in the last two innings.

31 Homers on the Road

A breakdown of Maris' home-runs this year shows that he hit thirty-one on the road. The one he hit Sunday was his forty-ninth off a right-hander.

Mantle hit thirty of his fifty-four homers on the road. Mickey connected forty-two times off right-handers.

The New York Times

The 27-year-old outfielder walks to the top step of the Yankee dugout to acknowledge the cheers of 23,154 fans. Hit produced game's only run as Yanks shut out Red Sox.

"I just concentrate on my timing and my swing. If some of my hits are homers, so much the better."

(Maris with Sal Durante, who caught 61st home run)

AGILE FAN MAKES A $5,000 CATCH

Youth Offers Home Run Ball to Maris for Nothing

By GORDON S. WHITE Jr.

The ball that was hit by Roger Maris—and, as a result, was worth $5,000—sailed high before it began its descent toward the recovery area—Box 163 D in Section 33 of Yankee Stadium yesterday afternoon.

Ready for its arrival in the right-field seats were many fans and twice as many grasping hands. Among them was Sal Durante, a young man with quick reflexes. Durante leaped to the challenge, grabbed the ball on the fly with one hand and suddenly found that he had leaped into a prominence that left him flabbergasted.

The 19-year-old truck driver, who lives at 1418 Neptune Avenue in the Coney Island section of Brooklyn, had bought a seat in the right-field sector for the same reason that thousands of others did yesterday, the day before and Friday night. They all were hoping to earn the $5,000 offered by Sam Gordon, a Sacramento (Calif.) restaurant owner, for Maris' sixty-first home run ball.

Like the others, Durante admitted he really felt he had little chance. When the chance came, however, he was ready.

When the ball came down, it was apparent that all within reach of Durante wanted a crack at getting it. They never had a chance. Playing it like an outfielder, Durante jumped onto his seat, reached up and caught the ball one-handed, according to his own version and that of his fiancée, Rosemarie Calabrese.

The Scramble Is On

For a moment, Durante and others fell into a heap, the ball was lost from sight and the scramble was on. Sal stuck to his guns, withstood some punches from his nearest box-seat neighbors and came up within seconds holding the prize high.

From then on, there was a whirl of excitement that Durante hadn't fully reckoned with when he bought his tickets. Miss Calabrese said, "He jumped up and said, 'I got it, I got it,' and before I knew just what he meant, the cops had him and were taking him away toward the Yankee bull pen."

The Stadium police came to the young man's rescue quickly, protecting him from other fans who were trying to take the ball away and then whisking him to television cameras, newspaper interviews and a meeting with the real hero of the day—Maris.

Durante said he knew something of the $5,000 offer, but didn't think too much of it. "All I want to do is give the ball to Maris," he said.

But Roger, who left the dugout to meet Durante while the Yanks batted in the fifth inning, said, "If they made the offer, then he (Durante) should get what's coming to him. I'll even fly out to the coast with him to that restaurant."

Gordon on Way Here

A West Coast trip by Maris and Durante won't be necessary, however. Gordon was flying to New York last night to present a $5,000 check to the Brooklyn youth on the CBS-TV program "Calendar," which will start at 10 A. M. locally.

Durante's offer to give up the ball impressed Maris. The Yankee slugger told Russ Nixon, the Boston catcher, about it when Maris came to bat again in the eighth inning.

"What do you think of that kid?" Maris asked. "The boy is planning to get married and he can use the money, but he still wanted to give the ball back to me for nothing. It shows there's some good people left in this world after all."

Gordon intends to pay the money and then turn the ball over to Maris. Maris had his hands on the ball at least a couple of dozen times yesterday afternoon, though he won't get full possession of it for a few days. He will get the ball, however.

Durante bought a ticket for himself and Miss Calabrese Tuesday night in Section 21, the first section in the Stadium inside fair territory in right field. He said, "while we were there Tuesday night, all the hitters, including Maris, seemed

CASH AND CLEMENTE GAIN BATTING TITLES

Norm Cash of the Detroit Tigers and Roberto Clemente of the Pittsburgh Pirates won the 1961 major league batting championships yesterday.

Cash collected two hits in three tries in his final game to capture the American League title with a .361 average. Clemente took the National League crown with a .351 mark after being sidelined the last five games with an arm injury.

Other American League leaders were: doubles, Al Kaline, Detroit, forty-one; triples, Jake Wood, Detroit, fourteen; stolen bases, Luis Aparicio, Chicago, fifty-three; highest won-lost pitching percentage, Whitey Ford, Yankees, 25—4, .862; strikeouts, Camilo Pascual, Minnesota, 221.

Other National League leaders were: hits, Pinson, 208; doubles, Hank Aaron, Milwaukee, thirty-nine; triples, George Altman, Chicago, twelve; stolen bases, Maury Wills, Los Angeles, thirty-five; highest won-lost percentage, Johnny Podres, Los Angeles, 18—5, .783; strikeouts, Sandy Koufax, Los Angeles, 269.

Orlando Cepeda of the Giants led the National League in homers with forty-six and runs batted in with 142. Roger Maris of the Yanks led the American League in those departments with sixty-one and 142.

STENGEL PRAISES MARIS

Mets' Manager Arrives Here and Calls Slugger 'Great'

Casey Stengel, let go last fall as manager of the New York Yankees, arrived last night to take up his duties as manager of the New York Mets of the National League.

Stengel, accompanied by his wife, Edna, and Babe Herman, West Coast scout for the new National League club, landed at Idlewild Airport in Queens.

Casey heard the news of Roger Maris' sixty-first home run just before he boarded the plane in Los Angeles.

"I'm happy for him," Stengel said. "He's a great player. He hit thirty-nine for me last year in only half a season. He played more than that, but he was hurt a lot of the time and couldn't swing right."

WARRIORS DOWN KNICKS, 169-147

Chamberlain Hits 36 Field Goals and 28 Foul Shots in Setting Pro Mark

HERSHEY, Pa., March 2 (AP)—Wilt Chamberlain set a National Basketball Association scoring record of 100 points tonight as the Philadelphia Warriors defeated the New York Knickerbockers, 169—147. The combined score was an association record, too.

Chamberlain toppled many records with his awesome display. The 7-foot-1-inch Warrior center set a league record for field goals (36), free throws (28 of 32), most points for a quarter (31), and most points for a half (59).

The 316 points by the two teams surpassed the record of 312 made in Boston's victory over Minneapolis on Feb. 27, 1959, at Boston. The Celtics set a single-team record in that game, when they beat the Lakers, 173—139.

Crowd Roots for Wilt

The crowd of 4,124 shrieked, "Give it to Wilt, give it to Wilt," as the Philadelphian scored again and again on his fallaway shots.

The Warriors realized early that Chamberlain was hot. So they fed him the ball repeatedly. The Knicks tried to stall and then tried to mob Chamberlain with defense in an effort to slow his scoring.

In the final perior Darrall Imhoff, who had been assigned to guard Chamberlain most of the night, fouled out.

When Wilt hit 100, a few seconds before the end, the fans swarmed onto the court. The game was held up until they were removed.

The Warriors seemed determined to run away with the game, scrambling to a 19-3 advantage. However with Richie Guerin hitting, the Knicks drew closer and it was 79-68 at the half. But Guerin, with 39 points, Cleveland Buckner (33) and Willie Naulls (31) couldn't overcome the lift given the Warriors by Wilt. Chamberlaind had twenty-five rebounds.

Chamberlain's effort broke the league scoring record of 78 points, a mark he had set earlier this season.

The recognized collegiate scoring record also is 100, set by Frank Selvy for Furman against Newberry in 1954. Selvy now plays for the Los Angeles Lakers.

Two over-100 efforts — by Paul Arizin of Villanova and Bevo Francis of Rio Grande (Ohio) College—are not recognized by the National Collegiate Athletic Association because they were made against junior-college teams.

Among the records set tonight was one by the Knickerbockers. Their 147 points was the most ever scored by a losing team, topping the previous mark of 139 by Minneapolis against Boston in 1959.

Wilt said, "I wasn't even thinking of hitting 100, but after putting in nine straight free throws I was thinking about a foul-shooting record. It was my greatest game."

PHILA. (169)	G.	F.	PF.	P.
Arizin	7	2	0	16
Meschery	7	2	4	16
Chamb'n	36	28	2	100
Rodgers	1	9	5	11
Attles	8	1	4	17
Larese	4	1	5	9
Conlin	0	0	1	0
Ruklick	0	0	2	0
Luckenbill	0	0	2	0
Total	63	43	25	169

KNICKS (147)	G	F	PF.	P
Naulls	9	13	5	31
Green	3	0	5	6
Imhoff	3	1	6	7
Guerin	13	13		39
Butler	4	0	1	8
Budd	6	1	1	13
Butcher	3	4	5	10
Buckner	16	1	4	33
Total	57	33	32	147

Philadelphia	42	37	46	44—169
Knicks	26	42	38	41—147

Free throws missed — Chamberlain 4, Rodgers 3, Ruklick 2, Naulls 2, Guerin 4, Butcher 2.

Attendance—4,124.

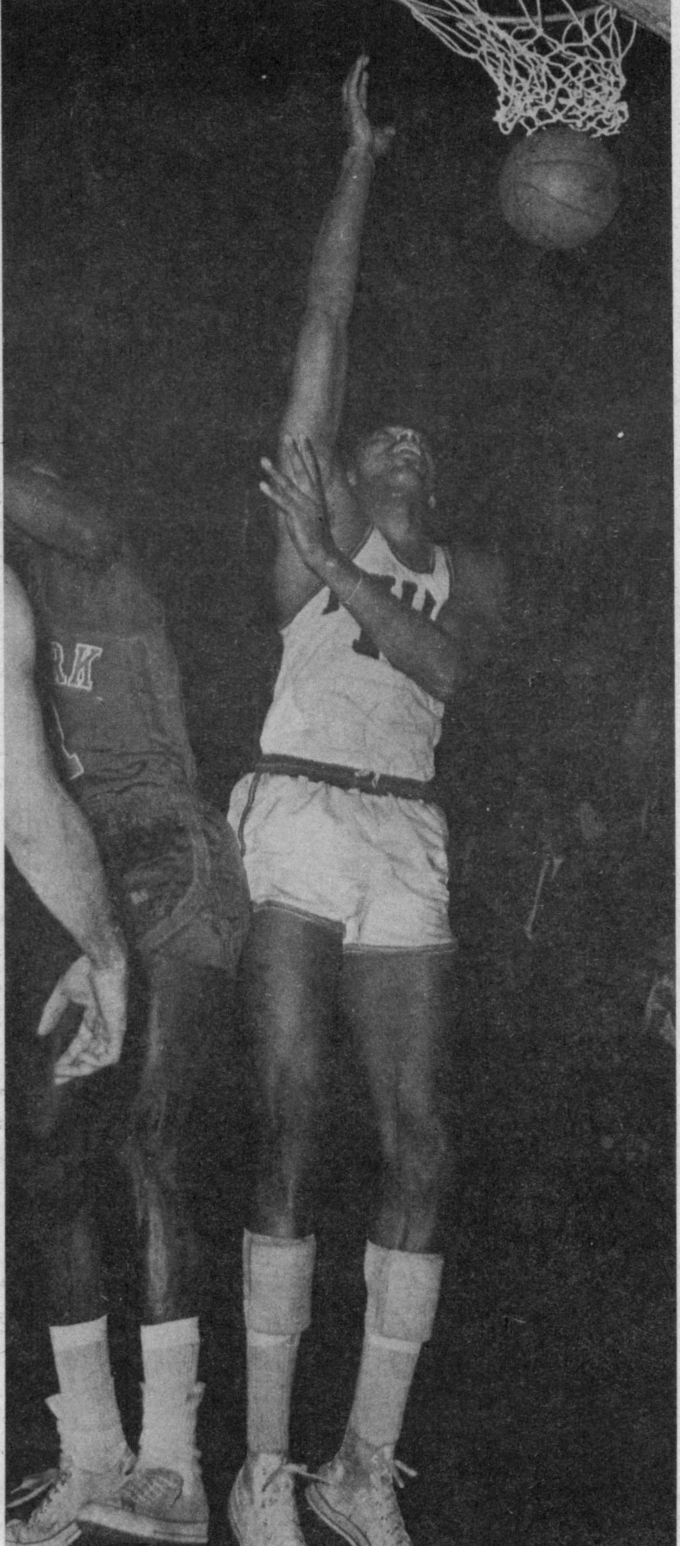

Wide World Photos

Wilt Chamberlain, right, of the Philadelphia Warriors, sinks a goal for his 100th point.

LOYOLA ACE TAKES MILE HERE IN 4:05.6

O'Hara First From Start—Gubner Puts Shot 63 Feet —Tomeo and Kerr Win

By JOSEPH M. SHEEHAN

Tom O'Hara, who pushed Jim Beatty in a 4:00.9 mile two weeks ago, proved last night he could force pace as well as follow it. The plucky, 19-year-old Loyola of Chicago sophomore, in front for all eleven laps, took the Frank A. Brennan Columbian mile in 4 minutes 5.6 seconds.

His commendable performance was among the highlights of the forty-third annual games of the New York Chapter of the Knights of Columbus. The meet, the final invitation track and field carnival of the local season, attracted 11,578 spectators to Madison Square Garden.

Two meet records were broken and three were equaled. It was another night of thrills for the railbirds, who never have had it so good as they have during this absorbing indoor track season.

Gary Gubner, New York University's big sophomore, contributed a meet shot-put mark of 63 feet. Frank Tomeo of Fordham set a meet record of 1:51.8 in the John J. Downing Memorial 880. Later he produced a 1:51.4 half-mile in anchoring the Ram two-mile relay team to a meet-record-equalling 7:34 victory.

Budd Wins 15th in Row

In extending their long winning streaks, Frank Budd and Hayes Jones, respectively, tied the meet records for the 60-yard dash and 60-yard high hurdles. Budd, who has won fifteen straight races, was clocked in 6.1 seconds. Jones, whose streak reached twenty-nine, was timed in 0:07.1.

Other individual racing victors were George Kerr, who took the 600 in 1:11; Ed Moran, who captured the 1,000 in 2:11.4, and Bruce Kidd, who ran off with the two-mile race in 8:58.8.

N. Y. U. and Morgan State reeled off the fastest mile relay times of 3:18.4 and 3:18.8, respectively. Manhattan's two-mile relay team won a college race in 7:37.

John Uelses, back in health but still not at his best, won the pole vault at 15 feet 4 inches on a tally of misses. Rolando Cruz, Henry Wadsworth and John Belitza also cleared that height. John Thomas was the high jump victor at 6 feet 10 inches.

In the hop, step and jump, which dragged on nearly an hour after the rest of the program had been completed, Ralph Boston, te great broad jumper from Tennessee State, won at 50 feet $1\frac{1}{2}$ inches.

Vinton Second in Mile

It was completely a do-it-yourself effort in the mile for O'Hara. The red-haired Chicagoan took the lead at the start, by default, and was in front every step of the way.

He wore out his rivals by running at a constantly accelerating pace. He stepped his successive quarters in 63.4, 62, 60.9 and 59.3 seconds.

Lieut. Pete Close of the Marines held on until the three-quarter-mile mark, then fell back. At the end, some thirty yards in back of O'Hara. Bob Vinton, the former Georgetown runner, was second. Larry Rawson of Boston College was third, ahead of Close. Vinton's 4:09.8 and Rawson's 4:10.6 were their best indoor clockings.

Only Ron Delany, who set the still-listed world indoor record of 4:01.4 in this meet in 1959, and Istvan Rozsavolgyi of Hungary, who did 4:01.8 last year, have bettered O'Hara's time in the Columbian Mile. The youngster will have another go at Beatty, behind whom he ran 4:02.3 at the New York A. C. Games, in Chicago next Friday.

In the 880 for metropolitan collegians, Tomeo stormed to the front with two laps to go and rolled home a ten-yard winner from Bob Carinci of Manhattan in 1:51.8. That first-class time clipped 2.1 seconds off the meet record set by Ed McAllister of Manhattan in 1959.

Though sharper than in winning the national title the previous Saturday, Gubner fell well short of his peak indoor record effort of 64 feet $11\frac{3}{4}$ inches in the New York Athletic Club Games two weeks ago. His six-put series was 61—$4\frac{1}{2}$, 62—7, 61—$11\frac{1}{2}$, foul, 61—$10\frac{1}{4}$ and 63. Behind him, Villanova's improving fullback, Billy Joe, achieved a personal best of 58—$5\frac{1}{4}$.

Jones in an :07.1 Rut

When Herb Carper, co-holder of the official indoor record of 0:06, pulled up lame in his semi-final of the 60-yard dash, Budd was left without effective opposition. Although he did not get off particularly well, Villanova's chunky speedster breezed home five feet in front of James Gee Johnson, a "sleeper" from Virginia State. Bob Mattis, Manhattan's rising sophomore, took third.

In the hurdles, Jones, on top all the way, scored by seven feet over Russ Rogers of Maryland State. Rogers nipped Bill Johnson, the Maryland alumnus. It was the fifth straight year that Jones had taken the K. of C. hurdles — and always in 0:07.1.

The Casey 600 lost its anticipated wallop when Crothers, who had won the national title handily the previous Saturday, stumbled and almost fell flat coming off the Eighth Avenue turn while out in front on the next-to-last lap.

By the time the bespectacled Canadian recovered his balance, Kerr had charged by and opened a five-yard lead. Crothers made a brave effort to get back into contention but closed the gap by only a yard. Don Webster, the Villanova freshman, was a close third, ahead of Dick Edmunds, now of Quantico.

In this meet a year ago, Kerr set his world indoor record of 1:09.3. Fast time went out the window early last night when Webster and Edmunds, who broke on top from the staggered start, just eased through the first 300 yards. Crothers then bolted from the rear and seemed to have the race well in hand until his casualty.

Taking charge early, Moran won the 1,000 easily. The husky Penn State graduate eased home ten yards in front of Thad Talley, the Southern Conference 880-yard champion from Furman. Talley charged up at the end and overhauled Charlie Durant of the Boston A. A.

Don O'Connor, Tom Kenney and Doug Tynan preceded Tomeo on Fordham's record-equaling two-mile relay team, which beat the reconstituted Irish team by ten yards and left Canada and Georgetown far behind.

Derek McCleane and Basil Clifford kept the Irish on top for the first two legs. But Tynan, ripping off his half-mile in 1:51, beat Noel Carroll and handed a three-yard lead to Tomeo. The Ram anchor man poured on the pace all the way and trebled this margin over Moran, who substituted for the hobbled Delany.

The 18-year-old Kidd ran in his usually erratic fashion in the two-mile. He stayed at the rear of the four-man field for nine gently covered laps, then took off. Sprinting the straightaways, with arms pumping wildly, and coasting the turns, he opened a huge gap in short order and won by more than 100 yards from Tom O'Riordan, the Irishman from Tralee by way of Idaho.

In the pole vault, Uelses had a miss at 14—6 but hit 15 and 15—4 on his first tries. This gave him the edge over his rivals. Of the four who jumped at 15—8, however, Cruz came closest to getting over. He missed by a whisker on his second try.

PRATT TRIUMPHS, 64-49

Mazria's 27 Points Help Beat Brooklyn Poly Quintet

Ed Mazria scored 27 points and hauled down twenty-eight rebounds to lead Pratt to a 64-49 basketball victory over Brooklyn Poly last night at the Thirteenth Regiment Armory in Brooklyn. The triumph gave Pratt a final season record of eighteen victories and four defeats. Brooklyn Poly has a 1-18 won-lost record.

PRATT (64)	G.	F.	PF.	P.
Mazria	12	3	2	27
Lange	10	4	1	24
Proto	1	2	2	4
Pirnie	1	1	2	3
Vitto	1	0	5	2
Ryan	1	0	0	2
McDonald	1	0	0	2
Scarpati	0	0	0	0
Total	27	10	12	64

BKLYN. POLY (49)	G.	F.	PF.	P.
Leuchs		1	2	7
Malinka	0	[illegible]	[illegible]	4
DeRosa	5	0	2	10
Avoy	[illegible]	[illegible]	3	6
Nagler	4	[illegible]	[illegible]	14
Schilling	3	0	1	6
DePompa	1	0	0	2
Total	18	13	15	49

Half-time score—Pratt 33, Brooklyn Poly 17.

SWIM RECORDS SET IN BIG TEN EVENT

BLOOMINGTON, Ind., March 2 (AP)—Michigan State's free-style relay team led an assault today on American swimming records in the Big Ten championships.

The Spartan team did 400 yards in 3 minutes 15.5 seconds in the afternoon trials for a national record and barely missed lowering the mark another full second in the evening final when Doug Rowe missed a hand touch.

Mike Troy and Tom Stock of Indiana set American records in the 200-yard butterfly and back-stroke events, respectively.

The previous relay mark of 3:15.9 was recorded by the Yale freshman team last year.

Troy lowered his American mark of 1:57.3 to 1:56.9 in the butterfly. Stock reduced the 200-yard backstroke record to 1:56.2. The former American record of 1:57.1 was set by Charles Bittick of Southern California in 1961.

Steve Jackman of Minnesota set a national record in the 50-yard free-style in 21.1 seconds in the trials. He held the old record of 21.4. He won the final in 21.3.

Laver Defeats Emerson to Win U. S. Title and Complete Tennis Grand Slam

AUSSIE'S SWEEP FIRST SINCE 1938

Laver Wins, 6-2, 6-4, 5-7, 6-4, in Tennis Final—Margaret Smith Beats Miss Hard

By ALLISON DANZIG

Rodney Laver of Australia achieved the first grand slam in men's tennis since 1938 when he won the national championship yesterday. For the first time, the women's title also went to an Australian player.

The holder of the Wimbledon, Australian and French championships, the red-haired, left-handed Laver completed his sweep of the world's four major titles by defeating his Davis Cup team-mate, Roy Emerson, in the final round. The scores were 6—2, 6—4, 5—7, 6—4.

A year ago, Emerson had beaten Laver in the final here in three sets.

The gallery of 9,000 in the Forest Hills stadium of the West Side Tennis Club acclaimed the 24-year-old champion with a standing ovation as he walked off the court.

Waiting to congratulate him as he reached the marquee was Donald Budge, also a redhead, and the only other player to achieve the grand slam.

Laver was born the same year that Budge won four titles.

"I feel so happy, I don't know what to say," said Laver after the championship cup had been presented to him by James B. Dickey, the first vice president of the United States Lawn Tennis Association. "I only wish I may be able to come back next year and defend this cup."

The Tongue in Check

Emerson, whom Laver had also defeated in the Australian French and Italian championship finals, said: "I would like to congratulate Rod for his fantastic record in matching Don Budge in winning the four major championships."

"He has beaten some great players in the finals," he added, as the crowd roared in appreciation.

Budge, called to the microphone, said, "If any one ever deserved winning the grand slam, Rod Laver certainly deserved to win it. I was lucky in not having to compete against such a player as Rod, and Roy's sportsmanship has been impeccable. A lot of our boys and players from other countries could learn something from them."

Margaret Smith is the Australian girl who made history in carrying off the women's crown. Like Laver, she too is red-haired.

The tall, 20-year-old Miss Smith ended the two-year reign of Darlene Hard of Long Beach, Calif., defeating her, 9-7, 6-4, in the final after saving set point in the fourteenth game.

Only once before had an Australian reached the women's final. Nancy Wynne of Australia was the runner-up to Alice Marble in 1938.

Miss Hard, who practically ruined her chances of winning with sixteen double-faults, was so emotionally distraught that she gave way to tears after losing the sixth game of the second set.

Miss Hard had been aggravated by close calls on the lines against her, as well as by her lost opportunity in the first set and her five double-faults in the third game of the second set. She found it too much when another call went against her in the sixth game.

Fighting to break service and get back on even terms in the set, she had volleyed the ball deep at advantage point for Miss Smith in the game. Miss Hard was going back to receive service, thinking she had won the point, when the official on the base line belatedly called the ball out.

Miss Hard stopped in her tracks as if stunned by the call, which gave the game to Miss Smith. She put her hand to her eyes and wept. Then she walked to the rear of the court and stood with her face to the canvas backstop, continuing to weep.

It was a trying ordeal for Miss Smith, and it became more difficult for her when the gallery roared its encouragement to Miss Hard as the American got back into the fight and won the seventh game with her skillfully turned volleys.

In the next game, the Australian girl broke badly. After Miss Hard had scored with a return of service, Miss Smith double-faulted and missed twice on her fine backhand, which had been so steadfast and had scored so often for her. She lost her service at love.

Miss Smith Fights Back

It seemed that the defending champion was strongly back in the running. Miss Smith, however, regaining her composure and, returning service beautifully from both sides, broke through easily in the ninth game as the California double-faulted.

Miss Smith then ran out the last game at love with her powerful service, which had been so big a factor in her victory along with her strong backhand volley. Miss Hard appeared to slam her last two returns of service carelessly out of court and into the net, as if in a hurry to have the match over with.

Laver, for the first two sets of the men's final, was almost as irresistible as he had been in overwhelming Rafael Osuna of Mexico in the semi-finals.

Emerson is one of the world's toughest competitors. He had led Laver, two sets to none, in the French final, and two sets to one in the Italian. He was not serving at his best, however, and he could not cope with Laver's rifle-fire return of service, failing on his lift volleys.

Laver, even though he was not getting his scorching first service in play as often as usual, was completely in command in the first two sets. He was both chipping and stroking his backhand return and hitting his forehand with topspin. At the net, he was ruthless with his volley and overhead.

Laver Breaks Though

In the very first game, Rocket Rod hit four of his fearful backhand returns of service and broke through. He broke service again in the eighth as Emerson double-faulted three times, and his emphatic volleys ended the set in the tenth.

Emerson's service improved in the second set and he showed what a masterly volleyer he is. He won his games decisively, but he had one letdown and yielded the long seventh game to Laver's cracking backhand returns of service.

Emerson had not once reached 40 on Laver's service, and it appeared he would never do so. Then Rod began to weaken in his serving and return of service. The gallery cheered Emerson on as he broke through for the first time in the eighth game of the third set. Two lucky net-cord shots helped.

Roy's two double-faults in the ninth enabled Laver to retaliate, and the latter saved three set points to even the score at 5—all. Then in the twelfth game, Emerson returned service from the backhand in the fashion of Laver, both chipping and stroking for winners, and he won the set. It was only the second set Laver had yielded in the entire tournament.

The crowd applauded Emerson enthusiastically as he left for the rest period, and it continued to cheer him as he broke Laver's service in the fourth game of the fourth set to get back on even terms after losing the first game.

The Big Break

Then came the break that sent Laver on his way to victory. Emerson faltered in his volleying, missing twice on high backhands as Laver tossed up lobs, and yielded the fifth game.

Emerson had one chance to save himself. He got to 40—30 in the last game, scoring with a marvelous cross-court forehand passing shot. Then Laver ran the next three points and it was over. He had his grand slam.

The mixed-doubles championship also went to Australia. In the final, Miss Smith and Fred Stolle defeated Lesley Turner of Australia and Frank Froehling 3d of Coral Gables, Fla., 7—5, 6—2.

Froehling and Miss Turner had defeated Ron Holmberg, of West Point, N. Y., and Jan Lehane of Australia, 6—4, 6—2, in a semi-final match. Stolle and Miss Smith had defeated James McManus of Berkeley, Calif., and Miss Hard in the other semi-final, 6—3, 6—4.

So ended the most exciting and most international championships held in recent years. Thanks to Col. Edward P. F. Eagan's People-to-People Sports Committee, which airlifted some seventy players from Europe in a chartered plane, thirty-five nations were represented in the tournament. The Soviet Union sent players here for the first time.

The attendance far exceeded last year's Colonel Eagan presented a citation to Mrs. Gladys Heldman, the editor and publisher of World Tennis, who represented his committee in marshaling the players, raising the funds for their transportation and housing and dining them for two weeks.

The New York Times

Rod Laver makes a forehand shot.

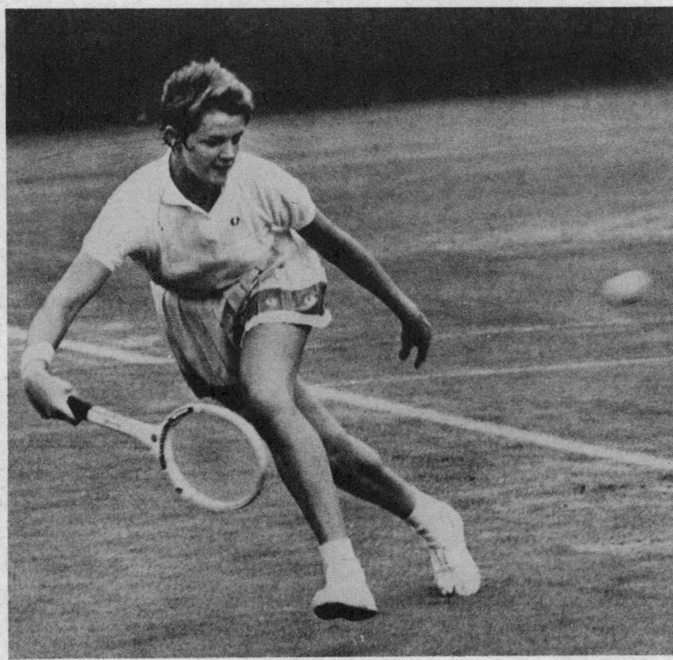

The New York Times

SMASHING SUCCESS: Margaret Smith of Australia races to make forehand return of shot by Darlene Hard of U.S. Miss Smith took women's title by winning in straight sets.

"All the News That's Fit to Print"

The New York Times.

THE WEATHER
Los Angeles: Considerable cloudiness.
San Francisco: Cloudy with a chance of rain.
Seattle: Clouds with intermittent showers.

VOL. CXII....No. 38,327. © 1962 by The New York Times Company. NEW YORK, MONDAY, DECEMBER 31, 1962. Air delivery to Alaska & Hawaii 25 cents; Air delivery in Canada & Mexico 15 cents P TEN CENTS

U.N. DRIVES ON IN KATANGA, VOWING END OF SECESSION; TSHOMBE OUT OF COUNTRY

AIRLINE SERVICE IS CASTRO'S PRICE TO FREE EMIGRES

Says Pan American Must Resume Flights Before He Allows More to Leave

KENNEDY IS ATTACKED

Havana Radio Ridicules His Speech to Ex-Prisoners at Ceremony in Miami

By The Associated Press.

KEY WEST, Fla., Dec. 30 — Cuba announced today that additional relatives of the ransomed and invasion prisoners could leave only if Pan American Airways resumed service to Cuba.

The new policy was reported by the Havana radio as an offical communique of Premier Fidel Castro's government. It was broadcast after the government-controlled station had ridiculed President Kennedy's participation in a ceremony greeting the prisoners in Miami yesterday.

The Castro communique said: "The Revolutionary government will maintain its policy to authorize the departure from the country of all those desiring to leave as soon as the Pan American Airways resumes its flights from Cuba, which it suspended by a decision of North American authorities." There was no elaboration of the statement.

Flights Still Banned

Private and commercial fights to and over the island were banned by the United States during the recent Cuban missile crisis because of the danger envolved. The ban still stands although it was temporarily lifted while flying out the ransomed prisoners.

A Pan American spokesman in New York said that the airline had little desire to resume normal service to Cuba. He explained that restrictions and limited travel had resulted in heavy losses on Cuban flights in the last several years.

Commenting on Mr. Kennedy's visit to Miami yesterday to greet the prisoners, the Havana radio said: "Kennedy admitted his participation and contribution in all steps related to satisfy the indemnification demanded by Cuban revolutionary justice to free the mercenaries."

The station described Mr. Kennedy as "an aristocratic and discriminating Yankee, who persists in his aggressive policy toward Cuba, in open violation of the United Nations Charter.

Committed to Freedom

"Kennedy made a real effort to forget his Yankee aristocratic prejudices when he called as brothers these contemptable Latin Americans born in Cuba," the radio said. It said the Cubans who packed the Orange Bowl Stadium were "men and women without a country."

Members of the Cuban invasion brigade shouted "guerra!" [war] during the ceremony, the Havana radio said, "while back in April, 1961, they were full of terror and implored for peace."

The President, in his address to the 40,000 people in the stadium, stopped considerably

Continued on Page 3, Column 5

Castro Rule, 4 Years Old, Beset by Severe Problems

Internal and International Strain Plagues the Cuban Regime, but It Retains Its Hold—Economy Still Declining

By TAD SZULC

Special to The New York Times.

WASHINGTON, Dec. 30 The Castro regime in Cuba will enter its fifth year Tuesday in the midst of deep domestic and international tensions and problems.

Cuba's economic situation continues to deteriorate. Production in all fields remains completely inadequate and shortages go on growing

Last October's crisis over the installation of Soviet missiles has deepened the cleavage between Dr. Castro's "new Communists" and the "old guard Communists." Reports from Cuba speak of increasing friction on all levels between the two main power groups.

Friction is said to exist within the top leadership, in lower ranks of Government, in the armed forces, and even within the Havana University, which has traditionally been Dr. Castro's personal ideological fortress.

But the Premier's tightly controlled Government apparatus still seems able to maintain its hold over the island. His secret police—the G-2—continues to smash all efforts at rebuilding the anti-regime underground.

Dr. Castro has yet to evolve a new relationship with the Soviet Union and assure himself of the sustained economic assistance that may be necessary if his revolution is to survive another year.

The missiles crisis has unquestionably damaged Havana-Moscow ties seriously. Intelligence reports from Cuba indicate that Dr. Castro is still greatly resentful that Premier Khrushchev removed the missiles from the island without first consulting him.

While on the surface both Havana and Moscow insist their

Continued on Page 3, Column 6

Californians Celebrating Disputed Claim of 'First'

By GLADWIN HILL

Special to The New York Times.

LOS ANGELES, Dec. 30—California this weekend embarked on a far-flung round of festivities commemorating its claimed—but disputed—accession to first rank among the 50 states in poulation.

The weekend's observances will culminate in a nominal state holiday tomorrow — although its lustre will be dimmed somewhat by a little political sniping, business un-interest, and total lack of public experience in celebrating such a milestone.

According to Californians, the state now has some 17,393,000 inhabitants, against an estimated 17,341,000 for New York.

However, New York's Governor Rockefeller contends California won't pass New York until next fall. The United States Census Bureau has put the juncture some time in the first three months of 1963.

Gov. Edmund G. Brown's proclamation of a state holiday tomorrow will mean mainly that state employes get a day off. Business people generally demurred at his suggestion that it be made a business holiday, and banks, stores, many offices, and securities exchanges will operate.

Los Angeles, the state's largest metropolis, followed the Democratic executive's suggestion that county and city officials likewise declare it an official holiday.

But in San Francisco, Mayor George Christopher—recent un-

Continued on Page 4, Column 6

VAN ALLEN SEES SCIENCE 'CLIQUE'

Says Data on Radiation Belt Reflect Hasty Judgment by Government Insiders

By WALTER SULLIVAN

Special to The New York Times.

PHILADELPHIA, Dec. 30 — Dr. James A. Van Allen, discoverer of the earth's encircling radiation belts that bear his name, voiced strong critcism today of President Kennedy's Science Advisory Committee.

He said its announcement of the creation of an unexpectedly severe and enduring radiation belt by the hydrogen bomb fired in space on July 9 was "hasty and ill-considered."

He and a fellow scientist told the American Association for the Advancement of Science that information was already available showing the belt to be far smaller than indicated by that announcement.

Furthermore, he agreed with his companion on the platform who said that the President's

Continued on Page 7, Column 4

BRAZIL OUTLINES ECONOMIC GOALS; FIGHTS INFLATION

3-Year Plan Seeks 7 Per Cent Annual Growth Rate and Curbs on Price Rises

By JUAN DE ONIS

Special to The New York Times.

RIO DE JANEIRO, Dec. 30 — The government made public today a three-year national development plan designed to keep Brazil's economy growing while inflation is shoved down.

The plan foresees a 7 per cent annual increase in Brazil's gross national product, with the principal emphasis on industry. To obtain this rate of growth, the blue-print calls for investment of about $7,000,000,000 for the 1963-65 period.

Measures to be taken against Brazil's serious inflation include a reduction in public expenditures in the 1963 budget and the floating of treasury notes to finance work not covered by revenues, in spite of recent tax increasing.

The return to relative monetary stability is expected to be gradual, however. Next year the plan aims at reducing by one half the 1962 price-increase rate of 60 per cent for 1965. The rate of price increases projected by the plan is 10 per cent.

Furtado Drafted Plan

The plan, which was published as a document of 850 pages, has been pulled together on an emergency schedule in less than three months under the supervision of Dr. Celso Furtado, minister without portfolio.

Dr. Furtado is well known in Washington as a director of Brazil's northeast regional development program. The United States is participating in that program under a $131,000,000 Alliance for Progress aid plan.

A northeast cooperative effort and all other forms of Alliance for Progress action here have been seriously hobbled by the inflationary erosion of development investments, as well as by administrative friction between United States and Brazilian officials.

The plan is similar in concept to the national development programs drawn up in Chile, Colombia and Bolivia. The latter plans already have been submitted to Alliance for Progress experts for global financing.

Brazil's plan diverges considerably, however, from the rigorous monetary and credit rules laid down by the International Monetary Fund for financing stabilization programs. Brazil's immediate need for foreign financing is considerable.

Planners here estimate that Brazil will have a favorable trade balance of about $700,000,000 in the 1963-65 period,

Continued on Page 3, Column 4

CAPITAL EXPECTS WORLD PROBLEMS TO REMAIN TOUGH

Diplomats See Less Tension in '63 But Little Easing of East-West Issues

By MAX FRANKEL

Special to The New York Times.

WASHINGTON, Dec. 30 — To the men who carry out United States foreign policy from State Department offices, it appears 1963 will be as tough, but not quite so tense, as 1962.

The world appears to them to be in an exciting state of flux, with the Western alliance straining for new forms of union and the old Communist bloc in unmistakable disarray, while the neutralisms of the world between become more difficult to define.

The department led by Secretary of State Dean Rusk rarely lingers long over the generalities of diplomacy. Even in the holiday season it was preoccupied with battles in the Katanga bush and negotiations over European Common Market vegetables. It sees the new year in terms not so much of past achievements as of the same old problems slightly transformed.

The biggest problems on the State Department's calendar are thought to require more attention than action, more manuever than battle. In relations with the allies, with the Russians and even with the Cubans, the mood at this moment is to wait and see and to "play it quietly" for a while.

Concern Over Europe

These are the problems and the apparent feelings here about them:

Washington is anxious about Britain's application of membership in the European Economic Community. It hopes Britain will join and stabilize Europe. It hopes the proposal to work toward a multi-national Atlantic nuclear force will speed the day of genuine interdependence of all the allied nations.

But officials seemed to believe that Europe has neither the need nor the means for developing any significant nuclear force. They are trying to prove as quickly and diplomatically as they can that Europe cannot afford the trappings of big-power defense and that it could and should rely upon the Americans' nuclear shield.

Perhaps not in the next year but soon, Washington believes, Europe will welcome Britain and scoff at France's insistence on separate national nuclear forces.

Increasingly Washington expects a prosperous Europe to contribute more generously to the conventional force requirements of the alliance, to Western aid programs for underdeveloped nations and to the rational realignment of free world trade patterns.

The dismaying problem hanging over the alliance stems from the realization that though all its members could be implicated in a bitter war by virtually any one of them, they are still a long way from finding methods to conduct properly coordinated and consistent foreign policies.

The West's difficulties are thought to be minimal beside

Continued on Page 2, Column 6

Associated Press Radiophoto

PROTEST IN BRUSSELS: Pro-Katanga demonstrators gather outside Belgian-Katanga Friendship Society to protest against U.N. "offensive" in the secessionist Congo province.

Congo Gains Lift U.S. Hope Of Ending Katanga Schism

By DAVID BINDER

Special to The New York Times.

WASHINGTON, Dec. 30—Reports of new gains by United Nations forces in Katanga led Government officials today to express cautious optimism about the chances of ending the secession of the Congo province.

The officials said the fighting around Elisabethville during the last six days had been something of a surprise development.

More surprising, they said, was the apparent demoralization of the 20,000 mercenary troops of the Katanga President, Moise Tshombe, that had retreated steadily before the United Nations forces.

"The situation is completely different from the one a year ago," one authority said. "It seems as if the mercenaries have finally got fed up with their lot."

U.S. to Wait and See

The official position of the United States at this point in the struggle is: Wait and see.

This is a change from the position a few days ago, when Government officials were talking about a substantial increase in United States support of the United Nations effort in the Congo.

Plans had already been drafted for an airlift of military supplies for the United Nations forces — especially transportation equipment. Some officials were suggesting privately that the United States might even send troops to bolster the 18,000-man command.

Other sources remarked that both the supply shipments and the suggestion that American units might be flown in were designed to intimidate Mr. Tshombe and to put pressure on the Katanga leader to end his secession.

Now the success of the United Nations forces seems to

Continued on Page 2, Column 8

PEKING SAYS INDIA MAKES WAR PLANS

Chinese Memorandum Calls Cease-Fire 'Unstable'—Peace Envoy in Canton

By Reuters.

PEKING, Dec. 30 — Communist China accused India today of "stepping up arms expansion and war preparation" and warned that the present cease-fire in their border conflict was "unstable."

The Chinese warning was made in a long memorandum issued on the eve of the arrival here of Prime Minister Sirimavo Bandaranaike of Ceylon on a peace-making mission.

Mrs. Bandaranaike who arrived in Canton today by way of Hong Kong, planned to discuss with Chinese Communist leaders the peace proposals drawn up in Colombo earlier this month by six nonaligned African and Asian countries.

Before leaving Hong Kong, Mrs. Bandaranaike said in a statement that the six nonaligned countries were confident that their proposals would help bring Communist China and India to the conference table, although they were not "intended to be a solution" to the territorial dispute.

Subandrio Also Expected

Mrs. Bandaranaike is expected to stay in Peking eight days before going to New Delhi to discuss the proposals with Prime Minister Jawaharlal Nehru.

Well-informed Asian sources said Foreign Minister Subandrio of Indonesia was expected in Peking on Wednesday to join Mrs. Bandaranaike in discussions.

The African-Asian proposals have not been officially disclosed but are reported to include suggestions for the withdrawal of Chinese troops and the establishment of a buffer zone in Ladakh, Indian's northern front.

The new Chinese memorandum replied to one from India 11 days ago. The Chinese said India's "non-impedement" of China's unilateral cease-fire last month was not the same as India's formal agreement to a cease-fire.

The memorandum again rejected as "absolutely unacceptable what it called India's "pre-

Continued on Page 3, Column 3

Holiday Notice

The New York Times Western Edition will not be printed tomorrow, Jan. 1, New Year's Day.

RESISTANCE EBBS

Key Towns Captured—Leader of Province Remains Defiant

By J. ANTHONY LUKAS

Special to The New York Times.

LEOPOLDVILLE, The Congo, Dec. 30 — The United Nations command set up its offensive in Katanga today and vowed it would continue until the province's cessation was ended.

(President Moise Tshombe of Katanga arrived in Salisbury, Southern Rhodesia, Sunday, the Associated Press reported. He denied that he had fled Katanga. He charged that the United Nations was trying to force a solution on his cessessationists province.)

As United Nations forces continued to advance virtually unresisted, Robert K. A. Gardiner, the organization's chief officer in the Congo, declared, "We are not going to make the mistake this time of stopping short."

To Press for Decision

"This is going to be as decisive as we can make it," he said at a news conference at United Nations headquarters here.

This was the first firm statement of United Nations policy in the third round of fighting with Katangese forces. It indicated that the United Nations would not stop short of total victory, as it did in September and December of last year.

Reports from commanders in the field indicated that the United Nations forces were well on the way to that victory.

Late in the afternoon, the United Nations announced that a Ghanaian battalion had captured Kamina, 270 miles northeast of Elizabethville. The

Continued on Page 2, Column 5

Packers Top Giants, 16-7, to Keep Pro Football Title

United Press International Telephoto

As Bob Skoronski of Green Bay takes out Andy Robustelli of Giants, Jim Taylor scores

By ROBERT L. TEAGUE

Special to The New York Times.

NEW YORK.

Yankee Stadium was no place for a warm-blooded mammal today especially Y. A. Tittle of the New York Giants. His passing arm was as cold as a popsicle. Hence, the Green Bay Packers scored a 16-7 triumph and captured the National Football League crown for the second straight year. Field goals of 26, 29 and 30 yards—all by Jerry Kramer—provided the margin of victory. A capacity gathering of 64,892 witnessed this exciting, closely contested affair. The most conspicuous witness in attendance was Old Man Winter. His temperature ranged from 20 to 17 degrees and he exhaled frigid, swirling gusts of wind

Continued on Page 8, Column 1

Agency Redefines Space Contracts

By JOHN W. FINNEY

Special to The New York Times.

WASHINGTON, Dec. 30 The space agency believes it has finally resolved a long-standing conflict-of-interest problem involving the General Electric Company and the program to land a manned expedition on the moon.

In the process, the space agency has established an important precedent defining and limiting the right of industry to bid on and receive Government contracts. Somewhat cautiously but deliberately, the agency, the National Aeronautics and Space Administration, is laying down a far-reaching policy. It specifies that a company cannot serve in the dual and potentially conflicting role of technical manager and hardware producer.

The potential conflict-of-in-

Continued on Page 7, Column 8

Pier Talks Pushed; Strike Loss Grows

Special to The New York Times.

NEW YORK.

Federal mediation efforts in the week-old longshoreman strike continued in New York yesterday amid a state of conflicting rumors. As losses in the Atlantic and Gulf coast walkout mounted, Secretary of Labor W. Willard Wirtz kept the disputing dockmen and employers in session separately at the Commodore Hotel.

The rumors ranged from pessimism to guarded optimism. Their volume was attributed in part to the fact that Mr. Wirtz had silenced the spokesmen for the New York Shipping Association and the International Longshoremen's Association. Each side agreed to leave all the talking to Mr. Wirtz or to designated aides in his headquarters in the hotel.

At a late hour Mr. Wirtz had

Continued on Page 4, Column 3

Kennedy Says Communist Myth Of Certain Victory Is Rebutted

By The Associated Press.

NEW YORK.

President Kennedy said today that history "has already refuted the myth of the inevitability of Communist victory."

Writing in the current issue of Look Magazine, the President said the Communists would lose their "bet" that the future will be a Communist world—"that the inexorable processes of history must send all nations, some early, some late, through the Marxist wringer."

Mr. Kennedy said "our bet" is that the future will be a world community of independent nations, with a diversity of economic, political and religious systems, united by a common respect for the rights of others." He continued:

"But history is what men make of it and we would be foolish to think that we can realize our own vision of a free and diverse future without unceasing vigilance, discipline and labor."

The President added that "above all, we must both demonstrate and develop the affirmative power of the democratic ideal—remembering always that nations are great, not for what they are against, but what they are for."

He summarized his view of the world by regions, saying:

Western Europe "The success of a Common Market symbolizes a united and astonish-

Continued on Page 2, Column 2

NEWS INDEX

Packers Beat Giants, 16-7, Keep Pro Football Title

FIELD GOALS WIN DEFENSIVE GAME

Kramer Boots 3 and Taylor Gets Touchdown—Giants Block Kick to Score

Continued from Page 1, Col. 4

that frequently reached 30 miles an hour.

Weather and wind seemed to wreak greater hardships on Tittle than on any man on the field. On at least 10 occasions, the 36-year-old quarterback overthrew or underthrew open targets far down the field.

It was a miserable day for Tittle. He rarely looked like the same chap who had established a league record of 33 touchdown passes during the regular season. The New York score was made when Erich Barnes blocked a Packer punt and Jim Collier recovered it in the end zone.

All told, Tittle connected on 18 of 41 aerials for 197 yards. His longest completion was a 21-yard pitch to Del Shofner in the first quarter. Too many of Yat's tosses went for short gains, and the Giants did not have the kind of rushing power that consistently could penetrate the Packer line.

Packer Rush Formidable

Part of Tittle's trouble stemmed from a formidable rush by the Green Bay forwards, notably Bill Quinlan, Willie Davis and Ray Nitschke, a blitzing middle linebacker.

Nitschke always seemed to be in the right place at the right time. He recovered two fumbles that led to Green Bay scores.

Even so, the Giants acquitted themselves far better than they had in Green Bay last year, when the Packers crushed them, 37-0, in the playoff. In fact, they could have won today except for two heartbreaking incidents.

In the first quarter, Tittle guided them from their 38 to a first down on the Packer 16. But then Tittle tried to pass to Joe Walton, alone on the goal line. Nitschke deflected the ball, however, and Dan Currie intercepted for Green Bay at the 15 and returned it 24 yards.

A touchdown for the Giants at that point would have put them ahead, 7-3, and might have made a big difference in the final result.

Bad luck thwarted the New Yorkers again in the third quarter. This time, a pass interference penalty called against Willie Wood of the Packers, plus a personal foul by the same player, gave a first down to the Giants on the Packer 18.

Wood's foul was an abrupt, violent turn toward the official who had just called interference, back judge Tom Kelleher of Holy Cross. He knocked Kelleher to the ground and was ejected.

But immediately after that break, two penalties for pushing and holding set the Giants back to their 40. The New Yorkers had got their touchdown earlier in the period, narrowing the deficit to 10-7. Had they been able to capitalize on Wood's misdemeanors here they would have gone ahead, perhaps to stay.

On still another occasion, the Giants narrowly missed a touchdown. This happened late in the first quarter after Jim Taylor had put the Packer lead at 10-0 with an 8-yard burst through center.

Johnny Counts received the ensuing kick-off on his 9 and appeared headed for a touchdown. But the last Green Bay defender—Wood, tackled him on the Giant 41. No one else was near enough to have caught the fleet rookie from behind.

Minutes later, Don Chandler of the Giants missed a fieldgoal attempt from 47 yards out seconds before the halftime gun.

A major factor in Green Bay's success was the determined rushing of the 215-pound Taylor. He was especially competent in third-down situations, usually picking up the yardage necessary to keep Packer drives under way.

Taylor gained 85 yards on 14 carries from scrimmage. He frequently found no holes in the line, but slid off tacklers and found running room on the outside.

Paul Hornung and Tom Moore also turned in first-down runs from time to time, helping the Packers amass 148 yards on the ground.

Bart Starr, Green Bay's quarterback, was not rushed so hard as Tittle, as a general rule. He completed 9 of 21 tosses for 85 yards, concentrating on screens and flares with an occasional longer pitch to Boyd Dowler, Max McGee and Ron Kramer.

It Was a Cold Day at Yankee Stadium—Especially for Giant Fans

United Press International Telephotos

While it was the kick that provided Green Bay's margin of victory, it also was a kick that provided the Giants with their only touchdown, if indirectly. Giant Erich Barnes, right, blocked punt by Packer Max McGee (85) with his chest in the third period. Jim Collier of the New Yorkers then fell on the ball in end zone for the touchdown.

TOP-RATED TEAMS IN BOWL FOOTBALL

U.S.C. Wisconsin Among 4 Major Games Tomorrow

By The Associated Press.

NEW YORK.

Eight of the nation's top 10 college football teams play tomorrow amid a profusion of roses, oranges, sugar and cotton as the big four of the bowl extravaganzas step front and center on a stage replete with all-Americans.

Preceding the big games, West Texas State, with eight victories and two defeats, meets Ohio University, also 8-2, in the Sun Bowl today.

In the Rose Bowl at Pasadena, Calif., tomorrow, top-ranked Southern California, with a 10-0 record, opposes No. 2 Wisconsin, 8-1. This oldest of all bowl games will be televised by the National Broadcasting Company. All-Americans on display will be a Trojan guard, Damon Bame, and a Badger end, Pat Richter.

In the Sugar Bowl at New Orleans, third-rated Mississippi, 9-0, will tackle Arkansas, 9-1 and sixth-ranked. N.B.C. will televise this before the Rose Bowl contest.

Texas Ranked No. 4

No. 4 Texas, with nine triumphs and one tie, will clash with Louisiana State, 8-1-1 and seventh-ranked, in the Cotton Bowl at Dallas. The Columbia Broadcasting System will televise this game. All-Americans sharing the spotlight will be a Longhorn guard, John Treadwell, and a Tiger halfback, Jerry Stovall.

In the Orange Bowl at Miami, Alabama, 9-1 and No. 5, will oppose Oklahoma, 8-2 and No. 8. This will be telecast by the American Broadcasting Company.

One all-American will be on the field, the Crimson Tide center, Lee Roy Jordan. In the stands will be President Kennedy.

On Saturday, Florida upset Penn State, 17-7, in the Gator Bowl on two touchdown passes by Tommy Shannon. The East defeated the West, 25-19, in the Shrine game; the Blue whipped the Gray, 10-6, and the Small College All-Stars topped the Major College All-Stars, 14-13, in the All-American Bowl.

A crowd of 100,000 is expected in the Rose Bowl. There Southern Cal's first national champions since 1939 will battle a Wisconsin team seeking revenge for a 44-8 humiliation at the hands of Washington in 1960.

ALERT U.S.C. DEFEATS WISCONSIN IN ROSE BOWL, 42-37; L.S.U., MISSISSIPPI AND ALABAMA WIN OTHER CONTESTS

TIGERS TOP TEXAS

Louisiana State Wins, 13-0, Before 75,504 in Cotton Bowl

By The Associated Press.

DALLAS, Jan. 1—Lynn Amedee's field goals of 23 and 37 yards and Jimmy Field's 22-yard touchdown gave Louisiana State a 13-0 victory over Texas in the Cotton Bowl today.

The Longhorns never got closer than the L.S.U. 25-yard line. On their only chance for a score, their shoeless kicker, Tony Brosby, missed a field goal from the Tiger 32.

The magnificent Louisiana State defense thwarted every Texas effort as the Tigers kept their goal lines uncrossed by rushing in 17 straight games. L.S.U. also intercepted three Texas passes.

The nation's No. 7 team beat the No. 4 team with comparative ease and finished with a record of 9-1-1 and its first victory in the Cotton Bowl in two tries.

The other time L.S.U. played here it fought to a scoreless tie with Arkansas in 1947. It was Texas' third Cotton Bowl loss.

Record Broken Twice

Amedee broke the Cotton Bowl field-goal record of 22 yards with his first 23-yard boot in the second period. His 37-yarder in the closing minutes broke it again.

A crowd of 75,504 sat in Indian summer weather as the expected tight defensive struggle turned into an offensive show on the part of Louisiana State. The Bayou Tigers tried 21 passes, about 11 more than they ordinarily attempt.

Jerry Stovall, an all-American, was overshadowed by other L.S.U. backs except for his excellent kicking. As the game ended, Stovall met St. Louis Cardinals' representatives on the 40-yard line and signed a contract with the National Football League Club.

Louisiana State got 132 yards in the air and 127 on the ground compared to 80 rushing and 92 passing for Texas.

Texas got to the L.S.U. 25, 32 and 30, but never could puncture the rough Louisiana State line and glittering secondary when danger appeared.

Texas Interferes on Pass

The first of two pass interference penalties against Texas helped the Tigers on their drive to the first field goal. But it was 33 yards in passing and 10 running by Amedee that did the most damage.

Charley Cranford ran for 13 in the 75-yard drive. With only 8 seconds left in the half Amedee booted the field goal.

The touchdown early in the third period was set up when Jerry Cook fumbled the kickoff on the Texas 37 and Amedee recovered.

Field's 11-yard pass to Gene Sikes got the Tigers moving. Field went back to pass on the Texas 22, saw he was covered so he just ran around left end for the touchdown.

L.S.U. rolled to the Texas 7 late in the third period on Field's passing, but Texas stopped this drive.

Amedee's passing to Bill Truax set up the second field goal with four minutes left in the game. Amedee completed 9 of 13 passes for 93 yards.

Cook Leads Gainers

Cook fumbled twice, but was the leading ground-gainer with 39 yards. Stovall topped L.S.U. with 36 in 12 runs. Stovall kicked for a fine average of 41.8 but Ernie Koy, the Texas sophomore, outdid him with 46.8. Stovall, however, was hampered by two bad center passes.

Amedee was named the outstanding back in a vote by the writers. He got 37 votes to four for Stovall and two for Field.

Johnny Treadwell, Texas' All-America guard, was the top lineman. He got 20 votes. Jack Gates, Louisiana State end, was second with 7½.

Ray Poage, the Texas full-

Continued on Page 10, Col. 4

NO. 1 FAN: President Kennedy tosses the coin (arrow) from his box in Orange Bowl prior to start of the game.

Associated Press

PASADENA: Fullback Ben Wilson smashes over Wisconsin line for USC's second touchdown in the Rose Bowl game. The Trojans staved off a sensational last-quarter rally by the Badgers to preserve their perfect record, 42-37.

100,000 THRILLED

Unbeaten, Top-Ranked Trojans Withstand Badgers' Rally

By BILL BECKER
Special to The New York Times.

PASADENA, Calif., Jan. 1—Southern California's national champion Trojans scored early and often and then hung on for dear life to edge the University of Wisconsin, 42 to 37, today in the all-time high-scoring parade in the Rose Bowl.

The Badgers, Big Ten champions and rated second only to the Trojans, almost ran U.S.C. out of the Pasadena pasture with 23 points in the final quarter. But they just couldn't catch up.

The wild finish, sparked by a superb quarterback, Ron Vanderkelen, had 98,698 spectators limp and hoarse. The total of 79 points far surpassed the previous Rose Bowl record set in 1930 when U.S.C. defeated Pittsburgh, 47-14.

Vanderkelen, magnificient in adversity, set another Rose Bowl record by completing 33 of 48 passes for 401 yards, including two touchdowns. He also scored on a 17-yard run himself.

But Pete Beathard, his opposing quarterback, was almost as flashy, if not as prolific. Beathard threw four touchdown passes in completing eight of 12. That gave him a record, too.

The touchdowns and records were as plentiful as popcorn as the two top elevens put on a genuine professional show. Wisconsin ran up 32 first downs to 15 for the Trojans and got only the consolation of chalking up another for the books.

Richter, Bedsole Score

Vanderkelen's payoff passes went 19 yards to his favorite target, Pat Richter, the All-America end, and four yards to Gary Kroner, a workhorse halfback.

Beathard's scoring shots went 57 and 23 to Hal Bedsole, Troy's All-America wingman; 13 yards to Fred Hill, another end; and 13 yards to Ron Butcher, a tackle who was eligible on a shift.

The last enumerated brought Troy's first touchdown in the first five minutes 37 seconds and set the tenor for the rest of the long, wild afternoon.

Vanderkelen and Beathard were named co-players of the game, quite deservedly, by a board of sportswriters.

The 11-touchdown extravaganza was an offensive coach's delight and a statistician's nightmare. It was topped by 11 successful conversions and even a safety. Only a field goal was lacking.

A poor pass from center Larry Sagouspe sailed over Ernie Jones' head as he tried to punt and he was downed in his end zone by Ernie Von Heimburg, Wisconsin guard, for a two pointer.

Trojans Killed Clock

That made it possible, mathematically, for the Badgers to pull the game out. There were still five minutes left to play.

But Vanderkelen and his fighting mates could only get one touchdown. The game ended with the thankful Trojans running backward deliberately to kill the clock and then punting on the final play.

Besides Beathard and Bedsole, Willie (the Wisp) Brown, a fleet halfback, stood out for the men of Troy. Brown made several fine receptions, kickoff runbacks of 41 and 31 yards and stopped one Badger drive with an interception for a touchback in the end zone.

Richter caught 11 passes for 163 yards total for one of his finest days. Little Lou Holland grabbed eight for 72 yards and scored on a 13-yard scamper around end.

Vanderkeln wound up with five net yards gained by rushing to give him a total of 406

Continued on Page 10, Col. 5

NEW ORLEANS: Billy Moore, Arkansas quarterback, takes 5-yard loss in Sugar Bowl as he is lifted off feet by Buck Randall of Mississippi. Ole Miss scored 17-13 victory.

Associated Press Wirephoto

MIAMI: Oklahoma fullback Jim Grisham plows up middle for 22-yard gain in Orange Bowl game against Alabama. Oklahoma was mostly contained as Alabama won, 17-0.

Rebels Defeat Arkansas In Sugar Bowl, 17 to 13

By United Press International

NEW ORLEANS, Jan 1—Glynn Griffing passed for 242 yards, scored one touchdown and threw for another today to lead Mississippi to a 17-13 victory over Arkansas in the Sugar Bowl.

Griffing, a 6-foot 1-inch 200-pound senior, closed his college football career with his finest performance before 82,500 fans.

The Ole Miss quarterback passed to Louis Guy for one touchdown and plunged for another. He was named the outstanding player in leading the Rebels to their first undefeated and untied season in 70 years. They won 10 games.

Arkansas, the runner-up to Texas in the Southwest Conference made a game showing. The Razorbacks' 13 points were the most scored against the Rebels this season.

Three Sugar Bowl records were set in the 29th annual contest. Griffing's 242 yards passing were the most ever garnered. Tom McKnelly's two field goals set another. And a 68-yard pass from the Arkansas quarterback, Bill Gray, to an end, Jerry Lamb, was the longest in the history of the series.

Irwin Kicks Field Goal

Mississippi took a 3-0 lead in the opening minutes of the second quarter when Billy Carl Irwin kicked a 30-yard field goal to cap a 49-yard drive. Arkansas tied it up with five minutes to go in the half on a 30-yard field goal by McKnelly. The Razorbacks' score was set up by the Gray-to-Lamb pass which carried to the Rebel 13.

Mississippi made it 10-3 at half time, scoring the first touchdown 2 minutes 13 seconds before the intermission on Griffing's 33-yard toss to Guy. The touchdown was set up by a 17-yard Griffing-to-Chuck Morris pass and Irwin kicked the extra point.

Early in the second half, the Razorbacks recovered a Buck Randall fumble at the Mississippi 18, and scored in two plays. Gesse Branch hit left tackle for 13 yards, breaking away from would-be tacklers four times. Billy Moore threw to Branch for five yards and the touchdown and McKnelly kicked the tying point.

Mississippi took the ensuing kick-off and drove 80 yards in 10 plays with Griffing completing passes of 18 and 35 yards to Guy and carrying over from the 1. Irwin's kick made it 17-10.

Parker Excels on Defense

Arkansas cut the margin to 17-13 on McKnelly's 32-yard field goal shortly before the end of the third quarter. The key play in the 70-yard Razorback march were passes of 30 and 9 yards from Moore to Lamb.

Mississippi barely missed another score in the final period because of the brilliant defensive work of Mike Parker, a halfback who batted down two Griffing passes in the Arkansas end zone. The threat ended with Ole Miss on the Razorback 3.

Mississippi threatened again in the final two minutes, with Griffing running and passing to

Continued on Page 10, Col. 1

ACCEPTANCE HINT BY A.A.U. IS GIVEN

Arbitration by MacArthur Looms as Next Move in N.C.A.A. Conflict

By United Press International

NEW YORK.

The National Collegiate Athletic Association today awaited word from President Kennedy whether the National Amateur Athletic Union would accept Gen. Douglas MacArthur's arbitration in the dispute between the country's leading amateur sports bodies.

Col. Donald Hull, the executive director of the A. A. U., wired the President at Palm Beach, Fla., yesterday his organization's answer, but refused to divulge the contents.

Attorney General Robert F. Kennedy interceded in the squabble in mid-November, when it was thought an acceptable agreement had been reached.

Friction erupted again in Detroit when the A. A. U. complained the N. C. A. A. federations had refused to accept the coalition plan which offered a vote and voice in track and field.

On Dec. 13, Hull recommended that his executive committee seek arbitration. President Kennedy responded by asking General MacArthur to arbitrate the dispute.

The President warned the feuding organizations that the amateur sports war threatened to weaken the United State's

Continued on Page 10, Col. 3

U.S. IN AGREEMENT OF FIGHT RECEIPTS

$400,000 Still to Be Held From Liston, Patterson in a Tax Dispute

By United Press International

NEW YORK.

The Federal Government confirmed yesterday that its $2,000,000 tax crackdown on receipts of the September Sonny Liston-Floyd Patterson heavyweight title fight had resulted in an agreement among all parties concerned.

Patterson will receive his $997,500 purse in payments already made in 1962 and to be made in 1963 instead of being spread over 17 years.

Championship Sports Inc., promoter of the fight, will accept the tax responsibility on all "ancillary" monies from television, radio, movies, etc., received by Graff, Reiner and Smith Enterprises, which the Government claims actually was a C.S.I. corporation.

Meanwhile the Government is holding $207,000 of Liston's purse until it determines the amount of taxes.

Patterson who already had received some of his purse, was paid an additional $210,000 by the Internal Revenue Service yesterday.

The terms of the stipulation, filed late Monday in Manhattan Federal Court and signed by all concerned, disclosed that the Government would hold $400,000 of the still frozen $1,379,000 receipts until it determines exactly how much was owed by C.S.I.

Tide Trounces Oklahoma In Orange Bowl, 17 to 0

By United Press International

MIAMI, Jan. 1—Rangy Joe Namath, operating behind a lightning-fast line, pitched and raced Alabama to a 17-0 Orange Bowl victory over ill-fated Oklahoma today before a shirt-sleeved crowd of 73,380 headed by President Kennedy.

Namuth put Alabama's 3-point favorites in front with a 25-yard touchdown pass to Dick Williamson in the first quarter. His passing and running set up Cotton Clark's 15-yard touchdown bolt in the second quarter. Tim Davis booted the two extra points as well as a 19-yard field goal in the third period.

Oklahoma gave it a gallant try in mid-70 temperature but was halted on the 7 and 8 on fumbles by Jim Grisham, a big fullback who was outstanding in defeat. On other occasions, the Sooners were halted on the 10 and 16.

Line Play Decisive

The line, led by All-America center Lee Roy Jordan, turned the tables in favor of the Crimsón Tide. Outweighed almost 10 pounds to the man, the mobile Alabama linemen opened huge holes for a host of racing backs and throttled every Oklahoma threat in the same manner in which they had yielded only 39 points all season.

Alabama smashed 61 yards for a touchdown the second time it received the ball. Namuth passes and the running of Ed Versprille and Clark took the ball to the Oklahoma 25. From there Namuth hit Williamson in the end zone.

Oklahoma gained 81 yards on three plays to the Alabama 7. Grisham got 3 and then 23 before Ron Fletcher hit Al Baumgartdner with a 55 yard pass. Then Grisham fumbled and Mike Hopper recovered for Alabama on his 6.

Versprille fumbled back shortly afterward, Oklahoma's John Porterfield recovering on the Tide 31. Oklahoma banged to the 18 and then Grisham, slashing into the line, fumbled the ball a second time and Dan Kearley recovered for Alabama on his 8.

Clark Punts Out on 8

Alabama padded its lead in the second quarter after Clark had punted out of bounds on the Oklahoma 8. The Sooners were driven back to their 4 and fleet Billy Piper took Joe Don Looney's punt from the Oklahoma 47 to the 34. Namath pinpointed Williamson with a 23-yard pass to the 13, Alabama lost 2 and then Clark lanced through tackle to score.

Looney's punting was outstanding, but his 5-yard kick set up the third period field goal. The punt went out of bounds off the side of his foot on the Oklahoma 32. Alabama drove to the 2 and, on fourth down, Davis kicked his field goal from the 9. Oklahoma marched from its 35 to the Alabama 16 in the last quarter, but the Tide line threw the Sooners back to the 20.

Oklahoma's tall Paul Lea broke loose on a 36-yard scamper in the waning moments to the Alabama 18, from where

Continued on Page 10, Col. 2

Cincinnati U. Five Tops 2 Polls Again

Special to The New York Times.

NEW YORK.

For the second straight week, Cincinnati was the unanimous choice of 35 coaches as the nation's best college basketball team in the United Press International poll yesterday. Cincinnati also topped The Associated Press poll again.

Cincinnati has won nine straight games. In both polls, Loyola of Chicago was rated second. Illinois rose to third place.

Arizona State, the University of California at Los Angeles, Ohio State, Kentucky, Wichita, Duke, and Oregon State, in the order named, complete the coaches' top ten. The writers spelled out the first ten with Arizona State, Ohio State, Kentucky, Duke, Wichita, U.C.L.A. and Auburn.

Dusky Damion Wins Santa Anita Race

By United Press International

ARCADIA, Calif., Jan. 1—Dusky Damion, a 6-year-old Washington State-bred gelding, scored a length-and-a-quarter victory today in the $27,500 San Gabriel Handicap at Santa Anita Park. The Axe II, the even-money favorite under Willie Shoemaker, finished fifth in the Seven-Horse field.

Dusky Damion, ridden by Ismael Valenzuela, paid $14.60, $6.20 and $4 for $2 across the board. Rablero was second, paying $8.20 and $4.80. Pardao was third at $3.20.

Dusky Damion's victory was worth $16,300 to the Swiftsure Stable. He ran the mile and an eighth on the turf in 1:48-3/5.

ALERT U.S.C. NIPS WISCONSIN, 42-37

Continued from Page 9, Col. 8

yards gained, surpassing the previous high of 279 yards set by Bob Chappuis of Michigan in 1948. The young man's coolness with a garland of Trojans around his neck was colossal.

Big Ben Wilson, fullback, led ground gainers with 57 yards in 17 carries. But Brown carried for 19 and caught three passes for 108 yards, the longest a 45-yard gainer from Bill Nelson, Beathard's alternate. Bedsole snagged four passes for 101 yards.

The marches were legion, and though the action occasionally was bogged down by 170 yards in penalties, the game never lacked for offensive thrills.

Doubtless the 5,500 Badger rooters who came from Wisconsin for the game will discuss a second-quarter called-back touchdown the rest of the winter. Vanderkelen completed a 30-yard pass to Holland in the end zone, but a Badger was detected clipping and the score was nullified.

That left the halftime score 21-7 in favor of U.S.C. Anything closer could have meant ultimate victory for Wisconsin's persistent Badgers.

Southern California closed out its first all-winning season in 30 years with 11 victories in 11 games. Wisconsin wound up with an 8-2 record and still is looking for its first Rose Bowl triumph.

Wisconsin lost 7 to 0 to U.S.C. in 1953 and 44 to 8 to Washington in 1960 in two previous appearances.

Troy's most successful Rose record now reads 10 wins and three defeats.

SCORING SUMMARY:

Southern Cal: Touchdowns—Butcher (13-yard pass from Beathard), Wilson (1-yard plunge), Heller (25-yard run), Bedsole 2 [illegible] 23-yard pass from Beathard), F. Hill (13-yard pass from Beathard). Conversions—Lupo 6 (all placekicks).

Wisconsin: touchdowns — Kurek (1-yard plunge), Vanderkelen (17-yard run), Holland (13-yard run), Kroner (4-yard pass, Vanderkelen), Richter (19-yard pass, Vanderkelen). Conversions — Kroner 5 (all placekicks). Safety — Ernie Jones, tackled by Von Heimburg in end zone.

By Quarters:

Wisconsin	7	0	7	23—37
U. S. C.	[illegible]	[illegible]	[illegible]	7—42

STATISTICS OF THE GAME

	Wisc.	USC
First Downs	32	15
Net Yards, Rushing	67	114
Net Yards, Passing	419	253
Total Yards Gained	486	367
Passes Atempted	49	20
Passes Completed	34	10
Passes Intercepted by	0	3
Punts—Average	4-40.25	5-40.40
Fumbles Lost	0	
Yards Penalized	77	93

WISCONSIN

LE—Leafblad, Carlson, Ezerins; LT—Pillath, Bernet; LG—Gross, Paar, Monk; C—Bowman, Heckl, Bruhn; RG—Underwood, Schenk; RT—Woidula, Jacobazzi; RE—Richter, Howard; QB—Norvell, Vanderkelen, Frain, Reichardt; LH—Holland, Nettles, Silvestri; RH—Kroner, W. Smith, R. Smith; FB—Kurek, Purnell, Norvell

USC

LE—Bedsole, Hoover, E. Jones, Thurlow; LT—Kirner, Byrd, Butcher; LG—Fisk, Johnson, Svihus, Ratliff; C—Sagouspe, Schmidt, Sanchez; RG—Lubisich, Smedley, Gonta; RT—Marionovich, Eaton, R. Jones, Gonta; RE—Pye, Brownwood, F. Hill, Potter, Austin; [illegible] Brown, Clark, G. Hill; RH—Del Conte, Heller, Hunt; FB—Byrd, Bame, Wilson, McMahon, E. Jones, Pye

GAME AND PARADE ARE BIG BUSINESS

Millions of Dollars Involved in Pasadena Extravaganza

Special to The New York Times.

PASADENA, Calif., Jan. 1—The Rose Bowl game and parade constitute one of Pasadena's major industries: millions of roses, millions of dollars—perhaps not a dollar for every rose, but almost.

The Tournament of Roses Association, the sponsoring group, works year-round on the New Year's Day extravaganza. It has taken 74 years to build the project into its status as the nation's biggest and most publicized welcome to the New Year.

"And that's what makes the work and expense worthwhile," says Max Colwell, manager of the association. "Nobody can begin to figure the number of people who have come to Pasadena because of the parade and game."

This figure, too, runs into the millions. Colwell predicted nearly 1,250,000 would be in Pasadena today for the parade, with 100,000 staying for the game. The city's normal population: 125,000.

The Tournament of Roses Parade began in 1889. This year's parade is the 74th in the long string. The Rose Bowl games did not start until 1902. Since there have been several lapses over the years, today's game was the 49th in the Rose Bowl series.

The game is the money-maker. It defrays the cost of the parade and supplies most of the association's annual budget.

Today's gross gate was $1,000,000, plus or minus a few cents. Of this, $500,000 came from television and radio rights, with the bulk of this from the National Broadcasting Company for the video broadcast.

Another $500,000 was assured from ticket sales, programs and other concessions at the Bowl. Tickets are $6 apiece for the general public; $3 each for undergraduates of the two universities involved.

The Tournament Association built the stadium in 1922 on city property and after organization deeded it to the city.

A $400,000 press box was completed in 1961. The Badgers and Trojans today enjoyed new $30,000 dressing rooms.

The Tournament Association, which has no affiliation with the city or the chamber of commerce, is a self-supporting civic group. It exists on 15 per cent of the net gate receipts from the game.

ACCEPTANCE HINT BY A.A.U. IS GIVEN

Continued from Page 9, Col. 4

chances for a good showing in the 1964 Olympic Games at Tokyo.

Hull hinted that his telegram to the President would mean that the A. A. U. had agreed to arbitration within certain limits when he said, "We are willing to mediate or arbitrate to reconcile the difficulties that the N. C. A. A. attack has caused."

But the executive director added, "We cannot and will not under any circumstances knowingly violate the rules." Hull charged that the N. C. A. A. leaders "have doublecrossed their own athletic directors and coaches as well as their athletes in making a power grab to take over control of all amateur athletics in the United States."

"The N. C. A. A. power grab is in direct conflict with established rules and the N. C. A. A. leaders know it," Hull asserted.

ALABAMA DEFEATS OKLAHOMA, 17 TO 0

Continued from Page 9, Col. 7

four cracks at the line carried only to the 10.

Alabama	7	7	3	0—17
Oklahoma	0	0	0	0— 0

Ala.—Williamson, 25, [illegible] from Namath (Davis kick)

Ala.—Clark, 15, run (Davis kick)

Ala.—Davis, F. G., 19

Attendance—73,380

STATISTICS OF THE GAME

	Ala.	Okla.
First downs	10	6
Rushing yardage	166	196
Passing yardage	86	106
Passes	9-17	4-8
Passes intercepted by	1	0
Punts	8-40.5	10-34
Fumbles lost	1	2
Yards penalized	12	5

Sports of The Times

The Fabled Bronk

By ARTHUR DALEY

Special to The New York Times.

NEW YORK.

Out of the past have come the storied heroes of old in nostalgic parade. They have moved in review before the critical gaze of the selection committee for the pro football Hall of Fame at Canton, Ohio, and some of these gridiron glamor boys already are on their way to niches in the shrine. One hulking figure in the forefront as an obvious choice would have to be Bronko Nagurski of the Chicago Bears.

The Bronk was once described as "the most devastating one-man thundering herd ever seen in football." He was a fullback who blasted with such unbelievable power that the defense had to use an unorthodox method to halt him. The first man slowed him down; the second spilled him and the third pinned him to earth.

"See these knobs on my head?" Steve Owen of the Giants used to ask, offering his noggin for scrutiny. "I got most of them from trying to stop the Bronk. The others came from trying to tackle the old Indian, Jim Thorpe."

One of the oldest football gags concerns the ball carrier who shouted to his blockers, "Interference, follow me." The Bronk didn't need interference and his blockers were safer following him than getting in his way.

Tacklers Sprayed Aside

Rated by the oversize standards of the modern football player, the Bronk wasn't big. But he was a 230-pound fullback in an era when few linemen weighed that much. He ran so close to the ground that he supplied no target area for tacklers and he sprayed them aside like a superdreadnaught plowing through the seas. He had a pecular knack of raising a shoulder when hit. It was like the jolt of an uppercut.

There is the story of the time he ripped over center against the Redskins, knocking two linebackers in opposite directions. He stomped over the defensive halfback and unconcernedly felled the safety man like a laborer dropping a bag of cement. Then he caromed off the goalposts and crashed to a shuddering halt against the brick wall. Wobbly but undeterred, he staggered back on the field.

"That last guy hit me awfully hard," he said.

In another game an overflow crowd was kept under control by a squadron of mounted policemen. The Bears kept hammering into scoring territory. Then the Bronk got the ball. He went catapulting over the goal line with such momentum that he knocked over a horse.

A horse? That brings to mind another story. Doc Spears, the coach at the University of Minnesota, was driving past a farm when he saw a muscular boy plowing a field — without a horse. When Doc asked for directions, the boy pointed — with the plow. So Spears brought him to Minnesota. It was the Bronk, of course. Doc asked what position he played.

"Everything," said the Bronk. "When the other team has the ball, they put me where I can make the most tackles. When we have the ball, I carry it."

The Doc followed the same system. In Nagurski's senior year he was chosen for every All-American team named. But some selectors picked him as tackle and others as fullback. Both were correct. The Bronk was at tackle on defense and fullback on offense.

Paul Bunyan From the North

Nagurski was heralded as a Paul Bunyan from the Northlands when he reported to the Chicago Bears. Old-timers were skeptical that anyone could be that strong, that tough, that indestructible. One such skeptic was Cal Hubbard, the 270-pound terror of the Green Bay Packers and the best lineman in the league. Just before the Monsters of the Midway went into punt formation early in the first meeting between the two team, Hubbard propositioned Red Grange, one of the Bear's protective blockers.

"I promise you I won't block the kick, Red," said the huge Hub. "But you'd do me a favor if you'd step aside and let me get a clean shot at Nagurski. I want to test him out."

Grange obediently let Hubbard through. Nagurski met Hubbard head on and Cal felt as though the grandstand had collapsed atop him. He landed on his ear, upside down.

"Please don't do me any more favors, Red," said Hubbard. "Now I know."

The Bronk was one of the fabled heroes of yesteryear. No Hall of Fame would be worthy of the name without him.

N.B.A. EYES STARS FROM RIVAL LOOP

But Kansas City Clubowner Considers Bid to Revive the American League

CHICAGO, Jan. 1 (AP) — With all clubs operating in the red, the American Basketball League has suspended operations and thrown some 100 players on the market as free agents.

"Not a single club was operating in the black," said Commissioner Abe Saperstein. He announced the decision to suspend yesterday after telephone conferences with club directors.

Several National Basketball Association Club's reportedly are in touch with A.B.L. players to whom they have N.B.A. rights through draft and trade procedure.

St. Louis Hawks are said to be interested in Bill Bridges of Kansas City, the A.B.L. top scorer, and his six-foot-nine teammate, Gene Tormohlen.

King Drafted by Zephyrs

Larry Staverman and Morris King of Kansas City and Roger Kaiser of Pittsburgh are said to be on the shopping list of the Chicago Zephyrs. the Zephyrs drafted Kaiser and King and traded Dave Piontek to Cincinnati for the rights to Staverman.

Syracuse is said to be anxious to get Ben Worley of Long Beach, drafted last summer. San Francisco is interested in Wille Spraggins of Philadelphia, a Warrior draftee last year.

The prize catch may be the former Ohio State All-American Jerry Lucas. The rights are held by the Cleveland Pipers, who withdrew from the A.B.L. and sought an NBA franchise without avail.

Lucas has not played a pro game so far. He was a draft choice of the N.B.A.'s Cincinnati Royals.

Some reports place losses of the A.B.L. at $1,000,000 last year and $250,000 this season.

Ken Krueger, owner of the Kansas City Steers, said he would try to reorganize the A. B. L. A Pittsburgh Rens spokesman said that team would seek an N.B.A. franchise.

Krueger Gives Plans

Of reorganization plans, Krueger said in St. Louis: "Oakland and Long Beach want to continue and a Pittsburgh representative has indicated that club might want to stay in the new set-up. I have suggested that Johnny Dee, the Kansas City coach, be appointed commissioner under any such new realignment. We might be able to move the Philadelphia franchise to another city."

The six-team loop, founded by Saperstein two years ago, had games scheduled through March 17.

Saperstein declared the second-year champion to be Kansas City with a 22-9 record. Long Beach finished 16-8, Pittsburgh 12-10, Oakland 11-4, Philadelphia 10-18, Chicago 8-20.

An A.B.L. innovation was the three-point field goal initiated for shots made 25 feet or more from the basket.

Two Teams Owned by Cohen

PHILADELPHIA, Jan 1 (AP) — Paul Cohen of New York, owner of the Philadelphia Tapers of the folded American Basketball League, disclosed today that he also owns the Pittsburgh Rens, another casualty of the collapse.

MISSISSIPPI TOPS ARKANSAS, 17-13

Continued from Page 9, Col. 3

the Arkansas 5. Then Tommy Moore, a halfback, intercepted a Griffing pass at the goal line.

Both teams missed on field-goal chances. McKnelly failed on a 43-yarder in the first quarter after a short Mississippi punt. Then Irwin tried one from 30 yards out with 1:46 left in the opening period, but it was wide.

The Mississippi tailback, Dave Jennings, was the leading rusher with 39 yards on nine carries, and his team mate, Jim Weatherly, Griffing's understudy at quarterback, was runner up with 36. Branch led the Razorbacks with 21 yards on seven tries.

Mississippi	0	10	7	0—17
Arkansas	0	3	10	0—13

Miss—f. g. Irwin, 30

Ark.—f. g. McKnelly, 30

Miss.—Guy, 33, pass from Griffing (Irwin kick)

Ark.—Ranch, 5, pass from Moore (McKnelly)

Miss.—Griffing, 1, run (Irwin kick)

Ark.—F. G. McKnelly, 22

Attendance: 82,500

STATISTICS OF THE GAME

	Miss.	Ark.
First Downs	22	7
Rushing Yardage	160	47
Passing Yardage	269	123
Passes	18-28	6-18
Passes Intercepted by	2	1
Punts	2-36	4-38.3
Fumbles Lost	1	0
Yards Penalized	40	13

LOUISIANA STATE TRIPS TEXAS, 13-0

Continued from Page 9, Col. 1

back who was expected to be a power, didn't carry the ball a single time. He was used as a decoy and for blocking.

Louisiana State	0	3	7	3—13
Texas	0	0	0	0—0

F. G., Amedee, 23

Field, 22, run (Amedee kick)

F. G., Amadee, 37

Attendance 75,504

STATISTICS OF THE GAME

	LSU	Texas
First Downs	17	9
Rushing Yardage	1[illegible]6	80
Passing Yardage	132	92
Passes	[illegible]-21	6-22
Passes Intercepted by	3	0
Punts	8-4[illegible].8	8-46.8
Fumbles Lost	0	2
Yards Penalized	1[illegible]	44

"All the News That's Fit to Print"

The New York Times.

LATE CITY EDITION
U.S. Weather Bureau Report (Page 70) Forecast: Variable cloudiness today; cloudy tonight. Fair and colder tomorrow.
Temp. Range: 42-30; yesterday: 34-19.

VOL. CXIII..No. 38,749. © 1964 by The New York Times Company. Times Square, New York, N.Y. 10036 — NEW YORK, WEDNESDAY, FEBRUARY 26, 1964. — TEN CENTS

58 ON JET KILLED IN CRASH IN LAKE AT NEW ORLEANS

Airliner on Way Here Falls Suddenly After Take-Off —No One Survives

U.N. AIDE AMONG DEAD

Widespread Debris Points to a Blast Either in Air or on Impact With Water

By The Associated Press

NEW ORLEANS, Feb. 25—An Eastern Air Lines jet carrying 58 persons on a flight to New York crashed in Lake Pontchartrain today soon after taking off from New Orleans. All aboard were killed.

The DC-8, Flight 304, left New Orleans International Airport for Atlanta at 3:01 A.M., Eastern Standard Time, and disappeared from radar at 3:10.

Visibility was good, although there was a light rain. The winds were calm.

The Coast Guard and other searchers sighted the wreckage around dawn in huge Lake Pontchartrain, about 20 miles northeast of New Orleans.

Explosion Indicated

Eastern said 51 passengers and a crew of seven were aboard. The flight had originated in Mexico City. At least 32 of the passengers were making the through trip. Fourteen got on in New Orleans. Fourteen were pass-riding Eastern employes.

The four-engined plane, capable of carrying 126 passengers, was due in Atlanta at 3:59 A.M., at Dulles Airport in Washington at 5:53 A.M. and at Kennedy Airport in New York at 7:10 A.M.

Twelve hours after the crash no bodies had been recovered. Debris floated over an area of several square miles of the lake. The main wreckage of the aircraft had not been located. The area of the pearshaped lake is about nine times that of the District of Columbia.

Delegate Is Victim

The victims included Mrs. Marie-Helene Lefaucheux, a member of the French delegation to the United Nations, who was active in women's and human rights activities of the world body.

The pilot, Capt. William B. Zeng, 47 years old, lived with his wife and seven children on a farm at Ringoes, N. J. Captain Zeng, with Eastern 21 years, had flown over five million miles. The co-pilot, Grant R. Newby, 40, of Manhattan, had almost two million miles on his flight log.

The Coast Guard recovered parts of the wreckage, clothing, luggage and what was described as bits of bodies from a wide-spread area centered six miles south of the north shore of the lake and about four miles east of the 27-mile-long Lake Pontchartrain causeway.

A Coast Guard pilot said there were indications that the plane had exploded either in the air or on impact. Eastern said that the crew had made the routine checks after take-off and that no alarm had been given.

An experienced Eastern pilot said the jet had probably reached a height of 16,000 feet shortly after it had got over the lake.

Lake Pontchartrain, 30 miles in diameter, has an average depth of 15 feet. Marshy land

Continued on Page 21, Column 1

Clay Wins Title in Seventh-Round Upset As Liston Is Halted by Shoulder Injury

Associated Press Wirephoto

Cassius Clay lands left to the head of Sonny Liston during first round of the title bout

Clay Is Exultant

By ROBERT LIPSYTE

Special to The New York Times

MIAMI BEACH, Feb. 25—Incredibly, the loud-mouthed bragging, insulting youngster had been telling the truth all along. Cassius Clay won the world heavyweight title tonight when a bleeding Sonny Liston, his left shoulder injured, was unable to answer the bell for the seventh round.

Immediately after he had been announced as the new heavyweight champion of the world, Clay yelled to the newsmen covering the fight: "Eat your words." Only three of 46 sports writers covering the fight had picked him to win.

A crowd of 8,297, on its feet through the early rounds at Convention Hall, sat stunned during the one-minute rest period between the sixth and seventh rounds. Only Clay seemed to know what had happened; he threw up his hands and danced a little jig in the center of the ring.

The victory was scored as a technical knockout in the seventh round, one round less than

Continued on Page 26, Column 1

Doctors' Findings

By The Associated Press

MIAMI BEACH, Wednesday, Feb. 26—A team of eight physicians said in a statement issued early this morning that the defeated heavyweight champion, Sonny Liston, had suffered an arm injury that would have prevented him from defending himself in his title fight with Cassius Clay.

Liston's purse had been held up pending the medical findings. The physicians' statement said a recommendation would be

Continued on Page 26, Column 8

TAX BILL IS VOTED IN HOUSE, 326-83; SENATE WILL ACT

Measure to Cut $11.5 Billion Due for Passage Today—G.O.P. Backs Legislation

By JOHN D. MORRIS

Special to The New York Times

WASHINGTON, Feb. 25—The House of Representatives approved the Administration's tax-reduction bill today, 326 to 83.

The Senate is expected to complete Congressional action on the measure tomorrow. Leaders obtained unanimous consent for a final Senate vote at 12:30 P.M.

The bill provides $11.5 billion in annual tax relief for individuals and corporations. It calls for top-to-bottom cuts in income-tax rates and various structural revisions or reforms in the Revenue Code.

Individuals, on the average, will get a tax cut of 19 per cent when the measure becomes fully effective in 1965.

Withholding to Drop

About two-thirds of the overall reduction applies to income received this year. The full reduction applies to income received in subsequent years. The new rates do not affect income for 1963, on which final tax returns are due April 15.

Today's action came on a compromise text devised by a conference committee appointed to adjust differences between versions passed by the House on Sept. 25 and the Senate on Feb. 7.

Senate approval of the conference agreement tomorrow, a virtual certainty, promises an increase early in March of $800 million a month in the take-home pay of the country's workers. This results from a cut in the 18 per cent income-tax withholding rate to 14 per cent, effective a week after President Johnson signs the bill.

A Boom Is Expected

The Administration is relying on the lower withholding rates to give the national economy the first big thrust toward goals it seeks to achieve through the tax bill. These include rises in consumer demand and business investment to stimulate increased employment and production, promote economic growth and avert future recessions.

The final bill cleared the House by a much larger margin than the earlier version, which had been passed by a vote of 271 to 155. Republican shifts accounted for most of the difference.

The changes had little relation to revisions made in the measure since its passage last September. Rather, they reflected what Republican spokesmen said was an improved outlook for curtailment of Federal spending.

On today's ballot, the bill was supported by 218 Democrats and 108 Republicans, while 63 Republicans and 20 Democrats opposed it.

On passage of the bill last September, 223 Democrats and 48 Republicans voted "aye." The measure was opposed then by 126 Republicans and 29 Democrats.

Representative John W.

Continued on Page 15, Column 5

Rusk Tells Why Policies Toward Red Lands Differ

He Says U.S. Aim Is to Encourage Some to Evolve Toward Independence—Critics Found to Sow Discord

By MAX FRANKEL

Special to The New York Times

WASHINGTON, Feb. 25—Secretary of State Dean Rusk said today that the United States treated different Communist countries differently to encourage the evolution of some of them toward national independence and internal freedom.

Some Communist regimes, Mr. Rusk asserted, have become

Excerpts from speech by Rusk are printed on Page 10.

more responsive to their peoples' aspirations, and even the Soviet Union has begun to recognize some of the risks of promoting Communism by force.

For that reason, the Secretary said, Washington distinguishes in its policies between the Soviet Union and Communist China, or between Poland and Cuba. For that reason also, he said, it is consistent to sell wheat to the Soviet Union while enforcing an embargo against Cuba.

Acknowledging that he was perturbed by suggestions here and abroad that the United States' foreign policies had become confused and inconsistent, Mr. Rusk devoted a major address to the Administration's view of the Communist world. He spoke at the annual conference on full citizenship and world affairs sponsored by the International Union of Electrical, Radio and Machine Workers (A.F.L.-C.I.O.).

The Secretary tried to cope with the criticism of foreign governments that the United States was applying a double

Continued on Page 10, Column 1

Dock Union Drops Boycott Of Wheat Bound for Soviet

By WILLIAM M. BLAIR

Special to The New York Times

WASHINGTON, Feb. 25—The White House announced today the end of the maritime union boycott of wheat shipments to the Soviet Union. President Johnson has issued orders that the Government must stick by its requirement that 50 per cent of the wheat sold under future export licenses be carried in United States-flag ships.

Settlement of the nine-day boycott appeared to be a victory for the International Longshoremen's Association, whose members refused to load wheat for Russia and other Soviet bloc countries.

It was understood that Thomas W. Gleason, president of the union, would direct union vice presidents in Atlantic and Gulf of Mexico ports to order a resumption of loading tomorrow. Eight ships are tied up in these ports and it is estimated that 25 to 30 ships are waiting offshore for the end of the boycott.

Soviet Wheat Covered

The President's orders cover the shipments to the Soviet Union only, which make up the bulk of the sales to Communist countries. The union's demand that the 50 per cent requirement also extend to other Soviet bloc countries and to other agricultural products, will be discussed at future meetings between Government and union representatives.

Meanwhile, a waiver of the 50 per cent requirement granted to the Continental Grain Company of New York will be permitted to stand because the company's sale of a million tons to Russia has been consummated and the export license has been granted.

Cargill, Inc., of Minneapolis also, and has been granted a license for 700 million tons of wheat to the Soviet Union but has not asked for a waiver of the shipping requirement. However, it is expected that a waiver may be granted if Car-

Continued on Page 14, Column 1

SOVIET WARNS U.S. NOT TO CARRY WAR TO NORTH VIETNAM

Vows 'Necessary Support' to Communists in South—Bids Americans Pull Out

CAPITAL'S HINTS SCORED

Chou, at News Conference in Pakistan, Also Demands Withdrawal of Forces

By HENRY TANNER

Special to The New York Times

MOSCOW, Feb. 25—The Soviet Union warned the United States today against extending the guerrilla war in South Vietnam to North Vietnam.

It said the Soviet people would render "the necessary assistance and support" to the "national liberation struggle" in South Vietnam. It called for a withdrawal of American troops and military equipment and for an end to American "interference" in the country's internal affairs.

[Premier Chou En-lai of Communist China, nearing the end of a week's visit to Pakistan, called for the removal of "United States forces of aggression and United States military personnel who are carrying out intervention in South Vietnam."]

The Soviet warning was in the form of an "authorized statement" made public tonight by Tass, the official press agency. This form of declaration is regarded here as only slightly less emphatic than a declaration by the Government itself.

Answer to Hints Seen

Western observers believed the statement was the Soviet Government's answer to recent hints by Administration officials at greater United States involvement in South Vietnam and at the possibility of South Vietnamese raids into North Vietnamese territory.

One such hint was given in a passage of a speech made by President Johnson last Friday. The President issued a warning to those who gave supplies and "external direction" to Communist guerrillas in South Vietnam and told them they were playing a "deeply dangerous game."

The Soviet statement declared that the "Government and the people of the Soviet Union" were giving their full support to the "just demands" of the Vietnamese people for an end of the American "intervention."

The statement charged that the "bloody war" waged by the United States was being stepped up and continued the

Continued on Page 3, Column 3

HILSMAN RESIGNS KEY POLICY POST

U.S. Adviser on Far East Plans Academic Career

Special to The New York Times

WASHINGTON, Feb. 25—The White House announced tonight the resignation of Roger Hilsman Jr. as Assistant Secretary of State for Far Eastern Affairs.

The announcement, which did not indicate when Mr. Hilsman would actually leave the State Department or who would replace him, said he had resigned to return to academic life.

The 44-year-old official, who holds a doctorate in political science, has been a key policy-making official in the Kennedy and the Johnson Administrations, first as head of the State Department's intelligence bureau and then as chief of Far Eastern policy.

He has played a crucial and controversial role in the formulation of United States policies in South Vietnam, particularly during last year's crisis when President Ngo Dinh Diem was assassinated and more recently in a re-evaluation of Washington's role in the war against the Communist guerrillas.

There has been major friction on Vietnam policy among various departments in the Administration. Many disagreements are still known to exist, notably over the possibility that the United States might assist

Continued on Page 3, Column 1

CYPRUS EXPANDS SECURITY FORCES

Makarios Allows 5,000-Man Rise—Impasse Reported at U.N. on Peace Unit

Excerpts from U.N. debate on Cyprus question, Page 4.

By W. GRANGER BLAIR

Special to The New York Times

NICOSIA, Cyprus, Feb. 25—Archbishop Makarios, President of Cyprus, announced tonight a sharp increase in the number of "legal" police forces needed to cope with "the abnormal situation" on the island.

The President said approval had been given for a temporary increase of up to 5,000 men in the special police.

[At the United Nations the Secretary General, U Thant, told the Security Council that an impasse had developed on the question of setting up a peace-keeping force for Cyprus. It was reported that the six elected member nations of the Council would step up efforts to reach agreement on the issue.]

Total Would Be 7,000

Before the crisis erupted Dec. 22, Greek Cypriote security forces — the police and gendarmerie — numbered 1,500 to 2,000 men, as permitted in the Constitution.

With an addition of 5,000 special policemen, the security forces would total 7,000 men at most, or roughly the equivalent of the British truce force now maintaining the shaky cease-fire on Cyprus.

The Archbishop also declared that "the instruments of the state responsible for maintenance of law and order have received instructions to disarm

Continued on Page 4, Column 1

Soviet Aide Urges Gain for Consumer

By THEODORE SHABAD

Special to The New York Times

MOSCOW, Feb. 25—An eminent Soviet economist called on planners today to set a more rapid rate of growth for consumer goods than for heavy industry. He pointed to the development of the United States economy as an example.

Writing in Pravda, the principal Communist party newspaper, Anushavan A. Arzumanyan denounced "Stalin's erroneous dogmas" that economic progress could be achieved at the expense of the consumer.

The major two-part article seemed to set the stage for a fundamental shift in economic

Continued on Page 10, Column 2

Bar Head Will Represent Oswald in Warren Inquiry

Special to The New York Times

WASHINGTON, Feb. 25—The Warren commission appointed an "independent lawyer" today to protect the interests of Lee H. Oswald, President Kennedy's accused assassin. Walter E. Craig of Phoenix, Ariz., the president of the American Bar Association, was selected for the job. He will not work for the commission but will be given access to all its materials.

The commission, headed by Chief Justice Earl Warren, explained the appointment at some length in a statement. The reason indicated was that Oswald had been killed and would never be able to defend himself at a trial.

But the statement said the commission was not, by this action, casting doubt on Oswald's guilt. It said that two months of investigation had "not caused the commission to doubt the reasonableness of the action of the authorities in charging Oswald."

Will Press for Facts

Mr. Craig, the commission said, will have the job of "examining every facet of the case pointing toward the involvement of Lee H. Oswald, in his absence, and in fairness to his family advise the commission in that regard."

The statement, perhaps reflecting some recent criticism of the commission's performance, said the panel would leave "no stone unturned in faithfully reporting all the facts surrounding the assassination."

The decision to appoint a special lawyer for Oswald's interests represents a change of view on the commission's part. The panel had rejected previous

Continued on Page 17, Column 3

GALAMISON MAPS INTEGRATION PLAN

Reaction of School Board to the New Proposal Will Determine Boycott Move

By LEONARD BUDER

The committee that ran the school boycott on Feb. 3 said yesterday it would submit its own integration proposals to the Board of Education soon.

The proposals would represent the views of groups affiliated with the Citywide Committee for Integrated Schools, including the New York Urban League and the Congress of Racial Equality.

If the school board fails to respond to the proposals in a way that the committee considers satisfactory, sources indicated, the committee will go ahead with plans for another boycott.

This strategy was outlined after the Rev. Milton A. Galamison, chairman of the committee, postponed the scheduled announcement of a date for a second boycott. On Monday, Mr. Galamison said he would announce the next day the date of the second boycott and probably the date of a third boycott.

The postponement was brought about by members of the committee who contended that the announcement at this time would diminish chances of working out a solution of the integration controversy with school authorities. The Urban League is known to feel that the committee's proposals may furnish the basis for fruitful negotiations with the school board.

However, opposition to the

Continued on Page 24, Column 5

BAKER IS SILENT IN SENATE INQUIRY

Cites Constitutional Ground —TV Cameras Barred on Demand of His Lawyer

By CABELL PHILLIPS

Special to The New York Times

WASHINGTON, Feb. 25—Robert G. Baker refused to tell the Senate Rules Committee about his private business affairs today, but he could not keep the members from putting into the record allusions to just about everything they know or suspect about his activities.

In a dramatic two-and-one-half-hour public appearance before the investigative panel, the former secretary of the Senate Democratic majority invoked constitutional immunity 121 times to avoid answering questions. But the questions themselves probed widely, not only into the established facts of Mr. Baker's career but also into the circumstantial areas of supposition and rumor as well.

The session, held before a standing-room-only crowd, and briefly before live television cameras, was marked by spirited legal skirmishes between committee members and Edward Bennett Williams, Mr. Baker's attorney.

Mr. Williams sought not only

Continued on Page 18, Column 3

A Rights Bill Move Scheduled in Senate

Special to The New York Times

WASHINGTON, Feb. 25—The opening skirmish in the Senate civil rights fight begins tomorrow.

Under a plan presented today by the Democratic leadership, the bill would be brought up for a second reading after a vote on the tax-reduction bill. The tax vote is set for 12:30 P.M.

The automatic second reading of the rights measure will bring a procedural debate. Southern Democrats will challenge the leadership plan to keep the bill out of the Judiciary Committee, where it could be held up.

The plan calls for the bill to

Continued on Page 15, Column 4

4 Clerics Mediate Racial Job Dispute

By JOSEPH LELYVELD

The city's religious leaders and institutions were urged yesterday to place themselves economically, as well as morally, behind the Negro's drive for equal employment opportunities.

The proposal, endorsed by the Metropolitan Conference on Religion and Race at the Americana hotel, called on churches and synagogues to review their own hiring, banking, insurance, investment and construction programs to make sure they did not support concerns that discriminated.

The conference was soon given an opportunity to practice what

Continued on Page 24, Column 7

Associated Press Wirephoto

APPEARS AT SENATE HEARING: Robert G. Baker, right, former Senate majority secretary, with his lawyer, Edward Bennett Williams, left. Mr. Baker refused to testify.

NEWS INDEX

Clay Wins Heavyweight Title as Injured Liston Fails to Come Out for 7th

SHOULDER INJURY LEADS TO THE END

Liston Tells Adviser He Is Unable to Continue After He Finishes 6th Round

Continued From Page 1, Col. 4

Clay had predicted. Liston seemingly had injured the shoulder in the first round while swinging and missing with jabs and hooks at the elusive 22-year-old.

The fight was Clay's from the start. The tall, swift youngster, his hands carelessly low, backed away from Liston's jabs, circled around Liston's dangerous left hook and opened a nasty gash under Liston's left eye.

He never let Liston tie him up for short, brutal body punches, and although he faltered several times, he refused to allow himself to be cornered. His long left jab kept bouncing off Liston's face. From the beginning, it was hard to believe.

The men had moved briskly into combat. Liston stalking, moving flat-footedly forward. He fell short with two jabs, brushed Clay back with a grazing right to the stomach and landed a solid right to the stomach. The crowd leaned forward for the imminent destruction of the young poet.

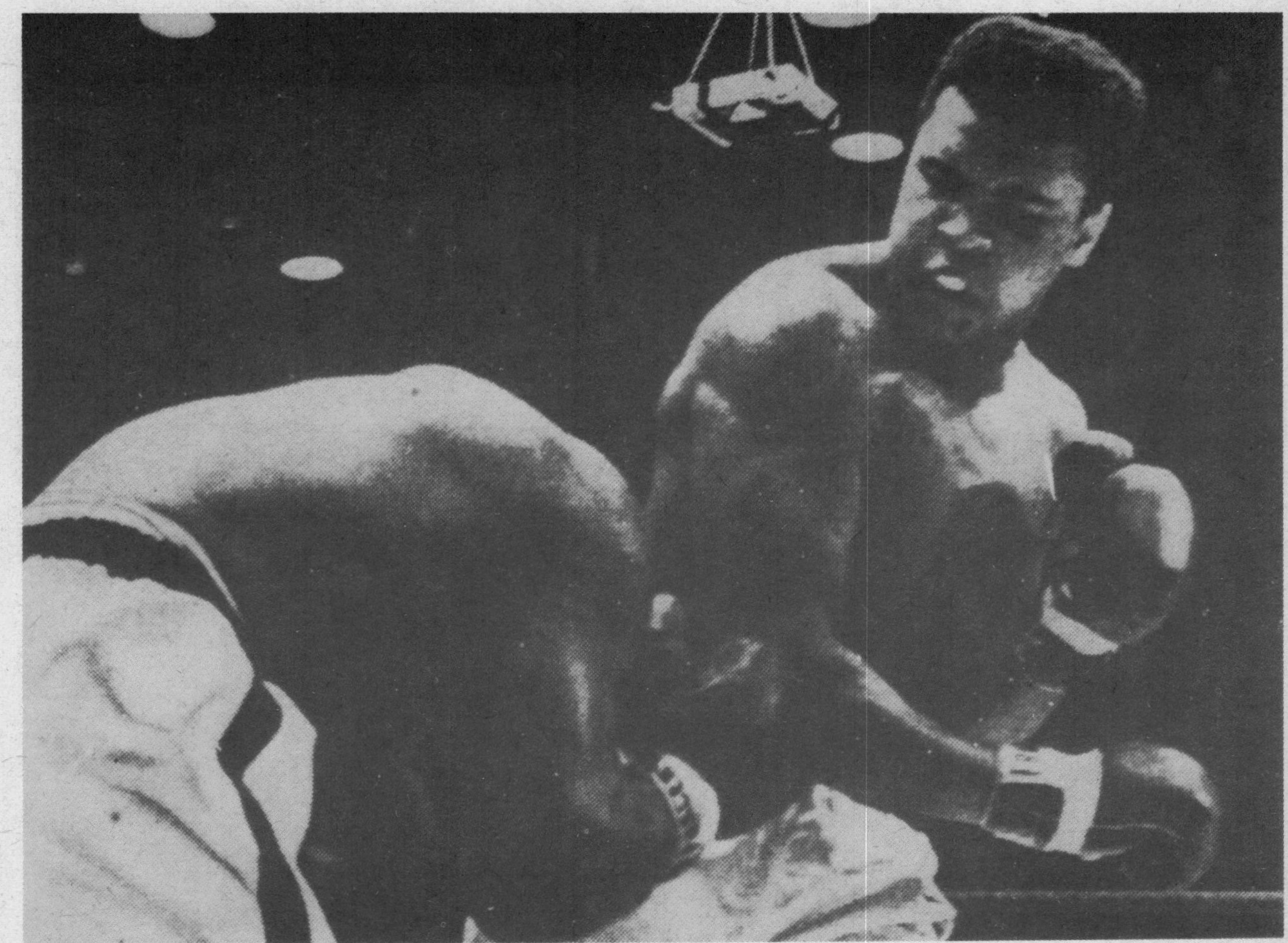

Associated Press Wirephoto

POWER: Cassius Clay lashes at Sonny Liston during the opening moments of their championship bout held in Miami

Hands Still Low

But the kid hadn't lied. All those interminable refrains of "float like a butterfly, sting like a bee," had been more than foolish songs. The kid was floating. He leaned back from Liston's jabs and hooks, backed into the ropes, then spun out and away. He moved clockwise around Liston, taunting that terrible left hook, his hands still low.

Then he stung, late in the first round, sticking his left in Liston's face and following with a quick barrage to Liston's head. They continued for long seconds after the bell, unable to hear the inadequate ring above the roar of the crowd.

It must have been somewhere in that round that Liston's shoulder was hurt.

[Jack Nilon, Liston's manager, said at the hospital that the former champion had hurt the shoulder during training. The Associated Press reported. He said Liston did not spar Feb. 3, 4, 5 and 14 because of the injury. Asked why he hadn't postponed the fight, Nilon said, "We thought we could get away with it."]

He strained forward with over-eager hooks that struck only air. For a moment, in the second round, Liston pummeled Clay against the ropes, but again, Cassius spun out and away.

Then the young man began to rumble as he had promised. His quick left jabs penetrated Liston's defenses, and he followed with right hands. He leaned forward as he fired rights and lefts at Liston's expressionless face. Liston began to bleed from a crescent-shaped cut high on the left cheekbone.

Liston Plunges Ahead

Like a bull hurt and maddened by the picadors' lances, Liston charged forward. The heavy muscles worked under his smooth, broad back as he virtually hurled his 218 pounds at the dodging, bobbing, dancing Clay.

His heavy arms swiped forward and he threw illegal backhand punches in his bear-like lunges. Once, Clay leaned the wrong way and Liston tagged him with a long left.

Cassius was staggered, but Liston was hurt and tired. He could not move in to press his advantage.

And now, a strange murmur began to ripple through the half-empty arena and people on blue metal chairs began to look at one another. Something like human electricity danced and flowed as the spectators suddenly realized that even if Cassius lost, he was no fraud. His style was unorthodox, but . . .

There was little action in the fourth, as Cassius continued to circle. Once he opened his eyes wide as a Liston jab fell short, and it seemed as if he were mocking the heavy-footed hunter. As it turned out, Cassius could barely see.

He began complaining to Angelo Dundee, his trainer, at the end of the round. Something had gotten into his eyes, from Liston's glove, from the sponge, somewhere. But he went out for the fifth anyway, and all Dundee could do was shout, "Stay way from him, stay away."

Clay tried to stay away. Sensing something, Liston bulled forward, slamming Cassius with a left hook in the nose and lefts and rights to the body. Blinking furiously, Clay kept circling away. He never hit back.

Both fighters were sluggish in the fifth round, breathing heavily. Liston's face was still impassive, but the grooves along his forehead seemed deeper, and the snorting breaths through his nose harsher.

He seemed even more tired in the sixth as Clay's eyes cleared and the younger man bore in, then leaped away, jabbing and hooking and landing a solid right to Liston's jaw. Clay's jabs were slipping through at will now, bouncing off that rock-like face, opening the cut under the left eye.

Liston walked heavily back to his corner at the end of the sixth. He did not sit down immediately. Then as Liston did sit down, Clay came dancing out to the center of the ring, waving his arms, all alone. It seemed like a long time before Drew (Bundini) Brown, his assistant trainer, was hugging him and Dundee was dancing up and down, and Jack Nilon, Liston's adviser, was wrapping yards of tape around the former champion's left shoulder.

"I just can't go back," a Liston aide reported Sonny to have said.

And then the crowd was cheering and booing, which is something like laughing and crying because it was the wildest thing they had ever seen. It didn't make sense. For weeks, Clay had played the fool and been tagged at will by unworthy sparring partners. This morning, at the weigh-in, he had acted bizarre and disturbed.

And tonight, he had been cool and fast and without fear.

Until the knockout, the officials had had the fight a draw. Referee Barney Felix had scored the six rounds 57—57 on the 10-point-must system. Judge Bill Lovitt scored it 58—56 for Liston, and Judge Gus Jacobsen 58—56 for Clay.

But points didn't really matter after all. Poetry and youth and joy had triumphed over the 8-1 odds. And until it had happened (and perhaps until they can look it up) people laughed at the thought that a night like this could happen...

The crowd had cheered lustily at 9:59 P.M., when Cassius came jogging down the aisle toward the ring, his face impassive, wearing a hip-length terry-cloth white robe on which was emblazoned The Lip. Nobody even snickered, for everyone knew Clay to be a braggart, not to be taken seriously.

He leaped through the ropes in a sudden motion, then waited in the ring for six minutes before Liston started down the aisle, shadow-boxing in a corner of the ring. He did not talk or shout. Liston, in a long, white robe, glared out from a white hood and climbed heavily through the ropes.

"Wipe my face off, hey, wipe my face off," said Clay to Dundee. The trainer was staring at the implacable Liston, and didn't hear Clay until he had repeated himself.

Both men stood in their corners, serenely as the inevitable parade of notables—Rocky Marciano, Sugar Ray Robinson, et al—shook their gloved hands. Sonny, in white trunks with a black stripe and his name across a thigh, seemed malevolent and invincible. Clay, in white trunks with red piping, seemed only big.

Earlier, rumors had swept Convention Hall that Cassius was not going to show, that the thin line of hysteria he had trod during the morning weigh-in had become full-scale fear.

But even as the rumor mounted (that he was in a plane, en route to Mexico), Cassius was standing quietly in a far corner of the arena. He was waiting for his brother, Rudolph Valentino Clay, to make his professional debut.

Few people noticed him. He was dressed in a tight-fitting black tropical suit and wore a black bow tie on his ruffled, white dress shirt.

Clay was surrounded by aides —Brown; Archie Robinson, his personal secretary, and Dundee. Dundee was carrying a blue suitcase and Bundini kept a hand on Clay's back, as if he might have to restrain him at any moment.

But Clay hardly moved. Despite his height (6 feet 3 inches) he often had to stand on tiptoe to watch the action in the far-off ring. Once, when Rudy floored his opponent, Chip Johnson of Naples, Fla., in the second round, Clay shouted some encouragement. Otherwise he was silent.

Even during the one-minute rest periods between rounds, Cassius stared at the ring. His face seemed tense and alert, but his body was unmoving. At the end of the four-round bout, when it was announced that Rudy had won, Cassius turned abruptly, without saying a word, and followed a phalanx of Miami policemen with flashy gunbutts out of the arena and into his dressing room.

Once there, at about 9:15 P.M., he was re-examined by Dr. Robbins.

At the weigh-in, Dr. Robbins had said that Clay's pulse rate was around 120, more than double his norm of 54. Forty-five minutes before the fight, Clay's pulse was 64, the same as Liston's. Sonny had arrived at the hall a few minutes after 8 P.M. and gone to his dressing room to rest.

DOCTORS CONFIRM INJURY TO LISTON

Continued From Page 1, Col. 4

made that the purse be released.

Dr. Alexander Robbins, chief physician of the Miami Beach Boxing Commission, read the statement at St. Francis Hospital after Liston had been with the doctors in an X-ray room for 3½ hours.

The statement read:

"We came to the conclusion that Sonny Liston suffered an injury to the long head to the biceps tendon of the left shoulder, with the result there is separation and tear of muscle fibers with some hemorrhage into the muscle belly. This condition would be sufficient to incapacitate him and prevent him from defending himself."

Dr. Robbins said no further examination by commission doctors was necessary and that he would recommend to the commission that Liston's purse be released.

Jack Nilon, Liston's adviser, said Liston also underwent plastic surgery beneath his left eye, where he had been cut. Six stitches were required to close the cut.

The Miami City Council had announced after the fight that it would conduct an investigation of the ending.

Cassius Is Angry for Being Long-Odds Underdog

CHAMPION'S VISION BLURRED IN FIFTH

Dundee Unable to Pinpoint Nature of Clay's Trouble Despite a Close Check

BY LEONARD KOPPETT

Special to The New York Times.

MIAMI BEACH, Feb. 25 — Cassius Clay seemed more angry than one would expect, but no less elated as he faced the press and cameras of the world as heavyweight champion for the first time.

He entered the interview room some 20 minutes after his victory. He mounted the steps to a platform with a battery of cameras at the center. He stood there silently, head thrown back, a pout of defiance on his handsome, unmarked face.

Then came the torrent.

"Whatcha gonna say now?" he shouted. "It won't last one round? He'll be out in two? How many heart attacks were there? Oh, am I pretty."

There was no chance to ask questions as the words just poured out.

'It's So-o-o Good'

"I beat him bad, and that's so-o-o good," Clay went on. "The Bear couldn't touch me, couldn't even get a good lick of me, I'm so pretty. He had linament on his gloves. I couldn't see, and still he couldn't hit me. There's not a mark on me.

"You can't call it a fix because I didn't stop the fight—the doctor stopped it. Oh, I'm so pretty. Watcha gonna say now, huh?

"I watched Sugar Ray Robinson and Jake LaMotta for eight months—the same fight, over and over. That's what I've been doing. I'm too quick for him, too fast, too fast for any heavyweight alive.

"You newspapersmen made it tough on Liston. Don't ever make a 7-to-1 favorite. Just let me go in even money."

Publicity men, trainers, handlers and friends were crowded around Clay, pawing at him, trying to make him keep still long enough to hear a question from the clamoring press corps.

Finally a query could be heard. Did he want to fight Liston again?

"If he wants a rematch he can have it, but I don't think he'll want it," shouted Clay. "Nothin' but a fool would want to fight me. No one can beat me. I'm too fast. Liston's a powerful man and I just chopped him up. He can have a rematch in three months if he wants it. Sonny was not even a match for me, but he must apologize. The man was dirty and he couldn't even hurt me."

Who did Clay want to fight?

"I'll fight any fighter the public wants me to fight," he yelled, "but nobody can beat me. What about you newspaperment? Where's justice? Let's hear it: Who's the greatest?"

A few applauded and called out, "You are."

'Who's the Greatest?'

At 22 years old Cassius is the second youngest fighter to win the heavyweight title. He was the fifth challenger to go into the ring unbeaten and take the crown. The others were John L. Sullivan, James J. Jeffries, Rocky Marciano and Ingemar Johansson.

"Let's really hear it, who's the greatest?" Clay insisted. "All you writers, I'll give you one more chance, who's the greatest?" This time there was a louder cheer.

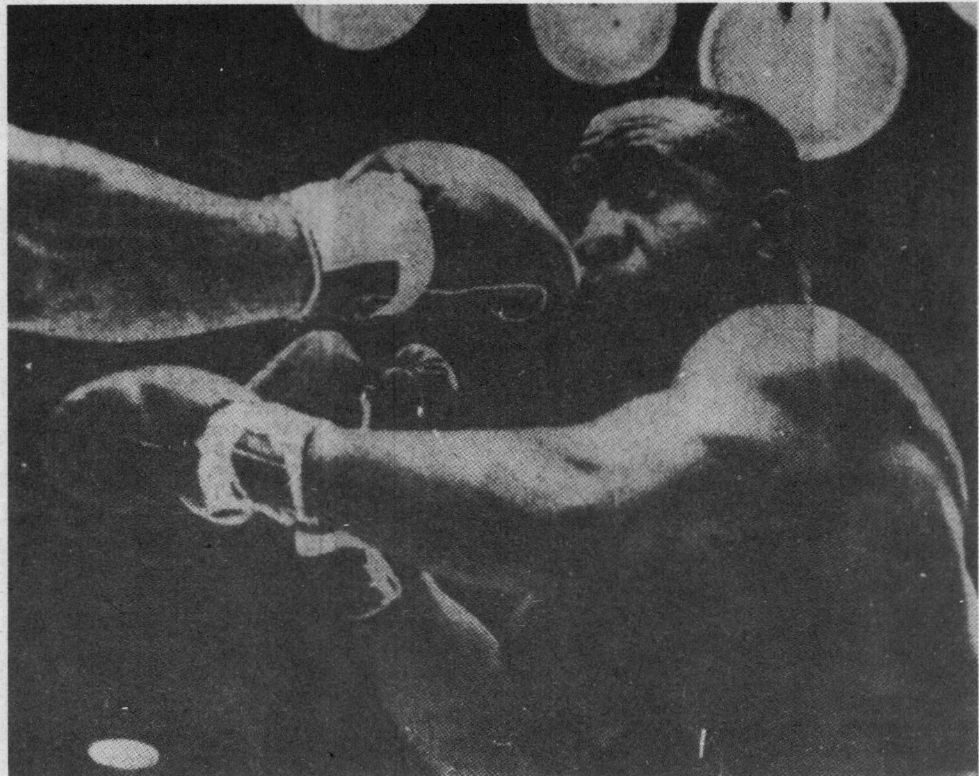

United Press International Telephoto

RIGHT TO THE HEAD: Cassius Clay looses a punch at Sonny Liston during the fourth

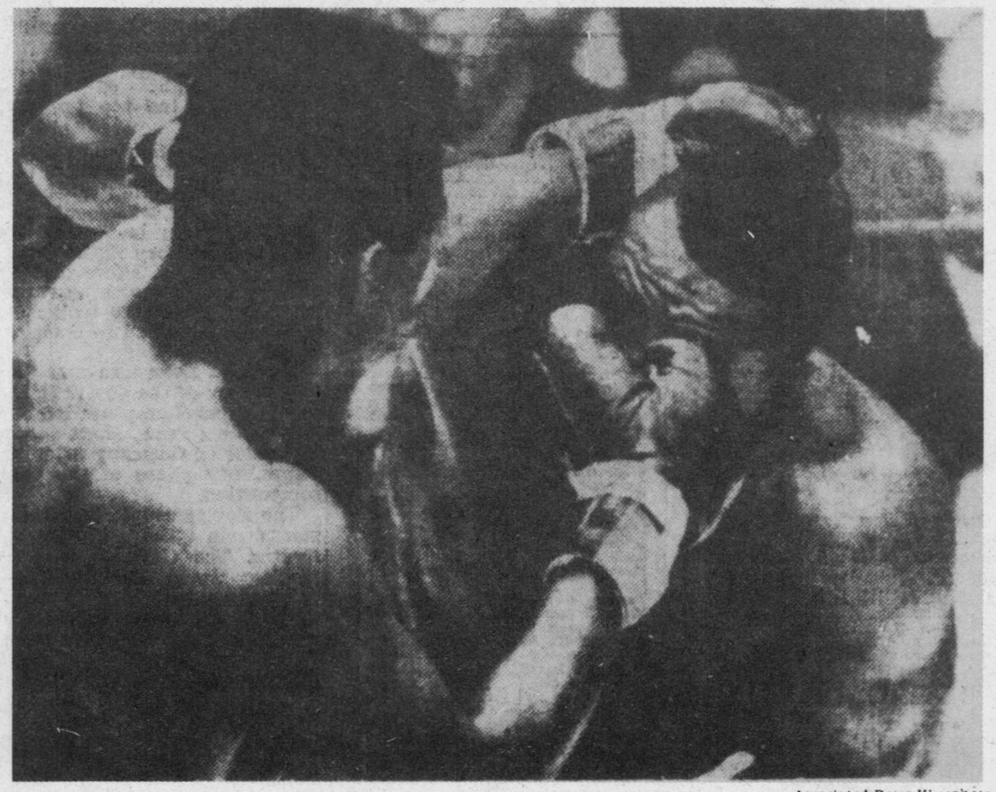

Associated Press Wirephoto

RAPID FIRE: Clay pounds away at Liston's left eye, cutting it and causing it to bleed

"Give some credit to Sugar Ray Robinson, all of you hypocrites," Cassius yelled. "You are hypocrites because none of you believed me."

Clay left and Angelo Dundee, his trainer, moved to the microphone to answer sensibly the unasked questions.

What had happened to Clay's eyes before and during the fifth round?

"Here's what it was," said Dundee. "It was something he picked up the round before. He came back and I wiped him with the sponge, then the towel. He started to blink, and I immediately checked the sponge and towel on my own face. There was nothing wrong with them."

Clay didn't respond visibly until a few seconds before the rest period ended. Then he jumped up, waving his arms, blinking painfully and having trouble with his mouthpiece.

'Maybe It'll Go 15'

"But it happened before that, he was complaining all through the rest period, even if you couldn't see it," Dundee repeated. "We thought it was something from Liston's glove—dirt, or something. We yelled at the referee to check Liston's gloves. I don't know if he did. I just watched Cassius then, and yelled at him to keep moving."

Late in the round, Clay's vision cleared.

"After that round, he was all right and I felt he'd end it in the next few rounds," Dundee said. "He kept saying to me, it's a long fight, it's 15 rounds, maybe it will go that long.

"Cassius was never hurt at any time. He just kept moving in his own inimitable way. It's like I told you last week, why should I try to change it? It's his own way and he can do it.

"I felt sure he had the style to stop Liston—the moves, the quick hands. It happened in the ring just the way I tried to tell you last Friday. I thought Clay was well ahead during the fight."

Was there any knowledge or suspicion of Liston's injured shoulder in the Clay corner?

"I don't know anything about that," said Dundee. "I don't think it showed in the ring. How did he throw all those punches? But I can't say about that."

When Clay first left the ring he went to his dressing room, where the press was not allowed in. He kept shouting, "I'm the greatest. I said I'd show the world and I did." His mother, father and Rudy, his younger brother, were in tears. It was this time a hysteria of pure joy.

To his mother he said:

"Mom, didn't I tell you I was the greatest. Here I am the champion of the world."

Cassius' Burden Lightened

Special to The New York Times

MIAMI BEACH, Feb. 25—At least one furrow will be removed from Cassius Clay's brow early in tonight's program. Rudy Clay, his 193-pound younger brother whose four-rounder with Chip Johnson had been scheduled just before the championship bout, will be in the No. 2 event (instead of No. 4) on the program. The switch was made this morning so that Cassius could have that worry off his mind sooner.

BOXING 'EXPERTS' GET EARS BOXED

Clay Picked to Win Title by Only 3 of 46 Writers

Special to The New York Times

MIAMI BEACH, Feb. 25—The boxing expert of Der Blick of Zurich was wrong. So were the men from the Aftonbladet and the Express of Stockholm.

But they were in good company tonight. Forty-three of 46 boxing writers at ringside were sure that Sonny Liston was going to win. Most of them said it would be by a knockout inside of six rounds.

The best laugh of the early evening was provided by the writer who announced, "It's even money Clay won't last the National Anthem."

Such pre-fight polls are a tradition at heavyweight championship bouts. United Press International, which conducted this one, said the vote was the most lopsided on record.

Only one of the writers picked Cassius Clay by a knockout. He was Bob Waters of Newsday, Garden City, L. I. Leonard Koppett of The New York Times also picked the new champion, but hedged on whether he would gain the crown by a knockout or decision. Bill Wise of True Magazine said Clay would score by a decision.

The fearless three were quietly respectful when their older and wiser colleagues called them "attention seekers" and "Johnny-Come-Latelys." Those who jeered did not stop to recall that Koppett had picked the Dodgers to win last year's World Series.

The wrong guessers were primarily influenced, of course, by Liston's pair of savage one-round knockouts of Floyd Patterson. And, although glad to have the ebullient Clay generate story after story, they preferred Liston's more traditional approach to the bout—long workouts, frequent scowls and few words.

Furthermore, many of the New York writers had seen Clay in action only once—his unconvincing 10-round decision over Doug Jones at Madison Square Garden last March.

As usual, Clay had the last word. In the ring, after his hand was raised in victory, he looked down at the hard-typing, mildly red-faced working press and shouted, "Eat your words."

Then, apparently believing that the man he dethroned had been too attentive to his press clippings, he aded, "All you reporters made it hard on Liston. Never write about me like that."

LOUISVILLE GLOVERS DANCE FOR CASSIUS

LOUISVILLE, Ky., Feb. 25 (AP)—They leaped to their feet, they shouted, they threw paper and hugged one another with glee.

They were Louisville fans reacting to Cassius Clay's victory over Sonny Liston in tonight's heavyweight championship fight.

About 10,000 persons crowded into Freedom Hall for the closed-circuit telecast from Miami.

The centerpiece for the huge gathering consisted of three boxing rings in place for the National Golden Gloves tournament being held here.

Sitting around the rings were the young Gloves contestants and when Clay, a 1960 Gloves winner, was assured of victory, they jumped up on the canvas and did wild dances of victory.

Hysterical Outbursts at Weigh-In Cost Clay $2,500

Tumultuous Prelude to Fight Leads to Punitive Action

Special to The New York Times

MIAMI BEACH, Feb. 25—Cassius Clay turned the weighing-in cermony—usually a perfunctory affair—into a tumultuous prelude to his heavyweight title challenge tonight against Sonny Liston. His ranting and jumping about brought punitive action from the Miami Beach Boxing Commission.

Clay was fined $2,500 for his noisy pre-fight weigh-in at the Cypress Room in Convention Hall. The examining physician, Dr. Alexander Robbins, said: "Clay is nervous and scared and he's burning up a lot of energy."

It came as a surprise when Clay's weight was announced as 210½ pounds. This was considered low, and Liston's 218 was about three pounds heavier than expected.

Clay's pulse rate was high, 120 beats a minute compared with his normal rate of 54.

While the 22-year-old contender was yelling at Liston, "You a chump, you a chump," Morris Klein, the chairman of the Miami Beach Boxing Commission, stepped to the microphone and shouted:

"Cassius Clay is fined $2,500." The fine, he said, was levied for Clay's conduct on the platform; the money, he added, would be withheld from Clay's purse. Clay was expected to gross about $600,000 and Liston about $1,360,000.

At precisely 10:30 A.M., the scheduled weigh-in time, Clay burst into the crowded room at the head of his retinue. The former Olympic champion from Louisville, Ky., was flanked by Sugar Ray Robinson and by Drew (Bundini) Brown, an assistant trainer and spiritual adviser.

Clay was wearing a blue denim work jacket with "Bear Huntin," written in red script across the back. He thumped the floor with a heavy wooden cane. Bundini wore a yellow plaid sport jacket and Robinson a maroon sport jacket.

Bundini and Robinson guided the challenger through the milling crowd, smiling as Clay kept shouting, in a hoarse and strained voice, "I'm ready to rumble. I'm the champ. I'm ready to rumble," over and over again.

Clay paused at the steps of the platform and turned to the throng.

"You can tell Sonny I'm here with Sugar Ray," he screamed. "Liston is flat-footed, and Joe Louis is flat-footed, but me and Sugar Ray are two pretty dancers."

Sugar Ray seemed to smile with embarrassment. Louis, who is attached to Liston's camp and had predicted Clay's early destruction, was not present. Cassius had always seemed resentful of Louis's alliance with the opposition.

"Round eight to prove I'm great," screamed Cassius. He turned to Bundini, a smiling, spaniel-eyed man, and they repeated their "Float like a butterfly, sting like a bee" routine.

At 10:37 A.M. Cassius and his entourage left the room to prepare for the weigh-in.

Supernumeraries on Stage

For the next half-hour, newsreel and television crews jockeyed for camera angles while officials and politicians jostled one another on the platform for positions in front of the cameras. Hundreds of newsmen milled about, and a Japanese journalist filled a notebook page with Oriental characters.

At 11:09 A.M. Cassius came roaring back, wearing a terry-cloth robe. He refused to climb up to the platform when uniformed guards stopped Bundini and Sugar Ray. "Let 'em up, this is my show, this is my show," he shouted.

Sugar Ray smiled and shook his head, but Bundini said: "I'll keep him quiet. I have to be up there to keep him quiet." The three men were finally waved up to the scale.

Two minutes later, Liston and his entourage silently entered the room to a smattering of applause. Cassius began jumping up and down gesticulating madly. Sugar Ray and Bundini patted him on the shoulders as if they were trying to calm a skittish colt.

Liston stepped on the scale, and the scale said 218. As the champion from Denver stepped off and replaced his gold-and-white silk robe, Cassius yelled from the other end of the platform: "Hey, sucker, you a chump, you a chump. Are you scared?"

A Rejoinder From Liston

Liston cupped his hands around his mouth and replied: "Don't let anybody know. Don't tell the world."

If there had been any fear the the weigh-in would explode into premature fisticuffs, it disappeared quickly. Liston was placid and in seeming control. Then Clay's weight was announced and the reaction was not favorable to the challenger.

Last Friday, when Clay ceased training, he weighed around 214.

Liston, whose normal resting pulse rate is 72, registered 80 on the platform. The physician refused to disclose blood pressure readings, and whether or not an electrocardiograph had been taken recently.

It was in the midst of one of Clay's yelling spells that Klein took the microphone to announce the $2,500 fine.

The boxing chairman said he had warned Clay earlier in the day that he would tolerate no ranting or raving. Furthermore, he said, "I told Clay I would withhold his purse if he acted up at the fight."

After the ceremonies, Clay was reunited with the rest of his entourage outside Convention Hall. It included four teen-age girls in a convertible, waving three picket-line-type signs. The signs read:

"Setting traps for big game," "Bear season opens February 25," and "Momma, can we little girls go to the fight?"

Cassius was still yelling, in the back seat of his own black Cadillac Fleetwood, as the little motorcade pulled away.

Dundee Sees No Fear

Later Angelo Dundee, Clay's trainer, disputed the conjecture that Clay was scared. "With that kind of fear I'd face a cage of lions," he said. "Cassius will win."

Dundee added that Liston had said nothing when he cupped his hands on the platform. "Liston was so shook up he couldn't talk. He just didn't know what to make of the kid."

Dundee said that Clay's high pulse rate was caused by the fine. The fine did seem rather hasty, since Clay's act had brought the fight its best publicity locally.

Jack Nilon, Liston's adviser, had still another version of the champion's on-platform remarks. Said Nilon: "Sonny said, 'You ain't afraid of me. You're afraid of my left hook.'"

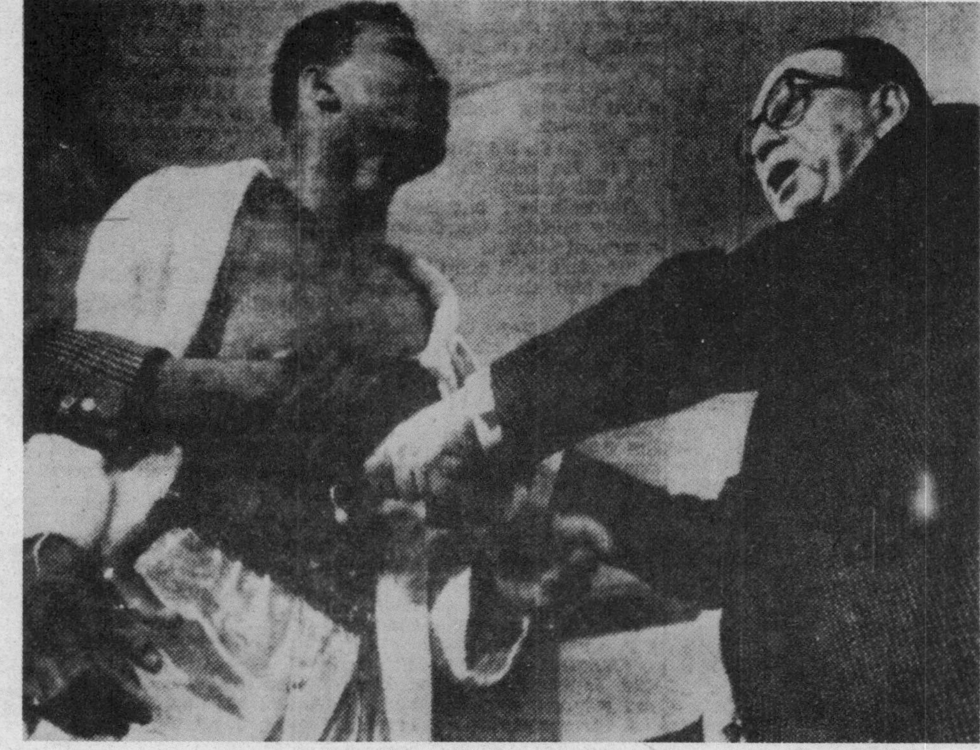

Associated Press Wirephoto

Clay is held back from Liston by Dr. Alexander Robbins, boxing commission physician

LOSS OF BICYCLE GOT CLAY ROLLING

He Learned to Fight After Thief Rode Away

By GERALD ESKENAZI

Somebody stole Cassius Marcellus Clay Jr.'s bicycle when Cassius was 12 years old. The theft launched the Louisville, Ky., youngster on his path to the heavyweight crown.

The angry Clay strode over to police sergeant Joe Martin. "I'm gonna beat up the guy that stole my bike," said young Cassius.

"First you'd better learn to box," replied the policeman.

Cassius learned. Although he never did find the bicycle thief, Cassius wound up with three Cadillacs, a neat house, a huge pile of rock 'n' roll records, and the championship.

While Sonny Liston frightened off interviewers with a scowl, Cassius Clay told an excitement-starved boxing world about himself:

"This is the story about a man
With iron fists and a beautiful tan,
He talks a lot and boasts indeed
Of a powerful punch and blinding speed."

Yet Clay, for all his big talk, his glib replies, his sophomoric trochees, may be more enigmatic than any recent heavyweight champion.

Cassius Clay was born on Jan. 18, 1942, to Odessa Grady Clay and Cassius Marcellus Clay. The original C.M.C. was a Kentuckian who had been the United States Ambassador to Russia. Young Cassius' great-great-grandfather had been a slave to the diplomat and had taken his name.

Young Clay's father was a frustrated artist who made a living as a sign painter. Even today, friends think of the older Clay as strange and Bohemian.

Managed by 11 Men

Perhaps it was his father's bitterness that caused him once to tell young Cassius: "See the color of your skin. You'll never be rich."

Clay's mother was the steady one in the house. She is known as a sweet, lovely woman.

Clay is an irreverent, brash, 22-year-old—in a crowd. He is shy with girls, yet he is supremely confident.

He is managed by a syndicate of 11 wealthy men from Louisville. His discoverer, and spokesman for the syndicate's executive board, is William Faversham Jr.

Faversham recalled yesterday that "even when he is sitting alone, Cassius shows the greatest of confidence."

"People sometimes tell me that Clay is a braggart, a show-off. I reply that he is no different than any other youngster would be who is making a half-million dollars a year."

Cassius apparently has little interests outside of himself. He has no sisters and only one brother, Rudolph Valentino Clay, with whom he is extremely close.

Clay turned professional in 1960 after a successful career as an amateur. In the simon-pure ranks he won the Olympic and Amateur Athletic Union light-heavyweight titles and the Golden Gloves heavyweight championship. In 19 bouts as a pro, before entering the ring with Liston, he was unbeaten, having scored 15 knockouts.

Clay has been accused of being a tool of the Black Muslim movement. He might even be a member of the black racist group. There has been talk that Archie Robinson, who was termed an adviser by Faversham, is actually a liaison man between Clay and the Muslims.

"I wouldn't care if Clay is a Muslim," Faversham said. "The boy is young, curious. He can say a lot of things and make believe he belong to a lot of groups if he thinks it would help him."

Maybe Clay is, after all, just a boy. He has told of his plans to build a utopian housing development—"filled with pretty boys and pretty girls for me to laugh and play with."

Prison Inmates Felt Liston 'Threw' Fight

JEFFERSON CITY, Mo., Feb. 25 (UPI)—Inmates at the Missouri State penitentiary, where the former heavyweight champion Sonny Liston served time, expressed disgust tonight with the results of Liston's title bout with Cassius Clay.

Howls erupted in the prison halls when Liston failed to respond to the seventh round bell. However, there were no incidents.

Ticket Sellers at Fight Spend Lonely Night at $250 Window

By JOE NICHOLS
Special to The New York Times

MIAMI BEACH, Feb. 25—"Who the hell's gonna pay $250 for a ticket to see that fight?" was the general reaction when the price scale for tonight's heavyweight championship was announced by the promoter, Bill MacDonald, some months back. The answer was forthcoming tonight: Not many.

What was intended originally as an approximation of the plush select circle at the Metropolitan Opera or at La Scala or at whatever symbol of elegance that might have come to MacDonald's mind, failed to attract anything at all resembling a capacity turnout.

There were about 400 seats at this price, but whether all those sitting there paid to do so, is a question that cannot be answered. As vigilant and thorough as the Andy Frain ushers were, they certainly could not be held accountable for every single person who sat in this fashionable enclave.

The $250 locations served to prove one thing, that the race track truism of "racing takes care of its own" has more than a little merit. MacDonald is a turf notable, as well as a baseball and boating aficionado.

He probably won't be much of a boxing buff after tonight's lack of paying interest. MacDonald came to national attention in the thoroughbred world a couple of seasons back when he gave $100,000 for a colt named Royal Native.

He also was a prominent figure at the various sales, most particularly the sales at Saratoga.

Mindful of his association with the turf world, a number of his co-owners "came to his rescue." Among those who "sprang" for $250 were Mrs. Liz Tippet, the owner of the famous Llangollen Farm; Raymond Guest, who owns the Kentucky Derby hopeful, Chieftain, and Mrs. Charles Shipman Payson.

Mrs. Payson is the co-owner, with her brother, John Hay Whitney, of the Greentree Stable and is more widely known as the owner of the New York Mets.

The occupants of the intended-to-be-plush locations were a rather subdued, if not self-conscious, lot. They stood up once in a while through the early part of the program, ostensibly for the purpose of stretching, but it could not be denied that the vanity motivating the expenditure of $250 was conducive to stretching, so those in the "cheaper" seats could see them.

"All the News That's Fit to Print"

The New York Times

LATE CITY EDITION
U.S. Weather Bureau Report (Page 90) forecasts: Fair and mild today and tonight. Fair and warm tomorrow.
Temp. Range: 72—58; yesterday: 69—52.

VOL. CXV . No. 39,346. NEW YORK, FRIDAY, OCTOBER 15, 1965. TEN CENTS

DODGERS TRIUMPH OVER TWINS, 2-0, AND TAKE SERIES

Koufax Fans 10 and Yields 3 Hits in Gaining His 2d Shutout in 4 Days

KAAT IS ROUTED IN 4TH

Johnson's Homer and Hits by Fairly and Parker Decide 7th Game

By LEONARD KOPPETT
Special to The New York Times

BLOOMINGTON, Minn., Oct. —Sandy Koufax completed a season of incredible personal accomplishment by pitching the Los Angeles Dodgers to a 2-0 victory over the Minnesota Twins today in the seventh and deciding game of the World Series.

Less than seven months ago, the 29-year-old left-hander from Brooklyn was afraid that his brilliant career was prematurely finished. He had discovered that he had a chronic arthritic condition in his left elbow, which was swollen and bent, and one week before the baseball season was to begin no one could tell whether Koufax would ever be able to pitch again.

Only 2 Days Rest

Today, pitching with only two days of rest, or one fewer than the ordinary healthy pitcher usually needs, he overpowered the Twins after a shaky beginning. He allowed only three hits, walked three men and struck out 10. He retired 14 of the last 15 batters he faced.

It was Koufax's second victory and second shutout of this series, and it put the ultimate embellishment on his year's work. During the regular season, he never missed a starting turn, won 26 games, set a season strike-out record, pitched a perfect game and did his best work during a stretch drive that enabled the Dodgers to win the pennant.

Including the World Series, Koufax pitched 360 innings and struck out 411 batters with an arm that needed constant medication.

His performance today, therefore, involved determination and response to pressure as much as sheer talent and skill. When it was over, he seemed too tired to show elation and even his teammates avoided the usual Series-ending ritual of mob congratulations.

End of Long Season

As Bob Allison swung and missed for the final out, Sandy walked wearily toward the dugout while the crowd of 50,596 —a record here at Metropolitan Stadium—seemed silent and depressed. It wasn't until he was across the third-base foul line that Koufax was joined by his fellow victors, and even then there was little leaping and back-pounding.

The most excited escort was Lou Johnson, who arrived late from his position in left field. It was his home run off Jim Kaat in the fourth inning that had provided the indispensable run.

A minor-leaguer most of his career, the 32-year-old Johnson went to the Dodgers last May only because Tommy Davis broke an ankle. He frequently powered the limited Dodger offense throughout the tight

Continued on Page 54, Column 5

United Press International Telephoto

WINNING FORM: Sandy Koufax of the Los Angeles Dodgers fires away at Minnesota Twins in ninth inning of final game of the World Series, which he won with a 2-0 shutout.

State Rebuffs Blue Cross On Request to Raise Rate

By MORRIS KAPLAN

The State Insurance Department rejected yesterday a Blue Cross request for rate increases affecting 7.5 million subscribers in New York City and 12 nearby counties.

Superintendent of Insurance Henry Root Stern Jr. asserted in his decision that "no rate increase for Associated Hospital Service [Blue Cross] will be necessary through 1966, at least."

State and Federal legislation, he explained, "dispenses with the need for any rate increase or change in the rating system of A.H.S. for the foreseeable future."

Blue Cross had applied last March 24 for rate increases ranging from 6 to 40 per cent. Its president, J. Douglas Colman, had also sought approval of a "current cost" system of determining subscriber rates.

Rating by Experience

His proposal would mean, in effect, an experience-rating system, under which various categories of subscribers would pay different premiums based on frequency of insurance use and other factors.

In disapproving the request, Mr. Stern referred to the Legislature's enactment last May of the Lent-Kelly bills, urged by Governor Rockefeller and to the subsequent passage of the Medicare program by Congress.

"Even without a departure

Continued on Page 33, Column 3

U. S. COURT BACKS GEORGIA NEGROES

Taliaferro's School System Is Declared Bankrupt—Receiver Appointed

By United Press International

AUGUSTA, Ga., Oct. 14—A Federal court today gave Crawfordville, Ga., Negroes a victory in their campaign against the closing of Taliaferro County's white schools and the busing of white students to segregated schools elsewhere.

In a highly unusual action, the three-judge panel declared the county school system bankrupt and named Claude Purcell, the state superintendent of schools, as receiver. He thus became a trustee representing the court, which retains jurisdiction in the case.

[In Mississippi Thursday, a Federal judge ordered school officials to halt enforcement of a state law requiring public school pupils to pay tuition if their parents do not live in the state. Page 27.]

Mr. Purcell will have the power to reopen Taliaferro County's white schools allegedly closed to avoid integration; order other counties to accept Taliaferro Negro students, "or come up with some other solution acceptable to the court," Presiding Judge Griffin Bell held.

Judge Bell directed opposing attorneys to draw up the formal orders that, in addition to put-

Continued on Page 27, Column 2

STUDENTS AT YALE TO JUDGE FACULTY

Plan Giving Them Voice on Tenure Would Recognize the Effective Teacher

By FRED M. HECHINGER

Yale University took the first step yesterday to give students an official voice in the appointment of faculty members to tenure positions.

In a move to give greater priority to teaching performance, the university authorities plan to invite academically high-ranking students to submit "a written appraisal of the strengths and weaknesses" of their educational experience in lectures, discussions and seminars.

The move, which is subject to faculty approval, is part of a complete review of the institution's system of faculty appointments. Central to the reappraisal was the threat that faculty members must "publish or perish." The new policy is an effort to turn the threat into a new admonition to "publish and teach—or perish."

It does not represent a surrender to those who oppose the publishing and research requirement for permanent appointment.

A statement on the new policy makes it clear that publication and original scholarship remain the vital requirements. It con-

Continued on Page 36, Column 2

ROCKEFELLER SAYS U.S. AID IN STATE BYPASSES ALBANY

Names Panel to Seek Ways of Coordinating Relations—Aldrich to Head It

By JOHN SIBLEY

Governor Rockefeller, disturbed that Federal aid has been bypassing Albany on its way to local areas, set up a special cabinet committee yesterday to look into Federal-state relations.

"Congress," he said, "has sanctioned increasing Federal intervention in matters that traditionally have been the responsibility of state and local governments."

The Governor is particularly concerned, a spokesman said, over Washington's growing tendency to deal directly with municipalities, organizations and individuals in the anti-poverty program.

Mr. Rockefeller named his executive assistant and cousin, Alexander Aldrich, to head the special committee and gave the group the following assignment:

¶"The exploration of areas in which recent and pending legislation bypasses or duplicates existing state machinery, thereby resulting in waste and disorder.

¶"The improvement of coordination between Federal and state governments.

¶"The development of ways to strengthen further the Federal system as an important and vital force in American life."

Clash at Hudson Hearing

A recent example of Federal-state conflict over a local issue was the clash at a Congressional subcommittee hearing in Yonkers last July 24 over the future of the Hudson River.

Conrad L. Wirth, executive director of the Governor's Hudson River Valley Commission, insisted at the hearing that there was no need for Federal intervention in preserving what remained of the river's beauty. He argued that the commission, comprising New York State residents, was doing an adequate job.

But critics of the Governor complained that his administration had done nothing to arrest the "spoliation" of the river. One of them, Representative Richard L. Ottinger, Democrat of Westchester, sponsored a bill for the creation of a national park to be called the Hudson Highlands Scenic Riverway.

The Governor, on June 5, called on the Legislature to support him in a vast conservation program for the Hudson valley area.

In his appeal, Mr. Rockefeller asserted that there was "no place here, and certainly no need, for the Federal Government, as has been suggested,

Continued on Page 30, Column 4

Tories Now Favor Ending Defense Role East of Suez

Powell Terms Commitments Too Heavy a Drain on Britain—Shift by Party Runs Counter to U.S. Policy

By ANTHONY LEWIS
Special to The New York Times

BRIGHTON, England, Oct. 14—The Conservative party, in a change of policy significant for American as well as British defense strategy, moved today toward a call for abandonment of Britain's military commitment east of Suez.

The Conservatives' defense spokesman, Enoch Powell, said in a speech to the party conference that the country's "military presence" in Asia and Africa might at some points be self-defeating.

He declared that it was too heavy a drain on Britain's resources and might hinder rather than help the policy of building up indigenous resistance to the advance of Communism.

Mr. Powell is so individualistic a thinker among the Tories that it was not clear at first whether his speech signaled a general shift in party policy. But tonight highest figures in the party confirmed that his views were those of the party hierarchy and had been scrutinized before they were delivered.

Any move for cutting the British commitment in the Middle East and the Far East would be a matter of the most serious concern to the United States State and Defense Departments.

They have urged Britain to maintain her traditional role east of Suez on the ground both that American resources are al-

Continued on Page 8, Column 4

Sections of Schema On Non-Christians Adopted by Bishops

Text of Vatican summary of declaration, Page 18.

By ROBERT C. DOTY
Special to The New York Times

ROME, Oct. 14 — The Roman Catholic hierarchy voted approval today for major passages of a declaration on the church's attitude toward non-Christians, probably including a controversial change in the section on the Jews.

The approvals covered the first passages containing an exoneration of the Jews collectively in the Crucifixion of Jesus and injunctions to Catholics to avoid scriptural misinterpretations that could foster anti-Jewish attitudes.

Months of controversy have resulted, however, in the deletion of a specific warning against applying the word "deicide" -- God-killing — to the Jews. This deletion was probably endorsed by the prelates in the Ecumenical Council today.

There is uncertainty on this point because results of the vote on the critical passage, taken late in the morning, were not announced before the end of the day's session.

Final Vote Is Due

There was virtual certainty, however, that all of the amendments to the text that received preliminary approval in November had now been accepted. The final amendments and the revised declaration itself were expected to be approved tomorrow.

In four ballots today — with a maximum of 2,185 prelates present —there were never more than 189 negative votes. Some were from those who sought to return to an earlier, stronger text and some from those who disapproved of any declaration on non-Christians.

In presenting the amendments, Augustin Cardinal Bea, the German Jesuit who heads the Secretariat for Christian Unity, alluded to both sources of pressure for changes that, in the view of many observers, chilled the tone of the document.

These pressures came first from bishops in Arab lands who feared possible anti-Catholic reprisals from Moslem Governments that might view the dec-

Continued on Page 18, Column 4

JAKARTA LEFTIST OUT AS ARMY CHIEF

Sukarno Announces Choice of Anti-Red Commander, a Foe of Coup Leaders

Special to The New York Times

SINGAPORE, Oct. 14—Command of the Indonesian Army was withdrawn from a leftist general tonight and given to an anti-Communist, Major General Suharto, who crushed the attempted coup d'état against President Sukarno on Oct. 1.

President Sukarno said over the Jakarta radio that General Suharto would replace Maj. Gen.

Associated Press

Major General Suharto

Pranoto Reksosamudro, the leftist he appointed immediately after the abortive coup. General Pranoto's next assignment was not announced.

The President said General Suharto would be made a Cabinet minister in addition to succeeding the army chief, Lieut. Gen. Achmad Yani, one of six anti-Communist generals killed by the rebels.

General Suharto, 44-year-old former commander of the army's strategic reserve, has been field commander of the army forces carrying out an anti-Communist drive under the Defense Minister, Gen. Abdul Haris Nasution.

In effect, General Suharto, a tough and able soldier, has led the army since the coup attempt, for General Pranoto has hardly been heard from. Western diplomatic sources in touch with Jakarta said General Nasution had given General Pranoto a back seat and had persuaded President Sukarno to name the new chief of staff.

Anti-Red Drive Suspended

SINGAPORE, Oct. 14 (Reuters)—The Indonesian Supreme Operations Command has ordered a temporary halt to action against elements involved in the coup attempt, the Jakarta radio reported tonight.

The broadcast said the order had been issued in the interest of maintaining peace and promoting investigations.

KUALA LUMPUR, Malaysia, Oct. 14 (AP) — The announcement of General Suharto's promotion today appeared to con-

Continued on Page 4, Column 3

DECEMBER DRAFT OF 45,224 BIGGEST SINCE KOREAN WAR

Call Issued as the Pentagon Builds Up Forces for U.S. Commitment in Vietnam

QUOTA INCREASES 8,774

Military Denies Any Plan to Mobilize Reserves Unless Situation Deteriorates

By JACK RAYMOND
Special to The New York Times

WASHINGTON, Oct. 14 — The Defense Department announced today a military draft call of 45,224 men for December, the biggest quota since the Korean War.

The request to the Selective Service System was 8,774 more than the November draft call.

It reflected the Administration's intensive effort to build up the armed forces, now numbering about 2,685,000 men, to a little over 3 million by next September.

The build-up itself is a consequence of the increasing war commitment in Vietnam, where United States forces now total nearly 145,000 and are expected to be increased to 200,000 by the end of the year.

Military conscription has risen steadily since the recent low of 3,000 men drafted last February. In May and June of 1961 no men were drafted.

Call-Up Plans Denied

At the peak of the Berlin crisis in 1961, the draft call rose to 25,000, a little more than half the latest draft call.

Pentagon officials stressed however, that the rise in the draft was consistent with the military personnel programs set last summer when President Johnson announced plans to increase the size of the armed forces.

Officials also insisted that, despite intensification of the training program for a newly designated force in the Army National Guard and Army Reserve, there were no plans for a reserve call-up.

The new Selected Reserve Force of 150,000 men, including three combat divisions and six combat brigades, was for the time being considered solely as a contingency force, officials stressed,

Wrong Assumption

They said it would be wrong to assume that the reserve force would be called to active duty unless the situation in Vietnam worsened considerably or a new, unexpected crisis demanded more military personnel.

When President Johnson announced last July 28 that American forces in Vietnam would be increased from 75,000 men to 125,000, he said that draft calls would be gradually raised to 35,000 a month from the then current 17,000.

However, the number of American troops in Vietnam has now exceeded the target set then, and the December draft call is more than 10,000 above the President's figure of July.

In connection with the draft call, the Army said that leave would be authorized for all personnel in Army training centers during Christmas week, Dec. 23 to 28.

Officials were asked why the reserves were not being called up, why the draft calls were not

Continued on Page 2, Column 4

Wingate Warns of Negro Revolt If Haryou's Program Is Curbed

By HOMER BIGART

Somber warnings of a Negro uprising in Harlem and other black ghettos if anything happens to Haryou-Act were voiced yesterday by Livingston L. Wingate, executive director of the controversial Harlem anti-poverty program.

The agency has been criticized for loose management and financial procedures, and about $1 million in future grants of Federal funds is being held up by the Office of Economic Opportunity pending a special audit.

Mr. Wingate made an impassioned denial of any misuse of public funds by Haryou-Act. He said his staff had committed "not one act of malfeasance." But he conceded the books were not in order.

His warnings of violence startled an Urban League regional conference on poverty in the Belmont Plaza Hotel. Later Mr. Wingate expanded on his revelation of a mysterious Harlem "movement" at an impromptu press conference.

He said the movement was composed of desperate youths who were "prepared to die" if the Haryou-Act project were halted.

He indicated that members of the movement were employed by Haryou-Act.

"Haryou-Act bought time with this movement," Mr. Wingate said, implying that his agency had forestalled rioting in Harlem last summer.

The police are sharply aware of the movement and want to crush it, Mr. Wingate said. But he said he had begged the police to withhold action until he had talked to the leaders of the movement and tried to appease

Continued on Page 36, Column 4

Cezanne Sold Here for $800,000

"Maisons a l'Estàque," a Cézanne landscape painted in 1880's, was sold for $800,000

By SANKA KNOX

A world auction record for a painting by Cézanne—$800,000—was set last night in the biggest money-making sale of impressionist and modern paintings.

The sale was held at the Parke-Bernet Galleries at 980 Madison Avenue, which was hooked by telephone to Sotheby's salesroom in New Bond Street, London. There was no telephonic competition from abroad for the great prize of the sale, and, so far as could be ascertained, just three bidders fought it out in the telling moments.

The winning bidder is an anonymous North American private collector, who won the picture, "Maisons à l'Estàque," through the agency of E. J. Roussuck, a paintings specialist here who acts as agent for several wealthy collectors.

His competitors were Hans Berggruen, the Paris dealer, and Knoedler & Co. of New York. The event last night, with 56 pictures from various owners, grossed $3,385,600. The previous record, established at Sotheby's in the William A. Cargill sale in 1963, brought $2,922,052 for 58 pictures.

The Cézanne painting, exe-

Continued on Page 40, Column 5

Nobel Prize Goes To 3 in Medicine

By CLYDE H. FARNSWORTH
Special to The New York Times

STOCKHOLM, Oct. 14 — Three French scientists were awarded the Nobel Prize for Medicine today.

They were honored for their discoveries in the late 1940's and 1950's of regulatory activities inside body cells that opened new frontiers of medical research and may lead to a practical cure for human cancer.

The three men — François Jacob, 45-year-old professor of cellular genetics at the Collège de France; André Lwoff, 53-year-old professor of microbiology at the Sorbonne, and Jacques Monod, 55-year-old professor of metabolic chemistry at the Faculté des Sciences, Paris —will divide an award worth $56,400 this year.

The annual Nobel Prizes for

Continued on Page 36, Column 1

U.S. Truce Efforts Rebuffed by Hanoi

By MAX FRANKEL
Special to The New York Times

WASHINGTON, Oct. 14—The United States appears to have failed in an intensive 10-week diplomatic effort to interest North Vietnam in an agreement to move gradually toward a cease-fire.

The Johnson Administration has virtually resigned itself to failure, although it has also backed away from a recent judgment that North Vietnam has stiffened its peace terms and moved still closer to Communist China.

Noting the year-long build-up in United States military efforts, including the bombing of North Vietnam and the commitment of nearly 150,000 American troops to South Vietnam, the Communist Government in Hanoi has described the proposing of a cease-fire

Continued on Page 3, Column 3

NEWS INDEX

News Summary and Index, Page 47

Koufax Holds Spotlight at Dodgers' Celebration

DODGERS WIN, 2-0, AND TAKE SERIES

Continued From Page 1, Col. 1

pennant race. Today, he made the most important hit of all and he is not the type of man to hide his emotions.

The second Dodger run came immediately after the homer, which hit the left-field foul-pole screen. It was produced by three other often unappreciated Dodgers: Ron Fairly, Wes Parker and Manager Walt Alston.

Fairly followed Johnson's drive with one just fair into the other corner of the field for a double. This was with nobody out in the fourth inning, so it was natural to expect the Dodgers to sacrifice Fairly to third, from where he could score on an out.

The Twins set their infield defense for this eventuality, but Alston, speaking to Parker before he went to the plate, told him to swing and try to hit the ball past the charging infield. Parker did exactly that. He bounced a single over the head of Don Mincher, the onrushing first baseman, and Fairly scored.

Thus the Dodgers became champions of the baseball world for the second time in three years, and for the fourth time in five chances under Alston's regime.

Alston became manager of the Dodgers when they were still in Brooklyn, and still had a star-studded line-up, in 1954. The next year, Brooklyn had its first and only world championship, thanks to a 2-0 victory in the seventh game at Yankee Stadium. The man who pitched that one — Johnny Podres — sat in the Dodger bull pen all day today, no longer needed.

In 1956, the Dodgers again battled the Yankees through seven games, but lost the last one. After the 1957 season, they moved to Los Angeles, and in 1959 won the pennant in a post-season playoff with Milwaukee. They then defeated the Chicago White Sox in the World Series, 4 games to 2.

In 1962, with fundamentally the same personnel now playing, the Dodgers lost a pennant playoff to the San Francisco Giants. But in 1963, they won the pennant handily and swept the Yankees, 4-0, with Koufax pitching two outstanding games. Last year, however, the Los Angeles club couldn't even win half its games and finished in a tie for sixth.

Koufax, Don Drysdale and Claude Osteen, plus Ron Perranoski and Bob Miller as relievers, gave the Dodgers superb pitching this year. And the bunt-run-steal-scamper attack led by Maury Wills produced enough runs.

That was the pattern used in this Series. In the first two games here, the attack didn't function. Drysdale and Koufax were not sharp, and the Twins won easily.

In the next three games in Los Angeles, Osteen pitched a shutout, Drysdale a five-hitter and Koufax a shutout — and the Dodger offense ran wild. Yesterday here, the offense died again and when Osteen made one bad pitch (which Allison hit for a two-run homer) the Series was all even.

It was, therefore, up to Koufax today. Drysdale was ready, however, to take over at any time. And three times in the first five innings it appeared that he would be needed.

Koufax almost had a run to work with at the start. Jim Gilliam singled with one out in the first and was bunted to second by Willie Davis. He was on his way home when Tony Oliva raced in and made a tumbling catch of Johnson's looper to right.

Control was Sandy's problem in the first. He was consistently high as he struck out Zoilo Versalles and retired Joe Nossek on a grounder. He walked Oliva on a full count and Harmon Killebrew on four pitches. Then he fired a third strike past Earl Battey and was out of the inning.

In the third, the Dodgers failed to score even though John Roseboro led off with a double and Koufax walked. Kaat made Wills bounce out, advancing the runners, and forced Gilliam to fly out to right field, too short for any attempt to score. Then he got Davis to foul out.

In the home half of the inning, Koufax had his second crisis, and he got a break. Versalles singled with one out and was trying to steal second when Nossek swung at a 1-1 pitch. In doing so Nossek clearly interfered with Roseboro's unsuccessful throw to second, so Umpire Ed Hurley declared Nossek out and sent Versalles back to first.

After getting his 2-0 lead, Koufax retired the Twins in order in the fourth, but had to struggle again in the fifth.

Frank Quilici lined a two-base hit off the fence in left-center with one out and Rich Rollins, a pinch-hitter for the pitcher, worked a full-count walk. The tying runs were on with one out and the top of the batting order was up.

Here Koufax got fielding support. Versalles mashed a sharp grounder down the third-base line. Gilliam, with a lunge, smothered it back-handed, scrambled to his feet and got over to the base in time for a forceout. Nossek's grounder to Wills then proved a third-out force at second.

From that point on, Koufax seemed to have much better control. Battey hit a line drive at Wills in the sixth and Versalles flied deep to left in the eighth, but no one got on base until Killebrew lined a single to left with one out in the ninth.

That meant a home run could tie the game and Koufax had to "reach back" for whatever strength he had left in his 360th inning.

He fired two strikes past Battey and hit the outside corner for a called strike three. Allison fouled the first pitch to him and took two balls, both high. Then he swung and missed for strike two. Finally Sandy reached back for the last time and threw strike three as Allison swung and missed.

It might have been an easier task for Koufax, but the Dodgers wasted three scoring opportunities after they had their runs.

In the fourth, Parker's single knocked out Kaat and Parker took second when Oliva bobbled the ball. Al Worthington relieved and made a fine catch on Dick Tracewski's pop bunt along the third-base line. Worthington walked Roseboro semi-intentionally, fielded Koufax's soft tap to the mound while the runners advanced, and made Wills foul out to Killebrew.

Parker tripled off Johnny Klippstein with one out in the sixth, but Tracewski bunted foul for the third strike on an attempted squeeze play. An intentional pass to Roseboro and a strike-out of Koufax ended the inning.

With one out in the seventh, Gilliam singled and Davis was hit on the foot by a pitch. Johnson's slow bounder to third left men on second and third with two out.

At that point Manager Sam Mele called Jim Merritt, a left-hander, in from the bull pen to face Fairly. It was an excellent decision because Fairly, who had been murdering Minnesota's right-handed pitchers, flied meekly to right field.

Koufax Is Voted Top Series Star For the 2d Time in Three Years

Special to The New York Times

BLOOMINGTON, Minn., Oct. 14 — Sanford Koufax will return to New York City, his home town, on Monday, just long enough to pick up one of the more tangible rewards for becoming "the outstanding player in the 62d World Series" — a new Corvette sports car.

It is the second time in three years that the star left-hander of the Los Angeles Dodgers has been voted by the editors of Sport Magazine as "the ball-player who did the most for his team" in the World Series.

The award was given to Bob Gibson of the St. Louis Cardinals last year, making him the ninth pitcher in 10 years to win it. The only non-pitcher and the only member of a losing team — to be selected was Bobby Richardson of the New York Yankees in 1960.

Koufax will get the keys to his trophy Monday after a luncheon at Cavanagh's Restaurant.

A Relaxed Wills

Maury Wills, relaxed and chatty, held a kind of press conference in the Dodger dugout before the big game and said he was glad to be around.

"This is my kind of game," said the captain of the Dodgers. "I like to think I'm at my best when everything rides on one game. I would gladly have paid any amount of money to get in."

He didn't have to pay, but the 50,596 fans in Metropolitan Stadium did. It was the biggest crowd in the history of the stadium, which was built on the farmlands south of Minneapolis and St. Paul 10 years ago in the expectation that the New York Giants would emigrate to Minnesota.

The Giants went to San Francisco, but in 1961 the Washington Senators franchise was moved here and a new Washington team was installed in the capital.

A Home-Rule Hassle

The problem of settling a baseball team in the Twin Cities area involved a home-rule hassle, since Minneapolis and St. Paul both had minor league traditions. The question was: The "Twin Cities" are equal, but is one more equal than the other?

The stadium finally was situated in Bloomington, the fourth largest city in Minnesota (pop. 68,000). Its history includes athletic contests between the early settlers and the Indians, far-ranging contests of strength and speed involving hundreds of men playing a kind of lacrosse all over the landscape.

Metropolitan Stadium's biggest crowd before this season was 41,034 for a night game between the New York Yankees and the Twins on July 17, 1963. The bigger crowds this year were made possible by the addition of a second deck in the left-field bleachers.

Master of the Mound

Sanford Koufax

Associated Press Wirephoto

IN the spring of 1953, the captain of the Lafayette High School basketball team in Brooklyn tried out for the baseball team.

The youth had a reputation as a promising sandlot pitcher. He made the high school team as a substitute first baseman. Coach Charlie Sheerin supposedly watched him pitch and said, "You'll never be a pitcher."

Man in the News

Sheerin said at his home in Valley Stream, L. I., yesterday that the incident didn't quite happen that way. "But I'll tell you this," he said. "I had a Boston Red Sox scout look at him, and maybe the scout said it because they never tried to sign him."

The pro-tem first baseman was Sanford (Sandy) Koufax, and for eight years the original verdict held up. Then two incidents in 1961 helped make Koufax the outstanding pitcher in baseball.

If any confirmation of that status was needed, Koufax provided it yesterday. With only two days of rest after shutting out the Minnesota Twins, 7-0, on four hits, he blanked them again, 2-0, on three hits in the deciding game of the World Series.

He was scheduled to pitch the opening game of the Series, which would have enabled him to get three days off between starts. But the first game fell on Yom Kippur, the holiest day of the year for Jews, and Koufax has never pitched on the holiday.

An Ironic Situation

It was ironic that the Los Angeles Dodgers chose Koufax to pitch even though Don Drysdale, a 23-game winner this year, was available and rested. In 1961, Koufax couldn't talk his way into a starting assignment.

In six seasons with the Dodgers, he had won 36 games. Then, in disgust, he had a conversation with General Manager Emil (Buzzie) Bavasi that went something like this:

"Why don't I pitch?"

"You can't get the ball over the plate."

"How can I get the ball over the plate if I don't pitch?"

After that, Koufax pitched more often. This was the first incident. Then his catcher, Norm Sherry, advised him to stop trying to blaze his fast ball, perhaps the fastest in baseball, past every batter on every pitch. Koufax took the advice and made the transformation from thrower to pitcher. In his last five seasons, he has won 102 games.

This year, he led the major leagues in victories (26), earned-run average (2.04) and strike-outs (382, the highest in history). He pitched his fourth no-hitter in four years, also a record, and it was a perfect game.

His record would be distinctive for a healthy man. For one who has undergone his physical tribulations, it is remarkable. In 1962, a circulatory ailment known as Reynaud's Phenomenon sidelined him for the last 2½ months of the season. Last spring, a traumatic arthritic condition in his left elbow (he is a left-handed pitcher) almost sidelined him from baseball forever.

Before he pitches, his left arm is massaged with a hot ointment to bring the blood to the surface. The arm swells as much as an inch during a game, and afterward the elbow is packed in ice for half an hour.

He Got $14,000 Bonus

As a youth, Sandy Koufax (his last name rhymes with Go Max) wanted to be an architect, not a baseball player. He was born on Dec. 30, 1935, in Brooklyn to Irving Koufax, a lawyer, and his wife, Evelyn. He went to the University of Cincinnati in 1953 on a basketball scholarship, but a year later he signed a baseball contract with the Brooklyn Dodgers for a $14,000 bonus and an annual salary of $6,000.

Now, at the age of 29, he earns an annual salary of $70,000, and the Dodgers have said they will raise that to $100,000 next year.

Though Koufax drinks and smokes (both in moderation), he has never endorsed cigarettes or liquor. He is careful of his public image.

He stands 6 feet 2 inches and weighs 205 pounds. He has dark hair, and when he doesn't shave, his beard is heavy. His rugged handsomeness is complemented by elegant sports clothes carefully chosen. His voice is deep and resonant, and his poise is seldom ruffled.

Unlike the stereotype of the lobby-sitting baseball player, he appreciates good books and good music. He lives in a two-bedroom ranch home in Studio City, Calif., outside Los Angeles, and he drives a convertible.

Though he has great natural baseball talent, he has become a thinking man's pitcher ("You have to have an idea, some sort of plan, on every pitch."). The combination is ideal. His future is limitless. As Ken Boyer of the St. Louis Cardinals put it:

"Koufax is just too damned much."

TV-RADIO COVERAGE OF SERIES A RECORD

The 1965 World Series between the Los Angeles Dodgers and Minnesota Twins received more television and radio exposure than any predecessor.

The National Broadcasting Company handled the television and radio broadcasts. In all, the telecast was carried by 306 stations. That figure includes 232 stations in the United States, among them (carrying the games on a delayed basis) three stations in Alaska and three in Hawaii.

In Canada, 42 stations carried the Series in English and 13 in French. The telecasts also were presented by the entire 16-station Telesistema network of Mexico and three stations in Puerto Rico. The total does not include stations in Saudi Arabia, which ordered kinescopes of the game for later broadcast.

The radio broadcast went out over 588 stations in the United States, Canada and Puerto Rico.

Packers Beat Colts on Hornung's 5 Touchdowns; Sayers Gets 6 as Bears Win

GREEN BAY GAINS 42-TO-27 VICTORY

Packers Take First Place in West—Ground Game Excels—Cuozzo Hurt

STATISTICS OF THE GAME

	Packers	Colts
First downs	18	21
Rushing yardage	144	74
Passing yardage	222	190
Passes	10-17	20-41
Interceptions by	3	1
Punts	3-44	4-35
Fumbles lost	2	0
Yards penalized	68	37

By WILLIAM N. WALLACE
Special to The New York Times

BALTIMORE, Dec. 12—Gary Cuozzo, young and impetuous, tried to fool the Green Bay defense, mature and disciplined, but failed today when Dave Robinson intercepted the Baltimore quarterback's little flip pass and ran 88 yards.

This big play late in the second period turned the game around and the Packers went on to defeat the Colts, 42-27. Paul Hornung, the Golden Boy who had been returned to the starting lineup for this big game, scored five touchdowns.

The victory jumped the Packers over the Colts into first place by half a game in the Western Conference of the National Football league.

The turning point came today in the fog of Baltimore Stadium when the 23-year-old Cuozzo, playing the biggest game of his life as a stand-in for the injured Johnny Unitas, went up to the line of scrimmage with his offensive unit. The Colts were 1 point behind, 14-13, and had a second down on the Green Bay 2-yard line, thanks to a recovered fumble.

Moore Fakes to Inside

It was an enviable situation. Cuozzo faked Lenny Moore, his halfback, to the inside. Jerry Hill, the fullback, tried to sneak outside to his right and Cuozzo lofted the football toward Hill.

But Willie Davis, the Packer right end, knew a pass was coming because the tackle opposite him, George Preas, had tipped it off. Robinson, the big linebacker playing just outside Davis, also had diagnosed the daring play.

Davis almost intercepted the pass, which went by his fingertips, and Robinson did, the ball hitting him chest high. Said a dejected Cuozzo later, "Robinson dropped off. I should have thrown the ball higher."

The Green Bay linebacker then raced 88 yards to the Colt 10-yard line. On the first play from there, with 19 seconds to go before half-time, Bart Starr passed deep to Boyd Dowler, his flanker, in the back of the end zone—and the Packers went to their locker room with an 8-point lead.

Less than a minute before they had been about to fall 6 points behind. So it goes in pro football.

In the third quarter, Green Bay opened up a 35-14 lead and the 60,238 Baltimore adherents in the stands were quiet as mice.

Returns After Injury

Cuozzo was hurt for one series and a halfback named Tom Matte had to play quarterback. Cuozzo's left shoulder was taped and he went into the locker room to be given a pain-killing shot.

Then he came back and attacked the Packers with a series of good passes. The youth with an injured shoulder completed 13 of 22 passes and took his team in for two touchdowns that closed the gap to 8 points with six minutes left to play.

It was a thrilling rally that had the fog-blanketed stadium in an uproar. But it all came to naught when Starr, the sound Green Bay quarterback, ended the nonsense by throwing a 65-yard touchdown pass to Hornung at 10:30 of the fourth period. That closed the scoring at 42-27.

On a third-and-9 situation, Hornung went up the middle against a blitzing Colt defense while Jimmy Taylor, the fullback, stayed back to block for Starr. Bart hit Hornung 15 yards downfield and he went all the way. Hornung was wide open because the blitzing middle linebacker, Dennis Gaubatz, had vacated the area.

In the first period, a similar play of 50 yards — Starr to Hornung — had given Green Bay a 14-3 lead. The Packers trailed only after a 14-yard field goal by Lou Michaels of the Colts had opened the scoring at 4:29 of the first quarter.

Hornung also scored on runs of 2, 9 and 3 yards, all off-tackle cutbacks in the typical Green Bay power style.

This was an old-fashioned Green Bay game — Hornung running outside and Taylor inside, with Starr throwing occasionally. It was elemental, fundamental football designed to destroy the other team's defense, which it did. On defense, Green Bay was sound and conservative, not even blitzing.

This was the best offensive game of the year for Green Bay, which has had a lot of trouble moving. Hornung, who was not a starter the last two games, had scored only three times and gained merely 231 yards. He got 61 yards running and 115 catching passes today.

The Colts? They show a tie and two losses for their last three games after winning eight in a row, and the bottom appears to have dropped out of their team.

Baltimore's best player today was Raymond Berry, the incomparable split end who caught 10 of Cuozzo's passes against the tight coverage of Doug Hart, but Berry could not do it alone against the mighty Packer defense that has carried Green Bay such a long way this season.

Green Bay Packers	14	7	14	7	42
Baltimore Colts	3	10	0	14	27

Balt.—FG, Michaels, 14.
G. B.—Hornung, 2, run (Chandler, kick).
G. B.—Hornung, 50, pass from Starr (Chandler, kick).
Balt.—FG, Michaels, 45.
Balt.—Moore, 3, run (Michaels, kick).
G. B.—Dowler, 10, pass from Starr (Chandler, kick).
G. B.—Hornung, 9, run (Chandler, kick).
G. B.—Hornung, 3, run (Chandler, kick).
Balt.—Hill, 1, run (Michaels, kick).
Balt.—Berry, 5, pass from Cuozzo (Michaels, kick).
G. B.—Hornung, 65, pass from Starr (Chandler, kick).

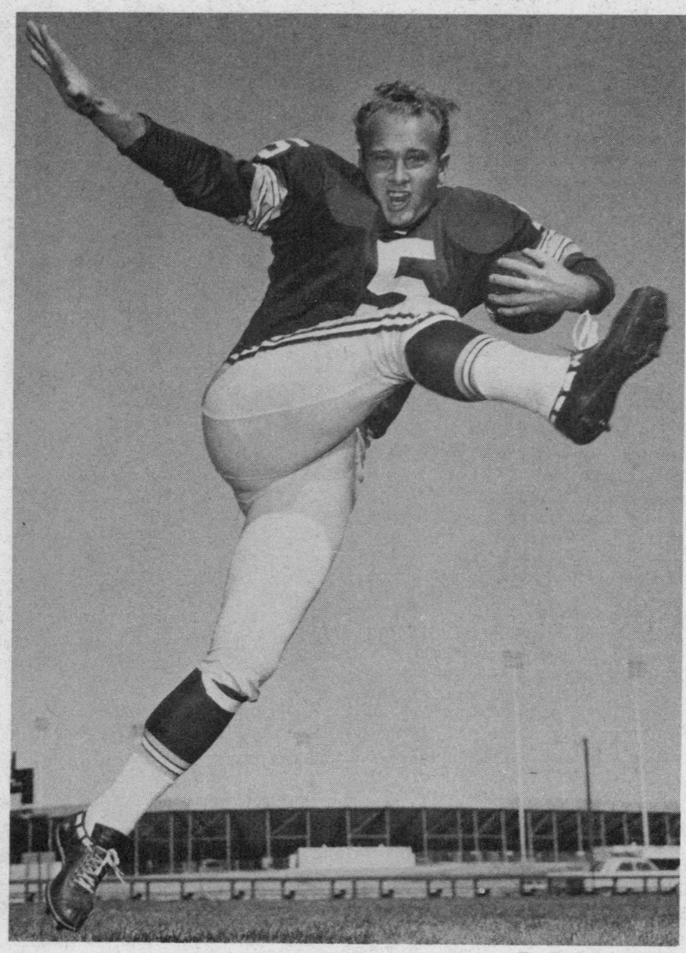
The Green Bay Packers
Paul Hornung

49ERS VANQUISHED IN CHICAGO, 61-20

Sayers Sets Season Mark With 21 Touchdowns and Ties Record for Game

STATISTICS OF THE GAME

	Bears	49ers
First downs	21	19
Rushing yardage	183	58
Passing yardage	401	272
Passes	17-33	23-44
Interceptions by	2	0
Punts	3-33	6-49
Fumbles lost	0	0
Yards penalized	30	14

CHICAGO, Dec. 12 (AP)—Gale Sayers scored six touchdowns today, raising his season total to 21—a National Football League record—as the Chicago Bears routed the San Francisco 49ers, 61-20.

Sayers established a Bear scoring record for one game and also matched the single game N.F.L. mark for touchdowns set by Ernie Nevers in 1929 and matched by Dub Jones in 1951.

Sayers's season total bettered the league record of 20 by Lenny Moore of the Baltimore Colts and matched this year by Jimmy Brown of the Cleveland Browns.

The triumph, avenging an opening-game 52-24 defeat at San Francisco, kept alive the Bears' chances of sharing the Western Conference title. They now have a 9-4 won-lost mark.

The remarkable rookie from Kansas scored in the first quarter, taking a screen pass from Rudy Bukich and running 80 yards.

In the second period, Sayers scored on runs of 21 and 7 yards.

Sayers cut through tackle and raced 50 yards in the third period. Later in this quarter, he dived over from the 1. His final touchdown, in the fourth quarter, came on a punt return of 85 yards.

Chicago Bears	13	14	13	21—61
San Francisco 49ers	0	13	0	7—20

Chi—Sayers, 80, pass from Bukich (pass failed).
Chi.—Ditka, 29, pass from Bukich (Leclerc, kick).
S.F.—Parks, 9, pass from Brodie (Davis, kick).
Chi.—Sayers, 21, (Leclerc, kick).
S.F.—Crow, 15, pass from Brodie (kick failed).
Chi.—Sayers, 7, run (Leclerc, kick).
Chi.—Sayers, 50, run (Leclerc, kick).
Chi.—Sayers, 1, run (run failed).
S.F.—Kopay, 2, run (Davis, kick).
Chi.—Jones, 8, pass from Bukich (Leclerc, kick).
Chi.—Sayers, 85, punt return (Leclerc, kick).
Chi.—Arnett, 2, run (Leclerc, kick).
Attendance—46,278.

Packers, Colts, Bears All in Title Contention

A victory by the Green Bay Packers next Sunday over the 49ers at San Francisco would give Green Bay the Western Conference championship and a chance to meet the Cleveland Browns for the National Football League championship at home on Jan. 2.

The Baltimore Colts will face the Rams Saturday in Los Angeles. A Baltimore victory coupled with a Green Bay defeat would enable the Colts to win it all.

The Chicago Bears are still alive, too, one game back of the Packers. The Bears could tie Green Bay for the Western title if they beat Minnesota, the 49ers beat Green Bay and the Colts lose. A tie would require a playoff in Green Bay on Dec. 26.

RAMS' AIR ATTACK TOPS BROWNS, 42-7

Gabriel Hurls 5 Touchdown Passes and Scores Once

STATISTICS OF THE GAME

	Rams	Browns
First downs	23	6
Rushing yardage	169	40
Passing yardage	300	79
Passes	15-31	11-27
Interceptions by	1	1
Punts	5-36	11-45
Fumbles lost	0	0
Yards penalized	35	85

LOS ANGELES, Dec. 12 (UPI)—Roman Gabriel, rated a second stringer at the season's start, threw five touchdown passes and scored on an 8-yard run today to lead the Los Angeles Rams to a 42-7 victory over the Cleveland Browns, champions of the National Football League's Eastern Conference.

This was the third straight for the Rams since Gabriel took over for injured Bill Munson. The other victories were over the Green Bay Packers and St. Louis Cardinals.

Three of Gabriel's touchdown passes were caught by Tommy McDonald, for 46, 43 and 42 yards. He also hit Willie Brown with a 22-yarder and passed 5 yards to Marlin McKeever.

The Browns played without their starting quarterback, Frank Ryan, who has a bad leg. His replacement, Jim Ninowski, connected with Ernie Green on a 3-yard pass for the only Cleveland touchdown.

The Rams made 23 first downs to six for Cleveland and held Jim Brown to a net of 20 yards in 13 carries.

Sayers Is First Bear to Get Game Ball Twice in Season

CHICAGO, Dec. 12 (UPI)—Gale Sayers, who set all kinds of records in the Chicago Bears' 61-20 rout of the San Francisco 49ers today, broke another in the dressing room after the game.

For the first time, a Chicago Bear was awarded the game ball twice in one season. The first time Sayers got it was for his four-touchdown performance against the Minnesota Vikings. But he scored six touchdowns today and his teammates just had to give him the ball again.

George Halas, the Bears' owner and coach, said: "It isn't often that the Bears break a tradition but this was the greatest football exhibition I have ever seen by one man in one game."

Sayers's 21 touchdowns for the season broke the N.F.L. record set by Lenny Moore of Baltimore last year. And his 126 points for the season broke a Bear record of 109 set by Johnny Lujack in 1950.

Sayers, who once said "I get my kicks running with the ball," had to concede this was his greatest thrill as a pro. But he wouldn't say whether he was more excited than he had been during his days as a high school star in Omaha, Neb., or as an all-America at the University of Kansas.

Sayers is 22 years old, 6 feet tall and weighs 200 pounds. He is described as an "instinctive" runner, relying more on his speed and shiftiness than sheer power. He is also a fine pass receiver.

In today's game, Sayers gained a total of 336 yards—113 rushing, 89 on receptions and 134 on punt returns.

Halas said he didn't make up his mind to take Sayers as one of his first-round draft choices until a few weeks before the N.F.L. draft. "We thought perhaps some of his performance was just luck," Halas said. "Then I saw a highlight film on him where he made two moves in one stride and ran 95 yards and that was it."

Celtics Defeat Lakers, 95-93, for Eighth Title in Row and 9th in 10 Years

RUSSELL PACES BOSTON'S ATTACK

Scores 25 Points, Gets 32 Rebounds—Baylor Held to One Basket in First Half

By GORDON S. WHITE Jr.
Special to The New York Times

BOSTON, April 28—The Boston Celtics won their eighth straight National Basketball Association title tonight by beating the Los Angeles Lakers, 95-93, and continued the longest championship reign in the history of major professional sports. This triumph in the seventh game of the final playoff gave the Celtics their ninth N.B.A. title in 10 years.

Thus they sent their retiring coach, Red Auerbach, out of the coaching business as a winner. The 48-year-old Auerbach lighted his last victory cigar—the sign that he is sure of winning a game—with 25 seconds to go after Sam Jones had sunk a 35-foot shot. And when he did, it sent the 13,909 fans filling Boston Garden into a screaming state of joy.

At the final buzzer, hundreds of fans stormed the court. With his shirt half torn off, Tom Sanders finally gave up and took what was left of it off and tossed it to the crowd.

It was a typical Boston triumph, one engineered through muscular strength on defense and fast-breaking attacks that lasted the full 48 minutes. Never were the Celtics behind and, after they got the first 10 points, the Lakers never got as close as 2 points until the last four seconds.

United Press International

Lakers' Elgin Baylor (L) drives around Celtics players (L-R) Tom Sanders; Bill Russell (6) and Sam Jones (24) during 1st quarter action of final game in the N.B.A. championship playoffs at Boston Garden.

The Boston Celtics

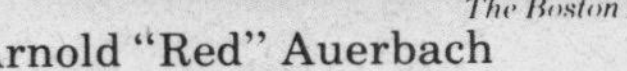

Arnold "Red" Auerbach

The Boston Celtics

Sam Jones

Russell at His Best

Bill Russell, the giant of the Celtics who will be the player-coach of the Celtics next season, played at his best, scoring 25 points (tops for the Celtics) and getting 32 rebounds (high for both teams).

The Celtics became the first team in 14 years to finish as the runner-up in the regular-season Eastern Division race and go on to the title. In fact, never before had the Celtics, who finished second to Philadelphia in the East, played in the semi-finals before going on to the championship.

Tonight Boston showed no signs of the ragged play that cost so dearly when, after the Celtics had led in the playoff, 3 games to 1, they lost two straight to the Lakers. Those defeats were the result of sloppy play on Boston's part as much as improved action by the Lakers.

But this time the Celtics shaped up and defended so well that Elgin Baylor, one of the Lakers' two big scorers, made only 18 points, and only 2 in the first half. Jerry West scored 36 points, high in the game, but the other Lakers couldn't penetrate Boston's defense.

Baylor Given No Chance

Baylor hit on only one of nine shots in the first half. He was forcing shots and missing because he never really was given a good chance by the Celtics.

From the moment John Havlicek hit on a short pop shot three seconds after the game-opening tap, there was a distinct feeling that Boston had things under control.

The Celtics built their lead to 19 points at the 2:01 mark of the third quarter when Sam Jones hit with a rebound for a 59-40 margin. It wasn't really downhill from then on, it was just a cagey game by Boston in which the Celtics managed to sit on a good lead for a long time.

Sam Jones scored 22 points and Havlicek made 16. Sanders and his replacement, Don Nelson, did most of the good defensive work on Baylor. Sanders, however, was forced to sit out a lot of the action. He drew three quick personal fouls and was up to five early in the third quarter.

Russell is the only member of the team who has played on all of the championship squads. Auerbach has been the coach of all of them.

BOSTON (95)	G.	F.	P.
Havlicek	6	4-6	16
Sanders	3	1-1	7
Russell	10	5-5	25
S. Jones	10	2-2	22
K. Jones	2	1-1	5
Siegfried	4	4-5	12
Nelson	2	4-4	8
Naulls	0	0-0	0
Totals	37	21-24	95

LOS ANGELES (93)	G.	F.	P.
Goodrich	2	2-3	6
King	1	0-1	2
Ellis	5	2-3	12
West	12	12-16	36
Baylor	6	6-6	18
Hazzard	5	2-5	12
Larusso	2	3-4	7
Imhoff	0	0-0	0
Boozer	0	0-0	0
Totals	33	27-38	93

Boston	27	26	23	19—95
Los Angeles	20	18	22	33—93

Attendance—13,909.

CANADIENS BEAT RED WINGS BY 4-2

Trim Detroit's Lead to 2-1 in Stanley Cup Finals

Special to The New York Times

DETROIT, April 28—The defending Stanley Cup champion Montreal Canadiens bounced back into title contention tonight by defeating the Detroit Red Wings, 4-2, in the third game of the Stanley Cup playoff finals. Detroit leads in the four-of-seven-game series, 2-1.

Although Montreal had heroes among its goal scorers, individual honors had to go to its goaltender, Lorne (Gump) Worsley.

After Capt. Jean Beliveau had given the Canadiens a 2-1 lead with a brilliant breakaway goal late in the first period, Worsley came to the fore in the second session.

The Red Wings, paced by Gordie Howe, Andy Bathgate, Alex Delvecchio and Dean Prentice, mounted many scoring advances at Worsley, who turned aside 15 shots.

The Canadiens clinched the decision early in the third period. Within four minutes of the start of action, Gilles Tremblay twice shot the puck past the Detroit goalie, Roger Crozier.

Detroit opened the scoring in the first period at 4:20 when Norm Ullman tallied on an individual effort, digging the puck out of the corner and skating in to beat Worsley.

Dave Balon put the Canadiens even at 15:40 when he slid the puck into the nets with Crozier flat on his back. Terry Harper and Henri Richard received assists.

Beliveau's tie-breaker came at 19:12. He retrieved the puck from Delvecchio in center ice and skated in on Crozier. He faked the net-minder neatly and slipped the puck over his prostrate form.

That was all the scoring for the winners until Tremblay's goals in the final period.

FIRST PERIOD—1, Detroit, Ullman (unassisted), 4:20; 2, Montreal, Balon (Harper, Richard), 15:40; 3, Montreal, Beliveau (unassisted), 19:12. Penalty: Backstrom (8:38). Shots on goal: Detroit 9, Montreal 9.

SECOND PERIOD—No scoring. Penalties: Rochfort (2:46), Howe (5:20), Prentice (11:31), Watson (18:23), Balon (5 minutes, 18:23). Shots on goal: Detroit 15, Montreal 9.

THIRD PERIOD—4, Montreal, G. Tremblay (Beliveau), 1:45; 5, Montreal, G. Tremblay (J. C. Tremblay, Rousseau), 3:21; 6, Detroit, Howe (Marshall, Delvecchio), 19:59. Penalties: Marshall (3:03), Balon (10:14), Ullman (10:14), Talbot (13:24), Detroit bench, served by McDonald (16:50). Shots on goal: Detroit 7, Montreal 13.

Referee—John Ashley. Linesmen—Matt Pavlich and John D'Amico.

Attendance—15,154.

Glad Rags Triumphs In Rich British Stakes

NEWMARKET, England, April 28 (AP)—Glad Rags finished a neck ahead of Berkeley Springs today for an upset victory in the 1,000 Guineas, a mile race for 3-year-old fillies. Both are American-owned.

Glad Rags went off at 100-6 odds while Berkeley Springs carried 100-8 odds.

The victory was worth $70,599 to Mrs. James P. Mills, owner of Hickory Tree Stables in Virginia. Paul Mellon of Pittsburgh owns Berkeley Springs.

FARMER OF HAWKS TO COACH BULLETS

BALTIMORE, April 28 (AP)—Mike Farmer, assistant coach and chief scout of the St. Louis Hawks, was named today as head coach of the Baltimore Bullets of the National Basketball Association.

Farmer, 29 years old, was given a two-year contract to succeed Paul Seymour, who resigned a month ago. Terms were not announced.

Farmer wound up a seven-year N.B.A. playing career with the Hawks last season after fracturing an ankle. He was named then as assistant to the St. Louis player-coach, Richie Guerin.

Section 5 | SPORTS BOATS AUTOMOBILES

The New York Times.

SPORTS SHIPPING NEWS SHOPPING GUIDE—DOGS | Section 5

S SUNDAY, NOVEMBER 20, 1966. L + S

NOTRE DAME AND MICHIGAN STATE PLAY 10-10 TIE; HARVARD, PRINCETON, DARTMOUTH SHARE IVY TITLE

CRIMSON WINS, 17-0

Leo Scores Twice and Defense Shuts Down on Yale Eleven

By JOSEPH DURSO

Special to The New York Times

CAMBRIDGE, Mass., Nov. 19 — Harvard captured a one-third share of the Ivy League's football championship today—and completed its best season in 46 years—by overpowering Yale, 17-0, before an overflow crowd of 41,000.

Bobby Leo scored two touchdowns and gained 106 yards rushing as the Crimson scored its eighth victory in nine games

FINAL IVY LEAGE STANDING

	W.	L.		W.	L.
Dartmouth	6	1	Yale	3	4
Harvard	6	1	Columbia	2	5
Princeton	6	1	Penn	1	6
Cornell	4	3	Brown	0	7

and marched into a triple tie with Princeton and Dartmouth for the league title.

By train, bus, station wagon they flocked to Harvard Stadium for The Game, the 83d in a series that started in 1875 and one of the most deliberately played.

Harvard, undefeated until it met Princeton two weeks ago, took dead aim on the team that knocked it out of the championship three years ago but had not beaten it since.

Held to 5 First Downs

It held Yale to five first downs and 82 yards on the ground, and played the entire game in Yale territory except for one stand on its own 20-yard line in the fourth quarter.

Meanwhile, the Crimson offensive unit seized a 3-0 lead in the opening moments of the second quarter on a 29-yard field goal by Jim Babcock.

Five minutes later Leo bucked across from 1 yard out, and early in the fourth quarter the senior halfback from Everett took a pitchout and sprinted 52 yards for another touchdown.

As a result Harvard scored its third straight victory in the series, something it had not achieved since 1928-29-30. It finished the season with 231 points, the most by a Harvard team since 1901, and lived up to the wildest expectations of Coach John Yovicsin, who had said:

"We are really on the edge of a good year. We've been pushed off once, but we're still in there. For us, this game is the difference between a good and a great season."

Thwarted at First

Leo, who made certain that Harvard was not pushed off the edge today, ended his varsity career in a barrage of statistics, too. He scored his eighth and ninth touchdowns of the season, and became the seventh Harvard player since 1875 to score four against Yale during his career. He also became the first to score against Yale in each of his three varsity seasons.

He was thwarted for the first 15 minutes as the teams, with one ear cocked for news of Princeton and Dartmouth, battled a 30-mile wind as tenaciously as they battled each other.

The wind was so strong out of the northwest that both teams were stymied through the air. Harvard's Ric Zimmerman completed only three of 11

Continued on Page 5, Column 3

THE TYING GOAL: Joe Azzaro of Notre Dame kicks ball in last quarter to make the score 10-10. George Chatlos gets there too late to block it. Associated Press Wirephoto

Irish Gain Standoff On Late Field Goal

By JOSEPH M. SHEEHAN

Special to The New York Times

EAST LANSING, Mich., Nov. 19—Who's the nation's No. 1 college football team now?

There was no immediate, clear answer to that burning question today after Notre Dame, which had been rated No. 1, and Michigan State, which had been rated No. 2, played to a 10-10 standstill before an emotion-wracked overflow crowd of 80,011 at Spartan Stadium.

Michigan State got in its scoring punches first. On a march initiated in the first quarter, the Spartans drove 73 yards to a touchdown in 10 plays. Regis Cavender smashed over for the score from 4 yards out at 1:40 of the second period.

About 7½ minutes later, after having penetrated to Notre Dame's 25 and having been set back to the 30, Michigan State tallied again, on a 47-yard field goal by Dick Kenney, the barefooted kicker from Hawaii who also had kicked the extra point after the touchdown.

Notre Dame Strikes Back

Notre Dame retaliated after the second Michigan State score by moving 54 yards to a touchdown on three successive pass completions by Coley O'Brien, a sophomore who took over at quarterback midway in the first period after his classmate, Terry Hanratty, had been knocked out of action by a shoulder separation.

The payoff toss was a 34-yard beauty into the end zone to Bob Gladieux, who filled in at left halfback for Nick Eddy, whose previously damaged shoulder would not permit him to play.

Joe Azzaro kicked the extra point after this touchdown and also made Notre Dame's equalizing field goal, from 28 yards out, on the first play of the fourth period after Notre Dame had moved the ball from its 20 to Michigan State's 12.

Azzaro, who had made all three of his previous field goal attempts this season, had a further chance to be a hero, but he muffed it.

With six minutes to play, Tom Schoen of Notre Dame made his second successive interception of a pass by Jimmy Raye, Michigan State's slick and nimble quarterback, and ran the ball from midfield to the Michigan State 18.

But the aroused Spartan defense threw the Irish back to the 24, forcing Azzaro to try a kick from 41 yards out. The kick was long enough, but it veered right and flew wide of the posts by a considerable margin.

This long-awaited clash of unbeaten and untied titans, which undoubtedly had one of the

Continued on Page 3, Column 3

Princeton Tops Cornell; Dartmouth 40-21 Victor

Tiger Wins, 7-0

By ALLISON DANZIG

Special to The New York Times

PRINCETON, N. J., Nov. 19—Ivy League football champion in 1964 and co-champion with Dartmouth in 1963, Princeton finished in a three-way tie for the title with Harvard and Dartmouth today in defeating Cornell, 7-0, in the season's finale.

There could hardly be a more equable division of the spoils, since Princeton defeated Harvard, Harvard beat Dartmouth and the Hanoverians, the defending champions, won from the Tiger.

Following the pattern of its victories over Yale and Harvard in its previous two outings, Princeton once again won in the final quarter of a game that was overwhelmingly dominated by the defense for three quarters.

Victims of Penalties

It was the fourth successive time that the Tiger has beaten the luckless Big Red, the victim of penalties and its own fumbling.

Princeton went for its touchdown on a drive of 51 yards after recovering the second of two Cornell fumbles within the space of a few minutes. The first bobble, on the completion of a pass, killed Cornell's advance to the Tiger 20 on the first play of the final quarter, and in the third period the Big Red had gone 43 yards to the Princeton 7-yard line and failed on a 24-yard field goal attempt, after being set back 15 yards on a personal foul.

In the opening quarter, a 15-yard penalty for holding stopped Cornell after it had gone to the 28.

Dick Bracken, the sophomore tailback in the Tiger single wing formation, scored the touchdown on a 5-yard sweep. Bracken was pretty much the whole show in the 51-yard drive, breaking away repeatedly and passing to Tad Howard, the blocking quarterback, for 9 yards. The pass, the only one

Continued on Page 4, Column 6

Penn Is Beaten

By MICHAEL STRAUSS

Special to The New York Times

PHILADELPHIA, Nov. 19—Dartmouth's heavily favored shock troops displayed expected power today as they swept past Pennsylvania and won, 40-21, to retain one-third of their Ivy League football crown.

The 1965 titleholders assured themselves of at least a first-place tie with Harvard and Princeton by taking a 21-0 lead early in the second period. Thereafter, however, their attack roared and stalled intermittently.

During these inconsistent phases of the Big Green's play the Quakers did some noise-making themselves. In charge of Penn's demonstrations was Bill Creeden.

To the delight of the Quaker rooters in the crowd of 10,582 sitting on the shaded side of Franklin Field, Creeden turned in a fine performance. He set up the first touchdown with passes and the second with a 15-yard keeper. Then he pro-

Continued on Page 5, Column 6

U.S.C. UPSET, 14-7, BY U.C.L.A. ELEVEN

Dow, Filling In for Beban, Gets One Score and Sets Up 4th-Period Clincher

By BILL BECKER

Special to The New York Times

LOS ANGELES, Nov. 19—The battling Bruins of the University of California, Los Angeles, upset the University of California Trojans today, 14-7, to step right back into the Rose Bowl picture.

Sparked by a substitute quarterback, Norman Dow, the Bruins swept past the favored Trojans with two second-half touchdowns. One was a 5-yard swing around end by Dow, who was playing in place of the injured Gary Beban.

The decisive score came midway in the fourth quarter on a 21-yard run by Cornell Champion, a right halfback who took the ball on a reverse from Dow.

A crowd of 81,980 in Memorial Coliseum watched the Bruins beat the Trojans for the second consecutive season, in smoggy, shirtsleeve weather.

The victory ended the U.C.L.A. season with nine victories and one defeat, while the Trojans are 7-2 with one game left—against Notre Dame next week.

Dow Moves Bruins

While U.S.C. sewed up the Pacific Eight championship with four conference victories against one defeat, the Bruins' 3-1 league record is good enough to make them "representative."

The athletic directors of the Pacific Eight will meet Monday in San Francisco to pick the Western representative in the Rose Bowl Jan. 2. Purdue will be the Big Ten's choice for the game.

Dow led his team to 229 yards rushing against the heavy Trojan line. The Bruins' ability to control the ball in the second half turned the tide after a scoreless first half.

The Trojans' score came late in the third period after Mike Hull, a fleet fullback, ran 57 yards to the Bruin 1-yard line.

Continued on Page 9, Column 2

Football Scores

East

Bowling Green 62	Temple 20
Boston College 14	Mass. 7
Boston Univ. 30	Rhode Island 14
Bridgeport 14	Montclair St. 0
Buffalo 25	Youngstown 16
Clarion 28	West Chester 26
Colgate 26	Rutgers 7
Columbia 40	Brown 33
Cornell J. V. 27	Princeton J. V. 22
Dartmouth 40	Pennsylvania 21
Delaware 45	Bucknell 20
Drexel Tech 28	Albright 27
Findlay 34	Susquehanna 20
Frank. & Marshall 14	Ursinus 6
Grove City 34	Thiel 0
Harvard 17	Yale 0
Holy Cross 16	Connecticut 0
Lafayette 16	Lehigh 0
Lebanon Valley 31	PMC Colleges 6
Maryland St. 18	So. Conn. St. 13
Moravian 14	Muhlenberg 7
Penn St. 48	Pittsburgh 24
Princeton 7	Cornell 0
Swarthmore 42	Haverford 6
Syracuse 34	West Virginia 7
Upsala 10	Wagner 7
Western Maryland 35	Johns Hopkins 7
Westminster (Pa.) 9	Mt. Union 7

South

Abilene Christian 28	San Angelo St. 18
Alcorn 52	Bishop 18
Arkansas St. 20	Trinity (Tex.) 7
Arkansas Tech 33	Southeast Mo. 21
Duke 41	North Carolina 25
Eastern Kentucky 14	Tampa 6
Fayetteville St. 22	Winston-Salem St. 18
Florida St. 28	Wake Forest 0
Georgetown (Ky.) 20	Emory & Henry 19
Hampden-Sydney 15	Randolph-Macon 14
Howard Payne 20	McMurry 0
Jackson St. 29	Miss. Valley St. 12
J. C. Smith 13	Livingstone 13
Louisville 29	Tulsa 18
Memphis St. 26	Cincinnati 14
Mississippi 34	Vanderbilt 0
No. Carolina St. 23	Clemson 14
Northern Michigan 7	Quantico Marines 7

Continued on Page 7, Column 7

AMBEROID SURGES FROM LAST TO WIN

Colt Takes Aqueduct Stakes by Length and Quarter—Exhibitionist Is Second

By JOE NICHOLS

Very few players in the crowd of 40,745 would have given anything for the chances of Reginald Webster's Amberoid early in the running of the $58,500 Queens County Handicap at Aqueduct yesterday. But those who had the courage to back the horse, before the 1⅛-mile race got under way, enjoyed a thrill and a profit when it was all over.

The space-eating Amberoid, under the guidance of Wally Blum, contributed a splendid exhibition in moving up from last in the field of a dozen to take the victory by a length and a quarter.

In second place came Mrs. Ethel D. Jacobs's Exhibitionist, with Isidor Bieber's Flag Raiser third. Those two ran as an

Continued on Page 8, Column 2

Tartan Horse First On Tartan Surface At Tropical Track

By STEVE CADY

Special to The New York Times

MIAMI, Nov. 19 — Dave Hidalgo, who won the third race with Barricado at $5.80 for $2, said his horse handled the track "nice and smooth."

Cecil Savis said his horse "took hold real good, even when he got tired." Jim Ruybali reported the track had no "give," that a rider would have to "play it by ear" until he and his mounts got used to it. And Barry Pearl said flatly and rather eloquently, "in my current frame of mind, I wouldn't want to ride on it again."

These were the quotes by jockeys today at Tropical Park, where the divided Hurricane Handicap got lost in the shuffle of thoroughbred racing's first pari-mutuel contest on the bouncy, non-skid, drip-dry synthetic track called Tartan.

A Hollywood script writer couldn't have come up with a better scenario than the one that developed in the debut of the $1-million Tartan surface, a 9/10-mile oval that circles the

Continued on Page 9, Column 6

205 BY DICKINSON LEADS AT HOUSTON

Palmer Second, Stroke Back—Geiberger and Goalby Tied for Third at 207

By LINCOLN A. WERDEN

Special to The New York Times

HOUSTON, Nov. 19—Gardner Dickinson, a 130-pounder, found himself challenging golf's heavyweights as the third-round leader in the $110,000 Houston Champions International tournament today. With a 54-hole total of 205, the slim professional from Lost Tree Village, Fla., held a stroke edge over Arnold Palmer.

As Dickinson scored a two-under-par 69 over the Champions course, he assumed the lead outright that he had shared with George Knudson of Toronto after yesterday's second round. Dickinson closed with birdies on the 17th and 18th to hold off Palmer's rush to the front. Palmer had been in a tie for fifth with seven others after 36 holes.

Palmer Three-Putts Once

Palmer, the winner with Jack Nicklaus of the Canada Cup team honors last Sunday in Tokyo, shot a 68 over the 7,118-yard par-71 course.

"It doesn't make any difference, no matter where I am, putting is my problem," said Palmer. "I had the same lack of confidence last week in Japan."

Palmer three-putted only once today for the sixth time in three days. After three birdies on the front half, he had nine straight pars, as repeated attempts to sink birdie putts failed.

Dickinson worried instead about his driving. As soon as he signed his scorecard, he went to the practice tee to cure a tendency to hook. Dickinson drove into the trees at five holes.

While Dickinson and Palmer were holding the attention of a gallery estimated at 16,000, Al Geiberger, the Professional Golfers' Association titleholder,

Continued on Page 1[illegible], Column 2

Columbia Scores Over Brown, 40-38

By DEANE McGOWEN

It was even wilder than expected — the Columbia-Brown Ivy League football game that was played before 5,187 thoroughly chilled fans in Baker Field yesterday.

In this battle to escape the league cellar, the Lions won, 40-38, after trailing by 18 points in the first quarter and by 19 points at the outset of the second.

It appeared that John McLaughry's club would finally get its first league triumph of the season, but that was before Martin Domres, the Lions' cool, poised quarterback, put Jim O'Connor to work.

O'Connor, a 19-year-old sophomore from Chicopee Falls,

Continued on Page 4, Column 4

Texas Tech Downs Arkansas, 21 to 16

By United Press International

LUBBOCK, Tex., Nov. 19—Texas Tech sent sixth-ranked Arkansas to a 21-16 defeat today that all but eliminated the Razorbacks' Cotton Bowl hopes.

The Red Raiders went into the game with a 1-5 Southwest Conference won-lost mark and the league's worst defensive record. But they posted their first victory over Arkansas in the 10-game series between the schools.

The decision dropped Arkansas to a mark of eight victories and one defeat for the season and 5-2 in Conference play, a half-game behind Southern Methodist, which needs only a victory over Texas Christian

Continued on Page 7, Column 3

United Press International Telephoto

WHAT, NO DUST? Not during the third race at Miami's Tropical Park, anyway. It was the first race ever to be run on Tartan, the new, non-skid, synthetic track covering.

NOTRE DAME TIES MICH. STATE, 10-10

Continued From Page 1

largest television audiences ever attracted by a sports event, was defense-dominated, as had been expected.

Michigan State had no other scoring opportunities other than those on which it capitalized and only once, other than on its scoring drives, did Notre Dame threaten. That was in the first period, when the Irish reached the home 37 on a 25-yard pass from Hanratty to Gladieux.

This march floundered on the 34 when rushes by Larry Conjar and Hanratty picked up only 4 yards and a pass by Hanratty missed connections.

Hanratty was injured on his running play. Charlie Thornhill, Michigan State's fine linebacker, slammed him down hard and 283-pound Bubba Smith, in hot pursuit, fell atop him.

For what it was worth, Michigan State had the better of the battle of the statistics. The Spartans had the edge in first downs, 13 to 10; in rushing, 142 yards net to 91; in passing, 142 yards to 128, and in total yards gained, 284 to 219.

But the Spartans gained most of their yardage in their own territory, in which they were kept pinned for much of the game by the superior punting of Kevin Hardy, Notre Dame's left-footed, 270-pound tackle.

While Raye could not keep his team moving consistently in attacking territory, he did a magnificent job of extricating the Spartans from sticky situations.

In the third quarter, for instance, Michigan State fumbled away the ball on its first play after the second-half kickoff. Notre Dame, in possession on the home 30, went to the air immediately, but the Spartans got the ball back right away when Jess Phillips picked off a pass by O'Brien intended for Rocky Bleier on the Michigan State 2.

This was a chance for the Irish to bottle up the Spartans —sit on them and play for a break.

But Raye, carrying three times himself, worked the ball out to a first down on the 13, passed to Gene Washington for another first down on the 28, and Notre Dame's territorial advantage was lost.

Michigan State's junior quarterback piloted his team out of danger again the next time the Spartans had the ball. Another booming punt by Hardy forced Michigan State back to its 5, and the Spartans once more were in trouble.

Raye met the challenge by tossing a 41-yard pass to Washington on first down and the Spartans were out of the pocket again.

Long Pass Starts Spartans

Another long first-down pass from Raye to Washington, this one for 42 yards, started Michigan State rolling to its first touchdown on the Spartans' third turn with the ball in the first period.

This play put Michigan State on Notre Dame's 30. Clint Jones and Raye punched out a first down on the 18 and, after the teams changed goals for the second quarter, Cavender roared 10 yards up the middle for another.

From the Notre Dame 8, Cavender bulled through to the 5, Jones hit over his left side for a yard and Cavender found a hole inside Notre Dame's left tackle and crashed through for the score.

Michigan State gave Notre Dame's vaunted tackles—Pete Duranko and Hardy—a working-over on this drive, but thereafter the Spartans were able to make only sporadic progress on the ground.

United Press International Telephotos

SPECIAL DELIVERY—ONE TOUCHDOWN: Regis Cavender gets 6 points for Spartans in second quarter of game

STATISTICS OF THE GAME

	M. S.	N. D.
First downs	13	10
Rushing yardage	142	91
Passing yardage	142	128
Passes	7-20	8-24
Interceptions by	1	3
Punts	8-38	8-42
Fumbles lost	1	1
Yards penalized	32	5

The next time it had the ball, on its 18, Michigan State began the drive to its field goal, which was a continuous drive only in a manner of speaking.

The slippery Raye got the Spartans moving with a 30-yard rollout sprint around end to his 48. Dwight Lee then broke around his left end for 16 yards to the Notre Dame 36.

After a short gain by Cavender, Jim Lynch, Notre Dame's stalwart linebacker, intercepted a pass by Raye. But before the play was over, Michigan State was back in possession, Jones tackling Lynch and knocking him loose from the ball.

A penalty set the Spartans back to the Notre Dame 43, but Raye passed to Washington for a first down on the 27. There the Irish braced and, after incurring a 5-yard motion penalty, Michigan State lined up on the Irish 30 for Kenny's field-goal attempt.

His boot split the uprights and gave him a total of 19 field goals for his three-year varsity career.

Tom Quinn's 38-yard return of the kickoff that followed Kenney's field goal put Notre Dame on the way to its touchdown. From his own 46, O'Brien opened up immediately.

Jim Seymour, Notre Dame's celebrated sophomore end (who didn't catch a pass today), dropped O'Brien's first throw. The next three connected.

Gladieux circled out of the backfield to take the first for a first down on Michigan State's 42. Bleier, from wingback, took the second for an 8-yard gain.

Then came the bomb to Gladieux. Again circling out of the backfield, but running a deeper pattern, Eddy's stand-in got behind the Spartans' deep defenders and O'Brien laid the ball in his arms in the end zone over a desperate lunge by Phillips, the safetyman.

O'Brien's passing also figured prominently in Notre Dame's drive to its field goal. Completions to Bleier for 10 yards, Conjar for 16, and Dave Haley for 24 swiftly moved the Irish from their 20 to Michigan State's 30.

Spartan Resistance Firm

After a Michigan State offside, Haley and Conjar punched out another first down on the home 17. But against Michigan State's stiffening resistance, Notre Dame could get no farther than the 10. It was from there, on the right-side hashmark, that they set up Azzaro for his field goal.

For the rest of the way, neither team made any substantial penetration of rival territory under its own momentum.

Notre Dame had its shot at victory on the Schoen interception—but missed the field goal—and then decided to settle for the tie, running out the clock with four running plays after getting the ball for the last time on its 35 with a minute and a half to play.

This was the end of the 1966 trail for Michigan State, Big Ten champion for the second straight year. Notre Dame has one game to play, against Southern California next Saturday.

The Line-up

MICHIGAN STATE (10)

Left Ends—Brenner, C. Smith, Chatlos.
Left Tackles—Przybycki, Ruminski, Bailey.
Left Guards—Conti, Bradley, Gallinaugh.
Centers—L. Smith, Ranieri, Redd, Richardson, Brawley.
Right Guards—Techlin, Pruiett, Jordan.
Right Tackles—West, McLoud, Hoag.
Right Ends—Washington, Haynes, Thornhill.
Quarterbacks—Raye, Wedemeyer, Kinney, Webster, Super.
Left Halfbacks—Lee, Berlinski, Summers, Lawson.
Right Halfbacks—C. Jones, Waters, Armstrong, J. Jones, Ware.
Fullbacks—Cavender, Phillips, Garrett, [illegible].

NOTRE DAME (10)

Left Ends—Seymour, Rhoads.
Left Tackles—Seiler, Duranko.
Left Guards—Regner, Hardy.
Centers—Goeddeke, Monty, Kelly, [illegible].
Right Guards—Swatland, Pergine.
Right Tackles—Kuechenberg, Lynch.
Right Ends—Gmitter, Stenger, Horney.
Quarterbacks—Hanratty, O'Brien, Martin, Azzaro.
Left Halfbacks—Gladieux, O'Leary, Bergener, Criniti.
Right Halfbacks—Bleier, Smithberger, Quinn, Haley.
Fullbacks—Conjar, Schoen, Dushiney.

Michigan State	0	10	0	0—10
Notre Dame	0	7	0	3—10

M.S.—Cavander, 4, run (Kenney, kick).
M.S.—FG., Kenney, 47.
N.D.—Gladieux, 34, pass from O'Brien (Azzaro, kick).
N.D.—FG., Azzaro, 28.
Attendance—80,011.

KENNEY'S KICKING FEARED BY IRISH

Notre Dame Refuses to Risk Setback on a Field Goal by Giving Up Ball

By DAVE ANDERSON

Special to The New York Times

EAST LANSING, Mich., Nov. 19—On his way out of Spartan Stadium, a Michigan State alumnus with a green-and-white blanket over his arm, snarled, "No guts, Parseghian had no guts."

It was a theory shared by probably all the Michigan State rooters today following the 10-10 tie with Notre Dame. In the closing seconds, the Irish had played it safe, a strategy that several Spartan players later would criticize as "sissy."

The question for Ara Parseghian was obvious: Why hadn't he ordered a possible touchdown pass on the last series?

In the low-ceilinged Notre Dame dressing room, Parseghian, still wearing his blue wool coach's sweater, had his back against a blackboard as two dozen newsmen jammed around him. As the newsmen came and went the question was asked. And every time Parseghian answered:

"It had to do with (Dick) Kenney's ability as a field-goal kicker. If it was early in the fourth quarter it would have been different, but we weren't going to give up the ball deep in our own territory and take a risk on losing the game after battling like we did."

With 1 minute 24 seconds to play, Notre Dame had the ball, first down on its own 30-yard line.

Three running plays moved the ball to the 39. On fourth down, Coley O'Brien, the quarterback who had replaced the injured Terry Hanratty, sneaked for a first down on the 41. On the next play, O'Brien was nailed for a 7-yard loss before he could pass. On the final play, with six seconds to go, O'Brien kept the ball and ran to the 39 but the gun sounded.

"At that stage," Parseghian said, "your strategy is dictated by the fact that you don't want to lose the game."

But why, on fourth down, had he risked O'Brien sneaking a yard for a first down? If the play had failed, the Spartans would have taken over and Kenney, presumably, the barefooted place-kicker, would have had an opportunity to make a field-goal from 56 yards, as remote as it was.

"We wanted to maintain possession," Parseghian explained. "At that time, the lesser risk was the quarterback sneak. If we had punted, we might have had a bad snap, or the punt blocked, or a long punt-return. The sneak was the lesser of the evils. And so was the possibility of Kenney being able to make a field-goal from that range."

On the last play, however, why didn't O'Brien go for the "bomb," a possible touchdown pass?

"Interception almost cost Michigan State the game," Parseghian said, "we weren't going to give it away cheaply."

Had he thought that a tie might maintain Notre Dame's No. 1 ranking in the national polls?

"The most remote thing in my thinking before the game was a tie," the coach replied. "I never thought about it. As for the polls, that's for the pollsters to decide."

Parseghian, ironically, votes in the United Press International's coaches poll. The Associated Press poll is a survey of football writers throughout the nation.

Elsewhere in the Notre Dame dressing room, the players did not appear disappointed by the tie salvaged despite three key injuries.

Nick Eddy, the breakaway halfback, disclosed that he had aggravated his ailing right shoulder when he tripped getting off the train that brought the team here yesterday. To avoid falling, he jerked his arm up quickly, slamming it against the steel car.

"All the News That's Fit to Print"

The New York Times.

LATE CITY EDITION

U. S. Weather Bureau Report (Page 29) forecasts: Fair today; increasingly cloudy tonight. Possible rain tomorrow. Temp. Range: 37—28; yesterday: 49—37.

VOL. CXVI..No. 39,804. NEW YORK, MONDAY, JANUARY 16, 1967. 10 CENTS

THANT ASKS ISRAEL AND SYRIA TO ACT TO PREVENT CLASH

Cites Military Build-up at Border and Voices Fear of an Imminent Outbreak

TRUCE SESSION SOUGHT

Israelis Say Syrians Fired on a Gunboat Escorting Galilee Sea Fishermen

By KATHLEEN McLAUGHLIN
Special to The New York Times

UNITED NATIONS, N. Y., Jan. 15 — Secretary General Thant moved today to lessen what he said was an imminent threat of a large-scale clash of military forces on the border between Syria and Israel.

He sent urgent appeals to both Governments to restrain their forces from any action that might produce such a conflict. He also asked them to accept "without delay or preconditions" a proposal for an emergency meeting of the Israel-Syria Mixed Armistice Commission and notified them that he had proposed reinforcement of United Nations military observers on both sides of the line.

[In Jerusalem, an Israeli spokesman reported that Syrians had opened fire on an Israeli gunboat escorting fishing vessels on the Sea of Galilee and that the gunboat had returned the fire. He said there had been no Israeli casualties.]

Mr. Thant also told Israel and Syria that he had taken "the unusual step" of immediately informing the members of the Security Council individually, as well as the Council itself, of the action he had taken. He requested from both Governments "a prompt and cooperative response."

Acts on Truce Reports

Mr. Thant's communications to the two governments were included in his message to the Security Council, which was made public this afternoon. Mr. Thant told the Council he had acted after reports this morning from Gen. Odd Bull, Chief of Staff of the United Nations Truce Supervision Organization.

These reports, he said, were "of such a disturbing nature as to impel me to communicate with Israel and Syria urgently."

The reports told of a build-up of heavy arms, armored vehicles and military personnel in the area within demilitarized zones on both sides of the line, the Secretary General said.

"It is clear," he added, "that the situation threatens to erupt at any moment into a large-scale clash of military forces in overt violation of Security Council

Continued on Page 12, Column 4

HANOI DENIES AIM IS TO ANNEX SOUTH

Program of North Is Found to Differ From Vietcong's

Following is the sixth article by an assistant managing editor of The New York Times summing up observations on his recent visit to North Vietnam.

By HARRISON E. SALISBURY
Special to The New York Times

HONG KONG, Jan. 11 — About 10 days ago Le Duan, First Secretary of the North Vietnamese Workers' (Communist) party, made a speech to army cadets, outlining the basis of party policy.

The party, he said, stands for "socialism in the North, democracy in the South."

His declaration was the talk of Hanoi, not because he had enunciated a new line, but because he had found it essential to restate the policy at this particular moment.

The party secretary's name is not well known outside North Vietnam. But there it is regarded as quite possibly even more important in party circles than that of Premier Pham Van Dong.

There are some who believe that if President Ho Chi Minh were to die, he would be succeeded either by Mr. Le Duan or another figure equally little known in the West, Truong

Continued on Page 10, Column 3

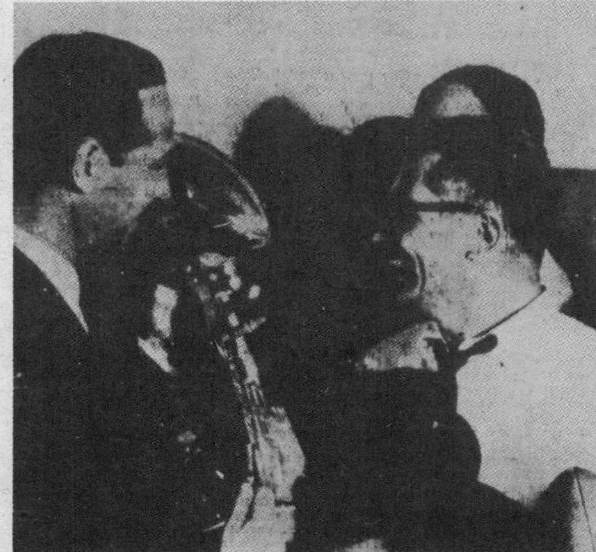

Associated Press Wirephoto

GREEN BAY'S PRIZE: Coach Vince Lombardi of Packers, right, receives trophy from Pete Rozelle, football commissioner, after victory over Kansas City in the Super Bowl.

Maoists See Turning Point In Ending Shanghai Revolt

Special to The New York Times

HONG KONG, Jan. 15—The forces of Mao Tse-tung, Chairman of the Chinese Communist party's Central Committee, and Defense Minister Lin Piao asserted today that the success of pro-Mao workers in crushing an opposition "counterattack" in Shanghai showed that the "cultural revolution" had reached a new turning point.

The assertion was made in an editorial in Hung Chi, a periodical published in the name of the Central Committee. It appeared to be an effort to rally the pro Mao forces against opposition elements.

"The principal aim of the proletarian cultural revolution is for proletarian forces to seize power from a handful of officials within the party who are following the capitalist road," the editorial declared, according to the Peking radio.

Purge of Foes Sought

The cultural revolution is the name of the campaign launched by Mr. Mao and Mr. Lin to purge their enemies and enforce their policies.

Supporters of Chairman Mao were urged yesterday to unite in a "great alliance" capable of taking control of the party and the nation's economy.

Hsinhua, the Chinese Communist press agency, reported today that "revolutionary rebel groups in all parts of China" were swiftly forming themselves into this alliance to "launch a general attack on the latest counteroffensive of the bourgeois reactionary line."

The possibility that the Red Guards, a militant youth movement formed by the Mao-Lin faction last year, might become more active was raised by an editorial in the Peking newspaper Jenmin Jih Pao today, which declared that their deeds had "shaken the world." The editorial called on the Red Guards to "destroy the old world and create a new one."

The pro-Mao Red Guards launched an attack on "bourgeois" persons and influences last year. Opposition elements

Continued on Page 3, Column 1

CHINA SAID TO SET 3 WAR CONDITIONS

French Editor Says Peking Will Stay Out of Vietnam If U.S. Observes Terms

By The Associated Press

WASHINGTON, Jan. 15—A French editor says that Communist China has set conditions for remaining out of the Vietnam war and that the United States is observing them.

René Dabernat, foreign editor of the magazine Paris-Match, says the Chinese assurances were relayed through the French Foreign Ministry.

The State Department declined to comment on the Dabernat statement made in a copyright interview in U. S. News & World Report.

"Last spring," Mr. Dabernat said, "a diplomat from the Red Chinese Embassy in Paris asked the Quai d'Orsay [the Foreign Ministry] to let Washington know that Peking would not enter the war on three conditions. These were that the U.S. not invade Red China, that it not invade North Vietnam and that it not bomb the dikes of the Red River in North Vietnam."

"France transmitted the message" he continued. "I verified this in Washington."

Signal to Peking

Mr. Dabernat added that a short time later President Johnson and other top-level United States officials "gave the necessary signals to Peking in various public speeches to show that they agreed to these conditions."

"I have to point out, however," Mr. Dabernat wrote "that all this happened before the Red Guards started running wild in China."

"Then," Mr. Dabernat wrote, "after the Manila conference Communist China was informed through diplomatic channels that President Johnson wanted to bring about a process of stabilization and peace in the Pacific, if only Red China did not try to use force to extend its influence in Asia."

At the Manila conference last October, South Vietnam and its

Continued on Page 5, Column 6

NEWS INDEX

The News Summary and Index is on Page 2; ships and weather on Page 29.

GREEN BAY WINS FOOTBALL TITLE

National League Champions Beat Kansas City, 35-10, in Super Bowl Game

By WILLIAM N. WALLACE
Special to The New York Times

LOS ANGELES, Jan. 15—Bryan Bartlett (Bart) Starr, the quarterback for the Green Bay Packers, led his team to a 35-10 victory over the Kansas City Chiefs today in the first professional football game between the champions of the National and American Leagues.

Doubt about the outcome disappeared in the third quarter when Starr's pretty passes made mere Indians out of the American League Chiefs and Green Bay scored twice.

Those 14 points stretched Green Bay's lead to 28-10 and during the final quarter many of the spectators in the crowd of 63,036 left Memorial Coli-

Continued on Page 32, Column 1

41 Held by Vietcong Reported Murdered

By The Associated Press

SAIGON, South Vietnam, Monday, Jan. 16 — Military sources said today that the Vietcong had shot and killed 41 of 48 prisoners at a Mekong River delta prison camp after the site was discovered by South Vietnamese troops.

United States mission officials said they were investigating and seeking further information. Officials said they assumed all the prisoners were Vietnamese, but there were no further details.

The killings were said to have occurred yesterday about 110 miles southwest of Saigon as Government troops approached the camp, which was guarded by Vietcong.

Of the seven other persons at the camp, two were reported to have been wounded and the five taken to 21st Division head-

Continued on Page 9, Column 4

U.S. OUTPUT IN '66 UP 5.4 PER CENT TO $739.5-BILLION

Nation's Total Product Tops Average Growth Rate—Military Items Mount

By EDWIN L. DALE Jr.
Special to The New York Times

WASHINGTON, Jan. 15—The nation's total output, after correcting for higher prices, rose 5.4 per cent last year, the Commerce Department reported today.

Today's report gave the preliminary figures for the gross national product, the output of all goods and services, for the fourth quarter and for all 1966.

The fourth quarter rise was $13.8-billion to an annual rate, seasonally adjusted, of $759.1-billion. Of the increase, $3.5-billion was in military purchases by the Government.

For the year as a whole the nation's product was $739.5-billion, $58.3-billion or 8.5 per cent above 1965. However, prices for the nation's entire output were about 3 per cent higher in 1966 than in 1965, leaving real growth at 5.4 per cent.

This was still far above the nation's long-term average growth. Last year's pace, it is widely agreed, cannot be maintained.

How Total Is Computed

The gross national measures output through purchases—by consumers, by business for investment in machines and structures, by government and by foreigners.

The most striking feature of 1966 was a rise of $10-billion over 1965 in the Government's national defense purchases. By the fourth quarter of last year these purchases, (which include only deliveries of finished military equipment as well as personnel costs) had reached an annual rate of $65.5-billion, up from $50-billion in 1964 before United States troops were so active in the war in Vietnam.

A major worrisome element of the fourth quarter figures was a huge rise in business inventories. They went up at an annual rate of $14.4-billion—or $15.6-billion, counting only nonfarm inventories. This was the

Continued on Page 70, Column 6

Eaton Joins Rockefellers To Spur Trade With Reds

Cleveland and New York Financiers to Set Up an East-West Exchange

By ROBERT E. BEDINGFIELD

An alliance of family fortunes linking Wall Street and the Midwest is going to try to build economic bridges between the free world and Communist Europe.

The International Basic Economy Corporation, controlled by the Rockefeller brothers, and Tower International, Inc., headed by Cyrus S. Eaton Jr., Cleveland financier, plan to cooperate in promoting trade between the Iron Curtain countries, including the Soviet Union, and the United States, Canada and Latin America.

The I.B.E.C. was organized in 1947 under the principal direction of Nelson A. Rockefeller, now New York's Governor. It was organized as an investment company specializing in enterprises in underdeveloped nations. The company already has interests in 29 foreign countries,

The New York Times

Cyrus S. Eaton Jr.

but none is in the Communist bloc.

Tower International is a wholly owned subsidiary of Tower Industries, a partnership

Continued on Page 67, Column 1

City Hospital Chief Admits Unapproved Experiments

By JOHN KIFNER

The Commissioner of Hospitals conceded yesterday that some unauthorized experiments had been carried out on patients in city hospitals without his knowledge or that of the hospitals' medical boards.

"This has come to my attention in the last few days," said Commissioner Joseph V. Terenzio. The department requires that approval for experiments in municipal hospitals be obtained from the Commissioner.

Mr. Terenzio did not say what type of experiments were involved. However, officials in his department said later that the experimentation might have involved the administering of new drugs to patients under private grants from drug companies, statistical studies, and studies of treatment and services outside the hospital.

"With a big system like this there's bound to be irregularity," the Commissioner said. "Sometimes people just don't think of it, and just haven't bothered to comply with the directives."

In other developments in the hospital dispute, State Senator Seymour R. Thaler said he intended to introduce legislation to give community groups a voice in the administration of city hospitals, and Mayor Lindsay issued a statement defending the controversial system under which private hospital administer city hospitals.

Senator Thaler, who charged last week that there was widespread experimentation on patients without their consent, continued his criticism yesterday, but said he was worried that he was destroying patients' "faith in what is second-class medicine, but is better than no medicine."

The Hospital Department issued a memorandum recently repeating a standing order that the Commissioner be informed of all research activities.

The normal procedure, Mr.

Continued on Page 70, Column 1

Joseph A. Harris for The New York Times

GLEAMING ALGIERS: Amid whitewashed apartment houses, Algerian men sit in Place des Martyrs near kasbah

Algeria Under Boumediene Struggles for Stability

By HENRY TANNER
Special to The New York Times

ALGIERS, Jan. 7 — When Col. Houari Boumediene removed President Ahmed Ben Bella in a military coup on June 19, 1965, the Algerian Army became the "guardian of government."

The Cabinet is still made up of civilian ministers, some of whom have real authority and considerable independence. But the ultimate power rests with the 24-man Revolutionary Council, made up chiefly of active army officers. The council acts as a super-government, initiating basic policies and setting the framework for Cabinet action. Colonel Boumediene is the President of the council and presides also at Cabinet meetings. The National Assembly is suspended.

The army's ambition, in taking over from Mr. Ben Bella, was to halt a gradual economic and administrative deterioration that had taken place since independence. It wanted to impose order, discipline and the kind of political stability that would enable the Government to meet the problems of building a nation.

Today, more than a year and a half later, the army-imposed stability endures. There have been no spectacular achievements. But most Algerians and foreigners agree that there is a new mood in the country and that for the first time since independence, an effort is being made to give Algeria serious and reasonably efficient government.

The principal question now is whether the army will continue to assure political stability.

Cliques and rivalries in the army threaten its unity.

Some of the members of the

Continued on Page 12, Column 4

PRESIDENT TO ASK $3.2-BILLION IN AID; FACES HARD TEST

Difficulties Expected in Both Houses, Although Figure Is Below '66 Request

OTHER CUTBACKS SEEN

Congress Leaders Assert Great Society Programs Are Also in Trouble

By FELIX BELAIR Jr.
Special to The New York Times

WASHINGTON, Jan. 15 — President Johnson is expected to ask Congress in his Budget Message later this month for about $3.2-billion to finance economic and military foreign aid in the fiscal year beginning July 1.

The amount would be below the $3.39-billion he requested a year ago but significantly more than the $2.94-billion appropriated by Congress. For this reason, among others, the request is expected to encounter determined opposition in the Senate and House.

Similar difficulty for Mr. Johnson's Great Society programs was also predicted today by Congressional leaders.

$2.5-Billion Economic Aid

The President's aid request for the new year would include nearly $2.5-billion for economic development loans, technical assistance and other grants. This is about the same amount the President requested for the current fiscal year but substantially more than the $2.14-billion approved in the final appropriation.

For military assistance programs, the President is expected to ask for about $700-million. This compares with last year's asking figure of $917-million and an appropriation of $790-million. But this reduction would reflect the transfer of military aid to Laos as well as Vietnam to the regular defense budget.

Military aid to Vietnam was shifted to the defense appropriation for the first time last year when it was running about $630-million annually. The amount going to Laos is a classified figure, but it is believed to exceed $100-million.

A Foregone Conclusion

A smaller economic aid program in the new fiscal year is a foregone conclusion even if Congress should do the unexpected and appropriate the full amount asked by the President. After a 13 per cent cut in funds for the current year, William S. Gaud, the aid administrator, complained that the Congressional action had been "pretty hard to swallow."

But he managed it because of a $320-million cushion resulting from the suspension of all economic and military aid to India and Pakistan following the border war between those countries. The money was carried over into this year's economic aid money but has now been spent or committed.

This was one reason why the Agency for International Development requested an even larger economic budget for the new year than the President sent up a year ago. This was

Continued on Page 2, Column 3

Welfare Strike Set, But Talks Continue

A strike by 7,500 city welfare Department workers was scheduled to begin at 7 A.M. today.

Although negotiations between the city and the Social Service Employes Union went on into the early morning hours, a union spokesman said at midnight, "We don't see how picket lines can be avoided."

Union leaders said that they would call a membership ratification meeting as quickly as possible if an agreement was reached, but that picketing would start automatically at 7 o'clock.

A strike by the caseworkers, homemakers, and children's counselors represented by the union would seriously affect the 600,000 persons who receive welfare assistance.

The negotiations were marred shortly after midnight by the discovery by union negotiators

Continued on Page 30, Column 7

Packers Rout Chiefs With 21-Point 2d Half and Win Super Bowl Game, 35-10

STARR COMPLETES 16 OF 23 PASSES

2 Go to McGee for Scores —Chiefs Pass Midfield Only Once in 2d Half

Continued From Page 1, Col. 4

seum, which had been only two-thirds filled.

The outcome served to settle the curiosity of the customers, who paid from $6 to $12 for tickets, and a television audience estimated at 60 million, regarding the worth of the Chiefs.

The final score was an honest one, meaning it correctly reflected what went on during the game. The great interest had led to naming the event the Super Bowl, but the contest was more ordinary than super.

McGee Catches 7 Passes

Starr, methodical and unruffled as ever, completed 16 of 23 passes, six producing first downs on key third-down plays. Seven completions went to Max McGee, a 34-year-old substitute end who was in action only because Boyd Dowler, the regular, was hurt on the game's sixth play.

McGee scored two of Green Bay's five touchdowns, the first one after an outstanding one-handed, hip-high catch of a pass thrown slightly behind him.

The Packers, who had been favored by two touchdowns, knew they were in a challenging game for at least half of the 2½-hour contest.

Kansas City played very well in the first two quarters and the half-time score, 14-10, made the teams just about even. Green Bay's offense was sluggish. Kansas City had stopped the Packer rushing game and Starr had not exploited the Chiefs' defensive men — Fred Williamson and Willie Mitchell —who looked vulnerable. Bart was to take care of that matter in the second half.

The Chiefs, with Lenny Dawson running the offense at quarterback, had found they could pass on Green Bay, so three times the team was in scoring range. Out of that came one touchdown, scored by the fullback, Curtis McClinton, on a 7-yard pass from Dawson, and a 31-yard field goal by Mike Mercer.

Packers Close the Doors

But that was all for Kansas City. In the second half the mighty Packer defense shut out the Chiefs, who were in the Green Bay half of the field only once—for one play. And they were only four yards into Packer territory.

The Packers changed their defensive tactics for the second half. They had not blitzed their linebackers during the first two periods and the four rushing linemen were unable to get at Dawson.

But the blitz came in the third period and Dawson found himself harassed.

Three times he was dropped for losses and once, under blitzing pressure, he threw a weak pass that Willie Wood intercepted for Green Bay and ran back 50 yards to the Kansas City 5-yard line.

Elijah Pitts, the halfback, scored on first down from the 5, running off left tackle behind a power block from Bob Skoronski, a tackle. That gave the Packers a 21-10 lead and they were in command for good.

The pass rush that led to Wood's interception was the key play. The Chiefs and Dawson never recovered. The Kansas City quarterback later left the field and Pete Beathard took his place in the fourth quarter.

Richest Sports Event

For their efforts the 40 Packer players won $15,000 each, with $7,500 going to each Chief. Gate receipts were estimated at $750,000 and the two television networks — the Columbia Broadcasting System and the National Broadcasting Company — paid $1-million apiece for the TV rights. So this was a $2,750,000 event, the richest for any American team sports event.

Starr was worth every cent of his $15,000. In the first period he took his team 80 yards in six quick plays for the opening score. The sixth play, on third down, was the 37-yard pass to McGee on which Max made his great catch.

Kansas City tied the score at 7-7 in the second quarter with a six-play, 66-yard drive featuring three passes by Dawson to Mike Garrett, Otis Taylor and McClinton, the one to McClinton for a touchdown.

Starr connected on a 64-yard touchdown pass play to Carroll Dale (on third down), but a Packer lineman was illegally in motion and the play was called back. That failed to bother Starr, who after 11 subsequent plays had the Packers over the Kansas City goal line.

It was a beautiful series of plays. On four third-down situations, Starr passed successfully for the first down. The score was made from 14 yards out by hard-running Jim Taylor on a sweep behind blocking by the guards, Fred Thurston and Jerry Kramer.

Just before the half, Kansas City drove to the Green Bay 31, but a pass to Garrett failed to pick up a first down and Mercer kicked a field goal that cut the N.F.L. team's lead to 14-10.

In the second half Starr concentrated on Mitchell, the cornerback who had had so much trouble covering McGee and Dale. Bart had great protection and on two touchdown drives that featured the pass, he probed at Mitchell's position successfully five times.

On these drives, one of 56 yards in the third quarter and one of 80 yards in the fourth, Starr completed seven of eight passes with cool precision. The Chiefs were helpless to stop him.

The first score was made by McGee from 13 yards out. He casually bobbled the ball, then caught it for six points, performing as if he were back in Green Bay during a routine practice on a Wednesday afternoon. McGee had caught only four passes during Green Bay's regular 14-game season.

The second touchdown went to Pitts, who slid off left tackle from a yard out as the Packer line closed down to the inside.

The Green Bay execution was as impeccable as ever. The only mistake was a harmless interception by Mitchell of a pass by Starr. It was the first interception against Starr since last Oct. 16. He had thrown 173 passes without an interception.

The Packer defense held the elusive Garrett to only 17 yards and Kansas City's offense had a net gain of only 239 yards. At the end the Packers were playing substitutes, but Paul Hornung never got in the game.

The Super Bowl games will now go on year after year, but it may be some time before an American League team will be good enough to win one, especially if the National League champion comes from Green Bay.

Associated Press Wirephoto

PULLING IT IN: Max McGee of Packers snares first-quarter pass from Bart Starr as Willie Mitchell (22) and Fred Williamson try to stop him on the Chiefs' 20-yard line.

GREEN BAY (35)

Ends—Dale, Fleming, Davis, Aldridge, Long, Anderson, B. Brown.
Tackles—Skoronski, Gregg, Kostelnik, Jordan, Wright, Weatherwax.
Guards—Thurston, Kramer, Gillingham.
Centers—Curry, Bowman.
Linebackers—D. Robinson, Nitschke, Caffey, Crutcher.
Quarterbacks—Starr, Bratkowski.
Offensive Backs—E. Pitts, J. Taylor, Dowler, McGee, Anderson, Mack, Vandersea, Grabowski.
Defensive Backs—Jeter, Adderly, T. Brown, Wood, Hart, Hathcock.
Kicker—Chandler.

KANSAS CITY (10)

Ends—Burford, Arbanas, Mays, Hurston, F. Pitts, Carolan, A. Brown.
Tackles—Tyrer, Hill, Rice, Buchanan, DiMidio.
Guards—Budde, Merz, Reynolds, Biodrowski.
Centers—Frazier, Gilliam.
Linebackers—Bell, Headrick, Holub, Corey, Abell, Stover.
Quarterbacks—Dawson, Beathard.
Offensive Backs—Garrett, McClinton, O. Taylor, Coan, Thomas.
Defensive Backs—Williamson, Mitchell, Hunt, J. Robinson, F. Smith, Ply.
Kickers—Mercer; Wilson.

Green Bay Packers ...	7	7	14	7—35
Kansas City Chiefs ..	0	10	0	0—10

G.B.—McGee, 37, pass from Starr (Chandler, kick).
K.C.—McClinton, 7, pass from Dawson (Mercer, kick).
G.B.—Taylor, 14, run (Chandler, kick).
K.C.—FG, Mercer, 31.
G.B.—Pitts, 5, run (Chandler, kick).
G.B.—McGee, 13, pass from Starr (Chandler, kick).
G.B.—Pitts, 1, run (Chandler, kick).
Attendance—63,036.

INDIVIDUAL STATISTICS

Rushing—G. B.: Taylor, 16 attempts for 53 yards; Pitts, 11 for 45; Anderson, 4 for 30; Grabowski, 2 for 2. K. C.: Dawson 3 for 24; Garrett 6 for 17; McClinton 6 for 16; Coan 3 for 1.

Passing—G. B.: Starr, 16 completions in 23 attempts for 250 yards; Bratkowski, 0 in 1. K. C.: Dawson 16 in 27 for 211; Beathard 1 in 5 for 17.

Receiving—G. B.: McGee, 7 receptions for 138 yards; Dale, 4 for 59; Fleming, 2 for 22; Pitts, 2 for 32. K. C.: Burford, 4 for 67; Taylor, 4 for 57; Garrett, 3 for 28; McClinton, 2 for 34; Arbanas, 2 for 30; Carolan, 1 for 7; Coan, 1 for 5.

STATISTICS OF THE GAME

	Packers	Chiefs
First downs	21	17
Rushing yardage	130	72
Passing yardage	228	167
Passes	16-24	17-32
Interceptions by	1	1
Punts	4-43	7-45
Fumbles lost	1	1
Yards penalized	40	26

Taylor, McGee and Hornung May Bid Adieu to Packers

Special to The New York Times

LOS ANGELES, Jan. 15—Three Green Bay Packers' stars probably ended their careers today in a blaze of glory as active players with the champions of professional football.

Jim Taylor, the fullback, played out his option. It is reported that the bruising back will become a member of the New Orleans team in the National Football League. However, Taylor plans to discuss his future plans with Vince Lombardi, the Packer coach.

Max McGee, the 34-year-old pass catching hero, insists that he will retire after 11 years in the N.F.L. Paul Hornung, the onetime Golden Boy of Green Bay, who has been handicapped by a pinched nerve in his neck and didn't play in the Packers 35-10 Super Bowl victory over the Kansas City Chiefs, may wind up with another N.F.L. club.

Chiefs Are Ahead At Least One Time —Entering Field

LOS ANGELES, Jan. 15 (AP) —When Mike Garrett, a longtime Los Angeles favorite, led his Kansas City Chief teammates through the tunnel from the dressing rooms onto the field of the Los Angeles Coliseum today for the first Super Bowl game, the Chiefs didn't know it but it would be the only time they would be ahead of the Green Bay Packers.

About four minutes later the first contingent of Packers trotted onto the gaudily decorated field. They were confronted immediately by several signs draped over the rails declaring fan support for the Chiefs.

Garrett, the former Heisman Trophy winner from Southern California, led the American League champion Chiefs to the right end of the field while the Green Bay place-kicking team took its place at the left end.

The Packers were squarely in front of a sign that read: "Go Chiefs—Scalp Packers."

And there was a reminder that:

"Today's Super Sunday Vince, But Wait 'Till Monday." This sign singled out Vince Lombardi, the Packer coach.

Meanwhile, the Chiefs' cheerleaders went to work in front of a crowd of about 6,500 Kansas City backers while War Paint, their mascot horse, trotted around the field.

The field was a profusion of color, with a wide white band with red-and-blue yard markers ringing the playing surface.

The yard-line markers on the field were alternately red and blue while each end zone was painted gold with the nickname of the clubs and the league insignia.

But the new harmony of the merger of the American and National Football Leagues was quietly in evidence at the 50-yard line on the field, where there was a blue, red and yellow combined N.F.L.-A.F.L. insignia.

Both the A.F.L. and N.F.L. footballs were used during the game while the six officials who were handling the game—three from each league—wore specially designed uniforms.

Because of slight differences in the two footballs, the Chiefs used the A.F.L. ball when they were on offense and the Packers used the N.F.L. ball when they were on offense. The A.F.L. ball is supposed to be easier to pass, the N.F.L. ball easier to kick.

The officials wore white pants with a black stripe down either side. The stockings were black with two white stripes across the calf. The shirt was black with white vertical stripes with a black collar with white numerals on each sleeve. The cap was white with a black bill.

And the penalty flags, naturally enough, were gold.

Lombardi Calls Chiefs Good Team But Not Equal to Top Elevens in N.F.L.

COACH MAINTAINS DALLAS IS BETTER

Starr Says Chiefs Stacked Defenses—McGee Bows Out in Blaze of Glory

By BILL BECKER

Special to The New York Times

LOS ANGELES, Jan. 15—"Kansas City is a good football team," Vince Lombardi, the Green Bay factotum, said generously today after his Packers had mopped up on the Chiefs. Then the gray, gruff coach added the kicker:

"But their team doesn't compare with the top National Football League teams. I think Dallas is a better football team."

Vince made the statement cooly while reporters and television men were losing their notes and equipment in the steamy Packers' dressing room. He punctuated his remarks by slamming a football from hand to hand.

"The boys gave me the game ball," said Vince proudly. "An N.F.L. ball," he added with eyes twinkling behind his heavy spectacles.

Chiefs' Speed Hailed

Regarding the Chiefs, he continued: "The Chiefs have great speed, but I'd have to say N.F.L. football is tougher."

He declined to specify how much tougher, or how many teams he rated higher than the Chiefs.

The Packers broke the game open in the second half by "getting more aggressive on defense and blitzing at least three or four times," Lombardi said. At half-time he told the defense they weren't tackling well and he expected a better rush in the third period.

"We got the message," said Willie Wood. Willie, the former Southern California Trojan, intercepted Len Dawson's pass and ran 50 yards shortly afterward to set up the Packers' third touchdown. From then on, the momentum was all Green Bay's.

Wood said that this was "the greatest run (if not the longest) I ever made in the Coliseum." Willie played all of his collegiate home games in this stadium. "But this has to be my biggest thrill in Los Angeles," he emphasized.

"I was stung by the pass Otis Taylor caught against me in the first half," said Wood, one of the N.F.L.'s stellar safety men. "So I was sort of waiting for a chance. We were all kind of anticipating a sideline pass on the third-down-and-five situation."

Wood cut in front of Fred Arbanas, the Chiefs' tight end, and nearly went all the way in the game's key play. Ironically, the man who kept him from scoring was another ex-Trojan, Mike Garrett. Garrett tackled Wood from behind on the Chiefs' 5-yard line.

Lauds Foe's Defense

Bart Starr, the Packers' directing genius, lauded the Kansas City defenses—up to a point. "We just didn't execute well in the first half," said Starr. "But we knew that their stacked defenses could not contain our passing all day."

Starr explained that the Chiefs, by stacking their linebackers in tight behind their line, exposed their flanks.

"The offensive end has the advantage in that he only has to worry about the cornerback," Bart said. "We have the ends that can beat anyone in a one-on-one situation."

And the man who did most of the catching in this fortuitous turn of events was Max McGee. This was McGee's final game as a pro, he said, adding: "I can't think of a nicer way to go."

McGee caught touchdown passes of 37 and 13 yards and set up a third score with another fine long reception. "I should have scored," he laughed, "but I darned near tripped over my tongue."

McGee, 34 years old, said Boyd Dowler's shoulder injury forced him to play "a lot more than I figured on and I got a little tired."

McGee said he might like to coach—"If Lombardi wants me."

Lamar Hunt, the Chiefs' owner, congratulated McGee on his great game and added: "Don't retire now. We want to come back and get you next year."

Low-Key Celebration

The Packer dressing room was relatively quiet compared to most championship chambers. Doug Hart, a defensive back, the first to come off the field, let out a tentative whoop or two.

Henry Jordan, the all-everything defensive tackle, came in singing softly, "Money, money, money" in the key of G, probably for greenbacks, $15,000 worth. That was what each Packer will get for the victory; each Chief will receive $7,500—a balm of sorts.

The spirit of the Packers, although perhaps they would be too blasé and professional to call it that, was exemplified by Elijah Pitts and Paul Hornung, the regular left halfback and the former regular left halfback.

Pitts scored two touchdowns, while Hornung didn't get into the game at all.

"Naturally, I would have liked to play," said Hornung, who remained mum on his future plans. "But it is great just to be associated with this team and these fellows."

Here he slapped Elijah on the back and Pitts, duly grateful, responded: "Paul helped me to become the player I was this season. His tips improved my running."

Wood's Steal Left Chiefs Stunned

Associated Press Wirephoto

Upended as jarringly as his entire team was, Chris Burford of Kansas City falls, still clutching ball he received on a 12-yard pass. Bob Jeter rolls after bringing him down.

Stram Terms Play the Turning Point —Starr Praised

By FRANK LITSKY

Special to The New York Times

LOS ANGELES, Jan. 15—The way the Kansas City Chiefs looked when they returned to their dressing room after today's 35-10 Super Bowl loss to the Green Bay Packers, it was difficult to tell whether they had won, lost, tied or even played.

There was no crying, no shoe-throwing, no outbursts of temper. There was disappointment with their performance and, to a lesser degree, there was praise for the Packers as a good—but not perfect—team.

But most of all, the Chiefs seemed stunned. They took the field thinking they could win, and they left at half-time sure they could win. Then, early in the third quarter, came the play that, they agreed to a man, broke their back.

It was Willie Wood's interception and 50-yard return that put the ball on the Chiefs' 5-yard line and set up the touchdown that put the Packers in front, 21-10.

Chiefs Break Down

"That play seemingly changed the personality of the game," said Coach Hank Stram of the Chiefs. "We played well in the first half and we got off to a good start in the second half," Stram said. "We were doing the things we should have been doing. Then came that one play. After that, we just broke down, and then they got to Len Dawson."

Until that interception, Dawson, the Chiefs' quarterback, had been having great success.

"The interception did it," said Dawson. "It gave them the momentum. Let's face it. Their offense took the ball and drove it down our throats. Do I blame myself? Yes, I generally blame myself when we get beat."

Many Chiefs were impressed by the way Bart Starr, the Green Bay quarterback, connected so often on third-down passes.

"We kept trying to change our defensive picture on third down," said Stram, "but he still pierced our areas."

"They pick out a weak spot and stay with it much better than any team I've seen," said Mike Garrett. "Which weak spot? Well, they were passing like mad on us and hitting those third-down plays, so there must have been a weakness in there somewhere."

Cornerbacks The Targets

The weaknesses appeared to be at cornerback, where Fred Williamson played the left side and Willie Mitchell the right.

The Packers' wide receivers caught 11 passes for 197 yards, and Max McGee spoiled Mitchell's day by beating him on two touchdown passes and a 37-yard completion that set up a third score.

"Were they picking on Mitchell?" Stram said. "Well, it was very evident that they were working on our right side in critical passing situations."

"Starr was throwing the ball as the receiver made his break," said Mitchell. "They seemed to run more or less a time pattern. I'll tell you — cornerback is the most embarrassing position to play. When you make a mistake, it is there for all to see."

Williamson, wearing only a frown, said he made a gross error in the second quarter. The result was a 64-yard touchdown pass that was called back because of a penalty.

United Press International Telephoto

Later in half, Otis Taylor of Chiefs hauls in pass from Len Dawson on Green Bay's 7-yard line as Tom Brown, left, and Willie Wood of the Packers move in. On the next play, the Chiefs scored their only touchdown of the game.

"It was third and one," said Williamson. "It was a running situation. He gambled on a pass, and the way he faked a run was tremendous. It fooled me."

The usually loquacious Williamson was knocked cold making a fourth-quarter tackle.

"A little rest and a little nighty-night will cure me," he said.

Williamson was one of three Chiefs who suffered minor aches. Fred Arbanas, the tight end, missed a few plays because of a leg cramp and a jarring of his slightly separated left shoulder. Sherrill Headrick banged up a knee but was quickly back in action.

Why did the Chiefs lose?

"We didn't play our kind of football long enough," said Stram.

"They made mistakes," said Mitchell, "but they made less than we did."

"We just made too many mistakes," said Buck Buchanan.

"We lost our poise after the interception," said Jerry Mays. "That's no excuse. Great teams don't lose poise."

Then Mays summed up the thousands of words that have been uttered and are yet to be uttered on what happened.

"The Packers," he said, "beat us in the first half. The Packers and the Packer mystique beat us in the second half. The Packers beat us. They beat the hell out of us."

ASTRONAUTS VIEW FOOTBALL STARS

Ten Are Among the Crowd at Super Bowl Contest

Special to The New York Times

LOS ANGELES, Jan. 15 — Real and low-level astronauts, New York Jets, New York Giants and players preparing for the National and American Football League all-star games were among the spectators at today's Super Bowl game.

The astronauts were Walter Schirra, Walt Cunningham, Don Eisele, Joe Shea, Dale Myers, Dave Scott, John Young, Ron Evans, Rusty Schweickert and Al Warden. Five sat in the stands behind the Green Bay Packers' bench and five behind the Kansas City Chiefs' bench.

The low-level astronauts were Robert F. Courter of Lewiston, N. Y., and William P. Suitor of Youngstown, N. Y. At halftime, they made a Rocket Belt double flight around the stadium.

They are a demonstration team for Textron's Bell Aerosystems Company of Buffalo and they travel around this and other lands giving exhibitions. They have flown through the air as fast as 60 miles an hour, as high as 80 feet and as far as 860 feet.

6 New York Jets, Too

A little closer to earth were Jets of another sort. At least six New York Jets — Verlon Biggs, Emerson Boozer, George Sauer, Sherman Plunkett, Larry Grantham and Johnny Sample — were in the stands. The first five will play in next Saturday's American League all-star game at Oakland, Calif.

Sample appeared on the National Broadcasting Company's one-hour pregame television show called "Showdown: The World's Football Championship." The show was written by Leo Levine, a former New York Herald Tribune sports writer.

One of the New York Giants here was Earl Morrall, the quarterback. Three weeks before the end of the National League season, he broke a small bone in the right wrist. The cast is still on, but it will be removed in two weeks.

"Then," said Morrall, "I will have to exercise it and start rebuilding strength. So far, everything looks promising."

Another quarterback recovering from injuries is Johnny Unitas of the Baltimore Colts. Tendonitis in the right shoulder plagued him all year.

Unitas on the Mend

"It's halfway recovered now," said Unitas. "By June, we hope, I will be myself again."

Unitas and other National League players felt sure the Packers would beat the Chiefs, but they agreed that the Chiefs' task wasn't impossible.

"The Packers are primarily pass-rushers," said Unitas. "The Chiefs will have to maintain control of the ball just the way the Packers do.

"You can run on the Packers," said Don Meredith, the Dallas quarterback. "We did. If I were Kansas City, I would give my backs the option to run and find a hole."

Norm Van Brocklin, the coach of the Minnesota Vikings, agreed.

"Everybody," he said, "runs on Green Bay."

Trade Talk in Lobbies

Los Angeles was crammed with pro football executives and coaches, and there was trade talk in many hotel lobbies. But Van Brocklin, who is quarterback-heavy, said he had no trades on the fire for any of them.

Persistent reports late in the season said that Van Brocklin would trade Fran Tarkenton, his No. 1 quarterback, because Van Brocklin had become disenchanted with him. The Vikings also have Ron VanderKelen Bob Berry and (on the taxi squad) John Hankinson.

Maestro of Offense

Bryan Bartlett Starr

UNLIKE some of his swinging teammates, Bryan Bartlett Starr, the quarterback for the Green Bay Packers, goes to bed early. He says, "yes, sir" to almost everyone and most notably his coach, Vince Lombardi. He works with a Boy Scout troop and if he has ever tried a cigarette or swallowed a beer there are no valid witnesses. At the same time, Bart Starr, as he is known to football fans, is a vicious competitor. He will find ways to beat people, as he showed yesterday in the Super Bowl against the Kansas City Chiefs. Starr runs the offense for the Packers, which is not their strongest asset (the defense is that), but a ruthlessly efficient one. Besides, Starr, who is 32 years old and in his 11th professional season, seems to be getting smarter all the time.

Man in the News

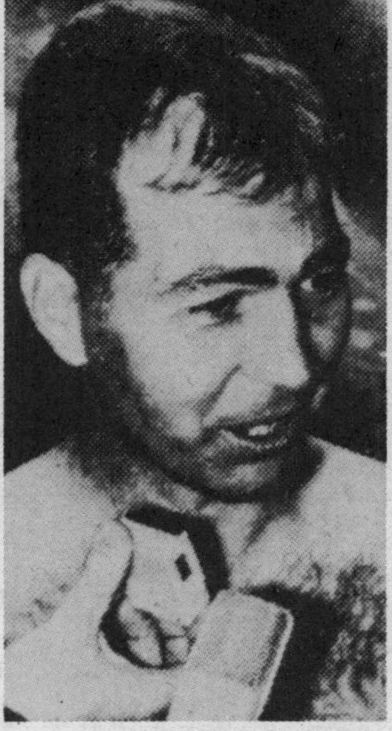

Associated Press Wirephoto

"Meat-and-potato plays"

(Bart Starr talks to reporters after the game.)

"It's not hard to read the Packer offense," a rival coach has said. "It's almost a Rinky-dink attack—not much imagination, simple meat-and-potato plays. But it is hard to read Starr. He takes those simple tools and uses them to the hilt. He has all kinds of guts, especially on third-down."

With yardage needed on third-down, the defense can move in for the kill. The offense is predictable, but not Starr's offense. In the National Football League's championship game in Dallas last New Year's Day, the one that matched the winning Packers and the Cowboys, Starr showed why he was acclaimed as pro football's best quarterback.

During the winning touchdown drive in the fourth period, Starr faced three third-down situations in which he had to gain 12 yards, 19 yards and 12 yards again. In each case this good-looking blond Alabaman coolly dropped back and waited for the pass receiver to break free, and then threw the football. The passes were pretty enough to belong in a museum. Each one was caught and each first down attained.

Following that exhibition there were few Starr doubters left. There have been many in the past largely because Starr came from humble football beginnings and he has never been the flashy athlete.

His first claim to fame was established on New Year's Day of 1953, when as a freshman quarterback he helped Alabama crush Syracuse, 61-6, in the Orange Bowl.

Starr later went into professional football, but nothing happened for a long time. When Lombardi arrived in Green Bay in 1959 to revive a dying franchise, Starr was a fourth-string quarterback behind Lamar McHan, Joe Francis and Paul Hornung. Lombardi made him first-string by 1960 because he was the best of a mediocre lot. Besides, he said, "yes sir," and followed this positive coach's orders to the letter.

In 1960, the Packers won the first of five division or league championships that were to come in the next seven seasons. Starr was good enough then and he has since become a lot better. He completes 55 per cent of his passes, a very high figure, and he is almost never intercepted.

"I don't know where the story began that Bart could not throw the long pass," said Lombardi yesterday. "That's ridiculous. He can throw with anyone. He's a fine quarterback and I'm delighted that he's finally getting the recognition that he has long deserved."

Starr's recognition last season included his third title as the N.F.L.'s best passer and the Jim Thorpe Trophy for being voted the most valuable player in the league.

Starr lives in Green Bay in a house half a mile from and within sight of the stadium and field house where the Packers work. A father of two young boys, this businessman recently stopped selling insurance and now spends his off-season time talking on speaking engagements and doing product endorsements. There is a stock brokerage firm in Milwaukee ready to give him a $100,000-a-year job when he gives up football.

Starr has been named "the man of the year" by numerous Wisconsin civic groups. He is chairman of a committee raising funds for a boys' Green Bay and when it comes to charity requests Starr is an easy mark. He is one of the state's best known personalities, respected from Oshkosh to Oconomowoc and beyond.

His teammates, some of them rowdy extroverts in contrast to Starr's quiet simplicity, have great respect for him. He is one of their leaders and he is the man who more than anyone else puts the points on the scoreboard that make winning a habit at Green Bay.

A Typical Coast Show

Super Bowl Is Unable to Measure Up To Advance Billing as TV Attraction

By JACK GOULD

THE Super Bowl yesterday was a representative example of most television dramas coming out of Los Angeles.

The advance build-up was more impressive than the show, and the script fell apart in the second act. Universal Pictures and Metro-Goldwyn-Mayer can comfort professional football. There is a million-dollar dud in every-one's closet.

The confrontation between the Green Bay Packers and Kansas City Chiefs reflected the usual difficulties of casting a TV special. The staring roles were methodically rendered by the Packers, but the bit parts were forlornly played by the Chiefs.

To the viewer untutored in the expertise of football, one conclusion seemed inescapable: Isn't it early to begin the 1967-68 exhibition-game schedule?

An omen of the anti-climax that might lay ahead came before the game. After all the rivalry, both networks carried the same introductory half-hour. The pooled 30 minutes were a lackluster interval bereft of excitement and seemingly designed only to accommodate additional spot announcements.

As for the championship game, the viewer at home had brief stirrings of hope in the first half when the Chiefs showed a touch of spirit. But thereafter it was downhill viewing all the way. The best TV sports of the afternoon, in fact, was the basketball game between the Boston Celtics and Philadelphia 76ers.

All the chitchat over the competition between commentators of C.B.S. and N.B.C. similarly proved to be malarkey. The play-by-play accounts of Curt Gowdy of N.B.C. and Jack Whitaker and Ray Scott of C.B.S. were almost the same, word for word. In the analysis it was a toss-up between Paul Christman of N.B.C. and Frank Gifford of C.B.S. Never were two networks more alike.

The iron-clad control that pro football exerts over its commentators was entertainingly illustrated on both networks. Each mentioned as briefly as possible that the attendance in the Coliseum was 63,036, but not a word about how that figure had fallen short of expectations. Sports reporting is not to be found on TV during a game.

In this regard, however, the director of the pooled TV coverage had a problem during the half-time ceremonies. The best shot of Al Hirt, the trumpeter, was from an angle that showed rows on rows of empty seats in the background.

The pictorial coverage was conventional, without any special shots or innovations for a championship.

But the afternoon did carry one immense blessing. With the game finally over, there will be no more of those Super Bowl commercials. The campaign of ballyhoo and promotional material was woefully overdone.

VINCE LOMBARDIS HAVE THEIR DAY

In the last year or so, people have been asking Vincent Lombardi, a 35-year-old school teacher, if he is *the* Vince Lombardi.

"And I say, yes, I'm *the* Vincent Lombardi."

Lombardi, the teacher, lives in Oakdale, L. I. He is not a football fan. But he happens to have the same name as the 53-year-old coach of the Green Bay Packers, whose team yesterday won the Super Bowl game in Los Angeles.

While the game was going on, the Long Island Lombardi was doing course work for a doctorate in history at New York University.

"Of course," he said, "I'm aware of the other Lombardi. But I'm strictly a baseball fan —the Yankees."

Another local Vincent Lombardi, of Ozone Park, Queens, puts up with plenty of ribbing.

"Just this afternoon," he said, "I walked into the bar and the guys said, 'What are you doing here? You're supposed to be on the Coast.'"

Satisfies Callers

The Queens Lombardi, 57, often makes long-distance telephone calls in his job with the Naval Department in New Jersey.

"I call and say I'm Vince Lombardi of Bayonne, and people ask me if I'm with the Packers, and I say sure."

Tomorroww Lombardi will get the usual razzing from his Navy co-workers.

"They'll tell me, 'Hey, coach, how did things come out?' and things like that. The funny thing is, when I put on my glasses, I do look a little like the coach."

Vincent Lombardi of Huntington, L. I., is engaged in management engineering. He is a bit bored having to explain again and again who he really is.

His allegiance?

"Who do you think I root for?" he asked rhetorically.

The 23-year-old Vincent Lombardi of Hartsdale, N. Y., who works in instrumental analysis, is too young to be mistaken for the coach. So people assume he must be a son, or nephew. He has taken to rooting for Green Bay.

"My first reason," he explained, "is because of the name. And secondly, they're a great team."

Associated Press Wirephoto

ANOTHER GREEN BAY SCORE: With Jim Taylor (31) running interference, Elijah Pitts, right, of the Packers heads for goal in the third period at Los Angeles.

Foyt Takes 500 as Jones, in Lead, Drops Out

FAULTY GEAR BOX CAUSE OF FAILURE

Foyt Sets Mark of 151.207 M.P.H. in Winning 3d Time —4 Cars in Last-Lap Spin

By FRANK M. BLUNK
Special to The New York Times

INDIANAPOLIS, May 31—A. J. Foyt Jr. of Houston won the 51st running of the 500-mile race today when auto racing's newest and fastest creation, a whispering turbine, went out of action with a broken ball-bearing holder in its gear box with only three laps to go and holding a 45-second lead.

Foyt, with previous victories here in 1961 and 1964, became the fourth man in the history of this race to wear the victory garland wreath three times. Louis Meyer, Mauri Rose and Wilbur Shaw were the others. The first two Foyt triumphs were in old front-mounted, Offenhauser-powered roadsters. Today he had a Ford engine in the rear end of a Coyote chassis, a racer of his own design.

Parnelli Jones of Torrance, Calif., was in charge of Andy Granatelli's STP Turbine Special. He had given notice yesterday that this car would be difficult to beat. It had caused a furor among other owners and drivers when it appeared on the track early this month. And there were many of the old-timers who said "wait and see." They knew that the turbine machine was having gear box and brake troubles.

Before the race was halted after 18 laps yesterday, Jones and the turbine special had thrown a scare into the rest of the field. The turbine's speed was superior to that of any of its piston-engine rivals. It moved into and out of the Speedway's corners silently and with ease.

Not 100 Per Cent Certain

The transmission of the turbine's smooth-flowing power to all four wheels had been a big problem for Granatelli, the car's builder, since its first running. Numerous gear boxes were used and finally, just before the first qualifying day on May 13, Granatelli announced that he had hit upon the correct set up.

Jones qualified early for the sixth place at 166.075 miles an hour and ran the machine sparingly during practice sessions that followed. This indicated that Granatelli was not 100 per cent certain that the new gear box would last. Still he stuck to his story and his confidence did not seem to be a pretense as the race progressed to its final stages today. There was quite a bit of excitement and confusion in the STP pit when Jones rolled in for his first fuel stop.

Some of the crewmen forgot, or were a bit late, in removing the two hoses that are attached to the pit tank and when Jones moved out there was a spilling of kerosene all over the pit. This mishap broke the hose coupling and a new hose was found to replace it.

Business in the pit then settled down and when Jones passed by on his 180th lap, Granatelli gave him a signal to "ease up." Jones was then 48 seconds ahead and had Foyt, running second, within view.

There had been no warning, Jones said later, of the gear trouble. "It just broke and all of a sudden I dropped from a 151 mile an hour leader to a nonfinishing also ran."

Dan Gurney of Costa Mesa, Calif., who had been running second to the turbine yesterday and Foyt who had been third, knew full well when the race was restarted today that their only chances to win depended upon the turbine's gear box. If the gear box held, the turbine car would win. It almost did. Jones had turned the corner to the main straight to end his 97th lap when the car gave the last gasp and slowed to a snail's pace.

Gurney had had mechanical troubles and was now on the sidelines. Foyt swept around the track with victory in sight. On the very last lap Foyt had another bit of good fortune. Four cars, driven by Chuck Hulse of Downey, Calif., Bob Grim of Indianapolis, Carl Williams of Grandview, Mo., and Larry Dickson of Marietta, Ohio, spun and hit the infield wall on the main straightaway. Foyt had to thread his way through the wrecks to take the checkered flag.

This chain-reaction series of spins brought out a red flag, stopping the action. Normally, all of the first 10 cars complete the 200 laps over the 2.5-mile course. Today Foyt was the only man to go the distance. All through the race Jones had been setting average speed records and now it was Foyt's turn. His 500-mile average was 151.207 miles an hour, eclipsing the 150.686 miles-an-hour mark set by Jim Clark of Scotland in 1965.

Second at the end today was Al Unser of Albuquerque, N. M., in a Lola-Ford owned by John Mecom Jr. of Houston. Unser was two laps behind Foyt. Third, at 197 laps, was Foyt's teammate, Joe Leonard of San Jose, Calif., in a Sheraton Thompson Special, also Ford powered.

Fourth was Denis Hulme of New Zealand, making his first appearance here in an Eagle-Ford built by Henry (Smokey) Yunick of Daytona Beach, Fla. Hulme won this year's Formula I race at Monte Carlo in a Brabham Repco. Yunick has been a successful preparer of stock cars on the National Association circuit. Hulme also completed 197 laps.

Jim McElreath of Arlington, Tex., placed fifth, also at 197 laps, with John Zink's Ford-powered track burner. Jones, having completed 196 laps, wound up in sixth place though he was not running at the finish. Hulse, involved in the last-lap spin, was seventh, with 195 laps. Art Pollard of Medford, Ore., also making his first start in the 500, also was credited with 195 laps in eighth place. Bobby Unser, Al's brother, was ninth, with 193 laps, and Bob Veith of Fort Bragg, Calif., was 10th, with 190 laps.

Jackie Stewart of Scotland who had to qualify twice to get into the race with a John Mecom Lola-Ford, worked his way from a 29th place at the start to a seemingly secure third place on the 168th lap. Then his engine gave out and he repeated his walk of 1966 from the fourth turn, where he parked the car, to the pits. Last year he finished sixth over all, with 190 laps. Today he took the 18th-place prize.

Gurney, whose hopes were so bright after qualifying second to Mario Andretti, had to give up after 160 laps. Graham Hill, last year's winner, went only 23 laps with a sick Lotus-Ford; Jim Clark, second in 1963, first in 1965, and second again last year, lasted 35 laps, also with a complaining Lotus.

Thus, Granatelli's team, with three of the top drivers and cars — Clark, Hill and Jones — drew another blank. And this may be his last chance with the turbine. There are reports here that before 1968 and May roll around, the United States Auto Club will have amended its rules to either bar or handicap turbine cars.

The only alternative would be for everyone to junk the piston engines and go to jets. And racing people fear an end to the sport if the roar of the piston engines is no longer heard.

Lloyd Ruby of Wichita Falls, Tex., who qualified in seventh place, had to abandon his turbo-charged Offenhauser after three laps yesterday. He had burned a piston. Today he started the continuation as a relief driver for George Snider of Fresno, Calif., in a Wagner-Lockheed Ford. This time he went 81 laps, giving the Snider car a total of 99, good for 26th place.

Andretti, the fastest qualifier now for two years, again failed to finish. Last year he quit after 27 laps with a burned piston. Yesterday he had to stop with a faulty clutch. The postponement of the race gave him time to install a new one and he was at the end of the single-file field of 32 for the restart.

After 50 laps today he lost a wheel and came to rest with his Dean Van Lines Hawk on the third turn. He wasn't hurt and no doubt will go on to compete in the remainder of this year's championship races and take the national championship for the straight year. His biggest rival, Foyt, who has four championships to his credit, now has a big lead on points, however.

Foyt's third triumph in the 500 halted, at least for a year, the domination of the race by foreign drivers. Clark's easy victory in a Lotus-Ford in 1965 and Hill's success in a Lola-Ford last year had the American boys talking to themselves. They just hated to see all that big prize money going overseas.

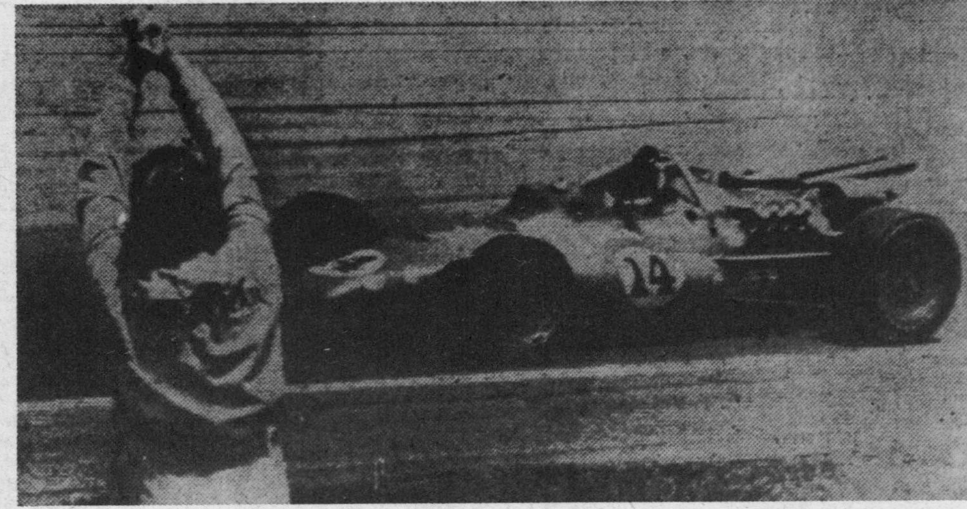

Associated Press Wirephoto

Gordon Johncock of Hastings, Mich., out of competition through a wreck, cheers Foyt on

500 See Theater TV Here With Rainchecks

About 500 of the 1,400 persons who had paid $6 on Tuesday to see the closed-circuit telecast of the Indianapolis 500-mile race at the DeMille Theater here used their rainchecks yesterday.

The race was postponed on Tuesday in the 19th lap because of rain. Some viewers in the theater demanded refunds, saying they would not be able to use their rainchecks. The management promised that they would get refunds if they mailed in their ticket stubs. Yesterday the theater sold 77 tickets.

A theater spokesman said he did not know what he would do if the 900 who had not used their tickets wrote for refunds.

Fate Is His Co-Driver

Anthony John Foyt Jr.

IT all started for Anthony John Foyt Jr. when he was 3 years old. He was presented with a blood-red miniature racing car.

"I thought it was the most beautiful thing that ever was," Foyt said in his soft Texas accent.

Man in the News

In his teens, everything with wheels was "beautiful" to A. J. — motorcycles, stock cars, midget racers, Indianapolis-type machines. Spinning from dirt track to asphalt, from backwoods ovals to high-powered competition, Foyt tried them all, any place, for any purse.

The small fortune the 32-year-old driver picked up yesterday for winning the Indianapolis 500-mile auto race for the third time will satisfy him for now. But after his last Indy triumph, in 1964, he flew to Bremen, Ohio, for a sprint-car race and then returned for the victory dinner to receive his $153,650 in prizes.

"It all adds up," explains A. J. "You drive the big ones and the little ones. This wasn't meant to be a soft sport."

He tries to make it as easy on himself as possible, though. "Dad likes to run second or third. He wants to keep in the race. I thought he had it all the way," said his 11-year-old son, A. J. Foyt 3d, in Houston yesterday.

Fate Sets the Rules

Foyt's three victories at Indianapolis were achieved after the leader had run into trouble. But Foyt doesn't back away from the challenge of auto racing. Instead, he accepts it, as nearly as possible, on fate's terms.

"Retire? The worst of us wait until we're driven to it, by injury or fear," he once said. "You have to want to drive so damn much, or else you wouldn't do it at all."

He entered auto racing quite naturally. His father was a successful builder of race cars in Houston, where A. J. was born on Jan. 16, 1935.

There is talk now that his father wants him to retire. The black-haired, brown-eyed Foyt Jr. is one of the few drivers who have become millionaires. Some friends insist that his wife, Lucy, whom he married in 1955, prays for him to quit.

When he is on the road he becomes edgy, and will get into all-night card games, losing himself among his colleagues and keeping away from the hundreds of well-wishers. He acknowledges that he gets homesick and that every day he calls his wife and children (besides A. J. 3d there are Terry Lynn, 8, and Jerry, 4).

"There is too much pressure on you from every side," he says. "I get homesick. But I love racing. I don't fear death. I don't think about it. I'm young. I'm at my best."

United Press International Telephoto

"I'm young. I'm at my best."
(Foyt after the race)

To become the best, Foyt would drive in as many as 50 races a year, sometimes wearing cowboy boots that became a trademark. He once failed to qualify for a race at Terre Haute, Ind., but prevailed upon one of the drivers to stay out. Foyt got in, and won.

Competing mostly in the sprint circuit in the Midwest, Foyt received a measure of national attention in 1957. The next year, he tried Indy. At 23, he was the youngest in the race. He failed. On his fourth attempt in 1961, he won.

He has consistently earned more than $100,000 a year since then. He lost $1,000 in 1962, however, after being fined by the United States Auto Club for threatening to punch a Milwaukee promoter. He was put on probation for a year. But after the year was up, he was suspended for hitting a driver following a race at Williams Grove, Pa., a contest with considerably less importance than the 500.

The quality of the competition, or the significance of the race, apparently don't matter. As he says, "It all adds up."

Ryun Sets a World Record of 3:51.1 in Mile Run

FIRST 7 FINISHERS UNDER 4 MINUTES

By WILLIAM N. WALLACE
Special to The New York Times

BAKERSFIELD, Calif., June 23—Jim Ryun, the precocious 20-year-old sophomore from the University of Kansas, set a world record for the one-mile run tonight at the Amateur Athletic Union's national track and field championships here.

Ryun, winning by some 40 yards, ran the classic distance in 3 minutes 51.1 seconds. That was two-tenths of a second better than Ryun's recognized world mark of 3:51.3, set a year ago at Berkeley, Calif.

It was a tremendous race that saw the first seven finishers run the distance in under four minutes. The seventh-place finisher, 17-year-old Martin Liqueri of Essex Catholic High School in Cedar Grove, N. J., posted a time of 3:59.8.

Jim Grelle, the seasoned miler from Portland, Ore., had a time of 3:56.1 for second place, then came Dave Willborn, University of Oregon, 3:56.2; Tom von Ruden, Oklahoma State, 3:56.9; Roscoe Divine, Oregon, 3:57.2; Sam Bair, Kent State, 3:58.6, and Liquori.

Paul Wilson, a 19-year-old sophomore at the University of Southern California, also set a world's record. In the pole vault event, Wilson cleared 17 feet 8 inches to eclipse the former mark of 17-7 set by his teammate, Bob Seagren, last June 10.

United Press International

Jim Ryun crosses the finish line in the world record time of 3:51.1.

A Blistering Finish

Ryun's quarter times were 59.2 seconds, 59.8, 58.6, and then a blasting 53.5 as he went for the world mark.

Ryun next took a leisurely jog around Bakersfield College's Memorial Stadium as the crowd of 10,000 cheered him mightily.

Ryun had taken the lead just after the start, a lead that grew longer and longer.

As the collective quarter times were announced over the public address system, the crowd sensed a record was at hand and urged on the slight, tall dark-haired Ryun.

Said Ryun afterwards, "I felt well and I wanted to run a fast race." That was succinct and simple.

On June 5, 1964 at Compton, Calif., eight men ran a mile race in under four minutes. Ryun. Then a 17-year-old junior at Wichita (Kan.) East High School, placed eighth. His time was 3:59.

Tonight's effort was Ryun's 12th mile run since then under four minutes and Grelle's 19th in his longer career.

Evans Takes Dash

Lee Evans, representing Santa Clara Youth Village, won the 440-yard dash just before the mile was run.

Evans, a 20-year-old junior at San Jose State College, where he loses only to a teammate, Tommie Smith, successfully defended his A.A.U. national title with an extreme effort in the stretch to hold off Vince Mathews of New York's Pioneer Club and Jim Kemp of the 49ers Track Club.

It was one of the fastest quarter miles ever run. Evans's time was 45.3 seconds, half a second under the A.A.U. meet record, which was also broken in the event by Mathews, Kemp and Elbert Stinson of Arkansas A.M. and N.

The pending world record, set by Tommie Smith, is 44.8.

Smith put away Jim Hines of Texas Southern, last night's 100-yard dash winner, in the finals of the 220-yard dash. The long-striding Smith, the world record-holder at the distance, posted a time of 20.4 seconds for a meet record—not bad for a man currently taking reserve officer training at Ft. Lewis, Wash.

Hines was two yards behind Smith at the finish, but inexplicably was given the same time, 20.4.

Wade Bell, the fine half-miler from the University of Oregon, ran away from the field in his event and won by 15 yards. His time was a remarkable 1 minute 46.1 seconds, a meet record and the fastest half-mile run in the United States this year. Bell won the N. C. A. A. championship last week in 1:47.6.

The two-mile walk went to Ron Laird of the New York Athletic Club and he missed an American record by only four-tenths of a second. The bespectacled Laird, the 1966 champion, went the distance with heel and toe in 13:41.4. This set an A.A.U. meet record and was over 11 seconds faster than Laird's effort at New York's Randalls Island a year ago.

TAYLOR CONQUERS DAVIDSON, 6-4, 6-4

Newcombe Puts Out Cooper, 6-1, 11-9—Nancy Richey Beats Miss Van Zyl

By FRED TUPPER
Special to The New York Times

LONDON, June 23 — Nancy Richey, ranked No. 2 in the United States, meets Kerry Melville, ranked second in Australia, for the London grass-court tennis title tomorrow. The little American slugger outlasted statuesque Annette Van Zyl of South Africa, 6-4, 7-5, in an interrupted match that was transferred from grass to wood because of a summer rainstorm.

Miss Melville, a pretty, athletic girl who loves to take a bash at the ball, prevailed over her teammate, Judy Tegart, 6-3, 10-8.

Roger Taylor, Britain's No. 1, defeated the new British coach, Owen Davidson of Australia, 6-4, 6-4, and meets John Newcombe, Australia's No. 3 and currently the American champion, in the final tomorrow.

Newcombe won from 20-year-old John Cooper, the brother of Ashley, the Wimbledon champion in 1955, although he squandered seven match points before scoring, 6-1, 11-9.

Newcombe Seeded Third

It has been a curious week at the Queens Club. Until today there hardly had been a predictable result. Manual Santana and Roy Emerson were beaten early and six of the men seeded players at Wimbledon disappeared before the semi-finals.

The burly Newcombe is seeded No. 3 at Wimbledon behind Santana and Emerson. Miss Richey is seeded No. 5 in the women's singles.

With Wimbledon opening next Monday, there were protests from the players about playing on wood. Mrs. Ann Jones and Virginia Wade, the top British pair, retired against Mrs. Billie Jean King and Rosemary Casals of the United States in a double semi-final. "It's a grass-court championship and we'll play only on grass," said Mrs. Jones.

Miss Richey was overpowering in beating Lesley Turner of Australia yesterday, but she had her anxious moments this afternoon.

A couple of service breaks at the beginning gave her the first set because she never stopped forcing the pace. At 2-3 in the second set, with Nancy serving, they moved indoors. Miss Richey lost that game and then her touch came back.

Hammering the ball from side to side, Nancy had Miss Van Zyl constantly on the stretch. Annette retrieved brilliantly but power paid off on the faster surface and Nancy finished her off with a couple of smashes from midcourt.

Three times Judy Tegart had points for the second set against Miss Melville and it took all of Kerry's intelligent command of the court to fob her off.

Miss Melville is a comer. She upset the Wimbledon champion, Mrs. King, at Forest Hills last year and seems destined to follow in Margaret Smith's footsteps as an Australian champion But wood is not her surface. Kerry was tentative with her ground strokes and too often she blew the point on attempted drop shots. She won thankfully on a Tegart overhit after double-faulting on her first match point.

The crowd was ecstatic over Taylor's victory. He becomes the first Briton to contest the final here since the legendary Bunny Austin won it in 1938. Taylor had his big kicking southpaw serve rocketing off the boards and today it was consistently more powerful than Davidson's.

MOTOR-SIZE LIMIT OF 3 LITERS VOTED

Sports Car Ruling Decided by International Body

PARIS, June 23 (AP) — Prototype sports cars racing for the manufacturers championship next year will be limited to motor sizes of three liters, according to a decision announced today.

The International Sporting Commission, which sets the rules for the manufacturers competition, made the decision at a closed meeting here June 13, just two days after a seven-liter Ford prototype, driven by Americans A. J. Foyt and Dan Gurney, won the 24-hour Le Mans race.

A spokesman for the International Automobile Federation, the sporting commission's parent group, said the decision had been under consideration since last year, when seven-liter Fords finished 1-2-3 at Le Mans.

French Weighed Limit

The spokesman said the five-nation commission made up its mind when it learned that the French government was considering setting a motor-size limit in the Le Mans race.

The three-liter limit translates to 183 cubic inches. Most standard United States six-cylinder auto engines run 220 cubic inches or larger.

Concerned with the speeds realized by the Fords — more than 214 miles-an-hour on the long Mulsanne straightaway—and by 4.7-liter Ferrari prototypes — 198.8 m.p.h. on the same stretch — the government was thinking about setting a two-liter maximum, the spokesman said.

"To head off government regulation, we decided to regulate ourselves," he said.

Representatives from all five countries — France, Germany, Italy, Britain and the United States—all agreed to the new rules, he said, "though the United States agreed with a certain reserve."

The decision affects all the races counting for the manufacturer championship—including Le Mans, Daytona Beach, Sebring, Targa Floria and Nurburgring.

The attitude of Ford, whose program of international sports cars racing is just coming to maturity, was not immediately known.

Hardest hit will be Texans Jim Hall and Hap Sharp, builders of the seven-liter Chaparral, a prototype with an automatic transmission and a movable air stabilizing wing fixed above the rear of their cars.

Red Sox Win Pennant by Beating Twins, 5-3

BOSTON RALLY LED BY YASTRZEMSKI

Star Bats Across 2 Tallies in 5-Run 6th and Gets 4 Hits—Lonborg Wins 22d

By JOSEPH DURSO
Special to The New York Times

BOSTON, Oct. 1—The Boston Red Sox completed one of baseball's great rags-to-riches stories today by defeating the Minnesota Twins, 5-3, and winning the tightest American League pennant race in history.

They won it before a roaring crowd of 35,770 persons in the 162d and final game of the season, one year after they had finished ninth in the league and 21 years after they had won their last pennant.

They also won it in a dramatic tale of two baseball cities with help from the California Angels, the final hurdle standing between the Detroit Tigers and a possible playoff.

But when the Tigers lost to the Angels, 8-5, in the second game of their double-header in Detroit—and in the last game of their season—the three-team free-for-all was finally ended. The Tigers and Twins finished in a tie for second, one game behind.

Series Starts Wednesday

As a result, the Red Sox—a second-division team for nine years — will open the 64th World Series on Wednesday against the St. Louis Cardinals.

They will open it in Fenway Park, where the Red Sox won their second straight game over Minnesota today behind the seven-hit pitching of Jim Lonborg and four straight hits by Carl Yastrzemski.

Yastrzemski, with three singles and a double, batted across two runs for the Red Sox. They were both scored in the sixth inning of a gripping struggle, when the Red Sox rallied for five runs and overcame a 2-0 lead that Minnesota had built for Dean Chance.

Two innings later, Yastrzemski made a key throw from left field to second base killing a counter-rally staged by Minnesota and ending two days of heroic performance that carried the Red Sox to the top.

For 5½ innings this afternoon, though, the gloom thickened in Fenway Park as the Red Sox and Twins fought it out under their rookie managers, Dick Williams and Cal Ermer.

Lonborg, gunning for his 22d victory, retired the first two batters, then walked Harmon Killebrew. Then came the first of two errors that put Minnesota ahead. Tony Oliva banked a line drive off the left-field fence just over Yastrzemski's head and the ball bounced toward center field.

Reggie Smith, in pursuit, picked it up and fired a good throw toward home plate. But George Scott, the first baseman, cut off the throw 25 feet in front of the plate and flung it high and wide to the screen as Killebrew scored.

In the third, trouble brewed for Boston again with two out. This time Lonborg walked Cesar Tovar, and Killebrew lined a single to left. Tovar normally would have stopped at second base, but when the ball skipped past Yastrzemski to the wall,

The Boston Red Sox
Rico Petrocelli

The Boston Red Sox
Carl Yastrzemski

he scored and it was 2-0, Minnesota.

And that's the way things stood until the sixth. Yastrzemski had singled in the first, Rico Petrocelli had singled in the second, Lonborg had singled in the third and Yastrzemski had doubled in the fourth—but still Chance had protected his 2-0 lead.

A Lucky Chance

The closest call for Minnesota developed in the fourth, when Yastrzemski led off with a lone drive off the left-field wall, just missing a home run. Ken Harrelson flied out to Oliva, but Scott ripped a vicious liner toward center field. However, Chance instintively reached up, clutched the ball in the netting of his glove, whirled and threw to second base to double up Yastrzemski.

Two innings later, the Red Sox abruptly broke through with a spectacular thrust that may rank with the Brink's robbery as one of the stunning events of Boston history. They sent 10 batters to the plate, four hit safely, one walked, one reached base on a fielder's choice, four advanced on a pair of wild pitches—and five scored.

Lonborg, who was pitching but losing a two-hitter at that point, started it all by curling a perfect bunt down the third-base line for a single. Jerry Adair hit the next pitch past the diving Rod Carew into center for a single. Dalton Jones, after fouling off the first pitch while trying to bunt, lined a single past third and the bases were loaded with nobody out.

The batter was Yastrzemski, who was leading the league in most offensive departments and who had hit two singles and a home run the day before.

Surrounded by deafening noise, he took a ball inside and then lined a single into center as Lonborg and Adair scored to tie the game and Fenway Park went wild.

The hit was the third straight of the game for Yastrzemski and his fifth in a row in the series. Before the game was over, he was to single again and run his streak to six hits in a row and seven for eight during the climactic weekend series. He also wound up with 121 runs batted in, and the feeling in Boston was unanimous that Nos. 120 and 121 were his most important.

Versalles Throws Home

While paper and streamers were still swirling through the air, Harrelson followed by chopping a high bouncer over the mound to the left of second base, where Zoilo Versalles grabbed it. He had a play at first but fired the ball instead to home plate, too late to intercept Jones, who was scoring the third run.

Chance, foiled in his bid for his 21st victory, was relieved by Al Worthington while José Tartabull went in as a pinch-runner for Harrelson, who had joined the Red Sox a month ago from the embroiled Kansas City Athletics.

There were still no outs and, when Scott squared away to bunt on the first pitch, Worthington pitched hard on the outside and off his catcher's glove. The runners each moved up a base.

Two pitches later, Worthington delivered another wild pitch into the dirt and, as it bounced into the front row boxes near the Boston dugout, Yastrzemski scored and Tartabull took third. Scott finally struck out.

Minnesota's hour of despair was not over, though. Rico Petrocelli walked, and Reggie Smith cracked a hard grounder off Killebrew's glove at first base. As the ball bounced into foul territory, Tartabull scored the fifth and final run of the inning.

MINNESOTA (A.)	ab.	r.	h.	bi.
Versalles, ss	3	0	0	0
Reese, lf	1	0	1	0
Tovar, 3b	3	1	0	0
Killebrew, 1b	2	2	2	0
Oliva, rf	3	0	2	0
Allison, lf	4	0	1	1
Hernandez, ss	0	0	0	0
Uhlaender, cf	4	0	1	0
Carew, 2b	4	0	0	0
Zimmerman, c	2	0	0	0
Nixon, c	1	0	0	0
Rollins, ph	1	0	0	0
Chance, p	2	0	0	0
Worthington, p	0	0	0	0
Kosco, ph	1	0	0	0
Roland, p	0	0	0	0
Grant, p	0	0	0	0
Total	31	3	7	1

BOSTON (A.)	ab.	r.	h.	bi.
Adair, 2b	4	1	2	0
Andrews, 2b	0	0	0	0
Jones, 3b	4	1	2	0
Yastrzemski, lf	4	1	4	2
Harrelson, rf	3	0	0	1
Tartabull, rf	1	1	0	0
Scott, 1b	4	0	0	0
Petrocelli, ss	3	0	1	0
Smith, cf	4	0	0	1
Gibson, c	2	0	0	0
Siebern, ph	1	0	0	0
Howard, c	1	0	1	0
Lonborg, p	4	1	2	0
Total	35	5	12	4

Minnesota	101	000	010	—3
Boston	000	005	00x	—5

E—Scott, Yastrzemski, Killebrew. DP—Minnesota 3, Boston 2. LOB—Minnesota 5, Boston 7. 2B—Oliva, Yastrzemski.

	IP.	H.	R.	ER.	BB.	SO.
Chance (L, 20-14)	5	8	5	5	0	2
Worthington	1	0	0	0	1	[illegible]
Roland	0	[illegible]	0	0	0	0
Grant	2	[illegible]	0	0	0	[illegible]
Lonborg (W, 22-9)	[illegible]	[illegible]	3	[illegible]	4	[illegible]

Wild pitches—Worthington 2.
T—2:25. A—35,770.

Sports of The Times

By ARTHUR DALEY

Toward a Date With Destiny

BOSTON, Oct. 1—Carl Yastrzemski stood in front of his locker before today's game and gazed longingly at the door leading to the playing field at Fenway Park.

"I want the feeling of coming through that door," he said with emotional fervor, "with the pennant won."

When he stepped blithely through that portal after the convincing beating that his Red Sox had administered to the Minnesota Twins, however, he wasn't completely sure whether the Bostons had a full grip on the championship or a partial one. A thousand miles away, the Detroit Tigers were tugging at the other end, needing to beat the California Angels in the second game of a double-header to tie for the lead.

The Red Sox players, nonetheless, behaved with all the exuberance of pennant winners. They doused each other with shaving cream foam and joyously poured beer over anyone within range. After the initial outburst they subsided to listen to the radio report from Detroit, whooping it up for every Angel run. Meanwhile, they thoughtfully sipped a beer, a beverage that even losers drink. They were waiting for the champagne.

Belief in a Mystique

The bubble water was on ice, the stuff that only winners are entitled to drink. The Fenway millionaires expected in full confidence that they'd be drinking it, too. In this absolutely insane section of the land they had been labeled destiny's darlings and Tom Yawkey's flannelled heroes had been swept up in the mystique. They believed it.

They had been overwhelmed by Boston's madness when the game ended. The fans cascaded out of the stands and mobbed Jim Lonborg, the winning pitcher. He was hoisted to eager shoulders, a chip tossed on a sea of happiness, and that sea surged unrestrainedly.

"I got scared after a while," he acknowledged afterward. "They ripped the buttons off my uniform shirt and kept plucking away at my sweatshirt. By the time I escaped all I had left of it was the cloth around my wrists."

"I made a total escape," said Yaz. "I did an end run around the mob, running alongside the Minnesota dugout until I could slip into ours. What a day! What a day!"

"Wowee," shrieked George Scott, tastfully attired in only a pair of shorts. "The Angels just picked up three more runs."

Red Sox Not in a Rush

The champagne kept getting colder but the Red Sox were not too impatient. They were savoring every anticipatory moment as they marked time before the big explosion, the final word that they really had won the pennant.

It was an unbelievable thing. This was a team that had finished only half a game out of 10th and last place the year before. Now it was a championship ballclub, doing it the hard way by taking the final two games against the Twins in a head-to-head showdown.

But the Red Sox had been doing it the hard way all season as they brought back to the older Bostonians the memories of the last time anything like it had ever happened. It was in 1914 that the Boston Braves were last on the Fourth of July, the halfway point in the baseball year, and they had rocketed up from there, not only to a pennant but also a victory over the supposedly invincible Philadelphia Athletics in the World Series. They beat the A's four straight, too.

No one ever will convince this new breed of Boston indomitables that it can't happen again when they square off against the St. Louis Cardinals in the opening game of another World Series here at the Fens on Wednesday.

Final Day Jitters

Sandy Koufax, a man not unfamiliar with last day pennant pressures, stood behind the batting cage before today's showdown and cast sympathetic glances in the alternate directions of the two starters, Lonberg and Lean Chance of the Twins. Both looked tense.

"I know how they feel," said Sandy. "The funny thing about last year, though, was that I went into the final game totally unconcerned. I never expected to be in it. But when we lost the opener of the Sunday double-header, I got the call. And I also got a big lead and that always helps. By the ninth inning I was ahead, 6-0, and thought I could just throw the ball past the hitters. I should have known better but I didn't. They got three runs before we ended it to clinch the pennant."

Staid Bostonians are so head-over-heels in love with Yastrzemski that they are totally blind to the virtues of Harmon Killebrew, a very nice guy. To them the Killer is a villain and they boo him with a venomous passion every time he comes to bat. Their beloved Yaz is gunning for the Triple Crown and Killebrew threatens his supremacy as the home run leader. Yesterday Yaz stroked his 44th in the seventh only to have the Killer draw abreast of him with a titanic blast with two outs in the ninth.

The Twins' muscular first baseman never would have gone to the plate if the weatherman hadn't given him some help. The man ahead of him in the batting order, Cesar Tovar, gave him life by dropping a soft double inside the left-field foul line.

"If the grass hadn't been so slippery from the rains," sadly recounted Yaz today, "I would have caught the ball and ended the game. But when I didn't, Harmon got to bat. I had an immediate premonition that he'd hit a home run. And he did."

"All the News That's Fit to Print"

The New York Times

LATE CITY EDITION

Weather: Fair, very cold today and tonight. Chance of snow tomorrow. Temp. range: today 24-14; Sunday 33-26. Full U.S. report on Page 30.

VOL. CXVII . No. 40,154 NEW YORK, MONDAY, JANUARY 1, 1968 — 10 CENTS

Saigon Looks to the New Year: Some Trust in Flowers, Others in Arms

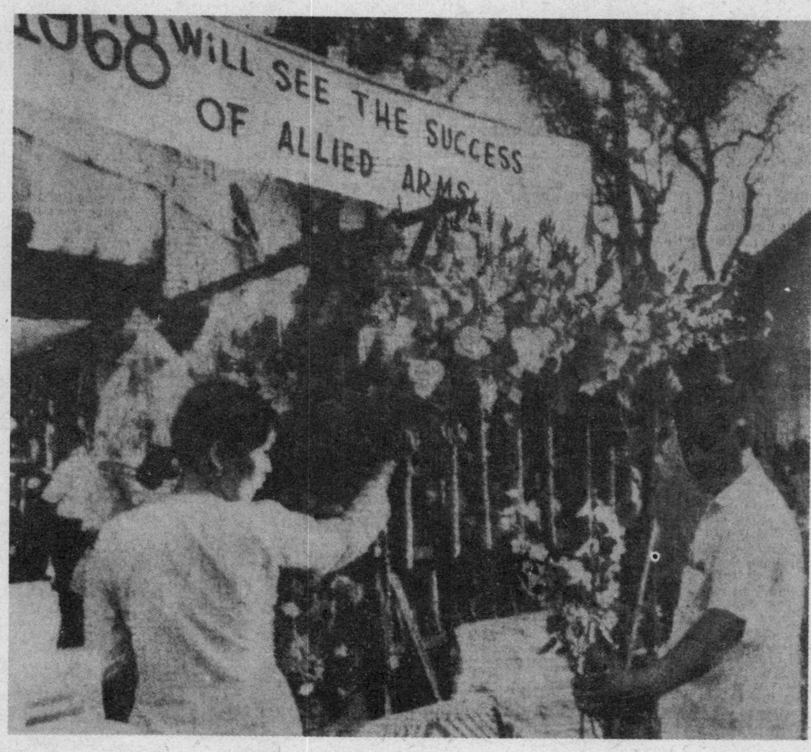

Associated Press Radiophoto

On New Year's Eve in Saigon, a man buys a branch of fresh young blossoms, symbol of the beginning of a new year. Sign above flower stall, predicting military success in 1968, was erected by the South Vietnamese Government.

MEDIATORS HOPE TO AVERT TRANSIT WALKOUT TODAY; SOME PROGRESS REPORTED

United Press International

TRANSIT MEDIATION PANEL: Theodore W. Kheel, flanked by Vincent D. McDonnell, left, and Joseph E. O'Grady, discussing the negotiations at a news conference yesterday.

TWO BASIC ISSUES

Unions Seek Half-Pay Pension and a Raise —Lindsay on Hand

By DAMON STETSON

Two of the mediators trying to avert a citywide strike scheduled for today said shortly before midnight that difficult issues remained but that there was "time enough to resolve them."

Vincent D. McDonnell and Theodore W. Kheel, the mediators, said they were giving their report on the crucial bargaining at the request of Mayor Lindsay. The third mediator, Joseph E. O'Grady, was continuing to meet with members of the Transit Authority.

"At this time," Mr. Kheel said, "we can report that there have been exchanges between the parties and that negotiations are as intensive as any I have taken part in. There are difficult issues to resolve, but there is time enough to resolve them."

Hints of Progress

The mediator said that the "exchanges" involved all matters in the negotiations, but he would not discuss any specific issues, including the union proposal for retirement at half pay after 20 years' service and the demand for a substantial wage increase.

However, persons familiar with the talks said that there had been some progress on the pension issue but that serious problems remained. Progress was also reported in resolving some of the other major demands of the union, but the wage question was expected to await final resolution of the pension issue.

Later this morning an official of the Transport Workers Union said, "Progress is being made." He expressed the opinion that once the pension issue was settled the rest would fall into place.

'Enough Time' for Pact

Negotiations were still being pressed at 3 A.M.

At the short news conference of the two mediators, Mr. Kheel declined to look beyond the 5 A.M. deadline, saying: "We're not going to think of after 5 A.M. We have enough time to reach a settlement."

Earlier in the negotiations, Matthew Guinan, president of the Transport Workers Union, said that if an agreement appeared imminent at the 5 A.M. deadline, the old contract might be extended a half-hour or an hour at a time. Four years ago the negotiations went beyond

Continued on Page 8, Column 1

G.O.P. LEADERS SAY ONLY ROCKEFELLER CAN BEAT JOHNSON

50-State Check Finds Nixon Close Loser, and Reagan and Romney Routed

By WARREN WEAVER Jr.
Special to The New York Times

WASHINGTON, Dec. 31 — Governor Rockefeller of New York is the only major Republican Presidential possibility who would defeat President Johnson if the 1968 election were held today, a national survey of party leaders and observers indicates.

These officials were asked by New York Times correspondents in the 50 states whether, as circumstances now stand, they believed the President would carry their state against each of the four possible Republican contenders.

Their answers, broken down into electoral votes, showed Mr. Johnson beating former Vice President Richard M. Nixon by a relatively narrow margin and Gov. Ronald Reagan of California and Gov. George Romney of Michigan decisively.

However, they had Governor Rockefeller carrying states with 378 electoral votes to 100 for Mr. Johnson and 60 for former Gov. George C. Wallace of Alabama.

A Few Imponderables

The survey did not attempt to predict how issues may shift or how candidates may rise and fall during 1968. It was designed to give the best available picture of the Presidential race, as it appears to politicians, as the election year opens.

Mr. Wallace represents the chief imponderable in any current effort to assess the election 11 months in advance. The Times survey includes an attempt to measure the effect of his candidacy in the South but not in other areas where his success in getting on the ballot has not yet been determined.

Even this limited treatment of the Wallace third party candidacy affects the results, as foreseen by the political experts.

Mr. Nixon shades President Johnson in a two-man race, 271 to 267, but when Mr. Wallace is included, the President pulls ahead, 301 to 210 with 27 for Mr. Wallace.

Wallace Backing Noted

Generally, this is because Mr. Wallace is expected to attract anti-Johnson votes in the Southern states that would otherwise go to the Republican candidate.

Mr. Rockefeller said earlier this month that he would consider acceding to a draft if a genuine movement arose.

When the President was matched against Governor Rockefeller, the politicians questioned saw the Democratic ticket carrying only Rhode Island, Georgia, Florida, Arkansas, Kentucky, Texas, Colorado, Arizona, Oklahoma, Utah and Hawaii.

The New York Governor demonstrated unusual strength

Continued on Page 7, Column 5

U.S. Said to Press Sharply For Good Vietnam Reports

By R. W. APPLE Jr.
Special to The New York Times

SAIGON, South Vietnam, Dec. 31—American officials at almost all levels, both in Saigon and in the provinces, say they are under steadily increasing pressure from Washington to produce convincing evidence of progress, especially by the South Vietnamese, in the next few months.

The pressure began to increase about three months ago, the officials report, and became more intense in December. They expect no lessening, and probably a further increase, as the American elections approach.

"I was in a briefing the other day," a middle-level civilian said, "and the man briefing us came out and said it: 'An election year is about to begin. And the people we work for are in the business of re-electing President Johnson in November.'"

Washington's latest campaign for "results" appears to differ from some in the past in that it is directed more toward South Vietnamese, military and civilian, than Americans.

A well-informed Saigon source said that recent cablegrams from the State Department and the Pentagon had been full of such instructions as these:

¶Get the South Vietnamese Army moving. Not only the regulars but the militia and the national guardsmen. And get the idea across to the American public that they are fighting well.

¶Do something — anything — about Government corruption.

¶Get President Nguyen Van Thieu to demonstrate his commitment to the war as well as his determination to demand sacrifices from the public.

"What it all adds up to," an officer in the American Embassy said, "is a simple, straightforward message: Washington is telling us that the American people will no longer tolerate

Continued on Page 3, Column 6

TRUCE DISRUPTED BY SHARP BATTLE

19 Government Troops and 30 Vietcong Reported Killed Near Saigon

By TOM BUCKLEY
Special to The New York Times

SAIGON, South Vietnam, Monday, Jan. 1—Striking out of the paddy fields at 10 minutes after midnight, while church bells in the nearby delta city of Mytho were still pealing the arrival of the new year, a Vietcong unit savagely mauled the headquarters elements of the South Vietnamese Second Marine Battalion early today.

The attack, by far the most serious violation so far in the 36-hour allied truce and the 72-hour cease-fire announced by the guerrillas, left 19 South Vietnamese marines dead and 47 wounded. Thirty of the enemy were reported to have been killed.

A Vietnamese military source said that the marines had been on a sweep 10 miles northwest of Caibe, in Dinhtuong Province, southwest of Saigon, when the cease-fire began at 6 P.M. last night (5 A.M. yesterday. Eastern standard time).

Marines in Bivouac

The marines then bivouacked for the night, the source said. While most of them slept, he added, the Vietcong, who were believed to have approached in sampans along the canals that lace the area, fired a 250-round rocket barrage.

They then began a ground attack on the marine positions, the source said. It could not be learned immediately whether they had broken through the South Vietnamese perimeter.

The American command, meanwhile, reported 16 violations of the truce during its first 12 hours.

Seven of the incidents, described as "significant" because they led to injury or death, left 14 Americans wounded and seven of the enemy dead, the command said. [A Government spokesman said 39 South Vietnamese soldiers had been killed in violations, Reuters reported.]

In the most serious encounter involving Americans, seven members of the 25th Infantry

Continued on Page 3, Column 7

World Bids Adieu To a Violent Year; City Gets Snowfall

By MURRAY SCHUMACH

Central Park vied with Times Square last night for the New Year's Eve spotlight here as the world greeted 1968 with revelry and prayer, with hope and apprehension.

As midnight arrived, thousands of horn-blowing revelers in snowy Times Square, most of them young people, embraced, screamed "Happy New Year!" and exploded firecrackers. Some even fired flares as the ball on the Allied Chemical Tower slid down the flagpole at midnight to mark the start of the new year—a leap year.

In Central Park, people drank mulled wine amid snow-draped trees.

To Department of Sanitation officials, however, the snowy New Year's Eve was work.

Condition of Streets Good

Early in the afternoon they began sending out equipment, and, when the Weather Bureau said expectations were for up to four inches of snow, 200 sanding and salting trucks were dispatched.

Snow-removal trucks were not needed, however, and the Department of Sanitation was satisfied that all major roads in the city would be in drivable condition through the night.

Outside the city, fresh snow falling on already icy highways made driving hazardous in the suburbs to the west and north.

More typical of the holiday was the contrast between Times

Continued on Page 31, Column 1

Owners Call 15c Increase In Taxi Fares Insufficient

By EMANUEL PERLMUTTER

A spokesman for the fleet taxi owners said yesterday that strikes by drivers were inevitable if the City Council adopted Mayor Lindsay's proposal to increase the cost of the average cab ride 15 cents, which he called "insufficient."

The warning came from Philip Rosenblum, treasurer of the Metropolitan Taxicab Board of Trade. The board negotiated a new contract for 74 fleets last month that would give 29,000 unionized drivers wage raises contingent upon fare increases.

Commenting on the Mayor's plan, Mr. Rosenblum said:

"If this proposal should somehow blindly be accepted, then we are in no position to sign the contract. The union, I seriously doubt, will continue to work without a contract. The result seems to be inevitable, unfortunately."

The owners have been seeking fare increases that would in effect increase the present average $1.05 ride to $1.80, according to Investigation Commissioner Arnold G. Fraiman, the head of the Mayor's taxi task force.

Specifically, the Mayor's plan calls for the first one-fifth of a mile to be increased to 40 cents from 35 cents and the waiting time for each 90 seconds to be doubled to 10 cents from 5 cents.

The owners had wanted the first fifth increased to 40 cents and the cost of additional fifths of a mile raised to 10 cents from 5 cents.

Union representatives declined yesterday to say whether the drivers were dissatisfied with Mr. Lindsay's proposal or whether they might strike.

Harry Van Arsdale Jr., president of Local 3036 of the New York City Taxi Drivers Union, had an informal discussion with some fleet owners at the Americana hotel, but refused to divulge the nature of the talks.

However, Mr. Van Arsdale said Saturday that if the drivers heeded their union leaders they would not strike.

Cautioned on Haste

Arthur A. Scherr, chairman of the Taxi Owners Division of Local 3036, said after talking with Mr. Van Arsdale last night:

"We are instructing all our owner-drivers to hold off and not take any hasty action and give us a chance to work toward a fare increase that will give them a livelihood."

The union represents 2,100 of the city's 2,900 independent owner-drivers.

Mr. Van Arsdale, who is co-chairman of the Labor-Management Council of New York City, has been staying at the Americana for possible assistance in the transit contract talks taking place there.

In November, the employers made public a 30-page survey of the taxi industry by Price Waterhouse & Co., the accounting concern. The survey, based on an audit of three of the city's 48 fleet companies, contended that the gross earnings

Continued on Page 9, Column 1

PACKERS, RAIDERS GAIN SUPER BOWL

Green Bay Tops Cowboys— Oakland Routs Oilers

The Green Bay Packers and the Oakland Raiders won their league championships yesterday and set the stage for their confrontation in the Super Bowl.

The weather was cold (13 below zero) in Green Bay, but Bart Starr's passing and running set a sizzling pace for the Packers as they defeated the Dallas Cowboys, 21-17, for their third straight National Football League title.

The Raiders played under sunny skies at Oakland and routed the Oilers, 40-7, in the American League championship game.

Starr, who had passed for two touchdowns earlier in the game, scored on a quarterback sneak with 13 seconds left to play to give Green Bay its victory.

The American Football League championship turned out to be a mismatch as Daryle Lamonica, calling his plays and passing brilliantly, led the Raiders to an easy triumph.

George Blanda, a former Oiler, kicked four field goals in the game, while Lamonica threw two touchdown passes.

Details on Pages 18 and 19

Shifts in the Kremlin Could Be Obstacle To Cultural Accord

By PETER GROSE
Special to The New York Times

WASHINGTON, Dec. 31—United States officials are concerned that a smoldering dispute in the Kremlin may have thrown up a new obstacle to continuation of the 10-year-old Soviet-American cultural exchange program.

Analysts of Soviet affairs interpret the abolition a week ago of a key cultural committee as the latest step in what United States officials call a "Brezhnev-style purge."

Through administrative reorganization, according to this analysis, the Soviet Communist party leader, Leonid I. Brezhnev, is gradually suppressing a faction that could challenge his leadership. This is the so-called Komsomol group, headed by Aleksandr N. Shelepin, a Politburo member.

An incidental consequence of this reshuffle is uncertainty among both Russian and American officials about how to negotiate a new cultural exchange agreement to replace the two-year pact expiring today. Talks on a new pact have not yet begun.

The abolished agency, called the State Committee for Cultural Relations With Foreign Countries, had been the Soviet unit responsible for cultural-

Continued on Page 4, Column 2

NEWS INDEX

Johnson's Press Secretary Is 'Unflappable' as Ever

Associated Press

George Christian

By MAX FRANKEL
Special to The New York Times

SAN ANTONIO, Dec. 31—"We've decided to unleash Christian," said George Christian with a faint smile and shrug as he contemplated his full-fledged debut on national television today.

It was a typical remark for the man President Johnson affectionately calls "Unflappable George," a man who mocks the publicity hoopla out of which he has built a career in politics and yet a man who deflates his own importance.

It was a fairly typical performance that Mr. Christian gave on the Columbia Broadcasting System's "Face the Nation" on his first anniversary as the White House press secretary.

It was a low-key but faithful transmission of the President's views and at the same time an alert defense against even the most oblique criticism of his employer.

For example:

¶"I don't think the reputation of being a hard man to work for is earned. [Mr. Johnson] is a hard-driving man. You do have to run to keep up with his walk."

¶"I think the question of the credibility gap is something that puzzles me as much as it does anyone. This has happened to other Presidents. It is, in a political sense, a smart thing to do, to discredit your President. I think it is incumbent on all of us people in government, people in the press, to do the very best we can to be accurate. I think there are mistakes made on both sides."

¶"I do enjoy working for the President. I happen to be very fond of him personally. I think I know him. I think I understand what motivates him. I agree with what he is trying to do for this country. I couldn't ask for a higher calling in my opinion as a more or less professional press secretary."

That is the George Christian that the White House press corps sees at least twice a day, and who, it believes, will succeed and survive in a job from which three better known national figures had been driven to various degrees of despair—Pierre E. Salinger, George E. Reedy and Bill D. Moyers.

The essence of Mr. Christian's success is a willingness to bury the ego, the willingness even to look foolish, if necessary, to carry out the President's usual wish to present a picture of serenity and order at the White House.

In his first months in office Mr. Christian inspired a

Continued on Page 6, Column 3

Packers Beat Cowboys, 21-17, for N.F.L. Title on Score in Last 13 Seconds

STARR'S PLUNGE ON 3D DOWN WINS

Quarterback Also Passes for 2 Scores as Packers Gain Record 3d Title in Row

STATISTICS OF THE GAME

	Cowb.	Packers
First downs	11	18
Rushing yardage	92	80
Passing yardage	100	115
Return yardage	43	44
Passes	11-26	14-24
Interceptions by	0	1
Punts	8-39	8-29
Fumbles lost	1	2
Yards penalized	58	10

By WILLIAM N. WALLACE

Special to The New York Times

GREEN BAY, Wis., Dec. 31—There had never been a football game like this one. Everyone agreed—Vince Lombardi, the winning coach; Tom Landry, the losing coach; Chuck Howley, the Dallas linebacker who symbolized the losers; Bart Starr, the quarterback who scored the winning touchdown with 13 seconds left to play.

The Green Bay Packers, frustrated and punished for 40 of the 60 minutes it takes to play these games, won their third straight championship of the National Football League by defeating the Dallas Cowboys, 21-17, before a capacity crowd of 50,861 at Lambeau Field.

The temperature was 14 degrees below zero at the start of the game and 12 degrees below at the end. And on top of that there was a 14-knot northwest breeze blowing down from the Yukon.

"It was terrible out there," said Landry, "terrible for both sides. That in itself made this game distinctive from any other."

A Game of Distinction

The fact that the teams, champions of the Western and Eastern conferences of the N. F. L., were able to play such capable football was remarkable. It was remarkable too that the stadium was filled and nobody went home before the outcome was decided. The customers, who paid as much as $12 for their tickets, received full worth.

No team in the 47-year history of the N.F.L. has ever before won three straight championships. But the Packers came within 13 seconds of missing this achievement. On third down from the 1-yard line Starr drove over right guard behind Jerry Kramer's block to score the winning touchdown.

This touchdown came at the end of an exciting 68-yard drive against the gallant Cowboys and the clock. Football players are mortal like the rest of us and they have fear. "I was scared we had thrown it all away," said Henry Jordan, the Packers' defensive tackle who played a magnificent game.

The Packers won $8,000 apiece today and now they move on to the Super Bowl at Miami on Jan. 14 to play the American League champion.

Jordan Paces Defense

Jordan and his mates on the defensive unit kept the Packers in the game by holding the rampant Cowboys numerous times in the second half. They made victory possible. The Green Bay offense was in trouble most of the time and had ground to a halt after opening a 14-0 lead in the first 18 minutes.

Starr, pressured relentlessly by the Cowboy front four, was thrown eight times, while attempting to pass, for losses totaling 76 yards.

But Bart and all the Packers have come back so many times from the depths of adversity. They did so again by mustering their last scoring drive.

The temperature was too cold for the "electric blanket"—the heating system under the turf—to work and the field became progressively harder and harder. This was to the Packers' advantage.

Starr began to throw short wide passes to his backs, Donnie Anderson and Chuck Mercein. The linebackers covering them, Dave Edward and Howley, who is an All-Pro performer, could not react swiftly enough to tackle the attackers in the open field. "There was no traction," said Howley. "The advantage had gone to the offense."

Compassion for Freezing Fans

Starr passed to Anderson for 6 yards, to Anderson again for 12 to the Dallas 39 and then a big one to Mercein for 19 to the Cowboy 11. Mercein, a fullback, who was a New York Giants' reject, stormed to the 3. Anderson was stopped twice and then Starr tried the quarterback sneak to score.

If he had failed would the Packers have had time to kick a field goal on fourth down to tie the score and send the game into a sudden-death overtime? Their time-outs were used up.

"It would have been close," said Lombardi. "We didn't want a tie. We had compassion for those spectators. We wanted to send them home right then."

The Packers seemed to have a much more positive attitude at the beginning of the game and seemed to worry less about the cold. Boyd Dowler scored on two touchdown passes from Starr, the first worked against Mike Johnson, the Dallas cornerback who is half a foot shorter than Dowler and proved to be a weak link in the early going. The first scoring pass was short, 8 yards, the second long, 46 yards.

Dallas scored to trail, 14-7, when Willie Townes dropped Starr for a 19-yard loss and Bart fumbled the football. George Andrie, the defensive end, picked it up and ran with it for a score from the 7. But Dallas in the first half gained only 42 yards and Don Meredith completed only four of 13 pass attempts. Meredith's passes for the most part were dreadful.

Halfback Throws a 'Bomb'

But Dallas made 3 points just before the half on a 21-yard field goal by Dan Villanueva after Willie Wood of Green Bay had fumbled away a punt.

Meredith and his offense finally began to show something in the third period. A big play at the top of the fourth quarter suddenly put the Cowboys ahead, 17-14. It was the halfback pass, Dan Reeves to Lance Rentzel for 50 yards. Rentzel, the flankerback was wide open, and the Packers—rarely tricked—had been fooled completely.

By then it looked as if Dallas could win because Townes, Andrie, Jethroe Pugh and Bob Lilly were dropping Starr as often as he tried to pass.

With five minutes left in the game, the Green Bay offense, so sorely tried all season and weakened by injuries, began the winning drive. It was to be a fatal one to the Cowboys and one that would enable the Packers to remain as champions once more.

"Those last five minutes are what the Packers are all about," said Lombardi. "They do it because they respect each other. They are selfless."

It Was a Long, Cold Afternoon for Packer Fans

Associated Press Wirephotos and United Press [illegible]

Bart Starr (15), left, is over by a head to score the winning touchdown.

Green Bay Scoring

Dallas Cowboys	0	10	0	7—17
Green Bay Packers	7	7	0	7—21

G.B.—Dowler, 8, pass from Starr (Chandler, kick).

G.B.—Dowler, 46, pass from Starr (Chandler, kick).

Dal.—Andrie, 7, return of fumble recovery (Villanueva, kick).

Dal.—FG, Villanueva, 21.

Dal.—Rentzel, 50, pass from Reeves (Villanueva, kick).

G.B.—Starr, 1, run (Chandler, kick).

Attendance 50,861.

INDIVIDUAL STATISTICS

RUSHES—G.B.: Anderson, 18 for 35 yards; Mercein, 6 for 20; Williams, 4 for 13; Wilson, 3 for 11; Starr, 1 for 1. Dal.: Perkins, 17 for 51; Reeves, 13 for 42; Baynham, 1 for minus 1; Clarke, 1 for minus 8; Meredith, 1 for 9.

PASSES—G.B.: Starr, 14 of 24 for 191 yards. Dal.: Meredith, 10 of 25 for 59; Reeves, 1 of 1 for 50.

RECEPTIONS—G.B.: Dowler, 4 for 77 yards; Anderson, 4 for 44; Dale, 3 for 44; Mercein, 2 for 22; Williams, 1 for 4. Dal.: Hayes, 3 for 16; Reeves, 3 for 11; Clarke, 2 for 24; Rentzel, 2 for 61; Baynham, 1 for 3.

GREEN BAY FANS ARE RUGGED, TOO

50,861 Brave Cold—Many Find Cars Are 'Frozen'

GREEN BAY, Wis., Dec. 31 (UPI)—The football fans are rugged up here.

They had to be today to sit through the National Football League title game in 13 degrees below zero weather.

It was the coldest N.F.L. title game—the first played in below zero temperatures.

By comparison, the previous coldest title game was in 1945 in a "warm" 5 degrees above.

The crowd was announced as a sell-out 50,861 and it did not appear as if any of the fans missed seeing the Packers win their third successive title.

There were some empty seats during the game as people sought a warm spot in the stadium or went to their cars to warm the engines and themselves.

But most stayed to the finish. Several hundred fans stayed to tear down the goal posts and many others had no choice when they got outside. Their cars wouldn't start.

On the field, the Packers and their opponents, the Dallas Cowboys, managed to keep warm on the sidelines, huddling in makeshift dugouts with liquid gas heaters.

And the hundreds of reporters covering the game from the heated press box encountered some difficulty, too. The windows frosted up and the writers had difficulty following the action. One man was kept busy scraping off the ice.

Raiders Rout Oilers, 40-7, for A.F.L. Crown

Meanwhile, in the Other Game, Oakland Was Out in Front All the Way

George Blanda, an ex-Oiler, kicking 40-yard field goal for the Raiders in second quarter. Daryle Lamonica holds.

United Press International Telephotos

Zeke Moore (22) climbs over fellow Oiler Walt Suggs (76) to make a nine-yard kickoff return in the second quarter.

DIXON'S 144 YARDS SET RUSHING PACE

3 Scores Involve Lamonica —Blanda Gets 16 Points, Kicking 4 Field Goals

STATISTICS OF THE GAME

	Oilers	Raiders
First downs	11	18
Rushing yardage	38	263
Passing yardage	108	101
Return yardage	215	135
Passes	15-35	10-26
Interceptions by	0	1
Punts	11-39	4-44
Fumbles lost	2	0
Yards penalized	45	69

By DAVE ANDERSON

Special to The New York Times

OAKLAND, Calif., Dec. 31—The Foreign Legion of pro football, the Oakland Raiders, qualified today to challenge the game's monarchs, the Green Bay Packers, in the Super Bowl.

In a 40-7 rout of the Houston Oilers in the American Football League championship game, the Raiders were magnificent, particularly several players who were deemed expendable by rival teams but coveted by Al Davis, known locally as "The Genius."

Hewritt Dixon, a 220-pounder Davis converted from tight end to fullback after obtaining him from the Denver Broncos, provided the play that broke open the game — a 69-yard touchdown run on a sweep around left end early in the second quarter.

Dixon rumbled for a total of 144 yards, his biggest day in a career that began when, as a 6-foot, 205-pound, 14-year-old freshman, he beat out his uncle Rufus as the first-string fullback at Lacross (Fla.) High School.

Lamonica at the Helm

Guiding the offense was Daryle Lamonica, a 25-year-old quarterback acquired from the Buffalo Bills, where he served his apprenticeship behind Jack Kemp. During the recent season, Lamonica took over as the Raider leader and threw 30 touchdown passes.

He threw two more today—a looping 16-yard toss to Dave Kocourek on a fake field-goal attempt that put the Raiders in command, 17-0, at half-time, and a 12-yard flip to Bill Miller for the final touchdown. He also scored on a 1-yard keeper.

Kocourek and Miller arrived in trades, too: Kocourek from the Miami Dolphins, Miller from Buffalo. But the coup de grâce for the Raiders was applied intermittently, and with relish, by another unwanted performer, 40-year-old George Blanda.

The Oilers, ironically, attempted to release Blanda following last season, but waivers were required. Davis, the former Raider coach whose title now is managing general partner, claimed the aging, but still accurate, field-goal specialist.

Blanda Makes His Points

Blanda kicked four field goals, of 37, 40, 42 and 36 yards. He is a year older than his coach, Johnny Rauch, and when he was a rookie quarterback with the Chicago Bears two decades ago, Sid Luckman and Johnny Lujack turned him into a linebacker.

Blanda even retired after the 1958 season, but he joined the Oilers for their first A.F.L. season in 1960.

His 16 points, including four conversions, set a league title game record. He now has 31 points in title games, another record. He had been the quarterback and place-kicker for the Oilers when they won league titles in 1960 and 1961.

Except for Pete Beathard's 5-yard touchdown pass to Charlie Frazier in the fourth quarter after the Raiders had run up a 30-0 lead, the Oilers were unable to penetrate a defense that was virtually as flawless as the diversified offense.

The Raiders did not fumble and not one of their passes was intercepted. The defensive line, led by Tom Keating and Ike Lassiter, punished Beahard, tackling him three times for a total loss of 34 yards, and controlled the 230-pound fullback, Hoyle Granger.

The Oilers entrusted their ball-control offense to Granger in finishing ahead of the New York Jets for the Eastern Division title, but the Raiders limited him to a net total of 19 yards. The Raiders had a scare, though, when Keating limped off.

His injury was diagnosed later as a sprained right ankle, but he predicted that he would oppose the Packers. He had problems with the same ankle when he, too, was with Buffalo. But not all the Raiders are members of the "Foreign Legion."

Dan Connors, the middle linebacker, provided a big play that sabotaged an early Oiler drive. He stole the ball from the grasp of Alvin Reed, the tight end, at the Raiders' 39-yard line.

Connors a Draftee

Unlike many of his teammates, Connors was a quality draftee, a No. 2 selection in 1964 from Miami, Fla. University. This year's No. 1 choice, Gene Upshaw, the rookie guard from Texas A. and I., provided the block that sprang Dixon loose.

Oakland Scoring

Houston Oilers	0	0	0	7—7
Oakland Raiders	3	14	10	13—40

Oak.—FG, Blanda, 37.

Oak.—Kocourek, 18, pass from Lamonica (Blanda, kick).

Oak.—Lamonica, 1, run (Blanda, kick).

Oak.—FG, Blanda, 40.

Oak.—FG, Blanda, 42.

Hou.—Frazier, 5, pass from Beathard (Wittenborn, kick).

Oak.—FG, Blanda, 36.

Oak.—Miller, 12, pass from Lamonica (Blanda, kick).

Attendance—53,330.

INDIVIDUAL STATISTICS

RUSHES—Oak: Dixon, 21 for 144 yards; Banaszak, 15 for 116; Lamonica, 5 for 22. Hou: Grangr, 14 for 19; Campbell, 6 for 15.

PASSES—Lamonica, 10 of 24 for 111 yards. Hou: Beathard, 15 of 35 for 142.

RECEPTIONS—Oak: Miller, 3 for 32 yards; Biletnikoff, 2 for 19; Cannon, 2 for 31; Banaszak, 1 for 4; Kocourek, 1 for 17; Dixon, 1 for 8. Hou: Taylor, 1 for 6; Frazier, 7 for 81; Campbell, 4 for 60; Granger, 1 for minus 10.

Upshaw had been permitted, reluctantly, to get married yesterday in San Antonio, Tex., after Davis had bristled that "You can do it by phone, I checked that out." The major domo feared that Upshaw, a 255-pound deer, might let his concentration wander.

Instead, Upshaw scattered Oiler tacklers as if they had absconded with his bride.

Another well-rated draftee, Pete Banaszak, a No. 5 choice from Miami in 1966, ran for 114 yards. He has performed with elan ever since he moved into the first unit following a broken ankle suffered by Clem Daniels.

Throughout the joyous afternoon, the 53,330 spectators, a league title-game record, were in celebration. The team across the big bay, the San Francisco 49ers, have never won a title, either in the N.F.L. or the old All-America Conference. And now the Raiders from "Li'l ol' Oakland," as Davis likes to say, had surpassed their more sophisticated neighbors.

OAKLAND PLAYERS SUPER CONFIDENT

By BILL BECKER

Special to The New York Times

OAKLAND, Calif., Dec. 31—Victor and vanquished alike expressed the belief today that the Oakland Raiders would give the Green Bay Packers a genuine test in the Super Bowl Jan. 14 in Miami.

"This is the best team I've ever played on" said 40-year-old George Blanda, the Raider kicking specialist. "And I've played on 18 of 'em."

Blanda, who accounted for 16 points, a record, today, once starred for the Chicago Bears in the National Football League.

"This team is not going to roll over and play dead," Blanda continued in the boisterous Raider dressing room. "We're not awed by the Packers. We'll give a good account of ourselves."

Starr Is in His Eyes

Daryle Lamonica, the Oakland quarterback, said he was looking forward to the test against the Packers' ace, Bart Starr.

Lamonica recalled that he was drafted by Green Bay when he was graduated from Notre Dame, but chose instead to go with the young American League.

"Some people have compared me with Bart Starr," said the 25-year-old Lamonica, who finally blossomed into stardom in his fifth pro season. "I don't copy anyone, much as I admire Starr. But I consider it a real privilege to play against a man who is rated tops in the business."

Lamonica believes that the Raiders have the team depth to cope with the Packers.

"If we play like we did today," said Daryle, "there is no reason why we can't beat the best. If we do beat the best, we'll have to be considered the best."

Pete Beathard, the Houston quarterback, compared Oakland "very favorably" with the Kansas City Chiefs, last year's A.F.L. champions. Beathard was a member of the Chiefs, who lost to Green Bay, 34-10, in the first Super Bowl last January.

"I think this year's game will be closer," Beathard said in the Houston lockerroom. "The Packers are terrific and tough, but I have great respect for the Raiders. They are very explosive and well balanced."

Oakland's coach, John Rauch, was understandably elated by his squad's performance.

"This was our best all-round game," said Rauch, a title winner in his second season as head man "Our over-all execution — particularly our ball-carrying and downfield blocking—was the best of the year."

Can the Raiders keep their fine edge for another fortnight?

"This team has a great deal of confidence," Rauch stressed. "It has grown in confidence from week to week. The men on this team, I am sure, will respond to one more challenge, like taking on the very best in football."

Hewritt Dixon, the big fullback who was the game's running star, conceded that he had played his best of the season. On his 69-yard touchdown run, Dixon said, he knew that "I had it made when I turned the corner." Dixon credited Gene Upshaw, a huge rookie guard, and Pete Banaszak, the halfback, with "a heluva job" on key blocks.

Automobiles, Boats
Dogs and Other Pets
Shipping News
Shopping Guide

The New York Times

SPORTS

Section 5

Sunday, January 21, 1968

Associated Press

A CLOSE CALL FOR DAMASCUS: Damascus, foreground, crossing finish line two lengths ahead of Most Host, right rear, in San Fernando Stakes at Santa Anita. Willie Shoemaker was aboard Damascus. Ruken, outside, was third.

DAMASCUS SCORES ON STRETCH RUN

Wins by 2 Lengths and Pays $2.20, Record Low at Santa Anita—Most Host Second

By BILL BECKER
Special to The New York Times

ARCADIA, Calif., Jan. 20—The 1967 dandy of the turf world, Damascus, made it two straight in '68 with a two-length victory in the $56,950 San Fernando Stakes today at Santa Anita Park.

Mrs. Edith W. Bancroft's 4-year-old bay colt, backed down to 1-10 favoritism in the six-horse race, returned the shortest win price in Santa Anita history—$2.20.

A crowd estimated at 53,000, lured by the 80-degree weather and the promise of a "sure thing," saw the son of Sword Dancer and Kerala cover the mile-and-one-eighth distance in 1:48 4/5.

Ridden as usual by Bill Shoemaker, Damascus pulled away steadily in the stretch from the runner-up, Most Host, a 22-1 shot, and Ruken (9-1), the third-place finisher.

Minus Pool Results

Most Host, ridden by William Harmatz, edged Ruken, Fernando Alvarez up, by a head in a photo finish. Behind them were Field Master, Rivet and Jungle Road.

The mutuel payoffs read $2.20, $2.20 and $2.10 for Damascus, $5.80 and $2.10 for Most Host and $2.10 for Ruken.

Santa Anita took a $7,177.92 loss on the race, when the show pool turned up minus, or overdrawn. It would have been much worse if California had not passed a new law allowing tracks to break down their payoffs to a dime. Last year Santa Anita had a $50,000 minus show pool on one of Buckpasser's victories.

A minus pool is created when the amount of money the track pays out exceeds 86 per cent of the total wagered on a race in this state. The California racing coce gives the state 7 per cent

Continued on Page 7, Column 6

Italian Driver Killed In Monte Carlo Rally

By United Press International

MONTE CARLO, Jan. 20—An Italian driver, Luciano Lombardini, was killed and his teammate, Sandro Munari, was seriously injured today when their Lancia-Fulvia sideswiped a passenger car in the 37th Monte Carlo Rally.

Lombardini was the co-driver of Munari's car which sideswiped a passenger car while trying to pass on the right and then slammed head-on into a truck near Skoplje, Yugoslavia. The accident occurred 12 hours into the 60-hour first stage of the rally.

Rally officials first announced that both Lombardini and

Continued on Page 10, Column 2

Forward Pass, 5-1, Is 5-Length Victor In Hibiscus Stakes

Special to The New York Times

MIAMI, Jan. 20 — Calumet Farm's Forward Pass won the $32,750 Hibiscus Stakes in convincing fashion at Hialeah Park today, crossing the wire 5 lengths in front of his nearest competitor, Isidor Bieber's Wise Exchange.

The On-And-On colt won only three of 10 races as a juvenile, but handled today's field of 12 3-year-olds with apparent ease. This was his first start of the year.

The winner covered the seven-furlong distance in 1:22 3-5, the fastest time for the Hibiscus since it was lengthened from six furlongs four years ago. He carried 117 pounds. He returned $12.20, $5.40 and $5.20 for $2 across the board.

End of Dry Spell

For Calumet Farms, the victory by the 5-1 shot marked the end of a dry spell that began in 1966. Kentucky Jug's victory in the Turf Cup in that year was the stable's last previous stakes victory at Hialeah.

Donald Brumfield, who has ridden Forward Pass in all but one of his previous starts, said he has been high on the colt since the first time he rode him. "This horse is going to get better as we go along," he said. "I felt I had a strong horse under me at the end."

The feature was marred by the late withdrawal of Carolawn Farm's sparkling colt, Subpet, who had drawn top

Continued on Page 7, Column 2

MARR'S 67 FOR 204 LEADS BY 2 SHOTS IN KAISER TOURNEY

Archer Is Next, With Littler Third at 207 in $125,000 Open Golf on Coast

By LINCOLN A. WERDEN
Special to The New York Times

NAPA, Calif., Jan. 20—Dave Marr finished in 78th place last Sunday in the Bing Crosby tourney, but today he continued to lead the $125,000 Kaiser international open field. With this third consecutive round in the 60's, Marr brought his 54-hole aggregate to 204 with a 67.

"I don't remember when I ever shot 68, 69 and 67 in succession," said the dapper professional from Larchmont, N.Y. "Maybe it was in prewar days," he suggested with a grin.

"But the big change in my playing here from last week at Pebble Beach is partly due to Arnold Palmer. In a practice round here Tuesday, Arnie gave me some advice. He told me I was standing too far from the ball and I was hitting everything to the right. When we came in, we talked about my golf. It's been a lot better since I made changes he suggested."

Palmer Cards a 74

Marr's golf was so improved that he enjoyed a two-stroke lead over rangy George Archer, the ex-cowboy. Archer, after a 68, was at 206. But Palmer, now credited with an assist for Marr's improved play, was down at 217, 13 strokes back of Marr, following a 74.

Gene Littler, who said a recent layoff helped his game, put together a 66 that consisted of six birdies and 12 pars. "I'm not much of a mechanic, but I have been tinkering in my off hours with Model A and Model T Fords I have at home," he noted. "It's a rest from golf."

"I've been restoring them. The Model A is as old as I am, it's 37 years old."

Littler's seemingly effortless golf, in which he had birdies on four of the last five holes for an inward 32, brought a smile from Kermit Zarley. Zarley, who was one above Littler's 207 and tied with Jacky Cupit at 208, said "the only thing that bothered Littler today was he got tired tipping his hat. The crowd kept applauding his birdies and pars."

Play began at 10 A.M. and, in contrast to frosty greens and the use of a helicopter to thaw them yesterday, the putting surfaces were normal. The course dried in the sunshine before the first group teed off.

This first Kaiser open at the Silverado Country Club attracted 12,105 spectators.

Lee Trevino of El Paso, Tex., the 1967 rookie-of-the-year, equaled Littler's 66 to share

Continued on Page 4, Column 2

Associated Press

FLOOR FIGHT: Lew Alcindor of U.C.L.A. clings to the ball as Ken Spain of Houston makes a diving lunge for it, just a second too late. Coming in to cover the play are Don Chaney (24), left, and Elvin Hayes, right, of the Cougars.

BALFANZ TRIUMPHS AT OLYMPIC TRIAL

Wins in Michigan and Gains Berth on Jumping Squad —Watt Takes Second

By MICHAEL STRAUSS
Special to The New York Times

IRON MOUNTAIN, Mich., Jan. 20—John Balfanz, the seasoned campaigner from Denver, turned in two stylish leaps this afternoon to capture the Kiwanis Trophy and insure himself of a berth on the American Olympic special jumping squad.

The 27-year-old ski salesman, the national champion in 1964, soared 286 and 285 feet to post 206.4 points.

Second best was Adrian Watt, 20, of Duluth, with flights of 284 and 299 feet for 202.7 points. Dave Norby of Madison, Wis., followed with 198.2 points, as a result of trips of 264 and 295 feet.

A crowd of 5,000 turned out for the opening of the two-day meet being held at this small city's towering 90-meter hill to determine American Olympic jumping team berths. It was treated to some stylish performances. Distances, however were not impressive.

The day's longest jump was turned in by one of the few Easterners in the 25-man field—Jay Rand, 17, of Lake Placid, N. Y. Jay flew 309 feet in the practice round and then moved into second place behind Bal-

Continued on Page 6, Column 3

United Press International

GOING UP FROM DOWN UNDER: Elvin Hayes easing in a basket from underneath the hoop in the first quarter.

Wood Takes Senior Title In National Figure Skating

By THOMAS ROGERS
Special to The New York Times

PHILADELPHIA, Jan. 20—The United States crowned its figure-skating champions at the Spectrum today and prepared to send one of its strongest teams in talent and depth to the Winter Olympics at Grenoble, France.

Peggy Fleming of Colorado Springs gave those who acclaim her as the greatest woman skater America has produced reason to point again with pride.

She won her fifth senior championship with a four-minute free-skating exhibition of surpassing talent and poise before an evening audience of 14,216 that rose to give her a 30-second ovation as she glided off the ice.

Only a Third Place

In the afternoon, the crowd also stood for half a minute to cheer John Misha Petkevich of Great Falls, Mont., who had dazzled it with a blur of leaps and corkscrew spins.

But Petkevich's stunning exhibition could earn him only third place in the senior men's class. The title went to Tim Wood of Bloomfield Hills, Mich., a 19-year-old college student who combined a strong

Continued on Page 6, Column 2

Rangers Win, 3-0, As Giacomin Stars

By United Press International

OAKLAND, Galif. Jan. 20—Ed Giacomin posted his fourth shutout of the season tonight and his second over the Seals as the New York Rangers defeated Oakland, 3-0, in a National Hockey League game.

Giacomin, a product of the New York Rovers, never was badly pressed by the Seals.

There was a bruising fight in the first period between Roger Fleming of the Rangers and a Seals rookie, Tracy Pratt, son of the former Ranger Hall of Fame star, Babe Pratt, that lasted a minute.

Both antagonists kept their feet throughout the melee and

Continued on Page 9, Column 8

COLUMBIA ROUTS CORNELL, 93 TO 51

Newmark, With Help From Walaszek and McMillian, Paces League Victory

By GORDON S. WHITE Jr.

Columbia played a game its basketball coach, Jack Rohan, called "our best basketball of the year" in trouncing a strong Cornell team, 93-51, in University Hall yesterday.

The Lions, who matured as they moved through the Holiday Festival in December for that tourney's title, reached a high point of the season to date to the cimplete enjoyment of most of the 1,756 persons jammed into the small gymnasium on Morningside Heights.

It was an important game in the Ivy League. If it had been possible, 10,000 persons or more would have been present for one of the best Columbia games in many seasons.

The Lions Become One

As is was the small crowd roared loud enough to indicate this may be the winter when that usually quiet pussy cat—the Columbia Lion—becomes a roaring, strong giant of basketball.

By winning easily, Columbia moved into a tie for second place in the Ivy race only a half game behind the defending champion, Princeton.

Cornell was certainly a big challenge for the Lions. The Big Red had beaten the Lions on Dec. 15 to start the Columbia team on a three-game losing streak. But here, in their home gym, the Lions continued their winning ways by gaining their seventh straight victory.

It was a good team effort by

Continued on Page 5, Column 2

HOUSTON BREAKS 47-GAME STREAK OF U.C.L.A., 71-69

Hayes, With 39 Points, Gets Final Two Free Throws—Alcindor Is Held to 15

By The Associated Press

HOUSTON, Jan. 20 — Houston's inspired Cougars, led by Elvin Hayes, toppled the University of California, Los Angeles, 71-69, tonight and ended the Bruins' myth of invincibility in college basketball.

A howling, happy crowd of 52,693 in the Astrodome—a record for a basketball game—saw Hayes, Houston's all-American, toss in 39 points and help put the defensive clamp on Lew Alcindor.

Appropriately enough, it was Hayes's two free throws with 28 seconds remaining that broke a 69-69 tie—and U.C.L.A.'s 47-game winning streak, second longest in history.

The Cougars, ranked No. 2 in the nation with a 16-0 won-lost mark going into their showdown with the top-ranked Bruins, turned U.C.L.A.'s own weapons on them—an outstanding performance by a superstar and a tenacious defense.

Cougars Lead by 3 at Half

Houston, sparked by Hayes' 29 points, established a 46-43 margin at intermission and spent the second half fighting off challenge after challenge by the cold-shooting Bruins.

When it was over, the delirious Houston fans and cheerleaders stormed onto the court, hoisted their heroes to their shoulders and began a rhythmic chant, "We're No. 1, we're No. 1."

If they are, they can thank their poise, which never broke in the face of the famous U.C.L.A. press defense.

Houston moved into a 13-12 lead with 13:45 to go in the first half on a basket by George Reynolds. The Cougars didn't trail again, although the game was tied three times.

The last deadlock occurred when Lucious Allen, the high scorer for the Bruins with 25 points, dropped in two free throws with 44 seconds to go. The Cougars then brought the ball down court, and when Hayes was fouled by Jim Nielson they went ahead to stay.

Bruins Lose the Ball

U.C.I.A. had one more chance, but blew it on an uncharacteristic mixup in signals on which Mike Warren of the Bruins tipped the ball out of bounds. Houston took over with 12 seconds left and ran out the clock.

"Isn't that Hayes great?" exulted the Houston coach, Guy Lewis. "Almost every game he plays is great."

"Houston played a tremendous game," said John Wooden, coach of U.C.L.A. "We'll just have to start over again."

It was a sweet revenge for Houston, whose last loss was to U.C.L.A. in the semi-finals of the national championship in Louisville, Ky., last March, 73-58.

If the Bruins had an excuse.

Continued on Page 5, Column 3

Cincinnati Quintet 82-72 Victor; Auburn Upsets Kentucky, 74-73

Louisville Beaten

By The Associated Press

CINCINNATI, Jan. 20 — The slow - starting University of Cincinnati Bearcats coupled Dean Foster's offensive play with brilliant defensive teamwork today to upset Louisville, the Missouri Valley Basketball Conference leader, 82-72.

The victory moved Cincinnati into the first place in the conference.

Managing to steal the ball at least 10 times on hard press maneuvers, the Bearcats broke loose for a 10-point lead late in the first half after trailing the Cardinals since the opening minutes. The half-time score was 42-32, and the Bearcats held their 10-point lead most of the remainder of the game.

Wesley Unseld, Louisville's all-America, scored a game-high of 26 points.

Cincinnati played without the services of two regulars. Jim Ard, a forward, has been hos-

Continued on Page 4, Column [illegible]

Perry's Shot Decides

By United Press International

AUBURN, Ala., Jan. 20—Tom Perry scored on a free throw with 36 seconds left today to give Auburn a 74-73 upset victory over eighth-ranked Kentucky in a Southeastern Conference game today.

Alex Howell got 25 points to pace the Auburn attack, which left Adolph Rupp of Kentucky still looking for victory No. 771, which would tie him with Forrest (Phog) Allen of Kansas as the coaches with the most triumphs in history.

After Perry's conversion, Kentucky raced back downcourt and with five seconds left Steve Clevenger made a desperation push shot behind a Wildcat screen. The ball just brushed the rim and time ran out.

The lead changed hands 18 times during the close battle, and the first half ended with Kentucky ahead, 32-30.

But Auburn forced the Wild-

Continued on Page 4, Column [illegible]

Associated Press

WATCHING THE BIRDIE: Dave Marr and fans waiting for his putt to drop into the cup for a birdie on the eighth hole at the Kaiser open tourney. Marr, who leads the field, had three other birdies on the front nine yesterday.

Army Sets Back Dartmouth, 76-58, for Fifth Straight Basketball Victory

CADET TRACKMEN DEFEAT COLGATE

Army Triumphs in Fencing, Loses in Hockey, 3 to 2, and in Gymnastics

Special to The New York Times

WEST POINT, N. Y., Jan. 20—Army turned a close game into a rout tonight as it rolled to a 76-58 victory over Dartmouth. It was the fifth straight victory for the cadets and their 11th in 14 games.

Dartmouth was in contention for the first five minutes, when a pair of baskets and a free throw by Joe Colgan had the Indians leading by a 5-4 margin. Back-to-back baskets by Bill Schutsky and Steve Hunt sent the cadets ahead as Army began to find the range.

A string of 13 consecutive points, coupled with a Dartmouth drought which saw the Indians go scoreless for 8 minutes 43 seconds, lifted Army into a comfortable lead with 5:22 remaining in the half. Army hit on 14 of 30 attempts from the floor in the first half while Dartmouth could manage only four field goals in 15 attempts.

Hunt and Noonan led Army with 11 points each. Henry Tyson was high for the Indians with 14.

The cadets also triumphed in a track meet, trouncing Colgate, 97-12, this afternoon.

Larry Hart put the shot 56 feet 3 inches, matching the distance he had a week ago against St. John's and New York University in setting a Military Academy indoor mark.

Thomas Albright, who gained Colgate's only first place, won the 600-yard run in 1 minute 11 seconds, bettering the Academy record of 1:11.1 set by Hal Jenkins in 1964. Bob Foos of Army was second in 1:11.1.

Army had three double winners. Hart also won the 35-pound weight throw, Van Evers took the 60-yard dash and long jump, and the team captain, Greg Camp, won the mile and 1,000-yard run. Camp also anchored Army's winning two-mile relay team.

The cadets gained 12 firsts and swept seven events for their fourth straight indoor track triumph.

Army's unbeaten fencers made Pace their fourth victim, 17-10, as Steve Murphy and Dave Madux posted 3-0 marks in the foil and Tom Watson won three in the épée.

Penn State swept seven events in handing the Cadet gymnasts a 184.70-174.60 defeat.

A goal by Tom Earl, his third of the game, with 3:24 remaining lifted Colgate to a 3-2 hockey victory over Army tonight. The Cadets had a 2-0 lead in the second period before Colgate started its rally.

Both Army goals were scored by Dave Merhar.

BASKETBALL

ARMY (76)	G.	F.	P.	DARTMOUTH (58)	G.	F.	P.
Schutsky	2	0-0	4	Colgan	2	6-9	10
Noonan	3	5-6	11	Tyson	3	8-9	14
Hunt	5	1-4	11	Reddy	0	0-0	0
Knyzewski	2	1-2	5	Pickering	1	2-5	4
Oxley	3	2-4	8	Burnham	2	2-4	6
George	1	3-3	5	Winn	1	0-0	2
Urban	2	1-1	5	Stableford	3	3-5	9
Simmons	1	4-4	6	Felmeister	0	2-2	2
Kremenak	3	3-4	9	Penberthy	1	1-1	3
Miller	0	0-2	0	Mathias	2	0-0	4
Joyce	2	5-6	9	Neal	0	0-0	0
Fenty	1	1-3	3	Steinmanis	2	0-2	4
Franke	0	0-0	0				
Total	25	26-39	76	Total	17	24-37	58

Half-time score—Army 37, Dartmouth 14.
Fouled out—Winn.
Attendance—3,000.

FIELD EVENTS

35-Pound Weight Throw—1, Larry Hart, Army, 61 feet 3¼ inches; 2, Bob Wallis, Army, 54-7½; 3, Dale Frederick, Army, 51-6¼.
Shot-Put—1, Hart, Army, 56-3; 2, Dan Seebart, Army, 54-9; 3, Helmuth Haas, Army, 51-6.
High Jump—1, Bob Keller, Army, 6-4¾; 2, John Armstrong, Army, 6-4¾; 3, B. N. Peifler, Army, 6-2¾.
Long Jump—1, Van Evans, Army, 21-11½; 2, Dave Phelan, Army, 21-11; 3, Peter O'Neill, Colgate, 21-7¾.
Pole Vault—1, John Rountree, Army, 15-1½; 2, Gil Bolvin, Colgate, 13-0; 3, Kerry Goodier, Army, 13-0.

TRACK

TRACK EVENTS

One-Mile Run—1, Greg Camp, Army, 4:12.5; 2, Jon Nolan, Army, 4:19.2; 3, Bob McDonald, Army, 4:24.5.
600-Yard Run—1, Thomas Albright, Colgate, 1:11; 2, Bob Foos, Army, 1:11.1; 3, Ron King, Army, 1:12.8.
60-Yard High Hurdles—1, Sheridan Groves, Army, 0:07.9; 2, D. C. Vahlbracht, Army; 3, Steve Fails, Army.
60-Yard Dash—1, Evans, Army, 0:06.3; 2, Mike Williams, Army; 3, Groves, Army.
1,000-Yard Run—1, Camp, Army, 2:13.8; 2, Jim Merrill, Colgate, 2:15.2; 3, Bruce Helmich, Army, 2:15.4.
Two-Mile Run—1, James Kee, Army, 9:35.6; 2, Dennis Tighe, Army, 9:36.1; 3, Nick Sebastian, Army, 9:40.
One-Mile Relay—Army (George Forsythe, Foos, Brian Morrill, King). Time—3:18.1.
Two-Mile Relay—Army (Peter Billia, Jim Osman, John Jaccard, Camp. Time—7:57.9.

Flyers Transfer Courcy From Quebec to Seattle Six

BOSTON, Jan. 20 (UPI)—The Philadelphia Flyers of the National Hockey League sent Bob Courcy from their top farm at Quebec to Seattle today.

The transfer from the American Hockey League Aces to the Western Hockey League Totems completes a deal under which Philadelphia promised to lend Seattle five players for a year with the right to recall them.

Courcy, a 5-foot-11-inch 170-pounder, had 32 goals and 28 assists with Cleveland last year.

A Flyers' spokesman said John Hanna had been recalled from Quebec. Hanna has been with Quebec for four years.

Currie Gets Varsity Post

HANOVER, N. H., Jan., 20 (UPI)—Quentin P. Currie, the freshman line coach at Dartmouth the last two years, was elevated today to the school's varsity football coaching staff to fill a vacancy created when John F. Anderson resigned to accept a position at Boston College.

The New York Times (by Robert Walker)

ALL EYES, LITTLE ACTION: Everyone was looking at the ball, but Columbia's Jim McMillian, light jersey at right, was the only player going after this rebound in the first quarter of the Columbia-Cornell game. Lions won, 93-51.

COLUMBIA ROUTS CORNELL, 93 TO 51

Continued From Page 1

Columbia, which ranks 10th in the nation. But the men who contributed most were Dave Newmark, Jim McMillian and Roger Walaszek.

Problems for Newmark

Newmark, a 7-foot junior, had his problems early in the season He began to shape up in the festival and yesterday moved as he has never done before for Columbia. He handed off well for layup shots by his mates, took his own selected shots though forced farther away from the basket than he wanted to be, and generally controlled the play of both Columbia and Cornell.

While doing these, Newmark was getting the help of some fancy play by McMillian and Walaszek. McMillian hit from the corners, drove in for some shots on passes from Newmark and managed 22 points. Newmark had 20.

But Walaszek was the big surprise. He had his best effort of the season. Though the star of the team a year ago when Newmark sat out, Walaszek has been sporatic. This game was his best performance of the winter by far. He led the scorers with 23 points.

Heyward Dotson also did very well, particularly on defense against Greg Morris of Cornell.

Cornell was all set to use a collapsing defense against the Lions. The Big Red planned to cave in on Newmark any time the ball was heading in the giant's direction. The Lions handled that problem with ease.

Rohan had his men, in turn, ready for just such a maneuver by Cornell. While three men bunched in around Newmark, Columbia's outside shooting was excellent. The drives around the closed defense also paid off for Columbia.

Strangely enough, Cornell refused to come out of this collapsing defense even though the Big Red never had the lead and trailed at half-time by 39-23.

Cornell was somewhat hampered by minor injuries. Its high scorer, Hank South, twisted a knee a few days ago but started. He made 10 points. Bill Schwarzkopf, another starter, suffered a broken nose in practice early this week. He played 30 minutes of the game, but his vision was obviously hampered by a big protective guard over his nose.

Newmark's effort was exceptional in that he had to struggle against three men most of the game. But the profits were great for Columbia.

Time and again the fast outside Lions took advantage. They stole the ball so much and set up a fast break so often that the collapsing defense was never in use before the Lions scored. Many times Newmark wasn't even up court before his mates turned a steal into a score.

The Lions forced 23 turnovers from the upstaters while committing only 14 themselves. After seven minutes of play there was no doubt which team was heading for the victory.

COLUMBIA (93)	G.	F.	P.	CORNELL (51)	G.	F.	P.
Walaszek	8	7-8	23	Schwarzkopf	1	4-5	6
McMillian	7	6-7	20	Otto	6	0-1	12
Newmark	10	2-5	22	Esdaile	1	0-1	2
Dotson	5	2-2	12	Morris	3	2-7	8
Ames	2	5-5	9	South	4	2-2	10
Metz	0	0-0	0	Frye	2	1-1	5
Schiller	1	2-2	4	Chapman	3	0-0	6
Thomas	0	0-0	0	Sessions	0	0-0	0
Fogel	0	0-0	0	Pope	0	2-2	2
Garnevicus	0	1-2	1				
Brown	0	2-2	2	Total	20	11-19	51
Detwiler	0	0-0	0				
Sponner	0	0-0	0				
Total	33	27-33	93				

Half-time score—Columbia 38, Cornell 23.
Fouled out—Schwarzkopf.
Attendance—1,756.

IVY LEAGUE BASKETBALL

	W.	L.		W.	L.
Princeton	3	0	Cornell	2	2
Columbia	3	1	Penn	1	2
Yale	3	1	Harvard	0	3
Dartmouth	2	1	Brown	0	0

Cougars Followed Game Plan: Stopped Alcindor Shots, Passes

HOUSTON, Jan. 20 (AP)—Guy Lewis, the victorious Houston coach, said rigid following of their game plan enabled the Cougars to upset previously unbeaten and top-ranked University of California, Los Angeles, 71-69, tonight.

"Our plan was to bottle up Alcindor and shut off his passing lanes to [Mike] Lynn and [Lynn] Shackelford," Lewis said.

"That's what we did, and that's what won it."

In the stunned silence of the U.C.L.A. dressing room, Lew Alcindor, the 7-foot-1½-inch center, said only:

"We lost to a better team."

John Wooden, their coach, emphasized the Bruins' poor shooting of only 33.6 per cent.

"I thought that the conditions—the lights, the pressure and the crowd—would make for poor shooting. But they shot well and there's no reason we shouldn't have."

Lewis said he devised his plan after the Cougars lost to U.C.L.A., 73-58, in the National Collegiate Athletic Association semi-finals last March in Louisville.

"Lynn Shackelford and Mike Lynn killed us from the corners in last year's game," he said. "We know we had to stop Alcindor and we had to stop his feeds to the corner men."

Elvin Hayes and Ken Spain were the chief defensive architects on the struggling Alcindor.

"It has to be the greatest thrill in my life," said Lewis. "I was scared to death all the time. In the last 12 seconds, I told them to get it to Hayes.

"When the chips are down, I can't think of anyone who I would rather have the ball."

HOUSTON UPSETS U.C.L.A., 71 TO 69

Continued From Page 1

it was poor shooting and a subpar Alcindor. The giant center missed the Bruins' last two games with an eye injury and was obviously off form. He finished with 15 points, but had only four field goals in 18 attempts.

Hayes and the 6-foot-9-inch Cougar center, Ken Spain, took turns giving big Lew the miseries. Hayes blocked three of Alcicndor's shots. stole the ball from him twice and Spain teased him into an unusual and unnecessary foul.

Hayes Plays Outstanding Game

Hayes was magnificent. He finished with 17 field goals in 25 attemptts, grabbed 15 rebounds and blocked four shots, although playing the last 11 minutes with four fouls.

Alcindor had 12 rebounds in the nationally televised game.

Reynolds, a tricky backcourt man and suddenly a tough defender, finished with 13 points for Houston and Don Chaney had 11. Warren had 13 and Lynn Shackelford 10 for U.C.L.A.

The Bruins hit on only 26 of 77 field-goal attempts, a 33.6 percentage as compared with its season average of 50 per cent. Houston was 30 for 66 and 45.6 per cent.

U.C.L.A.'s winning streak fell 13 short of the record of 60 set by the University of San Francisco 12 years ago.

The game started in characteristic fashion for the Bruins. They spotted Houston a 5-1 lead and then appeared as if they were going to run off and hide. They forced Houston into four consecutive backcourt errors and established an 8-5 lead.

Houston Battles Back

But the Cougars refused to wilt, however, and, trailing 12-11, put on a 16-6 scoring burst for a 27-18 lead and never trailed again.

Reynolds scored 6 of those points and Hayes the rest, the last two on a long jumper over the reaching hand of Alcindor.

U.C.L.A. finally caught up at 54-54, but Reynolds broke the tie with a free throw. The Bruins tied it again at 65-65, but Hayes snapped it with a jumper.

U.C.L.A. (69)	G.	F.	P.	HOUSTON (71)	G.	F.	P.
Allen	10	5-9	25	Hayes	17	5-7	39
Warren	5	3-3	13	Spain	1	0-1	2
Alcindor	4	7-8	15	Lee	1	2-4	4
Lacey	0	0-0	0	Chaney	5	1-3	11
Shackelford	4	2-2	10	Reynolds	5	3-3	13
Lynn	2	0-0	4	Gribben	1	0-0	2
Nielsen	1	0-0	2	Lewis	0	0-0	0
Totals	26	17-22	69	Totals	30	11-18	71

Half-time score—Houston 46, U.C.L.A. 43.
Attendance—52,693.

National Basketball Ass'n

LAST NIGHT'S GAMES

Baltimore 118, Boston 115.
Cincinnati 128, Detroit 120.
Philadelphia 135, Chicago 111.
St. Louis 120, Seattle 115.
Los Angeles 151, San Francisco 122.

FRIDAY NIGHT'S GAMES

Boston 120, New York 114.
Detroit 133, Seattle 119.
San Francisco 131, Philadelphia 120.

STANDING OF THE CLUBS

Eastern Division	W.	L.	Pc.	Western Division	W.	L.	Pc.
Phila.	35	14	.714	St. Louis	36	14	.720
Boston	32	14	.696	San Fran.	32	20	.615
Detroit	26	24	.520	L. Angeles	24	22	.522
Cincinnati	24	23	.511	Chicago	18	32	.360
New York	22	28	.440	San Diego	14	36	.280
Baltimore	17	30	.362	Seattle	14	37	.275

TODAY'S GAMES

New York at Detroit.
San Diego at Boston.
Chicago at St. Louis.
Seattle at Los Angeles (n).

KINGS POINT ROUTS TRINITY FIVE, 107-76

Special to The New York Times

KINGS POINT, L. I., Jan. 20—The Kings Point Mariners opened an early 10-point lead and were never headed as they trounced Trinity College, 107-76, today.

After the home team had piled up a 61-31 lead early in the second half, Coach Don Kennedy cleared his bench.

Ed Waryas, a 5-foot-8-inch sophomore, was the offensive leader for the Mariners as he poured in 27 points while playing 28 minutes.

Mark Schecter, a reserve, was strong on defense, pulling in 15 rebounds while hitting for 14 points.

KINGS POINT (107)	G.	F.	P.	TRINITY (76)	G.	F.	P.
Brown	3	5-7	11	Godfrey	4	0-1	8
Waryas	10	7-11	27	Zillmer	6	2-4	14
Miller	5	5-7	15	Clark	3	0-0	6
Gilligan	0	2-2	2	Kenworthy	2	0-2	4
Hoffman	4	2-3	10	Payne	1	2-3	4
Plauche	2	0-0	4	DePrez	0	1-1	13
Harren	5	1-2	11	Heimf'tner	1	1-2	3
Erickson	1	0-0	2	Elkins	1	0-1	2
Trahan	3	0-1	6	Newell	1	0-1	2
Roberts	2	2-2	5	Martin	1	5-5	7
Schechter	6	2-4	14	Stuhlman	4	3-7	11
				Maryeski	1	0-0	2
Total	41	25-39	107	Total	31	14-27	76

Thurmond of Warriors Has Surgery on Knee

SAN FRANCISCO, Jan. 20 (UPI)—Nate Thurmond, the San Francisco Warriors' center, was operated on today for a torn ligament in his right knee.

Dr. James Raggio said the surgery was a success and the 6 foot 11 inch center would be able to resume National Basketball Association play next season. However, the doctor said the Warriors' top scorer and rebounder might be able to play in the N.B.A. playoffs, scheduled to start in late March.

Thurmond was injured Friday night during the Warriors' 131-120 victory over the Philadelphia 76ers.

The injury was the fourth in four seasons for Thurmond, who entered the N.B.A. five years ago from Bowling Green. He suffered a broken hand last season and had back trouble the two previous years.

ROYALS VANQUISH PISTONS, 128-120

Extend Winning String to 6 as Robertson Stars

CINCINNATI, Jan. 20 (UPI)—Oscar Robertson scored 32 points tonight as the Cincinnati Royals ran their winning streak to six games with a 128-120 victory over the Detroit Pistons in a National Basketball Association game.

The Royals, hitting 53 per cent of their shots, had five men in double figures as they pulled within a half-game of the third-place Pistons in the Eastern Division.

Utilizing the fast break, the Royals jumped to a 35-24 first-period lead and led at half-time, 64-48.

The Royals led by 20 points when Robertson and Jerry Lucas left the game midway in the fourth period. Bob Love came off the bench to score 14 points in the fourth period for the Royals.

CINCINNATI (128)	G.	F.	P.	DETROIT (120)	G.	F.	P.
Dierking	8	2-4	18	Bing	9	12-13	30
Gray	1	0-0	2	Chappell	5	5-7	15
Fox	0	0-0	0	DeB'ssch're	7	2-2	16
Hairston	7	5-7	19	Dischinger	2	0-0	4
Love	7	0-0	14	Miles	10	4-6	24
Lucas	8	4-4	20	Patterson	3	2-2	8
Robertson	11	10-10	32	Strawder	0	0-0	0
Smith	3	3-3	9	Tresvant	2	0-0	4
Rodgers	4	0-0	8	VanArsdale	1	6-10	8
Wesley	2	2-4	6	Walker	4	3-4	11
Total	51	26-32	128	Total	43	34-44	120

Detroit	24	24	28	44—120
Cincinnati	35	29	27	37—128

Attendance—4,811.

Hawks TopSonics, 120-115

ST. LOUIS, Jan. 20 (AP)—Len Wilkens poured in 39 points and chalked up 18 assists to lead the St. Louis Hawks in a second-half surge that downed the Seattle Supersonics, 120-115, tonight.

Wilkens set a new team and Kiel Auditorium high with his 18 assists. Seattle, hitting on 60 per cent of its shots in the first half, led the Western Division leaders by as much as 9 points before Wilkens got hot in the third period.

SEATTLE (115)	G.	F.	P.	ST. LOUIS (120)	G.	F.	P.
Meschery	3	3-6	9	Bridges	6	2-2	14
Tucker	6	2-2	14	Silas	2	2-3	6
Rule	2	2-3	6	Beaty	6	8-10	20
Hazzard	11	3-8	25	Caldwell	11	1-2	23
Kron	4	5-7	13	Wilkens	13	13-13	39
Akin	1	3-6	5	Davis	1	0-0	2
Lott	0	2-2	2	Lehmann	0	0-0	0
Murrey	2	2-4	6	Hudson	0	0-0	0
Olsen	0	0-0	0	Snyder	3	4-6	10
Weiss	5	3-3	13	Tormohlen	3	0-0	6
Wilyson	2	0-2	4				
Thorn	6	6-8	18	Total	45	30-36	120
Total	42	31-51	115				

Seattle	33	29	17	36—115
St. Louis	25	31	33	31—120

Attendance—5,118.

76ers Trounce Bulls

CHICAGO, Jan. 20 (AP)—The Philadelphia 76ers raced to an early 10-0 lead, then went on to a 135-111 triumph over the Chicago Bulls tonight.

The victory enabled the league champions to increase their Eastern Division lead over the Boston Celtics to 1½ games.

Six Philadelphia players scored at least 14 points each, with Hal Greer winding up with 26 and Chet Walker with 24.

PHILA. (135)	G.	F.	P.	CHICAGO (111)	G.	F.	P.
Chambrlin	8	2-6	18	Robinson	9	5-6	23
Guokas	5	4-4	14	Washngtn	6	3-4	15
Greer	12	2-2	26	Schellhase	1	0-0	2
Green	2	2-3	6	Haskins	3	0-0	6
Jones	4	1-1	9	Barnes	1	2-2	4
Walker	8	8-9	24	Erickson	4	3-3	11
Cnninghm	7	3-5	17	Clemens	3	1-1	7
Jackson	5	5-5	15	McLemore	7	2-2	16
Melehonni	3	0-0	6	Boozer	11	5-5	27
				Spitzer	0	0-0	0
Total	54	27-35	135	Total	45	21-23	111

Philadelphia	33	42	26	34—135
Chicago	21	37	29	24—111

Fouled out—Erickson.
Attendance—6,544.

Bullets Down Celtics

BALTIMORE, Jan. 20 (AP)—The Baltimore Bullets broke a seven-game losing streak tonight by whipping Boston, 118-115, and ended the Celtics' winning streak at four games.

BOSTON (115)	G.	F.	P.	BALTIMORE (118)	G.	F.	P.
Jones	14	10-12	38	Monroe	14	4-5	32
Graham	0	0-0	0	Ohl	8	5-5	21
Russell	5	2-5	12	Ellis	1	4-4	6
Howell	3	4-5	10	Johnson	14	5-6	33
Sanders	4	3-6	11	Scott	6	4-4	16
Havlicek	13	3-5	29	Loughery	3	0-2	6
Nelson	4	5-7	13	Marin	0	4-4	4
Thacker	0	0-0	0	Egan	0	0-0	0
Embry	1	0-1	2				
Total	44	27-41	115	Total	46	26-30	118

BOSTON	16	31	38	30—115
BALTIMORE	34	26	30	28—118

Attendance—4,344.

E.L.T.A. PUTS OFF OPEN TENNIS VOTE

Favors Keeping Distinction Between Amateur and Pro

By ALLISON DANZIG

The Eastern Lawn Tennis Association made it unmistakably clear yesterday that it favored an open tournament, but did not go so far as to recommend that permission be given to the amateur players of this country to compete in an open Wimbledon next June.

The association was overwhelmingly against abolishing the distinction between amateurs and professionals.

In annual session at the Princeton Club, the delegates of the largest of the 17 sectional organizations in the United States Lawn Tennis Association authorized their delegate to the annual meeting of the national body Feb. 3 in Coronado, Calif., to vote to table the proposal that would allow our players to enter an open Wimbledon.

Should the proposal come to a vote, the Eastern delegate, Henry Benisch of Forest Hills, Queens, was uninstructed, which meant he would exercise his judgment.

Unanimous Action

A clarifying resolution offered by Lawrence Krieger of Summit, N. J., read:

"Resolved that the Eastern Lawn Tennis Association does favor the principle of open tennis and be it further resolved that its delegate work within the framework of the U.S.L.T.A. and the International Lawn Tennis Federation to procure this result."

The vote against abolishing the distinction between amateur and pro was unanimous. The delegates also voted as one in favor of the U.S.L.T.A.'s negotiating to bring the pros under its administration.

The Eastern's action follows the vote of the Western and Texas associations in favor of sanctioning players to compete in an open Wimbledon and opposing abolition of the pro, amateur distinction.

The position to be taken by the U.S.L.T.A. at Coronado and by the Australian Lawn Tennis Association at its meeting Jan. 30 is anxiously awaited as a possible influence on the International Federation's plan to suspend the British Lawn Tennis Association for defying federation rules in declaring Wimbledon open.

On Dec. 14 the British voted by 295-5 to conduct Wimbledon as an open championship and end the distinction between amateurs and pros. They did so, they said, to end the dishonesty and sham of amateur tennis in paying big sums to players as expenses.

The British acted after the federation, on July 12, had again turned down their annual request to be allowed to hold Wimbledon as an open.

The international body, which takes in some 80 countries, announced that the B.L.T.A. would be suspended April 22, when the British plan to conduct their first open tournament — the hard-court championships at Bournemouth.

Robert J. Kelleher of Beverly Hills, Calif., president of the U.S.L.T.A. hopes the crisis can be resolved and the suspension averted by calling a special meeting of the federation in April. Sweden has advocated such a meeting and the executive committee of the U.S.L.T.A. has approved.. Benisch, the retiring president of the E.L.T.A., said his group strongly supported Kelleher on this move.

"We want to do everything possible to give Kelleher a strong hand if such a meeting is held," said Benisch. "We want an open tournament, but whatever we do, we want to do it in the light of maintaining amateur tennis.

"Kelleher feels that the United States, France, Australia and Britain can resolve this problem and bring about the open legally."

To call such a meeting 60 votes are required and it must be held within 70 days of filing the request. This means that the necessary votes must be mustered by Feb. 12. The United States has 12 votes in the federation, as do France, Australia and Britain. Sweden has five.

The Eastern's decision to seek to table the proposal permitting the players to compete in an open Wimbledon came when it seemed the delegates were leaning toward rejecting the proposal. Only the intervention of Alastair B. Martin, the vice president of the U.S.L.T.A., dissuaded them.

Martin pleaded for tabling, saying that otherwise it would appear the Eastern was against open tournaments and that Kelleher's hands would be tied in his delicate task of trying to bring about a compromise between the British and the federation.

Pimentel Loses Title Bid

TOKYO,, Jan. 20 (UPI)—The Japan Boxing Commission said today it had been informed by the World Boxing Association that Jesus Pimentel of Mexico had lost his chance to challenge Fighting Harada, the world bantamweight champion, for the title. The match had been scheduled for Feb. 27 here. The W.B.A. said Pimentel had not come to terms on a contract.

Sports Today

BASKETBALL

Knicks vs. Pistons, at Detroit. (Television—Channel 7, 2 P.M.) (Radio—WHN, 1:55 P.M.)

FOOTBALL

National Football League Pro Bowl, Eastern Conference All-Stars vs. Western Conference All-Stars, at Los Angeles. (Television—Channel 2, 4 P.M.)
American Football League All-Star game, East vs. West, at Jacksonville, Fla. (Television—Channel 4, 1:30 P.M.)

HOCKEY

Long Island Ducks vs. New Jersey Devils, at Commack, L. I., 3:15 P.M.

ROAD-RUNNING

Road-Runners Club 12-mile event, at Ogden and Sedgwick Avenues, the Bronx, Noon.

SKIING

Ramapo Mountain jumping tournament, at Bear Mountain (N. Y.) State Park, 2 P.M.

SOCCER

German-American League six-a-side tournament, at Westchester County Center, White Plains, 12:45 P.M.

TENNIS

Bobby Riggs's Masters invitation tournament, at Bobby Riggs Racquet Club and Boulevard Gardens Tennis Courts, 51-26 Broadway, Woodside, Queens, 2 P.M.

MISS PALL CAPTURES GIANT SLALOM RACE

MARIBOR, Yugoslavia, Jan. 20 (UPI) — Olga Pall, Austria's newest skiing whiz, displayed unusual skill and stamina today in racing to victory in the Golden Fox giant slalom.

Miss Pall, who helps her mother pumps gas at the family service station, nearly ran out of gas in the gruelling 53-gate 1,520-meter course.

She, exhausted at the end of the race, won in the time of 1 minute 47.41 seconds.

Gertraud Gabl of Austria was second in 1:47.6 and Isabella Mir of France third in 1:47.63. Suzy Chaffee of Rutland, Vt., was fourth in 1:49.07.

Penny McCoy of Bishop, Calif., was 14th in 1:51.56 and Kiki Cutter of Bend, Ore., 15th in 1:51.77. Judy Nagel of Enumclaw, Wash., was 19th in 1:52.8, followed by Erika Singer of Stowe, Vt., 20th in 1:52.8 and Sandra Shellworth, Boise, Idaho, 21st in 1:53.36.

About 90 women from 18 countries, including several champion skiers, competed in the opening run of the two-day event.

Race conditions were hazardous with the icy slopes causing several spills.

"The course wasn't wide enough and in some parts it was very difficult," said Miss Pall.

One skier, Brigitta Seiwald, was hospitalized with minor injuries when she fell a few gates from the finish.

Heidi Zimmermann of Austria and Robin Morning of the United States, also fell but continued the race, finishing near the end.

BRITAIN AND FRANCE DRAWN AS CUP FOES

MELBOURNE, Australia, Jan. 20 (UPI)—Britain was drawn today to meet France in the first round of the 1968 Davis Cup European zone tennis competition, but the match is unlikely to take place.

Britain probably will be suspended by the International Lawn Tennis Federation on April 22, the opening day of the British hard-court championships, and will be banned from the Davis Cup competition. The British hard court championsships will be Britain's best venture into the prohibited area of open tennis for both professionals and amateurs.

If Britain is suspended, France will have a bye in the opening round.

Spain, which unsuccessfully challenged Australia for the Davis Cup in Brisbane last month, is expected to have an easy time in the first round against the Netherlands, and South Africa, another top contender for the challenge round this year, takes on Austria.

Russia is favored over Greece. The United States and Venezuela are the only entries so far in the American Zone, which closes on Feb. 10.

Mathis Goes Into Training For His Bout With Frazier

Special to The New York Times

HYDE PARK, N.Y., Jan. 20—Buster Mathis, who says he will throw four punches to Joe Frazier's one, opened training camp today for his March 4 bout with Frazier that will determine, in New York's view the world heavyweight champion.

Mathis weighed 248 pounds as he went three rounds with Eddie Vick of Corona, Queens, 56 pounds lighter. Mathis expects to weigh 235 when he enters the ring at Madison Square Garden to meet Frazier. The bout will follow a world middleweight title fight on the same card between Emile Griffith and Nino Benvenuti, the challenger.

Observers at Mathis's camp said today he was exceptionally fast in footwork and in throwing combinations.

JAPANESE SKATER TAKES WIDE LEAD

Miss Ohkawa Outdistances University Games' Rivals

INNSBRUCK, Austria, Jan. 20 (UPI)—Kumiko Ohkawa, a 21-year-old Japanese student, and Vladimir Kurenbine of the Soviet Union dominated figure-skating competition today in the Winter University Games.

Miss Ohkawa accumulated 488.5 points for the five compulsory figures in women's competition. Helli Turner-Sengstschmid of Austria was second with 447.

Kurenbine increased his lead in the men's division in the last two compulsory figures. He has 452.3 points for six figures to 432.7 for Guenther Anderl of Austria.

Bohunka Sramkova and Jan Sramek of Czechoslovakia led the pairs event in compulsory skating with 53.4 points.

In hockey, Canada trounced Austria, 10-1, for its first victory in the six-nation competition. Last night the Canadians lost, 8-4, to Czechoslovakia while the defending champion, the Soviet Union, trounced Austria, 21-0.

ENGLAND'S BATSMEN LEAD CRICKET TEST

PORT OF SPAIN, Trinidad, Jan. 20 (Reuters) — English English batsmen scored 302 runs today on top of a first-day total of 224 against the West Indies cricket team and virtually guaranteed a victory in the five-day test.

England still faces the task of getting the West Indies out twice in the remaining three days.

Ken Barrington scored 143 runs for England and Tom Graveney got 118. At the end of the day England had 526 runs with three of its 10 first-innings wickets still to lose.

Graveney and Barrington batting together scored 188 runs in 215 minutes before Barrington was caught out by Charlie Griffith off bowler Lance Gibbs.

Gibbs, although he gave 147 runs, also bowled out Graveney, in addition to having taken one of the two English wickets lost yesterday.

Florida Regatta Put Off

STURAT, Fla., Jan. 20 (AP)—Eight races in the Stuart sailfish regatta were postponed after rough water caused one boat to disintegrate, injuring the driver, and sent other craft bouncing haphazardly across waves. Theodore Panaretos, 39 years old, of Detroit, received multiple bruises, several cuts and a possible chest injury when he was thrown from his craft.

AMERICAN HOCKEY LEAGUE

LAST NIGHT'S GAMES

Buffalo 2, Cleveland 1.
Hershey 2, Portland (W.H.L.) 2.
Springfield 5, San Diego (W.H.L.) 3.

STANDING OF THE CLUBS

Eastern Division	W.	L.	T.	Pts.	Western Division	W.	L.	T.	Pts.
Springfield	21	19	5	46	Cleveland	21	13	6	48
Hershey	19	15	5	43	Rochester	19	16	7	44
Baltimore	16	16	7	39	Buffalo	18	18	7	43
Providence	16	19	6	38	Quebec	16	16	8	40

Skating Brother Chosen But It's a Close Shave

BALLSTON SPA, N. Y., Jan. 20 (AP)—Two Wurster brothers now are on the United States Olympic speed-skating team.

"If you get yourself a shave, I'll put you on the Olympic team," a former Olympic coach, Lee Freisinger, told Richie Wurster last night.

Richie, a 25-year-old native of this village, shaved. The skater had been passed over when the 11-man squad was selected earlier in the week. His brother, John, 20, was named to the team then. It's the first brother combination for an American Olympic speed-skating team.

Automobiles, Boats
Dogs and Other Pets
Household Employment
Shopping Guide
Situations Wanted

The New York Times

Section 5
L++

SPORTS

Sunday, February 18, 1968

KILLY GAINS OLYMPIC TRIPLE; SOVIET HOCKEY VICTOR; SETTE BELLO, $100, WINS WIDENER HANDICAP BY HEAD

The New York Times

HOME, SWEET HOME: Manager Gil Hodges in uniform (number 14) at Shea Stadium

Baseball: The Picture for 1968

By JOSEPH M. SHEEHAN

Baseball's annual rite of spring training begins this week. Advance elements of the Baltimore Orioles and Washington Senators go to work today. Other major league teams will muster daily in Florida, Arizona and California until March 1, when the full squad of California Angels checks in at Palm Springs, Calif., to complete the roll-call.

Seven weeks of huffing and puffing, stretching and bending, throwing and batting, fielding and running are on the agenda for the 1,000-odd players in the accelerated competition for the 500 places available on the 20 major league teams when the season opens April 9.

This year, for the first time, the major league teams, permitted to carry 40 players plus certain exempted supernumeraries on their winter rosters, must cut down to the in-season limit of 25 by opening day. In previous years, they could carry three extra players for the season's first month. Accordingly, there's extra urgency on the scramble for marginal jobs.

To a rookie breaking in, a roster place means an upgraded (from $7,000) minimum salary of $10,000 and, more important, a toehold on a career. To a Willie Mays, for instance, it means another year of $125,000 affluence.

There has been only one change in baseball's major league line-up since 1967—the Athletics will be based in Oakland instead of Kansas City. But this has more significance than just another franchise shift because it represents the first step in the major leagues' second round of expansion.

In permitting Charles O. Finley to move his Athletics, the American League concurrently voted to award franchises to new clubs in Kansas City and Seattle. These teams will become operative in 1969. The National League,

Continued on Page 10, Column 1

DEAD HEAT FOR 2D

Favorable Turn and Bold Hour Are Tied in $143,000 Race

By JOE NICHOLS

Special to The New York Times

MIAMI, Feb. 17 — Robert Lehman's Sette Bello came up the winner in $143,000 Widener Handicap today. With Earlie Fires giving him a rail-grazing ride, the 6-year-old son of Ribot scored by a head in the mile-and-a-quarter fixture.

The outcome was a proper surprise, as Sette Bello, the next to the outsider in betting, returned $100 for $2 in the win spot.

The runner-up spot was shared by George D. Widener's Bold Hour and Herbert Allen's Favorable Turn. This pair was locked in a dead heat, three lengths in front of J. R. H. Thouron's Rixdal.

The crowd of 30,169 established Bold Hour and his stablemate, Ring Twice, the favorite, by a close margin over the Darby Dan Farm's Proud Clarion, who won the Kentucky Derby last May. Ring Twice won the Widener last year. Neither of these stars impressed today. Proud Clarion finishing sixth and Ring Twice next to last.

Closing Rally Decides

Sette Bello—Beautiful Seven to those who are up on their Italian—had to make a dramatic closing rally to take the winner's share of $92,950. Through the early going he was way back in the field of eleven, as Peter Piper and then Favorable Turn made the pace.

As the field hit the stretch on the fast track it appeared that Favorable Turn was on his way to victory. With Angel Cordero riding him, he shook himself loose of the others and had a clear margin of more than a length halfway to the wire. Then Bold Hour sprang up to challenge him and this pair battled it out.

At the same time Sette Bello, overlooked by almost everybody in the park, made his speedy rush forward, from sixth place to fourth, and then into the lead at the wire. The time of the winner, who carried 110 pounds, was 2:01 3/5.

Conway Is Confident

The victory was the second of the season, in three attempts, for the Kentucky-bred Sette Bello, whose trainer is Jimmy Conway. Although the horse had never won a stakes before, he had three successes and was in the money nine times in 21 starts last year, earning $48,564 for his owner, a Wall Street investment broker. Lehman likes to give his horses Italian names. Among others, he owned the successful Prego of a few seasons back.

Conway, in his post-race comment, said that he thought his horse had a good chance, that he could not get going properly in his previous race. In that effort, the Seminole, he finished sixth, the first three being Favorable Turn, Rixdal and In Reality. The last named was a withdrawal from the

Continued on Page 6, Column 2

Associated Press

HOW SWEET IT WAS . . . AND HOW BRIEF: Karl Schranz of Austria, center, waves after finishing the men's special slalom in 99.22 seconds, faster than Jean-Claude Killy of France, right. Two hours later, the judges disqualified Schranz for missing a gate and they awarded first place to the Frenchman. At the left is Toni Sailer of Austria, who, like Killy this year, won the triple crown of Alpine skiing in the 1956 Olympics.

Associated Press

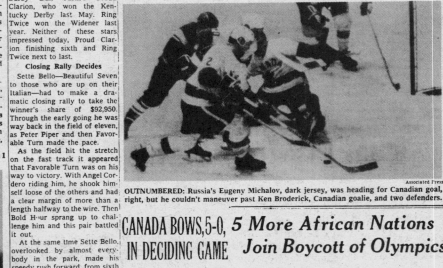

OUTNUMBERED: Russia's Eugeny Michalov, dark jersey, was heading for Canadian goal, right, but he couldn't maneuver past Ken Broderick, Canadian goalie, and two defenders.

VICTOR IN SLALOM

Frenchman Is Placed First After 2 Rivals Are Disqualified

By FRED TUPPER

Special to The New York Times

GRENOBLE, France, Feb. 17 —Jean-Claude Killy won the triple crown of Alpine skiing at the Winter Olympics today, but it took a jury's decision to make it official.

In the slalom race the idol of France, who had previously won the downhill and giant slalom, plunged through 131 gates on the 1,040-meter course in dense, icy fog for a two-heat time of 99.75 seconds.

He had the fastest time in the first heat, from which he had started in the 15th position.

In the second he was the first man down. Now all he could do was wait. It was agonizing.

Haakon Mjoen of Norway had better times, but was disqualified for having missed gates. The other men who might have beaten Killy had come and gone, and the thousands of fans peering through the mists were waiting for the seasoned Karl Schranz of Austria. He could be the danger.

Schranz had been third in the

Continued on Page 3, Column 1

CANADA BOWS, 5-0, IN DECIDING GAME

Russians Take Gold Medal —U.S. Six Ties Finns, 1-1, and Finishes 6th

By MICHAEL STRAUSS

Special to The New York Times

GRENOBLE, France, Feb. 17 —The winner is still champion, for the sixth straight year.

A scrappy, fast Soviet Union sextet kept the world amateur ice-hockey crown and won an Olympic gold medal tonight by beating Canada, 5-0, in a one-sided contest.

The game, the final Olympic event in the Ice Stadium, drew an enthusiastic standing-room crowd of 13,000. Tomorrow the final ceremonies of the Winter Games will be held under the same roof.

Earlier Czechoslovakia blew its chance to dethrone the red-shirted Russians by playing a 2-2 tie with Sweden. A victory would have given the Czechs

Continued on Page 3, Column 6

5 More African Nations Join Boycott of Olympics

By The Associated Press

GRENOBLE, France, Feb. 17 —A boycott of the Summer Olympic Games in Mexico City built up today when four more African countries withdrew and the Soviet Union reiterated its threat to follow suit in a protest over the readmission of South Africa.

Tanzania, Uganda, the Republic of Mali, Ghana and the United Arab Republic announced they would not send their athletes to Mexico next October. They joined Ethiopia and Algeria, which acted yesterday. Nigeria and several other African nations are expected to withdraw.

The U.A.R. said it would propose a collective African boycott to a foreign ministers' conference of the Organization for African Unity, scheduled to start Monday in Addis Ababa, Ethiopia.

The development followed Thursday's vote of the International Olympic Committee to readmit South Africa to the Games. South Africa had been ousted from the Olympic movement in 1963 because of its national segregationist policy.

The first reaction from Moscow left Olympic officials concerned about the possibility that the Soviet Union, too, would withdraw.

'This decision is a flagrant violation of the charter of the I.O.C. that forbids discrimination of athletes for political, racial or religious reasons," said a Soviet Olympic Committee statement.

A spokesman for the Soviet committee indicated however, that action might be delayed until after the South African team was selected.

The South Africans have assured the I.O.C. their team will be multiracial, will be chosen by a multiracial committee, will travel and live together and will march under the same flag in ceremonies before and after the games.

However, the athletes will be

Continued on Page 2, Column 2

United Press International

YES, IT'S THAT TIME OF YEAR AGAIN: Tom Seaver, pitcher for the Mets, throwing during a workout in St. Petersburg, Fla. The Met batteries are not expected to report for their spring training until Wednesday, but Seaver is getting an early start.

KNICKS TURN BACK SONICS BY 134-111

'Water Bugs' in New Garden Require Toweling of Court

By DAVE ANDERSON

The new Madison Square Garden developed "water bugs" last night that resulted in a 20-minute delay and intermittent toweling of the basketball court during a 134-111 victory for the New York Knickerbockers over the Seattle Supersonics.

During the third quarter of the schoolboy preliminary game, a heavy "rain" began to descend from the roof. Wide puddles soon formed on the court from outside the Seventh Avenue foul circle to across midcourt. The "rain" lasted about 10 minutes.

While three maintenance men mopped the floor, the "rain" ceased except for occasional drops outside the foul circle. Adding to the confusion, a pigeon fluttered across the arena.

After the delay, Collegiate School went on to defeat McBurney School, 59-52. Every few minutes, however, one of the Collegiate student managers used a towel to wipe the water on the court near the Seventh

Continued on Page 4, Column 3

St. John's Subdues Fordham, 75 to 71; Bogad Is Standout

By DEANE McGOWEN

Rudy Bogad, the St. John's center, played one of the better games of his varsity basketball career in Alumni Hall last night as the Redmen squeezed by Fordham, 75-71, before a wildly cheering but apprehensive capacity crowd of 6,002.

Lou Carnesecca, St. John's lively little coach, paid tribute to his 6-foot-7-inch center, saying, "If he had not had the game he did, we would have lost." Carnesecca was wholly correct.

The Redmen led just before half-time by 12 points and by 10 with almost eight minutes to play in the game. Then they ran into a drought from the floor that melted their advantage to a point.

In fact, over those final eight minutes the Redmen failed to score a field goal. Their last 9 points were from the free-throw line on opportunities presented by the overzealous guarding of the Rams.

And it was Bogad, working off the low post and completely dominating Dennis Witkowski, who calmly sank 4 of those last

Continued on Page 4, Column 2

PASARELL UPSET IN TITLE TENNIS

Defending Champion Beaten by Graebner in 5 Sets

By ALLISON DANZIG

Special to The New York Times

SALISBURY, Md., Feb. 17—Charles Pasarell's two-year reign as United States indoor tennis champion came to an end today.

Less than 15 hours after he and Ronald Holmberg of Highland Falls, N. Y., had been beaten in a record-breaking doubles marathon of 6 hours and 20 minutes last night by Bobby Wilson and Mark Cox of Britain, 26-24, 17-19, 30-28, Pasarell, the top-ranking player of the country, lost to Clark Graebner of Beachwood, Ohio. This semi-final match lasted three hours and 12 minutes.

A full house of 4,000 at the Civic Center saw the defending title holder from Puerto Rico go down again in the ultimate set, 16-14, 4-6, 8-6, 4-6, 6-3. In all, Pasarell played 217 games in just over 24 hours, and that must stand as a record in a national championship tournament.

Graebner ranks fourth in the country. He defeated Roy Emer-

Continued on Page Column 2

Associated Press

WINNING THE WIDENER: Sette Bello, right rear, is in front by a head to take the Widener Handicap at Hialeah. Bold Hour (1A) and Favorable Turn, center, were in a dead heat for the second spot. Earlie Fires rode the winner.

RANGERS DEFEAT MAPLE LEAFS, 3-2

Toronto Fails in Late Bid to Tie Before 15,896 Fans

Special to The New York Times

TORONTO, Feb. 17—The Toronto Maple Leafs lost another tough game to the New York Rangers, 3-2, tonight.

With less than three seconds left in the game, the Leafs made a desperate effort to tie as Frank Mahovlich passed to Bob Pulford in the middle, only a few yards out.

Pulford shot for the goal and the disk appeared to zip by the New York goalie, Ed Giacomin, at the very instant the automatic blue light signaling the end of the period—and the game—flashed. Then the red goal light, which is manually operated, went on.

The 15,896 fans in Maple Leaf Gardens and the Toronto players shouted for joy. A tie, at least, would have kept the gap between the fifth place Leafs and the fourth-place New Yorkers at 6 points.

But Referee Bill Friday ruled that the disk had crossed the goal line after the game had ended.

The victory increased the

Continued on Page 5 Column 2

Killy Captures Slalom Race for Olympic Triple

FRENCHMAN'S TIME IS 99.75 SECONDS

Schranz and Mjoen Finish Faster, but Miss Gates —Austria Protests

Continued From Page 1

first heat. A spectator interfered on his second run and Schranz pulled off the course. He sidestepped back to the top and was given permission to go again.

This time he was spectacular, darting and swiveling through the flags with such controlled abandon that his two-heat time was 99.22.

That should have been it. The Austrian had won. But had he?

He was reported for missing a gate before the interference by the spectator. If so he would automatically be disqualified, and that was the way the jury ruled in the end. The bulletin was flashed two hours after the race.

So Killy, the darkly handsome customs officer from Val D'Isere, has brought all those magazine covers back to life. He has won the triple, a memorable feat achieved only by Toni Sailer of Austria in 1956 at Cortina.

The Austrians, who were still protesting the decision, got the silver and bronze medals, anyway. Hubert Huber was timed in 9.82 and the youngster, Alfred Matt, in 100.09.

From an almost impossible starting position in the second 15, Spider Sabich of Kyburz, Calif., finished fifth. Jim Heuga of Squaw Valley, Calif., was seventh and Rick Chaffee of Rutland, Vt., ninth.

At the Games in Innsbruck four years ago, Billy Kidd of Stowe, Vt., and Heuga were second and third, respectively, as the United States took four medals in Alpine skiing. This time it won none. Kidd caught a ski tip and crashed today on the first run.

There were other heroes. That wonderful redhead, Eugenio Monti, had done it again. The 40-year-old ski-lift operator from Cortina, a miracle of plastic surgery after his years of derring-do, piloted his way smoothly down the twisting over the 1,600-meter ice chute to give the Italian four-man bobsled team a victory in the two-heat time of 2:17.39, nine-hundredths of a second faster than Ervin Thaler and the Austrian sled.

The Swiss, driven by Jean Wicki, were third, with a course record in the second heat.

The accolade was expected. Monti is loved by the men who ride sleds.

The Master Hailed

"The best bobber there is," said Thaler. "If we must lose, we're glad it's to Monti."

"I came here to learn from the master," said Boris Said of Fair Haven, Vt., pilot of the American sled that came in 10th.

"My men did it," said Monti, pointing to Roberto Zardonella, Mario Armand and the brakeman, Luciano de Paoles.

"We're going to do it tonight," said Armand. "After all these weeks of no wine, there will be rivers of Chianti flowing."

And so the old redhead now retires. He had two bronze medals at Innsbruck, two silvers at Cortina and now, with his first in the two-man sled here, the two golds he had always longed for. In between he has won nine world championships.

Norway, the medal leader, had its sixth gold one as Ole Ellefsaeter won the 50-kilometer cross-country, the most grueling race in all sport.

A tree-chopper from Nybygda, Ole panted and poled over those 30-odd miles and was still running on his skis at the end, long after the field had disappeared behind him.

Down that last right turn out of the pine trees he came, legs of steel pistoning for the gate. He was through in 2:28:45.8, the leader from the 15-kilometer post onward.

"My skis were soaked," said Ole. "The wax was torn off in the last few kilometers and it was slow going."

Viatches Vendenine had been gaining rapidly. Tenth halfway and third at 40 kilometers, the Russian had faster wax but lost time passing the also-rans and was 17 seconds behind at the end.

Josef Haas of Switzerland won the bronze medal for third, and Mike Gallagher of Killington, Vt., finished 22d.

An icy wind was blowing down from the peaks and across the speed-skating rink this morning. The world record-holder, Fred Anton Maier of Norway, was reputedly the man to beat in the 10,000-meter race. He started first, wheeling steadily around in the cold, with a schedule to meet of 37 seconds per lap. He came home flying in 15:25.9, the Olympic and his own world marks shattered.

Surprisingly, it wasn't good enough. The other great names attacked it and failed, but Johnny Hoeglin of Sweden had picked up a second on Maier's time along the way, when the gusts died down, and still had that margin at the bell lap. And he beat Maier with 15:23.6.

"I was hoping for fifth," he said. "I've never been under 15:40 in my life." Hoeglin was not well enough to compete in the European championships two weeks ago.

Third was Oerjan Sandler, also of Sweden, as the Dutch, for once, did not get a medal.

Bill Lanigan of the Bronx, New York, was 21st, exactly tying the old Olympic mark of 16:50.1.

With only one more event, the 90-meter ski jump, scheduled for the final day tomorrow, Norway has won the Games. Her six gold medals cannot be matched by any other country, and in Olympic competition only first places count.

RUSSIAN SEXTET WINS GOLD MEDAL

Continued From Page 1

the title regardless of the Soviet-Canada finale.

The Canadians put up a stubborn fight for one and a half periods, then started wilting. The Russians, after having scored a goal in each of the first two periods, broke the game open in the final session with a three-goal burst.

Before tonight's action the Soviet Union, Canada and Czechoslovakia were tied for first with five victories and one loss apiece. But in the technical standing the Russians were in trouble because they had been beaten by the Czechs.

Then, with the Czechs out of the way as a result of their tie, the Russians took up their task quickly. They scored the first goal shortly after the halfway mark in the opening session, although outnumbered on the ice by one man. The tally was made by Anatoli Firsov, who also got the final goal.

Shoot from up Close

All the goals were scored from up close, after the Russians had worked the puck in. That's the usual Soviet technique.

In contrast the Canadians did most of their attacking from outside. In the second period they put the pressure on the champions, storming the net repeatedly.

But Viktor Konovalenko, the Soviet goalie, was invincible. He stopped shots sent at him from all directions, using his stick, skates and gloves.

The Canadians made their peak effort in the second period, during which the action became so wild that seven sticks were broken within four minutes.

As for the United States, it was held to a 1-1 tie by Finland in the battle for fifth place. By finishing sixth, the Americans posted their poorest record in Olympic hockey—two victories, four defeats and a tie.

The second-place silver medal went to the Czechs and the Canadians won the bronze.

SOVIET UNION (5)—Goal, Konovalenko, Zinger; defense, Ragulin, Blinov, Davidov, Zaitsev, Romichevski, Kuzkin; forwards, Polupanov, Mayorov, Michakov, Ionov, Firsov, Vikulov, Starshinov, Zimin, Moiseyev, Alexandrov.

CANADA (0)—Goal, Broderick, Stephenson; defense, Johnston, Hargreaves, MacKenzie, O'Malley, Glennie, Conlin; forwards, Dineen, Monteith, Pinder, Huck, Cadieux, Mott, Bourbonnais, MacMillan, O'Shea.

FIRST PERIOD—1, Soviet Union, Firsov (Vikulov), 14:51. Penalties—Mott 9:28; O'Shea 11:57; Zimin 13:56; Pinder 15:03.

SECOND PERIOD—2, Soviet Union, Michakov (Moiseyev), 12:44. Penalties—MacKenzie 0:38; Polupanov 0:50; Johnson 16·43.

THIRD PERIOD—3, Soviet Union, Starshinov (unassisted), 1:21; 4, Soviet Union, Zimin (Starshinov, Davidov) 8·44; 5, Soviet Union, Firsov (Vikulov), 13:59. Penalty—Huck 8:18.

Soviet Union	1	1	3—5
Canada	0	0	0—0

Referees—Trumble of United States and Dahlberg of Sweden.

Shots on goal—Soviet Union: 11, 5, 16—32. Canada: 7, 12, 6—25.

Attendance—13,000.

UNITED STATES (1)—Goal, Rupp; defense, Nanne, Riutta; forwards, Pleau, Morrison, Lilyholm, alternates, Ross, Gaudreau, Paradise, Volmar, Dale, Cunniff, P. Hurley, T. Hurley, Stordahl, Brooks.

FINLAND (1)—Goal, Ylonen; defense, Partinen, Rantasila; forwards, Keinonen, Wahlston; Johanson; alternates, Koskela, Linstrom, Tirkkonen, Harju, Ketola, Oksanen, E. Peltonen, J. Peltonen, Leimu, Revnamaki.

FIRST PERIOD—1, United States—Volmar (P. Hurley), 9.08; 2, Finland—Wahlsten (unassisted), 10.47. Penalties—None.

SECOND PERIOD—No Scoring. Penalty—Nanne 1:10.

THIRD PERIOD—No scoring. Penalty—Ruitta 2:37.

United States	1	0	0—1
Finland	1	0	0—1

Referees—Kubinec of Canada and Seglin of the Soviet Union.

CZECHOSLOVAKIA (2)—Goal, Dzurila, Nadrchal; defense, Machac, Pospichil, Suchy, Horesovsky, Masopust; forwards, Golonka, Sevcik, Jirik, Nedomansky, Hrbaty, Holik, Hejma, Havel, Cerny, Klapac.

SWEDEN (2)—Goal, Holmqvist, Dahlloef; defense, Svedberg, Carlsson, Johansson, Nordlander, Sjoberg; forwards, Oberg, Nilsson, Wichberg, Lundstrom, Henriksson, Olsson, Hedlund, Graholf, Palmqvist, Bengtsson.

FIRST PERIOD—1, Sweden, Bengtsson (Lundstrom), 4:09; 2, Czechoslovakia, Golonka (Jirik, Sevcik), 15:29. Penalties—none.

SECOND PERIOD—3, Sweden, Henriksson (S. Svedberg), 15:40. Penalties—Carlsson 10:25, Sevcik 11:03.

THIRD PERIOD—4, Czechoslovakia, Hrbaty (unassisted), 6:22. Penalties—Hedlund 9:17.

Czechoslovakia	1	0	1—2
Sweden	1	1	0—2

Referese—Trumble of United States and Sillankowa of Finland.

Luge Doubles Set Today After Delays by Weather

VILLARD-de-LANS, France, Feb. 17 (AP) — The jury for the Olympic luge competition decided tonight to hold one practice run tomorrow morning and immediately follow with the two official heats for the two-man sleds.

The two-man event was originally scheduled for Thursday, but has been postponed because of warm weather that softened the ice on the track. The Games end tomorrow.

Associated Press

Jean-Claude Killy swings through a gate during the men's slalom. He finished third, but was awarded gold medal when the leaders were disqualified for missing gates.

Slalom Fans, Peering in Mist, Ask, 'Did Schranz Really Lose?'

Special to The New York Times

CHAMBROUSSE, France, Feb. 17—This was a day that started and ended with a question as the Alpine phase of the Winter Olympics was completed.

The first question, posed before the slalom, was "Why are they holding the race in such a fog?" The second: "Did Karl Schranz really lose?"

Officials seemed to have no difficulty in coping with the first. They merely explained that while a thick mist might present difficulties for the racers, the conditions would be the same for all.

The Schranz matter, however, came in for careful scrutiny. The Austrian rates as one of the top Alpine performers in the world. He is known as an athlete who wants to win only on his merits. The controversy over his disqualification today seemed certain to last for years.

The conference of the race jury that decided the outcome was closed. But during the press briefing held immediately after the two-run contest, the Austrian was pressed by reporters.

"Tell us about the episode with the spectator on the course and the discussion with the starting judge," he was asked.

"I was descending and I saw a dark shadow ahead of me," he answered. "I wanted to avoid it, and I stopped. It was apparently a ski policeman."

"Did the officials on top see what happened?"

"No, it occurred down the slope at about the 10th gate. The Soviet trainer was there, and he suggested I return to the top for another start. He climbed up with me."

"Did it disturb you to have to climb up the slope again?"

"Yes, when I got up there I was very tired. My goggles were fogged, and I was given permission to rest for a short while."

"They say that you missed a gate before the incident with the spectator. Is that true?"

"It is possible, but if I did I didn't realize it. I was hypnotized by the dark shadow I saw ahead. It is possible that for the moment I missed a gate to avoid it."

International Ski Federation rules stipulate that a racer who suffers interference on the course is automatically entitled to a rerun. Actually the officials on top had no choice. Conditions on a slalom course deteriorate quickly. They could not take time out to hold court on the mountain.

There was no question, however, about Haakon Mjoen of Norway, who had been credited with the event's fastest time after the second descent. He disqualified himself by explaining that he had missed gates.

Actually only the gatekeepers, stationed close to the flag-topped poles that zigzag down the course, could have seen the violations, except in the few areas where the mist was a little thinner.

The jury's decision helped to save the reputation of Jean-Claude Killy, the winner, as "a man with a clock in his head." Repeatedly he has exerted himself just enough in the second descent to back a first-run lead.

When the second descent had been completed and it was learned he trailed Mjoen, a moan was heard from his supporters. The announcement of Schranz's clocking sent a similar ripple through the crowd. Now Killy was third.

"The clock, it has stopped working," said a railbird. But that judgment proved premature.

U.C.L.A. Routs Houston to Gain N.C.A.A. Final

COUGARS' STREAK IS SNAPPED AT 32

U.C.L.A. Dominant From the Start — Hayes Is Checked —Ohio St. Bows, 80-66

By GORDON S. WHITE Jr.
Special to The New York Times

LOS ANGELES, March 22—The big rematch in college baskketball that fans were looking forward to became the most astonishing mismatch in the history of the National Collegiate Athletic Association championships as the University of California, Los Angeles, overwhelmed Houston, 101-69, tonight in an N.C.A.A. semi-final contest.

Now the Bruins will face North Carolina in the final of the tournament with what appears an easy chance to gain their second straight N.C.A.A. title and fourth in the last five years.

North Carolina gained the dubious distinction of being the Bruins' opponent by beating Ohio State, 80-66, in the first semi-final before 15,742 persons at the Los Angeles Sports Arena.

Cincinnati was the only team to win a semi-final game by more points than the Bruins did when it whipped Oregon State by 34 points in the next-to-last round in 1963. But tonight's game was supposed to have been a tight test, one between the team rated No. 1, Houston, and the No. 2 team, U.C.L.A.

In a Class by Themselves

There was little doubt in the minds of the fans present and those who wateched the national telecast that the polls have made a mistake this time. U.C.L.A. was in a class by itself tonight.

From the outset the Bruins had the game completely under control and Houston completely bottled up. Each of the Bruins did an outstanding job. No one man stood alone in the hero role. Defense, as well as offense, was well executed by Coach John Wooden's crew of Lew Alcindor, Lucius Allen, Mike Warren, Mike Lynn and Lynn Shackleford.

The match within the match—Alcindor vs. Elvin Hayes—was no more a contest than the game itself was. Hayes was handcuffed by a tenacious defense that didn't permit him to get his hands on the ball very often. The "player of the year" scored only 10 points after averaging 37.7 a game in leading Houston through an undefeated regular season.

The loss was the first for the Cougars in 33 games. They hadn't been beaten since U.C.L.A. stopped them, 73-58, in last year's semi-final. Houston handed the Bruin's their only loss this season, 71-69, last January in Houston.

But then U.C.L.A. wasn't completely healthy. Operating on all cylinders tonight, however, the Bruins laid claim to being the best team in the land, even if they won't get a No. 1 rating since polls are finished for the year.

Alcindor, with his hook shots and easy underneath tosses, scored 19 points as did Lynn, primarily on sets, and Allen, mainly on driving layups when Alcindor, the 7-foot-1½-inch star, cleared the lane for him.

UCLA Bruins

Lew Alcindor

U.C.L.A. could easily have rolled up the biggest margin of victory in a semi-final N.C.A.A. test. But Wooden and his team proved their point as they gained a 44-point lead toward the end of the game. Wooden then took his stars out one by one and Houston cut the margin from very embarrassing to just embarrassing.

As Alcindor left the game with 2:04 to go, he raised his long right arm with the index finger extended to indicate No. 1. No one could argue with him and the U.C.L.A. fans

When Jim Nielsen drove in for a layup to give U.C.L.A. its 100th and 101st points, the fans loved it. The U.C.L.A. team that won the title in 1965 is the only other team to score 100 or more points in a semi-final game. The 1965 Bruins beat Wichita State, 108-89, in the semi-finals. No team has scored 100 points in an N.C.A.A. final.

Coach Guy Lewis of Houston said, "That was the greatest exhibition of basketball I've ever seen in my life. They could have beaten anybody — I mean anybody."

Defense and some good breakaways when the opportunity arose were the keys to North Carolina's success that carried the Tar Heels to the National final for the first time since they won the title in 1957.

OHIO STATE (66)	G.	F.	P.
Howell	6	1-2	13
Hosket	4	6-9	14
Sorenson	5	1-3	11
Schnabel	0	0-0	0
Meadors	3	2-2	8
Finney	8	0-2	16
Smith	2	0-0	4
Barclay	0	0-0	0
Geddes	0	0-0	0
Totals	28	10-18	66

NO. CAROLINA (80)	G.	F.	P.
Miller	10	0-1	20
Bunting	4	9-10	17
Clark	7	1-1	15
Scott	6	1-4	13
Gruber	4	3-3	11
Fogler	1	0-0	2
Braun	0	0-0	0
Tuttle	1	0-1	2
Totals	33	14-20	80

Half-time score—North Carolina 34, Ohio State 27.
Fouled out—Hosket.

U.C.L.A. (101)	G.	F.	P.
Shackelford	6	5-5	17
Lynn	8	3-3	19
Alcindor	7	5-6	19
Warren	7	0-0	14
Allen	9	1-2	19
Nielsen	2	0-0	4
Heitz	3	1-1	7
Saner	0	0-0	0
Sutherland	0	0-0	0
Sweek	1	0-1	2
Total	43	15-18	101

HOUSTON (69)	G.	F.	P.
Lee	2	0-0	4
Hayes	3	4-7	10
Spain	4	7-10	15
Chaney	5	5-7	15
Lewis	2	2-2	6
Hamood	3	4-6	10
Gribben	0	0-1	0
Bell	3	3-4	9
Total	22	25-37	69

Half-time score—U.C.L.A. 53, Houston 31.
Atendance—15,742.

DAYTON COUNTING ON A CORNERMAN

May Is Expected to Offset White of Kansas in N.I.T.

By DAVE ANDERSON

Basketball skills that were nurtured a decade ago in a driveway by Don May and on a sidewalk by Jo Jo White will be on display at Madison Square Garden today, when Dayton University opposes Kansas University for the championship of the 31st National Invitation Tournament.

Although no tickets are available, the game will be televised in the metropolitan area on Channel 2, at 2 P.M. There will be no radio description.

The basic elements have been established. Dayton will try to set up May, a 6-foot-4-inch cornerman who has averaged 28 points in three previous N.I.T. games. Kansas will look for guidance from White, a smooth 6-3 playmaker, in positioning its deliberate offense.

May, the shooter, and White, the dribbler, are the leading candidates for the tourney's individual prize, the most valuable-player trophy. But they began to earn such stature years ago.

"When I was about 11," May said before practice yesterday, "I started shooting at a basket on a garage in a neighbor's driveway a few doors up the street, Kiefaber Street, in Dayton. I lived about two blocks from the Dayton campus, and I still live there."

In those years, he had a newspaper route that forced him to wake up at 5 A.M.

"I'd get home about 7, and go over and shoot before I went to school," he said, smiling at the recollection, "and then I'd shoot after school. And sometimes I'd shoot at night, by the porch light. I guess they wanted to shoot me, but they were nice about it."

White learned to play basketball in a schoolyard on the south side of St. Louis.

"You had to be able to handle the ball to play there," he said. "I always liked to dribble my basketball. I remember when my mother used to send me to the store, about two blocks away, I'd dribble all the way to keep me from getting mad about it."

As a high-school star, he often observed National Basketball Association players in St. Louis.

"I always liked Guy Rodgers. I thought he was really special," said White. "I watched Bob Cousy, too, and Oscar [Robertson]. Oscar says you should dribble hard, but I never think about how I dribble, I just do it. I never plan how I'm dribbling."

Kansas is appearing in its first N.I.T., but Dayton has qualified for the N.I.T. final for the seventh time in 11 appearances. The Flyers won in 1962.

With another sellout crowd of 19,500 assured, the tournament will have averaged 17,343 spectators for eight sessions, the highest average since 1950. The record average is 18,743, established in 1946 with four sessions. There were eight teams in 1946 instead of the 16 currently chosen.

Dayton will be risking a 13-game winning streak after St. Peter's goes against Notre Dame in the third-place game, starting at noon.

FIRST GAME—NOON

ST. PETER'S		NOTRE DAME
(24) MacMahon	L.F.	Murphy (33)
(30) Webster	R.F.	Arnzen (40)
(22) O'Dea	C.	Whitmore (53)
(14) Laurie	L.G.	M. O'Connell (20)
(10) Leckie	R.G.	Derrig (31)

SUBSTITUTES

St. Peter's—G. O'Connell (12), Wilk (20), DePiano (32), Grant (40), Drew (44), Schwester (50), Finnegan (52), Twyman (54).

Notre Dame—Gallagher (11), Freeman (30), Franger (32), Restovich (34), Keller (41), McKirchy (42), Quinn (44), Vignali (52), Ziznewski (55).

TV-CHANNEL 2, 2 P.M.

DAYTON		KANSAS
(33) Sadlier	L.F.	Sloan (31)
(21) May	R.F.	Bohnenstiehl (35)
(31) Obrovac	C.	Nash (13)
(42) Hooper	L.G.	Harmon (10)
(13) J. Gottcshall	R.G.	White (15)

SUBSTITUTES

Dayton — Waterman (22), Wannemacher (23), Jerry Gottschall (24), Leffel (30), Janky (35), Blevins (40), Torain (43), Sharpenter (45).

Kansas — Bradshaw (12), Douglas (20), Lawrence (22), Thomas (25), Vanoy (32), Arndt (33).

76ERS TURN BACK KNICKS, 118 TO 110

Chamberlain Nets 37 Points in Eastern Playoff Game

By LEONARD KOPPETT
Special to The New York Times

PHILADELPHIA, March 22—Wilt Chamberlain, who has a painfully bruised big toe on his right foot, scored 37 points tonight and hauled in 29 rebounds as he led the Philadelphia 76ers to a 118-110 victory over the New York Knickerbockers in the first game of the National Basketball Association playoffs.

His performance was almost matched by Willis Reed, who scored 38 points for New York and had 23 rebounds. But despite these statistics, the game witnessed by 5,093 in Convention Hall was not a man-against-man show.

The 76ers, last year's league champions, this year's Eastern Division leaders and favored to win the playoffs again, had to use all their experience and team balance to overcome the Knicks, who put up a fierce struggle and were beaten off only in the closing minutes. And it was New York's favorite team weapon, the zone press, that gave the Knicks the upper hand they held in the middle of the game.

Meet Again Today

Tomorrow night, the teams will meet again at Madison Square Garden in New York, in the second game of this four-of-seven opening round.

Just how effective Chamberlain might be was in doubt until the game began. His foot was stepped on during the final game of the regular season, and although X-rays showed no break, he did need treatment yesterday and today. Since his presence is the basis of Philadelphia's success, considerable importance can be attached to even a minor injury if it puts him below par.

But this one didn't. He scored 13 points in the first quarter, which Philadelphia dominated until the closing moments, and 13 of the last 25 points the 76ers scored.

From the Knick point of view, the defeat boiled down to poor shooting when the shots were there. The rookies—Walt Frazier, Phil Jackson and Bill Bradley—were unable to contribute their share upon the first exposure to the ferocity and pace of pro playoff basketball, which is far more intense then regular-season action.

Thanks to the press, the Knicks turned a 40-34 deficit into a 53-46 lead during the second half of the second period. It had three effects: It neutralized Chamberlain's power underneath, it kept the 76ers from setting up Hal Greer (who wound up with only 8 points), and it seemed to make the 76ers forget to play defense themselves.

Four minutes into the second half, the Knicks led, 69-59. But this time, the 76ers did keep their own defense tight, and the Knicks offense disappeared. New York scored only 7 points in the last 8 minutes 46 seconds of the third period, and the 76ers emerged with an 82-76 lead.

Now the 76ers were playing their own game, but the Knicks weren't beaten yet. They fought back to within one point and were trailing by only 93-92 with six minutes to go in the game.

But Chet Walker, who had scored his team's first 8 points and only 3 more since, scored two baskets in 10 seconds. Jump shots by Luke Jackson and Wally Jones made it 101-94, and then Wilt took charge. He spun in for one goal, rebounded for a 3-pointer, and dunked another rebound. That made it 109-96 with 2:40 to play and that was enough.

Cazzie Russell, who finished with 18 points, scored 10 of them after that, and helped bring the Knicks to within 112-106 with 1:16 left. But Wilt and Walker scored again, in quick succession.

NEW YORK (110)	G.	F.	P.
Reed	14	10-11	38
VanArsdale	1	1-2	3
Bellamy	4	6-11	14
Komives	2	0-1	4
Barnett	12	5-5	29
Bradley	1	0-0	2
Bryant	0	0-0	0
Frazier	1	0-0	2
P. Jackson	0	0-0	0
Russell	7	4-4	18
Total	42	26-34	110

PHILADELPHIA (118)	G.	F.	P.
L. Jackson	7	2-2	16
Walker	7	5-9	19
Chamb'ln	17	3-5	37
Greer	4	0-0	8
Jones	8	7-9	23
Cunningham	6	3-5	15
Green	0	0-0	0
Guokas	0	0-0	0
Total	49	20-30	118

New York	28	27	21	34—110
Philadelphia	27	25	30	36—118

Fouled out—L. Jackson.
Attendance—5,093.

Tournament Basketball

N. C. A. A.
(Semi-Final Round)

U.C.L.A. 101 .... Houston 69
No. Carolina 80 .... Ohio St. 66

NAT'L JR COLLEGE
(Losers Bracket)

Miami-Dade (Fla.) 86 .... Christian Coll. (Tex.) 75
Iowa Central 85 .... Boise 68
Robert Morris (Ill.) 68 Peducah (Ky.) 61

(Semi-Final Round)

Mercer C.C. (N.J.) 80 Vincennes (Ind.) 72

Trevino Wins U.S. Open by 4 Shots With 69 for Record-Tying Total of 275

LEG WORK: Lee Trevino sinking birdie on 12th hole

PUNCHING IT IN: Trevino after putting for birdie on the 11th. Ball dropped into cup.

Associated Press

VICTORY SMILE: Trevino after triumph gets congratulations from Bert Yancey. Yancey led for three rounds in U.S. Open played at the Oak Hill Country Club, Rochester, N.Y.

NICKLAUS FINISHES SECOND AFTER A 67

Yancey Fades to 76 for 281 and Third—Trevino Gains First Tourney Victory

By LINCOLN A. WERDEN

Special to The New York Times

ROCHESTER, June 16—Lee Trevino, a rookie recruit on golf's professional circuit last year, won the United States Open championship today with a record-equaling total of 275.

The voluble 28-year-old from Horizon City, Tex., who is of Mexican descent, scored a concluding 69 and beat Jack Nicklaus, the defending champion, by four strokes.

After receiving the victor's check of $30,000 from the $190,000 purse, Trevino conceded that he had never dreamed of being so successful. "I'm the happiest Mexican in the world right now. I never thought it would happen to me. But show me a guy who wouldn't feel great winning the United States Open."

Trevino did not continue in a serious vein for many minutes after his smashing triumph with a score that matched that of Nicklaus when he won last year at Baltusrol in Springfield, N. J.

Job on Par-3 Course

"I'll make a lot of money," predicted Trevino, who worked as a clerk on a par-3 Dallas public course before joining the Marines. "This makes me eligible for the World Series of golf and a $50,000 first prize, but it would be my luck to have them cancel that tournament. That would be like owning a pumpkin farm and they called off Halloween, wouldn't it?"

Although this was only Trevino's third bid for the big title, he outplayed an international field and rallied to overtake and pass Bert Yancey, the ex-West Pointer, who had set the pace for three successive rounds. With a 69, 68, 69 and his one-under-par performance today over the 6,962-yard Oak Hill Country Club course, Trevino became the first in 68 years of Open championships to play all four rounds under par.

Yancey and Trevino made this a head-to-head tussle until the last nine, and Yancey faded to 76 for 281 and third. Before starting, Yancey said it reminded him of a match-play event. But when the former Army golf captain required 38 to Trevino's one-over-par 36 going out, the ebullient Texan went one stroke ahead.

Palmer in Last Group

Thousands sat around the greens to catch a glimpse of the dark-haired Trevino with black hat, red shirt and socks and black slacks. But they also waited for Arnold Palmer, the golfing millionaire, who had an unusual role today. Palmer was in the last group, paired with two amateurs, Jack Lewis, a 20-year-old Wake Forest senior, and 18-year-old Jimmy Simons of Butler, Pa.

Palmer's 226 for 54 holes was responsible for his being listed at the end of today's field according to the United States Golf Association pairings.

The crowd wanted to see him, although Palmer was not pleased with his scoring and said so. He finished with a 75 for 301, only four places out of the cellar position, which went to young Simons, who had 310.

Nicklaus put together his best round, a 67, in an effort to move closer to the top. He was in the twosome just ahead of Yancey and Trevino, who were able to watch Nicklaus and Charles Coody putting as they waited on the fairways repeatedly.

Bobby Nichols, with a 69, was fourth at 282 while Steve Spray and Don Bies had 284's. Bob Charles and Jerry Pittman were at 285 and Sam Snead, the 56-year-old campaigner, and Billy Casper, the pretournament favorite, were in the group at 286.

The first indication that Trevino might break through came at the third hole. At this par 3, Yancey hooked his shot close to a tree and holed out with a bogey 4. The Texan's 3 put them on an even basis, erasing Yancey's one-stroke advantage beginning the round.

Two holes later Trevino went one ahead as Yancey was bunkered and carded a bogey 4. But he did not hold the advantage long. Yancey drew even again with a birdie 3 at the sixth.

Yancey took a bogey 5 after being bunkered at the ninth and Trevino's 4 there gave him a one-stroke lead that he subsequently increased steadily. Trevino had a 36 out, Yancey a 38 and Nicklaus, attempting a comeback, took only 33.

As his friends yelled encouragement, Trevino added a stroke a hole against Yancey over the next four. Two of these were pars, but he ran in a 35-footer for a deuce at the 11th and one of 22 feet for a birdie 3 at the 12th.

Only at one hole after that did Yancey outscore Trevino. That was at the 14th when he holed a 2-footer for a 3 to his rival's 4.

Yancey, however, lost ground when he three-putted at the 16th for a bogey 5 to the Texan's 4. At the final hole, Yancey was bunkered for another bogey, but Trevino, in the rough twice, salvaged a par 4 on a 4-foot putt.

The new champion, flushed with success, said he had no contracts with manufacturers of golf equipment. He is now part owner of the Horizon Hills Country Club, part of a housing development outside El Paso. "There'll be free booze there until midnight," he announced. "I'm a little nervous," he conceded later.

"I didn't telephone my wife. She knows about it by now from watching television. She'll get my check by Thursday. If I don't mail it, I'll hear about it. I expect to play in the Canadian open next week and I intend to play golf as long as I can until I'm a hundred years old."

As he came off the 13th green, he turned to Joseph C. Dey Jr., executive director of the U.S.G.A., who was accompanying him, and remarked, "I'm trying to get a big enough lead, so I won't choke."

Others who have scored their first tournament victory in the Open where Nicklaus in 1962 and Jack Fleck in 1955.

Trevino, who used a broomstick as his first golf club and was especially adept against opponents when he played with a soft-drink bottle while they used standard clubs on the par-3 course where he was employed, had finished second in Houston and Atlanta on the tour this year.

He said his grandfather a grave-digger, was responsible for rearing him. One of his habits on the pro tour has been to skip rope in his motel room to keep in trim. "But I didn't do that this week, I just practiced hitting golf balls," he said.

U.S. Open Scores

Lee Trevino	69	68	69	69—275	$30,000
Jack Nicklaus	72	70	70	67—279	$15,000
Bert Yancey	67	68	70	76—281	$10,000
Bobby Nichols	74	71	68	69—282	$7,500
Don Bies	70	70	75	69—284	$5,500
Steve Spray	73	75	71	65—284	$5,500
Bob Charles	73	69	72	71—285	$3,750
Jerry Pittman	73	67	74	71—285	$3,750
Bruce Devlin	71	69	75	71—286	$2,516
Billy Casper	75	68	71	72—286	$2,516
Gay Brewer	71	71	75	69—286	$2,516
Al Geiberger	72	74	68	72—286	$2,516
David Stockton	72	73	69	72—286	$2,516
Sam Snead	73	71	74	68—286	$2,516
Dan Sikes	71	71	73	72—287	$1,900
Rod Funseth	74	72	69	73—288	$1,633
Julius Boros	71	71	71	75—288	$1,633
Charles Coody	69	71	72	76—288	$1,633
Gary Player	76	69	70	73—288	$1,633
Dave Hill	74	68	74	72—288	$1,633
George Archer	74	72	73	69—288	$1,633
Hugh Royer	75	72	73	69—289	$1,425
Benson McLendon	72	76	70	71—289	$1,425
Miller Barber	76	68	78	70—290	$1,203
Don January	71	75	71	73—290	$1,203
Tom Weiskopf	75	72	70	73—290	$1,203
R. de Vicenzo	72	76	72	70—290	$1,203
Pat Schwab	76	70	75	69—290	$1,203
Bob Lunn	74	73	73	70—290	$1,203
Bob Erickson	75	68	72	75—290	$1,203
Larry Ziegler	71	71	74	74—290	$1,203
Dave Marr	70	72	74	75—291	$1,020
Robert Murphy	76	71	70	74—291	$1,020
Bill Collins	71	72	76	72—291	$1,020
Charles Sifford	75	69	75	72—291	$1,020
Terry Dill	74	71	73	73—291	$1,020
Harold Henning	75	68	76	73—292	$950
Doug Sanders	73	72	73	74—292	$950
Bob Boalby	76	71	73	73—293	$897
Gibby Gilbert	73	72	76	72—293	$897
Billy Farrell	70	72	74	77—293	$897
Mac Hunter	75	73	74	71—293	$897
D. Eichelberger	74	73	76	71—294	$856
Labron Harris Jr.	70	72	77	75—294	$856
Al Balding	70	76	71	77—294	$856
Bob Dickson	76	70	75	74—295	$835
Bruce Crampton	75	72	75	73—295	$835
Ronnie Reif	72	74	74	76—296	$815
Bob Stone	75	72	75	74—296	$815
Art Wall	74	74	75	74—297	$795
Monty Kaser	73	72	75	77—297	$795
Kel Nagle	72	75	76	75—298	$765
H. Blancas Jr.	72	75	74	77—298	$765
Frank Beard	76	72	73	77—298	$765
Billy Maxwell	72	74	78	74—298	$765
Gene Borek	73	74	76	76—299	$740
*Richard Siderowf	71	76	76	77—300	—
Paul Harney	74	73	78	75—300	$730
Arnold Palmer	73	74	79	75—301	$720
Al Chandler	74	72	78	78—302	$710
*Jack Lewis Jr.	73	75	80	74—302	—
Johnny Pott	76	72	76	79—303	$700
*James Simons	75	73	81	81—310	—

*Denotes amateur.

CARDS OF THE LEADERS

PAR FOR THE COURSE				
Out	4 4 3	5 3 4	4 4 4—35	
In	4 3 4	5 4 3	4 4 4—35—70	
LEE TREVINO				
Out	5 4 3	5 3 4	4 4 4—36	
In	4 2 3	5 4 3	4 4 4—33—69	
JACK NICKLAUS				
Out	4 4 2	4 3 4	4 4 4—33	
In	4 3 4	5 3 3	4 4 4—34—67	
BERT YANCEY				
Out	5 4 4	5 4 3	4 4 5—38	
In	5 3 4	6 3 3	5 4 5—38—76	

Golf's No. 1 Extrovert

Lee Buck Trevino

Man in the News

THE 28-year-old Mexican-American who pocketed $30,000 yesterday for his triumph in the United States Open golf tournament at Rochester is an aggressive, amiable, talkative, emotional, confident ex-marine who now, presumably, considers himself a Spaniard. "You never see a rich Mexican," Lee Trevino said earlier this week. "If you have money, you're a Spaniard." In the last year, Lee Buck Trevino has epitomized the old American success story. As a $30-a-week assistant pro at the Horizon Hills Country Club near El Paso, Tex., he made his debut on the professional tour in the 1967 Open at Baltusrol in Springfield, N. J.

"If I hadn't won any money, I'd have whipped back home," Trevino said then after winning $6,000 for his fifth-place finish.

Since Baltusrol, the muscular, smiling Trevino has been one of the consistent moneymakers on the pro tour, although yesterday's victory was his first. His official career earnings are now $110,899.85.

But Trevino's triumph in the Open will further pad his bank account with rich fees for endorsements, appearances and any personal promotions he may care to make.

Self-Taught Golfer

"It means a whole bunch of money," he said when asked what the victory meant.

The son of Mexican-American peasants near Dallas, Trevino found his first golf club in a field of hay at the age of 6. He set up his own two-hole course in a pasture and proceeded to teach himself the sport.

His self-instruction is evident even today to golfing purists who flinch while watching his flat swing, which many think would be more effective in the National Baseball League than on a golf course.

"I have a lot of confidence in my game, even though I have a bad swing," Trevino said the other day in an admission rare among the golfing fraternity.

Trevino's first serious golfing was undertaken during his service with the marines on Okinawa.

Beating the Colonels

"I didn't do anything but play golf with the colonels," he said. "That's when I really learned to play. I started out as a private, but after beating the colonels a few times, I rose to sergeant."

Following his discharge, Trevino operated a pitch-and-putt course and, to pick up extra money, won bets from customers by playing the game with a large soft-drink bottle.

"I wrapped the bottle with adhesive tape and made a good hitting surface," he explained. "I got to the point where I could drive a ball 150 yards with the bottle and could hit a tree from that distance almost every time. I putted with the bottle as I would with a cue stick. I could shoot around 56 or 58 and I could win most of my bets."

Later, Trevino got a job as assistant pro to Don Whittington at the Horizon Hills course and further shaped his game to accommodate the sand-filled winds that swept the scrubby, heat-baked fairways. Often playing with scuba-diver goggles, he learned to stroke the ball low, out of the gale-like gusts.

His wife, Claudia, has been the family financial administrator since he married her while running the pitch-and-putt course. Their family includes a daughter, Lesley, who is 3, and two dogs.

Charmer of Galleries

In his one year on the pro tour, the 5-foot-10-inch, 185-pound Trevino has charmed the galleries with his talkative exuberance, his smiling, determined stride and his ever-present lucky coin to which he attributes his good fortune.

His fans are known around the circuit as "Lee's Fleas" as opposed to "Arnie's Army," the worshiping horde that follows Arnold Palmer.

Observers on the pro tour think that the colorful Trevino may eventually replace Palmer as the idol of the galleries.

If so, his fans, who shout "Ole!" at each good shot, may be in for a long, happy reign.

"My goal is to play as good as I can for as long as I can," he said yesterday. "I'm going to keep practicing and playing until I get about 100 years old."

And, like the late "Champagne" Tony Lema, Trevino is a free-spending happy-go-lucky winner who said, "The booze will be free all night tonight at the Horizon Hills Country Club," where several hundred members watched the Open on five television sets.

His wife's bookkeeping may also grow more complex. Speaking of the $30,000 prize, he said, "My wife will let me keep $300."

United Press International

Lucky piece worth $30,000

SPRAY'S 65 TIES RECORD FOR OPEN

His 30 for Nine Holes Also Equals Tourney Mark

ROCHESTER, June 16 (AP)—Steve Spray, a 27-year-old touring pro, shot a five-under-par 65 today in the final round and tied two United States Open golf championship records.

His score of 30 on the incoming nine matched the record for the lowest nine-hole score, held by Ken Venturi, Arnold Palmer and James McHale Jr.

The score also tied the record for the lowest closing round, held by Walter Burkemo, Palmer and Jack Nicklaus.

Spray's fine round included eight birdies and three bogeys. Two of the birdies came on putts of 35 feet, and he had five other putts of 10 to 18 feet. He had 11 one-putt greens and only 25 putts for the round.

Spray finished the tourney with a 284 total after previous rounds of 73, 75 and 71.

Yancey Avoids Questions

Special to The New York Times

ROCHESTER, June 16—Several minutes after completing his round of 76 that dropped him into a third-place finish today, Bert Yancey, emerged today from the locker room of the Oak Hill Country Club. He was carrying a traveling bag and he was hurying toward the parking lot.

"Bring the clubs out to the car," Yancey told his caddie, 22-year-old John Teegardin. "I'll see how much money I got in my pocket."

After leading the United States Open championship during the first three rounds with a total of 205, Yancey's game had soured. Hoping for an explanation, a newsman asked him:

"May I bother you with a few questions?"

"I'd rather not, you don't mind, do you," he answered and he hastened into the parking lot.

His putting presumably had disturbed him. After the third round yesterday, he had said, "I've putted real well for three years. I putted well today, and I'll putt well tomorrow. I always do."

But he didn't.

Yancey required 35 putts, including three-putt greens on the 13th and 16th holes. His most significant misses were a pair of 3-foot putts that produced bogeys on the third and fifth holes and enabled Lee Trevino to take the lead without any birdies at that point.

Tipperary Tops All-Stars And Takes Hurling Title

Tipperary, the Irish Home League champion, defeated the New York All-Stars yesterday before 8,541 at Gaelic Park in the Bronx in the showdown match for the National league Hurling title. Tipperary got four goals and 14 singles for a total of 26 points to New York's two goals and eight singles for 14 points.

Tipperary went into the game trailing by one point in the two-game total aggregate championship, as a result of New York's 20-19 victory Saturday.

Miss Bardahl Takes Honors In Wisconsin Hydro Race

MADISON, Wis., June 16 (AP) — Bill Schumacher of Seattle, piloted the unlimited hydroplane, Miss Bardahl, to victory today in the first Wisconsin Cup race on Lake Monona.

Schumacher averaged 96.73 miles an hour in beating four other high-powered boats in the final heat over the 15-mile course before a crowd of 25,000. He earned $4,500 for the victory.

Vera Korsakova Sets Mark

MOSCOW, June 16 (Reuters)—Vera Korsakova, 26 years old, broke the women's world record for the 80-meter hurdles at Riga today, being clocked in 10.2 seconds in the Riga Cup meet.

Victorious Trevino Is Singing My Heart Belongs to Caddie

By DAVE ANDERSON

Special to The New York Times

ROCHESTER, June 16 — When his 20-foot putt plopped into the cup on the 12th green for a birdie 3 and a four-stroke lead, Lee Trevino stood on his left foot, swung his right foot and flashed his right fist at the sky in a symbol of triumph.

"Hole me down," Trevino said to his caddie on their way to the next tee, "hole me down."

His caddie, 18-year-old Kevin Quinn, who will begin his sophomore year at Cornell University in the fall, was tipped $2,000 by Trevino, once a caddie himself, for psychologically guiding him to glory today in the United States Open golf championship.

"This kid is a great kid," Trevino said later. "You'd think I was the caddie and he was the pro, he had me under control."

Caddie Seconds Motion

Most of the time, whenever Trevino picked an iron out of his white leather bag, the freckled-faced caddie would reassure him.

"He'd say, 'That's the club,'" the new champion explained later, "and just the way he said it made me feel it was the proper club. This boy controlled me. You want a little encouragement, you want somebody to tell you it's the right club."

On the 15th tee, as Trevino laughed later, "the kid choked for the only time" in 72 holes.

"He told me, 'It's a smooth 5-iron,'" Trevino said, recalling the 163-yard par 3, "but I said to him, 'if I hit a 5, I'm going to put it in that TV tower behind the green. Bert [Yancey] used an 8 and he's pin-high. I got to use an 8 here.'"

Trevino's 8-iron shot hit the pin, but his caddie did not lose his confidence in selecting the champion's club.

After hitting a good drive on the 463-yard 17th hole, the longest par-4 on the Oak Hill Country Club course, Trevino was confronted with choosing the proper long iron.

"I think it's a 1-iron," the golfer said.

It's really a hard 2," the caddie said.

Swinging a 2-iron, Trevino mis-hit the ball. Never attaining its proper trajectory, it landed perhaps 50 yards short of the green and stopped short of the putting surface.

He Remains Confident

"No problem," the caddie said, undaunted. "Just a chip in and one putt."

And that's exactly what Trevino did to preserve his par on the hole.

With a 4-shot lead at the 18th tee, Trevino was told by his caddie to "go for broke, go for the record." He needed a birdie 3 to set an open record score of 284 for 72 holes. And in that situation, Trevino agreed. But he pulled his drive into the rough.

"After that, I made the decisions," Trevino said with a laugh. "Ordinarily, I wouldn't have used a 6-iron with the lie I had, but I didn't want to be remembered as the U.S. Open champion who laid up with a wedge, so I hit the 6, but not far."

Within wedge distance on his next shot, he "hit it as hard as I could," and the ball stopped 3 feet from the cup.

Trevino holed the putt, another testimonial to his caddie. Throughout the 72 holes, he never had a 3-putt green.

"That kid was tremendous," the new champion said. "I wouldn't have won this tournament without him there with me."

Lourdes Rugby Victor

TOULOUSE, France, June 16 (Reuters)—The number of tries scored decided the French Rugby Union Club championship today after Lourdes and Toulon had tied, 9-9, after extra time. Lourdes was declared the winners by scoring two tries during the match. Toulon's points came from goal kicking.

MISS WRIGHT'S 212 WINS BY 3 SHOTS

Speedway Victory Is 4th on Tour—Miss Whitworth 2d

INDIANAPOLIS, June 16 (AP)—Mickey Wright clipped four strokes off par with a 68 today and won the Speedway open golf tournament with a 59-hole total of 212.

The fourth victory for Miss Wright tied her with Carol Mann for most triumphs this season. Miss Mann was forced to withdraw from the final round when back spasms prevented her from turning her neck.

Kathy Whitworth, who led entering the final round, shot a 73 for a 215 and second place at the Speedway Club.

The leading scores:

Mickey Wright	70	74	68—212	$2,250
Kathy Whitworth	71	71	73—215	$1,750
*Mrs. Alice Dye	75	73	73—221	—
Donna Caponi	78	70	74—222	$1,450
Sandra Haynie	72	77	74—223	$1,150
Mary Mills	74	73	77—224	$875
Marilyn Smith	76	77	71—224	$875
Sandra Spuzich	77	74	74—225	$595
Mrs. Murle Lindstrom	73	77	75—225	$595
Margie Masters	76	73	76—225	$595
Sharon Miller	80	73	74—227	$475
Sharron Moran	77	74	77—228	$392
JoAnn Prentice	76	78	74—228	$392
Sandra Palmer	76	76	76—228	$392
Gerda Whalen	71	82	77—230	$302
Jane Woodworth	74	82	74—230	$302

*Denotes amateur.

Westbury Polo Team Wins From Bethpage, 6 to 3

Special to The New York Times

BETHPAGE, L. I., June 16—Westbury evened its season polo series with Bethpage at one-victory each today by turning back the host club, 6-3, at Bethpage State Park.

WESTBURY (6)	BETHPAGE (3)
1—Ted Brinkman	1—Al Bianco
2—Fred Zeller	2—John Greenleaf
3—Alan Corey 3d.	3—Dave Rizzo
Back—Fred Guest	Back—Ted Shapiro

Westbury	5	0	0	0	0	1—6
Bethpage	0	1	1	0	1	0—3

Goals—Westbury: Brinkman 1, Corey 3, Guest 1, by handicap 1. Bethpage: Greenleaf 1, Shapiro 2.

Referee—John Rice.

Gottliebs Win Net Title

Special to The New York Times

SOUTHAMPTON, L. I., June 16—William Gottlieb of Hollis, Queens, and his son, Steve, No. 1 player for Columbia University's team this season, won the Eastern father-and-son grass court tennis championship today at the Meadow Club. They upset Philip and Donald Steckler of Scarsdale, N.Y. 6-4, 6-1.

The New York Times
SPORTS
Section 5
Sunday, September 15, 1968

M'LAIN DEFEATS ATHLETICS, 5-4, FOR 30TH VICTORY; EVANS SETS WORLD 400-METER RECORD IN U.S. TRIALS

United Press International

SECOND BY A STEP: Jim Ryun of Kansas being beaten out at the tape by Roscoe Divine of Oregon in the first heat of the qualifying trials for the Olympic 1,500-meter run yesterday in South Lake Tahoe, Calif. Both were clocked at 3:58.3, and qualified for semi-final round today.

CLOCKING IS 0:44

Evans Defeats James In Olympic Trial—Beamon Is Victor

By NEIL AMDUR

Special to The New York Times

SOUTH LAKE TAHOE, Calif., Sept. 14—The world record tone resumed today in the final United States Olympic track trials when Lee Evans posted a 44.-second time in the 400-meter dash.

Catching Larry James of White Plains, N. Y., with less than 10 meters left, the 21-year-old Evans wiped out the recognized world standard held by Tommie Smith, his San Jose State College teammate, by five-tenths of a second and beat Vince Matthews's pending time of 44.4 seconds.

The long-striding James, who led around the final turn, said he "tightened up" in the last straightaway and "had a hard time moving." But the Villanova University standout's time of 0:44.1 made the race the fastest 400 in history, a point of reference that is becoming quite common in this high-altitude warm-up for the Mexico City games.

4 World Marks Set

Four world records have been set in the meet: in the 400-meter intermediate hurdles, pole vault, 200-meter dash and today's 400-meter. Still to come are the 1,500 meters, with Jim Ryun and Dave Patrick, and the high jump.

Another world record was blown off the record books by the wind. Bob Beamon, the world record-holder in the long jump, leaped 27—6½ on his first attempt in today's final and won a berth on America's Olympic squad. But a 7.1-mile an-hour wind wiped out Beamon's chance for a world record.

Ralph Boston, the 1960 Olympic gold medal winner, joined Beamon on the team with a 27—1 leap. Charlie Mays, the 27-year-old from Jersey City, won the third spot with a career-high 26—9¼.

If Beamon was somewhat disappointed by the wind, Evans was not disturbed over whether his record would be approved. Evans wore the new all-weather track shoes with 68 small brush-type spikes on the sole, the same type shoes worn by John Carlos in his record-setting 200-meter dash.

"I think the shoes will be approved," Evans said. "They helped me run closer to the line and they also helped because they have no shoelaces and I have a tender bone in my foot."

James who lost to Evans in three qualifying races and the final, wore the conventional four-spike sole shoes.

"I know I can beat Lee,"

Continued on Page 9, Column 2

Ellis, Nose Broken, Retains Title

Associated Press

Floyd Patterson being dragged to the canvas by Jimmy Ellis, who slipped in the 14th round of their title bout

Decision Over Patterson Angers Crowd of 25,000 in Stockholm

By ANTHONY LEWIS

Special to The New York Times

STOCKHOLM, Sept. 14—Jimmy Ellis retained his World Boxing Association heavyweight title tonight with a 15-round decision over Floyd Patterson.

The referee, Harold Valan of Brooklyn, scored it nine rounds for the 28-year-old champion and six for Patterson. There were no judges. Most ringside reporters had it a bit closer. The New York Times scored it seven to six for Ellis, with two rounds even.

The crowd of 30,000—cheering all the way for Patterson, an old Swedish favorite — furiously jeered the decision.

The fans chanted "Floyd champ! Floyd champ!" in English, and they surged in on the boxers as they left the ring. For a moment it looked rough and some of the ringside spectators were thrown onto their chairs, but a police squad cleared

Continued on Page 4, Column 6

RALLY IN 9TH WINS

Tigers' Pitcher First to Achieve Feat Since Dean in 1934

By LEONARD KOPPETT

Special to The New York Times

DETROIT, Sept. 14—What no major league pitcher had been able to do since 1934 and what only two had accomplished in the last 48 years was achieved by Dennis Dale McLain of the Detroit Tigers today when he posted his 30th victory of the season.

The 24-year-old right-handed extrovert won it sitting on the bench, because he had been removed for a pinch-hitter in the home half of the ninth inning. The pinch-hitter, Al Kaline, walked and set off a two-run rally that gave the Tigers a 5-4 victory over the Oakland Athletics.

Grove Did It in '31

But the dramatic finish, typical of a Tiger team that has moved within four victories of clinching the American League pennant, in no way minimized McLain's triumph. He had pitched a strong game, hurt only by two home runs by Reggie Jackson, Oakland's budding star, and by the only walk he issued, which was turned into a run. McLain struck out 10 men and pitched his 27th complete game in 38 starts.

All the significance was packed into the "30." A 20-game winner is a member of baseball's elite. Only a handful of pitchers have won 30. The last had been Dizzy Dean, who hurled the St. Louis Cardinals to the 1934 National League pennant with a 30-7 record. Bob (Lefty) Grove of the Philadelphia Athletics was the last in the American League with a 31-4 season in 1931. No one else had won 30 since 1920.

When Willie Horton's drive over the left fielder's head

Continued on Page 4, Column 5

Tennessee Passes In Final Seconds Tie Georgia, 17-17

By STEVE CADY

Special to The New York Times

KNOXVILLE, Tenn., Sept. 14—In a wildly exciting game that will be remembered by football historians both for how it was played and what it was played on, Tennessee gained an incredible 17-17 tie with Georgia today at Neyland Stadium.

The orange-clad Volunteers did it by scoring a touchdown on the last play of the game, then adding two points with a conversion pass.

A crowd of 60,603, largest to view a football contest in the state of Tennessee, roared deliriously as Bubba Wyche hit Gary Kreis with a 21-yard pass for the touchdown. They lost control of themselves completely as Wyche, a senior quarterback from Atlanta, faded back and flipped the tying conversion pass to Kenny DeLong, a junior end from Norfolk, Va.

On Firm Ground

The improbable finish to this nationally televised Southeastern Conference opener proved that football on Tartan Turf, the newest synthetic playing surface, can be just as exciting as football on regular grass.

The rug-like Tartan surface, making its debut, provided a vividly green background for the record crowd at recently expanded Neyland Stadium and for perhaps 25 million television viewers across the nation. Looking like the world's biggest billiards table, the Tartan Turf indicated in its debut that defenders and punters, as well as run-

Continued on Page 2, Column 2

Yanks Top Senators For 9th in Row, 4-1, And Gain Tie for 3d

By JOSEPH DURSO

Special to The New York Times

WASHINGTON, Sept. 14—The New York Yankees, who must be eating catnip, won their ninth straight game today, tied a major league record, broke another and climbed into a tie for third place in the American League.

They did all this while defeating the Washington Senators, 4-1, behind the six-hit pitching of Al Downing. It was the first complete game of the season for Downing, who has been a patient more often than a pitcher, but is now sharing the Yankee's dramaaic revival.

As a result, the Yankees moved from fifth place past the Cleveland Indians, who lost to Baltimore, and they tied last year's cinderella team, the Bos-

Continued on Page 5, Column 2

DAMASCUS SECOND AS NODOUBLE WINS

Runner-Up Is 19th Favorite in 20 Runnings of Detroit Race to Be Defeated

By The Associated Press

DETROIT, Sept. 14—The graveyard of champions—the Michigan Mile and One-Eighth—proved too much today for Damascus.

The millionaire 4-year-old colt finished second to the 3-year-old Nodouble in the $123,300 race.

Damascus joined 19 favorites who had failed to win the race. Beau Prince in 1962 was the only favorite to win the 20-year-old classic at Detroit Race Course.

Finishing in a photo finish with Damascus was Misty Run, owned by Mrs. Anne Ford's Watermill Farms.

Nodoble paid $37.20, $5.40, $2.60 across the board for a $2 ticket. Damascus returned $2.40 and $2.40 and Misty Run paid $4.60.

Nodouble's time was 1:49 as ehe won by 2¾ lengths.

Damascus, the winner of 21 of 29 previous starts, and his stable-mate, Hedevar, owned by Mrs. Edith W. Bancroft, were jammed among horses rounding the first turn. Damascus looked like a beaten horse turn-

Continued on Page 6, Column 2

Gamely Captures $81,850 Beldame By Nose at Big A

By JOE NICHOLS

It took longer to inspect the photo of the finish than it did to run the $81,850 Beldame at Aqueduct yesterday. Then, after the officials spent almost three minutes deciding that William Haggin Perry's Gamely was first across the wire, by a nose in front of the Bohemia Stable's Politely, more time was required to consider a foul claim against Gamely.

At length the result stood, with Gamely the winner, Politely the runner-up and the Rokeby Stable's Amerigo Lady third in the field of five. The race was for fillies and mares 3 years old and up, at a distance of 1⅛ miles. Laffit Pincay was on the winner, who was the strong favorite with the crowd of 47,291. As such she paid $3.40 for $2 after covering the course in 1:49 3/5. Her burden, like that of the rest of the field, was 123 pounds.

The race worked up to a crescendo of excitement after

Continued on Page 6, Column 6

BRILES OF CARDS HALTS ASTROS, 8-0

Posts 18th Triumph With 8-Hitter—McCarver Star

By United Press International

HOUSTON, Sept. 14—Nelson Briles pitched an eight-hit shutout for his 18th victory and Tim McCarver his catcher, slammed a double and a triple today to lead the St. Louis Cardinals to an 8-0 victory over the Houston Astros.

Briles, keeping alive his chances to win 20 games for the first time in his career, struck out nine and walked only one. He pitched out of trouble three times—with bases filled in the first inning and with men on first and third in both the fifth and sixth.

The Cardinals scored two runs in the third on a walk to Dal Maxvill, Lou Brock's triple and a single by Curt Flood. They added another run in the fourth on McCarver's double with Harney, a native of Worcester, moved ahead after nine and a single by Mike Shannon.

The Cardinals scored twice in the fifth when Flood doubled

Continued on Page 4, Column 3

PIRATES TRIUMPH OVER METS BY 6-0

Clemente Cracks 2 Homers as Veale Hurls 8-Hitter

By GEORGE VECSEY

Roberto Clemente recently added up his dependents and found them to be 13. It was at that point that the great Pirate right fielder decided that he could not afford to retire from baseball, even if his right shoulder gives him pain.

Therefore, Clemente will continue to earn his $100,000 during the summer for having occasional evenings like last night when he hit two home runs to help Bob Veale and Pittsburgh beat the New York Mets, 6-0.

Although Clemente has sometimes seemed to dramatize his aches and pains, he is a high-strung athlete who suffers from insomnia and has also suffered from a bad back and malaria in his 14 years with the Pirates.

This year the 34-year-old star had a more pronounced injury. He fell off his back porch while working on his home in Carolina, P. R., a week before spring

Continued on Page 5, Column 5

United Press International

RARE PAIR: Denny McLain of the Tigers getting a hug from Dizzy Dean, a 30-game winning pitcher 34 years ago.

It's Kickoff Time for Giants and Jets

The New York Times — Fran Tarkenton; United Press International — Homer Jones; The New York Times — Joe Namath; Emerson Boozer

Steelers Underdogs Today

By WILLIAM N. WALLACE

Special to The New York Times

PITTSBURGH, Sept. 14—It was in this city last October that Francis Tarkenton, a man of drama, threw a spectacular last-minute touchdown pass following a fake end-around run and a lateral to win the game for the New York Giants over the Pittsburgh Steelers.

The play was typical of the Giants' season, one of peaks and valleys that wound up at the .500 level—seven victories, seven defeats. This year the Giants hope to be

Boozer to Start Against Chiefs

By DAVE ANDERSON

Special to The New York Times

KANSAS CITY, Sept. 14—The New York Jets open their 1968 American Football League season where, in retrospect, their 1967 season ended.

In last year's game here, Emerson Boozer, speeding toward the left sideline, turned and caught a pass from Joe Namath, but a few strides later he was tackled by two red-shirted members of the Kansas City Chiefs. When the Jet halfback arose, he was wobbling on his right knee.

Continued on Page 3, Column 3

Cardigan Bay Wins, Goes Over Million

Special to The New York Times

FREEHOLD, N. J., Sept. 14—Cardigan Bay became the first horse in the history of harness racing to win $1-million in purses today as he took the first- place purse of $7,500 in the Freehold Special at Freehold Raceway.

The 12-year-old gelding ran his total winnings to $1,000,671 by scoring by 1½ lengths in the one-mile pace. Cardigan Bay, driven by Stanley Dancer, covered the mile in 2 minutes 1 second — the fastest time of the current meeting.

Dancer said after the race that he was retiring the gelding to his farm at New Egypt, N. J., and that he would be returned next year to Mrs. Audrey Dean of Aukland, New

Continued on Page 7, Column 3

Moody, With 67 for 206, Takes One-Shot Lead in Kemper Open

By LINCOLN A. WERDEN

Special to The New York Times

SUTTON, Mass., Sept. 14—Orville Moody, a heavyweight ex-Army sergeant who is a 34-year-old rookie on the golf tour, led the Kemper open today with a 54-hole aggregate of 206.

The easy-going ex-serviceman, who was an enlisted man for 14 years, scored a third-round 67 over the Pleasant Valley Country Club course to gain a one-stroke edge over Bruce Crampton in the $150,000 event, the newest on the circuit. During his tour of duty, Moody won the Korean open three times and the American all-service championship among other golfing honors.

Since March, however, he has been competing among the experienced tourists and this afternoon, with one of the largest New England crowds streaming over the hilly 7,230-yard layout, he clicked off six birdies. The estimated attendance was 27,500 and if that figure seemed high, there was no doubt it was one of the most impressive turnouts of the season in the opinion of Professional Golfers' Association officials and all observers.

Arnold Palmer and Doug Sanders tied for third at 209.

Crampton shot a 67, which included a birdie 3 at the 11th, where he rolled in a putt of 100 feet. "It may have been longer," said the Australian later, "You know how huge the greens are here."

Palmer and Sanders each had

Continued on Page 9, Column 6

Major League Baseball

Sunday, Sept. 15, 1968

National League

YESTERDAY'S GAMES

Pittsburgh 6, New York 0.
Los Angeles 3, Atlanta 0.
Philadelphia 4, Chicago 1.
San Francisco 9, Cincinnati 1.
St. Louis 8, Houston 0.

FRIDAY NIGHT

New York 2, Pittsburgh 0.
Chicago 9, Philadelphia 1 (2d).
Cincinnati 6, San Francisco 3.
Houston 4, St. Louis 2.
Los Angeles 2, Atlanta 0.

	W.	L.	Pc.	G.B.
St. Louis	92	58	.613	—
San Francisco	80	69	.537	11½
Cincinnati	77	70	.524	13½
Chicago	77	74	.510	15½
Atlanta	75	74	.503	16½
Pittsburgh	72	76	.486	19
Philadelphia	71	78	.477	20½
Los Angeles	68	81	.456	23½
New York	67	83	.447	25
Houston	67	83	.447	25

American League

YESTERDAY'S GAMES

New York 4, Washington 1.
Baltimore 5, Cleveland 3.
California 5, Chicago 4 (10 inn.).
Minnesota 7, Boston 3.
Detroit 5, Oakland 4.

FRIDAY NIGHT

New York 2, Washington 1 (2d).
Boston 3, Minnesota 0.
Chicago 2, California 1.
Cleveland 10, Baltimore 2.
Detroit 5, Oakland 4.

	W.	L.	Pc.	G.B.
Detroit	95	54	.638	—
Baltimore	86	64	.573	9½
New York	79	70	.530	16
Boston	79	70	.530	16
Cleveland	80	72	.530	16½
Oakland	76	74	.507	19½
Minnesota	70	79	.470	23
California	64	86	.427	30½
Chicago	62	88	.413	33½
Washington	58	92	.387	37½

TODAY'S PROBABLE PITCHERS

Pittsburgh at New York (2 P.M.)—Blass (15-5) vs. Cardwell (7-12).
Atlanta at Los Angeles—Santorini (0-1) vs. Moeller (1-0).
Chicago at Philadelphia—Jenkins (17-14) vs. G. Jackson (1-5).
Cincinnati at San Francisco—Queen (0-1) vs. Marichal (25-8).
St. Louis at Houston — Carlton (12-10) vs. Wilson (13-14).

New York at Washington—Peterson (11-9) vs. Moore (2-6) or Pascual (12-11).
Baltimore at Cleveland—Hardin (18-10) vs. Williams (11-10).
California at Chicago—Messersmith (3-1) vs. Nyman (2-0).
Minnesota at Boston—Kaat (12-11) vs. Lonborg (5-7).
Oakland at Detroit — Krausse (11-11) vs. Lolich (14-9).

(Figures in parentheses are this season's won-lost records).

M'LAIN WINS 30TH ON TIGERS' RALLY

Continued From Page 1

ended the game by knocking in the tie-breaking run with one out, a wild scene erupted. It was an appropriate climax to an event carried by the National Broadcasting Company to millions of home television screens, and no set of scriptwriters could have surpassed what reality had provided.

In the stands were 44,087 people, 33,688 of them paying customers and the rest children admitted in groups, and they became part of the show.

His Mates Mob Him

As Horton's hit fell safe, McLain raced out of the dugout to embrace the teammates who had brought him his prize after it had passed out of his own power to gain. They, in turn, surrounded and lifted him, precariously, in a march to the dugout. Photographers, television crews and fans started to converge on the scene and there was a terrific crush near the third-base dugout.

Finally, McLain was able to say a few words on camera with Dean, who was present for the occasion, and with Sandy Koufax, who retired two years ago and removed himself from the glory McLain had attained.

On a personal level, there is the record itself, the argument for a $100,000 contract next year and the limitless possibilities for outside income for McLain and his organ-playing career.

But on a team basis, his superb season made possible the pennant the Tigers failed to win last year only on the last day, so the jubilation did not stem merely from statistics.

'We Want Denny!'

When McLain finally disappeared into the clubhouse, the crowd remained, chanting, "We want Denny!" When he heard about it, he insisted on going out again to wave, acknowledge the cheers and pose for more pictures. Half an hour later he was still gleefully answering questions inside while the clubhouse door was besieged by admirers.

The game, which lasted 3 hours 3 minutes, formed a perfect build-up. Jackson's first homer, with a man on, had put Oakland ahead, 2-0, in the fourth inning. But Norm Cash hit one with two on in the Tigers' half, and McLain had a 3-2 lead.

He lost it in the fifth to a leadoff walk, a sacrifice and a single by Bert Campaneris, and with two out in the sixth, Jackson hit another homer, the 28th of his first full major league campaign.

Now it was up to Diego Segui, Oakland's fourth pitcher, to hold off the Tigers, and he did for three innings.

With two out in the eighth, a walk and an infield single, on which Segui had failed to cover first, gave Detroit two men on with two out. Gates Brown, the Tigers' best pinch-hitter, bounced out on the first pitch. Had he walked, McLain would have had to be removed for a hitter right then, with unknown results.

Kaline Draws a Walk

As it happened, though, McLain breezed through the ninth and Kaline led off for him in the home half. Fouling off two 3-2 pitches, Kaline drew a hard-earned walk. Dick McAuliffe, after fouling back two bunt attempts, popped out on a foul, but Mickey Stanley grounded the next pitch through the box

United Press International

WHOOPING JOY: Denny McLain, right, and Al Kaline celebrate as the winning run driven in by Willie Horton, crosses the plate. The run gave McLain his 30th victory this season.

Tigers' Box Score

OAKLAND (A.)	ab	r	h	bi
Campaneris, ss	4	0	1	1
Monday, cf	4	0	1	0
Cater, 1b	4	1	2	0
Bando, 3b	3	0	0	0
Jackson, rf	4	2	2	3
Green, 2b	4	0	0	0
Keough, lf	3	0	0	0
Gosger, lf	0	0	0	0
Duncan, c	2	1	0	0
Dobson, p	1	0	0	0
Aker, p	0	0	0	0
Lindblad, p	0	0	0	0
Donaldson, ph	0	0	0	0
Segui, p	1	0	0	0
Total	30	4	6	4

DETROIT (A.)	ab	r	h	bi
McAuliffe, 2b	5	0	1	0
Stanley, cf	5	1	2	0
Northrup, rf	4	1	0	0
Horton, lf	5	1	2	1
Cash, 1b	4	1	2	3
Freehan, c	3	0	1	0
Matchick, ss	4	0	1	0
Wert, 3b	2	0	0	0
Brown, ph	1	0	0	0
Tracewski, 3b	0	0	0	0
McLain, p	1	0	0	0
Kaline, ph	0	1	0	0
Total	34	5	9	4

Oakland ....000 211 000—4
Detroit ....000 300 002—5

E—Matchick, Bando, Cater. DP—Detroit 1. LOB—Oakland 2, Detroit 10. HR—Jackson 2 (28), Cash (21). S—McLain, Bando, Donaldson.

	IP.	H.	R.	ER.	BB.	SO.
Dobson	3⅔	4	3	3	2	4
Aker	0	0	0	0	1	0
Lindblad	⅓	0	0	0	0	1
Segui (L, 5-5)	*4⅓	5	2	1	2	1
McLain (W, 30-5)	9	6	4	4	1	10

*One out when winning run was scored.
Wild pitch—Aker.
T—3:00. A—33,688.

into center for a single and Kaline hustled into third.

Bob Kennedy, the Oakland manager who had checked Detroit's fourth-inning rally by using two reliefers to pitch to one man each, now went out to discuss matters with Segui. Jim Northrup, a left-handed pull-hitter, was up, and a home run was a real danger. But Kennedy left Segui in and, from a pitching point of view, events did not prove him wrong.

But with the infield drawn in to try to cut down the tying run at the plate, Northrup bounced to Danny Cater, the first baseman. There was plenty of time to get Kaline, but Cater's throw was high and wild, and while Kaline scored Stanley raced around to third.

In the dugout McLain, who had been watching quietly most of the inning, leaped up and shouted. He thought Stanley, too, might score on the overthrow.

"Calm down, calm down," drawled Manager Mayo Smith. McLain laughed and calmed down.

Now it was up to Horton. Only the man on third counted, and both the ield and outfield played close, since a long fly-out would be as decisive as a home run. Segui put up quite a battle, until Horton smacked a 2-2 pitch beyond Jim Gosger's reach.

ELLIS KEEPS TITLE AS CROWD JEERS

Continued From Page 1

the way to the dressing room.

Ellis fought with a broken nose, smashed in the first round with what looked like a good right hook.

Afterward, though, Ellis's manager, Angelo Dundee, said his boxer's nose had been broken by a butt—two, in fact. But he said he was not suggesting the butts were deliberate.

Floyd Stumps Experts

For Patterson, twice the world heavyweight champion, it was a creditable performance at the age of 33. Many experts doubted he would last the distance. Had he connected more he might have won. He missed often with wild hooks or reached out with long left jabs as Ellis just danced disdainfully backward.

In some close rounds where no one was hurt, the referee said he had to give Ellis the edge because he attacked more and landed more punches.

Patterson, always the gentleman resigned to his fate, refused to take issue.

"I do feel that I won," he said afterward, "but I can't complain. I don't count the punches."

Valan said the disappointment of the crowd did not bother him.

"I know the people were all for Floyd," he said. "He's a nice guy. But the other guy's a nice guy, and I'm not interested in who's nicer."

Patterson had one first-class round, the 14th. He began it by landing his favorite punch in this fight, a long, leaping left. He led a moment later with his right, then scored with a left uppercut to the jaw. Then he landed a hard right to the head. Ellis looked dazed and held on.

In a flurry of punches, Ellis sank to his knees. Patterson seemed to be trying to help him up, in a gentlemanly gesture that confused everyone. Then Valan waved Patterson aside and had Ellis stand against the ropes while he seemed to be counting to the mandatory eight.

But after the fight Valan said it had not been a knockdown. He said Ellis had slipped and Patterson had pushed him down. In fact, there were no knockdowns in the bout. Patterson slipped to the canvas three times.

Most everyone agreed that Muhammad Ali could have taken either fighter, or both of them together, if necessary. Ali, alias Cassius Clay, was dethroned as champion because of his troubles with the draft.

In the early rounds, Ellis did most of the forcing. Patterson bounced and shuffled, crouching when Ellis aimed at his head. In the sixth, there was a nice parody of the Cassius Clay theatrical style, Ellis clowned, dancing around and suddenly throwing a flurry of fake punches. Patterson mimicked him right back.

Patterson in Retreat

In that round, Patterson caught Ellis in a corner and hurt him with a sudden left hook to the jaw. But Ellis got away, counterpunching and sending Patterson into retreat.

Then, as throughout the fight, Patterson's punches did not seem to have enough behind them to hurt Ellis and really open him up as a target. The only exception was the 14th round.

By the 15th, Patterson looked exhausted—but Ellis was unable to mount an attack that could hurt him.

Ellis, who at 198 outweighed Patterson by 9½ pounds, said the broken nose gave him trouble breathing.

"I was all messed up," he said.

BRILES OF CARDS HALTS ASTROS, 8-0

Continued From Page 1

and came home on Orlando Cepeda's grounder between Doug Rader's legs. Cepeda stole second, took third on a wild pitch and scored on McCarver's sacrifice fly.

St. Louis added two more runs in the seventh on a single by Brock, his 54th stolen base, and consecutive triples by Cepeda and McCarver. The Cards scored their final run in the ninth when Shannon singled home Cepeda.

Briles and Tom Dukes, a Houston reliever, engaged in a brief throwing duel in the eighth inning and Umpire Shag Crawford went halfway to the mound to talk to Briles after he hit Norm Miller in the side. Dukes had hit Maxvill on the left arm in the top of the inning.

SLUGGER KNOCKS 4 TALLIES ACROSS

Collects Nos. 20 and 21—Bolin Loses His Shutout in 8th on Perez's Smash

SAN FRANCISCO, Sept. 14 (AP)—Willie Mays smashed two home runs and Bob Bolin pitched a five-hitter, leading the San Francisco Giants to a 9-1 romp over the Cincinnati Reds today.

Mays opened the scoring with a 420-foot homer off Gerry Arrigo in the fourth inning. He hit a three-run clout off Arrigo in the fifth, giving him 21 for the season.

Bolin lifted his won-lost record to 9-4, but lost a shutout when Tony Perez hit his 18th homer in the eighth.

Dodgers Top Braves, 3-0

LOS ANGELES, Sept. 14 (UPI) — Tom Haller doubled twice and knocked in two runs as the Los Angeles Dodgers scored a 3-0 victory today over the Atlanta Braves. Don Sutton pitched a six-hitter for Los Angeles. It was his second straight shutout.

Milt Pappas, the Braves' starter, objected so violently in the third inning that Haller's second double was foul that he was thrown out of the game by Umpire Frank Secory.

Willie Davis teamed with Haller in the early innings to give the Dodgers their scoring punch. In the first Davis singled and stole second before Haller's double drove him in. Two walks loaded the bases and Jim Lefebvre's sacrifice fly scored Haller.

"All the News That's Fit to Print"

The New York Times

LATE CITY EDITION

Weather: Cloudy, showers likely through tonight. Fair tomorrow. Temp. range: today 75-65; Wed. 85-66. Full U.S. report on Page 93.

VOL. CXVIII.. No. 40,430 — NEW YORK, THURSDAY, OCTOBER 3, 1968 — 10 CENTS

ST. LOUIS WINS, 4-0, IN SERIES OPENER; GIBSON SETS MARK

Cardinal Hurler Strikes Out 17 Tigers to Break Record of 15 Held by Koufax

M'LAIN LEAVES IN SIXTH

Winners Score Three Runs in Fourth—Brock Clouts a Home Run in Seventh

By JOSEPH DURSO

Special to The New York Times

ST. LOUIS, Oct. 2 — Bob Gibson outpitched Denny McLain, overpowered the rest of the Detroit Tigers and struck out 17 batters today as the St. Louis Cardinals won the opening game of the World Series, 4-0.

The 32-year-old Nebraskan broke the Series strike-out record of 15, set by Sandy Koufax of the Los Angeles Dodgers against the New York Yankees in 1963. He allowed five hits and resolved baseball's "pitching duel of the century" before the game was half over.

He was the man of the hour on this summery afternoon as 54,692 persons in Busch Memorial Stadium and a national television audience watched. He left no questions unanswered as he conquered McLain, the first man to win 31 games in the major leagues in 37 years.

By winning his sixth straight game in three Series in five years, he tied the record set by Lefty Gomez and Red Ruffing of the Yankees between 1932 and 1942.

Another Record Falls

By working his sixth straight complete game in Series competition, he broke the record set by Ruffing for pitchers who finish what they start when the money is on the table.

Gibson, who started life in the slums of Omaha and now earns $90,000 a year, pitched to only 32 Detroit hitters. He also became the National League's No. 1 World Series winner. Other pitchers have won more games—Whitey Ford leads everybody with 10 victories during the Yankee era—but nobody has won more for the senior league than Gibson in 65 World Series.

He got all the runs needed for all this statistical success during one inning. It was the fourth, an inning marked by a fatal loss of control by McLain, who had walked only 63 batters in 336 innings this season.

This time the fresh-faced extrovert and organist walked two batters on the minimum total of eight pitches. Then Mike Shannon and Julian Javier singled and Gibson suddenly was staked to a three-run lead.

The other run was produced in the seventh inning by Lou Brock, who was Gibson's chief ally in the Cardinals' victory last fall against the Boston Red Sox. He bombed a 3-and-2 pitch into the center-field bleachers off Pat Dobson for a 400-foot home run.

But the essence of the day was Gibson's overwhelming fast ball and his surprisingly sharp curve.

He had won 22 games and

Continued on Page 60, Column 2

Handshake for Great Performance

Associated Press

Bob Gibson, Cardinals' pitcher, being congratulated by Tim McCarver after striking out 17 in St. Louis yesterday.

Schools Reopening Today On a Note of Uncertainty

By M. A. FARBER

The head of the teachers' union said yesterday that there was "better than a 50-50 chance" of a new citywide teachers' strike over the disruptions in the Ocean Hill-Brownsville district.

"If I were a betting man," said Albert Shanker, president of the United Federation of Teachers, "I'd put my money on it."

All city public schools were closed yesterday because of the Jewish holiday of Yom Kippur. Whatever the likelihood of a strike tomorrow or next week, Mr. Shanker said teachers throughout the city would be on the job today when schools are scheduled to reopen.

Mr. Shanker's assessment of the possibility of a strike came as Mayor Lindsay met with Police Commissioner Howard R. Leary and members of a special subcommittee of the Board of Education at Gracie Mansion to discuss compliance by the Brooklyn demonstration district with an order to return 83 disputed teachers to their posts.

Mr. Lindsay declined to comment at the end of the four-hour session at 8:30. John Doar, chairman of the special subcommittee, said: "We're prepared to meet our responsibility to see that there is compliance" with the city board's edict.

"I'm hopeful about what will happen tomorrow," he added.

Mr. Doar called Mr. Shanker from Gracie Mansion after the conference there. However, the union leader said afterward that his earlier assessment of a strike possibility remained valid. He said that the union executive board would meet on the issue tonight.

In a telegram Mr. Shanker sent to the city board at 10 P.M., he charged it with having failed to improve the situation in Ocean Hill-Brownsville.

He said that the union had been "patient" and had shown "restraint." But, he went on, "unless a normal situation pertains for teachers in this district, we will have no choice" but to conduct another citywide walkout.

"It is time for the board to act," his telegram said.

The reinstatement of the disputed 83 teachers to regular teaching duties in the predominantly Negro and Puerto Rican district—despite the re-

Continued on Page 50, Column 1

AT LEAST 20 DEAD AS MEXICO STRIFE REACHES A PEAK

Troops Fire Machine Guns and Rifles at Students—More Than 100 Hurt

By PAUL L. MONTGOMERY

Special to The New York Times

MEXICO CITY, Oct. 2—Federal troops fired on a student rally with rifles and machine guns tonight, killing at least 20 people and wounding more than 100.

The troops moved on a rally of 3,000 people in the square of a vast housing project just as night was falling. In an inferno of firing that lasted an hour, the army strafed the area with machine guns mounted on jeeps and tanks.

About 1,000 troops took part in the action. Tanks, armored cars and jeeps followed them, spurting .30- and .50-caliber machine-gun fire.

Buses, trolley cars and other vehicles were set on fire at several places in the city. Ambulances screamed through the rainy night.

Many women and children were among the dead and injured.

Games Cast Into Doubt

Also injured was Gen. José Hernández Toledo, a paratroop commander who has led troops into university campuses three times over the last two years. He was undergoing surgery tonight for a stomach wound.

According to the army, at least one soldier was killed and 12 were wounded by sniper fire from apartment buildings towering over the square.

The night's events cast into serious question the prospects for the Olympic Games, which are scheduled to begin here on Oct. 12. Until the troops moved in, it seemed that both the Government and the city's rebellious students were working to establish an atmosphere of calm after some 10 weeks of struggling.

In a statement tonight, the Defense Minister, Gen. Marcelino García Barragán, said that the troops had moved on the rally after snipers fired on the Federal District riot police guarding the nearby Foreign Ministry and a vocational school. The general's statement was disputed by many witnesses.

Hospital Full of Wounded

The army moved immediately to keep reporters from the Red Cross hospital, near the housing project, three miles north of the center of Mexico City. But an interne in the hospital said that it was full of wounded, all of them civilians. Army ambulances took the dead and many other wounded to the Military Hospital, which was closed to reporters.

Witnesses described the widespread killing in the square. Six dead—two of them women—could be counted by this correspondent in a small section of the square.

The clash was the worst in student demonstrations that have been going on in the capital since July 23.

In the last serious fighting, two weeks ago, at least 7 and perhaps 17 people, most of them students, were killed. High-school and university students have been on strike here

Continued on Page 11, Column 1

Soviet Diplomats Hear Moscow Denounced at U.N.

The New York Times (by Carl T. Gossett Jr.)

Yakov A. Malik, left, chief Soviet representative at the U.N., and Andrei A. Gromyko, Soviet Foreign Minister, listen as Secretary of State Dean Rusk addresses U.N. General Assembly. Mr. Rusk assailed the Soviet bloc for its military action in Czechoslovakia.

SENATE REJECTS MISSILES DELAY

Funds to Begin Deployment of Sentinel Defensive Net Retained by 45 to 25

By JOHN W. FINNEY

Special to The New York Times

WASHINGTON, Oct. 2—The Senate, after an unusual secret session, overwhelmingly rejected today what was probably the final effort to delay deployment of a multibillion-dollar missile defense system.

By a vote of 45 to 25, it defeated an amendment by Senator John Sherman Cooper, Republican of Kentucky, that would have eliminated $387.4-million requested by the Administration to start deployment of the Sentinel anti-ballistic missile system.

The funds are included in a $71.8-billion defense appropriations bill—the largest appropriations bill in the nation's history.

Final Action Put Off

The Senate put off until tomorrow final action on the bill as Senator Joseph S. Clark, Democrat of Pennsylvania, began offering a series of obviously doomed amendments to cut the military appropriations for the current fiscal year by as much as $8-billion.

The crucial vote on the Cooper amendment came after the Kentucky Senator had called a closed session to discuss secret intelligence information on Chinese and Soviet missile developments.

With spectators and the press removed from the gallery and the large wooden doors to the

Continued on Page 10, Column 1

Rusk, at U.N., Reaffirms NATO's Defense of Bonn

Secretary Warns Soviet

By DREW MIDDLETON

Special to The New York Times

UNITED NATIONS, N. Y., Oct. 2—Secretary of State Dean Rusk warned Moscow anew today that any military action against West Germany would bring immediate military reaction by the North Atlantic Treaty Organization powers.

Mr. Rusk's warning that force would be met with force was delivered before the United Nations General Assembly. This was the first time a Secretary

Excerpts from Rusk's address will be found on Page 14.

of State had addressed the Assembly since Christian A. Herter spoke here Sept. 17, 1959.

Foreign Minister Andrei A. Gromyko of the Soviet Union sat expressionless while Mr. Rusk denounced the invasion and occupation of Czechoslovakia by the Soviet Union, East Germany, Poland, Hungary and Bulgaria.

A demonstration against the Vietnam war by nine persons in the gallery who interrupted Mr. Rusk with cries of "Stop the war in Vietnam, bring the troops home!" failed to alter Mr. Gromyko's expression.

Mr. Rusk's charge that the Soviet Union was defying the Charter of the United Nations was also heard in denunciations of Moscow's actions by Foreign Minister Torsten Nilsson of Sweden, José de Magalhães Pinto of Brazil and Fernando A. Amiama-Tio of the Dominican Republic.

Mr. Nillson said that if the use of force did not achieve a

Continued on Page 15, Column 1

Paris Accuses Moscow

By HENRY TANNER

Special to The New York Times

PARIS, Oct. 2—France declared today that the Soviet Union had unleashed a violent campaign against West Germany as a diversionary maneuver to obscure the consequences of Soviet military intervention in Czechoslovakia.

Foreign Minister Michel Debré, addressing the National Assembly in a major speech approved earlier in the day by President de Gaulle and the Cabinet, paid an unusual tribute to the West German Government. It would be supremely unjust, he said, not to recognize the peaceful intentions of the present West German leaders.

The statement was the strongest made by any French official so far about the Czechoslovak crisis. Mr. Debré deplored the fact that Soviet tanks had not yet been withdrawn, that the Czechoslovaks had not yet been allowed "to regain their freedom of action" and that the rights of the individual were being held in contempt in Eastern Europe.

A Choice for Paris

The Premier's statement struck diplomatic observers as significant for two reasons.

It was viewed as the first indication that President de Gaulle might be coming to the conclusion that he must choose between good relations with Moscow and good relations with the governments and peoples of Eastern Europe that are seeking greater independence from Moscow.

The general is known to have hoped to be able to carry out these two policies simultaneously. But today Mr. Debré spoke more strongly than ever for the Eastern Europeans' right to sovereignty and, for the first time, he resumed efforts toward a relaxation of East-West relations contingent on the Soviet Union's respect for its independence.

Further, Mr. Debré's speech was viewed as evidence that the French felt the need to soothe the feelings of the West German leaders. Many West German officials and commentators have been expressing

Continued on Page 16, Column 1

FORTAS ABANDONS NOMINATION FIGHT; NAME WITHDRAWN

Justice, in Letter to Johnson, Says Senate Attacks Might Mar Court's New Term

DILEMMA FOR PRESIDENT

He May Try Another Man, Risking a Second Rebuff, or Yield to Successor

Texts of Fortas letter and Johnson statement, Page 42.

By FRED P. GRAHAM

Special to The New York Times

WASHINGTON, Oct. 2—Associate Justice Abe Fortas withdrew today as President Johnson's nominee for the office of Chief Justice, clearing the way for the President to submit a possible second nomination to the Senate.

In a letter that concluded with a prayer for "fairness and justice and moderation," Justice Fortas asked Mr. Johnson to withdraw his name to end the "destructive and extreme assaults upon the Court."

The President promptly complied with Mr. Fortas's request. He called the Senate's action in blocking the nomination "historically and constitutionally tragic."

The day's events also served to terminate Mr. Johnson's nomination of Judge Homer W. Thornberry of the United States Court of Appeals for the Fifth Circuit to succeed Mr. Fortas as associate justice. There is now no vacancy for Mr. Thornberry to fill.

Fortas Stays on Court

Mr. Fortas made it clear that he would remain on the Supreme Court as an Associate Justice, at least during the term that begins next Monday.

Sources in the White House reported this afternoon that Mr. Johnson was consulting with legal advisers about his next move.

The President was said to be undecided whether to drop the matter and leave the appointment to the next President, or to send up the nomination of a noncontroversial figure who might win confirmation in the fading days of the Congressional session.

Capitol Hill was swept with rumors of possible nominees.

Continued on Page 42, Column 1

HUMPHREY SHOWS POPULISTS' ZEST

He Shuns Stress on TV for Personal Ties With Voters

By R. W. APPLE Jr.

Special to The New York Times

CHARLOTTE, N. C., Oct. 2—One of the strongest strains in Hubert H. Humphrey's personality is prairie populism—the tradition of Robert LaFollette and George Norris and Sockless Jerry Simpson—with its celebration of the common man, its distrust of slickness, its fondness for simple pleasures.

This afternoon in the midst of yet another discussion of Vietnam and law and order in this country, that side of the Vice President burst forth.

A television interviewer in Jacksonville, Fla., asked the Democratic Presidential nominee whether he thought personal campaigning was too costly and too exhausting. Might not a campaign waged mainly through the media be a more reasonable approach in 1968? he was asked.

Mr. Humphrey replied that he was perfectly willing to use television, but said he thought the people wanted to get to know a candidate personally—"to look at him, feel him, touch him, smell him" — and contended that Madison Avenue could never provide that.

"Madison Avenue isn't America," the Vice President said, and continued:

"I've seen neighbors in Min-

Continued on Page 40, Column 2

NIXON FEARS LOSS OF NAVY'S MIGHT

Administration Complacent on Soviet Fleet, He Says

By HOMER BIGART

Special to The New York Times

NORFOLK, Va., Oct. 2—Richard M. Nixon accused the Administration tonight of complacency in the face of a Soviet naval build-up that, he said, threatened American superiority on the seas.

He charged that the Defense Department had defaulted on what he called former President Dwight D. Eisenhower's commitment to a nuclear-powered Navy.

He condemned the decision to equip the newest aircraft carrier, John F. Kennedy, with conventional rather than nuclear power.

He also said that the country's naval strength had been compromised by a freeze on nuclear submarines, which set the upper limit at 69, despite the Navy's request for 105.

He denounced the Administration's decision last summer to remove 50 ships and 100 naval aircraft from active service.

He charged that the Administration had withheld authority to proceed with "the super-quiet attack submarine, the one the Navy's planners and Admiral Rickover contend is the most important."

And finally, he said, the Soviet has built a merchant fleet that threatens to surpass Amer-

Continued on Page 40, Column 6

Wallace Aides Shift Rally to the Garden

By SYDNEY H. SCHANBERG

Campaign organizers for George C. Wallace, third-party Presidential candidate, yesterday canceled their plans for a rally next Wednesday in Shea Stadium in the face of the Lindsay administration's opposition and rescheduled the event at the smaller Madison Square Garden on Oct. 24.

Accusing the Lindsay administration of "a sorry exercise in political trickery," the Wallace organizers said they were forced to make the switch because of the city's decision to appeal a court ruling Tuesday that had upheld Mr. Wallace's right to rent Shea Stadium. The

Continued on Page 40, Column 2

16,000 in Air Guard To Be Deactivated

By The Associated Press

WASHINGTON, Oct. 2—The Pentagon announced tonight that all 16,000 Air National Guardsmen and reservists mobilized after the Pueblo incident would be returned to civilian life by June 30, 1969.

Four squadrons will be released by the end of this year and the rest during next April, May and June, the announcement said.

The Pentagon cautioned that the demobilization plans "could be changed, of course, if unforeseen circumstances arise." It did not say what such circumstances might be.

Some 37,000 Air Reservists, Naval Reservists and Army Na-

Continued on Page 4, Column 4

Marcel Duchamp Is Dead at 81; Enigmatic Giant of Modern Art

Special to The New York Times

PARIS, Oct. 2—Marcel Duchamp, one of the most influential artists of the century, died last night in his studio in the Paris suburb of Neuilly. He collapsed just after having had dinner with his wife and some friends.

Duchamp, who was 81 years old, was a naturalized American citizen. He maintained homes here and in New York. Funeral arrangements have not yet been announced.

The Grand Dada

By ALEXANDER KENEAS

Like the smile of the Mona Lisa, which he retouched with mustache and goatee, Marcel Duchamp remained an enigma.

Thrust into the international limelight by the 1913 Armory Show, he abandoned his career only a decade later, at the age of 36. Yet in half a century the enfant terrible who had thumbed his nose at the pantheon of art grew up to become the spiritual father of the pop generation — and Marcel Duchamp the artist had blossomed into Marcel Duchamp the idea.

The idea, however, posed more questions about the nature of art than it answered, for at its roots it was the idea of rejection.

"I'm afraid I'm an agnostic

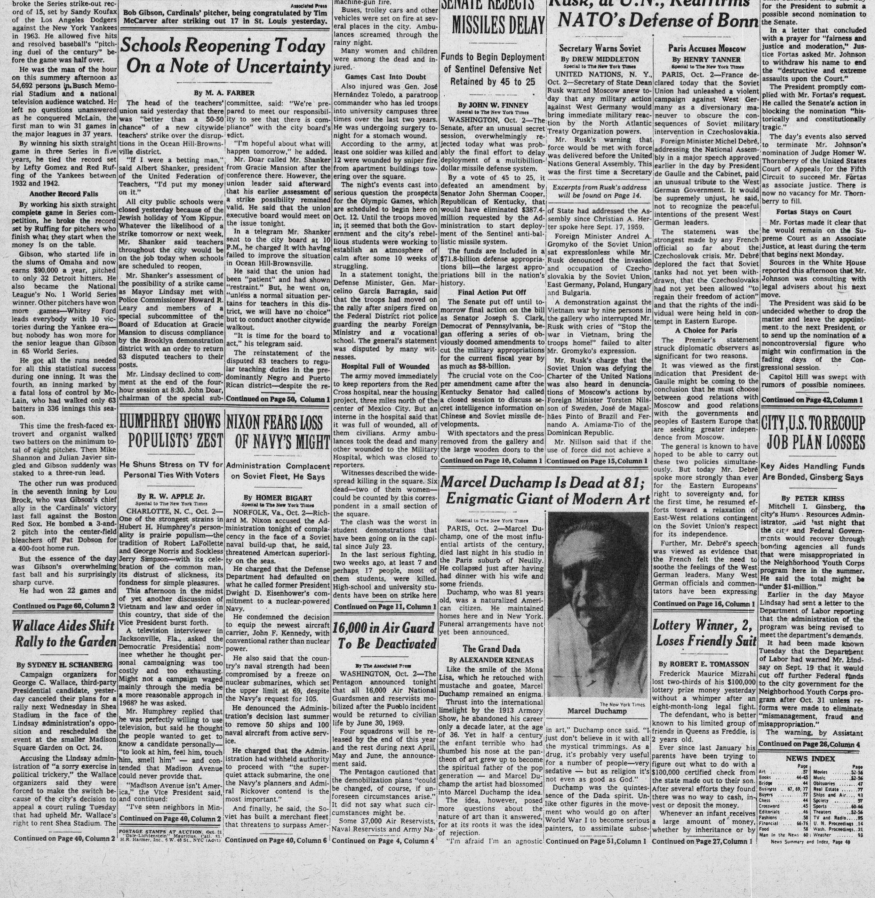

The New York Times

Marcel Duchamp

in art," Duchamp once said. "I just don't believe in it with all the mystical trimmings. As a drug, it's probably very useful for a number of people—very sedative — but as religion it's not even as good as God."

Duchamp was the quintessence of the Dada spirit. Unlike other figures in the movement who would go on after World War I to become serious painters, to assimilate subse-

Continued on Page 51, Column 1

Lottery Winner, 2, Loses Friendly Suit

By ROBERT E. TOMASSON

Frederick Maurice Mizrahi lost two-thirds of his $100,000 lottery prize money yesterday without a whimper after an eight-month-long legal fight.

The defendant, who is better known to his limited group of friends in Queens as Freddie, is 2 years old.

Ever since last January his parents have been trying to figure out what to do with a $100,000 certified check from the state made out to their son. After several efforts they found there was no way to cash, invest or deposit the money.

Whenever an infant receives a large amount of money, whether by inheritance or by

Continued on Page 27, Column 1

CITY, U.S. TO RECOUP JOB PLAN LOSSES

Key Aides Handling Funds Are Bonded, Ginsberg Says

By PETER KIHSS

Mitchell I. Ginsberg, the city's Human Resources Administrator, said last night that the city and Federal Governments would recover through bonding agencies all funds that were misappropriated in the Neighborhood Youth Corps program here in the summer. He said the total might be "under $1-million."

Earlier in the day Mayor Lindsay had sent a letter to the Department of Labor reporting that the administration of the program was being revised to meet the department's demands.

It had been made known Tuesday that the Department of Labor had warned Mr. Lindsay on Sept. 19 that it would cut off further Federal funds to the city government for the Neighborhood Youth Corps program after Oct. 31 unless reforms were made to eliminate "mismanagement, fraud and misappropriation."

The warning, by Assistant

Continued on Page 26, Column 4

NEWS INDEX

Gibson Unaware of Breaking Record Until Message Flashes on Scoreboard

CARDS 4-0 VICTORS IN SERIES OPENER

Continued From Page 1, Col. 1

lost nine this year, with 15 victories in a row, 13 shutouts and a league record for efficiency — allowing only 1.12 earned runs a game. He also had won three games in the World Series last year, including the final one. So today he was back at the old stand.

He walked one man and gave up four singles and one double. He struck out Dick McAuliffe to open the game, then added Al Kaline. He fanned Norm Cash, Willie Horton and Jim Northrup in the second inning, then got Bill Freehan and McLain in the third. So he struck out seven of the first nine men, including five in a row.

He struck out everybody in the Detroit line-up and he took care of the renowned Kaline three times and the power-hitting left-hander, Norm Cash, three times.

By the ninth inning, he had 14 strike-outs and needed one more to tie Koufax's memorable performance in Yankee Stadium five years ago.

Stanley Delays Inevitable

There was a pause while Mickey Stanley singled to center field, raising some faint thoughts about the Tigers' talent for raising a rumpus late in ball games. Thirty times this year they had won games in their final turn at bat. But not today.

Kaline, playing in his first series in a 16-year career, then swiped at a 1-and-2 pitch and missed for strike-out No. 15. Gibson seemed serenely unaware of the milestone he had reached, but many persons in the crowd knew, especially those with transistor radios.

They rose and gave him a standing ovation. A bit startled, Gibson peered over his shoulder just in time to see the news flashed on the right-field scoreboard.

Then he struck out Cash on a 2-and-2 pitch and got another standing ovation. And finally, for good measure, he threw a curveball past Horton for his 17th strike-out and the final out of the day.

While all this was going on, what of McLain, the 24-year-old man-child of Detroit, the musician and self-styled mercenary soldier, the prime mover in Detroit's first American League title in 23 years?

He had approached his confrontation with Gibson without losing his flair. He was not unduly upset by reports that he had top billing on the Cardinals' clubhouse bulletin board for his remark: "I want to humiliate the Cardinals."

On the eve of battle, he even packed the lobby of a downtown hotel by sitting down at an organ in a lounge and giving an impromptu recital. He played appropriate mood music like "Stardust," then soared into ad-lib rock tempos. Then this afternoon he met Gibson.

The result: McLain pitched five innings before leaving for a pinch-hitter. He allowed three hits and three walks, struck out three Cardinals and saw three runs cross the plate. His "thing" with the number 3 included errors—the Tigers committed three behind him.

He almost jumped off to a fast start when Stanley singled solidly to left field with one down in the first inning.

This was the young Stanley, the best center fielder in the league, who had been switched to shortstop in order to make room for more bats in the Tiger line-up. Playing with a borrowed infielder's mitt, he behaved professionally at shortstop and got two of the five hits off Gibson.

However, Stanley tried to steal second base on the next pitch after his single and was thrown out by Tim McCarver. Then Gibson struck out Kaline, and so much for McLain's fast start.

McLain, meanwhile, retired the first four Cardinals. Then, with one down in the second, McCarver lined the first pitch into the alley in right-center. He gambled that he could beat the relay and he did when McAuliffe's throw to third base went wide and McCarver wound up with a triple. But McLain struck out Mike Shannon and Javier to end the threat.

However, that turned out to be McLain's finest hour. In the third, he flirted with trouble by walking Dal Maxvill. Then Gibson bunted Maxvill to second. Brock followed with a grounder to McLain, who turned and stalked Maxvill between second and third, finally throwing him out with Stanley covering second.

Brock, who had been safe during this maneuvering, promptly stole second base for his eighth steal in eight Series games over the last two years. When Freehan's throw skipped into right field, Brock made it to third. But he was still there when Curt Flood popped up to Stanley.

The inning proved indecisive, though it may haunt the Cardinals before the Series ends. Brock jammed his right shoulder while sliding into second base and required some deep-freeze spray to ease the pain.

Then came the fourth inning and big trouble for the man-child. McLain opened the inning by throwing four straight balls to Roger Maris, who will retire after the Series and become a beer distributor in Florida. Then McLain threw two balls to Orlando Cepeda and immediately had company on the mound—Manager Mayo Smith.

Smith returned to the dugout and Cepeda fouled out. But McLain threw four straight balls to McCarver, Shannon lined a 2-and-2 pitch to left for one run and, when Horton bobbled the ball, McCarver took third base and Shannon second.

On the next pitch, Javier grounded a single into right field and both runners scored. That made it 3-0 and then McLain got Maxvill on a fly to left and Gibson on a strike-out.

Denny was followed by Pat Dobson of Depew, N. Y., who worked the next two innings, and by Don McMahon of Brooklyn, who worked the last two. They kept order except for the seventh-inning home run by Brock, who hit .414 in the Series last year with 12 hits, including a home run.

When it was all over — at least until Gibson and McLain meet again on Sunday—Gibson said he had relied chiefly on his fastball.

"But I had a good breaking ball," he said. "I think I was more of a surprise to them than anything else."

McLain conceded he had hurt himself with eye-high pitches that were called balls.

"That bad inning was typical of me," he said, not quite speechless. "A couple of walks, then the whole thing comes undone."

Associated Press

Bob Gibson bearing down in yesterday's opening game. His 17 strike-outs set record.

Cool Pitcher and Victor Over Pain

Robert Gibson

Man in the News

CASUALLY, but typically, Robert Gibson existed quite normally the night before he struck out 17 batters to set a World Series record.

"One of my daughters, Rene, she's 11, flew down from Omaha for the game," the ace right-hander of the St. Louis Cardinals said after yesterday's opener. "I picked her up at the airport, but she wasn't particularly excited about the game. She was more concerned with what she was going to wear."

Like father, like daughter. Of all the superstars in baseball today, Bob Gibson is perhaps the smoothest—no matter what the pressure, no matter what the pain.

"I don't get excited before a game," he has said. "I suppose I may feel it and not be aware of it. I know that I can't sleep *after* I pitch, so maybe that's how it shows itself. I sleep fine before I'm going to pitch. In a game, I get a certain satisfaction out of getting a man out, but I wouldn't call it fun."

In outpitching Denny McLain yesterday, Gibson must have attained more than his usual amount of satisfaction.

Not long ago McLain, the flamboyant organ player who won 31 games for Detroit this year, was quoted as saying that the Tigers wouldn't merely defeat the Cardinals, they would "humiliate" them. Informed of McLain's prediction, Gibson smoldered.

"Winning is important, not humiliating somebody," Gibson said firmly. "I can't understand why a person would want to feel that way, but if that's the way he feels, he's going to get his chance."

In the match-up between baseball's two leading pitchers, Gibson virtually humiliated McLain and the Tigers, but to students of the 32-year-old Cardinal, his superiority was not surprising. One of his Cardinal managers, the late Johnny Keane, perhaps described him best in a phrase: "He's a thoroughbred."

And like a true thoroughbred, he wins despite ailments that would deter others. Yesterday, for example, his pitching arm ached with arthritis in the elbow.

"It hurts in three places," he said, pointing to the top, bottom and back of the elbow. "Other times it hurts in just one or two places, but the pain never goes away. But I'll be ready whenever he [Red Schoendienst, the Cardinal manager] wants me."

Gibson is accustomed to pain. As an infant in Omaha, where he was born on Nov. 9, 1935, he required daily sun treatments to help a severe case of rickets. At the age of 3, he was hospitalized with pneumonia. He also had a rheumatic heart.

Although too skinny to play high-school football, he developed into an all-state basketball performer. He went on to Creighton University in Omaha as a pitcher and shortstop, in addition to continuing his career in basketball.

In 1957, he married the former Charline Johnson. They have a 9-year-old daughter, Anrette, in addition to Rene.

He later traveled with the Harlem Globetrotters' basketball team before settling into the Cardinal organization. He won 18 games in 1963, and 19 in 1964, when he also pitched the Cardinals to victory in the World Series with the Yankees.

"In the seventh game," Keane said at the time, "he pitched the last three innings on guts, but I had a commitment to his heart."

Gibson was a 20-game winner in 1966 and he presumably would have won at least 20 last year if he had not suffered a broken leg when struck by a line drive in midseason. He faced three more batters before surrendering to the pain, but his won-lost record was 13-7.

He returned to win three World Series games against the Boston Red Sox, and earned for the second time the sports car awarded by Sport magazine to the outstanding Series performer.

In compiling a 22-9 record and 13 shutouts during the recently concluded season, Gibson recorded the lowest earned-run average, 1.12, in National League history. Midway in the schedule he put together 92 innings in which he permitted only two runs. Over that span, he began a streak of 15 consecutive victories.

"Nobody," Schoendienst said at the time, "has ever pitched better than Bob Gibson."

In the off-season, he makes his pitch on his own radio show in Omaha, where friends call him Hoot, after the late cowboy actor. For relaxation, he listens to music, preferably jazz.

Six Arrested at St. Louis As Alleged Series Scalpers

ST. LOUIS, Oct. 2, (AP)—The police arrested four adults and two juveniles today for allegedy scalping World Series tickets in the Busch Memorial Stadium area.

The police said the adults identified themselves as Bennie Hale, 40 years old, of St. Louis; John R. Munger, 28, of Kansas City, Mo.; Robert D. Madkin, 50, of Seattle, and Daniel W. Dennis, 55, of Independence, Mo.

Witnesses were said to have reported some people offering tickets for sale asked as much as $30 for a $2 bleacher seat. Others reportedly asked the same amount for an $8 stadium seat. The lowest price reportedly asked was $9 for a $4 standing-room ticket.

WINNING IS RATED FIRST BY PITCHER

Gibson Also Says Outs Are More Important to Him Than Strike-Outs

By GEORGE VECSEY
Special to The New York Times

ST. LOUIS, Oct. 2—According to Bob Gibson, who has been there, it is possible for a man to stand on a mound in the center of an arena and not be aware of the passion of 54,692 people.

Still sweating, his Cardinal cap tilted slightly to the right, the pitcher bounded into his clubhouse today after striking out 17 Tigers to break the World Series record.

Under questioning, Gibson admitted that he had become aware of breaking Sandy Koufax's record of 15 strike-outs.

"I didn't know what was happening until I saw Tim [Tim McCarver, the catcher,] come out in front of the plate. Then I saw the message on the scoreboard. No, I don't remember what it said."

This happened in the ninth inning, when Gibson struck out Al Kaline to tie the record, Norm Cash to break it and Willie Horton to end the 4-0 victory. Yet Gibson claimed to be oblivious to another drama of the ninth inning, which was the fans rooting for foul balls to fall into the stands and not into the fielders' gloves.

No Outs Like Strike-Outs

Whenever a ball was popped into the air, the fans would instinctively flinch, their body english helping the ball into the stands. They didn't want to see pop-foul outs; they wanted to see strike-outs. They wanted more than victory; they wanted history and records.

Yet Gibson said he did not know of this. "I just want outs," he said. "I just want to win the game. The fans want the same thing. I wasn't aware of anything special. You don't see those things from the field."

The Cardinals, while glad for any kind of out, were aware of Gibson's strike-outs because Ed Spiezion, a bright-eyed substitute infielder, had been counting them.

"I heard when Gibby got 13 in the seventh [inning]," said Orlando Cepeda. "I know Sandy got 15 in the World Series for the record. But I don't say anything to him."

None of the Cardinals said anything to Gibson. "It's like a guy with a no-hitter," Curt Flood said. "You don't tell them. It's bad luck. As a matter of fact, we were talking about whether it was a good idea to put it on the message board."

Cepeda sat in the clubhouse and regarded the mob round his teammate, who has now pitched six complete-game victories in the World Series.

"He's got to be the best," Cepeda said. "Who else? Sandy. . . . Well, nobody was ever any better than Gibby."

The Cardinals seemed delighted at beating Detroit's winner of 31 games, Dennis McLain, who had said two weeks ago, "I want to humiliate the Cardinals."

That clipping was posted on the Cardinal bulletin board today.

McLain's Faults Found

The Cardinals felt they had beaten McLain two different ways, both as a consequence of their scouting reports: They had laid off McLain's high fastball and they had stolen three bases off McLain's motion.

"Gee, He can't hold anybody on base," Flood said. "He has to make his mind up early to throw to first base. If he doesn't, you can run on him."

A Cardinal scout, Mo Mozzali, had reported that McLain's fastball would rise out of the strike zone. With a National League umpire, Tom Gorman, working behind home plate today, the Cardinals did not swing at McLain's high, hard one.

"You get a higher strike in the American League," Flood said. "We definitely had that on our minds today." Flood noted that an American League umpire would be behind the plate for the fourth game, when McLain figures to pitch again. "We'll have to see what they're calling strikes that day," Flood added.

Roger Maris of the Cardinals scoring the first run in the fourth inning. Mike Shannon, who singled, goes to second on an outfield error. Denny McLain (17), the Tigers' pitcher, and Bill Freehan, the catcher, follow the action.

YOU'VE SEEN BEST, SMITH TELLS TEAM

Cash, Kaline Call Gibson Great—McDowell, Tiant Faster, Says Horton

By LEONARD KOPPETT
Special to The New York Times

ST. LOUIS, Oct. 2—"Dazzled" would not be exactly the word to describe the reaction of the Detroit Tigers to Bob Gibson's pitching, nor "stunned" nor "impressed" nor, in the other direction, "defiant." The best word, probably, would be "convinced."

"What can you say!" said Mayo Smith, the Tiger manager, affable and controlled as he settled into his desk chair. "I've seen that fellow pitch a lot but I never saw him like this. No one could have done anything against him. The one thing you know, as I told them [his players] just now, is that he can't even be any better. They've seen the best."

Before the game, Willie Horton and a group of teammates were talking about the night before their first World Series game. "My wife finally got tired of hearing Gibson's name all over the place," said Horton cheerfully. "Me, I can't wait to see if he really is superman."

They saw.

"I think McDowell [Sam, of Cleveland] and Tiant [Luis, also of Cleveland] maybe throw harder than he does," said Horton, "and I got a couple of pitches I should have hit. I'd like to have my third time up back again. But the thing about him is that he comes at you, and keeps coming at you, with every pitch to every hitter.

"Heck, he had super effort today," said Norm Cash. It was Cash, striking out for the third time with one out in the ninth inning, who provided the 16th and record-breaking strike-out for Gibson. "But I don't care about striking out. We got beat and if he didn't strike out any and we still got beat, it would be just as bad."

Al Kaline, finally playing in a World Series for the first time after 16 years of stardom in the American League, also struck out three times but hit a double to left in the sixth inning, when the Tigers came closest to scoring.

"To me, he threw breaking balls the first three times up and fast balls the fourth," said Kaline, "but I have to say, he sure got them all over. He was just plain good."

Wally Moses, the Tiger batting coach, analyzed it a little further. "He struck out quite a few with that change-up, a breaking ball. Then he has that hard slider and the real good fastball. And control. He's tough. With two strikes on you, he can use any of the three pitches. You just don't see a man pitch much better."

Johnny Sain, the pitching coach, agreed. "I remember when Koufax struck out 15 Yankees. I wouldn't say this was any more impressive than that—but it wasn't any less impressive, either."

Denny McLain, the losing pitcher, held court as cooperatively as ever, but his manner was totally subdued, serious—frankly glum. The fourth inning, in which St. Louis scored three runs, was the story.

In winning 31 games this season, McLain didn't have many troublesome innings, but when he did, this was the pattern: He'd walk a couple of men and a damaging hit would follow.

"I started doing something wrong, something mechanical," he said. "I'm pretty sure I know what it was, and I can correct, but you can't always correct right then and there. In the next inning, I thought I was all right again."

"He started to rush a little bit," said Smith, explaining why he went out to the mound after McLain had walked Roger Maris and thrown two balls to Orlando Cepeda. "That's typical of him when he gets into trouble. His control goes a little off."

But Mayo, like all the Tigers, simply felt there was nothing to discuss. You can't talk "ifs" and post-mortems when your team is stifled so thoroughly. Gibson had given a classic example of a fundamental baseball truth: When a great pitcher is in good form, that's it.

"That's right," said Mayo. "When a pitcher is like that, the hitters are just not going to get him. But we'll show up tomorrow. There'll be no forfeits in this series."

Smith's plans are unchanged. Mickey Stanley will stay at short ("I'm certainly glad the first one is over, and I'll feel much better there now," said Stanley); Mickey Lolich and Earl Wilson will pitch the next two games and McLain will face Gibson again on Sunday in Detroit. The Tigers are sure Denny can be better. The question is whether Gibson can somehow be worse.

Box Score of First Series Game

DETROIT (A.)	AB.	R.	H.	RBI.	PO.	A.
McAuliffe, 2b	4	0	1	0	3	0
Stanley, ss	4	0	2	0	3	2
Kaline, rf	4	0	1	0	2	0
Cash, 1b	4	0	0	0	7	1
Horton, lf	4	0	0	0	2	0
Northrup, cf	3	0	0	0	2	0
Freehan, c	2	0	0	0	4	1
Wert, 3b	2	0	1	0	0	1
bMathews, ph	1	0	0	0	0	0
Tracewski, 3b	0	0	0	0	0	0
McLain, p	1	0	0	0	0	2
aMatchick, ph	1	0	0	0	0	0
Dobson, p	0	0	0	0	0	0
cBrown, ph	1	0	0	0	0	0
McMahon, p	0	0	0	0	1	0
Total	31	0	5	0	24	7

ST. LOUIS (N.)	AB.	R.	H.	RBI.	PO.	A.
Brock, lf	4	1	1	1	2	0
Flood, cf	4	0	1	0	1	0
Maris, rf	3	1	0	0	1	0
Cepeda, 1b	4	0	0	0	1	1
McCarver, c	3	1	1	0	17	1
Shannon, 3b	4	1	2	1	0	0
Javier, 2b	3	0	1	2	2	0
Maxvill, ss	2	0	0	0	2	0
Gibson, p	2	0	0	0	1	0
Total	29	4	6	4	27	2

aGrounded out for McLain in 6th.
bStruck out for Wert in 8th.
cFlied out for Dobson in 8th.

Detroit (A.)	0	0	0	0	0	0	0	0	0—0
St. Louis (N.)	0	0	0	3	0	0	1	0	x—4

Errors—Freehan, Horton, Cash. Left on bases—Detroit 5, St. Louis 6. Two-base hit—Kaline. Three-base hit—McCarver. Home run—Brock. Stolen bases—Brock, Javier, Flood. Sacrifice—Gibson.

	IP.	H.	R.	ER.	BB.	SO.	HBP.	WP.	Bks.
McLain—L	5	3	3	2	3	3	0	0	0
Dobson	2	2	1	1	1	0	0	0	0
McMahon	1	1	0	0	0	0	0	0	0
Gibson—W	9	5	0	0	1	17	0	0	0

Bases on balls off McLain 3 (Maxvill, Maris, McCarver), Dobson 1 (Javier), McMahon (none), Gibson 1 (Freehan). Struck out by McLain 3 (Shannon, Javier, Gibson), Dobson (none), McMahon (none), Gibson 17 (McAuliffe, Kaline 3, Cash 3, Horton 2, Northrup 2, Freehan 2, McLain, Wert, Stanley, Mathews).

Umpires—Gorman (N.) plate; Honochick (A.) first base; Landes (N.) second base; Kinnamon (A.) third base; Harvey (N.) left field; Haller (A.) right field. Time of game—2:29. Attendance—54,692.

The 17 Strike-Outs

ST. LOUIS, Oct. 2 (AP) — Here's the way Bob Gibson of the St. Louis Cardinals broke the World Series strike-out record in pitching to a 4-0 victory today over the Detroit Tigers (S stands for swinging third strike; C for called third strike):

First Inning
Dick McAuliffe—S
Al Kaline—S

Second Inning
Norm Cash—S
Willie Horton—C
Jim Northrup—S

Third Inning
Bill Freehan—C
Denny McLain—bunted foul on third strike.

Fourth Inning
Kaline—C

Fifth Inning
Don Wert—C

Sixth Inning
Mickey Stanley—S
Cash—S

Seventh Inning
Northrup—S
Freehan—S

Eighth Inning
Ed Mathews—S

Ninth Inning
Kaline—S
Cash—S
Horton—C

Beamon's 29-2½ Long Jump and Evans's 43.8-Second 400 Set World Marks

AMERICANS SWEEP RUNNING EVENT

James Is Second, Freeman Third—Beamon's Leap Startles Olympic Fans

By NEIL AMDUR

Special to The New York Times

MEXICO CITY, Oct. 18—Two astonishing track and field achievements—a 29-foot-2½-inch long jump and a 43.8-second sprint in the 400-meter run — dramatically reaffirmed today the tenacity and competitive spirit of United States athletes.

Faced with mounting mental and social pressures that could have cost them coveted places on the Olympic awards platform, Bob Beamon and Lee Evans responded with gold-medal performances that rivaled the first 4-minute mile and the first 17-foot pole vault for breath-taking spontaneity.

The 21-year-old Evans scored a driving, determined triumph in the 400-meter run with his 0:43.8, which was an amazing seven-tenths of a second under the recognized world record and two-tenths better than Evans's pending performance at South Lake Tahoe, Calif., last month.

Larry James of White Plains, N. Y., finished inches behind Evans in 0:43.9, Ron Freeman of Elizabeth, N. J., was third and the United States gained its first 1-2-3 medal sweep in track since 1960.

Beamon Stuns Crowd

Beamon, 22, from Jamaica, Queens, startled the crowd of 45,000 in Olympic Stadium with an unbelievable opening attempt in the long jump. The world record for the event was 27-4¾, but Beamon, with his speed, height off the board and the thinner air at the 7,350-foot altitude here, flew by 27 feet, 28 feet and past 29 feet with a mark that may stand for years. Ralph Boston, Beamon's teammate, who share the listed world record with Igor Ter-Ovanesyan of the Soviet Union, was third, behind Klaus Beer of East Germany.

"I figured the pressure was on me and Ralph, so I knew I had to go 100 per cent," the 6-foot-3-inch Beamon said afterward. Beamon's best jump before today had been a wind-aided 27-6½.

That Beamon and Evans performed so marvelously was a tribute to their instinctive will to win. American athletes—blackk and white — had been under enormous pressure in the last 24 hours as a result of a United States Olympic Committee ruling that stripped Tommie Smith and John Carlos, the two Negro sprinters, of of their Olympic credentials.

Evans is a close friend of the pair and was one of the early leaders in the protest plans for an Olympic boycott by Negro athletes. Evans wore a pair of black socks as a silent sign of protest today. But once the gun sounded in the final, he moved out from lane No. 6 with the same fierce individual pride that earned him a berth on this strongest and most individualistic of American track teams.

Evans is unorthodox as quarter-milers go. He is stocky and seems to beat up a track rather than glide over it as the smooth-striding James or Freeman do.

After the three Negro runners crossed the finish line, they huddled for a few moments and then placed their left arms on each other's shoulders and walked a few more yards in unison.

Beamon got tremendous height on his opening jump. His arms flapped like a bird and he seemed to take off like one. When the numbers 8.90 [meters] were placed on the scoreboard in front of the long-jump area, the metric figures corresponding to 29-2½, the crowd let out an unbelieving roar and Beamon jumped up and down in front of the stands.

Mrs. Irena Szewinska of Poland broke her own world record in the women's 200-meter dash with a time of 0:22.5. Three American girls finished fourth, sixth and seventh in the event.

Maureen Caird of Australia won the 80-meter hurdles in an Olympic-record time of 0:10.3. Her time tied the world record set by Irina Press of the Soviet Union.

Lia Manoliu of Rumania won the women's discus gold medal with a toss of 191-2½.

Jim Ryun answered the question of whether he is ready to win the first United States gold medal in the 1,500 meters since 1908. Helped by a strong early pace and his own decisive kick, Ryun won his opening preliminary heat in 3:45.7, the best qualifying time.

Joining Ryun in tomorrow's second round of trials will be Martin Liquori and Tom Von Ruden.

Another obscured American athlete was Bill Toomey, the 29-year-old California schoolteacher, who is chasing the supreme title in track, the decathlon. With the final five events of the 10-event competition scheduled for tomorrow, Toomey is in excellent position to win it all.

United Press International

LOOK OUT BELOW! Bob Beamon of the U.S. squad in mid-flight during his leap of 29 feet 2½ inches in Olympic long jump final at Mexico City yesterday. Beamon's extra-long leap bettered the world record by almost two feet and won him the gold medal.

SUE GOSSICK WINS OLYMPIC DIVING

American Takes Gold Medal in 3-Meter Event

MEXICO CITY, Oct. 18 (UPI)—Sue Gossick of Tarzana, Calif., won the Olympic 3-meter springboard championship tonight and Tamara Pogozheva of the Soviet Union, with a great final dive, took the silver medal from Keala O'Sullivan of Honolulu.

Lieut. Micki King of Pontiac, Mich., who had been in the lead as tonight's final free diving began, had a poor final dive and dropped into fourth place.

Miss Gossick took the lead on her second dive, a reverse 1½ layout, which gave her 131.79 points to 129.58 for Miss King, who also did a reverse 1½ layout.

Many in the crowd thought that Miss King had performed well on this dive and there were loud boos as two of the judges gave her only 4's.

Miss Pogozheva did a reverse 1½ twist which gave her 20.28 points for a final total of 145.30 points to 150.77 for Miss Gossick. Miss King, knowing she needed a high score to win, did a reverse 1½ somersault twist and entered the water at the wrong angle for a low 7.80 score that gave her a 137.38 total compared with 145.23 for Miss O'Sullivan.

Defender Is Fifth

The defending champion in this event—Mrs. Ingrid Kramer Gulbin of East Germany, who was a double gold medal winner in diving eight years ago—was fifth with 135.82 and Zera Baklanova of the Soviet Union was sixth at 132.31 in the 12-girl field.

Michael Wenden of Australia broke the Olympic record of 53.4 seconds in the 100-meter free-style semi-finals in 0:52.9. Zach Zorn of Buena Park, Calif., had tied the record in an earlier previous heat. The mark was set by Don Schollander of Jacksonville, Fla., in 1964. Bob McGregor of Britain also won his semi-final heat in 0:53.8.

Mark Spitz of Santa Clara, Calif., Schollander's heir apparent as the United States Olympic swimming king, finished second to Wenden in 0:53.8.

Sue Pedersen of Sacramento, Calif.; Jan Henne of Oakland, Calif., and Marion Lay of Canada won the first three heats of the women's 100-meter free-style.

Miss Norbis Breaks Mark

Ana Marie Norbis of Uruguay lowered the women's 100-meter breast-stroke record to 1:16.7 in the second heat of the semi-finals, breaking the mark of 1:16.8 by Sharon Wichman of Fort Wayne, Ind., set in the first heat.

Miss Norbis had set a record for the new Olympic event at 1:17.4 in the first round earlier in the day. Catie Ball of Jacksonville, Fla., was second to Miss Norbis in the semi-final in 1:16.8.

C.C.N.Y. 5-0 Soccer Victor

Two first-period goals by Cirino Alvarado, a sophomore, paced City College to a 5-0 Metropolitan Soccer League victory over C. W. Post yesterday at Lewisohn Stadium.

Sports of The Times

The Poor Relations

By ROBERT LIPSYTE

MEXICO CITY, Oct. 18—"Our biggest problem is morale," said Phan Nhu My with a sad smile. "We must constantly repeat the Olympic slogan to the team: 'It is more important to compete than to win.' We remind them how much more fortunate they are than thousands of Vietnamese back home."

Sometimes it helps. Often it does not. The two cyclists on the Republic of South Vietnam team have had virtually no altitude training and the two girl swimmers trained in Paris, Tokyo and Singapore on their fathers' money. The entrant in the decathlon prefers to work out when no one is around to laugh at him. The fencer was eliminated early, as have been most Vietnamese athletes since 1952, the first time they came as a national team.

"We do not have a great tradition in sports," admits My, editor of the Vietnam Press Agency, secretary of his country's Olympic Committee and chief of its mission here. "When the French came to our country, they imported the European sports—cycling, tennis, football, rowing. We have a little wrestling art of our own, and some boxing, like Thai boxing. We allow kicking, bare knuckles and elbowing."

He shrugged and lighted another cigarette.

"The president and the prime minister agreed that we have to be here," said My, "to show the world that even a country at war is trying to normalize its life."

Le Tour de Vietnam

With their presence planned as a political gesture, the Vietnamese began planning for this Olympics in mid-1967 and allocated 5 million piastres ($42,500) for the team. Selection was not difficult: Virtually all Vietnamese athletes are either in American universities or living in Saigon.

Of the 10-member team, the three shooters are Saigon policemen, the two track-and-field men are students at San Fernando State College in California, and the fencer, an army major, recently returned from Texas. The two girls—one a doctor's daughter, the other a shipowner's daughter—learned to swim in the 30-meter pool of the exclusive Cercle Sportif Saigonnais. To prepare for competition in the Olympic 50-meter pool, the girls' fathers sent them abroad.

One of the two cyclists is a soldier, the other a 17-year-old who, says My, will be a soldier soon. Once quite popular, competitive cycling has never been the same since the Tour de Vietnam was canceled five years ago because the government could no longer control the roads.

South Vietnam has won a few medals in the Southeast Asia Games from time to time, particularly with its fine teams in volleyball, table tennis and soccer, the national sport. Despite coaching and equipment from the American military, sports training remains out of the question for most Vietnamese. There is, for example, a well-equipped rowing club on the Saigon River that has an affiliation with the world rowing organization, but the wealthy Vietnamese businessmen who belong to the club row only for pleasure and have no interest in training young oarsmen or scullers.

Preparation for these Olympic Games was halted for five months by last January's Tet offensive and then the allocation was cut in half. My said that even with the originally promised 5 million piastres there was no thought of bringing more athletes, or even training them better. The additional money would have gone for public relations.

Finding Friends

The two weeks they have spent here have not been bleak, however. Apprehensive about coming to a country they knew only from American Western movies, the Vietnamese were delighted by the ovation they received as they marched into the Olympic Stadium last Saturday and were charmed by the sympathy and kindness of the Mexicans.

Another bright spot, according to My, has been the continuing friendship of other Asian countries. Just yesterday, the Filipinos, Thais, Koreans, Malaysians and Vietnamese formed a mutual defense pact for next week's 196-kilometer cycling road race to offset the tacit European ententes.

The greatest frustration, said My, has been encountered while trying to overcome the inferiority complexes of the athletes. After time-consuming negotiations, the coach persuaded the decathlon man to train with athletes from other countries. But then the athlete insisted upon placing the pole vault bar considerably higher than 11 feet 6 inches, which was his limit.

The youth explained that he would be humiliated if the other athletes knew he could vault no higher than that. He would rather keep knocking off the bar, giving the impression he was just having a bad day.

"We made him understand," said My, "that we are not here to win, or even do well, but to learn and give our most. Then, if the situation comes to a normal state, if peace should come at the end of this year, or next year, we will be ready to make rapid progress in sport and take our place among the other nations of Asia."

EVANS PUTS ASIDE RACIAL PROBLEMS

Felt Boycott Pressure, but Concentrated on Winning

Special to The New York Times

MEXICO CITY, Oct. 18—"I did feel the pressure," Lee Evans said today in a crowded news conference after his thrilling record-setting performance in the 400-meter run.

"A lot of things were on my mind. But I just had to push them out of my mind and concentrate on winning the gold medal just like a friend of mine did."

Evans's friend is Tommie Smith, the United States sprinter and gold medalist in the 200-meter dash. Smith and John Carlos, another sprinter, were stripped of their Olympic credentials for their victory-stand gestures.

Evans won the 400 in the world-record time of 43.8 seconds. Larry James and Ron Freeman, who finished second and third, respectively, joined Evans at the news conference.

Medal of Significance

Evans said he felt the gold medal had special significance for him.

"I feel I won this gold medal for black people in the United States and black people all over the world," he said, echoing the news conference sentiments of Smith and Carlos after their 1-3 finish in the 200.

A reporter asked Evans whether he had profited from his experiences of the last year, and if so how?

"Tommie Smith and I have grown a lot," the 21-year-old San Jose State athlete said. "I learned a lot about people by being in the boycott movement. If I had it to do all over again, I'd support the movement. I never knew people until I supported something people were against."

Among the mysteries of the ceremonies were the black berets worn by Evans, James and Freeman. Did the berets represent a private social message?

"It was rainin'," Evans said with a smile. "We didn't want to get wet."

Evans turned to James and they exchanged grins. In a polite, casual way, this was a champion's manner of telling the press that it was none of their business.

Friday's Gold Medalists

MEN'S TRACK AND FIELD

400-Meter Run—Lee Evans, San Jose, Calif.

Long Jump—Bob Beamon, Jamaica, Queens.

WOMEN'S TRACK AND FIELD

80-Meter Hurdles—Maureen Caird, Australia.

200-Meter Dash—Irene Szewinska, Poland.

Discus Throw—Lia Manoliu, Rumania.

WOMEN'S SWIMMING

Three-Meter Dive—Sue Gossick, Tarzana, Calif.

SHOOTING

Free Pistol—Grigory Kosych, Soviet Union.

WEIGHT LIFTING

Middle Heavyweight—Kaarlo Kancasniemi, Finland.

The Summaries of Competition in the 19th Olympic Games at Mexico City

Friday

BASKETBALL

GROUP A

United States 95, Panama 60.
Spain 64, Senegal 54.
Puerto Rico 89 Philippines 65.

United States (95)	G.	F.	P.	Panama (60)	G.	F.	P.
Clawson	2	2	6	Checa	0	0	0
Spain	0	0	0	Osorio	1	0	2
White	5	3	13	Blades	2	0	4
Barrett	4	0	8	Malcon	0	0	0
Haywood	12	3	27	Alvarado	1	0	2
Scott	4	4	12	Agard	8	1	17
Hosket	1	0	2	Reyes	1	0	2
Fowler	0	0	0	Paralta	3	0	6
Silliman	6	2	14	Seebo	3	0	6
Saulters	3	2	8	Sinclair	1	1	3
King	0	0	0	Rivas	3	1	7
Dee	2	1	5	Ellis	5	1	11
Total	38	17	95	Total	28	4	60

Half-time score—United States 61, Panama 33.

GROUP B

Poland 85, Morocco 49.
Soviet Union 100, Cuba 66.
Mexico 73, Bulgaria 63.
Brazil 91, Korea 59.

BOXING

LIGHT-FLYWEIGHT CLASS

Francisco Rodriguez, Venezuela, outpointed Rafael Carbonel, Cuba. Hubert Skrzypczak, Poland, outpointed Tahar Asiz, Morocco; Joseph Donovan, Australia, outpointed Robert Urretivizcaya, Argentina; Albertto Morales, Mexico, knocked out Bernd Englmeier, East Germany, first round; Yong Lee, South Korea, otpointed Victor Zaporozhets, U.S.S.R.

LIGHT-WELTERWEIGHT CLASS

Nelson Ruiz, Venezuela, outpointed Niyom Prasertson, Thailand; Jerzy Kulej, Poland, outpointed Janos Kaidi, Hungary; Jaime Lozano, Mexico, outpointed Emmanuel Lawson, Ghana; Sa Kim, South Korea, outpointed Enrique Gonsalez, Chile; James Wallington, U.S.A., knocked out Donato Cartagena, Dominican Republic, in first round; Alex Odhiambo, Uganda, knocked out Mariano Perez, Spain, in first round; Issaka Dabore, Nigeria, outpointed Jose Martin, Costa Rica; Peter Tiepold, East Germany, outpointed Vladimir Kucera, Czechoslovakia; liubinko Veselinovic, Yugoslavia, outpointed Samuel Valencia, Ecuador; Petar Stoitchev, Bulgaria, outpointed Ali Kilicoglu, Turkey.

LIGHT-HEAVYWEIGHT CLASS

Bernard Malherbe, France, outpointed Efstathios Alexopoulos, Greece; Evgeny Frolov, U.S.S.R., outpointed Raymond Maguire, Australia; Antoniu Vasile, Rumania, walkover; Enrique Regueiferos, Cuba, bye.

CYCLING

SCRATCH SPRINT
First Round

(Winner qualify for second round, losers race in repechages.)

FIRST HEAT—1, Daniel Morelon, France, time over last 200 meters 11:24 seconds; 2, Juan Reyes, Cuba; 3, Alberto Roxas, Philippines.

SECOND HEAT—1, Pierre Trentin, France, 11.61; 2, Jaime Galeano, Colombia; 3, Pakanit Boriharnvanakhet, Thailand.

THIRD HEAT—1, Giordano Turrini, Italy, 11:34; 2, Sawji Inou, Japan; 3, Alva Reece, Barbados.

FOURTH HEAT — 1, Omar Pkhazadze, U.S.S.R., 11.30; 2, Jose Pittaro, Argentina; 3, Tarek Abou-Zahab, Lebanon.

FIFTH HEAT—1, Roger Gibbon, Trinidad and Tobago, 11.15; 2, Jurgen Kissner, West Germany; 3, Yue-tao Fan, Taiwan.

SIXTH HEAT — 1, Robert Van Lancker, Belgium, 11.37; 2, Hector Urrego, Colombia; 3, Kim Kwang Sun, South Korea.

SEVENTH HEAT—1, Reg Barnett, Britain, 11.34; 2, Bob Boucher, Canada; 3, George Artin, Iraq.

EIGHTH HEAT—1, Johannes Jensen, Netherlands, 11.10; 2, Arturo Garcia, Mexico; 3, Constantin Kamemba, Congo Kinshasa.

Repechage

(Winners qualify for second repechage)

FIRST HEAT—1, Barth, West Germany, 10.98; 2, Van Lancker, Belgium; 3, Barnett, Britain.

SECOND HEAT—1, Loevesijn, Netherlands, 10.66; 2, Gibbon, Trinidad and Tobago; 3, Kravtsov, U.S.S.R.

THIRD HEAT—1, Simes, United States, 10.92; 2, Fredborg, Denmark; 3, King Trinidad and Tobago.

FOURTH HEAT—1, Mountford, United States, 10.79; 2, Johnson, Australia; 3, Kucirek, Czechoslovakia.

Repechage

(Winners qualify for second round.)

FIRST HEAT—1, Inoue, Japan, 11.60; 2, Boriharnvanakhet, Thailand; 3, Urrego, Columbia.

SECOND HEAT—1, Pittaro, Argentina, 11.41; 2, Roxas, Philippines; 3, Bryce, Guyana.

THIRD HEAT—1, Mountford, United States, 11.03; 2, Kim, South Korea; 3, Galeano, Colombia.

FOURTH HEAT—1, King, Trinidad and Tobago, 11.35; 2, Reyes, Cuba; 3, Kwon, South Korea.

FIFTH HEAT—1, Lovell, Canada, 11.30; 2, Garcia, Mexico; 3, Guaves, Philippines.

SIXTH HEAT—1, Baranyecz, Hungary, 11.08; 2, Varavudhi, Thailand.

SEVENTH HEAT—1, Mercado, Mexico, 11.27; 2, Reece, Barbados.

EIGHTH HEAT—1, Roqueiro, Argentina, 11.15; 2, Torres, Puerto Rico.

NINTH HEAT—1, Alsop, Britain, 11:19; 2, Boucher, Canada.

TENTH HEAT—1, Goens, Belgium, 11.81; 2, Fan, Taiwan.

ELEVENTH HEAT—1, Kravtsov, U.S.S.R., 11.56; 2, Vazquez, Cuba.

TWELFTH HEAT—1, Nicholson, Australia, 11.09; 2, Sutherland, British Honduras.

Second Round

(Winners Qualify for Quarter-Finals, Losers in Repechage)

FIRST HEAT—1, Morelon, France, 10.94; 2, Mountford, United States.

SECOND HEAT—1, Trentin, France, 10.91; 2, Inoue, Japan; 3, King, Trinidad and Tobago.

THIRD HEAT—1, Turrini, Italy, 11.47; 2, Pittaro, Argentina; 3, Lovell, Canada.

FOURTH HEAT—1, Pkhakadze, U.S.S.R., 11.26; 2, Jelinek, Czechoslovakia; 3, Alsop, Britain.

FIFTH HEAT—1, Gibbon, Trinidad and Tobago, 10.70; 2, Pedersen, Denmark; 3, Baranyecz, Hungary.

SIXTH HEAT—1, Simes, United States, 10.72; 2, Van Lancker, Belgium; 3, Kravtsov, U.S.S.R.

SEVENTH HEAT—1, Kucirek, Czechoslovakia, 11.38; 2, Barnett, Britain; 3, Mercado, Mexico.

EIGHTH HEAT—1, Johnson, Australia, 11:06; 2, Jansen, Netherlands; 3, Roqueiro, Argentina.

NINTH HEAT—1, Barth, West Germany, 10.95; 2, Verzini, Italy; 3, Nicholson, Australia.

TENTH HEAT—1, Fredborg, Denmark, 11:09; 2, Loevesijn, Netherlands; 3, Goens, Belgium.

REPECHAGE

(Winners Enter Quarter-Finals)

FIRST HEAT—1, Kravtsov, U.S.S.R., 10.87; 2, Inoue, Japan; 3, Jelinek, Czechoslovakia.

SECOND HEAT—1, King, Trinidad and Tobago, 11.16; 2, Mercado, Mexico; 3, Alsop, Britain.

THIRD HEAT—1, Pedersen, Denmark, 11:31; 2, Mountford, United States.

FOURTH HEAT—1, Van Lancker, Belgium, 10.99; 2, Baranyecz, Hungary.

FIFTH HEAT—1, Barnett, Britain, 11.01; 2, Nicholson, Australia.

SIXTH HEAT—1, Jansen, Netherlands, 11.13; 2, Goens, Belgium; 3, Pittaro, Argentina.

SEVENTH HEAT—1, Verzini, Italy, 11.04; 2, Roqueiro, Argentina.

EIGHTH HEAT—1, Loevesijn, Netherlands, 11.9; 2, Lovell, Canada.

Eighths Finals

(Winners qualify for quarter-finals)

FIRST HEAT—1, Morelon, France, 11.0; 2, King, Trinidad and Tobago; 3, Barnett, Britain.

SECOND HEAT—1, Trentin, France, 10.96; 2, Kravtsov, U.S.S.R.; 3, Van Lancker, Belgium.

THIRD HEAT—1, Turrini, Italy, 10.96; 2, Barth, West Germany; 3, Loevesijn, Netherlands.

FOURTH HEAT — 1, Pkhakadze, U.S.S.R., 10.94; 2, Fredborg, Denmark; 3, Mountford, United States.

FIFTH HEAT—1, Jansen, Netherlands, 11.06; 2, Gibbon, Trinidad and Tobago; 3, Johnson, Australia.

SIXTH HEAT—1, Verzini, Italy, 10.81; 2, Simes, United States; 3, Kucirek, Czechoslovakia.

Third Place

1, Xaver Kurmann, Switzerland, 4:39.42 (bronze medal); 2, John Bylsma, Australia.

4,000-METER RACE
Individual Pursuit
Quarter-Final Round

(Winners qualify for semi-finals.)

Kurmann, Switzerland (4:45.94), beat Crapez, Belgium; Bylsma, Australia (4:41.66), beat Trevino, Mexico; Rebillard, France (4:39.87), beat Kratzer, West Germany; Jensen, Denmark (4:37.54), beat Chemello, Italy.

SEMI-FINALS

(WINNERS QUALIFY FOR FINAL)

FIRST HEAT—1, Hogens Jens, Denmark, 4 minutes 42.05 seconds; 2, Xaver Kurmann, Switzerland.

SECOND HEAT—1, Daniel Ribillard, France, 4:41.80; 2, John Bylsma, Australia.

FINAL

1, Waniel Ribillard, France, 4:14.71; 2, Mogens Jensen, Denmark, 4:42.43.

EQUESTRIAN

TREE-DAY DRESSAGE

1, Gasumov, U.S.S.R., 49.50 points; 2, Moratonio, Argentina, 68.01; 3, Purser, Ireland, 72.51; 4, Guyon, France, 73.01; 5, Moreton, Ireland, 74.01; 6, Flank, East Germany, 79.01; 7, LeGoupil, France, 83.01; 8, Argenton, Italy, 83.51; 9, Allhusen, Britain, 85.01; 10, tie between Bullen, Britain and Glushkov, U.S.S.R., 86.51; 15, Wofford, U.S., 101.51; 18, Page, U.S., 107.51.

FIELD HOCKEY

GROUP A

East Germany 1, Japan 0.
India 2, Belgium 1.
Spain 3, Mexico 0.
West Germany 0, New Zealand 0.

STANDING OF THE TEAMS

	W.	L.	T.	Pts.	G.F.	G.A.
India	4	1	0	8	14	4
New Zealand	3	0	2	8	6	2
West Germany	3	1	1	7	8	4
Spain	2	1	2	6	6	2
Belgium	2	3	0	4	9	6
East Germany	1	2	2	4	5	9
Japan	1	3	1	3	2	5
Mexico	0	5	0	0	1	19

FENCING

TEAM FOILS

POOL A—Cuba 9, Mexico 7.
POOL B—Britain 9, United States 7.
POOL C—Japan 13, United Arab Republic 3.
POOL D—Hungary 14, Argentina 2.
POOL E—West Germany 13, Canada 3; Italy 15, Ireland 1.

SECOND ROUND—Poland 11, Argentina 5; Hungary 15, Venezuela 1; France 12, Mexico 4; West Germany 15, Ireland 1; Italy 15, Canada 1; U.S.S.R. 12, United States 4; Rumania 13, U.A.R. 3.

THIRD ROUND—U.S.S.R. 9, Britain 0; Japan 8, Rumania 8; France 9, Cuba 3; Poland 9, Hungary 4.

FOURTH ROUND—Hungary 9, Cuba 2 (for 7th and 10th places); Britain 8, Japan 8 (or 8th and 9th places); Poland 9, West Germany 4 (for 4th and 5th places).

Medal Standing

	Gold	Silver	Bronze	Total
United States	12	4	8	24
Soviet Union	6	9	6	21
Hungary	3	4	6	13
Rumania	3	1	0	4
Poland	3	0	6	9
France	3	0	1	4
Australia	2	4	2	8
Kenya	2	3	1	6
West Germany	1	4	1	6
East Germany	1	2	2	5
Britain	1	2	1	4
Japan	1	1	1	3
Sweden	1	1	1	3
Finland	1	1	0	2
Iran	1	1	0	2
Czechoslovakia	1	0	1	2
Tunisia	1	0	1	2
Netherlands	1	0	0	1
Denmark	0	2	0	2
Austria	0	1	1	2
Brazil	0	1	0	1
Ethiopia	0	1	0	1
Jamaica	0	1	0	1
Mexico	0	1	0	1
Italy	0	0	3	3
Switzerland	0	0	1	1
Formosa	0	0	1	1

MEN'S TRACK AND FIELD

1,500-METER RUN
First Round

First five in each heat qualify for semi-finals.

FIRST HEAT—1, Kipchoge Keino, Kenya, 3 minutes 46.9 seconds; 2, Bodo Tummler, West Germany, 3:51.5; 3, John Boulter, Britain, 3:51.6; 4, Jorge Grosser, Chile, 3:51.7; 5, Francesco Arese, Italy 3:51.8; 6, David Bailey, Canada, 3:52.1; 7, Rober Honti, Hungary, 3:54.9; 8, Rudolf Klaban, Austria, 3:54.9; 9, Julio Quevedo, Guatemala, 4:03.1; 10, Edouard Sagna, Senegal, 5.04.1; 11, Emilio Barahona, Honduras, 4:56.0.

SECOND HEAT—Thomas Von Ruden, United States, 3:59.1; 2, Andre de Hartogue, Belgium, 3:59.3; 3, Henryk Szordykowski, Poland, 3:59.3; 4, Claude Nicolas, France, 3:59.3; 5, Arnd Kruger, West Germany, 3:59.3; 6, Renzo Finelli, Italy, 3:59.5; 7, Ove Berg, Sweden, 4:00.4; 8, Tom Hansen, Denmark, 4:01.4; 9, Subramaniom Ramasamy, Malaysia, 4:06.4; 10, Miguel Nunez, Dominican Republic, 4:23.6.

THIRD HEAT—1, Ben Jipcho, Kenya, 3:46.4; 2, Oleg Raiko, U.S.S.R., 3:46.8; 3, Harold Norpoth, West Germany, 3:46.9; 4, Josef Odlozil, Czechoslovakia, 3:47.4; 5, Jacques Boxberger, France, 3:47.5; 6, Jose Neri, Mexico, 3:47.5; 7, Jorge Gonzalez, Spain, 3:50.4; 8, Ioannis Virvilis, Greece, 3:55.5; 9, Xavier Frick, Liechenstein, 4:15.3; 10, Alfredo Cubias, El Salvador, 4:32.5.

FOURTH HEAT—1, Jim Ryun, United States, 3:45.7; 2, Hamadi Ben Haddou, Morocco, 3:47; 3, Edgard Salve, Belgium, 3:47.1; 4, Arne Kvalheim, Norway, 3:47.4; 5, Norman Trerise, Canada, 3:47.6; 7, Peter Watson, Australia, 3:55.4; 8, Maurice Benn, Britain, 3:56.4; 9, Pekka Vasala, Finland, 4:08.5; 10, Willie Rios, Puerto Rico, 4:14.4; 11, Jeffey Payne, Bermuda, 4:18.9.

FIFTH HEAT—1, Martin Liquori, United States, 3:52.7; 2, Hansruedi Knill, Switzerland, 3:52.8; 3, John Whetton, Britain, 3:53; 4, Ahmet Issa, Chad, 3:53.1; 5, Mikail Zhelobovsky, U.S.S.R., 3:53.2; 6, Matios Habtemichael, Ethiopia, 3:53.2; 7, Anders Gardesud, Sweden, 3:54.2; 8, Byron Dyce, Jamaica, 3:54.6; 9, Jerzy Maluski, Poland, 3:54.8; 10, Frank Murphy, Ireland, 3:54.8; 11, Rudi Simon, Belgium, 4:06.9; 12, Luis Cordova, Honduras, 5:18.9.

400-METER RUN
Final

1, Lee Evans, United States, 43.8 seconds (betters official world and Olympic records); previous world record 0:44.5 by Tommie Smith, United States, 1967; previous Olympic record by Evans in preleminants); 2, Larry James, United States, 0:43.9; 3, Ronald Freeman, United States, 0:44.4; 4, Amadou Gakou, Senegal, 0:45; 5, Martin Jellingshaus, West Germany, 0:45.3; 6, Tegene Bezabeh, Ethiopia, 0:45.4; 8, Amos Omolo, Uganda, 0:47.6.

DECATHLON
100-Meter Dash

FIRST HEAT—1, Rein Aun, U.S.S.R. 10.8 seconds, 853 points; 2, Clive Longe, Britain, 0:10.9, 828; 3, Werner von Moltke, Moltke, West Germany, 0:11.1, 780; 4, Werner Duttweiler, Switzerland, 0:11.2, 756; 5, A-Min Wu, Taiwan, 0:11.3; 733.

SECOND HEAT—1, Nickolay Avilov, U.S.S.R, 0:10.9, 828; 2, Manfred Tiedtke, East Germany, 0:10.9, 828; 3, Spas Djourov, Bulgaria, 0:10.9, 828; 4, Eduard de Noordlander, Netherlands, 0:11.1, 780; 5, Dominique Rakotorahalahy, Madagascar, 0:11.5, 687.

THIRD HEAT—1, Bill Toomey, United States, 0:10.4, 959; 2, Roberto Carmona, Mexico, 0:10.9, 828; 3, Valbiorn Tholaksson, Iceland, 0:11.1, 780; 4, Lennart Hedmark, Sweden, 0:11.1, 780; 5, Horst Mandl, Austria, 0:11.2, 756.

FOURTH HEAT—1, Kurt Bendlin, West Germany, 0:10.7, 879; 2, Chuan Che, Taiwan, 0:10.8, 853; 3, Steen Smidt-Jensen, Denmark, 0:10.9, 828; Thomas Waddell, United States, 0:11.3, 733; 5, Franz Biedermann, Liechtenstein, 0:11.5, 687.

FIFTH HEAT—1, Gert Herrunter, Austria, 0:10.5, 932, 2, Joachim Kirst, East Germany, 0:10.5, 932; 3, Yanis Lanka, U.S.S.R. 0:10.9, 828; 4, Charlemagne Anyamah, France, 0:11.2, 756; 5, Donald Velez, Nicaragua, 0:11.5, 687.

SIXTH HEAT—1, Hans Walde, West Germany, 0:10.9, 828; 2, Hansruedi Kunz, Switzerland, 0:11, 804; 3, Urs Trautmann, Switzerland, 0:11.2, 756; 4, Henh Ho, South Vietnam, 0:11.9, 601.

SEVENTH HEAT—1, Walter Riessl, Austria, 0:10.7, 879; 2, Herbert Wessel, East Germany, 0:10.8, 853; 3, Roger Lespegnard, Belguim, 0:11.1, 780; 4, Dichard Sloan, United States, 0:11.2, 756.

Long Jump

GROUP A—1, Toomey, 25 feet 9¾ inches, 994 points, 1,953 total points; 2, Avilov, 25-0¾, 949, 1,177; 3, Walde, 25-0¾, 949, 1,777; 4, Aun, 24-3¼, 901, 1,754; 5, Wessel, 24-3, 899, 1,752; 6, Hedmark, 23-11, 879, 1,659; 7, Smidt-Jensen, 23-6¼, 855, 1,683; 8, Lespagnard, 22-9¼, 808, 1,588; 9, Coarmona, 22-8¾, 806, 1,634; 10, De Noorlander, 22-7¾, 800, 1,580; 11, Longe, 22-6, 791, 1,619; 12, Chen 22-3, 774, 1,627; 13, Herunter, 22-1¾, 767, 1,699; 14, Sloan, 22-0½, 761, 1,517; 15, Velez, 21-9, 742, 1,429; 16, Rakotorahalahy, 21-8¾, 740, 1,427; 17, Anyamah, 19-9½, 611, 1,363; 18, Duttweiler, 17-5, 446, 1,202.

GROUP B—1, Kirst, 24-11¾, 943, 1,875; 2, Bendlin, 24-9¾, 933, 1,812; 3, Waddell, 24-6, 915, 1,648; 4, Tiedtke, 24-5¾, 913, 1,714; 5, Diessl, 24-4¼, 905, 1,784; 6, Wu, 24-3¼, 901, 1,634; 7, Djourov, 24-3¼, 901, 1,729; 8, Lanka, 23-5½, 850, 1,687; 9, Mandl, 23-1¼, 828, 1,584; 10, Trautmann, 22-10, 812, 1,568; 11, Thorlaksson, 22-2¼, 770, 1,550; 12, Kunz, 21-5½, 723, 1,527; 13, Biedermann, 20-8, 671, 1,358; 14, Ho, 20-2½, 640, 1,241; 15, Von Moltke, 20-1¾, 635, 1,415.

LONG-JUMP
Final

1, Bob Beamon, United States, 29 feet 2½ inches; world and Olympic record; previous world record, 27-4¾ by Ralph Boston 1965; previous Olympic record 27-1½ by Boston in preliminaries; 2, Klaus Beer, East Germany, 26-10½; 3, Ralph Boston, United States, 26-9¼; 4, Igor Ter-Ovanesian, U.S.S.R., 26-7¾; 5, Tynu Lepik, U.S.S.R., 26-6½; 6, Allen Crawley, Australia, 26-3¾; 7, Jack Pani, France, 26-1¾; 8, Andrzel Stalmach, Poland, 26-0½; 9, Lynn Davies, Britain, 26-0½; 10, Hiroomi Yamada, Japan, 26-0¼; 11, Leonid Borkovsky, U.S.S.R., 25-11; 12, Renhold Boschert, West Germany, 25-10¾; 13, Michael Ahey, Ghana, 25-3½; 14, Lars-Olof Hook, Sweden, 25-1½; 15, Victor Brooks, Jamaica, 24-7¾; 16, Gerard Ugolini, France, 24-5.

Shot-Put

GROUP A—1, Kirst, 53 feet 11 inches, 872 points, 2,747 total points; 2, Lanka, 50-2¾, 807, 2,485; 3, Trautmann, 49-9, 798, 2,366; 4, Longe, 49-6½, 795, 2,414; 5, Bendlin, 48-4¼, 773, 2,585; 6, Diessl, 46-11¾, 747, 2,531; 7, Hedmark, 46-2¼, 733 2,392; 8, Sloan, 46-2, 733, 2,250; 9, Anyamah, 45-11¼, 728, 2,095; 10, Djourov, 45-10¾, 727, 2,456; 11, Wessel, 44-11½, 709, 2,461; 12, Kunz, 44-10½, 708, 2,235; 13, Mandl, 43-9½, 687, 2,271; 14, Chen, 40-7½, 624, 2,251; 15, Biedermann, 35-10¾, 528, 1,886; 16, Von Moltke, no points, 1,415; 17, Rokotorahalahy, no points, 1,427.

GROUP B—1, Tiedtke, 51—9, 834, 2,575; 2, Walder, 49—7¾, 796, 2,573; 3, Aun, 48—4¾, 774, 2,528; 4, Waddell, 47—5, 757, 2,405; 5, Carmona, 47—1¾, 751, 2,389; 6, Herunter, 45—8½, 723, 2,422; 7, De Noorlander, 45—7, 721, 2,301; 8, Toomey, 45—1¼, 712, 2,665; 9, Avilov, 44—691, 2,468; 10, Smidt-Jensen, 42—9, 667, 2,350; 11, Thorlaksson, 41—8, 645, 2,195; 12, Lespagnard, 41—3¼, 638, 2,226; 13, Wu, 39—7½, 604, 2,238; 14, Ho, 39—1¾, 594, 1,835; 15, Velez, 34—9¼, 504, 1,933; 16, Duttweiler, No points, 1,202.

400-Meter Run

FIRST HEAT—1, Bendlin, 48.3 seconds, 884 points, 4,149 total points; Carmona, 0:50.5, 784, 3,757; Anyamah, 0:50.9, 766,3,541; Wessel, 0:53.4, 663, 3,858.

SECOND HEAT—Herunter, 0:49.7, 819, 3,948; Chen, 0:50.9, 766, 3,605; Diessl, 0:51.6, 695, 3,933; Aun, did not finish, 3,208.

THIRD HEAT—Kunz, 0:49.1, 847, 3,622; Lanka, 0:49.9, 810, 3,975; Hedmark, 0:51.3, 749, 3,901; Horlaksson, 0:53.2, 671, 3,454.

FOURTH HEAT—Longe, 0:49.3, 838, 3,840; Biedermann, 0:51.4, 744, 3,218; Wu, 0:52.2, 712, 3,630; Velez, 0:53.1, 675, 3,148.

FIFTH HEAT—Toomey, 0:45.6, 1,021, 4,499; Avilov, 0:49.9, 810, 4,195; Smidt-Jensen, 0:50.2, 787, 3,960; Kirst, 0:50.2, 797, 4,384; Waddell, 0:51.2, 753, 4,023; Trautmann, 1:03.9, 831, 3,497.

SIXTH HEAT—Walde, 0:49.0, 852, 4,290; Tiedtke, 0:50.0, 805, 4,193; Djourov, 0:50.2, 797, 4,013; Lespagnard, 0:50.2, 797, 3,836; De Norlander, 0:50.5, 784, 3,898; Sloan, 0:51.0, 762, 3,954.

WOMEN'S TRACK AND FIELD

80-METER HURDLES
Semi-Finals

(First four in each heat qualify for final)

FIRST HEAT—1, Maureen Caird, Australia, 10.5 seconds; 2, Patty von Wolvelaere, United States, 0:10.6; 3, Tatiana Talysheva, U.S.S.R., 10.7; 4, Karin Balzer, East Germany, 10.8; 5, Vera Karsakova, U.S.S.R., 10.8; 6, Teresa Sukniewicz, Poland, 10.9; 7, Valerie Bufanu Rumania, 0:11; 8, Inge Aigner, Austria, 0:11.1.

SECOND HEAT—1, Pam Kilborn, Australia, 10.4 seconds (equals olympic record record set by Pam Kilbourn, in preliminaries); 2, Cheng Chi-Taiwan, 0:10.5; 3, Damuta Straszynska, Poland, 0:10.5; 4, Elzbieta Zebrowski, Poland, 0:10.6; 5, Mamie allins, United States, 0:10.6; 6, Julia Dyer, United States, 0:10.8; 7, Ingeborg Schell, West Germany, 0:10.8; 8, Maria Kiss, Hungary, 0:11.2.

FINAL

1, Maureen Caird, Australia, 0:10.3 (equals official world record set by Irena Preas, U.S.S.R., 1965; Olympic record); 2, Pam Kilborn, Australia, 0:10.4; 3, Chi Cheng, Taiwan, 0:10.4; 4, Pat Van Wolvelaere, United States, 0:10.5; 5, Karin Balzer, East Germany, 0:10.6; 6, Damuta Straszynska, Poland, 0:10.6; 7, Elzbieta Zebrowska, Poland, 0:10.6; 8, Tatiana Talysheva, U.S.S.R., 0:10.7.

200-METER DASH
Final

1, Irena Szewinska, Poland, 22.5 seconds (betters official world record of 0:22.7 set by Miss Szewinska, 1965 and Olympic record of 0:[illegible]8 set in semi-final by Barbara Ferrell, United States); 2, Raelene Boyle, Australia, 0:22.7; 3, Jennifer Lamy, Australia, 0:22.8; 4, Barbara Ferrell, United States, 0:22.9; 5, Nicole Montandon, France, 0:23; 6, Wyomia Tyus, United States, 0:23; 7, Mrs. Margaret Bailes, United States, 0:23.1; 8, Jutta Stock, West Germany, 0:23.2.

800-METER RUN
Semi-Finals

(First Four in Each Heat Qualify for Final)

FIRST HEAT—1, Madeline Manning, United States, 2:05.8; 2, Ilona Silai, Rumania, 2:05.9; 3, Pat Lowe, Britain, 2:06.6; 4, Abigail Hoffman, Canada, 2:07; 5, Karin Burneleit, East Germany, 2:08.4; 6, Anna Zimina, U.S.S.R., 2:08.5; 7, Ilja Keizer, Netherlands, 2:14.8; 8, Vera Nikolic, Yugoslavia, did not run.

SECOND HEAT—1, Maria Gommer, Netherlands, 2:05.1; 2, Doris Brown, United States, 2:05.2; 3, Sheila Taylor, Britain, 2:05.2; 4, Marie Dupureu, France, 2:05.5; 5, Laine Erik, U.S.S.R., 2:06; 6, Sylvia Potts, New Zealand, 2:07.2; 7, Paola Pigni, Italy, 2:07.8; 8, Jaroslava Jehlickova, Czechoslovakia, 2:13.5.

DISCUSS THROW
Final

1, Lia Manoliu, Rumania, 191 feet 2½ inches (Olympic record; previous record 187-10½, E. Gorchakova, U.S.S.R., 1964; 2 Kiesel Westerman, West Germany, 189-6; 3, Kleiber Kontsek, Hungary, 180-1½; 4, Anita Otto, East Germany, 178-5½; 5, Antonia Popova, U.S.S.R., 175-3; 6, Olga Connolly, United States, 173-9; 7, Christine Spielberg, East Germany, 173-5; 8, Brigitte Berendonk, West Germany, 173-2½; 9, Liudmila Muravjeva, U.S.S.R., 171-5½; 10, Karen Illgen, East Germany, 171-2½; 11, Judit Stugner, Hungary, 170-10½; 12, Namjilmaadshzeveg, Mongolia, 166-6½; 13, Olimpia Catarama, Rumania, 164-8½; 14, Carol Moseke, United States, 158-4½; 15, Jean Roberts, Australia, 151-9.

MEN'S SWIMMING

100-METER BREAST-STROKE
First Round

FIRST HEAT—1, Nickolay Pankin, U.S.S.R., 1 minute 8.9 seconds; 2, Klaus Katzur, East Germany, 1:09.4; 3, David Percowski, United States, 1:09.5; 4, Michael Gunther, West Germany, 1:10.3; 5, Osamu Tsurumine, Japan, 1:10.5; 6, Nicolas Gilliard, Switzerland, 1:12.8; 7, Eduardo Moreno, Mexico, 1:13.7.

SECOND HEAT—1, Nobutaka Taguchi, Japan, 1:09.8; 2, Vladimir Koseinsky, U.S.S.R., 1:10; 3, Kenneth Merten, United States, 1:10.6; 4, Liam Ball, Ireland, 1:12.1; 5, Leiknir Jonsson, Iceland, 1:16.3; 6, Abel Munoz, El Salvador, 1:19.4; (Massimo Sacchi of Italy did not compete).

THIRD HEAT—1, Egon Henninger, East Germany, 1:09.6; 2, Ladislau Koszta, Romania, 1:10.1; 3, Jozef Klukowski, Poland, 1:11.0; 4, Thomas Aretz, West Germany, 1:11.1; 5, Sandor Szabo, Hungary, 1:11.3; 6, Stuart Roberts, Britain, 1:12.7; 7, Ivan Gonima, Colombia, 1:15.1.

FOURTH HEAT—1, Joe Fiolo, Brazil, 1:09.5; 2, Gregor Betz, West Germany, 1:10.3; 3, Amman Jalmaani, Phillippines, 1:10.6; 4, Slavko Kurbanovic, Yugoslavia, 1:11.6; 5, Roger Roberts, Britain, 1:11.7; 6, Leroy Goff, Philippines, 1:13.7; 7, Arturo Carranza, El Salvador, 1:28.0.

FIFTH HEAT—1, Donald McKenzie, United States, 1:08.1; 2, Eugeny Mikhailov, U.S.S.R., 1:09.3; 3, William Mahony, Canada, 1:09.7; 4, Osvaldo Boretto, Argentina, 1:10.3; 5, Felipe Munoz, Mexico, 1:10.6; 6, Johan Kende, Israel, 1:12.3; (King-Ming Chan of Taiwan did not compete).

SIXTH HEAT—1, Ian O'Brien, Australia, 1:08.9; 2, Alberto Forelli, Argentina, 1:09.3; 3, Per Johnsson, Sweden, 1:10; 4, Jose Duran, Spain, 1:12.3; 5, Javier Jimenez, Mexico, 1:10.3; 6, Eduadro Ramos, El Salvador, 1:31.2; (Istvan Zsadanyi of Hungary did not compete).

Semi-Finals

(Fastest eight qualify for final.)

FIRST HEAT—1, Henninger, 1:08.9; 2, O'Brien, 1:09; 3, Gunther, 1:09.7; 4, Katzur, 1:09.9; 5, Tsurumine, 1:10.3; 6, Jalmaani, 1:10.4; 7, Johnsson, 1:10.9; 8, Szabo, 1:11.1.

SECOND HEAT—1, Pankin, 1:08.1 (equals Olympic recor set by Dan McKenzie in first round); 2, Forelli, 1:08.9; 3, Perkowsky, 1:09; 4, Munoz, 1:09.4; 5, Koszta, 1:09.8; 6, Aretz, 1:11.2; 7, Boretto, 1:11.8; 8, Taguchi, disqualified.

THIRD HEAT—1, Kisinsky, 1:07.9 (betters Olympic record of 1:08.1 set by McKenzie and Pankin in earlier heats); 2, McKenzie, 1:08.1; 3, Fiolo, 1:08.6; 4, Mikhailov, 1:08.8; 5, Mahony, 1:09.7; 6, Betz, 1:09.8; 7, Klukowsky, 1:10.9; 8, Merten, 1:11.6.

100-METER FREE-STYLE
First Round

FIRST HEAT—1, Michel Rosseau, France, 54.9 seconds; 2, Erik Eriksson, Sweden, 0:55.2; 3, Bernard Guener, France, 0:56.2; 4, Pano Caperonis, Switzerland, 0:56.2; 5, Orjan Madsen, Norway, 0:56.3; 6, Donnacha O'Dea, Ireland, 0:59.5; 7, Tong-Shing Lee, Taiwan, 1:01; 8, Jose Alvarado, El Salvador, 1:02.

SECOND HEAT—1, Yanuzzi Nicolao, Argentina, 0:54.6; 2, Robert McGregor, Britain, 0:55.1; 3, Gregory Rogers, Australia, 0:55.4; 4, Jose Diniz, Brazil, 0:56.8; 5, Mario Santibanez, Mexico, 0:57.

THIRD HEAT—1, Leonid Ilychev, U.S.S.R., 0:54.9; 2, Kunihiro Iwasaki, Japan, 0:55.5; 3, Gary Goodner, Puerto Rico, 0:55.7; 4, Rafael Cal y Mayor, Mexico, 0:56.5; 5, Peter Schmid, Austria, 0:57.1.

FOURTH HEAT—1, Zachary Zorn, United States, 0:54.3; 2, Wolfgang Kremer, West Germany, 0:55. 3, Gabor Kucsera, Hungary, 0:55.1; 4, Csaba Csatlos, Hungary, 0:56.6; 5, Herman Verbauwen, Belgium, 57.5.

FIFTH HEAT—1, Mark Spitz, United States, 0:54.6; 2, José Chicoy, Spain, 0:54.9; 3, Francois Simons, Belgium, 0:55.5; 4, Roosevelt Abdulgafur, Philipines, 0:55.8; 5, Carlos Van Der Naath, Argentina, 0:56.4; 6, Angus Edghill, Barbados, 0:58.1; 7, Michael Goodner, Puerto Rico, 0:58.2; 8, Salvador Vilanoa, El Salvador, 0:59.6.

SIXTH HEAT—1, Sergei Gusev, U.S.S.R., 0:54.8; 2, John Gilchrist, Canada, 0:55.4; 3, Michele D'Oppido, Italy, 0:57.3; 4, Gregorio Fiallo Salazarte, Cuba, 0:58.2; 5, Geoffrey Ferreira, Trinidad-Tobago, 0:58.9; 6, Robert Loh, Hong Kong, 1:101.1. Karl Eriksson of Sweden did not compete.

SEVENTH HEAT—1, Georgy Kulikov, U.S.S.R., 0:54.3; 2, Pietro Boscaini, Italy, 0:55.7; 3, Olaf von Shilling, West Germany, 0:55.8; 4, Luis Ayesa, Philippines 0:56.2; 5, Salvador Ruiz de Cavez, Mexico, 0:56.4; 6, Paul Nash, Jamaica, 0:59; 7, Jose Martinez, Cuba, 1:00.4.

EIGHTH HEAT—1, Michael Wenden, Australia, 0:53.6; 2, Robert Windle, Australia, 0:54.8; 3, Mike Turner, Britain, 0:55.8; 4, Glen Finch, Canada, 0:56; 5, Jose Ferriouli, Puerto Rico, 0:56.1. 6, Ricardo Gonzalez, Colombia, 57.

NINTH HEAT—1, Ken Walsh, United States, 0:55.7; 2, Masayuki Oshawa, Japan, 0:56.5; 3, Anthony Jarvis, Britain, 0:56.5; 4, Peter Schorning, West Germany, 0:56.9; 5, Gerard Letast, France, 0:57.2; 6, Amnon Krauz, Israel, 0:57.2; 7, Guomundur Gislason, Iceland, 0:58.6; 8, Ernesto Duron, El Salvador, 1:03.8.

Semi-Finals

(Eight fastest qualify for final.)

FIRST HEAT—1, McGregor, 0:53.8; 2, Ilchev, 0:53.8; 3, Kulikov, 0:54.1; 4, Rogers, 0:54.9; 5, Gusev, 0:55.2; 6, Iwasaki, 0:55.8; 7, Goodner, 0:55.8; 8, Von Schilling, 0:55.9.

SECOND HEAT—1, Zorn, 0:53.4; 2, Yanuzzi, 0:53.8; 3, Walsh, 0:53.9; 4, Kremer, 0:54.3; 5, Eriksson, 0:54.9; 6, Chicoy, 0:54.9; 7, Simons, 0:55.3; 8, Abdulgafur, 0:55.9.

THIRD HEAT—1, Wenden, 0:52.9 (Olympic record; previous record 0:53.4 by Don Scollander, United States, 1964; 2, Spitz, 0:53.8; 3, Rousseau, 0:54.5; 4, Windle, 0:54.6; 5, Gilchrist, 0:54.8; 6, Kucsera, 0:55; 7, Boscaini, 0:55.6; 8, Turner, 0:55.6.

Continued on Page 45, Column 1

The New York Times

SPORTS

Section 5

Sunday, October 20, 1968
L++

TOOMEY OF U.S. TRIUMPHS IN OLYMPIC DECATHLON; MADELINE MANNING TAKES 800-METER TITLE IN RUN

United Press International

HEAVY AIR TRAFFIC OVER MEXICO CITY: Two athletes competing in the pole-vaulting part of the decathlon event pass each other in mid-flight. They were vaulting from adjoining pits. In front is Joachim Kirst, East Germany. At rear is A-Min Wu, Taiwan.

Americans Set 5 Records And Gain 4 Gold Medals

By JOSEPH DURSO

The United States reaped four gold medals and five records yesterday as the Olympic Games reached the halfway mark in Mexico City.

The gold medals were won in the decathlon by Bill Toomey, in swimming by Jan Henne and Donald McKenzie and in track by Madeline Manning. The records were set in swimming by McKenzie and Debbie Meyer, in track by Miss Manning and the women's 400-meter relay team and in the decathlon by Toomey.

They combined to give the United States its best day in the Olympics this year and to raise its trove of gold medals to 16. The Soviet Union is next in first-place finishes with eight.

The United States, though, suffered a stunning setback in rowing. West Germany's crew won the eight-oared race, while Harvard University finished last among the six starters. It was only the second time since 1900 that an American crew had not won the event.

The glamour event of the day went to Toomey, a 29-year-old teacher from Laguna Beach, Calif. He set an Olympic decathlon record of 8,193 points and gave strong performances in the final five events on the second day of competition—hurdles, discus throw, pole vault, javelin throw and 1,500-meter run.

He shared the spotlight with Miss Manning, who won the 800-meter run. The 20-year-old Cleveland girl took the final in

Continued on Page 3, Column 8

Associated Press

BUT AT THE FINISH, Tiedtke was ahead. Toomey won the overall competition though.

Toomey Gets 8,193 Points

By NEIL AMDUR

Special to The New York Times

MEXICO CITY, Oct. 19—Bill Toomey, a 29-year-old teacher of English won the grueling decathlon with an Olympic record of 8,193 points tonight and gained the 11th track and field gold medal for the United States.

Helped by a pressure performance in the pole vault and strong showings in the running aspects of the 10-event competition, Toomey beat three Germans—Kurt Bendlin, Hans-Joachim Walde and Manfred Tiedtke—for the most prestigious title in sports: a crown worn by such prominent American athletes as Jim Thorpe, Bob Mathias, Milt Campbell and Rafer Johnson.

Toomey, born in Philadelphia but a resident of Laguna Beach, Calif., needed a solid time in the final event, the 1,500-meter run, to assure himself of what some observers believe is the determinant of the "world's greatest athlete."

Toomey led Bendlin, a West German and the world record-holder, by 56 points, 7,764 to 7,708, and needed a time of 4 minutes 35.1 seconds in his

Continued on Page 3, Column 5

U.S. Crews Fail to Win

By STEVE CADY

Special to The New York Times

MEXICO CITY, Oct. 19—Oarsmen from the United States fired a record seven-round salvo in today's Olympic rowing finals but wound up hitting only two minor targets.

Never had a single nation put boats into all seven finals as the Americans did today on the magnificent 2,000-meter course at Xochimilco. And never had the United States gone back to the boathouse with such a meager collection of medals.

For the first time in Olympic rowing history, Americans failed to win a gold medal. Their last chance evaporated under a sizzling Mexican sun when Harvard's weakened eight-oared shell struggled home last in the final won by West Germany's superbly synchronized Ratzeburg crew.

The only times the Stars and Stripes were raised came after the races for pairs without coxswain and the double sculls. Larry Hough and Tony Johnson took a silver medal in the coxless pairs, losing by a scant four feet to East Germany's pair after looking like apparent

Continued on Page 3, Column 1

Yale Tops Columbia, 29-7, For 12th Triumph in Row

By GERALD ESKENAZI

Special to The New York Times

NEW HAVEN, Oct. 19—What was to have been a confrontation between the best quarterbacks in the East, Marty Domres of Columbia and Brian Dowling of Yale, became instead a battle of amphibious forces today, and the surer-footed Elis sloshed their way to a 29-7 victory over their oldest football rivals. In stretching its victory string to 12, the longest of any major college, Yale fumbled nine times, fighting a slippery ball and muddied turf more than the weak Columbia line.

Ultimately it was Dowling's options that gave the defending Ivy league champions the victory. Domres tried to do most of the work himself in a frustrating game, but couldn't. In the second quarter, for example, he passed or ran 15 times in the Lions' 18 plays.

The senior quarterback, who had ripped apart defenses in Columbia's three previous, though losing, efforts on drier

Continued on Page 6, Column 4

HARVARD DOWNS CORNELL BY 10-0

Undefeated Crimson Wins 4th Time as Hornblower and Gatto Pace Attack

By DEANE McGOWEN

Special to The New York Times

CAMBRIDGE, Mass., Oct. 19—Harvard University's lighter but faster football team smashed down Cornell's vaunted defenses today to score a 10-0 victory over the Big Red.

The victory was the fourth of the season for the undefeated Crimson squad of Coach John Yovicsin. The loss marked the third in succession that Coach Jack Musick had suffered at the hands of a Crimson team and left Cornell with a 2-2 won-lost record. It was Cornell's second league loss and put a serious cramp in its title hopes.

Harvard's victory, its second in Ivy League competition, was accomplished in a rainstorm that should have hampered the Crimson's swift halfbacks.

But the weather conditions

Continued on Page 6, Column 2

Princeton Subdued By Colgate, 14 to 7

By FRANK S. ADAMS

Special to The New York Times

PRINCETON, N.J. Oct. 19—Led by Ron Burton, a slender, 170-pound quarterback from Montclair, N.J., the Colgate football team downed favored Princeton in the rain today, 14-7.

Burton, the hero of Colgate's 7-0 victory here two years ago, scored the first Red Raider touchdown on a squirming 7-yard run around left end.

He was the mainspring of the Colgate attack throughout the game, but he had plenty of help from Gene Detwiler and Don Fisher, two hard-running backs. Detwiler's touchdown

Continued on Page 6, Column 8

Football Scores

East

Adelphi F.C. 30	St. Bonaventure F.C. 0
Albright 10	Delaware Valley 6
American Int'l 50	Bates 19
Amherst 26	Rochester 0
Army 24	Rutgers 0
Boston Univ. 7	Holy Cross 7
Bridgeport 20	Montclair St. 3
Carnegie-Mellon 48	Allegheny 18
Colgate 14	Princeton 7
Connecticut 29	Maine 0
Dartmouth 48	Brown 0
Delaware 28	West Chester St 0
Delaware St. 25	St Paul's 0
F. & M. 24	Dickinson 7
Fordham F.C. 41	Fairfield F.C. 0
Gettysburg 12	Bucknell 7
Hamilton 18	Middlebury 14
Harvard 10	Cornell 0
Hobart 14	Alfred 7
Indiana (Pa.) 18	Clarion 13
Johns Hopkins 42	Haverford 0
Juniata 25	Lycoming 7
Kings Point 16	C.W. Post 7
Kutztown St. 44	Cheyney St. 19
Lafayette 27	Drexel Tech 0
Muhlenberg 45	Ursinus 6
Navy 17	Pittsburgh 16
Northeastern 10	Springfield 7
Norwich 10	St. Lawrence 0
Pennsylvania 34	Lehigh 0
PMC Colleges 7	Moravian 2
Rhode Island 14	Massachusetts 9
St. John's F.C. 26	Pace F.C. 0
Trinity 35	Colby 6
Tufts 17	Wagner 10
Upsala 16	Susquehanna 9
Union 24	R.P.I. 14
Vermont 12	New Hampshire 10
Villanova 28	Buffalo 7
Waynesburg 49	Geneva 0
Wesleyan 29	Worcester Tech 6
Westminster 20	Union 6
W. Virginia St. 29	Howard 0
Wilkes 28	Ithaca 19
Williams 14	Bowdoin 7
Yale 29	Columbia 7

South

Arkansas AM&N 25	Wiley 19
Baldwin-Wallace 49	Otterbein 0
Chattanooga 16	E. Tennessee 6
Clemson 39	Duke 22

Continued on Page 9, Column 7

CZAR ALEXANDER TAKES MAN O' WAR

Fort Marcy Is 3½ Lengths Behind in $116,200 Race —Victor Pays $24.80

By JOE NICHOLS

Czar Alexander won the $116,200 Man O'War on the soft turf at Belmont Park yesterday, taking the 1½-mile event by 3½ lengths from Fort Marcy, with Advocator next in the field of 12. Owned by Gustave Ring and ridden by Jorge Velesquez, Czar Alexander was the third 3-year-old in a row to take the rich grass stakes. His purse of $75,730 marked a record for the Man O'War, by the slim margin of $65, which last year's winner, Ruffled Feathers, took down.

Carrying the comparatively light burden of 121 pounds, as against the 126 toted by older horses, Czar Alexander covered the distance in 2:30 4/5. The record for the distance and the stakes is 2:28 3/5 set by Beau Purple in taking the 1962 renewal.

Because of the presence of several more respected contestants in the race, Czar was only tepidly played, and his straight return in the mutuels was $24.80 for $2 for those in the crowd of 35,142 who backed him.

High Hat, ridden by Ray Broussard, gradually slowed down at that point, leaving Fort Marcy and Advocator to vie for the lead, with Czar Alexander gradually moving

Continued on Page 10, Column 6

Victorious Jockey After the Race

The New York Times (by Michael Evans)

Jorge Velasquez, rear, is congratulated by a friend after riding Czar Alexander to victory in the Man o'War at Belmont. In picture below, Velasquez and Czar Alexander near the finish well ahead of Fort Marcy, who was second.

ARMY VANQUISHES RUTGERS BY 24-0

Cadets Use Strong Ground Attack on Wet Field—Intercept 4 Passes

By GORDON S. WHITE Jr.

Special to The New York Times

NEW BRUNSWICK, N.J., Oct. 19—Steven Lindell, Army's quarterback, wisely ordered a running game in the heavy rain at Rutgers Stadium today. Then Charlie Jarvis, Billy Hunter and Lynn Moore replied, "Roger, Wilco," and proceeded to give Army its best ground attack of the season as the Black Knights crushed Rutgers, 24-0, before 28,000 persons huddled under umbrellas and plastic sheets.

Moore and Hunter each scored a touchdown and Jarvis ran for 153 yards as the trio of Cadet backs ran and slid for 284 yards, the highest combined total for the three men this fall. Jarvis, the strong fullback, increased his career total to 1,678 yards, only 82 yards short of a mile.

The defense, which was the bulwark of the Army team the last two weeks against Missouri and California, got into the act with some heroics of its own. Tom Haller turned one of Army's four interceptions into a touchdown when he stole a Bruce Van Ness pass and scampered 29 yards into the end zone in the first period.

Also, Dennis Hutchinson had two interceptions. Hutchinson also intercepted twice against Missouri. Dick Luecke, the de-

Continued on Page 4, Column 4

Ohio State Power Scores Over Northwestern, 45-21

By LINCOLN A. WERDEN

Special to The New York Times

COLUMBUS, Ohio, Oct. 19—Ohio State's football team pleased a homecoming crowd of 83,454 on this sunny afternoon by scoring in every period to beat Northwestern, 45 to 21.

A week ago the Buckeyes surprised Purdue, ranked then as No. 1 nationally in the writers' and coaches' opinion polls. During the practice sessions since then Coach Woody Hayes had been apprehensive. He cautioned against a letdown against the visiting Wildcats here today after losses in all four of their previous games.

For a while the coach's fears seemed justified. Northwestern took a 7-6 lead in the first quarter and came back subsequently to tie at 14-14 and put on an offense that kept this Big Ten meeting a tussle. The Buckeye power proved too much for the visitors in the final quarter as they passed and rushed for three touchdowns.

As 14 sophomores moved

Continued on Page 4, Column 7

PURDUE TRIUMPHS WITH RALLY, 28-27

Wake Forest Pounded for Two Late Touchdowns

By The Associated Press

LAFAYETTE, Ind., Oct. 19—Purdue's Boilermakers, the nation's No. 5 ranked college football team, scored two touchdowns in the last seven minutes today to win, 28-27, from a Wake Forest team that hasn't won once this season.

Leroy Keyes of Purdue lost the ball four times on fumbles, then redeemed himself by knifing through from the Deacons' 2 for the final touchdown with 1 minute 16 seconds to play.

Keyes carried the ball 214 yards in 25 rushes.

A sophomore, Jeff Jones, kicked 4 extra points for Purdue, including the winner.

Purdue trailed until the final minutes after Tom Deacon kicked a 28-yard field goal for Wake Forest in the first quarter.

Jimmy Johnson gave the Deacons a comfortable lead in the second quarter with a 24-yard scoring run. Purdue came back on a 3-yard scoring

Continued on Page 4, Column 1

TENNESSEE BEATS ALABAMA, 10 TO 9

Kremser's Record 54-Yard Field Goal in the Fourth Quarter Proves Decisive

By The Associated Press

KNOXVILLE, Tenn., Oct. 19—Karl Kremser kicked a 54-yard field goal—a Southeastern Conference record—today that gave Tennessee a 10-9 football victory over Alabama.

The game, played before an overflow throng of 63,392, while millions watched on regional television, wasn't decided until the last play, when Mike Dean's field-goal attempt with five seconds left was blocked by Jim Weatherford of Tennessee.

The victory was Tennessee's fourth in a row after a tie in its season-opener with Georgia.

The loss was Alabama's second and marked the first time in 10 years any team had beaten the Crimson Tide two straight years. Tennessee de-

Continued on Page 5, Column 8

Lakers Rout Knicks At Garden, 118-96

By LEONARD KOPPETT

The New York Knickerbockers, who needed only one game this season to go into a slump, fell deeper into it last night as they were crushed by the Los Angeles Lakers, 118-96, before a crowd of 16,433 at Madison Square Garden.

The Lakers are supposed to be a super-team now that they have Wilt Chamberlain at center to go with Elgin Baylor and Jerry West, their perennial stars. Friday night in Philadelphia, they lost their first game. But last night they needed only the first 11 minutes to show what the National Basketball Association can expect once

Continued on Page 14, Column 8

TOOMEY NOTCHES DECATHLON MARK

Continued From Page 1

heat of the 1,500 meters to set a world record. But he settled for a victorious 4:57.1.

As Toomey entered the final stretch ahead by eight meters, a big smile swept across his handsome face and he pointed his fingers up as a sign of victory. His Olympic record beat the mark of 8,001 points set in the 1960 Games by Johnson.

Toomey's victory capped another marvelous day for American track and field athletes, who have one afternoon left to top their record haul of 15 gold medals at the 1956 Games in Melbourne.

Madeline Manning, a 20-year-old from Cleveland, gave the United States its 10th gold medal and sixth world record with a victory in the women's 800-meter run. Miss Manning's time of 2:00.9 outdistanced the field of eight finalists by 15 meters and gave America its first gold medalist in the event.

The United States also qualified its three relay teams for tomorrow's finals, and three athletes each in the 1,500-meter run and high jump.

Jim Ryun gave a convincing demonstration in the 1,500 meters by winning his semi-final heat in 3:51.2. He was joined by Martin Liquori and Tom Van Ruden.

The decathlon consumed two days and two nights. When Toomey finished the 1,500 today, more than half of the crowd of 60,000 already had departed Olympic Stadium. But their absence could not detract from the artistic, physical and mental brilliance of Toomey's effort.

The decathlon is determined on a point scale rather than individual competition and athletes receive a specified number of points for each performance in the 10 events. The better the performance, the more points an athlete can receive.

Thus, when Toomey missed his first two jumps at the opening height in the pole vault, he faced the possibility of receiving no points in the event if he failed on his third attempt. He succeeded and reached 13 feet 9½ inches.

Demanding Assignment

Toomey's best showings came in the 100-meter dash, 400-meter run, high jump and 110-meter high hurdles where he either led his 30 rivals or was close to the top.

His exceptional 45.6 time in the 400 gave him 1,021 points. His best throw in the discus—143-3½—produced only 757 points, however.

Bendlin's world record in the decathlon is 8,319 points.

Toomey was a long jumper and quarter-miler at the University of Colorado when he decided to switch to the decathlon five years ago. Track observers told him to think twice. After all, they said, wasn't that rather late in life to begin such a physically and mentally demanding assignment? Mathias was 18 when he won an Olympic gold medal in 1948 and Campbell and Johnson also were considerably younger.

But Toomey's speed and versatility were his strongest assets en route to four National Amateur Athletic Union titles and a gold medal in the Pan-American Games and they were his strengths today. He probably would have established a world record except that he lost precious seconds in the 1,500-meter run, the final event, because of the high altitude here of 7,350 feet above sea level.

To appreciate Toomey's athletic achievements, it is worth comparing his performances of the last two days with those of Johnson, the 1960 gold medalist. Here is a statistical breakdown of the 10 events and how the two athletes fared in their respective Olympic performances:

	Toomey	Johnson
100-Meter Dash	10.4	10.9
Shot-put	45-1¼	51-10¾
High Jump	6-4¾	6-¾
400-Meter Run	45.6	48.3
Long Jump	25-9¾	24-1½
110-Meter High Hurdles	14.9	15.3
Javelin Throw	206-4½	223-10½
Pole Valut	13-9½	13-5½
Discus Throw	143-3½	159-1
1,500-Meter Run	4:57.1	4:49.7

Toomey led outright in six events; Johnson's forte was in the weights. Toomey proved a truly remarkable athlete.

Ryun continues to dominate the qualifying for the 1,500-meter run, and only a forceful pace tomorrow may keep him from becoming America's first gold medalist in the event since 1908.

Kenya has two runners in the final, Kipchoge Keino and B. W. Jipcho, and there is some speculation that the Kenyans may send out a tactical "rabbit"—possibly Jipcho—to set a strong, early pace and keep Ryun from laying back until the last lap.

Today, the pace for the first 400 meters was a crawling 1:08. At the 800 mark, it was 2:12.7 and with 300 meters left, the time was 3:11.9.

In typical fashion, Ryun settled in comfortably behind the pack until the last lap when he took the lead on the final turn. He moved into a 5-meter lead over Keino in the stretch and loked over his shoulder twice while coasting past the finish line.

Liquori, however, seemed pressed to finish fourth. The 19-year-old Villanova University sophomore, one of the youngest members of the American track team, made his move early at the end of the backstretch. When he finished in 3:52.1, he looked considerably more fatigued then Ryun.

Von Ruden, a 24-year-old from San Pedro, Calif., finished third in the first heat, which was even slower (1:07.6, 2:14.9, 3:14.6) than Ryun's.

Bodo Tummler of East Germany, who had the fastest 1,500 time in the world this year (3:36.5) led the qualifying and may be Ryun's chief rival tomorrow.

After the hectic world-record pace of yesterday, when Bob Beamon and Lee Evans shattered standards in the long jump and 400-meter run, respectively, one would have expected a let-up today. Not so.

In the opening event of the afternoon, the United States 400-meter relay women's team chopped two-tenths of a second from the world mark with a preliminary time of 43.4 seconds. The Netherlands recorded the same time in the second heat and set up an interesting final tomorrow.

The American men almost botched a berth in tomorrow's final when Charlie Greene and Mel Pender missed running out of the exchange zone by inches in the second heat of the semi-finals.

The United States was clocked in 38.6 seconds, but Jamaica, led by Lennox Miller's strong anchor leg, stole the show with a world-record clocking of 38.3.

How well the United States does tomorrow will depend on flawless baton passes and Greene, who ran the opening leg today, with both thighs heavily bandaged. Jim Hines, the gold medalist in the 100, is the strongest runner in the field, but will be hard-pressed to overtake Miller or Enrique Figuerola of Cuba if the United States trails too deeply into the final 100 meters.

Only an unbelievable comeback by Bob Hayes on the anchor leg at Tokyo saved the United States in 1964. The lone team to beat the Americans in the 400 relay in the last five Olympic Games was Jamaica, in 1952.

The 1,600-meter relay is considered America's safest gold medal bet tomorrow. The first three finishers in yesterday's thrilling 400 meters, Evans, Larry James and Ron Freeman, were joined by Vince Matthews for the 1,600. The foursome ran an Olympic record-tying 3:00.7. All four athletes also wore black socks.

AMERICANS GAIN FOUR GOLD MEDALS

Continued From Page 1

2 minutes .9 seconds, a world record.

The only other American who won a gold medal and broke a record was McKenzie, who is from Woodlands, Calif. He took the 100-meter breast-stroke race in 1:07.7 for an Olympic mark. He also defeated two Soviet swimmers, Vladimir Kosinsky and Nickolay Pankin.

The fourth gold medal went to Miss Henne, who is from Oakland, Calif., in the women's 100-meter free-style, with Sue Pedersen of Sacramento second.

The other American records were established by Miss Meyer in 400-meter free-style swimming and by the 400-meter relay track team of Barbara Ferrell, Mrs. Margaret Bailes, Mildrette Netter and Wyomia Tyus, a world mark.

Miss Meyer, who is 16 years old, and is from Sacramento, broke the mark the first time she entered the water in the trial heats.

Jim Ryun of Kansas also raced into the picture by winning a semi-final heat in the men's 1,500-meter run. He defeated Kipchoge Keino of Kenya, with Martin Liquori of New Jersey fourth.

As the first week of the XIX Olympiad ended, the furor over racial protests appeared to be subsiding.

Negro athletes on the United States team were still generally resentful of the suspension of the two sprinting stars, Tommie Smith and John Carlos. But a cooling trend was reported after Lee Evans, Larry James and Ron Freeman had swept the 400-meter dash Friday and then had made only token gestures of protest from the winners' stand.

Major Events of Day

These were the chief developments of the day's competition, as reported by The New York Times, The Associated Press, United Press International and Reuters:

¶The United States failed to win any of the seven finals on the rowing porgram but did manage to take one silver medal and one bronze. The silver medal went to Lawrence Hough and Anthony Johnson of Arlington, Va., for second place in the pairs without coxswain—an event they had been favored to win.

The bronze went to John Nunn of Cincinnati and William Maher of Detroit for third place in the double sculls.

¶The Soviet Union took its first gold medal in rowing when Anatoly Sass and Alexander Timoshinin won the double sculls. They withstood a formidable finishing sprint by Leondert van Dis and Henrious Droog of the Netherlands.

¶In wrestling, Dick Sanders of Portland, Ore., scored his second victory by pinning Boris Dimovski of Yugoslavia in an Olympic free-style match. The victory put the 23-year-old Sanders ahead in the flyweight division after three rounds with one bye and two falls.

¶Other American wrestlers gained ground, too, evoking reports that the American team might be the "sleeper" of Olympic wrestling this year. Thomas Peckham of Ames, Iowa, advanced in the middle-weight division by scoring a quick fall over Umberto Marcheggiani of Italy. Steven Combs of Deerfield, Ill., won his second straight bout by defeating Suk Suh Young of Korea in the welterweight class. Wayne Wells of Houston, meanwhile, pinned Stefanos Ionnidis of Greece in a lightweight match.

¶Jan Kurka, of Czechoslovakia, won a gold medal for shooting the small-bore rifle, his country's second gold at the Games. Kurka equaled the world record of 598 points of a possible 600. Laezlo Hammerl, of Hungary, was second and Ian Roy Ballinger, of New Zealand, third.

For the first time in the Olympic Games, women joined men on the firing range for the shooting competition.

The pioneers were Eulalia Rolinnka, a 22-year-old student from Poland, and Gladys de Seminario, a 3-year-old dentist from Peru. They took part under a change of rules adopted last year and they immediately proved themselves Annie Oakleys. Both scored 99 points of 100, firing 60 rounds, and both outshot most of the men in the match.

In trapshooting, John Braithwaite, of Britain, picked off the gold medal, equaling the Olympic record with a score of 198. Thomas Carrigus, of Hillsboro, Ore., was second and Kurt Czekalla, of East Germany, third.

The tempering of the racial protests by American athletes, meanwhile, was accompanied by indications the controversy might wind up in court.

E. GERMANS TAKE TWO GOLD MEDALS

W. Germany Eight Is Victor —Americans Take One Silver and a Bronze

Continued From Page 1

winners. In the double sculls, John Nunn and Bill Maher closed strongly but had to settle for third place in back of the Soviet Union and the Netherlands.

That was it: one silver, one bronze. East Germany, with boats in six of the seven finals, wound up with two gold and one silver.

The regatta, staged with ceremonial white-gloved pomp, was watched by a crowd of 20,000 that included the No. 2 admiral in Mexico's five-admiral navy. Smartly garbed sailors stood particularly erect on the red-carpeted dock for the benefit of Vice Admiral G. C. Gabriel Lagos Beltran, "Commandante General de la Armade de Mexico."

A 40-piece band that didn't spare the crashing cymbals and rippling trumpets provided the music for between-races ceremonies.

In the races themselves, the American oarsmen could have used some of the American-made Evinrude outboard motors that powered the officials' launches smoothly and steadily. Most observers had expected the United States to win gold medals in coxless pairs and double sculls and to make a creditable showing in the 8-oared final.

New Zealand in Front

United States eights had won nine of the previous Olympic medals in that glamour division, 11 in all. But Harvard obviously was hurting, even after its strong showing in a repechage last Tuesday. Today it was West Germany safely in front, with fast-closing Australia taking second and the Soviet Union third.

New Zealand's black-jerseyed rowers went to the front at the start of the six-boat final as the shells bucked a head-wind that sent the flags of the 39 nations in Olympic rowing flapping. Czechoslovakia trailed the leaders by less than a second, with Harvard a close third.

As the fractional time for the 500 meters was flashed on the electric scoreboard, apprehension grew among the American rooters. Harvard was doing what it did last Sunday, when it battled for the early lead and then wilted to fifth place in its opening heat.

In the repechage, with Steve Brooks at stroke in place of the ailing Arthur Evans, the Crimson had stayed off the pace, then closed powerfully to get the second-place finish it needed to gain the final.

Fast Pace Hurts Harvard

Today's fast pace apparently took its toll on Harvard, a crew bothered by sore throats, backaches and other ailments since it arrived here. At the halfway mark on this 150-meter-wide, man made canal, Harvard was still third, but West Germany had moved up to second to challenge New Zealand.

The Ratzeburg crew uses a shell some 75 pounds lighter than the others, with odd-numbered and even-numbered oars aligned on the same side in a break with traditional concepts. With 500 meters to go, the Germans took a clear lead as New Zealand faded to an eventual fourth-place finish.

Czechoslovakia, the other early contender, wound up fifth. Moral: At Xochimilco it pays to take your time.

In addition to winning the coxless pairs, East Germany took the gold medal in the race for coxless fours. The other golds went to the Netherlands (single sculls), Italy (coxed pairs), the Soviet Union (double sculls) and New Zealand (coxed fours.

The first jolt to the United States's gold-medal aspirations came when Hough and Johnson failed to hold off East Germany in the race for coxless pairs.

Americans Take Lead

Fourth for the first 1,000 meters, the Americans were soon described by the British translator of the public address call as "fighting very severely." With 300 meters to go, Hough and Johnson had taken the lead.

With 150 meters to go, they were ahead by open water, apparently on their way to the victory most of the experts had predicted.

But the East German combination of Jorg Lucke and Heinz-Jurgen Bothe, digging hard, suddenly loomed as a threat in the final 10 meters the American boat slowed noticeably. The Germans, with momentum on their side, slid past in the last few strokes.

JUDY RANKIN LEADS BY 2 SHOTS WITH 140

WACO, Tex., Oct. 19 (AP)—Judy Rankin took a two-stroke lead today in the $12,500 Quality Chekd golf tournament at the Lake Waco Country Club with a second round two-under-par 70 for 140.

Carol Mann, who led after yesterday's opening round, developed putting problems on the back nine and dropped three strokes back.

Kathy Ahern moved into second place with a 72.

The New York Times
SPORTS
Section 5
Sunday, November 24, 1968

HARVARD TIES YALE, 29-29, ON LAST PLAY OF THE GAME; OHIO STATE AND U.S.C. TRIUMPH

MICHIGAN ROUTED

Buckeyes Win, 50-14, as Otis Stars—Take Big Ten Title

By GEORGE VECSEY
Special to The New York Times

COLUMBUS, Ohio, Nov. 23—An undefeated season, a trip to the Rose Bowl and the Big Ten championship all came to Ohio State today. The Buckeyes defeated Michigan, 50-14, in perhaps the most significant meeting between the old rivals.

Ohio State and Michigan had met 64 times before today, in sunshine and in blizzards, with titles or Rose Bowl trips at stake for one or the other—but everything was at stake today. The winner would be unfeated in the Big Ten and would play Southern California in the Rose Bowl on Jan. 1. Only a loss to California in its nonleague opener had marred Michigan's record.

But Ohio State, with hard running inside and outside, and a defense that forced fumbles and interceptions broke a 14-14 tie with 36 seconds left in the first half, increased the lead to 27-14 after three quarters and then scored three more touchdowns and a field goal in the final period to completely overwhelm the losers.

Otis Scores 4 Times

Jim Otis, a junior fullback, gained 143 yards in 34 carries and scored four touchdowns to further the bond between his father, a doctor in Celina, Ohio, and the Ohio State coach, Woodrow Wilson (Woody) Hayes. Otis's father and the coach were roommates at Denison College.

But Otis was hardly the only star for the Buckeyes before a record crowd of 85,371. Rex Kern, a 180-pound quarterback, ran with the ball and handed it off, the way quarterbacks are supposed to do at Ohio State, and Larry Zelina supplied the powerful outside running threat.

Kern gained 96 yards and Zelina gained 92, often behind the blocking of 245-pound Rufus Mayes, who alternated between right and left tackle.

The defense was just as good. John Tatum, a sophomore cornerback from Passaic, N. J., produced one fumble with a hard tackle, intercepted a pass that bounced away from Gill Harris of Michigan, and chased the Michigan ball-carriers all day. He caught Ron Johnson, the Michigan ace, from behind once, and he wrestled Johnson from running out of bounds at a moment when time was still important.

Johnson, who had set a Big Ten record by gaining 347 yards and scoring five touchdowns against Wisconsin last week,

Continued on Page 3, Column 3

United Press International
JOYRIDE: Coach Woody Hayes of Ohio State is carried off the field by two of his players, Brad Neilsen, left, and James Roman, after undefeated Buckeyes routed Michigan, 50-14.

Columbia Crushes Brown On Domres Aerials, 46-20

By LEONARD KOPPETT

Marty Domres, the 6-foot-5-inch quarterback with an apparently tireless arm, ended his remarkable Columbia career yesterday by completing 30 of 54 passes in leading the Lions to a 46-20 victory over Brown at Baker Field.

The 21-year-old anthropology student, who hopes to play professional football before settling down to the study of other primitive cultures, left in his wake enough statistical accomplishments to keep a computer busy for weeks.

Among the more significant marks were:

¶A three-year career total of 1,133 offensive plays (runs or passes), the most in the history of major college football.

¶Ivy League and Columbia career records for passes thrown and completed, passing yardage and total offense.

¶Single-game Ivy and Columbia records for the same four categories.

¶A career total of 5,345 yards gained by running and passing, the fifth best record in major college annals.

These and other records were products of the most single-minded game plan a Columbia team had ever produced. In the first half, while Columbia built a 26-6 lead after Brown had scored first, Domres threw 26

Continued on Page 4, Column 6

GALLANT FOX WON BY FUNNY FELLOW

Principe Trails Favorite by Neck in $58,500 Handicap —Chompion Is Third

By JOE NICHOLS

Funny Fellow gave his backers a thrill instead of a laugh as he won the $58,500 Gallant Fox Handicap at Aqueduct yesterday. The 3-year-old Wheatley Stable colt was the favorite with the crowd of 42,388 to take the mile-and-five-eighths test, and he did.

His margin, however, was slim and his manner of accomplishing the success was far from easy. He scored by a neck over the King Ranch's Principe at the finish of the grueling event, with C. V. Whitney's Chompion next 1½ lengths behind Principe.

Funny Fellow, who was ridden by Braulio Baeza, had to rally from way back in the field of 10 to achieve his victory, and until the final few yards there was doubt that he could do it.

He engaged the pace-setting Principe in a tense closing duel and for a moment it appeared that Principe, with Mike Venezia riding, would slip back

Continued on Page 9, Column 5

PENN 26-21 VICTOR OVER DARTMOUTH

Quakers, 3d in Ivy League, Register 7th Triumph in Best Year Since 1959

By DEANE McGOWEN
Special to The New York Times

PHILADELPHIA, Nov. 23—Pennsylvania's finest football team since its championship year of 1959 staved off Dartmouth in the closing minutes today to score a 26-21 Ivy League victory before 50,188 fans.

The crowd included 25,000 Cub and Boy Scouts and members of 23 high school bands in the Philadelphia area. The fans gave old Franklin Field a look it has not had since Penn's former days of gridiron power.

But this 1968 team of Coach Bob Odell finished the season with a 7-2, won-lost record, best since 1959, and took third place in the league standing after years of reesidence in the second division.

For Coach Bob Blackman of Dartmouth, the final result gave the Hanover Indians a 4-5 campaign, Blackman's first losing season since he became head coach in 1955. It was also Dartmouth's first finish below the

Continued on Page 4, Column 2

U.C.L.A. DEFEATED

Simpson's 3 Scores Spark Trojans to 28-16 Victory

By WILLIAM N. WALLACE
Special to The New York Times

LOS ANGELES, Nov. 23—Neither smog nor smugness kept O. J. Simpson from his appointed rounds today as Southern California continued its unbeaten season by defeating the University of California, Los Angeles, 28-16, before 75,066 peering spectators in the Coliseum.

The Trojans, two-touchdown favorites against a foe that had lost six of nine games, seemed somnambulant for a great part of the afternoon, but Simpson did his work. Forty times Orange Juice squeezed the football to his chest and ploughed ahead. He gained 200 yards and scored three touchdowns.

Along the way the brilliant senior halfback with the skinny ankles and the wide shoulders set two major college records. With two games to go—against Notre Dame here next Saturday and against Ohio State in the Rose Bowl on New Year's Day—Simpson has carried the ball more times than anyone else in a single season and gained the most yards. His rushes total 334 (an average of 37 a game) and his yards 1,654.

U. C. L. A. Poses Threat

Simpson and his teammates, ranked as the No. 1 team in the nation, were definitely in a game today. U. C. L. A. led twice in the first half, 3-0 and 10-7. In the fourth quarter the Bruins were at the Trojan 1-yard line and behind by only 5 points, 21-16.

But the Trojans have often found themselves in similar straits this season and seem not to care. Their defense dug in; U. C. L. A. failed to score, and it was Simpson once more who bailed out the men of Troy. Starting at his 3, O. J. carried six straight times to the 27. U. S. C. punted, U. C. L. A. threatened again, but Jim Snow, a fine linebacker, intercepted a pass by Jim Nader at Southern Cal's 43 with 1 minute 55 seconds to go.

O. J. Too Successful

Although the smog by then was thick within the stadium and on the screens of millions of television sets, Simpson put on a show. He cut through the gallant and groping Bruin defense for 17 yards and then slashed for 26 to the foe's 4. His last play was a sprint around left end for an easy touchdown, his 22d of the season setting a U.S.C. record.

That five-play drive took only 90 seconds. Its purpose was to kill the clock so that U.C.L.A. would not get the ball back. But O. J. outran the clock and U.C.L.A. got in three more plays before the game ended.

It is amazing that Simpson has survived this season without injury since he has been a target so many times. "He's so fast, they never get a good shot at him; they can't get set," said Frank Gifford, a U.S.C. star of

Continued on Page 12, Column 3

United Press International
Frank Champi, Harvard quarterback, leading the Crimson to their last-minute comeback

Crimson Tallies Twice in 42 Seconds

By STEVE CADY
Special to The New York Times

CAMBRIDGE, Mass., Nov. 23—Unbeaten Harvard turned The Game into The Miracle today by scoring 16 points in the last 42 seconds and gaining a hysterical 29-29 tie with unbeaten Yale.

If the capacity crowd of 40,280 still can't believe what it saw, it could hardly be blamed.

With the ball on the Yale 38, the score 29-13 and the Eli stands chanting "We're No. 1," most of the record corps of 400 reporters in the press box already had their accounts of the game well under way.

Then Frank Champi, a second-string Harvard quarterback who had already thrown one touchdown pass, decided that maybe he, not Brian Dowling of Yale, really was the reincarnation of Frank Merriwell.

Just Enough Just in Time

His 15-yard scoring pass to Bruce Freeman and a 2-point conversion run by Gus Crim put the Crimson within tying range. Then, on the last regular play of the game, after a fumbled onside kickoff had given the Crimson possession, Champi hit Vic Gatto with an 8-yard scoring pass.

After the field had been cleared of demonstrative Harvard fans, the substitute quarterback threw a perfect 2-point conversion strike to Peter Varney.

Out came the paper in the press-box typewriters, out came articles that had begun, "Brian Dowling completed a spectacular Yale football career today by passing for two touchdowns and running for two more . . ."

Dowling, the 21-year-old senior who would have been playing for Ohio State against Michigan today if he had not decided to go to Yale, was spectacular beyond the wildest expectations of his admirers. Calvin Hill, too, had a big day for Yale, for he scored one touchdown and passed the fabled Albie Booth for most points (144) in a Yale career.

Dowling, who closed his career with eight Yale records, completed 13 of his 21 passes for 116 yards. He sent the Elis ahead by running 3 yards on a bootleg play in the first period, and in the second he threw a 3-yard touchdown pass to Hill and a 5-yarder to Del Marting. And after Harvard had scored on a 1-yard plunge by Crim in the third, his 5-yard touchdown run in the fourth looked like the clincher.

Just the Move Just in Time

But it was Champi, completing six of 15 passes for 82 yards and three touchdowns, who sent ancient Harvard Stadium into bedlam and turned a plaintive plea of "10,000 men of Harvard want victory today" into a boisterously understanding, if slightly inaccurate, mass singing of "With Crimson in triumph flashing."

Champi, a 5-foot-11 junior from Everett, Mass., replaced George Lalich late in the first half after Yale had taken a 22-0 lead.

With 44 seconds to go in the half, he managed to put the Crimson on the scoreboard with a 15-yard pass to Freeman, a second-string end. The conversion kick was muffed, and Yale went to the dressing room with a comfortable 22-6 lead.

This was the first time in 59 years the two schools had gone into their traditional showdown undefeated and untied. The un-

Continued on Page 4, Column 2

KANSAS DEFEATS MISSOURI, 21-19

62,200 See Tigers Rally in 4th Period Fall Short

By NEIL AMDUR
Special to The New York Times

COLUMBIA, Mo., Nov. 23—A blocked extra point attempt in the first quarter stood as the significant symbol of victory today in the latest chapter of the Missouri-Kansas football rivalry.

Kansas won, 21-19, before the largest crowd ever to witness a sports event in Memorial Stadium, 62,200. The national corn shucking contest, held on Nov. 4, 1937, in Marshall, Mo., was said to have drawn a crowd of 75,000. But Ran Hanson's reported feat of shucking 21.30 bushels of corn in 80 minutes could hardly have matched the excitement of today's 77th game in this intense and unpredictable series, which for the 17th time was decided by fewer than 4 points.

Kansas, headed for the

Continued on Page 3, Column 7

Best Of All Wins $98,132 Realization

By LOUIS EFFRAT
Special to The New York Times

WESTBURY, L. I., Nov. 23—At no stage during tonight's $98,132.42 Realization Pace was Best Of All anything but the best in the 1 1/16-mile classic before 27,112 fans at Roosevelt Raceway.

In front every step of the race for 4-year-olds, Samuel Huttenbauer's bay son of Good Time and Besta Hanover, lived up to his name and his 3-to-10 billing, beating Shipshape Lobell by 3¾ lengths. Hodgen Special supplemented for $10,000, finished 1½ lengths behind the place horse.

Bob Williams, his driver,

Continued on Page 12, Column 6

OUT IN FRONT: Funny Fellow edging out Principe, right, to win the $58,500 Gallant Fox Handicap at Aqueduct. Braulio Baeza was aboard winner. Chompion was third.

Football Scores

East

Boston College 21	Massachusetts 6
Buffalo 13	Boston Univ. 10
Columbia 46	Brown 20
Dayton 35	Temple 17
Delaware 38	Bucknell 12
Fordham F.C. 49	Catholic U. F.C. 22
Harvard 29	Yale 29
Haverford 17	Swarthmore 6
Holy Cross 27	Connecticut 24
Johns Hopkins 46	W. Maryland 23
Lehigh 21	Lafayette 6
LeMoyne 33	St. John Fisher 0
Moravian 47	Muhlenberg 15
Penn 26	Dartmouth 21
Penn St. 65	Pittsburgh 9
Princeton 41	Cornell 13
Rutgers 55	Colgate 34
Siena F.C. 25	Niagara F.C. 16
Villanova 63	West Chester 3
W. Virginia 23	Syracuse 6
Wittenberg 45	Wagner 7

Freshmen

[illegible]	[illegible]

South

[illegible] 42	[illegible]
[illegible] St. [illegible]	[illegible] 22
Chattanooga 40	[illegible] 7
Delta St. 63	Centenary 0
[illegible] 23	[illegible] 14
[illegible] Tennessee 17	Austin Peay 8

Continued on Page 5, Column 3

PENN STATE ROUTS PITTSBURGH, 65-9

Pittman Paces Nittany Lion Offense With 3 Tallies

By GORDON S. WHITE Jr.
Special to The New York Times

PITTSBURGH, Nov. 23—Joe Paterno, the coach of the undefeated Penn State football team, admonished his second-string quarterback, Mike Cooper, when the player tossed a 19-yard touchdown pass against Pittsburgh today. After all, that aerial in the third quarter raised the count to 58-9 for Penn State and Paterno didn't want to rub it in.

But there was really no holding the Nittany Lions, third ranked and headed for the Orange Bowl. They scored once more and gained their easiest victory in years with a 65-9 decision over the hapless Pittsburgh team. All Paterno could do was send in players who didn't play this season and order a halt to passes.

The score was the highest for the winning team in the 68 football games between the schools.

Penn State proved its point when it scored five touchdowns in the second period, with Charlie Pittman making three of those second-quarter scores. Pittsburgh was helpless then against a team so superior that

Continued on Page 5, Column 6

McCullough Excels As Princeton Scores Over Cornell, 41-13

By LINCOLN A. WERDEN
Special to The New York Times

PRINCETON, N. J., Nov. 23—Brian McCullough, a sophomore tailback, scored three touchdowns as Princeton ended its football season today with a 41-13 victory over Cornell.

The 20-year-old-son of a former Cornell back and assistant coach ran and passed for 202 yards and became the third sophomore in Tiger history to surpass the 1,000-yard mark in a season. As his team clinched fourth place in the Ivy League standing, McCullough brought his gains to 1,100 yards.

Only Royce Flippin in 1953, with 1,103 yards, and Dick Kazmaier in 1949, with 1,155, have been in a class with the speedy 6-foot, 180-pound McCullough from Doylestown, Pa.

Coach Dick Colman alternated McCullough and Scott MacBean, a junior, at the tailback spot in what was a smooth-clicking single-wing offense in this finale for both teams. The Tigers finished with a 4-3 won-lost record in the circuit, while Cornell's mark was 1-6.

Rolling to 217 yards along the ground while the Ithacans chalked only 4 yards rushing in the first half, Princeton had

Continued on Page 4, Column 5

BRUINS TRIUMPH OVER RANGERS, 5-1

Boston Completely Outplays Losers in Rough Contest

Special to The New York Times

BOSTON, Nov. 23 — In an ugly game that didn't do the Rangers, sportsmanship or the bellowing Boston fans proud, the New Yorkers were trounced by the Bruins tonight, 5-1.

Quite simply, it was Boston all the way, hitting both ways, and stopped only by Ed Giacomin, who probably had his finest game of the season despite the goals he allowed.

But with the action were cross-currents, some hidden, in this National Hockey League game reminiscent of early Ranger-Bruin games of last season, when the Bostonians trounced the Rangers in their first five meetings.

Ted Green set the tone for his club (the New Yorkers never followed suit) by slamming Dave Balon to the ice after the Ranger speared Don Awrey. While Balon was down Green hit him, as he had hit Larry Jeffrey a year ago here while Jeffrey's back was turned. Balon went to the penalty box, where the attendant, known to people at the Boston Garden as "Windy," acknowledged the boos and curses leveled at

Continued on Page 7, Column 8

Harvard Fans Roar Over Those Final 42 Seconds

Harvard Rallies to Tie Yale, 29 to 29

Continued From Page 1

expected result left each with a won-lost-tied mark of 8-0-1 and a share of the Ivy League title on league records of 6-0-1.

Harvard, salvaging its first unbeaten season since 1920, has never won the Ivy crown outright.

Today's eagerly awaited clash was the 85th in a series that began in 1875, and the deadlock was the first since 1951.

Ironically, it was Harvard's belatedly inspired offense, not its top-ranked defense, that saved the day and prevented Dowling from completing a perfect 23-0 record at Yale for games in which he played.

Dowling, a 195-pounder from Cleveland, missed 11 games in his four years at Yale because of injuries. Watched by pro scouts today, he has been described as a "born winner."

But he couldn't do anything to stop Harvard today in the last frantic 42 seconds. Like Hill, he was sitting on the bench.

A Boston Massacre Fails

Harvard's defense, stingiest in the nation among major colleges in the matter of points allowed, had been advertised in widely distributed handbills here as being "wanted for massacring Yale's offensive football team on Saturday, Nov. 23, 1968."

But the way Dowling and Hill operated, that billing would hardly have stood up in court. The evidence, particularly in the first half, was somewhat circumstantial.

In the final desperate moments, it was the neglected Harvard offense that turned Yale jubilation into frustration.

And it was a bad break for Yale, which had been getting most of the good ones, that set the stage for the wildest finish in the 63-year history of this concrete horseshoe.

Dowling, in charge as completely as Merriwell, Yale's fictional supedstar, flipped a screen pass from the Harvard 32 to an open receiver, who started toward the goal line. But the receiver fumbled and Steve Ranere of Harvard pounced on the ball at the Crimson 14.

Champi then got the Crimson going on the nine-play, 86-yard drive that resulted in the first of the miracle touchdowns. The big gainer, again reflecting the sudden turn of fortune, came on a fumble by Champi.

Fritz Reed, a junior who had been switched from end to tackle this season, grabbed the ball and took off toward the Yale goal. He might have thought he was an end again and had just caught a pass. Anyway, he rambled from the Yale 32 to the 15.

Nobody paid much attention, because only 42 seconds remained. In the Yale stands across the field from the press box, old Blues and young Blues waved white handkerchiefs and chanted, "We're No. 1" (in the Big Three, in the Ivy League and to some of the more dedicated football buffs, in the nation). Even Percy Haughton Harvard's legendary coach, might not have had the courage to ask a Crimson team to pull one out in that situation.

But Champi must have been listening to Mr. Merriwell. On the next play, he looked for an open receiver, failed to find one, tried to lateral, dodged some white-jerseyed Elis—and threw to his right. Freeman, the sophomore end, snagged the pass on the Yale 3 and went into the end zone.

The 2-point plunge by Crim, a junior fullback, reduced the volume of the "We're No. 1."

Now Harvard tried what it had to try—an onside kick. It worked. Yale fumbled the skittering kick and Bill Kelly, another Harvard sophomore, recovered on the Yale 49.

Champi, apparently trapped on a pass attempt, decided to do what Dowling had been doing with remarkable success most of the chilly, but clear, afternoon. He ran. He went for 14 yards to the Yale 35 and a face-mask penalty against the Elis advanced the ball to the 20.

Time remaining: 32 seconds. Harvard fans: in an uproar. Yale fans: apprehensive.

8 They Want, and 8 They Get

Champi threw two passes into the end-zone. Both were broken up. Champi surprised everybody, including Yale, by sending Crim up the middle on a draw play. It went for 14 yards to the Eli 6.

"We want 8," the Harvards screamed.

Champi, trapped trying to pass, was nailed on the 8 for a 2-yard loss. Four seconds remained, enough for one play.

Trapped again, the amazing substitute played ring-around-a-rosy with Yale's defenders. He tried to lateral, as he had attempted to do on the previous drive. He ran around in circles for what seemed like 10 seconds before spotting Gatto alone in the end zone. Gatto, the senior captain and the first back in Harvard history to rush for 2,000 yards, clutched the ball surely in the most dramatic moment of a dramatic career. Touchdown!

Spectators swarmed onto the field to mob the Harvard captain.

"Quiet, please!" the public-address announcer implored the fans. The field was cleared. Champi fired a bullet pass into Varney's midsection.

Merriwell couldn't have done it any better.

Yale	7	15	0	7—29
Harvard	0	6	7	16—29

Yale—Dowling, 3, run (Bayless, kick).
Yale—Hill, 3, pass from Dowling (Bayless, kick).
Yale—Marting, 5, pass from Dowling (Marting, pass from Dowling).
Harv.—Freeman, 15, pass from Champi (kick failed).
Harv.—Crim, 1, run (Szaro, kick).
Yale—Dowling, 5, run (Bayless, kick).
Harv.—Freeman, 15, pass from Champi (Crim, run).
Harv.—Gatto, 8, pass from Champi (Varney, pass from Champi).
Attendance—40,280.

STATISTICS OF THE GAME

	Yale	Harvard
First downs	19	17
Rushing yardage	251	118
Passing yardage	116	104
Return yardage	60	30
Passes	13-23	8-22
Interceptions by	0	1
Punts	3-36	8-36
Fumbles lost	6	1
Yards penalized	66	30

Columbia Beats Brown, 46-20

Continued From Page 1

times, ran when he had to three times (once for a touchdown) and called only 12 real running plays.

Then, during a scoreless third quarter that led to a Columbia touchdown in the second minute of the fourth, he called for a pass on 21 of 22 plays. Leading to the touchdown, he called 23 pass plays in succession, although on a couple he was unable to throw.

And for all this aerial work, Domres wasn't really sharp until the fourth quarter, and never completely consistent. It was a hard-hitting game, and Brown often covered his receivers and at other times put on a good rush. But sheer quantity wore the visitors down.

When it was over, Columbia had completed its first season under Coach Frank Navarro with two victories and seven defeats—exactly its record in the last two seasons under Coach Buff Donelli.

The Lions did, however, consign Brown to the Ivy cellar with an 0-7 record, while finishing fifth with 2-5, also ahead of Cornell (1-6), their only other victim this season. Brown won two nonleague games, from Rhode Island and Colgate.

The game had lots of action and no suspense once Columbia took command midway through the first quarter. It was further confused by terribly inconsistent officiating that victimized each team in turn. Brown wound up with 196 yards penalized, an Ivy record, of which 125 were on four pass-interference calls.

The penalties and other Brown mistakes set up most of Columbia's scoring opportunities, and the Lions made the most of them early.

Brown marched 70 yards from the opening kickoff, on eight running plays, to take a 6-0 lead on Steve Wormith's plunge from 1 yard out. Columbia was forced to punt, recovered the ball on the Brown 35 when Bill O'Donnell fumbled the kick, and soon settled for a 23-yard field goal by Rick Rose.

Kick Partly Blocked

Late in the period, after an exchange of punts, a kick by Harold Phillips of Brown was partly blocked and went out of bounds on the Brown 28. Domres missed twice, then hit Bill Wazevich for 13 yards and Bob Werner for 15 for the touchdown that put Columbia ahead.

On the next-to-last play of the quarter, pass interference gave Columbia a first down on Brown's 13. On the third play of the next period, Domres sneaked over from the 1.

In the closing minutes of the half, a holding penalty added to a doubtful completion kept a 74-yard drive going, moving the ball to Brown's 18. Domres, unable to find a receiver, circled his left end and scored. Right after that, Jeff Blake blocked a Brown punt on Brown's 7, and on the last play of the half another field goal by Rose made it 26-6.

For all the action in the third quarter, nothing changed. The fourth began with Columbia starting from its 33. Domres, trapped, ran for 6 yards, then hit Ken Alexander for gains of 21 and 39 yards on successive plays. Paul Burlingame ran over from the 3.

About three minutes later, Columbia recovered a fumble on its 48. A pass-interference call put the ball on Brown's 21 and Domres passed to Kevin Brown for the touchdown and a 39-6 lead.

Only then did Brown score again, on a Phillips-to-Jim Lukens pass that covered the last 12 yards of a 71-yard march.

Domres started the next sequence, but retired after Columbia had reached the Brown 21. Robbie Wroe, his sophomore replacement, lobbed a 29-yard pass to Jim O'Connor for the last Columbia touchdown.

Brown came back with its last score on an 18-yard pass from Phillips to Gerald Hart.

PENN TURNS BACK DARTMOUTH, 26-21

Continued From Page 1

top four teams since the league went formal in 1956.

Penn, losing only to Yale and Harvard, built its fine season around Bernie Zbrzeznj, a junior quarterback, and Gerry Santini, one of the league's finest running backs.

And it was their combined talents this sunny afternoon that propelled the Red and Blue to victory. Santini, a 195-pound fullback from Syracuse, N. Y., scored one touchdown and gained a total of 133 yards on 29 carries to become the single-season and career total offensive leader.

Indians Score First

Santini's season rushing mark of 880 yards broke the mark of 830, set by Cabot Knowlton a year ago. Santini's career mark of 1,593 yards broke the former standard of Fred Doelling, 1,558 yards, set from 1957 through 1959.

Zbrzeznj fired one scoring pass to his split end, Pete Blumenthal and finished his day's work with 13 completions in 24 attempts for 176 yards. Blumenthal, and Dave Graham, the tight end, were Zbrzeznj's principal targets in a game that produced long pass completions, a few long runs and missed opportunities by both.

Blumenthal finished with five receptions for 72 yards and Graham caught four for 56 yards.

Dartmouth's strength was its ground game primarily, although Bill Koenig finished with 138 aerial yards on five of 12 attempts.

But Penn's balanced attack of passing and running plus its stronger defensive secondary provided the Quakers with their triumph.

Both teams scored the first times they got possession of the ball, Dartmouth driving 73 yards in 10 plays capped by Clark Beier's 2-yard scoring burst. Blumenthal capped Penn's initial drive of 83 yards in nine plays by his 13-yard reception of Zbrzeznj's pass.

At the half the score was 14-14. The Indians scored from the 4 following a 22-yard interception by Joe Adams. Penn, earlier in the period had missed an Eliot Berry field goal attempt from the 19. But the Quakers tied the score just before the half with another march of 73 yards in 11 plays as Santini registered the touchdown from the 2.

Berry put the Quakers ahead after the intermission with his 11th field goal of the season from the 23-yard line. Beier took the kickoff 55 yards, but Jim Chasey, Dartmouth's sophomore quarterback, could not capitalize on Beier's fine run.

Zbrzeznj then marched the Quakers 80 yards and tossed his second touchdown pass to Ken Dunn from the 9.

Dartmouth was stopped by John Brown's interception and 42-yard runback early in the final period. The Quakers bogged down and Bill Sudhaus punted. Dunn and Bill Burdt tackled Dartmouth's Tom Quinn in the end zone for a safety.

But the Indians were not finished yet. A 58-yard Koenig to Jack Wimsatt pass put Dartmouth on the Penn 20. That was as far as they got. Two rushes and two incomplete passes by Koenig ended Dartmouth's final hope.

PRINCETON TRIMS CORNELL BY 41-13

Continued From Page 1

a 27-7 edge at intermission. A year ago Cornell won by 34 points, 47-13, and until the last minute it seemed that this spread would be duplicated in this 51st meeting in the 77-year-old series.

Cornell, held to a touchdown in the first quarter after Bill Robertson's pass to Dick Furbush was good for 70 yards, put on another bid through the air that brought its second touchdown. Bill Arthur, who replaced Robertson, covered the last 27 yards on a toss to Bill Davies in the fourth period. The Tigers failed to score in the final quarter.

The "M's" in the Princeton backfield had a satisfactory afternoon as Ellis Moore, a fullback, tallied twice, MacBean rushed for 125 yards and completed four passes for 35, while McCullough gained 150 yards on 26 carries and hit on five of eight passes for 52 yards.

His dad, Hal McCullough, was a Cornell star in 1939, '40 and '41 and later coached under Lefty James at Ithaca.

The first period indicated this might be a high-scoring contest as Moore dashed through tackle at 5:05 for the final 24 yards in Princeton's opening drive that covered 75 yards.

Bordley Goes 73 Yards

Robinson Bordley, a 155-pounder, scooted 73 yards on a punt return to make it 13-0 and then came the long Cornell pass that put the ball on the Tiger 3 as Furbush was forced out of bounds by Keith Mauvney. On second down, Chris Ritter plunged from the 3 for the Cornell score.

McCullough, who shuffled in and out of the backfield with MacBean, carried over from the 9 in the 40-yard drive in his team's fourth touchdown drive. After Arnold Holtberg's conversion kick made the score 27-7, Princeton threatened again before the period ended.

"All the News That's Fit to Print"

The New York Times

LATE CITY EDITION

Weather: Sunny, cold today; clear, cold tonight. Fair, warmer tomorrow. Temp. range: today 35-21; Sunday 34-20. Full U.S. report on Page 93.

VOL. CXVIII... No. 40,532 NEW YORK, MONDAY, JANUARY 13, 1969 10 CENTS

JETS UPSET COLTS BY 16-7 FOR TITLE IN THE SUPER BOWL

A.F.L. Club Wins for First Time as Namath Pierces Baltimore Defense

MILLIONS WATCH GAME

Morrall Is Harried Into 3 Interceptions by Rushers —Snell Is Standout

By DAVE ANDERSON
Special to The New York Times

MIAMI, Jan. 12—In a memorable upset that astonished virtually everyone in the football realm, the New York Jets of the American League conquered the Baltimore Colts, the supposedly impregnable National League champions, 16-7, today for the Super Bowl prestige and paycheck.

Joe Namath, the quarterback whose optimism proved to be contagious to his teammates, directed the Jets to a 4-yard touchdown run by Matt Snell, the workhorse fullback, and field goals by Jim Turner from 32, 30 and 9 yards.

Equally important, the Jet defensive unit dominated the Colt offense. Led by Gerry Philbin, the Jet pass-rushers hurried Earl Morrall, selected as the N.F.L.'s most valuable player, into throwing three interceptions in the first half.

Namath Best Quarterback

Midway in the third quarter, Morrall was benched and Johnny Unitas, the sore-armed master, took over at quarterback. With about 3½ minutes remaining in the game, the Colts scored on a 1-yard run by Jerry Hill, but by that time the Jets were in command.

In the A.F.L.'s ninth season, the Jets convinced 75,377 stunned spectators in the Orange Bowl and a television audience of perhaps 60 million that they deserved parity with the best teams in the N.F.L. and that Namath had developed into pro football's best quarterback.

In the two previous Super Bowl games, the Green Bay Packers had maintained the N.F.L. aura of invincibility by decisively defeating their A.F.L. opponents — 35-10 over the Kansas City Chiefs two years ago, 33-14 over the Oakland Raiders a year ago. And the Colts had been expected to continue that supremacy.

In the point-spread type of betting, the Colts were favored by 18 to 20 points. Without a point spread, the Colts were a 7-to-1 choice.

The outcome put the Jets on

Continued on Page 32, Column 5

United Press International

SUPER PASS NEEDED: With Bubba Smith of the Colts about to smother him, Joe Namath of the Jets looks for a receiver before passing in the second quarter of the Super Bowl.

Johnson-to-Nixon Transition Smooth

By MAX FRANKEL
Special to The New York Times

WASHINGTON, Jan. 12—The only shrill sound of transition here is that of the carpenter's drill on Pennsylvania Avenue. To the arriving Republicans, the scaffolding looks like a grandstand for a grand old party and parade. To the departing Democrats, as one of them remarked, it looks a little too much like a gallows.

But the workmen, like many of the other hired professionals here, are not about to draw any distinctions. They have put up a sign begging forgiveness for all the inconvenience by explaining that "we are making way for another great man." And that is certainly the spirit in which Lyndon B. Johnson and Richard M. Nixon have conducted themselves as they move into the 10th and final week of changeover here.

The President, by the testimony of his Administration's successors, has extended every courtesy and has set no booby traps in the files or partisan obstacles in the budgets and regulations that he leaves behind. And the President-elect, by the testimony of the predecessors of the new Administration, has treated their programs and leading personalities with all the respect and cautious deference that they had any right to expect, indeed with much more than they had expected.

At the State Department, William P. Rogers, the next Secretary, is being celebrated as a warm and friendly man who is asking all the right questions while leaping to no conclusions. He is said to be searching carefully for good men who might be asked to stay longer than another transitional month or two.

At the Department of Health, Education and Welfare, Robert H. Finch is said to have brought cheer and hope to fretful officials who only a few weeks ago feared

Continued on Page 14, Column 7

KEY ISSUE SETTLED IN DOCKER STRIKE

A Role for I.L.A. in Filling and Stripping Containers Clears Way for Pacts

By EDWARD A. MORROW

The major hurdle to a settlement of the 23-day-old waterfront strike was cleared late yesterday by negotiators for the New York Shipping Association and the International Longshoremen's Association. They reached an agreement on how container shipments would be handled.

David L. Cole, Presidential mediator, described the development as "the key breakthrough" in the negotiations. He expressed the hope that before the end of the week longshoremen would again be handling the more than 300 ships that have been tied up in Atlantic Coast ports and thus permit a resumption of oceanborne foreign trading.

Mr. Cole announced that the union committee, which represents longshoremen in ports from Maine to Virginia, had accepted unanimously a new clause in the master contract covering container shipments.

Union negotiators from other cities immediately started returning to their home ports to negotiate minor clauses, which are not covered in the master agreement.

The projected three-year contract provides a $1.60-an-hour package for wages, pensions, welfare, vacations and holidays.

It is the costliest package ever offered by the association, which represents 140 New York employers. Over the three-year period a longshoreman's wages will rise by 98 cents to $4.60 a hour.

Although this increase has

Continued on Page 93, Column 4

Negroes at Brandeis Seek New Talk on 'Racist' Issue

By JOHN H. FENTON
Special to The New York Times

WALTHAM, Mass., Jan. 12—A narrow strip of campus between the communications center and the administration building at Brandeis University has become an amphitheater for an academic drama of turmoil among students.

The production might be entitled "Truth Even Unto Its Innermost Parts," for that is the motto of the university, which has nurtured liberal inquiry in the 20 years it has been here.

The central figure is Morris Berthold Abram, president of Brandeis since Sept. 1. Mr. Abram, one of a new breed of university presidents, from the field of law, is undergoing an agonizing time of testing.

In the face of a series of tense situations in the last few days, Mr. Abram has impressed observers with his flexibility, his endurance and his ability to keep the rest of the university functioning smoothly.

This was the fifth day of a siege of Ford Hall, the communications center, since it was seized at 2 P.M. last Wednesday by 15 Negroes.

The day opened with the Negroes suggesting another meeting with Mr. Abram because of "the way that this situation is escalating."

Both sides exchanged messages seeking an agreement on ground rules. Meantime, the student council, an elective group, unanimously adopted a resolution opposing "any call for a student strike at this time." Such a move had been discussed by the white students. Ford Hall is a rather non-

Continued on Page 18, Column 4

NEWS INDEX

The News Summary and Index appears on Page 2; Regular financial news is on Pages 37 to 44.

Cannons Identified As Captain Cook's Found Off Australia

By ROBERT D. McFADDEN

On Aug. 26, 1768, Capt. James Cook, in command of H.M.S. Endeavour, set sail from Plymouth, England, on his first circumnavigation of the world, with a royal commission to make astronomical and botanical observations of the South Seas.

The Endeavour, an armed transport of 400 tons with half a dozen naturalists and a crew of 30 aboard, rounded Cape Horn, touched at Tahiti and New Zealand and reached Australia without serious incident.

But on the night of June 10, 1770, while sailing up the Great Barrier Reef that shelters Australia's east coast, the ship ran onto jagged coral, settling with a gaping hole in her hull. [illegible] the vessel, Captain [illegible] ordered her armament, [illegible] cannons, hurled overboard.

[illegible] next year the Endeavour, [illegible] and limping, reached [illegible] — and great acclaim.

Continued on Page 10, Column 3

U.S. Bids City Clean Up Poverty Agency; Ginsberg Defends It, Asks More Power

H.R.A. Gets 6 Months to Act or Federal Trustee Will Take Over

This report on the Human Resources Administration was prepared by Richard Reeves, Barnard L. Collier, Richard Phalon and Richard Severo.

The Federal Government has warned the city that a trustee will be appointed to manage local antipoverty programs if corruption and administrative chaos in the city's Human Resources Administration are not cleaned up within the next six months.

This "last chance" deadline, it was learned yesterday was given to the superagency's Administrator, Mitchell I. Ginsberg, two weeks ago by Assistant Secretary of Labor Stanley H. Ruttenberg.

The Labor Department's first choice for a trustee was former Associate Justice Arthur J. Goldberg, who said he could not take the assignment but would help select another man.

The trusteeship proposal, which was bitterly protested by city officials, was made last month after consultation with representatives of the incoming Administration of Richard M. Nixon, according to Mr. Ruttenberg, who will leave office next week.

Mr. Ruttenberg said in an interview yesterday that the Labor Department and the Office

The New York Times

Stanley H. Ruttenberg

of Economic Opportunity — two Federal agencies that largely finance local poverty programs — began discussing the idea of placing a trustee over some H.R.A. operations as early as last May.

The idea was officially presented to Mr. Ginsberg and representatives of Mayor Lindsay last month, but, according to Mr. Ruttenberg, Mr. Ginsberg said trusteeship would be "the last blow" for his troubled agency.

After a month of negotiation, the Labor Department agreed last Dec. 31 not to install a trustee over the Mayor's ob-

Continued on Page 23, Column 1

Official Denies Cheating of the Poor Reached Cost of Millions

Transcript of Ginsberg news conference is on Page 22.

By MARTIN TOLCHIN

Mitchell I. Ginsberg, the city's Human Resources Administrator, defended his agency yesterday against disclosures in The New York Times of corruption and inefficiency that have cheated the city's poor of uncounted millions of dollars.

"The overwhelming proportion of funds—from both Federal and city sources — have been expended for their designated purpose," Mr. Ginsberg, visibly upset, told a news conference at his office at 40 Worth Street.

Mr. Ginsberg, who charged The Times with "serious distortions," conceded during a question-and-answer period, however, that the multimillion-dollar agency had lacked "appropriate management systems." He commented: "We often have had to operate like a corner candy store."

The Times article brought demands for reform from some of the city's leading Democrats.

A proposal that the H.R.A. be placed in "receivership" was made by both City Council President Francis X. Smith

Continued on Page 22, Column 1

Western Envoys in Beirut See Need for U.S. Action

By DANA ADAMS SCHMIDT
Special to The New York Times

BEIRUT, Lebanon, Jan. 12—Top-ranking Western diplomats here are now satisfied in their view that unless and until the United States makes its weight felt in the Middle East there will be continuing danger of war.

The diplomats are telling their governments that it is essential for the United States to come to an understanding with the Soviet Union on terms that could lead to a four-power approach to the Arab-Israeli conflict. They fear that another incident like the Israeli reprisal raid on the Beirut airport Dec. 28 could touch off major fighting.

These diplomats judge the moment favorable because, according to diplomatic information, the Russians seem willing to make some concessions at this time to the West. Moscow is willing to do so, it is said, because it wants to avoid the confrontation between East and West that might result from a renewal of active war between Israel and the Arabs.

[A statement issued in Cairo by Al Fatah, the Arab guerrilla organization, reiterated the group's rejection of any political settlement in the Middle East.]

The latest Soviet plan, in essence, suggests collaboration with the United States in achieving a "just and lasting peace" in the Middle East through Dr. Gunnar V. Jarring of Sweden, the United Nations special envoy, in accordance with the Security Council resolution of Nov. 22, 1967.

The Russians envision initial Israeli withdrawal from all Arab areas occupied during the 1967 war, a United Nations buffer force and a document by Israel and the Arab nations ending their state of war, which has existed since 1948.

Because of the present Soviet attitude the diplomats think it would be worthwhile for Washington to give renewed consid-

Continued on Page 8, Column 3

FOE'S COMMANDOS RAID CANTHO BASE

8 Americans Die in Attack on U.S. Airfield in Delta—3 Copters Destroyed

By United Press International

SAIGON, South Vietnam, Monday, Jan. 13—Enemy commandos burst through the barbed-wire defenses of the Cantho air base before dawn today, hurling explosive satchel charges into 18 helicopters. Eight Americans were killed and 15 wounded.

First reports said the enemy wrecked three helicopters and damaged the 15 others. Military spokesman said American defenders drove them out of the base within minutes, but at high cost. The air base, 75 miles southwest of Saigon, is the largest in the Mekong Delta.

Bodies of five enemy soldiers were found after the base was cleared. The raiders melted into the countryside after the

Continued on Page 12, Column 3

VANCE REBUFFED IN NEW MEETING WITH HANOI AIDES

Allies' Two Proposals on the Design of a Conference Table Are Assailed

U.S. REQUESTED SESSION

Another Parley Before Shift of Administration Jan. 20 Is Believed Doubtful

By PAUL HOFMANN
Special to The New York Times

PARIS, Jan. 12—United States and North Vietnamese negotiators met this afternoon for the first time in 10 days in a futile effort to break the procedural impasse that has been delaying broadened Vietnam talks here.

In a 2-hour-and-15-minute private session at a secret site in the southern suburbs of Paris, the American side submitted new proposals on the design of the conference table and the order of speakers at proposed four-way negotiations. North Vietnamese representatives would not accept the proposals.

The meeting was called by the United States delegation in what seemed to be a last-minute effort by the Johnson Administration, which will be replaced Jan. 20, to end a 10-week deadlock in the talks.

Another Session Doubted

The deputy heads of the United States and the North Vietnamese delegations, Cyrus R. Vance and Colonel Ha Van Lau, were the ranking participants at today's session. They left with the understanding that they would meet again at the request of either side. No new date was set.

An American official declined to speculate later whether another session could be arranged during the Johnson Administration's final week. Privately, United States delegation sources said it was very unlikely.

The American official stressed that the latest proposals, submitted in two packages, had not been formally rejected by Colonel Lau. The official said that the North Vietnamese negotiator had made it plain, however, that his side could not accept the new suggestions.

Mr. Vance was said to have urged the North Vietnamese to reconsider the latest allied proposals.

Table's Sides at Issue

The North Vietnamese delegation asserted tonight in a statement that the United States had not submitted new proposals, but merely reformulated its own and South Vietnam's "absurd" views. The statement quoted Colonel Lau as having deplored what he termed United States obstinacy in refusing to accept North Vietnam's "reasonable and logical" proposals.

The impasse mainly revolves around the design of the table, with the United States and South Vietnam favoring one

Continued on Page 11, Column 1

Government to Grow Marijuana for Tests

By SANDRA BLAKESLEE

The Federal Government has decided to grow its own marijuana—at a top-secret site.

The reason: It needs pure marijuana for experimental purposes, and confiscated supplies vary greatly in quality, potency and toxicity.

Also, the demand for high-quality marijuana by other legitimate research groups throughout the country cannot be met by what Government agents seize in raids alone.

To meet the problem, the National Institute of Mental Health, a research arm of the Government, announced yesterday the award of seven contracts to research laboratories to produce high-quality marijuana and pure synthetic THC over the next year. The con-

Continued on Page 76, Column 2

Violence Erupts as 5,000 March in London to Protest Racial Bias

United Press International

Police resisting the rush of a crowd of youths trying to take over Rhodesia House, far right, in London yesterday

By THOMAS A. JOHNSON
Special to The New York Times

LONDON, Jan. 12—Violence flared in central London today after about 5,000 people marched to dramatize charges of racial discrimination in Britain against non-white immigrants. Hundreds of primarily youthful demonstrators engaged in shoving contests with policemen in Trafalgar Square and on nearby streets. There were frequent fist fights, and here and there picket signs were used as weapons. Bottles and coins were also tossed at the police. Thirty-one persons had been arrested by 8 P.M. Seventeen persons were injured, but none were seriously hurt. The demonstration, called a "march for dignity," was sponsored by the Black Peoples' Alliance, an amalgamation of militant Negro and Asian immigrant organizations. The alliance was formed last April in

Continued on Page 3, Column 1

Ewbank Says Jets Made No Errors in Beating Colts

The New York Times (by Meyer Liebowitz)

HANDOFF: Joe Namath, giving the ball to Matt Snell, left foreground, his fullback, for a short gain on a first-half play. Snell also scored the Jets' only touchdown of the game.

JETS UPSET COLTS BY 16-7 FOR TITLE

Continued From Page 1, Col. 1

a plateau with such other famous upsetmakers in sports as Cassius Clay, knocking out Sonny Liston for the world heavyweight title as an 8-1 underdog in 1964, and the racehorse, Upset, defeating Man o' War in 1919 for that thoroughbred's only loss.

But the upset did not surprise Namath, the Jets' positive thinker. Despite his reputation as a playboy, he also is a serious student of football. As he observed the Colts in game films during the week, he noticed weaknesses in their vaunted zone pass-defense that he hoped to exploit. It is one thing to see the weaknesses as the film is flashed on a hotel-room wall, it is quite another to penetrate that defense on the field.

Namath accomplished it with his lariat arm, a scientific split end named George Sauer Jr. and a fullback, Snell, whose power running established the ground game that enabled the celebrated $400,000 quarterback to keep the Colts uncertain as to what play he would call next.

Namath, Sauer and Snell accumulated impressive statistics, but the members of the Jets' offensive line—Winston Hill, Bob Talamini, John Schmitt, Randy Rasmussen and Dave Herman—provided the blocking that produced those statistics.

Protected from the vaunted Colt pass-rush as if he were a rare jewel, Namath completed 17 of 28 passes for 206 yards. Sauer caught eight for 133 yards, a significant statistic because the Jets' other wide receiver, Don Maynard, was shut out. Snell rushed for 121 yards and caught four passes for 40 more.

Jets Keep Poise

In earning $15,000 apiece, double the reward for each Colt, the Jets kept their poise in moments of crisis as demanded by their coach, Weeb Ewbank, once dismissed by Baltimore.

Late in the scoreless first quarter, Sauer fumbled a sideline pass when tackled by Lenny Lyles, and the loose ball was pounced on by Ron Porter, a Colt linebacker, at the Jets' 12-yard line. On third down at the 6, Morrall's pass bounced high into the air off his intended receiver, Tom Mitchell. Randy Beverly, the Jets' cornerback who had been outmaneuvered by Mitchell, intercepted. Touchback. Jet ball.

Starting at the Jets' 20, Namath used Snell on four consecutive running plays aimed at the Colts' right side. Ordell Braase, the end, and Don Shinnick, the linebacker, were victimized for a total of 26 yards, providing Namath with a first down at the Jets' 46, good field position.

After an incompletion and a short pass to Bill Mathis, a third-and-4 situation confronted Namath, but he drilled a 14-yard pass to Sauer, who had fooled Lyles, for the first down.

Another pass to Sauer moved the Jets to the Colts' 23. Then a 2-yard gain by Emerson Boozer, a 12-yard pass to Snell, a 5-yard gain by Snell and Snell's sweep produced a touchdown.

Sample Makes Interception

Not long after that, Tom Matte, who ran for a total of 116 yards, put the Colts at the Jets' 16 with a 58-yard dash down the right sideline.

On first down, Morrall threw toward Willie Richardson, his flanker, but Johnny Sample, once a Colt, zipped across to intercept the pass at the 2.

In the final minute of the first half, Morrall committed his worst mistake. At the Jets' 45, he handed off to Matte, who turned and tossed a backward pass to Morrall as the split end, Jimmy Orr, drifted beyond Beverly toward the end zone.

Orr was alone near the goal-line, with no Jet within 20 yards, but Morrall apparently never saw him. He threw toward Jerry Hill, his fullback, who was in front of the goal posts, but Jim Hudson, the Jets' strongside safetyman, intercepted at the 12, assuring a 7-0 half-time lead.

Another mistake, a fumble by Matte on the first play from scrimmage of the second half, turned the ball over to the Jets at the Colts' 33, in position for Turner's first field goal.

After three unsuccessful passes by Morrall on the next Colt series, Namath hit Sauer for two 14-yard gains to set up Turner's second field goal for a 13-0 lead with about 4 minutes remaining in the third quarter.

When the Colt offensive took the field, Unitas had replaced Morrall. Unable to throw long because of his tender right elbow, Unitas misfired twice on short passes to Matte and Orr.

When the third quarter ended, Namath was guiding the team to Turner's final field goal and the Colts had been limited to only eight plays, including two punts, in that period.

But early in the final quarter, Matte and Hill moved the Colts to the Jets' 25, but Unitas was unable to deliver. After overthrowing Richardson, the 35-year-old quarterback found Orr in the end zone, but the pass was intercepted by Beverly.

In his next opportunity, Unitas generated an 80-yard drive, sparked by a fourth-down pass to Orr from his own 20.

After the Colts avoided a shutout on Hill's touchdown, they recovered an onside kickoff at the Jets' 44. When Unitas hit Orr and Richardson to move the ball to the 24, the Jets began to wonder if Unitas would work the magic he had performed for so many years when his right arm was healthy.

But again, the Jet pass-defenders, not the Colt pass-receivers, made the big play. Sample tipped away a pass intended for Richardson. After the Jet rush harassed Unitas into throwing short to Orr and then too longs a fourth-down pass intended for Orr was batted beyond his reach by Larry Grantham, the linebacker.

After that, Snell carried on six consecutive plays, providing a needed first down that enabled the Jets to exhaust the final 2 minutes 21 seconds and frustrate the Colts.

Namath was awarded a Dodge Charger by Sport magazine as the game's most valuable player, but Snell appeared to be equally deserving. So did all the offensive linemen. In the most significant victory in A.F.L. history, the battle had been won where it usually is in football—in the trenches.

Super Bowl Scoring

NEW YORK JETS (16)

Ends—Sauer, Maynard, Lammons, B. Turner, Rademacher, Philbin, Biggs.
Tackles—Hill, Herman, Richardson, Walton, Rochester, Elliott, McAdams.
Guards—Talamini, Rasmussen.
Centers—Schmitt, Crane.
Linebackers — Baker, Atkinson, Grantham, Neidert.
Quarterbacks—Namath, Parilli.
Offensive Backs—Boozer, Snell, Mathis, Smolinski.
Defensive Backs—Sample, Beverly, Hudson, Baird, Christy, D'Amato, Richard, Dockery.
Kickers—J. Turner, Curley Johnson.

BALTIMORE COLTS (7)

Ends—Orr, Richardson, Mackey, Perkins, Hawkins, Mitchell, Bubba Smith, Braase, Michaels.
Tackles—Vogel, Ball, J. Williams, Billy Ray Smith, Miller, Hilton.
Guards—Ressler, Sullivan, Cornelius Johnson.
Centers—Curry, Szymanski.
Linebackers—Curtis, Gaubatz, Shinnick, S. Williams, Porter.
Quarterbacks—Morrall, Unitas.
Offensive Backs—Matte, Hill, Brown, Pearson, Cole.
Defensive Backs—Boyd, Lyles, Logan, Volk, Stukes, Austin.
Kicker—Lee.

New York Jets	0	7	6	3—16
Baltimore Colts	0	0	0	7— 7

N. Y.—Snell, 4, run (Turner, kick).
N. Y.—FG, Turner, 32.
N. Y.—FG, Turner, 30.
N. Y.—FG, Turner, 9.
Balt.—Hill, 1, run (Michaels, kick).
Attendance—75,377.

STATISTICS OF THE GAME

	Jets	Colts
First downs	21	18
Rushing yardage	142	143
Passing yardage	206	181
Return yardage	34	139
Passes	17-29	17-41
Interceptions by	4	0
Punts	4-39	3-44
Fumbles lost	1	1
Yards penalized	28	23

FEAT ACCLAIMED AS TEAM VICTORY

Players Label Themselves as "the Greatest" and Praise Each Other

By FRANK LITSKY
Special to The New York Times

MIAMI, Jan. 12—In case anyone watching in person or on television failed to get the message, the New York Jets left no doubt how they felt after beating the Baltimore Colts in today's Super Bowl game.

"We are a great team and this is the start of a new era," a happy Coach Weeb Ewbank said. "Ball control did it. We didn't make any errors. Joe Namath called a great game. He was fabulous, and he had great pass protection."

Johnny Sample, the Jet cornerback, defensive captain and No. 1 cheerleader, agreed.

"We're the greatest team," said Sample. "We put the Baltimore offense and defense to shame. When Earl Morrall released the ball, our defensive backs were racing to the ball. We read him pretty good. And I'll tell you, I feel pretty good. I've been thinking about this game for three years — every day."

Many Heroes on Club

Sample, with one interception and fine coverage of the dangerous Willie Richardson, was one of the many Jet heroes. So was Namath and Randy Beverly and Gerry Philbin and Matt Snell and George Sauer and so many others. The victory, as so many Jets pointed out, belonged to them all.

"It was execution," said assistant coach Walt Michaels, the architect of the Jet defense, "and great play by our safetymen. And I can't say enough about our linebackers. We sacrificed by letting the linebackers help out against passes. We didn't think their runners could go all the way. And they didn't."

"It was the offensive line with that straight-ahead blocking," said Snell, who had a big day at fullback.

"It was our defense," said Emerson Boozer, the halfback. "Our defense broke their backs."

"How about our defensive backs?" said John Elliott, the defensive tackle. "They played one hell of a game. I want to know who's got the No. 1 defense now."

Ewbank, too, had great praise for the defensive unit. "When our defense had to come through, it did, with the big play, with interceptions," he said.

Jets Are Jubilant

The Jets were not exactly humble in victory, and they didn't feel they had to be.

"We taught them out there," said Larry Grantham, who has been with the Jets since 1960, when they were the laughable Titans. "Now we're the first American League team to be taken seriously."

"I just hope," said Philbin, "this changes some people's minds about our league."

"It was a long time coming," said Namath, "a long time coming for the whole league."

Namath has a flair for the dramatic off the field, too. The team voted him the game ball. He promptly said he would give it to the American League. Sport magazine said it would give him a Dodge Charger, its prize for the game's outstanding player.

"Is that one of those things I have to give back after a year?" Namath asked.

"You keep it forever," he was told.

"That's more like it," Namath said.

Namath sat in the trainer's room cutting the yards of tape off his legs and knees. His wet hair flopping over his face, the wisecrackers coming fast and easily, he was as usual, king of the hill.

"Are you more exhilarated than usual after winning a big game?" he was asked.

"That's a big word," he said. "They didn't teach us that in school."

Did his right thumb, injured in the third quarter, hurt?

"Nothing hurts now," he said.

Was he really so confident of victory when he "promised" earlier in the week that the Jets would win?

"I always had confidence we would win," he said. "But I didn't know what to expect. But I had a good time. When you go out and play football, you're supposed to have a good time. When you're losing, you're not having a good time, so we went out and won."

Nearby, Babe Parilli, Namath's seldom-used substitute, raved about the job Namath had done.

"He caught them off balance," said Parilli, who has been a pro quarterback for 15 years. "He called the right play at the right time. He read the safety blitz, and he read their pass coverage. What else is there?"

John Namath, Joe's father, said he wasn't excited because "I was sure they would win."

A. M. Mathis, the father of Bill Mathis, the Jet halfback, said he tried to stay calm because of his heart condition, but his throat was sore from hollering.

Unexpectedly, there was little hollering in the Jet dressing room. The players had believed they would win, so they were not as surprised as almost everyone else. "We didn't make us three-touchdown underdogs," said Philbin.

Through it all, the Jets were looking forward to their winners' checks of $15,000 a man. The favored Baltimore players wound up with only $7,500 as the losers' shares.

United Press International

TO THE GROUND: Fred Miller of Colts leaps on Pete Lammons of Jets, who caught an 11-yard pass from Joe Namath in third quarter. Lenny Lyles of Baltimore was other tackler.

DEFENSE ACCEPTS BLAME FOR LOSS

Rushers 'Couldn't Quite' Get to Passer—'Didn't Make Big Plays,' Says Shula

By WILLIAM N. WALLACE
Special to The New York Times

MIAMI, Jan. 12—The many moods of the Baltimore Colts, following their loss today to the Jets in the Super Bowl, were in this order:

Disgust at themselves for having played a disappointing game, sky-high praise for Joe Namath and begrudging admiration for the other Jets.

Namath was the man the Colts remembered best. Said Billy Ray Smith, who before the game had suggested that Joe Willie might learn a little humility:

"He did it all. He threw the ball short a little. He threw the ball long a little. He ran the ball a little. He had it all going and so they won. I just couldn't quite get to him."

Smith was sitting half-undressed on a locker bench, perspiration on his upper body and dirt around his eyes. Ordell Braase, who like Smith could not get to Namath, said, "He was everything we expected."

Blitz Fails in 3d Period

Don Shula, the Baltimore coach, echoed his two pass-rushers.

"He was all we had heard," he said. "A fine football player."

"The story of the game was simple," added Shula. "We didn't do it and they did. We had all the opportunities, especially in the first half. We didn't make the big plays we've made all season. We had a lot of dropped balls. We just didn't do it. They deserved it.

"We'll have to be men enough to do it."

In Shula's estimation Namath clearly won the battle of the blitz. The Colts, beginning in the second period, began to blitz Namath, charging with one of the safetymen, Rick Volk or Jerry Logan, in combination with Dennis Gaubatz or Mike Curtis of the linebacking corps. It was no good.

"He beat us," said Shula. "He beat our blitz three or four times and we beat him only once."

Namath beat the blitz by unloading the ball quickly, usually to George Sauer, before the attackers could reach him.

Smith, at 33 years of age an old-timer on the highly praised Colt defense, blamed that unit for the defeat.

"It was us," he said. "We let down our teammates and the entire National Football League. My pride is bent."

Bill Curry, the center, said the Colts in their league had played "10 or 12 teams as good as the Jets."

"I don't mean that as sour grapes," he said, "but we didn't play our game. The turnovers were the story of the game. We had them. They didn't."

Curry's reference was to the four interceptions of Baltimore passes.

A downcast Earl Morrall repented for a missed opportunity at the end of the second period.

On a "flea flicker" play, in which he took a lateral pass from Tom Matte, then threw deep downfield, Morrall picked the wrong receiver, Jerry Hill.

Jim Hudson of the Jets stepped in front of Hill and intercepted the pass. Jimmy Orr, the Colt split end, had been wide open elsewhere.

Said Morrall: "The way I caught the ball from Matte, I was turned to the right and didn't see Orr."

Earlier in the second quarter, Morrall's pass bounced off Tom Mitchell's shoulder into the hands of Randy Beverly of the Jets for an end-zone interception. It would have been a tough touchdown catch for Mitchell.

"I think a linebacker tipped the ball and I think I threw it too hard," said Morrall.

John Unitas was not as visibly upset as Morrall. Said Unitas:

"I've been in football a long time. You always hate to lose. But a football player can't feel sorry for himself."

Shula said he had planned at half-time, after the Colts had gained only 71 yards passing and three of Morrall's passes had been intercepted, to replace Morrall with Unitas following one series of downs in the third period.

"I wanted to try to get something going," he said, "but we had a fumble (by Matte) on the first series and I kept Earl in."

In action for the final 19 minutes, Unitas completed 11 of 24 passes, but only two were beyond 20 yards and tested the power of his ailing arm. Neither was complete. The first went toward Jim Orr and was intercepted in the end zone by the ubiquitous Randy Beverly. The second, Unitas's final pass of the game, was overthrown to Orr in the end zone on fourth down.

"That's what happens when you don't practice much," said Unitas.

GAME'S STAR FELT RELAXED AT START

Namath Told A Teammate Arm Was 'Real Loose'

MIAMI, Jan. 12 (UPI)—Some of the New York Jets were a bit edgy going into their showdown today with the highly touted Baltimore Colts in the Super Bowl, but not Joe Namath.

Before trotting out on the field for the start of the game, he turned to one of his teammates and said: "I feel loose, real loose. My arm is so loose I think it's gonna fall off."

A pre-game ceremony was capped by the appearance of the three astronauts who had circumnavigated the moon. The trio — Capt. James A. Lovell, Col. Frank Borman and Lieut. Col. William A. Anders — recited over the loud-speaker system the Pledge of Allegiance. Their appearance must have further inspired Namath to put the Jets into orbit.

Probably no one on the Jets savored their 16-7 upset victory more than Larry Grantham, the weary 30-year-old linebacker who first signed nine years ago with the club when it was known as the New York Titans and something of a laughing stock throughout the A.F.L.

"Not in my wildest dreams did I ever imagine anything like this happening to me when I signed with the Titans in 1960," said Grantham. "We didn't know of any Joe Namath then, but things got different when he came along. I don't see how any team can defense against him. He hits you where it hurts."

Another happy member of the Jets was Walt Michaels, their defensive backfield coach. Michaels's brother, Lou is the Colts' place-kicking specialist and was involved in a near-fight in a Fort Lauderdale restaurant a week ago. But Walt smilingly had no comment about that incident.

"It was simply two hard-headed Pennsylvania ballplayers getting together,'" Michaels grinned, referring to Namath and his brother.

Sports of The Times

Broadway Joe Is No. 1

By ROBERT LIPSYTE

MIAMI, Jan. 12—Five years ago, a few miles from here, a young, loud-mouthed, confident charmer named Cassius Clay prepared to meet Sonny Liston for the world boxing championship. Hardly anyone would bet on the fight because Clay was at least a 7-1 underdog, and there was some harsh talk about the greediness of a sport and of a television industry that would allow such a good-natured kid to risk his life against the most powerful puncher of all time.

Sonny the Bear would let Cassius hit him a few times, a rubber ball against a brick wall, then beat the boy blue.

People were not terribly upset by this prospect because Liston, ex-convict, labor goon, intimidator, represented the kind of solid, silent brutality they had come to expect, even demand, in a champion. Clay was a pop-off, he was gay, he was magical, he went his way and told the truth. He said he was sorry for Liston, built up so big he would fall a long way and he said he was going to win. Incredibly, he did.

And last Thursday night, with a double scotch in his hand, Joe Namath of the Jets said: "We'll win. I guarantee it." It was neither the first nor the last time he promised victory, provoking laughter from fans of the Baltimore Colts, of the National Football League, of the Columbia Broadcasting System, of history, nostalgia, propaganda, logic and from the gamblers who made the Colts at least a 16-point favorite.

Clay told the world how he would win: he was going to jab and move and cut the beast to pieces. Namath said he was going to establish a running game so the Colts could not concentrate entirely on stopping his vaunted "bomb," the game-busting pass to his wide receivers, George Sauer and. especially, Don Maynard. Clay warned the world not to sell his defenses short, Liston would never touch him. And Namath said that the Colts' second-string quarterback, Earl Morrall, was not the best the Jets had faced, and would not do well against their defense.

Packaging the Smith Brothers

Ultimately, the talk had to stop, and it did on a mild and breezy afternoon in the Orange Bowl. The Jets won the toss and elected to receive. and Namath ran his fullback, Matt Snell, twice into the right side of the Colts line. Snell gained 3 yards the first time, 9 the second, and knocked Rick Volk, the right safety, rubber-legged. Namath had established his running game.

Morrall did little against the Jets' defense, as predicted. A journeyman quarterback, thrust into fame by an injury to Johnny Unitas, long considered the greatest, Morrall did not seem able to get the grinding, inexorable Baltimore touchdown machine moving. As the game moved into the second quarter, scoreless, the air began to visibly seep out of the Baltimore balloon. The Baltimore defense, including the Smiths, Bubba and Billy Ray, who are supposed to rise out of the turf on game days to swallow quarterbacks whole, was being contained. And Snell, playing the greatest game of his pro career, was bucking through that right side.

After the big boxing match, with Liston hurt and sitting on his stool, people said the Bear was a quitter. No one will say the Colts quit, but there came a time when the snap and crack were gone from their game. It may have happened sometime in that second quarter when Namath, in the midst of an 80-yard drive, gave Snell a breather and went to his receivers.

He passed to Sauer for 14 yards, and Lenny Lyles, the Colts' right cornerback, brought Sauer down. Namath, on the very next play, went to Sauer again, and Lyles took a chance. He flashed in front of Sauer in a wild attempt to pick the pass out of the air. He missed. Volk brought Sauer down with only a 1-yard gain, but it was another first down, and it was only a few minutes before Snell ran through that Colts' right side again and gave the Jets a lead they never lost.

Who Is the Greatest?

The game was not over, but it sometimes threatened to disintegrate into the kind of taunting with which Clay maddened Liston. Johnny Sample, the Jets' cornerback, intercepted a pass in that second quarter and tapped the intended receiver, Willie Richardson, on the head with it. No such nonsense for Namath, cool and professional and well-protected. It was deep into the third period before Bubba Smith finally got through. But it hardly mattered by then.

And then, with the score 13-0, John Unitas went into the game. If anyone in the world could turn it around and stop the upstarts and push Broadway Joe down for another few years, it would be Johnny U., even with that swinging chain of a right arm now a rag.

But the kid hadn't lied. Johnny U., his passes wobbly and short, managed to get the Colts moving and even onto the scoreboard. And with about 3 minutes left, trailing, 16-7, the Colts recovered their onside kick and threatened again. But time was against them, and Namath jogged off the field, his right forefinger waggling over head. The Jets were world champions, and he was No. 1.

In the locker room, like Clay that magical night, Namath hectored a press corps that had predicted him a loud-mouthed loser.

Those men of little faith could now eat their words, as they were told to five years ago. Or they could go across town and eat hamburgers. In the great new athletic rendition of the American dream, both Namath and Clay have their fast-food shops in Miami. Namath has his Broadway Joe's, and, not too far away, Clay has his Champburgers.

Laver Beats Roche in U.S. Open Final and Gains His 2d Tennis Grand Slam

RECORD ACHIEVED IN 4-SET TRIUMPH

Favorite Takes $16,000 Top Prize and 4th Major Title by 7-9, 6-1, 6-2, 6-2

By NEIL AMDUR

Rod Laver achieved the second grand slam of his tennis career yesterday.

With all the competitive trademarks of the true champion, the 31-year-old king of the court overcame Tony Roche, his 24-year-old Australian countryman, 7-9, 6-1, 6-2, 6-2, in the final of the United States Open championship at the West Side Tennis Club in Forest Hills, Queens.

With the $16,000 first prize, the richest singles payoff in the sport, Laver lifted his professional earnings this year to a record $106,000. He also entered the record books as the only player to have achieved two sweeps of the Australian, French, British and American championships, the international events that make up the grand slam.

Budge Did It First

Don Budge registered the first slam in 1938. Laver completed his initial sweep in 1962, but as an amateur and with such established pros as Richard (Pancho) Gonzales, Ken Rosewall, Lew Hoad and Tony Trabert ineligible for the competition. That situation has been changed with the approval of open tournaments.

"Tenniswise, winning this slam was a lot tougher because of all the good players," the modest, freckle-faced redhead said.

"Pressurewise, I don't think it was any tougher. There's always pressure when you're playing for something over nine months."

Laver and Roche had to wait 1 hour 35 minutes until a rented helicopter could dry the center court, which had been dampened by the morning rain.

"The playing conditions made it very difficult," Laver said. "The ground was very soft, the speeds of the bounce made it tough to return and you were sliding all over."

Switches to Spikes

Before the 10th game of the first set, after having lost his serve at 5-4 on Roche's backhand passing shot down the middle and three errors off his first volley, Laver made a strategic switch from sneakers to spiked shoes.

"The spikes helped me considerably," he said. "I lost the first set using them but I felt good and I was able to move better." Roche wore sneakers throughout.

The fine line that separates Laver from Roche, Arthur Ashe, Roy Emerson and others is his ability to concentrate on the big serve or decisive volley at 15-30 or 30-40.

Laver trailed, 30-40, in the opening game of the second set. A service break at this point could have carried Roche to a two-set lead. But three strong first serves saved the game. Laver won the last three service games of the set at love.

The crucial moment in the match, when it seemed to turn dramatically, came in the second game of the third set, after play had been suspended by rain.

Roche had won his serve at love for a 1-0 lead. When the players returned 30 minutes later, the pressure was on Laver. On Sunday he saw the result of the strain of serving first following a delay. At 12-12 in the third set of his match with Ashe, Arthur had to serve the first game. Laver broke him immediately and won the match in the next game.

Roche pushed Laver to deuce twice in that second game. But two more big serves, hopping deep to Roche's backhand, gave Laver the impetus to hold service and then break Roche in the next game, in which he was helped by Tony's netted forehand approach volley and long overhead at deuce.

Laver hefts U.S. Lawn Tennis Association's Open trophy

Runner-Up Gets $8,000

"Tony didn't seem to be digging in as much," Laver said of the player who had beaten him in five of their seven previous meetings. "I felt his concentration was off."

Roche, who collected $8,000 as runner-up, could have felt the physical strain of his three-hour, five-set semifinal with John Newcombe on Sunday, particularly after the 30-minute cooling-off period in the third set (he never got beyond 30 on Laver's last six serves).

But when the big money goes on the line, the winning strokes are Laver's. Except for last year's first Open here, when he lost to Cliff Drysdale in the quarter finals, Laver has won every major tennis money event in the world.

Alastair B. Martin, president of the United States Lawn Tennis Association, called Laver "the greatest player ever," and the 5-foot-9-inch, 155-pounder said "that makes me feel humble and proud and grateful."

Comparing Laver with the stars of other eras—Gonzales, Jack Kramer, Budge and Tilden—might be treasonous in tennis's sacrosanct society, but the Rocket has met every challenge with the discipline and dedication worthy of a place in the hall of heroes.

"Red showed this year that he's still the best," said Roche, who is considered Laver's successor. "He's won so much money this year that maybe the money might slow him down."

Laver has three years to go on a five-year, $450,000 contract with the National Tennis League. He keeps whatever amount he makes in prize money above his guarantee.

The pressure began for him last January after he had beaten Emerson, Fred Stolle, Roche and Andres Gimeno en route to the Australian title. In the French and Wimbledon championships, he trailed, two sets to love, twice in the early rounds, but salvaged each match and went on to the crowns despite persistent pains in his left elbow.

In winning here at Forest Hills, the richest tournament in the world with its $137,000 purse, Laver overcame psychological hazards as well as such quality pros as Dennis Ralston, Emerson, Ashe and Roche, his chief tormentor this year. Rain had washed out two complete sessions and delayed the final one day. His tense semifinal match with Ashe had been halted by darkness in the third set and finished the following day.

Meanwhile, in Newport Beach, Calif., Laver's wife, Mary, had also been experiencing delays. The couple's first child was three days' overdue and Laver had been calling every morning to make sure everything was all right.

Mrs. Laver reported yesterday by phone before her husband walked onto the stadium court for the final. "I've been telling him everything's fine and to concentrate on his tennis," she said.

If there was a touch of nostalgia to this tournament, it came in the women's doubles final yesterday, in which Francoise Durr and 33-year-old Darlene Hard upset the top-seeded team of Mrs. Margaret Court and Virginia Wade, 0-6, 6-4, 6-4.

The crowd of 3,708 (6,200 tickets had actually been sold) cheered lustily, particularly for Miss Hard, a former national champion who had replaced Miss Durr's regular partner, Mrs. Ann Haydon Jones.

"I guess Frankie (Miss Durr's nickname) cried when she saw my name on the doubles list," said Miss Hard, who is a teaching pro in Los Angeles and lost to Miss Durr in the second round of singles. "But everything worked out great, and a win like this convinces me I should get back to full-time tennis."

One day remains in the tournament to complete the men's doubles. Naturally Laver is still playing for the $3,000 top doubles prize, even though his mind is elsewhere.

"I want to get home as soon as possible," he said, flashing a familiar half-smile. "If you had a baby on the way, wouldn't you?"

The Summaries

MEN'S SINGLES

FINAL ROUND

Rod Laver, Australia, defeated Tony Roche, Australia, 7-9, 6-1, 6-2, 6-2.

MIXED DOUBLES

QUARTERFINAL ROUND

Dennis Ralston, Bakersfield, Calif., and Francoise Durr, France, defeated Richard Crealy, Australia and Virginia Wade, Britain, 6-4, 6-3; Marty Riessen, Evanston, Ill., and Mrs. Margaret Court, Australia, defeated Ken Rosewall, Australia, and Rosemary Casals, San Francisco, 6-4, 6-3.

WOMEN'S DOUBLES

FINAL ROUND

Darlene Hard, Los Angeles, and Francoise Durr, France, defeated Mrs. Margaret Court, Australia, and Virginia Wade, Britain, 0-6, 6-3, 6-4.

SEMIFINAL ROUND

Riessen and Mrs. Court defeated Torben Ulrich, Denmark, and Julie Heldman, New York, 6-3, 6-2.

MEN'S SENIOR DOUBLES

FINAL ROUND

Bobby Riggs, Plandome, L.I., and Emery Neale, Portland, Ore., won by default from Jaroslav Drobny, Britain, and Vic Seixas, Philadelphia (Drobny sprained ankle).

EXCEPT FOR RAIN, 'TWAS FINE TENNIS

2d U.S. Open Had More of Everything, It Seems

By PARTON KEESE

There was more of everything at the United States Open tennis championships in Forest Hills this year—prize money, gate receipts, cohesion, scheduling, promotion, enthusiasm, great matches and, of course, more rain.

There is even more of the tournament, with mixed doubles and men's doubles to be completed today starting at 11 A.M. Admission is $3; for students $1.

In spite of the rain, an aura surrounded this second Open, which most people will remember as the one that brought Rod Laver of Australia his second grand slam. But it was also a delight to the people involved with it. Here were some of their reactions:

Mike Gibson, the referee:

"It was the worst tournament for rain I've ever experienced. Even last year at Wimbledon we had rain the first five days but managed to play some of the matches every day. English grass is so much better, with its clay base. But then in England we have two tent covers and six regular tarpaulins to protect the courts. We need that here.

"Of course in the future you must go to artificial grass, especially with such big money involved. It was terrible to see the bad bounces in the Fred Stolle-John Newcombe match, for instance."

Mike Dunn, head umpire:

"There was more enthusiasm in serving as linesman or umpire this year than I've seen.

Tony Roche trying to stave off his fellow Australian

"All the News That's Fit to Print"

The New York Times

LATE CITY EDITION

Weather: Variable cloudiness today. Mostly fair tonight and tomorrow. Temp. range: today 61-50; Thurs. 64-47. Full U.S. report on Page 94.

VOL. CXIX ... No. 40,809 © 1969 The New York Times Company. NEW YORK, FRIDAY, OCTOBER 17, 1969 10 CENTS

PRESIDENT IS FIRM ON PUSHING POLICY TO CURB INFLATION

He Will Address Nation on Radio Today—Burns Says 'We Will Not Budge'

SURTAX MEASURE GAINS

Nixon Meets With Leaders of Congress to Press His Views on the Economy

By EILEEN SHANAHAN
Special to The New York Times

WASHINGTON, Oct. 16—The Nixon Administration pledged today to "persevere" in its anti-inflationary policies until they yield results.

"We in this Administration will very definitely persevere in the present policy of restraint," Dr. Arthur F. Burns, counselor to the President, said. "We will not budge from it."

President Nixon will explain his anti-inflationary policies to the American people tomorrow, the White House announced, in a radio address on the subject at 4 P.M.

Continuation of the anti-inflationary policies, so far as the Federal budget is concerned, will require not only a strict rein on federal expenditures but also a continuation of the income tax surcharge, at the reduced rate of 5 per cent, from January through next June, Dr. Burns said. The present rate is 10 per cent.

Sees Congressional Chiefs

Both these points were made by President Nixon in a meeting this morning with Congressional leaders and the ranking Democrats and Republicans on the Congressional tax and appropriations committees, Dr. Burns disclosed at a briefing.

The Senate Finance Committee, meanwhile, voted the surtax extension as requested. Its chairman, Senator Russell B. Long, Democrat of Louisiana, said that the vote had not been influenced by the President's statements. [Page 18.]

Monetary restraint as well as budgetary restraint "will continue for the present," Dr. Burns said.

But, at the same time, he predicted that interest rates would "move down sometime soon.'"

Paul W. McCracken, chair-

Continued on Page 19, Column 1

PROCACCINO VOWS JAIL FOR MAFIOSI

Pledges an 'Unprecedented Attack' on Syndicate

By DOUGLAS ROBINSON

Controller Mario A. Procaccino pledged yesterday that if elected he would unleash an "unprecedented attack" on the Mafia and said he was fully aware of its "infiltration into legitimate businesses and into labor unions."

In his first formal campaign statement on organized crime, which he coupled with a scathing attack on Mayor Lindsay, the Democratic candidate for Mayor promised to jail Mafia men.

"It is claimed there are about 5,000 members of the Mafia in these United States, 5,000 punks or bums or whatever you want to call them, who have besmirched the reputations of millions of decent, honest, hard-working Italian-Americans," he said.

"I will fight them, I will beat them, and put them behind bars."

Mr. Procaccino made known his stand on organized crime in a short statement and in a lengthy position paper distributed at a news conference

Continued on Page 50, Column 3

NEWS INDEX

Nixon's Draft Lottery Plan Approved by House Panel

Laird Praises 31-0 Vote on Proposal to Induct 19-Year-Olds First

By JOHN W. FINNEY
Special to The New York Times

WASHINGTON, Oct. 16—The House Armed Services Committee unexpectedly approved today, 31 to 0, the Administration's proposal of drafting 19-year-olds first through a random selection, or lottery, system.

The committee, however, refusing to go beyond this reform, rejected a proposal by a committee minority to end deferments for college students.

In an informal discussion with Pentagon newsmen, Defense Secretary Melvin R. Laird described the House committee's action as "a most heartening step to eliminate some of the inequities in the draft." He expressed hope that a lottery system could be inaugurated early next year.

The House committee had been regarded as the main obstacle to implementation of a lottery selection system, which was specifically prohibited in the 1967 draft law. But it is not certain whether the way is now clear for Congressional approval of the lottery this session.

Associated Press
Melvin R. Laird

With the unanimous approval of the House committee, the lottery proposal is certain to be approved by the House, perhaps as early as next week. What remained uncertain was whether the Senate Armed Services Committee, and thus

Continued on Page 23, Column 1

Moratorium Backers Say Nixon Will Have to React

By JOHN HERBERS

Some of the prominent supporters of Wednesday's Vietnam moratorium say that the massive outpourings of Americans opposed to the war will force President Nixon to alter his policy, even though the White House insists it will not.

This was the central issue emerging from the moratorium—whether mass demonstrations of unprecedented size will, or should, precipitate a major change in the nation's Vietnam policy.

In Washington, leaders of the moratorium were attempting to puzzle out what they had accomplished. "I think it was a good start," Sam Brown, one of the prime movers, remarked.

A number of newspapers around the country expressed concern in editorials that the country seemed to be moving into an era in which foreign policy was being made in the streets rather than through established channels of government.

Harriman Sums It Up

Supporters of the moratorium, however, said such a procedure was both proper and effective—a view summed up by W. Averell Harriman Wednesday night at a rally of 15,000 in East Meadow, L. I., and repeated yesterday by a number of prominent political leaders.

"I've been working for peace for four years," said Mr. Harriman, former chief negotiator at the Paris peace talks. "Now you've started something and nobody can stop you. President Nixon said he wouldn't pay attention to your voices. Now he's going to have to pay attention."

In Washington, Mike Mansfield of Montana, the Senate

Continued on Page 20, Column 3

A 'RESIDUAL FORCE' IN VIETNAM HINTED

Laird Sees Need to Maintain Small Group to Train and Advise After the War

By WILLIAM BEECHER
Special to The New York Times

WASHINGTON, Oct. 16—Secretary of Defense Melvin R. Laird said today that he expected the United States to maintain several thousand military men for training and advisory duty in South Vietnam after the fighting had ended.

But Mr. Laird, speaking at an informal news conference in the Pentagon, said he did not want to give the impression that the Nixon Administration contemplated keeping in Vietnam for any indefinite period anything like the 300,000 men in Europe or the 50,000 in South Korea.

The Secretary got into the matter of postwar planning while answering questions about the next defense budget, currently under preparation. He asserted that the Administration was trying to give more realistic planning guidance to the armed services in drawing up their budget proposals.

The premise in previous budget guidance, he said, has been to provide forces to fight two major wars and one brush-fire war simultaneously, but

Continued on Page 3, Column 5

$500-Million Development Plan For Brooklyn Shown by Mayor

By DAVID K. SHIPLER

Mayor Lindsay yesterday unveiled a master plan designed to remake downtown Brooklyn with $500-million worth of office buildings, department stores and apartment houses connected by an underground network of pedestrian passages.

Unlike some ambitious plans, this one appears likely to be realized, planners say, since numerous private investors are anxious to build there.

Six major department stores, including Alexander's and S. Klein, have expressed interest, according to Jonathan Barnett, director of the City Planning Department's Urban Design Group. A $14-million office building has already been scheduled for construction by private builders.

Downtown Brooklyn is now the city's second busiest retail hub, after Herald Square in Manhattan.

The New York Times Oct. 17, 1969
Area of redevelopment

But for several blocks on each side of Fulton Street, which is well developed with some major department stores,

Continued on Page 52, Column 4

HANOI PROPOSES U.S. AND VIETCONG NEGOTIATE ALONE

Calls, in Paris, for Secret and Immediate Talks—Plan Is Barred in Washington

By HENRY GINIGER
Special to The New York Times

PARIS, Oct. 16 — North Vietnam today proposed direct and secret peace talks, to begin immediately, between the United States and the South Vietnamese Communist forces.

The proposal, which would eliminate the South Vietnamese Government as a party to a settlement, was countered by the United States. Its chief delegate to the Paris peace talks, Henry Cabot Lodge, called for secret talks among all four participants at the conference here.

[In Washington, the White House said that "We would not meet alone with the Vietcong," but that the United States was ready to meet "with all the parties together in any format."

[In Saigon, allied spokesmen reported that 82 Americans were killed in battle last week, one of the lowest levels of the last three years. Page 3.]

Move Believed Tactical

North Vietnam has sought before to bring together the United States and the Vietcong without the Saigon Government. The latest move at the peace conference appeared to be a tactical one designed to take advantage of antiwar feelings in the United States, which reached a high point yesterday.

Hanoi's move followed the peace moratorium in the United States, which the North Vietnamese chief delegate, Xuan Thuy, and the Vietcong chief delegate, Mrs. Nguyen Thi Binh, hailed.

Mr. Thuy said President Nixon had not lived up to his promises of peace and now had to face "a movement of protest of the American people, a movement of national character, vigorous and widespread and without precedent in the United States."

In an unusually strong attack on the Saigon Government, Mr. Thuy referred to it as "traitorous" and warned that "as long

Continued on Page 3, Column 1

BOY AND GIRL DIE IN ANTIWAR PACT

Commit Suicide in Jersey After Moratorium Rally

By BERNARD WEINRAUB
Special to The New York Times

BLACKWOOD, N. J., Oct. 16—Two high school classmates who had attended the Vietnam Moratorium at nearby Glassboro State College yesterday were found dead this morning in a locked car cluttered with 24 notes urging peace and brotherhood for mankind.

The teen-agers, whose deaths were ruled suicides, were Craig Badiali, the president of the Highland Regional High School Dramatic Society, and Joan Fox, a cheerleader at the high school. The bodies of the two 17-year-olds were found in the front seat of a blue 1962 Ford Falcon owned by the Badiali family.

This morning the dead youth's 21-year-old brother Bernard Jr. said:

"My brother died for his convictions. He was against the war."

Thomas R. Daley, the medical investigator for the Camden County Medical Examiner's Office, gave the following account of the suicides in this community 10 miles from Philadelphia:

"They hooked a vacuum cleaner hose to the exhaust and drilled a hole through the rear floor of the car and brought the hose in through there.

"We found 24 notes in the car addressed to parents and close friends," he went on. "The

Continued on Page 22, Column 4

Mets Win, 5-3, Take the Series, And a Grateful City Goes Wild

The New York Times (by Michael Evans)
JUBILEE: Broad and Wall Streets at 4 P.M. yesterday after Mets stock hit all-time high

FANS STORM FIELD

Thousands Rip Up Turf After a Late Rally Defeats Orioles

By JOSEPH DURSO

The Mets entered the promised land yesterday after seven years of wandering through the wilderness of baseball.

In a tumultuous game before a record crowd of 57,397 in Shea Stadium, they defeated the Baltimore Orioles, 5-3, for their fourth straight victory of the 66th World Series and captured the championship of a sport that had long ranked them as comical losers.

They did it with a full and final dose of the magic that had spiced their unthinkable climb from ninth place in the National League — 100-to-1 shots who scraped and scrounged their way to the pinacle as the waifs of the major leagues.

Thumbnail sketches and pictures of all the Mets will be found on Page 57.

At 3:17 o'clock on a cool and often sunny afternoon, their impossible dream came true when Cleon Jones caught a fly ball hit by Dave Johnson to left field. And they immediately touched off one of the great, riotous scenes in sports history, as thousands of persons swarmed from their seats and tore up the patch of ground where the Mets had made history.

Lovable Winners Now

It was 10 days after they had won the National League pennant in a three-game sweep of the Atlanta Braves. It was 22 days after they had won the Eastern title of the league over the Chicago Cubs. It was eight years after they had started business under Casey Stengel as the lovable losers of all sports.

They reached the top, moreover, in the best and most far-fetched manner of Met baseball.

They spotted the Orioles three runs in the third inning when Dave McNally and Frank Robinson hit home runs off Jerry Koosman.

But then they stormed back with two runs in the sixth inning on a home run by Donn Clendenon, another in the seventh on a home run by Al Weis and two more in the eighth on two doubles and two errors.

The deciding run was batted

Continued on Page 58, Column 4

3 AMERICANS GET NOBEL IN MEDICINE

Share Prize for Discoveries Concerning Reproductive Mechanism of Viruses

By JOHN M. LEE
Special to The New York Times

STOCKHOLM, Oct. 16—Three American scientists were jointly awarded the 1969 Nobel Prize in Physiology or Medicine today for their discoveries concerning viruses and viral diseases.

The winners are:

Dr. Max Delbrück, 63-year-old professor of biology at the California Institute of Technology, Pasadena.

Dr. Alfred D. Hershey, 60, director of the Carnegie Institution's genetics research unit, Cold Spring Harbor, L. I.

Dr. Salvador E. Luria, 57, Sedgwick Professor of Microbiology, Massachusetts Institute of Technology, Cambridge.

The three men, who will

Continued on Page 24, Column 4

A Paper Blizzard Wraps City in a Blanket of Joy

By WILLIAM BORDERS

With the kind of jubilation it reserves for its special heroes, New York yesterday went pleasantly mad over the Mets.

From the sleek skyscrapers of Wall Street, where a spontaneous tickertape blizzard greeted the World Series victory, to the undistinguished bars of a hundred neighborhoods, where the toasts were in draft beer, the shouted cry was:

"We're Number One!"

Teachers suspended classes, because their transistor-equipped students were not paying attention anyway; bosses closed offices early for the same reason, and even policemen shrugged happily as they despaired of keeping order in the streets.

Celebrators, wading through paper that was ankle-deep in Wall Street and midtown Manhattan, hopelessly clogged traffic during the evening rush, an hour after the game ended.

But the mood was happy, and even the stalled motorists seemed not to mind.

The news from Shea Stadium occasioned largesse on the part of some New Yorkers, like the Madison Avenue bus driver who stopped collecting fares, informing startled passengers: "Everyone on free!"

It was a sign of hope for others, like Isaac Stern, the violinist, who said:

"If the Mets can win the Series, anything can happen—even peace."

In the financial district, where the police were forced to close part of Broad Street for an hour because of the crowds, old-timers compared the celebration to that honoring Col. Charles A. Lindbergh in 1927, after his solo flight across the Atlantic.

Shoulder to shoulder, the tycoons and the clerks poured out of their offices and into the narrow streets to cheer their team. From windows high above them, secretaries threw whatever paper was handy — tickertape, stationery, or shredded computer cards.

There, as in midtown, the

Continued on Page 60, Column 3

THE IMPOSSIBLE DREAM: Ed Charles dances for joy as Jerry Koosman, pitcher, jumps on Jerry Grote after last out

Mets' 3d Victory Celebration in 22 Days Is Biggest

METS WIN BY 5-3 AND TAKE SERIES

Continued From Page 1, Col. 8

home by Ron Swoboda, who joined the Met mystique in 1965 when the team was losing 112 games and was finishing last for the fourth straight time.

But, like most of the Mets' victories in their year to remember, the decision was a collective achievement by the youngest team in baseball, under Manager Gil Hodges—who had suffered a heart attack a year ago after the Mets "surged" into ninth place.

The wild, final chapter in the story was written against the desperate efforts of the Orioles, who had swept to the American League pennant by 19 games as one of the most powerful teams in modern times.

Orioles' Wings Clipped

The Orioles had not won since the opening game last Saturday in Baltimore and needed three straight victories to survive. In the third inning, they lashed out at Koosman with three runs and erased the memory of the six no-hit innings he had pitched against them Sunday.

Mark Belanger led off with a looping single over first base. He was nearly caught off the base by Jerry Grote, the New York catcher, who was backing up the play. But in a brief shoving contest, Belanger was called safe as he scrambled back to the base, where Grote took a throw from Swoboda.

On the next pitch, McNally hit a home run into the Baltimore bull pen in left field and the Orioles led, 2-0.

McNally, who had lost the second game to Koosman, is a 27-year-old left-hander who can hit as well as pitch. He didn't lose a game this season until Aug. 3, then finished with 20 victories. He also hit three home runs last year, including a grand slam, and another this year.

His drive off Koosman was the first extra-base hit for Baltimore in 35 innings and it cast a pall over the fans who had come to see the Mets reach the stars. Two outs later, Frank Robinson bombed Koosman's first pitch over the center-field fence, Baltimore led by 3-0 and the Mets' magic suddenly seemed remote.

But Koosman settled down after that and checkmated the Orioles on one single for the final six innings. He retired 19 of the last 21 batters, closed with a five-hitter and even swung a mean bat when the Mets began to do their "thing."

They almost revived in the third when Koosman doubled past third base. Nothing came of it because McNally knocked off the next three batters, but it was an omen: Koosman had made only four hits in 84 times at bat all season.

Then, in the sixth, another omen appeared. Each team argued in turn that a batter had been hit by a pitched ball. The Orioles, though, lost their argument; the Mets won theirs. And the game veered inexorably toward the "team of destiny."

Motion Is Denied

The Orioles pleaded their case first. With one out in the top of the sixth, an inside fastball plunked Frank Robinson on his right thigh. The home-plate umpire, Lou DiMuro, ruled that it had glanced off the bat first for strike two. Baltimore's volatile manager, Earl Weaver, who had been banished from Wednesday's game argued that it had simply struck Robinson, who already had started for first base.

When the Orioles were overruled, Robinson disappeared into the runway behind the dugout for five minutes while the trainer sprayed his thigh with a freezing medication and while everybody in the stadium waited. Then he returned, was greeted by a sea of waving handkerchiefs and struck out.

In the bottom of the sixth, it was the Mets' turn to plead an identical case and, in the amazing spirit of their new fortune, they won it on an appeal.

Jones was the leadoff batter and he was struck on the right instep by a dropping curveball. The umpire called it a ball; Jones insisted he had been hit. Hodges, the old hero of Ebbets Field, retrieved the ball from the Mets' dugout, where it had bounced, and executed the old "look-at-the-ball-trick."

DiMuro duly looked at the ball, detected a swatch of shoe polish on its cover, reversed himself and waved Jones to first base. Now Weaver shot out of the dugout to voice his indignation, but lost his point and soon his ball game.

The next batter, Clendenon, went to a count of two balls and two strikes, then whacked a home run off the auxiliary scoreboard on the facing of the left field loge seats.

It was his third home run in three games (he had hit 16 during the regular schedule) and it punctuated a remarkable season for the 34-year-old ex-student of law.

His homer yesterday, which put him one short of the Series record of four shared by Babe Ruth, Lou Gehrig, Hank Bauer and Duke Snider, put the Mets back in business. In the next inning, Al Weis brought them even on McNally's second pitch.

Weis, the silent supersub, drove the pitch over the 371-foot sign in left-center as the crowd rocked the stadium, and the game was tied, 3-3. It marked another achievement for the right-handed platoon that Hodges deploys against left-handed pitching and it was no mean achievement for Weis.

During Weis's two seasons with the Mets, 212 home runs had been hit in Shea Stadium—none by Al. He had hit only two all year, both in Chicago in July. But in the World Series, the quiet little infielder turned tiger with four walks, four singles and one historic home run.

Finally, the stage was set for the last full measure of Met magic.

In the eighth, with Eddie Watt pitching for Baltimore, Jones looked at three straight balls and then a strike. Then he lined the 3-and-1 pitch off the center-field fence for a double.

Clendenon, who was voted the outstanding player in the Series, fouled off two attempts to bunt. Then he lined a long fly into the right-field corner, just foul, then bounced out to Brooks Robinson, with Jones holding second base.

The next batter was Swoboda and, with first base open, the Orioles might have walked him intentionally. But they elected to challenge him and Swoboda drilled the second pitch down the left-field line, where Don Buford almost made a brilliant backhand catch off the grass. But the ball dropped in for a double as Jones streaked for home to put the Mets in front. 4-3, and tumult broke out across Flushing Meadow.

Ed Charles lifted a fly to Buford for the second out. But Grote followed with a low line drive toward John Powell and the 250-pound first baseman booted it for an error. He chased the ball, though, to his right and lobbed it to Watt, who was rusing over from the mound to cover first base.

By this time, Grote was flashing across the bag and, when Watt juggled the throw and dropped it, Swoboda was flashing across the plate with the second run of the inning.

That made it 5-3 and the Mets were three outs from fantasy. There was a brief delay when Frank Robinson opened the ninth, with a walk. But then Powell forced him at second base, Brooks Robinson flied out to Swoboda in right and—at 3:17 P.M.—Johnson lifted a fly to Jones in left-center.

Jones made the catch with a flourish, then he and his old high-school mate from Mobile, Tommie Agee, turned and streaked across the outfield to the Mets' bull pen in right.

The beat the avalanche by a split second and, as they ducked into the safety of the stadium's caverns, the crowd let go. Children, housewives, mature men, all swarmed onto the field where the Mets had marched. They tore up home plate, captured the bases, ripped gaping holes from the turf, set off orange flares and firecrackers and chalked the wooden outfield fence with the signs of success.

The Mets were the champions of the world on Oct. 16, 1969.

"I never saw anything like it," said Joe DiMaggio, the old Yankee, who had thrown out the first ball.

A BRAND-NEW BALL GAME: Al Weis, first batter up for the Mets in the seventh, returns to the dugout after tying the game, 3-3, with a homer. Tommie Agee welcomes him home.

The New York Times

Results of Series

FIRST GAME

				R.	H.	E.
New York Mets	000	000	100	1	6	1
Baltimore Orioles	100	300	00x	4	6	0

Batteries—Seaver, Cardwell (6), Taylor (7) and Grote; Cuellar and Hendricks.
Winning pitcher—Cuellar. Losing pitcher—Seaver.
Home run—Baltimore: Buford.

SECOND GAME

				R.	H.	E.
New York Mets	000	100	001	2	6	0
Balt. Orioles	000	000	100	1	2	0

Batteries—Koosman, Taylor (9) and Grote. McNally and Etchebarren.
Winning pitcher—Koosman.
Losing pitcher—McNally.
Home run—New York, Clendenon.

THIRD GAME

				R.	H.	E.
Baltimore Orioles	000	000	000	0	4	1
New York Mets	120	001	01x	5	6	0

Batteries—Palmer, Leonhard (7) and Hendricks; Gentry, Ryan (7), and Grote.
Winning pitcher—Gentry. Losing pitcher—Palmer.
Home runs—New York: Agee, Kranepool.

FOURTH GAME

					R.	H.	E.
Balt. Orioles	000	000	001	0	1	6	1
N.Y. Mets	010	000	000	1	2	10	1

Batteries—Cuellar, Watt (8), Hall (10), Richert (10) and Hendricks; Seaver and Grote.
Winning pitcher—Seaver.
Losing pitcher—Hall.
Home run—New York: Clendenon.

FIFTH GAME

				R.	H.	E.
Baltimore Orioles	003	000	000	3	5	2
N.Y. Mets	000	002	12x	5	7	0

Batteries—McNally, Watt (8) and Etchebarren. Koosman and Grote.
Winning pitcher—Koosman. Losing pitcher Watt.
Home runs—Baltimore: McNally, F. Robinson; New York: Clendenon, Weis.

MET SPECULATION TAKES BIG PROFIT

Wall Street's Most Active Issue Is Storm of Paper

By RICHARD PHALON

The avalanche broke over Wall Street in the same electrifying instant that the final out disappeared into Cleon Jones's glove—an avalanche of ticker tape, computer print-outs, toilet paper, Dow Jones broad tape, and over-the-counter pink sheets. It piled up ankle-deep along the curbs.

It became knee-deep in some spots along Wall Street, and continued to fall in slowly diminishing amounts from windows high overhead for the better part of an hour. The crowd that built up on the steps of the old Sub-Treasury Building went deliciously whacky to a beat pounded out on the bottom of an upended coffee urn.

The urn, thumped by a succession of young men with appropriately long hair, appeared to have been commandeered from a Schrafft's lunch cart.

BAM-BAM-BAM. "Let's Go Mets . . . Let's Go Mets," the crowd chanted. There were variations on the theme. To the "Battle Hymn of the Republic," the Mets went marching on.

The crowd was mostly young. There were more miniskirts and blazers around than Brooks Brothers worsteds.

Along about 4:40 P.M., the police did shoo about 50 delirious fans from their perch on the Sub-Treasury steps, but not before some wag had put in the hand of the statue of George Washington there a beautifully scripted sign that read: "God is Not Dead. He is Alive and Playing for the Mets."

There was another sign (red paint on brown wrapping paper that said simply, "No. 1."

Orioles Had Reputation, but Mets Had Momentum

'THIS IS SUMMIT,' CHARLES SHOUTS

Champagne Flows Freely in Clubhouse Crammed With Well-Wishers

By LEONARD KOPPETT

"We did it all."

Ron Swoboda said it, and in saying it, he said it all. The New York Mets had their biggest, their longest, their noisiest, their sweetest and their third victory celebration in 22 days at Shea Stadium yesterday.

On Wednesday night, Sept. 24, they clinched first place in National League East. Champagne splashed like bath water, and everyone got splashed by it.

On Monday afternoon, Oct. 6, they completed a three-game sweep of Atlanta in the first "championship series" to determine the National League pennant winner. The activity was similar, but the intensity was less, and the World Series loomed ahead.

And now, on a mid-October Thursday a good two weeks before Halloween, they had won the World Series and this was positively the last—and wildest—champagne shower.

"This is the summit," cried Ed Charles, 36 years old and until a couple of months ago beyond hoping for this particular thrill. "We're No. 1 in the world and you just can't get any bigger than this."

Did What Had to Be Done

"Some people still might not believe in us," said Cleon Jones, "but then, some people still think the world is flat."

"It boiled down to this," declared Bud Harrelson. "When it had to be done, we did it and they didn't."

The tumult was augmented by the crowded condition of an otherwise ample dressing room. This time, the crush of interviewers, cameramen and others carrying various equipment was as dense as the subway at peak rush hour, far denser than on the other two occasions. No one could move a full step in any direction without pushing someone else aside.

That was the main dressing room. But the office of the manager, which is to the left of the entrance door (while the corridor leading into the rest of the clubhouse leads off to the right) was an oasis of order.

Manager Gil Hodges at first was in the mob outside. The first one into the empty office was Gil Jr., the C. W. Post College student, who hastily climbed out of his civilian clothes and into his Met uniform for the sweaty hour to follow.

Then came his mother, and the older two of his three sisters.

"We're champions," cried out Joan Hodges, who has lived through her husband's baseball triumphs and setbacks with such fervor all these years. "Imagine, we did it!"

Gathering of the Clan

A moment later, the head of the family entered, and Joan hugged him and squealed:

"You know what we are? You know? Champions. We're champions of the world."

Hodges hugged her back, and his daughters. And they kissed him, and he grinned, and Gil Jr. put his arms around them from behind while the Met photographer snapped a family portrait.

And then the stream of interviewers began to trickle in, filling the office with bodies but not with any of the hysteria outside. Hodges, as he has always been, was calm, speaking softly but distinctly, mopping his face, listening attentively, answering carefully, smiling quickly — working, in a way, harder than during a game.

Mrs. Joan Payson arrived too. "Oh my, oh my," she kept repeating. "oh my." Donald Grant, the chairman of the board, was there, and then Johnny Murphy, who actually ran the club as general manager, and George Weiss who had started it, and other members of the Met family.

"Yes, it's the same and it's different," said Hodges, trying to answer questions about how this victory felt alongside other World Series triumphs he experienced in 1955 and 1959. "As a player, and as a manager, it's different — it's hard to explain. In a way this means more. I'm so proud of them all."

Did he think Donn Clendenon was the most valuable player, worthy of the car given for that distinction?

"That's not my job," said Gil. "I think of all 25 of them — and four coaches. Let's see, that's 29."

"And the manager," someone suggested.

"No, no, not the manager," demurred Hodges.

"The manager already has a car," a voice interrupted, and everyone laughed, including Hodges.

Later it became celebrity time — Pearl Bailey, who kissed Hodges, called him a "cool cat," and wound up dancing in the main room with Charlie while a record-player blared the sing-along record the Met squad had made two weeks ago; Robert Merrill, the opera star, who sat with the Met party all three days at Shea and was still shaking. Bill Shea, who set the whole thing in motion and for whom the stadium is named, saying "in my lifetime — they did it in my lifetime!"

After an hour or more, Joan Hodges was casting anxious glances at her husband — who, after all, had suffered a heart attack only 13 months before and whose marvelous discipline and recovery can't eliminate worry. Only two days ago, however, a doctor's examination had shown Gil in fine shape.

But sporadic yelling and singing were still going on in the clubhouse, the floor slippery, the room less crowded, but few players dressed. In another hour or two, they would go upstairs to the Diamond Club for a real party, with their wives and the whole Met official family.

"It's the first one," Swoboda had shouted at the beginning, "and the sweetest, and because it's the first nothing can ever be that sweet again."

'LITTLE MEN' HURT, JOHNSON ASSERTS

Mets Outdid Themselves and Gained Confidence, Says Baltimore 2d Baseman

By MURRAY CHASS

While Frank Robinson and Dave McNally told a few dozen listeners about home run pitches and pitches that did or didn't hit batters, Dave Johnson sat on the fringe of the crowd yesterday and talked about the Mets and the Orioles, the Jets and the Colts.

There is, the Orioles' scholarly second baseman theorized, a striking similarity in the way both New York teams upset both Baltimore teams.

It's Johnson's mushroom theory, and he postulates it this way:

"When you're expected to do things and you don't, it messes you up. But when you aren't expected to do things and you do them, they pick you up."

"It's part of momentum, it has a mushrooming effect in both directions," said the 26-year-old infielder who is studying mathematics at Trinity College in Texas.

"It's part of the thing that happened to the Colts. In fact, Tom Matte [the Baltimore football team's running back] said something similar to what I'm saying after the Super Bowl.

"Take our situation. The Mets were one of the few clubs we played this year that when they walked onto the field they felt they could beat us. Then their players went out and did more than they were supposed to. At the same time, the guys on our club didn't do as much as they were supposed to.

"They outdid themselves and did the unexpected. We did the unexpected, too—we didn't do what we should've done.

"One of our problems was all of our guys felt they had to do it themselves. When you have a team on which everyone in the starting line-up but Brooksie (Brooks Robinson) batted better than .280, they feel they should hit better than .280. When they went up to bat, they felt everyone expected them to hit that well.

"But most of the Mets had .218 averages, and the small guys were expected to make outs. When they did something else it was a kick in the rear end for everyone else. The Mets felt anything they did was a contribution, and that fired everyone else up.

'A Series for Little Men'

"When you're not supposed to do something, everthing you do is a plus. If you don't do it, you're not embarrassed. They made some catches, like Swoboda's yesterday, that they weren't expected to make. And their .200 hitters became 400 hitters. It was a Series for the little men.

"On the other hand, we didn't do what we were expected to do, and it hurt us. Things like balls dropping in and other balls going over guys' heads, plays we should have made and usually do make."

Johnson, a .280 hitter during the season who managed only one hit in 16 at-bats in the Series, is convinced that if the Mets would play an All-Star team this year they would win. But, he added, next year likely will be a different story.

"I'd be very surprised if they could do next year what they did this year," he said. "I don't think they can repeat what they did this year day-in and day-out. I don't think they can get all that from everyone again."

But the Mets did get it this year, and the Orioles readily admitted it.

As had been their style throughout this Series, the Orioles, from Earl Weaver, the manager, on down, offered no excuses, pleaded no alibis, refused to blame anyone else for their losses.

As they did following their first three losses, they sat in front of their lockers rather than running away and hiding as sometimes has been the custom with other losing teams. They patiently answered the same questions five and 10 times and never became irked.

They also declined to hide their praise for the Mets.

"The Mets are a good ball club," Weaver said. "You guys have been wrong all year saying they're lucky and they have gremlins going for them.

"No other pitching staff has contained us this well over the course of the year. I would say the only thing that surprised me in the Series was that we didn't get more runs, and you have to give their pitchers credit."

Series Standing, Figures

	W.	L.	Pc.
Mets	4	1	.800
Orioles	1	4	.200

Fifth-Game Statistics

Paid attendance	57,397
Total receipts	$618,173.09
Commissioner's share	$92,725.96
Clubs' and leagues' share	$131,361.78

Five-Game Totals

Paid attendance	272,378
Total receipts	$2,857,782.78
Commissioner's share	$428,667.41
Players' share (first four games only)	$1,142,200.93
Clubs and leagues' share	$321,728.61

Clendenon Spreads His Most Valuable Title Around

Donn Clendenon won the car that Sport Magazine gives to the Most Valuable Player of the World Series, and he'll take it, but he disagrees with the designation.

"There is no most valuable player on this team—we've got lots of them," he said.

In fact, he is surprised he was a player at all.

"It seems so strange to me," he said, "when I didn't think I'd be playing ball at all this year. I had retired, and I meant it. And I want to thank Arthur Harris of the Scripto Company, and John McHale of the Montreal club, and Commissioner Bowie Kuhn, who is a great commissioner and who is going to prove it to people who may not think so yet. They made it possible for me to come back and be part of this."

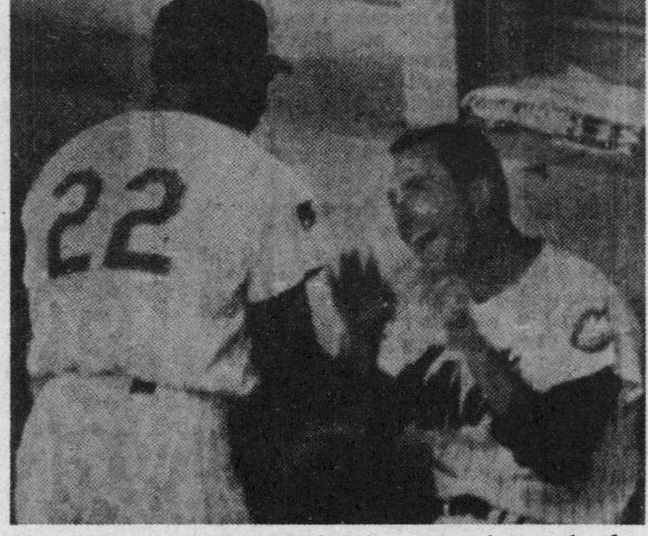

Donn Clendenon (22) and Al Weis congratulate each other. Clendenon hit homer in sixth inning, Weis in the seventh.

Clendenon had played his entire major league career with the Pittsburgh Pirates, through last season. He had also developed various business interests—a small nightclub in Atlanta, and most of all an executive position in public relations and selling for Scripto pens. That was the job he intended to devote all his time to when the Montreal Expos, who took him in the expansion draft from Pittsburgh, traded his contract to Houston as part of a trade for Rusty Staub.

But Clendenon's retirement put the trade into limbo, caused a technical baseball controversy, and left Clendenon struggling with indecision.

"Finally Mr. Harris said to me that the press wouldn't leave me alone and let me work," Clendenon explained, "so he offered to let me go back to baseball, keeping the same money and fringe benefits I had. Then I called Commissioner Kuhn, and he and McHale helped me get back.

"What a year. Five days of spring training, and a not very good start in Montreal—and now this."

On June 15, the day of the trading deadline, the Mets acquired Clendenon from Montreal for four players—Kevin Collins, an infielder briefly with the Mets; Steve Renko, a highly regarded minor-league pitcher, and two lesser minor leaguers. At that point, the Mets had just completed an 11-game winning streak that put them firmly above .500 for the first time in their history.

But it was obvious they couldn't go much further without more scoring punch. This was the difference Clendenon supplied for the rest of the season, not only with his own home runs and runs batted in, but indirectly for his effect on men hitting ahead of him (who couldn't be pitched around) or on the bench (as a pinch-hitter himself, or by making someone else available to pinch hit).

And in the World Series—three home runs, a .357 average—he was the big gun.

Next year? "I signed a two-year contract when I joined the Mets and I'll honor it, as I intended all along," he said. "Then we'll see."

And he grinned.

Paper Blizzard Wraps City in a Blanket of Joy

TRAFFIC CLOGGED DURING RUSH HOUR

Met Victory Creates Mood of Joy as Exuberant Fans Chant, 'We're No. 1'

Continued From Page 1, Col. 7

cascades of paper filled the air like a snowstorm.

At the intersection of 40th Street and Madison Avenue, where the paper was knee high, celebrators tied rolls of toilet paper to the radio aerials of automobiles that were inching through the crowd.

Perched atop mailboxes on the corner, two men drank from bottles of champagne, pausing between sips to squirt passers-by.

"Blow your horn," the crowd around them chanted at passing motorists, and the motorists complied — some, no doubt, just to get through the crowd, but many clearly expressing New York's joy.

Work at a Standstill

The wildness began shortly after 3:15, when Cleon Jones caught the fly ball that ended the game. But most work around town had stopped well before that, on the afternoon when nearly everyone became a fan.

At The New York Times, as in thousands of other offices, typewriters fell silent and desks were emptied, as employes clustered around television sets to watch the final innings, cheering lustily at the good news and wincing together at the bad.

In the seventh inning, when Al Weis's home run suddenly tied the score in a game that many New Yorkers had been ready to concede, excitement began to spread through the streets.

On East 14th Street, one flank of the pedestrian current turned abruptly, as if on signal, into the White Rose Bar, filling the place.

"I'd never been in a bar before, but I mean, I just had to see it on TV," said Ronald Strauss, a peppery little sophomore from Stuyvesant High School.

It did not matter that Ronald is only 14 years old, because during the eighth and ninth innings yesterday everyone was about the same age, and anyway, the air was so tense that the drinking all but stopped.

"Win it, Mets, win it!" he shrieked. And when they did, he jumped in the air with the whoop heard all over town, then rushed back into the street as the celebration began.

At this point, Grand Central Terminal erupted into cheers, three secretaries raced cheering through the lobby of the Time & Life Building, and a crowd of teen-agers in Times Square took up the chant, "Gil Hodges for Mayor."

The joy reached even to the United Nations, where the trees were quickly festooned with streamers thrown from the windows.

Estimates of how much paper had fallen came almost as fast as the paper itself. A waiter at the Harvard Club peered out at the blizzard on West 44th Street and pronounced the celebration "bigger than the astronauts'."

But the Sanitation Department, which keeps records going back to the 1,750 tons of paper that were thrown down on Lindbergh on June 13, 1927, wasn't sure.

The tickertape record, a department spokesman said, is 5,438 tons, which fluttered down on V-J day, Aug. 14, 1945. The record in a personal tribute is held by John Glenn, the astronaut, on whom 3,472 tons were showered on March 1, 1962.

To clean up and weigh yesterday's litter, the department early in the evening called into service the new Night Mobile Task Force consisting of 100 sanitationmen, then later because the problem was "approaching a serious magnitude" 150 additional men were assigned to the force, which sweeps the streets on a midnight-to-8 A.M. shift.

Governor Rockefeller, in a statement, said: "Tonight, everybody is a New York Met."

"The magnificent Mets have performed a baseball miracle" the Governor said. "But they've done a lot more. They've taught us again the great lessons of this country—that you never say die, you don't give up."

Associated Press

VIEW FROM THE TOP: Two workmen on a ledge of the Bankers Trust Building watch the pandemonium along Wall St. Their brooms could have been put to good use below.

In All Respects It Was A Shining Performance

The shoe polish that provided convincing evidence that a pitch had hit Cleon Jones on the foot yesterday had been applied the night before—to all Met shoes—by Nick Torman, the clubhouseman.

The ball bounced off Jones's foot into the Met dugout, where Jerry Grote caught it. Manager Gil Hodges was starting for home plate to plead the case with the umpire, Lou DiMuro, and Grote flipped the ball to Hodges. The umpire was convinced and Jones was given first base.

Did Hodges keep the ball as a souvenir?

"I wouldn't keep a thing like that," Hodges replied, with mock horror. "First thing you know, one of you fellows would say that it wasn't shoe polish and we'd have a controversy. This way you have to take our word for it."

Box Score of Fifth Series Game

BALTIMORE (A.)	AB.	R.	H.	RBI.	NEW YORK (N.)	AB.	R.	H.	RBI.
Buford, lf	4	0	0	0	Agee, cf	3	0	1	0
Blair, cf	4	0	0	0	Harrelson, ss	4	0	0	0
F. Robinson, rf	3	1	1	1	Jones, lf	3	2	[illegible]	0
Powell, lb	4	0	1	0	Clendenon, lb	3	1	1	2
Salmon, pr	0	0	0	0	Swoboda, rf	4	1	2	1
B. Robinson, 3b	4	0	0	0	Charles, 3b	4	0	0	0
Johnson, 2b	4	0	1	0	Grote, c	4	0	0	0
Belanger, ss	3	1	1	0	Weis, 2b	4	1	1	1
Etchebarren, c	3	0	0	0	Koosman, p	3	0	1	0
McNally, p	2	1	1	2	Total	32	5	7	4
Motton, ph	1	0	0	0					
Watt, p	0	0	0	0					
Total	32	3	5	3					

Baltimore (A.)	0	0	3	0	0	0	0	0	0—3
New York (N.)	0	0	0	0	0	2	1	2	..—5

Errors—Powell, Watt. Left on base—Baltimore 3, New York 6. Doubles—Koosman, Jones, Swoboda. Home runs—McNally (1), F. Robinson (1), Clendenon (3), Weis (1). Stolen base—Agee.

	IP.	H.	R.	ER.	BB.	SO.
McNally	7	5	3	3	2	6
Watt (L, 0—1)	1	2	2	1	0	1
Koosman (W, 2—0)	9	5	3	3	1	5

Hit by pitch—by McNally (Jones)

Time of game—2:14. Attendance—57,397.

After the Game, Delirious Rooters Tear Up Field

By GEORGE VECSEY

They came over the barricades like extras in a pirate movie, all hot-eyed and eager to plunder. Their hands were empty and their hearts were full and they were champions of the world—fan division.

For half an hour they sacked Shea Stadium yesterday afternoon and when they were done great gaps of dirt appeared in the grass and there were craters where the fans had clawed at home plate and the pitching mounds.

The ground crew stared at the wreckage and promised that the field would be ready — somehow — for the first home game of the New York Jets by next Monday night.

Rally Lifts Spirits

It will take four days of hard work to repair the damage of half an hour, but nobody can say it was not fun. The fans did have one eye on the television cameras, and they had obviously rehearsed in two previous clinching victories in Shea. But when the Mets rallied in those last glorious inings, the younger fans got the spirit all over again.

It is a cliché about the World Series that the true fans do not have the pull or the money to obtain tickets to a game. Yet the wild-eyed fans who poured on the field yesterday certainly seemed like the same inspired madmen who discovered the Mets at the Polo Grounds in 1962 and transferred out to Shea in 1964.

In the front rows, the Somewhat Important People cowered in their seats as the younger fans jostled past them. One elderly man deliberately tripped a youngster who was climbing through his section.

Once on the field, the young fans dived into the turf, clawing it out with fingernails, prying it out with pens. Some threw the clods of dirt in the air to fall on other heads and shoulders. But others neatly tucked a clod under their arms and marched away.

"This is a historic moment," said Jack Ginsberg of Middle Village, Queens. "I'm a fan since 1930 and I'm going to save this. You never know what might happen next year. They might turn into schlumps again."

Champagne and Youth

Not all the champagne was in the Met clubhouse. Scott Barry, 16½ years old, drained the last bubbles from his six ounces of Bleuve clicquot Ponsardin (Reims) and waved the bottle in the air.

"Ever since I was a little kid" he shouted, "back at the Polo Grounds, I've waited for this moment. Now I don't know what to say."

Most of the young fans pranced up and down, holding their forefingers in the air, chanting "One-One-One," like some mystical incantation.

Children of the communications age, they also sought out photographers and interviewers.

"Tell your paper we're No. 1," a young fan shouted.

"Aw, he already knows that," his friend said.

"Bring on the Astros," the first one shouted.

"I don't know if we can handle them," his friend muttered.

Weaver Bows Again to Umpire, But Keeps His Seat on Bench

Earl Weaver, innocent in appearance but fiery in action, had only one discussion with an umpire in the fourth World Series game Wednesday and was ejected.

In yesterday's fifth game he had two discussions but managed to stay around for the entire nine innings.

Each argument centered on sixth-inning pitches that did or didn't hit batters.

The first situation occurred in the top of the sixth when Jerry Koosman threw a fastball close to Frank Robinson. The Orioles contended the ball struck Robinson on the right thigh, but Lou DiMuro, the home-plate umpire, said it hit Robinson's bat.

"We asked him to ask the umpire at first what he thought," the Baltimore manager related afterward, "but he insisted he saw the play. Then when Frank came into the dugout he [DiMuro] just stood there. He should have come down and have seen what Frank was doing."

Robinson was receiving treatment on the spot where DiMuro said the ball didn't hit him.

Ralph Salvon, the Baltimore trainer, "froze" the spot with ethyl chloride and placed an ice pack on it, and it was more than five minutes before Robinson came out from the dugout.

"I wasn't in any rush to go out," Robinson said. "It would have been a good idea for him to come down and look at it, but if he's not going to ask another umpire about the pitch, I'm sure he's not going to come down and look at my leg."

Several minutes later Weaver was out of the dugout again, this time about a pitch that DiMuro ruled hit Cleon Jones.

"The ball hit him," Weaver said. "Everyone in the park knew it. But he didn't call it until they showed him the ball with shoe polish on it. I just wanted to ask him if he knew the ball had gone into their dugout. He said he did."

"I thought he umpired a good game," the manager said. "That call on Robinson was the only thing that hurt us."

Rangers Rout Penguins, for Sawchuk's 103d Shutout

The New York Times

Rangers and Penguins at Madison Square Garden.

BALON REGISTERS FIRST 3-GOAL FEAT

Runs Season Total to 21

By GERALD ESKENAZI

Brad Park planted a kiss on the scar tissue that serves as Terry Sawchuk's forehead and the pair danced off the Madison Square Garden ice last night to a standing ovation.

The 40-year-old Sawchuk, who said afterward, "I'm old and I'm tired but I try my best," had just turned in the 103d shutout of a topsy-turvy but mostly brilliant career as the Rangers blasted the Pittsburgh Penguins, 6-0.

Sawchuk, picked up by the New Yorkers to give Ed Giacomin a rest in the critical, nerve-wracking late stages of the National Hockey League season, shared idol-of-the-night honors with Dave Balon, who had the first three-goal game of his career.

Just about a year ago, when Emile Francis regained the Rangers, coaching reins, he placed Balon on the same line with Walt Tkaczuk. Before the move, Balon had been a utility player and, he said, "it got to the point where I started to lose my confidence."

Ratelle's Feat Overshadowed

Balon now has 21 goals this season, has scored more points than ever before and is among the leading scorers. There was some irony in his feat last night, for it overshadowed Jean Ratelle's two goals. Before Tkaczuk and his partners, Balon and Billy Fairbairn, became the highest-scoring line in the league, Ratelle's trio, which includes Rod Gilbert and Vic Hadfield, was No. 1 for New York.

Fairbairn also reached a high-water mark. His three assists gave him 42 points, a record for a Ranger rookie. It broke Camille Henry's mark of 39 set during the 1953-54 campaign. "Don't tell me about records," said Fairbairn.

Sawchuk, with more shutouts than anyone who ever played the game, had not had one since the 1967-68 season, when he played for the Los Angeles Kings. Giacomin injured his thigh last Wednesday (during the red light-green light game in Los Angeles) and Sawchuck was in the nets last Friday against the Oakland Seals.

RANGERS (6)		PITTSBURG (0)
Sawchuk	Goal	Smith
Park	Defense	Watson
Brown	Defense	Morrison
Tkaczuk	Center	Hextall
Fairbairn	Wing	Schinkel
Balon	Wing	Prentice
Gilbert	Forward	Fonteyne
Nevin	Forward	McCreary
Hadfield	Forward	Harbaruk
Stewart	Forward	Sather
Ratelle	Forward	Schock
Widing	Forward	Boyer
Marshall	Forward	Pronovost
Kurtenbach	Forward	Briere
Hamilton	Defense	Rupp
Neilson	Defense	Woytowich
Seiling	Defense	Pratt
Giacomin	Goal	Daley

New York Rangers	2	0	4—6
Pittsburgh Penguins	0	0	0—0

First Period

1—Rangers, Balon (19) (Park, Fairbairn) 5.44
2—Rangers, Balon (20) (Fairbairn, Tkaczuk) 18:50

Second Period

No scoring.

Third Period

3—Rangers, Ratelle (21) (Hadfield, Neilson) 1:36
4—Rangers, Ratelle (22) (Hadfield, Gilbert) 7:40
5—Rangers, Park (9) (Widing, Marshall) 9:21
6—Rangers, Balon (21) (Tkaczuk, Fairbairn) 11:15

PENALTY—First period: None. Second period: Tkaczuk (17:55). Third period: None.

SHOTS ON GOAL—Rangers: 14, 9, 13—36; Pittsburgh: 6, 11, 12—29.

Referee—Art Skov. Linesmen—John D'Amico and Willard Norris.

Attendance—17,250.

Bruins Down Maple Leafs, 7-6, In Game Marked by Brawling

BOSTON, Feb. 1 (UPI)—John McKenzie's goal midway in the third period today gave the Boston Bruins a 7-6 victory over the Toronto Maple Leafs, in a nationally televised National Hockey League game marked by fights among the players.

McKenzie received a minute-long standing ovation from a capacity crowd at Boston Garden after he broke a 6-6 tie at 9 minutes 24 seconds of the third period in a game that saw all the players on both squads take part in one major brawl. The goal was McKenzie's second of the game.

A total of 84 penalty minutes was assessed, 54 of them during the second period in which seven of the 13 goals were scored.

Several Players Score

Bobby Orr, Phil Esposito, Fred Stanfield, Wayne Cashman and Don Marcotte scored the five other Boston goals. Mike Walton with two, Norm Ullman, Jim McKenny, Jim Harrison and Dave Keon did the Toronto scoring.

The game twice erupted into fighting during the secon period, finally breaking into a Donnybrook that drew penalties totaling 35 minutes from Referee Bill Friday.

A fight between Orr and Pat Quinn ignited the struggle in which players from both benches jumped the boards to take part. Bryan Glennie drew a 10-minute misconduct for leaving the penalty box as Toronto's Rick Ley led the charge of bench players though he personally escaped notice.

About four minutes after the midperiod brawl, Ken Hodge collided with the Leaf's goalie, Bruce Gamble, and touched off a fight between Hodge and Tim Horton, a Toronto defenseman. The scrap produced 10 more minutes in penalties.

Orr, in scoring 3 points in the game on his 17th goal and two assists, increased his league-leading point total to 77.

Boston Bruins	3	3	1—7
Toronto Maple Leafs	1	4	1—6

First Period—1, Boston, Stanfield (18) (Orr, McKenzie) 1:56; 2, Boston, Esposito (29) (Carlton, D. Smith) 3:26; 3, Toronto, Walton (13) (Henderson) 12:06; 4, Boston, Orr (17) (McKenzie, Stanfield) 18:15. Penalties: Quinn, Toronto (0:27); Awrey, Boston (5:51); Lorentz, Boston (10:32); Carlton (14:34); Pulford, Toronto (16:48).

Second Period—5, Boston, Westfall (10) (unassisted) 5:25; 6, Toronto, Ullman (9) (Henderson, McKenney) 7:08; 7, Toronto, Harrison (10) (Selby, McKenney) 9:07; 8, Toronto, Walton (14) (McKenney, Oliver) 10:35; 9, Boston, Marcotte (2) (D. Smith, Westfall) 15:07; 10, Boston, Cashman (8) (Bailey, Doak) 16:11; 11, Toronto, McKenney (10) (Ullman, Henderson) 18:40. Penalties: McKenzie (5:47); Lorentz, Boston (9:26); Pulford (9:49); Awrey (9:49); Glennie, Toronto (11:15); Quinn, Toronto (7 minutes) (12:33); McKenzie (7 minutes) (12:33) Selby (5 minutes) (12:33); Orr (5 minutes) (12:33) Glennie (10 minutes) (12:33); Horton, Toronto (5 minutes) (16:01); Hodge, Boston (5 minutes) (16:01).

Third Period—12, Toronto, Keon (21) (Oliver, Walton) 3:43; 13, Boston, McKenzie (16) (Bucyk, Orr) 9:24. Penalties: Bailey, Boston (12 minutes) (2:58); Horton (4:57); Glennie (8:33); Harrison, Toronto (10:37); Walton (19:53).

Shots on goal by—Toronto: 13, 14, 11—38. Boston: 13, 18, 12—43.

Goalies—Toronto: Gamble; Boston: Cheevers.

Attendance—14,835.

CANADIENS' RALLY BEATS FLYERS, 5-2

4 Goals Scored Late in 3d Period—Backstrom Gets 3

PHILADELPHIA, Feb. 1 (UPI)—Ralph Backstrom registered three goals to help the Montreal Canadiens gain a 5-2 victory over the Philadelphia Flyers tonight in a National Hockey League game.

The Canadiens were trailing, 2-1, with 7 minutes 18 seconds left in the game when they rallied for four goals. Mickey Redmond tied the game with his 17th goal and Backstrom followed four minutes later with his second of the night to put the Canadiens ahead for the first time, 3-2.

Philadelphia removed its goalie, Bernie Parent, in the final minute and Claude Provost put the puck into an empty net with 45 seconds remaining. With Parent back in the net, Backstrom got his third goal with eight seconds left.

Montreal Canadiens	0	1	4—5
Philadelphia Flyers	1	0	1—2

First Period—1, Philadelphia, Heiskala (6) (Clarke, W. Hillman) 5:42. Penalties: Harris, Montreal (7:09); Harris (16:19); W. Hillman (18:07).

Second Period—2, Montreal, Backstrom (12) (Harris, Harper) 19:13). Penalties: Peters, Philadelphia (0:15); Heiskala, Philadelphia (12:50); Harris (16:41).

Third Period—3, Philadelphia, Lacroix (17) (Nolet, L. Hillman) 3:56; 4, Montreal, Redmond (17) (Richard, Harper) 12:42; 5, Montreal, Backstrom (13) (Harper) 16:57; 6, Montreal, Provost (10) LaPerriere, Savard) 19:15; 7, Montreal, Backstrom (14) (Bordeleau, Harris) 19:52. Penalties: Heiskala, Philadelphia (8:32); Richard, Montreal (9:21); LaPerriere (13:05); Redmond (18:42); Nolet (18:42).

Shots on Goal—Montreal, 15, 13, 12—40; Philadelphia, 12, 13, 10—35.

Goalies—Montreal: Vahon; Philadelphia: Parent.

Attendance—14,606.

Hawks Turn Back Stars

CHICAGO, Feb. 1 (UPI)—Jim Pappin registered the third three-goal game of his pro career and Stan Mikita scored two goals and had three assists tonight to lead the Chicago Black Hawks to a 7-4 victory over the Minnesota North Stars.

Hawks Turn Back Leafs, 4-0, To Tie Bruins for First Place

CHICAGO, March 29 (UPI)—Tony Esposito, the record-setting goalie, got his 15th shutout tonight as the Chicago Black Hawks skated to a 4-0 victory over the Toronto Maple Leafs.

The victory moved the Hawks into a tie with Boston for first place in the National Hockey League's East Division.

By extending their unbeaten string to five games, the Hawks clinched a playoff position. It was their 43d victory of the season and assured them of finishing with more triumphs than any other team, an important factor should they tie for a playoff position in the final standing. In such a case the team with the most victories gains the higher position.

Esposito, who set a record for shutouts in a season with his 14th against Detroit Thursday, racked up his third in the last four games. He has allowed only one goal during the 240 minutes, and is almost certain to win the Vezina Trophy that goes to the net tender allowing the fewest goals during a season. The Hawks have allowed only 162.

Esposito had to kick away 23 shots. The Hawks got 35 shots on the Toronto goalie, Marv Edwards.

Gerry Pinder scored the first two goals in the opening period, snapping in a rebound of his shot after 21 seconds and driving in a short blast after a breakaway

Bobby Hull put in the last two goals, both in the third period, as he tallied on a power play from 15 feet and then drove a 30-footer between Edwards's pads on a breakaway. He has 36 for the season.

Chicago Black Hawks	2	0	2—4
Toronto Maple Leafs	0	0	0—0

First Period—1, Chicago, Pinder (15) (Pappin, Martin) 0:21; 2, Chicago, Pinder (16) (Pappin, Magnuson) 15:46. Penalties: None.
Second Period—No scoring. Penalties: Dorey, Toronto (1:15); Chicago bench penalty (12:40); Dorey (17:42).
Third Period—3, Chicago, R. Hull (35) (Mikita, Mohns) 7:45; 4, Chicago, R. Hull (36) (Pappin) 16:47. Penalties: Spencer, Toronto (6:15); Maki, Chicago (9:03).
Shots on Goal—Toronto, 8, 8, 7—23; Chicago, 8, 15, 12—35.
Goalies—Toronto: Edwards; Chicago: Esposito.
Attendance—20,500.

National Hockey League

Tony Esposito

DETROIT TALLIES ON POWER PLAYS

DETROIT, March 29 (AP)—The Boston Bruins and Detroit Red Wings fought to a 2-2 tie today in a battle between East Division teams in the National Hockey League.

The Red Wings cashed in on two power-play goals before a crowd of 14,188 and a national television audience.

Taking up where they left off in a 5-5 deadlock in Boston yesterday, the two teams checked fiercely and often. The Bruins slipped to a first-place tie with Chicago in the East race for Stanley Cup playoff berths.

Alex Delvecchio, spearheading the team's bid for one of the four playoff spots, slammed in his 19th goal of the season midway in the third period to give the Wings the tie after they had trailed 2-1 after two periods.

For Delvecchio, it was his 394th career goal, putting him fifth in N.H.L. scoring history.

The Bruins struck first as Don Awrey netted his third goal of the season at 6:55 of the opening period. But Garry Unger got that one back quickly as he scored his 41st goal on a power play.

Don Marcotte sent the Bruins out in front at 2-1 at the 8:03 mark of the second period after being set up by Jim Lorentz and Bobby Orr.

The Wings buzzed around the Boston goalie, Gerry Cheevers, before Delvecchio tipped in the tying goal, with Frank Mahovlich and Gordie Howe getting the assists.

Boston Bruins	1	1	0—2
Detroit Red Wings	1	0	1—2

First Period—1, Boston, Awrey (3) (Orr) 6:55; 2, Detroit, Unger (41) (Connelly, MacGregor) 15:48. Penalties—Hatoum, Detroit (9:08); Orr, Boston (15:05); McKenzie, Boston (4 minutes, 16:26); Libbett, Detroit (16:26).
Second Period—3, Boston, Marcotte (9) (Lorentz, Orr) 8:03. Penalties: Stemkowski, Detroit (5:31); R. Smith, Boston (9:40); D. Smith, Boston (16:54).
Third Period—4, Delvecchio (19) (Mahovlich, Howe) 9:49. Penalty: Awrey, Boston (9:27).
Shots On Goal—Boston, 8, 8, 8—24. Detroit, 12, 12, 10—34.
Goalies—Boston: Cheevers; Detroit: Edwards.
Attendance—14,188.

NEW YORK CLOSES TO A POINT OF 4TH

Ratelle Tallies 2 Unassisted Goals—Park and Nevin Also Score at Garden

By GERALD ESKENAZI

Suddenly, the Rangers are no longer comatose.

With a fundamental attack reminiscent of their best games, they crept to within 1 point of a playoff berth last night with a deadly-perfect 4-1 thrashing of the Montreal Canadiens.

Jean Ratelle, who had been almost a forgotten man when he was overshadowed by Walt Tkaczuk earlier this National Hockey League season, paced the Rangers with two goals, both unassisted.

But perhaps overshadowing everyone else was a player who saw little action: Brad Park. It was his first Madison Square Garden game since Feb. 19.

On Saturday night, he returned to the line-up and the Rangers and Frenchmen skated to a 1-1 tie. So with Park back, the New Yorkers are undefeated in two games.

Weekend Showdown Looms

Three games remain for the Rangers, who are in fifth place in the East Division. If they can get past Toronto on Wednesday, the race for them will come down to the final weekend, when they play the Detroit Red Wings, who have a 1-point edge in fourth place, consecutive games.

"That's all we needed was a little togetherness," said Coach Emile Francis, trying to explain the weekend, which the Rangers had entered with one victory in 13 games. "That 10 hours on the bus kept us together."

He was referring to the Friday night incident, when their bus driver deserted them in Queens en route to Montreal.

The Canadiens were never in the game. They were belted out of it after the first body check and the Rangers sustained the momentum they had failed to generate since Park's injury.

Ed Giacomin made only one mistake in the Rangers' net. With nine seconds remaining, he tried to clear the disk by passing it out in front. Henri Richard intercepted it and scored.

Music to Fans' Ears

As each Canadien hit the boards—especially John Ferguson or the huge Pete Mahovlich—the fans applauded madly, as though they were opera buffs cheering an aria.

This was the type of play they had waited more than a month to see. The Walt Tkaczuk line carried the puck in deep, and didn't have to dump the disk in and chase it. With Rod Gilbert playing with his old verve, Rogatien Vachon was forced to make saves in self-protection.

The fans even cheered Bob Nevin lustily. The right wing played a key first period, always swarming around the puck and getting the disk away quickly with long, booming shots.

Whenever the Rangers dominate, the fans look for little things to appreciate: Tkaczuk exchanging elbows with Richard (who used to save his fighting for Vic Hadfield), or Rod Seiling, five inches shorter, trying to reach Mahovlich's face with his fist.

Nevin Starts It Rolling

Nevin opened the scoring with a roller that was set up by Don Luce in the first period. Then Ratelle intercepted a J. C. Tremblay pass in the second session and his hard shot went in.

That set the stage for Park. Twenty-five seconds later, he smashed in a 60-footer, and the club acted as if the last month had never happened.

RANGERS (4)		MONTREAL (1)
Giacomin	Goal	Vachon
Horton	Defense	Tremblay
Neilson	Defense	Harris
Tkaczuk	Center	Richard
Balon	Wing	Mahovlich
Fairbairn	Wing	Redmond
Gilbert	Forward	Beliveau
Nevin	Forward	Backstrom
Stewart	Forward	Mickey
Luce	Forward	Cournoyer
Ratelle	Forward	Provost
Kurtenbach	Forward	Ferguson
Irvine	Foward	Lemaire
Egers	Forward	Pleau
Park	Defense	Laperriere
A. Brown	Defense	Harper
Seiling	Defense	—
Sawchuk	Goal	Myre

New York Rangers	1	2	1—4
Montreal Canadiens	0	0	1—1

First Period

1—Rangers, Nevin (17) (Luce, Irvine) 5:41

Second Period

2—Rangers, Ratelle (30) (unassisted) 8:57
3—Rangers, Park (11) (Neilson, Ratelle) 9:22

Third Period

4—Rangers, Ratelle (31) (unassisted) 13:47
5—Montreal, Richard (16) (unassisted) 19:51

PENALTIES—First Period: Tkaczuk (0:35), Ferguson (2:56), A. Brown (7:59), Mahovlich (12:45), Tkaczuk (17:00). Second Period: Irvine (3:03), Harper (3:03), Ratelle (6:43), Laperriere (9:18), LeMaire (14:52). Third Period: Steward (16:49).

SHOTS ON GOAL—Rangers: 16, 14, 10—40. Montreal: 7:14, 14-35.

Referee—Art Skov. Linesmen—Matt Pavelich and Willard Norris.

Attendance—17,250.

The New York Times

ON TARGET: Shot by Jean Ratelle, rear, finds it mark and slips by Canadiens' Rogatien Vachon into the net. Walter Tkaczuk, right, cheers the second-period tally, which made the score 2-0. It was Ratelle's 30th goal of the season.

"All the News That's Fit to Print"

The New York Times

LATE CITY EDITION

Weather: Partly sunny, mild today; fair tonight. Cloudy tomorrow. Temp. range: today 78-53: Friday 72-50. Full U.S. report on Page 48.

VOL. CXIX. No. 41,013 © 1970 The New York Times Company. NEW YORK, SATURDAY, MAY 9, 1970 10 CENTS

NIXON DEFENDS CAMBODIA DRIVE AS AIDING STUDENTS' PEACE AIM; SAYS PULLOUT WILL BEGIN SOON

IN FINANCIAL AREA: Hard-hatted construction workers breaking up an antiwar rally at the Subtreasury Building

The New York Times (by Carl T. Gossett Jr.)

SEES SHORTER WAR

Voices Understanding of Critics and Seeks Theirs in Return

Transcript of the President's news conference. Page 8.

By MAX FRANKEL

Special to The New York Times

WASHINGTON, May 8 — Strongly defending the United States troop movement into Cambodia, which has evoked a storm of protest by students and others throughout the country, President Nixon said tonight that the operation would win six to eight months of time for the further training of South Vietnamese forces and thus shorten the war for the Americans.

He said that most American troops would be out of Cambodia by the middle of June, and that the first units would leave in the middle of next week.

Mr. Nixon said that he shared the objectives of his critics and that time would prove him to have served the cause of peace. He expressed understanding of the protesters and asked their understanding in return.

Visibly Nervous

The President, visibly nervous at his first televised news conference in more than three months, said that he was not surprised by the intensity of the protest, but placed the blame on a misunderstanding of his intentions. He disclaimed responsibility for the war in Vietnam and reiterated that he had no intention of expanding it. [Question 8, Page 3.]

The Cambodian operation was proceeding well ahead of schedule he said, denying "rockets by the thousands and small arms by the millions" to the enemy forces. The promised withdrawal of 150,000 additional American soldiers from South Vietnam by next spring will thus be achieved, Mr. Nixon said, and if various attempts at negotiations bear fruit, the pullout may be even faster.

No Revolt Expected

Mr. Nixon said he foresaw neither revolt nor repression in the United States, citing his tolerance of dissent and efforts to communicate with younger Americans as the necessary "safety valve." He expressed a hope that while the action was hot, everyone's rhetoric would remain cool, but insisted that he would not "muzzle" Vice President Agnew or other members of his "open" Administration. [Question 21.]

The President offered, somewhat tentatively, to receive some of the demonstrators who were massing in the capital tonight for the protest rally outside the White House tomorrow. He thought that they were seeking peace, an end of the killing, an end of the draft and American withdrawal from Vietnam,

Continued on Page 9, Column 7

Knicks Take First Title, Beating Lakers, 113 to 99

Frazier Scores 36 Points, Reed Excels on Defense Despite Ailing Knee

By LEONARD KOPPETT

The New York Knickerbockers, displaying their finest qualities with the limited physical but important spiritual aid of a limping Willis Reed, won the championship of the National Basketball Association last night by routing the Los Angeles Lakers, 113-99, at Madison Square Garden.

Walt Frazier, with 36 points and 19 assists, was the most brilliant individual, but this, like most Knick successes, was basically a team enterprise.

Darlings of the basketball world and a subject of national sports interest since November, when they set a league record by winning 18 games in a row, the Knicks finally achieved the first title in their 24-year history by winning the seventh game of the final round of the playoffs. It was their 101st game this season.

By winning, the Knicks gave

Continued on Page 29, Column 1

The New York Times

Walt Frazier in the game

NATION IS WARNED TO RETAIN ITS LEAD IN SCIENCE FIELDS

Study Group Contends U.S. Progress Is Dependent on Excellence in Technology

By HAROLD M. SCHMECK Jr.

Special to The New York Times

WASHINGTON, May 8—The White House released today a Presidential study group report that calls continuing leadership in science and technology a vital national goal.

The report was released at a time when the Administration appeared to be reconciled to the United States being in second place in some fields of science for the time being at least.

"Our national progress will become ever more critically dependent upon the excellence of our science and technology," the report stated. "A vigorous, high-quality program aimed at advancing our scientific and technological capabilities (including the social, economic and behavioral components) is vital to all national goals and purposes."

Such a program is especially vital to national defense and security and to the nation's international posture generally, it was said.

Economic Growth Effect

"It is generally recognized that the economic growth of highly industrialized countries in the Western world has been heavily dependent on the technological developments which have been incorporated into their societies," the report said. "In the past half-century the economic growth of the United States has been as much determined by new technology as it has by the continuous investment of capital."

The study group recommended that the President call for—as one national goal—continuing leadership in science and in the technology relevant to the nation's other goals.

Last month at the annual meeting of the National Academy of Sciences, two science advisers to the President conceded that the United States does not lead, presently, in all major fields of science.

Dr. Lee A. DuBridge, the President's chief science adviser told that meeting that an upswing in other countries had put the United States behind in such fields as radio and optical astronomy.

Patrick E. Haggerty, board chairman of Texas Instruments, Inc., of Dallas and a member of the President's Science Advisory Committee, said then that the United States was not going to dominate science in the world in the way it used to.

Inflation Effect Cited

The Administration posture seems to be that of weighing priorities in science to get the most from the limited funds available.

At a briefing on the report today, Dr. Hubert Heffner, deputy to Dr. Dubridge, said the science policy of the Administration "is constrained by the necessity to balance the budget."

The report noted that Federal funds for basic research had actually decreased in recent years when the effects of inflation were taken into account.

It recommended that the

Continued on Page 42, Column 2

7 PANTHERS FREED IN CHICAGO CLASH

State's Attorney Cites Lack of Proof of Shooting as Charges Are Dropped

By SETH S. KING

Special to The New York Times

CHICAGO, May 8 — All criminal charges were dropped today against the seven Black Panthers who survived a shooting incident with Chicago policemen last December.

State's Attorney Edward V. Hanrahan said there was not sufficient proof that any of the defendants had fired a weapon at the police.

The seven had been indicted by a Cook County Grand Jury on charges of attempted murder, armed violence, unlawful possession of weapons and unlawful use of weapons.

In a statement explaining his action, Mr. Hanrahan also said that the methods used in gathering evidence might have prevented "our satisfying judicial standards of proof."

Early last Dec. 4, a special detail of policemen from Mr. Hanrahan's office, carrying a warrant to search for weapons, broke into an apartment in which the Panthers were sleeping.

In the shooting that followed, Fred Hampton, 21-year-old leader of the Black Panther party in Illinois, and Mark Clark, 22, an-

Continued on Page 21, Column 1

PANEL ON POLICE MAY BE REPLACED

Mayor Is Expected to Name a Larger Unit on Graft That Excludes Leary

By DAVID BURNHAM

Mayor Lindsay plans to disband the special five-man committee established two weeks ago to investigate corruption in the Police Department and replace it with a larger panel, sources in the Lindsay administration reported yesterday.

The special committee was formed by Mr. Lindsay two weeks ago when he learned that The New York Times was preparing a survey on police corruption. The survey included reports of charges that the police received millions of dollars a year in graft and that high officials in city government had failed to investigate specific cases of corruption called to their attention.

Reason for Move

One reason for disbanding the present committee and forming a new one, according to the sources, would be to find a graceful method to remove Police Commissioner Howard R. Leary from a group charged with judging the performance of his own department.

Mr. Leary's presence on the committee, especially after he

Continued on Page 28, Column 1

STUDENTS STEP UP PROTESTS ON WAR

Marches and Strikes Held Amid Some Violence—200 Colleges Closed

By ROBERT D. McFADDEN

College students across the nation intensified the renewed antiwar movement yesterday with mass marches and rallies, widened school strikes and scattered incidents of violence.

More than 200 colleges and universities were closed in the spreading protest against the United States military involvement in Indochina and the fatal shooting of four Kent State University students by National Guardsmen last Monday.

Some 400 of the nation's 2,500 higher academic institutions were affected by strikes, many of them with faculty and administration support. Demonstrations continued to curtail classes at hundreds of other schools.

The vast majority of college campuses yesterday were peaceful. And at many schools antiwar activities took constructive form, with discussion seminars supplanting regular classwork and students gathering petitions to send to Congress and Mr. Nixon.

Movements were also under way to reopen some of the schools shut down in the protest.

While most campuses were

Continued on Page 9, Column 1

War Foes Here Attacked By Construction Workers

City Hall Is Stormed

By HOMER BIGART

Helmeted construction workers broke up a student antiwar demonstration in Wall Street yesterday, chasing youths through the canyons of the financial district in a wild noontime melee that left about 70 persons injured.

The workers then stormed City Hall, cowing policemen and forcing officials to raise the American flag to full staff from half staff, where it had been placed in mourning for the four students killed at Kent State University on Monday.

At nearby Pace College a group of construction workers who said they had been pelted with missiles by students from the roof, twice invaded a building, smashing windows with clubs and crowbars and beating up students.

Earlier the workers ripped a Red Cross banner from the gates of Trinity Church and tried to tear down the flag of the Episcopal Church.

"This is senseless," said the Rev. Dr. John Vernon Butler, rector of Trinity Parish. "I suppose they thought it was a Vietcong flag."

Twice Father Butler ordered the gates closed against menacing construction workers.

Inside the church, doctors and nurses from the New York University Medical Center had

Continued on Page 10, Column 4

Police Were Told of Plan

By MARTIN ARNOLD

City Hall and the Police Department received warnings yesterday morning that several hundred construction workers, organized into a band on Thursday, would attack peace demonstrators in lower Manhattan.

The warnings came from, among others, the office of Representative Allard K. Lowenstein, Democrat of Nassau County, and from construction workers who did not approve of the impending attack.

Tom Morgan, Mayor Lindsay's press secretary, said last night that many reports of probable confrontation between students and opposing groups were received at City Hall Thursday night and yesterday morning. All were referred to the Police Department, he said.

With the exception of the lower Manhattan warnings, he said, none were "considered valid."

After violence between construction workers and students broke out at noontime yesterday, the police said they did not have the manpower to control the workers.

Mayor Lindsay summoned Police Commissioner Howard R. Leary, First Deputy Commissioner John R. Walsh and other

Continued on Page 10, Column 7

PRESIDENT BACKS RIGHT TO DISSENT

Asserts He Shares Goals of Students—Denies Curbs on Agnew's Comments

By ROBERT B. SEMPLE Jr.

Special to The New York Times

WASHINGTON, May 8—President Nixon told the nation tonight that he shared the goals and concerns of student protesters.

He defended their right to dissent and said, at his news conference, that he would allow the members of his own Cabinet full freedom of speech. [Questions 3 and 7, Page 8.]

Contradicting reports from a spokesman for eight university presidents who conferred with Mr. Nixon yesterday, the President said that he would not "censor" Vice President Agnew. But he said that, when "the action is hot," he hoped his colleagues in the Government would "keep the rhetoric cool."

Earlier in the day, the Administration agreed to permit a mass antiwar rally tomorrow on the Ellipse, an area south of the White House that was previously declared out of bounds.

And, in another move to portray concern over campus dissent, Mr. Nixon appointed a prominent university administrator, G. Alexander Heard, chancellor of Vanderbilt University, as his personal adviser on campus problems.

At the news conference, Mr. Nixon also suggested that he would make no effort to restrain Secretary of the Interior Walter J. Hickel, who two days ago accused the Administration of insensitivity to student con-

Continued on Page 8, Column 6

U.S. Health Official Will Head New City Hospitals Corporation

By EDWARD RANZAL

Dr. Joseph T. English, a 37-year-old psychiatrist, was named yesterday as the first president of the New York City Health and Hospitals Corporation, the largest non-Federal health system in the nation.

Although no salary was announced — the details are still being worked out, a spokesman said — it is expected that Dr. English will receive about $70,000 a year. This would make him the highest paid city official, receiving $20,000 more than Mayor Lindsay.

Dr. English will leave a high position in the Federal Health, Education and Welfare Department to take the job here, where his immediate responsibility will be the operation of the city's 18 hospitals. His role is expected to be extended to include some health services now provided by the Health Department.

Dr. English will be working with a $600-million expense budget and a capital budget of $1-billion for new construction.

He will assume his new position on July 1. Until then, Joseph V. Terenzio, acting president of the corporation, will continue to serve in that capacity.

Mr. Terenzio resigned as Hospitals Commissioner earlier this year, but agreed to stay on until someone was selected to lead the health corporation.

Last Tuesday it was disclosed that two physicians had turned down offers to head the corporation.

One of the men, Dr. Peter Rogatz, a specialist in community medicine and a professor at the State University Center at Stony Brook, L.I. and director of University Hospital there, said he had turned the post down for "all kinds of personal reasons." A major consideration, he said, would have been "the impact on my family."

Dr. John H. Knowles, director of the Massachusetts General Hospital, said that he had asked that his name not be

Continued on Page 36, Column 4

NEWS INDEX

250 in State Dept. Sign a War Protest

By PETER GROSE

Special to The New York Times

WASHINGTON, May 8—More than 250 State Department and foreign-aid employes have signed a letter to Secretary of State William P. Rogers criticizing the United States military involvement in Cambodia.

Mr. Rogers accepted the petitions, but was reliably reported to have urged that there be no public dissent among career diplomats that could embarrass the Administration.

In addition, at the Peace Corps, about a dozen antiwar demonstrators today occupied part of one floor of the headquarters building, overlooking Lafayette Square in front of

Continued on Page 7, Column 1

The New York Times (by Neal Boenzi)

BATTLE ON BROADWAY: A construction worker aims blow at a youth near Fulton Street

Agnew Tones Down His Speech After Viewing President on TV

By United Press International

BOISE, Idaho, May 8—Vice President Agnew, delivering a speech tonight, toned down a text that came down hard on America's dissenters, saying he wanted "in some small way" to help cool the temper of the nation.

Mr. Agnew's office had released his prepared speech in advance. In it he turned his fire from student dissenters to the "tired, embittered elders" who oppose the Administration.

But, after watching President Nixon's news conference on television, he told his audience at a Republican dinner that he no longer wanted to say what the text said.

The Vice President said he did not "author these paragraphs" that were released by his office, but neither would he apologize for them. He said they reflected his thinking, but "the rhetoric was not mine."

He denied that Mr. Nixon had "muzzled" him but said he was following the President's advice in an attempt to "help cool in some small way" the situation facing the nation.

'Jeremiahs' Assailed

By ROBERT M. SMITH

Special to The New York Times

WASHINGTON, May 8—Vice President Agnew's prepared text had said that a group of

Continued on Page 12, Column 5

Knicks Trounce Lakers and Gain N.B.A. Crown

The New York Times

HOW SWEET THE VICTORY: Wilt Chamberlain of the Los Angeles Lakers is a forgotten man as jubilant New York Knicks sweep past him proclaiming their victory. From left are Don May, Mike Riordan and Cazzie Russell.

FRAZIER TALLIES 36 POINTS IN ROUT

Reed, Despite Ailing Knee, Bottles Up Chamberlain and Inspires Knicks

Continued From Page 1, Col. 1

New York's happy sports fans their third professional world championship in 16 months. The football Jets won the Super Bowl game in January, 1969, and the baseball Mets took the World Series last fall.

For the 19,500 screaming spectators, the Knicks produced a staggeringly effective defense, their trademark throughout the season. In addition, their shooting was deadly in the first quarter as they built a 38-24 lead.

Soon they had a 51-31 margin and it didn't dip below 20 points until the closing minutes.

Reed, as always, was an indispensable element, but in an unusual fashion. He had injured a muscle in his right leg that runs from the pelvis to below the knee early in the fifth game of the series, when the series was tied in games, 2-2. His injury seemed to doom the Knicks to defeat, because it left them with no counterweapon to Wilt Chamberlain, the 7-foot-2-inch giant who is the Laker center and the greatest scorer in basketball history.

But the Knicks rallied to win that game, which meant they were still alive when Chamberlain and the Lakers crushed them in Los Angeles on Wednesday night, while Reed sat on the bench. If Reed had been unable to play last night, the Knicks would not have been expected to win.

Reed Gets First Basket

As it turned out, after a late-afternoon examination by Dr. James Parkes, some pain-killing injections, a few minutes of shooting practice and another injection just before the game began, Reed was able to start. He took the first shot at the basket, with the game 18 seconds old, and made it.

A minute later, he hit another, making the score 5-2, and the effect on his teammates was electric.

"He gave us a tremendous lift, just going out there," said Coach Red Holzman afterward. "He couldn't play his normal game, but he did a lot of things out there and he means a lot to the spirit of the other players."

What Reed did was occupy Chamberlain. He presented enough of a defensive problem to keep the big man within bounds—and the other four Knicks simply ran away from the other four Lakers.

The Knicks shot better, defended better, hustled more, defended better, hustled more, ran faster, jumped higher, passed more accurately and stole the ball more often.

Reed Wins Award

When it was all over, Reed's line in the box score was unimpressive: just those two baskets in five shots, no free-throw attempts, three rebounds, four personal fouls. But his season-long contribution was taken into consideration and he was given the car that Sport magazine awards to the outstanding player of the final round of the playoffs.

As the game wore on, Reed felt more pain, and moved more slowly, even though he had another shot of pain-killer at half-time. But the early momentum he helped give the Knicks was enough.

Frazier in particular, and the team in general, showed a characteristic the Knicks had displayed before: the ability to fire their best effort in the most important situation. The three best performances they gave in six weeks of post-season competition were in the seventh game of the Baltimore series, which got them past that most serious hurdle; the fifth game against Milwaukee, which wrapped up the series against Lew Alcindor's team, 4 games to 1, and this one.

Dave DeBusschere, the rugged forward whose arrival from Detroit more than a year ago transformed the Knicks into a great team (by allowing Reed to move to center as well as by DeBusschere's own contributions) had another superb game. He had to do the heavy rebounding, taking down 17, and scoring 18 points.

Dick Barnett, the oldest Knick, scored 21. As Frazier's partner in backcourt, he had provided the outside shooting the Knicks always needed. He was the only Knick who had played in a final round before, with the Lakers in 1962 when they lost to Boston in seven games. The victory was especially sweet to him.

Bill Bradley, not at his best in much of the series, was in top form this time, with 17 points and five assists. And the much-appreciated Knick bench—Nate Bowman as Reed's relief, Dave Stallworth, Cazzie Russell and Mike Riordan—did its share, although only Bowman played as much as usual (and more).

For Coach Red Holzman, who also took over as general manager last March, it was a complete triumph. He succeeded Dick McGuire as coach halfway through the 1967-68 season, and the Knicks have been winning regularly ever since. Eddie Donovan, who built the team as general manager before resigning to take over the new Buffalo club, was also present to enjoy the victory.

And probably no one enjoyed it more than Ned Irish, original and present president of the club, who saw the Knicks fail in the final round in 1951, 1952 and 1953 before going into a long decline that Donovan finally reversed.

For the Lakers, the result was bitter disappointment. They have now reached the final round, and lost, seven times in the last nine years. All their previous defeats were at the hands of the Boston Celtics, led by Bill Russell. Now they had failed again, even though Reed—who is not, for all his virtues, the equal of Russell at his best—was hurt.

Elgin Baylor and Jerry West, who played on all those teams, must now carry the cruel "loser" label another year, along with Chamberlain, who has been on one title-winner in his 11-year career.

Lakers Play Poorly

And the fact is, the Lakers played badly. They had one tiny chance to make a game of it, when the Knicks started missing their shots in the third quarter, but couldn't generate a sustained offense. They became progressively disorganized as the Knicks harried and outran them. They didn't make their own good shots, and they gave the Knicks too many good ones.

Chamberlain finished with 24 rebounds and 21 points, West with 28 points, Baylor with 19; but these were just numbers. Joe Mullaney, their first-year coach, thought they tried too hard to catch up too quickly after New York's hot start.

"We fell into a faster tempo," he said, "instead of trying to get back 2 points at a time. We just can't play that kind of pace against a team like the Knicks."

To reach the final, the Lakers defeated Phoenix in seven games and Atlanta in four straight.

The New York Times

Willis Reed (19) guarding Wilt Chamberlain at the Garden.

The Line-Up

KNICKS (113)

	min	fgm	fga	ftm	fta	reb	a	pf	pts
Barnett	42	9	20	3	3	0	2	4	21
Bowman	21	3	5	0	1	5	0	5	6
Bradley	42	8	18	1	1	4	5	3	17
DeB'schre	37	8	15	2	2	17	1	1	18
Frazier	44	12	17	12	12	7	19	3	36
Reed	27	2	5	0	0	3	1	4	4
Riordan	10	2	3	1	2	2	1	2	5
Russell	6	1	4	0	0	3	0	0	2
Stallworth	11	1	5	2	2	2	1	3	4
Total	240	46	92	21	23	43	30	25	113

LOS ANGELES LAKERS (99)

	min	fgm	fga	ftm	fta	reb	a	pf	pts
Baylor	35	9	17	1	2	5	1	2	19
Chamb'l'n	48	10	16	1	11	24	4	1	21
Egan	1	0	2	0	0	0	0	2	0
Erickson	36	5	10	4	6	6	6	3	14
Garrett	34	3	10	2	2	4	1	4	8
Hairston	15	2	5	2	2	2	0	1	6
Tresvant	12	0	4	3	3	2	0	2	3
West	48	9	19	10	12	6	5	4	28
Total	240	38	83	23	38	49	17	19	99

Min.—Minutes played. FGM—Field goals made. FGA—Field goals attempted. FTM—Free throws made. FTA—Free throws attempted. Reb.—Rebounds. A—Assists. PF—Personal fouls. Pts.—Points scored.

Knicks	38	31	25	19—113
Los Angeles	24	18	27	30— 99

Referees—Mendy Rudolph and Richie Powers.

Attendance—19,500.

Lindsay Salutes Knicks For a 'Feast of Victory'

After the New York Knicks' victory last night, Mayor Lindsay, who was not at the game, sent a telegram to the team's locker room.

"After 24 years of famine, your superb basketball has given this city a feast of victory," the Mayor said.

Lindsay added, "I only hope I can do half as well as Mayor as you have played in this championship series against another great team."

Copies of the telegram, the Mayor told the Knicks, were sent to Gov. Ronald Reagan of California and Mayor Sam Yorty of Los Angeles.

Mrs. Court Completes Grand Slam at Forest Hills

ROCHE IS BEATEN IN U.S. OPEN FINAL

Mrs. Court Gains Her 4th Major Title of Year by Defeating Miss Casals

By NEIL AMDUR

Mrs Margaret Court swept everything, including her grand slam in singles, and little Ken Rosewall collected his biggest payday as a professional on the final day of the $160,000 United States Open tennis championships yesterday.

The 35-year-old Rosewall, who received a gold ball and a handshake for winning the National Amateur event 14 years ago, drove out of the West Side Tennis Club in Forest Hills, Queens, with a new Ford Pinto and a check for $20,000 after his 2-6, 6-4, 7-6, 6-3 victory over Tony Roche. It was the biggest payoff for a tournament since the Open era began in tennis three years ago.

Roche, the Australian left-hander beaten by Rosewall in the semifinals at Wimbledon and seeded fourth here, received $10,000 as the runner-up for a second straight year.

"I felt the pressure quite a bit at times," Mrs. Court said after her final. "I played very tentative, but I sort of made myself concentrate. I'm tired. I guess I haven't realized that it's all over."

Victor in Mixed Doubles

Mrs. Court, who at 5 feet 9 inches is two inches taller than Rosewall, overshadowed the women's field. She achieved the last leg of her singles grand slam with a 6-2, 2-6, 6-1 triumph over Rosemary Casals, a victory worth $7,500; teamed with Marty Riessen for the mixed doubles crown, 6-4, 6-4, over Mrs. Judy Dalton and Frew McMillan, worth $1,000, and received $1,000 more from Saturday's women's doubles championship.

In a move that may help to make her the first woman athlete to earn $100,000 in a single year, Mrs. Court received another 500 shares of stock from her racquet manufacturer, the Chemold Corporation of Jamaica, Queens. In addition to the victory, coupled with her titles in the Australian, French and Wimbledon championships, Mrs. Court has at least 2,000 shares of stock, currently valued at about $1.50 a share, a new contract for 1971 and countless opportunities for commercial endorsements.

The only other woman player to win the grand slam was the late Maureen Connolly as an amateur in 1953. Mrs. Court had won three of the four amateur events three times in the past. Two men, Rod Laver and Don Budge, have successfully completed the men's grand slam, Budge in 1938, Laver in 1962 and last year.

Rosewall's comeback delighted the record crowd of 14,502, the second sellout in two days. Not since Bill Tilden, at the age of 36, beat Francis T. Hunter in the 1929 amateur final here, has a player so late in his career successfully withstood the physical and mental pressures of potential five-set matches on grass courts over 12 long days.

Added Pressures on Rosewall

The pressure on Rosewall was compounded by the record prize money, the institution of the sudden-death nine-point tiebreaker and the depth of the professional talent in the 108-player field.

Yesterday, the dark-haired Australian survived the loss of the first set, three break points at 5-6 in the third set, a tense sudden-death playoff and a cracked frame in his favorite wooden racquet, which he continued to use because of its marvelous touch.

"It's my biggest win," said the modest soft-spoken Australian, who reached the semifinals here at the age of 18 in 1953 and ended Lew Hoad's bid for a grand slam in the 1956 final. "I'm very touched. It's such a long time between wins."

For the 25-year-old Roche, who grew up watching Rosewall play Davis Cup matches, defeat brought intense disappointment. Though he is considered one of the world's top five singles players, the blocky left-hander has yet to win a major grass-court championship.

"This is getting to be a bad habit for me," he said. "I thought I was going along well there, but Kenny hit some great shots."

As so often happened during the tournament, the momentum seemed to sway during the tie-breaker for the third set, after Rosewall held service for 6-all with a running forehand placement down the line and Roche's forehand error at deuce.

Roche had won all four of his previous tiebreaker sets during the tournament, including one in a straight-set victory over Cliff Richey in the semifinals. But the third-seeded Rosewall employed his strongest weapons, ground strokes and the return of serve, to push his rival out of position and take an early 2-0 lead in the playoff, with Roche serving the first 2 points.

The shot that brought the tense crowd to its feet was a forehand cross-court placement at 3-1, a ground stroke that Rosewall executed time after time in knocking down Charles Pasarell, Nikki Pilic, Stan Smith and John Newcombe, the Wimbledon champion, en route to the final.

With Roche attacking, Rosewall dug the ball out of the browned turf, refused to jerk the motion or top it, but fluently lifted it into an open spot, as if he were reproducing it from an instructional guide. The tie-breaker ended, 5-2, with Roche driving a backhand return of serve wide.

"That's what happens when you do 'Muscles' a favor," Roche said afterward of his Australian countryman. "I did his laundry for him yesterday and look what he does to me."

In winning the second set, the 21-year-old Miss Casals became the first player in two years here to take a set against Mrs. Court.

Both women appeared nervous and admitted afterward that the play had been "tentative and spotty" because of the stakes.

"I had a lot of trouble with my serve," said Miss Casals, a Californian who won $3,750 as the runner-up. "And Margaret has such long arms that they seemed to go all around the court."

Mrs. Court broke Miss Casals inthe second and sixth games of the third set, concentrating her attack on her rival's backhand volley and driving deeply off the ground.

"There was a lot of tension," she said. "I was praying on that last serve that Rosie hit into the net."

Mrs. Court's husband, Barry, was one of the first to congratulate her after the match.

"What was the first thing she said to you afterward?" a friend asked Barry.

"She said she couldn't believe it," he answered.

Road to the Slam

AUSTRALIAN OPEN

Defeated Evonne Goolagong, 6-3, 6-1; Karen Krantzcke, 6-1, 6-3, and Kerry Melville, 6-3, 6-1.

FRENCH OPEN

Defeated Marijke Schaar-Jansen, 6-1, 6-1; Olga Morozova, 3-6, 8-6, 6-1; Lesley Hunt, 6-2, 6-1; Rosemary Casals, 7-5, 6-2; Julie Heldman, 6-0, 6-2, and Helga Niessen, 6-2, 6-4.

WIMBLEDON OPEN

Defeated Sue Alexander, 6-0, 6-1; Maria Guzman, 6-0, 6-1; Vlasta Vopickova, 6-3, 6-3; Helga Niessen, 6-8, 6-0, 6-0; Rosemary Casals, 6-4, 6-1, and Mrs. Billie Jean King, 14-12, 11-9.

UNITED STATES OPEN

Defeated Pam Austin, 6-1, 6-0; Patti Hogan, 6-1, 6-1; Patricia Faulkner, 6-10, 6-2; Helen Gourlay, 6-2, 6-2; Nancy Richey, 6-1, 6-3, and Rosemary Casals, 6-2, 2-6, 6-1.

SENIOR DOUBLES FINAL

Straight Clark, Villanova, Pa., and Vic Seixas, Philadelphia, defeated Bobby Riggs, Plandome, L.I., and Emory Neale, Portland, Ore., 6-1, 6-2.

SENIOR SINGLES FINAL

Bob Howe, Britain, defeated Seixas, 6-4, 6-3.

The New York Times

Mrs. Margaret Court smashing a forehand to Rosemary Casals in final.

The New York Times

Rosewall and Roche after the match.

The New York Times

Ken Rosewall of Australia returns ball to Tony Roche in men's final.

Notre Dame Snaps Texas Streak With 24-11 Victory

THEISMANN RUNS FOR TWO SCORES

Back Also Passes for Tally —Irish Recover 5 Texas Fumbles in Cotton Bowl

STATISTICS OF THE GAME

	Notre Dame	Texas
First downs	16	20
Rushing yardage	146	216
Passing yardage	213	210
Return yardage	0	26
Passes	9-19	10-27
Interceptions by	1	1
Punts	8-46	5-33
Fumbles lost	1	5
Yards penalized	52	33

By NEIL AMDUR

Special to The New York Times

DALLAS, Jan. 1—A wishbone defense stopped the wishbone offense today, as Notre Dame ended college football's third longest winning streak with a 24-11 victory over Texas in the 35th annual Cotton Bowl game.

Lining up on defense to mirror the offensive players in the Texas backfield, the inspired, underdog Irish reversed last year's 21-17 loss to the Longhorns and snapped a 30-game Texas victory string that had spanned three seasons.

Also ended was the modest record of five consecutive post-season bowl triumphs for Coach Darrell Royal.

The victory marked the second time in the last 25 years that Notre Dame played the role of spoiler against teams with long victory streaks. On Nov. 16, 1957, the Irish ended Oklahoma's national collegiate record 47-game string by winning 7-0, in Norman Okla.

Today's game, viewed by a somewhat stunned capacity crowd of 73,000, was a strange turnabout from the thrilling 1970 finish that highlighted the Longhorns' comeback in the final 68 seconds. After its first series of plays last year Texas trailed, 10-0; today the Longhorns led, 3-0, after their first series—on a 23-yard field goal by Happy Feller.

Texans Need a Shamrock

But Notre Dame countered with three touchdowns in the next 13 minutes on a 26-yard pass from Joe Theismann to Tom Gatewood, and two Theismann runs of 3 and 15 yards.

The Texas Wishbone-T, which had averaged 41 points and 374 yards rushing through 10 regular-season victories needed a shamrock in the backfield today. The Longhorns were limited to 216 yards on the ground, fumbled nine times and lost five, had one pass intercepted and failed to convert the big possession plays that had characterized their dramatic victories in the last two seasons. On 19 occasions, the Notre Dame defense stopped Texas with no more than a 1-yard gain.

Steve Worster, the all-America fullback, showed the effects of a knee injury that had limited his practice time in recent weeks. Worster fumbled four of his 16 carries and gained only 42 yards against an aroused Irish squad, which had yielded 331 yards on the ground last year.

The 11 points were the lowest scoring total for Texas in three years. The Longhorns' last loss was to Texas Tech, 31-22, in the second game of the 1968 season.

Opportunities Abound

"We had our opportunities," said Royal, who was bidding for a second successive national championship. "They were there. We were not beaten so bad that we did not have opportunities."

Notre Dame produced a group of surprising heroes, besides the defense and Theismann, who completed nine of 16 passes for 176 yards.

The Irish played without Gatewood for most of the game, after the all-America junior strained a hamstring muscle running out the fourth-down touchdown toss from Theismann with 7 minutes 58 seconds left in the first quarter.

A 74-yard quick-kick by Jim Yoder midway through the second quarter stunned Texas and forced the Longhorns to spend the next seven minutes driving 86 yards for a touchdown. A 2-yard pitchout from Eddie Phillips, the courageous quarterback, to Jim Bertelsen accounted for the Texas score.

But rather than settle for a 21-11 half-time lead, Notre Dame came out throwing in the last 105 seconds. The big gainer that helped produce a 36-yard field goal was not a Theismann-to-Gatewood pass, but a Jim Bulger-to-Clarence Ellis hookup.

Bulger, a 6-foot, 5-inch, 200-pound sophomore quarterback from Pittsburgh, made his first appearance of the season with 54 seconds left. He came into the line-up after Theismann injured some fingers on his throwing hand.

Ellis, named the game's outstanding defensive player at cornerback, also ran into the line-up with Bulger and then raced behind a Texas defender to catch a 37-yard pass. It was the first appearance on offense ered on the Longhorn 13-yard line. Theismann scored six plays later on a rollout from the 3.

The strength of the Notre Dame defense was particularly evident early in the second half. When Texas reached the Irish 35-yard line needing 1 yard for a first down, the Longhorns gambled and Bertelsen cracked at left guard.

But Jim Musuraca, another Irish sophomore, closed up the hole and pushed Bertelsen back.

"They changed their defensive pattern and threw a lot of beef at us on that play," Royal said. "It worked."

United Press International

Notre Dame quarterback Joe Theismann (7) keeps the ball and goes 4 yards for the Irish's 2nd touchdown against Texas during the Cotton Bowl.

Irish Victory Formula: Theismann and Defense

Special to The New York Times

DALLAS, Jan. 1—"I haven't been so happy since I was married," Joe Theismann said with a wide grin, "and that was only three weeks ago."

Theismann, the 6-foot, 170-pound quarterback, scored two touchdowns and passed 26 yards for another in Notre Dame's 24-11 upset of Texas in the Cotton Bowl today.

"We really started getting mentally ready yesterday," Theismann said. "It started in practice and you could just feel it. We had a good week of practice and it all reached a peak today."

If Theismann carried the offense in the absence of Tom Gatewood, who was injured in the first quarter, the Notre Dame defense rebounded from its poor showing in the 38-28 loss to Southern California in the final game of the regular season.

Battle of Lines

"The defense gave it away in the Southern Cal game," said Greg Mark, a sophomore defensive tackle. "We had a lot to prove, to people and to ourselves."

Marx said that the battle for supremacy came in the line.

"We figured that we had to win the battle of the yard," he said, referring to the distance between the two lines. "Arkansas (beaten, 42-7, by Texas last month) sat back and let Texas charge. We knew that we couldn't do that. We had to hit and go after their backs."

Notre Dame's size frustrated the Longhorns' vaunted wishbone-T offense.

"They were large enough physically inside that we couldn't get a crease for [Steve] Worster," said Darrell Royal, the Texas coach. "They are a big, tough football team. That's a lot of beef they throw at you in the middle."

Royal also praised Clarence Ellis, the Irish cornerback, and Walt Patulski, the 6-foot-5-inch, 235-pound defensive end.

"Their end was boxing up on the keep, forcing Eddie Phillips to run all the time," he said. "I thought Ellis was tremendous, especially early in the game. We had passes perfectly on target, but he was so active and fast he just got back there and knocked the ball down."

Worster, the all-America fullback, was at a loss to explain his four fumbles and inability to shake loose. His timing and confidence may have been affected by a knee injury.

"They were hitting well and tackling the ball some," He said. "It seems like we were driving enough to win. We just couldn't follow through."

Fumbles Galore

Added Bobby Wuensch, the all-America Texas tackle: "I was horrible. We fumbled, fumbled, fumbled. We fumbled on drives, we fumbled a kickoff, we fumbled everything. They said they were gonna whip us and they did."

Coach Ara Parseghian said Notre Dame used a new defensive alignment for the game in an attempt to control the various options off the wishbone.

"We used an eight-man front, but we camouflaged this real well with different adjustments," he said. "We had our people in the middle of the defensive unit line up just like the offensive players in the wishbone. There's no way you can cover them with the typical defenses."

Parseghian said he told Royal after the game that Texas should be proud of its 30-game winning streak. But Notre Dame players also must have been thinking streaks. Long after the game, someone had replaced the X's and O's on the blackboard in the dressing room with this cryptic message: "We may never lose again."

SCOTT'S PASSING STUNS AIR FORCE

STATISTICS OF THE GAME

	Tenn.	Air Force
First downs	24	15
Rushing yardage	86	—12
Passing yardage	148	239
Return yardage	148	52
Passes	24-46	23-46
Interceptions	4	2
Punts	5-31	8-35
Fumbles lost	3	4
Yards penalized	74	0

NEW ORLEANS, Jan. 1 (AP) —Tennessee junked its strong running game and confused the Air Force with Bobby Scott's slingshot passing today to win the Sugar Bowl game, 34-13.

A crowd of 78,655 watched the Volunteers take a 24-point lead before Air Force could score.

Scott had Air Force defenders off balance throughout the first period. The Volunteers sailed to a touchdown on their opening series, with Scott's passing doing most of the damage, and scored on their next two possessions.

Scott completed 22 of 40 passes for 288 yards, and was named the game's most valuable player.

McLeary Scores Twice

Don McLeary punctured the Falcon line on a 5-yard smash for the first Tennessee touchdown and George Hunt's 30-yard field goal minutes later made it 10-0. McLeary went 20 yards on Tennessee's next series for another touchdown.

Jamie Rotella's recovery of a fumble by Brian Bream, the Air Force fullback, started the Vols going again late in the first quarter. Scott hit Gary Theiler with a 10-yard strike to give the Volunteers a 24-0 cushion.

Air Force scored when Scott bobbled a snap from center late in the first quarter and Darryl Haas recovered for the touchdown.

Bobby Majors of Tennessee scored with a 57-yard punt return in the third period. Air Force got one more score on a 27-yard pass from Bob Parker to Bob Bassa.

Hunt added a 33-yard field goal for the Vols.

Scott had opened with a withering passing attack in the first quarter and Air Force simply couldn't cope.

Scott connected with Joe Thompson for 18, hit Thompson for another 25 and whipped a strike to Les McLain for 14 yards to move the ball to the Falcons 5, where McLeary slammed over on the next play.

Scott ate up 19 yards with a pass to McLain to the Air Force 20 and McLeary darted through a gaping hole at left tackle for his second touchdown.

Scott passed to Stan Trott for 14 yards to the Falcon 11, and then fired to Theiler for Tennessee's third touchdown.

U. of Tennessee President Asks New Pact for Battle

NEW ORLEANS, Jan. 1 (AP) —The president of the University of Tennessee said tonight he would recommend that Coach Bill Battle be given a new five-year contract with a substantial pay rise.

The announcement by Dr. Edward J. Boling came a few hours after Battle's Vols beat Air Force, 34-13, in the Sugar Bowl.

Battle, 29 years old, just completed his first year under a four-year contract at Tennessee.

"All the News That's Fit to Print"

The New York Times

LATE CITY EDITION

Weather: Mostly sunny, cold today; fair and cold tonight, tomorrow. Temp. range today 26-13; Sunday 24-18. Full U.S. report on Page 78.

VOL. CXX... No. 41,267 © 1971 The New York Times Company NEW YORK, MONDAY, JANUARY 18, 1971 15 CENTS

Baltimore Field Goal in Last 5 Seconds Defeats Dallas in Super Bowl, 16 to 13

By WILLIAM N. WALLACE

Special to The New York Times

MIAMI, Jan. 17—The Baltimore Colts beat the Dallas Cowboys, 16-13, and won the Super Bowl game today. The National Football League headquarters will soon be sending the winners their $15,000 checks. But it will be difficult to convince the Cowboys and many of the viewers that anybody won this game, the climactic contest of the pro football season.

The contest was full of errors made by both offensive teams and one Baltimore touchdown play, a 75-yard pass-run, John Unitas to John Mackey, was controversial if not illegal.

The winning points were scored with only five seconds to play when Jim O'Brien, a Baltimore rookie, kicked a 32-yard field goal, breaking a 13-13 tie and eliminating the possibility of a sudden-death overtime period.

It might have been a good idea to start all over again with everyone even.

The Cowboys led, 13-6, at half-time, but the Colts scored a touchdown and a field goal in the fourth quarter. Interceptions set up both scoring opportunities. Those were two of the 11 turnovers, resulting from an intercepted pass or a lost fumble, in the game, seen by 80,055 in the Orange Bowl and an estimated 64 million on television.

The Colts lost four fumbles to the Cowboys and had three

Continued on Page 30, Column 1

United Press International

Jim O'Brien kicking the 32-yard field goal that won the Super Bowl for Baltimore Colts. Earl Morrall holds ball.

TEAMSTER STRIKE CLOSES 4 DEPOTS FOR PRODUCE HERE

Effect on Stocks Is Expected to Be Acute by Weekend —Negotiations Continue

By ROBERT E. TOMASSON

The four produce markets that handle most of the city's fresh and frozen fruit and vegetables were closed yesterday by a teamster strike.

Both the city, which runs three of the markets, and Local 202 of the International Brotherhood of Teamsters said last night that if the strike continued stores in the city would begin to feel the effects tomorrow in diminished supplies, with an acute shortage of fruit and vegetables developing toward the end of the week.

Charles Ullrich, president of the union, estimated that the four markets handled "between 90 and 95 per cent" of the city's supply of all fruit and vegetables. Patrick F. Crossman, Commissioner of Ports and Terminals, termed the estimate "too high," but he said that the amount "was very substantial."

1,600 Workers Involved

The strike was set off by about 1,600 members of the union who work for food wholesalers operating in the markets. The men unload the fresh produce that is brought in by railroad and truck, sort it and reload it on other trucks for distribution to other wholesalers and grocery chains.

By late afternoon a picket line had been set up at the Hunts Point Market, the largest produce terminal in the world, which sprawls over 126 acres in the East Bronx.

City and union officials said that many truckers apparently had sufficient warning of the strike for them to cancel their runs to the four markets here.

Sunday night is normally one of the busiest nights for the produce dealers, with many hundreds of trucks rolling into the city starting around 11 P.M.

Backlog Built Up

The impact to the consumer of the markets' closing will not be felt for at least another day, union and city officials said, because wholesalers and the chain stores have a backlog that was processed through the terminals Friday night. The markets are closed Saturdays.

The strike by the teamster local was directed against nine produce associations. They could not be reached for comment last night.

Their contract expired Friday, and on Saturday warehousemen and drivers who operate trucks inside the markets rejected a new contract offer by a vote of 394 to 45. Even though this assured a strike by the entire local, other members of the local — men who mainly handle frozen food —voted 177 to 118 yesterday to accept a new contract offered to them.

The warehousemen and drivers who voted against a new contract receive a base pay of $2.90 an hour, with all work done before 5 A.M. at time-and-a-half rates. Mr. Ulrich said

Continued on Page 11, Column 1

POLICE STRIKE TALKS DEADLOCKED; FIRE AND SANITATION UNIONS REBUFF CITY ON A 17.4% 3-YEAR WAGE OFFER

The New York Times/Barton Silverman

FEDERAL GUARDS ON DUTY: Deputy Chief Earl L. Drescher of the Executive Protective Service on patrol outside the Soviet Mission to the United Nations on East 67th Street.

LINDSAY IS CALM

Says Safety of City Is 'Assured'—No Rise in Crime Reported

By ROBERT D. McFADDEN

Negotiations to end the citywide policemen's strike were reported to be "gravely deadlocked" yesterday as the wildcat walkout deprived New York of 85 per cent of its patrolmen for a fourth successive day.

At least 25 per cent of the Transit Authority patrolmen assigned to yesterday's 4 P.M.-to-midnight shift refused to work, in sympathy with the strikers and in defiance of the transit union leadership.

The Transit Authority reported that, despite the partial walkout, adequate patrols were being maintained in the subways. But spot checks found only two transit patrolmen on duty in more than a dozen stations in Manhattan and Brooklyn and none on a series of trains.

Strike Is Endured

With no apparent increase in crime and with essential police services being maintained by detectives, uniformed officers and probationary patrolmen, New Yorkers appeared yesterday to be enduring the strike calmly but cautiously.

Mayor Lindsay, in an afternoon news conference at City Hall, said that the strike situation had not deteriorated, that schools would be open as usual today despite the absence of police protection and that the "safety of the city appears to be assured."

Police Commissioner Patrick V. Murphy, at the Mayor's side, said there had been "no serious problems" with crime and repeated his assertion that the present limited emergency service could be sustained "for several more days."

Cold Keeps People In

The cold weather that the Commissioner had called an "ally" of the police continued to hold down the number of people on the streets, and Federal guards helped out by protecting the Soviet Mission to the United Nations against demonstrations by the Jewish Defense League.

At the Americana Hotel, where negotiations between the city and its uniformed services have been intensified at the Mayor's request, the firemen's and sanitationmen's unions were offered, and promptly rejected, a 17.4 per cent pay increase over three years, almost double the city's previous offer.

Herbert L. Haber, director of the city's Office of Collective Bargaining, said the wage offer, which was tied to increases in productivity, would subsequent-

Continued on Page 18, Column 3

Foreign Policy: Decision Power Ebbing at the State Department

After two years in office, President Nixon has fashioned his own style in foreign policy and in the use of his staff. Correspondents of The New York Times have explored this foreign policy machinery, the power of the President's advisers and the impact of Washington's major institutions on foreign policy decisions. The role of the State Department is explored today in the first of a series of articles.

By TERENCE SMITH

Special to The New York Times

WASHINGTON, Jan. 17—The Department of State, once the proud and undisputed steward of foreign policy, has finally acknowledged what others have long been saying: that it is no longer in charge of the United States' foreign affairs and that it cannot reasonably expect to be so again.

By its own admission as well as the testimony of its critics, the department has been losing ground in the bureaucracy for a generation. In the opinion of many people in the department and outside, the erosion has accelerated sharply during the first two years of the Nixon Administration.

As President Nixon pledged during his campaign, he has gathered more and more of the business of foreign affairs in the White House. He has taken a personal hand in both the broad scope and mechanical details of foreign policy, from proclaiming the Nixon Doctrine on the American stance abroad to composing the Government's official condolences to France on the death of de Gaulle.

The centralization of the formulation of foreign policy in the White House has been a characteristic of the nuclear age, when the issues have become so complex and the consequences of error so grave. It has, in fact, been the pattern since the days of President Franklin D. Roosevelt.

Particularly strong Secretaries of State arrested the trend during the Truman and Eisenhower years, but since the death of John Foster Dulles in 1959, Presidents have dominated the foreign-policy scene.

The centralization has been most striking under President Nixon, who regards foreign affairs as his field of special competence. His detailed personal involvement has often been at the expense of the State Department. The 1970 message on the state of the world was a case in point.

The idea for a major year-end summary of the Administra-

Continued on Page 14, Column 3

The New York Times/George Tames

William P. Rogers, Secretary of State. His department has lost ground during the Nixon Administration.

'Nobody Could Have Stopped It'

By JOSEPH LELYVELD

"No, sir, I ain't working."

That was Patrolman Wallace Page's response when the desk officer in the 43d Precinct in the quiet Parkchester section of the Bronx started calling the roll for the 4-to-12 shift Thursday afternoon.

The decision to start a wildcat "job action" in the precinct was taken spontaneously by the 40 men on that shift, Patrolman Page said yesterday, after they learned of the Court of Appeals decision on the parity issue that blasted their hopes for early payment of an anticipated $2,700 in back pay.

"Nobody was leading it. Nobody could have stopped it," he declared.

Angry rumblings of wildcat action were being heard in station houses throughout the city; in the 78th and 84th Precincts in Brooklyn patrolmen had already refused orders to work. But the 43d Precinct was to play a pivotal role in the spreading stoppage because of a deadline set by Patrolman Page's shift.

Local leaders of the Patrolmen's Benevolent Association — the "delegates" as they are known in the precincts — urged the men to give the union a chance to take a stand. Assistant Chief Inspector Alfred Anger, who took command two weeks ago of all uniformed forces in the Bronx, hurried to the station and implored them to do their duty and not rush into something they would later regret.

Faced with these appeals, the 4-to-12 shift agreed finally to go on patrol but only until 7 P.M. By then, they

Continued on Page 18, Column 7

3 SEIZED IN SALE OF LICENSE TEST

State Cancels Chiropractic Exam Scheduled for Today After Arrests in Bronx

By PETER KIHSS

The breakup of a ring engaged in the theft and sale of state licensing examinations for chiropractors was reported yesterday by Bronx District Attorney Burton B. Roberts. As a result, the state canceled tests scheduled for today for more than 400 candidates.

Mr. Roberts announced three persons had been arrested after a chiropractor cooperating with his office passed $2,000 in marked bills, dusted with fluorescent powder, in exchange for sections of today's test with checked-off answers.

The Bronx prosecutor said investigation had indicated "a minimum of five chiropractors involved in sale of the examinations." A grand jury will investigate "what public official or officials may be responsible for theft of the examinations."

Continued on Page 21, Column 1

DeLury Scorns 'Pennies' But Maye Is Encouraged

By EMANUEL PERLMUTTER

The city virtually doubled its pay offer to firemen and sanitationmen yesterday, raising it to a 17.4 per cent increase over three years provided they agree to work rule changes for improved efficiency. The unions promptly rejected it.

"I'm looking for bread, not a slice," said John J. DeLury, president of the Uniformed Sanitationmen's Association, in commenting on the new offer. "I'm looking for dollars, not pennies. I won't even present the offer to my men."

Michael J. Maye, president of the Uniformed Firefighters Association, declared: "The city's offer is totally unacceptable." He added, however, that "we find encouragement in that the city has finally decided to move."

Both men said that despite their rejection of the proposals they would continue their negotiations with the city at the Americana hotel, where negotiations with the police are also being conducted.

The contracts with all three unions expired Dec. 31.

The new city offer would raise firemen's salaries by $1,900 from their present base maximum of $10,950. Sanitationmen would gain $1,711 over their present base pay of $9,871.

First-grade firemen's salaries

Continued on Page 18, Column 3

Army Spied on 18,000 Civilians in 2-Year Operation

By RICHARD HALLORAN

Special to The New York Times

WASHINGTON, Jan. 17—The United States Army fed the names of about 18,000 American civilians into its computers, dossiers and files in a wide-ranging intelligence operation during the tumultuous days of civil disturbances from the summer of 1967 through the fall of 1969.

In the operation, which was ordered ended last year, 1,000 Army agents gathered personal and political information on obscure persons, as well as the prominent, on advocates of violent protest and participants in legitimate political activity, on the National Association for the Advancement of Colored People and the John Birch Society, on the Black Panthers and the Ku Klux Klan, on the Students for a Democratic Society and the Daughters of the American Revolution. The emphasis was on radicals, black militants and dissenters against the war in Vietnam.

The military intelligence operation picked up much of its information from local police officials and the Federal Bureau of Investigation, but supplemented that data and collected its own through agents posing as members of the groups under surveillance, as newsmen, or merely as interested bystanders.

Thus, a black agent registered at New York University in 1968 to report on students taking a course in black studies. Another agent joined the Youth International party, or Yippies, and slept alongside its candidate, a pig named "Pigasus," during the counter-inaugural demonstration here in January, 1969.

The Army now authorizes only limited intelligence gathering on incidents that might lead to a Presidential call for Federal troops. But attention was sharply focused last month on the Army operation when Senator Sam J. Ervin Jr., Democrat of North Carolina, contended that prominent political figures in Illinois had been under military surveillance since 1968.

Senator Ervin is skeptical of the Army's announcement about halting the spying and has scheduled hearings by the Subcommittee on Constitutional Rights, of which he is chairman, to begin Feb. 23. He said the Army "must disclose in full what happened and what has been done to insure that it will never happen again."

Details of the operation, known as Continental United States Intelligence, or Conus Intel, emerged from interviews with civilian and uniformed Pentagon officials, Congressional sources, agents of the Secret Service and former agents, and from a study of Army documents and files.

The findings included the following:

¶Directives from Cabinet-level officials, authorizing intelligence gathering to help the Army carry out its mission of

Continued on Page 22, Column 1

NEWS INDEX

The News Summary and Index appears on Page 2. Obituary news, Page 35.

Nixon Steel Tactic: Put Off Import Talks

By EDWIN L. DALE Jr.

Special to The New York Times

WASHINGTON, Jan. 17—A key White House tactic in its confrontation with the steel industry over prices last week was cancellation of a negotiating session scheduled with foreign countries aimed at continuing an arrangement that limits steel imports.

The cancellation was made known to parts of the industry in midweek. The negotiating session had been scheduled for Frankfurt, West Germany, on Jan. 24, though this had not been publicly announced.

The agreement that limits imports of steel from Japan and the six countries of the European Common Market runs out at the end of this year. According to reliable official sources, the cancellation of the negotiations to renew the agreement — and perhaps make it more favorable to the domestic industry —caused great concern in those segments of the industry that knew about it.

Yesterday, the United States Steel Corporation, after conferring with officials in Washington in the morning, announced the decision to raise prices of structural steel products by 6.8 per cent, well under the 12 per cent announced last Monday by the Bethlehem Steel Corporation.

Government officials have indicated strongly that this reduction of the price problem will be satisfactory.

Tonight, the Kaiser Steel Corporation said that it planned to raise prices on some of its major construction products, matching the increases by United States Steel. It thus became the first producer to fall into line with the action by that company. [Details on Page 63.]

President Nixon, through his press secretary, Ronald L. Ziegler, had condemned the Bethlehem Steel increase. Last Tuesday, Mr. Ziegler raised the possibility of permitting more imports as a means of exerting downward pressure on domestic steel prices.

It has been learned on good authority that the White House suggested to the State Department that the negotiating session in Frankfurt be canceled

Continued on Page 64, Column 5

Colts Beat Cowboys, 16-13, on 32-Yard Field Goal

KICK IS DELIVERED IN LAST 5 SECONDS

Score Set Up By Curtis's Interception in Contest Marked by Errors

Continued From Page 1, Col. 3

passes intercepted. Two of these were thrown by Unitas and one by Earl Morrall. Unitas was hurt (bruised ribs) in the second period and Morrall took over.

There is an adage that a team cannot win when it turns the ball over to its opponent half a dozen times or more. But this game defied a lot of adages. Three Cowboy passes, all by Craig Morton, were also intercepted, and Dallas lost a fumble on the Baltimore 1-yard line. The ball was knocked loose from Duane Thomas's grip in a pile-up.

"We beat ourselves," said Tom Landry, the Dallas coach. "The fumble and two interceptions killed us."

Did Cowboys Touch Pass?

So did some kind of fate. The Dallas defense was outstanding, and the Colts, with Unitas, made no early progress. Then Unitas threw a pass 20 yards deep and high to Eddie Hinton, who got his finger tips on the ball but could not hold it or stop it. The ball passed over or through a Dallas player's finger tips and into the hands of Mackey, who ran 45 yards for a score that tied the game at 6-6 in the second quarter.

STATISTICS OF THE GAME

	Colts	Cowboys
First downs	14	9
Rushing yardage	69	104
Passing yardage	260	113
Return yardage	159	65
Passes	11-25	12-26
Interceptions by	3	3
Punts	4-42	9-39
Fumbles lost	4	1
Yards penalized	44	120

A pass is incomplete if two offensive players touch the ball successively without a defensive player intervening. The ruling on this play was that a Dallas defender had touched the football. Which defender?

"Not me," said Charlie Waters, the safetyman. "I was 10 yards away," said Cornell Green, the other safety. "I don't know," said Mel Renfro, the cornerback. "I didn't think I did," he added, and then to another questioner, he said, "maybe my finger nail."

The replay shown on television was inconclusive because of a poor camera angle. The official's instant decision was that the ball had been touched by a Cowboy and the call will stand.

Another pass grazed the finger tips of Walt Garrison, the Cowboy fullback, when Dallas was ahead, 13-6, in the fourth quarter and comfortably in control.

Rick Volk, the Colt's safety, made the interception on the Dallas 33 and ran to the 3. Tom Nowatzke scored on second down and the game was tied, 13-13, with half the period still to play.

With a minute left more fingers came into play. Morton's pass to Dan Reeves, the halfback, bounced off his hands when he was hit by Jerry Logan. The football careened into the hands of Mike Curtis, the Baltimore linebacker, and he returned this interception 13 yards to the Dallas 28.

The Colts ran two plays and then O'Brien, a nervous 23-year-old, came in and kicked his field goal. It represented the $7,500 difference between a winning and losing share for himself and his 39 teammates.

Interception by Howley

The Colts failed on three prior scoring chances. Hinton fumbled after catching a pass from Sam Havrilak, a halfback, in the final period. The ball rolled from the Dallas 5 through the end zone and out of bounds. Because the Colts were the last team to have possession, the play resulted in a touchback and Dallas took over at its 20.

Chuck Howley intercepted a pass by Morrall in the Cowboy end zone at the start of the fourth quarter and the Colts failed to score in four downs at the Dallas 2 just before the half-time intermission.

Dallas missed its touchdown chances early in the game. Recovery of a Baltimore fumble—Ron Gardin dropped a punt—put the Cowboys on the Colt 9, but Morton overthrew Reggie Rucker in the end zone. Dallas settled for a field goal by Mike Clark.

Morton missed on two more passes a little later from the Baltimore 7 and, following a penalty, Clark kicked a 30-yard field goal for a 6-0 lead.

The Colts tied the game when Mackey scored on the controversial play and O'Brien's attempted conversion kick was blocked by Mark Washington.

INDIVIDUAL STATISTICS

RUSHES—Balt.: Nowatzke, 10 for 33 yards; Bulaich, 18 for 28; Unitas, 1 for 4; Havrilak, 1 for 3; Morrall, 1 for 1. Dal.: Garrison, 12 for 65; Thomas, 18 for 37; Morton, 1 for 2.

PASSES — Balt.: Morrall, 7 of 15 for 147 yards; Unitas, 3 of 9 for 88; Havrilak, 1 of 1 for 25. Dal.: Morton, 12 of 26 for 127.

RECEPTIONS — Balt.: Jefferson, 3 for 52 yards; Mackey, 2 for 80; Hinton, 2 for 51; Havrilak, 2 for 27; Bulaich, 1 for 5; Nowatzke, 1 for 45. Dal.: Reeves, 5 for 46; Thomas, 4 for 21; Garrison, 2 for 19; Hayes, 1 for 41.

A fumble by Unitas at his 28 set up the Cowboy touchdown, scored on a 7-yard pass by Morton to Thomas in the second period.

The Colt defense tightened in the second half and the Cowboys' big runner, Thomas, gained only 37 yards in all.

Curtis was the outstanding defender.

Morton again left much to be desired as a passer. So did Unitas, who completed only three of nine passes and made only two first downs. Morrall was the best quarterback, although he had little to do with winning the game apart from holding the ball for O'Brien's field goal.

Somebody upstairs seemed to take care of the winning and losing. "You can say that again," said Renfro.

One Cowboy Wins: Howley Gets Award

Special to The New York Times

MIAMI, Jan. 17—Chuck Howley, the Dallas Cowboys' linebacker, was the surprise winner today of Sport Magazine's award of a 1971 Dodge Charger as the outstanding player in the Super Bowl game.

"The award is tremendous, but I wish it were the world championship," Howley said. "They go hand in hand."

Howley made two interceptions and also jarred loose a fumble by John Unitas, the Colt quarterback, early in the game.

"Howley was in on everything on defense," Al Silverman, editor of Sport, explained. "We thought he was the best over-all player."

United Press International

SUPER BOOT: Jim O'Brien (80) kicking the 32-yard field goal that gave the Colts victory as Dallas defenders struggled desperately to break through the Baltimore line.

Cowboys: Thomas Fumble Hurt

Special to The New York Times

MIAMI, Jan. 17 — When the Dallas Cowboys returned to their dressing room today, what did Tom Landry say to them?

"You can't say anything," heir coach explained. "I tried, out I can't say anything after a game like this."

Landry branded Duane Thomas's lost fumble at the Colts' 1-yard line early in the third quarter as the "big play" of the game from the Cowboys' viewpoint. The fumble occurred on first down. Had the Cowboys scored a touchdown, they would have opened a 20-6 lead.

"If he'd scored," Landry said, "they would've had a lot of catching up to do. We would have been in firm control. But he fumbled because of his second effort on the play."

Passing the Credit

Jerry Logan, a Colt safetyman, was credited with the tackle on Thomas, the Cowboys' star runner. But the Colt cornerback, Jim Duncan, who recovered the loose ball at the 1-yard line, thought that Ray May, the Colt linebacker on that side, had caused the fumble with a jarring tackle.

"I hit him," May said, "but I think Billy Ray Smith jerked the ball loose.

"If he says I jerked the ball loose, then I guess I did," Smith said, smiling.

Thomas was unavailable for comment. He dressed and departed before newsmen were permitted to enter the dressing room.

"We beat ourselves," Landry said. "The fumble and the two interceptions killed us."

Landry said the interceptions that enabled the Colts to rally with a touchdown and field goal in the final quarter were the result of deflected passes, and so was the Colts' first touchdown on the controversial deflection of a pass from John Unitas to John Mackey.

"The ball was bouncing off us, instead of them," Landry said. "That's a hard way to lose."

Quietly, the Cowboy coach discussed his disappointment in the hushed atmosphere.

"We were emotionally up, we were working and hustling," Landry said. "It was just one of those games. So many penalties."

Not far away, Lee Roy Jordan, a Cowboy linebacker, also discussed officiating.

"We had to overcome a lot of people today," Jordan said, "including the officials."

Morton Is Crushed

Craig Morton, who completed only 12 of 26 passes for 127 yards, was deflated by the defeat.

"We just made too many mistakes," said Morton, perhaps thinking of his three last-quarter interceptions. "Their defenses didn't do anything we didn't expect. But they shut down our run, especially in the second half. And we've been a running team. I don't know what they did—maybe they changed up front."

Landry sent in virtually all the Cowboy plays to Morton, but not the pass play on which Mike Curtis interceped to position the Colts' winning field goal.

"We were in our 2-minute offense at the time, Craig knew what plays I wanted. This hurts pretty bad. We fought uphill for eight weeks, —nobody could play defense the way we have for the last eight weeks. You can't measure our disappointment."

One More Disappointment

Landry, who was finally able to bring the Cowboys into the Super Bowl after years of frustration, said: "We had our opportunities to control the game in the first half, but we missed the big plays on a couple of occasions and had to settle for field goals. In the third period we moved the ball well downfield only to be stopped by Thomas's fumble."

Dan Reeves, a player-coach with Dallas, said: "This was the biggest game we ever played. I just wish we could have won it. What hurts most was giving up 10 points on two tipped plays."

Reeves explained as follows the pass that tipped his fingers only to be caught by Curtis, setting up the Colts' victory: "A back fresh out of college could have caught it. I went as high as I could, but it went through my hands.

"I don't take the blame for the loss. We lost it as a team. O'Brien did a great job. I didn't think a rookie could make a kick like that under such pressure."

"All the News That's Fit to Print"

The New York Times

LATE CITY EDITION

Weather: Partly sunny today; clear and cold tonight. Sunny tomorrow. Temp. range: today 37-23; Monday 36-31. Full U.S. report on Page 73.

VOL. CXX . No. 41,317 — © 1971 The New York Times Company. — NEW YORK, TUESDAY, MARCH 9, 1971 — 15 CENTS

Frazier Outpoints Ali and Keeps Title

United Press International

Muhammad Ali starting toward the canvas after taking a hard left hook from Joe Frazier in 15th round of title bout

TRIAL OF MEDINA ORDERED BY ARMY

Captain Accused of Killing at Least 100 Vietnamese —He Denies Mylai Guilt

By ROBERT M. SMITH
Special to The New York Times

WASHINGTON, March 8—Capt. Ernest L. Medina, the commander of the infantry company that swept through the hamlet of Mylai 4, was ordered today to stand trial on charges of premeditated murder and assault with a dangerous weapon.

One of the specifications brought against him by the Army alleges that he murdered "an unknown number of unidentified Vietnamese persons, not less than 100, by means of shooting [them] with machine guns, rifles and other weapons."

The specifications of assault allege that he shot at an unidentified Vietnamese twice "while interrogating suspected enemy personnel."

If he is found guilty, the 34-year-old Army captain could be sentenced to death or life imprisonment. A death sentence could not be carried out without the approval of President Nixon.

The decision to court-martial Captain Medina was made by his commander, Lieut. Gen. Albert O. Connor, the commanding general of the Third Army, at Fort McPherson, Ga.

The announcement of the general's decision was made at Fort McPherson and at the Pentagon. The Army said that no date had been set for the court-martial.

In a statement issued at Fort McPherson, Captain Medina said:

"I am innocent of the charges. I am surprised and dismayed that the Army has taken this action. Now pending before the United States Court of Military

Continued on Page 6, Column 1

Champion Floors His Rival With Left Hook in the 15th

By DAVE ANDERSON

In a classic 15-round battle, Joe Frazier broke the wings of the butterfly and smashed the stinger of the bee last night in winning a unanimous 15-round decision over Muhammad Ali at Madison Square Garden.

Defying an anonymous "lose or else" death threat, Frazier settled the controversy over the world heavyweight championship by handing Ali his first defeat with a savage attack that culminated in a thudding knockdown of the deposed titleholder from a hammerlike left hook in the final round.

During the classic brawl, one man in the sellout throng of 20,455 died of a heart attack.

When the verdict was announced, Ali, also known as Cassius Clay, accepted it stoically.

Hurried to his dressing room rather than the postfight interview area, Ali remained there for about half an hour. Suddenly, he departed for Flower-Fifth Avenue Hospital for X-rays of the severely swollen jaw. He was released from the hospital after 40 minutes and left unbandaged.

But even before Ali's jaw began to bloat, the unbeaten Frazier had dulled the vaunted weapons of his rival in recording his 27th victory, although he failed in his quest for his 24th knockout. Ali's defeat ended his winning streak after 31 triumphs, with 25 knockouts.

"I always knew who the champion was," Frazier, his brow swollen above each eye, said later with a smile.

The officials agreed with the Philadelphia slugger. Judge Bill Recht awarded him 11 rounds to four for Ali, while the other judge, Artie Aidala, had Frazier ahead by 9-6. Referee Arthur Mercante had it the closest, 8-6

Continued on Page 29, Column 4

KIDNAPPERS FREE 4 G.I.'S IN TURKEY

Airmen Back After 5 Days —Both Governments Say They Didn't Negotiate

By The Associated Press

ANKARA, Turkey, March 8—Four United States airmen were freed unharmed tonight after five days in the hands of leftist kidnappers. The airmen walked into their billets in Ankara just before midnight.

The kidnappers, members of a left-wing group known as the Turkish People's Liberation Army, had demanded $400,000 ransom, threatening to put the Americans before a firing squad if it was not paid by last Saturday morning. United States and Turkish spokesman said the two Governments had refused to negotiate.

The United States Ambassador, William J. Handley, issued a statement on the release, saying: "I am happy that reason has prevailed and that a senseless tragedy has been averted. I am sure that people everywhere share the joy of the families of the four airmen at their safe return."

The airmen were abducted by five armed Turks on Thursday as they were driving in a military car from a radar base where they worked outside Ankara to their billets.

The airmen are Sgt. Jimmie J. Sexton of San Angelo, Tex.,

Continued on Page 14, Column 1

Military Governor's Oath Blocked in East Pakistan

By TILLMAN DURDIN
Special to The New York Times

DACCA, Pakistan, March 8—The Chief Justice of the High Court here refused today to swear in the new military governor for East Pakistan appointed in West Pakistan last week by President Agha Mohammad Yahya Khan.

The Chief Justice, B. A. Siddiqui, was complying with yesterday's call by Sheik Mujibur Rahman, the East Pakistani nationalist leader, for a weeklong strike in Government offices and the courts against the military administration of this eastern province. The new governor, Gen. Tikka Khan, arrived last night.

Since today was a Moslem holiday here, Government offices and businesses were already scheduled to be closed. A major confrontation with the military administration appears likely tomorrow.

In appointing the new military governor, President Yahya Khan ordered the Pakistani armed forces to uphold the integrity and security of the country in the face of the swelling East Pakistan movement to assert self-rule.

Fearful of widespread violence, many foreign residents of East Pakistan have started to leave. A West German Government plane took out more than 100 Germans today, and may return tomorrow for the rest of the 200 German residents. A

Continued on Page 10, Column 1

Protests Interrupt City Welcome for Astronauts

By PAUL L. MONTGOMERY

The Apollo 14 astronauts, interrupted occasionally by demonstrations for better schools and welfare housing, received the honors of the city yesterday.

The chilled, smiling adventurers—Capt. Alan B. Shepard Jr., Capt. Edgar D. Mitchell and Lieut. Col. Stuart A. Roosa—rode in a motorcade past scattered crowds on Fifth Avenue and Broadway and were presented with the city's gold medal by Mayor Lindsay on the steps of City Hall.

"What I'm saying today is give us a break," Captain Shepard said at the presentation ceremony as demonstrators in the background chanted "Crumbs for the children and millions for the moon" and held up signs saying "Welfare hotels—the new-style concentration camps."

"When total budget is discussed, take a look at what's spent to improve our domestic conditions and what's spent on space," Captain Shepard said. "You'll be surprised at the ratio."

The leader of last month's voyage to the moon gave no specific figures. The $229.2-billion Federal budget for the 1972 fiscal year estimates that 42 per cent of the funds will be spent on "human resources" such as health, education and social security while 1.4 per cent will go to space research and technology.

"The management skills and the technological ingenuity which sent you to the moon and back can also help to bring our cities back," Mayor Lindsay told the astronauts. "We see a chance to use our resources — and yours — here at home, not by ending the space effort but by expanding its scope and purpose. Perhaps the worst enemy of our best hopes is the belief that we cannot succeed."

The astronauts, accompanied

Continued on Page 34, Column 2

NEWS INDEX

Harold Lloyd, Screen Comedian, Dead

By The Associated Press

HOLLYWOOD, March 8—Harold Lloyd, whose portrayals of a bumbling, bespectacled youth in impossible situations made him one of the great comedians of silent films and later of the talkies, died today of cancer at the age of 77.

He leaves three children, Harold Lloyd Jr., Mrs. Peggy Patten and Mrs. Gloria Guasti. His wife, the former Mildred Davis, was his leading lady in the twenties. She died in 1969.

A funeral service is scheduled for Thursday morning at the Scottish Rite Temple in Los Angeles, followed by burial at Forest Lawn Memorial-Park, Glendale.

Associated Press

Harold Lloyd in 1971 photo

Horn-Rims His Trademark

By MURRAY ILLSON

A pair of inexpensive, horn-rimmed eyeglass frames without lenses, the shy expression of a somewhat bewildered adolescent and a single-track ambition made Harold Clayton Lloyd the highest-paid screen actor in Hollywood's golden age of the nineteen twenties.

Mr. Lloyd's closest rivals during that dazzling decade were Charlie Chaplin, Douglas Fairbanks, Mary Pickford and Gloria Swanson. But before the horn-rimmed spectacles were to become his trademark, known wherever movies were shown two generations ago, Mr. Lloyd had been a lowly paid extra and a run-of-the-mill slapstick comedian.

After having experimented with various character roles, Mr. Lloyd, in 1917, donned the lensless frames that were to make him the fumbling but lovable silent-screen youth who overcame peril

Gene Korman

Mr. Lloyd as he was known to millions of moviegoers.

and frustration just in time to win the girl in the last reel.

Americans of all ages and audiences the world over ate it up, so much so that by 1926 a news story from Hollywood reported that Mr. Lloyd's earnings had advanced to "about $40,000 a week, or $2-million a year." And this was at a time when income taxes were low. He made nearly 300 films, from one reel to full-length, which earned more than $35-mil-

Continued on Page 40, Column 1

U. S. BACKS THANT ON BID TO ISRAEL FOR WITHDRAWAL

Comment Is Said to Parallel Private Efforts for Full Pullout From Egypt

By HEDRICK SMITH
Special to The New York Times

WASHINGTON, March 8—The United States today endorsed Secretary General Thant's appeal for a pledge by Israel to withdraw her forces from all Egyptian territory.

The public comment from the State Department was understood to have echoed the private approaches already made to induce Israel to be more flexible.

Well-placed diplomats said they expected that the next move would be a diplomatic inquiry to Israel by Dr. Gunnar V. Jarring, the United Nations intermediary, probably accompanied by American approaches to the Israelis.

President Zalman Shazar of Israel, who is visiting the United States in connection with Israeli fund-raising drives, paid a 30-minute courtesy call on President Nixon today. The details of their conversation were not disclosed.

No Early Combat Expected

The prevailing view in the Nixon Administration was that the formal expiration of the Middle East cease-fire yesterday was unlikely to bring an early return to combat between the United Arab Republic and Israel.

Robert J. McCloskey, the State Department spokesman, said that the United States was "counseling restraint against any resumption of fighting in the area" and was informed by the Soviet Union that Moscow was also urging restraint.

In answer to a question, Mr. McCloskey said that the United States supported in full Mr. Thant's report last Friday urging both sides to withhold fire and calling for Israel to "respond favorably" to Dr. Jarring's request for a commitment to withdraw all Israeli forces to Egypt's international boundary. Neutral diplomats interpreted this as meaning withdrawal from the entire Sinai Peninsula, but not necessarily the Gaza Strip, which was never formally a part of Egypt.

Declines at First

When asked if he was specifically endorsing Mr. Thant's appeal for Israel to reconsider her position on the withdrawal question, Mr. McCloskey initially declined comment. A second reporter asked if he was excluding that part from his earlier endorsement of Mr. Thant's report. Mr. McCloskey said that he was not, but he was seeking to avoid any public comment that would "prejudice the

Continued on Page 10, Column 1

Court Forbids Job Tests That Screen Out Negroes

Rules, 8 to 0, That '64 Rights Law Bars Examinations That Do Not Relate to Qualifications to Perform Work

Special to The New York Times

WASHINGTON, March 8—The Supreme Court ruled 8 to 0 today that employers cannot use job tests that screen out Negroes without realistically measuring their qualifications to do the work.

In the Court's first interpretation of the provisions of the equal employment section of the Civil Rights Act of 1964 relating to racial bias, the Justices sharply curtailed employers' discretion to use tests in hiring and promotions.

At issue was the interpretation to be given to an exception that was written into the civil rights law at the urging of Senators who wanted to preserve the employers' right to use testing.

The exception declared that it would not be illegal to use "any professionally developed ability test," provided that it was not designed or used to discriminate against a certain group.

Today's case grew out of applications for promotion by 13 black laborers at the Duke Power Company's Dan River Power Station at Draper, N. C.

Before the civil rights law was passed, the company employed Negroes only as laborers. When these Negroes asked to move up to jobs as coal miners, they were confronted with new requirements that they pass high school equiva-

Continued on Page 21, Column 1

Beame Suggests Schools Spend '72 Funds in Crisis

By ANDREW H. MALCOLM

Controller Abraham D. Beame proposed yesterday to transfer $25-million of this year's school personnel expenses into the budget for next year. The effect would be to "save" $25-million for the financially hard-pressed school system this year.

At the same time, Board of Education officials lowered their estimate of the budget deficit this year, making it $36.2-million instead of $40-million.

Mr. Beame's proposal, which he made at a news conference as 10 members of his staff began a "crash investigation" of the board's books, would charge teachers' salaries for the last half of June against the next fiscal year, which begins July 1.

Practice Called 'Unsound'

In an immediate reaction, Mayor Lindsay called the proposal a "device," "stopgap financial juggling," and "unsound fiscal practice."

Noting that the Controller had authority to take such steps without the Mayor's approval, Mr. Lindsay said the transfer would mortgage the next budget and would not "correct the [board's] overspending which produced the problem."

And the Mayor promised support for state legislation to give the city greater financial control over the board's spending.

The board's president, Murry Bergtraum, meanwhile, said he welcomed "any proposal which would avoid these cuts and their consequent chaos."

He was alluding to a series of severe economy measures the board ordered last week to bridge a projected deficit of

Continued on Page 44, Column 2

ELECTION DAY SALE OF LIQUOR BACKED

Assembly Clears and Sends to Rockefeller Measure Ending 50-Year Ban

By FRANK LYNN
Special to The New York Times

ALBANY, March 8—The Assembly gave final legislative approval today to a bill repealing the long-time ban on the sale of alcoholic beverages on primary and election days.

Assemblyman George Cincotta, Democrat-Liberal of Brooklyn, co-sponsor of the measure, predicted that Governor Rockefeller would sign the measure and end a tradition that began more than 50 years ago.

The Governor vetoed a repeal bill last year, but cited a local-option feature as the major reason for his disapproval. The measure approved today would apply statewide and not permit any option by local legislative bodies, such as the New York City Council.

The bill was approved in the Assembly 107-33 with almost no debate. Most of the opponents were upstate Republicans, but about a dozen New York City Democrats also opposed the bill in a show of hands. The State Senate had approved repeal last month.

Mr. Cincotta said that the major pressure for repeal had come from restaurant owners rather than proprietors of neighborhood bars, who, he said, "enjoy the two days off." He noted that, unlike the bars, restaurants did not generally close, although they cannot serve beer and liquor while the polls are open.

The Brooklyn legislator added that the drive for repeal gained

Continued on Page 41, Column 5

DRAFT EXEMPTION BARRED TO CRITICS OF A SINGLE WAR

High Court Rules Objection Cannot Be Based on the Vietnam Action Alone

DECISION ON AN 8-1 VOTE

Douglas Calls Guarantee of Religious Freedom Shield Against 'Unjust' Conflict

Excerpts from Court opinions are printed on Page 20.

By FRED P. GRAHAM
Special to The New York Times

WASHINGTON, March 8—The Supreme Court ruled today that young men were not entitled to draft exemptions as conscientious objectors if they objected only to the Vietnam conflict as an "unjust war" and did not oppose all wars.

In an 8-to-1 decision, the Court held that Congress had acted constitutionally when it ruled out "selective" conscientious objection by authorizing exemptions only for those men who were "conscientiously opposed to participation in war in any form."

The majority opinion, written by Justice Thurgood Marshall, said that this did not unconstitutionally favor religious denominations that teach total pacifism or did not infringe the freedom of religion of those who believe that only "unjust" wars must be opposed.

Rule Called Neutral

Justice Marshall declared that the rule against selective conscientious objection was essentially neutral in its treatment of various religious faiths and that any "incidental burdens" felt by particular draftees were justified by "the Government's interest in procuring the manpower necessary for military purposes."

The lone dissenter, Justice William O. Douglas, said: "I had assumed that the welfare of the single human soul was the ultimate test of the vitality of the First Amendment."

He argued that whether an individual's abhorrence of killing was the product of religious faith or individual conscience, the First Amendment's guarantee of freedom of religion should shield him from conscription into a war that he believed to be unjust.

In the two cases that were decided today, the Government conceded that each young man was sincere in his conscientious objection to the Vietnam war, but it insisted that they did not qualify for the C.O. exemption created by Congress because they did not oppose all wars.

Appellant From Yonkers

One appellant, Guy Porter Gillette of Yonkers, had told his draft board that his belief in the religion of humanism prevented him from serving in the military during the Vietnam war, which he considered unjust.

He was denied conscientious objector status because he conceded that he would fight in defense of the United States or in a peace-keeping effort by the United Nations. He was

Continued on Page 20, Column 1

Ramsey Clark and Paul O'Dwyer Join Defense in Berrigan Case

By LINDA CHARLTON

A team of four lawyers—Ramsey Clark, Paul O'Dwyer, Leonard Boudin and Addison Bowman—has agreed to undertake the defense of the Rev. Philip F. Berrigan and his five co-defendants when they stand trial on charges of conspiring to kidnap a Presidential aide and blow up heating tunnels in Government buildings in Washington.

Reports of a tentative agreement among three of the lawyers were confirmed last night by Mr. Boudin, who spoke in a telephone interview from Cambridge, Mass., where he is living during a year of teaching advanced constitutional litigation at Harvard Law School.

There is "nothing tentative" about the agreement, he said. He said also that Mr. Bowman, a lawyer practicing in Baltimore and Washington, would represent the Rev. Joseph R. Wenderoth, one of the six defendants.

Mr. Boudin said that while he had been associated with Mr. O'Dwyer "in several cases before," he had not previously been associated with Mr. Clark "except in the sense that, of course, he was Attorney General during the time of the Spock case, so I suppose that's an association."

Mr. Boudin represented Dr.

Continued on Page 22, Column 1

Frazier Floors Ali in 15th and Keeps Title

Continued From Page 1, Col. 3

for Frazier with one round even. During his uncharacteristic postfight silence, Ali sent this word to newsmen through Drew (Bundini) Brown, his assistant trainer: "Don't worry, we'll be back, we ain't through yet." But regarding a possible return bout, Frazier said, "I don't think Clay will want one."

Ali had predicted Frazier would fall "in six rounds" and he had maintained that there was "no way" the recognized champion could outpoint him. But the swarming Philadelphia brawler, battering his Cherry Hill, N. J., neighbor, ended the 29-year-old Ali's credibility as a prophet.

At the age of 27, Frazier justified his reign for all the world to see on a television network with an audience estimated at 300 million. Each fighter will receive $2.5-million from a posible $25-million in total worldwide receipts. The $1,352,951 gate at the Garden was a record for an indoor bout.

Ali remained unscratched, except for a slightly bloodied nose, but his jaw began to swell on both sides in the late rounds from Frazier's persistent hammering.

In the final round, Frazier landed a wild left hook that send Ali sprawling onto his back in a corner. But the 6-to-5 betting underdog was up almost instantly and took the mandatory eight-count on unsteady feet. Moments later, Frazier jolted his 215-pound rival with another left hook. But time was running out on the 205½-pound champion.

With a minute remaining, Ali desperately tried for a knockout, but his punches had virtually no effect. With the crowd roaring in the final seconds, the bell rang and Frazier playfully cuffed Ali across his head, bowed in apparent defeat.

Ali's strategy obviously had been to let Frazier grow armweary while pummeling him. But the chunky champion, despite a 6½-inch disadvantage in reach, defied Ali's tiring jab and moved in under it to convince the Garden audience he deserved the decision.

When the decision was announced, a patter of boos erupted, but the cheers soon thundered above them.

Except for the first round, when the red tassels on Ali's high white shoes flopped in rhythm to his ballerina moves, the deposed titleholder primarily used a flat-footed stance, a radical departure from his floating, stinging style prior to his 3½-year exile that ended last year.

Claiming exemption as a Muslim minister, Ali refused induction in the armed forces on April 28, 1967. He promptly was stripped of his title and license to box by the New York State Athletic Commission and the World Boxing Association, which governs boxing in most of the other states.

Not long after that, Ali was convicted of draft evasion. His sentence was five years in prison, plus a $10,000 fine, but an appeal currently is before the Supreme Court.

While his exile matured Ali's physique, it sabotaged his speed. But in red velvet trunks, he was as arrogant as ever even before the midring instructions. Twice he shouldered Frazier, in green-and-gold brocade trunks, as he whirled around the ring. And twice Frazier glared in contempt.

During the early rounds, Frazier pounded his left hook into Ali's midsection, but several times the deposed champion shook his head in the clinch as if to reassure his idolators.

At the end of the second round, Ali waved his right glove in derision at Frazier as they walked to their corners. And during that intermission, he showed his disdain by refusing to rest on his stool and moving threateningly to the center of the ring before the bell rang for the third.

Moments later, Ali's voice could be heard through the microphone hanging over the ring. Mercante warned Ali that "no talking" would be tolerated.

Soon, Ali wasn't talking anymore. Near the end of the fourth, Frazier's left hook bloodied Ali's nose. And in the fifth, Frazier strayed from his taciturn character. Holding his hands low, he permitted Ali to punch him at will in a demonstration of the blow's apparent

Frazier literally was laughing in Ali's face now and he was in command. When the bell ended the fifth round, Frazier cuffed Ali across the top of the head.

In the tremendous tempo, Frazier was fulfilling his strategy to "kill the body and the head will die." But somehow, Ali's head remained alive through the middle rounds as his sixth-round prediction was unfulfilled. But before the eighth round, a chant of "Ali, Ali, Ali" began.

Momentarily inspired, Ali waved to the crowd and pointed to them as if to show Frazier it was his audience. But after the round, a roar of "Joe, Joe, Joe" disputed Ali's confidence.

More willing to trade punches, Ali slowed Frazier's pace. The champion's legs were weaving instead of churning. Sensing a knockout opportunity, Ali pounced but Frazier, in his typical fury, fought him off. In the 10th, Ali glanced at the ringside and shouted, "He's out," in a reference to Frazier's weariness.

In the 11th, Ali slipped to the canvas momentarily. Near the end of the round, he was made wobbly by a left hook. Frazier's savage flurry sent him stumbling into the ropes. He flopped around the ring on rubber legs, but appeared to be playing possum, perhaps to frustrate Frazier further.

But in the 12th, Frazier, strengthened by the surging of joy he receives from punishing an opponent, resumed his frantic pace—but soon it slowed. Each boxer was moving securely, but slowly, until Frazier uncoiled the left hook that dropped Ali in the final round.

It was only the third time Ali had been knocked down in his decade of competition. Sonny Banks floored him in 1962 during his 11th bout and Henry Cooper flattened him in 1963 during his 19th bout.

But the knockdown by Frazier was the final embarrassment for the deposed champion, the sixth ex-heavyweight champion to fail in an attempt to regain his title. The others were Joe Louis, Jack Dempsey, Jim Jeffries, Bob Fitzsimmons and James J. Corbett. Only Floyd Patterson has succeeded in regaining it.

In his failure, Ali not only lost, but more embarrassing, he was silenced.

The New York Times

Frazier standing over Ali after knocking undefeated heavyweight to canvas in 15th round. Ali, after a three-year layoff, lost a decision to Frazier.

Frazier Says Blows to Body Won

By DEANE McGOWEN

Joe Frazier is the master of the boxing world. The 27 year-old Philadelphian realized his dream last night when he won undisputed claim to the heavyweight championship.

Before 20,455 fans and a record gate of $1,352,951 plus an estimated 300-million more fans who saw the bout on closed circuit television and via the satellite, Frazier removed the final obstacle to his dream, Muhammad Ali.

The chunky Frazier, punching with savagery, stunned Ali in the 11th round with a smashing right hand, then knocked the Louisville fighter to the ring floor with his blitzing left hook to the chin in the 15th and final round.

By then Ali, also known as Cassius Clay, knew that his return to the ring had ended in failure. Ali had been stripped of his title by boxing commissions and federations round the world in 1967 and refusing to enter the armed forces of the United States.

This was the third time Frazier had had to prove his right to sport's greatest prize. He knocked out Buster Mathis in the brand new garden ring to win New York State recognition. Then he knocked out Jimmy Ellis, the World Boxing Association titleholder, to clear up the dual situation.

But along came Ali, and Frazier had to prove himself once more—this time against a boxing master who was undefeated in 31 fights.

Frazier, who gave away almost seven inches in reach to Ali, divulged his fight plans. Yancey (Yank) Durham, his manager, sent Joe out to get Ali's head as soon as possible.

But that tactic was changed in the middle of the fight because Ali's long-range boxing, footwork and all-round skill was keeping the short, squat Frazier from doing any serious damage.

Frazier Switches Attack

So Frazier went to the body where the boxing adage says, "kill the body and the head will fall."

Over the final eight rounds Ali visibly wilted under the tremendous pressure to his mid-section.

But it was a badly-bruised Frazier who answered questions after the bout.

Frazier said, "He called me a lot of names. I wanted him to come to me after the fight and apologize. But he just mumbled something and turned to his corner."

A few times in the early round Frazier stuck his chin out deliberately. His reason? "I stuck it out to let him know he couldn't hurt me."

In the later rounds, Ali appeared to be playing with Frazier. As Frazier pinned him to the ropes, Ali was tapping him on the top of the head and punching Frazier very lightly in the face. Was Ali clowning? "Clowning? He couldn't move. Those body shots had slowed him down."

But Frazier's face was lumpy on both sides from Ali's solid short lefts and rights. Ali never really hurt him, however, except in the ninth round when he lathered Frazier's face with jolting left hooks and short rights that stunned the champion late in the round.

In the 10th Frazier had motioned toward the referee, Arthur Mercante, and called something to his corner. "Mercante had accidentally hit me in the eye, and I hollered to Durham to let him know. Mercante apologized to me almost immediately.

Frazier 'To Live a Little'

Would Frazier retire now? "No I'm going home and live a little. It's been tough, this business."

What about a rematch with Ali? "Sure, any time, but Yank's (Durham) the boss. I'll do what he thinks is best."

And finally—without a question being asked, Frazier volunteered, "What are you guys going to say now? You've been writing about the great Ali and what he was going to do to me. I can read, you know. Now let me go and get my face straightened out."

Joe Frazier departed laughing—all the way to the bank.

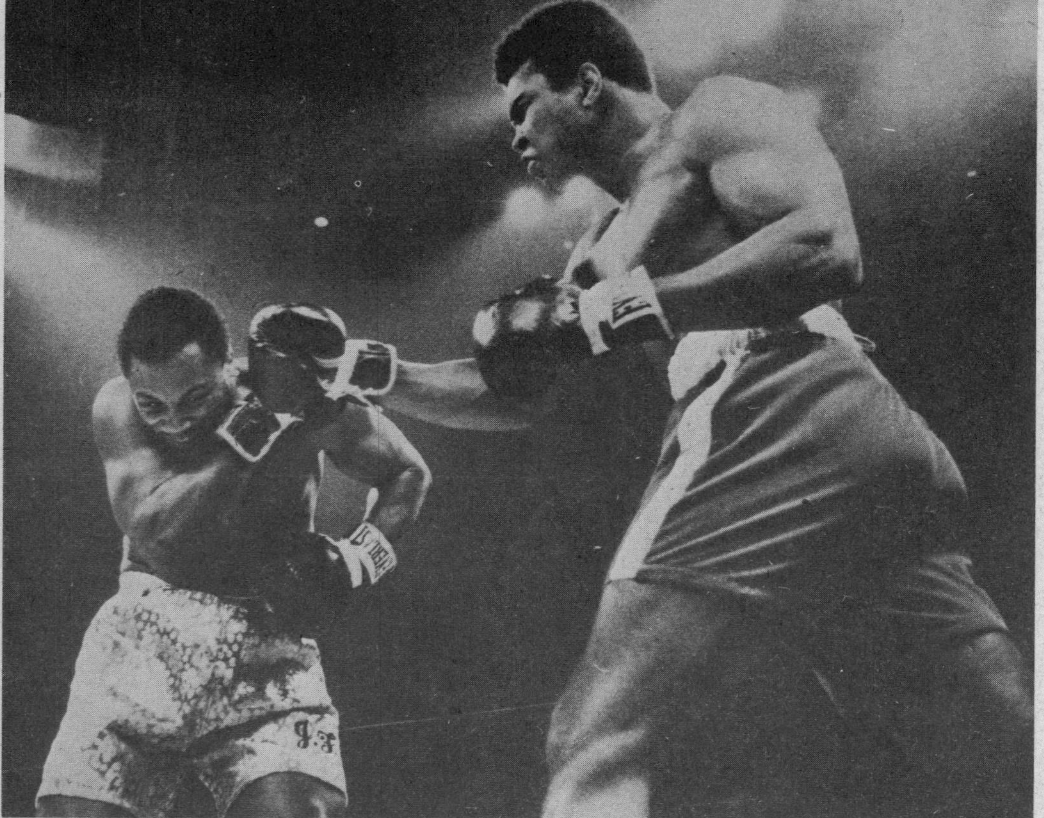

The New York Times

Muhammad Ali landing with a right to force Joe Frazier to cover up during the first round of championship bout.

The New York Times

Muhammad Ali on the canvas after taking Joe Frazier's wicked left hook in the final round of the heavyweight championship bout at Madison Square Garden. He rose quicky and put on a final flurry, but lost on a unanimous decision.

Ali Is Silent on Way to Hospital

By NEIL AMDUR

Muhammad Ali left his dressing room after his fight with Joe Frazier last night the same way he entered earlier in the day—surrounded by bodyguards.

But Ali's destination after the fight was to a hospital, not a hideway. The right side of his jaw was puffed out, the result of a hematoma of the right massater muscle according to Dr. E. A. Campbell, a physician who visited Ali's dressing room.

"We'll get it X-rayed to find out how bad it is," Angelo Dundee, Ali's trainer, said as his fighter moved through a crowd of followers to an awaiting car. "I can't tell right now."

Ali was taken to Flower Fifth Avenue Hospital for an examination and he left shortly thereafter.

The mood outside Ali's dressing room was considerably more restrained than the tumultuous greetings that had followed his earlier bouts and triumphs.

"You know we got robbed," Stacks Edwards, a friend of Ali, said of the unanimous decision in favor of Frazier. "You just know it."

"It's a government thing," another black follower said. "They out to get Ali and they got him."

Dundee, however, saw the fight differently.

"The other guy [Frazier] fought a great fight," Dundee said. "You can't take it away from him."

Dundee said he had tried to caution Ali between rounds to keep moving, but the speed, the Ali trademark before his ring exile, was simply not there.

Drew (Bundini) Brown, the assistant trainer, said Ali's long exile before his return contributed to his downfall.

"Joe put up a great fight," said Brown, who appeared at the postfight news conference in place of Ali, who was en route to the hospital. "Muhammad just been out three years [sic]."

Brown said the defeat did not represent a concession by Ali.

"We ain't through yet," he said. "It was one of the greatest fights."

Did Ali discuss the fight with Brown, he was asked?

"He just want you to know that it as a hard 15 rounds," Brown replied.

Leaving the dressing room, Ali appeared as calm as he did entering Madison Square Garden for the weigh-in earlier in the afternoon.

His early-morning exit capped a hectic day, that began with a chaotic ride from the New Yorker Hotel to the Garden. Ali's outburst at the weigh-in and another brief barrage of poems and predictions before he took up residence in the press lounge on the first promenade before the fight.

Sports of The Times

Epic Worth the Price

By ARTHUR DALEY

The multimillion dollar fight in Madison Square Garden last night was worth every glorious, heartbreaking penny. Rarely does anything so expensive live up to advance billing or exceed expectations. But the wildly exciting exhibition of primitive savagery that Joe Frazier and Muhammad Ali put on over 15 exhausting rounds was an epic that fit the price tag.

Frazier won a decision because he punched himself out so completely that he just didn't have that extra little zing to put into the one wallop that would have finished it by a knockout earlier. And Ali was still vertical at the end because he was just too proud a man, too magnificent an athlete and too gutsy a warrior to let himself stay down.

He had been toppled in the 15th round by one of those uncountable Frazier left hooks that disarranged and puffed up the right side of the Ali face until it looked as though the former Cassius Clay had been stricken by a bad case of the mumps. But Frazier was no bargain at the final bell. His right eye was almost closed and his profile was a mass of welts.

The margin of superiority was reasonably clear-cut with Frazier ahead on the cards of all three ring officials. Nor did the crowd react in angry disapproval as is normally the case when the spectators let wishful thinking misdirect their emotions. Everyone sensed that Ali had failed.

Bee Is Stung Often

He failed gloriously, though, in a strange sort of bout where he neither floated like a butterfly nor stung like a bee, supposedly his normal method of operations. His dancing speed fled early. He was hit more often by Frazier in 15 rounds than he had been hit by all his other opponents together in a hitherto unbeaten career.

In the 11th round, the relentless Frazier—he attacks with the ceaseless whirr of a buzzsaw—began to take Ali cruelly apart with those ferocious left hooks. He exploded one and Ali went wobbling all over the ring, staggering woozily at the end of the round as Frazier's flailing left kept missing the finisher.

He was still missing it through the 12th and 13th when he had an inviting target in front of him, an Ali whose defenses were feeble and whose own punching fires were hardly embers. But in the 14th, Ali unexpectedly came back from the dead, pounded the startled Frazier and detoured his trip to oblivion. He almost went out again in the last round, but survived in some miraculous fashion.

Wait a minute. It wasn't a miracle. Frazier was just too tired to complete a job that had begun to look easy. As the hands of the clock advanced toward the finish of the fight, Frazier pinned Ali in a corner and leaned against him, his face a mask of weariness and his grin a bloody smirk.

If everything about this fight was not in accordance with the original ideas that had been plotted for it by the experts, it took on a new and appealing character of its own. There were times when Ali looked absolutely helpless. He flicked feeble little teasers at the never-stop foe. The man who had danced out of harm's way for all his fistic life stopped stepping even though there were two at hand to tango.

'Sticks and Stones'

He let Frazier corner him and pin him against the ropes. At times he even stood there snarling, sneering and offering taunts. Frazier merely thought an old boyhood thought: "Sticks and stones can break my bones, but names will never hurt me." Maybe it was a quirk in the Ali defense mechanism, brought on by the unexpectedness of something that never had happened to him before.

How much his entire mental attitude was warped by the way his jaw was flailed by the Frazier hooks is beyond conjecture. This also was a new experience, and a trip to the hospital afterwards for X-rays and diagnosis was proof positive that it was a physical handicap of unquestionable severity.

It was a thriller all the way, jam-packed with suspense and tingling from start to finish with the special brand of drama inherent in all heavyweight championship bouts. Not until the last third of the fight—if it is proper to partition it that way—did Frazier's thumping hooks carry him definitely into the lead.

So breathless was the pace that awed ringsiders sometimes were wondering near the end how either of them could still reach deeply within for a galvanic outburst that provided another electric shock of excitement. Thanks to the last-round knockdown, it was to stay exciting to the end.

Frazier left the ring with undisputed possession of the heavyweight championship of the world, a claim that always had rested in the shadow of his unfrocked predecessor, Muhammad Ali. The cash customers undoubtedly had to feel that they got their money's worth in a magnificent bout that was prize fighting at its best.

Referee Mercante Calls Punches Best He's Seen

The man closest to the action, Arthur Mercante, the referee, came away surprised that it lasted so long after watching "some of the best punches I've ever seen."

"The way they were hitting each other I was surprised that it went 15," he said. "I thought it would be more wide open on Ali's part. I was surprised to see him in close so much, slugging toe to toe.

"But it was a beautifully fought fight, and they threw some of the best punches I've ever seen. They both could take it."

Mrs. King Defeats Chris Evert, 6-3, 6-2

The New York Times by EDWARD HAUSNER

Miss Evert following through after completing a forehand drive against Mrs. King

Miss Casals Also Reaches U.S. Tennis Final Round

By NEIL AMDUR

The endless summer came to a halt for Chris Evert yesterday, before the brilliance of Mrs. Billie Jean King.

Reaffirming her status as one of the sport's most versatile players, the top-seeded Mrs. King rushed past the unseeded 16-year-old Cinderella girl of the United States Open tennis championships, 6-3, 6-2.

The bespectacled 27-year-old Californian, who needs less than $25,000 to become the first woman professional to top $100,000 in a single year, will play a familiar face, Rosemary Casals, tomorrow for the $5,000 first prize.

The second-seeded Miss Casals played her best match of the tournament, beating Kerry Melville, 6-4, 6-3, in the first of the women's semifinal matches. But she will have to play even better in the final to handle an inspired, eager Mrs. King, who has lost only one of their 10 meetings this year.

Smith Gains Semifinals

A crowd of 13,647, the largest of the tournament, jammed the West Side Tennis Club in Forest Hills, Queens, lured primarily by the King-Evert match. But the spectators, including Vice President Agnew, also may have got a glimpse of the men's champion — Stan Smith.

The second-seeded 6-foot-4-inch Californian, the runner-up to John Newcombe at Wimbledon, overpowered Marty Riessen, 7-6, 6-2, 7-6, winning a pair of tiebreakers. Smith will play fourth-seeded Tom Okker today in one men's semifinal and third-seeded Ashe will face the unseeded Czech, Jan Kodes, in the other.

Smith won the first tiebreaker with a backhand volley serving the ninth point of the tiebreaker. The fifth-seeded Riessen rallied from 3-5 in the third set to reach another "sudden-death" playoff.

But the 24-year-old Smith, currently serving a two-year tour of duty in the Army, won his fourth consecutive tiebreaker in the tournament, this time, 5 points to 1.

The drama of the afternoon, however, belonged to the women, just as it had when Miss Evert had dominated the stadium and captivated the crowds during her four other appearances.

The high school student from Fort Lauderdale, Fla., had not lost a singles match since last February—a string of 46 consecutive victories—and one of her victims had been Mrs. King, who was forced to default a match in St. Petersburg because of cramps.

Schoolmates at St. Thomas Aquinas High School in Fort Lauderdale sent Miss Evert a telegram with more than 700 signatures wishing her well. But from the opening game, in which Mrs. King won the first three points on Chrissie's serve, it was apparent that Miss Evert would need more than moral support.

Mrs. King, who watched last year's tournament as a frustrated spectator after knee surgery, lost the opportunity for the opening-game break. As Miss Evert scored five straight points—but the Californian squandered few other chances, twice scrambled back from love-30 on service and never allowed Miss Evert a break-point on her serve.

"I didn't hit out as much as I wanted," the personable Mrs. King said. "But I wanted to hit the ball short on my approach instead of deep so the ball would bounce lower and make it more difficult for her to return."

Spin Serve Is Effective

Mrs. King faulted 21 of 50 first serves, a respectable percentage for accuracy. But it was a diverse second spin serve wide to Chrissie's forehand that moved Miss Evert out of position and helped Mrs. King establish position for the important first volley, which she played deep and decisive to nullify her opponent's strong ground strokes.

When Miss Evert tried to lob, Mrs. King answered with the overhead, confident and crisp. Her drop shots and touch volleys further pressured Chrissie's normally potent passing game.

Mrs. King was particularly impressive receiving service. As she has done with Mrs. Nancy Richey Gunter in their memorable duels, Billie Jean stayed at the baseline and skillfully changed pace during long rallies with an assortment of chips, topped drives, slices and spins that kept Miss Evert from finding a stroking groove.

To employ such skills demands almost total concentration. Mrs. King, who can be her own worst enemy, was committed yesterday, and had the repertory to execute her plans.

"I felt by staying back I wouldn't give her a target," Billie Jean said. But I also felt there was pressure on me."

There was. The stadium, as it had been for Miss Evert's other matches, again seemed tense and anxious. A power failure shut off the electric scoreboard and added to the anxiety.

On several exciting rallies, particularly when Mrs. King broke service for the first time in the seventh game, the crowd noise was so strong that the players could not hear the umpire's calls.

"I thought Chrissie learned a lot," said Jimmy Evert, her father, a teaching professional in Fort Lauderdale, who flew in for the match. "She should have come in more on some shots, but she stuck to what she thought had been good to her."

"I think I played well," said the soft-spoken Miss Evert, who admitted before the match that she had no illusions about winning the tournament. "Billie Jean is just too tough."

"I'm glad we can go back to reality," Chrissie's mother, Mrs. Colette Evert, sighed. She is relieved that the phone calls during dinner, and the flurry of attention will subside until next summer, when Wimbledon will beckon.

Sports of The Times

Naked Tennis

By ROBERT LIPSYTE

The sky was evenly overcast, no glints to dazzle the eye, and the breeze only wrinkled the flags above the stadium. Two young girls in white came down the steps of the green awninged marquee, and high on the horseshoe's rim someone asked, "Which one is her, is that her?" Someone else said, "No, no, she has long blond hair." The crowd stayed on its feet as the two girls, who were ball girls, took places alongside the grass court and turned toward the marquee, waiting also.

Chrissie Evert emerged first, shaking hands with Vice President Agnew, then moving serenely across the court, a slim girl in a demure white dress, her hair caught in a white ribbon. Her legs were smooth, without heavy muscle, and her narrow, thin-lipped face seemed purposeful. Billie Jean King, a step behind at the marquee, passed her on the court, her thigh and calf muscles bunching with each step. Her shaggy brown hair is longer now, she is slimmer, and more glamorous in wire-rimmed glasses and a lace dress, but she was an old face beside the child who packed the West Side Tennis Club yesterday for a women's semifinal match.

Chrissie Evert is 16 years old, which was why the stands were filled yesterday; she had won her first four matches in the Forest Hills tournament, more with consistency and poise than brilliance, and if she could beat Billie Jean she would probably win the tournament. The heat of publicity had mounted through the week and the crowd was obviously excited by the possibilities—a relatively unknown child making history and perhaps offering the world a message about dedication, obedience and good grooming that would help straighten it out.

Not a Hitch or a Twitch

Billie Jean, who might have been as good at 16, but was not nearly so famous, was not having much of the daydream. At 27, Billie Jean is the leading woman player, an outspoken promoter of tennis and herself, and a veteran of long tours and crippling injury. A scrambling, energetic athlete, emotional and fierce on court, Billie Jean attacked Chrissie's mild serves from the start.

But Chrissie held her serve in the match's first game and began to set the early rhythm, long, deep rallies that kept Billie Jean away from the net, where her smashing is deadly. Stroke by stroke, point by point, Chrissie is not overpoweringly impressive; her forehand sometimes seems pacific and without guileful slices and spins.

But in the course of a set her strengths are real and perhaps maddening. She hits everything right back and hits it to different places, into the corners, down the lines, cross-court. She shows little expression and no emotion, her face set, her body almost mechanical, without excess hitch or twitch. She seems to check-list her moves before each serve and she is always ready, racquet back, body turned, the teacher's pet.

The crowd was demonstrative and sometimes noisy. Billy Jean has always called for passion from the stands and Chrissie's sweet control seems to demand it. The crowd, which had been Chrissie's through the first four matches, was divided. Billie Jean gives so much on the court it is hard to root against her, and there were those who felt that a 16-year-old could always wait a year or two.

Victory in Chops and Slices

Chrissie forced Billie Jean to play her game, the deep, ground-stroking, baseline game, because a rush to the net would leave the sidelines open for passing shots. Billie Jean won the first set, 6-3, but only because of her extraordinary quickness. Chrissie played on, dogged, untiring, unflappable. Up in the stands, men yelled, "C'mon, baby," and no one turned, scandalized, with a finger to his lips.

In the second and last set, Billie Jean smelled her victory and came into net more often. She had solved the long rallying game by mixing up the speed of her strokes, slicing and chopping until Chrissie would hit short or have to lob. Then Billie Jean attacked, overhead smashes that were unreturnable. It was naked tennis, easy to watch; the ball slow enough to watch from racquet to racquet, the strategy and tactics simple to follow.

When it was over, Billie Jean was outgoing and unreserved; if Chrissie didn't burn herself out or let other people run her life, if she found quiet hideaways where her thoughts and her feelings wouldn't be interrupted, she could go far and enjoy it. Chrissie was sweet and cool.

"I had a really good summer," she said, "and I hate to see it end."

Nebraska, on Late Rally, Stops Oklahoma for 21st in Row, 35-31

4th Touchdown by Kinney Is Difference

STATISTICS OF THE GAME

	Neb.	Okla.
First downs	19	22
Rushing yardage	59-297	64-279
Passing yardage	65	188
Return yardage	80	7
Passes	6-13	6-11
Interceptions by	0	0
Punts	5-36	3-36
Fumbles lost	1	3
Yards penalized	5	0

By NEIL AMDUR
Special to The New York Times

NORMAN, Okla., Nov. 25—Unbeaten, top-ranked Nebraska scored a touchdown in the final 98 seconds today to outlast Oklahoma, its national challenger, 35-31, in a college football classic that surpassed expectations for Thanksgiving Day excitement.

The Orange Bowl-bound Cornhuskers, who had never trailed through 10 previous victories, had to come from behind twice to register their 21st consecutive victory and 30 game without a loss.

It took a pressure-filled 74-yard drive that consumed more than five minutes of the final period for Nebraska to regain the lead from the aroused Sooners, who also had trailed, by as many as 11 points, earlier in the game.

Jeff Kinney, a 6-foot-2-inch, 210-pound running back who seems destined for greater achievements as a professional, carried the last four times and 15 yards in the drive, including the final 2 for the decisive touchdown through a hole carved by Larry Rupert, the all-America guard.

It was Kinney's fourth touchdown of the afternoon, and he finished with a shredded white jersey, 174 yards rushing in 30 bruising carries and totally "exhausted."

Oklahoma, with a 9-1 won-lost record and headed for the Sugar Bowl on New Year's Day against Auburn, had one final chance at its 19-yard line after the fifth Nebraska score.

But Nebraska made a strategic change in its defensive secondary and applied a hard rush on Jack Mildren, the Sooner quarterback. On fourth down, Rich Glover, a junior middle guard from Jersey City, and a standout all day, rushed Mildren and deflected his attempt to throw long to Jon Harrison, his fleet wide receiver.

A record and raucous Owen Field crowd of 63,385 and an international television audience (the game was beamed by satellite to Europe and the Far East) had little time to let their midday holiday meals settle.

Johnny Rodgers, the Cornhuskers' explosive back, weaved 72 yards for a touchdown on a thrilling punt return after the Sooners' first offensive series. The furious pace continued for the entire game.

Almost No Foul Play

The two teams accounted for nine touchdowns and 829 yards total offense, including 311 in the first half by Oklahoma, which scored with five seconds left to take a 17-14 halftime lead on a 24-yard pass from Mildren to Harrison, his high school teammate from Abilene, Tex.

In a tribute to the consistency and quality of play throughout, only five yards in penalties were assessed against both schools.

Nebraska, the nation's No. 1 defensive team, spent 10 days trying to defense the various options and subtleties of the Oklahoma Wishbone offense. Yet Mildren, the 6-foot, 190-pound senior, was magnificent in defeat, running for touchdowns of 2 and 3 yards, throwing to Harrison behind a frustrated cornerback, Bill Kosch, for two more and amassing 267 yards total offense.

The Cornhuskers limited Greg Pruitt, Oklahoma's speedy all-America back, to his lowest output of the season, 53 yards in 10 carries. But Mildren's efficiency on the option and his ability to sustain long drives with crucial third-down calls reaffirmed the efficacy of the Sooners' attack.

Oklahoma scoring drives covered 70, 80, 78, 73 and 69 yards, and the Sooners averaged over 6 yards a play, incredible statistics against a team that had not yielded more than 17 points in a single game and had been called by Chuck Fairbanks, the Oklahoma coach, "one of the most complete college football teams ever assembled."

Nebraska has been termed "unemotional and efficient" in its tactical approach, and the two words summarized the Cornhuskers' comebacks, particularly on the last march.

Two Sooner fumbles led to Nebraska scores. But four Cornhusker touchdowns came on respectable marches af 54, 53 and 61 yards in addition to the winning 12-play drive after Harrison's second touchdown reception (17 yards) with 7:05 left had made it, 31-28, Oklahoma.

Twice on important third-down plays, Nebraska managed to avoid technical mistakes and maintain momentum. Kinney, who rushed for 154 yards in the second half, swept 17 yards on third-and-1 at the Cornhusker 35.

The biggest play of the game may have been Jerry Tagge's 11-yard pass to Rodgers on third-and-8 from the O.U. 46. Rodgers caught the ball lying on the ground.

"It's the greatest victory of my career," Coach Bob Devaney said afterward. "When we were down, 31-28, I thought we could score because our offense had been moving the ball in the second half."

In defeat Fairbanks acknowledged that it was a "classic game, the greatest one I've ever been involved in."

The Lost Chance

Oklahoma fans still thought the Sooners had a chance from the 19. But Devaney shifted Joe Blahak, the safety, to cornerback in place of Kosch, who had been victimized by Harrison for four catches and 115 yards.

In fairness to Kosch, it was the first time he had played cornerback in his varsity career. Normally a safety, he was shifted to play Harrison one-on-one in order to put Blahak, a strong tackler, closer to the Sooners' offensive muscle.

Mildren overthrew Harrison deep on first down, kept for 4 yards and was smothered by Larry Jacobson, a 250-pound all-America tackle, for an 8-yard loss before Glover, who was in on 22 tackles, batted the last ball away to send the Cornhuskers to the Orange Bowl with a chance for a second successive national title.

Nebraska	7	7	14	7—35
Oklahoma	3	14	7	7—31

Neb.—Rodgers, 72, punt return (Sanger, kick).
Okla.—FG, Carroll, 30.
Neb.—Kinney, 1, run (Sanger, kick).
Okla.—Mildren, 3, run (Carroll, kick).
Okla.—Harrison, 24, pass from Mildren (Carroll, kick).
Neb.—Kinney, 3, run (Sanger, kick).
Neb.—Kinney, 1, run (Sanger, kick).
Okla.—Mildren, 3, run (Carroll, kick).
Okla.—Harrison, 16, pass from Mildren (Carroll, kick).
Neb.—Kinney, 2, run (Sanger, kick).
Attendance—63,385.

Associated Press

NEBRASKA FANS WERE THANKFUL for Jeff Kinney, shown going over Oklahoma line as he scored the first of his four touchdowns in Nebraska's 35-31 triumph.

IRWIN'S 68 LEADS HERITAGE BY SHOT

Palmer and Eichelberger Share 2d at 2 Under Par —Trevino Cards a 78

By LINCOLN A. WERDEN
Special to The New York Times

HILTON HEAD ISLAND, S. C., Nov. 25—In cold and wind that reminded him of his football playing days at the University of Colorado, Hale Irwin led the opening round of the $110,000 Heritage Golf Classic with a 68 today.

The three-under-par score over the Harbour Town Golf Links enabled the 26-year-old former National Collegiate golf champion to lead Arnold Palmer and Dave Eichelberger by one stroke. The 68 also gave Irwin a surprising 10-stroke edge over Lee Trevino, the United States and British Open champion and the tour's leading money-winner.

Trevino had a disastrous 78 that equaled his highest score on the circuit this year. It included an unusual 8 at the 152-yard, par-3 14th, one of the picturesque water holes of this 6,655-yard course. There the creek is to the right of a green that is shored by railroad ties.

'Not Like El Paso'

Trevino said the cold "stiffened" him and was "not like it is back in warm El Paso" after he knocked two balls from the tee into the water. He was bunkered on his fifth stroke before recovering from the sand and two-putting for the 8.

After that Trevino hit a ball into the small pond at the 15th, where he took a bogey 6. He played the back nine first in 42 and was even with par of 36 on the front side. Trevino's previous 78 this year was in the Crosby tournament at Pebble Beach, Calif., last January.

Jack Nicklaus, who is co-designer of this course and is second to Trevino in 1971 earnings, was even with par after an incoming 33.

"I have no complaints about my game, only my score," said Nicklaus when he finished.

Rod Curl, a Wintuw Indian, and Bob Smith, a California amateur champion, were ahead of Nicklaus with 70's. Others at 71 were Deane Beman, Lou Graham, Bob Lunn, Mack McLendon and a rookie, Len Thompson.

Palmer had a chance to catch Irwin until the last hole. Now third in the money tabulation, Palmer began at the first hole, as did half the field. After a nine of 33, Palmer registered a succession of pars until the 18th, where the unprotected fairway is boardered on the left by Caliboque Sound.

Bogey-5 on 18th

Palmer's second shot at this 458-yard hole cleared the marsh grass but tumbled into a bunker short of the green before he holed out with a bogey 5. This kept him one stroke from a tying 68.

Eichelberger, winner of the Milwaukee open, had 35 on the back nine then a 34 that included four birdies and two bogeys.

Irwin had a 32 on the back nine to start today. Then he stayed even with par on the other half of the course. It was the first time he led a tournament this year.

THE LEADING SCORES

Hale Irwin	36	32—68
Arnold Palmer	33	36—69
Dave Eichelberger	34	35—69
Bob Smith	33	37—70
Rod Curl	36	34—70
Jack Nicklaus	38	33—71
Lou Graham	36	35—71
Mack McLendon	34	37—71
Deane Beman	37	34—71
Bob Lunn	34	37—71
Leonard Thompson	33	38—71
[illegible]	35	37—72
Homero Blancas	32	40—72
[illegible]	36	36—72
Don January	36	37—73
Larry Wood	37	36—73
Dow Finsterwald	35	38—73
[illegible]	36	37—73
Terry Dill	38	35—73
Bobby Mitchell	35	38—73
Ted Hayes	38	36—74
[illegible]	35	39—74

Bucks End Laker Streak at 33

Fast Break Cut Off in 120-104 Triumph

By THOMAS ROGERS
Special to The New York Times

MILWAUKEE, Jan. 9 — The offensive brilliance of Kareem Abdul-Jabbar plus an impromptu "get-back" defense devised by Coach Larry Costello of Milwaukee brought an end today to the longest winning streak in the modern history of professional team sports.

The Milwaukee Bucks, defending champions of the National Basketball Association, broke away from the Los Angeles Lakers midway in the fourth quarter at Milwaukee Arena and posted a 120-104 triumph. The setback ended a 33-game streak for the Lakers, who had last tasted defeat on Oct. 31, five days before the streak started.

A capacity crowd of 10,746 and a national television audience saw Abdul-Jabbar, formerly known as Lew Alcindor, score 39 points on a variety of shots. It was the 7-foot-2-inch center who ignited a decisive 18-2 Milwaukee burst midway in the final quarter with a pair of baskets from close to the hoop.

The Lakers led, 28-26, after one quarter, but then fell steadily behind and their deficit reached 9 points at 84-75 in the final seconds of the third period.

Flynn Robinson and Jim McMillian began to hit in the fourth quarter and drew the Lakers within 2 points at 94-92 with 6 minutes 52 seconds remaining.

Abdul-Jabbar then took a feed pass from Oscar Robertson and drove for a stuff shot basket. Moments later, Abdul-Jabbar tipped in the carom of his shot and the Bucks were zooming to victory.

Lucius Allen, who credited Costello with devising the defense that nullified the Lakers' fast break, scored the fifth and sixth straight Milwaukee points on a breakaway basket.

After Jerry West got Los Angeles' only basket in a stretch of 4 minutes 21 seconds, the Bucks sealed the triumph with a 12-0 spurt. Abdul-Jabbar ended the burst with a jump shot from the lane that made the score 112-94. It gave last season's most valuable player his 39th point and Milwaukee a certain triumph with 2:48 to play.

"Larry scouted the Lakers when they won their 33d in Atlanta Friday night and came up with a get-back defense to cut off their break," said Allen, who scored 18 points on 9-of-13 floor shooting in 19 minutes of play.

"We only used Kareem and one forward to rebound offensively," he said. "We kept the other forward at the foul line to prevent them from beating us down court."

"You have to give them credit for a fine defense," said West, who led Los Angeles in scoring with 20 points. "I don't think we hit one breakaway basket, unless it was on a 20-foot jump shot."

Most of the Lakers and Bucks also credited Abdul-Jabbar for a fine rebounding effort that at least neutralized the board strength of Wilt Chamberlain. Abdul-Jabbar pulled down 20 rebounds, eight more than Chamberlain and two more than Los Angeles's Happy Hairston, who topped the Lakers with 18.

"Our guys were really charged up," said Costello. "I could feel it in the locker room before the game."

"We were sort of dead out there, especially in the first half," said West of the Lakers, who made only 39 per cent of their floor shots (35 of 89), 10 per cent less than their usual figure.

As usual, Robertson was an important factor in the Milwaukee triumph, although he scored only 17 points. He directed the Bucks' offense, though, and was credited with nine assists.

"Oscar's usually the guy who gets the ball to you when the pressure's on and it's a big play," said Allen.

The Bucks were pleased, but not jubilant, over the triumph.

"They are our toughest competition in the league and it gives us a sense of accomplishment in beating them," said Abdul-Jabbar.

"Their streak was a fantastic accomplishment," said Costello. "But I'm glad it was our team that ended it."

"We knew it had to end sometime," said Coach Bill Sharman of the Lakers. "It was one of our weakest games in quite a while, but I think we learned something from it. It's hard to learn when you win."

Asked if he felt any relief that the streak was ended, West replied: "No, it was really a lot of fun. You just don't like to see it end this way, when we played so poorly."

"We've just finished a streak that I don't believe any other team is going to break," said McMillian, forgetting for the moment the cliché reason for the existence of records.

LOS ANGELES (104)

	min	fgm	fga	ftm	fta	reb	a	pf	pts
Ch'mb'rlin	48	7	11	1	3	12	2	4	15
Goodrich	40	5	20	8	9	9	4	3	18
Hairston	40	5	10	8	9	18	0	4	18
McMillian	44	7	19	4	5	4	3	3	18
Riley	9	0	2	0	0	2	1	0	0
Robinson	16	6	11	3	3	0	1	1	15
West	43	5	16	10	11	1	6	3	20
Total	240	35	89	34	40	46	17	18	104

MILWAUKEE (120)

	min	fgm	fga	ftm	fta	reb	a	pf	pts
Allen	19	9	13	0	0	0	3	4	18
Block	26	7	11	3	3	10	3	6	17
Dandridge	37	4	18	3	3	9	0	4	11
Jabbar	47	18	34	3	5	20	5	4	39
Jones	24	1	5	5	5	3	1	2	7
Kimball	1	0	0	0	0	0	0	0	0
McGlocklin	14	2	6	0	0	0	2	1	4
Perry	33	3	5	1	1	10	3	3	7
Robertson	39	5	14	7	7	6	9	2	17
Total	240	49	106	22	24	58	26	28	120

United Press International

BATTLE OF THE CENTERS: Kareem Abdul-Jabbar of the Bucks hooking the ball over Wilt Chamberlain of Lakers in game at Milwaukee. Jim McMillian of Lakers is at left.

Associated Press

EXCITED: Larry Costello, Bucks' coach, shouts to his players during Los Angeles game

RANGERS WIN, 8-0, AS RATELLE GAINS PRIZE FOR SCORING

Center Gets 5 Points Against Kings for 2d Game in Row and Earns $500 Award

By GERALD ESKENAZI

Erupting as if the Stanley Cup had finally returned, the fans at Madison Square Garden last night showered Jean Ratelle with applause, hats and ticker-tape as the rangy Ranger center turned in a 5-point performance that gave him the National Hockey League's scoring title for the first half of the season with 71 points.

Perhaps the fans wouldn't have been so excited in Montreal of Chicago or Boston. But there have been precious few honors the Rangers have earned in the last 30 years, and no New Yorker had led at the midway point since Andy Bathgate did 10 years ago.

Ratelle's performance, in an 8-0 rout of the Los Angeles Kings, was made under clutch circumstances. He knew that Phil Esposito of the Boston Bruins had a 4-point edge.

Typical Ratelle Maneuver

Even if Ratele amassed 4 points (an improbable total to expect, even against hockey's worst team), Esposito would win the $500 prize on the basis of more goals scored.

"The guys told me I needed the five," said Ratelle later.

He got the fifth point on a typical Ratelle maneuver. Midway through the final session he found himself alone with the disk in front of Rogatien Vachon, the goalie with a 4-16 won-lost record. Ratelle feinted, but Vachon wouldn't give. "Shoot!" cried the fans. "Shoot!" shouted Coach Emile Francis behind the New Yorkers' bench. Finally, Ratelle spotted Vic Hadfield to his left. He fed him the disk, and Hadfield punched it home.

In the last two games, Ratelle accounted for 10 points to 4 by Esposito. There had been speculation that in the last game he played, Ratelle received a tainted assist. However, the Rangers say that films of that game showed that Ratelle did deflect the puck to set up a goal.

Ratelle began his night's work with a score after 70 seconds of play. Subsequently, he earned four assists on two goals apiece by his linemates, Hadfield and Rod Gilbert.

"It's funny," said Hadfield. "When you know you need something, that's usually when you don't get it."

Recognition Overdue

Virtually overshadowed by Ratelle's performance was the fact that the New Yorkers are back in first place in the East Division (by 1 point over the Bruins) and that Gilles Villemure played a superb game as he turned in his second shutout of the campaign.

The Rangers must begin the second half of what has been their brightest season on the road. Their next six games are away.

Four points or fewer would have given Ratelle $250 as the runner-up. At the end of the season, the over-all winner receives $1,000. More than the

Continued on Page 41, Column 5

The New York Times
SPORTS
Section 5
Sunday, May 28, 1972
L + - -

DONOHUE SETS RECORD IN WINNING INDIANAPOLIS 500; TIGERS DEFEAT YANKEES, 2-1; METS DOWN CARDS, 4-1

United Press International

LATE STARTER: A. J. Foyt, bottom, leaving pit apron at Indianapolis to join rivals as the pace car, extreme right, pulled into pit area. Foyt's car had stalled at the starting line and was ordered pushed to the end of the pits. When Foyt's crew managed to start the car, it went in at the back of the pack.

Grant Finishes Second

By JOHN S. RADOSTA

Special to The New York Times

INDIANAPOLIS, May 27—Mark Donohue won the Indianapolis 500 this afternoon in a theatrical finish, taking the lead just 13 laps from the end after his teammate and another driver ran into trouble.

The race also ended in disagreement, with Dan Gurney's All American Racers convinced their driver, Jerry Grant, had won. If Gurney decided to protest, he cannot do that until official results are posted at 8 A.M. tomorrow.

In the provisional results Grant was credited with second place, 47.1 seconds, nearly a lap, behind Donohue.

The other provisional leaders were: third, Al Unser, the 1970 and 1971 winner, in a Parnelli-Offenhauser; fourth, Joe Leonard, the current United States Auto Club champion, in another Parnelli-Offy, and fifth, Sammy Sessions in a Lola-Ford.

Sam Posey was the leading rookie, finishing sixth in an Eagle-Offy.

Thirty-three cars started the race, and only 15 were running at the finish.

Donohue, driving one of Roger Penske's dark blue Sunoco McLaren-Offys, was running third, apparently out of contention, when disaster struck the men ahead of him.

His teammate Gary Bettenhausen, after leading comfortably most of the afternoon in another McLaren-Offy, stalled with malfunctioning ignition, yielding the lead to Grant in Gurney's "mystery" Eagle-Offy.

Minutes later Grant's left front tire was flattened by a three-inch piece of metal debris from someone's gearbox. The slow running on the flat tire caused his spark plugs to foul and when he returned to the track after the tire change, his engine just didn't respond.

In the greatest victory of an illustrious 13-year career that began with road racing, Donohue set a record for the 500 covering the distance in 3 hours 3 minutes 31.55 seconds for an average speed of 163.465 miles an hour. This is 5.73 quicker than the record that Al Unser set in 1971.

THE SMILE OF VICTORY: Mark Donohue in Victory Lane

It was perfect racing weather, with temperatures in the 70's and a light breeze. The management of Indianapolis Motor Speedway never discloses attendance figures, but the consensus put the crowd at more than 275,000.

This was a rough day for other leaders and front runners besides Bettenhausen and Grant. Bobby Unser, the 1968 winner and today's pre-race favorite, retired after 30 laps with broken ignition in his Olsonite Eagle-Offy. Mike Mosley was eliminated in an accident, and Peter Revsen, who started from second place, was forced out with a broken gear box in his Gulf McLaren-Offy.

The race began according to script, with Bobby Unser starting from the pole position and setting the early pace. Bettenhausen, the No. 2 driver on the Penske team, who had started from fourth position, took the lead when Bobby Unser went out and settled there for what seemed an easy cruise for the rest of the day.

Bettenhausen led 116 of the 200 laps around the 2½-mile speedway and won more than $20,000 in lap prizes.

With less than 65 miles to go, Bettenhausen was holding off Grant's challenge when, on

Continued on Page 6, Column 5

Associated Press

EVASIVE ACTION: Gary Bettenhausen, right, drives his Penske McLaren-Offenhauser racer past Mike Mosley. Mosley careened off the wall while leading and was burned in the cash. He is in satisfactory condition.

Tigers Score Two in Fifth, With Help of a Wild Pitch

By MURRAY CHASS

The Yankees, who escaped unscathed following a three-base wild pitch three weeks ago, perpetrated a two-base wild pitch yesterday and it resulted in a 2-1 loss to Detroit.

In a game against Minnesota, the since-traded Jack Aker threw a pitch for ball four that eluded Thurman Munson, and while the catcher walked after the ball (he thought it was only ball three), Cesar Tovar alertly raced all the way from home plate to third base.

In yesterday's situation, Mickey Stanley of the Tigers was at first base on a walk in the fifth inning when Mel Stottlemyre fired a pitch into the dirt. The ball skipped off Munson's glove, soared about 15 feet into the air and headed for the screen in front of the stands.

This time Munson ran toward the ball, but it stayed in the air long enough for Stanley to scoot to third. That extra base turned out to be a key one because on the next pitch Manager Billy Martin called for a suicide squeeze play.

Ed Brinkman followed orders perfectly. As Stanley darted for the plate, Brinkman pushed a bunt between the first-base line and the pitcher's mound. Ron Blomberg fielded the ball but couldn't make a play on Stanley at home. By the time he turned to throw to first, he had no play there either, and Brinkman had a single.

Joe Coleman, the pitcher, followed with another bunt, sacrificing Brinkman to second, and Dick McAuliffe then lined a Stottlemyre pitch to left for Detroit's second run.

The Tigers threatened to score additional runs in the inning when Stottlemyre hit Aurelio Rodriguez with a pitch and walked Norm Cash. But Paul Jata ended the inning by grounding into a force play.

The Yankees' run came in the seventh when Jerry Kenney, playing short while Gene Michael rested, singled and scored all the way from first on Horace Clarke's single. Clarke has driven in all the runs—three—the Yankees have scored in two games against Detroit.

Kenney was able to score from first on a single for two seasons.

The first was that the hit came on a two-out, 3-2 pitch, which meant Kenney was running with the pitch from Coleman. The second was that Jata, playing right field for Al Kaline, who strained a muscle in his right calf, fielded Clarke's hit and threw to second base instead of tossing the ball in the direction of the plate.

As soon as Dick Howser, the third-base coach, saw Jata start to throw to second he waved

Continued on Page 2, Column 6

M'ANDREW VICTOR WITH A SIX-HITTER

Right-Hander Pitches First Complete Game in 2 Years, Allows Bull Pen to Rest

By JOSEPH DURSO

Special to The New York Times

ST. LOUIS, May 27—Jim McAndrew, the high-brow of the New York Mets, pitched his first complete game in two seasons tonight as the Mets defeated the St. Louis Cardinals, 4-1.

For the Mets, who had lost three of their last four starts, McAndrew's new durability supplied something the team's bull pen needed as badly as a victory: time off. For McAndrew, who had not gone the distance since Sept. 12, 1970, the urgency was even greater: job.

The 28-year-old right-hander from Lost Nation, Iowa, has been the "odd man" of the Mets since he arrived in 1968. Off the field, he was the team intellectual — a psychology graduate of the University of Iowa, the quiet one of the clubhouse, the loner. But on the field, he was even more isolated than that—the sixth man in a five-man rotation, the hard-luck pitcher nobody scored any runs for, the "trade bait" whenever deals were discussed.

Tonight, though, the quiet man had his hour. He worked nine strong innings while the

Continued on Page 2, Column 5

French Confounded As N.F.L. Players Make Their Debut

By MICHAEL KATZ

Special to The New York Times

PARIS, May 27—An American accent at the Stade de Charléty screamed from the grandstand, "Hey, how about some football?"

And for the first time in French history, professional halfbacks ran through "trous" ("holes") created by "bloquers" ("tackles") and "gardes" ("guards"), Bob Hayes caught "une bombe" and Parisians in the crowd of about 8,000 were confounded by "le rugby Americain."

As the highlight of American Sports Week, 41 National Football League players gave a simulated exhibition of what is considered America's most popular spectator sport during half-time of a rugby match.

When it was over, the French couldn't understand why the "Blue" team always had the ball and why, contrary to glimpses of football they had seen in movies like "M.A.S.H.," there weren't any "pretty girls to stimulate the teams."

Because N.F.L. owners were wary of their valuable property taking part in this charity "contest" to benefit the American Hospital of Paris, the announcer told the crowd that what they were

Continued on Page 12, Column 4

GARY PLAYER'S 70 TIES LUNN AT 206

Lead Is 2 Shots—Nicklaus at 209 in Atlanta After a 75, His Worst of Year

By LINCOLN A. WERDEN

Special to The New York Times

ATLANTA, May 27 — Gary Player tied Bob Lunn for the 54-hole lead in the $130,000 Atlanta Golf Classic today as Jack Nicklaus soared to his highest round of the year, a 75.

The co-leaders brought their aggregates to 206, two strokes ahead of the field. Nicklaus, taking three putts at three greens on the back nine of the Atlanta Country Club course, dropped three strokes back at 209 in a tie for sixth.

Following his spectacular 64 that equaled the course record yesterday, Nicklaus's score today was 11 strokes higher. He explained it by saying, "I missed eight putts of from three to eight feet. Yesterday, I was holing them and that made the difference."

Nicklaus declared that tomorrow he would end his preliminary competitive play for the United States Open championship, which starts June 15 at Pebble Beach, Calif.

Player, who was paired with Nicklaus, was two under par with a 35 on each side for a 70. Lunn, just ahead of them, had an edge of three strokes over

Continued on Page 5, Column 3

Penn Takes I.C.4-A Track Title

By NEIL AMDUR

Special to The New York Times

PHILADELPHIA, May 27—Without help from some of its more touted talent, Pennsylvania ended a 52-year famine today by winning the 96th annual I. C. 4-A outdoor track and field championships.

Relying on another strong individual performance from Bruce Collins and their enormous balance and depth, the Quakers outdistanced their state rivals, Penn State, as well as Villanova and Pittsburgh in a two-day meet that may be remembered more for its perfect weather and the top athletes who did not compete.

Penn finished with 53 points. Penn State, with its best showing in recent years, wound up second with 40.

Collins won his specialty, the 440-yard intermediate hurdles, and the 220-yard dash. He joined Bill Rea, the Pitt long jumper-triple jumper, as the meet's only double winners. His 21.2-second effort in the 220 and one-yard victory over Jim Rudasill of Brown confirmed Collins's strength and stamina as he prepares for the National Collegiate championships and United States Olympic Trials.

In an Olympic year, when performances traditionally improve, today's program saw only one meet record, by Chris Dunn of Colgate. Continuing his string of fine high jumping, Dunn cleared 7 feet 2 inches on his first "Fosbury Flop" and stamped himself as a challenger for one of the three berths on the American team.

Unquestionably, the closeness of the N.C.A.A. meet next week affected the training strategy of coaches and athletes and the quality of the 65-college competition here.

Missing from the meet to rest for the Nationals were Bob Wheeler, the Duke miler; Fred Samara, the Penn decathlete, and Joe Lucas, the Georgetown steeplechaser.

Mike Keogh, the 5-foot-7-inch, 124-pound Manhattan distance runner, dropped from his specialty, the three-mile, to the mile. He proceeded to outrun Tom Gregan of Villanova and Bruce Fischer of Syracuse en route to a three-yard victory in 4:01.6, a career-best.

Keogh's triumph ended a six-year string of mile titles by Villanova. The Wildcats extended their gold-medal streak

Continued on Page 4, Column 4

Major League Baseball

Sunday, May 28, 1972

American League

YESTERDAY'S GAMES

Detroit 2, New York 1.
Oakland 6, Chicago 3.
Baltimore 4, Cleveland 2 (n.).
California 4, Kansas City 2 (n.).
Boston 9, Milwaukee 3 (n.).
Texas 16, Minnesota 2.

FRIDAY NIGHT

Detroit 8, New York 2.
Baltimore 2, Cleveland 0.
California 10, Kansas City 5.
Boston 5, Milwaukee 4.
Minnesota 7, Texas 0.
Oakland 4, Chicago 2.

STANDING OF THE TEAMS

Eastern Division

	W.	L.	Pct.	G.B.
Detroit	19	14	.576	—
Cleveland	18	14	.563	½
Baltimore	18	15	.545	1
New York	14	18	.438	4½
Boston	13	18	.419	5
Milwaukee	10	20	.333	7½

Western Division

	W.	L.	Pct.	G.B.
Oakland	21	11	.656	—
Chicago	21	12	.636	½
Minnesota	20	12	.625	1
Texas	16	20	.444	7
California	14	22	.389	9
Kansas City	13	21	.382	9

National League

YESTERDAY'S GAMES

New York 4, St. Louis 1 (n.).
Los Angeles 7, Houston 3 (n.).
Chicago 5, Montreal 3.
Philadelphia 2, Pittsburgh 1 (12 inn., n.).
Cincinnati 9, San Diego 4 (n.).
San Francisco 11, Atlanta 9 (n.).

FRIDAY NIGHT

St. Louis 6, New York 2.
Atlanta 9, San Francisco 4.
Cincinnati 4, San Diego 0.
Houston 5, Los Angeles 3.
Pittsburgh 6, Philadelphia 4.

STANDING OF THE TEAMS

Eastern Division

	W.	L.	Pct.	G.B.
New York	27	10	.730	—
Pittsburgh	21	14	.600	5
Chicago	19	16	.543	7
Philadelphia	16	20	.444	10½
Montreal	16	21	.432	11
St. Louis	14	24	.368	13½

Western Division

	W.	L.	Pct.	G.B.
Houston	24	13	.649	—
Los Angeles	22	16	.579	2½
Cincinnati	20	17	.541	4
Atlanta	15	21	.417	8½
San Diego	15	24	.385	10
San Francisco	14	27	.341	12

TODAY'S PROBABLE PITCHERS

Detroit at New York (2 P.M.)—Cain (0-3) vs. Hinton (1-0).
Chicago at Oakland—Bradley (5-2) vs. Blue (0-1).
Cleveland at Baltimore — Colbert (0-1) vs. Palmer (4-3).
Kansas City at California—Drago (2-3) vs. Rose (1-0).
Milwaukee at Boston — Lonborg (2-1) vs. Krausse (1-2).
Texas at Minnesota — Gogolewski (3-3) vs. Kaat (5-1).

New York at St. Louis — Gentry (3-1) vs. Cleveland (3-3).
Los Angeles at Houston—John (3-3) vs. Dierker (4-2).
Montreal at Chicago — Stoneman (4-4) vs. Hooton (4-4).
Philadelphia at Pittsburgh — Selma (1-5) vs. Blass (5-1).
San Diego at Cincinnati — Grief (3-6) vs. Grimsley (2-0).
San Francisco at Atlanta (2) — Bryant (2-3) and Stone (1-4) vs. Kelley (3-4) and Schueler (1-0).

(Figures in parentheses are season's won-lost records.)

WANDA TRIUMPHS IN MOTHER GOOSE

Susan's Girl Beaten a Neck After 7 Victories in Row

By JOE NICHOLS

Wanda of the Niblick Stable came through with a dramatic and surprising victory in the $84,600 Mother Goose at Belmont Park yesterday.

The Kentucky-bred daughter of Cornish Prince registered a distinct upset in taking the 1⅛-mile test for 3-year-old fillies, for she beat the heavily favored Susan's Girl, the runner-up in the field of eight, by a neck. In third place, six lengths back, came Summer Guest.

Under the guidance of Jorge Velasquez, Wanda raced in front all the way, and posted the impressive time of 1:48 2/5. This figure is a record for the stakes, surpassing the former standard of 1:49 2/5 met by Quill in 1959 and equaled by Dark Mirage in 1968. Hesitantly backed by the crowd of 38,894, Wanda returned $17.60, $3.60 and $2.80 for $2 across the board.

The Mother Goose is the middle jewel in the triple crown for fillies between the Acorn of one mile and the Coaching Club American Oaks at 1½ miles, listed for Belmont Park

Continued on Page 8, Column 2

. . . TUMBLED on back, but kept control of ball. Next batter, Mickey Stanley, came . . .

. . . RUNNING UP to protest the play, but with no result

Donohue Takes Indy 500 at Speed of 163.465 M.P.H.

VICTOR GAINS LEAD 13 LAPS FROM END

Bettenhausen Is Forced Out Near Finish After Setting Pace—Al Unser Is 3d

Continued From Page 1

lap 174, there was a yellow flag to permit track workers to pick up some debris.

Running at the slow 80 miles an hour required by a new rule, Bettenhausen's engine overheated, affecting the ignition. When the greeen light went on again on lap 176, Bettenhausen hit the throttle, but the engine simply popped, sounding very sick.

He slowed down so much that Grant lapped him within four circuits of the track. Eventually Bettenhausen stalled and had to park on the grass border. Grant took the lead and Donohue moved to second.

With Grant now in front, there was confusion in the pits and the announcing tower. Gurney's crew signaled Grant to "cool it" because they thought he was a lap ahead of Donohue. But when they saw Donohue's crew telling him to hurry, teammate Bobby Unser stepped over the pit wall into the roadway to signal Grant to "go."

The track announcing system also had to correct itself. First it had Grant ahead by a lap and five seconds; in a moment this lead was changed to five seconds.

It was here that disaster struck Grant, with the debris cutting his left front tire, he drove into the pit, frantically waving to indicate he needed a tire change. While Grant was sweating it out in the pit, Donohue just breezed by, taking the lead on Lap 188.

That was the race, with his plugs fouled by the slow running on the flat tire, Grant had no speed left to chase Donohue.

Donohue Led 13 Laps

Donohue was credited with leading just 13 laps, numbers 188 through 200, inclusive, but they were the ones that counted most. He made the required four pit stops but also had to make a fifth stop because the pit fueler was not working properly. That seemed to be the only trouble Donohue had.

Donohue's car was not at its best. He figured it was running 200 horsepower less than it did when he qualified last Sunday.

Donohue, the No. 1 driver of the Penske team, has raced here only four times before. His best previous finish was second place in 1970. Last year he was leading when his gear box broke down.

In road racing he has won the Trans-American championship three times, the United States road racing championship twice, and a host of other races. This season he is the leading threat to the superiority of the Gulf-McLaren team in the Can-Am road racing series. Donohue will drive a Porsche.

Today's purse is expected to total more than $1-million, depending on gate receipts, when it is announced tomorrow afternoon. Donohue's share may be about $250,000.

The race was a relatively safe one, with only one accident of consequence. Mosley leading on lap 56 in an Eagle-Offy, lost his right front wheel on the exit of Turn 4 and hit the wall twice.

He struggled out of the car and fell to the pavement and was immediately picked up by safety personnel.

Mosley suffered second and third degree burns on both feet and minor burns on the face and hands. He was flown by helicopter to Methodist Hospital, where his condition was reported to be satisfactory.

Turn 4 is the same place where Mosley hit the wall in 1971, when he broke a leg.

Wally Dallenbach's STP Lola-Ford caught fire twice in the pits, but he was not hurt and the finished the race in 14th position.

As for the controversy, Gurney said this evening that his position was not formally a protest, at least, not yet. "We don't want to protest anybody," he said. "We want to find out who won the race."

In fact, Gurney's team also was the subject of protest when Grant came in to change that tire, his crew connected a fueling rig to his car from teammate Bobby Unser's pit reservoir. The Penske people protested, but Frank Del Roy, the chairman of the technical committee, ruled that no fuel had been drawn.

Today's race was the third of this season's United States Auto Club Championship Trail. Bobby Unser won the opener on March 18 at Phoenix and Bettenhausen won the second, on April 23 at Trenton.

The Indianapolis 500 also is the first triple crown of 500-milers, the others being at Pocono in July and at Ontario, Calif., in September.

GERMAN AMATEURS ALLEGED TO BE PAID

A shadowy figure known as "Santa Claus" has systematically been paying off East German amateur athletes after significant track and field victories, Time magazine charges in its forthcoming issue.

The magazine also asserts that after Margitta Gummel captured the women's shot-put event in the 1968 Olympic Games in Mexico City she was given a $5,600 Wartburg automobile.

"Santa Claus" reportedly shows up "soon after an East German has won a big event or broken a record." The magazine says he then opens a briefcase, removes an envelope and counts out money, which he then hands over to the athlete.

The country's world-class swimmers, charges the magazine, are given special living quarters while attending school and often practice up to 35 hours a week.

The athletes also are given "sham" jobs for which they do nothing, yet pick up salaries, according to the article. Reportedly, there is a sliding scale of payments, depending on the importance of the event and whether a record is broken.

Tarport Skipper Scores

Special to The New York Times

FREEHOLD, N. J., May 27—Tarport Skipper, a 4-year-old bay colt owned by Del Miller and Hugh Grant of Meadowlands, Pa., turned in the first sub two-minute mile of the Atlantic City Raceway meeting at Freehold this season when he won the $12,500 Wenonah Pace by two lengths today. Tarport Skipper, driven by John Chapman, was timed in 1:59.4 and paid $3.20.

United Press International

INTO VICTORY LANE: Donohue on the way to collect the Borg-Warner trophy, right

Dave Anderson

'Not Meant for a Bettenhausen'

Associated Press

Gary Bettenhausen drives past crash of Mike Mosley's Eagle-Offenhauser (98)

INDIANAPOLIS, May 27—Eleven years ago, Tony Bettenhausen was sitting in the pits at the Indianapolis 500 during a practice day when another driver, Paul Russo, approached.

"Something's wrong with my car but I can't figure out what," Russo said. "Could you take it out for a few laps?"

Sports of The Times

Bettenhausen knew that his wife, Valerie, had asked him not to drive any car other than his own. But the previous winter, on his farm in Tinley Park, Ill., he had built a grain-curing bin with Russo's help as a welder. To return the favor, he agreed to test Russo's racing car.

"Excuse me," he told a friend that day in the pits, "I'll be right back."

Minutes later, on the main straight at the Speedway, a 5-cent pin in the steering system came loose. The car veered into the outside wall and soared 150 yards, landing upside down and burning. Tony Bettenhausen, who had driven in the 500 here 14 times without winning, died instantly. But today, he returned as he had promised. At least the memory of Tony Bettenhausen returned, because, with about 60 miles remaining, his 30-year-old son, Gary, in his fifth 500, was leading the race, his blue "Sunoco" car roaring down the same main straight when the motor began popping.

"Running to slow is what caused it," he would say later.

Pieces of Metal

Three laps earlier, the yellow caution flag ordered the drivers to slow to 80 miles per hour while pieces of metal from undertermined cars were being cleared from the No. 3 turn. During the slowdown, the water temperature rose on the small gauge at the bottom right of his dashboard.

"It kept getting hotter all day," he would explain. "It went up to 200, then 230, then over 240 when the yellow flag was on. The motor began poppin' and bangin', and when we got the green flag, I lost the motor. I knew 80 was too slow. You can get out and walk faster."

During the drivers' meeting the other day he had been among those requesting that 120 m.p.h. was enough of a slowdown.

"They told us at the meeting that it'd probably be 120," he said, "and then they told us the next day that it was 80. My engine just got hot and burned a piston. Until that yellow flag, my car was just perfect. I could've run a lot harder. They never would've known where I went. I passed guys every place—on the outside, through the corner, near the grass, anywhere I wanted to go."

Instead, when the motor went, he'd glided onto the grass near the No. 3 turn. "I got out of the car and sat awhile," he recalled. "Somebody gave me a beer."

He was in his wood-paneled garage now, his red helmet off, a blue baseball cap above his reddish hair, his asbestos underwear showing below his brown driver's suit, weariness in his sharply handsome face, sadness in his greenish eyes.

"I felt like crying," he said.

"Did you?" somebody asked him.

"Yeah," he said. "I guess it's not meant for a Bettenhausen to win here. I thought of him quite a few times during the race—when I was going good, and when the motor went. I know how much he wanted to win here.

Mrs. Berning Recaptures U.S. Open Golf Crown

Associated Press

AND TO THE WINNER, a kiss from her husband and a trophy for Susie Maxwell Berning after victory in the women's Open tourney at the Winged Foot course.

By LINCOLN A. WERDEN

Special to The New York Times

MAMARONECK, N.Y., July 2—Mrs. Susie Maxwell Berning, who won the title in 1968, before her 19-month-old daughter was born, recaptured the United States Women's Open golf championship today.

The 30-year-old matron from Lake Tahoe, Nev., who was a member of the men's golf team when she attended Oklahoma City University, closed with a one-under-par 71 for a 72-hole total of 299.

The 71st hole, or 17th, a par 3 of 200 yards at the Winged Foot Golf Club's east course, proved the turning point in the dramatic ending of the tourney.

Mrs. Berning rolled in a 20-foot putt there for a deuce and a birdie. Minutes later Pam Barnett carded a bogey 4 on the hole. The two-stroke swing gave Mrs. Berning a one-stroke lead that she held when Miss Barnett finished with a 76 for 300.

The Charlotte, N.C., professional, who had led yesterday after 54 holes, dropped into a second-place tie with Mrs. Judy Rankin and Kathy Ahern.

Miss Ahern, the Ladies Professional Golf Association champion, reeled off the low score of the championship with a 34, 36-70, over the 6,100-yard course that players and officials agreed furnished perhaps the toughest test in women's open championship history.

Miss Englehorn Cards 307

Betty Burfeindt trailed at 302 after a 75, while Mickey Wright, a four-time champion, went around in 71 in what she described as "my best from tee to green, but I three-putted three times." Miss Wright was in the 304 bracket as a consequence with Gloria Ehret and the leading amateur, Mrs. Jane Bastanchury Booth, the North and South champion who equaled the par of 72.

Janie Blalock, who is the center of controversy in the women's ranks because of her $5-million suit against the L.P.G.A. following a charge of cheating, was in a tie for fourteenth at 307 with Shirley Engelhorn, who led after the first and the second rounds.

Mrs. JoAnne Gunderson Carner, who won the Open by seven strokes last year at Erie, Pa., posted a 79 for 312, while Betsy Rawls, also a four-time winner, had an 81 for 308.

Mrs. Berning, who is 5 feet 2 inches and weighs 115 pounds, as does Miss Barnett, used a driver from the tee at the crucial 17th "to get home" but Miss Barnett used a No. 4 wood. Earlier, however, Miss Barnett, who began with birdies on the first and second holes, saw a five-stroke advantage vanish as her second shot went offline. She had successive bogeys at the eighth, ninth and 10th holes.

Mrs. Berning's share of the $40,000 purse was $6,000, considerably more than the $465 she earned by being in a tie for 23d in the 1971 championship. In 1970 she played "but I was five months pregnant then and didn't make the cut to qualify for the last 36 holes."

Asked if she and her husband had golfing plans for their daughter, Mrs. Berning said, "No, we won't push her."

Dale Berning and his wife travel in modern style on the tour in a motor home. They have a permanent baby-sitter for their youngster as they go from one tourney site to another. They estimate they travel 20,000 miles to tourneys in this fashion.

Outgoing Card of 34

Mrs. Berning's spurt to victory was unusual since her 79 was the highest opening round score of anyone who has gone on to win. After that she had a 73 but the third round of 76 included a triple bogey 8 at the 12th hole. "I didn't see how I could ever win the championship with an 8 at one hole," she said.

But today she had a 34, the best front nine of any of the leaders, and was within one stroke then of Miss Barnett. On the incoming half she missed the green for a bogey 5 at the 10th and after four pars took three putts for another bogey 5 at the 15th.

Undaunted she holed a 7-footer to save par at the next. She pulled her driver out of the golf bag and "let it go" at the 17th. When she downed the 20-foot putt she was told she was even with Miss Barnett.

After a 4 at the home hole, Mrs. Berning sat on the clubhouse terrace to await reports of what Miss Barnett was doing.

She smiled slightly when she heard she was ahead because of Miss Barnett's sixth bogey. Dale Berning came over and kissed his wife as the new champion. "She's been playing fantastic golf for the last two months and scoring so rotten. I knew she'd have to get the breaks some day," he said.

Scores on Page 13.

METS LOSE, 4 TO 3, ON A WALK IN 9TH

Rauch Passes Expos' Fairly With Bases Loaded to Force In Decisive Run

By DEANE McGOWEN

Special to The New York Times

MONTREAL, July 2—The New York Mets, who had beaten the Expos six successive times, went down to a 4-3 defeat today in Jarry Park, but it was not robust hitting that ended New York's streak.

A bases-loaded walk by Bob Rauch, the third Met pitcher, to Ron Fairly, in the last of the ninth inning with two outs turned the trick.

The setback, coupled with Pittsburgh's 7-4 victory over the Chicago Cubs, dropped the Mets one game behind the Pirates in the National League Eastern Division.

Rauch, who joined the Mets at the start of this seven-game trip in Philadelphia last Wednesday from the Mets' Tidewater farm team, pitched the final inning in relief of Tug McGraw.

Willie Mays, batting for McGraw in the top of the inning, singled to center, with two out and two runs home, to score Wayne Garrett with the tying run.

But Rauch, a lanky fastball pitcher, was unable to hold off the Expos. Terry Humphrey led off the inning with a walk, then Carl Morton ran for the Montreal catcher. Clyde Mashore, who had gone to left field for defensive purposes in the ninth, then sacrificed Morton to second.

Hunt Hit 186th Time

Ron Hunt was hit by a Rauch pitch (for the 186th time in his career). Mike Jorgensen, a former Met, also walked to fill the bases, and the Montreal fans in the crowd of 21,389 set the compact park rocking with their expectant cheers.

Bob Bailey, who had gone into the game in the eighth as a runner and remained to play third base, became the second out but not before Rauch had gone to a 3-and-2 count. Then Bailey fanned.

That left it squarely up to either Fairly or Rauch, and the Expo right fielder, who had already collected three singles and two runs batted in, won the battle at the plate.

Rauch, who had pitched one

Continued on Page 12, Column 8

Shoe Company Offered Bribe, Trackman Charges

Special to The New York Times

EUGENE, Ore., July 2—The signs of another major money scandal in track and field have appeared at the United States Olympic trials.

The latest charge comes from an American athlete, Gene White, a world-class high jumper, who contends that a representative from a West German shoe concern was prepared to offer him money if he wore the company's shoes in the American trials here and again at Munich if he qualified for the Olympics.

White outlined details of the alleged bribe attempt in a letter to members of the men's track and field committee of the United States Olympic Committee. American officials have refused to comment on the charge, although Bob Giegengack, the chairman, acknowledged that "we're gathering facts" on the case.

White's typewritten letter, a carbon of which he gave to The New York Times, is dated June 30. The alleged bribe attempt, according to White, took place on June 28 and involved a representative of Adidas, a a large West German manufacturer of athletic shoes and equipment.

Charges and Counter-Charges

"His name, as I recall, was Mr. Brinks," White wrote. "Mr. Brinks . . . took me into the room and talked to me about Adidas equipment and the possibility of wearing their shoes. Then he said that if he could do me any favors, for me to come to him. Next he said that something can be worked out in terms of money if I wore the Adidas shoes at the Olympic Trials, and if I made the United States Olympic team and wore the shoes in Munich also. As he talked about this,

Continued on Page 13, Column 2

The New York Times

Gene White, high jumper

Slow-Pitch Softball Is Fast With Runs

By GERALD ESKENAZI

Special to The New York Times

BALDWIN, L. I., July 2—The pitch floats down from an arc as high as 10 feet, coming in as big as a pumpkin. Jim Galloway at home plate is relaxed, muscles apparently limp, watching the ball as if he had all the time in the world. A second later the ball is gone, beyond the 290-foot fence, bouncing on top of a hill where it scatters picnickers.

In the world of slow-pitch softball, Galloway is king. He has a huge number of subjects. The people that follow slow-pitch say that it is this country's No. 1 participant sport, having passed bowling last year. Here on Long Island alone there are 1,000 teams registered with the Amateur Softball Association of America and there are more than 30,000 teams in the United States, each team with at least 15 players.

One of the best, Fallon's Empire City Astros of Levittown, defeated the Chattanooga Cards, 14-8, today and won the Rheingold Slow-Pitch Tournament of Champions for the third straight year. A major reason for their success was Galloway's 11 home runs in 23 times at bat during the round-robin tourney.

10th Man on the Field

It looks easy to stroke a slow-pitch ball. True, Galloway is hitting about .690 this season and will wind up with 70 to 80 homers in 40 games. But he's the best. The pitch is delivered underhand from 46½ feet away. It must reach the plate on a downward trajectory after reaching a height of at least three feet but no higher than 10 feet.

"Sure, it looks simple

Continued on Page 12, Column 6

B. Warren Brown

High-arcing slow-pitch ball approaches Piledrivers' batter during tournament at Baldwin Park on Long Island.

Seagren's 18-5¾ Vault Sets World Mark

Mann Captures 400 Hurdles, Shattering American Record

By NEIL AMDUR

Special to The New York Times

EUGENE, Ore., July 2—Reaffirming his status as one of track and field's supreme competitors, Bob Seagren cleared 18 feet 5¾ inches on his final attempt tonight and regained sole possession of the world record in the pole vault.

A Hayward Field crowd of 12,000 roared excitedly as the 1968 Olympic champion cleared the height, while the crossbar quivered dramatically for almost five seconds on his descent to the pit.

Seagren's effort capped another remarkable day of performances at the Olympic trials, which also saw the triumphant return of Ralph Mann and 18-foot pole vaults by Steve Smith and Jan Johnson.

It was the greatest exhibition of vaulting ever and confirmed that Americans were not yet ready to concede their gold-medal place to European challengers.

Roberts Clears 17-8½

The three 18-foot vaults eliminated a performance by Dave Roberts that almost certainly would have qualified on any other Olympic team. Roberts cleared 17-8½ but missed three attempts at 18-½ which Seagren, Smith and Johnson cleared, Johnson on his last jump.

Seagren's climb back to the top, ahead of Kjell Isaksson of Sweden, with whom he had shared the record at 18-4¼, was as dramatic as his performance four years ago when he got out of a hospital bed and set the world standard in the final American trials at South Lake Tahoe, Calif., en route to the gold medal.

This time around, a knee injury had kept the handsome Californian out of the competition for over a year, while Isaksson and others shattered the 18-foot barrier. Now, six vaulters have cleared 18 feet, and four are Americans.

Equally as dramatic and satisfying was Mann's victory in the 400-meter intermediate hurdles.

One month ago the 23-year-old Mann sat on the infield grass at the Los Angeles Coliseum, his head buried between his legs and a beaten fifth-place finisher in the Compton invitation meet.

"I don't know what's wrong," Mann pleaded at the time. "Tell me what to do."

Today, running in the far

Continued on Page 13, Column 5

The New York Times/Ernest Sisto

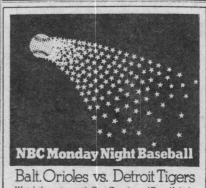

TWO-POINT LANDING: Bobby Murcer scoring in first inning of first game with Cleveland as Ray Fosse missed ball. Murcer scored from second on a single by Roy White.

Yanks Defeat Indians, 6-1 and 5-2

Lyle Registers 16th Save and Lowers E.R.A. to 0.96

By LEONARD KOPPETT

In the House That Ruth Built, formally named Yankee Stadium, the big moment these days comes when a guy steps out of a car in front of the Yankee dugout. Even before he emerges to stride confidently to the mound, the crowd knows he is Albert W. (Sparky) Lyle, relief pitcher extraordinary, and when he showed up on schedule yesterday, noisy anticipation quickly became happy reality. He nailed down a victory that enabled the Yankees to sweep a doubleheader from the Cleveland Indians, 6-1 and 5-2.

Fritz Peterson had pitched the first game for New York, set up nicely by four runs in the first two innings. And Rob Gardner, given his first start of the season, pitched the six innings Manager Ralph Houk hoped for effectively. He was trailing, 2-1, when the Yankees went to bat in the sixth, but four seeing-eye singles with two out created a 3-2 lead and Lyle was ready to be unleashed.

He is, right now, as hot a relief pitcher as anyone can imagine. The old Yankee traditions of home runs and championships aren't being sustained these days, but Lyle has matched, in half a season, anything done in a comparable stretch by Johnny Murphy, Joe Page, Luis Arroyo or half a dozen other notable relievers.

Yields Single in 7th

In his 23d appearance of the season, Lyle faced 10 batters for nine outs, yielding only a two-out single in the seventh. It was his 16th save, matching the total he posted all last year for the Boston Red Sox, and exceeding by four the total the entire Yankee staff got in 1971. He also has two victories (and one defeat) and an earned-run average of 0.96.

But the most illuminating statistic is this: the Yankees have won 31 games. In 12 of them, the starting pitcher worked a complete game. In the other 19, Lyle was there to get the final out in 18 of them (Fred Beene accounted for the other).

So the Yankee outlook, which looked so bleak in mid-May and turned depressing again last week, is suddenly brightening again. The four-game sweep of the Indians gave the Yankees 11 victories in their last 16 games and brought them within three games of .500. For all their agonies, they are in third place, with only four more losses than Baltimore and five more than Detroit.

Aside from Lyle and Peterson, yesterday's heroes were those who get relatively little publicity. Bobby Murcer knocked in three runs in the opener and Ron Blomberg hit his fifth homer and a game-tying infield single in the second, but they generally get their shares of headlines. John Ellis, Celerino Sanchez, Bernie Allen and Gardner do not.

Ellis made the key play in the second game. With the score 1-1 in the fifth, the In-

Continued on Page 12, Column 5

American League

Monday, July 3, 1972

YESTERDAY'S GAMES

New York 6, Cleveland 1 (1st).
New York 5, Cleveland 2 (2d).
Baltimore 7, Detroit 2.
Boston 15, Milwaukee 4 (1st).
Boston 3, Milwaukee 2 (2d, 11 inn.)
Minnesota 6, Chicago 4 (1st).
Chicago 2, Minnesota 1 (2d).
Oakland 3, California 1 (twi.)
Texas 7, Kansas City 5 (1st, 10 inn.).
Kansas City 8, Texas 3 (2d).

SATURDAY NIGHT

California 5, Oakland 3.

STANDING OF THE TEAMS

Eastern Division

	W.	L.	Pct.	G.B.
Detroit	37	29	.561	—
Baltimore	36	30	.545	1
New York	31	34	.477	5½
Boston	30	34	.469	6
Cleveland	27	39	.409	10
Milwaukee	26	40	.394	11

Western Division

	W.	L.	Pct.	G.B.
Oakland	44	24	.647	—
Chicago	41	28	.594	3½
Minnesota	36	31	.537	7½
Kansas City	33	34	.493	10½
California	32	38	.457	13
Texas	28	40	.412	16

TODAY'S PITCHERS

Baltimore at Detroit (n.)—Palmer (10-4) vs. Timmerman (6-6).
Minnesota at Boston (n.)—Blyleven (8-9) vs. Siebert (7-4.)
Oakland at California (n.)—Hunter (8-4) vs. May (2-5).
Texas at Kansas City (twi.)—Paul (2-2) vs. Drago (6-6).

Other teams not scheduled.
(Season's won-lost records in parentheses.)

National League

Monday, July 3, 1972

YESTERDAY'S GAMES

Montreal 4, New York 3.
Cincinnati 12, San Diego 2.
Houston 5, Atlanta 4.
Pittsburgh 7, Chicago 4.
St. Louis 7, Philadelphia 3.
San Francisco 9, Los Angeles 3.

LATE SATURDAY

New York 2, Montreal 0.
Cincinnati 3, San Diego 2.
Houston 4, Atlanta 2.
St. Louis 6, Philadelphia 4 (1st).
St. Louis 1, Philadelphia 0 (2d).
San Francisco 8, Los Angeles 5.

STANDING OF THE TEAMS

Eastern Division

	W.	L.	Pct.	G.B.
Pittsburgh	42	25	.627	—
New York	42	27	.609	1
Chicago	37	31	.544	5½
St. Louis	37	33	.529	6½
Montreal	30	39	.435	13
Philadelphia	24	45	.348	19

Western Division

	W.	L.	Pct.	G.B.
Cincinnati	43	27	.614	—
Houston	43	28	.606	½
Los Angeles	36	34	.514	7
Atlanta	31	38	.449	11½
San Francisco	30	46	.395	16
San Diego	24	46	.343	19

TODAY'S PITCHERS

New York at Montreal (2)—Seaver (10-4) and Capra (3-2) vs. Morton (3-7) and McAnally (1-10).
Atlanta at Houston (n.)—Stone (1-6) vs. Reuss (5-7).
Chicago at Pittsburgh (n.)—Hooton (6-6) vs. Blass (9-2).
St. Louis at Cincinnati (n.)—Wise (8-7) vs. Gullett (2-3).
San Francisco at Philadelphia (n.)—Carrithers (2-5) vs. Carlton (9-6).

Other teams not scheduled.
(Season's won-lost records in parentheses.)

WADKINS, HINSON IN TIE WITH 206'S

Lead by Shot at Cleveland —Homenuik Scores Ace

CLEVELAND, July 2 (AP)—Lanny Wadkins shot a four-under-par 67 today and moved into a tie with Larry Hinson for the lead after three rounds of the rain-delayed $150,000 Cleveland open tournament.

Hinson, who has been first or shared the lead since the opening round, shot a 69 today. The two pace-setters had 54-hole scores of 206 heading into tomorrow's final 18 over the 6,907-yard, par-71 course of the Tanglewood Country Club.

Stroking a putter that Lee Trevino used a year ago in winning the United States, Canadian and British Open titles, Cesar Sanudo carded a 67 and was all alone at 207.

Bruce Devlin, the former master plumber from Australia, shot a sparkling 66 and moved up with a 208. He needed only 29 strokes on the greens with a putter that a Cleveland plumbing firm gives free to good customers.

Another Aussie, David Graham, posted a 68 for 209 and was tied with a Canadian, Wilf Homenuik, and Brian Allin. Graham was using a putter that he obtained by trading away a set of clubs he'd gotten from Arnold Palmer.

Homenuik, who shot a 68, scored a hole-in-one on the 165-yard third hole. He used a No. 5 iron "and it took a couple of bounces and went

Continued on Page 12, Column 4

Red Smith

New, Slow Boy on the Baseball Beat

By his own admission, Richard Milhous Nixon has always had a suppressed ambition to be a sports writer, and now in his 60th year he has had the thrill of seeing his byline over a piece in the sports section. Allowing the cub two or three times as much space as a staff member would get, The New York Times published his essay in full Sunday, all 2,800 cliche-ridden words. Frankly, the new boy has a long way to go if he's ever going to cut it in this department.

Sports of The Times

He's got to tighten up his prose, squeeze the wind out, and say in 900 words what took him 2,800. He's got to kick those threadbare platitudes that he uses over and over, like "get the nod." He'll have to bone up on the mother tongue and learn, for instance, not to say "due to the fact" when he means "because" (see New York Times Style Book and American Heritage Dictionary Usage Panel).

He'll have to get out of the act. Posing as an objective authority, he disqualifies himself when he picked Harmon Killebrew as a first baseman because Senator Herman Welker of Idaho introduced them when Killebrew was a teen-ager, selects Nellie Fox over better second basemen because he knew Fox personally as a coach in Washington, and put Bobo Newsom on his pitching staff for similar personal reasons.

Above all, he's got to cover the assignment. He was asked to pick his all-time all-star baseball team and he blew it. He picked four teams, with spares.

Touching All Bases

Perhaps he should not be blamed for that, however. This is an election year when he could not afford to slight any segment of the electorate. He has, therefore, saluted young and old, white and black, Latin and Nordic, left-hander and right-hander, Catholic and Wasp, Jew and the Amercan Indian (Early Wynn). He has chosen fastball pitchers, curveball pitchers, a master of the knuckleball (Hoyt Wilhelm), and even a specialist in a politically unappetizing spitball (Burleigh Grimes).

To be sure, he is not above demagogy. Among the five starting pitchers on his postwar American League team is Satchel Paige. Beyond doubt, Old Satch could start pitching where most of the others left off, but no conscientious selector could choose him as a star in the American League, where his lifetime record was 28 games won and 31 lost. Paige might be regarded as the Strom Thurmond of 1972, bellwether of the Southern strategy.

As a sports writer, Richard might do for a weekly like Sports Illustrated but he'd have to step up his pace to qualify in the daily press. He started on the assignment Sunday, June 25, and even though he had professional help (David Eisenhower, a son-in-law who worked for the Washington Senators when there was such a team), he missed every edition until Sunday, July 2.

Even after all that time, he discredited himself as an authority. Nobody who saw Hack Wilson play the outfield could pick the fat man over Joe Medwick, not even the year Hack batted in 190 runs. Perhaps Mr. Nixon never heard of Jimmy Wilson, whose wondrous skills as a catcher he ignores in favor of lumbering, lovable old Ernie Lombardi. And as for relegating Frank Frisch to a utility role—well, words fail.

The Churchly Vote

One dislikes to be captious. To be sure, Branch Rickey, tapped as manager of the prewar National League team, was about as bad as managers get. He got nowhere with the St. Louis Browns in 1914 and 1915 and floundered for six years with the Cardinals, who won the world championship the summer after he was replaced. Still, he was a brilliant man and a holy one from Ohio. More than leadership and inspiration, we need the churchly vote of Middle America.

In the sports writing fraternity, borrowing from other sports writers is standard practice, and not everybody is scrupulous about crediting his sources. Thus it is perfectly all right for Mr. Nixon, hailing Lou Gehrig as the bravest of players, to call him "Mr. Profile in Courage." Funny he should think of that title, though.

The man wrote that picking these teams was one of the hardest jobs he ever attempted. Doing a fair critique of his performance is no easier. When you regard him as a sports writer, you can't help feeling that he really ought to go back to being President of the United States. That's a dreadful, difficult line to write.

SEAGREN'S 18-5¾ A VAULT RECORD

Continued From Page 11

outside lane where he had to make his own pace, Mann's rhythm and timing were impeccable, the result of recent workouts with Jim Bush, track coach at the University of California at Los Angeles. Mann's time, 48:4 seconds, was the second fastest ever, ahead of Dick Bruggeman (48:6) and Jim Seymour (49:3).

Bruce Collins, the National Collegiate champion from Pennsylvania, appeared to be headed for one of the berths but stumbled after hitting the seventh hurdle. Unable to regain his customary rhythm and drive, Collins faded to fourth in 49.5.

"He really tumbled," Jim Tuppeny, the Penn coach, said of his sophomore. "If he had gone over it, there would have been no question he might have won it."

Mann, the world recordholder at 440 yards and No. 1-ranked internationally, was ecstatic with his victory on a synthetic track that was 20 degrees hotter than the 94-degree temperature.

"People said I wasn't in shape," Mann said. "Now I know I'm in shape. I worked for two months to get into this type of shape."

Equally as elated was Milt Sonsky, the javelin thrower from Brooklyn, who celebrated his 31st birthday by finishing second with a toss of 267 feet 11 inches to qualify for the team.

A breezy tailwind, fast runway, enthusiastic crowd support and the close competition contributed to Seagren's third successful 18-foot jump. Wisely, after almost five hours, Seagren bypassed further attempts and decided to let 19 feet await another day, perhaps in Munich.

The hot weather took its toll. Joe Lucas, the N. C. A. A. steeplechase champion from Georgetown, finished 12th in the final, far behind Mike Manley, Doug Brown and Steve Savage.

Frank Shorter, America's premier long-distance runner, ran away from the field in the 10,000-meter run, using a 4:25.6 opening mile to destroy Greg Fredericks, the Penn State graduate who had outkicked Shorter on the final lap of the national championships last month en route to an American record.

Unfamiliar with the tactics of long-distance racing, the 22-year-old Fredericks tried to stay with Shorter in the early going rather than run a deliberate race. The strategy proved costly and could strip Fredericks of any significant stamina and speed in the 5,000-meter run next week, if he decides to try to qualify in the event.

FIELD EVENTS

Pole Vault (Final)—1, Bob Seagren, Southern California Striders, 18 feet 5¾ inches (World Record; previous record, pending acceptance, 18-4¼ by Seagren and Kjell Isaksson, Sweden, at El Paso, May 23, 1972); 2, Steve Smith, Long Beach State, 18-½; 3, Jan Johnson, Alabama, 18-½; 4, Dave Roberts, Rice, 17-8½; 5, Tom Blair, Philadelphia Pioneer Club, 17-¾; 6, Mike Wedman, Colorado, 17-¾; 7, Vince Struble, Maryland, 17-¾; 8, Roland Carter, unattached, Houston, 17-¾. Others included Bud Williamson, New York A. C., no height.

Javelin Throw (Final)—1, Bill Schmidt, U.S. Army, 270 feet 6 inches; 2, Milt Sonsky, New York A.C., 267-11; 3, Fred Luke, Husky T.C., 267-9; 4, Jack Bacon, New York A.C., 259-11; 5, Lez Tipton, Oregon T.C., 257-1; 6, Bob Wallis, U.S. Army, 255-7; 7, Cary Feldman, Husky T.C., 255-2; 8, Mark Murro, Pacific Coast Club, 247-1.

TRACK EVENTS

3,000-Meter Steeplechase (Final)—1, Mike Manley, Oregon T.C., 8:29.8; 2, Doug Brown, Tennessee, 8:31.8; 3, Steve Savage, Oregon T.C., 8:32; 4, Jim Dare, U. S. Navy, 8:33.6; 5, Cliff Clark, U. S. Air Force, 8:36.6; 6, Don Timm, Minnesota, 8:41.4; 7, Bill Reilly, New York A. C., 8:42; 8, Bob Richards, U. S. Air Force, 8:44. Others included 12, Joe Lucas, Georgetown, 9:13.

10,000-Meter Run (Final)—1, Frank Shorter, Florida T.C., 28:35.6; 2, Jeff Galloway, Florida T.C., 28:48.8; 3, Jon Anderson, Oregon T.C., 29:08.2; 4, Tom Laris, New York A.C., 29:43; 5, Bill Clark, West Valley T.C., 29:57; 6, Don Kardong, West Valley T.C., 30:21.2; 7, Greg Fredericks, Penn State, 30:37.6; 8, Dave Antognoli, Edinboro State, 30:39.6; 9, Charles Maguire, Penn State, 31:24.8. Jack Bacheler, Florida T.C., finished fourth in 29:09.8 but was disqualified.

400-Meter Intermediate Hurdles (Final)—1, Ralph Mann, Southern Calif. Striders, 0:48.4 (American Record; previous record 0:48.8 by Geoff Vanderstock, Southern Calif. Striders, at South Lake Tahoe, Calif., September 11, 1968, and Mann, Brigham Young, at Des Moines, June 20, 1970); 2, Dick Bruggeman, Ohio T.C., 0:48.6; 3, Jim Seymour, Southern Calif. Striders, 0:49.3; 4, Bruce Collins, Pennsylvania, 0:49.5; 5, Bob Casselman, Michigan State, 0:49.5; 6, Jim Bolding, Oklahoma State, 0:49.7; 7, Bob Steele, unattached, East Lansing, Mich., 0:50.2; 8, Carl Wood, Richmond, 0:50.2.

Associated Press

Bob Seagren clearing the bar at 18 feet 5¾ inches in the pole vault at Eugene, Ore.

OFFERED BRIBE, TRACKMAN SAYS

Continued From Page 11

he kept reminding me to keep this quiet."

Hans Brinks, the Adidas representative charged with the attempted bribe, denied White's allegation.

"The word money was never mentioned in our talks," said Brinks, who is supported by the company's American representative, Mike Larrabee, the 1964 Olympic 400-meter champoin. "I would be foolish to talk to him about money. We are not interested in paying money to any athletes."

White disagreed and said that Brinks also had threatened him.

"After he found out that I had reported it," White related today, "he came up to me yesterday and said. 'What would you do if I filed a complaint against you saying you took $200?' I said, 'You can't do that, because I haven't taken any money.'" Brinks termed this exchange "ridiculous."

Serving Jail Sentence

A touch of irony accompanies White's involvement. The 21-year-old black from Bristol, Pa., currently is serving a two-month-to-two-year sentence for forgery at the Centre County Jail in Bellefonte, Pa., and was granted a furlough by a judge and prison officials in order to try out for the American team.

Asked why he had reported the charge, White said, "Most athletes are afraid to speak up here. They're unnder a lot of pressure to switch shoe companies, but they don't want to blow a good thing later by talking now."

Adidas is one of two German companies that account for almost all of the shoes worn by track and field athletes around the world. The other manufacturer is Puma.

At the 1968 Olympics in Mexico City, the companies became embroiled in a battle for the favors of athletes, particularly Americans. Reports of large amounts of money being left in the track shoes of certain competitors were made to the United States Olympic Committee and several American athletes reportedly bought cars and clothes with their payoffs. No action was taken against either the athletes or the companies after the games.

The outrage in Mexico City prompted international officials to propose that white shoes, without any trademarks be worn in future Olympics and even at major international meets. Both shoe companies fought the plan, which was to have been instituted in 1969 and the proposal was defeated.

To guard against future payoffs, Adidas and Puma said they signed agreements with the Amateur Athletic Union. One of the provisions in the agreement called for either company to forfeit $25,000 to the A.A.U., as a fine for any bribe attempts.

Under international rules, athletes are allowed to receive a "reasonable amount of equipment" from companies.

PRICE OF BLACKOUT IS PUT AT $200,000

Special to The New York Times

WESTBURY, L. I., July 2—The "nervous breakdown" that short-circuited Roosevelt Raceway's computers last night, and cut betting and racing down to a minimum, was virtually cured today following hours of repairs.

"If nothing else was corrected by Monday night, we'd still be able to give the fans everything but potential daily-double and exacta payoffs," said George Morton Levy, the track's octogenarian president.

Levy said that 90 per cent of the malfunction had been fixed. He said the engineers "gave me some long electronic name for what happened." According to Levy, the troubles began when the result board was tested before the races.

"To test the board you have to put in a lot of punch cards," said Levy. "All the cards blew out, and then that blew out the entire board."

The result left fans bewildered—but relatively well-behaved. There was betting only on the daily double, the second race, and the triple in the fourth race. Only five of nine scheduled races were staged, with the card canceled after the fifth race, the $50,000 American Trotting championship.

Owners Are Paid

Normally, a percentage of the handle goes toward purse money. But Roosevelt paid the owners of horses that finished in the money even though no betting was done. Levy estimated that the track lost about $200,000. That would include purse money, admissions, food and parking. All fans who remained for the fifth race were given rain checks and parking stubs.

Although the track isn't insured for such a loss, Levy indicated that it was covered through its contract with the American Totalisator Company, the outfit that runs the tote board.

More than $750,000 was bet on the card with Offtrack Betting. An OTB official said today that about half-a-million dollars probably would have to be refunded. All those holding tickets on the card can have their refunds tomorrow.

ARCADIUS CAPTURES 2 DRESSAGE EVENTS

Special to The New York Times

DARIEN, Conn., July 2 — Jordan Miller of Ossining, N. Y., and Mrs. Lois Stephens's Arcadius formed an unbeatable combination today and won the two leading events in the Ox Ridge Hunt Club all-dressage horse show.

Miller, whose father manages Mrs. Stephens's Starbrook Farm, and Arcadius captured the intermediare with a 61.4 average and the grand prix, the most testing event in dressage, with a 64.6 mark.

Mrs. Berning Praised by Caddie

By STEVE CADY

Special to The New York Times

MAMARONECK, N. Y., July 2—"I don't care what she pays me," Mrs. Susie Maxwell Berning's caddie said today as he trudged off the 18th green at Winged Foot Golf Club. "She's the most consistent golfer I've ever worked for, male or female. Maybe not the longest hitter, but the most consistent."

That was Russ Barton's appraisal of his four-hour walk in the sun as he accompanied Mrs. Berning to her dramatic second United States Open championship.

"She's a fine lady and a smart one, too," said Barton, who stands to make up to $600 from the winner's $6,000 purse. "I know the greens here, and she was taking advantage of what I know. She listened to me on all the putts, and we put our heads together on most of the other clubs, too. I guess two heads are better than one."

Mrs. Berning agreed.

"If it wasn't for my caddie, I couldn't have won," said the 30-year-old golfer from Lake Tahoe, Nev. "He helped me read the greens. They're tricky, and he knew them like a book. If I didn't think he did, I wouldn't have taken his advice."

Though he started the day tied for fifth, Barton wound up as the big winner among an all-male colony of 150 caddies whose numbers were drawn out of a fishbowl by the contestants before the start of the four-day event.

He carried No. 94 on his back. The tough-luck number belonged to Pam Barnett's caddie, 17-year-old John Lennon. Miss Barnett began the day with a three-stroke lead, and Lennon was snapping his fingers as she sank birdie putts on the first two holes.

Later, Miss Barnett's game started melting under a blistering sun, until she needed a birdie on the 18th to tie Mrs. Berning. She didn't get it, and had to settle for a three-way tie for second.

The tournament golf bags lugged by the caddies weighed between 40 and 50 pounds—too heavy a burden for girl caddies, in the opinion of most golf people.

"Two girls applied for jobs here this season," said Gene Hayden, the cigar-smoking caddie master at Winged Foot. "I hired 'em because I was afraid they were testers from some Women's Lib group. We're not supposed to discriminate in our advertisements."

According to Hayden, the two high-school girls lasted only one round. "They had blisters on their hands, and they were exhausted. They never came back."

Two weeks ago, a girl was barred from being a caddie at Metacomet Country Club in East Providence, R. I., on the grounds that the golf course was no place for a girl caddie, "she'd hear a lot of things she shouldn't."

Female caddies are virtually non-existent in the United States, but they are used frequently in France and Japan.

"The girls couldn't make it," said Paul Deedy, a 15-year-old from Larchmont, N. Y., who rode a 70 by Cathy Ahern to a second-place tie in the Open. "The girls might be able to carry a regular golf bag, around 25 pounds, but they couldn't carry double."

Hayden, who maintains a staff of 250 caddies at Winged Foot, recalled that girls were used at Oak Ridge Country Club, Eastchester, N. Y., in 1920 for about two weeks when the male caddies went on strike.

Lugging a heavy golf bag five miles isn't the only obstacle for would-be girl caddies. A member of the local colony, John (Call Me Shank) Castellano, pointed out that women golfers might argue too much with girl caddies.

"Can you imagine two women discussing what club to use?" said Castellano. "They could argue for 20 minutes."

Kodes Upset by Amateur In Tennis at Forest Hills

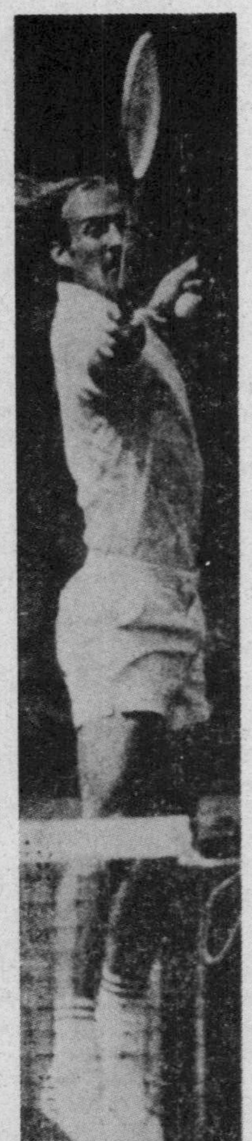

Stan Smith returning a corner net shot to Clark Graebner at Forest Hills.

Mrs. Gunter Is Beaten by Miss Sawamatsu —Smith Is Victor

By PARTON KEESE

The initial shock of last year's United States open tennis championships came when Jan Kodes of Czechoslovakia beat the defending champion, John Newcombe, in the first round. Yesterday, the first shock of this year's tournament in Forest Hills, Queens, occurred when Kodes lost in the second round to Alex Mayer Jr. of Wayne, N. J.

The reason the tourney is called an "open" is that amateurs can play professionals. About one-sixth of the 148 men entered are amateurs, and they cannot accept prize money. Shock occurs in an open when an amateur like the 20-year-old Mayer beats one of the world's top pros, such as Kodes, seeded No. 8 here and a finalist last year. The scores yesterday were 6-7, 3-6, 7-6, 6-3, 6-1.

Another huge surprise took place in the women's singles when Kazudo Sawamatsu of Japan defeated Mrs. Nancy Richey Gunter, 6-4, 4-6, 6-3. Mrs. Gunter twice has been a runner-up in the nationals. She was seeded [illegible] 6 here.

Two Key Points

Unfortunately for a large portion of the 10,332 spectators who remained glued to their stadium seats, none of the fireworks happened on the stadium courts. Mayer battled Kodes on the grandstand court while Mrs. Gunter was taking her lumps near the clubhouse.

In the stadium, Andres Gimeno of Spain was matter-of-factly defeating Owen Davidson of Australia, 6-4, 4-6, 6-4, 6-1; Stan Smith was mauling Clark Graebner of New York, 6-1, 6-4, 6-7, 6-0, and Mrs. Margaret Court was routing Janice Metcalf of Claremont, Calif., 6-2, 6-1. Center court was, in effect, dullsville.

The existing Mayer - Kodes match revolved around a couple of key points. Mayer (his nickname is Sandy) might well

Continued on Page 12, Column 5

United Press International

Pat Corrales, San Diego Padres' catcher, grabbing Rick Monday's face during a fourth-inning mixup yesterday In Chicago. Both were ejected. Details, Page 13.

Yancey Cards 63, to Lead Wethersfield Golf by One

By LINCOLN A. WERDEN

Special to The New York Times

WETHERSFIELD, Conn., Sept. 1 — Many people take a week off from business to play golf. But Bert Yancey, after leading in the $125,000 Greater Hartford open today with a 63, said that he took a vacation from the pro golf tour last week so he could relax.

Against a pastoral setting at the Wethersfield Country Club, with a herd of Holsteins grazing beyond the practice area, youngsters selling 10-cent lemonade off the fairways and snow cones a favorite at the 18th-hole refreshment stand, Yancey played eight-under-par golf. The score was 3 shots above the course record set by Tommy Bolt in 1954. Yancey's total led by one stroke.

"It was the best score of the year," said the 34-year-old professional, who recently won the American golf classic at Akron, Ohio. "The greens were good and had perfect speed." So was Yancey's putting good. He rolled in a six-footer at the home green for his sixth birdie on the back nine to cap an incoming score of 30.

Sharing second place at 64 were Lee Trevino, the British Open champion, and Lee Elder, the black professional from Washington, who recently finished second at Sutton, Mass.

"It was my best this year," said Trevino. "That goes for me, too," added Elder.

Elder, the Nigerian champion, had eight birdies also, but he had a bogey at the eighth hole where his drive struck a tree. He said the small greens and the short iron shots, instead of long ones, contributed to the low scoring.

Trevino had 31, 33 over the 6,598-yard course while Elder had 32 on both sides. Trevino attributed his good scoring to his improved physical condition following recent infections and an attack of bronchitis.

"I'm doing a lot of running these days," he reported. "I'll be running a mile a day at the Wethersfield High School track this week. Then he said he knew little about track as a

Continued on Page 12, Column 2

The New York Times/Edward Hausner

Jeanne Evert making a two-hand return to Lesley Hunt. Miss Evert lost, 6-2 and 6-1.

Borzov Gives the Soviet Union Its First Olympic Sprint Crown

Taylor Second—Rare Setback for the U.S.

By NEIL AMDUR

Special to The New York Times

MUNICH, West Germany, Sept. 1—Valery Borzov, a 22-year-old sprinter from the Soviet Union who said he wasn't even running at full speed, won the Olympic gold medal today in the 100-meter dash, long a symbol of the United States pride in track and field.

Confident from the second he left the starting blocks until the moment he reached the finish line with arms raised, the 5-foot-11½-inch Ukrainian outran America's only finalist, Robert Taylor, by a yard in 10.1 seconds.

The 22-year-old Taylor, a student at Texas Southern University, salvaged the silver medal by beating Lennox Miller of Jamaica, the 1968 runner-up. Miller came from behind in the last 10 meters and lunged ahead of another Soviet finalist, Aleksandr Kornelyuk, for third place.

'I Gave 90 Per Cent'

Borzov's triumph, before another capacity crowd of 80,000 in the Olympic Stadium, marked the first gold medal for the Soviet Union in a track and field event below 5,000 meters. It also was only the second time in the last nine Olympics, and the fifth time over-all, that the United States had been shut out of the top spot in the 100.

"I made the greatest effort in the finals and I gave 90 per cent of what I had to give," Borzov said through an interpreter, in what seemed a dig at the competitive quality of the field.

Asked for his evaluation of America's sprint situation, Borzov again took the opportunity to swipe at some United States rivals who had maintained earlier this year that "Borzov won't win nothin' in Munich."

"It seems," the Soviet physical education student said cynically, "that American sprinters are suffering from stagnation, while Europeans are making progress."

Wottle Qualifies

The 100 final was run with almost no wind, in slightly chilly weather and under overcast skies that seemed to reflect the somber mood of the American team.

The most surprising United States performance of the day, in fact, came from an 18-year-old woman javelin thrower, Kathy Schmidt of Long Beach, Calif., who took the bronze medal behind two East Germans, Ruth Fuchs and Jacquelin Todten. It was the first American medal in the javelin since the 1932 gold of the legendary Mildred (Babe) Didrikson.

Dave Wottle qualified for the final of the 800-meter run, and Ralph Mann and Jim Seymour reached the last stage of the 400-intermediate hurdles. But all will be pressed to gain a third place, let alone challenge for gold medals.

Wottle, finding some of the form that characterized his strong performances at the United States trials, won his semifinal heat of the 800 in 1:48.7, helped by a 55.3-second opening 400 pace that played into his closing kick.

The 21-year-old Bowling Green University senior, however, must contend with two Kenyans (Robert Ouko and Mike Boit), who are certain to set a fast pace and two East Europeans (Yevgeny Arzhanov and Dieter Fromm) who are strong kickers.

Mann, the world record-holder in the 440-yard hurdles and America's top intermediate hurdler, finished second to John Akii-Bua of Uganda in his semifinal but seemed to lack the rhythm and relaxation he displayed at the United States trials in Eugene, Ore., earlier this summer.

"I hope Ralph can put it together one more time," said Jim Bush, the track coach at the University of California, Los Angeles, who helped Mann regain his confidence before the American trials and is here for the Games. "Right now, though, he doesn't look like the same runner he was at Eugene."

All three American steeplechasers were outrun by Africans and Europeans, the first time an American failed to qualify for the final of the steeplechase since the event joined the Olympics in 1920.

The United States lost another possible medalist when Ken Swenson, a top half-miler, pulled up lame 300 meters into his 800 semifinal. Mrs. Madeline Manning Jackson, the 1968 women's 800-meter champion.

Continued on Page 11, Column 1

United Press International

Bob Seagren of Pomona, Calif., qualifying at 16 feet 8¾ inches with an "old-style" pole

Other Olympic Highlights

BASKETBALL — The United States breezed past Egypt, 96-31, for its 60th consecutive victory in the Olympics. Mike Bantom of Philadelphia scored 17 points and Tom McMillen of Mansfield, Pa., had 16 points and 15 rebounds. Aleksandr Belov scored 37 points to lead the Soviet Union team to a 100-87 victory over Puerto Rico. It was Puerto Rico's first loss.

BOXING—James Busceme, a lightweight from Beaumont, Tex., got off the floor to score a unanimous decision over Prai-a-Nan Vichit of Thailand. Only one American fighter has been eliminated.

EQUESTRIAN—Richard Meade of Britain, who has been linked romantically with Princess Anne, won the gold medal in the three-day event. Among the spectators: Princess Anne.

GYMNASTICS—Japan dominated the six finals in men's competition, taking three gold medals, four silver and five bronze.

WATER POLO—West Germany tied the unbeaten United States team, 4-4, with the aid of a goal tipped in by Jim Ferguson of Santa Clara, Calif. The United States lost a 4-1 lead. In a bitter contest Hungary defeated Italy, 8-7, scoring the winning goal in the last minute when five of the seven Italians were in the penalty box.

Olympic summaries on Page 10.

SHANE GOULD WINS THIRD GOLD MEDAL

Australian, 15, Registers a World Mark of 2:03.56 in 200 Free-Style

MUNICH, West Germany, Sept. 1 (AP)—Shane Gould's third Olympic gold medal dangled from her neck as the 15-year-old Australian said, "I reckon I'm fit enough to do another good one."

Miss Gould shattered her third world record tonight with a time of 2 minutes 3.56 seconds in the 200-meter free-style and looked ahead to a fourth golden opportunity in Sunday's 800-meter free-style.

The United States' moment of glory came when 16-year-old Rick De Mont of San Rafael, Calif., rallied from last place and won the 400-meter free-style in 4:00.26.

Shirley Babashoff of Fountain Valley, Calif., also broke the world record—her own, set in the Olympic trials in Chicago —in taking the silver medal behind Shane with a time of 2:04.92. Miss Babashoff's previous record was 2:05.2.

Mayumi Aoki, Japan's Madam Butterfly, stroked to a world record 1:03.34 in the 100-meter butterfly for her country's first women's swimming gold since Hideko Maehata won the 200-meter breaststroke in the 1936 Games in Berlin.

Miss Gould's victory gave the Aussies their fifth gold medal. The Americans have won only two in women's events.

"I don't make many predictions," said Miss Gould, a Sydney schoolgirl, "but I think the two-minute barrier will be broken by a woman in the 200, probably at the 1976 Olympics at Montreal."

Asked if that woman might be a 19-year-old Shane Gould, she grinned and answered, "I certainly hope so."

De Mont lagged through the first 100 meters of his championship performance in the 400-meter free-style, turning last and three seconds behind front-running Werner Lampe of West Germany. Lampe faded quickly, finishing eighth, and Brad Cooper of Australia grabbed the lead with De Mont closing to sixth at the 200-meter mark.

Cooper still led 100 meters from home, but De Mont was second and charging. The pair splashed stroke for stroke for the finish and De Mont won by 1/100 of a second.

"I've been swimming come-from-behind style since I be-

Continued on Page 11, Column 7

Red Smith

The Fastest Human Is a Commie

Sports of The Times

MUNICH, West Germany, Sept. 1—When the race was over, not one tan hair in the winner's wavy coiffure was out of place. As befits a clean-cut citizen of the Union of Soviet Socialist Republics, the coiffure was parted to the left.

Halfway around the clubhouse turn, the winner pulled to a stop. He stood there just long enough to draw one deep breath. Then he walked slowly back toward the finish line, his neat, sharp features composed and expressionless. Cameramen formed a phalanx in front of him, snapping their shutters, backing a step or so, snapping again. The winner just strolled along, not smiling, not frowning, not posing for pictures, Now and then he lifted a hand in acknowledgement of applause. He wore a red undershirt, white drawers, red, white and blue socks. Near the finish line, a man stuck a microphone in his face, some Muscovite Howard Cosell, no doubt. The winner spoke a few words, then disappeared under the stands.

The fastest human pro tem is a graduate student of footracing out of Novaya Kachovka in the Ukraine, the first sprinter of world class ever developed in the Soviet Union and the first Soviet runner to win an Olympic gold medal at less than 5,000 meters.

Of All Sad Words

His name is Valery Borzov. In a race that was mechanically perfect and in no respect remarkable, he won the 100-meter championship today by a fat yard over Robert Taylor, a flanker on the Texas Southern football team who was America's No. 3 man in the event and, because of a monumental blunder by his coach, the only United States runner eligible for the final.

As everybody not living in a cave knows by now, the coach is Stan Wright of Sacramento State, an Olympic veteran who managed the Malaysian track team in 1964, was assistant to Peyton Jordan with the United States team in 1968 and is handling the dash men for Bill Bowerman at this clambake. Wright is good at keeping runners fit and getting them off the marks fast, weak at telling time on a 24-hour clock. Noting that yesterday's 100-meter qualifying heats would start at 16:15, he read that as 6:15 P.M. for the benefit of America's three sprinters. Result: Eddie Hart and Reynaud Robinson, America's first and second candidates, were disqualified for tardiness.

Of all sad words of tongue or pen, as the man says. Nobody will ever know what might have been if Hart and Robinson had made the final, but both tied the world record of 0:09.9 qualifying for the American team. Comparisons are inevitable between their best time and Borzov's 10.1 clocking today.

On the other hand, before these Games started Borzov had beaten American sprinters six times in six matches. He didn't pick on patsies, either.

At one time or another he has finished in front of Dr. Delano Meriwether, Ivory Crockett, Ben Vaughan, Jim Green and Herb Washington.

Thus it was distinguished company that Bob Taylor joined today when he finished second. He gave it the old Texas Southern try. He chased the rapid Russky and drew just about even with him after 60 meters but couldn't contain Borzov after that.

But Can He Catch a Pass?

The fastest human is 22, in his first year as a graduate student at the Institute of Physical Culture in Kiev. He trains three hours a day and his trim body shows it; at 5 feet 11 inches and 175 pounds, he is handsomely proportioned, muscular but not bulgy.

Son of an officer in the Red Army, he has given his time to track and field since he was 13. He started as a long jumper but Boris Voitas, his coach, insisted that sprinting was his bag. At 17 he was doing 10.5 for 100 meters and 22 seconds for 200. Last year he was clocked in 10 seconds flat in a meet in Kiev, and he did the 200 in 20.2 winning the U.S.S.R. championship.

He is the Soviet Union's first European champion in the sprints. Chances are his gold medal will be placed on public display in the Kremlin right alongside Lenin's well preserved cadaver, for the dashes have been a capitalistic monopoly. In the eight Olympic Games between 1928 and now, the only non-Yank to win the century was Germany's Armin Hary in 1960.

Borzov will became a Soviet deity. Americans who win the Olympic 100 get to be pass receivers like Bob Hayes of the Dallas Cowboys. Probably Bob Taylor will, too.

National League

Saturday, September 2, 1972

YESTERDAY'S GAMES

Houston 8, New York 0 (n.).
Chicago 14, San Diego 3.
St. Louis 5, Los Angeles 1 (st. twi.).
Los Angeles 2, St. Louis 1 (2d, n).
Cincinnati 1, Montreal 0 (12 inn., n.).
Philadelphia 11, Atlanta 1 (1st. twi.).
Atlanta 11, Philadelphia 5 (2d, n.)
Pittsburgh 10, San Francisco 6 (n.).

THURSDAY NIGHT

Houston 5, Philadelphia 1.

STANDING OF THE TEAMS

Eastern Division

	W.	L.	Pct.	G.B.
Pittsburgh	78	46	.629	—
Chicago	68	58	.540	11
New York	63	59	.516	14
St. Louis	61	64	.488	17½
Montreal	57	66	.463	20½
Philadelphia	45	80	.360	33½

Western Division

	W.	L.	Pct.	G.B.
Cincinnati	79	46	.632	—
Houston	73	54	.575	7
Los Angeles	67	58	.536	12
Atlanta	58	70	.453	22½
San Francisco	56	71	.441	24
San Diego	46	79	.368	33

TODAY'S PITCHERS

New York at Houston (n.)—Strom (0-2) vs. Wilson (10-8).

Los Angeles at St. Louis—Strahler (0-2) vs. Durham (2-6).

Montreal at Cincinnati (n.)—Torrez (13-9) vs. Nolan (14-2).

Philadelphia at Atlanta (2, twi.-n.)—Brandon (5-5) and Niebauer (0-2) vs. Stone (5-10) and McQueen (0-1).

San Diego at Chicago—Caldwell (6-7) vs. Pappas (11-7).

San Francisco at Pittsburgh (n.)—McDowell (8-7) vs. Briles (12-6).

(Season's won-lost records in parentheses.)

YANKS TURN BACK WHITE SOX BY 4-0

Stottlemyre Hurls 4-Hitter —Spikes Stars in Debut

By MURRAY CHASS

In defeating the pennant-minded Chicago White Sox, 4-0, last night, the pennant-minded Yankees celebrated the birth of a potential star and the rebirth of an established star.

Mel Stottlemyre, who's been plagued with pitching problems the past six weeks, experienced the rebirth, shutting out the White Sox on a brilliant four-hitter for his first victory since Aug. 13 and his first complete game since July 21.

Aiding the right-hander in what perhaps was his most satisfying victory of the season was Charlie Spikes, a 21-year-old outfielder who, in his major league debut, singled and scored the first run, singled across the third run, and made a diving catch that helped Stottlemyre escape the only jam he encountered all night.

The catch by Spikes, on a sinking, slicing line drive to right field by Mike Andrews, came in the fourth with runners at first and second, one out and the Yankees leading, 2-0. Stottlemyre followed that

Continued on Page 13, Column 4

American League

Saturday, September 2, 1972

LAST NIGHT'S GAMES

New York 4, Chicago 0.
Baltimore 3, California 2.
Minnesota 5, Cleveland 4 (10 inn.)
Oakland 4, Detroit 1.
Boston 1, Kansas City 0.
Milwaukee 3, Texas 0.

THURSDAY NIGHT

Milwaukee 7, Kansas City 3.
California 4, Detroit 0.

STANDING OF THE TEAMS

Eastern Division

	W.	L.	Pct.	G.B.
Baltimore	68	57	.544	—
New York	67	59	.532	1½
Detroit	67	59	.532	1½
Boston	65	58	.528	2
Cleveland	58	67	.464	10
Milwaukee	50	75	.400	18

Western Division

	W.	L.	Pct.	G.B.
Oakland	74	51	.592	—
Chicago	71	53	.573	2½
Minnesota	62	60	.508	10½
Kansas City	60	64	.484	13½
California	57	67	.460	16½
Texas	49	77	.389	25½

TODAY'S PITCHERS

Chicago at New York (2:15 P.M.)—Bradley (13-11) vs. Kline (14-5).

Baltimore at California (n.)—Palmer (18-6) vs. May (6-10).

Cleveland at Minnesota—Dunning (3-2) vs. Woodson (11-12).

Detroit at Oakland—Lolich (19-11) vs. Blue (5-7).

Kansas City at Boston—Hedlund (4-6) vs. Siebert (10-11).

Milwaukee at Texas (n.)—Parsons (9-12) vs. Broberg (5-11).

(Season's won-lost records in parentheses.)

SHANE GOULD WINS THIRD GOLD MEDAL

Continued From Page 9

gan," said the young Californian.

Steve Genter of Lakewood, Calif., beat Tom McBreen of San Mateo, Calif., for the bronze with a clocking of 4:01.94.

"At the United States Olympic trials, I was strictly thinking of the 1,500-meters," said De Mont, "but now I love the 400 . . . especially after tonight."

Genter now has a gold in the 800-meter free-style relay, a silver in the 200 free-style to Spitz and a bronze in the 200.

BORZOV TAKES 100 FOR SOVIET UNION

Continued From Page 9

also was eliminated in semi-finals dominated by East European half-milers.

As if these problems, coupled with yesterday's sprint controversy, were not enough headaches, American pole vaulters spent more time defending the legitimacy of their fiberglass poles today than qualifying for the final.

Bob Seagren, the 1968 Olympic champion, had four of his poles barred from the competition by Klaus Lehnertz, the German pole vault judge and the 1964 bronze medalist. Jan Johnson, another American who has cleared 18 feet, was forced to rustle up a light pole used by decathlon entries to clear his qualifying height and join Seagren in the final.

Steve Smith, the third American vaulter, was less fortunate and failed to clear the qualifying height. So did Kjell Isaksson of Sweden, the world's second 18-foot pole vaulter, who seemed a certain medalist earlier this year but has been hindered in recent weeks by a leg injury.

The Fastest Ukrainian

"This whole thing is ridiculous," Seagren said, angry over recent rulings that have banned, readmitted and then banned again a newer, lighter pole.

For Borzov, however, the absence of two American rivals, Rey Robinson and Eddie Hart, served only to solidify his confidence. Robinson and Hart were eliminated after failing to show up on time for their second-round heats yesterday.

"There were unfortunate circumstances," said Borzov, who has a perfect record against American sprinters in six races. "But it's generally acknowledged that the winner of the Olympic Games is also considered the world's fastest human."

Americans may scoff at such talk, especially after viewing the bullish tactics of a Bob Hayes or the clean, classic lines of a Bobby Morrow or Jim Hines. But Borzov is a polished sprinter in the three areas that count—start, pickup and finish—as he displayed today in refusing to yield to Taylor's closing lift and acceleration.

"What changes will there be in your life when you return to the Soviet Union as a gold medalist?" Borzov was asked.

"Oh, I'll probably have to give more autographs," Borzov said, in perhaps the understatement of the Games.

Borzov showed typical humility and party loyalty in crediting country, coach and compatriots over himself. But he also reflected the confidence and composure requisite for survival at the starting line for sprinters.

Wide World Photos

Australia's Shane Gould powers to victory in the 200-meter freestyle final.

Olympic Personalities: Bikila Returns in a Wheelchair

The first black African ever to win a medal in Olympic Games competition, **Abebe Bikila** of Ethiopia, was greeted with cheers and applause yesterday as he visited the Olympic Stadium in a wheelchair.

Bikila, running barefooted, won the gold medal in the marathon in the 1960 Olympics at Rome. He won the marathon four years later in Tokyo—with shoes on. He is the only man ever to win the Olympic marathon twice.

Shortly after the 1964 Games he was paralyzed below the waist as a result of an automobile accident. A countryman, Mamo Wolde, gave Ethiopia a third marathon gold medal at Mexico in 1968.

●

Ho Minh Thu of South Vietnam might be the only happy loser in the Olympic Games. It didn't mater so much that he lost in the free pistol competition; what was important to Thu was that he used his gun for sport, not war.

"I happy to be here because I no shoot at bodies, only shoot at bullseyes," said the 43-year-old marksman. He finished 49th among 56.

A captain on the Saigon police force, Thu teaches apprentice policemen how to handle a gun. "There so much shooting in my country," he said. "Many killings. I don't care I no win here. I please to be in place where shooting is only a game."

South Vietnam sent only two representatives to the Olympics. North Vietnam did not enter.

"Everybody in Vietnam must fight now," he said. "If not, we would send many people to Olympics. We would compete in football, swimming, cycling, judo . . . I no like to go home where there no games played."

●

Mrs. Olga Connolly, who has been known to have an opinion or two, was immediately available for comment—naturally—after the colossal blunder that knocked two American sprinters, **Eddie Hart** and **Rey Robinson**, out of the 100-meter dash. Nobody has ever run 100 meters faster than Hart and Robinson, but they lost their chance for a gold medal because they didn't get to the starting blocks in time for their heats. A coach had given them the wrong starting time.

"I hear they cried like babies," said Mrs. Connolly, the controversial discus thrower and flag-bearer, rushing into one of the United States executive offices. "It's tragic. It's sick. How can you blame one man for this stupid business? It's the fault of the whole setup. This backs up what I have been saying all the time."

A member of the United States Olympic brass, in his monogrammed blue jacket and gray striped slacks, overheard the brief conversation.

"Trouble-maker," he mumbled under his breath. "A damned trouble-maker."

●

Vince Matthews, a 400 meter runner from Brooklyn, criticized the assistant coach, Stan Wright, for removing Robinson from the 400-meter relay team.

"Rey definitely wanted to run on the team," said Matthews. "To show his desire he went to Brunswick, Me., to work on the stick pass even though he didn't have to show up. He was bumped in Oslo when he got beat out of the blocks by a Russian. . . . They told the press he couldn't run on a curve. There are two straightaways in the 400. Why didn't he get one of those? Most countries here would give half of their athletes in bondage to get a 9.9 sprinter. Robinson could still be returned to the relay team.

"I think he will say no if they ask him," said Matthews. "It's his spot and they gave it away. He's got pride, you know, and I don't think he will run."

●

After the best showing ever by American wrestlers in the Olympics, **Dan Gable** relaxed enough to smile and say it was undoubtedly the happiest moment of his life. The intense young man from Waterloo, Iowa, had thought about the gold medal for three years, sweating through at least three grueling workouts a day to prepare himself.

With the medal around his neck, for a decisive victory in the 149.5-pound class, Gable, 23, said he might celebrate by restricting himself to "a couple of days of light workouts."

Then it will be back to the grind, especially if he decides to try again in Montreal in 1976.

"I'll never try it unless I'm the best-conditioned and best-trained guy around," Gable said.

Some members of the United States basketball team were not all that pleased with the amount of work forced on them by Coach **Hank Iba** before the Games, but there is little questioning now with five straight victories.

"If we come out and play as a team we cannot lose," said **Mike Bantom** of Philadelphia. "And all of that work was to get us playing together as a team. The only way we can lose is if we go against the way the coach wants us to go. I have great respect for the way the coach is coaching us."

United Press International

Australia's Shane Gould bends over to receive the gold medal for the 200-meter freestyle swim for women, in which she set a new world mark of 2:03.56 min. in Olympic competition.

Greece's Sprint Star Misses Start of Race

MUNICH, West Germany, Sept. 1 (Reuters) — Another Olympic sprint star was scratched from the 100-meter event today for failing to arrive on time for a heat.

Vassilios Papageorgopoulos of Greece, the European co-record-holder, who was expected to press the favorites in the final, was eliminated without starting when he failed to arrive for his semi-final.

Officials said there was no immediate explanation of why he had not turned up.

Spitz Swims to His Seventh Gold Medal; Doping Charge Bars DeMont From 1,500

The New York Times/Michael Evans

Pam Teeguarden of Los Angeles, top, during her match at Forest Hills against Evonne Goolagong, bottom.

Pam Teeguarden Upsets Miss Goolagong, 7-5, 6-1

By CHARLES FRIEDMAN

Frustrated by an incredible string of errors, unable to grasp what had gone wrong, Evonne Goolagong was eliminated in the third round of the United States Open tennis championships yesterday by Pam Teeguarden of Los Angeles, the 18th-ranked American, 7-5, 6-1.

The exit of the second-seeded Australian capped a day of upsets in the $160,000 tournament at the West Side Tennis Club in Forest Hills.

Roscoe Tanner, a 20-year-old Tennessean with a huge serve, sent seventh-seeded Tom Okker to the sidelines by 6-4, 3-6, 7-5, 6-3; Okker was bombed with 21 aces by the Stanford senior, who also showed a surprisingly firm volleying attack under which the Dutchman, a contract pro, gradually succumbed.

In a struggle between two former United States champions, Fred Stolle toppled John Newcombe, seeded No. 5, by 7-6, 6-4, 5-7, 7-6. Stolle, 33 years old, unseeded, played the kind of tennis that carried him to the title in 1966, when, also unseeded, he beat Newcombe in an all-Australian final.

The match was played in a spirit of sportsmanship as befitting old friends and rivals, and the crowd of 10,994 warmly applauded both men.

Stolle was unrelenting on service and volleyed with steel-like strength from above and below the level of the net. In both tiebreaker games he quickly forced the issue, winning the first by 5-1 and the second by 5-3.

Still unable to find his form, Manuel Orantes, the stylish Spanish southpaw, seeded 10th and a semifinalist at Wimbledon, yielded to John Cooper of Australia, 7-6, 6-4, 6-4.

Cooper, another tremendous server, had previously eliminated Gerald Battrick, the high-ranking Briton, and Onny Parun, the No. 1 New Zealander. He was too strong off the ground for Orantes, who could not quite keep his attacking shots under control. He next plays Tanner in a match that should produce the heaviest bombardment of the tournament.

Mark Cox, the conqueror of Ken Rosewall, found his moment of glory all too brief as young Dick Stockton solved the Briton's big weapon, the serve, and put so much pressure on him that he wilted in the last two sets. The scores were 6-7, 6-2, 4-6, 6-2, 6-2.

Stockton, the National Collegiate champion from Port Washington, L.I., is one of a group of "hungry" young players, including Tanner, Alex Mayer and Paul Gerken, who may be about ready to push out the established stars.

The rest of the men's third round went according to form as Bob Hewitt of South Africa defeated Patricio Cornejo of Chile, 6-4, 6-4, 3-6, 6-4; Cliff Drysdale of South Africa blunted Charlie Pasarell's artillery in a 7-5, 4-6, 6-4, 6-3 triumph; Tom Gorman of Seattle took care of the tempestuous Nikki Pilic of Yugoslavia with a service break in each set, winning by 6,4, 6-4, 6-4, and Ilie Nastase of Rumania put on another great shotmaking exhibition as he downed Patrice

Continued on Page 49, Column 6

JENKINS DEFEATS METS ON 4-HITTER

Posts 19th Victory, 2-0—Cubs Drop 2d Game, 7-2, as Gentry Hurls Eight

By LEONARD KOPPETT

Ferguson Jenkins, the tall, talented gentleman from Canada who dabbled in baseball and hockey before he found his niche pitching for the Chicago Cubs, moved within one step of one of baseball's greatest achievements yesterday while his team was splitting a double-header with the New York Mets.

A crowd of 36,004 at Shea Stadium saw Jenkins post his 19th victory of the season with a four-hit 2-0 shutout in the first game. The Mets took the second, 7-2, and remained two games behind Chicago in their battle for second place in National League East.

Last year, Jenkins won 24 games, his fifth straight 20-victory season for the Cubs. If he wins one more this season, he will move into select company indeed. Since baseball's modern era began in 1920 with the introduction of the lively ball, only three men have been able to win 20 or more games for six consecutive seasons.

Lefty Grove did it for a seven-year stretch, 1927 to 1933, in the American League. Robin Roberts, from 1950 to 1955 with Philadelphia, and Warren Spahn, from 1956 to 1961 with Milwaukee, had six-year runs.

In fact, all the way back to 1900, only two other pitchers had longer streaks: Christy Mathewson went 12 straight years, 1903 to 1914, and Walter Johnson 10, 1910 to 1919. Both are original Hall of Famers, along with Grove, and Roberts and Spahn are considered certain to be elected when eligible.

So Jenkins, who is still only 28 years old, has proved himself a model of consistency for a team that plays its home games in a park (Wrigley Field) that favors hitters. His current won-lost record is 19-10 in 33 starts, and he is scheduled for at least six more starts.

He was in top form against

Continued on Page 50, Column 4

YANKEES WIN, 5-2, AFTER A 4-3 LOSS

Split With Orioles Leaves New Yorkers a Half-Game Out of First in East

By MURRAY CHASS

Special to The New York Times

BALTIMORE, Sept. 4—The positive elements balanced out the negative aspects of New York's double-header with Baltimore tonight. When it was over, the Yankees were as near, or far, from first place as when they started—half a game.

The Orioles won the opener, 4-3, as Andy Etchebarren and Paul Blair, two of the weakest of the team's generally weak hitters, struck key blows.

Then the Yankees won the second game, 5-2, behind the hitting of Bobby Murcer and the pitching of Rob Gardner and Sparky Lyle. The combination left the Yankees in fourth place, a percentage point behind Boston and four behind Baltimore and Detroit.

On the negative side, Fritz Peterson let Etchebarren, a .189 hitter, sock a three-run homer, only his second home run of the season, in the seventh inning of the opener, and Lyle suffered his fourth loss when Blair, batting .219, drove in a run in the eighth with a double which was aided by Roy White, the Yankee left fielder.

The Positive Side

On the positive side were the developments in the second game. First, Murcer, who entered the contest hitless in 16 times at bat, lashed three hits, including his 26th home run and a run-scoring single that snapped a 2-2 tie as the Yankees erupted for three runs in the eighth.

Second, Gardner pitched another strong game, scattering eight hits before Lyle relieved him in the ninth and secured the left-hander's sixth victory in seven decisions as a starter.

And third was Lyle himself. The plucky relief ace bounced back from his opening-game defeat and gained a club record 30th save by retiring Boog Powell and Blair after Brooks Robinson doubled off Gardner with one out.

None of the three pitchers the Orioles tried in the eighth inning was successful. Pat Dobson, the starter, departed after Horace Clarke led off with a single and Bernie Allen reached first when Powell fumbled his grounder.

Manager Earl Weaver brought in Grant Jackson, a left-hander, to pitch to Murcer, but the left-handed hitter lined Jackson's first pitch to right for a single that brought in Clarke.

Jackson struck out the next two batters, White and Johnny Callison, but Felipe Alou, playing both games because Ron Blomberg was home, sick with a virus, singled to center for another run.

That's when Weaver called for Eddie Watt, but the second reliever of the inning also was greeted by a run-scoring single, this by John Ellis.

Fritz Peterson was making a strong bid in the opener for his second straight shutout until the seventh. But Boog Powell singled and went to second on a wild pitch, Blair walked

Continued on Page 50, Column 2

Associated Press

Mark Spitz being carried by his teammates after the U.S. won the 400-meter medley relay. He is on the shoulders of Tom Bruce, left, and Mike Stamm. Jerry Heidenreich is at the right.

LOUD CAPTURES GOVERNOR STAKE

Scores by Head, Survives Foul Claim, Pays $22.80—Autobiography Is 2d

By JOE NICHOLS

Loud withstood a claim of foul and won the $118,600 Governor Stakes at Belmont Park yesterday. A good runner once he gets going, Loud advanced steadily under the guidance of Jacinto Vasquez and took the 1 1-8-mile event by a head.

In second place among the dozen that competed in the fourth running of the stakes was Autobiography, who finished ahead of his entrymate, Hitchcock. Loud is owned by William Haggin Perry, and the entry races in the silks of Sigmund Sommer.

Before the result was official, Loud had to withstand a claim of foul by Eddie Belmonte, who rode Hitchcock. He protested that Loud had interfered with his mount in the stretch drive.

The fine weather and the attractive holiday program drew a crowd of 51,769 fans, and these players made Tentam of the Cragwood Stables the favorite, and the Sommer entry the second choice. Loud, relatively ignored by the bettors, paid $22.80 for $2, while the entry returned $5.80 to place and $6.40 to show. Under 114 pounds, Loud covered the distance in 1:48 1/5.

George Cassidy sent the large field away almost in a line. Loud dropped back almost to the end of the pack in the early going, while Spanish Riddle and Droll Role set the pace. Approaching the far turn, Autobiography, ridden by Angel Cordero assumed the lead, and Loud raced with the pack.

When the field straightened out in the stretch the Sommer entry was running 1, 2, but Loud, flashing the closing outside rush that has been one of his characteristics, came along to score in the last stride. Autobiography had the margin

Continued on Page 50, Column 5

Other Olympic Highlights

BOXING—Two Americans advanced but another lost, dropping the team's performance below its showing at the 1968 Games. Marvin Johnson and Ray Seales, a light-welterweight celebrating his 20th birthday, were the winners. Davey Armstrong, youngest member of the squad at 17, lost a unanimous decision.

WEIGHTLIFTING—Exasperated by the unexpected collapse of their lifters, Soviet officials sent home all but three members of the team. One of the remaining Russians, Yan Talts, promptly went out and won the gold medal in the heavyweight class.

YACHTING—Harry Melges of Wisconsin moved closer to a gold medal in the Soling Class by winning for the second time in five races at Keil.

National League

Tuesday, September 5, 1972

YESTERDAY'S GAMES

Chicago 2, New York 0 (1st).
New York 7, Chicago 2 (2d).
Atlanta 6, Houston 5 (n.).
Los Angeles 6, Cincinnati 5 (n.).
Cincinnati at Los Angeles (2d, n.).
Montreal 1, St. Louis 0 (1st).
St. Louis 8, Montreal 7 (2d).
Pittsburgh 10, Philadelphia 0 (1st).
Pittsburgh 5, Philadelphia 1 (2d).
San Diego 1, San Francisco 0 (n.).

STANDING OF THE TEAMS

Eastern Division

	W.	L.	Pct.	G.B.
Pittsburgh	82	46	.641	—
Chicago	70	60	.538	13
New York	66	60	.524	15
St. Louis	62	67	.481	20½
Montreal	59	68	.465	22½
Philadelphia	47	83	.362	36

Western Division

	W.	L.	Pct.	G.B.
Cincinnati	80	48	.626	—
Houston	73	57	.562	8
Los Angeles	70	58	.547	10
Atlanta	60	72	.455	22
San Francisco	56	74	.431	25
San Diego	48	80	.375	32

(Last night's 2d Cinc.-L.A. game not incl.)

TONIGHT'S PITCHERS

Chicago at New York (8:05 P.M.)—Hands (10-8) vs. Seaver (16-10).
Atlanta at Houston—Reed (11-13) vs. Roberts (11-6).
Cincinnati at Los Angeles—Gullett (7-7) vs. Sutton (14-9).
Montreal at St. Louis—Stoneman (10-10) vs. Wise (13-14).
San Francisco at San Diego—Marichal (5-15) vs. Arlin (8-18).
Other teams not scheduled.
(Season's won-lost records in parentheses.)

American League

Tuesday, September 5, 1972

YESTERDAY'S GAMES

Baltimore 4, New York 3 (1st, twi.).
New York 5, Baltimore 2 (2d, n.)
Boston 2, Milwaukee 0 (1st).
Milwaukee 5, Boston 2 (2d).
Oakland 10, California 5 (1st).
California 2, Oakland 1 (2d).
Detroit 2, Cleveland 1 (n.).
Kansas City 4, Texas 3 (n.).
Minnesota 2, Chicago 1 (1st).
Minnesota 4, Chicago 0 (2d).

STANDING OF THE TEAMS

Eastern Division

	W.	L.	Pct.	G.B.
Baltimore	69	60	.535	—
Detroit	69	60	.535	—
Boston	67	59	.532	½
New York	69	61	.531	½
Cleveland	60	68	.469	8½
Milwaukee	52	77	.403	17

Western Division

	W.	L.	Pct.	G.B.
Oakland	76	53	.589	—
Chicago	72	56	.563	3½
Minnesota	64	62	.508	10½
Kansas City	61	65	.484	13½
California	60	69	.465	16
Texas	50	79	.388	26

Remaining games: Baltimore 26; Boston 29; Detroit 27; New York 25.

TONIGHT'S PITCHERS

New York at Baltimore—Stottlemyre (13-15) vs. McNally (13-13).
Boston at Milwaukee—Pattin (14-12) vs. Lockwood (7-10).
Cleveland at Detroit—Wilcox (7-11) vs. Coleman (14-12).
Kansas City at Texas—Splittorff (10-10) vs. Gogolewski (3-8).
Minnesota at Chicago—Goltz (3-0) vs. Fisher (4-6).
Other teams not scheduled.
(Season's won-lost records in parentheses.)

MEDICATION RULE TRIPS U.S. YOUTH

DeMont Is Disqualified Over Asthma Aid—Spitz Relay Team Sets World Mark

By NEIL AMDUR

Special to The New York Times

MUNICH, West Germany, Sept. 4—To nobody's surprise, Mark Spitz won his seventh gold medal of the Olympics tonight with a seventh world-record swimming performance.

But the luster of Spitz's final race and subsequent world-record victories by Mike Burton, Melissa Belote and Karen Moe were tarnished by the stunning disqualification of an asthmatic American swimming gold medalist on drugging charges.

The 22-year-old Spitz, in what may have been his final race before he retires to pursue a career in dentistry, swam the butterfly leg in the 400-meter medley relay. The Californian turned a tight team duel with East Germany into a two-body-length lead for Jerry Heidenreich on the anchor free-style leg, as the Americans clocked 3 minutes 48.16 seconds.

The victory in the concluding race of the swimming competition gave Spitz four individual golds [100 and 200-free-style and 100 and 200-butterfly] and three relay titles—an achievement unequaled by a single athlete in one Olympics.

But even as Spitz and his teammates received a standing ovation from the capacity crowd of 10,000, some members of the American team were in tears over the disqualification of Rick DeMont, a

Continued on Page 49, Column 1

Arthur Daley

Decathlon Marvel in Miniature

MUNICH, West Germany, Sept. 4—When Bill Toomey was winning the final tryouts en route to his Olympic decathlon championship four years ago, he made a sympathetic appraisal of the talents of Jeff Bennett, the fifth-place finisher.

"It's too bad he isn't bigger," said Toomey. "He does many things so well. If he only had more size, he could go far as a decathlon man."

Sports of The Times

Bennett hasn't changed much in the intervening years. He's still 5 feet 8 inches tall. According to his own proud admission, however, his weight has ballooned from 148 pounds to 152. But his stature as an all-round performer has so increased that he now ranks among the best in the world. This means he definitely is a contender for the decathlon championship in the two-day gruelling grind that starts on the morrow.

One of the more interesting aspects of a competition whose winner is traditionally hailed as the greatest of all Olympic athletes is that it offers two types of performers. Toomey once described them as "the speed guys and the strength guys." He himself was a speed guy. So is Bennett.

Man of Muscle

But the other top American contender for decathlon honors, Jeff Bannister, is a muscular powerhouse who relies more on strength. He's 6 feet 3 inches tall and a solid 205 pounds.

"I'm not great at any of the 10 events," he says. "But I'm consistent. Balance is the name of my game."

Little Bennett is an engaging black man with a straggly little beard and some events that are explosive. He has pole-vaulted 16 feet 7 inches, long-jumped more than 25 feet, run the 400 meters in 46.4 and hit 4:06 in the climactic 1,500-meter run, astonishing time for an exhausted athlete to fashion.

"I drop as many as four of five places after the shot and discus," he says with a carefree shrug of his shoulders, "but I pick them all up in the pole vault. It's a skilled event and a good vaulter can score more than 1,000 points. No shot-putter or discus thrower ever can go over 1,000. If I ever could put all my best decathlon performances together, I'd be up around the world record."

A hurdler and long jumper in high school, he became a pole vaulter and intermediate hurdler—what an extraordinary combination—at Oklahoma Christian, one of the top small-college track schools. Coach Ray Vaughn noticed this bundle of energy fooling around with shot and discus. It gave him an idea.

"Would you be interested in trying the decathlon at the Drake Relays?" asked the coach of his midget marvel. Bennett tried it, didn't do especially well, but found himself bitten by the decathlon bug.

"When the Olympic Committee established a training camp at Lake Tahoe in 1968," he said, "I wanted to go there more than anything in this world. I figured I could qualify for an invitation by doing well in the small-college championships as an intermediate hurdler. I fell on my face—literally. I went down at the ninth hurdle. That finished me there. But the next week the national decathlon championships were being held, and I took a whirl at it. I qualified in fourth place and decided that my future was in the all-around. I've stayed with it ever since."

Cross-Handed Vaulter

The other top American contender, Bannister, was minding his own business as a basketball player a half-dozen years ago when the national pentathlon, or five-event competition, was held in Westbrook, Maine. The promotors wanted some local color to dress up their project and they invited Bannister. He finished third but came under the influence of Toomey, the winner.

"Toomey was only a name to me then," he was to say, "but he became an inspiration to me later on. The one event that killed me in the decathlon was the pole vault. Up to a few years ago I knew so little about it that I actually was vaulting cross-handed."

Both Bennett and Bannister have gone over 8,000 points, the major dividing line for separating the men from the boys. Bennett beat Bannister in the national championships and Bannister beat Bennett in the final tryouts. They rank with Johann Kirst of East Germany and Nicolai Avilov of the Soviet Union, both strength guys, among the favorites.

Small persons everywhere would rejoice if Bennett, the little man in a big mans game, were to emerge as the Olympic decathlon champion.

Canadians Conquer Soviet Six, 4 to 1

By GERALD ESKENAZI

Special to The New York Times

TORONTO, Sept. 4—Team Canada remembered to shake hands tonight.

The squad, composed of the National Hockey League's finest players, brought themselves and their country back to respectability with a solid 4-1 victory over the Soviet Union's national squad. It came two days after a humiliating 7-3 loss in the first meeting between the teams, and following that game the Canadians left the ice without the traditional handshakes.

It was different tonight as John Ferguson, the Canadian assistant coach, had promised. To break the Soviet's pattern, the most famous hockey players in the world had to adopt a defensive posture. That meant they would shoot the puck in and chase it, rather

Continued on Page 49, Column 3

Ukrainian First to Gain Double in 16 Years

MUNICH, West Germany, Sept. 4 (Reuters)—Valery Borzov of the Soviet Union became the first man in 16 years to score an Olympic sprint double today when he added the 200-meter crown to his 100-meter title. He was clocked in 20 seconds flat.

Borzov, a 22-year-old Ukrainian, thus solidified his claim to the title "fastest man on earth."

Kipchoge Keino of Kenya, the maestro of middle-distance running, accomplished the remarkable feat of winning the 3,000-meter steeplechase in his first season of serious competition in the event.

Keino, who defends his Olympic 1,500-meter title later this week, ran his first real steeplechase last May. But his superb judgment and tactical know-how proved sufficient today to bring him the title in an Olympic record time of 8 minutes 23.6 seconds.

World Mark Tied

Ulrike Meyfarth, a 16-year-old high school student, scored a big upset for West Germany by winning the women's high jump with a leap of 6 feet 3½ inches, equaling the world record.

It was a double triumph for the jaunty Kenyan squad in the steeplechase as 29-year-old Ben Jipcho took the silver medal ahead of Tapio Kantinen of Finland, who was edged by only a fraction of a second.

The only thing that prevented an overwhelming triumph for Kenya was the failure of the defender, Amos Biwott, to retain his title. Biwott finished sixth.

Keino, a 32-year-old police inspector who had been the main driving force behind the upsurge in African track and field performances over the past decade, let the rest of the field take turns setting the pace while he lingered in the middle of the pack. He timed his winning move to perfection.

Keino was momentarily shaken when one of his spikes caught a barrier three laps from home. He staggered but regained his balance and remained tucked in safely in the middle of the pack.

The Kenyan made his big move shortly before the bell lap, followed by Jipcho and Bronislaw Malinowski of Poland.

He made a long sustained drive down the backstretch, with Jipcho and Kantinen in close pursuit until the final bend, when Keino pulled away.

Borzov, a post-graduate student at the Kiev State Institute of Physical Culture, was annoyed by suggestions that his 100-meter triumph was a hollow victory because the American stars, Eddie Hart and Rey Robinson, did not run.

The 100-meter and 200-meter double was last accomplished by Bobby Morrow of the United States at Melbourne, Australia, in 1956.

Borzov came out of his blocks in a blur of motion today. As he came off the turn into the stretch, Larry Black of the United States and Pietro Mennea of Italy closed for a brief moment, but the Russian moved back into top gear and crossed the line ahead of Black.

The tall, slender Miss Meyfarth held the attention of the floodlit Stadium crowd as she Fosbury-flopped her way to the high-jump title before going on to tie the world mark set by Ilona Gusenbauer of Austria.

Miss Guenbauer finished second today and Yordan Blagoeva of Bulgaria was third.

Victor Saneev of the Soviet Union became the first athlete to retain his title in Munich when he won the triple jump with 56 feet 11¼ inches.

The talented United States 110-meter hurdles trio ran their way into tomorrow's final. Rod Milburn, the fastest hurdler in the world over 120 yards, led the way with a time of 13.44 seconds despite knocking over two barriers.

Willie Davenport, the defender, was third to Milburn without much trouble in 13.73. The strength of the American entry was illustrated in the opening semifinal when Tom Hill found himself trailing the French star, Guy Drut, at the final hurdle. Hill put his head down and brought his knees up as he sped across the line for the first place in 13.47 seconds.

Spitz Captures 7th Gold; Drug Rule Bars DeMont

Continued From Page 47

16-year-old high school senior from San Rafael, Calif.

De Mont, who won the 400-meter free-style earlier in the competition, was dropped from the finals of the 1,500 minutes before the race tonight because his doping test had turned up positive following the 400.

Kenneth Treadway, manager of the men's team, said that De Mont regularly takes a prescription known as Malax, which contains an ephedrine.

De Mont listed the special medication on his Olympic forms during final processing in the United States, but American team doctors apparently did not clear the prescription with the medical committee of the International Olympic Committee.

"He's been taking that medicine since he was a little boy," said Mrs. Betty De Mont, who tried to comfort her tearful son when he was informed of the disqualification at poolside.

According to the drug-control manual of the I.O.C. Medical Committee, ephedrine is included among a group of drugs or related amphetamines that can affect an athlete's performance.

"They have a particular point of attack in the vegatative nervous system, in addition to their central stimulating effect and the resulting elimination of fatigue," the manual, printed earlier this summer, states on the reason for the ban. "These drugs, as well as some of different pharmaceutical nature, which act similarly such as ephedrine . . . increase the fonicity of the sympathetic nerves which must be active in any great exertion."

The decision to disqualify De Mont was made after a recheck of his urinalysis today, and a second meeting of the I.O.C. Medical Committee. His first urinalysis after the 400 had proved positive.

The committee granted De Mont an opportunity to explain the situation earlier today, but ruled that he was to be disqualified from the 1,500.

"The question of whether he will have to return his medal will be submitted to the I.O.C. Executive Committee," Prince Alexandre de Merode, chairman of the Medical Committee, said.

The tests proved positive 12 parts in a million—a trace one doctor here described as an "infinitesimal amount."

Nevertheless, officials of the I.O.C. Medical Committee urged that "the persons accompanying the athlete should be punished according to the recommendations of the I.O.C. Medical Committee, since they were clearly co-responsible for the incident."

If the I.O.C. strips De Mont of his medal, the gold will go to Brad Cooper of Australia, the runner-up in the 400. Steve Genter, another American, finished third.

United Press International

Karen Moe of Santa Clara, Calif., taking a deep breath after winning the fourth heat of the 200-meter butterfly.

De Mont had qualified easily for the final of the 1,500 and was counted on to challenge Cooper, Graham Windeatt of Australia and Burton for first place.

In defending his title and setting a world record, in 15:52.57, Burton proved that his nickname as "The Old Man" is deceiving. He is 25 years old.

"I was right where I wanted to be at 400," said Burton, who was in the lead. "Graham sprinted to try and drop me off, but I think he tried to put on the sprint too early."

Miss Belote, a 15-year-old from Springfield, Va., followed up her triumph in the 100-backstroke with a sweep and world mark (2:19.19) in the 200. Susie Atwood, a teammate, was second.

Miss Moe, a 20-year-old Californian, let Ellie Daniel, a teammate, and Rosemarie Kother of East Germany battle for the lead in the 200-butterfly final before moving in front in the last 50 meters. She won by about a body length in 2:15.57.

In the men's 10-meter platform diving, Richard Rydze of Pittsburgh rallied from fifth place to take the silver medal back of Italy's Klaus DiBiasi. Franco Cagnotto, also of Italy, took the bronze.

DiBiasi, the defender, took an insurmountable lead with a 3½-somersault dive on the ninth of 10 efforts.

American men wound up with 10 of the 15 gold medals. They grabbed eight silvers and eight bronzes. Over all, world marks were clocked in 23 of 29 events.

CANADIANS DOWN SOVIET SIX, 4 TO 1

Continued From Page 47

than attempt to stickhandle into the attacking zone.

The Canadian wings also helped out, going in deep in their own zone to battle the visitors, who had been so tough to dislodge from the disk two nights ago.

The crowd of 16,475 at Maple Leaf Gardens was a microcosm of Canadiana. The fans came from all over the country after receiving their tickets (only two to a lucky winner) in a national drawing.

It was an angry and disillusioned bunch of Canadians who took the ice tonight, and Rod Gilbert perhaps summed up their feelings best.

"Now it's not country against country any more," he said. "It's us against them."

The crowd, too, wanted revenge. Strangely, it behaved like an underdog, like expansion hockey crowds do against the Establishment. Whenever a Soviet pass was broken up, the fans—normally the quietest in the N.H.L.—cheered lustily. If a Team Canada forward merely had the disk on his stick, ready to began a goalward thrust, there were roars of approval.

When the first period ended with both teams off the scoreboard, a sort of moral victory had taken place. The Soviets, though, brought "oohh's" from the big crowd with their extraordinary passing and their controlled shot-making.

The Soviets held off the hosts until a little more than seven minutes went by in the second session. Then the Canadians capitalized on a break. Wayne Cashman, one of the new players in a major line-up shake-up, crashed into a Soviet so hard that he lost his stick. Brad Park got off a shot while the visitors were a stick short, and Emil Esposito banged home the rebound.

The Stanley Cup hadn't come back to Toronto, but the crowd reacted as if it had. The players hugged one another.

The session ended with the Canadians leading 1-0, as they outshot the Soviets by 16-5 in the 20 minutes.

After 79 seconds of the final period, Yvan Cournoyer did what Coach Harry Sinden had demanded—he shot the puck. It went in after he made a big move down the right side and the Canadians led by 2-0. Alexander Yakushev soon cut the score to 2-1, but the Soviet six failed to impress.

First Period

No scoring.

Second Period

1—Canada, Esposito (2) (Park, Cashman) 7:14

Third Period

2—Canada, Cournoyer (1) (Park).....1:19

3—Soviet Union, Yakushev (2) (Liapkin, Zimin) 5:53

4—Canada, P. Mahovlich (1) (Esposito) 6:47

5—Canada, F. Mahovlich (1) (Mikita, Cournoyer) 8:59

MISS GOOLAGONG IS UPSET IN OPEN

Continued From Page 47

Dominguez of France, 6-3, 5-7, 6-2, 6-4.

Arthur Ashe also entered the fourth round by polishing off Ross Case of Australia, 6-4, 6-4, 3-6, 6-1, the match being carried over after three sets had been completed Sunday evening. Ross surrendered very quickly and was not nearly the player who had knocked out John Alexander of Australia in the second round.

Miss Goolagong's setback could hardly have been imagined as she coasted to a 5-3 lead, breaking service in the fifth game when Miss Teegarden, a Virginia Slims tour player, double-faulted twice and seemed resigned to defeat.

But the Australian, one of the four top world players, made the mistake of letting down, either through overconfidence or carelessness. Suddenly she was spraying shots out of court. Her beautifully rhythmic game disintegrated as she lost her groove.

The crowd in the stadium sat in stunned disbelief as the points came rolling in for Miss Teeguarden. She sensed her opportunity and began to lash out more confidently with her sharp flat forehand, and low, heavily sliced backhand. She went to the net more quickly to saw off the volleys, sending Evonne scurrying for recoveries, her yellow-trimmed skirt swirling in the wind.

There was nothing to stem the flood. Miss Teeguarden took five games running. She simply would not miss and Miss Goolagong, as the stream of winners went past her, could only shake her head numbly or nod vigorously in approval of her opponent's play.

At 1-3, in the second set, she tried valiantly to gather her remaining resources. But in a long game with several deuces, she finally hit a volley long and seemed visibly to shrink.

The champion had run her course. She had nothing more to fight back with. Miss Teffguarden, on the first match point, slashed a forehead volley across court for the clincher.

Evonne had no excuses. Shaking her curly head, she said: "I've played better. I thought I could get back, but Pam didn't give me a chance."

An Olympian Rhubarb

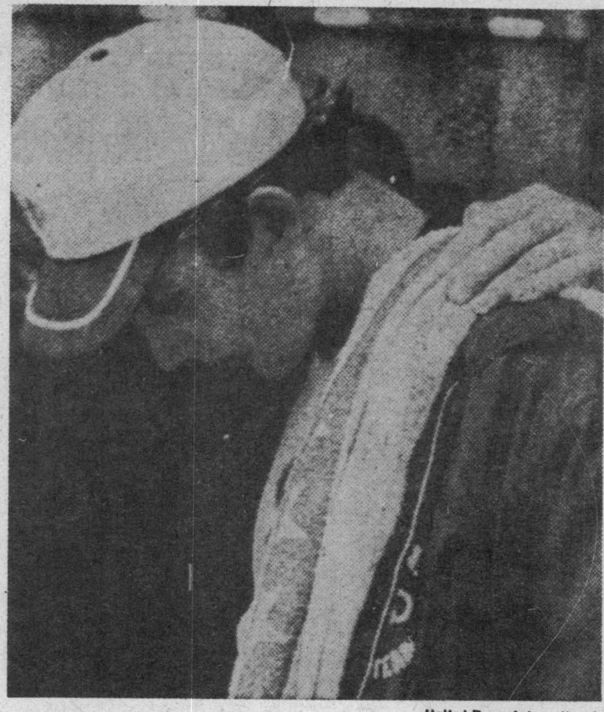

United Press International

Rick DeMont of San Rafael, Calif., after he was disqualified in the 1,500-meter free-style event.

DeMont's Case Is Latest Controversy Involving American Games Officials

By NEIL AMDUR

Special to The New York Times

MUNICH, West Germany, Sept. 4—Instead of basking in the glow of its most impressive single-day show in swimming at the 20th Olympic Games, the United States Olympic Committee found itself involved tonight in another major crisis.

News Analysis

This time, the offense is considerably more serious and embarrassing than a coach forgetting the time of a heat in a 100-meter dash — the human error that eliminated two American potential gold medalists, Rey Robinson and Eddie Hart, before they could reach the starting blocks last Thursday.

Tonight's problem involved a gold medal and an apparent failure to understand and follow specific rules set down by the medical committee of the International Olympic Committee regarding the use of medical prescriptions for athletes.

As an athlete with a chronic history of asthma, Rick DeMont, a 16-year-old swimmer from San Rafael, Calif., had been taking a prescription known as Malax "since he was a little boy," his mother said.

But the prescription is an ephedrine, and I. O. C. medical rules clearly state that such drugs are not allowed, except in situations where the dosage is significantly small and has been previously approved.

Whether U.S.O.C. medical officials chose to ignore the rule, forgot to request special dispensation or failed to follow up in DeMont's behalf is not important.

"Unfortunately," Ken Treadway, the manager of the swim team, acknowledged, "there must have been a failure on the part of someone."

Prince Alexandre de Merode, chairman of the I.O.C. medical committee, was less than enthusiastic with the American behavior and even suggested that the burden of responsibility belonged as much with U.S.O.C. officials as with DeMont, a soft-spoken, pleasant teen-ager who probably couldn't tell the difference between marijuana and L.S.D.

This case is not the first medical foul-up involving American medalists. George Woods, the 305-pound shot-putter, still carries bitter memories of the 1968 Games when American team doctors neglected to tell Woods that he could request special consideration to tape his tender wrists during the finals.

Woods, who won the 1968 trials, finished second at Mexico City.

Mrs. Olga Connolly, the five-time Olympian and an outspoken critic of the alleged neglect by American officials, decided to seek medical advice on her ailing knee from doctors attached to the Czechoslovak delegation because, she felt, "the Americans weren't giving me the help I thought I needed."

Other United States athletes also have met secretly with Czech doctors for treatments since the competition began.

It has been no secret that German organizers are distressed and, in some cases, angry over the attitude of United States officials and coaches.

On several occasions, as with the sprint controversy, German officials have contended that American officials "lied in order to save face."

They point to early contentions by American officials that the sprinters were caught in traffic and could not reach the stadium and a later announcement that the coaches were following a time schedule drawn up 18 months ago.

"How come every other team seems to follow the rules?" one German official asked. "The Americans just seem to go their own way."

John Smith, the quarter-miler, went so far as to suggest today that American losses in the 100 and 200 meter dashes to Valeriy Borzov of the Soviet Union could have been averted.

"All the News That's Fit to Print"

The New York Times

LATE CITY EDITION

Weather: Cloudy, quite cool today; cold tonight. Fair, mild tomorrow. Temp. range: today 33-40; Sunday 26-39. Full U.S. report on Page 59.

VOL. CXXII ... No. 41,995 — NEW YORK, MONDAY, JANUARY 15, 1973 — 15 CENTS

United Press International

Referee signaling touchdown, scored by Howard Twilley of the Dolphins on a pass play, in the first quarter of the Super Bowl. Pat Fischer of Redskins is at right.

Miami Wins in Bowl for Perfect Season

By WILLIAM N. WALLACE

Special to The New York Times

LOS ANGELES, Jan. 14—The big scoreboard in the Coliseum flashed the message over and over, "The Dolphins Are Super," at the end of the Super Bowl contest today, and indeed the Miami team had played an almost perfect game in defeating the Washington Redskins, 14-7, for a perfect season and the championship.

The game was watched by millions on national television.

[Many television sets in the metropolitan New York area were affected by atmospheric disturbances that interrupted the program.]

The score of the undefeated Dolphins' 17th victory could easily have been a more decisive 21-0 or 17-0 except for a single botched Miami play near the end of the game. That play featured little Garo Yepremian, the soccer-kicking specialist from Cyprus, attempting the skills of the big fellows, passing and tackling. Yepremian tried futilely to throw a pass after his 42-yard field-goal attempt had been blocked.

This pass was intercepted by Mike Bass, the cornerback, who ran 49 yards for the Redskins' only touchdown with 2 minutes 7 seconds left to play. The 155-pound Yepremian missed the tackle. This score put some suspense into a game that otherwise had generated little ex-

Continued on Page 35, Column 1

OPPOSITION RISES TO AMENDMENT ON EQUAL RIGHTS

Ratification Is Uncertain as Foes Marshal Arguments For State Legislators

By EILEEN SHANAHAN

Special to The New York Times

WASHINGTON, Jan. 14—Ratification of the equal rights amendment to the Constitution no longer looks like a sure thing.

Well organized and seemingly well financed opposition groups have appeared, and they are making arguments against the amendment that many state legislators find persuasive. There was little organized opposition last year, when 22 of the 38 states necessary for ratification approved the amendment.

The amendment would outlaw all forms of sex discrimination that are based on law or Governmental action. Congress passed it early last year.

Foes' 2 Arguments

Opponents are making their mark with two key assertions: that the amendment would subject women to the draft and that it would abrogate laws that require men to support their families.

Supporters of the amendment say that the statement about the draft is true but irrelevant, since the draft is about to end, and that the argument about support is simply false.

Enactment of the amendment is necessary, they say, if such discrimination as differing entrance requirements for males and females to tax-supported schools is to be eliminated.

While the advocates of ratification do not concede the possibility of failure, they do agree with opponents that the battle will be closer than seemed likely just a short time ago.

Finds Momentum Faded

Doris Meissner, executive director of the National Women's Political Caucus, one of several large, pro-amendment groups, said in an interview:

"The momentum for passage of the amendment has sort of worn out, because it has already gone through in most of the states where it was a natural. Also, it's going to be tougher to get the last 16 states we need because there's a natural backlash setting in toward the gains that women are making."

Mrs. Meissner nonetheless predicts victory.

The apparent leader of the opposition forces, Phyllis Schlafly, a political conservative who formerly held high posts

Continued on Page 12, Column 3

Associated Press

Henry A. Kissinger, right, talking with President Nixon and Gen. Alexander M. Haig Jr. at the Presidential home in Key Biscayne, Fla., yesterday afternoon.

NIXON SENDS HAIG TO SAIGON TO TALK ABOUT CEASE-FIRE

Aide Leaves to Consult With Thieu After Kissinger Sees the President

LONG FLORIDA BRIEFING

General Is Also Expected to Make Stops in Thailand, Cambodia and Laos

By JOHN HERBERS

Special to The New York Times

KEY BISCAYNE, Fla., Jan. 14—President Nixon sent Gen. Alexander M. Haig Jr. to Saigon tonight to consult with President Nguyen Van Thieu about the Paris negotiations on a Vietnam cease-fire.

General Haig, one of the chief participants in the American efforts to reach a settlement in Southeast Asia, left for South Vietnam only a few hours after Henry A. Kissinger arrived from Paris early this morning and reported to the President on his six days of meetings with Le Duc Tho, the North Vietnamese negotiator.

"General Haig is going to Southeast Asia for the purpose of consulting with President Thieu on the negotiations," Ronald L. Ziegler, the White House press secretary, told reporters this morning outside the President's waterfront home, as Mr. Nixon, Mr. Kissinger and General Haig were meeting inside. "While in Southeast Asia, he also will go to Thailand, Cambodia and Laos."

3 Meetings With Nixon

Mr. Kissinger left Paris last night after describing the negotiations as "very useful." His plane stopped in Washington and picked up General Haig, deputy chief of staff of the Army who was formerly the President's chief military aide. Mr. Kissinger and General Haig arrived at the Presidential compound at 1:15 A.M. and met immediately with the President for more than an hour before retiring. They met again for four hours, beginning shortly after 10 A.M. [President Nixon met again with Mr. Kissinger for 75 minutes Sunday evening, United Press International reported.]

Mr. Ziegler said the President would remain here tomorrow for further talks with Mr. Kissinger.

Mr. Kissinger has made no public statement about the negotiations since he left Orly Airport in Paris last evening. There he said that after reporting to Mr. Nixon, "The President will then decide what next step should be taken to achieve a peace of justice and conciliation."

The North Vietnamese delegation issued a statement in Paris last night saying that the private talks had "made prog-

Continued on Page 3, Column 1

Pressures to Plead Guilty Alleged in Watergate Case

By SEYMOUR M. HERSH

Special to The New York Times

WASHINGTON, Jan. 14—A source close to the Watergate case said today that four of the five defendants were under what he termed "great pressure" to plead guilty to charges of eavesdropping on the Democratic National Committee headquarters in Washington last June.

The source, who has provided other reliable information about the case in the past, refused to name those who were said to be putting pressure on the defendants—all of whom are from the Miami area—but he did say that a substantial promise of money had been made to the men.

In essence, the source was confirming a Time magazine report that the Watergate defendants had been promised a cash settlement as high as $1,000 a month if they pleaded guilty and took a jail sentence. Additional funds would be paid to the men upon their release, Time said. The article did not cite the source of the information.

The New York Times source, however, said, "It's not really a question of money—just pressure."

"It is not a bribe," he added. "Just a lot of promises."

The four men—Frank A. Sturgis, Virgilio R. Gonzales, Bernard L. Barker and Eugenio Rolando Martinez—are represented by Henry R. Rothblatt, a New York lawyer.

Mr. Rothblatt refused to discuss the reports of "pressure" during a brief telephone interview today, but did acknowledge that he would withdraw from the case if the four men decided to plead guilty.

"I have repeatedly said that I will not be a party to any plea of guilty," he said.

The Watergate trial, held in United States District Court here, was recessed Friday by Chief Judge John J. Sirica until

Continued on Page 13, Column 1

New Orleans Sniper

A week after six persons were slain by sniper fire at a New Orleans hotel, two questions are unanswered: Was there more than one sniper? If so, how was an escape made past a swarm of policemen? A study of what is known about the case appears on Page 18.

MRS. MEIR TO VISIT POPE PAUL TODAY

To Make First Such Call by an Israeli Premier—Italy Provides Heavy Security

By PAUL HOFMANN

Special to The New York Times

ROME, Jan. 14—Premier Golda Meir of Israel will meet with Pope Paul VI tomorrow in the first visit to the head of the Roman Catholic Church by a head of the Israeli Government.

Hundreds of Italian policemen were mobilized to provide security for Mrs. Meir, who arrived here tonight from Paris, where she had been attending a meeting of the Socialist International.

[Running clashes between demonstrators and the police continued through the day in the Latin Quarter of Paris, near the Senate building in which the Socialist leaders were meeting.]

Vatican Invited Her

The papal audience that Mrs. Meir is scheduled to have tomorrow morning follows a formal invitation from the Vatican. Israel and the Vatican maintain no diplomatic relations, but informal contacts have been going on for a long time.

Sources in the Vatican said today that the Pope and Premier Meir would discuss above all the status of the holy places in Jerusalem and in other parts of the Holy Land and the chances for a peaceful settlement of the Middle East conflict.

Ever since the birth of Israel,

Continued on Page 5, Column 2

U.S. CRIME REPORT CALLS FOR REFORM

End of Plea Bargaining in 5 Years Among Hundreds of Changes Urged in Study

Special to The New York Times

WASHINGTON, Jan. 14—The National Advisory Commission on Criminal Justice Standards and Goals, in a report issued today, recommended the elimination of plea bargaining within the next five years as one of hundreds of recommendations for change in the nation's courts, police forces, corrections systems and community attitudes.

Plea bargaining is the practice of permitting a criminal defendant to plead guilty to a lesser charge than the one with which he is charged, enabling the state to avoid the expense and uncertainty of a trial. The practice has become a matter of controversy in several states, including New York, where Governor Rockefeller proposes eliminating plea bargaining for those accused of selling hard narcotics.

Further Discussion Planned

The 750-page report, which is divided into four sections, was compiled by the commission under the auspices of the Justice Department's Law Enforcement Assistance Administration and will be presented later this month to the National Conference on Criminal Justice for discussion and possible amendment.

Still to come from the commission are its recommendations on gun control and drug-abuse control. But the commission report states that if its recommendations in four areas — the police, the corrections system, the courts and community crime prevention — were implemented in full, crime

Continued on Page 16, Column 5

Northeast Is Bracing Itself For Possible Energy Crisis

By GENE SMITH

The much-talked-about "energy crisis" became a reality last week in some other areas of the nation, and it could still happen in the Northeast if the weather turns sharply colder.

However, last night the prediction for Wednesday through Friday in the New York area was for mild weather, with daytime highs generally in the 40's.

Locally, utilities have had a chance to build up reserves of oil and gas, as no real cold weather hit until last week. However, utilities in the Boston area have been granted approval to import liquefied natural gas from Algeria for their own use later this heating season. The Government recently ordered increased quotas for imported heating oil.

The Petroleum Industry Research Foundation said that to its knowledge no homeowner in the Northeast had yet been deprived of fuel oil. But, the foundation added, the situation could get serious should the cold weather persist. It noted that with temperatures in the first seven days of this year colder than normal, particularly in the Northeast and Midwest, stocks of light home heating oil had dropped to 147 million barrels from 178 million a year ago.

A spokesman for the foundation said an increase in the price of No. 2 oil was needed to bring about increased production.

Meanwhile thousands of

Continued on Page 46, Column 1

NEWS INDEX

	Page		Page
Books	27	Music	20-23
Bridge	26	Obituaries	32
Business	41-46	Op-Ed	29
Crossword	37	Society	24
Editorials	28	Sports	34-41
Family/Style	24-25	Theaters	20-23
Financial	41-46	Television-Radio	59
Going Out Guide	20	[illegible]	60-61
Man in the News	37	U.N. Proceedings	7
Movies	20-23	Weather	59

News Summary and Index, Page 31

South Bronx: A Jungle Stalked by Fear, Seized by Rage

This is the first of four articles on the South Bronx. The series is based on a four-week study of the community, interviews with hundreds of residents and officials, and visits to dozens of the community's institutions.

By MARTIN TOLCHIN

The fire hydrants are open, even in this biting cold weather—town pumps that provide the sole water supply for drinking, washing and sanitation for thousands of tenants in 20 per cent of the housing in the area. When one hydrant freezes over, the residents pry open another.

Packs of wild dogs pick through the rubble and roam the streets, sometimes attacking residents. As protection, many mailmen, health workers and deliverers carry dog repellent.

A drug pusher is murdered by a youth gang acting on a $30 contract from a rival pusher. A youngster is nearly stomped to death outside a school in an argument over a soda bottle. Merchants close their stores at sunset even though many are armed and some conduct business inside their stores behind bullet-proof glass.

This is the South Bronx today—violent, drugged, burned out, graffiti-splattered and abandoned. Forty per cent of the 400,000 residents are on welfare, and 30 per cent of the employables are unemployed.

Over the last 10 years, middle-class whites have fled the South Bronx, which is now home to a young, shifting population that is 65 per cent Puerto Ricans and other Hispanics and the remainder blacks. Its vague borders are Park Avenue on the west, the Cross Bronx Expressway on the north and the Bronx River on the east, encompassing such neighborhoods as Mott Haven, Morrisania, Bathgate and Hunts Point.

Even for a native New Yorker, the voyage across the Willis Avenue Bridge is a journey to a foreign country where fear is the overriding emotion in a landscape of despair. The residents, who have long been afraid to go out at night, are now afraid to go out during the day into streets menaced by 20,000 drug addicts and 9,500 gang members.

"The South Bronx is a necropolis—a city of death," says Dr. Harold Wise, founder of the Martin Luther King Jr.

Continued on Page 19, Column 1

The New York Times/Neal Boenzi

Miss Dorothy River, o[illegible]e tenants remaining in her building on Tiffany Street, rear, draws water [illegible]n hydrant, like 80,000 others in the South Bronx.

Martin Luther King Day

Public schools will be closed today here and in numerous cities, including Newark, Chicago, Los Angeles, St. Louis and Atlanta, to mark the birthday of the late Rev. Dr. Martin Luther King Jr. Details are on Page 32.

Divorce Insurance Gains Varied Support in State

By ENID NEMY

The idea of divorce insurance, to be taken out immediately before or after marriage, is gaining increasing interest among feminists, lawyers and legislators. The insurance would be used primarily to insure adequate child support in the event of a divorce, but it could also be used by childless divorced couples and, should the marriage be a lasting one, be converted to other uses.

"It's as logical as protecting oneself with accident, fire or life insurance," said State Senator Donald Halperin, who has drafted a bill that would establish a study commission on offering such insurance for sale in this state.

The bill, originally introduced by the Brooklyn Democrat last year, never got out of committee, but the Senator plans to resubmit it during the current legislative session.

"I think it will be in a much better position now because of increased public pressure," he said.

The public pressure is coming from such organizations as the National Organization to Improve Support Enforcement (NOISE), founded more than a year ago to restructure the concept of child support "in new and realistic terms."

The group, which works closely with feminist committees active in divorce, alimony and support questions, now has a mailing list of more than 7,000 interested men and women.

"We're out to alleviate the suffering of the silent, middle-income woman," said Mrs. Diana Du Broff, a fellow of the Academy of Matrimonial Lawyers and founder of NOISE. A 62-year-old grandmother, who conceived the idea of the organization after decades of "thorough disgust and frustration" with

Continued on Page 25, Column 1

Dolphins Take Super Bowl, 14-7, and Cap Record 17-0 Season

Miami Defense Thwarts Redskins, Larry Brown

Continued From Page 1, Col. 3

citement because Miami was the dominant team from the start.

The Redskins had the ball one more time with 74 seconds remaining, but the Dolphin defense harassed Bill Kilmer, the Washington quarterback, and the final play was symbolic. Kilmer was dropped by Bill Stanfill and Vern Den Herder for a 9-yard loss on his 17-yard line.

Larry Csonka ran for 112 yards for Miami, 9 short of the Super Bowl record set by Matt Snell of the New York Jets in 1969, while Larry Brown, the Redskins' No. 1 carrier, scratched out 72 in 22 carries. His average was 3.3 yards, a yard below his standard during the regular season. Brown's longest run was for 11 yards while Csonka had one of 49 yards, the most yards the Redskins' defense had given up on a single ground play all season.

Csonka's running mate, Jim Kiick, scored the second Miami touchdown on a 1-yard run in the second period and Howard Twilley, the wide receiver, made the first on a dazzling play in the opening quarter. Twilley, cutting inside and then outside, caught a pass from Bob Griese on the 5 and scored to complete a 28-yard play. Twilley turned the defending back, Pat Fischer, all the way around on his fake.

Jake Scott, the Miami free safety, won the automobile when he was voted the game's outstanding player by a panel on the basis of his two interceptions. The choice of Scott was hardly a clear-cut one because all 11 players on the Dolphin defense were outstanding.

George Allen, the Redskin coach, had anticipated his defense giving Miami 14 or even 17 points, but his hope for victory expired because his offense was shut out rather than scoring the expected 21 or 24 points.

Allen said: "We felt we had to get on the board early against them because when they get ahead they have the talent to hold the ball and ground it out." That is what happened before the crowd of 81,706.

Allen added: "There was great pressure on Kilmer because we were unable to run as we would have liked to. It was a difficult day for him. But he brought us where we are today. They stopped our running better than I thought they would."

This attack, with Brown held in check, never moved into Miami territory until the third quarter began. That drive failed when Curt Knight's 33-yard field-goal try went wide.

The Redskins' only other drive, in the final period, ended when Kilmer's pass on third down to Charlie Taylor was intercepted by Scott in his end zone.

Kilmer had little luck when attempting to pass into the middle of the Miami zone defense. His first effort in the second quarter was intercepted by Scott and his second, in the same period, was picked off by Nick Buoniconti.

Washington had four turnover errors, the three interceptions and a lost fumble, to just one, an interception, for Miami. This interception, of a Griese pass by Brig Owens in his own end zone, prevented a Miami touchdown late in the third quarter that would have put the game out of Washington's sights with a 21-0 score.

The early Miami touchdowns came after a six-play, 63-yard drive, which ended with the Twilley score, and a 27-yard drive following Buoniconti's interception and 32-yard return. Kiick slammed over the goal from the 1 behind a block by Csonka to make it 14-0 at halftime.

So Miami became the first team in the 53-year history of the National Football League to go through a season undefeated and untied. For the coach, Don Shula, a Super Bowl victory had been some time in coming. His two earlier qualifiers, the 1969 Baltimore Colts and last year's Dolphins, had lost, to the Jets and to the Dallas Cowboys.

"I'm 0-2," said Shula last week, "and on Sunday night I intend to be 1-2." He made it.

For Allen and the Redskins, there was disappointment at the end of a glorious season that had carried the coach and the Washington entry to the Super Bowl for the first time.

Form held up. The Dolphins were the fourth team to win the Super Bowl on the second try after losing on the first. The others were Kansas City in 1970, Baltimore in 1971 and Dallas last year.

In the locker room, Shula said: "There is no empty feeling this year. This is the ultimate."

Griese added: "I'm really happy for Don Shula. This year we won it for him."

Each of the 40 Dolphins also won for themselves $15,000, the Super Bowl prize money. The Redskins will receive half as much.

A downcast Allen commented: "It doesn't do any good to play in the Super Bowl if you don't win. We just lost to a team that played a better game."

Allen said the Redskin kicking game "was not up to par," a reference to Mike Bragg's weak 31-yard punting average and Knight's missed field-goal attempt.

Then Allen said: "I can't get out of here [Los Angeles] fast enough. There will be a lot of hours of agony tonight.' George will start working on next season tomorrow.

Shula will linger to savor the victory. "This team," he said of the Dolphins, "is the greatest I have been associated with. It went undefeated and won at the end and they have to be given credit for their achievement."

Miami Dolphins	7	7	0	0	—14
Washington Redskins	0	0	0	7	— 7

Mia.—Twilley, 28, pass from Griese (Yepremian, kick).

Mia.—Kiick, 1, run (Yepremian, kick).

Wash.—Bass, 49, fumble recovery return (Knight, kick).

Attendance—81,706.

INDIVIDUAL STATISTICS

RUSHES—Mia.: Csonka, 15 for 112 yards; Kiick, 12 for 38; Morris, 10 for 34. Wash.: Brown, 22 for 72; Harraway, 10 for 37; Kilmer, 2 for 18.

PASSES—Mia.: Griese, 8 of 11 for 88 yards. Wash.: Kilmer, 14 of 28 for 104.

The Miami Dolphins

Mercury Morris

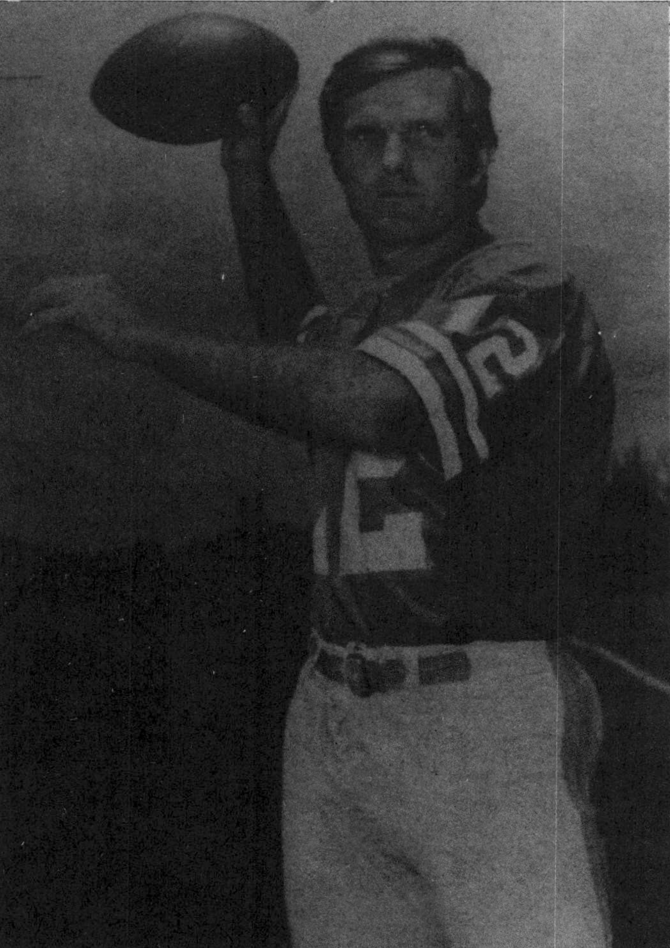

The Miami Dolphins

Bob Griese

RECEPTIONS—Mia.: Warfield, 3 for 36 yards; Kiick, 2 for 6; Twilley, 1 for 28; Mandich, 1 for 19; Csonka, 1 for minus 1. Wash.: Jefferson, 5 for 50; Brown, 5 for 26; C. Taylor, 2 for 20; J. Smith, 1 for 11; Harraway, 1 for minus 3.

STATISTICS OF THE GAME

	Dolphins	Reds.
First downs	12	16
Rushing yardage	37-184	36-141
Passing yardage	69	87
Passes	8-11	14-28
Interceptions by	3	1
Punts	7-43	5-31
Fumbles lost	1	0
Yards penalized	35	25

Blackout Ammunition: 8,476 Unused Tickets

Special to The New York Times

LOS ANGELES, Jan. 14—Although the Super Bowl crowd today was recorded as 90,182, the National Football League announced that 8,476 ticket-holders did not watch the game at the Coliseum.

"There were 8,476 no-shows," an N.F.L. spokesman said.

Although the N.F.L. did not mention the absence of a local TV blackout, the number of "no-shows" surely will be used as ammunition in its campaign to maintain the blackout policy. The blackout for this Super Bowl game was lifted 10 days ago when the game was a sellout, as promised by Commissioner Pete Rozelle.

The actual Coliseum attendance today was 81,706, although 90,182 tickets were sold. The actual crowd still set a Super Bowl record, breaking the 80,591 mark in Miami last year.

NIXON SENDS WIRES TO SHULA AND ALLEN

KEY BISCAYNE, Fla., Jan. 14 (UPI) — President Nixon sent telegrams tonight to both Super Bowl coaches, offering congratulations to Don Shula and his Dolphins and condolences to George Allen and the Redskins.

The telegram to Shula read: "Today's victory was a smashing climax to a truly perfect season. You and all the Dolphins have my heartiest congratulations. It was a great victory for all of your players, for all of your devoted followers throughout the country, and especially for you, Don — the man who brought the Vince Lombardi Trophy to Miami. Once again my congratulations and warmest personal regards to you and all the Dolphins."

He wired Allen that the loss was "a keen disappointment for all Redskins fans but it certainly has done nothing to diminish our admiration and love for the team that you have coached so masterfully this season."

"The Redskins played gallantly from the opening kickoff this fall through the final seconds in the Coliseum, bringing a new sense of pride to the entire Washington community. You will never be 'over the hill' in our book and we'll all be in there rooting for you next season, fully confident you can go all the way."

Losers Win The Battle Of Banners

LOS ANGELES, Jan. 14 (AP) — If the bedsheet brigade meant anything, Washington was the overwhelming favorite among the fans today. And in the pregame workout nearly an hour before kickoff, the Redskins drew loud cheers from the half-filled stands when they took the field. Minutes later, when Miami appeared, booing was the predominant sound.

"Over the Hill-King of the Hill," one bedsheet-fashioned sign said, referring to the seasoned Redskins, many of them former Los Angeles Rams. Others had these comments:

"Welcome to the Super Bowl Fish Fry."

"Redskins" Menu: Filet Dolphin."

'Thought I Gave Game Away,' Says Yepremian

Kicker's 'Mind Went Blank' as Miscue Let Foe Score

By DAVE ANDERSON
Special to The New York Times

LOS ANGELES, Jan. 14—In his relief over the Miami victory today, Garo Yepremian sighed.

"I never prayed so much," the Cyprus-born place-kicker acknowledged, 'And God came through for me."

Yepremian was discussing the aborted field-goal attempt from the Washington Redskins' 42-yard line with about two minutes remaining that resulted in Mike Bass's 49-yard run for a touchdown. Another Redskin touchdown and extra point would have produced overtime.

"I thought I gave the game away," Yepremian said. "I picked up the blocked kick, but my mind went blank. I tried to throw a pass. I just saw some of our uniforms downfield, I don't know who they were. But the ball slipped out of my hand."

Scolded by Coach

As the baldish, 5-foot-8-inch kicker trotted to the sideline after having been outrun by Bass for the touchdown, he was scolded by Coach Don Shula.

Following the Redskin kick after the touchdown, the Dolphin offense went on the field with 1:57 remaining and first down on the Miami 16.

"In the huddle I said that we knew that this was what we'd been working for since July," said Larry Csonka, the big running back. "We knew we had to get a couple of first downs to kill the clock and keep the ball away from them. And then Norm Evans said: 'We don't have to say it. We all know what we have to do now. So let's just do it.'"

In a second-and-7 situation, Bob Griese threw a sideline pass to Paul Warfield for a first down at the Dolphin 30.

"That was a big play," Shula said. "Mike Bass, the cornerback, was lined up way inside Warfield. Bob and I talked about it. Bob had the confidence to do it, and I had the confidence to let him do it. When it worked, it gave us two extra plays to help kill the clock with."

Back to Yepremian.

"Shula told me I should've fallen on the ball," he said. "I knew that, but I didn't think fast enough to do it. But the guys on the sideline came up to me and told me not to worry about it—Norm Evans, Larry Ball, Tim Foley, Larry Seiple.

Snap Was Low

On the field-goal attempt, Howard Kindig's snap was low, forcing Earl Morrall, the holder, to position it quickly.

"Garo hit it good," Morrall said, "but the ball didn't get up in the air fast enough; they penetrated to block it."

Yepremian recalled a similar situation during a victory over the St. Louis Cardinals.

"I picked the ball up and fumbled it," the 28-year-old soccer-style kicker said. "I'm not used to throwing. I kick with my left foot, but I throw with my right hand, like I tried to. The ball just slipped. The only time I throw the ball is in practice when I throw to the guys just for fun. This wasn't fun."

Shula said the game plan was to exploit the Redskin pass defense in various situations.

"Like the pass to Warfield for the touchdown that was nullified," the coach said. "In that situation we thought the Redskins wouldn't be looking for that. And the pass to Jim Mandich that set up the second touchdown. On the first touchdown, Howard Twilley got away from Pat Fischer on the bump and run. Howard likes that."

3 Standouts in Line

As for the Dolphins' defensive plan, as designed by Bill Arnsparger, an assistant coach, Shula mentioned the line led by Manny Fernandez, Bill Stanfill and Vern Den Herder.

"We felt that if we could whip 'em up front and stay in our pursuit lanes, we'd have somebody there when Larry Brown looked to cut back," he said. And that's what we did. We wanted to contain their running game to short gains and make 'em pass more than they wanted to."

After two Super Bowl losses as coach of the Baltimore Colts four years ago and the Dolphins last year, Shula was delighted.

"It's the greatest moment of my coaching career," he said. "All along I've had an empty feeling of not having accomplished the ultimate.

"With a 17-0 record, I don't know what we can do for an encore. But right now I'm just going to sit back and relish this for a while.

Miami Is Wild With Joy; Hopes Dashed in Capital

MIAMI, Jan. 14 (AP)—The chilly air was filled with sounds of firecrackers, horns and chants of "We're No. 1!" as Miamians took to the streets tonight to celebrate the Dolphins' Super Bowl victory.

"I loved it, we were shouting and yelling," said Virginia Miller, a cashier at the exclusive Jockey Club, the home away from home for many professional athletes who winter in Florida.

"We're Numero Uno! shouted a Cuban exile, Francisco Garcia, after watching the game at the Little Havana Bar in the southwest section. "The Dolphins sure showed 'em."

The police reported some traffic congestion, but said there were no real problems.

"I think it's great, everybody's going wild," said Sgt. L. Griffin, who watched the game on a portable television set up in the police station.

"The defense did it," said Patrolman Ken Borchers of Miami Beach.

Like many throughout the city, Chuck Honkonen and his wife Brucie, watched the game with a group of neighbors who decided to make a party of it.

"It's nice to see a team that was always being accused of having a weak schedule finally play an acknowedged tough team," he said. "That no-name defense ought to have their numbers engraved in stone."

Week of Tension Ends

By JAMES T. WOOTEN
Special to The New York Times

WASHINGTON, Jan. 14 — Sundays are generally quiet here—a siren or two each hour, church chimes spreading in the dirty air and little more—but today brought a new low to the city's noise level.

In the early afternoon a few tourists stared curiously at the inaugural stands being raised in front of the White House, police cars rolled slowly past the stores and shops on nearby Constitution Avenue and in Lafayette Park a pair of young lovers sat by themselves watching the squirrels play at the French general's statue.

"I've never seen it quite like this," an elderly woman, passing by, said. "It's like the whole town has just stopped."

In a way it had stopped, for this was the day the beloved Redskins, Washington's venerable National Football League entrant, was to get a shot at the world's championship in the seventh Super Bowl game, a continent away in Los Angeles.

From Virginia's rolling suburbs to counterparts in Maryland, the metropolitan area had awakened to the prospects of victory, and the priority of the day was a free afternoon, a place to sit and a television set in working order.

Hotel bellmen were tense, waiters nervous, bartenders distracted and even a policeman walking a Georgetown beat wanted to talk more about the game than the directions for which he had been asked.

"I didn't have to drive today," a woman cabbie said as she steered her taxi around the near-deserted downtown streets. "But my old man had all his friends in and they were whooping and hollering, so that I just had to get out."

It was the same throughout the area: a doomsday silence, punctuated through open apartment windows with the sound of the crowd's clamor and the commentator's wisdom chattering from radios and television sets.

The pigeons in the park went unmolested and unfed. At Scott Circle a beggar circled a vacant corner wondering why business had gone so bad.

For two solid weeks the entire area had been subjected to a massive, media promotion of the game. With each day, the newspapers and television and radio stations escalated their own excitement with reams of Super Bowl stories, documentaries, interviews and some rather shameless examples of unabashed cheerleading.

Further, it had become fashionable in White House-influenced circles to take more than a passing interest in the fortunes of the Redskins. President Nixon had set the pace, and even though he flew to Florida to his Key Biscayne villa to watch the game, what was good enough to fascinate the occupant of the Oval office was good enough to fascinate the thousands of those working in lesser offices nearby.

Arthur Daley

Success on the Second Time Around

LOS ANGELES, Jan. 14—It's cause and effect rather than coincidence, but one inescapable Super Bowl fact remains: Every team making a return visit to the Super Bowl made good on the second chance by winning. If anyone so desires, he even can count Vince Lombardi's Green Bay Packers, who started the series with two thumping victories. By taking their second game as easily as they had their first, they proved the point. It was a return visit, wasn't it?

Sports of The Times

Kansas City lost the first, but came back to win the fourth. Baltimore dropped the historic third Super Bowl game to the Jets, but took the fifth from Dallas, which knocked off Miami in the sixth. Today the Dolphins completed the sequence by crushing the Washington Redskins, 14 to 7.

Don't let that score fool you. It wasn't that close a game. The Dolphins dominated all the way, yielded a freakish touchdown late in the action and practically yawned their way through to complete a perfect season of 17 and 0. For Coach Don Shula it was particularly precious because he had been on the wrong end twice, once with Baltimore and last year with Miami. He's finally on the alkaline side.

A Fluke From the Past

That second time around may even be worthy of a psychological study. When a team makes its debut in the Super Bowl, everyone says, "Wow, we made it." An objective has been attained, blurring the essential objective, a Super victory. But the losers readjust their sights and shoot for the moon, the stars and victory. Thus far, everyone of them has achieved it.

Once the Dolphins entered the swim with a slick touchdown late in the first quarter and tacked on another late in the second quarter, the Redskins were barely able to get out of the glub. They made not one penetration of any consequence in the entire first half, had one abortive attempt in the third quarter and had to believe that nothing ever would work for them.

Here's a sample: In the final period the Redskins engineered their most noble effort of the game, driving down to the Dolphins' 10. Then a strange thing happened, something that had historians blinking their eyes in amazement. Jerry Smith broke clear in the end zone and Bill Kilmer fired a pass right at him. But the ball hit the upright. It was no dice. On the next play the Dolphins intercepted to avert the threat.

But what made trusty historians do a mental flip-flop was a recollection of a costly similar play in the 1945 championship playoff, the last one in which the Redskins were involved. Backed into his end zone, the incomparable Sammy Baugh threw an escape pass. It also hit the upright and bounced back through the end zone. According to the rules then in effect, it was a safety. It also meant the difference between victory and defeat because the 'Skins lost, 15 to 14.

Kicker Violates Precept

However, nothing much would have saved the Redskins today. When they scored, they did it on a freakish play that is even a little fuzzy to eye-witnesses and may not be clear in everyone's mind until the official movies are premiered. Garo Yepremian, the left-footed Cypriot who manufactures ties and field goals, attempted a 42-yarder. Bill Brundige blocked it and the ball bounced off crazily to Yepremian's right.

In hot pursuit was the baldish little kicker who is supposed to shun all active combat. He violated all union rules. Instead of following the precepts found in the kickers' handbook, he went for the ball. Since he is far more used to touching it with his foot than with his hands, he juggled that hot potato while fire-eating Redskin monsters bore down on him. It looked as if he were trying to throw a forward pass—of all things. Whatever it was, it was ruled a fumble.

Mike Bass plunked the ball out of the air and raced downfield for the goal line. Miami defenders were totally out of position. The only one in the neighborhood was Yepremian, the non-combatant. He violated the union code again. He tried to make a tackle. He missed, and the Redskins' cornerback streaked down the sideline for a touchdown.

Thus did the Redskins finally get into the swim, far too late for it to help them much. By the time the researchers had completed all their chores, they were able to offer the observation that the touchdowns were scored by two Dolphins and one Bass. It could be from a script plucked out of an old Lloyd Bridges underwater series.

The crowd in the cavernous Coliseum, a mere 81,706 for a record, was unashamedly in favor of the Redskins because Coach George Allen and so many of his elderly Over the Hill Gang had once been Los Angeles Rams. Seated in the stands, however, were most of the owners and coaches of the National Football League. They definitely were not rooting for Allen, the low man in their hit parade.

When it all was over, Allen was saying something that most first-time coaches in the Super Bowl said in the past. It was:

"We all probably learned something."

Associated Press

Don Shula being carried off the field in Los Angeles after guiding the Dolphins to undefeated season

No. 1 Fan Dismayed By Defeat

KEY BISCAYNE, Fla., Jan. 14 (AP) — President Nixon watched with dismay today as his favorite football team, the Washington Redskins, lost to Miami, 14-7, in what he called "One of the best Super Bowl games ever."

"That was a fine game," the President said, in comments relayed by a deputy press secretary, Neal Ball, ". . . because there was suspense right up to the end."

"The people of Washington and the people of Miami can both be proud of their teams," he added. "They played well."

Scores of motorists drove past the Nixon compound after the game blowing their horns to "show their resentment at Nixon's support for the Redskins," one motorist explained.

The Coach Who Has the Last Laugh

Donald Shula

By MICHAEL KATZ

In the often overdramatic world of professional football, where coaches exhort their teams each week "to win one for the Gipper," and where locker-room truisms like "Winning Is Everything" are hailed as philosophy, Don Shula usually cooled it.

Man in the News

All week long, the coach of the Miami Dolphins had reacted to the pressures of Super Bowl week with a loose, graceful humor, a refreshing contrast to the gung-ho George Allen, his counterpart with the Washington Redskins.

And the joking, relaxed Shula set the tone for his team, which defeated the tense Redskins, 14-7, yesterday in Super Bowl VII and capped a season in which it won everything—all 14 regular-season games, two playoff contests and the Super Bowl.

For the 42-year-old Shula, yesterday's triumph was the "ultimate" one after he twice before coached losing teams in the Super Bowl.

Filling a Void

"All along I've had an empty feeling," admitted Shula afterwards in the winners' locker room, "of not having accomplished the ultimate."

"And this right here," he said tapping the Vince Lombardi Trophy for the National Football League championship, which had been presented to him moments before by Commissioner Pete Rozelle, "is the ultimate."

This was the third time around for Shula, whose Baltimore Colts lost the 1969 Super Bowl to the New York Jets and whose Dolphins were defeated last season by the Dallas Cowboys.

Even Then, He Knew

"I hadn't done too well in my first two [Super Bowl games], as a lot of people kept reminding me," he said.

Shula doesn't have to remind anyone about his professional coaching record—five times he has been voted somebody's coach of the year and he is the first coach to win 100 games in only 10 N.F.L. seasons. In his 10 seasons, his won-lost-tied record, including playoffs, is 109-33-5.

He did it mainly with a tough, practical, professional approach. In a way, Donald Shula, the son of an immigrant Hungarian nurseryman and dock worker, had been preparing himself to be a professional football coach as early as childhood.

"As a kid, I was the one who organized the games," he has said of the sandlot football he played in the lots around Painesville, Ohio, a Cleveland suburb. "In grade school I chose the line-ups. In high school I knew what everyone was supposed to do and I corrected their mistakes. That's my background."

That background included the ubiquitous "will to win."

"He hates to lose," said his mother, Mary, who accompanied his father, Dan, to the Los Angeles Coliseum yesterday. "When he was 8 years old, he would play cards with his grandmother. If he lost, he would tear up the cards and run and hide under the porch. You couldn't pry him out for supper."

Shula didn't tear up his playbook when the Dolphins lost last year's Super Bowl. "You set a goal to be the best and then work hard every hour, every day striving to reach that goal," he has said.

He worked the Dolphins hard, too. It has been said that the key to Shula's success as a coach is repetition—he makes his players practice the same thing over and over until he finally is satisfied. His teams seldom make mistakes.

Shula, who played halfback at John Carroll University in Cleveland and had an undistinguished seven-year N.F.L. career as a defensive back with the Cleveland Browns, Baltimore Colts and Washington Redskins, began his coaching career in 1958 as an assistant at the University of Virginia. He also was an assistant at the University of Kentucky and with the Detroit Lions before becoming the Colts' head coach in 1963.

He took over the Dolphins in 1970 after a falling out with Carroll Rosenbloom, the Colts' owner, and built the expansion club into a contender in his first season at Miami.

Thinking Unbeaten

The Dolphins followed their relaxed leader loyally all season and were able to resist the growing pressures of their winning streak.

"We weren't thinking about being 13-0, 14-0, 15-0 or 16-0," Shula said yesterday. "We were only thinking about being 17-0, like right now."

Next week, the Dolphins won't have to worry about being 18-0. "Next," said Shula, "is relaxation and enjoyment."

Shula will relax with his wife Dorothy and their five children — David, Donna, Sharon Lee, Ann Marie and Michael. Winning isn't everything.

'We'll Be Back,' Says Allen After Uttering Prepared Alibi

By LEONARD KOPPETT

Special to The New York Times

LOS ANGELES Jan. 14—It took George Allen, the Washington coach, only a few sentences to put before the American public his carefully prepared alibi after his team's 14-7 loss to undefeated Miami today—but many of his players spent the next hour pointedly rejecting the idea.

After a few remarks to Kyle Rote, his post-game television interviewer, about Miami showing "just about what we expected" on offense and defense, Allen slid smoothly into the position he had been preparing all week and, in effect, all season.

"I don't want to make excuses," he said, "but our team wasn't as sharp as it had been against Green Bay and Dallas, and I think the carnival atmosphere that's here makes it hard for a team like ours."

During the week-long publicity build-up for Super Bowl VII intended to maximize the television rating since all tickets to the Coliseum were long since sold—Allen had complained about the "distractions" his players had been subjected to. Among these he included the presence of the players' wives for even one day prior to the game, and "media" interviews demanded by his ultimate employer, the National Football League.

But the Washington players, who actually had to play the game, shrugged off the distraction theory.

"I wasn't distracted," declared Bill Kilmer, the Redskin quarterback, "This was the biggest game of my life. How could I not be up? You execute or you don't execute, that's what football's about, and today we lost."

In other cubbyholes around the dressing room, which is unusual in its construction in that there are little roomettes for each two players, similar sentiments were being expressed. The Redskins were disappointed that they had lost, but unwilling to give up the pride they felt in earning the right to be in the championship game.

And even in Allen there was a subtle shift in emphasis. All week the theme had been "nothing means anything unless you win this last one." Now he was conceding, in later interviews at least, a tacit pride in what had been achieved.

"I want to emphasize one thing most of all," he said: "We'll be back."

Solace from Owners

As he spoke, two of the owners of his team came up to offer solace and congratulations: Edward Bennett Williams, the glamorous Washington attorney who is president of the Redskins, and Jack Kent Cooke, the one-man sports cartel who owns the largest individual share (about 25 per cent). Cooke also owns the basketball Lakers (world champions), hockey Kings, the Los Angeles Forum and some residual rights for another heavyweight championship fight.

New Auto Right Make For Scott

Special to The New York Times

LOS ANGELES, Jan. 14—Jake Scott, whose two interceptions sparked the defensive unit in the Miami Dolphins' 14-7 victory, was awarded a Dodge Charger by Sport magazine today as the most valuable player of the Super Bowl game.

"That's great," the free safetyman said, grinning. "I work for a Dodge dealer in Miami."

Scott performed spectacularly despite a sore right shoulder that required a pregame injection of Xylocaine as a pain-killer and despite bone chips in his right wrist that will require surgery.

"I didn't practice for two weeks," he said. "But my shoulder only hurt me once, when I landed on it covering a pass."

Scott's first interception occurred early in the second quarter at midfield, halting a Redskin drive when the Dolphins had a 7-0 lead. In the fourth quarter, he ran his second interception out of the end zone to the Redskins' 48-yard line.

"I was lucky on the first one," he said. "I batted the ball in the air and caught it. On the second, Lloyd Mumphord and I were covering Charlie Taylor, with Lloyd outside and me inside, but Bill Kilmer didn't see me cut over and the ball came to me."

Scott was drafted by the Dolphins in 1970 after he had played in the Canadian Football League for one season.

"I wasn't eligible for the N.F.L. draft, and I had a year of eligibility left at Georgia, but all my buddies had graduated," he recalled. "And when Vancouver of the Canadian League made me an offer I couldn't refuse, I took it."

Oddly, the 27-year-old native of Athens, Ga., was a wide receiver in the C.F.L., not a defensive back.

"Then they traded me to Montreal, but several N.F.L. teams were interested in drafting me. The Dallas Cowboys talked to me, but then nobody took me until the Dolphins did on the seventh round. I had to take a $5,000 pay cut to join them."

Scott's reasoning was that he preferred to compete in the N.F.L. rather than remain in Canada.

The New York Times

SPORTS

Section 5

L+++

Sunday, June 10, 1973

Secretariat Sweeps to Triple Crown by 31 Lengths

The New York Times/Barton Silverman

The 3-year-old champion being brought into the winners' circle in front of the grandstand at Belmont. Ron Turcotte is in the saddle.

A BELMONT MARK

Secretariat Races 1½ Miles in 2:24 Before Crowd of 69,138

By JOE NICHOLS

Secretariat won the Belmont Stakes yesterday with a finality that was incredible. The Meadow Stable star flashed to success in the 1½-mile event by the improbable margin of 31 lengths over Twice a Prince, his runner-up, and, even with the big margin, he set a track record time of 2:24.

The performance was executed under a splendid ride by Ron Turcotte, and was most noteworthy in that it enabled Secretariat to become the ninth winner of the Triple Crown for 3-year-olds.

A quarter of a century ago Citation turned the trick, and Secretariat is the first since then to do so. He won the Kentucky Derby at 1¼ miles on May 5, and the Preakness at 1³⁄₁₆ miles on May 19.

Sham Finishes Last

A crowd of 69,138, the second largest turnout to see a Belmont Stakes, attended the 105th running of the race. It had five contestants, and the advance indications were that it would turn out to be a duel between Secretariat, whose payoff at the end was $2.20 for $2 to win and $2.40 to place, and Sham, who competes in the silks of Sigmund Sommer.

Sham was in there for a while, but he found the going too tough as the contest went on, and he wound up in the most unlikely spot—last place. The colt that finished back of Twice a Prince was Arthur Appleton's My Gallant, who was a half-length out of second place and 13 lengths ahead of C. V. Whitney's Pvt. Smiles. Sham trailed that one by three-quarters of a length.

The exacta of Secretariat and Twice a Prince returned $35.20 for $2. The OTB letters were A and E.

The race had a gross value of $150,200, with the five starters, and the share to the winner, who is trained by Lucien Laurin, was $90,120.

In the day or two preceding the Belmont, Sham's trainer, Frank (Pancho) Martin, had said he would send a "rabbit," Knightly Dawn, into the race, to test Secretariat with an early

Continued on Page 3, Column 5

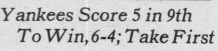

The New York Times/Meyer Liebowitz

All alone, Secretariat was guided across the finish in the Belmont Stakes yesterday by Ron Turcotte

Belmont Stakes Chart

EIGHTH—The Belmont Stakes, $125,000 added, 3YO, 1½ M. Start good. Won ridden out. Off, 5:38. Winner, ch. c. by Bold Ruler—Somethingroyal, by Princequillo. Trainer, L. Laurin. Value to winner, $90,120, second, $33,044, third, $18,024; fourth, $9,012. Times—23 3/5; 46 1/5; 1:09 4/5; 1:34 1/5; 1:59; 2:24 (track record).

OTB	Starters	Wt.	PP	¼	½	1m	1¼	Str.	Fin.	Jockeys	—Mutuels— St.	Pl.	Sh.	Dollar Odds
A	Secretariat	126	1	1hd	1hd	1[illegible]	1[20]	1[28]	1[31]	R Turcotte	2.20	2.40	out	.10
F	Twice a Prince	126	5	4[5]	4[10]	3hd	2hd	3[illegible]	2½	Baeza		4.60	out	17.30
C	My Gallant	126	3	3[3]	3hd	4[7]	3[2]	2hd	3[13]	A Cordero Jr.				12.40
B	Pvt. Smiles	126	2	5	5	[illegible]	5	5	4¾	Gargan				[illegible]
F	Sham	126	[illegible]	2[5]	2[10]	2[7]	4[8]	4½	5	Pincay Jr.				5.10

Scratched—Knightly Dawn.
Exacta (2-5, A-E) paid $35.20.

Owners—1, Meadow Stable; 2, Elmendorf; 3, A. I. Appleton; 4, C. V. Whitney; 5, Sommer.

Mrs. John B. Tweedy watching Secretariat early in the race yesterday . . .

. . . and, as race neared end, she became visibly happier.

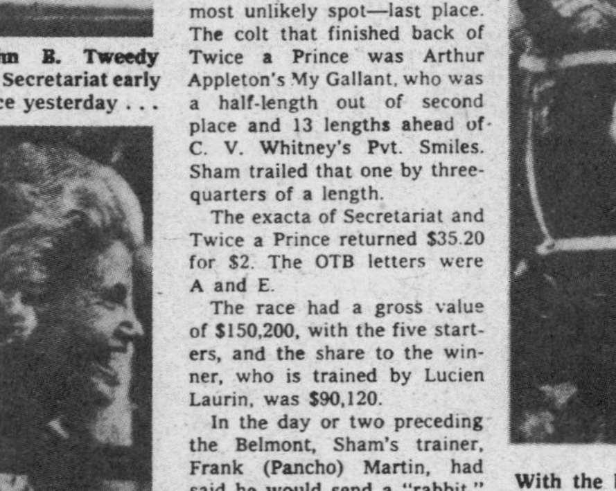

The New York Times

With the blanket of carnations draped over his withers, the chestnut and Turcotte are led around the winners' circle.

Photographs for The New York Times by MICHAEL EVANS

The Belmont Stakes won, Mrs. Tweedy and her husband, in glasses, and Secretariat's trainer, Lucien Laurin, in white suit, smiled broadly and waved in moment of victory.

Wottle Takes Mile; 8 Better 4 Minutes

By NEIL AMDUR

Special to The New York Times

BATON ROUGE, La., June 9—Eight runners smashed the 4-minute barrier in the one-mile run at the National Collegiate outdoor track and field championships today, but it was Dave Wottle and his familiar white golf hat who flashed across the finish line first in 3 minutes 57.1 seconds.

In the final race of his collegiate career, on the day that he was to have been graduated and commissioned a second lieutenant in the Air Force, the Bowling Green University senior uncorked a decisive sprint in the last 120 yards. He outkicked two North Carolina runners, Tony Waldrop and Reg McAfee. It was Wottle's fastest career mile and a meet record for this 52d annual championship.

"I'm not as confident as I used to be on my kick, and I've been getting outkicked in some races lately," the soft-spoken Olympic 800-meter champion said. "But it worked out fine today."

Waldrop, a junior, who said he would have been satisfied with sixth place, finished second in 3:57.3. He was two yards behind Wottle and four yards in front of his teammate, McAfee, who was clocked in 3:57.8, his third sub-four-minute performance of the spring.

"I was surprised with my performance," said Waldrop, an admitted "country boy," who used to train on baseball and football fields because his high school in Columbus, N. C., had no track. "Until this year, I had run only two mile races in college."

The University of California at Los Angeles won its third consecutive team title, as expected.

But the team competition on

Continued on Page 2, Column 3

Major League Baseball

Sunday, June 10, 1973

National League

YESTERDAY'S GAMES

New York 4, Los Angeles 2.
Cincinnati 8, Chicago 4.
Pittsburgh 4, Houston 1 (n.).
Atlanta 8, St. Louis 2 (twi.).
Philadelphia 4, San Diego 1 (n.).
Montreal 9, San Francisco 3 (n.).

FRIDAY NIGHT

Los Angeles 5, New York 3.
Atlanta 5, St. Louis 3.
Houston 4, Pittsburgh 3.
Montreal 17, San Francisco 3.
Philadelphia 5, San Diego 1.

STANDING OF THE TEAMS

Eastern Division

	W.	L.	Pct.	G.B.
Chicago	33	23	.588	—
Montreal	24	25	.490	5½
Pittsburgh	24	25	.490	5½
St. Louis	24	28	.462	7
New York	23	27	.460	7
Philadelphia	22	32	.407	10

Western Division

	W.	L.	Pct.	G.B.
San Francisco	38	22	.633	—
Los Angeles	34	23	.596	2½
Cincinnati	31	24	.564	4½
Houston	32	27	.542	5½
Atlanta	22	33	.400	13½
San Diego	20	38	.345	17

American League

YESTERDAY'S GAMES

New York 6, Kansas City 4 (n.).
Boston 12, Texas 1 (n.).
Chicago 6, Cleveland 3 (twi.).
Oakland 4, Detroit 0.
Milwaukee 1, California 0 (n.).
Baltimore 7, Minnesota 4 (n.).

FRIDAY NIGHT

New York 8, Kansas City 1.
Chicago 5, Cleveland 2.
Detroit 4, Oakland 1.
Milwaukee 8, California 2.
Minnesota 2, Baltimore 0.
Texas 5, Boston 2.

STANDING OF THE TEAMS

Eastern Division

	W.	L.	Pct.	G.B.
New York	30	25	.545	—
Detroit	29	25	.537	½
Baltimore	25	24	.510	2
Milwaukee	26	27	.491	3
Boston	25	26	.490	3
Cleveland	20	34	.370	9½

Western Division

	W.	L.	Pct.	G.B.
Chicago	30	20	.600	—
Minnesota	29	22	.569	1½
California	27	25	.519	4
Kansas City	30	28	.517	4
Oakland	28	28	.500	5
Texas	18	33	.353	12½

TODAY'S PROBABLE PITCHERS

Los Angeles at New York (2:05 P.M.)—Osteen (6-3) vs. Koosman (5-4).
Cincinnati at Chicago — Nelson (2-2) vs. Hooton (6-3).
Pittsburgh at Houston—Briles (3-5) vs. Reuss (6-4).
St. Louis at Atlanta (2) — Foster (3-3) and Murphy (0-0) vs. Gentry (4-5) and Harrison (0-2).
San Diego at Philadelphia—Kirby (2-6) vs. Twitchell (4-2).
San Francisco at Montreal—Bryant (9-3) vs. Stoneman (1-2).

New York at Kansas City—Stottlemyre (7-5) vs. Busby (3-7).
Boston at Texas (n.)—Lee (6-2) vs. Siebert (3-4).
Chicago at Cleveland (2)—Bahnsen (6-5) and Stone (1-1) vs. Bosman (2-6) and Tidrow (4-5).
Detroit at Oakland — Coleman (10-4) vs. Hunter (7-3).
Milwaukee at California — Short (2-1) vs. Singer (10-2).
Minnesota at Baltimore—Woodson (4-3) vs. Alexander (5-1).

(Figures in parentheses are season's won-lost records.)

Mays's Homer, 'Circus' Catch Help Mets Beat Dodgers, 4-2

By JOSEPH DURSO

Willie Mays, the old man of the major leagues, staged a one-man Old-timers' Day before 47,800 persons at Shea Stadium yesterday afternoon as the New York Mets defeated the Los Angeles Dodgers, 4-2.

He took over the stage not long after the legendary "old-timers" from the Mets' and Dodgers' past had held their reunion on the field before the biggest crowd of the season there. And he did it despite two bad knees, a sore shoulder and other erosion damage from a 22-year career in baseball.

The 42-year-old outfielder—older than a dozen of the guest old-timers—made a tumbling catch in deepest center field in the top of the third inning, with the score tied at 2-all. Then, half an inning later, he put the Mets in front with his first home run since last Aug. 18, and No. 655 in a career that has been threatened lately by the toll of time.

Staub Lends a Hand

As a result, the Mets momentarily checked a slide that had cost them 10 games in their last 13 and Jon Matlack checked a personal slide that had cost him five defeats in a row. In fact, he had not won since April 28, and for the last month he has been pitching with a foam-rubber pad protecting his forehead, which was cracked May 8 by a line drive.

Matlack got plenty of help from Rusty Staub, who batted in two runs in the first inning with a double and who played a lead role during a six-man rundown of two Dodgers in the seventh. But the front man was Mays, making his second start in a month of speculation that his career might finally have ended.

It was also Willie's first start at home since his birthday, May 6, after which he settled onto the disabled list for three weeks. But yesterday, he shook down a few echoes himself—becoming, with his home run, the third man in baseball history to pass 6,000 total bases at bat.

He finished the day with 6,003 total bases on 3,244 hits. The only ones ahead of him are Henry Aaron of Atlanta, still going strong at 39, and Stan Musial, who retired from the St. Louis Cardinals a decade ago.

For the Dodgers, who had won 10 of their last 13 games, it was an afternoon of both nostalgia and frustration—and the frustration began in the first inning just after the nostalgia had left the field.

Dave Lopes led off the game

Continued on Page 6, Column 1

Yankees Score 5 in 9th To Win, 6-4; Take First

By MURRAY CHASS

Special to The New York Times

KANSAS CITY, June 9—With a Detroit World Series ring on the ring finger of his right hand and a Baltimore World Series ring on the little finger of his left hand, Pat Dobson joined the Yankees today, looking for another ring and regular work.

The newcomer from Atlanta found work immediately and immediately heightened hopes for postseason work for all the Yankees.

Manager Ralph Houk probably would've been satisfied if all he could've had was Dobson's one-hit, five-inning relief pitching tonight. But he got even more when the Yankees rallied for five runs in the ninth and a 6-4 victory over the Kansas City Royals that vaulted them into first place.

Horace Clarke, whose error on an inning-ending double-play ball paved the way for four Royal runs against Fred Beene in the third, highlighted the rally with a two-out, bases-loaded single that drove in the fifth and sixth runs. Sparky Lyle then pitched to three batters in the bottom of the ninth, picked up his 13th save and secured Dobson's first victory as a Yankee.

"The win was great," an ecstatic Houk said, "but the greatest thing of the night was seeing Dobson pitch like the Dobson we know."

When the 31-year-old right-hander met with Houk before the game, the manager told him he would become one-fifth of a five-man starting rotation begining next Saturday against California. First, though, he wanted Dobson to pitch in relief.

The chance popped up tonight, and Dobson, who had pitched only two innings in the previous 17 days, responded by retiring the first nine batters he faced.

He wound up shutting out the Royals, walking one and

Continued on Page 7, Column 3

Former Mets' Inabilities Have Dimmed With Age

By LEONARD KOPPETT

A group of New York Met alumni, clearly improving with age, routed a group of survivors from championship Brooklyn Dodger and New York Yankee teams, 1-0, in the annual two-inning, Old-Timers Day game at Shea Stadium yesterday.

In the festivities, dedicated to the memory of Gil Hodges, the teams were formed by those who had played with, against or for the late Dodger and Met first baseman, who was the only Met pennant-winning manager.

The formal retirement of Gil's No. 14 uniform, a brief speech by Mrs. Hodges and the presence of their four children helped emphasize that feature of the celebration.

But the way Rod Kanehl, Frank Thomas, Jay Hook, Alvin Jackson and Richie Ashburn, along with other Original Mets, tore into the famous Ebbets Field vintage Dodgers, buttressed by Joe DiMaggio and Whitey Ford, warmed the hearts of true Mets followers.

That the only run was driven home by Yogi Berra's clean single off Carl Erskine didn't dilute anything, because Yogi ended his playing career with a few games as a Met in a period of classic ineptness early in 1965.

One could say that this proved how baseball was constantly improving, since the tenth-place Mets of the 1960's were able to crush the Dodgers of the 1940's and 1950's. One could also say, of course, that it proved nothing of the sort, or anything else.

What it did prove, as it does every year, is that baseball fans love this organized nostalgia and the participants love it even more.

"But I don't see why they

Continued on Page 6, Column 6

Ferraris and Matra Duel for Honors at Le Mans Race

By BERNARD KIRSCH

Special to The New York Times

LE MANS, France, June 9—French and Italian cars, as they have been known to do throughout Europe, hogged the roads here today and made the 24 Hours of Le Mans a two-factory race for publicity.

The Italian Ferraris and French Matra Simcas, starting from the first rows in the 55-car field, roared away at the start as if it were a two-hour Formula One grand prix, while the rest of the field played the waiting game and hoped for attrition.

Among the hopefuls in auto racing's most exhausting publicity campaign were the two-car Gulf-Mirage team of John Wyer and the one-car entry of Frankie Mir, owner of a repair shop in Santa Monica, Calif., and repair man for the cars of Hollywood stars. Two months ago Frankie bought a Ferrari Daytona for this race, billed as "the world's most prestigious endurance test."

At the halfway point, a Ferrari driven by Jacky Ickx of Belgium and Brian Redman of Britain was eight minutes in front of the only surviving Matra, piloted by Henri Pescarolo and Gerard Larrousse. But the two Frenchmen were gaining with each lap. Another Ferrari, driven by the early leaders, Carlos Pace of Argentina, and Arturo Merzario of Italy, was fourth, behind an Alfa Romeo driven by Carlo Facetti of Italy.

The Ickx-Redman Ferrari took over the lead when their stablemates, Carlos Reutemann of Argentina and Tim Schenken of Australia, had to withdraw with an oil failure. Reutemann's Ferrari had been in the lead for almost five hours.

After 12 hours, Mir's machine was in 18th place and both Gulf-Mirages were out of the race.

Before the start, Mir, born in Argentina, said: "I've had my shop for seven years and I've had nothing in publicity. This is the first time I've spent some money in advertising. I just hope it's tax-deductible."

Mir spent $70,000 to get his car to the circuit, and hired two Argentines, Nestor Jesus Garcia Veiga and Luis di Palma, to handle his Ferrari after his neighbor, Phil Hill, had turned down a proposition to drive.

That was exactly what Wyer, who first won here in 1959, said he intended to do. Also like Mir, he said his Gulf-Mirages were here for publicity.

"It is an undisputed fact that Le Mans has worldwide prestige," said Mirage's Wyer. "In the United States, the name Le Mans means something. I don't think there's any question that if your object is publicity, that is, a lasting effect, something that lives in the public's memory, then you go to Le Mans more than any other race, or more than all the other races put together.

"Publicity is the object of

Continued on Page 9, Column 7

Secretariat's Record Romp Electrifies His Fans

Continued From Page 1

pace, but yesterday morning Martin changed his mind and withdrew Knightly Dawn.

The race, as regards tight competition, was hardly a tingler, considering the huge margin of victory. But it held continuous excitement because of the superequine achievement of Secretariat.

At the start he went to the front with Sham, who was ridden by Laffit Pincay, and for a spell the pair raced together, the others being "nowhere."

Turcotte Takes Off

Approaching the three-quarter pole, Turcotte turned around to spot his pursuer, who was two lengths behind. Assured that his margin was a comfortable one, Turcotte just sped away to the score, which had to be the easiest one of Secretariat's career, while Sham cracked completely under the fast pace.

The fractional times, most of them set by Secretariat, were 0:23 4/5, 0:46 1/5, 1:09 4/5 and 1:59. The mark that Secretariat shattered was 2:26 3/5, set by Gallant Man in the Belmont Stakes in 1957. Each horse in the Belmont carried scale weight of 126 pounds.

It was obvious through the going that Turcotte was out for the record with Secretariat, just as he did in the Kentucky Derby of 1¼ miles. In that race Secretariat, in beating Sham by 2½ lengths, was timed in 1:59 2/5, beating the standard of 2:00.

In the Preakness of 1 3/16 miles there was a misunderstanding about Secretariat's time, and the matter was finally resolved with a clocking of 1:54 2/5, as against the standard of 1:54. Some clockers caught Secretariat in 1:53 2/5. In that race Sham also was the runner-up, again by 2½ lengths.

When he returned to the winner's circle yesterday Turcotte corroborated the speculation that he was record-conscious. He said, "When we got to the stretch, and I saw those figures on the tote board, I knew that I was going to a record."

American Record Set

Incidentally, the world record for a mile and a half (on turf, and not on the dirt, like the Belmont), is 2:23, set by Fiddle Isle at Santa Anita in 1970. The American record on dirt, which was broken yesterday, was 2:26 1/5, set by Going Abroad at Aqueduct in 1964.

The occasion of the Belmont Stakes was one of complete joy, glory and accomplishment for Mrs. John (Penny) Tweedy, who directs the activities of the Meadow interests founded by her late father, Christopher T. Chenery; for Turcotte, who has ridden Secretariat in all but the first two of the colt's 15 races, and for Laurin, who trains for the Meadow interests.

For this Belmont marked consecutive successes for these track notables. Riva Ridge of the Meadow Stable won the Belmont Stakes last year.

Secretariat is a Virginia-bred son of Bold Ruler and Somethingroyal, and now has a record of 12 victories in his 15 races. His share of yesterday's gross purse was $90,120. This sum raised his season's earnings to $438,838, and his career earnings, over the last two years total $895,242.

Gov. Nelson A. Rockefeller, along with Gov. Lynwood Holton of Virginia, presented the Triple Crown trophy to Mrs. Tweedy. Governor Rockefeller also presented the Belmont Trophy to Mrs. Margaret Chenery Carmichael, vice president of the Meadow Stable.

Secretariat entered the race with so formidable a record that he became the prohibitive favorite all through the betting, which was on win and place only. The place price on Twice a Prince was $4.60.

The Triple Crown has now been won nine times, starting with Sir Barton in 1919. He was followed by Gallant Fox in 1930, Omaha in 1935, War Admiral in 1937, Whirlaway in 1941, Count Fleet in 1943, Assault in 1946, and then Citation.

There were several instances following Citation in which horses won the first two legs, only to falter on the third, that it was ventured in some quarters that the Triple was a modern impossibility. Secretariat has now put that theory to rest.

Secretariat now figures quite highly in the economic scheme of things in the thoroughbred world. He has been syndicated for breeding purposes for $6,080,000, his career in that field to begin when his racing days are over, late this year.

Mrs. Tweedy, a-tingle over the victory for some time after it happened, said "That horse is wonderful, and the reason he is, is because he has been trained magnificently."

Laurin, hearing this, gave credit to the breeding and the ownership, and to Turcotte, whose record-breaking ride pleased the trainer no end. Asked if Secretariat was the best horse in his recollection, Laurin said, "Positively."

Pincay, of Sham, said, "I was following the trainer's instructions in trying to go to the front, but I couldn't pass Secretariat. My horse just didn't run the first mile, and I never could get him started. I didn't use my horse in the stretch as I was not going to abuse him. He was not the same horse that ran in the Kentucky Derby."

Commenting further on his ride on Secretariat, Turcotte said, "he's just the complete horse. I let him run a bit early to get position to the first turn. Once he got in front of Sham he wasn't about to give anything away."

Cause for Celebration

Laurin's further comments were, "I wondered a bit when I saw those early figures, wondered if he was going too fast. But I told myself that Ronnie [Turcotte] knows the horse, and that made me feel better. And I felt better all through the stretch when he was drawing out and still running like a gem."

Baeza, of Twice a Prince, said, "My horse ran a better race than expected, but Secretariat is a superhorse."

Angel Cordero, who rode My Gallant, said, "That winner is a real runner. When he and Sham hooked up early I thought to myself that they would run each other into the ground and that I had a chance. But that all changed when Secretariat ran off by himself. He's the best I've ever seen."

Dan Gargan, of Pvt. Smiles, said, "Secretariat is a hell of a horse. My horse disappointed, but there will be another day."

The Belmont, named for the horse owner and financier in the latter part of the 19th century, had its first running in 1867, and was won by a filly named Ruthless. The second Belmont went to General Duke and the third was the one that was won by Fenian, who raced in the silks of Belmont himself.

Secretariat Sweeps to Triple Crown by 31 Lengths

By STEVE CADY

"Three . . . two . . . one—ignition!"

It was racing's version of a moon shot, and the crowd of nearly 70,000 at Belmont Park never stopped yelling yesterday as Secretariat roared off the launching pad and streaked to the first Triple Crown in 25 years.

Any other horse who set the kind of pace he set in the 1½-mile Belmont Stakes would have come home in a horse ambulance. Secretariat came to the wire in glory, a 31-length winner of the fastest dirt-course mile and a half ever run in America.

"I just let him run his own way," said an obviously relieved Ron Turcotte after riding the Meadow Stable colt down geranium-lined Victory Lane to collect the blanket of white carnations. "All of us had a lot of pressure, but I guess I carried the last couple of minutes of it."

Secretariat's "own way" was to run the first six furlongs in 1:09 4/5, the mile in 1:34 1/5 and the mile and a quarter in 1:59. That was faster than his record time in the 1¼-mile Kentucky Derby last month—and he still had the toughest quarter-mile in American racing ahead of him.

By then, though, he was 20 lengths in front, and doubters were beginning to think maybe he really was the reincarnation of Pegasus.

This was the kind of race when even the losers could shout, "How sweet it is"—and mean it. It was the kind of unbelievable performance that sent seasoned horsemen babbling incoherently into radio and television microphones.

On all sides owners and trainers and Governors were saying the 2:24 Belmont was the greatest effort in racing they had ever seen.

"He broke the Belmont Stakes record by 2 3/5 seconds," noted John Finney, president of Fasig-Tipton, "and he did it all by himself. It took three horses to set that old 1957 record—Bold Hero for the first half, Bold Ruler for the mile and Gallant Man for the mile and a half."

On a television stand near the winner's enclosure, Mrs. Penny Tweedy's hands shook at her sides as she watched the videotape rerun.

"I'm so excited," said the syndicated colt's proprietor. "It was such a strain. We wanted this badly. **He's** really tired now."

Turcotte, committed to ride a horse for **Rokeby** Stable in the race immediately after the Belmont, didn't have time to let acclaim interfere with business.

Cut on the bridge of his nose when Secretariat's girth snapped back at the unsaddling, the 31-year-old Canadian-bred jockey stayed on the television stand only long enough to watch one rerun.

His Day Is Not Over

He carried a single white carnation in his right hand. Then he hurried off to the jockey room to exchange the blue and white Meadow Stable silks for Rokeby's gray and yellow.

In the paddock, the Rokeby trainer, Elliott Burch, had his hand extended. "I never saw anything like that is my life, Ronnie."

"I kept looking back," said Turcotte. "The last 70 yards or so, I seen on the toteboard teletimer I was breaking the record pretty good, so I let him go on a little. Just a hand ride. I never hit him once."

Finally, Burch drew Turcotte aside. "We gotta talk strategy, man." Whatever strategy was outlined, it didn't work. Head of the River, Turcotte's mount in the ninth, finished fifth. That left racing's hottest jockey with three winners and three losers for the day.

The New York Times

Secretariat, Ron Turcotte up, passing the one-quarter pole on the course at Belmont Park.

"All the News That's Fit to Print"

The New York Times

LATE CITY EDITION

Weather: Partly cloudy today, clear and cool tonight. Fair tomorrow. Temp. range: today 52-68, Thurs 57-72. Degree Days yesterday: 0 Additional Details on Page 81.

VOL. CXXIII ... No. 42,244 © 1973 The New York Times Company NEW YORK, FRIDAY, SEPTEMBER 21, 1973 15 CENTS

Philharmonic Hall Gets Gift of $8-Million

Is Renamed for Avery Fisher, the Donor

By DONAL HENAHAN

Philharmonic Hall, which opened 11 years ago this month, yesterday was renamed Avery Fisher Hall in appreciation of a "major gift" of undisclosed size by a pioneer manufacturer of high-fidelity phonograph and radio equipment. Informed sources in musical and financial circles here immediately estimated the over-all gift at $8-million to $10-million.

Mr. Fisher, who founded Fisher Radio in 1937 and became famous as a maker of high-fidelity components for music listeners who demanded better sound than the ordinary console sets could then provide, sold his firm for $30-million two years ago to the Emerson Electric Company of St. Louis. He still has a large interest in the company and acts as consultant.

Described As Breakthrough

Amyas Ames, chairman of the board of Lincoln Center and the New York Philharmonic, announced the benefaction at a news conference in the lobby of the 2,836-seat hall. He described it as a breakthrough in the field of arts patronage.

While major donors have traditionally tagged their gifts for glamorous purposes such as buildings or new opera productions, 80 per cent of the Fisher grant will be used chiefly to help meet the hall's housekeeping expenses—the annual maintenance and operating deficit, which Mr. Ames said amounted to about $500,000 a year.

But the gift, while it will alleviate the financial burden of one constituent of Lincoln Center, throws into sharp relief the extraordinary dimensions of the fiscal crises of all of the center's cultural components.

Standing under a hastily erected gold-lettered glass sign proclaiming the new name, Mr. Ames said that Mr. Fisher's grant, which one observer of the fund-raising scene termed "a pretty sophisticated kind of gift," would help the hall pay for such mundane expenses as window washing, security, electricity and the like.

Although most of the grant goes to meet the maintainance deficit, 20 per cent will finance a program close to Mr. Fisher's heart: a fellowship project designed to give impetus to the careers of young American instrumentalists. "We intend to scour the country for talent," Mr. Fisher said, "but we will not subject the young artists to contests." He added, "I have been totally opposed to competitions, which a worthy runner-up may be 'scarred for life' by losing."

In an interview, Mr. Fisher, a 67-year-old amateur violinist and chamber-music fanatic, explained his reason for choosing Philharmonic Hall as recipient of his high-fidelity millions: "I owe it all to live music and live musicians. They made everything possible for me." He added that his is "a major

Continued on Page 50, Column 4

The New York Times/William E. Sauro

Avery Fisher in his apartment on Park Avenue

SENATE UNIT FINDS VERY LITTLE BASIS FOR 17 WIRETAPS

Committee Backs Kissinger but Assails 'Infringement of Individual Rights'

By BERNARD GWERTZMAN
Special to The New York Times

WASHINGTON, Sept. 20—The Senate Foreign Relations Committee said today that "very little, if any, justification, was presented in most instances" for the White House-sanctioned wiretapping of the phones of 13 officials and four newsmen from 1969 to 1971.

In a formal report to the Senate recommending the confirmation of Henry A. Kissinger as Secretary of State—the vote is set for tomorrow—the committee leveled the harshest official criticism against the wiretapping. President Nixon has defended it as necessary to find the source of leaks of sensitive national security information.

The report repeated that that committee, in examining the wiretapping record, had found no ground to bar Mr. Kissinger as Secretary of State. It added:

"The committee was deeply concerned, however, over the pattern of casual and arbitrary infringement of individual rights which this inquiry brought to light."

Mitchell Gave Approval

Mr. Kissinger had testified before the committee — which voted on Tuesday to approve his nomination — that his role in the wiretapping was to provide the names of people who had access to information that had been leaked to the press.

The actual wiretapping was carried out by the Federal Bureau of Investigation, with the approval of John N. Mitchell, who was then Attorney General.

The committee was permitted to study an F.B.I. report on the wiretaps, but it decided not to make public any of the details of the wiretapping, such as the names of those under surveillance.

These names, however, have appeared in the press, and some of them seem to have had little connection with national security matters.

"Examination of the F.B.I. report on these wiretaps revealed that very little, if any, justification was presented in most instances, and that the Attorney General's review was routine," the report said.

"At the time of the surveillance in question, adequate standards of probable cause were not applied and adequate procedural safeguards with respect to authorizing and termination of the taps were not observed," it said.

The committee, noting that

Continued on Page 8, Column 4

NIXON AIDES AND COX FAIL TO GET ACCORD ON TAPES; TEST IN HIGH COURT SEEN

3 SESSIONS HELD

Letters to Judges Cite 'Sincere Efforts' to Meet Request

By JOHN HERBERS
Special to The New York Times

WASHINGTON, Sept. 20 — President Nixon's lawyers and Archibald Cox, the special prosecutor in the Watergate case, informed the United States Court of Appeals here today that they had failed to reach a compromise on access to Presidential tape recordings bearing on the Watergate crimes.

In similar letters filed with the appeals court for the District of Columbia, both sides said they had met on three occasions this week in an effort

The texts of Wright and Cox letters are on Page 18.

to reach an out-of-court settlement, as the panel of judges had requested, but regretted to report that "these sincere efforts were not fruitful."

This means that the constitutional issue of whether a President must yield records of private conversations with his aides for purposes of criminal prosecution must be decided by the appeals court and is virtually certain to go to the Supreme Court for final settlement.

Nixon Draws Limits

President Nixon has added to the drama by saying, through his spokesmen, that he would obey only a "definitive" Supreme Court decision but would not define what he meant by definitive.

Last week, the seven members of the nine-man court who are hearing the case suggested, in an unusual memorandum, that a constitutional confrontation between the branches of Government might be avoided if the President, his lawyers and Mr. Cox reviewed in private the tapes that the prosecution has been seeking as possible evidence for a grand jury.

Both parties were asked by the court to discuss the idea and report back by today as to whether their meetings had been "fruitful."

The letters filed today said that Mr. Cox and J. Fred Buzhardt, special White House counsel, met on Monday and Tuesday. A final, lengthy meeting was held today and was attended by Charles Alan Wright, special legal consultant to the

Continued on Page 18, Column 5

Any Agnew Replacement May Face Bar on '76 Bid

By JAMES M. NAUGHTON
Special to The New York Times

WASHINGTON, Sept. 20—Democratic leaders of the House of Representatives have reportedly made plans to insist, if Vice President Agnew leaves office before his term expires, that his successor pledge not to seek election as President in 1976.

Authoritative members of Congress said today that the "contingency" plans were discussed at a private meeting yesterday between the House leaders and a group of Democratic freshmen in the office of House Speaker Carl Albert.

"The will of the leadership, as expressed to the freshmen, was to strive for a stand-in Vice President who would be committed to bypass the 1976 election," one participant said today.

The discussion was prompted by reports—vigorously disputed by associates of the Vice President — that Mr. Agnew was considering resigning, and by Democratic concern over the political complications of the method for choosing a midterm Vice President if the choice became necessary.

The 25th Amendment to the Consitution, which took effect in 1967, stipulates that when there is a vacancy in the Vice Presidency the President must nominate a candidate who is subject to confirmation by a majority vote in both houses of Congress.

"We're not going to be a party to picking somebody who is going to run against us three years from now," one of the Democratic officials said.

His concern was underscored today by Robert Strauss, the chairman of the Democratic National Committee. He said that if Mr. Nixon should be required to select a new Vice President he should avoid a "tricky, treacherous situation" by choosing a "nonpresidential" person.

Speculation about Mr. Agnew's possible resignation or impeachment and removal from office, has been a principal topic in the White House and elsewhere because of a Federal grand jury investigation into allegations that Mr.

Continued on Page 20, Column 4

Most Aides to Rockefeller Urge Drive for Presidency

By FRANK LYNN

A majority of Governor Rockefeller's closest advisers are recommending that he not seek a fifth term and instead concentrate all his efforts on a bid for the Republican Presidential nomination in 1976.

The Governor is playing his cards close to the vest. Not one of 10 close advisers would say flatly whether he would run next year, and a reporter who spent an hour in a background discussion with the Governor could not detect even a tentative decision on a fifth term.

Publicly, Mr. Rockefeller has said repeatedly that he is keeping his options open on both the governorship and Presidency, and his aides say that is also his private position.

But his advisers are equally convinced that he is already running for President and that a bid for another term in Albany would merely be a means to that end.

Mr. Rockefeller leaves little doubt about his national aspirations. "I'm interested in serving in whatever way I can," the Governor responded to the now standard question on his Presidential ambitions in Los Angeles a week ago. The fairly candid response was tantamount to a declaration of candidacy at this point, three years before the Presidential election.

The Governor's aides say that he would "grab at" a Vice Presidential appointment now—again as a route to the White House—even though he has in the past dismissed the Vice Presidency as "stand-by equipment."

Mr. Rockefeller, who has carefully cultivated his ties with President Nixon after years of strained relations, has been widely mentioned as a possible Nixon appointee to succeed Vice President Agnew if he is forced to resign.

However, Rockefeller aides believe that John B. Connally, the former Texas Governor and Secretary of the Treasury who recently switched to the Republican party, has the edge on any Vice Presidential ap-

Continued on Page 54, Column 1

Israel Expects a New Bid By U.S. to End Stalemate

Kissinger Drive Seen

By TERENCE SMITH
Special to The New York Times

JERUSALEM, Sept. 20 — Israel expects a renewed American effort to get the Middle East stalemate off dead center later this year.

Although the Israelis harbor mixed feelings about any renewal of political activity that could bring pressure on them, the expected United States move has stimulated sentiment within the top leadership that—at least for the sake of her image abroad — Israel should be prepared to adopt a flexible approach toward any American-sponsored initiative.

From the recent statements of President Nixon about the "priority" he attaches to the Middle East, Government officials here have concluded that the Secretary of State-designate, Henry A. Kissinger, will begin a major new effort to get negotiations started, probably in December. Half-jokingly, officials in the Foreign Ministry are talking about "Kissinger's winter offensive."

A number of Israeli leaders have expressed this view privately in recent days, including two men who frequently differ on political questions: Defense Minister Moshe

Continued on Page 6, Column 3

Arabs Shaping New Unity

By HENRY TANNER
Special to The New York Times

CAIRO, Sept. 20—The pragmatic moderate and conservative Arab leaders who control most of the area between the Nile and the Persian Gulf are fashioning a new solidarity.

Arab unity in the exalted terms of Libya's leader, Col. Muammar el-Qaddafi, remains as elusive as ever, but events of the last few weeks have brought a new sense of excitement in Cairo, Amman, Beirut and other capitals. This movement has fostered a feeling that, for the first time since the 1967 war, events seem favorable to the Arab cause.

Seasoned European diplomats believe that the Arabs have substantially strengthened their bargaining power in the political maneuvering that is expected this fall.

The Middle East debate that will start at the United Nations soon will find Israel and the United States more isolated than ever if some African leaders keep promises made to the Arabs at the recent Algiers conference of nonaligned nations.

In addition the Arabs are girding for what Mohammed

Continued on Page 6, Column 5

INTERVIEWS CLOSE 1 IN 5 RELIEF CASES

State Cuts 8.908 From Rolls in First 2 Months of Plan —City Chided as Lax

By PETER KIHSS

One of every five welfare cases investigated in the state has been closed in the first two months of face-to-face interviews with welfare families, the State Department of Social Services announced yesterday.

The interviews, ordered so that eligibility could be recertified, resulted in the elimination from relief rolls of 8,908 cases involving 30,480 people.

However, State Commissione Abe Lavine said that because New York City had scheduled interviews for only 3.6 per cent of the 130,531 cases the state had required, he would impose a penalty on the city. The penalty, he said, could approach $750,000 for the last two weeks of August.

Commissioner Lavine said he had warned the city that the penalty could climb to $1.5-million a month starting this month and to $9-million a month starting in November if the city continued to ignore state mandates and timetables. The penalty involves the withholding of

Continued on Page 82, Column 2

Officer in Albany Says Fellow Police Joined in Thievery

By RALPH BLUMENTHAL
Special to The New York Times

ALBANY, Sept. 20—An Albany policeman told the State Commission of Investigation today that he had carried out "many" burglaries and larcenies with fellow policemen and said that "to remain in good standing" with his colleagues he had felt compelled to pretend that he was stealing even more than he was.

Then, "my position in the squad improved," he said. "I was more accepted. I wasn't harassed or anything."

The testimony, at a public hearing of the commission, was piped in from an adjoining room to conceal the identity of the policeman.

The policeman became the first active member of the department to testify about police burglaries and other corruption.

Yesterday, a former police-

Continued on Page 54, Column 3

A Supersonic Concorde Lands in Texas

By RICHARD WITKIN
Special to The New York Times

GRAPEVINE, Tex., Sept. 20—In the first visit of a supersonic airliner to the United States, a French-British Concorde flew here today from Caracas, Venezuela, to provide an extra dimension to Saturday's dedication of the world's largest jetport.

A second aim of the trip was to start trying to convince the American public that, as a top British airline official said in midflight, "the plane is not the monster many people think it is."

Carrying 32 officials and newsmen plus a special crew of 10, the Concorde made the 2,559-mile flight in about two hours and a half, a major portion of which was flown at twice the speed of sound. The speed of sound at high altitudes is 660 miles an hour.

The same passengers made the flight from Dallas to Caracas yesterday in a subsonic Boeing 707 of Braniff International. That flight took over four and a half hours. The contrast was exhilarating and difficult to comprehend. It was the first time that the Concorde had been publicly demonstrated over a city-to-city route to passengers who had just made the reverse run in a conventional jet.

The initiative for the Concorde's first trip to North America came some months ago from officials of the new Dallas-Fort Worth Regional Airport. It is about the size of Manhattan, or twice the size of any jetport built before it. Sprawled across the prairie half-way between Dallas and Fort Worth, the facility will, it is hoped, serve as a model for how to make airport life easier for today's often confused, frenetic, and baggage-burdened passengers.

By accepting the idea of coming here on the Concorde's first United States trip, the manufacturers needed have little concern for stirring the passions of airport neighbors with the plane's landing and take-off noises. The jetport is so vast that residences are well beyond high-nose areas.

"We didn't want to disturb

Continued on Page 81, Column 3

NEWS INDEX

Mrs. King Defeats Riggs, 6-4, 6-3, 6-3, Amid a Circus Atmosphere

By NEIL AMDUR
Special to The New York Times

HOUSTON, Sept. 20—Mrs. Billie Jean King struck a proud blow for herself and women around the world with a crushing 6-4, 6-3, 6-3 rout of Bobby Riggs tonight in their $100,000 winner-take-all tennis match at the Astrodome.

In an atmosphere more suited for a circus than a sports event, the 29-year-old Mrs. King ended the bizarre saga of the 55-year-old hustler, who had bolted to national prominence with his blunt putdowns of women's tennis and the role of today's female.

Mrs. King, a five-time Wimbledon champion and the most familiar face in the women's athletic movement, needed only 2 hours 4 minutes to reaffirm her status as one of the gifted and tenacious competitors in sport, female or male.

A crowd of 30,492, some paying as much as $100 a seat, watched the best-three-of-five set struggle, the largest single attendance ever for a tennis match. Millions more viewed the event on national television. The match also was seen in 36 foreign countries via satellite.

Mrs. King squashed Riggs with tools synonymous with men's tennis, the serve and volley. She beat Bobby to the ball, dominated the net and ran him around the baseline to the point of near exhaustion in the third set, when he suffered hand cramps and trailed, 2-4.

Most important, perhaps for women everywhere, she convinced skeptics that a female athlete can survive pressure-filled situations and that men are as susceptible to nerves as women.

It was Riggs, for example, who only yesterday had claimed "I have no nerves," who double-faulted at 4-5, 30-40 to decide the first set.

And it was another Riggs double-fault, at deuce in the ninth game of the final set, that gave Mrs. King her third match point. An uproar of cheers followed when Riggs drove a high backhand volley into the net.

Later, away from the tumult and the shouting,

Continued on Page 31, Column 5

Associated Press

Mrs. Billie Jean King making a return to Bobby Riggs in the Astrodome

Mrs. King Trounces Mr. Riggs

Continued From Page 1, Col. 5

Mrs. King admitted that she, too, had suffered cramps in her leg in the sixth game of the final set.

"It was a combination of nerves and just all that running," she said. "When I felt the first twinge, I said, 'Oh God, not now—not this close.' I was really worried."

Riggs did not leave the match empty-handed. Like Mrs. King, he was guaranteed a minimum of $75,000 for ancillary rights to the promotion. His other endorsements and contracts should swell his take to over $300,000.

Mrs. King, the biggest money-winner in the history of women's athletics and the foremost spokesman for equality in sport, is certain to reap even greater financial returns from tonight's victory. But as she said yesterday, "pride matters a lot more than money."

Riggs, who had hoped to use another triumph as a springboard to greater riches, praised Mrs. King.

"She was too good," said the 1939 Wimbledon singles champion. "She played too well. She was playing well within herself, and I couldn't get the most out of my game. It was over too quickly."

In the first set alone, in what represented an incredible testimony to her quality of play, Mrs. King won 26 of her 34 points with outright winners, balls which Riggs never touched with his racquet.

After having lost her serve to open the second set, she immediately broke back at 30 with the shot she relishes, the running backhand crosscourt.

As he pressed to put more pace on his serve and first volley, Riggs's game gradually deteriorated. He found himself being passed on return of serve, chasing lobs that HE was supposed to be stroking, and stretching in vain for Billie Jean's assortment of passing shots and deadly volleys.

At the finish, Mrs. King's statistics spoke for themselves: 70 of the 109 points she won, or over 64 per cent, were outright winners. Such perfection might compare favorably with a quarterback who completes 20 of 24 passes for six touchdowns.

Even before the first ball was struck, it became even more evident that this was to be no ordinary tennis event.

Instead of the traditional walk onto to the court, the players entered the stadium with the flourish of something out of a Cecil B. DeMille movie.

Mrs. King came first on a Cleopatra-style gold litter that was held aloft by four muscular track-and-field athletes from nearby Rice University and an Astrodome employe. One of the togo-clad carriers was Dave Roberts, one of the world's finest pole vaulters.

Riggs was transported into the stadium in a gold-wheeled rickshaw pulled by six professional models in tight red and gold outfits who had been dubbed "Bobby's Bosom Buddies" during his stay here. It was apparent why.

A band, seated behind what would have been home plate for baseball, blared brassy march music while brightly colored costumed characters from Astroworld frolicked for the large crowd.

Large banners, seldom displayed at staid country clubs where tennis languished as a sport for the classes for much of this century, were sprinkled throughout the stadium.

The circus atmosphere contrasted sharply not only with conventional tennis events but with the challenge match between Riggs and Mrs. Margaret Court last Mother's Day.

That match, which Riggs won in a 6-2, 6-1 rout, was held at a wilderness site in Ramona, Calif., before 3,000 fans sitting in make-shift seats.

Tonight's courtside crowd sat in $100 seats sipping champagne from several improvised bars. Some spectators arrived in suits or evening dresses.

Mrs. King even went one-up on Riggs at the courtside introductions. After Bobby had presented Billie Jean with a large candy sucker (he had given Mrs. Court a bouquet of roses before their match), Mrs. King gave her gift—a brown baby pig.

Wide World Photos

Bobby Riggs races in to make a return of a shot by Billie Jean King in their $100,000 winner-take-all match.

The New York Times

Billie Jean King

New Post for Mulzoff

CHERRY HILL, N. J., Sept. 20 (AP)—Frank Mulzoff, former basketball coach at St. John's University, was named today as coach of the new Cherry Hill Rookies of the Eastern Basketball Association. Rich Iannarella, Cherry Hill's general manager, said Mulzoff, who coached St. John's from 1970 to this year, signed a one-year contract.

Rangers Send Down 22

KITCHENER, Ont., Sept. 20 (AP)—The New York Rangers assigned today 22 players, including goalie Peter McDuffe and forwards Rick Middletown and Al Blanchard, to their Providence club of the American Hockey League.

Mrs. King Calls Victory 'Culmination' of Career

By GRACE LICHTENSTEIN
Special to The New York Times

HOUSTON, Sept. 20—She flung her racquet high toward the girded roof of the Astrodome and then collapsed, tears in her eyes, in her husband's arms. Mrs. Billie Jean King had just beaten the lady-killer of women's tennis and all of a sudden, she was a champion, a woman and a little girl at the same time.

As Larry, her husband, lifted her onto a table at courtside, Mrs. King held the $100,000 winner's trophy high in the air, blowing kisses to the crowd. She stuck her tongue at Dennis van de Meer, her coach. She held up a fist to some friends.

For Billie Jean, it was in her own words, "the culmination of 19 years of tennis." But as she walked into the Houston Astros' dressing room for the postmatch press conference, she was still so keyed up she insisted on taking her blue suede sneakers off and walking around barefooted on the raised platform for a moment to calm herself.

Referring to her opponent playfully as "Roberta," Billie Jean revealed that she had gotten careful advice from Mrs. Margaret Court, the champion who had lost so badly to Riggs last May, and who, ever since, had implied that she and Mrs. King were not on the best of terms.

"Margaret told me that you really can't roll over his backhand, that you could only pass him with a flat shot or an undercut on his backhand," she said.

Asked whether the carnival atmosphere bothered her, Mrs. King gave an emphatic no. "I've always said I like bands, I like cheers," she replied. And indeed, throughout the two hours, this was an event with more of the spirit of a Super Bowl game than a lawn tennis match.

The Billie Jean King fans screamed "Atta Boy, Billie!" The Bobby Riggs fans yelled "Kill, Kill!" Mrs. King's 55-year-old father, Bill Moffitt, leaped out of his seat at the Astrodome last night screaming "Go, baby go!" at every King point. George Foreman, the heavyweight champion, did the same.

When Mrs. King won the first set, Stella Lachowicz, the public relations chief for the Virginia Slims women's tennis circuit, trotted around courtside handing out printed invitations to "The Bobby Riggs Bridge Jump." She was reminding spectators that Riggs had promised to jump off a California bridge if he lost to her.

Mrs. King's colleagues on the Slims circuit, who were squatting together in a corner of the court snapping pictures and chewing Sugar Daddies handed out by Riggs supporters, were nearly beside themselves with glee by the time Billie Jean had taken the second set. "Bye, Bye Bobbie," they yelled, while waving green placards.

"Oh, Bobby, I can't wait to spend your $100,000," shouted 16-year-old Kathy Kuykendall, a frequent practice partner of Mrs. King.

Perhaps the calmest person in the house throughout the match was a 25-year-old pale, willowy blonde, a former hairdresser from Beverly Hills, Calif. She sat on the sidelines in a flowered halter dress next to Billie Jean, when the player rested.

She was Marilyn Barnett, Mrs. King's secretary, who earlier in the day had said that she had "good vibrations." And so, for the big event, she wore a dress that was brown and blue. "In yoga," she said in explanation, "brown stands for money and blue stands for spirit."

"All the News That's Fit to Print"

The New York Times

LATE CITY EDITION

Weather: Sunny, mild today; fair tonight. Fair, seasonable tomorrow. Temp. range: today 55-79. Monday 55-74. Additional details on Page 92.

VOL. CXXIII ... No. 42,262 — NEW YORK, TUESDAY, OCTOBER 9, 1973 — 15 CENTS

ISRAEL REPORTS 2-FRONT DRIVE BACK TO OLD CEASE-FIRE LINES; EGYPTIANS CLAIM GAIN IN SINAI

United Press International

Egyptian soldiers atop a tank near the eastern end of one of the bridges thrown across the Suez Canal on Saturday, the first day of fighting between Arab and Israeli forces. Israel said yesterday all bridges were cut.

FIGHTING IS BITTER

Resistance by Arabs Heavier Than Many Israelis Expected

By TERENCE SMITH

Special to The New York Times

TEL AVIV, Tuesday, Oct. 9—Reinforced Israeli units have opened major counterattacks on two broad fronts, throwing the Syrian and Egyptian Armies back to the cease-fire lines in heavy fighting, a military spokesman said last night.

The counteroffensive reportedly got under way at dawn and was preceded by heavy

Excerpts from Israeli news conference. Page 17.

Israeli air attacks against military airfields, missile sites and other targets deep inside Egypt and Syria. By midday, an Israeli military spokesman reported that a total of 90 Egyptian and Syrian aircraft had been downed, including about a dozen troop-carrying helicopters.

Although the Israelis apparently succeeded in largely reversing the combined Arab advances by nightfall, their counterattack was clearly encountering heavier resistance than many Israeli commanders had expected.

Syrian Strength in Heights

The fighting was especially bitter, senior commanders said, on the Golan heights, where the Syrians had amassed a force of some 800 tanks and driven three deep wedges into Israeli-held territory.

One military source said that while the fighting on the Egyptian front might be largely over in another day or so, heavier resistance was expected in the Golan heights.

Lieut. Gen. David Elazar, the Israeli Chief of Staff, told newsmen this evening that Israel was determined to "break and destroy" the Syrian and Egyptian forces.

"We have begun the destruction of the Egyptian Army," General Elazar said at a news conference.

Asked if the Israelis would carry their offensive beyond the cease-fire lines established in 1967, the general replied forcefully that "I have to remind you that the cease-fire lines are not marked in the terrain." He said: "We are attacking the enemy wherever it is necessary. And we shall

Continued on Page 17, Column

Agnew's Charge on Leaks Denied by Justice Agency

Court Memo Calls His Stand 'Frivolous' and Scores Newsmen's Subpoenas —Reporters Rebuffed on Delay

By ANTHONY RIPLEY

Special to The New York Times

WASHINGTON, Oct. 8—The Justice Department branded as "frivolous" today Vice President Agnew's allegation that it had engaged in a campaign of news leaks directed against him and said that subpoenas to newsmen to prove there was a campaign were merely "fishing expeditions."

In a memorandum delivered to United States District Judge Walter E. Hoffman, the department declared its opposition to Mr. Agnew's efforts to call off the Baltimore grand jury that is looking into possible criminality on his part. Nevertheless, the department said it did not intend to fight the subpoenas its officers had received.

At the same time, lawyers for 11 reporters and news organizations called the subpoenas "virtually unprecedented" in their sweep and indicated today they would attempt to have the court throw them out.

They filed a motion asking for a week's delay in responding to the subpoenas, from Thursday to Oct. 18, but the request was summarily rejected by Judge Hoffman.

Several of the 10 lawyers involved said that they did not know of any ground on which the motion was rejected and that they were considering a possible appeal of the judge's action.

The rejected motion was filed in Federal District Court in Baltimore where the grand jury has been sitting since January investigating scandals in suburban Baltimore County and in the state of Maryland. Mr. Agnew served as elected Executive of the county from 1962 to 1966 and as Maryland's Governor from 1966 to 1968.

The Vice President was notified by letter Aug. 1 that he was under investigation for possible bribery, extortion and tax fraud. He has denied the charges.

The newsmen argued that one of the key issues at stake was the "right and duty of the press to alert the voters and their representatives to activities which may constitute grounds for impeachment."

Mr. Agnew's lawyers have argued that he cannot be indicted by the grand jury but must be removed from office

Continued on Page 33, Column 1

METS WIN, 9 TO 2, AS FIGHT ERUPTS; LEAD PLAYOFF, 2-1

Fans Hurl Debris, Forcing Reds to Evacuate Field —Staub Hits 2 Homers

By JOSEPH DURSO

Fists, cups, beer cans, assorted debris and even whisky bottles filled the clamorous afternoon air at Shea Stadium yesterday as the Mets and their public fought the Cincinnati Reds in one of baseball's memorably riotous games.

The game was won by the Mets, 9-2, which brought them within one victory of completing a five-week march from last place to the National League pennant. But they had to fight their way to that milestone before 53,967 roaring, cheering and booing fans in a series of skirmishes and two fistfights.

Pete Rose of the Reds and Bud Harrelson of the Mets fought the main event after Rose had barreled into second base trying to break up a double play in the fifth inning. Pedro Borbon of the Reds and Buzz Capra threw punches while 50 players rolled and milled around.

Warned of Forfeit

The fans pelted Rose with flying objects, the Reds evacuated the field and New York was warned that it would forfeit the game unless order was restored.

Then, while Mayor Lindsay and the rest of the crowd watched in amazement, Yogi Berra led a peace delegation across the outfield lawn to quiet the fans—Tom Seaver, Cleon Jones, Rusty Staub and 42-year-old Willie Mays.

They stood in the no man's land in left field, where Rose had just ducked a whisky bottle and where the Cincinnati outfielder had pegged junk back at the box-seat customers.

With his arms outstretched, Mays made his first appearance since announcing his retirement two weeks ago, and appealed with feeling for calm. Then the mission marched back to the dugout 100 yards away, nine attendants cleared the debris and the game continued.

He Rips a Cap

Before it was over, though, the president of the National League left his box to intervene; the umpires suggested Rose be switched to center field; Borbon found that he somehow was wearing a Met cap, bit it and ripped it in half, and the crowd stood and roared for the embattled home team.

"I'll be honest, I was trying to knock him into left field," the 200-pound Rose said later. "I play to win. In 1970, all I did was try to score a run in the All-Star game by running through the catcher, and I've been criticized for three years."

The 146-pound Harrelson said: "They've been coming in

Continued on Page 55, Column 6

Subway Maintenance Is Better Than It Was

By VICTOR K. McELHENY

The collapse of a concrete tunnel-ceiling in which one subway passenger was killed and 1,000 other Flushing-line riders were forced to wait 80 minutes for rescue in 115-degree heat last Aug. 28 immediately revived questions about the safety and efficiency of New York City's subways.

The questions had reached a peak of intensity in 1970, when train accidents killed New York subway passengers for the first time since 1938.

An outside review board

This is the second in a series of reports on the New York City subways.

named amid the 1970 outcry reported that "there has been a deterioration in the performance record of the system as a whole in the five years 1965 to 1969" and proposed a sharply increased emphasis on subway-car maintenance.

Partly in response to the board's recommendations, subway-car maintenance spending has doubled in the last five years, the maintenance staff has increased about 50 per cent, regular overhaul schedules have been started for all cars, motors and air compressors, and a large inventory of spare parts has been built up, according to Transit Authority officials interviewed during a New York Times survey of subway performance.

Observers of the subways interviewed by The New York Times agreed that the system is inherently very safe and has been somewhat better maintained in the last few years than previously.

According to them, the low rates of accidents and injuries, with only a handful of fatalities in the last 45 years, are achieved by special automatic controls—such as trip arms to operate a trains's brakes from outside if the train runs a red light—and by the diligence of the subway staff.

Joe Asher, a New York-based transit writer who has visited most of the world's subway systems, said of the New York system: "It's very safe. That's a well-known fact."

Of the maintenance, Mr. Asher said, "I think it's better, but not hugely better. A lot

Continued on Page 92, Column 1

Secretariat Scores

Secretariat set another Belmont Park record yesterday in winning the $113,600 Man o' War Stakes by five lengths in 2:25 4/5. Details, Page 55.

U.S., in U.N., Urges A Mideast Pullback To Cease-Fire Line

By ROBERT ALDEN

Special to The New York Times

UNITED NATIONS, N. Y., Oct. 8—The United States asked the Security Council tonight to bring an end to hostilities in the Middle East and to restore the cease-fire line that existed before the new war.

Speaking at a special session that the United States had requested, John A. Scali, the American delegate, said that the United States hoped that the Council would act in such a way that "the present tragedy can be made a new beginning rather than simply another lost opportunity."

Preposterous, China Says

Huang Hua, the representative of China, one of five Council members with veto power, said that it was "preposterous" for the United States to propose that Egypt and Syria withdraw to the cease-fire lines of 1967. He said it was "perfectly just" for the Arab countries to "rise in resistance to the invading enemies of their own sacred territories."

Yakov A. Malik of the Soviet Union criticized the Council for meeting at all and expressed his support for Egypt and Syria. However, Sir Donald Maitland of Britain called for an end to the fighting, as did Mr. Scali.

The Council adjourned without any decision until tomorrow.

Mr. Scali told the Council that United Nations reports appeared to indicate that Syrian

Continued on Page 16, Column 2

U.S. AND SOVIET DISCUSS MIDEAST

White House Says Nixon and Brezhnev Conferred on Limiting the Conflict

By BERNARD GWERTZMAN

Special to The New York Times

WASHINGTON, Oct. 8—Administration officials said today that the Soviet Union had indicated that it shared the American desire to limit the conflict in the Middle East.

Although Washington still regarded the fighting as serious, officials expressed general satisfaction that a consensus seemed to have developed not to let the conflict seriously damage relations between Moscow and Washington.

This view was made known after the disclosure by the White House this morning that President Nixon and Leonid I. Brezhnev, the Soviet Communist party leader, had exchanged private messages last night through regular diplomatic channels.

Ronald L. Ziegler, the White House press secretary, said the emergency hot line between Moscow and Washington, which was used during the 1967 war, was not used by Mr. Nixon and Mr. Brezhnev.

The Senate, meanwhile, approved a resolution calling for a cease-fire and a return of Arab and Israeli forces to the positions they occupied before the outbreak of hostilities Saturday. [Details on Page 18.]

Officials refused to provide

Continued on Page 17, Column 1

Cairo Says It Has Raided Oil Fields Held by Israel

By HENRY TANNER

Special to The New York Times

CAIRO, Tuesday, Oct. 9—The Egyptian command announced last night that Egyptian troops had raided the Israeli-occupied Egyptian oilfields at Balayim, on the Gulf of Suez, and set large fires.

The raid was personally ordered by President Anwar el-Sadat, the command said.

At the same time, the command announced that Israeli planes had strafed Port Said, on the Mediterranean, destroying houses and some installations.

[In Israel, the military said that the air force had struck surface-to-air missile sites and other targets around Port Said.]

Under Israeli occupation the production of Sinai oil has been six million tons of crude a year, producing a large part of Israel's domestic consumption.

In a communiqué, the command said that tanks and infantry reinforcements were crossing to the eastern bank of the Suez Canal for the third consecutive day.

The command reported yesterday afternoon that its forces were holding the entire length of the 100-mile canal from Port Fuad, at the northern end, to a point south of Suez city, in the south, and that Israeli counterattacks Sunday and yesterday had been repulsed.

The command reported, over the Cairo radio as usual, that 24 Israeli Phantom and Skyhawk jets were shot down and 36 Israeli tanks were destroyed yesterday on the Egyptian front, along with an unspecified number of helicopters and vehicles. Several Israeli pilots and 45 soldiers were taken prisoner, the command said.

It acknowledged 10 Egyptian planes lost.

Against the background of reports of military success in what is called here the "new war," Egyptian officials have stated for the first time that the goal of the military operation is the liberation of all the Egyptian territory occupied by Israel in the June, 1967, war.

Ashraf Ghorbal, an adviser to President Sadat, said on Cairo television that all that Egypt wanted was recovery of occupied territory in the Sinai Peninsula and recognition of the basic rights of the Palestinians.

Mr. Ghorbal's purpose, diplomats here felt, was to make it clear that Egypt had no ag-

Continued on Page 16, Column 2

Israelis Back From Golan Tell of 2-Day Tank Duel

This dispatch was written by Sol Stern, an American freelance writer who is in Israel for research on a book.

Special to The New York Times

TIBERIAS, Israel, Oct. 8—The first two days of fighting in the Golan heights consisted of seesaw tank battles with small isolated Israeli units often surrounded by great concentrations of Syrian armor.

This was the description of the fighting given by Israeli soldiers coming out of the battle zones today.

Although Israeli Army authorities have not yet allowed foreign reporters into the Golan heights to view the battle, Israeli soldiers who were at the front talked freely about their experience.

A young infantry sergeant, his face covered with dust, his eyes glazed from three nights without sleep, was interviewed at Ein Gev on the eastern shore of the Sea of Galilee, where he was resting after 40 hours of almost continuous battle.

His unit of regular army soldiers had been close to the frontier when the Syrians attacked on Saturday after-

Continued on Page 19, Column 1

NEWS INDEX

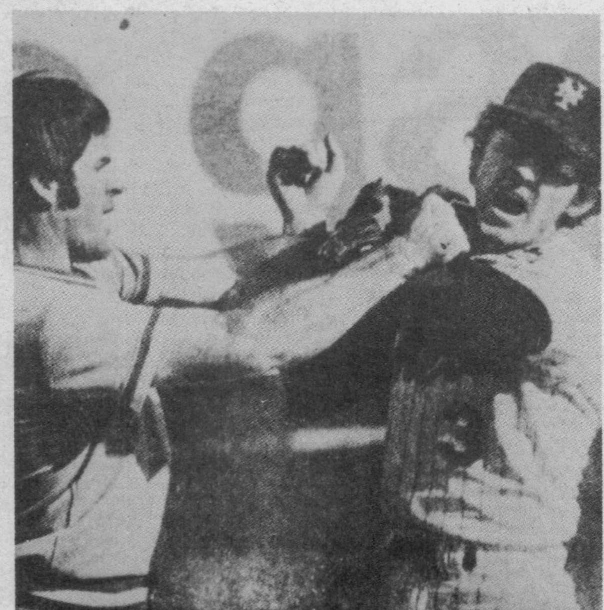

Associated Press

Pete Rose of the Reds, left, and Bud Harrelson of the Mets in a fracas at second base following a double play in the top of the fifth inning at Shea Stadium.

United Press International

Israeli Defense Minister Moshe Dayan confers in the Sinai with generals. Seated with him are Maj. Gen. Rehavam Zeevi, left, and Maj. Gen. Shmuel Gonen, right.

Mets Beat Reds, Fight Erupts; Lead Playoff, 2-1

Continued From Page 1, Col. 3

hard all year. I thought he came in hard and I didn't like it. I said something, he turned and asked, 'What?' and it suddenly became a shoving match."

Said Sparky Anderson, manager of the Reds: "It's awful dangerous to throw a whisky bottle at a player. I can't believe that in America today a man would do that. Pete came in and told me, 'Spark, they just threw a whisky bottle out,' and I said, 'That's enough for today.' Then an umpire said we better get this straightened out, and I replied, 'Let me know when you do.'"

Charles (Chub) Feeney, president of the league, said: "I went into the dugout and asked Yogi and Willie Mays to come out and talk to the fans. They'll recognize Willie, but if I went out there, they'd probably throw things at me."

For Berra, whose team stood last in the Eastern Division on Aug. 30, the immediate issue was urgent: quiet the crowd or forfeit a 9-2 lead in the fifth inning.

To Johnny Bench, the Cincinnati catcher, the issue was urgent, too — the Reds were dropping their second game in a row to the underdog Mets and were in danger of dropping the playoff for the pennant in one more afternoon.

"Here we are," he said in the stunned locker room. "It was a small battle, but we're losing the war."

They began losing the war Sunday in Cincinnati, when the Mets bounced back from a 2-1 defeat in the opening game Saturday and scored a 5-0 victory to square the series.

Then, in the first inning yesterday, Staub drove Ross Grimsley's 2-and-2 pitch over the right-field fence with two down and the war started slipping away from the Reds again.

This was the Mets' first appearance in postseason play at Shea Stadium since Oct. 16, 1969, when they dramatically won the World Series from the Baltimore Orioles. Since then, they had spent three seasons in third place and most of this summer in last place.

Their pitcher yesterday was Jerry Koosman, who also pitched that October game four years ago. This time the left-hander from the Minnesota farm country got plenty of early support before the fighting broke out.

The Mets batted around in the second inning on four hits and two walks, and cashed five more runs.

They opened with a walk to Jerry Grote and a single to right by Don Hahn, one of the hottest October bats. Harrelson flied out, but Koosman curled a bunt toward the mound and, when Grimsley slipped and fell on the grass, everybody was safe with the bases loaded.

Wayne Garrett followed with a fly to center for one run and Felix Millan singled to right for another. Then Anderson rescued Grimsley and called for his slender left-handed relief pitcher Tom Hall, who had faced seven batters in two days and got only one out.

Hall threw one strike to Staub before lightning struck again. Staub, who played with two damaged hands this season, pulled a high home

Mets' Bud Harrelson completes double play in fifth inning as Reds' Pete Rose slides into bag. As Rose got up . . .

Photographs for The New York Times by BARTON SILVERMAN

. . . and Harrelson followed through, they collided and . . .

Mets' Box Score

CINCINNATI (N.)	ab	r	h	bi
Rose, lf	4	0	2	0
Morgan, 2b	4	0	1	1
Perez, 1b	4	0	0	0
Bench, c	4	0	1	0
Kosco, rf	4	0	0	0
Armbr'ster, cf	4	0	1	0
Menke, 3b	4	1	1	1
Chaney, ss	3	0	0	0
Gagliano, ph	1	0	0	0
Grimsley, p	0	0	0	0
Hall, p	0	0	0	0
Stahl, ph	1	1	1	0
Tomlin, p	0	0	0	0
Nelson, p	1	0	0	0
King, ph	1	0	1	0
Borbon, p	0	0	0	0
Total	35	2	8	2

METS (N.)	ab	r	h	bi
Garrett, 3b	4	0	0	1
Millan, 2b	3	2	1	1
Staub, rf	5	2	2	4
Jones, lf	3	1	2	0
Milner, 1b	4	0	1	1
Grote, c	3	2	1	0
Hahn, cf	4	1	2	0
Harrelson, ss	4	0	0	0
Koosman, p	4	1	2	1
Total	34	9	11	8

Cincinnati . . . . . 002 000 000—2
Mets . . . . . 151 200 00x—9

E—Kosco, Garrett. DP—Mets 1. LOB—Cincinnati 6, Mets 6. 2B—Jones, Bench. HRs—Staub 2, (3), Menke (1). SF—Garrett.

	IP.	H.	R.	ER.	BB.	SO
Grimsley (L, 0-1)	1⅔	5	5	5	1	2
Hall	⅓	1	1	1	1	1
Tomlin	1⅔	5	3	3	1	1
Nelson	2⅓	0	0	0	1	0
Borbon	2	0	0	0	0	2
Koosman (W, 1-0)	9	8	2	2	0	9

T—2:48. A—53,967.

run off the facing of the loge seats down the right-field line, his second in two innings and third in two days, and three more runs crossed.

Half an inning later, the Reds finally got stirring when Denis Menke hit a home run into the left-field bull pen. Then Larry Stahl pinch-hit a single, Rose added a single to left and Joe Morgan singled to right, making it 6-2.

But the Mets were high as kites for this one, and they retaliated with another run in the bottom of the third and two more in the fourth.

They made it 7-2 in the third on singles by Grote and Koosman, then completed the job in the fourth on a walk, a double by Jones, an outfield error and singles by John Milner and Hahn.

Then the teams were in the fifth and, with one down, the irrepressible Rose singled through the middle for his second hit. Morgan, who had been hitless the first two games, bounced one wide of first, where Milner fielded the ball and started a photo-finish double play by way of Harrelson at second.

That was when Rose slid into the bag, coming up hands-high as Harrelson fired back to Milner for the second out.

By the time order had finally been restored, most of the fight seemed to have been drained out of the teams. The Reds made only two hits off Koosman over the last four innings and the Mets made none off the fourth and fifth Cincinnati pitchers.

Nobody was thrown out of the game by the officials, and the crowd kept a noisy sort of order the rest of the afternoon. The police, though, packed the left-field foul line and left-field grandstand porch to prevent new outbreaks. And when the Reds left the stadium by chartered bus, they had a police escort for their trip back to Manhattan while several hundred fans booed and shouted.

The melee on the field was wilder than last year's in Oakland, when Bert Campaneris of the A's threw a bat at Lerrin Lagrow of Detroit in the American League playoff. And it resembled, in some tempestuous ways, the garbage-throwing blast aimed at Joe Medwick of the St. Louis Cardinals in the 1934 World Series.

The playoff continues at 2 o'clock this afternoon, with Fred Norman pitching for Cincinnati and George Stone for New York. Both sides said they would try to behave better in their fight for the pennant.

. . . squared off. Harrelson's back is to the camera.

Associated Press

Rose tossing back some of the debris that landed near him.

Photographs for The New York Times by ROBERT WALKER

Rose, the larger man, gained the upper hand before both sprawled on the grass and the dugouts emptied.

Feeney's Peace Party Calms Left-Field Fans

By RED SMITH

It's a little late in the year for outdoor fights, but they had a lovely day for it at Shea Stadium. The National League's pennant playoff had been so orderly it could have been held in the aisle of a cathedral—no errors, no difficult plays, no arguments and hardly any hitting or scoring.

"Big deal," a man said to Yogi Berra yesterday. "You've creamed 'em with 10 hits in 18 innings."

"They got eight," said the manager of the Mets, "they" being the Cincinnati Reds.

Then it was the fifth inning of the third game, and New York's Bud Harrelson, 146 pounds, and Cincinnati's Pete Rose, 200, were clutching each other's eyeballs and rolling in the dirt near second base.

As belligerents raced out of dugouts and bull pens, all on fisticuffs bent, a hero cop rushed into the breach. He leaped from his seat behind a television cameraman and assumed a defensive crouch in front of Bowie Kuhn, the commissioner of all baseball. Not until an uneasy peace had been effected was the high priest left unguarded.

The cease fire was only temporary. When Rose returned to his post in left field, a whisky bottle whizzed past his head and a beer can struck Gary Nolan in the bull pen nearby. Up leaped the minion of the law once more and again the commissioner had a bodyguard.

When, at long last, final peace terms were signed and casualty lists compiled, Harrelson had a scratch over an eye, and the Mets' Buzz Capra a bruise where Cincinnati's Pedro Borbon had slugged him, but not a hair in Bowie's coiffure was out of place.

Also unmarked was Larry Stahl, the Reds' spare outfielder who used to be a Met. Held in the fell clutch of divided loyalty, he had dawdled on the bench until the last blow was missed.

Inevitably, historians compared the affair with the untidy scenes that helped make the seventh game of the 1934 World Series memorable. With Dizzy Dean and the St. Louis Cardinals holding a lead of 11-0, the Cardinal outfielder, Joe Medwick, slid hard into the Detroit third baseman, Marv Owen, who let fly fistful of knuckles.

Cargo of Obsolete Eggs

It was the seventh inning, and when Medwick returned to left field the Detroit crowd unloaded such a cargo of obsolete eggs and melancholy vegetation that Kenesaw Mountain Landis, the Bowie Kuhn of his day, ordered Medwick removed so the series could be completed.

When the bottle landed near Rose yesterday and Sparky Anderson pulled his troops off the field, Chub Feeney, the president of the National League, took even more Solomonic measures than Landis. Bareheaded and unguarded, he walked onto the field and appointed a commission to negotiate a peace.

Although the owners in his league have stubbornly refused to adopt the designated-hitter rule, he chose Willie Mays as designated peacemaker and asked Berra to serve as a Henry Kissinger in knickers. Tom Seaver was an obvious choice as secretary-general. Cleon Jones joined up because he is the resident leftfielder and it was in his territory the garbage was falling. Rusty Staub, hero-of-the-day on the strength of two home runs in his first two times at bat, completed the mission.

"We'd been talking about Willie and Yogi going out there," Jones said later, because we figured if the fans saw Willie they'd quiet down. Then Chub came along and said Willie was a good choice

"They were cheering when we walked out. They hadn't seen Willie in quite a while and they were happy to see him."

Arthur Daley

Fight and Frolic

For most of the time it had been a fun afternoon. The merry villagers jammed Shea Stadium to the gunwales and chortled in delight as their beloved Mets humiliated the formidable Cincinnati Reds in the third game of their playoff series. They enjoyed it so much that they pounded their palms and screamed like the true Metsomaniacs they are as their heroes kept piling up the hits and the runs.

Sports of The Times

But suddenly this afternoon of sheer bliss turned ugly. That eternal hustler, Pete Rose, let his frustrations warp his judgment. Out on a force play at second base in the fifth inning with the Reds seven runs behind, Pete angrily pushed little Bud Harrelson to trigger a free-for-all of sprawling immensity. Players spilled out of dugouts and bull pens to join in the action.

There were private fights as well as impersonal wild-swinging melees. The area at second base was populated by fighters, peace-makers and players who hoped no one would mistake them for other than what they were, innocent bystanders. Somehow or other they sorted themselves out and eventually dispersed.

But the populace remained inflamed even after the Reds took to the field. Because the 200-pound Rose had assaulted one of their pets, the 146-pound Harrelson, the multitude flung imprecations at the fiery Pete and then they began to fling garbage. He threw back beer cans at them; attendants came out to tidy up the lawn, and Sparky Anderson, the manager, ordered his troops off the field until the unruly multitude became more ruly.

Chub Feeney, president of the National League, conferred with the umpires and finally a peace committee was dispatched to calm the natives. In it were Yogi Berra, Willie Mays, Rusty Staub (bat in hand), Cleon Jones and Tom Seaver. The United Nations should have much efficient committees. The crowd subsided in sullen silence.

Everything had been so festive up to that point. The fanatics who root so unrestrainedly for the Mets were finally given their first glimpse once again of their demigods in the flesh. They had seen them on the tube over the weekend in Cincinnati and were almost satisfied. They had seen Seaver pitch magnificently but lose and they had seen Jon Matlack spin off a gaudy two-hitter and win. Now they had the enemy on their own turf. Maybe the coup de grace could be delivered within the friendly confines of Shea Stadium to send the amazing Mets into an unexpected berth in the World Series.

With Jerry Koosman, another of those superior Met pitchers, about to pitch, the crowd bubbled with anticipation, gay and happy on a glorious afternoon. Even the Reds seemed to sense that crowd reaction could be an extra spur, an advantage to a hopped-up ball club.

Johnny Bench, a merry jape, was babbling away before the game with the mischief shining from his eyes.

Sparky gave us a pep talk," he said, tongue in cheek. He said: 'The way you guys are going it won't be long now. This is my way of saving good-by fellows.' Don't believe it, though. I made it all up."

But it can be a lot later than the Cincinnati optimists originally believed. The Mets need only one more victory to wrap up the playoffs. If they can't do it with George Stone pitching today, they should do it with the awesome Seaver tomorrow. The Reds, once considered the superior club, face extinction.

Seaver had lost a heartbreaker on Saturday through two late-inning homers. Matlack had won a spine-tingler on Sunday with the pressure not easing on him until the very end. Koosman had a laugher.

Rusty Staub crashed a homer in the first inning and five more Met runs came tumbling in in the second. Hence Koosman was able to relax and enjoy such munificence That also went for the crowd. Kooz bore down on those baffled Red batters only as hard as was necessary—but no more. Half of the hits he yielded, four, came in the one inning when the Reds got their two runs, but he struck out nine and was in command.

He was making it a fun afternoon until Rose became a thorny problem for Harrelson and others in the fifth. It certainly brought a new element into the insanities that have distinguished Shea Stadium since it was created.

The New York Times/Larry Morris

Sparky Anderson, center, Reds' manager, leading Pete Rose, right, and other players off the field in the bottom of the fifth inning following disturbance in left field.

When Bottle Flew From Shea Stands, Rose, Anderson, Other Reds Saw Red

By MURRAY CHASS

Pete Rose and his manager, Sparky Anderson, couldn't agree if the bottle was Jack Daniel or Johnnie Walker, but whatever the label said, the bottle created a fuss at Shea Stadium yesterday that was cooled only after a five-man Mets' peace delegation visited the battle zone.

The empty whisky bottle, heaved from the left field stands not long after Rose and Bud Harrelson triggered a fight between the Mets and the Reds, sent Rose from the field and prompted Anderson to take his entire team into the safety of the clubhouse for nearly 20 minutes.

"It zoomed right past my head," said Rose, the Reds' gutty left fielder. "I told Ed [Umpire Ed Sudol] I didn't mind the booing and some of the other things like the cups and the programs, but when the whisky bottles start coming, I don't like that. I want to play baseball tomorrow. I don't want my eye put out with a whisky bottle."

The bottle marked the culmination of the deluge of debris, from programs to apples and cans that zealous Met fans tossed on the field in Rose's area. Gary Nolan, a Cincinnati relief pitcher stationed in the bull pen, was struck by a beer can but wasn't hurt.

The whisky bottle, Jack or Johnnie, descended from the stands with Felix Millan at bat and two out in the bottom of he fifth inning. Rose's fight with Harrelson occurred in the top half of the inning.

After the bottle whizzed past his head, Rose called time and started walking in toward the dugout. Anderson, whose snow-white hair belies his 39 years of age, walked out to meet him.

"Spark, they just threw a whisky bottle out," Rose said.

"That's enough for us today," the manager replied. "Let's go."

"Well get this straightened out," Chris Pelekoudas, an umpire, told Anderson.

"Let me know when you do," Anderson replied and walked off, his players trailing him.

Charles (Chub) Feeney, the National League president, immediately got out of his box seat next to the Met dugout, walked onto the field and conferred with the six-man umpiring crew.

They decided the best idea would be to have some of the Mets go out to the embattled area and talk to the fans. Manager Yogi Berra and Willie Mays led the delegation which also included Tom Seaver, Cleon Jones and Rusty Staub.

Simpson Breaks Mark as Bills Rout Jets, 34 to 14

O.J. Gains 200 Yards for Total 2,003—Ewbank Says Good-by

By MURRAY CHASS

On a day that combined the happiest moments of O. J. Simpson's career and the most emotional of Weeb Ewbank's, the Buffalo Bills defeated the Jets yesterday, 34-14, at Shea Stadium.

Simpson was happy because he had shattered Jim Brown's rushing record and become the first runner in the National Football League to gain over 2,000 yards in a season. Ewbank was emotional because he retired after 20 years of coaching pro football.

As the outcome indicated, the emotion stirred by Ewbank's retirement was no match for the offense ignited by Simpson's magnificent running.

In gaining 200 yards on a snow-covered field and leading the Bills to their ninth victory against five defeats (the Jets finished with a 4-10 record) Simpson reached that lofty yardage level for a record third time this season (Brown did it twice in 1963).

With the rest of the Buffalo offensive unit geared to make sure O. J. got the record—he needed 61 yards—Simpson ran for 200 on 34 carries. He wound up the season with 2,003, well ahead of the 1,863 Brown amassed in 1963.

In addition, the indomitable Simpson surpassed Brown's record for the number of carries in a season—332 to 305. He also helped the Bills set a league record for total yards rushing by a team, 3,088 to 2,960 the Miami Dolphins gained last season.

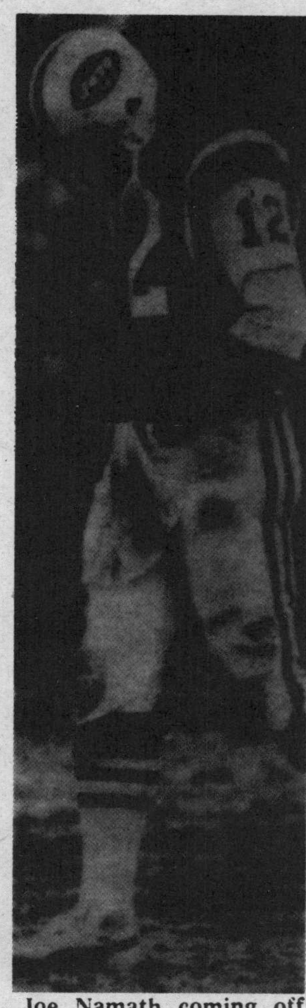

Joe Namath coming off the field in fourth quarter of Jets' final game.

The New York Times

Simpson hitting a hole in the first quarter against the Jets to break Jim Brown's record of 1,863 yards. Simpson carried the ball 34 times for 200 yards.

As for the significance of Simpson's yardage in the game itself, he ran for 57 of the team's 71 on the first touchdown drive and scored the second touchdown on a nifty 13-yard burst through the left side of the line.

"We tried to mix our defenses like always, but we weren't successful," Charlie Winner, Ewbank's designated successor, said. "We were embarrassed that he got so much yardage against us. We gun." The Jets had such little success stopping Simpson that he gained the record on the first play after Bills got the ball for the second time.

With Joe DeLamielleure, the rookie right guard, knocking Mark Lomas, the right end, out of the way, Simpson broke through the left side and gained 6 yards before John Little tackled him from behind with 10:34 gone in the first quarter.

The game was stopped, the other offensive players pounded Simpson on the back and hugged him. An official handed the ball to Simpson, who took it to the Bills' bench, where he was mobbed.

"We thought they'd give the ball to the fullback more, figuring we would key on O.J.," explained Ralph Baker the linebacker who calls defensive signals. "But they didn't. They came right out to get the record."

"We were saying let's get it in the first quarter," said Simpson, who also experienced his record, 11th 100-yard game of the season and surpassed the 5,000-yard mark for his five-year career. "But after we got it, we relaxed and I fumbled."

The fumble came on the play immediately after the one on which he broke the record. Two plays after that, Joe Namath—who may have been playing his last game — connected with Jerome Barkum for the tying touchdown on a 48-yard pass play.

But Simpson's 13-yard scoring burst with 1:12 left in the first half snapped the tie, and 48 seconds later Bill Cahill took Julian Fagan's 26-yard punt and scooted 51 yards for another Buffalo touchdown.

The Bills then spent the second half focusing on the attempt to raise O. J. to the unheard-of plateau of 2,000 yards. At one point early in the fourth quarter, Simpson related, "Joe Ferguson [the rookie quarterback] came in and said I needed 50 yards for 2,000. We broke 20 off right away and we were going after it then."

With 6:28 left in the game, Simpson reached the mark on a 7-yard smash through left guard to the Jet 13. This time he went to the sideline and was lifted to the shoulders of his excited teammates. He did not return to the game.

The clock, meanwhile, ticked off the final minutes of Ewbank's noted career. When it was over and the Jets were in the seclusion of their locker room, away from the onslaughts of Simpson, they held a ceremony of their own.

First, Winston Hill led the team in the traditional post game prayer. Kneeling and with his hefty arm around

The New York Times

Teammates cheering O. J. Simpson (32) of Bills as announcement was made yesterday at Shea Stadium that he had set a new N.F.L. record of 2,003 yards gained in a season.

the roly-poly coach, the tackle said: "Thanks, Lord, for our rich relationship with Weeb. We want to thank you for Weeb."

Then, another long-time Jet, Dave Herman, gave Ewbank a gold watch.

"When you look at this watch, just think of what you have meant to us," Herman said in his brief presentation. As he finished, the players crowded together in a semi-circle, applauded heartily and Ewbank began crying profusely. The players cried, too.

"It's a great game, it's a great life," the 66-year-old coach responded in a broken voice. "I let you down. It's been good to me. Don't let things like this get you down. We've had good days here and we've had bad days. You're still great. Come back next year and win 'em all."

Then Ewbank, tears still rolling down his chunky face, walked around the room, stopping at each locker to hug and shake hands with each player.

"I don't like to cry," Namath said later. "But I coulda cried. I had to fight back the tears."

"I'm really disappointed," Ewbank said of the game, his eyes red and moist "I'm sorry we didn't do better. But the kids tried. I wouldn't fault anybody. We just have to take our hats off to a great halfback.

United Press International
Notre Dame's Wayne Bullock slamming past Wayne Hall (50) and the Alabama line for the Irish's first touchdown

Notre Dame Defeats Alabama, 24 to 23, In Bid for National Title in Sugar Bowl

Thomas's 19-Yard Field Goal Gives Irish Victory

By NEIL AMDUR
Special to The New York Times

NEW ORLEANS, Dec. 31—Notre Dame won the right to claim a national college football title with a 24-23 victory over Alabama tonight in a Sugar Bowl classic that surpassed expectations for sustained excitement.

A 19-yard field goal by Bob Thomas with 4 minutes 26 seconds left became the final points for the unbeaten Irish before a game-record crowd of 85,161 and millions more who watched on national television.

Notre Dame then showed even more courage, in the tradition of a championship team, by running out the clock in the final three minutes with two first downs. One of the first downs came when Tom Clements, on third and 8 from his own 2-yard line, dropped back into the end zone and completed a 35-yard pass to Dave Weber, a sophomore tight end.

It was the 11th consecutive victory for Notre Dame, a 7-point underdog. Alabama, rated No. 1 nationally before the game, suffered its first setback in 12 games and extended its victoryless post-season record to seven successive games.

But the Crimson Tide had nothing to be ashamed of with tonight's showing, coming from behind on three occasions to take the lead.

The quality of play rivaled the 1971 Nebraska-Oklahoma Thanksgiving Day classic, and the emotional pitch was so intense throughout the stadium that almost the entire Notre Dame team poured onto the field after Al Hunter's 93-yard kickoff return had erased a 7-6 Alabama lead midway into the second quarter.

Even the officials seemed caught up in the swirl of excitement. On at least two occasions in the opening quarter, Ennis Grundmeyer, the clock operator, inadvertently failed to stop the clock after two routine punts and used up a total of 47 seconds.

Associated Press
Bullock picks up a first down against David McMakin (18)

Missed Placement, Turnovers Hurt Tide in 2d Half

Almost as bizarre was the missed extra point by Bill Davis, the regular 'Bama place-kicker, after the third Tide touchdown on a 25-yard trick pass play from a halfback, Mike Stock, to Richard Todd, a quarterback. The score had moved Alabama back in front, 23-21.

Davis had missed only 2 of 53 extra point attempts this season and only 10 of 145 in a three-year career. But the 6-foot-2-inch, 192-pound senior, after a high snap from center, may have misjudged the intensity of swirling winds, and his kick sailed wide.

Thomas' game-winning kick followed an Irish drive from their 19-yard line to the Alabama 2. Clements, voted the game's most valuable player, delivered the crucial completion with a 15-yard to Dave Casper, the all-America tight end, on third and 1 from the Alabama 45.

Notre Dame held 'Bama's prolific wishbone offense for three plays following the field goal. A roughing-the-kicker penalty was called

Continued on Page 26, Column 3

Dolphins Compared to Packers of 1960's

Shula's Record of 53-11-1 Is Cited

By MURRAY CHASS

The Oakland Raiders say they're committed to excellence, but it's the Miami Dolphins who are the epitome of excellence. And now it's the Minnesota Vikings, turn to get a sample of that excellence.

Since the National and American Football Leagues realigned in 1970, a four-year period that parallels Don Shula's tenure as coach of the Dolphins, Miami has won 53 games, lost 11 and tied one. No other team comes close to that record, which is why it has become natural to think of the Dolphins in terms of the Green Bay Packers of the 1960's.

"But instead of us being the Packers of the 70's," one Miami official suggested, perhaps only half-jokingly, "why not call the Packers the Dolphins of the 60's?"

Even Shula, who generally shies away from comparisons, talks about his team in terms of Green Bay, which won its league's ultimate championship five times in seven seasons.

"The Packers are the only team that's won two Super Bowls in a row," the highly successful coach said yesterday, still savoring his team's

Continued on Page 26, Column 5

United Press International
Don Shula after the Dolphins beat the Raiders Sunday

Skill of Newcomers Bolsters Vikings

The Miami Dolphins have been established in an early betting line from Las Vegas, Nev., as 6-point favorites over the Minnesota Vikings for the Super Bowl game in Houston Jan. 13. That seems fair enough. The Dolphins are an imperturbable crowd going into their third straight Super Bowl. It will be another game for them and they are accustomed to winning, with 31 victories in their last 33 games.

Minnesota does not have such reassurance. The Vikings' 27-10 triumph over Dallas on Sunday was the team's best effort of the season against a formidable foe and it pleased the players immensely. However, it was the kind of performance the Dolphins turn out weekly and never get excited about.

The Vikings last played in the Super Bowl four seasons ago with Joe Kapp at quarterback, losing to Kansas City, 23-7, at New Orleans. The team has changed since then with new starters at 10 of the 24 positions which includes the two kickers.

There are seven new players on offense, including Fran Tarkenton at quarterback, athletes who improved the attack and gave the club

Continued on Page 26, Column 3

Cedeno Released on Bail After Charge Is Reduced

SANTO DOMINGO, Dec. 31 (UPI)—Cesar Cedeno, the Houston Astro center fielder, was freed on bail today to await trial for involuntary manslaughter in the fatal shooting of a 19-year-old woman in a motel room here.

Cedeno, who had been imprisoned at La Fe Precinct jail since he turned himself in to the police about eight hours after the Dec. 11 shooting, could be finished with the judicial process before spring training starts, according to Dominican legal experts.

District Attorney Maximo Henriquez Saladin, who had brought a charge of "voluntary manslaughter" against Cedeno, reported that Magistrate Socrates Diaz Curiel had reduced the charge to involuntary manslaughter.

Persons charged with the more serious offense, which is roughly the equivalent of second-degree murder in the United States, are not permitted to go free on bond under Dominican law.

The reduced charge not only freed Cedeno from jail but also reduced the maximum penalty he could face — from 10 years' to three years' imprisonment. Under Dominican law, even if he were convicted of involuntary manslaughter, the judge could absolve him.

The charge of involuntary manslaughter will be heard in a "correctional court" and will likely be a much shorter proceeding than would a trial in criminal court, the legal experts said.

The $10,000 bail set by Diaz Curiel was posted by his lawyer and Cedeno left jail

Continued on Page 26, Column 5

Parseghian Is Still Able to Refuse Any Offer

Special to The New York Times

NEW ORLEANS, Dec. 31—At least once every year since he arrived at Notre Dame a decade ago, Ara Parseghian has either been offered a job as a pro coach or patiently put down erroneous reports of offers.

Last year, a weekly football publication, without ever contacting Parseghian to confirm one rumor, reported that he was about to accept a $1-million deal as coach and general manager of the Philadelphia Eagles.

This fall, Parseghian has already denied privately that he was about to retire or that he had been contacted about the coaching vacancy with the New York Giants.

"My position has been pretty clear for the last 10 years," the coach of the Irish said before tonight's victory in the national championship Sugar Bowl game with top-ranked Alabama. "I've maintained that I'm very happy at Notre Dame, I like the environment, the school, everything about my job."

What would it take for Parseghian to leave South Bend?

"If the policies of the administration suddenly changed toward football," he said, "or if the policies in intercollegiate football change, such as a return to single-platoon football or a broad de-emphasis, then I would probably have to re-evaluate my position."

Like Paul (Bear) Bryant, his colleague at Alabama, Parseghian enjoys rare status for a college coach. He draws an excellent salary at Notre Dame, has numerous fringe benefits within the school and has been allowed leeway in outside ventures such as commercial endorsements for the Ford Motor Company and a pending promotional contract with the Deltona Corporation for next year.

"I'm flattered that my name comes up in job discussions," he said. "But sometimes I think that people bring it up just to complicate my relationship at Notre Dame. Every time I'm linked with a job, I have to reassure the school, my staff, my players and even potential prospects."

What does Parseghian tell high school seniors who are considering Notre Dame?

"I just say that my record speaks for itself," he continued. "I've been here for 10 years, and my policy has never wavered."

Parseghian has posted an impressive record at Notre Dame, including this year's 10-0 mark, the first perfect regular season won-lost record at the school in 25 years. Yet in some minds, such as Ellis Beck, the No. 1 fullback at Alabama, Parseghian is re-

Continued on Page 26, Column 5

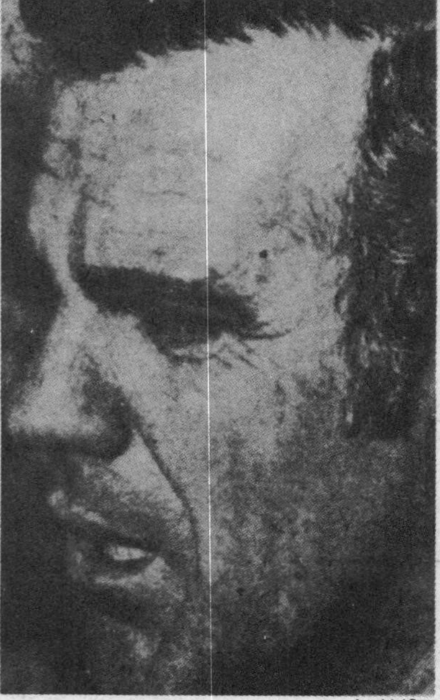
Associated Press
Ara Parseghian, the coach of Notre Dame

Arthur Daley

Possession Is 9 Points of the Law

Back in the old days the Chicago Bears were the most awesome team in the entire football world. They ripped off so much yardage and ran up so many points that someone asked Jimmy Conzelman, the droll coach of the [then Chicago] Cardinals, what kind of defense the Bears had.

"I dunno," he said. "They're never on defense. They always have the ball."

Sports of The Times

When the Miami Dolphins and Minnesota Vikings were flattening final obstacles to the Super Bowl on Sunday, they left the identical impression that they always had the ball. The long-standing juridical principle that possession is nine points of the law has even weightier connotations when applied to football. Although it isn't exactly impossible for one team to score while the other team has possession of the ball, it is not a procedure normally recommended by the more brilliant football strategists. It can be done—but not often—by means of pass interceptions, recovered fumbles, blocked kicks, and what else is there? Kick returns don't count because this becomes an offensive play by the receiving team.

There is no quality in football more important than possessiveness. The Vikings, for instance, rolled 74 yards for an apparent touchdown the first time they were handed the ball. A holding penalty nullified this sortie into the end zone. But they had hogged the ball for nine minutes before settling for a field goal. The next time they took over they went 87 yards and used up six minutes more. They led, 10-0, before the Cowboys could even get their lassos untangled.

The Foot Soldiers

Miami defied Oakland all the way. Although the Raiders led the conference in defense against running, the Dolphins called on their infantry for old-fashioned hand-to-hand combat, striking at enemy strength. With Larry Csonka serving as platoon sergeant, these troops mauled the Raiders for an embarrassing yield of 266 yards along the ground. In the first half they marched, with stately tread, distances of 64 and 63 yards for touchdowns, consuming time and denying possession to Oakland.

The most shocking phase of this game, perhaps, was the way Miami abjured air support for the ground troops. It was almost as if Dolphin strategy had been dictated by Woody Hayes of Ohio State who seems to consider the forward pass an invention of the Devil and resists practically all temptation to use it.

But Don Shula, the Dolphins coaching genius, has no compunctions about the free employment of the pass as an integral part of his attack. In Bob Griese he even has one of the better practitioners of the art. But once Miami began jamming the ball down reluctant Oakland throats by running at them or over them or around them, the urgency disappeared for putting the ball in the air. So Griese threw only six, completing three for 26 yards, unbelievably low figures for a championship game. It might even be one of those left-handed records, the kind that delights collectors of trivia.

This was to produce a corollary oddity. Griese, the non-passing passer, gained more yardage by his personal running as he picked up 39 with his feet as contrasted with a mere 26 with his arm. One run in particular was a strategic gem, an artfully planned and consummately executed quarterback draw play, the kind Otto Graham once used so effectively with the Cleveland Browns. It led to a field goal that lifted the pressure just as Oakland had begun to make a few menacing gestures. The Raider defenders had planted the idea in the Griese think tank by their adhesive coverage of potential Miami receivers.

"They had everybody covered but the quarterback," said Griese in explanation. Some grandstand quarterbacks thought this was the key play of the game.

The Other General

But Griese was not the only field general in this elimination tournament to perform with superior skills. The Vikings had one of their own in Francis Asbury Tarkenton, the often maligned scrambler. He silenced his critics this year by leading the Vikes into the Super Bowl, and he waved a fist triumphantly overhead as he made his exit march from the field after hornswoggling the Cowboys all afternoon.

Dallas is a methodical, unemotional team that reflects its coach, Tom Landry. Everything is carefully planned to the last detail. But Fran was positively disruptive. He threw passes on first downs which he isn't supposed to do and crossed up the Cowboy defense constantly with redesigned running plays and pass patterns. And he ran just enough himself to keep the enemy honest.

It has been a great year for Fran. His ambition had been to make it to the Super Bowl and he had requested a return in 1972 to his old team, the Vikings, after five unproductive seasons with the Giants. But the Vikes let him down and had a bad 7-7 finish. This year Bud Grant had his heroes percolating again, and Fran was the cream in the coffee. His 54-yard touchdown pass to John Gilliam broke apart the game with the Cowboys. But Fran had controlled that game most of the way because he made sure the Vikes kept possession of the ball. It's still the best possible system for ensuring victory.

Penn State Slight Orange Bowl Favorite Over L.S.U.

By GORDON S. WHITE Jr.
Special to The New York Times

MIAMI, Dec. 31 — In the Orange Bowl where the No. 1 collegiate ranking is not at stake, Penn State, undefeated and untied, is about a one-touchdown favorite to beat Louisiana State University tomorrow night.

The only time Penn State was favored to win in its 11 previous bowl appearances, the Nittany Lions lost to Florida, 17-7, in the 1962 Gator Bowl. But that year Penn State officials made the mistake of insisting their team participate in a bowl against the wishes of the players.

Times have changed, and now Penn State players enter each season with priorities that include a bowl game at the end of the campaign. The big Nittany Lions, with a perfect 11-0 record, are playing this one because they feel they deserve it and because they want it.

Coach Charlie McClendon's Tigers from Baton Rouge also had a perfect record when they accepted this Orange Bowl bid. But they lost to Alabama and Tulane after that and now go against the much bigger Nittany Lions with a 9-2 season mark.

The game will start at 8 P.M., E.S.T., and will be nationally telecast by the National Broadcasting Company (Channel 4 in New York).

This is Penn State's sixth bowl in eight seasons under coach Joe Paterno with three victories, one loss and a tie in his other bowl games. McClendon's 12th L.S.U. team is his 10th to play in bowl games. L.S.U. has won six and lost three bowl tests under McClendon.

Paterno said, "If this is a high-scoring game we won't win it. I would think it would be a game of three scores to two scores."

McClendon said, "I'm hoping it is a low scoring game. That way you are not going to be making many mistakes, those things that hurt."

Louisiana State's problem appears to be trying to stop the Heisman Trophy winner of 1973, John Cappelletti. This unusually big tailback, at 6 feet 1 inch and 210 pounds, will go at the Tigers in the middle or on sweeps from his I-position. He will do so behind "the biggest line we've had since I've been at Penn State," according to Paterno.

The Tigers' defense is not nearly as big as Penn State's offense.

The Nittany Lions' chief problem will be presented by a quick and varied offense that can call on four good L.S.U. tailbacks. Each of these runners is considerably smaller than Cappelletti, but each is fast. Brad Davis is the primary man at the L.S.U. tailback position.

Both teams have solid quarterbacks with Tom Shuman for Penn State and Mike Miley for L.S.U.

Penn State suffered prestige and, as a result, position in the ranking because of what some persons felt was a weak schedule in 1973. The best the Lions could do was reach No. 5 in the weekly polls at midseason. Now they are sixth. Victory probably would not vault them to the top in the final Associated Press vote.

L.S.U., a member of the Southeastern Conference, is considered to have played a more difficult schedule. But the Tigers, who were right behind Penn State in the weekly rankings for nine weeks, slipped considerably when beaten, and now are at 14.

United Press International
Joe Paterno, left, Penn State coach, and Tom Shuman, quarterback, at workout last week in Miami.

Ohio State Choice To Defeat U.S.C.

By BILL BECKER
Special to The New York Times

PASADENA, Calif., Dec. 31 — Ohio State, bent on restoring the Big Ten's prestige, seeks revenge tomorrow against Southern California in the 60th Rose Bowl game.

The Buckeyes (9-0-1 won-lost tied record) are rated 2-point favorites over the Trojans (9-1-1). A near-capacity crowd of 104,700 is expected for the nation's premier bowl attraction, dating back to 1902.

Woody Hayes's Buckeyes hope to break a string of four losses by the Big Ten, including the stinging 42-17 setback they suffered from the Trojans last New Year's Day. That triumph assured Southern Cal of the 1972 national championship.

Ohio State, led by Archie Griffin, a sophomore halfback, and John Hicks, an all-America tackle, crushed all opponents except Michigan. The Wolverines tied the Buckeyes, 10-10, to share the Big Ten title, but in a controversial 6-4 vote Ohio State was picked to represent the conference here again.

Southern Cal, coached by John McKay, won the Pacific Eight title by beating seven conference foes. The Trojans lost only to Notre Dame and were tied by Oklahoma.

This is McKay's seventh Rose Bowl squad in 14 years; it is Hayes's sixth in 23 years. The two coaches are even (1-1) against each other here, the Buckeyes topping the Trojans, 27-16, in 1969.

Ohio State will rely on its customary bruising ground game and a defense that yielded only 43 points while the Buckeyes were scoring 371. Randy Gradishar, an all-America linebacker, is the defensive anchorman.

Southern Cal's offensive weapons include the rushing of Anthony Davis and Rod McNeill, the passing of Pat Haden and the receiving and the punt-return skills of Lynn Swann. Davis is also a threat on kickoff returns, if they'll kick to him.

The Trojans scored 301 points to their opponents' 160. The defense has two all-Americans in Richard Wood at linebacker and Artimus Parker at safety.

The game probably will hinge on whether U. S. C. can disrupt Ohio State's ball-control tactics, built around Griffin, who rushed for 1,428 yards and a 6.3 average. Davis ran for 1,038 yards and a 4.0 average.

Haden completed 56 per cent of his passes, averaging 19 throws a game. Cornelius Greene and Greg Hare averaged eight passes and three completions a game for the slogging Buckeyes.

Should a field goal be needed, the call will go to Chris Limahelu of Indonesia, with a 12-for-15 record, for the Trojans and Blair Conway, 5 for 10, for the Bucks.

RECORDS OF THE TEAMS

OHIO STATE (9-0-1)		SO. CALIF. (9-1-1)	
56—Minnesota	7	17—Arkansas	0
37—T.C.U.	3	23—Georgia Tech	6
27—Washington St.	3	7—Oklahoma	7
24—Wisconsin	0	21—Oregon St.	7
37—Indiana	7	46—Washington St.	35
60—Northwestern	0	31—Oregon	10
30—Illinois	0	14—Notre Dame	23
35—Michigan St.	0	50—California	14
55—Iowa	13	27—Stanford	26
10—Michigan	10	42—Washington	19
		23—U.C.L.A.	13

Texas-Nebraska Match A Case of Rush vs. Pass

DALLAS, Dec. 31 (AP) — Texas, ranked No. 8, and Nebraska, No. 12, high-scoring teams with little in common except bad losses to Oklahoma, meet tomorrow in the 38th Cotton Bowl classic.

The game matches the Longhorn's bruising ground game with the Cornhusker's potent air attack.

It will be nationally televised at 2 P.M., E.S.T. (Channel 2, New York).

"We'd like to be champions of something, and the Cotton Bowl is all we have left," said Frosty Anderson, Nebraska's wide receiver, of the clash between the champions of the Southwest Conference and the Cornhuskers, Big Eight runner-up.

Texas is rated a slight favorite in the game which is expected to draw 72,000 fans, including some 18,000 rooters from Nebraska.

Texas compiled an 8-2 won-lost record with its Wishbone-T offense, capturing the S.W.C. title for the sixth consecutive years.

The Cornhuskers were 8-2-1 under Tom Osborne, their freshman head coach.

While Texas runs a grind-it-out offense behind a sophomore quarterback, Marty Akins, and an all-America fullback, Roosevelt Leaks, Nebraska is an airminded outfit in the slot-I formation.

David Humm, the Nebraska quarterback, has an excellent receiver corps, spearheaded by Anderson and Tony Davis, a breakaway running back.

Texas, which plays a split-four defense, has been vulnerable to the pass this year.

Under Coach Darrell Royal, the Longhorns have been to bowl games in 14 of 17 years. Texas whipped Alabama last year in the Cotton Bowl while Nebraska, hopefulof running its string of bowl victories to five in a row, routed Notre Dame in the Orange Bowl.

In the last 12 years, Nebraska and Texas have the best records nationally—the Cornhuskers with an 82.9 winning percentage and Texas, 82.2 per cent.

"There's no secret to what we've got to do," said Bell. "We've got to stop Leaks and he's a great player."

Leaks scored 14 touchdowns, gained 1,415 yards, and averaged 6.2 yards a carry for the Longhorns.

RECORDS OF THE TEAMS

NEBRASKA (8-2-1)		TEXAS (8-2)	
40—U.C.L.A.	13	15—Miami (Fla.)	20
31—No. Caro. St.	14	28—Texas Tech	12
20—Wisconsin	16	41—Wake Forest	0
48—Minnesota	7	13—Oklahoma	52
12—Missouri	13	34—Arkansas	6
10—Kansas	9	55—Rice	13
17—Oklahoma St.	17	42—S.M.U.	14
28—Colorado	16	42—Baylor	6
31—Iowa St.	7	52—T.C.U.	7
50—Kansas St.	21	42—Texas A&M	13
0—Oklahoma	27		

The Sugar Was Sweet, Indeed

By WILLIAM N. WALLACE
Special to The New York Times

NEW ORLEANS, Dec. 31—The hero of Notre Dame's thrilling victory over Alabama for the college football championship of the land was Tom Clements, the Irish junior quarterback from McKees Rock, Pa. Clements made two big plays in the final quarter, one which brought the victors into position for the winning field goal by Bob Thomas and the other which kept Alabama from getting its sticky fingers on the football one last time.

Both plays were passes by Clements to tight ends and they came in desperate situations. The first came on third down at the Alabama 45-yard line with Notre Dame behind and the pass, a wobbly one, went to Dave Casper for a 30-yard gain to the 15.

The second came near the end with Notre Dame down at its 2-yard line, third down and 8 yards needed for the precious first down with two minutes to play. Clements dropped back into his end zone and risked a long pass to Robin Weber, Casper's substitute. It was complete way out to the Notre Dame 38 and the Irish team then was able to run out the clock.

The first play then was an offensive attacking one, the second defensive in nature. Without them, Alabama wins the game.

Clements said that both play calls came from the bench, from Coach Ara Parseghian. "I rolled right," Clements said of the first pass to Casper. "Art Best threw a good block so I had a little time. I got the ball off but it wasn't a very god pass. Dave had to come back for it. But it worked."

In truth the Alabama defense was laggard and the ball might well have been intercepted.

"On the pass to Weber," Clements continued, "Coach said we might as well take the chance to throw. If it didn't work, we'd punt out on fourth down and see what happened. Weber got wide open and I threw it as hard as I could.

"It was a great play" he said and that was an understatement.

Did Clements consider the terrible risk of an interception? He shook his head. "You have to take chances to win," he said.

Sugar Bowl at a Glance

Ala.	N.D.	
		FIRST QUARTER
0	6	Bullock, 1-yard run at 11:41. 64-yard drive in 7 plays. Key gains: Demmerle, 19, 26 and 14 yards on passes from Clements. Conversion failed when high pass from center was fumbled.
		SECOND QUARTER
7	6	Billingsley, 6-yard run at 7:30. 52-yard drive in 7 plays. Key gains: Stock, 15, pass from Rutledge; Rutledge, 12-yard run. Davis, kick.
7	14	Hunter, 93-yard return of kickoff at 7:43. Demmerle, pass from Clements for 2-point conversion.
10	14	Davis. 39-yard field goal at 14:29. 60-yard drive in 7 plays. Key gain: Jackson, 21-yard run.
		THIRD QUARTER
17	14	Jackson, 5-yard run at 3:48. 93-yard drive in 10 plays. Key gains: Rutledge passes to Jackson, 21, and Wheeler, 13. Davis, kick.
17	21	Penick, 12-yard run at 12:30. First play after Mahilic recovered fumble by Sharpless. Thomas, kick.
		FOURTH QUARTER
23	21	Todd, 26-yard pass from Stock at 5:21. 39-yard drive in five plays after Bullock's fumble. Key gain: Billingsely, 9-yard run. Davis, kick.
23	24	Thomas, 19-yard field goal at 10:34. 78-yard drive in 11 plays. Key gain: Casper, 29-yard pass from Clements.

Basketball Scoring
NATIONAL ASSOCIATION

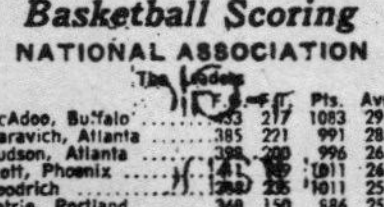

The Leaders

	F.G.	F.T.	Pts.	Ave.
McAdoo, Buffalo	[illegible]	217	1083	29.3
Maravich, Atlanta	385	221	991	28.3
Hudson, Atlanta	398	200	996	26.9
Scott, Phoenix	[illegible]	[illegible]	[illegible]	26.6
Goodrich	[illegible]	[illegible]	1011	25.3
Petrie, Portland	368	150	886	25.3
Abdul-Jabbar, Milwaukee	418	122	958	25.2

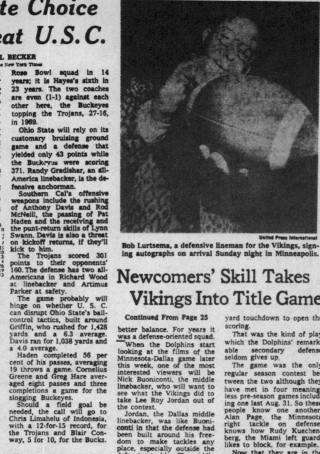

United Press International

Bob Lurtsema, a defensive lineman for the Vikings, signing autographs on arrival Sunday night in Minneapolis.

Newcomers' Skill Takes Vikings Into Title Game

Continued From Page 25

better balance. For years it was a defense-oriented squad.

When the Dolphins start looking at the films of the Minnesota-Dallas game later this week, one of the most interested viewers will be Nick Buoniconti, the middle linebacker, who will want to see what the Vikings did to take Lee Roy Jordan out of the contest.

Jordan, the Dallas middle linebacker, was like Buoniconti in that the defense had been built around his freedom to make tackles any place, especially outside the defensive tackles. The middle linebacker was not to be blocked, an essential of the standard pro 4-3 defense which Tom Landry first evolved for the New York Giants in the 1950's with Sam Huff as the middle linebacker.

It is unlikely that Buoniconti will be surprised. Teams have thrown every imaginable blocking combination at Nick, a lawyer and Notre Dame alumnus, over the years. There is no memory of him being wiped out of a key contest like Jordan was.

The Dolphins and Vikings did not meet this season but they did play in 1972. It was the third game of the year, at Bloomington, Minn., and it was close. Miami winning 16-14 with 10 points in the fourth quarter. The Minnesota home-run combination, Tarkenton, passing long to John Gilliam, was in action as they combined for a 56-yard touchdown to open the scoring.

That was the kind of play which the Dolphins' remarkable secondary defense seldom gives up.

The game was the only regular season contest between the two although they have met in four meaningless pre-season games including one last Aug. 31. So these people know one another. Alan Page, the Minnesota right tackle on defense, knows how Rudy Kuechenberg, the Miami left guard, likes to block, for example.

Now that they are in the Super Bowl, the Vikings have three players to be especially thankful about: Chuck Foreman, Nate Wright and Jeff Wright, all new starters for them.

At the end of last season, when Minnesota as a favorite to gain the Super Bowl, dropped shockingly to .500, the need for a superb running back with speed was apparent. It seemed three were available in the draft, Otis Armstrong from Purdue; Sam Cunningham of Southern California and Foreman of the University of Miami. In the first round, Denver took Armstrong as the ninth selection. New England took Cunningham 11th and Minnesota chose Foreman as No. 12.

Foreman had a fine rookie season and after a minor slump showed all that great speed again against Dallas. He will concern Buoniconti a little bit.

Notre Dame Turns Back Alabama for Title, 24-23

Continued From Page 25

against the Irish on fourth down, which forced Alabama into a crucial decision: Take the field position on the punt, which rolled dead at the Irish 1-yard line, or consider gambling on what would have been fourth and 3 at its 45.

With three minutes left, the Tide decided to trust their defense to regain a final shot for the offense. It might have worked, but Clements hit Weber and then followed with a 7-yard keeper, again on third down, that sealed the third national title for Coach Ara Parseghian and satisfying sequel to the controversial 1966 tie game with Michigan State.

Alabama's Bryant acknowledged that "the long pass right at the end beat us."

"If we get the ball back, we're going to win the game," Bryant added. "At least on a field goal. When we had them backed up to the 1yard line, if I'd been a betting man, I'd have bet you anything we were going to win."

Parseghian, in perhaps the finest hour of his 10-year coaching career at Notre Dame, also agreed that the Clements-to-Weber pass was "the key to the win."

"It was a win or punt situation," said Parseghian, who may have squelched forever any notion that he is anything less than a championship coach. "If we hadn't made the first down, Alabama would surely have been in field goal position with us punting from our end zone. That was the same pattern we scored the extra 2 points on earlier in the game."

Both coaches could find little fault with the performances of their players, despite the nine fumbles, many caused by a synthetic Poly-Turf still spongy from heavy rains as late as an hour before the opening kickoff.

"I don't really feel like we lost, just that time ran out on us," Bryant said. "Notre Dame came up with a lot of big plays, which means they did a better job of coaching."

Parseghian expressed little doubt over Notre Dame's status as national champion.

"I definitely feel we're the national champion," he said. "We beat the leading scoring team in the nation and the team that was leading in offensive yardage. They are an excellently disciplined team. We beat a great football team and they lost to a great football team."

Notre Dame	6	8	7	3—24
Alabama	0	10	7	6—23

N.D.—Bullock, 1, run (kick, failed).
Ala.—Billingsley, 6, run (Davis, kick).
N.D.—Hunter, 93, kickoff return (Demmerle, pass from Clements).
Ala.—FG, Davis, 39.
Ala.—Jackson, 5, run (Davis, kick).
N.D.—Penick, 12, run (Thomas, kick).
Ala.—Todd, 25, pass from Stock (kick failed).
N.D.—FG, Thomas, 19.
Attendance—85,161.

Lorentz Scores 3 In Sabre Victory

DETROIT, Dec. 31 (AP)—Jim Lorentz scored three goals helping the Buffalo Sabres to a 6-5 victory over the Detroit Red Wings in the National Hockey League tonight.

Buffalo Sabres	2	2	2—6
Detroit Red Wings	3	2	0—5

FIRST PERIOD—1, Buffalo, McNab (3) (Carriere), 3:52. 2, Detroit, Charron (15) (Bailey), 4:50. 3, Detroit, Libett (16) (Collins, Hughes), 5:24. 4, Buffalo, Lorentz (12) (Berreault, Roberts), 11:16. 5, Detroit, Charron (16), 18:58. Penalties—Libett, Detroit, (9:23); Collins, Detroit, (18:26).

SECOND PERIOD—6, Buffalo, Lorentz (13) (McNab, Korab), 6:17. 7, Detroit, Dionne (6) (Stackhouse, Roberts), 10:55. 8, Detroit, Berenson (9) (Johnston, Collins), 12:54; 9, Buffalo, Lorentz (14) (Korab, McNab), 14:30. Penalties—Harris, Detroit, (16:00); Atkinson, Buffalo, (17:48).

THIRD PERIOD—10, Buffalo, Terbenche (1) (Luce), 3:48. 11, Buffalo, Dudley (7) (Luce) (Ramsey), 10:40. Penalties—Martin, Buffalo, 5:43; Johnson, Detroit, 6:45.

Shots on goal—Buffalo: 16, 13, 12—41. Detroit: 9, 9, 13—31.

Goalies—Dryden and McKenzie.

Attendance—13,864.

Dolphins Favored By 6 Points

Continued From Page 25

decisive 27-10 victory over Oakland for the American Conference championship.

"The Packers, under Vince Lombardi, were talked about as The team in professional football and their consistency was admired by everybody. We'd like to be the team everybody talks about next."

Most football people already are talking about the Dolphins, who will make their third straight Super Bowl appearance against the Vikings on Jan. 13 in Houston's Rice Stadium.

The Vikings have been there before, having lost to Kansas City four years ago. If Super Bowl history prevails, the Vikings should win because no team that's been there once and lost has also lost in its second try (i.e. Baltimore, Kansas City, Dallas and Miami).

However, no team ever has played in the Super Bowl three times so history may get a little confused.

By no means are the Dolphins assured of a victory, of course, and Shula will not permit his players to think the game already is wrapped up.

"We've been down that road before where you get there and you don't win," said the coach who lost his first Singer Bowl with Baltimore in 1969 and then again with Miami in 1972. "The only team they talk about is the team that wins. Minnesota is a fine poised group of professional football players.

"A lot of them have been in the Super Bowl and some of them have been great all-pros. They're solid in every department and they're a team that's very businesslike, very much like the Miami Dolphins. They go about getting the job done. That's why they're in the Super Bowl."

Shula said a big difference in the Vikings this year as compared with last is that this is Fran Tarkenton's second year back with them.

"He has continually come up with the big plays for them, plays that have kept them in games and helped them win games," Shula said. "He knows exactly what he wants to do with the offense."

The teams met in an exhibition game this year, and the Vikings won, 20-17, on a last-second Fred Cox field goal. That gave Minnesota a 3-1 won-lost record with Miami in exhibitions.

However, in their one regular-season encounter last season, the Dolphins won, 16-14, on Bob Griese's 3-yard touchdown pass to Jim Mandich with a minute 28 seconds left.

Parseghian Still Happy With Irish

Continued From Page 25

membered most for the 1966 tie game with Michigan State.

"I remember it, even though I was an Auburn fan back then," said Beck. "I thought Ara made a fool of himself going for the tie—you hold that against him."

"There's no question that this could be the most important game ever, certainly since Ara Parseghian has been here," Edward (Moose) Krause, the Notre Dame Athletic director was quoted earlier.

Parseghian will never be vindicated in the minds of some skeptics or opponents of the subway alumni, who are almost equally intense in their disregard for the Irish as Notre Dame fans in their support. Nor is the speculation about future pro jobs likely to end.

Cedeno Out Of Prison

Continued From Page 25

"emotionally calm," but did not make any public statement, according to a court clerk.

Trial date was expected to be set later this week.

Cedeno, accompanied by his father, turned himself in about eight hours after Altagracia de la Cruz, was shot in the head with Cedeno's .38 caliber pistol.

A police report described the shooting as accidental and said the bullet apparently had been fired when Miss de la Cruz picked up the pistol to admire it and Cedeno tried to take it away from her.

The baseball star, 22, faces civil suits brought by relatives of Miss de la Cruz and Saladin has suggested the possibility that another criminal action could be brought against him if he did not hold a license for the pistol.

RECORDS OF THE TEAMS

PENN STATE (11-0)		L.S.U. (9-2)	
20—Stanford	6	17—Colorado	6
39—Navy	0	28—Texas A. & M.	23
27—Iowa	8	24—Rice	9
19—Air Force	9	24—Florida	3
54—Army	3	20—Auburn	6
49—Syracuse	6	28—Kentucky	21
62—West Virginia	14	33—South Carolina	29
42—Maryland	22	51—Mississippi	14
35—No. Car. St.	29	26—Mississippi St.	7
49—Ohio U.	10	7—Alabama	21
35—Pittsburgh	13	0—Tulane	12

Celtics Win 7th Straight, 106-97

BOSTON, Dec. 31 (AP)—The Boston Celtics, led by their workhorse center, Dave Cowens, pulled together after a slow start and scored their seventh consecutive victory today, 106-97, over the Philadelphia 76ers.

It was the only game in the National Basketball Association today, played before a small crowd for Boston, 9,365 fans.

Cowen, the N.B.A.'s most valuable player last season, scored 23 points and grabbed 24 rebounds to help lift the Celtics' won-lost record to 29-6, the best in the league.

The 76ers, who have an 11-27 mark, took advantage of 13 Boston turnovers to take a 56-51 half-time lead.

They widened the advantage to 58-51 on a pair of free throws by Leroy Ellis after Cowens picked up his fourth personal foul at the start of the second half.

Lead See-Saws

Then Cowens ignited the Celtics with a short jumper. He and Jo Jo White each scored 8 points as Boston took a 75-70 lead at the end of the third period.

The 76ers managed to regain the lead at 78-77 in the first two minutes of the final period. But then the Celtics outscored Philadelphia, 12-2, to pull away for good.

John Havlicek scored 22 points and Don Nelson 18 for the Celtics. Paul Silas had only 10 points but grabbed 15 rebounds.

The 76ers were led by Tom Van Arsdale with 27 and Fred Carter with 17.

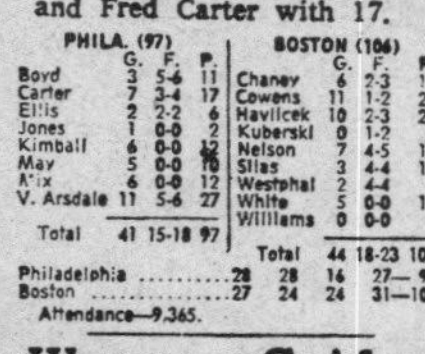

PHILA. (97)	G.	F.	P.
Boyd	3	5-6	11
Carter	7	3-4	17
Ellis	2	2-2	6
Jones	1	0-0	2
Kimball	6	0-0	12
May	5	0-0	10
Mix	6	0-0	12
V. Arsdale	11	5-6	27
Total	41	15-18	97

BOSTON (106)	G.	F.	P.
Chaney	6	2-3	14
Cowens	11	1-2	23
Havlicek	10	2-3	22
Kuberski	0	1-2	1
Nelson	7	4-5	18
Silas	3	4-4	10
Westphal	2	4-4	8
White	5	0-0	10
Williams	0	0-0	0
Total	44	18-23	106

Philadelphia	28	28	16	27—97
Boston	27	24	24	31—106

Attendance—9,365.

Associated Press

Steve Kuberski squeezing between Tom Van Arsdale, front, and Steve Mix of the 76ers yesterday to shoot for Celtics at the Boston Garden. The Celtics won, 106-97.

Woman Guides Rutgers Victory

Rutgers University overcame a New York Athletic Club lead in the last 500 meters yesterday and won the featured eight-oared race of the New Year's Eve Regatta on the Orchard Beach Lagoon in the Bronx.

Tom Reith understroked the Winged Foot crew 32 to 36 in the body of the 1,500-meter event and the Scarlet moved away to a three-length margin at the finish.

Reith also stroked the Rutgers fours with coxswains, but lost both in the elite and senior races by three-length margins to the higher stroking New Yorkers.

The coxswain for the Rutgers crews was Susy Weinstein of Trenton. She seemed to withstand the 35-degree blustery, wet weather better than her male companions and her voice could be heard for over a half-mile, urging the Scarlet oarsmen to row harder.

Dr. Larry Klecatsky won his 37th race of the season in the elite singles by four lengths. Sandy Killen of John Jay College finished second. Killen led for about 200 meters but Klecatsky, rowing a long 29, took the lead with about 600 meters remaining. Frank Pisani was third and John Sonberg fourth.

All competitors in the singles event were current national champions in at least one event.

1,500-METER EVENT

Eight-Oared Shells—1, Rutgers, 5 minutes 6.4 seconds; 2, New York A.C., 5:20.9.

1,000-METER EVENTS

Junior Singles—1, Turgay Kadioglu, New York A.C., 4:13.3; 2, Larry Cantemessa, New York A.C., 4:30.

Elite Singles—1, Dr. Larry Klecatsky, New York A.C., 3:36.9; 2, Sandy Killen, John Jay College, 3:44.9; 3, Frank Pisani, New York State University at Purchase, 3:48.9; 4, John Sonberg, New York A.C., 3:52.9.

Senior Fours with Coxswains—1, New York A.C., 3:47.4; 2, Rutgers, 3:53.4.

Elite Fours with Coxswains—1, New York A.C., 3:43.7; 2, Rutgers, 3:50.

College, School Results

BASKETBALL
Colleges

Georgia 80		Vermont 55
L.S.U.-New Orl. 130		Chicago St. 109
Memphis St. 67	('t)	Murray St. 65
Mercer 86		Delaware 73
Southern Illinois 108		Mo. Western 69
Texas Tech 75		Utah St. 65

Knicks Ready for Hawks Led by Maravich, Hudson

By SAM GOLDAPER

With his slight grin or a sly look from the corner of his eye Bill Bradley has a way of putting one on. When the Rhodes' scholar is in a good mood he offers treasured prose, often with double meanings.

Such was the case Sunday night after the Knicks overwhelmed the Kansas City-Omaha Kings, 102-85.

"I thought it was N.B.A. basketball at its best," said Bradley.

Teams like the Kings are good for the Knicks' future planning. New York has not been involved in too many one-sided games this season. Coach Red Holzman would like to see more games in which his team is ahead by 33 points with nine minutes of play remaining. It gives him a chance to give Mel Davis, Harthorne Wingo and John Gianelli the playing time they need to develop.

Dave DeBusschere, who scored 34 points Sunday and is having his finest offensive season, is retiring. Bradley has been signing year-to-year contracts, and no one knows when he will decide on his retirement. Willis Reed has been injury-prone the last few seasons and Jerry Lucas is getting along in playing years.

Holzman is also aware the college senior crop is not a strong one this season, and by the time the Knicks get to pick, there will be little available.

Madison Square Garden must have a winner to keep its seats filled. There are 13,000 season-ticket holders to keep happy and that means winning. If Bradley joins De Busschere in retirement and injuries persist in hampering Reed, the Knicks really will be hurt in the front court.

The Knicks, winners of seven of their last nine games, oppose Atlanta in the Garden tonight. For the Hawks, struggling to stay over the .500 mark, it's the same old story, a lot of scoring power and too little defense. Atlanta is the second best scoring team in the National Basketball Association and next to the worst in defense.

Atlant brought its won-lost record to 19-18 Sunday night when it defeated the Cleveland Cavaliers, 99-95. It was a game in which Pete Maravich, the league's second best scorer, was not in the starting line-up. Instead, Cotton Fitzsimmons, the Hawks' coach, turned Maravich loose in the second quarter and he finished with 29 points.

"We have five games in six days and I thought I would let Pete sit out the first period," said Fitzsimmons. "After all, you don't win N.B.A. games in the first quarter."

The Hawks almost didn't win the game in four quarters. Through the locked dressing room doors, Fitzsimmons was heard to scream, "There is no reason to blow an 18-point lead. We lost basics and made too many mistakes."

Maravich was supported offensively by Lou Hudson, who scored 27 points.

It's been that way all season, Maravich and Hudson, the best one-two scoring punch in the N.B.A. Hudson is the league's third best scorer.

Sweet Lou, as he has become known around the league, is smooth, efficient and unemotional.

Hudson went into this, his eighth season (five as an All-Star) with a 22.9 scoring average.

Knicks' Line-Up

AT GARDEN—7:30 P.M.

KNICKS	ATLANTA
6—Riker	3—Gilliam
7—Meminger	8—Bellamy
10—Frazier	12—Washington
15—Monroe	13—Jones
17—Bibby	20—Bracey
18—Jackson	22—Tschogl
22—DeBusschere	23—Hudson
24—Bradley	24—Ingelsby
31—Davis	33—Wetzel
32—Lucas	44—Maravich
40—Gianelli	50—Brown
43—Wingo	54—Schlueter

Sports Today

BASKETBALL

Knicks vs. Atlanta Hawks, at Madison Square Garden, Eighth Avenue and 33d Street, 7:30 P.M.
(Television — Channel 10 (cable, 7:30 P.M.) (Radio—WNBC-AM, 7:25 P.M.)

FOOTBALL

Cotton Bowl, Texas vs. Nebraska, at Dallas.
(Television — Channel 2, 2 P.M.)

Rose Bowl. Ohio State vs. Southern California, at Pasadena, Calif.
(Television — Channel 4, 4:45 P.M.)

Orange Bowl, Penn State vs. L.S.U., at Miami.
(Television — Channel 4, 8 P.M.)

HARNESS RACING

Monticello (N. Y.) Raceway, 8 P.M.

Basketball, Hockey Standings

Nat'l Hockey League

LAST NIGHT'S GAME
Buffalo 6, Detroit 5.

SUNDAY NIGHT'S GAMES
N.Y. Rangers 4, Minnesota 3.
Boston 8, California 1.
Detroit 4, Atlanta 2.
Philadelphia 5, Buffalo 4.
Toronto 4, Chicago 3.

STANDING OF THE TEAMS

East Division	G.P.	W.	L.	T.	Pts.	Goals For	Goals Agst.
Boston	33	24	6	3	51	155	90
Montreal	34	20	8	6	46	119	89
N.Y. Rangers	37	17	11	9	43	132	113
Toronto	37	17	13	7	41	132	106
Buffalo	36	17	15	4	38	120	119
Detroit	37	14	19	4	32	117	153
N.Y. Islanders	35	7	17	11	25	83	109
Vancouver	34	8	20	6	22	91	131
West Division							
Philadelphia	33	21	8	4	46	104	58
Chicago	34	16	7	11	43	115	69
Atlanta	36	15	14	7	37	91	98
St. Louis	33	15	14	[illegible]	[illegible]	91	[illegible]
Minnesota	35	11	16	8	30	100	115
Los Angeles	35	11	17	6	28	99	116
Pittsburgh	35	9	21	5	23	80	120
California	36	7	24	5	19	85	144

TONIGHT'S GAME
Boston at Vancouver.

Amer. Basketball Ass'n

SUNDAY NIGHT'S GAMES
Indiana 109, San Diego 100.

STANDING OF THE TEAMS

Eastern Division	W.	L.	Pct.	Western Division	W.	L.	Pct.
Carolina	25	15	.625	Utah	22	15	.595
Kentucky	23	14	.622	Indiana	21	18	.538
New York	23	16	.590	San Antonio	20	19	.513
Virginia	11	23	.324	Denver	17	18	.486
Memphis	10	29	.256	San Diego	18	23	.439

TOMORROW NIGHT'S GAMES
Carolinas vs. New York at Nassau Coliseum, Uniondale, L.I., 7:35 P.M.
Uniondale, L.I., 7:35 P.M.
San Antonio at Denver.
Virginia at Memphis.

Nat'l Basketball Ass'n

YESTERDAY'S GAME
Boston 106, Philadelphia 97.

SUNDAY NIGHT'S GAMES
New York 102, K.C.-Omaha 85.
Atlanta 99, Cleveland 94.
Detroit 98, Milwaukee 91.
Los Angeles 108, Buffalo 105.
Portland 99, Chicago 92.
Seattle 96, Golden State 92.

STANDING OF THE TEAMS
EASTERN CONFERENCE

Atlantic	W.	L.	Pct.	Central	W.	L.	Pct.
Boston	29	6	.829	Capital	20	15	.571
New York	23	16	.590	Atlanta	19	18	.514
Buffalo	16	22	.421	Cleveland	14	27	.341
Phila.	11	27	.289	Houston	12	27	.308

WESTERN CONFERENCE

Midwest	W.	L.	Pct.	Pacific	W.	L.	Pct.
Milwaukee	30	8	.789	L. Angeles	22	18	.550
Chicago	28	12	.700	Golden St.	17	17	.500
Detroit	24	16	.600	Portland	17	21	.447
KC-Omaha	14	27	.341	Seattle	17	27	.386
				Phoenix	15	24	.385

TONIGHT'S GAMES
Atlanta vs. New York at Madison Square Garden, 7:30 P.M.
Buffalo at Portland.
Chicago at Golden State.

World Hockey Ass'n

SUNDAY NIGHT'S GAMES
Chicago 5, Minnesota 3.
Houston 6, Los Angeles 4.
Toronto 5, Winnipeg 2.

STANDING OF THE TEAMS

East Division	G.P.	W.	L.	T.	Pts.	Goals For	Goals Agst.
New England	37	22	14	1	45	138	119
Toronto	40	19	18	3	41	151	131
Cleveland	36	17	15	4	38	112	115
Quebec	38	17	18	3	37	140	128
Chicago	34	16	16	2	34	114	119
Jersey	37	15	20	2	32	99	128
West Division							
Houston	35	19	12	4	42	137	102
Edmonton	35	20	15	0	40	123	110
Minnesota	37	19	17	1	39	134	130
Winnipeg	39	17	18	4	38	128	[illegible]
Vancouver	37	15	22	0	30	127	148
Los Angeles	37	13	24	0	26	110	149

TONIGHT'S GAMES
Cleveland at Toronto.
Vancouver at Chicago.
Winnipeg at Edmonton.

The New York Times

SPORTS

Section 5

Sunday, January 20, 1974

Notre Dame Beats U.C.L.A. in Last 29 Seconds, Ending Streak at 88

Adrian Dantley of Notre Dame pulling down basketball net after U.C.L.A. lost at South Bend, Ind. The defeat ended the Bruins' victory streak at 88.

Clay's Shot Wins, 71-70, as Irish Rally From 11-Point Deficit With 3:32 to Go

By GORDON S. WHITE Jr.

Special to The New York Times

SOUTH BEND, Ind., Jan. 19—U.C.L.A.'s record 88-game basketball winning streak came to an end today on the same court where the Bruins had last lost three years ago.

In a surprising and thrilling finish, unbeaten Notre Dame turned an 11-point deficit and apparent defeat in the last 3 minutes 32 seconds into a 71-70 victory.

Dwight Clay took a jump shot from the right corner and the ball went through for the winning points. With 29 seconds remaining, the Irish held on in a wild finale to beat the school that has been the National Collegiate champion for the last seven years and nine of the last 10.

The crowd of 11,343 fans in Notre Dame's Athletic and Convocation Center was almost stunned. It was a few seconds before belief registered, apparently, and then the fans swarmed on the court, smothering the Irish players and Coach Digger Phelps with wild undergraduate enthusiasm.

The Irish will obviously move up from No. 2 to No. 1 in the weekly polls, replacing U.C.L.A., which has been No. 1 since the semifinals of the 1968 National Collegiate Athletic Association championship tournament. The victory came 20 days after Notre Dame's football team became the No. 1 team by beating Alabama in an equally exciting Sugar Bowl game.

However, the basketball team will have to fight to retain its lofty spot because it meets U.C.L.A. in a return game a week from tonight at Pauley Pavilion in Los Angeles.

What made the victory more impressive was that the Irish beat the "Walton Gang," with Bill Walton playing the entire 40 minutes and playing very well. That U.C.L.A. could not get the ball to the big redhead at the end was a telling factor after Clay's shot.

Walton injured his back

Continued on Page 4, Column 6

Associated Press

Digger Phelps, right, Irish coach, with Bob Whitmore, former player, after the game

Rangers Close Trip With a 3-2 Victory

By PARTON KEESE

Special to The New York Times

CHICAGO, Jan. 19—A last-period aggressiveness, which seemed to be missing until Emile Francis returned as coach, paid off today for the New York Rangers with a 3-2 victory over the Chicago Black Hawks. The triumph before a national television audience brought the Rangers' six-game trip to a fruitful climax with three victories and a tie.

Pete Stemkowski engineered the winning goal, taking the puck into the Hawks' zone after Brad Park had stopped a Chicago drive. Stemmer skated straight for Tony Esposito in the goal, darted to his right and fired. The puck hit Esposito's glove and kept going for the winning score at 11:56.

Park, who had been both hero and goat earlier in the game, gained an assist on that final tally, which with a first-period goal and another assist gave him the club lead in points with 49. Park also kept alive a Ranger record for defensemen, having scored at least one point in his last nine games.

Brad came up with the contest's first score with a long shot from the blue line, one that Esposito probably never saw. Walt Tkaczuk had labored to keep the puck in the zone, finally getting it out to Gilles Marotte. Marotte passed cross-rink to Park, who gained his 14th goal.

Chico Maki took charge after that, scoring both Chicago goals in the second period. The first one came after 24 seconds of play. The 5-foot-10-inch right wing took the puck away from Park in front of Eddie Giacomin and, after bringing the Ranger goaltender to his knees, calmly lofted the disk over him.

Less than six minutes later, Maki scored again, this time taking a perfect pass from J. P. Bordeleau in front of the goal.

But the Rangers, fired up by a couple of fights, were able to enter their favorite period (the third) with a 2-2 tie when Ted Irvine scored his 16th goal of the season. It took a ballerina step by Park, plus an assist by the all-star defenseman, to give Irvine shooting room.

Tkaczuk and Dick Redmund engaged in a mild wrestling bout in the second period. Later Steve Vickers landed some solid punches on Len Frig's head in another battle. All four served time in the penalty box.

Starring for the Rangers unexpectedly in the afternoon game was Billy Fairbairn, who had bruised his left knee so badly in Thursday night's game with St. Louis Blues that Francis had called up Jerry Butler from the Providence Reds of the American Hockey League to replace him.

Farbairn who has earned a reputation for not missing games despite injuries, admitted he didn't like to sit out "if I can help it."

'Calling up a man to take my place also makes me more eager to keep going and not lose my position to anybody else,'' Billy said.

The Rangers were delighted with this victory, which to

Continued on Page 5, Column 1

Associated Press

Tony Esposito, Black Hawks' goalie, about to slap away from the net a shot by the Rangers. Keith Magnuson, rear, manages to keep Vic Hadfield away from rebound.

Suns Rout Knicks by 112 to 89

By LEONARD KOPPETT

Special to The New York Times

PHOENIX, Ariz., Jan. 19—Having scored something of a victory merely by reaching Phoenix, after three plane cancellations, an unscheduled sleepover in the Houston Airport's luxurious hotel and a route through San Antonio, the New York Knicks faced the Phoenix Suns tonight in the last game of a two-week road trip.

After all that travail, the result, perhaps, was predictable as the Knicks lost, 112-89, giving them a .500 mark for the six away games.

Whether from road-weariness or other causes, the Knicks seemed generally flat throughout the first three quarters, during which they trailed by as much as 15 points and seldom by less than 9. Sniping at the referees, which began early in the game, became a standard occupation of both teams, and this had something to do with the fact that no clear pattern emerged.

The Suns, who had taken command by being more aggressive and running through spotty Knick defenses, had as much trouble getting anything rolling in the third period as the Knicks did.

With two minutes to go in the third quarter, however, the Knicks were trailing by only 73-65, and not

Continued on Page 4, Column 8

Whole New Game for Giants

By NEIL AMDUR

The assistant equipment manager, a black youth in his early 20's, spotted Bill Arnsparger seated at a table with Don Shula and several friends at the Miami Dolphins' Super Bowl victory party last Sunday night in Houston.

The youth walked toward the table, sat next to Arnsparger, whispered something to him and began crying, as if he could not believe the report that Arnsparger was leaving the Dolphins to become the head coach of the New York Giants. Arnsparger, a father of two, put his hand on the back of the youth's neck and held it there for almost five minutes consoling him with kindness.

"It'll be my most impressive memory of Bill," a person seated at the table recalled the other day. "It was a very touching scene and told me as much about Arnsparger as anything he did for the Dolphins' defense."

There will be more than a kind face in charge of rebuilding the confidence and character of the Giants next season. An entirely new attitude is likely to emerge among relationships involving not only management and coach but also coach and players.

Each of the last four Giant head coaches (Alex Webster, Allie Sherman, Jim Lee Howell and Steve Owen) took the traditional family route from assistant to the top spot. As such, all may have felt grateful and, in some cases, subservient to management for their promotion and position.

Arnsparger was recruited for the job, not because he was identified with anything in the Giants' proud past, but because he was identified with winners wherever he had worked as an assistant—from Ohio State under Woody Hayes to the Dolphins under Don Shula.

It is for this reason that Arnsparger's presence represents a significant cutting of the cord—a break acknowledged as necessary even by Andy Robustelli, old No. 81, now the director of Giant operations.

"Maybe we needed to hang onto it," Robustelli said on why the Giants attached their spirit to the past so strongly in recent years. "But these players have got to play for what they are now."

In assessing Arnsparger's coaching qualities, he has been characterized as patient, soft-spoken, easy-going, with a sleepy-eyed, introspective manner that

Continued on Page 3, Column 2

Johnny Miller's Lead Falls to 2 Shots

By LINCOLN A. WERDEN

Special to The New York Times

TUCSON, Ariz., Jan. 19—Johnny Miller still led after 54 holes in the $150,000 Dean Martin-Tucson open today but his edge diminished to two strokes.

Complaining of a sore throat, the 26-year-old United States Open champion finished with a 71, his 10th subpar round of the current campaign and brought his three-round aggregate to 204. Three challengers in a tie at 206 had cut his margin in half.

"Honestly, I'm so tired I hope to muster enough energy to win tomorrow," said Miller. "I have a cold and it's getting worse and it's wearing me down. I've got to be realistic, I'm tired. I'm no superman—trying to win three in a row is something."

Miller, who has won the Crosby and the Phoenix open tournaments, the preceding two events on the year's schedule, added, "It was ridiculous. We had to wait on every shot. It took too long to play, four-and-a-half hours or more."

Although he spoke in almost a whisper during his press interview, he said, "I'll have to shoot in the sixties to win. Those guys," meaning J. C. Snead, who won this tournament in 1971; Ben Crenshaw, the spectacular rookie who became 22 years old last week, and Allen Miller, no relation, "are hungrier than I am."

Snead scored a seven-un-

Continued on Page 2, Column 5

Ali's Hand Treatments Stir a Mystery in Camp

By GERALD ESKENAZI

Special to The New York Times

DEER LAKE, Pa.—Every day since last October, an oversized jar of Theraffin is opened and its contents are smeared over Muhammad Ali's right hand.

Ali has used the hand hardly at all against sparring partners, but on Jan. 28 it will have to be exposed against Joe Frazier's jaw in their heralded rematch at Madison Square Garden.

Is there anything wrong with Ali's hand?

The Theraffin is a waxy substance that those around Ali claim toughens his hand, which was hurt last September against Ken Norton. Ali never had used the Theraffin before on a daily basis.

When asked about it the ex-champion lowers his voice half a dozen decibels and whispers, "Joe Frazier is gonna feel the hand."

But Dr. Edwin Campbell of the State Athletic Commission expressed surprise when told that Ali had been using the wax treatments every day.

"It's an astringent," said the doctor. "It's supposed to be used to stop inflammation. I know that Ali's had problems before with the cartilage around his right knuckle, but I hadn't heard of anything lately."

The doctor will be examining Ali on Wednesday. "I'll X-ray the hand," he said.

Willie Pep, the former featherweight champion, was a visitor here the other day.

"I never seen a guy train that way," said Pep. "He's not throwing no punches."

"Oh, the champ's the worst gymnasium fighter in the world," said Angelo Dundee, Ali's trainer. "What's he got

Continued on Page 3, Column 2

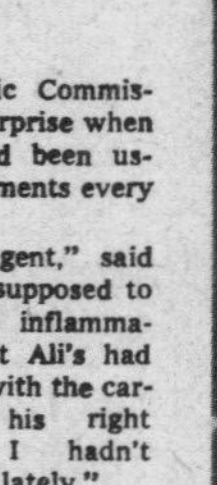

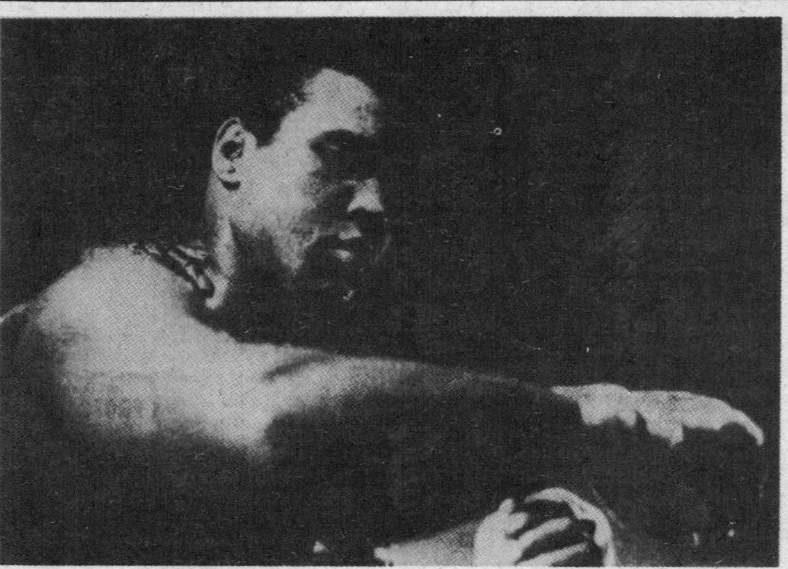

The New York Times/Robert Walker

Muhammad Ali taping his right hand for a training session last week at his camp at Deer Lake, Pa.

Inside Information

U.C.L.A. Winning Streak Ended by Irish, 71 to 70

Continued From Page 1

seriously in a fall during a game at Washington State last Monday, and had missed the last three U.C.L.A victories. He played today with an elastic corset. He scored 24 points, had nine rebounds and intimidated Notre Dame throughout.

This was the first time Walton or any of the other Bruins had tasted defeat as varsity players. Walton, Tommy Curtis and Keith Wilkes are the outstanding seniors who went a long time before losing.

Phelps, in his third year as Notre Dame coach after leaving Fordham, said:

"This was great for college basketball. I'm sure everyone was rooting for us the way they used to root against the New York Yankees. The win was special for Notre Dame, for the kids, for my staff, for my mother and father [who were present] and for us all."

Describing the action of the final three minutes, Phelps said:

"We thought we had to to go to really pressing again, and so I put in Ray Martin [freshman from Long Island City, Queens] for Bill Paterno [freshman from Spring Lake, N. J.]. The kids never gave up and were incredible, just unbelievable."

The other Notre Dame players who went down the wire in the press when the Irish got their first and only lead of the game were Clay, John Shumate (defending against Walton), Adrian Dantley (a freshman from Washington) and Gary Brokaw, who led the game scoring with 25 points.

Big Leads Dwindle

U.C.L.A., which led by 17 points twice in the first half, and by 43-34 at the intermission, was in front, 70-59 with 3 minutes 32 seconds to go. Phelps ordered time-out 10 seconds later and set up a press, replacing Paterno with Martin.

Shumate connected on a hook shot over Walton with 3:07 remaining. But nobody could believe that this was the beginning of the end for the national champions.

Shumate, strong and quick at 6 feet 9 inches and 235 pounds, stole the ensuing U.C.L.A. inbounds pass right under the basket and easily scored again. Now the crowd sensed something and began hollering, "Shoo! Shoo!" for Shumate.

U.C.L.A. made the inbounds pass this time, but at midcourt Dantley, an amazing freshman, stole the ball from Curtis and went in unchallenged for the basket that cut the margin to 70-65.

Another Turnover

U.C.L.A. tried something different, with Wilkes making a long, upcourt pass to Curtis. Curtis was behind Martin, who fell. But when Curtis got the ball, he ran with it and Notre Dame gained possession on the turnover.

The Irish worked for a good shot by Brokaw, the junior from New Brunswick, N. J., and the score was 70-67. Dave Meyers went in for a layup for U.C.L.A., but was charged with traveling. Again Notre Dame scored on the turnover as Brokaw hit a short jumper. The place went wild.

Now Wilkes tried to score on a drive, but he fouled Brokaw in the process for the fifth U.C.L.A. turnover in those final minutes.

The Irish wanted to work the ball to Shumate with less than 45 seconds remaining. But Shumate wasn't open, so Brokaw got the ball to the open man, Clay, who hit on the jump shot and fell into the crowd as he came down.

The Bruins, at a signal from Coach John Wooden, called time-out with 21 seconds to go, plenty of time for them to get the winning shot. But Curtis shot from 25 feet and missed, Meyers missed a tip-in of the rebound and Walton got his hands on the ball, but not enough to control it for a good shot.

After a Notre Dame player knocked the ball out of bounds with 6 seconds to play, U.C.L.A. worked the ball to Walton, who was off on a 12-foot shot. Two Bruins missed follow-up shots as time ran out.

Thus U.C.L.A., which set the collegiate record with 61 victories in a row by winning here a year ago, was doomed to have its new record end here.

After the game Clay said:

"It was one of the greatest feelings I've ever had. I looked out at Gary [Brokaw] with the ball when he was trying to get it into Shoo. Then I saw the defense shift in to Gary and I was alone, so I called to him for the ball."

Shumate, who played well against Walton despite the big man's excellent performance, said: "Walton's a devastating player. He's got everything." Then he raised his arm and pointed, "We're No. 1."

Phelps said: "When they shot 70 per cent in the first half, they were something. Whew! They're a great team, just great. Now we have to get ready for Kansas Tuesday night and then St. Francis Thursday night, and then we get ready for U.C.L.A. again.

"Sure it was a great victory, but what we want most of all is a bid to the N.C.A.A. championship, so each game means as much as each other game as they approach. Undefeated isn't so much as not losing too many to lose that bid."

Then he added with a laugh: "I hope I get a call from President Nixon saying we shouldn't fly to Los Angeles because of the fuel shortage."

Notre Dame has a 10-0 record and U.C.L.A. is 13-1. This was only the sixth defeat for U.C.L.A. in the last eight seasons during which Wooden's Bruins have won 218 games.

Wooden said:

"Once we got the game to break the record, it was relatively meaningless. We knew it would end sometime. Now we have to win our conference to defend our national title."

Then the coach added. "The travel call against Curtis and the charge call on Wilkes were important."

Asked if he had objected to the officials' calls on those late key plays, Wooden replied, "They were close and could have gone the other way."

Wooden refused to permit reporters to talk to his players after the game. "Only winners talk," he said. However, he had repeatedly closed the dressing room to reporters after his teams had won N.C.A.A. championship games.

U.C.L.A. (70): Wilkes [illegible] 6-7, 18; Trgovich 3, [illegible] 7; Walton 12, 0-0, 24; Curtis 3, 3-4, [illegible]; Meyers 5, 0-[illegible], 10; Lee 0, [illegible], 2; Johnson 0, 0-0, 0. Totals 29, 12-16.

NOTRE DAME (71)—Brokaw 10, 5-7, 25; Clay 2, 3-4, 7; Shumate 11, 2-4, 24; Dantley 4, 1-[illegible], 9; Novak 0, 0-0, 0; Paterno 2, 0-0, 4; Martin 1, 0-0, 2. Totals—30, 11-16.

Half-time score—U.C.L.A. 43, Notre Dame 34.

Technical fouls—Meyers, Brokaw.

Attendance—11,343.

Wide World Photos

Bill Walton of U.C.L.A. fights for a rebound with Notre Dame's Adrian Dantley.

The U.C.L.A. Dynasty: One Era Comes to End But Another Is on Way

The U.C.L.A. basketball dynasty, under Coach John Wooden, has been a succession of "mini-eras" spanning a quarter-century of unequaled success. Yesterday the latest of the mini-eras ended. More such eras will probably come.

The record National Collegiate Athletic Association victory string started by the University of California, Los Angeles, on Jan. 30, 1971, finally ran out at 88 straight as a result of the 71-70 loss to Notre Dame.

Most of the streak has been called the "Era of the Walton Gang," since Big Bill Walton has been the most important player from victory No. 16 (Dec. 3, 1971) onward. The Walton Gang won the last two of U.C.L.A.'s seven straight N.C.A.A. championships. In all U.C.L.A. has won nine of the last 10 titles.

Notre Dame was the last team to beat Wooden's Bruins before they began the victory string that might become one of the most durable records in sports. On Jan. 23, 1971, Austin Carr led an Irish attack on a tired band of traveling U.C.L.A. players, and Notre Dame won, 89-82.

U.C.L.A. had beaten Loyola of Chicago in Chicago Stadium, 87-62, on a Friday night and then had to meet Notre Dame at South Bend, Ind., the next afternoon. Sidney Wicks was the Bruins' star of that season, Steve Patterson was the big man and Henry Bibby the best guard. They and the other Bruins showed weariness when a strong Irish team pressed them.

As a result, Wooden insisted afterward that the annual trip to Chicago and South Bend consist of a Thursday night game at Chicago Stadium, not Friday night. Never again, he vowed, would U.C.L.A. have a tired team facing Notre Dame.

Rested and ready, U.C.L.A. easily beat the University of California, Santa Barbara, 74-61, a week after losing to Notre Dame that year, and the Bruins were off on what was believed to be the longest victory streak in United States team sports.

The Wicks-Patterson Era team went on to win its last 15 games of the 1970-71 season and the N.C.A.A. championship. It was the seventh national title and fifth in a row for Coach Wooden.

The coach said: "Amazing poise, incredible courage and extraordinary discipline were qualities consistently exemplified by the 1971 champions."

Walton entered the scene as a sophomore in the opening game of the 1971-72 season, in which U.C.L.A. routed The Citadel, 105-49. Two years after the loss to Notre Dame, the Walton Gang established a new collegiate streak of 61, also gaining revenge.

The 61st triumph, on Jan. 27, 1973, was an 82-63 decision over Notre Dame at South Bend that broke the previous N.C.A.A. record of 60 set by San Francisco when Bill Russell played for the Dons (1955-57). Until yesterday, U.C.L.A. had just kept adding to the record.

The Walton Gang won the eighth and ninth of Wooden's N.C.A.A. championships in 1972 and 1973. The coach said, "The 1972 championship team probably was the most versatile of all my teams."

Wooden suffered a "mild heart condition" at the start of the 1972-73 season. After winning the title again, he said: "This season was one of the most trying in my experience. However, the end result was extremely gratifying."

Walton turned in what some persons considered to be the greatest individual performance in N.C.A.A. playoff history when U.C.L.A. beat Memphis State, 87-66, in the 1973 title game. The big redhead connected on 21 of 22 floor shots, scored 44 points, took 13 rebounds and blocked many shots.

Wooden's first national title at U.C.L.A. came in 1964 at the height of the Hazzard-Goodrich Era. Walt Hazzard and Gail Goodrich were the superstars of a band of comparative midgets. Though small, the team was skilled and exemplified Wooden discipline.

The coach, looking back, said:

"The fact that this was my first N.C.A.A. championship team is reason enough for it to be my favorite, but there are other factors. It was the shortest of all N.C.A.A. champions, it used the exciting press defense exceptionally well and it was a very colorful and fascinating team to watch."

The next year Hazzard was gone, but Goodrich led the Bruins to their second national championship. They didn't win the following season, but the Alcindor Era began in the 1966-67 season. It was the start of a string of nine national crowns. For three years Lew Alcindor led the parade.

Wooden said, "I was pleased to learn that I could work an unusually tall and talented superstar, Lewis Alcindor, into my idea of team play without his teammates losing their identity." Alcindor changed his name to Kareem Abdul-Jabbar after graduation.

The Wicks-Patterson Era came next, followed by the Winning Streak Era and the Walton Gang.

Wooden's first 15 years at U.C.L.A. (1948-1963) were the Era of Preparation, although he never had a losing season. Once that period was over, U.C.L.A. went on to four undefeated seasons.

The New York Times
SPORTS
Section 5
Sunday, March 24, 1974

N.C. State Ends U.C.L.A.'s 7-Year Reign, 80-77; Purdue and Utah Fives Capture N.I.T. Semifinals

Favorite American Pastimes
Total Popularity (Projected Estimate In Millions)

Swimming	107,191,000
Bicycling	65,613,000
Fishing	61,263,000
Camping	54,435,000
Bowling	38,218,000
Table Tennis	33,501,000
Pool and billiards	32,920,000
Boating (other than sailing)	32,629,000
Softball	26,362,000
Ice Skating	24,875,000

Source: A. C. Nielsen Co.
The New York Times/March 23, 1974

Swimming Still Rated Top Participant Sport; Camping on Increase

By NEIL AMDUR

The next time your wife or girl friend tries to talk you into a camping trip, don't laugh: camping is second only to swimming in the sporting hearts and habits of American women.

This interesting statistic has emerged with thousands of others in a detailed survey of the participant sports tastes of Americans—from children-under-12 to adults.

The study was compiled late last year by the A. C. Nielsen Company, a prominent market research firm, in telephone interviews with 2,000 survey households involving 6,375 persons across the country. Nielsen has been selling its volumes of statistics to manufacturers, advertisers, analysts and potential sports investors.

Among some of its more surprising findings are the following:

¶While swimming remains the most popular participant sports pastime (it was No. 1 in an informal Nielsen survey fours years ago), Americans swim less with age. Only 47 per cent of men 18-and-over, and 39 per cent among adult women, said they swam "from time to time," a significant drop from the 80 per cent level recorded among the 12-to-17-year-olds.

¶Tennis, once a sport for the classes, finally

Continued on Page 6, Column 5

Jacksonville Bows, 78-63–B.C. Loses in 117-93 Battle

By SAM GOLDAPER

Utah, the highest scoring and hottest shooting team, and Purdue, the most poised and disciplined, gained the final round of the National Invitation Tournament at Madison Square Garden yesterday.

The Utes, with their three-man Eastern contingent again on target (74 points) battered Boston College, 117-93, after Purdue had eliminated Jacksonville, 78-63, before 12,105 basketball fans and a national television audience. Both winners needed strong second halves to put the games out of reach.

Utah and Purdue will meet today in the final at 1 P.M., with Jacksonville and Boston College playing the consolation game at 11 A.M. It will be the second meeting of the finalists this season. Utah won the first on a shot at the buzzer by Ticky Burden at Salt Lake City last Jan. 1.

The 117 points Utah ran up gave the Westerners a three-game total of 311, bettering the N.I.T. record of 294 set by the 1957 Bradley team. The Utes' 48 field goals yesterday was also a tournament record.

Utah, which shot 52 per cent, broke out with a 69-point second half after it had led Boston College, 48-45, at the intermission. The Eagles were able to keep the game close in the first half primarily on the shooting of Bob Carrington, a 6-foot-6-

Continued on Page 4, Column 5

United Press International

David Thompson of North Carolina State pulling in a rebound despite attempts of Dave Meyers of U.C.L.A. to get it. Play came during semifinal of N.C.A.A. tournament in Greensboro, N. C.

2 Overtimes Needed –Marquette Beats Kansas, 64-51

By GORDON S. WHITE Jr.
Special to The New York Times

GREENSBORO, N.C., March 23—For the first time in eight years, and only the second time in the last 11, there will be a new National Collegiate basketball champion crowned Monday night.

The University of California, Los Angeles, was dethroned today by North Carolina State in a thrilling double-overtime contest, 80-77, in the semifinals of the N.C.A.A. tournament. Thus, either N.C. State or Marquette will replace U.C.L.A. as champion. Marquette won the other semifinal game by beating Kansas, 64-51, in a regulation 40-minute game.

North Carolina State and Marquette will meet Monday night in the final at Greensboro Coliseum, where 15,829 fans, most of them N.C. State partisans, were treated this afternoon to one of the most exciting tourney games on record.

Trailing by 7 points with 3 minutes 27 seconds to go in the second five-minute overtime period, N.C. State showed no signs of panic. The Wolfpack came back to win on 6 points by David Thompson, 3 by Tommy Burleson, the biggest player on the court, and 4 by Monte Towe, the smallest player in the 36th annual N.C.A.A. tournament.

As a result, there will be a new champion for the first time since Texas Western (now the University of Tex-

Continued on Page 4, Column 1

Forego Wins Widener At Hialeah

By JAMES TUITE
Special to The New York Times

MIAMI, March 23—Like a fading dowager queen whose sand castle has been eroded by time and circumstance, Hialeah Park reached out today for a touch of its lost glory, and a horse named Forego helped her achieve this by winning the 37th running of the venerable Widener Handicap.

With a burst of speed at the top of the stretch, Forego of the Lazy F. Ranch showed some of the class that marked such Widener winners as War Admiral (1938) and Armed (1947). He swept to a length victory over arch-rival True Knight for a $3.60 return on a $2 ticket. True Knight was two lengths ahead of Play the Field and More Horsepower was fourth.

Forego, in taking the $76,635 winner's share of the $117,900 purse, was timed in 2:01 1-5 for the mile and a quarter.

Six times from the stretch turn to the wire, Heliodoro Gustines turned on Forego to look back for True Knight, whose late charge was a bit tardy. When True Knight hove into view with Angel Cordero driving him, the race was on.

Gustines gave one quick flick of his whip and the contest was over. Many of the 17,279 fans on hand who had bet the odds-on choice hap-

Continued on Page 10, Column 6

The New York Times/Robert Walker

Sharon Ireland cheering for Jacksonville during the N.I.T. semifinal with Purdue at the Garden yesterday afternoon

John Miller Cards Ace, Leads by 4

By JOHN S. RADOSTA
Special to The New York Times

HILTON HEAD ISLAND, S. C., March 23—What was Johnny Miller thinking about as he undid himself with three bogeys and a double-bogey in five holes? Not his golf, not his lead, but the basketball game in which the University of California, Los Angeles, lost to North Carolina State.

Keeping abreast of the game with reports from his gallery, Miller lost his concentration. The result was one of his worst nine-hole scores in recent years, a dismal 40 after a superb 32 for a round of 72, one over par for the Harbour Town Golf Links.

And so Miller, the whiz kid of the pro golf tour, protected his lead, though not too securely, after three rounds of the $200,000 Heritage Golf Classic. He finished the day with a 72 and 206 for 54 holes, four under par.

"I'll give you guys a good story tomorrow," he said, "if I blow the biggest lead of the year."

Starting the third round

Continued on Page 9, Column 8

Kings Overcome Knicks; Rangers Beaten by Wings

Victors by 107-106

By THOMAS ROGERS

Making up for more than three years of frustration at Madison Square Garden, the Kansas City-Omaha Kings tore back from a 20-point half-time deficit to upset the Knicks, 107-106, last night before the usual capacity crowd of 19,694. The Kings had not won a game at the Garden since Nov. 19, 1970, when the franchise was operating out of Cincinnati as the Royals.

The loss, one of the Knicks' most embarrassing of the season, momentarily prevented the New Yorkers from clinching the home-court advantage against the Capital Bullets in the first round of the National Basketball Association playoffs which begin on Friday.

But 20 minutes after the end of the game, the Knicks

Continued on Page 4, Column 6

Lose, 5-3, After 3-1 Lead

By PARTON KEESE
Special to The New York Times

DETROIT, March 23—Tonight's 5-3 loss to Detroit was supposed to mark the beginning of an unofficial "Don't Arouse The Red Wings" period for the New York Rangers as the two teams played the first of three games against each other with just eight remaining on the season schedule. The results could well determine the fortunes of New York: second or third place.

But the Detroiters got themselves aroused anyway, all because of their scoring leader, Mickey Redmond. Although the sixth-place Wings are going nowhere this season, they psyched themselves up trying to help Redmond get 50 goals and become only the third player in National Hockey League history to

Continued on Page 5, Column 5

Yanks Buy Maddox From Rangers, Then Lose, 9-8

Special to The New York Times

POMPANO BEACH, Fla., March 23—The Yankees, suddenly collecting outfielders as some people collect bottle caps, welcomed one new outfielder to the club today, then bought another while he sat in the Texas Rangers' bull pen.

A couple of hours after Walt Williams checked in, the Yankees purchased Elliott Maddox from the Rangers for about $40,000, prompting an ecstatic reaction from the 25-year-old, who grew up in Union, N.J.

Combined with Manager Bill Virdon's decision to use Ron Blomberg in right field instead of first base, the addition of Williams and Maddox makes the Yankees well stocked with outfielders. Maddox is clearly the best defensive outfielder and figures to play primarily in defensive situations.

The trade was made too late for Maddox to change uniforms for the game, but Williams, more a hitter than a fielder, singled on the first pitch he saw as a Yankee.

The Yankees lost the game, 9-8, when Tom Grieve scored a two-run home run off Roger Hambright in the ninth inning. Mike Hegan had put the Yankees in front, 8-7, with a two-run, inside-the-park homer in the eighth. A grand-slam homer by Jeff Burroughs off Wayne Granger had sent the Rangers ahead, 7-6, in the seventh.

Maddox was so primed to escape from the Rangers, as soon as he saw a group of writers heading toward the Ranger bull pen, he started shaking hands and saying good-by to his teammates.

Continued on Page 3, Column 1

After 2 Years, Nassau Coliseum Is More of a Complement Than Satellite to Garden

By GERALD ESKENAZI

A pair of anniversaries are coming up in a few weeks—the birthdays of the Nassau Coliseum and Madison Square Garden. Almost 100 years ago, P. T. Barnum put up his grand Hippodrome, which became Madison Square Garden I. And two years ago, a major league arena came to Nassau County when the Coliseum officially opened.

Both are big. The Garden, of course, is No. 1 in the world. It probably is identified with the city more than any other indoor arena. The Coliseum? In 24 months it has become the third busiest arena in the United States, behind that Greek-inspired Los Angeles palace that was given a Roman name—the Forum.

The Garden's identity is easy.

"We pulse with the blood of New York," said Mike Burke, the dashing president of the Garden. "It's an earthy place. We're not dealing here with an intrinsic value. We're dealing with a state of mind."

Out of the Island, meanwhile, the search for an identity hasn't been easy—but it's coming. No one ever said it would be simple to merge the big city and the suburbs.

When the building opened, the County Executive, Ralph G. Caso, spoke of it as "a people's place." But he also wanted the sophistication of the Garden. He was tired of Nassau County being considered a satellite of New York, and he didn't want the Coliseum to be a satellite of Madison Square Garden.

When the basketball Nets moved into the building, one of Caso's first orders was to stop the Nets' practice of giving 10 gallons of gasoine to anyone who scored a 3-point goal. That was a bush-league image.

But today there still is a Dairy Barn most valuable player in Nets and Islanders games.

"That would be a non-sequitur in the Garden," said Burke, reflecting on the difference in attitude. Apparently, the fans at basketball and hockey games at the Coliseum don't mind. They are not the expense-account crowd the Garden attracts (primarily because of the high price of season seats). It is a younger, blue-collar crowd.

There are pluses in the Coliseum that the Garden may never equal. There's the parking. For $1 you park in the 6,000-space lot. And you get in and out as easily as going shopping. There are no 45-minute or one-hour waits for cars, as at the private parking lots surrounding the Garden.

The ticket-takers smile more at the Coliseum. The ushers appear to be friendlier. Yet, strangely, many of the ushers also work at the Garden.

"I guess we've tried to create a sort of Disneyland East in the way the workers here treat the public," explained Jack Globenfelt, the Coliseum's operations manager. "But it may be more than that. Perhaps the fans here are politer than they are in New York, and the ushers react to that. Also, a lot of our ushers live on the Island and they've got a vested interest in this place."

The image of the ushers

Continued on Page 6, Column 5

Inside Information

N.C. State Ends Reign Of U.C.L.A.

Continued From Page 1

as, El Paso) beat Kentucky for the title in 1966. U.C.L.A. had won the title in 1964 and 1965 and then won it seven straight times from 1967 through 1973.

This 1973-74 U.C.L.A. season will probably become better known for the four losses the Bruins suffered than for any of the 25 victories they achieved. The first of these defeats came on Jan. 19, when Notre Dame beat Coach John Wooden's team, 71-70, to end the U.C.L.A. record winning streak of 88 games that spanned three seasons. The next two losses were on a dark weekend in Oregon, when U.C.L.A. lost to Oregon State and then Oregon. And finally there was today's loss to N.C. State, the team ranked No. 1 in the nation that was playing before the home folks in North Carolina.

Norm Sloan, N.C. State's coach, said: "This is one of our best wins but not our best. If we win Monday night, that will be our greatest victory."

The 63-year-old Wooden, coach of all the U.C.L.A. title teams, did not consider this the end of a dynasty.

"I never considered it a dynasty," he said. "There were different teams, and many things broke our way in games."

But this was the end of the Walton Gang as a major power, because Bill Walton, the big, red-haired leader of the team, is finishing his senior season. He played well today, scoring 29 points, more than anyone on the floor, but couldn't do it alone.

When N.C. State was beaten by U.C.L.A. early this season (Dec. 15 in St. Louis), Walton played only 19 minutes but completely dominated Burleson, the 7-foot-4-inch center for the Wolfpack. Walton did not handle Burleson that easily today, and Sloan said, "I've seen both of 'em play better."

The game was not only tied, 65-65, after 40 minutes and 67-67 after the first overtime period, but it was also tied at half-time, 35-35. Dave Meyers of U.C.L.A. made that tie possible when he scored on a desperation 40-foot shot at the buzzer ending the first half.

Then, in the first 10 minutes of the second half, N. C. State twice fell 11 points behind. But a streak of 10 straight points by the Wolfpack cut the second big deficit considerably. U.C.L.A., meanwhile, was attempting long, wild shots and was unable to work the ball into Walton.

Then, the game went nip and tuck to the wire. Walton scored to give U.C.L.A. a 65-63 lead with 2:22 left in regulation, but Thompson scored the tying points with 2 minutes to go on a quick inside pass from Tim Stoddard.

Thompson showed no effects from the head injury he suffered in the quarterfinal round victory over Pittsburgh just a week ago.

He and the other Carolinians [Thompson is a native of the Tar Heel State] controlled the ball most of the final 2 minutes of regulation, and Stoddard took a baseline shot from the right side with 9 seconds to go. He missed and thus the first overtime.

Burleson and Greg Lee traded baskets, and N.C. State controlled the ball again for most of the first extra period. But then, in the second overtime, Walton got 4 quick points and Keith Wilkes got 3 to put U.C.L.A. ahead, 74-67, and it seemed all over for North Carolina State.

The Wolfpack, however, turned the game around in a frantic finish, using an interception of a U.C.L.A. pass, a couple of missed U.C.L.A. shots and some good shooting and playmaking of their own, much of it from Towe, who is only 5-feet-5½ inches tall. After the score was 75-69, Thompson's 6 points led a spree of points by the Wolfpack that won the game.

Coach Al McGuire's Marquette team became the first squad from the Milwaukee university to reach an N.C.A.A. final in nine attempts, the last six under the direction of McGuire, an admitted "dictator."

As usual, Marquette did its job in a slow and meticulous fashion, waiting for the opening to strike and then dealing the death blo wto the Big Eight Conference champion during a four-minute stretch early in the second half. This drive made up for first-half lapses, during which Marquette lost a 7-point lead and went into the dressing room at half-time behind by 1 point, 24-23.

It was there, in the seclusion of the locker room, that things changed a bit for Marquette.

McGuire said: "We went at each other (coach vs. players) pretty hard at half-time. There were a couple of things, and it had nothing to do with basketball."

Whatever was said in there, the Warriors, young but composed, came out and crept back to take the lead at 30-29 with 16½ minutes remaining in the game. Never again was Marquette behind in the semifinal match.

U.C.L.A. (77)	G.	F.	P.
Meyers	6	0-1	12
Wilkes	5	5-5	15
Walton	13	3-3	29
Curtis	4	3-4	11
Lee	4	0-0	8
Johnson	0	0-0	0
McCarter	1	0-0	2
Total	33	11-13	77

N. C. State (80)	G.	F.	P.
Stoddard	4	1-2	9
Thompson	12	4-6	28
Burleson	9	2-6	20
Rivers	3	1-2	7
Towne	4	4-4	12
Spence	2	0-0	4
Hawkins	0	0-0	0
Total	34	12-20	80

Half-time score—U.C.L.A. 35, N.C. State 35.
Regulation—U.C.L.A. 65, NC State 65
First overtime—U.C.L.A. 67, N.C. State 67.
Officials—Rick Weiler, Paul Galvin.
Fouled out—Wilkes, Curtis, Stoddard.
Attendance—15,829.

KANSAS (51)	G.	F.	P.
Cook	1	2-4	4
Morn'gstar	5	0-0	10
Knight	0	0-0	0
Greenlee	3	0-0	6
Kivisto	2	2-5	6
Suttle	8	3-4	19
Smith	3	0-0	6
Total	22	7-13	51

MARQUETTE (64)	G.	F.	P.
Ellis	2	1-2	5
Tatum	5	4-6	14
Lucas	7	4-4	18
Walton	2	3-4	7
Washingt'n	5	6-11	16
Daniels	0	0-0	0
Campbell	0	0-0	0
Homan	1	0-0	2
Delsman	0	2-2	2
Total	22	20-29	64

Half-time score—Kansas 24, Marquette 23.
Officials—Irv Brown, Jim Howell.
Fouled Out—Kansas: Cook.
Attendance: 15,000.

L.I. Lutheran Five, St. Anthony Gain

Special to The New York Times

HEMPSTEAD, L. I. March 23—Long Island Lutheran and St. Anthony of Smithtown will meet in the final of the Top Eight Classic here tomorrow night as a result of defeating St. Agnes and Molloy, respectively, at Hofstra University tonight.

Wayne McKoy led Long Island Lutheran with 44 points and 18 rebounds as Lutheran beat St. Agnes, 99-87. Al Eford added 17 points and pulled down 13 rebounds for Lutheran, while Mike Palma led St. Agnes with 34 points. Lutheran will go into the final with 19 victories in 20 games this year.

St. Anthony's posted its 20th victory of the year and its 38th in a row by trouncing Molloy, 51-35. Ken Kolakowski tallied 26 points for St. Anthony's and Ken Wallace led the losers with 17 points.

Kings Down Knicks; Frazier Injured

Continued From Page 1

learned that the Bullets had lost in Atlanta. The defeat for Capital ended any chance for the Bullets to finish with a better record than the Knicks. Thus, the playoffs will start here on Friday with the home court alternating until one team has won four games.

As well as emerging with reddened cheeks from their poor second-half play, the Knicks may have suffered a more serious blow. Walt Frazier twisted his ankle early in the fourth quarter and went to the bench with 10:37 remaining in the game. He sat there and watched as the Kings were outscrapping the Knicks in the final minutes. He did not accompany the team to Cleveland for a game there tonight against the Cavaliers.

"I came down on somebody's foot after a jump shot and twisted my right ankle," said Frazier while soaking his lower leg in a bucket of ice water. "I couldn't have played after that. It was too painful."

Frazier was missed in the exciting fourth quarter after the Kings had bounced back from a 58-38 half-time deficit by scoring 43 points in the third quarter. They held the suddenly lifeless Knicks to 20 points in the period and went into the final minutes with an 81-78 lead.

Led by Jimmy Walker, who scored 14 of his 28 points in the third quarter, the Royals hit 17 of 22 shots. Don Kojis, with 13 points, and Ron Behagen, with 10, helped Walker bedevil the Knicks with a running attack that led to a bevy of open shots.

The Knicks seemed to recover their composure midway in the fourth period when they scored 8 points in a row to regain the lead at 98-95. But Behagen, a rookie from Minnesota, and Walker refused to turn off the current. They scored all but one of the Kings' 12 points in the final 3½ minutes when the lead was changing hands three times. The final switch came with 11 seconds left on one of two free tosses by Mike D'Antoni, another rookie, breaking a 104-104 tie.

After a New York time-out, the Knicks lost possession when Earl Monroe dribbled the ball off his foot and it went out of bounds. Dave DeBusschere promptly fouled Walker, who gave Kansas City-Omaha a 2-point lead, 106-104, by hitting the second of two free throws with 4 seconds remaining.

The Knicks then called time out for the fourth time in the quarter, one more than is legally permitted. Walker sank the free throw on the technical foul and the Knicks were conscious it would cost ket at the buzzer only cut the margin.

"I told them to take the time out," admitted Coach Red Holzman afterward. "We weer conscious it would cost us a technical foul, but we thought we had to gamble. It didn't turn out too well. we thought that four seconds wasn't enough time to come all the way up court and get off a shot. We were hoping that they would miss the technical, but they didn't."

Willis Reed, playing in his second game since recovering from a knee operation, logged 13 uneventful minutes, missing two shots from the floor, hitting a pair from the foul line and grabbing four rebounds.

"I would liked to have played more, but it wasn't the type of game where I could get time," he said. "Maybe tomorrow night. I think I could go about 20 minutes if I get the chance. Everything felt fine tonight."

Later, at the airport, Reed learned that not only will he get more playing time in Cleveland but that he also will start the game because John Giaanelli suffered a bruise on his left thigh and is not expected to play.

Knicks' Box Score

K.C.-OMAHA (107)

	min	fgm	fga	ftm	fta	reb	a	pf	pts
Behagen	39	9	17	4	4	8	4	4	22
Kojis	31	9	11	3	3	4	0	2	21
Lacey	40	4	10	2	2	12	2	3	10
Walker	46	10	20	8	11	4	4	4	28
Williams	26	7	13	1	2	4	2	4	15
Block	10	0	3	0	0	1	0	0	0
Moore	8	1	2	0	0	2	1	0	2
D'Antoni	29	1	8	1	2	2	4	3	3
Durrett	7	3	4	0	0	1	0	1	6
Komives	2	0	2	0	0	0	0	0	0
McNeill	2	0	0	0	0	0	0	0	0
Total	240	44	89	19	24	38	17	21	107

KNICKS (106)

	min	fgm	fga	ftm	fta	reb	a	pf	pts
Bradley	31	8	17	2	2	5	0	4	18
DeB'chere	37	9	17	1	1	13	3	2	19
Gianelli	22	1	3	1	2	6	4	1	3
Frazier	24	8	12	2	2	4	6	2	18
Monroe	35	8	12	4	6	1	2	4	20
Jackson	26	6	9	2	2	7	2	3	14
Lucas	13	0	2	0	0	1	3	0	0
Meminger	33	5	9	2	3	3	1	3	12
Reed	13	0	2	2	2	4	0	1	2
Bibby	4	0	2	0	0	0	0	1	0
Wingo	2	0	1	0	0	1	0	0	0
Total	240	45	86	16	20	45	21	21	106

K.C.-Omaha	23	15	43	26—107
Knicks	31	27	20	28—106

min—Minutes played. fgm—Field goals made. fga—Field goals attempted. ftm—Free throws made. fta—Free throws attempted. reb—Rebounds. a—Assists pf—Personal fouls pts—Total points.

Referees—Bob Rakeland and Len Wirtz.
Attendance—19,694.

Utah Gains N.I.T. Final With Purdue

Continued From Page 1

inch sophomore, who scored 25 of his 33 points in the first 20 minutes.

In the second half the Utes came out running. They found a way to cool off Carrington's hot hand by getting by the screens set for him. And offensively, Burden, their 6-1 sophomore from Albany, regained his shooting touch.

Burden, who came into the game as the tournament's leading scorer with 64 points, scored 24 of his 29 points in the second half. He shot 2 for 11 in the first half and 8 for 16 thereafter to bring his three-game mark to 91.

"That Weldon guy did a hell of a job on me in the first half," said Burden, referring to Mel Weldon, Boston College's 6-foot guard who chased him up and down the floor.

"He was picking me up real well and kept me from getting the ball. This was the first time in my life I saw him, and I don't like these pesky little guys like him guarding me."

Mike Sojourner, the 6-8 strongman from Philadelphia, was Utah's top scorer with 29 points and Tyrone Medley, Burden's backcourt mate, who is from Camden, N.J., scored 17 and had six assists.

Sojourner was overpowering with his inside play and intimidating defensively. He gave Utah control of the boards. His 19 rebounds were half as many as B.C.'s total.

"His rebounding was super," said Bill Foster, the Utah coach. "He just cleared th boards and we were able to get men downcourt in droves during the second half."

Defensively, Sojourner clogged the middle and it became precarious for any Eagle to drive through it. He blocked about nine shots. Jere Nolan, the Eagles' backcourt star whose specialty is driving, made only one basket in six attempts in the first half and was 4 for 12 for the game.

The Utah coach, watching Purdue win, said: "The nicest thing I can say about them is they have great individual personnel that play as one. They are a team, and a sound one at that. They do so many things well."

How did Foster like his chances against Purdue?

"Our chances of winning this thing get better all the time," he said smilingly.

The Purdue-Jacksonville game could best be described as a matchup between a boxer and slugger. The Boilermakers, in the role of boxer, had the power, finesse and the experienced coaching of Fred Schaus.

Jacksonville, the slugger, is a run-and-shoot team with overwhelming natural talent, but the Dolphins yesterday shot wildly, did not pass off and showed that they still had to learn that defense is an integral part of basketball.

The best Jacksonville player is Henry Williams, a 6-6, 220-pound junior forward, who was drafted by the Nets last season. But his is an unharnessed talent. He forgot about his teammates and shot almost every time he got the ball.

The same was true for Leon Benbow, who scored 20 points. Between them they took 50 shots and made 17.

Williams, who scored 18 points, shot 8 for 26, while Benbow, after a hot 6 for 9 in the first half, suddenly turned cold, hitting only 3 for 15 in the second half.

Hawks Post 3-1 Triumph Over Flyers

PHILADELPHIA, March 23 (AP) — Dick Redmond's second-period goal clinched a 3-1 Chicago victory over the Philadelphia Flyers and enabled the Black Hawks to keep their flickering pennant hopes alive in the N.A.L. West.

The victory pulled the Hawks to within 8 points of the division-leading Flyers, and broke Philadelphia's 11-game unbeaten string.

Chicago Black Hawks	1	1	1—3
Philadelphia Flyers	0	1	0—1

FIRST PERIOD—1, Chicago, Rota (19) (Russell), 5:00. Penalties—Pappin, Chicago (1:10); Frig, Chicago ([illegible]:35); Clarke, Philadelphia ([illegible]:25); Dupont, Philadelphia (3:04); Flett, Philadelphia (9:4[illegible]); Marks, Chicago 1([illegible]:24); Frig, Chicago (8:43).

SECOND PERIOD—2, Chicago, Redmond (1[illegible]) (Mikita, Gagnon), 4:0[illegible]; 3, Philadelphia, Dornhoefer (10) (Crisp, Saleski), 18:09. Penalties—[illegible], Philadelphia ([illegible]); [illegible] 13:02); Barber, Philadelphia ([illegible]:48); Redmond, Chicago (15:45); Dornhoefer, Philadelphia (18:43).

THIRD PERIOD—4, Chicago, Mikita (27), 19:17. Penalties—Dornhoefer, Philadelphia (2:01); Talon, Chicago (8:37); [illegible], Chicago, (11:32); Dupont, Philadelphia ([illegible]3:[illegible]9).

Shots on goal—Chicago 12, 4, 7—23. Philadelphia 12, 11, [illegible]—34.

Goalies—Esposito and Parent.

Attendance 17,007.

Shiftways Is Victor In Horse Show

Special to The New York Times

SUFFERN, N. Y., March 23—Shiftways, owned and handled by Amy Friedman of Glen Head, L.I., captured one championship and finished as reserve titleholder in another division today at the Catamount Hunt Club horse show.

"All the News That's Fit to Print"

The New York Times

LATE CITY EDITION

Weather: Rain likely today; cold tonight. Partly cloudy tomorrow. Temp. range: today 38-45; Monday 44-50. Additional details on Page 81.

VOL. CXXIII ... No. 42,444 | © 1974 The New York Times Company | NEW YORK, TUESDAY, APRIL 9, 1974 | 20¢ beyond 50-mile radius of New York City, except Long Island. Higher in air delivery cities. | 15 CENTS

Aaron Hits 715th, Passes Babe Ruth

United Press International

Henry Aaron being hugged by his mother after homer in Atlanta. At right is the prized ball, held by Tom House, Braves' relief pitcher who caught it in the bullpen.

By JOSEPH DURSO
Special to The New York Times

ATLANTA, April 8—Henry Aaron ended the great chase tonight and passed Babe Ruth as the leading home-run hitter in baseball history when he hit No. 715 before a national television audience and 53,775 persons in Atlanta Stadium.

The 40-year-old outfielder for the Atlanta Braves broke the record on his second time at bat, but on his first swing of a clamorous evening. It was a soaring drive in the fourth inning off Al Downing of the Los Angeles Dodgers, and it cleared the fence in left-center field, 385 feet from home plate.

Skyrockets arched over the jammed stadium in the rain as the man from Mobile trotted around the bases for the 715th time in a career that began a quarter of a century ago with the Indianapolis Clowns in the old Negro leagues.

It was 9:07 o'clock, 39 years after Ruth had hit his 714th and four days after Aaron had hit his 714th on his first swing of the bat in the opening game of the season.

The history-making home

Continued on Page 49, Column 5

NIXON TAX STUDY IN HOUSE TO TOUCH ON POSSIBLE FRAUD

Doar Asserts His Staff Has Requested I.R.S. Data on President's Returns

By BILL KOVACH
Special to The New York Times

WASHINGTON, April 8—The impeachment inquiry staff of the House Judiciary Committee is investigating whether fraud may have been involved in President Nixon's handling of his income taxes.

John M. Doar, chief counsel of the staff, told committee members at a briefing today that the question of fraud was clearly part of their investigation. He said records of the Internal Revenue Service dealing with the President's tax matters had been requested along with other tax information.

Several members of the committee have said that they would regard any evidence of criminal fraud in the President's tax returns as potential grounds for impeachment.

Earlier statements by the Judiciary Committee chairman, Representative Peter W. Rodino, a New Jersey Democrat, and other senior committee members had indicated the committee was not prepared to consider the question of fraud but would concentrate instead on whether the President's handling of his personal tax matters had diminished confidence in the internal revenue system.

No Judgment

The Joint Committee on Internal Revenue Taxation, whose staff found that Mr. Nixon's returns included a deficiency of $440,000, refrained from any judgment on the question of fraud. The I.R.S., which has ordered that he pay $432,000 in back taxes and penalties, said it had found no basis for assessing a fraud penalty.

The fraud investigation was disclosed at a briefing in which Mr. Doar also reported that the White House has agreed to reply by tomorrow to the committee's request for tapes of 41 or 42 Presidential conversations involving the Watergate cover-up.

The White House is expected to agree, at least in part, to the request and thus head off a major confrontation with Congress. Mr. Rodino had been prepared to seek authority to issue a subpoena should the White House fail to meet the deadline for a yes-or-no answer set for tomorrow.

May Consider Subpoena

In fact, Mr. Rodino said he would schedule a meeting of the full committee for later this week to consider a subpoena should the White House response tomorrow be unsatisfactory. However, a source familiar with the recent dialogue between staff members and the White House said that the response "will probably eliminate the need for any consideration of a subpoena."

Republican Congressmen were predicting over the weekend that the White House would

Continued on Page 19, Column 1

Associated Press

Senator Lowell P. Weicker Jr., Connecticut Republican, testifies at Senate hearing on White House actions.

Weicker Says Nixon Used I.R.S. Records in Politics

By JAMES M. NAUGHTON
Special to The New York Times

WASHINGTON, April 8—Senator Lowell P. Weicker Jr., in a sequel to the Senate Watergate hearings, made public today documents showing that the White House had frequent access to confidential Internal Revenue Service files on political friends and foes of President Nixon.

The Republican Senator from Connecticut told three Senate subcommittees holding joint hearings on government surveillance activities that "the I.R.S. was acting like a public lending library for the White House."

Reading from a thick stack of documents obtained last year by the Senate Watergate committee, of which he is a member, Mr. Weicker recited a number of new details about alleged White House improprieties. They included the following charges:

¶An Administration study group set up in mid-1969 to gather tax information on "activist organizations" collected files on some 10,000 taxpayers before the unit was disbanded last August.

¶John J. Caulfield, a former Treasury Department and White House official, gave John W. Dean 3d, the former White House counsel, information in 1971 on Internal Revenue Service audits of the Rev. Billy Graham, the evangelist and John Wayne, the film star, two political supporters of Mr. Nixon.

¶A series of 1971 memos from Mr. Caulfield to Mr. Dean described preparations the White House could undertake

Continued on Page 19, Column 1

PRESIDENT SIGNS RISE IN PAY BASE TO $2.30 AN HOUR

He Cites 'Reservations' But Says Higher Minimum Can 'No Longer Be Delayed'

BILL VETOED LAST FALL

Increases in Stages Are Extended to 7 Million, Including Domestics

By R. W. APPLE Jr.
Special to The New York Times

WASHINGTON, April 8—President Nixon signed today a bill that will increase the minimum wage for American men and women by stages from the present $1.60 to $2.30 an hour.

Mr. Nixon, who vetoed similar legislation last year, said that he had "some reservations" about this year's bill but added that "raising the minimum wage is now a matter of justice that can no longer be fairly delayed."

In a statement issued by the White House, the President did not explain why he had chosen to disregard the inflationary impact of the bill, which he cited in a veto message last Sept. 5. But politicians in both parties suggested that, with possible impeachment hanging over his head, Mr. Nixon could not afford to risk a second veto.

Many More Covered

For about 36 million workers covered under the provisions of the 1966 Minimum Wage Law, the new measure will provide an increase from $1.60 to $2 next month, with further increases to $2.10 on Jan. 1, 1975, and $2.30 Jan. 1, 1976.

The new law also extends Federal minimum wage and overtime requirements to between seven and eight million workers not previously covered, including all state and local government employes, most domestic servants, certain employes of chain stores, telegraph agency employes and others.

When the law takes full effect, 55-million American workers will be protected by minimum wage standards.

Series of Steps-Ups

Mr. Nixon signed the bill in his Oval Office with Secretary of Labor Peter J. Brennan sitting beside him. Appearing in a jovial mood, the President slid the pen across his desk to Mr. Brennan and then dropped the legislation in his "out" box.

The bill was passed by the Senate and House with large majorities, and Mr. Nixon was told by his Congressional nosecounters that there was little chance of sustaining a veto. Congress failed in an effort to override last year's veto.

In addition to providing for workers covered under the 1966 act, the new law provides for other groups in the following manner:

¶For about 19 million nonfarm workers covered under amendments to the 1966 act,

Continued on Page 16, Column 6

OIL-PLOT CHARGES HELD 'PREMATURE'

U.S. Regional Energy Chief Declines to Back Turetsky Report of Price Cheating

By DAVID BIRD

The new regional head of the Federal Energy Office backed away yesterday from his predecessor's charges that some oil companies had "lied" and "cheated" and had illegally manipulated prices to take advantage of the energy crisis.

Alfred Kleinfeld, who took over yesterday as the acting regional administrator of the office, said that "we're just a little premature" in accusing the companies of wrongdoing. Mr. Kleinfeld, a 47-year-old career civil servant, had been deputy regional director. His appointment was announced yesterday by John C. Sawhill, the deputy director of the Federal Energy Office, in a news conference at the Waldorf-Astoria Hotel.

Investigation Planned

Seated on a damask settee next to Mr. Kleinfeld, Mr. Sawhill also played down the allegation made by Gerald J. Turetsky, the former regional chief who resigned last week.

"We have discussed the basis of this charge," Mr. Sawhill said, "and will be investigating this charge." He added: "I haven't reviewed the evidence."

Early last month Mr. Turetsky charged that several oil companies had "lied" and had "cheated" in reports they had

Continued on Page 30, Column 4

Nixon's Demeanor During Paris Visit Draws Sharp Criticism From French

By NAN ROBERTSON
Special to The New York Times

PARIS, April 8—President Nixon's talks with world leaders and his activities on the streets of Paris this weekend brought sharp criticism in France today, as well as some grudging acknowledgment of continuing United States power.

On three occasions on Saturday and Sunday, Mr. Nixon plunged through police lines to shake hands and talk with curbside crowds. This was in addition to talks with foreign leaders assembled here to honor the memory of President Georges Pompidou, who died on Tuesday.

A letter circulated to journalists and made available today to the bureau of The New York Times by a high official of a French ministry said Mr. Nixon had "shamelessly substituted a publicity campaign for the mourning of an entire nation, introducing an atmosphere of loud feverishness, the discourtesy of which is equaled only by its clumsiness."

Le Monde, the most respected newspaper in France, joined in the indignation in a front-page editorial titled "The Nixon Festival." But it added that the American President had spectacularly demonstrated his continuing ability to dominate international politics — even without the presence of Secretary of State Kissinger.

The paper said that Mr. Nixon had asked for and received the allegiance of the European statesmen he saw one after the other and that he had continued the "superpower dialogue" with President Nikolai V. Podgorny of the Soviet Union.

The mass-circulation daily

Continued on Page 2, Column 5

PRIME RATE IS 10% AT BANKERS TRUST

Key Charge Equals High—Stock Prices Decline

By JOHN H. ALLAN

The Bankers Trust Company raised yesterday its prime rate on loans to corporations to 10 per cent, and a large New Jersey bank joined it.

This basic lending rate had been as high once before—briefly last fall—but currently there is some feeling in financial circles that it may go even higher unless it is arrested by political considerations.

There has been an extraordinarily sharp increase in all short-term interest rates since early February, raising the cost to banks of "buying" money in the open market.

Stock prices declined yesterday in the wake of the announcement of the higher prime rate. The Dow Jones industrial average fell 7.58 points to close at its lowest level since mid-February.

The underlying reasons for the steep rise in interest rates are strong demand by business

Continued on Page 66, Column 1

Wilson Faces Parliament In Storm Over Land Deal

By ALVIN SHUSTER
Special to The New York Times

LONDON, April 8 — Prime Minister Wilson went before the House of Commons today in an effort to calm a raging political controversy over property dealings involving his private secretary and members of her family.

Mr. Wilson said that Mrs. Marcia Williams, his secretary for 18 years, was not guilty of any wrongdoing, attacked newspapers for "sensationalizing" the property transactions and denied that he himself had been involved in any way. He said there was no evidence that any of the dealings were "illegal or improper."

It was one of Mr. Wilson's most delicate moments since he came to power five weeks ago. The controversy, arising from newspaper reports, has been particularly embarrassing for the Prime Minister because the Labor party, which he heads, attacked "property speculators" and "tax havens" during the election campaign.

At issue are about 90 acres of derelict land at Ince-in-Makerfield in Lancashire on which an iron and steel plant once stood. Some 30 acres of the land were bought in 1967 by Anthony Field, Mrs. Williams's brother, who worked for Mr. Wilson for two years until last June.

Mrs. Williams, who is known as an influential figure in Mr. Wilson's retinue, and her sister, Miss Peggy Field, a former aide to the Prime Minister's wife, were partners in the company that sold the property at a substantial profit last year. Mr. Field's company is also engaged in selling the remaining

Continued on Page 9, Column 1

City Adopts System to Test Effectiveness of Its Schools

By LEONARD BUDER

A pioneering system of school accountability, which would provide a yardstick for judging the educational effectiveness of the city's 950 public schools, will be introduced here next fall, School Chancellor Irving Anker said yesterday.

The accountability project will begin experimentally in two or three schools in each of the city's 32 decentralized community school districts, as well as in certain high schools. The program, believed to be the first ever attempted on such a scale, was developed after three years of study by the Educational Testing Service of Princeton, N. J., and a committee of educators and organizational representatives, including those from groups that traditionally do not see eye-to-eye on school issues.

Mr. Anker said that a top-level official would soon be appointed to direct implementation of the project, which will eventually encompass all schools in the city system.

The 62-year-old educator, who attended the city schools and has spent 40 years in the system as a teacher, principal and administrator, discussed the new project during an interview with editors and reporters of The New York Times. Among other points Mr. Anker made during the two-hour session, were the following:

¶The over-all "score is not yet in" on school decentralization, started here in 1970, and which has helped to "diffuse confrontation" and make possible greater parent and community participation in school affairs. But it

Continued on Page 29, Column 2

Con Ed Bills Stay

The Consolidated Edison Company said yesterday that fuel adjustment charges in April electric bills would not be cut by 10 per cent as announced, but that the reduction instead would be minuscule or nonexistent. Page 43.

Yale Asks 370-Million

Yale University yesterday announced a $370-million drive, the largest fund-raising effort ever attempted by an American university. Page 29.

U.S. Acts to Help Meat Packers Diversify Into Other Businesses

By ROBERT J. COLE

The Department of Justice, in a significant display of current antitrust policy, took a direct hand yesterday in helping three leading meat packers diversify into other areas.

The Government agency said that it had joined Swift & Co., Armour & Co. and the Cudahy Company in asking a Federal court judge to modify a 54-year-old consent decree that the three had signed.

Attorney General William B. Saxbe said the proposed modification, placed before Judge Julius J. Hoffman of the United States District Court in Chicago, would become final 30 days after approval.

Based on Judge Hoffman's approval of a prior modification in 1971, also approved by the Department of Justic, the latest modification is expected to receive quick approval.

Thomas E. Kauper, Assistant Attorney General in charge of the antitrust division, said the entry of the three companies into product lines now pro-

Continued on Page 64, Column 5

NEWS INDEX

The New York Times/George Tames

Albert E. Jenner Jr., left, impeachment inquiry's minority counsel, and John M. Doar, chief counsel, examining a minority report yesterday. Also reading the report, at rear, are Mr. Doar's sons Robert, 13, left, and Burke, 10.

Cooke and 10 Deaf Children Stuck in Elevator an Hour

By IRVING SPIEGEL

Cardinal Cooke, four other adults and 10 deaf children were trapped for more than an hour yesterday afternoon in an elevator stalled between the first and second floors of a Times Square building.

While maintenance men and finally a police emergency crew worked to get the elevator cab down six feet to street level, a priest and a nun inside kept up a running account of the rescue effort in sign language to reassure the children.

The children finally scampered up a ladder to freedom, while Cardinal Cooke squirmed out an opening between the floor of the elevator and the lobby ceiling, into the arms of rescuers. He told reporters:

"The children were wonderful, no panic—they couldn't get away fast enough to eat hot dogs."

Later, an aide said the Cardinal "did not offer any prayer—there was no need."

The incident took place at 1481 Broadway, between 42d and 43d Streets. Cardinal Cooke, with a background of 70 young choristers, had just taped an Easter mass in a

Continued on Page 82, Column 1

Jammed Park Goes Wild Over Historic Clout

Continued From Page 1, Col. 4

run carried into the Atlanta bull pen, where a relief pitcher named Tom House made a dazzling one-handed catch against the auxiliary scoreboard. He clutched it against the boards, far below the grandstand seats, where the customers in "Home-Run Alley" were massed, waiting to retrieve a cowhide ball that in recent days had been valued as high as $25,000 on the auction market.

So Aaron not only ended the great home-run derby, but also ended the controversy that had surrounded it. His employers had wanted him to hit No. 715 in Atlanta, and had even benched him on alien soil in Cincinnati.

The commissioner of baseball, Bowie Kuhn, ordered the Braves to start their star yesterday or face "serious penalties." And tonight the dispute and the marathon finally came home to Atlanta in a razzle-dazzle setting.

The stadium was packed with its largest crowd since the Braves left Milwaukee and brought major league baseball to the Deep South nine years ago. Pearl Bailey sang the national anthem; the Jonesboro High School band marched; balloons and fireworks filled the overcast sky before the game: Aaron's life was dramatized on a huge color map of the United States painted across the outfield grass, and Bad Henry was serenaded by the Atlanta Boy Choir, which now includes girls.

The commissioner was missing, pleading that a "previous commitment" required his presence tomorrow in Cleveland, and his emissary was roundly booed when he mentioned Kuhn's name. But Gov. Jimmy Carter was there, along with Mayor Maynard Jackson, Sammy Davis Jr. and broadcasters and writers from as far away as Japan, South America and Britain.

To many Atlantans, it was like the city's festive premiére of "Gone With the Wind" during the 1930's when Babe Ruth was still the hero of the New York Yankees and the titan of professional sports. All that was needed to complete the evening was home run No. 715, and Aaron supplied that.

The first time he batted, leading off the second inning, Aaron never got the bat off his shoulder. Downing, a one-time pitcher for the Yankees, wearing No. 44, threw a ball and a called strike and then three more balls. Aaron, wearing his own No. 44, watched them all and then took first base while the crowd hooted and booed because their home town hero had been walked.

A few moments later, Henry scored on a double by Dusty Baker and an error in left field, and even made a little history doing that.

It was the 2,063d time he had crossed home plate in his 21-year career in the majors, breaking the National League record held by Willie Mays and placing Aaron behind Ty Cobb and Ruth, both American Leaguers.

Then came the fourth inning, with the Dodgers leading by 3-1 and the rain falling, with colored umbrellas raised in the stands and the crowd roaring every time Aaron appeared. Darrell Evans led off for Atlanta with a grounder behind second base that the shortstop, Bill Russell, juggled long enough for an error. And up came Henry for the eighth time this season and the second this evening.

Downing pitched ball one inside, and Aaron watched impassively. Then came the second pitch, and this time Henry took his first cut of the night. The ball rose high toward left-center as the crowd came to its feet shouting, and as it dropped over the inside fence separating the outfield from the bull pen area, the skyrockets were fired and the scoreboard lights flashed in six-foot numerals: "715."

Aaron, head slightly bowed and elbows turned out, slowly circled the bases as the uproar grew. At second base he received a handshake from Dave Lopes of the Dodgers, and between second and third from Russell.

By now two young men from the seats had joined Aaron, but did not interfere with his 360-foot trip around the bases into the record books.

As he neared home plate, the rest of the Atlanta team had already massed beyond it as a welcoming delegation. But Aaron's 65-year-old father, Herbert Aaron Sr., had jumped out of the family's special field-level box and outraced everybody to the man who had broken Babe Ruth's record.

By then the entire Atlanta bull pen corps had started to race in to join the fun, with House leading them, the ball gripped tightly in his hand. He delivered it to Aaron, who was besieged on the grass about 20 feet in front of the field boxes near the Braves' dugout.

Besides the ball, Henry received a plaque from the owner of the team, Bill Bartholomay; congratulations from Monte Irvin, the emissary from Commissioner Kuhn, and a howling, standing ovation from the crowd.

The game was interrupted for 11 minutes during all the commotion, after which the Braves got back to work and went on to win their second straight, this time by 7-4. The Dodgers, apparently shaken by history, made six errors and lost their first game after three straight victories.

"It was a fastball, right down the middle of the upper part of the plate," Downing said later. "I was trying to get it down to him, but I didn't and he hit it good—as he would."

"When he first hit it, I didn't think it might be going. But like a great hitter, when he picks his pitch, chances are he's going to hit it pretty good."

Afterward the Braves locked their clubhouse for a time so that they could toast Aaron in champagne. Then the new home-run king reflected on his feat and on some intimations that he had not been "trying" to break the record in Cincinnati.

"I have never gone out on a ball field and given less than my level best," he said. "When I hit it tonight, all I thought about was that I wanted to touch all the bases."

> "I have never gone out on a ball field and given less than my level best. When I hit it tonight, all I thought about was that I wanted to touch all the bases."
> —Henry Aaron

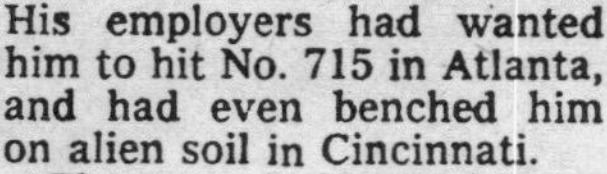

The Atlanta Braves

Hank Aaron

Aaron Is Congratulated By Nixon After Homer

ATLANTA, April 8 (AP)—President Nixon telephoned congratulations to Henry Aaron shortly after the 40-year-old slugger smashed his record 715th career home run tonight.

Dave Anderson

The Sound of 715

ATLANTA, April 8—In the decades to come, the memory of the scene might blur. But the memory of the sound will remain with everyone who was here. Not the sound of the cheers, or the sound of Henry Aaron saying, "I'm thankful to God it's all over," but the sound of Henry Aaron's bat when it hit the baseball tonight. The sound that's baseball's version of a thunderclap, the sound of a home run, in his case the sound of the 715th home run. The sound momentarily was the only sound in the expectant silence of 53,775 customers at Atlanta Stadium and then, as the sound faded, the ball soared high and deep toward the left-center-field fence. And over it. On the infield basepaths, Henry Aaron was trotting now, trotting past Babe Ruth into history in his 21st season. On his first swing in tonight's game, the 40-year-old outfielder of the Atlanta Braves had hit another home run, just as he had hit his record-tying home run on his first swing at Cincinnati in last Thursday's season opener. At home plate, surrounded by an ovation that came down around him as if it were a waterfall of appreciation, he was met by his teammates who attempted to lift him onto their shoulders. But he slipped off into the arms of his father, Herbert Sr., and his mother, Estella, who had hurried out of the special box for the Aaron family near the Braves' dugout.

Sports of The Times

"I never knew," Aaron would say later, "that my mother could hug so tight."

The Missing Commissioner

Moments later he was accepting a diamond wristwatch from the commissioner of baseball, Bowie Kuhn, but not from Kuhn himself. Rather than expose himself to the boos of the Atlanta populace, Kuhn had dispatched an ambassador, Monte Irvin, to the scene of the pregame festivities in the event the 715th home run occurred. When it did, Irvin presented the watch and when he was introduced as being from the commissioner's office, the boos roared. In his jubilation, Henry Aaron smiled.

"I was smiling from the boos," he would say later. That's all he would say because that's the way Henry Aaron is. Henry Aaron doesn't gloat. Quietly, he has resented Kuhn's attitude toward him, whether real or imagined. It began when Kuhn ignored his 700th home run last season and it simmered when Kuhn ordered Eddie Mathews to use him in the starting line-up in Cincinnati yesterday after the Braves' manager had planned to preserve him for the Atlanta audience. Kuhn was correct in that ultimatum, because the Braves were defying the integrity of baseball.

But the commissioner was wrong tonight in not being here. He had stood up gallantly, but suddenly he had sat down again. Henry Aaron should have ordered the commissioner to be here.

"I thought the line-up card was taken out of Eddie Matthew's hand," the man with 715 home runs said. "I believe I should've been given the privilege of deciding for myself."

It's unfortunate that controversy somewhat clouded Henry Aaron's moment. It's also untypical. Of all our superstars, Henry Aaron has been perhaps the most uncontroversial. But time will blow those clouds away. Soon only his home runs will be important, not where he hit them, not where the commissioner was. His eventual total of home runs will be his monument, although they represent only a portion of his stature as a hitter.

Convincing the Skeptics

With a normally productive season, in what he insists will be his last, Henry Aaron probably will hold six major-league career records for home runs, runs batted in, total bases, extra base hits, games and times at bat. Ty Cobb will retain the records for hits, runs, batting average and stolen bases. Babe Ruth will hold the records for slugging average and walks. Through the years, Cobb and the Babe were the ultimate in hitting, but now they must move over.

"With a good year," Henry Aaron has said, "I'll hold six records, Cobb will hold four and Ruth two."

Perhaps that will convince the skeptics who minimize his accomplishments as a hitter. Some of the skeptics are traditionalists, some are racists. Statistically, their argument is that Henry Aaron needed 2,896 more times at bat than Babe Ruth in order to break the home-run record. Those skeptics ignore Henry Aaron's durability and consistency, attributes as important as Babe Ruth's charisma. And when his 715th home run soared over the fence tonight, Henry Aaron never lost his dignity, his essence as a person.

"You don't know what a weight it was off my shoulders," he said later, "a tremendous weight."

Now the weight will be transferred to the hitter who someday challenges Henry Aaron, if that hitter appears.

"All the News That's Fit to Print"

The New York Times

LATE CITY EDITION

Weather: Partly sunny today; mild tonight. Fair and warm tomorrow. Temp. range: today 68-85; Friday 73-89. Highest Temp.-Hum. Index yesterday: 80. Details on Page 44.

VOL. CXXIII ... No. 42,532 NEW YORK, SATURDAY, JULY 6, 1974

20c beyond 50-mile radius of New York City except Long Island. Higher in air delivery cities.

15 CENTS

Associated Press

Chris Evert smiling as she tossed her racquet into the air yesterday after winning the final match at Wimbledon. Miss Evert defeated Olga Morozova of Soviet Union, 6-0, 6-4.

Chris Evert Captures The Wimbledon Title

By FRED TUPPER

Special to The New York Times

WIMBLEDON, England, July 5—This is the year of Chris Evert. I., just an hour today she defeated Olga Morozova of the Soviet Union, 6-0, 6-4, and added the Wimbledon tennis title to the Italian and French titles that she won a few weeks ago. She was the runner-up a year ago in all three of these tournaments.

At the age of 19, Miss Evert of Fort Lauderdale, Fla., became the youngest winner of the women's singles here since Maureen Connolly took the title in 1952 at 17.

Miss Evert, who was beaten in two sets by Mrs. Billie Jean King in the 1973 championship round, said she was surprised at winning this year. "I know I'll be playing at Wimbledon for years to come. But I was thinking a few years ahead when Billie Jean and Margaret [Court] might retire. I never expected to win Wimbledon this year."

To her baseline accomplishments she put on parade today a volley and overhead game. That was the deciding factor in those last minutes down the stretch, when the Russian had pulled up from 2-4 to 4-all in the second set just as she had rallied yesterday in upsetting Virginia Wade.

In the men's singles final tomorrow, Jimmy Connors of Belleville, Ill., will play Ken Rosewall, who left center court in a state of shock when he came out of the abyss to win a match that had seemed irretrievably lost. Here was little Ken, semi-retired and approaching 40, two sets and match point down to Stan Smith, the 1972 champion, from Sea Pines, S.C. The script looks incredible, but it's now on the record, a tale of tennis to be told in years to come as the Australian triumphed, 6-8, 4-6, 9-8, 6-1, 6-3.

Henri Cochet came from two sets and 1-5 down to beat Bill Tilden here in 1927, but not from match point.

Connors reached the final by stopping young Dick Stockton of Dallas, 4-6, 6-2, 6-3, 6-4.

A sentimental journey with his family had seemed the reason for Rosewall's presence. He was seeded ninth on his reputation, not on his recent record. He had quit the World Championship Tennis circuit this year,

Continued on Page 11, Column 1

'PLUMBERS' JUDGE REFUSES TO QUASH CALL TO KISSINGER

Directs Him to Be Ready to Testify for Defense—Prosecution Rests Case

By LINDA CHARLTON

Special to The New York Times

WASHINGTON, July 5—The prosecution rested its case today in the conspiracy trial of John D. Ehrlichman and three others, and the judge ordered Secretary of State Kissinger to "hold himself in readiness" for a possible appearance as a defense witness.

Mr. Kissinger had been subpoenaed to appear today, presumably to testify that he had no knowledge of or interest in the preparation of a "psychological profile" of Dr. Daniel Ellsberg in the summer of 1971, and thus undercut the credibility of David R. Young Jr., a co-director of the White House "plumbers" unit and a major prosecution witness.

Lawyers for Mr. Kissinger presented a motion to quash the subpoena on the ground that he had no information relating to the break-in at the office of Dr. Lewis J. Fielding, Dr. Ellsberg's former psychiatrist. The break-in is the central incident on which the conspiracy charge is based.

'Unduly Oppressive'

In addition, the motion contended that it would be "unduly oppressive and injurious to the public interest to require Dr. Kissinger to appear at this time."

"Such an order would require Dr. Kissinger to abruptly terminate his official mission abroad, including critical meetings with United States allies and various NATO officials in Europe," the motion said.

William S. Frates, the Miami lawyer who heads Mr. Ehrlichman's four-man defense team, told Judge Gerhard A. Gesell in United States District Court that the defense was "not trying to call Dr. Kissinger just to have Dr. Kissinger here."

"Mr. Young has testified that the psychological profile was ordered by Dr. Kissinger and John Ehrlichman," he said. "We expect the evidence to show that is not true."

Judge Gesell, commenting on the motion to quash, said, "I understand he's [Mr. Kissinger] presently seeing the Pope. I wouldn't want to interfere with that."

However, after learning that Mr. Kissinger was due back in the United States Wednesday,

Continued on Page 6, Column 5

Associated Press

Mrs. John D. Ehrlichman being comforted by her husband after she was accidentally struck on the head by a TV camera as they left Federal Court yesterday in Washington.

RATE OF JOBLESS REMAINS STABLE FOR FIFTH MONTH

June Unemployment, 5.2%, Is Essentially Unchanged From Level for May

CONFLICT IN STATISTICS

A Discrepancy Is Reported in Results of Different Surveys of Jobholders

By EILEEN SHANAHAN

Special to The New York Times

WASHINGTON, July 5—The unemployment rate remained unchanged at 5.2 per cent in June, a level that has held essentially stable for five straight months, the Labor Department reported today.

Herbert Stein, chairman of the President's Council of Economic Advisers, said in a statement that the stability of the unemployment rate "is one of the more gratifying economic developments of 1974 so far."

He noted that the council itself had expected a somewhat higher unemployment rate by midyear when it made its annual forecast in January and that many private forecasters had, at that time, thought the council's prediction of unemployment, although not specified, was too low.

Categories Unchanged

Not only the over-all unemployment rate but also most of its subdivisions were essentially unchanged from the levels of May.

The jobless rates for heads of households, at 3.1 per cent, adult men, 3.5 per cent, adult women, 5.1 per cent, and teenagers, 15.6 per cent, were all the same or nearly the same as in the preceding month.

There was at least one puzzling conflict in the figures, however.

The Labor Department makes two separate surveys of the number of employed persons. One is done through a sample of households and the other through a sample of employers.

The survey of households for June showed an increase of nearly 200,000 in the number of jobholders, whereas the survey of employers showed a decline of 48,000.

The two surveys do not cover exactly the same workers, since the survey of employers excludes workers in agriculture and persons who are not on a formal payroll, such as domestic workers.

Similar Discrepancy

Nevertheless, some experts felt that the discrepancy was unusually large, particularly since there was a similar, though smaller, discrepancy in May.

Whether the unemployment rate will start to rise again may depend on whether one of these figures—and, if so, which one—is in error.

The Labor Department's monthly report also showed that wages were continuing to rise rapidly, but not so much as in May, which was the first month following the end of wage controls.

The department's index of hourly earnings for all nonsupervisory workers outside of

Continued on Page 7, Column 1

LIGHTNING KILLS GIRL, 15, IN PARK

Connecticut Boy Also Dies in Storms That Drench Metropolitan Area

By ROBERT D. McFADDEN

Lightning struck and killed a 15-year-old girl and injured two young sisters, one of them critically, near a small lake at the north end of Central Park yesterday afternoon during a brief but severe thunderstorm that blackened the skies and drenched the metropolitan area.

In Connecticut, a 12-year-old Brookfield boy also was struck and killed by lightning while he was trying to find cover at Candlewood Lake in New Milford.

A woman emerging from a taxicab on Fifth Avenue was injured by falling bricks dislodged by a lightning bolt. In addition to lightning, hailstones pounded several sections of the city and suburbs.

The storm, which ended a four-day heat wave with a downpour of nearly a half-inch of rain in an hour, snarled homebound traffic by flooding low-lying highways and numerous subway tunnels. It also forced three private planes to make emergency landings in

Continued on Page 44, Column 8

MORTGAGE RATES INCREASED TO 9¾%

New Level for F.H.A.- and V.A.-Insured Homes Aims at Greater Lending

By ROBERT J. COLE

Interest rates on Federally insured home mortgages were allowed yesterday to rise to 9 per cent in a move designed to encourage lenders to grant them.

The move, announced simultaneously by both the Department of Housing and Urban Development and the Veterans Administration, would raise rates on mortgages insured by the V. A. and the Federal Housing Administration to the new level next Monday. The rates are now 8¼ per cent.

Although the higher rate was expected to help somewhat, initial reaction suggested that consumers would still find resistance.

Arthur C. Langsdorf, senior vice president of the Manufacturers Hanover Trust Company, said his bank would "entertain" both F.H.A.- and V.A.-insured mortgages at the new rate—in New York and in New Jersey—but that with the maximum loan permitted by the F.H.A. at about $33,000, it would mean that buyers who want a 90

Continued on Page 23, Column 1

U.S. Calls Back Its Envoy In Turkish Opium Dispute

By BERNARD GWERTZMAN

Special to The New York Times

WASHINGTON, July 5—The State Department said today that the United States Ambassador to Turkey had been called back for consultation because of strained Turkish-American relations resulting from the Turkish decision to resume the cultivation and sale of opium poppies, once the main source of illegal heroin in this country.

John F. King, a department spokesman, said that Ambassador William B. Macomber Jr. had been ordered back to Washington "to review the situation arising from the July 1 decision of the Turkish Government."

On Monday, Turkey lifted her ban—imposed in 1971 as part of an agreement with the United States—on cultivation of the poppy. Under the 1971 accord, Turkey agreed to ban the poppy in return for an American pledge to give Turkey $35.7-million over a four-year period, as compensation for losses incurred.

Before 1971, Turkey was one of the world's largest producers of legal opium for the medical market. Both morphine and heroin are derived from opium.

But illegally grown poppies, processed into opium and shiped clandestinely to France, became the largest single source of illegal heroin sold in

Continued on Page 2, Column 1

Mistrial Declared In Case Involving Dun & Bradstreet

By MORRIS KAPLAN

A mistrial was declared yesterday in the case against Dun & Bradstreet and one of its former district managers, who had been charged with conspiring to defraud the Federal Housing Administration and making false statements that enabled the poor to buy houses with F.H.A.-insured mortgages.

Federal Judge Anthony J. Travia declared the mistrial after a second note from the jury of nine men and three women stated that it had failed to agree after 14 days of deliberation. One of the jurors said later that the panel had stood 10 to 2 for acquittal since last Wednesday.

The United States Attorney's office in Brooklyn had no immediate comment on whether it would seek a retrial of the case, which began last Oct. 1. "We have made no decision on that," said Edward R. Korman, the chief assistant to David G. Trager, the United States Attorney.

A statement by Dun & Bradstreet, the largest private credit-rating concern in the country, said the Government had failed to prove its case.

"We are naturally disappointed that the jury did not return

Continued on Page 23, Column 3

Drug Ring Broken

The Justice Department says a drug ring that smuggled $32.7-million in cocaine into the United States by using Chilean diplomatic pouches and military flights has been disrupted with the arrests of 22 persons. Page 7.

State to Restudy L.I. Expressway Plan

By EDWARD C. BURKS

State Transportation Commissioner Raymond T. Schuler yesterday ordered the suspension of further planning to double the number of lanes or otherwise expand the capacity of the Long Island Expressway in Queens.

He called instead for a thorough study by a transportation task force joined by community groups to "develop a wide range of alternatives" to present to a public hearing by late 1975.

He said that the order, issued at the direction of Governor Wilson, was in keeping with the state's current policy of "striving to find ways to hold down the number of vehicles on major roadways."

The Long Island Expressway already carries 150,000 vehicles a day in Queens. Mr. Schuler added that engineering studies have shown "how difficult it would be to expand capacity of the road without creating damage to the environment and housing."

Alternative methods of improving use of the corridor, he said, could include exclusive lanes for buses and vehicles in car pools, bus and rail transit expansion, and rail improvements to provide far-greater rail freight access to Long Island, especially piggyback trains, to lighten the truck load on the highway.

In particular, Mr. Schuler's order applies to a long-considered city-state plan that would have doubled the number of lanes for nearly three and one-half miles of the expressway through the heart of Queens by either outward expansion or double-decking. That stretch extends eastward from Maurice Avenue in the Maspeth section, where double-decking now ends, to Grand Central Parkway in Flushing Meadow Park.

At the time of the ill-fated $2-billion state transportation bond issue proposal last fall, the city's Transportation Administration listed the dualization—or lane doubling—plan as one of five major highway projects to be paid for with the bonds.

Even with the failure of the bond issue, the dualization plan remained very much alive because the Long Island Expressway through Queens is part

Continued on Page 44, Column 6

NEWS INDEX

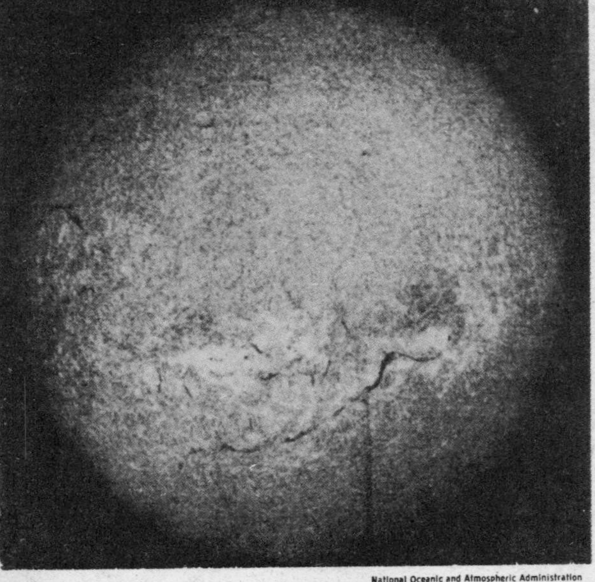

National Oceanic and Atmospheric Administration

THE SUN FLARES UP: Recent heavy activity on the sun is shown in this unusual picture. White areas are solar flares and black areas are filaments of relatively cool gas. Photo was taken by red light through telescope at Boulder, Colo. Details, Page 44.

Enclosed Sidewalk Cafes Facing Closer Regulation

By JOHN DARNTON

Sidewalk cafes are flourishing in New York this summer, and while officials still welcome new open-air cafes that add a flair to the city's streets, the same officials are considering tighter guidelines for enclosed cafes that take up sidewalk space.

Unlike the open-air institutions of leisure along the Boulevard St. Germain, the Via Veneto and Vienna's Ringstrasse, New York's cafes that are doing a booming business are retreating behind protective enclosures, which seem to grow larger, more opaque and, grammar aside, more permanent. They are causing increasing complaints from pedestrians, nearby retailers, and esthetes.

And so, after a decade of encouragement of cafes of any kind, city officials are now turning to the idea of stricter regulations and more stringent enforcement to control their location and design.

Since February, the Board of Estimate, which rules on all matters concerning city property—in this case, sidewalks—has not granted a single new franchise for an enclosed cafe. (Open cafes, apparently endorsed by all, are not in question.)

The board's moratorium, in effect while new guidelines are being drafted, was imposed largely at the urging of Manhattan Borough President Percy E. Sutton. For at least a year now, Mr. Sut-

Continued on Page 22, Column 3

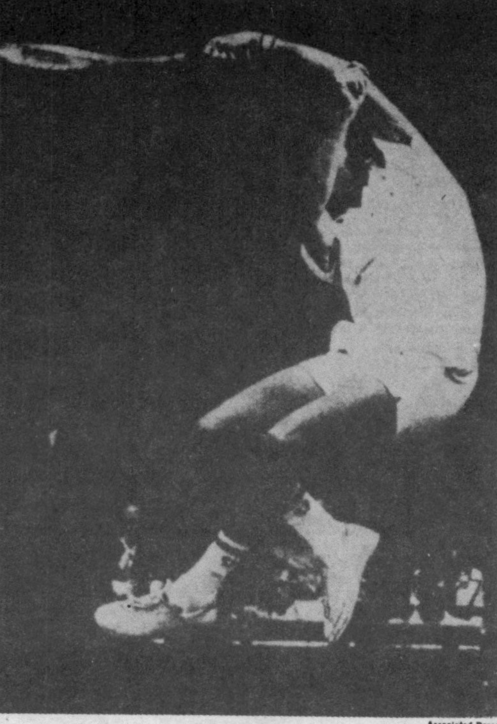

Associated Press

Ken Rosewall, left, defeating Stan Smith, and Jimmy Connors downing Dick Stockton yesterday at Wimbledon. They meet today in final.

Chris Evert Captures Title; Connors and Rosewall Reach Final

Continued From Page 1, Col. 2

played one tournament back in March and came back in May to be a manager-player of Pittsburgh in World Team Tennis.

He knocked out John Newcombe, the top-seeded player and three-time champion to gain the semifinal round here. Today he was 6-8, 4-6 and 4-5 down with big Stan serving for the match. Ken had played well earlier with a point to break to 5-3 in the first set.

But then it had been all Smith. The American served harder, volleyed better and was invincible overhead. Even the vast crowd, Rosewall lovers since he first enchanted this stadium at 17, was beginning to drift away.

So 6-fot-4-inch Smith toed the line and served, and Ken changed his tactics. Instead of trying to pass on the flanks, he dinked a return to the feet as Stan charged in for the volley. Twice Smith fluffed the short ball and the third caromed off his shoetops and Rosewall reached 15-40. Stan half-volleyed the next return and Rosewall backhanded the ball to the far corner and tied the game at 5-all.

It didn't seem that important then and in the tiebreak that followed at 8-8. Smith reached match point at 6-5 and backhanded into the net. Then that Rosewall backhand streaked across court and he had that set 9-8. He broke in the first game, again in the third and once more in the seventh and had the fourth set at 6-1 with the stadium a well of sound.

Stan was shaken, his confidence fading. At 1-2 serving in the fifth set he missed a simple smash at the net and netted again as another backhand flew by him. Ken now was serving for the match at 5-3 and 40-0. Almost by script a backhand return like a shaft of lightning seared the chalk. The last shot had gone from the Australians' sling, the giant had been slain.

Rosewall is in a Wimbledon final for the fourth time over 20 years, winning in five sets in 3 hours 8 minutes. Now he has another chance for the one big title that has always escaped him. There was a standing, cheering ovation as he and Smith trudged off court.

Connors proved the better man on the big occasion. Stockton, who had upset Ilie Nastase and Alex Metreveli, a 1973 Wimbledon finalist, started the stronger. A couple of volley errors, a lob that spun over his head and a lob that he hit out cost Jimmy a break in the third game and then the first set at 6-4.

They exchanged service breaks. Another timely lob, as Connors charged in, put Stockton at 2-1. But suddenly his game disintegrated. Jimmy had slowed the pace a bit and seemed to be more flexible on the volley. The games came running. He had eight in a row now and the match comfortably by taking the next three sets.

Asked about Rosewall, who played before he was born, Connors said: "How do you play a legend?"

Connors got no help from Newcombe and Tony Roche, the Australian doubles team, which lost the first two sets and won in five from Nastase and Connors in the semifinals. They were hitting most of the balls to Jimmy.

Connors and Miss Evert are engaged to be married. The wedding is scheduled for November. A tradition of Wimbledon is the ball that follows completion of play at which the men's singles champion and the women's champion dance the first dance. Chris is hoping that the first dance tomorrow night will be with Jimmy.

Miss Evert has beaten Miss Morozova repeatedly, in a semifinal at Rome, in the final at Paris and over three tough sets on grass in a tune-up at Eastbourne, which seemed the key to today's play.

The Russian has a game of serve and volley built for a fast surface such as Wimbledon's, and she came to center court tired but confident after dethroning Mrs. King and eliminating Miss Wade.

In a long first game that lasted 13 minutes with Olga three times at advantage, Chris won and raced to 6-0 in 14 more minutes. On clay she lobs continually, today she was hitting her ground strokes deep and making occasional sorties to the net. Her overhead was sharp and her volley deadly placed in the direction Olga was not going. Quickly she reached 4-2 in the second set, breaking service at love.

Miss Morozova was still in the hunt. She hit a blazing forehand passing shot and a forehand volley to break to 4-3 and held her own service with a drop shot and a deep smash for 4-all.

At 30-all in the ninth game, a vital stage, Miss Evers hit a forehand cross-court shot for an outright winner. That did it. The Russian volleyed over the line and then double-faulted on match point, 6-0, 6-4.

"To beat her you have to win all the points," said Olga later. "There is no other way."

Miss Evert missed out on a chance to share another title. Paired with Miss Morozova, she was beaten in doubles by Evonne Goolagong of Australia and Margaret Michel of Pacific Palisades, Calif., in the semifinals, 7-5, 6-2.

Summaries on Page 12.

Associated Press

Chris Evert shows the trophy she won at Wimbledon

Mets' Koosman Beats Giants On Hitting of Schneck, 3-2

By AL HARVIN

To get two hits, knock in two runs and be a hero in the New York Mets' 3-2 victory over San Francisco was all just a bonus for Dave Schneck last night, the icing on the cake.

"I was happy just to be platooning again," said Schneck, after getting off the Met bench for the first time in more than two weeks after having alternated with Don Hahn in center field. "I don't blame them for benching me though, because I wasn't hitting anything."

He came into the game at Shea Stadium with one hit in his last 31 at bats, none in his last 16 and no runs batted in since May 21 and then gave Jerry Koosman nearly all the support the Met left-hander needed.

Schneck's single to center in the second inning drove in Cleon Jones with the first Met run of the game after Jones had reached on an error and gone to second on an infield out.

And Schneck's single over the glove of Chris Speier at shortstop knocked in the first of two Met runs in the fourth, scoring John Milner, who had walked and gone to third on Jerry Grote's single.

Teddy Martinez then knocked in the final Met run with a double, giving Koosman a 3-0 advantage on his way to his ninth victory against five defeats.

Koosman struck out seven and walked three. He stranded only five men, but worked his way out of a couple of tight spots in picking up his seventh complete game, the most on the club.

The Giants got both their runs off Koosman in the sixth inning after Tito Fuentes opened with a double.

Rusty Staub then misjudged a high fly hit by Speier. The right-fielder slipped, tried to recover and the ball bounced off his glove for a triple and the first Giant run. Koosman let in the other run with a wild pitch to Bobby Bonds.

"I was trying to throw a low breaking ball to Bonds and it hit a piece of sand in front of the plate and just bounced away," said Koosman, happy that he held the most dangerous Giant hitter and the man he thought

Continued on Page 12, Column 5

The New York Times/Larry Morris

Tito Fuentes of the Giants firing to first to catch Felix Millan of the Mets after having put out Wayne Garrett at second. Play, with bases filled and one out, ended fifth inning of game at Shea. Mets won, 3-2.

Yanks Get 20 Hits, Beat Rangers, 14-2

By MICHAEL STRAUSS

Special to The New York Times

ARLINGTON, Tex., June 5—Any similiarity between the Yankees of a few nights ago, who were then finding it difficult to put few hits together, and the Yankees who took on the Rangers tonight must have proved a revelation for even their manager, Bill Virdon.

As a follow-up on its 6-to-4 victory over Detroit, which ended a seven-game losing streak, New York went on a batting spree tonight that provided a new high for total runs and hits this season as it swamped the Texans, 14-2.

The Yankees emerged with 20 hits that included successive home runs by Thurman Munson and Graig Nettles in the fifth inning. For Munson it was his seventh circuit clout and for Nettles, who had started the season with an explosive home-run sequence, it was No. 13. The third baseman's round-trip clout was his first since June 9.

Other highlights in the bombardment included a collection of four singles by Elliott Maddox in his first five trips to the plate: four consecutive hits by Munson and two hits by Bobby Murcer. Murcer and Bill Sudiakis sat out the last three innings.

Rudy May, the southpaw the Yankees obtained from the Angels last month for a

Continued on Page 12, Column 6

Soviet Men, Women Lead U.S. in Track

By NEIL AMDUR

Special to The New York Times

DURHAM, N. C., July 5—Tom Byers insisted he was fouled from behind, 100 yards from victory. Jimmy Carnes, the United States coach, agreed.

But their appeal on a last-lap dispute in the 1,500-meter run was turned down today and the Soviet Union posted a commanding 90-75 lead over the United States in a rainy opener of this two-day track and field duel at Wallace Wade Stadium.

Surprising victories in the shot put, pole vault and the controversial 1,500 by a last-minute substitute, Vladimir Ponomared, helped the Soviet men to a 54-49 lead over the Americans, who have never lost to the Russians outdoors in this country. The Soviet women led, 36-26.

The bizarre events, before a crowd of 27,000, also included a peaceful protest outside the stadium against the treatment of Soviet Jews and a male streaker who darted across the grassy Duke University football field, hurdled a wooden fence and escaped into the woods.

No time was announced for the streaker, but it was considerably slower than Reggie Jones's victory in the 100-meter dash (10.23 seconds).

The 20-year-old Jones, refusing to let steady late afternoon showers and the absence of Valery Borzov, the Olympic champion, dampen his spirits, exploded off the blocks, beat Steve Williams by 2 feet and then anchored the victorious American 440-yard relay team.

If Jones, the National Collegiate champion from Tennessee, appeared satisfied with his performance and the prospect of facing Borzov in the 200 tomorrow afternoon, Byers was emotionally upset with his third-place finish in the 1,500.

The 19-year-old Ohio State freshman, who had swept the 800 and 1,500 events at the recent United States-Soviet junior meet, led throughout until he stumbled and broke stride coming off the last tnrn into the stretch.

"The little guy who came in second clipped me twice

Continued on Page 13, Column 3

Top Rookie Of Chargers Joins Strike

SAN DIEGO, July 5 (AP)—The striking National Football League Players Association won a victory of sorts today in its three-day-old strike when Dan Goode, one of the San Diego Chargers' first-round draft choices, left the training camp and joined the picket line.

"I don't know if anyone will follow me," said Goode, a linebacker. "Some are willing but they have doubts in their minds."

Goode was the second Charger to leave camp and join the strike. The first was Coleman Zeno, a wide receiver and free agent, who left late yesterday.

Another free agent, Jerry Dunigan, who was cut from the Chargers' team today, also joined the pickets a few hours later. "I was the ringleader who told the rookies to come down and mingle with the vets," said Dunigan, a linebacker, adding he believed that his advice affected the decision to cut him after the second practice.

"I don't know why I did it," Goode said when he arrived to picket. "I just didn't get the assurance I wanted up on the hill."

Goode said he advised Coach Tommy Prothro of his decision last night. "He told me to wait and hear what management had to say," Goode said. "So I did. I listened to Gene Klein [owner of the Chargers] and their lawyer [J. Stacey Sullivan]. But I still wasn't satisfied.

"I figured by coming down here I might be able to hurry

Continued on Page 12, Column 4

Dave Anderson

Kyle Rote Jr. Views the World Cup

Sports of The Times

To most Americans, the World Cup is a trophy in another world, one where soccer is supreme. But as the United States' best known soccer player, Kyle Rote Jr. understand that world. He also foresees the time when the United States will be a contender. In that connection he talks admiringly of the Netherlands team that will oppose West Germany in Munich tomorrow for the World Cup title.

"I'm for Holland," says Rote, "because of their team play. They've gone at the World Cup more scientifically than the others."

Rote remembers a recent World Cup game when seven Dutch players suddenly surrounded a Uruguay player who had the ball at midfield.

"They stole the ball from him," Rote says. "He had received a pass and was confronted with seven Dutch players. I was watching it on closed-circuit TV with several of my teammates on the Dallas Tornado and we couldn't get over it. But that's what I mean about the tremendous coaching advantage that the Dutch team has. Strategically, the Dutch are doing things that no other teams are doing. But someday I believe the United States will be a factor and eventually a contender because of coaching and because of the psychology of the American athlete. There's something about an American athlete—determination, hustle, willingness to learn. As soon as our young talent develops, I'm speaking now of kids 13 or 14 years old now, we'll have a world-class team. There was no soccer in Dallas until 1967, but now there are 40,000 kids playing. There are programs all over the country. Once the kids develop and you combine them with American coaching technique, we'll dominate."

$53,400 of Identity

Rote provided soccer with an identity it had never known in the United States when he won $53,400 last winter in the Superstars tournament. Not many Americans know what a corner kick means, but they all know what $53,400 means.

"The whole dedication of American coaching has to be a factor eventually," says the son of the former New York Giants' football player. "The detail in which a player has to be involved in football is far beyond what a soccer player is concerned with, at least up until the Dutch team came along. Most soccer coaches are willing to let a player develop by himself. Soccer teams don't use films yet, for example. We've spent 30 minutes at practice arguing where a player was on a certain play. If we had films, we wouldn't waste that time."

In the World Cup, a nation's players must be citizens of that nation, but a coach can be a foreigner. Early this year a team of Americans registered a 1-0 victory over Poland's team that went to the World Cup semifinal Wednesday before losing to West Germany, 1-0.

"It was quite a shock, not only to them but also to us," says Rote, on that team along with several North American Soccer League players including Al Trost of the St. Louis Stars, Bob Smith of the Philadelphia Atoms and Roy Turner of the Tornado. "I think we can organize a good American team for the 1978 World Cup, but if we get into the last 16 in Argentina we'll be doing well. I think it'll take two or three more World Cups before we have a team that's really capable of winning it."

For now the World Cup provides Americans with an opportunity to display ethnic pride at the closed-circuit TV sites every four years.

"We'll do more than $5-millon gross," says Rene Anselmo, the 48-year-old theatrical impresario with TV locations in 45 cities in the United States and Canada. "We would've done over $6-million if Brazil had made the final, over $7-million if Italy had made it."

Americans watch the World Cup in order to root for the old country, not for their current country. Most of them probably don't realize that at the first World Cup in 1930 the United States was a semifinalist, its best showing. also its most humorous showing. During the 6-0 loss to Argentina, an American trainer ran onto the field to protest a foul call. In his anger with the referee, he flung his medicine box to the ground. The bag opened. Several bottles broke, including the one that contained chloroform. The fumes dazed the trainer, who had to be helped from the field.

The Olympic Spinoff

Perhaps the United States' most memorable World Cup moment was a 1-0 upset over England in 1950 at Brazil, but it hasn't qualified for the final round of 16 teams since then.

The World Cup originated as a spinoff to Olympic soccer. According to Brian Glanville's "The History of the World Cup" (Collier, $4.95), one of its organizers, Henri Delauney, proclaimed in 1926, "International football can no longer be held within the confines of the Olympics; and many countries where professionalism is now recognized and organized cannot any longer be represented there by their best players." Henri Delauney was a realist, not a dreamer. So is Kyle Rote Jr.

"I don't foresee the United States as the site of the World Cup finals for many, many years," Rote says. "Most people here don't have an appreciation for it that the people of the host country must have. But perhaps someday they will."

40-Foot Birdie Putt at 16 Helps Nicklaus Win His 5th Masters

Weiskopf and Miller 2d After Misses on 18th

By JOHN S. RADOSTA

Special to The New York Times

AUGUSTA, Ga., April 13—Jack Nicklaus, who likes to live dangerously and has a sense of show business, set up one of the most exciting finishes today in the history of the Masters golf tournament.

It came down to the last two putts on the last green, and when the delirious shouting was over, Nicklaus has fended a thrilling charge by two of the best players in the game, Johnny Miller and Tom Weiskopf—and he beat them each by a shot. And the shot he beat them with was a 40-foot putt that broke two ways before dropping for a birdie on the 16th green.

Nicklaus, widely accepted as the greatest golfer in history, became the first man to win the symbolic green jacket a fifth time. To get there he shot a final round of 68 for a 72-hole total of 276. Only two other scores have been better—Nicklous's record 271 in 1965 and Ben Hogan's 274 in 1953.

But what a finish! Miller, in a drive that he himself calls "berserk," shot a six-under-par 66 to finish at 277. Weiskopf shot a 70 for his 277.

Irwin Shoots a 64

Miller's 66, with yesterday's 65, set a record of 131 for the final 36 holes, two shots better than the record Nicklaus set in 1965. With Friday's 71, Miller set a record 202 for the final 54 holes, breaking by two the record held by Nicklaus and Hogan.

And speaking of records, there was Hale Irwin, who had been playing disappointingly all week, who shot a 64 to tie the course record shared by Nicklaus, Maurice Bembridge and Lloyd Mangrum.

No finish could have been more theatrical. The lead had swung between Nicklaus and Weiskopf three times. Twice they shared the lead. At no time was Miller in front, but with birdies at the 15th and 17th holes, he came to within one shot of the lead.

So there was Nicklaus on the 18th green—on in two, with a 10-foot putt that had to break left about 18 inches. Nicklaus misguaged the amount of break, and the ball slid past the hole. A tap-in for par-4, and Nicklaus was in, 12 under par for the tournament.

"I wanted to end the tournament right there," Nicklaus said, "but I just couldn't get that putt in. I figured a break of about a foot, and it broke at least a foot and a half."

As Nicklaus watched from the scorer's tent near the **18th green, Weiskopf and Miller marched up the hill, each 11 under. Miller hit a 9-iron 20 feet from the hole; Weiskopf's shot was about 8 feet away.**

Miller knew it was a hard putt. He missed. There was no way Weiskopf could understand how he missed. Even watching a replay on television, he was convinced his ball would go in—but it didn't.

United Press International

Jack Nicklaus, wearing the green jacket of the Masters winner, winking as he signed an autograph at the end of the tournament yesterday in Augusta, Ga.

Any time Jack Nicklaus wins a Masters, the question comes up: Can he win the other components of the grand slam—the United States and British Opens and the championship of the Professional golfers' Association—all in one year?

He was asked today if he felt like facing the question. "Absolutely," he replied with a happy smile.

Nicklaus has accomplished the grand slam, although not in one year. He has won a record 15 "major" tournaments, **including three United States Opens, two British Opens, three P.G.A. championships and two United States Amateur titles. His previous Masters victories came in 1963, 1965, 1966 and 1972.**

Weiskopf had a heart-breaking day. This was the fourth time he had tied for second place in the Masters.

"I can't say now how I feel," he said. "How do you describe pain?"

"Nobody in golf has a better swing than I have," the lanky Ohioan continued. "Shouldn't I be disappointed? I never played any hole all week without confidence. I never doubted I was going to win.

"My next goal is the U.S. Open, that's what's on my mind."

Miller was close to defiant. He won eight tournaments last year and has won three this year, but is constantly reminded that he has won only one major, the United States Open.

He said he was determined to play well to show them he was there."

"I'm no Jack Nicklaus, but I'm not bad either," he said.

"I've won one U.S. Open, placed second twice in the Masters and been second in the British Open.

"I'm not upset. I'm funny this way. I don't get down on myself when I don't win. I gave it my best, and 66 and 65 are not too shabby."

The competition between Weiskopf and Nicklaus was not unlike a motor race in which one development or another forces changes in the lead.

Nicklaus had led at the 36-hole stage, but he shot a poor 73 yesterday while Weiskopf was scoring a 66. When the final round began today, **Weiskopf was leading at nine under par and Nicklaus was eight under.**

Nicklaus had trouble at the start today. He opened with a poor drive, and that cost him a bogey on the first hole. In the twosome behind, Weiskopf parred the first hole. Nicklaus birdied the par-5 second by blasting out of a bunker to three feet from the hole to return to eight under. Then he birdied the third to go nine under and the sixth to go 10 under.

But Weiskopf was not loafing back there. He had birdies at Nos. 3 and 6, and after six holes he still had a one-shot lead. **Nicklaus finally tied Weiskopf at the ninth by holing a 15-foot birdie putt. They were both 11 under.**

Weiskopf lost the lead with a bogey on 11, where he went into the water. No. 14 became a swing hole. Nicklaus missed the green and picked up a bogey to slip to 10 under; Weiskopf's birdie there put him 11 under and he had a one-shot lead again.

Both birdied the par-5 15th. The par-3 16th then became the next and last swing hole—Nicklaus's birdie put him 12 under and Weiskopf three-putted for a bogey to go 11 under. That was how they finished.

Nicklaus's putt on 16 was a masterpiece. He knew from the instant it left his putter it was good, and when his caddie jumped up and down, that confirmed it.

The caddie's jumping was nothing compared with Nicklaus's reaction. He held his club in the air and jogged around the green as though he were doing a war dance.

Later Miller was asked if he had seen that putt from the 16th tee. "See it?" Miller replied. "I had to, walk through the bear prints."

Miller was, as the golfers say, shooting out the lights. He started the day at four strokes behind Weiskopf and three behind Nicklaus. Miller shot five birdies and one bogey on the front nine to make the turn at 32, only two shots over the record 30 he scored yesterday. He gave ground by three-putting 11, but returned to nine under par with a bird on 13 and went 10 under with another bird on 15.

He closed in on Weiskopf and Nicklaus with a birdie putt of 20 feet on the 17th. The putt was so sure, so true, so pure, that he raised is hand in an exuberant wave even before the ball reached the hole. He had it made, and he knew it.

If either Miller or Weiskopf had sunk the birdie putt on 18, there would have been an 18-hole playoff tomorrow. The last playoff here was in 1970, when Bill Casper defeated Gene Littler.

"I've dreamed of a finish like this since I was a kid," said Miller. "You can't imagine how exciting that last putt was on 18 unless you were in my shoes, trying it."

Said Weiskopf, "The Masters is one of the greatest spectacles in sport, and I will win it some day. Adversity is part of this game, and the guy who beats adversity is the champion, and should be."

Said Nicklaus, "I don't think there's ever been a more exciting day. Any one of the three of us could have won. All that action on 18—my putt and theirs—that's the fun of this game."

The others were not quite inclined to consider it fun.

But there they were, the three leading money-winners on the tour this year, the rich getting richer. Nicklaus's $40,000 purse increased his season's winings to $149,242. Miller's $21,250 kept him in the lead, at $149,476. Weiskopf's $21,250 raised his winnings to $112,488.

Hale Irwin was the unsung hero of the day. Because he was at 218 after 54 holes, two over par, he was an early starter, and did not have much of a gallery.

But as the red numbers were added to the leader boards, spectactors abandoned their stations to find him on the course. It was a flawless round, 32, 32—64, with four birdies on each nine and no bogeys. Most of the birdies were scored on giant-size putts, 25 and 30 feet.

But all it got Irwin, a former United States Open champion, was a tie for fourth place in what turned out to be a three-man race. His total of 282 was six shots behind Nicklaus's and the same as Bobby Nichols's. Nichols had a 69 today.

Final Scores

Jack Nicklaus	68 67 73 68—276	$40,000
Tom Weiskopf	69 72 66 70—277	21,250
Johnny Miller	75 71 65 66—277	21,250
Hale Irwin	73 74 71 64—282	12,500
Bobby Nichols	67 74 72 69—282	12,500
Billy Casper	70 70 73 70—283	7,500
Dave Hill	75 71 70 68—284	6,000
Tom Watson	70 70 72 73—285	4,500
Hubert Green	74 71 70 70—285	4,500
Lee Trevino	71 70 74 71—286	3,600
J. C. Snead	67 72 75 70—286	3,600
Tom Kite	72 74 71 69—286	3,600
Arnold Palmer	69 71 75 72—287	3,250
Larry Ziegler	71 73 74 69—287	3,250
Allen Miller	68 75 72 73—288	2,900
Bobby Cole	73 71 73 71—288	2,900
Bruce Devlin	72 70 76 70—288	2,900
Art Wall	72 74 72 70—288	2,900
Rod Curl	72 70 76 70—288	2,900
Bud Allin	73 69 73 74—289	2,550
Ralph Johnston	74 73 69 73—289	2,550
Graham Marsh	75 70 74 71—290	2,250
Pat Fitzsimons	73 68 79 70—290	2,250
Gene Littler	72 72 72 74—290	2,250
Hugh Baiocchi	76 72 72 70—290	2,250
Dave Stockton	72 72 73 74—291	$2,000
Jerry Heard	71 75 72 73—291	$2,000
Miller Barber	74 72 72 73—291	$2,000
Maurice Bembridge	75 72 75 69—291	$2,000
Ben Crenshaw	72 71 75 74—292	$1,850
Forrest Fezler	76 71 71 74—292	$1,850
Gary Player	72 74 73 73—292	$1,850
Bert Yancey	74 71 74 73—292	$1,850
Vic Regalado	76 72 72 72—292	$1,850
Ray Floyd	72 73 79 68—292	$1,850
*George Burns	72 72 76 72—292	
*Jerry Pate	71 75 78 69—293	
Gary Groh	72 76 71 75—294	$1,775
Tommy Aaron	71 75 76 72—294	$1,775
Charles Coody	72 75 75 73—295	$1,700
Lou Graham	72 72 77 74—295	$1,700
Bob Murphy	70 72 80 74—296	$1,700
Lu Liang-Huan	73 74 78 72—297	$1,700
Homero Blancas	72 69 79 77—297	$1,700
Jumbo Ozaki	73 69 79 77—297	$1,700
Richie Karl	72 75 79 76—302	$1,700

*Amateur

Flyers Capture Seventh Game, 4-1, and Foil Islander Comeback

MacLeish's 3 Goals Put Cup Defenders in Final

By ROBIN HERMAN
Special to The New York Times

PHILADELPHIA, May 13—The inspiring saga of the three-year-old New York Islanders came to a close tonight as the Philadelphia Flyers finally let out the tiger and roared into the Stanley Cup finals with a 4-1 victory.

After having held a lead in games in the semifinal series, it took the defending National Hockey League champions four more games to subdue a team that passionately believed in itself. The Flyers thus earned the right to meet the Buffalo Sabres in a four-of-seven-game final round beginning here at the Spectrum Thursday night.

The Islanders' comeback dreams ended with Rick MacLeish's empty-net goal with 68 seconds to play. It gave the brilliant Flyer forward a three-goal hat trick and caused the faces of 20 Islanders to fall in unison.

The Islanders had survived eight other critical playoff contests in which a loss would have meant elimination. They had rallied twice from three-game deficits and they had won two playoff games in overtime. They had, in short, done far more than could have been predicted for a third-year expansion club carrying nine players 23 years old or younger.

But they could not cope when the Flyers finally decided to play with some verve and hunger.

Flyers Dominate

The game was really decided in the first seven minutes, when the Flyers exploded to a 3-1 lead. Behind so early, the Islanders could not afford to play their usual conservative style. In the end, the Flyers' domination was spelled out in the shots-on-goal advantage: 35-15.

Although the Islanders' captain, Ed Westfall, had presented flowers to Kate Smith before she sang "God Bless America", and each member of the New York team had shaken her hand, the mollifying gestures failed to dampen the revival spirit that surged through the crowd and the Flyers.

As the 17,077 fans responded to Miss Smith's song with tumultuous cheers, the Flyers responded by blitzing the Islanders. They pounded Glenn Resch with nine shots in the space of 2½ minutes, scoring a goal on Gary Dornhoefer's shot just 19 seconds into the game.

MacLeish tipped in a 55-foot shot by Bill Barber 2 minutes, 8 seconds later on a power play. The Flyers had failed to score on the previous 18 power plays in this series.

MacLeish added a power-play goal at 7:11 of the period. It offset the Islanders' only tally, by Jude Drouin, also on a power play at 5:02.

First Goal Is Key

"I can't stress enough the importance of that first goal," said Resch, who led the Islanders through 10 of their last 11 contests. "It changes your whole game plan. The thing that frustrates me is that I got a piece of it. You should be able to stop the ones you get a piece of."

Dornhoefer's clean 40-foot shot beat Resch on the gloved side.

"The whole secret to winning this game was to shut the door in the first period," Resch explained, "and give us time to regroup. We're slow starters. We never got the chance."

From the drop of the puck the Flyers were skating with the dynamism of old and seemed to be wherever the puck wandered. The Islanders couldn't move out of their zone, and the few times they did, Flyer defensemen stood at the blue line to stop them.

Resch's hardest saves in the first period came during Islander power plays, when he had to stop Ross Lonsberry and Bill Barber on dangerous breakaways. He would have had to face a third breakaway during the last Islander power play of that period, but Denis Potvin hooked MacLeish, drawing a penalty to stop the fluid-skating center.

After a scoreless second period, the Flyers were able to alter their strategy in the third period, taking fewer risk-filled rushes in order to protect their lead.

"It's good to get the lead," said New York's Clark Gillies. "You can tighten up a little and get careful. When we got down, we had to pull out all the stops and go after them. We were bound to leave a few positions open. They stormed us in the first period. Everyone on their team was hustling."

A Glowing Future

Although the Islander locker room was solemn, the players found a lot of which to be proud. They also realized that the team's prospects for next year are golden.

"We proved a lot to ourselves," said Gillies "This extra month that we played is going to give us extra experience for next year. We have it in our heads that we can get all the way in."

Bert Marshall, a 31-year-old defenseman, said he had learned this season that, "Every guy on this team can do the job in the season and the playoffs. I have to take my hat off to them all. Many of them are young guys who hadn't experienced before the lifestyle changes that come with the playoffs. There's definitely a future for this team."

First Period — 1, Philadelphia, Dornhoefer 3 (Jim Watson), 0:19. 2, Philadelphia, MacLeish 8 (Barber, Clarke), 2:27. 3, New York, Drouin 6 (D. Potvin, Westfall), 5:02. 4, Philadelphia, MacLeish 9 (Goodenough), 7:11. Penalties — Hart, NY, 1:40; Jim Watson, Phi, 4:09; Dupont, Phi, 4:56; D. Potvin, NY, 6:08; Schultz, Phi, 8:12; D. Potvin, NY, 8:12; Joe Watson, Phi, 12:29; Saleski, Phi, 15:27; Van Impe, Phi, 17:34; D. Potvin, NY, 18:28.

Second Period — None. Penalties — Marshall, NY, 8:02; Leach, Phi, 13:04; Drouin, NY, 13:22; D. Potvin, NY, 18:35.

Third Period — 5, Philadelphia, MacLeish 10 (Saleski), 18:52. Penalties — Dupont, Phi, 1:50; D. Potvin, NY, 9:43.

Shots on Goal: New York 4-5-6 — 15. Philadelphia 15-11-9 — 35. Goalies: New York, Resch. Philadelphia, Parent. A. 17,077.

The Philadelphia Flyers

Rick MacLeish

A Giant Misses Buddies

By MURRAY CHASS

Throughout the years in sports there have been cries of "break up the Yankees" and "break up the Celtics" and "break up the Packers." These teams, of course, had long strings of success.

No one, however, has suggested that someone should break up the San Francisco Giants for similar reasons.

Nevertheless, as soon as the 1974 season ended, they started breaking up the Gians. It started with the trade of Bobby Bonds to the Yankees and was still going strong last week when they traded Garry Maddox to Philadelphia.

"I suppose they're just trying to get a winner," said Mike Phillips, the shortstop the Mets recently acquired on waivers from the Giants. "Mr. [Horace] Stoneham needs a winner bad. They say he needs money. I guess they changed the whole face of the team to try and get a winner."

Kate Smith Calls the Tune For Islanders' Swan Song

By PARTON KEESE
Special to The New York Times

PHILADELPHIA, May 13—The New York Islanders' miracle ended tonight. There were a lot of reasons: the law of averages, the Philadelphia Flyers' special meeting, Rick MacLeish's three goals, the rabid fans, home ice, Denis Potvin's five penalties. But maybe most of all, it was Kate Smith, in person.

When the Spectrum has substituted the recording of "God Bless America," for the national anthem, the Flyers have scored 41 victories and one tie against oinly three losses in the last six years. But when the 66-year-old singer had sung in person, the Flyers were not only unbeaten, they hadn't been scored upon.

The Islanders broke that scoring jinx tonight with Jude Drouin's first-period goal. But they couldn't break the others as they fell, 4-1, to Miss Smith's Spectrum magic. With Miss Smith watching in person, the Flyers are 4-0 at home.

New York did what it could to break the spell, skating out en masse before she sang. Captain Ed Westfall gave her a bouquet of flowers and all the Islanders players shook her hand. It didn't work as Miss Smith, a fanatic Flyer fan, drove the already fevered crowd into a frenzy.

"She's a nice lady," said Westfall. "We wanted to do something nice, so we decided to give her flowers. It didn't help us win, but at least I got to meet her."

Clarke Important, Too

Gerry Hart didn't see Kate Smith as the key to the game, though. None of the Islanders did. "It was Bobby Clarke who brought them through," said Hart. "With the series tied, 3 to 3, he called the Flyer players together, put them all in a motel last night and laid it on the line.

"Then he went out on the ice and showed them how to do it. He deserved the star of the game before he even stepped on the ice."

When the time came to line up and shake hands, Clarke and Hart stopped and chatted for a moment at center ice. "We set up a golf match in Flin Flon the end of June," Hart explained. "Bobby's sister is graduating from high school, and we're going up there."

Denis Potvin, the Islanders' star defenseman, didn't see Kate Smith's presence influencing anything, either. "I said before the game they'd have to beat us on the ice," Potvin said. "And that's what they did, beat us on the ice. No excuses from me."

But Potvin was peeved over Referee Lloyd Gilmour's five penalties against him. "Three times I never even touched the guy and he calls me for tripping or hooking. That's the part of the game I can't stand," he said.

Dissatisfied with losing the seventh game ("I have a funny feeling we were looking ahead to Buffalo," said Denis Potvin), the Islanders appeared satisfied with their over-all playoff record.

"We've established pride in ourselves," said Hart. "We can look each other in the eye all summer now and look to next year with anticipation.

Wait Till Next Year

"Everyone thought we were a surprise and called us a Cinderella team," Hart went on, "but they forgot what the playoffs are all about. It's a brand new season, and we gave it the extra effort that it calls for.

"Three months ago we got together and decided we were a better team than we thought we were. We didn't play over our heads at all, and next year we'll play even better."

Coach Al Arbour looked more relaxed than at any time since the Islander miracle began. As the Islanders kept pulling incredible feats, Arbour kept repeating how "my kids never quit."

The Islander coach praised "his kids" again tonight, saying, "They're the youngest in the league, but they've gained so much maturity. They're better now and they're more eager. Why, if I called a practice next week, every one of thme would show up."

The New York Times

SPORTS

Section 5

Sunday, September 7, 1975

The New York Times/Robert Walker

Chris Evert during her final match in the U.S. Open at Forest Hills against Evonne Goolagong

Miss Evert Takes Open Crown; Connors, Orantes Reach Final

By PARTON KEESE

Chris Evert won her first United States Open singles championship on her fifth attempt yesterday, defeating Evonne Goolagong of Australia, 5-7, 6-4, 6-2.

Before her victory, worth $25,000, Jimmy Connors beat Bjorn Borg to gain the men's final. And then, in a 3-hour-44-minute match under the lights in the Forest Hills stadium, Manuel Orantes outlasted Guillermo Vilas in the second semifinal to earn the right to meet Connors.

A crowd of 15,720 braved a threat of rain to see Miss Evert and Connors move one victory away from duplicating their "lovebird" Wimbledon triumphs in singles last year. The three matches yesterday lasted more than nine hours, however, forcing many persons to leave early and tournament officials to postpone the men's doubles final until this afternoon.

Connors defeated his Swedish rival 7-5, 7-5, 7-5. The sets not only were identical in the number of games, but also in the manner that Connors succeeded. In each instance, the top-seeded American broke Borg's service in the 12th game to take an otherwise even set.

Orantes, a Spaniard, made an amazing comeback against the second-seeded Vilas of Argentina. Trailing by two sets to one and down 0-5, in the fourth set, Orantes saved 5 match points before winning, 4-6, 1-6, 6-2, 7-5, 6-4, in the longest match of the tournament.

Cheered on by his followers, Orantes simply lasted longer than his exhausted foe. Seeded third, he contin-

Continued on Page 5, Column 4

The New York Times

Jimmy Connors slamming ball back to Bjorn Borg during semifinals at the U.S. Open

Met Errors Help Cardinals Triumph, 6-3

By JOSEPH DURSO

The Mets took themselves out of a ballgame and possibly out of a pennant race yesterday when they made two errors in the first inning, staked the St. Louis Cardinals to a 6-3 victory and lapsed back into fourth place with only 22 games left to play.

Capitalizing on the Mets' charity, the Cardinals combined the two errors with two walks and two hits for four fast runs off Jerry Koosman, and then the Mets spent the rest of the afternoon at Shea Stadium trying to catch up. But they were checked by Bob Forsch, a onetime third baseman who became a pitcher five years ago, and Al Hrabosky, the "Mad Hungarian" of the St. Louis bull pen.

Afterward, Koosman reflected on the wastefulness of it all—a fly ball lost in the sun, a futile throw to the plate, a pickoff throw that got away—and said with some feeling:

"To win a pennant, you've got to play nearly errorless ball. You can't spot anybody anything, especially the guys you're contending with for the pennant. We should've been out of that inning with no runs scored, but instead things went wrong and it took us out of the ballgame. I'll be damned if I know why these things happen. But they've been happening to me for eight seasons."

Koosman allowed only two singles in the five other innings he worked, but by then the Mets had undermined the best asset they own in their pursuit of the Pittsburgh Pirates: pitching. It was ironic because Manager Red Schoendienst of the Cardinals, surveying the final three weeks of the race in the National League's East Division, had observed:

"We have speed, the Mets have pitching and the Pirates have a five-game lead. That's about it, I guess. But we have a problem, too: We can't catch the ball. Been giving away too many runs. We've already made 147 errors."

That's more than one error a game, because yesterday's game was No. 140 for both teams. The Mets' meantime,

Continued on Page 4, Column 3

National League

St. Louis 6, New York 3.
Chicago 7, Philadelphia 6 (n.).
Atlanta 3, Los Angeles 2 (n.).
Pittsburgh 12, Montreal 5 (11 inn, n.).
San Diego 2, Houston 1 (n.).
Cincinnati 3, San Francisco 2 (n.).

Standing on Page 4.

Chris: 'Never Thought I'd Win'

By STEVE CADY

"This has to be the year's biggest upset," a champion of underdogs said gleefully yesterday after Evonne Goolagong beat Chris Evert in the opening set of their United States Open tennis final yesterday.

"It hasn't transpired yet," the man's companion shot back.

It never did. But even Miss Evert, nailing down the title that had escaped her for so long, was surprised the upset had not taken place.

"All through the match I never thought I'd win," the 20-year-old Florida slugger said afterward. "I was pretty down the whole way."

When it was over, with Miss Evert having worn down her 24-year-old Australian opponent, 5-7, 6-4, 6-2, everything seemed almost routine. The queen of women's tennis had won her 84th straight match on clay over 2½ years. She had increased her 1975 earnings to $280,027, and the victory had prompted some of those in the crowd of 15,720 at the West Side Tennis Club in Forest Hills, Queens, to say jokingly: "What a surprise! Chris Evert won."

Yet this was a match that could be understood by athletes who know about momentum and competitive fires. Miss Goolagong, playing what some of the experts considered the finest match of her career, had Miss Evert hanging on the ropes like a wobbly fighter whose punches had lost their sting.

The favorite's devastating, two-fisted backhand wasn't doing much damage, her occasional trips to the net weren't producing winners—and Miss Goolagong was getting everything back. When the Australian took a 2-1 lead in the third set on a service break, the upset script appeared ready to run its course.

That's when Miss Evert got more aggressive, when Miss Goolagong's concentration began slipping and when the crowd began cheering for the top-seeded Floridian as a kind of one-time underdog. She wrapped it up by winning five straight games.

"I was thinking to myself that maybe she'll have one of her walkabouts, or whatever, where she loses concentration," Chris said. "So I stayed in there."

Miss Evert had been trying to win the Open since 1971, when at 16 she became the youngest player to reach the semifinals. She had never got past the semifinals.

For winning, she received a small treasure: the $25,000 first-place prize; a red Ford

Continued on Page 5, Column 5

The New York Times/Paul Hosefros

Cards' Bake McBride crossing the plate on a wild pitch by Jerry Koosman of the Mets, who covered the plate in the first inning at Shea yesterday.

Yankees Beaten in 13th by 7-6

By PAUL L. MONTGOMERY
Special to The New York Times

BALTIMORE, Sept. 6—In a game that had more chapters than "War and Peace" and more dramatic reversals than "King Lear," the Baltimore Orioles scratched out a 13-inning 7-6 victory over the Yankees tonight at Memorial Stadium.

It was 3-hours 56 minutes of baseball entertainment for 19,236 people in attendance. In the ninth inning alone, both managers, Billy Martin and Baltimore's Earl Weaver, were thrown out of the game, as well as Thurman Munson, the Yankee catcher. The ejections, believe it or not, oc-

Continued on Page 4, Column 6

American League

Baltimore 7, New York 6 (13 inn. n.).
Boston 20, Milwaukee 6.
Cleveland 4, Detroit 2.
Kansas City 4, California 3 (1st. twi.).
Kansas City 6, California 3 (2d n.).
Chicago 5, Minnesota 2 (n.).
Oakland 2, Texas 1.

Standing on Page 4.

Watson Leads by 3 With 69

United Press International

Tom Weiskopf sends ball out of woods on second hole of first round at Akron, Ohio

By JOHN S. RADOSTA
Special to The New York Times

AKRON, Ohio, Sept. 6—Tom Watson, the 26-year-old British Open champion with the Huck Finn image, shot a 69 today to lead the first round of the 36-hole, four-man World Series of Golf.

Watson's score, one under par for the difficult and rain-soaked South Course of the Firestone Country Club, gave him a three-stroke lead over Jack Nicklaus, who won the Professional Golfers' Association Championship Aug. 10 on this course. Nicklaus's 72 included four bogeys, two of them in sequence, and two consecutive birdies.

Tom Weiskopf, just returned and still tired from working on a television film series in Scotlnad, shot 75. In one sequence he carded double bogey, bogey, bogey.

Lou Graham brought up the rear at 76 with six bogeys and no birdies.

The World Series, a television showcase for the winners of the four major tournaments this year, was hardly classical in quality today. The four players combined shot only six birdies, and those were more than offset by 16 bogeys and Weiskopf's double bogey.

The competitors agreed the over-par scores resulted from a combination of poor playing—lackadaisical, really—and difficult playing conditions on a "soft" golf course where many iron shots were flyers or jumpers.

On the 15th hole, a par 3

Continued on Page 11, Column 6

Miss Navratilova Asks U.S. Asylum

Martina Navratilova, the 18-year-old tennis star from Czechoslovakia, asked for political asylum in the United States last night, the State Department announced.

A department spokesman said that Miss Navratilova, who reached the semiminals of the United States Open before being eliminated yesterday was granted a temporary residence while the Justice Department considers her request.

A spokesman for the Immigration and Naturalization Service said the processing of Miss Navratilova's application for asylum "will be very routine."

He added: "She's from a Communist country. If she wants to stay here she'll be permitted to stay."

A Justice Department spokesman said Miss Navratilova appeared at an Immigration and Naturalization Service office in New York City last night to ask for asylum.

"She was told her request would be taken under advisement and she would be allowed to remain in this country pending a decision on her request," the Justice Department spokesman said. "The decision is made by the district commissioner of the Immigration Service in New York City after a review of the matter," he said. "Sometimes there is some background checking."

The spokesman said Miss Navratilova entered the United States Aug. 15 with a Czechoslovak passport and was given permission then to remain in the country until Oct. 31.

Miss Navratilova, an exuberant personality given to gesturing, screaming and glaring while on the court, was named a rookie-of-the-

Continued on Page 5, Column 5

Hunting as a Sport: A View From Behind the Gun

By NELSON BRYANT

Wood, Field and Stream

If one were planning to portray the glories of love between woman and man in a television documentary, then devoted the entire show to the antics of a drunken clod in a bordello, one would achieve the same level of truth realized in the CBS News 90-minute film, "The Guns of Autumn."

Purporting to be a fair examination of hunting in America, the show instead focused on the shooting of bears in a city dump, the hurly-burly of opening day on a public waterfowl hunting area, running a bear with hounds, Jeeps and two-way radios, then keeping the animal treed until the women and youngsters can gather about to witness the kill, and the slaughter of exotic big-game animals in a mile-square private shooting preserve on the outskirts of Detroit.

Make no mistake about it, "The Guns of Autumn," shown last Friday night, was powerful stuff and the fragment of the hunting scene it portrays is accurate, but because it is only a fragment the final result is propaganda.

I find it necessary to become personal to describe some of my thoughts on hunting.

When, for example, the film showed an army of gun-waving men and boys blasting away before dawn at Canada geese and mallards, I thought of a winter day that I spent alone on a salt marsh. All day long I heard no sound save the wind in brown grass and the surf on the distant beach. All day long I saw ducks and geese, but they were too distant for me to shoot at them. Then, just before sunset, a small flock of black ducks

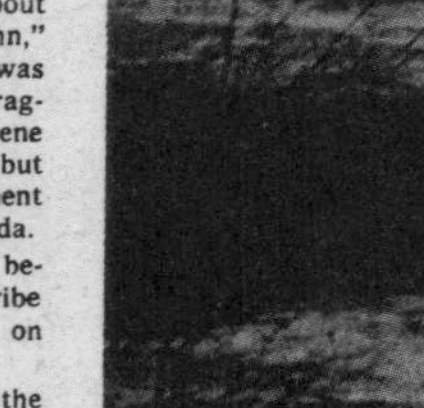

came in low out of the last light. I stood to shoot, but they looked so lovely I hesitated. They talked to each other as they descended and I lowered my shotgun, neither, at that time, wanting to kill nor to shatter the soft, sweet sound of the wind and waves.

And when the film showed a band of out-of-shape hunters puffing along the barbed wire fence of the aforementioned preserve, I thought of a log cabin in the wilderness of northern New Hampshire, where, at dawn, the several of us who hunt from that spot go forth, each his separate way, into the snow-covered mountains, and

Continued on Page 6, Column 6

Futurity Victory To Vasquez

By MICHAEL STRAUSS

Soy Numero Uno, which even a beginning student of Spanish knows means "I Am Number One," demonstrated yesterday in the 86th running of the rich Futurity at Belmont Park that he was just that—and with something to spare.

Competing in only the second race of his career and the first in stakes competition, the 2-year-old son of Damascus sped to an impressive victory. His winning margin — over Elmendorf's Jackknife—in the $117,680 contest was 2¾ lengths.

Third in the 6½-furlong fixture was Fred W. Hooper's 17-to-1 Beau Talent. Calumet's Turn to Turia, with an unbeaten record in five ca-

Continued on Page 11, Column 5

Inside Information

Miss Evert Takes First Open Title

Continued From Page 1

ued his jinx over Vilas with his fourth victory in four meetings this year.

Today's final program will start at 11:30 A.M. with the Hall of Fame doubles, followed by the women's doubles and the men's singles, the men's doubles, in which Connars will also play, and the mixed doubles.

Miss Evert's victory stretched her winning streak on clay to 84 matches and increased her year's earnings to $280,027. In her keen rivalry with Miss Goolagong over the last three years, she has won 12 of 21 matches.

Both were battling for a title they had never won, but had come close to winning. Chris had reached the semifinals four times before this year, her furthest advance, while Evonne had played in the final without success in 1974 and 1973.

FINAL MATCHES TODAY

STADIUM COURT

11:30 A.M. Bob Hewitt-Bob Howe vs. Neale Fraser-Fred Stolle (Hall of Fame).

Second Match—Billie Jean King-Rosemary Casals vs. Margaret Court-Virginia Wade.

Second Match—Jimmy Connors vs. Manuel Orantes.

Fourth Match—Connors-Ilie Nastase vs. Tom Okker-Marty Riessen.

Fifth Match—Miss Casals-Dick Stockton vs. Mrs. King-Fred Stolle.

Though she outdueled Miss Consistency from the baseline to take the opening set and barely lost the second on the only service break, Miss Goolagong faded badly in the third set, winning a otal of only 3 points in the last three games.

"I felt sort of tennised out," she said afterward. "She was getting too much back, and I'm not patient enough to play that type of game and keep going."

Capturing the last five games with little resistance, Miss Evert raced on to a triumph she termed "more satisfying than Wimbledon."

Not that she wasn't worried and even "quite down on myself" when Miss Goolagong looked as if she would win in straight sets.

"I had two thoughts when things were really tight," Miss Evert said. "The first one was how Evonne always seemed to win our close matches. The second one was on how hard I'd worked to come this far and lose."

There was little to choose between Connors, 22, and the 19-year-old Borg except in the final game of each set. The defending champion hit the ball consistently harder and flatter than his rival, but Borg's tremendously accurate topspin returns and placements matched everything Connors could hurl at him.

Credit Connors with figuring out what to do.

"Every time Bjorn passed me in the beginning," he said, "it was on a helluva shot. Then, after 30 of these shots it began to dawn on me. They were all hit down the line. When I realized this, I was there when it counted and cut them off."

Jimmy started in his normally cocky way, joking with the crowd, which seemed to favor Borg. When a baby cried loudly in the stands, Connors shouted, "I hope it isn't mine!"

In the second set he showed some anger. He had hit two straight shots into the net, and on the second asked to see the ball. Feeling it, he contended it was too soft and tossed it to Frank Hammond, the umpire, to confirm this and perhaps replay the point.

Hammond agreed on a new ball but not the point, letting it stand, and the crowd began getting on Connors, who shouted at one heckler, "Shut up!" Then, when he took the court again, he held up his little finger derisively as the stands hooted. But that was the end of the show.

'Never Thought I'd Win,' Admits U.S. Open Queen

Continued From Page 1

Mustang II Stallion from Virginia Slims; a bouquet of red roses; a tennis pin from the diamond industry; a lifetime supply of something or other from the City of New York.

But the best reward must have been the knowledge that she had turned in a courageous performance to win "my own country's title" for the first time.

"I was really confident in the last game," she said. "I was looking at my friends and family. I knew my father was back home in Florida watching on TV. He's there because my younger brother and sister are starting school, and my father doesn't think it's fair to ignore the rest of the family."

Compared to the ferocity of the earlier men's semifinal, in which Jimmy Connors beat Bjorn Borg of Sweden, the women's final had a pattycake placidness at times as the two players stayed back for lengthy baseline rallies. Some of the exchanges had 20 or more hits, the kind of back-and-forth sparring that gives sideline spectators sore necks.

Miss Goolagong, mixing patience with daring, looked like a winner until she apparently lost her patience.

"Yes, I felt it was monotonous," she said. "Getting everything back isn't my type of game."

A broken racquet string in the eighth game of the second set also slowed Miss Goolagong's momentum. "You get a favorite racquet and you don't feel as confident after the strings break and you have to use another one," she said.

The slow pace of the women's final stirred some debate about the relative merits of men's and women's tennis.

"Is this exciting or boring?" a man asked a women friend after the first set.

"It's exciting," the woman answered. "It's great."

"I think its terrible," he said.

Czechoslovak Net Star Asks to Remain in U.S.

Continued From Page 1

year last year by Tennis magazine.

This year, she has continued to enhance her reputation as one of the world's best young players while amassing earnings of $119,363.

Although a Communist country, Czechoslovakia has allowed its top tennis players to keep a percentage of earnings. Twenty per cent of her purses, after expenses, goes to her Government.

In recent years, when the first wave of Eastern European players came to the United States, many were accompanied by coaches and security people. But in the last two years, because of the international nature of the tennis circuit, it is almost impossible for authorities to keep a complete grip on players.

Alex Metreveli, the top-ranking men's player in the Soviet Union, has been allowed to play on the World Championship Tennis tour here. World Championship Tennis is an America-based organization owned by Lamar Hunt, the millionaire sportsman from Dallas.

One of the biggest fears of the Eastern European countries is the so-called "Westernization" of their athletes. Miss Navratilova, for example, is a very free-spirited, free-thinking individual whose tastes range from a love of American hamburgers to off-beat outfits.

During the United States Open, she wore a new dress especially designed for her for the tournament by Ted Tinling, the renowned British tennis fashion designer.

The outfit was a brightly colored floral print, which Martina described as "my favorite dress." The reason—"because it's like my personality—wild!"

Another possible reason for her attempt to defect is the opportunity for large-scale commercial endorsements. Under proper management, Miss Navratilova could accrue as much as $100,000 to $200,000 a year in endorsements and also sign potentially lucrative contracts with World Team Tennis, another American-based organization.

Although Eastern European players were selected by numerous franchises in W.T.T. each year, the national federations frowned on such participation because the W.T.T. summer schedule conflicted with the European circuit.

One of Miss Navratilova's closest friends is Chris Evert, the new United States Open champion, who defeated her in the semifinals last Friday, 6-4, 6-4.

The two young players, both single, are double partners and "talk a lot," according to Miss Evert.

"She's very sensitive," Miss Evert remarked only two days ago, referring to Martina's personality. "She wants to know about a lot of things."

The fact that Miss Navratilova could become the game's dominant player in the next decade also may have affected her decision.

Under the stricter jurisdiction of her home federation, she faced the possibility of continued scrutiny, particularly on travel plans, her personal life and any long-term professional goals.

Tennis federations in Europe, particularly in such Eastern European countries as the Soviet Union, Rumania, Yugoslavia, and Czechoslovakia, have considerably more control over the destiny of players than the United States Tennis Association or those in Britain or France.

Miss Navratilova, a left-hander, has had a spectacular surge to the top of the international game, unusual for a sport like tennis that stresses extensive junior participation.

One factor for her success is a 5-foot-7-inch, 137-pound husky frame, which has provided her wtih a strong, definitive game. Her only drawback, in the minds of most tennis observers, is her temperament, which often succumbs to outbursts that have cost her games, sets and matches.

In last Friday's semifinal loss to Miss Evert, Miss Navratilova lost the last nine points of the match after balking over a questionable line call.

Defections among athletes from Eastern European nations have diminished in recent years, particularly with the liberalization of international travel and less internal pressure. However, tennis is not an Olympic sport — an area of intense concentration by the Communist bloc nations—and its unusual status as a professional game has allowed players like Miss Navratilova; Jan Kodes, a countryman; Ilie Nastase, of Rumania, and Nikki Pilic, of Yugoslovia, to benefit materially.

For most amateur athletes in Eastern European countries, the only benefits are travel, perhaps an apartment, state-subsidized training, and the opportunity for permanent jobs that will allow for athletic participation.

Athletes from the Soviet Union and other Communist-bloc countries have been known to shop extensively while abroad and then resell their purchases at considerably higher prices upon clearing customs back home. But even this practice has drawn critical responses from authorities in recent years.

Growing Pains Afflicting Open at Forest Hills

By NEIL AMDUR

Last Thursday, while hundreds of fans futilely sought tickets for the United States Open tennis championships, a security guard was stashing his pockets with $10 bills at the gates of the West Side Tennis Club in Forest Hills, Queens.

"The matches were sold out, but this guard was letting people in for the right price," said a criminal attorney from Manhattan, who had driven out for the men's quarterfinals but left in disgust after refusing to pay that price. "The guy must have made $200 for the day. If he did the same thing on other sellouts, he probably took home more than most players for the tournament."

Growing pains have set in for the Open, in between the record crowds, exciting competition and the controversial innovations this year.

Once content to cater to the country-club set and loyal fans, the world's richest tournament, in the words of Bill Talbert, "now is with the people who ride the subways."

As unsalaried tournament director, Talbert calls the bulging prize money ($309,430), six sellouts in 12 days and the successful introduction of night play (50,003 for eight sessions) a successful sign of the times.

Yet even with the sport enjoying unsurpassed popularity at the participant and spectator level, unpleasant murmurs have echoed from West Side during the last two weeks.

The complaints range as follows: players "You can't get a practice court; it's worse than either Wimbledon or Paris"); spectators ("It's too crowded and commercial; you can't see a match outside of the stadium); linesman ("Why should we take all that abuse?"); media ("Everybody's accredited except the right people").

Talbert, one of the first tournament directors to institute tiebreaker playoffs, upgrade prize money for women and push for the expanded night program, is aware and concerned about the rumblings.

Two Thursday ago, in a quiet experiment on the second day of the tournament, Talbert authorized the sale of 800 ground-admission tickets at $3 each to satisfy spectators shut out because of a sellout. The tickets did not qualify for seats in the stadium but allowed the holders to wander around the grandstand and 10 field courts, a practice allowed successfully at Wimbledon.

"I'd like to do this more often during the tournament," Talbert said the other day. "But I don't think you can. New York crowds are not as orderly as British crowds."

The pressure of big money also has added fuel to the feud between players and umpires. Yet, although the prize-money circuit now exceeds $7-million, no significant funds are set aside by any of the player groups for umpires or the schooling of crews to respond under pressure.

"People talk about it, but they don't take any action," Chris Evert, the new president of the Women's Tennis Association, conceded. How then can the players expect any sympathy on a bad call when they are too selfish to treat officiating seriously?

$1 an Hour

The United States Open has used about 100 persons to officiate this year's matches, according to Bill Bigelow, the chairman of umpires. The meager total of only $6,000 was allocated to the umpires, which averages out to about $7 a day pay.

Each linesman received nightly dinner stubs, a drink chit and two guest tickets for the first nine days, plus one ticket a day for the remaining three days. But in terms of actual officiating conditions, with some working as many as five matches a day. Bigelow estimated their salary at about $1 an hour.

As a possible alternative, Talbert is looking into an electronic system that was set up on the grandstand court during the week. Under such a setup, a match could be worked by three officials instead of the current complement of 12.

Even meticulous officiating, however, may not satisfy fans who fel that escalating prices for parking and food and dull, skimpy evening programs are examples of how commercialism is the tournament's new priority.

"All the News That's Fit to Print"

The New York Times

LATE CITY EDITION

Weather: Partly cloudy today; fair and mild tonight and tomorrow. Temperature range: today 62-77; Sunday 61-73. Details on Page 61.

VOL. CXXIV . No. 42,961 — NEW YORK, MONDAY, SEPTEMBER 8, 1975 — Price higher in air delivery cities. — 20 CENTS

G.O.P. Picks Kansas City For Its 1976 Convention

Full Committee Is Expected to Ratify Selection Unit's Choice Today—Ford Is Said to Have Favored Mid-West

By WARREN WEAVER Jr.

Special to The New York Times

ARLINGTON, Va., Sept. 7—The Republican party's site selection committee voted unanimously tonight to hold the 1976 G.O.P. convention in Kansas City, Mo. The full national committee is expected to ratify the choice tomorrow.

Mary Louise Smith, the Republican National Chairman and head of the site committee, said that it had been "a difficult decision." The other contenders in the final committee debate and balloting were Miami Beach and Cleveland.

The Republicans have not held a Presidential nominating convention in Kansas City since 1928, when they chose Herbert C. Hoover.

Tonight's closed meeting took more than 3½ hours because of spirited lobbying for all three cities by state and local officials and members of Congress.

President Ford was reported to favor holding the nominating session in the friendly Middle West, rather than returning to Miami Beach, where Richard M. Nixon was chosen in 1968 and 1972.

The seven-member site selection committee met in closed session on the matter with the expectation that its choice would be ratified tomorrow by the 159-member Republican National Committee at the opening of a two-day session in the Washington suburb here.

The Democrats have agreed to hold their 1976 convention in New York City. They will convene on July 12, and Republicans on Aug. 16. The party that expects to oppose an incumbent President customarily nominates earlier to give its challenger a longer campaign.

Republican state chairmen and national committeemen held preliminary meetings in the Twin Bridges Marriott Hotel here, discussing the assets of the three cities.

Governor Is Hopeful

Kansas City has the Kemper Arena, a sports center used for basketball, which has 10,500 permanent seats and can accommodate 5,000 temporary ones on the floor, more than adequate for a convention with about 4,500 delegates and alternates.

Backers of Kansas City contended that there were 13,000 first-class hotel rooms available

Continued on Page 42, Column 1

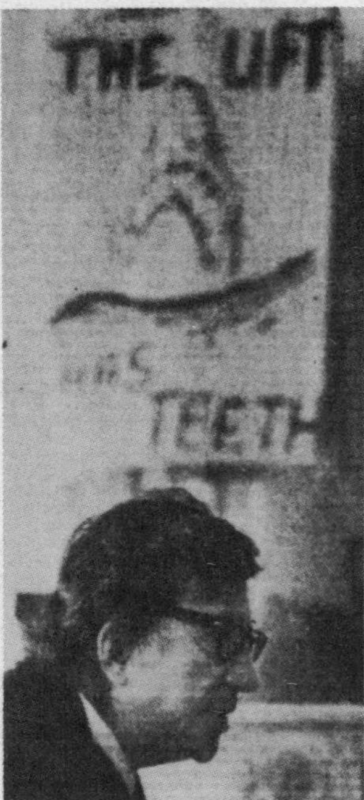

Albert Shanker, teachers' union leader, consulting with aides yesterday.

Harold Newman, the chief conciliator for the state, said the contract situation was a "cliff-hanger."

Louis Yagoda, state mediator, discussing the possibility of a strike in his room at the Plaza Hotel.

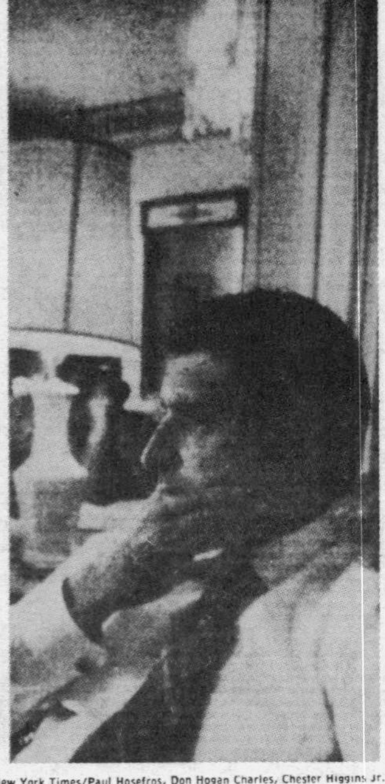

The New York Times/Paul Hosefros, Don Hogan Charles, Chester Higgins Jr.

Dr. Robert J. Christen, Board of Education negotiator, ponders the issues.

ANDERSON PLEADS CITY'S CASE TODAY WITH FORD'S AIDES

State Senate Leader to See Simon on Washington Visit About U.S. Loan Backing

SECRETARY IS ADAMANT

He Is Against Federal Role in Helping Municipalities With Fiscal Problems

By MAURICE CARROLL

Warren M. Anderson, the majority leader of the State Senate, will press on the Ford Administration in Washington today a proposal for Federal insurance for some municipal borrowing, then return to Albany to try to pass a state program to help money-short New York City past its next brush with default.

Mr. Anderson, the most powerful Republican in the state government, will move into the middle of the effort to ease the city's troubles by linking the short-term Albany package, designed to raise enough money to pay the city's bills until December, with a long-term Federal program to get the city back into the borrowing market.

The Senator, through a spokesman, gave a hint of the argument he will make to his Washington host, Treasury Secretary William E. Simon, who said yesterday on a television interview program that such insurance would set "an intolerable precedent," a Federal intrusion in local affairs that would have local-government advocates like Thomas Jefferson "twirling in their graves."

City Economies Urged

Frowning earnestly into a camera, Mr. Simon said the city needed to take strong economy actions, so that welfare, for instance, would go to "the needy, not the greedy."

Mr. Anderson's spokesman listened to the show, then said:

"It's not enough to talk about serving the needy, not the greedy. We assume that's being done. By December, we will have done everything that is humanly possible."

The possibilities in both Washington and Albany are permeated by political considerations. Mr. Anderson will be trying to talk his fellow Republicans into something that

Continued on Page 23, Column 1

Authoritarian Rule Gains Wide Acceptance in India

By WILLIAM BORDERS

Special to The New York Times

NEW DELHI, Sept. 7—Two months ago, when the Government of the world's most populous democracy declared a state of emergency and began arresting thousands of its opponents, there were confident predictions that the new authoritarian position would not be tolerated.

Among opposition groups here, as well as among people who care about India in places like London and New York, many foresaw the emergence of an underground resistance movement, whose disruptive activities would force Prime Minister Indira Gandhi to relent.

From a hideout in southern India, one underground figure called for a wave of general strikes in protest; another issued a mimeographed sheet urging the people to "paralyze the functioning of the Government."

But the calls have largely gone unheeded and no resistance movement has developed.

In the cities and in the countryside, in the regions of the isolated rich and of the many, many, poor, India is almost completely at peace, and Prime Minister Gandhi, in the opinion of knowledgeable people here, is as firmly in control as she has ever been.

What happened?

"Much as I hate to admit it, the state of emergency is popular," said a disappointed opponent of the Government, who had hoped for more signs of resistance. "If the people are for it, the fact that a few chaps like me are actively against it does not make much difference."

The reasons that people give for supporting—or at least not actively opposing—the Government's crackdown are as diverse as India herself. Here are some of the principal ones:

¶The feeling, apparently growing in some quarters, that India's problems are so huge that they require drastic, nondemocratic solutions.

¶The pervasive Indian tradition of nonviolence, which dis-

Continued on Page 19, Column 1

Israel Shopping for Arms To Meet Changes in Sinai

By DREW MIDDLETON

Israeli arms procurement in the United States is about to accelerate, focusing on weapons to cope with the change in the military situation in the Middle East caused by the signing last week of an agreement on Sinai.

Israeli Government sources reported over the weekend that the United States had ended the ban on long-term arms sales it imposed after the failure of its efforts to negotiate a Sinai agreement between Israel and Egypt last March.

The Israeli sources said negotiations had resumed on a shopping list that includes:

¶F-15 fighter planes to match the MIG-23's deployed by Egypt and Syria.

¶Hundreds of tanks and armored personnel carriers to defend the Sinai plain east of the Mitla and Gidi passes, from which Israel has agreed to withdraw.

¶Surface-to-surface missiles to balance those in Arab countries.

¶The most advanced electronic countermeasures and laser-guided munitions, or "smart bombs."

Israeli arms acquisitions are expected to cost more than $2.2-billion, according to Defense Department estimates, and will involve some hard choices.

The Israelis must measure proven weapons now available against more sophisticated arms coming into production in five years. They may be asking more from the American arms industry than it is now capable of providing, some Defense Department sources cautioned. Defense authorities, however, do not believe that Israeli requirements will slow the flow of new weapons to the United

Continued on Page 2, Column 4

12 Killed in Lebanon

Twelve people were reported taken from a bus in Tripoli, Lebanon, and shot to death by gunmen from the nearby town of Zgharta in a renewal of communal fighting. Page 3.

CITY IS RATED HIGH IN TEACHER PAY

National Study Shows Fringe Benefits Also Rank Well—Work Conditions Poorer

By EDWARD B. FISKE

New York City public-school teachers are, on the average, better paid than their counterparts in other large cities, and they rank at or near the top in major fringe benefits such as pensions, insurance and contributions to the union welfare fund. They also have the shortest working day.

At the same time, teachers here are called upon to handle larger maximum classes than those elsewhere, have fewer paid days off for illness and personal business and face relatively high living costs. As a group, New York teachers come to their work with more graduate training than teachers in other cities.

These were the major conclusions of a survey by The New York Times of teacher benefits in New York City and in the five next-largest cities in both the United States and New York State.

Teachers here are now in the process of negotiating with the Board of Education on their salary and other benefits for the coming year. Schools are scheduled to open tomorrow. and the United Federation of Teachers, the teachers' union. has threatened to go on strike

Continued on Page 38, Column 1

City Schools Open Today, Face a Strike Tomorrow

By LEONARD BUDER

The city's public schools will open for the new term this morning facing the possibility of a teachers' strike tomorrow and with over-all educational prospects the gloomiest in many years because of the fiscal crisis.

Negotiators for both the Board of Education and the United Federation of Teachers continued into the early morning to attempt to work out a new contract that would lift the threat of a strike.

Albert Shanker, president of the teachers' union, said at 10 o'clock last night:

"A strike is inevitable. They just don't think that teachers are going to strike. They won't believe it until tomorrow when we vote to strike."

Harold Newman, chief of conciliation for the state's Public Employment Relations Board, described the contract situation as "a cliff-hanger."

At 2 A.M., Mr. Newman, looking weary, said that he and Louis Yagoda, state mediator, would "push through the night" in the hope of bringing both parties together. But, he added, "there very well could be a strike."

Dr. Robert J. Christen, chief of the board's negotiating team, said that he expected state-appointed fact-finders to make their recommendations later and that he hoped that these would lead to a settlement.

He said that the main stumbling block was money. Sources close to the talks have said that the money issue, which does not fundamentally involve salary matters, was complicated by the city's fiscal predicament — that the board was uncertain how much money it could commit to a contract.

The union has scheduled a general membership meeting for 6 P.M. today at Madison Square Garden. Ned Hopkins, a spokesman for the U.F.T., said the members would be asked to vote on a proposed contract—if an agreement has been worked out before then—or to invoke the union's "no contract, no work" policy.

Even as the Board of Education contract-settlement efforts

Continued on Page 38, Column 4

Guardsmen in Boston for Busing Today

By JOHN KIFNER

Special to The New York Times

BOSTON, Monday, Sept. 8—A hotly disputed court-ordered busing program takes effect today with National Guardsmen standing by to help the police if need be.

Elaborate safety plans drawn up by city, state and Federal officials were shaken by a sudden "blue flu" epidemic as hundreds of policemen called in sick in a dispute involving overtime and shift changes.

Last night a rock-and-bottle throwing clash between whites and the police and guardsmen broke out in South Boston near the Old Navy Yard Annex Building where the guardsmen are stationed.

South Boston residents carrying flags and signs were on hand as the guardsmen arrived. and one guardsman was injured in the confrontation. In a later incident near South Boston High School, a motorcycle policeman was struck with a broken bottle. There were several arrests.

Early today United States marshals moved into South Boston for the first time in the conflict. Two carloads of them arrived at the high school shortly after 1 A.M. to investigate the injury of the motorcycle policeman. One hundred marshals are detailed in Boston.

Also early today, the state police began to assemble hours earlier than had been planned for their role in maintaining order as the schools opened.

Police Commissioner Robert DiGrazia said that 258 city policemen had called in sick after being ordered to report for overtime duty and that attempts to reach 187 other policemen had been unsuccessful.

Yesterday afternoon, 6,000 chanting, singing opponents of busing, mostly from the South Boston and Charlestown neighborhoods, rallied on the broad brick plaza in front of City Hall.

As word of the arrests reached a rally being held near South Boston High School, local residents rushed to the pier area. Additional police were brought in, and the crowd of about 500 persons faced the helmeted line until shortly before 11 when they left in response to the urgings of community leaders and a rumor that blacks were entering their neighborhood.

The crowd, led by youths who sped through the narrow streets in cars and trucks, reassembled at the high school

Continued on Page 22, Column 1

United Press International

Members of National Guard Military Police unit marching at Camp Curtiss Guild in Reading, Mass., a suburb of Boston, before they were called into the city.

Chavez and Teamsters Intensify Fight

By JON NORDHEIMER

Special to The New York Times

SALINAS, Calif., Sept. 7—The job of the cortadore, the man who cuts lettuce from its thick roots, is hard work, even for the young men with strong backs who toil in the broad green fields of the Salinas Valley.

Jose Morales knows this harvest work very well. He has labored in the lettuce fields of California and Arizona during harvests since 1962 when he and his brothers and sisters came here from Mexico.

This is the first lettuce crop in the Salinas Valley in 13 years that Mr. Morales will not help to pick. But he is in the fields every day, moving among the rows of workers, seeking a different harvest.

Mr. Morales, 37 years old, is campaigning for votes for the United Farm Workers of America in the decisive union elections that are being held this month in the Salinas Valley and other farm centers of central California.

New Law in Effect

California's unusual farm labor law, which went into effect the week before last, has thrown the entire collective-bargaining future of the state's 250,000 farm workers up for grabs. All existing labor contracts can be challenged if a majority of the workers on a farm petition for an election at harvest time.

The state's two principal farm labor representatives, the United Farm Workers and the International Brotherhood of Teamsters, are now locked in a struggle in the central valleys of the state in dozens of union elections, a broad contest that will continue through the changing seasons as the harvest moves to other parts of the 800-mile-long state.

It is a debate carried into the fields and work camps of the laborers, a dialogue that holds the potential to give one union dominance in the future and banish the other.

"Listen," Mr. Morales said in Spanish the other day to a knot of cortadores who had moved far enough ahead of the packaging machines that follow them to take a break, "this election is everything that we have been working for. Everything will be different after we vote. Wages, working conditions, everything."

The men nodded their heads and smoked cigarettes. A few asked questions. "Are you sure the vote will be secret?" asked one man nervously.

"Yes, yes," Mr. Morales responded. "A secret ballot. It is the new law."

Both sides have opened propaganda campaigns that contain a dizzying amount of charges, and it is difficult in the short lifespan of a campaign—an election must be held within seven days after the filing of a petition—to ferret out scurrilous claims from legitimate ones.

The mood here is that the last-minute activity is of little value anyway. The whole farm

Continued on Page 42, Column 1

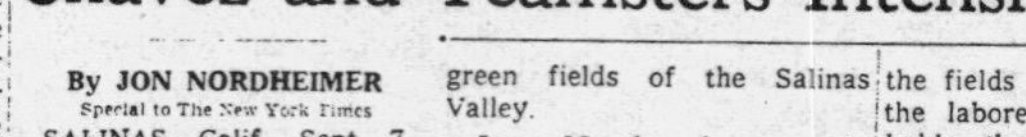

The New York Times/William E. Sauro

UPSETS CONNORS AT FOREST HILLS: Manuel Orantes of Spain falls to his knees in ecstasy after defeating Jimmy Connors, the favorite, in U.S. Open, 6-4, 6-3, 6-3. Details on Page 25; a profile of Orantes is on Page 26.

NEWS INDEX

Orantes Takes U.S. Open Title, Beating Connors by 6-4, 6-3, 6-3

By NEIL AMDUR

Like a matador taunting a bull, Manuel Orantes destroyed Jimmy Connors, 6-4, 6-3, 6-3, yesterday for the men's singles title in the United States Open tennis championships.

Less than 18 hours after he had survived five match points in an exhausting five-set struggle with second-seeded Guillermo Vilas, the 26-year-old Spanish left-hander brought the top-seeded Connors to his knees before a stunned crowd of 15,669 at the West Side Tennis Club in Forest Hills, Queens.

Off-speed ground strokes and passing shots from both sides were two of the tactics that blunted the bullish tactics of the defending champion. But Orantes's most devastating weapon was the forehand topspin lob, a shot that typified the tone of a tournament that had switched from grass to the clay-like Har-Tru surface.

Time and again, with time to spare on a slower playing surface, Orantes looped the deceiving lobs over his net-rushing rival for outright winners, while cheers and chants of "Viva Orantes" emanated from a small, but vocal rooting section high above Portal 9.

"If he wins, do you think they'll give him one of Jimmy's ears?" a spectator in a courtside box joked after Orantes broke Connors in the opening game of the third set with two winning lobs.

The third-seeded Orantes collected $25,000 and a Pinto automobile for his biggest tournament achievement. More important, the gracious self-effacing Spaniard finally may have achieved the respect and recognition due him after being almost totally ignored and shunted to obscure field courts in the early rounds of the 12-day event.

How Orantes managed to control the tempo against Connors after his 3-hour-44-minute match with Vilas and a sleepless night at his midtown hotel was a tribute to the Spaniard's competitive instinct and clay-court artistry.

The Vilas struggle did not end until 10:28 P.M. Saturday and only after Orantes had rallied from two sets to one down and 0-5 in the fourth set. He ate no dinner after the match, did not reach the Roosevelt Hotel until 2 A.M. yesterday and could not get to sleep until 3 A.M. because of running water in the bathroom that forced him to summon a plumber.

"It was a very hard night," he said.

Connors, seeking to become the first two-time singles winner since Neale Fraser 15 years ago, had outslugged Bjorn Borg of Sweden in a straight-set Saturday afternoon semifinal. But just as Arthur Ashe had changed speeds and kept Connors from finding a hitting groove in the Wimbledon final on grass, Orantes left him uncomfortable in pursuit of a pattern.

"I tried to give him soft balls," said the soft-spoken Spaniard who joined his countryman, Manuel Santana, as a champion here. "Let

The New York Times
Orantes exulting after the final point at Forest Hills

him do everything. I know he is not as consistent that way, and I am lucky he miss so many shots."

Connors had said after his first match that "everyone's a challenger on clay." Subconsciously, however, he may have wondered how Orantes could recover from the Vilas encounter.

"He played unbelievably," Jimmy told the stadium gathering, after receiving his runner-up check for $12,000. "I didn't think it would be possible for him to play the way he did and hit the kind of passing shots he did. Unfortunately for me, he did."

Connors started with a flourish by breaking his rival at love and holding at 15 for 2-0. But Orantes turned matador, his drop-shots and slicing backhands teasing Connors with the same effect as a red cape.

Jimmy netted a routine forehand approach that brought Orantes to 2-all. He stroked a forehand volley past the baseline at 30-40 that moved Orantes ahead, 4-2.

A forehand passing shot down the line gave the Spaniard the first set after Connors tried to attack on a weak approach shot.

Orantes appeared ready for the kill at 3-1, 40-love in the second set only to have Connors charge back to 3-all. But the earlier matches against such clay-court proponents as François Jauffert, Ilie Nastase and Vilas had toughened Orantes, and he broke for 5-3 by blocking a serve with a forehand that bounced on the baseline.

Connors strung together 13 straight points in the third set to reach 3-all and continued to banter with the crowd, responding to pleas of "C'mon Jimmy," with "I'm comin' baby!"

Orantes was too deliberate, conserving energy and patience just as Chris Evert, another clay-court specialist, had done in beating Evonne Goolagong for the women's singles crown.

"I had a point for 4-2 and blew it," Connors noted, referring to a netted forehand service return that got Orantes to deuce from 30-40.

Orantes delivered the final blows with successive service breaks in the seventh and ninth games, each time with forehand passing shots down the line.

Connors was boring in on the second match point when Orantes took the big backswing for the clincher, a shot that might not have been possible with a skidding ball on a faster surface such as grass.

As the ball landed for the final winner, Orantes dropped to his knees, smiled in relief and turned immediately toward his wife, who was seated at courtside.

"Another day, another final, another loss," Connors lamented, of his defeats in the Australian, Wimbledon and United States Open finals.

Asked about the tirelessly effective play of his rival, Connors said, "A lot of times it happens that way. The guy is still playing from the night before. You forget to sleep, you forget to eat. I don't think he had time to get tired."

Connors returned and teamed with Nastase for a 6-4, 7-6 victory over Tom Okker and Marty Riessen in the men's doubles final. Afterward, he said that Orantes had become the top opponent for next February's $250,000 challenge match in Las Vegas.

Connors did not appear pleased with the partisan Orantes crowd, although underdogs generally draw considerable support from West Side galleries, even against Americans.

"The American public is spoiled with its tennis players," America's top-ranking player said. "There are too many good tennis players now."

The women's doubles title was won by Margaret Court and Virginia Wade over Rosemary Casals and Billie Jean King, 7-5, 2-6, 7-6. In mixed doubles, Miss Casals and Dick Stockton beat Mrs. King and Fred Stolle, 6-3, 6-7, 6-3.

A Popular Champion

Manuel Orantes Corral

By PARTON KEESE

The stocky, dark-eyed player who won the men's singles title yesterday at the United States Open tennis championships in Forest Hills is one of the most popular competitors in the game. Not only opponents, but also officials and fans throughout the world have come to admire Manuel Orantes, the 26-year-old left-hander from Barcelona, Spain. His infectious smile, constant cheerfulness whether winning or losing and gracious Latin manners on and off the court have given him a reputation to complement his racquet artistry. Even when he is capturing tournament after tournament—eight on clay this year—his foes find it difficult to vent their anger at a man who applauds their best shots, won't argue about close calls and purposely misses a point if he feels a wrong call has hurt his opponent.

Man in the News

The New York Times
Upset winner
(Manuel Orantes with trophy at Forest Hills yesterday.)

"My business is to play tennis," Orantes says, "not argue about points. I dislike arguments."

In the quarterfinals of the Open against Ilie Nastase, the temperamental Rumanian, Orantes gave a point away at the beginning and, incredibly, gave away the final point of the third set because he felt Nastase's shot had been erroneously called out.

"If I saw the ball very clear," he added, "I would do it even in the fifth set."

Because of his unassuming behavior, he has been overshadowed by the flamboyant players.

For Manuel Orantes Corral, born Feb. 6, 1949, in Granada, the son of an optician, the tennis boom proved a salvation. He grew up in a period when Spain was deliriously taken with another tennis hero, Manuel (Manolo) Santana, who won the Wimbledon championship in 1966 and the United States title in 1965.

With every Spanish boy wanting to be a tennis champion, Orantes (pronounced O-RANN-tays) became a ball-boy at the age of 10 at the Royal Tennis Club of Barcelona.

He won the Orange Bowl junior singles at 18 and the De Gallea Cup for youths under 21. As a substitute on the Spanish Davis Cup team (Santana and Juan Gisbert were the principal players) he played his first match in 1968 against Italy.

For Orantes in those days, however, there were still heavy pressure and worries. He was expected to live up to the first Manolo and found that trying to do so made him "choke" in major tournaments. He was too nice, he once confessed, and lacked the killer instinct.

Besides, he had problems with his back, which would grow stiff after long, arduous matches. Last winter he decided to do something about it. He left the tennis circuit and consulted the physician of the Barcelona soccer club. Advised to undertake special exercises, which he still does religiously every night, he finally overcame the problem.

"That's the big difference this year," he said. "I no longer have to worry about my back and it has made me a much better player. This year I am very well prepared."

Until this year the only major world title he had won was the Italian in 1972. But he had been a semifinalist several times and had led the Spanish Davis Cup team to several series victories, although Spain has never won the cup. He and Gisbert are one of the world's best doubles teams.

Orantes was married last year and his wife, Virginia, also Spanish, has helped to clear his mind for tennis. He has been nearly unstoppable on clay courts this season. His amazing consistency has rescued him from defeat so often that his fans have learned never to give up on him.

During his path to the championship at Forest Hills, a large group of Spanish-speaking fans shouted "oles" and "vivas" and kept yelling in Spanish, "Manolo, Manolo, you're the greatest!" In the semifinals, such support helped him save 5 match points against Guillermo Vilas and then go on to win in one of the greatest comebacks ever seen at Forest Hills.

As perilous as his position was then, his composure never varied, and he never failed to applaud his opponent's good shots. As one fan said, "If Orantes were a bullfighter, he'd be so busy clapping for the bull he'd be gored to death."

"All the News That's Fit to Print"

The New York Times

LATE CITY EDITION

Weather: Partly sunny today; cool tonight. Chance of rain tomorrow. Temperature range: today 60-76; Tuesday 56-73. Details on Page 89.

VOL. CXXV..No. 42,984 · NEW YORK, WEDNESDAY, OCTOBER 1, 1975 · 25 cents beyond 50-mile zone from New York City, except Long Island. Higher in air delivery cities. · 20 CENTS

Associated Press

EMPEROR HIROHITO GREETED IN VIRGINIA: The Emperor being welcomed by women in colonial costumes in Newport News yesterday. It is the first time a reigning Japanese monarch has made official visit to United States. Page 9.

PRESIDENT ASKS $13-MILLION MORE FOR PROTECTION

Tells Chicago Audience That He Will Continue Travel by 'Every Prudent Means'

By JAMES M. NAUGHTON

Special to The New York Times

CHICAGO, Sept. 30—President Ford, after asking Congress today for $13.5-million more this year for Secret Service protection, said tonight that he would continue traveling across the country "not in any foolhardy spirit, but by every prudent and practical means."

Mr. Ford told a Republican fund-raising dinner at the Conrad Hilton Hotel here that his travels were intended to help him "talk straight to the American people."

"I have also done a lot of listening," Mr. Ford added. He called "two-way communications with my friends and fellow Americans" an essential part of the Presidency. The 1,500 persons who attended the $125-a-plate dinner gave the President a standing ovation.

Spending Request

In a supplemental spending request submitted before Mr. Ford left Washington late today, James T. Lynn, director of the Office of Management and Budget, said that the $13.5-million would provide 150 additional Secret Service agents. The request would also pay for additional travel costs for protective details to be assigned beginning tomorrow to Democratic Presidential candidates.

"I intend to keep my communications open, not in any foolhardy spirit, but by every prudent and practical means," the President said in his dinner address.

Woman Had Permit

The tension surrounding the President's trip to Chicago was heigthened about a half-hour before Mr. Ford's arrival, when the police learned that a woman near the Conrad Hilton Hotel was carrying a handgun in her purse.

The woman was said by the White House to have a permit to carry the weapon in connection with her job in a downtown currency exchange.

Ron Nessen, the White House press secretary, said the woman was being questioned by Secret Service agents and the Chicago police, but that she "does not appear to be any sort of threat to the President." He said that she was cooperative

Continued on Page 18, Column 4

A State Financing Agency Finds Loan Market Is Shut

With $69-Million Needed in the Next 2 Weeks, Banks' Position Perils Many Kinds of Construction

By FRANCIS X. CLINES

Officials of the state's Housing Finance Agency, facing the need to raise $69-million in the next two weeks, have been told by bankers that the borrowing market is closed to it for the foreseeable future.

The situation, which is even more critical in time than the threatened default by the city, is now at an impasse, according to officials of the huge agency, who said yesterday that they were hoping the Governor and Legislature could come up with some sort of emergency help.

Default would mean the stopping of work at dozens of projects statewide, including a variety of housing, hospital and university construction, officials said.

Beyond that, the failure of the borrowing agency would strike at the credit rating of the state itself and precisely when it is hoping its healthier status can be used to prop up the city.

The difficulty at the Housing Finance Agency, which must borrow at the rate of about $100-million a month, represents the entwinement of the state and city credit problems, in the view of harried state officials.

The agency has a good credit rating and revenue flow, but it has been caught in what State Controller Arthur Levitt termed the "irrational emotional" reaction of potential investors against all offerings from New York, regardless of relative quality.

The city's credit failure and the earlier default on notes by the state's Urban Development Corporation have unfairly tarred the Housing Finance Agency, state officials complain. Regardless, the market is now closed, according to

Continued on Page 29, Column 1

Split on School Pact

The Board of Education challenged Governor Carey's labor consultants to substantiate their contention that the new teacher's contract could cost the city $140-million this year. Page 27.

BANKS RESISTING NEW STATE ISSUE OF NOTES FOR CITY

Stand Further Jeopardizes Legislative Package Aimed at Staving Off Default

CAREY ASKS LEVITT AID

Fails to Persuade Controller to Invest Pension Funds Despite Court Ruling

By LINDA GREENHOUSE

A second crucial element in the financial package for staving off a New York City default appeared jeopardized yesterday by a growing unwillingness of bankers to buy the $500-million in short-term notes the state is due to issue over the next two months on the city's behalf.

"The marketability of that state paper is problematic at this point," Felix G. Rohatyn, chairman of the Municipal Assistance Corporation, said after a long meeting with Governor Carey and other members of the M.A.C. board here.

On Monday, the State Court of Appeals threw out a section of the emergency plan that required State Controller Arthur Levitt to invest $125-million from two state pension funds in M.A.C. bonds. The Governor met with Mr. Levitt for more than two hours yesterday, but failed to persuade him to make the investment voluntarily.

Rescue in Doubt

With these rapid consecutive blows—the loss of $125-million in pension investments and the prospect of failure of the $500-million note sale—the intricate $2.3-billion rescue package that the Legislature patched together in a special session three weeks ago appeared close to coming apart.

The setbacks for the city triggered yet another drop in the prices of New York State-related bonds and notes, and trading activity was virtually halted. Some bonds of the Municipal Assistance Corporation were trading as low as 75 cents on the dollar, while general-obligation state bonds sold at prices that yielded up to 9 per cent. [Page 29.]

Review of Federal Funds

The only cheerful news for the city was the announcement by President Ford that, at the request of Senator James L. Buckley, he had ordered two Cabinet officers to review Federal allocations to the city and make sure that they were being given fairly. [Page 29.]

The meeting in the Governor's office yesterday afternoon ended with no public statements and apparently without a decision on what to do next. Mr. Carey will fly to Washington this morning to brief members of the state's Congressional delegation on

Continued on Page 28, Column 4

Miss Moore Tried to Call Ford Guards Five Times

By RICHARD D. LYONS

Special to The New York Times

WASHINGTON, Sept. 30—Top Secret Service agents told a Congressional hearing today that only a few hours before Sara Jane Moore allegedly tried to assassinate President Ford she made five attempts to telephone the agents protecting him but was never able to reach them.

The officials testified that Miss Moore, who was questioned by Secret Service agents the night before the shooting, made her first call to them at 8 A.M. on Sept. 22, the day of the incident, but there was no one on duty in the San Francisco district office and the call was taken by a telephone answering service.

H. Stuart Knight, the Secret Service Director, and James T. Burke, Assistant Director for Intelligence, said in response to questions that Miss Moore made two further calls to the Secret Service later that morning, one to the Federal Bureau of Investigation and one to the San Francisco Police Department.

But they added that the calls—or the fact that they had been made—were not relayed to the agents who questioned Miss Moore and that her attempts to telephone them were not discovered until after the shooting incident in front of the St. Francis Hotel about 3:30 P.M.

The two agents and other Federal law enforcement chiefs who testified today said that

Continued on Page 19, Column 1

Ex-Im Bank Head Put Stock in Trust, Profited on Its Sale

By EDWIN L. DALE Jr.

Special to The New York Times

WASHINGTON, Sept. 30—Henry Kearns, when he was head of the Government's Export-Import Bank in 1972, promoted an apparently highly profitable sale of stock he had placed in a "blind trust" and received some of the proceeds of the sale, it was disclosed today.

The disclosure came in a letter from Richard L. Thornburgh, Assistant Attorney General in charge of the Criminal Division, to Senator William Proxmire, Democrat of Wisconsin, who made the letter public.

Mr. Thornburgh wrote that "insufficient evidence has been developed to date to support criminal charges." But Senator Proxmire said he was "flabbergasted" by that conclusion and asked Attorney General Edward H. Levi to overturn "the outrageous decision."

While declining to press criminal charges, Mr. Thornburgh did say that "it would appear

Continued on Page 21, Column 1

Lisbon Lifts Troops

Portgual's Premier removed troops occupying leftist-controlled radio and television stations. In reversing the step he took two days ago to prevent the suspension of civil liberties, the Premier said he was "confident that it would not be necessary to reimpose emergency measures." Page 3.

MADRID REJECTS FOREIGN PROTESTS

Premier Defends Executions and Accuses Critics of 'Intolerable Aggression'

By HENRY GINIGER

Special to The New York Times

MADRID, Sept. 30—Premier Carlos Arias Navarro tonight angrily denounced international protests against Spain over the execution of five terrorists and called on the Spanish people to unite behind Generalissimo Francisco Franco and the Government.

In his first public appearance since Saturday when the terrorists, two of them Basque separatists, were put to death, the Premier attacked the numerous protests from abroad as "an intolerable aggression against Spanish sovereignty."

[In London, the organization Amnesty International issued a report asserting that it had evidence that Spanish authorities used torture on Basque detainees on a large scale. Page 5.]

Speaking of the expressions of hostility from many countries, the Premier said, "We do not desire to be alone but the possibility of isolation does not intimidate us."

Mass Rally Planned

The Premier's 15-minute address was preceded through the day by numerous official and semiofficial calls for a mass rally tomorrow in Madrid in support of General Franco's regime. It will be the fourth such rally since World War II, each held when the regime felt itself in danger from internal and external sources.

The various appeals pictured

Continued on Page 4, Column 4

U.S. Will Let Vietnamese Who Ask to Go Back Do So

By RICHARD HALLORAN

Special to The New York Times

ASAN, Guam, Sept. 30—The United States has decided to allow 1,600 Vietnamese refugees here to return to their homeland as they have requested despite the new Saigon Government's apparent reluctance to accept them.

About 100 others who are in the United States and who also want to go home are due to be flown here, and all are to sail for South Vietnam in two or three weeks aboard a Vietnamese ship that brought refugees here five months ago.

Robert V. Keeley, an official of the Interagency Task Force on Indochina Refugees, told reporters that the United States decision was made at "the insistent request of the repatriates" but without the concurrence of the new Government in Saigon.

"We are assuming," he went on, "that the South Vietnamese authorities will not turn back their own citizens."

Other American officials here said the decision had been made to avoid any further violence as a result of the refugees' impatience with their lot. A month ago, two buildings in their compound were burned down, and four United States marshals were injured during a protest demonstration.

Leaders of the 1,600 refugees here, informed of the decision by Mr. Keeley during a meeting tonight in a shed with a corrugated iron roof, broke into cheers and applause. The news brought hundreds of other refugees streaming out of the compound's ramshackle former hospital barracks into the warm humid night to cheer and talk excitedly.

Banners had been strung around the camp reading: "We

Continued on Page 12, Column 4

C.I.A. YIELDS DATA TO HOUSE INQUIRY

Provides All but 50 Words of Materials Panel Sought in Battle With Ford

By JOHN M. CREWDSON

Special to The New York Times

WASHINGTON, Sept. 30—The Central Intelligence Agency delivered tonight the bulk of the national security documents subpoenaed two weeks ago by the House Select Committee on Intelligence. The move appeared to resolve the stalemate between the committee and President Ford, committee sources said.

The C.I.A. made available all but 50 words of materials on the intelligence community's reports prior to the Tet offensive in South Vietnam in 1968.

Material was delivered with a covering letter stipulating conditions upon which the Ford Administration was making the documents available.

They included the condition that the House committee must provide "reasonable notice" if it planned to make any portion of the secret material public. The intelligence community, according to the condition, would have a right to argue the case for continued secrecy and there would be "a final appeal" to the President.

The conditions will be presented to the full committee at a meeting at 10 A.M. tomorrow. With the approval of the two senior members, however, it is expected the committee will vote to accept Mr. Ford's proposal.

Committee sources said that the chairman, Representative Otis G. Pike, personally took possession of the documents late today. The material delivered represents pre-Tet reports by the C.I.A., the defense intelligence agency, and the national security agency. Committee sources said, however, that this did not include information from the Department of State and that that controversy would be handled separately.

A source close to the com-

Continued on Page 21, Column 1

An Alleged Gift by N.M.U. To Ford Splits 2 Agencies

By M. A. FARBER

The United States Attorney for New Jersey and the Internal Revenue Service have become embroiled in an intense dispute over each agency's handling of an allegation that Gerald R. Ford may have received an unusual payment from leaders of the National Maritime Union around 1968.

The prosecutor, Jonathan L. Goldstein, is investigating whether the I.R.S. failed to pursue the allegation after it was made, apparently in early 1974, by a former leader of the union. At the same time, the I.R.S. says it acted "appropriately." And some officials of the tax agency contend that the United States Attorney's office had known of the charge by the fall of 1974 and had dismissed it out of hand.

Neither Mr. Goldstein's office nor the I.R.S. is believed to have any evidence at this stage that the alleged transaction involving President Ford when he was a Congressman ever occurred. Nor has any such evidence emerged in a detailed investigation by The New York Times.

What has developed, however, is a conflict over the treatment of the allegation between two Government agencies that, in a post-Watergate atmosphere, are particularly sensitive to any charge of a cover-up.

An anatomy of their conflict, which comes during a period of heightened public and Congressional interest in the integrity and techniques of Federal investigative agencies, illustrates how two major law-enforcement agencies—ostensibly working together—can come to challenge each other's motives, actions and memory.

The story has two threads

Continued on Page 90, Column 1

Yale Sets Up School Of Administration With Dual Purpose

By MICHAEL KNIGHT

Yale University will announce today the establishment of a Graduate School of Organization and Management to train leaders for both business and government service.

Named to head the school, which is expected to open next fall, will be William H. Donaldson, former Under Secretary of State and Wall Street "whiz kid." In the nineteen-sixties, as a partner in Donaldson, Lufkin, Jenrette, Inc., he helped transform institutional investors into a major force in the securities market and he amassed a personal fortune in excess of $10-million.

The new graduate school is expected to combine the study of business administration and public management techniques—increasingly needed by the growing corps of executives who shuttle between jobs in industry and government.

"I think the lines between the private and public sectors are blurring more and more,"

Continued on Page 57, Column 1

Stengel's Death at 85 Widely Mourned

By JOSEPH DURSO

Casey Stengel, who died Monday night in California at the age of 85, was mourned yesterday by a public that had marveled for more than 60 years at his antics and achievements as a baseball player, coach, manager and nonstop showman.

Tributes poured in during the hours after "the Ol' Professor" died in Glendale Memorial Hospital from around the country—from public officials like Governor Carey and Mayor Beame, who recalled that he had worked for all four of New York's major league teams in this century, to former players like Yogi Berra, who remembered him as "a great man."

Mr. Stengel died at 10:58 P.M., Pacific Time, only a few hours after a family spokesman disclosed that he was suffering from cancer of the lymph glands. He had entered the hospital two weeks earlier for tests, not far from the home he had shared for half a century with his wife, Edna, who was in a nursing home nearby.

The legends that he had created continued long after his retirement 10 years ago and, as recently as June, he enlivened the Mets' annual old-timers' reunion by riding into Shea Stadium in a Roman chariot dressed in a toga and gladiator's helmet.

"Casey Stengel had the baseball mind ofa genius," Governor Carey said yesterday, "the heart of Santa Claus and St. Francis, and the face of a clown, and something very good has gone from our lives."

"Casey Stengel will be ranked in the history of baseball with such great managers as John McGraw, Connie Mack and Joe McCarthy. And New Yorkers will always hold him in their hearts, with warm memory, because he is the only baseball figure who wore the uniforms

Continued on Page 30, Column 1

NEWS INDEX

Associated Press

ALI RETAINS TITLE: Joe Frazier recoiling from a blow to the head by Muhammad Ali in heavyweight championship bout in Manila. Ali won on a technical knockout after 14 rounds. Details, Page 31.

Ali Retains Title, Fight Stopped After 14th

Battered Frazier's Pilot Ends Brutal Manila Bout

By DAVE ANDERSON
Special to The New York Times

MANILA, Wednesday, Oct. 1—In the most brutal confrontation of their five-year rivalry, Muhammad Ali retained the world heavyweight boxing championship today when Joe Frazier's manager, Eddie Futch, surrendered from the corner moments before the bell was to ring for the 15th round.

Frazier, dominating the middle rounds with the fury of his youth, had been battered by the champion throughout the three rounds prior to Futch's merciful decision.

"I stopped it," Futch explained, "because Joe was starting to get hit with too many clean shots. He couldn't see out of his right eye. He couldn't see the left hands coming."

Ali was far ahead on the scoreboards of the three officials. Using the 5-point must scoring system, referee Carlos Padilla Jr. had the champion ahead, 66-60. Judge Alfredo Quiazon had it 67-62 and Judge Larry Nadayag had it 66-62. On a rounds basis, Quiazon had Ali ahead 8-3, with three even. The others each had it 8-4-2.

Ali's victory was recorded as a knockout in the 14th round since the bell had not rung for the final round.

"My guy sucked it up," said Ali's trainer, Angelo Dundee. "When he looked completely out of gas, he put on another gas tank. I thought we were in front. My guy was hitting him better shots."

Futch believed that Frazier was ahead, which only added to the humanity of his decision to surrender.

"Joe had two bad rounds in a row," Futch said. "Even with three minutes to go, he was going downhill. And that opened up the possibility in that situation that he could've been seriously hurt."

Wearing dark glasses to hide his puffed eyes, especially his right eye, Frazier agreed with Futch.

"I didn't want to be stopped, I wanted to go on," Frazier said, "but I'd never go against Eddie."

Frazier dismissed questions about retirement, saying, "I'm not thinking that way now." But the weary champion indicated that the "trilla in Manila" might have been his last fight.

"You may have seen the last of Ali," the champion said. "I want to get out of it. I'm tired and on top. What you saw tonight was next to death. He's the toughest man in the world."

Ali attempted to register the early knockout he had predicted while dominating the early rounds. But then Frazier, in his relentless attack, smashed and slowed the 33-year-old champion. They resembled two old bull moose who had to stand and slam each other because they couldn't get away from each other.

Through the middle rounds, Frazier took command. On the two scorecards of the New York Times, the 31-year-old challenger won eight of the first 11 rounds. But then Ali searched for the knockout punch that would assure the retention of the title.

Moving on weary legs, Ali began to measure Frazier in the 12th with a flurry of punches to Frazier's face, which resembled a squashed chocolate marshmallow. In the 13th, the champion quickly knocked out Frazier's mouthpiece with a long left hook, then landed a left-right combination.

Frazier was shaken now, wobblign on his stumpy legs, but his heart kept him going. But then Ali's straight right hand sent Frazier stumbling backward to the center of the ring but somehow the former champion kept his feet. His mouthpiece gone, Frazier kept spitting blood as he resumed his assault moments before the bell.

Associated Press

Joe Frazier after being defeated in Manila contest by Muhammad Ali. At right, Frazier taking a punch to the head before fight was stopped.

In the 14th round Frazier hopped out quickly but Ali shook him with a hard right, then jolted him with several left-right combinations before the bell and Frazier stumbled to his corner.

Moments later, Futch waved his surrender to the referee. On the stool in his corner. Frazier appeared exhausted. He didn't protest.

Unlike their first two fights, Ali-Frazier III maintained a level of boxing violence seldom seen. During their 1971 classic, Frazier earned a 15-round unanimous decision and undisputed possession of the title with a relentless assault as Ali often clowned. In their 12-round nontitle bout early last year, Ali's holding tactics detracted from his unanimous decision.

But from the opening bell in the Philippine Coliseum, the estimated crowd of 25,000, including President Ferdinand Marcos and his wife, realized that Ali had not come to dance. Moving out flat-footed, he shook Frazier with several right hands in the early rounds but Frazier kept attacking.

At the bell, Ali came out, hands high in a semipeekaboo. He stood flat-footed rather than dancing, as if looking for the early knockout he had predicted. Frazier, in contrast, moved in aggressively, trying to unload his left hook but the champion tied him up effectively in two clinches.

Ali landed a left-right combination, then jarred Frazier with a left hook that sent him against the ropes. Ali also landed a hard right hand before the bell.

In the second round, Ali remained flat-footed, using his pawing jab to keep Frazier at bay. When he cupped his left glove around Frazier's head, the referee warned the champion. Ali then landed a hard right to the head that shook Frazier, then landed two more as Frazier kept coming in.

Ali covered up against the ropes, then easily pushed Frazier away, displaying complete control of the tempo. But suddenly, Frazier landed a hard left hook to Ali's jaw before the bell.

Before the third round, Ali bowed and blew kisses to President Marcos and his wife. Ali then taunted Frazier with his pawing jab, using his six-inch advantage in reach to keep Frazier away. Ali landed a series of hard punches to the head, but Frazier burrowed through them to land a left.

Ali covered up against the ropes, and when Frazier stepped back, Ali waved his right glove at Frazier, as if inviting him to return. Ali was talking to Frazier now, then burst out of his cocoon with a flurry of lefts and rights in a toe-to-toe exchange that had the spectators in a frenzy.

But in the fourth round Ali's tempo slowed as Frazier's increased. By the fifth round, a chant of "Frazier, Frazier" filled the round arena. As the struggle continued, the crowd sounded as if it favored Frazier, one of the few times that Ali hasn't converted the live audience into cheering for him.

Ali, at 224½ pounds at last Saturday's weigh-in, had been the 9-to-5 betting favorite in the United States but he was a 6-to-5 choice here. Frazier had weighed 214½ at the ceremonial weigh-in.

Ali's won-lost record is now 49-2 with 34 knockouts. He has lost only to Frazier in 1971 and to Ken Norton, who broke Ali's jaw in winning a 12-round decision that Ali later reversed. Frazier's record is now 32-3, losing to Ali twice and being dethroned as champion by George Foreman in 1973.

In the decades to come, Ali and Frazier will be remembered as two of boxing's classic rivals through 42 rounds. As memorable as their first two fights were in Madison Square Garden, their masterpiece developed halfway around the world from where their rivalry began.

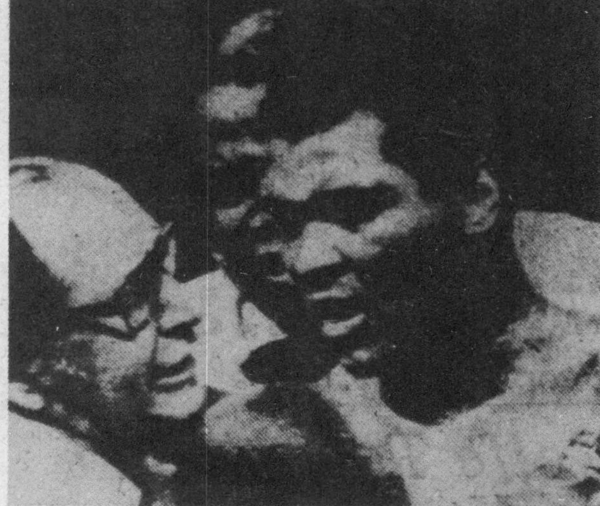

Associated Press

Muhammad Ali after being declared victor in bout

United Press International

Joe Frazier reaching out with a left as Muhammad Ali ducks away in the first round of their title bout.

United Press International

Heavyweight champ Muhammad Ali glances a right off Joe Frazier during the 7th round.

Manila Excited; Fans Searched

MANILA, Wednesday, Oct. 1 (AP) — Everybody was searched at tho gate.

Policemen in brown uniforms, guns hanging loosely on their hips, stood by grimly as security personnel opened women's purses and examined every parcel.

Sirens rang out in the early morning air. Police cars with red lights flashing careened down the wide boulevards. It was a city in high excitement and on the move.

It was only a fight, but it was perhaps the biggest one ever held, witnessed, promoters said, by 700 million people around the world, the television picture relayed off satellites over the Pacific and Indian Oceans.

This sprawling metropolis of 4.5 million normally awaken early, but on this day of the third meeting between Muhammad Ali, the heavyweight champion of the world, and tough, bearded Joe Frazier, it pulsated with high drama.

Among those at ringside were President Ferdinand Marcos, his wife, Imelda, and their daughter. They sat in the third row, the President in a red velvet chair with a high gold back.

A fight before noon would have been unheard of a few years ago, but that has now become common in Don King's new concept of promoting his shows in exotic places.

It was hazy and humid and the streets were bustling when the vanguard of visitors began pouring down Magsaysay Boulevard to the modern, air-conditioned structure where the fight took place.

Colorful jitneys—elaborateately painted jeeps, relics of the last war — carried passengers for 30 centavos, the equivalent of an American nickel. Motorcycle policemen and squad cars with lights flashing and sirens screaming escorted the fighters to the scene followed by black limousines bearing their huge entourages.

Youngsters went unwillingly to school. Some played hookey to go to the fight. Many had saved for weeks and months for the 30-peso seat $4 in the gallery.

A Chastened, Sore Ali Praises His Rival

MANILA, Wednesday, Oct. 1 (AP)—"He could have whupped anybody in the world except me," a chastened Muhammad Ali said after having successfully defeated his world heavyweight boxing crown today with a 14th-round knockout against a game Joe Frazier.

"He is great," Ali said. "He is greater than I thought he was. He is the best there is except me."

The champion first declined to go to the interview area, saying, "I am too tired, I don't want to talk to anybody."

But later, after a battered Frazier had swallowed his pride and appeared and after trainers of both fighters had given interviews, Ali agreed to show up.

"My arms are sore, my legs are sore, my sides are sore," he said. "I am so tired I want to rest for a week."

He said Frazier had shaken him up a few times with left hooks, but he never felt he was in too much trouble.

"I couldn't take the punches he took," the champion said.

Frazier had a large bruise under his right eye. His mouth was bloody.

"It was one heck of a fight," he said. "I thought I was ahead when they stopped it. Sure, I was disappointed, but I never argue with what Eddie does."

Eddie Futch, Frazier's trainer, walked to the center of the ring at the end of the 14th round and told the referee that his man had taken "a lot of shots and I didn't think he could win in the condition he was in, and I saw no use in risking an ijury to him."

Angelo Dundee, Ali's trainer, said durability was the key to the outcome.

"My guy has a knack for taking it, sucking it up," he said. "I knew he was good in the stretch."

He said Ali had been hurt by a left hook in the 10th round and his legs had become wobbly.

"It was the same punch that decked him in their first fight," he said. But Frazier ran out of gas, he added, and "my man had that extra gas tank; he always has it."

Frazier and Futch shrugged off suggestions that it might have been Joe's last fight.

"I want to kick it around a little more," Frazier said.

Futch added, "We will talk it over."

Red Smith

Joe Was Still Coming In

MANILA, Wednesday, Oct. 1—When time has cooled the violent passions of the sweltering day and the definitive history is written of the five-year war between Muhammad Ali and Joe Frazier, the objective historian will remember that Joe was still coming in at the finish. For more than 40 minutes, the former heavyweight champion of the world, who was now the challenger, attacked the two-time champion with abandoned, almost joyous, ferocity. For seven rounds in a row he bludgeoned his man with hooks, hounding him into corners, nailing him to the ropes. And then, when Ali seemed hopelessly beaten, he came on like the good champion he is. In the 12th round, the 13th and all through a cruel 14th, Ali punched the shapeless, grinning mask that pursued him until Eddie Futch could take no more.

Sports of The Times

After 14 rounds of one of the roughest matches ever fought for the heavyweight championship. Frazier's trainer, Futch, gave up. At his signal, the referee stopped the fight with Ali still champion.

All three Filipino officials had Ali leading on points at the end, but in The New York Times book, Futch snatched defeat from the jaws of victory. On The Times' two scorecards, Frazier had won eight of the first 13 rounds when he walked into the blows that beat him stupid. He lost while winning, yet little Eddie was right to negotiate the surrender. Frazier's $2-million guarantee wasn't enough to compensate him for another round like the last.

So now the saga ended. It began on March 8, 1971, when Ali and Frazier met for the first time, both undefeated as professionals, both with valid claims to the championship, both in the glory and strength of youth. That time Frazier won it all. They fought again on Jan. 28, 1974, when both were ex-champions and Ali got a debatable decision. Today's might have been debatable, too, if a decision had been needed.

Many-Digit Inflation

It has been a series both men can remember with pride—and pride has been the spur for both. All three meetings were happenings, memorable chapters in the annals of the ring, and in many respects this was the best of the three. It will be some time before anybody knows whether the gross revenue from the live gate, closed-circuit and home television around the world will equal the $20-million drawn for their first encounter, but this day's business in the Philippine Coliseum may have broken all records for an indoor fight. Attendance was estimated at 25,000, with a gate of something like $1.5-million at $333 tops.

If a price can be put on the suffering of brave men, this returned a dollar in pain for every dollar involved. Curiously, the winner's suffering was the greater. Not many men could have stood up under the punishment Ali took from the fifth round through the 11th.

Yet Ali not only endured when he had taken all that Frazier could deliver, but he also had enough to win. Say what one will about this noisy extrovert, this swaggering, preening, play-acting slice of theatrical ham: the man is a gladiator. He was a callow braggart of 22 when Sonny Liston surrendered the title to him 11 years ago. At the ripe age of 33, he is a champion of genuine quality.

He has been saying he would have one more fight, probably with George Foreman, and then retire as the greatest of all time. It is not wise to accept his promises or faith, but he must take his leave some day. When he does, he will be remembered as one of the good ones.

Loser, and Still Champion

Whatever can be said to Ali's credit must be said with equal emphasis about Joe Frazier. This man was a good champion in his own right. He is the best man Ali ever fought, an opponent who searched Ali's inner depths and brought out qualities Ali never had to reveal to any other man.

It was Joe, rather than Muhammad, who made this a great fight. In the early round, Ali made half-hearted attempts to strut and posture the way he has done against men like Joe Bugner and Chuck Wepner, but Frazier's persistent advance brooked no such nonsense. Ali's faster hands and circling retreat held Joe off for a while. Joe was remorseless, though, and single-minded.

He brushed pawing gloves aside, rolled in under punches, bore straight ahead and slugged, and by the fifth round he was getting the message across. It was hook, hook, hook—into the belly to draw Ali's hands down, then up to the head against the ropes.

He beat the everlasting whey out of Ali. His attack would have reduced another man to putty. The guy in the white trunks was not another man. He was the champion, and this time he proved it.

Duran Beats Viruet

By **GERALD ESKENAZI**

Special to The New York Times

UNIONDALE, L. I., Sept. 30—In a startling, often comic, never dull 10-round nontitle fight, Roberto Duran, the lightweight champion, won a unanimous decision tonight from Edwin Viruet, his dancing, mimicking opponent.

A crowd of 14,396 at Nassau Coliseum paid $241,106, a Coliseum record, to see the live bout and the Muhammad Ali-Joe Frazier battle that followed on closed-circuit television.

When the Duran-Viruet fight ended, the crowd stood and applauded. For reasons of heart and not logic, they had expected Viruet to get the decision.

But all smiles stopped together when it was announced that Duran had won. The New York Times scorecard gave one round to Viruet, the third, and called two rounds even.

Viruet was shocked. "Duran called me a piece of nothing," said the New Yorker later. "I said to him: 'You some champ. I can't even break an egg, but you can't knock me out.'"

About the only thing the fighters had in common was their age: 24 years. Duran is from Panama City. Viruet, a pigeon fancier, is from Manhattan. At the end, one of his neighbors released two white pigeons, which quickly fluttered down because a weight had been attached to their tails.